DICTIONARY OF AMERICAN BIOGRAPHY

AMERICAN
COUNCIL
★ OF ★
LEARNED
SOCIETIES
★

DICTIONARY

OF

AMERICAN BIOGRAPHY

PUBLISHED UNDER THE AUSPICES OF
THE AMERICAN COUNCIL OF LEARNED SOCIETIES

The American Council of Learned Societies, organized in 1919 for the purpose of advancing the study of the humanities and of the humanistic aspects of the social sciences, is a nonprofit federation comprising forty national scholarly groups. The Council represents the humanities in the United States in the International Union of Academies, provides fellowships and grants-in-aid, supports research-and-planning conferences and symposia, and sponsors special projects and scholarly publications.

MEMBER ORGANIZATIONS
AMERICAN PHILOSOPHICAL SOCIETY, 1743
AMERICAN ACADEMY OF ARTS AND SCIENCES, 1780
AMERICAN ANTIQUARIAN SOCIETY, 1812
AMERICAN ORIENTAL SOCIETY, 1842
AMERICAN NUMISMATIC SOCIETY, 1858
AMERICAN PHILOLOGICAL ASSOCIATION, 1869
ARCHAEOLOGICAL INSTITUTE OF AMERICA, 1879
SOCIETY OF BIBLICAL LITERATURE, 1880
MODERN LANGUAGE ASSOCIATION OF AMERICA, 1883
AMERICAN HISTORICAL ASSOCIATION, 1884
AMERICAN ECONOMIC ASSOCIATION, 1885
AMERICAN FOLKLORE SOCIETY, 1888
AMERICAN DIALECT SOCIETY, 1889
AMERICAN PSYCHOLOGICAL ASSOCIATION, 1892
ASSOCIATION OF AMERICAN LAW SCHOOLS, 1900
AMERICAN PHILOSOPHICAL ASSOCIATION, 1901
AMERICAN ANTHROPOLOGICAL ASSOCIATION, 1902
AMERICAN POLITICAL SCIENCE ASSOCIATION, 1903
BIBLIOGRAPHICAL SOCIETY OF AMERICA, 1904
ASSOCIATION OF AMERICAN GEOGRAPHERS, 1904
THE HISPANIC SOCIETY OF AMERICA, 1904
AMERICAN SOCIOLOGICAL ASSOCIATION, 1905
AMERICAN SOCIETY OF INTERNATIONAL LAW, 1906
ORGANIZATION OF AMERICAN HISTORIANS, 1907
COLLEGE ART ASSOCIATION OF AMERICA, 1912
HISTORY OF SCIENCE SOCIETY, 1924
LINGUISTIC SOCIETY OF AMERICA, 1924
MEDIAEVAL ACADEMY OF AMERICA, 1925
AMERICAN MUSICOLOGICAL SOCIETY, 1934
SOCIETY OF ARCHITECTURAL HISTORIANS, 1940
ECONOMIC HISTORY ASSOCIATION, 1940
ASSOCIATION FOR ASIAN STUDIES, 1941
AMERICAN SOCIETY FOR AESTHETICS, 1942
METAPHYSICAL SOCIETY OF AMERICA, 1950
AMERICAN STUDIES ASSOCIATION, 1950
RENAISSANCE SOCIETY OF AMERICA, 1954
SOCIETY FOR ETHNOMUSICOLOGY, 1955
AMERICAN SOCIETY FOR LEGAL HISTORY, 1956
SOCIETY FOR THE HISTORY OF TECHNOLOGY, 1958
AMERICAN COMPARATIVE LITERATURE ASSOCIATION, 1960

DICTIONARY
OF
American Biography

Supplement Four

1946–1950

John A. Garraty, *Editor*

Edward T. James, *Editor*

WITH AN INDEX GUIDE TO THE SUPPLEMENTS

Charles Scribner's Sons

NEW YORK

The preparation and publication of Supplement Four of the *DICTIO-NARY OF AMERICAN BIOGRAPHY* has been made possible in part by the generosity of the New York Times Company. The preparation of the original twenty volumes of the Dictionary was made possible by the public-spirited action of the New York Times Company and its President, the late Adolph S. Ochs, in furnishing a large subvention. Entire responsibility for the contents of the Dictionary and its Supplements rests with the American Council of Learned Societies.

American Council of Learned Societies Committee on the
Dictionary of American Biography

Editorial Staff

ELISABETH P. KRABISCH, *Managing Editor*

FREDERIC C. BEIL III, *Assistant Editor*

LYLE CHURCHILL, *Assistant Editor*

MARY GREENBERG, *Editorial Assistant*

ROSE MOSELLE, *Editorial Assistant*

DOROTHY UPJOHN LEWIS, *Copy Editor*

LELAND S. LOWTHER, *Copy Editor*

MICHAEL KNIBBS, *Proofreader*

DORIS ANNE SULLIVAN, *Proofreader*

MARSHALL DE BRUHL, *Director, Reference Editorial*

PREFACE

This volume extends the coverage of the *Dictionary of American Biography* from January 1, 1946, through December 31, 1950. It contains 561 biographies; thus the *Dictionary* as a whole now describes the lives of 16,004 persons who have made distinctive contributions to one or another aspect of American life. These new sketches were written by 437 authors, each an expert on the subject or on the subject's field of work. In deciding upon the persons included and in commissioning the biographies, we called upon many scholars and specialists for advice. These experts served without compensation other than the knowledge that they were contributing to a worthy and venerable enterprise.

A change in the editorship occurred in August 1973 when the work was transferred from Cambridge, Massachusetts, to New York City. My predecessor, Edward T. James, supervised the gathering of the names of potential subjects, collected and collated the opinions of experts, and drew up the final list of entries. He also recruited all but a handful of the contributors, and he and his staff, with Philip De Vencentes as assistant editor, did the bulk of the editing of about 300 of the biographies and checked them for accuracy of detail. The rest of the editorial work—including copy editing of the entire manuscript and most of the inevitable negotiations with contributors regarding changes— was under my direction. Thus, while Dr. James has given the volume its basic shape and is responsible for any errors in judgment regarding inclusions and omissions, we share responsibility for any factual errors that may have slipped through the editorial net. (We respectfully request, however, that readers who disagree with any of the interpretations of the lives of the subjects should blame the authors of the biographies, who had the final say about such matters!)

Many scholars, librarians, and other experts have helped us in our editorial work, verifying obscure facts, adding missing details, and providing critical readings of many of the biographies. Students of librarianship at Brown University, Carnegie Library School (now the Library School of the University of Pittsburgh), Columbia University, Emory University, the University of Illinois, Louisiana State University, the University of Texas, and both the Madison and Milwaukee branches of the University of Wisconsin drafted biobibliographies of prospective *Dictionary* subjects for the use of both the contributors and the editorial staff. We are, of course, most grateful for the assistance of all these persons.

Finally, I wish to thank Frederick Burkhardt of the American Council of Learned Societies and the members of the council's board for the *Dictionary* for their many kindnesses and their wise guidance during the period of editorial transition.

JOHN A. GARRATY

DICTIONARY OF

AMERICAN BIOGRAPHY

Abel-Henderson—Youmans

**ABEL-HENDERSON, ANNIE HELO-
ISE** (Feb. 18, 1873-Mar. 14, 1947), teacher
and historian, was born in Fernhurst, Sussex,
England, the first daughter and the third of
seven children of George Abel and Amelia
Anne (Hogben) Abel. Her parents made a
brief trip to Kansas in the 1870's but quickly
tired of frontier life and went back to England.
Part of the family, including the father, who
was a gardener, returned to Salina, Kans., in
1884; Annie and two younger sisters followed
in 1885. Here she completed high school, taught
for two years, then went to the University of
Kansas, where she graduated in 1898. After
another year of teaching at Colby, Kans., high
school, she returned to the university, earning
a master's degree in history, philosophy, and
English in 1900. Her major professor, Frank
Heywood Hodder, called her the most brilliant
history student he had ever known and sent her
to Cornell for the doctorate, but for lack of
funds she returned to Kansas after a year to
teach history in a high school in Lawrence. Her
free time was spent in graduate study with
Hodder at the University of Kansas, doing research on United States Indian policy. In 1903
the university published her study of Kansas
Indian reservations, which attracted wide scholarly attention. Both Yale and Columbia offered
her scholarships. She accepted Yale's Bulkley
fellowship, and, after two years of study under
Edward Gaylord Bourne and George Burton
Adams, she received the Ph.D. in 1905.

Abel's first year out of Yale was spent as
instructor of history in Wells College, Aurora,
N.Y. In 1906 she became history instructor
in the Women's College of Baltimore, now
Goucher College. She was tall and plain, a
careful scholar, but painfully shy. Her lectures
tended toward dull formality, yet she was warm
and witty with small groups. Despite her retiring nature, scholarly recognition came early.
Her revised doctoral dissertation, "The History
of Events Resulting in Indian Consolidation
West of the Mississippi River," won the Justin
Winsor Prize for 1906, and was published in
that year's *Annual Report* of the American
Historical Association. A tendency toward long
and rambling footnotes was curbed in this
study, still her most readable work. In her
book reviews she checked every source consulted, plus many the author failed to find.
Francis Browne, editor of *The Dial,* once
wrote to ask her why, if the book in question
was really "one of the most important historical
works of the season," it was necessary to include a catalogue of shortcomings that went on
for nine pages.

Acting on a suggestion of Professor Bourne,
Abel began to study American treatment of the
California Indians. At the Indian Bureau in
Washington, she poked into dusty bundles of
official records, making copious longhand notes
and careful typescript copies. The Smithsonian
Institution originally planned to publish her
California Indian documents, but she withdrew
the manuscript when the Smithsonian insisted
on deleting all reference to politics. The California material was never published, though
other important studies were, including a massive three-volume history of the Five Civilized
Tribes during the Civil War, *The Slaveholding
Indians* (1915-1925). In 1913 she received a
brief presidential appointment as official historian of the Bureau of Indian Affairs. In order
to show the sort of valuable material buried in
government files and thus generate public support for a national archives, she edited (and

I

the government published) *The Official Correspondence of James S. Calhoun . . .* (1915).

At Goucher, Abel rose to full professor and head of the history department, at the same time teaching English history at Johns Hopkins University Teachers College. She also served as president of the Maryland branch of the College Equal Suffrage League. In 1915 she moved to Smith College as associate professor of history, becoming full professor the next year.

By 1921 her interest in the American West had begun to fade. With a sabbatical from Smith for 1921-1922, she went to Great Britain, then to New Zealand and Australia to study the British native policy. At the University of Adelaide she met George Cockburn Henderson, a history professor, whom she married on Oct. 27, 1922, after resigning her Smith College professorship. She was then almost fifty years old, her husband fifty-two; neither was able to adjust after so many years of independence. In 1924, she returned to the United States on a trial separation and taught for a year at Sweet Briar College.

In 1925 the American Association of University Women awarded her the Alice Freeman Palmer traveling fellowship, which enabled her to go to England to continue her research. One result of this work was the publication in 1927 of the Lewis Tappan Papers, which she edited with Frank J. Klingberg. Finishing her research in London, she sailed for Adelaide in an attempt at reconciliation with her husband. When it became obvious they would be happier apart, she returned to America. An Australian friend suggested she hyphenate her surname, and, after 1927, she did so, calling herself Annie Heloise Abel-Henderson, though she often dropped the Henderson in scholarly publications.

In the fall of 1928 Abel-Henderson was appointed professor of history at the University of Kansas, and the following year, after receiving a grant from the Social Science Research Council, she went to Ottawa, Canada, for further research into British native policy. This led to her finishing her work on *Chardon's Journal at Fort Clark, 1834-1839* (1932) and on *Tabeau's Narrative of Loisel's Expedition to the Upper Missouri* (1939). After 1930, though insisting she had retired, Abel-Henderson continued to lecture, do research, and write for another fifteen years. During World War II, in spite of ill health, she worked for British-American War Relief in Seattle and helped to organize a chapter of the Daughters of the British Empire. In 1946 the British government decorated her for this work. She died of cancer at Aberdeen, Wash., on Mar. 14, 1947, and was buried with Episcopal rites in Wynooche Cemetery near Aberdeen.

In her final years, Abel-Henderson planned to write a comparative study of British and American policy toward native peoples, but the research was never completed. She considered *The Slaveholding Indians* her most valuable work, but probably her greatest service to scholars was the publication of great masses of original documents.

[There is a brief autobiographical statement in a letter from A.H.A. to George H. Martin, c. Jan. 1904, Manuscript Collect., Kans. State Hist. Soc., Topeka. The *Kansas City Journal*, Sept. 6, 1903, p. 24, also has helpful information. There are letters, clippings, and notebooks in the Abel-Henderson Papers at the Washington State Univ. Arch. and in the National Arch. There is a good deal of biographical information in introductions to her books and journal articles, especially a note to "Indian Reservations in Kansas and Extinguishment of Their Title," *Trans. of the Kans. State Hist. Soc.* 8 (1903-1904): 72, which erroneously describes the article as her M.A. thesis; the correct title of her thesis was "Pessimism in Modern Thought." There are fairly accurate obituaries in Yale Univ., *Obituary Record of Graduates, 1946-1947* (1948), pp. 177-178; and "Necrology," *The Graduate Magazine: University of Kansas* 46 (1948): 32. See also Marjorie R. Casson, "George Cockburn Henderson, A Memoir," *South Australiana* Mar. 1964, pp. 35-37, 50. Harry Kelsey, "Annie Heloise Abel-Henderson, 1873-1947," *Arizona and the West*, 15 (1973): 1-4, contains a photograph of Dr. Abel-Henderson.]

HARRY KELSEY

ADAMS, JAMES TRUSLOW (Oct. 18, 1878-May 18, 1949), historian, was born in Brooklyn, N.Y., the second son and youngest of three children of William Newton Adams, Jr., and Elizabeth Harper (Truslow) Adams. He was of Virginia ancestry, his Adams forebear—an indentured servant who rose to landowner—having settled there in the seventeenth century. He had a Spanish grandmother, for William Adams, Sr., while representing an American mercantile firm in Latin America, had married the daughter of a prominent family in Caracas, Venezuela. Both of Adams' grandfathers were prosperous businessmen. His father, by contrast, was an unsuccessful Wall Street broker, whose precarious financial condition closely defined the course of Adams' education and early career. For reasons of economy, he attended the Brooklyn Polytechnic School (1890-1894) and its Institute (1894-1898), from which he received the A.B. degree in 1898. His graduation as class president, valedictorian, and poet gave evidence of his intellectual and literary talent.

Drawn at first to philosophy, Adams spent

an uninspiring year at Yale, for which he received a pro forma M.A. (1900). He then began a routine and ever more unappealing business career in New York that culminated in twelve years in a Wall Street brokerage house. In 1912, having amassed a sum he considered sufficient to give him independence, he withdrew from business and moved to Bridgehampton, L.I., to devote himself to study and writing. His first books—*Memorials of Old Bridgehampton* (1916) and *History of the Town of Southampton* (1918)—clearly demonstrated his skill as a writer and scholar and brought him to the attention of professional historians. During World War I, because of his increasingly recognized talents, he was appointed to "The Inquiry," a commission gathered by Col. Edward M. House, President Wilson's adviser, to assemble data for use at the Paris Peace Conference, and he attended the conference as cartographer in the American delegation.

In the postwar years, Adams undertook the four books that gained him his national reputation as a writer of American history. These were the so-called New England trilogy—*The Founding of New England* (1921), *Revolutionary New England, 1691-1776* (1923), and *New England in the Republic, 1776-1850* (1926)—and *Provincial Society, 1690-1763* (1927), a volume in the History of American Life series edited by Dixon Ryan Fox and Arthur M. Schlesinger, Sr. What gave the books their distinction was Adams' increasingly refined literary ability, his capacity for seeing events in broad perspective, and his presentation of themes that were, in their day, fresh and challenging. He arraigned the Puritans for their bigotry and greed, attributing their migration to America more to economic than to religious motives. He redeemed the antagonists of the Puritans, including the Indians and the British imperial administrators. He stressed the growth of secular ideals and of a uniquely American culture during the later colonial and early national periods. And in both periods he considered central the conflict between men of wealth and common people.

As his fame grew, Adams was invited by the editors of some of the major journals to write articles on timely issues. Collected in two volumes—*Our Business Civilization: Some Aspects of American Culture* (1929) and *The Tempo of Modern Life* (1931)—the articles expounded more or less the same theme: that Americans were materialistic, provincial in outlook, lacking in grace and manners, losing their moral fiber, and more and more disrespectful of the law. This theme he reiterated in *The Epic of America* (1931), by far his most popular volume. A broad survey of the nation's past, it traced the evolution of what he called "the American dream" of a better, richer, and fuller life for everyone. Realizing that the dream was in danger, Adams concluded that it could be saved only by a refinement of American values, an improvement of the quality of American life. From his vantage ground in London, where he lived from 1927 to 1935, he felt particularly qualified to see his homeland in clearer perspective.

The historical writings of Adams' later years dealt with subjects that held an ever-growing interest for him. He drew a lively, sympathetic, yet honest portrait of four generations of the great Massachusetts Adamses in one of his most widely read books, *The Adams Family* (1930). In *America's Tragedy* (1934), he saw the Civil War as a product of forces he considered fundamental to the nation's history: the frontier and sectionalism. A devout Anglophile, he sought to show in the two volumes of his history of the British empire—*Building the British Empire* (1938) and *Empire on the Seven Seas* (1940)—what expanding British ideas and institutions had contributed to the world. Adams' continuous and deepening preoccupation with making himself financially secure involved him in a series of publications that were remunerative, if far from being his best efforts. Some of these, for which he served as editor, were nevertheless useful reference works, such as the *Dictionary of American History* (5 vols., 1940), the *Atlas of American History* (1943), and the *Album of American History* (4 vols., 1944-1949).

More a popularizer than an original mind, Adams expressed consummately the attitudes and ideas that commanded respect among intellectuals in the 1920's. His histories adopted the progressive outlook that had been given currency by the works of Charles A. Beard, Carl Becker, Frederick Jackson Turner, and Arthur Schlesinger. His essays echoed criticisms of American life that had been sounded by Sinclair Lewis, F. Scott Fitzgerald, H. L. Mencken, Lewis Mumford, and Van Wyck Brooks, among others. The popularity of his achievement was amply evidenced by the many awards and honors he received, including the Pulitzer Prize in history in 1922 (for *The Founding of New England*), election to the American Academy of Arts and Letters, and the conferment of honorary degrees by several notable universities. But when the depression came, his critique of American life, because it was genteel rather than radical, nostalgic rather than truly reformist, rapidly lost appeal. Unlike many returning expatriates, who saw the New Deal as an attempt to redeem American life, Adams became an increasingly conservative and embittered enemy of Roosevelt's reform programs. With the passage of time, his histories also became outmoded, as the rather simplified progressive interpretation they set forth began to lose ground and as the writings of Samuel Eliot Morison and Perry Miller rehabilitated the Puritans as founders of the American experience.

Reserved and shy, Adams avoided giving public speeches and turned down the teaching offers some colleges had extended him. He remained a bachelor until he was forty-eight. On Jan. 18, 1927, he married Kathryn M. Seely, a young nurse who had attended him during an illness three years earlier. In the interim he had come to depend more and more on her friendship, but much soul-searching and anxiety preceded his final, happy decision to marry. He and his wife had no children. Adams was an Episcopalian in religion. He died of a stroke at his home in Southport, Conn., and was buried in Greenwood Cemetery in Brooklyn.

[The principal source is Allan Nevins, *James Truslow Adams* (1968), consisting of a memoir by Nevins and some 200 pages of selected correspondence. Other sources of information include: Michael Kraus, *A Hist. of Am. Hist.* (1937); memoir by Roy F. Nichols in Am. Philosophical Soc., *Year Book*, 1949; *Current Biog.*, 1941; *Nat. Cyc. Am. Biog.*, XXXVI, 72-73. Adams' papers (20 boxes) are at Columbia Univ.]

A. S. Eisenstadt

ADAMS, JOSEPH QUINCY (Mar. 23, 1881-Nov. 10, 1946), Shakespeare scholar, was born in Greenville, S.C., the first of three sons of Rev. Joseph Quincy Adams and Mamie Fouchée (Davis) Adams, both natives of South Carolina. His father was a Southern Baptist minister who held pastorates during the 1880's in a succession of South Carolina towns and then in Asheville and Wadesboro, N.C. Joseph's mother died when he was in his teens. The boy's early schooling must have been irregular because of the family's frequent moves, but in due course he attended Wake Forest College, taking the A.B. degree with honors in 1900 and the M.A. in 1901. For the next year he served as principal of the Raleigh (N.C.) Male Academy. After graduate study at the University of Chicago (1902-1903) under John Matthews Manly, at Cornell University (1903-1904)

under James Morgan Hart, and at the University of London (1904-1905), Adams received the Ph.D. degree in 1906 from Cornell, where in 1905 he had been appointed an instructor in English. He studied at the University of Berlin in the summer of 1907. In 1909 he became assistant professor at Cornell and in 1919, professor.

Adams gave early promise of a productive scholarly career when in 1904 he published the first of his many contributions to learned journals. Within a few years he had acquired a thorough knowledge of both the English stage and the English drama from the beginnings through the eighteenth century, as well as of sixteenth-century nondramatic literature. His productivity and the soundness of his scholarship were due in great part to self-discipline and the systematic gathering of material. Soon after he joined the Cornell teaching staff, finding the university library inadequate for his needs, Adams secured a grant of several thousand dollars to spend at his discretion for additions to the library. So productive were the results that the grant was increased several times, and Cornell's resources for the study of Renaissance drama and theatrical history attained outstanding excellence.

Among Adams' works, four, published within a span of eight years, established his international reputation: *Shakespearean Playhouses: A History of English Theatres from the Beginning to the Restoration* (1917), *The Dramatic Records of Sir Henry Herbert* (1917), *A Life of William Shakespeare* (1923), which was highly regarded and was several times reprinted, and *Chief Pre-Shakespearean Dramas* (1924). These attracted students to the Cornell English department, where Adams' gifts of organization and style made his lectures popular, and the breadth of his knowledge and the ability to impart it drew many graduate students to enroll under his guidance. As director of dissertations and graduate studies he was unfailingly generous with his time, and he had the knack of communicating to his students something of his scholarly integrity.

In 1931 Adams announced his decision to leave Cornell and accept the position of supervisor of research at the Folger Shakespeare Library in Washington, D.C. The wealth of Shakespearean materials in this institution, then just taking shape as directed by the will of Henry Clay Folger, and the promise of having a major hand in its future development seemed to Adams an opportunity not to be missed. Folger had left an unparalleled collection for the study of Shakespeare and his times, together with a building, still unfinished in 1931, to house it. Though himself interested solely in Shakespeare, Folger had yet seen that an understanding of Shakespeare must rest on a knowledge of his age, and had collected thousands of early books and manuscripts broadly illustrative of that period.

Soon after assuming his new duties, Adams saw that the breadth of Folger's collecting had made the library valuable for students of the English Renaissance in general, and that future expansion must be in this direction. During the first years of the Folger Library, the Great Depression made Folger's ample endowment virtually unproductive and prevented Adams from taking advantage of the rich buyers' market in books. But by 1937 financial conditions were improving, and Adams, who had been elevated to the directorship in 1934, saw a great opportunity. The death of the noted collector Sir Leicester Harmsworth suggested the remote possibility of obtaining his collection of early English books—the largest ever gathered by one man. With the vigor and imagination that he had exhibited as a Cornell instructor, Adams persuaded the Harmsworth heirs to sell and the trustees of the Folger Library to raise the necessary funds to buy. In the end he carried away the prize from under the noses of other and more affluent contestants, including Harvard University. It was a coup that placed the Folger second only to the British Museum for its collection of English books printed before 1641.

In the same year, 1938, Adams added to the library the important Loseley Collection of theatrical manuscripts of the sixteenth century and a collection of Dryden unequaled elsewhere. These were the major purchases, but Adams believed that market conditions not likely to endure offered the last chance to acquire significant numbers of Renaissance books, and for the next few years he devoted his energies mainly to their purchase, until the outbreak of World War II dried up the sources. The task he had marked out for himself was finished. In 1944 Adams suffered a heart attack that imposed on him a slower pace, and he died two years later, at the age of sixty-five, in Washington. He was buried in Washington's Rock Creek Cemetery. Adams had never allowed himself the luxury of family life until the age of forty-nine, when, on Jan. 29, 1931, he married Helen Banks of Ithaca, N.Y. She died four years later. They had one daughter, Helen Banks.

[Joseph Q. Adams, *The Folger Shakespeare Memorial Lib.: A Report on Progress, 1931–1941* (1942); biographical foreword by Adams' lifelong friend Lane Cooper in James G. McManaway, Giles E. Dawson, and Edwin E. Willoughby, eds., *Joseph Quincy Adams Memorial Studies* (1948), also reprinted in Cooper's *Late Harvest* (1952); information from archives of Cornell Univ. and from Adams' daughter, Mrs. J. K. Morrison; personal knowledge. See also memoir by St. George L. Sioussat in Am. Philosophical Soc., *Year Book*, 1947. On his father, see obituary in *Baptist Courier* (Greenville, S.C.), Mar. 10, 1921 (courtesy of J. Glenwood Clayton, Special Collections Librarian, Furman Univ.).]
GILES E. DAWSON

ADKINS, HOMER BURTON (Jan. 16, 1892-Aug. 10, 1949), chemist, was born near Newport, Ohio, the second son and the youngest of the three children of Alvin Adkins and Emily (Middleswart) Adkins. His parents operated a farm lying in a bend of the Ohio River.

The Adkins family was descended from English immigrants who settled in Saratoga County, N.Y., late in the eighteenth century. The Middleswart family emigrated from the Netherlands before 1800 and migrated first from New Jersey, to Pennsylvania, and finally settled in the Ohio Valley. Emily Middleswart studied at Shepherd College and was a country schoolteacher before her marriage.

Homer attended Denison University, earning his expenses during summer vacations on the family farm by raising melons, which were shipped by river packets to Wheeling, W.Va., and Pittsburgh. Upon graduating with the B.S. in 1915, he entered Ohio State University where he received the M.S. in 1916. The following year, on Feb. 21, 1917, he married Louise Spivey, who had been a Denison classmate and then taught high school mathematics. They had three children: Susanne Dorothea, Nancé, and Roger. Continuing his postgraduate work, he took his Ph.D. in 1918. His major professor was William Lloyd Evans; his doctoral thesis dealt with the oxidation of organic compounds by alkaline permanganate. After completion of his doctorate, Adkins served briefly as a chemist in the War Department, held an instructorship in organic chemistry at Ohio State, and held a summer position with the Du Pont Company before joining the chemistry department at the University of Wisconsin in the fall of 1919.

During Adkins' thirty-year career at Wisconsin his leadership in research and teaching quickly brought him national and international recognition and placed him among such American leaders of organic chemistry as James B. Conant, Roger Adams, Frank Whitmore, Henry Gilman, and S. M. McElvain. Early in his career he was ambitious to develop broad generalizations around which the facts of organic chemistry might be organized, but he soon lost faith in the prospect of recognizing such generalizations before a more substantial body of experimental facts was available. He then concentrated his research program on gathering such facts. More and more he became an empiricist.

Early in his career Adkins undertook the study of catalytic reactions, particularly those involving hydrogenation of organic compounds. The study of various catalysts revealed the different natures of products formed from a given starting material and the difference in the pathways of the reactions. Preparation of aluminum oxide catalysts by heating various aluminum alkoxides led to catalysts with different surface structures dependent upon the organic groups present in the starting material. His studies on metal oxide catalysts also led to recognition of the role of trace impurities and to the value of mixed oxides. He developed a copper-chromium oxide catalyst of particular value in the conversion of organic esters to alcohols, a process he termed hydrogenolysis. He also worked with metallic catalysts, Raney nickel in particular. His work led him to the use of higher and higher pressures. He showed great ingenuity in the design of heavy-walled reaction vessels and agitators for studies of reactions in which hydrogen was dissolved under high pressure in liquid reactants with the solid catalyst held in suspension.

Late in his career Adkins began to study the reactions of organic compounds with carbon monoxide under high pressure in the presence of catalysts. He was able to convert alcohols to acids with one additional carbon atom, a process termed carbonylation. He was always interested in comparative chemical reactivities. He clearly distinguished between equilibrium and reaction rate and pointed out that various authors differed widely in the criteria used for comparing reactivities of different compounds. Several of his reviews of the subject had broad influence.

Between 1940 and 1946 Adkins and his associates were deeply involved in military research programs. His laboratory staff in Madison, Wis., worked on chemical warfare agents and on chemicals of value as protective agents against toxic gases and vesicants. Synthetic work was also done on potential antimalarial agents. His administrative duties and extensive travels during this period undoubtedly had a detrimental effect on his health. After the war President Truman awarded him the Medal of Merit for his administration of investigations for the Office of Scientific Research and Development.

In the classroom Adkins was a master of clear and well-organized presentation. His critical evaluations were spiced with wit. His "Survey of Advanced Organic Chemistry" was a milestone course. Until World War II he regularly took his turn in presenting the undergraduate organic course. It was in the research laboratory, however, that his teaching skill stood out and he was responsible for the direction of more than 100 doctoral candidates. He worked in the research laboratory routinely and was in close touch with the progress of his students, many of whom went on to distinguished careers in industry and the academic world.

His professional expertise was widely sought. He served as a consultant to several chemical corporations and was active in the American Chemical Society, in which he held several local and national offices. At the time of his death he was about to become a nominee for the society's presidency.

Throughout his life, Adkins read widely, with particular interest in the philosophy of science and in the Civil War. He also had a deep interest in social and political affairs, toward which he took a moderately liberal position. He grew up in a family of devout Baptists but became a member of the First Congregational Church in Madison.

Adkins was tall and thin, vigorous and intense in his actions, personally charming and witty. He never hesitated to take an unpopular position, especially when he believed an injustice was being done. He was skeptical of routinely accepted dogmas in science and in social and educational areas and was intolerant of inefficiency and lack of candor.

On June 20, 1949, during a meeting of the Eleventh National Organic Chemistry Symposium in Madison, Adkins suffered a coronary occlusion. He died on Aug. 10, 1949, after what had appeared to be a promising recovery, and was buried in the Forest Hill Cemetery in Madison.

[Farrington Daniels' memorial in Nat. Acad. Sci., *Biog. Memoirs*, XXVII (1952), pp. 293–317, carries a full bibliography of Adkins' journal articles, as well as reference to his many honors and the titles of his wartime contracts with the Office of Scientific Research and Development and the Committee on Medical Research. He was the author of the following books: with S. M. McElvain, *Practice of Organic Chemistry* (1925); 2nd ed. (1933); with McElvain and M. W. Klein, 3rd ed. (1940); with S. M. McElvain, *Elementary Organic Chemistry* (1928): and *Reactions of Hydrogen with Organic Compounds over Copper-Chro-*

mium Oxide and Nickel Catalysts (1937). Also see Aaron J. Ihde in W. D. Miles, ed., Dictionary of American Chemists, in press.]

AARON J. IHDE

ALDRICH, CHARLES ANDERSON (Mar. 4, 1888–Oct. 6, 1949), pediatrician and educator, was born in Plymouth, Mass., the first of three children of David Emulus Aldrich and Laura Linwood (Perkins) Aldrich. His father, a native of Providence, R. I., was a businessman; his mother, born in Plymouth, Mass., devoted herself to the rearing of her three sons, the youngest of them a semi-invalid. "Andy" attended the public schools of Boston and New York City, where his family lived before settling in Evanston, Ill. After several years of sales work, undertaken in deference to his father's wishes, he turned with characteristic single-mindedness to the study of medicine, his ambition from the time of a childhood bout with diphtheria. When his father continued to oppose his career choice after his graduation from Northwestern University in 1914, he worked his way through Northwestern University Medical School (M.D., 1915), making an excellent academic record while tutoring and running a bookstore. Following internship at Evanston Hospital (1915-1916), he joined Frank H. Blatchford of Winnetka in general practice, first as an assistant, then as full partner, while continuing to do much of the X-ray work of the Evanston Hospital. On Oct. 3, 1916, he married Mary McCague of Omaha, Nebr., a graduate of Northwestern University School of Music and an experienced teacher whose interest in the nursery school movement meshed with Aldrich's growing attraction toward pediatrics. Of their three children, both sons entered medicine.

After graduate training in 1920-1921 at the New York Nursery and Children's Hospital and at the Children's Hospital and Massachusetts General Hospital in Boston, Aldrich returned to the Chicago area and began what was for the next twenty years a large and busy pediatric practice. To parents with children under one year, he offered prepaid care, including periodic examinations, full immunization, and house calls. When prepayment later became a point of controversy, he defended it as essential to preventive pediatrics, stating that he had never known a family to abuse it. Beginning in 1922 he held various staff appointments at the Evanston Hospital and at Children's Memorial Hospital in Chicago, where, in 1941, he succeeded Joseph Brennemann as chief of staff. In the same year he became professor of pediatrics at Northwestern University Medical School, where he had taught since 1934. From 1944 until his death, he combined the teaching of pediatrics with the study of the developmental and preventive aspects of child care as director of the Rochester Child Health Institute of the Mayo Clinic, a long-term experiment in the pooling of community resources for preventive psychiatric and child care and for community education in physical and mental health. His able staff made a series of important contributions to the medical literature and in 1948 acknowledged his excellence as a teacher by proposing him for the Lasker Award, which he received for "outstanding accomplishments in the education of the physician in the psychologic aspects of the practice of medicine."

A gift for clinical observation and a readiness for innovation are revealed in his numerous publications, which are devoted to prevention and to treatment between 1923 and 1944, and thereafter to the development of health procedures and prevention. Out of his experience in treating kidney disease he wrote fifteen papers on nephritis, proposed a system of clinical classification to facilitate its description and study, and contributed the chapter on nephritis to Brennemann's Practice of Pediatrics (1936). In collaboration with William Bradbury McClure, he devised a simple skin test to measure edema, then a little-studied phenomenon (JAMA, July 28, 1923, and May 3, 1924; Klinische Wochenschrift, June 18, 1927). In 1928 he designed a test for hearing in the newborn, which has been called "one of the earliest attempts to utilize the concept of the conditioned reflex in diagnosis" (Archives of Disease in Childhood, 36 [1961], 50).

His major contribution lay in bringing child development studies into pediatric thought, causing a profound shift away from the rigid and arbitrary child-rearing practices that had evolved apace with expanding scientific knowledge. In the field of nutrition these inflexible methods, far from bringing the expected millennium, had caused a widespread incidence of eating problems, estimated in 1930 at 80 percent of pediatric practice in prosperous communities. Applying the findings of Arnold Gesell and others to his own observations, he discerned the existence of an inborn mechanism, now called the appestat, designed to inform the infant of the amounts of food needed. He accordingly implemented a program for educating parents to avoid even the most subtle forms of coercion at mealtime. His conclusions, published first in *Mental Hygiene* in October 1926 (the subject of a *New York Times* editorial column, Jan. 1, 1927) and in *JAMA,* Sept. 17, 1927, reached a wide public as *Cultivating the Child's Appetite* (1927), which was revised and retitled *Feeding Our Old-Fashioned Children* (1941), with Mary M. Aldrich; a humanistic antidote to ultrascientific feeding techniques.

Even more widely read was *Babies Are Human Beings: An Interpretation of Growth* (1938), written with Mary M. Aldrich, a masterful presentation in lay terms of pertinent data from medicine, physiology, biology, psychology, philosophy, anthropology, and education. To help parents sort through the mixture of folklore, taboo, and often conflicting scientific doctrine surrounding parenthood, the Aldriches presented the facts of growth and development as the key to understanding children as products of their evolutionary past, as dynamic creatures, and as potential adults. Compassionately viewing parents as buffers "between the young barbarian and the amenities of culture," they argued that child-rearing should be a "collaboration with growth," a series of compromises between the baby's needs and the expectations of society. Such an approach, they believed, offered a far safer and more certain path to healthy maturity than did pressure toward premature conformity. The Aldriches advocated the restoration of lullabies, fondling, and rocking—all time-honored customs rejected in the early twentieth century. They considered thumb-sucking a "pre-natal sport" likely to be prolonged only if the baby's routine was somehow unsatisfactory; it should therefore be treated by modified methods of feeding or handling, rather than by physical restraint. Observing that sexual development begins in infancy and that accepted conventions deviated drastically from nature's intentions, they asserted that later concepts of sexual relations might be jeopardized by punishment for genital exploration or masturbation.

Aldrich's articles in such journals as *Parents Magazine,* frequently the basis for the parent-child page of the Sunday *New York Times Magazine* (1946-1948), informed a large audience that feeding or toilet-training schedules enforced without regard for innate individual rhythms give rise to undesirable conflicts and sometimes to lasting disturbances of the sensitive, intricate controls provided by nature. To charges that he advocated "tyranny by autocratic children," Aldrich answered in terms of "self-regulation" and the idea that truly spoiled children are those who, as babies, are denied essential gratifications in a mistaken attempt to force them into a regimen. Pressing his heretical ideas with imperturbable good humor and with "a perseverance that never irritates, but never gives up" (Baehr, p. 124), he contributed to a "revolution in pediatrics." A recent historian has noted that the commonsense *laissez-faire* attitude that has come to characterize feeding theory is "directly traceable" to Aldrich and to his mentor, Brennemann, and that "the independence—in the best sense—of the modern American child owes much to Aldrich's influence" (Faber and McIntosh, pp. 158, 251).

His impact on pediatric thought and on such representatives of the younger generation as Benjamin Spock was enhanced by his position of professional leadership: secretary of the American Medical Association Section on Diseases of Children from 1927 to 1930, and chairman 1930-1931; president of the American Pediatric Society in 1946. In 1929 he played an important role in organizing the American Academy of Pediatrics and was secretary of the American Board of Pediatrics from 1934 to 1944 and president in 1945-1947. His humanizing and liberating influence pervaded the pediatric literature through his active service on the editorial boards of the *Journal of Pediatrics* (1941-1947) and of *Pediatrics* (1948-1949) and through his editorship of the pediatric section of *Psychosomatic Medicine* from 1940 to 1947.

Despite the onset of rather severe Parkinsonism in his late forties, he continued to carry a full work load, making the tremor a point of interest for his young patients; and he persisted in a fondness for tennis, swimming, and fishing until his death from pancreatic carcinoma at St. Mary's Hospital, Rochester, Minn. After Episcopal services, he was buried in Oakwood Cemetery.

[Biographical information is taken from Borden S. Veeder, ed., *Pediatric Profiles* (1957), pp. 669–674 by Henry F. Helmholz, and from the following obituaries: George F. Munns, *Child Development,* Dec. 1949; Benjamin Spock, *Psychosomatic Medicine,* Sept.–Oct. 1949, with photograph; *Pediatrics,* Dec. 1949; *The Clinic Bulletin* (Rochester), Oct. 8, 1949; and *JAMA,* Nov. 26, 1949. Additional information was provided through correspondence by Mrs. Charles Anderson Aldrich, and by Dr. Stephen L. Aldrich, Dr. Robert A. Aldrich, and Dr. Benjamin Spock. Aldrich's publications were located through the *Quarterly Cumulative Index Medicus* and the *Reader's Guide to Periodical Literature.* A full account of the Lasker Award, with the citation by George Baehr, appeared in *Mental Hygiene,* Jan. 1949. The detailed workings of the Rochester Child Health Project are described in Miriam E. Lowenberg, "A Community Program for Child Development," *Childhood Education,* Sept. 1948. Assessments of his contribution appear throughout the pediatric literature: see particularly Leo Kanner, *Child Psychiatry* (1957); Alfred Washburn, "All Human Beings Start Life as Babies," remarks on receiving the C. Anderson Aldrich Award in Child Development, *Pediatrics,* May 1966; Marshall Carlton Pease, *American Academy of Pediatrics 1930–1951* (1951); Harold Kniest Faber and Rustin McIntosh, *History of the American Pediatric Society 1887–1965* (1966). Birth record from the Massachusetts Div. of Vital Statistics; death certificate from the Minnesota Dept. of Health, Minneapolis.]

PATRICIA SPAIN WARD

ALEXANDER, GROVER CLEVELAND (Feb. 26, 1887–Nov. 4, 1950), baseball player, was born on a farm at Elba, Howard County, Nebr., youngest of thirteen children, twelve boys and a girl. His parents were William Alexander, a native of Clinton County, Iowa, and Maggie (Cooty) Alexander, born in Kenosha, Wis. He attended public school in the neighboring town of St. Paul and at the age of nineteen took a job as a telephone lineman to help support the large family. He also began to play baseball on local town teams and with independent Nebraska clubs, where he developed his skill as a pitcher.

Alexander signed his first contract in organized baseball in 1909, with the Galesburg, Ill., club. Toward the end of the season Galesburg sold his contract to the Indianapolis club, a member of the American Association; it in turn sent him to Syracuse in the New York State League, for which he won twenty-nine games in 1910. The Philadelphia club of the National League drafted him for the 1911 season, paying his former club $750 for the privilege. That year Alexander won twenty-eight games for the Phillies, a record for a major-league freshman pitcher that was still unmatched six decades later. He stayed with the Philadelphia club until the end of the 1917 season, when he was traded to the Chicago Cubs, but after pitching in only three games, he was drafted into the army in April 1918. On June 1 of that year he married Aimée Arrant of Omaha, a childhood friend. They were divorced in 1929, later remarried, and were again divorced; they had no children.

During World War I, Alexander served in France as a sergeant in the 342nd Artillery. After his discharge in 1919 he resumed pitching for the Cubs. He often broke training rules, was addicted to alcohol, and by 1926 had become such a disciplinary problem that the team's new manager, Joe McCarthy, disposed of his contract in mid-season to the St. Louis

Cardinals for the waiver price of only $4,000. Alexander pitched well for the Cardinals. Without the nine victories he turned in during the second half of the season they could not have won the 1926 pennant, and his successes against the New York Yankees in the World Series that fall were vital in bringing the world championship to St. Louis. The following season Alexander received $17,500, his peak salary, and at the age of forty he won twenty-one games for St. Louis. He enjoyed another good year in 1928, winning sixteen games, but in the following year, because of his drinking, the club paid him off in full and sent him home six weeks before the close of the season. That winter he was traded to Philadelphia, where for the first time he lost more games than he won. When the club released him in mid-1930, his major-league career had come to an end.

From then on Alexander drifted downhill. He played briefly for the Dallas club of the Texas League, pitched for various semiprofessional outfits, including the well-known House of David team in Benton Harbor, Mich., and, when he could no longer pitch, took various jobs such as selling tickets at a racetrack and working in a flea circus on 42nd Street in New York. His health declined; on two occasions he was found lying unconscious in the street; and he suffered a heart attack after watching a World Series game in 1946. He finally settled in a rooming house in St. Paul, Nebr., subsisting on his meager war pension and small sums provided by the National League. He died there, probably of cardiac failure, at the age of sixty-three, and was buried at Elmwood Cemetery in St. Paul.

Alexander ranks among the best pitchers of American baseball history and among its most tragic folk heroes. Despite alcoholism and the epilepsy from which he also suffered, he shares with Christy Mathewson the National League record for most games won, 373. The ninety shutout games he pitched (sixteen in the 1916 season alone) also set a National League record. He set the major-league record for the lowest lifetime average of runs earned against him in games where he pitched—2.56—and only two other National League pitchers have bettered his 1915 earned-run average of 1.22. He also led his league five times in this category, thus establishing a record matched only by Sandy Koufax. Seven times Alexander led in innings pitched, setting another major-league record, and he pitched 440 complete games, a total exceeded by only three other players. He never pitched a no-hit game, but he shares with two others the National League record for one-hitters—five.

It was not a game he won, however, but a game he saved that made Alexander an enduring hero in the folklore of baseball. In the seventh inning of the seventh and deciding game of the 1926 World Series, with the Cardinals leading 3-2, the Yankees filled the bases with two out and with Tony Lazzeri, a dangerous power hitter, next at bat. In this tense situation, manager Rogers Hornsby removed the starting pitcher, Jesse Haines, and called in Alexander. "Old Pete," as the players called him, had already defeated the Yankees for the second time in the series the day before, and had apparently celebrated appropriately that night—although he always denied it. He ambled slowly from the bull pen and, with hardly any warm-up, struck out Lazzeri. He then held the Yankees scoreless for the remaining two innings, and the Cardinals became world champions.

As a pitcher, Alexander was an artist who relied upon skill more than brawn. His delivery was smooth and effortless, and he possessed remarkable control that enabled him to throw his sinking fast ball, his sharp, quick curve, and his screwball with pinpoint accuracy and economy of pitches. Rather than try to strike batters out, he concentrated on forcing them to hit the kind of pitch he wanted them to. He wasted no time between pitches, and often he would retire the side on five or six pitches in an inning; once he finished a game in fifty-eight minutes.

Alexander was easily distinguishable on the field in those days before players wore identifying numbers on their uniforms. He was six feet one inch tall and weighed about 175 pounds; he had reddish-brown hair and a freckled red face, prematurely seamed. He walked slightly knock-kneed, and wore his cap, which always seemed too small, perched on the top of his head like a peanut shell. In private life he was soft-spoken and kindly. His hobby was hunting, and he was a member of the American Legion and the Masons. He was among the first players chosen for the Baseball Hall of Fame at Cooperstown, N.Y. A movie based on his life, *The Winning Team,* appeared in 1952.

[Files of *N.Y. Times* and *Sporting News* (St. Louis); Thomas Meany, *Baseball's Greatest Pitchers* (1951); *Who's Who in Am. Sports* (1928); Christy Walsh, ed., *Baseball's Greatest Lineup* (1952); *The Little Red Book of Major League Baseball* (1971); Robert M. Broeg, *Super Stars of Baseball* (1971); Harold Seymour, *Baseball: The Golden Age* (1971); "Certificate of Delayed Birth Registration" and death record from Nebr. State Dept. of Health.]

HAROLD SEYMOUR

ALLEN, EDWARD ELLIS (Aug. 1, 1861-Apr. 14, 1950), educator of the blind, was born in West Newton, Mass., the oldest of the four children of James Theodore Allen and Caroline Augusta (Kittredge) Allen. He was descended from Pilgrim forebears; the first of his paternal line in America was James Allen, who settled in Medfield, Mass., in 1649. From both parents he gained a heritage of social consciousness and respect for learning. James Allen was a teacher in the English and Classical School, the first school in America to have a kindergarten, which had been founded by his brother Nathaniel. Caroline Allen, who traced her ancestry to William Bradford, was a quiet, studious woman who had been a pupil at Brook Farm, a transcendentalist community established by George Ripley. Allen was educated at his uncle's school and for two years (1872-1874) at German schools in Leipzig and Zurich. He entered Harvard College in 1880 and received the A.B. degree in 1884. Yielding to his mother's desire that he study medicine, Allen then entered Harvard Medical School. After a year he began to question his choice of a career and accepted an offer to teach at the Royal Normal College in Upper Norwood, London, England, under the direction of Dr. (later Sir) Francis J. Campbell, a remarkable blind American who had formerly taught at the Perkins Institution for the Blind (now Perkins School for the Blind) in South Boston.

Allen found teaching more rewarding and better suited to his taste than practicing medicine, and he acquired an enthusiasm for providing blind persons with a chance to live independent lives without the need of charitable assistance. He returned to the United States in 1888 and became the headmaster of the boys' school of Perkins Institution. There he worked with Michael Anagnos, the son-in-law and successor to Samuel Gridley Howe, who had established the school in 1831. In 1890, at the age of twenty-nine, Allen was named principal of the Pennsylvania Institution for the Blind in Philadelphia. Although his premature baldness had led the trustees to believe they were hiring an older man, his performance soon justified their initial confidence. The following year, on July 9, Allen married Katharine Francena Gibbs of Westfield, Mass., a teacher at Perkins. They had three children: Isabel Sturtevant, Caroline Kittredge, and Edward Ellis.

In his seventeen years as principal, Allen transformed what had been a cheerless charitable home into a vibrant educational institution. Allowing the department of manufactures and sales to languish and die, he stressed instead reading, music, nature study, and athletics; and he initiated a program to help graduates of the school to find employment. He replaced the widely used Howe type with the New York Point type, which blind students found easier to learn and which, unlike Howe, they could write as well as read. Allen was also an early and enthusiastic advocate of the introduction of Braille. Determined to broaden his knowledge of the psychology of educating handicapped children, he spent the summers of 1895 and 1896 studying with G. Stanley Hall at Clark University, and he formed a close working relationship with Edward R. Johnstone, director of the Vineland (N.J.) Training School for the feebleminded. One of Allen's most important contributions was to move the Pennsylvania Institution from inadequate and overcrowded facilities in Philadelphia to new, well-designed quarters in suburban Overbrook.

In 1907, following the death of Michael Anagnos, Allen was appointed director of the Perkins Institution. Here at least he did not have to create a "new spirit" as he had in Pennsylvania. Under Howe and Anagnos, ideals were established which brought a sense of dignity and purpose to blind men and women, and a standard of dedication to their teachers.

Allen moved Perkins to a suburban estate in Watertown, Mass., where it became a standard for many similar institutions. Believing with the school's founder that the successful socialization of blind students would only emerge from a family environment, he reestablished at the new facility the "cottage-family" plan. In this way, students, teachers, and, frequently, guests could live, eat, and play together.

Allen's concern for the proper educational guidance of the blind led him to sponsor scientific research into the psychology of blindness and to attempt to raise the teaching of the blind to the level of a profession.

In 1916, in cooperation with his successor at the Pennsylvania Institution at Overbrook, he interested Samuel P. Hayes, professor of psychology at Mount Holyoke College, to devote part of his time to the development of tests and measurements for use with the blind students. The resulting Hayes-Binet Intelligence Tests helped dispel the popular belief that blind people in general are mentally defective and for the first time permitted the accurate classification of blind pupils.

In 1920 Allen cooperated with Harvard University in presenting a series of extension lectures on the education of the blind, a series which laid the groundwork for the subsequent introduction of graduate courses on the education of the blind by universities throughout America. His other activities on behalf of the blind included participation in programs for the prevention of blindness, the establishment of classes for the partially seeing (he helped to establish the first such school in the United States in Boston), and, in 1932, the establishment of a summer camp for the blind in Manchester, N.H.

In his lifelong crusade for educational reform for the blind, Allen used many forums. Beginning in 1909 he served three terms as a member of the Massachusetts Commission for the Blind; he was president of the department of special education of the National Education Association, and the Massachusetts Association of Instructors of the Blind (1915). He was also a prolific contributor of scholarly papers to journals and the conventions of professional societies. In 1931 Allen was involuntarily retired as director of the Perkins Institution because of his age and the onset of deafness. He carried on his writing and his professional activities until his death of uremia at Muhlenburg Hospital in Plainfield, N.J. His remains were buried in Newton Cemetery, Newton Center, Mass.

[The Research Lib. at the Perkins School possesses a large body of material pertaining to Allen, including all his speeches and journal articles. The annual reports of both the Overbrook School and the Perkins School also contain useful information. The Harvard Class of 1884, *Twenty-fifth Anniversary Report* (1909), pp. 18–22, contains a largely autobiographical sketch by Allen. The only full biography of Allen is Katharine G. Allen, *Edward Ellis Allen* (1940), which contains a portrait. See also Ishbel Ross, *Journey into Light* (1951), and Gabriel Farrell, *The Story of Blindness* (1956), Harvard Class of 1884, *Fiftieth Anniversary Report* (1934); and *Who Was Who in America*, III (1960).]

EDWARD J. WATERHOUSE

ALLEN, HENRY JUSTIN (Sept. 11, 1868-Jan. 17, 1950), newspaper publisher, governor of Kansas, was born in Pittsfield, Warren County, Pa., the second of four children and elder of two sons of John and Rebecca Elizabeth (Goodwin) Allen. Both parents were natives of Pennsylvania, the father of Scottish, the mother of English ancestry. In 1870 John Allen moved his family to a farm in Clay County, Kans., but lost it through a mortgage foreclosure in 1879, an event that soured his son on agriculture. After graduating from high school and working as a barber to earn his way, Henry Allen entered Baker University, Baldwin City, Kans., in 1890, but left after two years to begin newspaper work. On Oct. 19, 1892, he married Elsie Jane Nuzman of Circleville, Kans., whom he had met at Baker. Of their four children, only one, Henrietta, survived childhood.

Allen's first job was as a reporter on the *Salina* (Kans.) *Daily-Republican,* published by Joseph L. Bristow. He soon assumed the duties of chief editorial writer and advertising manager. In 1895 he joined Bristow in buying the *Ottawa* (Kans.) *Herald,* and in 1903 the *Salina Daily Republican-Journal*; Allen also bought interests in three other papers on his own. During these years his editorial efforts to revitalize the Republican party in Kansas contributed to the decline of the Populists. The partnership with Bristow was dissolved in 1905, and Allen assumed full ownership of the *Herald*; but two years later he sold all his newspaper interests and bought the *Wichita* (Kans.) *Beacon,* which he held until 1928. A crusading journalist, he used the *Beacon* as a means of exposing local corruption, suppressing saloons and the red-light district, and promoting the city-manager form of government.

Although previously a staunch Republican, Allen bolted the party in 1912 to support the Progressive presidential candidate Theodore Roosevelt. Two years later he ran unsuccessfully as the Progressive candidate for governor, but with that party's decline he joined his fellow editor William Allen White and other prominent Kansas Progressives in returning to the G.O.P. in 1916. Allen was an advocate of military preparedness, and in 1917, after America's entry into World War I, he and White went together to France as Red Cross officers. Allen's criticism of the military for its slowness in communicating with relatives of the dead and wounded nearly got him cashiered, but with White's assistance he was transferred to duty with the Y.M.C.A.

Meanwhile, in 1918, Allen won the Republican nomination for governor of Kansas; and although he was in France during the campaign, he was elected by the record margin of 150,000 votes. He was reelected in 1920. As governor, Allen advocated a number of reforms, including a bill to help farm tenants purchase land, a workmen's compensation law, and a new state constitutional convention, but little of his program passed the legislature. An enemy of the Ku Klux Klan, he instituted a suit in 1922 to oust the society from Kansas.

Allen was perhaps best known for the controversial Kansas Industrial Act of 1920, passed by a special session of the legislature after a prolonged miners' strike had brought a statewide shortage of coal. The measure effectively forbade strikes in a number of industries, including food production and fuel mining. It also created a court of industrial relations empowered to hear and settle labor disputes, and even to set minimum wages and maximum hours. Organized labor attacked the law as an instrument of "indentured servitude," but Allen, in a notable debate with A.F. of L. president Samuel Gompers in New York City in 1920, defended the measure as a necessary safeguard of the public's rights. The act had already fallen into disuse when the United States Supreme Court in 1923 ruled that its power to fix wages deprived an employer of his rights of property and liberty of contract without due process of law (*Wolff Packing Company* v. *Court of Industrial Relations* [262 U.S. 522]). Some observers have seen the law as a forerunner of the federal Taft-Hartley Act of 1947.

Following tradition, Allen did not seek reelection as governor in 1922, but he remained active in both politics and publishing. He served in 1923 as a commissioner for Near East Relief, surveying the problems of refugees, and in 1926-1927 as head of the department of journalism of the University World Travel School, a converted cruise ship. He was appointed to the United States Senate in 1929 to fill the unexpired term of Charles Curtis, who had just been elected vice-president, but lost to a Democrat when running for election to a full term in the depression year of 1930. Active in every presidential campaign through 1944, Allen served as national publicity director for the G.O.P. in 1928 and 1932.

Allen sold the *Wichita Beacon* in 1928, but from 1935 to 1940 he was part owner and editor of the *Topeka* (Kans.) *State Journal.* As a world traveler during the 1930's, Allen published several articles on international affairs. In 1941, as honorary national chairman of the Save the Children Federation, he visited nurseries established in England with American aid.

Small, portly, and bald, the genial Allen was considered a gifted orator throughout his career. Hard-won affluence and cultural enthusiasm were reflected in the Allens' patronage of art in Wichita and in the home designed for them in 1917 by the architect Frank Lloyd Wright. Allen was a Methodist. He died of a cerebral thrombosis in Wichita at the age of eighty-one and left an estate of more than $2.5 million.

[Allen's official papers as governor, and photographs of him, are at the Kans. State Hist. Soc., Topeka; his personal papers are in the Lib. of Cong.

Extensive newspaper clippings are at the Wichita Pub. Lib. and the Kans. State Lib., Topeka. Allen's activities in Europe during World War I are humorously recounted in William Allen White, *The Martial Adventures of Henry and Me* (1918); see also White's *Autobiog.* (1946). Helpful secondary works include John D. Bright, ed., *Kans.: The First Century,* II (1956), chaps. xxv and xxvi; William E. Connelley, ed., *Hist. of Kans.,* II (1928); Domenico Gagliardo, *The Kans. Industrial Court* (1941); Donald R. McCoy, *Landon of Kans.* (1966); Walter Johnson, *William Allen White's America* (1947); Homer E. Socolofsky, *Arthur Capper* (1962); A. Bower Sageser, *Joseph L. Bristow* (1968); and Francis W. Schruben, *Kans. in Turmoil: 1930–1936* (1969). Useful newspaper appraisals are in the *Wichita Beacon,* Apr. 7, 1929 and Jan. 17, 1950; *Topeka State Jour.,* Jan. 17, 1950; *Topeka Daily Capital,* Jan. 18, 1950; and *Wichita Eagle,* Jan. 21, 1962. Family data from Warren County (Pa.) Hist. Soc. and Kans. State Hist. Soc.]

FRANCIS W. SCHRUBEN

ALLEN, HERVEY (Dec. 8, 1889-Dec. 28, 1949), poet, teacher, biographer, historical novelist, was born in Pittsburgh, Pa., and christened William Hervey Allen, Jr.; he was the eldest of the three sons and two daughters of William Hervey Allen, the inventor of an automatic stoker for blast furnaces, and Helen Eby (Myers) Allen. His paternal grandparents, Edward Jay Allen and Elizabeth (Robinson) Allen, were of western Pennsylvania pioneer stock and English descent. Allen received his early education in Pittsburgh schools and entered the United States Naval Academy at Annapolis in 1909. Two years later he withdrew because of injuries sustained in athletics, though he once told an interviewer, Robert van Gelder, probably in jest, that he was "kicked out." In 1915 he received the B.S. degree with honors from the University of Pittsburgh.

Allen enlisted in the Pennsylvania National Guard in 1915 and served with an infantry company on the Mexican border. Although he had been writing poetry for some time, none had had the success of the pamphlets he published during these years, *Ballads of the Border* (1916), which sold very well on nearby college campuses. During World War I, he was a first lieutenant in the 111th Infantry, 28th Division, A.E.F. Wounded during the battle for a bridgehead at Fismes, he afterward took part in the attack on Montfaucon in the Meuse-Argonne drive. His experiences are realistically narrated in his *Toward the Flame: A War Diary* (1926; rev. ed., 1934), a work described by the critic Herbert F. West as "among the best books on World War I" (p. 207).

After a period of graduate study at Harvard in 1920, Allen settled in Charleston, S.C., where he taught English in a high school and became a close friend of DuBose Heyward. He and Heyward founded the Poetry Society of South Carolina, and collaborated on a book of poems about the legends of Charleston, *Carolina Chansons* (1922). Earlier Allen had published *Wampum and Old Gold* (1921), containing probably his best known poem, "The Blind Man," a somber war ballad; *Blind Man* was published separately in 1923. Among his eight books of verse are *Earth Moods and Other Poems* (1925), praised by Harriet Monroe, and *New Legends* (1929). Allen's outstanding reputation as a poet in the 1920's did not endure.

Allen was a member of the department of English at Columbia University (1925-1926), lectured on American literature at Vassar (1926-1927), and for a number of years after 1929 he lectured on poetry at the Bread Loaf Writers' Conference in Middlebury, Vt. He married Annette Hyde Andrews, daughter of Charles W. Andrews, a Syracuse attorney, on June 30, 1927, at Cazenovia, N.Y. She had attended Allen's lectures while a student at Vassar. They had three children: Marcia Andrews, Mary Ann, and Richard Francis.

Allen's most important work of nonfiction is the two-volume, enormously detailed biography *Israfel: The Life and Times of Edgar Allen Poe* (1926). The work, an impressive contribution to American literary biography, went through a number of printings and was praised by most reviewers. It was an attempt, Allen said, "to tell the story of Poe's life in more than usual detail; to get the essential narrative of time, place, events and personalities . . . in proper sequence and truthful relationship." Poe specialists, conceding the book's eminent readability, tend to find it too romantic and vividly written, misleading because it "lacks balance and sobriety" (Craig, p. cxxl). Allen collaborated with Thomas O. Mabbott in editing *Poe's Brother: The Poems of William Henry Leonard Poe* (1926).

In 1933 Allen published *Anthony Adverse,* a historical novel he had worked on for five years while living in Bermuda. The novel is "a throwback to the ancient and honorable picaresque tradition, tracing a handsome hero through the wars and bedrooms of the Napoleonic era in 1,224 pages of expertly-tailored prose," said literary historian Russel B. Nye (p. 46). The book was significant as the first in a number of long, adventure-packed historical novels highly popular in the United States through the period that saw Margaret Mitchell's *Gone With the Wind* (1936) and Kathleen Winsor's *Forever Amber* (1944). Allen's treatment of sexual themes was advanced for the times. His novel, one of the best selling historical novels of all times, sold 395,000 copies the first year (in the midst of the depression), and was eventually translated into eighteen foreign languages. By 1968 total sales were nearly 3,000,000. In an article, "The Sources of *Anthony Adverse*," in the *Saturday Review of Literature* (Jan. 13, 1934), Allen replied heatedly to accusations that he had misused historical source material.

With royalties from *Anthony Adverse*, Allen bought Bonfield Manor, an estate on the eastern shore of Maryland, near the village of Oxford. His next novel, *Action at Aquila* (1938), a Civil War story, narrated the adventures of Col. Nathaniel Franklin of the 6th Pennsylvania Cavalry. The book, which lacked the flamboyance and complexity of *Anthony Adverse*, failed to repeat that great popular success, as did *It Was Like This* (1940), composed of two starkly realistic war stories about the Western Front during the summer of 1918. Allen then began a projected five-volume series of novels about Colonial America, with an eighteenth-century protagonist, Salathiel Albine, a soldier and adventurer on the western Pennsylvania frontier. The complete series was to be called *The Disinherited*. Three volumes were published: *The Forest and the Fort* (1943), *Bedford Village* (1944), and *Toward the Morning* (1948). The author was working on the fourth volume, *City in the Dawn* (1950), when he died of a heart attack at his home, The Glades Estate, Miami, Fla. He was buried in the National Cemetery at Arlington with full military rites.

Allen's claim to lasting recognition as a man of letters may ultimately rest upon his biography of Poe, rather than his poetry and novels, skillfully written and popular as the latter were. His fiction, notable for historical authenticity and episodic sweep, has been for the most part ignored by serious literary critics. An energetic and prolific writer, Allen characterized himself as a "Jeffersonian democrat" and a "methodical person," who wrote slowly "a few paragraphs a day."

Allen was portrayed by an acquaintance as "a tall (six feet, four inches), florid, blond man, partly bald, who resembles an English country gentleman." In World War II, he worked with the War Manpower Commission. From 1943 until his death, he edited, with Carl Carmer, the *Rivers of America* series. He was on the original staff of the *Saturday Review of Literature*. Allen was affiliated with the Episcopal church, and served on the board of governors of St. John's College, Annapolis, and as a trustee of the University of Miami and Cazenovia (N.Y.) Junior College.

[Allen's personal papers, books, correspondence, and manuscripts are at the Univ. of Pittsburgh. A genealogy compiled by Allen and in his hand is in the archives, Univ. of Miami, Coral Gables, Fla. For an appreciation of Allen as a teacher, by a former high school student, see James I. Wallace, *Literary Digest*, Aug. 11, 1934. *Nat. Cyc. Am. Biog.*, XXXVII, 67; Stanley J. Kunitz, ed., *Twentieth Century Authors* (1950); Harry R. Warfel, *American Novelists of Today* (1951); Dilly Tante, ed., *Living Authors* (1937); James D. Hart, *The Popular Book* (1950); J. S. Wilson, "Poe and the Biographers," *Virginia Quarterly Rev.*, Apr. 1927; Edward Davison (who taught with Allen at Vassar), "Hervey Allen," *The Carrell*, June 1960; Harriet Monroe, "Epic Moods," *Poetry*, Nov. 1925; Robert van Gelder, *N.Y. Times Book Review*, July 6, 1941; Herbert F. West, *The Mind on the Wing* (1947); Hardin Craig, *E. A. Poe* (1935); Russel B. Nye, *The Unembarrassed Muse* (1970); Montgomery M. Culver, Jr. "Hervey Allen, Historical Novelist" (Ph.D. dissertation, Univ. of Illinois, 1959); obituaries in the *N.Y. Times*, Dec. 29, 1949, and *Miami Herald*, Dec. 29 and 30, 1949.]

WILLIAM McCANN

ALLEN, VIOLA EMILY (Oct. 27, 1867–May 9, 1948), actress—named for the heroine of Shakespeare's *Twelfth Night*—was born in Huntsville, Ala., the elder daughter and the first of the four children of C[harles] Leslie Allen and Sarah Jane (Lyon) Allen, both of the stage. Her father, whose great-grandfather had emigrated from England to Braintree, Mass., in 1752, was a native of Boston. Her mother was born in England. When Viola was about three, the family settled in Boston, where her father became a member of the Boston Theatre stock company. She was educated in a local school in suburban Boston, in Wyckham Hall, a church school in Toronto, Canada, and in Miss Cornell's School for Girls in New York City, when her father became a member of the Madison Square Theatre company.

At that theater, on July 4, 1882, Viola Allen made her professional debut as an ingenue, replacing Annie Russell in the title role in *Esmeralda*, by William Gillette (adapted from Frances Hodgson Burnett's novel). Although only fourteen and relying mainly on her father's coaching in Shakespearean roles, she was a success, and she toured in a road company of the play the following season, then briefly supported Mrs. D. P. Powers and William E. Sheridan. In 1883–1884 she joined tragedian John McCullough on his final tour, playing Shakespearean and classical roles (Cordelia, Desdemona, Portia, Imogen, Lady Anne; Julia in *The Hunchback*, Julia in *The Gladiator*, Tarquinia in *Brutus*, Virginia in *Virginius*, and Parthenia in *Ingomar*). Subsequent seasons found her playing comedy and dramatic roles at various theaters; then resuming her classical repertoire, she toured as leading lady successively to Lawrence Barrett,

Tomasso Salvini, and Frederic de Belleville. During the 1888-1889 season, she played several leading parts with the Boston Museum stock company, including Mrs. Errol (Dearest) in Frances Hodgson Burnett's *Little Lord Fauntleroy* and Gertrude Ellingham in Bronson Howard's Civil War drama *Shenandoah*. She returned to New York in the latter play (Star Theatre, Sept. 9, 1889), but was forced to leave the company because of a prior commitment to Joseph Jefferson and W. J. Florence, with whose comedy troupe she toured, notably as Lydia Languish in *The Rivals* and Cicely Homespun in *The Heir-at-Law*. She next appeared in New York in *The Merchant* (1891) and in *Aristocracy* (1892).

A beautiful girl with large, expressive eyes and an air of refinement, Viola Allen became leading lady at Charles Frohman's Empire Theatre in New York in 1893. She created nearly a score of roles during the next five seasons, but left Frohman in 1898 over a contract dispute: objecting to her assignment in *The Conquerors,* she wanted the right to refuse a part on moral grounds. She advanced to stardom under the management of George Tyler as Glory Quayle in Hall Caine's *The Christian* (Knickerbocker Theatre, Oct. 10, 1898). During 1900-1901 she starred in Lorimer Stoddard's romantic drama *In the Palace of the King*; and in 1902 she played Julia in the all-star revival of *The Hunchback* and Roma in Caine's *The Eternal City.* She then toured (under the management of her brother, Charles W. Allen) in a series of opulent Shakespearean revivals: as Viola in *Twelfth Night* (1903-1904), as Hermione and Perdita in *The Winter's Tale* (1904-1905), as Rosalind in *As You Like It* (1905), and as Imogen in *Cymbeline* (1906-1907).

On Aug. 16, 1905, in Louisville, Ky., Viola Allen secretly married Peter Edward Cornell Duryea, the Brooklyn-born co-owner of a stock farm near Lexington, Ky., where he bred and trained champion trotting horses.

In May 1906 the actress opened in New York in Clyde Fitch's *The Toast of the Town* and during the ensuing decade she appeared in a succession of classical, romantic, and contemporary parts. *The White Sister* was her single unimpressive venture into motion pictures (Essanay Company, 1915). Neither *Macbeth* (co-starring with James K. Hackett) nor the Shakespeare Tercentenary *Merry Wives of Windsor* (as Mistress Ford), both in 1916, achieved popular success; and critic Brander Matthews found Lady Macbeth "little more

fitted to her temperament than Juliet would be to that of Marie Dressler" (*New York Telegraph,* Feb. 8, 1916). Her last stage appearance was as Margaret Russell in a single benefit performance of *When a Feller Needs a Friend* (New Amsterdam Theatre, New York, Dec. 1, 1918).

Following her retirement, Allen and her husband spent much time abroad before his death in December 1944. She actively supported several theatrical and charitable organizations; she was a member of the Episcopal Actors Guild; and horseback riding, motoring, and book-collecting were her favorite recreations. She died on May 9, 1948, at her New York City home and was buried in Sleepy Hollow Cemetery, Tarrytown, N.Y.

Journalist Henry Tyrrell generously ranked Viola Allen with Maude Adams, Minnie Maddern Fiske, Julia Marlowe, and Ada Rehan among the "small but supreme group of our native actresses" (*Cosmopolitan,* Feb. 1913, p. 410). She sustained star status through a transition from classical to realistic acting style, sometimes alternating between the two in a single season. Eschewing the advancing Ibsen school, she established herself chiefly in Shakespearean and costume parts. As she put it in 1903, "I like to play the real—the dramatized truth clothed with some of those idealistic verities we all possess. A little romance in these days of materialism does much to lighten and leaven the whole" (Coward, *Theatre,* Feb. 1903).

[A MS. autobiography in the Museum of the City of New York, clippings in the Harvard Theatre Collect., and press books and the Robinson Locke Scrapbooks, N.Y. Public Lib., Theatre Collect., Lib for the Performing Arts, Lincoln Center, are basic sources. Articles by Viola Allen include "Life Is Tedious," *N.Y. Herald,* Jan. 31, 1897, 4th Sect., p. 10, with a drawing of Viola Allen; "What It Means to Be an Actress," *Ladies Home Jour.,* May 1899; "The Actor's Chances for Fame," *Pittsburgh Gazette Home Jour.,* Apr. 10, 1904; "My Beginnings," *Theatre,* Apr. 1906; "My Yesterdays," *Bohemian,* Feb. 1907; Edward Fales Coward, "An Interview with Viola Allen," *Theatre,* Feb. 1903; and F. Elderkin Fyles, "Viola Allen," *Leslie's Monthly,* July 1, 1903. Also by Viola Allen are "On the Making of an Actress," *Cosmopolitan,* Aug. 1901, and "Changing Styles of Acting," *The Green Book, Album,* June 1909. Other articles and books about Allen and interviews with her include: "Miss Viola Allen's Quest for 'Atmosphere,'" *N.Y. Telegraph,* Sept. 14, 1902; "Viola Allen, Fair Apostle of Joyousness," *N.Y. Telegraph,* Feb. 14, 1904; Walter Browne and E. De Roy Koch, eds., *Who's Who on Stage,* 1908, pp. 12-14 (1908); John Bouvé Clapp and Edwin Francis Edget, *Players of the Present,* p. 622 (1901; reissued 1970); Margherita Hamm, "Viola Allen: Her Domestic Gods," in *Eminent Actors in Their Homes,* pp. 139-149 (1902); Grace E. Drew, "Stars Seen by Day: Viola Allen at Home," *Ev'ry Month,* Jan. 1, 1899; Ward Morehouse, "Viola Allen's Remarkable

Career," *N.Y. Sun*, Feb. 22, 1935 (a chronology of the actress' stage career, prepared by Johnson Briscoe); Helen Ormsbee, "Miss Viola Allen, Past and Present," *N.Y. Herald Tribune*, Jan. 19, 1941; Chauncey L. Parsons, "Viola Allen: Classical, Historical and Modern Plays," *N.Y. Dramatic Mirror*, Mar. 20, 1912; Robert H. Prall, "Viola Allen's Cup of Life Brims Full," *N.Y. World-Telegram*, Oct. 19, 1946; May Davenport Seymour, "Viola Allen," *Shakespeare Assoc. Bull.*, July 1948; Lewis C. Strong, *Actresses of the Day in America*, First Series (1899) and Second Series (1901); William Winter, *The Wallet of Time* (1913), Vol. II; and *Woman's Who's Who of America* (1914–1915); George C. D. Odell, *Annals of the New York Stage*, vols. XI-XV (1939–1940); *Nat. Cyc. Am. Biog.*, XXXIV, 462–463; Andrew B. Myers in *Notable Am. Women*, I (1971).

Obituaries appeared in the May 10, 1948, issues of the *N.Y. Herald-Tribune*, the *N.Y. Sun*, and the *N.Y. Times*, and in *Variety*, on May 12, 1948.

Photographs abound in the Robinson Locke Scrapbooks, in many of the articles and books here cited, in Marie Burroughs, *Stage Celebrities*, and in the Crawford Theatre Collect., Yale Univ.

Miss Allen gave her press books and photographs to the N.Y. Public Lib. (Lib. for the Performing Arts, Lincoln Center, N.Y.); her stage costumes and memorabilia to the Museum of the City of N.Y. Voice recordings are in the Hist. Sound Recordings Collect., Yale Univ.]

PAT M. RYAN

AMES, OAKES (Sept. 26, 1874-Apr. 28, 1950), botanist, was born in North Easton, Mass., the second son and youngest of six children of Oliver Ames (1831-1895), financier and governor of Massachusetts, and Anna Coffin (Ray) Ames; he was a grandson of Oakes Ames, one of the builders of the Union Pacific Railroad. As a boy, Ames became interested in botany when he collected wildflowers with his father, and he was fascinated by the colorful beauty of the orchids grown in the family greenhouses. After preparing at Hopkinson's School in Boston, he entered Harvard, determined to make the study of orchids his lifework. He received the A.B. degree in 1898 and then joined the Harvard faculty as assistant in botany, receiving the A.M. degree in 1899. He served as instructor (1900-1910), assistant professor (1915-1926), professor (1926-1932), and Arnold professor of botany (1932–1935), and in 1935 was appointed research professor of botany, a post he retained until his retirement in 1941.

During his long association with Harvard, Ames held a number of other positions, many of them administrative. His intimate knowledge of the university's extensive botanical "empire" —the Botanical Garden and the Botanical Museum in Cambridge and the Arnold Arboretum in Jamaica Plain—served him well in his various capacities. As early as 1899 he became assistant director of the Botanical Garden, and in 1900, in collaboration with George Lincoln Goodale, he brought about the founding of

Harvard's Atkins' Garden in Cuba. In 1909 Ames succeeded Goodale as director of the Botanical Garden, a post he held until 1922. He was successively curator (1923-1927), supervisor (1927-1937), and director (1937-1945) of the Botanical Museum. When he became director, its activities were at a low ebb; when he relinquished his active administrative duties, he had firmly established the museum as one of the world's foremost research institutions in paleobotany, orchidology, and economic botany. In the years 1926-1935 Ames also exerted important leadership as chairman of two university bodies: the council of botanical collections, and the committee to consider the university's future work and needs in biology. His administrative ability and his skill at fund-raising found full play in the planning and construction of Harvard's Biological Laboratories, a large, modern plant housing most of the university's experimental biology. He was also instrumental in the difficult task of amalgamating the various departments of botany and zoology into the single department of biology. During this same period, as supervisor of the Arnold Arboretum (1927-1935), Ames more than doubled its endowment, broadened its research activities to include work in genetics, forest pathology, and plant ecology, and brought members of the Arboretum staff within the teaching framework of the university.

In spite of these heavy responsibilities, Ames never neglected his chief interest, orchids. As an undergraduate he had visited various orchid collections in Europe. Aware of the chaotic condition of orchid taxonomy, in 1905 he embarked with his assistants on a study tour that included the Lindley Herbarium at Kew, the Muséum d'Histoire Naturelle in Paris, and the Rijksherbarium in Leiden. In 1908 he wrote the section on the Orchidaceae for the seventh edition of *Gray's New Manual of Botany,* and his interests gradually widened to include the orchids of the Philippines, Florida, the Caribbean, and Central and South America. From the beginning, he collected on a large scale both living and herbarium specimens; these collections formed the basis of the Ames Botanical Laboratory at North Easton. The living collection was later given to the New York Botanical Garden, and the herbarium was transferred to the Botanical Museum at Harvard, where, under Ames's direction and endowment, it became one of the two world centers for studying the taxonomy and evolution of the Orchidaceae. The herbarium is unique in having an extensive collection of critically identified floral dissections preserved in glycerine on glass slides—a valuable innovation by Ames for rapid consultation. It is also rich in type specimens, and Ames himself described more than a thousand species new to science. The unusually inclusive library of orchid literature which he amassed forms an integral working part of the herbarium.

Ames won almost equal recognition as a pioneer in the interdisciplinary field of economic botany, which he defined broadly as the study of plants useful or harmful to man in relation to human progress. He first taught a course in this subject in 1909-1910; and his interest took a firm hold five years later when Edward Murray East asked him to teach a course in medical botany at Harvard's Bussey Institution (a graduate school of applied biology). From these beginnings grew the course in economic botany that Ames taught regularly in the department of biology at Harvard. Over the years he assembled his own herbarium of cultivated and useful plants, together with an extensive collection of plant products and a library covering all aspects of useful plants, exclusive of ornamentals. These, too, he donated to Harvard's Botanical Museum. Ames's own *Economic Annuals and Human Cultures* (1939) has become one of the classics that has helped orient modern thinking in economic botany. His thesis, at that time unorthodox, that civilization had been directly dependent on the angiosperm seed and the annual growth habit that the angiosperms developed, and that agriculture was far older than anthropologists then allowed, was subsequently supported by several archaeological finds.

On May 15, 1900, Ames married Blanche Ames of Lowell, Mass.—daughter of Adelbert Ames, Reconstruction governor of Mississippi and granddaughter of Gen. Benjamin F. Butler—and shortly thereafter established their lifelong home, "Borderland," at North Easton. Their four children were Pauline, Oliver, Amyas, and Evelyn. Blanche Ames became a leading botanical artist and drew the illustrations for many of her husband's publications. Their joint book, *Drawings of Florida Orchids,* appeared in 1947.

Many honors came to Ames, among them the Centennial Medal (1929) and the George Robert White Medal (1935) of the Massachusetts Horticultural Society, an honorary degree (1938) from Washington University in St. Louis, and, the honor he valued the most, election as a fellow of the Linnean Society of London (1905). Ames's interests were broad and

included music, literature, and sports, particularly baseball and football, which he had played on Harvard teams as an undergraduate. Like many New Englanders, Ames was conservative in politics and liberal in religion, a lifelong Republican and a Unitarian. He found little or no conflict between his religious philosophy and his science, and more than once told his students that his views in both fields might be summed up in Tennyson's "Flower in the Crannied Wall." Ames died of heart failure at the age of seventy-five at his winter home, "The Whim," at Ormond, Fla. He was buried in the Ames family plot in the cemetery at North Easton.

[Biographical sketch by Paul C. Mangelsdorf in Oakes Ames, *Orchids in Retrospect* (1948), which also includes a bibliography of Ames's publications; obituary by Richard Evans Schultes in *Rhodora*, Mar. 1951, and in Linnean Soc. of London, *Proc.* (1949-1950), pt. 2, 223-228; *Nat. Cyc. Am. Biog.*, LXXX, 569-570, 573 (on Ames and his wife); conversations and correspondence with Mrs. Francis T. P. Plimpton; personal knowledge.]
                                    RICHARD EVANS SCHULTES

ANDERSON, BENJAMIN McALESTER

(May 1, 1886-Jan. 19, 1949), economist, was born in Columbia, Mo., the second of four children and only son of Benjamin McLean Anderson and Mary Frances (Bowling) Anderson. Both parents were natives of Missouri and were descended from families which had moved west from Virginia. His father ran a successful livestock and livery business and traded in real estate; he was active in the Southern Methodist Church and also in politics, serving as presiding judge of the Boone County court and as a state senator (1897-1899). From the many political conferences young Benjamin witnessed at home, he absorbed a keen interest in political and economic issues.

After graduating from the Columbia high school in 1902, he entered the University of Missouri in Columbia, from which he received the A.B. degree in 1906. While in college he taught history during the summer of 1905 at the State Normal School at Cape Girardeau, Mo., and during the following academic year at the Columbia high school. Upon graduating he became professor of political economy and sociology at Missouri Valley College in Marshall (1906-1907), and then head of the department of history and political economy at the State Normal School at Springfield. On May 27, 1909, he married Margaret Louise Crenshaw of St. Louis. Their four children were Benjamin McAlester (who died in infancy), John Crenshaw, William Bent, and Mary Louise.

Anderson took a leave of absence from teaching in 1909 to pursue graduate studies in economics. He received an A.M. degree from the University of Illinois in 1910 and a Ph.D. the following year from Columbia University, where he was influenced by John Dewey, John Bates Clark, and E. R. A. Seligman. Part of his doctoral dissertation won the Hart, Schaffner & Marx economics prize in 1910; it was published as *Social Value: A Study in Economic Theory, Critical and Constructive* (1911). Anderson looked upon his theory of social value as a substitute for the individualistic marginal utility theory as developed by the Austrian school. But as Henry Hazlitt pointed out in the book's foreword, it was actually an explanation of the "essentially social conditions which go to form both the individual's marginal valuations and prices in the Market" (p. v).

Anderson stayed on at Columbia as instructor in economics (1911), with promotion in 1913 to assistant professor. That fall he moved to Harvard, where for the next five years (again as assistant professor) he gave courses in money and banking, commercial crises, economic theory, and sociology. He left academic life in 1918 to become economic adviser to the National Bank of Commerce in New York City. Two years later he moved to the Chase National Bank as economist. There, until his resignation in 1939, he wrote and edited seventeen volumes of the influential *Chase Economic Bulletin*. Over the years Anderson used the *Bulletin* as a vehicle for his economic views, which he expressed at times with dogmatic conviction. He criticized the quantity theory of money as set forth by Irving Fisher, contending that the quantity of money and credit was less important than the quality, and that one of the theory's faults was that it retarded investigation of the underlying factors in the business situation. A staunch advocate of the gold standard and gold redemption, he opposed the gold exchange standard. He found little of substance in Keynesian doctrines or in the economic practices of the New Deal. In 1933 he was one of a group of forty-four economists who organized the Economists' National Committee on Monetary Policy, of which he later (1948) became president. National and world prosperity, Anderson believed, depended on free markets and a reduction in trade barriers. In his opinion, cheap money, deficit financing, and the substitution of bank credit for savings laid the basis for economic maladjustments and inflation.

Anderson left the Chase National Bank in 1939 to become professor of economics at the University of California at Los Angeles, and in 1946 he became Connell professor of banking. He died of a heart attack at the Santa Monica (Calif.) Hospital at the age of sixty-two and was buried in the Columbia (Mo.) Cemetery. Anderson's clear, forceful writings exerted great influence on the attitudes of the business community during the 1920's and 1930's, and he became one of the best-known economists of his generation.

[Anderson's books include *The Value of Money* (1917), *Effects of the War on Money, Credit and Banking in France and the U.S.* (1919), and *Economics and the Public Welfare* (1949). For family background, see the article on his father in Howard L. Conard, ed., *Encyc. of the Hist. of Mo.*, I, 40–41 (1901). Biographical material is scant: an unpublished memorial adopted by the Southern Section of the Academic Senate, Univ. of Calif., Oct. 25, 1949; obituary and editorial in the *N.Y. Times*, Jan. 20, 1949; and *Who Was Who in America*, II (1950). The author received the help of many people in gathering data, including Mrs. Elizabeth Comfort, reference librarian, State Hist. Soc. of Mo.; Alice H. Bonnell, curator, Columbiana Collection, Columbia Univ.; John D. Wilson of the Chase Manhattan Bank; Henry Hazlitt, Wilton, Conn.; and Prof. Dudley F. Pegrum, Univ. of Calif., Los Angeles.]

BENJAMIN HAGGOTT BECKHART

ANDERSON, EDWIN HATFIELD (Sept. 27, 1861–Apr. 29, 1947), librarian, was born in Zionsville, Ind., the seventh of the ten children of Philander and Emma Amanda (Duzan) Anderson. His father, a physician, was a Pennsylvanian of Scottish ancestry; his mother, of French descent, was a native of Tennessee. The Andersons, strict Presbyterians, named their son for a minister of that denomination, Edwin Hatfield. An older brother, Albert Barnes Anderson (named for the Rev. Albert Barnes), became a federal district court judge. During Edwin's childhood the family moved to Anthony, Kans., where he completed his public school education. He entered Wabash College in Crawfordsville, Ind.—his father's alma mater—in 1879 and graduated four years later with an A.B. degree.

Anderson once said that he decided to become a librarian while in college, but it was not until the fall of 1890 that he entered the pioneering New York State Library School at Albany, N.Y., which had been founded shortly before by Melvil Dewey. He spent the intervening years reading law, writing for a Sunday school paper and for Chicago newspapers, and teaching school in Chicago. At Albany he worked part-time in the library of the Y.M.C.A. to help pay his expenses. Family needs called him home in May 1891 before the completion of his first year of study, but he had managed to attend many of the lectures given before the second-year or senior class.

Anderson's career as a professional librarian began in June 1891 when he was hired by the Newberry Library in Chicago as a cataloguer. On December 22 of that year he married Frances R. Plummer of Glencoe, Ill., a sister of the librarian Mary Wright Plummer. The couple had no children of their own, but after World War I adopted two French girls, Cecile and Charlotte. Anderson remained at the Newberry through April 1892, and in the following month became librarian of the Carnegie Free Library, Braddock, Pa., the second of the many public libraries set up with funds given by Andrew Carnegie. In 1895 he was called to Pittsburgh to organize that city's Carnegie Library. There, over the next nine years, Anderson planned the new library, even designing many of the furnishings and arrangements. He assembled a remarkable staff, organized strong departments for children and for the study of science and technology, and developed a system of branch libraries. In 1900, again through the generosity of Carnegie, he established a training school for children's librarians which was to become pre-eminent in its field. It later became the Carnegie Library School, affiliated with the Carnegie Institute of Technology.

Anderson left library work in 1904 to become a partner in a zinc and lead mining enterprise at Carthage, Mo. He returned to his profession two years later, however, as director of the New York State Library and Library School in Albany, succeeding Melvil Dewey. In 1908 he moved to New York City as assistant director of the New York Public Library. He became director in May 1913, succeeding John Shaw Billings.

Anderson gave much of his time during his first years at the New York Public Library to the development of the fast-growing branch system. In the branches, and in the reference department at the main library, he displayed his remarkable ability to develop a strong staff, bringing in able, scholarly men and women who were trained in library procedures. His long administration saw the introduction of a number of new departments, including a reader's advisory service, theatre and picture collections, a municipal reference library, and traveling bookmobiles. In 1911, again with funds given by Carnegie, Anderson organized a library school at the New York Public Library (with Mary Wright Plummer as principal),

which trained many of the future leading experts in the reference and circulation work of the period. He later (1926) took an active part in organizing the School of Library Service of Columbia University, formed through the consolidation of the New York State Library School and the Library School of the New York Public Library.

Anderson was a handsome, genial man, full of humorous stories which he told with gusto, but he was reticent about his personal life and reserved in his statements about library policy. Because of his strong distaste for personal publicity, he was little known outside his profession. He was active in professional organizations and served as president of the American Library Association in 1913-1914. He received honorary degrees from Carnegie Institute of Technology, New York University, Wabash College, and Columbia.

Anderson retired as director of the New York Public Library in 1934, at the age of seventy-three. He had lived in Scarsdale, N.Y., during much of the time he was with the library and ascribed his exceptionally good health to his regular cross-country walks in Westchester County. He had long maintained a summer home in Dorset, Vt., and it became his permanent address until the last year of his life, when he and his wife moved to a new home in Williamsburg, Va. Anderson died of a coronary thrombosis in 1947 while on a visit to one of his daughters in Evanston, Ill., and was cremated, without service or burial.

[*The First Quarter Century of the N.Y. State Lib. School, 1887-1912* (1912) contains Anderson's recollections as a student. For memorials, see H. M. Lydenberg (Anderson's successor as director of the N.Y. Public Lib.) in *N.Y. Libraries*, Nov. 1834; Am. Lib. Assoc., *Bull.*, Aug. 1947, and *Lib. Jour.*, Sept. 15, 1947; and F. F. Hopper in N.Y. Public Lib., *Bull.*, June 1947. Brief biographies appeared in *Who's Who in Lib. Service*, 2nd ed. (1943); *Who Was Who in America*, II (1950); N.Y. State Lib. School Assoc., *Register, 1887-1926* (1959); *Nat. Cyc. Am. Biog.*, Current Vol. D, 56-57; and *N.Y. Times*, May 1, 1947 (obituary). See also profile in the *New Yorker*, Dec. 21, 1929. An unpublished biobibliography by Max M. Gilstrap (Emory Univ., 1963) is on file at the N.Y. Public Lib. Anderson's contributions to professional education are recorded in Sarah K. Vann, *Training for Librarianship Before 1923* (1961); and Ray Trautman, *A Hist. of the School of Lib. Service, Columbia Univ.* (1954). Information on Anderson's family background and his early years was provided by his daughter Charlotte (Mrs. John W. Green, Jr.), Danbury, Conn., and Gerald R. Dreyer, Public Information Director, Wabash College.]

EDWARD G. FREEHAFER

ANGELL, JAMES ROWLAND (May 8, 1869-Mar. 4, 1949), psychologist and college president, was born in Burlington, Vt., where his father, James Burrill Angell, was then president of the state university. Two years later his father became president of the University of Michigan at Ann Arbor, where the son spent most of his boyhood. His mother, the former Sarah Swope Caswell, was the daughter of Alexis Caswell, president of Brown University. The youngest of three children, with a sister six years older and a brother twelve years older, he spent much time alone, and he perhaps lacked something in robustness, partly as a result of an early attack of scarlet fever, which left him deaf in one ear. He recalled having been "rather oversensitive" and "somewhat timid and unassertive." But he appears to have relished the atmosphere in his father's home, where notables often visited. For a year and a half, when he was eleven, the family lived in Peking, where his father was United States minister to China. The boy's diary regarding the Far East reveals a precisely observant mind, enthusiastic but conventional.

Except for this single interruption, Angell attended public schools in Ann Arbor. He received the B.A. from the University of Michigan in 1890 and the M.A. in 1891. Despite a strong attraction toward athletics, he did very well academically. He took the classical course and elected logic and psychology. His definite sense of intellectual commitment came when he read John Dewey's textbook on psychology (published in 1886) perhaps at the time of Dewey's arrival at Michigan as a professor in 1889. This book, he later recalled, "instantly opened up a new world, which it seemed to me I had been waiting for" (Murchison, III, 5). He now plunged into the major branches of philosophy, but found himself most greatly stimulated during his graduate year by a seminar with Dewey on the *Principles of Psychology* by William James, a book which he said "unquestionably affected my thinking for the next 20 years more profoundly than any other" (*ibid.*). Nonetheless, in that still unspecialized era his master's thesis was a study of imagery in certain English poets, and he minored in economics and American history.

Angell selected scholarship as a profession after an initial hesitation about his abilities which no doubt masked an intense desire to excel. His decision also meant a choice of remaining within the orbit of his father's personal contacts and advice or going to other areas. During the years that followed, his father (who continued as president at Michigan until 1909) did not hesitate to offer definite suggestions at every stage and to use his influence to sound out possible academic openings for his son. During Angell's first year of teaching, moreover, his father wrote (Nov. 4, 1893) urging him to "observe & study . . . the questions of administration. . . . There is a great lack of good administrators of colleges." More than once thereafter, the older man would pointedly joke with his son about the time when he, too, would become a college president. Yet Angell declared his independence in certain respects. His father was a devout Congregationalist; his son soon made it clear that he could not accept many traditional Christian dogmas, despite the grief which his doubts gave the older man. Still, he never became an avowed skeptic, carefully dissociating himself from the label of "materialist." He retained his Congregational membership all his life and attended church often.

During 1891-1892 Angell studied at Harvard under William James and Josiah Royce, dividing his time between philosophy and psychology. He enjoyed warm relations with James, temporarily becoming his research assistant. After receiving a second M.A. degree, he left for Europe in the summer of 1892. Unable to gain a place in Wilhelm Wundt's famous psychology laboratory, he spent a few months at Berlin studying under Hermann Ebbinghaus and Friedrich Paulsen; then he moved to Halle to study psychology with Benno Erdmann, and Kant with Hans Vaihinger. Much to his eventual regret, he never completed the Ph.D. degree: the offer of an instructorship at the University of Minnesota kindled a desire to return home and marry. Yet at that time a mere year of study in Germany crucially advanced one's American academic reputation. On Dec. 18, 1894, a year and a half after his return, he married Marion Isabel Watrous, a Michigan classmate from a prosperous Des Moines family, to whom he had been engaged since 1890. They had two children, James Waterhouse, later an economist at Columbia, and Marion Waterhouse Caswell.

After only a year at Minnesota, Angell accepted an invitation to become an assistant professor of philosophy at the University of Chicago. He was to be in charge of the psychology laboratory. At first his teaching duties were arduous, made more so by the summer sessions he taught to gain added income. For seven years he received no increase in rank or salary, perhaps because of his close tie with Dewey, who was not liked by President William Rainey Harper. Then, as he began to get tempting offers from elsewhere, he was promoted, first to associate professor in 1901, next to professor (1904), and to chairman of the newly independent department of psychology (for which he had previously fought) in 1905. A year later, at an unusually young age, he was elected president of the American Psychological Association. As a teacher, Angell was popular among advanced students for his intellectual keenness, his judiciousness in assessing controversial issues, and his witty flow of words. Graduate students in his laboratory, who included John B. Watson and Harvey Carr, were inspired to respectful affection by his warm, stimulating interest in their personal development.

Though Angell published half a dozen empirical research papers which were well received, his renown as a psychologist stemmed from his promotion of the Chicago school of psychology known as "functionalism," and from his telling criticisms of rival perspectives. His position was set forth in three books and a dozen articles, all written between 1903 and 1916. In *The Relations of Structural and Functional Psychology to Philosophy* (1903) he attacked the abstractly formalistic "structuralism" of the dogmatic Wundtian, Edward B. Titchener of Cornell, arguing that "structure and function represent simply two phases of a single fact." He urged psychologists to pay more attention to the dynamic flow of life; they should study longer temporal sequences of behavior and not chop up their observations into artificially tiny bits. They should stop trying to define what consciousness is and start inquiring about what it does. Adopting a biological analogy, as was appropriate for a believer in psychophysical parallelism, Angell said that consciousness is "really an efficient agent in the furtherance of the life-activities of the organism," springing into existence only when an adjustment of some kind, whether slight or large, becomes functionally necessary for the individual's survival.

Angell's widely used textbook, *Psychology* (1904), promoted Jamesian viewpoints in a more conventional language and arrangement. A series of lectures he gave at Union College, *Chapters from Modern Psychology* (1912), surveyed the entire field of academic psychology. Their tone was strongly positivistic throughout. In them and for the rest of his life Angell rejected Freudianism with evident distaste, though he sometimes grudgingly admitted the importance of the passions in motivating human action. However, though initially intrigued by

John B. Watson's experiments with animals, Angell grew into an equally outspoken critic of behaviorism. Well before his death he came to recognize that functionalism had not survived as a viable school of psychology, although he continued to argue for its value as a dynamic, comprehensive outlook and correctly viewed it as a significant development during a critical period in the growth of American psychology.

Angell eventually parted company with much of the thinking of William James, sending James several bluntly critical letters about the pragmatic theory of truth. Angell's own writings were hardly Jamesian at their core; they revealed no acceptance of intellectual relativism, no fascination with the complex inner texture of thought, and no feeling for the quality of ambivalence. Unlike James, Angell had a compelling desire for intellectual tidiness. His cheerful scientific rationalism was much closer to the mood of John Dewey, though even here Angell's mind remained far more deeply imprisoned in the absolutistic German ethos of "pure" research, which long predated pragmatism. As an educator, Angell, unlike Dewey, was not strongly utilitarian. He believed in the value of intellectual curiosity disciplined by scientific training.

His father, not James or Dewey, remained the most powerful influence in Angell's life. In 1908 Angell was strongly tempted to become president of Dartmouth College when that position was offered to him. Instead, he was made dean of the Senior College at the University of Chicago, and in 1911 "dean of the faculties," a post next in rank to that of president. Thereafter, although from 1912 to 1922 he edited an important psychological monographs series, he lost touch with the world of scholarship. During World War I he served on two army committees in Washington and then returned to Chicago as acting president of the university in 1918. But the return of President Harry Pratt Judson and the requirement that Chicago have a Baptist president (a provision subsequently dropped) blocked Angell's rise to the top. He grew restive, and in 1919 became chairman of the National Research Council. The next year he was elected to the National Academy of Sciences. In 1920 he accepted the presidency of the Carnegie Corporation, the holding organization for all the Carnegie philanthropies, even though it meant moving to New York.

A year later Angell was invited to become president of Yale University. The offer was made to him because of his extremely high reputation as an executive, and because a deadlock among rival candidates had made it seem wise to move toward an outsider. Still, from the perspective of Yale traditions it was a strange choice. Only one previous president of Yale, in the mid-eighteenth century, had not been a Yale graduate. Moreover, Angell's Midwestern background, scientific outlook, and intellectual seriousness all grated against the prevailing atmosphere of gentlemanly conservatism in New Haven. There are hints that Angell later regretted having accepted the position, but in 1921 he willingly did so, even though it meant a drop to half his former salary. The wish to be remembered, like his father, as president of a leading university perhaps influenced this decision.

Power at Yale had long resided in an oligarchy of the senior professors; the presidency was weak, particularly in the government of Yale College. Moreover, Angell remained overly self-conscious of his position as an outsider. Though he was not as self-effacing as his predecessor, Arthur T. Hadley, he did not strongly push forward his own viewpoints on most practical questions of policy. His desires to raise intellectual standards, develop graduate education, curb the excesses of intercollegiate football, and improve the tone of student life were all well known. But he lacked the personal thrust, and the united support, which would have allowed him to make a decided impact. Thus, though his intentions were not entirely unlike those of Robert Hutchins at Chicago or Alexander Meiklejohn at Amherst, he was not in their league as an influence in American higher education. During his sixteen-year term as its head, Yale transformed itself physically and increased its endowment more than fourfold. But the moving forces remained the trustees, the senior faculty, and a few rather ill-informed and arbitrary private philanthropists. More broadly, Yale College, which had experienced a long period of intellectual decline when Angell arrived, changed only slightly in the last few years of his administration. Angell's major personal achievements were the founding of the Yale Nursing School in 1923 and the Institute of Psychology in 1924 (which was expanded into the Institute of Human Relations in 1929). The professional schools and the graduate school of arts and sciences (the latter headed by Wilbur L. Cross) gained more autonomy and strength, and Angell helped push professorial appointments in a more scholarly direction.

The major physical change at Yale during Angell's administration, the adoption of a residential college plan for undergraduates in imitation of Oxford and Cambridge, resulted from an enormous gift by Edward S. Harkness, the oil millionaire. Beyond any doubt Angell sympathized with the basic college scheme, despite his seemingly contrary Germanic view of the university. But his unusually slow and meticulous involvement of the faculty in the matter and, still more remarkably, his personal lethargy —or second thoughts—while negotiating directly with Harkness created a delay in accepting the gift which very nearly cost Yale the money. Angell became *persona non grata* with Harkness, and the negotiations had to be completed by the provost Charles Seymour, later Angell's successor. Harkness' benefactions set the architectural stamp of pseudo-Georgian on Harvard; to Yale they brought the elaborate pseudo-Gothic of James Gamble Rogers.

On the everyday level Angell became a rather popular president. Though his democratic openness of manner repelled many associated with the university, he was admired for his after-dinner wit, his businesslike clarity and impartiality, and his way of keeping everyone equally at a distance. Around 1933 his politics may have offended some, for he gave measured support to the New Deal and the NRA, fearing much greater authoritarianism if they were to fail. But by 1936 he had become far more conservative. Unlike John Dewey, he said that the best cure for America's economic ills was a moral and spiritual regeneration. Further, there was a vagueness about many of his opinions. He even told his wife that his training as a psychologist prevented him from taking definite stands on issues and forced him to see all sides of everything. He did believe strongly in academic freedom. And he firmly opposed nazism as well as communism, although in 1935 he accepted a decoration from Mussolini's Italy. Many of his speeches were collected in *American Education* (1937).

Angell's first wife died on June 23, 1931, and on Aug. 2, 1932, he married Mrs. Katharine (Cramer) Woodman, of Ardmore, Pa. Retiring from Yale in 1937, he was offered a nomination as senator from Connecticut but declined to enter politics. Instead he became a full-time educational consultant to the National Broadcasting Company. He was national president of the English-Speaking Union from 1939 and director or trustee of several major museums. He died in his eightieth year, of recurrent carcinoma, at his home in Hamden, Conn., and was buried in the Grove Street Cemetery, New Haven.

[A useful brief autobiography by Angell is in Carl Murchison, ed., *A Hist. of Psychology in Autobiog.*, III, 1–38 (1936). A biographical sketch by Walter S. Hunter, emphasizing his psychological work, is in Nat. Acad. Sci., *Biog. Memoirs*, XXVI (1951); it includes a bibliography of his publications. See also, on his work in psychology, Darnell Rucker, *The Chicago Pragmatists* (1969). The major indispensable source for Angell's Yale years is George W. Pierson, *Yale: College and University, 1871–1937* (1955). A perceptive undergraduate sketch of Angell as Yale president is Maynard Mack, "Portraits from a Family Album," *Yale Literary Mag.*, Nov. 1931. A very complete obituary is in the *Yale Alumni Mag.*, Apr. 1949. An interview with Mrs. Angell was useful. Angell's extensive papers are at Yale. They contain few personal letters by him, but include his father's long series of letters to him. Large numbers of Angell's letters are in other collections: his father's papers at the Univ. of Mich.; the President's Papers at the Univ. of Chicago (for his letters to Harper); and the papers of a number of other prominent professors at Michigan and Chicago. A dozen letters to William James, in the James Papers at Harvard, reveal his reactions to Germany and his eventual open disagreement with James over the pragmatic theory of truth; in intellectual terms, they may be the most important documents of his entire life. A letter to George H. Howison, Jan 7, 1905, in the Howison Papers, Univ. of Calif., Berkeley, is important for showing how insistently he resented the label of "materialist" despite the positivistic tenor of many of his views.]

LAURENCE VEYSEY

ANTIN, MARY (June 13, 1881–May 17, 1949), author, social worker, and lecturer, was born in Polotsk, Russia, a city within Russia's "Pale of Settlement." She was the second daughter and second of six children of Israel and Esther (Weltman) Antin. Her father was trained as a rabbi, but at the time of Mary's birth he was a storekeeper. Her male ancestors, both paternal and maternal, achieved moderate business successes, and her paternal grandfather, Hayim, gained fame among Hasidic Jews as a holy man. Unlike most Jewish girls of the time, Mary and her elder sister received some education. As a child, Mary faced the horrors of the pogroms and the harsh realities of religious persecution and, before she was thirteen, she found it "very strange that the Czar and the police should want all of Russia for themselves." Physically delicate, Mary was also intellectually inquisitive and strongly independent. Probably influenced by her father's liberal rejection of orthodoxy, she questioned literal interpretations of ancient scriptures, and at one time declared herself an atheist. Later, she summed up her questioning by declaring, "I . . . think it doubtful if the conversion of the Jew to any alien belief or disbelief is thoroughly accomplished."

In 1891, Mary's father immigrated to America, settling in the Boston suburb of Chelsea, where he became a grocer. The family followed in 1894. There, young Mary enjoyed the benefits of free, public education, and then went on to a brilliant academic career at the Boston Latin School, at Teachers College of Columbia University, and at Barnard College. While at Barnard, on Oct. 6, 1901, she married Amadeus W. Grabau, son of a Lutheran minister, and a well-known geologist and onetime Columbia University professor. They had one daughter, Josephine, but separated in 1919 when her husband was forced to leave Columbia because of his pro-German position during World War I and moved to China.

Her autobiography, *The Promised Land,* was published in 1912. This book, an account of Jewish life in Czarist Russia and of that of a Jewish-American in Boston's slums, expressed the dreams and fears of many illiterate hyphenated Americans who could not speak or write for themselves. It won her a place as a commentator on Jewish immigrant life, equal to that of playwright Israel Zangwill, author of *The Melting Pot,* and Morris Rosenfeld, ghetto poet. But *The Promised Land,* which sold almost 85,000 copies, also appealed to native-born Americans, who sought reassurance that the great American "melting pot" could absorb the foreign-born without imperiling traditional national concepts of freedom, democracy, and hard work. Antin stated that her book told the story of Americanization—the "upheaval preceding the state of repose." If the Antins' conflicts over adoption of American religious and cultural practices illustrated the difficulties of immigrant adjustment, their staunch patriotism and eager acceptance of freedoms and opportunities denied them as Jews in Russia assured longer-time residents that America was, indeed, the promised land. Antin believed that her life story proved "what a real thing is this American freedom." The book so successfully convinced Americans of their nation's greatness that public schools continued using it as a civics class text as late as 1949.

Although she received many civic and literary honors in her lifetime, Mary Antin had the reputation of being an "unwilling celebrity." For six years after the publication of *The Promised Land,* she traveled about the country lecturing on America's meaning to the immigrant. Her last book, *They Who Knock at Our Gates,* confirmed her faith in "the sinew and bone of immigrants of all nations," and her belief in social reform rather than restriction of immigration as a solution to social and economic ills. Although she was not as well known as Jane Addams and a number of other women progressives, Antin aligned herself with the reformers by supporting the initiative, the referendum, conservation, and urban anti-slum, park, and playground movements.

On May 17, 1949, Antin died in Suffern, N.Y., after a long illness.

[The most detailed account of Mary Antin's early life, which contains pictures of the author, is *The Promised Land* (1912); her first book, *From Polotzk to Boston* (1899), is a series of letters written to her uncle in Russia about her experiences on the journey from Polotsk to Boston. Articles by Mary Antin include "The Soundless Trumpet," *The Atlantic*, April 1937, pp. 560–569, which focuses on individual improvement and the value of personal meditation as a means to understanding one's self, and "This Is Ours: The Treasure of Our Public Schools," *Women's Home Companion*, Nov. 1913, p. 16, which stresses the value of public education. Mary Antin's correspondence with Margaret Prescott Montague (author, 1876–1955) is to be found in the W. Va. Univ. Lib., and with Rabbi Maximillian Heller (1860–1929) in the Am. Jewish Arch., Cincinnati, Ohio. A portrait of Antin as a young woman may be found in the selection, "Mary Antin," by Mary H. Wade in *Pilgrims of Today* (1920), pp. 112–141. Obituaries appeared in the *N.Y. Herald Tribune* and the *N.Y. Times*, both on May 18, 1949, and in *Publisher's Weekly*, June 11, 1949, p. 2396.]

VIRGINIA McLAUGHLIN YANS

APPLETON, WILLIAM SUMNER (May 29, 1874-Nov. 24, 1947), antiquarian, was born in Boston, the only son and the second of five children of William Sumner Appleton and Edith (Stuart) Appleton. His father, a Unitarian, was a lawyer and an antiquarian, an authority on numismatics, heraldry, and geneaology.

The Appletons had been a prominent family in Massachusetts since the 1630's. One branch of the family moved, in about 1750, to New Ipswich, N.H., whence two brothers, Samuel and Nathan, came to Boston by 1794 and established themselves as merchants. Prosperity in trade enabled the brothers to participate in financing the emergent textile industry. Nathan, William's grandfather, also served several terms as a Whig congressman.

William grew up in the Beacon Street house his grandfather had built. Poor health impeded his progress at St. Paul's School and at Harvard. A condition of hypermetropic astigmatism was a major cause of a breakdown that ended participation in a real estate partnership Appleton had formed with a classmate after graduating from Harvard in 1896. Thereafter, for a decade, he felt limited in what he could do, and the decision of his father to leave the family wealth in trust seemed to Appleton an additional barrier between himself and the world of business. The impasse was left unchanged by

three tries at graduate school. In 1905-1906 Appleton attended the Bussey Institution, a school for agriculture attached to Harvard. The following year he studied architecture at the Harvard Graduate School of Arts and Sciences, and in 1907-1908 he was a student in the department of mining and metallurgy. Meanwhile, he pursued the rounds of the Boston gentleman, including service with several antiquarian organizations.

Indecision ended abruptly in 1910 with Appleton's founding of the Society for the Preservation of New England Antiquities (SPNEA). The immediate purpose of the society lay in acquiring and preserving historic buildings. Appleton foresaw that local groups, each preoccupied with a single structure or town, would always lack the freedom and power of a regional agency. Money and members came in slowly at the start, but by 1911 the society had acquired its first building. Forty more were added in Appleton's lifetime, most of them houses that dated from the seventeenth and eighteenth centuries.

The founding of the SPNEA coincided with a general awakening of sympathy for the arts and architecture of the colonial period. Appleton was instinctively drawn to houses of this period; as he later said in explaining the origins of the SPNEA, he had never known a time when he was not interested in the New England past. Of more specific influence on his interest were his participation in 1909 in the successful effort to save the Paul Revere house and his course in architecture with Denman Ross. Appleton was capable of valuing old houses both for their ancestral associations and for their place in the history of architecture. His interest in agriculture played an important part in determining the choice of buildings he wanted to preserve. It led him also to emphasize the collecting of archival materials relating to the history of architecture. The archives of the SPNEA soon came to rival its list of properties in value.

Appleton was less successful in developing a point of view on restoration. He was ahead of his time in appreciating the accretions time could add to a historic house, and he detested pretentious, ill-documented restorations. Yet he also sanctioned the contemporary practice of returning old buildings to their original condition. As preservation became a national movement and as projects on the scale of colonial Williamsburg seized attention, the SPNEA remained a personal instrument, sharing the strengths and weaknesses of its director. Appleton's single-mindedness and energy were coupled with a modesty and a zeal for thrift that at times became compulsive. He never married. Conservative in personal and political tastes, Appleton exemplified the narrowing relationship between certain upper-class Bostonians and the world about them. Late in the fall of 1947, Appleton died of a stroke and was buried in Mount Auburn Cemetery, Cambridge.

[The personal and professional papers of Appleton are at the SPNEA. The personal papers include diaries for the years 1906–1910 and occasional periods thereafter. Appleton's annual reports as corresponding secretary may be found in *Bull. of the Soc. for the Preservation of New England Antiquities*, 1910–1919, and thereafter in *Old-Time New England*, which replaced the *Bulletin*. Appleton contributed autobiographical sketches to successive editions of his Harvard College classbook, *Harvard University Class of 1896* (1899), *et seq.* A memorial notice appears in *Proc.* of the Mass. Hist. Soc., 69 (1956): 422–425, written by Bertram K. Little, who succeeded Appleton as director of the SPNEA. Little also contributed an essay on Appleton to Clifford L. Lord, ed., *Keepers of the Past* (1965). A chapter in Charles B. Hosmer, *Presence of the Past* (1965), describes the founding and development of the SPNEA. Louise Hall Tharp has written an informal history of the family, *The Appletons of Beacon Hill* (1973).]

DAVID D. HALL

ARLISS, GEORGE (April 10, 1868–Feb. 5, 1946), actor and playwright, was born in London, England, as George Augustus Andrews. He was the youngest of three boys and a girl born to William Arliss-Andrews. (His mother's name is not known.) The elder Andrews, a printer and publisher, was known for his liberality toward his drinking companions, a group of eccentrics and literati who frequented the British Museum nearby the Andrews home in middle-class Bloomsbury. This coterie of gentlemen served George Arliss well in later life when he searched for details to round out his many elegantly fashioned stage characterizations.

Stage-struck from the age of twelve, when at a children's Christmas party he was rushed into a part vacated by a sick friend, Arliss threw himself into the frequent dramatic impromptus given by Joseph and Henry Soutar (both of whom later became actors) on a makeshift stage in their cellar. Even in these juvenile experiments, Arliss was the character actor, that indispensable member of the nineteenth-century stock company who would "get up" the old men, the professors, the villains and fops. Several years later, in a provincial company, he realized that these parts best utilized his particular theatrical gifts and devoted the remainder of his long career to refining the craft of the character man into a fine art. In his autobiography, *Up the Years*

from Bloomsbury (1927), Arliss emphasized the versatility he regarded as the essence of his acting when, rebutting a manager determined to type-cast a certain role, he explained, "Of course it didn't really need a big man. All that was necessary was a decent character actor" (p. 176).

Young Arliss, however, seemed condemned to work in his father's business while surreptitiously presenting entertainments and recitations at workingmen's clubs. Fortunately, he ultimately won his family's support for an attack on his true vocation, the theater. Actor relatives of the brothers Soutar convinced J. A. Cave, manager of the old-fashioned Elephant and Castle stock company, to take on the two boys and Arliss, who was then eighteen years old, as extra gentlemen, nonspeaking walk-ons who filled out the crowd scenes.

The traditional route for an English actor who aspired to reach the West End of London led first to the provinces, and within a year, George Arliss joined a second-rate "Irish Repertory Company" that toured through the north of England. In his first week with the company, he played sizable parts in six different plays in as many nights. He received invaluable instruction in all facets of the stage, from tricks of makeup to bits of business, and he never ceased to praise the experience of playing stock in repertory: "The regular audience that has paid for its seat is, in my opinion, the great teacher and the almost infallible critic" (Arliss, *Up the Years*, p. 128).

Following this engagement, Arliss spent several years in and out of agents' offices, where he was occasionally hired for pickup touring companies of such melodramas as *The Vicar of Wakefield* and *The Captain of the Vulture*. A season at the Theatre Royal, Margate, a better grade of stock company, gave him an opportunity to play the great character parts in such classic old comedies as *The School for Scandal* and *She Stoops to Conquer*. (Although he was trained in the nineteenth-century style of acting, with its emphasis on effects, meaningful stillnesses and gestures, Arliss was never a classical actor in terms of the parts he played). While at Margate, he met his future wife and leading lady, Florence Montgomery.

By this point able to secure steady employment in provincial theaters, he played a musical comedy judge in a touring company of *The Gaiety Girl* and, as a significant step forward, took over the part of the Duke of St. Olpherts in the touring company of Sir Arthur Pinero's acclaimed *The Notorious Mrs. Ebbsmith*. On this tour, Arliss wrote a farce entitled *There and Back,* which was presented successfully in England and the United States for many years.

Though he had appeared in the West End as early as 1890, Arliss first became a West End actor in 1898, when he took the small part of Brumaire in *On and Off* at the Vaudeville Theatre. Having reached this pinnacle of his ambition, he married Florence Montgomery on Sept. 16, 1899. After two years in *On and Off,* he joined Mrs. Patrick Campbell, who managed her own company at the Royalty Theatre. He appeared in a translation of Edmond Rostand's *Les Romanesques* and supported Mrs. Campbell in her notable productions of *The Notorious Mrs. Ebbsmith,* in which Arliss again played the duke, and *The Second Mrs. Tanqueray* (also by Pinero), in which he played Cayley Drummle (both, 1900-1901).

In 1901 Arliss and his wife accompanied the Campbell company to the United States. Arliss was somewhat skeptical of leaving London so soon after achieving recognition in the West End, but his greatest successes lay before him in America. Reviewers in Chicago and New York soon hailed his performances in the two Pinero roles. These notices led David Belasco, the eccentric genius of the American theater, to sign Arliss to play the minister of war in Belasco's exotic Japanese play *The Darling of the Gods* (1902; on tour, 1903), starring Blanche Bates, in which he was again warmly received. Then began a pattern for the Arlisses that was to continue with slight variation throughout the remainder of his stage career: acting in America autumn to spring, summer vacations in England.

In 1904, Arliss entered the company of Mrs. Fiske, the artistic and moral leader of the American stage; once again he played important supporting roles. His perfectly villainous Marquis of Steyne in *Becky Sharp* (1904) and his amoral Judge Brack in Ibsen's *Hedda Gabler* (1904) won a place in American theatrical memory. In the *American Magazine* for January 1912, Walter Prichard Eaton described Arliss' portrayal of the marquis as he entered a crowded ballroom at the top of the center stairs: "... a smallish figure immaculate in black silk hose and breeches and coat, with a curiously crafty, malicious and domineering face framed between its dark whiskers and over a high white stock. The keen eyes were glancing down the bare shoulders of the women. A smile played upon the sensuous lips. But the figure neither moved nor spoke. . . . When all eyes were fixed upon him, the figure moved. He stepped with the grace of a panther down the stairs, and it was as if a dark shadow of evil, of tragedy, settled on the gay scene" (p. 361).

Arliss also appeared with Mrs. Fiske in *Leah Kleschna* (1904, 1907), *The New York Idea* (1906), *Tess of the D'Urbervilles* (1907), as Ulric Brendel in Ibsen's *Rosmersholm* (1907), and on tour (1907-1908). Since Mrs. Fiske was at this time battling the theatrical monopoly of the producers Klaw and Erlanger, such a tour meant the hardships of playing ill-fitted theaters and lodge halls in small towns throughout America. Arliss greatly admired Mrs. Fiske as an actress and co-worker, and he adopted her strong antivivisectionist sentiments.

Arliss now had the impetus to become a star in his own right, but his leading performances as the sinister title character in Ferenc Molnár's *The Devil* (1908) and as an absent-minded inventor in the dramatization of W. J. Locke's novel *Septimus* (1909) did not produce the overwhelming public response he sought. George Tyler, who had brought Mrs. Campbell to America, acted on Arliss' suggestion for a play about the diplomatic triumphs of Benjamin Disraeli, Victoria's prime minister, and persuaded English dramatist Louis Parker to write it. *Disraeli* opened in Montreal on Jan. 23, 1911, and soon moved to Chicago. Although the play barely survived the first few months, it slowly grew in popularity, and by its Sept. 18, 1911, opening at Wallack's Theatre in New York, "George Arliss in *Disraeli*" was fast becoming a catch phrase. As the *New York World* rhapsodized, "Not since the curtain was drawn on the careers of Henry Irving and Richard Mansfield has a New York audience witnessed a performance that could approach it."

Disraeli made Arliss a true celebrity and linked his name with the play as inextricably as that of Otis Skinner with *Kismet* or James O'Neill with *The Count of Monte Cristo.* The dapper Arliss, with his long, narrow face, pointed nose, patent leather hair stretched over a bony head, and a monocle habitually placed in his right eye, added in makeup curls, a small goatee, and a high, bald forehead to achieve a picture-book resemblance to Disraeli. In 1925, Stark Young, in the *New York Times,* described Arliss' acting in *Old English* and his words apply to *Disraeli* as well: "... it is marked by dry humor, precision in effects, subtle and deliberate tempo. . . . Mr. Arliss' art belongs to the realm of social comedy."

After five seasons of *Disraeli,* Arliss played title roles in Edward Knoblock's *Paganini* (Chicago, 1915; New York, 1916), James Barrie's *The Professor's Love Story* (1917), and in *Hamilton* (1917; on tour, 1918), which he wrote with Mary Hamlin. In 1918 he joined such stage luminaries as George M. Cohan, Laurette Taylor, and Mrs. Fiske in *Out There,* which toured abroad to entertain American servicemen. His more notable stage performances after the war were as a French scientist in *Jacques Duval* (1920), a Russian in Booth Tarkington's *Poldikin* (1920), a rajah in William Archer's *The Green Goddess* (New York, 1921-1923; London, 1924, his first appearance there in more than twenty years), and the old curmudgeon Sylvanus Heythorp in John Galsworthy's comedy *Old English* (1924; on tour, 1925-1927). The latter two plays provided Arliss with two of his most popular roles, both of which he later re-created in films of the same names. Arliss' last formal stage appearance came as Shylock in *The Merchant of Venice* (1928; on tour, 1928-1929), with Peggy Wood as Portia. As opposed to his sympathetic portrayal of a real Jew in *Disraeli,* Arliss managed to convey chilling hatred and cunning in an old-fashioned depiction of Shakespeare's Jew.

Arliss' film career officially began in 1920, and there was a silent version of *Disraeli* in 1921, but it was the 1929 talking version of his most famous vehicle that transformed him into a major motion picture star and earned him that year's Photoplay Gold Medal for the outstanding performance by an actor. He now began a second career, making over twenty films during the following decade.

His best films divide themselves between portraits of characters, frequently wise old men: *The Millionaire* (1931); *The Working Man* (1933); *The Last Gentleman* (1934); *Mister Hobo* (1936); *The Green Goddess* (1923, silent; 1930, talking); and *Old English* (1931) and portraits of famous men of history, in addition to *Disraeli*: *Voltaire* (1933); *The House of Rothschild* (1934), playing both Meyer and Nathan Rothschild; *The Iron Duke* (1935), playing Wellington; and *Cardinal Richelieu* (1935). In *The House of Rothschild,* perhaps his finest film, Arliss drew on his wit and dignity as well as his Semitic features to offer a stirring likeness of Jews who conquered religious prejudice through their intelligence; at least one critic found the film powerful

propaganda against the Nazis. His last picture was *Dr. Syn* (1937).

George Arliss was elected a fellow of the Royal Society of Arts in 1934 and awarded an honorary M.A. by Columbia University, the first actor so honored. He lived in England during his final years and died in London of a bronchial ailment when he was seventy-seven.

For more than forty years, George Arliss created villains, charming old men, and great historical leaders with a subtlety and effortlessness which masked his painstaking devotion to the techniques of the traditional actor's art.

[The excellent collection of newspaper and magazine clippings on Arliss and *Disraeli* in the Harvard Theatre Coll. and Arliss' well-written autobiography *Up the Years from Bloomsbury* (1927), which gives a real sense of the man's serene humor, are the primary sources. Also see Arliss' second volume of autobiography, *My Ten Years in the Studios* (1940), and his obituary in the *N.Y. Times*, Feb. 6, 1946. Recommended strongly for descriptions of Arliss' important roles with Mrs. Fiske is Archie Binns, *Mrs. Fiske and the American Stage* (1955), which, in addition, is one of those rare theater history books that are just plain good. For a good likeness of Arliss, see the photograph of the Charles Sneed Williams painting which serves as the frontispiece of *Up the Years.*]

GEORGE PHILIP BIRNBAUM

ARNOLD, HENRY HARLEY (June 25, 1886-Jan. 15, 1950), army air officer, was born at Gladwyne, Pa., near Philadelphia. He was one of five children and the second of four sons of Dr. Herbert Alonzo Arnold, a general practitioner, and Anna Louise (Harley) Arnold. The families of both parents were rooted in the area from pre-Revolutionary days; the Arnolds had come from England in 1740. Henry attended public school in nearby Lower Merion. After considering medicine and the Baptist ministry as possible careers, he entered West Point in 1903 on an appointment originally intended for his older brother, Thomas. At the academy, Arnold won the nickname "Happy"—later shortened to "Hap"—but achieved little military or academic distinction; he graduated in 1907 in the middle of his class of 110. In spite of a passionate preference for the cavalry, he was commissioned a second lieutenant in the infantry and served with the 29th Regiment in the Philippines (1907-1909) and on Governors Island in New York harbor (1909-1911).

Dissatisfied with the dull routine and slow promotion of his service, Arnold volunteered for flight training in the fledgling Aviation Section of the Signal Corps. In April 1911 he reported to the flying school operated by Wilbur and Orville Wright at Dayton, Ohio, where he became familiar with many of the pioneers of American aviation. After completing the two-month course, he was assigned as an instructor to the new Signal Corps Aviation School at College Park, Md. The following year he was awarded one of the first military aviator's badges to be issued. Arnold became a skillful and daring pilot, developing a lifelong interest in experimentation. He established numerous records and in 1912 won the new Mackay Trophy, awarded by the War Department for the year's outstanding military flight. In November 1913, now a first lieutenant, he was assigned to the 13th Infantry in the Philippines. In 1916, as captain, he was returned to the Aviation Section and sent to Rockwell Field, San Diego. Early in 1917 he was ordered to organize the 7th Aero Squadron for defense of the Canal Zone, but when the United States entered World War I, he was recalled to Washington for duty in the Signal Corps's Air Division.

In the disorderly expansion of the air arm, Arnold rose rapidly in rank, becoming the army's youngest colonel (temporary) in August 1917. Widespread criticism of the lagging aviation program brought a reorganization in May 1918 and Arnold was made assistant director of military aeronautics and the ranking rated pilot in Washington. Unhappily, his increased responsibilities blocked his constant efforts to get overseas. When finally he wangled a trip to France to persuade Gen. John J. Pershing to use an experimental flying bomb (the "Bug"), Arnold was delayed in England by an attack of pneumonia and barely reached the front as an observer by Armistice Day.

During the two decades between the Armistice and Munich, the fundamental concepts of American air power were formulated. Air power enthusiasts, notably Gen. William ("Billy") Mitchell, haunted by memories of wartime errors but thwarted by conservative civilian and military officials, turned away from conventional channels for support. Arnold, like many professional aviators, supported Mitchell, a personal friend, in his fight for an independent air force, but he lacked Mitchell's crusading temperament. He was stationed in California (in aviation posts at San Diego and San Francisco) from January 1919 until autumn 1924, and thus missed most of the controversy at Washington. When an assignment to attend the Army Industrial College brought him to the capital as the fight reached its climax, he testified in Mitchell's favor at the latter's court-martial, but his advocacy was not such as to prejudice seriously his own career.

Leaving Washington in March 1926, Arnold spent five years in the Middle West. He himself considered his tour at Fort Riley, Kans., a cavalry post, punishment for the Mitchell incident, but his subsequent assignment to attend the Command and General Staff School at Fort Leavenworth (1928-1929) marked him as a field-grade officer of promise. After commands at Fairfield and Wright Field, Ohio, Arnold was promoted to lieutenant colonel in February 1931, and later the same year was sent back to California with a challenging mission: to transform March Field at Riverside from a primary training school into an operational base housing both bomber and pursuit units. As more and better planes became available, he was able to intensify unit training, continue experimentation with matériel and tactics, and increase the scope and realism of maneuvers.

In March 1933 Arnold was given command of the 1st Fighter Wing, with components in various California airfields. Some of his tasks of this period fell outside the normal purview of military aviation, as when, in May 1933, he was given responsibility for housing members of the Civilian Conservation Corps in the West, eventually commanding thirty camps. More to his liking was his command of the successful flight of ten Martin B-10's, the first "modern" bomber, from Washington, D.C., to Fairbanks, Alaska, and back, for which he received the Distinguished Flying Cross and his second Mackay Trophy. In March 1935, as a sop to proponents of a separate air arm, the General Headquarters Air Force was established as a striking force independent of the corps areas. Arnold, as temporary brigadier general, was given command of its 1st Wing, one of three components, with headquarters still at March Field. But his days with combat units were numbered; in January 1936 he returned to Washington as assistant chief of the Air Corps, and in September 1938, now a major general, he was promoted to chief.

As Europe headed toward war, Arnold was frozen in a Washington desk job as inexorably as in World War I. Earlier than most, he realized the danger to the United States, and with the aid of Harry Hopkins he encouraged President Roosevelt's intention of expanding vastly the basic elements of United States air power. Without appropriations or contract orders to back him, Arnold persuaded the American aircraft industry to begin the radical changes required for production goals that were to escalate rapidly. Similarly, before funds had been appropriated for expansion of pilot training, he persuaded a number of private flying schools to make the considerable investments necessary to turn their establishments into contract schools for primary flight training. After September 1939, as German victories proved redundantly the importance of air power and the present perils of the Western powers, one of Arnold's most difficult tasks was to allocate aircraft production between our expanding army and navy air forces and those of our potential allies. When the lend-lease program intensified this problem in the spring of 1941, Arnold went to England to reach acceptable agreements, and while there established friendly relations with Royal Air Force leaders that would be reflected in the close cooperation of the war years. The war plan prepared under his direction in September 1941 gave a remarkably accurate preview of the air phase of World War II, in strategy as well as in logistics.

Changes in the organization of the air arm gave token of its growing importance in defense. In October 1940 Arnold was given the additional position of deputy chief of staff of the army, for air matters, and with the establishment in 1941 of the Army Air Forces, he was made their chief. The army's chief of staff was Gen. George C. Marshall, a friend whose growing realization of the role of air power and confidence in Arnold's ability made for close and cordial cooperation throughout the war. When, in August, President Roosevelt and British Prime Minister Winston Churchill held their historic Atlantic Charter conference off the coast of Newfoundland to plan a possible alliance, Arnold was Roosevelt's chief advisor on air warfare. When war came, Arnold, advanced to lieutenant general, played a similar role in the "Arcadia" conference at Washington, at which the heads of government agreed on the strategy for the Allies. The informal procedures of these two conferences now crystallized in the Combined Chiefs of Staff; in its American half, the U.S. Joint Chiefs of Staff, Arnold was the air member. His powers were rounded out with the army reorganization of March 1942, which created three equal components, Army Ground, Service, and Air Forces, of which last Arnold was made commanding general.

As head of the Army Air Forces, Arnold was responsible for building the air arm at home; as Deputy Chief of Staff and member of the J.C.S. and C.C.S. he helped formulate policy and strategic plans for conduct of the war in its several theatres. In the army he was deputy to General Marshall, but in the J.C.S. and C.C.S. he sat as peer, and soon the Army Air Forces took on a quasi-independence that went beyond the letter of army regulations. Thus Arnold's large and capable staff became a rival rather than a subordinate of the army staff. Promotions to general (March 1943) and general of the army (December 1944)—a newly created rank he shared only with Marshall, Douglas MacArthur, and Dwight D. Eisenhower—recognized rather than increased his power. Part of Arnold's influence on combat operations stemmed from his personal ties with air commanders in the overseas theatres.

Arnold finally got a combat job in April 1944 as commanding general of the Twentieth Air Force, whose B-29 bombers were to hasten the defeat of Japan; but his headquarters was still in the Pentagon and his orders for bombardment missions were issued via radio. Still, Arnold was no chair-borne general. He traveled frequently in the Zone of the Interior and made a number of flights abroad to observe and settle air problems in the various theatres. He attended, too, the great conferences of the Combined Chiefs of Staff which charted the course of the war: Casablanca (January 1943), Quebec (August 1943 and September 1944), London (June 1944), and Potsdam (July 1945). The meeting at Washington (May 1943) he missed because of heart trouble, and those at Malta and Yalta because of a serious heart attack that required a long hospitalization. He continued to drive himself hard, with the desire both to end the war quickly and to ensure a proper role for the Air Forces in postwar years. The collapse of Japan in 1945 after Arnold's B-29's had dropped atom bombs on Hiroshima and Nagasaki allowed him in good conscience to ask for relief, and early the following year he turned over his command to Gen Carl A. Spaatz, one of his most successful theatre air commanders.

In March, Arnold retired to a small ranch he had bought in the Valley of the Moon near Sonoma, Calif. Retirement did not mean inaction. He carried on a heavy correspondence from a part-time office at nearby Hamilton Field and also wrote for publication. He continued to work for a strong national defense in which air power would play a leading role, but he understood clearly the significance of technological advances that had already made obsolete the weapons and some of the ideas of World War II. Of the many honors of his long career, he especially cherished his last promotion to permanent general of the air force (May 1949), since it symbolized the creation, in 1947, of the independent Air Force he had long advocated. Arnold died at his ranch home in 1950 of a coronary occlusion, the fifth such attack. He was buried with full military honors at Arlington National Cemetery, in a funeral attended by President Truman and ranking officers of all services. Arnold was survived by his wife, Eleanor A. Pool of Rochester, N.Y., whom he had married in Philadelphia on Sept. 10, 1913, and by their four children: Lois Eleanor (1915), Henry Harley (1917), William Bruce (1918), and David Lee (1927). All three sons graduated from West Point and received commissions; the daughter married Commander Ernest M. Snowden, a distinguished navy pilot.

Arnold was neither an original strategist nor a great organizer, but he was in a very real sense the builder of the greatest air force the world had seen. In 1938 he inherited some obsolescent planes, a few B-17's, other aircraft in various stages of development, and a small but highly competent officer corps which he imbued with the team spirit. Before he retired, the Army Air Forces had reached a wartime peak of actual operational strength of 243 combat groups, with 63,715 planes on hand, and 2,411,294 personnel. The A.A.F., with the aid of the Royal Air Force, had completely destroyed the German and Italian air forces, and with the navy had knocked out the Japanese air force. The A.A.F. tactical units had contributed to the defeat of enemy armies, and its program of strategic bombardment, which Arnold had so vigorously urged, had led to the overall collapse of the enemy. Arnold drove his men as he drove himself; he had little patience for incompetence or excuses. Of volatile temperament, he could explode instantly, exchanging the famous Hap Arnold grin for the dreaded General Arnold frown. His favorite motto was: "A second-best air force is like a second-best poker hand—no good at all." By his single-minded persistence he ensured that the United States held the best cards.

[Besides articles in technical and popular magazines, Arnold wrote several books: *Airmen and Aircraft: An Introduction to Aeronautics* (1926); the Aviator Series ("Bill Bruce" Series) of half a dozen juvenile books (1928); and three volumes with Ira C. Eaker as co-author: *This Flying Game* (1936), *Winged Warfare* (1941), and *Army Flyer* (1942). The three *Reports* to the commanding general of the Army Air Forces to the secretary of war (Jan. 4, 1944, Feb. 27, 1945, and Nov. 12, 1945), later collected in *The War Reports of Gen. of the Army George C. Marshall . . . Gen. of the Army H. H. Arnold . . . [and] Fleet Adm. Ernest J. King* (1947), were written by his staff, but give his official views of the air war. There is no adequate biography of General Arnold. His autobiography, *Global Mission* (1949), is useful, but

is episodic rather than reflective and far from complete. Most of the memoirs of top World War II leaders and many of the narrative histories of that war contain references to Arnold of varying degrees of usefulness. On his death and funeral, see *N.Y. Times*, Jan. 16-20, 1950. The Archives of the Research Studies Inst., Maxwell Air Force Base, Ala., has a useful file (K-141-2421 Arnold) containing news releases, newspaper clippings, and miscellaneous personal information. For Arnold's activities of 1939–1945, Wesley Frank Craven and James Lea Cate, eds., *The Army Air Forces in World War II*, 7 vols. (1948–1958), provides the fullest record, and the footnotes supply for the serious student by far the most detailed index to the vast collections of unpublished sources in various government archives.]

JAMES LEA CATE

ATHERTON, GERTRUDE FRANKLIN (HORN) (Oct. 30, 1857-June 14, 1948), novelist, was born in San Francisco, Calif., the only child of Thomas Lodowick Horn and Gertrude (Franklin) Horn. Her father came from a Stonington, Conn., family, established there for 200 years in the shipping business. Her mother was the daughter of Stephen Franklin, a San Francisco newspaper editor and later bank secretary, who came to California after business failure in New Orleans, La.; his granduncle was Benjamin Franklin. Gertrude's mother, brought up on a Louisiana plantation, hated her arranged marriage and was divorced after three years. Her second marriage, to John Frederick Uhlhorne in 1865, gave Gertrude two stepsisters, but it too ended badly. Brought up in various houses in San Francisco and on a ranch near San Jose, Gertrude, a fiercely independent girl, felt the influences of her beautiful, but irresponsible, mother and her grandfather, who forced her to read serious books and paid for her education. She attended St. Mary's Hall in Benecia, Calif., and at the age of seventeen went to the Sayre Institute in Lexington, Ky., residing with her Presbyterian uncle's family. After a restless year and engagements to two men, she was sent home. She met George Henry Bowen Atherton, then twenty-four, at her mother's ranch, and they eloped and were married by a Catholic priest in 1876. Gertrude went to live on the Atherton estate in Fair Oaks (now Atherton), Calif. Never much in love with her husband, she spent an unhappy decade in the wealthy Atherton clan and bore two children, George Goñi, who died at six years of age, and Muriel Florence. Reading and writing afforded her the only means of escape from the demands of marriage, the family, and the boredom of Menlo Park society. Her first novel, *The Randolphs of Redwoods* (c. 1882), serialized in the San Francisco *Argonaut*, derived from a contemporary scandal over a wellborn girl who succumbed to alcoholism. Its anonymous publication infuriated her husband, family, and society. "A brutal revival," one reviewer said, "of a deplorable scandal that every decent citizen was only too willing to bury." Revised, it became *A Daughter of the Vine* in 1899.

Unsuccessful in every business venture, George Atherton died on a trip to Chile in 1887. Gertrude promptly sought her fortune in New York, using her journalistic experience, her various family connections, and $1,000 from her loyal grandfather. There she published *What Dreams May Come* (1888) and *Hermia Suydam* (1889), quickly establishing a reputation for liberated female characters, romantic melodrama, and sexual candor. New York critics heaped scorn on her work, and she determined to find wider horizons, but not before issuing *A Question of Time* (1891), about a woman of sixty who loves a man half her age. Her name came to be linked with Amelie Rives, Ella Wheeler Wilcox, Laura Daintry, and Edgar Saltus, all of whom demonstrated in their writing that American women could put love and pleasure before marriage, family, or religion. She went to England in 1895 and met, among others, Henry James (whom she had long admired), James MacNeill Whistler, Thomas Hardy, and George Moore. The English welcomed her works as revelations of the American character and eagerly sought copies of *Patience Sparhawk and Her Times* (1897), about a woman who murders her husband; *His Fortunate Grace* (1897), about an American girl who marries a shabby English duke; and *American Wives and English Husbands* (1898), about "the Californian view of the 'relation of the sexes,'" as Henry James remarked. The last was her greatest success in this genre and was later retitled *Transplanted* (1919). She wrote *The Doomswoman,* a novel of Spanish life in old California, in 1892 and continued to explore this theme throughout her career, sometimes interlinking characters in Balzacian fashion. Best known of these works are *The Californians* (1898); *The Splendid Idle Forties,* a collection of stories (1902); *Ancestors* (1907); and *Sleeping Fires* (1922). Her most ambitious and successful works, however, were fictionalized biographies: *The Conqueror,* about Alexander Hamilton (1902); *Rezánov,* about Nikolai Petrovich Rezánov (1906); and *The Immortal Marriage,* about Pericles and Aspasia (1927). During World War I she worked energetically for hospital relief charities, producing *The Living Present* (1917), about the war work of Frenchwomen, and *The White*

Morning (1918), a novel about German women. She earned several medals for her effective publicity. Always daring and enterprising, she traveled alone in Europe and around the Mediterranean; went to Washington, D.C., to prepare her *Senator North* (1900); to the Adirondacks for *The Aristocrats* (1901); to the British West Indies to do research on Hamilton's early life; and to prepare for *The Gorgeous Isle* (1908), a fictional account of Algernon Charles Swinburne. After undergoing Eugen Steinach's rejuvenation therapy, she wrote *Black Oxen* (1923), popularizing the treatment in the United States. Even into her eighties she was a tall and handsome blonde woman, active in San Francisco life. There she died of old age and was buried. She was the author of a total of fifty-six books.

"Practically every one of her novels," Lionel Stevenson wrote, "centers upon a woman who claims the right to think and act for herself, to play a part in the political and intellectual world and to be no more ashamed of her sexual impulses than men are" (*The Bookman,* July 1929). And Henry James, who found both her and her books vulgar, once remarked, "I abominate the woman" (Theodora Bosanquet, *Henry James at Work,* 1924). Between these two observations lies the judgment that Gertrude Atherton was a magnificently energetic propagandist for her sex, an adventurous woman who pursued her career with an intense will, yet a writer who was seldom more than a popularizer, who had no subtlety in style, no instinct for form, and little originality in psychological insight or in plot.

[The prime source is her lively autobiography, *Adventures of a Novelist* (1932). This may be supplemented by the *Nat. Cyc. of Am. Biog.,* vol. XXXVI; *Twentieth-Century Authors,* which contains pungent remarks by the author; and the *Reader's Encyc. of Am. Lit.* (1962), all of which contain photographs of her. Major holdings of her manuscripts and correspondence are located in the Lib. of Cong., Mills College Lib., Stanford Univ. Lib., and Oakland (Calif.) Free Lib. Criticism, apart from innumerable contemporary reviews of individual works, is almost nonexistent. Lionel Stevenson's essay, "Atherton Versus Grundy: The Forty Years' War" (*The Bookman,* July 1929, pp. 464–472), is invaluable. And Henry James's review comments, reprinted in Leon Edel, ed., *Am. Essays of Henry James,* 205–207, 218–219 (1956), are useful. Her history of California, *California: An Intimate Hist.* (1914), and her book of personal essays, *Can Women Be Gentlemen?* (1938), further reveal her character and abilities.]

DEAN FLOWER

ATWOOD, WALLACE WALTER (Oct. 1, 1872-July 24, 1949), geologist, geographer, and university president, was born in Chicago, Ill., the oldest of three children of Thomas Greene Atwood and Adelaide Adelia (Rich-

ards) Atwood. Both parents were natives of
Massachusetts. Thomas Atwood, a descendant
of John Wood (or Atwood), who had settled
in Plymouth Colony in 1635, owned a planing
mill in Chicago, having come there from Pittsfield, Mass., where he had been a builder and
contractor. Wallace Atwood graduated from
Chicago's West Division High School and
entered the University of Chicago, where as a
student of Rollin D. Salisbury, he developed a
strong interest in the geographical aspects of
geology. After receiving the S.B. degree in
1897, he stayed on for graduate study in geology, teaching at various Chicago schools to help
earn his way. He also served under Salisbury
as a junior assistant on the New Jersey Geological Survey (1897) and the Wisconsin Natural History Survey (1898-1899). On Sept. 22,
1900, he married Harriet Towle Bradley,
daughter of a Chicago lawyer. Mrs. Atwood
later regularly accompanied her husband on his
worldwide travels and field researches. They
had four children: Rollin Salisbury, Wallace
Richards (later Wallace Walter, Jr.), Harriet
Towle, and Mary Fessenden.

Atwood was appointed an instructor in the
University of Chicago geology department in
1902, and the following year, after submitting
a dissertation on the glaciation of the Uinta
Mountains, he received the Ph.D. degree. Like
Salisbury, Atwood became a superb field
teacher, coupling discovery methods with insistence on careful reasoning and clear writing.
He also obtained appointments with the Illinois
State Geological Survey and the United States
Geological Survey; he held the rank of geologist in the latter service from 1909 until his
death. In 1913, having risen to the rank of
associate professor, Atwood left Chicago to become professor of physiography at Harvard.

Atwood's principal scientific contributions
grew out of the fieldwork of his Chicago and
Harvard years. He chose to work in physiography (later called geomorphology), a research
area primarily pursued by geologists, but cultivated for educational purposes by geographers,
who perceived it as the foundation of human
and regional geography. It was still largely a
field science, in the distinctively American empirical tradition of the nineteenth-century
topographical surveys of the West. Atwood,
one of the last geologist-geographers to work
in this tradition, picked the Rocky Mountains,
particularly the San Juan Mountains in southwestern Colorado, as his area of investigation.
Between 1909 and 1948 he spent over twenty-
five seasons in or near the Rockies, exploring,

studying, and recording their geological and
geographical characteristics, and getting to
know them better than any other scientist then
living.

A popular teacher at Harvard, Atwood frequently led his students on local excursions and
advanced field studies. His generous grading
policies and an inadequately supervised field
trip to Mount Monadnock, however, put Atwood in the bad graces of President A. Lawrence Lowell, and when Lowell resisted his
proposals for a school of geography, Atwood
grew dissatisfied. He had meanwhile become
interested in writing school texts, and in 1916
signed a contract with Ginn and Company. One
of the Ginn executives, Charles Thurber, was
also chairman of the board of trustees of Clark
University in Worcester, Mass. When in 1919-
1920 the Clark trustees were looking for a
president to succeed both G. Stanley Hall in
the university and Edmund C. Sanford in Clark
College, Atwood was offered the combined
posts, and with it a mandate to establish graduate and undergraduate programs in geography
under his personal direction. He took up his
new duties in September 1920.

Atwood's presidency of Clark was marked by
periodic outbreaks of controversy with students
and faculty. Initial distrust was aroused by the
grandiose plans for the new Graduate School of
Geography. Its first year (1921-1922) budget
exceeded 40 percent of all departmental appropriations put together, and Atwood announced
at the same time, without consulting the faculty,
plans to discontinue graduate work in several
other fields. Then in 1922 the "Nearing incident," when Atwood personally stopped a public
lecture being given by the radical socialist Scott
Nearing, transformed the issue from one of
internal differences over educational policies
into the broader one of academic freedom, and
polarized students, faculty, alumni, and the
larger community. For two years the campus
was rent by agitation, and several prominent
scholars publicly resigned; Atwood and the
conservative trustees perceived the difficulties
as a conspiracy organized by radical students
and faculty. Relations between Atwood and his
faculty stabilized during the 1930's, although
internal disorders occurred in mid-decade in
the psychology department and in the early
1940's in biology, in each case leading to the
departure of nationally recognized scholars
from Clark.

During Atwood's administration, the undergraduate Clark College was extended from a
three-year program to the standard four years,

an intercollegiate athletics program was begun, and a program in business administration was instituted. Enrollments increased significantly, as did the school's physical plant. In 1942 the Women's College was established, and later a Division of Nursing Education. The Division of International Affairs was set up at the graduate level. The development of geography, however, was clearly Atwood's primary interest at Clark; in retrospect, the fact of his being president and at the same time the head of a major graduate department had unfortunate consequences for Atwood and for the university.

To the science of geography, Atwood made three principal contributions. The first was the establishment of the Graduate School of Geography at Clark. This was only the second fully staffed, independent doctoral program in geography in any American university, and it remained for over fifty years the leading producer of geography doctorates, originally placing special emphasis on fieldwork, firsthand observation, land use studies, and geographic education. Atwood himself taught regularly both in the field and in the classroom, and was notable for his infectious enthusiasm, his easy style of lecturing, and his technique of sketching landforms on the blackboard using both hands at once. Among the school's innovations for which he was partly or fully responsible were the founding in 1925 of *Economic Geography,* a professional journal of worldwide circulation; a fall field camp for graduate students and faculty; and a widely imitated geography workroom, with an associated map library and cartographic facilities.

Atwood's second contribution was to geographic education at the grade school level. His series of geographies for elementary and junior high school students, most of them written in collaboration with Helen Goss Thomas, began in 1920 and by the time of his death had sold well over ten million copies. Also useful for getting the new geography directly into the hands of teachers were Clark's home-study department, set up to provide correspondence courses, the Clark summer school, and a professorship in the teaching of geography. Atwood spoke before teachers' groups in every state, worked closely with the Worcester school system, and served a term as president of the National Council of Geography Teachers.

Atwood made his third contribution to geography as a skillful scientific popularizer. His extensive research in the Rockies and his ability to write lucidly were tailored to the general reader's taste in *The Rocky Mountains* (1945),

and he filled many nonprofessional speaking engagements. His lifelong interest in conservation found reflection in his membership in the National Parks Association (president 1929-1933), the National Forestry Association, the Sierra Club, and the Save-the-Redwoods League. His dignified appearance, interest in all types of audiences, and air of being a cultivated man of the world all helped him carry off his role as a salesman for geography among nonprofessional groups. Within the profession, he served as president of the Association of American Geographers in 1933-1934.

Atwood's retirement in 1946 occasioned little lessening of his activity. That same year he was an incorporator and chairman of the board of trustees of the new Utopia College in Eureka, Kans. He also worked with the American Council on Education on a project to develop teaching films in world geography. Atwood belonged to the Unitarian church and was a Republican in politics. In May 1949, at seventy-six, he was told that he was suffering from a malignancy which could not be successfully treated. He died at his summer home in Annisquam, Mass., and was buried in Mount Auburn Cemetery, Cambridge, Mass.

[Atwood's papers are in the Clark Univ. Arch.; other manuscripts are at the Am. Geographical Soc., N.Y. City; the Assoc. of Am. Geographers, Washington, D.C.; the Univ. of Chicago, and Harvard. There is no critical biographical study. Memorial sketches of varying degrees of value are those of George B. Cressey in the *Annals* of the Assoc. of Am. Geographers, Dec. 1949, with a bibliography of Atwood's writings; Clarence S. Brigham in the *Proc.* of the Am. Antiquarian Soc., LIX, 174-176 (1949); Kirtley F. Mather in Geol. Soc. of America, *Proc.*, 1949; and Samuel Van Valkenburg in *Geographical Rev.*, Oct. 1949. Basic details are in *Who Was Who in America,* II (1950); and the *Nat. Cyc. Am. Biog.*, XXXVII, 46-48. Less accessible, but useful, are the *Memorial Service Honoring Wallace Walter Atwood, 1872-1949* (1950) and "Bibliography of Wallace W. Atwood," Clark Univ. Lib., *Publications*, Feb. 1945. The most significant of Atwood's scientific publications is *Physiography and Quaternary Geology of the San Juan Mountains, Colo.* (with Kirtley F. Mather), U.S. Geological Survey, Professional Papers, no. 166 (1932). His ideas concerning geography are best set forth in his inaugural address, "The New Meaning of Geography in Am. Education," Clark Univ. Lib., *Publications,* Apr. 1921 (reprinted in *School and Society,* Feb. 19, 1921); and in his presidential address to the Assoc. of Am. Geographers, in their *Annals,* Mar. 1935. Two of Atwood's many accounts of his own work at Clark are valuable if used with care: his "Administrative Report, 1920-1945," Clark Univ. Lib., *Publications,* May 1945; and *The Clark Graduate School of Geography: Our First Twenty-Five Years, 1921-1946* (1946). These should be supplemented by Arthur O. Lovejoy et al., "Report of Committee of Inquiry Concerning Clark Univ.," Am. Assoc. of Univ. Professors, *Bull.*, Oct. 1924. Death record from Mass. Registrar of Vital Statistics. An oil portrait of Atwood by John C. Johansen (1925) is at Clark Univ.]

WILLIAM A. KOELSCH

AUER, JOHN (Mar. 30, 1875-Apr. 30, 1948), pharmacologist and physiologist, was born in Rochester, N.Y., the son of Henry Auer and Luise (Hummel) Auer. Henry Auer, a native of Germany, was a brewer.

Auer received the degree of bachelor of science from the University of Michigan in 1898. He studied medicine at the Johns Hopkins University, taking the M.D. degree in 1902. In 1902-1903 he was a resident house officer (intern) at the Johns Hopkins Hospital. The next year he joined the recently established Rockefeller Institute for Medical Research (now Rockefeller University) in New York City, first as fellow, then on the permanent roll as assistant in the laboratory of the physiologist Samuel J. Meltzer. During the eighteen years of his connection with the institute the two men were closely associated personally and in research.

On Oct. 1, 1903, Auer married Meltzer's daughter Clara (also a fellow of the institute); they had three children, James, Helen, and John. And, from that time on, most of his scientific contributions were published jointly with his father-in-law, to whose imaginative program of research Auer brought experimental skill of high order. They collaborated on twenty-five papers dealing with the anesthetic and relaxative effects of magnesium sulphate, administered intravenously, with findings that were widely used in the treatment of tetanus, eclampsia, and other spasmodic conditions.

In 1906 the Rockefeller Institute sent Auer to Harvard University for a year to gain experience in physiological methods. In 1900-1910 Meltzer and Auer, seeking ways to counteract a side effect of magnesium anesthesia which made it dangerous for use in surgery, namely inhibition of the respiratory center in the brain, hit upon the method of ventilating the lungs by a stream of air blown into them through the trachea. By this means the blood can be aerated without breathing movements of the chest, and, by including ether or some other anesthetic vapor into the airstream, an animal or a human patient can be kept under surgical anesthesia, even after the chest is opened. This invention promptly found worldwide use in thoracic surgery. Other joint investigations by Meltzer and Auer dealt with absorption from muscle, and with movements of the stomach and intestines and their control by the vagus and splanchnic nerves.

Auer's first independent publication (1906) described hitherto unnoticed inclusions ("Auer bodies") in the large lymphocytes in acute leukemia. With a junior colleague, Paul A. Lewis, he studied the phenomenon of anaphylaxis in guinea pigs, making the important discovery that sudden death from anaphylactic shock is caused by spasm of the bronchial musculature. This observation led Meltzer to propose the hypothesis, now universally accepted, that bronchial asthma results from anaphylactic sensitivity to foreign proteins. When in World War I the Rockefeller Institute was officially constituted U.S. Auxiliary Laboratory No. 1, Auer was enrolled in the Medical Reserve Corps of the army with the rank of major. He studied the effects of poison gases, but with little or no practical results.

Auer was a tall man of studious appearance and broad intellectual interests, outgoing, and fond of argument. He would often linger at the Rockefeller Institute's lunch table to talk with the younger men, frequently espousing unpopular causes. He was, for example, a great enthusiast for Matisse at a time when the post-impressionist painters were regarded as extremists.

When S. J. Meltzer died in 1920, his laboratory was discontinued and Auer, who had reached the rank of associate member of the institute, accepted a call to the chair of pharmacology at St. Louis University School of Medicine. His activity as an experimental scientist was much hampered by this transfer from a research-oriented environment to that of a professorship in a school not yet strong in research. He was absorbed in organizing his courses and published nothing for eleven years. He then resumed work in the laboratory mostly with the assistance of his junior staff, studying the motor functions of the digestive and urinary systems. In these later years he remained a devoted and unselfish teacher, deeply concerned with the interests of his students, and an example to them of the humane physician-scientist. He was an ardent reader of French, German, and Latin classics, deeply interested in music and art, and in his spare time, an amateur painter. He was one of the organizers of the American Society of Pharmacology and Experimental Therapeutics and served as its secretary (1912-1916), vice-president (1917-1918), and president (1924-1928).

[For Auer's more than 140 scientific papers, see *Index Medicus, passim*, 1904-1948. For his research 1903-1921, see George W. Corner, *Hist. of the Rockefeller Inst.* (1964). Memoirs by Ralph Kinsella, *Trans. of the Assoc. of Am. Physicians* 61 (1948): 5, by George B. Roth, *Jour. of Pharmacology and Experimental Therapeutics* 95 (1949): 285-286 (portrait), and by Alphonse J. Schwitalla in the files of St. Louis Univ. School of Medicine. Personal information from Michael Heidelberger, Ph.D., N.Y.]

GEORGE W. CORNER

AYRES, LEONARD PORTER (Sept. 15, 1879-Oct. 29, 1946), statistician, research administrator, economist, was born in Niantic, Conn., the son of Milan Church Ayres and Georgiana (Gall) Ayres. The family moved to the Boston area during Leonard's early childhood, and he received his early education in the public schools of Newton, Mass. His father, a journalist, lecturer, clergyman, and author, was for many years editor of the *Boston Advertiser*. After receiving the Ph.B. degree from the College of Liberal Arts of Boston University in 1902, Ayres began his career as a teacher in Puerto Rico. As a young man, his interests were divided among statistics, educational administration, and bicycling. A champion long-distance racer, he also gained attention as a bicycle dealer, advertising wheels to match the colors of dresses. He rose rapidly in the Puerto Rican school system, becoming superintendent in Caguas in 1903 and in San Juan in 1904. Two years later, Ayres was named general superintendent of schools of the island and organized the Insular Bureau of Statistics.

Returning to the United States in 1907, he attended Teachers' College of Columbia University briefly and then earned the M.A. (1909) and Ph.D. (1910) degrees from Boston University. In 1908, he joined the staff of the Russell Sage Foundation and began to earn a reputation as an innovator in the areas of research administration and the application of statistical methods to educational and social research. The Russell Sage Foundation was the first major philanthropic organization to undertake exhaustive research in social welfare and education. Ayres, as director of the departments of education and statistics, participated in numerous landmark studies in the development of applied social research in the twentieth century. An early book, *Laggards in Our Schools* (1909), based on research on backward schoolchildren conducted by Ayres and Dr. Luther Halsey Gulick of the foundation was reprinted three times in the next four years. Ayres and Gulick argued that the most important causes of retardation were environmental. Ayres's later studies of intelligence tests and his recommendations of yardsticks for measuring the problems and progress of children in elementary schools also attracted wide attention. He applied to education the survey techniques developed by the foundation for the investigation of slum conditions in Pittsburgh and other cities. The school surveys made a double contribution: they enabled Ayres and his associates to test and promote new tools for testing ability in

handwriting, spelling, arithmetic, and reading; and they created the ethics of contemporary management consultation in education, by establishing the principle that drafts of reports—findings and recommendations— would be discussed with local officials and a strategy for implementation devised before publication.

Between 1917 and 1920, Ayres applied the techniques of social research to national defense, war, and peacemaking while holding important public positions. In April 1917, volunteering with eight members of his staff on behalf of the Russell Sage Foundation, Ayres organized the Division of Statistics of the Council of National Defense. Six months later, Ayres had acquired responsibility for statistical reporting and analysis for the War Industries Board, the Priorities Committee, and the Allies' Purchasing Committee. In addition, he provided services to the army, which had no statistical office until early 1918, when Ayres's work was put under military auspices and he was made a lieutenant colonel. With a staff of fifty, he directed the Statistics Branch of the General Staff, preparing confidential reports for the military leadership and President Wilson, applying methods of research, analysis, and presentation that he had developed at the foundation. Later that year, he joined General Pershing in France with a statistical staff that had grown to 250 people. His statistical summary, *The War with Germany* (1919), brought him considerable public recognition. Following a brief period in the United States after the armistice, Ayres returned to France as chief statistical officer to the American Commission to Negotiate Peace. In 1924, when he served as economic advisor to the Dawes Plan Commission to examine reparations issues, it was widely noted that he was the only member of that group who had also served with the commission to negotiate peace. On his return to the United States he was promoted to colonel and awarded a Distinguished Service Medal.

After his return from Versailles in 1920, Ayres became vice-president and chief economist of the Cleveland Trust Company, in charge of statistics. He also edited a monthly economic review. The Cleveland offer, chosen in preference to several opportunities to teach and serve as an administrator in a university, was made by former Secretary of War Newton D. Baker and the bank president Frederick A. Goff, who, as leader of the Cleveland Foundation, the prototype of modern community trusts and foundations, had commissioned Ayres to conduct a school survey before the war. During his Cleveland years, Ayres wrote prolifically, mostly on economic questions, and achieved a national reputation for his opinions and predictions. After making pessimistic analyses of the state of the economy in the late 1920's, for example, he was one of the few economists to insist that the 1929 stock market crash foreshadowed a major depression. In the 1930's he argued in favor of public regulation of banking, minimized the influence of abandoning the gold standard on recovery, and criticized the National Recovery Act, urging instead legislation to stimulate business to price and profit competition. These ideas were developed in a widely read book, *The Economics of Recovery* (1933).

Ayres remained in Cleveland, writing and speaking to local and national audiences for the rest of his life, except for a return to active military service as a brigadier general from 1940 to 1942. He was chairman of the Economic Policy Commission of the American Bankers Association for two terms, 1932-1941 and 1944-1946, and also served as an officer of the American Statistical Association, the American Economic Association, and the American Association for the Advancement of Science.

Ayres's views reached a wide audience through the *Business Bulletin* of the Cleveland Trust Company, which the *New York Times* described as having a style unique for what may perhaps be described as "its penetrating simplicity" (Oct. 30, 1946). Particular attention was paid the *Bulletin*'s year-end business review and forecast. Ayres's forecasts also appeared in such national periodicals as *Banker's Magazine* and *World's Work*. He published seven books, numerous addresses and periodical articles, and many widely read reports. His reports in his Cleveland years included "The Automobile Industry and its Future" (1921), and "The Chief Cause of This and Other Depressions" (1935). He also directed studies on such topics as "The Earning Power of Banks" (1931) and "The Bank Chartering History and Policies of the United States" (1935). In 1931 he published a chart of American business activity since 1790, which he revised annually until 1946. He died of a heart attack while reading his morning newspaper in Cleveland, when he was sixty-seven, and was buried in the National Cemetery at Arlington.

Ayres was a "harmless looking man of modest build" who lived quietly and remained unmarried. He suffered the posthumous oblivion that is the fate of many generalists in an increasingly professionalized and stratified society. It is curious that the innovations he pioneered

in research methods and administration have been particularized by the disciplines to which he contributed, rather than remaining the set of general principles and applications which energized his work.

[The best secondary source for Ayres's early work is John M. Glen, Lilian Brandt, F. Emerson Andrews, *Russell Sage Foundation, 1907-1946*, 2 vols. (1947). Ayres's prolific writings, and the few interviews and articles that touch on his personal life, are listed in Business Information Bureau, Cleveland Public Library, *Leonard Porter Ayres: A List of His Published Works* (1947). Scanty details about his personal life can be gleaned from clippings in the archives of Boston Univ. A warm interpretation of his character and achievement was written by J.W.L., "Neighbors," *Survey*, July 1, 1924, pp. 417-418.]
                                    DANIEL M. FOX

BABCOCK, HOWARD EDWARD (Feb. 23, 1889-July 12, 1950), farm cooperative leader and agricultural educator, was born on a farm near Gilbertsville in Chenango County, N.Y., the only child of Mary Emma (Donahue) and Howard Worden Babcock. His father, a native of Vermont, was descended from a family which had settled in Rhode Island before the American Revolution; his mother was born in New York City, the daughter of a Protestant Irish father and an English mother. Babcock early shared in farm chores. After graduating from the Gilbertsville high school, he spent two years in farm work before entering Syracuse University. There he planned to study law but became interested in botany instead.

After receiving his B.A. degree in 1911, Babcock took a summer course at Cornell University to qualify for teaching vocational agriculture in high schools, a newly opening field. His first positions were at Albion, N.Y. (1911-1912), and at the Elmira Free Academy (1912-1913), where he was head of the biology department. At that time the movement for promoting better farming practices through demonstration work in the field, begun in 1903 by Seaman A. Knapp, was gaining a foothold in New York. Aided by state and federal funds, a system of county demonstration agents quickly grew up, linked to the extension department of the State College of Agriculture at Cornell and supported by county organizations of farmers known as farm bureaus. Babcock in 1913 became county agent for Cattaraugus County. His work was of such high quality that within a few months he was called to Ithaca as county agent for Tompkins County. On Oct. 23, 1913, he married Hilda Wall Butler, who had been a fellow teacher in Albion. They had three children: Howard Edward, Barbara Elizabeth, and John Butler.

Babcock became assistant state leader of county agents in 1914 and state leader two years later. The farm bureau system expanded rapidly under his direction, and in 1917 he fostered the establishment of the New York State Federation of County Farm Bureaus (later called the New York Farm Bureau Federation), of which he was secretary until 1921. From 1918 to 1920 he was also secretary of the New York Conference Board of Farm Organizations. While serving as state food commissioner during World War I, Babcock had become interested, as he later wrote, in "what farmers might do for themselves through a cooperative" (Ranney, p. 46). Thus, in 1920, he was instrumental in having the Board of Farm Organizations sponsor the founding of the Cooperative Grange League Federation Exchange (the G.L.F.) as a statewide cooperative purchasing organization. Babcock was one of the original directors of the G.L.F., and took charge of its "million-dollar" stock selling drive, which was a phenomenal success. He gave up his position as state county agent leader in 1920 to develop his own expanding farming interests near Ithaca. Later in the year he was persuaded by George F. Warren, head of the department of agricultural economics at Cornell University, to take a position there as professor of marketing. His innovative and stimulating courses attracted a large following of men who were soon to become key leaders in the G.L.F. and in agriculture.

When the G.L.F. faltered after two years of uncertain and inept management, Babcock was drafted to take charge as general manager. Under his leadership, it soon became the outstanding regional purchasing cooperative in the United States, and its pathfinding procedures made it the model for cooperatives throughout the nation. Babcock expanded the field sales force, upgraded the system of local distributive agencies, and made imaginative use of advertising to interest farmers in G.L.F. feed, seed, and fertilizer. He also established vital and lasting links with academic specialists in rural sociology, marketing, and agricultural sciences at Cornell and other land-grant universities. Babcock managed the G.L.F. from 1922 to 1932, and again from 1935 to 1937. He continued to give direction to the organization's marketing, research, and educational programs until 1945, by which time the G.L.F. had developed a business volume of $174 million and assets of over $34 million.

Babcock regarded the G.L.F. not only as a purchasing and marketing cooperative, but also as a great research and educational institution. Thus he helped establish the "University of the G.L.F.," which became the G.L.F. School of Cooperative Administration, and served as director from 1940 to 1943. This was the first major personnel training school sponsored by an American cooperative organization. Babcock also served on the board of trustees of Cornell University from 1930 until his death. As chairman, 1939-1946, he presided over the university's wartime expansion and, working with President Edmund E. Day and with New York Gov. Thomas E. Dewey, was instrumental in founding the Schools of Nutrition, Business Administration, and Labor Relations. Babcock's leadership, along with that of the first director, Leonard A. Maynard, made the School of Nutrition one of the best in the world.

Slender and bespectacled, Babcock was a man of restless energy, intellectual drive, and saving common sense. These qualities, together with his lucidity in oral and written expression, made him a national leader in American agriculture as early as 1919, when he helped organize the American Farm Bureau Federation. In 1933 he was called to Washington by the Roosevelt administration to help unscramble the Federal Farm Board and put the Farm Credit Administration on a sound operating basis. He was one of the first directors of the F.C.A.'s Central Bank for Cooperatives. As president of the National Council of Farmer Cooperatives in 1941, Babcock helped mobilize the work of cooperatives to meet wartime agricultural needs. Many honors came his way, including honorary doctorates from Syracuse University and Michigan State University. In 1946 the American Farm Bureau Federation granted Babcock its highest award for "Distinguished Service to American Agriculture."

Babcock made his own farm, "Sunnygables," something of an experimental laboratory in promoting advancements like grass silage, assembly-line milking, home freezers in the interest of better nutrition, and interchangeable wheels for farm equipment. While hospitalized in New York City following a minor operation, he died of a heart attack at the age of sixty-one. He was buried in East Lawn Cemetery, Ithaca, N.Y. Babcock had a profound and beneficial influence on the agricultural character of the United States, both through his demonstration of the possibilities and values of strong democratic cooperative organizations, and in his pioneering leadership in the fields of animal and human nutrition and in improved farm business and cultural practices.

[*Howard Edward Babcock* (mimeo., Cornell Univ., 1950) ; Joseph G. Knapp, *Seeds That Grew: A Hist. of the Grange League Federation Exchange* (1960) ; Thomas E. Milliman, *The GLF Story* (1964) ; Warren A. Ranney, "Howard Edward Babcock," in Joseph G. Knapp et al., *Great Am. Cooperators* (1967) ; Ruby Green Smith, *The People's Colleges: A Hist. of the N.Y. State Extension Service in Cornell Univ.* (1949) ; Gould P. Colman, *Education & Agriculture: A Hist. of the N.Y. State College of Agriculture at Cornell Univ.* (1963) ; information from Mrs. Babcock and Dr. William I. Myers. A portrait of Babcock by Bob Childress is at the School of Nutrition, Cornell Univ.; one by Bradford Crandall is in the trustee meeting room in Day Hall, Cornell.]
JOSEPH G. KNAPP

BACHELLER, IRVING (Sept. 26, 1859-Feb. 24, 1950), popular novelist, was born in Pierrepont, St. Lawrence County, N.Y., the son of Sanford Paul Bacheller and Achsah Ann (Buckland) Bacheller. Named Addison Irving, he was the fourth son and sixth of seven children. His father, born in Vermont, had grown up on a farm in the St. Lawrence Valley frontier. He met his wife while he was working in Springfield, Mass., and the couple returned to the North Country to farm and raise cattle.

Bacheller has described his youth as "bookbound and happy" (*Coming up the Road*, p. 73). After earlier schooling in Pierrepont, he attended the Canton (N.Y.) Academy when his family moved to that nearby town. Between the ages of thirteen and seventeen he was in and out of school and was employed variously as a telegraph operator, road gang worker, post office clerk, bookkeeper, salesman, and teacher. Although he had not completed high school, he was admitted to St. Lawrence University in 1878 as a special student. He received the B.S. degree in 1882, having been president of the college literary society and active in debate and oratory.

Following graduation, Bacheller went to New York City, where after working for a time on a hotel trade journal he joined the staff of the *Brooklyn Daily Times*, first as military and then as drama editor. In 1884 he arranged for the simultaneous publication by newspapers in several American cities of a series of interviews of literary notables by the English novelist Joseph Hatton. This led to the formation later that year of the New York Press Syndicate, directed by Bacheller in partnership with James W. Johnson—the first such enterprise in metropolitan journalism. (Previous syndicates had supplied inside pages to country weeklies.) Bacheller's syndicate grew rapidly and within a decade was sending fiction and feature stories to nearly all the leading newspapers in the United States. It was the first to publish *The Red Badge of Courage* by Stephen Crane, serializing it in 1893. Bacheller introduced Sir Arthur Conan Doyle and Rudyard Kipling to the American reading public and contracted with other leading contemporary writers, including Joseph Conrad, Hamlin Garland, and Anthony Hope.

After publishing the literary works of others, Bacheller decided to explore his own creative talents. He began with a ballad, "Whisperin' Bill," published in the *Independent* of July 17, 1890, a simple tale of the Civil War and its damaging effect on a particular soldier (modeled on someone Bacheller had known in his youth). This was followed by a short story, "A Passion Study" (*Cosmopolitan*, January 1897; published in book form as *The Story of a Passion*, 1899). A tale of nostalgia and local color, it foreshadowed Bacheller's later writings in both theme and style. His first novel, *The Master of Silence* (1892), sold only 600 copies; the next, *The Still House of O'Darrow* (1894), was published only in England.

Fearing the consequences of depression and growing competition, Bacheller sold his newspaper syndicate in 1896 to John Brisben Walker, the owner of *Cosmopolitan*. He soon began working on a new novel but had to put it aside when Joseph Pulitzer called him in 1898 to be Sunday editor of the New York *World*. After a year and a half Bacheller took a leave of absence to complete the novel, which was published in July 1900 as *Eben Holden*. This romantic tale about pioneers in the St. Lawrence Valley during the nineteenth century, which drew upon Bacheller's own childhood experiences, won praise from William Dean Howells, E. C. Stedman, and Walter Hines Page and became an immediate best seller, with total sales estimated at 750,000. Bacheller himself described the book as meeting a public demand for something "clean, strong, sincere, uplifting, and American" (*Critic*, October 1904, p. 298). The central characters are Eben Holden, a hired man who combines the characteristics of jovial Yankee and rustic philosopher, and the small boy Willie. The sole survivors of a devastated home in Vermont, they travel to the St. Lawrence Valley and find a new life, and Willie grows up to become a Civil War reporter for the *New York Tribune*.

Bacheller's next novel, *D'ri and I* (1901), was also a success. A similar blending of patriotism, humor, and romance, it describes the adventures of a soldier, Ramon Bell, and his hired man, D'ri (Darius Olin), during and following the War of 1812. Ramon Bell is the romantic hero; his foil is D'ri, a Yankee patriot whose "frugal wit" is "expressed in grinning idioms" (*Independent*, Sept. 5, 1901, p. 2117).

Over the next forty years (with the exception of service in 1917 as a war correspondent in France) Bacheller devoted his time to his own writing, publishing more than thirty novels and numerous short stories, essays, and poems. These ranged in setting and subject from the time of Christ (*Dawn*, 1927) and ancient Rome (*Vergilius*, 1904) to his familiar North Country (*The Light in the Clearing*, 1917), and included romances and historical novels. Three books are devoted to stages in the life of Abraham Lincoln—*A Man for the Ages* (1919), *Father Abraham* (1925), and *A Boy for the Ages* (1937). *In the Days of Poor Richard* (1922) centers on Benjamin Franklin; *The Master of Chaos* (1932), a tale of the Revolution, on George Washington. Three volumes comprise Bacheller's reminiscences of his own life and express his lighthearted philosophy: *Coming up the Road* (1928), which tells of his boyhood, *Opinions of a Cheerful Yankee* (1926), and the anecdotal *From Stores of Memory* (1938).

Bacheller was of athletic build, a devotee of nature and the outdoor life. Renowned for his after-dinner storytelling, he was quiet and easygoing, yet filled with what a friend called "judicial determination" (*Opinions of a Cheerful Yankee*, p. 224). Although not officially a church member until late in life, he followed his mother's Universalist faith. Bacheller married Anna Detmar Schultz of Brooklyn on Dec. 13, 1883. She died in 1924, and on June 25, 1925, he married a widow, Mary Elizabeth (Leonard) Sollace of Flushing, N.Y., who died in 1949. He had an adopted son, Paul. From 1905 to 1917 Bacheller lived in Riverside, Conn.; he then moved to Winter Park, Fla., but returned to Riverside for the summers. He died of bronchopneumonia at the age of ninety at the Westchester Division of the New York Hospital in White Plains, N.Y., and was buried in Kensico Cemetery, Valhalla, N.Y.

Bacheller's works provided millions of readers with vivid portraits of American pioneers and frontier life. Their popularity stemmed initially from their expression of national pride and cheerful optimism at a time of patriotic nostalgia following the Spanish-American War. Although little read a generation later, Bacheller was praised in his day. Hamlin Garland wrote of him, he "not only keeps his native land in memory: he has put it imperishably into American fiction. In his [works] . . . you may find the finest types and the best traditions of 'The North Country' " (*American Magazine*, April 1918, p. 19).

[Sketchy biographical information from Bacheller's *Coming up the Road, From Stores of Memory*, and *Opinions of a Cheerful Yankee* is supplemented by *Nat. Cyc. Am. Biog.*, XL, 10–11; Stanley J. Kunitz and Howard Haycraft, eds., *Twentieth Century Authors* (1942); and Alberta Lawrence, ed., *Who's Who among North American Authors*, 1936–1939. See also contemporary accounts in *Current Literature*, Oct. 1904, pp. 323–325; the *Critic*, Oct. 1904, pp. 294–298; *Bookman*, Nov. 1900, pp. 218–221; *Everybody's Mag.*, June 1919, p. 43; Robert van Gelder, "An Interview with Irving Bacheller," *N.Y. Times Book Rev.*, Dec. 21, 1941; Edward F. Harkins in *Literary World*, July 1903; Hamlin Garland in *American Mag.*, Apr. 1918; and reviews of his principal novels. Bacheller expresses his philosophy in several essays, of which the most useful are "The Rungs in My Little Ladder," *American Mag.*, Apr. 1918; "What's the Matter?" *Outlook*, Jan. 25, 1922; and "The Idiotic Era," *Rev. of Revs.*, May 1932. A. J. Hanna, *A Bibliog. of the Writings of Irving Bacheller* (1939), includes all of Bacheller's writings up to the time of publication, with a chronology and interpretive essay. See also, for background and references to Bacheller, Frank L. Mott, *Am. Journalism* (1941) and *Golden Multitudes* (1947); James D. Hart, *The Popular Book* (1950); Ernest E. Leisy, *The Am. Historical Novel* (1950); and Elmo S. Watson, *A Hist. of Newspaper Syndicates in the U.S. 1865–1935* (1936). Death record from N.Y. State Dept. of Health.]

OLIVIA A. HAEHN

BAGLEY, WILLIAM CHANDLER (Mar. 15, 1874–July 1, 1946), educator, was born in Detroit, Mich., to Ruth (Walker) and William Chase Bagley. Both parents were natives of Massachusetts; his father was for many years superintendent of the Harper Hospital in Detroit. Bagley attended elementary school in Worcester, Mass., and high school in Detroit and entered the Michigan Agricultural College in 1891. Upon graduation in 1895, finding no opening for a specialist in scientific agriculture, he took a job in a one-teacher school in the lumbering town of Garth in Michigan's Upper Peninsula.

Bagley enjoyed teaching and early sought to learn more about the principles of education. In the summer of 1896 he took courses at the University of Chicago in psychology and in the physiology of the nervous system. After his second year at Garth, he borrowed enough money to study at the University of Wisconsin under Joseph Jastrow, Michael Vincent O'Shea, and John William Stearns and received the M.S. degree in 1898. He then began doctoral work in psychology and education at Cornell under the tutelage of Edward Bradford Titchener. Bagley received his Ph.D. in 1900 with a dissertation on "The Apperception of the Spoken Sentence"—one of the first doctorates to be completed in Titchener's famed psychological laboratory. In the winter of 1901 he accepted the principalship of the Meramec

Elementary School in St. Louis, Mo., and on August 14 of that year he married Florence MacLean Winger of Lincoln, Nebr. They had four children: Ruth Winger, Joseph Winger, William Chandler, and Florence Winger.

Seeking a healthier climate for his wife, Bagley in 1902 moved to the Montana State Normal College at Dillon as professor of psychology and pedagogy and director of its training department. He subsequently became vice-president of the college and superintendent of the Dillon public schools, where he instituted the employment of practice teachers, as well as the use of maps, sandtables, globes, and aquariums in the classroom. Bagley left Dillon in 1906 for a position at the State Normal School in Oswego, N.Y., but two years later went to the University of Illinois as professor of education, becoming director of the School of Education in 1909. He worked closely with the university's progressive president, Edmund Janes James, to build a strong faculty and a strong program in education. In 1914 Bagley began working part-time on a survey of teacher training in Missouri sponsored by the Carnegie Foundation and directed by William S. Learned. He left the University of Illinois in 1917 to accept a professorship at Teachers College, Columbia University, but first took a year's leave of absence for further work on the survey. At Teachers College, Bagley organized a department for the study of normal schools and teachers' training classes. He continued at Teachers College until his retirement in 1939.

Bagley was concerned with two goals: defining a general theory of education and professionalizing teacher training. At first he was confident that psychological and biological research would discover and verify fundamental principles upon which a science of education could be built. This view was reflected in his books *The Educative Process* (1905) and *Classroom Management* (1907). In 1910 Bagley joined J. Carleton Bell, Carl E. Seashore, and Guy Montrose Whipple in the founding and editing of the *Journal of Educational Psychology*. By 1911, however, when he published *Educational Values*, Bagley had begun to lose his faith in psychology. Seven years later he had concluded that teaching was not an applied science but an art.

Bagley devoted most of his career to improving the professional preparation of public school teachers, through his participation in school surveys, through his writings and public addresses, and through his work on teacher-training curricula. His most successful book,

Classroom Management, sought to equip novice teachers with the skills and techniques necessary for effective control of the classroom. Bagley was author or co-author of a number of books aimed at upgrading the teaching profession, such as *Craftsmanship in Teaching* (1911). He also collaborated on several grade school textbooks, among them a *History of the American People,* written with Charles A. Beard. His concern for professionalization led him, early in his career (1905), to found the *Inter-Mountain Educator,* the first such school journal in the northern Rocky Mountain region. He edited *School and Home Education* from 1912 to 1914 and the *Journal of the National Education Association* from 1920 to 1925. When he retired from teaching, Bagley worked with the Carnegie Foundation to organize the Society for the Advancement of Education and was editor until his death of its journal, *School and Society.*

Fundamental to Bagley's thought was his emphasis on the collective social good as opposed to the satisfaction of individual desires. This concern contributed to his critical attitude toward progressive education. In a much-publicized address of 1938, "An Essentialist's Platform for the Advancement of American Education," Bagley voiced the opinion of an influential group within the teaching profession who deplored many of the current innovations in curriculum and teaching practice. To their mind, progressive educators were prone to overvalue every scientific and philosophical innovation and to substitute fads and panaceas for sound, continuing practices. Language and arithmetical skills were the essentials around which any viable program must be built. For Bagley, especially, it was imperative to make use of the "social heritage," to provide a socially useful education for citizenship. But though critical of the progressivists, Bagley was by no means a reactionary. He spoke out, for example, in his *Determinism in Education* (1925) against those who would restrict educational opportunity on the basis of the currently popular intelligence tests.

Students remember Bagley as vigorous, energetic, and forward-looking. He died in New York City at the age of seventy-two. His remains were cremated.

[I. L. Kandel, *William Chandler Bagley: Stalwart Educator* (1961); Erwin V. Johanningmeier, "William Chandler Bagley's Changing Views on the Relationship Between Psychology and Education," *Hist. of Education Quart.,* Spring 1969; Henry C. Johnson, Jr., and Erwin V. Johanningmeier, *Teachers for the Prairie: The Univ. of Ill. and the Schools, 1868–1945* (1972). See also: *Nat. Cyc. Am. Biog.,* XXXV, 227–228. An official portrait of Bagley hangs in the Founders Room of the national headquarters of Kappa Delta Pi in Lafayette, Ind. For an earlier likeness, see the photograph published in the *Kadelpian Rev.*, Mar. 1928.]

ERWIN V. JOHANNINGMEIER

BAILEY, FLORENCE AUGUSTA MERRIAM (Aug. 8, 1863-Sept. 22, 1948), ornithologist, writer, and teacher, was born at Locust Grove, a village two miles southwest of Port Leyden, Lewis County, N.Y. She was the last of four children of Clinton Levi Merriam and Caroline (Hart) Merriam. Her father, a merchant and banker in Utica and later in New York City, retired to his Lewis County estate, Homewood, about the time she was born, and from 1871 to 1875 served two terms in the U.S. House of Representatives. His ancestry traced back to Joseph Merriam, who came to Concord, Mass., from Kent, England, about 1636. Her mother was the daughter of Levi Hart, an early settler of the area who became a county judge and state assemblyman; she was a graduate of the Rutgers Female Institute, New York City. Florence's uncle Augustus Merriam was a professor of classical archaeology at Columbia, and her older brother Dr. Clinton Hart Merriam (1855-1942) served for many years as chief of the U.S. Biological Survey.

At Homewood her early education was obtained from her family. From the unspoiled surroundings of the western foothills of the Adirondacks she acquired the love of wild nature, which became the dominant force of her life. At Smith College, which she entered in 1882 after preparatory studies at Mrs. Pratt's Seminary in Utica, she helped to found one of the first Audubon Society chapters in the country, getting valuable aid in conducting bird walks from naturalist John Burroughs.

Merriam attended Smith as a special student, with English as a particular area of concentration, reflecting her desire to become a writer. She left Smith in 1886 without a degree (finally awarded in 1921), but she had already begun writing a series of articles on birds for publication in *Audubon Magazine*. These were collected and much augmented to make up her first book, *Birds Through an Opera Glass* (1889), which was reprinted a number of times. In a style which continued to mark most of her work, she combined in this book close observation with a warm enthusiasm for her subjects, and a desire to enlighten and entertain her readers.

Family trips to California and Bermuda offered new fields of nature study. She attended for one month during the summer of 1891 a school started for Chicago working girls as a branch of Jane Addams' Hull House, and the following winter she was employed in one of Grace Dodge's working girls' clubs. In the midst of these activities she became ill with tuberculosis, and in 1893 was forced to seek a better climate in the West—thus beginning, as it turned out, the important western phase of her career.

My Summer in a Mormon Village (1894) was a sensitively written book, far more concerned with the social realities and complexities of Mormon life (especially with regard to polygamy) than with natural scenes or creatures. *A-birding on a Bronco* (1896), recounting her outdoor studies in the Southwest—and implicitly her return to health—was the first of her western bird books. The others were *Handbook of Birds of the Western United States* (1902), *Birds of New Mexico* (1928), and *Among the Birds in the Grand Canyon National Park Country* (1939). Both the *Handbook* and the New Mexico volume were major achievements. The former was a counterpart to Frank Chapman's *Handbook of Birds of Eastern North America* (1895) and, like that work, soon became a standard reference in its field, succinct and technical, but with informative remarks and illustrations for nearly all of its many hundreds of species and races. The New Mexico work, originally planned as part of a Biological Survey report, in her hands was greatly revised and enlarged to become a comprehensive book of general use and interest. For it she received the Brewster Medal of the American Ornithologists' Union, the first woman so honored.

Both books were to some extent collaborative efforts, with much work contributed by Vernon Bailey (1864-1942), a biologist for the U. S. Biological Survey, whom Merriam met at her brother's home in Washington, D.C., and married on Dec. 16, 1899. From then on, Florence Merriam Bailey often shared in her husband's field trips, and each helped with the other's books. By rail or wagon, by pack train or afoot, they traveled and camped from Texas to Washington state, in Glacier Park, in North Dakota, Minnesota, and Wisconsin, in the Mammoth Cave region of Kentucky, and in the Adirondacks. Clearly theirs was a marriage of warmly shared devotion to the natural world, and of deep personal affection.

Though her travels testify to Bailey's physical vigor and intrepid spirit, and her published works to her need for assertion and achievement, those who knew her tell also of gentler, more traditionally feminine attributes. Field trips and outdoor living restored her health, but she remained delicate in appearance and artlessly direct in her responses to natural creatures. To select one example from among many, she wrote this caption for a photograph of a New Mexico owl: "The old mother on the edge of the nest. Surely she will not let the beautiful eggs get cold."

For many years the Bailey home in Washington, D.C., was a gathering place for natural history professionals and amateurs, young and old. Childless herself, she hoped always to impart to young people her love for birds. Her first book, for example, was included in a series of juveniles, and her fourth, *Birds of Village and Field* (1898), was subtitled *A Bird Book for Beginners.*

She died of myocardial degeneration in Washington in her eighty-sixth year, and was buried at the Homewood estate.

[Other titles by Bailey include *How Birds Affect the Farm and Garden* (1896), *Some Needs of Public Education in the District of Columbia* (1905), and *Birds Recorded from the Santa Rita Mountains in Southern Arizona* (1923); with Vernon Bailey, *Wild Animals of Glacier Park* (1918); and *Cave Life of Kentucky* (1933). Beginning about 1890, many of her articles appeared in *The Auk, Bird-Lore,* and *The Condor.*
Paul H. Oehser, who knew Bailey in her later years, contributed the biographical essay in *Notable Am. Women,* I, 82–83, and memorial articles in *Nature Mag.,* Mar. 1950, and *The Auk,* Jan. 1952. Other secondary sources: *Biog. Cyc. Am. Women,* II, 206–211; *Nat. Cyc. Am. Biog.,* XIII, 263–264.]
ROBERT H. WELKER

BAILEY, JOSIAH WILLIAM (Sept. 14, 1873-Dec. 15, 1946), United States senator, was born in Warrenton, N.C., the second son and third of five children of Christopher Thomas and Annie Sarah (Bailey) Bailey. Both parents were natives of Virginia. The father, a Baptist minister, soon moved his family to Raleigh, N.C., where he edited the *Biblical Recorder,* a Baptist weekly newspaper with the second largest circulation of any periodical in the state. Bailey attended local schools, the Raleigh Male Academy, and Wake Forest College, where he read extensively in the English classics and studied Greek. After graduating with the B.A. degree in 1893, he took over the editorial duties of his father, who had suffered a stroke; he officially became editor of the *Recorder* after his father's death two years later.

Almost immediately Bailey became involved in the attempt to improve North Carolina's public schools, a crusade begun under the leadership of such reformers as Charles D. McIver and Edwin A. Alderman, but Bailey followed his own course. In his editorials he proposed financing public schools through legislative appropriation, instead of through local taxes as the reformers preferred, and he advocated a compulsory four-month school term. His campaign drew him into political life. Although a Democrat, he was appointed in 1895 by the Republican-Populist fusion governor, David L. Russell, to the state Board of Agriculture. Bailey resigned three years later and allied himself with the state Democratic chairman, Furnifold M. Simmons, in the successful "white supremacy" campaign which that year broke the political control of the fusionist alliance. In return, Simmons saw to it that the legislature enacted Bailey's educational proposals in 1899. A prohibitionist, Bailey served as chairman of the executive committee of North Carolina's Anti-Saloon League (1903-1907), but resigned when the league abandoned support of local option in favor of state prohibition.

Bailey was never happy as an editor, and in 1905, believing that a legal career provided the best foundation for politics, he began to study law. He resigned as editor of the *Biblical Recorder* in 1907, was admitted to the bar the following year, and set up a law practice in Raleigh. As his political activity increased, he served on the Wake County Board of Education (1909-1911) and as chairman of the state Child Labor Committee (1911-1913). Although a lieutenant in the Simmons machine, Bailey gained a reputation for progressivism by urging the adoption of state election reforms, helping to establish a commission form of government for Raleigh, and working to improve the law limiting child labor. In 1914 he led a concerted attempt to induce the state Democratic convention to adopt a program of progressive measures, but without success. Meanwhile President Woodrow Wilson, whom Bailey firmly supported, had in 1913 appointed him collector of internal revenue for the eastern district of North Carolina, a post (broadened in 1919 to cover the whole state) that Bailey held for eight years and administered with marked efficiency. His marriage on Aug. 16, 1916, to Edith Walker Pou allied him with one of the state's most influential families. They had five children: James Hinton Pou, Annie Elizabeth, Josiah William, Edith Pou, and Sally.

Bailey had continued his close ties with the political organization of Senator Simmons, but during the 1920's he came to feel he could achieve higher office only by breaking away. He therefore waged an independent, but unsuccessful, race for the Democratic gubernatorial nomination in 1924. In the presidential campaign of 1928, when Simmons bolted the party and backed Herbert Hoover, Bailey loyally supported Alfred E. Smith. Two years later, taking advantage of Simmons' irregularity, Bailey ran against him in the primary and won Simmons' seat in the United States Senate. He remained in the Senate until his death.

An early supporter of Franklin D. Roosevelt, Bailey acquiesced in much of the early New Deal legislation, including the National Industrial Recovery Act (1933) and the Emergency Relief Appropriation Act (1935). Increasingly, however, he grew uneasy over the New Deal's tendency toward centralization. A solemn, dignified man who saw politics as the clash of moral and constitutional principles (he was dubbed "Holy Joe" by the press), Bailey believed in the traditional virtues of states' rights, self-help, and balanced budgets. After 1936, declaring himself a "conservative by nature," he began actively to oppose the administration on such measures as the Wagner-Steagall Housing Act (1937) and the Fair Labor Standards Act (1938). He also played a major role in the defeat of Roosevelt's "court-packing" plan in 1937. By then a leading spokesman for a bipartisan group of anti-New Deal senators, Bailey drafted, with Sen. Arthur H. Vandenberg, a "conservative manifesto" expressing the group's determination to limit government intervention in the free enterprise system.

Bailey nevertheless remained on good terms with Roosevelt and consistently, if tacitly, endorsed him in his reelection campaigns. In foreign affairs, Bailey abandoned a lifelong isolationism to support the president's policy of preparedness. He backed both increased defense expenditures and the Selective Service Act in 1940, and the following year worked diligently for passage of the Lend-Lease Bill. During World War II, antagonized by labor strikes, he repeatedly but unsuccessfully promoted a "work or fight" law to draft civilians who were exempt from military service into essential war industries. As chairman of the Senate Commerce Committee, Bailey throughout the war played an important part in overseeing the acquisition of merchant vessels for defense purposes and in determining national maritime policy. Following the war he strongly championed the establishment of the United Nations.

Never robust, Bailey suffered throughout his career from migraine headaches. During much of 1945 and 1946 illness kept him from his work in the Senate. He died of a cerebral hemorrhage at his home in Raleigh, and was buried in that city's Oakwood Cemetery.

[A large collection of Bailey's papers is at Duke Univ. John Robert Moore, *Senator Josiah William Bailey of N.C.* (1968), is a detailed analysis of his career and contains an extensive bibliography. Elmer L. Puryear, *Democratic Party Dissension in N.C., 1928–1936* (1962); James T. Patterson, *Congressional Conservatism and the New Deal* (1967); Joseph F. Steelman, "The Progressive Democratic Convention of 1914 in N.C.," *N.C. Hist. Rev.*, Spring 1969; and Richard L. Watson, Jr., "A Southern Democratic Primary: Simmons *vs.* Bailey in 1930," *ibid.*, Winter 1965.]

JOHN ROBERT MOORE

BAKER, HUGH POTTER (Jan. 20, 1878–May 24, 1950), forester and college president, was born in St. Croix Falls, Polk County, Wis. He was the fifth of the six sons of Joseph Stannard Baker, real estate agent and owner of extensive timberland, and Alice (Potter) Baker. One brother was the journalist Ray Stannard Baker; another, Charles Fuller Baker (1872–1927), became a zoologist and botanist of some note. After local schooling, Hugh entered Macalester College, St. Paul, Minn., but transferred after a year to Michigan Agricultural College, where he received the B.S. degree in 1901. He earned the master of forestry degree at Yale University in 1904 and the degree of doctor of economics at the University of Munich in 1910.

Meanwhile, in 1901, Hugh and his brother Fred (later a professor of forestry at Michigan Agricultural College) had begun part-time duty as assistants in the federal Bureau of Forestry headed by Gifford Pinchot. Over the next six years Hugh Baker participated in the preparation of forest management plans for the owners of private timberland and helped compile data for the possible forestation of sand dunes at various shore points on the Atlantic and Pacific coasts and the Great Lakes. Pinchot regarded him highly and apparently would have been pleased to have him as a full-time employee, but Baker decided instead on a teaching career. In 1904, after receiving his master's degree, he became an assistant professor of forestry at Iowa State College in Ames, and, on December 27 of that year, he married Fleta Paddock of Three Oaks, Mich. Three years later he moved to Pennsylvania State College as professor of forestry, succeeding Bernhard E. Fernow, a pioneer in American forestry. Building upon Fernow's early efforts, Baker raised the forestry department to major status within the college of agriculture, with access to a 7,000-acre state forest reserve for study and demonstration work.

Baker's achievements attracted the attention of officials at Syracuse University, who in 1911, after a long contest with Cornell University, had secured the location of New York's new State College of Forestry on their campus. Early in 1912 they persuaded him to become the college's first dean. Aided by a generous state appropriation, Baker soon made it one of the leading schools of forestry in the United States. He developed a five-year program leading to the degree of master of forestry, and established summer courses in forest ecology, botany, soils, geology, and woodcraft. He also helped establish the New York State Ranger School in a 2,000-acre forest in the Adirondacks. A subsidiary unit of the State College of Forestry, the school by 1913 was offering one- and two-year courses training men for positions as rangers, guards, forest estate managers, tree planting experts, and nursery foremen, the first such technical institution in America.

In 1920, evidently tired of constant struggles with the state legislature for financial support, Baker resigned from Syracuse University to become executive secretary of the American Paper and Pulp Association in New York City. He regarded this position as an opportunity to bring the principles of scientific forestry into a major organization of manufacturers dependent upon forest resources. During this phase of his career he was also a member of the National Forestry Program Committee, an industry-oriented group that encouraged forestation and protection against fire through cooperation of the federal government, the states, and private timber owners. He undertook similar work in 1928 as manager of the trade association department of the Chamber of Commerce of the United States, an appointment that evidenced the growing commercial concern for better forest management during the 1920's. He later (1931-1932) served as a member of the advisory committee of the Timber Conservation Board appointed by Secretary of Commerce Robert P. Lamont.

Baker returned to academic activities in 1930 when he again became dean of the New York State College of Forestry at Syracuse University. Three years later he was chosen president of Massachusetts State College in Amherst. His administration saw a significant expansion of the programs and facilities of what had been until 1931 the Massachusetts Agricultural College. Moving conservatively in response to pressures from students and the outside community, Baker presided over a gradual broadening of the agricultural curriculum marked by the in-

troduction in 1938 of the A.B. degree and the creation of separate departments in such fields as economics, psychology, and engineering. The building of new dormitories made possible a modest expansion in enrollment on the eve of World War II. Postwar pressures for state-supported higher education brought the official transformation of the college into the University of Massachusetts in 1947, the year Baker retired from the presidency.

Baker and his first wife had three children: Carolyn, Stephen Paddock, and Clarence Potter. In 1928 Fleta Baker died, and on Nov. 27, 1929, Baker married Richarda Sahla of Bückeburg, Germany.

In poor health Baker spent the last months of his life in a sanatorium in Orlando, Fla., where he died of cancer at the age of seventy-two. He was buried at St. Croix Falls, Wis.

[Published biographical material is meager: sketches in *Who Was Who in America*, III (1960), *Am. Men of Sci.*, 8th ed. (1949), and the *Nat. Cyc. Am. Biog.*, XXXIX, 421–422; brief obituaries in the *Jour. of Forestry*, July 1950, and the *N.Y. Times*, May 25, 1950. Records of the U.S. Forest Service in the Nat. Archives, Washington, D.C., document Baker's part-time work for the service from 1901 to 1907; records of the Dept. of Agriculture in the same institution contain scattered references concerning other aspects of his career. His academic role is set forth in W. Freeman Galpin, *Syracuse Univ.*, II, *The Growing Years* (1960); and Harold W. Cary, *The Univ. of Mass.: A Hist. of 100 Years* (1962). Death record from Fla. Bureau of Vital Statistics.]

HAROLD T. PINKETT

BAKER, OLIVER EDWIN (Sept. 10, 1883-Dec. 2, 1949), agricultural and economic geographer, was born in Tiffin, Ohio, the only child of Edwin Baker and Martha Ranney (Thomas) Baker. His father, a descendant of Rev. Nicholas Baker, who emigrated from England to Massachusetts in 1635, was a seafaring man from Cape Cod who moved to Tiffin and became a carpet merchant; his mother, also born in New England, had been a teacher. She looked after much of her son's early education, for he was a frail child and was often forced to miss school.

Although asthma and other health problems plagued him, Baker obtained a broad education. He attended Tiffin's Heidelberg University, a small liberal-arts college affiliated with the United Church of Christ, and earned a bachelor's degree in 1903, emphasizing mathematics, history, and botany, and a master's degree the following year, in sociology and philosophy. He then earned a second master's degree at Columbia University in 1905, this time in political science, and studied forestry at Yale in

1907-1908. Next, he became a graduate student in agriculture at the University of Wisconsin, specializing in soils and doing research on the effects of climate on Wisconsin agriculture. Long interested in geography, he developed maps of climates and soils and studied Henry C. Taylor's mapping of agricultural production. When William J. Spillman of the Office of Farm Management, U.S. Department of Agriculture, became interested in exploring a geographical approach to farm problems, Taylor recommended Baker for the job. Joining the department in 1912, Baker embarked upon several significant, long-term projects delineating agricultural regions and mapping the physical basis of agriculture, agricultural production, and agricultural trade.

As his geographical work moved forward, Baker enlarged the economic dimension. Encouraged by Taylor, a pioneer in agricultural economics, he returned to the University of Wisconsin and earned a Ph.D. in economics in 1921 with a dissertation on land utilization. When the USDA's Bureau of Agricultural Economics was established in 1922, with Taylor as chief, Baker became a member. During the next decade, he published extensively on land utilization, working closely with L. C. Gray and contributing to the changes taking place in thinking about land policy.

Before the end of the 1920's, Baker began to shift his attention to population problems, influenced by the farm crisis, the shift of population to the cities, and the sharp drop in the birthrate. That drop had, he believed, brought to an end an era of extraordinary increase in population and of agricultural expansion. Now, he suggested, instead of the food scarcities that had been feared, food supply exceeded demand in the United States and seemed likely to continue to do so, for soon the population would begin to decline. His conclusions influenced the Hoover and Roosevelt administrations, contributing to their attempts at land-use planning and to their efforts to cut back on agricultural production and to develop new communities.

Baker hoped to reverse undesirable trends. Worried that society would soon not have enough leaders, he urged well-educated people to have more children. Very critical of city life, he called for improvements in rural living that would make it more attractive to able people, and he advocated a "rurban" civilization that would combine industrial and commercial employment with life in villages and suburbs and part-time farming. Such developments would, he was convinced, strengthen family ties, improve land-use practices, and increase the birthrate.

Baker's own marriage came rather late, and his choice of a wife, the size of his family, and their style of life conformed with his theories. Already forty-two, he married Alice Hargrave Crew, the daughter of a distinguished physicist, on Dec. 30, 1925. They had three daughters, Helen Thomas, Sabra Zilpha, and Mildred Coale, and one son, Edwin Crew. The family lived on a large suburban plot that enabled them to raise chickens and cows and cultivate a garden.

A research leader as well as a research worker, Baker had a personality that suited him for both roles. Although he was not physically strong, he worked hard and creatively. He accepted suggestions from those who worked with him, was interested in their work, and inspired, encouraged, and helped them.

As a geographer, he did pioneering work of basic significance, helped to broaden the discipline, and carried his research and theories into the policy-making arena. His contributions were widely recognized. He taught and lectured at several universities, including Clark and Chicago, and, in 1932, became president of the Association of American Geographers. In 1937, he received an honorary Ph.D. from Göttingen University.

Baker left the Department of Agriculture in 1942 to become professor and department chairman at the University of Maryland. He created and developed the department of geography, building it into an important part of the profession. He remained active in research, assisting in the development of an atlas of the world's natural resources and another on China. And, although the "baby boom" had begun, his concern with population trends persisted. As the cold war began, he warned that within a century the United States would be dominated by Russia because of America's declining birthrate and luxury living.

Baker resigned as department chairman in July 1949, hoping to push his research forward, but he died suddenly, of a coronary occlusion, at his home in College Park, Md., on Dec. 2, 1949. Although he had been raised as a Methodist and regarded the church as a valuable institution, he had not been a member. His funeral service was held in his home, and his ashes were scattered over his large farm, near New Market, Va., where he had pursued his interests in soil conservation.

[The records of the B.A.E. in the Nat. Arch. contain Baker's official papers. Much of his career can be traced in the USDA *Yearbooks* from 1915 to 1938. His most important contributions as a geographer include a *Geography of the World's Agriculture* (Gov. Printing Office, 1917); a series on "Agricultural Regions of North America" published in *Economic Geography* from 1926 to 1933; several graphic summaries of American agriculture published in the *Yearbooks* and other government publications, and the monumental *Atlas of American Agriculture* that developed under his direction over two decades and was published in final form by the Gov. Printing Office in 1936. His presidential address, "Rural-Urban Migration and the National Welfare," *Annals of the Assoc. of Am. Geographers, Annals* 40 (1950) : 328–334. For Baker, Ralph Barsodi, and M. L. Wilson, *Agriculture in Modern Life* (1939), are especially valuable on his work and ideas in the 1930's. Two of his close associates, S. S. Visher and Charles Y. Hu, published a perceptive summary of his career with a photograph of him and a bibliography of his work for the Assoc. of Am. Geographers, *Annals* 40 (1950) : 328–334. For appraisals of his contributions, Richard Hartshorne, "The Nature of Geography : A Critical Survey of Current Thought in the Light of the Past," Assoc. of Am. Geographers, *Annals* 29 (1939), 450 ; Leonard A. Salter, Jr., *A Critical Rev. of Research in Land Economics* (1948) ; Howard Odum, *American Sociology: The Story of Sociology in the United States Through 1950* (1951) ; Henry C. and Anne Dewees Taylor, *The Story of Agricultural Economics in the United States, 1840–1932* (1952) ; and Richard S. Kirkendall, "L. C. Gray and the Supply of Agricultural Land," *Agricultural Hist.* 37 (1963) : 208.]

RICHARD S. KIRKENDALL

BAKER, RAY STANNARD (Apr. 17, 1870–July 12, 1946), journalist and author, was born in Lansing, Mich., the first of the six sons of Joseph Stannard Baker and Alice (Potter) Baker. Of primarily English stock, he was descended on his father's side from Alexander Baker, who came to Massachusetts in 1635, and Joseph Stannard, who settled in Connecticut in 1662. Over the centuries Baker's forebears gained some fame if no great fortune. Capt. Remember Baker, his great-great-grandfather, led the Green Mountain Boys with his cousins Ira and Ethan Allen. Baker's father during the Civil War joined the Secret Service under La Fayette C. Baker, a cousin, and subsequently earned distinction as commander of a cavalry company. After the war, Joseph Baker left his birthplace in Genesee County in western New York for Michigan. He eventually secured a job as agent for the land interests of Caleb Cushing and settled his growing family in St. Croix Falls, Wis.

Ray Baker, cherishing his pioneer heritage, later credited his faith in democracy to the rough egalitarianism of life on the Wisconsin frontier. Yet other influences also shaped his character and vision. Joseph Baker, gruffly honest, sometimes dogmatic, usually cautious, provided his son a model of principled moderation. Both father and mother had attended college: he, Oberlin and Wisconsin; she, Olivet. Their sizable library enriched young Ray's leisure hours, and their devotion to good literature introduced him to the best of a culture only a later generation would call "genteel." Devout Presbyterians, they bequeathed a religious faith which Baker would modify but never abandon. The senior Baker fought a running battle with the lumbering interests whose dams flooded his lands, thus providing his son an early illustration of the plight of the individual in a corporate society. Although never wealthy, the Bakers enjoyed a comfortable living and considerable prestige in the small community.

After a year of high school, Ray Baker entered Michigan Agricultural College in East Lansing. He took a wide range of courses but most enjoyed his science classes, especially those with the botanist William James Beal, whose call for careful observation contributed directly to Baker's later success as a reporter. Active in the Y.M.C.A., a fraternity man (Phi Delta Theta), and editor of the school newspaper, Baker evidenced the driving energy that characterized his entire career. After receiving a B.S. degree in 1889, he reluctantly returned home to help his father in business. He entered law school at the University of Michigan in January 1892, but after a few months abandoned these studies to audit courses in literature, among them a pioneering seminar in journalism conducted by Fred Newton Scott. In June, disillusioned with business and law, he went to Chicago, determined to find literary work, and secured a job as a reporter on the influential *Chicago News-Record* of Victor F. Lawson. Since he planned to write the "Great American Novel," Baker initially gave little thought to a career in journalism, much less in reform. His experiences, however, with the poverty of the depression years, with Coxey's Army, and with the Pullman Strike awakened him to social realities, and Lawson's liberal policies encouraged full and sympathetic reporting of these events.

Baker left the *Record* in 1898 to join the staff of *McClure's,* a leader in the "New Journalism" that was revolutionizing the magazine world. The staff, led by editors Samuel S. McClure and John S. Phillips, included Ida M. Tarbell and Lincoln Steffens. A versatile reporter, Baker in his early years at *McClure's* celebrated American imperialism, chronicled the vigorous and expanding American economy, and described the latest scientific discoveries. Attracted by the "vitality" of great men, he penned glowing character sketches of such new American heroes as Theodore Roosevelt and J. P. Morgan. Baker developed into a "muckraker" (a label he disliked) almost by accident. For the January 1903 *McClure's* he wrote an angry account of violence against nonstriking miners during the anthracite coal strike in Pennsylvania, an article which, along with others by Tarbell and Steffens, launched the magazine's celebrated crusade against lawlessness and corruption. Though doubtful at first about organized labor, Baker in subsequent articles took a more favorable view of unions and criticized employer abuses in the New York garment trade. This series, as well as one on the need for greater regulation of the railroads, gained national attention. On several ocasions President Roosevelt, whom Baker then admired, requested his advice, most notably during the fight for the Hepburn Bill (1905-1906) regulating railroads.

Roosevelt's attack on "muckraking" in the spring of 1906 destroyed this mutual confidence and marked a broader national turn of sentiment away from the literature of exposure. At the same time, an imbroglio at *McClure's* led Baker and several associates to resign and buy the *American Magazine,* which they sought to make an organ of optimism and constructive reporting in contrast to the shrill factuality of *McClure's.*

One manifestation of the new spirit was Baker's alter ego, which first made its appearance in the November 1906 issue of the *American.* Writing under the pseudonym "David Grayson," Baker penned a highly popular series of "adventures in contentment." Grayson, a gentleman farmer, sang the joys and beauties of life as he tramped the countryside, an antidote to the troubling realities the muckraker was reporting. Indulging a philosophical penchant the reporter never entirely suppressed, Grayson preached a cosmic idealism, Emersonian in tone. Although few critics praised their literary merits, the Grayson stories inspired countless letters from grateful readers over five decades. Published in nine volumes between 1907 and 1942, they eventually sold more than two million copies in America and the British Commonwealth, and in several foreign languages.

Yet Baker did not abandon his interest in America's problems. He wrote a series collected as *Following the Color Line* (1908), a pioneer field report on race relations, liberal by the standards of the day. This was followed by *The Spiritual Unrest* (1910), an exposure of lassitude in some churches, coupled with praise for the Social Gospel movement. An inner tension during these years between his inherited creed of individualism and laissez-faire and his urge toward reform drove him briefly into a romance with Fabian socialism, and in a report on the Lawrence, Mass., textile strike of 1912 he strongly criticized the mill management. But a more characteristic moderation prevailed. Meanwhile, Baker's enthusiastic reports on political insurgency, between 1909 and 1912, had served to mobilize public opinion behind insurgents in both parties. He supported Sen. Robert M. La Follette in 1911 and aided in the preparation of La Follette's *Autobiography.* In 1912, irritated by Theodore Roosevelt's shunting aside of La Follette's presidential candidacy, Baker refused to support the Bull Moose movement and, uneasily, voted for Wilson. By 1914 he was a confirmed Wilsonian.

This loyalty to Wilson matured during World War I into a lifetime commitment. At first opposed to the war, Baker supported America's entry in 1917. In 1918 he served as special agent for the State Department in England. At the peace conference he was director of the American delegation's press bureau—a type of presidential press secretary—and during the battle over the Versailles Treaty he championed Wilson's cause in *What Wilson Did at Paris* (1919). He later prepared a three-volume account of *Woodrow Wilson and World Settlement* (1922) and, with William E. Dodd, edited *The Public Papers of Woodrow Wilson* (6 vols., 1925-1927). Designated by President Wilson as his authorized biographer, Baker devoted fifteen years to preparing the eight-volume *Woodrow Wilson: Life and Letters* (1927-1939). The early volumes were praised by historians and sold very well, but toward the end changing historical judgments of Wilson combined with Baker's failing health caused sales to fall off and critical complaints to rise. Nevertheless, the series was awarded a Pulitzer Prize in 1940.

Baker had resigned from the *American Magazine* in 1915, and most of his time after 1920 was devoted to his writing. Soft-spoken, seemingly shy, he disliked the public platform, and despite brief excursions into politics preferred to monitor national affairs from the sidelines. He was disgusted with the "normalcy" of the 1920's. During the 1930's, although he admired the vigor and decisiveness of Franklin D. Roosevelt, his inbred individualism resurfaced, and he opposed most New Deal programs.

On Jan. 1, 1896, Baker had married Jessie Irene Beal, daughter of his former botany professor. They had four children: Alice Beal, James Stannard, Roger Denio, and Rachel

Moore. Rejecting the bustle of New York City, he moved his family to East Lansing, Mich., in 1902 and to Amherst, Mass., in 1910. During the final years of his life he prepared two volumes of autobiography, *Native American* (1941) and *American Chronicle* (1945). Written against the background of World War II, they remain testaments of the best in a "native" America that was fast disappearing. Baker died in Amherst of heart disease that had plagued him for the final decade of his life. He was buried in Wildwood Cemetery, Amherst, near the Massachusetts hills he loved to roam.

An avowed popularizer, Ray Stannard Baker laid no claim to original thought. "That a man is 'ahead of his time' or 'behind his time,' " he once remarked, "is an admission that he is second rate." His several hundred articles, crisp and accurate in detail, balanced in judgment, earned him a reputation as "America's Number 1 Reporter." Although his refusal to specify remedies in the early *McClure's* pieces infuriated some critics, and his unflagging optimism seemed to a later generation sanguine, even naive, his commitment to both high professional standards and the public good remains a model of the journalist-reformer.

[There is a voluminous collection of Baker Papers in the Lib. of Cong., and smaller ones in the Jones Lib., Amherst, and in the Princeton Univ. Lib. Two book-length studies drawing on these materials are Robert C. Bannister, Jr., *Ray Stannard Baker: The Mind and Thought of a Progressive* (1966), which considers Baker's ideas against a background of his entire life; and John E. Semonche, *Ray Stannard Baker: A Quest for Democracy in Modern America* (1969), a scholarly study of his career through early 1918. David Chalmers, "Ray Stannard Baker's Search for Reform," *Jour. of the Hist. of Ideas*, June 1958, describes Baker's "romance with socialism." Frank P. Rand, *The Story of David Grayson* (1963), mingles "fact with some fancy" in a sentimental revisit to the Grayson stories. See also, on Baker's muckraking career, David M. Chalmers, *The Social and Political Ideas of the Muckrakers* (1964); Peter Lyon, *Success Story: The Life and Times of S. S. McClure* (1963); and Harold S. Wilson, *McClure's Mag. and the Muckrakers* (1970). An excellent unpublished bibliography of Baker's writings by Rachel B. Napier (copies at Lib. of Cong. and Princeton Univ.) may be supplemented by that of Andrew K. Peters (Jones Lib., Amherst, 1935).]

ROBERT C. BANNISTER, JR.

BALDWIN, EDWARD ROBINSON (Sept. 8, 1864–May 6, 1947), physician, pioneer in tuberculosis research in the United States, was born in Bethel, Conn., the first of four children, all sons, of Elijah Clark Baldwin, a Congregational minister, and Frances Marsh (Hutchinson) Baldwin, daughter of a physician. Both parents were of old New England stock, with strict standards of discipline. Although the family's income was modest, the children received a sound education. Baldwin attended the Hillhouse High School in New Haven, intending to enter Yale, but at the age of sixteen left school to work in the magazine and hardware business in order to contribute to the financial resources of the family. In 1887 he entered the Yale Medical School, where he served as a laboratory assistant and received the M.D. degree in 1890.

After an internship in the Hartford (Conn.) Hospital (1891-1892), Baldwin opened a general practice in Cromwell, Conn. Within a few months, however, he began to suspect that he had contracted pulmonary tuberculosis and confirmed the diagnosis by examining his sputum under the microscope and identifying tubercle bacilli. In the winter of 1892, hoping to regain his health, he went to the Adirondack Cottage Sanatorium, later the Trudeau Sanatorium, near Saranac Lake, N.Y., where the physician-in-charge, Edward L. Trudeau, had a growing reputation in the outdoor and hygienic treatment of tuberculosis. Only a decade had elapsed since Robert Koch had announced his discovery of the tubercle bacillus, and many physicians still refused to accept its role in producing the disease. Trudeau, impressed with Baldwin's scientific abilities, accepted him as a patient and put him on a regimen of combined rest and cautious, part-time scientific investigation in the sanatorium laboratory—the first to be established in the United States for experimental research in tuberculosis. Baldwin assisted in the clinical duties, but gave his chief attention to the problems of native and acquired resistance to tuberculosis, making animal experiments with various kinds of tuberculin. He was able to spend part of the years 1901 and 1902 studying under Koch and other leaders of German medical research. By 1908, when the Sixth International Congress on Tuberculosis, then dominated by Europeans, met in Washington, D.C., Baldwin had become recognized as a leader in the field and shared the platform with outstanding scientists such as Koch and Albert Leon Charles Calmette of France, known for his part in developing a vaccine against tuberculosis. In his paper "The Problem of Immunity in Tuberculosis," Baldwin displayed extraordinary familiarity with the literature in the field and reported his own significant experiments on inherent and acquired resistance, emphasizing the role played by mild infection or even inoculation with dead tubercle bacilli in stimulating strong resistance to more serious infection. In succeeding years Baldwin developed this theme extensively. And, just as Trudeau had stimulated him, he in turn strongly influenced a younger researcher, Allen K. Krause, who clarified the relations of allergy, or hypersensitivity, and infection. The concepts of these three men on the mechanism of resistance to tuberculosis dominated American thought for a quarter of a century.

Baldwin epitomized his views in a widely circulated text, *Tuberculosis: Bacteriology, Pathology and Laboratory Diagnosis* (1927), written with two laboratory associates, S. A. Petroff and L. U. Gardner. This monograph strongly emphasized the role of hypersensitivity in heightening inflammatory reactivity to tubercle bacilli and stressed its implementation by "an acquired specific digestive power" of sensitized and thereby immunized phagocytic cells, a concept in which Baldwin was influenced by the maturing views of his own student Krause. Most of the research on which these views were based was carried out in the Saranac Laboratory, which Baldwin directed until 1926. During these years Saranac Lake had become world-renowned in the study of tuberculosis. Baldwin, as dean of the laboratory group, and Lawrason Brown as leader of the clinical group, together with Krause and others resident or trained at Saranac Lake, carried out a program of practical and advanced teaching in what was designated the Trudeau School of Tuberculosis. In association with Walter B. James in 1915, Baldwin inaugurated and initially directed the Edward Livingston Trudeau Foundation, which gave strong support to tuberculosis research.

Baldwin published more than a hundred papers on tuberculosis, several of which were of encyclopedic character and appeared in leading medical texts. He was editor-in-chief (1916-1921) of the newly founded *American Review of Tuberculosis*. Active in the national and international control of tuberculosis, Baldwin served as president of the American Clinical and Climatological Association (1910) and the National Tuberculosis Association (1916-1917). After World War I he was a delegate at a conference sponsored by the League of Red Cross Societies at Cannes, France, which set the stage for renewed cooperation among nations in tuberculosis control. Baldwin was awarded the Trudeau Medal of the National Tuberculosis Association in 1927 and the Kober Medal of the Association of American Physicians in 1936, and received honorary degrees from Yale (1914) and Dartmouth (1937).

Baldwin is remembered as a physician and laboratory investigator with rigorous professional standards. Uncomplicated in personality, he was cautious and thoughtful in reaching decisions, but firm in his convictions when they were made. He was also a leader in the civic activities of Saranac Lake and in its Presbyterian church. Spare and almost frail in appearance, he gave his strength without reservation to the health and welfare of his community, with deep sympathy for suffering and misfortune, but without display of emotion. Busy as he was in his work, he was devoted to nature and found enjoyment in the forest and mountain lake country around him.

Baldwin had married Mary Caroline Ives of Cheshire, Conn., on June 1, 1895. They had one child, Henry, who became prominent in the field of forestry. Baldwin died of pneumonia at Saranac Lake at the age of eighty-two and was buried there in the Pine Grove Cemetery.

[E. L. Trudeau, *An Autobiog.* (1916); J. A. Miller, "Edward R. Baldwin, 1864–1947," *Am. Rev. of Tuberculosis* 56 (1947): 261–265, photograph of a portrait by Wilford S. Conrow is included; "Bibliography of E. R. Baldwin," *Am. Rev. of Tuberculosis* 62 (1950): 114–119; E. R. Long, "The Concept of Resistance to Tuberculosis, with Special Reference to the Contributions of Edward R. Baldwin," *Am. Rev. of Tuberculosis* 62 (1950): 3–12; E. R. Baldwin, "The Problem of Immunity in Tuberculosis," *Trans. of the Sixth International Cong. on Tuberculosis,* (1908) *1,* Part 1, 174, also in *Am. Jour. of the Medical Sciences* 137 (1909): 103. E. R. Baldwin, "Studies in Immunity to Tuberculosis," *Jour. of Medical Research* 22 (1910): 189–256. E. R. Baldwin and L. U. Gardner, "Reinfection in Tuberculosis, Experimental Arrested Tuberculosis and Subsequent Infections," *Am. Rev. of Tuberculosis* 5 (121): 429–517. E. R. Baldwin, S. A. Petroff, and L. U. Gardner, *Tuberculosis: Bacteriology and Laboratory Diagnosis* (1927). The writer is indebted to Baldwin's son, Henry Ives Baldwin, for essential information recorded in this biography, and for checking the accuracy of items derived from other sources listed.]

ESMOND R. LONG

BANKHEAD, JOHN HOLLIS (July 8, 1872-June 12, 1946), lawyer and United States senator, was born in Moscow, Lamar County, Ala., the third of five children and eldest of three sons of John Hollis Bankhead and Tallulah James (Brockman) Bankhead. He was a brother of William Brockman Bankhead. His father, whose political career took him to the state legislature and the House of Representatives and Senate, also founded, in 1886, the Bankhead Coal Company in Jasper, Ala., from which he derived sufficient wealth to give his family economic advantages denied most Alabamians of the time. Young John, after attending local public schools, entered the University of Alabama in 1887 and received the B.A. degree in 1891. He then went to Washington, D.C., where his father—then in Congress—got him a job as a clerk for a congressional committee. Although a devout Methodist, he attended night classes at Georgetown University Law School, a Roman Catholic institution, from which he received the LL.B. in 1893.

After graduation, Bankhead returned to Jasper to enter law practice with Ezra W. Coleman, a business associate of his father. The firm enjoyed a lucrative practice, handling the affairs of the family coal company and representing the Louisville & Nashville Railroad, the Alabama Power Company, and other large corporations. On Dec. 26, 1894, Bankhead married Musa Harkins, a childhood friend, in Fayette, Ala. They had three children: Marion, Walter Will, and Louise.

Bankhead wanted to follow his father and later his brother into politics, but felt the public might resent three Bankheads holding political office. Thus, although he served one term in the lower house of the state legislature (1903-1905), during which he wrote the new suffrage law of 1903 aimed at disenfranchising Negroes, he devoted his talents chiefly to the law and the family business, forming a law partnership with his brother William in 1904. Bankhead did, however, serve as his family's campaign manager, and in 1915 he drew up and lobbied through the legislature a gerrymandered congressional district that ensured a safe seat for his brother. Despite his family's political conservatism and business connections, John Bankhead recognized the popularity of more radical leaders, and pragmatically urged his father to modify some of his positions to ensure political survival.

In 1926, six years after his father's death, Bankhead sought the United States Senate seat being vacated by Oscar W. Underwood, but lost in a bitter four-way primary to Hugo L. Black, a Birmingham attorney. Convinced that his long association with large corporations had harmed him, Bankhead determined to devote his attention to farming interests, especially cotton farmers, the state's largest single bloc of voters. He tried again in 1930, when Senator J. Thomas Heflin was declared ineligible to run for reelection as a Democrat because of his support of Herbert Hoover in 1928. Bankhead defeated a weaker opponent in the Democratic primary, and went on to defeat Heflin (running as a "Jeffersonian Democrat") in the general election. He was to continue in the Senate until his death.

As senator, Bankhead was an influential advocate of agricultural interests, particularly those of the cotton grower. Overcoming his basic conservatism, he supported the presiden-

tial candidacy of Franklin D. Roosevelt and embraced the early New Deal program with enthusiasm. His stand, which he based on party loyalty and economic necessity, assured him a voice in agricultural policy. He thus became one of the most powerful men in the farm bloc, much closer, for example, to Roosevelt and to Secretary of Agriculture Henry A. Wallace than Chairman Ellison D. Smith of the Senate Agriculture Committee.

A leading advocate of federally enforced production controls, Bankhead played an important role in the passage of the Agricultural Adjustment Act of 1933. He was influential the same year in getting the administration to extend to farmers willing to cut back production a loan of ten cents a pound on cotton, which would then be stored to await higher prices. This principle was institutionalized for all basic commodities the following year with the establishment of the Commodity Credit Corporation. Convinced that acreage reduction alone was incapable of raising prices, Bankhead pushed through the Cotton Control Act (1934), which established marketing quotas for large farmers. This act was repealed in 1936 after the Supreme Court declared the AAA unconstitutional. But as one of the leaders of the Senate farm bloc, Bankhead worked closely with the Roosevelt administration for other measures favorable to agriculture, including the second Agricultural Adjustment Act of 1938 and federal crop insurance.

Unlike most of his Southern colleagues, Bankhead sought to benefit the tenant farmer and sharecropper as well as the large commercial producer. The subsistence homestead amendment he succeeded in adding to the National Industrial Recovery Act in 1933 became the basis for the Resettlement Administration, established in 1935, which was designed to aid poor farmers and help resettle the urban destitute on farm lands. The Bankhead-Jones Farm Tenant Act of 1937 reorganized the Resettlement Administration into the Farm Security Administration, empowered to lend money to tenants wishing to purchase their own land, rehabilitate small farms, and aid migrant workers.

During World War II, Bankhead accepted the president's military and diplomatic leadership. Although he refused to join more conservative colleagues in trying to dismantle many New Deal structures, he bitterly attacked the administration's wartime efforts to hold down farm prices. Convinced that farmers were not sharing equitably in the new prosperity, Bankhead and his colleagues in the farm bloc, closely allied with the Farm Bureau Federation and National Grange, pushed a number of bills through Congress that would have seriously modified existing policy, but were unable to obtain the necessary votes to override Roosevelt's vetoes. They did manage, however, to exact a number of concessions, forcing the administration to sell surplus crops at parity prices and to agree to maintain farm price supports for two years after the war ended. The most acrimonious conflict centered on the subsidies which the administration granted to processors in an effort to roll back rising food prices. Asserting that the public should become accustomed to higher prices for food and fiber, Bankhead and his friends tried unsuccessfully to put through legislation ending the subsidies.

Like other rural conservatives, Bankhead disliked the growing liberal influence of labor in the Democratic party. In 1944 he sought the Democratic vice-presidential nomination, but threw his support to Harry S. Truman to prevent the renomination of Henry A. Wallace. When Truman became president in 1945, Bankhead opposed his domestic program. In the midst of the battle to prevent the continuation of price controls, Bankhead collapsed in May 1946. A victim of heart disease and chronic bronchial illness, he died the next month at the Bethesda (Md.) Naval Hospital. He was buried in Oak Hill Cemetery in Jasper, Ala.

A serious, somewhat solemn man, Bankhead shared the racial attitudes of many of his Southern colleagues, but never ran on an openly racist platform. He was an effective legislator. Although he seldom achieved a national perspective, he was more than a spokesman for parochial interests.

[Bankhead Family Papers, in the Dept. of Archives and Hist., Montgomery, Ala. (those of John H. Bankhead, Jr., are incomplete, many having been destroyed at the time of his death); J. B. Key, "John H. Bankhead, Jr: Creative Conservative" (Ph.D. diss., Johns Hopkins Univ., 1964); interviews with Hugo L. Black, Lister Hill, and Marvin Jones. Published accounts include: Thomas McA. Owen, *Hist. of Ala. and Dict. of Ala. Biog.*, III, 92–93 (1921); *Current Biog.*, 1943; *Nat. Cyc Am. Biog.*, XLIII, 495–496; obituaries in *N.Y. Times* and *Montgomery* (Ala.) *Advertiser*, June 13, 1946.]

J. B. KEY

BARBOUR, THOMAS (Aug. 19, 1884–Jan. 8, 1946), naturalist, herpetologist, museum director, was born on Martha's Vineyard, Mass., the eldest of the four sons of William and Julia Adelaide (Sprague) Barbour. His father was president of Barbour Brothers, a flax-spinning company, a director of the linen mills of William Barbour and Sons in northern Ireland,

and head of many other firms in many fields of business. His paternal great-great-grandfather, John, of Paisley, Scotland, set up a flax-spinning plant in Lisburn, Ireland, in 1768, "the oldest linen thread manufacturing establishment in the world." His grandfather, Thomas, together with his greatuncle, Robert, came to America in 1855 to establish the family business here. Barbour's mother came from a prominent New York family; his brother, William Warren Barbour, became a United States senator from New Jersey.

Barbour's interest in natural history developed at an early age. It was nurtured by his father, a lover of the out-of-doors, who, taking the family with him on many of his business trips abroad, exposed the children to nearly all the major natural history museums in Europe. Observation of creatures in the wild was also encouraged by his father, who had a large estate on Tupper Lake in the Adirondacks, where Thomas spent many vacations in his youth, and by his paternal grandmother, whom he visited a number of times at her home, Walden Cottage, at Eau Gallie, on the then almost unsettled east coast of Florida. He was an enthusiastic fisherman and hunter all his life, but he tended even as a boy toward the scientific study of animals, particularly reptiles and amphibians, the field of herpetology. During his youth the New York Zoological Society's zoo in Bronx Park was under development, and Thomas promptly made the acquaintance of the staff members there when he began a herpetological collection.

After an attack of typhoid fever in his early teens, Thomas was privately tutored by Dr. Theodore W. Moses before preparing for college at the Browning School in New York. Crucial to his career was a visit, when he was fifteen, to Harvard's Museum of Comparative Zoology, the "Agassiz Museum." He decided then and there that he would someday become director of that institution.

Barbour entered Harvard in 1902 and from that moment to the end of his life the M.C.Z. was the center of his work and interests. He took his bachelor's degree in 1906. On October 1 of that year he married Rosamond Pierce of Brookline, Mass., a strong-minded New England girl. On their round-the-world wedding trip—to India, Burma, China, Japan, and the islands of the Far East—they gathered specimens of all classes of vertebrates and insects to send back to the Harvard Museum. They had six children, three of whom reached maturity: Mary Bigelow, Julia Adelaide, and Louisa

Bowditch. Barbour, like his father, was raised a Presbyterian, but he was confirmed in the Episcopal church and later served on the vestry of Trinity Church, Boston.

Returning to Harvard after his honeymoon, Barbour settled down to work on his Ph.D., which he achieved in 1910. He was then appointed an associate curator of reptiles and amphibians at the M.C.Z.; some years later he was promoted to full curator.

At the time of Barbour's first appointment the Harvard Museum was entering upon a period of decline. It had been founded by the famous naturalist Louis Agassiz, and his son Alexander continued in charge until his death in 1910. Seventeen stagnating years for the museum followed until, in 1927, Barbour was made director, a post which he held until his death.

Barbour was a striking figure—a "genial giant," some 6 feet 5 inches in height and weighing nearly 300 pounds. He had a massive head, crowned by a mop of curly hair, broad shoulders, and a great barrel of a trunk, tapering to relatively tiny feet. He was a facile and charming conversationalist, outspoken but possessing a keen sense of humor, abundant enthusiasm, and much restless energy. In any organization or project in which he became interested he played a major and often dominant role. "I like to run things," he said.

Under him the museum was rejuvenated. "Glory-holes" of useless material were emptied; the collections were put in much improved order; and exhibits were revised. Barbour made every effort to encourage the research of the scientific staff, so that the M.C.Z. achieved an enviable reputation among its workers in systematic zoology. Barbour interested himself in all fields of museum activity. An example was his encouragement of vertebrate paleontology, notably the Thomas Farm project in Florida. The material brought up in digging a well on this abandoned property was found to contain remains of fossil mammals. The farm was purchased and for a dozen years actively explored, resulting in the discovery of one of the most important sites for fossil mammals in the eastern United States.

Barbour's energies were not confined to the museum; major external interests were the development of the Atkins' Garden in Cuba and the Barro Colorado tropical station in the Panama Canal Zone. The Atkins family of Massachusetts owned a large sugar plantation at Soledad, near Cienfuegos, Cuba. They gave Harvard a plot of land which at first was uti-

lized for experimenting in the improvement of Cuban sugar canes. Barbour became interested, and this area was enlarged and developed as a botanic garden where was to be found any type of tree or shrub that would flourish in the Cuban climate; two buildings were erected to house resident and visiting scientists and to provide quarters for research.

With the building of the Gatun Dam of the Panama Canal, a hill, Barro Colorado, enclosed within the lake formed by the dam, became an island of about eight square miles of tropical jungle with magnificent flora and fauna. This was made a natural reserve by the U.S. government. Barbour became executive officer; under his supervision a laboratory building was erected and a series of nature trails laid out; as a result Barro Colorado became a major American center for the study of tropical natural history.

Barbour's own work lay mainly in systematic zoology, and for the most part in herpetology. Over the years, he described 274 species representing 120 genera. A major work was *A Check List of North American Amphibians and Reptiles;* the first edition appeared under joint authorship with Leonhard Stejneger in 1917; four revised editions were published during Barbour's lifetime. He was much interested in Cuban birds and published two books on this subject.

Arising naturally out of his work in systematic zoology was an interest in the geographical distribution of animals. His Ph.D. thesis was a memoir on the zoogeography of the East Indies, published in 1912. This was followed two years later by a similar work on the West Indies, and he remained actively concerned throughout his life in the geographical history of the Caribbean-West Indian region.

Barbour was an inveterate traveler throughout his life. In later years he went to South America and Africa on several occasions, but Florida and the West Indies, particularly Cuba, were areas of especial interest and these he visited almost every winter.

As he grew older, Barbour developed a hypertensive arteriosclerotic heart disease. He died on Jan. 8, 1946, at Massachusetts General Hospital in Boston, after suffering a cerebral hemorrhage. He was buried at Mount Auburn Cemetery, Cambridge, Mass.

[Much information on Barbour's life is to be found in his four popular books written during his later years: *Naturalist at Large* (1943); *That Vanishing Eden; a Naturalist's Florida* (1944); *A Naturalist in Cuba* (1945); *A Naturalist's Scrapbook* (1946), in all of which, except the third, photographs are included.

In *Naturalist at Large* there is a reproduction of the portrait of Rosamond and Thomas Barbour painted by John Singer Sargent in 1919. An appreciative sketch is H. B. Bigelow, "Thomas Barbour, 1884–1946," in *Nat. Acad. Sc., Biog. Memoirs*, XXVII (1952), in which there is a photograph. Articles about Barbour in magazines and newspapers are numerous, including : E. D. Merrill, "Dr. Thomas Barbour," *The American Naturalist*, Mar. 1, 1946, pp. 214–216, with a portrait on the cover; J. L. Peters, "Thomas Barbour, 1884–1946," *The Auk*, July 1948, pp. 432–438; F. E. Wright, "The Annual Meeting of the National Academy of Sciences," *Scientific Monthly*, June 1933, pp. 572–578. In the latter two there are pictures. Obituaries appeared in all major newspapers, including the *N.Y. Times*, Jan. 9, 1946, which carries a photograph.]

ALFRED S. ROMER

BARRETT, JANIE PORTER (Aug. 9, 1865–Aug. 27, 1948), social worker and educator, was born in Athens, Ga. Much of her childhood was spent living in the Macon, Ga., home of a wealthy white family named Skinner, where her mother, Julia Porter, was employed as a housemaid and seamstress. The Skinner children in this transplanted New York family were her age and became her close friends. When Janie reached her teens, her mother and stepfather, a railroad shop worker, insisted that she attend a school for blacks rather than go north to a white school with the Skinner children, as Mrs. Skinner had suggested.

She enrolled at Hampton Institute in Hampton, Va., graduating in 1884. Janie Porter then taught in the small rural community of Dawson in southwest Georgia for two terms before returning to Hampton Institute in 1886–1887 to teach domestic science. She next taught at Haines Normal and Industrial School in Augusta for two terms. On Oct. 31, 1889, she married Harris Barrett, a former Hampton schoolmate, who was a cashier and bookkeeper at the institute. They had four children: May Porter, Harris, Julia Louise, and Catherine.

Shortly after her marriage Janie Barrett began an informal day care center for the children in her Hampton neighborhood. Money saved for improvements on the Barrett's home was spent on a neighborhood clubhouse, and in 1890 the Locust Street Social Settlement was founded, the first of its type for blacks. There Barrett taught young girls laundering and sewing. As financial support and cooperation came from teachers and students at Hampton, the settlement's activities spread to encompass entire families and neighborhoods. An 1895 picnic held at Bay Shore, a local beach resort, attracted over 800 children and their parents. At the settlement, mothers were taught child care, and their experience was broadened through health clubs and reading clubs and classes in sewing, flower care, general homemaking, and poultry-raising. Further financial support for the endeavor came from white philanthropists who became acquainted with the project through contacts Barrett made as she traveled with the Hampton Quartette. Neighborhood activities included annual family outings, Easter egg hunts, and musical contests.

Barrett involved students and local clubwomen in her search to improve community life for the people. Shocked by the number of children and adolescents in the local jail, Barrett organized a committee to assist in her campaign to get every child out of jail and into a home. She gave vigorous support to the juvenile court movement by promoting petitions for such a facility to the Newport News City Council.

In 1908 Barrett was the prime force in organizing the Virginia State Federation of Colored Women's Clubs. As president she traveled throughout the state collecting an initial $10 pledge from each club to finance a home for delinquent girls. The federation raised $5,300 in three years. The Negro Organization Society held a tag day in 1913 that alone netted $600 for the project. Barrett studied the information she could find on setting up an industrial home school, seeking advice from the child welfare department of the Russell Sage Foundation and visiting the Slayton Farm near Philadelphia.

A 140-acre farm was finally purchased at Peake (also known as Peaks Turnout), Va., eighteen miles from Richmond. The Virginia Industrial School for Colored Girls opened on Jan. 19, 1915. From an initial enrollment of twenty-eight girls between the ages of eleven and eighteen, the school grew to house an average of 100 girls a year. Emphasis was placed on cleanliness, hard work, discipline, and respect for oneself and one another.

Upon entering, a girl was assigned a "big sister," a place in a cottage, and membership in a small group suitable to her temperament and interests. A series of small rewards of graded clubs and uniforms of different colors earned by exemplary behavior were intended to be outward signs of inward growth of character. Each resident was expected to stay a minimum of two years at the school. When the honor level was maintained for a full year, with its privileges of wearing a white dress and enjoying special eating and sleeping accommodations, a student was eligible for parole. Parolees were placed in selected black or white homes where protection and supervision were promised and paid employment provided. Each girl was referred to a local minister to help with the aftercare seen as an important part of the school's training. Follow-up letters and *The Booster,* a newspaper edited by the students, were sent to former students. A savings account at the school held part of a parolee's earnings until she reached her twenty-first birthday. Personal responsibility was encouraged, and the severest punishment was consignment to the "thinking room" to meditate on one's behavior. The girls themselves handled much of the discipline on lower levels through the club structure and a demerit system.

In 1915, after her husband's death, Barrett took her own three daughters to Peake and became superintendent of the school. Matching state and federal grants and privately raised funds aided in enlarging the school and in providing additional facilities for the girls. In 1920 the State Federation of Colored Women's Clubs accepted the state's offer to assume financial responsibility for the school, but shared control until 1942 when it was placed under the state Department of Welfare and Institutions. Under Barrett's direction, the school became a model of its type; the Russell Sage Foundation rated it among the top five institutions of its kind.

Barrett received the William E. Harmon Award for Distinguished Achievement among Negroes in 1929. In 1930 she was a delegate to the White House Conference on Child Health and Protection called by President Hoover. *Crisis,* the magazine of the NAACP, named her fifth of the "First Ladies of Colored America" in 1943. She served on the executive board of the Richmond Urban League and was a member of the Virginia Commission on Interracial Cooperation and the Southern Commission on Interracial Cooperation. In 1940 Barrett retired and returned to her home at Hampton where she lived until her death of diabetes mellitus. She was buried at Elmerton Cemetery in Hampton. In 1950 the Virginia Industrial School for Colored Girls was renamed the Janie Porter Barrett School for Girls.

[Sources include Sadie Iola Daniel, *Women Builders* (1931); J. E. Davis, "Fertilizing Barren Souls: The Industrial Home School for Delinquent Colored Girls of Virginia," *The Southern Workman,* Aug. 1916; Sarah Collins Fernandis, "A Colored Social Settlement," *The Southern Workman,* June 1904; Winona R. Hall, "Janie Porter Barrett: Her Life and Contributions to Social Welfare in Virginia" (Master's thesis, Howard Univ., 1954). See also L. H. Hammond, *In the Vanguard of the Race,* Council of Women for Home Missions and Missionary Education Movement of the United States and Canada and annual reports of the Janie Porter Barrett School for Girls.]
        LETITIA BROWN

BARRY, PHILIP JAMES QUINN (June 18, 1896-Dec. 3, 1949), playwright, was born in Rochester, N.Y., the third son and youngest of four children of James Corbett Barry and Mary Agnes (Quinn) Barry. James Barry, a well-to-do marble and tile contractor, had been brought to the United States at the age of ten from a failing farm in Ireland. His wife, also of Irish descent, was a Philadelphian, daughter of the proprietor of a lumber business. The family was Roman Catholic. James Barry died the year after Philip's birth, but Philip's inheritance enabled him, after attending Catholic and public schools in Rochester, to go on in 1913 to Yale. He had begun to write at the age of nine, and had read widely in childhood. At Yale he contributed to the *Daily News* and the *Literary Magazine* and wrote a one-act play, *Autonomy,* for the dramatic club. When the United States entered World War I, Barry sought to enlist, but was rejected for poor eyesight and had to content himself with service in the State Department and in the American embassy in London, after which he returned to complete his B.A. in 1919.

That autumn Barry enrolled in the famous English 47 Workshop of George Pierce Baker at Harvard. Immediately he set to work on a play, *A Punch for Judy,* which with Baker's aid and encouragement was performed in New York (Apr. 19 and 20, 1921) under the auspices of the League of Pen Women. To finance further study, Barry worked for a year in a New York advertising firm and then returned to the workshop in October 1921. His next two plays, both comedies of character, won professional performance on Broadway. *You and I* opened in February 1923 and was still drawing large audiences five months later. *The Youngest* (December 1924) ran for 104 performances. Even before this success Barry had blithely assumed the support of a wife: Ellen Marshall Semple of Mount Kisco, N.Y. on July 15, 1922. They had two sons, Philip Semple (1923) and Jonathan Peter (1926); a daughter born in 1933 died in infancy.

The success of *You and I* and *The Youngest* launched Barry on a Broadway career that lasted through three decades. Critics came to regard high comedy as his forte, but he was determined to experiment and to write what he wanted to write. Thus during the remainder of the 1920's he wrote not only two highly successful sophisticated comedies, *Paris Bound* (1927) and *Holiday* (1928)—the latter a scintillating attack on materialism—but also a fantasy about a street cleaner (*White Wings,*

1926) and a tragedy concerning John the Baptist (*John,* 1927). In collaboration with Elmer Rice he also wrote a murder mystery (*Cock Robin,* 1928). He established a home in Cannes, France, where he did most of his writing, but lived in Mount Kisco from September to January each year, with excursions to New York when his plays were in production.

Neither Barry nor his writing was much influenced by the surface glitter of the Jazz Age. If his plays of the 1920's reflect the period at all, it is in the slang of the young people, the casual acceptance of wealth, and the equally casual acceptance of alcohol.

Barry was not greatly affected by the Great Depression of the 1930's. His first play in the 1930's, *Hotel Universe* (1930), lost money. It was a poetic fantasy with a serious philosophical message which critics found interesting but baffling. But *Tomorrow and Tomorrow* (1931), another serious drama, was a surprise hit. Money came easily during the decade—from his successful plays and, most generously, from Hollywood.

He returned to drawing-room comedy with *The Animal Kingdom* (1932), which like *Paris Bound* and *Tomorrow and Tomorrow* concerned marriage and illicit love; its success was in part owing to the skill of the leading actor, Leslie Howard. Barry's next three plays were failures, but the damage to his reputation was at least partially repaired by *Here Come the Clowns* (1938), a serious study of good and evil in the universe, adapted from his only novel, *War in Heaven* (1938). *The Philadelphia Story,* which followed (1939), was the crowning example of his success with high comedy and Barry's biggest hit by far. It was credited with saving the Theatre Guild from financial disaster and with reestablishing Katharine Hepburn as a major star.

In the 1940's Barry wrote three plays reflecting in varying degrees his concern with the war—*Liberty Jones* (1941), *Without Love* (1942), and *Foolish Notion* (1945). He had finished the first draft of a final play, *Second Threshold,* when he died of a coronary thrombosis in New York City in 1949, at the age of fifty-three. He was buried in St. Philomena's Cemetery, East Hampton, Long Island.

Even in his drawing-room comedies Barry had worked with serious themes, and he remains a playwright of substantial achievement. Robert E. Sherwood, who completed *Second Threshold* for production, found in it the beginning of a synthesis of Barry's "Irish, impish sense of comedy, and his profound, and also

Irish, sense of the ultimate sadness of life on earth, the 'endless assault' of evil upon good." He was one of the first American dramatists to experiment with Freudian psychology and perhaps the first to produce (in *Hotel Universe*) a true "psychodrama." He experimented with writing, acting, and stagecraft with considerable versatility; and he attempted almost every form of drama from farce through fantasy and satire to tragedy.

[Joseph Patrick Roppolo, *Philip Barry* (1965), a biographical and critical study, includes an extensive bibliography. Gerald Hamm, *The Drama of Philip Barry* (1948), is a comprehensive doctoral dissertation, especially valuable for biographical material obtained through interviews with Barry. Barry's papers are in the Am. Literature Collec. at Yale. See also Robert E. Sherwood's introduction to Barry's *Second Threshold* (1951). The *N.Y. Times* obituary, Dec. 4, 1949, reproduces a portrait of Barry by his wife.]

JOSEPH PATRICK ROPPOLO

BASSETT, EDWARD MURRAY (Feb. 7, 1863-Oct. 27, 1948), lawyer and city planner, was born in Brooklyn, N.Y., the second of five children and younger of two sons of Charles Ralph and Elvira (Rogers) Bassett. His father, who came from Massachusetts, was a traveling peddler; his mother, a native of New York state, had taught school. Edward grew up in Watertown, N.Y., where the family moved when he was seven. He graduated from the Watertown high school and entered Hamilton College in Clinton, N.Y., on a scholarship, but transferred for his senior year to Amherst, from which he received the A.B. degree in 1884. While teaching at a private school in Brooklyn, he attended afternoon and evening classes at Columbia Law School and earned an LL.B. degree in 1886. Bassett then joined his brother in a contracting firm to build waterworks in upstate New York cities, with headquarters in Buffalo. On May 14, 1890, he married Annie Rebecca Preston, daughter of a Congregational minister of Bath, N.Y. They had five children: Preston Rogers, Marion Preston, Isabel Deming, Howard Murray, and Helen Preston.

Bassett's business prospered, but in 1892 he returned to Brooklyn and began a law practice. Ten years later he formed the firm of Bassett and Thompson (later Bassett, Thompson and Gilpatric), with which he was to be associated for four decades. Long interested in civic and political affairs, Bassett joined the local Democratic organization and was elected to the Kings County (Brooklyn) Democratic Committee, on which he served until 1907. He was elected to Congress in 1902 but did not seek reelection.

In his law practice, Bassett specialized in bankruptcy and real estate cases. This experience, together with his civic concern, gave him an awareness of the physical problems of the city. In 1905 he became secretary of the Citizen's Central Committee of Brooklyn, which advocated the construction of more bridges and tunnels across the East River to handle the increasing interborough traffic. Between 1907 and 1911 he served on the newly created Public Service Commission (for the district including New York City and Long Island), to which he was appointed by Gov. Charles Evans Hughes, a former Columbia classmate. Here he helped devise plans for new subway systems which greatly expanded the city's rapid transit facilities. Applying methods developed in other cities, he recommended the replacement of "stub-end" terminals, which became congested at peak hours, with a "pendulum" system by which trains would move from outlying areas through the central city and into outlying areas on the opposite side. This would better distribute the passenger load to several stations and help create a two-way traffic flow.

Increasingly, Bassett became interested in city planning. He visited several German cities in 1908 to examine their pioneering work in zoning, and the following year he attended the first National Conference on City Planning held in Washington, D.C. The planning movement put him in the company of architects, engineers, and enlightened legislators with whom, as he later wrote, he felt "more at home than in . . . ordinary political associations" (*Autobiography*, p. 117). In 1911 he joined with Alfred T. White and Frederic B. Pratt to form the Brooklyn City Plan Committee, and during the next two years he worked with reformers like Lawson Purdy and George McAneny to develop ways to protect the city from unrestricted growth. An expanded transit system, he realized, by bringing greater numbers of workers into downtown Manhattan, would lead to increased construction of skyscrapers and a consequent decrease in available light and air. Regulation of such building through zoning seemed essential.

Zoning at this time was also winning the support of financial and realty interests, led by the powerful Fifth Avenue Association, which had waged a long publicity campaign for a law to protect the valuable shopping area north of 34th Street from the encroachment of garment factories and lofts. The convergence of the two movements brought the creation in 1913 of an official Heights of Buildings Commission (including both reformers and Association members), and Bassett was appointed its chairman. Within months the commission recommended that the city be divided into districts, each with stipulated standards for maximum building height and bulk, and also for building use. Such regulations, the commission contended, could be enforced under the government's police power to protect the health and welfare of its citizens. An amendment to the city charter in 1914 granted New York the right to zone, and in the same year Bassett was named chairman of the new Commission on Building Districts and Restrictions, which drew up New York City's zoning ordinance of 1916—the first comprehensive zoning law in the United States and one which quickly became a model for the rest of the country.

Yet the New York law fell short of the hopes of many reformers who viewed zoning as the cornerstone of a broader urban plan. Bassett, determined to frame an ordinance that would not be overruled in the courts on constitutional grounds, had minimized the restrictions it imposed. It stressed neighborhood "stability" and applied limits to future development, but exempted existing nonconforming land uses, such as factories in residential areas. The law reflected Bassett's fundamental conception of the purposes of zoning. Standing between advanced social planners on the one hand and special interest groups on the other, he saw zoning as a means of improving the quality of urban life. "My interest in zoning," he later wrote, "was largely based on sunlight" (*ibid.*, p. 134). To this extent the ordinance was a success. Its height regulations in high-bulk areas led to extended use of the "setback" design for skyscrapers still evident in New York City.

Over the next two decades, Bassett continued his advocacy of zoning through writings, lectures, and consulting work. From 1916 to 1946 he served as counsel for the privately organized Zoning Committee of New York, and in 1917 he became a charter member of the American City Planning Institute (later the American Institute of Planners). He also served as counsel to the Regional Plan of New York and Its Environs (1922-1928), for which he wrote a series of reports on zoning. In 1922, as chairman of a federal advisory committee, he drafted a Standard City Enabling Act for the guidance of state and local governments desiring to enact zoning. Given this encouragement by the federal government, and aided by a favorable Supreme

Court decision upholding the constitutionality of zoning (*Euclid* v. *Ambler*, 1926), the zoning movement spread rapidly; by 1931 over 80 percent of America's largest cities had enacted zoning ordinances.

During these years, however, it became increasingly clear that zoning ordinances, which were often circumvented by powerful interests, were having a negligible effect on the development of large cities. Even Bassett began to suggest in the 1930's that the real impact of zoning would be on the unbuilt periphery of the city and on the suburbs. Yet critics complained that zoning was being used in many wealthy suburbs to achieve wasteful lot size and residential exclusiveness. Bassett remained unconverted by the social planning schemes of the 1930's. In his most theoretical book, *The Master Plan* (1938), he expressed a wariness of public housing. Planning, he felt, should be primarily a regulatory function; he opposed positive government action.

Hailed in later years as the "father of modern zoning," Bassett received honorary degrees from Hamilton College and Harvard and was elected president of the National Conference on City Planning for 1928-1929. He loved to travel, and was an active layman in the Congregational church. He died in Brooklyn at the age of eighty-five and was buried in Ashfield, Mass.

[Bassett's *Autobiog.* (1939), an anecdotal account intended for his family, is useful on his early life. He also wrote *Zoning: The Laws, Administration, and Court Decisions during the First Twenty Years* (1936); and, with Frank B. Williams, Alfred Bettmann, and Robert Whitten, *Model Laws for Planning Cities, Counties, and States* (1935). Thomas Adams, *Outline of Town and City Planning* (1935), makes favorable mention of Bassett, as does Seymour I. Toll, *Zoned American* (1969); more critical is Mel Scott, *Am. City Planning since 1890* (1969). See also Stanley J. Makielski, Jr., *The Politics of Zoning: The N.Y. Experience* (1966); Belle Preston, *Bassett-Preston Ancestors* (1930); *N.Y. Times* obituary, Oct. 28, 1948; and *Nat. Cyc. Am. Biog.*, XLIV, 548–549.]

STANLEY BUDER

BATEMAN, HARRY (May 29, 1882-Jan. 21, 1946), mathematician, expert in mathematical physics, was born in Manchester, England, and spent his early childhood mainly in Oldham, Lancashire. He was the third and youngest child of Samuel Bateman and Marnie Elizabeth (Bond) Bateman. His father, a pharmaceutical chemist, was born in England, and his mother was born in New York City; her father, a native of England, had been a planter in the West Indies. The family were Episcopalians.

After some schooling at home, Bateman attended, from 1891 to 1900, board school and grammar school in Manchester and held Manchester City Council and Langworthy scholarships. He showed proficiency in mathematics from the first and won a Derby scholarship and sizarship at Trinity College, Cambridge. He also participated, when eighteen years old, in a chess tournament between England and the United States.

In Cambridge, after winning a major scholarship in 1902, he took the B.A. in 1903, being bracketed senior wrangler with P. E. Marrack. In 1904 he won the Smith Prize and became a fellow of Trinity College, meanwhile marking papers for the Briggs Correspondence School and coaching candidates for the mathematical tripos. In 1905 and 1906 he studied in Paris and Göttingen, then served for a year as a lecturer at Liverpool University, before becoming (1907) a reader in mathematical physics at Manchester University. In 1910 he accepted a position in the United States as lecturer at Bryn Mawr College, where an Englishwoman, Charlotte Angas Scott, was head of the department of mathematics. In that same year, he prepared for the British Association for the Advancement of Science a paper entitled *Report on the History and Present State of the Theory of Integral Equations.*

On July 11, 1912, Bateman married Ethel Horner Dodd, who was also a native of Manchester, England. A son, Harry Graham, was born in 1914 and after his early death in 1917 the Batemans adopted a girl, Joan Margaret. In the early years of Bateman's marriage, in order to supplement his small income, he taught at the Bureau of Standards and at Mount Saint Agnes College and reviewed papers for the Weather Bureau.

At this time (1912-1917) Bateman was connected with Johns Hopkins University at Baltimore, where to took the Ph.D. in 1913 and where he was a Johnston scholar until 1915 and a lecturer from then to 1917.

In 1917 Bateman was appointed professor of theoretical physics and aeronautics at the California Institute of Technology, then called Throop College, and it is with the institute that his name is most frequently associated.

Bateman's first mathematical papers were in geometry and algebraic geometry. This mathematical field had been cultivated masterfully in Britain in the nineteenth century by Arthur Cayley and George Salmon. Bateman undoubtedly caught the spirit of this kind of mathematics, and he would occasionally turn and return to it for decades to come. But Bateman specialized in the analytical mathematical idiom and instrument of mathematical physics, especially of the undulatory theories of electrodynamical physics and of hydro- and aerodynamics. There is no evidence that he was equally interested in thermodynamics. Electrodynamics lured him first, and understandably so. Around 1900 the electromagnetic theory of James Clerk Maxwell was not yet properly developed, especially not in many special cases; and after 1900 the emerging special theory of relativity, which is an offshoot and completion of Maxwell's theory, raised or suggested additional problems. Bateman reacted to this challenge by introducing special functions to solve special differential equations, and there are, in fact, so-called Bateman functions and Bateman expansions. In 1915 he had gathered up many of these results in his book *The Mathematical Analysis of Electrical and Optical Wave Motion on the Basis of Maxwell's Equation.* This 159-page book is packed with details, special cases, insight, and references. Bateman preferred the illuminating detail, which he made very illuminating indeed, to the general theory, the pertinent applications of a theory to fine points of justification, its physical explication to its metaphysical foundation. But, at times, he had anticipated philosophical interpretations too, as he rightly pointed out himself in 1919 in his brief article, "On General Relativity," *Philosophical Magazine* 161 (1919): 219-223.

Electrodynamical theory is modeled in part on the older hydrodynamical theory. In the 1920's Bateman turned to this theory, and he displayed his knowledge of it by composing most of the voluminous report *Hydrodynamics,* which constituted a 1932 *Bulletin* of the National Research Council in Washington, D.C. This was the most dazzlingly erudite of all his works.

But his finest large-scale work, also published in 1932, was his monograph *Partial Differential Equations of Mathematical Physics,* which extended to four dimensions many mathematical analyses that were done before for two or three dimensions only.

Bateman was also an editor of technical journals and a cofounder of the *Quarterly of Applied Mathematics.* In 1928 he was elected to the Royal Society of London, and in 1930 to the National Academy of Sciences in Washington, D.C.

Bateman died of coronary thrombosis in Utah on Jan. 21, 1946, while traveling by train to New York, where he was to be honored with Einstein and other leading scientists by the Insti-

tute of Aeronautical Science for outstanding work. His remains were buried in Mountain View Cemetery in Retadena. After his death, the Office of Naval Research sponsored the Bateman Manuscript Project, which aimed to prepare for publication Bateman's manuscripts, files, and index cards, which were teeming with information on special functions and integrals that solve partial differential equations. A large number of volumes ensued.

[Two tributes to Harry Bateman and his work are by Arthur Erdelyi, "Harry Bateman 1882–1946," *Obituary Notices of Fellows of the Royal Society,* 5 (1947), 591–618, and by F. D. Murnaghan, "Harry Bateman," *Bull. of the Am. Mathematical Soc.,* 54 (1948), 88–103. An article by C. S. Fisher is in *Dict. Sci. Biog.* I, 499–500. An obituary appeared in the *N.Y. Times* on Jan. 24, 1946.]

SALOMON BOCHNER

BAZETT, HENRY CUTHBERT (June 25, 1885-July 12, 1950), physiologist, was born in Gravesend, England, the second of two children of Henry Bazett, a clergyman, later a physician, and Eliza Ann (Cruickshank) Bazett. Bazett attended Dover College and Wadham College, Oxford, from which he received the B.A. in 1908, M.S. in 1913, and M.D. in 1919. He received his clinical training at St. Thomas's Hospital, attaining qualification in 1910. After holding house appointments and a demonstratorship at St. Thomas's he received the Cheselden Medal in 1911. While he was studying medicine, his father also decided to become a physician.

In 1912 Bazett was granted a Radcliffe traveling fellowship, which enabled him to spend a year in postgraduate study at Harvard University. He returned to England in 1913. During World War I Bazett served as a member of the Royal Army Medical Corps in France. He received the M.C., was mentioned three times in dispatches, and on demobilization was appointed an officer, Order of the British Empire, in 1918. While serving as a medical officer at advanced posts he became much interested in wound shock as well as in the sensation and effects of cold. During the first battle of Ypres he suffered an attack of acute appendicitis. He was operated on in a tent at the front and the appendiceal abscess drained. He was not expected to survive, and the number of wounded to be evacuated was so great that he was left unattended in the unheated tent until found by a friend of his own unit, who had him transferred to a base hospital. Bazett regarded his experience as a fine test of the effect of cold on shock.

After demobilization, Bazett returned to Oxford as Christopher Welch lecturer in clinical pathology and was appointed fellow of Magdalen College. During this period he served as Sir Charles Sherrington's assistant. It was under the supervision of Sherrington that Bazett and W. G. Penfield undertook one of their first major research projects, "A Study of the Sherrington Decerebrate Animal in the Chronic as well as in the Acute Condition" (*Brain*, 1922). Bazett's interests, however, were in the clinical aspects of physiology and, on being unable to obtain the post he desired, he accepted in 1921 the professorship of physiology at the University of Pennsylvania, a position he retained until his death. Here he thought he would have an opportunity to do research and teach the appropriate mixture of basic and clinical physiology.

After initial work on nervous system function, Bazett turned to the study of circulation, blood volume, temperature sense, and body temperature regulations. For some years he was the author of the section on cardiovascular physiology in Macleod's *Physiology and Biochemistry in Modern Medicine* (8th ed., 1938; 9th ed., 1941). He made a major contribution to the discovery of "counter current" effects, which show how the anatomical arrangement of veins and arteries provides an excellent mechanism for the exchange of heat. Cold venous blood from an extremity may, through this exchange, be at thermal neutrality before reaching the body core, there being thus a conservation of heat and an easier protection of core temperature. Bazett studied acclimatization in man and was the first to establish clearly that an increase in blood volume occurs in adaptation to a hot environment.

He had a penchant for making drastic experiments on himself; in his studies of thermal sense and body temperature control, he had thermocouples inserted under his skin at various depths and in nearly every available blood vessel. His contributions in this field were considerable and he reviewed many of them in a chapter on temperature regulation in *The Physiology of Temperature Regulation and the Science of Clothing,* edited by L. H. Newburgh (1949). His work on blood flow and temperature change in arteries and veins is still considered important.

Bazett always retained his British nationality and felt some responsibility for all English-speaking peoples. In 1940, when the United States was not yet at war, he took a leave of absence from Pennsylvania to do aviation medical research in Canada. After the death of Sir Frederick Banting left that research effort without a leader, Bazett headed the Canadian Committee on Aviation Medical Research from 1941

to 1943. His advice was continually requested on both sides of the Atlantic during World War II. He was a temporary member of the British Medical Research Council and carried out a mission to India and Burma in 1944 for consultation with the R.A.F. and Royal Navy, after which he was made a commander of the Order of the British Empire (1946); he also served with the U.S. Office of Scientific Research and Development. He was a member of the council of the American Physiological Society (president-elect at the time of his death) and was also one of the founders of the International Union of Physiological Sciences.

Bazett was highly competitive, and this characteristic plus his curiosity and disregard of his own safety caused his friends considerable anxiety on his behalf. When he was engaged in his early studies of the effects of gravity, he would seek out the most daring R.C.A.F. pilots and insist they "take him up" and demonstrate what was required to make him "black out." He was soon officially grounded. He was a swimmer and liked competition, frequently beating much younger men. At one Physiology Society discussion the question was raised as to how long a man could stay under water. The prevailing opinion was that one minute was about the limit for an untrained man. Bazett took the group to a swimming pool where he swam under water for two minutes. This demonstration unfortunately precipitated his first heart attack. As a laboratory teacher Bazett was excellent and inspired enthusiasm in his students. As a lecturer he was sometimes brilliant but at other times would become sidetracked into somewhat tedious mathematical formulations. Nevertheless his perpetually youthful spirit and his alertness of mind made him popular with his associates and students.

On Mar. 10, 1917, Bazett married Dorothy Livesey; they had two children, Hazel and Donald John.

Bazett died of a heart attack on board the *Queen Mary* while en route to a conference of physiologists at Copenhagen. He was a member of the Church of England and was buried in a small cemetery in Oxford, England.

[Obituaries appear in *The Lancet*, Aug. 19, 1950; *British Medical Jour.*, July 22, 1950; and Am. Neurological Assoc., *Trans.*, 77 (1952). See also a memoir by Francis Heed Adler in *Trans. and Studies*, College of Physicians of Philadelphia, 19 (1952).]

CHANDLER McC. BROOKS

BEACH, REX (Sept. 1, 1877–Dec. 7, 1949), novelist, scenarist, was born in Atwood, Antrim County, Mich. Christened Rex Ellingwood

Beach, he was the third of the three sons of Henry Walter Beach and Eva Eunice (Canfield) Beach, who came to Michigan from New York state. His father was a diligent, modestly successful farmer; his mother, who had been a schoolteacher, was well educated and wrote poetry. Their fruit farm near Lake Michigan was insufficiently productive, and when Beach was nine his parents sailed to Florida with neighbors on a schooner and settled on a farm near Tampa. Beach went to the preparatory department of Rollins College, Winter Park, when he was fifteen. He was at Rollins four years, working in a laundry for his tuition. In 1896 he left, without graduating, to study law at the Chicago College of Law, joining his two older brothers, who were lawyers there. However, lured by the Klondike gold rush in 1897, he abandoned law and spent much of the next five years prospecting and mining in Alaska without remarkable success.

While in Alaska, Beach read a collection of short stories by Jack London, and was awakened to the possibilities of turning his own experiences to fictional account. He sold his first story, "The Mule Driver and the Garrulous Mute," to *McClure's Magazine* for $50 and became a frequent contributor. His first book, *Pardners* (1905), was a collection of ten stories of life in Alaska and the West. His next, a novel, *The Spoilers* (1906), became a best seller (more than 700,000 copies). It was a story about Alaskan prospectors cheated of valuable claims by chicanery. "I wrote it," Beach said, "as an exposure of corrupt judges and lawyers." His second novel, *The Barrier* (1907), also about Alaska, was superior to the first in technique and sold nearly as well.

In 1907 in New York City Beach married Edith Greta Crater, an actress and daughter of George E. Crater, a Denver, Colo., businessman and former superintendent of the Denver Mint. They had met in Nome, where she owned and operated a small hotel. The marriage was childless.

Beach continued to write popular "red-blooded" Alaskan novels—*The Silver Horde* (1909), a tale of the salmon fisheries, and *The Net* (1912). "My early novels were Alaskan, and they stamped me with a brand as distinctive as the label on a sardine can," Beach said. However, he turned to other subjects and backgrounds—the Canal Zone, for instance, in *The Ne'er-do-Well* (1911), and New York City in *The Auction Block* (1914). Beach, like James Oliver Curwood and Stewart Edward White (the three were all born in Michigan; all came to prominence early in the century, and were on best-seller lists into the 1920's), used his material romantically and sentimentally to illustrate the virtues of courage, hard work, and personal integrity. His stories were infused with authentic knowledge of the scenes described and a love for outdoor life. By 1926, Beach's publisher could advertise that more than 3,000,000 copies of his books had been sold.

Beach was the first American author to insert a clause about movie rights in his contracts, securing for himself a footnote in film history and a great deal of additional revenue. By refusing to sell the novel outright, he profited each time *The Spoilers* was filmed (with William Farnum in 1914, Milton Sills in 1922, Gary Cooper in 1930, and John Wayne in 1942). Fourteen of his novels and sixteen of his original scenarios were made into motion pictures. In 1948, he sold the film rights to his last novel, *Woman in Ambush* (1951)—not quite completed at the time of his death—for $100,000, the highest price paid by Hollywood producers up to that time for an unpublished manuscript.

After making one fortune from novels and motion pictures, Beach went on in his later years to make another from flower and vegetable growing—he grossed $200,000 in one season from the sale of bulbs alone. Eventually he sold this farm to his employees and began raising cattle. He once owned 7,000 acres near Sebring and 2,000 acres near Avon Park. He shrewdly followed the advice of specialists on farming methods and soil problems. Though he continued to write fiction on a reduced scale, he also wrote about soil conservation, human and animal nutrition, and other subjects that concerned him. His interest in Alaska never waned and he proposed government-financed projects for American youth to develop the territory. In 1927, he received honorary B.S. and Litt.D. degrees from Rollins College.

Beach was described by a friend, Cosmo Hamilton, as "a man standing six-feet-one in his socks, ... with a back as broad as a door, a hand like a leg of mutton, a deep, vibrating voice, soft blue eyes with a twinkle." An athlete and sportsman, Beach played football for the Chicago Athletic Association and participated as a swimmer in the Olympic Games at St. Louis, Mo., in 1904. He had a humorous temper and was warmly regarded by his neighbors and farm employees. "It has always been my failing," he once wrote, "to quit the thing I am doing before it is well or completely done and try something new."

In his later years Beach suffered acutely from throat cancer and from failing eyesight. He endured four eye operations, and for two years breathed through a tube inserted in his throat, with nerve-block surgery to relieve pain. Finally, at age seventy-two, he committed suicide at his home in Sebring. His body was cremated; his ashes and those of his wife (who had died on Apr. 15, 1947) were buried on the campus of Rollins College. Rites of the Episcopal church were read at the funeral in Sebring.

[The Beach manuscript collection, papers, correspondence, and memorabilia are at Rollins Coll., Winter Park, Fla. Additional material is available at Syracuse Univ. Beach's autobiography, *Personal Exposures* (1941), is a succession of rambling reminiscences but provides significant insights into his activities and personality. See also *Nat. Cyc. Am. Biog.*, XIV, 58; Robert van Gelder, *Writers and Writing* (1946); C. C. Baldwin, *The Men Who Make Our Novels* (1952); Russel B. Nye, *The Unembarrassed Muse* (1970); Louis Nizer, "The Most Unforgettable Character I've Met," *Readers' Digest*, Jan. 1951; Rex Beach, "My Adventures as a Rolling Stone," *American Mag.*, Aug. 1924; Howard Haycraft and Stanley J. Kunitz, eds., *Twentieth Century Authors* (1942; and first supplement, 1955) includes a list of Beach's numerous books, with publication dates; obituaries in *N.Y. Times*, Dec. 8, 1949, and *Time*, Dec. 19, 1949; see *Bookman*, Sept. 1911, p. 8, for a good photographic portrait.]

WILLAM McCANN

BEARD, CHARLES AUSTIN (Nov. 27, 1874-Sept. 1, 1948), historian, political scientist, public figure, was born on a farm near Knightstown, Ind., the younger of the two sons of William Henry Harrison Beard and Mary J. (Payne) Beard. Independence of spirit was a family tradition. Nathan Beard, Charles's Quaker grandfather, was read out of meeting in his native North Carolina for marrying a Methodist, and once hid fugitive slaves on his farm. His only son, William, fled because of his Unionist sentiments to Indiana, where he married the daughter of Hoosier pioneers. William Beard possessed an adventurous spirit and an inquisitive mind. A schoolteacher, building contractor, and real estate speculator as well as a farmer, he made a considerable fortune.

Charles Beard attended Spiceland Academy, a Quaker school near his home, and enjoyed his agnostic father's large library. For a time, in the early 1890's, he and his brother Clarence edited the *Knightstown Banner*, a local newspaper their father had bought for them. Insistence on economic and intellectual independence, a firm humanitarian conscience, and a fluent competence in writing were characteristics formed early. Inheriting a Republican family tradition, Beard entered the Methodist-affiliated DePauw University in Greencastle, Ind., in

1895 and there encountered the stimulating teaching of Col. James R. Weaver, who opened up the vistas of a social reformation prophesied by Karl Marx, John Ruskin, Lester Frank Ward, and others. On a trip to Chicago, Beard visited Hull House, listened to the Populist-inspired oratory of William Jennings Bryan, and had a firsthand glimpse of urban poverty. As a member of the DePauw debating team, he spoke in support of a federal income tax and the right of labor to unionize.

After receiving a Ph.B. degree from DePauw in 1898 and trying unsuccessfully to volunteer for service in the Spanish-American War, Beard went to Oxford University for a year's study of English constitutional history. In his graduate work he displayed the combination of intellectual energy and passion for reform that would mark his entire career. Studying under F. York Powell (who found him "the nicest American I ever knew"), he also responded deeply to the social movement that had produced J. Keir Hardie's Independent Labour party. In 1899 he joined with Walter Vrooman, a Kansas socialist, whose wife put up $60,000 for the purpose, in founding Ruskin Hall, a workers' college at Oxford—named for John Ruskin, whose *Unto This Last*, an ethical and aesthetic critique of capitalism, Beard often carried in his pocket. Back in America, Beard enrolled for the fall term at Cornell University, and then, on Mar. 8, 1900, married Mary Ritter of Indianapolis, whom he had first met at DePauw. They had two children, Miriam and William.

Beard took his bride to Ruskin Hall, where as secretary he wrote a series of articles for *Young Oxford*, the school's journal, in which he expressed hope for the gradual amelioration of social conditions without class warfare. Exploring the "black country" of industrial England, he preached the ideal of workers' education to the cooperative movement. His first book, *The Industrial Revolution* (1901), written in the cause of this ideal, struck a dominant chord of his thought in finding "the central theme of history" in man's increasing assertion of "his right and power to determine his own religion and politics, and corporately to control every form of his material environment." This optimistic rationalism drew heavily on the Victorian idea that technology, substituting "the tireless power of Nature" for manual labor, would provide "the material key to man's spiritual progress" (pp. 86, 42).

Beard returned to the United States in 1902 and resumed graduate work, this time at Columbia University, where he received his

A.M. (1903) and Ph.D. (1904) degrees. His master's thesis, "The Present Status of Civil Service Reform in the United States," reflected the impact of the pioneering work in public administration of Frank J. Goodnow; his doctoral dissertation, "The Office of Justice of the Peace in England in Its Origin and Development" (1904), mirrored the more traditional constitutional history favored by John W. Burgess. In the fall of 1904 Beard himself joined the Columbia faculty as a lecturer in European and English history. Three years later he moved to the department of public law, where he rose through the ranks to become professor of politics in 1915. Two of his Columbia colleagues, James Harvey Robinson and Harry Elmer Barnes, were promoting "the New History," and Beard collaborated with the former on *The Development of Modern Europe* (2 vols., 1907-1908), which, in the spirit of the current Progressive Era, aimed to use the past to explain the present in the faith that "men of science, not kings, or warriors, or even statesmen are to be the heroes of the future" (II, 421). Beard was also familiar with the antiformalist historiography of Frederick Jackson Turner, who in 1904 called for the study of "the vital forces" that lay "behind institutions"; with Arthur F. Bentley's study of interest-group politics, *The Process of Government* (1908); and with *The Economic Interpretation of History* (1902) by Edwin R. A. Seligman.

In 1913 Beard published *An Economic Interpretation of the Constitution of the United States*, in which he cited Seligman's assertion that changes in social structure, conditioning the relations of classes, must be traced "in the last instance" to economic causes. An earlier work by James Allen Smith, *The Spirit of American Government* (1907), had already prepared Progressives for the image of the framers of the Constitution as political reactionaries. Beard's treatise—one of the most controversial and influential ever written—argued that members of the Constitutional Convention were not working "under the guidance of abstract principles of political science" but rather represented "distinct groups whose economic interests they understood and felt in concrete, definite form through their own personal experience with identical property rights" (p. 73), a conclusion he based on his research in the debt-funding records of Washington's administration. Beard admired the realistic statecraft of the framers, but his thesis strongly hinted at conspiratorial motivation and was seized upon by both Progressives and their enemies as a "muckraking" exposé of the Founding Fathers. Beard went on to apply an economic interpretation to a later historical period in his *Economic Origins of Jeffersonian Democracy* (1915) and to all of American history in *The Rise of American Civilization* (1927).

The storm that raged over Beard's publication made him as popular with students as it made him notorious to conventional conservatives. At Columbia he virtually created the undergraduate curriculum in political science, using as a focus his *American Government and Politics* (1910 and later editions), a pioneering textbook in the field. He also stressed the importance of studying public administration and gave a course on municipal government. Beard's eloquence as a lecturer inspired and challenged his students; and in his recounting of America's historical achievements and failures, he displayed a range of emotions from hopeful pride to humorous irony and withering wrath. Lanky, with striking blue eyes, red hair, and an aquiline nose which, according to one biographer, "in grave moments could give him the aspect of a worried eagle" (Hofstadter, p. 179), Beard despised pretense and treated his students with the same friendliness and courtesy he showed his colleagues.

Characteristically, Beard left academic life on an issue of principle. With the entrance of the United States into World War I, President Nicholas Murray Butler and the Columbia trustees attempted to suppress any faculty criticism of American intervention. Beard supported the war effort, but he saw its repressive impact on free speech. In 1917 Leon Fraser, a young instructor in Beard's department, was denied reappointment, along with two prominent anti-war members of other departments—James McKeen Cattell in psychology and Henry Wadsworth Longfellow Dana in literature. That October, Beard resigned his own position to protest, as he wrote in a strong letter to Butler, the domination of the university by trustees "who have no standing in the world of education, who are reactionary and visionless in politics, narrow and medieval in religion." Beard remained ever after a courageous spokesman for academic freedom and civil liberties. He was called on in 1925 by the American Civil Liberties Union to protest a State Department effort to muzzle the exiled Count Michael Károlyi, former socialist premier of Hungary, and by the National Education Association in 1935 to attack a red-baiting effort of the newspaper publisher William Randolph Hearst to discredit public school teachers.

After leaving Columbia, Beard moved to New Milford, Conn. He never again held a regular academic appointment, but he remained active as a writer and public figure. During his teaching years he had taken an active part in municipal affairs as a member of both the National Municipal League and the New York City Bureau of Municipal Research. As director of the Bureau's Training School for Public Service (1917–1922), he introduced many students to the scientific approach to public administration, and emphasized the need for close relationships between the academic disciplines and the world of practical politics. As a writer, he insisted that public surveys and reports be presented in clear language, comprehensible to the ordinary citizen. Beard drafted important phases of the report of the New York State Reconstruction Commission, which was presented in 1919 to Gov. Alfred E. Smith. In 1922, on the invitation of the mayor of Tokyo, he aided in organizing a Japanese Bureau of Municipal Research, and he returned after the earthquake of 1923 to advise on the rebuilding of Tokyo.

Beard's devotion to education and the writing of history remained strong. He joined with John Dewey, Alvin S. Johnson, and James Harvey Robinson to found the New School for Social Research in 1919, and two years later he helped organize the Workers Education Bureau of America. He remained active in scholarly circles, serving as president of both the American Political Science Association (1926) and the American Historical Association (1933). In 1927, in collaboration with his wife, he published *The Rise of American Civilization*, a work dominated by his dialectic of a recurring conflict between province and metropolis, agriculture and business, which "figured in every great national crisis" (I, 202). This polarizing scheme was resonant with the contemporary literary history of Vernon L. Parrington, who insisted on a recurrent conflict between liberal "realists" and conservative "romantics."

In his middle years Beard both lived the role of a man of public affairs and returned to the rustic, farmer's life that he had known as a boy, combining these disparate styles with considerable success. Since leaving Columbia, he had lived on his writings and on investments. In 1929 he purchased a large dairy farm in Connecticut, and he thereafter divided his time between the farm and a residence in Washington, D.C., where he spent several months each year writing on current affairs and advising congressmen and cabinet officers. Despite increasing deafness, he played an active part in events. He supported the planning aspects of the early New Deal, helped settle a strike by milk producers in Connecticut, and as a bondholder of the Missouri-Pacific Railway secured an investigation of the Van Sweringen railroad empire by the Senate Committee on Interstate Commerce.

During the last two decades of his life, Beard became increasingly concerned with foreign affairs and the issue of American neutrality. He went to Europe in 1921 to examine the disenchanting revelations from the government archives opened by Germany, Austria, and Russia, but as late as 1926 he still believed that American intervention in World War I had been justified to prevent a German victory that would have threatened Washington. His recoil from intervention was, however, a spring stretched taut over fifteen years. In the early 1930's Beard responded to the crisis of the depression by revising his economic interpretation of politics, his belief in objective scholarship, and his concern for the balance of power in Europe. Fascism emphasized military power rather than economic factors; New Deal planning dramatized the need for a more-than-economic sense of civilization; and Beard's son-in-law, Alfred Vagts, directed his attention to European thinkers who had challenged the idea of scientific history that had dazzled American historians since the 1880's. In 1931 Carl L. Becker, whom Beard admired as a congenial disturber of the professional peace, attacked historical positivism and emphasized the historian's duty to mirror present hopes and fears. Beard's presidential address to the American Historical Association in 1933, "Written History as an Act of Faith," added the reformer's idea that the historian had to guide his work by an idea of progress, entailing a statesmanlike commitment to a specific future.

Beard's own "act of faith" was in a "collectivist democracy" rooted in a relatively self-sufficient, nationally planned economy, disentangled from imperial ambitions and European alliances. In *The Idea of National Interest* and *The Open Door at Home*, both written in 1934 with George H. E. Smith, Beard argued that the current economic crisis afforded the United States an excellent opportunity to reevaluate its world relationships in the light of national self-interest and to seek an independent course of recovery. (He applauded President Roosevelt's intervention in 1933 to thwart the London Economic Conference.) Beard approved the inquiry into the munitions industry begun in

1934 by a Senate investigating committee headed by Gerald P. Nye, an ardent Midwestern isolationist. The findings of the Nye Committee persuaded Beard that "powerful economic and political personalities," conspiring to tie America closer to Great Britain through credit arrangements, had forced the United States into war in 1917, and he worried that history would repeat itself. In *The Devil Theory of War* (1936), he attacked the idea of wicked warmakers as a fiction, while at the same time asserting that bankers had pressured Wilson into war. Beard warned that Roosevelt would exploit an incident in the Pacific to the advantage of Allied imperialism ("National Politics and War," *Scribner's,* February 1935).

An opponent of naval expansion, the lend-lease program, and universal military training, Beard was often called to testify before congressional committees, and he advised the minority on the committee investigating the Pearl Harbor disaster. He endorsed the isolationist platform of the America First Committee, though he refused to join the committee when he saw it becoming a forum for "native fascists." In accord with his earlier prophecy, his last book, *President Roosevelt and the Coming of the War, 1941* (1948), argued that Roosevelt had deliberately maneuvered Japan into attacking the United States. Meanwhile he had revised his views of the Founding Fathers. In *The Republic: Conversations on Fundamentals* (1943) he saw them as men imbued with a deep sense of social responsibility for national unity and constitutional government—his own goals. Active until the end, he died in a New Haven hospital at the age of seventy-three, of aplastic anemia. He was buried in Ferncliff Cemetery, Hartsdale, N.Y.

Beard's economic interpretations of the Constitutional Convention, the Civil War, and the Fourteenth Amendment have proved highly vulnerable to criticism, and his revolt against scientific history was marred by a residual nineteenth-century deterministic view of science. Yet despite his skepticism, he was, like Henry Adams, "a searcher for the key to things," and if the sage of New Milford, with his belief in nationality, republicanism, technology, and "realism," sometimes sounded like the Connecticut Yankee in King Arthur's Court, at his best Beard answered Emerson's demand for "a tyrannous eye" that would know "the incomparable value of our materials." In the classroom Beard alternated a mordant sense of historical fate with an indignant idealism, and this double vision characterized his whole

career like a personal signature. Prodigious in output (twenty-nine histories, fifteen theoretical studies, fifteen textbooks), "Uncle Charlie" was a salty Socratic gadfly to two professions, a defender of academic freedom and civil liberties, and probably the most widely read of American scholars.

[Mary R. Beard has collected some biographical material in *The Making of Charles A. Beard* (1955). Howard K. Beale edited a collection of articles by thirteen prominent friends, *Charles A. Beard: An Appraisal* (1954), which treats him as historian, political scientist, reformer, and teacher. It also includes sales figures and a complete bibliography of his works. Beard's ideas regarding relativism, economic determinism, and the idea of progress are examined in relation to the positivistic tradition and to pragmatism in Cushing Strout, *The Pragmatic Revolt in Am. Hist.: Carl Becker and Charles Beard* (1958; reprinted with new preface, 1966). Bernard C. Borning traces in detail three phases of Beard's development in *The Political and Social Thought of Charles A. Beard* (1962). Lee Benson closely analyzes the methodological weaknesses of Beard and his critics, Robert Brown and Forrest McDonald, regarding the Constitutional Convention in *Turner and Beard: Am. Historical Writing Reconsidered* (1960). Richard Hofstadter assimilates the important critical literature on Beard and integrates it with biographical material in *The Progressive Historians* (1968). See also memorial reminiscence by Matthew Josephson in *Va. Quart. Rev.,* Autumn 1949; and obituary by Arthur W. Macmahon in *Am. Political Sci. Rev.,* Dec. 1948. There is no available collection of Beard papers. The most extensive set of letters belongs to Harry Elmer Barnes and is in the library of the Univ. of Wyo. I have also benefited from interviews with Mary Beard and Alfred Vagts.]

CUSHING STROUT

BEARD, MARY (Nov. 14, 1876–Dec. 4, 1946), administrator and educator in nursing and public health, was born in Dover, N.H., where her father was an Episcopal rector. The third daughter and fourth of five children born to Ithamar Warren Beard and Marcy (Foster) Beard, she grew up in a cultivated but modest home, where social service and education were highly valued and where she acquired a lifelong habit of wide reading. In childhood when she was very ill with diphtheria, a trained nurse, the first she had ever seen, came from New York to supervise her convalescence. So greatly was she impressed by this nurse that she decided to be a nurse when she grew up. After being educated in the public schools of Dover, she held a tutoring position in a private home in Boston and, in 1899, at the age of twenty-three, she entered the New York Hospital School of Nursing.

Following graduation in 1903, when there were fewer than 150 public health nurses, she became a visiting nurse with the Waterbury (Conn.) Visiting Nurse Association (1904–1909). After a brief interlude in the Laboratory of Surgical Pathology, College of Physicians and Surgeons, Columbia University (1910-1912), she returned to nursing in response to an appeal by Ella Phillips Crandall. "There was so great a need for active public health nurses that I must consider seriously the special 'call' she brought me," Beard decided (*Public Health Nursing* 30 (1938) : 726-727).

As director of the Boston Instructive District Nursing Association (1912-1922), Beard was a persuasive advocate for preventive health services. Her conviction that voluntary and official agencies should plan jointly to eliminate duplication of services and uneconomical use of health resources and her skill in working with community groups were key factors in bringing about a merger with the Baby Hygiene Association. For two years she served as general director of the combined Community Health Association (1922-1924), during which period the association succeeded in convincing the city of Boston to assume a large part of the work with babies. She then decided that the diminishing program called for a different personality as director.

In 1924 Beard accepted a short-term appointment to conduct a study of maternal health care in England for the Rockefeller Foundation. Her later positions were special assistant to the director of the division of studies (1925-1927), assistant to the director of the division of medical education (1927-1930), and associate director, international health division (1931-1938). During the years that she directed its nursing program from the New York office, the foundation spent over $4 million on nursing projects. Beard's responsibilities included numerous projects to advance education and public health nursing in the United States and abroad. This work took her to European, Middle Eastern, and Asian countries for conferences with representatives of governments, health professions, and educational institutions and for some extensive studies of nursing. Always strongly supportive of university-based schools of nursing that would attract educated women and teach preventive health, she used her influence with the foundation, schools of nursing, allied health groups, and nursing leaders to encourage sound experiments in nursing education and service. A crucial resource for these innovative programs was the nurses whose preparation for leadership positions was strengthened through foundation-supported fellowships; Beard arranged travel and study programs for approximately 428 nurses from thirty-eight countries and eighty-three nurse leaders from the United States.

After leaving the foundation she embarked at at the age of sixty-two on yet another challenging position as director of the newly consolidated nursing service of the American Red Cross (1938-1944). An enrolled Red Cross nurse since 1912, she directed a massive wartime program to recruit graduate nurses for military and civilian services and represented the Red Cross in collaborative efforts to expand and utilize wisely the nation's nursing resources, both as a member of the National Nursing Council and as the first chairman of the subcommittee on nursing of the health and medical committee of the Office of Defense Health and Welfare Services. Having learned through her experience in World War I of the hazards of leaving the civilian population without adequate nursing service, she advocated policies that would meet military needs and yet keep public health nurses and nursing instructors at their posts. The strains and complexities of her task increased as the Red Cross Nursing Service tried to reconcile its recruitment and service functions with those of a growing number of federal agencies and professional organizations. Nevertheless, by 1944, when she resigned because of illness, 50,000 nurses had been recruited for military service and expanded home nursing programs and a new volunteer nurse's aide program were helping to meet civilian needs.

Beard was one of the best-known nurses in the world. A founder of the National Organization for Public Health Nursing, she was its president during World War I, chairman of the subcommittee on public health nursing of the General Medical Board of the Council of National Defense, and a member of the National Committee on Red Cross Nursing Service. Other memberships included the Rockefeller Foundation Committee for the Study of Nursing and Nursing Education, which produced the Winslow-Goldmark Report, *Nursing and Nursing Education in the United States,* the nursing committee of the Henry Street Nursing Service, and the advisory committee on nursing, New York City Department of Health. In addition to honorary membership in the Grand Council of the International Council of Nurses, the "Old International Association," and the Association of Collegiate Schools of Nursing, she received honorary doctoral degrees from the University of New Hampshire (1934) and Smith College (1945). After an illness of several weeks, Mary Beard died in New York Hospital on Dec. 4, 1946, at the age of seventy.

Although her professional life was intense and demanding, she found time to enjoy friendships, the countryside of her New Hampshire home, and to write, paint, and read. Tall and erect, she made an imposing appearance with her lively expression, light hair, and blue eyes; an aura of warmth and concern in her direct, attentive look made people feel at ease.

[Beard's publications include *The Nurse in Public Health* (1929); "Midwifery in England," *The Public Health Nurse,* Dec. 1926 and Jan. 1927; "Creative Nursing," *Am. Jour. of Nursing,* Jan. 1936; "Some Contrasting Systems of Nursing Education as Seen by a Traveller in Europe, Asia and America," in *International Aspects of Nursing Education* (1932); "Wanted, 10,000 Nurses," *Am. Jour. of Nursing,* Mar. 1939; "The American Red Cross Nursing Service," *Public Health Nursing,* Oct. 1939. See also biographical sketches with portraits in "Specialists in Internationalism," *Am. Jour. of Nursing,* Dec. 1931 and Oct. 1938; Genevieve Forbes Herrick, *Country Gentlemen,* June 1939; Beth Blaine, *Washington Star,* Sept. 7, 1942; S. J. Woolf, *N.Y. Times,* Dec. 1, 1940; obituary in *N.Y. Times,* Dec. 5, 1946; Alan Gregg, "Mary Beard—Humanist," *Am. Jour. of Nursing,* Feb. 1947. Other information from letters and documents filed in the archives of the Rockefeller Foundation, the American Red Cross, and the Cornell Univ. Lib.; from Mary M. Roberts, *American Nursing: History and Interpretation* (1954); and from colleagues of Beard.]
ALICE J. GIFFORD

BEERY, WALLACE FITZGERALD (Apr. 1, 1885-Apr. 15, 1949), stage and screen actor, was born in Kansas City, Mo., the youngest of the three sons of Noah Webster Beery, a policeman, and Margaret (Fitzgerald) Beery. A husky child, poor at schoolwork, he chafed under the nickname "Jumbo" given him by his schoolmates and under the piano lessons imposed by his mother. In his early teens he ran away from home, and though he soon returned, he never went back to school. After working as a railroad section hand and roundhouseman, he joined the Forepaugh-Sells circus as an elephant handler and later became the head elephant trainer for the Ringling Brothers circus.

While with the circus, Beery learned some dance steps and developed an interest in acting. On the advice of his brother Noah, who had embarked on a stage career in musical comedy, he left the circus in 1904 and secured a job in the chorus of the musical comedy company of Henry W. Savage in New York. Among the productions in which he appeared were *Babes in Toyland, The Prince of Pilsen,* and *The Student King.* Between engagements with Savage, he worked in Midwestern summer stock. His first break came in 1907 when he temporarily replaced the popular musical star Raymond Hitchcock in *A Yankee Tourist.* It was at this time that he began to develop the jowly face

and burly figure that the film camera was later to make internationally famous.

As early as 1908 Beery worked as a movie extra in New Rochelle, N.Y. In 1913, after closing in Chicago with *The Balkan Princess,* he left the stage and signed with a Chicago film-producing company, Essanay, to write and direct. In his first Essanay film he played the comic role of a Swedish housemaid, the effectiveness of the impersonation owing much to his six-foot-one-inch height and 250-pound bulk. So successful was the picture that Beery made an extended series of "Sweedie" films, as well as many other Essanay comedies. Among the actors in the company were Ben Turpin and sixteen-year-old Gloria Swanson. In 1915 G. M. "Bronco Billy" Anderson, co-founder of Essanay, sent Beery to Niles, Calif., to manage a new studio. This was not successful, however, and the next year Beery went to Hollywood, where he found work as an actor and director at Universal Pictures. From Universal he moved to Keystone. Here he again met Gloria Swanson. They were married in February 1916 and divorced about two years later.

Beery's career was now at a standstill. He was rescued from neglect by the director Marshall Neilan who cast him as a vicious German in the war picture *The Unpardonable Sin* (1919). Thus after years of comedy Beery became a leading screen villain. In the early 1920's he acted for many major Hollywood studios, appearing in such popular films as *The Four Horsemen of the Apocalypse* (1921), with Rudolph Valentino, and *Robin Hood* (1922), with Douglas Fairbanks. In 1925 he began a five-year association with Paramount Pictures during which he made, among other films, a series of comedies with Raymond Hatton. Meanwhile, on Aug. 4, 1924, he had married Mary Arieta Gilman, known as Rita Gilman, an actress whom he had met during the filming of *Robin Hood;* they adopted a daughter, Carol Ann. Beery and his second wife were divorced in 1939.

Lacking confidence in Beery's ability to achieve popularity in sound pictures, Paramount dropped him in 1929. This, as it turned out, was the making of his fortune, for he went at once to Metro-Goldwyn-Mayer, where he soon developed into a major attraction. Under M-G-M guidance, Beery adopted the screen image of a lovable low character, often drunk and even dangerous, but at the same time warmly human. With his large frame, he was convincing as the convict who leads a prison uprising in *The Big House* (1930), a down-and-out prizefighter in

The Champ (1931), a champion wrestler in *Flesh* (1932), and a Mexican revolutionary leader in *Viva Villa!* (1934). Co-starring with Marie Dressler, whose waning career had also been saved by M-G-M, he played in two popular comedies of rowdy middle-aged affection, *Min and Bill* (1930) and *Tugboat Annie* (1933). When permitted, Beery proved that he could still portray the villain effectively, as in the all-star *Grand Hotel* (1932) and *Dinner at Eight* (1933). A good performer with children, he was teamed repeatedly with M-G-M's numerous child stars and was especially successful with Jackie Cooper in *The Champ* and *Treasure Island* (1934) and with Mickey Rooney in *Stablemates* (1938).

Beery enjoyed the outdoor life in his leisure hours and owned ranches in Wyoming and Idaho. Though one Hollywood historian has described him as "petty, testy, and mean" off screen (Crowther, *Hollywood Rajah*, p. 230), he was a devoted family man. In his last decade, the spell of his gruff manner and rasping voice began to fade. The studio's attempts to sustain his popularity by casting him with new juvenile actors and the character actress Marjorie Main did not fulfill expectations. In 1949, shortly after the completion of *Big Jack* with Miss Main, he died at his Beverly Hills home of a long-standing heart ailment. He was buried in Forest Lawn Memorial Park in Glendale. He left an estate reported to be in excess of $2 million.

Though an uneven actor, Beery made an important contribution to the screen in the 1930's. With the possible exception of Marie Dressler, none of the M-G-M stars outshone him at his best. His talent won recognition from his peers in the form of an Academy Award for his role in *The Champ*. His following among filmgoers put him among the ten foremost moneymaking stars from 1932 through 1935 and again in 1940, and earned his studio an estimated $50 million.

[Accounts of Beery's life disagree in details of the early years. The following are the most useful: Leonard Maltin in *Film Fan Monthly*, July–Aug. 1967 (includes a Beery filmography, omitting, through an oversight, *Grand Hotel*); Earl Anderson in *Films in Rev.*, June–July 1973 (with filmography by Richard Braff); David Shipman, *The Great Movie Stars: The Golden Years* (1970), pp. 53–56; Wallace Beery, "It's Funny about My Face," *American Mag.*, June 1934 (probably ghostwritten); profile by Alva Johnston in *New Yorker*, Nov. 9, 1935. Comments of interest on Beery's life and work appear in the *N.Y. Times*, Aug. 17, 1924, sec. 7; Dec. 18, 1932, sec. 10; May 2, 1939; and Apr. 17, 1949 (obituary). On M-G-M, see Bosley Crowther, *The Lion's Share* (1957) and *Hollywood Rajah* (1960). Beery's birth year was established by his death certificate and by correspondence with Noah Beery, Jr. Photographs of Beery in famous roles appear in the Maltin and Ship-

man references above, and in such books as Richard Griffith and Arthur Mayer, *The Movies* (1957), and Richard Schickel, *The Stars* (1962).]
                        MALCOLM GOLDSTEIN

BEESON, CHARLES HENRY (Oct. 2, 1870–Dec. 26, 1949), classical scholar, medievalist, and paleographer, was born in Columbia City, Ind., the only son and first of three children of Henry Norris Beeson, a descendant of Penn emigrants from Lancashire, England, and his second wife, Magdelena (Wekerle) Beeson, daughter of a German emigrant. Henry Beeson, a blacksmith from boyhood, became proprietor of a successful drugstore in his early forties.

The appearance and demeanor of young Charles may be surmised from the nickname "Deac" (deacon), given him by schoolmates. From high school he attended Indiana University at Bloomington. Majoring in classics, he attained election to Phi Beta Kappa, Phi Kappa Psi, two degrees (B.A. 1893, M.A. 1895), and a teaching assignment (tutor, 1893-1895; instructor in Latin, 1895-1896). During two summers (1892-1893), he participated in a biological survey of Indiana, exploring the Eel and Maumee river basins, cataloguing the fish of each.

Early in the autumn of 1894 Beeson met a newly appointed instructor in Latin and Greek, Mabel Banta, who had recently studied at Cornell University and the University of Chicago under William Gardner Hale. Responding to her appreciation of Hale's challenging theories on syntax and innovations in the teaching of Latin, Beeson matriculated in the graduate school at Chicago in 1896.

His first contact with Hale was initiation into problems of text, through a new critical study of Catullus prompted by Hale's recent discovery of MS R (Ottobonianus 1829). The second was participation in a teachers' training course, which led to his appointment as head instructor of Latin and Greek in Peoria (Ill.) high school (1897-1901), and to collaboration with both Hale and F. J. Miller in preparation of the Hale-Buck *Latin Grammar* (1903) and the Miller-Beeson *Second Latin Book* (1900, rev. Beeson-Scott, 1902)—and similar cooperation on other school texts, ending with the Sanford-Scott-Beeson *Third Latin Book* (1923).

On Nov. 23, 1897, Beeson and Mabel Banta were married. She henceforth resigned the classroom but not the role of colleague in her husband's career. She compiled the vocabulary for the Miller-Beeson reader, proofread copy, transcribed or collated Latin manuscripts in European libraries, and, for twenty years, taught by correspondence in the Extension Division of the University of Chicago.

Beeson resumed work at Chicago as fellow in Latin (1901-1903) and later took his degree, Ph.D. summa cum laude, at the Royal Ludwig-Maximilians Universität in Munich (1907). He was drawn to Munich by the great medievalist and paleographer Ludwig Traube, to acquire from him new directions in the Latin literature, philology, and scripts of the Middle Ages. Then began his exploration into the influence of classical upon medieval authors, into lexicography and grammar, and his development of the technique that discovers in the transmission of texts traces of an Anglo-Saxon or Irish intermediary. Between pupil and master arose a mutual affection and respect that Traube acknowledged by inviting the Beesons to live in his home and accepting Mabel Beeson's assistance in cataloguing his library.

Beeson returned to the University of Chicago as instructor, then became assistant professor (1909), associate professor (1911), and professor of Latin (1918). In 1930-1931 he served as annual professor in the School of Classical Studies at the American Academy in Rome. He edited *Classical Philology* from October 1934 through 1938, although he retired from teaching in 1935. He received an LL.D. from Indiana University in 1939.

His skill in detecting sources of textual error brought Beeson into the staff assembled by his colleague John M. Manly in Washington, D.C., for service in codes and ciphers during World War I. He was commissioned a captain, Military Intelligence Division, General Staff, U.S. Army, July 1918. In February 1919, he was detailed by the War Department as assistant to the military attaché in Paris.

Beeson taught with enthusiasm and an informal manner that belied his impatience with carelessness and his resentment of repeated error. He directed numerous M.A. theses and doctoral dissertations concerning the lexicography and syntax of post-classical authors, paleographical treatises, and critical studies of medieval grammars. The latter he proposed to incorporate into a series, together with the text discussed in his "Ars Grammatica of Julian of Toledo" (1924).

While his prime interest came to be the Insular element in medieval culture, he also treated such diverse subjects as "The Vocabulary of the Annales Fuldenses" (1926), "The Oldest Manuscript of Paulus Diaconus" (1929),

"The Authorship of 'Quid sit ceroma'" (1938), "The Text History of the Corpus Caesarianum" (1940), "The Collectaneum of Hadoard" (1945), "The Palimpsests of Bobbio" (1946), "The Manuscripts of Bede" (1947). His achievements may be epitomized in four books. *Hegemonius: Acta Archelai* is the definitive edition of a Greek patristic text which, surviving entire in a Latin version only, is the main source of almost all Western accounts of Manichaeism. In the Prussian Academy's series of Greek Christian writers (vol. 16, 1906), it is the first American contribution. *Isidor-Studien* (1913) catalogues the extant manuscripts and reveals the dissemination, outside Spain, of works attributed to Isidore of Seville. *A Primer of Mediaeval Latin* (1925) is an anthology compiled to promote acquaintance with and some appreciation of the contribution of the Middle Ages to Western culture. The introduction offers the most succinct summary available of the differences between classical and medieval Latin. *Lupus of Ferrières as Scribe and Text Critic* (1930) is a detailed demonstration of a ninth-century monk's interest in classical Latin literature and occupation with the transmission and survival of Letters, comparable to Beeson's own.

Beeson was fellow, president of the fellows (1929-1932), and president (1936-1939) of the Mediaeval Academy of America, fellow of the American Academy of Arts and Sciences, and member of the American Philosophical Society. He acted as delegate of the Mediaeval Academy to the American Council of Learned Societies and four times as the council's delegate to the Union Académique Internationale at Brussels. He was chairman of the American committee on the revision of DuCange sponsored by the Union throughout that enterprise. For recreation he liked to camp, fish, or tramp with camera in hand, in the Rockies, Minnesota woods, British Columbia, and Alpine country; in residence he chose billiards, cards, detective fiction, and music.

He died in Chicago of a cerebral hemorrhage, two months after his wife's death. Services for each, in turn, were followed by cremation in Oakwoods Cemetery.

[Personal acquaintance and papers in Beeson's files; Jasper L. Beeson, *Beeson Genealogy* (1925); Weston A. Goodspeed and Charles Blanchard, eds., *Counties of Whitley and Noble, Ind.* (1882); *Annual Register of the Univ. of Chicago* 1891-1925; *Who Was Who in America*, II (1950). A photograph of Beeson hangs in a corridor of Hiram Kelly Memorial (Classics Building), Univ. of Chicago; Indiana Univ. possesses another. Newspaper notices with photographs appear in the *Chicago Times*, Dec. 30, 1937, and in the

Indianapolis News, June 5, 1939. Contributions to honorary volumes, in addition to four articles mentioned above (dated 1924, 1929, 1938 and 1946), include "Roger Bacon and the 'Dialogues of Seneca,'" *The Manly Anniversary Studies in Language and Literature* (1923); "Paris 7530 A Study of Insular Symptoms," *Raccolta di Scritti in onore di Felice Ramorino* (Milan, 1927); "Insular Influence in the Quaestiones and Locutiones of Augustine," *Mélanges Mandonnet II* (Paris, 1930); "Insular Symptoms in the Commentaries on Vergil," *Studi Medievali V, Nuova Serie* (Turin, 1932).]

BLANCHE B. BOYER

BELLANCA, DOROTHY JACOBS (Aug. 10, 1894-Aug. 16, 1946), labor leader and social reformer, was born in Zemel, Latvia (then a part of the Russian Empire), the youngest of four daughters of Harry and Bernice Edith (Levinson) Jacobs. Her father, a Russian Jew, immigrated with his family to the United States in 1900 and worked as a tailor in Baltimore. Dorothy attended Baltimore public schools but left at the age of thirteen to work as a hand buttonhole maker in the Baltimore men's clothing industry. Thereafter her formal education was limited to occasional attendance in evening schools.

From the start of her working life, Dorothy Jacobs sought to organize fellow workers into a trade union, and in 1912 she led a walkout by Baltimore hand buttonhole makers that soon developed into an industry-wide strike. Two years later she assumed a more prominent role in the trade union movement as a result of a split in what was then the leading union in the men's clothing industry—the United Garment Workers of America—between the younger, more militant Jewish and Italian immigrant members and the union leadership, which consisted of an older generation of more conservative and acculturated workers. An idealistic reformer and typical of her generation of immigrant Jewish workers, she cast her lot with the union insurgents, who late in 1914 founded the Amalgamated Clothing Workers of America (A.C.W.A.) as an independent trade union dedicated to socialist principles and goals. A delegate to the A.C.W.A.'s founding convention, Dorothy Jacobs served its Baltimore affiliates first as an elected member of the city's joint board and then as secretary of the board in October 1915. Her union activity extended beyond the Baltimore area. Assigned to the organization of female workers, she participated in major organizing campaigns in Chicago in 1915 and in Philadelphia and New York City in 1917. She was also elected as the A.C.W.A.'s first female general executive board member in 1916, a position in which she urged a more equal role for women in the union. Reelected in 1918, she soon resigned after her marriage in August of that year to August Bellanca, a leader among the Italian immigrant workers in the men's clothing industry and himself a member of the general executive board.

Shortly after her marriage, which was childless, Dorothy Bellanca resumed an active union career, joining with her husband a special committee established in 1920 to organize shops which had fled the union geographically by moving their production facilities out of the major cities and into depressed areas with surplus labor, especially in the Pennsylvania anthracite country. During the early 1920's she also served as an organizer in New York City, Utica, N.Y., Philadelphia, and Baltimore. And when in 1924 the A.C.W.A. established a Women's Bureau, Bellanca headed it until its dissolution in 1926. The bureau's failure to survive more than two years caused her to oppose its reestablishment in 1928. Indeed, as the only woman in the union hierarchy, she found it difficult to explain women's demands to her male colleagues. As she wrote to another woman unionist in 1925: ". . . women came into the trade and into the organization on grounds that were already established and fought out. One cannot expect equal consideration from men members . . . where such conditions exist without being patient and waiting for proper opportunities" (to Bessie Malac, Sept. 2, 1925, A.C.W.A. files). Not an uncritical advocate of women's rights, Bellanca believed that the cause of the union must supersede that of particular members, that the larger issues (class and economic) must transcend the smaller ones (sexual and social).

During the union resurgence triggered by the New Deal in 1933-1934, Bellanca acted as an exceptional organizer of women and children shirt workers in the more rural regions of Pennsylvania, New Jersey, New York, and Connecticut. She also participated in the massive 1934 general strike in the textile industry and later (1937-1938) as a special organizer for the C.I.O.'s Textile Workers' Organizing Committee among Southern workers. She was again elected to the general executive board of the A.C.W.A. in 1934 and continued thereafter to serve as the union's sole female vice-president until her death.

Like most needle-trades unionists of her generation, Bellanca did not restrict her reform efforts to the labor movement. She participated in local, state, and national politics, joining in the creation of the American Labor party in 1936 and serving on its state executive committee. In 1938 she ran unsuccessfully for Congress from a Brooklyn district with the endorsement of the American Labor and Republican parties. Her political contributions and her trade-union standing brought her numerous appointments to public committees and agencies. In a single year, 1941, she was a member of the Labor Advisory Committee of the federal Department of Labor, labor advisor to the International Labor Organization conference, and a member of the New York State Council on Discrimination in Employment. She was appointed to the New York State War Council Committee on Discrimination in Employment in 1943, but resigned the following year—together with seven other members—in protest against Gov. Thomas E. Dewey's refusal to support antidiscrimination legislation.

At the peak of her union career Dorothy Bellanca was struck by multiple myeloma, a disease of the bone marrow. Once a slender, strikingly attractive woman with sparkling black eyes, she had become at the time of her final illness a shell of a person racked by constant pain. After a confinement of several months, she died at Memorial Hospital in New York City in 1946, at the age of fifty-two. Her body was cremated at Ferncliff Cemetery in Ardsley, N.Y. As the *Nation* remarked at the time of her death, Mrs. Bellanca "was possessed by an unflagging and passionate concern for the sufferings of others. Without question she was the ablest woman organizer in the American labor movement."

[The best source of information on the life and career of Dorothy Bellanca is the files of the Amalgamated Clothing Workers of America's Research Dept. in N.Y.C. These include her correspondence, copies of her writings in union publications, and full biographical data. The biennial reports of the A.C.W.A.'s convention proceedings and of its Gen. Executive Board, 1914–1946, published initially under the title *Documentary Hist.*, as well as the A.C.W.A. journal, *Advance*, for the same years, contain scores of articles and speeches by Bellanca. See also Herbert G. Gutman in *Notable Am. Women*, I; 124–126; *N.Y. Times* obituary, Aug. 17, 1946; and editorial appreciation in the *Nation*, Aug. 31, 1946. Matthew Josephson, *Sidney Hillman* (1852), is the best history of the A.C.W.A. and the people who led it. Joel I. Seidman, *The Needle Trades* (1942), is a useful general survey of the union movement in the clothing trades.]
MELVYN DUBOFSKY

BENEDICT, RUTH FULTON (June 5, 1887–Sept. 17, 1948), anthropologist, was born in New York City, the older of two daughters of Bertrice Joanna (Shattuck) and Frederick Samuel Fulton, both of "old American" farming stock. Her father, a surgeon who did cancer research, died in 1889, and the early years of

her "rigorously frugal" childhood were spent on the farm of her maternal grandparents in the Chenango Valley near Norwich, N.Y. After 1892 she lived (largely in the care of a maternal aunt) in Norwich, St. Joseph, Mo., and Owatonna, Minn., where her mother, an early Vassar graduate, held a series of teaching jobs before settling in Buffalo, N.Y., as a librarian in 1899. By her own later account, the most important event of her childhood (her "primal scene") was the death of her father, and her mother's hysterical grief, ritually repeated upon each anniversary. From early childhood she "recognized two worlds"—"the world of my father, which was the world of death and which was beautiful, and the world of confusion and explosive weeping which I repudiated." Reared on the King James version in a staunchly Baptist family, she created "her world" largely from the Bible, peopling it with Blakean figures "of a strange dignity and grace," among whom her father was identified with Christ. The world outside was a difficult one; partially deaf from infancy, Benedict suffered regularly recurring "bilious attacks," and was "deviled" by tantrums and depressions. No one—not even the grandfather whom she loved above all others—really got past her "physical and emotional aloofness."

In 1905 Benedict matriculated at Vassar, where as a freshman she abandoned formal religious belief for Walter Pater's humanistic vision of culture, and as a senior she lamented the loss of "the sense of reverence and awe" in the realistic "Modern Age." After graduation (1909), a year in Europe with two friends, and another doing charity work in Buffalo, she moved in 1911 to California, where she taught for three years in girls' schools in Los Angeles and Pasadena. Neither social work nor teaching, however, offered a way to cope with "the very terrible thing" of being a woman. On June 18, 1914, having decided "a woman has one supreme power—to love," she married Stanley Rossiter Benedict, a brilliant biochemist, and began the life of a housewife in the suburbs of New York City.

At first she dabbled with literary projects— poetry, "chemical detective stories" that she hoped to publish under the pseudonym "Stanhope," and a manuscript on "New Women of Three Centuries," for which she completed only the section on Mary Wollstonecraft. Denied by fate the "man-child" who might "call a truce to the promptings" of self-fulfillment and unwilling to "twist" herself into "a doubtfully useful footstool," she soon found that marriage in its turn "did not hold me." "Stanhope" died, to be reborn later as "Anne Singleton."

Searching for expedients "to get through the days," Benedict turned again to social work, to modern dance, and finally, almost by chance, to anthropology. In 1919 she began attending lectures at the New School for Social Research, whose faculty included two anthropologists— the wealthy feminist Elsie Clews Parsons, and the erratically brilliant Alexander Goldenweiser. To one whose psyche was built on an opposition between emotional worlds, and whose life experience had undercut the value-absolutes buttressing the central institution of her culture, the implicit relativism of the anthropological approach offered a principle of order, and in 1921 Benedict went uptown to Columbia to study for a doctorate under Franz Boas. Quickly sensing the vigorously imaginative mind veiled by her "painfully shy" demeanor, Boas waived credit requirements to hurry her through to the Ph.D. she received in 1923. She in turn felt grandfatherly resonances behind his rigorous and somewhat authoritarian reserve, and became for her younger fellow students the medium by which he was transformed from Dr. Boas into "Papa Franz."

Benedict's doctoral dissertation was a library study of American Indian religion. Rejecting all generalized origin theories, she undertook a Boasian analysis of the "observed behavior" of a single "well-recognized cultural trait"—the guardian spirit concept—over a "fairly wide area." She found that its associations with other cultural elements were a series of "essentially fortuitous" and "fluid recombinations" defying any single causal explanation. At the same time, it is worth noting that, for Benedict, the "religious thrill" of the vision-experience itself was more important than its specific theological reformulation in the guardian spirit idea. Furthermore, in any given culture, the vision-complex was "formalized" into definite "patterns" under the influence of dominant values and activities (*The Concept of the Guardian Spirit in North America,* American Anthropological Association, *Memoir* No. 29, 1923).

From 1923 to 1931 Benedict held a series of one-year appointments as lecturer in anthropology at Columbia. During this period she did anthropological fieldwork among the remnants of the Serrano in California (1922), and then among several southwestern tribes: the Zuñi (1924-1925), the Cochiti (1925), and the Pima (1927). Hampered by deafness, Benedict did not find fieldwork easy, though working through interpreters she collected hundreds of pages of myths and tales (*Tales of the Cochiti Indians,* 1931; *Zuñi Mythology,* 2 vols., 1935). Nevertheless, her field experience, especially at Zuñi, was to have a considerable impact on her subsequent anthropology. Still relatively whole and functioning, sharply differentiated in psychological tone from its neighbors in the same environment, Zuñi culture seems to have had a great attraction for Benedict—as indeed Pueblo culture in general had for a number of alienated intellectuals.

During these same years, Benedict found for the first time friends with whom to share an intellectual communion and a certain emotional intimacy. The most important was the brilliant linguistic anthropologist Edward Sapir, also an aspiring poet, with whom for some years she regularly exchanged poems. Sapir found her poetry "finely within the [Puritan] tradition . . . but with a notable access of modernity," though he was upset by the "toying" with "dissociation" implicit in her publishing her poems under the pseudonym "Anne Singleton." At the same time, Sapir, who was interested in the implications of the newer psychological viewpoints (Freud, Jung, and Kurt Koffka) for anthropology, pushed Benedict toward a psychological analysis of the integration of whole cultures. Her eventual approach was developed in close interaction with another poet-confidante, Margaret Mead, who had been her first student when she was Boas' assistant at Barnard in 1922. The specific stimulus was the sharp contrast Benedict felt between the Pima and the Zuñi, which she elaborated during the winter of 1927 in terms of two Nietzschean "psychological types," the Dionysian and the Apollonian. Zuñi culture was the product of a "fundamental psychological set" which, "institutionalized" over centuries, had bent borrowed elements "to its own uses," and "created an intricate cultural pattern" to express "the Apollonian delight in formality" ("Psychological Types in the Cultures of the Southwest," 23rd International Congress of Americanists, *Proceedings,* 1928).

Elaborated over the next several years, Benedict's "configurational" viewpoint was presented at length in *Patterns of Culture* (1934). Posing the Apollonian Zuñi against the "paranoid" Dobu and the "megalomaniac" Kwakiutl, Benedict saw cultures as "personality writ large," and argued that each one selected and elaborated a "certain segment of the great arc of potential human purposes and motivations." Psychological normality was thus culturally defined, and "the misfit is the person whose disposition is not capitalized by his culture." Benedict ended her classic statement of "cultural relativity" with a plea for tolerance of all "the coexisting and equally valid patterns of life which mankind has created for itself." Nevertheless, her own preference for the Zuñi—so reminiscent of the Blakean figures of her own adolescent other world —was evident throughout, and the response her book evoked among American intellectuals cannot have been unrelated to her comparison of the dour, prudish Dobuans to American Puritans, or her suggestion that the potlatching Kwakiutl provided "a parody on our own economic arrangements." Not surprisingly, *Patterns of Culture* was later sharply criticized by anthropologists familiar with the psychological variation within the cultures Benedict described in somewhat archetypical terms.

In 1931, the year after Benedict finally separated from her husband, Boas got her a regular appointment as assistant professor at Columbia, and for the next few years she assumed much of the burden of his anthropological activity. She had already taken over the editorship of the *Journal of American Folklore* (1925-1940), as well as much of Boas' teaching, and henceforth she was in effect responsible for the conduct of the Columbia department—a position that was formalized after Boas' retirement (and her promotion to associate professor) in 1936, when she served for three years as departmental "executive officer." During these same years she followed Boas into the arena of public struggle against racism and intolerance, publishing a small volume, *Race: Science and Politics* (1940), as well as numerous articles in popular journals.

As World War II approached, Benedict found her position at Columbia increasingly frustrating under Boas' successor, Ralph Linton (whose appointment she had opposed), and she began to find a more satisfying outlet for her energies in anthropological activities connected with the war effort. In 1943 she went to Washington as head of the Basic Analysis Section, Bureau of Overseas Intelligence, Office of War Information. Along with Mead and other anthropologists, she pioneered in the application of anthropological methods to complex societies and the study of culture "at a distance," working through documentary materials and interviews with emigré informants in a series of "national character" studies. The last of these became *The Chrysanthemum and the Sword* (1946), a study of our "most alien enemy." Laying bare the complicated Japanese system of *on* (obligation), Benedict explicated

for Americans the apparent contradictions of the Japanese "ethic of alternatives." Once again, her work was criticized for neglecting subcultural variation, but it remains one of the best accounts of Japanese culture by a Westerner, and even Japanese found in it new understanding. Here at last the two halves of Benedict's own being finally merged in a book that, as Mead suggested, combined a sense of the strength and integrity of cultural pattern with the "special poignancy of the human spirit trapped always in ways which limit its full expression."

Benedict returned in 1946 to Columbia, where, with the aid of a large grant from the Office of Naval Research, she helped organize and became director of a project for Research in Contemporary Cultures. During the summer of 1948 she attended a UNESCO seminar in Czechoslovakia, partly in order to have firsthand experience of some of the cultures being studied. After her return to New York she suffered a sudden and fatal coronary thrombosis, "staying quietly alive" for five days until her long-time friend and companion, Ruth Valentine, returned to her deathbed from California. Shortly before her death she had finally been promoted to the full professorship long denied her because she was a woman. The previous year she had served as president of the American Anthropological Association. Among her various other offices and honors were the presidency of the American Ethnological Society (1927-1929), the vice-presidency of the American Psychopathological Association (1946), and the Achievement Award of the American Association of University Women (1946).

Benedict came to anthropology at a point when Boas had decided that "diffusion was done." Her own anthropological work was a creative elaboration of the holistic "other half" of the Boasian impulse, which, attacking racial determinism, sought a cultural explanation of the "geniuses" of peoples. Although her earlier psychological interpretation of culture focused on the total emotional patterning of particular cultures, and she was never very receptive to psychoanalytic approaches, her later writing showed a greater concern for the processes by which children in different cultural situations were molded into different personality types. Taken as a whole, her work provided a large part of the foundation of the modern culture and personality movement. Benedict often spoke of anthropology as a science, but her own work was an expression of its fundamental humanistic strain. An antinomian rebel within the Puritan tradition, she found in the anthropological concept of culture a fuller realization of Pater's humanistic ideal, and she was without doubt its most effective advocate. *Patterns of Culture,* frequently reprinted and translated into fourteen languages, remains today the single most influential work by a twentieth-century American anthropologist.

[The crucial source is Margaret Mead's *An Anthropologist at Work: Writings of Ruth Benedict* (1959), which includes biographical chapters by Mead and both published and unpublished writings by Benedict, as well as selections from correspondence in the Benedict Papers at Vassar College, the Boas Papers in the Am. Philosophical Soc., and letters in Mead's own possession. Mead's volume also contains photographs. For Benedict's bibliography, consult the obituary by Mead in the *Am. Anthropologist,* July–Sept. 1949, or the Viking Fund's *Ruth Fulton Benedict: A Memorial* (1949). For the professional reaction to her major works, see Victor Barnouw, *Culture and Personality* (1963); John W. Bennett and Michio Nagai, "The Japanese Critique of the Methodology of Benedict's 'Chrysanthemum and the Sword,'" *Am. Anthropologist,* Aug. 1953; and Alfred G. Smith, "The Dionysian Innovation," *ibid.,* Apr. 1964. For general anthropological context, see David F. Aberle, "The Influence of Linguistics on Early Culture and Personality Theory," in Gertrude E. Dole and Robert L. Carneiro, *Essays in the Science of Culture* (1960); and George Stocking, Jr., *Race, Culture, and Evolution* (1968).]

GEORGE W. STOCKING, JR.

BENÉT, WILLIAM ROSE (Feb. 2, 1886-May 4, 1950), poet, editor, and author, the oldest of three children, two sons and a daughter, was born at Fort Hamilton, N.Y., to James Walker Benét and Frances Neill (Rose) Benét. His great-grandfather, Esteban Benét, a master mariner in the Spanish merchant marine, emigrated from Minorca, Spain, to St. Augustine, Fla., in the 1780's. Benét's grandfather and father were officers of ordnance in the United States Army; James Walker Benét retired as a colonel in 1921.

As a boy, William was read to by his father, who inspired him with his love of poetry. Nevertheless, after graduating from the Albany (N.Y.) Academy in 1904, Benét went on to the Sheffield Scientific School at Yale University, from which he was graduated in 1907. He became editor of the *Yale Record* and the *Yale Courant* and pursued "the most earnest desire" of his life, writing poetry, from this time forward. He joined the *Century* magazine in 1911, rising to assistant editor before volunteering for army service during World War I; he served during 1918 as a second lieutenant in the aviation (nonflying) section of the U. S. Signal Corps.

After the war he was assistant editor of *The Nation's Business,* and in 1920 joined the New York *Evening Post Book Review,* which became the *Literary Review,* with Benét as one of its founders. It subsequently was named the *Saturday Review of Literature,* in 1924, published by Time, Inc. In 1926 the group associated with Benét bought Time's interest in the magazine. Benét remained an editor, reviewer, and columnist for the *Saturday Review* until his death, writing under several pseudonyms, among them Kenelm Digby, and originating the "Phoenix Nest" column of the magazine.

Benét's first book of poetry, *Merchants From Cathay* (1913), with its oriental exotica and lush imagery, placed him among the romantic poets of the day. In three more books during the next six years he turned to the American scene and its vernaculars, rendering the atmosphere of the barroom, the quick-lunch counter, and the waterfront. During the 1920's his lifelong absorption in historical subjects (he was a collector of old books) led him to narrative poetry, notably "Jesse James: American Myth." His ballads showed the influence of Stephen Vincent Benét, his younger brother by twelve years, whose work he promoted and admired and whose success he welcomed— although with wry humor over his own eventual reputation as the older brother of a famous poet. Benét's novel, *The First Person Singular* (1922), combined mystery, romance, and a Sherwood Anderson-like critique of small-town America.

In the 1930's Benét developed a mystical and philosophical strain. John Crowe Ransom singled out for praise his "romantic poems . . . of birds, giraffes, horses, dolphins, and dirigibles" and called "Whale" "a distinguished little addition to our poetry" (*Saturday Review,* July 27, 1935, p. 6). During World War II, Benét published two books of patriotic verse. In all of his books, love poetry was prominent. *Perpetual Light* (1919) was a memorial to his first wife, who also figured importantly in earlier books, as did other women in later ones. Benét's admirers were the first to admit his "extravagance." "He drenched, and sometimes drowned, the meaning in the music," wrote Louis Untermeyer, who concluded, "His poetry was the man: generous, sometimes too lavish, overflowing with forthrightness and brotherly good will" (*Saturday Review,* May 20, 1950, pp. 13-14).

The gentle graciousness and trustfulness that endeared Benét to his friends were evident in his writing. In "Man Possessed," a poem on the death of his first wife, he wrote: "I hardly know what I believe or what I mean/ Save there is a sweetness round my heart and the world a screen/ Of interwoven mystery to a world unseen." In his collection of light essays, *Wild Goslings* (1927), he declared himself in favor of "emotionalism and sentimentality." *The Dust Which Is God,* an autobiography in verse, won the Pulitzer Prize for 1941; in it Benét frankly detailed his temporary refuge in drinking (and consequent heart attack) over the loss of his second wife, the novelist and poet Elinor Wylie, and his divorce from his third wife, Lora Baxter, an actress. He set these private events against a Dos Passos-like chronicle of the darkening 1930's. Yet, in this work, too, he arrived at hope for "Man's soul."

Benét's strongest feelings were balanced by humor, often expressed in cartoons and light verse. Although aroused by injustice and attracted to causes, he never became a joiner or lost faith in his country. Benét was tall and lean through his twenties, but in later years he grew heavier and his face appeared to radiate an "instinctive happiness" (Louis Untermeyer in Kunitz, 118).

Benét married Teresa Frances Thompson, a sister of Kathleen Norris, the novelist, on Sept. 3, 1912; she died in 1919. Their children were James Walker, Frances Rosemary, and Kathleen Anne. Benét was married three more times: to Elinor Wylie (Oct. 5, 1923), who died in 1928; to Lora Baxter (Mar. 15, 1932), from whom he was divorced in 1937; and to Marjorie Flack (June 21, 1941), who was an author and illustrator of children's books and with whom he often collaborated.

Benét received an honorary M.A. degree from Yale University (1921), a Litt.D. from Dickinson College (1933), and a National Playwrighting Award for *Day's End: A Fantasia in One Act* after it was produced by the Dock Street Theatre in Charleston, S.C., in 1939.

Benét died of a heart attack in New York City while on his way to a meeting at the National Institute of Arts and Letters, of which he was secretary. He is buried in Pigeon Cove, Mass.

[Other books of poetry by Benét include *The Falconer of God and Other Poems* (1914), *The Burglar of the Zodiac and Other Poems* (1918), *Rip Tide, A Novel in Verse* (1932), *Starry Harness* (1933), *Golden Fleece* (1935), *Day of Deliverance, A Book of Poems in Wartime* (1944), *The Stairway of Surprise* (1947), and *The Spirit of the Scene* (1951). His manuscripts are at the Yale Univ. Lib. Benét edited numerous anthologies and guides to reading, among them *The Oxford Anthology of Am. Lit.* with Norman Holmes Pearson (1938), *The Poetry of Freedom,* with Norman Cousins (1945), and *The Reader's Ency.* (1948). A photograph accompanies the *N. Y. Times* obituary, May 5, 1950.]

PETER SHAW

BERRY, GEORGE LEONARD (Sept. 12, 1882-Dec. 4, 1948), labor leader, briefly senator from Tennessee, was born in Lee Valley, Hawkins County, Tenn., one of at least two children of Thomas Jefferson Berry and Cornelia (Trent) Berry. In Berry's evidently romanticized version of his background, his father was a Civil War captain, state legislator, and county official, and was killed in 1884 while serving as a deputy United States marshal. State legislative and Civil War records do not list his name. When George's mother was unable to keep the family together, the boy was placed in an orphanage and then in a foster home in Mississippi. By his own account, he ran away at the age of nine to Jackson, Miss., where he worked for five years at the *Evening News* learning the printing trade. He had only brief stints at school. After serving as a private in the Spanish-American War, Berry found employment in the pressroom of the *St. Louis Globe-Democrat.* He then moved to San Francisco, where, besides working as a printer, he did exhibition boxing to supplement his income, and later prospected for gold in Nevada. By 1907 he had become superintendent of a large commercial printing plant in San Francisco. On August 7 of that year he married Marie Margaret Gehres; they had no children.

Berry had joined the fledgling International Printing Pressmen and Assistants' Union in 1899. He became secretary and business agent of its San Francisco branch and served as president of the city's Central Labor Council. In 1907, because of a deadlock between contending factions, the twenty-four-year-old Berry was elected president of the Pressmen's Union, a position he was to hold until his death. By 1910 he had moved the union's national headquarters from Cincinnati, Ohio, to a permanent site near Rogersville, Tenn. There Berry established the Pressmen's Home, a retirement residence for union members, together with a tuberculosis sanatorium and a trade school to improve the members' technical skills. He also reformed the union's election and convention procedures; inaugurated an old-age pension fund; founded, with other crafts, the International Allied Printing Trades Association, with a union label; and extended the union's jurisdiction over lithographic offset printing. During World War I, Berry served with the Engineer Corps in France and attained the rank of major, a title by which he was commonly known thereafter. After the Armistice he was named a labor adviser to the Paris Peace Commission.

A tough, blunt man, Berry nevertheless believed in conciliation and labor peace. His thought closely followed the "business unionism" of Samuel Gompers. Viewing labor's prosperity as dependent on that of business, Berry insisted upon arbitration and abhorred strikes. He secured nationwide arbitration agreements with newspaper publishers and employing printers. Twice he broke wildcat strikes of his own locals to enforce the sanctity of contract, and he frequently attacked radicalism, defending what he called the "American way" of "profit and exchange."

At Rogersville, Berry built up extensive holdings of farmland and other property, both for his union and himself. Indeed, he seems to have viewed the two interests as interchangeable. During World War I, he transferred $165,000 from the union's pension fund to build a privately owned electric plant to provide cheaper power to the Pressmen's Home. A federal court in 1921 ordered him to return the money, but Berry, then as at other times, had the loyal support of union members, and the case was subsequently dismissed. In 1927, with authorization from the union's convention, Berry organized the International Playing Card and Label Company at Rogersville to compete with nonunion firms in the field. A successful venture which employed several hundred workers, it was financed by union loans of nearly $900,000, on the understanding that Berry would leave his interest in the company to the union at his death.

Berry, a lifelong Democrat, took some part in Tennessee politics. He unsuccessfully sought the nomination for governor in 1914 and United States senator in 1916. In 1924, perhaps as a reflection of the recent upsurge in labor political activity, he came within three votes of receiving the Democratic vice-presidential nomination. In 1928 he campaigned vigorously for Alfred E. Smith. During the New Deal, Berry served as a labor representative on two boards of the National Recovery Administration and as a divisional administrator. In 1936 he joined Sidney Hillman and John L. Lewis in organizing Labor's Non-Partisan League, a political action group dedicated to the reelection of President Franklin Roosevelt, and served as its first president.

Berry's prominence in the 1936 campaign led to mention of him as a possible cabinet appointee. The following year he was appointed by the governor of Tennessee to an unexpired term in the United States Senate, but he was defeated for renomination in the Democratic primary of 1938. By this time Berry had begun to withdraw support from the New Deal, and even came to refer to it as "state socialism." He supported Wendell Willkie in the 1940 presidential race, and during the 1940's he became a spokesman for the most conservative faction of the A.F. of L.

Stocky and balding, with shell-rimmed glasses, always impeccably groomed, Berry was a dignified and persuasive figure. He was a Southern Baptist in religion and a member of many fraternal orders. He died of a gastric hemorrhage at the Pressmen's Home in Rogersville in 1948 and was buried in the cemetery there. His will left extensive real estate and a half-ownership of a local newspaper to the Pressmen's Union, but not his interest in the playing card company. The bequests proved of little practical value, since Berry had been convicted shortly before his death of income tax evasion, and the fine took all of his estate and more.

Appraisals of Berry have differed. Some saw him as a symbol of autocratic and corrupt union leadership. A congressional investigation after his death concluded that he had indeed "misused" union funds and had employed "economic compulsion" against protesting locals, but hesitated to question either his motives or the success of his union in promoting its members' interests (Baker, pp. 399, 494 n., 496).

[The best source of biographical information on Berry is the *Rogersville Rev.*, a newspaper he owned, especially the issues of Sept. 26 and Oct. 3, 1935, and Dec. 9, 1848. For an extensive account of his union activities, see Elizabeth Faulkner Baker, *Printers and Technology: A Hist. of the Internat. Printing Pressmen and Assistants' Union* (1957); see also references in Irving Bernstein, *The Lean Years* (1960) and *Turbulent Years* (1970). Contemporary articles on Berry include George Creel in *Collier's*, Aug. 28, 1937; and *Newsweek*, June 6, 1949, pp. 63–64. See also *Current Biog.*, 1948; *Nat. Cyc. Am. Biog.*, XXXVI, 477–478; *Who's Who in Labor*, 1946; *Who Was Who in America*, II (1950). For the charges against Berry, see U.S. House of Representatives, 81 Cong., 1 and 2 Sess., *Hearings on Union Democracy before a Special Subcommittee of the Committee on Education and Labor* (1950). Death record from Tenn. Dept. of Public Health.]

JAMES A. HODGES

BERRYMAN, CLIFFORD KENNEDY (Apr. 2, 1869-Dec. 11, 1949), editorial cartoonist, was born near Versailles, Woodford County, Ky., the sixth of seven sons of James Thomas Berryman, a commission merchant, and his second wife, Sallie Church; there were also two sons and two daughters by the first marriage. Both parents were descended from English and Scottish families that had settled in Virginia before 1726. Even as a youth Berryman loved to draw, a skill he taught himself. A sketch he made of Joseph C. S. Blackburn so pleased the Kentucky congressman that when Berryman graduated in 1886 from Professor Henry's School for Boys in Versailles, Blackburn secured him a job as draftsman in the United States Patent Office in Washington.

While working in the Patent Office, Berryman in 1889 began contributing sketches to the *Washington Post,* which soon made him a regular illustrator. Visual content in newspapers was then increasing, spurred by intense journalistic competition and the availability of a rapid means of reproduction. Berryman at first drew news sketches and advertising art; he became the *Post*'s editorial cartoonist in 1896.

In 1902 the young artist learned of President Theodore Roosevelt's bear-hunting expedition in Mississippi. The party had no luck, but one attendant dragged a bear cub into camp on the end of a rope. Roosevelt commented, "If I shot that little fellow, I couldn't look my boys in the face again." Seizing on the incident, Berryman sketched a cartoon, "Drawing the Line in Mississippi" (Nov. 16, 1902), showing T.R. refusing to shoot the cub. The woeful little bear was an immediate success and brought thousands of requests for reprints. A New York toy manufacturer put out a stuffed "Teddy bear," and the idea caught on, creating what was to become a standard item for generations of children to come—though the artist was always quick to point out that he got none of the profits.

The Teddy bear, which Berryman repeated in later drawings of Roosevelt, made him one of the nation's best-known political and editorial cartoonists. His work was frequently reprinted in such publications as *Life,* the *Review of Reviews,* and *World's Work.* In 1907 he left the *Washington Post* to become editorial cartoonist for the Washington *Evening Star,* and he remained with that newspaper until his death.

Berryman drew his figures in a more realistic style than most cartoonists of the day. He was not influenced by the grease-pencil school created by liberal and radical artists. Neither in concept nor in execution did Berryman's work have the bite of such great political cartoonists as Thomas Nast or Rollin Kirby. He was more in the folksy tradition of his con-

temporaries J. N. "Ding" Darling and John T. McCutcheon. One of his best-known cartoon series was "Squash Center," in which a group of old-time countrymen gathered around a stove in a village grocery store.

Six feet tall and broad-shouldered, white-haired and pink-cheeked in later years, courtly in manner, Berryman had a gentle, whimsical nature that found expression in his work. Only rarely were his opinions sharp, as in a 1938 cartoon which portrayed the American farmer goosestepping in front of Secretary of Agriculture Henry A. Wallace, depicted as the "Fuehrer." He was, however, often critical of President Franklin D. Roosevelt and later of Harry S. Truman, who nonetheless admired him. A cartoon of 1943, "But Where Is the Boat Going?" showing Roosevelt in a rowboat, the "U.S.S. Manpower Mobilization," with government officials and labor leaders all pulling in different directions, won a Pulitzer Prize.

Cartoonists have not generally been well integrated into the journalistic community, but Berryman was elected to Washington's prestigious Gridiron Club and was its president in 1926. He was honored as the city's "outstanding citizen" by the Cosmopolitan Club in 1949. He was also a frequent and popular giver of "chalk talks"—lectures illustrated by blackboard sketches.

Berryman was married on July 5, 1893, in Washington, to Kate Geddes Durfee, the daughter of an engraver. They had three children: Mary Belle, who died in infancy; Florence Seville, later an art critic for the Washington *Evening Star;* and James Thomas, who succeeded his father as cartoonist on the *Star.* Indeed, Jim Berryman, originally a sports cartoonist, had begun sharing the editorial cartooning as early as 1935, though the similarity of their styles made the change little noticed. Clifford Berryman died of a heart ailment in Washington at the age of eighty and was buried in Glenwood Cemetery, Washington.

[The largest collection of Berryman originals, nearly 2,000 drawings, is in the Lib. of Cong.; see description and biographical account in the library's *Quart. Jour. of Current Acquisitions,* Feb. 1946. Collections of Berryman's work in book form are *Berryman Cartoons* (1900) and *Berryman's Cartoons of the 58th House* (1903), in which he sketched every member of the current House of Representatives. He also published a short monograph, *Development of the Cartoon* (Univ. of Mo. *Bull.,* Journalism Series, 1926). For comments on his work see: Richard Spencer, *Pulitzer Prize Cartoons,* 2nd ed. (1953); and Stephen Hess and Milton Kaplan, *The Ungentlemanly Art* (1968). See also feature story in the Washington *Sunday Star,* Apr. 2, 1939; the lengthy obituary in the *Evening Star,* Dec. 12, 1949. Other obituaries and articles appear in *N.Y. Times,* May 2, 1944, Dec. 12,

1949; *Washington Post*, Dec. 12, 1949; *Newsweek*, Nov. 29, 1948, p. 56; *Time*, Aug. 21, 1944, pp. 56–57; *Who Was Who in America*, II (1950); and, on the origins of the toy, Peter Bull, *The Teddy Bear Book* (1970).]

EVERETTE E. DENNIS

BIGELOW, HARRY AUGUSTUS (Sept. 22, 1874–Jan. 8, 1950), law educator, was born in Norwood, Mass., one of three children and the only son of Erwin Augustus Bigelow, a merchant, and Amie Leighton (Fisher) Bigelow, natives respectively of Boxboro and Salem, Mass. The family, though not wealthy, was comfortably situated. Bigelow attended the Norwood high school, Harvard College (A.B. 1896), and the Harvard Law School, where he was an editor of the *Law Review* and received the LL.B. degree in 1899. He worked for some months as a law clerk in a conveyancing office in Boston and as a part-time instructor in criminal law at the Harvard Law School. In 1900 he moved to Honolulu, Hawaii, where he began a legal practice.

In 1904 he gave up his practice in Hawaii and settled at the University of Chicago. There he helped President William Rainey Harper and Joseph Henry Beale, who was on leave from Harvard, in establishing a law school at the university. Bigelow was appointed to the faculty, was admitted to the bar in Illinois in 1908, and became professor of law in 1909 and dean of the law school in 1929.

His highly analytical mind and his gift for presenting material with freshness and clarity soon earned him a reputation as a brilliant teacher. His students learned to regard him with affection, in spite of the scathing intellectual reprimands he often administered to those guilty of confused or careless preparation. Bigelow became an authority on the law of real estate and personal property, and his reputation as a legal scholar was strengthened by his publication of a third edition of *May on Criminal Law* (1905) and of casebooks on *The Law of Personal Property* (1917, 1930, 1942), *The Law of Rights in Land* (1919, 1933, 1945), and *The Law of Property* (1942, with Ralph W. Aigler and Richard R. B. Powell). The casebooks became standard material in the classroom, extending Bigelow's influence on students in many law schools.

Bigelow himself was masterly in his use of the case method of instruction; he soon recognized, nevertheless, that in some aspects of the law it was so cumbersome and time-consuming as to be ineffective. Also he came to realize that studies of legal questions, based only on the materials in the law reports, were often sterile and that textbooks would be a valid aid to the student. Although this view was unorthodox at the time, he wrote an *Introduction to the Law of Real Property* (1919, 1934, 1945), a brief historical survey that proved to be an invaluable tool for the student of modern land law. Bigelow also believed that an effective understanding of law required a knowledge of subjects which traditionally had been excluded from law school curricula. Under his tenure as dean, he effected a revision of the curriculum at the University of Chicago Law School so that it included accounting, economics, and psychology. He also encouraged the development of a tutorial program which greatly enriched the training that the school afforded its students.

After the organization of the American Law Institute in 1923, Bigelow played a key role in the preparation of its *Restatement of the Conflict of Laws* (1934) and *Restatement of the Law of Property* (1936). In 1933 he was appointed trustee in bankruptcy of Insull Utility Investments, Inc. In the liquidation of the ill-fated enterprise of Samuel Insull, Bigelow's shrewd comprehension of the issues involved commanded the respect of both businessmen and lawyers. Although Bigelow retired as dean of the University of Chicago Law School in 1939, he did not give up his classes in conflict of laws and in property. In 1947 President Harry S. Truman appointed him a member of the National Loyalty Review Board, and he devoted the last years of his life to the work of that agency.

On Apr. 12, 1902, in Honolulu, Bigelow married Mary Parker of Georgetown, Colo. They had no children, and she died in 1920. Bigelow was a Universalist. He had a lively interest in the arts and in travel. His collection of Japanese prints was an excellent one. In 1924-1925, with his Chicago friends Herbert and Mary Hastings Bradley, he took part in the first expedition to cross the unexplored country west of Lake Edward in the Belgian Congo.

Bigelow died in a Chicago hospital on January 8, 1950, of pulmonary edema, while hospitalized for cirrhosis of the liver. In his memory, the University of Chicago established a Harry A. Bigelow Professorship and Bigelow Tutorial Fellowships.

[Data in the archives of the Univ. of Chicago; *Class Reports* of Harvard College Class of 1896; obituaries in *Chicago Bar Record*, Sept. 1950, and Assoc. of Am. Law Schools, *Proc.* (1950); death record from Ill. Dept. of Public Health; author's personal acquaintance.]

SHELDON TEFFT

BILBO, THEODORE GILMORE (Oct. 13, 1877-Aug. 21, 1947), governor of Mississippi, United States senator, was born on a farm at Juniper Grove, Poplarville, Pearl River County, Miss., the youngest of the nine children of James Oliver and Beedy (Wallace) Bilbo. His father, a Confederate veteran, was a moderately well-to-do farmer. Young Bilbo graduated from the Poplarville high school in 1896 and for three years (1897-1900) attended Peabody Normal College in Nashville, Tenn. For the next several years he taught Latin and mathematics in schools in south Mississippi. He also studied law at Vanderbilt University (1905-1907) and the University of Michigan (summer, 1908), after which he began a legal practice in Mississippi. He was twice married: on May 25, 1898, to Lillian S. Herrington, who died in 1900; and on Jan. 27, 1903, to Linda R. Gaddy. The second marriage ended in divorce in 1938. Bilbo had a daughter, Jessie Forrest, by his first wife, and a son, Theodore Gilmore, by his second.

A short, stocky man with a rustic wit and a penchant for garish clothes, Bilbo early displayed an aptitude for politics. He developed a colorful, sometimes bawdy, style of oratory which he used with skill against his enemies. In the state senate, where he served from 1908 to 1912, he became a supporter of former governor James K. Vardaman, race-baiting champion of the underprivileged workers and farmers in the hill country and piney woods, as against the aristocratic Delta planters, the railroads, and the corporations. In 1910 the legislature was faced with the duty of filling an unexpired term in the United States Senate. The chief candidates were Vardaman and LeRoy Percy, the latter a corporation lawyer and Delta plantation owner; after a long "secret caucus," the aristocratic Percy was chosen. Bilbo was accused of having accepted a $645 bribe to cast his vote for Percy. Although he claimed to have accepted the money only to expose the corruption of the anti-Vardaman forces, the senate came within one vote of expelling him, and did adopt a resolution of censure requesting him to resign. Bilbo, however, remained in the legislature, assumed the role of a persecuted folk hero, and, with the secret caucus as his chief issue, immediately sought election as lieutenant governor. In a particularly vituperative campaign, Bilbo ("the man of the people") galvanized the crowds with slashing attacks on his opponents. Embodying what one Southern commentator, Wilbur J. Cash, has described as "the whole bold,

dashing, hell-of-a-fellow complex," he won election.

As lieutenant governor from 1912 to 1916, Bilbo emerged as a leader of the masses equal to Vardaman. He feuded with Gov. Earl Brewer and again posed as a martyr when he was indicted on another bribery charge, for which he was tried and acquitted in 1914. The following year he was elected governor. He proved to be an energetic and constructive administrator, one who did not fear to increase the state's fiscal indebtedness. He brought Mississippi a series of important reforms, including the creation of a highway commission and a board of pardons; the establishment of a tuberculosis sanatorium; the addition of manual training and farm mechanics to school curricula; and the introduction of a program to combat ticks, and thus reduce the incidence of Texas fever among livestock. Perhaps his most important contribution was a tax equalization law by which a central board was empowered to revise property assessments it felt were undervalued by county officials under the control of corporations or large planters.

By 1920 the Bilbo-Vardaman faction of the Democratic party had begun to weaken, and when Bilbo, unable to succeed himself as governor, sought a congressional seat, he was badly beaten in the primary. Failing in 1923 in a bid for a second term as governor, he began to edit the *Mississippi Free Lance,* a widely distributed political weekly, in preparation for the campaign of 1927. He was returned to the governorship that year, but his second administration was a fiasco. His highway building program was riddled with scandal; he debased the state college system by appointing political allies to academic posts; and although the state was nearly bankrupt, he began to build for himself a controversial and expensive home, "Dream House," near Poplarville. Thoroughly discredited by the end of his term, in 1933 he was forced to accept a position with the Agricultural Adjustment Administration clipping newspapers (one wag dubbed him the "Pastemaster General").

In 1934, however, Bilbo returned to the political wars and after a whirlwind campaign won a seat in the United States Senate. "The Man," as he called himself, now promised to "raise more hell than Huey Long" in the Senate. But he served unobtrusively until the late 1930's, supporting most New Deal measures and working hard for his constituents. Toward the end of the decade, however, he became increasingly preoccupied with racial matters. He denounced a federal antilynching bill in 1938, advocated the resettlement of American Negroes in Africa, and attacked a Washington, D.C., law permitting racial intermarriage, claiming the offspring of such a union would be a "motley melee of miscegenated mongrels." Reelected in 1940, he joined in filibusters against anti-polltax measures in 1942 and 1944. With one eye on his next campaign, he dramatized himself as a bulwark against the wartime Fair Employment Practices Committee and the threat of Negro voting in Mississippi. Other objects of his vilification were "kikes," "dagoes," Communists, and labor unions.

Although Bilbo was again elected in 1946, the Senate Republican Steering Committee sought to deny the Mississippian his seat when the Eightieth Congress convened in 1947. He had been investigated by two Senate committees, one of which censured him for personal gain in connection with war contracts and campaign funds. Since Bilbo was ill, a compromise was arranged whereby his credentials would lie on the table without prejudice until he could return to defend himself. This he was never able to do, for that August, after three operations for cancer of the mouth, he died of a heart ailment in a New Orleans hospital. A funeral service was held in the Juniper Grove Baptist Church, of which he was a member, and he was buried in the church cemetery.

Bilbo's turbulent and melodramatic career in many ways fitted the stereotype of the demagogue. There was much that was twisted and unsavory in his record, including the racism of his later years. Yet he was a genuine reform governor in the World War I era, and there was a basic thread of consistency in his concern for the plebeian masses and in his conviction that government could render practical help to ordinary people.

[A large collection of Bilbo's papers is at the Univ. of Southern Miss., its use subject to special permission. Bilbo's book, *Take Your Choice: Separation or Mongrelization* (1947), elaborates his racial views. The only biography, A. Wigfall Green, *The Man Bilbo* (1963), is useful and generally reliable, but hardly more than a biographical sketch. Three helpful essays on Bilbo are those by Reinhard H. Luthin in his *Am. Demagogues: Twentieth Century* (1954); by Roman J. Zorn in J. T. Salter, ed., *Public Men in and out of Office* (1946); and by Allan A. Michie and Frank Ryhlick in their *Dixie Demagogues* (1939). Albert D. Kirwan's *Revolt of the Rednecks: Miss. Politics, 1876–1925* (1951), is indispensable for the political background of Bilbo's earlier career. A perspicacious interpretation of the later period is contained in chap. xi of V. O. Key, Jr., *Southern Politics in State and Nation* (1949). For a caustic characterization of "The Man" by a Delta critic, see William A. Percy, *Lanterns on the Levee* (1841), chap. xiii. On the 1910 charges against Bilbo, see *Investigation by the Senate of the State of Miss. of the Charges of Bribery in the Election of a U.S. Senator* (1910). For the Senate investigation of Bilbo's campaign of 1946, see 79 Cong., 2 Sess., U.S. Senate, *Hearings before the Special Committee to Investigate Senatorial Campaign Expenditures, 1946* (1947). Among the best of the many periodical articles on Bilbo are Clarence E. Cason in *Va. Quart. Rev.*, Apr. 1931; Louis Cochran in *Outlook and Independent*, June 17, 1931; Hilton Butler in *North Am. Rev.*, Dec. 1931; Hugh Russell Fraser in *Am. Mercury*, Aug. 1936; Hodding Carter in *N.Y. Times Mag.*, June 30, 1946; and "Senator Bilbo Meets the Press," *Am. Mercury*, Nov. 1946. Brief biographical sketches can be found in the *Biog. Directory Am. Cong.* (1961) and N.Y. *Times*, Aug. 22, 1947. See also *Phila. Record*, Jan. 13-18, 1946; and the Congressional *Memorial Services* for Bilbo, 80 Cong., 2 Sess. (1950).]

DEWEY W. GRANTHAM

BILLIKOPF, JACOB (June 1, 1883-Dec. 31, 1950), social worker, welfare leader, and labor arbitrator, was born in Vilna, Russia, the youngest of three sons and fifth of six children of Louis Bielikov and Glika (Katzenelenbogen) Bielikov. When he was thirteen his family immigrated to Richmond, Va., where his older sister had settled. Jacob knew no English and thus was placed in the first grade. But he learned the language rapidly and three years later was awarded a high school diploma. He supported himself while attending Richmond College by working in grocery stores and selling wares from door to door. His article in the college *Messenger* won him a fellowship from the National Council of Jews to the University of Chicago, where he received the degree of bachelor of philanthropy in 1903. He undertook graduate study at the University of Chicago and then at the New York School of Philanthropy (1905).

Meanwhile in 1904, he had taken his first position in social and welfare work, beginning a career remarkable for its geographical reach as well as for its many facets. After serving as superintendent of a Jewish settlement in Cincinnati (1904-1905), he moved to Milwaukee as superintendent of United Jewish Charities (1905-1907) before transferring to Kansas City, Mo., where he became a recognized community figure as superintendent of United Jewish Charities. He applied his energies in Kansas City to public night schools, municipal baths, a legal aid bureau and a remedial loan agency. Seeing the need for a systematic approach to these undertakings, he took the lead in the establishment of the pioneering Kansas City Board of Public Welfare, on which he served as a member. He was also vice-president of the Kansas City Board of Pardons and Paroles, president of the Missouri State Conference on Charities, and secretary of the Municipal Recreation Commission. During this period he also lectured on sociology at the University of Missouri and was director of the Jewish Educational Institute in Kansas City and president of the National Conference of Jewish Social Workers.

In 1918 Billikopf moved to New York City, where he was placed in charge of a national campaign to collect $25 million for Jewish victims of World War I. While so engaged, Billikopf met Ruth Marshall, a junior at Barnard College and the daughter of a campaign official, Louis Marshall. They were married on Feb. 23, 1920, and had two children, Florence and David Marshall.

After his marriage Billikopf moved to Philadelphia as the executive director of the Federation of Jewish Charities. In addition to fund-raising on a broad scale, he was an impartial mediator of labor disputes, serving such major clients as the men's clothing industry of New York and the women's garment industry in Philadelphia. His notable success in reconciling employees and management led to his appointment in the New Deal era as chairman of the Regional Labor Relations Board of Philadelphia (1933-1936). Earlier in the depression he had served as chairman of the Committee of One Hundred for Unemployment Relief and as a member of the Pennsylvania State Welfare Commission.

In 1933 Billikopf sounded one of the first warnings in the United States against Hitler's potential threat to world peace. He gave eager support to the "University in Exile" for German refugee scholars at the New School for Social Research, helping to raise large sums of money, and became executive director of the national committee to coordinate relief efforts for refugees from Germany and Italy. He was also chairman of the executive committee of the board of trustees of Howard University, a member of the New School's advisory committee, and a trustee of *The Nation* and *Survey* magazines. He displayed an early concern for the welfare of the elderly and was an officer of the American Association for Old Age Security. Another interest was reflected in his civilian chairmanship of a Special Military Clemency Board during World War II.

The University of Chicago Alumni Association cited him for "service to the community, nation and the world," and the *Richmond Times-Dispatch* placed him on its Virginia honor roll, both in 1942. He was an honorary member of Phi Beta Kappa and received an LL.D. from the University of Richmond. Known to friends as "Billie," he was especially

effective in bringing diverse groups together in communal activities. After his first wife's death in 1936, he married Esther Freeman, a teacher, on Jan. 8, 1942. He died in University Hospital, Philadelphia, in his sixty-eighth year from stomach cancer and was buried in Philadelphia. Paul Kellogg wrote (*Survey*, Feb. 1951) that "few . . . Americans have put their hands to anything like as many good causes."

[*Who Was Who in Am.*, III (1960) ; Paul U. Kellogg, "Jacob Billikopf," *Survey*, Feb. 1951 ; Philadelphia *Enquirer*, Jan. 1, 1951 ; Philadelphia *Bulletin*, Jan. 1, 1951 ; *N.Y. Times*, Jan. 1, 1951 ; *N.Y. Herald-Tribune*, Jan. 1, 1951 ; *Jewish Exponent* (Philadelphia), Jan. 5, 1951 ; biographical account prepared by his son, David M. Billikopf of New Canaan, Conn. ; personal acquaintance ; assistance of George W. Corner of Philadelphia gratefully acknowledged ; an example of Billikopf's writing in the area of his speciality, "The Social Duty to the Unemployed," appeared in the *Annals Am. Acad. of Political Sci.*, Mar. 1931.]

IRVING DILLIARD

BILLINGS, ASA WHITE KENNEY (Feb. 8, 1876-Nov. 3, 1949), civil and electrical engineer, was born in Omaha, Nebr., the son of Albert Stearns Billings and Abbie (Park) Billings, both natives of New England. By 1887, when he was eleven, alternating-current generators had begun to make long-distance power transmission feasible, trolley cars were appearing, and to an avid reader like young Billings, the electric light must have been a dazzling symbol of a new frontier. When he entered Omaha high school that year, he was already set on being an electrical engineer, and so, for love more than for money, he began working in his spare time as a laborer in the local power station. At fifteen he entered Harvard as a physics major; and though the youngest member of the class of 1895, he tied for first place at graduation, going on to receive his master's degree in 1896.

During the summers Billings had worked for electrical companies, and in his spare time he had learned Spanish. This background enabled him to get a job in street railway and steam power plant construction in Pittsburgh and then, in 1899, an assignment to electrify a streetcar system in Havana. He continued in Cuban electric transit and steam power construction until 1909, when he joined a New York engineering firm. In 1911, F. S. Pearson, a leading New York consulting engineer and entrepreneur of power projects, persuaded him to supervise a Texas irrigation project requiring a massive concrete dam. His careful study of the composition and mixing of concrete for this project served him well then and thereafter. In 1912 he took charge of another of Pearson's far-flung projects, Talarn Dam in Spain. When it was finished in 1916, it was the highest dam in Europe. By then Billings had drawn plans for a still higher one, Camarasa Dam, also in Spain. In 1917 he joined the U.S. Navy Corps of Civil Engineers, building airplane and dirigible bases in Europe and rising to the rank of commander. For his work, he received the U.S. Distinguished Service Cross and was made a chevalier of the French Legion of Honor. After the war he served as consultant on Camarasa Dam until its completion in 1920.

Pearson died in 1915 aboard the *Lusitania,* but Billings remained associated with Pearson's congeries of Spanish, Mexican, and Brazilian power companies. In 1921 he became construction manager of a Canadian company that served the group in design and purchasing. After getting a Mexican power project under way, he investigated a Brazilian enterprise, the largest electric company in Brazil, operated by a Canadian corporation, named the Brazilian Traction, Light and Power Company, and known to Brazilians as "The Light." There, in 1922, he found the opportunity that absorbed the remaining quarter-century of his career as a pioneer in hydroelectricity.

Brazil, though poor in coal and oil, was the world's fourth-richest nation in potential hydroelectric power. Along 1,300 miles of coast from the southern border to Espiritu Santo, an escarpment called the Serra do Mar rises 1,000 to 2,500 feet from a tropical shore to a temperate, healthy, fertile plateau, well-suited for cattle and grain. The nineteenth-century coffee boom and a railroad to the port of Santos had turned the plateau town of São Paulo into a fast-growing city. Lack of power hampered São Paulo's manufacturing development. But the advent of hydroelectricity had already suggested to more than one engineer that the Serra do Mar might be a bulwark as well as a barrier, that inland-flowing rivers, rising near its edge and fed by extraordinarily heavy rainfall, might be diverted to flow over it and generate enormous power.

Billings' first Brazilian triumphs demonstrated the engineering courage and resourcefulness needed for such a project. Ninety miles north of power-starved Rio de Janeiro, at Ilho dos Pombos, F. S. Hyde, a company reconnaissance engineer, had discerned a promising site for a "run-of-river" power plant (i.e., one without a storage reservoir). Billings revitalized the stalled project in 1922, meeting the government's insistence on a minimum downstream flow with three of the largest concrete sector gates ever built. Ilho dos Pombos power began lighting Rio in 1924. In that year, Billings became vice-president of The Light.

Hyde had also proposed diverting water from the inland-flowing Rio Grande to a reservoir that would supply water for a drop of 2,350 feet from the crest of the Serra to generators at Cubatão, near São Paulo. Sophisticated in the ways of financiers and governments, Billings at first hesitated. Then he committed himself to the project. He won over officials by pointing out the dividends of flood control that would open new land for São Paulo's expansion, and especially of cheaper transport through a canal, locks, and inclined rails. (The flood control plan was realized; the freight system, though sound, was forestalled by a new railroad and outmoded by a mid-century highway and pipeline.) Undeterred by a local revolutionary outbreak and a drought, Billings brought the first two generators into operation in 1927 and then began creating the largest artificial lake in South America. The worldwide depression stopped work from 1931 to 1934, but the Serra project was completed in 1937. Billings at once began a project to divert flow from a second large reservoir into the Serra system. During the 1930's and 1940's he also significantly enlarged the capacity of the Rio de Janeiro system, but he regarded the Serra development as his crowning achievement.

Billings' engineering achievements were notable in themselves. The range and depth of his technical knowledge impressed civil, mechanical, and electrical engineers alike. He developed an ingenious, multipurpose system of low-head pumping in stages from the large reservoirs to the head of the penstocks, the great pipes that conveyed water down the Serra escarpment to the Cubatão generators. Perceiving that the standard penstock design rested on faulty hydraulic theory, he collected reports from over the world, worked out a new mathematical analysis, and confirmed it with extensive tests, making a large saving possible. His 1933 paper, "High Head Penstock Design," became a classic on the subject. In raising the height of a dam in the Rio system from 105 to 197 feet, he saved a third of the usual cement requirements by building great buttresses in a daring and unprecedented design. He used the highest head reaction turbines and the largest impulse turbines in the world at that time.

As a project planner, Billings showed foresight, flexibility, and readiness to incorporate new engineering and other ideas. He made the most of corollary benefits such as navigation, flood control, fish culture, water supply, irrigation, and recreation. With notable success, he organized antimalaria studies and programs. Hoping to anticipate long-range trends in rainfall, he initiated and directed hydrological and meteorological studies of the region. This engaged him in his chief hobby, the study of the correlation between sunspots and rainfall cycles.

Meanwhile, during the 1930's, Billings contended with Brazilian governmental hostility toward foreign utility companies, dramatized by the Water Act of 1934, which prohibited further power concessions to the foreign companies and limited their profits so much as to dry up investment. After a six-year campaign, pleading his cause before organizations and officials as being that not only of The Light but also of Brazil (for which his concern was genuine and evident), Billings obtained modifications that, with some engineering ingenuity, permitted expansion of existing projects. As an administrator and promoter, Billings had to be versed not only in local, national, and international politics, but also in banking, foreign trade, and Brazilian commercial law.

Billings was a friendly, modest man whose full, clean-shaven face conveyed both good humor and quiet forcefulness. This aspect, along with his capacity for details and sustained work (often seven days a week), won the respect and liking of employees, although he asked much of them. His age and the problems created by World War II, which cut off sources of equipment, had their effect after 1940. He reluctantly accepted The Light's presidency in 1944, but he retired in 1946 to serve as consulting engineer. During his career, Billings added half a million kilowatts to Brazil's power supply, more than a third of the total; and projects that he had under way or planned in 1946 eventually added another million. In the summer of that year he was awarded the National Order of the Southern Cross, Brazil's highest civilian decoration, and in May 1949 the great reservoir was named Lake Billings.

Billings and his wife, Josephine, planned to settle in La Jolla, Calif., but he died there of a heart attack in a hotel room a few weeks after arriving. He was buried in New York City. In addition to his wife, he was survived by his son, Asa, Jr., and his daughter, Mary. His work had been vital in advancing São Paulo's role as the largest city and leading industrial center of Brazil.

[The chief sources are Asa W. K. Billings, "Water Power in Brazil," *Civil Engineering*, Aug. 1938, and Adolph J. Ackerman, *Billings and Water Power in Brazil* (1953), full and authoritative, although laudatory, on his career; there is no mention of his personal life. Obituaries in the *San Diego Union*, Nov. 5, 1949, and *Civil Engineering*, Dec. 1949, add a few details. The Brazilian background may be found in Warren Dean, *The Industrialization of São Paulo, 1880–1945* (1969); Simon Kuznets, Wilbert E. Moore, and Joseph J. Spengler, eds., *Economic Growth: Brazil, India, Japan* (1955); Brazilian Embassy, Washington, D.C., *Survey of the Brazilian Economy* (1965); and especially Institute of Inter-American Affairs, *The Development of Brazil* (1955).]

ROBERT V. BRUCE

BINGA, JESSE (Apr. 10, 1865–June 13, 1950), banker and realtor, was born in Detroit, Mich., the youngest of eight girls and two boys of William W. Binga, a barber, and Adelphia (Powers) Binga. His parents, both of whom were freeborn, came to Detroit in the 1840's where his father eventually became sufficiently prosperous to invest in real estate and housing.

Jesse Binga attended public school in Detroit and completed two years of high school. While in school he learned barbering from his father, and also collected rents and helped maintain his father's properties. After leaving school, he worked for a young black attorney, and in 1885 he embarked on an eight-year journey as an itinerant barber and transient entrepreneur. He went to Chicago, worked as a barber in Kansas City, Mo., then stopped in St. Paul, Minn., and in Helena and Missoula, Mont., where his uncle owned a restaurant and real estate. In Tacoma, Wash., he opened a barber shop, and moved on to Seattle, where he again set up a shop. He sold out soon after and traveled to Oakland, Calif., where he was employed as a barber. Then he entered the service of the Southern Pacific Railroad as a porter on the coastal runs. Disillusioned with life on the west coast, he moved to Ogden, Utah, where he worked as a Pullman porter. He invested in land on a former Indian reservation near Pocatello, Idaho, and when he arrived in Chicago shortly before the World's Columbian Exposition of 1893, he had accumulated capital from his profitable land dealings.

Binga's subsequent career paralleled the rise and fall of the dream of developing a black metropolis on Chicago's south side. His rise from huckster to businessman for more than twenty years and the ensuing collapse of his financial empire at the start of the depression serve as a parable of black Chicago.

In 1898 he opened a real estate office on south State Street. With his clientele drawn from the rapidly growing black community, Binga prospered by seeking rental property throughout the south side, regardless of discriminatory traditions. Thus he helped open up better quality housing to blacks. In 1905 he leased a seven-story building on State Street and opened it to black tenants. In 1908 he opened the Binga Bank in a newly constructed office building next door; it was the first bank owned, managed, directed, or controlled by blacks in the North.

With the great migration of blacks to Chicago initiated during World War I, Binga grew successful and rich. At one time he owned 1,200 apartment leaseholds, and by 1926 he owned more property on State Street south of Twelfth Street than any other person. In 1921 his bank was chartered by the state, and as the Binga State Bank opened in January 1921, with a capital and surplus of $120,000. Although the board of directors comprised leading black businessmen, Binga was the major stockholder and it was still considered Binga's bank, under his personal control, the shift from private to state bank notwithstanding. Binga continued to run it as if it were privately owned and under single proprietorship.

In the 1920's his realty company expanded, and the capital and surplus of the Binga State Bank increased to $235,000 in 1924. He organized the Binga Safe Deposit Company and promoted a black insurance company. In 1929 he constructed the Binga Arcade as his banking headquarters and as a central office building in the black belt. Binga's name became synonymous with black business and success. He promoted interracial business associations to encourage other black as well as white investment on the south side. A single-minded businessman, he stressed an ideology of hard work and thrift, as in his pamphlet of aphorisms, *Certain Sayings of Jesse Binga*. Although not an active civil-rights leader, his concern for enlarging his business and opening up black opportunity placed him in the center of racial turmoil that followed World War I.

Binga's activities brought him into direct confrontation with the traditional color line in Chicago. As the black population expanded, Binga leased apartments and funded mortgages in south side areas previously barred to blacks. White homeowners and renters fought to maintain the restrictions, but Binga was not intimidated by verbal threats or bombs. In March and November 1919, his real estate office was bombed, and in 1919 and 1920 five attempts were made to bomb his home (three of them successful) despite police guard. Binga pledged to continue representing his clients: "I will not run. The race is at stake and not myself" (Chicago Commission on Race Relations, p. 131).

What bombs could not do, however, the collapse of the economy did. On July 31, 1930, the state auditor ordered Binga's bank closed because its liabilities exceeded assets by over $500,000. The major cause of the closing had been the deflation of real estate values on the south side; other contributing factors had been the decline in deposits, the large amount of unsecured loans, and the excessive investment in the bank building and site. The bank's problems had been evident for more than a year, but Binga would not give up control of the bank to save it; he tried to do so by himself and failed. Eventually almost every neighborhood bank outside the Loop also closed. The failure of the Binga State Bank ended the dream of a black metropolis, and with Binga's loss of his personal fortune, estimated at $400,000, the savings of thousands of working-class blacks also disappeared. The average deposit at the bank's closing in 1930 was $66.12; over 80 percent were under $100.00.

After the bank failure, its practices came under close scrutiny and Binga was indicted for embezzlement. The first trial ended in a hung jury, but in 1933 Binga was convicted of five counts of embezzlement for the issuance of fraudulent loans. After serving three years in jail, he was paroled in 1938 to work as a handyman at St. Anselm's Catholic Church. During his imprisonment, south side leaders had campaigned for a pardon for him.

On Feb. 20, 1912, Binga married Eudora Johnson, sister of a Chicago gambling lord. She died of a cerebral hemorrhage in March 1933, during his trial. Eudora Binga had inherited her brother's $200,000 estate and worked actively in charitable and benevolent institutions. They had no children. Binga died on June 13, 1950, in St. Luke's Hospital, Chicago, after suffering a stroke and falling down a staircase in his house. He was buried in Oakwood Cemetery. His career symbolized the optimism of black business in the 1910's and 1920's. Despite his downfall, his achievements inspired pride, and his life was important to large numbers of black Americans.

[Carl R. Osthaus, "The Rise and Fall of Jesse Binga, Black Financier," *Jour. of Negro Hist.*, Jan. 1973, pp. 39–60, provides a thorough although somewhat negative overview of Binga's career. Inez V. Cantey, "Jesse Binga," *Crisis*, Dec. 1927, pp. 329, 350–352, is a rags-to-riches summary of his early background and success. Cantey was indicted along with Binga and turned state's witness at the second trial. St. Clair Drake and Horace R. Cayton, *Black*

Metropolis: A Study of Negro Life in a Northern City (1945), and Allan H. Spear, *Black Chicago: The Making of a Negro Ghetto, 1890–1920* (1967), deal with the rise of black Chicago and refer to Binga's role as its preeminent businessman. A detailed financial analysis of the Binga State Bank can be found in Abram L. Harris, *The Negro as Capitalist: A Study of Banking and Business Among Am. Negroes* (1936). Frank Cyril James, *The Growth of Chicago Banks,* II (1938), examines the Binga bank within the perspective of Chicago banking. The Chicago Commission on Race Relations, *The Negro in Chicago: A Study of Race Relations and a Race Riot* (1922), and William M. Tuttle, Jr., *Race Riot: Chicago in the Red Summer of 1919* (1970), describe Binga as the target of racial violence in Chicago. The measure of his importance to black America can be seen in two editorials on the bank's closing: "A Negro Bank Closes Its Doors," *Opportunity*, Sept. 1930, p. 264, and W. E. B. DuBois, "Postscript: Binga," *Crisis*, Dec. 1930, pp. 425–426. His banking career and trial can be traced in the Chicago *Defender*, the Mar. 5, 1938, issue summarizes his career and legal problems; the June 17, 1950, issue contains his obituary. Portraits of Binga appear with the Cantey article, in J. L. Nichols and William H. Crogman, *Progress of a Race* (1925), and with many of the *Defender* articles (e.g., Dec. 13, 1919, p. 1; Apr. 13, 1935, p. 1).]

DAVID M. KATZMAN

BIRGE, EDWARD ASAHEL (Sept. 7, 1851–June 9, 1950), limnologist and university administrator, was born in Troy, N.Y., the older of two sons and second of three children who survived infancy. Both parents, Edward White Birge and Ann (Stevens) Birge, were of New England stock dating back to the 1630's. The father, a carpenter, in 1851 turned for reasons of health to dairy farming in Hamden, Conn., but moved back to Troy when his son was about twelve and became a partner in a bakery. He was an ardent Christian but, in the absence of a Congregational church in Troy, a reluctant Presbyterian. The family were accustomed to discuss theological problems under his guidance.

Before entering the Troy high school, where he enrolled in the classical course, young Birge had taken private lessons in Greek and Latin. After graduating in 1869, he entered Williams College in Williamstown, Mass., where he studied philosophy under Mark Hopkins and John Bascom, whom he regarded as major influences in his development. Birge graduated with the A.B. degree in 1873, second in his class. Having developed a strong interest in zoology, he went to Harvard's Museum of Comparative Zoology to study under Louis Agassiz and later did graduate work there. In December 1875, he accepted an instructorsip in natural philosophy at the University of Wisconsin. In Cambridge he had begun a study of the systematics of Cladocera, the minute crustaceans known as water fleas. For this work he received the Ph.D. from Harvard in 1878 and the following year

was made professor of zoology at Wisconsin. On July 15, 1880, he married Anna Wilhelmina Grant. They had two children, Edward Grant and Anna Grant. After his marriage he spent a year (1880–1881) in Leipzig studying histology and physiology and then returned to Wisconsin, where he remained for the rest of his life as teacher, research scientist, and administrator.

Birge greatly enlarged the scope of Wisconsin's instruction in biology. He had brought with him from Germany new histological apparatus and research techniques that enabled him to institute laboratory courses in bacteriology and physiology, and in 1887 he established the first premedical course given at Wisconsin. His teaching was marked by clarity of presentation, tremendous breadth of knowledge, the ability to stimulate the student's investigative interests, and an uncanny instinct for the particular topics about which a student was hazy. He won the enthusiastic regard of large numbers of future physicians and scientists, some of whom rated him as their finest teacher.

Although Birge continued his research on Cladocera after going to Wisconsin and became an authority on their taxonomy, to biologists he is known chiefly as a pioneer limnologist. Before 1910, when he finished his synopsis of the Cladocera of North America, he had enlarged the scope of his research to include their lake habitat and the physical and chemical factors that conditioned their movements, biological productivity, and life history. As director (1897–1919) of the Wisconsin Geological and Natural History Survey, he supervised a variety of research projects and carried on his own classic studies of Wisconsin lakes as individual, integrated entities. About 1905 he began a long collaboration with Chancey Juday. Birge had earlier investigated the vertical and seasonal distribution of a lake's microorganisms, insects, and fish. His research with Juday did much to elucidate how that distribution was affected by thermal strata in the lake waters, by transmitted solar radiation, and by dissolved gases. Birge published nearly seventy papers, many with Juday, the last appearing when he was nearly ninety.

Birge's research time was limited by his teaching and administrative responsibilities. In 1891 he was appointed the first dean of the College of Letters and Sciences. At the beginning he dealt chiefly with student problems, but his duties soon expanded to include academic matters and working with the faculty on appointments, curricula, and policy. The "common law" applied by later deans stemmed largely from Birge's initial decisions. He not only championed but exemplified the spirit of liberal education. One of his most important achievements came during the period 1914-1915, when the university was under attack from a survey authorized by the state legislature. The survey savagely criticized the current practices and advocated a rigid restructuring of the university. Birge's reasoned and persuasive contribution to the defense was a major factor not only in the defeat of the survey's recommendations but in vindicating the university's reputation.

In 1918, on the death of Charles Van Hise, Birge, who had earlier served as acting president of the university (1900-1903), was elected president, a post he held until his retirement in 1925. Although his incumbency was not marked by innovation, he consolidated the changes of the Van Hise regime, successfully coped with the problems of postwar inflation, and obtained better salaries for the faculty. He skillfully cultivated the services of the university's regents, and was more effective than visible.

In 1921-1922 Birge became involved in a public dispute with William Jennings Bryan, who attacked him for defending the theory of evolution. Birge believed in a developing revelation of which both Darwin and St. Paul were apostles, and felt as strongly that Bryan was a blasphemer as Bryan felt that Birge was. Birge's adult Bible class was a notable feature of the Congregational church of which he was a member. At the age of seventy-nine he began a series of annual sermons on St. Paul, given at a local Episcopal church, which revealed a mind confident of Christianity and also of its own power. Birge was an articulate person with both tongue and pen and was a master essayist. The combination of an extremely retentive memory and amazing reading speed, along with breadth of interests, created a phenomenally informed individual. He was basically both kind and just, but not to the extent of curbing his tart wit. Nor was he a merciful opponent in debate. His activities were diverse, but he did not easily tolerate distractions and hence at times appeared brusque. He was slight of stature, quick of motion, and had piercing black eyes. One always stayed alert in his presence.

In 1925, after his retirement, Birge devoted more time to his research and with Juday established the Trout Lake Limnological Laboratory near Minocqua, Wis. There he continued to work at what is probably his most important investigation, the penetration of light into lake water. Birge served as president of the American Microscopical Society (1902) and the American Fisheries Society (1907), and he and Juday together were posthumously awarded the Naumann Medal of the International Association of Limnology. Birge died of pneumonia at his home in Madison in his ninety-ninth year. He was buried in Forest Hill Cemetery, Madison.

[The fullest biographical treatment is George C. Sellery, *E. A. Birge* (1956), which includes an appraisal of his contributions to limnology by C. H. Mortimer. Another critical assessment of Birge's scientific work is David G. Frey, "Wisconsin: The Birge-Juday Era," in Frey, ed., *Limnology in North America* (1963). See also memoir by John L. Brooks et al. in *Archiv für Hydrobiologie*, 45 (1951): 235-243; and Edwin B. Fred in Am. Philosophical Soc., *Year Book*, 1950. On Birge's presidency, see Merle Curti and Vernon Carstensen, *The Univ. of Wis., 1848-1925*, 2 vols. (1949); and Irvin G. Wyllie, "Bryan, Birge, and the Wis. Evolution Controversy, 1921-1922," *Wis. Mag. of Hist.*, Summer 1952. Birge's papers, including autobiographical material and a biobibliography by Diane Dumdey, are in the State Hist. Soc. of Wis. Paintings of Birge are in South Hall and Birge Hall, Univ. of Wis.]

MARK H. INGRAHAM

BLACKWELL, ALICE STONE (Sept. 14, 1857-Mar. 15, 1950), woman's rights editor and humanitarian, was born in Orange, N.J., the only child of Henry Browne Blackwell and Lucy Stone. Her father, who at various times sold hardware, speculated in real estate, and tried to raise sugar beets in Maine, was sympathetic to a wide range of reforms before he met and married Lucy Stone, the Oberlin-educated suffrage leader. One of Blackwell's aunts, Elizabeth Blackwell, was the first American woman to graduate from medical school; another, Antoinette Brown Blackwell, was the first regularly ordained woman minister in the United States. As a child, Alice Blackwell remembered hating the incessant talk of woman's rights in her home, but by the time she was twelve she was already "bristling up like a hen in defense of her chickens" when anyone dared question the justice of her family's cause.

After attending Chauncy Hall School in Boston and graduating from Boston University, Phi Beta Kappa, in 1881, she joined her parents as an editor of the *Woman's Journal*, a magazine Lucy Stone had founded to serve as the official organ of the American Woman Suffrage Association. The rival National Association, which published for a brief time its own periodical, *Revolution*, was dominated by Elizabeth Cady Stanton and Susan B. Anthony, women who were more than willing to offend polite sensibilities for the sake of feminist principles. Lucy Stone was not. And it was only through the efforts of her daughter, Alice, that she was finally persuaded in 1890 to close ranks with those outspoken suffragists who had exposed themselves to the charge of advocating free love. Many years later, Jane Addams suggested that Blackwell's equanimity in the face of a second split in the suffrage movement between militants and conservatives before World War I grew out of her historical perspective. This is not to say that she never took sides. In her biography of her mother, *Lucy Stone: Pioneer of Woman's Rights* (1930), for example, Blackwell accused Stanton of having been willing to sacrifice woman's best interests in order to get even with orthodox clergymen. More broadminded than her mother, she still wasted no sympathy on those feminists who refused to concentrate on legal reforms.

For thirty-five years Alice Blackwell edited the *Woman's Journal*, gathering copy, reading proof, and writing long arguments in favor of equal rights. Beginning in 1887 she also edited the *Woman's Column*, a bulletin of suffrage news sent out to newspapers across the country. She produced several volumes of poetry translated from Spanish, Armenian, Yiddish, Hungarian, and Russian, in some cases by herself, more often by friends whose prose versions of the original poems she put into verse. In addition to her biography of her mother, she edited a life of Catherine Breshkovsky, *The Little Grandmother of the Russian Revolution* (1917). It was in these translations and tributes that she was able to express her deepest feelings of outrage and sympathy for the oppressed; her writings in behalf of contemporary women were less tender and more trenchant.

Blackwell's seriousness and intensity led her mother to hope that she would be able to understand jokes in the next world. Her father was famous for his nimble wit, and although Blackwell inherited her father's cleverness, she could never accept his philosophy of life. Shortly after her college graduation he confided to her that nothing was worth doing except as a diversion. Unable to share the humorless singlemindedness that marked her mother's lifelong crusade and yet shocked by her father's avowed opportunism, Blackwell cultivated a cutting intelligence in the woman's cause and expressed her strongest humanitarian feelings in behalf of others.

A Unitarian, she was active in the Woman's Christian Temperance Union (describing herself as "almost a rabid dry"), the Women's Trade Union League, the National Association for the Advancement of Colored People, the Anti-Vivisection League, the American Peace Society, the Armenian General Benevolent

Union, and the Friends of Russian Freedom, as well as serving as recording secretary of the amalgamated National American Woman Suffrage Association for nearly two decades after 1890, and, later, becoming a founding member of the Massachusetts League of Women Voters. After retiring from the *Woman's Journal* shortly before the Nineteenth Amendment was ratified, she reported that her main recreation was writing letters to other editors in support of unpopular causes. A socialist but never a party member, she backed Robert M. La Follette for president in 1924, espoused the cause of Nicola Sacco and Bartolomeo Vanzetti and protested everything from President Franklin Roosevelt's deficit spending to the trend toward longer skirts after World War II. In the early 1930's she was particularly active in a Massachusetts League of Women Voters campaign against the policy of firing married women from municipal jobs to make room for family men.

Like many prominent suffragists, Blackwell had hoped that women voters would outlaw drink, child labor, and war, and was disturbed to find that they were just as bellicose, as unresponsive to human need, and as vulnerable to the appeal of party politics as men. She felt that it was generally a misfortune when young mothers went to work: like her own mother, she was a staunch believer in home, maternal duty, and monogamy. Yet she had little patience with those housebound women who lacked the "gumption" to organize against sex-based discrimination, or any other infringement of civil liberties.

Blackwell died of arteriosclerotic heart disease at the age of ninety-two in Cambridge, Mass. Her mother had been the first New England resident to be cremated, and in this as in so many other things she followed the family tradition. Her ashes were placed in the Lower Columbarium at Forest Hills Cemetery, Boston. Alice Blackwell's final self-abnegating wish was that her biography of her mother be placed in the library of every woman's college, and that her parents' papers be indexed for future historians.

[The Alice Stone Blackwell Papers are in the Lib. of Cong. Additional letters can be found in the Blackwell Family Papers, Schlesinger Lib., Radcliffe Coll., and the Sophia Smith Collect. at Smith Coll. The files of the *Woman's Journal* and the *Woman's Column* are provocative, as is *A Bubble Pricked: A Reply to "The Case Against Woman Suffrage,"* a pamphlet Blackwell published in 1916. Biographical details appear in *Woman's Who's Who of America*, 1914–1915; *N.Y. Times*, Mar. 16, 1950; and in the sketch by Geoffrey Blodgett in *Notable Am. Women*, I, 156–158. Further information can be found in Blackwell's *Lucy Stone,* in Elinor Rice Hays' *Morning Star: A Biography of Lucy Stone* (1961), and in Lois B. Merk's "Mass. and the Woman-Suffrage Movement" (microfilm, Schlesinger Lib., 1961). The city clerk of Cambridge, Mass., supplied a death record.]

GAIL THAIN PARKER

BLISS, CORNELIUS NEWTON (Apr. 13, 1874-Apr. 5, 1949), philanthropist and businessman, was born in New York City, the only surviving son of the four children of Cornelius Newton Bliss and Elizabeth M. (Plumer) Bliss; the second of his two older sisters, Lizzie Plumer Bliss (1864-1931), was one of the founders of the Museum of Modern Art in New York City. His father had come to New York in the 1860's from Fall River, Mass., and engaged successfully first in the manufacture of textiles, then in the wholesale dry-goods business. The elder Bliss was also active in Republican politics, serving as secretary of the interior in 1897-1898 under President William McKinley.

Cornelius Bliss the younger was educated at the Cutler School and then at Harvard, from which he received his B.A. in 1897. He entered his father's business, Bliss, Fabyan and Company, and was made a partner in 1899. On Apr. 26, 1906, he married Zaidee C. Cobb of Washington, D.C. They had three children: Elizabeth Addison, Cornelius Newton, Jr., and Anthony Addison. Throughout his life, Bliss was an Episcopalian and a member of the Republican party.

Bliss had a solid business career, achieving election as president of the Associated Merchants and United Dry Goods companies in 1914, becoming a director of the Banker's Trust in 1916, a board member of the Radio Corporation of America in 1927, and remaining prominent in Bliss, Fabyan until it closed in 1940. His political career was similarly substantial. After serving as an alternate delegate to the National Republican Convention in 1916, he became national treasurer of the Republican party during the campaign of Charles Evans Hughes for the presidency in 1916. His father had also been national treasurer. In 1920 he endorsed Gen. Leonard Wood for the presidency, and thereafter limited his political activities to the Republican party in New York state.

Bliss's most important contributions, however, were in philanthropy. He divided his concerns between the poor and the fine arts. In 1920 he became associated with the New York Association for Improving the Condition of the Poor, serving as president from 1913-1934. In this period the association was moving from marginal role to obsolescence among the city's philanthropic organizations. Bliss was aware of the need for new measures and sources of funds to relieve suffering. In 1931, at the depth of the depression, he chaired a commission, appointed by Mayor James J. Walker, to administer a $15 million relief fund. He remained committed to the idea that private charity had a role to play in relief for the unemployed. He supported block committees for mutual help and campaigned to raise money for relief. From 1938, he served as vice-president of the Community Service Society of New York, an organization seeking to provide social service to poor and helpless citizens whose cash needs were met from public relief. Bliss was also active in the American Red Cross in both world wars.

Bliss's involvement with music and the visual arts began later in life, but became his most important philanthropic achievement. In the 1920's he was active in the company that owned the Metropolitan Opera House. In 1933, after joining the board of the Metropolitan Opera Company, he chaired the first national campaign for funds to sustain the organization in the midst of the depression. He was elected chairman of the board of the Metropolitan Opera Association in 1938 and was responsible for publishing its first detailed financial statement in 1942. He also served as a trustee of the Metropolitan Museum of Art and the Museum of Modern Art in the 1930's.

Bliss died of undisclosed causes, after an illness of ten days, in New York City, on Apr. 5, 1949, and was buried at Woodlawn Cemetery. His greatest achievement was his measured mediation between the worlds of business and philanthropy. Not a dominant figure, he nevertheless helped to establish public-spiritedness rather than self-indulgence as a model for others of his class.

[A private man, Bliss appears to have left no papers and to have inspired no lengthy verbal portraits. His life was part of the story of his class and his city and is recorded in most detail in the pages of the *N.Y. Times* and the *N.Y. Herald Tribune*; it is accessible through the indexes to these papers. Other references to him appear in national and specialized biographical dictionaries, and in the house organs and sponsored histories of the institutions and agencies he served.]

DANIEL M. FOX

BLOOM, SOL (Mar. 9, 1870-Mar. 7, 1949), congressman from New York, earlier a showman, music publisher, and real estate operator, was born in Pekin, Tazewell County, Ill., the third son and youngest of the six children of Gershon (or Garrison) and Sarah (or Sara) Bloom. His Jewish parents had migrated sometime before 1860 from Schirpitz, West Prussia (Szyrpcz, Poland). Bloom's heritage was one of piety and poverty. In 1875 his father opened a small clothing store in Peoria, Ill., but it failed, and later that year the family moved to San Francisco. Although the elder Bloom was industrious and fairly well educated, he was irregularly employed and frequently peddled from door to door to eke out a living. The "real head" of the family, Sol recalled, was his strong-willed, deeply religious mother, who valued knowledge and taught him to read both Hebrew and English. His formal schooling was limited. Self-reliant and already an experienced peddler, he got his first steady job at the age of seven in a San Francisco brush factory. The following year he began to augment his earnings with evening work at the theater, where he made additional money by selling free programs and by other forms of "legitimate chiseling." He was fascinated with numbers and prices and picked up arithmetic during his lunch hour. At the age of ten he began keeping the brush factory's accounts.

At fifteen Bloom abandoned the brush factory for show business when he became assistant treasurer of the Alcazar Theatre, owned by the San Francisco newspaper publisher H. H. de Young. Bloom also produced plays, arranged tours, and built his first theater. At nineteen, having saved $80,000, he visited the 1889 Paris Exposition and booked the North African sword swallowers, glass and scorpion eaters, and belly dancers for an American tour. Perhaps through de Young's connections, he was asked to supervise the amusement section of the World's Columbian Exposition held at Chicago in 1893. Bloom brought order out of chaos and gave America the Algerian Village with the "Hootchy Kootchy" dance, whose classic tune he originated.

Remaining in Chicago, Bloom invested in commodities, but was wiped out when his dairy products spoiled on the tracks during the 1894 Pullman strike. Never down for long, he became manager of the music department at Rothschild's department store and on the side began publishing sheet music, and then selling music and instruments by mail. Advertising himself widely as "Sol Bloom, the Music Man," he built a chain of eighty music departments in stores around the country, and a new fortune. Bloom married Evelyn Hechheimer, an aspiring songwriter from San Francisco, on June 22, 1897, and the following year their only child, Vera, was born. Since New York had by then become the center of his operations, Bloom in 1903 moved his family there, where among other things he was the national distributor of

Victor talking machines. By 1910 Bloom had withdrawn from the music business to concentrate on real estate investments and building construction. Buying and selling extensively in midtown Manhattan, he helped assemble the property on which Pennsylvania Station was erected. He also built or renovated close to a dozen theaters, and publicized his transactions to enhance property values and his reputation.

At fifty, tired of business routine, Bloom started to withdraw from his enterprises "to do something noble" (*Autobiography,* p. 198). He was a longtime Democrat, and his opportunity came when Charles F. Murphy, the leader of Tammany Hall, asked him to run for Congress in the special January 1923 election in the normally Republican 19th Congressional District. Narrowly winning the hard-fought election, the amiable, accessible Bloom became enormously popular in his district (later the 20th) and served in the House of Representatives until his death.

Until 1939 Bloom's congressional career was routine and occasionally bordered on the ludicrous. Although he consistently opposed "blue" laws and immigration restriction, he was essentially a garrulous, flamboyant, publicity-seeking showman, whose political philosophy extended little beyond venerating the Founding Fathers (particularly Washington), the Constitution, and the flag. Bloom was small (five feet six inches), but he stood out in a crowd; he had a lively, mobile face, dressed colorfully, and always wore a pince-nez on a broad, black ribbon. He was a loyal supporter of Franklin Roosevelt's New Deal, and he usually enjoyed the support of New York's American Labor party; but he was chiefly renowned for his prodigious and effective work as director of commissions for the observance of George Washington's bicentennial and the sesquicentennial of the federal Constitution.

In 1939 Bloom, a staunch interventionist, became by seniority head of the crucial Foreign Affairs Committee. He soon dispelled apprehension concerning his capacity for the job. A hardworking chairman who quickly established a nonpartisan and cordial atmosphere, Bloom decided issues after consultations with the State Department, wide reading, and committee discussions. Seemingly aware of his limitations, he neither innovated policy nor molded public opinion, but he was a superb strategist in securing legislation implementing Roosevelt's policies. He adroitly steered the Lend-Lease Act through the House in 1941, supported extension of the draft, and sponsored legislation to arm American merchant ships and allow them to carry cargo to belligerent ports. He was assailed as a "Jewish warmonger" both in and out of Congress. Bloom was also a firm supporter of the United Nations. He helped secure passage of the 1943 Fulbright resolution calling for a postwar international organization and in 1945 was a delegate to the San Francisco Conference which drew up the United Nations Charter.

Bloom also helped those dispossessed by World War II. During the winter of 1943-1944 his skillful conduct of hearings and his sponsoring of legislation supporting the United Nations Relief and Rehabilitation Administration destroyed effective congressional opposition to that international agency. After the war Bloom fought to extend UNRRA, represented the United States on the UNRRA committee, and sought homes for displaced persons.

In the postwar years Bloom supported foreign aid and Zionism. He attacked British policies in Palestine and in 1948 worked to extend private and public aid to the newly sovereign nation of Israel. In March 1947, Bloom favored President Harry Truman's proposals to aid Greece and Turkey and in the spring of 1948 supported the European Recovery (Marshall Plan) Program as part of an omnibus aid bill. The next year he entered the United States Naval Hospital at Bethesda, Md., with a severe cold, and while there died of a coronary thrombosis. He was buried in Mount Eden Cemetery, Pleasantville, N.Y.

[Bloom's papers are in the N.Y. Public Lib. His *Autobiog.* (1948) is a basic source. See also Hugh A. Bone, "Sol Bloom: 'Supersalesman of Patriotism,' " in John T. Salter, ed., *Public Men in and out of Office* (1946); Samuel Dickson *The Streets of San Francisco* (1955); *Current Biog.* (1943); *Biog. Directory Am. Cong.* (1961); *Who's Who in Am. Jewry* (1938-1939); and *N.Y. Times* obituary, Mar. 8, 1949. A biobibliography of Bloom, prepared by Gretchen Dettwiler at the Univ. of Wis. Lib. School, was helpful.]
ARI HOOGENBOOM

BLOOMFIELD, LEONARD (Apr. 1, 1887-Apr. 18, 1949), American linguist, was born in Chicago, one of three children of Sigmund Bloomfield and Carola (Buber) Bloomfield, nephew of the indologist Maurice Bloomfield and of the concert pianist Fannie Bloomfield Zeisler. His father's parents had come from Austria to Chicago in 1868; the family belonged to the economically depressed intellectual aristocracy of the German-speaking Jewish immigrants of the period. He was raised bilingually, but with no religious affiliation.

His childhood years were divided between Chicago and Elkhart Lake, Wis., where his father ran a small resort hotel, except for two winters in Europe (1898-1899 and 1900-1901). Graduated from Chicago's North Division School in 1903, he entered Harvard College, receiving the B.A. in 1906. He then went to the University of Wisconsin as graduate assistant in German. Arriving with no precise study plans, he was quickly persuaded by the ingenuous enthusiasm of Eduard Prokosch to dedicate his life to linguistics. After two years he transferred to the University of Chicago, to earn the Ph.D. in 1909 under Francis A. Wood. On Mar. 18, 1909, he married Alice Sayers of St. Louis; there was no issue, but they adopted two children, Robert Monteur and James Sheldon.

His ensuing academic itinerary: 1909-1910, instructor in German, University of Cincinnati; 1910-1913, same, University of Illinois; 1913-1914, on leave, at Leipzig and Göttingen; 1914-1921, assistant professor of comparative philology and German, Illinois; summers of 1920 and 1921, with the Menomini Indians of Wisconsin; 1921-1927, professor of German and linguistics, Ohio State University; summer of 1925, with the Cree Indians of Sweet Grass Reserve, Saskatchewan; 1927-1940, professor of Germanic philology, University of Chicago; summers of 1937, 1938, and 1939, the Linguistic Institute (of the Linguistic Society of America) at the University of Michigan; summer of 1941, same at the University of North Carolina; from 1940, Sterling professor of linguistics, Yale University. His work was stopped May 27, 1946, by a massive stroke; lesser ones followed and his life ended in New Haven three years later.

In Bloomfield's day an American linguist was obliged to earn his living as a foreign-language teacher. Bloomfield accepted this as challenge, not chore. His *First German Book* (1923) was ahead of its time. When World War II made much practical work for linguists, he uncomplainingly shouldered a large share, guiding younger men and himself preparing teaching materials in Russian and in Dutch. "About Foreign Language Teaching" (1945) is a masterful summary of findings and prospects.

Another applied area to receive Bloomfield's touch is teaching children to read. His materials were prepared and tested in the 1930's, but published only in 1961. "Linguistics and Reading" (1942) sets forth the procedure and its scientific basis: The child already knows the language, and has only to learn the ways in which spellings represent sounds. He should be started with materials in which the spelling-to-sound correspondences are regular, and only after the mastery of these should he be moved on to irregularly spelled forms, introduced on the basis of decreasing frequency and importance.

Bloomfield came to linguistics when it was regarded in the United States chiefly as the dilettantish preoccupation of scholars who could not make the grade in literary studies. He left it a branch of science, the branch that "attempts to define the place of language in the universe." The quoted phrase is from his 1927 article "On Recent Work in General Linguistics"; other key writings on the issue include, in addition to the books to be mentioned later, his review of Jespersen (1922), "Linguistics as a Science" (1930), "Linguistic Aspects of Science" (1935); "Language or Ideas?" (1936), the monograph *Linguistic Aspects of Science* (1939), "Philosophical Aspects of Language" (1942), and the latter part of "Secondary and Tertiary Responses to Language" (1944).

Bloomfield insisted that science must be empirical ("the only useful generalizations about language are inductive generalizations," 1933, p. 10), that it is cumulative, and that it is not its own justification: "We have acquired understanding and the power of prediction and control and have reaped vast benefit in the domains where we have developed non-animistic and non-teleologic science. We remain ignorant and helpless in the domains where we have failed to develop that kind of science, namely, in human affairs" (1944). But he saw in our small body of reliable information about language an exception to the stricture, and hoped that it might point the way to greater objectivity and success in the examination and management of other aspects of human life.

In his search to understand "the place of language in the universe," Bloomfield first mastered the achievements of his predecessors. He knew Indo-European well, and spoke as a specialist on several of its branches (Indic, Greek, Germanic, Slavic). In 1914 this led to a book, *An Introduction to the Study of Language*, intended to cover all the reliable findings of linguistics. It turned out, however, that the empirical basis was too narrow and the approach faulty.

Finding the accounts of "exotic" languages by missionaries and travelers largely unusable, Bloomfield sought opportunities to deal with some of them directly. He worked with a speaker of Tagalog (Philippines) in Urbana (results published 1917); this was his baptism in field methods, and the context of his discovery of the phonemic principle, also discovered about the same time by several others. The phonemic principle is the recognition that, although in our speaking we produce all manner of sounds that a trained ear can identify, only certain distinctions among the sounds are heeded by the users of any one language, and are thus communicatively relevant for them, other audible effects being due to diverse momentary extraneous factors. Thus, although all languages use the same vocal apparatus, each has its own *sound system,* determinable only through empirical study.

After Tagalog, Bloomfield examined the reports on Algonquian, and eventually did field work with three languages of this aboriginal North American family. *The Menomini Language* (1962) is among the handful of truly thorough language descriptions we have, and the comparative Algonquian sketch of 1946 (replacing his preliminary version of 1925) is an exemplar.

In his 1914 book, Bloomfield had assumed that linguistics must rest on psychology, and had therefore turned to what he understood to be the most reliable psychological theory then available: that of Wilhelm Wundt. Subsequently, through careful restudy of the Wundt-Delbrück debate of 1901 (see Bloomfield, 1933, p. 18; Esper, 1968, pp. 15-81) and, more pointedly, through his close association at Ohio State with the psychologist Albert P. Weiss, he came to realize that the methods and findings of linguistics are quite independent of any particular psychological theory.

His empirical base thus broadened and his approach liberated, Bloomfield issued, in 1933, the integrated treatise *Language,* which has not yet been superseded. He covers all the positive findings of students of language from the ancient Hindu, Greek, and Roman scholars, through the medieval grammarians, through the philosophical-descriptive and historical-comparative traditions of the nineteenth century, to the ongoing researches of his contemporaries. He describes first how language can be studied fruitfully, then how languages work, then how they change with the passage of time, and finally, in brief and modest fashion, the areas of possible practical application of the accumulated knowledge. There are some errors of detail, none of broad perspective. (The one major flaw is technical and hidden: under close scrutiny, his version of the phonemic principle proves incompatible with his unimpeachable interpretation of regularity of sound change in language history.)

Bloomfield's greatest discovery, made jointly with Weiss, is not fully presented in the 1933 book. Forerunners (see Esper) had suspected that in the analysis of human conduct it is as useless and misleading to speak of a non-physical "mind" as it is, in discussing light, to posit a "luminiferous aether." Bloomfield and Weiss argued, not through philosophical speculation but with the empirical tools of science, that this is so—but *only if language is taken into account*. A linguistically naïve monism or physicalism is as impotent as any dualism: it cannot explain the differences between human behavior and that of other animals. Determining "the place of language in the universe" thus carries us a long way toward understanding man's place in nature.

The impact of Bloomfield's work cannot yet be fully assessed. The marked improvement of foreign-language instruction in the United States in the 1950's and 1960's surely owed much to his stimulus. On the other hand, thirty-odd years after his germinal research, the sorts of materials he recommended for teaching children to read are still not used in our schools. And his hard-won and plainly expressed objective views on the nature of language and its role in human affairs have been overshadowed by alternative approaches and fads; it is too early to say whether that is temporary or will constitute a tragic permanent failure of science to be cumulative.

[*A Leonard Bloomfield Anthology* (1970) reprints many articles and reviews from his pen (including all those cited above), a complete bibliography of his writings, reviews of his work by others, obituaries, and extensive biographical data. Tagalog: *Tagalog Texts with Grammatical Analysis* (*Univ. of Illinois Studies in Language and Literature*, vol. 3, Nos. 2–4, 1917). Teaching reading: (with Clarence L. Barnhart) *Let's Read: A Linguistic Approach* (1961). By other authors: Albert P. Weiss, *A Theoretical Basis of Human Behavior* (1925; rev. ed., 1929); Erwin A. Esper, *Mentalism and Objectivism in Linguistics* (1968).]

CHARLES F. HOCKETT

BOARDMAN, MABEL THORP (Oct. 12, 1860–Mar. 17, 1946), Red Cross leader, was born in Cleveland, Ohio. Both her parents, William Jarvis Boardman and Florence (Sheffield) Boardman, had distinguished antecedents. William Boardman, a wealthy Ohio businessman and lawyer, numbered among his ancestors Gov. William Bradford of Plymouth Colony; John Mason, colonial soldier and Indian fighter; and Elijah Boardman, Revolutionary soldier and senator from Connecticut, whose son immigrated to Ohio's Western Reserve. Mabel's mother was the daughter of the wealthy New Haven merchant Joseph Earl Sheffield, benefactor of the Sheffield Scientific School at Yale. Mabel Boardman, the first of three daughters and three sons, studied and traveled in Europe after attending private schools in Cleveland and New York. From 1889-1893 she lived in Germany, where she enjoyed the social life of the kaiser's court as the guest of her uncle William Walter Phelps, United States minister to Germany. On her return she settled in Washington, D.C. In Cleveland she had done volunteer work at the Children's Day Nursery, and in Washington she served on the board of Children's Hospital. During the Spanish-American War she recruited army nurses.

At this time public confidence in the American Red Cross was at an ebb; charges were rife of unbusinesslike management by the dedicated but aging founder Clara Barton. When in 1900 the Red Cross received a formal federal charter, Boardman's name appeared on the list of incorporators—without, she always said, her consent. She nevertheless assumed an active role. Accepting membership on the executive committee, she studied foreign Red Cross societies and concluded that further changes in the American association were necessary. Weak in organization and operation, it had never established branches throughout the country. Complaints persisted, moreover, that Barton made important decisions without consulting her executive committee and received disaster funds directly rather than through the treasurer. A struggle for control ensued, with one side loyally supporting Barton and the other moving forward under Boardman's leadership. Barton won the first round, but President McKinley's death removed a strong supporter and brought into office a new president, Theodore Roosevelt, whose sister Anna (Roosevelt) Cowles was in the Boardman camp. Early in 1903 Roosevelt withdrew government support from the Red Cross, and the conflict broke into the public realm. After a complex series of maneuvers, victory went to the proponents of change. Barton retired gracefully, and Congress in 1905 enacted a new organizational structure under which Boardman emerged as the dominant figure, with her good friend William Howard Taft as the society's president. The Red Cross was now a quasi-governmental organization; the president of the United States appointed the chairman as well as five members of the eighteen-member central committee. The society's financial records, moreover, were audited by the War Department.

Although Boardman was unwilling to accept either the presidency or the central committee chairmanship ("The public," she explained, "has more confidence in men executives"), her control until 1917 was as complete as that of her predecessor. Both the central committee and its steering group, the executive committee, accepted her recommendations as a matter of course. Even her nominal superior, Taft, remarked, "She is not the president—she is not the chairman—she *is* the Red Cross." Again like her predecessor, Boardman never married and made the Red Cross the focal point of her time and energy. An important difference was her refusal to participate personally in relief efforts; her place, she believed, was in Washington organizing resources. Another difference was the emphasis that Boardman placed upon leadership by the socially elite as a means of inspiring public confidence.

Termed the "administrative genius" of the Red Cross, Boardman transformed a society that had scarcely existed between disasters into a continuing national organization. She was indefatigable in her efforts; as unpaid secretary she worked with untiring zeal at her Washington desk and faithfully attended meetings of the executive committee, on which she held continuous membership until 1918. Her intensive campaign and success in obtaining a permanent endowment fund put the society on a sound financial basis. Boardman created or improved the Red Cross life-saving, first-aid, and nursing services—the latter through a fruitful affiliation with the American Nurses' Association. In 1908 she adopted a suggestion for an antituberculosis Christmas seal project, which, after a decade of successful sales through Red Cross volunteers, was turned over to the National Tuberculosis Association. Several times she served as delegate to international Red Cross conferences, and after the Russo-Japanese War she toured Japan, where the nation's four million Red Cross members inspired her to build a national organization that would rival foreign societies. Moving from a one-room office to quarters in the War Department provided by Taft and then in 1913 to temporary larger accommodations, Boardman launched a campaign for adequate permanent headquarters. She obtained a federal appropriation matched by private contributions, and in 1917 saw the opening of the Red Cross's massive "marble palace" on a block of federal land. When the society outgrew this building, she raised funds for a larger structure behind the first. In 1930 she was similarly successful in financing the construction of a fine building for the District of Columbia chapter.

An advisory role was impossible for Boardman; she expected her instructions to be followed to the letter. Apparently unable to delegate responsibility, she handled matters down to the finest detail. In accepting the new position of central committee vice-chairman in 1915, Eliot Wadsworth did so on condition of "freedom from domination of one not having express authority." It was not until the United States entered World War I, however, that Boardman's control faded. The wartime crisis produced a sudden expansion in membership as well as a flood of offers from eager volunteers. Neither an overwhelmed headquarters staff nor the society's financial resources seemed adequate to meet the emergency. Duplications and delays, moreover, resulted from lack of any clear definition of officers' functions. At Wadsworth's request President Wilson called a meeting of leading businessmen and bankers, and as a result of this conference a new group assumed control. The central committee temporarily delegated its executive committee's authority to a war council, the chairmanship of which went to a member of the J. P. Morgan banking firm, Henry P. Davison. Boardman was relegated, as the *Washington Post* later put it, to the society's "shadowy background." At the close of the war the new group's influence led to President Wilson's appointment of Livingston Farrand as the executive committee's first salaried chairman, and Taft, who resigned, failed to achieve Boardman's appointment to the executive committee. The aim of the Red Cross was thenceforth professional social work.

Boardman briefly turned her considerable energies to another quarter. In 1920 she accepted President Wilson's appointment to a term on the three-member District of Columbia Board of Commissioners, the first woman to be appointed to the District's governing body. Given charge of the area's charitable institutions, she visited them all personally. By 1921, however, she was back on the Red Cross executive committee as national secretary. At the 1922 convention she took a strong stand against the trend toward professional leadership and against the professionals' view that the society should engage in social welfare work in the intervals between emergencies. She was destined to lose; soon afterward the central committee stated unequivocally that while military and disaster aid were primary concerns, the nursing and family welfare programs would continue.

Boardman now carried her conviction regarding the importance of volunteer leadership into a new Red Cross project, the Volunteer Service, later renamed Volunteer Special Services, of which she became director in 1923. Her purpose was to maintain specific volunteer community services and to keep volunteers trained through regular activity for prompt disaster service. Successful applicants, drawn primarily from the ranks of the social elite, pledged a minimum number of hours to their chosen service. Of the nine corps that were established, the Gray Ladies, serving in veterans' hospitals, and the Nurses's Aides became especially well-known. Upon her retirement from the directorship of the Volunteer Special Services in 1940, the membership roll totaled 2,720,000.

A tall, impressive figure with a broad, firm mouth and lively blue eyes, Boardman carried herself with "majestic dignity." She was described as "straight as a ramrod, and at ease, but with a touch of military tension." Fashionably dressed and fond of jewelry, she wore her hair in a pompadour reminiscent of the 1890's and pinned a hat atop it in Victorian style. Her appearance bore such a marked resemblance to the dowager Queen Mary of England that the former Prince of Wales, seeing her in 1919, was startled into comment on it. She entertained graciously in her spacious Washington mansion; an invitation to her home was almost as significant in Washington social circles as an invitation to the White House.

Continuing as national secretary and central committee member, Boardman directed relief projects during World War II until her retirement in December 1944, at which time she was awarded the Red Cross's first Distinguished Service Medal. During her forty-five years of service she also received many other awards, including decorations from foreign governments and honorary degrees from Yale, Western Reserve, and George Washington universities and Smith College. In 1946, at eighty-five, she died of a coronary thrombosis at her Washington home. An Episcopalian and a member of Washington's St. John's Church, she was buried at the National Cathedral.

[Mabel Boardman's papers are at the Lib. of Cong. The library of the Am. Red Cross headquarters in Washington, D.C., has articles and clippings by and about her, as well as a 49-volume series of unpublished monographs on the history of the Am. Red Cross; particularly useful are chap. iv of vol. II, all of vol. III, and portions of vol. IV, all by Gustave R. Gaeddert. Foster Rhea Dulles based his useful *The Am. Red Cross: A Hist.* (1950) on this monograph series. See also two personal accounts by Ernest P. Bicknell, a close associate of Boardman—*Pioneering with the Red Cross* (1935) and *In War's Wake, 1914-1915* (1936)—and Boardman's *Under the Red Cross Flag at Home and Abroad* (1915), a brief account of the society's origin and development. Charlotte Goldthwaite, *Boardman Genealogy, 1525-1895* (1895), gives the family background.]

MARY R. DEARING

BOND, CARRIE JACOBS (Aug. 11, 1862-Dec. 28, 1946), composer of popular songs, was born in Janesville, Wis., the only child of Hannibal Cyrus Jacobs and Mary Emogene (Davis) Jacobs, both natives of Vermont. When Hannibal Jacobs, a prosperous dealer in grain and produce, lost his business and died in 1873, Carrie and her mother moved into a Janesville hotel owned by Mrs. Jacobs' father. Educated in the local Episcopal school, Carrie early displayed musical talent, being able to pick out and harmonize on the piano tunes that she had heard. At nine she could play by ear a recognizable version of Liszt's popular Hungarian Rhapsody no. 2. Between the ages of nine and seventeen, she took piano lessons with local teachers ("the sort one would find in a town like Janesville fifty years ago," she later wrote), but never received any training in music theory.

On Dec. 25, 1880, in Racine, Wis., she married Edward J. Smith, who worked in a local men's clothing store. One child, Fred Jacobs Smith, was born seven months later on July 23, 1881. The couple separated in 1887 and were divorced the next year. On June 10, 1889, Carrie married a childhood friend, Frank Lewis Bond, a physician considerably older than she. They moved to Iron River, a mining town in northern Michigan. These were happy years for Carrie Jacobs Bond, whose creative talent was encouraged by her second husband, but they were ended by Dr. Bond's financial collapse in 1893 and his accidental death early in 1895. Nearly impoverished but faced with the need to support herself and her son, she decided to market her talent. Several months before her husband's death she had traveled to Chicago and there managed to publish two of her songs. Now, after a short stay in Janesville (where she composed "I Love You Truly," later to become one of her most popular efforts), she moved with her son into a Chicago rooming house.

In the decade after 1895 Bond employed every opportunity to popularize her songs. Initially she sold them to a local publisher for royalties, but she quickly came to see that "nothing much could be accomplished till I had created a very real demand for my music."

To create such a demand she began to perform her songs in private parlor recitals and public concerts and even to publish them herself and peddle them to Chicago stores. All the while she cultivated a widening circle of increasingly influential friends who provided her with crucial assistance. As her hometown obituary later put it, Bond "had the faculty of making contacts that led to recognition." In 1901, aided by a loan from contralto Jessie Bartlett Davis, she published a collection, *Seven Songs as Unpretentious as the Wild Rose,* including "I Love You Truly" and "Just a-Wearyin' for You." Shortly afterward she set up the Bond Shop as her business headquarters in one of the two rooms she now occupied with her son, who now became her business manager. At about the same time she began to perform outside Chicago. Several friends arranged in her behalf a testimonial concert attended by Illinois governor Richard Yates. On the invitation of the author Elbert Hubbard she went east; another friend arranged a trip to England, where she performed at a parlor recital on the same program with the then relatively unknown Enrico Caruso; the actress Margaret Anglin arranged three recitals in New York City in 1906 and 1907. This phase of Bond's career crested when some of her "kind friends" won her an invitation to sing for President Theodore Roosevelt at the White House.

Despite such successes, her music did not sell well, and by 1906 Bond found herself deeply in debt. This discovery led to a brief period of physical and emotional collapse—she had long considered herself an "invalid"—that was relieved by a substantial investment loan from an old family friend. Bond paid off her debts, moved the Bond Shop to a fashionable location, and incorporated as Carrie Jacobs Bond and Son. At this same time her music caught on for the first time with the piano-owning public. By 1910 she was wealthy enough to travel around the world and to move to Hollywood, Calif., where she had previously wintered for reasons of health. She also built a mountain retreat, Nestorest, near San Diego. In 1910 her creative career climaxed with the composition of the song with which her name became chiefly connected, "The End of a Perfect Day." Employing the image of a beautiful sunset to suggest the parting of "dear friends" at "the end of a journey," with a hint of death and eventual reunion, this song appeared at what Bond herself called "*the* psychological moment." Popularized as

were many of her songs by the baritone David Bispham, its fame and resonance were heightened during World War I, when it took on a special poignancy for American soldiers (for whom Bond occasionally sang it at training camps) and their families. By the early 1920's "A Perfect Day" had sold more than five million copies, along with phonograph records and piano rolls.

Carrie Jacobs Bond's very popularity, along with the more cynical ambience of the postwar years, subjected her to a critical scrutiny and even ridicule she had always feared, since "A Perfect Day" was also a perfect vehicle for parody. In her autobiography, *The Roads of Melody,* published in 1927 after serialization in the *Ladies' Home Journal,* Bond tried to deal with this ridicule. While she flatly denied rumors that she did not compose her own accompaniments and even that she could not read music at all, she did acknowledge that it was "difficult" for her to write out her own songs and that for most of her career she dictated them to a professional musician. She also acknowledged the "lurking feeling" that she "ought to have done better things" and insisted that hers was "a greater talent than the world knows anything about." At times she attributed this failure to the fact that economic pressure had forced her to write "little songs that would sell." At other points she ascribed it to the fact that nobody in provincial Janesville had recognized the need to provide her with technical training in theory. But in the end Bond tried to make a virtue of her lack of cultivation—just as she had done in the double-edged title of her first collection, *Songs as Unpretentious as the Wild Rose.* She insisted, "I had my gift—and my music did not need correction."

Carrie Jacobs Bond continued to compose until the end of her life—there were some 400 songs in all, of which about 170 got published—but "A Perfect Day" was her last big success. Mrs. Bond's music was written to be played and sung rather than simply listened to, and the slow ebbing of her popularity after 1920 can be attributed in part to the fact that parlor pianos (and the decadent form of chamber music they represented) were being replaced at this time by phonograph records and radios as domestic music gradually became a spectator sport in middle-class households. In these years Bond began to write books. Besides her autobiography and numerous magazine pieces, she published three children's volumes and a collection of miscellanies, *The End of the*

Road (1940). A final tragedy of her life was the suicide in 1928 of her son. She spent the last decade of her life in semiretirement in California and died at eighty-four of heart failure following a cerebral hemorrhage. She was buried in Forest Lawn Memorial Park, Glendale, where she is honored with a plaque bearing a tribute from Herbert Hoover.

[In addition to Bond's autobiography, the most useful sources are William Lichtenwanger's biography in *Notable Am. Women,* I (1971) and the obituary in the *Janesville Daily Gazette,* Dec. 30, 1946. See also the articles by Neil M. Clark in *Am. Mag.,* Jan. 1924; Dorothy Walworth in *Independent Woman,* Nov. 1945; and the anonymous biography in *Music Jour.,* Sept. 1955. Of additional interest is Bond's "Music Composition as a Field for Women," *Etude,* Sept. 1920. A sketch in *Billboard,* Jan. 22, 1949, contains a list of her works.]

STEPHEN NISSENBAUM

BOOTH, EVANGELINE CORY (Dec. 25, 1865-July 17, 1950), Salvation Army general, was born in the London suburb of Hackney, the seventh of the three sons and five daughters of William Booth and Catherine (Mumford) Booth, founders of the Salvation Army. Christened Evelyne, she was called Eva after Harriet Beecher Stowe's seraphic heroine; her middle name honored the brothers Cory, early supporters of General Booth, whose Methodistic gospel Thomas Huxley derided as "corybantic Christianity." The comfortable but conscientiously plain and strict Booth home was a combination nursery, seminary, and general headquarters, where all activities and thoughts centered on the battle for souls and the Booths' part in that battle. Discipleship is the key to Eva Booth's life. She revered her mother, whose feminism had a distinctly pietistic source, as the embodiment of energetic yet self-effacing womanhood. Her father was, after his fashion, one of the most eminent Victorians, brimming with nervous energy and great plans —nearly all of which came to fruition. He was an emotional, even hypnotic preacher, and a dyspeptic, who once sighed, "What a worrying thing 'Booth blood' is." The children were tutored at home, where they played at being revivalists, and early assumed serious Army responsibilities.

Eva became a sergeant at fifteen, selling the *War Cry* on the streets. At seventeen, assigned to the Marylebone district, she learned first-hand how the poor lived by donning a disguise and working as a flower girl. Her musical talent was put to service in composing Army hymns, of which the best known is "The World for God." Her field work came to an end when she was placed in charge of the International Training College—a sort of grammar school and induction center—and was made field comissioner of the home counties. Only twenty-three, she had proved herself the equal of her older brothers and sisters.

Before the century was out, some of the Booths became schismatics. The death in 1890 of Catherine Booth may have contributed to the weakening of family bonds. Six years later Eva's brother Ballington, the American commander, and his wife, Maud Ballington Booth, broke away to form the Volunteers of America. Eva, now calling herself Evangeline, had been dispatched to the United States to prevent the rupture. She arrived too late, but prevented further erosion during the interim between Ballington's defection and his replacement by their sister Emma Moss Booth-Tucker as joint commander, with her husband, of the American forces. Evangeline then became field commander of Canada (1896), reorganizing headquarters in Toronto, taking Army contingents to the Klondike gold rush, and missionizing the Alaskan Indians. In 1902 two other members of the Booth family cut their ties to the Army. A year later Emma Booth-Tucker died. Her husband was too prostrated to continue, and in 1904 the office of American commander-in-chief passed to Evangeline, who filled the role with decision and imagination.

By this time the Army had carved out a secure niche as a relief agency and city missions operation; the years of bitter and sometime violent opposition were past. Evangeline, like Ballington before her, increased the independence of the American Salvation Army. She greatly expanded its institutional structure, building training colleges, orphanages, rescue missions, shelters for the homeless and intemperate, homes for the aged, infirmaries, and hospitals. When the earthquake struck San Francisco in 1906 she personally supervised disaster relief there. San Quentin State Prison received an Army mission that worked to rehabilitate its inmates. Immigrants were also enlisted under the Army banner, with special Russian, Italian, and Chinese corps in major cities. With characteristic Army flair and without mincing words, Booth commanded "sieges" to convert special groups by campaigns such as Notorious Sinners and Drunkards' Week.

As in England, the Army caught the public imagination and became a highly popular philanthropy, applauded by politicians and churchmen alike. Commander Booth's tremendous achievements and her very evident popularity forced her brother Bramwell, their father's successor as general, to waive the Army's rotation rule, and she held the American command for thirty years. World War I saw American Salvationists accept official designation as a denomination, something the movement had long avoided. Booth was awarded the Distinguished Service Medal in 1919 for her own and the Salvation Army's services to the troops in France and in the war effort generally. The Salvation Army underwent other important changes under her command. Booth had long considered the mendicant aspect of the Army a too quaint and wasteful use of personnel; she abolished street begging and established a national fund-raising apparatus in its stead. She divided the American command into four territories and, while consolidating gains in the rest of the country, launched an assault on the deep South. In 1923 she became a United States citizen, thus formalizing her profound attachment to the country she felt was her real home.

On two issues she was especially outspoken: woman suffrage and teetotalism. She advocated the first, but was not a militant. She enlisted the Army behind the second, and in fact linked the two reforms. Efforts to repeal prohibition she characterized as "a fight on the part of the selfish few to reimpose the subjection of innumerable women and children to a masculine indulgence in liquor, medieval and degrading as the veil and purdah" (*To Be or Not To Be*, temperance pamphlet, 1930, p. 24). Political issues were otherwise avoided by the Salvationists, and while complex social issues were treated in an emotionally charged, moralistic fashion, the emphasis was always on reclaiming and fellowshipping, not merely denouncing, the sinner and his corrupters. As the twentieth century wore on, the Army's origins in the Methodist holiness movement were played down, and the social relief operations burgeoned to a point where remaining Army peculiarities—the uniforms, brass bands, and Christmas kettles—became largely symbolic to the American public.

The deposition in 1929 of Bramwell Booth climaxed a long and painful struggle over succession to the Salvation Army generalship, in which Evangeline Booth sided with her brother's opponents. In 1934 she was elected general, succeeding Edward J. Higgins. Returning to England, she was an effective, tireless supervisor of the Army's global operations. Upon her retirement in 1939 her home in Hartsdale, N.Y., and her Lake George cottage reclaimed her, and she remained active, athletic, and concerned for others well into old age. She

died of coronary thrombosis at Hartsdale at the age of eighty-four and was buried in Kensico Cemetery, Valhalla, N.Y. No one knew better than Evangeline Booth that the Salvation Army was born of and nurtured by a family of powerful and often contentious personalities. She also believed that the Army had a special mission that transcended these origins. Of this larger role she wrote: "Wherever human life is in moral peril, wherever the human mind is contemplating self-destruction, wherever material circumstances have extinguished the last spark of hope, there is our mission of service. . . . We are . . . a revolutionary force in religion."

[Philip W. Wilson's authorized biography, *Gen. Evangeline Booth* (1948), is the fullest source, and less hagiographical than other publications by the Army or its officers. A good short treatment is the article by Herbert A. Wisbey, Jr., in *Notable Am. Women*, I, 204–207. On the family, see Harold Begbie, *Life of William Booth*, 2 vols. (1920), and St. John Ervine, *God's Soldier*, 2 vols. (1934). The most useful histories of the Army are Herbert A. Wisbey, Jr., *Soldiers Without Swords* (1955) and the official *Hist. of the Salvation Army*, 4 vols. (1964–1968) of which the last volume, by Arch Wiggins, treats the period of Evangeline Booth's generalship. Bernard Watson, *A Hundred Years' War* (1964), describes the current work of the Army. Grace Livingston Hill co-authored Evangeline Booth's chatty account of the Army's World War I service, *The War Romance of the Salvation Army* (1919). Other books by Evangeline Booth are *Love is All* (1908), a collection of essays; *Toward A Better World* (1928), a volume of sermons; *Songs of the Evangel* (1927), a collection of her hymn compositions.]

MARIE CASKEY

BOWES, EDWARD J. (June 14, 1874– June 13, 1946), real estate entrepreneur, theater owner, conductor of the popular radio program "Major Bowes' Amateur Hour," was born in San Francisco. He was the oldest of three children and the only son of John M. and Caroline Amelia (Ford) Bowes; the family also included four children by his mother's previous marriage. Both parents were of Irish stock, the mother having been born in Ireland, the father in Illinois. A public cargo weigher, John Bowes was killed in an accident on the San Francisco docks in 1880. To help support the family, Edward left school at the age of thirteen and went to work as an office boy in a real estate firm.

San Francisco was enjoying remarkable growth, and Bowes was quick to sense the opportunity for profit. By the early years of the twentieth century he had built up a flourishing real estate enterprise and was a prominent member of the city's business community. A close friend of Fremont Older, reformist editor of the *San Francisco Bulletin*, Bowes was named in 1904 to the grand jury chosen to investigate the graft-ridden regime of Mayor Eugene E. Schmitz and the political boss Abraham Ruef. As chairman of the jury's police committee, Bowes provided Older with evidence for his crusade against corruption; and with Older he carried out the audacious kidnapping of Chan Cheng, a Chinatown vice lord, in order to compel his appearance before the grand jury. Bowes also served as the editor's handpicked representative on the Republican League, an organization formed to solidify the fusion coalition which in 1905 sought unsuccessfully to unseat Mayor Schmitz. It was a subsequent grand jury, however, in 1906, which returned indictments against Ruef, Schmitz, and several traction executives, including Patrick Calhoun.

Although Bowes lost most of his real estate holdings in the San Francisco earthquake of 1906, he began rebuilding immediately and soon recouped his fortune. His career, however, entered a new phase with his marriage on Nov. 14, 1909, to Margaret Illington, an actress recently divorced from the theatrical producer Daniel Frohman. Besides taking over the active management of his wife's career, Bowes discovered a way to combine his business acumen with his love of the theater. Moving east, he joined John Cort and Peter McCourt in buying and operating the Cort Theatre in New York City and the Park Square Theatre in Boston. In 1918 he became a partner in the construction of the Capitol Theatre, one of New York's earliest movie "palaces," and assumed the post of managing director. In 1922 he was also named a vice-president of Goldwyn Pictures Corporation, and he retained that office with the formation two years later of Metro-Goldwyn-Mayer, with which the Capitol Theatre became affiliated.

Bowes's radio career grew out of his association with the Capitol, which in 1922 became the home of "Roxy and His Gang," a weekly variety and audience-participation broadcast conducted by Samuel L. Rothafel. Bowes took over the program in 1925 and, using the army reserve title he had gained as an entertainment specialist during World War I, renamed it "Major Bowes' Capitol Family." While retaining the basic format, he punctuated the show's proceedings with his own brand of homely wisdom and sentimentality. Bowes next began to consider a radio showcase for amateur talent. In 1934, after becoming manager of station WHN (owned by Metro-Goldwyn-Mayer), he inaugurated "Major Bowes' Amateur Hour." The show proved an instant success. Resigning

from M-G-M the following year, he assured the "Amateur Hour" network distribution by moving it first to NBC and then, in 1936, to CBS, where it was sponsored by the Chrysler Corporation.

In the midst of the depression, the "Amateur Hour" offered the hope of instant stardom to the thousands of would-be contestants who flocked to New York for an audition. A warning in 1935 by the New York Emergency Relief Bureau that each week 300 such hopefuls were stranded in the city led to the establishment of regional auditions. It was occasionally charged that despite the amateur "oath" required of the performers, many out-of-work professionals auditioned in order to get the $10 stipend paid to all contestants and the minimum of $50 per week received by the winners who were sent on tour. For the program's huge radio audience, the weekly parade of talent—a hodgepodge of operatic sopranos, mimics, tap dancers, and the inevitable players of jugs, saws, and "bones"— was heralded by the unctuous voice of Bowes announcing: "The wheel of fortune goes 'round and 'round and where she stops nobody knows." The "Amateur Hour" was produced before a live audience, and the votes of radio listeners were recorded by banks of telephone operators.

A keen judge of talent, Bowes participated directly in the selection of contestants. On the air his manner ranged from folksy to gruff, and he often exchanged acidulous wisecracks with the performers. His familiar "All right, all right," to spur the show along, became a national catchphrase. Adapting the principle of the vaudeville "hook," he used a gong to toll a merciful end to failing acts. Yet Bowes was genuinely sympathetic to real talent, and his show launched the careers of many new performers, including the opera singers Rosa Ponselle, John Charles Thomas, and Clyde Barrie. Because its format was widely imitated, the "Amateur Hour" eventually added the word "Original" to its title.

A heavy-set man with "orange-blond" hair and a prominent nose, Bowes enjoyed the monetary fruits of his success. His income, from radio shows, tours, and movie features, was estimated in 1939 to be as high as $35,000 a week. He dressed stylishly, owned a stable of racehorses, and employed four chefs at his homes in New York City and Rumson, N.J. A collector of books, wines, and art, he enjoyed sailing his sixty-one-ton yacht Edmar, which in 1940 he turned over to the United States Navy. His many philanthropies included lavish gifts to his own Roman Catholic church and the donation of a Westchester County estate for a retreat to the Lutheran church. In ill health for some time, Bowes retired from radio in 1945. He died of arteriosclerotic heart disease at his Rumson estate on the eve of his seventy-second birthday. After services at New York's St. Patrick's Cathedral, he was buried in Sleepy Hollow Cemetery, Tarrytown, N.Y. His wife had died twelve years earlier, and he had no children. He left the bulk of his $4.5 million estate to charity.

[Information supplied by the Calif. State Lib., Sacramento, including census data, was helpful on Bowes's family background. His California career is touched on briefly in Fremont Older, *My Own Story*, new ed. (1926), and Walton Bean, *Boss Ruef's San Francisco* (1952). Aspects of his later career are treated in Ray D. Porter, "From Amateur to Star," *Delineator* (Dec. 1935); Francis Chase, Jr., *Sound and Fury: An Informal Hist. of Broadcasting* (1942), pp. 226–227; Gleason L. Archer, *Big Business and Radio* (1939); and articles in *Current Biog.*, 1941, and *Etude*, Dec. 1939. See also *Who Was Who in America*, II (1950); *Am. Catholic Who's Who*, 1942–1943; and *Internat. Motion Picture Almanac*, 1942–1943. A detailed obituary appears in the *N.Y. Times*, June 14, 1946. Other useful newspaper items are in the *N.Y. Times*, Oct. 29, 1939, Apr. 22, 1945, July 2 and Nov. 2, 1946; and the *San Francisco Chronicle*, Aug. 25, 1935, June 14, 1946. Death record from N.J. Dept. of Health.]

PHILIP DE VENCENTES

BOWMAN, ISAIAH (Dec. 26, 1878-Jan. 6, 1950), geographer and university president, was born in Waterloo, Ontario, Canada, the third of eight children and elder of two sons of Samuel Cressman Bowman, a farmer and former teacher, and Emily (Shantz) Bowman. His paternal ancestors, originally named Baumann, had left southeast Germany, probably in 1689, and come to Ontario via brief settlement in the Netherlands and the eastern Appalachians. His father was a farmer and was seeking land in eastern Michigan when Isaiah was born. In February 1879 Isaiah was transported in a horse-drawn sleigh to a log cabin near Brown City, where the family managed a 140-acre farm. He attended the one-room school located on the farm grounds and lived the simple farm life, knowing its hours, demands, and rewards. This spirit of earnest and hard work, facilitated by a good physique, characterized his lifework, along with his enthusiastic, imaginative curiosity, self-reliance, and articulateness.

In 1896 Bowman began teaching in the rural schools of St. Clair County, Mich., for $15 a month. There he heard Charles T. McFarlane of the Michigan State Normal College, "giving his enthusiastic speeches on geography." During the next three years he attended summer institutes and in 1900-1901 enrolled as a full-

time student at Ferris Institute (Big Rapids, Mich.), where he studied under one of McFarlane's students, Harlan H. Barrows. In 1901 he enrolled at the Normal College in Ypsilanti, but was disappointed to learn that McFarlane had been called to the New York State Normal School at Brockport. Mark S. W. Jefferson had taken McFarlane's post, so Bowman studied geography under Jefferson. He studied local rivers with his mentor and they became good friends. Many years later, on Mar. 16, 1949, Bowman wrote to his former teacher:

When I went to the State Normal College in 1901 you were to me an altogether extraordinary person because of the range of your experience and interests and a certain sophistication which these had brought. We all felt stimulated by your lectures and were aided by your broad point of view. The most important single event of that first year was your suggestion that I go to Harvard and study under [William Morris] Davis.

After studying under Jefferson, 1901-1902, Bowman took a year's work at Harvard under William Morris Davis, 1902-1903; he than returned to Ypsilanti to teach alongside Jefferson, 1903-1904, accumulating enough savings to finance his senior year at Harvard, 1904-1905. Davis was then perhaps at the height of his career. Bowman elected all the work that he could from Davis, made Davisian "mud-pie models" to illustrate fluvial processes, and took breakfast with him on the days of Davis' lectures. In 1904 Bowman was appointed assistant to Davis and was also an assistant to Albrecht Penck when the latter gave the Lowell lectures at Harvard that same year. During his two years at Cambridge Bowman came to know students Henrie Baulig, James W. Goldthwait, Ellsworth Huntington, Vilhjalmur Stefansson, and Walter S. Tower. Goldthwait introduced Bowman both to the ocean, and to his sister Cora, whom Bowman married on June 28, 1909. They had three children, Walter Parker, Robert Goldthwait, and Olive.

Upon Bowman's graduation from Harvard in 1905, Davis placed him under Herbert E. Gregory at Yale, where he remained until 1915. There he worked in a department of geology that produced five presidents of the Association of American Geographers. His close associates were Herbert E. Gregory, Joseph Barrell, Charles Schuchert, Richard S. Lull, Edward S. Dana, and Ellsworth Huntington. He offered courses in physiography, physiography of the United States, physical and commercial geography, anthropogeography, principles of geography, political geography, the geography of North America, and the geography of South America. During the summers of 1903-1906 he studied water supply problems for the United States and Indiana state geological surveys, thereby gaining invaluable field experience and seeing much of the country. In his Yale years, Bowman participated in three expeditions to South America —1907, 1911, and 1913: he was leader of the first and third of these expeditions. *South America: A Geography Reader* (1915), *The Andes of Southern Peru* (1916), *Desert Trails of Atacama* (1924), and numerous articles were directly attributable to his South American experiences. He also wrote a textbook— *Forest Physiography: Physiography of the United States and Principles of Soils in Relation to Forestry* (1911)—for a course he was teaching in the Yale Forestry School; it was the first thorough treatment of the landforms of the United States. He was instructor, 1905-1909, but upon completion of his Ph.D. dissertation, "The Geography of the Central Andes," in 1909, he was promoted to assistant professor.

In 1915 Bowman was named director of the American Geographical Society. He redesigned the society's *Bulletin,* gave it a new title *(The Geographical Review),* provided a new format and a new direction for the publication, created a monograph series, and began *The Map of Hispanic America on the Scale of One to One Million,* which, when completed in 1945, consisted of 107 sheets extending to 320 square feet. He corresponded with geographers and explorers the world over, directly aided many of them, and indirectly aided many more. Byrd, Mawson, Riiser-Larsen, Ellsworth, Rasmussen, Stefansson, Forbes, Bartlett, and Finn Ronne were only some of those whose work he urged the society to support. When World War I broke out, he placed the society's facilities, including its large map collection, at the disposal of the government. When Woodrow Wilson asked Col. Edward M. House to organize data for the redrawing of European boundaries at the projected peace conference, the American Geographical Society became home to the "Inquiry." Approximately 150 experts worked at preparing base maps, block diagrams, and assembling data in flexible form, which was then transported to Paris. At the Peace Conference in Paris, Bowman was chief territorial specialist for the American delegation; he also served on a number of other commissions,

gained much valuable experience, and created many lasting friendships. After the war, inspired by the need for Americans to understand the international questions of the time, he wrote *The New World: Problems in Political Geography* (1921). The book went through four editions and was translated into French and Chinese. There was also a Braille edition, and a special reprinting was made for armed services training units studying the causes of World War II. As another result of his peace conference experience, Bowman became a founding member of the Council on Foreign Relations, serving from the beginning as one of the council's Board of Directors and on the editorial advisory board of its periodical *Foreign Affairs.*

Bowman was a prolific author (seventeen books and more than 170 articles) and notwithstanding his many and varied duties he wrote much of enduring worth. Especially noteworthy was his advocacy of, and contribution to, "a science of settlement." He made journeys in 1912 and 1921 to Montana and Oregon, to the Great Plains of Kansas and Nebraska in 1930, and to the northwest of Edmonton ("the fringe of the fringe") in 1932. *The Pioneer Fringe* (1931) was perhaps the most significant of his several contributions on the subject. He also wrote *Geography in Relation to the Social Sciences* (1934), an explanation of something of the nature and purpose of geography.

In 1935 Bowman accepted a call to the presidency of the Johns Hopkins University, serving until his retirement on Dec. 31, 1948. In the wake of the depression, he managed to lift the institution out of debt. After 1941 he helped deploy the institution's resources to serve the war effort. He continually insisted on a place of prominence for the graduate school and for research. He explained his academic posture in *A Design for Scholarship* (1936), a small volume of academic addresses. Some modifications to his thought on pedagogics, the place of research, and the role of the university were rendered in numerous addresses that followed and in several issues of the annual "Report of the President" to the university. *The Graduate School in American Democracy* (1939), the product of his own thought and correspondence with many administrators and scholars throughout the United States, remains a vital part of the literature on that subject.

With nazism emergent, a political refugee problem loomed. President Franklin D. Roosevelt frequently requested information from Bowman for his Advisory Committee on Political Refugees. During World War II, Bowman commuted from nearby Johns Hopkins to Washington once or twice a week to serve in the State Department as a special advisor to Secretary Cordell Hull, as a member of the political and policy committee of the department, and as chairman of its territorial committee. He was much involved in the "M Project" (M for migration), which task resembled somewhat his earlier work with the "Inquiry." He was a member of both the Stettinius Mission to London (1944) and the American delegation to the Dumbarton Oaks Conference on World Peace and Security, and he contributed to the plans for permanent world organization both privately in Washington and officially at the San Francisco Conference that founded the United Nations (1945); there he served as an advisor to the secretary of state and chairman of the group of advisors for the American delegation. Following retirement from Johns Hopkins University (1948), Bowman gave much of his time to the Economic Cooperation Administration, which left little time for the six books he had planned— "Who Are You?," "Where Do You Live?," "What Do You Do?," "How Do You Do?," "What Do You Say?," "What Do You Believe?" Essays on each had been commenced at the time of his death, in Baltimore, of a coronary occlusion.

Isaiah Bowman made substantial contributions as scholar and administrator to the development of twentieth century American geography. His accomplishment was recognized nationally and internationally: nine medals, seventeen honorary degrees, and thirteen memberships or corresponding memberships in national and international societies. He was president of the Association of American Geographers (1931); president of the International Geographical Union (1931-1934); chairman of the National Research Council (1933-1935); vice-chairman and director of the Science Advisory Board to President Roosevelt (1933-1935); vice-president of the National Academy of Sciences (1941-1945); president of the American Association for the Advancement of Science (1943). Bowman Bay in Baffin Island and Bowman Coast, Island, and Glacier in Antarctica were named respectively by explorers Putnam, Wilkins, Mawson, and Byrd.

[The papers of Isaiah Bowman are located in three places: the Am. Geog. Soc.; Johns Hopkins Univ.; and in a private holding of Robert Bowman. Useful secondary accounts include George A. Knadler's "Isaiah Bowman: Backgrounds of His Contribution to Thought" (Ph.D. diss., Indiana Univ., 1959); Lawrence E. Gelfand, The Inquiry: American Preparation for Peace 1917-1919 (1963); John K. Wright, Geography in the Making: The American Geographical Society, 1851-1951 (1952); and Geoffrey J. Martin, Mark Jefferson: Geographer (1968). A biography, The Life and Thought of Isaiah Bowman by Geoffrey Martin, is currently in progress. Useful obituaries and memoirs are John K. Wright and George F. Carter, "Isaiah Bowman, December 26, 1878–January 6, 1950," Nat. Acad. Sci., Biog. Memoirs, XXXIII (1959); Gladys M. Wrigley, "Isaiah Bowman," Geog. Rev., Jan. 1951; Am. Philosophical Soc. Year Book, 1951; and George F. Carter in Annals of the Assoc. of Am. Geographers, Dec. 1950, which contains a full bibliography of Bowman's writings.]

GEOFFREY J. MARTIN

BRACKETT, JEFFREY RICHARDSON (Oct. 20, 1860–Dec. 4, 1949), social work educator, was born in Quincy, Mass., the second son and only surviving child of Jeffrey Richardson Brackett, a merchant, and Sarah Cordelia (Richardson) Brackett. Both parents came of old New England families which had prospered in banking and trade. Orphaned at the age of sixteen when his parents died within six months of each other, young Jeffrey went to live at the home of a boyhood friend. A comfortable inheritance allowed him such later luxuries as a large yacht and a summer home on Penobscot Bay, but he was sensible about the use of his money. After graduating from Adams Academy, Quincy, in 1879, he entered Harvard, from which he received the A.B. degree in 1883. He next spent a year in study and travel in Europe, and then began graduate work in history and political science at Johns Hopkins University, where he wrote a dissertation on The Negro in Maryland: A Study of the Institution of Slavery (1889) and received the Ph.D. in 1889. On June 16, 1886, Brackett married Susan Katharine Jones, the daughter of a Virginia planter. They had no children.

Settling in Baltimore after receiving his doctorate, Brackett became interested in the work of the city's Charity Organization Society, founded in 1881 by President Daniel Coit Gilman of Johns Hopkins; and in the early 1890's, like a number of others at the university, he became a volunteer "friendly visitor" to the poor. From 1897 to 1904 he was chairman of the society's executive committee. From 1899 to 1904 he served also as lecturer on public aid, charity, and correction at Johns Hopkins.

The charity organization movement extolled the moral virtues of work over public home relief and prided itself on its "scientific" dedication to gathering individual data about the poor and helping them regain their self-sufficiency. Although Brackett accepted most of these principles, he was never a doctrinaire. As chairman of the executive committee of the Baltimore Central Relief Committee, a citizens' work project established during the 1893 depression, he came to see the need for closer cooperation between public and private charity. Individual casework alone, he declared, would not attack the "roots" of poverty, which lay in the "social economy of the time, in industrial conditions, lack of vocational training, social barriers and public apathy" (Hardwick, p. 28). In 1897, furthermore, he was chairman of a city committee which recommended reforms in the care of public dependents, and which resulted in the creation of a Board of Supervisors of City Charities. In 1900 Brackett was named the chairman of this board, as well as head of the Department of Charities and Correction, positions he held until 1904. He was chairman of the City Relief Committee after the great Baltimore fire of 1904. Brackett's leading role in the welfare movement was recognized when he was elected president of the influential National Conference of Charities and Correction (later the National Conference of Social Work, now the National Conference on Social Welfare) for the year 1904.

Perhaps Brackett's most important contribution was his consistent advocacy of formal training for professional social workers. Unlike some of his colleagues in the Baltimore Charity Organization Society—such as Mary E. Richmond and John M. Glenn—who stressed teaching the methodology of scientific charity, Brackett insisted on a broad academic program as a necessary foundation for professional training. In 1904, aided by members of the Boston Associated Charities, he organized the Boston School for Social Workers (later the Boston School of Social Work). Formed under the joint sponsorship of Harvard University (which withdrew in 1916) and Simmons College, this was the first such institution under university auspices and the first to offer full-time training combining academic and field work. As director until his retirement in 1920, Brackett worked closely with Boston's "progressive" welfare agencies. Zilpha Smith of the Boston Associated Charities was associate director of the school and Alice Higgins Lothrop lectured there. Brackett gave important guidance to the pioneering social service department established at the Massachusetts General Hospital under the leadership of Dr. Richard C. Cabot and in 1912 added a special second year at the School of Social Work for the training of medical social workers.

Both before and after his retirement, Brackett was active in other areas of social work. As a member of the Massachusetts State Board of Charity from 1906 to 1919 and subsequently of the advisory board of its successor, the Massachusetts Board of Public Welfare (1920-1934), he worked to modernize and professionalize public assistance, to improve the foster children program, and to transform state workhouses into infirmaries for the aged. Although his attempts to decentralize state welfare activities by opening district offices were defeated by political pressure, he helped secure passage of a state mother's aid law (1912) and an old-age assistance law (1931). Brackett was an incorporator of the American Red Cross in 1911 and chairman of the Boston Associated Charities in 1913. Although considering himself "a nonsectarian Christian," he served for many years as a vestryman of Trinity Church (Episcopal) in Boston, and was chairman of the Social Service Department of the Protestant Episcopal Diocese of Massachusetts from 1922 to 1929.

Brackett's first wife died in 1931, and on June 22, 1935, he married Louisa de Bernière Bacot, headmistress of St. Catherine's School for Girls in Richmond, Va. After living in Richmond for a time, they retired to her native home, Charleston, S.C. There Brackett died of an intestinal disorder. Following cremation, his ashes were buried in Mount Wollaston Cemetery, Quincy, Mass.

[The principal biographical source is Katharine D. Hardwick et al., *Jeffrey Richardson Brackett: "Everyday Puritan"* (privately printed, 1956), which includes a bibliography of his writings. See also: autobiographical statements in Harvard Class of 1883, *Thirtieth Anniversary Report* (1913) and *Fiftieth Anniversary Report* (1933); sketch by Ralph E. Pumphrey in Harry L. Lurie, ed., *Encyc. of Social Work* (1965); *Nat. Cyc. Am. Biog.*, XXXVIII, 515–516; *N.Y. Times* obituary, Dec. 6, 1949; and Roy Lubove, *The Professional Altruist: The Emergence of Social Work as a Career, 1880–1930* (1965). Death record from S.C. Bureau of Vital Statistics.]

         BLANCHE D. COLL

BRADFORD, ROARK WHITNEY WICKLIFFE (Aug. 21, 1896–Nov. 13, 1948), novelist, short story writer, and journalist, was born on his family's cotton plantation near the Mississippi River in Lauderdale County, Tenn., the eighth of the eleven children of Richard Clarence and Patricia Adelaide (Tillman) Bradford, both of whom were descended from families prominent in colonial and southern history. A well-to-do lawyer-planter, Richard Bradford not only supervised his plantation of six hundred acres, which was worked by about twenty Negro families, but was in the lumber business and was justice of the peace in his community.

Like all boys of his time and social status, Roark spent a gregarious childhood, mingling as freely with black children as with his brothers and sisters. In fact, he seems to have spent most of his boyhood with black companions, three in particular, Algie, Ed, and Sweet. With a hound dog named Rattler, the four boys wandered in the fields where the hands were picking cotton and visited in the Negro quarters. If young Roark showed any unusual intellectual curiosity, it was about the local Negro church and its minister, Uncle Wes Henning. Here, in addition to the songs and stories common in the fields and homes of the plantation blacks, he heard Uncle Wes's versions of biblical stories. Bradford's informal education in the world of the southern plantation, which was to become the basis of his literary career, was supplemented by instruction in a one-room local school, and later by a more substantial formal schooling in Halls, Tenn.

When the United States entered World War I, Bradford volunteered for service and, upon completing the officers' training program, was commissioned a first lieutenant in the U.S. Army Artillery Reserve and was assigned to Balboa, Canal Zone. He was ordered to France in October 1918, but the armistice was declared before he sailed. His further military service included duty as an instructor in military science and tactics at Mississippi Agricultural and Mechanical College. He was honorably discharged in 1920. Meanwhile, he had married Lydia Sehorn of Columbia, Miss. After her death several years later he married Mary Rose (Sciarra) Himler of Indianapolis, Ind. A son, Richard Roark, was born of this second marriage.

Bradford spent the years 1920-1926 as a journalist, working successively as a reporter on the *Atlanta Georgian,* the *Macon* (Ga.) *Telegraph,* and the *Lafayette* (La.) *Daily Advertiser,* and moved up in 1924, to night city editor on the *New Orleans Times-Picayune.* Although he was soon promoted to the editorship of the *Picayune*'s Sunday edition, Bradford decided in 1926 to attempt a new career as a free-lance writer.

While he was in Lafayette, La., Bradford again came into contact with an environment in which folk storytellers were prominent, in this case the Cajun raconteurs. In New Orleans he found himself back in touch with a Negro community—one more varied and richer in musicians, singers, preachers, and storytellers than he had known before—the world of Rampart Street and the Mississippi River front. One day he discovered an old Negro fishing with a line equipped with a spring alarm clock that sounded when a fish yanked on the line. He wrote a story based on the incident and sold it to the *New York World.* Encouraged by this success, he wrote a more ambitious story about Negro life, "Child of God," which was accepted by *Harper's* magazine and was awarded first prize in the O. Henry Memorial competition for 1927. Soon Bradford had written enough stories in a similar vein—tales that were essentially adaptations of biblical stories by uneducated Negroes —to make up the book *Ol' Man Adam an' His Chillun* (1928). A dramatic version of this work by Marc Connelly, entitled *Green Pastures* (1930), was a theatrical triumph, and Bradford and Connelly were jointly awarded a Pulitzer Prize that year. From that time, Bradford became a widely popular writer. Except for one novel, *The Three-Headed Angel* (1937), about the first settlers in the Cumberland Mountains of Tennessee, he made Negro life the focus of his work. *Kingdom Coming* (1933), a novel about the struggles of the freed slaves in the aftermath of the Civil War, attempted to show the American Negro in historical perspective, as did an earlier novel, *This Side of Jordan* (1929), a portrayal of the invasion of the plantation world by the machine age. The larger part of Bradford's fictional representation of the Negro, however, fell within the realm of sentimental comedy. This was true of two further collections of short stories, *Ol' King David and the Philistine Boys* (1930) and *Let the Band Play Dixie* (1934), as well as of the many uncollected stories (most of which appeared in *Collier's*) about life on Little Bee Bend Plantation and the life of the river roustabouts. Bradford's one play, *How Come Christmas* (1930), was filled with comic pathos. Only *John Henry* (1930), a collection of stories about a legendary Negro roustabout that are more folklore than fiction, escaped the sentimental.

Bradford interrupted his writing career in 1942-1946 to serve as a lieutenant in the U.S. Naval Reserve with an assignment to the Bureau of Aeronautics Training, Navy Department, and, in 1946, he accepted a position as visiting lecturer in the English department of Tulane University, which he held until 1948. In the fall of that year he died at his home in New Orleans—of an amoebic infection contracted while he was serving in the navy off the coast of Africa—and, after cremation, as he had requested, his ashes were scattered on the waters of the Mississippi River. At the time it seemed that his stories interpreting the life of the Mississippi River valley, notably of its black people, would be as permanent as those of Mark Twain. Not only did they enjoy a large popular audience, but they had won favorable critical commendation. But Bradford's death coincided with the beginnings of the first major civil rights revolution in the United States, during which stereotyped images of the American Negro were challenged as never before. This challenge revealed clearly how much Bradford was indebted to sentimental and comic stereotypes of the Negro and how little he conceived of the Negro as a person in his own right. He had unintentionally made this clear as early as 1927 in an essay called "Notes on the Negro" (*Forum*, Nov. 1927). In this analysis Bradford divided the black race in America into three groups: "niggers," "colored persons," and Negroes (with a capital N). The last group he saw as having a certain independence of mind because they had acquired an ironic comprehension of the white man's civilization. He apparently felt that this was a liberation sufficient in itself.

[Ruth Louise Durrett, "Roark Bradford's Portrayal of the Negro" (master's thesis, Louisiana State Univ., 1950); David L. Cohn, "Strictly Personal: Roark Bradford's Revenge," *Saturday Rev.*, June 24, 1944, pp. 13–14; David L. Cohn, "Straight to Heaven," *Saturday Rev.*, Dec. 4, 1948, pp. 20–21; Meigs O. Frost, "The Man Who Put God in a Role on the Stage," *New Orleans States*, May 18, 1930, pp. 1–2; Kenneth Thomas Knoblock, "Uncle Roark," *The New Orleanian*, Jan. 15, 1931, pp. 19–20, 38–39; Grace Leake, "Old Man Fortune and the Bradford Boy," *Holland's*, Nov. 1930, pp. 18, 34; "Roark Bradford," *New Orleans Times-Picayune*, Nov. 15, 1948, p. 12; Harrison Smith, "Roark Bradford," *Saturday Rev.*, Nov. 27, 1948; Lewis P. Simpson, "Roark Bradford," in Louis D. Rubin, Jr., ed., *A Bibliog. Guide to the Study of Southern Literature*, pp. 159–160 (1969).]

LEWIS P. SIMPSON

BRADY, WILLIAM ALOYSIUS (June 19, 1863–Jan. 6, 1950), theatrical manager and producer, was born in San Francisco, Calif., apparently the only child of Terence A. and Catherine (O'Keefe) Brady. His father was a newspaper editor who had landed in San Francisco in 1856 from Dublin, Ireland, and had founded the Catholic *Monitor*; his mother was "the most famous singer on the Coast in her day." The elder Brady was a fervent secessionist during the Civil War and his newspaper was wrecked. He was also, according to William, a scholar who educated his son on Shakespeare. When William was about three, his parents separated. His father "kidnapped" him and took him to New York, where they lived on the city's Lower East Side. During the elder Brady's periodic unemployment as a free-lance writer, William sold newspapers and shined shoes. He early abandoned public school in favor of haunting the theaters. When he was about fifteen his father was killed, apparently by a fall under an elevated train. The New York Press Club hired the youth as a day steward, but shortly thereafter he returned to California, aided by the Press Club and by working as a "peanut butcher" or vendor on trains.

Once in San Francisco, young Brady earned a living by running a newsstand. He spent his spare time "chasing the theatrical will-of-the-wisp" until he landed a job as call boy with author-producer Bartley Campbell's production of the melodrama *The White Slave* in 1882. He made his professional debut when he took over the role for an indisposed actor. Campbell next sent him to Sacramento to join the troupe of Joseph R. Grismer as a utility man. During his barnstorming days in the West he married, at the age of twenty-two, a Paris-born dancer, Marie René ("In the Spotlight for Forty Years"); they had two children: Alice and William A. Brady, Jr., who died at the age of five.

William Brady's break into management on his own had a good deal to do, as he later wrote, with "the old-time tradition of piracy and plagiarism." Elated over the success of his own rewritten and dramatized version of H. Rider Haggard's popular adventure novel *She*, he decided to book it east. He abandoned it in St. Paul (or Minneapolis), Minn., however, when confronted by the more elaborate production of Charles Frohman heading west and starring William Gillette. Instead, Brady resolved to storm New York with the melodrama *After Dark*, the rights to which he had purchased for $1,100 from the author Dion Boucicault while trouping on the West Coast. *After Dark* opened at the People's Theatre in the Bowery in April 1889 with Brady in the part of the boatman Old Tom and Marie René as a "transformation dancer." Producer Augustin Daly immediately served him with an injunction, claiming that the big scene in the play—the rescue by the heroine of a man bound to the rails in the path of an onrushing train—had been plagiarized by Boucicault from Daly's own *Under the Gaslight*. In spite of litigation lasting more than a decade and finally settled against him, Brady enjoyed several successful years with *After Dark*, especially after introducing into the cast the prizefighter James J. Corbett, whom he later managed and for whom he coauthored the play *Gentleman Jack* (1892).

Brady's next venture, his biggest money-maker, was *Way Down East*, the tale of a country girl betrayed into a mock marriage. Titled *Annie Laurie* by the author Lottie Blair Parker and turned down by nearly every important Broadway manager, the script was renamed and elaborated upon by Brady's partner Joseph R. Grismer and produced by Brady and Florenz Ziegfeld at the Manhattan Theatre on Feb. 7, 1898. Ziegfeld shortly withdrew from the undertaking leaving Brady to reap a fortune with the play, which toured for more than twenty years and whose screen rights David W. Griffith purchased.

On Jan. 8, 1899, some three years after his first wife's death, Brady married the actress Grace George, by whom he had a son (also William A. Brady, Jr.), who followed in his father's footsteps as a producer. Brady succeeded in his ambition to make his wife a star. In 1911 she opened the playhouse he built with *Sauce for the Goose*, followed by a series of plays including *Divorçons*, a comedy by Victorien Sardou and Emile de Najāc (1913), and George Bernard Shaw's *Major Barbara* (1915) and *Captain Brassbound's Conversion* (1916). His daughter, Alice Brady, also scored in several of her father's productions, among them *Little Women* (as Meg, 1912) and Owen Davis' *Forever After* (1918). Brady helped many other players on their way to stardom. Of his early "discoveries" he considered his "most notable," David Warfield, whom he had met on the West Coast and who first appeared on Broadway in 1891 in Brady's production *The Inspector*. Robert B. Mantell claimed to have learned more about Shakespeare from Brady than he had "in all his studies" (Colgate Baker in *New York Review*. Aug. 5, 1911). Grace George called her husband's attention to Douglas Fairbanks, who appeared under Brady's management in several plays including *All for a Girl* (1908), his initial starring role, *A Gentleman from Mississippi* (1908), and *The Cub* (1910), where he first conspicuously utilized his acrobatic talent. It was Grace George who suggested the young Helen Hayes for the role of Maggie in *What Every Woman Knows* (1926). When Broadway turned a deaf ear to Katharine Cornell, Brady gave her an opportunity in one of his road companies of *The Man Who Came Back* in 1918-1919, her first touring experience.

Of his more than 250 productions Brady lost a fortune on the one of which he was most proud: *The World We Live In* by Josef and Karel Čapek, adapted by Owen Davis (1922), a fantasy concerning a drunken philosopher who falls asleep in a forest and discerns an analogy between the lives of insects and men. His longest Broadway run came at an ebb in his fortunes and toward the end of his career. Most of the important New York managers had turned down Elmer Rice's *Street Scene* with its cast of fifty as too elaborate. But Brady, though often known for his penuriousness, envisioned the possibilities of its setting: a dingy New York street dominated by a brownstone house with whose occupants the play dealt. Lee Shubert furnished the financial backing and Jo Mielziner, then at the beginning of his career, designed the set. According to Brady (*Showman*, p. 277) the production cost him $6,000, with profits reaching $500,000 and movie rights selling for $165,000. *Street Scene*, which opened in January 1929, captured a Pulitzer Prize.

William Brady won and lost many fortunes during his life, not only in the theater but, especially in his early days, as a sports promoter. (In addition to Corbett, he managed James J. Jeffries.) He also played a role in the film world, serving for a few years beginning in 1915 as head of the National Association of the Motion Picture Industry. In his thirties he was pictured as having the physique of an athlete with clear, shrewd, blue eyes and a ringing laugh; in his later years he assumed somewhat the look of a gangster, seldom appearing without a cigar in the corner of his mouth. He had an "uncanny instinct for drama." At rehearsals he would "roar a reading of a line" that was "electric" and "the whole stage would light up" (McClintic, p. 150). He died of a heart ailment at his New York home at the age of eighty-six and was buried in Sleepy Hollow Cemetery, Tarrytown, N.Y.

[The following books and articles by Brady deal largely with his early career: *The Fighting Man* (1916); *Showman* (1937); "In the Spotlight for Forty Years," *Pictorial Rev.*, Sept. 1824–Mar. 1925; "I've Always Been a Gambler" (as told to John B. Kennedy), *Collier's*, Dec. 14, 1929; "Drama in Homespun," *Stage*, Jan. 1937.

Books that shed tangential light on Brady are: Channing Pollock, *Harvest of My Years* (1943); Ralph Hancock and Letitia Fairbanks, *Douglas Fairbanks* (1953), pp. 83–95 (pages given because book is not indexed); James J. Corbett, *The Roar of the Crowd* (1954 ed.); Guthrie McClintic, *Me and Kit* (1955); Elmer Rice, *The Living Theatre* (1959), for *Street Scene*; Bernard Sobel, ed., *The New Theatre Handbook* (1959); John L. Toohey, *A History of the Pulitzer Prize Plays* (1967), pp. 68–75, for *Street Scene*.

Articles on Brady's career are to be found in: Colgate Baker, "William A. Brady," *N.Y. Rev.*, Aug. 5, 1911; Robert B. Mantell, "Personal Reminiscences," *Theatre*, Oct. 1916; *N.Y. Herald Tribune*, May 18, 1930; George C. D. Odell, *Annals of the N.Y. Stage*, XIV (1945) and XV (1949).

Information on Brady's first son may be found in *N.Y. Dramatic Mirror*, Mar. 3, 1899.

For Brady's involvement in the movies, see Terry Ramsaye, *A Million and One Nights*, II (1926).
Obituaries in *N.Y. Times*, Jan. 8, 1950, and *Variety*, Jan. 11, 1950.]

ELIZABETH F. HOXIE

BRAGDON, CLAUDE FAYETTE (Aug. 1, 1866-Sept. 17, 1946), architect, author, and lecturer, was born of native stock in Oberlin, Ohio, the only son of George C. and Katherine (Shipherd) Bragdon. He had a sister, May. Both parents had attended Oberlin College, which was founded by his mother's uncle. At the time Claude was born, his father was a journalist, and this profession soon took the family to New York. They were living in Oswego when Claude, at the age of sixteen, took a job as a letterer, in after-school hours, for A. J. Hopkins, the only architect in town. For a time he intended to become a wood-engraver, and he also tried his hand as a cartoonist. When his family moved to Rochester in 1884, he apprenticed himself as a draftsman in the office of L. P. Rogers and, upon demonstrating an exceptional talent, was recruited by the firm of Charles Ellis to become their head draftsman. According to Bragdon's memoirs, it was Harvey Ellis, brother to the head of the firm, who was most influential in leading Bragdon toward expressing his own ideas in sketches and paintings. At the urging of Ellis, he went to New York City in the first stage of a period of wandering. Unsuccessful in establishing himself there and then in Buffalo as an architect, he traveled abroad, observing the art and life of Rome, Paris, and London.

Returning to Rochester in 1901, he settled down as an architect working in upper New York state and the adjoining provinces of Canada. On Nov. 3, 1902, he married Charlotte Coffyn Wilkinson. They had two sons, Henry W. and Chandler. After his wife's death, he married Eugenie Macaulay Julier, on July 13, 1912; she died in 1920.

The architectural project recalled most vividly in Bragdon's memoirs was the New York Central Railroad Station in Rochester, completed in 1913. In accord with Bragdon's belief that architecture must obey the law of organisms—that form must follow and express function—the façade of this building drew its inspiration from the five large driving wheels of the steam-driven locomotives of the era. An innovative use of concrete, expressive of its unique qualities, was manifest in his design for the Hunter Bridge across the Otonobee River in Ontario (1918). In pressing his idea that color added a further dimension to architectural design, Bragdon ran afoul of the industrialist George Eastman. Viewing the unfinished interior of the Rochester Chamber of Commerce Building, Eastman decided that he could save money by leaving the white plaster bare. Bragdon immediately dissociated himself from the project. Other prominent structures which he designed were the Genesee Valley Club in Rochester, the Livingston County Court House, and the parapet of the York-Leaside Viaduct in Toronto. Bragdon's retrospective view was that prevailing eclectic and materialistic tastes in architecture were the fruits of a "vicious and depraved form of feudalism," but as a practicing architect he had to accede to the demands for Italianate churches and castellated railroad stations. His achievements were considerable and won him wide recognition, including three President's Medals of the Architectural League of New York.

Bragdon first expressed his admiration for the bold functionalism of Louis Sullivan in an article published in 1903. Later he edited Sullivan's *Kindergarten Chats on Architecture, Education and Democracy* and wrote a preface to *The Autobiography of an Idea* (1924). To the pragmatic functionalism of Sullivan, Bragdon added his own more transcendental illuminations. For him a skyscraper was "only a symbol . . . a condition of consciousness"; all life was a sacrament, full of "ulterior meaning." The laws of the universe were revealed in pure mathematics and the color spectrum. These ideas led him to a theory of "projective ornament" (mathematically derived designs) and to the use of ceramics in ornamentation.

While pursuing his career as an architect—he received an M.Arch. from the University of Michigan—Bragdon had also become a writer and lecturer. He published a volume of poetry, *The Golden Person of the Heart* (1898, 1908), and wrote an introduction to Adelaide Crapsey's collection, *Verse* (1915). In 1903 he was the featured speaker at the annual meeting of the Architectural League of America, held in St. Louis. In 1915 he gave the Scammon Lectures at the Chicago Art Institute. In 1934, at the Princeton Architectural School, he gave a series of lectures titled "Design in Space."

His interest in theosophy was fully developed by 1909, when he published *A Brief Life of Annie Besant*. A year later he brought out *The Beautiful Necessity: Seven Essays on Theosophy and Architecture*. In all, he published sixteen books, on subjects ranging from theatrical set design to yoga, and contributed dozens of articles to periodicals. Among his most notable works were *A Primer of Higher Space*

(1913), *Architecture and Democracy* (1918), *Old Lamps for New* (1925), *Merely Players* (1929), and *The Frozen Fountain* (1932). In collaboration with Nicholas Bessaraboff, he translated one of the leading apologies for the theosophical philosophy, P. Ouspensky's *Tertium Organum* (1920).

Through a friendship with the actor-producer Walter Hampden, Bragdon became interested in set design. In 1919, at Hampden's urging, he designed the set for his friend's production of *Hamlet*. When, in 1923, he decided to give up his practice in Rochester and to move to New York, he became much involved in designing sets for Hampden productions, among them *Cyrano de Bergerac, Macbeth, Othello,* and *The Merchant of Venice.*

During his later years, Bragdon lived at the Shelton Hotel in New York, where he was known for his sunrise exercises in yoga. He died in his hotel room at the age of eighty of natural causes.

Throughout his life, Bragdon had spoken for the artistic conscience, resisting at every turn the debasing of beauty and formal values in the name of material progress, and positing as achievable goals the discoveries of the spiritual life. From two decades as a practicing architect he had turned to stage design and self-expression, merging the functionalism of Louis Sullivan and the theosophy of Annie Besant into a personal credo.

[Bragdon gives a full account of his early career in a series of articles, "Salvaged from Time," in *American Architect and Architecture* (1936–1937), and in expanded form in *More Lives than One* (1938). Obituaries in the *N.Y. Times*, Sept. 18, 1946, and in the *Am. Inst. of Architects Jour.*, Nov. 1946, review the highlights of his career. Data on his family were obtained from the archives of Oberlin College.]
ALBERT F. McLEAN

BRECKINRIDGE, SOPHONISBA PRESTON (Apr. 1, 1866-July 30, 1948), social worker, was born in Lexington, Ky., the second of seven children of William Campbell Preston Breckinridge, a lawyer, editor, United States congressman, and colonel in the Confederate Army, and his second wife, Issa (Desha) Breckinridge. Isba, as she was called by family and friends, was strongly influenced by the long family tradition of public service and support of education. She never lost her aristocratic appearance or southern accent. One of the first generation of college women, she graduated from Wellesley in 1888 and, like most of her contemporaries, searched restlessly for several years before finding a career. After teaching at a Washington, D.C., high school

while her father was a congressman, she returned with him to Kentucky and studied in his law office. In 1895 she became the first woman admitted to the Kentucky bar, an achievement that did not end her search for a meaningful career.

In 1895 she became an assistant to Marion Talbot, dean of women at the University of Chicago. She also began graduate work in political science, earning the Ph.D. in 1901 for a thesis on legal tender. She then entered the University of Chicago Law School, where she received her J.D. in 1904. That year she became an instructor in the department of political economy at the university, where she taught until 1942. Teaching and administration occupied only a portion of her time. About 1905 she met Jane Addams of Hull House, Margaret Dreier Robins of the Women's Trade Union League, and others engaged in social research and reform in Chicago. Through them she discovered a way to combine her interest in scholarship, teaching, and social reform. She became a resident of Hull House in 1907 and for the next fourteen years she spent part of her time at the settlement. Also in 1907 she began to teach at the Chicago School of Civics and Philanthropy, organized in 1903 by Graham Taylor. She became dean of the school and director of research, and in 1920 she was responsible for the school's incorporation into the University of Chicago as the Graduate School of Social Service Administration.

Breckinridge, who never married, appeared delicate and sickly; she had a pale, thin face and weighted only ninety pounds. But her appearance was deceiving. She had tremendous energy, an engaging sense of humor, and total commitment to her careers. Her great capacity for research and writing was expressed in an impressive array of articles and books, all heavily loaded with charts, graphs, and statistics documenting the squalid conditions she observed. She collaborated with Edith Abbott, who also taught at the University of Chicago, on *The Delinquent Child and the Home* (1912), *Truancy and Non-Attendance in the Chicago Schools* (1917), and *The Tenements of Chicago* (1936). Her lifelong concern with the role of women in American society was reflected in two articles published in 1906 in the *Journal of Political Economy* on the legal aspects of the employment of women in industry and in *Marriage and the Civic Rights of Women: Separate Domicile and Independent Citizenship* (1931), and *Women in the Twentieth Century: A Study of Their Political, Social and Eco-*

nomic Activities (1933). Her research drew her into participation in many reform movements. Her principal role was that of advisor and expert, often utilizing her legal training, but she also took part in a whirlwind of conferences, campaigns, and causes. She helped organize and was the first secretary of Chicago's Immigrant Protective League and was an early member of the National Association for the Advancement of Colored People and vice-president of the National Woman's Suffrage Association. She served on the executive committee of the Illinois Consumers League and advised Julia Lathrop and Grace Abbott on policy at the Children's Bureau. She was president of the Woman's City Club of Chicago and an officer of the American Association of University Women. She helped to draft the Progressive party platform in 1912, aided in the campaign to launch a federal investigation of women and children in industry, and was a delegate to the International Congress of Women at The Hague in 1915.

Her chief importance was as a teacher of social work and as one of the first generation of professional women. Working closely with Edith Abbott, she shaped the School of Social Service Administration into one of the country's leading institutions. She maintained that social workers should be not merely philanthropists or technicians but professionals. She emphasized the need for the federal and state governments to promote social welfare in *New Homes for Old* (1921), *Family Welfare Work in a Metropolitan Community* (1924), *Public Welfare Administration in the United States* (1927), *The Family and the State* (1934), and *The Social Service Review,* a journal that she helped found in 1927. In 1933 President Franklin D. Roosevelt appointed her a delegate to the Pan American Congress, the first woman to receive such an honor, and in 1934 she was elected president of the American Association of Schools of Social Work. After her retirement in 1942 she continued to teach and to write until a few months before her death at the age of eighty-two from a combination of arteriosclerosis and a perforated ulcer. An aristocrat who had sympathy and understanding for those less fortunate, Breckinridge was a pioneer in social welfare administration and teaching, a researcher with great energy, and one of the first professional women in America.

[There are voluminous personal papers in the Breckinridge family MSS in the Lib. of Cong. There are biographical articles in *Notable Am. Women,* I (1971); and *Nat. Cyc. Am. Biog.,* XXXVII, 65. Tributes appear in *Social Service Rev.,* Dec. 1948 and Mar. 1949. Other information is included in Helen R. Wright, "Three Against Time," *Social Service Rev.,* Mar. 1954. In addition to books mentioned above she also wrote *Madeline McDowell Breckinridge* (1921), a biography of her sister-in-law; *Social Work and the Courts* (1934); and *The Illinois Poor Law and Its Administration* (1939).]

ALLEN F. DAVIS

BRILL, ABRAHAM ARDEN (Oct. 12, 1874-Mar. 2, 1948), psychoanalyst, was born in Kanczuga in the Austro-Hungarian province of Galicia, the son of Philip Brill, a noncommissioned army officer, and Esther (Seitelbach) Brill. It is not known whether there were other children. The family had moved about a great deal, and young Brill felt "stifled" in his home by his father's authoritarianism. At the age of fifteen Brill obtained permission to immigrate alone to America and arrived without resources in New York City, where he made his home for the rest of his life. Possessed of unusual ability to apply himself, he set about learning English and adapting to the new country; he was naturalized in 1899. He at first supported himself by working in the clothing trade. He graduated from the public schools and in 1892 entered the City College of New York. Because he had to earn his way, his education was frequently interrupted. In 1901 he took the Ph.B. from New York University, and in 1903 he obtained the M.D. from the College of Physicians and Surgeons at Columbia University and began the practice of medicine.

Brill's mother had wanted him to become a rabbi, but as a young man in America he turned away from the Jewish faith, even thinking briefly of a clerical life with the Methodists or Roman Catholics. However, in later years he maintained a strong Jewish identity. His humane interests led him to obtain a liberal education before taking up medicine. Psychiatry had early attracted him, and upon obtaining the M.D. he began work at the New York State Hospital at Central Islip, Long Island. There he came into the first special class of Adolf Meyer, who was introducing dynamic viewpoints and high standards of clinical procedure into American psychiatry. In 1907 Brill sought further training in Paris, but he found the work there sterile, and at the suggestion of his old teacher and patron, the eminent New York psychiatrist Frederick Peterson, he spent the winter of 1907-1908 in Zurich, where he received a third assistant physician's appointment with Eugen Bleuler at the Burghölzli. Bleuler and others there were working with Freud's new theories, and Brill discovered in both his psychotic patients and his own dreams evidence of the validity of Freud's contention that psychological mechanisms contain and express forbidden unconscious desires. Brill met other neophyte analysts and found in psychoanalysis his life's work. He traveled from Switzerland to a psychoanalytic congress and to Vienna to visit Freud. Before he left Zurich, Brill had undertaken to translate a new psychoanalytic book on dementia praecox (schizophrenia) by Carl Jung, the most enthusiastic of the Swiss Freudians, and had obtained permission to translate Freud's works.

Arriving back in New York in 1908, Brill married another physician, Kitty Rose Owen, in Brooklyn, on May 21. They had two children, Edmund and Gioia.

He then opened a private practice, becoming the first psychoanalyst in America. Peterson sponsored him and referred patients to him. He obtained clinical appointments in the Vanderbilt Clinic and Bellevue Hospital and in the succeeding years held other increasingly prestigious clinical appointments at various New York institutions, in nervous and mental disease services. Ultimately he became a lecturer at Columbia University.

Unlike many other analysts, especially those in Europe, Brill came into psychoanalysis with a background in psychiatry rather than neurology, and he maintained an interest in psychotic patients all of his life. He differed from Freud in favoring a medical background for analysts, and he tended to work within the American medical—and in particular, psychiatric—institutions rather than set up an independent psychoanalytic discipline as Freud attempted in Europe.

Soon after Brill arrived home, the English analyst Ernest Jones came to Toronto for a few years, and the two of them in effect divided the continent between themselves, Jones seeking converts in the north and west and Brill centering his attention on the New York metropolitan area. Because the practice of psychoanalysis was spread almost exclusively by means of personal persuasion, Brill's persistent proselytizing was of very great importance. Unlike others who stayed close to their practices, Brill was constantly talking to other physicians. He early converted the editor of the important *Journal of Nervous and Mental Disease*, Smith Ely Jelliffe, who in 1913 was cofounder of the first English-language psychoanalytic periodical, *The Psychoanalytic Review*. Many young physicians from the New York State hospital system came to meetings of the New York Psychoanalytic Society, which Brill founded in 1911 and which often met in his home. He thought of himself as "Professor Freud's official representative in America," and he was depressed for several years around World War I when he imagined that Freud was displeased with him. Until the émigré analysts arrived in considerable force in the 1930's—with Brill's encouragement—Brill was in closer touch with the formal Freudian psychoanalytic movement in Europe than any other American. He worked to change the open American psychoanalytic organizations into exclusive scientific-educational certification bodies on a European model and succeeded in the early 1930's.

Brill also carried the Freudian message to the general public and, in particular, influential cultural groups. Himself an admirer of cultural activities, he had many friends and analysands among the influential New York literati and intelligentsia. His own children went to an early progressive school where the teachers were influenced by psychoanalytic ideas. He often wrote for a public forum as well as medical specialists—but in both cases always as the proponent of psychoanalysis. Before World War I he knew personally many of America's intellectual elite, and in years afterward his proximity to New York groups permitted him a substantial influence on the country's culture.

It is much more difficult to calculate the influence of Brill's writings than his personal influence. His medical papers are almost entirely basic expositions of psychoanalysis as he understood it at the time. These writings did not win practitioners over to psychoanalysis but rather familiarized members of the profession with psychoanalysis and helped combat misunderstandings and misrepresentations that were rife. Brill's expositions were clear and straightforward, without any subtlety—indeed, they often represented considerable simplification. In the early days simplification was of little moment, but in later years, when theory came to have much greater significance, Brill's good, but sometimes limited, understanding was not as useful as it had been.

Brill's chief fame was as translator of Freud's works. Beginning in 1909, he made available in English most of Freud's books and a number of papers. All of the translations appeared under Brill's name, although some of the work was done by patients and impecunious literary friends. Moreover, when translation was difficult (e.g., of a pun), Brill made up his own examples and substituted them for Freud's:

perhaps a quarter of *The Psychopathology of Everyday Life* was omitted or changed in Brill's 1914 English version. Jones, especially, was distressed by the rough-and-ready renderings, charging that Brill was at home in neither English nor German. Freud simply commented that he preferred to have a good friend than a good translator, and in fact Jones did not undertake the task himself. Brill on his part observed, "I made no effort to produce literary excellencies; I was only interested in conveying these new ideas into comprehensible English" ("A Psychoanalyst Scans His Past," p. 539-540). Having Freud's own works available was particularly important in America, where most educated people did not read foreign languages. Errors of interpretation became momentous only many years later. The book that introduced the most Americans to Freud's teachings was Brill's collection of his translations in the Modern Library series, *The Basic Writings of Sigmund Freud* (1938).

Brill's personality was extremely influential not only in his own career but in the reception that Freud's teachings received in the United States because he so often presented himself—or was taken as—the spokesman for the psychoanalytic point of view. His absolute honesty, buoyant good humor, quick wit, and ability to make fun of himself blunted any personal offense that he might have given as a bellicose defender of Freudianism. His immense energy once led him to characterize his own personality type as "schizoid manic." He was genuinely interested in people and humanity. One of his early patients, Mabel Dodge Luhan, hostess to a generation of intellectuals, remembered him as "all for action. . . . Apparently nothing counted unless it was painted, written down, or formulated into some life pattern composed of persons and their movements" (pp. 505-506, 512). This warmth of character, coupled with loyalty and tolerance of everyone's frailties, served him well in personal and group relationships. In the realm of ideas, his preoccupation with the grossly sexual and his insensitivity to intellectual subtleties gave much of American psychoanalysis both a sensational and simplistic tendency for some years. At the same time, these qualities, coupled with his thoroughgoing candor, won for Freud's work an audience in both medical and, more generally, intellectual circles that ultimately made the United States the center of psychoanalytic thought and practice.

Brill was a member of many societies and received many honors, particularly from New York specialty groups where he was best known. When he was not speaking, writing, or attending to his large practice, he was an avid bird watcher. Active to the end of his life, he died in New York of coronary thrombosis.

[Brill's writings are listed in "Bibliography of A. A. Brill," *Psychoanal. Quart.*, 17 (1948), 164–172. The *N.Y. Times* index indicates that he appeared in print on many occasions not recorded in the formal bibliography. The Brill Papers are in the Lib. of Congress.
Autobiographical material is to be found in A. A. Brill, "A Psychoanalyst Scans His Past," *Jour. Nerv. Ment. Dis.*, 95 (1942), 537–549; in letters printed in Nathan G. Hale, *Freud and the Americans: The Beginnings of Psychoanalysis in the U.S., 1876–1917* (1971); and in comments scattered throughout his writings, especially *Freud's Contribution to Psychiatry* (1944) and "Reminiscences of Freud," *Psychoanal. Quart.*, 9 (1940), 177–183.
Secondary sources include Paula Fass, "A. A. Brill—Pioneer and Prophet" (M.A. thesis, Columbia Univ., 1969); Mabel Dodge Luhan, *Movers and Shakers* (1936); May E. Romm, "Abraham Arden Brill, 1874–1948, First American Translator of Freud," in Franz Alexander, Samuel Eisenstein, and Martin Grotjahn, eds., *Psychoanalytic Pioneers*, pp. 210–223 (1966); *Nat. Cyc. Am. Biog.*, Current Vol. E, p. 526; John C. Burnham, *Psychoanalysis and American Medicine, 1894–1917: Medicine, Science, and Culture* (1967); C. P. Oberndorf, *A History of Psychoanalysis in America* (1953); Ernest Jones, *The Life and Work of Sigmund Freud*, 3 vols. (1953–1957). Helpful obituaries are found in *Psychoanal. Quart.*, 17 (1948), 146–172; *Psychoanal. Rev.*, 35 (1948), 394–402; and *N.Y. Times*, Mar. 3, 1948.]

JOHN C. BURNHAM

BROOKE, CHARLES FREDERICK TUCKER (June 4, 1883-June 22, 1946), Shakespearean scholar, was born in Morgantown, W.Va., the oldest of three children, and first of two sons, of Henry St. George Tucker Brooke and Mary Harrison (Brown) Brooke. His father, a native of Charlottesville, Va., was professor of law at West Virginia University; his mother was from Charles Town, W.Va. Tucker Brooke (as he was known) was descended from Robert Brooke, who came from England in 1650 and settled in Maryland. Through his paternal grandmother he was also related to the prominent and extensive Tucker family of Virginia.

Brooke attended West Virginia University, graduating at the early age of eighteen. He received the B.A. in 1901 and the M.A. in 1902. Although he had been strongly interested in botany while he was in college, it was in German that he did his graduate work from 1901 to 1904 at the University of Chicago. In 1904 he also received a Rhodes scholarship and proceeded to Oxford, where his most formative years as a scholar were spent. Arriving at St. John's College, he changed his field again and took the B.A. and the B.Litt. in English literature, gaining the latter degree in 1907. At this time he came under the influence and encouragement of the famous Shakespearean scholar Sir Walter Raleigh, who led him into the field of Elizabethan drama.

In 1908 he became an instructor at Cornell; the following year he moved to Yale, where he was to spend the rest of his life. His scholarly reputation had preceded him, and he soon was teaching courses in the graduate school. In 1919 he first gave the seminar in Shakespeare which soon became one of the most popular courses for graduate students. In 1921 he was made a full professor and in 1931 he was appointed to one of the newly endowed Sterling professorships, the second member of the faculty to receive this honor.

In 1907-1908 he gave the series of lectures on Elizabethan drama which formed the basis of his book *The Tudor Drama* (1911). This study was so thorough and authoritative that it is still considered one of the most useful treatments of the subject.

Brooke's publications were voluminous and were produced without interruption throughout his whole career. He became particularly well known in his early years for his work on Christopher Marlowe. In 1910 he published the standard text, for those days, of Marlowe's plays. In addition, he wrote a series of impressive articles on the plays and in 1930 wrote a life of Marlowe that appeared in the first volume of a new English edition of the works. Those who heard his lectures on Marlowe enjoyed a rare privilege. Brooke was known above all, however, as a Shakespeare editor and scholar. While he was at Yale he became involved in the Yale edition of Shakespeare; he edited a number of individual plays and was made general editor of the series. His crowning work was his magnificent edition of the sonnets in 1936. His original essays for the *Yale Review* on Shakespeare's life, character, and plays were later collected under the title *Essays on Shakespeare and Other Elizabethans* (1948).

During the last decade of his life Brooke was occupied with two pieces of work of which the results only appeared posthumously. One was the section on the Renaissance for the Appleton-Century *Literary History of England* (1948). This was a distinguished piece of literary history and was sprinkled with memorable epigrammatic comments. The other work to which he devoted many hours was the preparation of a complete edition of the Latin poems and plays of the sixteenth-century Oxford don William Gager. It was nearly finished at the time of his death, but only one part, the biographical sketch of Gager's life, was published (American Philo-,

sophical Society, *Proceedings*, 1951). It is unfortunate that this interesting work seems destined to obscurity for it is the crowning product of a lifelong enthusiasm for Neo-Latin poetry. As early as 1914 Brooke had offered a course on this subject at the Yale graduate school, a course which he continued to offer from time to time during the rest of his career. The increasing importance of this field of study owes not a little to Brooke's pioneering work.

On July 27, 1909, Brooke married Grace Elizabeth Drakeford, daughter of Alfred Drakeford of Warwickshire, England. They had three children; Elizabeth Grace Tucker, Henry St. George Tucker, and Alfred Drakeford.

Brooke died on June 22, 1946, in New Haven, Conn., of a sudden heart attack. An Episcopalian, he was buried in the churchyard of Zion Church in Charles Town, W.Va.

[Personal knowledge and information from former students. *Nat. Cyc. Am. Biog.*, XXXVI, 396–397. See also the memoir by Chauncy B. Tinker and Robert D. French in Am. Philosophical Soc., *Year Book* (1946). The complete MS of Brooke's edition of William Gager's works is in the library of the Am. Philosophical Soc.]

LEICESTER BRADNER

BROWN, CHARLES REYNOLDS (Oct. 1, 1862–Nov. 28, 1950), Congregational clergyman, was born near the town of Bethany in what was then Virginia, but the year after his birth became West Virginia. He was the oldest child of Benjamin F. Brown and Sarah Jane (Kinkade) Brown, and his family traced their ancestors to the original settlers at Jamestown. His father was a farmer who moved the family to a farm in Washington County, Iowa, in 1866.

Young Brown worked on the farm and attended a one-room school near his home. His mother played a central role in the education of her children during Brown's childhood. She read aloud every day for them and required each child to memorize ten verses of scripture every Sunday. His mother had been a Presbyterian but joined her husband in the Methodist church, in which Brown was baptized.

After finishing primary and grammar school he attended Washington Academy and then the University of Iowa in Iowa City, from which he was graduated in 1883. Brown was interested in law at this point and in order to get enough money to attend law school he took a job as a stenographer in the law offices of Sweeney, Jackson and Walker in Rock Island, Ill., and later in the law offices of Davis and Lane in Davenport, Iowa. Gradually, however, he decided it was not law, but the ministry which was to be his lifework. He worked for a year in the home office of the Hawkeye Insurance Company of Des Moines to accumulate tuition money and then entered the School of Theology at Boston University in the fall of 1886.

After receiving the S.T.B. degree in 1889, he was appointed minister of the Wesley Chapel in Cincinnati. After three years of a rather successful pastorate there, he became a Congregationalist and accepted a call to the Winthrop Church in the Charlestown section of Boston, Mass.

On Sept. 23, 1896, Brown married Alice Tufts, who was then a student at Radcliffe College. After his marriage he moved to the First Congregational Church in Oakland, Calif., where he carried on an active ministry for nearly fifteen years. For a number of years he also taught a course at Stanford University, alternating between teaching the Old Testament and social ethics. For more than ten years he was president of the board of trustees of Mills College in Oakland. Brown's social concern was expressed in part through his involvement with the labor movement. For a number of years he was a delegate to the Central Labor Council in Oakland and did a good deal of work on boards of arbitration. The Beecher Lectures which he gave at Yale in 1906 were entitled *The Social Message of the Modern Pulpit* and dealt with the relation between religion and labor.

In the spring of 1911, Brown was named dean of the Divinity School at Yale University, a post which he held until his retirement in 1928. For eleven years he also served as pastor of the University Church at Yale. Brown, as dean, brought new life to the Divinity School, which was evidenced by a marked increase in its enrollment and faculty as well as by increased financial resources. Although he was a strong leader of the Divinity School, Brown was perhaps most prominent as a preacher; over the course of the years he preached almost every Sunday in countless college chapels and pulpits. In a poll of 25,000 ministers in 1924, he was voted one of twenty-five "foremost living American preachers." He was elected moderator of the National Council of Congregational Churches in 1913 and served a two-year term. He was also a well-known lecturer at universities. Many of these lectures were published in book form. Altogether, Brown was the author of thirty-nine books.

After his retirement he continued to live in New Haven, and he died there on Nov. 28, 1950. He was buried in Washington, Iowa.

[The following books written by Brown probably best express his personal philosophy: *The Art of*

Preaching (1922); *Have We Outgrown Religion?* (1932); *The Modern Man's Religion* (1911); *The Social Message of the Modern Pulpit* (1906); and *What is Your Name?* (1924). Sources concerning the life and work of Charles R. Brown include Charles R. Brown, *My Own Yesterdays* (1931); James Glover Johnson, "The Yale Divinity School 1899–1928" (Ph.D. diss., Yale Univ., 1928); references to Brown in *Yale Divinity News*, "Biographical Sketch," Jan. 1921; "Retirement of Dean Brown," Mar. 1928; "The Dean and the Dean-Elect," Mar. 1928; "Charles Reynolds Brown," Jan. 1951.]

HARRY B. ADAMS

BROWN, PERCY (Nov. 24, 1875–Oct. 8, 1950), physician and roentgenologist, was born in Cambridge, Mass., to Isaac Henry and Mary Elizabeth (Kennedy) Brown. He was a descendant of patrician New England families including Pierces and Emersons. He was christened Percy Emerson Brown, but in early manhood he legally dropped his middle name— an act not intended, however, to be disrespectful to his distinguished ancestor Ralph Waldo Emerson. After graduating from the Browne and Nichols School, Brown in 1893 took three years of premedical study at the Lawrence Scientific School. He entered Harvard Medical School and received the M.D. degree in 1900; for two years he interned at Boston Children's Hospital. During this period he first became interested in roentgen rays. In 1904 he started his own private practice, and on December 7 he married Bernice Mayhew; they had no children.

From the very beginning of his professional career, Brown employed X rays for medical purposes. At that time Roentgen's discovery had been known for only six or seven years and the clinical application of X rays had barely begun. Brown exerted a strong and continuing influence, both in personal contacts and in professional affiliations, including the American Roentgen Ray Society, which he joined in 1902, to establish professional standards and training for physicians practicing roentgenology, now more familiarly known as radiology. As a measure of the continually growing importance of X rays in medical diagnosis and therapeutics, and of his role in their application and practice, he held clinical teaching appointments at Harvard Medical School from 1911 to 1922, first as assistant in the use of the roentgen ray and later as instructor in roentgenology.

In World War I, Brown, serving as a major in the Army Medical Corps, was appointed chief of X-ray service to Base Hospital No. 5, which operated in France as the Harvard Unit from Peter Bent Brigham Hospital. In this capacity he worked with Harvey Cushing, Elliott C. Cutler, Roger I. Lee, and other colleagues who became famous figures in American medicine.

Brown had worked with X rays during his student days and internship, and soon after establishing his own practice he had noticed lesions on his face and hands which he came to recognize were the result of overexposure to radiation. Although they began to cause him some concern, he nevertheless insisted on serving with the base hospital where much fluoroscopy had to be done on the wounded under conditions that afforded inadequate protection to the examiner.

On his return from the war, he abandoned his practice and became associated with various large clinics as a roentgenologist. His longest service (1924-1929) was at St. Luke's Hospital in New York City, but he also served at the Jackson Clinic, Madison, Wis., Grunow Clinic in Phoenix, Ariz., and as roentgenologist-in-chief at the Western Pennsylvania Hospital of Pittsburgh (1923). Always closely allied with the American Roentgen Ray Society, he served as its Caldwell Lecturer in 1923 (he had been president of the society in 1911) and as its historian until shortly before his death. In 1923 he received the Gold Medal of the Radiological Society of North America. Although he published numerous articles in medical journals, he is best remembered for his book *American Martyrs to American Science Through the Roentgen Rays* (1935), an account of twenty-eight physicians, physicists, and engineers, the majority known by the author, whose deaths resulted from overexposure to radiation during the pioneering days of X rays.

In time the lesions on his hands became progressively worse, eventually forcing his retirement from active practice in 1934. Although he underwent over fifty operations for the control of cancer, he neither complained nor indulged in self-pity. Former medical students remember his willingness to have his lesions demonstrated to classes. Intimates describe him as a lovable, gifted, and modest physician. In his seventy-fifth year Brown died of a cardiac ailment in the village of Egypt near Scituate, Mass., and was buried in the Congregational cemetery at West Tisbury on Martha's Vineyard.

Brown was one of the most important advocates of a small but influential group of American physicians of the early twentieth century who elevated the use of X ray for diagnosis and therapy to the status of a separate medical specialty. He, as much as any other American physician of his period, was responsible for

taking the application of Roentgen's invention out of the hands of hospital photographers and electricians, to whom it had been relegated initially, and placing it in charge of physicians versed in the physics of radiation. In addition he also designed several pieces of apparatus used in the operation of the roentgen ray. Due in large part to his efforts, diagnosis and therapeutics through X irradiation came to be carried on in a scientific manner, and principles were laid down upon which rests much of modern medical radiology.

[Personal recollections and communications of Dr. Lloyd E. Hawes, Boston; George and Helen Levene, Martha's Vineyard; Mrs. Rosalie Powell, Vineyard Haven. Obituary articles and notices in *Am. Jour. of Roentgenology*, 65 (1951), 122–123 (with photograph); *Annals of Internal Medicine*, 33 (1950), 1532–1533; *Radiology*, 55 (1950), 898 (with photograph); and the *Boston Herald*, Oct. 9, 1950. Photographs, publications and reprints, and some manuscript materials by and about Brown are preserved in the Lloyd E. Hawes Collect. on the hist. of radiology and in the Harvard Medic. Arch., both in The Francis A. Countway Lib. of Medicine, Boston.]

PAUL C. HODGES

BROWN, RALPH HALL (Jan. 12, 1898-Feb. 23, 1948), historical geographer, was born in Ayer, Mass., the third son and fourth of five children of William Brown and Nellie Eliza (Leavitt) Brown. His paternal grandfather, Michael Brown, had emigrated from County Clare, Ireland, in 1848; his mother was descended from an old New Hampshire family. The father was a Roman Catholic, the mother a Congregationalist, and Ralph was reared in his mother's church. As a child he was a somewhat solitary student of nature. He attended the Ayer public schools and entered Massachusetts State College in Amherst in 1915, but left two years later. After working for a time in his father's drugstore, he enrolled at the University of Pennsylvania, where he specialized in history and graduated with the B.S. degree in 1921. He then began graduate work in geography at the University of Wisconsin, receiving the Ph.D. in 1925 with a dissertation entitled "The Economic Geography of the Middle Connecticut Valley." On Mar. 21, 1924, he married Eunice Rasmussen. They had three children: George Burton, Nancy Eleanor, and Laura Leavitt.

Brown began his teaching career at the University of Colorado, as instructor (1925-1927) and later assistant professor (1927-1929). His early research, continuing through the mid-1930's, included pioneering attempts to apply the current field methods of cultural geography, developed in humid areas, to the mountain and piedmont regions of the semiarid West. His move to the University of Minnesota in 1929 as assistant professor of geography initiated the major phase of his life's work. He was asked to initiate a course in historical geography, and during a year's leave spent in East Coast libraries (1936-1937) he made a comprehensive examination of the geographical writings of Americans and of European commentators on America during the late colonial and early national eras. Half a dozen substantive articles, a lengthy study of the geographies of Jedidiah Morse, and an important statement of his critical method, "Materials Bearing upon the Geography of the Atlantic Seaboard, 1790 to 1810" (*Annals* of the Association of American Geographers, September 1938), led to Brown's major scholarly work, *Mirror for Americans: Likeness of the Eastern Seaboard, 1810* (1943), a landmark in American geography for its technical scholarship, distinctive historical method, and literary presentation. A synoptic cross-sectional view of the area's systematic and regional geography as seen through the eyes of an imagined Jeffersonian savant, "Thomas Pownall Keystone," this carefully annotated work demonstrated that geographic analysis of a region could profitably include images and concepts—how people perceived the geographical environment and how those perceptions affected behavior—as well as the actual material conditions.

Brown was promoted to associate professor at Minnesota in 1938 and to professor in 1945. He served the Association of American Geographers as secretary (1942-1945), a post made extraordinarily burdensome by the war, and as editor of its *Annals* beginning in 1947. In the midst of these professional labors he worked on his second major book, *Historical Geography of the United States*. Published a week before his death in 1948, this has remained the basic text in the field. The coverage is uneven, reflecting to a large degree what Brown himself had been able to accomplish in field and library work. Prominent themes were man's modification of the biotic environment and patterns of settlement, agriculture, and commerce, viewed from a strongly regional perspective. As in his *Mirror*, Brown relied heavily on contemporary maps and eyewitness accounts, and suggestively emphasized the role of concepts, true and false, about the land in each period.

Brown's childhood love of the outdoors and of making things was continued in his later avocations of camping, hiking, fishing, working with hand tools and gardening. A modest, self-effacing scholar, always generous of his time,

he was a congenial colleague. His lectures were well organized and meaty, but appealed primarily to advanced students. Brown died of an apparent heart attack. Rumors of possible suicide arising after his death were countered immediately by an official investigation of the University of Minnesota. He was buried in Sunset Memorial Park in Minnesota. Few students continued his scholarly explorations, perhaps because his methods and researches reflected too closely his own special interests; but during the 1960's a newer generation of geographers came to recognize the validity of Brown's dictum that "Men at all times have been influenced quite as much by beliefs as by facts." He was thus an important antecedent of the perceptual approach to historical geography.

[No comprehensive biographical or critical study of Brown exists. This sketch is based on a study of his writings, reviews of his books, manuscript materials in the archives of the Assoc. of Am. Geographers in Washington and the Am. Geographical Soc. in N.Y., the unpublished memorial read by Richard Hartshorne to the Assoc. of Am. Geographers, Dec. 30, 1948, and on correspondence with family and associates. Additional Brown MSS are at the Univ. of Minnesota, in the Ralph Hall Brown Room of the Social Sci. Tower. Published biographical accounts include the memoir by Stanley D. Dodge in the *Annals* of the Assoc. of Am. Geographers, Dec. 1948 (with a photograph and a bibliography of Brown's writings); and briefer notices in *Geog. Rev.*, July 1948, and *Jour. of Geog.*, May 1948. For appraisals of Brown's work, see the especially perceptive review of *Mirror for Americans* by Woodrow W. Borah in the *William and Mary Quart.*, Apr. 1946; and Andrew H. Clark in *Die Erde*, V, 148–152 (1953) and in Preston E. James and Clarence F. Jones, eds., *Am. Geography: Inventory and Prospect* (1954). Death record from Minn. State Board of Health.]
WILLIAM A. KOELSCH

BROWNE, CHARLES ALBERT (Aug. 12, 1870-Feb. 3, 1947), chemist, was born in North Adams, Mass., the oldest of five children, two of them boys, of Charles Albert and Susan (MacCallum) Browne. Both parents were natives of Massachusetts; the father was descended from the Rev. Chad Browne, who came to Boston from England in 1638. A tradition of scientific inventiveness was part of the family heritage; through his paternal grandmother, Browne was related to Benjamin Talbot Babbitt and Isaac Babbitt. His father, trained as a bookkeeper, was a self-taught chemist and inventor who devised and manufactured a successful electric blasting fuse. Although blinded in a chemical explosion the year before his son's birth, he continued an active interest in business, inventing, and—through the family farm—agriculture.

Young Charles attended Drury Academy in North Adams and Williams College, from which he received the B.A. degree in 1892.

While in college he developed a strong interest in Greek and upon graduation considered following a career in either chemistry or the classics. His first offer of employment, from an analytical laboratory in New York City, tipped the balance in favor of chemistry. In 1895 he went to Pennsylvania State College as assistant in the chemistry laboratory and a year later became chemist at the Pennsylvania Agricultural Experiment Station, where he was able to pursue his interest in agricultural chemistry. Going to Germany for further study, Browne enrolled in 1900 at the University of Göttingen, where Bernhard Tollens had built up an outstanding center for the study of agricultural chemistry and plant physiology. Under Tollens' direction, Browne began his investigations of sugar chemistry and received the Ph.D. degree in 1902.

His next employment was as a research chemist at the Louisiana Agricultural Experiment Station in New Orleans. His work there was so successful that in 1906 he was appointed chief of the Sugar Division in the Bureau of Chemistry of the Department of Agriculture in Washington. Here he was closely associated with Harvey W. Wiley, head of the bureau. Browne resigned a year later, however, to establish the New York Sugar Trade Laboratory, set up by the sugar industry to test imported cane sugar for producers and refiners as a means of quality control. He continued as director until 1923, when he returned to the Department of Agriculture as chief of the Bureau of Chemistry. When the combined Bureau of Chemistry and Soils was set up in 1927, Browne became chief of chemical and technological research (after 1935, supervisor of chemical research). He retired in 1940.

Most of Browne's own scientific research was concerned with the chemistry of sugar, a field in which he was a recognized authority. His interests extended, however, to general problems of agricultural biochemistry. He made many studies of the function of enzymes in agricultural products. He also investigated the economic phases of agriculture, such as the loss of sugar (and hence of nutritive value) in hay and the prevention of spontaneous combustion in this crop. In the study of plant nutrition, he was an early advocate of greater emphasis on foliary diagnosis and the effect of trace elements. To augment his research, he made many trips throughout the world to investigate agricultural procedures and policies.

In 1908 Browne began the second of his major activities, the study of the history of chemistry. As might have been expected from his classical background, he began with several papers on Greek philosophy and science, but he soon combined his scientific and historical interests to write on early phases of agriculture. During the decade from 1910 to 1920 he built up an excellent library on historical subjects and started to devote himself chiefly to the history of chemistry in America. This brought him into contact with Edgar Fahs Smith of the University of Pennsylvania, also an avid book collector and historian of American chemistry. In 1921 the two founded the Division of the History of Chemistry in the American Chemical Society. After Smith's death in 1928, Browne greatly aided the University of Pennsylvania in setting up the Edgar Fahs Smith Collection in the History of Chemistry, a notable research center for historical studies, to which he subsequently donated a large part of his own library. He served as president of the History of Science Society in 1935-1936.

Browne was a prolific writer, and the list of his publications runs into the hundreds. His books ranged from *A Handbook of Sugar Analysis* (1912) to *Thomas Jefferson and the Scientific Trends of His Time* (1943). His crowning achievement, however, was probably *A Source Book of Agricultural Chemistry* (1944), which combined his classical, historical, and scientific interests.

Browne has been described as "an exact, painstaking, and very systematic worker" with a "charming and rather complex personality" and a lively sense of humor. "He had a cool logical mind with oddly warm corners in it" (Balls, p. xi). On Feb. 9, 1918, Browne married Louise McDanell of Gallatin County, Ky., a graduate of Stanford who had recently completed the Ph.D. in physiological chemistry at Yale. They had one daughter, Caroline Louise. Browne was a Unitarian. When the University of Pennsylvania undertook to publish *Chymia*, an annual in the history of chemistry, Browne was named editor-in-chief, but failing health limited his activity and he died before the publication of the first issue. Early in 1947 Browne succumbed to a coronary thrombosis and bronchopneumonia at Emergency Hospital in Washington, D.C. He was cremated at Fort Lincoln Cemetery.

[The best account of Browne's scientific career is the obituary by Arnold Kent Balls in the *Jour. of the Assoc. of Official Agricultural Chemists* (Aug. 1947). Browne's historical work is discussed by Herbert S. Klickstein and Henry M. Leicester in the *Jour. of Chemical Education,* June 1948, and by Claude K. Deischer in *Chymia*, 1948. Each of the last two papers contains a bibliography of Browne's historical writings, and *Chymia* includes a portrait. See also sketches of Browne and his father in the *Nat. Cyc. Am. Biog.*, XXXV, 56–57, and XXIX, 214; Browne's letters in his Williams College class reports; *Who Was Who in America*, II (1950); *N.Y. Times* obit., Feb. 4, 1947; and in his genealogy, William B. Browne, *Babbitt Family History* (1912), pp. 552–553. Death record from D.C. Dept. of Human Resources.]

HENRY M. LEICESTER

BROWNE, HERBERT WHEILDON COTTON (Nov. 22, 1860–Apr. 29, 1946), architect, was born in Boston, Mass., the son of Thomas Quincy Browne, a merchant, and Juliet Frances (Wheildon) Browne. Educated at Noble's Classical School, the Boston Museum of Fine Arts School, and the Massachusetts Institute of Technology, he traveled extensively in Europe, studying painting in Paris and, in 1883, with Fabio Fabii in Florence. After working as a student (1888–1890) in the Boston architectural office of Andrews and Jacques, he joined Arthur Little of Salem, Mass., in establishing the Boston firm of Little and Browne.

Little was one of the early exponents of the "colonial revival" in American architecture. Browne had a deep feeling for the New England past, as well as a strong affection for Italian architecture of the baroque and Empire periods and for Italy and its people. He thought grandly in terms of marbles, bas-reliefs, busts, statues, and bronze ornaments. Little and Browne specialized in large and elegant city and country houses. Like Richard Morris Hunt, Charles F. McKim, Stanford White, and Ogden Codman, who was a close friend of Browne's, they created great houses that were sometimes more tasteful than their owners.

A sociable bachelor, Browne wore a small beard *à la Richelieu,* had many friends, and was in great demand in Boston as a dinner companion. His flair for elegance would have endeared him to Italian grand dukes or German princes of an earlier period. He worked closely with his clients, who were also his friends, to provide handsome settings for their lives. One such example is Faulkner Farm, a house on a hillside in Brookline, Mass., which he designed early in his career for Mrs. Charles F. Sprague (later Mrs. Edward D. Brandegee), and which is now the home of the American Academy of Arts and Sciences. In its first form, it was a rectangular, two-story, frame structure, clapboarded and painted white, which stood in large Italianate gardens designed by Charles A. Platt. Early in this century, the house was encased in red brick, and a third story and large wings were added. In one of the wings was a ballroom with mirrors designed to enhance a set of French tapestries and four colossal marble columns that Browne had found in Italy; at one end a lower circular Empire room with painted paneling, brought by him from Mantua, served as an anteroom to the garden. Although Faulkner Farm was a complete and handsome house in its first stage, it had clearly been planned with the subsequent enlargement in mind. His ideas involved a subtle and tasteful collaboration between architect and client, both of whom enjoyed working with fine materials to create a European setting.

About 1900 Browne designed Mrs. Wirt Dexter's house in Chicago and later a house for her on Commonwealth Ave. in Boston. He designed a Washington house for Sen. Stephen B. Elkins of West Virginia, a country house in Hamilton, Mass., for Ambassador George von L. Meyer, and many houses in Boston. In later years it saddened him that, after the deaths of the friends for whom he had designed them, some of his houses were demolished because of their scale. That was the case with Weld, the Brookline country house of Mr. and Mrs. Larz Anderson, which was near Faulkner Farm. The Washington house that he built for the Andersons at 2118 Massachusetts Ave., N.W., in 1902-1904 has survived as the headquarters of the Society of the Cincinnati.

Browne was a fellow of the American Institute of Architects, and a life member and long a trustee of the Society for the Preservation of New England Antiquities. After the society in 1916 acquired the 1795 house built by Charles Bulfinch for Harrison Gray Otis at the corner of Cambridge and Lynde Streets in Boston, Browne restored and remodeled the building. Following the death of Arthur Little in 1925, Browne continued the practice under the firm's name in partnership with Lester Couch. On Couch's death in 1939, Browne retired and the firm came to an end.

Browne's apartment at 66 Beacon Street was crowded with the Italian furniture, marbles, and medallions that he loved. It was cared for by Francesco Benfante, a manservant whom he had brought from Italy early in the century, who for decades came daily from his home in Somerville to look after his master. A devout Anglo-Catholic, Browne was from 1926 a member of the corporation of the Church of the Advent. As a skilled watercolorist of Italian landscapes and gardens, whether he depicted villas on Lake Como, the Roman aqueduct at Acqui, or Sicilian streets or temples, he painted with an endearing profusion of lively colors. When he died in his eighty-sixth year, he bequeathed his collection of early architectural books to the Society for the Preservation of New England Antiquities. He was buried in Sleepy Hollow Cemetery, Concord, Mass. A memorial exhibition of his watercolors was held in 1948 at the Boston Athenaeum, of which he had been a proprietor since 1903.

[His notebooks containing the record of his works are preserved, with his architectural library, at the Soc. for the Preservation of New England Antiquities, Boston. Henry E. and Elsie R. Withey, *Biog. Dict. of Am. Architects* (1956); *Athenaeum Items,* June 1948; *Who Was Who in America,* vol. II (1950); personal conversations and correspondence.]

WALTER MUIR WHITEHILL

BRUCE, WILLIAM CABELL (Mar. 12, 1860–May 9, 1946), municipal reformer, United States senator, biographer, was born at Staunton Hill, his father's plantation in Charlotte County, Va. He was the sixth of eight surviving children and the fifth of six sons of Charles and Sarah Alexander (Seddon) Bruce, both members of wealthy, established Virginia families. An older brother was the historian Philip Alexander Bruce. Much of the family's wealth had been lost in the Civil War, yet William Bruce grew up in a milieu of servants, tutors, and a vigorous outdoor sporting life. The strong religious influence of his mother was also present. After attending private schools, he entered the University of Virginia in 1879, but left the following year to study at the University of Maryland School of Law in Baltimore. He received the LL.B. in 1882, began practice in Baltimore, and in 1887 formed a partnership with William A. Fisher, then judge of the supreme bench of Baltimore, and Fisher's son, David Kirkpatrick Este Fisher. On Oct. 15 of that year Bruce married Louise Este Fisher, his senior partner's daughter. They had three sons: William Cabell died young, but James and David Kirkpatrick Este lived to maturity.

Politically, Bruce considered himself a Jeffersonian and a Cleveland Democrat. He became active in support of civil service reform in the 1880's and later joined the Baltimore Reform League, working for honesty, efficiency, and economy in municipal government. In 1893, when reformers were initiating one of their periodic challenges to the local political machine, Bruce ran for the state senate. His victory in that election, followed two years later by the statewide defeat of the machine of Arthur Pue Gorman, led to Bruce's election as president of the state senate in 1896. He helped insurgents pass a major reform in the election law and a limited civil service bill. When the machine subsequently regained power in 1897,

Bruce did not seek reelection, but returned to private practice. He became general counsel for the local gas, electric light, and power utility in 1901.

Following his support of a victorious reform candidate, Robert McLane, for mayor of Baltimore in 1903, Bruce was appointed city solicitor. Over the next five years he drafted enabling acts to permit the floating of bond issues needed to finance municipal improvements. He was also one of nine commissioners appointed in 1909 to draft a new city charter which strengthened governmental powers, increased efficiency, and enlarged services. The following year he was named the first general counsel of the state Public Service Commission, newly established to regulate public utilities, a post which he held until 1922. Bruce's record during the Progressive Era was that of a moderate seeking to improve the existing system, with emphasis on structural rather than social reform. He backed the candidacy of Woodrow Wilson in 1912, and subsequently became a strong internationalist supporting the League of Nations.

Bruce made an unsuccessful bid for the United States Senate in 1914, and a successful one in 1922. During his single term, he defended individual rights and opposed prohibition, lynching, the Ku Klux Klan, and the expanding powers of the federal government. Prohibition and the Klan he characterized as twin fruits of "sectarian bigotry." A tall, formal man, Bruce had a keen, independent mind, a sharp tongue, and an occasionally explosive temper. His hopes of reelection were thwarted in the Republican landslide of 1928, and he returned to his Baltimore law practice. During the New Deal period, Bruce abandoned the Democratic party and opposed the reelection of Franklin Roosevelt in 1936.

At interims in his political career Bruce turned to historical writing. His *Benjamin Franklin, Self-Revealed* (1917), a well-written and comprehensive popular biography, won a Pulitzer Prize. His *John Randolph of Roanoke* (1922) undertook to defend the Virginia agrarian from what Bruce considered to be character assassination on the part of Henry Adams in the latter's biography in the American Statesmen series. After retiring from law practice in 1937, Bruce devoted much of his time to a biography of Thomas Jefferson, which was never completed. He died of myocarditis at his home in the Baltimore suburb of Ruxton at the age of eighty-six. An Episcopalian, he was buried in the cemetery of St. Thomas's Church in Garrison, Md.

[Bruce's papers are on deposit in the Univ. of Va. Lib., Charlottesville. Genealogical information is in Alexander Brown, *The Cabells and Their Kin* (1895). Bruce's early years are best described in his *Recollections* (1936). His career as municipal reformer is covered in James B. Crooks, *Politics and Progress: The Rise of Urban Progressivism in Baltimore, 1895 to 1911* (1968). His senatorial career can be followed in the *N.Y. Times* and *Cong. Record*, as indexed. Brief biographical sketches are in the *Nat. Cyc. Am. Biog.*, XXXV, 17; Stanley J. Kunitz and Howard Haycraft, eds., *Twentieth Century Authors* (1942); and *N.Y. Times*, May 10, 1946. Death record from Md. Division of Vital Records.]

JAMES B. CROOKS

BRUNSWICK, RUTH MACK (Feb. 17, 1897-Jan. 24, 1946), psychoanalyst, was born in Chicago, Ill., the only child of Julian William Mack, lawyer and spokesman for liberal Jewry, and Jessie (Fox) Mack, both of German-Jewish descent. Her father was elected to the recently established Cook County juvenile court when his daughter was entering grade school, and he soon became identified nationally with Reform Judaism and public-minded activism. The circumstances of Ruth Mack's early years prepared her for the cosmopolitan surroundings in which she would spend her life.

In 1914 Brunswick entered Radcliffe College, where she studied philosophy and psychology. Although not an outstanding student, her interest in psychiatry led her to work with Elmer Ernest Southard at the Boston Psychopathic Hospital while yet an undergraduate. She was a slight, vivacious, and much admired young woman, active in college affairs and responsive to opportunities for intellectual and social leadership. She sang in the choral society and was elected May Queen; along with two classmates, Estelle Frankfurter and Elizabeth Brandeis, she helped found Radcliffe's chapter of Menorah and served as its president. In the summer of her junior year she married Herrman L. Blumgart, a student at Harvard Medical School, and following graduation from Radcliffe in 1918, she entered Tufts Medical School, completing the program with honors four years later.

When, in 1923, Blumgart received a Mosely traveling fellowship for further medical study in London, Brunswick went to Vienna to pursue her interest in psychoanalysis. She was fortunate in being able to commence her training as Freud's analysand, and when her marriage ended in divorce in 1924, she stayed on in Vienna. During the next thirteen years her energies were first focused on her own instruction in psychoanalytic methods and then on the guidance of other students who had come to Vienna to study under Freud. She was a member of the Vienna Psychoanalytic Society and a teacher at the Psychoanalytic Institute. Meanwhile, she maintained ties across the Atlantic, becoming an editor of the *Psychoanalytic Quarterly* when it was established in the United States in 1932.

Brunswick was an intimate associate of Freud's family, as well as a devoted and talented student whose gifts as a sensitive analyst and contributor to psychoanalytic theory were quickly recognized. Freud selected her to continue treatment of one of his best-known patients, the Wolf-man, whose initial treatment he described in *History of an Infantile Neurosis*. Brunswick saw this patient from October 1926 through February 1927, and her vivid narrative of the analysis and treatment she undertook is a brilliant model of a didactic case history. Published originally in the *International Journal of Psycho-Analysis* (1928), it is a classic exposition of the task of the mature and affective analyst and remains the work for which she is best known.

Immersed in her work, closely tied to Freud yet still with many friends and colleagues in the resident American colony, Brunswick enjoyed a considerable professional reputation. Vienna during the 1920's was a magnet for American intellectuals and artists who enjoyed the congenial and stimulating milieu of a European urban culture in which "advanced" ideas were accepted and assimilated. Among her American associates were two cousins of her former husband: David Brunswick, a student of psychoanalysis, and his brother Mark, a composer-musician whom Ruth married in 1928. The couple returned briefly to the United States in 1929 spending the year in New York City, where their daughter, Mathilda Juliana, was born; they reestablished residence in Vienna in 1930.

The happy and productive years that followed ended abruptly in 1938, when the Nazis entered Vienna. The Brunswicks, faced with the necessity of relocating their home and work, chose to settle permanently in New York City, where Brunswick continued to practice psychoanalysis as a member of the New York Psychoanalytic Society. These were years also spent giving aid and encouragement to European refugees from Nazism.

The move to New York was attended by other problems; poor health diminished her energies and curtailed her active professional role. Her name is not listed as an editor of the *Psychoanalytic Quarterly* from 1938 to 1944, when she resumed that position on the masthead of the journal. Her divorce from Mark Brunswick in 1945 seemed to be accompanied by renewed vitality, and her colleagues at the Psychoanalytic Institute anticipated her increased contribution to their work. This expectation heightened the shock of her sudden death shortly after apparent recovery from pneumonia. Her body was cremated, and in accordance with her wishes, no memorial service was held at the time.

Ruth Mack Brunswick's contribution to psychoanalysis rests in part on the few appealing and instructive articles she published. "The Analysis of a Case of Paranoia" (*Journal of Nervous and Mental Disease,* 70 [1929]) and "The Preoedipal Phase of the Libido Development" (*Psychoanalytic Quarterly,* 9 [1940]) are representative of the sensitive way she drew from her own practice to illuminate the active role of the analyst. Both articles also indicate the critical importance of Freud's collaboration in Brunswick's work.

Brunswick's contribution to psychoanalysis, however, extended beyond these writings. Her close association with Freud from the outset of her career identified Brunswick as an unusually gifted and perceptive analytic practitioner. Her special concern was the treatment of the severely ill, those whose symptoms others had seen as intractable to psychoanalytic techniques. Much of her work focused on the elaboration of unresolved childhood trauma in adult life, a subject of major concern in the development of psychoanalytic theory. Her most important influence was on other analysts; in this small, intense person her colleagues perceived the warmth, the humane consideration of patients' needs, and the unswerving adherence to psychoanalytic theory that was believed to embody the best qualities of scientific psychoanalysis.

[There is a good short biographical note on Brunswick by John C. Burnham in *Notable Am. Women,* II (1971); for a moving tribute to her talents as psychoanalyst, see the memorial address by Herman Nunberg in *Psychoanal. Quart.,* 15 (1946). Biographical information from these sources was supplemented with details from the *Radcliffe Yearbook* (1918) and by correspondence and interviews with Dr. Raymond Gosselin, Dr. David Brunswick, and Mathilda Brunswick Stewart. Albert Grinstein, *Index of Psychoanalytic Writings,* I, 263–264 (1958), provides a complete list of Brunswick's published papers. A small collection of Brunswick's notes and papers are in the Freud Archives at the National Archives, Washington, D.C.]

BARBARA GUTMANN ROSENKRANTZ

BRYAN, KIRK (July 22, 1888-Aug. 22, 1950), geologist, geomorphologist, was born in Albuquerque, N. Mex., the oldest of the three sons of Richard William Dickinson Bryan and Susannah Hunter (Patten) Bryan. Both parents were descendants of Scotch-Irish Presbyterians who had emigrated from Ireland to the New England colonies in the mid-eighteenth century. Kirk's mother had come to Albuquerque from Little Rock, Ark., to teach at the Pueblo Indian Industrial School, run under Presbyterian auspices. His father, born in Rye, N.Y., and descended from George Bryan, a leader in Pennsylvania politics during the Revolutionary period, had graduated from Lafayette College in Pennsylvania. After serving as astronomer on the final arctic expedition of Charles Francis Hall, he received a degree in law at Columbian (later George Washington) University. An appointment as superintendent of the Pueblo Indian school took him in 1882 to Albuquerque, where he later practiced law and was a founder and regent of the University of New Mexico.

Kirk Bryan attended the Albuquerque public schools, spent a year at Blair Academy in Blairstown, N.J., and then entered the University of New Mexico. Studying under William G. Tight, president of the university and professor of geology, he became interested in earth science and made his first field trip. He received the B.A. degree in 1909 and then went on to Yale, where he studied geology under Herbert E. Gregory and Joseph Barrell. After receiving a second B.A. in 1910, he remained at Yale for two years of graduate work (he received the Ph.D. in 1920) and in 1912 joined the United States Geological Survey, with which he was to be associated until 1927. During this period he also served as instructor in geology at Yale (1914-1917) and saw wartime duty in France with the geologic section of the Army Corps of Engineers (1918-1919). In 1927 he joined the Harvard faculty as an assistant professor, becoming professor of physiography in 1943, a post he held until his death.

Bryan's early fieldwork for the Geological Survey, carried out in the Sacramento Valley of California and in the Southwest, dealt with groundwater supplies in arid and semiarid country. In the fall of 1917 he made a four-month study of the desert watering places of the Papago country in southern Arizona which served as the basis of his doctoral dissertation. In this and later papers he described piedmont plains cut in rock; calling them "pediments," he attributed them to lateral corrasion by streams rather than to the weathering process favored by William M. Davis. Bryan emphasized the sharp junction between the low angles of the pediment slopes and the high angles of the mountain slopes, angles that persist as the mountain slopes recede and the pediments spread. Later he observed erosion surfaces that extend from mountain rock onto basin fill and cover wide areas in many basins with through-flowing streams. He enlarged the concept of pediment to include them. As his work on hydrology continued, Bryan became an authority on the geology of water conservation and dam sites, and on several occasions served as consultant to the Mexican government on the construction of dams and reservoirs for reclamation projects.

In the summer of 1923 Bryan served as geologist on an archaeological expedition (repeated in 1924 and 1925) to the Chaco Canyon area of New Mexico, sponsored by the National Geographic Society. Thus began what became a major interest: geological research as an aid to archaeological and anthropological investigation. "In this field," he remarked in 1940, "the two sciences merge and the broken pieces of pottery and other relics of man become fossils recording geologic events." In the Southwest he recognized three episodes of alluviation and two interims of erosion. His correlations—without benefit of carbon-14 dating—of alluviums, cave deposits bearing artifacts, moraines, and till helped establish the antiquity of man in North America.

In developing his theories of land formation, Bryan disagreed with Davis' conviction that geomorphic cycles were initiated by uplift, and championed the views of Walther Penck, the Austrian geologist, who emphasized continuing rather than initial uplift. Bryan did not discount the geomorphic effects of tectonism, but he called attention to change of climate as an initiating factor. He recognized polygenetic soils and demonstrated the value of soils and paleosols as stratigraphic markers. He brought into focus the distinctiveness of Arctic denudational processes and their possible former role in now temperate climates. Bryan recognized six alternating climate-induced epicycles of alluviation and erosion in the Southwest, the first represented by the youngest Pleistocene alluvium and the sixth by the present arroyo cutting, which began about 1880. He discredited overgrazing as the cause of the last erosion. As a son of the unyielding desert, Bryan espoused environmental determinism and underestimated prolific, industrial man as a destructive geological agent.

Bryan was highly intuitive both in teaching and research, and he loved to talk. The union of individuality, family tradition, and environment gave him a "love of wild gorges and bare plains," a pioneer spirit, stubbornness, and a friendly common touch. His field dress consisted of khakis, the customary blue shirt, and a dilapidated Western hat. His major contribution was the training of students. He organized field camps in New Mexico for graduate and undergraduate students from 1931 to 1934, and later in other parts of the Southwest and in the Rocky Mountains. Within twenty years after his death geomorphology in America had come to be dominated by his former students, both in universities and in the Geological Survey.

Bryan married Mary Catherine MacArthur, a Smith College graduate of Wagon Mound, N. Mex., on July 11, 1923. They had four children: Richard Conger, Mary Catherine, Kirk, and Margaret Stuart. Bryan died at the age of sixty-two of a heart attack at Cody, Wyo., while on a field trip with a group of archaeologists. He was buried in the family plot in Fairview Cemetery, Albuquerque. In 1951 the Geological Society of America established the Kirk Bryan Award for significant published contributions to geomorphology.

[Appreciations by geologists: Esper S. Larsen, Jr., in Geological Soc. of America, *Proc.*, 1950, with extensive but incomplete bibliography; L. L. Ray in *Geographical Rev.*, Jan. 1951; and Sheldon Judson in *Dict. Sci. Biog.*, II, 548–549. A memoir by a geographer, Derwent Whittlesey, is in Assoc. of Am. Geographers, *Annals*, Mar. 1951 (with portrait). See also, for appreciations by archaeologists, Frederick Johnson in *Am. Antiquity*, Jan. 1951; and Neil M. Judd's foreword to Bryan's "The Geology of Chaco Canyon, N. Mex.," *Smithsonian Miscellaneous Collections*, LXXII, no. 7 (1954); and, for an estimate by colleagues, *Harvard Univ. Gazette*, Dec 16, 1950. For a photograph of Bryan in field clothes, see *Harvard Alumni Bull.*, Mar. 17, 1933, p. 634. On his father, see *Biog. Catalogue of Lafayette College, 1832–1912* (1913), p. 158.]

RONALD K. DeFORD

BUCK, FRANKLYN HOWARD (Mar. 17, 1884–Mar. 25, 1950), better known as Frank Buck, wild animal entrepreneur and showman, was born in Gainesville, Tex., one of the four children of Howard D. and Ada (Sites) Buck. Howard Buck was a wagon-yard operator, and when Frank was three years old the family moved to Dallas, where the elder Buck worked in the local agency of the Studebaker wagon and carriage company. Leaving school after the seventh grade, Frank spent a knockabout youth, with intervals as a cowboy, a carnival concessionaire, and a freight-train vagabond. In 1901, while working as a bellhop in Chicago, he married Lillie West (known professionally as Amy Leslie), a *Chicago Daily News* drama critic and former light-opera star who was twenty-nine years his senior. Through his wife's connections Buck became assistant to the owner of the Western Vaudeville Managers Association and Western representative of the *New York Telegraph,* a theatrical and sports daily.

In 1911, having separated from his wife (they were divorced in 1916), Buck traveled to Bahia, Brazil, where he purchased a large collection of tropical birds which he subsequently sold, at a considerable profit, to zoos and dealers in New York City. When a second Brazilian bird trip—this one terminating in London—proved equally lucrative, Buck began to recognize the commercial potential of what had hitherto been an avocation. Establishing his headquarters in Singapore, he soon became a major supplier of Asian fauna to zoos, circuses, and exhibitors in the United States. Among his customers were the New York Zoological Park; the Lincoln Park Zoo in Chicago; the Ringling Brothers, Barnum & Bailey circus; and the Al G. Barnes touring wild-animal show. Only infrequently did Buck actually participate in the capture of his specimens; his more usual method was to purchase them from dealers in Singapore, Calcutta, or other major centers. By the end of the 1920's, in more than forty Pacific crossings, he had brought to the United States thousands of animals, including thirty-nine elephants, sixty tigers, sixty-two leopards, and fifty-two orangutans.

In 1928 Buck married Muriel Reilly (Riley); they had one daughter, Barbara Muriel.

Frank Buck's greatest talent was for publicity. As early as 1915 he had worked as public-relations director for the amusement zone of the San Francisco exposition and, briefly, for the Mack Sennett motion picture company in Hollywood. In the 1930's, his business hard hit by the depression, he turned this promotional gift to good advantage, parlaying what had been a colorful but hardly remarkable career into a reputation of national proportions. In a series of adventure books written with various collaborators—beginning with the best-seller *Bring 'em Back Alive* (1930) and continuing through *Wild Cargo* (1932), *Fang and Claw* (1935), *On the Jungle Trails* (1937), and *Animals Are Like That!* (1st ed., 1939)—Buck infused with maximum dramatic interest the incidents and escapades of his life. The same formula proved effective in several shorter books, magazine articles, lectures, radio talks, and in the six wild-animal movies he produced and appeared in, which included three based on his own books. In 1937-1938 he toured with the Ringling circus, and in 1939-1940 he exhibited at the New York World's Fair. For several years he was also the impresario of Jungle Land, a wild-animal zoo in Amityville, L.I. The image of the intrepid explorer and trapper was furthered by his strong and rugged features, his black moustache, and a pith helmet which he invariably wore in publicity photographs. By the time of World War II, Frank—"Bring 'em Back Alive"—Buck had become a household name, familiar to adults and a host of youthful admirers.

Buck moved in the late 1940's from New York to San Angelo, Tex. He was sixty-six when he died of a lung ailment at the Texas Medical Center in Houston.

[Frank Buck with Ferrin Fraser, *All in a Lifetime* (1941); *N.Y. Times,* Mar. 26, 1950; *Current Biog.,* 1943, pp. 84–88; *Who's Who in Am., 1942–1943; Notable Am. Women,* II, 389–390 (on Amy Leslie).]
                                        PAUL BOYER

BUDD, EDWARD GOWEN (Dec. 28, 1870-Nov. 30, 1946), industrialist, was born in Smyrna, Del., the youngest of four children and second son of Henry George and Caroline (Kettell) Budd. His father was descended from William Budd, a Quaker who left England in the late seventeenth century and settled in New Jersey; his mother was the daughter of a New England clergyman. Edward Budd attended public school in Smyrna, where his father was justice of the peace, and completed high school in 1887. After working briefly as a machinist's apprentice at the Taylor Iron Works in Smyrna, he moved to Philadelphia, at that time one of the principal metalworking centers in the country. For the rest of his life Philadelphia was the setting for his business career. He began as a machinist's apprentice in the shops of Bement, Miles and Company, and was subsequently named drafting office foreman of the hydraulic press design group. Meanwhile, he furthered his education in engineering through evening classes and correspondence courses at the University of Pennsylvania and the Franklin Institute.

In 1899 Budd became factory manager of the American Pulley Company. His role in the design and fabrication of an innovative sheet-metal pulley gave him an insight into the capabilities of press- and die-formed light-gauge sheet-metal stampings as an alternative to forgings and castings. One of the first Americans to grasp the superior structural characteristics of such stampings, Budd drew from this experience the impetus for his later pioneer contributions as a manufacturer of transportation equipment. In 1902 he became general manager of the Hale and Kilburn Company, a leading maker of railroad car seats and interior trimmings for Pullman and other firms. The all-steel passenger car was then being developed to replace wooden coaches. Instead of castings and forgings, Budd introduced pressed steel parts joined by oxyacetylene welding. During this time he obtained from France the first autogenous gas-welding equipment ever used in the United States.

Under Budd's supervision, Hale and Kilburn in 1909 manufactured welded pressed steel panels for automobile bodies used by the Hupp Motor Car Company. About this time the spread of integrated manufacture among Pullman and other makers resulted in declining demand for railway car components. Looking to the emergent motorcar industry to take up the slack, Budd submitted to the business managers of Hale and Kilburn a proposal for constructing all-steel automobile bodies on a commercial basis. When the proposal was rejected, Budd resigned in 1912 and, with the help of two outside investors, organized the Edward G. Budd Manufacturing Company, with himself as president. The initial capitalization of $100,000 was increased to $500,000 within the first year, but the company from the start was short of capital; its rented shop in northeast Philadelphia was so small that a large stamping press had to be housed outdoors under a rented circus tent. Underfinancing continued to be a recurring problem for Budd over the next twenty-five years or more, chiefly because of large capital expenditures and sharp fluctuations in the business cycle.

With an expert staff, Budd organized his company as a producer of sheet-metal stampings, but before long the firm added a line of steel truck and auto bodies. He initially met indifference both from automobile manufacturers, hobbled by conservatism and inertia, and from body makers, most of whom had started as carriage makers and were content to produce bodies made primarily of wood. But in 1912 General Motors ordered welded all-steel touring-car bodies for the Oakland Motor Company, and three years later Budd also became exclusive supplier of touring-car and roadster bodies for the newly formed Dodge firm. Dodge soon became Budd's largest customer, and its orders enabled him to move into expanded quarters. Other new customers included Willys-Overland, Studebaker, Cadillac, and Franklin.

During World War I, Budd made a variety of military equipment, including army truck bodies, mobile field kitchens, helmets, shells, and bombs. He returned to automobile work after the Armistice and added an all-steel sedan body to his line. In the early 1920's, when other companies were still using wood, Budd conducted experiments that resulted in large one-piece steel components, such as floors, roof panels, and inside and outside door panels with integral window frames. This "monopiece" construction, which by shifting most of the stress to the outer surface ensured greater strength and rigidity, came in time to be generally adopted by the automobile industry.

Budd held patent rights on his steel body, but waived them in the American market in the belief that customer goodwill and a large backlog of orders were preferable to royalties and the likelihood of patent litigation. This left the field open to larger competitors, notably the Fisher, Briggs, and Murray companies. Budd, however, promoted sales of his all-steel body with an imaginative campaign of stunts to dramatize its superiority. The acquisition of new accounts, among them Ford and Chrysler, encouraged him to open a body division in Detroit in 1925. In 1916 Budd had established a separate Budd Wheel Corporation (reincorporated in 1921 as the Budd Wheel Company), and this, too, he transferred to Detroit in 1925. The company, which in 1919 had begun to manufacture the tapered steel disk wheel under a license agreement with the Michelin Company of France, became a leading supplier for makers of trucks, buses, and passenger cars, and later diversified its production to include the artillery type of steel disk wheel made from a single stamping.

The Great Depression of the 1930's, with its severe contraction of auto output, led Budd into his next pioneering venture, the fabrication of stainless steel. Technical obstacles had prevented the use of this alloy in large structures, but Budd's chief engineer, Col. Earl J. W. Ragsdale, devised the "Shotweld" method of controlled-resistance welding, which made it possible to join stainless steel without impairing its structural strength. The effectiveness of the process was demonstrated in 1931 when Budd built the first stainless steel airplane. Three years later he constructed a stainless steel railroad streamliner, the Pioneer Zephyr, which was put into service by the Chicago, Burlington and Quincy Railroad. Although the automotive industry remained the major source of income for the Budd company, the building of streamliners contributed materially to a restoration of the firm's profitability in the late 1930's. By December 1941 the Budd concern had sold nearly 500 lightweight railroad passenger cars.

During World War II the Budd facilities were once again fully converted to the production of war equipment. The company was the original maker of the bazooka (antitank) projectile and the rifle grenade, and turned out millions of fragmentation bombs and shells. In 1946 the Edward G. Budd Manufacturing Company and the Budd Wheel Company were merged into the Budd Company.

Tall and erect, with penetrating blue eyes, Budd was a man of driving energy whose impact upon the organization was primarily that of a catalyst. He was formal and courtly in manner, and his social views befitted an economic individualist and self-made man. In a crucial dispute with the National Labor Board in 1933-1934, he successfully prevented the United Automobile Workers from organizing his plant. In religion Budd was a Methodist. On May 16, 1899, he married Mary Louisa Wright of Philadelphia. They had five children: Edward Gowen, Archibald Wright, Mary, Katharine, and Francenia Allibone. Budd died of a coronary occlusion at his home in Germantown, Pa., a month before his seventy-sixth birthday, and was buried in West Laurel Hill Cemetery, Philadelphia. His honors included the John Scott Medal, awarded in 1932 for his work on stainless steel as a structural material, and, in 1944, the medal of the American Society of Mechanical Engineers for "outstanding engineering achievements."

[G. L. Kelley, "The Life and Work of Edward Gowen Budd," *Jour. of the Franklin Inst.*, May 1949; Edward G. Budd, Jr., *Edward G. Budd (1870-1946), "Father of the Streamliners," and the Budd Company* (Newcomen Soc. pamphlet, 1950); "Pioneer without Profit," *Fortune*, Feb. 1937 (with portrait); J. D. Ratcliff, "Old Man in a Hurry," *Liberty*, Dec. 19, 1942; *Time*, Jan. 8, 1940, pp. 49-50; Lloyd E. Griscom in *Antique Automobile*, Jan.-Feb. 1971; obituaries in *N.Y. Times*, Dec. 2, 1946, and *Railway Age*, Dec. 7, 1946; *Nat. Cyc. Am. Biog.*, XXXVI, 17-19; Sidney Fine, *The Automobile under the Blue Eagle* (1963); Lewis L. Lorwin and Arthur Wubnig, *Labor Relations Boards* (1935); death certificate from Pa. Dept. of Health; information from Mr. Paul O. Sichert, Jr., of the Budd Co.]
WILLIAM GREENLEAF

BULLARD, ROBERT LEE (Jan. 15, 1861-Sept. 11, 1947), army officer, the eleventh of twelve children and second son of Daniel and Susan (Mizell) Bullard, was born on his father's homestead near Opelika, Lee County, Ala. He was christened William Robert, but changed his name as a boy in honor of the Confederate general. His father was a North Carolinian of Scottish and English ancestry; his mother, the daughter of a Methodist circuit

rider, was of Georgia Huguenot stock. They were pioneer settlers in eastern Alabama, where Daniel Bullard raised cotton, sold cotton gins, and speculated in farm land. Robert, a shy and sickly youth, was educated by his family and a series of temporary schoolmasters. He attended the Agricultural and Mechanical College of Alabama (later Auburn University) for one year. In 1881, having won a competitive examination, he entered the United States Military Academy at West Point. The Civil War had given him romantic notions about soldiering, but his immediate motive was to finish college without going into debt.

Bullard's academic record at West Point was undistinguished, and after graduating in 1885, twenty-seventh in a class of thirty-nine, he was assigned, like other low-ranking graduates, to the infantry. For most of the next thirteen years Bullard served with the 10th Infantry, chiefly in the Southwest. On Apr. 17, 1888, at Fort Wingate, N. Mex., he married Rose Douglass Brabson, daughter of a Tennessee congressman and stepdaughter of an army surgeon. They had four children: Robert Lee, Peter Cleary, Rose, and Charles Keith.

Weary of frontier duty and disturbed by his stagnant career (he was still a first lieutenant at thirty-seven), Bullard arranged a transfer to the Commissary Department in 1898 as a captain. During the Spanish-American War, with the temporary rank of colonel, he commanded the 3rd Alabama Regiment, made up of black volunteers, and later the 39th Volunteer Infantry Regiment, which engaged in guerrilla and open warfare in the Philippines in 1900-1901 and won a reputation for aggressiveness and determination in the face of sickness and the Filipinos' stubborn resistance. The regiment's qualities were those of its colonel. When his regiment was mustered out, Bullard stayed in the Philippines as a commissary, but arranged a transfer back to the Infantry in 1902 at the rank of major, thus "jumping" more than a hundred of his peers in seniority. To silence his critics, he volunteered for more combat service against the Moros on Mindanao, where he served as a battalion commander and district governor until 1904. He became a protégé of Gen. Leonard Wood.

In the decade prior to World War I, Bullard sought varied and challenging service which enhanced his reputation. Between 1906 and 1909 he was an official in the provisional government of Cuba, then under army occupation; in 1911 he went into revolutionary Mexico to search for Japanese naval bases. After graduating from the Army War College in 1912, he was promoted to colonel and picked by Chief of Staff Wood and Secretary of War Henry L. Stimson to command the 26th Infantry. Bullard made this regiment combat-ready during the Mexican civil war, and in 1915 it helped keep the peace in the lower Rio Grande Valley. The following year he commanded a brigade of National Guard regiments from Louisiana, South Dakota, and Oklahoma, mobilized for service on the Mexican border. His militiamen found Bullard demanding, but a personable officer with little taste for formality and an appetite for polo, hunting, and field training.

In June 1917, after American entry into World War I, Bullard was promoted to brigadier general—a rank for which he had lobbied for fifteen years—and was placed in command of the 2nd Brigade of the 1st Division. He accompanied the division to France, where Gen. John J. Pershing soon made him commandant of the infantry officer specialist schools of the American Expeditionary Forces as major general (August 1917). In December Pershing gave him the command of the 1st Division; its successful attack on Cantigny in late May of 1918 demonstrated for the Germans and the Allies the offensive ability of an American division. Bullard was an able and popular commander. He gathered an exceptional group of officers around him, including three future Chiefs of Staff, and his ability to speak French helped him to get along with his French superiors. In July 1918 he assumed command of the III Corps. During the summer this unit took part in the Aisne-Marne counteroffensive along the Vesle River, battering the Germans, who finally retreated in early September. Bullard then led the III Corps into the Meuse-Argonne sector, where they again fought creditably. Promoted to lieutenant general, Bullard took charge of the Second Army in October, shortly before the Armistice. His role in the war won him the Distinguished Service Medal and several foreign decorations.

Returning to the United States in May 1919, Bullard became commanding general of the II Corps area at Fort Jay, Governors Island, N.Y., where he served until his compulsory retirement in 1925. His first wife died in 1921, and on Aug. 24, 1927, he married Mrs. Ella (Reiff) Wall, a widow from Philadelphia.

Tall, slender, athletic, patrician in appearance, Bullard was a popular speaker. After his retirement he sought to promote public interest in military affairs through lectures, articles for the Hearst press, and the work of the National Security League, of which he became president in 1925. A dogged nativist and isolationist, conservative in his philosophy, he was a strong critic of the New Deal; in 1935 he suggested that the Communists were using the relief system to undermine the United States. Reared as a Methodist, he had in 1901 become a convert to Roman Catholicism, the religion of his first wife. He died of a cerebral hemorrhage at the Fort Jay Hospital in New York City and was buried in the Military Academy Cemetery at West Point.

Bullard built his military reputation on his ability as a field commander of citizen-soldiers, his loyalty to both his superiors and his subordinates, and his thorough knowledge of troop morale, logistics, tactics, communications, and administration. He was typical of the largely anonymous but talented officers who ended their careers as generals in the American Expeditionary Forces.

[Bullard Papers, Lib. of Cong., including diaries, notebooks, correspondence, and an unpublished autobiography; army personnel records; Bullard material in the archives of Auburn Univ. and Alpha Tau Omega fraternity, Chicago; sketch of Bullard in Thomas McA. Owen, ed., *Hist. of Ala. and Dict. of Ala. Biog.*, III, 254 (1921); obit. in *Assembly* (journal of the West Point Alumni Assoc.), July 1948; Joseph C. Chase, *Soldiers All: Portraits and Sketches of the Men of the A.E.F.* (1920), pp. 29–30; Edward S. Holden and Wirt Robinson, eds., *Gen. Cullum's Biog. Register of the Officers and Graduates of the U.S. Military Acad.*, Supplements, IV–VI (1920–1921). See also Edward M. Coffman, *The War to End All Wars: The Am. Military Experience in World War I* (1968). Bullard's memoir, *Personalities and Reminiscences of the War* (1925), is a candid source of information on the A.E.F.]
ALLAN R. MILLETT

BURGESS, W(ILLIAM) STARLING (Dec. 25, 1878–Mar. 19, 1947), inventor, naval architect, airplane manufacturer, and poet, was born into a prominent Boston family, the oldest of two sons of Edward Burgess, renowned Boston yacht designer whose father Benjamin Franklin Burgess had been a notable New England merchant, and Caroline Louisa (Sullivant) Burgess of Columbus, Ohio, daughter of William Starling Sullivant of an old Virginia family. Starling Burgess' early years exposed him to yachting at home and abroad, especially during the 1880's, when his father designed the three *America's Cup* defenders, the awards from which the elder Burgess earned sufficient funds for his sons' educations. Burgess, who received his B.A. from Harvard in 1901, inherited his father's mechanical instincts and love of the sea and poetry and hoped one day to emulate the father's accomplishments in yachting. After service aboard the auxiliary cruiser *Prairie* as a gunner's mate during the Spanish-American War, Burgess was tempted to follow his lively artistic imagination, influenced by the works of John Ruskin, into a literary career. "Poetry was the foundation of accomplishment, he contended, and it carried him to his love of the wind and the sea" (*N.Y. Times,* Mar. 20, 1947).

In the first of several partnerships (1900) and single business ventures (1904) in the design and construction of yachts and commercial vessels in the Marblehead-Boston area, Burgess exhibited a flair for experimentation and created impressive, fast vessels, as in the scow-type "skimming dishes" like *Outlook* (1902), the Sonder and Q and R Universal Rule class yachts, the largest five-masted sailing schooner ever built, the *Jane Palmer* (1904), and the less successful fast fishing schooner *Elizabeth Silsbee* (1905).

"With a restless mind that was attracted by almost any sort of engineering problem" (Taylor, *Yachting*, 80), he fell under the spell of aviation in 1909, when a Wright brothers plane flew over the New York hospital in which he was recovering from a major operation. With Norman Prince, subsequent founder of the Lafayette Escadrille, Burgess took flying lessons from the Wrights and in 1910 opened his own airplane manufacturing company at Marblehead. Utilizing the designs of his only two competitors, the Wright and Glenn H. Curtiss companies, his firm shared with them many early American and British government contracts; its stocks were purchased by the Curtiss company early in 1916. Burgess' fertile mind succeeded best when he was able to apply his knowledge of the sea to naval "hydroaeroplanes" (seaplanes), first with pontoon floats for land planes, then with the D-1 flying boat (1913), and finally his adapting of Englishman J. W. Dunne's revolutionary delta-shaped, swept-wing tailless design into the Burgess-Dunne seaplane, earning him the 1915 Collier Trophy for that year's "greatest progress in aviation." He and his brother Charles Paine Burgess joined the navy during World War I to design dirigibles: Starling for the duration as a lieutenant commander, Charles for the rest of his life as the navy's leading authority in airship design.

After the war Burgess returned to yacht designing, into which he introduced innovations to hulls, rigging, and sails—notably the "staysail rig," first used on the schooner *Advance* (1924). Operating from Boston as the partner of Frank C. Paine (1922-1926) and

after 1927 from New York in several short-lived partnerships, he designed all sizes of sailing vessels but most notably large, fast, racing craft, like the Gloucester fishing schooner *Mayflower* (1922), criticized as a racing yacht in disguise, the forty-six-foot rating Class M sloop *Prestige* (1927) of Harold S. Vanderbilt, and the famous ocean racing schooner *Niña* (1928).

Burgess dominated American yachting during the 1930's by utilizing modern aerodynamic and industrial techniques. Assisted initially by his brother Charles, he designed the three seventy-six-foot rating Class J sloops which successfully defended the America's Cup. With Vanderbilt as captain and Burgess in the after guard to tend his brother's revolutionary duralumin mast and rigging, their *Enterprise* handily defeated three other Cup contenders and then Sir Thomas Lipton's *Shamrock V* in 1930; their *Rainbow* (designed with Henry Gruber) beat two of the older contenders and T. O. M. Sopwith's *Endeavour I* in close Cup competition in 1934; and their welded-hull *Ranger* (designed with Olin J. Stephens), "far and away the fastest all-around Class J sloop ever built" (Taylor *Yachting*, 81) and probably "the fastest racing yacht of all times" (Baader, p. 314), easily defeated Sopwith's *Endeavour II* in 1937.

Burgess also designed R. Buckminster Fuller's three-wheeled, bullet-shaped Dymaxion car based on reduced air flow in 1933 and anti-submarine devices for the navy during World War II. He died at Hoboken while studying damage control for the navy at the Stevens Institute of Technology.

Described as "a genius in every sense of the word" (Taylor, *Yachtsman's Yearbook*, 401), a "jack of all trades in which mechanical skill counted" (*N.Y. Times*, Mar. 20, 1947), with "hazy, but brilliant conceptions" (Hoyt, p. 284), Burgess in many ways typified the inventor who bridged two technological ages by marrying the aerodynamic features of sail and aviation in his yachts and seaplanes. Ignoring the accusations of his all-sail critics that he employed too many modern devices and mechanic-crewmen on his Class J yachts, he applied modern metals, air flow principles and water tank tests with models in the design of over 2,000 superior yachts. Something of "a remarkable and lovable character" (Herreshoff, p. 179), wiry and mustached, Burgess as a young man reputedly stood on his head without using his hands to recite his friend A. C. Swinburne's ballads and even late in life followed his father's habit of turning a double somersault on the deck of his winning yacht as it crossed the finish line.

His first wife, Helene Adams Willard (1901), died after one year of marriage, while his second, Rosamund Tudor (1904), bore him two sons, Edward and Frederick Tudor and a daughter, Tasha Tudor, before the marriage ended in divorce (1925). In 1925 he married Elsie Janet Foos; they had two daughters, Ann and Diana. Their marriage ended in divorce (1933). Two other marriages followed, to Anna Dale Biddle (1933) and Marjorie Gladding Young (1945). He is buried in Boston.

[William H. Taylor has provided the most complete information on Burgess: "W. Starling Burgess," *Yachting*, May 1947, pp. 80–81, with photograph, and "Who is America's Leading Skipper?" in Alfred F. Loomis, ed., *The Yachtsman's Yearbook 1934*, pp. 35–44, with photograph; Harold S. Vanderbilt, *Enterprise* (1930), with photograph; Howard I. Chapelle, *The American Fishing Schooners, 1825–1935* (1973); William P. Stephens, *Traditions and Memories of American Yachting* (rev. ed., 1945); Jerome E. Brooks, *The $30,000,000 Cup* (1958); L. Francis Herreshoff, *An Introduction to Yachting* (1963); Juan Baader, *The Sailing Yacht* (1965); C. Sherman Hoyt, *Memoirs* (1950); and Paul C. Morris, *American Sailing Coasters of the North Atlantic* (1973). For Burgess' aircraft and automobile, see George van Deurs, *Wings for the Fleet* (1966), and Robert W. Marks, *The Dymaxion World of Buckminster Fuller* (1960), with photographs. See also *N.Y. Times*, Apr. 14, 1930, for a partial account of his sailing career and *N.Y. Times*, Mar. 20, 1947, obituary, with photograph. Burgess' poetry may be sampled in his *The Eternal Laughter, and Other Poems* (1903). His nephew, Edward D. Burgess, provided important data.]

CLARK G. REYNOLDS

BURLEIGH, HENRY THACKER (Dec. 2, 1866–Sept. 12, 1949), singer and composer, was born in Erie, Pa., the younger of the two sons of Henry Thacker Burleigh and Elizabeth (Waters) Burleigh. His father, a laborer, was a native of Newburgh, N.Y. Burleigh's maternal grandfather, Hamilton Waters, had been born a slave in Somerset County, Md.; freed after being blinded by punishments received for his attempts to escape, he settled in Erie and became the town crier. From his grandfather, young Harry (as Burleigh was known) acquired an early familiarity with Negro folksongs. His mother, a graduate of a teachers' college, sang well and encouraged her son's interest in music. Since the family was very poor, Harry worked from early childhood, running errands, selling newspapers, and lighting street lamps. He sang constantly and attended musical events whenever possible. His mother worked as a domestic at the home of a family named Russell, where well-known musical artists often performed. After Harry had once stood knee-deep in snow for hours outside the Russell home listening to the pianist Rafael

Joseffy, his mother arranged for him to serve as a doorman when musical events took place.

Burleigh graduated from the Erie high school, where he presumably learned typing and stenography, since for a time he worked as a stenographer. As he grew older he built up a local reputation as a singer and was able in that way to supplement his earnings. At the age of twenty-six he went to New York City, planning to attend the National Conservatory of Music, which offered free tuition for those who could pass the stringent entrance examinations. He failed on his first try, but was given a second opportunity upon the recommendation of the registrar, Frances (Knapp) MacDowell, mother of the composer Edward MacDowell, who remembered him as the young doorman at the Russell musicales. During his four years at the conservatory, Burleigh studied voice with Christian Fritsch, harmony with Rubin Goldmark, and counterpoint with John White and Max Spicker. He played double bass and tympani in the conservatory orchestra. To support himself, he helped Mrs. MacDowell with clerical tasks, copied music scores, gave piano and voice lessons, and served as the orchestra librarian. Burleigh also grew close to the Czech composer Antonín Dvořák, who was director of the National Conservatory from 1892 to 1895. Dvořák was a leading exponent of nationalistic music, and Burleigh spent many hours in the composer's apartment, singing Negro folksongs for him and discussing their significance. Burleigh's influence is reflected in three of Dvořák's works which employ Negro folk idioms: Symphony no. 5 (*From the New World*), and two chamber works (op. 96 and op. 97).

In 1894 Burleigh secured the position of baritone soloist at New York's St. George's Protestant Episcopal Church, winning in competition with fifty-nine white candidates. His appointment caused considerable consternation among the parishioners, but his talent earned him acceptance and he remained there for fifty-two years. He established two traditions: he sang Fauré's "The Palms" every Easter Suday, and beginning in 1923 he conducted an annual service of Negro spirituals. In 1900 Burleigh also became the first black soloist at Temple Emanu-El, serving until 1946. Over the years Burleigh toured extensively as a concert singer in the United States and Europe; his appearances included command performances for King Edward VII of England, Prince Henry of Prussia, Theodore Roosevelt, and many other notables. In 1898 he had a brief fling with vaudeville, being persuaded to play in the orchestra for a show by the black comedians Bert Williams and George Walker.

Burleigh first began to compose about 1898. His art songs and sentimental ballads became popular with the most celebrated singers of the time, including John McCormack, Lucrezia Bori, and Ernestine Schumann-Heink. Most frequently performed were "Jean" (1903), "The Prayer" (1915), "Little Mother of Mine" (1917), "In the Great Somewhere" (1919), and "Just You" (1921). Italian troops used his song "The Young Warrior" (1914), a setting of a poem by James Weldon Johnson, as their marching song during World War I. From 1911 until his death Burleigh was a music editor for the firm of G. Ricordi and Company.

Burleigh made his great contribution to American music with his artistic settings of Negro spirituals. Before Burleigh, spirituals had been available only in ensemble and choral arrangements. His "Deep River" (1916), the first concert arrangement of a spiritual for solo voice, was immensely popular. Other popular arrangements over the years were: "Weeping Mary," "By and By," "You May Bury Me in de Eas'" (all 1917); "Sometimes I Feel Like a Motherless Child," "My Lord What a Morning" (1918); "There is a Balm in Gilead" (1919); "Were You There," "Every Time I Feel the Spirit" (1924); "Joshua Fit de Battle of Jericho" (1935). In addition to arranging approximately 100 spirituals for solo voice and chorus, Burleigh composed more than 250 art songs and miscellaneous choral pieces, arranged plantation melodies for violin and piano, and published the *Old Songs Hymnal* (1929). His style varies according to the musical form, but typically is characterized by a basically diatonic harmonic texture discreetly flavored with chromatic coloring. His accompaniments are never obtrusive, but support and sustain the moods of the texts. On the whole, the solo songs are superior to the choral pieces, the art songs and spirituals more imaginative than the ballads.

Burleigh was a short, dignified, dapper man who looked twenty or more years younger than his age. He was noted for his infectious enthusiasm for life, music, and poetry—which he read in French, Latin, German, Italian, and Hebrew—and for his generosity to struggling black musicians. He counted among his protégés Roland Hayes, Paul Robeson, and Marian Anderson. A charter member of the American Society of Composers, Authors, and Publishers (ASCAP) in 1914, Burleigh was elected to its board of directors in 1941. His many honors include the Spingarn Medal (1917) and a Harmon Foundation Award (1929). Burleigh married Louise Alston on Feb. 9, 1898. They had one son, Alston Waters. Burleigh died of a heart attack at the age of eighty-two in Stamford, Conn., and was buried in Mount Hope Cemetery, Hastings, N.Y. Burleigh was a leader of the group of "nationalistic" black composers that included R. Nathaniel Dett, Clarence C. White, and Will Marion Cook.

[The Burleigh Collection of magazine and newspaper articles, located in the Schomburg Collection of the N.Y. Public Lib.; Maud Cuney-Hare, *Negro Musicians and Their Music* (1936); Eileen Southern, *The Music of Black Americans* (1971); Ellsworth Janifer, "H. T. Burleigh Ten Years Later," *Phylon*, Summer 1960; Henry Lee, "Swing Low, Sweet Chariot," *Coronet*, July 1947; Alain Locke, *The Negro and His Music* (1936); Benjamin Brawley, *The Negro Genius* (1940); *The ASCAP Biog. Dict. of Composers, Authors and Publishers*, 3rd ed. (1966); obituaries in *Jour. of Negro Hist.*, Jan. 1950, and *N.Y. Times*, Sept. 13, 1949. Alston Burleigh provided information about his father in personal interviews. Reproductions of photographs are to be found in the Cuney-Hare and Southern books.]

EILEEN SOUTHERN

BURNHAM, FREDERICK RUSSELL May 11, 1861–Sept. 1, 1947), explorer, scout, soldier of fortune, was born in Tivoli (near Mankato), Minn., a small settlement on an Indian reservation. He was the elder of the two sons of the Rev. Edwin Otway Burnham, a Congregational minister and missionary, and Rebecca (Russell) Burnham. His father was a native of Kentucky; his mother's family had come from England around 1832 and had settled in Iowa. The elder Burnham, a graduate of Union Theological Seminary, was also a homesteader and farmer, and though he retained, as Frederick Burnham later wrote, the "narrow Puritanical ideas of his scholastic environment," he introduced his son to the pleasures of woodcraft, tracking, and nature study. Burnham was chiefly educated at home, where he learned the "three R's" and memorized Bible passages. His mother told him adventure stories, but these often paled beside the family's own frontier experiences, which included at least one narrow escape from an Indian war party. When Burnham was nine his father suffered a lung injury in a barnbuilding accident and moved his family to Los Angeles, Calif.—then a small ranching town. After his father's death in 1873, Burnham decided to remain in the West rather than return east with his mother and brother.

Already he was determined to lead the life of a scout, and he set out systematically to learn his craft. Beginning at the age of thirteen as a horseback messenger for the Western Union

Telegraph Company, he spent the next two decades ranging widely over the Southwest and Mexico. Except for an unhappy year living with an uncle and attending high school in Clinton, Iowa, he hunted and sold big game, prospected for gold, fought Apaches, served as a deputy sheriff, and was even a hired gunhand in an Arizona range war. Above all, Burnham sought out the best scouts living in the Southwest, including one who had worked for Gen. George Crook, and closely studied their methods. Girding himself for the rigors of his vocation, he studied military strategy, learned to subsist on minimal rations of food and water, and even gave up smoking in order to heighten his sense of smell. In the course of learning the "signs of the trail," Burnham acquired a knowledge of botany, meteorology, and geology, which provided a solid foundation for his future prospecting ventures.

Burnham had been intrigued since childhood by tales of Africa, and he greatly admired the exploits of the British colonialist Cecil Rhodes. Summoned by an "irresistible call," Burnham went to Matabeleland (later part of Rhodesia) in 1893 on the eve of a bloody rebellion by the Matabeles, an offshoot of the Zulu nation, against the colonial settlers. As a scout for Rhodes' British South Africa Company, Burnham gained considerable fame when he sought unsuccessfully to relieve a force commanded by Major Allan Wilson that had been attacked by a large band of Kaffir warriors. Wilson's force was killed to a man, but their fight for survival and Burnham's rescue attempt were quickly legendized in the press and in *Wilson's Last Stand,* a popular London stage play.

In the second Matabele rebellion in 1896, Burnham's heroic image was enhanced by an episode in which he supposedly killed the M'Limo, believed by the settlers to be a deified tribal prophet who had inflamed the Matabele against the whites. The M'Limo seems actually to have been an invisible spirit whose commands were interpreted by a number of native priest-oracles. In a daring raid, Burnham tracked one of the most provocative of these oracles to his sacred cave in the Matopo mountains and there killed him, apparently in cold blood. Subsequent popular legend regarded this act as instrumental in ending the rebellion, but its real effect is difficult to judge.

When not helping to quash native uprisings, Burnham led several expeditions from his home in Bulawayo, the principal settlement of southern Rhodesia, to explore the area north of the Zambesi River, where Rhodes had granted him an unpegged claim of one hundred square miles. A friend of the adventure novelist H. Rider Haggard, the romantic Burnham hoped to locate the Englishman's fabled "King Solomon's Mines." Though failing in this, he mapped previously uncharted regions, located significant African ruins, and discovered important copper deposits. His expeditions also provided Rhodes with geographical and geological information necessary to complete the projected Cape-to-Cairo railroad; it was Burnham who came upon the rich Wankie coal fields, a vital factor in the future economic development of Rhodesia.

Although he returned to North America in 1897 to mine gold in the Klondike, Burnham was recalled to South Africa early in 1899 with the outbreak of the Boer War. Named chief of scouts in the field for the British army, he was twice captured by the Boers and was wounded in a thwarted attempt to sever the Pretoria-Delagoa Bay railway line before being invalided to England in June 1900. There he was given the rank of major, was widely feted by London society, and was awarded both the Distinguished Service Order and the South African Medal. Returning to Africa in 1901, he explored the Volta River in West Africa and later, as a representative of the British East Africa Company, the vast territory between the Indian Ocean and Victoria Nyanza. One of his parties discovered Lake Magadi, a rich source of carbonate of soda.

Burnham returned to the United States in 1904, and over the next decades engaged in several prospecting and exploring ventures. Spurred by tales of buried cities, he led archaeological expeditions into Mexico, and his discoveries added to the knowledge of Mayan civilization. With the mining engineer John Hays Hammond, whom he had first met in Africa, he launched a project to irrigate and cultivate the Yaqui River valley of northern Mexico, a plan frustrated by the onset of the Mexican civil war of 1912. More successful was the Burnham Exploration Company, an oil venture established with Hammond in 1919, which developed the highly productive Dominguez Hill field in California. Concerned with the preservation of the American wilderness, Burnham was one of the original members of the California park commission, and in his later years he lived on a cattle ranch in the High Sierras near Sequoia National Park.

In neither personality nor physique did Burnham fit the rough-and-tumble stereotype of the frontier scout. A slight, though muscular man, handsome, with a bronzed complexion, and penetrating light-blue eyes, he was nicknamed "He-Who-Sees-in-the-Dark" by African natives and "Hawkeye" by his colleague-in-arms Sir Robert Baden-Powell, founder of the Boy Scouts, who regarded Burnham as a model for emulation by the young. Quiet, courteous, and well informed, he possessed a personal modesty rare in one of his calling. Perhaps most untypical was the fact that Burnham's adventures were all carried out *en famille*. After his marriage in March 1884 to Blanche Blick of Clinton, Iowa, he was accompanied everywhere both by his wife and by a bevy of in-laws. Burnham's daughter Nada (named after the heroine of a Haggard story) was the first white child born in Bulawayo. He also had two sons: Roderick and Bruce. Burnham's wife died in 1938, and on Oct. 28, 1943, he married Ilo K. Willits. Burnham died of a coronary thrombosis in Santa Barbara, Calif., at the age of eighty-six, and was buried in Three Rivers, Tulare County, Calif., near his ranch. His important scouting career in Africa had begun just as the American frontier was coming to a close. As he once commented: "It is the constructive side of frontier life that most appeals to me, the building up of a country . . . ; when the place is finally settled I don't seem to enjoy it very long" (Davis, p. 215).

[After spurning publishers' offers for decades, Burnham finally set down the story of his life in two autobiographical volumes: *Scouting on Two Continents* (1926) and *Taking Chances* (1944). His name and exploits figured prominently in several contemporary memoirs, including: H. Rider Haggard, *The Days of My Life*, 2 vols. (1926); Robert S. S. Baden-Powell, *The Matabele Campaign, 1896* (1897); Frederick C. Selous, *Sunshine and Storm in Rhodesia* (1896); and John Hays Hammond, *Autobiog.*, 2 vols. (1935) and "South African Memories: Rhodes-Barnato-Burnham," *Scribner's Mag.*, Mar. 1921. See also Richard Harding Davis, *Real Soldiers of Fortune* (1912). A contemporary biography for young readers is James E. West and Peter O. Lamb, *He-Who-Sees-in-the-Dark: The Boys' Story of Frederick Burnham, the Am. Scout* (1932). Useful secondary sources include: Robert Cary, *A Time to Die*, 2nd ed. (1969), which contains a somewhat debunking account of Burnham's Rhodesian exploits; Stafford Glass, *The Matabele War* (1968); L. S. Amery, ed., *The Times Hist. of the War in South Africa, 1899–1902*, 7 vols. (1900–1909); Sir (John) Frederick Maurice, comp., *Hist of the War in South Africa, 1899–1902*, 4 vols. (1906–1910); and R. R. Money, "The Greatest Scout," *Blackwood's Mag.*, Jan. 1962. See also *Who Was Who in America*, II (1950); and *Nat. Cyc. Am. Biog.*, XXXVI, 100–101. Obituaries appeared in the *N.Y. Times*, Sept. 2, 1947, and *The Times* (London), Sept. 4, 1947. On Burnham's father, see Union Theological Seminary, *Alumni Catalogue, 1836–1926* (1926).]

PHILIP DE VENCENTES

BURROUGHS, EDGAR RICE (Sept. 1, 1875–Mar. 19, 1950), author, was born in Chicago, Ill., the youngest of the four sons of George Tyler Burroughs, a wealthy businessman, and Mary Evaline (Zieger) Burroughs.

The father was descended from early English settlers of Massachusetts; the mother was of Pennsylvania German ancestry. George Burroughs had been a captain in the Union Army, and his son remembered him as retaining a "very stern and military" aspect. Mrs. Burroughs was warm and good-humored. Ed was an uncomplicated boy, fond of outdoor sports, but a poor student. He learned to shoot and ride on his brothers' Idaho ranch, where he relished the camaraderie of cowboy life. Educated at various private schools in Chicago, he was sent to Phillips Academy, Andover, Mass., to prepare for Yale, but was expelled, confirming his father's bitter predictions of failure. The pattern of the next two decades was one of high striving and low attainment.

Burroughs continued his schooling at the Michigan Military Academy in Orchard Lake, Mich., whose novel-writing commandant fulfilled his youthful ideal of the gallant fighting man. He perfected his horsemanship and decided on a military career. When he failed the examination for West Point he was forced to return to Orchard Lake, where he gave instruction in geology and the Gatling gun. In 1896 Burroughs enlisted in the U.S. cavalry but was soon discharged, ostensibly for a weak heart. The years from 1897 to 1911 saw a long succession of mostly petty jobs and aborted small business ventures in Idaho and Chicago. When he needed money to marry his childhood sweetheart, he took a job with his father's American Battery Company, but the friction between father and son worsened. Burroughs married Emma Centennia Hulbert, the daughter of a Chicago hotel owner, on Jan. 31, 1900; they had three children: Joan, Hulbert, and John Coleman. The newlyweds headed west to share in the mining ventures of Burroughs' luckless brothers. Reared in affluence, the couple soon found themselves in less-than-genteel poverty. In 1905 they returned to Chicago, reduced to living in George Burroughs' house while Ed held down a series of low-paying jobs. One of his assignments was the placing of advertisements in pulp magazines. Claiming that a novice could equal the top pulp authors, he was soon writing fiction to relieve his boredom.

In 1911 Burroughs tossed off his first novel and sold it to one of the leading science fiction and adventure magazines, *All-Story*, which ran it as a serial the following year. "Under the Moons of Mars" by "Norman Bean" (a nom de plume later happily discarded) was highly successful, and Burroughs turned to writing full time. By the time the novel was published in book form as *A Princess of Mars* (1917), he had nineteen other works in print, most of them serialized in *All-Story* before book publication. Burroughs is best known for three long series. The Martian novels, beginning with *A Princess of Mars,* concern the conquest of Barsoom (Mars) by "John Carter, gentleman," an ageless swordsman from Virginia. In the Pellucidar series, which began in 1922 with *At the Earth's Core,* David Innes, a wealthy Yale graduate, becomes emperor of a prehistoric world deep within the globe. His most famous series, Tarzan of the Apes, began with the novel of that title in 1914. There the scion of an ancient English family, whose parents were shipwrecked on the African coast, survives their death to grow up in the bosom of a tribe of prehominid apes. In the sequel Tarzan makes the transit from jungle to civilization, recovers the title of Lord Greystoke, and wins the hand of the beautiful Jane Porter.

Though set in different worlds, these series are alike in their essentials. The hero is a fighting man, quick-witted, resourceful, and inured to the hardships and terrors of an unexplored continent or a retrograde civilization on a dying planet. He has a capacity for great violence, even bloodlust, but lives by a code of honor that exalts him above the mass of his fellow creatures, whom he rules by strength of character or vanquishes by righteous conquest. His only vulnerability is a chivalrous recklessness, especially when he follows the promptings of an enamored heart. His womanly ideal—his "mate" or "princess"—is imperious and willful, but ultimately yielding. The love story is naively romantic rather than erotic, despite Burroughs' celebration of "the primeval woman." Lest too much be made of Burroughs' fondness for unsullied nature, it must be pointed out that there is more of the weird and horrifying strain of Rider Haggard than the innocent vision of Rousseau. Certain themes recur in Burroughs' novels. The virtues of physical courage and militarism are pointed up by his fascination with the decline of civilizations through luxury, effeminacy, and the tyranny of debauched priesthoods. The Africa of Tarzan abounds with lost civilizations ruled by ruthless queens and priestly cabals. Barsoom is wracked by genocidal wars waged by several races, each more degenerate than the last. A related theme is the importance of heredity—positively, as in the impeccable lineage of a Lord Greystoke, and negatively, as in the atavistic races and monstrous hybrids of man and beast. *Tarzan and the Lion Man* (1934) features a demented Victorian geneticist who calls himself God and produces an English-speaking race of gorillas through infusions of Tudor chromosomes.

Burroughs' writing is uneven and often amateurish. His technique in the Tarzan tales of following parallel lines of action through the eyes of various characters has been compared to cinematic cross-cutting, and he often succeeds through a racy, headlong descriptive power. The feral child rapt in the discovery of a written language, his animal delight in hurtling through the "upper terrace" of the rain forest, and the orgiastic ritual Dum Dum of the apes are Burroughs at his best. But he often stumbles in characterization and dialogue. Thus Lady Greystoke to the villain bent on raping her: "What is the use . . . of expatiating upon the depths to which your vengeful nature can sink?" (*The Beasts of Tarzan,* 1916). Burroughs occasionally scores when he writes in a satirical vein, particularly in *Tarzan and the Ant Men* (1924), but he is more often clumsy than not. His shortcomings as a writer are most apparent in *Beyond Thirty* (*All Around* magazine, 1916; published in book form, 1957), whose theme is the reversion of England and Western Europe to wilderness. Just when the story promises to be more than a potboiler, it grinds to a halt, as though Burroughs' invention had flagged.

Burroughs' sudden success enabled him to move to Hollywood, where he could supervise the filming of the immensely popular Tarzan movies. In 1919 he bought an estate near Hollywood, in what would later be named Tarzana, Calif., which he operated at a heavy loss as a "rancho." Always pressed for money, he averaged three novels a year, producing some sixty-eight titles in all. He was an inveterate plunger, and his bad investments reduced his fortune. His financial interests expanded so rapidly that in 1923 he took the unprecedented step of incorporating himself. A *Tarzan* comic strip began in 1929 and was still being published in the 1970's. Tarzan products ranging from gasoline to coloring books proliferated. A radio serial starring his daughter and son-in-law (a former movie Tarzan) enjoyed great popularity. Tarzan of the films was, of course, the most successful of these by-products, though Burroughs was pained to see his multilingual aristocrat reduced to a lumpish commoner grunting in pidgin English, bereft of both intellect and irony.

Burroughs' first marriage ended in divorce on Dec. 6, 1934, and on Apr. 4, 1935, he married Florence (Gilbert) Dearholt in Las Vegas,

Nev. They were divorced on May 4, 1942. The outbreak of World War II prompted Burroughs to write a series of morale-boosting pieces for the *Advertiser* of Honolulu, where he was then living. Returning to California in late 1944, he fell prey to Parkinson's disease. He died at the age of seventy-four, in Encino, Calif., of heart disease and hardening of the arteries. His ashes were placed in the Chapel of the Pines Crematorium in Los Angeles.

Burroughs was no Kipling or H. G. Wells, but he was one of the most successful popular novelists America has ever produced. The 1960's saw a revival of interest in his work. His better science fiction novels continue to be well regarded, both here and abroad, and his partisans form a cult rivaling that of Sherlock Holmes—a fitting tribute to the man who gave the world Tarzan.

[Robert W. Fenton, *The Big Swingers* (1967), is the only full-length biography of Burroughs. The entry on his brother George Tyler Burroughs, Jr., in the *Hist of the Class of 1889*, Sheffield Scientific School, Yale Univ., III (1934), provides information on the family background. Richard A. Lupoff, *Edgar Rice Burroughs: Master of Adventure*, rev. ed. (1968), is a sympathetic and exhaustive treatment of all of his writings. Henry H. Heins, *A Golden Anniversary Bibliog. of Edgar Rice Burroughs*, rev. ed. (1964), includes illustrations from the original *All-Story* serials, as well as many other examples of Burroughsiana. There have been a number of semischolarly treatments of Burroughs, among them "To Barsoom and Back with Edgar Rice Burroughs," in Sam Moskowitz, *Explorers of the Infinite* (1963). Rudolph Altrocchi's "Ancestors of Tarzan," in his *Sleuthing in the Stacks* (1944), traces a long literary tradition of men living among the beasts and attempts to resolve the question of Burroughs' indebtedness. There have been as many as seventeen periodicals, many of them short-lived, published by his fans in England, Canada, Australia, and the U.S. The culmination of this sort of writing is Philip J. Farmer's *Tarzan Alive* (1972), which purports, in the tradition of Baring-Gould on Sherlock Holmes, to be a "definitive biography" of the actual Lord Greystoke. See also Gabe Essoe's pictorial history, *Tarzan of the Movies* (1968).]
MARIE CASKEY

BURROW, TRIGANT (Sept. 7, 1875–May 24, 1950), phylobiologist and psychiatrist, was born in Norfolk, Va., the youngest of the four children of John W. Burrow and Anastasia (Devereaux) Burrow. He had an older sister and two older brothers. His father was a wholesale druggist. The family was of mainly French extraction. Burrow was educated in Norfolk until he was sent to St. Francis Xavier Academy in New York City and then to Fordham University. Later he drifted away from his Roman Catholic upbringing. After graduating in the classical curriculum at Fordham in 1895, he prepared himself for the study of medicine for a year and in 1896 entered the medical

school of the University of Virginia. Burrow took his M.D. in 1899 and stayed on for a year as demonstrator in biology. In 1900 he and his roommate, Cornelius C. Wholey, who himself became an eminent psychiatrist, spent the year in medical centers in Europe.

The two young physicians then settled in Baltimore, and Burrow began study at Johns Hopkins University. He married Emily Sherwood Bryan, a nurse, on Aug. 9, 1904. They had two children, John Devereaux and Emily Sherwood.

Burrow took his Ph.D. in experimental psychology in 1909, working on an aspect of attention. He then began work under the preeminent Adolf Meyer at the New York State Psychiatric Institute at Ward's Island. Before the year was out, Burrow was on his way to Zurich to study with Carl Jung. In 1910 Burrow opened an analytic practice in Baltimore—"the first man of American birth to take up this work, and the second man in America," as he remarked at the time.

Burrow was not only one of the earliest but, until well into the 1920's, one of the purest Freudians (despite his training with Jung) in the United States. He had the backing of the powerful Meyer, who was then at Johns Hopkins, and he retained a clinical appointment there until 1927. His practice flourished, and he published papers regularly. In one he reported his finding of the human infant's initial feeling of identity with its mother.

In 1918 Burrow began studying interpersonal relationships with an analysand, Clarence Shields. Burrow withdrew from practice in 1921 and with the help of Shields built up a new approach to curing nervous disorders. When Burrow took up practice again, it included group meetings with students and patients. Burrow reported his new group analysis in papers and in *The Social Basis of Consciousness* (1927). There he explained that he was not analyzing individuals in a group setting, but the group was analyzing itself, an appropriate procedure, he said, because neurosis is a social phenomenon.

Burrow's ideas after about 1921 were relatively consistent; in later years they developed rather than changed. His procedure was based on eliminating the physiological-psychological affective elements that usually intrude upon social relationships. He did not attempt to treat individual maladaptations as such but rather to remove the cause of neurosis generally, the social-biological heritage of all men. Freud asked once, "Does Burrow think he is going to cure the world?" but that was exactly what Burrow had in mind through "phyloanalysis." He believed that man collectively does have the power to shape his own destiny.

Burrow moved his practice to New York in 1927, working within the Lifwynn Foundation for Laboratory Research in Analytic and Social Psychiatry (named after the Adirondack camp where he continued his research each summer). He developed his ideas in numerous scientific papers and a series of books published between 1932 and (posthumously) 1964. In 1945 the foundation moved to Westport, Conn., near Burrow's home. He considered group analysis a laboratory investigation, and in 1937 he and his colleagues began a number of more conventional laboratory experiments on the physiological concomitants of the social neurosis.

The work of Burrow and the Lifwynn Foundation did not receive the attention and corroboration for which he had hoped. Although Burrow was a founder of the American Psychoanalytic Association and president in 1925-1926, his criticism of conventional techniques alienated him from the tight-knit analytic group, and a reorganization finally excluded him formally in 1933. Since he was even more critical of anti-Freudians, he increasingly was limited to his own group and general scientific forums. Because he and his students did not operate within mainline psychiatric or scientific elite, the personal influences that would have been essential to widespread study and acceptance were absent. Major medical and academic institutions received continuous dramatic increases in mental health research funds in which the Lifwynn Foundation did not share. Burrow's work tended to get lost in the avalanche of high quality publications in the field. Lacking both effective institutional and personal influence, he was unable to win for his ideas the attention that they deserved.

Despite Burrow's disappointment, he had a considerable impact. In his earlier years he not only helped domesticate psychoanalysis in the United States but on his own influenced the thinking of writers D. H. Lawrence and Sherwood Anderson. As Burrow's ideas evolved into a system, however, other intellectuals found them increasingly difficult to integrate into the eclecticism that prevailed in psychiatry and related disciplines, although a number of important psychiatric teachers such as Harry Stack Sullivan adopted ideas from Burrow. Burrow's thinking was not consonant with that of his contemporaries. While the psychoanalysts were developing individual epigenetic explanations, Burrow was emphasizing the total physical and mental reaction of not only one holistic human

being but the entire human race. Indeed, Burrow's vision was so radical as to lead him to reject much of conventional Western culture, such as the idea that normality is healthy, just at a time in the 1930's and 1940's when most American intellectuals were reaffirming traditional values.

Only later did many modes in which Burrow thought appear of great importance—the significance of nonverbal behavior, analysis of a holistic group, the pathogenic potential of the person's concept of the self, interdisciplinary approaches to neurosis, the psychophysiological study of eye movements, breathing, and EEG. Much of his importance lay, therefore, beyond his own day, in the way in which his writings gave courage to a later generation of pioneers in a number of different areas in psychological-psychiatric research. His example at first encouraged a number of workers to try a group setting for individual psychotherapy, and much later in his writings were an inspiration to organic group analysts, particularly in the family analysis movement of the 1960's.

Burrow was a well-bred Southern gentleman who never knew what it meant to be without servants. Of medium height with blue eyes and brown hair, he was a trim, youthful-looking person who liked drama, music (he had perfect pitch), poetry, riding, and tennis. He died at home in Greens Farms, Conn., on May 24, 1950, of malignant lymphoma. His body was cremated.

[The Burrow Papers, which have been microfilmed, are in the Lifwynn Foundation, Westport, Conn. William E. Galt, et al., eds., *A Search for Man's Sanity, The Selected Letters of Trigant Burrow, with Biographical Notes* (1958), gives both facts and insight and contains a full list of Burrow's publications. Among Burrow's books are *The Structure of Insanity* (1932) and *The Biology of Human Conflict* (1937). Basic facts are in *Who Was Who in America*, III (1950); *The Psychological Register 2* (1929): 32–33; *N.Y. Times*, May 26, 1950. W. Riese, "The Brain of Dr. Trigant Burrow, Physician, Scientist, and Author . . . ," *Jour. of Comparative Neurology* 100 (1954): 525–568. Important evaluations are W. Riese, "Phyloanalysis (Burrow)—Its Historical and Philosophical Implications," *Acta Psychotherapeutica et Psychosomatica* II (Suppl. 1963): 5–36; H. Syz, "Reflections on Group- or Phylo-Analysis," *ibid.*, 37–88; Alfreda S. Galt, "Therapy in the Context of Trigant Burrow's Group Analysis," *Group Process* (forthcoming); John C. Burnham, *Psychoanalysis and American Medicine, 1894–1917: Medicine, Science, and Culture* (1967). Personal communication from Alfreda S. Galt.]
JOHN C. BURNHAM

BUTLER, BURRIDGE DAVENAL (Feb. 5, 1868-Mar. 30, 1948), agricultural publisher, was born in Louisville, Ky., the second of four surviving children and oldest son of Thomas Davenal Butler, a minister of the Christian (Disciples of Christ) Church, and Marie Burridge (Radcliffe) Butler. His mother had been born in New York state and reared in Ohio; his father, a native of Shrewsbury, England, had come to America in 1859. In personality, Butler's parents were polar opposites, the father a brusque, temperamental, overbearing figure, the mother a quiet, gentle woman who wrote poetry.

Butler's early childhood was insecure, with his father often away from home. Thereafter the family moved frequently to new pastorates: Detroit and Grand Rapids, Mich.; a small town in Ontario; Akron, Ohio; Johnstown, Pa. Butler's formal education was limited to grammar school. Leaving home after his mother's death in 1884, he held a variety of jobs in Louisville and Cincinnati but was increasingly drawn toward journalism. He returned to Grand Rapids and became a reporter for the *Morning Democrat* in 1886. Regarded by associates as a "born newspaperman, a tremendous worker and an intense partisan," he had risen to the position of state editor when he resigned in 1894 to take an advertising position with a stove company in St. Louis. A year later he moved to Chicago and in 1896 joined the sales office of the Scripps-McRae League, a newspaper group being formed by Edward W. Scripps. Butler soon adopted the Scripps philosophy of editorial crusading for the common man, low subscription rates, and hard-boiled business management, a philosophy he was to apply throughout his career.

In 1899 Butler and two other Scripps employees left to build a newspaper chain of their own, Clover Leaf Newspapers. Butler became editor of their first paper, the *Omaha Daily News,* but returned to Chicago around the end of 1900 to help staff Clover Leaf's advertising office. In 1903, for the partnership, he established the *Minneapolis Daily News,* becoming president and publisher. Clover Leaf enjoyed spectacular early growth, and by 1907 was publishing seven Midwestern dailies and two rural mail-order papers. Two years later, however, owing partly to conflict among the partners, Butler left the chain. In the settlement he acquired ownership of the semimonthly *Prairie Farmer,* an ailing farm paper located in Chicago, which had been purchased by Clover Leaf in 1908. He was to remain its publisher until his death.

Under Butler and Clifford V. Gregory, the young editor he hired in 1911, the *Prairie Farmer* gained a reputation as a crusading farm journal. Gregory set the editorial policies, but part of the paper's warmth and human interest reflected Butler's family feeling toward his readers. Of particular interest to Butler were the *Prairie Farmer's* campaigns against rural crime and deception, from chicken stealing to fraudulent mail-order and stock sales. Over his four decades of ownership, circulation rose from about 50,000 to more than 365,000 in Illinois and neighboring states.

Butler added a new dimension in 1928 when the *Prairie Farmer* purchased radio station WLS in Chicago. He insisted that both media operate as a team to serve farm families. Starting the broadcasting day at 5 A.M. for its early-rising audience, WLS offered news reports, women's features, and a folksy noontime show called "Dinnerbell," which dealt with the joys and trials of individual listeners. The station's most successful program was the National Barn Dance, begun in 1924 and broadcast every Saturday night. Combining country music, rural humor, and hymn singing, the show provided an early forum for entertainers like Gene Autry and Fibber McGee and Molly. The National Barn Dance played to live audiences at Chicago's Eighth Street Theatre and was seen by nearly two million people between 1932 and 1948.

After 1928 Butler, who suffered from arthritis, began to divide his time between Chicago and a home in Phoenix, Ariz. In his later years he acquired radio stations in Phoenix and Tucson and another agricultural journal, the *Arizona Farmer.* Widely recognized as an innovative journalist and a shrewd businessman, the tall, round-faced Butler was a personal enigma, alternately kind and bullying, generous and niggardly, religious but critical of organized religion. Although displaying a fatherly regard for his staff as well as his readers, he was known on occasion to throw furniture about in a fit of temper. Yet his human sympathy was reflected in his interest in aiding disadvantaged youth. He was a trustee of Blackburn College, whose self-help program appealed to him; a member of the national council of the Boy Scouts of America (1925-1930); and a member of the national board of the Boys' Clubs of America (1920-1948).

Butler was married twice: on Dec. 22, 1890, to Winifred L. Whitfield of Grand Rapids, and, after her death in 1904, to Ina Hamilton Busey of New York City on July 30, 1906. He had no children. He died at the age of eighty in Phoenix of injuries sustained in a fall. His body was cremated and the ashes interred at the North Shore Garden of Memories, Chicago. Under the terms of his will, a large share of his $5 million estate went to youth-oriented charities in Illinois and Arizona.

[James F. Evans, *Prairie Farmer and WLS: The Burridge D. Butler Years* (1969), is a detailed study of both Butler and his business enterprises; it includes photographs and a bibliography of sources. Also useful are Neil M. Clark, "I've Never Lost Money by Calling a Spade a Spade," *American Mag.*, June 1931; *Who Was Who in America*, II (1950); and obituaries in *N.Y. Times*, Mar. 31, 1948, and *Broadcasting*, Apr. 5, 1948.]

JAMES F. EVANS

BUTLER, NICHOLAS MURRAY (Apr. 2, 1862-Dec. 7, 1947), president of Columbia University, was born in his maternal grandmother's home in Elizabeth, N.J., the eldest of the three sons and two daughters surviving infancy of Henry Leny Butler and Mary Jones (Murray) Butler. His father was a textile importer and manufacturer in Paterson, N.J. The boy was named for his late maternal grandfather, Nicholas Murray, an old school Calvinist clergyman, sometimes dubbed the "Presbyterian Pope." Most of Butler's ancestors (who were English, Welsh, Scottish, and Irish) came to the United States after the American Revolution, and all settled in the Middle Atlantic states. His grandparents emigrated from England in 1835 when his father was two. At that time the family name was changed from Buchanan to Butler.

Murray grew up in an affectionate, secure, middle-class home, with many relatives nearby. He began his formal education in 1867 at a private ungraded school in Paterson, shifting to the public schools three years later and graduating from Paterson high school at the age of thirteen. Although he returned for a postgraduate year, the school's curriculum was not designed for college preparation, and he continued his studies privately before entering Columbia College in 1878. He largely supported himself by teaching and newspaper writing. Butler was a leader in undergraduate activities, particularly journalism. He was popular among his fellow students, although his self-confidence and ambition sometimes rankled. His independence also expressed itself in religion. Although he had attended Presbyterian churches as a child, he shifted to Episcopalianism and was confirmed in Calvary Church, New York, about 1882.

Butler's original career intentions, law and politics, were changed by conferences with the president of the college, Frederick A. P. Barnard, who urged him to do something distinctive by developing the neglected field of education. Another strong influence was John W. Burgess, whose classes on constitutional history instilled the distinction between "the sphere of government" and "the sphere of liberty."

Throughout his undergraduate years, Butler won honors in a wide variety of subjects, and upon graduation in 1882 he received a three-year fellowship in letters from Columbia. Working principally under Archibald Alexander, Butler earned an M.A. in 1883 with a thesis on "The Permanent Influence of Immanuel Kant," and a Ph.D. in 1884 with "An Outline of the History of Logical Doctrine" as his dissertation. In a student philosophical society that he organized, he expressed his allegiance to neo-Kantianism as the way out of both skepticism and dogmatism. From June 1884 to June 1885, Butler traveled and studied in Europe. During a winter in Berlin, he especially profited from the teaching in philosophy and educational theory of Eduard Zeller and Friedrich Paulsen.

Returning to Columbia in 1885 as assistant in philosophy, Butler rose rapidly through the teaching ranks, becoming in 1890 professor of philosophy, ethics, and psychology and lecturer in education (after 1895 professor of philosophy and education). As a teacher, regularly offering history of philosophy, history and principles of education, and modern British and German philosophies, Butler was noted for his lucidity, and it was said that students could not tell where he himself stood philosophically. The announcement that President Barnard would retire in 1889 brought to a climax the struggle between the "university-minded" among Columbia's faculty and trustees and the "college-minded." Butler, emphatically on the "university" side, recommended following the pattern set by the faculty of political science since 1880: creating parallel faculties of philosophy and natural science to provide advanced training, not only for candidates for graduate degrees, but also for Columbia College seniors. His ideas were presented in a letter to the trustees and in 1890 at a gathering of the whole teaching body ordered by Seth Low, the new president, whose installation foretold victory for the university advocates. "As the junior officer . . . [Butler] was called upon . . . to open the discussion. . . . No one in the opposition answered or could answer his arguments. His convincing presentation . . . gave the university party the greatest encouragement" (Burgess, p. 239). The plan adopted was close to Butler's, and in May 1890 his colleagues in the new faculty of philosophy elected him its dean. Continuing to concern himself with the whole university, Butler participated in the selection of the new Morningside Heights site and was chiefly responsible for the flourishing summer school established in 1900.

In 1887 Butler was chosen president of the Industrial Education Association, a group of New York philanthropists seeking to promote the training of public school children in domestic and manual arts. Butler at once put emphasis on a program of general professional training of public school teachers and gave courses himself. The organization's school was chartered in 1889 as the degree-granting New York College for the Training of Teachers (Teachers College after 1892). Although he resigned as president of the college in 1891, Butler remained on its board of trustees and pressed for its affiliation with Columbia, obtained in 1893, originally as an adjunct of the faculty of philosophy.

Before shifting his residence to New York in 1894, Butler participated in drafting the act of 1886 that reorganized the New Jersey public library system. He also aided in resystematizing the Library of Congress in the 1890's and the Vatican Library in the 1920's. He served on the New Jersey State Board of Education, 1887-1895, encouraging nonpartisan control of education, removal of teacher certification from local authorities, and the introduction of manual training courses. In 1892-1893 he was president of the Paterson Board of Education.

In New York, too, Butler argued that the old educational system was mired in mindless routine and corrupted by political appointment of teachers. He played the leading role in the "School War" of 1895-1896, which led to a state law abolishing ward school boards in the city of New York. Further centralization and the creation of a city superintendent of schools came in the Greater New York charter of 1897, of which Butler was a leading advocate. The same centralizing and professionalizing spirit underlay Butler's behind-the-scenes participation in the passage of the 1904 law to unify the New York state educational system and establish a powerful commission of education. These achievements identify Butler with part of the amalgam usually called "progressive education." But for the child-centered tendencies in progressivism, often associated with Teachers College, he had little sympathy.

In the National Education Association, of which he was president in 1894-1895, Butler helped create and publicize both the Committee of Ten and the Committee on College Entrance Requirements, precedent-setters in the developing of nationwide standards and definitions by professional organizations. Although unhappy with the rising power of classroom teachers in NEA, Butler remained largely responsible for managing its endowment as chairman of the board of trustees. When charges of delinquencies were raised by the NEA president Ella Flagg Young, Butler waited until an audit proved them baseless and then in 1911 resigned as a trustee. In the search for a flexible yet clearly defined articulation between secondary and higher education, Butler contributed probably more than any of his contemporaries. He led in the founding of the College Entrance Examination Board (1900), was its first secretary, and from 1901-1914 its chairman.

From the mid-1880's on, Butler was much in demand as a consultant, speaker, and editor in the field of education. Effective as a publicist, he produced no important work of scholarship. Of the approximately twenty books he wrote, most consisted of his addresses. As founder and editor (1891-1919) of *Educational Review,* Butler provided a regular outlet for his views. The journal stressed professionalism in administration and teaching, but was open to proponents of other reform ideas of the Progressive era.

When Low resigned as president of Columbia in 1901, Butler succeeded him, first as acting president, then as president (installed Apr. 19, 1902). Columbia had already undergone the major transformations that made it a university, and Butler's remarkable executive talents were devoted principally to consolidating these developments. During his first decade as president, advanced work in the arts and sciences grew dramatically. Such scholars as John Dewey in philosophy and Thomas Hunt Morgan in zoology were added to an already distinguished faculty. Soon Butler could credibly claim Columbia as the American university that gave greatest emphasis to graduate work, and Morningside Heights was sometimes referred to as "the American Acropolis." Butler tightened Columbia's bonds with its professional schools and directed the creation of new ones (or the affiliation of independent schools). With 7,500 students by 1911, Columbia was the largest university in the world, and by 1914 it had the largest endowment of any American university. The increased administrative centralization that accompanied this growth tended to heighten Butler's power (e.g., after 1905 deans were appointed rather than elected by their colleagues), and faculty complaints reached the press. Butler defended the changes on grounds of business-like efficiency and freeing teachers from irksome administrative chores.

Butler's attitude toward the undergraduate program is suggested by his remark of 1912,

"It was fortunately not necessary that Columbia College should die in order that Columbia University might be born" (Summerscales, p. 117). He repeatedly pressed for shortening the length of the college course. In a step that showed both his power and his suspicion of undergraduate activities, Butler abolished intercollegiate football at Columbia in 1905, after a series of fatalities. Columbia was the only major university to take so drastic a step. In spite of student protest, the game was not restored until 1915. Complaints of the college's diminished role and its budgetary subservience to the university, never completely stilled, were strongly reasserted in 1941 in the Condon Report (issued by the Class of 1921, under the leadership of Lawrence R. Condon).

Butler's early years in office were marred by charges of violations of academic freedom in a series of dismissals and resignations of professors: George E. Woodberry (1904), Edward A. MacDowell (1904), Harry Thurston Peck (1910), and Joel E. Spingarn (1911). On Oct. 1, 1917, Henry W. L. Dana, assistant professor of comparative literature, and J. McKeen Cattell, professor of psychology since 1891, were peremptorily dismissed, the former after speaking against the Conscription Act, the latter (who had been the object of earlier dismissal efforts) after urging that draftees not be sent overseas against their will. Several faculty members resigned in protest, most conspicuously the historian Charles A. Beard, who claimed to discern a pattern in which "a small group of trustees (unhindered, if not aided, by Mr. Butler) [sought] to take advantage of the state of war to drive out or humiliate every man who held progressive, liberal, or unconventional views on political matters" (Summerscales, p. 96). Critics saw Butler's role in this series of cases as that of an increasingly autocratic executive who confused intellectual disagreement with bad manners, failed to see the value of protecting nonconformists, and showed himself an unmitigated nationalist in wartime. Butler's defense was implied in his argument that *Lehrfreiheit* applied to the thought and expression of a scholar in his field of competence and not to violations of generally accepted moral and social standards. After World War I, there were no further flagrant violations of academic freedom at Columbia; in fact, the wide variety of personal styles and political views at the university made it one of the most stimulating academic communities in America.

Influenced by his politically active father, Butler was a Republican from boyhood. In most respects a party regular, he was a delegate to the Republican national convention in 1888 and from 1904-1932. An "insider of insiders," he helped draft platforms, campaigned for nominees, and sought to influence the policies of those elected. He declined opportunities to run for mayor of New York as early as 1897 and as late as 1925 and for governor in 1904, but served as informal adviser to the state constitutional conventions of 1894 and 1915, and as a member of the state and city commissions on administrative reorganization (his forte) which reported in 1926 and 1928 respectively.

Although he had been consulted by McKinley, it was the presidency of Theodore Roosevelt that brought Butler his fullest access to a national leader. As governor of New York, Roosevelt regarded Butler as "one of my right-hand men" (Morison, II, 1640), and in the White House he continued to welcome both Butler's counsel and his companionship. Reflecting the views of the New York corporation lawyers and investment bankers whom he knew well, Butler urged Roosevelt to temper his anti-trust pronouncements and to press for tariff reduction. By 1906 the relationship had cooled, and after Roosevelt's special message of Jan. 31, 1908, proposing greater federal control of the economy, Butler virtually broke with him. Butler often advised President Taft on party and foreign policy matters and in 1912, both at the New York State Republican Convention, where he presided, and at the national convention, he helped fight off Roosevelt's efforts to regain office. Although not Taft's running mate, Butler did receive the eight Republican electoral votes for vice-president after vice-presidential candidate James S. Sherman died during the campaign.

Butler regarded himself as a Hamiltonian and likened his approach to that of England's Tory reformers. Although a persistent tinkerer with organizational mechanisms, he believed society to be essentially "an organism, not a machine" (Veysey, p. 364). At the climax of the Progressive era, for all his eclecticism and adroitness at political compromise, his essential conservatism stood out in sharp relief. Opposed to direct democracy, he wanted government by the trained and enlightened elite; accordingly, he opposed the direct primary, direct election of senators, and initiative, recall, and referendum, while supporting the "short ballot." Stressing the ideal of limited government, he opposed the income tax, the Child Labor Amendment, and the Adamson Eight-Hour Act. On both domestic and foreign affairs, Butler adhered closely to the views of his friend Elihu Root, but failed in his efforts to win the presidential nomination for Root in 1916.

Butler's most serious attempt to win the nomination for himself came in 1920. Before the convention, he obtained considerable publicity through interviews, and his organized supporters urged the Republicans to "Pick Nick for a Picnic in November." He declared that he was a serious candidate and not merely a favorite son, but after the first ballot, on which he won sixty-nine and one-half votes (sixty-eight of them from New York), he lost strength rapidly. During the campaign, Butler was one of the "Thirty-One Republicans" who declared that Harding's election would be the best way to get the United States into the League of Nations. After Harding's victory, Butler enjoyed an influential position with a president such as he had not had since Roosevelt's day and was not to have again. He was among those who encouraged Harding to call the Washington Conference on the limitation of armaments.

Much of Butler's growing dissatisfaction with his party during the 1920's sprang from its support of the nation's experiment with prohibition, since he considered the Eighteenth Amendment a revolutionary step that carried government beyond its proper sphere and bred hypocrisy and lawlessness. In 1924 Butler began aggressively seeking converts to this view, and in 1928 declared himself a candidate for the presidency, principally to dramatize his support for repeal, which he tried unsuccessfully to get into the Republican platform. Also straining his party loyalty were his long-standing dislike for Herbert Hoover and Republican resistance to tariff reduction—not that the New Deal attracted him. Although proud of the role of Columbia scholars in the Brain Trust, which seemed to fit his definition of the university as a "powerhouse of scholarship and service," he upbraided Franklin D. Roosevelt in public pronouncements and personal letters for imposing new taxes on the wealthy, wasting public money, and threatening the survival of individualism.

Butler's international activities constituted virtually a second career. He exerted considerable influence through trips to Europe, often as an unofficial presidential envoy. Indeed, he was more highly regarded in Europe than in the United States, and H. G. Wells aptly labeled Butler "the champion international visitor and retriever of foreign orders and degrees" (Johnston, p. 220). In 1905 he began to see himself as a moderator of British-German relations. In Germany he gained the ear of Kaiser Wilhelm

II, while in Britain he was often consulted by committees of Parliament and by informal governmental conferences. In France he developed a friendship with a leading advocate of international conciliation, Paul-Henri-Benjamin d'Estournelles de Constant.

The addresses Butler gave as president of the Lake Mohonk Conference on International Arbitration in 1907 and 1909-1912, published as *The International Mind* (1912), helped give currency to the term "internationalism." He saw lasting peace as following from enlightened public opinion, armament limitations, and an independent international judiciary. A stronger base for his internationalist activities was created in 1910, when Andrew Carnegie, after closely consulting with Butler, established the Carnegie Endowment for International Peace with a $10 million gift. Butler served on the executive committee, directed the division of intercourse and education, and in 1925 succeeded Elihu Root as president of the endowment. (The American Association for International Conciliation, which Butler organized in 1907, became virtually a subsidiary of the new foundation.) The Carnegie funds at his disposal greatly enhanced Butler's influence. On his 1911 trip abroad he claimed to have seen "all the cranks, and half the wise men of Europe" (Lutzker, p. 155). Without much success, he sought to use the endowment to centralize and coordinate the activities of various American peace groups, many of which resented the conservative course to which Carnegie's gift was directed. Butler also helped the Carnegie Foundation for the Advancement of Teaching and the Carnegie Corporation, of which he was chairman (1937-1945).

Caught in Europe at the outbreak of World War I, Butler proved highly resourceful in getting his family back to the United States by commandeering a railway car and chartering a ship. Although at first continuing to aim his comments at "militarism" in all nations, Butler was soon urging American involvement on the side of the Allies. In a series of articles in the *New York Times,* published in book form as *The Basis of Durable Peace* (1917), he developed his ideas for postwar international organization, stressing clearly formulated international law based on principles of right and justice. Although he refused to join the League to Enforce Peace, he did not entirely rule out sanctions and suggested that international agreements not be limited by reservations concerning national honor or vital interests. The struggle over American entry into the League of Nations in 1919 found him allied with the mild reservationists.

After the war, Butler was more welcome than ever in Europe. The Carnegie Endowment rebuilt libraries, sponsored exchanges of professors, students, and journalists, and financed courses on international relations in American universities. Although Butler felt his primary mission was to help keep Britain and France from drifting apart, he revisited Germany in 1926 as a guest of the government and worked for the removal of Allied troops from the west bank of the Rhine. Upon his return from his frequent European trips, his comments on the international situation were usually front-page news.

Butler was closely involved in the creation of the Kellogg-Briand Pact. In 1927, when Aristide Briand, the French foreign minister, made his initial suggestion to the United States for a bilateral renunciation of war, Butler called for a favorable response to be followed by an opening of the plan to all nations. Reacting to his pressure, the State Department asked him to draft a treaty, a task Butler delegated to two Columbia professors, Joseph P. Chamberlain and James T. Shotwell. Believing that Secretary of State Frank Kellogg was not deeply committed, Butler launched a public-speaking campaign, which probably helped bring Senate ratification. As the culmination of his efforts, he won the support of Pope Pius XI for the treaty. Butler's hand was strengthened for his international labors by his receiving the Nobel Peace Prize for 1931, which he shared with Jane Addams.

Balancing the optimistic legalism of his activities for the Kellogg-Briand Pact was Butler's increasing concern for international economic conditions. He began to argue that economic nationalism was the greatest threat to peace. In an address to the German Reichstag in 1931, he proposed an economic "United States of Europe." Distressed by the failure of the London Economic Conference of 1933, he suggested regional understandings as an alternative, particularly a Danubian economic union. Through the Carnegie Endowment, he sponsored the Chatham House Conference of 1935 in London, where citizens of ten nations suggested easing the burdens of debtor nations and lowering tariffs. Butler saw colonialism as politically appropriate and economically stimulating. He urged American retention of the Philippines and in one of several conversations with Mussolini suggested that Italy buy the Portuguese colonies in West Africa. Butler considered the

American neutrality acts of the 1930's folly, and he roundly attacked isolationists. During World War II, he characteristically urged those proposing America's entry into an international peace-keeping organization to consolidate their efforts.

Balding and moustached, round-faced and of medium height, Butler with his commanding presence could be mistaken for a British military officer out of uniform. Though he struck some as pompous, his conviviality was prodigious. He relished social clubs and dinner parties and often dominated the conversation with anecdotes which linked him to famous persons. He was conspicuously a New York urbanite, the quintessence of what a later generation would call "the Eastern Establishment." Revealingly, he cited William Jennings Bryan as his opposite on nearly every issue.

Assertive and energetic, "Nicholas Miraculous" displayed ready political ingenuity and a considerable rhetorical gift. Although his thought lacked originality, he sometimes managed to symbolize a movement in his own person or in an apt phrase. Perhaps Butler's fight against prohibition best fulfilled his avowed allegiance to the sphere of liberty. More typically, he sought to bring individual, inchoate, or overlapping activities into rationalized institutional form. His internationalism could be traced in large measure to his distaste for a world of nations uncontrolled by law.

On Feb. 8, 1887, Butler married Susanna Edwards Schuyler of Bergen Point, N.J.; she died in 1903. From his marriage came Butler's only child, Sarah Schuyler Butler, who was active for many years in the Republican party of New York State. Butler married Kate La Montagne of New York, a wealthy Roman Catholic, on Mar. 5, 1907.

Plagued by approaching blindness and increasing deafness, Butler stayed on as Columbia's president until the age of eighty-three, retiring on Oct. 1, 1945, and leaving the presidency of the Carnegie Endowment two months later. In June 1947, he commended the Columbia trustees' choice of Dwight D. Eisenhower as his successor. Butler died in New York of bronchopneumonia and was buried in Cedar Lawn Cemetery, Paterson, N.J.

[The two principal repositories of Butler's correspondence are the Butler Papers, Special Collect., Butler Lib., Columbia Univ., and the files covering the years of his presidency in the Columbia Univ. Arch., Low Lib. The former contains many volumes of clippings. In the Columbiana Room, Low Lib., are bound addresses by Butler. His autobiography, *Across the Busy Years: Recollections and Reflections*, 2 vols. (1939–1940), although burdened by anecdotage, is the best single source on his life. Its bibliography supplements M. Halsey Thomas' *Bibliography of Nicholas Murray Butler, 1872–1932: A Check List* (1934). Two scholarly assessments of Butler's educational activities are Richard Whittemore, *Nicholas Murray Butler and Public Education, 1862–1911* (1970) and William Summerscales, *Affirmation and Dissent: Columbia's Response to the Crisis of World War I* (1970). Both offer general characterizations of the man. Horace Coon's irreverent *Columbia: Colossus on the Hudson* (1947) reveals much about the closing years of Butler's presidency. More detailed are the various volumes in *The Bicentennial History of Columbia University*, gen. ed. Dwight C. Miner, 15 vols. (1954–1957). Butler's annual reports to Columbia's trustees reveal not only the development of the university, but also his changing opinions on public issues. Columbia at the peak of Butler's success as a university-builder is portrayed in Edwin E. Slosson, *Great American Universities* (1910). Among autobiographies of his academic contemporaries, see particularly the highly sympathetic treatment of Butler in John W. Burgess, *Reminiscences of an American Scholar* (1934) and the carefully balanced appraisal in John Erskine, *The Memory of Certain Persons* (1947) and *My Life as a Teacher* (1948). Laurence R. Veysey's *The Emergence of the American University* (1965) places Butler in the wing of the university movement that stressed institutional aggrandizement rather than fulfillment of particular ideals. Butler's international activities are treated in Warren F. Kuehl, *Seeking World Order: The United States and International Organization to 1920* (1969) and in the annual reports of the Carnegie Endowment. His political activities can be partly discerned in the collected letters and biographies of leading politicians, notably Elting E. Morison, ed., *The Letters of Theodore Roosevelt*, 8 vols. (1951–1954), and in Ray B. Smith, ed., *History of the State of New York: Political and Governmental*, vol. IV (1922). Butler emerges importantly in two of the essays in Jerry Israel, ed., *Building the Organizational Society: Essays on Associational Activities in Modern America* (1972), that of David B. Tyack on urban schools and that of Michael A. Lutzker on the peace movement. For further details, see the files of *Columbia Univ. Quart., Columbia Monthly,* and *Columbia Alumni News*; Alva Johnston, "Cosmos," in *Profiles from the New Yorker* (1938), and the *N. Y. Times,* Dec. 7–8, 1947.]

HUGH HAWKINS

CADMAN, CHARLES WAKEFIELD (Dec. 24, 1881–Dec. 30, 1946), composer, organist, and pianist, was born in Johnstown, Pa., the son of William Cadman and Caroline (Wakefield) Cadman. He had a younger sister named Mabel. His father was a metallurgist at the Carnegie Steel Company, and his mother was an accomplished choir singer; both their families had lived in America since colonial times.

Cadman showed musical talent at the age of nine and at thirteen began to take piano and organ lessons. In 1901 he met Nelle Richmond Eberhart, who wrote the lyrics for most of his songs, as well as the libretti for his operas. In 1903, when the family moved to Duquesne, Pa., he left school and for the next three years worked as a messenger in the steel plant of Charles M. Schwab, in order to supplement the family income. The family subsequently moved to Homestead, Pa., where Cadman

worked as a church organist. He pursued musical studies in Pittsburgh with Edwin Walker (piano), Leo Oehmler (organ, harmony), W. K. Steiner (organ), Emil Paur (composition), and Luigi von Kunitz (orchestration).

His interest in American Indian music was aroused at this time by reading the ethnological studies of Alice Fletcher and Francis La Flesche. In 1909 he made phonograph recordings of the songs and flageolet love calls of the Omaha and Winnebago tribes. He used these melodies in his first opera on Indian themes, *Daoma, or The Land of Misty Water* (1912), to a libretto by Eberhart and La Flesche.

Cadman was organist of the East Liberty Presbyterian Church in Pittsburgh until 1910 and music critic for the Pittsburgh *Dispatch,* from 1908 to 1910. Never in robust health, he became ill in 1910 and took a rest cure in Colorado. He returned to Pittsburgh to attend a testimonial concert of his compositions on Dec. 22, 1910, but soon returned to Colorado, where he was church organist in Denver. He continued his studies of Indian music among the Pima and Isleta tribes of Arizona and New Mexico. From 1909 to 1923 he gave lecture recitals on Indian music, often assisted by the mezzo-soprano Tsianina Redfeather, with whom he appeared in Paris and London in 1910.

Cadman's song "At Dawning" (1906) was sung with tremendous success by the tenor John McCormack and eventually sold more than a million copies. "From the Land of the Sky-blue Water" (1908) was popularized by the soprano Lillian Nordica. Cadman wrote about 180 songs, but his chief interest was in opera. His two-act opera *Shanewis* (The Robin Woman) was produced at the Metropolitan Opera House in New York on Mar. 23, 1918, and was performed three times during the following season—the first American opera to be presented there for two consecutive seasons. Another opera on Indian themes, *The Sunset Trail,* was produced in Denver in 1922. His third important opera, *A Witch of Salem* (1924), was produced by the Chicago Civic Opera on Dec. 8, 1926. His one-act opera, *The Garden of Mystery* (1915), based on Hawthorne's tale *Rappaccini's Daughter,* was performed at Carnegie Hall in New York, in 1925.

Among his instrumental works based on Indian themes are the Idealized Indian Themes, for piano (1912), and Thunderbird Suite, for orchestra (1914). After 1925 his interest in American Indian music waned. His later works include Dark Dancers of the Mardi Gras, for piano and orchestra (1933), and Symphony no. 1 in E Minor (*Pennsylvania* Symphony). A depiction of the history of Pennylvania from early times to the industrial boom years, it was first performed in Los Angeles on Mar. 7, 1940.

From 1917 Cadman lived in California, mostly in Los Angeles. He was a founder of the Hollywood Bowl Concerts and a member of its board of directors. His many honors and distinctions included membership in the National Academy of Arts and Letters and honorary degrees (doctor of music) from the Wolcott Conservatory of Music in Denver and the University of Southern California. In 1929 he was awarded the David Bispham Memorial Medal by the American Opera Association. Filled with nervous energy and always in a hurry, he was also affable, friendly, and helpful to young musicians. He never married. He died in Los Angeles, Calif., of a heart attack and was buried in Forest Lawn Cemetery, Glendale, Calif.

Cadman owes his niche in history to a combination of three factors: his prominent role in the "Indianist" movement, which remains historically significant; the extraordinary success of his two songs "At Dawning" and "From the Land of the Sky-blue Water"; his many-sided organizational activities, especially in promoting American music. His compositions are conventional in style, often melodically pleasing, but lacking any marked originality.

[No biography or critical study of Cadman exists. A scrapbook of clippings concerning his music is in the music department of the Carnegie Lib., Pittsburgh. A catalog of his musical works was compiled by Charles W. Wakefield in the 1930's; see also Lulu Sanford-Teft, *Little Intimate Stories of C.W.C.* (1926). He is included in E. E. Hipsher, *Am. Opera and Its Composers* (1927), and Grace Overmyer, *Famous Am. Composers* (1944). Portraits are in Guy McCoy, *Portraits of the World's Best-Known Musicians* (1940), David Ewen, *Am. Composers Today* (1944), *The Oxford Companion to Music* (1955), and J. T. Howard, *Our Am. Music* (1965). See also Cadman's article, "The 'Idealization' of Indian Music," in *The Musical Quart.*, July 1915, pp. 387–396.]
GILBERT CHASE

CALDWELL, OTIS WILLIAM (Dec. 18, 1869-July 5, 1947), educator, was born in Lebanon, Boone County, Ind., the third of four children and second of three sons of Theodore Robert Caldwell, a farmer, and Isabella (Brenton) Caldwell. Both parents had firm family roots in the county: his mother's forebears had settled there in the 1820's; his father, of Scottish ancestry, was descended from Pennsylvanians who had come to Indiana by way of Kentucky. Otis Caldwell attended local district schools and nearby Franklin College, graduating with the B.S. degree in 1894. After a year as high school principal at Nineveh, Ind., near Franklin, he began graduate study in botany at the University of Chicago, receiving the Ph.D. in 1898. On Aug. 25, 1897, he married Cora Burke of Portland, Ind. They had two children: Helen (who died in childhood) and Esther.

In 1899 Caldwell became head of the biology department at Eastern Illinois State Normal School in Charleston, where he remained until 1907. He then moved to the University of Chicago as associate professor of botany, becoming professor in 1913. He served also as head of the department of natural sciences in the School of Education and as dean of the University College (1913-1917). Caldwell was a firm proponent of the educational value of science and campaigned to upgrade its position in public school curricula. While studying the science program in the Gary, Ind., public schools as part of a survey conducted by the General Education Board, he became acquainted with Abraham Flexner, co-director of the project. When in 1917 the Board, at Flexner's urging, provided funds to establish the Lincoln School, an experimental elementary and secondary school affiliated with Teachers College at Columbia University, Flexner hired Caldwell as director and then presented him to the dean at Teachers College, where he was made professor a month later.

Historians of the progressive education movement agree that under Caldwell's ten-year administration the Lincoln School may well have been the finest progressive school in the country. It exemplified and perhaps even established that movement's curricular tenets. Caldwell hired the ablest faculty available, told them that each teacher must be an experimenter, and assessed their various proposals at first skeptically and then approvingly. He attracted to Lincoln such outstanding teachers as Hughes Mearns in English, Laura Zirbes in reading, and Harold Rugg (a former colleague at Chicago) in social studies. The influence of Lincoln's curriculum reforms on the nation can be seen in the immediate and widespread acceptance of the social studies materials assembled by Rugg. The twelve-volume text sold more than 100,000 copies the first year, and by 1929 more than 600,000 were in use in forty states.

The principles that appeared to guide Caldwell in his educational reforms were those that he applied to his own efforts to establish science as an essential element of the curriculum. Course material, Caldwell believed, should be based on the most important principles in the field, and should be related, if possible, to practical and familiar experiences of the students. Thus general science courses, for example, would include material on diet, hygiene, and home economics. At the Lincoln School there was much use of the "unit approach," involving the combining in one course of the concepts and techniques of several traditional disciplines. Unlike many of his colleagues on the Teachers College faculty, Caldwell did not have strong views on such major theoretical themes of the progressive education movement as the child-centered school, the testing movement, and the reformist goal of using the schools to expand the social consciousness of students. Rather, he eschewed theory and opted for teaching youngsters as clearly and dynamically as possible.

Caldwell's relations with Dean James Earl Russell and the Teachers College administration were generally cordial. By the mid-1920's, however, certain tensions developed as it became apparent that Caldwell was suffering from overwork and exhaustion. In 1927, therefore, control of the Lincoln School was divided; Jesse H. Newlon was hired to take over administrative duties, and Caldwell was made director of the newly formed Lincoln Institute of School Experimentation. Unable to adjust to this new arrangement, he was given an extended leave of absence in 1928, during which the institute was severed from the Lincoln School. He retired from the Teachers College faculty in 1935.

Throughout his career, Caldwell was active in professional organizations. A longtime member of the American Association for the Advancement of Science, he served as its general secretary (with offices at the Boyce Thompson Institute for Plant Research in Yonkers, N.Y.) from 1935 until his death. He was also president of the National Association for Research in Science Teaching (1940). Caldwell's writings were mainly on the teaching of science. His textbook, *Elements of General Science* (1914), written with William L. Eikenberry, exerted a strong influence on the development of general science courses and went through several editions. His other principal interest, on which he wrote several books, was the disproof of superstitions through science. Originally a Baptist, Caldwell became a Presbyterian and later a Congregationalist. In 1931 he moved from New York City to New Milford, Conn. He died there in 1947 of a cerebral hemorrhage and was buried in the town's Center Cemetery.

Caldwell's lifetime commitment was to science and to practicality. He was uninterested in either educational or scientific theories. His childhood experiences on an Indiana farm taught him early to appreciate the useful applications of science. He was reared in an environment as free of economic and racial divisions as it was of literary or cultural traditions. In such an environment, science, with its astonishing new discoveries, could indeed seem, as he believed to the end of his life, more important than any other aspect of human learning.

[Peter Buttenwieser, "The Lincoln School and Its Times, 1917-1948" (Ed.D. dissertation, Teachers College, Columbia Univ., 1969); obituaries in *School Science and Mathematics*, Oct. 1947, *Science Education*, Dec. 1947, *Scientific Monthly*, Dec. 1947, *Science*, Dec. 12, 1947, and *N.Y. Times*, July 6, 1947; *Nat. Cyc. Am. Biog.*, XXXV, 495; Teachers College faculty records; interview with Esther Caldwell Harrop; data on family background from 1870 and 1880 censuses and from county histories (courtesy of Jean E. Singleton, Ind. State Lib.).]

PATRICIA ALBJERG GRAHAM

CAPONE, ALPHONSE (Jan. 17, 1899-Jan. 25, 1947), Chicago bootlegger who became a symbol of lawlessness in the 1920's, was born in Brooklyn, N.Y., the fourth son and fourth of nine children of Gabriel and Teresa (Riolia) Capone (originally Caponi). His parents had emigrated from Naples, Italy, in 1893, and his father worked as a small shopkeeper. Al dropped out of the Brooklyn public schools at fourteen, held various odd jobs, joined a street gang, and was arrested on several charges, including suspicion of murder. While working as a bartender and bouncer, he received the knife wound that later earned him the newspaper nickname of "Scarface." On Dec. 30, 1918, he married Mary (Mae) Coughlin, the daughter of a construction laborer. They had one child, Albert Francis.

In late 1919 or early 1920 Capone moved to Chicago to join John Torrio, a former New Yorker then rising in the Chicago underworld. Born near Naples, reared in New York's slums, Torrio was a nephew and partner of James ("Big Jim") Colosimo. While Big Jim operated a restaurant in Chicago's famous Levee (the South Side red-light district), Torrio managed their vice resorts there and in such working-class suburbs as Stickney and Burnham. With the coming of prohibition in January 1920, the resorts needed liquor. Colosimo was mysteriously assassinated in May 1920, leaving Torrio free to build, with considerable entrepreneurial skill, a major bootlegging organization.

In that organization, Capone moved rapidly into a leadership position. At first he was an employee and later manager of the Four Deuces at 2222 South Wabash Avenue, a combination saloon, gambling den, whorehouse, and headquarters for the growing Torrio businesses. Central to the Torrio enterprises was a system of liquor distribution in the Chicago Loop, the Levee, and the suburbs where he had cabarets and resorts. Along with other entrepreneurs, including the Irish gangsters Frankie Lake and Terry Druggan, Torrio invested in breweries and distilleries. Because neither local nor federal officials made serious efforts to enforce prohibition laws before 1923, the syndicate was one of many in Chicago that easily established corrupt relations with politicians and police.

In the spring of 1924, when the Torrio syndicate decided to extend its influence into suburban Cicero, Capone began to capture the headlines that would soon bring him international notoriety. He led the gunmen who controlled the Cicero polls on election day; in a shootout with police, Capone's brother Frank was killed. (After his father's death in 1921, Capone had brought his mother to Chicago and provided positions in the syndicate for his older brothers, Ralph and Frank.) The Capone candidates won, and the Torrio organization, with headquarters at the Hawthorne Inn, coordinated bootlegging and gambling in Cicero. Meanwhile, in Chicago itself, rivalries were breaking out within the underworld. A series of gangland killings led to the critical wounding of Torrio in an assassination attempt in 1925. With Torrio hospitalized, Capone took temporary charge of his enterprises. Torrio had meanwhile been given a nine-month prison sentence for bootlegging. Upon his release, he took an extended European "vacation," leaving Capone, at the age of twenty-six, a leading figure in a coalition of entrepreneurs who operated a major bootlegging and entertainment syndicate in the nation's second largest city.

Much of Capone's reputation stemmed from the highly publicized beer wars that, from 1923 to 1930, left hundreds dead in the streets of Chicago or nearby suburbs. Even though some killings were the result of competition among other bootlegging groups, Capone's organization was strengthened by the decimation of rival gangs, and his men became known as efficient and remorseless assassins. Among those murdered were Dion O'Banion, a leader in the North Side gang (1924), three of the six Genna brothers, leaders of the Genna gang (1925); Assistant State's Attorney William H. McSwiggin (1926), killed while he was socializing with gangsters; and a *Chicago Tribune* reporter Jake Lingle (1930), who had probable underworld connections. Chicago opinion was also shocked by the bombings and killings that marked the so-called "pineapple primary" election in the spring of 1928 ("pineapple" being a current slang term for bomb), as well as by the famous St. Valentine's Day massacre in 1929, in which seven members of the North Side gang were machine-gunned in a garage, by Capone gunmen. The numerous killings, the grand jury and police investigations, and the failure to convict the perpetrators—all created the image of a lawless city and made Capone the symbol of a lawless decade.

Capone also became a symbol because he was good newspaper copy. A heavy-set man, five feet ten inches tall, weighing over 250 pounds, with blunt features and a cigar protruding from his mouth, he looked the gangster. Riding in his custom-built, $30,000 Cadillac, preceded and followed by cars containing bodyguards, he was a tourist attraction. By the early 1930's he was the subject of several books and popular movies. In 1928 he purchased a mansion on Palm Island at Miami, Fla., where he entertained newspapermen, athletes, show-business personalities, and others who found his company glamorous or useful. He attended the racetracks (betting heavily), baseball games, and boxing matches in Chicago and Florida. He also engaged in extensive charitable activities. In a number of interviews he expounded his philosophy that he was just a businessman supplying a consumer want. Believing politics and business to be a system of deals and favors, he agreed that his activities were illegitimate but argued that everyone else's were too.

Behind the headlines, the Capone syndicate grew and diversified, but Capone never became as important as the myth made him out to be. Basically, the organization operated through partnerships, the senior partners being Al and his brother Ralph, Frank Nitti, and Jack Guzik. The syndicate had its business headquarters and living accommodations at Chicago's Metropole Hotel beginning in 1925 and at the Lexington Hotel beginning in 1928. With the election in 1927 of Mayor William Hale ("Big Bill") Thompson, some of whose followers were closely linked to the Capone partners, the syndicate operated with relatively little interference from local police. In Cicero the partners shared the profits of the major gambling houses from 1924 on. They also extended their investments in Chicago gambling and in suburban slot machines, and in 1927 became secret owners of a profitable dog track near Cicero. As a result of such investments, the income from various gambling activities by 1930 probably approached the income from bootlegging.

Bootlegging also expanded, however. Under Frank Nitti the organization provided booze for suburban roadhouses and speakeasies and, by the late 1920's, was expanding its territory in South Side Chicago. After the St. Valentine's Day massacre, Capone members also began to supply liquor for the important nightclub district on the near North Side, probably insisting upon a share of the profits from several night spots there. In suburban Stickney and Burnham, as well as in parts of Chicago, Capone leaders continued to offer houses of prostitution. By 1928, too, several labor racketeers had become associated with Capone leaders, and some Capone members began to move into labor racketeering—long a fertile source of profits for gunmen.

Although Capone in 1927 appeared to be entering his years of greatest influence, he was in increasing difficulty and seldom exercised day-to-day supervision of the organization. That winter he moved to Florida, in part a reflection of growing affluence but partly also an informal exile, since Mayor Thompson, nursing unrealistic presidential ambitions and bothered by the bad publicity Capone provided, wanted him out of the city. Then in May 1929, after attending a conference of top bootleggers from New York, New Jersey, Philadelphia, and Chicago held in Atlantic City, Capone was arrested in Philadelphia for carrying a concealed weapon and sentenced to a year in jail. The federal government was meanwhile moving against Capone through Prohibition Bureau and Treasury Department investigations. By 1930 several of his partners, including Ralph Capone and Jack Guzik, had been convicted of income tax violations, and in June 1931 Capone himself was indicted for income tax fraud and for conspiring to violate federal prohibition laws. He was found guilty on five counts in October 1931 and sentenced to eleven years in prison, plus fines and court costs of $80,000. At the age of thirty-two, his career was over, but not his reputation. The coalition of gunmen and entrepreneurs survived his departure and continued for years to be known as the Capone organization.

For about a year, while his case was on appeal, Capone lived in style in the Cook County Jail. When the appeal failed in 1932, he entered the federal penitentiary in Atlanta, Ga.; later he was moved to the newly opened Alcatraz penitentiary. In February 1938 he was found to have advanced syphilis of the brain; for the remainder of his life, periods of partial lucidity alternated with mental derangement.

Capone was released from prison in November 1939 (his sentence reduced for good behavior), and after several months as an outpatient in Baltimore, he retired to Miami. There, surrounded by his wife, son, and a few close relatives and associates, he spent his final years. In January 1947 he collapsed with a brain hemorrhage, contracted bronchial pneumonia, and died six days later. He was buried in Mount Olivet Cemetery in Chicago. In 1952, after the death of his mother, his grave was moved near hers in Mount Carmel Cemetery, away from the tourists.

[Capone has been the subject of innumerable journalistic books dealing with Chicago bootlegging gangs of the 1920's. By far the most complete and accurate is John Kobler, *Capone* (1971). Also useful for its information on the early development of the Torrio syndicate is Jack McPhaul, *Johnny Torrio* (1970). A few of the other journalistic books, largely anecdotal but often quite accurate, are: Fred D. Pasley, *Al Capone* (1930); James O'Donnell Bennett, *Chicago Gang Land: The True Story of Chicago Crime* (1929); Walter N. Burns, *The One-Way Ride: The Red Trail of Chicago Gangland from Prohibition to Jake Lingle* (1931); and Edward D. Sullivan, *Rattling the Cup on Chicago Crime* (1929) and *Chicago Surrenders* (1930). Two books that place the 1920's in the longer history of Chicago crime, but remain largely anecdotal rather than analytical, are Virgil W. Petersons, *Barbarians in Our Midst* (1952), and Herbert Asbury, *Gem of the Prairie: An Informal Hist. of the Chicago Underworld* (1940). A number of works are useful because they illuminate particular aspects of Capone's life and activities. Humbert S. Nelli, *Italians in Chicago, 1880–1930: A Study in Ethnic Mobility* (1970), especially chap. vii, places Capone's activities in the context of the Chicago Italian community. John Landesco, *Organized Crime in Chicago*, 2nd ed. (1968), chaps. iv-xi, is a thoughtful analysis of the place of organized crime in the politics and ethnic life of the city. Ovid Demaris, *Captive City* (1969), is particularly good in describing the political ties of the gangs and tracing the ties to the present. Elmer L. Irey, *The Tax Dodgers: The Inside Story of the T-Men's War with America's Political and Underworld Hoodlums* (1948), chap ii, tells something of the investigation that resulted in Capone's conviction for tax evasion. Robert Ross, *The Trial of Al Capone* (1933), has excerpts and summaries of the trials and appeals. There is a good selection of photographs in Kobler, *Capone*; see also *Life of Al Capone in Pictures, and Chicago's Gang Wars* (1931). Information about Capone's marriage was supplied by the City Clerk, Brooklyn, N.Y. Two major sources of documents for the study of Capone's career and the development of organized crime in Chicago during the 1920's are the files of the Chicago Crime Commission and those of the U.S. Treasury Dept., which assembled massive documentation on Capone's business activities and expenditures. Some interesting information on the movement of Capone men into labor racketeering can be gleaned from the Victor A. Olander Papers at the Univ. of Ill., Chicago Circle.]

MARK H. HALLER

CAPPS, EDWARD (Dec. 21, 1866-Aug. 21, 1950), classicist, was born in Jacksonville, Ill., the third son and the third of nine children of Stephen Reid Capps and Rhoda Smith (Tomlin) Capps. The family was Methodist. His father, an 1857 graduate of Illinois College in Jacksonville, was a prominent and philanthropic manufacturer, an excellent Greek student, and trustee of the Illinois School for the Deaf and of Illinois Women's College. He was a descendant of William Capps, who emigrated from England in 1610 and settled in Virginia. His mother's forebears had come from England and Wales before the Revolution and settled in New Jersey, later moving to Winchester, Ky. By about 1837 his parents' families had settled in Jacksonville. One of Capps's brothers, Stephen Reid Capps, became a geologist with the U.S. Geological Survey; another, Dr. Joseph Almarin Capps, became professor of clinical medicine at the University of Chicago; and a sister, Rhoda Jeanette, married Charles H. Rammelkamp, later president of Illinois College.

Capps attended Whipple Academy in Jacksonville before entering Illinois College, from which he graduated in 1887. Edward B. Clapp, later (1890-1892) his colleague at Yale, secured him for classics. He also long remembered the Latin instruction of Harold W. Johnston. The young alumnus was appointed instructor in classics at Jacksonville in 1887 but the next year went on at Clapp's urging to graduate work at Yale, where he was appointed tutor in Latin (1890-1892). Unlike most young classicists of the day, he preferred a domestic degree to a German one. His dissertation, "The Stage in the Greek Theatre" (Yale, 1891), published in *Transactions of the American Philological Association*, 22 (1891), 5-80, reflected Clapp's interests in tragedy and argued expertly from the texts against the existence of a raised stage in classical Greece. His dissertation determined his subsequent scholarly investigations. At Yale, where he studied with Tracy Peck and Thomas Day Seymour, he met William Rainey Harper. Harper took him to the University of Chicago at its founding in 1892, where he became assistant professor of Greek language and literature in the department headed by Paul Shorey. In 1893-1894 he was a student at the American School of Classical Studies at Athens. In 1903-1904 he heard Carl Robert at Halle and visited the universities at Berlin and Munich. Capps became editor-in-chief of the University of Chicago Decennial Publications (29 vols.) in 1902 and the first managing editor of *Classical Philology* in 1906. In 1901 he published an elementary history of Greek literature, *From Homer to Theocritus*. This was the period of his most enduring work in Greek drama. He published articles on "Vitruvius and the Greek Stage," University of Chicago Studies in Classical Philology (1893) and "The Introduction of Comedy into the City Dionysia," University of Chicago Decennial Publications (1903). He directed three famous dissertations on aspects of Greek acting by Kelley Rees, F. W. Dignan, and J. B. O'Connor. In 1903 he lectured on the Greek theater at Harvard. In 1907, after Harper's death, he sued the University of Chicago over a question of salary. The case was notorious and was decided in Capps's favor by the Supreme Court of Illinois.

Capps left Chicago that year for Princeton, where he was professor of Greek until his retirement in 1936. He arrived during the struggle between Woodrow Wilson and Dean Andrew Fleming West over the question of the location of the new graduate school. In the crucial decision of his life, Capps astutely chose to support Wilson against his classical colleague West. He became a lifelong Democrat in a Republican family and won the enduring loyalty of Wilson, who once said of him: "I would trust his judgment most of the time and his intentions always." In 1910 he published a text and commentary to four fragmentary plays of Menander. The exegesis of certain passages has remained of permanent value. In 1914 Capps was appointed an American editor of the Loeb Classical Library and was elected president of the American Philological Association. The appointment signaled his international reputation as scholar and editor but resulted in his devoting the best years of his scholarly life to improving the work of others. He often regretted the post, and the year 1914 marks the end of his creative scholarly period and the transition to administration.

In 1918 Wilson supported Capps's candidacy as American Red Cross commissioner to Greece, which he held (1918-1919) with the rank of lieutenant colonel. In 1920-1921 he served as Wilson's envoy extraordinary and ambassador plenipotentiary to Greece and Montenegro. He met men like Eleutherios Venizelos, the prime minister, who would ease his later work in Greece. He worked for the founding of Athens College, an American-Greek boys' school, which until 1967 boasted an alumnus in every Greek cabinet. He was a founder of the American Association of University Professors in 1915 and served as its first president in 1920.

In 1918 Capps was elected chairman of the Managing Committee of the American School of Classical Studies at Athens and served from

Dec. 1, 1919, to May 13, 1939. His abiding achievements were four. He increased the school's endowment more than tenfold. He secured in 1922 the library of Dr. J. Gennadius for the school and raised the considerable funds needed to house it. With the permission of the Greek government, he secured for the school in 1928 the excavation of the Agora at Athens, comparable in importance only to the Forum at Rome. Through his friendship with Dr. Abraham Flexner he obtained Rockefeller funding and supervised the appointment of the original staff. The importance of the subsequent excavations by the school makes this the greatest contribution of Capps's career. Finally he mercilessly insisted on prompt, competent publication of finds. A long series of expert volumes and the journal *Hesperia,* founded in 1937, resulted.

His most controversial act was firing B. H. Hill, for twenty years director of the school, a brilliant field archaeologist who was unable and unwilling to publish the results of his excavations. The decision, painful and necessary, alienated the archaeologist Carl Blegen, Hill's friend, and resulted in Blegen's excavating Troy and in Pylos not being a school dig.

Capps fostered select careers—Oscar Broneer, Rhys Carpenter, B. D. Meritt, T. Leslie Shear—and demanded loyalty. He secured Princetonian hegemony over the school for some fifty years. He possessed the energy often found in many short men and had a rare gift for imparting enthusiasm. He chose friends astutely. A stubborn fighter for what he thought right, he was justly called "the second founder of the school." He was an impeccable scholar who deserted scholarship for successful administration.

Capps received honorary degrees from Illinois College (LL.D. 1911), Oberlin College (Litt.D. 1923), Harvard (L.H.D. 1924), the University of Michigan (Litt.D. 1931), the University of Athens (LL.D. 1937), and Oxford (Litt.D. 1946); and was thrice decorated by the Greek government.

Capps married Grace Alexander of Greenville, Ill., on July 20, 1892. She died at Princeton in 1937. They had four children, Priscilla, Edward, Jr., Alexander, and Rhoda. Capps died in Princeton after a long illness, and his ashes were interred in the Diamond Grove Cemetery in Jacksonville.

[Sources include L. E. Lord, "The Chairmanship of Edward Capps," *A Hist. of the Am. School of Classical Studies at Athens* (1947), with photograph; and "Edward Capps: In Memoriam," *Sixty-ninth*

Annual Report of the Am. School of Classical Studies at Athens (1949–50), with photograph; obituary in the *N. Y. Times,* Aug. 22, 1950; *Who Was Who in Am.,* III (1950); G. H. Chase, *Am. Jour. of Archaeology,* 55 (1951), 101; B. D. Meritt, *Trans. and Proc. of the Am. Philological Assoc.,* 81 (1950), xiv–xv; photograph in *Classical Studies Presented to Edward Capps on His Seventieth Birthday* (1936). Personal information was supplied by Priscilla Capps Hill, Edward Capps, Jr., Louise Capps Scranton, W. K. Pritchett, and Homer A. Thompson.]

WILLIAM M. CALDER III

CARAWAY, HATTIE OPHELIA WYATT (Feb. 1, 1878–Dec. 21, 1950), United States senator, was born on a farm near Bakerville (Humphreys County), Tenn., one of four children of William Carroll Wyatt and Lucy Mildred (Burch) Wyatt. Her father's family (of English origin) came from Virginia and North Carolina; her mother's were natives of North Carolina and Tennessee. When Hattie was four, the Wyatts moved to Hustburg, Tenn., where her father farmed and ran a general store. At the age of fourteen she entered Dickson (Tenn.) Normal College, where she earned a B.A. in 1896. After teaching briefly in local schools, she married a classmate, Thaddeus Horatius Caraway, on Feb. 5, 1902.

While Thaddeus practiced law in Jonesboro, Ark., and embarked on a political career, Hattie devoted herself to domestic duties, tending a kitchen garden, helping to manage the family cotton plantation, and raising three sons, Paul Wyatt, Forrest, and Robert Easley. The Caraways moved to Washington following Thaddeus' election to the House of Representatives in 1912. Hattie (who described herself as a "homebody") remained in the background, caring for her family and their home, the historic Calvert mansion in Riverdale, Md.

When Thaddeus Caraway died in November 1931, in the fifth year of his second term as U.S. senator from Arkansas, Governor Harvey Parnell appointed Hattie Caraway to the seat. On Jan. 12, 1932, she won a special election for the remainder of the term, thus becoming the first woman ever elected to the Senate (Rebecca Latimer Felton of Georgia had served a "courtesy" appointment for two days in 1922). Everyone expected her to bow gracefully out of politics when her term expired, but she confounded the politicians by standing for election to a regular term. "I am going to fight for my place in the sun," she declared. "The time has passed when a woman should be placed in a position and kept there only while someone else is being groomed for the job"(*Arkansas Democrat,* July 14, 1932). She was given little chance of winning, for her six opponents in the August Democratic primary included a former governor, a former senator, and the Democratic national committeeman. But, in July, Sen. Huey P. Long of Louisiana announced that he would come to Arkansas and conduct a whirlwind campaign in her behalf. She had supported Long's proposals for wealth redistribution, and the foray gave him an opportunity to embarrass his political foe, Arkansas's senior senator Joseph Robinson.

Long barnstormed Arkansas on August 1, launching what the *Arkansas Democrat* later called "perhaps the most spectacular political tour the state ever witnessed" (Aug. 10, 1932). Leading a caravan of sound trucks and literature vans, he crisscrossed the state for nine days in behalf of "the little widow woman." His theme was the struggle between "the money power" and "the people"; Caraway, he claimed, was an "unbossed" candidate who had repeatedly defied Wall Street to vote the interests of the common man. Warming to the campaign, the candidate herself made some speeches defending her record and attacking the Hoover administration.

She won a decisive primary victory and in November was elected to a full term in the Senate. In her thirteen years in that body, she compiled a series of other firsts for women: first to preside over the Senate, first to conduct a Senate committee hearing, first committee chairman (Enrolled Bills), first senior senator.

Despite her pioneering role, Senator Caraway consistently shunned the limelight. A short, plump woman, invariably dressed in black, she sat quietly at her desk, sometimes working crossword puzzles during Senate debates. Typically described as "diminutive," "quiet," and "demure," she rarely spoke on the floor. "I haven't the heart to take a minute away from the men," she told George Creel. "The poor dears love it so." Nevertheless, she attended faithfully to her duties as a member of the Agriculture and Forestry, Commerce, Enrolled Bills, and Library committees, and she compiled a progressive voting record consistently supporting the New Deal. Occasionally her southern background was evident, as in her defense of prohibition (she was a lifelong Methodist) or her participation in the filibuster against the antilynching bill in 1938.

Senator Caraway's performance won her the backing of most federal employees, unions, and women's groups when she embarked upon "her first unchaperoned campaign for reelection" in 1938 (*N. Y. Times*, Aug. 8, 1938). After narrowly defeating Rep. John L. McClellan in a bitter primary contest, she easily won the general election. With the outbreak of war in Europe she spoke out against isolationism and voted for Administration policies, including lend-lease.

Never a feminist, Caraway at first displayed little interest in women's concerns. When the Nineteenth Amendment was ratified, she later told George Creel, "I just added voting to cooking and sewing and other household duties. Of course living in Arkansas helped a lot, for down there we don't have to bother about making a choice between two parties." Her election to the Senate occasioned widespread comment about the ability of a woman to do the job; the *New York Times* said at the time of her death that she had "proved that a woman could easily carry out the work that her male colleagues were called upon to do." Caraway was no doubt influenced by her success in politics; by 1936 she was saying that the time was past for treating women "as set apart by sex from any serious legislative qualifications" (*Washington Evening Star*, Apr. 7, 1936). In 1943 she cosponsored the Equal Rights Amendment, the first woman in Congress to do so.

Standing for reelection in 1944, Caraway was defeated in the Democratic primary by Rep. J. William Fulbright, who subsequently won her seat. In 1945 President Roosevelt nominated her to the Federal Employees' Compensation Commission; in July 1946 she became a member of the Employees' Compensation Appeals Board. She suffered a stroke in January 1950 and died eleven months later in a sanitorium in Falls Church, Va. She was buried in West Lawn Cemetery, Jonesboro, Ark.

[The principal primary source is the *N.Y. Times*, 1931–1945, and Dec. 22, 1950 (Senator Caraway's obituary). The *Arkansas Democrat* (Little Rock) is useful for campaign years; see especially July 14, 1932; see also Dec. 21 and 22, 1950. A radio broadcast on Caraway's activities as a senator is reprinted in the *Washington Evening Star*, Apr. 7, 1936. There are scattered references in the *Cong. Rec.* The most important general account is in *Notable Am. Women*, I, 284–286; see also *Current Biog.*, 1945 (which includes a photograph); George Creel, "The Woman Who Holds Her Tongue," *Colliers'*, Sept. 18, 1937, pp. 22, 55; "Last of the First," *Time*, Aug. 7, 1944, p. 19; and *Nat. Cyc. Am. Biog.*, Current Vol. D, 148–149. The best accounts of the 1932 campaign are Hermann B. Deutsch, "Hattie and Huey," *Saturday Evening Post*, Oct. 15, 1932, pp. 6–7, 88–90, 92 (which includes a photograph), and T. Harry Williams. *Huey Long* (1970), pp. 583–593. Studies that treat Caraway in the context of other women in politics include Hope Chamberlin, *A Minority of Members: Women in the U.S. Congress 1917–1972*, pp. 86–95 (1973); Annabel Paxton, *Women in Congress*, pp. 15–29 (1945); and Maxine Davis, "Five Democratic Women," *Ladies' Home Journal*, May 1933, pp. 114, 117.]

NANCY J. WEISS

CARLSON, EVANS FORDYCE (Feb. 26, 1896–May 27, 1947), soldier and author, was born in Sidney, N.Y., the first of four children of Rev. Thomas Alpine Carlson, a Congregational minister, and Joetta Viola (Evans) Carlson. Thomas Carlson, the son of a Norwegian immigrant who had prospected for gold and silver in the High Sierras, owed his middle name to the mountainous county in California where he was born in a mining camp. He had attended theological seminaries in San Francisco and Auburn, N.Y., and he maintained a strict household, but he was close to his son and told him stories about his youthful adventures. Joetta Carlson, whose Welsh forebears had come to America during the colonial period, was a sensitive, charming, self-possessed woman. Evans grew up in three New England towns where his father held pastorates: Shoreham, Vt., Dracut, Mass., and Peacham, Vt. A restless youth, he left home at fourteen to work on a farm near Vergennes, Vt., where he attended but did not graduate from the local high school. He found jobs as a laborer in Connecticut and New Jersey, and then, in 1912, joined the army. He was stationed in the Philippines and in Hawaii and was discharged with the rank of master sergeant in 1915.

Recalled to active duty in 1916 during border trouble with Mexico, Carlson served as an instructor to the National Guard Artillery at Fort Bliss in El Paso, Tex. After the entry of the United States into World War I, he was commissioned a second lieutenant and assigned to the 13th Field Artillery. Two promotions brought him to the rank of captain, and late in the war he served briefly in France on the staff of Gen. John J. Pershing. He resigned his commission in 1919, believing that life in the peacetime army would be too sedate. For the next two years he worked as a salesman for the California Packing Corporation, but he was not content and resolved to reenter the service. When he learned the army would only take him back as a second lieutenant, Carlson balked at the prospect of being outranked by former friends and, deciding to start afresh in a new branch, enlisted as a private in the Marine Corps in 1922.

It was primarily as a Marine that Carlson earned public distinction. Commissioned a second lieutenant in 1923, he held several domestic assignments over the next four years. From 1927 to 1929 and again from 1933 to 1935 he served as an operations and intelligence officer in China. In 1930 he was awarded the Navy Cross for heroism in combat against guerrillas in Nicaragua. Carlson

was promoted to captain in 1935 and was appointed second-in-command of the military guard at President Franklin D. Roosevelt's retreat in Warm Springs, Ga., a fortuitous circumstance that led to a personal relationship with the president. Carlson's interest in China grew during these years, and despite his lack of a college education at some time during this period he took graduate courses in international law at George Washington University in Washington, D.C.

Beginning in 1937, when Carlson returned to China, he carried on a private correspondence with Roosevelt, thereby providing the commander-in-chief with eyewitness accounts of Chinese developments. In pursuit of his attempt to gather information on the Sino-Japanese War, he became the first foreign military observer to scrutinize at first hand the operations of the Chinese Red Army, or as it was called at the time, the Eighth Route Army. He made two extended cross-country tours with this army in December 1937 and during 1938, often accompanying Communist guerrillas behind Japanese lines. Excited by his historic experiences, Carlson overstepped the bounds of his diplomatic position and granted extensive press interviews, in which he highly praised Communist military and political institutions. He was especially impressed by the unreciprocated willingness of the Communists to form a united front with the Nationalist government of Chiang Kai-shek to defeat their common foe, the Japanese; and he was highly critical of the selling of American supplies to Japan. Cautioned by his superiors to exercise more discretion, Carlson resigned from the Corps in 1938 in order "to be free to speak and write." He was requested to give his resignation further thought but he officially resigned Apr. 30, 1939.

Returning to the United States, Carlson for the next two years delivered anti-Japanese lectures, contributed pro-Chinese articles to magazines, and published two books: *The Chinese Army: Its Organization and Military Efficiency* (1940), a technical treatise, and *Twin Stars in China: A Behind-the-Scenes Story of China's Valiant Struggle for Existence by a U.S. Marine Who Lived and Moved with the People* (1940). The latter book, which tended to view the Chinese Communists as selfless democrats, aroused a good deal of attention. He visited China again as a civilian in 1940 and in 1941, primarily to study Chinese cooperatives, and returned to the United States to write and lecture on the movement.

Convinced that war with Japan was likely, Carlson returned to the Marine Corps and was commissioned a major in the Reserves in 1941. In 1942 he was promoted to the rank of lieutenant colonel and given command of the 2nd Marine Battalion, with the president's son, Major James Roosevelt, as his executive officer. This was the group that became known as "Carlson's Raiders." Drawing on the knowledge he had accumulated in China, Carlson patterned his battalion after the Eighth Route Army. The Raiders' rallying cry was "Gung Ho!"—an adaptation of the Chinese slogan for "working together." Insistent that every Raider subordinate himself for the harmony of the group, Carlson abolished officers' mess and other privileges, directed that all wear the same garb and live alike, invited suggestions about his battle plans in open discussions before each engagement, and afterward encouraged self-criticism. The "Old Man," as he was affectionately called, inspired intense loyalty among his men, both by his fearlessness and by his sympathetic and unpretentious manner. He was always at the "point" on the march; as one Raider said later, even when his tall, gaunt figure could not be seen through thick jungle foliage, the smell of his "wonderful, stinking, large-bowl pipe" gave reassurance to his men (Blankfort, p. 297).

Carlson's Raiders first saw action on Aug. 17, 1942, when they landed from submarines on Makin Island in the Gilberts, attacked the Japanese garrison there, and destroyed many installations. Although the Makin raid was not of great military consequence, American successes against Japan were then so rare that the Raiders captured the public imagination. Their only other significant military campaign came late in 1942 on Guadalcanal. Operating behind Japanese lines, they killed nearly 500 enemy troops while suffering but thirty-four casualties. A Marine historian has called this "one of the great combat patrols in the history of the Corps" (Heinl, p. 372).

Guadalcanal was Carlson's last assignment in combat leadership. His unorthodox methods did not please his superiors, and in 1943 the 2nd Battalion was merged with three others into a Marine Raider Regiment. The remainder of the war was anticlimactic for Carlson. In 1943 he was an official observer at the assault on Tarawa, and in 1944, while serving in the same capacity, he was seriously wounded on Saipan while rescuing an enlisted man. He retired from the Marine Corps on July 1, 1946, and at that time was given the rank of bri-

gadier general. Among his many citations were the Legion of Merit, three Navy Crosses, two Purple Hearts, and three Presidential Unit Citations.

During the last year of his life, Carlson became increasingly active in groups opposing the foreign policy of the cold war. He served as chairman of the Committee for a Democratic Far Eastern Policy, as co-chairman of the National Committee to Win the Peace, and as a vice-chairman of the National Citizens Political Action Committee. He was also a national vice-chairman of the Progressive Citizens of America, which in late 1947 became the Progressive party and endorsed the presidential candidacy of Henry A. Wallace. Carlson called for the immediate withdrawal of United States troops from China and the termination of all support for the regime of Chiang Kai-shek until Chiang agreed to establish a coalition government with the Chinese Communists. He also deplored the growing rift between the United States and the Soviet Union, asserting that they could peacefully coexist. When criticized for his defense of the Communists as the "only democratic force" in China, Carlson responded: "People in this country don't like that word, 'Communist.' But I've learned it's wise to go behind words and find out about action" (New York Times, Sept. 6, 1946).

Carlson married Dorothy Seccombe of Perris, Calif., in May 1916. They were divorced about six years later, and on Apr. 29, 1924, he married Etelle Sawyer. This second marriage also ended in divorce, in 1943, and on Feb. 29, 1944, he married Peggy (Tatum) Whyte, a divorcée and the daughter of an army colonel. Carlson had two children: Evans Charles by his first marriage, and Anthony John by his second. Following his retirement Carlson settled with his wife in Oregon on the slopes of Mt. Hood. In 1947, at the age of fifty-one, he suffered a fatal heart attack and died in Portland, Oreg. He was buried with full military honors in Arlington National Cemetery .

Less than five years after his death, Carlson's strong advocacy of the Chinese Communist movement led Sen. Joseph R. McCarthy to condemn him as a hero of international communism and a "disciple" of the radical journalist Agnes Smedley. Carlson had indeed been a close friend of Smedley in China, yet he was anything but a Marxist. He was, instead, a Bible-quoting New Englander who believed deeply in egalitarian democracy. Almost totally unconcerned about political dogma, he can be faulted for underestimating the ideological commitment of China's Communists, but he had realistically appraised their dynamism and their military potential. He was a talented professional soldier and a flinty individualist who espoused the brotherhood of man.

[Carlson letters can be found in the Nelson T. Johnson and Raymond Gram Swing papers, both in the Lib. of Cong., and in the Franklin D. Roosevelt Papers at Hyde Park, N.Y. Insight into Carlson's personality and career have been gained from correspondence with Michael Blankfort, Edgar Snow, and Helen Foster Snow. Memoirs and other works by his contemporaries that contain substantial information about Carlson include: James M. Bertram, *Beneath the Shadow: A New Zealander in the Far East, 1939-1946* (1947); Agnes Smedley, *Battle Hymn of China* (1943) and *China Fights Back: An American Woman with the Eighth Route Army* (1938); Edgar Snow, *Journey to the Beginning* (1958); Ilona Ralf Sues, *Shark's Fins and Millet* (1944); Freda Utley, *China at War* (1939) and *Odyssey of a Liberal: Memoirs* (1970); and Anna Wang, *Ich kämpfte für Mao* (1964). Sen. Joseph R. McCarthy's view of Carlson is stated in his *America's Retreat from Victory* (1951). Michael Blankfort, *The Big Yankee: The Life of Carlson of the Raiders* (1947), is a sympathetic biography written before Carlson's death and based on interviews and personal papers. Other useful secondary works include: Benis M. Frank and Henry I. Shaw, Jr., *Victory and Occupation: Hist. of U.S. Marine Corps Operations in World War II*, V (1958); Samuel B. Griffith II, *The Chinese People's Liberation Army* (1967); Robert D. Heinl, Jr., *Soldiers of the Sea: The U.S. Marine Corps, 1776-1962* (1962); Kenneth E. Shewmaker, *Americans and Chinese Communists, 1927-1945* (1971) and "The American Liberal Dream: Evans F. Carlson and the Chinese Communists, 1937-1947," *Pacific Hist. Rev.*, May 1969. See also *Current Biog.*, 1943; and the well-researched obituary in the *N.Y. Times*, May 28, 1947.]

KENNETH E. SHEWMAKER

CARRIER, WILLIS HAVILAND (Nov. 26, 1876-Oct. 7, 1950), mechanical engineer, pioneer in air conditioning, was born on a farm near Angola in western New York, the only child of Duane Williams Carrier and Elizabeth (Haviland) Carrier. His mother, who died when her son was eleven, was descended from Quakers who migrated to Massachusetts in the seventeenth century. His father traced his lineage to Thomas Carrier, who settled in Andover, Mass., about 1663. Willis presumably grew up as a Presbyterian, his affiliation of later years. Reared on the family farm, he early showed considerable mechanical aptitude. He attended district school, graduated from Angola Academy in 1894, and after two years of teaching school entered Central High School in nearby Buffalo in order to meet college entrance requirements. In the following spring he won a state scholarship to Cornell University. He graduated from Cornell in 1901 as a mechanical engineer.

Almost six feet tall, with powerful shoulders and impressive bearing, Carrier took a job with the Buffalo Forge Company, a manufacturer of blowers, exhausters, and heaters. Convinced by his first assignments that existing data were insufficient to permit the design of soundly based heating and ventilating systems, he began to derive such data for himself. In July 1902 the company recognized the value of this work by putting Carrier in charge of a new department of experimental engineering.

Carrier's career took more definite shape that same year when Buffalo Forge contracted to control humidity in the Sackett-Wilhelms Lithographing and Publishing Company plant in Brooklyn, N.Y. The objective was to hold the dimensions of paper constant so that colors would register properly in the printing process. Carrier designed a system which maintained a level of 55 degrees relative humidity throughout the year at a temperature of 70 degrees Fahrenheit in winter and 80 degrees in summer. He achieved humidification in winter by introducing low-pressure steam from the plant boilers into the airstream through perforated pipes. He accomplished dehumidification in summer by passing the air over two sets of coils, one cooled with water from an artesian well, the other refrigerated by an ammonia-compression machine.

Carrier next developed more flexible and efficient temperature and humidity controls. In 1904 he invented a central-station spray apparatus (Patent 808,897) in which a very fine mist of water, heated for humidification and cooled for dehumidification, served the function of the pipes and coils. In 1906 he developed dew point control (Patents 1,085,971, 1,095,156, and 1,101,784), a method of regulating relative humidity by altering at the apparatus the temperature at which moisture begins to condense. Concurrently, he undertook research to improve the design of air distribution systems. By the end of 1907 Carrier systems had been installed in several cotton mills, a worsted mill, two silk mills, a shoe factory, and a pharmaceutical plant.

Late in 1907 the Buffalo Forge Company established a wholly owned subsidiary, the Carrier Air Conditioning Company of America, to engineer and market complete systems. The term "air conditioning" was first used by Stuart W. Cramer, a Charlotte, N.C., mill owner and operator, but Carrier quickly adopted it, defining air conditioning as control of air humidity, temperature, purity, and circulation. Carrier spent six busy and fruitful years, serving as both vice-president of the new subsidiary and chief engineer and director of research for the parent firm. Carrier equipment was installed in industry after industry: tobacco, rayon, rubber, paper, pharmaceuticals, and food processing. Meanwhile, he continued his scientific and technical investigations. A milestone was reached in 1911 when he presented a paper on "Rational Psychrometric Formulae" at the annual meeting of the American Society of Mechanical Engineers (*Transactions,* XXXIII, 1911, pp. 1005-1039), in which he questioned generally accepted humidity measuring data, which were based on empirical formulas he found both incorrect and limited in range. The new formulas he proposed, based on accurate recent measurements, became the theoretical standard of the industry. Carrier's handbook on air movement and distribution, *Fan Engineering,* appeared in 1914.

In 1914 Buffalo Forge decided to limit itself to manufacturing and to withdraw from the business of engineering and installing air conditioning systems. Carrier and a handful of colleagues thereupon formed the Carrier Engineering Corporation (1915), with Carrier as president. Though started on a shoestring, the company prospered; by 1929 it had two plants in Newark, N.J., and a third in Allentown, Pa. Basic to its success was Carrier's development of a radical new refrigerating machine, the centrifugal compressor (Patents 1,575,817-18-19). Since it used safe, nontoxic refrigerants and could serve large installations cheaply, it opened the way for systems whose objective was human comfort. Carrier air-conditioned the J. L. Hudson department store in Detroit in 1924, the House and Senate chambers in the national Capitol in 1928-1929, and, by 1930, more than 300 theatres.

In 1930 the Carrier Engineering Corporation merged with two manufacturing firms, the Brunswick-Kroeschell Company, and the York Heating and Ventilating Corporation, to become the Carrier Corporation, with Carrier as chairman of the board. The coming of the depression of the 1930's forced Carrier to fight for business survival. He brought in financial expertise, cut costs, and centralized operations in Syracuse, N.Y. Taking a characteristically long and confident view, he insisted on continued investment in research and development. He turned to the problem of air-conditioning high-rise buildings, where space could not be sacrificed to bulky ducts. This led to his 1939 invention of a system in which conditioned air from a central station was piped through small steel conduits at high velocity to individual rooms. Here the air, released through nozzles, induced a secondary circulation over supplemental heating or cooling

coils, as the season required (Patents 2,353,144, 2,355,629, 2,363,294, and 2,363,945).

The air conditioning industry revived in the late 1930's, demonstrated its practical utility during the war, and flourished in the postwar years, when the time was ripe for a vast expansion into home installations. A heart ailment forced Carrier into retirement in 1948, and two years later he suffered a fatal heart attack in New York City. He was buried in Forest Lawn Cemetery in Buffalo.

At the time of his death air conditioning had come of age. Carrier had seen his company prosper and his systems for industrial and private purposes installed throughout much of the world. There were other firms, other inventors, and other engineers, but no one else had contributed so much across the whole range of the art (more than eighty patents) and had so closely identified his name with the new technology.

Carrier married Edith Claire Seymour, a classmate at Cornell, on Aug. 10, 1902. She died in 1912, and on Apr. 23, 1913, he married Jennie Tifft Martin of Angola, N.Y., who died in 1939. His third marriage, in 1941, was to Elizabeth Marsh Wise. Carrier had no children of his own but adopted two sons, Vernon and Earl.

[Papers relating to Carrier and the company he founded are in the Cornell Univ. Collect. of Regional Hist. and Univ. Archives. Carrier was the author of more than 100 articles which appeared between 1903 and 1953 in professional and trade journals, and co-author, with Realto E. Cherne and Walter A. Grant, of *Modern Air Conditioning, Heating and Ventilating* (1940). Margaret Ingels, *Willis Haviland Carrier: Father of Air Conditioning* (1952), is a good short biography which concentrates on Carrier's technical contributions; it includes a list of his writings. Cloud Wampler, *Dr. Willis H. Carrier: Father of Air Conditioning* (Newcomen Soc., pamphlets, 1949), is a short appreciation of the man and his work by a close business associate. A photograph of Carrier is reproduced in Ingels, a portrait in Wampler. See also obituaries in *N.Y. Times,* Oct. 8, 1950, and *Refrigerating Engineering,* Nov. 1, 1950, and, for his marriages, *Nat. Cyc. Am. Biog.,* Current Vol. E, pp. 24-25. For the larger context in which Carrier worked, see Oscar E. Anderson, *Refrigeration in America* (1953).]

OSCAR E. ANDERSON

CARROLL, EARL (Sept. 16, 1893-June 17, 1948), producer and director, was born in Pittsburgh, Pa., the son of James Carroll and Elizabeth (Wills) Carroll. He is believed to have had two brothers and one sister. His father was a tavernkeeper. Carroll's education apparently stopped at the grammar school level, and his early precocity in showmanship often brought him attention. At ten he was staging penny shows in his parent's basement and, shortly after, he began earning pocket money as a program boy at the Alvin Theatre in downtown Pittsburgh. In 1910 he became assistant treasurer of a leading theater, the Nixon, where he managed the box office. His work permitted him to mingle with the celebrities of the era, among them Sarah Bernhardt, Richard Mansfield, and Enrico Caruso. Evidently touched with wanderlust in his late adolescence, he traveled through the Orient for nearly a year.

He next settled briefly in New York, but returned to Pittsburgh to become treasurer of the Nixon Theatre. In 1912 he wrote a play, *Lady of the Night,* which he submitted to A. H. Wood, a New York producer. Upon receiving a favorable response from Wood, Carroll quickly returned to New York. When plans for the play's production dissolved, he took a job in the music publishing house of Leo Feist, clipping news items for the company scrapbooks. Under Feist's direction, he rose rapidly in the firm, meanwhile writing song lyrics on his own. Among his more than four hundred lyrics were some notable successes, especially "Dreams of Long Ago," composed for Caruso. Carroll's music and lyrics for *The Pretty Mrs. Smith* were seized upon by Oliver Morosco as a popular vehicle for his fast-rising young protégée, Fritzi Scheff. Others to take his songs to the Broadway stage were Charlotte Greenwood, who popularized "So Long, Letty," and Eddie Cantor, who included "Canary Cottage" in one of his shows. Carroll had developed a keen sense of the demands of the musical theater, and he admittedly followed the successful formula of David Belasco, using lavish costuming and stage sets.

Shortly before World War I, on Oct. 25, 1916, Carroll married Marcelle Hontabat. After the war, in which he served as a lieutenant in the Army Aviation Corps, he began producing his own shows on Broadway, among them two ephemeral entertainments called *Lady of the Lamp* (1920) and *Daddy Dumplings* (1921). In 1923, however, the first of *The Earl Carroll Vanities,* which he wrote, composed, directed, and produced, caught the imagination of the "Roaring Twenties." Profitable beyond all expectations, the *Vanities* spun off road companies to carry its gaudy message across the country. For thirteen successive seasons Carroll reworked this formula of girls, music, and pageantry into new "editions." Convinced that full control of a theater was essential to his style of showmanship, he constructed the first Earl Carroll Theatre in 1923, and a second in 1931.

Not all of New York City shared Carroll's sensuous appreciation of womanhood, however,

and he was once jailed for four days in the Tombs prison before being cleared of a charge that he had displayed indecent posters in the lobby of his theater. But it was a predawn party at the height of the prohibition era that caused the most serious reversal of his life. A nude show girl was alleged to have taken a bath in champagne during a private party on center stage. Rather than involve prominent friends in a scandal, Carroll lied ("like a gentleman," it was said) under oath, was subsequently convicted of perjury, and eventually served four months of a one-year sentence in the federal penitentiary in Atlanta, Ga.

Throughout his career, Carroll was responsible for over sixty theatrical productions. Among the best known were *White Cargo* (1924), *Sketchbook* (1935), and *Black Waters.* In 1936 he shifted the focus of his business activities from Broadway to Hollywood and soon built an Earl Carroll Theatre there, in which revues flourished for the next twelve years. Over the doorway of this theater he inscribed the proclamation, "Through these portals pass the most beautiful girls in the world." A self-proclaimed authority on feminine beauty, he ballyhooed his searches and auditions for chorus girls, and for many years served as a judge at the Atlantic City beauty pageants. During his years in Hollywood, Carroll produced about a dozen motion pictures, mostly adaptations of the *Vanities,* among them *Murder at the Vanities* (1934) and *A Night at Earl Carroll's* (1940).

Carroll was an active member of the show business fraternities, the Lambs, the Friars, and the Lotus Club. A founder of ASCAP, he eventually fell out with the powerful union leader, James Petrillo, and spent several years in bitter contention with him over union matters.

After his wife's death in 1936, Carroll did not remarry. His companion when he was killed in a commercial airline crash between San Diego and New York was Beryl Wallace, one of the stars of his revues. Following separate funeral services—Carroll's an ornate affair with displays of floral statues representing life-size chorus girls—the ashes of Earl Carroll and Beryl Wallace were placed together in a niche of the Forest Lawn Mausoleum, Beverly Hills, Calif.

At the time of his death, Earl Carroll had come to stand for that gaudy showmanship of the 1920's that was as much a naïve and patriotic salute to American affluence as it was a shrewdly commercial enterprise.

[Information on Earl Carroll may be found in articles by Charles Bochert, "The Most Beautiful Girls in the World," and "The Mecca of Beauty" in *The New York Magazine Program,* Oct. 1932, and miscellaneous clippings in the files of the Harvard Theatre Collect. Brief factual data on his life may be found in Bernard Sobel, ed., *The New Theatre Handbook* (1959) and *Who Was Who in America,* II (1950). Abel Green and Joe Laurie, Jr., *Show Biz* (1951) contains scattered pieces of information on the producer and his *Vanities,* as they appeared in the pages of the theatrical journal *Variety.* Obituaries appeared in the New York and Pittsburgh newspapers.]

ALBERT F. McLEAN, JR.

CASE, SHIRLEY JACKSON (Sept. 28, 1872–Dec. 5, 1947), historian and university administrator, was born in Hatfield Point, New Brunswick, Canada. He was the son of George F. Case and Maria (Jackson) Case. To maintain his family, the father worked exceptionally hard both as a farmer and as a carriage builder at the edge of the small village. By his own admission, Case had no love for farm life, but throughout his career he maintained an interest in woodworking, which he had learned from his father. He had a fine collection of tools, which he prized highly, and he was capable of producing exquisite wood pieces.

Both parents were active members of the Free Baptist Church, which represented the most liberal and open-minded branch of that denomination. Shirley Jackson Case was marked by this tradition for the remainder of his life.

Case enrolled in Acadia University, New Brunswick, and received the B.A. degree in 1893 and the M.A. degree in 1896. He specialized in classical studies and mathematics, and his first teaching position was in mathematics at St. Martin's Seminary and Horton Collegiate Academy in New Brunswick in 1896. In 1897 he moved to the United States, where for four years he taught Greek at the New Hampton Literary Institute in New Hampshire. In addition to his teaching responsibilities he served as pastor in the local community church. On June 29, 1899, he married Evelyn Hill, an accomplished musician and music teacher at the institute. They had no children. In 1901 he entered Yale University Divinity School, where he specialized in Biblical languages and received his B.D. degree *summa cum laude* in 1904. He then proceeded to work on his doctorate in the area of Biblical studies and early Christianity and he received the Ph.D. from Yale in 1906. While pursuing graduate work, he was also instructor in Greek at Yale for a year, pastor of the Congregational Church, Bethany, Conn. (1902–1903), and pastor of the United Church in Beacon Falls, Conn. (1903–1906).

His academic career commenced with his appointment in 1906 as professor of history and philosophy of religion at Bates College. In 1908 he was appointed assistant professor of New Testament interpretation in the University of Chicago Divinity School and was promoted to associate professor in 1913. In 1915 he became a full professor in the New Testament department at the divinity school, and in 1917 he was also appointed professor of early church history and received an honorary doctor of divinity degree from Yale. In 1923 he was named chairman of the church history department, and in 1925 he was given a new designation, professor of the history of early Christianity. In 1933 he was appointed dean of the divinity school at Chicago and served in that post until his retirement in 1938. In 1938–1939 he was a special lecturer in New Testament at Bexley Hall, the Episcopal Theological Seminary in Gambier, Ohio. In 1940 he became professor of religion at Florida Southern College and dean of the Florida School of Religion in Lakeland, where he remained until his death.

Case's career was marked by distinction both in the field of scholarship and in the area of academic administration. With his appointment as chairman of the church history department in the divinity school at Chicago, a new epoch was inaugurated. He gathered one of the most distinguished groups of church historians ever to teach on a single faculty in the United States, John T. McNeill, Wilhelm Pauck, Matthew Spinka, Charles Lyttle, and W. E. Garrison.

Perhaps Case's outstanding discovery was William Warren Sweet, who was brought to the university to carry on the work vacated by the resignation of Peter Mode in the area of the history of Christianity in America. Sweet was given special encouragement to gather and catalogue sources and to publish his findings in the area of religion in America. As a consequence, a new discipline developed at Chicago with Case's full support.

In 1924 he was elected president of the American Society of Church History. Under his leadership the organization was rejuvenated, the membership was greatly increased, *Church History* began regular publication, and Dr. Sweet's research work was transferred from Chicago to the American Society of Church History. Case also was responsible for recommending regional meetings of the society in order to strengthen its grass-roots support throughout the nation.

In 1925 he was elected president of the Chicago Society of Biblical Research, and in 1926 he was elected president of the national organization, the Society of Biblical Literature and Exegesis. In 1927 he became editor of the *Journal of Religion,* a publication of the Chicago Divinity School, and brought distinction to that journal through his editorial acumen.

From 1931 to 1932 he headed a special deputation to investigate the teaching of the history of Christianity in the various universities and schools developed by mission organizations throughout the Orient. His report became influential in modifying the way church history was taught throughout the mission field in the Orient.

Although his deanship lasted only five years, he carried on and strengthened the traditions developed under his predecessor and close friend, Shailer Matthews. He also chaired a special committee of the American Association of Theological Schools with regard to curriculum revision in the member institutions. Dean Case demonstrated a rare capacity for organizing scholarly activities and enhancing the contributions of individual scholars so that an impact might be made through their collaborative efforts.

Case's major contribution, however, was in the area of historical scholarship, both in the field of New Testament studies and the history of early Christianity. Along with Matthews he became a foremost exponent of the so-called sociohistorical method, which came to mark the entire divinity school faculty so that it was soon known both in the United States and abroad as the Chicago School. The sociohistorical method was marked by four basic concerns that were closely correlated in an effort to develop a fresh perspective in historical scholarship. First, there was an insistence on a rigorous use of the historical method, which involved careful observation of all of the facts, based on literary, archaeological, and other forms of evidence. The historian's task was to develop a hypothesis based upon a rigorous analysis of the facts properly tested by canons of evidence so that conclusions could be developed which stood close scrutiny by other scholars. Case and his colleagues were aware of the dialectic between presupposition and factual material. They insisted that an awareness of the historian's own assumptions and presuppositions was one of the best safeguards to prevent the misuse of the evidence at hand.

The distinctive mark of the Chicago School was a concern for the total environment in which any historic event occurred. Case was convinced that a true picture of Jesus could be obtained only by a proper understanding of the full context or setting in which Jesus' ministry occurred. The Chicago School sought to review carefully the economic, political, social, geographical, psychological, and philosophical dimensions of a given culture prior to the task of attempting to understand any documents. That is, documents were not to be studied either in isolation or with merely a polite bow in the direction of these other factors. The total environment in which a religious leader or group developed was to be meticulously analyzed and reconstructed. Thus the nature and history of an individual or group could be understood.

Case paid close attention to the various literary documents and archaeological evidence that history has left behind. Though these were to be studied carefully, and the latest methods were to be employed, documents also were to be seen in the broader total environmental context. Finally, Case and his Chicago colleagues felt that in the reconstruction of past history a genetic approach was essential. They had adopted an evolutionary hypothesis, and they tended to understand history as emerging from one epoch to another, or from lower forms to higher, more sophisticated forms.

Case had four basic centers of research. He was profoundly interested in the question of Jesus, his ministry, and his function and role in early Christianity and throughout Christian history. His first book, which appeared in 1912, was entitled *The Historicity of Jesus,* and in one way or another he continued that interest throughout his career. Perhaps his most famous book, and that which demonstrated most clearly his dependence on the sociohistorical method, appeared in 1927 and was entitled *Jesus: A New Biography.* This was followed in 1932 by a further study on *Jesus Through the Centuries.*

At the same time that Case was carrying on his research on Jesus, he was struggling with the overall question of the origin and nature of Christianity itself. In 1914 he published *The Evolution of Early Christianity: A Genetic Study of First Century Christianity in Relation to Its Religious Environment.* The title recapitulates the basic concerns of the Chicago School. In 1923 he pursued the question in greater depth in *The Social Origins of Christianity,* and that was followed ten years later by *The Social Triumph of the Ancient Church* (1933).

Another of Case's basic concerns was the element of the supernatural in early Christianity and its continuance in contemporary history. *The Book of Revelation* was published in 1918 and followed the same year by *The Millennial Hope: A Phase of Wartime Thinking.* In 1919 there appeared *The Revelation of John.* In these volumes he struggled with the question of the origin, nature, and role of apocalyptic thought in Christianity. In 1943 he wrote *The Christian Philosophy of History,* in which he attempted to outline a distinctive Christian view of the nature and meaning of history. His final book, *The Origins of Christian Supernaturalism* (1946), reflected his earlier concern with apocalyptic thought. Although he published several other works, each in its own way exhibited one of the four basic concerns developed above.

[Case provided an excellent account of his development in three separate articles: "Education in Liberalism," in Vergilius Ferm, ed., *Contemporary Am. Theology* (1932); "The Profits of Education," *Crozer Quart.,* 21 (1944); "Living in the Garden of Eden," *ibid.,* 22 (1945). A brief account of his life is by Louis B. Jennings, "Shirley Jackson Case," in *The Chronicle,* July 1948, and also in Jennings, *The Bibliography and Biography of Shirley Jackson Case* (1949). Also helpful is Jennings' study of Case's method in *Shirley Jackson Case: A Study in Methodology* (unpub. doctoral diss., Univ. of Chicago, 1964). An excellent large photograph of Case is in Swift Hall, Univ. of Chicago.]

JERALD C. BRAUER

CATHER, WILLA (Dec. 7, 1873–Apr. 24, 1947), author, was born in Back Creek Valley (later Gore), near Winchester, Va. When the family moved to Webster County, Nebr., in 1883, the change from Virginia was so shattering that on first encounter with the open flatlands she felt, she later said, "an erasure of personality." The prairie life stimulated her imagination; she absorbed stories told by immigrant neighbors in a photographic detail that would be reproduced lyrically in her mature art. But her persistent effort to reconcile past and present, Europe and America, primitive and civilized, originated in the move that forced her to grapple with this new land: the "happiness and curse" (her words) of her life.

The first of the Cathers in America—she was the fifth generation—came to Virginia after the Revolutionary War; apparently from Northern Ireland, though the family was originally Welsh. From Cather ancestors Willa inherited the physical stamina on which her creativity relied; in independence and combative will she resembled her mother, Mary Virginia (Boak) Cather, who dominated the family, in which Willa was the first of seven children. Her father, Charles

Fectigue Cather, was gentlemanly, unaggressive, conversational. Unlike his pioneering father, he preferred a farm loan business, in which his training in law proved helpful, to frontier farming. Willa was especially attached to him and to her two oldest brothers, as reflected in her sensitive studies of filial and sisterly relations, as well as to her grandmother Rachel (Seibert) Boak, who read her the Bible and *Pilgrim's Progress,* the origin of her cadenced style and allegorical bent of mind. Willa adopted her grandmother's maiden name, spelling it Sibert, for a middle name, though not retaining it publicly after 1920. Much of her apprentice and journalistic writing appeared under various pseudonyms. Recorded in the family Bible as Wilella, she later rewrote her name as Willa and subtracted three years from her age, revisions suggesting the urgency of her lifelong quest for permanence.

Willa's formal education began in Red Cloud. She attracted the sympathetic attention of teachers, though her adolescent nonconformity—vivisectionist experimentation and public defense of the practice, boyish clothes and haircut—caused comment. Red Cloud was raw, bleak, and jerry-built, but the spiritually cramped villages of her fiction were as much literary inventions as the Spoon River of Edgar Lee Masters or Sinclair Lewis' Gopher Prairie. The actual place was notable for its cultivated people who introduced her to French and German culture, classical languages, and music.

She entered the preparatory school of the University of Nebraska in 1890 and the university itself a year later. She made her literary debut before her freshman year with the publication in a Lincoln newspaper of a composition on Thomas Carlyle. The essay reveals her early commitment to art as a religious vocation, exacting sacrifice of love and marriage, and its publication encouraged her to channel her formidable energy and ambition into writing. She never married.

In addition to campus literary activities, she became a drama critic and columnist for Lincoln newspapers in 1893 and continued this work after receiving her A.B. in 1895. Having earned a statewide reputation for her bright, brash reviews, she left in June 1896 for Pittsburgh, Pa., where she tested her mettle first as an editor on a small magazine and then as a telegraph editor and reviewer on the *Daily Leader.* She had been publishing fiction and poetry all along, and, desiring a life more conducive to creative work, she turned in 1901 to high school teaching and moved into the well-appointed family home of a friend, Isabelle McClung, the daughter of a Pittsburgh judge. Her first book, *April Twilights* (1903), a collection of poems interesting primarily as a gloss to her fiction, was followed by *The Troll Garden* (1905), consisting of stories about artists, a subject that never ceased to engage her. Though overly schematic, these stories have a persuasiveness arising from her firsthand knowledge of theatrical and musical worlds. Her most ambitious fictional portrait of the artist, *The Song of the Lark* (1915), was inspired by the opera singer Olive Fremstad, but the imaginatively satisfying parts are re-creations of her Nebraska childhood. The lure of New York for the title character in "Paul's Case," the best of the early stories, was also autobiographical. When, in 1906, S. S. McClure offered Willa Cather a New York job on his muckraking magazine, her indifference to social questions did not deter her from promptly accepting.

After publishing her first novel, *Alexander's Bridge* (1912), neatly plotted with London and Boston settings in imitation of Henry James, she visited the Southwest, where exploration of canyons and ancient Indian cliff dwellings exhilarated her. The region became symbolically significant in several novels; more immediately, she returned East invigorated, ending both her journalistic career as an editor of *McClure's* and her long literary apprenticeship with the completion of *O Pioneers!* (1913), aptly titled after Whitman.

Encouraged by the advice and example of Sarah Orne Jewett, Cather had made unconventional use of Nebraska material as early as 1909 in "The Enchanted Bluff." *O Pioneers!* was, however, the first novel in which, using an intuitive, episodic approach, she recalled the pioneering experience affirmatively as a heroic enterprise of will and imagination against bitter odds. Unlike James Fenimore Cooper in his Leatherstocking series (in particular, *The Prairie*) or, later, F. Scott Fitzgerald in *The Great Gatsby,* who viewed the virgin land as inevitably contaminated by settlement, she believed in the possibility of a society aesthetically and ethically worthy of the land. Characteristically, in her frontier fiction, she locates this possibility in the European immigrants who bring with them rich cultural traditions and a love of life lacking in her native-born Americans, who are presented as contrastingly anemic in spirit, complacent, joyless.

Moving chronologically in these novels to the present, she became first increasingly elegiac in tone and then embittered as she saw the defeat of her cultural-agrarian ideal in actuality. In *My Antonia* (1918) the Bohemian heroine fulfills her vital nature on a farm in creative motherhood, but for the narrator, a New York lawyer whose story it is as much as hers, she exists finally as an image of a shared "incommunicable past." *A Lost Lady* (1923) portrays the end of the pioneering era in the declining years of a railroad builder whose "lady" lacks the moral fiber to resist the exploitative younger generation. Exemplifying the novel démeublé, Cather's phrase for the spare, imagistic style she critically upheld against reportorial realism, *A Lost Lady* followed a diffuse, slack book, *One of Ours,* which nevertheless won the Pulitzer Prize in 1922. Beginning before World War I, *One of Ours* shows the utter defeat of her social ideal in America: the young farmer with inchoate yearnings for a better life must go as a soldier to France to discover, just before his death, a world worth living for. Her depiction of the Nebraska countryside desecrated by the machine, resembling that of Sherwood Anderson in *Poor White* (1920), relates Cather to the wasteland spirit of postwar writing and signaled the near end for her of Nebraska as a literary resource.

The Professor's House (1925) and *My Mortal Enemy* (1926) were transitional to her discovery of the frontier spirit in history; as psychological studies of middle-age crises, they reflect her own unease, mitigated by her confirmation in the Episcopal church in 1922. Her Protestant-Baptist heritage prevented conversion to Catholicism, but an instinctive sympathy for its ritual beauty and discipline informs her last important works, in which the rock of the church and of the landscape fuse as symbols of permanent value. *Death Comes for the Archbishop* (1927) is a reconstruction from historical accounts of the middle-nineteenth-century missionary work of two French priests in the Southwest. It is her most artistically poised "narrative," a word she preferred for this book to "novel." Striving to emulate in prose Puvis de Chavannes's frescoes of the life of Saint Geneviève, she succeeded in creating an idyll that does not exclude but subsumes human failings. *Shadows on the Rock* (1931), an evocation of late-seventeenth-century Quebec under Frontenac's rule, is permeated by a simpler, more static piety. Its emphasis on the beauty of order and continuity, as epitomized by the rituals of French housekeeping, owes more to Cather's deep appreciation of France than to her touristic experience of Quebec.

The three long stories published in *Obscure Destinies* (1932), revisitations of her Nebraska youth in palpable detail, are unmarred by the sentimentalism and querulous tone of some of her other late writing. She returned to Virginia in her last novel, *Sapphira and the Slave Girl* (1940), which reflects the physical and creative diminishment of her last years. The title of the collection of critical essays and literary portraits which she published in 1936, *Not Under Forty*, warning off the younger generation, indicates her defensive sense of isolation, especially in the ideological 1930's. Considerable popularity and critical acclaim heightened her desire for privacy to the extent that in her will she prohibited publication of her letters. Her honors include the Prix Femina Américaine, gold medals from the American Academy of Arts and Letters and the National Institute of Arts and Letters, and honorary degrees from Nebraska, Michigan, Columbia, Yale, Princeton, California, and Smith.

Willa Cather was sustained in her latter years by ties with friends and family in Red Cloud as well as in New York, where she found new pleasure in music through the companionship of the Menuhin family, especially the children Hephzibah, Yaltah, and Yehudi, and by summer stays on Grand Manan Island, New Brunswick, and autumns in Jaffrey, N.H. She died of a cerebral hemorrhage in New York City and at her request was buried on a hillside in Jaffrey.

In her feeling for landscape and weather, in which she has been said to resemble Turgenev, Cather also invites comparison with Ernest Hemingway (in particular his Michigan stories) and F. Scott Fitzgerald in his descriptions of the Middle West. The juxtaposition throws into relief, however, her essentially nineteenth-century sensibility and her limitations: what she could not personally absorb—much of modern life—she either excluded or deplored. Her lasting works are recollective, those in which her intensely personal response to people, legends, and landscape have a communal, mythic resonance. Her thought was unsupple, without nuance; the strength of her romantic, idealistic vision lay in her broad human sympathies and in a stoic acceptance of the harshness of life, inequalities of chance, death itself.

[The most comprehensive bibliography is by Bernice Slote in *Fifteen Modern Am. Authors* (1969), ed. by Jackson R. Bryer; it includes sections on editions, MSS, and, especially useful, an interpretative summary of Cather criticism from early reviews of her work to date. Though not to be quoted from, letters may be seen in numerous libraries and historical societies throughout the country; I have made particular use of the Barrett Collect. of the Univ. of Virginia.

The Willa Cather Pioneer Memorial in Red Cloud, Nebr., has memorabilia and letters. Other collections of importance are named by Slote and by James Woodress in his *Willa Cather: Her Life and Art* (1970). Woodress makes excellent use of letters and other biographical and critical sources not available when E. K. Brown wrote his semiauthorized *Willa Cather: A Critical Biog.* (1953), completed by Leon Edel. The Brown-Edel biography is still valuable for its insights into her character and works. For the flavor of her personality, see also *Willa Cather Living* (1953), by Edith Lewis, her longtime companion, and Elizabeth Shepley Sergeant, *Willa Cather: A Memoir* (1953); and for her Red Cloud background, Mildred R. Bennett, *The World of Willa Cather* (1951; rev. ed. 1961). Of her works, the Library Edition, published by Houghton Mifflin, 1937–1941, is most complete and was supervised by Cather. Notable editions including uncollected writings are *The Old Beauty and Others* (1948); Bernice Slote, ed., *The Kingdom of Art: Willa Cather's First Principles and Critical Statements, 1893–1896* (1967); William M. Curtin, ed., *The World and the Parish: Willa Cather's Articles and Reviews, 1893–1902* (1970); Virginia Faulkner, ed., *Collected Short Fiction, 1892–1912* (1965); Bernice Slote, ed., *April Twilights* (1968); and Bernice Slote, ed., *Uncle Valentine and Other Stories: Willa Cather's Uncollected Short Fiction, 1915–1929* (1973). Recommended critical introductions are David Daiches, *Willa Cather* (1951); Dorothy Van Ghent, *Willa Cather* (Univ. of Minnesota Pamphlets on Am. Writers, 1964); and James Schroeter, ed., *Willa Cather and Her Critics* (1967). Helpful discussions of her place in American literary traditions appear in Alfred Kazin, *On Native Grounds* (1942); Morton Zabel, *Craft and Character: Texts, Method, and Vocation in Modern Fiction* (1957); and Warner Berthoff, *The Ferment of Realism* (1965). For special aspects of her art, see Edward A. and Lillian D. Bloom, *Willa Cather's Gift of Sympathy* (1962); and Richard Giannone, *Music in Willa Cather's Fiction* (1968). A portrait by Leon Bakst in the Omaha Public Lib. is reproduced, as well as photographs by Edward Steichen and others, in the popular biography by Barbara Bonham, *Willa Cather* (1970).]

VIOLA HOPKINS WINNER

CATT, CARRIE CLINTON LANE CHAPMAN (Jan. 9, 1859-Mar. 9, 1947), feminist, internationalist, and leader of the woman suffrage movement, was born in Ripon, Wis., the second of three children and the only daughter of Lucius Lane, a farmer, and Maria (Clinton) Lane. In 1866 the family joined the westward migration to northern Iowa and settled near Charles City. There in the frontier atmosphere Carrie Lane grew to be a spirited, self-reliant, and intellectually precocious girl, ambitious, and quick to challenge any suggestion that her sex was a handicap to achievement.

After she graduated from the Charles City high school, she taught school for a year, before enrolling at Iowa State College (Ames) as a sophomore in 1877. The curriculum emphasized science courses, and she thus obtained a thorough acquaintance with the theories of Darwin and Spencer. The result was a belief in evolutionary progress through social change which served as a lifelong "working faith"—furnishing both an interpretation of history and a philosophy of action. She left Ames with the B.S. degree in November 1880 and read law for a year, hoping to attend law school. In October 1881 she accepted the principalship of the Mason City high school. She still hoped to study law, but success as principal won her the superintendency of the Mason City schools in 1883, a post necessarily, although reluctantly, surrendered two years later (Feb. 12, 1885) when she married Leo Chapman, owner and editor of the *Mason City Republican*. As assistant editor of her husband's newspaper, she attended the 1885 convention of the Iowa Suffrage Association, and was readily converted to the suffrage cause.

In August 1886 Leo Chapman, while in California for the purpose of buying a larger newspaper, contracted typhoid fever. He died before she could reach him. Stranded in San Francisco, she found work on a trade paper and saw at first hand the wretched exploitation of working women. A year later an emotional crisis precipitated by frustration and despair ended in a resolve to devote her life to the emancipation of women—a resolve from which she never thereafter deviated. Returning to Iowa, she became recording secretary of the Iowa Suffrage Association (meanwhile earning a precarious living as a lyceum lecturer) and discovered her talent for organizational work.

In 1890 Carrie Chapman went to Washington, D.C., as an Iowa delegate to the historic national convention that reunited, after twenty years of schism, the sundered halves of the suffrage movement as the National American Woman Suffrage Association (NAWSA). Susan Anthony instantly sensed that the attractive young widow with the commanding platform presence, low-pitched voice of rare carrying power, and vigorous ideas was a valuable recruit, and engaged her to campaign in South Dakota for an approaching suffrage referendum. Before undertaking this task, however, Carrie Chapman married on June 10, 1890, a civil engineer, George William Catt, who had been a fellow student at Ames. Catt not only approved of his wife's dedication to reform but supported it by signing jointly with her a legally attested document providing that she would spend four months each year in suffrage work. They initially lived in Seattle, but left in 1892 for permanent residence in New York City, where Catt became president of a marine construction firm. The partnership whereby he earned the living for both while she did the reforming for both was a source of practical and psychological support to Carrie Chapman Catt

throughout her husband's life. At his death in 1905, he left her financially independent, able to devote the rest of her life to the woman suffrage movement.

From 1890 to 1895 Carrie Chapman Catt participated in a series of state suffrage referenda and congressional hearings on the federal suffrage amendment, under the tutelage of Susan Anthony. As she rose to leadership, she studied the social, economic, and political forces arrayed against woman suffrage, and also sharply analyzed the flaws in the reformers' efforts. It was a period of quickening political concerns among women, with the temperance and woman's club movements pressing for increased social consciousness and insurgent political parties drawing heavily on the moral energies of women. Yet the single-goaled woman suffrage movement, with aging leaders and meager resources, remained on the fringe, safely ignored by the major political parties. At Catt's suggestion, a national organization committee was set up in 1895 to intensify efforts to mobilize widespread latent support for woman suffrage. As chairman, she was director of operations, training and sending out organizers to establish new auxiliaries and galvanize old ones, raising funds, establishing administrative procedures, preparing carefully detailed plans of political work for auxiliaries, and attempting, against internal resistance, to coordinate the activities of state and local auxiliaries. In these years her extraordinary gift for executive leadership was coaxed forth and developed. When Susan Anthony, in her eightieth year, retired from the presidency in 1900, she chose Carrie Chapman Catt as her successor.

During the four years of her presidency, Carrie Chapman Catt worked vigorously to shift NAWSA emphasis from propaganda to political action. "The time has come to cease talking to women," she insisted, "and invade town meetings and caucuses. . . ." In the annual conventions she encouraged interest in political action by workshops in organizational and political techniques, and engaged convention speakers on electoral and government reforms such as the direct primary, the initiative and referendum and civil service reform in place of the traditional recitals of feminist grievances. Swinging the organization into the orbit of the progressive movement, she won allies among liberal and "social justice" reformers of both sexes and attracted many outstanding women, including Florence Kelley and Jane Addams, into active suffrage work. When she felt impelled to withdraw from the presidency in 1904 because of her husband's ill health, she left to her successor, Anna Howard Shaw, a thriving nationwide organization.

After her husband's death in October 1905, Catt divided her energies between suffrage activities in New York and international feminism. In New York City, beginning in 1908, she and a group of suffragists organized the New York Woman Suffrage Party—the name emphasizing its political character—on the basis of precincts, wards, and districts, consolidating the ward and district captains in the Interurban Suffrage Council. In 1913 the council served as the nucleus of the Empire State Campaign Committee, led by Catt, which conducted the brilliant though unsuccessful referendum campaign in 1915. Two years later an intensified effort by the same disciplined organization was successful in enfranchising the women of New York state, a decisive victory in the long struggle.

Catt's efforts in behalf of international feminism were a logical extension of her belief that evolutionary progress in Western society had made the eventual emancipation of women inevitable. Beginning in 1902, she had encouraged a sharper focus on woman suffrage among the affiliates of the International Council of Women, preparing the way for the establishment of the International Woman Suffrage Alliance at the Berlin Congress in 1904. Elected president, Catt was the acknowledged leader and chief fund raiser of the IWSA until 1923, presiding over congresses in Copenhagen (1906), London (1908), Amsterdam (1909), Stockholm (1911), and Budapest (1913). Accompanied by the Dutch feminist Dr. Aletta Jacobs, she toured the world (1911-1913), organizing feminists in several Asian and African countries, and increasing the affiliates of IWSA from nine to thirty-two. The outbreak of war in 1914 was a severe blow to international feminism. In January 1915, Catt joined Jane Addams in organizing 400 representatives of American women's organizations in a Woman's Peace Party to ally with a similar coalition of European feminists. This group pressed for mediation to end the war through a conference of neutrals, but circumstances proved intractable. Catt's global evangelism was rounded out in 1922-1923 by an organizing trip to South American countries, where women were not yet enfranchised.

When Carrie Chapman Catt yielded to demands that she return to the national presidency in December 1915, she faced a bleak situation. The organization was challenged on the one hand by the dynamic Midwestern suffrage organizations riding the progressive wave, and on the other by an ardently militant group led by Alice Paul, whom Shaw had named chairman of NAWSA's Congressional Committee in 1912, charged with lobbying for the federal woman's suffrage amendment. Paul played a dual role as chairman of the Congressional Committee, bound by NAWSA policies, and as the imaginative and charismatic leader of her personal followers in the Congressional Union, dedicated to promoting the federal amendment and holding the party in power, i.e., the Democrats, "accountable" for failure to pass it. Catt led the opposition to Paul's demand that all other efforts be abandoned in order to concentrate on the federal amendment. The delegates to the 1914 convention formally repudiated Paul's approach as politically unrealistic, because it flouted the support of friendly Democratic congressmen and was unacceptable to the southern auxiliaries with their insistence on suffrage by state action. This forced Paul and her followers to withdraw from NAWSA and thereafter go their own way as the National Woman's Party.

In 1916 with a board of her own choosing, Carrie Chapman Catt developed a comprehensive but flexible program: intensified lobbying pressure on Congress for passage of the federal amendment; pressure for state constitutional referenda in promising situations; pressure for action by state legislatures to grant women the right to vote for presidential electors, as in Illinois in 1913, the breakthrough that had turned the tide in the suffrage struggle; and pressure for the right to vote in primaries. The 1916 elections were approaching and both parties gave indications that women suffrage was an issue they could no longer evade. Party platforms carried suffrage planks, although not wholly satisfactory ones. Catt summoned delegates to a convention in September and invited the presidential candidates to speak. President Wilson accepted and made a notable speech. Catt later dated his "conversion" from this occasion, though it was nearly two years before his commitment to the federal amendment was unqualified. After the convention, Catt divulged the outline of her "Winning Plan" to the board and presidents of state auxiliaries. She had prepared a special task for each state. While the details were kept secret, the tactic was to force their opponents to fight on all fronts at once.

United States entry into the war in 1917 caused a partial suspension of plans, but Catt insisted that women must take part in war work as well as continue to fight for suffrage, which would assure their right to play a role in achieving a lasting peace. She herself set the example by continuing her suffrage work, while serving on the Women's Committee of the Council of National Defense. Her judgment and tact, enhanced by the realization of the part women voters had played in his reelection and reinforced by the string of suffrage victories in 1917 and 1918, including the spectacular New York victory, won Wilson's commitment to the suffrage amendment. In the meantime the suffrage cause had received an unexpected boon in 1914 when Carrie Chapman Catt was named chief legatee of Miriam Florence Folline Leslie's publishing fortune amounting to $2 million, with the stipulation that the money be expended to promote woman suffrage. Litigation by dissatisfied heirs and other claimants and legal fees cut the amount in half, but nearly $1 million became available to suffrage workers in 1917 and was spent in a nationwide educational and publicity campaign, creating the momentum that carried the movement to victory. The federal amendment passed the House of Representatives on Jan. 10, 1918, but did not finally pass the Senate until June 4, 1919. Fourteen additional months were consumed before ratification by the legislature of Tennessee, the thirty-sixth state, with one vote to spare, on Aug. 18, 1920. It was proclaimed part of the Constitution on August 26. Carrie Chapman Catt stands alongside Susan B. Anthony as one of the two great women whose lifework it was.

At the 1919 NAWSA Convention, Catt called for the women in the enfranchised states to organize a league of women voters to "finish the fight" and prepare women to play a political role. A year later the national League of Women Voters (LWV) was established, with officers drawn from the younger generation of suffragists. Catt exercised a strong and constructive influence on the league during its early years and always maintained friendly ties, although she did not conceal her disappointment that integrating women voters in a resistant political order proved too massive a task for rapid accomplishment. Soon after her death in 1947, a group of league members established the Carrie Chapman Catt Memorial Fund (now the Overseas Education Fund) to accelerate political participation among newly enfranchised women in foreign countries.

In 1921, with women suffrage a fact and the League of Women Voters established to promote women's political socialization, Mrs. Catt turned her talents to writing and speaking on behalf of the League of Nations. Dismayed by the Senate's rejection of the league, she made a dramatic appeal to the 1921 LWV Convention to organize the sentiment for peace existing among women and enlarge public understanding of the necessity for international cooperation to prevent war. Seizing the initiative, she invited leaders of national women's organizations to join her in calling upon women to use their political power to put an end to war and to bring the issue of peace out of the realm of "cloudy idealism" into the forum for study and discussion of war's causes and possible cures. Leaders of nine organizations signed the call to the first Conference on the Cause and Cure of War, which met in Washington, D.C., in 1925, and annually thereafter until 1939. Catt remained chairman of the Conference Committee until 1933.

After her husband's death, Carrie Chapman Catt shared her home with her close friend, Mary G. Hay, first in New York City, then on a farm near Ossining, N.Y. In 1928, shortly before Hay's death, they moved to a spacious house with gardens in New Rochelle, N.Y. A feminist to the end, Catt's last major project was the Women's Centennial Exposition, 1840-1940, held in New York in 1940, honoring distinguished women in a hundred professions not open to women in 1840. Seven years later she died of a heart attack at her home in her eighty-eighth year and was buried in Woodlawn Cemetery in New York City.

The most widely admired woman of her generation, Catt possessed throughout her life a distinction of person and manner, and also a certain aloofness suitable for "relations on a grand scale." The prototype of the professional career woman, she successfully integrated her private and public lives by the strength of her adaptive intelligence and resolute will. She was the recipient of many honors and awards, including a citation of honor from President Franklin D. Roosevelt (1936); the Cross of Merit of the Order of the White Rose (Finland, 1939); the Medal of the National Institute of Social Sciences (1940); and the National Achievement Award sponsored by Chi Omega (1941).

[The Carrie Chapman Catt Papers in the Manuscript Div., Lib. of Congress, is an extensive collection of correspondence, speeches, articles, diaries of world travels, and memoranda. Related manuscript materials in the Lib. of Congress include the papers of the Nat. Am. Woman Suffrage Assoc., the Leslie Commission, and the League of Women Voters. Also useful are the Blackwell Papers. Additional Catt correspondence is in the Schlesinger Lib., Radcliffe College, the Sophia Smith Collect., Smith College, and the New York Public Lib.

Also of value is Carrie Chapman Catt and Nettie S. Shuler, *Woman Suffrage and Politics* (1923). Her faith in evolutionary progress is discussed in "Why I Have Found Life Worth Living," *Christian Century,* Mar. 1928, and "Evolution—Fifty Years Later," *Woman Citizen,* July 11, 1925. Valuable for her criticism of isolationist foreign policy during the 1920's are her editorials in successive issues of the *Woman Citizen,* 1920-1927. See also "A Suffrage Team," *Woman Citizen,* Sept. 8, 1923.

The only biography of Carrie Chapman Catt is Mary Gray Peck, *Carrie Chapman Catt* (1944), an intimate and detailed portrayal by a devoted associate, with illustrations. Also helpful are Maud Wood Park, *Front Door Lobby* (1957); Lola C. Walker, "The Speeches and Speaking of Carrie Chapman Catt" (Ph.D. diss., Northwestern Univ., 1950); Rose Young, *The Leslie Commission: 1917-1929* (1929); Louise Degen, *History of the Woman's Peace Party* (1947); Elizabeth Cady Stanton et al., *History of Woman Suffrage,* vols IV-VI (1902-1922). The best interpretive treatment of Carrie Chapman Catt is Eleanor Flexner, *Century of Struggle: The Woman's Rights Movement in the U.S.* (1959); *N.Y. Times* obituary, Jan. 10, 1947.

Carrie Chapman Catt's feminist library (900 volumes) is deposited in the Rare Book Div., Lib. of Congress; her "Peace and War" collection (600 volumes) is in the library of her alma mater, Iowa State Univ., along with a collection of memorabilia.]

LOUISE M. YOUNG

CESARE, OSCAR EDWARD (Oct. 7, 1883-July 24, 1948), cartoonist, artist, and journalist, was born in Linköping, Ostergötland, Sweden, the second son and fourth child of the former Carolina Pehrsdotter, whose shoemaker husband, Carl Johan Caesar, used the common spelling of his last name. An enterprising as well as an artistic youth, Oscar was curious about the world that lay beyond his Methodist home in rural Scandinavia. After studying art in Paris, he immigrated to the United States in about 1901 (*Lexikon,* I, 302), following his older brother, Claes, who attended Cornell University. Oscar pursued art studies in Buffalo, N.Y., and then went to Chicago to report and draw for several newspapers, including the *Chicago Tribune,* to which he contributed cartoons.

After moving to New York, Cesare—he pronounced his name "See-sare"— served in succession on the staffs of the *World,* the *Sun,* and the *Evening Post.* He was influenced by Gustave Doré and Honoré Daumier and, in the United States, by Boardman Robinson. During the Theodore Roosevelt era, when his work was appearing in the *Outlook* and other magazines, he was established as a cartoonist of unusual pictorial strength and penetrating political insight. When World War I broke out,

he moved into the front rank of illustrators, with a steady flow of striking, powerful drawings that delineated the conflict's cost in lives and resources.

A collection of these works, largely from the *New York Sun* and *Harper's Weekly,* was published in 1916 with the title, *One Hundred Cartoons by Cesare.* Among them were three of his best-known drawings: "Dropping the Pilot" (*N.Y. Sun,* June 11, 1915), which showed President Wilson dumping Secretary of State William Jennings Bryan from the "Ship of State" into the sea, an adaptation of Tenniel's depiction in *Punch* of the kaiser dismissing Bismarck in 1890; an angry Atlas wresting the planet Earth from his shoulders and casting it from him; and a woman war victim, holding a small child before the guns of a battlefield in an appeal to "Cease Firing." An early war drawing showed an awakening "Spirit of Vesuvius" asking, "What Is That Rumbling I Hear on Earth?" Cesare was especially skilled at drawing ships and producing seascapes, as, for example, the sinking of the *Lusitania,* while his scenes of winter at the front conveyed feelings of bitter cold and privation.

During this period, Cesare married Margaret Worth Porter, daughter of O. Henry, but the marriage was not a happy one and it lasted less than a year. They were divorced in 1916.

In that year, Cesare began to draw for the *New York Evening Post,* then under the direction of Oswald Garrison Villard, whose pacific policies brought much criticism from the war's prosecutors. American cartoonists generally became "government cheerleaders" after the United States entered the war in 1917 (Hess and Kaplan, p. 140), but Cesare stood out against the trend. He held truth to be a wartime casualty and hit hard at military censorship. A 1918 *Evening Post* cartoon, combining humor and realism, pictured Trotsky, as the Brest-Litovsk peace negotiator for Russia, quaking at the edge of a crumbling precipice to which he had been pushed by a helmeted soldier, representing German armed might (Murrell, p. 194, 197-198). Throughout the war period, and later, *Cartoons* magazine (1913-1921) reproduced dozens of Cesare's drawings, and his work was reprinted in Europe probably more frequently than that of any other American cartoonist.

In 1920 Cesare became a regular contributor to the *New York Times.* His talents as a caricaturist, often of "magnificent insolence," were well displayed in Clinton Gilbert's *The Mirrors of Washington* (1921), for which

Cesare provided comic drawings of Wilson, Harding, Hoover, Hughes, Lodge, Borah, Root, Penrose, Baruch, and other political notables. For the *Times* Sunday magazine section he developed a feature that set him apart among journalists—the illustrated interview, with artist and reporter one and the same. The most celebrated of these picture-word interviews was one with Lenin at the Kremlin, arranged after weeks of effort. The interview, on Oct. 13, 1922, was reported as a news event on the first page of the *Times,* October 15. It was published, with a large portrait drawing of Lenin on the magazine cover, on December 24. Thus, at a time when Lenin was variously listed as sick or dead, Cesare presented him as friendly and smiling, with an "animated face" that "lights up vividly," and fully "absorbed in his work." Among other world figures whom Cesare interviewed and sketched were Mussolini, Lloyd George, Joseph Conrad, Louis Blériot, Orville Wright, and Sinclair Lewis. He was fond of the theater and sketched stage personalities such as Sarah Bernhardt, Ethel Barrymore, Alla Nazimova, Richard Mansfield, E. H. Sothern, and Arnold Daly. "A Baker's Dozen" of Democratic presidential hopefuls, as caricatured by Cesare, was published in the *Forum* for July 1924. A representative Cesare article, which he wrote as well as illustrated with seven head portraits, in *World's Work,* January 1927, was "Firebrands of Fascismo: Some Visits to the Men Who Marched on Rome."

In that year, 1927, Cesare married Ann (Valentine) Kelley of Richmond, Va. They had one son, Valentine.

Cesare was a student of European history, as his work reflected. He was attracted to Chinese art and adapted its broad strokes and firm outlines when they suited his subject. "Success," a drawing of unusual force, in *Harper's Weekly,* May 23, 1914, showed a gaunt, puzzled John D. Rockefeller surveying the smoldering site of the Ludlow, Colo., massacre. His portrayals of so diverse a gallery as Uncle Sam, Kaiser Wilhelm II, the British lion, and the hooded skeleton of death all had qualities of their own. By 1940 his work had been printed in a wide range of leading magazines: *The Review of Reviews, Collier's, Puck, Life, Nation's Business, Fortune, The Etcher.* When he painted in color, most often on travels abroad when he had more leisure, he possessed "a magic touch in a wider field." For pleasure he turned to etchings.

Cesare died after a long illness at his home in Stamford, Conn., in his sixty-fifth year. His body was cremated.

Although Cesare held "strong opinions," usually not orthodox, he had "a singular charm of manner" that, in the editorial appraisal of the *New York Times* (July 27, 1948), "commanded the affection no less than the admiration of his colleagues of all trades and every rank." The judgment of the *Dial* (Nov. 30, 1916) held firm after more than thirty years: "Aside from a splendid technique, Cesare is possessed of a poetic fervor, imagination, and a keen feeling for beauty. . . . Because of his power as much as his fine restraint, Cesare may be said to be an aristocrat among American cartoonists."

[In 1952 Mrs. Cesare established a collection of more than 200 of her husband's works at the Alderman Lib., Univ. of Virginia; Valentine Cesare retained many original drawings, and others are in the Art Wood Collect., Rockville, Md., the Lib. of Congress, and the N.Y. Public Lib. In addition to publications cited in the text, sources include: *Book Review Digest for 1916* (1917); William Murrell, *A Hist. of Amer. Graphic Humor: 1865–1938* (1938); Stephen Hess and Milton Kaplan, *The Ungentlemanly Art: A Hist. of Amer. Political Cartoons* (1968); *Svenskt Konstnärs Lexikon,* Bk. I, 302; *Allgemeines Lexicon Der Bildenden Kunstler,* V, 372; *N.Y. Times,* July 25 (with photograph) and 27, 1948; *Chicago Tribune,* July 25, 1948; *Time,* July 17, 1927. Valuable information came from Valentine Cesare, Stamford, Conn.; Priscilla Wells, York, Pa.; and Miriam L. Leslie, Philadelphia. Everette E. Dennis, Univ. of Minnesota, shared facts from his cartoon collection. A full-page drawing *Sketch of the Artist Himself* appears in *One Hundred Cartoons.* Personal recollection. Gudrun Westin-Göransson, Råå, Sweden, obtained and translated family data from Linköping parish records, which gave the birth year as 1883.]

WALTER PARTYMILLER
IRVING DILLIARD

CHERRINGTON, ERNEST HURST (Nov. 24, 1877–Mar. 13, 1950), temperance reformer and Methodist layman, was born in Hamden, Ohio, the son of George Cherrington and Elizabeth Ophelia (Paine) Cherrington. Reared in the small towns and rural communities of southern Ohio, where his father, a Methodist clergyman, held pastorates, Cherrington attended the preparatory department of Ohio Wesleyan University in Delaware (1893-1897). He taught school in Ross County, edited a small-town newspaper, the *Kingston Tribune,* and began speaking on Sundays for the Ohio Anti-Saloon League, which had been founded at Oberlin in 1893. In 1902 he became a full-time temperance worker as superintendent of the Canton district of the league. His effectiveness in field work soon attracted the attention of Purley A. Baker, the state superintendent, who the following year selected Cherrington as his assistant. On Mar. 17, 1903, Cherrington married Betty Clifford Denny of Greenville, Ill.;

they had two children, Ernest Hurst and Ann Elizabeth.

Ohio, the birthplace of the Anti-Saloon League, often served as a training ground for league work elsewhere. In 1905 Baker, now head of the national organization, sent Cherrington to Seattle as superintendent of the Washington league. There Cherrington brought new vigor to the temperance movement, building a powerful organization, editing the league's newspaper, the *Citizen,* and initiating a successful campaign for a state local-option law. The national league called Cherrington to Chicago in 1908 to become assistant editor of its new newspaper, the *American Issue.* The following year the league moved its headquarters to Westerville, Ohio, a town just north of Columbus, and built a large printing plant there. Recognizing Cherrington's ability, Baker selected him as editor of the *American Issue* and general manager of the Anti-Saloon League's publishing activities.

Under Cherrington's management the American Issue Publishing Company became a huge enterprise. During the following decade his presses produced in vast quantities the temperance propaganda so important to the success of the prohibition movement. While directing this enormous effort, Cherrington, a resourceful organizer and effective administrator whose energies could not be confined to one field, exerted a dominant influence upon many other policies and activities of the Anti-Saloon League. As secretary of the national executive committee he developed the league's fund-raising program, managed its finances, and organized its national speakers' bureau. The league's publisher, he was also its editor, statistician, and historian. He wrote three books and numerous pamphlets and articles, compiled the *Anti-Saloon League Yearbook* (1908-1932), and edited a six-volume reference work, the *Standard Encyclopedia of the Alcohol Problem* (1925-1930). On Cherrington's initiative, the league in June 1919 expanded its scope and founded the World League against Alcoholism, an organization to promote prohibition throughout the world. As general secretary, Cherrington made the direction of its work his chief concern after 1919.

Cherrington was the youngest of the Ohio leaders who, along with Bishop James Cannon, Jr., of Virginia, dominated the American prohibition movement. Handsome, well over six feet tall and of stout build, he was forthright but conciliatory in manner, and his moderation and sound judgment were valued in the league's often stormy inner councils. He shunned publicity and remained in the background while more flamboyant figures captured the headlines. Nevertheless, the huge propaganda effort he directed, the massive speaking campaigns he organized, and his businesslike management of the league's financial affairs were as important to the success of prohibition as the more spectacular legislative and political work of others. Recognizing these contributions, Bishop Cannon considered Cherrington the one man most responsible for the adoption of the Eighteenth Amendment.

The triumph of Cherrington and his colleagues was relatively short-lived, for economic depression and the repeal of prohibition dealt the temperance movement a harsh blow in the 1930's from which it never recovered. The Anti-Saloon League virtually collapsed, and its leaders, now powerless, were quickly forgotten, although Cherrington and others continued as best they could on a greatly reduced scale.

In addition to his temperance work, Cherrington was a prominent layman in the Methodist Episcopal church. He was elected to eight General Conferences (1916-1944), played a significant role in the movement for Methodist unification, and served on the executive committee of the Board of Home Missions (1920-1936); he held a similar post in the Federal Council of Churches (1920-1948). In 1936 Cherrington moved to Washington to become executive secretary of his church's Board of Temperance. There he edited the board's organ, the *Voice* (1936-1948), and by strenuous effort retired the large debt on the Methodist Building, the church's headquarters on Capital Hill.

Upon retirement in 1948, Cherrington returned to Westerville, the scene of his life's work. He died of cancer two years later in a sanitarium in nearby Worthington. After cremation, his remains were buried in Otterbein Cemetery, Westerville, where many of the other Anti-Saloon League leaders are also buried.

[Cherrington's books are *Hist. of the Anti-Saloon League* (1913), *The Evolution of Prohibition in the U.S.A.* (1920), and *America and the World Liquor Problem* (1922). The Temperance Education Foundation in Westerville, Ohio, has preserved his voluminous personal papers, along with extensive files of the *American Issue.* The article on Cherrington in his own *Standard Encyc. of the Alcohol Problem,* II, 565-566, and the warm tribute by his longtime secretary and assistant, Miss Ila Grindell, in *American Issue,* Apr. 1950, contain the most complete accounts of Cherrington's career. Also informative is the obituary in the *Westerville Public Opinion,* Mar. 16, 1950. Bishop James Cannon, Jr., in his autobiography, *Bishop Cannon's Own Story,* ed. Richard L. Watson, Jr. (1955), provides a generous estimate of Cherrington's contribution to the prohibition movement. Norman H. Clark, *The Dry Years: Prohibition and Social Change in Wash.* (1965), gives attention to Cherrington's accomplishments in that state. Peter H. Odegard, *Pressure Politics: The Story of the Anti-Saloon League* (1928), and James H. Timberlake, *Prohibition and the Progressive Movement, 1900–1920* (1963), both describe the significance of the American Issue Publishing Co. Good photographs of Cherrington may be found in Clark, facing p. 147, and in the *Standard Encyc. of the Alcohol Problem*, II, facing p. 564.]

ROBERT A. HOHNER

CHEYNEY, EDWARD POTTS (Jan. 17, 1861–Feb. 1, 1947), historian, was born in Wallingford, Delaware County, Pa., the fourth son and fourth of eight children of Waldron J. Cheyney and Fannie (Potts) Cheyney. His father, a descendant of English settlers of Chester County, Pa., was a businessman with chemical and mining interests. His mother's ancestors were Quakers who had come to Philadelphia in 1740. Edward Cheyney was educated in country schools, at Penn Charter School in Philadelphia, and at the University of Pennsylvania. He received his B.A. in 1883 and, after a trip to Europe, returned for further study in the university's new Wharton School of Finance, where he earned a bachelor of finance degree in 1884.

Cheyney apparently began his study of history under John Bach McMaster, who joined the Wharton School faculty in 1883. There were then few professional historians in the United States, and the prospects for such a career were not bright, which may explain why Cheyney never took the Ph.D. He began his teaching career at the University of Pennsylvania in 1884 as an instructor in history. After also teaching Latin and mathematics he became assistant professor of history in 1890, and professor in 1897. Cheyney's first publications were several monographs on American subjects. He soon turned to English history with his first significant book, *Social Changes in England in the Sixteenth Century* (1895), but, typical of his generation, he continued to focus on subjects that were common to both the European and American experiences, as in his *European Background of American History* (1904). In the late 1890's he began to edit, along with James Harvey Robinson and Dana C. Munro, the series entitled *Translations and Reprints from the Original Sources of European History*, which sought to make available to seminars the primary materials of history. His concern for improved teaching was also manifest in his publication of *Readings in English History* (1908), *An Introduction to the Industrial and Social History of England* (1901), and *A Short History of England* (1904), the latter long regarded as a standard text in the field.

Cheyney became a professional historian

when "scientific history" was the prevailing orthodoxy, and in his earliest writings he adhered to its canons of evidence, arguing that the dispassionate collection and arrangement of discrete facts constituted the historical enterprise. "The simple but arduous task of the historian is to collect facts, view them objectively, and arrange them as the facts themselves demanded, . . ." (AHA, *Annual Report*, I, 29). To this scrupulous concern for objectivity in the search for truth, he later added his commitment to the "New History" with its emphasis on the continuity of historical process, the broad range of man's interests and activities, and the use of the more advanced social science disciplines. These themes, along with his early acceptance of the implications of evolution and a progressive liberal's belief in order and progress in human affairs, were the sources for his well-known essay, "Law in History," the presidential address of the AHA in 1923. Cheyney said: "Human history, like the stars, had been controlled by immutable self-existent law" (*Law in History and Other Essays*, 1927, p. 8), which he expanded to include the laws of continuity, change, interdependence, democracy, control by free consent, and moral progress. He envisioned history as a practical tool for dealing with future problems, but he later warned of the dangers of exploiting historical materials "for purposes of supporting preconceived beliefs or strengthening one form or another of propaganda" (*ibid.*, p. 158).

Cheyney's most ambitious study, *A History of England, from the Defeat of the Armada to the Death of Elizabeth* (2 vols., 1914–1926), showed the strengths and weaknesses of his approach. In a study which purported to depict the whole life of the period, Cheyney nevertheless excluded from consideration literature, science, and religion, concentrating instead on government, great men and women, intrigues, explorations, and military adventures. But though largely a conventional narrative, with a tendency toward flatness, it was the product of meticulous research and filled a major gap in the existing historical literature.

Cheyney was one of the leading American historians of Europe of his generation, and he also contributed to the growth of the profession. He joined the young American Historical Association in 1890 and was an important member of an inner circle that helped build it into an important force. He helped to put down a "Young Turk" revolt within the AHA in 1915, and was elected its president in 1923. In 1912 he was elected to the board of editors of the then semi-independent *American Historical Review,* and he was one of those who welded that journal to the AHA in 1915. He was also active in the Social Science Research Council and late in his career was its choice to make a study of freedom of inquiry in the United States (later published in the *Annals of the American Academy,* 1938). Cheyney's contemporaries found him "kindly, lovable," and a "man of no pretense." He was a friendly, sympathetic counselor of young scholars and eager to find ways to help gifted students. Although impatient with careless performance he was at the same time tolerant (some said too tolerant) of the poor student who should be "let alone to get what he may or can" from his education (Lingelbach, p. 30).

His 1928 Lowell Institute lectures were later published as *Modern English Reform, From Individualism to Socialism* (1931), and he concluded his major publications with two interpretive works. In one, *Dawn of a New Era* (1936), he drew on his broad knowledge of early modern Europe to interpret the forces ushering in a new age. In his *History of the University of Pennsylvania* (1940) he brought to bear his long interest in higher education and his affection for his alma mater. Cheyney married Gertrude Levis Squires on June 8, 1886; they had three children: Alice S., Ernest Waldron, and Edward Ralph. A small, portly, vigorous man, Cheyney was rarely ill and continued to write and garden, after his retirement in 1934, at his country home, "the Schoolhouse," near Media, Pa. After Mrs. Cheyney's death, Feb. 10, 1918, his daughter, "Miss Alice," was her father's constant companion at his home and on his extensive travels. Living on to the age of eighty-six, he died of a heart attack in Crozer Hospital, Chester, Pa., while hospitalized for a broken hip, and was buried in the family cemetery in Cheyney, Pa.

[William E. Lingelbach, *Portrait of an Historian* (1935), a collection of tributes to Cheyney, includes a bibliography of his writings to that date and his witty "last Will and Testament (Academic)," which is useful in understanding his attitude toward the university and education. Other material from the obituary in *Am. Hist. Rev.,* Apr. 1947, pp. 647–648; *Who Was Who in America,* II (1950); Roy Nichols' autobiography, *A Historian's Progress* (1968), especially pp. 95–96; Elizabeth Donnan and Leo F. Stock, eds., *An Historian's World: Selections from the Correspondence of John Franklin Jameson* (1956); Joshua L. Chamberlain, ed., *Univ. of Pennsylvania Illustrated, 1740–1900* (1902), p. 415; interviews with family members. Cheyney's papers are in the Univ. of Pennsylvania Arch. A portrait (1972) by Adolph Borie, Jr., hangs in the Graduate History Lounge, College Hall, at the university.]

DANIEL R. GILBERT

CHURCHILL, WINSTON (Nov. 10, 1871–March 12, 1947), novelist and political reformer, was born in St. Louis, Mo., the only child of Edward Spaulding and Emma Bell (Blaine) Churchill. His father was descended from John Churchill, who emigrated from England to Plymouth in the 1640's, and from a long line of merchants in the West Indian trade who operated out of Portland, Maine. His mother came from a prominent St. Louis family of Southern origin and was also connected with the Dwight family of New England. Winston's mother died three weeks after his birth, and the boy saw little of his father, being raised in the upper-middle-class home of his mother's sister and her husband, the James B. Gazzams of St. Louis. In these circumstances he grew to place some value on his lineage, and in his novels later dwelt repeatedly on themes of inherited character and orphanage.

After training at Smith Academy in St. Louis (1879-1888), Churchill entered the Naval Academy at Annapolis in 1890. There he mustered a good academic record and starred in fencing and crew. Three months after graduation in 1894 he resigned his commission to try a career in writing. Following brief service as editor for the *Army and Navy Journal* and *The Cosmopolitan,* he married Mabel Harlakenden Hall, the daughter of a wealthy St. Louis iron manufacturer, on Oct. 22, 1895. They had three children: Mabel, John, and Creighton. His marriage brought Churchill the personal and financial security he needed to pursue his craft. He published *The Celebrity,* a lightweight social satire, in 1898, and then turned to the American past. Over the next six years he achieved national fame as a novelist, exploiting the turn-of-the-century taste for warm historical romance. In sequence, *Richard Carvel* (1899), *The Crisis* (1901), and *The Crossing* (1904), all best sellers, strode in leisurely style across the national landscape from eighteenth-century Maryland to Civil War St. Louis, their pages an appealing mix of well-researched historical pageantry and patrician moral melodrama. "I believe in healthy optimism in literature, not in a literature for literary men (and women) twisted into cults and governed by fads," he told his publisher. "What is historical romance if it is not taking a man to a strange country, which he longs to see and never can? And when he arrives there he must be given the best time possible; a full time. . . . A time to think of with a lingering delight when he has put down the book" (Churchill to George Brett, Dec. 3, 1897, Churchill Papers).

The air of sunny patriotism that brightened his fiction shifted abruptly in *Coniston* (1906), set in post-Civil War, small-town New England. This tale marked Churchill's transition from historical romance to the problem novel. In the character of Jethro Bass—one of his strongest creations, modeled after a semi-legendary New Hampshire party boss named Ruel Durkee—*Coniston* connected history to present politics. The problem was corruption.

The new concern reflected important changes in Churchill's own career. In 1898 Churchill and his wife bought a tract of hilly woodland along the Connecticut River near Cornish, N.H. There they built a sprawling neo-Georgian country place, their home for the next quarter-century. Named Harlakenden House, the sumptuous estate soon was a social focus for the local Cornish colony of writers and artists. Herbert Croly was a neighbor and became a particular friend. Churchill met Theodore Roosevelt, an admirer of his novels, in the summer of 1901, and dined at the White House later that year. The impact of the young president on Churchill, turning his mind toward public affairs, is manifest in the writer's letters of the period. His role as country squire also gave Churchill an elite consumer's interest in forest conservation, in better roads and bridges (he was an early automobile enthusiast), and in improving New Hampshire's attractions for summer residents. These new influences in his life, together with the novelist's curiosity for fresh experience, persuaded Churchill to run for the state legislature as a Republican in 1902.

He served two terms in the assembly at Concord, an ingenuous cosmopolitan amateur among seasoned professionals. Baffled, fascinated, and finally incensed by lobbyists' manipulations and the corrupting power of the Boston and Maine Railroad, he decided in 1906 to run for governor as an insurgent to catalyze reform energies against corporate control of the state. "We are going to . . . put the Republican party in New Hampshire where Theodore Roosevelt has put it before the nation," he announced to startled fellow legislators (undated circular letter, 1906, Churchill Papers). To one of them he added: "I can see no other way of clearing the atmosphere but to come out plainly and squarely with what I believe to be right, with what I have always tried to set forth in my books as right" (Churchill to Merrill Shurtleff, July 7, 1906, Churchill Papers).

Slim, handsome, and affable, driving through the villages in an open car with his Irish terrier, Churchill made a dashing candidate. Not one major newspaper in the state and, among established politicians, only the aging liberal, ex-U.S. Sen. William E. Chandler, supported him. Yet the coalition which Churchill's Lincoln Republican Club gathered among small-town lawyers, farmers, and college men came very close to winning at an exciting and disorderly party convention. It was, Churchill acknowledged privately, "the best fun I have ever indulged in" (Churchill to Finley Peter Dunne, Sept. 12, 1906, Churchill Papers). He promptly set to work employing the experience in his next novel, *Mr. Crewe's Career* (1908), which included a mocking self-parody in the character of Humphrey Crewe. But the movement he had launched was serious and effective. It soon broke the hold of the Boston and Maine, and reform laws began moving through the legislature in abundance. Churchill viewed the achievement with an urbane, paternal pride. While his campaigns remained largely symbolic —he ran unsuccessfully for governor again as a Bull Mooser in 1912—few doubted his crucial initiative in bringing progressivism to the state.

Meanwhile, Churchill's mind ranged outward in new directions. Like many friends of the New Nationalism he ventured bold assertions about the need for stronger federal authority, public ownership and control of industry, and attention to social injustice in order to advance the progressive millennium. But it was as a writer, not as a politician, that he pressed the search for better answers. "I am not merely writing a story," he said of one of his later novels, "I am giving a solution" (Churchill to Roland Phillips, June 22, 1912, Churchill Papers). Plot and character now moved more dutifully to the requirements of urgent social themes. Marriage, divorce, and the brutal ethics of modern business were salient preoccupations in both *A Modern Chronicle* (1910) and *A Far Country* (1915). The social gospel, and the chance for personal integration through moral rebirth, concerned *The Inside of the Cup* (1912)— perhaps the most durable of Churchill's problem novels, opening realms he would explore one way or another for the rest of his life.

Conscious of the domineering social purpose in his later novels, Churchill experienced growing difficulty in fitting new naturalistic themes to the dramatic conventions of his earlier work, where personal honor, genteel morality, and pleasant resolutions governed. His last novel, *The Dwelling Place of Light* (1917), a somber tale of blighted aspirations in a strife-torn New England mill town, closed on a note of vacuous acceptance.

Churchill

Churchill's reign as America's most popular novelist collapsed with the end of the Progressive era, the beginning of the war, and the sway of new tastes in postwar politics and literature. But the causes of his eclipse were also personal. The good life at Harlakenden House had begun to come apart years before. Marital troubles were compounded by his wife's breakdown in 1913. In 1917, after brief service in Washington as a naval propagandist, Churchill toured the European war zone, contracted a serious disease, and came home exhausted physically and psychologically. In convalescence he suffered what he later called a "severe neurosis" and underwent a number of mystical religious experiences. Thereafter his life took on a passive, almost posthumous quality. Extended amateur forays into biblical criticism, psychology, and evolutionary science alternated with carpentry and oil painting, which he pursued under the eye of his Cornish neighbor Maxfield Parrish. He found serenity in a personal philosophy of noncontention—a renunciation of willful resistance to perceived reality—and achieved nearly total detachment from his earlier career. After Harlakenden House burned in 1923, somehow confirming his break with the past, he moved into a simple farmhouse nearby. After two decades of meandering contemplation he published a distillation of his thoughts, *The Uncharted Way* (1940). It met with confused silence. He died of a heart attack in Winter Park, Fla., at age seventy-five and was buried beside his wife, who had died two years before, in a solitary lot on his estate overlooking the Connecticut River.

The boundaries of Churchill's importance were apparent even before his retreat from active life. Among the political figures of the Progressive era, he was the most gifted novelist, and among its novelists, the most skillful politician. In both callings his achievement was modest but clear. He was a fresh wind in New Hampshire politics, and however brief his influence it brought permanent structural change to the state. His fiction belongs to a shattered past, when middle-class families read novels together for improving entertainment, and a California schoolteacher could testify: "I have studied under you, Mr. Churchill, and my life is better and larger for your influence" (Gail Cleveland to Churchill, Sept. 29, 1910, Churchill Papers). He had that sort of audience and disappeared with it.

[The Churchill Papers at the Dartmouth College Library are a large and dense collection, part of which remains on restricted deposit. Churchill is the subject of several theses, one of which was published

Cloud

in shortened form by Warren I. Titus, *Winston Churchill* (1963). The best critical studies are found in Richard and Beatrice Hofstadter, "Winston Churchill: A Study in the Popular Novel," *American Quart.*, Spring 1950, pp. 12–28; Charles C. Walcutt, *American Literary Naturalism: A Divided Stream* (1956); and Robert W. Schneider, *Five Novelists of the Progressive Era* (1965). A fuller biography by Professor Schneider awaits publication. Useful background on New Hampshire politics is found in Leon B. Richardson, *William E. Chandler, Republican* (1940).]

GEOFFREY BLODGETT

CLOUD, HENRY ROE (Dec. 28, 1886–Feb. 9, 1950), educator and administrator, was born in Winnebago, Nebr., to Winnebago parents. His father's name was Na-Xi-Lay-Hunk-Kay; his mother's is given as "Hard-to-See." His own Winnebago name was Wo-Na-Xi-Lay-Hunka; the "Roe" in his English name is from his adoptive parents, Dr. and Mrs. Walter C. Roe, who, like many of the Caucasians who took an interest in Indian affairs in their day, were missionaries. Roe Cloud was educated at an Indian school at Genoa, Nebr., and at Mt. Hermon School in Massachusetts. He went on to become the first Indian person to graduate from Yale, receiving the B.A. degree in 1910. After studying sociology for a year at Oberlin, he earned the B.D. degree from Auburn Theological Seminary in 1913 and the M.A. from Yale in 1914. He was ordained in the Presbyterian ministry in 1913.

Roe Cloud early distinguished himself as a leader. He was chairman of a Winnebago delegation to meet with the president in 1912-1913, and a member of a survey commission on Indian education in 1914. Still in his twenties, he was an important leader in the Society of American Indians, predecessor of the pan-Indian National Council of American Indians. Most importantly, in 1915 he founded the Roe Indian Institute in Wichita, Kans., and for fifteen years thereafter was its superintendent. This institution, which became the American Indian Institute in 1920, was unique among Indians schools in its academic orientation; unlike other schools, which followed the Booker T. Washington-style idea that vocational education was most appropriate, Cloud's school trained Indian people to be leaders.

Cloud made another major contribution as a member of the staff of a survey of Indian affairs conducted by the Institute for Government Research (the Brookings Institution) in 1926-1927 and 1929-1930. He was coauthor of its report to the secretary of the interior, the Meriam Report (1928). This document, which revealed the shocking varieties of Indian poverty and deprivation, had some effect in the effort to redefine federal Indian policy under the New Deal.

Cloud spent two years as special regional representative in the Office of Indian Affairs (1931-1933), and then in August 1933 Franklin Roosevelt appointed him superintendent of Haskell Institute in Lawrence, Kans. This was to be the high point in Cloud's career. His appointment was part of what was intended as a clean sweep: Roosevelt's new secretary of the interior, Harold Ickes, was conceived of as a friend of the Indians, and his new head of the Bureau of Indian Affairs, John Collier, was committed to the preservation and even the nurturing of tribal cultures. The choice of Cloud to head Haskell Institute, a major Indian educational institution, was seen as part of an enlightened policy of using native administrators whenever possible.

Though Cloud as superintendent spoke with New Deal cheer of new directions in policy and bluntly described the failings of previous administrations, he shared with his white predecessors a belief that assimilation of the Indian into white society was coming, one way or another. He also tended to confuse missionary zeal with education. In his baccalaureate sermon of 1934, for example, a mixture of attitudes is apparent: "The once great and glorious past of the race has been held up disparagingly by many white teachers thinking thereby to coerce the young Indian student to abandon this reigning spirit of his forefathers. Mistakenly, teachers of the past believed that this was the only method left open for advancement into the white man's civilization." He did not say that such an "advance" might not be desirable. Believing in the "onward march in civilization," he felt that Indian peoples had their choice of being trampled under its feet or rising up to "join its forces in keeping with the mighty tread of all the races."

Cloud insisted, however, that the nature of the transition should be determined by Indian leaders. "Haskell Institute," he wrote, "today postulates as a reason for its continued existence its great task in the development of a native leadership for every Indian tribe in the United States." He felt that he and his institution were "definitely committed to the preservation of Indian race culture," and was therefore frustrated by Haskell's limiting vocational-oriented curriculum.

Cloud left Haskell Institute in 1936 to become assistant supervisor of Indian education at-large in the Office of Indian Affairs. His further posts were superintendent of the Umatilla Indian Agency, Pendleton, Oreg. (1947-1950); and regional representative, Grande Ronde and Siletz Indian Agency (1948-1950). He also served at one time as editor of the *Indian Outlook*.

On June 12, 1916, Roe Cloud married Elizabeth Georgian Bender, a part-Chippewa graduate of the Hampton Normal Training School, who assisted him in the founding and management of the American Indian Institute. They had four daughters, Elizabeth Marion, Anne Woesha, Lillian Alberta, Ramona Clarke, and a son, Henry Roe, who died in infancy. Cloud died of coronary thrombosis in Siletz, Oreg., and was buried in Crescent Grove Cemetery, Beaverton, Oreg. His wife remained active after his death in the National Council of American Indians.

Henry Roe Cloud stands as an important transitional figure, among the most eloquent and the best trained of the first generation of organized and educated Indian spokesmen, very different from current pan-Indian leaders yet committed to pride in the Indian heritage and to an Indian voice in the determination of Indian destiny in the United States.

[Marion Gridley, ed., *Indians of Today* (1936 and 1947 eds.); *Who Was Who in America*, in an addendum to, II (1950); Yale Univ., *Obituary Record*, 1949-1950; numerous references to Roe Cloud, as well as texts of his speeches as superintendent, in the *Indian Leader*, published by Haskell Institute; many items in the *Lawrence* (Kans.) *Daily Journal-World* during his superintendency; items in the *Quart. Jour.* (also known as the *American Indian Magazine*), Soc. of Am. Indians; Loretta May Granger, "Indian Education at Haskell Institute, 1884-1937" (master's thesis, Univ. of Nebraska, 1937); Hazel W. Hertzberg, *The Search for an American Indian Identity* (1971).]

STUART LEVINE

COCKERELL, THEODORE DRU ALISON (Aug. 22, 1866-Jan. 26, 1948), naturalist, was born in Norwood, a suburb of London, England, the eldest of the four sons and two daughters of Sydney John and Alice Elizabeth (Bennett) Cockerell. His father was a partner in the firm of George Cockerell and Company, coal merchants. The Cockerells were originally a Suffolk family of brewers, probably of Flemish origin (Cocquerel), and included several members of unusual ability. Theodore's brother Sydney Carlyle became director of the Fitzwilliam Museum in Cambridge; and a nephew, Christopher Cockerell, invented the Hovercraft.

Cockerell attended private schools in Beckenham, where his parents had moved in 1872. Encouraged by his father, he showed an early interest in the natural history displays at local museums and began collecting snails, caterpillars, and butterflies. After his father's death in 1877 the family was left in poor circumstances and moved to Margate. There on the shore, and two years later during a visit to Madeira with a family friend, the boy developed a strong enthusiasm for shells and insects. During his teens he briefly attended the Middlesex Hospital Medical School, joined the Socialist League, where he formed a friendship with William Morris, and earned his living by working for a firm of flour factors; but natural history remained a major interest. Before he was twenty-one he had published more than 160 brief notes, chiefly on shells.

Cockerell had never been too healthy, and, discovering that he had tuberculosis, he sailed in June 1887 for the United States and went directly to Colorado, where he joined a colony of English immigrants at Westcliffe, near the Sangre de Cristo Mountains. In this climate his health improved, and during the next three years the rich flora and fauna of the region apparently fixed his interest in biology. He founded and became secretary of the Colorado Biological Association, maintained an extensive correspondence with scientists, including Alfred Russel Wallace, and began to assemble records leading to a comprehensive catalogue of the entire biota of the Rocky Mountain region. After his return to England in 1890 he worked for a year at the British Museum (Natural History) and assisted Wallace in preparing the second edition of his *Island Life,* an experience that stimulated Cockerell's lifelong interest in the mechanisms of evolution.

On June 2, 1891, Cockerell married Annie S. Fenn and immediately sailed for Kingston, Jamaica, to become curator of the public museum there. Their first son, Austin, was born in Kingston but lived only a few days. In 1893 Cockerell, again in poor health, moved to Las Cruces, N. Mex., as professor of entomology and zoology at the New Mexico Agricultural College (he became a naturalized citizen in 1898). His wife died in September 1893, a few days after the birth of their second son, Martin, who died at the age of eight. On June 19, 1900, Cockerell married Wilmatte Porter, a graduate of Stanford and a biology teacher at the New Mexico Normal College. They had no children, and his wife actively assisted him in his research.

Although Cockerell had no earned university degree, he spent the rest of his professional life on the faculties of educational institutions in the Rocky Mountain region. He carried out research at the New Mexico Agricultural Experiment Station at Las Cruces (1893-1901), taught biology at the New Mexico Normal College at Las Vegas (1900-1903), served a year as curator of the museum of Colorado College in Colorado Springs, and in 1904 moved to the University of Colorado. There he remained until retirement, as lecturer in entomology (1904-1906), professor of systematic zoology (1906-1912), and professor of zoology (1912-1934). He received honorary degrees from Colorado College (1913) and the University of Denver (1942), served as president of the Entomological Society of America (1924), and was elected to the American Philosophical Society in 1928.

A naturalist in the broad tradition of the nineteenth century, Cockerell was best known for his work in entomology. He was a recognized authority on the taxonomy of bees in all parts of the world; he published more than five thousand new names for species, subspecies, and varieties, and 146 names for genera and subgenera. In botany, perhaps his most important contribution was "The North American Species of *Hymenoxys*" (Torrey Botanical Club, *Bulletin,* September 1904, pp. 461-509). He also published *Zoölogy* (1920), a textbook, and *Zoology of Colorado* (1927). Cockerell's interests were far-reaching, however, and the scope of his intellectual curiosity is reflected in the nearly 4,000 papers and notes he published, many no more than a few lines in length. His studies in systematic biology spanned a broad spectrum of organisms, including Mollusca, Lepidoptera, scale insects, fossil insects, gall wasps, the flowering plants, and Fungi, and he pioneered in the classification of fossil fish by their isolated scales. Aided by his wife, Cockerell discovered and worked out the genetics of a wine-red sunflower, *Helianthus annuus,* whose seeds were later put on the market. He made many collecting trips, including travels to Siberia and Japan (1923), South America (1925), Russia (1927), Australia (1928), and Africa (1931).

Cockerell's phenomenal output of papers brought strong criticism from his colleagues, who accused him of publishing hasty notes on trivial matters rather than waiting to accumulate enough material in a given area to produce a comprehensive paper. Cockerell explained his haste in publishing by stating his fears for his uncertain health; but a stronger factor was probably his eagerness to communicate his observations and ideas to interested colleagues without delay. Then too, from his experience in preparing lists and catalogues, he believed that much of the material reported in his short notes, each dealing with a single item, would have been lost by being submerged in longer publications bearing generalized titles.

By 1934, when Cockerell retired, the era of the well-rounded naturalist had largely given way to the new age of specialization. During his last years he was regarded on his campus as an eccentric, of little importance to the modern curriculum in biology. After his retirement he spent his winters in California, working in the Santa Barbara islands off the southern coast, and for a time (1941-1945) served as curator of the Desert Museum at Palm Springs, Calif. He died in San Diego of arteriosclerotic heart disease. Following cremation, his ashes were buried at Green Mountain Cemetery in Boulder.

[Cockerell's "Recollections of a Naturalist," published in fifteen installments in *Bios*, 6–11, 14 (1935–1948); William A. Weber, *Theodore Dru Alison Cockerell, 1866-1948* (Univ. of Colo. Studies, Series in Biblio. No. 1, 1965), a short biography, with a photograph, list of obituaries, and complete bibliography of Cockerell's publications; Joseph Ewan, *Rocky Mountain Naturalists* (1950), chap. x, on Cockerell; Wilfred Blunt, *Cockerell: Sydney Carlyle Cockerell, Friend of Ruskin and William Morris and Director of the Fitzwilliam Museum, Cambridge* (1964). Cockerell's Papers, 1895-1949 (approximately 11,500 items), are in the Western Hist. Collect. of the Univ. of Colorado. Many of his insect collections remain at the Univ. of Colorado Museum, but because he believed that specimens should belong to the scientific institution to whose geographical area and research specialties they are most relevant, much of the material he used to document his publications is dispersed and difficult to locate.]

WILLIAM A. WEBER

COHEN, MORRIS RAPHAEL (July 25, 1880-Jan. 28, 1947), philosopher, was born in Minsk, Russia, the fifth or sixth child of Abraham Mordecai Cohen and Bessie (Farfel) Cohen. His first twelve years were spent in impoverished circumstances in a culture whose traditions were predominantly medieval and religious. Throughout his life he retained a deep attachment to the humane wisdom of his early heritage, and especially to the instruction he had received from his maternal grandfather in Neshwies (Nesvizh), a town near Minsk. Brought to New York City by his parents in 1892, he attended the public schools of that city and received the B.S. from the College of the City of New York in 1900. After graduate work at Columbia University, he went to Harvard in 1904, where he obtained the Ph.D. in philosophy in 1906 with a doctoral dissertation on "Kant's Doctrine as to the Relation Between Duty and Happiness."

Cohen thus came to intellectual maturity in the atmosphere of modern science and in a social environment whose condition led him to question the dominant *laissez-faire* economic and social philosophy of the period. During his undergraduate days, he belonged to the Educational Alliance on the Lower East Side of New York, where he met Thomas Davidson, a wandering Scottish philosopher, who encouraged his philosophical interests. Davidson also inspired him to help establish a Breadwinner's College at that institution, to enable working people to pursue cultural studies in the evening. This venture was continued after Davidson's death in 1910, although it did not survive World War I, and it enabled Cohen to offer a variety of courses in history and the philosophy of civilization. He was an elementary-school teacher for a year after completing college, and during 1902-1904 and 1906-1912 he taught mathematics at Townshend Harris Hall, the preparatory division of the College of the City of New York. He married Mary Ryshpan on June 13, 1906; they had three children, Felix, Leonora, and Victor.

Cohen realized his ambition to become a professional teacher of philosophy in 1912, when he was appointed to the department of philosophy of the College of the City of New York, whose member he remained until his retirement in 1938. However, he was at various times visiting professor of philosophy at a number of institutions of higher learning, including Columbia, Yale, Harvard, and the University of Chicago; and he also was a lecturer at the Law School of St. John's College and the New School for Social Research, both in New York City. He helped organize the Conference on Legal and Social Philosophy in 1913 and was a cofounder in 1933 of the Conference on Jewish Relations, whose aim was to sponsor research on matters concerning Jews in Europe and elsewhere. Elected president of the American Philosophical Association (Eastern Division) in 1928, he later received the signal honor of giving a series of lectures on the Paul Carus Foundation at an annual meeting of the association. His lectures, delivered in 1941, were published as *The Meaning of Human History* (1947).

Cohen understood by philosophy not an inquiry directed, as are the special sciences, to discovering the facts of existence or the nature of things, but the disciplined critical reflection on the interpretations that men place on the primary materials of their experience—interpretations that are codified in the propositions certified by the positive sciences, in the norms contained in moral and legal rules, or in the evaluations and standards manifested in esthetic criticism. As he conceived it, philosophic reflection seeks to make explicit the logical articulation of claims to knowledge, the grounds on which their credibility rests, and the import of their content for a coherent view of nature and man. He was no philosophical system builder in the grand manner, and he confessed that he never felt quite at home in the imposing intellectual mansions that philosophers and theologians have built. He found no evidence for the frequent assumption that the universe is a unitary process, or even an integral pattern of different processes, conforming to the neatly arranged categories of any of the historical or contemporary systems of philosophy. He rejected as baseless the recurrent attempts to map the contours of existence in terms of anthropomorphic notions. He was unable to see any signs of inevitable progress in the events of biological or human history, but he could also find no reason in the fact that the universe is not organized to advance human aspirations either for attitudes of unrelieved despair or for postures of cosmic defiance. Cohen's philosophy was therefore a thoroughgoing naturalism, but informed by far-ranging studies of intellectual methods employed in the pursuit of reliably based knowledge. He was also a vigorous exponent of a liberal social philosophy that joined a faith in rational analysis with a willingness to use the instrumentalities of the state to achieve a more just society. He recognized as legitimate the traditional function of philosophy to supply an integrated and clarified vision of the nature of things. He also insisted, however, that the vision must not be a dogmatic projection of willful hopes and desires, but must be supported by the findings of competently conducted empirical inquiry and by the results of scrupulous logical analyses of their assumed interrelations.

Cohen often characterized himself as being primarily a logician, although with the understanding that logic is not to be identified with the theory of formal demonstrative inference. Indeed, he adopted William James's account of metaphysics to describe logic as nothing but an unusually obstinate effort to think clearly. This catholic conception of logic is evident in his attempts to clarify the major issues in discussions of scientific method, in philosophical assessments of the natural and social sciences, and in debates over legal, political, and ethical theories. These attempts at clarification appear in nearly all his writings and especially in his first and major book

Reason and Nature (1931), subtitled *An Essay on the Meaning of Scientific Method.* Cohen's reading of Bertrand Russell's *The Principles of Mathematics* shortly after its publication in 1903 emancipated him from the prevalent Kantian, Hegelian, and psychological interpretations of logic and mathematics. He was also a close student of the writings of Charles S. Peirce, the American logician and founder of pragmatism. The first collection of Peirce's writings to appear in book form was published by Cohen in 1923 as *Chance, Love and Logic.* He acquired from Peirce not only the conception of scientific laws as statements of genuinely objective relations in nature, but also the view that their logical import is to be found in the sensible states of affairs that can possibly verify them. Cohen therefore rejected all forms of *a priori* rationalism that try to deduce factual propositions from purely formal truths. But he was also a vigorous critic of atomistic empiricism, partly on the ground that its implicit denial of the objective reality of relations in nature is incompatible with the findings of the sciences, and partly because it misconceives the role of rationally constructed theories in scientific inquiry. He regarded the necessary truths of formal logic (such as the principle of contradiction) not only as the basis for valid inference, but also as formulations of absolute invariants present in all subject matters. On the other hand, he maintained that the laws of the positive sciences state relations that are invariant only under special types of changes, so that scientific laws are at best only contingently true. Cohen thus acknowledged a fundamental diversity of what he called the rational and empirical elements of nature, a diversity illustrating his general principle of polarity, according to which "opposites such as immediacy and mediation, unity and plurality, the fixed and the flux, . . . all involve each other when applied to any significant entity"; and he subjected to a spirited criticism philosophical doctrines that ignore one or the other of these polar aspects of nature. His essays in legal and social philosophy, which won for him an audience outside the circle of professional philosophers, exhibit a similar attempt to achieve a balance between polar contentions. For example, he was an early proponent of the view, at one time regarded as a heresy, that judges not only follow but also create the law. And although he was an eloquent spokesman for the use of rational methods in the pursuit of knowledge and the organization of human life, he was acutely aware that the life of reason is not only a difficult but also a precarious achievement. He did not hide his fears that the latent forces of unreason, uneasily dormant under the thin veneer of civilization, might be unleashed to destroy the most precious heritage of mankind.

Although Cohen wrote much, his frail health, a prolonged illness, and a relatively early death were obstacles to the fulfillment of his literary hopes. He did not realize his youthful ambition to produce a philosophic encyclopedia that would do for his century what d'Alembert and Diderot achieved for theirs. A number of the books he had planned were incomplete when he became incapacitated by illness, and several of them were published only posthumously. He died in Washington, D.C., and was buried in Mt. Zion Cemetery in Maspeth, N.Y.

[The main source for the biographical data in the foregoing is Cohen's autobiography *A Dreamer's Journey* (1949), which also contains a bibliography of his published writings, and Leonora Cohen Rosenfield, *Portrait of a Philosopher: Morris R. Cohen in Life & Letters* (1962). Five of Cohen's books which were published after his autobiography are *Studies in Philosophy and Science* (1949); *Reason and Law* (1950); *Reflections of a Wondering Jew* (1950); *King Saul's Daughter, A Biblical Dialogue* (1952); and *American Thought* (1954). Interpretations of Cohen's work include Sol Roth, "A Theory of Rationalism: An Examination of the Philosophy of Morris R. Cohen" (Ph.D. diss., Columbia Univ., 1966); Arturo Deregibus, *Il Razionalismo di Morris R. Cohen nella Filosofia Americana d'Oggi* (Turin, 1960); Joseph L. Blau, *Men and Movements in American Philosophy*, ch. 9 (1952); and Daniel J. Bronstein, "The Principle of Polarity in Cohen's Philosophy," Arthur F. Smullyan, "The Philosophical Method of Morris R. Cohen," and Philip P. Wiener, "Cohen's Philosophical Interpretations of the History of Science," all in *Freedom and Reason*, eds. Salo W. Baron, Ernest Nagel, and Koppel S. Pinson (1951).]

ERNEST NAGEL

COLBY, BAINBRIDGE (Dec. 22, 1869-Apr. 11, 1950), lawyer, secretary of state, was born in St. Louis, Mo., the older of two children and only son of John Peck Colby and Frances (Bainbridge) Colby. Both parents were descended from old New York families; his mother's forebears included Commodore William Bainbridge. Colby's father, after Civil War service in New York's 59th Regiment, moved to Missouri, where he practiced law. Young Colby was educated in public schools and at Williams College, from which he received the A.B. degree in 1890. He then entered the Columbia University Law School, but transferred after a year to the New York Law School, where he took the LL.B. in 1892.

Colby entered practice in New York City and rapidly achieved prominence, representing such well-known clients as Mark Twain and, later, William Randolph Hearst. On June 22,

1895, he married Nathalie Sedgwick of Stockbridge, Mass., who later became a novelist of some prominence. They had three children: Katherine Sedgwick, Nathalie Sedgwick, and Frances Bainbridge.

Initially a Republican in politics, Colby was elected on a fusion ticket to the New York state assembly in 1901. He declined renomination the next year, however, to return to his practice. Colby was an effective and much sought-after speaker, combining eloquence with wit and biting political satire. In 1912 he helped found the Progressive party and campaigned vigorously for Theodore Roosevelt. He ran as a Progressive for the United States Senate in 1914 but was defeated. Two years later, when Roosevelt urged a return to the GOP, Colby led a group of dissident Progressives who endorsed Woodrow Wilson, and soon afterward he joined the Democratic party. Colby thus won the gratitude of the new president, but his switch in political allegiance earned him much hostility and a not entirely undeserved reputation for instability.

Although offered an appointment by Wilson, Colby at first chose to remain in private practice. In 1917, however, with the United States at war, he accepted a position on the Shipping Board and, as part of a mission led by Col. Edward M. House, helped establish the Allied Maritime Transport Council to coordinate interallied shipping. He resigned from the Shipping Board in 1919. In March of the following year Wilson unexpectedly appointed him secretary of state to replace Robert Lansing. The ailing president admired and trusted Colby, and hoped that his appointment would aid in the fight for Senate approval of the Versailles Treaty. For his part, Colby idolized Wilson and, unlike Lansing, was uncritically flattering in his relations with the president. He alone of Wilson's three secretaries of state was able to establish a good working relationship with the White House.

As secretary of state, Colby vigorously defended Wilson's position on the League of Nations. He had ample warning that the only hope for Senate ratification of the peace treaty lay in compromise, but his unswerving personal loyalty to the president prevented him from urging concessions to Republican critics. Even before defeat of the treaty, Wilson had become embittered by the willingness of the Allies to proceed without the United States in working out details of the postwar settlement. As the instrument of Wilson's refusal to permit continuing American involvement in the Paris Peace

Conference, Colby presided over a transition from wartime internationalism to the neo-isolationism of the 1920's. Colby was strongly anti-Communist, and therefore also underwrote an American nonrecognition policy toward Soviet Russia in August 1920, a policy that was to last until 1933. He continued, in cooperation with Great Britain, Lansing's efforts to curb Japanese expansionism in Manchuria and Siberia, thus laying the basis for the Pacific treaty system established at the Washington Conference of 1921-1922.

Colby's most significant achievement involved Latin America. In a program foreshadowing the Good Neighbor policy of the 1930's, he avoided further armed intervention in the Caribbean, announced America's intention of withdrawing occupying forces from Haiti and the Dominican Republic, and toured Latin America explaining Wilsonian hemispheric goals and disavowing American imperialism. Negotiations with the Obregón regime in Mexico concerning the expropriation of foreign-owned oil and landed property laid the groundwork for a successful agreement in 1923. Thus, while his tenure as secretary was brief, Colby's record was a creditable one.

After leaving office with Wilson in 1921, Colby formed a law partnership in Washington with the former president (1921-1923). Thereafter he continued private practice until his retirement in 1936. He supported Franklin Roosevelt for president in 1932, but soon became repelled by New Deal "collectivism." He wrote numerous articles for the Hearst press, and in 1934 joined Alfred E. Smith and other conservative Democrats in founding the American Liberty League. He supported the Republican presidential candidates in 1936 and 1940.

Colby's first marriage was ended in divorce in 1929, and on November 1 of that year he married Anne (Ahlstrand) Ely, a widow, in New York City. He was an Episcopalian in religion. For several years Colby maintained a home at Bemus Point, Chautauqua County, N.Y., and it was there that he died, of arteriosclerotic heart disease. He was buried in the Bemus Point Cemetery.

[Abundant materials relating to Colby's life and diplomatic career are contained in the Colby Papers and the Wilson Papers in the Lib. of Cong. For published documents, see *Papers Relating to the Foreign Relations of the U. S., 1920* (3 vols., 1935-1936), and *1921* (2 vols., 1936). Colby was the author of *The Close of Woodrow Wilson's Administration and the Final Years* (1930). The most recent studies of Colby are Daniel M. Smith, "Bainbridge Colby and the Good Neighbor Policy, 1920-1921," *Miss. Valley Hist. Rev.*, June 1963, and *Aftermath of War: Bainbridge*

Colby and Wilsonian Diplomacy, 1920-1921 (1970). An older but useful short account by John Spargo is in Samuel Flagg Bemis, ed., *The Am. Secretaries of State and Their Diplomacy*, X (1929). Brief biographical sketches are in the *N.Y. Times*, Feb. 29, 1920, sec. 6, and Apr. 12, 1950; *Current Opinion*, Apr. 1920, pp. 479-482; *Nat. Cyc. Am. Biog.*, XLVIII, 10-11 (with a good portrait opposite p. 10); and *Who Was Who in America*, III (1960). Death record from N.Y. State Dept. of Health.]

DANIEL M. SMITH

COLCORD, LINCOLN ROSS (Aug. 14, 1883-Nov. 16, 1947), journalist and maritime historian, was born at sea off Cape Horn in the bark *Charlotte A. Littlefield*, commanded by his father, Captain Lincoln Alden Colcord of Searsport, Maine. His family had been seafarers for five generations. His mother, Jane French (Sweetser) Colcord, accompanied her husband on his distant voyages as a matter of course. Her two children, Joanna Carver, later a social worker at the Russell Sage Foundation, and Lincoln, were not only born but grew up on voyages to China, during which they were taught by their parents. Lincoln (who never used his middle name) did not come ashore until the age of fourteen. He was graduated from the Searsport High School in 1900 and attended the University of Maine intermittently from 1900 to 1906. Although he left in the middle of his junior year, the university awarded him an honorary M.A. in 1922 and elected him to Phi Beta Kappa in 1924.

Colcord worked in the Maine woods as a civil engineer with the Bangor and Aroostook Railroad from 1906 to 1909, when he settled in Searsport and began writing short stories for magazines. On May 4, 1910, he married Blanche T. Nickels, also of Searsport; they had a daughter, Inez Nickels Colcord. His book of sea stories, *The Drifting Diamond*, was published in 1912, and *The Game of Life and Death* appeared in 1914. The outbreak of World War I led him to write a 149-page poem, *Vision of War*, published in 1915. He soon plunged into the current of political reform, and by 1916 he had become a close ally of Col. Edward M. House, who sponsored him for the post of staff correspondent in the Washington bureau of the *Philadelphia Public Ledger*, which he held in 1917-1918. He took to journalism with the same passionate energy that he had suddenly developed for political activism in the radical liberal cause. "Colcord is still new in this business," H. B. Brougham, publisher of the *Ledger*, wrote to House on July 19, 1917. "If he is a cub he is a lion's cub, and waxing powerful. Since he came here I have watched his course with an amazed admiration which I find it difficult to conceal. He is a man of hungry and indomitable energy, and facts are his prey, which he devours and assimilates with a veritable rapacity after the truth."

By July 1918, Colcord had begun to lose faith in both House and President Wilson. "For Colcord, the Bolshevik revolution in November 1917 posed the decisive test of the administration's good faith. The failure to aid the revolution, followed by the decision to intervene in Siberia, convinced him that Wilson had gone over to the reactionaries" (Lasch, p. 248). In 1919-1920 he worked for Oswald Garrison Villard as associate editor of *The Nation* in New York. Thereafter the drama of national political reform began to fade, and Colcord returned to Searsport. His third collection of stories, *An Instrument of the Gods*, appeared in 1922. In his introduction to his sister Joanna's *Roll and Go, Songs of American Sailormen* (1924), he wrote: "We discern at last a great truth—that our secret feeling for sailing ships is based on deeper values than those of sentimental attachment or the perception of beauty. It is based on something very real in life, something so true, of such immense significance, that we hardly dare to face the issue. The sailing ship stood for a sociological achievement of the highest order. She stood for a medium whereby men were brought to their fullest development. She stood for a profession where only merit could endure. She stood for the efficiency of spirit and character. She stood for things that we could not afford to lose."

In the mid-1920's, after the death of his first wife, Colcord and their young daughter lived for a time in Minneapolis, where his sister was then working. There he became a friend of the Norwegian-born novelist O. E. Rölvaag, whom he assisted with the English translation of *Giants in the Earth, A Saga of the Prairie* (1927). This enormously successful novel owed much to Colcord's "real *labor amoris*," as Rölvaag characterized it, in unifying and rewriting the text. Colcord married Loomis Logan on Feb. 16, 1928; they were divorced on Jan. 7, 1929. On July 23 of that year he married Frances Brooks; they had one son, Brooks.

Colcord then returned to Searsport for good. To his house overlooking Penobscot Bay came sailors, scholars, publishers, painters, railroad presidents, film actors, and poets. The range of his ideas was boundless, and it did not discon-

cert him in the least to make a right-about-face in his arguments with neither warning nor apology. His literary style seldom reflected his conversational gifts, except in his book reviews for the *New York Herald-Tribune* and in his exuberant letters, which remain uncollected and unpublished. With his wife he compiled from Custom House documents a 225-page "Record of Vessels Built on Penobscot River and Bay," an appendix to George S. Wasson's *Sailing Days on the Penobscot* (1932).

When the Penobscot Marine Museum was created in Searsport in 1936 by his cousin, Clifford N. Carver, the Colcords were active in gathering paintings, models, and logs of local ships. Although Link's head was crammed with details about maritime history, it was next to impossible to persuade him to get down his information on paper. He was too busy comparing the earlier world of "real men" to their shabby successors. Although he wrote President Roosevelt seeking a patronage appointment for himself as a "deserving Democrat," he soon came to abhor the New Deal. The nearer the country moved to war, the more vociferously isolationist he became. Yet he would happily lend his friend Samuel Eliot Morison nineteenth-century blue-backed charts of the Pacific to take with him on his cruises as historian of United States naval operations.

As the undisputed "sage of Searsport," Colcord stirred others to action. In the fall of 1939 he spoke before the Peabody Museum Marine Associates, delivering an impassioned plea for founding a journal of maritime history similar to the *Mariner's Mirror*. *The American Neptune* began publication in January 1941.

Colcord died suddenly at Belfast, Maine, on Nov. 16, 1947, and was buried at Searsport. Few men have had so varied a career with so little conventional preparation; few have had so wide an influence simply by talking to their friends. He was a man of outstanding vitality and gusto. He met life eagerly, equally alert for the savor of a situation, a bowl of chowder, a bottle of rum, an idea, an anecdote, or a stretch of landscape. Whatever ills he gallantly encountered—and he had stood up to his fair share—boredom was not one of them. Through his boyhood at sea he had established, somehow, a private quarterdeck of the mind from which he passed judgment on men and things. With characteristic fairness, though, he was more than willing to allow each of his fellow men a similar retreat, because of his limitless respect for the rights of the individual. Much that was strange or perverse he could tolerate, provided only it arose from wholehearted conviction; contrariwise, his scorn for affectation and pettiness was blistering. This all-engrossing concern for the independence of the individual led him to decry our contemporary processes of regimentation, and to exalt the past, particularly the seafaring past of New England, which, to his imagination, had fostered the hardihood of man.

[Walter Muir Whitehill, *Analecta Biographica, A Handful of New England Portraits* (1969), ch. 6; *Who Was Who in Am.*, II (1950); personal conversations and correspondence; Christopher Lasch, *The New Radicalism in America, 1889–1963* (1965), ch. 7 for the friendship with House.]

WALTER MUIR WHITEHILL

COLPITTS, EDWIN HENRY (Jan. 9, 1872–Mar. 6, 1949), communications engineer, was born in Point de Bute, New Brunswick, Canada, the first of eight children of James Wallace Colpitts and Celia Eliza (Trueman) Colpitts. Although farming had been the occupation of this English Methodist family for generations, five of the Colpitts children sought scientific or teaching careers. Among them, Julia and Elmer Colpitts both earned Ph.D.'s in mathematics from Cornell and taught at the university level.

Planning to pursue a teaching career, Colpitts graduated from normal school at Fredericton, New Brunswick, 1890. A short stint in the schools of Newfoundland changed his plans. Returning to New Brunswick, he entered Mount Allison University and graduated in 1893 with a B.A. in science. He continued his scientific education at Harvard (B.A., 1896; M.S., 1897), concentrating in mathematics and physics. From 1897 to 1899 he served as an assistant to John Trowbridge, director of Harvard's Jefferson Physical Laboratory.

In 1899 Colpitts began his lifelong association with the American Bell Telephone Company, becoming one of the first trained scientists at Bell's Boston laboratory. His work spanned two eras of communications, the electromechanical era (until 1912) and the vacuum tube electronic era (1912–1945). In both, his main strength was his rare combination of scientific expertise and practical engineering judgment.

As his three main contributions to the first era show, his strengths were problem-solving and analysis. Applying the concepts of Michael Pupin and G. A. Campbell, his work on new "loading coils" helped extend the range of long-distance telephony. His new methods for measuring the mutual capacitance of neighboring telephone circuits helped reduce the problem

of crosstalk. And methods that he devised helped reduce the interference of electric power currents in telephone signals.

Colleagues of this early period describe Colpitts as a man of Yankee temperament, whose strengths were "directness . . . integrity . . . [and] keen analytical intellect," rather than brilliance or originality (*Western Electric News,* May 1924, p. 40). "There comes to mind," Frank B. Jewett wrote, "many a picture of Colpitts in the early morning hours, hard at work . . . we find Colpitts in the van, sometimes in the laboratory, but more frequently in rough clothes in the mountains of Pennsylvania or the bush of Georgia . . . always in quest of the facts needed for solution of the problem" (*Western Electric Engineer,* July 1960, p. 11).

By 1912, when Colpitts was director of the Research Laboratories of the Western Electric Company, telephone engineers had exhausted the possibilities of extending the range of long-distance telephony by electrical or mechanical means. To Colpitts and his staff fell the task of adapting Lee De Forest's "audion"—the first triode—for telephone use. The successful accomplishment of this job in 1915 marked the beginning of the electronics age in communications.

Colpitts' administrative contribution to this effort was to keep his team focused on the practical problems, dispelling fascination with techniques alone. He invented the Colpitts system of modulation, a key element in the pioneering AT&T radio system, which sent voice messages from Arlington, Va., to Paris in 1915. After serving in the U.S. Army Signal Corps in 1917–1918, however, he turned his attention from radio, having underestimated its commercial potential. His last technical efforts were in the field of frequency multiplex telephony (1918–1924). As a vice-president of AT&T (1924–1934) and Bell Labs (1934–1937), he supervised the commercial application of new ideas.

Colpitts disdained his most famous invention. In a casual conversation (about 1915) he suggested the principle behind the Colpitts oscillator, a building-block of radio circuitry. He promptly forgot the suggestion and, according to company tradition, had to be persuaded to sign the 1918 patent application that credited it to him.

On Aug. 17, 1899, Colpitts married Annie Dove Penney; they had one son, Donald Bethune. A niece recalls Colpitts in middle age as tall and quiet, somewhat "crusty on the outside" and tending to impose his own high standards on relatives and associates. Yet he was modest and generous, with a dry sense of humor. At his retirement in 1937 he had received twenty-four patents and had published ten technical papers without the dramatic climaxes or disappointments experienced by such communications pioneers as Bell, De Forest, or Reginald Fessenden.

World War II added a distinguished postscript to his career. He came out of retirement to serve as head technical aide of Division Six (antisubmarine warfare) of the National Defense Research Committee (1940-1946) and was awarded the Medal of Merit for his services.

After the death of his first wife in March 1940, Colpitts married Sarah Grace Penney. On Mar. 6, 1949, after a lengthy illness, he died at his home in Orange, N. J. He is buried in the family plot at Point de Bute.

[The principal sources are the files of the Western Electric Co. Lib. in New York City, and the Bell Telephone Laboratories in Murray Hill, N. J. See especially Colpitts' account of his 1915 radio work and the evaluations of his technical work by Lloyd Espenscheid, R. W. King, and other AT&T personnel. Articles of historical interest are E. H. Colpitts and O. B. Blackwell, "Carrier Current Telephony and Telegraphy," *Trans. of the Am. Inst. of Electrical Engineers* (1921); and E. B. Craft and E. H. Colpitts, "Radio Telephony," *ibid.* (1920). Family background and personal glimpses of Colpitts were kindly supplied by Evelyn Colpitts Henderson of Seattle, Wash.]

GEORGE WISE

CONE, ETTA (Nov. 30, 1870-Aug. 31, 1949), art collector, as an associate of her sister CLARIBEL CONE (Nov. 14, 1864-Sept. 20, 1929), who was likewise a collector of works of art, was the third daughter and the ninth of the thirteen children of Herman Cone (né Kahn) and Helen (Guggenheimer) Cone. Claribel was the second daughter and fifth child; Moses Herman Cone, merchant and textile manufacturer, was a brother. Their father, born in 1828 to a pious Jewish family in Altenstadt on the Iller, Bavaria, emigrated to America in 1846 and settled in Jonesboro, Tenn., where by the mid-1850's he had established himself as a successful merchant. His wife, born in Hürben, Württemberg, Germany, in 1838, had emigrated as a child to Virginia, settling with her family in Gilmores Mill near Natural Bridge. The couple were married in 1856, lived for a time in Jonesboro, where Claribel was born, and moved to Baltimore in 1870 just before Etta's birth there. Herman Cone established a wholesale cigar and grocery business and took his sons into the firm. The two eldest brothers, originally drummers for the family enterprise, acquired textile mills in the South and eventually became the leading producers of denim, corduroy, and flannelette. As the business prospered, they provided comfortable, steady incomes for Claribel and Etta, neither of whom ever married.

Claribel Cone graduated from Baltimore's Western Female High School in 1883 and, surmounting her father's objection to her "unladylike" ambition to become a doctor, entered the recently opened Woman's Medical College of Baltimore for the three-year course and obtained her medical degree in 1890. After an internship in Philadelphia, she returned to Baltimore in 1893 and taught at the Woman's Medical College intermittently until 1910 as a professor of pathology. During this period she did research at Johns Hopkins University and, from 1904 to 1907, in Europe: at the Senckenberg Institute in Frankfurt am Main, Germany, and briefly at the Pasteur Institute in Paris. She published a number of scientific articles, was active in the cause of birth registration, and served as president of the Women's Medical Society of Maryland (1925-1927). She never entered private practice.

That Etta's formal education ended with her graduation from high school belies the fact that she remained a student with lifelong pursuits in the study of art history and piano. In 1898, commissioned to decorate the family's Victorian-style parlor, she acquired five paintings by Theodore Robinson, an American who worked in the French Impressionist style. She thereby showed an early propensity for contemporary painting and began the collection which was to be the principal endeavor of her life.

A strong influence on the Cones' collecting was their friendship with Gertrude Stein and her family, which began when Gertrude and her brother Leo settled in Baltimore in 1892. Through the next four decades, both in the United States and in Europe, the Cones and Steins spent much time together. During the winter of 1905-1906, when Etta was living in Paris in the same house as Gertrude's brother Michael and his wife and was typing Gertrude's novel *Three Lives*, the Steins introduced her to their new friends Henri Matisse and Pablo Picasso, from whom first Etta and later Claribel purchased drawings and paintings at minimal cost. They remained close friends with Matisse, whose works form the core of the art collection which they gradually accumulated. The sisters also began collecting Japanese prints and various kinds of decorative art objects, such as textiles, laces, and jewelry, during their sojourns in Paris and on a trip around the world in 1906-1907.

After World War I, with Claribel's professional medical career at an end and with the knowledge that they were now well-to-do, the Cone sisters began making annual trips to Europe and became more active as collectors. They bought antique furniture and many paintings from the Stein family in Paris. Claribel also purchased from art dealers and auction houses such major works as Cézanne's "Mont Ste-Victoire Seen from Bibémus Quarry," Matisse's then controversial "Blue Nude" of 1907, and Van Gogh's "Shoes." Etta, whose taste was less bold, meanwhile acquired Cézanne's "Bathers," Renoir's gentle "Washerwomen," and numerous colorful Matisse oil paintings. They arranged their treasures in their apartments in Baltimore, filling the rooms almost to overflowing, yet avoiding a feeling of clutter by the combined warmth of the vivid colors of the paintings, rugs, and fabrics and the constant abundance of fresh flowers.

The sisters' stately appearance was enhanced by their long black Victorian clothing, adorned with precious old lace, Renaissance jewelry, and exotic Oriental shawls. Claribel, despite her imperious manner, emanated charm and charisma and always seemed to dominate those around her, whereas Etta, though dignified, kindly, intelligent, and especially well-informed, was more retiring. They participated in the cultural life of Baltimore but were considered eccentric by local society not only for their unconventional clothing but even more for their independent judgment and courage in amassing a collection of modern art long before the community in general had any understanding of their avant-garde taste.

Claribel died of pneumonia and cardiac insufficiency in Lausanne, Switzerland, in 1929. According to the terms of her will, her collection was left to Etta to be given to the art museum in the city which they had always considered home if "the spirit of appreciation of modern art in Baltimore becomes improved." In subsequent years, Etta strengthened the collection by purchasing important paintings by Corot, Manet, and Gauguin, as well as Picasso's 1922 "Mother and Child." She bought many works of Matisse directly from the artist, augmented her lace and textile collections, and expanded the already considerable art library that she and her sister had assembled. Ultimately the art collection included sixteen paintings and thirty-eight drawings by Picasso, mostly of his pink and blue periods. The Cones'

group of Matisses, which includes forty-three paintings, more than a hundred drawings, and eighteen pieces of sculpture, probably constitutes the most comprehensive collection of the artist's work anywhere.

Etta Cone, who survived her sister by twenty years, died of a coronary occlusion in Blowing Rock, N.C., in 1949. Both were buried in a family mausoleum in Druid Ridge Cemetery, Pikesville, Md. In accordance with Claribel's suggestion, Etta bequeathed their joint collection to the Baltimore Museum of Art.

[Barbara Pollack, The Collectors: Dr. Claribel and Miss Etta Cone (1962), including a word "portrait" of 1912, "Two Women," by Gertrude Stein; Ellen B. Hirschland, "The Cone Sisters and the Stein Family," in Four Americans in Paris: The Collections of Gertrude Stein and Her Family (Museum of Modern Art, 1970); Edward T. Cone, "The Miss Etta Cones, the Steins, and M'sieu Matisse," Am. Scholar, Summer 1973; Adelyn D. Breeskin in Notable Am. Women, I, 371-373; Aline B. Saarinen, The Proud Possessors (1958); interviews and correspondence with relatives and friends of the Cones. Concerning the collection, see also Etta Cone, The Cone Collection of Baltimore–Md.: Catalogue of Paintings–Drawings–Sculpture of the 19th and 20th Centuries (1934); Clive Bell, Modern French Paintings: The Cone Collection (1951); Baltimore Museum of Art, Paintings, Sculpture and Drawings in the Cone Collection (1967); Alfred H. Barr, Matisse: His Art and His Public (1951); John Rewald, "The Cone Collection in Baltimore," Art in America, Oct. 1944; Baltimore Museum of Art News, issues of Oct. 1949, Jan.–Feb. 1950, and Feb. 1957. Articles about Claribel Cone are in: Matthew P. Andrews, Tercentenary Hist. of Md., II, 350–354 (1925); Jour. Am. Medic. Women's Assoc., Nov. 1952; and Margie H. Luckett, Md. Women, I, 87–89 (1931). Photographs of Claribel and Etta Cone, a drawing of Claribel by Picasso (1922), and drawings of both sisters by Matisse (1933–1934) are reproduced in Paintings, Sculpture and Drawings in the Cone Collection. The Baltimore Museum also has a sculptured bust of Etta by William Zorach (1943). MS materials are in the Baltimore Museum of Art, Yale Univ., the Leo Baeck Inst., and the collections of various family members.]
                                        ELLEN B. HIRSCHLAND

CONNOR, ROBERT DIGGES WIMBERLY (Sept. 26, 1878–Feb. 25, 1950), historian and archivist, was born in Wilson, N.C., the third son and fourth of twelve children of Henry Groves Connor, a prominent state legislator and judge, and Kate (Whitfield) Connor. From his father young Connor acquired a deep and lifelong interest in the history of his native state. After attending the public schools of Wilson, he entered the University of North Carolina at Chapel Hill, from which he graduated with a Ph.B. degree in 1899, having served in his senior year as editor-in-chief of all three student publications.

Connor had hoped to take graduate work in history at Johns Hopkins University, but lack of funds precluded this, and he began a career in public school education. Starting as a high school teacher in Winston, N.C., he moved in 1902 to Oxford as superintendent of schools and in 1903 became principal of the Wilmington high school. On Dec. 23, 1902, he married a fellow teacher, Sadie Hanes of Mocksville, N.C.; they had no children. In his next post, as secretary (1904-1907) of the educational commission established during the administration of Gov. Charles B. Aycock, Connor conducted a statewide campaign for improved schools, higher teacher salaries, and better school libraries. He was secretary of the North Carolina Teachers Assembly from 1906 to 1912.

Meanwhile, in 1903, Connor had committed himself to a second career when he accepted the unsalaried secretaryship of the newly created North Carolina Historical Commission. Founded at the instigation of the State Literary and Historical Association, the commission sought to collect and preserve the state's historical records. Through Connor's efforts, encouraged by his study of the Alabama Department of Archives and History, established in 1901 under the leadership of Thomas McAdory Owen, the commission's authority and its appropriations were enlarged in 1907, at which time Connor was appointed its first full-time, salaried secretary. Over the next fourteen years, Connor laid the essential foundations of what was later characterized as "a model historical agency" (Leland, p. 46). During these years he also found time to undertake historical writing of his own. His *Cornelius Harnett: An Essay in North Carolina History* (1909) was well received, and his *Makers of North Carolina History* (1911) was for many years a basic public school text.

Connor had kept in close touch with the University of North Carolina, serving as secretary of its board of trustees (1915-1920) and president of its alumni association (1917-1921). In 1920 he was called to a professorship there and in preparation spent a year of graduate study in history at Columbia University. He took up his duties as Kenan Professor of History and Government in the fall of 1921. His carefully prepared lectures, presented with "clarity and wit," made him one of the university's most popular teachers (Lefler, p. 114). In 1929 Connor produced his most ambitious scholarly work, the two-volume *North Carolina: Rebuilding an Ancient Commonwealth,* the best standard history of the state published to that time.

Connor was called back to archival work in 1934 when President Franklin D. Roosevelt appointed him the first archivist of the United States. He had been recommended for the post by the historian J. Franklin Jameson, whose long campaign had brought the National Archives into being, and by the executive committee of the American Historical Association. An experienced administrator, Connor recruited an able staff (resisting political patronage pressures), worked out the organization of the new agency, and set high professional standards. His qualities of personal force and tact enabled him to establish good relations with Congress, thus ensuring adequate appropriations, and with the various government agencies which he had to persuade to part with their records—in some cases, as with the War and State departments, a difficult task. Connor also worked closely with the president in establishing the Franklin D. Roosevelt Library at Hyde Park, N.Y., the forerunner of subsequent institutions in the presidential library system administered by the National Archives.

Connor resigned in 1941 and returned to the University of North Carolina to occupy the newly established Craige Professorship of Jurisprudence and History. This position he held until his retirement in 1949. He maintained his interest in the archival profession, serving as president of the Society of American Archivists, 1941-1943, and as chairman of the North Carolina Historical Commission, 1942-1943, and of the executive board of its successor, the State Department of Archives and History, from 1943 until his death. He died of a cerebral hemorrhage in Durham, N.C., at the age of seventy-one and was buried in the Chapel Hill (N.C.) Cemetery.

[Connor's personal papers are in the Southern Hist. Collection of the Univ. of N.C. at Chapel Hill. His official correspondence as secretary of the N.C. Hist. Commission, 1903-1921, is in the State Archives at Raleigh; that as Archivist of the U.S. is in the Nat. Archives. See also the published biennial reports of the N.C. Hist. Commission, 1903-1922, and annual reports of the Archivist of the U.S., 1934-1942. The two best biographical sketches of Connor are those by Hugh T. Lefler, in Clifford L. Lord, ed., *Keepers of the Past* (1965); and Waldo G. Leland, in the *Am. Archivist,* Jan. 1953. See also *Who Was Who in America,* II (1950), p. 14; and *N.Y. Times* obituary, Feb. 26, 1950. An oil portrait of Connor by Mary Arnold Nash (1952) is in the Nat. Archives; one by William C. Fields (1972) is in the N.C. Office of Archives and Hist., Raleigh.]

H. G. JONES

COOMARASWAMY, ANANDA KENTISH (Aug. 22, 1877-Sept. 9, 1947), art historian and metaphysician, was born in Colombo, Ceylon, the only child of Sir Mutu Coomaraswamy and Lady Elizabeth (Beeby) Clay Coomaraswamy. Sir Mutu, a member of the Legislative Council of Ceylon, was the first

Asiatic to be called to the bar at Lincoln's Inn, and, as Knight Bachelor, to enjoy the highest honor that a British sovereign could bestow upon a colonial subject. A friend of Disraeli and widely esteemed in England, he died when Ananda Coomaraswamy was only two years old. Although the young Coomaraswamy can hardly be said to have known him, the father's reform spirit, internationalism, and abiding interest in Indian scripture and poetry all reappeared in the son. After Sir Mutu's death, Lady Coomaraswamy closed her house in Colombo and returned to England, where she settled with her son and her two sisters. The family was well-to-do. In later years, Coomaraswamy used his personal fortune to build a remarkable art collection and to support his scholarly work; he died a man primarily of inner wealth.

Coomaraswamy attended Wycliffe College in Gloucestershire, and then the University of London (B.Sc. in geology, with first class honors, 1900; D.Sc. in geology, 1906). He married two interests by returning to Ceylon in about 1903 to do research on its mineral deposits and succeeded so well in his first year that an official Mineralogical Survey of Ceylon was established; he served as its director until 1906. Traveling the length and breadth of Ceylon, he was increasingly outraged by the weakening of indigenous culture by the pervasive influence of English colonialism. He founded the Ceylon Social Reform Society, dedicated to the revival of Sinhalese and Tamil culture, and edited the *Ceylon National Review*, its principal means of expression. He also undertook research for a book on the pre-industrial, precolonial crafts of Ceylon, which he published in 1908 as *Mediaeval Sinhalese Art*. His English wife, Ethel, later to become a noted craftswoman, helped him extensively. By 1908, Coomaraswamy was no longer a geologist, but rather an Eastern William Morris, for it was this great Victorian craftsman, reformer, and socialist after whom Coomaraswamy modeled his actions and attitudes in this period. Even in the 1940's, when Coomaraswamy was much changed from his brash early years in Ceylon, he continued to express eloquently the views on art, industry, and the individual artist that Morris first proposed.

Coomaraswamy maintained a home in Broad Campden, England, near C. R. Ashbee's Guild and School of Handicraft at Chipping Campden. Although living in India for extended periods, he purchased from Ashbee the printing equipment of Essex House Press and established it in his own residence. Much of this equipment originally belonged to William Morris' Kelmscott Press. It was upon this hallowed press, in the company of some of Morris' former staff, that Coomaraswamy supervised the printing of *Mediaeval Sinhalese Art*.

In Calcutta and northward to the foothills of the Himalayas, in 1910-1914, Coomaraswamy investigated Indian painting and gathered his findings in his second major publication, *Rajput Painting* (1916). This book, which distinguished the Hindu art of Rajputana and the Punjab Hills from the Mogul art with which it had long been confused, further established Coomaraswamy's reputation as a pioneer of Indian art-historical scholarship, a field that had developed slowly and suffered from colonial prejudice until Roger Fry, E. B. Havell, Coomaraswamy, and others, in 1910, made a widely publicized reassessment of Indian art. But even at this point, Coomaraswamy was not only an art historian: his books *Myths of the Hindus and Buddhists* (1913) and *Buddha and the Gospel of Buddhism* (1916), well received upon publication and often reprinted, foreshadow the deeply religious writings of his later years.

Coomaraswamy became Keeper of Indian and Muhammadan Art at the Museum of Fine Arts, Boston, in 1917; he brought to the United States his vast collection of paintings, bronzes, and textiles, many of which were purchased for the museum by a leading patron, Denman W. Ross. One year later he published *The Dance of Shiva,* a series of essays on art, customs, religion, and erotic love in India, which more knowledgeably and gracefully than any similar literature of its time introduced Americans to Indian culture. Throughout the 1920's, however, Coomaraswamy's main concern was the scholarly interpretation of Indian art in monographs, articles, and catalogues that established new standards in his field.

Coomaraswamy was not a settled man until relatively late in life. By 1910 he had divorced his first wife and married an English singer of Indian songs, known on the stage as Ratan Devi. There were two children by this marriage, Narada and Rohini, but the union was ill-starred, and by 1922 they were divorced. In that year he married Stella Bloch, a beautiful and talented painter. This marriage was dissolved in 1930, at which time Coomaraswamy married Doña Luisa Runstein. They had a son, Rama, in 1932. The fourth Mrs. Coomaraswamy was the irreplaceable companion of his most creative period.

In the years 1929-1932, Coomaraswamy underwent a serious transformation. He immersed himself in the study of traditional metaphysics—that is to say, the spiritual traditions of Hinduism, Buddhism, Christianity, Islam, Platonism, Gnosticism, and the Kabbala. These traditions, and his intensive reflection upon them, were the basis of his writings in the period 1932-1947, which deal primarily with the philosophy of art and metaphysics, although also, and at length, with myth and folklore, the traditional theory of government, and conflicts between traditional and modern values. By prodigious work and intense inner transformation, he had achieved meticulous intellectuality and religious faith. His unique writings of this period have been somewhat neglected. While Coomaraswamy in his lifetime made a number of essay collections, the majority of his later essays have remained scattered in journals. This situation is currently being remedied by a publication program in the United States (perhaps to be joined by a similar program in India), which in 1974 will bring about the republication of more than seventy major essays on such diverse subjects as traditional Indian psychology, the concepts of divine play, transmigration, self-sacrifice, and numerous themes in the philosophy of art.

Through his essays, Coomaraswamy aimed at nothing short of the "re-education of the Western *literati*," as he once put it—reeducation to a point of view that makes the study of consciousness itself the preeminent concern, into which may be fitted all other studies both empirical and speculative. He believed that the structure of consciousness is authoritatively described in the scripture and commentary of many traditions, and that means are still available for man to understand himself in depth, and so free his energy for the Good. Since his writings are in part difficult to grasp, because of their abundance of quotation from ancient authors and their Scholastic terminology, he may never reach the masses; but this was rarely his intention. To seasoned, patient readers, he offers an inexhaustible knowledge of the traditional Indian view of art, metaphysics, psychology, and related subjects, presented in a literary style that varies from dispassionate exposition to ardent poetry.

Coomaraswamy died suddenly, from a heart attack, at his home in Needham, Mass., on Sept. 9, 1947. According to family custom, his ashes were scattered in the Ganges River.

[The principal biography of Coomaraswamy, in preparation by the present writer, will be published as *Signature and Significance: The Life and Writings of Ananda K. Coomaraswamy*; publication is expected in 1975. Meanwhile, much can be gleaned from S. Durai Raja Singam, ed., *Homage to Ananda Coomaraswamy, A Memorial Volume* (Kuala Lumpur, 1952), and from the film *The Dance of Shiva*, a study of Coomaraswamy and Indian art produced by Chidamanda Das Gupta under the auspices of the United States Information Agency (1974; available for showing only outside the United States). A good bibliography of Coomaraswamy's writings is in *Ars Islamica* IX, 1943. His major books include *The Transformation of Nature in Art* (1934), *Elements of Buddhist Iconography* (1935), *Why Exhibit Works of Art?* (1943), *Hinduism and Buddhism* (1943), *Figures of Speech or Figures of Thought* (1946), *Am I My Brother's Keeper?* (1947), *Time and Eternity* (1947).]
ROGER LIPSEY

COOPER, JOHN MONTGOMERY (Oct. 28, 1881-May 22, 1949), ethnologist and Roman Catholic priest, was born in Rockville, Md., the youngest of three sons of James Cooper and Lillie (Tolou) Cooper. His father, an employee of the Pennsylvania Railroad, was descended from James Cooper, an English Quaker who had immigrated to Pennsylvania in 1684. He was a Roman Catholic, as was his wife, who came of a French family that had settled in Baltimore in 1810. The Coopers lived comfortably in Baltimore. There, having early decided to become a priest, John prepared for seminary at Calvert Hall. In 1897, he entered St. Charles College, Ellicott City (later Catonsville), Md. In 1899 he went to North American College in Rome, where he received the Ph.D. from St. Thomas Academy (1902) and the S.T.D. from Propaganda College (1905). After ordination in Rome, June 17, he was called to St. Matthew's Church, Washington, D.C., as curate; he served until 1918.

Cooper approached his parochial tasks with great dedication and with the zest he had earlier had for boxing and tennis. Social services, such as hospital work and dealing with the problems of youth, were of major concern to him, but his broad intention was to arouse people to the importance of a point of view on social problems rather than to use these services as a laboratory for research in sociology.

In 1909 he added to his parish duties the teaching of religious education at the Catholic University of America. Here his approach was similar. Feeling that religious education should meet the needs of the laity, he stressed the importance of social action as an extension of Christian love. His *Religious Outlines for Colleges*, published later (4 vols., 1924-1930), were based on this conviction and, while they met with some opposition at first, they soon were adopted as standard texts. His last contribution to applied sociology, also influential in the field of social work, was *Children's Institutions* (1931).

In the meantime, his interest in European archaeology and American social problems coalesced with his increasing attention to cultural anthropology, which arose from camping trips to Canada, where he became acquainted with the life of the Algonquian tribes. Ethnological study at the Smithsonian Institution absorbed him in his spare time, and he was encouraged in his work by John Reed Swanton, Frederick W. Hodge, and Ales Hrdlicka. His first notable contribution to ethnology was his *Analytical and Critical Bibliography of the Indians of Tierra del Fuego* (1917). This study revealed the qualities common to all his work—mastery of scholarly techniques, lucidity of expression, and critical judgment.

In 1918 Cooper was appointed secretary of the National Committee of Women's Activities of the National Catholic War Council (later the National Catholic Welfare Conference). In this position he managed an elaborate nationwide program of social group work. In 1920 he became a full-time instructor in religion at Catholic University. Three years later he was named associate professor of anthropology in the university's department of sociology; he became professor in 1928 and, in 1934, chairman of the newly organized department of anthropology, where he served until his death. Cooper was also on the faculties of Trinity and Sisters colleges in Washington and was the founder and head (1930-1937) of Catholic University's graduate department of religion.

Although he contributed to several areas of anthropology, Cooper was primarily an ethnologist and ethnographer. His fieldwork was done mostly among the Algonquians of the woodlands and plains of North America and he wrote numerous papers on various aspects of their culture. His last full-length monograph, *The Gros Ventres of Montana*, Part 2, on religion and ritual, was published posthumously in 1957.

His theoretical interests led him to grapple with questions of distribution and historical reconstruction. Although by the 1940's the trend in American anthropology was away from such problems, Cooper's paper "Areal and Temporal Aspects of Aboriginal South American Culture" (1942), inspired the over-all arrangement of the *Handbook of South American Indians,* edited by Julian H. Steward (7 vols., 1946-1959), to which Cooper contributed ten articles. His historical approach is clearly presented in *Temporal Sequence and*

Marginal Culture (1941), which argued that nonliterate peoples of the present are "tarriers," relatively unchanged from their prehistoric cultural state. He presented several canons of historical reconstruction, which, however, he recognized could not "yield a total all-embracing reconstruction of prehistoric culture." Considering both distribution and genetic factors, he worked out tentative sequences of cultural development in certain relatively limited geographical areas and proceeded only so far as he felt the evidence warranted. He rejected what he considered the inflated generalizations of the Vienna Kulturkreis theory, which tried to reconstruct original primeval human culture. Cooper founded and edited several periodicals, including *Primitive Man* (retitled *Anthropological Quarterly* in 1953). He never shirked professional responsibility and played an active role in many organizations, such as the American Anthropological Association, of which he was president in 1940.

His religious beliefs and his priestly vocation completely penetrated his life. He never felt that they interfered in any way with his scientific attitude as an anthropologist. Both sides of Cooper's life were welded together in his lifelong dedication to social work, social hygiene, and racial justice. He wrote many papers on these subjects and presented his views before various organizations of which he was an active supporter, including the National Conference of Social Work, the National Probation Association, the National Conference of Catholic Charities, and the American Social Hygiene Association.

Cooper himself, in the words of R. H. Lowie, "radiated mental health, tolerance, humanitarianism. He had a keen sense of the ludicrous and was an admirable raconteur . . . and his praise was singularly generous and wholesouled for so critical an intelligence." Cooper was made a monsignor in 1941. He died of a coronary thrombosis in Washington at sixty-seven and was buried in Rock Creek Cemetery, Washington, D.C.

[Cooper's correspondence is in the archives of Catholic Univ. of Am.; unpublished field notes in the possession of the author; author's obituary of Cooper with anthropological bibliography and photograph in *Am. Anthropologist,* 52 (1950), 64-74; memorial issue of *Primitive Man,* 23, no. 3 (1950), 35-65, with complete bibliography of Cooper's writings and articles about him by Leopold H. Tibesar, Alfred Métraux, and Paul H. Furfey. See also R. H. Lowie in *Boletin bibliográfico de antropologia americana* (1949); William N. Fenton in *Jour. of the Washington Acad. of Sci.,* 40 (1950), 64; *Internat. Encyc. of the Soc. Sci.; Am. Catholic Who's Who,*

1944–1945; *Encyc. Britannica*; *New Catholic Encyc.*, 4 (1967), 298; and *Amer. Men of Sci.* Cooper collection of African, American, Oceanian, and Philippine ethnological specimens in the U.S. National Museum.]

REGINA FLANNERY-HERZFELD

COPLEY, IRA CLIFTON (Oct. 25, 1864-Nov. 2, 1947), Illinois public utility executive, newspaper publisher, and congressman, was born in Copley Township (named for his father), Knox County, Ill., the third of five surviving children and younger of two sons of Ira Birdsall Copley, a farmer, and Ellen Madeline (Whiting) Copley. His mother had moved west from Connecticut; his father, a descendant of colonial Massachusetts settlers, had migrated to Illinois in 1854 from his native New York state. When young Ira was blinded at the age of two by scarlet fever, his parents moved to Aurora, Ill., to be near an eye specialist. There the elder Copley became part owner and manager of the moribund Aurora Gas Light Company. The son regained some vision after four years of treatment, but it remained impaired for the rest of his life. After graduating from West Aurora High School (1881) and attending the town's Jennings Seminary (1881-1883), he entered Yale University, from which he received the B.A. degree in 1887. He then studied at the Union College of Law in Chicago, supporting himself by tutoring in history and mathematics, and was awarded the LL.B. degree in 1889.

Although admitted to the Illinois bar, Copley never practiced law. Shortly before graduation he was called home to help run his father's failing gas company. Copley revived the utility by marketing gas as a fuel instead of as an illuminant. Building on this success, he went on to acquire several other utilities in Illinois, merging them in 1905 into the Western United Gas and Electric Company, of which he became president. Over the next two decades he expanded his holdings through the purchase of additional gas and electric companies and streetcar lines, and in 1914 organized a firm to market coke and coal tars. His utilities empire was consolidated in 1921 into the Western United Corporation.

Meanwhile, Copley had also built parallel careers in publishing and politics. As early as 1894 he was a member of the Republican state central committee and a lieutenant colonel in the Illinois National Guard. "Colonel" Copley, as he became known, served on the State Park Commission (1894-1898) and as an aide on the staff of Gov. Charles S. Deneen (1905-1913). Copley purchased his first newspaper, the *Aurora Beacon*, in 1905; by 1913 he also owned papers in nearby Elgin and Joliet.

A longtime foe of United States Senator Albert J. Hopkins, an Aurora neighbor and owner of a rival newspaper, Copley opposed his reelection by the state legislature in 1909. The political boss William Lorimer was chosen instead, but was later unseated as a result of charges that the position had been bought. Unsubstantiated rumors that Copley was a party to the bribery failed to thwart his own political career, and in 1910 he was elected to the first of six consecutive terms in the federal House of Representatives. Politically liberal, he supported the Progressive presidential candidacy of Theodore Roosevelt in 1912, but ran as a Progressive himself only in 1914. In Congress, he introduced a bill to prevent the interstate shipment of goods produced by child labor, supported a graduated income tax and a national referendum on prohibition, and advocated the regulation of public utilities.

Copley was defeated for renomination in the Republican primary of 1922 by farm unrest and antiprohibition sentiment, and thereafter returned to his business ventures. In 1926, after a long struggle for dominance in Illinois with the utilities magnate Samuel Insull, he sold his interest in the Western United Corporation to two investment firms. He was restless in retirement, however, and two years later, at the age of sixty-three, he bought up twenty-four newspapers in southern California, including the *San Diego Union* and the *San Diego Evening Tribune*, at a cost of $7.5 million. To oversee the finances of these journals he established the Copley Press, Inc., serving as president (1928-1942) and chairman (1942-1947); in 1939 his Illinois papers were brought into the corporation.

Copley's business career was guided by the principle that the safest investment is a monopoly serving many customers so well that it discourages competition. In applying this principle to journalism, he hastened the spread of newspaper monopolies. He preferred to operate in small and medium-sized cities; by the time of his death all his papers, except for those in San Diego, were in one-publisher cities. Copley was one of the few men to find the key to successful management of a large group of newspapers. Recognizing that each paper and each community has a distinct identity, he refused to do what he called mass thinking for his chain. He gave his publishers considerable autonomy and insisted that they publish all local news impartially. Thus Copley, who lacked editorial background, transferred managerial techniques from one industry to another.

Slight of build, with angular features, and always fashionably dressed, Copley was a complex man, friendly but formal, tolerant but authoritative. He contributed generously to several philanthropic causes, including the Wilmer Ophthalmological Institute at Johns Hopkins University and the Copley (later Copley Memorial) Hospital in Aurora. Reared as a Unitarian, he became a member of Aurora's Trinity Episcopal Church. Copley was married twice: on Mar. 3, 1892, to Edith Strohn of Los Angeles, who died in 1929; and in Paris, France, on Apr. 27, 1931, to Mrs. Chloe (Davidson) Worley, whom he had known in Aurora. Three children by Copley's first marriage died in infancy, and he later adopted two sons: James Strohn in 1920, who succeeded his father as head of the Copley Press, and William Nelson in 1921. He also had a stepdaughter, Eleanor Worley. Copley died of arteriosclerotic heart disease at Copley Hospital and was buried in Spring Lake Cemetery, Aurora.

[The only extensive source is Walter S. J. Swanson, *The Thin Gold Watch: A Personal Hist. of the Newspaper Copleys* (1964). There is a richly detailed, noneulogistic obituary in the *San Diego Union*, Nov. 3, 1947; other obituaries are either uninformative or inaccurate. See also Yale Univ., *Obituary Record of Graduates*, 1947–1948; and *Nat. Cyc. Am. Biog.*, XXXVI, 118–119.]

OLIVER KNIGHT

CORT, EDWIN CHARLES (Mar. 14, 1879-Jan. 10, 1950), Presbyterian medical missionary to Thailand, was born in Rochelle, Ill., the son of Joseph and Martha (Shaw) Cort. He attended Washington and Jefferson College, Washington, Pa., receiving the B.A. in 1901 and the M.A. in 1904. He graduated from the Johns Hopkins Medical School in 1907. Cort then applied to the Board of Foreign Missions of the Presbyterian Church in the U.S.A. and was appointed to the Thailand Mission in March 1908; he sailed in September. Mabel Gilson, of Zanesville, Ohio, was already in service in the mission, and she and Cort were married on Sept. 26, 1910.

The Corts were sent to the Lao country of northern Thailand and resided the first two years at Lampang and the second two at Prae. In 1914 Cort assumed control of McCormick Hospital in Chiengmai when James McKean decided to devote himself exclusively to leprosy work. This was to be Cort's assignment until retirement. Cort developed McCormick into a fully equipped, up-to-date hospital. The most

noted and influential foreign medical expert in Thailand, he was held in complete confidence by the government health service and had great influence with its officers. He directed many young Thai students to the Johns Hopkins Medical School and retained close contacts with them on their return to Thailand.

Medical education was a major concern of Dr. Cort. He began a medical school at Prince Royal's College in 1916 with the assistance of McKean and Claude Mason. Four men were graduated and licensed as M.D.'s by the Thai government, but the school was then discontinued because the government expanded the Royal Medical College in Bangkok. Nurses rarely served in the provinces and Cort founded the McCormick School for Nurses in 1923, the first such school outside the capital. The relocation and rebuilding of McCormick Hospital further contributed to the development of health care resources. The new hospital was formally opened on Feb. 13, 1925, by Prince Mahidol, heir-apparent to the throne. The prince had received his M.D. from Harvard University, and in 1927 he joined the hospital as an intern and resided with the Corts. He died before completing his internship, but his association with the hospital gave it great prestige in the minds of the people. A building was erected by the prince of Chiengmai in gratitude for Cort's personal care of the Princess Dara, his mother and a wife of King Chulalongkorn. Cort made friends with royalty, but he just as genuinely made friends and identified with the peasants of the countryside and the poor of the city. In addition to supervision of McCormick Hospital Dr. Cort took charge of the leprosarium whenever Dr. McKean was on leave, including the long period of 1915-1918. So thoroughly was Cort known and revered throughout the northern region that the popular name for him was *Phor Lieng* (foster-father).

When the Japanese troops occupied the country during World War II, Thailand was forced to join the Axis. Cort forestalled seizure of the hospital by the Japanese in 1941 by turning the institution over to the Thai government. He, his wife, and the other American missionaries fled across the border into Burma, and then went on into India. The Corts spent three years at Fatehgarh, where the doctor took charge of the hospital, raised funds for a new maternity ward, three child-health centers, and a nurses' dormitory. He also expanded the school for nurses.

Cort went to the United States to prepare for return at the earliest date and attack the health problems brought on by the war. He arranged with Church World Service for supplies and an emergency system of relief. He returned in April 1946 with a huge supply of drugs, as medical director of Church World Service for the country. Once again malaria was the principal scourge; and, employing the governmental agencies and the scores of doctors and nurses he had trained or aided, he set up a system which administered atabrine to 350,000 persons. The health of these people was so improved that they were able to bring in the rice harvest which had been expected to be lost. The government, through Prince Wan Waithayakon, presented a jeweled plaque to Church World Service. The government in this period also turned back to the Presbyterian Mission seven hospitals which it had held during the war years, and Cort rehabilitated them. He also began plans for a new Bangkok Christian Hospital.

Cort was a fellow of the American College of Physicians, the American College of Surgeons, and the Royal Society of Tropical Medicine. He contributed much to the knowledge of tropical medicine.

When the Corts retired in 1949 and returned to America, they were showered with honors and tributes in the Chiengmai area and in Bangkok. The king had bestowed on Dr. Cort in 1927 the honor of knight of the Order of the Crown for distinguished service in medicine, and now the king presented him with the highest honor, the Most Exalted Order of the White Elephant. Even though retired, he still kept busy with medicine—engaged in work at the Veterans' Hospital at Ft. Belvoir, Va. Dr. Cort died at Alexandria, Va. His wife died March 15, 1955.

[Kenneth E. Well, *History of Protestant Work in Thailand, 1828–1958;* Foreign Missions Arch. in the Presbyterian Historical Soc., Philadelphia; and Memorial Minute Adopted by the Presbyterian Board of Foreign Missions, Jan. 20, 1950.]

R. PIERCE BEAVER

CORTISSOZ, ROYAL (Feb. 10, 1869–Oct. 17, 1948), art critic, was born in Brooklyn, N.Y., apparently the only child of Francisco Emanuel and Julia da Costa (Mauri) Cortissoz. His father, although of Spanish descent, was a native of England who had immigrated to Brooklyn around 1855. His mother had come to America from Martinique. Cortissoz attended public schools in Brooklyn and sometime between 1883 and 1885 went to work at the firm of McKim, Mead, and White, architects, in

New York City, where his father may have been employed. A precocious writer from the age of fourteen, when he began to write weekly letters to a Kansas City newspaper, Cortissoz published his first article on art in January 1886, shortly before his eighteenth birthday. During the period of his employment with the architectural firm Cortissoz traveled to Italy with McKim, where they chose works in the Vatican sculpture gallery to be reproduced in plaster for display at the Chicago World's Fair in 1893. Cortissoz later wrote that McKim had played a significant role in his art education, and certainly the architect's commitment to the eclectic continuation of the classical tradition had a decisive influence on the formation of Cortissoz's tastes.

Cortissoz remained with McKim, Mead, and White until 1889 or 1890 and then accepted a position as an art critic on the *New York Commercial Advertiser.* In 1891 he became the art critic on the *New York Tribune,* a position he held for fifty-three years. In the 1890's, in addition to his newspaper work, he contributed articles regularly to *Harper's* and *Century* on such topics as the National Academy of Design and the American Academy in Rome. On June 1, 1897, he was married in London to Ellen MacKay Hutchinson, the literary editor of the *Tribune.* They had no children. Cortissoz and his wife shared the literary editorship of the newspaper from the time of their marriage until 1912 or 1913, and during this period he produced his first two books, *Augustus Saint-Gaudens* (1907) and *John La Farge: A Memoir and a Study* (1911). In these books Cortissoz praised both artists for their intelligent use of the classical tradition, and indeed he was able to understand their works fully, because they are as much a part of the Renaissance revival era in American taste as are the buildings of McKim, Mead, and White.

But after the sudden and definitive turning away from all aspects of the Renaissance tradition that was caused by the exhibition of Postimpressionist and Cubist works at the Armory Show of 1913, Cortissoz became an adversary of contemporary developments. He was unable to abandon the idea that art is an imitation of nature, and so in *Art and Common Sense* (1913), he wrongly described Van Gogh and Cézanne as Impressionists who had failed to achieve sufficiently naturalistic effects. Unbending in his resistance to modernism, Cortissoz continued throughout his life to attack the mainstream of twentieth-century art while praising the old masters and artists such as

George De Forest Brush and Paul Manship, who continued to adhere to the Renaissance idea of beauty.

Although Cortissoz had been elected to membership in the National Institute of Arts and Letters in 1908, it was not until the mid-1920's that he began to receive a steady stream of official and academic acknowledgments. In 1924 he was elected to membership in the American Academy of Arts and Letters and was appointed to the board of directors in 1930. In 1925 he was made an honorary fellow of the Metropolitan Museum of Art and in 1928 was elected to honorary membership in the American Institute of Architects. He received two honorary doctorates: from Wesleyan in 1927 and from Bowdoin in 1942. The 1920's and 1930's were also Cortissoz's most prolific period as an author. In 1923 he published *American Artists,* followed by *Personalities in Art* (1925), *The Painter's Craft* (1930), *Guy Pène du Bois* (1931), *Arthur B. Davies* (1932), *An Introduction to the Mellon Collection* (1937), and *The Works of Edwin Howland Blashfield* (1937). Cortissoz's wife, who had long been an invalid, died on August 13, 1933.

In December 1941 M. Knoedler and Co. held a loan exhibition of paintings in its gallery in honor of Cortissoz's fifty years as critic on the *Tribune.* The works for the show were chosen by Cortissoz himself; among them were favorite old master paintings by Botticelli, Rembrandt, Velasquez, and Vermeer, and American works by Whistler, La Farge, Sargent, and Bellows. Cortissoz continued to write regularly for the *Tribune* until 1944 when heart trouble caused his retirement. He died of heart failure in his home on Oct. 17, 1948. After an Episcopal service at the Church of the Ascension, he was buried at Woodlawn Cemetery in New York.

Cortissoz developed his principles of art criticism in the last decade of the nineteenth century, a decade during which he steeped himself in Gibbon's *Decline and Fall of the Roman Empire.* In a letter to Van Wyck Brooks he cited another nineteenth-century British writer, Matthew Arnold, as "the critic whom I regard as my own spiritual ancestor." Cortissoz looked to works of art not only for evidences of sound technique, intelligence, beauty, and refinement, but also for qualities of morality and character. It is in this respect that what he himself called his "Victorian temperament" shows itself most clearly in his criticism. Although Cortissoz's blindness to the values of modern art and the dogmatism of his attacks upon it are serious

flaws in his thinking, they by no means completely nullify his achievement. His narrowness may have reinforced the public's fear and distrust of modernism, but most of his long career was devoted to educating the public to the virtues of the old masters of the Renaissance and their tradition. Prolific and articulate, his impact on art education was probably a good deal broader than that of his friend Bernard Berenson, even if not quite so profound.

[The richest source of primary material on Cortissoz is the Royal Cortissoz Collect. of Letters, Yale Collect. of Am. Literature, Beinecke Rare Book and Manuscript Lib., Yale Univ. The collection consists of a great number of letters to and from Cortissoz, a small number of autobiographical notes, and a pamphlet and clipping file. Cortissoz's collection of scrapbooks as well as some loose clippings and reproductions are in the Arch. of Am. Art, Smithsonian Institution, Washington, D.C. Books by Cortissoz not mentioned in the text are *Life of Whitelaw Reid* (1921), *Nine Holes of Golf* (1922), and *The N.Y. Tribune* (1923). Some of the more interesting introductions written by Cortissoz were for *The Autobiog. of Benvenuto Cellini* (1906), *Don Quixote* (1906–1907), and *The Work of Charles A. Platt* (1913). The most complete discussions of his criticism can be found in Milton W. Brown's *American Painting from the Armory Show to the Depression* (1955) and *The Story of the Armory Show* (1963). Among the most detailed articles on his life and activities are *Time,* Mar. 10, 1930, *Newsweek,* Dec. 8, 1941, and *Nat. Cyc. Am. Biog.,* XXXVI, 549. Lengthy obituary notices appeared in the *N.Y. Times* and the *N.Y. Herald Tribune* on Oct. 18, 1948. M. Knoedler and Co. published a catalogue on the occasion of the fiftieth anniversary show that contains an introductory statement by Cortissoz as well as numerous reproductions of his favorite works. An oil painting of Cortissoz by Louis Betts is reproduced on the cover of *Art Digest,* May 1, 1944.]

JOHN H. BAKER

COTTRELL, FREDERICK GARDNER (Jan. 10, 1877–Nov. 16, 1948), physical chemist and inventor, was born in Oakland, Calif., the younger of two surviving sons of Henry and Cynthia L. (Durfee) Cottrell. Both parents were descended from English families that had settled in Rhode Island in the seventeenth century. The father had begun in the shipping business in New York, probably as a clerk, but in 1873 moved to San Francisco, where at the time of the boy's birth he was the paid secretary of the Union Club; he later worked for an oil company. A talented amateur photographer who developed and printed his own plates, he probably helped stimulate his son's later interest in chemistry. The mother's difficult personality led to an estrangement from her sons, and the household was managed by her older sister, Mary. Both "Aunt Mame" and Frederick's father encouraged the boy's enthusiasm for hobbies that included photography, electricity, telegraphy, job printing, and publishing a weekly newspaper, the *Boys' Workshop.* The intensity and diversity of these childhood interests were characteristic of Cottrell's later life as well.

After two years in the Oakland high school, he was admitted, by examination, to the University of California at Berkeley, where he completed the course requirements in three years and received the B.S. degree in 1896. Because of his outstanding work in chemistry and physics he was awarded a Le Conte Fellowship for a fourth year at the university. Three years of teaching chemistry at the Oakland high school enabled him to finance further graduate work in Germany. Convinced that the richest opportunity for fundamental new developments in science lay in the ill-defined border between two established disciplines, he chose the relatively new field of physical chemistry. He worked first (1900) under Jacob Henry van't Hoff in Berlin and the following year under Wilhelm Ostwald in Leipzig; he received the Ph.D. degree from Leipzig in 1902, summa cum laude, with a dissertation on the problem of determining diffusion rates of salts in solution by the use of electrolytic cells.

Returning to the United States in the autumn of 1902, Cottrell accepted a fellowship at Harvard and began studying under Theodore Richards; but, finding himself in a state of lassitude and irresolution, he resigned after a few weeks and returned to the University of California to become instructor in physical chemistry (1902–1906) and later assistant professor (1906-1911). As a teacher, Cottrell inspired his students with much of his own enthusiasm for research, but he sometimes overwhelmed them by the proliferation of his ideas. Similarly, in later years, scientists working under Cottrell's direction complained of his laying out a lifetime of research in a few minutes of consultation.

In 1905 Cottrell began studying ways of dealing with the corrosive fumes—particularly sulfuric acid—emitted by chemical and smelting plants in the vicinity of San Francisco Bay. By 1907 he was able to apply for a patent on a method that used electrical precipitation to dispose of the noxious particles in dust and smoke. Essentially, his technique involved passing a high-voltage direct current through a conductor or electrode from which the charge leaked, carrying the particulate matter with it, to the neighboring electrode. The deposited matter, in some installations, could be retrieved as valuable minerals or chemical compounds. To obtain financial backing for continuing and applying this research, Cottrell and a few associates

formed the International Precipitation Company. Over the next few decades his inventions found many commercial applications and reduced pollution from chemical plants and smelters. Cottrell also adapted the precipitation process to dehydrate petroleum. His patents covering the separation and collection of liquid and solid particles from gases and liquids proved extremely valuable.

Cottrell had a deep conviction, however, that the results of research should be used for the public good, not for private profit. He demonstrated the strength of this belief when in 1912 he created a nonprofit organization, the Research Corporation, and, with the consent of his associates, turned over to it all his patents. Administered by a distinguished board of directors who served without fee, the corporation used the income from its patents to support further research and the practical application of that research to benefit mankind. Over the years the corporation gave basic aid to such important projects as Ernest O. Lawrence's pioneer investigations of atomic nuclei, the development by Lawrence and others of the cyclotron, and Robert J. van de Graaff's development of the electrostatic generator. It also helped support the production of cortisone by Edward C. Kendall of the Mayo Clinic, and the synthesis of vitamin B_1 by Robert R. Williams and his associates. Patents derived from some of these and other projects were assigned to the Research Corporation, as Cottrell had hoped would be the case. By 1952, forty years after its founding, the corporation's annual grants were approximately $900,000.

Cottrell's strong interest in applied science led him to resign his professorship in 1911 in order to organize and administer the San Francisco office of the federal Bureau of Mines. In 1916 he was named the bureau's chief metallurgist and moved to Washington, D.C. During World War I he was one of a number of scientists and engineers who contributed to the development of a commercial process for the cheap production of helium for use in dirigibles. Newspapers, to his discomfort, exaggerated his role in the project, which brought a sensational reduction of the price of helium from $1,700 to one cent per cubic foot. Cottrell served for eight months in 1920 as temporary director of the Bureau of Mines, and then resigned to become salaried chairman (1921-1922) of the Division of Chemistry and Chemical Technology of the National Research Council. He then returned to government service as director of the Fixed Nitrogen Research Laboratory of the Department of Agriculture, where he directed the development of improved catalysts for the Haber-Bosch process and contributed to the utilization in the United States of this German technique for cheaply producing fertilizer. He resigned from the Agriculture Department in 1930 in order to take a more active part in the affairs of the Research Corporation. In all these positions he accepted a salary about one-fourth of what he could have earned in industry, but he chose work that he believed contributed most to the public welfare.

Cottrell was memorable for his eccentricities (he occasionally wore several pairs of dime-store glasses simultaneously), but even more so for his restless energy. Although intervals of nervous depression or ill health plagued him throughout his life, he always retained his enthusiasm for research and his dedication to social and scientific goals. Through his nitrogen research he became involved in the disposition of the government's wartime nitrogen plants at Muscle Shoals, Tenn., and the associated Wilson Dam; he greatly influenced the character of the legislation introduced by Sen. George W. Norris that set up the Tennessee Valley Authority in 1933. In an address to the Western Society of Engineers in 1937, when it presented to him the Washington Award for his social vision, Cottrell urged engineers to leave private corporations and associate themselves with enterprises, exemplified by his own Research Corporation, in which the profit motive could be subordinated to concern for social utility and improved working conditions. Another of his commitments was the promotion of international cooperation, especially by means of the international language Esperanto. Some of Cottrell's colleagues thought his interests spread too wide and his focus and concentration shifted too often.

Cottrell's work, nonetheless, won a variety of honors, including two awards in chemistry, the Perkin Medal (1919) and the Willard Gibbs Medal (1920). The American Society of Mechanical Engineers gave him its Holley Medal in 1937. Somewhat tardily, in 1939 the National Academy of Sciences elected him a member. In 1940 the National Association of Manufacturers named him as one of nineteen great American pioneers of invention.

Cottrell married Jessie Mae Fulton, a college classmate, on Jan. 1, 1904. Their only two children died at birth. If some of the burden of Cottrell's idealism—his lack of interest in wealth, his ceaseless work—at times fell upon his wife, it was because, as he once wrote, "I

. . . don't feel the ties of kinship in as forceful a way, compared to the ties of humanity as a whole, as many people" (Cameron, p. 175). The couple moved in 1944 from Washington to Palo Alto, Calif., where in spite of poor health Cottrell continued to work on problems of nitrogen fixation. He died of a coronary thrombosis at the age of seventy-one while attending a meeting of the National Academy of Sciences in Berkeley. His remains were cremated. A grove of California redwoods was dedicated to his memory.

[Frank Cameron, Cottrell: Samaritan of Science (1952), is a detailed biography that covers both his scientific and organizational activities and his character and personal relationships. See also Vannevar Bush in Nat. Acad. Sci., Biog. Memoirs, XXVII (1952), with a bibliography of Cottrell's writings; Farrington Daniels in Am. Philosophical Soc., Year Book, 1950; and three articles by Cottrell: "The Social Responsibility of the Engineer," Science, June 4, 11, 1937—the fullest account of his views on technology and society; "The Research Corporation, an Experiment in Public Administration of Patent Rights," Jour. of Industrial and Engineering Chemistry, Dec. 1912; and "Electrical Precipitation: Hist. Sketch," Am. Inst. of Electrical Engineers, Trans., 34, pt. 1 (1915): 387–396.]

THOMAS PARKE HUGHES

COUTARD, HENRI (Apr. 27, 1876–Mar. 16, 1950), radiologist, was born in Marolles-les-Braults, Sarthe, France, the son of Louis Coutard and Mélanie Marie Joséphine (Ragot) Coutard, both from neighboring agricultural villages. After finishing high school in Caen, Coutard entered the medical school of the University of Paris, graduating in 1902. Because he had developed pulmonary tuberculosis, he settled in a town in the Jura Mountains, where he practiced general medicine for several years and became an enthusiastic alpinist and skier. Having regained his health, he returned in 1912 to Paris and began research with radium at an experimental laboratory in Gif, a Paris suburb. During World War I he served in a radiological ambulance unit on the Eastern Front.

In 1919 Coutard joined the Radium Institute of the University of Paris, as chief of the X-ray department. His work first attracted attention at the International Congress of Oto-Rhino-Laryngology in Paris in 1921, where, with Claude Regaud, he reported the cases of six patients with advanced carcinoma of the larynx, which had been controlled by means of X radiation. This marked the beginning of the acceptance of roentgen therapy as a primary method of treatment, rather than a method to be used only when no other choice remained. Coutard was the first to publish on the diagnostic X-ray examination of the larynx; he constructed a photometric radiometer to improve the measurements of dosage; and he coined the term "radio-epithelitis" for the reaction observed during irradiation of a mucosa. Perhaps his most important contribution was teaching a generation of radiologists to observe their patients carefully and to record painstakingly the clinical course of treatment. Coutard was a pioneer in the practical application of the time-dose relationship in radiotherapy, known as fractionation or the protracted fractional method—the dividing of a given amount of radiation into several smaller doses administered at intervals of several days so as to allow recovery of the skin and mucosa—which came to be known as "Coutard's method." Coutard did not believe in rigid rules and never published any rigid standards for administering radiation, which he adjusted according to each patient's reaction.

During a tour of the United States in 1935, Coutard took part in a round-table discussion of radiotherapy at a meeting of the American College of Surgeons in San Francisco and was invited to give the McArthur Lecture before the Institute of Medicine in Chicago. Two years later he resigned his position in Paris and came to the United States. He worked for a short time with Robert A. Millikan at the California Institute of Technology, studying the use of high-voltage therapy, and then took up his post at the Chicago Tumor Institute, a short-lived institution founded by the histopathologist Max Cutler. There for the next three years Coutard carried on research, worked on the use of brief, concentrated radiation in treating carcinoma of the larynx, and taught well-attended graduate courses. During this period, on the invitation of his patient Spencer Penrose (who had installed an X-ray machine in his own home), he spent some time in Colorado Springs, treating Penrose for throat cancer. After Penrose's death in 1939 and the establishment of the Penrose Cancer Hospital (later the Glockner-Penrose Hospital), Coutard moved in 1941 to Colorado Springs as its first radiotherapist, although he had never obtained a license to practice in this country.

Meanwhile, however, a marked change had occurred in the direction of Coutard's professional interests, perhaps initiated by marital problems and a crisis in his personal life. After moving to Colorado he published no papers, seemed to have lost faith in accepted methods of radiation therapy, and devoted himself almost entirely to research that his medical associates regarded as strange. Those projects included X-ray filtration experiments that involved the use of a block of gold and slabs of aluminum, and the timing of irradiation to coincide with the height of the growth cycle of tumor cells. He postulated an extracellular antimitogenetic factor that confers radioresistance to neoplastic cells, contended that X rays could potentiate or even re-create the antimitogenetic factor, and insisted that patients having tumors with well-differentiated cells be treated with homeopathic doses of low-energy beta rays. Coutard's relations with the medical staff deteriorated, and he was finally asked to resign.

On Mar. 25, 1919, Coutard married Anne-Marie Adèle Rougier; they had no children. After her death in 1940, he married Suzanne Rosalie (Mathot) Jourgeon, the widow of a former patient. She died in France in 1949. That same year Coutard returned to France and published a book presenting the results of his experimental work in Colorado Springs. A rambling mixture of clinical observations, working hypotheses, and fantastic assumptions, the book was ignored by the medical journals and led some colleagues to doubt Coutard's sanity. Nevertheless, he journeyed to Copenhagen and enlisted the support of a former pupil, the radiotherapist Jens Nielsen, in arranging for clinical tests of his hypotheses. On the return flight, Coutard suffered a cerebral hemorrhage; he died a few months later at the home of his sister in Le Mans.

[Obituaries by Juan A. del Regato in *Radiology*, May 1950, and *Cancer*, May 1950; by François Baclesse in *Jour. de radiologies et d'électrologie*, 31 (1950): 475; and by Jean Lavedan in *Paris médical* 40 (1950): 345; Coutard's published papers (which number about thirty-five) and his book, *Aperçus roentgenthérapiques relatifs à divers modes d'involution cancéreuse, et méthodes de protection* (1949); conversations with Franz Buschke of San Francisco, Max Cutler of Beverly Hills, Calif., Stewart Harrison of Pasadena, James Wallace McMullen and Juan del Regato of Colorado Springs, and Edris Dale Trout of Corvallis, Oreg.; birth record from town of Marolles-les-Braults.]

E. R. N. GRIGG

COWL, JANE (Dec. 14, 1883–June 22, 1950), actress, playwright, director, and commentator, was born Grace Bailey in Boston, Mass. She was the daughter of Charles A. and Grace (Avery) Bailey. She reportedly characterized her family as "New England for generations" and herself as "an only child of only children." Her father, a native of Lowell, Mass., was identified variously as a provision dealer and a clerk and her mother, from Albany, N.Y., as a singer and a voice teacher. The family moved to Brooklyn, N.Y., when the girl was about three years old. She described her parents as very poor; however, her mother, whom she adored, took her to plays and concerts whenever possible.

Two years at Erasmus Hall topped off education in the public schools of Brooklyn. During the early days of her acting career (trying Cowles as a professional surname before settling for Cowl), she also attended classes at Columbia University.

In a civil ceremony June 18, 1906, Miss Cowl married Adolph E. Klauber (1869-1933), then drama critic of the *New York Times*. Later he joined Selwyn and Co. in producing many of the plays in which she appeared, and he acted as her personal manager. They had no children.

From May to August of 1907 she took her first European vacation, bicycling much to conserve funds. After achieving stardom, she vacationed abroad frequently—in the grand manner.

Jane Cowl never hesitated to take a stand and speak out on issues of the day, especially theatre issues. She served as vice-president of Actors Equity Association in 1927. With Selena Royal she founded and labored unstintingly at New York's Stage Door Canteen during World War II.

She died in Santa Monica, Calif., at age sixty-six, two weeks after an operation for cancer. Gregory Peck read the eulogy at her Episcopalian funeral service. She was buried in Valhalla Memorial Park, Burbank. Although she had earned fabulous sums, she had spent lavishly and given much away. Her effects, when auctioned, yielded $1,499.

Jane Cowl made her acting debut in December 1903 at Belasco's theatre in New York, as a walk-on in *Sweet Kitty Bellairs*, which starred Henrietta Crosman. She eagerly continued in bit parts, supporting one or another of Belasco's big names: David Warfield in *The Music Master* and *A Grand Army Man*, Frances Starr in *The Easiest Way* and *Rose of the Rancho*. Belasco, the mentor who influenced her most, rewarded her zeal in 1909 with her first major role, Fanny Perry in *Is Matrimony a Failure?* Critics welcomed the beautiful young comedienne, who shrewdly sharpened her skills by continuing to play one leading role after another—albeit during summers in the Hudson Theatre stock company of Union Hill, N.J. The plays, frequently ones seen in New York during the previous decade (*Her Own Way, Merely Mary Ann, Paid in Full*), provided varied and invaluable experience.

Leaving the Belasco fold, she began the 1910-1911 season in *The Upstart,* followed by *The Gamblers.* With her portrayal of the lead in the latter, a Charles Klein play, critics noted

an extension to her range: Jane Cowl could play serious drama as well as light. In the 1912-1913 season, as the wronged shopgirl of Bayard Veiller's *Within the Law,* she saw her name go up in lights above the title outside the Eltinge Theatre. The melodrama ran for 541 performances and spawned numerous road companies. Melodrama also provided her second starring vehicle and another success when in 1915 she played Ellen Neal in *Common Clay,* a Harvard prize play by Cleves Kinkead.

The year 1917 brought Jane Cowl two firsts: she appeared in a film, *The Spreading Dawn,* made in Fort Lee, N.J., and she co-authored, with Jane Murfin, a friend from her Belasco days, the highly successful *Lilac Time.* The Selwyns produced the war play February 6 at the Republic Theatre. Miss Cowl starred as Jeannine in the 176 New York performances and toured the production throughout the country to great acclaim.

In the next two seasons, the Cowl and Murfin team wrote a moderate success, *Daybreak,* for which Miss Cowl shared staging chores with Wilfred North, and *Information Please,* which survived only briefly, despite her own appearance in it as Lady Betty Desmond.

In the season of 1918-1919 Edgar Selwyn and Channing Pollack's *The Crowded Hour* provided her with a rewarding role, but Cowl herself, again with Miss Murfin, furnished the next of her top successes by fashioning the dual heroine Moonyean Clare and Kathleen Dungannon of *Smilin' Through.* Her "hauntingly beautiful" performance took New York by storm on next to the last day of 1919. The program listed the dramatist as Alan Langdon Martin, a pseudonym the ladies had adopted, suspecting that their previous disaster had resulted from sex discrimination.

Extended success sent Jane Cowl scurrying after new worlds to conquer. In the fall of 1922 she tried the title role of Malvoloca in a play by the Quintero brothers, with Rollo Peters as her leading man—an alliance that would endure. Not daunted by failure of the piece, she next threw in her lot with Shakespeare and triumphed with *Romeo and Juliet* from coast to coast in both byways and metropolises. In New York alone, with Peters as her Romeo and scenery designer, she racked up a record of 157 performances—this after Ethel Barrymore had failed as Juliet a month earlier. Critics spoke of "a miraculous vibrant production," "palpitant with life," "the greatest in memory." They looked for her to emerge as the premiere American actress of the decade.

Pushing on into uncharted seas, Jane Cowl next essayed Maeterlinck's *Pelleas and Melisande* (1923) and saw it pronounced dull and dreary. Back to Shakespeare, but nothing could please about *Antony and Cleopatra* (1924). Skirmishes with *The Depths* and *One Trip of the Silver Star* (both 1925) led nowhere.

Noel Coward's *Easy Virtue* came to the rescue. From a New York opening at the Empire in late December 1925, Miss Cowl as Larita moved triumphantly to a June 1926 opening at the Duke of York in London.

Returning to the United States in the fall, she tried vaudeville, then scored again early in 1927 as Amytis, the Roman lady who "conquered" Hannibal in Robert Sherwood's romp, *The Road to Rome.*

Indifferent and adverse reactions to *The Jealous Moon* (her own script), *Jenny,* and *Paolo and Francesca* preceded another major adventure. She threw herself into an attempt to revive repertory in the fall of 1930 by acting Cecilia in *Art and Mrs. Bottle* and Viola in *Twelfth Night,* and by designing an ingenious setting for the latter.

She tried out half a dozen scripts in as many cities before finding another long-lived vehicle, George Kaufman and Katherine Dayton's social satire, *First Lady.* Infusing Lucy Chase Wayne with her own charm and shrewdness at New York's Music Box in 1935, she later swept across the country for thirty-three and a half weeks, receiving a real-life First Lady's kind of attention.

She came back to New York in the waning days of 1938 to try Mrs. Levi of Thornton Wilder's *The Merchant of Yonkers* in a Max Reinhardt production which expired after five weeks.

In December 1940—thirty-seven years to the month after her first New York appearance—Jane Cowl opened as Katherine Markham in her last respectable box office draw, John Van Druten's *Old Acquaintance.* After touring in it she returned to New York November 17, 1941, for a disappointing ten-performance run of *Ring Around Elizabeth.*

In standard theatres and summer theatres around the country, she gamely experimented with a variety of scripts, often directing as well as acting in them. Revivals figured prominently among her efforts, including two Shaw titles, *Captain Brassbound's Conversion* and *Candida.* In 1943 she appeared in her first movie since 1917, playing herself in *Stage Door Canteen.* By 1949 she agreed to move to the West Coast to try her hand seriously at films.

She was assigned only featured roles in indifferent scripts such as *Once More, My Darling; The Lie; The Secret Fury.*

Jane Cowl, who played upward of fifty roles, was first and last a stage luminary in the great tradition, faultlessly theatrical on- or offstage. Her beauty—dark lustrous eyes, a fine figure—and a full-toned, well-modulated voice contributed to her magnetism and allure. Capricious, vain, and sometimes selfish, she often created pandemonium; yet she was liked by her colleagues and admired by the public. Her unerring dramatic instincts, inquiring mind, quick imagination, and conscientious industry moved her to the forefront of professional American actors at a time of staggering robustness in the theatre. The decade of her steadiest achievement, the 1920's, bristled with potent rivals for attention. In the year of her legendary Juliet alone, the Moscow Art Theatre visited, John Barrymore created his immortal Hamlet, and Jeanne Eagels swaggered through *Rain,* to name only three competitors. But Jane Cowl earned and held a position in the front rank, a totally committed leading lady.

[The New York Public Lib. Manuscript Div. and Theatre Collect., Lib. of Performing Arts, contain her diary, biographical and autobiographical notes, including a substantial typescript fragment of a book dictated to Frank Morse, legal documents, correspondence, clippings, photographs, programs, publicity releases, scrapbooks, and scripts. Jane Cowl, "Jane Cowl's Story," *Delineator,* Apr. 1924; Basil Dean, *Seven Ages* (1970); Crosby Gaige, *Footlights and Highlights* (1948); Tyrone Guthrie, *A Life in the Theatre* (1959); Ward Morehouse, *Matinee Tomorrow* (1949).]
CLARA M. BEHRINGER

COWLES, GARDNER (Feb. 28, 1861-Feb. 28, 1946), newspaper publisher, was born in Oskaloosa, Iowa, to Rev. William Fletcher Cowles (pronounced "Coles"), a Methodist clergyman, and his first wife, Maria Elizabeth LaMonte. He had an older brother and two half sisters by his father's second marriage. William Cowles, born in Detroit, Mich., of Puritan-Covenanter lineage, was twice appointed a collector of internal revenue in Iowa by President Lincoln. Gardner's mother, a teacher and a descendant of Richard Gardner, who crossed on the *Mayflower,* came of a family of northeast Iowa pioneers. She died when the boy was twelve. Reared in a home of piety and thrift where "idleness was akin to sin," Cowles worked his way through public school doing farm chores and odd jobs in a succession of Iowa communities where his father held pastorates. He attended Penn College in Oskaloosa for one year, then studied at Grinnell College for two years and, moving again, was graduated with the A.B. degree, from Iowa Wesleyan College in 1882. He later (1885) took the A.M. degree there.

While in college, Cowles had taught school, and for two years after graduating he served as superintendent of schools in Algona, Iowa. On Dec. 3, 1884, he married Florence Maud Call, a member of the teaching staff and the daughter of a local banker. They had six children: Helen, Russell, Bertha, Florence, John, and Gardner. For eighteen months (1883-1884) Cowles was a partner in publishing the weekly *Algona Republican* and, briefly, was the editor of the weekly *Advance*. For most of the next twenty years, however, he devoted himself to the variety of commercial opportunities that abounded in the developing agricultural region. Maintaining his home in Algona, he was at one time or another a rural mail contractor, real estate dealer, lender on land, and handler of investments, but particularly a banker, with as many as ten banks in northern Iowa under his control. Local prominence and esteem led to his election, as a Republican, to the Iowa house of representatives, where he served for two terms (1899-1903).

His principal career in journalism began somewhat inadvertently. In 1903, at the urging of Harvey Ingham (1858-1949), his admired onetime competitor as a newspaper editor in Algona, Cowles bought a majority interest in the *Des Moines Register and Leader,* of which Ingham was editor. The paper was in debt and had a circulation of only 14,000. By working long hours, personally answering complaints, handling business matters, and encouraging Ingham to shun partisanship and prejudice and to cultivate assiduously Iowa's opportunities and needs, Cowles reversed the downward trend. Success did not come easily, but in five years the *Register* was covering the Des Moines area thoroughly and reaching out into the state. In 1908 Cowles bought the newly established *Des Moines Tribune* and entered the afternoon field. Continuing this process over two decades, he absorbed two additional Des Moines papers: the Scripps *Daily News* in 1924 and the fifty-year-old *Capital* in 1927. By 1930 the centrally situated Cowles newspapers had enveloped the Iowa daily newspaper market, morning, evening, and Sunday. Their publisher insisted that his papers be available through home delivery service, and for many years he counted more on revenue from circulation than from advertising, a financial reliance that was most uncommon in American journalism. Moreover, Cowles rejected liquor advertisements and established a

bureau to screen other advertising for false claims and harmful effects and to assure accuracy and fair play.

Journalistic achievement went with business success. Under Ingham and William W. Waymack (1888-1960), handpicked by Cowles as managing editor, the Des Moines *Register* and *Tribune* were frequently on the Pulitzer Prize and other award lists. His formula, Cowles said, was that "the more honestly a paper is conducted, the more successful it will be." Though he believed in vigorous, independent editorial utterance, he believed equally in providing subscribers with ample space for their own opinions. His policies produced a combined circulation of 350,000 daily and 425,000 on Sunday. In 1925 the Cowles company engaged a young journalism instructor, George Gallup, to survey the preferences of *Register* and *Tribune* readers, thus inaugurating the Gallup opinion poll. Cowles also pioneered in the establishment of employees' group insurance, retirement, and stock purchase plans. An early advocate of news broadcasting, he set up the first of his three radio stations in 1928. Two of the Cowles sons, John and Gardner, Jr., followed their father into journalism. (The third became a painter.) Under their increasingly active direction, the Cowles company in the 1930's introduced picture transmission by airplane, started the Register and Tribune Syndicate, acquired and developed newspapers in Minneapolis, and in 1937 began publication of *Look* magazine, which by the time of Cowles's death had reached a circulation of 2.6 million.

Cowles found time for public service and philanthropy. He was a close friend of Herbert Hoover, who appointed him in 1929 a member of the Federal Commission on Conservation and Administration of the Public Domain and, during the banking crisis of 1932, a director of the Reconstruction Finance Corporation. In 1934, Cowles and his wife created the Gardner Cowles Foundation, primarily to provide financial assistance for twenty-eight private colleges and the principal hospitals in Iowa. One grant built a $100,000 Negro community center in Des Moines named in honor of Wendell L. Willkie.

Cowles was modest and conscientious, quiet and dignified, gentle but also firm. His word was as good as his signature. In later years he became a world traveler. Beset by chronic myocarditis, and both deaf and blind, he died at his Des Moines home on the eighty-fifth anniversary of his birth. Following cremation, burial was in Glendale Cemetery, Des Moines. He was, in the words of the Davenport *Times,* "as much a part of Iowa as its waving corn." Few newspaper publishers have allowed their staffs so much initiative, and few have won greater loyalty.

[The Register and Tribune Co. published in 1946 a memorial book, *Gardner Cowles: 1861–1946*, which reprinted many of the news articles, editorials, and tributes that followed Cowles's death. See also newspapers and news and opinion weeklies at that time; *N.Y. Times*, Mar. 1, 1946, p. 21; *Editor & Publisher*, Mar. 9, 1946; *Who Was Who in America*, II (1950); Frank L. Mott, *Am. Journalism* (1941); Kenneth Stewart and John Tebbel, *Makers of Modern Journalism* (1952); Edwin Emery, *The Press and America* (1962). Other information from Gardner Cowles, Jr., N.Y. City, from Cowles's death certificate, and from personal recollections. An oil portrait by his son Russell was placed on public view in the Register and Tribune Building, Des Moines.]

IRVING DILLIARD

CRANE, FREDERICK EVAN (Mar. 2, 1869–Nov. 21, 1947), lawyer and judge, was born in Brooklyn, N.Y., the son of Frederic William Hotchkiss Crane and Mary Elizabeth (Jones) Crane. His father was a manufacturer of printing presses. After attending Adelphi Academy, he went directly to Columbia Law School, where he received his LL.B. in 1889. The next year he was admitted to the bar and began work in Brooklyn with the law firm of Bailey and Bell. On Dec. 13, 1893, he married Gertrude Mary Craven, the daughter of a Montreal merchant. Three years later he left private practice to become assistant district attorney of Kings County. In 1901 he was elected county judge on the Republican ticket, and five years later became a trial judge on the state supreme court. In 1917 Gov. Charles S. Whitman elevated him to the Court of Appeals, the highest tribunal in the state. He was elected to a full fourteen-year term in 1920, with Democratic as well as Republican endorsement. As a result of another bipartisan nomination, he was elected chief judge of the court in 1934, serving from 1935 through 1939, when he was required to retire on account of age.

During his more than two decades on the Court of Appeals, Crane acquired a reputation as a judge of stature alongside such respected colleagues as Frank Harris Hiscock, Benjamin Cardozo, and Cuthbert W. Pound. In 1934, anticipating his promotion to the chief judgeship, the *New York Times* proclaimed it "a worthy—one would almost say apostolic—succession in this high judicial office." Although leery of being classified liberal or conservative in his judicial philosophy and critical of what he considered to be extremes espoused by the "ultra-utilitarian" and the "ossified construc-

tionist," Crane placed himself squarely in the middle of the broad movement to revise twentieth-century American law to meet new social needs. "The law," Crane observed in 1930, "following public opinion, is more interested today in the general welfare of society than in merely individual rights" (*New York Times*, June 13, 1930.) Curiously, two of his most publicized opinions as chief judge, in each case on behalf of the majority of a divided court, argued the constitutional necessity of voiding social legislation on narrow grounds, first the state NRA Act and then the state minimum-wage law for women (*Darweger* v. *Staats*, 1935. *People ex rel. Tipaldo* v. *Morehead*, 1936). More characteristic was his majority opinion declaring constitutional the state unemployment-insurance law. "Unless there is something radically wrong, striking at the very fundamentals of constitutional government," he contended, "courts should not interfere with these attempts in the exercise of the reserve power of the state to meet dangers which threaten the entire common weal and affect every home" (*W. H. H. Chamberlin, Inc.* v. *Andrews*, 1936).

Apart from his opinions as a member of the Court of Appeals, Crane's influence was felt in the field of judicial administration. Before he became chief judge he had regularly expressed concern over the cumbersome machinery of the courts and the "breakdown" of the criminal justice system, but his administrative interests intensified in 1935, when as chief judge he had to preside over a state judicial council created the previous year by the legislature. Under Crane's vigorous leadership the judicial council moved to improve the state court system by recommending such measures as severe restriction of the privilege of exemption from jury duty, extension of procedures for pretrial examination, and regulation of publicity during trials. By 1937 the council reported that delay in the state courts had been "substantially eliminated," following the passage of legislation proposed by Crane and others (*New York Times*, June 21, 1937).

Administration was congenial to Crane, it seemed. As a judge in Albany, he once observed that he felt "very much like a monk," and he considered isolation to be a vice of lawyers. "We hate to mix," he told a bar group in 1926; "we dislike the rough and tumble of public life, and we leave it to others" (*New York Times*, Mar. 24, 1926). Crane himself hesitated to plunge into the practical affairs of politics, yet often in his career he appeared on the verge of doing so. Early in 1924 his name figured prominently in speculation about a successor to Harry M. Daugherty, President Coolidge's attorney general. For a time that same year he was generally considered to be the front-runner in the preconvention scrambling for the Republican gubernatorial nomination. Eventually he professed disinterest, but the story was that he had been prepared to run until upstate rank-and-file party opposition made it clear that he could not have a unanimous nomination, despite promises to the contrary by party leaders (*New York Times,* July 29, Aug. 14, 1924; July 16, 1926). In 1925 he was mentioned as a candidate for mayor of New York, and the next year his name again surfaced in gubernatorial discussions. As late as 1938, in spite of his age, the governorship remained at least a remote possibility. Then, having been chosen by the Republican leadership to serve as president of the first state constitutional convention to be held since 1915, Crane was at the center of state politics for half a year. Although he spoke impressively of the convention as "an experiment in true democracy," undertaken at a time of world political crisis, he worked closely as president with the leaders of his party, who ran the proceedings much like an ordinary legislative session. Crane did make some effort to prevent excesses of patronage, and in the hectic last four weeks he pressed the delegates relentlessly toward votes, impatiently threatening at one moment to adjourn sine die if they did not mend their dilatory ways. In the end he neither gained nor lost reputation by his role in the convention, as a modest package of reform produced during the summer was ratified by the voters of the state in the fall (see Vernon A. O'Rourke and Douglas W. Campbell, *Constitution-Making in a Democracy,* 1943).

Two years later, after retiring as chief judge and resuming the practice of law, Crane was appointed Moreland Act commissioner to investigate state printing-contract frauds. Otherwise, he did not remain noticeably active in public life. He died in his home in Garden City. A former associate, Albert Conway, paying tribute to his memory, observed that for years he was "the most beloved lawyer and judge in Brooklyn." Crane had indeed been a judge of easily familiar manner, regarding it as important that there be less reserve between bench and bar than had been the custom. Tall and direct of speech, he sang regularly with the Apollo Glee Club in Brooklyn. He was an Episcopalian and participated in a wide range of community affairs. He was the father of two children, and an admirer of countless others. "Most of us here are living for the children," he told a statewide radio audience of school children in 1935 at the opening of a crime conference in Albany. It was unusual for a chief judge to address children as he did, but Crane's style was informal and affable. It was all a part, in his mind, of avoiding what was merely technical, in order "to get to the heart of the matter."

[See *N.Y. Times* obituary, Nov. 22, 1947. Crane's career is best followed through the *Times* and in his opinions. See, too, brief personal recollections by Irving Lehman, *Brooklyn Law Review,* 9 (1939–1940), 113–116, and Albert Conway, New York State Bar Association *Bulletin,* 20 (1948), 40–43.]

STEPHEN BOTEIN

CROCKER, WILLIAM (Jan. 27, 1874–Feb. 11, 1950), plant physiologist, was born on a farm at Montville, Medina County, Ohio, to Charles David and Catherine (House) Crocker. Of nine children, William and his twin sister, Nell, were considerably younger than their brothers and sisters. His father, a skillful woodsman and barn framer, was a descendant of Deacon Job Crocker who settled in Barnstable, Mass., in the early seventeenth century. Relations in the Crocker family were not entirely happy, and Crocker left home at the age of fourteen. He attended the preparatory school of Baldwin University (Berea, Ohio) and was graduated from the Illinois Normal University in 1898. For ten years, beginning at the age of nineteen, he taught in country schools. During that period he entered the University of Illinois, where he received a B.A. degree in 1902 and a M.A. in 1903. After teaching biology for two years at the Northern Illinois Normal School he began work in botany at the University of Chicago and received his Ph.D. in 1906. While there, he came under the influence of John Merle Coulter, in whose department he worked; first as a graduate student, as an assistant in 1906, and as an associate professor from 1915-1921. From 1913-1918 he was also plant physiologist and collaborator at the U.S. Department of Agriculture. He married Persis Dorothy Smallwood of Warsaw, N.Y., on September 3, 1910; they had two sons: John Smallwood, born in 1911, and David Rockwell, born in 1916.

When Colonel William Boyce Thompson, the mining magnate, donated over $10 million to establish a laboratory for the study of plants in Yonkers, N.Y., Crocker was appointed director (February 1921). He and Dr. John Arthur visited research laboratories in the United States and Europe, purchased books for a library, and assembled a staff; in the fall of 1924, the Boyce Thompson Institute, designed for research in plant physiology, plant pathology, and biochemistry, was opened.

Crocker was a big, handsome man with a great capacity for work. In addition to planning, building, organizing, and administering the institute, he carried on a program of research and, in his later years, devoted considerable time to local and national affairs. His major concern in research was the physiology of seed plants; and he was inclined to attack problems of practical importance. An endeavor, on which he had been associated with Percy White Zimmerman and Albert Edwin Hitchcock, to determine the cause of injury to greenhouse-grown carnations led to the discovery of the toxicity to plants of illuminating gas and to studies on the effects of ethylene and various other gases, such as carbon monoxide, sulfur dioxide, and mercury vapor, on plant life. Equally important were his studies on the dormancy and germination of seeds; he discovered a method of increasing the yield of hybrid rose seeds and a number of tree seeds. He was concerned with fertilizers (especially sulfur and iron), plant hormones, and the factors influencing the distribution of water plants which serve as duck food. He developed a method of preserving in storage seeds that would not last from year to year otherwise. Crocker was president of the Botanical Society of America in 1924, a fellow of the American Association for the Advancement of Science, and a member of other notable organizations. In 1932 he received a medal from the Institute of Arts and Sciences of New York and, with Zimmerman and Hitchcock, the A. Cressy Morrison prize in experimental biology from the New York Academy of Science, for initiation and stimulation of roots from exposure of plants to carbon monoxide.

Crocker also devoted much time to public service. He was a member of the Yonkers Board of Education for nine years, during seven of which he was president, and he served on many local committees. He was a member of the Advisory Committee on Gerontology of the U.S. Public Health Service and chairman of the Division of Biology and Agriculture of the National Research Council.

On Feb. 11, 1950, a year and a half after his first wife's death, Crocker married Neva Ray Brown Ankenbrand in Marietta, Ohio. Hours later, he died of a heart attack in an elevator on his way to his hotel room in Athens, Ohio. He was buried in Marietta, Ohio. Crocker combined the qualities of an honest, critical and imaginative scientist with the leadership and business sense of a great administrator.

[Crocker's honors are listed by Otto Kunkel in the *Year Book* (1950) of the Am. Philosophical Soc., pp. 277–280. His research and the programs he administered are covered in three books: *Growth of Plants: Twenty Years Research at the Boyce Thompson Institute* (1948); with Lela V. Barton, *Twenty Years of Seed Research at Boyce Thompson Institute for Plant Research* (1948); and also with Lela V. Barton, *Physiology of Seeds* (1953). A tribute to Dr. Crocker by Edmund W. Sinnott, "William Crocker—the Man and Scientist," is published in *Contributions to Boyce Thompson Institute*, Jan.–Mar. 1950. Obituary in the *N.Y. Times*, Feb. 12, 1950; see also *Nat. Cyc. Am. Biog.*, Current vol. D. Personal communications from his sons, David and John, and others to the author, as well as newspaper articles, and a limited number of personal papers are deposited at the Boyce Thompson Institute. Photographs of William Crocker are available at the Boyce Thompson Institute and an excellent pencil sketch by George Baekland, Jr., is in the possession of David R. Crocker.]

WILLIAM J. ROBBINS

CROMWELL, WILLIAM NELSON (Jan. 17, 1854-July 19, 1948), lawyer, was born in Brooklyn, the son of John Nelson Cromwell and Sarah M. (Brokaw) Cromwell. The family soon moved to Peoria, Ill., and in 1861 his father, a colonel with the Forty-seventh Illinois Volunteers, left for war and later was killed during Grant's advance on Vicksburg. The family returned to Brooklyn, where Cromwell attended public schools and then worked for several years as an accountant in a railroad office, to support a younger brother and his mother. In 1874 he secured an accounting job with the New York law firm of Sullivan, Kobbe and Fowler. With the encouragement of the firm's senior partner, Algernon Sydney Sullivan, an experienced trial lawyer from Cincinnati, Cromwell attended Columbia Law School on the side, graduating and being admitted to the bar in 1876. He continued with the Sullivan firm and soon was well enough established to marry Jennie Osgood Nichols, on Dec. 24, 1878. A year later, when Kobbe and Fowler withdrew from the firm, Sullivan invited Cromwell, just twenty-five years old, to become his partner, with a one-third interest in all fees. When Sullivan died in 1887, Cromwell became senior partner.

Under Cromwell's leadership the firm prospered and grew, employing twelve lawyers and six stenographers by 1902. Specializing in business law, Sullivan and Cromwell excelled at supplying legal advice to increasingly complex organizations that were trying to reach rapidly expanding markets. One of the most resourceful legal technicians in the country at the turn of the century, Cromwell was wizardly with figures, as befitted a former accountant. He was no orator, perhaps for lack of a college education, but he had a taste for facts, an aptitude for realistic economic analysis, and a flair for fast-talking argument. He was thus well equipped to manage such protracted and intricate affairs as the consolidation of sixteen of the largest American tube-manufacturing concerns into the National Tube Company, completed in 1899 and capitalized at $80 million, and E. H. Harriman's two-year proxy battle against Stuyvesant Fish for control of the Illinois Central Railroad Company, brought to a successful conclusion in 1908.

Cromwell was more interested in efficient results than in legal doctrine. "It profoundly irritated him," a young partner later recalled, "to be told . . . that there was no effective legal solution to a difficult economic problem" (Dean, pp. 96-97). For the sake of economic rationality, he urged corporations to make full public disclosure of their assets, to "win and hold the confidence of the investing public." To promote efficiency, too, he made his most important contribution to the practice of American business law, the so-called Cromwell plan, for salvaging enterprises in distress, from which he acquired a reputation as "the physician of Wall Street," adept at "rescue operations" (*American Bar Association Journal*, 34 [1948], 782). The essence of the Cromwell plan, which was especially well adapted to the fluctuating economic conditions of the late nineteenth century, was to arrange a voluntary agreement of creditors within the framework of the New York state insolvency laws, whereby a firm in difficulty could reorganize itself in order both to continue in business and to fulfill its obligations without a sacrifice sale of slow assets or of assets the value of which was temporarily depressed as a result of financial crisis. The Cromwell plan was originally developed in 1891, to save the failing New York brokerage house of Decker, Howell and Company, whose liabilities were in excess of $10 million; subsequently it was applied to other kinds of enterprise, including a group of large jewelry importing houses in danger of ruin during the panic of 1907.

Cromwell's practice also had an international dimension. Representing various European banks and bond syndicates, he played a part in stimulating the flow of European capital to the United States before World War I. Such was the scope of his international business that he

was said to aspire to become secretary of state, a position that eluded him despite his generous support of the Republican party and his cultivation of Republican presidents. His one dramatic achievement in the diplomatic arena was for the benefit of a client, the New Panama Canal Company of France, which first engaged him in 1896 and on whose behalf he tried to take advantage of what he called the "influences and relations" of Sullivan and Cromwell with "a considerable number of public men in political life, in financial circles, and on the press" (*Story of Panama*, p. 207.) In the course of some eight years of intensive lobbying, negotiating, and public relations work, Cromwell was instrumental in persuading influential Republican politicians to abandon support of a Nicaraguan canal and promote a plan by which the Colombian government would agree to allow the New Panama Canal Company to sell its Panamanian property to the United States and the company itself would agree to the sale at a price of $40 million. To opponents of the Spooner bill authorizing the Panama route, which Theodore Roosevelt signed in June 1902, and to critics of the American decision to support the secessionist movement in Panama the next year, Cromwell's motives and actions had of course been reprehensible throughout. According to one hostile observer, he was "the man whose masterful mind, whetted on the grindstone of corporation cunning, conceived and carried out the rape of the Isthmus" (Miner, p. 76).

After World War I, Cromwell retired from active legal practice, residing for long periods in France. An Episcopalian, he devoted himself to various charitable enterprises, among them fund-raising to aid the blind and efforts to restore the hand-lace industry in France. For all his involvement in the new industrial order, he had never been personally comfortable with modernity. His very appearance was flamboyantly reminiscent of a previous age, featuring as it did shaggy white locks and a Buffalo Bill mustache. Characteristically, he liked to conduct business not in his office on Wall Street but in his midtown Victorian home, crammed with paintings and statuettes. That home he clung to stubbornly, despite the best efforts and offers of the Rockefeller interests, who wanted the property for Rockefeller Center. There he died, in 1948, after a long illness. He was childless and his wife had died in 1931, so most of the nearly $19 million that he left went to philanthropic causes. In all he gave almost $5 million to law schools, bar associations, and legal research centers. Appropriately, for one whose law practice had been so outsized, it was the largest sum ever bequeathed by an individual to the legal profession.

[See *N.Y. Times* obituary, July 20, 1948. By far the most useful memorial to Cromwell is Arthur H. Dean's book-length *William Nelson Cromwell, 1854–1948: An American Pioneer in Corporation, Comparative, and International Law* (1957). Dwight Carroll Miner, *The Fight for the Panama Route: The Story of the Spooner Act and the Hay-Herrán Treaty* (1940), chs. 3–4, 8, and 10, has much detail on Cromwell. Supportive documentation is available in *The Story of Panama: Hearings on the Rainey Resolution before the Committee on Foreign Affairs of the House of Representatives* (1913). For general commentary on business law in the period, see Thomas C. Cochran, *Business in American Life: A History* (1972), ch. 12.]

STEPHEN BOTEIN

CROSS, CHARLES WHITMAN (Sept. 1, 1854-Apr. 20, 1949), geologist, petrologist, was born in Amherst, Mass., the son of Rev. Moses Kimball Cross, a Congregational minister, and his second wife, Maria Elizabeth (Mason) Cross. His father, a native of Danvers, Mass., was a graduate of Amherst College and attended Hartford and Andover theological seminaries; his mother was from Amboy, Ill. She died a year after her son's birth, but Moses Cross soon remarried. Whitman Cross (as he was known) grew up in Iowa, where his father held pastorates in Tipton (1855-1865), Washington (1865-1867), and Waverly (1867-1871). After attending the Waverly high school, he entered Amherst College, graduating with the B.S. degree in 1875. He spent a year in postgraduate study at Amherst and then went to Germany, where he studied geology at the universities of Göttingen (1877-1878) and Leipzig (1878-1880), receiving the Ph.D. from the latter in 1880.

Upon his return, Cross joined the U.S. Geological Survey, thus beginning an association that was to last for forty-five years. Assigned to the survey's Rocky Mountain Division, headed by Samuel F. Emmons, he made studies of the mineralogy of the rapidly developing mining region around Denver, some in collaboration with the chemist William F. Hillebrand. Around 1895, Cross focused his interest on the complex series of volcanic rocks in the San Juan region of southwestern Colorado, where he worked for many years. He proceeded from studies of such famous mining areas as Telluride, La Plata, Ouray, and Silverton to a detailed mapping of an area of about one hundred square miles. The going was rough; pack-horses transported his equipment, but often he made difficult climbs to places where no pack animal could go. Most petrologists at that time

were satisfied with describing and classifying the rocks they found, with little attempt at analysis. Cross was among the first to treat complex piles of igneous rocks as units which could be mapped in much the same way as sedimentary rocks. His efforts in this direction provided valuable information on the stratigraphy of the San Juan region, as well as its volcanic history.

In 1902 Cross collaborated with three younger petrologists—Joseph P. Iddings, Louis V. Pirsson, and Henry S. Washington—in devising a new system of classifying igneous rocks based on chemical and mineralogical structure. Their book, *Quantitative Classification of Igneous Rocks* (1903), became a standard work, and the "C.I.P.W." system (after the authors' initials) was still in use seventy years later. Cross's interest in classification was heightened by his service as chief of the section of petrology of the Geological Survey from 1903 to 1907, and later as secretary of the committee on petrographic names.

Cross precisely trimmed the rocks he collected to a uniform size and shape. To him any rock worth collecting was worthy of a chemical analysis and a thin section study. For each specimen he recorded on a card the locality, the type, and his petrographic finding, together with the chemical analysis and an attached thin section of the rock. These skillfully prepared cards, numbering more than 2,000, became the nucleus of the Smithsonian Institution's petrographic collection. The same concern with detail led Cross to insist that his campsites in the mountains be located where they could provide the best possible view.

Cross was president of the Geological Society of America in 1918. He was one of a group of scientists who successfully persuaded the Carnegie Institution of Washington to establish the Geophysical Laboratory for the study of rocks at high pressures and temperatures. He was elected to the National Academy of Sciences in 1908 and was its treasurer from 1911 to 1919. During the last two years he served in the same capacity for the National Research Council, which he helped organize.

After his retirement in 1925, Cross devoted himself almost exclusively to the cultivation of roses at his home in Chevy Chase, Md., and to arranging the annual rose shows held in the U.S. National Museum in Washington. Whenever he was invited to attend social affairs of that congress his reply was "I am fully engaged in rose culture." From his garden of over two thousand bushes, a Washington showplace, he produced several award-winning new varieties, some of which were commercially grown; among the most familiar were "Chevy Chase," "Mrs. Whitman Cross," and "Honorable Lady Lindsay." He was also known locally as an expert in investment and finance. Cross was very meticulous about his clothes and was not a flashy dresser. A quiet man, with a ready smile, he sometimes appeared shy. This he was not. He could never accept disparaging allusions to the classification of rocks, even when such remarks came from friends who intended them to be humorous. Any remark that sounded like a slur at rock classification to Cross was blasphemy. On Nov. 7, 1895, Cross married Virginia Stevens of North Andover, Mass. They had one child, Richard Stevens. In his last years Cross became ill and was moved to a sanatorium in Rockville, Md., where he died of kidney failure and pneumonia. He was buried in North Andover, Mass.

[The chief biographical accounts are those of Esper S. Larsen, Jr., in Nat. Acad. Sci., *Biog. Memoirs,* XXXII (1958), which includes a photograph and a bibliography of Cross's writings; and Clarence S. Ross in Wash. Acad. Sci., *Jour.,* Oct. 15, 1949. See also *Who Was Who in America,* II (1950); and the entries on Cross and his father in the *Amherst College Biog. Record* (1939). Death record from Md. Division of Vital Records.]

EDWARD P. HENDERSON

CROSS, SAMUEL HAZZARD (July 1, 1891-Oct. 14, 1946), professor of Slavic languages and literatures, was born in Westerly, R.I., the only child of Samuel Hazzard Cross and Jessie (Kerr) Cross. His father, who came of an old Rhode Island family, was a high school principal. He died in 1898, and Cross's mother, herself a high school teacher, moved with her son to New Bedford, Mass. A somewhat delicate child, Samuel was discouraged from rough play by his mother, who fostered a penchant for reading and served as his tutor. In 1908, after graduating from the New Bedford high school, he entered Harvard College, from which he received the A.B. degree in classics in 1912, summa cum laude. Fellowships enabled him to spend the next two years in Europe, where he studied German and Russian literature and historiography—the main fields of his later scholarly work—at Graz, Berlin, Freiburg, and St. Petersburg. In the fall of 1914 he began graduate work at Harvard in comparative literature. He received his Ph.D. in 1916 with a thesis on "The Contribution of G. F. Müller to Russian Historiography" and began teaching German at Western Reserve University.

When the United States entered World War I, Cross joined the army, and as an infantry officer spent a year and a half training machine gunners. In 1919 he went to Poland with the American Commission to Negotiate Peace. He left the army in January 1920 and in May became United States Trade Commissioner in Brussels, a post he held for nearly five years, serving also as commercial attaché to the American embassy to Belgium (from 1921) and to the American legation at The Hague (from 1923). Recalled to Washington in 1925 to be chief of the European Division of the Bureau of Foreign and Domestic Commerce, he soon decided that he was not suited to working "in a large bureaucratic organization," and resigned after a year to try his hand briefly at the securities business in Boston. "I shall probably never do worse at anything," he wrote later of this experience; it convinced him that his place was in academic work.

In the spring of 1928, accordingly, Cross returned to Harvard as lecturer in history. For the next two academic years he was instructor in German at Harvard and Tufts; in 1930, upon the retirement of Leo Wiener, he was made professor of Slavic languages and literatures at Harvard, a post he held until his death. A man of formidable energy, brilliant linguistic skills, and retentive memory, forthright in speech, helpful to gifted students but impatient with others, Cross offered a broad variety of courses. He taught Old Church Slavonic, Old Russian, modern Russian, Polish, Czech, and Serbo-Croatian; he lectured on Russian and Soviet literature—fiction, poetry, and drama—and maintained a more than amateur interest in Russian architecture and ballet.

The history of Slavic studies in America as well as his own gifts may be responsible for the unusual range of Cross's pedagogical activity. His generation of American Slavists (which he represented at its best) was a sparse one; because the field itself was new and tentatively defined, his work was primarily one of cultural mediation. He produced reliable translations, such as his pioneering rendition of *The Russian Primary Chronicle* (1930), and wrote informed accounts of some of the most important aspects of Slavic civilizations, notably in his *Slavic Civilization Through the Ages* (1948). At the same time he provided his students with the kind of linguistic training that would make possible the more discipline- and problem-oriented work of subsequent scholarly generations. Concerned throughout his career with language teaching, Cross consistently argued for what he termed a "more humane" and pragmatic approach against those who placed their faith in pedagogical systems and methodologies.

The volume of Cross's published scholarship —largely on medieval Russia—was limited by temperament and external factors alike. He was a popular and indefatigable lecturer to all sorts of groups outside the university; within it, he held a variety of administrative posts, including the chairmanship of the department of Germanic languages from 1935 to 1939 (concurrently with his de facto chairmanship of the program in Slavic languages and literatures). Beginning in 1929 he also served *Speculum,* the journal of the Mediaeval Academy of America, as assistant managing editor, managing editor (1931-1936), and editor (from 1936 until his death). During World War II he assumed additional editorial responsibilities in connection with the American stewardship of the *Slavonic and East European Review* (London) and *Byzantion* (Brussels), while spending considerable time responding to appeals from or on behalf of refugee Slavic scholars. He was, moreover, a frequent consultant to the U.S. government, and in the spring of 1942 acted as President Roosevelt's interpreter during the secret visit to Washington of the Soviet foreign minister, V. M. Molotov.

Short and stout, assured and emphatic, irascible and exuberant, Cross is remembered as a "boon companion" and "a kind of Elizabethan figure in his large capacity for the stuff of life" (Simmons and Pares, p. 568). He married Constance Curtis on June 28, 1918; they had three daughters: Caroline Lee, Ann Louise, and Ricarda. Cross was divorced in 1944. He was an Episcopalian in religion. He died of coronary thrombosis at the age of fifty-five in Cambridge, Mass., and was buried there in Mount Auburn Cemetery. A chair perpetuates his name at Harvard; and the vast expansion of American Slavic studies in the 1950's and 1960's may be seen as a further memorial to his activity.

[Cross's unpublished papers and correspondence are in the Harvard Univ. Archives. Autobiographical accounts may be found in the several *Reports* of the Harvard Class of 1912; the fullest, together with a bibliography to date and a portrait at the back, is in the 25th reunion volume (1937). On Cross's career: Faculty Minutes in *Harvard Univ. Gazette,* Feb. 15, 1947; memoirs by Ernest J. Simmons and Bernard Pares in the *Slavonic and East European Rev.,* Apr. 1947; *N.Y. Times* obituary, Oct. 15, 1946; Albert Parry, *America Learns Russian* (1967). Information was also obtained from relatives, associates, and friends: Mrs. George F. Limerick, Mrs. Peter R. Chase, Mrs. Katherine Benedict of Cambridge, Mass., Profs. B. J. Whiting and Horace G. Lunt of Harvard, Prof. William A. Coates, Kans. State Univ.]

DONALD FANGER

CROSS, WILBUR LUCIUS (Apr. 10, 1862-Oct. 5, 1948), English scholar and teacher, governor of Connecticut, was by long ancestry the "Connecticut Yankee" he called himself in his autobiography. Gurleyville, the tiny village within the town of Mansfield in which he was born, was named for his maternal great-grandfather, Ephraim Gurley, a descendant of William Gurley, who came to Massachusetts in 1679. His father's forebear William Cross had enlisted in the Pequot War at Wethersfield, Conn., in 1637. Wilbur was the third son and fourth of five children of Samuel and Harriet Maria (Gurley) Cross. Growing up in Gurleyville on a hill sloping steeply to the Fenton River, which turned the great wheel of Samuel Cross's grist- and sawmill, the boy attended a one-room red schoolhouse. At the same time he was being initiated into the world of grownups through helping in the general store which his older brother had opened. Pausing to listen between transactions at the counter, he learned the character of the neighbors and the speech of the Connecticut countryman. "As a boy," he later recalled, "I was most interested, except for politics, in horse trades, funny stories, and what are now called wisecracks." The experience proved ultimately to be of great importance for his career.

After graduating as valedictorian from Natchaug High School in nearby Willimantic, he taught for a year in a country school and then entered Yale College in 1881. The new disciplines of political economy and English literature were finding a place in the curriculum of this ancient stronghold of the classics, and Cross chose the later. For a year after receiving his B.A. in 1885, he served as principal of Staples High School in Westport, Conn. Then, with a Yale College fellowship, he returned to New Haven for three years of graduate study in English under Henry A. Beers and Thomas R. Lounsbury. Since no college position opened in 1889, when he received his Ph.D. degree, he accepted a post as master of English at Shady Side Academy in Pittsburgh, Pa. To that city he took his bride, Helen Baldwin Avery of Willimantic, whom he married on July 17, 1889. It was a happy marriage which ended in 1928 with her sudden death. They had four children: Wilbur Lucius, Samuel Avery, Elizabeth Baldwin, and Arthur William, of whom the last two died in childhood.

After five years in Pittsburgh, where in addition to his teaching he gave public lectures on the English novel, Cross in 1894 was appointed instructor in English at the Sheffield

Scientific School of Yale. He became professor of English in 1902 and in 1907, after Lounsbury retired, head of the department. With his appointment in 1916 as dean of the graduate school, he began teaching there also, though he retained his professorship in the Scientific School until his appointment as the first Sterling professor of English in 1922. He published his revised Pittsburgh lectures in 1899 under the title *The Development of the English Novel;* it became a standard college text. Research in England prepared the way for his edition in 1904 of the principal works of Laurence Sterne. This and his *The Life and Times of Laurence Sterne* (1909) revolutionized the critical appraisal of the hitherto little-regarded author of *Tristram Shandy* and established Sterne's position among the foremost humorists in English literature. In allusion to Sterne, students began to call Cross "Uncle Toby," a sobriquet by which he was affectionately known the rest of his life. In 1918 Cross brought out in three volumes *The History of Henry Fielding*—his favorite author—which combined, like the *Sterne,* painstaking research with narrative skill, and took its place as a standard biography.

Other duties came to him at Yale. In 1911 President Arthur T. Hadley asked Cross to assume the editorship of the *Yale Review,* at that time a journal of economics, and to transform it into a broad national quarterly of literature and public affairs. Cross quickly made the *Review* a significant force in American intellectual life; for twenty-nine years he gave it his close attention, reading all contributions in manuscript and proof. From 1916 until his retirement from the faculty in 1930 Cross served as dean of the Yale Graduate School. Hitherto a rather casual offshoot of Yale College, it attained under his leadership a status equal to the other professional schools, with its own faculty and a new Graduate Quadrangle. His prestige and wide acquaintance enabled him to draw to its faculty an unusually able group of scholar-teachers. Beyond the university, Cross served as chancellor of the American Academy of Arts and Letters (1931-1941) and as president (1931-1935) of its parent body, the National Institute of Arts and Letters.

In June 1930 Cross reached the mandatory retirement age of sixty-eight. That summer he accepted from the convention of Connecticut's habitually defeated Democratic party what all thought to be a pro forma nomination for governor. He campaigned with great success through the country villages of the state, discussing crops, swapping stories, and talking politics in the vernacular he had learned as a boy in Gurleyville. To the astonishment of the dominant Republican machine and the dismay of their Democratic opposite numbers, the voters elected Cross by a solid majority. As he took office in January 1931, he faced a legislature dominated by Republicans with whose machine psychology and methods the Democratic leadership had more sympathy than with the "one-man brain trust" their party had inadvertently installed in the capitol. With a combination of sense, firmness, and tact Cross defeated an early legislative move to deprive him of the power of appointment and established himself as a politician to be reckoned with; and he won election to three more terms. In the end, however, the party machines indirectly brought him down. When after eight years in office he ran for a fifth term in 1938, recently exposed scandals connected with the building of the Merritt Parkway and with the city of Waterbury tarred both party machines and brought out a heavy protest vote for the Socialist candidate for governor. Cross had dealt with the scandals in a forthright and effective manner; the protest was not directed against him. But it enabled the Republican candidate, Raymond E. Baldwin, to defeat him by a paper-thin plurality.

In his four terms Cross gave both strong and skillful leadership to the state in the dark years of the depression. Although by temperament and philosophy a believer in laissez-faire economics and Yankee moralism, he was enough of a pragmatist to respond to crisis. His humanitarian concern prompted him to institute generous public works and relief programs and to secure the abolition of child labor and the establishment of minimum wage scales and working standards for women, thus routing hitherto proliferating sweatshops. He lowered public utility rates and strengthened the state's regulatory commission. Reorganization of the state government brought more effective management of finances and the budget; a new civil service act improved the quality of state employees. He vigorously furthered new and better buildings for state institutions. In an age of rapidly expanding motor traffic he led in creating for Connecticut a proper highway system; later one of the principal parkways of the state received his name. His regime brought his Connecticut a "little New Deal."

Cross was a member of the Episcopal church. He died at his home in New Haven at the age of eighty-six of "pneumonia and a weakened heart." Academic and political notables gathered at his funeral, and he was buried in Evergreen Cemetery in New Haven.

[Cross's *Connecticut Yankee, An Autobiog.* (1943) is a compendium of information spiced with humorous stories. Albert E. Van Dusen, *Connecticut* (1961), contains a detailed and scholarly discussion of the administration of Governor Cross; his intellectual evolution is traced in Robert L. Woodbury, "Wilbur Cross: New Deal Ambassador to a Yankee Culture," *New England Quart.*, Sept. 1968. Chauncey Brewster Tinker appraises Cross's scholarship in *Commemorative Tributes of the Am. Acad. of Arts and Letters, 1942–1951* (1951); George W. Pierson assesses his work as dean of the graduate school in his *Yale: The Univ. College, 1921–1937* (1955). See also memoir by G. L. Hendrickson in Am. Philosophical Soc., *Year Book*, 1948; and obituary in *N.Y. Times*, Oct. 5, 1948. Cross's papers are in the Yale Univ. Lib.]

RALPH H. GABRIEL

CROWE, FRANCIS TRENHOLM (Oct. 12, 1882–Feb. 26, 1946), civil engineer, dam builder, was born in Trenholmville, Quebec, Canada, to John Crowe and Emma Jane (Wilkinson) Crowe. His father had come to the United States from England in 1869; his mother was a native of Brooklyn, N.Y. The couple were married in 1880 and soon afterward moved to Quebec, where John Crowe established and operated a woolen mill until 1888. He then returned to the United States and founded a similar mill in Fairfield, Iowa, but it failed after two years. During the next nine years he held mill superintendencies at Kezar Falls, Maine, and Picton, N.J., before settling in 1899 in Byfield, Mass.

Francis Crowe completed elementary school in Byfield and attended nearby Governor Dummer Academy, graduating in 1901. That fall he entered the University of Maine. Although his father urged him to pursue a medical career, he chose engineering, and received the B.S. degree in civil engineering in 1905. Inspired by a visiting lecturer, Frank E. Weymouth of the federal Reclamation Service, Crowe spent the summer of 1904 working for the service on a survey party in Montana. He was strongly attracted to the West, and after graduating he secured a regular position with the Reclamation Service. Except for three years (1906-1908, 1920) when he worked for private contractors, Crowe remained with the service for two decades, as assistant superintendent and superintendent of construction for several western dams. The Reclamation Service was reorganized in 1923 as the Bureau of Reclamation, and the following year Frank Crowe was named general supervisor of all construction activities in seventeen western states. In 1925, however, the bureau discontinued its construction force and began

to let out the work to private contractors, and Crowe, who disliked desk work and loved an active, outdoor role, resigned.

Fired by a dream of building supersized dams, Crowe joined the Morrison-Knudsen Company, a construction firm of Boise, Idaho. The United States was entering a period of extensive dam building, and Crowe served during the late 1920's as engineering supervisor of the Guernsey Dam in Wyoming, the Van Giesen (Coombe) Dam in California, and the Deadwood Dam in central Idaho. When the Reclamation Bureau requested bids for the 726-foot-high Boulder (later Hoover) Dam, to be constructed in Black Canyon on the Colorado River, Crowe successfully urged his employer, Harry W. Morrison, to promote a syndicate with other construction firms (including that of Henry J. Kaiser). The syndicate was named Six Companies, Inc., and submitted a bid. Crowe in 1919 had prepared cost estimates for a dam at Black Canyon for the Reclamation Service, and he was assigned the task of preparing the estimates for the Morrison firm. Each of the six companies drew up bids, but it was Crowe's figures that the syndicate submitted. Six Companies won the contract in 1931, and Crowe was named general superintendent in charge of construction.

After overcoming serious organizational difficulties among the syndicate's leaders, Crowe took firm command of the construction program. Besides the dam itself, he supervised the building of the dam's power plant and of the town of Boulder City, which housed the working force. His use of cableways to convey construction materials at the dam was a bold stroke for that time. So skillfully did he coordinate the men and the materials involved in a vast and complex project that the dam was completed in 1935, a record twenty-five months ahead of schedule.

Crowe and the syndicate continued their profitable relationship. In 1936 "The Old Man," as Crowe was affectionately known by his men, supervised the building of Parker Dam down river from the Hoover Dam. He also directed the building of two water storage dams in California in 1937 and 1938. In 1938 Six Companies was underbid for construction of the massive Shasta Dam, a key structure in the Central Valley Project of California, but Crowe was chosen by Pacific Constructors, Inc., winners of the contract, to supervise construction. The Shasta project—the second major project of Crowe's career—required all of his technical daring because of problems of terrain, foundation, and heavy seasonal rains. Here, since horizontal cableways were not suitable, Crowe designed a unique and widely acclaimed system of 25-ton-capacity radial cableways operating from a 460-foot tower to carry concrete and other materials to every area of the construction project. Crowe completed the project, which proved to be his last, in 1944, a few months ahead of schedule, despite the complications of wartime demands for labor and materials.

Crowe found time during his career for professional activity. He wrote frequent essays for engineering journals and for Bureau of Reclamation publications. The American Society of Civil Engineers, of which he had been a member since 1915, elevated him to honorary membership in 1943, a rank attained by very few engineers. Crowe first married Marie Sass, who died in 1911 shortly after the marriage. On Dec. 9, 1913, he married Linnie Korts of Boise, Idaho. He had two children by his second marriage: Patricia and Elizabeth Jean. Crowe was an Episcopalian. His hobby was raising Hereford cattle on a 20,000-acre ranch near Redding, Calif. He died of coronary thrombosis at Mercy Hospital in Redding, and was buried in the Redding Cemetery. Frank Crowe, said one contemporary, "changed the physical landscape perhaps more than any other individual in history." Few would challenge this assertion about the man who constructed nineteen dams over a period of forty years.

[Memoir by S. O. Harper, Walker R. Young, and W. V. Greeley in *Trans.* of the Am. Soc. of Civil Engineers 113 (1948): 1397–1403; J. C. Maguire, "The Old Man," in *Builders of Shasta Dam* (Pacific Constructors, Inc., 1964); *Nat. Cyc. Am. Biog.*, XXXIV, 494–495; "The Earth Movers," *Fortune*, Aug.–Sept. 1943; *N.Y. Times*, Feb. 28, 1946.]
WILMON H. DROZE

CROWNINSHIELD, FRANCIS WELCH (June 24, 1872–Dec. 28, 1947), better known as Frank, magazine editor and patron of the arts, was born in Paris, one of three children of Frederic Crowninshield and Helen Suzette (Fairbanks) Crowninshield. The father's American progenitor, Johannes von Kronenscheldt, had anglicized the name upon his emigration from Germany to Salem, Mass., in 1670. A more recent ancestor, Benjamin W. Crowninshield, was secretary of the navy under Presidents Madison and Monroe. Frederic Crowninshield, an artist specializing in watercolors, murals, and stained glass, was studying in Italy at the time of Frank's birth. From 1878 to 1885, with frequent interludes in Europe, the family lived in Boston, where Frederic Crowninshield taught in the museum school of the Museum of Fine Arts. Frank's early education was mainly in the hands of private tutors. In 1886 the family moved to New York City where Frank studied at Lyon's Academy. In 1890 he became a clerk in a Putnam's bookstore. His five years (1895-1900) as publisher of Dodd, Mead and Co.'s literary review *The Bookman* was the first of a succession of positions in the New York periodical world—assistant editor of *Metropolitan Magazine* (1900-1902) and of *Munsey's Magazine* (1903-1907), London literary agent for *Munsey's* (1908-1909), art editor of *Century Magazine* (1910-1913), and finally, in 1914, editor of *Dress and Vanity Fair,* an undistinguished ten-year-old periodical recently acquired by the dynamic publisher Condé Nast.

Shortening the name, Crowninshield quickly transformed *Vanity Fair* into a chic and slick reflection of his own sophisticated interests in modern art and literature, the theater, society, and sports—"the things people talk about at parties." Coming to *Vanity Fair* in the year of the Armory Show, Crowninshield for twenty-two years worked to win support and sympathy for the new in all branches of the arts among his select and affluent readership. He regularly published reproductions of the works of contemporary artists—especially French modernists such as Picasso, Matisse, Bonnard, and Rouault—and provided an outlet for young writers including Edna St. Vincent Millay, F. Scott Fitzgerald, Aldous Huxley, John Dos Passos, and Edmund Wilson. He was a founder (1929), first secretary, and lifelong trustee of New York's Museum of Modern Art. He himself owned a notable collection of contemporary paintings which he often lent for exhibit.

A tall, elegant, and urbane bachelor whose lapel was invariably adorned with a boutonniere, Crowninshield was exceptionally active in Manhattan social life as a toastmaster, party guest, cotillion leader, and after-dinner speaker. Indeed, his contemporary reputation seems to have rested as much on his style as on his journalistic achievements; "He could order a can of sardines," a friend once said, "and give you the impression it was a distinguished and festive thing to do." (He never touched alcohol, having, so he said, inadvertently taken the pledge at the age of ten while attending a Boston temperance rally with a female relative.) What became known as café society—a mingling of artists and writers with members of the traditional upper crust—

was in part his creation. "My interest in society," he once observed, "at times so pronounced that the word 'snob' comes a little to mind, derives from the fact that I like an immense number of things which society, money, and position bring in their train: painting, tapestries, rare books, smart dresses, dances, gardens, country houses, correct cuisine, and pretty women" (quoted in the *New Yorker,* Feb. 14, 1948, p. 72).

Inevitably, the Great Depression forced some difficult adjustments upon a man of Frank Crowninshield's outlook. *Vanity Fair* frequently operated at a loss even in the 1920's, and in the 1930's it faltered badly. In 1932 Condé Nast undercut Crowninshield's editorial autonomy by appointing two editorial advisors to give the magazine a more serious tone and to solicit a greater number of articles on politics and economics. Four years later, when Nast merged *Vanity Fair* with *Vogue,* another of his magazines, Crowninshield became art editor of *Vogue* and "literary advisor" to Condé Nast Publications, Inc. Many of his paintings and rare books were sold at auction in these years; one such sale, in 1943, netted more than $180,-000. After a five-week illness following an operation, he died at Roosevelt Hospital, New York, at the age of seventy-five. After services in St. James Protestant Episcopal Church, New York, he was buried in Mount Auburn Cemetery, Cambridge, Mass.

[*N.Y. Times,* Dec. 29, 1947, p. 17 (obituary with photograph); *New Yorker,* Sept. 19 and 26, 1942, Feb. 14, 1948; *Vogue,* Aug. 15, 1960; *Who Was Who in America,* II (1950); Cleveland Amory and Frederic Bradlee, eds., *Vanity Fair: Selections from America's Most Memorable Magazine* (1960); *Vogue's First Reader* (1942), includes several pieces by Crowninshield; Theodore Peterson, *Magazines in the Twentieth Century* (1964), pp. 269–271. Crowninshield published two books under the pseudonym Arthur Loring Bruce, *Manners of the Metropolis* (1908) and *The Bridge Fiend* (1909).]

PAUL BOYER

CULLEN, COUNTÉE PORTER (May 30, 1903-Jan. 9, 1946), poet, novelist, and essayist, was unofficially called "poet laureate" of the "Negro (Harlem) Renaissance," the term used to identify a period of intense cultural activity and productivity by black Americans during the 1920's. (Cullen's first name appears both with and without an acute accent; he pronounced it "Countay.") Facts about Cullen's parentage and place of birth are uncertain. Although Cullen's friends and his second wife have stated that he was born in Louisville, Ky., Cullen claimed as his birthplace New York City, where he lived after he was nine.

Cullen was reared by his grandmother Elizabeth Porter and, after her death, was adopted in 1918 by Rev. Frederick Cullen, minister at Salem Methodist Episcopal Church.

Cullen attended De Witt Clinton High School, where the student body was predominantly white. He won the Douglas Fairbanks oratorical contest; edited the Clinton *News*; served as associate editor of the *Magpie,* the school's literary magazine (1921); received first prize (for "I Have a Rendezvous with Life") in a citywide poetry contest; was vice-president of his senior class; maintained a grade-point average of 92; and earned a Regent's scholarship. At New York University, which he entered in 1922, he earned honorable mention for poems submitted in the nationwide Witter Bynner Undergraduate Poetry Contest of 1923 ("The Ballad of the Brown Girl") and 1924 ("Spirit-Birth," later called "The Shroud of Color"). In 1925, his "Poems" was unanimously awarded first prize in the Bynner competition. By 1926, a year after he graduated, Phi Beta Kappa, Cullen had received prizes from *Palms, Poetry, The Crisis* (writing under the name of Timothy Tumble), and *Opportunity* magazines and had published a volume, *Color* (1925).

After earning an M.A. degree in English from Harvard in 1926, Cullen accepted a position as assistant editor of *Opportunity, A Journal of Negro Life,* for which he wrote a monthly literary column, "The Dark Tower." In 1927 two new volumes of his poetry—*Copper Sun* and *The Ballad of the Brown Girl*—were published, as was *Caroling Dusk,* an anthology of Afro-American poetry that he edited. In 1927 he was honored for "distinguished achievement in literature by a Negro" with the first Harmon Award given by the National Association for the Advancement of Colored People, and he received a Guggenheim fellowship in 1928.

On Apr. 9, 1928, shortly before leaving for France to begin work on his Guggenheim project, Cullen married Nina Yolande DuBois, daughter of Dr. W. E. B. DuBois, the most respected Afro-American intellectual of the times. Despite their long friendship, temperamental differences between Cullen and his wife appeared almost immediately after the marriage. Their delayed honeymoon in Paris was aborted by her illness, which necessitated her return to the United States in the fall of that year while Cullen remained abroad. In the following year, she initiated divorce proceedings; the divorce was granted in March 1930.

Rather than completing his Guggenheim project, Cullen wrote a long poem and a number of shorter ones, *The Black Christ and Other Poems* (1929). The long title poem describes Christ sacrificing himself to save a black man from lynching. In 1929, he also published four essays in *The Crisis,* edited by W. E. B. DuBois. Although he had vociferously opposed the belief that Negro writers should limit themselves to Negro themes, Cullen again focused on black subjects in his next book, *One Way to Heaven* (1932), a novel written to reveal the beauty, tenderness, and joy of black life in Harlem.

Between 1929 and 1934 Cullen returned to the United States periodically. Then, in 1934, despite his affection for France, he permanently relocated in the United States and, refusing invitations to teach at black colleges in the South, accepted a position at Frederick Douglass Junior High School in New York, where he taught French, English, and creative writing until his death. On Sept. 27, 1940, he married Ida Mae Roberson.

Although his devotion to teaching young people limited his time, Cullen continued to write. After a poetic drama published as the title poem of *The Medea and Some Poems* (1935), he produced two works for children: *The Lost Zoo* (1940), a collection of poems about the animals left behind when Noah sailed, and *My Lives and How I Lost Them by Christopher Cat* (1942), the autobiography of a cat. His long interest in writing drama was finally rewarded professionally with the Broadway production of *St. Louis Woman,* based on Arna Bontemps' novel, *God Sends Sunday.* At the time of his death (from uremic poisoning), Cullen was revising his longest poem "The Unfinished Chronicle," preparing a book of children's literature, editing a collection of his poetry, and contemplating an autobiography, *The Sum of My Days.* The collection of poetry was published posthumously as *On These I Stand* (1947).

Throughout his poetic career, Cullen was a lyricist, best when writing subjectively and most effective when his feelings derived from subjects sufficiently universal to encourage a reader's interest and, possibly, identification. One of the few black writers to appear in American literature anthologies published before 1960, Cullen's creative genius and his devotion to teaching were commemorated by his name being given to a school in Harlem and to the Harlem branch of the New York Public Library.

[Cullen's other works include *The Third Fourth of July,* a play co-authored with Owen Dodson and reprinted in *Theatre Arts,* Aug. 1946. Cullen's papers are at Dilliard Univ. in New Orleans.

Full-length studies of Cullen are found in Stephen A. Bronz, *Roots of Racial Consciousness* (1964); Blanche E. Ferguson, *Countee Cullen and The Negro Renaissance* (1966); Margaret Perry, *A Bio-Bibliography of Countee P. Cullen* (1971); and Darwin T. Turner, *In a Minor Chord* (1971).

Long unpublished studies of Cullen's life and work are Helen Dinger, "A Study of Countee Cullen with Emphasis on His Poetical Works" (master's thesis, Columbia Univ., 1953); and Beulah Reimherr, "Countee Cullen: A Biographical and Critical Study" (master's thesis, Univ. of Maryland, 1960).

Studies of Cullen's fiction are in Robert Bone, *The Negro Novel in America* (rev. ed., 1965); Hugh M. Gloster, *Negro Voices in American Fiction* (1948); and Saunders Redding, *To Make a Poet Black* (1939). Examinations of Cullen's poetic themes can be found in Nicholas Canady, Jr., "Major Themes in the Poetry of Countee Cullen," A. Bontemps, ed., *The Harlem Renaissance Remembered,* pp. 103–125 (1972); Arthur P. Davis, "The Alien and Exile Theme in Countee Cullen's Racial Poems," *Phylon,* 14 (1953); 390–400.

Other useful insights are Arna Bontemps, "The Awakening: A Memoir," in *The Harlem Renaissance Remembered,* pp. 1–26; "Countee Cullen, American Poet," *The People's Voice,* Jan. 26, 1946, pp. 52–53; "The James Weldon Johnson Memorial Collection of Negro Arts and Letters," *Yale Univ. Lib. Gazette,* 18 (1943), 19–26; Sterling Brown, *Negro Poetry and Drama* (1937); Abraham Chapman, "The Harlem Renaissance in Literary History," *College Language Assn. Jour.,* 11 (1967), 38–58; Eugenia Collier, "I Do Not Marvel, Countee Cullen," *College Language Assn. Jour.,* 11 (1967), 73–87; David Dorsey, Jr., "Countee Cullen's Use of Greek Mythology," *College Language Assn. Jour.,* 13 (1969), 68–77; Nathan I. Huggins, *Harlem Renaissance* (1971); Langston Hughes, "The Negro Artist and the Racial Mountain," *Nation,* 122 (1926), 692–694; George Kent, "Patterns of the Harlem Renaissance," *The Harlem Renaissance Remembered,* pp. 27–50; James C. Kilgore, "Toward the Dark Tower" *Black World,* 19 (1970), 14–17; John S. Lash, "The Anthologist and the Negro Author," *Phylon,* 8 (1947), 68–76; Alain Locke, "Introduction," *Four Negro Poets* (1927); Beulah Reimherr, "Race Consciousness in Countee Cullen's Poetry," *Susquehanna Univ. Studies,* 7, no. 2 (1963), 65–82; Izetta W. Robb, "From the Darker Side," *Opportunity,* 4 (1926), 381–382; Harvey Webster, "A Difficult Career," *Poetry,* 70 (1947), 222–225; and Bertram Woodruff, "The Poetic Philosophy of Countee Cullen," *Phylon,* 1 (1940), 213–223. A portrait can be found in *Sat. Rev. of Lit.,* Mar. 22, 1947, pp. 12–13.]

DARWIN T. TURNER

CUNNINGHAM, KATE (RICHARDS) O'HARE. See O'HARE, KATE RICHARDS CUNNINGHAM.

CUPPY, WILLIAM JACOB (WILL) (Aug. 23, 1884–Sept. 19, 1949), humorist and literary critic, was born in Auburn, Ind., the second of three children and the older of two sons of Thomas Jefferson Cuppy and Mary Francis (Stahl) Cuppy. Of Huguenot origin, Will's paternal ancestors had migrated from South Carolina; his mother's forebears were Pennsylvania Dutch. His paternal grandfather, Abram Cuppy, was an Indiana state senator.

Cuppy's father sold sewing machines and worked as a cobbler. His mother ran a small shop in which she sold embroidery and other fancywork; she may also have taught school. She sang in the Presbyterian church while Will or his brother pumped the organ. Cuppy recalled happy childhood summers on his widowed grandmother's farm near South Whitley, Ind., "where I acquired my first knowledge of the birds and the flowers and all the other aspects of animate nature which I have treated none too kindly in some of my writings" (Kunitz, p. 182).

Cuppy graduated from Auburn high school in 1902 and in the same year entered the University of Chicago, where he worked as college reporter for the *Chicago Record-Herald,* the *Chicago Daily News,* and other newspapers. After receiving a Ph.B. in 1907, he worked toward a Ph.D. in English literature, meanwhile completing his first book in 1909, *Maroon Tales*—short stories of fraternity life written at the request of university authorities who desired that he create some "traditions" for the recently inaugurated fraternity system. Cuppy enjoyed the sheltered, scholarly life of a graduate student and lingered at Chicago until 1914, when he received his M.A. in English and went to New York City and began a career in journalism. In his later humorous writing, his favorite role was that of the diffident but intellectually assertive and rhetorically pompous pedant and scholar.

During World War I, Cuppy served as a second lieutenant in the Motor Transport Corps. After the war he worked on the *New York Herald-Tribune,* where in 1926 he began a new column in the Sunday book review section entitled "Light Reading," later renamed "Mystery and Adventure." Over the next twenty-three years he reviewed nearly 4,000 books, mostly detective fiction and true crime narratives. He did much of his writing in his isolated cabin on Jones Island, off Long Island, where he lived from 1921 to 1929 and which he revisited regularly for the rest of his life. In the sketches collected in his first humorous volume, *How to Be a Hermit* (1929), he ridiculed, despite much self-denigration, the pretensions of a gadget-oriented culture and maintained that "a hermit is simply a person to whom civilization has failed to adjust itself." Because of the recipes included in it, which he created while living in his cabin, the Library of Congress classified it under "culinary arts." Subsequent collections of essays and sketches, *How to Tell Your Friends from the Apes* (1931)—most of which appeared first in the *New Yorker*—*How to Become Ex-*

tinct (1941), and *How to Attract the Wombat* (1949), were, as he rightly implies, much more than "little pieces about animals." In the guise of a "bookish old recluse" obsessed with natural history, Cuppy attacked, on behalf of reason and tolerance, the gullibility and self-destructiveness of the "modern man or nervous wreck," the arrogance of specialists in science and the humanities, and the shallow optimism that dominated popular culture. Two posthumous volumes selected from Cuppy's notes by Fred Feldkamp, his friend and literary executor, were *The Decline and Fall of Practically Everybody* (1950)—satirical essays on historical figures from Cheops to Miles Standish—and *How to Get from January to December* (1951)—arranged as a comic almanac. He also wrote humorous footnotes for W. C. Sellar and R. J. Yeatman's *Garden Rubbish and Other Country Bumps* (1937) and edited collections of crime fiction: *Murder Without Tears* (1946), *The World's Great Detective Stories* (1943), and *The World's Great Mystery Stories* (1943).

Cuppy suffered from an inferiority complex that doubtless contributed to his perfectionism as a researcher. Before beginning to write even a short piece, he would read sometimes as many as twenty-five books on the subject, from which he would amass hundreds of note cards; *The Decline and Fall of Practically Everybody,* on which Cuppy started work in 1933, was distilled from about 15,000 such cards. This meticulousness had its compensations: naturalist William Beebe wrote that "When a scientist begins to read Will Cuppy's 'How to Become Extinct,' it doesn't seem as funny as he thought it would be because so much of it is scientifically correct"; but, "the scientist reader sort of comes to and realizes that Will Cuppy is saying what he always wanted to in class but never dared." In saying it with something of the iconoclasm of Ambrose Bierce and H. L. Mencken and in making skillful use of irony, anticlimax, free association, wordplay, and other devices exercised on a wider range of material by such humorists as Robert Benchley and James Thurber, Cuppy made a unique contribution to the sophisticated, urban-oriented humorous essay, which in the twentieth century has overshadowed the older tradition of rustic, crackerbarrel humor while preserving some of its neighborly informality.

Cuppy never married. Although he would work and live like a hermit for weeks at a time among his files in the Greenwich Village apartment where he lived during the last twenty years of his life, he had an unusual capacity for friendship and was in some demand as a lecturer. After a long period of failing health, he was found unconscious in his apartment on Sept. 9, 1949, and taken to St. Vincent's Hospital, where he died ten days later. The cause of death was variously reported as coronary arteriosclerosis and as barbiturate poisoning with complications. His remains were cremated in accordance with his wishes, and interred in a mausoleum near the grave of his mother in Woodlawn Cemetery, Auburn, Ind.

[Fred Feldkamp's Introductions to *The Decline and Fall of Practically Everybody* and *How to Get from January to December*; obituaries in the *N.Y. Times*, Sept. 20, 1949; *N.Y. Herald-Tribune*, Sept. 19, 1949, and Sept. 20, 1949. Stanley J. Kunitz, ed., *Authors Today and Yesterday* (1933), with autobiographical statements and photograph; Burton Rascoe, *Before I Forget* (1937); *Publisher's Weekly*, Oct. 1, 1949; William Rose Benét, *Saturday Rev. of Lit.*, Oct. 15, 1949; David Dempsey, "Humorist," *N.Y. Herald-Tribune Book Rev.*, Oct. 8, 1950. Evaluations include P. G. Wodehouse, *N.Y. Herald-Tribune Book Rev.*, Nov. 29, 1931; William Beebe, *N.Y. Herald-Tribune Book Rev.*, Nov. 16, 1941; E. F. Allen, *N.Y. Times Book Rev.*, Dec. 14, 1941; C. B. Palmer, *N.Y. Times Book Rev.*, Oct. 8, 1950; Will Davidson, *Chicago Sunday Tribune*, Dec. 18, 1949; Norris W. Yates, *The American Humorist* (1964), pp. 321-330. Also consulted were the death certificate of the New York City Department of Health and the hospital summary of St. Vincent's Hospital; James D. Kroemer, *Auburn* (Ind.) *Evening Star* for information about Cuppy's early life. Most of the family records are in the possession of Cuppy's niece, Frances Clark, Fort Wayne, Ind.]

NORRIS YATES

CURME, GEORGE OLIVER (Jan. 14, 1860–Apr. 29, 1948), scholar in German and English grammar, was born in Richmond, Ind., the oldest of the two sons and four daughters of Arthur Allen Curme and Elizabeth Jane (Nicholas) Curme. His mother was the daughter of a minister of the United Brethren Church in Cincinnati. His father, born in England, had come to the United States in childhood and after an apprenticeship as a tanner had gone into the leather business, where he prospered. He was also a licensed Methodist preacher and served for sixteen years on the Richmond city council.

Curme attended public schools and received four years of private instruction in Latin and Greek. He entered DePauw University in 1876, but because of business reverses suffered by his father was able to attend only irregularly until 1881, when he transferred to the University of Michigan. He had elected classical studies, but German, which he took initially as a tool language, became his dominant interest at Michigan under the influence of Calvin Thomas and George A. Hench. He received the B.A. degree from Michigan in 1882 and in 1885 the M.A. from DePauw, his highest earned degree. He spent a year studying at the University of Berlin in 1890.

Curme began his teaching career at Jennings Seminary in Aurora, Ill. (1882-1884) and later taught at the University of Washington (1884-1886) and Cornell College in Iowa (1886-1896). He then became professor of Germanic philology at Northwestern University, where he remained until his retirement in 1934. Curme initially taught Latin, Greek, French, and German; his first published book was an 1888 edition of *Selected Poems* by the French poet Lamartine. After 1887 he specialized in German. He enjoyed German literature—his admiration of Goethe had influenced his switch from the classics to German—and to the end of his career he taught both literature and language, although his scholarly research was confined to the latter.

The two works which won Curme an international reputation were his German and English grammars. His *Grammar of the German Language,* begun in 1886, went through many painstaking revisions before it was first published, at his own expense, in 1905. A second edition appeared in 1922 and a reprint in 1952. Distinctive in its use of original quotations from literary works, newspapers, and the spoken language, it was still the leading scholarly German grammar in English nearly seventy years after its original publication. A by-product of this work, a beginning text entitled *A First German Grammar* (1913), was too scholarly to be a popular success. Curme worked with equal dedication on his *Grammar of the English Language,* which was published in two volumes: *Syntax* (1931) and *Parts of Speech and Accidence* (1935). The English grammar slowly took its place alongside European studies of the subject, becoming influential largely after his death. Curme also wrote *College English Grammar* (1925) and *Principles and Practices of English Grammar* (1946).

After his retirement Curme became lecturer in German at the University of Southern California (1934-1939). Throughout his career he enjoyed contact with students, many of whom were captivated by his contagious enthusiasm. He received honorary doctoral degrees from DePauw (1908), Heidelberg (1926), University of Southern California (1935), and Northwestern (1937). Devoted to his work, which especially in later years, occupied him from morning until night, Curme had little social life, but he was an expert gardener. On July 14, 1881, he married Caroline Chenoweth

Smith of Perrysville, Ind. They had four children: Herta, Anna Gertrude, George Oliver (who became an industrial chemist known for his invention of Prestone antifreeze), and Henry Russell. When the children were grown, the parents separated, and Curme led a lonely life among his books. After 1939 he lived with his daughter Anna Gertrude in White Plains, N.Y., and it was there that he died, of myocardial failure; his remains were cremated.

[*Curme Vol. of Linguistic Studies* (1930), with biographical sketch and portrait; obituary in *Monatshefte*, 40 (1948): 290–295; introduction to 1952 reprint of Curme's *Grammar of the German Language*; family data from Mrs. Harriet E. Bard, Librarian, Morrison-Reeves Lib., Richmond, Ind.; death record from N.Y. State Dept. of Health.]

W. F. LEOPOLD

CURRY, JOHN STEUART (Nov. 14, 1897-Aug. 29, 1946), painter and illustrator, whose dramatic paintings of the American rural scene placed him with Grant Wood and Thomas Hart Benton as a leading exponent of Regionalism in the visual arts during the 1930's, was born near Dunavant, Jefferson County, Kans. He was the oldest of five children of Smith Curry, a farmer, and Margaret (Steuart) Curry. His father's lineage in America reached back four generations to the eighteenth century, when Samuel Curry emigrated from County Tyrone, Ireland, and settled in South Carolina. John Curry, as he later remembered it, was "raised on hard work and the Shorter Catechism." He was not a person to make friends easily, yet his childhood was not cramped. The family farm was prosperous, and both parents were college graduates. As befitting descendants of the Scottish Covenanters, Smith Curry had taken his bride on a wedding trip to Scotland. They brought back colored reproductions of the old masters, with which their children became familiar in the ensuing years. John was short and stockily built, and endowed with a voice that piped in the upper ranges. He attended a local grammar school and the high school in nearby Winchester, but he was an indifferent student and left after three years.

His education in the pictorial arts had its origins in some private lessons as a boy with a friend of his mother, and upon leaving high school he studied briefly at the Kansas City Art Institute. Seeking broader horizons, he drifted to Chicago, where he studied for two years at the Chicago Art Institute, earning his tuition by sweeping floors. After a tour of duty in the army during World War I, he entered Geneva College in Pennsylvania in 1918. There he distinguished himself as a foot-

ball player before dropping out in January 1920. Soon afterward he began a career as a magazine illustrator under the tutelage of Harvey Dunn of Tenafly, N.J. His first sale was an illustration of a locomotive for the *Saturday Evening Post,* and between 1921 and 1925 he filled numerous commissions for Wild West magazines.

By 1925 Curry had become interested in extending his range into more serious art. A loan from a banker who had bought some of his paintings enabled him to spend a year in Paris, and at the Russian Academy, under the tutelage of Basil Schoukhaieff, he acquired the vocabulary of imaginative art. On his return to New York in 1927 he continued his studies at the Art Students' League, where he was particularly influenced by Charles W. Locke and became noticed for his work in lithography.

In 1928 he emerged as a significant artist. His "Baptism in Kansas" was exhibited that year at the Corcoran Gallery in Washington, and Gertrude Vanderbilt Whitney began subsidizing his work. Two years later her Whitney Studio Club gave him a one-man show, which attracted much attention; and his "The Tornado" took second prize at the prestigious Carnegie International Exhibit in 1933. Other works of this period which brought him growing recognition were "State Fair" (1929) and "Hogs Killing a Rattlesnake" (1930), again large oils focusing upon intense moments of the rural life of his childhood. He declared that his intention was to bring to his subject matter sufficient form "so that the feeling and underlying motive that comes through will be sharpened and given its full dramatic power." When his paintings were displayed in Kansas in 1931, in an exhibition sponsored by the newspaper publisher William Allen White, local reviewers found them "drab" and "uncivic," but eastern critics, caught up in the current nativist enthusiasm for an American representational art uncorrupted by foreign "isms," boosted his reputation.

Curry traveled with the Ringling Brothers circus in 1932, finding dramatic subject matter for sketches, and later for oils of elephants and trapeze artists. In 1936 he was awarded the commission to paint a mural for the Department of Justice building in Washington, D.C., and subsequently for the General Land Office. He also designed and painted murals for the state capitol building in Topeka, Kans., inviting controversy by depicting John Brown in a pose reminiscent of Michelangelo's Deity on the ceiling of the Sistine Chapel. Although Curry never articulated his political views, his paintings of blacks in themes of slavery and emancipation suggest a sympathy with the incipient civil rights movement of the New Deal period.

For several years Curry taught painting at the Cooper Union in New York City and the Art Students' League, but in 1936 he moved from his home in Westport, Conn., to become artist in residence at the University of Wisconsin in Madison. With no formal duties, instructional or otherwise, he mingled freely with the undergraduates and roamed the Wisconsin countryside, painting undistinguished landscapes of the dairyland. His students would later recall him primarily for his friendly, bemused smile and the informality of his dress. Becoming interested in talent native to the region, he developed the Rural Art Project, an annual exhibition of largely amateur painters and sculptors. He died in Madison of a heart attack at the age of forty-eight and was buried in the family plot in the cemetery of the Reformed Presbyterian Church of Winchester, Kans. Curry was married twice: to Clara Derrick in New York City on Jan. 23, 1923, and after her death in 1932, to Kathleen Muriel Gould in Greenwich, Conn., on June 2, 1934.

By the mid-1930's, critical opinion had begun to turn away from the provincialism of the Regional school, and later estimates have called attention to much that was imitative in Curry's style. Although he was elected an academician of the National Academy of Design in 1943, his reputation had begun to wane before his death. A generation later he was recalled chiefly as part of a transitory artistic vogue for the American scene.

[Lawrence E. Schmeckebier, *John Steuart Curry's Pageant of America* (1943), gives a full coverage of Curry's life and work. Other biographical and critical material may be found in *John Steuart Curry* (1970), the catalogue of a retrospective exhibition held in the Kans. State Capitol (largely reprinted from the *Kans. Quart.*, Fall 1970). See also *Current Biog.*, 1941; *Nat. Cyc. Am. Biog.*, Current vol. F, pp. 448–449; and *N.Y. Times* obituary, Aug. 30, 1946. For conflicting appraisals of his work, see Margaret Bruening in *Studio*, June 1937, and John Canaday in the *N.Y. Times*, Nov. 1, 1970, sec. 2.]

ALBERT F. McLEAN

CUSHMAN, JOSEPH AUGUSTINE (Jan. 31, 1881–Apr. 16, 1949), micropaleontologist and prolific student of the single-celled living and fossil animals known as Foraminifera, was born in Bridgewater, Mass. He was of solid New England stock and could literally trace his ancestry to the *Mayflower* pilgrims. He was the second son of the second marriage of both his parents, Darius and Jane Frances (Fuller) (Pratt) Cushman. His father sold and repaired shoes in Bridgewater. Cushman

graduated from Bridgewater High School in 1897 and hoped to pursue a medical career, but his father's death forced a change in plans. He entered the Bridgewater Normal School and graduated in 1901. He received a scholarship from Harvard University and entered the Lawrence Scientific School with junior standing in the fall of 1901. He intended to pursue a career in cryptogamic botany, but fell under the influence of the great specialist in fossil echinoderms, Robert Tracy Jackson. He switched to paleontology and graduated magna cum laude in 1903.

In October 1903, he married Alice Edna Wilson of Fall River, Mass. They had three children: Robert Wilson, Alice Eleanor, and Ruth Allerton. She died of tuberculosis in 1912 and in September 1913, Cushman married Frieda Gerlach Billings.

After graduation, Cushman became a curator at the Boston Society of Natural History, where he remained until 1923. His studies of Foraminifera began during two summers' work (1904, 1905) at the U.S. Fish Commission in Woods Hole, Mass., where he undertook to study worldwide collections made by the commission's steamer *Albatross*. He worked with the U.S. Geological Survey from 1912-1921 and again from 1926 until his death in 1949. Late in 1922 he began to reap the considerable benefits available in consulting for the petroleum industry; he worked for the Marland Oil Company and continued consulting until the end of 1925. With the direct income from this venture and the returns from his uncanny skill in investment, he built his own laboratory in Sharon, Mass., in 1923. Here he remained, devoting himself entirely to research on Foraminifera, until his death. He offered the facilities of his laboratory to students at nearby Harvard, Radcliffe, and M.I.T. For twenty-three years he served as lecturer (without stipend) at Harvard University. In 1937 these services were recognized when Harvard conferred upon him the honorary degree of doctor of science. Among other honors and offices, he was elected honorary fellow of the Royal Microscopical Society of London in 1938; he received the Hayden Memorial Geological Award of the Academy of Natural Sciences of Philadelphia in 1945, served as president of the Society of Economic Paleontologists and Mineralogists in 1930-1931, and of the Paleontological Society in 1937. He was vice-president of the Geological Society of America in 1938 and editor of the *Journal of Paleontology* from 1927 to 1930.

Cushman was a prodigious researcher. His complete bibliography lists 557 items, more than 90 percent dealing with the systematics of Foraminifera. He founded his own journal at his laboratory in Sharon, *Contributions from the Cushman Laboratory for Foraminiferal Research*. It appeared in twenty-five volumes from 1925 to 1949. Upon his death, his unparalleled collection, including 12,000 primary and secondary type specimens, was bequeathed to the U.S. National Museum. His journal, first renamed *Contributions from the Cushman Foundation for Foraminiferal Research* (21 vols., 1950 to 1970), continues as the *Journal for Foraminiferal Research* (4th vol., 1974).

Cushman was no theorist. His work was squarely in the old tradition of empirical, descriptive, taxonomic paleontology. His thorough reclassification of the Foraminifera was first published in the 1927 volume of the *Contributions* and formed the basis for his famous text *Foraminifera, Their Classification and Economic Use* (4 eds., 1928, 1933, 1940, 1948). He recognized that previous classifications, based on external morphology of the outer shell or test, were poorly constructed since they confounded superficially similar forms of diverse evolutionary origin. He based his reclassification upon the structure of the test and upon the mode of its ontogenetic development, for he (correctly we would say) regarded these characters (1927, p. 4) as "fundamental" and as representing "deep-seated physiologic expression."

Cushman showed no originality in the evolutionary theory that he used to buttress his work. He supported faithfully the doctrines of recapitulation and racial life cycles taught by his mentor R. T. Jackson (who had learned them from his teacher, Alpheus Hyatt). His first major work (1902) applied Jackson's concept of localized stages to plants (an adjunct of recapitulation theory claiming that localized points of an adult organism repeat the phyletic history of its lineage just as the entire organism does in its total growth). He outlined his evolutionary thought in his only major theoretical work (1905): classification should be based on phylogeny; phylogeny can be inferred from adult ancestral stages repeated in correct sequence during the early growth of a descendant (recapitulation); lineages, like individuals, have life cycles with stages of youth, maturity, and old age; phyletic old age is marked by a series of senescent characters including loss of ornamentation, spinose and extravagant growth, and return to the features of youthful stages of the same organism (theory of racial senescence). These notions were already outdated when he based his classification of Foraminifera upon them in 1927; they were downright antiquated when he invoked them again without the slightest hint of change in his last theoretical paper of 1945. He accepted an inductive model of scientific progress and apparently believed with a good deal of moral fervor that the task of paleontology (and of the scientist in general) was simply to describe and document in an unbiased way (see his 1938 address on the future of paleontology).

He was an exemplar of normal science and we should not criticize him for lack of theoretical interest. His research was probably of more immediate practical importance than that of any other paleontologist working in this century; for Foraminifera and other microfossils held the key to stratigraphic and environmental interpretation needed by the oil industry. Large fossils are not found in sufficient numbers in drill cores, and microfossils must be used. When Cushman started his work, it was generally believed that Foraminifera could not be used for stratigraphic dating: they were, first of all, an obscure group that had inspired very little interest and even less recorded knowledge; moreover, they were seen as very primitive creatures that had not evolved since their first appearance; their morphologic variability was attributed not to evolution (which would permit their use in dating rocks) but to immediate influences of their surrounding environment. Cushman transformed the study of Foraminifera from an arcane pursuit to one of the most important and potent tools of the petroleum industry. This he did by recognizing minute but constant differences among forms from rocks of different ages. He was therefore able to establish a system of stratigraphic zonation based upon Foraminifera. He named thousands of species during his career—thus displaying a tendency for "splitting" of species much out of favor today. Yet, although his methods may not have represented good biology, they served both his practical needs and the economy well.

[Cushman's works include "Studies of Localized Stages of Growth in Some Common New England Plants," *American Naturalist,* 36 (1902), 865–885; "Developmental Stages in the Lagenidae," *ib'd.,* 39 (1905), 553–637; "An Outline of a Re-classification of the Foraminifera," *Contr. Cushman Lab. Foraminiferal Res.,* 3 (1927), 1–105; *Foraminifera, Their Classification and Economic Use* (1928; 4th ed., 1948); "The Future of Paleontology," *Bull. Geol. Soc. Am.,* 49 (1938), 359–366; "Parallel Evolution in the Foraminifera," *American Jour. Sci.,* 243A (1945), 117–121.

Eight articles about Cushman and a complete bibliography are in Ruth Todd et al., *Memorial Volume for Joseph Cushman* (1950); L. G. Henbest, "Joseph Augustine Cushman and the Contemporary Epoch in Micropaleontology," *Proc. Geol. Soc. America, Annual Report for 1951* (1952).]

STEPHEN JAY GOULD

CUSHMAN, VERA CHARLOTTE SCOTT (Sept. 19, 1876-Feb. 1, 1946), organizer and leader in the YWCA, was born in Ottawa, Ill., the only daughter and second of three children of Samuel Swann Scott and Anna Margaret (Tressler) Scott. Her father, an emigrant from Northern Ireland, founded, with his brothers, the dry goods stores in northern Illinois which eventually became the wholesale and department store firm of Carson Pirie Scott and Company. Her mother, a native of Loyville, Pa., and descendant of German and French families, devoted herself to church and community activities. Except for the years 1887-1891 when Samuel Scott served as president of a local bank in Salina, Kans., the family lived in the Chicago area.

The Scott family was deeply religious and had a strong feeling for foreign missions. Her youngest brother, Rev. George T. Scott, served for many years as assistant director, then executive secretary of the Presbyterian Board of Foreign Missions. From childhood Vera "was trained to think first of others' comfort, well-being and pleasure" and was "taught to regard thoughtfulness of others as an essential part of Christian character and courtesy." (Robinson, p. 68).

A beautiful girl of dignified bearing, with golden hair and violet eyes, Vera Scott graduated from Ferry Hall, Lake Forest, Ill., and from Smith College with the class of 1898. In her second year at Smith, she became ininterested in the student YWCA and served as its president. A natural leader, she continued her active interest in the YWCA after graduation. In 1905 she was appointed to the Joint Committee, chaired by philanthropist Grace H. Dodge, which in 1906 successfully brought together two YWCA organizations to form one national body, the YWCA of the U.S.A. Cushman served on the National Board from its formation until 1936.

On Oct. 15, 1901, Vera Scott married James Stewart Cushman, a New York businessman, engaged in real estate and paper manufacturing; he is credited with designing and building the Allerton Houses, residential hotels in New York City. They had no children. Vera Cushman became a famous and successful hostess, noted for her knack of bringing together people who had common interests.

At the same time both the national YWCA, established in 1906, and the YWCA of the City of New York claimed her talents and interest. She helped bring about the merger of all YWCA activities in New York City and was the first president of the YWCA of New York City and one of the leaders of the "Whirlwind Campaign," in which the YWCA and the YMCA of New York City raised $4 million in fourteen days. She served several terms as vice-president of the national organization between 1906 and 1936, but her chief contribution was as chairman of the War Work Council, created in May 1917 to carry the responsibility, designated by the government, as one of seven official war service organizations.

Under Cushman's direction, 140 Hostess Houses were built in the United States and Europe near training camps, naval stations, hospital camps, and embarkation and debarkation ports; these centers provided housing and recreational facilities for nurses, signal corps workers, and other women connected with the military services as well as women industrial workers. In addition, these centers became appropriate places for servicemen to meet wives, relatives, and friends. Over 400 women recruited by the council directed clubs, the Hostess Houses, and service centers in nine countries. In recognition of her war service Cushman was one of six women to receive the Distinguished Service Medal at a ceremony in Washington in the summer of 1919 and was chosen to christen *The Blue Triangle,* one of seven ships named in tribute to war service organizations.

Following the war, Cushman, an enthusiastic traveler, turned her attention to international activities. She served as vice-president of the World Council of the YWCA (1924-1938), was on the executive committee of the Presbyterian Women's Board of Foreign Missions (1920-1921), and was associated with the boards of the China Christian Colleges. She was vice-president of the League of Nations Non-Partisan Association (1923) and was a delegate to the International Suffrage Convention in Geneva, Switzerland in 1920.

Cushman died of coronary occlusion in Savannah, Ga., while en route to Florida for a holiday. Burial was in the Cushman vault at Trinity Cemetery, New York City.

In a letter to the *New York Times,* Oswald Garrison Villard, former editor of *The Nation,* called her "one of the city's greatest human assets, whose influence and radiance will continue to inspire others."

[Interviews with Charlotte Adams, the late Mrs. Cleveland E. Dodge, the late Margaret P. Mead, Mollie Sullivan (Mrs. C. A. Dowell). *Report*, YWCA War Work Council, 1917–1919; *Proc.*, 6th National Convention, YWCA of the U.S.A., Cleveland, Ohio, 1920; clippings, MSS, and other historical materials from the Lib. National Board of the YWCA, N.Y.C.; college and alumnae records, Smith College Arch. Marion O. Robinson, *Eight Women of the YWCA* (1966). Obituaries in *N.Y. Sun*, Feb. 2, 1946 and *N.Y. Times*, Feb. 2, 1946; Oswald Garrison Villard's letter to editor, *N.Y. Times*, Feb. 12, 1946; death record from Ga. Dept. of Public Health.]

MARION O. ROBINSON

CUTLER, ELLIOTT CARR (July 30, 1888–Aug. 16, 1947), surgeon and teacher, was born in Bangor, Maine, the second of five sons of George Chalmers Cutler, a lumber merchant, and Mary Franklin (Wilson) Cutler. Both parents were natives of Maine, and his father's first American ancestor had come to this country from England in 1635. Within a year of Elliott's birth, the family moved to Brookline, Mass., where Cutler attended Pierce grammar school. After preparing at the Volkmann School in Boston he enrolled at Harvard, during his senior year was captain of the crew, and received the B.A. degree in 1909. He then entered Harvard Medical School and, dissatisfied with the limitations of the training then offered, he spent his fourth year studying pathology in the laboratory of Frank B. Mallory at the Boston City Hospital. Cutler later looked back on that year as probably the most important of his training experience, in that it taught him the value of precise work, making and recording careful observations, and taking time to study a medical problem in all its aspects. He received the M.D. degree in 1913 and after a summer studying pathology at Heidelberg became a surgical intern under Harvey Cushing at the newly established Peter Bent Brigham Hospital.

In August 1915, Cutler went to Paris for a three-month period as resident surgeon with the American Ambulance Hospital, and then began a year as resident surgeon at Massachusetts General Hospital. Wishing to broaden his medical background, he then spent several months at the Rockefeller Institute in New York City, studying immunology with Simon Flexner. With America's entry into World War I, Cutler was commissioned a captain and returned to France as a member of the Harvard Unit, Base Hospital No. 5, with the American Expeditionary Forces. On detached duty under the trying conditions of trench warfare during various offensives, in which he assumed great

responsibility for the care and shelter of the wounded, he acquired a broad experience in surgery and was promoted to the rank of major. He returned to Boston at the end of the war to become resident surgeon, under Cushing, at Brigham. On May 24, 1919, Cutler married Caroline Pollard Parker, of Brookline, who had also served at Base Hospital No. 5. Their children were Elliott Carr, Jr., Thomas Pollard, David, Marjorie Parker (who died in childhood), and Tarrant.

In 1921 Cutler was appointed associate in surgery at Brigham Hospital and for two years served as director of the laboratory for surgical research and chairman of the department of surgery at Harvard Medical School. In 1924 he moved to Cleveland as professor of surgery at the Western Reserve University Medical School. In the eight years following, Cutler played an active role in the development of the school. He assumed a large share of the responsibility for the planning and construction of the new Lakeside Hospital, now a division of the University Hospitals in Cleveland, and was director of the surgical service.

In 1932, with the retirement of Cushing, Cutler was recalled by Harvard to become the Moseley Professor of Surgery and surgeon-in-chief of the Peter Bent Brigham Hospital, posts he held until his death. This active period of his life was devoted to surgical practice, teaching, and research.

As World War II approached, Cutler foresaw the needs of the civilian population as well as those of the military. As the head of the medical aid division of the Massachusetts Committee on Public Safety, he organized a system whereby in the event of disaster doctors could be mobilized, and he saw to it that every hospital was equipped to function as an emergency unit. This plan served as a model for the nation. He also assisted in organizing the Fifth General Hospital, the Harvard Unit in World War II. As a lieutenant colonel in the Army Medical Reserve Corps, Cutler was recalled to military duty again in 1942. With the rank of colonel he served as chief surgical consultant and subsequently as chief of the professional services division of the European Theater of Operations. He played a major role in establishing good military surgical practice and fostering the excellence of care for the wounded. In his liaison role with the British and the medical services of other countries, he organized the ETO Surgical Society for the dissemination of clinical lessons learned in combat surgery. He was instrumental in the procurement of blood supplies from the United States for use by military surgeons. In 1945 he was promoted to the rank of brigadier general and for his services was awarded the Distinguished Service Medal with an oak leaf cluster, the Legion of Merit, and the Order of the British Empire. For his efforts directed to the improvement of military surgery he also received the Croix de Guerre and the Liberation Cross of Norway.

All his life Cutler emphasized the need to broaden the training of medical students. His teaching clinics were masterpieces, designed to awaken the student's interest in the patient's illness and its management, and he delighted in demonstrating the art and science of diagnosis and surgical treatment. Demanding of his house officers and his students, he was no less demanding of himself. Each detail of a patient's clinical course was carefully evaluated so that, if possible, no matter was left to chance. Another aspect of his surgical program, then highly unusual, was the opportunity afforded his residents to work in the surgical research laboratory, where many a future investigator got his start. To the development of this laboratory he devoted much personal effort, directing the research and raising the funds for its support. The large number of his pupils who became professors and distinguished surgeons bear witness to the inspiration and effectiveness of his teaching.

As a surgeon, Cutler was meticulous, deliberate, and gentle in handling tissues, characteristics inherited from his studies under Cushing; his achievements were of solid importance in the art and science of surgical practice. Notable were his interests in thoracotomy, cardiac surgery, and the treatment of lung abscess. He was the first surgeon (1923) in the United States to perform a successful operation on a heart valve in a patient; he inserted an instrument into the left ventricle to divide the stenosed mitral valve, a procedure that antedated by nearly thirty years the development of similar techniques that became commonplace in the treatment of rheumatic heart disease. He also was the first on this continent to undertake the successful resection of the pericardium for constructive pericarditis. Among other innovative operations he devised was the relief of heart failure by total thyroidectomy. He published more than 260 papers, as well as the *Atlas of Surgical Operations*, written with Robert Zollinger, which remains a valuable source of information for young surgeons in training.

Cutler received honorary degrees from the universities of Strasbourg, Vermont, and Rochester. He belonged to a large number of professional societies, both here and abroad, which included the American Surgical Association (president, 1947), the American College of Surgeons, the American Association for Thoracic Surgery, the American Society for Clinical Investigation, the American Society for Experimental Pathology, the Society for Clinical Surgery (president, 1941-1946). He also served on the editorial board of several journals, including the *American Heart Journal, Journal of Clinical Investigation, Surgery, American Journal of Surgery,* and *British Journal of Surgery.*

Cutler was above medium height, of a lean, wiry build. His sharp features were topped by well-combed blond hair. The genuine interest he felt for his students and others who came into contact with him was manifested by the twinkle in his piercing blue eyes. A generation of students and house officers remember him typically as dressed in a scrub suit covered by a long white coat. A Unitarian in religion, his chief recreations were sailing and fishing.

When he returned from his war services in 1945, Cutler realized that he was in poor health. Examination showed that he was suffering from cancer of the prostate. In spite of continuing metastases, he continued to work with cheerfulness. Only a few weeks before his death, in a speech accepting the Bigelow Medal from the Boston Surgical Society, he reaffirmed his philosophy of teaching and his conviction that a broad background of laboratory training was necessary for the surgeon. He died at his home in Brookline, a few days after his fifty-ninth birthday. In his will he directed that after a complete autopsy, for the benefit of medical science, his body be cremated. The ashes were placed in Mount Auburn Cemetery, Cambridge, Mass.

[Autobiographical notes appear in Harvard Class of 1909, *Tenth Anniversary Report* (1919), p. 89 and *Twenty-fifth Anniversary Report* (1934), p. 150. Cutler's report on his operation of the valves of the heart can be found in *Arch. of Surgery* (1924); the remarks and his speech given on acceptance of the Henry Jacob Bigelow Gold Medal are reprinted in *The New England Jour. of Medicine*, Sept. 25, 1947, pp. 465–470. Other of his numerous publications include, with S. A. Levine, "Cardiotomy and Valvulotomy for Mitral Stenosis, Experimental Observations and Clinical Notes Concerning Operated Case with Recovery," *Boston Medical and Surgical Jour.* 188 (1923): 1023; and "Civilian Medical Defense in Massachusetts," *New England Jour. of Medicine* 227 (1940): 7. Brief biographical sketches appear in *Who Was Who in America*, II (1950); *Am. Men of Sci.* (1960); Sir D'Arcy Power and W. R. Le Fanu, *Lives of the Fellows of the Royal College of Surgeons of England,*

1930–1951 (1953), pp. 198–199. Obituary articles appear in *Surgery* 23 (1948): 863–866; *Jour. of Am. Medical Assoc.*, Sept. 6, 1947, p. 47; *Harvard Univ. Gazette*, XLIII (1948), p. 43–45; *New England Jour. of Medicine*, Oct. 30, 1947; Harvard Class of 1909, *Fortieth Anniversary Report* (1953), pp. 272–274; *N.Y. Times*, Aug. 17, 1947, and Aug. 24, 1947; *Military Surgery* 101 (1947): 351–352; *Brit. Jour. of Surgery* 35 (1947): 208–209; *Brit. Medical Jour.*, Aug. 23, 1947, 312.]

GEORGE H. A. CLOWES

DAMROSCH, WALTER JOHANNES (Jan. 30, 1862-Dec. 22, 1950), musical conductor and composer, was born in Breslau, Prussia (now Wrocław, Poland), the third son and the third of six children of Leopold Damrosch and Helene (von Heimburg) Damrosch. His parents had met in Weimar, where Leopold was concertmaster of the ducal court orchestra, conducted by Franz Liszt, and Helene was a leading singer of opera and lieder. The newlywed couple moved to Breslau in 1858, where Leopold was conductor of the symphony orchestra when Walter was born. Noted musicians who came to perform for the Breslau Orchesterverein often stayed in the Damrosch home, among them Franz Liszt, Richard Wagner, Hans von Bülow, Anton Rubinstein, Clara Schumann, Joseph Joachim, and Carl Tausig.

The Damrosches moved to New York in 1871, when Leopold accepted the directorship of the Arion Society, a German-American male chorus. Walter entered Public School No. 40 and continued his musical studies, which he had begun in Breslau, with a number of German musicians teaching in New York. His principal teacher, however, was his father, who remained his idol and inspiration throughout his career.

His early training as a conductor was mainly as apprentice to his father. (Later, in 1887, he spent three months at Frankfurt, Germany, studying with von Bülow the interpretation of Beethoven's symphonies.) From the age of fourteen he assisted in his father's performances with the Arion Society and with the Oratorio Society of New York and the New York Symphony Society, which Leopold organized in 1873 and in 1878, respectively. During these early years, too, he served as organist at Plymouth Church in Brooklyn (where Henry Ward Beecher was pastor), toured Southern cities (1878) as accompanist for the violinist August Wilhelmj, and was named permanent conductor of the 300-voice Newark Harmonic Society, which he had rehearsed for its part in his father's performance of Berlioz' massive *Requiem* in 1881. In the summer of 1882, he traveled to

Europe for the first time, to meet Liszt at Weimar and to hear the first performance of Wagner's *Parsifal* at Bayreuth.

When Leopold Damrosch undertook to produce German opera for the Metropolitan Opera Association in 1884, Walter served as assistant conductor. And when his father was stricken mortally ill the following winter, in the middle of a triumphant season, young Walter conducted the scheduled performances of *Die Walküre* and *Tannhäuser* and then shared the conducting duties for the remainder of the season.

The Symphony Society and Oratorio Society immediately invited Walter to carry on his father's work as their conductor. The management of the Metropolitan Opera, however, asked him to remain in the role of assistant. At the board's request, he traveled to Europe to engage principals for a second season of German opera at the Metropolitan, including the Wagnerian conductor Anton Seidl, to whom young Damrosch would have to take second place. Damrosch succeeded in gaining for the Metropolitan the services not only of Seidl but also of such outstanding singers as Lilli Lehmann, Max Alvary, and Emil Fischer. To his chagrin, however, he then had few opportunities to conduct the Wagnerian works, and when the Metropolitan in 1891 reverted to Italian and French opera, Damrosch chose to go his own way.

In the winter of 1893-1894 he staged his own production of Wagner's *Die Götterdämmerung* in a charity performance at Carnegie Hall. It was so well received that he went on to give *Die Walküre* and then to repeat both works. The success spurred him to a bolder step: he set out to form his own Wagnerian company, financing it by selling his house, launching a Wagner Society to help sell subscription tickets, and winning the support of William Steinway, then the head of the piano firm.

The Damrosch Opera Company made its debut in the spring of 1895 at the Metropolitan Opera House and for five seasons performed in New York and on tours that enabled audiences as far west as Denver to hear—often for the first time—the Wagnerian music dramas, Beethoven's *Fidelio,* and other works of the German repertoire. Damrosch's company included such singers as Johanna Gadski, Rosa Sucher, Marie Brema, Katharina Klafsky, Milka Ternina, Lehmann, Lillian Nordica, Fischer, Alvary, and the American baritone, David Bispham. Nellie Melba joined the roster in the last two seasons, when Damrosch formed a partnership with her manager, Charles Ellis.

Through these years, Damrosch later said,

he became increasingly doubtful about Wagner's dramatic theory and increasingly convinced that the music succeeded in spite of the drama. He did return to the Metropolitan to conduct the German repertoire for two seasons (1900-1902), but thereafter he devoted himself almost exclusively to symphonic conducting.

During the Damrosch Opera Company years, he also made his debut as a composer. He produced his opera *The Scarlet Letter* (with a libretto by Hawthorne's son-in-law George Parsons Lathrop) for the first time in 1896, in Boston. Although Damrosch himself noted the "overwhelming influence" of Wagner in the work, critics acknowledged signs of a genuine talent for composing in the thirty-four-year-old conductor. Damrosch soon began a second opera, *Cyrano* (libretto by W. J. Henderson), but did not complete it until 1913, when it was produced by the Metropolitan. In the meantime, he wrote a number of songs, among which "Danny Deever" (to Kipling's poem) remains the best known of all his compositions.

Having put opera-conducting behind him after the turn of the century, Damrosch determined to establish an orchestra on a permanent basis in New York, as Theodore Thomas had managed to do in Chicago a decade before. An invitation to conduct the Philharmonic Society in 1902 appeared to present an opportunity. The Philharmonic Society had been organized sixty years earlier on a cooperative basis and was always in financial difficulty. Damrosch proposed to place the orchestra under a permanent board of directors who would see to its financial stability. He proceeded to line up a prospective board, and when the Philharmonic Society's members rejected his plan, Damrosch persuaded his group of benefactors—led by Harry Harkness Flagler—to join in the reorganization of the New York Symphony Society instead. In 1903 he thus gained his permanent orchestra. With it, he performed in New York (introducing Sunday afternoon concerts) and in wide-ranging tours of the United States. Carrying on the pioneer work begun by Theodore Thomas in the 1860's and continued by his father, Walter Damrosch took the New York Symphony to every part of the United States, to cities where a symphony orchestra had never been heard. Often, he would present concerts for children or speak informally to his audiences to share with them his enthusiasm for a particular feature of the work at hand. He found it, he said, always "fascinating . . . to do pioneer work, either by organizing something new, introducing a new composer, or penetrating into

regions where symphonic music was not yet known" (*My Musical Life,* p. 189).

During World War I, Damrosch went to France to conduct concerts for American troops, and he remained to organize (with Gen. John J. Pershing's support) a school at Chaumont for training army bandmasters. The fruitful relationship established there between French and American musicians led Damrosch to urge his French friends to find a way to continue after the war—perhaps, he suggested, by founding a summer music school near Paris, where gifted young American musicians could come to work with French masters. The French responded by establishing the summer music school at Fontainebleau, which was to contribute to the training of a number of America's most distinguished composers. When the French government invited Damrosch to bring the New York Symphony to perform in France in 1920, Flagler's generosity made it possible for them to tour in five European countries. From France (where the schedule included a special concert at Fontainebleau), to Italy, to Belgium, to Holland, to England, Damrosch took his orchestra in triumph—the first American symphony orchestra to be heard in Europe.

Like his father, Walter Damrosch took pride in introducing musical works to the American public. Among the most significant pieces he performed for the first time in the United States were Liszt's oratorio *Christus,* Wagner's *Parsifal,* Tchaikovsky's Fourth and Sixth symphonies, Brahms's Fourth, Bruckner's Third, Mahler's Fourth, Saint-Saëns's *Samson et Dalila,* Vaughan Williams' *London* and *Pastoral* symphonies, Sibelius' *Tapiola* and Fourth Symphony, Ravel's *Daphnis et Chloë,* Honegger's *Pacific 231.* He gave the first performances anywhere of Bloch's *America,* Gershwin's Concerto in F (which Damrosch commissioned) and *An American in Paris,* and works by other American composers including George W. Chadwick, Henry K. Hadley, D. G. Mason, John Alden Carpenter, Deems Taylor, E. B. Hill, and Aaron Copland. In 1891, Damrosch arranged for Tchaikovsky to come to New York to conduct his own music during a festival with which Damrosch inaugurated a new concert hall built on Fifty-seventh Street by his friend Andrew Carnegie and later renamed Carnegie Hall. It was the first time a major European composer had visited the United States.

Damrosch's musical convictions were nevertheless conservative. If he was a musical missionary—and he was an ardent one—his gospel was the tradition of European classical and nineteenth-century music. Although he felt it his duty to conduct new music, he had no sympathy for the "ultra-modern." "There is no love in this music," he said, "no nobility, no God" (*N.Y. World-Telegram,* June 8, 1946). When in 1932 Leopold Stokowski proposed to have the Philadelphia Orchestra's performances of new music broadcast into school classrooms, Damrosch protested that "to force these experiments on helpless children is criminal" (*N.Y. Times,* Oct. 20, 1932).

Damrosch was himself a pioneer in giving concerts for children (only Theodore Thomas was earlier), having begun a series with the New York Symphony in 1891. In these concerts, as in the broadcasts he undertook in the last phase of his career, he aimed to bring his young listeners an understanding of the music of Beethoven, Mozart, Wagner, and other masters as examples of musical art but "above all, a love for it as an expression of their own inner lives."

In 1926, the New York Symphony merged with the Philharmonic Society to form the Philharmonic-Symphony of New York, under the conductorship of Arturo Toscanini. Damrosch at first retired to the family retreat at Bar Harbor, Maine, but soon emerged to pioneer in a new field: radio broadcasting. He had already, in 1925, conducted the New York Symphony in the first broadcast of an orchestral concert. The National Broadcasting Company (NBC) immediately asked him to broadcast a series of Saturday evening concerts in the winter of 1926-1927. In 1927, he was named musical counsel for NBC and that winter broadcast twenty-four concerts with explanatory comments as part of a new "University of the Air." Although radio was at that time technically incapable of transmitting with any fidelity the sound of a symphony orchestra, NBC's statisticians estimated a weekly audience of four million for the broadcasts, and Damrosch received as many as 30,000 letters a week from listeners.

That same year, he suggested that NBC try a series of musical programs for young people, to be broadcast into school classrooms on Friday mornings. Three test programs drew a promising response from selected studio audiences of teachers, and on Oct. 26, 1928, Damrosch launched the "NBC Music Appreciation Hour" broadcasts, which he narrated and conducted until they were discontinued in 1942. The first year's audience of some one and a half million grew to over seven million in the 1930's, and by 1941 nearly two million "teacher's manuals" for the broadcasts had been distributed.

The network of twenty-six stations that carried the original broadcast had grown to 137 by the time the series ended, and Damrosch's grandfatherly "Good morning, my dear children" not only was familiar in every part of the United States but was relayed by shortwave to Latin America, Africa, and Asia. Damrosch was particularly pleased to hear from listeners in rural areas, where some teachers regularly gathered their children around a radio-equipped automobile to hear "Papa" Damrosch talk about his beloved music and perform it for them.

In 1937, at seventy-five, Damrosch again appeared in the role of composer, when his opera *The Man Without a Country* (libretto by Arthur Guiterman) was performed first at the Metropolitan Opera and then at the Chicago City Opera. A revised version of *Cyrano* was presented in a concert of the New York Philharmonic in 1941, and in 1942 Damrosch produced a new work, *The Opera Cloak,* with a libretto by his daughter, Gretchen Finletter. His ballad for baritone voice, chorus, and orchestra, *Dunkirk* (text by R. Nathan), was performed in 1943.

Damrosch won lasting respect not so much through his achievements as an interpreter as through his historic work in bringing operatic and symphonic music to an ever-widening American public over a span of more than half a century. By means of his industry, initiative, tactical skill, organizational ability, personal charm, and infectious devotion to music, he contributed to the establishment of American musical institutions and to the growth of American audiences for music.

Damrosch died of a heart attack in his Manhattan home. He was buried in Bar Harbor, Maine, after funeral services in New York City. His wife, the former Margaret Blaine (whom he married on May 17, 1890), died in 1949. Damrosch was survived by their four daughters: Alice, Gretchen, Leopoldine ("Polly"), and Anita.

He received many honors during his lifetime. Among them were decorations from the French, Italian, Belgian, and Spanish governments; the silver medal of the Worshipful Company of Musicians of London; the gold medal of the National Institute of Arts and Letters; and honorary degrees from several universities. A concert given in 1922 in New York by his colleagues Josef Stransky, Artur Bodanzky, Albert Coates, Willem Mengelberg, and Leopold Stokowski served to raise funds for a Walter Damrosch Fellowship in Music at the American Academy in Rome. Damrosch was president of the National Institute of Arts and Letters (1927-1929 and 1936-1941), the American Academy of Arts and Letters (1941-1948), and also the first president (1933-1943) of the Musicians Emergency Fund, for which he gave numerous benefit performances.

In 1959, the City of New York established Damrosch Park in the Lincoln Center complex. The 2.5-acre site next to the Metropolitan Opera House is dedicated to the "distinguished family of musicians"—Leopold, Frank, and Walter Damrosch, Clara Damrosch Mannes (Walter's younger sister), and her husband, David Mannes, founder of the Mannes School of Music.

[The Lib. of Cong. has an extensive collection of Damrosch family papers. The principal published sources on Damrosch's life include his autobiography, *My Musical Life* (1923, with an additional chapter written for a new edition in 1930); W. J. Henderson, "Walter Damrosch," *Musical Quart.*, Jan. 1932; a controversial essay, "Walter Damrosch," signed "Martin Goodale"—evidently a pseudonym—in *Am. Mercury*, Mar. 1935; and a detailed, but in some points inaccurate, obituary in the *N.Y. Times*, Dec. 23, 1950.]

IRVING L. SABLOSKY

DANDY, WALTER EDWARD (Apr. 6, 1886-Apr. 19, 1946), neurological surgeon, was born in Sedalia, Mo., the only child of John and Rachel (Kilpatrick) Dandy, who had come to the United States two years earlier from Barrow-in-Furness, Lancashire, England. A member of the fundamentalist Plymouth Brethren, John Dandy had been a railroad man in England. In America he became a locomotive engineer on the Missouri-Kansas-Texas Railroad and in time the engineer of its celebrated passenger train, the Katy Flyer.

Growing up in Sedalia, Walter Dandy delivered newspapers, developed a skill at marbles, and graduated from the local high school at the head of his class. He enrolled at the University of Missouri, where he earned part of his expenses by working in the science laboratories and as an assistant to the zoologist Winterton C. Curtis. Dandy had probably already determined on a career in medicine, since he chose a number of classes in the biological sciences and while still an undergraduate took several preclinical courses at the university's medical school. Curtis and other Johns Hopkins alumni at Missouri urged him to continue his studies at the Johns Hopkins University School of Medicine; and with their aid, after receiving the A.B. degree in 1907, Dandy entered the second-year class at Johns Hopkins. Before graduating he published his first paper, a study of the nervous and vascular systems of a young hu-

man embryo. He received the M.D. degree in 1910 and was chosen by Harvey Cushing as his surgical assistant for the year 1910-1911 in the Hunterian Laboratory of Experimental Medicine. There, experimenting with dogs, Dandy began studying the blood and nerve supplies of the pituitary body, the subject of his second paper, published in 1911 with Emil Goetsch. His research earned him the M.A. degree that year and also an appointment to the house staff of the Johns Hopkins Hospital (where William S. Halsted was chief of surgery) to serve for a year as Cushing's clinical assistant in neurosurgery.

During Dandy's first year at the Hunterian, a series of clashes began between him and Cushing, which developed into a lifelong personal conflict. Dandy himself remembered that the first incident occurred when some experiments he had been carrying out on the production of glycosuria in rabbits by stimulation of the sympathetic nerves produced results that contradicted a theory of Cushing's. Both men were highly competitive, and later disagreements, stemming in part from arguments over priority and in part from marked differences in temperament, increasingly marred their relations. A careful study of the quarrel suggests that Cushing was the antagonist. In the judgment of his biographer, Cushing at times "seemed jealous of his own priority, and several who had difficulties while on his service have insisted that he could not face serious competition" (Fulton, p. 489).

In 1912, when Cushing left Johns Hopkins to become professor of surgery at Harvard and surgeon-in-chief at the new Peter Bent Brigham Hospital, he informed Dandy, with very little warning, that he was not being taken to Boston. Dandy was allowed to remain at the Johns Hopkins Hospital at first on an unofficial basis, but soon received an appointment to Halsted's service and later became resident surgeon (1916-1918). During these and the succeeding years he carried out the brilliant work that eventually brought him recognition as Cushing's equal in surgery.

At the Hunterian, Dandy had already begun research, in collaboration with Kenneth D. Blackfan, on the mechanism and pathology of hydrocephalus. In 1913 they published the first in a series of papers that demonstrated the mode of circulation of the cerebrospinal fluid and for the first time provided a physiological basis for diagnosing hydrocephalus and treating the disorder by surgery. The work gave Dandy an international reputation.

Dandy made even more important advances, when in 1918, after several years of research on brain tumors, he introduced ventriculography, a diagnostic method that many regard as the greatest single contribution ever made to neurological surgery. He showed by animal experiment that if some of the cerebrospinal fluid were removed from the cerebral ventricles and replaced by air, the outline of the ventricles would appear clearly on X-ray film. Abnormalities in contour could reveal the presence and exact location of lesions such as tumors, otherwise undetectable, so that early diagnosis and surgical removal would be possible. Some months later Dandy reported another important diagnostic procedure, pneumoencephalography, which by injecting air into the spinal canal made possible the study through X-ray films of the subarachnoid space, sometimes affected directly or indirectly by brain lesions.

In 1922 Dandy announced a new surgical approach to the removal of tumors of the acoustic nerve, a method that involved total extirpation of the tumor and greatly reduced the formerly high mortality rate. His successful surgical method for the treatment of trigeminal neuralgia, a disease characterized by excruciating facial pain, represents one of his most brilliant and original contributions. His procedure, reported in 1925, had a mortality rate close to zero and did not produce the facial palsies, corneal ulcers, and partial paralyses that had sometimes followed the classical operation. Two years later he introduced a curative operative procedure for glossopharyngeal neuralgia (tic douloureux), another form of facial neuralgia.

One of Dandy's greatest accomplishments was the development of an operation that would often permanently cure Ménière's disease, the symptoms of which include violent attacks of dizziness, nausea, and progressive deafness. In 1928 he reported nine such operations, all successful. The procedure involved dividing the fibers of the anterior part of the acoustic nerve and did not impair hearing. Among Dandy's other contributions were his surgical cures for intracranial aneurysms, his demonstration that a ruptured vertebral disk was often the cause of pain in the lower back and leg, and his devising of new diagnostic tests and operative procedures for this ailment. In addition to many papers, he published five books: *Benign Tumors in the Third Ventricle of the Brain: Diagnosis and Treatment* (1933), *Benign, Encapsulated Tumors in the Lateral Ventricles of the Brain: Diagnosis and Treatment* (1934), *Orbital Tumors: Results Following the Transcranial Op-* *erative Attack* (1941), *Intracranial Arterial Aneurysms* (1944), and *Surgery of the Brain* (1945), a monograph of more than six hundred pages.

Although after 1918 Dandy engaged in private practice, he retained a lifelong connection with the Johns Hopkins medical school, holding a succession of professorial posts in neurological surgery, and with the Johns Hopkins Hospital, where his last appointments were as visiting surgeon in neurosurgery (1928-1946) and neurosurgeon in the diagnostic clinic (1941-1946). Dandy was a brilliant diagnostician, and he displayed great originality and imagination in devising new surgical techniques, as well as courage in applying them. He possessed acute powers of observation and a beautiful surgical technique reflected in an economy of movement.

A complex man, Dandy was often hot-tempered and demanding, and at times petty. On other occasions he could be gracious and considerate to patients, residents, and medical students. He was a pragmatist by temperament and apparently had no interest in organized religion. At the age of thirty-eight, on Oct. 1, 1924, he married Sadie Estelle Martin of Baltimore. Their children were Walter Edward, Mary Ellen, Kathleen Louise, and Margaret Martin. Aside from his family and career, Dandy's interests centered in golf, which he played at least once a week, tennis, bridge, baseball, and boxing. He was an avid reader of history and biography, particularly of works dealing with the Civil War. As a baseball fan, he took pride in having developed during his later years a protective cap that had pockets on either side into which plastic cups could be inserted before a player came to bat.

Dandy never lost his scientific curiosity, and before his final illness was working to determine just where the center of consciousness was located in the brain, the subject of his last publication. He died in Johns Hopkins Hospital a few days after his sixtieth birthday, of a coronary occlusion, and was buried in Druid Ridge Cemetery, Baltimore.

[Most of Dandy's papers are in the possession of his widow; a small portion is in the Welch Medical Lab., Baltimore. Charles E. Troland and Frank J. Otenasek, eds., *Selected Writings of Walter E. Dandy* (1957), contains his most important professional papers. Published biographical accounts include: Samuel J. Crowe, *Halsted of Johns Hopkins: The Man and His Men* (1957), chap. v; memoir by Eldridge Campbell in *Jour. of Neurosurgery*, May 1951, an excellent summary of Dandy's professional accomplishments; and briefer sketches by Alfred Blalock in *Surgery*, May 1946, and by A. Earl Walker in Webb Haymaker, ed., *The Founders of Neurology* (1953). Mark A. Ravitch, ed., *The Papers of Alfred Blalock*, 2 vols. (1966), contains many references to Dandy;

there are several also in A. Earl Walker, ed., *A Hist. of Neurological Surgery* (1951), a valuable survey. John F. Fulton, *Harvey Cushing* (1946), provides insight into the Cushing-Dandy controversy. Ruth and Edward Brecher, *The Rays: A Hist. of Radiology in the U.S. and Canada* (1969), is valuable for its treatment of ventriculography in the context of radiological development.]

WILLIAM LLOYD FOX

DANIELS, JOSEPHUS (May 18, 1862-Jan. 15, 1948), newspaper editor, secretary of the navy, and diplomat, was born in Washington, N.C., the second of three surviving sons of Josephus Daniels and Mary Cleaves (Seabrook) Daniels. Both parents were of English descent, of families that had lived in North Carolina since the late eighteenth century. Mary Daniels, who had been orphaned at an early age, came from a background of small planters and professionals and thus was socially somewhat above the humbler status of her husband, a skilled shipwright. The elder Daniels, because of his political views as a Whig and Unionist, declined to serve in the Confederate armed forces, although he worked for a time building and repairing blockade runners in a Confederate yard at Wilmington, N.C., before being killed in an ambush in the closing months of the Civil War. His destitute widow moved with her three small sons to Wilson, N.C., where she earned a modest living as a seamstress and the village postmistress. Her piety and serene Methodist faith made an indelible impression on young Josephus, who remained a teetotaler throughout his life and regularly attended church and taught Sunday school. Educational opportunities were limited in postbellum rural North Carolina, but Daniels, with a naturally keen mind and gift of expression, made the most of his studies at Wilson's one-room school and in the nine-month term of the Wilson Collegiate Institute. His interest in journalism began at the age of sixteen when he and his younger brother, Charles, published an amateur newspaper, the *Cornucopia.* In 1880 Josephus left school to become local editor of the *Wilson Advance,* a small rural weekly, which he purchased two years later with borrowed money.

Daniels quickly developed his characteristic style of journalism, as a hard-hitting champion of reform and of the Democratic party. Warmly personable and open-hearted, personally incorruptible, he was well liked or at least respected even by many of those who were the object of his biting editorial criticism. His background was no doubt responsible for his concern for the underdog, which in the early 1880's was reflected in his campaigns for the establishment of a tax-supported graded school system, including federal aid to education, and for radical experiments in agricultural diversification. His strong commitment to his Methodist faith led him to advocate prohibition and to reject advertisements for lotteries. Daniels' staunch partisanship soon cost his mother her post office appointment, but the loss was balanced by the growing success of his newspaper work. By 1885 he had become a partner in two other rural weekly papers and was sufficiently known at the age of twenty-two to be elected president of the State Press Association.

Recruiting a friend to publish the *Advance* in his absence, Daniels spent the summer of 1885 in Chapel Hill, studying law at the University of North Carolina, his only formal experience with higher education. However brief his studies, he thereafter was one of the university's most devoted backers, immediately serving a term as secretary of the alumni association and subsequently as a university trustee for forty-seven years. Daniels passed the bar examination in October 1885, but he was destined never to practice law. Backed by Julian S. Carr, a wealthy Durham banker and tobacco manufacturer, he instead took over a struggling weekly newspaper in the state capital, the *Raleigh State Chronicle.* The paper was available because its previous editor, Walter Hines Page, had lost a fortune trying to turn it into a daily. Daniels' reform crusades and lively editorials, including regular articles submitted by Page from New York, soon revived the *State Chronicle* and attracted growing attention around the state to its outspoken young editor. Daniels also took an increasing interest in Democratic politics, so successfully cultivating influential legislators that in 1887 he was awarded the contract of state printer. In Raleigh he formed lifelong friendships with other young idealists, such as the educational reformers Edwin A. Alderman and Charles D. McIver, and he forcefully championed establishment of the new North Carolina State Normal and Industrial College (now the University of North Carolina at Greensboro), of which McIver became president in 1891. Another close associate was Charles B. Aycock, law partner of Daniels' older brother, Frank; Daniels always considered Aycock the greatest of North Carolina reform governors (1901-1905).

Daniels' modest prosperity enabled him on May 2, 1888, to marry Addie Worth Bagley, the nineteen-year-old granddaughter of Jonathan Worth, the first elected governor of North Carolina after the Civil War. The marriage was a supremely happy one, producing five children:

Adelaide, who died in infancy; Josephus; Worth Bagley; Jonathan Worth; and Frank Arthur. The following year Daniels began publishing the *State Chronicle* on a daily basis, but the paper lost money in the depressed early 1890's, and he was obliged to sell it in 1892. To keep his hand in North Carolina journalism and politics, he started a small weekly, the *North Carolinian,* and used his political connections to secure a government post in Washington in the Democratic administration of Grover Cleveland, first as chief of the appointments division and then as chief clerk in the Department of the Interior under Secretary Hoke Smith. Daniels used most of his salary to support the faltering *North Carolinian* and took advantage of his two years in Washington (1893-1895) to advance his contacts in national Democratic circles. He returned to North Carolina when one of the established Raleigh dailies, the *News and Observer,* went bankrupt in 1894; Daniels purchased it with the backing of his former patron, Julian Carr, and other friends.

For the rest of his life Daniels was associated with what North Carolinians soon nicknamed the "Nuisance and Disturber," which he made the leading voice of reform in North Carolina and the upper South and a fervent partisan of the progressive wing of the Democratic party. Under his guidance the paper achieved a growing statewide following; Daniels regularly inveighed against special interests, demanded more effective control of the trusts and railroads, exposed corruption, condemned vice and the liquor traffic and fought for better public schools, including Daniels' special concern, the state university at Chapel Hill. The *News and Observer* also played a leading role in the disfranchisement of North Carolina blacks in 1900, a "reform" Daniels believed necessary to remove a corrupt element from state politics and incidentally to assure the ascendancy of the lily-white Democratic party.

Beginning in 1896 Daniels served for many years on the Democratic National Committee, a post that gave him considerable influence in the party without the unpredictable hazards of seeking elective office, which he considered incompatible with his independence as a journalist. A close friend of William Jennings Bryan, he campaigned hard for the Great Commoner in his three unsuccessful bids for the presidency. His party loyalty also led him to take charge of publicity for the unfortunate presidential race of the conservative Democrat Alton B. Parker in 1904. Well before 1912, Daniels became an enthusiastic supporter of Woodrow Wilson, and

he was instrumental in getting North Carolina Democrats in that year to endorse the scholarly New Jersey governor for the presidency. He was also able to smooth strained relations between Wilson and Bryan, who happened to be visiting Daniels in Raleigh when Wilson's famous anti-Bryan Joline letter (wishing Bryan could be knocked "once and for all into a cocked hat") was leaked to the press. Daniels' further service as one of Wilson's floor managers at the Baltimore convention and as national director of publicity in the successful campaign that followed made him one of Wilson's top lieutenants; he was subsequently appointed secretary of the navy. Unlike some of the president's associates, Daniels remained a warm admirer throughout Wilson's life. He was one of only three cabinet members to serve throughout both of Wilson's terms, and only Gideon Welles under both Lincoln and Andrew Johnson held the navy secretaryship for as long a time.

Despite his lack of previous nautical experience, Daniels quickly demonstrated that he intended to be more than a figurehead navy chief. He instituted a number of significant personnel reforms, such as requiring sea service for promotion, providing compulsory schooling for illiterate and poorly educated sailors, improving the United States Naval Academy and opening it to enlisted men for the first time, strengthening the Naval War College, reforming the naval prisons, and replacing the unsatisfactory Council of Aids with a Chief of Naval Operations and a Secretary's Advisory Council of bureau chiefs, rather than the general-staff system advocated by some officers. He insisted on competitive bidding on navy contracts and used navy facilities as a yardstick for manufacturing costs, even persuading Congress to authorize a navy-owned armor-plate plant to assure fair prices from the three private armor-plate companies. Daniels vigilantly guarded the naval oil reserves from exploitation by private interests, as championed by Secretary of the Interior Franklin K. Lane, a fight that later came to a head in the notorious Teapot Dome oil scandals of the Harding administration. One of Daniels' imaginative innovations was the creation of the Navy Consulting Board, headed by Thomas A. Edison and consisting of prominent experts nominated by the leading scientific and engineering societies of the country to advise on technical problems.

Daniels was probably the most controversial member of Wilson's cabinet and, for a time, the most unpopular. Some of his reforms, such as his historic order of 1914 banning liquor from officers' messes and his alleged coddling of the enlisted men, made him highly unpopular with many naval officers and their civilian supporters in the influential Navy League, whose bitter feud with Daniels led him eventually to ban the league from all navy ships and shore installations. More serious were the complaints by big navy advocates that Daniels, a near pacifist, was inadequately preparing the navy for possible belligerency after the outbreak of World War I. Similar charges were made at the close of the war by Adm. William S. Sims, the commander of United States naval forces in Europe, and were investigated by a subcommittee of the Senate Naval Affairs Committee in 1920. The findings of the highly partisan hearing were, at worst, a standoff between the two chief protagonists, for Daniels could point to the undeniably creditable performance of the navy in the war. Daniels' enemies sometimes received quiet encouragement from his ambitious young assistant secretary, Franklin D. Roosevelt, whose social and yachting background made him more at home with the navy professionals than his landlubber chief. Daniels was aware of, but wisely chose to overlook, his subordinate's occasional disloyalty, and Roosevelt increasingly respected the older man's sound political judgment if not always his naval policies. Despite the controversy surrounding his administration, in retrospect it seems clear that Daniels must be regarded as one of the most innovative, and perhaps one of the few great, navy secretaries.

Returning to his Raleigh newspaper in 1921, Daniels continued to play a prominent role in state and national Democratic politics. At some cost of popularity in North Carolina, he fought the Ku Klux Klan and championed the Child Labor Amendment, the League of Nations, and the World Court. Ever a party loyalist, unlike many North Carolina Democrats he reluctantly supported Alfred E. Smith for president despite Smith's opposition to prohibition. Daniels gave much more enthusiastic backing to Franklin D. Roosevelt's successful bid for the presidency in 1932, for his affectionate regard for his former associate had deepened as he watched Roosevelt's courageous comeback from his attack of paralytic polio. Daniels was always "Chief" to Roosevelt and was one of the few intimate friends to have the president's permission to call him Franklin. The seventy-year-old Daniels hoped Roosevelt would offer him a cabinet post, preferably the secretaryship of the Navy Department, but after declining to head a proposed new transportation agency, he settled for the ambassadorship to Mexico.

Despite initial Mexican reservations over Daniels' role in the American occupation of Veracruz in 1914, he proved to be one of the most successful United States ambassadors ever sent to Mexico. As a lifelong progressive, he warmly supported the social and economic goals of the Mexican revolution, which he advised Roosevelt was Mexico's badly needed New Deal. During his nearly nine years in Mexico he remained an eloquent and consistent champion of neighborliness in a country that gave the Good Neighbor Policy its severest test. When Mexico's land-reform program affected American interests, Daniels tried to distinguish between the rights of small resident American landowners and those of large absentee landholders, some of whom he considered exploitative and far less deserving of sympathy. When the Mexican president Lázaro Cárdenas expropriated American oil holdings in 1938 after a long labor dispute, which the ambassador privately believed the companies had mishandled, Daniels almost singlehandedly prevented a diplomatic rupture between the two countries. His influence with President Roosevelt, in opposition to the harder line advocated by Secretary of State Cordell Hull and Undersecretary Sumner Welles, ultimately paved the way for the settlement of all major Mexican-American differences in November 1941 and assured a friendly neighbor to the south in World War II, in sharp contrast to the hostile situation in World War I.

Daniels reluctantly resigned his Mexican post late in 1941 because of his wife's deteriorating health and returned to Raleigh, where she died in 1943. He continued to take an active interest in the *News and Observer,* now edited by his son Jonathan, and in state and national affairs. His last years were as busy as ever—writing editorials and completing his five-volume autobiography, making speeches in various parts of the country, and regularly visiting Washington to confer with political leaders and to lobby for various liberal causes. In December 1946 he returned to Mexico as an honored guest at the inauguration of President Miguel Alemán. Less than a month before his death, in his eighty-sixth year, he was in Washington meeting with political leaders, including President Truman, and expressing his hopes for world peace and his fears of a revolt by Southern Democrats that might wreck the party in 1948. At the start of the new year he caught a cold that developed into pneumonia and caused his death two weeks later in Raleigh. After Methodist funeral services attended by many government officials, he was buried in Raleigh's Oakwood Cemetery.

[There are two major collections of Daniels' papers; one in the Lib. of Cong., and the other, in the Southern Hist. Collect. at the Univ. of N.C. His own recollections of his eventful life are given in the five volumes of memoirs: *Tar Heel Editor* (1939), *Editor in Politics* (1941), *The Wilson Era: Years of Peace* (1944), *The Wilson Era: Years of War and After* (1946), and *Shirt-Sleeve Diplomat* (1947). See also Jonathan Daniels' book on his father, *The End of Innocence* (1954); Joseph L. Morrison, *Josephus Daniels Says* (1962) and *Josephus Daniels: The Small-d Democrat* (1966); E. David Cronon, *Josephus Daniels in Mexico* (1960); and Cronon, ed., *The Cabinet Diaries of Josephus Daniels, 1913–1921* (1963).]

E. DAVID CRONON

DARTON, NELSON HORATIO (Dec. 17, 1865-Feb. 28, 1948), geologist, was born in Brooklyn, N.Y., the only child of William and Caroline Matilda (Thayer) Darton. His paternal grandparents had come from Devonshire, England, to Quebec in 1825 and had later settled in Charlestown, Mass. William Darton, a shipbuilder at the Brooklyn Navy Yard, served as a civilian navigator for the navy during the Civil War and later worked as a civil engineer; he helped his son learn higher mathematics. Young Nelson dropped out of school at the age of thirteen to enter the pharmaceutical laboratory of his uncle William Thayer in New York City, and never resumed formal education.

Darton was an extremely productive scientist. After two years in his uncle's firm, during which he learned practical chemistry, he opened his own shop at the age of fifteen, specializing in organic analyses and industrial chemistry, mainly sugar processing and tanning. The American Chemical Society, probably unaware of his age, elected him a member in 1881. Gradually, however, Darton's scientific passion was deflected from chemistry to geology. He was fascinated by his uncle's small mineral collection and began taking field trips in the New York area. As he read in the geological literature on the region he set up a card catalogue of references which led him to correspond with Grove Karl Gilbert of the United States Geological Survey. Gilbert needed a bibliographical project done for the entire Appalachian region, and in 1886 invited Darton to join the federal survey staff in Washington, D.C.

Darton's bibliographical project was expanded to a general catalogue of references from 1732 to 1891 on North American geology. This work, published in 1896 as the Geological Survey's Bulletin no. 172, initiated the indispensable annual series, *Index to North American Geology*, used by both geologists and historians of science. At the same time Darton also worked on Atlantic Coast field assignments, studying the Newark group of rocks in New Jersey (1886), running reconnaissances in West Virginia and Virginia (1887-1888), examining phosphate-bearing formations in Florida (1890), and reviewing water-bearing beds of the Coastal Plain (1895). In 1892-1893 he drew up a new state geological map for New York, in the process learning to construct his own topographical base maps.

Darton was transferred in 1895 to the hydrographic branch of the Geological Survey to study underground water resources in the Great Plains area. This work, which occupied him until 1907, necessarily required much basic research on the stratigraphy and structure of rock formations. He began in the Dakotas, paying particular attention to the Black Hills sequence, and worked south through Colorado, Nebraska, and Kansas, spending the winter seasons investigating Arizona and New Mexico. His results appeared as the *Preliminary Report on the Geology and Underground Water Resources of the Central Great Plains* (U.S.G.S. *Professional Paper* No. 52, 1905). Overlapping this work was his study of the Grand Canyon, summarized for a popular audience in the best-selling pamphlet, *Story of the Grand Canyon* (1917). In 1907 Darton transferred to the technologic branch of the survey, which in 1910 became the federal Bureau of Mines. For the bureau he investigated coal lands in the far west and in Pennsylvania. His studies of anthracite coal fields and of gas explosions in mines had practical consequences for the conservation movement and for mine safety.

In 1913 Darton rejoined the Geological Survey, where he remained until his retirement in 1936. He returned to the Southwest for six years to prepare a report on the red beds of New Mexico, strata notorious in geology for the controversies over the exact conditions of their deposition. A series of field trips outside the United States followed, to Cuba (1916) to study water-bearing rocks; to Santo Domingo (1919-1920), Baja California (1920), and Venezuela (1926-1927) for petroleum exploration; and to Mexico City (1924) to date archaeological remains from lava flows. He composed a topographical map and a geological map of Texas from 1925 to 1931. He then worked on a geological map of South Dakota and completed his study of Pennsylvania's coal fields. After retirement he continued to study the Atlantic Coastal Plain in the Maryland-Washington-Virginia area until he died in 1948.

In contrast to nineteenth-century American geologists, Darton cared little for studying fossils, using paleontology only when necessary for dating formations. His fascination with artesian waters, first acquired during his work as an industrial chemist when he investigated the well water of Brooklyn, ran through almost all of his geological career. Darton was a master at structural geology, having an uncanny ability to envision the configurations of formations which went deep into the earth, a skill he expressed in his structure contour maps. His achievements in reconnaissance geology were prodigious—he mapped about one-fifth of the nation topographically and about one-quarter geologically—although detailed mapping has since shown that errors crept in because of the scale in which he worked. Darton's accomplishments were recognized in his own time: The Geological Society of America (of which he was a founding member) awarded him its Penrose Medal in 1940; and the American Geographical Society, the Daly Medal in 1930.

Darton's first marriage, to Lucy Lee Harris of Baltimore, Md., on July 18, 1891, ended in divorce. On Nov. 3, 1903, he married Alice Weldon Wasserbach of Washington, D.C. He had one child by the first marriage, Horace Lee, and two by the second, Annunciata and Arthur Beaupre. He was a Roman Catholic. Dalton died of chronic myocarditis in Chevy Chase, Md., and was buried in Mount Olivet Cemetery, Chevy Chase.

[Philip B. King's memorial in Geological Soc. of America, *Proc.*, 1948, includes a list of Darton's publications, a photograph, and figures of the areas he mapped. It is a thorough and generally reliable evaluation of Darton's work, although uncritical in a few particulars. See also *N.Y. Times* obituary, Mar. 4, 1948; *Nat. Cyc. Am. Biog.*, XXXVII, 40–41; *Who Was Who in America*, II (1950); memorial by Watson W. Monroe in Am. Assoc. of Petroleum Geologists, *Bull.*, Jan. 1949, pp. 116–123; and "Presentation of the Penrose Medal," Geological Soc. of America, *Proc.*, 1940, pp. 81–88. Family data are from Horace L. Darton, Washington, D.C., and Arthur B. Darton, Tucson, Ariz. Darton's field notebooks are filed at the Denver office of the U.S. Geological Survey; his personal papers remain in family hands (1971). His death certificate is at the State Dept. of Health, Baltimore.]

MICHELE L. ALDRICH

DAVIS, JAMES JOHN (Oct. 27, 1873–Nov. 22, 1947), fraternal order leader, secretary of labor, senator from Pennsylvania, was born in Tredegar, South Wales, the oldest son and second of six children of David James Davies and Esther Ford (Nicholls) Davies. An immigration official changed the name to Davis when James's illiterate father came to America. The family joined him in April 1881, settling in Sharon, Pa., where the father worked in the iron mills, as he had in Wales.

Young Davis began full-time work at the age of eleven, but later continued his education in night school. After a year in a nail factory, he became a puddler's assistant in the iron mills and at sixteen a puddler. He thrived on the hard work and throughout life took pride in his muscular strength. In 1893, after brief employment in Pittsburgh and Birmingham, Ala., he moved to Elwood, Ind., where he worked in a tin mill, joined the Amalgamated Association of Iron, Steel, and Tin Workers of America, and as president of his local union established a reputation for good judgment among both workers and employers. A foe of free silver, he campaigned for William McKinley in the presidential election of 1896. He was elected city clerk of Elwood in 1898, and before assuming office spent several months attending business college. In 1902 he was elected recorder of Madison County, a post he held until 1907. During this period he also read law in an Elwood law firm.

Davis then began a career in fraternal affairs that was to occupy much of his life. He had joined the Loyal Order of Moose in 1906, and the following year he negotiated a contract with its officers that gave him the title of supreme organizer and the exclusive right to establish lodges and collect fees. He was named director general in 1907. Living in Pittsburgh, Davis devoted his full time to building the Moose as a traveling organizer of lodges. He also established a publishing concern, a jewelry firm to supply pins and insignia to the order, and a real estate firm to build and lease lodges, ventures which eventually provided him with an annual income that reached as high as $50,000. He helped found the order's vocational school for orphans at Mooseheart, Ill., in 1913 and was chairman of its governing body. His efforts were primarily responsible for the growth of the Moose to over 500,000 members by 1916. Davis was indicted in 1932 for violating federal lottery laws in connection with a Moose enterprise, and, though acquitted, he became less influential in the order thereafter, giving up his contract as organizer for a regular salary as director general.

In 1921 President Harding appointed Davis secretary of labor. Although Davis had maintained his union membership, he had had little contact with the labor movement since the 1890's, and his appointment was opposed by organized labor. A stocky, robust man, hearty and gregarious, "Puddler Jim" believed in the

American dream, with its virtues of hard work and self-help. He viewed trade unions more as benevolent associations than as opponents of capital, and felt that strikes were seldom justified. He distrusted doubters, radicals, and intellectuals and held fast to a philosophy compounded of Republicanism, fraternalism, conservative trade unionism, and his simple Welsh Baptist faith.

As secretary of labor, Davis nevertheless followed a conciliatory course, tempering antilabor opinion within the Republican party. Herbert Hoover, the secretary of commerce, was the dominant influence in the administration's domestic policy, and Davis' role was therefore limited, but his sympathy for labor's point of view and his opposition to antiunion pressures eventually won the grudging respect of organized labor. Reappointed by both Coolidge and Hoover, Davis served them and the party faithfully as a link to the labor movement and as an effective political campaigner. During his tenure the Labor Department became responsible for enforcing the new immigration laws. A supporter of restrictive legislation, Davis tried to thwart illegal entrants, but advocated humane methods of examination and processing of immigrants.

Davis left the cabinet in 1930 following his election to the United States Senate from Pennsylvania. Competing for the vacancy caused by the Senate's refusal to seat William S. Vare, he had won the Republican nomination by defeating the incumbent, Joseph Grundy, in a tangled primary. Davis was reelected to full six-year terms in 1932 and 1938. In the Senate, he sponsored one significant measure, the Davis-Bacon Act (1930), which required contractors to pay standard local wages for labor in federal construction. Although he frequently criticized the implementation of New Deal programs, Davis voted for the Social Security, Wagner, and Fair Labor Standards acts. He also supported the neutrality legislation of the 1930's, while at the same time favoring preparedness. Never a forceful figure in the Senate, Davis survived politically through a combination of folksiness, popularity among trade unionists and fraternal order members, and careful attention to issues important to Pennsylvania voters. In 1942 he unsuccessfully sought the Republican nomination for governor. Plagued by ill health and having steadily faded from public attention, he was narrowly defeated for reelection to the Senate in 1944.

Davis married Jean Rodenbaugh of Pittsburgh, Pa., on Nov. 26, 1914; they had five children: James John, Jane Elizabeth, Jean Allys, Joan, and Jewel. He died of nephritis at the Washington Sanitarium and Hospital in Takoma Park, Md., at the age of seventy-four. The Loyal Order of Moose honored him with a ceremonial funeral, and he was buried in Uniondale Cemetery in Pittsburgh.

[James J. Davis Papers, Lib. of Cong.; Davis' autobiography, *The Iron Puddler* (1922), and his *Selective Immigration* (1925); Joe M. Chapple, "*Our Jim": A Biog.* (1928); Alfred P. Dennis in *Saturday Evening Post*, Aug. 2, 1930; Warner Olivier, *Back of the Dream: The Story of the Loyal Order of Moose* (1952); Robert H. Zieger, *Republicans and Labor, 1919–1929* (1969) and "The Career of James J. Davis," *Pa. Mag. of Hist. and Biog.*, Jan. 1974; John B. Dudley, "James J. Davis: Secretary of Labor Under Three Presidents" (Ph.D. dissertation, Ball State Univ., 1972); *Biog. Directory Am. Congress* (1961); *Who Was Who in America*, II (1950); *N.Y. Times*, Nov. 22, 1947; *Cong. Record*, 80 Cong., 1 Sess., pp. 10,697–10,698, A3958–A3960.]

ROBERT H. ZIEGER

DAVIS, JOHN STAIGE (Jan. 15, 1872–Dec. 23, 1946), plastic surgeon and teacher, was born in Norfolk, Va., the only child of William Blackford Davis and Mary Jane (Howland) Davis, both descendants of Virginia colonists. His father and parental grandfather were physicians. At the time of John's birth, his father was assistant surgeon in the U.S. Naval Hospital at Portsmouth, Va.; his childhood was spent in a succession of frontier posts where his father served as a colonel in the Army Medical Corps. John spent a year (1887-1888) at the Episcopal High School of Virginia in Alexandria, and then entered St. Paul's School, a military school in Garden City, L. I., where he remained until his graduation in 1892. That year he entered the Sheffield Scientific School at Yale University, where he studied biology under Russell H. Chittenden and received the Ph.B. degree in 1895. He then enrolled in the Johns Hopkins University School of Medicine, and after receiving the M.D. in 1899 served a year as resident house officer at the Johns Hopkins Hospital, and three years (1900-1903) as resident surgeon and superintendent at the Union Protestant Infirmary (now the Union Memorial Hospital) under John M. T. Finney. On Oct. 26, 1907, Davis married Kathleen Gordon Bowdoin; their children were Kathleen Staige, William Bowdoin (who also became a physician and plastic surgeon of national prominence), and Howland Staige.

Davis began private practice in Baltimore in 1903 and by 1908 had limited his work to surgery. In his early clinical experience he had become curious about the processes of wound healing and scar formation, an interest that led him to investigate the use of surgical methods in repairing deformities and blemishes of the skin, whether congenital or acquired. He was particularly concerned with the psychological effects of such deformities on children. One of the first to devote all his time to the principles and techniques of general plastic and reconstructive surgery, he developed a number of methods for repair. He perfected the "Davis graft," in which small patches of healthy, full-thickness skin are transplanted to raw areas and allowed to grow together and cover the raw area, a technique still used in the treatment of certain badly infected wounds. He also devised methods in the design and movement of local skin flaps for reconstructing defects around the face and jaws. He never became especially adept at taking large sheets of split-thickness skin as free grafts—perhaps because of his own skill and genius in moving tissue by the flap technique. For about ten years he also carried on research in the Hunterian Laboratory of Experimental Surgery at Johns Hopkins on the physiology of circulation during skin transplantation. He was one of the first plastic surgeons to show experimentally the ingrowth of capillaries into skin grafts at approximately nine days after grafting. His work and methods were described in more than seventy papers, and in his book, *Plastic Surgery: Its Principles and Practice* (1919), for which his wife drew many of the illustrations. This was the first definitive textbook on plastic surgery and remains a classic.

Davis continued a close association with the Johns Hopkins University, serving as instructor in surgery (1909-1920), associate in clinical surgery (1920-1923), and associate professor of surgery (1923-1946). Under his patient, lucid direction, a large number of medical students, residents, and house officers learned the art of reconstructive surgery, and its possibilities in relieving the awesome effects of physical deformities.

From 1917-1919, Davis served as a captain in the Army Medical Corps, as consultant in plastic surgery to the surgeon general's office and as chairman of the examining board of the Medical, Sanitary and Veterinary Corps of Maryland. In World War II, he took an active part in organizing special units of the Medical Corps for the treatment of soldiers whose war injuries required plastic surgery. He also served on the subcommittee for plastic and maxillo-facial surgery of the division of medical science of the National Research Council, as con-

sultant to the secretary of war, and as consultant in plastic surgery to the surgeon general.

Davis was also on the staff of Johns Hopkins Hospital, serving successively as assistant visiting surgeon (plastic surgery), visiting surgeon, and surgeon-in-charge. He also served as visiting surgeon at the Union Memorial Hospital, the Children's Hospital School, the Robert Garrett Hospital, the Hospital for the Women of Maryland, and the Church Home and Hospital. He was a member of the American Surgical Association (vice-president, 1937), and was president of the Southern Surgical Association in 1940. He was a founder member of the American Association of Plastic Surgeons (president, 1945), a founder and chairman of the American Board of Plastic Surgery until the year before his death, and a founder, member and fellow of the American College of Surgeons. A member of the Episcopal church, he was a gentle, quiet-spoken man with unusual intellect, strong will, and sound judgment, and gave great sympathy to the many patients who sought his help. Advanced age and occasional fatigue never brought his work to a stop. On the morning of his death he had his usual office hours, operated at the Union Memorial Hospital, and lunched with a group of his colleagues at the Maryland Club. That afternoon, at home, he died in his sleep, of a coronary occlusion. He was buried in the Druid Ridge Cemetery, Baltimore.

[Notes taken from the author's files from a ceremony given in honor of Davis at Johns Hopkins University in about 1958; *Nat. Cyc. Am. Biog.*, XXXVI, 374-375; obituaries from *Southern Surgical Assoc. Trans.; Am. Surgical Assoc.* 65 (1947); 673-674; Yale Univ., *Obituary Record, 1946-1947*, p. 127; *Surgery* 22 (1947): 158-159; *Annals of Surgery* 126 (1947): 116-119; *Jour. of Am. Medical Assoc.*, Feb. 1, 1947, p. 338; *Plastic and Reconstruction Surgery* 2 (1947): 171-173. Information was also supplied by Davis's wife and son, Dr. Bowdoin Davis.]
MILTON T. EDGERTON

DEALEY, GEORGE BANNERMAN (Sept. 18, 1859-Feb. 26, 1946), Texas newspaper publisher, was born in Manchester, England, the fourth of nine surviving children and second of five sons of George Dealey, proprietor of a shoe shop, and Mary Ann (Nellins) Dealey. (Bannerman was the name of a family friend.) His father was a native of Liverpool, his mother of County Monaghan, Ireland; George was brought up as a Protestant. When he was about seven, the family moved to Liverpool, where he attended school and worked as a grocer's apprentice. His father's bankruptcy in 1870 led the family to embark for Galveston,

Texas, where relatives had settled. There the senior Dealey established a coffee and tea business.

In Texas, young George attended school reluctantly for a few years while holding jobs as an organ pumper, office boy, and messenger. In 1874 he became office boy at the *Galveston News*, where his older brother was employed. Under the eye of the proprietor, Col. Alfred H. Belo, George rose rapidly, becoming chief mailing clerk at the age of seventeen. To improve his education he attended evening classes at the Island City Business College. In 1882 Belo sent him to north Texas to survey the possibilities for a new newspaper there as an offshoot of the *Galveston News*. Dealey recommended the raw town of Dallas as the best site, and when the *Dallas Morning News* was founded three years later, he was appointed its business manager. Meanwhile, on Apr. 9, 1884, he had married Olivia Allen, the daughter of a newspaper publisher in Lexington, Mo. They had five children: Annie, Fannie, Walter Allen, Edward Musgrove, and Mary.

Dealey spent the rest of his career at the *Dallas Morning News*. In 1895 Colonel Belo made him manager of the entire newspaper, not merely the business side, and five years later Dealey began the daily conferences that established his influence over editorial policy. In 1902, after Belo's death, Dealey became a member of the board of directors for the Galveston and Dallas papers and, four years later, vice-president and general manager of the corporation. He became president in 1920.

In these years Dealey led the *News* into a gentlemanly, civic-minded journalism that was, as Adolph S. Ochs later asserted, the inspiration for the policies of the *New York Times*. Dealey turned down advertising he considered dishonest or immoral. Despite the loss of revenues, he banned hard-liquor advertisements, and during the booming 1920's he rejected oil-field promotions. Paternalistic toward his employees, he once settled by personal appeal a union stoppage that threatened publication of the initial issue of the *Journal*, an afternoon paper operated by the *News* from 1914 to 1938.

As Dallas expanded into a city, Dealey enlisted the *News* in efforts for planning and improvements. His campaign in 1899 led to formation of a Cleaner Dallas League, which attacked litter and sewage pollution. After a flood in 1908 Dealey pushed for a long-range city development plan; as an inspiration, the paper ran pictures of urban beauty from other cities. He aided in the building of a union rail-

road station and the removal of unsightly downtown tracks. In honor of his work, Dallas named a park for him: Dealey Plaza (the site of the assassination of President John F. Kennedy in 1963). Dealey was also active in publicizing Texas history and in urging aid to rural Texans.

Dealey always followed a policy of tolerance. The news columns, for example, were early cleansed of anti-Semitic references. The *News'* uncompromising resistance to the Ku Klux Klan in the early 1920's, at a time when Dallas was a Klan stronghold, cost hundreds of subscribers and, coupled with the business recession, forced the sale of the parent *Galveston News*.

With the decline of the K.K.K. in the mid-1920's, the company's outlook improved. Dealey sought in these years to become owner, as well as manager, of the *Morning News*. After intricate negotiations with Colonel Belo's heirs, a reorganization was effected in 1926 under which Dealey received a majority of the company's voting stock, while the Belo family was compensated with nonvoting securities.

Dealey cast a generally benevolent editorial eye on the New Deal, and the *News* supported Roosevelt's recognition of the Soviet Union. Over the years Dealey brought members of his family into the company. His son E. M. (Ted) replaced him as president in 1940 (Dealey at this time becoming chairman of the board), and his younger brother, James Quayle, a retired political scientist, became editor-in-chief in the 1930's. Dealey served on boards of nonprofit organizations (never on boards of other businesses), including Westminster Presbyterian Church in Dallas. He received honorary degrees, mostly notably from Southern Methodist University, which he had helped bring into existence. Still active at the age of eighty-six, Dealey died of a coronary occlusion in Dallas in 1946. The *News* continued under the leadership of his son and later of his grandson.

[Ernest Sharpe, *G. B. Dealey of the Dallas News* (1955), uses Dealey's papers but suffers from fictionalization; Sam Acheson, *35,000 Days in Texas: A Hist. of the Dallas News and Its Forebears* (1938), offers much of the same material more compactly. Also useful are Dealey's recollections in Aileese Parten, "The Dallas News" (master's essay, Graduate School of Journalism, Columbia Univ., 1932). On particular phases of the *News* under Dealey, see Kenneth T. Jackson, *The Ku Klux Klan in the City, 1915–1930* (1967), and Paul F. Boller, Jr., "The *Dallas Morning News* and Communist Russia," *Southwestern Social Sci. Quart.*, Mar. 1961. See also the Associated Press obituary, *N.Y. Times*, Feb. 27, 1946; and Ted Barrett's, in *Editor & Publisher*, Mar. 2, 1946. Portraits appear in Acheson (facing p. 303) and in the endpapers of Sharpe.]

JAMES BOYLAN

DE LUCA, GIUSEPPE (Dec. 25, 1876-Aug. 26, 1950), operatic baritone, was born in Rome, Italy, the first son and oldest of three children of Nicola and Lucia (De Filippi) De Luca. His father was a blacksmith. His mother, who had a beautiful soprano voice, fostered Giuseppe's musical education, beginning with the Schola Cantorum in Rome, to which he was admitted at the age of eight. As a boy soprano he sang in St. Peter's and before Pope Leo XIII. At fifteen, he began to study with Venceslao Persichini at the Royal Academy of St. Cecilia. During this time his father died, and he was obliged to take odd jobs to help support the family.

By Nov. 6, 1897, however, he was ready for his professional debut, at Piacenza, in the role of Valentin in Gounod's *Faust*. His success was immediate. He sang in Genoa, Ferrara, and Milan, first at the Teatro Lirico, where in 1902 he sang in the world premiere of Francesco Cilèa's *Adriana Lecouvreur* (with Arturo Toscanini conducting and Enrico Caruso in the cast), and later at La Scala, where in 1904 he sang in the world premiere of Giacomo Puccini's *Madama Butterfly*. He appeared in most European capitals and in South America. In 1903 he married Olimpia Fierro. They had one daughter, Wally Panni. After his wife's death in 1918 he married her sister Giulia on Oct. 22, 1922.

De Luca made his New York debut at the Metropolitan Opera House on Nov. 25, 1915, as Figaro in Rossini's *Barber of Seville*. Richard Aldrich wrote in the *New York Times*, "His voice has an excellent quality and resonance, though he showed last evening an unnecessary tendency to force it. He has . . . intelligence and comic power. . . ."

De Luca remained a member of the Metropolitan company until the summer of 1935. A perennial favorite, he sang some 100 roles in more than 800 performances (as many as 50 in a season). He then returned to Italy, as he had usually done in the summers (when he rested and preferred not to sing), until 1940. On Feb. 7, 1940, he sang again at the "Met" as Germont in *La Traviata*. Olin Downes wrote in the *New York Times*, "The first five notes made the pulses beat because of the art and beauty of the song. The quality of the legato, the perfection of the style, the sentiment which ennobled the melodic phrase, struck the whole audience." This was when De Luca was sixty-three years old, an age at which most singers hide away. On Nov. 7, 1947, to celebrate his fifty years as a public artist, he gave a Town Hall recital that was a great musical, as well as personal, success.

De Luca had never stopped singing, since, after his 1935 "retirement," he gave concerts and sang over the radio. (He spent the war years in Italy, but did not sing publicly.) After 1947 he taught privately and at the Juilliard School. He died in 1950 at Columbus Hospital, New York, after undergoing surgery, and was buried in Rome. He had apparently remained an Italian citizen.

De Luca was accurately described by the critic Howard Taubman as "the greatest living exponent of the [Italian] art of 'bel canto,' the tradition of technically perfect, beautiful singing." His voice was first of all beautiful; he controlled it perfectly, from very soft to full volume. His diction, whether in Italian or in French, was exceptionally clear. His phrasing was elegant, musically convincing, and emotionally moving. And, although only about five feet tall, he was an effective actor. He studied his roles not only as music but also as drama.

He was also increasingly a phenomenon because of his vocal longevity. This must be attributed partly to heredity, but flawless technique and careful physical discipline contributed. De Luca believed that his early success as a swimmer and his later devotion to daily physical culture before an open window, to vocal exercises (sometimes performed in the bath), and to regular habits were essential. A beautiful voice, then, exemplary training, physical prowess, and single-minded devotion to the singer's art made De Luca an outstanding singer for an extraordinary span of years. And his great achievements were accompanied by personal modesty and vivacious energy.

[*Baker's Biog. Dict.* and *Grove's Dict. of Music and Musicians* both list De Luca, as do the *Dizionario Ricordi*, the *Enciclopedia Italiana*, and *Musik in Geschichte und Gegenwart*. Numerous reviews are excerpted in W. H. Seltsam, *Metropolitan Opera Annals* (1947). David Ewen, *Living Musicians* (1940), presents a brief sketch and a good photograph. An earlier photograph appears with a valuable personal interview in Harriette Brower, *Vocal Mastery* (1920). Henry Pleasants, *The Great Singers* (1966), and Howard Taubman, "'Pazienza'—Recipe for 50 years of Singing" (an interview for the *N.Y. Times Mag.*, Nov. 2, 1947, p. 20 ff.), both give useful biographical details as well as informed critical estimates. An obituary is in the *N.Y. Times*, Aug. 28, 1950, p. 17. De Luca's birthday is sometimes given as Dec. 29. His biography in *Who Was Who in America*, III (1960), could not be verified before publication. His voice can be heard on many phonograph records, some still available in 1973.]

VERNON GOTWALS

DENNETT, TYLER (WILBUR) (June 13, 1883-Dec. 29, 1949), historian, government official, and college president, was born in Spencer, Wis., the first of four children and only son to survive infancy of Rev. William Eugene Dennett and Roxena (Tyler) Dennett. His father was a Baptist pastor. On his father's side he was descended from Alexander Dennett, who settled in Portsmouth, N.H., in 1662; on his mother's, from a family who arrived in Massachusetts in 1634. Soon after their son's birth, Dennett's parents moved to Pascoag, R.I., where the father, an advocate of hard work, self-denial, and self-reliance, served the Baptist church.

Dennett was educated in an ungraded one-room school in Pascoag and then at the Friends School, Providence. After a year at Bates College in Maine, he attended Willams College on a scholarship. There he achieved distinction as student, editor, and football player. He was graduated in 1904.

A year as secretary to Rev. John H. Dennison, retired clergyman and Williams professor, led Dennett to Union Theological Seminary, where he took the B.D. degree in 1908. There followed a pastoral assistantship in Washington, D.C., service in a Congregational mission in Seattle (1909-1910), and a call to the Congregational Church of Los Angeles (1910-1914). On Mar. 15, 1911, at Pasadena, he married Maybelle Raymond, daughter of Rev. George Lansing Raymond, a wealthy Williams graduate and former professor of aesthetics at Princeton. Between 1913 and 1926 four children were born: (George) Raymond, Tyler Eugene, Audrey, and Laurence.

The example and influence of his father-in-law and the conservatism of his Los Angeles parish persuaded Dennett to leave the ministry in 1914 to become a writer and editor. Between 1914 and 1920 employment by the Methodist Episcopal Board of Foreign Missions and the Inter-Church World Movement took him twice to Asia on extended tours of inspection, resulting in articles in *Asia* that stressed rising expectations in the Far East and the emergence of the United States as a world power with Far Eastern responsibilities. These articles were collected and published as *The Democratic Movement in Asia* (1918), illustrated with some remarkable photographs taken by the author.

In 1920 Dennett moved to Washington, where he worked in the archives of the Department of State, preparing memoranda on American policy in the Far East for the use of American commissioners at the Washington Disarmament Conference, 1921-1922. From these researches Dennett developed a pioneering study of United States policy toward China, Japan, and Korea in the nineteenth century (*Americans in Eastern Asia*, 1922). It established him as the preeminent expert in American diplomacy in the Far East. Fifty years later scholars were just beginning to move beyond the questions and framework with which Dennett had defined the field. Access to the papers of Theodore Roosevelt and a lectureship in American history at Johns Hopkins (1923-1924), which awarded him a Ph.D. degree in 1924, allowed him to continue his account of U.S.-Asian relations with *Roosevelt and the Russo-Japanese War* (1925). The culmination of his historical studies was the definitive biography *John Hay: From Poetry to Politics*, which won the Pulitzer Prize in biography for 1934. An edition of selections from Hay's diaries and letters, *Lincoln and the Civil War in the Diaries and Letters of John Hay*, followed in 1939.

In 1924 Secretary of State Charles Evans Hughes made Dennett chief of the division of publications and editor for the Department of State; he held this position, lecturing in 1927-1928 at Columbia University, until 1929, when he became historical advisor. Under Dennett's direction the publication of U.S. diplomatic correspondence in the World War I years was successfully undertaken. For the first time order rather than chaos, and competent, responsible editorial direction characterized the publications program of the department.

Dennett became professor of international relations in the School of Public and International Affairs at Princeton University in 1931 and three years later was elected president of Williams College. Williams was at the end of an era; for twenty-five years Harry Augustus Garfield had presided over a fashionable, academically weak institution catering to wealthy graduates of Eastern boarding schools. Dennett, a vigorous practitioner of the strenuous life, interpreted his election as an invitation to reform.

He was then fifty-one, a solid, square man with a massive head set on heavy shoulders. Alert, penetrating eyes, a ruddy wrinkled face, moved readily from quick smile to withering disgust. Of more than average height, he projected a sense of great power and energy. Soon the students were calling him "Tiger."

In his first year daily chapel was abolished, discipline tightened, the faculty winnowed, salaries selectively raised, the budget balanced. Student government and the college administration were reorganized. Then he pushed through curricular reforms supporting his definition of the liberal arts college as an environment for minds at work. His three tempestuous years at Williams were a course in contradictions. Headstrong and tactless, he insulted at least one tenured professor into retiring. He unobtrusively provided financial support to many deserving undergraduates and led the college community with great tenderness and sensitivity on two occasions when it was struck by sudden tragedy. He opposed the New Deal, but he welcomed instructors who were in trouble elsewhere because of their radical views. Some were intimidated by him, others were exhilarated. "He is a holy terror," one student wrote. "He is human and sincere. He is caustic and inconsiderate. He is a real man."

Two widely publicized episodes indicate that these contradictions derived from his fundamental belief in self-discipline, individuality, true merit, and hard work. In 1935 he refused to accept Federal Emergency Relief Administration grants for student scholarships. Many values were in contention, but none more important than individualism and self-reliance, both of which Dennett regarded as endangered by sentimental egalitarianism. The funds he refused, however, would have supported his desire to make Williams "a campus on which there is always going on an intellectual row between strong, consecrated men of good manners."

This aim was partially realized by a policy of faculty recruitment that led Howard Mumford Jones to say of Williams in *The Atlantic Monthly* (April 1940) that it possessed "the liveliest college faculty" in New England. But the student body, narrowly recruited and entrenched in a self-satisfied fraternity system, was another matter, and in a speech before Williams alumni in Boston, March 1937, Dennett said that there were too many "nice boys" at Williams. The remark was subject to misinterpretation, and it is doubtful whether Dennett ever successfully convinced his various constituencies that he objected not to "well-mannered, sophisticated, and generally well-disposed young men" but to the homogeneity that deprived the college of "an invigorating intellectual and social atmosphere." Dennett had insulted and threatened powerful segments of the college community, but he had recognized the college's responsibility as a privileged institution to be more "fully representative of the American people." Dennett and the board of trustees allowed themselves to fall into irreconcilable differences, over the locus of ultimate institutional power and decision, over who had the last word, who gave and who took

orders, whether the president was employee or leader. Dennett resigned.

To his last years Dennett remained sensitive to the movement of international affairs in the Far East and commented on them in leading journals. In 1938-1939, he was a Carnegie visiting lecturer in Australia and New Zealand. He died of a heart attack at Geneva, N.Y., and was buried in the Princeton Cemetery, Princeton, N.J.

Between 1920 and 1937, Dennett had responded to three important challenges: an unexplored and unrecognized area of international history, a chaotic publication program at the Department of State, and the stagnation of an old New England college. On all three he left an indelible stamp.

[Published and manuscript materials important to an assessment are at Williams College; few of the latter are catalogued. Two reliable biographical sketches are Richard M. Lovell, "Tyler Dennett—New England Frontiersman," *Sketch*, May 1939, an undergraduate essay written soon after Dennett's resignation; and James M. Cole, "The Dennett Hurricane" (1967), by a student of another generation drawing heavily on faculty reminiscences; both are at Williams. For ancestry and the early years, correspondence of importance is with his son, Tyler E. Dennett, and his sister, Mildred Dennett Mudgett, who possesses family papers, genealogies, and reminiscences. Dennett's role as a historian and editor can be developed from his books and from Dorothy Borg, ed., *Historians and American Far Eastern Policy* (1966), and Ernest R. May and James C. Thomson, Jr., eds., *American East Asian Relations: A Survey* (1972). Correspondence and interviews with Dennett's Williams contemporaries and researches for the author's projected "Rich Man's College: Williams College, 1872–1961" have been helpful.]

FREDERICK RUDOLPH

DE SYLVA, GEORGE GARD "BUDDY"

(Jan. 27, 1896-July 11, 1950), lyricist, librettist, producer, and director, was born in New York City, the only child of Aloysius Joseph De Sylva and Georgetta (Gard) De Sylva. His father was a lawyer who had appeared in vaudeville under the name of Hal de Forest. When George was two, his family moved to Los Angeles, where, as a child, he did a song-and-dance routine at the Grand Opera House, after which he toured the Keith vaudeville circuit. This did not interfere with his education in public schools in Los Angeles, at Citrus Union High School at Azusa, Calif., and at the University of Southern California. While attending high school, he supported himself by working as a shipping clerk, and at college by making public appearances with a Hawaiian band. While still in college, he started writing song lyrics, some of which he dispatched to Al Jolson. De Sylva's first lyric to be performed was "'N Everything," which Jolson set to music and introduced. Jolson continued to write music for De Sylva's lyrics and featured some of them in the Winter Garden extravaganza *Sinbad* in 1918, among these being "Avalon," "Chloe," and "By the Honeysuckle Rose." When De Sylva received his first royalty check, for $16,000, he decided to come to New York. There, in 1919, he worked as a staff lyricist for the music publishing house of J. H. Remick, and in collaboration with Arthur Jackson contributed the lyrics for George Gershwin's first Broadway musical, *La, La, Lucille,* whose principal song was "Nobody But You." In 1920 De Sylva worked with the composer Jerome Kern on the songs for *Sally,* a highly successful Broadway musical that yielded the song classic "Look for the Silver Lining," and for the *Ziegfeld Follies of 1921.* Between 1922 and 1924 De Sylva was George Gershwin's lyricist for the *George White Scandals.* Up to this time, his principal songs were "April Showers" (1921), music by Louis Silvers, popularized by Al Jolson in *Bombo;* "A Kiss in the Dark" (1922), music by Victor Herbert; with Ira Gershwin, "Stairway to Paradise" (1922), music by George Gershwin; and, with Al Jolson, "California, Here I Come," music by Joseph Meyer, introduced by Jolson in *Bombo* during its out-of-town tour in 1923. For the *George White Scandals of 1922,* De Sylva also wrote the libretto and lyrics for a one-act opera, *Blue Monday* (later renamed *135th Street*), music by George Gershwin.

On Apr. 15, 1925, De Sylva married Marie Wallace, a Ziegfeld girl; they had no children. That same year he joined lyricist Lew Brown and composer Ray Henderson to form one of the most successful songwriting teams in popular music history. They wrote all the songs for the *George White Scandals* in 1925, 1926, and 1928. The most successful score of these was the 1928 show, which included "Black Bottom," "The Birth of the Blues," "The Girl is You," and "Lucky Day." They also wrote the songs for four successful Broadway musical comedies, in all of which De Sylva also assisted in the writing of the libretto: *Good News* (1927), *Hold Everything* (1928), *Follow Thru* (1929), and *Flying High* (1930). In addition, they provided songs for two screen musicals, *The Singing Fool* and *Sunny Side Up,* both in 1929. The principal songs from these various productions were: "The Varsity Drag" and "The Best Things in Life Are Free" from *Good News;* "You're the Cream in My Coffee" from *Hold Everything;* "Button Up Your Overcoat" from *Follow Thru;* "Good For You,

Bad For Me" and "Wasn't It Beautiful?" from *Flying High;* "Sonny Boy" from *The Singing Fool;* and "If I Had a Talking Picture of You" and "Aren't We All?" from *Sunny Side Up.*

This remarkable songwriting combination broke up in 1930. De Sylva went to Hollywood as a producer for Fox, 20th Century-Fox and Paramount. His films included five starring Shirley Temple. Between 1933 and 1947 he directed nine of his stage musicals for motion pictures. At periodic intervals, he returned to Broadway as producer and colibrettist for such distinguished musicals as Cole Porter's *Du Barry Was a Lady* (1939) and *Panama Hattie* (1940), and Irving Berlin's *Louisiana Purchase* (1940). With these productions he achieved the distinction of becoming the first Broadway producer since Florenz Ziegfeld to have three musicals running simultaneously.

Late in 1942, with Johnny Mercer and Glenn Wallichs, he helped to found Capitol Records. De Sylva died of a heart attack in Hollywood on July 11, 1950. A romanticized film biography of De Sylva, Brown, and Henderson, *The Best Things in Life Are Free,* was released by 20th Century-Fox in 1956.

[*The Ascap Biographical Dictionary of Composers, Authors and Publishers* (1966); David Ewen, *Great Men of American Popular Songs* (1970); David Ewen, *New Complete Book of the American Musical Theatre* (1970); Irwin Stambler, *Encyclopedia of Popular Music* (1965); *Life,* Dec. 30, 1940; *Time,* July 24, 1950.]

DAVID EWEN

DEVINE, EDWARD THOMAS (May 6, 1867–Feb. 27, 1948), social worker, was born on a farm near Union, Hardin County, Iowa. He was the first of three children and the only son of John and Laura (Hall) Devine; his father also had eight children by a previous marriage. His mother, of New England descent, was a native of New York state. John Devine, brought from Ireland in infancy, had grown up in Ohio. Before settling down as an Iowa farmer, he served in the Texas War of Independence and the Mexican War, became a gold prospector, road builder, and tollgate operator in the West, and lost a leg in the Civil War.

Edward Devine acquired a solid classical education and seemed destined for a teaching career. A Methodist by upbringing, he attended that denomination's Albion (Iowa) Seminary and entered Cornell College, Mount Vernon, Iowa, as a sophomore in 1883. He graduated, A.B., in 1887, having interrupted his studies by a year's teaching in Albion and six months as principal of an Albion public school. He spent the following year in Marshalltown, Iowa, as high school teacher and principal of a grammar school and then became principal of the Mount Vernon public schools.

While at Marshalltown, Devine had met Simon Nelson Patten, who was teaching in a nearby village. Patten was soon appointed professor of political economy at the University of Pennsylvania and in 1890 encouraged Devine to enroll there for graduate work in economics. Upon arriving in Philadelphia, Devine found Patten temporarily absent and began work under Edmund J. James, but shortly departed, at James's suggestion, to study for a year at the University of Halle in Germany. Meanwhile, on Aug. 15, 1889, he married Harriet (Hattie) Evelyn Scovel, a college classmate. They had three children: Larry, who died in infancy; Thomas, who became a social worker; and Ruth.

Devine returned to the University of Pennsylvania in 1891 and continued his studies under Patten and James, earning a Ph.D. in 1893. While in Philadelphia he was also a staff lecturer in economics for the American Society for Extension of University Teaching, of which he was secretary, 1894-1896. In 1896, inspired by Patten, Devine helped organize a summer school for economists. One of those attending was Franklin H. Giddings, a member of the central council of the New York Charity Organization Society (C.O.S.), which was looking for a general secretary. Giddings was impressed with the success of the sessions, and after consulting Patten—who for several years had been seeking to interest his students in social work—recommended Devine for the post; he was appointed later that year.

Under Devine's leadership as general secretary (the title was changed in 1912 to secretary), the New York Charity Organization Society played a major role in the development of social work as a profession and in the enactment of social legislation. It established a summer school of philanthropy in 1898; this was expanded to a full-year curriculum in 1904 and became the New York School of Philanthropy (later the Columbia University School of Social Work). Devine, who twice served as director of the school (1904-1907 and 1912-1917), was also professor of social economy at Columbia, 1905-1919. He helped shape and interpret welfare policy throughout the nation by his strategic editorial and administrative responsibilities. Devine founded and edited *Charities*, published by the C.O.S. beginning in 1897; this absorbed in 1901 the *Charities Review*. *Charities* merged with the Chicago

Commons in 1905 and with *Jewish Charity* early in 1906, and finally, as the *Survey* (after 1909), became the leading national social work journal. Devine acted as editor until 1912 and associate editor until 1921. He exerted further influence as the prolific author of articles and books, gifted with a knack for popular exposition, and through his participation in the National Conference of Charities and Correction, of which he was president in 1906.

Reflecting Devine's preferences, the New York C.O.S. became a powerful lever of social reform. A tenement house committee under Lawrence Veiller was established within the C.O.S. in 1898; its work led to the New York State Tenement House Law of 1901 and the emergence of Veiller as the nation's leading housing expert. Devine was active in the creation of a tuberculosis committee in 1902 and a committee on criminal courts in 1910. Social reform activities of the C.O.S. were centralized through the formation of a Department for the Improvement of Social Conditions in 1907. Outside the C.O.S., Devine played a large role in the creation of the National Child Labor Committee and the National Association for the Study and Prevention of Tuberculosis, both in 1904. He also was a member of the advisory committee of the International Prison Congress in 1910, and chairman in 1912 of a committee of social workers which successfully lobbied for passage of an act creating the federal Commission on Industrial Relations.

Devine was an exceptionally versatile social worker whose interests encompassed virtually every social problem of the early twentieth century. Yet his point of view was consistent. He justified his career in terms of two religious principles: the infinite worth of the individual, and the lasting relevance of the Golden Rule as a guide to human relationships. From a secular perspective he was profoundly influenced by Simon Patten's economic thought, especially Patten's emphasis upon the transition from an economy of scarcity to one of abundance. A sufficient surplus existed, Devine believed, to ensure a minimum standard of living for all members of American society, and social workers could help attain this goal by pursuing a "constructive" or preventive policy. Constructive social work implied, first, the careful, scientific diagnosis of each case of dependency in order to establish a basis for permanent rehabilitation of the individual or family. Second and more important, it implied a commitment to environmental change or social legislation in order to eliminate the conditions which produced dependency. A line should be drawn below which competition would not be allowed to operate if it produced living standards lower than the community norm. Ultimately, the crucial test of any social institution or process was its effect upon family life—the source of individual and racial welfare.

Along with his duties at the Charity Organization Society, Devine undertook several missions in disaster relief for the Red Cross: in San Francisco, after the earthquake of 1906; in Dayton, Ohio, after the flood of 1913; and in 1917, during World War I, as chief of the Bureau of Refugees and Relief of the American Red Cross Commission to France. Upon his return from France, according to one observer, Devine seemed unable to "regain his old position of leadership in social work" (*Social Service Review*, June 1948), and that same year he resigned from the Charity Organization Society. He remained active for another two decades as an author and administrator. He was a member of the United States Coal Commission in 1922-1923, and from 1926 to 1928 he was professor of social economy and dean of the graduate school at American University, Washington, D.C. He then returned to New York to direct the Bellevue-Yorkville Health Demonstration, sponsored by the Milbank Memorial Fund, in 1929-1930. He became director of the Housing Association of New York, organized in 1930, and in 1931 vice-chairman of the New York Committee of 1,000, a private reform body organized to investigate political corruption in New York City. He served as executive director of the Nassau County (Long Island) Emergency Work Bureau, 1931-1933, and of the county Emergency Relief Bureau, 1933-1935. In the early 1930's he was active in several departments of the Federal Council of the Churches of Christ in America.

Devine is significant as a representative and transitional figure rather than as an original thinker. His talents lay in administration, synthesis, and interpretation. He balanced, better than most, the diverse and often contradictory forces which shaped the character of American social work in the twentieth century. Thus Devine embodied both its religious impulse and its aspiration for scientific, professional status. He was pragmatic, temperate, and experimental in attitude, but imbued with the moral idealism of the nineteenth century. Devine always paid tribute to the volunteer tradition of social service, but abhorred spontaneous, undisciplined, unorganized charity. He exemplified the social work commitment to "wholesale" or environ-

mental reform in the early twentieth century, but he devoted considerable attention to "retail" casework and relief techniques and, indeed, became an expert on disaster relief. An aggressive champion of social legislation, he favored compulsory social insurance, but opposed public assistance programs such as mothers' pensions. Voluntary agencies like his own, he believed, were superior in their capacity to combine relief with family rehabilitation; and in the old C.O.S. tradition, he was fearful of the effect of relief upon the incentives and disciplines which sustained the American work culture.

Devine spent his last years in Oak Park, Ill., the home of his daughter. He died there at the age of eighty of a coronary thrombosis associated with generalized arteriosclerosis. He was cremated and buried in Union, Iowa.

[Devine published dozens of articles and editorials in *Charities, Charities Rev., Charities and the Commons,* and *Survey,* particularly in the period 1897-1921. On the shift from production to consumption, see his "The Economic Function of Woman," Am. Acad. of Political and Social Sci., *Annals,* Nov. 1894. His general philosophy of charity and welfare is outlined in "The Dominant Note of the Modern Philanthropy," Nat. Conference of Charities and Correction, *Proc.,* 1906; "The New View of Charity," *Atlantic Monthly,* Dec. 1908; and "Social Ideals Implied in Present Am. Programs of Voluntary Philanthropy," Am. Sociological Soc., *Publications,* VII (1912), 177-188. On social work as a profession, see his "Education for Social Work," Nat. Conference of Charities and Correction, *Proc.,* 1915; and "A Profession in the Making," *Survey,* Jan. 1, 1916. Devine outlined his social philosophy and social work principles in more than a dozen books, among them: *The Practice of Charity: Individual, Associated and Organized* (1901), *The Principles of Relief* (1905), *Misery and Its Causes* (1909), *The Family and Social Work* (1912), *The Spirit of Social Work* (1912), *The Normal Life* (1915), and *Progressive Social Action* (1933). The *Reports* of the N.Y. Charity Organization Soc., 1896-1917, provide a good picture of that agency's development under Devine's leadership. Its work is also covered in Roy Lubove, *The Progressives and the Slums: Tenement House Reform in N.Y. City* (1962). For information on Devine's personal background and career, see his autobiographical *When Social Work Was Young* (1939); *Who Was Who in America,* II (1950); *Nat. Cyc. Am. Biog.,* XVIII, 214; and obituaries in *N.Y. Times,* Feb. 28, 1948; *Survey,* Mar. 1948, and *Social Service Rev.,* June 1949. A death certificate was obtained from the Ill. Dept. of Public Health. Mrs. Ruth Devine Hunt supplied family data.]

ROY LUBOVE

DE WOLFE, ELSIE (Dec. 20, 1865-July 12, 1950), actress, decorator, and hostess, was born Ella Anderson de Wolfe in New York City, the only daughter and second of five children of Stephen de Wolfe and Georgina (Copeland) de Wolfe. In the cluttered Victorian household maintained by her physician father's erratic finances, Elsie grew up with an oppressive sense of her own plainness, which she identified with the dowdiness around her. When, at age fourteen, she visited her father's French-style ancestral home in Wolfville, Nova Scotia, where the de Wolfes, an English family of Huguenot stock, had moved in 1761 from New England, she began to see an alternative to nineteenth-century design. Upon her return home, her Scottish-born mother sent her to live with a cousin, Dr. Archibald Charteris, in Edinburgh, where she attended school. Three years later Charteris, Queen Victoria's chaplain at Balmoral, arranged to have her presented at court. Elsie was awakened to her own potential for style and was launched on a social career in London and, upon her return in 1884, in the United States.

Elsie de Wolfe's energy and flair soon found an outlet in amateur theatricals, performed for charity. In 1890 she turned professional when her father's death left her family in need of money. Her first role was the lead in Victorien Sardou's *Thermidor,* for which she prepared at the Comédie Française before her debut, in 1891, at Proctor's Twenty-third Street Theater in New York. In 1894 she joined producer Charles Frohman's Empire Theatre stock company and gained a reputation as an actress of promise and as the best-dressed woman on the American stage. Despite her success in *The Bauble Shop* (1894), *The Marriage of Convenience* (1897), *Catherine* (1897) and later with her own company in *The Way of the World* (1901), which Clyde Fitch wrote for her, she was unable to escape a sense of her own mediocrity as an actress. Demanding more of herself and of life, she left the stage after the failure of *A Wife Without a Smile* in 1905. A period of uncertainty followed.

The career in which she would achieve distinction was one she created for herself and other women. At the suggestion of her closest friend, the agent Elisabeth Marbury, she turned her lifelong interest in design into a profession, becoming America's first female decorator. Her success in decorating the small Greek Revival house at Irving Place which she shared with Marbury established her reputation for taste, and she was soon launched. De Wolfe strove to provide homes for her clients that would afford, as she later put it, "breathing-space" from the jarring pace of America's development. Drawing her inspiration from eighteenth-century principles of unity, simplicity, and serenity, she added her own love of vibrant color and airiness to create her anti-Victorian interiors. The de Wolfe colors were greens and yellows and whites; her fabrics, muslins and chintzes. She favored mirrors for the effect of space and light

they provided and challenged the convention of uniformity of period by creating visual harmony among furniture of different styles. De Wolfe's revolt against the dark hangings and crowded arrangements of Victorian decor remained controversial until her imaginative decoration, in 1906, of New York's first women's social club, the Colony Club, established her reputation. With the publication of her *The House in Good Taste* (1913) she became an arbiter of American design.

Carrying her rebellion against drabness into her personal life, Elsie de Wolfe acquired a reputation for experimentation. She became, in 1908, one of the first women to fly, when she went up with Wilbur Wright in France. Although not generally interested in politics, she was an early supporter of the woman's suffrage movement, shocking her friends by marching up Fifth Avenue in the great spring parade of 1912. She devoted most of her leisure time, however, to the creation of a second home in France. Her great friendship with Elisabeth Marbury was rooted in a common love of French life. As early as the 1890's, they traveled regularly throughout the French countryside. When, in 1903, the opportunity arose to purchase the graceful Villa Trianon in Versailles, the two women, joined later by Anne Morgan, committed themselves to its restoration. As her firm prospered, de Wolfe spent more and more time at Versailles. With the coming of World War I, Elisabeth Marbury returned to the United States, eventually relinquishing her share in the villa. Determined to stay in France, de Wolfe distinguished herself at the Ambrine Mission for the care of gas burns and was awarded the Croix de Guerre and the Legion of Honor.

In the 1920's, Elsie de Wolfe's hospitality at Versailles became a cornerstone of international social life. Known for the inventiveness of her parties, she was hostess to diplomats, artists, and aristocrats and was a celebrity in her own right. On Mar. 10, 1926, she married Sir Charles Mendl, press attaché at the British Embassy. Sir Charles, a genial man devoted to Anglo-Saxon comforts, was unable to share his wife's passion for artistic affect. Theirs was a warm relationship, but they maintained the habits of a lifetime of independence. Lady Mendl presided at Versailles, and her husband continued to give his own quiet dinner parties at his apartment in Paris. With the outbreak of World War II, Sir Charles and Lady Mendl—who regained her citizenship by an act of Congress—moved to southern California. Ever youthful and determined, she re-created the life she had led at Versailles and inspired Ludwig Bemelmans' tribute, *To the One I Love Best* (1955). After the war she returned to Versailles, where she died five years later at the age of eighty-four.

[Aside from Ludwig Bemelmans' somewhat fictionalized *To the One I Love Best,* there is no full-length biography of de Wolfe. Her autobiography, *After All* (1935), supplemented by Elisabeth Marbury's *My Crystal Ball* (1923), provides the fullest record of her life through the 1920's and 1930's and includes several photographs of de Wolfe and examples of her design. See also *Notable Am. Women,* the *Dict. of Nat. Biog.* article on Sir Charles Mendl, and Janet Flanner, *An American in Paris,* pp. 103–118 (1940). Clippings from her stage career are included in the Players Collect. and the Robinson Locke Scrapbooks in the Theatre Collect., Lib. of Performing Arts, N.Y. Public Lib., Lincoln Center. Elsie de Wolfe was not a prolific writer, having published only a few articles from France in the 1890s—see, for example, *Cosmopolitan* 12 (1892): 653–658—before those she collected in *The House in Good Taste* (1913), and those in the *Touchstone,* Feb. 1921, and *Country Life,* Nov. 1921, published afterward. Obituaries appeared in the *N. Y. Times* and the *N. Y. Herald-Tribune* for July 13, 1950; *Le Monde,* July 14, 1950; *Time* and *Newsweek* for July 2, 1950; and *France Illustrated,* July 29, 1950.]

MARC PACHTER

DICKINSON, ROBERT LATOU (Feb. 21, 1861-Nov. 29, 1950), gynecologist, was born in Jersey City, N.J., one of five children of Horace Dickinson and Jeannette (Latou) Dickinson. His father, a hat manufacturer, was a descendant of Nathaniel Dickinson, who came from England to Massachusetts in 1634. His maternal grandfather had immigrated to the United States from Scotland in the early nineteenth century. Robert attended the Brooklyn Polytechnic Institute and studied for four years in Germany and Switzerland. He received his M.D. from Long Island College Hospital (later the Long Island College of Medicine) in Brooklyn in 1882, and after brief internships began a private practice in gynecology and obstetrics. On May 7, 1890, he married Sarah Truslow, daughter of a Brooklyn banker, who later helped found the Travelers' Aid Society and the national Y.W.C.A. They had three children: Margaret (who died in infancy), Dorothy, and Jean. Dickinson was a lifelong Episcopalian.

Beginning in 1883, Dickinson held a number of clinical and teaching positions at Long Island College Hospital. Although his first post was in the chest department dispensary, he became assistant obstetrician in 1884, lecturer in obstetrics in 1886, assistant professor of obstetrics in 1899, and professor of gynecology and obstetrics in 1918. He also served as obstetrician at King's County Hospital, Brooklyn (1894-1899); as

gynecologist surgeon (1897-1910), gynecologist (1910-1912), and eventually senior gynecologist (1912-1935) at Brooklyn Hospital; and as obstetrician-in-chief, Methodist Episcopal Hospital, Brooklyn (1905-1911). He was an examiner in 1885 for the Brooklyn Police Department and, in 1890-1897, for the Brooklyn Civil Service Commission. These experiences, together with his World War I service, probably contributed to his concern for establishing standards of "average" physical character and behavior. During World War I, he was the assistant chief of the medical section of the Council of National Defense (1917) and, with the rank of lieutenant colonel in the Army Medical Corps, served as medical advisor to the Army General Staff (1918-1919). In 1919 and in 1926, he headed missions to China for the U.S. Public Health Service. In 1940-1942, he lectured at Vassar College.

Dickinson was perhaps the most eminent American gynecologist of his day. He developed several new surgical techniques, including the use of electric cauterization in the treatment of cervicitis and in intrauterine sterilizations. He also was among the first physicians to use aseptic ligatures for tying the umbilical cord. He was co-editor of the *American Textbook of Obstetrics* (1895) and gained wide recognition as a teacher; at one time three of the four chairs in his specialty in New York City were occupied by his former assistants. Not content with the usual methods of instruction, Dickinson used his remarkable talents as a sculptor and illustrator in his teaching. To demonstrate the techniques of delivery, for example, he used "babies" made of rubber, and he taught female anatomy with the aid of his "gyneplacques" of the vagina and uterus. In 1939-1940, with the sculptor Abram Belskie, he developed the "Birth Series" exhibit for the New York World's Fair, a set of life-size sculpted models showing the development of a baby from fertilization to birth (published as *Birth Atlas,* 1941). He also created sculptures of the statistically average man and woman, naming them "Norman" and "Norma," and drew the illustrations for many of his own articles in medical journals.

Dickinson exemplified the concern for professionalism and specialization characteristic of so many areas of American life around the turn of the century. He was an active member of the American Medical Association and a founder of the American College of Surgeons in 1913. His presidential address to the American Gynecological Society, in 1920, noted with concern "the threat of eclipse of the gynecologic guild," especially by surgery. In a plea both to improve the quality of treatment and to preserve gynecology and obstetrics as distinct medical specialties, Dickinson urged the standardization of nomenclature, periodic recertification of specialists, and greater attention to women's interests —especially contraception—that gynecologists had theretofore largely ignored.

Dickinson strongly supported a number of feminist causes, including dress reform and contraception, and was among the most progressive male allies of the feminist movement. Few American physicians in the early 1900's approved his support for birth control, but his position followed naturally from a lifetime of advocating greater freedom for women. In the 1890's he wrote several articles demonstrating the harmful effects of the then fashionable styles of women's dress—especially steel-ribbed "health waists" and heavy, superfluous layers of underclothing. He also encouraged women to get more exercise than was then considered proper for genteel ladies. From at least 1890 onward, he fought against cultural taboos that inhibited women's erotic lives, including the notion that sexual urges were shameful, and against the general condemnation of autoeroticism as unnatural and unhealthy. Convinced by his experience as a practicing gynecologist that women were frequently the victims of sexual maladjustments deriving from ignorance and superstition, he early advocated a scientific program of sex education.

Dickinson was the single most important physician associated with the early birth-control movement. In 1923 he founded the Committee on Maternal Health (which in 1930 became the National Committee) to gather data on contraception. Throughout the rest of the decade, he tried repeatedly but unsuccessfully to persuade the birth-control leader Margaret Sanger to allow accredited physicians to play a more active role in her New York clinic. Sanger, reluctant to lose control of the clinic she had so laboriously built, rebuffed Dickinson, thus frustrating his efforts to gain greater respectability for birth control in the medical profession and to involve doctors more directly in the search for improved contraceptive techniques. Nevertheless, Dickinson's standing in his profession, his influential position as a fellow of the New York Academy of Medicine, and his publications under the auspices of the National Committee on Maternal Health—particularly *Control of Conception* (1931; 2nd ed., 1938) and, with Woodbridge Edwards Morris, *Techniques of Conception Control* (1941)—did much to secure eventual medical support for birth control.

Dickinson's National Committee concerned itself not only with problems of fertility and contraception, but with the whole range of sexual behavior. With Lura Beam, Dickinson published two important studies: *A Thousand Marriages* (1931) and *The Single Woman: A Medical Study in Sex Education* (1934). Both books drew principally upon the more than 5,000 case histories Dickinson had accumulated in his practice. They were among the handful of studies concerned with the sexual behavior of average people, as distinct from works such as Richard von Krafft-Ebing's *Psychopathia Sexualis,* which dealt primarily with deviance. That concern, the fact that his case histories often contained information gathered over an individual's lifetime, and the special diagnostic skills that Dickinson, as a gynecologist, brought to his interviews with patients, made his studies unique in the literature of sexual behavior. Later workers in the field have criticized the limitations of the population sample in Dickinson's studies (mostly middle- and upper-class women from New York), as well as their statistical crudity and occasional errors in calculation, but have recognized their value as pioneering efforts that made possible the subsequent, more thorough investigations of sexual behavior.

Dickinson's associates recognized him as a humane, enlightened gentleman who brought unusual intellectual vigor to his many professional concerns. The general public knew him as the author of *Palisades Interstate Park* (1921), about New Jersey's palisades on the Hudson River, which he knew and loved deeply, and the *New York Walk Book* (1923), written with Raymond H. Torrey and Frank Place (Dickinson also provided the pen and ink sketches). He was a member of the Planned Parenthood Federation, the American Association for the Study of Sterility, the American Association of Marriage Counselors, the Euthanasia Society (president, 1946-1949), the National Sculpture Society, and the American Geographical Society. In 1946 he received the Albert and Mary Lasker Foundation Award for his original work in birth control. He died of pleurisy at his daughter's home in Amherst, Mass.

[In his presidential address to the American Gynecological Society in 1920, Dickinson made a comprehensive statement of most of his important professional concerns; it is reprinted in *Am. Jour. of Obstetrics and Gynecology* I (1920): 2–10. Some of his papers, including medical case histories, are in the Inst. for Sex Research, Indiana Univ.; others are at the Countway Medical Lib., Boston, with a small collection at the N.Y. Acad. of Medicine. Two papers read before the Charaka Club were published in one volume, "Sketching Boats on the China Coast" and "Action and Humor in Han Dynasty Decoration." See also *Nat. Cyc. Am. Biog.*, XXXIX (1954), 485–486, with photograph; *N.Y. Times*, Nov. 30, 1950, p. 33; *Am. Jour. of Obstetrics and Gynecology* 61 (1951): 232; David M. Kennedy, *Birth Control in America: The Career of Margaret Sanger* (1970), chap. vii.]

DAVID M. KENNEDY

DIETZ, PETER ERNEST (July 10, 1878-Oct. 11, 1947), priest and early leader of the Roman Catholic social reform movement, was born in New York City, the second child in a family of ten. His parents, Frederick and Eva (Kern) Dietz, were German immigrants. Frederick Dietz, a varnisher by trade, was frequently unemployed, and his children grew up in considerable poverty. At an early age, Peter determined to enter the priesthood. He attended a parish school conducted by the German-based Redemptorist Fathers, and in 1894 entered St. Mary's, a Redemptorist college in North East, Pa. Ill health forced his withdrawal two years later but, after an interim as a paperhanger and painter, he studied at St. Francis Xavier College in Manhattan (1897-1899) and St. Bonaventure College in Allegany, N.Y. (1899-1900), in preparation for admission to a seminary.

In 1900, having become acquainted with several priests of the Society of the Divine Word, Dietz went to study at the society's seminary in Moedling, Germany. He had already decided to devote his priestly career to the cause of the workingman, responding to the call for such work by Pope Leo XIII in his 1891 encyclical *Rerum novarum*. A nervous, restless man, subject to headaches and fits of melancholy, Dietz was eager to begin his ministry and chafed at the cloistered life of the novitiate. He therefore returned to the United States in 1903 and continued his studies at Catholic University in Washington, D.C. There his interest in social problems was encouraged by his friendship with Walter H. R. Elliott, a liberal member of the Paulist Fathers, and William J. Kerby, a pioneer Catholic social scientist who in 1910 helped found the National Conference of Catholic Charities. Only reluctantly did Dietz reenter a seminary, St. Mary's in Baltimore, as a prerequisite to ordination.

Dietz was ordained a priest in December 1904 and was assigned as assistant pastor to a church in Elyria, Ohio. In a time of increasing opposition to organized labor, Dietz believed that trade unionism offered the surest road to the peaceful resolution of industrial problems. The Catholic church, he felt, must join in the

effort to eliminate social injustice if it wished to retain the loyalty of Catholic workers and stem the drift toward socialism. Among the chief elements of the program he evolved were the creation of a unified national Catholic reform movement, the organization within the trade union movement of Catholic workers to combat socialism, and the establishment of a Catholic school of social service. Dietz worked initially within the socially conscious Central Verein, a national federation of German Catholic beneficial societies. As English-language editor of the Verein's *Central Blatt and Social Justice* (1909-1910), he worked closely with the Ohio Federation of Labor on a legislative program and lobbied actively for its passage by the state legislature.

Dietz's national efforts began in 1909. Attending the convention of the American Federation of Labor that year, he was impressed by the success of the Presbyterian minister Charles Stelzle in establishing closer ties between the trade union movement and the Protestant churches. Dietz thereupon organized the Catholic delegates into the Militia of Christ for Social Service, of which he became executive secretary. Intended to include all Catholic unionists and to provide programs of social education and social action, the militia was endorsed by most Catholic bishops and labor leaders, who saw it as a useful ally in the A.F. of L.'s internal struggle against socialism. Yet, though the militia maintained a presence at national conventions, it remained a small organization (never attracting more than 700 members) and exerted little influence. It ceased to exist in 1914.

Meanwhile much of the militia's program had been adopted by the American Federation of Catholic Societies, which in 1911, at Dietz's urging, established a Social Service Commission with Dietz as executive secretary. Besides supporting the programs of organized labor, the commission concerned itself with the problems of immigration and scientific social work, and attempted to educate Catholics on the need for reform. In 1915 Dietz organized the American Academy of Christian Democracy, a school to train young Catholic women to become professional social workers. Originally established at Hot Springs, N.C., in facilities provided by a wealthy Catholic laywoman, the school was moved in 1917 to Cincinnati to afford students better opportunities for urban field work.

Following World War I the American Catholic bishops consolidated the church's social service activities into the National Catholic

Welfare Conference, a permanent organization of the type Dietz had long advocated. Dietz was consulted about the establishment of the body's Social Action Department but was offered no role. In the unfavorable atmosphere of the postwar period, his militancy and his partisanship toward labor gained him many enemies, as did his abrasive personality. Plagued by neuralgia, he was often irritable, abrupt, and suspicious. He lacked the social graces, and though his underlying qualities of sympathy and honesty won him many close friends, he frequently alienated more casual acquaintances.

Continuing in the leadership of his school, Dietz also became involved in Cincinnati trade union activities, acted as a mediator in several labor disputes, and helped set up an industrial council plan in the city's building trades. In 1922, at his American Academy of Christian Democracy, he established the National Labor College—the first of its kind in America— where unionists attended lectures, conferences, and retreats. Dietz hoped to imbue workers with the principles of moderation and the need for industrial peace. But opposition to his efforts by the Cincinnati Chamber of Commerce led in 1923 to his expulsion from the archdiocese by Archbishop Henry Moeller and the closing of the American Academy.

Dietz was never again active on the national scene. Appointed pastor in the rural community of Whitefish Bay, Wis., in the diocese of Milwaukee, he spent the rest of his life there, building up his parish, St. Monica's. He stayed in close touch with the labor movement, however, and in his community helped organize cooperatives and credit unions. In later years Dietz suffered from hypertension and at the time of his death was nearly blind. He died in Milwaukee at the age of sixty-nine. Though his pioneering efforts were short-lived, Dietz was a seminal figure in the Roman Catholic reform movement. Like his contemporary, the Rev. John A. Ryan, he jarred the church's social conscience, and made the church more responsive to the needs of workers in a modern, industrialized America.

[Mary Harrita Fox, *Peter E. Dietz, Labor Priest* (1953), is a full biography. Aaron I. Abell, *Am. Catholicism and Social Action* (1960), places Dietz in the context of the general reform movement. Also useful are: Marc Karson, *Am. Labor Unions and Politics, 1900–1918* (1958); David J. O'Brien, *Am. Catholics and Social Reform: The New Deal Years* (1968); and Sister M. Adele Francis Gorman, "Peter E. Dietz and the N.C.W.C.," Am. Catholic Hist. Soc. of Phila., *Records*, Dec. 1963.]

DAVID J. O'BRIEN

DIGGES, DUDLEY (June 9, 1880–Oct. 24, 1947), actor and director, was born to James Dudley Digges and Catherine (Forsythe) Digges in Dublin, Ireland. He was educated at the Christian Brothers' School (1886–1890) and St. Mary's College, Dublin (1890–1893), but thereafter he chose to study informally the craft of the theater under Frank J. Fay. Digges joined the Fay brothers' Ormonde Dramatic Society at its birth (1898) and by 1902 was sufficiently accomplished an actor to take his place among the charter members of the Irish National Theatre (later to take up residence at the Abbey Theatre), directed by W. B. Yeats and Lady Gregory. In that initial season Digges appeared in the premieres of Yeats's *Cathleen-ni-Houlihan* and AE's *Deirdre,* among other works, and shortly thereafter traveled with the company to London. The trip occasioned an invitation to Digges and some of his companions to play at the Louisiana Purchase Exposition in 1904 in St. Louis, Mo.

The Irish season at the exposition was a fiasco of sorts: the somberness of the repertoire was ill suited to the liveliness of the occasion to such an extent that the actors at one performance faced an audience consisting solely of a dozen or so Indians. Digges's part in the venture ended when he argued with the exposition's management over the inclusion of anti-Irish elements in the entertainment in violation of the troupe's contract. He then went to work as a clerk in St. Louis until the producer Arnold Daly signed him to appear at New York's Garrick Theater in Bernard Shaw's *John Bull's Other Island* (1904).

Digges remained in New York until 1907, playing with Mrs. Fiske, Ben Greet, and other noted actors of the day; on August 27 of that year he married Mary Roden Quinn, an actress. Thereafter he spent about four years touring with Greet's company. From 1911 to 1918 Digges served as stage manager for the company of George Arliss. Up to this point Dudley Digges had earned a fine reputation among his colleagues, if not with the public, and a place among the founders of America's first great producing organization, the Theatre Guild.

Perhaps the greatest compliment one could pay Digges would be to list the actors with whom he worked—as actor and director—in his long association with the guild from its inception in 1919 until shortly before his death; it would include many of the most respected names in the American theater. Digges appeared in the guild's very first production,

Jacinto Benavente's *The Bonds of Interest* (1919), whose cast, incidentally, included Edna St. Vincent Millay. But it was the second offering of the company that gave Digges what many considered his greatest role—James Caesar in St. John Ervine's *John Ferguson* (1919); his work was described as near-perfect by more than one critic and showed him to be one of the company's greatest assets. The public had ample opportunity to savor his work: because the Theatre Guild was the only producing organization to recognize the newly formed players' union Actors Equity, *John Ferguson* was for several months the only play on the boards in New York. Digges was of course quite at home in the work of his fellow countryman, but the seasons to follow were to lead both him and the Theatre Guild further afield.

In 1920 Digges undertook one of the leads in Strindberg's *Dance of Death,* a rather daring work for the period. His roles were many and diverse; they included Boss Magnan in Shaw's *Heartbreak House* (1920), a lead in Karel Čapek's *R.U.R.* (1922), Mr. Zero in Elmer Rice's *Adding Machine* (1923), a role in support of the Lunts in Ferenc Molnár's *The Guardsman* (1924), Volpone (to Alfred Lunt's Mosca) in Stefan Zweig's adaptation of Jonson's classic (1928), and Andrew Undershaft in Shaw's *Major Barbara* (1928). Digges's directorial duties for the guild included several memorable Shaw revivals that prompted the playwright to offer the Theatre Guild first refusal for the American productions of his later works. After 1930 Digges acted in several non-guild productions, achieving stardom as the grandfather who tangles with death in *On Borrowed Time* (1938). On one of the occasions when he returned to the Theatre Guild's fold, to play Emperor Franz Joseph in Maxwell Anderson's *Masque of Kings* (1937), he chalked up his three-thousandth performance under guild auspices.

Digges made the first of his more than fifty film appearances as the prison warden in *Condemned* (1929). Although he played such roles as the Chinese hotel manager in *The General Died at Dawn* (1936) and the ship's doctor in *Mutiny on the "Bounty"* (1935), he was more likely to be cast in films as an irascible, but lovable, grandfatherly character, a role that drew upon the natural warmth and intelligence of the private man. In 1946 Digges was reunited with the Theatre Guild when he masterfully assumed the role of the bar owner Harry Hope in Eugene O'Neill's *The Iceman Cometh.* It was to be his valediction to the theater, for he died of a stroke at his New York home the following year.

Digges was a member of the Lambs and Players clubs and was paid tribute in 1939 by the American-Irish Historical Society for his contributions to the theater of two nations, but at his death Digges was best eulogized by the poet Padraic Colum, who wrote, "The role we singled when we spoke his name/ Of instant goodness and deep faithfulness/ Will be sustained beyond the curtain fall."

[There is no biography of Digges; the Lib. for the Performing Arts at Lincoln Center in New York City has a file of clippings tracing his American career. The best source, textual and pictorial, is Norman Nadel, *Pictorial Hist. of the Theatre Guild* (1969). See also obituary in *N.Y. Times,* Oct. 25, 1947.]

LELAND S. LOWTHER

DIXON, THOMAS (Jan. 11, 1864-Apr. 3, 1946), clergyman, lecturer, author, theatrical and motion picture producer, known as Thomas Dixon, Jr., was born near Shelby, Cleveland County, N.C., the second of three sons and third of five children of Thomas Dixon, a Baptist minister and farmer, and Amanda Elizabeth (McAfee) Dixon. His mother was the daughter of a prosperous South Carolina planter; his father's forebears had come to North Carolina from Scotland and Germany before the American Revolution. Impoverished by the Civil War and unable to make a sufficient living from his pastoral duties, the elder Dixon opened a hardware store in Shelby in 1865, but seven years later returned to farming. Young Thomas, an impressionable boy during these difficult postwar years, learned to fear Negro domination and despise Radical Reconstruction. Watching the growth of the Ku Klux Klan, he quickly assimilated its doctrine of white supremacy and viewed its members as "knights of old, riding for their country, their women and their God." His father was a Klansman and an adored uncle, Col. Lee Roy McAfee, served as Grand Titan in western North Carolina.

Dixon received his early education in the country schools around Shelby and at Shelby Academy. A gifted student, he entered Wake Forest College at the age of fifteen and graduated in 1883 with an M.A. degree. His record won him a scholarship to Johns Hopkins University as a graduate student in history and politics. With the aid of his friend and fellow student Woodrow Wilson, Dixon secured a part-time job as drama critic of the *Baltimore Mirror.* After a few months, seized by stage fever, he left Johns Hopkins and went to New York City, where he studied acting and joined a Shakespearean road company. The manager absconded, leaving the troupe stranded in upstate New York, and Dixon returned to North Carolina. Though only twenty, he ran successfully in 1884 for the state legislature. Before beginning his two-year term he enrolled at the Greensboro (N.C.) Law School and received an LL.B. in 1886. But he found himself discontented with politics and disillusioned by the injustices of the law. After a period of uncertainty he felt a call to enter the Baptist ministry and was ordained in October 1886. Meanwhile, on Mar. 3, 1886, he had eloped with Harriet Bussey of Columbus, Ga. They were to have three children: Thomas, Charlotte Louise, and Jordan.

Dixon proved a spellbinding minister and moved quickly from his first pastorate in Goldsboro, N.C., to increasingly larger parishes in Raleigh, Boston, and New York City. He spent six successful years at the 23rd Street Church in New York, at the same time building both a reputation and a fortune as a public lecturer. In 1895, feeling confined by Baptist denominationalism, he founded his own "People's Church" for the "unaffiliated masses." His sermons, which drew large crowds, dealt not with the kingdom of heaven, but with the crookedness of Tammany politics in New York, the shortcomings of presidential candidate William Jennings Bryan, and the need for a strong policy against Spain. So violent were the reactions Dixon sometimes aroused that police had to be stationed in his church.

Continually restless, Dixon abruptly left both his church and the ministry in 1899 and withdrew to a 500-acre estate he had purchased in Gloucester County, Va., on Chesapeake Bay. There, along with hunting trips and outings on his yacht, he began to write historical novels of a highly polemical cast. *The Leopard's Spots* (1902) was followed by *The Clansman* (1905) and *The Traitor* (1907); this trilogy aimed at refuting the indictment of the South made by Harriet Beecher Stowe in *Uncle Tom's Cabin*. Set in the Reconstruction era, the novels pictured Negroes as bestial bogeymen threatening white society, and the Ku Klux Klan as valiantly trying to save the South from black domination. They had little literary merit but became best sellers. At a time when discrimination and Jim Crow legislation were increasing, they served to solidify racial hostility.

Dixon wrote seventeen other novels, all to correct what he saw as "social evils," as well as several nonfiction works, but none had the same impact. Another trilogy—*The One Woman* (1903), *Comrades* (1909), and *The Root of Evil* (1911)—attacked socialism; *The Foolish Virgin* (1915) criticized the emancipation of women, *The Fall of a Nation* (1916) indicted pacifism, and *The Flaming Sword* (1939) dealt with the dangers of miscegenation. In the meantime, as a further means of bringing his message to the people, Dixon had returned to the theater. He adapted *The Clansman* for the stage and in 1905-1906 produced it with two simultaneous touring companies. Dramatizations of other of his novels followed, and at times he acted in his own productions.

Dixon reached his widest audience when a fellow Southerner, the director D. W. Griffith, decided to make a film version of *The Clansman*. The result was a motion picture landmark, *The Birth of a Nation* (1915). An immense artistic and popular success, it demonstrated the vast potential of the new medium; but it also inflamed the public with its powerful anti-Negro propaganda. Opposition to the film was mounted in major cities by the National Association for the Advancement of Colored People, and four thousand Negroes protested its opening in Boston. Dixon was sometimes blamed for the rebirth of the Ku Klux Klan after World War I, but he condemned the new secret group as dangerous and unworthy of the traditions of the original Klan, a viewpoint expressed in his novel *The Black Hood* (1924).

The Birth of a Nation aroused Dixon's enthusiasm for moviemaking. He organized his own studio in Los Angeles in 1915 and produced five films based on his novels, including *The Fall of a Nation* (1916) and *The One Woman* (1918). None was critically or financially successful, and Dixon's career went into decline. Public taste was changing, and though he continued to write historical romances, most of his later works were repetitious and sold poorly. He estimated that he had earned over $1.2 million over the years, but by 1929 he was penniless, having lost heavily in the stock market during the panic of 1907, in the short-lived Florida land boom of 1925, and in an ambitious attempt in 1926 to develop a sort of Chautauqua center and artists' colony, "Wildacres," in the North Carolina mountains.

Dixon's interest in politics was reawakened in the 1930's when he collaborated with former Attorney General Harry M. Daugherty on *The Inside Story of the Harding Tragedy* (1932), written to counter *The Strange Death of President Harding* (1930), in which his sister May Dixon Thacker had misguidedly collaborated with Gaston B. Means. Dixon campaigned vigorously for Franklin D. Roosevelt in 1932, then undertook a nationwide speaking tour in 1934 as a special representative of the National Recovery Administration. But he turned away from Roosevelt in 1936, feeling that the New Deal had been infiltrated by Communist and other radical elements, and campaigned for the Republican candidate, Alfred M. Landon. The next year Dixon received a Republican appointment as clerk in the United States District Court in Raleigh. His first wife died in 1937, and on Mar. 20, 1939, he married Madelyn Donovan of Raleigh, who had acted in two of his motion pictures. Meanwhile, in February 1939, Dixon had suffered a cerebral hemorrhage. A semi-invalid for the rest of his life, he died in Raleigh in 1946, at the age of eighty-two. He was buried in Sunset Cemetery, Shelby, N.C.

[Two scholarly studies are Raymond A. Cook, *Fire from the Flint: The Amazing Careers of Thomas Dixon* (1968), and James Z. Wright, "Thomas Dixon: The Mind of a Southern Apologist" (Ph.D. dissertation, George Peabody Coll. for Teachers, 1966), which includes the most complete Dixon bibliography. Both draw extensively upon Dixon's MS autobiography, "Southern Horizons," which as of 1973 was in the possession of Mrs. Madelyn Donovan Dixon, Raleigh, N.C., and was not accessible. The largest single collection of Dixon Papers is at Duke Univ.; his personal library (including scrapbooks and photo albums) is at Gardner-Webb College, Boiling Springs, N.C. Other materials are in the hands of Dixon's niece Mrs. Clara Dixon Richardson; in the Dixon collection at the Park Square Public Lib., Asheville, N.C.; and in the papers of Dixon's brother Amzi Clarence Dixon, in the Dargan-Carver Lib. of the Baptist Sunday School Board, Nashville, Tenn.]

ANDREW BUNI

DOBIE, GILMOUR (Jan. 31, 1878–Dec. 23, 1948), football coach, was born in Hastings, Minn., the first son and third of four children of Robert Dobie, a well driller, and Ellen (Black) Dobie. He was probably named Robert Gilmour, but never used a first initial, though in news reports he was often erroneously called "J. Gilmour Dobie." Both parents had come to the United States in the early 1870's from Scotland. Dobie's mother died in 1882. His father remarried but died soon afterward, and Dobie, who was never close to his stepmother, left home as soon as he could support himself. He played football at the Hastings high school and at the University of Minnesota, which he entered in 1899. As varsity left end in his freshman year and first-string quarterback in his sophomore and junior years, he made an impressive record, the 1900 team being undefeated. He was light in weight but was known as a "ferocious" tackler.

Dobie began his coaching career in 1902. For the next four years he was assistant to Dr.

Henry L. Williams, Minnesota's football coach. In 1905 he also coached Minneapolis' South Side High School to a state championship. During these years Dobie studied law at the University of Minnesota, graduating in 1904. He was admitted to the bar, but apparently never practiced.

Dobie's appointment in 1906 as director of athletics and coach of all sports at North Dakota Agricultural College in Fargo marked the beginning of one of the most unusual coaching achievements in American collegiate history. For two years his football team was undefeated, and he maintained the same record as football coach at the University of Washington from 1908 through 1916, winning fifty-eight victories and gaining three ties and keeping his opponents scoreless in forty-two of the sixty-one games. For three seasons (1917-1919) Dobie was football coach at the United States Naval Academy at Annapolis. His teams won seventeen games and lost three. Navy's opponents were held scoreless in eleven games, and none scored more than a single touchdown. In 1920 he was called to Cornell University, where he was to remain for sixteen years.

As a coach, Dobie was not a creative innovator, but rather a perfectionist who demanded player dedication and extensive drill on fundamentals. He stressed power and timing, with precise coordination. The "off-tackle" play was his favorite, and his teams used the forward pass and deception only enough to keep the opposition "honest." Yet he sometimes surprised an opponent with a strong passing attack. Dobie always emphasized defense and prepared his teams carefully for each opposing team. At least through his first quarter-century of coaching, he seems to have earned and retained the loyalty as well as the respect of his players. His great teams and numerous All-American players, especially Eddie Kaw and George Pfann of Cornell, earned him national attention.

At Cornell, Dobie at first continued his amazing success. Reviving a lagging football program, he coached undefeated teams in 1921, 1922, and 1923. Gradually, however, Cornell's athletic prowess began to decline. Despite pressure from alumni, Dobie refused to engage in the aggressive recruiting of other college coaches; the depression and a rigid admissions policy hurt the athletic programs; undergraduates became more indifferent to sports; and losing seasons became more frequent. A hard taskmaster with a poor sense of public relations, Dobie came in for his share of the blame. His constant pessimism about his teams' prospects, which earned him the sobriquet "Gloomy Gil," was regarded by some as adversely affecting player morale. In 1935 Cornell unified control of intercollegiate and intramural athletics under a director of athletics and physical education, and after another losing season, Dobie resigned in 1936. He spent the next three years at Boston College, with moderate success, and in 1939 retired from coaching.

Despite his waning days at Cornell, Dobie left a unique record. In thirty-three years his teams won 179 games, lost forty-five and tied fifteen. He had fourteen undefeated seasons, eleven of them in succession. His devotion to football found expression in numerous magazine articles, many for the *American Boy,* and he taught for several summers in the football clinic at the University of Illinois. A charter member of the Football Coaches Association, he became one of its trustees in 1924 and its president in 1928. He was active in fraternal and Presbyterian church activities. Tall and lean, Dobie was known to friends as a rather shy man with a quiet sense of humor, one who was well read and could be a fascinating conversationalist, a hard-driving coach who yet accepted the importance of the academic, a citizen deeply concerned about the problems and the issues of his day. On Jan. 2, 1918, he married Eva M. Butler of Seattle. They had three children: Jane, Gilmour, and Louise. Mrs. Dobie died in 1927. In his last years Dobie made his home in Putnam, Conn., near his son. He died of a cerebral thrombosis in Hartford, Conn., and was buried in Lakeview Cemetery, Ithaca, N.Y.

[Extensive file of clippings, athletic department reports, etc., in Cornell Dept. of Manuscripts and Univ. Archives; files of *Cornell Alumni News,* 1920–1936; Morris Bishop, *A Hist. of Cornell* (1962); Allison Danzig, "Gilmour Dobie," *N.Y. Times,* Nov. 3, 1931; *Cornell Daily Sun,* Feb. 1, 1936; obituary in *Ithaca Jour.,* Dec. 24, 1948; death record from Conn. Dept. of Health; information from Univ. of Minn. Arch. and from athletic departments at Minn., Wash., and the Naval Acad.; correspondence with George Pfann of Ithaca, Mrs. Frank J. (Jane Dobie) Howatt of Ponte Vedra Beach, Fla., and John Dobie of St. Paul, Minn., a half brother.]
RALPH ADAMS BROWN

DODGE, HENRY CHEE (1860-Jan. 7, 1947), Indian leader, was given the name Adiits'a'ii ("one who hears and understands") by the Navajo. Although by descent he was only one-fourth Navajo, Dodge was raised among them and knew only their language up to the age of twelve. His father, Juan Cocinas

(sometimes called Juan Aneas), was a Mexican who had been captured by the Navajo when he was ten years old. Juan quickly learned the Navajo language and became an excellent silversmith. Because of his ability to speak both his native Spanish and Navajo, he was used frequently as an interpreter. He often worked for an American agent named Henry Dodge, after whom Henry Chee Dodge was named. "Chee" is the English spelling of the Navajo word *chii,* meaning "red." He was widely known as Chee Dodge.

Juan Cocinas married a woman who was half Navajo and half Jemez (a Pueblo tribe); Chee was their only child. His father was, ironically, killed by Mexican raiders when Chee was only one year old. Chee was cared for by his mother until he was three years old, when a large band of American soldiers, led by Kit Carson, compelled most of the Navajo to surrender by destroying their food supplies, killing their sheep, and burning their fields and fruit trees. Chee's mother left for the Hopi villages to try to obtain food for the family, but she never returned. Chee was then cared for by his mother's sisters. As the family continued to travel about searching for food, Chee grew weak from malnutrition. His mother's sisters finally found a family willing to feed and care for him while they continued their search for food. After the food supply of this second family ran short, Chee was given to a third family. Later he was left for a fourth family who never arrived to get him. He awoke one morning and found himself alone. After a frantic search for another human being, he was found by an eight-year-old girl who was traveling with her grandfather, searching for food and trying to avoid the American soldiers. Chee joined them, but they were soon captured and marched off some 500 miles to Fort Sumner with other Navajo.

Chee remained with his adopted sister and grandfather through the four years of captivity at Fort Sumner (1864-1868) and returned with them to Navajo country, where they made their new home just north of Fort Defiance. They acquired a few sheep, planted some fields, and began building a good life for themselves. This was the first time in his life that he felt free from hunger and fear.

When he was about twelve years old, Chee again met his mother's sister who had cared for him when he was three. She was now married to a white man who was a clerk at Fort Defiance. After spending a few months learning English in a Presbyterian school, Chee was given a job as a clerk's helper by his aunt's husband, Perry Williams. While working as an assistant stock clerk, Chee expanded his command of the English language, learned arithmetic, and acquired many skills that aided him in his later business endeavors. He also earned five dollars per week, which he did not spend until years later when he went into business for himself.

His increasing command of English enabled him to act frequently as an interpreter. When he was twenty years old, he was appointed official interpreter for the Navajo tribe. He was soon much more than just an interpreter. He had learned two ways of living and thinking, and he displayed unusual wisdom and skill in bringing the two together, settling disputes, correcting misunderstandings, and adjudicating rights and obligations. He continued in this role for nearly ten years, again saving nearly everything he earned.

At the age of thirty Chee realized that his savings had made him a relatively wealthy man. He decided to leave public service and go into business for himself, becoming a partner with Stephen Aldrich in operating the Round Rock Trading Post. He married Asdzaan Trinnijinnie and then established a home at Crystal, N.Mex. He soon built up a prosperous farm, expanded his herds of sheep and cattle, acquired hundreds of acres of grazing land, and became a successful rancher as well as a businessman.

Chee divorced his first wife because she habitually gambled away his wealth. He next married Nanabah, who was a daughter of the girl who had found him when he was four. He also took Nanabah's younger sister as his wife. He built an enormous beautiful house at the foot of the Chuska Mountains and continued to expand his business enterprises and his ranch holdings. At the age of thirty-nine, Nanabah's younger sister gave birth to his first son, Tom. Two years later Nanabah gave birth to his second son, Ben. Later Nanabah gave birth to his daughter Mary.

Nanabah proved to be Chee's equal in intelligence and business skill and soon acquired great wealth of her own in real estate and cattle. Their separate business interests often kept them apart for long periods of time. During one separation Chee took another wife, K'eehabah, who bore him a second daughter, Annie.

Chee was a concerned father and strong disciplinarian, determined to see his children become well educated and successful. He sent them to Salt Lake City to school during the winters. With the exception of Mary, all of Chee's children did well in school and became involved in Navajo politics. Tom became a lawyer and in 1932 was elected Chairman of the Navajo Tribe. Ben and Annie both became members of the Tribal Council. Annie became famous for her efforts to improve health conditions among American Indians. In 1963 Annie Dodge Wauneka was awarded the Presidential Medal of Freedom.

From 1864 to 1923 the Navajo had no central leadership or tribal government. They lived as dispersed extended families, bound together by wide-ranging clan and marriage ties and by a common language and culture. In 1923 the first Navajo Tribal Council was organized. Henry Chee Dodge became its first Chairman and held this position until 1928. The Tribal Council at this time was not given many important powers but did conduct much of the tribe's business with the United States government and business corporations that wanted to lease Navajo lands to exploit the oil and mineral reserves found there. Chee was an able leader who did everything he could to protect and assert the rights of his people.

In 1934 John Collier, commissioner of the Bureau of Indian Affairs, was told that the Navajo reservation was overgrazed. Being an ardent conservationist, Collier decided the Navajo had to reduce their livestock holdings by more than half. The Navajo understandably resisted. Chee Dodge tried to change Collier's mind and get government officials to understand the feelings and needs of the Navajo people, but his efforts were unsuccessful. Three-fourths of Chee's own herd was taken from him. Chee, like most Navajo, responded to the events with prolonged melancholy and intense bitterness. Others violently resisted the forced reduction and destruction; they were either imprisoned or killed.

Dodge was again elected Tribal Chairman in 1942 and thereafter spent most of his time trying to make government officials aware of the difficulties faced by the Navajo people, so that solutions could be worked out and problems resolved. These efforts ultimately proved valuable. Not long after World War II, many actions were taken by both the Navajo and the federal government to improve economic and health conditions. In addition, educational facilities and opportunities for the Navajo were improved and expanded.

Chee Dodge's greatness and importance cannot be found in any crucial decisions or actions that he took or in any far-reaching programs or policies that he initiated but rather in the quality of man he was. Rising from the depths of deprivation, despair, and bondage, he mastered the world of the white man while remaining true to the faith and character of the Navajo, ever sensitive to the needs of his people and ever willing to serve his people wherever there was a need.

At the age of 86 Dodge was elected Vice-Chairman of the Navajo Tribe in 1946. When he died in 1947, he was buried in the cemetery at Fort Defiance. His funeral was attended by hundreds of people from a variety of ethnic and cultural backgrounds who had come to know and respect him.

[*Navajo Biographies* (Rough Rock Demonstration School, 1970); interview with Annie Dodge Wauneka.]
GARY J. WITHERSPOON

DOUBLEDAY, NELSON (June 16, 1889-Jan. 11, 1949), book publisher, was born in Brooklyn, N.Y., the second of three children and younger son of Frank Nelson Doubleday and Neltje (De Graff) Doubleday. Growing up in Oyster Bay, N.Y., he was educated at the Friends School in New York City and Holbrook Military Academy in Ossining, N.Y., from which he was graduated in 1908. He then attended New York University for two years, but dropped out to pursue a career in book publishing and merchandising. The decision was a natural one, for his father had entered the publishing field when Nelson was only eight years old, and in the early years of the twentieth century, with his second partner, Walter Hines Page, was making the name Doubleday synonymous with the aggressive distribution of books. Nelson's mother, under the pen name "Neltje Blanchan," was the author of several nature books published under the Doubleday imprint.

Significantly, however, he did not join the family firm until he had established himself independently. In 1910 he started a "deferred subscription" business by which individuals could purchase unsold copies of current periodicals returned to publishers. With the profits from this venture he began to publish books under his own imprint, including a popular etiquette guide rewritten by his secretary from an earlier unsuccessful work issued by his father. In 1916 Nelson sold his father an interest in his enterprises, and in 1918, back from wartime service in Washington, D.C., as a naval lieutenant commander, he joined Doubleday, Page and Company as a junior partner. He rose rapidly, becoming vice-president in

1922 and president in 1928, a year after the firm merged with that of George H. Doran to become Doubleday, Doran and Company. With his father's death in 1934 he became chairman of the board as well.

Perfecting techniques already developed by his father, Doubleday concentrated on the mass production of inexpensive books and their distribution to the broadest possible market. Production was handled at the firm's Country Life Press in Garden City, L.I. Distribution was carried out through department stores and other high-volume outlets and through a variety of direct-mail book clubs and reprint divisions controlled by the parent firm: the Dollar Book Club, Garden City Reprints, the Famous Author Series, the Crime Club, Sun Dial Press, Windward House, the Mystery Guild, Doubleday Junior Books, and others. The corporation also owned a chain of twenty-six retail book stores, and in 1934 acquired full ownership of the Literary Guild of America, a book club which alone generated sales of a million books a year. A managerial genius, Nelson Doubleday exercised close supervision of these various enterprises and subdivisions, readily terminating any that proved unprofitable. In 1937 he moved the company's business and editorial offices from Garden City to New York City's Rockefeller Center.

The books Doubleday favored were those best adapted to mass-market distribution: popular fiction by such authors as Edna Ferber, Kenneth Roberts, and Daphne du Maurier; inspirational, reference, and "how-to" books; and cheap reprints of classics and established best sellers. By 1947, the firm's fiftieth anniversary year, Doubleday and Company (as it had become in 1945) was the largest publishing house in America, with 4,765 employees and annual sales of more than thirty million books. The expansion of public education, coupled with the cultural aspirations and status anxieties of a mass society, had created a vast new market for books, and Nelson Doubleday was one of the most successful entrepreneurs to tap that market. He enthusiastically embraced advertising techniques and market strategies already well established in other avenues of commerce but hitherto somewhat resisted in the book world, with its genteel and elitist traditions. He scorned the notion prevalent among publishers that theirs was an exalted calling somewhat akin to the ministry; "I sell books, I don't read them," he declared. Among those who found this philosophy abrasive was George Doran, who left the firm in 1930 and later wrote bitterly of his experiences as a Doubleday partner.

Nelson Doubleday's first marriage, on June 10, 1916, to Martha Jewett Nicholson of Providence, R.I., ended in divorce in 1931. On June 14, 1932, he married Ellen George (McCarter) Violett of Rumson, N.J., by whom he had two children: Nelson (later active in the family business) in 1933 and Neltje in 1934. Two daughters of his second wife by a former marriage also made their home with the Doubledays. Commanding in appearance and in size (he was six feet five inches tall), Doubleday was identified with few public activities apart from his business. His avocations were golf, horticulture, and high-powered automobiles. He was an Episcopalian in religion, a Republican in politics.

In 1943, already ill, Doubleday appointed the firm's chief legal officer, Douglas Black, as executive vice-president. He resigned the presidency to Black in 1946 but continued as chairman of the board. Doubleday died of cancer early in 1949, at the age of fifty-nine, in his Oyster Bay home. He was buried in the Locust Valley (Long Island) Cemetery.

[*N.Y. Times,* Jan. 12, 1949; *Publishers' Weekly,* Jan. 22, 1949, pp. 304–305; Russell Doubleday, "Nelson Doubleday: A Publisher in the Making," in Joseph A. Moore, *Famous Leaders of Industry,* Fifth Series (1945), pp. 33–47; *Nat. Cyc. Am. Biog.,* XXXVII, 36–37; Charles A. Madison, *Book Publishing in America* (1966); George H. Doran, *Chronicles of Barabbas* (1935).]

PAUL BOYER

DOVE, ARTHUR GARFIELD (Aug. 2, 1880–Nov. 23, 1946), painter, was born in Canandaigua, N.Y., and named for the candidates on the Republican presidential ticket in the year of his birth. He was the oldest of two sons and a daughter of William George Dove and Anna Elizabeth (Chipps) Dove. Both parents were natives of New York state. His father was a bricklayer and brick-manufacturer, who became a successful building contractor in Geneva, N.Y., where he later served as county clerk and fire chief. Arthur early displayed a talent for painting; at the age of seven a neighboring truck farmer, Newton Weatherby, who was an artist and interested in natural history took him on hunting and fishing trips and provided him with encouragement and painting supplies. A local teacher also gave him painting lessons. After attending private school and the Geneva high school, Dove entered Hobart College in Geneva. He transferred two years later to Cornell University; although his father insisted on a year of law, he studied art under Charles Wellington Furlong, a magazine illustrator.

Dove was influenced by Furlong's success. After graduating from Cornell in 1903, he went to New York City to become an illustrator. Equipped with a facile style, a flair for animation, and a buoyant sense of humor, he had little difficulty selling his work to magazines like *Harper's, Scribner's,* and the *Saturday Evening Post.* In 1904 (or 1905) Dove married Florence Louise Dorsey of Geneva, N.Y. They had one child, William Clinton.

Dove enjoyed the semi-bohemian artist life of New York City. Although he earned his living illustrating, he also painted and drew mostly with pastels. In 1908 he went to Paris to study; there he formed lasting friendships with several American artists including Alfred Maurer, who had recently given up painting portraits for a "modern" style. Dove had already been moving toward impressionism and he now began to reflect the influence of fauvism. He exhibited works in the Autumn Salon of 1908 and again the following year, with his entry *The Lobster.* Dove returned to the United States in 1909. Through Maurer he met the art dealer Alfred Stieglitz, one of the few men in the country aware of the changes taking place in twentieth century art. Stieglitz soon became the sponsor of three important modern painters: John Marin, Georgia O'Keeffe, and Dove.

Dove had his first one-man show in February 1912, at Stieglitz's "291" Gallery in New York City. He showed a series of pastel abstracts, which Stieglitz characterized as "beautiful . . . not reminiscent of anyone else." When the exhibit moved to Chicago, Dove called the group the "Ten Commandments," but the classification was later changed by Stieglitz to "Nature Symbolized" as a more accurate description. Abstract art was just beginning to emerge in different parts of the world, and Dove's offerings were important early examples of the form. "Abstractions 1 to 6," a part of the show, cannot, however, be called nonobjective; Dove did not follow the artistic course of Kandinsky or Mondrian, nor did he adopt the cubist style. He painted particular objects, but translated them into symbols of themselves. He was addicted to spirals and wave undulations or, by contrast, to brittle forms, characteristically with sharp sickle shapes. Although the Chicago show created a stir, it produced few sales, and Dove was forced to borrow money from his friend William S. Hart, the silent film star, for his fare back to New York.

Relative poverty plagued Dove throughout

his life. His father was appalled at his son's work and refused to subsidize his "madness." Fortunately, Dove enjoyed the simplicity of rural life, where he could live off the land and paint. In 1910 he managed to buy a farm in Westport, Conn., and began to raise chickens; when this proved unprofitable he turned briefly to lobster fishing. But his determined efforts to earn a living from nature did not afford him much time for his art, and for years he painted little. About 1920 Dove left his family permanently and moved to a scow on the Harlem River in New York City. Soon thereafter, with the help of William S. Hart, he bought a forty-two-foot yawl, the *Mona,* which became his home for the next seven years.

Painting on small canvases, Dove began to deal with cosmic themes: suns, moons, and great rolling and swirling wave forms dominated his work. He based his art on the theory that each object in nature possesses its own particular "condition of light," a special quality of color and form that defines the intangible essence beneath its physical appearance. To capture the condition of light and reveal an object's visual karma, Dove felt, required going beyond ordinary representational painting. For Dove, all objects were integral and self-defining. "Works of nature are abstract," he wrote in 1925, "they do not lean on other things for meaning." Expressing his love for the soil and sea, Dove used color and form to reveal the "shy interior life of things," from cows and pastures (a recurring theme) to sunrises and ships (Rosenfeld, *Port,* p. 171). Some of Dove's work during the 1920's was a significant digression from his main efforts, reflecting a spontaneous humor and the use of symbols. He executed, for example, symbolic collage "portraits"—of friends like Ralph Dusenberry (1924) and Stieglitz (1925). A collage entitled *Grandmother* (1925) was made of needlepoint, a Bible page, and pressed leaves. In the painting *George Gershwin's "Rhapsody in Blue," Part I* (1927) he employed the swirl of an unwound clockspring to set off a dynamic pattern that suggested Kandinsky.

Dove's professional and personal fortunes improved during the 1920's. He finally found a patron for his works in 1922 in the collector Duncan Phillips, founder of the Phillips Gallery in Washington, D.C. Beginning in 1925 his paintings were again displayed by Stieglitz—who had closed the "291" during World War I—at his new Intimate Gallery in New York. Dove was also encouraged by Helen (Reds) Torr, herself an artist and sailor, whom he married in 1932, three years after the death of his first wife. In 1933, following the death of his mother, Dove returned to Geneva to help liquidate his father's estate. Here he lived for four years, first in a succession of farmhouses on the family land, and later, when the land was sold for taxes, in a sports arena his father had built in the town of Geneva. In the midst of his losing financial struggles, he continued to paint. *Sunrise I* (1937) and *Moon* (1935) were magnificent flights of the imagination; *Holbrook's Bridge, Northwest* (1938), with its somber sepulchral feeling, was a major achievement.

An aloof, modest man with a broad forehead and wide candid mouth, Dove combined the outdoorsman's rugged stamina with the hermit's love of isolation. In the late 1930's, he began to suffer from heart trouble and Bright's disease. Moving to an abandoned post office in Centerport, L.I., he stubbornly continued to paint from his bed. His canvases in the 1940's were unquestionably his finest: more abstract, more arbitrary, revealing the ominous power of great natural forces; they also depicted a more cosmic geometry. *Square on the Pond* (1942), *Parabola* (1943), *High Noon* (1944), and *The Rising Tide* (1944) are typical examples. After the death of Stieglitz in July 1946, Dove's works were handled by Edith Halpert, whose Downtown Gallery showed only American art. Dove was beginning to enjoy considerable success, when he died of uremia at the age of sixty-six at the Huntington (L.I.) Hospital. He was buried in St. John's Cemetery in Cold Springs Harbor, L.I.

Dove's work was never sufficiently valued in his lifetime. Even the modest size of his paintings belied his significance. His abstract paintings differed from the intellectual designs of European abstract artists. As Paul Rosenfeld wrote, his paintings were not derived from the head. "They gush forth spontaneously as breath. They are easy and free as the swing of a body in motion" (*Port,* p. 170). With their rugged textures, bold patterns, and "dark, pungent, gritty hues," they derived from his American experience. Dove did not adhere to any formal school, but used abstract principles to create his own uniquely American form, which one critic called "visual music" and another described as a "sort of 'Leaves of Grass' through pigment" (Phillips, p. 509; Rosenfeld, *Port,* p. 169).

[*Index of Twentieth Century Artists,* pp. 512–513 (1936), with bibliography; Frederick S. Wight, *Arthur G. Dove* (1958); Alan R. Solomon, *Arthur G.*

Dove, 1880–1946: A Retrospective Exhibition (1954); Paul Rosenfeld, *Port of N.Y.*, pp. 167–174 (1924); Martha Davidson, "Arthur Dove: The Fulfillment of a Long Career," *Art News*, May 7, 1938, p. 16; Ben L. Summerford, "Arthur Dove Retrospective," *Right Angle*, June 1947, p. 6; Duncan Phillips, "The Art of Arthur Dove," *New Directions Annual* 11 (1949): 509–512; Robert Goldwater, "Dove: A Pioneer of Abstract Expressionism in American Art," *Perspectives U.S.A.*, no. 2, Winter 1952; Elizabeth McCausland, "Dove, Man and Painter," *Parnassus* 9 (1937): 3–6; James T. Soby, "Arthur Dove and Morris Graves," *Saturday Rev. of Lit.*, Apr. 7, 1956, pp. 32–33; Paul Rosenfeld, "The World of Arthur G. Dove," *Creative Arts*, June 1932.]

FREDERICK S. WIGHT

DREW, CHARLES RICHARD (June 3, 1904-Apr. 1, 1950), surgeon, pioneer in the production and preservation of blood plasma, was born in Washington, D.C., the eldest of the two sons and three daughters of Richard Thomas Drew and Nora Rosella (Burrell) Drew. His father, a high school graduate, was a carpet layer who earned only a modest income. Charles's mother was a graduate of Miner Normal School in Washington. Both parents were active members of the Baptist church and encouraged their children to get a good education.

Drew attended Dunbar High School in Washington, then perhaps the best secondary school for Negroes in the country, where he excelled in sports. Following the example of several other Dunbar graduates, including Charles H. Houston, he went to Amherst College, supporting himself by an athletic scholarship and by working as a waiter. At Amherst he was a star football player (Coach D. O. "Tuss" McLaughry later called him "the best player I ever coached") and captain of the track team, and at graduation he was awarded the Howard Hill Mossman Trophy as the man who had contributed most to athletics in the college during his four years. Although he did not achieve a notable academic record, he developed a strong interest in biology and resolved to make medicine his career. After receiving the B.A. in 1926, however, lack of money forced him to accept a post as director of athletics and instructor in biology and chemistry at Morgan College, Baltimore, Md.

In the fall of 1928 Drew was admitted to the medical school of McGill University, Montreal, Canada. A loan from a group of his Amherst classmates supplemented his earnings as a waiter, and in his third year he was given a scholarship. Although he continued to excel in sports, he increasingly devoted himself to his medical studies. He had the good fortune to gain the friendship of a young English doctor, John Beattie, who taught bacteriology. Through

Beattie, Drew became interested in blood groups and in the research of Karl Landsteiner. In 1933 Drew received the degrees of M.D. and C.M. (Master of Surgery). He served a year each as intern and resident at Montreal General Hospital, where he specialized in surgery, blood typing, and problems of transfusion.

Drew returned to Washington as instructor in pathology at Howard University Medical College in 1935, and in the following year became resident and instructor in surgery at Freedmen's Hospital, the university's teaching facility. Wth the aid of a grant from the General Education Board of the Rockefeller Foundation, Drew served for two years (1938-1940) as resident in surgery at Columbia-Presbyterian Medical Center, New York City. Under Dr. John Scudder, research director of the center, he carried out investigations in the preservation and storage of blood, a problem that had earlier been investigated in the Soviet Union and in Spain during the civil war but had received little attention in this country. He also investigated the use of plasma (blood with the cells removed) in transfusions, and in 1939 established the hospital's first blood bank, patterned on that set up by Dr. Bernard Fantus at Cook County Hospital in Chicago. In 1940 Drew received the Sc.D. degree from Columbia, with a thesis on banked blood and methods of blood preservation. His publications of this period, with Scudder and others, included "Plasma Potassium Content of Cardiac Blood at Death" (1939) and "Studies in Blood Preservation: Some Effects of Carbon Dioxide" (1940).

With the advent of World War II, Drew was appointed to a committee of the Blood Transfusion Association to consider means of supplying blood to the French armies. He strongly recommended the shipment of plasma rather than whole blood. After the fall of France in June 1940, he returned to Howard as assistant professor of surgery, but a few weeks later, after the bombing of Britain had begun, he was recalled to New York as medical supervisor and liaison officer between the board of the Blood Transfusion Association and the hospitals collecting blood for use in England. Drew and his co-workers established uniform procedures for procuring and processing the blood, shipping the plasma, and for minimizing the danger of bacterial contamination.

In February 1941, when the British were able to supply their own needs for blood and possible American involvement in the war had become apparent, Drew was appointed medical director of the American Red Cross blood bank program and assistant director of blood procurement for the National Research Council, which had charge of collecting blood for use by American armed forces. A few weeks later, however, the Red Cross received an official directive from the armed forces that the program must keep non-Caucasian blood separate from other blood donations. Although Drew and other scientists affirmed that the chemical differences in human blood depended only on blood type and not on race, the directive was accepted. Drew resigned and returned to Howard.

For the remaining nine years of his life he did no research, but devoted himself to surgery and teaching. In 1942 he was promoted to professor and head of the department of surgery at Howard and to chief surgeon at Freedmen's Hospital, where he subsequently became chief of staff (1944-1946) and medical director (1946-1948). In 1941 he was certified as diplomate by the American Board of Surgery, and in 1946 he was made a fellow of the International College of Surgery. Drew received the Spingarn Medal of the National Association for the Advancement of Colored People in 1944 and honorary degrees from Virginia State College (1945) and Amherst (1947). During the summer of 1949, as a surgical consultant to the army's surgeon general, Drew joined other physicians in a tour of hospitals in occupied Europe to improve the quality of medical care and instruction.

On Sept. 23, 1939, he married Minnie Lenore Robbins of Philadelphia, a teacher at Spelman College, Atlanta, Ga. Their children were Bebe Roberta, Charlene Rosella, Rhea Sylvia, and Charles Richard. Drew died at the untimely age of forty-five in an automobile accident near Burlington, N.C., while on his way to deliver a lecture at the annual John A. Andrew Memorial clinic at Tuskegee Institute. He was buried in Lincoln Memorial Cemetery, Suitland, Md.

[Richard Hardwick, *Charles Richard Drew, Pioneer in Blood Research* (1967); obituary by W. Montague Cobb in *Jour. Nat. Medical Assoc.*, July 1950, with a list of Drew's publications; briefer obituaries in *Negro Hist. Bull.*, June 1950 (by Dr. Cobb; also reprinted in *Jour. of Negro Hist.*, July 1950) and *Jour. Am. Medical Assoc.*, May 6, 1950; *Who's Who in Colored America*, 7th ed. (1950); interviews with Mrs. Charles R. Drew, Dr. Cobb, Dr. Frank Jones, and others; personal reminiscences. A portrait of Drew by Betsy Grove Reyneau was placed in the Am. Red Cross Building in Washington, D.C., in 1959.]
RAYFORD W. LOGAN

DURANT, WILLIAM CRAPO (Dec. 8, 1861-Mar. 18, 1947), automobile manufacturer and financier, was born in Boston, Mass., the only child of William Clark Durant and Rebecca Folger (Crapo) Durant. Little is known about his father, who is listed on the son's birth record as a clerk and a native of New Hampshire; he appears to have been a drifter who married into a wealthy family. Rebecca Durant was the daughter of Henry Howland Crapo, originally of New Bedford, Mass., who made a fortune in whaling, moved to Michigan, became a successful lumberman, and served as governor of Michigan from 1865 to 1869. Durant, nicknamed "Billy," grew up in his grandfather's home in Flint, Mich. He left high school at the age of sixteen to work in his grandfather's lumberyard, but soon left for a variety of other jobs, mainly in selling; at twenty he was manager of the Flint Water Works. Since Flint was one of the leading centers of carriage and wagon manufacturing, Durant was inevitably drawn into that business. He took his first major step in 1885 by buying the patent rights to a two-wheeled cart for $50 and organizing, in partnership with J. Dallas Dort, the Flint Road Cart Company, renamed the Durant-Dort Carriage Company a year later. The company rapidly became one of the country's leading manufacturers of horse-drawn vehicles. Its production methods anticipated the assembly system that later characterized the American automobile industry. Separate plants made the parts—wheels, bodies, axles, and even whip sockets—and these were assembled at the main factory in Flint.

Durant moved into the automobile business in 1904 when a fellow carriage manufacturer, James H. Whiting, decided he could no longer afford to support David D. Buick's effort to put the Buick car into production and persuaded Durant to buy him out. Durant did not possess the mechanical skills of the automotive pioneers, but he was an energetic promoter and an excellent administrator when he concentrated on the management of a single company. With a basically good design to sell, he quickly made the Buick Motor Car Company the largest automobile manufacturer in the United States. A fast-growing demand for cars offered promise of great profits in the still speculative industry, but the market was fought for by hundreds of small companies and the attrition rate was high. Durant became convinced that the formula for success was a large organization making a variety of models and controlling its own sources of parts. To this end he tried in 1908 to merge Buick with its three principal competitors: Ford, Maxwell-Briscoe, and Reo. The plan failed when Henry Ford and Ransom E. Olds of Reo each demanded $3 million in cash for their companies, which exceeded Durant's resources.

Durant's next move was to charter the General Motors Company in New Jersey in September 1908. It acquired a number of motor vehicle firms, the most important being Buick, Cadillac, Oakland (later Pontiac), and Oldsmobile, and several parts manufacturers. Durant himself was directly responsible for moving the Weston-Mott Axle Company from Utica, N.Y., to Flint and for financing Albert Champion's project for making porcelain spark plugs. He apparently made a second unsuccessful attempt to buy out Ford. General Motors soon ran into financial troubles. Unprofitable acquisitions, made because Durant wanted to cover all the possibilities of a still uncertain automotive technology, and expensive patent litigation accompanying the purchase of the Heany Lamp Company accentuated a lack of liquid capital. Regarded by the banking community as a speculator and a visionary, Durant discovered that his credit was inadequate when difficulties arose. In 1910 General Motors passed under the control of a bankers' trust headed by James J. Storrow of Boston's Lee, Higginson and Company, and Durant was forced out of active management.

He immediately joined Louis Chevrolet, a Swiss-born mechanic and racing driver for Buick, in a new automobile venture, organized in 1911 as the Chevrolet Motor Car Company. This company entered the popular-priced car market so successfully that Durant was able to recover control of General Motors by exchanging Chevrolet for General Motors stock, and after the bankers' trust terminated, he resumed the presidency in 1916. Beginning in 1914, Du Pont interests, notably Pierre S. du Pont and John J. Raskob, invested substantially in General Motors. Durant next organized the United Motors Corporation (1916), a holding company for a group of parts manufacturers including the Hyatt Roller Bearing Company and the Dayton Engineering Laboratories Company (Delco), with the important result that Alfred P. Sloan, Jr., and Charles F. Kettering were brought into the General Motors structure. At Du Pont's insistence, a new General Motors Corporation was chartered in Delaware in 1916 to absorb United Motors and rectify the anomaly of having the General Motors Company technically controlled by Chevrolet.

Durant again launched an ambitious program of expansion for General Motors. The Fisher Body Company was acquired in 1919 and in the same year the General Motors Acceptance Corporation was created to assist in financing dealers. The building of the General Motors Center in Detroit was also begun. The corporation became a manufacturer of electric refrigerators when Durant, as a personal enthusiasm, bought control of the Guardian Frigerator Company and later sold it to General Motors under the name of Frigidaire. Durant, however, allowed his energies to be dispersed in too many directions and gave the sprawling General Motors structure neither coherent organization nor consistent management. His determination to run all aspects of General Motors cost the company some of its best executives. Henry M. Leland, president of Cadillac, resigned in 1917 after failing to persuade Durant to convert Cadillac to aircraft engine production during World War I; and Walter P. Chrysler, president of Buick, left in 1920 when Durant persistently interfered in Buick affairs and, finally ignoring Chrysler's advice, involved General Motors in an unsuccessful attempt to build farm machinery. Alfred P. Sloan also seriously considered leaving the company.

The depression of 1920 caught General Motors in a confused financial condition. With poor central management procedures, division heads had greatly overrun their budgets; demand for automobiles was declining, and inventories were swollen. As the price of General Motors stock declined sharply, Durant sought to bolster it by making large purchases; buying on margin (he is reported to have had seventy separate brokerage accounts), he soon became overextended. As the crisis developed, the du Ponts, fearing the shattering effects of a margin call on Durant's accounts, moved to preserve the solvency of General Motors by paying off his debts in return for control of a large block of his General Motors stock. As part of the arrangement, Durant resigned as president of General Motors in December 1920 and was replaced by Pierre du Pont.

Early in 1921 Durant returned to the automobile industry by raising $7 million among friends and forming a new company named Durant Motors. It acquired various minor companies and produced some well-known cars— Durant, Flint, and a low-priced model called the Star. Although the Star enjoyed some popularity, Durant Motors was not a success; it lost money even at the peak of the boom period. Durant continued to plan new combinations that he confidently announced would rival General Motors, but none of these plans had real substance. Durant Motors could not survive the crash of 1929 and was liquidated in 1933. Durant filed a petition in bankruptcy in 1935, listing liabilities of $914,000 and assets of $250 (his clothes).

Yet although he was now in his seventies, his promotional zeal was undiminished. He opened a supermarket in Asbury Park, N.J., in 1936, and in 1940 he returned to Flint to launch a chain of bowling alleys designed for family recreation. The coming of the war blocked this project, and shortly afterward Durant's health broke down. He was able to be present in 1942 at a celebration of the production of the twenty-five-millionth General Motors car and received a well-deserved tribute, but this was his last public appearance. He died in New York City in 1947, at the age of eighty-five, and was buried in Woodlawn Cemetery in New York.

Surprisingly little is known about Durant's life apart from his business career; it appears, indeed, that he lived almost entirely for business. He was married twice: first to Clara Miller Pitt on June 17, 1885; second to Catherine Lederer on May 28, 1916. He and his first wife had two children, Russell Clifford and Margery; that marriage ended in divorce in 1908. He was a Republican in politics and affiliated at various times with both the Episcopal and Presbyterian churches. Durant had a warm, likable personality. Even those who disagreed with him on business matters acknowledged his personal charm; no one ever questioned his integrity. His aggressive temperament and small stature inevitably led to his being described as "Napoleonic." Despite his mistakes, he had a clear insight into the future of the automobile industry; its organization has followed the pattern that he initially adopted for General Motors.

[Biographical material on Durant is limited; a full-length book by Margery Durant, *My Father* (1929) is only moderately useful. A much better work is Lawrence R. Gustin, *Billy Durant, Creator of General Motors* (1973). There are references to Durant in Alfred B. Chandler, Jr., and Stephen Salsbury, *Pierre S. du Pont and the Making of the Modern Corporation* (1971); Alfred P. Sloan, Jr., *My Years with General Motors* (1964); and John B. Rae, *Am. Automobile Manufacturers: The First Forty Years* (1959). See also John B. Rae, "The Fabulous Billy Durant," *Business Hist. Rev.*, Autumn 1958, pp. 255–271. For brief biographical sketches, see *Time*, Mar. 31, 1947, p. 86; *Newsweek*, Mar. 31, 1947, p. 54; *Nat. Cyc. Am. Biog.*, XXXVI, 16–17; and the *N.Y. Times* obit., Mar. 19, 1947. Birth record from Mass. Registrar of Vital Statistics.]

JOHN B. RAE

DWIGHT, ARTHUR SMITH (Mar. 18, 1864–Apr. 1, 1946), mining and metallurgical engineer, was born in Taunton, Mass., the younger of two sons of Benjamin Pierce Smith,

a jewelry manufacturer, and Elizabeth Fiske (Dwight) Smith. His mother, whose father had been a deacon in Brooklyn, N.Y., was related to Timothy Dwight, clergyman and president of Yale. She died a year after Arthur's birth. He was christened Arthur Edwards Smith, but he and his older brother assumed their maternal surname by court authority when they came of age. In his choice of career, Dwight was influenced by his uncle Rossiter W. Raymond, who lived in Brooklyn and who was one of the founders and for over twenty years the secretary of the American Institute of Mining Engineers. There is very little information available about Dwight's childhood.

After graduating from Brooklyn Polytechnic Institute in 1882, Dwight entered the School of Mines at Columbia University and received the M.E. degree in 1885. Through Raymond's connections, he went to work as assayer and chemist for the Colorado Smelting Company at Pueblo, where he advanced rapidly, becoming general superintendent in charge of the concern's Colorado mining and smelting operations. After becoming manager, he left in 1896 to reorganize and superintend plants of the Consolidated Kansas City Smelting and Refining Company in Kansas, Colorado, and Texas. When properties of this firm were merged to form the American Smelting and Refining Company in 1899, Dwight was a member of the operating committee that had charge of technical direction of the twenty smelting plants included in the consolidation. In 1900 he went to Mexico as assistant to the president of the Compañía Metalúrgica Mexicana at San Luis Potosí. Three years later he moved to Cananea, Sonora, as consulting engineer and then general manager of the Greene Consolidated Copper Company plant. During his last year there, when revolutionary insurgents threatened to seize the mines, Dwight turned his organization into a military unit to protect American employees and the citizens of Cananea.

It was also at Cananea that Dwight and Richard Lewis Lloyd invented the Dwight-Lloyd sintering process, by which fine ore or flue dust was ignited on moving grates that passed over a down-draft, thus converting the ore or dust to a sinter or agglomerate which could be treated in a blast furnace. The process had two clear benefits: it salvaged ore that had previously been lost as waste, and, when applied to the lead industry, it reduced the hazard to workers of free-floating lead dust. Dwight returned to the United States in 1906 and set up a consulting practice in New York,

meanwhile patenting and perfecting the sintering process. With his co-inventor, he formed
the Dwight and Lloyd Metallurgical Company
in 1909 and the Dwight and Lloyd Sintering
Company in 1912 to improve the method and
equipment and to grant licenses for use of the
basic patents. Dwight was president of both
companies until his death. The down-draft
grates, originally designed for copper flue dust,
proved useful for lead concentrate and for iron
ores, and ultimately in 1923 were applied with
greatest importance to zinc.

With the outbreak of World War I, Dwight
became an ardent advocate of preparedness.
With a fellow engineer, William Barclay Parsons, he helped organize an engineer officers'
reserve corps, and was one of the first civilians
commissioned into the reserve ten weeks before
the United States entered the war. In July 1917,
the 11th Engineers (Railway), in which he was
a major, sailed for France. The first American
Expeditionary Forces unit to see action, it
fought at Cambrai, in the Arras sector, in the
Lys defensive, and in the Meuse-Argonne offensive. Later Dwight served as special metallurgical advisor to the French and as engineering
salvage officer for the A.E.F.; he was promoted
to the rank of colonel. After twenty-two months
in France, he was appointed chairman of the
minerals advisory committee in the secretary
of war's office in Washington.

Upon his return to civilian life in 1919, he
again established an office in New York City.
He now turned his attention to the study of
special metallurgical processes, the Dwight-
Lloyd companies, and others with which he was
involved: the American Ore Reclamation Company, the Thornewood Construction and Securities Corporation, and the Tirrill Gas Machine
Corporation. He was president of the American
Institute of Mining and Metallurgical Engineers
in 1922; twenty years later he received the
institute's James Douglas Medal for his work
on the sintering process. In addition to the
many patents he obtained, he wrote many technical articles, including the chapter on roasting
and sintering in Donald M. Liddell's *Handbook
of Non-Ferrous Metallurgy* (1926).

On June 4, 1895, Dwight married Jane Earl
Reed, daughter of Samuel B. Reed, chief engineer in the construction of the Union Pacific
railroad; after her death in 1929, he married
Anne (Howard) Chapin, a widow, on Mar. 15,
1930. He had no children. In religion he was
an Episcopalian. A genial, cultured, and generous man, Dwight died at his winter home,
"Beau Rivage," at Hobe Sound, Fla., of coro-

nary thrombosis. He was buried in Great Neck,
Long Island.

[For his own discussion of his work, see Dwight's,
"The Dwight and Lloyd Sintering Process," in Walter
R. Ingalls, *The Mineral Industry: Its Statistics, Technology and Trade during 1907*, pp. 380–395 (1908).
Biographical data can be found in *N.Y. Times*, Apr. 2
and 5, 1946; *Mining and Metallurgy*, Mar. 1922, pp.
17–18 and June 1946, pp. 383–384; *Who Was Who in
America*, II (1950); *Who's Who in Engineering*,
1941; Mining and Metallurgical Soc. of Am., *Bull.*, 39
(1946): 69–70; *Nat. Cyc. Am. Biog.* XXXIII, 16–17;
Engineering and Mining Jour., July 30, 1921, p. 178.]
                                        CLARK C. SPENCE

DYKSTRA, CLARENCE ADDISON (Feb.
25, 1883-May 6, 1950), public administrator,
educator, university president, and scholar in
the fields of education and government, was
born in Cleveland, Ohio, the second of six
children of Lawrence Dykstra and Margaret
(Barr) Dykstra. His father, a clergyman of
the Dutch Reformed Church, served in several
pastorates during Dykstra's childhood, but the
boy received much of his early education in the
Chicago public schools. An honor student at
Iowa State University in history, French, and
Greek, he was also active in debating, dramatics, and the college newspaper. It was at
Iowa that Dykstra first became interested in
municipal government, in which field he
achieved national fame as both a scholar and a
professional administrator. After receiving the
B.A. degree in 1903, Dykstra began graduate
work at the University of Chicago, where he
spent a year as a fellow in history and an
assistant in political science. During the next
two years he taught at private schools in
Pensacola, Fla., before returning to the University of Chicago in 1906 for additional advanced study. After a year (1908-1909) as an
instructor in history and government at Ohio
State University, he moved to the University of
Kansas, where at the age of thirty he became
head of the newly created department of political science.

At the University of Kansas (1909-1918),
Dykstra became recognized as a leading theoretician in state and municipal administration.
His first move into active participation in governmental affairs took place in 1918, when he
returned to Cleveland as executive secretary of
the Civic League. His prolonged but unsuccessful struggle in Cleveland with the Van Sweringen interests over the building of a union railway station marked him as a civic reformer. In
the next few years he moved on to similar positions in the Chicago and the Los Angeles city
clubs.

In 1926, Dykstra became a commissioner of the Los Angeles Department of Water and Power, contributing to the establishment of the Metropolitan Water District, the building of the $300 million aqueduct for the Los Angeles area, and the construction of hydroelectric plants. In the same year, he became the department's director of personnel and efficiency. In his spare time, he helped Dr. John D. Haynes, the father of direct legislation in California, to draw up plans for the Haynes Foundation, later a leading private civic research organization in the Pacific Southwest. He also resumed his academic career, serving as a part-time lecturer and professor of public administration at the newly created Los Angeles branch of the University of California.

In 1930 Dykstra was appointed city manager of Cincinnati, Ohio, the nation's most prestigious professional job in municipal management. Led by reformers Murray Seasongood and Henry Bentley, Cincinnati's "charter reform" movement had toppled the fabled Cox-Hynicka political machine in 1924, replacing boss control with the council-manager form of municipal government. Between 1926 and 1930, under the political leadership of Murray Seasongood as mayor and the capable administration of city manager Col. C. O. Sherrill, Cincinnati had become a model of efficient municipal administration and the "best-governed" city in the United States, according to political scientist Jerome Kerwin. Dykstra had been among the candidates for the first managership of the city in 1925, and when Sherrill resigned in 1930 to take a position with Procter and Gamble, he was quickly selected to replace him. Dykstra's identification with the successful "Cincinnati experiment" established his reputation as one of the country's leading professional administrators. In his seven years at Cincinnati, he carried forward the work begun by Seasongood and Sherrill, expanding and improving city services despite problems brought on by the depression. Although he instituted improvements in zoning, waste collection, purchasing, public works, and social programs, Cincinnati's tax rate remained the lowest in the nation for a city of its size.

At Cincinnati, the six-foot-three, two-hundred-pound Dykstra was at the height of his career. He served in important capacities in many organizations, such as president of the International Association of City Managers, member of the Technical Advisory Board of the National Emergency Public Works Administration, and president of the National Municipal League (1937-1940). Cool and unemotional, he lacked the charisma of Cincinnati reform mayors Seasongood and Russell Wilson. His speeches were direct, terse, deliberate, and lacking in humor. His only hobby was music, but even here he was once described as the type of man who after performing a better than average rendition of Debussy's *Clair de Lune* would get up from the piano saying, "The man we need for the police job is. . . ." Despite this detachment and apparent aloofness, citizens found Dykstra readily approachable. It was not at all unusual, it was reported, for a housewife to phone him if her garbage was not collected on time.

His greatest challenge in Cincinnati and the source of much of his popular fame came with the 1937 Ohio River flood. During the eight-day crisis, the City Council granted him unprecedented, even dictatorial, powers. He organized and coordinated flood relief and flood control with remarkable efficiency, staying at his desk for hours at a time and wading about flooded areas as he supervised emergency measures. Emerging from this ordeal as a national hero of sorts, he became known as "Cincinnati's Dyke."

Dykstra viewed his stint as a professional city manager as field experience for his academic career, and by April 1937 he returned to academic life as president of the University of Wisconsin. He assumed his post at a particularly difficult time in the university's history—the major handicaps stemmed from a bitter struggle between the regents and his predecessor, Glenn Frank. Although according to *Time,* he "kindled no fire among faculty or students," his leadership received generally favorable reaction as he applied the same techniques of administration that he had used to advantage in Cincinnati.

In 1940, President Roosevelt appointed Dykstra as the first director of the Selective Service System. In this capacity he organized the peacetime draft and devised the structure and policies that characterized the system throughout the war. Early in 1941, he left this position to become chairman of the newly formed National Defense Mediation Board, a forerunner of the War Labor Board.

Dykstra retained his university post while in Washington, and after leaving the Selective Service Board, he was able to devote more time to the university, although throughout the war he continued to serve on numerous national boards and committees. He played an especially significant role in developing the Army Special

Services and the Armed Forces Institute. In February 1945, he returned to the University of California at Los Angeles as provost and set about molding the loosely organized, rapidly growing, former teachers' college into a university. Beset by myriad postwar difficulties, his plans were only beginning to come to fruition at the time of his death in 1950.

Dykstra was married on July 31, 1909, to Ada M. Hartley, who died in 1926. They had one daughter, Elizabeth Sylvester. On Dec. 25, 1927, he married Lillian K. Rickaby, who had been dean of women of the Riverside School in California. He died at Laguna Beach, Calif., and was buried in the Inglewood, Calif., cemetery.

Dykstra provides the rare example of the academician who seized the opportunity to put his expertise to practical application. His reputation as a leading theoretician of state and municipal government administration and his tenure as a university president established him as a leading American educator, but it was as the manager of one of the nation's most efficiently governed cities that he has received a secure place in American urban history.

[Good accounts of Dykstra's life can be found in *Am. Political Sci. Rev.*, 44 (1950), 736–738; *N.Y. Times*, May 7, 1950, p. 106, with portrait; *Current Biog.*, 1941. For Dykstra's administration in Cincinnati, consult the Murray Seasongood Papers, the Russell Wilson Papers and the Henry Bentley Papers, all at the Cincinnati Hist. Soc.; the annual reports of the city manager, and Cincinnati newspapers for 1930–1937. Also useful are William A. Baughin, "Murray Seasongood: Twentieth-Century Urban Reformer" (doctoral diss., Univ. of Cincinnati, 1972); Charles P. Taft II, *City Management: The Cincinnati Experiment* (1933); W. Davenport, "Cincinnati's Dyke," *Collier's*, Apr. 10, 1937, p. 13; G. Seybold, "Dykstra of Cincinnati: Portrait of a Scholar in Action," *Survey Graphic*, Apr. 1937, 204–206; H. C. Hodges, "City Manager Steps into an Emergency: Flood at Cincinnati," *Nat. Municipal Rev.*, Feb. 1937, pp. 88–91. For other aspects of his career, see S. J. Woolf, "Dykstra Talks of Service and the Nation," *N.Y. Times Mag.*, Nov. 10, 1940, p. 9; "First Conscript," *Time*, Oct. 21, 1940, p. 23; "Dykstra to U.C.L.A.," *Time*, Nov. 6, 1944, p. 48; "Prexy Trouble," *Newsweek*, Nov. 13, 1944, p. 85; "Choice for University of Wisconsin Presidency," *Nation*, Mar. 20, 1937, p. 309; "Wisconsin Chooses Its New President," *Christian Century*, Mar. 24, 1937, pp. 373–374.

Among Dykstra's more notable publications are *The Commission Manager Plan of City Government* (1915); *Democracy and Education: Phi Beta Kappa Address* (1938); *Democracy and the Manpower Crisis* (1944). Dykstra was a frequent contributor to the *Nat. Municipal Rev.* and *Public Management*.]

WILLIAM A. BAUGHIN

ECKSTORM, FANNIE HARDY (June 18, 1865–Dec. 31, 1946), author, ornithologist, authority on the history, folk songs and Indians of Maine, was born in Brewer, Maine, the eldest of six children born to Manly Hardy and Emeline Freeman (Wheeler) Hardy. Ancestors on both sides were from old Penobscot River families. Benjamin Wheeler, her mother's ancestor, was the first settler of Hampden, Maine; her paternal grandparents moved from New Hampshire to Maine in 1811, and eventually settled in Brewer. Her grandfather, Jonathan Hardy, a fur trader with business interests in lumbering, land, and shipping, befriended the local Penobscot Indians and learned their language. Manly Hardy, who became the largest fur trader in Maine, continued this close relationship with the Indians and became an authority and writer on Maine birds and mammals. As her father's close companion Fannie learned the local Indian dialects early in her life and often accompanied him on trips to purchase furs. She attended high school in Bangor and later Abbott Academy in Andover, Mass. before entering Smith College in 1885. The summer after her graduation, she returned to Maine, where she traveled with her father on the first of many memorable canoe trips through the wilderness.

In Brewer she served from 1889–1891 as one of the first women superintendents of schools in Maine. During this period she began writing articles on her work. In 1891 her father enlisted her services in a crusade to fight for fish and game protection laws to control out-of-state hunters. She wrote two series of articles as a strong defender of Maine in what she conceived to be a battle with outside interests.

After completing her superintendency, she returned to Massachusetts as a reader of scientific manuscripts for the publishing firm of D. C. Heath in Boston. Here she met Rev. Jacob A. Eckstorm, an Episcopal clergyman of Norwegian parentage from Chicago, who served pastorates in Oregon. She went West and on Oct. 24, 1893, they were married in Portland. They lived in Oregon City until June 1894, when he obtained a pastorate in Eastport, Maine. Her experience in Oregon was documented in her early ornithological writing. A daughter, Katherine Hardy, born in 1894, lived only seven years. A son, Paul Frederick, was born in 1896 and died in 1945, a year before his mother. In 1898 the family moved to Providence, R.I., where her husband died on Dec. 23, 1899; she returned with her children to live in Brewer.

Shortly after her return she produced two major books on birds. *The Bird Book* (1901), a children's text, and *The Woodpeckers* (1901). *The Penobscot Man* (1904, rev. ed. 1924) celebrated the strong virtues of river drivers and woodsmen, to attack, by extension, the paper mills then taking over Maine's forests and rivers. Another lumbering book, a biography, followed, *David Libbey: Penobscot Woodsman and River Driver* (1907). A strong advocate of the local Indians, she wrote major articles based on surviving Indian legends to correct earlier records by whites. A major essay, "Thoreau's 'Maine Woods,'" published in *Atlantic Monthly* criticized Thoreau's skill as a scientific observer and ended in praising his poetic feeling for the woods.

In the 1920's she was senior author of two books collecting and analyzing folk songs: *Minstrelsy of Maine: Folk Songs and Ballads of the Woods and Coast* (1927) was written with Mary Winslow Smyth, and *British Ballads from Maine: The Development of Popular Songs, with Text and Airs* (1929), with Mary Winslow Smyth and Phillips Barry. Eckstorm's interest then turned to Indian philology, history, and handicrafts, first in *The Handicrafts of the Modern Indians of Maine* (1932). New and distinguished contributions in *Indian Place-names of the Penobscot Valley and the Maine Coast* (1941) established her as the leading authority on the Penobscot Indians. In this she also stated her belief (not held by her father or grandfather) in clairvoyance among the shamans. She memorialized her Indian acquaintances in her last book, *Old John Neptune and Other Maine Indian Shamans* (1945). She died of heart failure in her eighty-second year and is buried in Oak Hill Cemetery in Brewer.

Her work in ornithology, Northeast Indian philology, and Maine history continues to be a basic source for researchers. Her collections, annotations, and analysis of folk songs remain standard. Eckstorm's books are widely read and her views still greatly influence the written history of the state of Maine.

[The Eckstorm-Hardy manuscripts in the Bangor Public Lib. are the major manuscript source. There are 102 letters from Eckstorm to William Ganong (1916–1936) and a few in return (1904–1941) in the New Brunswick Museum, St. John, New Brunswick, Canada; these deal mainly with Indian place names. A collection of seventy-eight letters with Mary Wheelwright in the Maine State Lib. deals with Indian handicrafts (1930–1946). A few letters remain in the hands of local collectors, mainly James Vickery, Bangor Hist. Soc. A diary of an early canoe trip has been edited and published in *Appalachia*, by Benton L. Harch, "Down the West Branch of the Penobscot: August 12–22, 1889," 15 (1949): 480–498.

In addition to Eckstorm's own publications, the major work that deals with her is Elizabeth Ring, "Fannie Hardy Eckstorm: Maine Woods Historian," in *New England Quart.*, 26 (1953): 45–64. Jeanne Patten Whitten's unpublished master's thesis is the standard bibliographical guide, "Fannie Hardy Eckstorm: A Bibliographical Census of Her Published and Unpublished Writings" (Univ. of Maine, 1964). A recent edition of *The Penobscot Man* (1972) has an introduction by E. L. Ives. It reprints some examples of her photography. There are a number of photographs of Eckstorm herself, some as a young girl

taken by her father on the early canoe trips, and the best known, a studio portrait of later years, in the Bangor Public Lib. Ives reprinted two of these in the new edition.]

DAVID C. SMITH

ELSBERG, CHARLES ALBERT (Aug. 24, 1871–March 18, 1948), neurological surgeon, was born in New York City, one of six children of Albert Elsberg, a merchant and stagecoach operator, and Rebecca (Moses) Elsberg. Nathaniel Elsberg, Charles's paternal grandfather, came from Germany to New York City in 1848.

Charles's education, from the primary grades through medical school, was obtained in New York. In 1890, having graduated from the City College of New York with a B. A. degree and a Phi Beta Kappa key, he entered the College of Physicians and Surgeons, Columbia University, from which he received the M.D. degree three years later. Soon after his graduation from medical school, Elsberg briefly considered becoming a psychiatrist. He completed internships at Mount Sinai and Sloane hospitals in New York and, in turn, became assistant pathologist at Mount Sinai in 1895.

In 1895-1896 he studied under Dr. Johann von Mikulicz-Radecki in Breslau, where he developed the habit of resolving his clinical problems in the laboratory. Upon his return from Europe, he continued to work in surgical pathology while serving on the surgical staff at Mount Sinai Hospital, where he was adjunct surgeon in 1900, was made associate surgeon in 1911, and served as attending surgeon from 1914-1929.

Elsberg began his professional career as a general surgeon, as did all early neurosurgeons; he was largely self-taught in neurology and neurosurgery. Although the pioneers in neurological surgery in New York City were many, Charles Elsberg and Alfred Taylor did much to advance this surgical field there.

Elsberg's interest in laboratory research led in 1908 to his development of an improved blood cannula for transfusions. Two years later he designed a portable anesthesia apparatus for the administration of air and ether through intratracheal insufflation, making possible operations on the chest which could not have been performed earlier.

In 1909 the Neurological Institute of New York was established through the efforts of Drs. Joseph Collins and Joseph Fraenkel, who, in turn, invited Dr. Pearce Bailey and Elsberg to join them. Collins, Fraenkel, and Bailey were designated "physicians" and Elsberg "attending surgeon." The institute, one of the first of its kind in the United States, was devoted to the study and treatment of diseases of the nervous system. In 1937 it merged with Presbyterian Hospital.

Five years before the institute opened, Elsberg had published his first paper on neurological surgery, which described two cases of tumor of the cerebellopontine angle. By the time the institute was established, he had practically ceased handling general surgical cases, confining his attention to neurological surgery, especially that relating to diseases of the spinal cord. Although Elsberg served over the years as consultant surgeon to several hospitals, including Vassar Brothers Hospital in Poughkeepsie, Flower and Fifth Avenue Hospital, Knickerbocker Hospital, Montefiore Hospital, Columbia Presbyterian Medical Center, and Mount Sinai Hospital, and was successive professor of neurological surgery at Fordham University, professor of surgery at the New York University School of Medicine, and professor of neurological surgery at the College of Physicians and Surgeons, he conducted his research and performed most of his surgery at the Neurological Institute.

Within the first eight years of his association with the Neurological Institute, he published several articles and a book, *The Diagnosis and Treatment of Surgical Diseases of the Spinal Cord and Its Membranes* (1916). He also wrote *Tumors of the Spinal Cord and the Symptoms of Irritation and Compression of the Spinal Cord and Nerve Roots: Pathology, Symptomatology, Diagnosis and Treatment* (1925); *Surgical Diseases of the Spinal Cord, Membranes, and Nerve Roots: Symptoms, Diagnosis and Treatment* (1941); and *The Story of a Hospital: The Neurological Institute of New York 1909-1938* (1944), a short history of the institute from its beginnings to the time of its merger with Presbyterian Hospital. Elsberg's writings reflected a clear, graceful style. During his last six years at the institute, he edited the *Bulletin of the Neurological Institute of New York*.

After America's entry into World War I, the New York Neurosurgical School for Medical Officers of the U.S. Army was established at the Institute, and Elsberg was asked to serve in a civilian capacity as the military director. About 200 medical officers underwent instruction that included five courses of ten weeks each. Although a rather shy, retiring man revealing a slight hesitation of speech, he proved to be an excellent teacher in this program, as well as in the medical school with which he was associated.

In November 1935 Elsberg announced the development of a "scent detector" test for brain tumors. Realizing that certain brain tumors affect the olfactory sense, he found that if one held his breath and an odor was then injected directly into the olfactory nerve, the varying effects on normal and diseased persons could be measured. Elsberg found coffee and lemon oil especially suitable for a quantitative measurement of smell. This diagnostic test was never used widely, but by using a quantative determination of the sense of smell, he was able for the first time to measure what had previously been considered unmeasurable. It also revealed Elsberg's continued interest and research in the field during the last years of his active practice. Elsberg retired as chief of the department of neurosurgery at the institute in 1937.

On Oct. 3, 1937, Elsberg, then sixty-six, married Jane Stewart, the daughter of a Pittsburgh surgeon, and subsequently they moved to Stamford, Conn. Although Elsberg was reared as a Jew, he had held no ties with Judaism during his adult life, and in 1945 he converted to Roman Catholicism. He died at the age of seventy-six of coronary heart disease.

[Collected Papers of Charles A. Elsberg, 1897–1936, Lib. of the New York Academy of Medicine. Collection consists only of bound copies of reprints of articles by Elsberg. Joseph Hirsh and Beka Doherty, *The First Hundred Years of The Mount Sinai Hospital of New York: 1852–1952* (1952), contains several references to Elsberg's association with the hospital. Henry Alsop Riley, "The Neurological Institute of New York: The First Hospital in the Western hemisphere for the Treatment of Disorders of the Nervous System—The Intermediate Years," *Bull. of the N.Y. Acad. of Medicine* 42 (1966): 654–678, discusses the first steps toward integration of the Neurological Institute and the College of Physicians and Surgeons involving Elsberg's work. Byron Stookey, "The Neurological Institute and Early Neurosurgery in New York," *Jour. of Neurosurgery*, 17 (1960): 801–814, makes reference to the pioneers in New York neurosurgery and the second generation in the field including Elsberg. Frederick Tilney, "Foreword," *Bull. of the Neurological Inst. of N.Y.: Elsberg Anniversary Number* 5 (1936): 1–3, is a good, though brief, review of Elsberg's career. Arthur Earl Walker, ed., *A History of Neurological Surgery* (1951), is a valuable survey of neurosurgery from prehistoric times to the present, including a biographical sketch of Elsberg preceding a chapter on the "Surgery of the Spinal Cord and Vertebral Column," pp. 362–392. Obituary in the *N.Y. Times*, Mar. 19, 1948.]

WILLIAM LLOYD FOX

EMBREE, EDWIN ROGERS (July 31, 1883-Feb. 21, 1950), foundation executive and author, was born in Osceola, Nebr., the youngest of seven children of William Norris Embree and Laura Ann (Fee) Embree. His father, a telegrapher with the Union Pacific Railroad, moved the family westward as far as Wyoming. When Edwin was seven, his father died of "telegrapher's fever" (a form of slow electrocution). His widow and the three youngest children moved to Berea, Ky., where Berea College and Berea Academy had been founded by her grandfather, the abolitionist and preacher John Gregg Fee. Elihu Embree, founder of the first abolitionist newspaper in Tennessee, was a paternal ancestor.

Edwin's education and environment in Berea directed him toward a career in the ministry and accustomed him to racial integration. He lost interest in the ministry after his mother's death during his freshman year at Yale College. He graduated from Yale in 1906, with a B.A. in philosophy, and became a journalist, an occupation with which he had supported himself during college. After a year as a reporter for the New York *Sun* he returned to New Haven, where he served in various editorial positions on the *Yale Alumni Weekly,* which was owned by Clarence S. Day, Jr., who became Embree's close friend and advisor. From 1911 to 1917, he held various administrative positions at Yale concerned with alumni affairs and received the M.A. degree in 1914. On July 16, 1907, he married Kate Scott Clark of New Haven; they had three children: John Fee, Edwina Rogers, and Catherine Day.

Administrative duties at Yale brought Embree into contact with George Vincent, who became president of the Rockefeller Foundation in 1917 and invited Embree to join his staff. Embree spent ten years with the foundation, as secretary (1917-1923), director, Division of Studies (1924-1927), and vice-president (1927). During this period, the Rockefeller Foundation made important contributions in the areas of biomedical research, medical education, and public health. Embree's service included extensive work with the foundation's overseas projects, particularly in China to help organize six medical missions to Peking Medical Union College. He also traveled in Europe, Latin America, New Zealand, and Japan.

From 1928 to 1948, Embree made his most important contributions to philanthropy and institutional change as president of the Julius Rosenwald Fund. This fund, which was incorporated on Oct. 30, 1917, and began with 20,000 shares of Sears, Roebuck and Co. stock, was required by Rosenwald to expend its principal within twenty-five years of its founder's death. Under Embree's direction, until it dissolved on June 30, 1948, the fund pioneered in the fields of health and education, with particular emphasis on black Americans and social conditions in the South. A generation of black, and some Southern white, artists and scholars completed their training and launched important projects as Rosenwald Fellows; recipients included Marian Anderson, Langston Hughes, Willard Motley, William Smith, Charles Johnson (president of Fisk University), and Ralph McGill (editor of the *Atlanta Constitution*). At the fund's initiative, special positions were created in federal agencies during the New Deal to assure black representation in policy making. Robert Weaver, later the first black cabinet member, was a notable member of this group of administrators. The fund's institutional projects included building 5,357 rural schools for blacks and libraries, sustaining Negro colleges, supporting innovations in prepayment for hospital care and mass control of contagious diseases, and providing institutional settings for black physicians to receive training in medical specialties. The fund's activities in the field of health led directly to the development of the Blue Cross organization.

Embree's most significant contribution to public policy was his stimulation and organization of research and planning on farm tenancy in the 1930's. The fund's work in this area helped focus national attention on the exploitative labor and tenancy systems in the South and their harmful effects on the lives of both blacks and whites. Among the results of the fund's work was the creation and significant, if brief, life of the Farm Security Administration (1936-1941) under the direction of Embree's friend and colleague Dr. Will S. Alexander.

In addition to his work with the fund, Embree was one of the original supporters and the first chairman of the board of trustees of Roosevelt College in Chicago, chairman of the Chicago Mayor's Commission on Race Relations (1943-1948), and an officer of numerous educational and charitable organizations. He maintained an active writing career, producing books and articles on education, race relations, and foundations. His most noted works are *Brown America: The Story of a New Race* (1931); *Brown Americans: The Story of a Tenth of the Nation* (1943), and, with Charles S. Johnson and Will S. Alexander, *The Collapse of Cotton Tenancy* (1935). After the liquidation of the Rosenwald Fund in 1948, Embree served as president of the Liberian Foundation (1948-1949) and a consultant to the John Hay Whitney Foundation and the Greenwood Foundation (1949-1950). He died of a heart attack in New York City; his ashes were interred at his family summer home, Lake Rousseau, Ontario.

Embree was a descendant of abolitionists who participated actively in the secularization and bureaucratization of advocacy for black causes. Nurtured in Berea, he rejected the religious, moral, and political values of the town and became a cosmopolitan figure, an Episcopalian, and a Democrat. But he remained faithful to the idealism of Berea, and was a major actor in movements for social justice in his generation.

[In addition to those publications mentioned, Embree's other works include *American Negroes: A Handbook* (1942); *Indians of the Americas* (1939); and *Peoples of the Earth* (1948); portions of his unpublished, autobiographical manuscripts are in the Rockefeller Foundation Archives. Charles S. Johnson, "Edwin Rogers Embree," *Phylon* 7 (1946): 317–334, is the most comprehensive study. An account of the Rosenwald Fund's activities and a complete bibliography of Embree's writings is in Edwin R. Embree and Julia Waxman, *Investment in People: The Story of the Julius Rosenwald Fund* (1949). His activities with the Rockefeller Foundation are described in Raymond B. Fosdick, *The Story of the Rockefeller Foundation* (1952).]

DANIEL M. FOX

EMERSON, ROLLINS ADAMS (May 5, 1873-Dec. 8, 1947), agricultural scientist and geneticist, was born in Pillar Point, N.Y., near Sackets Harbor on the eastern end of Lake Ontario. He was the second of three children and older of two sons of Charles David Emerson, a farmer, and Mary Caroline (Adams) Emerson. Both parents were of seventeenth-century Massachusetts descent, his mother's forebear being the progenitor of the Adams family of Braintree. Rollins Emerson grew up on a farm in Kearney County, Nebr., to which his parents moved in 1880. They were strict Methodists, and they encouraged the education of their children, which for Rollins included attendance at the Franklin (Nebr.) Academy. Inspired by a physician in the neighborhood who was an ardent naturalist, he began as a boy to collect and identify local flora. An analytical interest in natural phenomena characterized the rest of his life.

In 1893 Emerson entered the agricultural college of the University of Nebraska, where he was strongly influenced by the noted teacher and botanist Charles E. Bessey. While still an undergraduate, Emerson was appointed assistant horticulturalist at the University's Agricultural Experiment Station and spoke at meetings of the Nebraska Academy of Science on subjects as diverse as the internal temperature of tree trunks and the horticultural setting of farmhouses. After receiving the B.Sc. degree in 1897, he moved to Washington, D.C., to become an assistant editor in the Experiment Station's Office of the Department of Agriculture. On

May 23, 1898, he married Harriet Theresa Hardin of Lincoln, Nebr.; their children were Thera, Sterling Howard, Eugene Hardin, and Myra. In 1899 Emerson moved back to the University of Nebraska as horticulturalist in the Experiment Station and assistant professor and head of the department of horticulture; he became professor in 1905.

Emerson carried on a remarkable variety of activities. His early publications show his concern with the improvement of sand cherries, better means of spraying orchards, and the beautification of school grounds. An innovative teacher, he fostered individualized practical work by students. Increasingly, however, his primary interests focused on plant breeding and genetics. His first major studies in heredity were carried out with garden beans. A preliminary report (1902) on variation in bean hybrids shows that he was familiar with Mendelian principles, which had been "rediscovered" in 1900 by European biologists. A major summary on the inheritance of seed color in the bean (1909) was not only thoroughly Mendelian but also dealt with genetic modifiers and environmental influences. At about this time some interesting and rather unexpected results roused Emerson's particular interest in maize, especially its quantitative characters such as ear length and row number. While at Harvard for graduate study (1910-1911), he worked with the plant geneticist Edward M. East, an authority on quantitative inheritance, and received the D.Sc. in 1913. In the same year he and East published an influential paper, *The Inheritance of Quantitative Characters in Maize* (Nebraska Agricultural Experiment Station, *Bulletin* No. 2), which remains a classic.

Emerson left Nebraska in 1914 to become professor and head of the department of plant breeding at Cornell University, positions he held until his retirement in 1942. At Cornell, Emerson and his students established maize as one of the best understood and most utilizable objects for genetic research. Although no single investigation by Emerson constituted a major breakthrough, the sum of his work was enormously important. He was notable for his rigorous, objective analysis of data, as exemplified in his *The Genetic Relations of Plant Color in Maize* (1921). *A Summary of Linkage Studies in Maize* (1935), written with George W. Beadle and Allan C. Fraser, catalogued over 300 genes of maize, included descriptions, designated the appropriate symbols, and, when available, gave the chromosomal locations of the genes. Much of the information was derived from investigations made by Emerson and his students.

Emerson, characteristically, was fascinated by the difficult genetic problems of his time, such as variegation and the inheritance of quantitative characters. Many of his efforts were directed against problems that remained recalcitrant long after, but he provided a firm base for subsequent research. Although his chief work dealt with the genetics of maize, he never lost interest in practical biology and was persistently active in breeding vegetables; even after retirement he continued to experiment with celery and beans.

Emerson had far greater influence on genetics than can be estimated by assessing his research. After his first years at Cornell he did little formal teaching but, particularly in the period from about 1920 to 1935, he directed a large number of graduate and postdoctoral students who became major participants in the next, dynamic generation of geneticists. An intellectual pedigree stemming directly from Emerson includes Beadle, later a Nobel laureate; Milislav Demerec, who became director of the influential Biological Laboratory at Cold Spring Harbor, N.Y.; Marcus M. Rhoades, the cytogeneticist; and George F. Sprague, geneticist and breeder of maize. Leaders in plant breeding as well as genetics emerged from Emerson's tutelage, and his foreign students became significant scientists in their own countries. Cornell was in an era of strength in biology, and exceptional students were drawn by other members of its distinguished faculty. One of these was the cytologist Lester W. Sharp, whose students, including the brilliant Barbara McClintock, interacted strongly with those in the Emerson group. But though Emerson's gifted students must have learned from one another, his own persistent and hard-headed research, together with his integrity and generous fairmindedness, provided the definitive intellectual environment.

In the same spirit, Emerson initiated the organization, in 1928, of a central clearinghouse for seed stocks and the exchange of unpublished data and ideas among maize geneticists both in the United States and abroad, initially by means of an annual mimeographed newsletter, which first appeared in 1932. This "Maize Genetics Cooperation," as it became known, was so helpful that geneticists working with other organisms used it as a model for the *Drosophila Information Service,* the *Microbial Genetics Bulletin,* and the *Neurospora Newsletter,* among others.

Never free of administrative duties, Emerson served as dean of the Cornell Graduate School from 1925 to 1931 and as faculty representative on the board of trustees from 1925 to 1928. He was a member of the National Research Council, and had major responsibility for the Sixth International Genetics Congress, which met at Cornell in 1932. Respect for Emerson's accomplishments was shown by his election to the presidencies of the American Society of Naturalists (1923) and of the Genetics Society of America (1933) and to membership in the National Academy of Sciences in 1927.

Emerson was more than six feet tall, physically powerful and energetic; his long hours in the cornfield and the pace of his work became legendary. In addition to the pleasures of research, he was devoted to his family and found time for nonprofessional interests. A keen hunter and fisherman, he also enjoyed bowling and watching intercollegiate sports. He was an enthusiastic amateur cook. After his wife died in 1942, he chose to do much of his own housework. His favorite poet is said to have been Rudyard Kipling.

During the summer of 1947 Emerson underwent surgery that revealed a carcinoma of the stomach. He continued to work, as much as he was able, until his death in Ithaca, N.Y., a few months later at the age of seventy-four. He was buried at East Lawn Cemetery, Ithaca. A major building at Cornell, dedicated in 1968, was given his name. His son Sterling also became a noted geneticist.

[The most extensive single treatment of Emerson is an unpublished paper by Rosalind Morris, available in the Cornell Univ. Arch. The chief published accounts are those of Marcus M. Rhoades in Nat. Acad. Sci., *Biog Memoirs,* XXV (1949), with photograph and a bibliography of his publications; and G. W. Beadle in *Genetics,* Jan. 1950. Arthur H. Sturtevant, *A Hist. of Genetics* (1965), includes an incomplete but nonetheless impressive intellectual pedigree for Emerson; a more complete one can be worked out from graduate school records in the Cornell Arch. A portrait photograph of Emerson is in the foyer off the entrance to Emerson Hall, Cornell. Death record from N.Y. State Dept. of Health.]

ADRIAN R. SRB

EUSTIS, DOROTHY LEIB HARRISON WOOD (May 30, 1886–Sept. 8, 1946), humanitarian, philanthropist, and founder of The Seeing Eye, the first training school in the United States for dog guides and their blind users, was born in Philadelphia, Pa., the youngest child of Charles Custis Harrison and Ellen Nixon (Waln) Harrison. She had three brothers and two sisters. Both parents were native Philadelphians and descendants of pre-Revolutionary settlers. Her father, the head of a sugar refining company, became provost of the University of Pennsylvania. Dorothy was edu-

cated at the Agnes Irwin School in Philadelphia and the Rathgowrie School in Eastbourne, England.

On Oct. 6, 1906, at Radnor, Pa., she married Walter Abbott Wood, head of a mowing and reaping machine company in Hoosick Falls, N.Y., and a state senator. Her later interest in animal genetics was probably fostered by the experimental dairy farm that they operated at Hoosick Falls. In conjunction with the state department of agriculture, the Woods farm demonstrated successfully that selective breeding could increase the milk production and commercial value of dairy cattle. The work continued until 1917.

In 1917, two years after Mr. Wood's death, she moved to Radnor, Pa., where she remained until 1922, when she moved to Vevey, Switzerland. At Hoosick Falls she had owned a German shepherd dog, Hans, of unusual intelligence and faithfulness. Now she decided to experiment with the scientific selection and breeding of these dogs at her estate, Fortunate Fields. With her second husband, George Morris Eustis, of Aiken, S.C., whom she married on June 23, 1923, and with Elliott S. ("Jack") Humphrey, an American horse breeder and trainer, she began a program of research and experimental breeding. A strain of German shepherds of seemingly exceptional qualities evolved, but it was soon evident that the effectiveness of the program could be measured only by the dogs' performance. A training program was added to the enterprise, and the "graduates" were soon rendering outstanding service to the Swiss army and to several European metropolitan police units.

Eustis became aware of the dogs' full potential when she visited a school in Potsdam, Germany, in 1927 and observed shepherd dogs being trained as guides for blinded war veterans. Deeply impressed, she wrote an article, "The Seeing Eye," for the Saturday Evening Post (Nov. 5, 1927). Many letters came to her from blind Americans, asking where such dogs could be procured. One letter was from Morris S. Frank, a young insurance salesman in Nashville, Tenn., who was willing to go to Switzerland to be trained. "Thousands of blind like me abhor being dependent on others," he wrote. "Help me and I will help them. Train me and I will bring back my dog and show people here how a blind man can be absolutely on his own." Eustis invited Frank to Fortunate Fields to work with the first dog guide trained there. Returning to the United States five weeks later, Frank and his dog, Buddy, re-

ceived much favorable publicity. Eustis then decided to establish a dog guide school in this country. The Seeing Eye was incorporated in 1929, and during its first year, in Nashville, seventeen blind men and women and their dogs were trained. The school moved the following year to Morristown, N.J., home of Willi Ebeling, a retired importer who raised German shepherds as a hobby and who joined the enterprise as a kind of financial manager. From 1929 to 1933 Eustis also presided over L'Oeil Qui Voit, a school she established in Switzerland to train instructors and to train dogs for other countries that might wish to organize more dog guide programs. Eustis early discovered that good instructors were not easy to find; many who imagined the work would be congenial lacked the dedication and perseverance to undergo the rigorous years (usually three to five were required) of apprenticeship. The dogs had to be educated rather than trained to learn to follow commands and also to be intelligently disobedient to commands that might endanger a sightless master. The instructor also had to have a sympathetic understanding of blind pupils.

A small, spirited woman of great intelligence and independent outlook, Eustis did not advocate placing dog guides with every blind person. "The dog guide," she said, "is suitable for the person who can use him in his daily life, who wants an aid in making himself a free economic unit in his community, and who wants a wider, freer life." She was impatient with the apathy and resignation that prevented many blind people from seeking a freer life, as impatient as she was with restrictions on the rights of Seeing Eye dogs and their masters to go wherever they wished. She and her coworkers, many of them blind, overcame barriers that had denied dog guides and their owners access to restaurants, hotels, and public transportation.

Yet even by the 1970's only about 1 percent of blind Americans used dog guides, less than half the number meeting the physical and emotional criteria for eligibility. The Seeing Eye limits applicants to persons between sixteen and fifty-five years of age, with some exceptions for younger people of unusual maturity and older persons of adequate physical strength as well as those seeking replacement dogs. Like other reputable dog guide schools, it will not provide dogs for mendicants or those with no work plans.

From the beginning Eustis approved the Seeing Eye policy requiring each student to pay for his dog, enhancing his sense of self-respect and responsibility, even though the organization could have assumed the financial responsibility, as it does for transportation, board, and lodging at the school during the student's month of training.

The Seeing Eye attracted immediate public support. By 1958 its funds were ample, and no further fund raising has been undertaken. At that time The Seeing Eye grants program was instituted. In its first fifteen years it allocated $5,885,719 to 128 different institutions, providing support for ophthalmic research, veterinary medicine, orientation and mobility training, and vocational and educational rehabilitation.

Eustis devoted much of her own fortune to The Seeing Eye, which remained her keenest interest. She served as president until 1940 and thereafter as honorary president. She herself trained many dogs. At her death The Seeing Eye had supplied over 1,300 dogs to the blind. The organization's social impact, which was always potentially broader than its training programs, has been frustrated by community attitudes of pity and overprotection toward the blind.

Eustis had two sons by her first marriage, Walter Abbott and Harrison; her second marriage ended in divorce in 1928. She was a Christian Scientist. She died of cancer at her home in New York City and was buried in the churchyard of St. David's Church, Wayne, Pa.

[*Notable Am. Women*, I (1971), and sources in that bibliog. Annual report, Grants Program report, and other material from The Seeing Eye, Morristown, N.J.; conversation with Morris S. Frank, Brookside, N.J.; correspondence with Walter A. Wood.]

PATRICIA READ

EVERLEIGH, MINNA (July 5 or 13, 1878-Sept. 16, 1948) and **ADA** (Feb. 15, 1876-Jan. 3, 1960), madams, were reportedly descendants of an old Virginia family of Welsh origin, whose relations included Edgar Allan Poe. Though popularly known by the name of Everleigh, the sisters are generally believed to have been the daughters of a Kentucky attorney named Lester, who was sufficiently prosperous to send the girls, two of his five children, to finishing school. A variant account, "The Scarlet Sisters Everleigh" (*Chicago Tribune*, Jan. 19, 1936), however, hints that the sisters hailed from Texas and their father might have been a one-time resident of Mexico. Admitted actresses, the sisters Everleigh presented themselves as aristocratic Southern belles, although Wallace (p. 50) won-

dered how much of Minna Everleigh's tale was "conscious pretense based on elementary caution and how much was the sublimation of an old lady who had come to believe in a dream identity. . . ."

After brief unhappy marriages, the sisters deserted their husbands and left their hometown to join a traveling theater troupe. During 1898, having come into a legacy of $35,000, the sisters invested in a high-class brothel in Omaha, Nebr., near the site of the booming Trans-Mississippi Exposition. When the fair closed, their investment had increased to $70,000, and, on the suggestion of madam Cleo Maitland of Washington, they went to Chicago, where the famous madam Effie Hankins sold them her business at 2131 South Dearborn Street.

The name "Everleigh" used during their Chicago years derived from their grandmother, who always concluded her letters "Everly Yours." Minna was frequently referred to as Minnie and was so listed in the Chicago city directory. Ada, who in later years used the name Aida, was listed in the city directory as Ray. In their declining years, the sisters used the family name of Lester.

What is known for certain is that their bordello, named the Everleigh Club, was "probably the most famous and luxurious house of prostitution in the country" (Chicago Vice Commission Report, *The Social Evil in Chicago*, 1911, p. 152). Before opening the club, the sisters recruited new girls, replaced the help with black servants, and furnished the house in a sumptuous manner. Downstairs was a ballroom with a $15,000 gold-leaf piano, a library of richly bound volumes, a dining room, and a buffet that reproduced the decor of a private Pullman car. Parlors decorated around a theme bore fanciful names, including the Silver Parlor, the Gold Parlor, the Japanese Throne Room, the Oriental Music Room, the Rose Parlor, and the Louis Quatorze Room. The downstairs rooms were generally used for group entertainment, while upstairs chambers such as the Blue Room with its bedroom alcove accommodated private pleasures. Overstuffed furniture and oriental carpets abounded, and $650 gold cuspidors were placed judiciously. Nude paintings and statuary reminded the visitor of the establishment's function. Early dinners and midnight suppers included menus with fried oysters, caviar, capon, crab, duck, and lobster.

At a time when the one-dollar disorderly house was the norm and a price of 25¢ for a prostitute was not unknown, the Everleigh Club was at the head of its trade. Ten dollars merely admitted one to the premises, $12 secured a bottle of wine, $50 paid for an evening with the hostess of one's choice. Nightly receipts at the club, which employed from twenty-five to thirty girls, averaged $2,000-$2,500. In eleven years of operation, the sisters reportedly accumulated $1 million, along with $200,000 in furnishings, a fortune in jewels, and $25,000 in receipts outstanding. What the captains of industry and finance were to regular business, the Everleigh sisters were to prostitution.

Their initial operation proved so successful that a "new Annex" at 2133 was opened Nov. 1, 1902. Fame over the years enabled the sisters to be more selective in their clientele and earned the club the epithet of the millionaires' bagnio. Advertising was an important business tool for the Everleighs. In 1902 the club subscribed to a half-page ad in the Cook County Republican Marching Club's Eighth Annual Reception souvenir booklet. Not to be partisan, the sisters attended the renowned First Ward Democratic ball given by the bosses ("Bathhouse John" Coughlin and Michael "Hinky-Dink" Kenna) of the South Side, red-light Levee district. The club published an illustrated brochure with thirty pictures of the interior and an introduction declaring "Fortunate indeed, with all the comforts of life surrounding them, are the members of the Everleigh Club."

Of the two sisters, Minna, the younger, was the dominant figure and generally handled business matters; Ada interviewed and managed the girls of the house. Minna, who greeted the customers with considerable wit and charm, was referred to as the speaking partner. She once described herself as "a student of tinsel and glitter—nothing more" (Washburn, p. 152). Both sisters were always the soul of discretion regarding their customers, but their fame and their pretensions set them apart from all their fellow madams.

As the club became a booming success, antivice crusaders, inspired by English reformers, determined to end official policies that permitted toleration of prostitution and its segregation in recognized districts. William T. Stead, English journalist and reformer, had tried to "awaken" Chicago in the 1890's, but it took the more immediate example of New York's struggles with prostitution in 1901 and 1905 to motivate Chicago's crusaders to form a loose coalition of clergymen, social workers, and urban reformers. Although politicians were slow to act, a municipal vice commission was finally appointed in 1910; and the report the commission published in April 1911 heralded the beginning

of the end for Chicago's red-light district.

The Everleigh Club's visibility and reputation made it a prime target for reformers. Minna Everleigh's arrogant attitude toward the commission did not help matters (Louise C. Wade, *Graham Taylor*, 1964, p. 199). At a time when a poor salesgirl earned $6 a week, there was considerable resentment of the silken-clad prostitute who presumed to mingle with society. The end came when Mayor Carter H. Harrison, Jr., was shown a copy of the club's illustrated brochure. Incensed by this audacity, he ordered the Everleigh Club closed as a signal that he meant to clean up the Levee. The club ran full blast the night of Oct. 24, 1911, until the order arrived, Minna noting "If the ship sinks we're going down with a cheer and a good drink under our belts anyway."

After the closing, the sisters traveled for six months in Europe before returning to Chicago to see if the furor had subsided. Mayor Harrison, who later claimed to have seen the sisters on the street, characterized them as "a painted, peroxided, bedizened pair." Deciding the furor would not cease, the sisters removed to New York and lived an anonymous life of poetry-reading and theatergoing. After Minna's death in 1948, Ada moved to Virginia, where she died in 1960. Both sisters are reputedly buried in a cemetery in that state.

[Biographical data on the sisters contained in Charles Washburn's *Come into My Parlor* (1934 or 1936) and Irving Wallace's *The Sunday Gentleman* (1965) are based on interviews given in the sisters' final years and are of questionable accuracy.

To these sources can be added Herman Kogan's article on the sisters in *Notable Am. Women*, I (1971). Like Washburn and Wallace, Kogan deals with the sisters as exemplars of the prostitute whose heart is gold. Herbert Asbury portrays them differently and includes pictures of them both, in his *Gem of the Prairie* (1940). Ray Hibbler's *Upstairs at the Everleigh Club* (n.d.), recounting a dialogue with a former girl of the house, has little redeeming value. The Chicago newspapers of the time are invaluable, as are the several retrospectives the Chicago newspapers have since published, including Charles Washburn's "Everleigh Sisters," *Chicago Tribune Mag.*, Nov. 1, 1953.]

R. RICHARD WAGNER

FAIRBURN, WILLIAM ARMSTRONG (Oct. 12, 1876-Oct. 1, 1947), naval architect, marine engineer, and corporate executive, was born in Huddersfield, England, the son of Thomas William Fairburn and Elizabeth (Frosdick) Fairburn. His father, a shipbuilder by trade from a seagoing family, immigrated with his family to Bath, Maine, late in the 1880's, where he was employed by the Bath Iron Works. Fairburn graduated from Bath public schools and became a mechanic apprentice at the iron works, acquiring master papers at the age of eighteen. During his apprenticeship he wrote articles for several technical magazines on marine engineering. In 1896 he entered the University of Glasgow, Scotland, and completed in one year a two-year program in naval architecture and marine engineering, standing at the head of his class. Returning to Maine, he became general superintendent and naval architect for the Bath Iron Works and at the age of twenty-three designed the first all-steel freighter built in America. By 1900 Fairburn had become an independent engineering consultant. Both James J. Hill, 1900-1903, and Edward H. Harriman, 1904-1908, employed him to design and supervise construction of cargo vessels when they expanded their railroad enterprises into shipping. Fairburn pioneered in applying the diesel to railroading, urging Harriman to adopt his design for a locomotive. Meanwhile Fairburn had served as a consultant for the Stirling Company and Babcock and Wilcock on steam boiler and marine manufacturing problems.

Executives in both companies, Ohio Columbus Barber and Edward R. Stettinius, Sr., were also officers in the Diamond Match Company, plagued by rising manufacturing costs, losses in related lumbering operations, and negative public attitudes toward its matches. The U.S. Bureau of Labor had publicly condemned the main ingredient of matches, white phosphorus, because it led to phosphorus necrosis among production workers and poisoned children who ate matches. Also railroad and insurance companies increasingly criticized match distribution and use because their handling posed a growing fire hazard. A safety match, already available on foreign markets, was free of white phosphorus and nonpoisonous, but it would strike only on a special surface and the American consumer was unfamiliar with its use. Additionally, American match producers had made considerable investments in white phosphorus by that time. However, public outcry to end the dangers of the white phosphorus match grew to such proportions that American manufacturers were threatened with loss of business to foreign producers of safety matches if they did not respond. Public demand as well as declining profits led Barber and Stettinius in 1909 to place Fairburn in charge of Diamond Match operations to reorganize production and solve the marketing and public relations problems.

In moving from consultation to management Fairburn joined a new breed of corporate executive, distinct from both the founder-entrepreneur and the banker-reorganizer types. His training in engineering inclined him to a sys-

tematic approach to business based on efficient use of technology. Given a free hand, Fairburn uncovered a company-owned, European-developed process for match production, using sesquisulfide rather than white phosphorus. Working with company chemists and using available patents owned by the company, Fairburn perfected the match in approximately two years. In 1911 he announced the development of the Diamond safety match at the time Congress was considering a prohibitive tax on white phosphorus matches. Opposition to the tax, which benefited the new safety match, was very strong among domestic match producers. President William H. Taft, therefore, intervened with Fairburn to waive Diamond's patent rights to the new process, to ease acceptance. The tax, which effectively prohibited the white phosphorus production process, was enacted in 1912, but without an increase in tariffs on matches to protect domestic producers against foreign competition. Fairburn also worked out new, safer container packaging and altered components of match heads to increase consumer safety. In 1914 Fairburn and Diamond received the Gold Medal of the American Museum of Safety; and both received the Louis Livingston Seaman Gold Medal in 1915 for elimination of industrial disease and achievements in the interest of labor. When Stettinius became a J. P. Morgan partner in 1915, Fairburn replaced him as the president of Diamond just in time to face the problems of World War I. A German cartel controlled chlorate of potash, an essential raw material for matches. Fairburn guided Diamond research chemists into opening new domestic sources. While these sources were considerably more expensive than the German prewar supplies, domestic match production was able to continue. Since the war also disrupted finished match importation, Fairburn moved quickly to expand production capacity. However, when peace restored international trade, foreign competition increased, leaving Diamond with an excess capacity.

Fairburn then addressed problems both of productive capacity and competitive pressures. He streamlined Diamond production, shutting down the most inefficient plants, reorganizing the administrative network, and diversifying into other household woodenware and paper products. Diversification helped Diamond maintain its profits during the 1920's and 1930's despite the pressures of foreign match competition. In 1915 all Diamond's earnings had come from match sales; by 1940 these constituted only half the company's revenues. To counter foreign competition Fairburn negotiated an agreement early in the 1920's with Ivan Kreuger, the Swedish "match king," for marketing foreign matches. Kreuger, however, grew restive with the agreement and attempted to purchase production facilities within the United States. Fairburn contained Kreuger's efforts to compete openly by reorganizing and recapitalizing Diamond in 1930 and selling Kreuger an interest in a Diamond-controlled subsidiary. When the Kreuger empire collapsed in 1932, Diamond's major competitive threat ceased. By 1939 Diamond controlled 90 percent of American match production and was very closely allied with major British and European match manufacturers.

Despite Fairburn's inclination toward developing an efficient, regularized organization at Diamond, he retained a strong sense of personal independence. He rarely worked at the New York Diamond headquarters, spending winters in Ojai, Calif. and summers in Kezar Lake, Maine, yet he tightly controlled company policy. He spent considerable time in England, where he was director of the British Match Company, among others. Each Diamond annual report reflected his personal philosophy and concern. Fairburn was a nominal Republican but inactive in public affairs. He abhorred New Deal labor practices, considering them destructive of his company's welfare policies. In private life he was a rugged outdoorsman and also intellectually inclined. He rode horses and played softball; he was fond of music and literature, collected primitive artifacts and ship models, remained active in several British and American scientific and engineering societies, and privately published over a dozen books on philosophy, history, and economics. On Sept. 17, 1904, he married Louise Ramsey, daughter of a Perth Amboy, N.J., shipbuilder. They maintained a home in Morristown, N.J., and had two sons, William Armstrong, Jr., and Robert Gordon. Upon his death at his Maine home and burial in Center Lovell, Maine, cemetery, Fairburn's younger son succeeded him as president of Diamond Match Company.

[Herbert Manchester, *William Armstrong Fairburn: A Factor in Human Progress* (1940) and "The Diamond Match Company," *Fortune*, May 1939, pp. 88–93, provide the most comprehensive information about a man who shunned publicity and for whom there is little information except of a general nature. *Nat. Cyc. Am. Biog.*, XXXVII, 24–25, supplies vital data. Among Fairburn's publications are *Human Chemistry* (1914), *The Individual and Society* (1915), *Mentality and Freedom* (1917), *A Diagnosis of the German Obsession* (1918), *Organization and Success* (1923), *Life and Work* (1925), *Loyalty* (1926), *Justice and Law* (1927), *Russian, the Utopia in Chains*

(1931), and *Work and Workers* (1933). He also began *Merchant Sail* (1945–1955), a 6-vol. history of ships in the development, growth, and prosperity of the U.S., published and distributed without charge by the Fairburn Marine Educational Foundation, Inc.; E. M. Ritchie edited the last four volumes. Obituary in *N.Y. Times*, Oct. 3, 1947.]

WILLIAM O. WAGNON, JR.

FAIRCHILD, MUIR STEPHEN (Sept. 2, 1894-Mar. 17, 1950), army and air force officer, was born in Bellingham, Wash., the only child of Harry Anson Fairchild, a lawyer, and Georgie Ann (Crockett) Fairchild. His father, born near Brantford, Ontario, had moved to the United States and settled in Washington in 1884. He served as chairman of the state Railroad Commission, and of the Public Service Commission which succeeded it, from 1905 until his death in 1911.

Young Fairchild attended public schools in Bellingham and Olympia, and in 1913 entered the University of Washington as a military cadet, concurrently enlisting in the Washington National Guard. His three and a half years at the university were interrupted by National Guard service as a radio platoon sergeant on the Mexican border in 1916, and he did not complete a degree. In June 1917, after American entry into World War I, Fairchild became a flying cadet in the Aviation Section of the Army Signal Corps. He received flight training at an Italian school in Foggia, where he completed a pilot and observer course and was commissioned in the U.S. Air Service in January 1918. He then flew night bombing missions with French air groups during the Aisne-Marne and St. Mihiel offensives until wounded by German antiaircraft artillery fire in October.

After a few months of civilian life, Fairchild sought and received a regular commission in the Air Service, and upon return to active duty with the rank of first lieutenant in 1920, he commanded a bombardment squadron (the 11th Aero) at Kelly Field, Texas. As one of the few American pilots with combat bombing experience, Fairchild might have been expected to give active support to the campaign of Gen. William "Billy" Mitchell for greater recognition of the importance of military air power. Such, however, was not Fairchild's temperament; he preferred anonymity, and sought to make a thorough study of any matter before passing judgment. He became a test pilot at McCook Field, Ohio, in February 1921, graduated from the maintenance engineer course there in 1923, and served in varied Air Corps engineer assignments at McCook Field, Mitchell Field, N.Y., Langley Field, Va., and Santa Monica, Calif., through the decade. As a notable exception to these technical duties, he flew on the Army Air Corps goodwill circumnavigation flight of South America from December 1926 to May 1927 and, as one of the ten officers of the mission, received the Distinguished Flying Cross—the first awards of the new decoration. Meanwhile, on Apr. 26, 1924, Fairchild had married Florence Alice Rossiter of Omaha, Nebr. They had one child, Betty Anne.

In 1934 Fairchild began several years of military professional education, completing courses at the Air Corps Tactical School at Maxwell Field, Ala. (1935), the Army Industrial College (1936), and the Army War College (1937). In 1937 he joined the faculty of the Air Corps Tactical School, where a group of instructors—soon to be wartime air leaders—were planning a strategic air warfare concept of air bombardment against the vital industrial fabric of a hostile nation. This effort generated American air warfare concepts of World War II, and Fairchild's associates credited him with bringing to the planning a deep understanding of national policy, particularly the role of air power as an instrument for the furtherance of national objectives.

In July 1940 Fairchild was transferred to the Office of Chief of Air Corps, the beginning of five years of staff duty in Washington during World War II. He was promoted to brigadier general in August 1941 and major general a year later. From November 1942 through December 1945 Fairchild was one of the three "elder statesmen" composing the Joint Strategic Survey Committee, the organization charged to advise the Joint Chiefs of Staff on "global and theater strategy, rather than area strategy and campaign plans." He was a member of the United States delegations to the Dumbarton Oaks and San Francisco United Nations conferences and placed great hope in the collective security aspects of the United Nations as a guarantor of postwar peace, especially the prospect that the Security Council would be supported by an international peace-keeping air force.

With the end of World War II and the impending establishment of a separate air force, Fairchild was assigned in January 1946 as the first commanding general of the Air University at Maxwell Air Force Base, Ala. Here he established the aim of the new military colleges of the Air University as "Truly to educate; not merely to train or indoctrinate." He insisted on the broadest academic freedom for students and faculties. Fairchild was appointed vice chief of staff of the Air Force in May 1948 and served

in this post, with promotion to the rank of general, until his death. He died at Fort Myer, Va., of a heart attack at the age of fifty-five, and was buried in Arlington National Cemetery. In the development of the U.S. Air Force, Fairchild may best be described as a judicious and stabilizing influence and as the "father" of Air Force postgraduate professional officer education.

[There is no biography of Fairchild. A collection of his personal papers is in the Albert F. Simpson Hist. Research Center at the Air Univ.; another collection, for 1948–1950, is in the Lib. of Cong.; and the Fairchild family retains photograph albums and personal diaries. Brief biographical sketches appear in Flint O. DuPre, U.S. Air Force Biog. Dict. (1965), and Nat. Cyc. Am. Biog., XXXIX, 432–433. There are passing appreciations of Fairchild in: Thomas H. Greer, The Development of Air Doctrine in the Army Air Arm, 1917–1941 (1955); Robert F. Futrell, Ideas, Concepts, Doctrine: A Hist. of Basic Thinking in the U.S. Air Force, 1907–1964 (1971); Perry McC. Smith, The Air Force Plans for Peace (1970); and Haywood S. Hansell, Jr., The Air Plan That Defeated Hitler (1972). A posthumous portrait of Fairchild is in the Fairchild Lib., Air Univ.]

ROBERT FRANK FUTRELL

FAIRLIE, JOHN ARCHIBALD (Oct. 30, 1872-Jan. 23, 1947), political scientist, educator, and public official, was born in Glasgow of an old Scottish family who held lands in Ayrshire and whose Fairlie Castle overlooked the Clyde near the village of Fairlie. His ancestors included farmers, tradesmen, and artisans at Bannockburn, Balfron, Killearn, and Glasgow. He was the second of five children and the first of three sons of James Mitchell Fairlie and Margaret Simpson (Miller) Fairlie. James Fairlie was a chemist (druggist) who left Glasgow in 1879 after the failure of a venture in soft-drink syrup manufacturing. He worked in New York City for two years and then opened a drugstore in Jacksonville, Fla., where he established his family when John was nine. Husband and wife were overwhelmed in relief efforts during the yellow fever epidemic of 1888 and both died that year.

The elder sister, Margaret, held the survivors together, and John worked as a shorthand typist for Jacksonville officials. He went to Harvard on a scholarship, graduated Phi Beta Kappa in 1895, and remained at Harvard for a master's degree, serving also as an assistant in history. He then decided on the study of governmental institutions for his career and entered Columbia University's graduate school where, under Frank J. Goodnow, he wrote a dissertation on state government in New York. This became Fairlie's first book, *Centralization of Administration in New York*

State, published in 1898, the year of his doctorate.

Local government was in low esteem—James Bryce had called it "the one conspicuous failure of the United States"—when Fairlie made it his major area of concern and research. His book, *Municipal Administration* (1901), was in the forefront of treatments of American city government and its problems. He became a specialist in a still more localized area through his book, *Counties, Towns and Villages* (1906). With the publication of his *Essays in Municipal Administration* (1908), Fairlie stood as a leading young authority on the country's burgeoning cities, their growing needs and the means of meeting them. This interest continued throughout his life and, in 1930, he and a junior colleague, Charles M. Kneier, brought out *County Government and Administration.* Fairlie directed public attention to the outmoded character of local units of government, asserting that counties, "established in the days of mud roads and ox carts, are too small for an age of motorcars and concrete highways" (*American Political Science Review,* Feb. 1930).

Meantime, Fairlie rose in the academic world. After holding the secretaryship of the New York State Commission on Canals, 1899-1900, under Gov. Theodore Roosevelt, and also concurrently a lectureship on municipal administration at Columbia University, he was appointed an assistant professor of administrative law at the University of Michigan. He continued at Ann Arbor until 1909, when he became associate professor of political science at the University of Illinois. Fairlie was promoted to professor in 1911 and served until his retirement in 1941. During his last years he was head of his large and distinguished department (1938-1941) and a member of the graduate faculty. He also taught public administration, administrative law, jurisprudence, and a course on the government of Britain. "He was at his best in the graduate seminar, guiding and directing the students in their researches and in writing of their theses" (Berdahl, p. 97).

To Fairlie the university was a proper base for related public service. While in Michigan he was elected a delegate on the Republican ticket to the 1907-1908 state constitutional convention. He was also secretary of the League of Michigan Municipalities, and when he went to Illinois, he became the chief founder of the Illinois Municipal League, of which he was also secretary. He directed the comprehensive work of the Illinois Efficiency and Economy Committee (1914-1915), established on the recommendation of Gov. Edward F. Dunne. Its proposals, in large part Fairlie's, became effective during the governorship of Frank O. Lowden and "set the pattern for state administrative reorganization in Illinois and numerous other states that undertook such reorganization" (Berdahl, p. 98). For six years he was an Urbana alderman. His other public posts included: special agent in the United States Bureau of Corporations, 1908-1909; chief clerk of the Illinois Tax Commission, 1909; and chief of the War Department's procurement section, 1918-1919. He also served as a member of the Illinois Public Aid Commission, 1941-1946.

Fairlie was a founder in 1905 of the American Political Science Association and managing editor of its *Review,* 1916-1925. He played a major role in the development of the National Municipal League's program for the reform of local and state government and was a leader in drafting the model city charter and the model state constitution. He served as president of APSA in 1929. His writings included *National Administration in the United States* (1905), *British War Administration* (1919), *Administrative Procedure in Great Britain* (1927), and a biography of his longtime colleague, James W. Garner, which was published in 1943. He was an editor of the University of Illinois Studies in the Social Sciences and served on many policy-determining committees.

In retirement, Fairlie was a visiting professor at the Ohio State University and remained an active member of the Illinois Public Aid Commission of the International Association of City Managers and the International Institute of Public Law. He was on the board of directors of the *Encyclopedia of the Social Sciences* (1930-1935).

In 1944 Fairlie had a major operation and, two years later, while in Atlanta, Ga., visiting his brother, Andrew, he died of stomach cancer. He was buried in Evergreen Cemetery in Jacksonville, Fla.

The Fairlie family was Presbyterian, but while at Harvard he joined friends in the Baptist church. He never married. Phenomenal memory made him a remarkable bridge player. Friends remember him with moustache and goatee-shaped beard, holding a hand of cards at the Faculty Club in Urbana, checking galley proofs, and reading a newspaper seemingly at the same time.

[Some sources give "fár-lǐ" as the pronunciation but members of the family say "fair-lǐ." Margaret C. Fairlie, a sister, compiled a family genealogy. *Who Was Who in Am.*, II (1950); B. A. Hinsdale, *History of the Univ. of Michigan* (1906) with sketch and portrait; C. A. Berdahl, memorial in *Am. Political Sci. Rev.*, Feb. 1947; *Univ. of Illinois Alumni News*, Feb. 1947; newspapers at the time of death, including *N.Y. Times*, Jan 27, 1947 (portrait). Information from his nephews, E. F. Ricketts, Chicago, and Barron Ricketts, Jackson, Miss.; from C. A. Berdahl and M. J. Bickford, Urbana, Ill.; R. J. Hathaway, Lansing, Mich.; and W. N. Cassella, New York, personal recollection. Fairlie's papers were placed in the Archives of the Univ. of Illinois. An oil portrait by Kate Flowards hangs in the Univ. of Illinois Library.]

IRVING DILLIARD

FALK, MAURICE (Dec. 15, 1866-Mar. 18, 1946), industrialist and philanthropist, was born in Old Allegheny, Pa., a small community near Pittsburgh, the first of seven children, two sons and five daughters. His parents were Charles Falk and Sarah (Sanders) Falk, both German Jews, natives of Erpol, a village near Frankfurt am Main in Hesse. They immigrated to the United States in 1850 shortly after marrying and settled in Old Allegheny, then largely populated by Germans and Scots-Irish. Charles Falk, an expert tailor, opened a clothing store. After a few years at Old Allegheny, the family moved to Irwin Station, a suburb of Pittsburgh. Maurice attended the public schools of both Irwin and Pittsburgh. At the age of fourteen he began working for his uncle, a merchant tailor, and eventually became a traveling salesman for him. On May 19, 1888, he married Laura Klinordlinger, a native of Pittsburgh. They had no children who survived beyond infancy; after the death of an infant son, Laura was invalided for life.

Probably as he traveled in the area around Pittsburgh, Falk saw abundant evidence of the opportunities in the burgeoning iron and steel industry. In any case, evidently without any experience in metal refining, he joined a brother-in-law, Henry Weiskopf, in 1893 in the establishment of the Duquesne Reduction Company for the smelting and refining of copper, brass, and other nonferrous metals. A few years later, his younger brother, Leon Falk, Sr., bought out Weiskopf's interest and entered the business.

The company prospered, becoming one of the largest enterprises of its kind in the region. Falk then turned to other ventures. In 1902 he organized the Crown Chemical Company, which produced tin oxide, zinc sulfate, and antimony oxide. He combined this company and the Duquesne company in 1924 into the Federated Metals Corporation, a firm that he had created originally for the refining of nonferrous junk metals. In the meantime, in 1908, he bought a substantial interest in the Phillips Sheet and Tin Company. It became the Weirton Steel Company in 1914 and later was merged with other companies to form the National Steel Company. He was also a large stockholder and director of the Blaw-Knox Company, the Farmers Deposit National Bank, the Reliance Life Insurance Company, and other corporations.

As he achieved success in the industrial world, Falk was able to initiate many philanthropic programs. Both he and his brother believed that men of means should share their wealth with their less fortunate neighbors. "I firmly believe," he once said, "that any great surplus of wealth which may come to a man is properly to be regarded as a trust that should be employed for the welfare of mankind, and I count myself fortunate in being able to translate this principle into practice during my lifetime." An early philanthropic effort came in 1912, when he and his brother assisted Rabbi J. Leonard Levy in organizing the Pittsburgh Federation of Jewish Philanthropies. During World War I they supported programs for extending assistance to European Jews. After giving important but piecemeal aid to charitable institutions in the next decade, the brothers made a gift of $500,000 to the University of Pittsburgh in 1928 for the establishment of an outpatient clinic known as the Falk Medical Clinic. A year later, after the death of Leon Falk, Sr., Maurice Falk and Leon Falk, Jr., who became his closest business associate, gave an additional $400,000 to the clinic. The same year, Maurice Falk, prompted by suggestions of John G. Bowman, chancellor of the University of Pittsburgh, created the Maurice and Laura Falk Foundation and endowed it with $10 million. Dedicated to his wife, who had died in 1928, the foundation was directed to support programs for "the uplifting and upbuilding of the afflicted, and the encouragement, improvement, and betterment of mankind." In its early years it engaged primarily in funding research in economic development. Some of its later recipients were the Carnegie Institute of Technology, to which funds were given for education and research in social problems, and, during the mid-1930's, the Brookings Institution, for a study that advocated the organization of vertical unions for steel workers; in 1943-1944, it supported studies in demobilization and reconstruction, the preparing of a commercial code, and possible changes in the federal tax system. By 1964 it had expended

$33 million for a wide range of projects in economic and medical research, political education, and cultural affairs.

With the coming of World War II, Falk increasingly addressed himself to the problems of the Jewish community in Europe. He made grants in 1939 and 1940 for the study of the feasibility of resettling Jewish refugees in the Caribbean and, along with Leon Falk, Jr., gave substantial sums of money to programs for relief of Jews in Europe. Owing to his philanthropic endeavors, Falk was often called the "Little Carnegie." While Falk led a quiet life, conducting his philanthropic work outside public view, he was well known around Pittsburgh; he was director of the Federation of Jewish Philanthropy, the Montefiore Hospital, and the Young Men's and Young Women's Hebrew Associations. Falk married his second wife, Selma K. Wertheimer of Pittsburgh, on Sept. 25, 1930. He died in 1946 at Miami Beach, Fla., after a lengthy illness, and was buried in West View Cemetery in Pittsburgh.

[*Universal Jewish Encyc.*, IV (1941); *Nat. Cyc. Am. Biog.*, current vol. D (1934); *Encyc. Judaica*, VI ((1971); *Britannica Book of the Year*, 1946 (1947); *Foundations Directory* (1964); *Who Was Who in America*, II (1950); *N.Y. Times*, Mar. 20, 1946. An important source for a description of the work of the Maurice and Laura Falk Foundation is Agnes Lynch Starrett, *The Maurice and Laura Falk Foundation* (1966). A portrait of Falk, painted in the early 1930's, hangs in the lobby of the Falk Clinic Building; another, painted in 1937 by Charles C. Curran, hangs in the Maurice Falk Auditorium of the Brookings Institution in Washington, D.C.]

CARL M. BECKER

FELS, SAMUEL SIMEON (Feb. 16, 1860–June 23, 1950), soap manufacturer and philanthropist, was born in Yanceyville, Caswell County, N.C., the sixth of seven children and the youngest of four sons of Lazarus and Susanna (Freiberg) Fels. His parents were Jewish emigrants from the Bavarian Palatinate who had left Germany after the revolution of 1848. Lazarus Fels, who had begun in America as an itinerant peddler, owned a general store in Yanceyville and prospered by trading in real estate and commodities, but was ruined by the Civil War. Moving his family to Baltimore, he began a soapmaking venture in 1866. This enterprise failed in 1870, and he moved on to Philadelphia in 1873. Samuel attended public schools in both cities but left high school with a "partial certificate" in 1876 to join the firm his brother Joseph had established that year for the manufacture and sale of toilet soaps. Both Samuel and his father became partners in the firm in 1881. On May 15, 1890, Fels married

Jennie M. May of New Haven, Conn. They had no children.

Barely five feet tall, Fels as a youth was nervous, impulsive, and somewhat sickly. He nevertheless took increasing authority over the manufacturing aspects of the business. Although the company initially made a wide variety of soaps, Joseph favored concentrating on one product, and in 1894 the family acquired the Philadelphia company of Charles Walter Stanton, who had succeeded in introducing a naphtha or benzine solvent into laundry soap. Thus began the manufacture of "Fels-Naptha" soap (the spelling simplified for convenience). Essentially depression-proof and marketed by seasoned promoters, it was an overnight success and built the family fortune. In 1914, after Joseph's death, Fels and Company was incorporated with Samuel as president, a post he held until his death. He once described himself as early inclined to be "sot" in his ways, a marked characteristic of his business leadership in later life.

His career as a civic leader and philanthropist, by contrast, displayed a wide-ranging curiosity and a venturesome and scientific turn of mind. Always a generous benefactor, he helped organize the Hebrew Immigrant Aid Society in 1884, the Federation of Jewish Charities in 1901, and the Allied Jewish Appeal in 1938. Although never an ardent Zionist, he made many contributions to projects in Palestine, and during the 1930's he assisted Jewish scientists fleeing Germany. He was a co-founder of the Big Brothers Association in Philadelphia and of the Crime Prevention Association. His lifelong goal to improve local government led him with others in 1904 to found the Committee of Seventy as a watchdog body of citizens, and in 1908 Philadelphia's Bureau of Municipal Research. In 1929 he helped establish the Regional Planning Federation of the Philadelphia Tri-State District, and in 1937 he served on the commission to draft a new city charter. Among his other interests were the Philadelphia Civil Liberties Committee and the Philadelphia Housing Association. His desire to "rouse a sense of participation in our universe" induced him in 1933 to give to the Franklin Institute the planetarium instrument that bears his name.

Fels's principal philanthropic medium was the Samuel S. Fels Fund, incorporated in Pennsylvania in 1935, which he founded to aid research projects, especially in the fields of medicine and government. Major activities sponsored by the fund over the years have included the Research Institute for the Study of Human

Development at Antioch College, the Research Institute of Temple University Medical School in Philadelphia, the Institute of Local and State Government of the University of Pennsylvania, programs at Philadelphia's Wistar Institute for the study of the aging process in rats and of human fertility problems, and the Dissertation Fellowship Program. Reputedly Fels donated more than $40 million to various causes during his lifetime. His philanthropies won him many honors, including the gold medal of the American Congress of Radiology, election to the American Philosophical Society, and in 1948 the Philadelphia Award. Spry, wiry, and mentally alert to the end of his life, Fels died at Temple University Hospital, Philadelphia, at the age of ninety, following a brief siege of acute hemorrhagic pancreatitis. His body was cremated, and his ashes deposited at the Chelten Hills Cemetery, Philadelphia.

[The early history of the Fels family must be pieced together from fragmentary sources and accounts, most of which are assembled in the Joseph Fels Papers at the Hist. Soc. of Pa. in Philadelphia. Dale Phalen, *Samuels Fels of Philadelphia* (1969), is a useful memoir, generously illustrated, based on the subject's personal papers in the files of the Samuel S. Fels Fund. The fund's biennial reports reveal the directions his philanthropic impulses and guidelines have taken. For a book of his own thoughts, see his *This Changing World—As I See Its Trend and Purpose* (1933). Obituaries appeared in the *N.Y. Times,* June 24, 1950; and in the Am. Philosophical Soc., *Year Book,* 1950. See also Arthur P. Dudden, *Joseph Fels and the Single-Tax Movement* (1971).]

ARTHUR POWER DUDDEN

FENICHEL, OTTO (Dec. 2, 1897-Jan. 22, 1946), psychoanalyst, was born in Vienna, the second son and youngest of three children of Leo Fenichel and Emma (Braun) Fenichel. His father, a native of Tarnow, Poland, was a lawyer in moderately wealthy circumstances. Otto demonstrated exceptional intellectual abilities as a boy attending the Gymnasium and at the University of Vienna, where he obtained his M.D. degree in 1921. His earlier ambition was to be a biologist, but he was persuaded by his father to enter medical school, where his interest led him to the biology and psychology of sexology. At seventeen he decided to become a psychoanalyst and began his training while still a medical student. In 1918 at the age of twenty-one he presented his first paper, "The Derivatives of the Incest Conflict."

In 1922 he moved to Berlin to complete his training at the Berlin Psychoanalytic Institute, the first established psychoanalytic training center. In 1923 he was appointed an assistant at the Berlin Psychoanalytic Clinic and in 1925 he was made a training analyst. Meanwhile, he

undertook postgraduate work in psychiatry and neurology under Karl Friedrich Bonhoeffer and Richard Cassirer. He led a seminar for younger students, which was looked upon askance by the elders of the movement because too many evenings were devoted to the relation of psychoanalysis to sociology and Marxism. His comment, "What of it? If you don't like the way we do it—let us be naughty children," led to the discussion group's becoming known as "The Children's Seminar."

Fenichel loved to teach, discuss, and lecture; he traveled widely, to wherever psychoanalytic training was in progress, and thus made friends all over the Continent. In 1929 and in 1932 he traveled to the Soviet Union, and in 1933 Fenichel went to Oslo to undertake the training of analysts. Two years later he was called to Prague to take charge of the teaching and training there. Finding the political climate in Central Europe under the Nazis inimical to psychoanalysis, he moved to Los Angeles in 1938, where he remained for the rest of his brief life.

Fenichel's way of scientific work was characterized by youthful enthusiasm and optimism. His early years in the youth movement in Austria evidenced his interest in social change. He was a confirmed Marxist, holding that psychoanalysis was dialectical materialism in psychology. Therefore he opposed epistemological idealism in psychoanalysis as he did in other fields of knowledge. He was not a Communist and could not agree with the small handful of colleagues in the Soviet Union he met on a trip there in 1929 and 1934 that the eradication of the bourgeois family would lead to the prevention of neurosis. He admired their efforts but felt them doomed to failure because of their doctrinaire political attitudes.

According to Fenichel, "Scientific psychology explains mental phenomena as the result of the interplay of primitive physical needs, rooted in the biological structure of man—and the influence of the environment on these needs. . . . As to the influence of the surroundings, these must be studied in detail, in their practical reality. There is no psychology of man in a vacuum— only a psychology of man in a certain concrete society and in a certain social setting within this concrete society." This credo guided his 100 published papers, 200 reviews, and 240 abstracts. His papers were marked by originality; his reviews were often essays in which he advanced new concepts. His productions reveal wide reading, clarity of thinking, an ability to judge the work of others dispassionately, and a prodigious memory. He made notes on almost everything he read, a trait useful in the writing of his encyclopedic works *The Outline of Clinical Psychoanalysis* (1934) and *The Psychoanalytic Theory of Neurosis* (1945). Once a student asked him if anything worthwhile had been written on psychoanalysis and economics; he immediately opened the top right-hand drawer of his ancient desk and removed one of the many batches of 3 x 5 slips of paper, all bound by rubber bands, and in about ten seconds extracted one slip with the names of the paper, author, and journal. He handed it over with a chuckle, saying, "It's very good, almost as good as the author thinks."

When *The Outline of Clinical Psychoanalysis* appeared it immediately became a standard reference, not only for psychoanalysis but also for the larger world of psychology, psychiatry, and the behavioral sciences. It was, however, more than replaced by *The Psychoanalytic Theory of Neurosis* (1945), which was characterized by colleagues as both a "labor of love" and "an encyclopedia of stupendous completeness." Its defect of not having complete case histories is in part made up for by Fenichel's clinical studies, reported in *Collected Papers of Otto Fenichel* (1953-1954). Another major book, *Problems of Psychoanalytic Technique* (1941), exerted considerable influence on subsequent psychoanalytic writers in its succinct statement of the issues, especially on the relatively unexplored area of the theory of technique.

As a youth, Fenichel was tall and thin; in later years he became portly. Quite myopic, one of his characteristic gestures was to lift his glasses in order to peruse his notes. Always fortified by a small notebook and a stub of a pencil, he would extract them and unobtrusively make a note when an idea occurred to him in the course of conversation or discussion. He loved conversation, friends, and travel. Once a patient in a particularly difficult part of his analysis told Fenichel a funny story, pertinent to his problems. Fenichel burst out laughing and then calmly remarked, "You know I like these stories. Why do you tell them to me?"

On May 10, 1926, Fenichel married Clare Nathansohn. They had one daughter, Hanna. This marriage ended in divorce in August 1940 and on September 30 of that year Fenichel married Hanna Heilborn, a lay analyst in Los Angeles.

Concerned by trends in psychoanalysis toward over-biologization on the one hand and toward attribution of behavior solely to cultural influences on the other, Fenichel decided that he should obtain a license to practice medicine in California, feeling that this legal formality would give his voice and reputation a sounder pragmatic basis. Accordingly, he began an internship at the Cedars of Lebanon Hospital in Los Angeles, a legal prerequisite to taking the medical board examinations. However, he died, during the internship, of a ruptured cerebral aneurysm. His ashes are in the care of his widow in Los Angeles.

[Personal appreciations of Fenichel are to be found in Bertram D. Lewin's introduction to David Rapaport and Hanna Fenichel, eds., *Collected Papers of Otto Fenichel* (1953); Ralph R. Greenson's article in F. Alexander, S. Eisenstein, and M. Grotjahn, eds., *Psychoanalytic Pioneers* (1966), pp. 439-449; E. Simmel, ed., *Anti-Semitism* (1946), p. xiv. A straightforward biographical sketch is given in *Encyclopedia Judaica*, VI, 1222-1223. W. Reich, in M. Higgins and C. M. Raphael, eds., *Reich Speaks of Freud* (1967), gives some vignettes and impressions of Fenichel, utterly distorted in some details and untrue in others.
An almost complete bibliography of Fenichel's writings exists in A. Grinstein, *Index of Psychoanalytic Writings*, I, 481-500 (1956); V 2757 (1960); VI 3177-3178 (1964); X 5345 (1971).
Fenichel sent mimeographed circular letters on psychoanalytic topics to colleagues for discussion; most of these are in the Freud Arch. Other data are in the custody of Dr. Hanna Fenichel of Los Angeles. A photograph hangs in the meeting room of the San Francisco Psychoanalytic Inst. A sketch of the young Fenichel may be found in O. Szekely-Kovacs and R. Bereny, *Caricatures of 88 Pioneers in Psychoanalysis* (1954).
Obituaries appeared in: E. E. Krapf, *Revista de psicoanalisis* (Buenos Aires), 4 (1946): 151-160; Rudolph Lowenstein, *Psychoanalytic Quart.* 15 (1946): 139-140; Ernest Simmel, *International Jour. of Psychoanalysis* 27 (1946): 67-71.]

NORMAN REIDER

FERGUSON, SAMUEL (Nov. 18, 1874-Feb. 10, 1950), utility executive, the first of the four children of Henry Ferguson and Emma Jane (Gardiner) Ferguson, was born in Exeter, N.H., where his father was rector of Christ Church. His paternal grandfather, John Ferguson, was a New York banker; his maternal grandfather, Frederic Gardiner of Gardiner, Maine, was a prominent religious educator. Due to journeys for his father's education and for his mother's health, he had traveled in Europe and Australia by the age of eight. His sister was to credit constant early travel for his childhood insecurity and later shyness. In 1893 his father accepted the post of professor of history at Trinity College, and the family settled in Hartford, Conn.

Ferguson attended Hartford Public High School and Trinity College. His dislike of the classics and the influence of an outstanding teacher at Trinity, William L. Robb, led him to take the B.S. in electrical engineering in 1896. Postgraduate work followed at Columbia University School of Mines, under another influential teacher, Michael I. Pupin. Ferguson graduated in 1899 with both the E.E. and M.A. degrees, having received extensive laboratory experience in electrical testing.

Late in 1899, after a few months with the Stone and Webster Engineering Company, he joined the test department of General Electric in Schenectady, N.Y. In 1902 he joined GE's new research laboratory, working on a mercury-arc rectifier for battery charging. He soon learned that his main talents were administrative, not technical. As the lab's administrative engineer from 1904 to 1912, he overcame some of his early shyness and blossomed as a diplomatic young man of few words and sound judgment. On Nov. 3, 1903, he married Ellen Margaret Price, the daughter of a Union College professor.

In 1912, Austin C. Dunham retired as president of the Hartford Electric Company (HELCO), which he had guided since its founding in 1882. Ferguson accepted the offer of a HELCO vice-presidency, and returned to his home city and to the company that he had served briefly in 1893 as a lineman and in 1898. The primary policy of his forty-four years at HELCO was an effort to gain the technological advantages of size without paying the penalties of unsound growth. This meant avoiding outside control, whether from a private holding company or from the federal government, and close personal attention to the needs and complaints of consumers.

Ferguson's early role was mainly technical. His work was capable, rather than creative; of HELCO's thirteen self-proclaimed "technical firsts," only one was achieved while he was with the company. His ambition, however, remained bounded. Born socially and financially secure, he was able to avoid the temptation to empire building that proved Samuel Insull's downfall.

His early problems at HELCO were local ones. He led an unsuccessful utility-company resistance to the state public utility commission's taxation policies (1916), while reconciling company policies with state regulation. After World War I, his progressive side emerged. While other utility leaders were condemning Ontario's public power experiment, he learned from it the "two-part rate" idea. A pioneering step in 1921, this method of encouraging power use by a rate that declines with increasing usage is standard today. Another bit of administrative pioneering followed (1920-1925): the Connecticut Power Exchange was an early effort at regional power supply. A typical Ferguson touch was to set up the exchange as a gentleman's agreement rather than as a contractual arrangement.

As Ferguson emerged as a regional, and then a national, power spokesman, the problem of the holding company increasingly occupied his time. In 1920, he personally arranged HELCO's purchase of the Connecticut Power Company, blocking expansion of the Stone and Webster group. After becoming president of HELCO in 1924, he repeatedly refused offers and countered the efforts of the Mellon and Morgan-Bonbright interests. Yet he did not oppose holding companies in principle—they had value when properly used, he said. This middle road was hard to defend. Twice in 1933 he took the public platform to answer charges—he preferred to call them "misunderstandings"—that HELCO was a puppet of the "power trust." In 1935 he fought the Wheeler-Rayburn Holding Company Act, which he considered an attack on free enterprise and a betrayal of an earlier power policy compromise that he had helped to arrange. For the rest of his career, he opposed the growing power of the Federal Power Commission.

By 1940 his former progressivism seemed conservative, but Ferguson was never reactionary. He sincerely sought to supply the public with reliable, low-cost power; his many speeches (none ghostwritten) were an honest attempt to educate the public in the complexities of utility regulation. He lived comfortably but never lavishly, sharing his main pleasures, such as fishing and bridge, with his son, Samuel, Jr., and his three daughters. He always came home for lunch. He served as a vestryman of St. John's Episcopal Church, in Hartford. In all he brought to a highly technical business environment the home-centered virtues of a simpler age.

Ferguson retired as president of HELCO in 1935, but the personal problems of his successor forced him to resume the office in 1939. His final retirement to board chairman came in 1946. He died on Feb. 10, 1950, of a heart attack suffered while on vacation at Lake Wales, Fla., and was buried in Schenectady.

[Principal sources are three published works: C. W. Kellogg, *Samuel Ferguson*, (1951), an uncritical memorial volume with reminiscences of family and friends; Samuel Ferguson, *Public Utility Papers*, 3 vols. (1947), which contains speeches, articles, and debates; and Glenn Weaver, The *Hartford Electric Light Co.* (1969), which contains much material on Ferguson. Also helpful are the *Hartford Courant*, Mar. 28–Apr. 1, 1935; and, for Ferguson's work at GE, reel 21 of laboratory reports in the library of the GE Research and Development Center, Schenectady, N.Y.]

GEORGE WISE

FERNALD, MERRITT LYNDON (Oct. 5, 1873-Sept. 22, 1950), botanist, was born in Orono, Maine, one of the five children of Merritt Caldwell Fernald and Mary Lovejoy (Heyward) Fernald. His father served two terms (1869-1871 and 1879-1893) as president of Maine State College of Agriculture and Mechanic Arts, which later became the University of Maine. Young Fernald became interested in botany at a very early age. During his years at Orono high school, he studied and collected plants from the fields and woods nearby and on Cape Elizabeth, Maine. Shortly after he entered Maine State College (1890) his first scientific paper was published. For more than sixty years he was a constant writer about the plants of eastern North America.

Fernald's training in botany began in earnest in the winter of 1891 when he became a junior assistant in the Gray Herbarium of Harvard University. Entering the Lawrence Scientific School that fall, he took courses on a reduced schedule in Harvard College while maintaining his position at the herbarium. He received a bachelor of science degree, magna cum laude, in 1897. During this period, he was essentially an apprentice to Sereno Watson, then curator of the Gray Herbarium, and to B. L. Robinson, who succeeded Watson as curator in 1891. Fernald's connection with Harvard and with the Gray Herbarium was continuous throughout his professional career. In the university he was successively instructor, assistant professor, and Fisher Professor of Natural History, the chair previously occupied by the famous botanist Asa Gray. He was curator of the Gray Herbarium from 1935-1937 and director from 1937-1947.

In his early botanical research, perhaps under Robinson's influence, Fernald dealt with plant collections made by others in Mexico. But it was soon clear that fieldwork was primary to his own interests and, when he had the opportunity, he went on his own exploring expeditions. In Maine, he spent time botanizing Mount Bigelow, Mount Katahdin, and the valleys of the St. John and Aroostook rivers. Farther afield, he explored the region of the Gulf of St. Lawrence, Newfoundland, southern Labrador, Nova Scotia, and the Magdalen Islands on repeated expeditions that were carefully planned and well executed. Eventually, Fernald took for his area of botanical concentration the region often called the Gray's Manual range. This included most of North America east of the Missouri and Mississippi rivers and north of the Carolinas. "I am attempting to attain and

record as exact an understanding as possible of the natural flora of this region and the geological and geographic conditions of the past under which the plants have reached their present habitats," he explained.

Fernald worked untiringly to fulfill this goal. In later years, when the vigor required for arduous mountain climbing and the exploration of remote areas was no longer at hand, he concentrated his field efforts along the coastal plain, particularly in southeastern Virginia. His botanical efforts combined field observations with laboratory and library study of the components of the natural vegetation of eastern America. These efforts led ultimately to the publication of the eighth (centennial) edition of *Gray's Manual of Botany* in 1950, which was his crowning achievement. This was a wholly new book, quite unlike the seven earlier editions.

Fernald made several generalizations of considerable botanical and geological significance. Although it had long been accepted by glacial geologists that Pleistocene ice covered eastern and northern North America to great depths and effectively obliterated all plant and animal life from the region, he saw much evidence from his plant studies that refuted such an assumption. He found many instances where species of plants appeared to have survived through the Pleistocene and from this he reasoned that refugia of some type must have existed in areas where glaciation was supposed to have been total. His ideas and the evidence supporting them were presented in a landmark paper entitled, "Persistence of Plants in Unglaciated Areas of Boreal America" (*Mem. Amer. Acad. Arts and Sci.* 15[1925]: 239-342).

The natural disjunction of plant species between eastern and western North America became a special study at one point in his career and this was followed by a wider interest in specific segregations and identities in the flora of eastern North America and that of the Old World. He was always interested in phytogeography; some of his most notable contributions were made in this area of botany. A book that he wrote with A. C. Kinsey (*Edible Wild Plants of Eastern North America*, 1943) provided the basic information upon which several subsequent popular books on edible wild plants were based. Soon out of print, it was reissued in revised form in 1958.

By far the largest part of Fernald's published work concerned questions of the identities, accurate definition, and geographic distribution of the vascular plants of his chosen area. Early in this work he discovered that botanists of an earlier period had not been careful enough about checking and properly correlating the names in use with the specimens upon which the names were originally based. Fernald was meticulous in these matters and often turned to classical specimens, usually conserved in European herbaria, for authentic comparative materials. He was exacting in his own work, and was also highly critical of inaccurate publications by others. As an editor and particularly as editor-in-chief of the journal *Rhodora* for twenty-one years, he was in a position to monitor the botanical literature of his field; and in dozens of reviews his talents as a critic were fully utilized; they often embodied critical analyses that only a master of the field could make.

Fernald was a member of the American Academy of Arts and Sciences, the National Academy of Sciences, and the American Philosophical Society as well as many botanical scientific organizations. He was president of the New England Botanical Club (1911-1914); president of the Botanical Society of America (1942); and president of the American Society of Plant Taxonomists (1938). He was elected a Foreign Member of the Linnean Society of London; Royal Science Society, Uppsala; Société Linnéenne de Lyon; Societas Phytogeographica Sueciana; Societas pro Fauna et Flora Fennica; and Norske Videnskaps Akademi. He was a recipient of the Leidy Gold Medal of the Academy of Natural Sciences, Philadelphia (1940), the Gold Medal of the Massachusetts Horticultural Society (1944), and the Marie-Victorin Medal awarded by the Fondation Marie-Victorin for outstanding services to botany in Canada.

Fernald married Margaret Howard Grant, of Providence, R.I., on Apr. 5, 1907. They had three children: Katharine, Henry Grant, and Mary. Fernald died of a coronary thrombosis in Cambridge, Mass., and was buried in Mount Auburn Cemetery.

[The primary biographical materials relating to the professional career of M. L. Fernald are in the Gray Herbarium of Harvard Univ. These include hundreds of letters in the historical file and copies of his published works in the library. A portrait hangs with those of other curators and directors of the Gray Herbarium. A series of five articles: "Merritt Lyndon Fernald 1873-1950," by Arthur Stanley Pease; "Fernald as a Teacher," by John M. Fogg, Jr.; "Fernald as a Reviser of *Gray's Manual*," by Harley Harris Bartlett; "Fernald as a Botanist," by Reed C. Rollins; and "Fernald in the Field," by Ludlow Griscom, make up an entire issue of *Rhodora* V 53 (1951): 33-65; a portrait faces the opening page. "A Biographical Memoir of Merritt Lyndon Fernald 1873-1950," by Elmer D. Merrill, was presented to the Nat. Acad. of Sci. and published in *Biog. Memoirs*, XXVIII (1954); this includes a full bibliography.]

REED C. ROLLINS

FETTER, FRANK ALBERT (Mar. 8, 1863-Mar. 21, 1949), economist, was born in Peru, Ind., the second of three children and only son of Harry George and Ellen (Cole) Fetter. His father, a photographer, was a native of Pennsylvania; his mother, of Indiana. After graduating from the Peru high school, Fetter entered Indiana University in 1879, but left after his junior year when the illness of his father made it necessary for him to help support the family. For seven years he operated a bookstore in Peru and informally continued his education by reading many of the works he kept in stock. Fetter returned to Indiana University in 1890 and received the A.B. degree the following year. He then pursued graduate studies in political economy at Cornell University (Ph.M. 1892), at the Sorbonne and the École de Droit in Paris (1892-1893), and at the University of Halle in Germany, where he studied under Johannes Conrad and received a Ph.D. in 1894, summa cum laude. His doctoral dissertation outlined a population theory based on a critique of the Malthusian principle. Upon his return to the United States, Fetter taught economics at Cornell (1894-1895), Indiana University (1895-1898), Stanford (1898-1900), and again at Cornell (1901-1911). In 1911 he became professor of political economy at Princeton, where he remained until his retirement in 1931, serving until 1922 as chairman of the department.

Fetter's economic thought—contained in six books and more than sixty articles—was distinguished by a devotion to simplicity and a creative skepticism toward established economic doctrines. Focusing on the practical elements of modern economic problems, he sought a revision of the whole theory of economic distribution. Although in his *Principles of Economics* (1904), he accepted the traditional concept of the "economic man," motivated by a pleasure-pain psychology, he grew increasingly critical of this approach and came to stress instead the mechanics of the market. Similarly, Fetter subjected to critical reexamination the prevailing theories of wages, interest, capital, rent, and value. In his *Economic Principles* (1915)—the first volume of a revision of his earlier work—he propounded a new statement of the theory of value which adopted modern volitional psychology and eliminated Benthamite utilitarianism and hedonism. The basis of value, he argued, was a "simple act of choice and not a calculation of utility." Fetter's writings also anticipated by several decades two important later economic issues: consumerism, and the interaction between population growth and economic welfare.

Fetter's major works, however, were concerned with the monopoly problem in the United States, the problem that dominated his writings during the last quarter-century of his life. In time, his style became more akin to that of Ida Tarbell and John Kenneth Galbraith than to that of the neoclassicists of his day. He was among the first of the professional economists to recognize the basing-point system of pricing as a price conspiracy at variance with the workings of the competitive marketplace. This system was epitomized by the famous "Pittsburgh plus" policy of the United States Steel Corporation, under which the manufacturer charged users of rolled steel products the Pittsburgh base price plus the freight from Pittsburgh, even if the steel were in fact produced at plants nearer the consumer. In 1923 Fetter attacked "Pittsburgh plus" in testimony before the Federal Trade Commission, which the following year ordered U.S. Steel to abandon the practice. His numerous articles on base pricing in general and his role as adviser to the FTC (1938-1939) laid the groundwork for court and commission decisions in the late 1940's declaring the system an unlawful price-fixing arrangement.

In *The Masquerade of Monopoly* (1931), Fetter took to task both the antitrust agencies and the courts for their failure to exorcise from the economy base pricing and other flagrant excesses of monopoly. He reviewed forty years of antitrust law enforcement and concluded that while millions of farmers and small businesses were subject to laws of competition, the giant combinations reaped the rewards of monopoly with immunity. Thus there was one law of the marketplace for the small and the poor, another for the big and the rich. In his last commentary on the monopoly problem, published nearly two decades later, Fetter found no reason to change his earlier views. "In the tug of war between competition and monopoly in the United States," he concluded, " 'the free competitive system' has on the whole, I fear, lost ground" (*American Economic Review,* June 1949. p. 695).

On other matters as well Fetter extended his personal commitment far beyond that of the detached scholar. An interest in social welfare found expression as early as 1900-1901 when, on leave from Stanford, he participated in a study of low-grade housing in Chicago. While at Cornell he was president of the Social Service League of Ithaca (1904-1911) and a member of the New York State Board of Charities

(1910-1911). While at Princeton he was president of the New Jersey Conference for Social Welfare (1918-1919) and, during a year's leave of absence, manager of the National War Camp Community Service during World War I. Fetter was vitally concerned with the issue of academic freedom and tenure, and participated actively in the deliberations and proceedings of the American Association of University Professors virtually from its founding.

Fetter earned the respect of his colleagues and students as a devoted teacher-scholar. Among the honors that came to him were the presidency of the American Economic Association (1912) and degrees from Occidental College and Colgate and Indiana universities. He married Martha Whitson of Atglen, Pa., on July 16, 1896. Of their three children—Frank Whitson, Ellen Cole, and Theodore Henry—the eldest followed his father in becoming a professor of economics. Fetter died at his Princeton home of cardiovascular disease two weeks after his eighty-sixth birthday, and was buried in the Princeton Cemetery.

[Memorial by J. Douglas Brown in *Am. Economic Rev.,* Sept. 1949; "birthday note" by Stanley E. Howard and E. W. Kemmerer, *ibid.,* Mar. 1943; Joseph Dorfman, *The Economic Mind in Am. Civilization,* III, especially pp. 360–365 (1949); Donald D. Egbert and Diane M. Lee, *Princeton Portraits* (1947), pp. 162–163; *Survey,* Aug. 19, 1911, pp. 744–745; *Who Was Who in America,* II (1950); family information from Prof. Frank W. Fetter, Hanover, N.H., and from the 1880 federal census (courtesy of Ind. State Lib.). Fetter's papers, dealing mainly with the monopoly problem, are at Indiana Univ. A photograph of Fetter is in the *Am. Economic Rev.,* June 1945, facing p. 263.]

JESSE WILLIAM MARKHAM

FIELD, FRED TARBELL (Dec. 24, 1876-July 23, 1950), chief justice of the Supreme Judicial Court of Massachusetts, was born in Springfield, Vt., the older of two children and only son of Frederic Griswold Field and Anna Melanie (Tarbell) Field. His family, for three generations, had participated in state, civic, and Baptist church affairs; his father ran a bank and a general store. Fred Field went to the local schools and to Vermont Academy in Saxton's River. After a year in his father's store, he attended Brown University (B.A., 1900).

Despite some discouragement from a greatly admired uncle, Walbridge A. Field, then chief justice of the Supreme Judicial Court of Massachusetts, Field correctly discerned his natural aptitude and entered the Harvard Law School. He received the LL.B. degree in 1903, cum laude, and then spent seven years (1905-1912) in the office of three successive attorneys general of Massachusetts. An able and diligent young lawyer, he quickly acquired broad experience in governmental law and gained a reputation as a thorough legal craftsman. The civil work of the attorney general was growing in complexity and importance. State administrative law was in a formative stage. New methods of taxation were being discussed and developed. Field inevitably was involved in this activity.

In 1912 he entered private practice in Boston and soon came to be recognized as an expert in tax matters and in litigation affecting educational, religious, and charitable institutions. (See, e.g., *Trustees of Andover Theological Seminary* v. *Visitors,* 253 Mass. 256, in which in 1924 he served as master appointed by the Supreme Judicial Court.) During World War I, as a member of the legal staff of the federal Bureau of Internal Revenue, Field helped develop policies and procedures for administering the then somewhat novel tax statutes expanded to meet the heavy cost of the war. He was persuaded to remain in Washington after the armistice to organize an advisory tax board in the Treasury Department. When this task was completed late in 1919, he left government service to become a partner of two law school contemporaries in the Boston firm of Goodwin, Procter, Field, and Hoar.

In 1929 Field, with widespread approval by the bar, was appointed an associate justice of the Supreme Judicial Court, thus achieving a long-held ambition to follow in his uncle's footsteps. The appointment, directly from the bar, of the first justice in twenty-four years without prior judicial service brought to the court a relatively young judge (he was then fifty-two) with extensive knowledge in increasingly important legal fields. Upon the death of Arthur Prentice Rugg in 1938, Field was appointed chief justice by Gov. Charles F. Hurley. In that office, with its heavy administrative responsibilities, he served until his resignation in 1947, three years before his death.

His term as chief justice coincided with a period of substantial litigation arising out of the depression of the early 1930's or dealing with novel social legislation. Some cases required consideration of the impact on state concerns of broadened federal regulation of business, both in peacetime and during World War II. In all these matters Field wisely led the court in meeting the needs and challenges of the changing social and governmental climate. His opinions, found in fifty-five volumes of Massachusetts court reports, were thorough and carefully reasoned. As was said in a memorial presented to the court in 1952, once he "had completed an opinion there was little else that could be said with profit on the point."

A devout Baptist layman, Field served as president of the American Baptist Foreign Mission Society in 1923 and 1924. He was also trustee, and for a time chairman of the board, of Newton Theological Institution. He received honorary degrees from Amherst, Boston University, Dartmouth, the University of Vermont, and Williams. Field married Gertrude Alice Montague, daughter of a Baptist clergyman, on Oct. 11, 1922. They had one child, Ann Montague. Field made his home in Newton, Mass., and it was there that he died of a cerebral hemorrhage and was buried.

[Memorials presented to the Supreme Judicial Court on Nov. 20, 1952, 329 Mass. 773; a memorial presented to the Curtis Club, Boston, Oct. 10, 1950; memoir in Am. Antiquarian Soc., *Proc.,* Oct. 18, 1950; *Who Was Who in America,* III (1960); *Nat. Cyc. Am. Biog.,* XXXVIII, 96–97; death record, Mass. Registrar of Vital Statistics.]

R. AMMI CUTTER

FIELDS, WILLIAM CLAUDE (Jan. 29, 1880–Dec. 25, 1946), stage and motion picture comedian, was born William Claude Dukenfield in Philadelphia, Pa., the first child among the three sons and two daughters of James C. Dukenfield and Kate (Felton) Dukenfield. His father, who had come to the United States from London, England, worked as a costermonger, hawking fruit and vegetables from a horse-drawn wagon. After four years of schooling, Claude went to work with his father. But they quarreled violently, and at the age of eleven the boy ran away from home. He lived for a time above a blacksmith shop and later stayed briefly with his maternal grandmother, working at odd jobs in a pool hall, on an ice wagon, in a department store, and as a newsboy.

In 1894, Fields began his career as a carnival juggler. From an early age he had been fascinated by the art of juggling, and he devoted hours of concentrated practice to perfecting his skills. By his teens, he had become an expert juggler with a comic routine built around the artful fumble. Dressed as a bewhiskered tramp, and with W. C. Fields as his stage name, he worked his way up from touring circus companies to a featured performer on the American vaudeville stage before he was twenty. From 1901 to the outbreak of World War I he made several European and world tours with his juggling act and with new comic routines as a billiards player and as a golfer—routines that he recorded in his first silent movie, *Pool Sharks* (1915), and his first sound film, *The Golf Specialist* (1930). Reconciled with his family, he took his father to England on one such tour.

Fields joined the Ziegfeld *Follies* in 1915 and played in the famed variety show through 1921. He spent the 1922 season in a similar show, George White's *Scandals*. The next year he took a starring role in the Broadway musical comedy *Poppy*, in a part that was to have a decisive influence on his later career. Fields played Eustace McGargle, an old-time country-fair performer, a juggler, a mountebank peddler of nostrums, a gambling trickster adept at the shell game and at cards. This role became Fields's comic persona, both as a performer and in private life—the confidence man in a top hat, muttering caustic asides, hostile not only to pretension and sentiment but to most of society, including (or especially) children and dogs. He repeated the role of Eustace McGargle in his first important silent movie performance in *Sally of the Sawdust* (1925), directed by D. W. Griffith, and in a sound version of *Poppy* (1936); he played similar characters in such films as *Tillie and Gus* (1933), *The Old-Fashioned Way* (1934), and *You Can't Cheat an Honest Man* (1939).

Except for his appearances in Earl Carroll's *Vanities* in 1928 and on a weekly radio program with the ventriloquist Edgar Bergen in the late 1930's, Fields devoted his career, after *Sally of the Sawdust,* to motion pictures. Altogether, Fields appeared in at least twelve silent and twenty-nine sound films between 1915 and 1944. He was one of the few silent motion picture comedians successfully to make the transition to sound comedy. Several other aspects of his career were also unusual. While his vaudeville and stage routines had been built on sight gags and were largely silent, his most famous movie performances relied almost exclusively on verbal humor. And although humor is closely tied to aggression, Fields's comic persona was far more openly and belligerently aggressive than that of other movie comedians. Moreover, his animus was rarely rooted in social or personal conflicts and often appeared to stem solely from malice.

Yet in the two films that are generally considered Fields's most effective contributions to the genre of motion picture comedy, *It's a Gift* (1934) and *The Bank Dick* (1940), Fields played a rather different role. In these he was the oppressed family man, dominated by a shrewish wife and selfish, mean-spirited children. His guile and cantankerous wit were thus rooted in a social context and served a purpose with which audiences could more easily identify. These two films and a third Fields domestic comedy, *The Man on the Flying Trapeze* (1935), are among the most pointed satires on family life ever made in Hollywood. He also portrayed a memorable Micawber in George Cukor's *David Copperfield* (1935).

Fields was reputed to be as misanthropic in private life as he was on the screen. His most famous personal foible was his suspicion of banks. With an income of more than $125,000 per motion picture at the height of his career, Fields was said to carry huge sums of cash on his person, and he reportedly opened scores of bank accounts around the country under various false names. His reputation as a drunk was probably exaggerated, but his capacities as a drinker were considerable. During his Hollywood years, according to Robert L. Taylor, he began drinking martinis before breakfast and consumed two quarts of gin a day.

Fields married Harriet Veronica Hughes on Apr. 8, 1900. They had one child, a son, William Claude Fields, Jr. They separated when Fields was still playing vaudeville, although they were still legally married at the time of Fields's death. Fields died of cirrhosis of the liver in a Pasadena, Calif., sanitarium and was buried in Forest Lawn Memorial Park, Glendale, Calif.

[The most complete, but not always accurate, account of Fields's life is Robert L. Taylor's anecdotal biography *W. C. Fields: His Follies and Fortunes* (1949). A more favorable view of the comedian's family relations is presented in *W. C. Fields by Himself* (1973), a collection of letters, notes, cartoons, and vaudeville sketches by Fields, compiled and annotated by a grandson, Ronald J. Fields. William K. Everson has written a useful critical study of Fields's films, *The Art of W. C. Fields* (1967). Donald Deschner, *The Films of W. C. Fields* (1966), contains several early photographs as well as stills, credits, and cast lists from his motion pictures and excerpts from reviews. Some of Fields's humorous sayings were gathered in *Drat!,* ed. Richard J. Anobile (1968). Fields's voice may be heard on several phonograph records made from radio programs and movie soundtracks. Many of his films are available on 16mm.]
ROBERT SKLAR

FILLMORE, CHARLES (Aug. 22, 1854–July 5, 1948), cofounder with his wife of the Unity School of Christianity, was born on an Indian Reservation near St. Cloud, Minn., where his father traded with the Chippewas. He was the older of two sons of Henry Gleason Fillmore, a native of Buffalo, N.Y., and Mary Georgeanna (Stone) Fillmore, from Nova Scotia. He was christened Charles Sherlock but never used his middle name. In the remote settlement where he grew up, Charles experienced more than the usual hardships of privation and limited schooling. When he was two years old, he was kidnapped by a band of marauding Sioux but was returned unharmed. When Charles was seven, his father left the family and moved to land ten miles north of their cabin; his mother provided for the children by taking up dressmaking. Five years after his father left, his younger brother ran away from home. Soon after that, Charles was left crippled in one hip as a result of a skating accident; the growth of the leg was stunted by rheumatism and badly cared for by doctors, but despite this handicap Charles helped support his mother. It was at about this time that he met Caroline Taylor, the wife of an army officer, who taught him literature, grammar, and writing.

Fillmore left home at nineteen for Oklahoma Territory. In the next few years he was successively a freight clerk, muleteer, assayer, and real estate developer in Colorado and Texas. As soon as he was able, he made arrangements for his mother to join him in Denison, Tex.; he had always been close to her and she remained with him throughout her later years. In Denison he met Myrtle Page, a schoolteacher nine years his senior, who, like him, had been searching for an alternative to the Protestant orthodoxy of the time. Born Aug. 6, 1845, in Pagetown, Ohio, the youngest of nine children of Mark Page and Lucy (Wheeler) Page, she had grown up in a Methodist household and had attended Oberlin College for a year before embarking on a teaching career. She and Fillmore were married in Clinton, Mo., on Mar. 29, 1881. They had three sons: Lowell Page, Waldo Rickert, and Royal.

Returning to Colorado, Fillmore turned to the field of real estate, which remained an abiding interest for the rest of his life; first in Gunnison and then in Pueblo, his fortunes improved, but the Pueblo boom collapsed in 1884. The Fillmores moved to Kansas City, Mo., to experience another cycle of prosperity and defeat. At the same time Myrtle Fillmore, whose tubercular condition had stabilized in the dry air of Colorado, found her health worsening in Kansas City and began seeking medical help, but to no avail. Later reminiscences would suggest that Fillmore, too, suffered severe ill health at this time, but it is clear that it was his wife who took the lead in studying methods of mental healing similar to those made famous by Mary Baker Eddy. Their most important teacher was Emma Curtis Hopkins of Chicago, who had led a breakaway movement from Mrs. Eddy's Christian Science. Myrtle Fillmore, her health greatly improved,

felt called upon to teach the new methods herself. Her husband, at first reluctant to credit this type of cure, himself benefited from mental healing—his withered leg, he claimed, began growing and strengthening miraculously. Together, in 1888-1889, the Fillmores made the decision that shaped the rest of their lives: they would devote themselves to spreading a practical Christianity able to overcome physical, mental, and financial ills alike.

The Fillmores' first venture was the publication of the magazine *Modern Thought* (later renamed *Unity*), launched in April 1889. In 1890 they organized the Society of Silent Unity, offering prayers for anyone who wrote in for them. These practical talents, more than anything else, lay at the heart of the Fillmores' success. They did not aim at founding a new denomination but at building a "school" to teach the unity of truth underlying all denominations. Nevertheless, success invited some organizational separation, and eventually there were to be separate Unity churches, hundreds of them, mostly in the Middle West and southern California, many served by women ministers. The movement's basic textbook, *Lessons in Truth,* was written by a woman, Dr. H. Emilie Cady, a homeopathic physician from New York City. By its sixtieth anniversary, the Unity School of Christianity claimed to have reached one million homes. Its vast operations were sustained by freewill offerings.

Shortly after World War I, Fillmore once more embarked upon land development, this time on behalf of Unity. At Lee's Summit, Mo., near Kansas City, he began building facilities for the movement's magazine and book publishing, for its prayer society, for the training of teachers and ministers, for radio broadcasting, and for its summer schools and year-round conferences. Low-cost houses were erected for Unity helpers and employees. The Fillmores themselves moved there and purchased more land, ultimately a total of 1,300 acres. Final transfer of all Unity operations to Unity Farm, as the development was named, was completed in 1949.

Fillmore wrote ten books, all of which explained practical Christianity. If at first this was presented as "modern" thought (until 1922 Unity was affiliated with the International New Thought Alliance), Fillmore soon turned, in a classic tropism of popular Protestantism, to proving that Unity was the true, scriptural Christianity. With the exception of the doctrines of reincarnation and the regeneration of the body, there was little in the Fillmores' teachings that was unacceptable to mainstream Protestants. Fillmore retained the emphasis upon personal health that was Mrs. Eddy's chief endowment to the turn-of-century mind-cure movement. By 1890, however, mind-cure writers were clearly responding to demands of a less existential, and more particularly cultural, nature. Fillmore took a special interest in demonstrating that Christian principles were conducive to business success (Braden, *Spirits*, p. 248). In his last book, *Prosperity* (1936), Fillmore explained the Great Depression, inevitably, as a result of negative thinking. "Increase," he wrote, comes not through "personal efforts" but "by the operation of a universal law, and our part is to keep that law." If men held faith together, booms need not collapse.

Fillmore's partnership with his wife ended upon her death at Unity Farm in 1931, at the age of eighty-six. This had been a partnership not only of man and wife but also of cofounders, coexecutives, coteachers, and leaders in a public life. In his personal readiness for equality, Fillmore displayed elements of that new attitude growing in certain late nineteenth-century Protestant circles, not of feminism but of greater uniformity between the sexes, an attribute Unity clearly expressed in its special use of women in its offices and ministry. Fillmore remarried on Dec. 31, 1933; he published one of his last books jointly with his second wife, Cora G. (Dedrick) Fillmore. By then his two surviving sons (Royal had died in 1923) had taken over much of the administration of the Unity operations. Fillmore died at his home at Unity Farm in 1948, not quite ninety-four years old. He had once wondered whether death itself, properly understood in light of universal plenty, might yield to thought.

[The Unity School has published versions of its history: James D. Freeman, *The Story of Unity* (1954); Dana Gatlin, ed., *Unity's Fifty Golden Years* (1939); James Decker, ed., *Unity's Seventy Years of Faith and Works* (1959). For biographical data on Fillmore, see *Nat. Cyc. Am. Biog.*, Current Vol. B, pp. 58–59; *Who Was Who in Am.*, III (1960); and on Myrtle Fillmore, Charles S. Braden, in *Notable Am. Women, 1607–1950*, I, 617–619. See also Marcus Bach, *They Have Found a Faith* (1946); Charles S. Braden, *These Also Believe* (1949) and *Spirits in Rebellion* (1963); and Donald Meyer, *The Positive Thinkers* (1965).]

DONALD MEYER

FISHER, IRVING (Feb. 27, 1867-Apr. 29, 1947), economist, was born in Saugerties, N.Y., the third of four children of George Whitefield Fisher and Ella (Wescott) Fisher. His father,

a Congregational minister, was a descendant of William Fisher, who settled near Troy, N.Y., in 1766 and who is believed to have come from a family of Palatinate Germans who migrated to Ireland in the sixteenth century and to New England in the eighteenth century. The Wescott family arrived in Connecticut about 1636. The two older children of George and Ella Fisher died young so that Irving grew up as the older child in the family. Shortly after his birth, the family moved to Peace Dale, R.I., where his father served as pastor of the Congregational church from 1868 to 1881. In the latter year the family moved to New Haven for a short stay and then to St. Louis. When his father died, in July 1884, Irving Fisher had just graduated from Smith Academy in St. Louis. The following September he entered Yale, where he excelled in mathematics, was elected to Phi Beta Kappa, and was chosen valedictorian of the class of 1888. Almost immediately, he received a grant for graduate study at Yale.

The two people who influenced him most in graduate school were Josiah Willard Gibbs, the theoretical physicist, and William Graham Sumner, the economist and sociologist. Academically, Fisher found himself drawn in two directions: to the beauty of mathematics on the one hand and to the practical significance of economics and social science on the other. He aspired to achieve distinction in both areas, and he succeeded. At the suggestion of Sumner, he devoted himself to the study of mathematical economics, and began teaching mathematics at Yale while still in graduate school. In 1891 he received the Ph.D. with a dissertation entitled "Mathematical Investigations in the Theory of Value and Prices." While his work had been anticipated by others, including Leon Walras and Francis Edgeworth, Fisher developed his ideas without knowledge of their work and his dissertation was recognized as a significant step in the development of the theory of utility and consumer choice. Fisher insisted that the theory of utility should be independent of the psychological and ethical hedonism to which several of his predecessors had tied it. At a later period he turned to attempts at empirical measurement of marginal utility, a problem that continues to defy solution.

After taking his doctoral degree, Fisher continued on the faculty at Yale. On June 24, 1893, he married Margaret Hazard, daughter of a well-to-do family of Peace Dale, R.I.; they had three children: Margaret, Caroline, and Irving Norton. The Fishers spent the year after their wedding abroad, where he studied in Berlin and Paris. During this stay he met many English and European economists, including such leaders in mathematical economics as Walras, Edgeworth, and Vilfredo Pareto.

Returning to Yale, Fisher continued his teaching in mathematics until 1895, when he transferred to the department of political economy. His economic studies in the period from 1895 to 1898 clearly foreshadowed the main outlines of his professional economic career. His doctoral dissertation was followed by several publications in mathematics related to his earlier interests and to his initial teaching responsibilities. It was, however, during these years that he began his investigations of monetary problems, capital and interest, and economic statistics, the themes that dominated his work in scientific economics and that constituted his principal contributions. In these years he clearly demonstrated his two interests: to develop the basic theory of his subject and to serve as a critic and advisor on economic policy. He was critical of scholarship for scholarship's sake and as he said much later, in a talk to the economics department at Harvard on the occasion of his seventy-fifth birthday, "I realize well that many pure studies like those of Gibbs are of inestimable practical importance and all the more because such students have not tried to apply them . . . but in general I think that education should stress not so much pure scholarship as harnessing up our universities for the world" (memorandum in the Irving Fisher Collect. at the Yale Sterling Memorial Lib).

Unfortunately in 1898 he was stricken with tuberculosis and forced to take three years' leave from Yale to restore his health at Saranac, N.Y., Colorado Springs, and Santa Barbara, Calif. When he returned to Yale, he resumed his work in economics with renewed vigor. A series of major publications followed, including *The Nature of Capital and Interest* (1906), *The Rate of Interest* (1907), *Elements of Economic Science* (1910), *The Purchasing Power of Money* (1911), *Stabilizing the Dollar* (1920), *The Making of Index Numbers* (1922), *The Theory of Interest* (1930), *Booms and Depressions* (1932), *Stable Money: A History of the Movement* (1934), and *100% Money* (1935). After 1920 his energies were increasingly devoted to the problem of monetary stability, a dominant theme of general economic discussion in the 1920's and a cause in the pursuit of which Fisher is said to have spent over $100,000 of his own resources.

The theory of income, capital, and interest occupied Fisher from an early period. While much of his work had been anticipated by others, he clarified the issues and emphasized the relations between the concepts themselves and their relation to the theory of money. He had considerable influence in reasserting the primacy of income as the central concept of economics and in pointing out that capital is simply the discounted value of future income streams. Analysis of the rate of discount led Fisher inevitably to the theory of interest. He made a distinction between the "normal" or money rate of interest and the "real" rate or rate measured in terms of goods. If the monetary standard were stable, he noted, the two rates would be the same, and if the fluctuations of the value were perfectly foreseen, the money rate and the real rate would diverge sufficiently to compensate for anticipated appreciation or depreciation of the currency. Since foresight is not perfect, "when prices are rising, the rate of interest tends to be high but not so high as it should be to compensate for the rise; and when prices are falling, the rate of interest tends to be low, but not so low as it should be to compensate for the fall" (*Theory of Interest,* p. 43). In conditions of stable prices the rate of interest is determined by two principal factors: impatience or the rate of time preference on the one hand, and investment opportunity or the rate of return over cost on the other. "The rate of interest is the mouthpiece at once of impatience to spend income without delay and of opportunity to increase income by delay" (*Theory of Interest,* p. 495). Fisher argued that society's investment opportunities are subject to change due chiefly to three circumstances: the increase or decrease in resources, the discovery of new resources or means of developing old ones, and change in political conditions. Time preferences, he believed, depend on six principal factors: the degree of foresight, the extent of self-control, habit, the prospective length and certainty of life, the love for offspring and regard for posterity, and fashion.

The contributions of Fisher's studies of money lie not in his theoretical innovations but rather in his effort at statistical verification and his advocacy of proposals for monetary stabilization. He formulated the equation of exchange $(MV + M'V' = PQ)$ in the form that became common to generations of students. At a time when the quantity theory of money was under widespread attack, Fisher espoused the theory in the sense that "the level of prices varies indirectly with the quantity of money in circulation, provided the velocity of circulation of that money and the volume of trade which it is obliged to perform are not changed" (*Purchasing Power of Money*, p. 14). But Fisher recognized that historically the price level and quantity of money do not in fact vary in direct proportion since velocity and the volume of trade do in fact change in periods of "transition." "The strictly proportional effect on prices of an increase in *M* is only the *normal* or *ultimate* effect after transition periods are over" (*Purchasing Power of Money*, p. 159).

Fisher's concern with the purchasing power of money led him to extensive studies of the best index number for measuring price changes. He recognized that the appropriate index number depends upon the purpose for which it is used. The "best" index for a standard of deferred payment, he concluded, is one which is based on the prices of "all goods *exchanged* during a given period" (*Purchasing Power of Money*, p. 233). Fisher also undertook extensive studies of the velocity of money, studies that were still in process at the time of his death (Sasuly, "Irving Fisher and Social Science," *Econometrica*).

In his discussion of index numbers, Fisher recognized that during the process of inflation or deflation there is a considerable dispersion of price change. He looked upon the index number as designed to measure essentially the center of gravity of this dispersion. In his *The Making of Index Numbers* (1922) he set up two criteria for an ideal number: first, the test of time reversal, i.e., that the percentage of change between two years should be the same no matter which year is used as the base; and second, the test of factor reversal, i.e., that the index of prices multiplied by the index of quantity should be equal to the change in the value during the time period. On this basis he determined that the geometric means of the Étienne Laspeyres and Hermann Paasche indexes were the best approximation to his ideal. There has been considerable criticism of this thesis (Ruggles in Fellner, *Ten Economic Studies*, p. 171, et seq.).

The practical significance of Fisher's work on the purchasing power of money lay in his proposals for stabilizing the value of the dollar. Recognizing the hold of the gold standard on people's imagination and the dangers of a paper currency, he advocated the "compensated dollar," a standard by which the gold content of the dollar would be varied inversely with changes in the index of deferred payments. Moreover, in order to avoid monetary instability resulting from the creation and destruction

of bank deposits, he advocated a system of 100 percent money by which a currency commission would purchase enough assets from every commercial bank in return for the commission's notes so that each bank would have a 100 percent reserve in cash or notes behind its checking deposits.

Fisher's interest in the quantification of economics and the development of various econometric models led him to extensive work in statistics. His contributions in this respect have been evaluated by Max Sasuly in the article cited earlier. Besides his work on index numbers and velocity, they include a critical appraisal of United States vital statistics, development of the concept of the distributed lag, and work on the problem of effective graduation of statistical series.

Fisher had a great gift for exposition of even the most technical matters, taking great pains to explain his economic propositions verbally with appropriate analogies and usually relegating his mathematical formulations to an appendix. His doctoral dissertation on value and prices was a distinctive contribution on a central problem of economic theory that remains of concern to contemporary economists. His work on income, capital, and interest, together with his work on the purchasing power of money, provided the components of a model of the economic system which, had it been expanded in detail, might have replaced the neoclassical model. But Fisher was in many ways ahead of his time and although his work has had an important influence on his successors, no Fisherian "school of economics" developed. He stood out among his contemporaries as uniquely prophetic of the methods that have become dominant among contemporary economists. In his support for the mathematical formulation of economic proportions and of empirical verification by quantitative means, he stood almost alone among his contemporaries in economics in the United States.

Fisher's influence at Yale, while substantial in his early years, was less than might have been expected. His interest in mathematical economics and econometrics brought a new dimension to economics in the United States, and he might have been expected to develop at Yale a leading center for the study of the fundamentals of economic science. But neither Yale nor the profession were ready. Although he tried to promote the establishment of a society for mathematical and statistical research in economics as early as 1912, these efforts did not bear fruit until the establishment of the

Econometric Society in 1930 with Fisher as its first president. In cooperation with Ragnar Frisch and Charles F. Roos, he persuaded Alfred Cowles to support the Cowles Commission for Research in Economics at Colorado Springs in 1932. The commission, which moved to Chicago in 1939 and to Yale in 1955, where it was renamed the Cowles Foundation, has been a major leader in econometric research in succeeding years.

While Fisher did not succeed in making Yale a center of econometrics during his lifetime, he did play a major role in college affairs until World War I. From 1896 to 1911 he served as editor of the *Yale Review,* which was then a major journal in the United States devoted to the social sciences. After World War I, his efforts at the university were limited generally to a half-course for graduate students on some topic closely related to his research. His energies were increasingly directed to various external activities, including his crusades for health, prohibition, and monetary reform and to his various business ventures. His reputation as an economist in the Yale community was overshadowed by these interests, and when in the Great Depression his confidence in the "new economic era" of the 1920's was shaken and he lost a major fortune, his reputation among his colleagues suffered. Neither at Yale nor in the profession at large was the significance of his contributions to the development of economics fully appreciated during his lifetime.

Fisher's continuing interest in problems of health began with his attack of tuberculosis in 1898. This led to an intensive study of problems of health and a crusade to improve the health not only of his family and his friends but also of the country and the world at large. He experimented with various diets and programs of exercise. With Harold Ley, he founded the Life Extension Institute to promote sane living and periodic physical examinations, and in collaboration with Dr. Eugene Lyman Fisk he wrote a book, *How To Live* (1915), which, running to twenty-one editions, became a standard text on hygiene in many schools and colleges. He became active in the temperance movement and wrote extensively in support of the country's "noble experiment" with prohibition.

Fisher's interest in peace went back to his days as a graduate student when he read a paper on the need for a league of nations. Upon the outbreak of World War I in 1914, with Hamilton Holt and others, he advocated the idea of an international organization to promote peace, which was embodied in Woodrow Wilson's proposal for the League of Nations, and well into the 1920's Fisher continued to urge the participation of the United States in the league (see his *League or War,* 1923, and *America's Interest in World Peace,* 1924).

Fisher had a strong penchant for the invention of mechanical gadgets. Perhaps the most famous was the hydrostatic mechanism he devised to illustrate the equilibrium principles of an exchange economy. During his early illness he designed a tent for tubercular convalescents. His inventions also included a sundial, a three-legged folding seat, an icosahedral world map to reduce distortion on a flat surface, and a visible card-index system. The latter invention was the basis of a company established in 1913, which in 1925 was merged with Remington Rand.

Fisher's wide interests led him to be associated with many organizations. He served as president of the American Economic Association (1918), the Econometric Society (1931-1933), the American Statistical Association (1932), the National Institute of Social Science (1917), the American Association for Labor Legislation (1915-1917), the Eugenic Research Association (1920), and the Pro-League Independents. He was secretary of the New Haven County Anti-Tuberculosis Association (1904-1914). In addition, he was a member of the American Association for the Advancement of Science, Royal Economic Society, Royal Statistic Society, the American Academy of Political and Social Science, Sigma Psi, American Philosophical Society, the American Ethnographical Society, International Free Trade Association, New England Free Trade League, National Association for Study and Prevention of Tuberculosis, American Association for Study and Prevention of Infant Mortality, National Consumers League, and League of Nations Association.

The day after a testimonial dinner on the occasion of his eightieth birthday held at the Yale Club in New York City, Fisher entered Gotham Hospital in New York suffering from cancer. He died two months later on Apr. 29, 1947, and was buried in Evergreen Cemetery in New Haven.

Irving Fisher was, in the opinion of many, the leading economic theorist in the United States during the first half of the twentieth century. Although his contributions to economic theory and to the development of econometrics ensure him a preeminent position among contemporary economists, he was a versatile man. In his day he was equally well-known as social philosopher, teacher, inventor, businessman, and passionate crusader for many social causes.

[I am indebted to Fisher's son, Irving Norton Fisher, for an intimate personal biography and for indexing and making available many private letters and unpublished documents; see *My Father: Irving Fisher* (1956). A rich collection of letters, MSS, and memorabilia available in the Sterling Memorial Lib. is described by I. N. Fisher, "The Irving Fisher Collection," *Yale Univ. Lib. Gazette* 36 (1961): 45–56. An exhaustive index of materials by I. N. Fisher is *A Bibliog. of the Writings of Irving Fisher* (Yale Univ. Lib. 1961; Suppl., 1972). This bibliography includes a brief chronology of Fisher's life and a list of all his known published works and manuscripts, reviews of his publications, press reports of speeches and interviews, obituaries, and memorials.
Among the more significant assessments of Fisher's position as an economist are: Paul H. Douglas, "Memorial to Irving Fisher," *Am. Economic Rev.* 37 (1947): 661–663; Ragnar Frisch, "Irving Fisher at Eighty," *Econometrica* 15 (1947): 71–73; Max Sasuly, "Irving Fisher and Social Science," *Econometrica* 15 (1947): 255–278; Joseph A. Schumpeter, "Irving Fisher's Econometrics," *Econometrica* 16 (1948): 219–231; Ray B. Westerfield, "Memorial to Irving Fisher," *Am. Economic Rev.* 37 (1947): 656–661. See also William Fellner, et al., *Ten Economic Studies in the Tradition of Irving Fisher* (1967).
For photographs of Fisher see I. N. Fisher, *My Father: Irving Fisher,* William Fellner, *ibid.,* and A. D. Gayer, ed., *The Lessons of Monetary Experience* (1937).
The principal publications in economics by Irving Fisher not cited earlier are "Mathematical Investigations in the Theory of Value and Prices," *Trans.* of the Connecticut Academy, July 1892, pp. 1–124, reprinted by Yale Univ. Press (1925); "Appreciation and Interest," *Publications* of the Am. Economic Assoc., Aug. 1896, pp. 331–442; *Elementary Principles of Economics* (1912). Publications illustrative of Fisher's interest in health include *Report on National Vitality, Its Wastes and Conservation,* Sen. Doc. No. 676, 60 Cong., 2 Sess., vol. 3, July 1909; and *Prohibition at Its Worst* (1926). Fisher's interest in peace and the League of Nations is reflected in the publications noted in the biography.]

JOHN PERRY MILLER

FISHER, WILLIAM ARMS (Apr. 27, 1861-Dec. 18, 1948), composer, music editor, and publisher, was born in San Francisco, Calif., the oldest of three children and only son of Luther Paine Fisher and Katharine Bruyn (Arms) Fisher. Both parents were descended from colonial Massachusetts families; they were natives, respectively, of Scotland, Conn., and Kingston, N.Y. Luther P. Fisher, who had come to San Francisco in the gold rush year of 1849, was for half a century the owner of a successful advertising agency. Young Fisher attended public and private schools in Oakland, where the family made its home, and began musical studies there under John P. Morgan. Moving east in 1890, he studied harmony with Horatio Parker in New York City and singing with William Shakespeare in London.
While teaching at the National Conservatory of Music in New York, then recently established by Jeannette M. Thurber, Fisher became a student and close friend of Antonín Dvořák, the noted Bohemian composer, who was director of the conservatory from 1892 to 1895. The young man was a guest of Dvořák at the first performance (Dec. 15, 1893) in Carnegie Hall of the symphony *From the New World.* He later wrote words to the slow movement of that work, and the song, published under the title "Goin' Home," achieved great popularity, many persons believing, erroneously, that it was a Negro spiritual. Fisher wrote popular arrangements of other noted melodies, including "Swing Low, Sweet Chariot," "Deep River," "Would I Were the Tender Appleblossom," "Steal Away," and "Passing By," all of which sold thousands of copies. Over the years he also composed about seventy-five part-songs and anthems, and many solo songs to sacred texts. Fisher's songs were solidly crafted and inclined to fullness of texture, reflecting the continuing Mendelssohnian tradition as influenced by Dvořák and Dudley Buck. The lack of simple, straightforward accompaniments or of easily conveyed melody somewhat limited their popularity. Written in a commendable pattern of their day, they were not trivial; but they did not outlast their time.

It was as an editor that Fisher exerted his greatest influence on American music. In 1897, after two years of teaching music in Boston, he became director of publications and editor for the Oliver Ditson Company, the largest music publisher and dealer in the United States. Hired to improve the company's output, Fisher eliminated outdated publications and began to produce a series of educational works including the Music Student's Library (begun 1897, numbering more than forty textbooks), the Musician's Library (1903, nearly 100 volumes), and the Music Student's Piano Course (1918, twenty books). He also edited *Sixty Irish Songs* (1915) and a volume of Negro spirituals. In a day when nearly every middle-class home had a piano and every neighborhood a music teacher, when churches were prospering and were maintaining large choirs and highly paid soloists, and when anthems and oratorios sung by local choral societies were often a mainstay in the musical life of the community, American music publishers enjoyed a strong market, and many began offering editions previously obtainable only from Europe. Boston firms—including those of C. C. Birchard, B. F. Wood, E. C. Schirmer, and Arthur P. Schmidt—then led the field, and Fisher was one of the most discerning of their editors. While the family of Oliver Ditson remained nominally in charge of the

Ditson company's far-flung enterprises (there were at various times branches in New York, Chicago, Cincinnati, and Philadelphia), the editorship of William A. Fisher was at the core of the firm's success. Fisher later (1926-1937) became vice-president, but by this time the golden age of music publishing had passed, and in 1931 the Ditson assets were sold to the Theodore Presser Company of Philadelphia.

Fisher claimed no authority as a musicologist (a term not widely used in that day), but his scholarship is proven by the orderly, continuous flow of accurate catalogues issued by the Ditson firm. His books, including *Notes on Music in Old Boston* (1918), an enlarged edition titled *One Hundred and Fifty Years of Music Publishing in the United States, 1783-1933* (1934), and *Music Festivals in the United States* (1934), were carefully researched and engagingly written and illustrated. In person Fisher was tall, slight of build, and quiet of manner, quick to support musical causes while eschewing personal leadership. He did, however, serve as president of the Music Teachers National Association and of the Music Publishers Association of America. On Feb. 14, 1922, at the age of sixty, Fisher married Mrs. Emma (Roderick) Hinkle of Waterloo, Iowa. They had no children. Mrs. Fisher, who survived her husband, was active in bringing professional musicians into contact with amateur talents, often through settlement schools. Although his wife was the daughter of a Methodist clergyman, Fisher was a Unitarian. He died of arteriosclerotic heart disease at his home in Brookline, Mass., at the age of eighty-seven and was cremated at Mount Auburn Cemetery in Cambridge.

[Fisher's concern for the history of music in America led him to undertake a systematic examination of early American newspapers from the Revolutionary period onward for musical data. The resulting notes are now in the Special Collect. of the Mugar Lib., Boston Univ. Besides his own writings, printed source material on Fisher is slight. But see John Tasker Howard, *Our Am. Music*, rev. ed. (1946); Am. Soc. of Composers, Authors, and Publishers, *Biog. Dict.*, 3rd ed. (1966); *Nat. Cyc. Am. Biog.*, XXXIX, 323-324; obituaries in *Etude*, Mar. 1949, *Musical America*, Jan. 1, 1949, *N.Y. Times*, Dec. 20, 1948, and *Boston Globe*, Dec. 20, 1948; with reference to Fisher's father, see Philip A. Fisher, *The Fisher Genealogy*, pp. 232-233 (1898). Death record from Mass. Registrar of Vital Statistics.]

H. EARLE JOHNSON

FITZGERALD, JOHN FRANCIS (Feb. 11, 1863-Oct. 2, 1950), politician and newspaper publisher, was born in a tenement near the Old North Church in Boston, Mass., the third son and third of eleven children of Thomas Fitzgerald and Rose Mary (Murray) Fitzgerald. His parents had left County Wexford, Ireland, during the potato famine of the 1840's and settled in Boston, where his father operated a grocery and liquor store. John was one of the first Irish Catholics to attend the Boston Latin School, where he captained the baseball and football teams, edited the school newspaper, and achieved high grades. Fitzgerald attended Harvard Medical School for one year, but dropped out to support his family when his father died, vowing "we'll never break up." He worked in the Boston customhouse, started an insurance and investment business, and plunged into politics. On Sept. 18, 1889, he married Mary Josephine "Josie" Hannon, a union which lasted sixty-one years and produced six children—Rose, Thomas, Agnes, John F., Jr., Eunice, and Frederick. Rose later married Joseph P. Kennedy, financier and ambassador to Great Britain; their children included President John Fitzgerald Kennedy and senators Robert F. and Edward M. Kennedy.

Fitzgerald was a short man but was handsome, dapper, immaculately dressed, and vigorously athletic. He was an avid reader, with a great capacity to retain details, and an eloquent speaker, able to produce about 200 words per minute of "Fitzblarney." He was so loquacious that a newspaper correspondent once penned a poem which began, "Honey Fitz can talk you blind on any subject you can find." He also possessed a fine singing voice and his rendition of "Sweet Adeline" became his political theme song and the unofficial anthem of his campaign to repeal prohibition, although he was a nondrinker. His voice and his "instinctive ability to dazzle a crowd with consummate Irish charm" earned him the nickname "Honey Fitz," and made him one of the most colorful and popular politicians in Boston history. Like many Irish Catholics of his day, he was determined to overcome prejudice and discrimination and to succeed in a Yankee Protestant city by "working harder than anyone else." He early adopted the slogan, "What I undertake, I do. What I want, I get." When asked by a Yankee opponent what right Jews and Italians had to this country, Fitzgerald snapped, "As much right as your father or mine. It was only a difference of a few ships."

Beginning as a city councilman in 1892, Fitzgerald became a state senator in 1893, leading the Boston Irish forces, defending the rights of immigrants and laborers, and chairing the committees on liquor and election laws. From 1895 to 1901 he served as congressman from the eleventh district; in his first session he was both the only Democrat and the only Catholic from New England in the House of Representatives. He helped persuade President Grover Cleveland to veto the literacy test for immigrants in 1897, defended civil rights legislation for Southern Blacks, and attacked the meat industry for shipping "embalmed beef" to feed troops during the Spanish-American War. Retiring from Congress, he bought a weekly newspaper, *The Republic,* which provided him with a substantial income and a public forum. From his base in the "dear Old North End," the "Napoleon of Ward Six" emerged as one of the powerful ward bosses who so dominated Boston Democratic politics that they were often referred to as the "mayor-makers." Shifting alliances in bewildering combinations, they even backed reformers and Republicans when it was politically advantageous. In December 1905 he was elected mayor, defeating the candidate of the Good Government Association, a Yankee reform group derisively referred to by the ward bosses as the "goo-goos." As chief executive, Fitzgerald backed organized labor and expanded urban services to the poor, but tolerated vice, circumvented civil service regulations, and tried to build a citywide political machine through patronage and the awarding of contracts. When the Good Government Association called his administration the most corrupt in Boston history and demanded an investigation, Fitzgerald appointed his own Finance Commission which included several association members. The commission produced a four-volume report which proposed more efficient and economical administration, reduction in urban services and the public payroll, nonpartisan elections, and the strengthening of the mayor against the city council, bailiwick of the ward bosses. Ironically, Fitzgerald became the first mayor elected to a four-year term under the new reform charter in 1910, defeating the Good Government Association's candidate by a mere 1,402 votes, despite a vitriolic campaign against "Fitzgeraldism." "Never," according to the historian John Henry Cutler, "was character assassination more brutally practiced in a Boston campaign."

In 1912 Fitzgerald was chairman of the Massachusetts delegation to the Democratic National Convention, where he supported the candidacy of Woodrow Wilson. His second administration was characterized by continuing charges of corruption and payroll padding and by the efforts of his fellow "mayor-makers" to prevent Fitzgerald from constructing a citywide

political organization. Faced with a probable defeat by James M. Curley in 1914, he withdrew from the race and jauntily joined the Good Government Association in backing city council president Thomas J. Kenny against the victorious Curley. In 1916 he lost his bid against Henry Cabot Lodge, for a seat in the United States Senate, but two years later apparently defeated Independent Democrat Peter Tague for his old congressional seat by a scant 238 votes. A congressional committee, however, found that Fitzgerald's backers had voted unqualified electors and supplied Tague voters with "ungummed stickers" which later fell off and invalidated their ballots. Tague was declared the official winner on Oct. 23, 1919. Three years later he ran for governor of Massachusetts and lost to Republican Channing Cox by 60,000 votes; in his campaign Fitzgerald supported organized labor and denounced prohibition and federal aid to education as "paternalistic." After campaigning vigorously for fellow Irish Catholic Al Smith for president in 1928, he helped found the Jefferson Club to work for "the principles of Alfred E. Smith," particularly economic reform and cultural pluralism. In 1930 he again sought the gubernatorial nomination in the Democratic primary, but became ill and lost to Joseph B. Ely. Thereafter, he devoted his attention to his various business interests, served on the Port Authority, and performed quadrennial tasks as a presidental elector, serving as chairman of the Massachusetts delegation in 1933 and 1945. In 1946, at eighty-three, he campaigned for his grandson and namesake, John Fitzgerald Kennedy, in his first Congressional campaign and sang the mandatory "Sweet Adeline" at the victory celebration. Four years later he died of circulatory problems and was buried in St. Joseph Cemetery in West Roxbury, Mass.

[The only full-scale biography of Fitzgerald is John Henry Cutler, *"Honey Fitz": Three Steps to the White House; the Life and Times of John F. "Honey Fitz" Fitzgerald* (1962). Much information about him can be found in biographies of his famous relatives and of his political contemporaries. See especially Rose Fitzgerald Kennedy, *Times to Remember* (1974); Gail Cameron, *Rose: A Biography of Rose Fitzgerald Kennedy* (1971); David E. Koskopf, *Joseph P. Kennedy: A Life and Times* (1974); James Michael Curley, *I'd Do It Again: A Record Of All My Uproarious Years* (1957); Kenneth P. O'Donnell and David F. Powers, with Joe McCarty, *"Johnny, We Hardly Knew Ye": Memories of John Fitzgerald Kennedy* (1973); and Leslie Ainley, *Boston Mahatma: The Public Career of Marten Lomasney* (1949). Fitzgerald also figures prominently in books on Massachusetts politics of his era such as J. Joseph Huthmacher, *Massachusetts People and Politics, 1919–1933* (1969); Richard Abrams, *Conservatism in a Progressive Era* (1964); and Michael E. Hennessy, *Four Decades of*

Massachusetts Politics, 1890–1935 (1935). Other information can be found in the *Biog. Direct. Am. Congress, 1774–1971* and in his obituaries in the *Boston Globe* and the *N.Y. Times,* Oct. 3, 1950. The John F. Kennedy Presidential Library has several oral history interviews with contemporaries of Fitzgerald who recall their association and two collections of portraits: *Mayors of Boston: An Illustrated Epitome of Who the Mayors Have Been and What They Have Done* (1914); and *Men of Massachusetts: A Collection of Portraits of Representative Men in the Commonwealth of Massachusetts* (1903).]

JOHN D. BUENKER

FITZPATRICK, JOHN (Apr. 21, 1870-Sept. 27, 1946), labor leader, was born in Athlone, Ireland, the youngest of five sons of John Fitzpatrick, a small farmer who also worked as a horseshoer, and Adelaide (Clarke) Fitzpatrick. The mother died when John was a year old, the father when he was ten, and his formal education in the local grammar school ended at that time. In 1882 he came to America to live in Chicago with an uncle, who, however, died before the boy could resume his schooling. Forced to go to work, John spent three years in the packing plant of Swift and Company in the Chicago stockyards. Settling on the trade of farrier, he joined the International Union of Journeymen Horseshoers in 1886, served out his apprenticeship, and became a full member of Local No. 4. But Fitzpatrick was not destined for a life in a smithy shop. Marked early as a leader, he served as vice-president, treasurer, president, and, for five years, business agent of his local. He was powerfully built, simple and direct in manner, and endowed with an Irish sense of humor and also an intense Irish nationalism. His leadership was characterized by rugged honesty, the absence of guile, and a total identification with the cause of the workingman. On June 29, 1892, he married Katherine McCreash, a schoolteacher, an invaluable ally who helped make up for the education he had missed as a boy. They had one son, John.

During the 1890's the Chicago labor movement was a battleground for rival ideologies and factions. Early in the decade William C. Pomeroy captured the Chicago Trades and Labor Assembly and converted that central body into a vehicle for his personal enrichment and for the peddling of political influence. Reform elements, unable to dislodge the wily Pomeroy from the Trades and Labor Assembly, formed a rival body that gained backing from the Illinois and American federations, thus launching in 1896 a new city central, the Chicago Federation of Labor. As the delegate from Horseshoers' Local No. 4, Fitzpatrick participated in the reform movement, and he emerged as one of its leaders. From 1899 to 1901 he served as president of the new federation. At this point the city central was again captured by graft-ridden elements, this time emanating from the building trades and headed by Martin B. ("Skinny") Madden, whose specialty was strong-arm tactics. Once more the struggle resumed to drive the rascals out. With citywide reform support behind him, including such progressives as Jane Addams and Raymond Robins, Fitzpatrick defeated the Madden forces and won reelection in 1905 to the presidency of the Chicago Federation of Labor, a post he held thereafter until his death.

With its national-union structure and economic focus, American trade unionism normally affords city leadership a very restricted field of action. Fitzpatrick stood virtually alone as a city official who became a labor leader of national consequence. The Chicago Federation of Labor under his leadership won a wide reputation for progressivism; it was, for example, one of the first labor organizations to take up the cause of the convicted West Coast labor radical Tom Mooney. Two particular contributions set Fitzpatrick apart. First, he figured heavily in the pre-New Deal efforts to bring mass-production workers into the craft-oriented American Federation of Labor. Despite a craft and ethnic background that inhibited his contemporaries in the labor movement, Fitzpatrick was notably free from bias against Slavic and black workers, deeply sympathetic to their plight in Chicago's factories, and genuinely committed to organizing them. When the Chicago garment workers went on strike in 1910, Fitzpatrick mobilized financial support and helped bring about the historic Hart, Shaffner and Marx agreement of 1911. He remained a good friend to the garment workers and their leader, Sidney Hillman, despite the fact that the union that emerged in 1914—the Amalgamated Clothing Workers of America—was a dual union outside the A.F. of L.

World War I made conditions ripe for a major organizing move. Utilizing the concept of federated unionism (since the A.F. of L. ruled out an industrial union structure), Fitzpatrick and William Z. Foster, a former member of the Industrial Workers of the World, in July 1917 organized the Stock Yards Labor Council, with Fitzpatrick as acting chairman. Representing all the local unions with jurisdiction in the Chicago stockyards, the S.Y.L.C. made rapid headway among the packinghouse workers and, with the aid of the President's Mediation Commission, forced the packers to operate under a system of arbitration (but without actual union recognition). The next year, on Aug. 1, 1918, Fitzpatrick and Foster utilized the same federated approach—this time, however, on a national basis—to form the National Committee for Organizing the Iron and Steel Workers, of which Fitzpatrick subsequently became chairman. The steel drive broke into open-shop territory even more spectacularly than had the packinghouse campaign. In the end, however, both ventures came to grief. The steel industry defeated the unions in the great steel strike of 1919. Packinghouse organization declined more slowly, suffering, among other ways, from conflicting authority between the S.Y.L.C. and the national unions. The collapse came with a national strike in 1921-1922. Still, this marked the high point before the New Deal of any A.F. of L. effort to reach the mass-production workers.

Fitzpatrick had meanwhile embarked on the second major undertaking of his career. He had early disagreed with the political views prevailing within the A.F. of L. Although never a socialist, Fitzpatrick did, as Raymond Robins observed in 1911, believe "in labor legislation and the direct political action of the workers." Encouraged by the example of the Labour party in England, and thoroughly disillusioned with the Wilson administration, Fitzpatrick started a movement in late 1918 to form a labor party in Illinois. In 1919 he ran unsuccessfully as the labor candidate for mayor of Chicago. Fitzpatrick now attempted to broaden the state movement into a national labor party, and simultaneously to widen its base of support. This led in 1920 to the formation of the Farmer-Labor party, which nominated a presidential ticket and entered Fitzpatrick (again unsuccessfully) in the Illinois senatorial race. Efforts to induce progressive elements, first the Committee of Forty-Eight in 1919-1920 and then the Conference for Progressive Political Action in 1922, to join in an independent party failed. Trying once again in 1923, Fitzpatrick issued a call to all labor and left-wing elements. The only fresh group to respond in force was the Communists, who, led by Fitzpatrick's former ally William Z. Foster, proceeded to take over the Chicago convention of July 1923 and to form a new Federated Farmer-Labor party. Fitzpatrick led his followers out of the convention and abandoned the idea of an American labor party.

The episode left Fitzpatrick thoroughly disheartened and the dynamic phase of his career came to an abrupt end. It had been testimony to the man's personal stature that, with virtually no power base of his own (he had been, in fact, a salaried A.F. of L. organizer since 1902), he had been able to take an independent line in organizing work and in politics which his conservative A.F. of L. superiors either felt ambivalent about or thoroughly opposed. Defeat forced Fitzpatrick to cave in, and after 1923 he was reduced to the conventional role of city labor functionary. Neither in the organizing ferment nor in the new politics of the Great Depression did he play a major or distinctive part. He died of a heart attack at his Chicago home in 1946 after suffering for some years from arteriosclerosis. A Catholic, he was buried in Calvary Cemetery in Evanston, Ill.

[The major study of Fitzpatrick is John Keiser, "John Fitzpatrick and Progressive Unionism, 1915–1925" (Ph.D. dist., Northwestern Univ., 1965). A valuable early account of his career by Raymond Robins is in *Life and Labor*, Feb. 1911; it includes a good photograph. Fitzpatrick's personal papers are at the Chicago Hist. Soc. Equally important is the official publication of the Chicago Federation of Labor, the *New Majority* (later retitled *Federation News*). Phases of Fitzpatrick's career can be studied in David Brody, *Steelworkers in America: The Nonunion Era* (1960) and *The Butcher Workmen: A Study of Unionization* (1964); William Z. Foster, *The Great Steel Strike and Its Lessons* (1920); James Weinstein, *The Decline of Socialism in America, 1912–1925* (1967); and Barbara Warne Newell, *Chicago and the Labor Movement: Metropolitan Unionism in the 1930's* (1961). See also Eugene Staley, *Hist. of the Ill. State Fed. of Labor* (1930). There are obituaries in the *Chicago Tribune*, Sept. 28, 1946, *Chicago Sun*, Sept. 28, 1946, and the *N.Y. Times*, Sept. 29, 1946, all with photographs.]

DAVID BRODY

FLAGG, ERNEST (Feb. 6, 1857-Apr. 10, 1947), architect, was born in Brooklyn, N.Y., the third son and third of six children of Rev. Jared Bradley Flagg, then rector of Grace (Episcopal) Church in Brooklyn Heights, and his second wife, Louisa Hart. The family had a strong artistic strain that extended back to the painter Washington Allston, Ernest's great-uncle. His father had been a prominent portrait painter before entering the ministry, and Ernest's half-brother Montague became a genre painter of recognized ability. Jared Flagg gave up the ministry in 1863 and returned to painting, living briefly in Minnesota and then in New Haven, Conn., before returning to New York. These family moves and his mother's death in 1867 made Ernest's childhood unsettled; he attended a total of ten different schools. Since times were hard for his family, he left school at fifteen to become an office boy for a Wall Street firm. In 1880, after unsuccessful attempts to establish businesses for the sale of salt fish and oleomargarine, Flagg joined the architect Philip G. Hubert in a real estate venture. Through advance sale of apartments, they financed the construction of two cooperative apartment buildings, one at 121 Madison Avenue and "The Knickerbocker" at 245 Fifth Avenue. Flagg designed the floor plans for the buildings, using a then novel scheme of two-story "duplex" apartments.

The success of the project prompted Cornelius Vanderbilt II, a cousin by marriage, to seek Flagg's aid in altering the plans of the mansion Vanderbilt was then building. The millionaire was so taken with the young man that he sent him to the Ecole des Beaux-Arts in Paris for architectural training where he studied in the atélier of Paul Blondel. Flagg absorbed the methods, outlook, and "principles of good taste" that characterized the Beaux-Arts style. Both the school's credo and contemporary trend in architecture stressed a logical balance between aesthetics and functional practicality. By contrast, Flagg found American architecture sentimental and enthralled by diverse revivals; he was especially appalled by the contemporary popularity of the "barbaric" Romanesque style, and felt there had not been a distinctively American architecture since the clean-cut, uncluttered structures erected by colonial craftsmen. Flagg was undoubtedly affected also by the great Paris Universal Exposition of 1889, the year he graduated from the École des Beaux-Arts. A Parisian influence was consistently revealed in his work, guided always by his own individualism.

Flagg's first commission after his return to America in 1891 was for St. Luke's Hospital on West 113th Street in New York City, facing the Cathedral of St. John the Divine; he won the commission in competition against some eighty contestants. With its large, domed central tower and pavilions, St. Luke's was neo-Baroque in style, as was St. Margaret's Hospital in Pittsburgh, which he began in the same year. In 1891 Flagg was chosen as architect of a new museum for the Corcoran Gallery of Art in Washington, D.C. The resulting building was remarkably open in plan, with a neo-Italian Renaissance exterior and a Greek Doric interior, built of marble. Flagg won the competition for the Washington State Capitol at Olympia in 1893, but the structure remained unfinished for thirty years and was then considerably altered from his original scheme.

In 1897 Flagg designed a fine Beaux-Arts-style building, at the northwest corner of Broadway and Liberty Street, for the Singer Sewing Machine Company. Soon thereafter he designed the Bourne Building to the west, which he later

(c. 1905) enlarged with a fourteen-story addition. In 1906-1908 these earlier structures were remodeled and integrated into Flagg's new forty-seven-story Singer Tower. At 612 feet this was for a time the tallest office building in the world. The vertical elegance of the new lobby, with its marble-clad columns edged in bronze supporting illuminated saucer domes, was the finest evocation of Flagg's inventive genius. In another commission for the Singer company, a twelve-story office building (1904) at Broadway and Spring Street, and in the Produce Exchange Bank Building (1905), Flagg chose to give expression to the basic steel structure, rather than to disguise it with traditional forms. The bank, with metal and terra cotta bay windows occupying most of the space between the structural columns, was one of his most radical designs. More conservative, but clearly Beaux-Arts in style, was the office building for Charles Scribner's Sons at 597 Fifth Avenue (1913), which sixty years later was still serving the firm and the purpose for which it was built.

Flagg designed many splendid town houses, including his own at 109 East 40th Street (c. 1906). One of the most Parisian was the four-story Oliver G. Jennings residence (c. 1900) at 7 East 72nd Street. Crowned by a convex mansard roof with copper crestings, it illustrated what could be done to make a house on a narrow city lot imposing. Much larger, and freestanding, was the three-story neo-Georgian Alfred Corning Clark house at the northeast corner of Riverside Drive and West 89th Street, built at the turn of the century. Flagg's most imposing country house was the great brick mansion he designed for Frederick G. Bourne (c. 1902) at Oakdale, L.I. His own country house, "Stone Court" (1898), at Dongan Hills on Staten Island, is a charming gambrel-roofed example of neo-Dutch Colonial architecture.

Flagg's greatest opportunity came with the commission that he received in 1896 to design a completely new campus for the United States Naval Academy at Annapolis. The ten main buildings (constructed 1899-1907), with their rusticated stonework and great steel and glass windows, are expressive of the Beaux-Arts style but are handled with Flagg's creative adaptability. This great, formal complex, centering on a domed chapel, gave many Americans their first taste of design in the grand manner.

From his Beaux-Arts training, Flagg also acquired an interest in rational plans for city living. Although his Singer tower was an early skyscraper, he sought zoning restrictions to prevent these giants from robbing their neighbors of light and turning streets into caverns. More important, he brought to the attention of his confreres the pressing need for low-cost housing, fireproofing, and modular design. Under a commission from the philanthropist Darius Ogden Mills, Flagg designed a series of low-cost "Mills hotels" for lower Manhattan, making use of interior courtyards joined by a central stairway with elevators. The model tenement houses he designed for the City and Suburban Homes Company (between 68th and 69th Streets west of Amsterdam Avenue) and for the New York Fireproof Association (between 41st and 42nd Streets and Tenth Avenue) were separated from each other by light-admitting courts. (Both were built before 1902.) In 1933 he designed the very extensive Flagg Court Apartments for low-income families in Bay Ridge, Brooklyn. Flagg also attempted to reduce the cost of small suburban homes with his "Ernest Flagg System" of stone-concrete construction, as set forth in his *Small Houses: Their Economic Design and Construction* (1922).

Save for one brief interval (c. 1895-1898) with Walter B. Chambers as an associate, Flagg headed his own firm without a partner. He was one of the few Beaux-Arts architects in this country who placed his own interpretative stamp on every design he created. His architectural work continually reflected an inventive gift. This gift was demonstrated in his ability to innovate in every phase of a building: lighting, furniture, staircases, and even the door handles and hinges. Distinguished in appearance and charmingly persuasive, he was highly regarded by his contemporaries. He was one of the founders of the Society of Beaux-Arts Architects in 1894, and was advanced to fellowship in the American Institute of Architects in 1926. On June 27, 1899, he married Margaret Elizabeth Bonnell, a great-granddaughter of John Harper, co-founder of the publishing firm which became Harper and Brothers. They had one child, Margaret Elizabeth. Flagg died of a heart attack at his New York City home and was buried in Evergreen Cemetery, New Haven, Conn.

[Writings by Flagg include *Genealogical Notes on the Founding of New England* (1926); also books on architecture, *Small Houses, Their Economic Design and Construction* (1922) and *Le Naos du Parthenon* (1928); "A Fish Story: An Autobiog. Sketch of the Education of an Architect," *Jour. Am. Inst. of Architects*, May 1945; "The Ecole des Beaux-Arts," *Architectural Rec.*, Jan.-Mar. through July-Sept. 1894; "Influences of the French School on Architecture in the U.S.," *ibid.*, Oct.-Dec. 1894; "Am. Architecture as Opposed to Architecture in America," *ibid.*, Oct. 1900; "The Limitation of Height and Area of Buildings in N.Y.," *Am. Architect and Building News*, Apr. 15, 1908; "New Buildings for the U.S. Naval Academy, Annapolis, Md.," *Am. Architect and Building News*, July 1 and 8, 1908; "Fireproof Tenements and the Building Law," *N.Y. Architect*, June 1911; and "The Module System in Architectural Design," *Architecture*, July 1920. The principal source on his architecture is "The Works of Ernest Flagg," *Architectural Rec.*, Apr. 1902, with extensive illustrations and an introduction by H. W. Desmond. See also Desmond's "A Rational Skyscraper," *ibid.*, Mar. 1904, a description of the Singer office building; Otto F. Semsch, ed., *A Hist. of the Singer Building Construction* (1908); Alan Burnham, "Forgotten Pioneering," *Architectural Forum*, Apr. 1957; "A New Type of City House," *Architectural Rec.*, Sept. 1907, on Flagg's own town house; Norman G. and Lucius C. S. Flagg, *Family Records of the Descendants of Gershom Flagg* (1907), on his genealogy; *Nat. Cyc. Am. Biog.*, Current Vol. E, 239-240 (with photograph); *N.Y. Times* obituary, Apr. 11, 1947.]

ALAN BURNHAM

FLANAGAN, EDWARD JOSEPH (July 13, 1886-May 15, 1948), Roman Catholic priest, founder of Boys Town, was born in Leabeg, County Roscommon, Ireland, where his father managed a farm. He was eighth among the eleven children of John and Honora (Larkin) Flanagan and the third of their four sons. A frail, studious child, he earned good grades at a nearby elementary school and at a boarding school in Sligo. Like his oldest brother, Patrick, he decided to prepare for the Catholic priesthood. He also followed others of his family in going to the United States, emigrating in 1904 and becoming a citizen in 1919. Supported by an uncle, Flanagan attended Mount St. Mary's College in Emmitsburg, Md., and received the B.A. degree in 1906 and the M.A. in 1908. After illnesses endangering his lungs forced him out of St. Joseph's Seminary in Dunwoodie, N.Y., and Rome's Gregorian University, he worked as a bookkeeper at Omaha, Nebr., where his brother was already a priest. In 1909 he entered the University of Innsbruck, Austria, and was ordained a priest there on July 26, 1912.

After serving briefly as a curate at O'Neill, Nebr., Father Flanagan was assigned to Omaha. Moved by the plight of itinerant workers and vagrants, he established there the Workingmen's Hotel, which provided free or cheap lodging to many from 1914 through 1917. He became adept at securing funds for his undertaking but was less successful in attempts to rehabilitate his tenants. Hence he turned to preventive work among homeless youths, who in those days were often sent to the reformatory. On Dec 12, 1917, he opened Father Flanagan's Home for Boys. He believed that his boys, most of whom had committed no crime, would respond favorably to an atmosphere like that of his own childhood home. He enforced rules paternally, soon abandoning corporal punishment, and relied upon his warmth, trust, and interest to win each boy's cooperation. Perforce, the director of the struggling home had the boys share in its work, thus also building group spirit. This he strengthened by an ambitious program of sports, music, and hobbies. Always he stressed the practice of religion. His policies were unoriginal but uncommonly humane. Combined with his winning personality, they made him a successful molder of boys.

Other attributes and abilities accounted for his increasing reputation within his region. Foremost was his democratic spirit. From the first, he welcomed boys of all races. In 1919, during the racial tensions which culminated in an especially savage lynching at Omaha, one of Flanagan's publicity photographs conspicuously paired a black and a white boy at his home. While the priest and the nuns who assisted him gave a Catholic tone to the institution, Father Flanagan accepted Protestant and Jewish boys and forbade denominational proselytizing. In consequence, he was able to secure general support in Omaha, the source of most of his original boys. A local Negro musician helped train his boys' band. His early contributors included not only Catholics encouraged by their bishop but also several Protestant ministers, Jewish merchants, and a leading Mason; one of his staunch supporters was Henry Monsky, later president of B'nai B'rith. Occasional opposition from the Ku Klux Klan of the hinterland only made Father Flanagan more appealing to tolerant Omahans of all sects and classes. He soon became a civic idol.

A master of publicity, he developed a formula which combined his own popularity with the sentimental appeal of homeless boys. He marched with his boys' band in Omaha parades and sent athletic teams and a troupe of entertainers throughout the area. From the towns and farms of the Midwest, Father Flanagan thus attracted additional boys. He reached for regional support for them through a magazine whose cover bore his picture and whose pages were filled with touching case histories and such slogans as "There is no such thing as a bad boy." Flanagan also proved to be a good business manager. To perpetuate what began as a one-man institution, he almost simultaneously heavily insured his life in its favor, built up a staff, and acquired a physical plant. In 1921, using a characteristic combination of borrowing and fund raising, he moved his home from rented quarters to a farm outside Omaha, where he gradually developed facilities for elementary, secondary, and vocational education. In 1935 he incorporated the home's property as the municipality of Boys Town and thereby gave an unusual legal status to the juvenile government which he allowed his 200 boys to institute. For his work, he received in 1937 the papal title of Monsignor.

Father Flanagan, as he continued to be called, became a nationally known figure in 1938, when Metro-Goldwyn-Mayer, attracted by his publicity, made the first of two popular films about Boys Town, starring Spencer Tracy and Mickey Rooney. Dark-haired and bespectacled, standing an inch over six feet, the solidly built cleric was a frequent recipient of degrees and other honors. He exploited his cinema fame to raise money for buildings that expanded the home's capacity to 500 boys and would double that number after his death. Through magazine articles and well-delivered speeches, he expounded his views on youth problems to an audience concerned by the disruption of families during World War II. He encouraged the towns for homeless children which sprang up in several devastated countries. By invitation of the United States War Department, he inspected child welfare facilities in Japan and Korea in 1947, and in Austria and Germany in 1948. While in Berlin he died of a heart attack. His body was placed in a sarcophagus in Boys Town's Dowd Chapel. Father Flanagan was important not only as the founder of a continuing institution but also as a pioneer in intergroup relations.

[Papers, records, and scrapbooks relating to Flanagan are at Boys Town, where also are nearly complete files of the very valuable *Father Flanagan's Boys' Home Jour.* and its successor, the *Boys Town Times.* The only biography, Fulton and Will Oursler, *Father Flanagan of Boys Town* (1949), is saccharine but generally accurate. Useful for biographical data are *Who Was Who in America,* II (1950), and a sketch in *Current Biog.,* 1941. Good obituaries are in the *N.Y. Times* and *Omaha Morning World-Herald,* May 15, 1948. For illuminating comments on Flanagan's practical side, see editorials in the *Omaha Evening World-Herald,* May 17, 1948, and the *Catholic Charities Rev.,* June 1948. The most detailed exposition of his theories is *Understanding Your Boy* (1950), published in his name "as told to Ford McCoy." See also Gladys Denny Shultz, "Boy-handling Tips from Boys Town," *Better Homes and Gardens,* Mar. 1940; and statement of Father Flanagan in U.S. Senate, 78 Cong., 1 Sess., *Wartime Health and Education,* Hearings before a Subcommittee of the Committee on Education and Labor, Nov. 30, 1943, pp. 66–71, 82–84. Elementary but illustrative of his international impact is Rosemarian V. Staudacher, *Children Welcome* (1963); see also Elisabeth Rotten, *Children's Communities* (Paris, 1949), and Georg Wagner, *Father Flanagan und seine Jungenstadt* (Vienna, 1957). Several officials at Boys Town, particularly Patrick J. Norton, supplied useful recollections.]

FRANK L. BYRNE

FLEISHER, BENJAMIN WILFRID (Jan. 6, 1870-April 29, 1946), newspaper publisher and editor, was born in Philadelphia, Pa., the oldest son of Simon B. Fleisher and Cecilia (Hoffheimer) Fleisher. The Fleishers were a Jewish family who emigrated from Memel in East Prussia during the 1830's. Benjamin's father and his uncle Moyer moved from Meadville, Pa., to Philadelphia and founded the Fleisher Yarn Company. His mother was born in New York state. Benjamin's younger brothers were to become active members of the Philadelphia community: Samuel S. as a businessman and philanthropist, Edwin A. as a patron and collector of music.

After Benjamin received the Ph.B. from the University of Pennsylvania in 1889 he entered the family business of manufacturing worsted yarns and in time became treasurer of the company. On Mar. 26, 1896, he married Marie Blanche Blum, whose family lived in France. Around the turn of the century he speculated heavily with both personal and company funds and ended by losing nearly $1 million. Disgraced and disowned by the Fleisher family, he took his wife and young children to Paris.

From Europe Fleisher traveled to Japan early in 1908, where he became associated with a small and struggling English-language newspaper published in Yokohama, the *Japan Advertiser*. He was so successful as a reporter and advertising salesman that in a short time he obtained financing and became the proprietor of the paper. He first attracted public attention and circulation by publishing a series of illustrated special editions at the time the United States fleet visited Japan in the fall of 1908.

This unexpected success committed Fleisher to the profession of journalism. From 1911 to 1913 he joined with Thomas F. Millard and Carl Crow in founding the *China Press*, a Shanghai newspaper reflecting an American point of view. Fleisher also served as Far Eastern correspondent for the United Press Association of America, for the *New York World,* the *New York Times,* and the *Philadelphia Public Ledger.* But his main efforts were devoted to building the *Japan Advertiser* into one of the leading English-language papers in Asia. By moving the plant to Tokyo in 1913 he was able to concentrate on national and international news, rather than the more parochial concerns of the foreign community. In comparison with competing papers under British management, the *Advertiser* was described as "a typical live, hustling, newsy, pithy, adaptable and resourceful American newspaper" (*Terry's Japanese Empire,* 1914 ed.). By American standards, however, the format and editorial policy were fairly conservative, for Fleisher consciously took the *New York Times* as his model. The paper's professional treatment of economic news also gained the respect and advertising support of both the foreign and the Japanese business communities. When Emperor Hirohito succeeded to the throne in 1928, Fleisher planned and published a handsomely bound special edition that was both an artistic and a commercial success. In 1919 Fleisher started to publish the *Trans-Pacific,* first a monthly and later a weekly magazine covering the political, economic, social, and cultural events of East Asia. Beginning in 1927 the *Advertiser* also published a yearbook of finance, industry, and commerce.

Fleisher imported the first linotype machines used in Japan and developed a first-rate printing plant. At the time of the great earthquakes of 1923 and again in an unexplained fire in 1930, his plant was burned to the ground; but in each case Fleisher succeeded in raising capital in Japan and the United States to rebuild. Through a close relationship with the University of Missouri School of Journalism, particularly with its first dean Walter Williams, Fleisher induced a number of promising young journalists to work on the *Advertiser*; from that base many of them became prominent foreign correspondents. In May 1933 the Missouri journalism school awarded its medal of honor to the *Advertiser.*

Always concerned with promoting good relations between Japan and the United States, Fleisher became in 1917 a founder and first vice-president of the America-Japan Society of Tokyo. He lavished great effort on a special America-Japan edition of the *Advertiser* published on July 9, 1922, and on another edition in 1931 on the occasion of the visit to Japan by Colonel and Mrs. Charles Lindbergh. At a testimonial dinner in New York, Elbert R. Gary, Charles R. Crane, and Thomas W. Lamont paid tribute to his service to American business interests.

After the Manchurian incident of 1931 Fleisher and his son Wilfrid, then managing editor of the *Advertiser,* found their work increasingly difficult. In an effort to control the news, the military elements in power issued numerous press bans forbidding discussion of certain subjects. Respect for the divinity of the emperor became a fetish; on one occasion the *Advertiser* was forced to tender a formal apology because one letter in the caption under a picture of members of the imperial family had been blurred. Police surveillance and pressure on both Japanese and American staff members became so intense that in October 1940 Fleisher finally sold out to the *Japan Times,* an English-language paper controlled by the Japanese Ministry of Foreign Affairs.

Fleisher then returned to the United States, after over three decades of residence in Japan. Despite the amputation of a leg that confined him to a wheelchair in later years, he and his wife had enjoyed a position of leadership in the foreign community of Tokyo and an active social life that brought them into contact with Japanese at the highest levels. As an avocation Fleisher collected Chinese art.

After returning to the United States, Fleisher and his wife lived in Beverly Hills, Calif., until her death; he then moved to Washington, D.C., near his three children: Wilfrid, Marion, and Simone. He died at the Mayo Clinic in Rochester, Minn., of Burger's disease, and was buried in Forest Lawn Memorial Park in Glendale, Calif.

[*Who's Who in the Orient* (1915); *N.Y. Times,* May 1, 1946; Demaree Bess, "Tokyo's Captive Yankee Newspaper," *Saturday Evening Post,* Feb. 6, 1943 (with photograph); Wilfrid Fleisher, *Volcanic Isle* (1941); Hachirō Ebihara, *Nihon ōji shimbun zasshi shi* (History of Western-Language Newspapers and Magazines in Japan, 1934); Sara Lockwood Williams, *Twenty Years of Education for Journalism: A History of the School of Journalism of the University of Missouri, Columbia, Missouri, U.S.A.* (1929); information from Fleisher's daughter, Mrs. William Stix Wasserman.]

ROBERT S. SCHWANTES

FLETCHER, JOHN GOULD (Jan. 3, 1886-May 10, 1950), poet, was born in Little Rock, Ark., the second of three children and only son of John Gould Fletcher and Adolphine (Krause) Fletcher. His father, son of a pioneer who had migrated from Tennessee to Arkansas in 1825, served in the Confederate Army, then became a successful banker and cotton broker in Little Rock and was three times a candidate for governor. Fletcher's mother was of Danish and German ancestry; from her he acquired a love of music, poetry, and art. When Fletcher was three, his father purchased the stately antebellum mansion that had been the home of Albert Pike, an early Arkansas scholar and poet. Confined to its grounds without playmates, the sensitive boy began to develop a romantic point of view that was to color his entire life and work. He received his early education from tutors and in a private local academy and graduated from the Little Rock high school in 1902. After a year in Phillips Academy at Andover, Mass., he was admitted to Harvard in the fall of 1903.

Predisposed toward the arts, and taking only a perfunctory interest in his other studies, Fletcher spent many hours in the Boston Museum of Fine Arts. He had been reared as an Episcopalian, but when a Nietzschean friend convinced him that he could no longer accept organized religion, he turned to poetry as a substitute. He wrote his first poems in the summer of 1905 while on a trip to the West Coast. During his junior year he discovered the English poet Arthur Symons, and through Symons the French symbolists. His father's death in 1906 brought promise of financial independence, and Fletcher gave up college in the middle of his senior year. For a time he pursued an interest in archaeology, but a field trip in the Southwest disenchanted him, and in the summer of 1908 he sailed for Europe. After a sojourn in Italy, he settled in London and threw himself into the Socialist movement. At the urging of a Fabian friend he began to read Whitman and to write poetry in a somewhat Whitmanesque vein.

In 1913, after publishing five small volumes of poetry at his own expense, Fletcher made his first important literary friendship: he met Ezra Pound, who introduced him to various London literary figures, among them the Imagist poets "H.D." (Hilda Doolittle) and Richard Aldington. At first unsympathetic to the aims of the Imagists, Fletcher refused Pound's invitation to contribute to his anthology *Des Imagistes,* but spent much time with Pound and his circle. In 1913, too, he began a liaison with Florence Emily Arbuthnot, wife of a photographer he had met in London. The poems Fletcher was now writing—"Irradiations" and the "symphony" poems, such as "Blue Symphony," "Green Symphony," and "Golden Symphony"—were all experimental in form and substance. In the "symphonies" he was trying to create a new material for poetry out of analogies between his own moods and those of nature, which he took to be the method of Zen Buddhism. He had been reading various orientalists as well as Chinese and Japanese poets, and henceforward much of his poetry was to show a pronounced strain of oriental thought, imagery, and symbolism. By the summer of 1914, when Amy Lowell took over the leadership of the Imagist group, he felt himself to be part of it, and contributed to each of the three Imagist anthologies she sponsored, published in 1915, 1916, and 1917. It was she who found an American publisher for his *Irradiations: Sand and Spray* (1915). Together they developed a kind of prose-poetry, which Fletcher named "polyphonic prose."

After the outbreak of war in 1914, Fletcher

made the first of several returns to the United States. He remained there for over a year, living chiefly in Boston, the friend and neighbor of Conrad Aiken. In Chicago he met Harriet Monroe, who had published his work in her magazine *Poetry*. He visited his boyhood home and there wrote "Ghosts of an Old House," published with the "symphonies" in *Goblins and Pagodas* (1916). A trip down the Mississippi and through the Southwest to California provided material for *Breakers and Granite* (1921). Resuming his life in England, Fletcher married "Daisy" Arbuthnot (who had divorced her first husband) on July 5, 1916. He met T. S. Eliot and contributed to his *Criterion*. When *The Tree of Life* and *Japanese Prints,* both published in 1918, received lukewarm reviews, Fletcher stopped writing verse for a time and devoted himself largely to art criticism. Besides articles on oriental and modern art he wrote a biography (1921) of Paul Gauguin, for whom he felt a considerable affinity as a rebel against a materialistic civilization. Next he turned to writing mystical religious poetry (some of it prose-poetry) published in *Parables* (1925), *Branches of Adam* (1926), and *The Black Rock* (1928).

Fletcher spent seven months in America in 1926 and realized that thenceforward his future lay in his native land. On a lecture tour through the South he spoke at Nashville, where he met John Crowe Ransom and Donald Davidson of the Fugitive group. A meeting with Allen Tate led to an invitation to contribute to the symposium *I'll Take My Stand: The South and the Agrarian Tradition* (1930). From this time on, Fletcher was to be deeply committed to regionalism and Southern agrarianism, which he saw as antidotes to the evils of a machine civilization. He left England in March 1933 to settle permanently in Little Rock, leaving behind his wife. They were divorced in 1936, and on January 18 of that year he married the recently divorced Charlie May (Hogue) Simon, a writer of children's books, and sometime thereafter was baptized in the Episcopal church. In 1939 Fletcher's *Selected Poems* won the Pulitzer Prize. Much interested in his native state, he organized the Arkansas Folklore Society and the Arkansas Historical Society and wrote poetry about the region. *South Star* (1941) contains his "Story of Arkansas," and much of *The Burning Mountain* (1946) is regional in theme or imagery; he published an excellent history of Arkansas in 1947. During World War II he also spent much time alleviating the distress of the Japanese-Americans interned in

a relocation camp in the state. Fletcher had suffered from recurrent mental illness, and in 1950, not long after a period of hospitalization, he drowned in a pond near his home, an apparent suicide. He was buried in Mount Holly Cemetery, Little Rock. He had no children.

Although Fletcher is remembered chiefly as an Imagist, he departed from that relatively narrow movement fairly early in his career and was always somewhat of a loner. In his early work he was an experimenter who sought to fuse the influences of Postimpressionist art and music in free verse. He went his own way in drawing upon oriental philosophy and imagery to express his personal mysticism. His style and themes changed notably in America, and though his Southern regional poetry, like the rest of his poetry, is uneven in quality, some feel that in it he achieved his greatest artistic success.

[Fletcher's autobiography, *Life Is My Song* (1937), is the principal biographical source; see also Charlie May Simon, *Johnswood* (1953), his second wife's account of their life together. Critical studies include: dissertations by William R. Osborne (George Peabody Coll. for Teachers, 1955), Bernard P. Zur (Northwestern Univ., 1958), and Edna B. Stephens (Univ. of Ark., 1961); Glenn Hughes, *Imagism and the Imagists* (1931); Stanley K. Coffman, *Imagism* (1951); Alfred Kreymborg, *A Hist. of Am. Poetry* (1934); Horace Gregory and Marya Zaturenska, *A Hist. of Am. Poetry, 1900–1940* (1946). See also references to Fletcher in Amy Lowell, *Tendencies in Modern Am. Poetry* (1917), and in Harriet Monroe's autobiography, *A Poet's Life* (1938). Fletcher's papers are at the Univ. of Ark. Significant Fletcher letters are in collections in other libraries: at Harvard (Amy Lowell, John Cournos), the Univ. of Chicago (Harriet Monroe), and the Huntington Lib. A collected edition of Fletcher's poems by E. Leighton Rudolph is in preparation. A photograph of Fletcher as a young man is in Lowell, *Tendencies*; one as an older man is in Stanley J. Kunitz and Howard Haycraft, eds., *Twentieth Century Authors* (1942).]

EDNA B. STEPHENS

FLEXNER, SIMON (Mar. 25, 1863–May 2, 1946), pathologist, director of the Rockefeller Institute for Medical Research, was born in Louisville, Ky., the fourth son and fourth of a remarkable family of nine children of Morris Flexner and Esther (Abraham) Flexner. Among his brothers were Bernard Flexner, lawyer and Zionist, and Abraham Flexner (1866-1959), author of an influential study of medical education and first director of the Institute for Advanced Study in Princeton, N.J. Morris Flexner, a wholesale merchant, had come to the United States from Bohemia; his wife was from Alsace. Simon, after attending public schools, was apprenticed to a druggist, who under the indenture sent him to the Louisville College of Pharmacy, where he was graduated in 1882. He then worked in his eldest brother's drugstore and studied medicine at the University of Louisville, taking the M.D. in 1889. At a time when the medical school had little provision for laboratory work, he acquired a microscope, taught himself how to use it, and began to do simple clinical tests for local physicians.

In 1890 he went to Baltimore to study pathology at the Johns Hopkins Hospital with William H. Welch, who was thereafter a major influence in his career. Despite his almost complete lack of scientific training, Flexner impressed his teacher so deeply that he was offered a fellowship for the following year. He soon began to publish valuable studies in pathology, and by 1892 he was Welch's first assistant; in that year he became associate in pathology in the newly opened Johns Hopkins Medical School. An epidemic of cerebrospinal meningitis in Western Maryland in 1893 gave him valuable experience in the study of acute infectious disease. Later in 1893 Flexner visited Europe briefly, studying pathology at Strasbourg and at Prague. Returning to Baltimore as resident pathologist at Johns Hopkins Hospital, he continued research in bacteriology and pathology. In the summer of 1895 he broadened his interests by collaborating with Jacques Loeb at the Marine Biological Laboratory, Woods Hole, Mass., on a problem in invertebrate biology. The Johns Hopkins University promoted him in 1895 to associate professor and in 1898 to professor of pathological anatomy. While at Manila the following year in charge of a small party studying the diseases of the Philippine Islands, he discovered a widespread strain of the dysentery bacillus since known as the Flexner type.

After his return from the Orient, Flexner was professor of pathology at the University of Pennsylvania from 1899 to 1903. Creating a strong department and equipping an admirable laboratory building, he carried on research on a wide variety of problems in pathology, bacteriology, and immunology. Among his co-workers was the young Japanese physician Hideyo Noguchi, who was much influenced by Flexner throughout his brilliant but uneven career. In 1901 Flexner took a month's leave to head a governmental commission investigating the presence of bubonic plague in San Francisco.

All this diverse experience in the newest and at that period the most rewarding field of medical science fittted Flexner for the opportunity opened by the creation in 1901 of the Rockefeller Institute for Medical Research (later Rockefeller University) in New York City. He became one of the seven members of the insti-

tute's board of scientific directors headed by William H. Welch, and was asked to organize and direct the laboratories. The idea of a corps of investigators devoting all their time to medical research was new to America. Beginning in 1943, with the advice of Welch and his board, Flexner organized the institute according to specifications he had himself drawn up at the board's request. In contrast to the program of its European prototypes, the institute did not limit its work to any particular subdivision of medical science. There were to be several laboratory departments, each headed by a competent scientist. The first of these carefully chosen men, brought together in temporary quarters in 1904 or early 1905, were (besides Flexner himself) the physiologist Samuel J. Meltzer, the biochemist P. A. T. Levene, and the pathologist Eugene L. Opie. Alexis Carrel, experimental surgeon, was added in 1906, Jacques Loeb in 1910.

In 1906 the Rockefeller Institute opened a permanent new laboratory building and in 1910 a modern research hospital under the direction of Rufus Cole. Made financially secure by Rockefeller endowments, it was becoming internationally famous. In this development Flexner, appointed ostensibly to direct the laboratories only, by his administrative skill and general wisdom had established himself as head of the whole organization. His own scientific achievements, moreover, first won public respect for the institute and the ever-increasing confidence of John D. Rockefeller and his son. This personal success began when in 1905 New York City was struck by a severe epidemic of cerebrospinal meningitis, the same disease that Flexner had studied in Maryland twelve years before. He now was able to transmit the infection to monkeys. A serum against it had been prepared in Europe and also in New York, but was not very effective. Flexner conceived the idea of placing the serum at the seat of the infection by injecting it into the spinal canal. This procedure reduced the mortality by half, and Flexner for several years produced the serum under his own supervision, distributing large quantities to public health officers throughout the country.

In 1907 America's first large epidemic of poliomyelitis spread through the eastern states. Flexner at once attempted to transmit the disease to monkeys, but without success. When he learned that in 1908 Karl Landsteiner, then at Vienna, had successfully infected a monkey, Flexner with Paul A. Lewis repeated the experiment (September 1909) and this time was able to transmit the disease from monkey to monkey. Having thus, so to speak, trapped the disease for laboratory study, he found that the infectious agent was a filterable virus rather than a bacterial organism. At that time no way was known to cultivate such viruses or to prepare vaccines against them. Flexner's work, however, laid the foundation for the development, forty years later, of protective vaccines.

During these early years at the institute, Flexner worked also with some of his juniors, not as a chief with assistants, but sharing problems with them. Noguchi and he in 1905 were among the first to confirm Fritz Schaudinn and Erich Hoffmann's sensational discovery of the microscopic parasite of syphilis, the spirochete now called *Treponema pallidum,* only sixty-six days after the first announcement. With J. W. Jobling, Flexner in 1906 found a transplantable malignant tumor of a rat, providing cancer investigators with a useful experimental process which nearly seventy years later was still flourishing in many laboratories.

Since the beginning of his career as an investigator Flexner had published, alone or with collaborators, a flood of major and minor reports on his research in pathology and bacteriology, more than 200 between 1890 and 1909. This productivity continued, but as his energies had to be expended more and more upon the direction of the flourishing institute, Flexner made his later contributions to research largely by stimulating and advising his juniors. To some of these he turned over key ideas; with others he actively collaborated as time permitted; with Hideyo Noguchi he maintained a fatherly relation, largely directing Noguchi's choice of topics for investigation. Although no longer himself opening up new lines of research, Flexner published many valuable survey articles and reviews in his own fields of experience, as well as discussions of policy in public health, education, and research organization. For nineteen years, beginning in 1904, he was the chief or sole editor of the *Journal of Experimental Medicine.*

Slight of build, self-contained, soft-spoken, Flexner presided vigorously over the manifold activities of the Rockefeller Institute, welding into a coherent whole his band of individualistic senior colleagues. One of the most critical among them, Carrel, wrote to Flexner, "The Rockefeller Institute is yourself. You are its mind." With quick insight and exceedingly keen judgment, he respected the diverse temperaments of the research staff. To men of independent genius, whether they came from other institutions or grew up in the institute, he gave a free hand; others he shepherded until they were ready for independent work. His attention to individual performance extended to the laboratory assistants and maintenance staff. Several of these men who rose to high rank owed their opportunity to Flexner's observation of their performance. He watched every administrative detail closely; stories are still told of careful economies and meticulous regulations resulting from his strong sense of duty regarding funds entrusted to him. But there are many more tales of generous decisions and personal kindness.

When, during World War I, the Rockefeller Institute became the headquarters of a military demonstration hospital, Flexner was commissioned a lieutenant colonel in the Army Medical Corps and went to Europe to inspect the medical laboratories of the expeditionary forces. After the war his responsibilities at the institute included general direction not only of the laboratories and hospital, but also of a large department of animal pathology at Princeton, N.J., under the immediate direction of Theobald Smith. In 1924 Flexner's de facto headship was recognized when the trustees formally named him director of the entire institution.

When Flexner began his work at the Rockefeller Institute his intellectual interests were almost wholly scientific, but through his marriage on Sept. 17, 1903, to Helen Whitall Thomas, sister of M. Carey Thomas, president of Bryn Mawr College, and a talented member of an outstanding Quaker family in Baltimore, he was introduced to the larger world of arts and letters. Friendship with the cultivated physician Christian A. Herter of the institute's board of scientific directors also broadened his intellectual range, and friendly relations with John D. Rockefeller, Jr., introduced him to the larger philanthropic movements of the time. Through his charter membership on the board of trustees of the Rockefeller Foundation, Flexner contributed much to its international public health program and to the support of American medical education. As a member of the China Medical Board he helped organize the Peking Union Medical College. A successful scheme of the National Research Council for postdoctoral fellowships in physics, chemistry, and the biological sciences, supported by the Rockefeller Foundation, was largely based on Flexner's plans.

His services as scientific and administrative counselor extended far beyond the Rockefeller group of benefactions. Flexner was a member and for many years chairman of the Public Health Council of New York state. He was also a trustee of the Johns Hopkins University and of the Carnegie Foundation of New York. In

1920 he was president of the American Association for the Advancement of Science. In addition to many foreign honors, including membership in the Royal Society of London, he was elected to the National Academy of Sciences, the American Philosophical Society, and the American Academy of Arts and Sciences. After his retirement from the Rockefeller Institute in 1935, Flexner was appointed Eastman Professor at Oxford University for 1937-1938 and was a helpful advisor in setting up the medical professorships endowed by Lord Nuffield at Oxford's Radcliffe Infirmary. A book, *The Evolution and Organization of the University Clinic* (1939), resulted from this visit. He spent two years in writing, with the collaboration of his son James T. Flexner, a distinguished biography of his late teacher and friend, *William Henry Welch and the Heroic Age of American Medicine* (1941). Simon Flexner died at the Presbyterian Hospital, New York City, at the age of eighty-three, of a coronary occlusion following surgery. He was survived by his wife and their two children, William Welch Flexner, mathematician and United Nations official, and James Carey Thomas Flexner, historian and author.

[Peyton Rous in *Obituary Notices of Fellows of the Royal Soc.*, VI, 409–445 (1948–1949), with portrait and complete bibliography; Stanhope Bayne-Jones in Am. Philosophical Soc., *Year Book*, 1946; *Memorial Meeting for Simon Flexner* (pamphlet, Rockefeller Inst., 1946), with personal characterizations by John D. Rockefeller, Jr., and others; George W. Corner, *Hist. of the Rockefeller Inst.* (1965). Flexner's papers are in the library of the Am. Philosophical Soc., Phila.]

GEORGE W. CORNER

FORCE, JULIANA RIESER (Dec. 25, 1876-Aug. 28, 1948), museum director, was born in Doylestown, Pa., a twin, and one of the nine children of Maximilian Rieser and Julie Ann (Schmutz) Rieser, both natives of Baden, Germany. Her father owned a haberdashery store. After being educated in local schools, Juliana supported herself, first by secretarial work and later as head of a secretarial school in New York, which she left to work as a secretary for Helen Hay (Mrs. Payne) Whitney. In 1912 she married Dr. Willard Burdette Force. They had no children.

Early in the 1900's Mrs. Whitney's sister-in-law, Gertrude Vanderbilt Whitney (Mrs. Harry Payne Whitney), sculptor and art patron, had begun giving informal and unpublicized exhibitions for young and unknown American artists in her studio on Macdougal Alley. In 1914 she decided to enlarge these activities and engaged Juliana Force as her assistant. Through this collaboration developed one of the most vital and germinating influences in the history of American art. The next year, Mrs. Whitney formed the Friends of the Young Artists and made Mrs. Force its director. Though lacking a formal background in art, Mrs. Force had other essential requirements —an instinct for quality, an innate good taste, and the ability to assimilate new ideas. Among Gertrude Whitney's friends were the foremost protagonists of the liberal movement in art—Robert Henri, John Sloan, Arthur B. Davies, William Glackens, Guy Pène duBois, and Forbes Watson, the art critic for *The World* and a leading champion of modern art and native artists. It was from her association with these artists, and not through academic study, that Juliana Force acquired her knowledge of American art. Out of the Friends of the Young Artists grew, in 1918, the Whitney Studio Club, with Mrs. Force as director, and, when it was seen that the club needed its own galleries, an old house on West 4th Street was purchased and remodeled. This was a place where the young and unrecognized artists, as well as the liberal leaders, could meet and exhibit their work. Among the artists of the rising generation of the 1920's to hold their first exhibitions at the Whitney Studio Club were Edward Hopper, Reginald Marsh, Henry Schnackenburg, and Stuart Davis. Mrs. Force took an active part in the club, not only as director, but as hostess and friend. Her vitality, her zest for life, and her warmhearted interest in the artists gave the club a quality of informality and friendliness.

By 1923, the club had outgrown the 4th Street house and it was moved to 10 West 8th Street. Two years later, when the membership mounted to 400, plus a large waiting list, Mrs. Whitney and Mrs. Force felt that the club had achieved its purpose of liberating American art and so it was disbanded. Its place was taken by the Whitney Studio Galleries at 8 West 8th Street, the primary purpose of which was to show the work of young and progressive artists. Exhibitions with a central theme were featured, among them the Circus Exhibition of paintings and sculptures related to the circus and Henry Schnackenburg's pioneering presentation of American folk art, which was to have so wide an influence on American taste. Such exhibitions were the forerunners of the many Whitney Museum discoveries of forgotten artists and forgotten periods of American art and design.

By 1928 uptown galleries were beginning to show the work of artists from the Whitney

Studio Galleries, and the purpose for which it had been founded was achieved.

The next year Mrs. Whitney decided to offer to the Metropolitan Museum her collection of more than 600 paintings and sculptures acquired through the years from the exhibitions of the Studio Club and the Studio Galleries. Mrs. Force was delegated to offer the collection to Dr. Edward Robinson, director of the Metropolitan Museum of Art, and to convey Mrs. Whitney's willingness to build and endow a wing to house it. The latter offer was never made, as Dr. Robinson flatly refused to accept the collection. As a result, Mrs. Whitney and Mrs. Force, with the advice of Forbes Watson, decided to establish a new museum. Mrs. Whitney insisted that Juliana Force should be the director and in 1930 the Whitney Museum of American Art was created in four houses on West 8th Street, remodeled for that purpose. The building followed no stereotyped museum architecture, and the interior reflected Mrs. Force's preference for informality and beauty of color and materials. An extensive program was launched centering on annual exhibitions of contemporary painting and sculpture. The winners received monetary awards drawn from a fund of $10,000 that was set aside every year to purchase paintings and sculpture.

Two important aspects of the museum's educational program were traveling exhibitions and publications. Exhibitions were sent to museums and universities throughout the United States and this activity was extended to Europe in 1935, when Mrs. Force was invited to send an exhibition of contemporary American art to the American Pavilion of the Biennial Exhibition in Venice. The Whitney Museum also pioneered, in 1931, in publishing a series of monographs and books on living American artists, including two full-length biographies, by Lloyd Goodrich, of Thomas Eakins and Winslow Homer.

With the opening of the Whitney Museum, Juliana Force's gifts as a hostess were given wider scope. A series of morning and evening lectures by eminent art historians, critics, artists, and museum directors were held in the museum galleries. The morning lectures were followed by buffet luncheons and the evening ones often ended in informal parties in her apartment above the museum. She was extremely gregarious and loved to entertain. She was a brilliant conversationalist, an inimitable mimic with a sharp-edged sense of humor and impatient with any show of pomposity or pretense. Her apartment, an eclectic combination of many styles and periods, reflected her love of elegance and her daring as a decorator. She was one of the first to revive an interest in Victorian furniture and objets d'art, which she combined effectively with contemporary painting and sculpture.

The Whitney Museum's steadily growing reputation was due in no small part to Mrs. Force's personality and activities. More than any of her contemporaries in the museum field, she knew the artists who produced the works in which she dealt. And as the prestige of the Whitney Museum grew, so did Juliana Force's influence as a museum director. Inevitably, she assumed other responsibilities in the field of American art. She was chairman of Region No. 2 of the Public Works of Art Project (1933-1934), which employed over 900 artists. She was also chairman of the committee for a New York State Art Program and a trustee and officer of the American Federation of Arts and the American Association of Museum Directors, the first woman to hold such posts.

Soon after Gertrude Vanderbilt Whitney's death in 1942, a merger with the Metropolitan Museum was again discussed and a tentative agreement was reached by the trustees of both museums. But when it became evident that differences of opinion, especially on the more advanced trend in contemporary painting, made it doubtful that the Whitney Museum's policies would be maintained, the trustees of the Whitney Museum decided against the coalition. Juliana Force had viewed the proposed coalition with considerable misgiving. Since 1943 she had been serving as unofficial advisor for the Metropolitan Museum's purchases of American art under the Hearn Fund and her misgivings were augmented when the Metropolitan rejected the selection of paintings she recommended. The trustees' decision to continue the Whitney Museum as an independent museum was a great comfort to her in the last months of her life. In July 1948 she was taken to Doctors Hospital in New York, where she died of cancer at the age of seventy-one. She was buried in Doylestown, Pa.

John Sloan summed up her contribution: "The Whitney Museum of American Art is really a memorial to the distinctive genius of Juliana Force but her memory is held dear in the hearts and minds of two generations of American artists."

[Two principal biographical sources are: *Juliana Force and American Art* (Whitney Museum of Am. Art, 1949), which contains essays by Herman More,

Ford

Lloyd Goodrich, John Sloan, Guy Pène duBois, Alexander Brook, and Forbes Watson; and Calvin Tomkin, *Merchants and Masterpieces* (New York, 1973). Articles may be found in *Notable Am. Women, 1607–1950*, I (1971); *Who Was Who in Am.*, II (1950); *Current Biog.*, 1941, pp. 294–296, which contains a portrait; and *Art Digest*, Sept. 15, 1948, p. 15. Obituary notices appeared in the *N.Y. Times*, Aug. 29, 1948; *Time Magazine*, Sept. 6, 1948; *Museum News*, Sept. 15, 1948; *Current Biog.*, 1948; *Magazine of Art*, Oct., 1948; and *Current Biog. Yearbook*, 1948 (1949). Death record from N.Y.C. Department of Health.]

HELEN APPLETON READ

FORD, HENRY (July 30, 1863–Apr. 7, 1947), automotive pioneer and industrialist, was born in a farmhouse in Greenfield Township (now in Dearborn), Wayne County, Mich. He was the second son and the second of eight children born to William Ford and Mary (Litogot) Ford. His grandfather, John Ford, was a Protestant tenant farmer on an estate in Kilmalooda parish near the town of Clonakilty in County Cork, Ireland, and was said to be descended from English freeholders who early in the seventeenth century colonized Irish lands confiscated by Queen Elizabeth. Three of John's brothers immigrated to the United States in 1832 and became farmers in the frontier townships of Greenfield, Redford, and Springwells, several miles west of Detroit in the area later comprising part of Dearborn. John Ford followed in 1847, accompanied by his wife, Thomasina, who died en route in Canada, and by his seven children, including his eldest son, William. In 1848 John Ford and his family settled on a farm along present-day Joy Road in Dearborn. While working on the farm of Patrick O'Hern, William met Mary Litogot. The daughter of a carpenter in Wyandotte, Mich., she had been born in 1839 and was adopted by the O'Herns after being orphaned at an early age. Mary was supposedly of Dutch or Belgian Flemish descent. She and William Ford were married in Detroit on Apr. 25, 1861. They had six sons and two daughters. Their first child, a son, died in infancy in January 1862; their last one, also a son, died at birth in 1876.

Young Henry, growing up on the family farm some two miles east of the River Rouge at the edge of thickly wooded country, learned to savor the sights and sounds of rural life. The deep attachment to the soil he formed at that time gave him an enduring affinity for the traditional past of agrarian America and its virtues of self-reliance, hard work, and thrift. His social outlook of individualism stemmed as much from his mother, who was the dominant influence on his boyhood, as it did from the moral precepts of the McGuffey Readers that were the staple of his formal education in the two rural schools he attended from 1871 to 1879. The death of his mother in March 1876, shortly after she had a stillborn child, had a profound effect upon him. "The house," he recalled, "was like a watch without a mainspring." Henry was fascinated by any kind of machinery, and by the time he was fifteen he had become expert in watch repairing, but he disliked the inefficient drudgery of farm life. "I never had any particular love for the farm," he said in 1923. "It was the mother on the farm I loved."

In December 1879 Ford went to Detroit and became an apprentice in the James Flower and Brothers Machine Shop. Paid only $2.50 a week, he had to take a night job in a jewelry shop, where he repaired watches, in order to meet his expenses. It was a propitious time for an apprentice to learn the trade of machinist, for Detroit, after the long depression of the 1870's, was enjoying a new burst of prosperity in its bustling industrial establishments. In the summer of 1880 Henry joined the Detroit Drydock Company, the largest shipbuilding firm in the city, and was assigned to the engine shop, where he acquired a firsthand knowledge of diverse types of power plants. Completing his apprenticeship in 1882, he became a road agent for the Westinghouse Engine Company and spent about a year servicing steam traction engines for farmers in southern Michigan. These self-propelled traction engines had a special interest for Ford, who first encountered one in July 1876, but his recollection (Ford and Crowther, *My Life and Work*, p. 23) that the road engine inspired his work in automotive transportation merits skepticism. More likely, it sharpened his dissatisfaction with the excessive hard labor of farming and reinforced his desire to work with machines. Over the years 1884–1886 Ford divided his time operating and repairing steam engines, reluctantly helping his father on the family farm, and occasionally working in Detroit factories during the winters. Early in 1885 he met Clara Bryant, daughter of a neighboring farmer, and at some time during their courtship, in 1886–1887, Ford accepted from his father an offer of a wooded tract situated on present-day Ford Road in Dearborn. William Ford retained title to the land, and the offer, according to Henry, was made on condition that he would abandon the machinist's trade and return to farming. Henry Ford and Clara Bryant were married in the Bryant house in Greenfield Township on Apr. 11, 1888. They moved into a house built by Henry from timber

291

cut by himself on a small portable sawmill. Ford made a small income from selling lumber and firewood. To his father's disappointment, he did not engage in farming, but instead used his spare time to experiment with steam and gas engines in a shop attached to his house.

Ford in the late 1880's was a young man with an intuitive understanding of machinery, who was trying to bring his primary interests into closer focus and was eager to grasp larger opportunities that would free him from the conventional legacy of farming and give him a foothold in the world of machine power. In the mid-1880's, while Ford was tinkering with steam engines, years of experimentation by the German automotive pioneers Gottlieb Daimler and Karl Benz culminated in their successful operation of self-propelled gasoline vehicles. An infant industry quickly sprang up in Western Europe, and by 1891 automobiles were being produced commercially by the French firm of Panhard et Levassor. At the same time a number of Americans, working independently, were groping their way toward the creation of an operable horseless carriage. As early as 1879 George B. Selden, a patent lawyer in Rochester, N.Y., filed an application for a patent on a "road locomotive" using an internal combustion engine. The first American-built gasoline automobile, made by the brothers Charles E. and J. Frank Duryea, was taken on its initial run by the latter at Springfield, Mass., in September 1893. Ford may have garnered fragmentary information about these early automotive achievements, but there is no evidence, despite his subsequent predated claims, that in the period 1888-1892 he designed or built a self-propelled gasoline vehicle or a workable motor for one. Nevertheless, he had more clearly defined this as his central aim and purpose. He abandoned farming and moved with his wife to Detroit, where in September 1891 he became a night engineer with the Edison Illuminating Company at a salary of $45 a month. In November 1893 he was transferred to its powerhouse in downtown Detroit and a short time later became chief engineer at a salary of $100 a month. On Nov. 6, 1893, a son and only child, Edsel Bryant Ford, was born to the couple.

Ford used his spare time for experimenting with a gasoline engine in an effort to find a portable power plant capable of being used as the motor of an automobile. From the end of 1893 to the spring of 1896 his experiments were conducted in a workshop set up in a small brick shed behind the two-family house at 58 Bagley Avenue, where the Fords had lived since De-

cember 1893. His work on small gasoline engines was stimulated by the technical advice of a young Detroit engineer, Charles B. King, and King's assistant, Oliver E. Barthel, both of whom made the first horseless carriage operated on the streets of Detroit. The test of the King car on Mar. 6, 1896, was witnessed by Ford. At about this time Ford completed a four-cycle, air-cooled gasoline motor with two cylinders of 2.5-inch bore and 6-inch stroke capable of delivering three to four horsepower. Ford mounted this engine on a chassis and body built with the assistance of a friend, James W. Bishop. The mechanical features of the quadricycle, as Ford called it, drew liberally on his firsthand observation of the King car and represented no advance over the work of contemporary pioneers. The car weighed 500 pounds, had a belt-and-chain transmission, two speeds and a neutral gear, and, except for the engine, axles, wheels, and steering rod, was made entirely of wood. The quadricycle made its first run in the pre-dawn hours of June 4, 1896. The success of the car encouraged Ford to press forward with his automotive experimentation. Late in 1896 he sold the quadricycle for $200 and began work on a second machine.

In developing his second car between 1897 and 1899, Ford received financial support from Mayor William C. Maybury of Detroit and three associates. Remaining in the full-time employ of the Edison Illuminating Company, Ford produced an operable car by mid-1899. This vehicle, a two-passenger car weighing 875 pounds, had fully enclosed mechanical elements, electric spark ignition, and chain-and sprocket transmission. It established his reputation as one of the automotive pioneers in the city. As the result of Ford's approach to William H. Murphy, a wealthy Detroit lumber merchant, Murphy and a group of other investors, including Maybury and his associates, formed the Detroit Automobile Company on Aug. 5, 1899. Capitalized at $150,000, and with a paid-in capital of $15,000, it was the first company organized in Detroit for the manufacture of motorcars. It was one of many similar enterprises, few of them destined to survive, launched on the wave of prosperity just after the Spanish-American War, when the automobile industry began to emerge in the United States. Ford's attempt to build a car with interchangeable gears and bodies was hampered by the relatively crude production methods then available. After turning out approximately twenty machines, the Detroit Automobile Company went out of business in the autumn of 1900. Its record, however, was better than those set by most of the other companies that mushroomed during this period. His experience as shop superintendent took Ford into the motorcar field on a full-time basis and gave him an insight into the essential requirements for building a light, sturdy, and durable gasoline automobile suitable for quantity production.

To gain a wider reputation, Ford turned to auto racing. Again with financial backing from William H. Murphy, and with technical assistance from Oliver Barthel and Edward S. Huff, Ford built a racer with a horizontal engine capable of generating 26 h.p. He entered it in a contest held at the Grosse Pointe, Mich., racetrack on Oct. 10, 1901, in which he was pitted against a more powerful machine handled by a more expert driver, the Cleveland automobile manufacturer Alexander Winton. Ford's victory revived the enthusiasm of some former stockholders of the Detroit Automobile Company and resulted in the reorganization of that firm on Nov. 30, 1901, as the Henry Ford Company. It was capitalized at $60,000, of which $30,500 was paid in. Ford contributed no cash. He was given a one-sixth interest of 1,000 shares ($10,000) and was appointed superintending engineer. Dissension soon broke out between Ford and the promoters, partly because he insisted on building a larger and faster racing car rather than a commercial model. These differences came to a head shortly after Henry M. Leland, of the Detroit engineering firm of Leland and Faulconer, was brought into the Henry Ford Company as a consultant. Ford resigned on Mar. 10, 1902, and the company, which agreed to discontinue using Ford's name, was reorganized later that year as the Cadillac Motor Car Co., with Leland as its production manager. In association with Tom Cooper, a former bicycle racing champion, Ford again turned to auto racing, and in May 1902 began constructing two racing cars, "The Arrow" and the "999." Cooper furnished most of the money for the project. The vehicles were built by Ford and a young assistant, C. Harold Wills, a gifted toolmaker, machinist, and metallurgist who became one of Ford's key associates. The "999," with a wheelbase of 9 feet 9 inches and a tread of 5 feet 2 inches, had a four-cylinder motor developing between 70 and 80 h.p. On Oct. 25, 1902, with Barney Oldfield at the wheel, the "999" won the Manufacturers' Challenge Cup at the Grosse Pointe racetrack, setting a new American record by traversing the five-mile course in 5 minutes 28 seconds. Save for a few more occasions up to 1907, Ford abandoned racing. On one of these, in January 1904, he and his mechanic, Ed "Spider" Huff, hurtled over the ice of Anchor Bay on Lake St. Clair to set a new record of 39.4 seconds for a measured mile.

In 1902, at thirty-nine, Ford had two unsuccessful automotive enterprises behind him, but he had a local standing as an authority on motor vehicles and a demonstrated ability to attract both investors and co-workers with confidence in his technical expertise. Moreover, he had arrived at a closer definition of his aims. In mid-1902 Ford began laying out rough designs for a pilot model capable of competing with such popular-priced cars as the Oldsmobile, which at this time was being manufactured in volume in Detroit and was designed as utility transportation in contrast to the main trend, especially as exemplified by Eastern manufacturers, that envisioned the automobile as a luxury product for the wealthy. Ford, requiring some $3,000 for development costs, approached Alexander Y. Malcomson, a leading Detroit coal dealer, and in April 1902 they formed a partnership to produce a marketable automobile. Ford agreed to contribute his designs and skills and took charge of manufacturing activities, while Malcomson financed the project and agreed to handle the business operations, which he delegated to his clerk and office manager, James Couzens. Ford, working alongside C. Harold Wills in a shop at 81 Park Place in Detroit, brought the model almost to completion by December 1902, but lacked the capital to start up quantity production. The high incidence of failures in the auto industry had made established investors, especially bankers, wary of supporting such ventures; but for those who succeeded, the rewards were great, and by 1903 the demand for automobiles was so strong that factories could hardly keep up with their orders. In April 1903 Ford and Malcomson moved their operation to larger quarters in a former wagon shop, 250 feet long by 50 feet wide, on Mack Avenue. A second and improved model had been built, and Ford had contracted with outside suppliers for parts and components. Foremost among these suppliers were the Dodge brothers, John F. and Horace E., owners of a large Detroit machine shop, who had agreed to deliver 650 chassis. Bodies were supplied by another local firm, the C. R. Wilson Carriage Company. The ease with which Detroit foundries, machine shops, and other manufacturing establishments could meet the needs of auto assembly plants contributed to the swift rise of that city as a motorcar center, although its abundance of skilled labor and excellent rail and water connections were also important. After successive rebuffs, Ford and Malcomson were able to persuade a number of investors to make definite commitments, and on June 16, 1903, the Ford Motor Company was incorporated with an authorized capitalization of $150,000, of which $100,000 was issued in stock, the balance being kept in reserve as treasury stock. Only $28,000 was paid in cash. The Ford-Malcomson partnership transferred its holdings to the new company for 510 shares equally divided between the two associates, who with 255 shares each became the largest individual shareholders. In all, including Ford and Malcomson, there were twelve stockholders: the Dodge brothers, 50 shares each; Malcomson's uncle, John S. Gray, president of the German-American Bank, who held 105 shares and became president of the company; Vernon C. Fry, Malcomson's cousin, 50 shares; Horace H. Rackham and John W. Anderson, Malcomson's attorneys, 50 shares each; Albert Strelow, a painting and building contractor, 50 shares; Charles J. Woodall, 10 shares; and James Couzens, 25 shares (including one owned by his sister, Mrs. Rosetta V. Hauss). Ford, who paid no cash for his stock, became vice-president; Malcomson became treasurer; and Couzens, who was made secretary, took charge of business operations and also did the work of treasurer. Ford and Couzens ran the company. As general manager, Ford was in charge of design, engineering, and production, while Couzens not only handled routine office activities but also negotiated contracts, attended to advertising, and laid the groundwork of a strong sales organization. The two men followed a policy of financing operations from profits to which the company adhered for the rest of Ford's lifetime.

The first Ford automobile, the Model A, was brought out in June 1903 and sold for $850. Equipped with a two-cylinder, eight h.p. engine and planetary transmission, this light touring car immediately attracted buyers, and 1,708 were sold in the first fifteen months. To keep up with the brisk demand, a second story was added to the Mack Avenue assembly plant. The higher-priced Models B, C, and F were offered in 1904-1905, when net profits amounted to $290,000, and in early 1905 manufacturing operations were transferred to a new and large plant at the junction of Piquette Avenue and Beaubien Street in Detroit. Two dividends of $100,000 each were declared in June and July 1905. Within the company, a dispute had broken out between Ford and Malcomson. Ford, supported by Couzens, advocated a standardized design for a cheap car suitable for quantity production and a mass market. Malcomson, who believed that the automobile would remain a luxury, favored the production of a heavy, expensive car. The Malcomson policy was exemplified by the Model B, brought out in 1905-1906 for $2,000. The outcome of the Ford-Malcomson controversy was a significant redistribution of power within the Ford Motor Company. Malcomson's overcommitments in outside investments left him in financial difficulty, and in July 1906 he accepted Ford's offer of $175,000 for the purchase of his 255 shares of company stock. Over the ensuing year three stockholders who had supported Malcomson disposed of their shares. Woodall sold his 10 shares to Ford; Bennett's 50 shares were divided between Couzens (35 shares) and Ford (15 shares); and Fry's 50 shares were bought by Ford. In addition, Couzens purchased Albert Strelow's 50 shares. Thus by the fall of 1907 the number of stockholders had been reduced to eight. Ford held 585 shares, or 58.5 percent, while Couzens, his close ally, held 110 shares. Moreover, Ford was president, having succeeded John S. Gray on his death in 1906, and Couzens had replaced Malcomson as treasurer.

No longer hindered by internal opposition, Ford proceeded to translate into reality his concept of a low-cost car for mass use. His first step was the Model N of 1906-1907, which he hailed as a car that would take the auto out of the luxury class. Ford told the press that it was "destined to revolutionize automobile construction," and he saw it as the answer to the problem of whether "a serviceable machine can be constructed at a price within the reach of many" (*Detroit Journal*, Jan. 5, 1906). Introduced at $600, but subsequently sold at $700, the Model N had a four-cylinder engine and a single standardized chassis. Ford hired Walter E. Flanders, an able machine tool and production expert, to make 10,000 units of the Model N in a single year; the standardized design enabled Flanders to meet this goal by exploiting the possibilities of sequential flow production techniques. The success of the Model N contrasted with the poor showing of the Model K which the company brought out at $2,800 in 1906. The Model N raised the net income of the company for the first time to more than $1 million, placed the firm at the forefront of the industry, and showed that Ford was correct in his view that the future of the industry belonged to the quantity-produced small car. Even as the Model N went into production, Ford was at work on a new design embodying the basic elements of a "universal car." No other company was so well-equipped to carry out the formula of the low-cost car to its logical conclusion. It had attracted some of the most ingenious production managers in the industry. As a mark of its steady growth, the company in late 1908 increased its capitalization to $2 million, divided into 20,000 shares at $100 each, of which $1.9 million was issued to shareholders as a stock dividend (each shareholder received twenty shares for each share held prior to Oct. 22, 1908, approved on Nov. 3, 1908). In 1906-1907, when it became clear that the recently built Piquette Avenue plant was no longer adequate for the rapidly expanding business, the company acquired a sixty-acre tract in Highland Park, immediately north of Detroit, and in 1908 began construction of the largest industrial plant in Michigan. Its foreign operations were initiated with the establishment of branches in Canada and Great Britain.

The Model T, introduced on Oct. 1, 1908, combined in a standardized utility vehicle the features of lightness, durability, economy of operation, efficiency, interchangeable parts, and low cost. Ford was responsible for the basic concept; the details were designed by him in collaboration with C. Harold Wills and another company engineer, Joseph Galamb, between 1905 and 1908. The car had a 100-inch wheelbase, a four-cylinder, twenty h.p. water-cooled engine cast in one block, planetary transmission, and, in place of dry-battery ignition, a magneto built into the flywheel. It weighed 1,200 pounds and used high-strength vanadium steel in the axles, crankshaft, and other components. The initial price of the Model T ranged between $850 and $1,000, but by Aug. 1, 1916, as a result of progressive price reductions based on cost-cutting production methods, Ford was able to offer the runabout at $345, the touring car at $360, and the chassis at $325. From its introduction until 1927, the Model T was the sole model built by the company. For most of these years its spare, angular body was painted black, but Ford's frequently quoted remark, "Any customer can have a car painted any color that he wants so long as it is black," did not apply to every Model T. The earliest ones were available in red, green, black, blue, and two shades of gray; starting in 1914 all left the factory painted black. Color options were reintroduced in 1926 and were continued through May 1927.

Ford designed the car for rural America. Admirably suited to travel over poor country roads, it quickly became the favorite in farm areas and small towns, especially in the large and untapped segment of the automobile market that lay in the Middle West and Plains states. Ford introduced the car at precisely the most auspicious historical moment, for between 1909 and 1916, when the Model T established its uncontested supremacy in the mass market, American agriculture was basking in the prosperity of its "golden age." Thus the rural market, with its strong purchasing power, its simple and utilitarian preferences, and its innumerable uses for the versatile Model T, gave the first sustained impetus to the car that was principally responsible for taking the automobile out of the luxury class and making it an inexpensive necessity for the common man. The far-reaching influence of this farmer's car put the nation on wheels, enormously accelerated the urbanization of America, and ultimately brought the motor transportation revolution to other countries. As the catalyst of the automobile age in the twentieth century, the Model T was undoubtedly "the greatest single vehicle in the history of world transportation" (Nevins and Hill, *Ford*, 1957, II, 377).

At the time that orders for the Model T were starting to pour in, the Ford Motor Company was still under the cloud of a patent infringement suit that had been lodged against it in 1903, when it defied the Association of Licensed Automobile Manufacturers (ALAM), a trade group that sought to impose a monopoly on the motorcar industry through its control of the Selden patent. The ALAM claimed that this allegedly basic patent, issued in 1895 to George B. Selden after a long delay in the Patent Office, covered any gasoline automobile made, sold, or used in the United States. Ford, capitalizing on contemporary hostility to business monopoly, assailed the "Auto Trust" and derided Selden's claims as having contributed nothing to the technology of the motor car. In the process of fighting for his own freedom to produce without paying tribute to the ALAM combination, Ford emerged as the foremost industry exponent of open competition in a free market system. Although he and the company received much valuable free publicity from the suit, Ford seems to have been temporarily discouraged by it. In 1908, and again in 1909, he and Couzens reportedly were prepared to sell their interests had William C. Durant been able to make a cash offer. Ford's central legal position in the case was that the Brayton two-cycle engine specified in the Selden patent did not cover the four-cycle Otto-type internal combustion engine in the Ford car. In 1909 a federal district court in

New York upheld the broad scope of the patent and found that Ford had infringed. With the Model T in production, back royalties under the patent, which was due to expire in 1912, would have been sizable. Ford appealed, and in January 1911 the U.S. Court of Appeals for the Second Circuit ruled that although the Selden patent was valid, its scope was restricted to vehicles incorporating the two-cycle engine, then used by few makers. Ford's long fight against the ALAM freed the industry from the threat of monopoly and gave him a reputation for independence. Neither the profitability nor the growth of the company was seriously affected by the Selden case. Up to Feb. 21, 1911, the firm's total cash dividends came to more than $4.8 million and from profits plowed back into the business the company built the Highland Park plant, which eventually covered 229 acres, including 52 acres of floor space. Nor did the Selden litigation hinder the soaring production of Ford cars, which went from 18,664 in 1909-1910 to 34,528 in 1910-1911 and 78,440 in 1911-1912, but its favorable outcome allowed the company to expand its facilities and to embark in 1912 on a program of branch assembly plant construction that by 1916 had brought twenty-eight branch units into existence. In addition, the sales organization was strengthened, and by 1913 there were some 7,000 dealers in the country, with at least one in every town of 2,000 or more.

In announcing that he would "build a motorcar for the great multitude," Ford became the first automobile manufacturer to concentrate on a single model with a standardized chassis made of interchangeable parts. This revolutionary departure imposed a new set of technological requirements, which were met in the Highland Park plant between 1910 and 1914. During those years Ford and his production engineers, among them Peter E. Martin, Charles E. Sorensen, Carl Emde, and Clarence W. Avery, laid down the foundations of automotive mass production and its culminating achievement of continuously moving assembly. After the company moved its operations to Highland Park early in 1910, Ford was often on the factory floor with his associates as they arranged machines, materials, and men in patterns that systematized "line" or sequential production, eliminated unnecessary motion, and cut factory costs. Machines were grouped according to their function in the plant process rather than by type or class of operation; materials were transported from one work station to another by overhead conveyors, gravity slides and tubes, endless belts, and other mechanical handling devices according to predetermined plan and without interrupting the progressive movement of parts, subassemblies, and assemblies into the feeder lines; the work was brought to the man, not the man to the work, in a manner that kept the moving lines of materials waist-high at all times, so that the worker, his operations having been simplified and specialized by a minute subdivision of labor, would not have to bend, stoop, or engage in any other movement interfering with his maximum efficiency and productivity. By empirical means, Ford and his production experts independently arrived at some of the same principles of work and motion management formulated by Frederick Winslow Taylor and Frank B. Gilbreth. A new phase in the history of accurately timed and coordinated industrial production began in the spring of 1913, when a continuously moving conveyor was installed for the subassembly of the flywheel magneto coil. This operation, originally requiring twenty minutes for completion by one man, was reduced to five minutes. After the new system was adapted to other subassemblies, workers on final assembly, where chassis were fixed in a stationary position, were unable to keep pace with the enormously increased output. To eliminate this bottleneck, engineers installed in the summer of 1913 a motor with a windlass and heavy rope on which a chassis was kept in continuous motion past workers and materials arranged according to sequence of operation. This was the progenitor of the continuously moving final assembly line, equipped with a mechanically powered endless chain, which went into operation on Dec. 1, 1913. By early January 1914 six main assembly lines were in use. The change from stationary to moving assembly in 1913-1914 yielded a reduction of the average assembly time for a chassis from 728 minutes to 93 minutes. The technological innovation of continuously moving mass production followed from the logic of a standardized design for an ever-expanding market, and it enabled Ford to raise his production from 248,307 in 1913-1914 to 472,350 in 1915-1916 and to 730,041 in 1916-1917. By 1916, when the millionth Model T rolled off the line, Ford production was averaging 2,000 cars a day.

Although it was Ford's intention to dispense with skilled labor, it did not concern him that the speed and monotony of mechanized mass production might dehumanize the worker. By 1913, however, it was evident that the subdivision of labor at Highland Park was generating restiveness and discontent. Faced with a serious problem of labor turnover, Ford and Couzens recognized that the vast market for the Model T could not be satisfied unless Ford workers had an incentive to submit to the new industrial discipline of the moving assembly line. Primarily from this motive, and partly for humanitarian reasons, the Ford Motor Company announced on Jan. 5, 1914, a basic wage of $5 a day for all eligible workers in the Ford plants, as well as a reduction in shift time from nine to eight hours. At this time the daily wage in Detroit automobile factories was $1.80 for unskilled labor and $2.50 for skilled workers. The announcement of the "Five Dollar Day" was front-page news and overnight made Henry Ford a national celebrity. The financial and business community considered the move as radical and utopian; the press and public opinion generally gave it overwhelming approval. Even though a substantial number of Ford workers were either flatly excluded, not immediately eligible, or never received more than the starting wage of $2.72 a day, the scheme was hailed as a landmark of labor-management policy. Ford was praised as the prophet of a new industrial order and high-consumption society when he pointed out that workers should be paid high wages so that they might buy the goods they produced. To administer the Five Dollar wage plan, the company established a Sociological Department in 1914. Headed by John R. Lee, who in 1915 was succeeded by Rev. Dr. Samuel S. Marquis, Dean of St. Paul's Episcopal Cathedral in Detroit, the Sociological Department in some respects performed useful social functions for Ford workers and their families, but in other ways it was a paternalistic and authoritarian organization that frequently intruded on the privacy of employees.

The Five Dollar Day signaled Ford's meteoric rise to fame, and for the first time linked the Ford name on the Model T to a recognizable image and a concrete personality. To most of the American people, he loomed as a benefactor and humanitarian who had placed his industrial enterprise and the arts of mass production at the service of the public and his employees. At that point the Ford legend had its beginnings. One immediate consequence was a change in his mode of life. Besieged by journalists and trailed by crowds, Ford was compelled to hire a guard for protection against supplicants for jobs, money, interviews, and favors. In pursuit of privacy, he gave up a comfortable house that he had built at 66 Edison Avenue in Detroit in 1907-1908 at a cost of $283,000, and in 1913-1915 built a mansion in his spacious Fair

Lane estate, on the banks of the River Rouge in Dearborn, at a cost of $2 million. Ford later acquired two winter homes, one at Fort Myers, Fla., and the other at Richmond Hill, Ga., along the Ogeechee River some twenty miles south of Savannah, on a plantation occupying 100 square miles.

In early 1914, Ford was fifty and at the height of his powers. Five feet nine inches tall, he had a spare, lithe, and sinewy figure, a thin and serene face, and extraordinarily brilliant light blue eyes that verged on pale green. He was clean-shaven, having discarded a handlebar moustache some ten years earlier, and his light brown hair, much of it already silver gray, was parted in the middle and brushed to the side. He gave a general impression of restless vitality and movement; his long, supple fingers were almost always in rippling motion. He loved to walk in the country, and on impulse might climb a tree, jump over a fence, or challenge a companion to a foot race. He did not care for small talk, was not a good conversationalist, and was an inept public speaker. He was completely self-assured in working with problems of mechanical construction and automotive manufacture, displaying here a gift of analytical insight tantamount almost to genius. He had little use for conventional formulas and expert authority and preferred to rely upon his own intuitive judgments, or "hunches," as he called them. But in applying his "hunches" to other fields for which he was ill-equipped either by education or knowledge, Ford exhibited a narrow materialism, utilitarianism, and anti-intellectualism. "I don't like to read books," he said. "They muss up my mind." He also said: "I wouldn't give five cents for all the art in the world." Outside his special province, his thought was unsystematic, fitful, impulsive, and arbitrary, and prey to his latent prejudices, dark suspicions, and unpredictable moodiness. "Well, I can't prove it, but I can smell it," was one of his sayings. His friend, the naturalist John Burroughs, remarked: "Ford has a big heart, but his head is not so large except in his own line." To virtually all of his associates, he was a complex and puzzling combination of disparate and discordant elements that were never properly integrated. Ford could be modest, idealistic, helpful, kind, and generous; he could also be vain, cynical, overbearing, harsh, and vindictive. His sudden rise to fame, by enhancing his self-importance, made him more inclined to interpret his success and its universal acclaim as proof of his unerring judgment. This predilection intimately affected his role in company and public affairs in 1915-1921 when Ford became involved in the most controversial episodes of his career.

Within the company, Ford's single-minded purpose and iron will became united to a drive for absolute power. He was dissatisfied with his minority stockholders, particularly the Dodge brothers, who were no longer active in the company and were financing the manufacture of their own car with Ford dividends. Ford had personal differences with Couzens, and relations between the two were broken in October 1915, when Couzens resigned in protest against Ford's use of company advertising to disseminate his antiwar views. Up to the end of 1915 the minority stockholders had collected a total of $25 million in cash dividends, and Ford hinted that they were "absentee owners" and "parasites." When Ford announced his intention to limit annual dividends to a total of $1.2 million (in 1914 alone, they had amounted to $9.2 million) so that he might reinvest most of the profits in plant expansion and further cut the price of the Model T, the Dodge brothers filed a stockholders' suit against him in November 1916 to block the expansion plans and force payment of a large dividend. Ford proclaimed his dedication to the principle of a small unit profit on volume production that would create additional jobs at good wages and allow more people to enjoy the use of a car. In October 1917 a Michigan circuit court ruled in favor of the Dodges and ordered Ford to pay a special dividend of $19,275,000. Ford appealed, and in February 1919 the Michigan superior court termed the withholding of dividends arbitrary and illegal, and ordered Ford to pay them with interest, bringing the total to more than $20 million. Determined to win an absolutely free hand over policy, Ford, having already resigned as president of the Ford Company on Dec. 30, 1918, left for California and in March 1919 gave out press interviews about his plans to organize a new and entirely family-owned firm to produce a car underselling the Model T. This shrewd stratagem sowed alarm and confusion among the minority stockholders. Meanwhile, Ford initiated confidential negotiations through third parties for acquisition of the 8,300 shares comprising the full minority interest of 41.5 percent. A price of $12,500 per share was set for all of the minority stockholders except Couzens, who was paid $13,444.43 per share. The Dodges received $25 million; Couzens $29,-308,857.90; and Rosetta V. Hauss (who held out for $13,000 per share) received $262,036.67 for her twenty shares. The total cost to Ford

was $105,820,894.57. To finance the purchase, Ford obtained a credit of $75 million (of which he actually used $60 million) from a financial syndicate of three Eastern banks. All of the Ford enterprises, including Henry Ford and Son, a Dearborn company established in 1915 to manufacture the Fordson tractor, were absorbed into the Ford Motor Company of Delaware in 1920, which then reissued stock. Henry Ford received 95,321 shares (55.2 percent); Clara Ford, 5,413 shares (3.1 percent); and Edsel Ford, 71,911 shares (41.7 percent). All of the Ford properties were thus combined in a single unit under the centralized control of Henry Ford, who wielded greater power over his corporate domain than either John D. Rockefeller, Sr., or Andrew Carnegie ever exercised over their own.

In 1915-1919, as Ford moved toward one-man control of the company, he also became involved in some of the most controversial episodes of his multifaceted career as a public personage. The outbreak of World War I in Europe reawakened his deep aversion to militarism and war. In the summer of 1915 he issued militant pacifist denunciations of war as murderous and wasteful. In November, the Hungarian feminist Rosika Schwimmer and the American pacifist Louis P. Lochner induced Ford to support a project for ending the war through "continuous mediation" by a proposed Conference of Neutrals. At his own expense, Ford chartered a Scandinavian ocean liner, *Oscar II*, to take the peace delegates to Europe. Impulsively, he told reporters, "We're going to try to get the boys out of the trenches before Christmas." In a more reflective moment, he conceded that he did not expect the peace expedition to end the war immediately, "The chief effect I look for is psychological." The "Peace Ship" was derided by most of the American press, and popular opinion, much of it pro-Allied, was generally hostile. The vessel, with Ford among the passengers, sailed from Hoboken, N.J., on Dec. 2, 1915, and docked at Christiania (Oslo), Norway, on December 18. Shortly afterward Ford abruptly quit the expedition and returned home, but he continued to give financial support to the work of the Neutral Conference for Continuous Mediation, to which he contributed a total of $465,000.

Throughout 1916 Ford continued to attack war "profiteers," but after diplomatic relations with Germany were broken in February 1917, he pledged that in the event of war he would place his factory at the disposal of the government and "operate without one cent of profit."

Following the declaration of war in April 1917, Ford filled government contracts for ambulances, trucks, light tanks, Liberty aircraft motors, Eagle boats (submarine chasers), gun caissons, shells, armor plate, and helmets. Despite repeated assurances by Ford and others, he never redeemed his promise to return his war profits.

Nominally a Republican, Ford participated only minimally in politics until 1916, when he enthusiastically supported President Woodrow Wilson for reelection. In June 1918, at Wilson's urging, Ford agreed to enter the Michigan race for the United States Senate. An advocate of the League of Nations and other Wilsonian proposals, Ford entered both the Democratic and Republican primaries as a non-partisan independent, calling himself "the President's candidate." His chief rival in the Republican primary was Truman H. Newberry, whose campaign organization spent money lavishly on publicity and advertising. Ford won the Democratic nomination, but Newberry's victory on the Republican side gave him the advantage in a normally Republican state. The election campaign was marked by scurrilous attacks on Ford's patriotism and by insinuations that his son Edsel was a draft-dodger. Ford lost the election by 7,567 votes (later reduced by a recount to 4,337). Stung by the abusive tactics of the opposition, Ford financed an undercover investigation of the Newberry organization. The evidence unearthed by his operatives was instrumental in bringing Newberry and his associates to trial for violating the Federal Corrupt Practices Act and in later driving Newberry to resign from the Senate.

Privately, Ford had attributed the European war to "international bankers" and his defeat in the Senate contest to Wall Street "interests" and to "the Jews." His latent bigotry, shaped primarily by his narrow education and his constricted rural origins, was reinforced in 1919 as a result of his celebrated million-dollar libel suit against the *Chicago Tribune,* which he sued for an editorial it had published on June 23, 1916, calling him an "anarchist" and "an ignorant idealist" because of his antipreparedness utterances. After about three years of legal maneuvering, the trial opened in May 1919 in Mt. Clemens, Mich. The exceptionally broad terms on which the judge decided to admit evidence gave the *Tribune* attorneys, headed by the formidable Elliott G. Stevenson, an opportunity to cross-examine Ford pitilessly and expose to reporters for the national press his ignorance in areas of general knowledge. In

August 1919 the jury found the *Tribune* guilty of libel and awarded Ford six cents. The trial was a humiliating personal ordeal for Ford, leaving him angry and disillusioned, and more disposed to be bitter and cynical rather than idealistic and hopeful.

The *Tribune* suit drove Ford deeper into intolerance and intellectual isolation and made him prey to a growing belief that his enemies were leagued against him in a sinister conspiracy. This view of social reality gradually came to dominate his thinking in the last thirty years of his life. Its most extreme instance involved the anti-Semitic campaign Ford undertook in the *Dearborn Independent,* which he acquired as a small country weekly in November 1918 with the intention of conducting it as his own journal of opinion in support of Wilson's principles of postwar reconstruction. The publication followed this editorial policy until the spring of 1920, when Ford, assisted by his personal secretary, Ernest G. Liebold, and by the new head of the editorial staff, William J. Cameron, launched an anti-Semitic tirade with an article, "The International Jew: The World's Problem." Ninety issues of the *Dearborn Independent* were devoted to this propaganda; a compilation of the articles entitled *The International Jew* was widely distributed in the United States and Europe. Ford resurrected the discredited forgery "The Protocols of the Wise Men of Zion," and in order to increase the circulation of the *Dearborn Independent,* which reached 472,500 in 1923, tried to force the journal on Ford dealers. In 1924-1925 Ford published a series of articles attacking Aaron Sapiro, a Chicago lawyer who responded by filing a suit for defamation of character asking $1 million in damages. Ford made an out-of-court settlement with Sapiro, and on July 7, 1927, issued a formal retraction of his attacks on the Jewish people, promised to refrain from publishing any more anti-Semitic material, and made a personal apology to Sapiro. The *Dearborn Independent* ceased publication at the end of 1927. A deficit operation, it had cost Ford $4,795,000.

Ford's excursions into pacifism, politics, and biogotry exposed his flaws and foibles, but did not seriously impair his popularity among small-town and rural Americans, who admired him as a self-made man and responded to his neo-Populist rhetoric against "profiteers" and "Wall Street." In the early 1920's Ford was seriously mentioned as a presidential possibility, and in a poll conducted by a national weekly in 1923 ran ahead of President Warren G. Harding, even in the latter's home state of Ohio. At the same time, Ford's world reputation continued to flourish. "Fordismus" became an international term connoting factory efficiency, high wages, and mass consumption. In the Soviet Union, where Ford's name was known to millions, "Fordizatsia" became a synonym of advanced industrial techniques. By and large, the Ford legend grew of its own accord, but after 1919 Ford's bent for self-advertisement led him to maintain a corps of company publicists, including Liebold and Cameron, who assiduously fostered favorable publicity. In the 1920's Ford reached a wide public as the nominal author of books and articles written by amanuenses, chief among them Samuel Crowther, who "collaborated" with Ford on *My Life and Work* (1922), which became a best seller in the United States and was translated into several European languages. A pirated and censored edition enjoyed a large circulation in the Soviet Union.

Upon taking full control of the company in 1919, Ford converted it into an organization completely responsive to his autocratic imperatives by forcing out his independent-minded lieutenants and retaining only those who followed his dictates unquestioningly. The spring of 1919 saw the departure of C. Harold Wills, John R. Lee, and the able sales manager Norval A. Hawkins; in the winter of 1920-1921 they were followed by William S. Knudsen, Rev. Dr. Samuel S. Marquis, and treasurer Frank L. Klingensmith. For the next decade power at the second echelon in the company was concentrated in the hard-driving production expert Charles E. Sorensen, and in the abrasive and overbearing Ernest G. Liebold, under whom the purging of managerial talent ultimately left a vacuum of leadership that seriously weakened the company. A harsher atmosphere came to prevail after Ford met the postwar recession of 1920-1921 with stringent measures that enabled him to fulfill his obligations when repayment of his bankers' loan fell due in April 1921. Ford responded to the business slump of mid-1920 by steeply reducing Model T prices in September, initiating ruthless internal economies, and shutting down for six weeks. Reopening his factory on Feb. 1, 1921, he assembled some 90,000 autos made of materials purchased at deflated prices and forced the cars on Ford dealers, who were generally able to obtain financing from their local bankers. By April 1921, Ford had realized $24.7 million from the sale of cars and parts, and had saved $28 million by reducing inventory; together with income from other sources and a cash reserve of $20 million, he had liquid assets of $87.3 million for paying debts amounting to some $58 million.

Emerging from the crisis of 1920-1921 with renewed vigor, the company embarked upon a period of dynamic growth at home and abroad. Between 1919 and 1927 Ford's most innovative technological contribution was his development of the immense River Rouge plant in Dearborn. Ford attempted to make this virtually self-contained industrial city covering 1,115 acres the focal point of a system of "moving inventory," whereby raw materials carried from distant points would be in process until their final embodiment as Ford cars or tractors. At the Rouge, Ford built an enormous complex of blast furnaces, coke ovens, dock facilities, the world's largest foundry, a glass plant, and other structures; and he acquired forests and iron mines in the Upper Peninsula of Michigan, and coal mines in Kentucky and West Virginia, to assure his supplies. Between 1924 and 1927 the principal car-making factories of Highland Park were transferred to the Rouge. However, Ford abandoned his scheme of comprehensive vertical integration at the Rouge when it proved economically and administratively impracticable, and Ford's later preoccupation with decentralized "village industries" in Michigan, Ohio, and other states was partly a token of his recognition that self-sufficiency on such a vast scale was not desirable. In the 1920's Ford's ambition to create a vast industrial empire took him into a variety of projects, most of them related to his automotive activities. He acquired a glass plant in Pennsylvania and established another in Minnesota; he developed a rubber plantation in Brazil to guarantee a rubber supply for his tire factory at the Rouge; in 1922 he purchased the Lincoln Motor Car Company at a sacrifice price, ousted the founders, Henry M. Leland and his son Wilfred, and for the first time diversified the Ford line of cars; he helped pioneer commercial aviation in the United States and set up a factory at Dearborn to manufacture the all-metal Ford monoplane popularly known as the "Tin Goose"; he bought the Detroit, Toledo and Ironton Railroad in 1920 and operated it successfully until 1929, when he sold it to the Pennsylvania Railroad, and until 1924 he publicized his controversial proposal to take over from the federal government the hydroelectric generating facilities it had built at Muscle Shoals on the Tennessee River during World War I.

The Rouge and its ancillary activities were central to Ford's larger design to maintain a position of leadership in the automotive industry. From the time that the five millionth Ford car was produced on May 28, 1921, the company continued to raise its output. In 1921 the Model T accounted for about 56 percent of all cars sold in the United States. But as the industry, which had learned its advanced techniques from Ford, increased its output, Ford failed to enlarge his share of the market despite sharp increases in his own production. Thus in the banner year of 1923, when Ford raised his output by 55 percent, his share of the market remained almost stationary, and by 1925 had fallen to 45 percent. Ford answered the challenge by cutting prices, but this once reliable formula proved inadequate. The Model T was outmoded, and the reasons for its decline were rooted mainly in the insulated mind of its creator and in the pattern of one-man rule he imposed on the company. In the 1920's, as the standards of an affluent consumer culture began to permeate American society, the Model T no longer satisfied the more sophisticated and cosmopolitan preferences of younger Americans from the cities and the mushrooming suburbs who looked for comfort, fashion, style, and status in their automobiles. Until 1919, Ford had been receptive to changes in the Model T, but after that time he clung obstinately to a utilitarian and functional view of the automobile and expressed his contempt for the planned obsolescence of competitive cars. By 1924 the principal threat to Ford's market supremacy was the Chevrolet, which, in 1922, as a lagging division of General Motors, had been taken in hand by William S. Knudsen. Even though the Chevrolet cost more than the Ford, its mechanical improvements, roomy interior, and color options attracted a legion of customers. A capable research and engineering facility might have helped Ford, but he discouraged any attempt to organize a systematic one and was intolerant of suggestions to introduce hydraulic brakes or to replace the planetary transmission. The company itself was ill-suited to respond to change. Under Ford's autocratic regime, it became a collection of fiefdoms without any clear lines of authority and responsibility. Edsel Ford, who on Dec. 31, 1918, succeeded his father as president, might have been able to modernize the administrative machinery, but he was president in name only, and his wise decisions were often countermanded or undermined by the elder Ford. The system of management instilled at General Motors under Alfred P. Sloan, Jr., was one of the factors that by the late 1920's gave it a competitive advantage over the Ford Motor Company.

Over the winter of 1925-1926 it became clear that neither radical restyling nor additional price cuts would save the Model T from extinction. In March 1926, when Ford production accounted for only 34 percent of the industry's output, it was the first time since 1918 that its share of the market had dropped below 40 percent. By the fall of 1926 the signs of a potentially ruinous situation could no longer be ignored, and Ford, despite the lack of advance planning, privately decided by the end of 1926 to bring out a new car. Public announcement was withheld until the following spring, when the fifteen millionth Model T came off the assembly line on May 26, 1927. At that time more than 11,300,000 Model T's were registered in the United States. All told, including engines for replacement, Ford produced over 15 million Model T's.

In May 1927, when Ford shut down his plants for a massive changeover, he was almost sixty-four. His creative energies were running down. The industry he revolutionized had caught up with him, and while General Motors had no single complex comparable to the Rouge, it had actually carried vertical integration farther. Ford's once dominant position, now shared with General Motors, would shortly face additional competition from the low-priced Plymouth made by the Chrysler Corporation. During the five-month shutdown Ford's rivals were eager to preempt his market, while his dealers, many of them disaffected, waited impatiently in empty showrooms. Ford threw all of his energies into designing a new car that was designated the Model A. A prototype, powered by a four-cylinder engine, was ready in August 1927 and the first Model A was assembled at the Rouge on Oct. 21, 1927. The estimated cost of the changeover, including lost profits of $42 million a month on new cars, came to about $250 million. Although conventional in design, the Model A included safety glass in the windshield, a distinctive feature in the low-priced field. The introduction of the car on Dec. 1, 1927 was one of the most tumultuous public events of the year, and within two weeks 400,000 orders had been taken. But production lags that persisted until the summer of 1928 proved costly, and Ford ended the year with only 15.4 percent of the market and a net loss of $74 million. A surge in production in 1929 enabled Ford to outstrip Chevrolet by about 400,000 units and take about 44 percent of the market, but the coming of the Great Depression, which had a crushing impact on the automotive industry, caused a precipitous decline in Model A sales. The car never fulfilled Ford's hope that its commercial life, like that of its predecessor, would be a long one. Barely four years after its introduction, the Model A had already encountered the same kind of buyer resistance that doomed the Model T. Meanwhile, the competitively priced Chevrolet and Plymouth brought out new models with more advanced engineering and styling. In August 1931 Ford discontinued the Model A. No longer the single most decisive influence in the industry, Ford had to conform to the new conditions of the automotive marketplace. In March 1932 he introduced a new eight-cylinder engine car, the Ford V-8, so called for its motor, which had two banks of four cylinders each set at an angle of ninety degrees and cast in a single piece with the crankcase. Ford sales remained low, and for the three worst years of the depression, 1931-1933, company losses amounted to $125 million. The V-8 engine was Ford's last automotive innovation. Ford sales improved in 1934 and 1935, but in 1936 the company settled back into third place in the industry.

As a leading public figure, Ford issued advice and homilies on how the country should cope with the depression. His favorite remedies were hard work, self-help, and frugality, and some of his prescriptions reflected his agrarian individualism. Opposed to organized charity and to government intervention in the economy, he advocated family gardens to prevent dependence on public relief rolls, and he rejected proposals for unemployment insurance as alien ideas diverging from "the principle that every man should take care of himself and be responsible to himself." His fierce individualism was illustrated by his refusal to sign the industry-wide code sanctioned by the National Recovery Administration and his unyielding defiance of the NRA, which by 1934 had made him the best-known symbol of unfettered rugged individualism. After 1932, however, Ford spent less time on company affairs, although he still controlled basic policy decisions. The outside project which absorbed most of his time was his historical museum and village in Dearborn, a venture in the preservation and reconstruction of the past, inspired mainly by the nostalgia for the vanishing rural America of his boyhood that overtook Ford in middle age. More immediately, this interest seems to have been crystallized by the *Chicago Tribune* trial of 1919, when the country became familiar with the statement Ford made to a reporter in 1916: "History is more or less bunk." Although Ford was abysmally ignorant of written history, he shrewdly divined some of its limitations, and in the early 1920's began to

amass a huge hoard of Americana and other artifacts with the aim of illustrating the advance of the peaceful arts in what he called his "living textbook of human and technical history." At the same time, in 1923, he acquired the seventeenth-century Wayside Inn at Sudbury, Mass., and restored it at a cost of more than $2 million. To house his collection of relics, Ford built at Dearborn a complex of museum and school buildings which in 1929 were dedicated as the Edison Institute in honor of his friend, the inventor Thomas A. Edison. An adjoining miniature rural community that Ford began to develop in 1928 was given the name of Greenfield Village. Both the museum and the village were opened to the public in June 1933. Most of the village had been completed by 1936, when fifty buildings were in place. In January 1952 the museum itself was formally designated as the Henry Ford Museum. Ford spent an estimated $30 million on the museum and village. His re-creation of history-in-the-round served as a model for similar ventures throughout the United States.

By the early 1930's Ford, as the aging head of an industrial despotism without parallel in the history of American industrial enterprise, had come to rely increasingly upon Harry H. Bennett, a tough, dapper ex-boxer whose swift rise in Ford's esteem began at the Rouge after World War I. "Harry," Ford once said, "gets things done in a hurry," and by 1930, when Liebold's standing with Ford began to wane, Bennett loomed as the only rival to Sorensen in the scramble for power. Bennett, as director of personnel and plant security, headed an organization that was in effect an intelligence apparatus; his Service Department was a force of plant police, labor spies, plug-uglies, and underworld figures. The passage of the Wagner Labor Relations Act in 1935 and the formation of the United Automobile Workers intensified Ford's near-paranoid fears that a conspiracy of labor unions, Communists, and international bankers was joined in an effort to destroy his enterprise. Throughout the 1920's and the depression the Ford Motor Company had one of the worst labor relations records in the industry. The Rouge became a byword for the speedup, job insecurity, and labor espionage. In 1929 Ford instituted a Seven Dollar Day, but this was cut back to $4 in 1932 and Ford wages were below those paid by his major competitors. After General Motors and Chrysler recognized the UAW in 1937, Ford remained the only holdout among the Big Three. His adamant hostility to the union, carried out brutally by Bennett, resulted in a campaign of violence in Dearborn, Dallas, and other centers, which in December 1937 led the National Labor Relations Board to condemn the Ford labor policies. For four years Ford persisted in using intimidation and terror against the UAW. At length, in an election held at the Rouge in May 1941, the UAW received 70 percent of the vote. Ford reportedly wanted to shut down the plant, but he finally accepted the contract, according to Sorensen, because Mrs. Ford threatened to leave him if he did not sign. The UAW victory made Ford more dependent on Bennett, who aggrandized his own power by speaking in Ford's name even when he did not have specific authority. This was abetted by the deterioration of Ford's health. In 1938 he suffered a stroke, and in 1941 this was followed by a second, more serious one. Ford's illnesses deepened his anxieties and made him turn to Bennett even more. Meanwhile, Bennett gradually undercut Sorensen's authority and began to replace his rival's subordinates with men loyal to himself.

At the outbreak of World War II in 1939, Ford urged American aloofness from the conflict, and later, through his friend Charles A. Lindbergh, Jr., supported the isolationist position of the America First Committee. Ford advocated national preparedness, but he balked at making Rolls-Royce aircraft engines destined for Great Britain. This brought accusations that he sympathized with Nazi Germany, his critics pointing to Ford's acceptance in 1938 of the Grand Cross of the German Eagle from the Hitler government. Ford was heavily involved in national defense production by the time the United States was drawn into the war in December 1941. The principal wartime accomplishment of the company was its huge facility at Willow Run, near Ypsilanti, Mich., for producing the B-24 Liberator bomber, with Sorensen playing the chief role in this feat. Upon the death of his son Edsel in May 1943, the aged and infirm father once more assumed the presidency, but it was Bennett who wielded the power. With the ouster of Sorensen in March 1944, Bennett secretly took steps to wrest effective control of the company in his hands for ten years following the death of Ford, but this scheme for a regency was undone by Henry Ford II, eldest grandson of the founder, who joined the company in August 1943, obtained the resignation of his grandfather in September 1945, and as the new president removed Harry Bennett from the company. In all of this, Henry Ford took no part. The billion-dollar corporation he created had been brought to a precarious

state by years of autocratic rule, and it would remain for others to rebuild it. Ford slipped quietly into retirement, dividing his time between his Fair Lane estate and his Georgia plantation. Shortly before midnight on Apr. 7, 1947, he died at Fair Lane of a massive cerebral hemorrhage. He died by the light of candles and an oil lamp, for the River Rouge, then in flood, had knocked out the power plant on his estate. More than 100,000 persons viewed his body as it lay at Greenfield Village. Ford, who was a nominal Episcopalian, was buried from St. Paul's Cathedral in Detroit, and on the day of his funeral workers in industrial shops throughout Michigan observed a moment of silence in his honor. He was buried in the Ford Cemetery on Joy Road between Greenfield and Southfield roads in Dearborn, on the site of the farm settled by his grandfather, John Ford.

After his death most of Ford's fortune, consisting mainly of company stock, went to the Ford Foundation. Although Ford was bitterly hostile to organized philanthropy, during his lifetime he nevertheless gave $37 million to philanthropic causes, notably the Henry Ford Hospital in Detroit, to which he donated more than $10.5 million. The Ford Foundation, established by Henry and Edsel Ford on Jan. 15, 1936, as a small family foundation, was organized principally to ensure preservation of family control of the Ford Motor Company after ownership passed to the foundation for compelling tax reasons. The 172,645 shares of company stock held by the Fords were converted into 3,452,000 shares, of which 95 percent was Class A nonvoting stock and 5 percent was Class B voting stock. Henry and Edsel Ford left their Class A stock to the foundation and their Class B stock to their family heirs. Thus the foundation received a 95 percent equity in the company. Had the foundation not received most of the two estates, the Ford heirs would have paid an estimated federal estate tax of $321 million after the government agreed to a valuation of $135 per share. The foundation, as residuary legatee, paid the estate taxes on the voting shares; effective family control of the company remained intact; and the outcome was the transformation of a small family philanthropy into the richest private foundation in the world.

Despite shortcomings mostly attributable to a narrow provincialism, Ford is a figure in world history, and will probably be remembered as the greatest revolutionary of the machine age. His principle of moving mass production was the most momentous innovation of the Industrial Revolution since its dawn in the eighteenth century; in his own lifetime it spread around the globe as a basic principle for the organization of industrial activity, with far-reaching effects upon economic and social life. In the United States he became a national folk hero largely because his career epitomized some of the traits its people identified as peculiarly American. At his creative best, Ford's distrust of dogmas and theoretical preconceptions in the world of mechanics appealed to a deep-seated practicality. His vast fortune was not resented, for it was seen as having been earned fairly, in keeping with accepted ideas of equality of opportunity and free competition. In an age of impersonal business corporations and absentee ownership, his personal stamp upon his enterprise set him apart, while his public image was that of the common man. The Five Dollar Day made him a popular symbol of abundance, high wages, and a decent standard of living. His democratization of the automobile, hitherto the toy of the wealthy, accorded with American notions of an open, classless society. Above all, his car for the masses initiated a motorcar revolution whose central feature of individual transportation harmonized with two dominant characteristics of early twentieth-century America: a longing for technological mastery of time and space, and a yearning for personal freedom inseparable from the expansionism and exuberance of the American frontier experience.

[The most extensive collection of documentary materials on the life and career of Henry Ford is in the Ford Archives, formerly a part of the Ford Motor Company and now located in the Henry Ford Museum at Dearborn, Mich. This collection, consisting of several million pieces, includes family records, personal correspondence, diaries and memoranda, company minute books, cables and telegrams, production, financial, sales, and legal records, blueprints, photographs, and transcripts of hundreds of tape-recorded reminiscences of associates of Ford and friends and relatives of the Fords. The Ford Archives also houses a valuable collection of newspaper clippings, magazine articles, pamphlets, and books dealing with Ford, the company, and the automotive industry.

The most detailed, authoritative, and closely documented work on Ford and his protean activities is a three-volume history by Allan Nevins and Frank Ernest Hill based on sources in the Ford Archives and other collections: Ford: The Times, the Man, the Company (1954); Ford: Expansion and Challenge, 1915–1933 (1957); Ford: Decline and Rebirth, 1933–1962 (1963). These contain likenesses of Ford from childhood to old age.

For some thirty years after he was suddenly lifted to national and world prominence, many of the books on Ford were uncritical, laudatory, or pietistic. Early examples of this genre are Rose Wilder Lane, Henry Ford's Own Story (1917), Sarah T. Bushnell, The Truth about Henry Ford (1922), and Allan L. Benson, The New Henry Ford (1923); a typical later one is William A. Simonds, Henry Ford (1943). Ford was the nominal coauthor of the following, all written in collaboration with Samuel Crowther, My Life and Work (1922), Today and Tomorrow (1926), and Moving Forward (1931). All of the books inspired or

written by Ford must be used with care because of inaccuracies, bias, or significant omissions. The first carefully researched account of Ford and his career was Keith Sward, The Legend of Henry Ford (1948). Despite minor errors, it is a landmark effort that inaugurated a new phase in the study of its subject. Roger Burlingame, Henry Ford (1954), utilizing materials in the Ford Archives, is a balanced short account. John Rae, ed., Henry Ford (1969) is an informative compilation. Useful bibliographies may be found in Sward, Burlingame, and Rae, as well as in Nevins-Hill, Ford (1954).

The published literature on Ford is vast, and only a brief sampling can be listed here. Samuel S. Marquis, Henry Ford: An Interpretation (1923) and Edwin G. Pipp, Henry Ford: Both Sides of Him (1926) are personal accounts by individuals who observed Ford at close range; the Marquis book is the best psychological portrait of Ford based on direct evidence. William C. Richards, The Last Billionaire (1948) contains much anecdotal material. The best account of Highland Park technology at the height of the mass production revolution is the classic by Horace L. Arnold and Fay L. Faurote, Ford Methods and Ford Shops (1915). Two valuable series of articles on the development and operation of the River Rouge plant are John H. Van Deventer, in Industrial Management, 64–65, Sept. 1922–Sept. 1923, and Fay L. Faurote, in Factory and Industrial Management, 74–75, Oct. 1927–June 1928. Christy Borth, Masters of Mass Production (1945) has good portraits of Knudsen and Sorensen. Harry Bennett, We Never Called Him Henry (1951) should be used with caution. Garet Garrett, The Wild Wheel (1952) is an incisive interpretation by a journalist who knew Ford from 1914 on. Charles E. Sorensen, My Forty Years with Ford (1956) is indispensable. R. L. Bruckberger, Image of America (1959) is interesting as an example of the durable impression left on the minds of foreigners by "the Ford Revolution" and should be read in conjunction with the earlier appraisal by an American journalist, Charles Merz, And Then Came Ford (1929). William Greenleaf, Monopoly on Wheels: Henry Ford and the Selden Automobile Patent (1961) is a scholarly monograph. The international scope of Ford operations is traced in Mira Wilkins and Frank Ernest Hill, American Business Abroad: Ford on Six Continents (1964). A full account of Ford's involvement in such projects as the Henry Ford Hospital, the Edison Institute, and Greenfield Village, and an examination of Ford's views on philanthropy, is William Greenleaf, From These Beginnings: The Early Philanthropies of Henry Ford and Edsel Ford, 1911–1936 (1964), which may be supplemented by Roger Butterfield, in Proc. of the Mass. Hist. Soc. 77: (1965). Alfred D. Chandler, Jr., ed., Giant Enterprise: Ford, General Motors, and the Automobile Industry (1964) places Ford in a larger context. Anne Jardim, The First Henry Ford, A Study in Personality and Business Leadership (1970) is an exercise in psychohistory. Charles A. Lindbergh, The Wartime Journals of Charles A. Lindbergh (1970) has some fascinating glimpses of Ford, Sorensen, and Bennett in the early 1940's. Reynold M. Wik, Henry Ford and Grass-roots America (1972) measures the impact of Ford on his rural constituency.]

WILLIAM GREENLEAF

FORRESTAL, JAMES VINCENT (Feb. 15, 1892–May 22, 1949), investment banker, public servant, under secretary and secretary of the navy, and first secretary of defense, was born in Matteawan (now part of Beacon), N.Y., the youngest of the three sons of James Forrestal and Mary (Toohey) Forrestal. His father was a first-generation Irish immigrant, as was his maternal grandfather, Mathias Toohey. Both had prospered in the land of their adoption, Toohey as a farmer and landholder and the elder Forrestal as owner of a prospering construction company and small-town Democratic politician. But it was Mary Forrestal who dominated the household and dictated the raising of the children. A devout Roman Catholic, she was a strict disciplinarian who tolerated few lapses by her sons in either religious observance or personal conduct.

From this stern atmosphere of Irish-American puritanism young James was the only son to emancipate himself, first by going to college and then by ceasing to be a practicing Catholic. He attended Dartmouth College (1911–1912) and then transferred to Princeton University at the beginning of his sophomore year. At Princeton success came quickly. Active in sports, chosen to the select and prestigious Cottage Club, editor of the *Daily Princetonian*, Forrestal was, by prevailing undergraduate standards, a distinguished member of the class of 1915. Yet, on failing one English course, he abruptly abandoned college six weeks before graduating.

In 1916 he entered the investment banking house of William A. Read and Company (shortly to become Dillon, Read and Company), where he was to remain, except for a short tour of duty during World War I as a commissioned naval aviator, until 1940—first as bond salesman, then as partner (1923), as vice-president (1926), and as president (1938). On Wall Street, Forrestal achieved wealth, power, and social position, all of which he had coveted. A strenuous and compulsive worker; a superb administrator; pugnacious both intellectually and physically (witness his outsized nose, broken in a boxing match); aggressive in manner yet in fact shy and introspective; reflective, philosophic, sensitive, solitary; and in many respects emotionally insecure in spite of his many achievements—these are the traits and contradictions that characterized the adult James Forrestal. On Oct. 12, 1926, he married Josephine Ogden of Huntington, W. Va. (it was her second marriage). They had two children: Michael and Peter.

In June 1940 Forrestal was called to Washington to serve President Franklin D. Roosevelt as special administrative assistant. The administration was seeking the services of businessmen, in the face of the growing likelihood of United States involvement in World War II. Forrestal was an obvious choice: he was a Democrat; his Wall Street credentials were impeccable, yet he was unorthodox enough to have supported the Securities and Exchange Commission; and he enjoyed the reputation of being a highly effective administrator. However, he served in the White House for less than two months. In August 1940 he was sworn in to the newly created post of undersecretary of the navy, second in command to Secretary Frank Knox. Moving on to the secretaryship in May 1944, following Knox's death, Forrestal remained in the Navy Department for almost seven years—the years of World War II and its aftermath.

As undersecretary, he became the chief matériel coordinating agent of the Navy Department, and under his leadership, this office became the nerve center of the navy's wartime procurement program. It was Forrestal, more than any other single person, who was responsible for "buying" the fleet that won the war. In the period roughly covering his tenure as undersecretary, 9 new battleships, over 70 aircraft carriers, 20 cruisers, more than 500 destroyers and destroyer escorts, over 100 submarines, and about 34,500 airplanes were constructed. In the same period uniformed naval personnel grew in number from 189,000 to 3,600,000.

Yet his career in the Navy Department was not untroubled. His relationships with Fleet Commander-in-Chief and Chief of Naval Operations Adm. Ernest J. King were often strained. At issue was the question of civilian versus military dominance in the Navy Department. King wanted operational control of all naval logistics including procurement; Forrestal resisted and succeeded in retaining control himself. Forrestal relieved Adm. Harold R. Stark from duty for his alleged partial responsibility for the navy's unpreparedness for the Japanese attack on Pearl Harbor; King was outraged. Partly to escape from these and other Washington pressures, Forrestal paid periodic visits to the navy's combat zones: the Southwest Pacific in 1942; Kwajalein Atoll in 1944; and Iwo Jima in February 1945, to observe the U.S. Marines landing operation at close range.

The war in the Pacific ended, but another war of a different nature was soon to begin—this one in Washington over the issue of unification of the U.S. armed services. When the proposal to unify the army, navy, and a separate air force first came before Congress in 1944, Forrestal opposed it, partly out of fear that the navy's role in the new defense establishment would be diminished. Bowing to the inevitable after the war, he accepted the principle of unification but fought for a large measure of service autonomy within the new Department of Defense created by the National Security Act of 1947. Although a separate air force was established, naval aviation remained under the Navy Department, and the continued existence of the Marine Corps within the naval service was guaranteed by law, much as Forrestal had insisted. Then in July 1947 he was named to be the nation's first secretary of defense.

Almost immediately upon assuming office in September he became involved in the struggle between the navy and the air force over their respective roles and missions with respect to strategic bombing. He quarreled with W. Stuart Symington, the new secretary of air; he was bitterly disappointed with Congress' failure in 1948 to provide for a defense establishment of "balanced forces" as against one heavily weighted in favor of air power; and most of all he became estranged from President Harry Truman himself. The heart of the issue between them was the size of Truman's defense budget, which Forrestal felt to be unrealistically low. Also, Forrestal opposed the partition of Palestine, which Truman supported. He favored ultimate military control over atomic weapons, whereas the president supported civilian control through the Atomic Energy Commission. He worked to strengthen the hand of the National Security Council, which Truman feared as a threat to presidential authority. Finally, the president came to suspect the secretary's loyalty and to doubt his enthusiasm for Truman's reelection. Forrestal was, in fact, skeptical of Truman's chances for reelection and presumably did make at least one financial contribution to Thomas E. Dewey's campaign. In any case, two months after the unexpected Democratic victory of November 1948, Forrestal was asked to start grooming as his successor Louis Johnson, the 1948 Democratic campaign fund-raising chairman. Then on Mar. 1, 1949, he was abruptly summoned to the White House and asked for an immediate letter of resignation.

Never one of Truman's intimate advisors, Forrestal nonetheless was one of the shapers of American foreign policy during the early cold war years. Well before the end of World War II he had become fearful of the Soviet Union's postwar intentions, convinced of its inveterate hostility to the United States, and suspicious of Vice-President Wallace's apparent pro-Soviet leanings; he therefore opposed Wallace's renomination on the 1944 Democratic ticket and later rejoiced when Truman forced

Wallace to resign as secretary of commerce. Further, Forrestal seconded ambassador to Moscow W. Averell Harriman's moves to harden the State Department's attitude toward the Soviet Union; and it was Forrestal who persuaded George Kennan to publish the "Mr. X" article in the July 1947 issue of *Foreign Affairs,* which first publicly articulated the United States policy of containment.

On Mar. 28, 1949, Forrestal, as requested, officially left the office of secretary of defense. For about a year previous, he had shown signs of mental and physical exhaustion, presumably attributable to his excessive, if self-imposed, work load; constant conflicts over the size and nature of the defense establishment; endless bureaucratic and political frustrations; the apparent loss of presidential confidence; and the open hostility of air-power enthusiasts, Zionists, Wallaceites and other liberals, and sundry Washington and New York journalists. On the day of his departure from the Pentagon, Forrestal began to break down. Symptoms of extreme depression and paranoia were obvious enough to induce friends to persuade him to fly to Hobe Sound, Fla., for a rest. There the symptoms worsened, and he attempted suicide. He was flown back to Washington on April 2 and admitted to Bethesda Naval Hospital for intensive treatment for involutional melancholia.

In the early morning hours of May 22, 1949, Forrestal plunged to his death from an unguarded window on the hospital's sixteenth floor. His last recorded act was to copy on a hospital memo pad a few lines from the *Ajax* of Sophocles; among them these: "Worn by the waste of time—/Comfortless, nameless, hopeless save/In the dark prospect of the yawning grave. . . ." Three days later Forrestal was buried with full military honors in Arlington National Cemetery.

[The major sources are the Forrestal Papers, Princeton Univ. Lib.; Walter Millis, ed., *The Forrestal Diaries: A Study of Personality, Politics, and Policy* (1963); Carl W. Borklund, *Men of the Pentagon: From Forrestal to McNamara* (1966); Robert H. Connery, *The Navy and Industrial Mobilization in World War II* (1951); Robert G. Albion and Robert H. Connery, *Forrestal and the Navy* (1962); Demetrios Caraley, *The Politics of Military Unification* (1966); Paul Y. Hammond, *Organizing for Defense: The American Military Establishment in the Twentieth Century* (1961).]

PHILIP A. CROWL

FOSTER, WILLIAM TRUFANT (Jan. 18, 1879–Oct. 8, 1950), college president, economist, was born in Boston, Mass., the youngest of three children and only son of William Henry Foster and Sarah Jane (Trufant)

Foster. His father was a native of Boston, his mother of Lewiston, Maine. Foster inherited the protesting spirit of Puritan ancestors but not the prosperity of his early forebears. His father, who had worked for a merchant relative before the Civil War, returned an invalid and died when Foster was a child, leaving the family, as Foster later recalled, impoverished. Foster worked his way through Boston's Roxbury High School and through Harvard, from which he graduated magna cum laude in 1901. After teaching for two years at Bates College in Lewiston, he took an M.A. in English at Harvard (1904) and went to Bowdoin College as instructor in English and argumentation. Within a year his success as an inspiring teacher and his interest in organizing a department of education won him promotion (1905) to full professor, reputedly the youngest of this rank in the nation. His *Argumentation and Debating* (1908) was the first of several widely used texts.

During the academic year 1909-1910 Foster was a fellow and lecturer in education at Teachers College, Columbia University, where he received a Ph.D. in 1911. His conception of "the ideal college" set out in the concluding chapter of his dissertation, "Administration of the College Curriculum" (1911), was a major factor in his election as first president of Reed College in Portland, Oreg. He was given a free hand to create the type of institution he envisioned: a college which, among other things, would combat the "laziness, superficiality . . . [and] excessive indulgence in what we are pleased to call college life," and have the "requisite insight and courage to become a Johns Hopkins for undergraduates. . . ." (pp. 330, 334).

He first attracted widespread attention by announcing that Reed College rejected competitive intercollegiate sports, fraternities, and sororities in favor of a democratic and intellectual environment. With emphasis upon a close working relation between high-quality teachers and selected students, Foster and his faculty adapted to undergraduate instruction practices usually associated with graduate education: comprehensive examinations in the junior year, senior seminars, theses, and final orals.

Foster's successes as an administrator were undermined by financial stringency, by conflict over academic priorities, and by local reaction to his pacifism on the eve of World War I. During the war he served as an inspector of the Red Cross in France (1917), and after his return to the college he instituted the nation's first program to train reconstruction aides for military hospitals. Administrative anxieties and overwork seriously jeopardized his health, and in December 1919 he resigned the presidency of Reed.

The following year Foster began a new career as director (1920-1950) of the Pollak Foundation of Economic Research, established in Newton, Mass., by his Harvard classmate Waddill Catchings for the study of economic problems, particularly the causes and cures of depressions. In a mutually stimulating collaboration, Foster and Catchings wrote four related books on this subject: *Money* (1923), *Profits* (1925), *Business without a Buyer* (1927), and *The Road to Plenty* (1928). Abandoning laissez-faire theory, which relied on free market forces to effect an equilibrium between production and consumption, they held that since underconsumption was the chief cause of depression, adequate consumer income was the chief remedy. Unlike other underconsumption theorists, they proposed to maintain dynamic economic growth through control of the volume and flow of money by means of fiscal policy. Developed in the 1920's, this school of thought preceded "the Keynesian theory of income determination and post-Keynesian growth economics" (Gleason, p. 157).

The Foster-Catchings theses—purposely expounded in lay language for lay audiences—were criticized as oversimplified and lacking in precise terminology and in supporting statistical analysis. Nevertheless, a number of the authors' constructs, particularly the circular flow of money with institutional offsets—such as public spending—were accepted by bankers and business executives and had some effect on public policy. In 1928 President Herbert Hoover requested that state and federal governments cooperate in public expenditures to sustain business and prevent unemployment, and he cited Foster and Catchings' *The Road to Plenty* as an aid in their planning (*New York World,* Nov. 24, 1929; see also E. C. Harwood, ed., *Cause and Control of the Business Cycle,* p. 91 [1957]). A parallel has been noted between their proposals for harnessing the business cycle and Roosevelt's initial efforts to resuscitate the economy, later implemented in the Full Employment Act of 1946 (Gleason, p. 170).

Foster's concern as an economist was for the public as consumers. He was chairman of the Committee on Consumer Credit set up in 1935 by the Massachusetts legislature. He was one of the original small group which organized the privately supported Committee on the Costs of Medical Care; and he prepared its final report,

Medical Care for the American People (1932), which recommended organization of the medical profession to contract with lay groups for "better medical care at less cost" through voluntary insurance. From 1933 to 1935 Foster also served as a member of the Consumers' Advisory Board of the National Recovery Administration. To educate the public on economic issues, he lectured throughout the country and for three years wrote a syndicated daily newspaper column on economics for laymen.

A handsome man, witty and charming, Foster was an impressive speaker and prolific writer. Self-confident and impatient, with a restlessly inquiring and fertile mind, he was in his own words "a born rebel" and a crusader. But whatever the social ills he identified and attacked, he proposed constructive, if not always popular, solutions. Foster married Bessie Lucile Russell of Lewiston, Maine, on Dec. 25, 1905. They had four children: Russell Trufant, LeBaron Russell, Faith, and Trufant (originally named William Russell). Foster died of coronary occlusion at his summer home in Jaffrey, N.H., at the age of seventy-one. A memorial service was held at the Jaffrey Center Congregational Church, and his ashes were scattered over the lake on the Reed College campus.

[*Writings of William Trufant Foster,* privately printed in 1938, provides a bibliography of his works, which include several widely used texts on debating. Biographical data, checked by family members, have been drawn from Foster's MS autobiography, left incomplete at the time of his death, and from other of his papers, relating both to his college presidency and to the Pollak Foundation, in the Reed College Arch. For an interpretation of Foster's role in shaping Reed College, see Burton R. Clark, *The Distinctive College: Antioch, Reed and Swarthmore* (1970). On his economic writings, see Alan H. Gleason, "Foster and Catchings: A Reappraisal," *Jour of Political Economy,* Apr. 1959. Brief notices are in *Leaders in Education,* 1948; *Who Was Who in America,* III (1960); Harvard Class of 1901, *Twenty-fifth Anniversary Report* (1926); and obituaries in the (Portland) *Oregonian, N.Y. Herald Tribune,* and *N.Y. Times* of Oct. 9, 1950. *World's Work,* Sept. 1910, contains an excellent photograph of the young college president. A later oil portrait by Winifred Rieber is in the possession of Russell T. Foster, West Hartford, Conn.; an oil copy hangs in the Reed College chapel.]

DOROTHY O. JOHANSEN

FRAZIER, LYNN JOSEPH (Dec. 21, 1874-Jan. 11, 1947), farmer, teacher, and politician, was born in Steele County, Minn., the son of Thomas Frazier, a farmer, and Lois (Nile) Frazier, natives of Rangeley, Maine, and descendants of early Minnesota pioneers; Thomas Frazier traced his ancestry to Simon Frasher, a British army general in the American Revolution. In 1881 his parents took him to Pembina County, Dakota Territory, where they built a sod

house. His father died before he graduated from high school, and he and his brother had to manage the family farm. After teaching high school for a brief period, he entered the Normal School in Mayville, N. Dak. from which he graduated in 1895. In 1897, at the age of twenty-three, Frazier enrolled in the University of North Dakota, where he achieved a good scholastic record, became captain of the football team, and graduated in 1901. Although Lynn wanted to become a professional man, his mother persuaded him to return to the farm, the brother in charge having died. On Nov. 26, 1903, Frazier married Lottie J. Stafford in Hoople, N. Dak.; they had five children: twins, Unie Mae (Mrs. Emerson G. Church) and Versie Fae (Mrs. Stanley H. Gaines), and Vernon, Willis, and Lucille. Lottie Frazier died on Jan. 14, 1935. On Sept. 7, 1937, he married Cathrine W. Paulson, a widow and daughter of Christopher Behrens, a miller, of Redwing, Minn.

Before the formation of the Nonpartisan League in 1915, Frazier was better known as a successful farmer and advocate of farmer's rights, who neither smoked, drank, nor used profane language, than as a politician. Yet he was endorsed for governor by the league in 1916, nominated in the primary on the Republican ticket, and, along with other league candidates, was swept into office. During his first term as governor, laws were passed to establish a new grain grading system; guarantee bank deposits; shift more of the tax burden onto corporations, industry, and trade; grant suffrage rights to women; use the initiative and referendum; and adopt the Torrens system in the registration of land titles.

In 1918 Frazier was reelected by a handsome majority. During his second administration the legislature enacted more laws than he called for; they included the creation of an industrial commission to operate utilities and properties established, owned, or operated by the state, except those of a charitable, educational, or penal character; and the establishment and operation of a state-owned bank in which were to be deposited all state, county, township, municipal, and school district funds. Also enacted were laws for the creation of the North Dakota Mill and Elevator Association, a state-owned and operated warehouse, elevator, and flour-mill system; a state hail insurance plan; a program providing homes for residents of the state; a state inspector of grades, weights, and measures; a workmen's compensation act; the regulation of coal mines; and state income and inheritance taxes.

Frazier's third administration was beset with difficulties. Resistance to his policies hardened. Limits were placed on the amount of public funds to be deposited in the state bank, and the building of state-owned projects slackened. Frazier refused to confine the operations of the state bank to rural credits; and his refusal, along with that of other leaguers, led to the circulation of petitions for the recall of the members of the industrial commission of which he was a member. In the special election of 1921, Frazier, William Lemke, the attorney general, and John H. Hagan, the commissioner of agriculture, were recalled.

In 1922, in a drive to unseat Porter McCumber from the United States Senate and right some of the wrong done in the recall election of 1921, a combination of progressive Republicans, leaguers, and others who considered Frazier an honest man, nominated and elected him to the Senate by a substantial majority. In the Senate he sought legislation to give the producers of wheat, corn, and cotton their cost of production plus a fair profit; to transfer the administration of the Packers and Stockyards Act from the Department of Agriculture to the Federal Trade Commission; and to require members of Congress and employees of the federal government to file statements of stocks, bonds, and other securities owned by them or members of their families in industrial, mining, oil, and other operations. In 1924 Frazier and three of his colleagues in the Senate, Robert M. La Follette of Wisconsin, Edwin C. Ladd of North Dakota, and Smith W. Brookhart of Iowa, were branded by the regular Republicans as "renegades," who were not to be invited to further Republican conferences or named to vacancies on Senate committees.

Reelected to the Senate in 1928 and again in 1934, Frazier continued his campaign for agricultural price supports and also supported prohition, the payment of a cash bonus to World War I veterans, and disarmament. He served on various committees, including agriculture and forestry, banking and currency, civil service, and Indian affairs. In the Senate he is best remembered as a coauthor of the Frazier-Lemke Amendment to the Farm Bankruptcy Act of 1934, which postponed interest payments on farm mortgages for three years. A revised amendment in 1935 was upheld by the Supreme Court in 1937.

By 1940 his long antimilitary record came under severe attack from opponents who accused him of selling America short. He also was opposed for reelection by William Langer, who himself had been antiwar in the 1930's but now wanted Frazier's seat in the Senate. Conservatives also rallied against him because of his hostility to banks and insurance companies.

Frazier was a product of his agricultural environment and the various protest movements that swirled about him. Almost bovine in appearance, he was thoroughly committed to the farmers and their cause and fought a rearguard action in attempting to resist the encroachments of industry, finance, transportation, and their allies on agriculture. An antiwar man throughout his career, he exposed himself to attacks from political adversaries, rivals, and others who believed him insensitive to the dangers of the hour.

A member of the Methodist church and Modern Woodmen of America, his chief hobbies were walking and coin collecting. He died in Riverdale, Md., while on a visit. Interment was in Park Cemetery, Hoople, N. Dak.

[A book-length biography of Frazier still remains to be written; but brief biographical sketches of him are in *Nat. Cyc. Am. Biog.*, Current Vol. B, pp. 189–190; *ibid.*, Current Vol. E, pp. 155–157; *ibid.*, 58–59; *Biog. Direct. of Am. Congress* (1961); and the *N.Y. Times*, Jan. 12, 1947. Materials pertaining to him are to be found in Edward C. Blackorby, *Prairie Rebel: The Public Life of William Lemke* (1963); Elwyn B. Robinson, *History of North Dakota* (1966); Charles E. Russell, *The Story of the Nonpartisan League* (1920); Herbert E. Gaston, *The Nonpartisan League* (1920); Robert L. Morlan, *Political Prairie Fire* (1955); and Theodore Saloutos, "The Rise of the Nonpartisan League in North Dakota, 1915–1917," *Agricultural Hist.* 20 (1946) : 43–61. The back files of *The Nonpartisan Leader* are indispensable to anyone interested in his administrations as governor of North Dakota and the role he played as a member of the Nonpartisan League, as are the papers of the Nonpartisan League, 1915–1917, located in the Minn. Hist. Soc.]

THEODORE SALOUTOS

GÁG, WANDA (HAZEL) (Mar. 11, 1893–June 27, 1946), artist and writer, was born in New Ulm, Minn., the oldest of the seven children of Anton Gág and Elizabeth (Biebl) Gág. Her father was born in Neustadt, in Bohemia; her mother, although a native of this country, also had a Bohemian background. New Ulm in the 1890's was a small town inhabited chiefly by German and Austrian immigrants, who gave a faintly European tone to its culture. The children thus grew up in an atmosphere of Old World customs, legends, and folksongs. Their father was a mural decorator of churches and similar buildings, and their mother came from a family with traditions of woodworking and folk art.

Wanda was strongly inclined toward a career

in the arts, although the way to Parnassus turned out to be arduous. In her fifteenth year her father died of tuberculosis, leaving the family practically destitute. The story of Wanda's struggle to keep her family together and give all the children an education and herself four years of technical training at art schools in St. Paul and Minneapolis is edifying but harrowing. That she did it at all is a tribute to her determination and resourcefulness, for her gentle, delicate mother was unequal to the task and died in 1917. (Wanda gave a glimpse of those desperate years in an autobiographical fragment published anonymously in *The Nation* in 1927, and in the transcript of her diaries in *Growing Pains,* 1940.)

In 1917 she came to New York on a scholarship from the Art Students' League. For several years she was one of many art students earning a precarious living making batiks and fashion drawings and painting lampshades. Gradually she became more successful; she brought her brother and sisters to New York one by one, and even saved a small amount of money. In 1923 she made a momentous decision. She gave up all her commercial ties and went to live in a shack in Connecticut and later, in 1924-1930, in an old farmhouse named "Tumble Timbers" near Glen Gardner, N.J. One of the factors that impelled her to "go native" was the reading of Henry David Thoreau's *Walden* and Knut Hamsun's *Growth of the Soil.* Another and more important reason was the pressure of certain innate drives for self-expression that had been stifled by her commercial work. Now she set about slowly and deliberately to build a new aesthetic principle and to forge her own personal style.

The Weyhe Gallery of New York encouraged her by buying some of her drawings and gave her an exhibition of prints and drawings in 1926, followed by others in 1928, 1930, and 1940. She became a popular and artistic success. Artists respected her talent and originality; laymen were impressed by the vividness and intensity of her vision—a "still life" that was not still, a "tired" bed, cats and flowers, a garden, or a hillside. Reviews were favorable. Henry McBride, one of the keenest critics of the time, wrote in *The Sun* (Nov. 6, 1926): "Her work is clear, strong and individual. She draws with intensity and mats her designs together so that her little pictures have the unity of a die. There is just a touch of cubism here and there in the discreet American fashion."

Her production of prints, drawings, and watercolors during the next few years was abundant. Among her best lithographs were *Elevated Station, Spring in the Garden, Lamplight, Stone Crusher,* and *Backyard Corner;* among wood engravings, *The Franklin Stove* and *Cats at Window.*

In 1928 an alert literary agent, Ernestine Evans, having seen her exhibition of drawings, surmised that she might make a good illustrator of children's books. When she met the artist, she discovered that she was also an author. The first of her ten children's books, *Millions of Cats,* was published that year. Again the artist-author received both popular and critical acclaim. She inaugurated a new style of children's book in which the illustration was an integral part of the hand-lettered text. Such a layout made for a handsome and exciting page, but obviously it could be made only by one who was both an author and an artist. She also translated and illustrated four volumes of tales from Grimm's *Kinder und Hausmärchen.* Anne Carroll Moore, the influential head of the children's department of the New York Public Library, has summed up Gág's achievement in the *Horn Book Memorial*: "A kinship with all children made her respect their intelligence, and gave them at once ease and joy in her company. With as sure an instinct for the right word for the ear, as for the right line for the eye, Wanda Gág became quite unconsciously a regenerative force in the field of children's books."

Having prospered modestly with her books and pictures, she bought, in 1930, a farm located in the Muscanetcong Mountain Range near Milford, N.J. This place, named "All Creation," was to be her home (with occasional intervals in an apartment in New York) for the rest of her life. It was at about this time, also, that she married her long-time friend, Earle Humphreys. They had no children of their own, but they shared "All Creation" with Howard and Flavia, Wanda's youngest brother and sister. In the early 1940's her interest in printmaking and especially oil painting revived. She became fascinated by the interplay of complex repetitive rhythms, and in another vein her touch became broader and more artistic in color values. Such lithographs of 1944 as the enigmatic *Whodunit* and the beautifully organized *Philodendron* still life are tokens of what might have happened had she lived longer.

Early in 1945 she became seriously ill with what was diagnosed as a bronchial infection. Actually, it was cancer. She died in New York; her remains were cremated and her ashes were spread over the farm by her husband.

Wanda Gág's achievement in art, in one

sense, was only a promise: she never attained mastery in oil painting, the only pictorial medium respected as major by the critical establishment. Furthermore, her pictures, along with those of many artists of her generation, began to appear "dated" as public tastes in art changed over the years. Secondly, it is undeniable that books for children belong to a limited category. There are indications that she was moving toward involvement with books and plays on the adult level. For all her moral integrity and passion for perfection, however, she must be rated a minor figure. She did have some measure of fame and success in her day. It did not spoil her; she consistently resisted pressure from publishers to repeat previous successes. "One does not laugh," she would say, "at the same joke a second time."

[Wanda Gág's own books and her prints, drawings, and watercolors are, in a sense, her best autobiography. Three autobiographical publications are: *Growing Pains: Diaries and Drawings for the Years 1908–1917* (1940), the story of her early years; "These Modern Women: A Hotbed of Feminism," *Nation*, June 22, 1927, pp. 691–693; "I Like Fairy Tales," *Horn Book Magazine*, Mar.–Apr. 1939, pp. 74–80. *Batiking at Home* (1923) is a pamphlet. Biographical sketches are numerous, especially: Alma Scott, *Wanda Gág, the Story of an Artist* (1949), primary source material by a schoolmate and lifelong friend, illustrated; "Tribute to Wanda Gág," *Horn Book Magazine*, May–June 1947, entire issue, important source material with articles by Anne Carroll Moore, Alma Scott, Carl Zigrosser, Ernestine Evans, Rose Dobbs, Lynd Ward, and Earle Humphreys, illustrated; Carl Zigrosser, "Wanda Gág," *The Artist in America* (1942), pp. 33–44, a critique based upon firsthand knowledge; Marya Mannes, "Wanda Gág, Individualist," *Creative Art*, Dec. 1927, pp. xxix–xxxii, a portrait based on personal interviews, six illustrations including one color plate; Weyhe Gallery, "Wanda Gág Number," *Checkerboard*, Jan. 1930, illustrated with seven original wood and linoleum cuts, containing press notices and checklist of prints to date, issued in connection with artist's exhibition in 1930; College Art Association, "Wanda Gág," *Index of Twentieth Century Artists*, III, no. 7, 273–274, plus supplement and bibliographical references; Elizabeth Luther Cary, "Peggy Bacon and Wanda Gág, Artists," *Prints*, Mar. 1931, pp. 13–24, illustrated; Rose Dobbs, " 'All Creation,' Wanda Gág and Her Family," *Horn Book Magazine*, Nov.–Dec. 1935, pp. 367–373; Minneapolis Institute of Arts, "Prints by Wanda Gág," *Minneapolis Institute of Arts Bull.*, Dec. 1946, pp. 153–159; "Wanda Gág," in Mahoney, Latimer, and Folinsbee, *Illustrators of Children's Books* (1947), pp. 309–310, 411; "Wanda Gág," in S. J. Kunitz and H. Haycraft, eds., *Twentieth Century Authors*, pp. 508–509 (1942); *Notable Am. Women*, II, 1–2; S. J. Kunitz and H. Haycraft, *The Junior Book of Authors*, pp. 134–136, 2nd ed. rev. (1951); "Wanda Gág," in Hans Vollmer, *Allgemeines Lexikon der bildende Kunstler des XX Jahrhunderts*, 184–185 (Leipzig, 1955), slightly inaccurate in information. Gág's books for children are: *Millions of Cats* (1928), *The Funny Thing* (1929), *Snippy and Snappy* (1931), *A.B.C. Bunny* (1933), *Gone Is Gone* (1935), *Nothing at All* (1941). Her translations from Grimm are: *Tales from Grimm* (1936), *Snow White and the Seven Dwarfs* (1938), *Three Gay Tales from Grimm* (1943), *More Tales from Grimm* (1947).

Prints, drawings, and watercolors may be found in various museums and public libraries in the U.S., notably: Cleveland Museum of Art; Lib. of Cong., Prints Division, Washington, D.C.; Metropolitan Museum of Art, N.Y.; Minneapolis Inst. of Arts; Newark Public Lib.; N.J. State Museum, Trenton; New Ulm Public Lib., New Ulm, Minn.; N.Y. Public Lib. The most complete collection of her work is at the Philadelphia Museum of Art. There are also substantial groups of her prints and drawings in the British Museum in London, in the Bibliothèque Nationale in Paris, and in the Pushkin Museum in Moscow. Letters to the artist and the complete sequence of her notebooks and diaries (sealed and inaccessible until 1985) are deposited in the Univ. of Pa. Lib., which also has a group of letters from Wanda Gág to Carl Zigrosser, among the latter's papers. Wanda's brother-in-law, Robert Janssen, an expert photographer, has a substantial file of photographs of the artist.]

CARL ZIGROSSER

GALPIN, CHARLES JOSIAH (Mar. 16, 1864-June 1, 1947), rural sociologist, was born in Hamilton, Madison County, N.Y., the oldest of the three sons and one daughter of Leman Quintilian Galpin and Frances Cordelia (Look) Galpin. On his father's side he was of French and Welsh origin; on his mother's, of English. His father, a graduate of Madison (later Colgate) University and Colgate Theological Seminary, was a Baptist minister who served rural parishes in Michigan and in central New York. As Galpin later noted in his autobiography, a rural milieu was his native habitat. Both parents had grown up on farms, his father in Virginia and his mother in New York state, and most of his closest relatives were farmers. Religious constraint was a daily companion, interpreted in the home as active obligation to others.

After attending schools in rural areas in central New York, Galpin entered Colgate Academy and then Colgate University, from which he received the B.A. degree in 1885. For the next three years he taught science and mathematics at Union Academy, a secondary school in Belleville, N.Y. In 1888 he received an M.A. from Colgate and took a position teaching history and English at Kalamazoo College in Michigan. He returned in 1891 to Union Academy, where, save for a year of study at Harvard where he received an M.A. in philosophy in 1895, he served as principal until 1901.

Union Academy was run much like a Scandinavian folk school, and most of the students were the children of dairy farmers. Learning about the potential scientific character of agriculture, Galpin established in 1901 a department to teach agriculture, possibly the first in a high school in the United States. Persistent insomnia, however, prompted him to resign his principalship that year, and for three years he operated a forty-acre cutover farm in Michigan. He next spent a year in Walworth County, Wis., where he established a new milk plant in which one of his brothers, a chemist, had a business interest. In 1905 another brother, then a Baptist minister in Madison, Wis., persuaded Galpin to become Baptist "university pastor," to work with students at the University of Wisconsin. He held this post for six years.

At Wisconsin, Galpin became acquainted with Henry C. Taylor, chairman of the department of agricultural economics, who stimulated him to pursue his natural curiosity about the social aspects of rural life. In a paper presented before the Wisconsin Country Life Association in 1911, Galpin mapped the "social topography" of his former residence, Belleville, N.Y., in order to show the social relationships which existed between the farm and village homes in the area. On the basis of this report, and with Taylor's backing, Galpin joined the faculty of the University of Wisconsin in 1911 to teach courses in problems of country life. Thus, at the age of forty-seven, he drifted into the work which was to make him one of the pioneers in the sociology of rural life. Because of the lack of useful texts on this subject, he began work on two of his own, later published as *Rural Life* (1918) and *Rural Social Problems* (1924).

Galpin sought firsthand knowledge to better understand the uncharted realm of rural social forces. Devising a questionnaire and employing a sampling technique, he conducted a broad study of Wisconsin's Walworth County. His report, published by the university's Agricultural Experiment Station in 1915 as *The Social Anatomy of an Agricultural Community*, had a lasting influence on rural sociology and social ecology. It identified by means of a striking set of maps the "social watersheds" of what Galpin came to see as the basic, repeating social unit emerging in rural society, a natural community of farm and village (or small city) families. Although he was later criticized for placing too great an emphasis on trade as the most important form of "rurban" interdependence, Galpin also noted the community-forming influences of shared nationality, religion, and associational activities. Galpin was not the first to detect a social connection between farm and town, but he was a pioneer in attempting to define scientifically both the nature and scope of this connection.

In 1919 Galpin left Wisconsin for federal service in Washington at the invitation of Taylor, now head of the Office of Farm Management, the economic research arm of the United States Department of Agriculture. Galpin established a

unit in the department for research into the sociological phases of farm life, known initially as the Division of Farm Life Studies, which he headed until his retirement in 1934. He gave great impetus to the development of the special discipline of rural sociology, in part through research by his own small staff, but especially by encouraging rural life studies at colleges and universities in thirty-seven states, including the agricultural experiment stations at the state colleges of agriculture. Further, Galpin almost singlehandedly persuaded the United States Bureau of the Census to divide the rural population into "rural farm" and "rural non-farm" in the collection and publication of population statistics beginning in 1920.

On several trips abroad, Galpin came into contact with rural life in European countries. At the International Conference on Rural Life (1927) he was decorated by the Belgian king for his contributions to the country life movement. Galpin married Zoe N. Wickwire of Hamilton, N.Y., on June 22, 1887. They had no children. He died of myocarditis at his home in Falls Church, Va., at the age of eighty-three.

[Galpin's autobiography, *My Drift into Rural Sociology* (1938), and the June 1948 issue of *Rural Sociology*, a memorial issue with articles by Henry C. Taylor, J. H. Kolb, and Carl C. Taylor, are the basic sources. See also: chapter on Galpin in Lowry Nelson, *Rural Sociology: Its Origin and Growth in the U.S.* (1969); *Who Was Who in America*, IV (1968); L. H. and Ethel Zoe Bailey, eds., *RUS: A Biog. Register of Rural Leadership in the U.S. and Canada* (1918 and 1930 eds.); *A Gen. Catalogue of Colgate Univ.* (1913); and obituaries in *Rural Sociology*, Sept. 1947, *Washington Post*, June 3, 1947, and *Evening Star* (Washington), June 3, 1947. For a listing of Galpin's addresses and publications, see *Dict. Catalog of the Nat. Agricultural Lib., 1862–1965* 26 (1968): 278–280.]

OLAF F. LARSON

GARDNER, HELEN (Mar. 17, 1878–June 4, 1946), art historian and teacher, was born in Manchester, N.H., the youngest of four children. Her father was Charles Frederick Gardner, a native of Hingham, Mass., and her mother Martha W. (Cunningham) Gardner of Swanville, Maine. She had two sisters and a brother, who died in infancy. In 1891 her father, a merchant tailor and Baptist deacon, moved his family to Chicago, Ill., where he conducted a successful business until he died in 1899.

Helen attended the Hyde Park High School in Chicago and the University of Chicago. In high school she excelled in the classics and was a member of a speaking and writing club; at the university she was elected to Phi Beta Kappa and graduated with the B.A. degree in Latin and Greek in 1901. After graduation she taught at Brooks Classical School in Chicago, where her sister Effie was principal; she served as assistant principal from 1905-1910. It was during these years evidently that her deep interest in art history developed. In 1915 she entered the University of Chicago graduate school; she received the M.A. degree in 1917 and was granted a fellowship in the department of art history from 1917-1918. Until 1922 she continued to audit or take for credit a succession of art history courses.

Around 1919 the Ryerson Library of the Art Institute of Chicago appointed Gardner head of the photograph and lantern slide department, and with the wealth of visual material she encountered there her ambitious plan to combine art of all ages into a single survey volume began to take shape. At the Art Institute School in the fall of 1920 she established a lecture course in world art. Two years later she resigned from her library position and devoted all her time to teaching, writing, and developing a curriculum for the study of art history. Until 1943 she continued to teach at the school, the last ten years as full professor and chairman of the history of art department. In 1927 she was a guest lecturer at the University of California in Los Angeles and in 1928 at the University of Chicago.

Until Gardner published *Art Through the Ages* in 1926, there had been no comparable single-volume art history text of such breadth and clarity. J. M. Hopkins' *Great Epochs in Art History* (1901) and W. H. Goodyear's *History of Art for Classes, Art-Students, and Tourists in Europe* (1889) were typical of those available and while useful were lacking in illustrations, contents, and readability. It is no wonder that *Art Through the Ages* was seized upon eagerly as a text for many college and high school art courses; indeed, at this time history of art courses appeared in numerous high schools largely because Helen Gardner's book was available. There were good reasons for the success of the new book: scholarly insight into both the history and aesthetic quality of the subject; a careful screening of the most significant examples of each age of art with a summary and bibliography at the end of each chapter; the fine illustrations made possible by Gardner's travels in Europe and Egypt; and her knowledge of photography. In 1932 in her zeal to attract a wider audience to art appreciation, her *Understanding the Arts* was published. Now out of print, it was the first of a torrent of "introductions" that examined the basic qualities as well as the purposes of art. It ranged beyond the fields of painting, sculpture, and architecture to include such topics as the art of the garden and the art of city planning.

Continuing popularity of *Art Through the Ages* led Gardner to prepare two further editions. The revised and enlarged second edition appeared in 1936. Running to almost 800 pages, it included an introduction with diagrams summarizing the visual elements of artistic expression, new maps and a pronouncing index, plus new chapters on medieval Russian, baroque, and modern art. During World War II this edition, which had already gone through four printings, was chosen as a text (paperbound) for the armed service schools. The third edition (1948) came closest to fulfilling Gardner's dream of a single art text on all fields and ages. She completed it shortly before her death, leaving unfinished a book she had planned on the arts of the Americas. An operation for breast cancer in 1944, not wholly successful, had left her in poor health, and she died of bronchopneumonia in 1946 at Presbyterian Hospital in Chicago. She was buried in the family plot in Oak Woods Cemetery, Chicago.

Another version of *Art Through the Ages,* prepared by the history of art department at Yale, appeared in 1958; it offered somewhat more emphasis on stylistic developments. Still another edition, revised by Horst de la Croix and Richard G. Tansey, was published in 1970. This lavishly illustrated fifth edition concentrated on the art of Europe and its ancient antecedents.

Gardner was a small, energetic woman with endless enthusiasm, deep humanity, and a missionary zeal. Singleness of purpose left little time for other activities, but she was a member of the American Association of University Women, the American Society of Aesthetics, and Midland Authors. Her life was dedicated to bringing the enriching effects of art in all its aspects to a wide audience and in this she was notably successful.

[Harold Allen's sketch in *Notable Am. Women,* II (1971) is a good account of Gardner; see also *Direc. of Am. Scholars,* 1st ed. (1942); *Who Was Who in America,* II, 1950; prefaces in 1st–5th editions of *Art Through the Ages.*]

WILLIAM M. JEWELL

GARDNER, LEROY UPSON (Dec. 9, 1888-Oct. 24, 1946), pathologist and authority on tuberculosis and silicosis, was born in New Britain, Conn., the eldest in a family of four sons and two daughters of Irving Isaac Gardner and Inez Baldwin (Upson) Gardner. His father, a real estate and insurance broker, was descended from Scottish-Irish forebears who settled in the United States early in the seventeenth century; his mother was of French-English lineage. As a boy, Gardner enjoyed collecting plants and minerals and become a skillful woodworker. He attended public schools in Meriden, Conn., graduated with the B.A. degree from Yale College in 1912, and then entered the Yale School of Medicine. He developd a strong interest in pathology and after receiving the M.D. degree in 1914, became an intern in the laboratories of Frank B. Mallory, professor of pathology at Harvard Medical School, whose base of operations was the Boston City Hospital. In 1916 Gardner was made instructor in pathology at the medical school, where he continued the histopathologic research he had started under Mallory.

In 1917 Gardner was appointed assistant professor of pathology in the Yale School of Medicine. As the United States mobilized for its entry into World War I, however, he entered military service and was assigned, as first lieutenant in the Army Medical Corps, to Camp Devens, Mass. There it was discovered that he had pulmonary tuberculosis. He was discharged from service and entered the Trudeau Sanatorium near Saranac Lake, N.Y., a pioneer institution famous for its treatment of tuberculosis. As a patient, he developed a deep concern with the disease, which determined the course of his professional career. In 1918, while still under medical observation, he moved to the Saranac Laboratory, in the town of Saranac Lake, as pathologist of the Edward L. Trudeau Foundation to carry out research in tuberculosis. Early in this service, he became interested in the striking disparity between the high death rate from tuberculosis among granite cutters in the nearby quarries of Barre, Vt., and the relatively low mortality from the same cause among marble cutters. This difference led him to investigate the role of mineral dusts in tuberculosis. In carefully planned experiments using tuberculous and normal guinea pigs, he showed that the inhalation of granite dust injured the lungs and hastened the progress of tuberculosis. His first report, published in 1920, remains a medical classic. In a series of later experiments, he demonstrated that the silica particles in the dust to which granite cutters were exposed were responsible for activating the slight latent tuberculosis common at that time to persons in all walks of life and stimulating the progress of active disease.

Gardner was a mechanical genius in devising research apparatus, and his organization of equipment for producing silicosis in laboratory animals by the inhalation of dust soon became a model for similar experimental studies in other laboratories. He showed unequivocally that inhalation of silica dust caused progress of tuberculosis in guinea pigs previously infected with mild, nonprogressive forms of the disease, whereas latent tuberculosis remained stable in animals not exposed to silica dust. Later he developed many ramifications of these experiments and investigated the pathogenicity of a variety of mineral dusts. His work received strong encouragement from industry and labor and was an important factor in the devising and imposing of safety measures to mitigate dust hazards in mining operations. His advice and assistance were sought by research institutions in many parts of the world.

True to his original training, Gardner remained a pathologist in his outlook. He was not satisfied with the important results of his investigations for the diagnosis, prevention, and practical control of tuberculosis and silicosis, but went deeply into the basic pathologic mechanisms through which silica exerted its damaging effects. He also studied possible ameliorating influences in the treatment of silicosis, such as the apparently favorable role of aluminum therapy. His more than 100 published papers included fundamental observations on the pathogenesis of the two diseases. His book, *Tuberculosis: Bacteriology, Pathology, and Laboratory Diagnosis,* written with Edward R. Baldwin and S. A. Petroff, appeared in 1927.

Although Gardner was primarily a laboratory investigator, administrative responsibilities were steadly pressed upon him. He was made director of the Saranac Laboratory for Tuberculosis in 1927, and in 1938 he became director of the Trudeau Foundation, succeeding the noted tuberculosis investigator Edward R. Baldwin. He organized a series of symposia there on silicosis and tuberculosis in industry, which attracted large numbers of physicians and scientific investigators, many of whom later became leaders in the field. Gardner traveled abroad repeatedly as a consultant on the prevention and control of diseases caused by mineral dust. For several years he was special consultant for the U.S. Department of Health. He served as a United States delegate to the first international conference on silicosis (1930) in South Africa, where the disease was rampant among miners, and to international labor conferences in London and Geneva. He was actively associated with the National Tuberculosis Association, which awarded him its Trudeau Medal in 1935. He also received the Knudsen Award (1940) of the American Association of Industrial Physicians and Surgeons, and was a charter member (1946) of the American Academy of Industrial Medicine. Intensely loyal to the village of Saranac Lake, he served as a trustee of the village and a trustee of the Presbyterian church. His wide influence in professional and administrative affairs was favored by a remarkably warm and genial personality. His many staunch friends valued him as reliable and utterly trustworthy.

On June 22, 1915, Gardner married Carabelle McKenzie; they had two children, Margaret and Dorothy. The family were Presbyterians. Gardner died suddenly at the age of fifty-seven at his home in Saranac Lake of coronary thrombosis and was buried at St. John's in the Wilderness at Paul Smith's, N.Y., not far from Saranac Lake.

[The first of Gardner's studies on the relation of mineral dusts to tuberculosis was published in *Am. Rev. of Tuberculosis* 4 (1920); 734–755; an exhaustive series of articles followed during the next twelve years. Also, "The Pneumoconioses," appears as a chapter in *Nelson Looseleaf Medicine* (1941). A definitive biography by Edward R. Baldwin, "Leroy U. Gardner (December 9, 1888–October 24, 1946)," appears in *Am. Rev. of Tuberculosis* 54 (1946): 585–587. Tributes to Gardner from colleagues in industrial medical research are in *Occupational Medicine* 4 (1947): 1–12.]

ESMOND R. LONG

GARDNER, OLIVER MAXWELL (Mar. 22, 1882-Feb. 6, 1947), known as O. Max Gardner, governor of North Carolina and influential Democrat, was born in Shelby, Cleveland County, N.C. He was the youngest of ten children of Oliver Perry Gardner and his second wife, Margaret (Young) Gardner; there were also two children of his father's first marriage. Gardner's father, who had served as a Whig member of the state legislature and as an officer in the Confederate Army, was a struggling country physician and farmer. His mother died when he was ten, and he was reared largely by his older sisters. After attending the Shelby high school, he entered North Carolina College of Agriculture and Mechanic Arts (now North Carolina State University at Raleigh), where he majored in chemistry; he received the B.S. degree in 1903, and stayed on for two years as an instructor. He had begun to read' law in Raleigh, and after a year in the law school of the University of North Carolina at Chapel Hill, he began a practice in Shelby on Jan. 1, 1907. On November 6 of that year he married Fay Lamar Webb of Shelby. They had four children: Margaret Love, James Webb, Ralph Webb, and Oliver Maxwell. Gardner's wife was the daughter of James L. Webb, judge of the local superior court, and a niece of Congressman E. Yates Webb. Gardner's brother Junius was mayor of Shelby, and his sister Bess had married Clyde R. Hoey, local newspaper owner and later governor and United States senator. These alliances created the so-called "Shelby dynasty," which was to be a power in North Carolina politics for the next forty years.

Gardner entered politics in 1907 as chairman of the county Democratic committee. He was elected to the state senate in 1910 and 1914 (he did not run in 1912). A moderately progressive spokesman for the new South, Gardner supported state prohibition in 1908 and a statewide primary law in 1915. He was elected lieutenant governor in 1916. He was a leading candidate for governor in 1920 but was defeated in both the first and the second primary by a political ally of Furnifold M. Simmons, North Carolina's veteran political leader. Meanwhile, Gardner had begun to build a personal fortune. Besides his successful law practice, he invested in real estate, raised cotton, and in 1926 became half-owner of the Cleveland Cloth Mills, a rayon mill which became a multimillion-dollar company. In his purchase and rehabilitation of run-down farms, he became known as an advocate of scientific agriculture; and he helped organize local cooperatives to bring rural electrification and establish a creamery.

In 1928, having wisely decided not to challenge Simmons' organization in 1924, Gardner received the gubernatorial nomination unopposed; and despite his cautious support of Alfred E. Smith, whose presidential candidacy split the state's Democratic party, he was easily elected. Although his hopes for a tranquil administration were upset by the impact of the depression, he governed according to the slogan "reorganization, retrenchment, and consolidation." He pushed through the legislature an Australian ballot bill and a workmen's compensation act. He secured important measures to centralize and improve the state's administrative machinery and to consolidate the University of North Carolina, North Carolina State College, and North Carolina College for Women into a single state system. He achieved state responsibility for maintaining roads and for the public school system, and successfully fought against a sales tax. At least partly because of his personal reputation, the state's credit was sustained during a period of financial stringency. During the violent labor unrest at the textile towns of Gastonia and Marion in 1929, Gardner attempted to see that justice was done in the courts, insisted that Communists had the right of protection by the law, attacked obstinate employers, and won attention by his firm assertion, "We cannot build a prosperous citizenship on low wages." Gardner, whose own mill workers were among the best paid in the South, emerged from these crises with a favorable national reputation.

Gardner's term as governor ended in 1932; that year he supported Franklin D. Roosevelt for president, and during the New Deal their acquaintanceship, begun when they both were governors, ripened into friendship. In 1933 Gardner opened a law office in Washington specializing in tax matters. With contacts in both the political and business worlds, he became one of Washington's most effective lobbyists, serving among others the Cotton Textile Institute, the Rayon Producers Association, Pan-American Airways, and Coca-Cola. During these years Gardner had easy access to the White House. He served on the Commerce Department's advisory and long-range planning committee, negotiated the government's airmail contract with private carriers, and frequently contributed speech material to the president and other government officials. Still a political force in his home state, Gardner also exerted an influence on North Carolina patronage decisions. Although he supported much of the New Deal, he opposed Roosevelt's Supreme Court "packing" plan, and was so upset by the attempt to purge anti-New Deal senators in 1938 that he quietly organized the successful reelection campaign of Georgia's Sen. Walter F. George.

During World War II, as chairman of an advisory board to the Office of War Mobilization and Reconversion (1944-1946), Gardner acted as a liaison between Congress and the White House. President Truman appointed him under secretary of the treasury in 1946. In this post Gardner supported the British loan and freer trade with England. He worked to reorganize the Bureau of Internal Revenue and the Bureau of Customs and to prepare the way for a joint accounting system that would coordinate the Treasury, the Bureau of the Budget, and the General Accounting Office.

A tall, rugged, handsome man, Gardner was tactful and pragmatic. His probity of character, genius for friendship, and love of entertaining aided his success in business and politics. Yet he was also modest, and he was characteristically uncomfortable when Boiling Spring Junior College in North Carolina, of which he

was a benefactor, changed its name to Gardner-Webb. In religion he was a devout Baptist. In December 1946 Gardner was appointed ambassador to Great Britain. In poor health for several years, he died of a coronary thrombosis in New York City two months later, on the day he was to set sail for his new post. After funeral services at the First Baptist Church in Shelby, he was buried in the town's Sunset Cemetery.

[Gardner's personal papers are in the Southern Hist. Collect. at the Univ. of N.C., Chapel Hill; his gubernatorial papers are in the State Dept. of Arch. and Hist. in Raleigh. Other useful MSS are those of E. Yates Webb in the Southern Hist. Collect. and of F. M. Simmons, Josiah Bailey, and Clyde Hoey at Duke Univ. The basic biographical study, based on these and other sources, is Joseph L. Morrison, *Gov. O. Max Gardner* (1971). Edwin Gill and David L. Corbitt, eds., the *Public Papers and Letters of Oliver Max Gardner, Governor of N.C.* (1937), contains a biographical sketch by Allen Jay Maxwell. Gardner's state career is seen in perspective in Hugh T. Lefler, *Hist. of N.C.*, II (1956); and Elmer L. Puryear, *Democratic Party Dissension in N.C., 1928–1936* (1962). Gardner described his governorship in "One State Cleans House," *Saturday Evening Post*, Jan. 2, 1932. See also Richard L. Watson, Jr., "A Political Leader Bolts—F. M. Simmons in the Presidential Election of 1928," *N.C. Hist. Rev.*, Oct. 1960; "A Southern Democratic Primary: Simmons vs. Bailey in 1930," *ibid.*, Winter 1965, and "Furnifold M. Simmons: 'Jehovah of the Tar Heels?'," *ibid.*, Spring 1967; and obituaries of Gardner in *N.Y. Times*, Feb. 7, 1947, and *Durham Morning Herald*, Feb. 7-9, 1947.]
RICHARD L. WATSON, JR.

GARFIELD, JAMES RUDOLPH (Oct. 17, 1865-Mar. 24, 1950), secretary of the interior under President Theodore Roosevelt, Ohio state senator, lawyer, and Rooseveltian Progressive, was born in Hiram, Ohio, the third child and second son of James Abram Garfield, the twentieth president of the United States, and Lucretia (Rudolph) Garfield. During Jim Garfield's youth, his father was a congressman, and the family moved back and forth between Washington, D.C., and Ohio—first Hiram, then, after 1877, Mentor, which he regarded as "home" for the rest of his life. There were seven children in the family, two of whom died in infancy. Jim's older brother, Harry Augustus, became president of Williams College and fuel administrator during World War I. As soon as they were old enough, Jim and Harry accompanied their father on the summer campaign trail in Ohio. They were educated together, sometimes in school, sometimes at home. Both boys attended St. Paul's School, Concord, N.H., for a year and again were tutored in Washington, D.C., after Garfield's election as president in the fall of 1880.

In September 1881, after Garfield's assassination, Jim and Harry entered Williams College.

James confided in his journal that he had had "a grand and glorious time and made many friends," but he also lamented "that intellectually my course is not one to view with pleasure. . . ." He had leanings toward medicine and law and pursued both during the winter of 1886, but by fall he had definitely decided on the law. He entered Columbia Law School and simultaneously the law firm of Bangs and Stetson in New York City. Early in 1888 he returned to Ohio, passed the bar examination, and in July opened a law office with his brother Harry in Cleveland. The partners concentrated on estate and corporation law, especially railroads. They added Frederic C. Howe as a partner in 1898. On Dec. 30, 1890, James married Helen Newell of Chicago, daughter of John Newell, president of the Lake Shore Railroad. They had four sons: John Newell, James Abram, Newell, and Rudolph Hills.

Politically, Garfield was committed to the Republican party of his father, but he was also predisposed to reform it. He wished, however, to introduce political and administrative improvements, not to change the economic order. He belonged to the group of upper-middle-class reformers who believed that leadership by men of their own class would promote justice and efficiency in government. He was twice elected to the Ohio state senate (1895 and 1897), where he initiated a Corrupt Practices Act, a civil service bill that failed of adoption, and he worked for home rule for cities. In the session of 1898 he supported the election of Mark Hanna to the United States Senate by the Ohio General Assembly and defended Hanna in the face of bribery charges against him.

Garfield twice sought the Republican nomination for congressman from Ohio's Twentieth Congressional District, in 1898 and 1900, and was defeated both times. In the second try he also lost Hanna's support, and it appeared that his political career was at a standstill. His return to public life came not by election but by his appointment to the United States Civil Service Commission in 1902 by President Theodore Roosevelt.

The appointment began a close political association that continued as long as Roosevelt was active in politics. Garfield was promptly brought into the president's inner circle—"the tennis cabinet." The next year Roosevelt chose him for the new post of commissioner of the Bureau of Corporations because he respected his ability as an administrator and because the two shared the view that the proper way to deal with the trust problem was through federal regulation, not

through trust-busting. During Garfield's tenure the bureau's most notable investigations were those into the beef and oil industries. He was criticized for not being zealous enough in the first but was praised in the second for the searching examination he made of the Standard Oil Company, which led to an antitrust suit. An investigation was initiated against the United States Steel Corporation, but in the view of the president and the commissioner this was a "good trust." They reached a "gentlemen's agreement" with the officers of the steel corporation: the company agreed to provide information on its operations and finances and to correct any illegal or bad practices in return for a guarantee against prosecution. The agreement has been criticized as being too considerate of the company and not considerate enough of the public welfare.

Roosevelt promoted Garfield to secretary of the interior in 1907. Although inexperienced in conservation problems, he readily adopted the views of Roosevelt and the federal forester Gifford Pinchot that there should be a program of scientific land management of the federal domain, and that the use of broad discretionary power was necessary to implement such a program. During Garfield's term the department established national parks, reclaimed arid lands, withdrew coal, oil, gas, and phosphate lands from private sale for classification and investigation, took steps to prevent the monopolization of water and electric power, and improved waterways.

After William H. Taft was elected president, Garfield returned to Ohio in March 1909, not only to practice law but also to further his own political ambitions. Early in 1910 he was talked about as a Republican candidate for governor, and in the spring he drew up what he considered "a progressive platform" on which he would stand. He was drawn to progressivism because of its mounting popularity and because Roosevelt was identified with it. Garfield, however, had done nothing to organize his forces in advance, and he and the Progressives were routed by the regulars at the Republican state convention in July 1910.

For the next year Garfield followed Roosevelt's advice to support Progressives, oppose Taft, but keep open the choice of a substitute presidential candidate. He joined the National Progressive Republican League but argued against linking league support to Sen. Robert M. La Follette. As soon as Roosevelt announced his willingness to run again for the presidency, Garfield came out for him. He was prominent in the movement that bolted the Republican party after it renominated Taft and formed the new Progressive party to back Roosevelt. Garfield was the keynote speaker at the Ohio state Progressive convention, and he stumped for "Teddy" outside of Ohio. In 1914 he was the Progressive party candidate for governor, but was defeated. The precipitous drop in the party's polling strength in the 1914 elections made Garfield and other Progressive leaders determined to rejoin the Republican party on honorable terms. The Ohioan was a leader in the harmony movement. He helped Roosevelt draft the public letter refusing the Progressive nomination in 1916 and served as one of the six Progressives on the special election committee of the Republican candidate, Charles Evans Hughes. After the 1916 election Garfield formally announced his return to the Republican party, from which he did not stray again. By this time he had transferred his attention from domestic reform to issues related to World War I—"preparedness and Americanism." He was a partisan of America's entry into the war on the side of the Allies and was critical of President Woodrow Wilson for not being firm enough against Germany.

Garfield's participation in politics subsided after the war, and he devoted himself more to his law practice in the firm of Garfield, MacGregor, and Baldwin. He became involved in Mexican affairs as counsel for an American land and cattle company that owned two million acres in northern Mexico, at a time when the Carranza government threatened foreign landowners with expropriation. But he maintained his concern for conservation, speaking against the proposal of Henry Ford to buy Muscle Shoals on the ground that it did not protect the public interest. He accepted the chairmanship of the Commission on Conservation and the Public Domain appointed by President Herbert Hoover in 1929. Garfield supported Calvin Coolidge for president in 1924, joining with other former Rooseveltian Progressives in denouncing La Follette's bid for the presidency. He campaigned for Hoover in 1928 and in 1932 was chairman of the Republican Resolutions Committee. His last notable public statement was a report to the American Bar Association in 1940 attacking the usurpation of judicial functions by administrative tribunals in Franklin D. Roosevelt's administration.

Garfield's greatest service was as secretary of the interior. He undertook to reorganize the complex department according to a plan he and Pinchot had devised. He sought to prove that the federal bureaucracy could be operated as effectively as any private corporation and was praised as the best secretary the department ever had. He brought to the task the spirit of the efficiency expert, the hallmark of the Rooseveltian reformer.

Throughout his later years Garfield was active in educational and civic affairs as a trustee of Williams College, president of the board of trustees of Lake Erie College, cofounder of the Cleveland Community Fund, director of the Welfare Federation of Cleveland, trustee and president of the Cleveland Hearing and Speech Center (founded by his wife), and president of the Roosevelt Memorial Association.

His wife died in an automobile accident in 1930. Sometime thereafter he went to live with his brother Abram, a prominent Cleveland architect; this arrangement lasted until his final illness. He died of pneumonia in a nursing home in Cleveland and was buried in the Mentor, Ohio, cemetery.

[The sources on Garfield are: the James R. Garfield Papers, Lib. of Cong., which include his lifelong journal, correspondence, speeches, political and legal files, and the draft of chapters for a book on conservation in which he and Pinchot collaborated; diaries and family letters in the James A. Garfield Papers, Lib. of Cong.; Harry J. Brown and Frederick D. Williams, eds., *The Diary of James A. Garfield* (in progress); *Reports* of the Commissioner of Corporations on the Beef Industry and on the Transportation of Petroleum; annual *Reports* of the U.S. Civil Service Commission, 1902–1903, and of the Secretary of the Interior, 1907–1909; Elting E. Morison et al., eds., *The Letters of Theodore Roosevelt;* files of the *Cleveland Plain Dealer* and of the *N.Y. Times.*
Garfield's own major articles are "A Review of President Roosevelt's Administration: Economic and Industrial Influences," *Outlook* 91 (1909): 389–393; "How President Taft Pledged Himself to Follow the Roosevelt Policies—and Failed," *Outlook* 101 (1912): 116–122; "Publicity in Affairs of Industrial Combinations," *Annals* of the Am. Acad. of Political and Social Sci. 42 (1912): 140–146. Secondary sources include Jack M. Thompson, "James R. Garfield: The Career of a Rooseveltian Progressive, 1895–1916" (Ph.D. diss., Univ. of South Carolina, 1958); Lucretia Garfield Comer, *Harry Garfield's First Forty Years* (1965); Gaillard Hunt, "The First Commissioner of Corporations," *Outlook* 82 (1906): 676–680; "Report of the Commissioner of Corporations," *Harper's Weekly* 49 (1905): 8–9; "The Best Secretary of the Interior We Have Ever Had," *Current Literature,* 43: 151–152; *Nat. Cyc. of Am. Biog.* (includes portrait); *Encyc. of Am. Biog.;* Gabriel Kolko, *The Triumph of Conservatism;* Samuel P. Hayes, *Conservation and the Gospel of Efficiency;* Judson King, *The Conservation Fight;* Gifford Pinchot, *Breaking New Ground.*]
                                        HOYT LANDON WARNER

GATES, CALEB FRANK (Oct. 18, 1857–Apr. 9, 1946), missionary and college president, was born in Chicago, Ill., the third son of Caleb Gates and Elizabeth (Hutchins) Gates. His early education was a mixture of private schooling and parental tutoring, and in September

1866 he entered the preparatory department of Wheaton College. Following graduation from Beloit College in 1877, he worked in a bank with his father but soon decided to study for the ministry, graduating from the Chicago Theological School in 1881. At an early age Caleb's mother had taught him the Greek alphabet—the early development of a linguistic talent which later mastered Arabic, Armenian, and Turkish.

Following graduation in 1881 he accepted an invitation from the American Board of Foreign Missions to join their station at Mardin in Turkey. He returned to the United States in 1883, and on May 31 of that year, he married Mary Ellen Moore of Chicago and took his bride back to Mardin, where, from 1885 to 1894, he was connected with a boys' high school. In 1894 he was elected to succeed Dr. Crosby H. Wheeler as president of Euphrates College at Harput. When trouble broke out in the area two years later, eight of the school's twelve buildings were burned; yet Caleb Gates carried on and not only rebuilt the school but doubled the size of the student body.

Though Harput lay deep in remote Anatolia, Gates's work did not go unnoticed. In 1897 Knox College conferred on him an honorary D.D. and in 1899 the University of Edinburgh gave him an honorary LL.D. At this time, John S. Kennedy, chairman of the board of Robert College, located in Constantinople, began to press Gates to accept the presidency of that institution. In 1903 Gates accepted that post and moved to Constantinople with his family.

Gates, short of stature and of stocky build, was forty-six when he arrived at Robert College. A colleague has described him as a deeply religious man with a keen sense of social justice, who, during World War I, organized a soup kitchen on the campus to help feed the local villagers. He was a man of strong will, a superb diplomat, with a keen sense of humor. He was an excellent athlete and from time to time could be found in the gymnasium with the students.

Despite the fact that the Ottoman government frowned upon Turkish students attending Western schools, the first pupil graduated from Robert just before Gates arrived. Gates made the mastering of the Turkish language one of his first priorities. This helped to win him the respect of the government and to smooth the way in many a difficulty.

On Oct. 31, 1909, Kennedy died, leaving a bequest of $1.5 million to Robert College. Gates was summoned to New York to discuss with the board how this money should be used. He proposed the establishment of an engineering school, explaining that the only engineering school in the Ottoman Empire was restricted to the military and taught only civil engineering. The country, he felt, badly needed a school that would teach electrical, mechanical, mining, and civil engineering. Gates's proposal was accepted and the Robert College School of Engineering opened in September 1912.

During World War I, in which Turkey was allied with the Central Powers, the American ambassador advised all Americans in Turkey to leave the country. Although most of the Robert College faculty did so, he stayed on along with the dean of engineering and a few other diehards. Several times in the next few years the college buildings came close to being taken over for the military. Each time Gates succeeded in gaining permission to keep the college open. That Robert College survived World War I was due in large measure to his courage.

After the armistice of 1918 ended, Gates spent a year in the United States but then returned to Turkey to face the business crisis of 1921-1922 and the fall of the Ottoman Empire. As the armies of Kemal Ataturk swept across the Anatolian plateau, the fear in Constantinople was that the Bosphorus area would become a battleground. Thousands fled the city but Robert College remained open.

In 1922-1923 Gates served as adviser to Adm. Mark Bristol, who had been American high commissioner in Constantinople, at the peace conference in Lausanne, Switzerland. Adm. Bristol had been named one of the American representatives. On August 6, 1923, President Coolidge signed the treaty which restored commerce and relations between the two countries. Gates was a principal in the long battle for ratification, which failed in the United States Senate. Gates's diplomacy and fluent Turkish helped to smooth out the situation in Turkey in the face of this rebuff.

The new Turkish Republic was established by Ataturk in 1923. He was determined to modernize the country and it is not surprising that 1924 saw the first large influx of Turkish students to Robert College.

Caleb Gates retired in 1932 at the age of seventy-four. He returned to Turkey in 1938 for the seventy-fifth anniversary of the college. In his twenty-six years as president, he had built six new buildings, as well as additional faculty housing, and expanded the campus property from a few acres to more than a hundred.

He died in Denver, Col., at the age of eighty-eight.

[Information in the Robert College files and from various colleagues of Gates.]

KATHERINE ROSE

GATES, THOMAS SOVEREIGN (Mar. 21, 1873-Apr. 8, 1948) investment banker and university president, was born in Germantown, Pa., the younger of two sons of Jabez Gates and Isabel (Sovereign) Gates. Both parents were natives of Germantown; the father, an established merchant, later became president of the Mutual Fire Insurance Company of Germantown. Thomas Gates attended Germantown Academy, spent two years at Haverford College, and then entered the University of Pennsylvania, graduating from the Wharton School of Finance in 1893 with the Ph.B. degree. He next enrolled in the university's law school, working part-time (1893-1894) in the law office of Sen. George Wharton Pepper. After graduating (LL.B.) in 1896 he practiced law in the office of John G. Johnson, at the same time taking graduate evening courses in philosophy at the University of Pennsylvania for which he ultimately (1946) received the Ph.D. degree.

In 1906 Gates joined the Pennsylvania Company for Insurance on Lives and Granting Annuities as trust officer to advise in the settlement of estates. He rose to vice-president, but resigned in 1912 to become president of the Philadelphia Trust Company. Since trust companies often provided short-term loans to investment bankers, Gates soon came to the attention of Drexel and Company, the Philadelphia branch of the banking house of J. P. Morgan. Gates became a Drexel partner in 1918, and three years later joined J. P. Morgan and Company of New York, as a partner.

Gates entered investment banking as the field was undergoing rapid expansion both at home and abroad. During the 1920's the Drexel firm was primarily a bond wholesaler, with a volume that ranked it among the top ten investment houses. As a resident partner in Philadelphia, Gates promoted bonds and advised businesses, particularly railroads, on reorganization. He also served on the boards of a number of companies identified with the Morgan banking interests, including the Pennsylvania Railroad, the Baldwin Locomotive Works, and several Pennsylvania and New Jersey utility companies, commercial banks, and insurance firms. Throughout the 1920's he chaired the Eastern Pennsylvania Group, a regional organization of the Investment Bankers Association.

During his banking career Gates had retained his interest in higher education. He became a trustee of the University of Pennsylvania in 1921, and in the mid-1920's he raised $16 million in an endowment fund drive. In 1929 he assumed chairmanship of the executive board of the trustees, which supervised the twelve schools and related activities comprising the university. In 1930, at the age of fifty-seven, he retired from the Drexel and Morgan firms to accept the university's presidency, an office recently separated from that of provost.

Serving without salary, Gates set to work to improve the University of Pennsylvania's financial structure, battered by the depression. He reorganized its finances, combining the indebtedness of various schools and consolidating various trust funds. Through rigid economies he balanced the budget and reduced expenditures. His most notable savings came through reorganizing the athletic program. He removed intercollegiate sports from the control of the alumni association and placed them in the hands of a newly created department of physical education, intercollegiate athletics, and student health, thus bringing athletic funds and financial aid to student athletes under the university's direct control. This became known as the Gates Plan and was widely emulated by other colleges. Gates gave greater emphasis to academics by inaugurating the "Cultural Olympics," an annual series of intellectual and artistic contests among colleges of the middle states. He launched an experimental college at Valley Forge, Pa., and provided increased funds for research, scholarships, and libraries. He conducted a new endowment drive in 1937 which raised $12 million. Gates retired as president in 1944, but in the new office of chairman of the university, and later as chairman of the trustees, he remained active in policy making until his death.

Tall and spare, with a buoyant personality, Gates lived unassumingly in spite of his wealth. He was active throughout his career in the civic life of Philadelphia. He headed the Philadelphia Orchestra Association, was president (1945-1948) of the American Philosophical Society, and chaired both local and national community chest drives. A prominent Episcopalian, he also served as treasurer of the diocese of Pennsylvania. In 1940 he received the Bok Prize as Philadelphia's outstanding citizen. Although a lifelong Republican, Gates advocated United States membership in the League of Nations, the recognition of the Soviet Union, and a lowering of the barriers to international trade. He married three times: on June 3, 1905, in Fairfield, Conn., to Marie Rogers, who died in 1906; on Jan. 6, 1910, to Mary Emma Gibson of Philadelphia, who died in 1925; and on July 18, 1929, to Mrs. Emma Barton (Brewster) Waller, Jr., a Philadelphia widow. Gates had one child, Thomas Sovereign, by his first marriage, and two children, Jay Gibson and Virginia Ewing, by his second; he also had a stepson, James. Gates died in his sleep at the age of seventy-five, probably of a cerebral hemorrhage, while at his summer home in Osterville, Mass., on Cape Cod. He was buried in the churchyard of the Church of the Redeemer in Bryn Mawr, Pa.

[Gates's university career is recounted in Edward P. Cheyney, *Hist. of the Univ. of Pa., 1740–1940* (1940). Obituaries in the *N.Y. Times* and *Phila. Inquirer*, Apr. 9, 1948, are sketchy; more helpful are Lawrence Davies, "A Banker Rejoins His Old University," *N.Y. Times Mag.*, Aug. 3, 1930; and the memoir by George W. McClelland in Am. Philosophical Soc., *Year Book*, 1948. See also *Who Was Who in America*, II (1950); and *Nat. Cyc. Am. Biog.*, XLII, 324–325. Death record from Mass. Registrar of Vital Statistics.]
WILLIAM O. WAGNON, JR.

GAY, EDWIN FRANCIS (Oct. 27, 1867–Feb. 8, 1946), economic historian, was born in Detroit, Mich., the first of three children and only son of Aaron Francis and Mary Lucena (Loud) Gay. Both parents came of New England colonial stock. The mother was a Methodist, the father a Unitarian; Gay ended up in his father's denomination. Mary Gay, the daughter of a clergyman who turned to business in later life, was born in Ohio, but she spent much of her youth in Massachusetts, where her father held pastorates. Aaron Gay, a native of Boston, left an inherited stationery store there to become a partner in a Michigan lumber business established by his wife's father. Shortly after Edwin's birth, the family moved to Au Sable, a small village near the firm's timber tracts north of Detroit.

Because of the meager educational opportunities in Au Sable, Gay and his sisters were sent to Europe for three years of schooling beginning in 1878—years that accentuated Gay's social aloofness. On their return the family settled in Ann Arbor, where Gay attended the public high school, graduating in 1886, and the University of Michigan. He studied philosophy, English literature, and history and received the A.B. degree in 1890. Having briefly considered becoming a physician, he decided instead on an academic career and went to the University of Berlin for graduate study in medieval history.

Gay had planned to complete his doctoral studies in four semesters, but his insatiable intellectual curiosity and continued indecision about his goals stretched his stay to twelve years. During this time he studied at several universities and followed an intensive program of independent reading. He worked under many prominent scholars, including Gustav Schmoller at Berlin, founder of the New German Historical School, under whom he received his Ph.D., with highest honors, in 1902. His dissertation, on the English enclosure movement, challenged traditional assumptions about the extent and evil consequences of enclosures, and his subsequent article, "Inclosures in England in the Sixteenth Century" (*Quarterly Journal of Economics*, August 1903), was a major revisionist study. The chief weakness of Gay's German training was the lack of rigorous instruction in economic analysis—squeezed out of German universities in his day by historicism—as a result of which he never fully understood the self-regulating functions of a free market economy.

Gay began his professional career in 1902 as an instructor in economics at Harvard, rising to the rank of professor and chairman of the department in 1906. President Charles W. Eliot, impressed by Gay's knowledge and administrative ability, relied heavily on his advice in planning Harvard's Graduate School of Business Administration, and appointed him its first dean when the school opened in 1908. Despite a total lack of business experience, Gay formulated a general policy for the school, worked out a budget, planned a curriculum, and assembled an illustrious faculty, which included William M. Cole (accounting), Oliver M. W. Sprague (banking), Melvin T. Copeland (marketing), and William J. Cunningham (transportation). He also initiated the case method of instruction to which the school owed much of its success.

World War I drew Gay into government service. In December 1917 he left Harvard to serve as a full-time advisor to the United States Shipping Board, then coping with the critical problem of securing the ship tonnage needed to carry war supplies and American troops to Europe. His first report was so impressive that he was asked to summarize it at a meeting of President Wilson's cabinet in January; within a few months he was appointed a member of the Shipping Board and director of the joint Division of Planning and Statistics of the Shipping and War Trade boards. The statistical data and policy recommendations supplied by Gay for restricting imports and controlling ship utilization were largely responsible for a million additional tons of shipping for war use; they earned him a reputation as one of the "miracle men" of the war. As director of the government's Central Bureau of Planning and Statistics, set up in June 1918, he helped prepare the economic data used by American representatives at the Versailles peace conference.

At the conclusion of the war Gay decided not to return to Harvard but instead, in 1919, accepted an offer from Thomas W. Lamont, the new owner of the ailing New York *Evening Post,* to become the newspaper's editor and president. He had found administration to his liking, and the position offered him the opportunity to help mold public opinion on important national issues like the League of Nations, in which he strongly believed. With Lamont's financial backing, Gay enlivened the *Post's* staid format, expanded its news and feature staff, bringing in such able writers as Mark Sullivan and Christopher Morley, and established an influential literary supplement to the Saturday edition, which later evolved into the *Saturday Review of Literature.* Unfortunately, these costly improvements did not boost circulation enough to offset the paper's shaky finances, nor did the economy drive that followed. In 1924 the *Post* went under, with heavy losses to Gay and many of his friends, and was sold to the Philadelphia publisher Cyrus H. K. Curtis.

Disappointed and exhausted, Gay returned that same year to Harvard as professor of economic history; he remained until his retirement in 1936. Gay was an inspiring if exacting teacher, insisting on painstaking research as a preliminary to writing, and he trained many of the ablest economic historians of the postwar years. Partly as a result of the care he devoted to supervising the work of his students, his own scholarly production was meager, amounting to only a few published articles. A projected history of the Industrial Revolution never materialized because of his unwillingness to write without having examined all pertinent manuscript collections in the British archives.

Throughout his career Gay took an active part in professional and public affairs organizations. Through the American Association for Labor Legislation he had helped secure an improved factory inspection act in Massachusetts in 1912. He was a founder of the National Bureau of Economic Research in 1919 and served as its first president. As the bureau's

director of research (1924-1933), he coordinated the writing and assembling of the two-volume study *Recent Economic Changes* (1929), an important source of information on American social and economic life in the 1920's. Gay served as the first secretary-treasurer of the Council on Foreign Relations (1921-1933) and was chiefly responsible for the establishment of its quarterly journal, *Foreign Affairs,* in 1922. Although he was more respected among historians than among economists, Gay served as president of the American Economic Association (1929) and as the first president of the Economic History Association (1940).

After his retirement from Harvard, Gay joined the research staff of the Huntington Library in San Marino, Calif. Although afflicted with diabetes in his later years, he continued to work until the time of his death. On Aug. 24, 1892, Gay married Louise Fitz Randolph, a high school and college classmate. They had two children: Edward Randolph and Margaret Randolph. Gay died of pneumonia at the Huntington Memorial Hospital in Pasadena at the age of seventy-eight. His body was cremated and the remains buried at Forest Hills Cemetery, Boston. In the judgment of his colleague Frank W. Taussig, Gay had directed "the best economic research ever done in the United States."

[Herbert Heaton, *A Scholar in Action: Edwin F. Gay* (1952); memoirs by N. S. B. Gras in *Economic Hist. Rev.,* 16 (1946), 60–62, and Earl J. Hamilton in *Am. Economic Rev.,* June 1947; preface to *Facts and Factors in Economic Hist.* (1932), a volume of essays in Gay's honor by former students; personal recollections. See also Melvin T. Copeland, *And Mark an Era: The Story of the Harvard Business School* (1958), chaps. i and ii.]

EARL J. HAMILTON

GEIGER, ROY STANLEY (Jan. 25, 1885-Jan. 23, 1947), Marine Corps officer and naval aviator, was born in Middleburg, Fla., the youngest of four sons and sixth of seven children of Marion Francis and Josephine (Prevatt) Geiger. His father's ancestors had migrated in the early eighteenth century from Austria to Philadelphia; their descendants moved progressively southward, settling finally in the timber-growing regions south of Jacksonville, Fla. Geiger's father was a local tax assessor and superintendent of the Clay County schools, but the family had limited means, and Geiger had to struggle to support and educate himself. He worked his way through Florida State Normal School and in 1904 entered John B. Stetson University in Florida, from which he received the LL.B. degree in 1907. He was admitted to the bar the same year, but soon became discouraged with the prospects of the legal profession in a rural community. Restless, and longing for physical outdoor activity, that November he enlisted in the Marine Corps.

After fifteen months in the ranks, Geiger won his commission as a second lieutenant in February 1909. Officers' training and two years of sea duty followed, after which he had nearly four consecutive years of foreign field service, including combat duty in Nicaragua. By the time of his promotion to first lieutenant in 1915, Geiger had earned the reputation of an efficient and dynamic troop leader, an outstanding swimmer and diver, and an expert rifleman and equestrian. In March 1916 he reported to the Navy Flying School at Pensacola, Fla. In June 1917, having successfully completed flight training in seaplanes and free balloons, Geiger, now a captain, was officially designated a naval aviator, the fifth Marine Corps officer to win the coveted gold wings.

The United States was at war with Germany, but Geiger did not get to France until July 1918, when, promoted to major, he was assigned as one of four squadron commanders of the 1st Marine Aviation Force. He led several bombing raids against enemy installations and front lines in northern France and Belgium, for which he subsequently received the Navy Cross. Geiger's duty over the ensuing two peacetime decades included both aviation commands and advanced training billets. After several briefer assignments at home and overseas, he spent three and a half years (1921–1924) at Quantico, Va., as the commanding officer of the 1st Aviation Group attached to the 3rd Marine Brigade. Considerable flying was involved, as his group took part in all of the brigade's frequent maneuvers, and also participated fully in the navy's annual fleet problems in the Caribbean. In 1923 he led a flight of four heavy bombers safely across the continent from the West Coast.

To increase his professional knowledge, Geiger attended the army's Command and General Staff School at Fort Leavenworth, Kans., from which he was graduated with distinction in 1925. Two years later, after a tour of duty in Haiti, he returned to Quantico to command its air station. In 1928 he enrolled at the Army War College, at Washington, and on graduation a year later he was designated commanding officer, Aircraft Squadrons, East Coast Expeditionary Force, based at Quantico. During his two years in that command, Geiger flew two noteworthy long-distance rescue missions: one to Santo Domingo with relief supplies for hurricane victims, the other to Nicaragua to aid a

capital devastated by earthquake and fire. Adjudged the Marines' most experienced pilot, Geiger served at its Washington headquarters from 1931 to 1935 as officer-in-charge of Marine Corps aviation, attaining the rank of lieutenant colonel in 1934.

His next assignment was commanding officer, Marine Air Group One, a component of the 1st Marine Brigade, Fleet Marine Force, at Quantico. From this four-year tour of duty, Geiger, now a colonel, gained a reputation as a highly skilled instrument pilot-navigator. He then spent nearly two years (June 1939 to March 1941) at the Naval War College in Newport, where he completed both the senior and advanced courses. For part of 1941 he was detailed as an official observer with British Military commands engaged in combat in the Mediterranean and North Africa, as well as on maneuvers in the United Kingdom. He returned to Quantico later that year to become commanding general of the 1st Marine Aircraft Wing, Fleet Marine Force.

With the United States' entrance into World War II, Geiger, after months of intensive training in southern California, flew to Guadalcanal in the Solomon Islands, where he directed the operations of his wing and all allied aircraft based at Henderson Field during September and October 1942. An experienced organizer, Geiger greatly improved staff operations, and his group, which reinforced elements of the 1st Marine Division, played a vital role in repelling repeated Japanese attempts to recapture Guadalcanal as part of their advance toward New Guinea. His command shot down nearly 300 Japanese planes and sank or severely damaged more than a score of enemy vessels.

Geiger, now a major general, was recalled to Marine Corps headquarters in Washington in May 1943 to become director of aviation, but he returned in November to the Southwest Pacific as commanding general, First Marine Amphibious Corps, which he led until mid-December during the occupation and defense of Cape Torokina, Bougainville. He commanded the Third Marine Amphibious Corps in the invasion and recapture of Guam (July–August 1943) and the Southern Palau Islands (September–October). In the spring of 1945 Geiger again led his Third Corps, now a part of the Tenth Army, into action in the assault and occupation of Okinawa. On the death of Gen. Simon Bolivar Buckner in combat, Geiger as his deputy succeeded to the command of the Tenth Army, the first Marine officer and the first American aviator to be so honored. His new command brought promotion to lieutenant general. For his courage and tenacity during the South Pacific operations, Geiger was awarded a number of combat decorations, including Distinguished Service medals from both the army and the navy and the navy's Distinguished Flying Cross.

In July 1945 Geiger was named commanding general of the Fleet Marine Force, Pacific, at Pearl Harbor, and as such supervised Marine forces in the occupation of China and Japan. He was transferred to Washington in November 1946, but his health was failing. He entered the Naval Medical Center at Bethesda, Md., in January 1947 suffering from inflammation of the veins, and died there later that month. He was buried in Arlington National Cemetery. By a special act of Congress he was posthumously elevated to the rank of full general.

Geiger married Eunice Renshaw Thompson of Pensacola on July 12, 1917. They had two children: Joyce Renshaw, the wife of a Marine aviator, and Roy Stanley, a career army artillery officer.

Throughout his career in the Marine Corps, Geiger thought of himself primarily as a line officer, additionally qualified as a naval aviator. An utterly fearless soldier, he was a man bursting with self-confidence, and his aggressive approach to all problems could not help but create antagonism on the part of some of his associates. But his character and conduct served as an inspiration to at least one generation of Marines.

[Geiger's personal papers are in the Marine Corps Museum, Quantico, Va. This article is based on the author's biography of Geiger, *Unaccustomed to Fear* (1968), which draws upon Geiger's papers, official records, and interviews with his family and surviving associates. Published material on Geiger includes: Robert Sherrod, *Hist. of Marine Corps Aviation in World War II* (1952); sketches in *Newsweek*, Dec. 21, 1942, p. 21, *Time*, Nov. 22, 1943, p. 65, *Current Biog.*, 1945 and 1947, and *Nat. Cyc. Am. Biog.*, XXXVI, 349-350; and obituaries in the *Leatherneck*, May 1947, and *N.Y. Times* and *N.Y. Herald Tribune*, Jan. 24, 1947.]

ROGER WILLOCK

GIANNINI, AMADEO PETER (May 6, 1870-June 3, 1949), banker and financier, was born in San Jose, Calif., the first of three sons of Luigi Giannini and Virginia (Demartini) Giannini, Italian immigrant farmers from Genoa. Early in 1877 a disgruntled workman shot and killed Luigi Giannini; several months later his widow married Lorenzo Scatena, a self-employed teamster who had worked his way from Italy to San Jose. Scatena moved the family in 1882 to San Francisco, where he took a job

with one of the city's produce firms. Less than a year later he opened his own wholesale produce business, which in time became one of the leading firms in the city. Amadeo Giannini started working in his stepfather's business at age twelve, often leaving home at midnight and returning only in time to get ready for classes at Washington Grammar School. Although he was a superior student, he preferred business to school, and after finishing the eighth grade, he completed his formal education with five months at Heald's Business College.

For the next eighteen years (1883-1901) Giannini devoted himself to his stepfather's produce business. A "huge youth, bull strong and tireless" (he was over six feet tall and weighed 170 pounds at age fifteen), Giannini contributed materially to the growth of L. Scatena and Company. He traveled with horse and wagon throughout Santa Clara, San Joaquin, and Napa counties buying fruit and vegetables, and took trips as far south as Los Angeles to contract for commodities. So successful was he in cultivating new business that in 1889 his stepfather made him a partner with a one-third interest, which was increased two years later to one-half. On Sept. 14, 1892, Giannini married Clorinda Agnes Cuneo, daughter of Joseph Cuneo, an Italian immigrant who had made a fortune in real estate. They had six children, of whom three survived childhood: Lawrence Mario, Virgil David, and Claire Evelyn. In 1901, at the age of thirty-one, Giannini retired from the produce business. By then his savings, invested in real estate, netted him a monthly income of $250. This, together with his half-interest in L. Scatena and Company, which he sold to several of the firm's employees for some $100,000, was more than sufficient for his family's needs. "I don't want to be rich," he asserted. "No man actually owns a fortune; it owns him" (James and James, p. 9).

It was his father-in-law's death in 1902 that forced Giannini out of retirement and started him on his banking career. Joseph Cuneo died intestate, and his family asked Giannini to manage the estate, worth approximately $500,000. Among Cuneo's holdings were some shares in the Columbus Savings and Loan Society, a small community bank in North Beach, San Francisco's Italian quarter. Cuneo had been a director of the bank, a position to which Giannini succeeded. The Columbus bank, founded in 1893 by John F. Fugazi, one of the most prominent Italian-Americans in the United States, provided North Beach residents with a convenient and safe place to keep their money and assisted the community's businessmen with loans; but like most banks at the time, it did little to accommodate small borrowers. To serve them, Andrea A. Sbarboro, one of the organizers of the Italian-Swiss Colony winery at Asti, Calif., had founded the Italian-American Bank in 1899. Noting the rapid growth of this competitor, Giannini sought to persuade the directors of the Columbus bank to make more small loans, to help workers buy their own houses or go into business for themselves. When his efforts failed, Giannini and five other directors resigned and, along with Giannini's stepfather and four friends (all but one of Italian descent), organized the Bank of Italy.

Capitalized at $300,000, the new bank opened in October 1904. It was located in a one-room renovated saloon in the North Beach community, and nearly all its stock was owned by local residents. Though the bank started out serving mostly small tradesmen, merchants, farmers, and workers of Italian origin (an Italian Department was set up to aid non-English-speaking depositors), Giannini intended it to serve clients of every nationality, social position, and income, a principle he adhered to throughout his career. From the start the Bank of Italy offered complete banking services; it accepted both savings and commercial (checking) accounts, pursued an easy lending policy, and, alone among San Francisco's banks, encouraged small loans, some amounting to as little as $25. Recognizing that if the bank was to lend money it had to increase deposits, Giannini was as unorthodox in soliciting accounts as he was in extending credit. A friendly, outgoing, unceremonious man, he walked the streets of North Beach looking for prospective depositors. Many that he enlisted were Italian immigrants who had previously kept their money hidden at home in gold and silver coins. Giannini spoke to them in Italian, won their confidence, and made them lifelong clients. He also instituted a program of popular, eye-catching advertisements. His informal methods shocked established bankers, but the bank's steady progress convinced him that he was satisfying a public need. By the end of December 1904, less than three months after it had opened, the Bank of Italy's loans amounted to $178,400 and its deposits stood at $134,413; a year later the figures were $883,522 and $703,024.

Giannini's bold and resourceful behavior during the great San Francisco earthquake and fire of April 1906 boosted his stature among the city's business and civic leaders and enhanced the reputation of his bank, which until then had been almost totally ignored outside of North Beach. As fire spread across the city, Giannini borrowed two teams and wagons from his stepfather's produce firm, loaded them with some $80,000 of the bank's coin and currency, covered the money pouches with fruit and vegetables, and transported them to the safety of his own house in suburban San Mateo. Four days later, with one-third of San Francisco burned out and much of it still smoldering, Giannini circularized the bank's depositors, announcing that their funds were safe. Using a "plank counter" for an office, he made loans and accepted deposits days before the city's other banks had resumed operations. When the financial panic of 1907 hit San Francisco late the following year, most of the city's banks were forced to use clearinghouse certificates, but the Bank of Italy continued to issue currency. Anticipating trouble months before the panic, Giannini had been accumulating gold, which he was now able to pay out on demand. Nor did the Bank of Italy place a limit on withdrawals. Its readiness to meet customers' demands inspired confidence, and by the end of the year the bank's deposits had increased by some $311,000.

At meetings of the state and national bankers' associations in 1908, Giannini heard Lyman J. Gage, the former secretary of the treasury, and Woodrow Wilson, then president of Princeton University, extol the benefits of branch banking. Wilson contended that branch banking would open wider credit channels to local merchants and farmers and would improve the image of banking among the general public. Save for a few large metropolitan bankers, not many of those present agreed. Giannini—already familiar with Canada's branch system—was one who did. In 1909 California enacted a new banking law authorizing the state superintendent of banks to approve branches when in his opinion they satisfied "the public convenience and advantage." That statute provided the legal basis upon which Giannini started his vast banking empire.

The first Bank of Italy branch outside San Francisco opened at San Jose in October 1909, just three months after the new law went into effect. The technique employed in acquiring that branch—buying a small bank and converting it into a branch of the Bank of Italy—was continued until mid-1917, when Giannini started using corporate affiliates and holding companies to facilitate his acquisitions. By the end of 1918, with twenty-four branches scattered throughout California and total resources of more than $93 million, the Bank of Italy had become the first statewide branch-banking system in the United

States and California's fourth largest bank in assets.

Giannini's phenomenal success aroused strong opposition among California bankers, both large and small, many of whom disapproved of branch banking. Their combined efforts, aided by state officials who shared similar views, delayed but failed to stop Giannini, whose goal was a transcontinental and worldwide system. His first step in this direction came in 1919, when he organized Bancitaly Corporation, a holding company that purchased the East River National Bank in New York City and later acquired a branch system in Italy. In 1924, at the age of fifty-four, Giannini retired as president of the Bank of Italy, but remained a director and chairman of its executive committee, as well as president of Bancitaly. These posts, he said, would allow him "to concentrate on major policies," the most important of which was the acquisition of new banks.

When the McFadden Act, passed by Congress in 1927, greatly extended the previously circumscribed functions of national banks, Giannini decided to protect his state-chartered Bank of Italy from additional competition by joining the national banking system. The result was the creation, in March 1927, of the Bank of Italy National Trust and Savings Association. Giannini also noted that the McFadden law permitted a national bank to absorb other banks with headquarters in the same city. This included all branches of the absorbed banks, regardless of location, which had existed prior to passage of the act. Using this provision, Giannini quickly acquired a new network of branch banks and by 1928 had unified them under the name of Bank of America of California. Two years later Giannini and the directors of Transamerica Corporation—the holding company which succeeded Bancitaly in 1928—merged the Bank of Italy and the Bank of America of California into the Bank of America National Trust and Savings Association. Several other banks controlled by the corporation but ineligible for inclusion were united in a new state bank called simply the Bank of America. This, in turn was later merged into the parent Bank of America N.T. and S.A. under terms of the Banking Act of 1933.

The expansion of the 1920's, however, was halted by the stock market crash of 1929. As the depression deepened, Transamerica's new president, Elisha Walker, inaugurated a program of contraction which included selling some bank properties. Outraged, and determined to save his empire from liquidation, the then-ailing sixty-

two-year-old Giannini waged a successful proxy fight in 1932, ousted Walker and his allies from Transamerica's board of directors, and resumed the position of chairman of the board of both Transamerica and the Bank of America N.T. and S.A. Working long hours, he cut operating costs, campaigned for new accounts, and steered the bank successfully through the financial crisis of March 1933.

Bank of America's spectacular recovery—total resources climbed from $876,300,000 in 1932 to upwards of $1.6 billion in 1939—aroused considerable opposition. Single-unit bankers, long opposed to branch banking, continued to fight Giannini's expansionist policies, but the most serious and widely circulated attacks against the Bank of America during the 1930's focused on its dealings with California's farmers. The bank and its affiliate, California Lands, Inc., were accused of collusion with the state's large landowners in exploiting migratory field workers and frustrating their efforts at unionization. The bank also was criticized for its farm mortgage policies. Carey McWilliams, in his *Factories in the Field* (1939), asserted that the Bank of America "controlled" some 50 percent of the farm lands in Central and Northern California. The bank provided statistical data showing that at no time did it hold more than 10 percent of the farm mortgages in the counties McWilliams had listed. Nor did the other charges made against the Bank of America survive close scrutiny (James and James, pp. 411-413).

Though he never realized his goal of worldwide branch banks, Giannini established an impressive state system that led in developing many new banking trends, particularly in the area of personal and agricultural credits. He retired in 1934 as chairman of the board of Bank of America, but continued as board chairman of Transamerica Corporation. By this time, Bank of America had grown into the world's largest commercial bank, with 493 branches in California and assets of more than $5 billion. A Federal Reserve Board investigation, begun in December 1948, into charges that Transamerica had violated the antimonopoly provisions of the Clayton Anti-Trust Act led to an order in 1951 that the holding company divest itself of all banking stock except for that of Bank of America.

Giannini did not live to learn the results of the government's action. He died of a heart attack at his home in San Mateo at the age of seventy-nine. A lifelong Roman Catholic, he was buried in Holy Cross Cemetery in nearby

Colma. His son Lawrence Mario was president of the Bank of America from January 1936 until his death in 1952, and Giannini's daughter, Claire, the wife of Clifford P. Hoffman, succeeded to her father's place on the bank's board. Giannini left an estate of $439,278, all but $9,000 of which he assigned to the Bank of America-Giannini Foundation. He had established the foundation in 1945 with a gift of $509,235, a sum which then represented half of his personal fortune, to finance medical research and provide educational scholarships for the bank's employees. These bequests, together with a gift in 1927 of $1.5 million to the University of California, which was used to establish the Giannini Foundation of Agricultural Economics, were his major benefactions.

[The largest collection of primary materials, including personal and business correspondence, is in the Bank of America's San Francisco headquarters. Other papers dealing with banking developments in California are in the Bancroft Lib., Univ. of Calif., Berkeley. The standard study of the Bank of America is Marquis James and Bessie R. James, *Biography of a Bank: The Story of Bank of America N.T. and S.A.* (1954). Julian Dana, *A. P. Giannini* (1947), is a lively, undocumented account. George W. Dowrie, "Hist. of the Bank of Italy in Calif.," *Jour. of Economic and Business Hist.,* Feb. 1930, and Howard H. Preston, "Bank of America," *ibid.,* Feb. 1932, are useful corporate histories of Giannini's banks. See also Joseph Giovinco, "Democracy in Banking: The Bank of Italy and California's Italians," *Calif. Hist. Soc. Quart.,* Sept. 1968. Other useful works include Gerald C. Fischer, *Bank Holding Companies* (1961), and S. D. Southworth, *Branch Banking in the U.S.* (1928). Obituaries appeared in all the important California newspapers and in the *N.Y. Times,* June 4, 1949. There is a good oil painting of Giannini in the Bank of America's San Francisco headquarters.]

VINCENT P. CAROSSO

GIBSON, JOSHUA (Dec. 21, 1911–Jan. 20, 1947), baseball player, was born in Buena Vista, Ga., the first of three children (two sons and a daughter) of Mark Gibson and Nancey (Woodlock) Gibson. His father scratched out a bare living by farming a small patch of ground. Hoping to provide a better life for his young family, he moved north in 1923 to Pittsburgh, Pa., where he took a job as a laborer for the Carnegie-Illinois Steel Company. The following year he sent for his family and they settled in Pleasant Valley, a Negro enclave in Pittsburgh's North Side.

There young Josh was introduced to sports and developed a strong interest in baseball and swimming. His natural talent as a hitter made him first choice of the captains in neighborhood pickup baseball games, and as a swimmer he won several playground medals. He had attended a segregated elementary school in Georgia through the first five grades, and he continued his education in Pittsburgh's schools. At sixteen he joined his first organized baseball team, the Gimbels A.C., an all-Negro amateur club which played in and around Pittsburgh. He dropped out of school after completing the ninth grade in Allegheny Pre-Vocational School, where he had begun to learn the rudiments of the electrician's trade, and took a job as an apprentice in an air-brake manufacturing company.

It was becoming evident, however, that baseball would be his real vocation. Since the major leagues held to an unwritten rule that excluded black players, he was confined to the segregated world of black sports. In 1929 and 1930, while in his late teens, Gibson played with the semiprofessional Crawford Colored Giants of Pittsburgh, his growing reputation as a slugger drawing crowds as large as 5,000. He also attracted the attention of the Homestead (Pa.) Grays, one of the most powerful all-Negro professional clubs. On July 25, 1930, when their regular catcher was injured during a game against the all-black Kansas City Monarchs at Pittsburgh's Forbes Field, the Grays called Gibson out of the stands to fill in as catcher. This marked the start of Gibson's career in the Negro "big leagues." Although he was not a polished catcher, his powerful hitting quickly made him a regular on the team.

In 1931, as the Homestead Grays barnstormed through Pennsylvania, West Virginia, Ohio, and New York, meeting black teams and white semipro teams, Josh Gibson was credited with seventy-five home runs. From then until his death he was the black Babe Ruth, the most famous black ballplayer next to the legendary Satchel Paige. Because Negro clubs and leagues did not keep complete records, his home run total and batting averages are not known. His highest reported number of home runs for a single season was eighty-nine. The few statistics available and the recollections of men who played on Negro teams indicate that during his seventeen years in professional baseball Gibson hit more than 800 homers in regular season play. His longest measured home run traveled 512 feet, but others were without doubt considerably longer. Some old ballplayers claim that in a Negro league game in New York's Yankee Stadium, Gibson hit a drive that cleared the third tier of the grandstand beside the left field bullpen, the only fair ball ever hit out of Yankee Stadium, which has been the home of such sluggers as Babe Ruth, Lou Gehrig, Joe DiMaggio, and Mickey Mantle.

During his career Gibson played not only for the Grays but for the Pittsburgh Crawfords (named for the earlier Crawford Giants), an outstanding all-black club that boasted Satchel Paige and several other of the greatest stars of Negro baseball. From 1933 through 1945 he also played each winter with teams in Puerto Rico, Cuba, Mexico, or Venezuela. His highest salary in the United States was about $6,000 a season, and he earned an additional $3,000 in winter baseball during his peak years; among black players, only Satchel Paige earned more in baseball's preintegration era.

Gibson, a right-handed batter and thrower, stood six feet one inch tall and weighed 215 pounds in his prime. He had a moon-round face and a heavily muscled body in the athlete's classic mold. His amiable disposition won him the affection of both teammates and opponents, and his power earned their awe.

While in his late teens Gibson married Helen Mason. She died in August 1930, at the age of eighteen, while giving birth to Gibson's only children, the twins Helen and Joshua. In 1940 he married a second wife, Hattie, from whom he was later separated. As early as 1942 Gibson began to experience severe, recurrent headaches. He was hospitalized in January 1943 after suffering a blackout and was found to have a brain tumor. He refused, however, to permit an operation, fearing that he would become "a vegetable," and during the last four years of his life he continued to play ball despite the persistent headaches. He died at the age of thirty-five of a cerebral hemorrhage at his widowed mother's Pittsburgh home, just three months before Jackie Robinson finally broke the major league color bar.

Gibson was one of the greatest stars of Negro baseball and a rival of Babe Ruth as the preeminent slugger in baseball history. There is virtual unanimity among white players who saw him perform that in the major leagues he would have been an outstanding star. In 1972 he was elected to baseball's Hall of Fame.

[Robert Peterson, *Only the Ball Was White* (1970), a history of Negro baseball; *Time,* July 19, 1943, pp. 75–76; sports pages of *Pittsburgh Courier* and *Chicago Defender,* 1930–1947; death record from Pa. Dept. of Health; interviews with Mrs. Annie Mahaffey, Pittsburgh, Gibson's sister; Mrs. Helen Dixon, Pittsburgh, daughter; and the following former players: J. W. Crutchfield, Chicago; William J. (Judy) Johnson, Wilmington, Del.; William J. Yancey, Moorestown, N.J.; William (Jack) Marshall, Chicago.]
ROBERT PETERSON

GILLETT, HORACE WADSWORTH (Dec. 12, 1883–Mar. 2, 1950), metallurgist, was born near Penn Yan in Steuben County, N.Y., the only child of Edward Chauncey Gillett and Mary Elizabeth (Doolittle) Gillett. The families of both parents had come to the Finger Lakes region from New England in the early nineteenth century; the father was a modestly prosperous farmer who had briefly served in the New York legislature. Horace Gillett developed an interest in chemistry while a student at Cornell University. After graduating with the B.A. degree in 1906, he spent the summer in the laboratory of the inventor Thomas A. Edison, who commended his analytical skill, and then returned to Cornell as a graduate student and instructor in physical chemistry and electrochemistry. In subsequent summers and vacations he worked for the industrial research firm of Arthur D. Little. Gillett received the Ph.D. in chemistry in 1910.

For the next two years Gillett was manager of the research department of the Aluminum Castings Company, Detroit, Mich. In 1912 he moved to the U. S. Bureau of Mines as chief alloy chemist in charge of the field station at Ithaca, N.Y., a post he occupied until 1924. It was during this period that Gillett's main interest turned from chemistry to metallurgy. One aspect of his work at the bureau led to the development of the rocking arc electric furnace for melting brass and other metals, a development for which he received, in 1915, the first of his thirteen patents. Gillett moved to the Bureau of Standards in Washington, D.C., in 1924 as chief of the Division of Metallurgy, where his reputation continued to grow. He was one of the founders in 1929 of the magazine *Metals and Alloys* and served as its editorial director until 1943.

In 1929 Gillett was chosen as the first director of the new Battelle Memorial Institute in Columbus, Ohio, established by a grant from the will of Gordon Battelle "for the encouragement of creative research . . . and the making of discoveries and inventions." A thin, wiry man in a baggy sweater and with an ever-present pipe, "Gil," as his associates affectionately knew him, was well qualified to organize and initiate a program of active and significant research. He had a quick perception and an awesome reading ability capable of detecting the smallest detail or error in a manuscript at a glance, an ability which extended to a half-dozen foreign languages, which he had taught himself. It was Gillett who determined that the Battelle Institute should concentrate on metallurgical research and—though his own interests and knowledge covered every aspect of metallurgy—on "practical" applications rather than abstract theory.

He began by surrounding himself with outstanding individuals from every branch of

Gillett · Glaspell

metallurgy and physical science, drawing on the long associations he had made at the Bureau of Mines and the Bureau of Standards. Over the next several years the institute under his guidance carried on research in such areas as blast furnace technology, ceramics, and the use of electron diffraction to determine the surface properties of metals, quickly establishing a reputation as a world leader in metallurgical research. During these years Gillett continued to write prolifically for *Metals and Alloys* and other technical journals. At the time of his death, his list of publications included six books and over two hundred articles covering nearly every phase of the practice of metallurgy.

Gillett was first and foremost a scientist and he begrudged the time away from his research demanded by the promotional and administrative aspects of the director's post. In 1934 he persuaded the Battelle Institute trustees to let him step down in favor of Clyde E. Williams, a chemist whom he had recruited from industry in 1930. Gillett remained at the institute as chief technical advisor under Williams. He continued his work with alloy steels, foundry problems, and heat treatment, and also studied metal fatigue, an important factor in aircraft structures. His pioneering study of the "creep" of metals, their gradual deformation and failure under stress at high temperatures, played a role in future space technology.

In his research Gillett was able to draw upon, and sometimes to obtain fresh insights from a vast store of erudition which extended well beyond the field of metallurgy. Throughout his long career he urged the value of a broad general knowledge and opposed the increasing tendency toward specialization in the scientific fields. He retired from the Battelle Institute in 1949 but remained a consultant until his death.

The recipient of numerous professional awards, including the McFadden Gold Medal of the American Foundrymen's Society, Gillett remained a modest man. Among his hobbies were hunting, fishing, and the training of English setters. He listed his religious affiliation as Baptist. Gillett had married Carrie Louise Pratt, the daughter of a local manufacturer, at Penn Yan, N.Y., on Apr. 18, 1911. They had three children: Guertha Mary, Edward Pratt, and Horace Wadsworth. Gillett died of a cerebral hemorrhage near Nicholasville, Ky., while returning from a hunting trip in the South. His remains were cremated and buried in the family plot at Penn Yan.

[*In Memoriam: Horace Wadsworth Gillett, 1883–1950* (Battelle Memorial Inst., 1952), which includes a complete list of Gillett's patents, publications, and awards; *Nat. Cyc. Am. Biog.,* XXXIX, 319; information on family history and on Gillett's personal interests from Edward P. Gillett, Bethlehem, Pa.; information on Gillett's professional career from interviews with Robert Adams and Russell Dayton at the Battelle Memorial Inst.; death record from Ky. State Dept. of Health. See also: George A. W. Boehm and Alex Groner, *Science in the Service of Mankind: The Battelle Story* (1972); Bertram D. Thomas, *The Legacy of Science: The Story of Battelle Memorial Inst.* (Newcomen Soc., 1963); article on Gillett in *Metal Progress,* Mar. 1939 (with photograph); *Who's Who in Engineering,* 1948; obituaries in *N.Y. Times,* Mar. 5, 1950, *Jour. of Metals,* 1950, pp. 733–734, and *Materials and Methods,* Apr. 1950, p. 48. An oil painting of Gillett by David Philip Wilson (1969) is at Battelle Memorial Inst.]

JAMES A. MULHOLLAND

GLASPELL, SUSAN KEATING (July 1, 1876–July 27, 1948), author, was born in Davenport, Iowa, the second of three children and only daughter of Elmer S. Glaspell and Alice (Keating) Glaspell. Her mother was born in New York City of Irish parents recently arrived from Dublin. The Glaspells were early Americans of English descent and among the first white settlers in Iowa. A dealer in hay and feed who never earned much, Elmer Glaspell was unable to give his daughter material advantages, but being a man of sharp contradictions—he was devoutly religious (a member of the Disciples of Christ) yet a fervent admirer of racehorses; he prayed and he swore with equal relish—he unwittingly gave the future author a running lesson in the complexities of human nature. Accompanying him to farms in their home state and in the Dakotas, Susan early developed "a feeling of the wideness and richness" of the region, a love of the land and its plain people that would be incarnated in the many idealized, if not sentimentalized, Midwesterners who throng her writings.

A bright pupil in the schools of Davenport, Susan was generally expected to be a teacher, but she early dreamed of a literary career and on completing high school became a reporter at $3 a week for her hometown paper. At Drake University in Des Moines, Iowa, she helped pay her way as college correspondent for a local newspaper, and, in 1899, immediately after graduating with a Ph.B. degree, she went to work for the *Des Moines Daily News.* Slightly built, with brown eyes and light brown hair demurely parted in the middle, she appeared almost otherworldly, but she was shrewdly observant and had great drive. After covering politics, murder trials, and "other excitements" for less than two years, she felt she had accumulated so much story material that, in her words, "I recklessly gave up my job and went home to Davenport to have a try at the magazines."

329

While still on the *News* she had sold several short stories to *Youth's Companion*; from 1903 until she abandoned the genre in 1922, her stories became a familiar feature in leading magazines. More than half of her tales—she published forty-three in all—were set in "Freeport" (Davenport), enabling her to freshen what all too often were stale situations and conventional plots with local color and realistic detail. *Lifted Masks* (1912), a collection of her magazine stories, is typical of her writing in this period. In 1909 her first novel was published, *The Glory of the Conquered,* a romantic bonbon similar in quality to her magazine pieces. By the time she wrote *The Visioning* (1911), a better work, she had lived abroad a year and had come under the influence of George Cram Cook, the strange, rebellious son of a prominent Davenport family. Echoing his radicalism, though in a softer key, she sympathetically depicted a socialist in *The Visioning.* Essentially, however, she remained a grassroots idealist, an apolitical libertarian. She and Cook were married on April 14, 1913, and settled in Provincetown, Mass.

While continuing to sell magazine stories for a living, Susan Glaspell readily fell under the sway of the untrammeled, yet earnest, spirit of her husband's circle, which came to include Hutchins Hapgood and John Reed, the radical journalist. Under Cook's leadership a theater was founded in Provincetown in 1915. The following year, after Eugene O'Neill had joined the group, the Provincetown Players moved to Greenwich Village. Among those who wrote and acted in the plays was Edna St. Vincent Millay. A bulwark of the playhouse, second only to O'Neill, Glaspell between 1915 and 1922 wrote seven short plays, including, in collaboration with Cook, the popular *Suppressed Desires* (1915), which deflated the chic but naïve Freudianism of Village sophisticates. Of her four long plays of this period, the best were *Inheritors* (1921), a drama of social protest at a Midwestern college, and *The Verge* (1922), a study of a Nietzschean woman.

The Cooks devoted their winters to the playhouse and passed their summers in Provincetown, with Cook's two children by a previous marriage. During their second summer Glaspell learned that she had a heart condition and, later, that she was unable to bear children. Her restless husband found the success of the Provincetown Playhouse unsettling, and in 1922 they moved to Greece, where they lived happily until his untimely death in 1924.

Returning to Cape Cod, Glaspell resumed her writing. As a playwright she had served a public more demanding than her magazine readers. Under this new discipline her stories became more substantive, but only in "Jury of Her Peers" (1917) did she write one of lasting quality; significantly, this somber little gem was adapted from *Trifles* (1916), her finest one-act play. Her remaining plays were *The Comic Artist* (1928), written with Norman Matson, whom she married in 1925 and divorced six years later, and *Alison's House* (1930), a drama inspired by the life of Emily Dickinson that won the 1931 Pulitzer Prize.

After *Fidelity* (1915), Glaspell did not publish another novel until *Brook Evans* (1928), which was more artfully constructed than her previous ones but displayed no improvement in literary grace. The heightened skill derived from writing plays is more evident in *Ambrose Holt and Family* (1931), *The Morning Is Near Us* (1939), and *Judd Rankin's Daughter* (1945). All three, like so much of her writing, have a distinct regional feeling, and each centers on a Midwestern woman trying to reconcile the traditional and nurturing values of the American past with the demands of the present. Probably her finest work is neither a novel nor a play but *The Road to the Temple* (1927), an informal biography of George Cram Cook. In 1948 Glaspell died in Provincetown of a pulmonary embolism and was cremated in Boston.

[Arthur E. Waterman, *Susan Glaspell* (1966), and his sketch in *Notable Am. Women,* II, 49–51 ; Glaspell's *The Road to the Temple;* Helen Deutsch and Stella Hanau, *The Provincetown* (1931); the Cook-Glaspell papers in the Berg Collect., N.Y. Public Lib.; Louis Sheaffer, *O'Neill, Son and Playwright* (1968); information from Rev. Albert Glaspell, a cousin. Though Miss Glaspell always gave 1882 as her birth year, the Iowa state census of May 1895, which lists her as 18, and the enrollment records of Drake University establish that she was born in 1876.]
                                    LOUIS SHEAFFER

GLASS, CARTER (Jan. 4, 1858–May 28, 1946), newspaper publisher, United States senator, and secretary of the treasury, was born in Lynchburg, Va., the fourth son and youngest of five children of Robert Henry Glass and Augusta (Christian) Glass. Both parents were of Scots-Irish ancestry, their forebears having settled in Virginia before the American Revolution. His mother died when he was two, but his father promptly remarried; he and his second wife had seven children. Robert Glass was part-owner and publisher of the *Lynchburg Republican* and a prominent figure in local Democratic politics. Postwar stringency forced him to sell the *Republican,* but he became editor of another local paper, the *Intelligencer,* in 1869, and subsequently of papers in Petersburg and Danville, Va.

It was Carter Glass's ambition to follow in his father's footsteps. When he left school at the age of fourteen, he became a printer's devil on his father's paper. In 1880, after working briefly as an auditor's clerk for a railroad, he became a reporter for the *Lynchburg News*. Appointed editor in 1887, he purchased the paper the following year with the help of a loan from friends. By 1895 he had acquired two other Lynchburg papers, the *Virginian* (which he merged with the *News*) and the afternoon *Advance*.

At maturity Glass stood only five feet four inches tall and weighed barely a hundred pounds. Perhaps in compensation he had an intense, combative personality. An unruly shock of red hair seemed to accentuate his quick, often waspish, temper. He worked indefatigably and suffered from recurring bouts of hypertension and physical exhaustion. His nervous disposition was emphasized by his peculiar habit of speaking through the drooped left corner of his mouth. Glass's political and social values bore the stamp of the Reconstruction era in which he grew to maturity. Believing the South to have been treated with insufferable arrogance after the Civil War, he became an unflagging defender of the special heritage of the region and of its states' rights tradition. Strongly negrophobic, he waged incessant warfare in the columns of his newspapers against anyone who advocated the acceptance of Negro suffrage and popular democracy.

Glass was a lifelong member of the Democratic party, and as his newspapers prospered he took a more active role in politics. A staunch advocate of the free coinage of silver, he wrote caustic editorials attacking the monetary policies of President Grover Cleveland, and in 1896 joined the free-silver crusade of William Jennings Bryan, a step which he later regretted. Glass served one term (1899-1903) in the state senate; but it was as a delegate to the Virginia constitutional convention of 1901-1902 that he first gained political prominence. This body was convened to replace the state's Reconstruction constitution, particularly the provision for universal manhood suffrage. Like many Virginians, Glass believed that the political corruption then rampant in his and other Southern states was caused by a system that allowed the ignorant to vote and tolerated fraudulent election practices to counteract their votes. The only solution, he concluded, was the imposition of such electoral controls as the literacy test and the poll tax, and it was largely through his powers of persuasion that the convention adopted these measures. Although Glass, like other spokesmen for disfranchisement, publicly stressed the Negro as the source of corruption, he was equally intent on eliminating the votes of poor and illiterate whites.

The constitution of 1902, when implemented, reduced the Virginia electorate by more than half and opened the way for one-party domination of the state. Glass, as one of the chief architects of the new system, was elected to Congress in 1902, where he served for the next sixteen years. He was assigned to the House Committee on Banking and Currency. Though knowing little of economics, he read diligently and within a matter of years was recognized as one of the leading congressional authorities in this field.

When Woodrow Wilson became president in 1913, Glass as banking committee chairman was given responsibility for the administration's measure to reform the nation's banking and currency system. With the aid of H. Parker Willis, a former professor of economics at Washington and Lee University in Virginia, Glass prepared a draft measure providing for a system of reserve banks under the control of the banking industry. The draft raised an outcry among progressive Democrats, and Wilson, urged by Louis D. Brandeis and others, then insisted that the government must control both the currency and the banking system through an independent federal board. Though himself favoring a decentralized, private system of reserve banks, Glass loyally accepted these revisions and guided the president's bill through Congress in 1913. In later years he took pride in his title as "Father of the Federal Reserve System."

At the beginning of 1919 Wilson appointed Glass secretary of the treasury to succeed William G. McAdoo. Glass's most notable accomplishment was the successful floating of a $5 billion Victory Loan to help liquidate the expense of World War I. He left the Treasury in February 1920, having been appointed to fill a vacancy in the United States Senate created by the death of Thomas S. Martin. He was elected without opposition later that year, and remained in the Senate until his death. An ardent champion of the League of Nations, Glass drafted the 1920 Democratic platform, which gave strong endorsement to the league.

A new Democratic administration took office in 1933, but Glass, now seventy-five, felt out of tune with the time. Although personally fond of Franklin D. Roosevelt, he refused an appointment as Roosevelt's secretary of the treasury, fearing that the president would advocate inflationary fiscal policies. Glass cooperated with Roosevelt in passing the Emergency Banking Act (1933) and he cosponsored the Banking Act of 1933 (the Glass-Steagall Act), which established the Federal Deposit Insurance Corporation and separated the functions of commercial and investment banks. He broke with the administration over Roosevelt's decision to decrease the gold value of the dollar, and for the rest of his career was an implacable foe of the New Deal. He bemoaned the decline of individualism and states' rights and damned the growth of government spending and bureaucracy. He declared that he would never display the NRA blue eagle (or "buzzard" as he called it) at his newspaper offices, and he bitterly opposed the Banking Act of 1935, which sought to reorganize the Federal Reserve System and provide greater government control. He delighted in Roosevelt's description of him as an "unreconstructed old rebel." In his reelection race in 1936 Glass openly opposed the New Deal (one of the few Southern senators powerful enough to do so), and in the late 1930's he emerged as a leader of the bipartisan "conservative coalition" in Congress that sought to block further New Deal legislation.

In matters of foreign policy, Glass had been an ardent internationalist since the days of the Wilson administration. As early as January 1941 he advocated United States intervention in the European war. He was a sponsor of the Fight for Freedom Committee, an organization formed to counter the isolationist views of the America First Committee. He called for repeal of the Neutrality Act, and stated he would personally like the opportunity to "shoot hell" out of the Germans. After Pearl Harbor, Glass supported Roosevelt's war measures and as chairman of the Senate Appropriations Committee hastened the passage of many of the administration's bills. Thus in a time of war, Glass and Roosevelt were reconciled.

Although he devoted himself to publishing and politics with nearly single-minded dedication, Glass did find moments of relaxation on his "Montview Farms" near Lynchburg, where he raised pedigreed Jersey cattle. He was also an insatiable reader of literature, one who took the Baconian side in the controversy over the authorship of Shakespeare's plays. Glass was a lifelong member of the Court Street Methodist Church in Lynchburg. On Jan. 12, 1886, he married Aurelia McDearmon Caldwell of Lynchburg. They had four children: Paulus

Powell, Mary Archer, Carter, and Augusta Christian. His first wife died in 1937, and on June 22, 1940, he married the widowed Mary (Scott) Meade of Amherst, Va.

Glass was elected president pro tempore of the Senate in 1941. Owing to old age and illness, he did not make an appearance in the Senate chamber after June 1942, although he retained his seat until his death nearly four years later. He died of heart failure in Washington, D.C., and was buried in Spring Hill Cemetery in Lynchburg.

[Glass's papers are at the Alderman Lib., Univ. of Va. His book, *An Adventure in Constructive Finance* (1927), recounts his role in the drafting and passage of the Federal Reserve Act. There is no scholarly biography of Glass. Two contemporary popular biographies are James E. Palmer, Jr., *Carter Glass: Unreconstructed Rebel* (1938), and Rixey Smith and Norman Beasley, *Carter Glass* (1939). See also Marquis James, "The Gentleman from Va.," *Saturday Evening Post*, Aug. 28, 1937; and Harry E. Poindexter, "From Copy Desk to Congress: The Pre-Congressional Career of Carter Glass" (Ph.D. diss., Univ. of Va., 1966). There is useful material on Glass in Allen W. Moger, *Virginia: Bourbonism to Byrd, 1870–1925* (1968); Raymond H. Pulley, *Old Virginia Restored: An Interpretation of the Progressive Impulse, 1870–1930* (1968); Arthur S. Link, *Wilson: The New Freedom* (1956); and James T. Patterson, *Congressional Conservatism and the New Deal* (1967).]
RAYMOND H. PULLEY

GLENN, JOHN MARK (Oct. 28, 1858–Apr. 20, 1950), social work leader and foundation director, was born in Baltimore, Md., the eldest of two boys and a girl (who died in childhood) of William Wilkins Glenn and Ellen Mark (Smith) Glenn. His father's family, of Scottish origin, had settled in New York state in colonial times, but this particular branch had migrated to Maryland early in the eighteenth century. John Glenn's grandfather (also John Glenn) was one of four Bank of Maryland partners who were targets of the mob in the Baltimore riot of 1835. Three generations of his family had produced lawyers, but Glenn's father added to his law practice his work as an iron commission merchant and his interests in a newspaper, a tobacco brokerage, extensive real estate holdings, a mine in Colorado, race horses, and a race course. The family owned slaves and were ardent supporters of the Confederacy. His mother died when he was six years old, and Glenn was reared by his grandmother and an unmarried aunt. His father was out of the home for long periods of time, mostly in Colorado; he died in Baltimore when Glenn was seventeen.

Glenn attended a small Episcopal school near his home in the outskirts of Baltimore and in 1874 entered Washington and Lee

University, from which he received the B.A. degree in 1878 and the M.A. the following year. After an additional year of graduate work at the Johns Hopkins University, he transferred to the University of Maryland, where he took a law degree in 1882; he was admitted to the bar in the same year. For the next several years he devoted most of his time to managing the family businesses in Baltimore and Colorado, relieving his blind and aging uncle, John Glenn, of responsibilities he had assumed on the death of Glenn's father. The Colorado mine was always highly speculative and eventually failed, but the Baltimore real estate paid off handsomely as the city expanded rapidly after the Civil War.

By the 1890's Glenn was free to follow his uncle in volunteering an increasing amount of time to charitable work. Locally, the focal point of this work was the Charity Organization Society (COS), which had been founded in 1881 under the leadership of Daniel Coit Gilman, president of Johns Hopkins University. As part of the COS movement, the Baltimore agency sought to mobilize all the charitable resources of the city to replace indiscriminate almsgiving by careful investigation and individualized treatment of the needy. The COS also expressed interest in studying the causes of poverty and pauperism and later advocated some economic and social reforms, particularly in housing and public health.

Glenn's knowledge of law and his business experience soon brought him administrative positions in charitable work. He became chairman of the finance committee of the Baltimore COS. But unlike many in the movement, he retained an open mind about public charity. (One of the most important tenets of the COS movement was its opposition to public charity.) In 1898, when Baltimore adopted a new system for administering its public charities, he was appointed one of nine supervisors of City Charities; in 1904 he became president and served until 1907. Meanwhile, he had been elected president (1901-1902) of the influential National Conference of Charities and Correction, an organization composed of representatives of both public and private charities and correctional institutions. He was also at various times director of the Maryland School for the Blind, a member of the council of the state Tuberculosis Commission, a trustee of the Johns Hopkins Hospital, and a lecturer on philanthropy at Johns Hopkins. A devoted Episcopalian, he was also a director of St. Paul's Guild House, a Baltimore residence and educational-recreational center for young men.

On May 21, 1902, he married Mary Willcox Brown, Baltimore social worker who had headed the Henry Watson Children's Aid Society and was then the general secretary of the COS. The couple had no children and Mary Glenn, who continued active in social work, became president of the National Conference of Charities and Correction in 1915.

During the late nineteenth and early twentieth centuries, a time of great expansion and interest in social work, increasing attention was given to professionalization, to social research, and, to some degree, to social reform. In 1907, Margaret Olivia Sage, widow of railroad financier Russell Sage, established the Russell Sage Foundation with an endowment of $10 million for "the improvement of social and living conditions in the United States." Glenn was among the leaders of the charity movement consulted by her while the foundation was being planned and, in May 1907, he was named its director. The foundation's board of trustees had great freedom of choice in dispensing the annual income of approximately $450,000, but agreed with Glenn's view that "the first object of the fund should be investigation; the next education, chiefly by publication." Grants were made with the idea of giving a start to a good cause or helping at a strategic moment. One early grant was in aid of the Pittsburgh Survey, a pioneer field investigation of economic and social conditions of the working class. Early schools of social work—the New York School of Philanthropy, Chicago School of Civics and Philanthropy, and the Boston School of Social Works—received five-year grants from the new foundation, and their representatives were brought together for joint planning and consultation. Only in a few instances, notably in the development of the Forest Hills Gardens housing project in New York City did the foundation engage in independent projects.

Glenn quickly concluded that the foundation should acquire a permanent staff of highly qualified individuals organized to permit the foundation itself to carry on social investigative activities. "To educate and lead the public," he said, "so that it will assume its share of responsibility and have a clear vision of its opportunities and the best methods of seizing them, will in the long run accomplish more than too much direct giving." Although the foundation continued to make some grants, within two years, Glenn set the course toward the organization of departments and divisions with responsibility for various fields; child helping, charity organization, industrial studies, recreation, and surveys and exhibits were the most important. Following a survey of the unscrupulous practices of loan-sharks who preyed upon the working classes, a division of remedial loans was set up in 1910 to assist in establishing associations offering loans at reasonable interest rates. Technical aid for all divisions was furnished through the departments of statistics and publications. The staff was small—two to three professionals to a department—but it fully met Glenn's high standards of scholarship and leadership. During the twenty-four years of Glenn's tenure, the foundation published eighty-four books (many written by members of the staff) as well as hundreds of pamphlets. Among the projects pursued during his term of office, the child welfare and child-placing services were expanded and a study of women's work in industries was established.

After his retirement as director in 1931, Glenn remained a member of the board of trustees of Russell Sage for another sixteen years. Throughout his career, he also saw long service on the boards of such agencies as the National Society for the Prevention of Blindness, the Federal Council of Churches of Christ in America, and the National Urban League. A modest man who hated showiness, Glenn nevertheless had a deep appreciation of the social uses of money. After retirement he returned his pension to the Russell Sage Foundation to help support its programs. He died at the age of ninety-one at New York Hospital and was buried in the cemetery at St. Timothy's Church, Catonsville, Md.

[*Charities Record,* I–VII, 1893–1895 and 1905–1907; "The Executive of the New Foundation," *Charities and The Commons,* May 18, 1907; John M. Glenn, "The Church and Social Work," National Conference of Charities and Correction, *Proc.,* 1913; "The Need of Organization in Charity Work," *Proc.,* 1899; John M. Glenn, Lilian Brandt, and F. Emerson Andrews, *Russell Sage Foundation; 1907–1946* (2 vols., 1947); John M. Glenn, "Social Service in the Episcopal Church," *Survey,* Nov. 5, 1910; David Grimsted, "Rioting in Its Jacksonian Setting," *Am. Hist. Rev.,* Apr. 1972; "Mrs. John M. Glenn," *Survey,* Nov. 1940; Shelby M. Harrison, "John Mark Glenn," *Survey,* June 1950; Shelby M. Harrison, "John Mark Glenn and Some First Steps toward Better Living Conditions," unpub. MS.; obituaries in *Am. Sociological Rev.,* Oct. 1950; *Social Service Rev.,* June 1950; and *N.Y. Times,* Apr. 21, 1950.]

BLANCHE D. COLL

GLENNON, JOHN JOSEPH (June 14, 1862–Mar. 9, 1946), cardinal-archbishop of St. Louis, was born near Kinnegad, County Meath, Ireland, the first of eight children of Matthew Glennon and Catherine (Rafferty) Glennon. His father immigrated to the United States in 1851, working for a time for the Pennsylvania Railroad before returning to Ireland in 1859 and marrying the following year. Young John spent his boyhood on the family's sixty-acre farm, attended the local primary school in Kinnegad, the diocesan college of St. Mary's in Mullingar, and completed his philosophical and theological studies for the priesthood at All Hallows College in Dublin. At the invitation of Bishop John Hogan of Kansas City, he came to the United States in the fall of 1883 and was ordained for the diocese of Kansas City by special dispensation at the early age of twenty-two on Dec. 20, 1884.

Father Glennon served first as an assistant in St. Patrick's Church in Kansas City for three years and then returned to Europe for several months to visit his family in Ireland, to enroll in classes at the University of Bonn, and to study the German language so common among the Roman Catholics of Missouri. On his return, he was appointed secretary to the bishop and rector of the cathedral, and, in 1892, vicar-general of the diocese. Because of failing health, Bishop Hogan petitioned Rome for assistance and on June 29, 1896, Father Glennon was consecrated coadjutor bishop of Kansas City. Seven years later, on Apr. 27, 1903, he was appointed coadjutor to Archbishop John Kain of St. Louis, a larger jurisdiction of approximately 32,000 square miles and 225,000 Roman Catholics. When Archbishop Kain died on October 13 of that same year, Glennon succeeded as archbishop, a position he held until his death.

Glennon soon proved himself an able builder and administrator. On May 1, 1907, he broke ground for a new cathedral, the largest Roman Catholic church in North America at the time. He dedicated the new Kenrick Seminary in 1916 and the St. Louis Preparatory Seminary in 1931. Conservative in finance, he was a builder but not a borrower. "It is a bad thing," he once remarked, "to have a mortgage between you and the Almighty." In establishing new parishes, he anticipated population trends and the direction of suburban growth. In his long tenure, he erected ninety-five parishes, five hospitals, and almost a hundred schools.

A traditionalist in education, he favored neither coeducation nor the attendance of Roman Catholic children in public schools. He centralized the administration of the parochial school system by establishing the office of Archdiocesan Superintendent of Schools in

1910. He was a supporter of The Catholic University of America, serving on its board of trustees for forty years, taking special interest in its library holdings, and initiating fund drives. Within his own archdiocese, he took a keen interest in St. Louis University, helped to organize the Catholic Historical Society of St. Louis, and was instrumental in the establishment of three colleges for women, Fontbonne, Webster, and Maryville College of the Sacred Heart.

On public issues, Glennon was an opponent of both prohibition and the Child Labor Amendment. He had hoped that America could avoid World War I, but, when war was declared, he was one of the first to sign Cardinal Gibbons' resolution of support for President Wilson. Avoiding fanaticism, however, he refused to prohibit the use of German in his national parishes: "As I understand it, we are making war, not on languages, but on false principles." An outspoken champion of Irish independence, he opposed Article X of the Treaty of Versailles because he feared it might perpetuate the existent division of Ireland.

The problems of the poor and the immigrant were of special concern to him. He was a sponsor of the American Colonization Society and other efforts to settle Roman Catholic immigrant groups on farm lands in the Southwest, and he gave his warm support to Father Peter Dunne's Newsboys' Home and Protectorate, to Father Timothy Dempsey's Hotel for Homeless Men, and to other charities. He erected parishes and catechism centers for the black Roman Catholics of his archdiocese, but his successes in this area, like those of many of his fellow bishops in the early twentieth century, were limited.

It was said of Archbishop Glennon that "those who did not know him were never in danger of mistaking his rank and those who knew him well were never reminded of it." He was tall, erect, and dignified, yet never forgot his humble origins nor lost his ready sense of humor. He enjoyed sports, a good cigar, and informal visits with friends and neighbors. An outstanding orator, he was invited to preach on some of the most memorable occasions of the American Roman Catholic church, including the centenary of the Baltimore cathedral in 1906, the consecration of St. Patrick's Cathedral in New York in 1910, and the funeral service for Cardinal Gibbons in 1922.

In 1945, at the age of eighty-three, Glennon was named a cardinal by Pope Pius XII and invested with the robes of his new office on Feb. 21, 1946, in Rome. While visiting Ireland before returning to St. Louis, he contracted pneumonia, followed by uremic poisoning, and died at the home of President Sean O'Kelly in Dublin. His body was returned to St. Louis on March 13, and he was buried in the crypt under the Chapel of All Souls in the cathedral he had built and of which he was so justly proud.

[Cardinal Glennon's papers are preserved in the archives of the Archdiocese of St. Louis. The most complete biography is Nicholas Schneider, *The Life of John Cardinal Glennon, Archbishop of St. Louis* (1971). Shorter accounts can be found in Thomas B. Morgan, *Speaking of Cardinals* (1946); Brendan A. Finn, *Twenty-Four American Cardinals* (1947); Francis B. Thornton, *Our American Princes* (1963); Rev. John Rothensteiner, *History of the Archdiocese of St. Louis,* II (1928); and William Faherty, *Dream by the River* (1973). Helpful also are F. P. Kenkel, "Cardinal Glennon: A Rural-Minded Prelate," *Land and Home* (1946), and Cyril Clemens, "Cardinal Glennon of St. Louis," *Ave Maria* (1947). Glennon's addresses, speeches, and pastoral letters can be found in *The St. Louis Register, The Catholic Herald* (of St. Louis), and *The Oriflamme,* the monthly bulletin of the St. Louis Cathedral.]

THOMAS E. BLANTZ

GOMBERG, MOSES (Feb. 8, 1866-Feb. 12, 1947), organic chemist who discovered stable free radicals, was born in Elisavetgrad (now Kirovograd), Russia, where his parents, George Gomberg and Marie Ethel (Resnikoff) Gomberg, possessed a small estate. Very little is known of the family except that there was a younger sister, Sonja. In 1884 Moses' father, an anti-Czarist, was accused of being involved in a political conspiracy and his property was confiscated. He fled to America, where he settled in Chicago. Members of his family either accompanied him or followed soon thereafter. Moses had been a student in the Nicolau Gymnasium in Elisavetgrad from 1878 until this time. He and his father, neither with a prior knowledge of English, supported themselves by menial work, partly in the Chicago stockyards. Years later, after Upton Sinclair published *The Jungle,* Gomberg would tell friends that the allegations in the novel regarding sanitation and working conditions were not exaggerated.

Gomberg managed to complete high school in Chicago, and in 1886 entered the University of Michigan, where he earned his expenses by janitorial work. After receiving the B.S. in 1890 he received an assistantship which enabled him to pursue graduate studies in organic chemistry. His major professor, Albert B. Prescott, who was frequently called upon by industrial firms as a consultant, assigned tasks of analyzing materials to Gomberg, which enabled him to reinforce his meager finances. This experience gave him a profound respect for careful analysis, since he sometimes had to serve as an expert witness in court cases.

Gomberg earned his M.S. degree in 1892, the Ph.D. in 1894, his doctoral dissertation dealing with the chemistry of caffeine. In 1893 he was appointed instructor in chemistry at Michigan. Except for several brief leaves of absence, he was associated with the university until his retirement in 1936. He was made assistant professor of organic chemistry in 1899 and full professor in 1904. From 1927 until retirement he served as chairman of the department, following two years as acting chairman.

Accumulated savings enabled Gomberg to take a leave of absence in 1896-1897 for study in Germany. He looked forward to this opportunity, since his studies under Prescott had emphasized the analytical rather than the synthetic side of organic chemistry. He spent two terms in Munich where he worked in the laboratory of Adolf von Baeyer on isonitramino- and nitrosoisobutyric acids. A third term was spent with Victor Meyer in Heidelberg, where he undertook the preparation of tetraphenylmethane $(C_6H_5)_4C$. Although Meyer sought to dissuade him from this goal because well-established chemists had failed, Gomberg was successful in obtaining the compound.

On returning to Michigan in the fall of 1897 he undertook the preparation of hexaphenylethane $(C_6H_5)_6C_2$, the next fully phenylated member of the hydrocarbon series. He undertook to bring about the reaction of triphenylmethyl halides with sodium but was unsuccessful. Substitution of silver for sodium yielded a colorless compound which was assumed to be hexaphenylethane. Analysis for carbon and hydrogen gave low results, and it was later found that oxidation had occurred during the reaction. By utilizing apparatus of his own design, which enabled him to exclude air and to carry out the reaction in the presence of carbon dioxide, he was successful in obtaining what appeared to be the desired product.

This hydrocarbon, instead of being the inert product which had been expected, proved to be highly reactive. In solution it was yellow and, surprisingly, it readily absorbed chlorine, bromine, and even iodine. On exposure to air it formed a stable peroxide. In his first paper on the subject in 1900 he reported, "The experimental evidence . . . forces me to the conclusion that we have to deal here with a free radical, triphenylmethyl, $(C_6H_5)_3C$. On this assumption alone do the results described above become intelligible and receive an adequate explanation."

The announcement of the discovery of a stable free radical was received with skepticism by organic chemists and much of Gomberg's research effort during the rest of his life was aimed toward demonstrating the soundness of his interpretation and in gaining new knowledge of organic free radicals. Free radicals had been postulated by various investigators up to 1850, but the development of valence theory and its application to structural theory of organic compounds after 1860 rendered free radical concepts unacceptable. Furthermore, a free radical such as triphenylmethyl suggested trivalence for carbon, an element which was considered to combine only in the tetravalent state. It was now necessary to establish that free radicals were possible, at least for compounds such as triphenylmethyl where the dimer, hexaphenylethane, might be rendered unstable because of bulkiness associated with six phenyl groups attached to a pair of carbon atoms.

Gomberg based his conclusion that the compound was a free radical on the fact that the reactivity was unusually great toward oxygen and halogens whereas hexaphenylethane should be unreactive. Others were not in agreement. Vladimir Markovnikov in Moscow argued in 1902 that Gomberg had prepared hexaphenylethane and that the compound was simply more reactive than had been expected. Paul Jacobson in Berlin postulated a quinoid structure which would explain color without recourse to a free radical hypothesis. Molecular weight determinations by Lee H. Cone in Gomberg's laboratory produced values close to double the values calculated for the triphenylmethyl radical. On the basis of these facts, Gomberg postulated the existence of an equilibrium mixture of dimer (hexaphenylethane) and monomer (triphenylmethyl), the color and reactivity being attributable to the latter, even though present in the solution in small concentration. Although the equilibrium hypothesis was in reasonable agreement with the experimental facts, there were a number of leading chemists who were unconvinced, and the subject of stable free radicals remained controversial for many years. Gomberg's equilibrium hypothesis received new support around 1910, when Wilhelm Schlenk in Munich prepared a series of ethanes combined with biphenyl and other groups more complicated than phenyl. These compounds were clearly split into free radicals to a major degree.

During this period, Gomberg became uncertain regarding the identity of the so-called hexaphenylethane dimer and favored the Jacobson quinoid formula. However, he ultimately abandoned this formula in favor of the simple hexaphenylethane structure, despite existing chemical evidence favoring the Jacobson structure. Gomberg's choice found general support among organic chemists until 1968 when T. Nauta and his associates in Holland demonstrated the validity of the Jacobson structure on the basis of nuclear magnetic resonance and ultraviolet spectral data. Such analytical techniques had not been available during Gomberg's lifetime. Despite Gomberg's failure to understand clearly the nature of the dimer, he was correct in recognizing the presence of free radicals in solution. He thereby opened up a fruitful field of chemistry, which would have extensive development later in the twentieth century. Not only did work continue on the multiaryl type of free radicals, which Gomberg and Schlenk had prepared, but evidence began to accumulate for transitory free radicals of very simple constitution. Fritz Paneth obtained evidence for free methyl radicals in 1929 in Berlin, and this work was extended by Francis O. Rice at Johns Hopkins University. Rice and Karl Hertzfeld developed the theoretical aspects of free radical mechanisms and Morris Kharasch at the University of Chicago was a leader in utilizing free radical mechanisms for the understanding of various organic reactions, particularly photochemical reactions. Such concepts, while resisted in many quarters at first, became widely utilized in both organic and inorganic chemistry after Gomberg's death.

In addition to his work on organic free radicals, Gomberg carried out studies on the reducing action on organic compounds of magnesium-iodide mixture, the synthesis of certain dyes, the properties of the perchlorate radical, and the synthesis of biaryls (Gomberg reaction).

During World War I he participated in gas warfare research directed by the U.S. Bureau of Mines. His work on the synthesis of ethylene chlorohydrin led to a commercial method for the preparation of this compound, an intermediate in the manufacture of mustard gas. Although he was opposed in principle to gas warfare, he entered into the research because he deplored the prospect of a German victory. Later during the war he became a major in the Ordnance Department, where he served as an advisor on the manufacture of high explosives and smokeless powder.

Gomberg's life was centered on chemistry. As a student he read the principal journal of chemistry, the *Berichte der deutschen chemischen gesellschaft,* starting with volume one (published in 1868) and working through the set.

His phenomenal memory enabled him to retain much of what he read. He recommended such studies to his graduate students. Contrary to the practice of many leading organic chemists he discouraged night work in the laboratory, insisting that the evenings were more appropriately used for reading. He arrived at his office early in the morning and expected his students to be at work when he arrived. They might expect visits from him several times a day for discussion of their work.

Gomberg was a highly reserved person, with great sensitivity and much personal charm. Despite a slight accent, he spoke English with clarity; his lectures were characterized by remarkable organization and vivid presentation. A man of average height and build, he was remembered for his soft-spoken firmness, his courtly manners, and his concentration on the business at hand. One of his last graduate students, John Bailar, characterized him as ". . . extremely interesting as an individual—brilliant, yet modest; shy, yet friendly; famous, yet humble." He never married and forbade his graduate students to do so before finishing their degrees. His unmarried sister, Sonja, served as his housekeeper.

He was elected to the National Academy of Sciences in 1914 and served as president of the American Chemical Society in 1931. Other honors included the Nichols Medal (1914), the Willard Gibbs Medal (1925), the Chandler Medal (1927), honorary Sc.D. degrees from the University of Chicago (1929) and Brooklyn Polytechnic Institute (1932), and the LL.D. from the University of Michigan (1937).

Following his retirement in 1936 he failed to pursue plans for research and travel because of a decline in his health and that of his sister. He died of a heart ailment in Ann Arbor.

[The obituary of C. S. Schoepfle and W. E. Bachmann, *Jour. Am. Chemical Soc.* 69 (1947): 2921–2925, carries a full bibliography of Gomberg's publications; as does John Bailar, Nat. Acad. Sciences, *Biog. Memoirs,* XLI (1970), pp. 141–173. Most of his papers were published in *Jour. of the Am. Chemical Soc.* Gomberg published review articles on free radical chemistry in *Chemical Reviews* 1 (1924): 91–141 and 2 (1925): 301–314; *Jour. of Industrial and Engineering Chemistry* 20 (1928): 159–164; *Jour. of Chemical Education* 9 (1932): 439–451; *Science* 74 (1931): 553–557. His role as a pioneer in free radical chemistry is evaluated by A. J. Ihde in *Pure and Applied Chemistry* 15 (1967): 1–13; reprinted in International Union of Pure and Applied Chemistry, *Free Radicals in Solution,* pp. 1–13 (1967). Short sketches are A. H. White, *Industrial and Engineering Chemistry* 23 (1931): 116–117; A. J. Ihde, *Dict. Sci. Biog.,* V, 464–466.]

AARON J. IHDE

GORE, THOMAS PRYOR (Dec. 10, 1870–Mar. 16, 1949), United States senator from

Oklahoma, known as the "Blind Orator," was born in Old Choctaw (later Webster) County, near Embry, Miss., the first son and second of four children of Thomas Madison Gore and Caroline Elizabeth (Wingo) Gore. One of his father's English ancestors had come from Ireland before the American Revolution and had settled in Maryland; other members of the family moved to South Carolina and later to Alabama before arriving in Mississippi prior to the Civil War. Gore's father was a farmer and lawyer in the poor north-central section of Mississippi.

In an accident at the age of eight, Gore lost the sight of one eye and severely injured the other. Three years later blindness was already overtaking the damaged eye, and, at the age of twenty, Gore was totally blind. Resisting his father's suggestion that he attend a school for the blind, he continued in the public schools of Walthall, Miss., while classmates and members of the family read his lessons to him. After graduating in 1888 from high school, he studied two additional years, took a "scientific course," obtained a license to teach, and in 1890-1891 assisted his sister as a public school teacher. He then entered the law school of Cumberland University in Lebanon, Tenn., where a close friend took the course with him and acted as his amanuensis; he received his law degree in 1892.

Following the lead of his father and other relatives, Gore became an active Populist, one of that protest party's ablest and best-known stump speakers. When the Mississippi Populists were soundly defeated in 1895, the "Blind Orator" moved to Corsicana, Tex., where he struggled to make a living as a lawyer. Opportunistic enough to appreciate the declining fortunes of populism, he joined the Democratic party in 1899. With the change of allegiance a change of scene seemed to offer a better hope, and with the encouragement of his wife, Nina Kay, daughter of a Texas cotton planter, whom he married on Dec. 27, 1900, he determined to join those pioneers who were moving northward to the new territory of Oklahoma.

In 1902, a year after he settled in Oklahoma Territory, Gore was elected to the territorial council. Rising rapidly through his driving ambition, his superb oratorical ability, and the support of the powerful *Daily Oklahoman* in Oklahoma City, he became the territory's leading politician; in 1907, when the Oklahoma and Indian territories joined to form the new state of Oklahoma, Gore was one of its first two senators. He was also the first totally

blind man to sit in the United States Senate.

Gore aligned himself with the Senate's progressive members in the pre-World War I period, attacking the trusts, the tariff, and monopolies, especially the railroads. One of the important early supporters of the presidential candidacy of Woodrow Wilson, he helped elect Wilson in 1912 and endorsed his domestic legislative program. With the coming of World War I, however, Gore revealed a growing pacifism, economic conservatism, and isolationism. During the controversy over American neutral rights in 1916 he sponsored a Senate resolution warning American citizens that they traveled on armed belligerent ships at their own risk. This precipitated a serious legislative revolt against Wilson's foreign policy, which was quelled only with difficulty. Gore opposed American entry into the war in 1917, although illness prevented him from voting against the war resolution in Congress. During the war he was against military conscription and pensions, the food administration, emergency governmental control of transportation and communication facilities, and deficit financing. His stand against Wilson's wartime policies, coupled with his opposition to the League of Nations, resulted in his defeat by a Wilson supporter in the Democratic primary of 1920.

Gore was returned to the Senate for a final term in 1930, during which he opposed the policies of both a Republican and a Democratic president. After assisting with the election of Franklin D. Roosevelt in 1932, Gore found himself out of step with the New Deal. He was a strong advocate of a balanced budget in a period when the administration was moving toward deficit spending, and he was a vigorous opponent of Roosevelt's social measures, which he felt stifled private initiative and enterprise. For the second time in his public career his opposition to the program of a popular president was responsible for his defeat in his 1936 reelection bid. As he had done in the 1920's, Gore practiced law in Washington, D.C., during the final thirteen years of his life, specializing in tax matters and Indian affairs. Stricken with a cerebral hemorrhage in late February 1949, he died in his Washington apartment three weeks later. He was buried in Oklahoma City's Rose Hill Cemetery. In religion he was a Methodist but was not a regular churchgoer.

Although best known for the Gore Resolution of 1916, Gore made his most tangible legislative contributions in the areas of agriculture, Indian affairs, and oil. As chairman of the Senate Agriculture and Forestry Committee during the Wilson administration, he played an important role in passing agricultural appropriations and other proposals (including the Federal Farm Loan Act of 1916) to aid the farmers and rural areas of the country. Throughout his career, he was a persistent advocate of soil conservation. He gave considerable attention to his large Indian constituency, especially during his early years in the Senate. Interested in the welfare of the oil industry so prominent in Oklahoma, Gore was the author of an amendment to the Revenue Act of 1918, which provided oil companies with exemptions from income tax on a stipulated portion of the proceeds from oil that represented capital. Known as the discovery-depletion allowance, this concept was later revised, but the basic principle has been retained and has been applied to scores of other mineral industries. More broadly, perhaps Gore's greatest single contribution was the inspiration his successful career gave to persons with a similar handicap.

[The Gore Papers in the Univ. of Okla. Lib. are the basic source. Monroe Billington, *Thomas P. Gore* (1967), is a biographical study with a full bibliography.]

                    MONROE BILLINGTON

GORKY, ARSHILE (b. 1904 or 1905-July 1, 1948), painter, was born Vosdanig Adoian in Khorkom Vari Haiyotz Dzor, a village on Lake Van in Turkish Armenia, the third of four children and the only son of Sedrag Adoian and Sushanig Adoian. His father, a wheat trader and carpenter, fled Turkish military service in 1908, abandoned his family, and, eventually, immigrated to the United States. His mother was descended from a long line of distinguished priests in the Gregorian Apostolic church. When Gorky was four the family moved to Aykestan, a suburb of the city of Van. Gorky did not speak before the age of five, when a tutor successfully alarmed him into protest by convincingly threatening to jump off a cliff. During the World War I massacres of Armenians by Turks, Gorky's mother moved the family to Russian Transcaucasia where they settled in Erivan in 1914. Gorky attended secondary school while working at such trades as typesetting, bookbinding, carpentering and comb-making. For a short time, living in Tiflis, he studied engineering and received his first formal art educaton. His mother died in 1918, and in 1920 he and his younger sister immigrated to the United States. First settling in Massachusetts, he lived with his older sister and worked at Hood Rubber Company. His father

was living in Providence, R.I., and Gorky attended various schools in Boston and in Providence: the Providence Technical High School, where he prepared for Brown University's school of engineering, the Rhode Island School of Design, and the New School of Design in Boston, where he became an instructor in 1924. He conducted his own apprenticeship, however, learning more from galleries and books than from classes.

In 1925 he changed his name to Gorky ("the bitter one" in Russian) and moved to Greenwich Village, New York City. He both studied and taught at the Grand Central School of Art until 1931. Productive friendships with other painters formed during this period—Stuart Davis, John Graham, and, later, Willem de Kooning. In his painting he had almost passed through what Julian Levy aptly characterized as his "arduous years of self-imposed apprenticeship," years in which he successfully identified himself so intently with the work of the impressionists, the postimpressionists, the cubists, and the nonfigurative painters of the 1930's that he seemed almost to paint in their style rather than to create his own. Yet William Seitz, in the perspective of time, has estimated that "derivative though these works are, they stand on their own." Gorky's portraiture, which covered the period from 1926 to 1936, has also gained in stature and may well be his most original contribution. *The Artist and His Mother* in the Whitney Museum of Art, for which Gorky worked on studies throughout the entire ten years, has become one of the enduring images of twentieth-century American art.

Gorky's fourth decade, which brought a coalescence of styles, was marked by increasing recognition, exhibitions, and commissions. His first one-man show took place at the Mellon Galleries in Philadelphia, in 1934; his first one-man show in New York, at the Boyer Galleries in 1938. In 1941 the San Francisco Museum of Art presented a retrospective exhibition of twenty of his paintings. Meanwhile he had executed mural commissions for the WPA Federal Art Project, beginning in 1935; for the Aviation Building at the New York World's Fair in 1939; and for Ben Marden's Riviera nightclub in Fort Lee, N.J. in 1941. In 1937 the Whitney Museum of Modern Art purchased his still life in abstract forms, *Painting, 1936-1937*. In 1941 the Museum of Modern Art acquired *Garden in Sochi* (1941), a biomorphic abstraction in which, according to Seitz, Gorky finally assimilated the influences of Picasso and Miro and transformed them into something of his own. Gorky's first marriage, to Marny George in 1935, ended in divorce the same year; on Sept. 15, 1941, he married Agnes Magruder in Virginia City, Nev. They had two children, Maro and Natasha.

In the 1940's Gorky's work took on a new and more open form. From 1942 on, he achieved his finest drawings and major canvases, painted in transparent washes and in lines as fine as his pencil drawings. Their content showed the almost microscopic study of nature, which followed upon his visits to the Virginia farm of his wife's parents, and a new surrealist imagery, resulting from his meeting with André Breton and other surrealist artists in 1944. Kandinsky's work was particularly appealing to him at this time and led Gorky to the improvisational aspects of his last work, which was impressive for its freedom and complexity. The various versions and preparatory sketches for the following works, mostly in private collections, illustrated this culminating phrase: *Summation* (1946), *The Plough and the Song* (1946-1947), and *Dark Green Painting* (1946-1948).

After 1945, Gorky's work was shown annually at the Julian Levy Gallery in New York. Levy saw Gorky as "a very camouflaged man" for whom "art was religion." As long as they had known each other, Gorky "wore a patched coat . . . in winter a ragged overcoat much too long." Gorky was tall and lean, his face dark, even fierce, with a "ferocious black moustache," which concealed a softer, not easily approachable quality. (Levy in Seitz, p. 7) Gorky's last years were troubled by the loss by fire of twenty-seven paintings and about 300 drawings in his Connecticut studio in January 1946, by an operation in February 1946 to remove cancer, by an automobile accident in June 1948 in which his neck was broken and his painting arm was injured, and by feelings that he had been thrice rejected—"in his love, in his health, and in his art" (Levy, in Seitz, p. 9). He committed suicide by hanging himself in Sherman, Conn., in 1948. Gorky's legacy of painting explored "psychological space" and laid much of the groundwork for abstract expressionism, which in the decade following his death became America's significant contribution to world art. In 1962 Gorky was accorded a retrospective exhibition at the Venice Bienniale; his work has received growing interest from painters and critics.

[Ethel K. Schwabacher, *Arshile Gorky* (1957), bibliography; William Chapin Seitz, *Arshile Gorky: Paintings, Drawings, Studies* (1962), chronology, selected references, catalogue, and portrait; Julian Levy, *Arshile Gorky* (1966), a perceptive appreciation.]
ROBERT BARTLETT HAAS

GOSS, ALBERT SIMON (Oct. 14, 1882-Oct. 25, 1950), agricultural leader, was born in Rochester, N.Y., the youngest of the four children (two boys and two girls) of John Weaver Goss and Flora M. (Alling) Goss. His father, who had a substantial hardware business, moved his family in 1889 to Spokane, Wash., and in 1897 to Portland, Oreg., where he operated a flour-milling business. Albert graduated from high school in Portland and attended Holmes Business College. After his father's death, he and his brother took over their father's business in Portland and in Lamar and Tacoma, Wash., and managed it until about 1914. Albert also ran a small country store and a telephone company. His marriage to Minnie E. Hand, on Dec. 21, 1907, resulted in the birth of three children: Ruth Dorothy, Warren Hand, and Betty Jane.

Goss had a better appreciation of the business phases of farming than most farmers even before he himself took up farming. Beginning in 1914 he operated a dairy farm in Kennewick, Benton County, Wash., and became active in the Grange. He served as master of a local Grange (1916-1918) and as a member of several committees of the Washington State Grange. After the passage of the Federal Farm Loan Act in 1916, Goss called together farmers in his neighborhood, to organize a cooperative farm loan association (of which he was to become the first president), which would enable them to apply to the Federal Loan Bank at Spokane for loans.

From 1920 to 1922 Goss was manager of the Grange Cooperative Wholesale Society in Seattle; he worked for the amalgamation of the scattered Grange warehouses into a cooperative buying unit, established a central system of bookkeeping and auditing, and stressed the potentialities of producer and consumer cooperatives. He was very alert to the cooperative business needs of the farmers.

Goss's climb up the Grange ladder was assured. In 1922 he became master of the Washington State Grange, a position he held for the next eleven years. As master he worked to heal the breach that had been caused by the aggressive reformism of his predecessor; to encourage cooperatives; and to emphasize the need for improved rural schools, roads, tax reform, and power development. He was critical of the eastern outlook of the National Grange and its failure to consider the problems of the western states and to furnish help to the locals. His elevation to the executive committee of the National Grange probably was inspired by his trenchant criticisms. Later as chairman of the same committee, he pressed for changes in Federal Land Bank policy to broaden the services of the federal land banks. Goss was one of a group of consultants who worked on the draft of the Emergency Farm Mortgage Act of 1933. As director of the Federal Land Bank in Spokane from 1927 to 1933, he drafted a program of cooperative farm credit that subsequently became a model for the Farm Credit Administration (FCA). As land bank commissioner of the FCA from 1933 to 1940, Goss probably derived much satisfaction from seeing a cooperative credit system that he helped develop at the local level being placed at the national.

Goss resigned as land bank commissioner when President Roosevelt ordered the consolidation of the FCA with the Department of Agriculture and ordered changes in its functions. He argued that the FCA had been useful in sustained emergencies caused by the failure of the federal government to develop a workable farm policy.

In 1941 Goss was elected master of the National Grange, which gave him an opportunity to seek reforms he had been advocating, such as helping make the locals more effective and extending the influence of the National Grange within the federal government. A critic of Roosevelt's wartime price-control program and later of subsidies for the farmers, Goss believed that a broader farm program and price controls would eliminate these difficulties and benefit the farmers.

After World War II, Goss became an advisor to the United Nations Food and Agricultural Organization and a founder and member of the executive committee of the International Federation of Agricultural Producers. He was critical of programs that restricted production to maintain prices in the midst of acute food shortages, believing that under a strong program farmers could produce abundantly and still get fair prices. He served as a member of the Land Management Commission of the War Power Administration, the War Mobilization and Reconversion Advisory Board, the advisory board of the Federation for Railway Progress, and the Public Advisory Board. Death came from a heart attack minutes after he finished a speech on mobilization policy at the 1950 *New York Herald Tribune* Forum at the Waldorf-Astoria in New York. Burial was at Forest Lawn Cemetery, Glendale, Calif.

Goss was a moderate on matters of farm policy and in step with the quiet, conservative approach of the Grange. His views were those of one who was more responsive to the needs of the better-placed farmers. As head of an organization that pioneered in cooperatives, farm credit reforms, and lobbying at the congressional level, he was far more influenced by his business experiences and the thinking of agricultural leaders of the Far West and Washington, D.C., who were sensitive to the needs of the commercial farmers in an urban-industrial state.

[Brief, but useful, biographical sketches are to be found in Charles M. Gardner, *The Grange, Friend of the Farmer, 1867–1947* (1947), and the National Grange, *A Tribute to the Memory of Albert S. Goss* (1950). See also Harriet Ann Crawford, *The Wash. State Grange, 1889–1924* (1940); *Current Biog.*, 1945; and *N.Y. Times*, Nov. 18, 1941, and Oct. 26, 1950. For a convenient summary of Goss's views on agricultural policy, see the annual *Proc. Nat. Grange*, esp. 1922–1932, for his reports as master, and 1942–1950.]
                                    THEODORE SALOUTOS

GOUDY, FREDERIC WILLIAM (Mar. 8, 1865–May 11, 1947), lettering artist, type designer, and printer, was born in Bloomington, Ill., the younger son and one of at least three children of John Fleming Gowdy and Amanda Melvina (Truesdell) Gowdy. His father, who changed the spelling of the family name to Goudy about 1883, was of Scottish descent and a native of Ohio. By the time Frederic was eleven, his family had lived in a succession of Illinois towns where his father was schoolmaster, principal, or superintendent of schools. As a boy, he liked best to copy the wood engravings in *Harper's Weekly*. After graduating from the two-year Shelbyville, Ill., high school in 1883, he worked for a sign painter and then for a photographer in Springfield. His father hoped that Frederic would become a civil engineer, but the younger Goudy lacked the entrance qualifications and, in any case, was not keen for more school. In 1884 his family moved to the prairie cow-town of Highmore in Dakota Territory, where his father entered the real estate business and later became county treasurer, probate court judge, and county superintendent of schools. In his father's real estate office, he taught himself bookkeeping and occasionally arranged type or lettered real estate advertising pieces. Striking off on his own in 1888, he first worked in Minneapolis as a cashier in a department store (1888-1889); he then joined a real estate office in Springfield (1889-1890), where again he could lay out advertisements.

In January 1890, Goudy moved to Chicago, where he worked for a financial broker. He was then employed by a real estate office where his advertising designs won recognition and later by A. C. McClurg's bookstore, a position that put him in touch with the private press movement. In 1891 he persuaded a friend, Cyrus Lauron Hooper, an English teacher, to back a small magazine, *Modern Advertising*; when that failed, he and Hooper joined in forming Camelot Press (initially called Booklet Press) in 1895. Camelot Press put its imprint on *Chapbook*, a small magazine, and reprinted in book form *The Black Art*, an article by D. Berkeley Updike. Although the press failed in 1896, his experience with it and with the magazine was valuable.

On June 2, 1897, Goudy married Bertha Matilda Sprinks in Berwyn, Ill. They left the same night for Detroit and Goudy's new position as bookkeeper for the *Michigan Farmer*. They were able to leave only through the sale and prompt collection of payment for a type design, enabling Goudy to pay his few debts. On the strength of such sales and better earnings from commercial lettering, Goudy swore off bookkeeping for life in 1899 when he lost the Detroit job. Returning to Chicago, he prepared advertising for firms like Hart, Schaffner, and Marx and Marshall Field, and in 1900 he began teaching at the Frank Holme School of Illustration, the first of a number of school appointments. At this time their son Frederic Truesdell was born, and in 1903 they moved to Park Ridge, Ill., where there was a barn suitable for a press. That year the long-lived Village Press was established, and it figured heavily in their moves to the colorful village of Hingham, Mass., in 1904 and then, because of declining business, to New York City in 1906. The Parker Building fire of Jan. 10, 1908, wiped out the press, but it was revived two years later in a Brooklyn apartment.

Goudy paid his first visit to Europe in the summer of 1909 and the next year went again with his wife and son. During the winter of 1910-1911, on commission by Mitchell Kennerley, he produced the acclaimed Kennerley typeface and a fine book (H. G. Wells, *The Door in the Wall*) to show it. The new face was warmly received by Bernard Newdigate, and the Caslon firm bought both the British and continental rights. D. B. Updike thought "the curves are perhaps too round and soft, and lack a certain snap and acidity," but it was popular. In 1911 Goudy formed Village Letter Foundery to sell Kennerley, Forum, and other faces, as he designed them. From 1920 to 1940 he was art director of Lanston Monotype Machine Company, which owned American rights for many of his designs. Honors came in the form of medals from the American Institute of Graphic Arts (1920), the American Institute of Architects (1922), the Architectural League of New York (1927), and eventually degrees *honoris causa*—L.H.D., Syracuse (1939); Litt.D., Mills (1941); and LL.D., California (1942). In 1916 he became an honorary member of the Society of Printers, Boston, which in 1937 spoofed him with awards of T.D.P. (Type Designer Prolific) and R.E. (Raconteur Extraordinary), representing the best-known holes in his armor.

In 1914 the Goudys moved the Village Press from Brooklyn to Forest Hills Gardens, L.I., which remained their comfortable base of operations for nine years. Their last move was in 1923 to Marlboro, N.Y., to an old farmhouse with a mill and brook in a park-like setting on the bank of the Hudson River. At Deepdene (as they named their "estate") they wrestled with and conquered the problems of cutting matrices and casting fonts, a family concern with no outside aid. The joyous day, in Goudy's words, on which they overcame these difficulties was somewhat tempered by the discovery that he had lost the sight of his right eye overnight. His wife, who had learned to ink-in the drawings, set the type, operate the pantograph engraving machine, and shape cutters for it, died in 1935. On Jan. 26, 1939, the mill and workshop burned down. Since all he needed to design type was a pencil and an idea, Goudy worked on till his count of typefaces tallied 116. He taught lettering at the Arts Students League in New York (1916-1924) and graphic arts at New York University (1927-1929). Goudy wrote several books and articles on his craft. His greatest contribution, however, was the introduction of a number of his sound designs into the mainstream of typographic communication. Goudy died at Deepdene of a heart attack at the age of eighty-two. After a funeral service in New York, he was cremated and his ashes were placed beside those of his wife in Evergreen Cemetery, Chicago.

[A collection of Goudy material is at the Grolier Club, N.Y., and information is in various issues of the *News-Letter* of the Am. Inst. of Graphic Arts. Goudy's own book, *A Half-Century of Type Design and Typography, 1895-1945* (2 vols., 1926), contains much autobiographical information, a record of his type designs, and a bibliography. He also discusses his work in *Typologia: Studies in Type Design and Type Making* (1940). The output of Village Press is described in Melbert B. Cary, *Bibliog. of the Village Press* (1938). See also Vrest Orton, *Goudy: Master of Letters* (1939); Bernard Lewis, *Behind the Type: The Life Story of Frederic W. Goudy* (1941); and Peter Beilenson, *The Story of Frederic W. Goudy* (1939; 1965); and obituary in *N.Y. Times*, May 12, 1947.]

RAY NASH

GRABAU, AMADEUS WILLIAM (Jan. 9, 1870–Mar. 20, 1946), geologist and paleontologist, was born in Cedarburgh, Wis., the third of ten children of Rev. William H. Grabau, a Lutheran minister, and Maria (von Rohr) Grabau. His grandfathers, Rev. Johannes A. A. Grabau and Henry von Rohr, led a group of German Lutherans to Buffalo, N.Y., for the sake of religious freedom. During a bitter ecclesiastical controversy, William Grabau resigned his Buffalo pastorate and moved to Wisconsin. Amadeus grew up in a family with a strongly Germanic outlook. His mother died when he was six, but he became deeply attached to his stepmother, who encouraged his intellectual pursuits. He at first attended his father's parochial school but was later enrolled in the Cedarburgh high school.

In 1885 Grabau's father was recalled to Buffalo to take charge of the Buffalo (later Martin Luther) Seminary. For a time the boy attended a high school in Buffalo; after he was apprenticed to a bookbinder, he continued his education through evening classes. Botany was his favorite study in Wisconsin, but in Buffalo he was attracted to the well-preserved Middle Devonian fossils of the region and became active in the Buffalo Society of the Natural Sciences. His performance in a correspondence course in mineralogy caught the eye of geologist William Otis Crosby, a curator of the Boston Society of Natural History, who in 1890 gave him a job in the society's mineral supply department. This appointment also enabled Grabau to become a special student at the Massachusetts Institute of Technology. After additional preparation at the Boston Latin School, he matriculated at M.I.T. in 1891 and received the B.S. degree in 1896. The following year he taught paleontology at M.I.T. He next received a fellowship from Harvard, where he took an M.S. degree in 1898 and a D.Sc. degree in 1900. While finishing his graduate studies, he taught geology at Tufts College and at Rensselaer Polytechnic Institute. After a year (1900-1901) as professor of geology at Rensselaer, he went to Columbia University as lecturer in paleontology, becoming in turn adjunct professor (1902) and professor of paleontology (1905). On Oct. 5, 1901, he married a Barnard student, Mary Antin, later

the author of *The Promised Land*. They had one daughter, Josephine Esther.

Although his earliest interests had been in the physiography of the glaciated areas near Buffalo, Grabau's attraction to fossils and their stratigraphic position become paramount. In Boston he was strongly influenced by Alpheus Hyatt and R. T. Jackson, who emphasized the biological aspects of paleontology. Work in the Devonian of western New York led to study of the Devonian of Michigan, and through it to inquiry into lateral changes in rock type and fauna. The Silurian rocks underlying the Devonian, and forming the falls at Niagara, also attracted his attention. While at Columbia, Grabau published many papers concerned primarily with the stratigraphy of the Silurian and Devonian of the northeastern United States but including some investigations in other areas and disciplines. He was, for example, one of the first persons to write extensively on deltaic and continental sedimentation. A series of short papers on gastropods attempted to support the idea of ontogeny as a reflection of phylogeny, and other speculative aspects of Darwinian evolution. These were not always well received. However, his magnificent two-volume work with Hervey W. Shimer, *The North American Index of Fossils* (1909-1910), is both a compilation of ranges and a classification which in some points was superior to the classic work of Karl von Zittel in this field; no one attempted to revise the work for more than thirty years.

Grabau's concepts of correlation (age equivalency of rock units) put him in direct conflict with E. O. Ulrich and they often argued heatedly at meetings of the Geological Society of America. Grabau maintained that the general rise and fall of sea level was responsible for the distribution of certain rock strata, whereas Ulrich argued that tilting of the continent and deposition limited to particular basins was more important: neither was entirely correct. Although Grabau had a good grasp of Devonian and Silurian rocks, his correlations at time were in error. In paleontology his view of species tended to exceed the generally accepted limits of variation; he was a "splitter" rather than a "lumper."

Grabau was methodical in the classic Teutonic model. The elaborate terminology of his *Geology of the Nonmetallic Mineral Deposits Other Than Silicates* (1920) tended to confuse the reader, and he never established a "school" of followers. His two-volume *Textbook of Geology* (1920-1921) compares favorably with contemporary texts, and his earlier *Principles of Stratigraphy* (1913; 2nd ed., 1924) possibly contains more material for the stratigrapher, paleontologist, and sedimentologist than any other single work.

Anti-German sentiment in the United States, coupled with his pro-German pronouncements during World War I, forced Grabau to leave Columbia University in 1919. His views also led to a family estrangement, and he migrated to China. Though years later there was reconciliation, his wife and daughter never visited him in his adopted country.

From 1920 on, Grabau made his home in Peking. He was a professor of paleontology in the National University of Peking and simultaneously chief paleontologist of the National Geological Survey of China. For two decades, while in charge of the survey's paleontological laboratory, he trained stratigraphers and paleontologists. A man of prodigious energy, within three years he had written a 500-page book, *Stratigraphy of China* (1923), a basic work revised five years later. While he continued to emphasize the Devonian and its fossils—publishing another 500-page monograph on Devonian brachiopods in 1931—his writing ranged throughout the subject of the Paleozoic rocks of China. He produced major works on Chinese Permian brachiopods as well as a volume on this subject for the American Museum's Natural History of Central Asia. He also contributed several large papers on corals, while continuing a steady stream of shorter works.

Grabau attended the 1933 International Geological Congress in Washington, D.C. Following his return to China he continued to write on specific topics in paleontology and stratigraphy, but his principal effort went into elaboration of his pulsation hypothesis, the idea that most of the prominent changes in the geologic column (vertical sequence of rock types) were a consequence of worldwide transgressions and regressions of marine waters resulting from changes in sea level. Further, he suggested that there was movement of the continents alternately toward and away from the poles to account for glacial and mild climates. His four books documenting these ideas with the geologic record of Cambrian and Ordovician strata show an amazing grasp of the world literature. These concepts as they applied throughout the geologic record are summarized in his last major work, *The Rhythm of the Ages* (1940). It is worth noting that this summary volume was produced in essential isolation. In 1937, when the Japanese took Peking, Grabau remained behind because of illness and lack of communica-

tion facilities; according to some reports, he prevented the despoiling of geological collections and libraries. After 1941 he was interned. Crippled by arthritis and suffering from ill health and insufficient food, Grabau declined both mentally and physically. Although he lived to survive the war, his career had ended. He died in Peking at the age of seventy-six of internal hemorrhage and was buried in the compound of the geological department of the National University of Peking.

Because of World War II, Grabau's ideas never received the critical study they deserved. He is an excellent example of a scientist who wrote voluminously with meticulous detail but had little immediate impact, perhaps because he was ahead of his time. Some of his speculative ideas have proven incorrect; others which were totally ignored, such as his notions on paleogeography and polar wandering, apparently contain elements of truth; still others, such as the close tie between stratigraphy and sedimentation, were prophetic. Grabau's contributions to better knowledge of the paleontology and stratigraphy of the United States would have assured a respected place for him in science. These pale beside later efforts, for his work on the Paleozoic rocks of China is fundamental, and it is a just title when he is referred to as "the father of Chinese geology."

[A number of biographical notices have been written, including H. D. Thomas, *Nature* 158 (1946): 89–91; H. W. Shimer, *Am. Jour. of Science* 244 (1946): 735–736 (with bibliography); H. W. Shimer, Geological Soc. of America, *Proc.*, 1947, pp. 155–166; V. K. Ting, in Geological Society of China, *Bull.* 10 (1931): ix–xviii (also cited as *Grabau Anniversary*, the commemorative vol. presented to Grabau on his fiftieth birthday); Y. C. Sun, in Geological Society of China, *Bull.* 27 (1947): 1026, includes a bibliography of 291 titles.]

ELLIS Y. YOCHELSON

GREENE, BELLE DA COSTA (Dec. 13, 1883–May 10, 1950), library director and bibliographer, was born in Alexandria, Va., the third of five children and second daughter of Richard Greene and Genevieve (Van Vliet) Greene. Belle Greene's determined reticence about her antecedents, her olive complexion, and the name da Costa led to the widely held assumption that she was foreign born; da Costa was her maternal grandmother's name. The Greene children received their schooling in Princeton, N.J., where their Virginia-born mother, apparently separated from her husband, supported them by giving music lessons. A college education was beyond their limited means, and Belle Greene went to work at the Princeton University library. She served her apprenticeship in the cataloguing and reference departments, soon showing her budding passion for rare and beautiful books and manuscripts. Ernest C. Richardson, the university librarian and professor of bibliography, was the first of several mentors from whom she eagerly learned her craft. Vivacious and attractive, she drew the attention of a Princeton man, Junius Spencer Morgan, a collector of manuscripts and rare books. His uncle, J. Pierpont Morgan, needed someone to take charge of his splendid but haphazard collection of rare books and manuscripts, soon to be housed in a new building. Belle Greene began work at the Pierpont Morgan Library in 1905, and for three years she guided the collecting and organizing of the coordinated treasures that made it one of the world's greatest libraries.

Greene and Morgan soon proved deeply compatible, and by 1908 she had acquired so much knowledge and responsibility that he sent her abroad as his agent. In England she came under the sympathetic tutelage of Sydney Cockerell, director of the Fitzwilliam Museum at Cambridge University, who also furnished her with introductions to the foremost European scholars. Increasing in confidence and with a sure feel for the quality of a rare object, she nonetheless never decided on the desirability of an acquisition without seeking the opinion of experts. The final decision to purchase was always Morgan's. She was soon known and respected in museums, galleries, libraries, and aristocratic houses all over Europe. It was during the appraisal of the estate following Morgan's death in 1913 that she met Bernard Berenson, who became an important influence and a lifelong friend.

J. P. Morgan, Jr., was at first indifferent to enlarging the collection, and Greene became involved in World War I work with characteristic intensity. Having brought her mother with her to New York, she now took into her home a war-widowed sister, whose son, Robert Mackenzie Leveridge, was born there. When the sister remarried, Belle Greene legally adopted the child.

By 1920, Morgan had become interested in enriching and enlarging the collection, and Greene soon resumed her professional trips to Europe. Then, in 1924, Morgan incorporated the library as an educational institution dedicated to the memory of his father. Greene was named director, a position she held until her retirement on Nov. 30, 1948. The new status of the library called for a revised orientation: the organization of its material for service to scholarship, a task for which Greene revealed a special genius, had to be equal in importance to the continuing expansion of the collections. Her dedication to making the library useful resulted in a generous lending policy and information and photographic services, which made its resources world famous. In addition, innumerable visiting scholars from around the world found that she personally took a ready and discerning interest in their work.

Belle Greene's standing as one of the great figures in the art and bibliophile world earned her wide recognition. The French, Belgian, and Italian governments decorated her. She was named to the Committee for the Restoration of the University of Louvain Library, the Librarian's Advisory Council of the Library of Congress, and the advisory board of the Index Society, and served as a consultant to the trustees of the Walters Art Gallery in Baltimore. She was one of the first women to become a fellow of the Mediaeval Academy of America and a fellow in perpetuity of the Metropolitan Museum of New York; she also served on the editorial boards of the *Gazette des Beaux-Arts* and *Art News*. Tribute was paid her by a retrospective exhibition in the Pierpont Morgan Library in 1949, and in 1954 by a volume of essays, *Studies in Art and Literature for Belle da Costa Greene*, contributed by internationally eminent scholars.

Short, gray-eyed, and black-haired, Belle da Costa Greene had a vivid personality and a strong sense of her role. When representing the Morgans abroad, she wore couturier clothes and patronized luxury hotels; while working in the library in her early years, she dressed in Renaissance gowns with appropriate jewelry. She was witty, racy in her speech, unconventional, and impulsive, and could be witheringly imperious when faced with pretentiousness and pomposity. She made and kept friends easily, and she inspired loyalty and dedication in her staff.

Although a mishap resulting in a broken arm had made her increasingly fearful of falling, she continued for some time to go daily to the library after her retirement. At sixty-six she died of cancer in New York. Funeral services were held at St. Thomas Church (Episcopal), of which she was a member, and her ashes were buried in Kensico Cemetery, Valhalla, N.Y.

[*Notable Am. Women*, II, 83–85; Pierpont Morgan Lib., *The First Quarter Century of the Pierpont Morgan Lib.: A Retrospective Exhibition in Honor of Belle da Costa Greene* (1949), includes a portrait; "Belle of the Books," *Time*, Apr. 11, 1949, includes a portrait; Dorothy Miner, ed., *Studies in Art and*

Literature for Belle da Costa Greene (1954), includes a portrait; letter of W. G. Constable, *N.Y. Times,* July 3, 1950; "Morgan Librarian," *Times Lit. Supp.,* Nov. 13, 1948; Aline B. Louchheim, "The Morgan Library and Miss Greene," *N.Y. Times,* Apr. 17, 1949; Curt F. Bühler, "Belle da Costa Greene," *Speculum,* July 1957 (reprinted in his *Early Books and Manuscripts, Forty Years of Research,* 1973); *Publishers Weekly,* June 10, 1950; recollections of Rudolph Ruzicka and Henry Allen Moe. For the development of the library under her leadership, see Pierpont Morgan Lib., *A Rev. of the Growth, Development and Activities of the Lib.* . . . for 1924–1929 (1930) and similar reviews for 1930–1935 (1937), 1936–1940 (1941), and 1941–1948 (1949). A portrait of Greene hangs in the library.]

MARY TOLFORD WILSON

GREENE, ROGER SHERMAN (May 29, 1881–Mar. 27, 1947), diplomat, foundation official, medical administrator in China, national leader in affairs relating to East Asia, was the fourth son and sixth of eight children of Rev. Daniel Crosby Greene, a Congregational minister, and Mary Jane (Forbes) Greene. His parents, descendants of colonial Massachusetts families, had been among the earliest American missionaries in Japan, arriving in 1869 and serving until their deaths (the mother's in 1910, the father's in 1913); they were deeply involved in bringing modern Western education to the Japanese during the Meiji era. Two of their other children achieved prominence, Evarts Boutell as an American historian at Columbia and Jerome Davis as a foundation administrator, banker, and secretary of the Corporation of Harvard University.

Roger Greene was born in Westborough, Mass., while his parents were on furlough in the United States. After earlier schooling in Japan, he entered Harvard, from which he received a B.A. degree in 1901 and an M.A. the following year. He then obtained a position with the consular service and over the next twelve years held posts in Brazil, Japan, Siberia, Manchuria, and China; at Hankow (1911-1914) he performed with distinction as consul general during the Chinese revolution. Perhaps as a result of his missionary heritage, Greene became uncomfortable in his role as agent of the interests of the United States, feeling an obligation to mankind more broadly conceived. He therefore surrendered a highly promising diplomatic career to accept, in 1914, an opportunity to join in the philanthropic activities of the Rockefeller Foundation, of which his brother Jerome was then secretary.

Greene began as a member of the foundation's commission which surveyed the medical and public health needs of China. The commission's recommendations led to the establishment, later in 1914, of the China Medical Board, to foster medical education in China through the improvement of hospitals and medical schools and the granting of fellowships to missionary and Chinese physicians. Wallace Buttrick of the General Education Board accepted the directorship of the board, and Greene was made resident director in China. He remained in China until 1935, becoming director of the China Medical Board in 1921 and serving from 1927 to 1929 as vice-president of the Rockefeller Foundation in the Far East. He also took a particular interest in one of the board's projects, the Peking Union Medical College, and became acting director in 1927.

During his years with the China Medical Board, Greene developed close ties with China's westernized intellectuals, most notably the philosopher-diplomat Hu Shih. He was deeply involved in projects directed toward the modernization of China, especially in the field of public health. He also kept up a steady correspondence with members of the Department of State responsible for American policy toward China. With China torn by civil strife in the 1920's, Greene urged a policy of noninterference, arguing that the Chinese were entitled to the freedom that Americans had enjoyed in the 1860's: the freedom to fight their civil war until one side won a decisive victory and could unify and determine the future of the country. In 1927-1928 he led a group of Americans in Peking, mostly missionaries, who successfully opposed a plan by the American minister for intervention in cooperation with the other great powers. Greene's opinion carried special weight at this time because Nelson T. Johnson, his former protégé in the consular service, had taken over responsibility for East Asian affairs within the State Department.

Tension developed, however, between Greene and the Rockefeller Foundation. This was partly the result of Greene's character and style. To many he seemed the archetypical New Englander, austere, righteous, and rigid; and he was, indeed, highly principled and uncompromising. He regarded with contempt the increasing involvement of John D. Rockefeller III in China Medical Board affairs and would do nothing to appease that young man's sensibilities. A host of financial issues, born of the board's depression-ridden desire to cut expenses, served as irritants, but the major issue became the future of the department of religion at Peking Union Medical College. In founding the college in 1916, John D. Rockefeller, Jr., had acquired the facilities of a British missionary medical school and had declared his intention to continue the school's religious atmosphere. Greene, however, had come to believe that the effort to instill Christianity in medical and nursing students was an anachronism in modern China. As Chinese nationalism grew more intense in the 1920's and 1930's, both students and faculty objected to the department of religion. Regarding the department as expendable during the budget crisis, Greene fought hard for his beliefs, but lost out in a confrontation with the Rockefellers. He resigned from the China Medical Board in 1934, and later the same year, by direction of the board, submitted his resignation from the Peking Union Medical College as of July 1935.

Greene emerged from semiretirement in the late 1930's as a leader in organizations formed to work for the support of China and Great Britain against Japan and Germany. From 1938 to 1941 he served as chairman of the American Committee for Non-Participation in Japanese Aggression and from 1940 to 1941 as associate director of William Allen White's Committee to Defend America by Aiding the Allies. For both organizations he lobbied with federal officials for American assistance to China. More than any other private citizen, Greene had the attention of Stanley K. Hornbeck, the State Department's powerful senior advisor for Far Eastern Affairs. Almost alone, he kept the Committee to Defend America from focusing its entire campaign on the war in Europe.

Ill health curtailed Greene's activities shortly before Pearl Harbor, but he was able during the war to serve part-time as a consultant to the State Department's Division of Cultural Relations. He maintained a deep interest in Chinese affairs, and while he gradually, with misgivings, came to regard the Kuomintang as China's best hope, he was outraged by the attacks on John S. Service and other Americans who had reported favorably on Chinese Communist activities. He also lent active encouragement to the development of East Asian studies in the United States. Greene's home in his later years was Worcester, Mass. He died in West Palm Beach, Fla., of cardiac failure and chronic nephritis and was buried in Westborough, Mass. He was survived by his wife, Kate Brown, whom he had married on May 8, 1920, and their two children, Edward Forbes and Katharine Curtis.

[Greene's papers, at Harvard, are a basic source. There is MS material also in the files of the State Dept. (Nat. Arch.); of the China Medical Board and Rockefeller Foundation, N.Y. City; of the Am. Committee for Non-Participation in Japanese Aggression (Harvard); and of the Committee to Defend America by Aiding the Allies (Princeton). Greene's activities in China can be traced in the *Annual Reports* of the Rockefeller Foundation. Other references include Mary E. Ferguson, *China Medical Board and Peking Union Medical College* (1970); *Who Was Who in America,* II (1950); obituary (with photograph) in *N.Y. Times,* Mar. 29, 1947. Information on family background can be found in Evarts B. Greene's biography of his father, *A New-Englander in Japan* (1927). Death record from Fla. Bureau of Vital Statistics.]

WARREN I. COHEN

GREGG, JOHN ROBERT (June 17, 1867- Feb. 23, 1948), inventor of a system of shorthand, was born in Shantonagh, County Monaghan, Northern Ireland. He was the youngest among the four sons and one daughter of George Gregg, a railroad stationmaster in nearby Rockcorry, and Margaret Courtney (Johnston) Gregg. As a schoolboy, Gregg suffered permanent damage to his hearing when he was struck by one of his teachers. His subsequent poor academic record was mistakenly attributed to dull-wittedness by his parents, who soon lost hope of his achieving the academic success of their other children. At the age of ten, however, Gregg was introduced to shorthand by a family friend and mastered it with greater facility than his siblings. "I suddenly determined to stick to shorthand," he later wrote. "It was my last chance" (Symonds, pp. 4-5).

Gregg moved with his family to Glasgow, Scotland, about 1878, and after some additional schooling, he became a clerk in a law office. He used the free time accorded by his employer's incapacitating bouts of drunkenness to study closely the historical development of the many English and foreign-language shorthand systems and to correspond with shorthand teachers and innovators all over the world. Disappointed with the existing systems, Gregg while still a teenager worked out the principles for a method that was at once fast, natural, and easy to learn. In 1887 he moved to Liverpool, where his brother was established as an architect, and opened a one-room shorthand school. The following year, with $50 he had borrowed from his brother, he published *Light-Line Phonography,* a twenty-eight-page pamphlet that was the first of many editions of the Gregg shorthand system.

Believing that writing should always be fluid and curvilinear, Gregg constructed his shorthand on the components of the ellipse, using the slant of normal longhand, rather than the circle employed by such contemporary systems as that of Isaac and Benn Pitman. Gregg's sense of linguistic symmetry was also offended by the positioning of disjointed signs (usually representing vowels) above or below the writing line, and by the practice of altering a symbol's meaning merely by thickening its outline. By joining vowels to consonants in the text line and eliminating shading, he increased speed and reduced the possibility of error in transcription. Although many existing shorthands adopted one or another of these principles, Gregg's was the first to incorporate them all. His system, like Pitman's, was phonetic but attached much greater significance to the vowel sounds. Gregg made a scientific study of the relationship and occurrence of these sounds, aided by his sister Fanny, a teacher of the deaf and dumb. He was also the first shorthand inventor to allocate his characters so as to permit the smoothest joinings between the most frequently occurring letter combinations.

In 1893, having suffered a further deterioration of his hearing and being concerned about his American copyrights, Gregg sold his business and immigrated to the United States. He arrived at the beginning of a severe business depression. After operating a shorthand school in Boston for two years, he moved to Chicago, where he was more successful. An eloquent and persuasive self-advertiser, he offered free correspondence courses to potential Gregg teachers and sent his most capable students to demonstrate the system throughout the country. Demand for business skills was rising and Gregg shorthand was quickly adopted by private business colleges attracted by its logic and simplicity. Somewhat more slowly, it also found its way into the curricula of public secondary schools, where the Pitman system was firmly entrenched. In the early 1900's Gregg began to open a chain of his own schools throughout the United States, Canada, and Great Britain. His reputation was enhanced as Gregg-trained stenographers won numerous international shorthand competitions and established the world's highest speed records.

Once his business was established, Gregg did little teaching himself, but he took an active and paternal interest in its affairs. He edited his organization's house journals, the *Gregg Writer* (founded in 1899) and the *American Shorthand Teacher* (1920; renamed in 1933 the *Business Education World*); and he was president of the Gregg Publishing Company, which printed manuals, drills, and home study courses. Interest in the simplification of communication led him to champion the artificial international language Esperanto, one of thirteen languages to which his shorthand was adapted. By the time

of Gregg's death, it was estimated that 18,000,-000 people had learned his shorthand system.

A handsome man with blue eyes and long white hair, Gregg possessed a quiet charm and modesty, a droll wit, a driving enthusiasm, and an occasional taste for sartorial eccentricity. In his dedication to shorthand, he was both an evangelist and an astute businessman who, according to one associate, attempted to negotiate out of the market any stenographic system that threatened to become competitive. Regarding shorthand skill as a ladder to commercial success, he especially urged young men to acquire it, pointing out that American industrialists like George Cortelyou, Samuel Insull, and John J. Raskob had begun their careers as stenographers.

Outside his business, Gregg's principal interests were art, theater, and travel. He collected paintings and served for many years as treasurer and then as president of the National Arts Club in New York. Gregg was married twice: on July 3, 1899 to Maida Wasson of Hannibal, Mo., who died in 1928; and on Oct. 23, 1930 to Janet Fraser Kinley, daughter of President David Kinley of the University of Illinois. He and his second wife had two children, Katherine Kinley and John Robert. Gregg was an Episcopalian. He died of a heart ailment in New York City at the age of eighty, a week after undergoing surgery, and was buried in New Canaan, Conn., near his home in Cannondale.

[The Oral Hist. Collect. at Columbia Univ. has reminiscences of Gregg by his widow, Mrs. Alfred C. Howell, and his former associates, which can be used with Mrs. Howell's permission. There is material about the Gregg system in the extensive shorthand collection Gregg gave to the N.Y. Public Lib.; see Karl Brown and Daniel C. Haskell, *The Shorthand Collection in the N.Y. Public Lib.* (1935). Frequent articles by Gregg on shorthand and its history appear in his periodical, *Business Education World*. Other sources include *The Story of Gregg Shorthand as Told by John Robert Gregg* (1913); David McKevitt, "Galloping Words," *American Mag.*, Nov. 1930; F. Addington Symonds, *John Robert Gregg: The Man and His Work* (1963); Louis A. Leslie, *The Story of Gregg Shorthand, Based on the Writings of John Robert Gregg* (1964); *Nat. Cyc. Am. Biog.*, Current Vol. C, p. 273; and obituaries in the *N.Y. Times*, Feb. 24, 1948, and *Jour. of Business Education*, Mar. 1948. The Leslie book reproduces many photographs of Gregg and two portraits.]

PHILIP DE VENCENTES

GRIFFITH, DAVID WARK (Jan. 22, 1875-July 23, 1948), motion picture director, was born near Beard's Station (later Crestwood), Oldham County, Ky., the third of four sons and sixth of seven children of Jacob Wark Griffith and Mary Perkins (Oglesby) Griffith. His father's forebears had settled in Maryland

and moved after the Revolution to western Virginia, where Jacob Griffith was born; his mother came from a Virginia family. Jacob Griffith successively practiced medicine in Kentucky, fought in the Mexican War, spent two years in California during the Gold Rush, served in the Kentucky legislature, and became a slaveholder and plantation owner. He was a colonel in the Kentucky cavalry during the Civil War. The war left the family impoverished, with their land heavily mortgaged. David's father died in 1882, and his mother presently settled in Louisville, where she ran a boarding house. Griffith had attended country schools and briefly continued his schooling in Louisville, but he soon left high school to go to work in a dry goods store and then as a clerk in a bookstore.

As a young man Griffith planned to be a writer, but his deep voice and slightly flamboyant manner also drew him to the theater. In 1895 he joined an amateur theatrical company that toured in Kentucky and Indiana. Minor roles followed in several professional companies based in Louisville, and by the turn of the century he was an itinerant and not very successful stock company actor, playing bits parts throughout the United States, at first under the name "Lawrence Brayington," then as "Lawrence Griffith." Occasionally he was stranded when companies went broke or folded, and he worked in a steel mill, as a hop picker, and on a lumber schooner off the Pacific Coast, earning money to pay his way back to Louisville or to New York, where stock companies were formed. On May 14, 1906, while playing in Boston, he married Linda Arvidson Johnson, an actress whom he had met in San Francisco. They had no children.

At the time of their marriage, as his wife later described him, Griffith in his early thirties was a man with lofty ambitions but no direction, and thus a tendency to drift. Between acting assignments he began writing plays, short stories, and poems, signing them with his family name. He sold a story to *Cosmopolitan* and a poem to *Leslie's Weekly*. A play he wrote about California hop pickers, *The Fool and the Girl,* was purchased by the producer James K. Hackett for $1,000; it opened Sept. 30, 1907, in Washington, D.C. Though it lasted only a week there and a week in Baltimore, it demonstrated Griffith's feeling for movement and lighting and his ability to portray everyday life.

Returning to New York, he resumed his stage name and, at a friend's suggestion, offered story ideas to motion picture studios. At the Edison Company he was hired to act in *Rescued from*

an Eagle's Nest, directed by Edwin S. Porter, the pioneer director of the famous 1903 film *The Great Train Robbery.* The Biograph Company bought several of Griffith's film synopses and also used him as an actor. In June 1908 he was offered a trial assignment to direct for Biograph. His first films were successful, and Biograph hired him as its principal director.

During his five years at Biograph, from 1908 to 1913, Griffith demonstrated increasing mastery of the motion picture medium, moving his camera closer to his actors, including more separate shots in his films, breaking the motion picture play free from the conventions of the theater. Biograph films became highly popular among the motion picture's then predominantly working-class audience, and Griffith gradually sensed the significance of his directorial work. On his third annual contract he crossed out the name Lawrence and inked in David; his fourth contract was made to David Wark Griffith. Griffith directed nearly five hundred one- and two-reel films for Biograph, often turning out more than two per week. He became known as a skilled judge and teacher of actors and actresses. Among the players he developed into stars were Mary Pickford, Lillian and Dorothy Gish, Henry B. Walthall, Mae Marsh, and Blanche Sweet. Although his own acting style had been bombastic, as a director Griffith pioneered a new style of acting, with emotion expressed not by large gestures but by restraint, by small movements and subtle expressions. It is not too much to claim, as Griffith himself asserted in a trade-paper advertisement when he left Biograph in 1913, that in his five years as a director he had succeeded in "revolutionizing Motion Picture drama and founding the modern techniques of the art."

As his personal innovations Griffith listed close-up and long shots, the "switchback" or parallel montage for suspense, the fade-out, and restraint in expression. Motion picture historians have subsequently discovered that nearly every new technique claimed for Griffith and his cameramen, G. W. "Billy" Bitzer and Arthur Marvin, had in fact been used by other film makers before 1908. Griffith's achievement, instead, was to explore and develop such techniques in a systematic and increasingly effective way, thus freeing the motion picture from the spatial limitations of the stage and re-creating it as a new and unique art form, able to control and use time, space, and movement for its own visual and dramatic ends. Griffith also established the primacy of the director, rather than the cameraman, as the principal artistic figure in the making of commercial motion pictures.

Griffith left Biograph in 1913 when the company resisted his desire to take the lead in the making of longer films, a trend at this time among European film makers as well. He became director of production for Reliance-Majestic, producing companies for the Mutual Film Corporation, and quickly directed four films of from five to seven reels in length, both to fulfill his contractual obligations and to raise money for a film he wanted to make about the American Civil War.

This film, *The Birth of a Nation,* made in 1914 and released in 1915, filled twelve reels; it was the longest and most expensive motion picture up to that time and was to become perhaps the most famous and controversial film in the first half-century of the screen. Griffith's epic depiction of the struggle between North and South, based on the novel and play *The Clansman* by Thomas Dixon, ends with the reconciliation of the sections through white racial solidarity, symbolized in the emotionally overpowering final scenes of the hooded clansmen riding to the rescue of a Northern white girl threatened by a black man. The film was enormously popular with white middle-class audiences, many of whom were won over to motion pictures as respectable entertainment, or as a significant art form. But Negro groups vigorously protested the film's racism, an attack which provoked Griffith to defend his right of self-expression in a pamphlet, *The Rise and Fall of Free Speech in America* (1916).

With his profits from *The Birth of a Nation,* Griffith immediately began an even more ambitious historical epic, *Intolerance,* released in 1916. It portrayed not one but four historical epochs and places—modern United States, sixteenth-century Paris, Palestine in the time of Christ, and ancient Babylon—and interspersed episodes from each period in the completed film. For the Babylonian sequence Griffith built enormous, lavishly decorated sets that dominated the Hollywood landscape. *Intolerance* was not as popular as *The Birth of a Nation,* but it had even greater influence on other film makers, who studied the remarkable buildup of dramatic tension through parallel cutting in the modern American sequence and the vast grandeur and crowd movement of the Babylonian shots. In *The Birth of a Nation* and *Intolerance* Griffith made two of the most important films in motion picture history and established the motion picture as a medium capable of artistic excellence and historical significance.

Griffith's achievements at Biograph and in his two great epics helped create dramatic forms and the wide audience for what was rapidly becoming a major mass entertainment industry. In the period of World War I, the big studios were forming in Hollywood, and many directors followed in Griffith's path, making long films using themes and styles he had pioneered. Griffith devoted a considerable part of his energy to establishing an independent financial position in the industry. In 1917 he signed with the producer Adolph Zukor to make a series of pictures for the Artcraft Corporation, and in 1919 he joined with Charles Chaplin, Douglas Fairbanks, Sr., and Mary Pickford to form the United Artists Corporation. Meanwhile, he built his own studio in Mamaroneck, N.Y., and made films for other studios to finance his independent ventures. His business deals were exceedingly complicated, and Griffith did not always keep pace with changing patterns of film production and distribution. By 1925 he could no longer maintain the expense of his own studio and staff. He gave up his independence and became a studio director under Zukor at Paramount Pictures.

Throughout this period of rapid change in the motion picture industry Griffith continued to demonstrate his mastery of the medium and his skill as an innovator. In *Broken Blossoms* (1919) he astonished critics and audiences by creating a film radically different from his epic style, an intimate, subtle film emphasizing atmosphere, lighting, and pictorial composition. *Isn't Life Wonderful!* (1924) was an unusually effective drama of social realism photographed on location in postwar Germany. Griffith's most popular motion picture in this period was *Way Down East* (1920), a film version of a well-known stage melodrama; also memorable were *True Heart Susie* (1919) and *Orphans of the Storm* (1921). In all, he directed some eighteen films between 1917 and 1924, half of them major efforts, the others hurried productions to fulfill contracts or raise money.

Griffith's experience as a studio director was an unhappy one. In 1925 and 1926 he directed three films for Paramount, and the relationship then broke off in discord. Thereafter he signed as a director with Joseph Schenck's Art Cinema Corporation and returned to Hollywood in 1927 for the first time since 1919. But the studio system, with its array of administrators and artistic tinkerers, made Griffith truculent and sullen, and the three silent films he directed for Schenck were poorly received. *Abraham Lincoln,* Griffith's first sound film, made for

Schenck in 1930, was a somewhat slow and static yet deeply engaging character study of the Civil War president, with Walter Huston in the title role. In 1931 Griffith reactivated his old independent company and made *The Struggle,* a temperance-oriented film so disastrously unpopular that it brought Griffith's career as a film maker to an end.

Tall, thin, erect in posture, and customarily wearing a wide-brimmed hat, Griffith was an imposing and impassive figure to his fellow workers. Some saw him as an aloof and self-contained genius from an earlier, more romantic era; others as an intuitive but naïve artist who could not fully understand the complex changes in the motion picture industry and hence became increasingly cynical and embittered. Even his close associates called him "Mr. Griffith." After 1931 he lived mainly in Hollywood, where he tried unsuccessfully to find backing for several motion picture projects. He divorced his first wife on Feb. 28, 1936, after a separation of twenty-five years, and on March 2 married Evelyn Marjorie Baldwin. They were divorced in November 1947. Griffith died of a cerebral hemorrhage in Los Angeles and was buried in Mount Tabor Cemetery, Centerfield, Oldham County, Ky.

D. W. Griffith was the first important creative artist in the motion pictures. His influence on world cinema was enormous, ranging from the young Soviet directors, who screened *Intolerance* over and over before making their first films, to the many Hollywood directors who worked for Griffith or studied his techniques. His epics *The Birth of a Nation* and *Intolerance* laid the foundation for an entertainment industry centered in Hollywood that sent its films to every country, shaping images and habits throughout the world. As time gives greater perspective to the development of mass technological culture in the first half of the twentieth century, it is likely that Griffith's historical importance will continue to grow.

[Robert M. Henderson, *D. W. Griffith: His Life and Work* (1972), the first scholarly biography, establishes the factual background to Griffith's career. An autobiographical fragment has been published by Griffith's collaborator James Hart, as *The Man Who Invented Hollywood* (1972), with a memoir and notes. See also Iris Barry, *D. W. Griffith: Am. Film Master* (1940; reprinted, 1965) with important additional material by Eileen Bowser; and Robert M. Henderson, *D. W. Griffith: The Years at Biograph* (1970). Seymour Stern, "Griffith: 1—'The Birth of a Nation,'" *Film Culture*, Spring-Summer 1965, gives extensive detail about that film. Several memoirs are concerned with Griffith, including one by his first wife, Linda Arvidson Johnson, *When the Movies Were Young* (1925), and Lillian Gish's *The Movies, Mr. Griffith and Me* (1969). Most of the above contain many illustrations

of Griffith and stills from films. Anita Loos provides perceptive insights into Griffith's character in her autobiography, *A Girl Like I* (1966). Ezra Goodman, *The Fifty-Year Decline and Fall of Hollywood* (1961), depicts Griffith in his last year. Lewis Jacobs' discussion of Griffith in *The Rise of the Am. Film* (1939), though outdated, remains one of the few over-all treatments of his career. The Mass. Registrar of Vital Statistics has a record of Griffith's first marriage. Considerable additional Griffith material is in the D. W. Griffith Arch., Film Dept., Museum of Modern Art, N.Y. City. The museum has the most comprehensive collection of Griffith films; many films from the Biograph period are also in the Motion Picture Section of the Lib. of Cong. Several Griffith films may be rented from 16 mm. rental firms.]

ROBERT SKLAR

GUGGENHEIM, SOLOMON ROBERT (Feb. 2, 1861–Nov. 3, 1949), mining magnate, art collector, and museum founder, was born in Philadelphia, the fourth of the eight sons and eleven children of Meyer Guggenheim and Barbara (Myers) Guggenheim. Educated at first in public schools in Philadelphia, he was sent at fourteen, in the interest of stricter discipline, to the Concordia Institute in Zurich, Switzerland—the country from which his parents had emigrated in 1847. At twenty, he joined his three elder brothers, Isaac, Daniel, and Murry, as a partner in M. Guggenheim's Sons, a Swiss embroidery manufacturing and importing company financed by their father. Sol, as he was called, trained at its factory in St. Gall, Switzerland, and presently set up and took charge of a branch establishment in the textile-milling town of Plauen, Saxony. In the late 1880's his father, now a power in copper and silver mines in Colorado, advised the Sons to turn to metallurgy; the embroidery business was liquidated, and the sale of its factories was handled by Sol.

Back in America in 1889, he spent a year in Leadville, Colo., familiarizing himself with the mining industry and was then sent to Monterrey, Mexico, to take charge of the building of that country's first silver-lead smelter. In 1891 he supervised the erection of a copper smelter, also Guggenheim-owned, at Aguascalientes. He continued to work in Mexico, often under primitive conditions in undeveloped regions, until 1895, when he returned to New York, now the family's headquarters. "Solomon, the 'good fellow' of the family, became the popular contact man," William, his youngest brother, wrote in his autobiography (p. 67).

In 1901, when the Guggenheims won control of the reorganized American Smelting and Refining Company, thus becoming one of the foremost refiners of metals in the world, Sol joined the board of directors. Less dominant in the firm than his brother Daniel, he was nevertheless an eminent working Guggenheim—president of the Braden Copper Company in Chile and a director of such other family properties as the Chile Copper Company, the Utah Copper Company, and the Guggenheim Exploration Company, formed to gain control of the sources of ore supply. He founded the Yukon Gold Company in Alaska, which was succeeded by the Pacific Tin Company in Malaya. "When courage was given out," Bernard M. Baruch once said, "Sol was sitting in the front pew. . . . He had very pronounced ideas, and when he decided to do something, he insisted on doing it his own way and would brook no interference" (Lomask, p. 25).

Solomon Guggenheim retired from full-time business activity in 1919. His second—and, conceivably, greater—claim to fame was now in a seminal stage. He had on Apr. 3, 1895, married Irene M. Rothschild, who interested him in collecting paintings, mostly in such established fields as the Barbizon school, American and Italian landscapes, and Italian, Dutch, and German primitives. All this began to change in 1926 when, at sixty-five, he met the Baroness Hilla Rebay von Erhenweisen, an Alsatian-born artist twenty-nine years his junior, with whom he formed an enduring friendship. A relentless champion of nonobjective art, she opened Guggenheim's eyes to the attractions of modern painting. Forming a liking for such artists as Vasily Kandinsky, Ladislaus Moholy-Nagy, Fernand Léger, Paul Klee, Marc Chagall, and Picasso, he began to collect these and other modernists on a grand scale. In 1937 he established the Solomon R. Guggenheim Foundation "for the promotion of art and education in art and the enlightenment of the public especially in the field of art." The foundation set up a temporary museum, the Museum of Non-Objective Paintings, in rented quarters in New York with several hundred selections from Guggenheim's collection and with the Baroness as curator. The museum suffered somewhat from her idiosyncratic tastes; Guggenheim's own private collection was considered superior. In 1943 he commissioned Frank Lloyd Wright to design and build a permanent museum on upper Fifth Avenue. Sixteen stormy years elapsed between the original plans and the completion of this great, shell-like, architecturally controversial structure, which came to house more than three thousand modern paintings and sculptures. Its construction and land cost more than $4 million. Guggenheim did not live to see his monument, which opened in 1959, ten years after his death. To the founda-

tion that administered it, he left $8 million.

Guggenheim was a small, elegant, tough, methodical, sociable, hospitable man with large features, a rather quizzical expression, and deep-set eyes under a high brow. He had a gourmet's taste and an earthy sense of humor. A generous donor, especially to hospitals, he was a conservative Republican in his social outlook. A lover of property, and an active sportsman well into his eighties, he had, at various times, eight homes, or homes away from home: a suite at the Plaza Hotel, full of paintings; Trillora Court, a Sands Point, L.I., estate with a private golf course; another country house at Elberon, N.J., and a shooting place nearby; a winter house on the Battery at Charleston, S.C., and a ten-thousand-acre plantation nearby; a twenty-thousand-acre cattle ranch and hunting preserve in Idaho; and a shooting lodge in Scotland. He and his wife had three daughters: Eleanor May, Gertrude Renée, and Barbara Josephine. Guggenheim died of cancer at Trillora Court and was buried in the Guggenheim mausoleum in Temple Emanu-El's Salem Fields Cemetery in Brooklyn.

[Milton Lomask, *Seed Money: The Guggenheim Story* (1964); Harvey O'Connor, *The Guggenheims: The Making of an Am. Dynasty* (1937); Edwin P. Hoyt, Jr., *The Guggenheims and the Am. Dream* (1967); *William Guggenheim* (1934), an autobiography written under the pen name "Gatenby Williams"; Peggy Guggenheim, *Confessions of an Art Addict* (1960), which has a few comments on her uncle's art collecting; Geoffrey T. Hellman, "Getting the Guggenheims into Focus," *New Yorker*, July 25, 1953; information supplied by Guggenheim Brothers and the Solomon R. Guggenheim Museum; interview with Peter Lawson-Johnson, Guggenheim's grandson. Pertinent correspondence is in the files of the Solomon R. Guggenheim Foundation and the Guggenheim Museum. There is a portrait of S. R. Guggenheim at Guggenheim Brothers.]

GEOFFREY T. HELLMAN

GUILDAY, PETER KEENAN (Mar. 25, 1884-July 31, 1947), Roman Catholic priest and church historian, was born in Chester, Pa., the second son and second in a family of twelve children of Peter Wilfred Guilday and Ellen Teresa (Keenan) Guilday. His father came from Waterford, Ireland; his mother, of Irish descent, was a native of Chester. A foreman in a textile plant, the elder Guilday earned enough to raise his large family in a reasonably comfortable manner. Young Guilday was educated in a Chester parochial school and at the Roman Catholic High School in Philadelphia. In 1902 he enrolled at St. Charles Borromeo Seminary in the Overbrook section of Philadelphia as a candidate for the priesthood. After completing his studies in philosophy and theology, he was awarded a scholarship to the American College at the University of Louvain in Belgium for his final two years' study of theology. There, on July 11, 1909, Guilday was ordained to the priesthood. He returned to the United States and spent nine months as a curate in Philadelphia churches and then returned to Europe for graduate work in history—briefly at the University of Bonn and then at Louvain, where his major professor was Canon Alfred Cauchie, to whom he was always deeply devoted. Upon the publication in 1914 of his dissertation, "The English Catholic Refugees on the Continent, 1558-1795," he was awarded the doctorate by Louvain.

On returning to the United States in the fall of 1914, Guilday was assigned to the faculty of the Catholic University of America in Washington, D.C., at the request of its rector, Bishop Thomas J. Shahan, himself a church historian. Guilday began as instructor in history and rose through successive promotions to professor in 1923. Realizing that the history of the Catholic church had, at that time, little professional standing in the United States, having languished since the death of John Gilmary Shea in 1892, Guilday decided to concentrate on that field. His contributions to it, during his thirty-three years at Catholic University, took a variety of forms. The earliest was the *Catholic Historical Review,* a quarterly journal launched in April 1915, to which Bishop Shahan lent the prestige of his name as editor-in-chief; five of the university's professors served as editors, but Guilday had the most active role. The first six volumes of the *Review* were devoted exclusively to the history of American Catholicism, but after 1921 the scope was widened to embrace the history of the Catholic church throughout the world. Guilday continued as the principal editor until 1941, when failing health compelled his practical retirement, though he remained nominally the editor-in-chief.

A second major contribution was the founding of the American Catholic Historical Association, organized on Guilday's initiative in December 1919. The association held annual meetings of scholars and teachers to further interest in Catholic history, then largely neglected by professional historians, and to coordinate the work of local Catholic historical societies. Guilday served as its secretary until 1941, and the *Catholic Historical Review* became its chief organ. By the time of its founder's death the original group of fifty members had grown to about 800.

At Catholic University, Guilday inaugurated a graduate program in church history that was for many years unique in American Catholic higher educational circles. Between 1922 and 1943, thirty-five of the doctoral dissertations he directed were published. His own writings gave great impetus to the revival in American Catholic history. Once he had become firmly established in a field that he was first compelled to master himself, a steady stream of scholarly publications flowed from his pen, beginning with *The Life and Times of John Carrol, Archbishop of Baltimore* (1922) and followed by *An Introduction to Church History* (1925), a manual of historical method for beginners; *The Life and Times of John English, First Bishop of Charleston* (1927), perhaps his best work; and the useful general account, *A History of the Councils of Baltimore 1791-1884* (1932). Besides these publications, Guilday edited in 1923 the joint pastorals of the American hierarchy and wrote the only complete biography of John Gilmary Shea (1926).

Guilday was a man of medium height, rather stout in his years of vigorous health, with a handsome and dignified bearing. His ability as a speaker brought him many invitations for sermons and lectures, in which he displayed a forceful delivery and a fine command of language. To his students he was a kindly mentor, open and friendly in manner. He was at his best in introducing them to the literature in the field, by stimulating them to research, and in correcting the early drafts of their graduate theses. But he offered little or no content in his courses, believing that to be the student's responsibility; for that reason a number of students found his classes a disappointment.

Formal recognition of Guilday's achievements included eight honorary degrees, and decoration by the king of Belgium for his efforts toward the restoration of the Louvain library. In 1935 he was made a domestic prelate by Pope Pius XI. The latter years of Guilday's life were clouded by a period of suffering from diabetes marked by failing eyesight and the amputation of one leg and part of the other foot. He died of pneumonia in Providence Hospital in Washington, D.C. According to his expressed wishes, his funeral took place from the National Shrine of the Immaculate Conception; he was buried in the university lot in Mount Olivet Cemetery in Washington.

Peter Guilday deserves to rank after John Gilmary Shea as a founder of American Catholic history. Re-creating, as it were, a field that had been allowed to lapse, he gained for it a respectability in scholarly circles that it had not previously known and left it in a flourishing condition for those who came after him.

[John Tracy Ellis in *Cath. Hist. Rev.*, Oct. 1947; James J. Kortendick, S.S., in *Cath. Lib. World*, May 1941; files of *Cath. Hist. Rev.*; author's personal recollections. See also William J. Lallow in *Am. Ecclesiastical Rev.*, Jan. 1948; and Mother Richard Marie Fitz Gibbons, "The Am. Catholic Hist. Assoc. Secretaryship of Peter Guilday, 1919–1941," *Am. Catholic Hist. Soc. of Phila., Records*, Dec. 1966.]
JOHN TRACY ELLIS

HAMILTON, CLAYTON (Nov. 14, 1881-Sept. 17, 1946), teacher, critic, playwright, was born in Brooklyn, N.Y., the only child of George Alexander Hamilton, a Brooklyn merchant, and Susan Amelia (Corey) Hamilton. Originally named Clayton Meeker Hamilton, he deleted Meeker from his name before he was twenty-one. As a teenager he sent his writing to various periodicals, receiving a $15 check for a short story when he was fourteen, thereby reinforcing his desire to be a writer. He was graduated from Polytechnic Preparatory School in Brooklyn in 1896. In 1900 he received his B.A. from Polytechnic Institute of Brooklyn, and in 1901 his M.A. from Columbia University.

From 1901-1904 he tutored in English at Barnard and Columbia and served as first assistant to Prof. Brander Matthews at Columbia. In 1903 Hamilton established one of the first academic courses in the United States designed to study current theater. Over the next twenty years thousands of students attended his Saturday morning lectures on contemporary drama at Columbia Extension School. He held lectureships on drama and literature at several private New York schools, the Brooklyn Institute of Arts and Sciences (1913-1919), Dartmouth College (summers, 1916-1917), Bread Loaf Summer Conference (1931-1933), and the Mohawk Drama Festival (1935-1936, 1938-1939), among others. He conducted two lecture tours of the United States (1924-1926, 1932-1933), which took him to every state except Florida and many parts of Canada.

As a drama critic and editor, Hamilton was distinguished in his focus on the structures and themes of plays rather than critical analyses of acting or productions. He was dramatic critic and associate editor of *Forum* (1907-1909), and dramatic editor of *The Bookman* (1910-1918), *Everybody's Magazine* (1911-1913), *Vogue* (1912-1920), and *Vanity Fair* for one year. As well as writing numerous introductions to plays and books and contributing many articles to periodicals, he wrote eleven books of his own: *Materials and Methods of Fiction* (1908)—

twice revised as *A Manual on the Art of Fiction* (1918), and *The Art of Fiction* (1939); *The Theory of the Theater* (1910); *Studies in Stagecraft* (1914); *On the Trial of Stevenson* (1915); *Problems of the Playwright* (1917); *Seen on the Stage* (1920); *Conversations on Contemporary Drama* (1924); *Wanderings* (1925); and *So You're Writing a Play* (1935).

Unlike most critics, Hamilton wrote or co-authored plays of his own: *A Night at the Inn,* produced on Broadway when he was twenty-one; *The Love that Blinds* with Grace Isabel Colbron, *Heart of Punchinello,* and *It'll All Come Out in the Wash* with Gilbert Emery (all in 1906); *The Stranger at the Inn* (1913); *The Big Idea* with Augustus Thomas (1914, published 1917); *The Morning Star* with Bernard Voight (1915); *Thirty Days* with Augustus Thomas (1916, published 1923); *The Better Understanding* with Augustus Thomas (1917, published 1924); and *Friend Indeed* with Bernard Voight (1926, published 1926).

Among his other activities, he was literary advisor to the actor Richard Mansfield (1906-1907); associate story editor for Goldwyn Studios, Hollywood (1920-1922); director of education for Palmer Photoplay Corporation (1922-1925); president of Palmer Institute of Authorship (1925-1929); administrative assistant for U.S.O. Camp Shows, Inc. (1940); radio commentator for WOR-Mutual (1945); and during the 1920's he was associated in theater production with such people as George Crouse Tyler, Minnie Maddern Fiske, Walter Hampden, William Gillette, and Norman Bel Geddes.

In 1912 he became one of the youngest members ever admitted to the National Institute of Arts and Letters, eventually serving as secretary and vice-president. For sixteen seasons between 1912 and 1934 he was a member of the three-man Pulitzer Prize Committee in drama. As chairman in 1934 he became involved in the only public controversy of his career. He, playwright Austin Strong, and Prof. Walter Prichard Eaton chose Maxwell Anderson's *Mary of Scotland,* but the advisory board of Columbia's School of Journalism, ignoring that recommendation, awarded the prize to Sidney Kingsley's *Men in White.* The conflict that ensued resulted in the resignation of the entire committee. In 1932 Hamilton received the Columbia Medal for Service, and he was named Honorary Fellow in Drama, Union College, Schenectady, N.Y., in 1936. He was a member of The Players, joining in 1903, and served as secretary three terms; P.E.N. in New York;

and Writers in Hollywood. On May 24, 1913, he married Gladys Coates of Kansas City, Mo., the daughter of Arthur Coates of New York; they had two children, Donald Clayton and Gordon Clayton. He worked diligently throughout his life, yet he often bemoaned his laziness. A stout man with strong features, multiple chins, and thick white hair, he relaxed by swimming, yachting, and playing bridge. He traveled extensively, often in unconventional ways—by tramp steamer, foot, donkey, and canal boat. In private conversation he preferred to talk about his personal experiences rather than drama, theory, or literature. He is best known as one of the first Americans to write seriously about the art and institution of the theater, successfully combining academic theory with popular criticism. In his encouragement of American playwriting, he was among the first to recognize Eugene O'Neill's *Beyond the Horizon* (1920) as the first great tragedy from a native dramatist. As Professor F. D. Hunter has said, he replaced former standards of criticism based upon revealed personality, eloquence, and moral propriety with new criteria which encouraged firm technical analyses of plays as they related to audiences. Hunter also points out, however, that Hamilton's criticism was perhaps too colloquial, too vacillating, and too impressed with inconsequential factors to assume greatness. He enjoyed a life of good health until his sudden death of coronary thrombosis at his home in New York City.

[For an analysis of Hamilton's criticism, see F. J. Hunter, "Technical Criticism of Clayton Meeker Hamilton," *Educational Theatre Jour.*, Dec. 1955; For biographical and critical information, see obituaries in *N.Y. Times*, Sept. 18, 1946; *Publisher's Weekly*, Nov. 9, 1946; *Time*, Sept. 30, 1946; *Twentieth Century Authors*, First Supp. (1955); *Twentieth Century Authors* (1942); *Who Was Who in America*, II (1950); "Who's Who Among Columbia Alumni," *Columbia Alumni News*, Sept. 25, 1936; *Who's Who in New York*, 10th ed. (1938); *Who's Who in the Theater*, 9th ed. (1939); "So You're Writing a Play," *Literary Digest*, Oct. 12, 1935; "Prominent Critics," *N.Y. Dramatic Mirror*, May 5, 1913; "Clayton Hamilton," *Bookman*, June 1908; "Clayton Hamilton, the Editor," *Bookman*, June 1908; Virginia B. Lee, "An Experiment," *Overland Monthly and Outwest Magazine*, Feb. 1925; regarding the Pulitzer controversy, see Clayton Hamilton, "Poor Pulitzer Prize," *American Mercury*, May 1935; and "Refuses to Serve on Pulitzer Prize Drama Jury," *N.Y. Times*, Oct. 4, 1935.]

JAMES R. MILLER

HANNEGAN, ROBERT EMMET (June 30, 1903-Oct. 6, 1949), politician and government official, was born in St. Louis, Mo., the second of four children and the second of three sons of John Patrick Hannegan and Anna (Holden) Hannegan. His father, who became chief of detectives in the St. Louis police department, followed in a strongly Catholic line and named his black-haired boy for the executed eighteenth-century Irish nationalist. Bob Hannegan, as he was known throughout his life, was a tall youth and nearly succeeded in enlisting in the Marines at the age of fourteen. A star athlete, he won letters in football, basketball, baseball, track, and swimming at St. Louis University, from which he graduated in law with honors in 1925. He backed up his early legal practice by playing football and minor-league baseball and coaching at his alma mater. Hannegan's climb on the political ladder began with his appointment in 1933 to fill a vacancy from his ward on the St. Louis Democratic City Central Committee. Like the city, the traditionally Republican ward went Democratic shortly afterward, and Hannegan shared the credit for his party's victory. His election as chairman of the committee in 1934 made him a power in the city administration of the new Democratic mayor, Bernard F. Dickmann.

Factional strife led to Hannegan's ouster from the chairmanship in 1935, but he was reinstated a year later when Dickmann's forces regained control. After Hannegan managed Dickmann's reelection campaign in 1937, the mayor's organization became known in the newspapers as the "Dickmann-Hannegan machine" and Hannegan as a political force to be reckoned with. A significantly successful venture in 1940-1941 was followed by a serious blunder. Hannegan made a secret agreement with Harry S. Truman to support him for renomination to the Senate even though the St. Louis Democratic organization was outwardly supporting Gov. Lloyd C. Stark. Hannegan switched publicly just before the primary and his precinct workers, carrying out his plan, managed to put Truman over narrowly in St. Louis, the local margin being slightly more than Truman's statewide edge. Hannegan's undercover deal thus saved Truman's Senate seat. But in November 1940, when the Democrats lost a close race for the governorship, Hannegan and his associates concocted a scheme to prevent the elected Republican, Forrest C. Donnell, from taking office. The state Democratic committee filed a petition charging "fraud and irregularities" that held up official certification of the election results. Governor Stark condemned the device as "a shameless steal." The perpetrators were routed by the press, public opinion, and the Missouri Supreme Court, but only after six weeks of political upheaval during which Hannegan and all other Democratic participants were strongly criticized throughout the region.

Only a few months later, in 1942, Senator Truman proposed Hannegan for presidential appointment as collector of internal revenue for the Eastern District of Missouri. The St. Louis press denounced the choice almost without restraint, charging "disgraceful plum-passing." Truman was adamant: "Hannegan carried St. Louis three times for the President and me. If he is not nominated, there will be no collector at St. Louis" (*N.Y. Times*, Oct. 7, 1949). Roosevelt sent Hannegan's name to the Senate, and he was confirmed over strong and vocal opposition. In the fall of 1943, again with Truman's sponsorship, Hannegan was advanced to commissioner of internal revenue, the top post in the revenue service in Washington. On Jan. 22, 1944, with Truman's effective support, Hannegan was installed as chairman of the Democratic national committee, in charge of Roosevelt's fourth-term campaign.

Hannegan simultaneously gave the party machinery a thorough dusting and set about repaying Truman for his favors. He was now in a position to maneuver his fellow Missourian into front rank as Roosevelt's running mate, in place of Vice-President Henry A. Wallace, and he made the most of it. He obtained from the president a written statement that he would be "glad to run with either Bill Douglas (Justice William O. Douglas) or Harry Truman." When this was copied for circulation at the convention, it read "Harry Truman or Bill Douglas" (Rodell, p. 134). Hannegan also had to maneuver Truman's nomination around Sidney Hillman, a Roosevelt labor favorite, whose CIO ranks were strongly behind Wallace. In less than a year, Truman was nominated, elected, and elevated to the presidency. For Truman's first cabinet appointment he nominated Hannegan as postmaster general, effective June 30. Former Gov. Donnell, now United States senator, sought unsuccessfully to block confirmation.

Hannegan did not devote all his energies to party politics. He worked beneficial changes in the collector's office at St. Louis, leading Secretary of the Treasury Henry Morgenthau, Jr., to call him "the best Collector of Revenue in the country" (Truman, p. 324). As postmaster general, he confounded his critics by supporting liberal legislation and progressive appointments (Rodell, p. 135). Whether in the Post Office Department or the Internal Revenue Service, he insisted on efficiency and courteous treatment of taxpayers and patrons. As postmaster general, Hannegan traveled around the world in 1946 on behalf of an international postal rate agreement for airmail. Democratic losses in the congressional election that year provoked complaints against the national chairman, but President Truman defended him.

Suffering from a serious back ailment, Hannegan resigned his governmental and party posts on Nov. 25, 1947. He announced that he was quitting politics to go into business as an owner of the St. Louis Cardinals baseball team. Early in 1948 he declared: "I have dropped the curtain completely on political activity of any kind." He took no public part in Truman's 1948 reelection campaign and later there was speculation that differences had come between them (*N.Y. Times*, Oct. 7, 1949; *St. Louis Globe-Democrat*, Oct. 11, 1949). To devote himself to his declining health, Hannegan sold his interest in the baseball team for a reported $1 million in January 1949. After repeated heart attacks he died, in his forty-seventh year, at his home in St. Louis. He was buried in Calvary Cemetery, St. Louis.

Although Truman and Hannegan were together at a dinner only a few days earlier, it was widely noted that Truman did not attend the last rites. He was survived by his wife, the former Irma Protzmann of St. Louis, whom he married on Nov. 14, 1929, and by two sons, Robert Emmet, Jr., and William, and two daughters, Patricia and Sally. His activities in lay Roman Catholic circles were recognized in 1946 by Pope Pius XII, who made him a Knight of St. Gregory, Grand Order of the Holy Cross. Edward T. Folliard quoted Hannegan as having said, "When I die, I would like to have one thing put on my headstone— that I was the man who kept Henry Wallace from becoming President of the United States" (*Washington Post*, Oct. 7, 1949).

[The many articles on and references to Hannegan and his activities that appeared in the political literature of the 1930's and 1940's have been reviewed at appropriate occasions by the press, particularly in St. Louis, Kansas City, and Washington. The Missouri newspaper campaigns against Hannegan were led by the *St. Louis Post-Dispatch* and the *St. Louis Globe-Democrat*. Hannegan appears frequently in memoirs and biographies, including *Memoirs by Harry S. Truman: Years of Decision* (1955); Bert Cochran, *Truman and the Crisis Presidency* (1973); Margaret Truman, *Harry S. Truman* (1973); Merle Miller, *Plain Speaking: An Oral Biography of Harry S. Truman* (1974). Representative magazine articles are Rufus Jarman, "Truman's Political Quarterback," *Saturday Evening Post*, Mar. 2, 1946; and Fred Rodell, "Robert E. Hannegan," *Am. Mercury*, Aug. 1946. See also *St. Louis Post-Dispatch*, Oct. 6, 7, 1949; *N.Y. Times*, Oct. 7, 1949; *St. Louis Globe-Democrat*, Oct. 7, 1949; *Washington Post*, Oct. 7, 1949; *Kansas City*

Star, Oct. 7, 1949. Other sources are *Cong. Directory*, 80th Cong., 1st Sess. (1947), p. 346, *Who Was Who in America*, II (1950); *Biog. Directory of the Am. Cong.: 1774–1961* (1961); *Cong. Record*; and *Annual Report of the Postmaster General*, 1946. Assistance of Roy T. King, Mary Mewes, and William Pettus of St. Louis gratefully acknowledged. Personal recollection.]

IRVING DILLIARD

HANSEN, NIELS EBBESEN (Jan. 4, 1866-Oct. 5, 1950), horticulturist and plant explorer, was born on a farm near Ribe, Denmark, the youngest of three children and only son of Andreas Hansen and Bodil (Midtgaard) Hansen. His father, a mural decorator and altar painter, immigrated to the United States in 1873. After living for three years in New York and New Jersey, he settled his family in Des Moines, Iowa, where he found work in the decoration of the new state capitol building.

Niels Hansen showed an early interest in nature and took long walks in the woods collecting natural history specimens. At Iowa State College at Ames, he was influenced by Joseph L. Budd, head of the department of horticulture, and after receiving the B.S. degree in 1887, he spent several years working for commercial nurseries in Iowa. In 1891 he returned to Iowa State College as assistant professor of horticulture, and in 1895 received an M.S. degree. That same year he was named professor of horticulture at the South Dakota State College in Brookings and a staff member of the Agricultural Experiment Station there, positions that he retained until his retirement in 1937.

Hansen was responsible for the introduction and development of new varieties of grains, forage crops, and fruits in the Western prairies and Great Plains of the United States. Much of his work involved a search for fodder plants that could withstand the cold, dry climate of this region. Early in his career he established the principle that hardiness could not be bred into plants by selection alone, but rather through hybridizing (cross-breeding) with existing cold-resistant strains. Beginning in 1894 he made several trips to northern Europe and Asia seeking suitable plants. On one such trip in 1897, made at the request of Secretary of Agriculture James Wilson, who had known him at Iowa State College, Hansen discovered the bacterial-wilt-resistant, blue-flowered Turkestan alfalfa, suitable for a cold, northern climate. On later trips, undertaken for the Department of Agriculture or for the state of South Dakota, he collected the yellow-flowered alfalfa, which grew even farther north, and discovered a natural hybrid of the blue and yellow varieties. He also brought back seeds and plants of many other types, including crested wheat grass, which became a major forage crop on the northern American plans. He also brought with him the Siberian fat-rumped sheep.

Hansen carried on experiments in hybridization and selection at his horticultural plant at Brookings, which included one of the world's first greenhouses for fruit breeding. Here he originated Hansen hybrid plums and improved many varieties of such fruits as apples, pears, grapes, and melons for growth in the prairies and plains. Hansen's worldwide reputation led the Lenin Academy of Agricultural Sciences to invite him in 1934 to the Soviet Union to advise on agriculture and horticulture.

During his long and productive life, Hansen received many honors and awards, including the George Robert White Gold Medal "for eminent service to horticulture" from the Massachusetts Horticultural Society (1917) and the Marshall P. Wilder Silver Medal "for new fruits" from the American Pomological Society (1929). Hansen was married twice: on Nov. 16, 1898, to Emma Elise Pammel, sister of Louis H. Pammel, head of the botany department at Iowa State College; and after her death in 1904, to her sister, Dora Sophie Pammel, on Aug. 27, 1907. He had two children by his first marriage, Eva Pammel and Carl Andreas. Hansen died in Brookings of chronic myocarditis at the age of eighty-four and was buried in that city's Greenwood Cemetery.

Broad in his interests, patient and philosophic by temperament, Hansen believed that man could succeed by working with nature. Although he once modestly referred to the horticulturist Luther Burbank as the "master of us all," he had himself enriched the prairies and the plains with new varieties of alfalfa, wheat, millet, and fruits.

[Niels E. Hansen, "Fifty Years Work as Agricultural Explorer and Plant Breeder," Iowa State Horticultural Soc., *Trans.*, 79 (1944): 28–49; Mrs. H. J. (Rose) Taylor, *To Plant the Prairies and the Plains: The Life and Work of Niels Ebbesen Hansen* (1941); and three articles by William P. Kirkwood: "The Romantic Story of a Scientist," *World's Work*, Apr. 1908; "The North Pole of Alfalfa," *Outlook*, May 28, 1910; and "Hansen, America's First Plant Explorer," *Rev. of Reviews*, Oct. 1913. See also *Who Was Who in America*, III (1960). Death record from S. Dak. State Dept. of Health.]

WAYNE D. RASMUSSEN

HANSEN, WILLIAM WEBSTER (May 27, 1909-May 23, 1949), physicist, was born in Fresno, Calif., the older of two surviving sons of William George Hansen and Laura Louise (Gillogly) Hansen. His paternal grandfather had immigrated to the United States from Denmark after the German annexation of Schleswig-Holstein. His mother, the daughter of a non-Mormon missionary to Utah, encouraged her children to be independent. Hansen as a boy showed a precocious interest in electrical devices and a special aptitude for mathematics. From his father, a hardware merchant, he acquired a familiarity with and love for machine tools. He completed his high school course in two years, at the age of fourteen, but stayed on for an additional year at the Fresno Technical High School before entering Stanford University in 1925. Except for one year at Fresno State College, he remained at Stanford, where he began studying electrical engineering but shifted to physics; he received the A.B. degree in 1929 and the Ph.D. in January 1933. Appointed a National Research Fellow, he spent eighteen months studying at the Massachusetts Institute of Technology and at the University of Michigan, and returned to Stanford in 1934 as assistant professor of physics. He was made associate professor in 1937 and professor in 1942.

At M.I.T., Hansen became interested in mathematical methods of analyzing emission and absorption of atomic radiation. At the time of his return to Stanford, plans were being made for research on atomic nuclei by bombarding them with particles accelerated to energies of about a million volts. Hansen proposed to attain this voltage by means of electromagnetic resonance at very high radio frequencies, using a cavity resonator that he conceived for the purpose. The "rhumbatron," as he called it, was to consist of a hollow space bounded with copper walls. Just as Hansen was well started on the design of such an accelerator, his close friend Russell H. Varian saw the possibility of using two rhumbatrons as resonators in a new device—which he called the "klystron"—to generate radio frequency energy at very short wavelengths. Hansen's interest was challenged, and he quickly designed and built a tube that demonstrated Varian's ideas to be highly practical. For the first time (1937), a substantial amount of "radio" energy became available at wavelengths of the order of 10 cm. One immediate practical application of the klystron was the use of reflected radio waves to locate aircraft, the system now called radar. A group headed by Hansen and Varian, with support from the Sperry Gyroscope Company, vigorously pursued this concept at Stanford until early in 1941, when they moved east to Sperry's plant on Long Island.

With the increasing probability of American entry into World War II, the klystron research took on new importance. Promptly after his arrival in the East, Hansen was invited to M.I.T.'s Radiation Laboratory, which had been formed the previous fall to exploit the possibilities of microwave radar. From then until the end of the war he commuted between Cambridge and Long Island almost every week, while simultaneously carrying full-time responsibility in Sperry's microwave radar program. At the Radiation Laboratory, Hansen performed a unique role. The laboratory's leadership consisted of a group of brilliant physicists and engineers who had worked on cyclotrons and X-rays, but who in general knew little or nothing about microwaves. In a very real sense, Hansen became their tutor, at weekly lectures and informal conferences. In the summer of 1943 he also spent some weeks at the University of California as consultant on aspects of atomic energy problems for the Manhattan Project.

After the war ended, Hansen returned to Stanford as director of the microwave laboratory being established there. In the first months he took time out from his own research to help in an investigation being carried out by Felix Bloch, a Stanford colleague. Hansen devised the instrumentation Bloch used in discovering the existence of nuclear magnetic resonance and made many valuable suggestions that contributed to the successful demonstration of the method of nuclear induction in 1946. Bloch subsequently (1952) received the Nobel Prize for work in this field.

Hansen realized that the microwave technology he had helped create could be used to make an electron accelerator far superior to anything he had dreamed of a decade earlier, when he invented the cavity resonator. A relatively short accelerator built in the spring of 1947 proved the soundness of his underlying ideas and was soon followed by a longer section. Late in 1948 the Office of Naval Research agreed to finance the construction of a linear accelerator 220 feet in length, designed to produce about 750 million electron volts. In early 1949 Stanford started construction of a building to house this machine, with its associated shops, laboratories, and offices. Finished after Hansen's death, it became the model for Stanford's later 10,000-foot, $110 million linear electron accelerator.

Hansen possessed a remarkable spectrum of talents well exemplified in his twenty-nine published papers. He had great originality, and his inventiveness always had a practical quality.

He was an excellent theoretical physicist but, unlike most theoreticians, was also skilled with apparatus, had extraordinary knowledge of shop processes, and superb ability as a design engineer. His pioneering contributions to the technology of microwave electronics resulted from this unusual combination of qualities. He was also an excellent classroom teacher, whose lucid and stimulating lectures excited even the Ph.D. physicists at M.I.T.'s Radiation Laboratory. The value of his work was recognized by the award of the Morris N. Liebmann Prize of the Institute of Radio Engineers in 1945 and by his election to the National Academy of Sciences in 1949.

On Oct. 18, 1938, Hansen married Betsy Ann Ross, the younger daughter of Prof. Perley A. Ross of Stanford, with whom he had collaborated in X-ray studies as a graduate student. Their only child, a son born in 1947, died six weeks after birth. Since his youth Hansen had suffered periods of illness, the result of bronchiectasis and fibrosis of the lungs. The disease was progressive, and he died of a heart attack at his home on the Stanford campus a few days before his fortieth birthday. His ashes were scattered from an airplane over the Golden Gate area.

[A more extensive biography of Hansen by Felix Bloch, with a complete bibliography, appears in Nat. Acad. Sci., *Biog. Memoirs*, XXVII (1952). There is relevant material in the archives of Stanford Univ., especially a brochure, *The Uncommon Man* (1951).]
FREDERICK E. TERMAN

HARBORD, JAMES GUTHRIE (Mar. 21, 1866-Aug. 20, 1947), army officer and corporation executive, was born near Bloomington, Ill., the oldest of three children and only son of George Washington Harbord, a farmer of modest means, and Effie Critton (Gault) Harbord. His father's forebears had come from Virginia and had lived in Kentucky before settling in Illinois in 1823. The Gaults had migrated from Maryland to Pennsylvania and then to Ohio, where his mother was born. During James's boyhood his family moved to Pettis County, Mo., and in 1878 to Lyon County, Kans.

An avid reader, James was encouraged by his parents to continue his education beyond the local schools. He entered Kansas State Agricultural College, where he learned telegraphy and typewriting. He had planned to be a telegrapher, but the military training he took as an undergraduate made him decide to become a professional soldier. Upon graduating with the B.S. degree in 1886, he tried unsuccessfully to obtain an appointment to the United States Military Academy at West Point, and in January 1889, after an interim of teaching, he enlisted as a private in the 4th Infantry Regiment.

Harbord's skill as a typist, a rarity in the army at that time, brought him rapid promotion through the ranks to quartermaster sergeant. In August 1891, after passing the required examinations, he became a second lieutenant in the 5th Cavalry Regiment. He graduated from the Infantry and Cavalry School in 1895 and earned the M.S. degree at his alma mater the same year. During the Spanish-American War, Harbord served as a major in the 2nd Volunteer Cavalry ("Torrey's Terrors"), a cowboy regiment organized in Wyoming, which did not see combat. Meanwhile, promotion in the regular army to first lieutenant (July 1898) brought about his transfer to the 10th Cavalry, where in the fall of 1899 he met and formed a friendship with a senior first lieutenant, John J. Pershing.

After a round of administrative assignments in Cuba and in Washington, D.C., Harbord, by this time a captain, went to the Philippines in 1902. The next year he became an assistant chief of the Philippine Constabulary with the equivalent rank of a colonel. This position provided an unusual opportunity to exercise authority and responsibility far beyond that of a cavalry troop commander. He was most successful in his first mission of increasing the constabulary by recruiting the warlike Moros and remained on this duty until January 1914, when he was assigned to the 1st Cavalry. Promoted to major in December 1914, he entered the Army War College; he was a student there when the United States entered World War I in April 1917. It is a significant indication of his reputation that Theodore Roosevelt selected hm as one of the three brigade commanders for his projected volunteer division.

On May 15, 1917, Harbord was named chief of staff to General Pershing, the newly designated commander of the American Expeditionary Forces. Over the next twelve months he helped his commander pick and organize a staff, then plan and supervise the development of the A.E.F. Decisive, frank, and completely loyal to his chief, he performed an invaluable service. Two brief but important combat assignments followed. In May 1918 Harbord—a brigadier general since the previous August—took over command of the Marine brigade in the 2nd Division and led it during the victorious battle of Belleau Wood, one of the most famous battles in Marine Corps history. In July, newly promoted to major general, he was given command of the entire 2nd Division, which played a crucial role in the counteroffensive at Soissons. Harbord won high praise from both subordinates and superiors. Nevertheless, a detailed study of his role in the battles of Belleau Wood and Soissons shows that, at times, he did not have his units under close control, and that the success of his commands resulted from the raw courage of the men rather than from his use of maneuver and firepower.

Pershing, fearing a War Department plan to take the logistical forces from him, asked his favorite officer on July 28 to take command of the Services of Supply. This move not only kept the S.O.S. within Pershing's sphere but also placed a more dynamic leader in charge. For the remainder of the war, Harbord spent much time checking on his network of installations and attempting to speed up the distribution of supplies. When the war ended, he had under his command 386,000 soldiers, in addition to thousands of civilian laborers and German prisoners. He deserved and received much of the credit for the effective operation of the S.O.S. in the last three and a half months of the war.

Harbord left the S.O.S. in 1919 and, after a brief second tour as Pershing's chief of staff, became chief of the American Military Mission to Armenia, sent to study the possibility of establishing an American mandate under League of Nations auspices. His report was favorable, but Congress rejected the plan. Upon his return to the United States, Harbord again commanded the 2nd Division. When Pershing became the army's chief of staff in July 1921, he named Harbord his executive assistant. During the next eighteen months Harbord carried much of the administrative load of the Office of Chief of Staff and helped reorganize the General Staff on the same pattern as the A.E.F. General Staff. Harbord retired from the army in December 1922 and in January began a new career as president of the Radio Corporation of America. At this time R.C.A. was involved in many disputes with other corporations as well as with the federal government. Since Owen D. Young, the chairman of the board, already had a most effective general manager in the young David Sarnoff, he wanted a president who could act not as an operating head but as a highly respected spokesman. Harbord, a distinguished soldier with broad administrative experience ideally suited the role. He served as president until 1930 and then as chairman of the board until his retirement in 1947. During these years he held membership on the boards of several other corporations and played some part in pol-

itics. He was president of the National Republican Club in 1931, and his name was placed in nomination for vice-president at the 1932 convention. Throughout the remainder of his life he continued to be a close friend and advisor of Pershing. He was promoted on the retired list to lieutenant general in 1942.

A large man, red-haired but bald by middle age, Harbord was impressive in appearance and forceful in personality. He was an Episcopalian in religion. He married twice: to Emma Yeatman Ovenshine on Jan. 21, 1899, and, after her death in 1937, to Mrs. Anne (Lee) Brown, a widow, on Dec. 31, 1938. He had no children. Harbord died of a coronary thrombosis at his home in Rye, N.Y., and was buried in Arlington National Cemetery. Although he received numerous decorations, honorary degrees, and other awards, his highest accolade was Pershing's appraisal in his efficiency report for 1922—"the ablest officer I know."

[Harbord's papers are in the Lib. of Cong. and the Nat. Arch.; his correspondence with Pershing is in the latter's papers, also in the Lib. of Cong. An index file at the Kans. State Univ. Arch. is of particular value on his early life, as is Christian Gauss, "The Education of General Harbord," *Saturday Evening Post*, July 30, 1932. For his service in World War I, see his own books, *Leaves from a War Diary* (1925) and *The American Army in France, 1917–1919* (1936); John J. Pershing, *My Experiences in the World War*, 2 vols. (1931); John Hagood, *The Services of Supply* (1927); Frederick Palmer, *Our Greatest Battle* (1919); and Edward M. Coffman, *The War to End All Wars* (1968). For his business career, see Erik Barnouw, *A Tower in Babel* (1966); Gleason L. Archer, *Hist. of Radio to 1926* (1938) and *Big Business and Radio* (1939); and Eugene Lyons, *David Sarnoff* (1966). Biographical information is in the appropriate volumes of the *Official Army Register* and *Who's Who in America*, and in *Nat. Cyc. Am. Biog.*, XXXVI, 493–494.]

EDWARD M. COFFMAN

HARE, JAMES H. (Oct. 3, 1856–June 24, 1946), news photographer and war correspondent, was born in London, England, one of two children and the only son of George Hare and Margaret (Ball) Hare. A poor student, he briefly attended St. John College, London (1870–1871), and then went to work for his father, a manufacturer of handmade cameras that were highly regarded for their quality. When the elder Hare, a Yorkshire Quaker, stubbornly resisted new developments in photography, for example, the transition from wet to dry plates, James joined another firm. At the same time he began taking pictures as a hobby. He soon made his hobby a profession by furnishing photographs of public gatherings and sporting events for use in drawing illustrations for periodicals, in the days before the adoption of the halftone process. He was a pioneer in taking snapshots, a technique he hit upon by accident. The heavy cameras of the period were mounted on tripods, but Hare, in trying to photograph a balloon ascension, lifted his camera as the craft moved upward, pointed it over the heads of the crowd, and snapped the shutter. He obtained a clear picture and thereafter was a devotee of the hand-held camera.

Hare was quick to adopt American photographic innovations—the dry plate, cut film made by spreading emulsion on celluloid, the film pack on a paper-covered roll, and small cameras—and in 1889, he went to the United States to accept a position as technical advisor to a New York City firm. He quit after a year to produce his own handmade, quality cameras. Only moderately successful, he then became a photographer for the *Illustrated American* and a free-lance contributor to newspapers. Early in February 1898 the offices of the *Illustrated American* were destroyed by fire and Hare was out of a job. Soon afterward, when the battleship *Maine* blew up in Havana harbor, Hare rushed to the office of *Collier's Weekly* and persuaded Robert J. Collier to send him to Cuba to take pictures.

The Spanish-American War launched Hare on a new career in which he gained fame as one of the most daring and resourceful of battlefield news photographers. With the *New York World's* famous correspondent Sylvester Scovel, Hare made a trip into the interior of Cuba to interview the rebel leader Gen. Máximo Gómez. He later covered events leading up to the siege of Santiago and photographed the battles of San Juan Hill and El Caney. In the early years of the twentieth century, *Collier's* sent Hare to report revolutions in Haiti, Venezuela, Panama, and Mexico, the Russo-Japanese War (1904-1905), and the Balkan wars of 1912-1913. So often was he on hand to photograph revolution and strife that the noted correspondent Richard Harding Davis said of him, "No war is official until Jimmy Hare is there to cover it."

When *Collier's* refused to send Hare to Europe in 1914 to report World War I, he went to work for *Leslie's Weekly*. Over the next several years he traveled throughout Europe covering the war in France, Italy, Greece, and Russia. A small, wiry man, Hare withstood the rigors of warfare better than more robust men. No risk was too great when he was seeking a picture of battle action. In the Russo-Japanese War, told by officials to stay clear of the fighting, he replied: "I might as well set my camera up on Broadway and point it toward Man-

churia as to be five miles from a fight." Although he knew no foreign language, he was understood almost everywhere because of his mastery of pantomime and his sublime impudence.

Hare was also a pioneer in aerial photography. Intrigued by aviation since his days in England, he ascended in a balloon in 1906 and took the first aerial photographs of New York City. Two years later he snapped the first picture of an airplane in flight, that of Orville and Wilbur Wright at Kitty Hawk, N.C. In 1914, when United States Marines occupied Veracruz, Mexico, Hare flew in the two rattletrap aircraft used for reconnaissance, and during World War I in France he was taken aloft by a French fighter pilot. After the war, in 1919, he covered the first transatlantic flight made by the United States Navy from Newfoundland.

Leslie's Weekly ceased publication in 1922, and Hare, now sixty-five, thereafter devoted himself to giving lectures, making guest appearances on radio, and contributing occasional articles and photographs to magazines. On Aug. 2, 1879, he married a Yorkshire girl, Ellen Crapper. They had five children: George James, Harry, Margaret Ellen, Dorothy, and Ruth Kate. In religion he was an Episcopalian. Hare died of heart disease at the home of a daughter in Teaneck, N.J., and was buried in Mount Olivet Cemetery, Brooklyn. He taught a whole generation the art of news photography.

[The chief source is Cecil Carnes, *Jimmy Hare, News Photographer* (1940), which draws on letters, clippings, and Hare's diaries. See also R. W. Ritchie in *American Mag.*, Feb. 1913; *News-Week*, Oct. 7, 1933, p. 17; *Business Week*, Dec. 14, 1940, p. 67; Amy Porter, "The Week's Work," *Collier's*, Sept. 29, 1945; *Who Was Who in America*, II (1950); obituaries in *N.Y. Times* and *N.Y. Herald Tribune*, June 25, 1946. Death record from N.J. State Dept. of Health.]

CHARLES H. BROWN

HARRIS, PAUL PERCY (Apr. 19, 1868-Jan 27, 1947), founder of Rotary International, was born in Racine, Wis., one of six children of George Howard Harris and Cornelia (Bryan) Harris. At the age of three, his father's drugstore business having failed, Paul was sent to live with his paternal grandparents, Howard and Pamela (Rustin) Harris, in Wallingford, Vt. His subsequent contact with his parents, whom he later characterized as improvident and flighty, was confined to brief family reunions. After a boyhood that he sentimentalized in his autobiographical writings, Harris attended high school in Rutland, Vt., and then transferred to Black River Academy in Ludlow, from which he was expelled for his pranks. Concluding his secondary education at Vermont Academy, a military school in Saxton's River, he enrolled at the University of Vermont in Burlington in 1885, only to be expelled once again for disruptive behavior, midway through his sophomore year. He next attended Princeton College for a year (1887-1888), and in 1889, after working briefly for a marble company in West Rutland, he heeded his grandmother's advice to go West. Settling first in Iowa, he read law in Des Moines and in 1891 received a law degree from the state university at Iowa City. In 1919, by vote of the Vermont trustees, he was retroactively awarded the Ph.B. degree as of 1899.

A wanderer for the next five years, Harris worked as a reporter in San Francisco, a business-college teacher in Los Angeles, an actor in Denver, and a fruit picker in Louisiana. He made two trips to England, first as stockboy on a cattleboat and then as salesman for a marble and granite company. Settling in Chicago in 1896, be began to practice law, but with only modest success. "Desperately lonely" (*Road to Rotary*, p. 230) and still unmarried, he lived in thirty different residences over the next fourteen years and attended various churches but still made few friends. On Feb. 23, 1905, he brought together three other young businessmen of his acquaintance into a club for friendship and civic activity. The name "Rotary" was chosen because the weekly luncheons (then and later the heart of the movement) were initially held in rotation at the various members' places of business. Harris founded a second club in San Francisco in 1908, and by 1910, when the National Association of Rotary Clubs was organized in Chicago, sixteen local clubs had been established. Founded at a moment when an emergent urban middle class was discovering itself and coming together for a variety of civic and social purposes, Rotary caught on at once. Many of the early members, like Harris himself, were young business or professional men of rural or small-town origins who had few ties or associations in the cities where they were trying to make their fortunes. For them, Rotary provided a circle of friends, business contacts, and a sense of meaningful involvement with a large-scale movement that espoused a variety of worthy philanthropic and civic causes.

From the first, Paul Harris threw himself into the new movement. He served as first president of the national association, and in 1912, when deteriorating health forced his resignation, he became president emeritus. Although still technically head of his Chicago law firm (which after various permutations became Harris, Reinhardt and Bebb), he in fact spent almost all his time addressing clubs around the world, writing regularly for *The Rotarian,* and serving as Rotary's principal public spokesman. With Chesley R. Perry, secretary of Rotary International from 1910 to 1942, he tirelessly preached the dual gospel of sociability and service that gave the movement such appeal. Indeed, with his own unsettled and peripatetic background, gregariousness, civic idealism, nondogmatic religiosity, and Republican politics, Harris was in many respects the quintessential Rotarian. He lived to see the movement grow to some quarter of a million members in more than seventy countries and was the recipient of many awards, honors, and citations, including the Silver Buffalo of the Boy Scouts of America (1934) and the French Legion of Honor (1937). Paul Harris died in Chicago in 1947, at seventy-eight, after several years of failing health. He was survived by Jean Thomson Harris, a native of Edinburgh, whom he married in Chicago on July 2, 1910.

[The most useful sources are Harris's own autobiographical writings, *The Founder of Rotary* (1928) and *My Road to Rotary* (1948), and the files of *The Rotarian,* esp. Mar. 1947, May 1947, and Feb. 1948. See also *N.Y. Times,* Jan. 28, 1947 (obituary); *Who Was Who in Am.,* II (1950); *Who's Who in Chicago and Illinois* (1945); and, for the larger social context, Charles F. Marden, *Rotary and Its Brothers* (1935); Charles W. Ferguson, *Fifty Million Brothers: A Panorama of American Lodges and Clubs* (1937); Arthur M. Schlesinger, Sr., "Biography of a Nation of Joiners," in *Paths to the Present* (1949); and Robert H. Wiebe, *The Search for Order, 1877–1920* (1967). Information from University of Vermont archives.]

PAUL BOYER

HART, WILLIAM SURREY (Dec. 6, 1862?-June 23, 1946), motion picture actor and director, perhaps the most important early Western movie star, was born in Newburgh, N.Y., the second son and second of eight children of British parents, Nicolas Hart and Rose (McCauley) Hart. His father had emigrated from Liverpool; his mother, born in northern Ireland, had grown up in Newburgh. Nicolas Hart, a miller who specialized in locating sites for grain mills and supervising their construction, headed west with his family soon after William's birth; never staying long in one place, he moved from town to town across the plains states, from Illinois to the Dakotas. Illness twice took William's mother back to Newburgh for protracted periods, but William spent much time with his father in the West. He lived alongside the Sioux in Minnesota and the Dakotas, learning their language, and in the frontier towns of Kansas during the days of the cattle drives. In his later life and work he tried to re-create the authentic flavor of experience in what he called "the unbroken West."

Hart's father returned to the East in the middle 1870's, and the reunited family moved to West Farms in the suburbs of New York and then into the city. William had his only formal schooling at West Farms, attending public school after a brief interval at a private school in Morrisania. In the city he worked as a messenger boy for hotels, as a drugstore cashier, and for a longer period as a postal clerk. He was drawn to athletic events and showed considerable skill at distance running and walking races, becoming a member of the Manhattan Athletic Club's track team. After working his way to England, he won several international races there.

As a young man in New York, Hart developed an ambition to become an actor. He was by then over six feet tall, lean and rugged-looking, with the high cheekbones and stark features that were to become more prominent with age and even then seemed to justify his self-image as a "white Indian boy." On a second trip to England he began to study acting, and he continued his training on his return to New York. In the fall of 1888 he found a place in a touring company headed by Daniel E. Bandmann. By coincidence, he made his stage debut in Newburgh; the company opened in New York City in January.

Thus began a phase of Hart's career that was to last a quarter-century, until 1914. Becoming a journeyman actor in the last years of the American theater before competition from the movies, he barnstormed from coast to coast, rehearsed without pay, bought his own wardrobe, and played one-night stands of melodrama and Shakespeare. In 1897 he made his first tour with star billing in *The Man in the Iron Mask,* and two years later he played Messala in the New York production of *Ben Hur,* in which he drove a chariot across the stage. Hart's acting fortunes took a downward turn in 1903 and 1904, and he was forced to support himself by working for a private detective agency. But the following year he was engaged to play Cash Hawkins in Edwin Milton Royle's Western melodrama *The Squaw Man,* and thereafter he united his passion for the West with his career. He became the quintessential cowboy of the American stage, playing Broadway and touring in such Westerns as *The Virginian, The Bar-*

rier (1910), and *The Trail of the Lonesome Pine* (1912).

"While playing in Cleveland," Hart wrote in his autobiography, "I attended a picture show. I saw a Western picture. It was awful!" So Hart describes the moment he determined to leave the stage and enter motion picture work. He saw at once, so he recalled, that his skills as an actor and his knowledge of the West gave him the perfect qualifications for success in Western movies. On a theatrical tour in California he learned that an old friend, Thomas H. Ince, was in charge of production for the New York Motion Picture Company in Santa Monica. Though Ince was not particularly encouraging, Hart persevered, and began movie work in the summer of 1914. After playing villains in two short films, he starred that year in a five-reel feature, *The Bargain,* which made an immediate hit with audiences. In his early fifties, though disguising his age by as much as fifteen years, Hart became a famous cowboy star in a screen career that was to last a dozen years.

His success was built on several attributes of his work as actor and as director of his own Westerns—the authenticity of costumes, settings, and techniques; the quality of his acting, a fusion of intensity and restraint that gave him a commanding presence on the screen; and, perhaps most important, the popular formula he followed in his movie stories of realistic action combined with sentimental morality. His own characterizations were at the heart of this skillful combination. Typically he played a "good badman," an outlaw or outsider whose instincts are good despite his record or reputation, and who invariably performs a brave and honest act to ensure a happy ending. In the early 1920's, however, the formula began to lose its appeal, in part because of changing audience tastes, in part because Hart's effort to play heroes half his age became more and more an anomaly.

As with D. W. Griffith and other early filmmakers, Hart's creative work was frequently complicated and sometimes undermined by complex financial dealings. Ince took advantage of Hart's ignorance by signing him to a contract in 1914 at $125 a week when comparable actors at the same studio were earning $2,000 and more weekly. In 1915, along with Ince, Hart moved to Triangle Pictures, and two years later he shifted again to Adolph Zukor's Artcraft Productions. In the 1920's he formed his own company, William S. Hart Productions, and signed with Zukor's Famous Players for distribution. But Zukor soon demanded he make

films under studio supervision because of the
declining box office appeal of his independent
films, and Hart severed relations. He made his
last film, *Tumbleweeds,* in 1925, capping his
career with a spectacular sequence depicting the
Oklahoma land rush. But despite good reviews
and large audiences for its New York opening,
the distributor, United Artists, took little interest in the film, and Hart lost money on it.

Hart nevertheless became wealthy from his
movie work. He owned a large estate in West
Hollywood and an eight-acre ranch in Newhall,
north of Los Angeles, which he stocked with
cattle and filled with authentic Western artifacts
and memorabilia. At his death he willed his
Hollywood estate to Los Angeles for use as a
park and his ranch to Los Angeles County as a
public park and museum.

Hollywood legend has it that Hart fell in
love with and proposed to many of his leading
ladies. His one marriage, to Winifred Westover,
who played opposite him in *John Petticoats,*
lasted only briefly. They were married Dec. 7,
1921, and separated May 10, 1922; Mrs. Hart
obtained a divorce on Feb. 11, 1927, on grounds
of desertion. They had one child, William S.
Hart, Jr. For most of his adult life Hart lived
with his sister Mary, who died in 1943. Three
years later Hart died in California Lutheran
Hospital, Los Angeles, of acute pyelonephritis.
After Episcopal funeral services—the denomination to which he belonged throughout his life—
he was buried in Greenwood Cemetery, Brooklyn, N.Y. He left most of his estate for public
and private charitable purposes.

[Hart's autobiography, *My Life East and West*
(1929), remains the most complete account of his life
and career. The only substantial treatment of his
motion picture work is George N. Fenin and William
K. Everson, *The Western: From Silents to Cinerama,*
pp. 74–107 (1962); the book is dedicated to Hart.
The former contains many photographs, the latter
many film stills. See also George Mitchell, "William S.
Hart," *Films in Rev.,* Apr. 1955. Though Hart in
later years gave his birth year as anywhere from
1870 to 1876, his death record has the year as 1864;
internal evidence in his autobiography, as well as
hospital records at his death, suggests 1862 as the
correct date. Hart wrote several books of Western
stories, some in collaboration with his sister Mary.
An extensive collection of material pertaining to Hart
(1,150 pieces), gathered by Gatewood W. Dunstan, is
in the Lib. of Cong. Newspaper reports of Hart's
death and court actions pertaining to his will are at
the library of the Acad. of Motion Picture Arts and
Sciences, Los Angeles. Several Hart Westerns in 16
mm. prints are circulated by the Film Dept., Museum
of Modern Art, N.Y. City.]

ROBERT SKLAR

HATCHER, ORIE LATHAM (Dec. 10,
1868-Apr. 1, 1946), pioneer in vocational guidance, was born in Petersburg, Va., the first

of three daughters of Rev. William Eldridge
and Oranie Virginia (Snead) Hatcher. The
family later moved to Richmond, where Latham
was, at fifteen, the youngest graduate of the
Richmond Female Institute. She then became
one of the very first women from Virginia
to venture to a northern college. At Vassar
she developed a consuming interest in Renaissance and sixteenth-century literature. This passion survived years of teaching at Miss Belle
Peers's School in Kentucky and months of
labor at the Richmond Female Seminary, where
she helped expand the curriculum, and eventually brought her to the University of Chicago
(1903-1904) for graduate work. At Chicago
she developed close ties with a group of graduate students, two women and four men, whom
she remembered, the men especially, as "all
my colleagues and friends." She never married,
and she seems never to have grown personally
close to any man in her circle of professional
associates.

Hatcher's brilliant work at Chicago led to
a teaching appointment at Bryn Mawr in 1904.
In 1910 she became the first chairman of
the department of comparative literature, a post
she held until 1915.

Gradually, however, it became clear that Bryn
Mawr could not hold her. No member of her
family and no close associate could ever fully
explain Hatcher's decision in 1914 to leave
Bryn Mawr. Certainly her return to the South
was prompted by no failure of scholarly zeal
and initially by no conversion to the cause
of the downtrodden. A trip abroad in the
summer of 1914 was devoted to research on
Italian Renaissance poetry and to the beginnings of a volume of translations that was
permanently interrupted by World War I. Yet
the work she undertook on her return to
Richmond was focused not on her own scholarly
achievements, but on the pursuit of higher education by talented young women. Through her
Virginia Association of Colleges and Schools
for Girls, she sought to standardize the requirements in Virginia junior colleges and to secure
for their outstanding graduates admission to
the major women's colleges of the Northeast.

Hatcher and her colleagues had at this stage
no interest in precollegiate work or vocational
education, although she did allow, in 1919,
that "a sound full academic education" seemed
"the best possible foundation for any vocation
or profession." Women might certainly hold
responsible positions outside the home; she
could hardly deny to others what she had
chosen for herself. But, as with her standards

for the higher education of talented secondary school graduates, her career models were of the northeastern variety. With this change in position, she renamed her organization the Virginia Bureau of Vocations for Women and advocated, besides better education for prospective businesswomen, the establishment of vocational counseling services in southern women's colleges and surveys of vocations for women. Preparing women for managerial positions was the goal. Those incapable of filling such positions got short shrift. The problems of high schools and students who would not receive advanced training were not then her concern.

The early 1920's, however, saw both the expansion of Hatcher's efforts and a radical change in the outlook of her Virginia organization. Its name was changed again, to the Southern Woman's Educational Alliance. The headquarters were in Richmond and she opened a branch in New York City. By 1925, she had changed her view of her region's real needs. No longer would the emphasis be on sending talented women to northern schools; now, she sought funds "to use in the rural sections of Georgia, Virginia and North Carolina."

One of the most lasting of alliance contributions was a series of studies, begun in the 1920's and continuing through the depression years, which documents conditions in the rural South and the problems of rural youth seeking work in southern cities. Out of these studies, Hatcher hoped, would come new techniques for providing "rural girls individual help" and for aiding "the capable, ambitious rural girl."

During the depression the alliance moved toward a deeper concern for and service to a broader constituency. By 1932, Hatcher was proposing measures for "emergency guidance": recreation and guidance centers for mountain girls and boys, shop-trucks to provide instruction and shop training in schools with limited budgets and scanty equipment, county vocational schools, and symposia and traveling seminars to assist mountain missions in setting up schools more appropriate to the region. Noting the current work of missions in the Appalachian south, Hatcher lamented that "such schools tend to overstress college education and professional occupations. Adequate courses for practically minded boys and girls of average intelligence are urgently needed" (*Some Forms of Emergency Guidance,* Apr. 25, 1932, Papers of the Alliance for the Guidance of Rural Youth).

This change in direction was formalized during the early 1930's by the creation of a "rural section" of the Southern Woman's Educational Alliance and finally by a change of name in 1937 to the Alliance for the Guidance of Rural Youth. Throughout the decade, Hatcher constantly sought funds and publicity for her various rural projects.

The expansion of alliance activities in the 1930's brought the organization into open conflict with both the educational establishment and local school authorities. Boys were brought within the purview of alliance programs when local school officials insisted; but the problems with the theorists were less easily resolved.

A conflict emerged over the nature of guidance and its scope and function in the schools. Staff members of Teachers College, Columbia University, particularly, complained that Hatcher and her associates had inappropriately expanded the functions of guidance, by offering in its name a broad range of social services and counseling.

Among alliance projects in the 1930's, the one that attracted most attention was in Breathitt County, Ky., where a broadly acclaimed demonstration school had been created. Eleanor Roosevelt made a much-publicized visit to the school. The real contribution of the alliance was not in the creation of the school, but in the strengthening of the local county council, and in encouraging local citizens to take an active part in school affairs. Still, weaknesses remained, and even Hatcher's vigorous urging failed to produce enough local efforts to win Federal Emergency Relief Administration funds. The Breathitt County demonstration did, however, focus fleeting national attention on Appalachia; it provided a locus for the training of teachers in summer institutes; it offered a laboratory from which the alliance could gather facts for future efforts. Hatcher regarded it as perhaps the most important of her accomplishments.

Hatcher's efforts won both national publicity for the alliance and an increasing role in national committees and conferences for herself. She served on the National Advertising Council on Radio in Education, on the executive board of the National Council of Women (1932-1935), on the National Occupational Conference (1933-1939), and on the board of trustees of the National Vocational Guidance Association (1933-1937). In 1934, she was a consultant to the Youth Conference of the Department of the Interior, and, from 1936 to 1942, technical director of the Pine Mountain Guidance Institute, in Harlan, Ky.

Not until the late 1930's was the alliance able to shift its attention and resources to a problem that had haunted Hatcher for nearly a decade. As opportunities in the rural areas contracted, rural youth left the farms and migrated North and East, arriving in the cities penniless and without the skills needed to fill even the few jobs available. Homeless and bewildered, they added to the mass of unemployed in the cities; lacking skills for survival in an urban environment, they posed special problems for welfare workers and social agencies. In 1938 the alliance set up Youth Migration Institutes in New York, Washington, Richmond, and Durham, N.C. These institutes provided a haven and gave practical advice to farm youngsters coming to the cities for work.

Hatcher's work was diverted by World War II and by the need to fit young people for jobs suddenly vacated by older citizens fighting overseas. Continuing to seek national support for her programs, Hatcher spent more and more time in Washington. From teas at the White House to luncheon meetings of workers in the field to the more formal White House Conference on Children in a Democracy (1940-1944), she found herself, well into her seventies, still the most active and prominent leader of her movement. When she suffered a cerebral hemorrhage, in late March 1946, she was just beginning to coordinate the efforts of agencies serving handicapped youth in rural areas.

Hatcher had, indeed, so dominated her movement that her death, on Apr. 1, 1946, left her followers without the direction and the leadership they needed to continue the work. She had trained no one to succeed her. Funeral services were held in the apartment-office she had maintained and burial was in Richmond's Hollywood Cemetery.

[Papers of the Alliance for the Guidance of Rural Youth are located at Duke Univ.; there are approximately 23,000 items, many of them letters from Hatcher to professional associates and friends. In the picture files at Duke are two photographs of Hatcher dating from the late nineteenth and early twentieth centuries. The best photograph readily available, which depicts her in her mature years, appears in the *Richmond Times–Dispatch*, Apr. 2, 1946, accompanying an obituary article. A second obituary appeared in the *Times–Dispatch*, Apr. 3, 1946; see also *Who Was Who in Am.*, II (1950). Hatcher's own publications are a valuable source of information about her work, and together with the manuscripts remain indispensable unless a full biography appears. In addition to her doctoral dissertation, she published in the field of Renaissance literature *A Book for Shakespeare Plays and Pageants* (1916). Her other publications include *Occupations for Women; a Study*

Made for the Southern Woman's Educational Alliance (1927); *Rural Girls in the City for Work* (1930); *A Mountain School; a Study Made by the Southern Woman's Educational Alliance* (1930); and *Guiding Rural Boys and Girls: Flexible Guidance for Use by Rural Schools and Related Agencies* (1930). The last and a revised edition published in 1943 with Ruth May Strang (*Child Development and Guidance in Rural Schools*) were perhaps the most significant of Hatcher's works.]

ELIZABETH S. NATHANS

HECHT, SELIG (Feb. 8, 1892-Sept. 18, 1947), physiologist, biophysicist, was born in the village of Glogow, then a part of Austrian Poland, the eldest of five children (four of them boys) of Mandel Hecht and Mary (Mresse) Hecht. In 1898 the family emigrated to the Lower East Side of New York City, where the elder Hecht became a foreman in the men's clothing industry. Selig attended local public and Hebrew schools and at home was taught Hebrew by his father, a man of strong scholarly interests. To help pay his way through high school and college he worked as a bookkeeper in a woolen business. At the College of the City of New York he concentrated at first in mathematics, but a course in zoology turned his interest to that field. He received the B.S. degree in 1913, having spent the previous summer on a fellowship at the U. S. Bureau of Fisheries station at Beaufort, N.C. After graduation he worked briefly as a chemist in an industrial laboratory and then (1913-1914) as a pharmacologist with the Department of Agriculture in Washington. In 1915 he entered the graduate school at Harvard, where, working under the zoologist George H. Parker, he received the Ph.D. in 1917 with a thesis on the physiology of the marine organism *Ascidia atra* Lesueur. On June 3, 1917, Hecht married Cecilia Huebschman, whom he had met as an undergraduate. They had one daughter, Maressa.

After a summer at the Scripps Oceanographic Institute at La Jolla, Calif., Hecht moved to Omaha, Nebr., as assistant professor of physiology at the medical school of Creighton University, a post he held until 1921. Here he had neither time nor facilities for research, but he was able to spend his summers working at the Marine Biological Laboratory at Woods Hole, Mass., where acquaintance with Jacques Loeb exercised a profound influence on his scientific development. With Loeb as sponsor, Hecht received a National Research Council fellowship in biology (1921-1924), followed by one from the General Education Board (1924-1926). During this period he carried out research with the photochemist E. C. C. Baly in Liverpool;

with Lawrence J. Henderson at Harvard; at the zoological station in Naples; and with the physiologist Joseph Barcroft at Cambridge University. In 1926, after five years without an academic post, Hecht was appointed associate professor and in 1928 professor of biophysics at Columbia University, where he remained for the rest of his life. In the biophysics laboratory that he organized there, he and his students investigated a variety of problems relating to visual functions, particularly in man, including dark adaptation, pattern vision, brightness discrimination, and color vision.

Hecht had an indelible effect on the development of the scientific understanding of photoreception. He brought into this field for the first time the clear concept that visual responses take place through physical and chemical processes amenable to quantitative study. He pointed out that all photoreception must begin with the absorption of light by a visual pigment (S) in the retina; that this pigment must be transformed by light to products (P); and that the economy of the system demanded that P revert to S, so establishing a steady state in the light permitting vision to go on, and the regeneration of S from P in darkness as the basis of dark adaptation. This simple paradigm served as model for a lifetime of experimentation.

Hecht's fundamental notion was that accurate measurements of visual responses in organisms ranging from clams to man should become explicable in terms of such a model. With his students, he provided an enormous body of exemplary measurements of visual functions, in the hope that whenever some aspect of visual physiology had been measured in his laboratory, the work would be so complete that it would never have to be repeated. Researchers in vision still refer to those measurements as among the most reliable and detailed that we possess. Another great contribution from his laboratory was the study of the minimum amount of light necessary to stimulate vision. His findings pointed to the fundamental conclusion that a dark-adapted rod in the human eye can be excited by absorbing one quantum of light—one photon—presumably by a single molecule of visual pigment. This concept of the ultimate limit of visual sensitivity has dominated much later thinking on the mechanisms of visual excitation.

During World War II Hecht carried out research for the armed forces, particularly on problems of night vision. He received the Frederick Ives Medal of the Optical Society of America in 1941 and was elected to the National Academy of Sciences in 1944. His concern with the effort to abolish the military uses of atomic energy led him to become an active member of the Emergency Committee of Atomic Scientists, and to produce an excellent book for the layman, *Explaining the Atom* (1947).

Hecht pursued his relaxations as seriously as his science. He understood music as do few nonprofessional musicians and was a talented painter in watercolors. He died at his home in New York City at the age of fifty-five, of a coronary thrombosis. After cremation at the Ferncliffe Crematory, his ashes were scattered.

[Obituaries in *Jour. of General Physiology*, Sept. 20, 1948 (by George Wald), *Am. Jour. of Psychology*, Jan. 1948 (by C. H. Graham), *Science*, Jan. 30, 1948, *Nature*, May 1, 1948, and *N.Y. Times*, Sept. 19, 1947; *Who Was Who in America*, II (1950); information from Mrs. Hecht.]

GEORGE WALD

HENDRICK, BURTON JESSE (Dec. 8, 1870–Mar. 23, 1949), journalist, biographer, and historian, was born in New Haven, Conn., the fourth son and fifth of six children of Charles Buddington Hendrick and Mary Elizabeth (Johnson) Hendrick. The families of both parents had long resided in the New Haven area. The father, a watchmaker and inventor, was descended from Hendrik Hendrickson, who had come from the Netherlands to New Amsterdam in 1650 and had moved soon after 1664 to Connecticut. Encouraged by an older sister who was a librarian, Burton Hendrick early showed an interest in literature and a talent for writing. He attended New Haven's Hillhouse High School, where he edited the literary magazine, but had to defer college until he had earned the tuition by working at various clerking jobs. He entered Yale when he was nearly twenty-one and quickly distinguished himself as a writer, becoming editor of both the *Banner* and the *Courant* and financial editor of the *Yale Literary Magazine*. He graduated with the B.A. degree in 1895.

Hendrick's initial ambition was to become a literary scholar, and it was to finance further study that he entered newspaper work. In 1896, after brief reportorial assignments, he became editor of the *New Haven Morning News* and at the same time began graduate work in English at Yale under the direction of Henry A. Beers. On Dec. 29 of that year he married Bertha Jane Ives, the daughter of a New Haven manufacturer and a graduate of Mount Holyoke College. They had two sons, Ives and Hobart Johnson. To help finance his second year of graduate study, Hendrick accepted an assignment as the ghost-writer of *Dragons and*

Cherry Blossoms (1896), an account of travels in Japan by Alice Parmelee Morris.

In 1897 he received the M.A. degree from Yale, and a few months later the *Morning News* ceased publication. Hendrick, unable to obtain an academic position, accepted a job in 1899 as staff reporter on the New York *Evening Post.* Here, under the tutelage first of E. L. Godkin and later of Horace White, he learned well the skills of accurate and detailed reporting that would give distinction to his later work. An article he submitted to *McClure's Magazine* caught the attention of the publisher, S. S. McClure, who in 1905 asked Hendrick to join the staff at the then lavish salary of $100 a week.

Hendrick entered a distinguished company of writers, including such investigative reporters as Lincoln Steffens, Ida Tarbell, and Ray Stannard Baker, who were making *McClure's* a national pulpit for progressivism. Although a series of articles that he wrote in 1906 on the scandals revealed by legislative investigation of the New York life insurance industry was as valuable to the cause of reform as any other exposé published by the magazine, Hendrick never regarded himself as a muckraker in the same category as Steffens and Tarbell, and his articles were generally less imprecatory. When Steffens and others left *McClure's* in 1906 to take over the *American Magazine,* Hendrick declined to join them.

He remained with *McClure's* until 1913, when he became associate editor and chief editorial writer of *World's Work,* then edited by Arthur Page, son of the founder and former editor Walter Hines Page, who had just been appointed ambassador to Great Britain. Hendrick found the more leisurely, less sensational tone of *World's Work* more congenial to his temperament than the frenzied editorial offices of *McClure's.* For two decades he faithfully reported on the American political scene during one of its most lively eras, but he remained curiously apolitical, a detached commentator on, rather than a participant in, progressive reform. Although he strongly supported the antimonopoly philosophy inherent in Woodrow Wilson's New Freedom (including its application to organized labor), Charles Evans Hughes, whom he had first met as the chief government counsel in the life insurance investigations, was the only national political figure to win his unqualified support.

Hendrick is perhaps best known as a biographer and popular historian. After ghostwriting the autobiography (1919) of Ambassador Henry Morgenthau, he published his first book under his own name, *The Age of Big Business* (1919), a volume in the Yale Chronicles of America series. During the 1920's he won three Pulitzer Prizes: for *The Victory at Sea* (1920), the wartime memoirs of Adm. William S. Sims, on which Hendrick "collaborated"; for *The Life and Letters of Walter Hines Page* (3 vols., 1922-1925), on Page's wartime ambassadorship; and for *The Training of an American* (1928), on Page's earlier years. Hendrick resigned from *World's Work* in 1927 to devote all his time to writing biography and history. With a large subsidy from Louise (Whitfield) Carnegie, widow of Andrew Carnegie, he spent five years in researching and writing *The Life of Andrew Carnegie* (1932). There followed *The Lees of Virginia* (1935); *Bulwark of the Republic* (1937), a "biography" of the Constitution; *Statesmen of the Lost Cause* (1939), on the leaders of the Confederacy; and *Lincoln's War Cabinet* (1946).

All of these works, carefully researched and marked by a felicity of style that gave them wide popularity, showed Hendrick's early journalistic training; they were accurate and detailed, but lacked sharp, critical evaluation. His subjects all emerged as heroes. Hendrick nonetheless won recognition, even within the historical profession. He served on the Pulitzer Prize jury in history from 1930 to 1938, and on the jury for biography from 1940 until his death. He was elected in 1923 to the National Institute of Arts and Letters and was its secretary from 1926 to 1932.

During the last several years of his life, Hendrick and his wife were separated, by mutual consent, and he took up permanent residence in the Yale Club of New York. He was engaged in writing a biography of Louise Carnegie when he died in New York City of a coronary occlusion. He was buried in Evergreen Cemetery, New Haven, Conn.

[The most useful source is Hendrick's memoir in the Oral History Collect., Columbia Univ. For his career at *McClure's*, see Peter Lyon, *Success Story: The Life and Times of S. S. McClure* (1963), and Harold S. Wilson, *McClure's Mag. and the Muckrakers* (1970). Other sources: Yale Univ., *Obituary Record of Graduates,* 1948-1949; Stanley J. Kunitz and Howard Haycraft, eds., *Twentieth Century Authors* (1942); *N.Y. Times* obituary, Mar. 25, 1949; interview with Dr. Ives Hendrick of Boston.]

JOSEPH FRAZIER WALL

HERNE, CHRYSTAL KATHARINE (June 17, 1882-Sept. 19, 1950), actress, was born in the Ashmont section of Dorchester, Mass., a town since annexed by Boston. She was the second of four children—three daughters followed by a son—of James A. Herne and Katharine (Corcoran) Herne, both well-known actors and both of Irish descent. For several years after their marriage, the couple trouped across the country together, and when Herne began his career as a playwright, he wrote almost all of the female leads for his wife. The success of his melodrama *Hearts of Oak* made possible the comfortable suburban home in Ashmont where Chrystal spent her first nine years, until the family moved to New York City.

Chrystal's formal education ended before she reached high school, but her home life was intellectually stimulating to an unusual degree. Her parents were avid readers of the best authors of the period—William Dean Howells, Henry James, Tolstoy, and Thomas Hardy, among others. Hamlin Garland, then a drama critic in Boston, was a frequent visitor and introduced the Hernes to the dramas of the European realists Henrik Ibsen, Gerhart Hauptmann, and Hermann Sudermann. It was during these years that Chrystal was drawn to the works of George Bernard Shaw; she later starred in many of his plays.

In 1891 Chrystal and her sister Julie distributed placards in Boston announcing their father's new play, *Margaret Fleming*, the first example of Ibsenesque realism on the American stage. The writing of the play and its production greatly excited her parents, and their more than usual attention to the play stimulated her interest. Listening to her mother rehearse the part of Margaret, she early learned the importance of an actor's "reading" of a line—how the wrong emphasis could be as fatal as a false note by a singer.

In 1899 she first acted in her father's plays *The Reverend Griffith Davenport* and *Sag Harbor*. She profited greatly from his direction, learning the value of good diction and the art of expressing emotion through suggestion, keeping gestures and facial expressions to a minimum.

Her exceptional training, combined with her beauty and grace, attracted the attention of producers. In 1902, a year after her father died, she played Gertrude in E. H. Sothern's production of *Hamlet,* and in 1903, the part of Huguette in *If I Were King.* She later appeared with Nat Goodwin in *A Midsummer Night's Dream.* Her first engagement as a leading lady came in November 1903, in Clyde Fitch's *Major André.*

Her intellectual depth and sophistication made her the inevitable choice of Arnold Daly to play leading roles in a series of Shaw's plays that he introduced to the American public in 1905-1906: *Candida, You Never Can Tell, John Bull's Other Island,* and the then-sensational *Mrs. Warren's Profession.* Critics attributed much of the success of Daly's financially hazardous venture to the ability of his leading lady to project Shaw's intellectually daring women.

Almost every season thereafter she played a leading part in a prominent play, among them Vera Ravendal in Israel Zangwill's *The Melting Pot* (1908), Mrs. Clayton in Augustus Thomas' *As a Man Thinks* (1911), and Lady Grayston in Somerset Maugham's *Our Betters* (1917). She won the acclaim of critics and public alike in George Kelly's *Craig's Wife,* which was awarded the Pulitzer Prize for 1925. But Kelly's work lacked the breadth, depth, and wit of Shaw, and the tragedy of Chrystal Herne's career was that her great talent was wasted during her later years on inferior plays. Her last appearance was in the role of Beatrice Crandall in *A Room in Red and White* (1936).

In Los Angeles, on Aug. 31, 1914, she married Harold Stanley Pollard, chief editoral writer for the *New York Evening World,* and spent much of her later years at their country home in Harvard, Mass. They had no children. She was stricken with cancer and died at the Massachusetts General Hospital in Boston.

[The major biographical sources are the Herne Papers at the Univ. of Maine, Orono; Herbert J. Edwards and Julie A. Herne, *James A. Herne: The Rise of Realism in the Am. Drama* (1964); Hamlin Garland, "On the Road with James A. Herne," *Century,* Aug. 1914; John Parker, *Who's Who in the Theatre* (10th ed., 1947); clippings in Harvard Theatre Collect.; and obituaries in the *N.Y. Times* and *Boston Herald,* Sept. 20, 1950. Photographs tracing her career are in Daniel Blum, *A Pictorial Hist. of the Am. Theatre* (1950).]

HERBERT J. EDWARDS

HILL, ERNEST ROWLAND (Jan. 29, 1872-Aug. 25, 1948), electrical engineer, known as E. Rowland Hill, was born in Pompton, N.J., one of at least three children of Benjamin Rowland Hill, a wheelwright, and Hetty Maria (Van Duyne) Hill. Both parents were of English colonial stock. Hill was educated at Pratt Institute in Brooklyn, N.Y., and at Cornell University, where he graduated in 1893 with the degrees of mechanical engineer and electrical engineer. He then joined the Westinghouse Electric and Manufacturing Company, entering the general shop and engineering training course, which involved the mechanical and electrical inspection of machinery manufactured by the company. In 1895 he became a special assistant to George Westinghouse and was placed in charge of the installation and initial operation of all of Westinghouse's heavy railway and multiple-unit train equipment.

Hill went to London in 1901 as engineer-in-chief of the British Westinghouse Electric and Manufacturing Company; in that position he directed all of the company's engineering work, with particular attention to railway electrification. In London he came in close contact with George Gibbs, with whom he formed a lifelong personal and professional association. Hill returned to the United States in 1906 and for the next five years served as Gibbs's chief assistant in the construction and electrification of Pennsylvania Station in New York City and its related complex of tracks and tunnels. In 1911 the two engineers formed a partnership, which in 1923 was incorporated as Gibbs & Hill.

The firm's primary work during its first quarter century was the electrification of steam railways. Gibbs & Hill were in charge of the electrification of sixty-three miles of the Norfolk and Western Railway (1915) and of 134 miles of the Virginian Railway (1925), both coal-carrying roads with difficult grades. In each case electrification permitted higher speeds and more flexible and efficient operations; it also permitted the Virginian to postpone expensive double-tracking of a portion of its line. Gibbs & Hill helped modify the electrical equipment of the New York, New Haven and Hartford Railroad and electrified the Chicago suburban trackage of the Illinois Central. The largest and most complex electrification job was that of the Pennsylvania Railroad. The process began in New York in 1910 with tracks between Manhattan Transfer and the Sunnyside, L.I., coach yards. It continued in 1915 with the Broad Street Station and suburban service in Philadelphia. And it was completed between 1928 and 1938 with main-line service between New York, Washington, and Harrisburg. The railroad invested some $150 million to electrify 2,200 miles of track along 670 miles of its route.

In later years, particularly after Gibbs's death in 1940, the firm broadened its activities and undertook a variety of consulting, design, and construction assignments for industries, public utilities, rapid transit systems, and government bodies both in the United States and abroad. Hill managed virtually all Gibbs & Hill activities until shortly before his death; Gibbs, the senior partner, served mainly as a contact with clients and directed engineering on special prob-

lems. A demanding administrator, Hill was noted for his "unswerving adherence to the ethics of the profession" and for an "unusual aptitude for discarding quickly any outmoded design or engineering concept, in favor of more advanced, but proven, techniques." He was an "old school" administrator, enforcing discipline and demanding "a full day's work for a full day's pay" (Sloan, p. 22).

Hill married Grace Gibson Crider of Pittsburgh, Pa., on June 1, 1904. They had one child, Jean Swan, who married Ernest Clayton Johnson, Hill's successor as president of Gibbs & Hill. Unlike his senior partner, George Gibbs, who had been described as "a man of the world," Hill was inclined to be introspective and reserved. He was nevertheless active in community affairs in East Orange, N.J., his longtime residence; he was also a prohibitionist and an active Presbyterian layman. He died of heart disease at the Orange (N.J.) Memorial Hospital and was buried in Union Dale Cemetery, Pittsburgh. Hill's work, like that of many engineers, was essentially anonymous, and it is difficult to appraise his contributions relative to those of his associates. His contemporaries regarded him as a pioneer in railway electrification and as an engineer of the highest quality.

[David B. Sloan, George Gibbs, M.E., D.Eng. (1861–1940), E. Rowland Hill, M.E., E.E. (1872–1948), Pioneers in Railroad Electrification (Newcomen Soc. pamphlet, 1957); Nat. Cyc. Am. Biog., XXXVII, 160; memoir in Am. Soc. of Mechanical Engineers, Trans., 1949; Who Was Who in America, II (1950); obituary in N.Y. Times, Aug. 26, 1948; death record from N.J. State Dept. of Health. The progress of many of Gibbs & Hill's projects can be followed in trade journals such as Railway Age.]
KENDALL BIRR

HILL, GEORGE WASHINGTON (Oct. 22, 1884-Sept. 13, 1946), tobacco executive, was born in Philadelphia, Pa., the only son among the three children of Percival Smith and Cassie Rowland (Milnes) Hill. His mother was the daughter of a Philadelphia coal merchant and his father, the son of a Philadelphia cotton and woolen goods jobber. George was named for his paternal grandfather, who became president of the American Life Insurance Company and a national bank in Philadelphia. When George was six, his father sold his carpet business to John Wanamaker and entered the tobacco business as sales manager for the Blackwell Durham Tobacco Company. Percival Hill expanded Blackwell's sales, bought a partnership in the company, and then sold the firm to James P. Duke's American Tobacco Company in about

1898. He became one of Duke's executives and moved his family to New York City, where George graduated from Horace Mann School in 1902. After two years at Williams College young Hill married Lucie Langhorne Cobb and took a job with the American Tobacco Company in its factory and leaf market operations in North Carolina. They had two children, Mary Gertrude and George W., Jr. This marriage ended in divorce in 1920.

In 1907 Percival and George Hill purchased the tobacco firm of Butler and Butler. As head of the company George took over merchandising its principal product, Pall Mall cigarettes, and boosted sales to first place among higher-priced Turkish brands. Promoting tobacco, particularly cigarettes, through advertising became the young Hill's consuming concern. In the wake of reorganizing the American Tobacco trust, 1911-1912, Duke named Percival Hill its president, and George became vice-president and sales manager of the cigarette division. He proved to be an effective executive, providing the company with an efficient, flexible merchandising organization, including reorganizing the division's sales and distribution system and developing a proficiency in advertising promotion.

Prior to World War I, the demand for machine-made cigarettes was limited to local markets with brands of single kinds of tobacco not selling well in more than one market. Then, in 1913, R. J. Reynolds launched Camel, a nationally advertised blended cigarette. American Tobacco, preoccupied with its established products, initially ignored this. However George Hill began to realize the importance of concentrating on a particular product and succeeded in convincing his father that they too should develop a competitor for Camels, then uncontested in the national market. In 1917 they introduced on a national scale their own Lucky Strike. The younger Hill personally supervised every facet of its promotion from the design of its packaging to the slogan "It's toasted." His bold, vigorous, and sometimes controversial campaigns, coupled with an expanded war and postwar demand for cigarettes, boosted sales of Lucky Strikes continually. One of the more effective, controversial campaigns, known as "Reach for a Lucky instead of a sweet," implied the healthfulness of smoking as opposed to obesity. Hill also sponsored personalities such as Walter Winchell on nationwide radio. In 1927 he appealed to potential women customers, using testimonials as inducements.

When Percival Hill died in December 1925

his son replaced him as president of the American Tobacco Company, but George's energy and interest continued to focus on advertising Luckies. In 1930 he briefly achieved his goal of supplanting Camels with Luckies as the nation's leading cigarette seller. The magnitude of his advertising budget was unique, the first to expend $20 million a year for a single product. Hill was also regarded as a corporate genius in the early 1930's because his company consistently made money during the depression when most firms operated with deficits. As a result he was one of the nation's highest paid executives, averaging nearly half a million dollars a year in salary and bonuses over his tenure as American Tobacco's president. But Hill was not an innovator as much as a successful exploiter of the proven. Advertising as the key to tobacco sales was first used by James Duke. The idea of concentrating on one brand in a national market belonged to Reynolds. Moreover, Hill only reluctantly used radio as a medium. His basic assumption behind his campaigns, appealing to animal rather than aesthetic senses, drew heavily from patent medicine promotion. But advertising as the primary thrust of business competition did represent another stage in the evolution of American business practices. Unlike Duke, who built the American Tobacco trust in an attempt to bring order out of competitive chaos, Hill succeeded at market penetration within the confines of oligopolistic control and the threat of government restrictions. Hill, as a product of this new generation of corporate executives, proved especially skillful in this altered environment.

In his private life Hill avoided public exposure. Most of his energy was focused on promoting his tobacco products, and he drew his friends from among those who shared his zeal. His approach to people was easy and direct, and he acted on informed instinct. He was uninterested in civic affairs; fishing and dancing constituted his only outside diversions. In 1922 Hill married Aquinas M. Heller, who died in 1925. They had two children, Percival Smith and Mary. On July 8, 1935 he married Mary Barnes, his secretary, in a civil ceremony at Caxton Hall registry office in London. They had no children. Until 1942 they lived at his country estate in Irvington, N.Y., where tobacco plants and a bronze statue of the Bull Durham bull adorned the formal landscaping. Hill died of a heart attack at his private fishing camp near Matapedia, Quebec, and was buried in Sleepy Hollow Cemetery, North Tarrytown, N.Y.

[As a guide to Hill's thinking about advertising, see his privately published 1917 manual, *Selling Principles of Demonstration*; H. L. Stephen, "How Hill Advertises Is at Last Revealed," *Printers' Ink*, Nov. 17, 1938, pp. 11–14, 89–103; and Edward H. Pearson, "Gone—One of Advertising's Great Teachers," *Printers' Ink*, Oct. 4, 1946, p. 156. Useful were George H. Allen, "He Makes America Sit Up and Buy," *Forbes*, Jan. 1, 1933, pp. 12–14; and "American Tobacco Company, Which Is More than Two-Thirds Lucky Strike: A Story of Advertising," *Fortune*, Dec. 1936, pp. 96–102, 154, 156, 158, 160; and the obituary, *N.Y. Times*, Sept. 14, 1946. For a fictional, best-selling characterization of Hill see Frederic Wakeman, *The Hucksters* (1946). Particularly helpful was a biobibliography compiled by Robert L. Volz, Univ. of Wisconsin Lib. School.]

WILLIAM O. WAGNON, JR.

HILL, GRACE LIVINGSTON (Apr. 16, 1865-Feb. 23, 1947), author of popular fiction, was born in Wellsville, N.Y., the only daughter of Charles Montgomery Livingston and Marcia (Macdonald) Livingston. An older brother had died in infancy. Her father, a stern Presbyterian minister descended from the Schuyler family, was one of seven clergymen in the immediate family. Her name, Grace, was chosen for its theological meaning. She was educated at home and in public schools in New York, New Jersey, and Ohio; she also studied at the Cincinnati Art School and at Elmira College, Elmira, N.Y.

From childhood, literary inclinations were dominant. Her mother, a writer of children's stories, was a helpful critic; her aunt, Isabella Macdonald Alden, who wrote juvenile religious literature under the pen name Pansy, was Grace's inspiration and idol. At the age of twenty-two, Hill published her first book, *A Chautauqua Idyl* (1887), previously printed as a magazine serial. Based on her regular attendance at chautauquas in the company of older members of her family, the story described a meadow of flowers that organized its own chautauqua. Her allegory enjoyed the prestige of a preface by Edward Everett Hale.

On Dec. 8, 1892, she married Rev. Thomas Guthrie Franklin Hill of Pittsburgh, in Hyattsville, Md. They had two daughters, Margaret Livingston and Ruth Glover. After seven years of marriage, her husband's death in 1899 from appendicitis forced her to write to support herself and her small daughters. At her comfortable stone home in Swarthmore, Pa., she settled into a prodigious career, soon averaging two novels a year. Surrounded by books and magazines in her second-floor study, she wrote tirelessly amid interruptions and disturbances. Early in her career, she made a highly satisfactory publishing agreement with the Philadelphia firm of J. B. Lippincott Co. This mutually helpful association continued throughout most of her career.

Although she claimed to have no set formula, Hill "used the same ingredients over and over again, mixing romance, adventure, conflict and religion" (*N.Y. Times*, Feb. 24, 1947). Her innocuous, simplistic stories were essentially pleasant tracts filled with strict morality and religion. Having withstood social temptations and evil influences, her heroines were rewarded with happiness and fulfillment. Her stories all closed in accordance with her homily "I feel that there is enough sadness and sorrow in the world, so I try to end all my books as beautifully as possible" (*Wilson Lib. Bull.*, April 1947). Her biographer, Jean Karr, characterized her novels as "more than a pleasant pastime for thousands of people; they were object lessons in clean living and thinking" (Karr, p. 5). Most of her novels were issued under her own name, but she also used the pen name Marcia Macdonald and for a brief period she wrote as Grace Livingston Hill Lutz, after having married Flavius Josephus Lutz in Swarthmore, Pa., on Oct. 31, 1904. The marriage ended in a separation.

Although her novels sold nearly four million copies during her lifetime and were translated into many languages, none of them ever reached the annual best-seller lists. Typical titles included *The Angel of His Presence* (1902), *The Story of a Whim* (1902), *The Girl from Montana* (1907), *Marcia Schuyler* (1908), *Dawn of the Morning* (1910), *The Best Man* (1914), *Cloudy Jewel* (1920), *The Tryst* (1921), *The Prodigal Girl* (1929), *Happiness Hill* (1932), *Matched Pearls* (1933), *Rainbow Cottage* (1934), *April Gold* (1936), *Stranger Within the Gates* (1939), *Crimson Mountain* (1942), and *A Girl to Come Home To* (1945). Her two most popular novels were *The Witness* (1917) and *The Enchanted Barn* (1918). She also wrote a religious column, "The Christian Endeavor Hour," for newspapers in Philadelphia, Washington, and New York. An active supporter of the Salvation Army, she contributed to its service in World War I by collaborating with Evangeline Booth in the writing of *The War Romance of the Salvation Army* (1918).

Hill supported a Presbyterian mission Sunday school organized in an abandoned rural church near her home, in addition to lecturing before church and young people's groups. Particularly concerned with the moral development of her younger readers, she personally answered their letters seeking advice. She spoke without fee, for her royalties provided an altogether comfortable living. Her main luxury was a chauffeur-driven Lincoln. She disliked motion pictures and advised against them. Lively and energetic, with a firm voice and deep laugh, she never sought a secluded, contemplative life. In her youth she enjoyed tennis and horseback riding. She died of cancer in Swarthmore, Pa., in her eighty-second year and was buried in the family plot in the Johnstown, N.Y., cemetery. Her eightieth novel, on which she was working at the time of her death, was completed by her daughter, Ruth Munce.

[Jean Karr, *Grace Livingston Hill, Her Story and Her Writings* (1948), includes a chronological bibliography of her books; *Who Was Who in Am.*, II (1950); *Nat. Cyc. Am. Biog.*, XL; Stanley Kunitz, ed., *Twentieth Century Authors* (1942) and *First Supplement* (1955); *Notable Am. Women*, II (1971); Durward Howes, ed, *Am. Women, 1935–1936;* foreword in Isabella Macdonald Alden, *An Interrupted Night* (1929). See also *N.Y. Times*, Feb. 24, 1947, with portrait; *Publisher's Weekly*, Mar. 8, 1947; *Wilson Lib. Bull.*, Apr. 1947.]
MARY SUE DILLIARD SCHUSKY

HILL, PATTY SMITH (Mar. 27, 1868–May 25, 1946), kindergarten and nursery school educator, was born in Anchorage, near Louisville, Ky., the third of four daughters and fourth of six children of Dr. William Wallace Hill and Martha (Smith) Hill. Her father, a Princeton graduate and a Presbyterian minister, had been editor of the *Presbyterian Herald* before the Civil War, then turned to the education of young women, first as principal of the Bellewood Female Seminary in Anchorage, Ky., then as president of the Female College at Fulton, Mo. He and his wife, a well-educated Southern woman, encouraged their daughters as well as their sons to pursue careers in order to achieve economic independence and personal fulfillment.

Thus aided by her parents to seek higher education, Patty attended the Louisville Collegiate Institute and, after graduating in 1887, enrolled in the only kindergarten training class in Louisville, started that year by Anna Bryan. Upon completion of the courses, she took charge of the school's demonstration kindergarten and, with Bryan's urging, regarded it as an educational laboratory, leaving behind a strictly Froebelian approach and trying new methods and materials. Hill accompanied her mentor to a National Educational Association meeting in 1890 where they presented some of their innovative ideas and word circulated quickly about their exciting classes and pro-

vocative experiments. Three years later, after Anna Bryan's return to her home city of Chicago, Patty Hill became head of the Louisville Training School for Kindergarten and Primary Teachers, a position she held for twelve years. In the summer of 1896, she and Anna Bryan went to Clark University to study under psychologist G. Stanley Hall and pedagogist William Burnham. Her work in Louisville attracted such wide attention that, in 1905, she was invited by Dean James Earl Russell to accept a post at Teachers College, Columbia University, New York. Russell had chosen her carefully as the person to challenge Susan Blow, the conservative, aging champion of adhering strictly to the Froebelian system of kindergartening, who was then a member of the Teachers College staff.

As a popular, attractive lecturer with a dynamic personality, exciting new ideas, and the support of Dean Russell, Patty Hill quickly succeeded in spreading and implementing her progressive ideas about the kindergarten. She thought that the kindergarten, which was originated by Friedrich Froebel in Germany in the early nineteenth century, had become rigidly formalized in the United States by the beginning of the twentieth century. In the last three decades of the nineteenth century, kindergarten teachers had been fifty years ahead of their time educationally in stressing the need for beautiful rooms and school grounds, excursions, music, games, and well-educated and well-prepared teachers; by the time the kindergarten movement won both public and educational acceptance, Froebel's ideas had been formalized to excess. Hill believed that Froebel had used his materials in a natural, innovative manner in his daily contact with children and that it was time to return to a more fluid procedure in the classroom in order to search in new directions for the best activities and methods for preschool learning.

Throughout her career, Hill constantly sought the experience, help, advice, and stimulation of those in the forefront of education. For example, with the aid of Colonel Francis Parker, the head of Cook County Normal School and an early progressive educator, she worked to unify the kindergarten and primary curricula, hoping to avoid wasteful gaps, but vociferously fighting the growing tendency to inflict upon kindergarten children such disciplines of the primary curriculum as beginning reading.

She fought an uphill battle to provide kindergartens with the kind of psychological and medical help stressed so heavily in her studies with Hall and Burnham. At the same time, she became involved in nursery school education, hoping that, without traditions or public school affiliation, the nursery school could provide the best of prekindergarten care to two- to four-year-olds and establish a strong foundation of mental and physical health and well-being.

She relied heavily on John Dewey's concept of socialization in education and his use of the project method. She saw how much a child could learn, for example, in the process of playing with and building things for a favorite doll. However, her realization that a more quantitative approach was valuable to educators led her to lean more toward behaviorism in the newer kindergarten program of the 1920's and 1930's. After keeping careful records of children's individual and social progress in the Teachers College laboratory kindergartens between 1915 and 1921, Hill asked her colleagues, in particular Edward Lee Thorndike, for help and criticism in evaluating the record sheets. They replied that the values were too qualitative and that they needed more "objective outcomes." This behavioristic approach to education as formulated by men like Thorndike urged educators to see the purpose of education as changed behavior, that is, to develop desirable habits and traits in children. Accordingly, Hill enlisted the aid of three to four hundred specialists in early childhood to devise a list of specific habits that children should form and the activities and subjects to develop these habits. Published in 1923, this "habit inventory" soon became the basis of many kindergarten curricula.

Hill did not abandon her humanistic approach to kindergarten education and she warned teachers against a tightly structured approach to each day's classroom work and against the effort to be too empirical, advising that "There are values that still escape our formulas" (Amidon, p. 523). She saw the need for new songs, stories, games, and materials that would maintain a child's attention without coercion from the teacher. She designed new blocks for children, so large that they could actually play inside the structures they built, and she wrote songs for young children in collaboration with her sister, Mildred Hill, including the well-known "Happy Birthday to You." Written originally in 1893 as "Good Morning to You," this song was sung without permission in the 1921 Irving Berlin and Moss Hart Broadway production As Thousands Cheer. A successful plagiarism lawsuit ensued.

Hill had a long and productive career at Teachers College, serving as the major spokesman in preschool education for several decades. Without a formal college degree she became a full professor in 1922, one of the first three women at Teacher's College to be so designated; she received the honorary degree of Litt.D. in 1929; and after retirement in 1935 she became one of the first women to be named professor emeritus from Columbia University. After 1935 she concentrated her attention on the Hilltop Community Center in New York City, which a few years earlier she had helped to organize. At the age of seventy-eight, she died of a long illness at her home in New York.

[Patty Hill discusses her early career in Louisville in "Anna E. Bryan," *Pioneers of the Kindergarten in America*, pp. 223–230 (1924); Hill and Finnie Burton, "The Work of Anna E. Bryan in Louisville, Kentucky," *Kindergarten Magazine*, 13 (1901), 436–438; and in the *Annual Reports of the Louisville Free Kindergarten Association*. Statements explaining her educational views on kindergartening can be found in such articles as: "Some Conservative and Progressive Phases of Kindergarten Education," *Nat. Soc. for the Scientific Study of Education Sixth Yearbook*, Part II (1907), 61–86; "The Future of the Kindergarten," *Teachers College Record*, 10 (1909), 29–56; "Introduction," *Teachers College Record*, 15 (1914), 1–8; "Kindergartens of Yesterday and Tomorrow," *The Kindergarten-Primary Mag.*, 29 (1916), 4–6; "The Functions of the Kindergarten," *Nat. Education Assoc. Proc.*, 64 (1926), 685–694; and "Changes in Curricula and Method in Kindergarten Education," *Childhood Education*, 2 (1925), 99–106. She presents her ideas in contrast with the strict Froebelians in *The Kindergarten*, published by the International Kindergarten Union Committee of Nineteen (1913), and she presents her views on behaviorism in introduction to Agnes Burke, et al., *A Conduct Curriculum* (1923).
Accounts of Hill's experience at Teachers College are found in Lawrence Cremin, et al., *A History of Teachers College Columbia* (1954) and in James Earl Russell, *Founding Teachers College* (New York, 1937). Beulah Amidon's lengthy interview with Miss Hill, "Forty Years in Kindergarten," *Survey Graphic*, 2 (1927), 506–509, contains several lengthy quotes from Miss Hill, shedding insight on a variety of subjects from her early home and family life through her retirement from Teachers College. A biobibliography prepared by Stefan Moses at Columbia Lib. School in 1959 lists many facts about Miss Hill's career and her publications.
The *N.Y. Times* ran several articles either by or about Patty Hill, among them, "Shy Women Teachers Who Wrote Child's Ditty . . . ," Aug. 15, 1934, referring to her lawsuit over the song "Happy Birthday to You." The *N.Y. Times* also carried an obituary on May 26, 1946, which included a portrait of Miss Hill.]
ELIZABETH D. ROSS

HILLMAN, SIDNEY (Mar. 23, 1887–July 10, 1946), labor leader, was born in Zagare, a market village in Lithuania, the second son and second of the seven children of Samuel Hillman and Judith (Paiken) Hillman. For generations the Hillman family had produced rabbis in this region of the Jewish Pale, including Sidney's grandfather, Mordecai. Samuel Hillman was a grain and flour merchant, but more given to devoutness than to enterprise. When his business dwindled, his wife, who came of a family with a flair for trade, opened a grocery shop in the front room of their house and became the primary breadwinner.

Sidney (originally Simcha) was the most studious of the Hillman sons, and he was early marked to carry on the family's rabbinical tradition. In 1901, at the age of fourteen, he went to study at the famous Hebrew seminary in Kovno. But Talmudic training did not satisfy him for long. Falling under the spell of the powerful secularizing and revolutionary forces then gripping Russian Jewry, he left the seminary and at the age of sixteen began organizing the typesetters of Kovno for the Bund, the outlawed Jewish trade union movement. Hillman was imprisoned in 1904 for participating in a labor parade, and again during the revolution of 1905 while working for the Social Democratic party. When the revolution collapsed the following year, he left Russia and, after a brief stay in England, sailed for the United States.

Hillman settled in Chicago, where he found a job as a stock clerk at the mail-order plant of Sears, Roebuck and Company. After a layoff in the spring of 1909, he went to work as an apprentice cutter at the men's clothing factory of Hart, Shaffner and Marx. At first he hoped for more education and for a professional career, but his shop experience rekindled his activist sympathies for the cause of labor. On Sept. 28, 1910, the simmering discontent at Hart, Shaffner and Marx boiled over into a spontaneous strike of female workers, spread slowly throughout the factory, and by the end of October had engulfed the entire Chicago men's clothing industry. Hillman emerged as one of the principal strike leaders, and was instrumental in persuading the Hart, Shaffner and Marx workers to accept a compromise calling for arbitration of the dispute. He was promptly elected business agent of the newly formed Local 39, United Garment Workers of America. His moderation and realism, evident throughout the strike, now made the arbitration plan work. Hillman satisfied his own followers, gained the trust of the Hart, Shaffner and Marx management, and meanwhile put the union on a solid footing. With a growing reputation as a young "statesman of labor," Hillman was called to New York City in February 1914 by the International Ladies Garment Workers Union to serve as chief clerk for its famous Protocol of Peace, the settlement that ended the garment strike of 1910-1911.

The move to New York proved fortuitous. A revolt had long been brewing in the major manufacturing centers against the old-line craft-oriented national leadership of the United Garment Workers. In 1914 a group of disaffected locals, including Hillman's Chicago unions, seceded and formed a new organization, subsequently named the Amalgamated Clothing Workers of America. Hillman, absent during the climactic months and hence above the battle and free of any suspicion of personal ambition, was the logical choice to become president of the new union. He was to hold the post until his death.

The first years were devoted to organizing the clothing workers. The industry was highly competitive, fragmented, and seasonal, and hence offered a thorny field for unionization. Since the Amalgamated, as a rival of the United Garment Workers, was regarded by the American Federation of Labor as an illegitimate dual union, it could not command the full support of organized labor. Hillman shrewdly mixed militancy and reasonable negotiation in a sustained organizing campaign, fighting a series of bloody strikes in Baltimore, Chicago, and elsewhere. World War I finished the job. Asserting his union's full support for the war and maneuvering energetically in Washington, Hillman helped bring into being a federal Board of Control and Labor Standards for Army Clothing. This regulatory board, as he had anticipated, contributed greatly to the union's wartime growth. By 1920 the Amalgamated boasted a membership of 177,000, contracts covering 85 percent of the industry, and a significant rise in labor standards, including the forty-four-hour week. On May 3, 1916, Hillman married Bessie Abramowitz, a fellow worker and labor leader at Hart, Shaffner and Marx. Although she resigned as business agent of Local 152 after their marriage, she remained active in the affairs of the Amalgamated and in the career of her husband. They had two daughters, Philoine and Selma.

With the union-building job largely completed, Hillman moved during the 1920's to transcend the narrow job consciousness of American business unionism. To the industry's employers he offered a program of active cooperation. To the members of his union he offered educational and social programs, low-cost housing, and the union's own banks. In collective bargaining, the Amalgamated pioneered in gaining unemployment insurance for its members. The New Unionism, as it became known in the 1920's, fitted the Amalgamated's immigrant membership, its adherence to industrial unionism, and its strong strain of social idealism. But Hillman refused to identify the New Unionism as the avenue to social revolution. "I have no ultimate program," he insisted in 1920. "In time of leisure . . . I indulge in dreams, but I don't permit them to become the policy of the organization" (Josephson, p. 208). With his regard for efficient administration, his frank respect for the uses of power, and his eagerness for day-to-day gains, Sidney Hillman stood closer ideologically to President Samuel Gompers of the A.F. of L. than to the Socialists in his own union. A slight, intense man, a speaker who won his audiences by clarity and logic rather than flamboyance, Hillman was completely devoted to the cause of the clothing workers. He became a revered figure within his own union and (at a time when there was little competition) the preeminent progressive unionist of the prosperity decade.

The Great Depression opened a new phase in Hillman's career. Only government action, he concluded, could solve the nation's economic problems. A champion of the National Industrial Recovery Act (1933), he served on the NRA Labor Advisory Board (1933-1935) and on the National Industrial Recovery Board that took over the NRA after the resignation of Gen. Hugh Johnson in 1934. This Washington experience had a profound impact on Hillman. With the Amalgamated Clothing Workers at last admitted to the A.F. of L. in 1933, he aligned himself with John L. Lewis and other labor progressives urging industrial unionism for the mass production industries. As he saw it, not only did government protection of labor's rights now make such unionization possible, but an enlarged movement was essential to reap the political benefits generated by the New Deal. Collaborating closely with Lewis, Hillman helped launch the Committee for Industrial Organization in 1935 and took a leading part in its brilliant organizing campaign in the mass-production fields. When conflict with the parent A.F. of L. became irreconcilable, Hillman helped establish the Congress of Industrial Organizations as a full-fledged rival, becoming vice-president. The C.I.O. drive in the textile industry, which began in 1937, fell wholly to Hillman's direction.

Hillman now entered national politics as well. In April 1936 he and Lewis established Labor's Non-Partisan League to mobilize union support for the reelection of President Franklin D. Roosevelt. Despite his hints that the league might lead to a labor party, the practical Hillman in fact committed himself to a continuing alliance with Roosevelt and the Democratic

party. (This held true even in New York state, although he and his allies found it necessary there to organize the American Labor party independent of the regular Democratic machine.) For Hillman personally, this strategy proved its merit, above all, in his successful lobbying for the passage of the Fair Labor Standards Act of 1938. Although he was overshadowed initially by John L. Lewis, Hillman's political star rose when Lewis' fell. As the erratic Lewis broke with Roosevelt, Hillman became the key labor figure in Washington. In June 1940 Roosevelt appointed Hillman the labor member of the National Defense Advisory Commission, set up to plan the production of armaments, and in December, associate director general (with William S. Knudsen) of the Office of Production Management. He worked prodigiously, if not with entire success, in handling thorny labor disputes and developing a manpower program for the defense industries, often becoming the target of union criticism by his refusal to act as labor's partisan.

Wartime reorganizations eased Hillman out of administrative power in May 1942. He left Washington ill and disappointed, and resumed his role as union president. The following year he became chairman and director of the C.I.O.'s Political Action Committee, formed to mobilize organized labor for the upcoming presidential election. The P.A.C. developed into a potent nationwide organization, and its leaders consequently carried much weight within Democratic party counsels. Although formally committed to the renomination of Vice-President Henry A. Wallace, Hillman and other P.A.C. leaders accepted Harry Truman, and hence helped assure his nomination. Hillman's influence (Roosevelt's remark regarding the selection of a running mate, "Clear it with Sidney," became a Republican rallying cry) made him a prime political target in the hot campaign that followed.

As World War II drew to a close, Hillman turned his attention to international labor affairs, and was instrumental in the formation of the World Federation of Trade Unions in 1945. As so often in the past, he played the part of conciliator, composing intractable factional and ideological differences, and succeeding—if only for a brief time—in uniting the labor movements of Communist and non-Communist nations in a single world organization. In frail health since a severe attack of pneumonia in 1937, Hillman refused to spare himself. He suffered the first of several heart attacks in April 1942. Four years later, at the age of fifty-nine, he died at his summer cottage at Point Lookout, L. I. He was buried in Westchester Hills Cemetery, Hastings, N.Y.

[Hillman's personal papers are at the national office of the Amalgamated Clothing Workers of America in New York City. His public career can be studied in the NRA and defense agency records in the Nat. Archives and in the Franklin D. Roosevelt Papers at Hyde Park, N.Y. Although he rarely wrote for publication, one important statement of his labor philosophy is in a brief essay, "Labor Attitudes," in J. B. S. Hardman, ed., *Am. Labor Dynamics* (1928). The major biography is Matthew Josephson, *Sidney Hillman: Statesman of Am. Labor* (1952), uncritical, but detailed and based on full use of the sources. George Soule, *Sidney Hillman* (1939), covers only his earlier career; it reproduces a painting of Hillman by Carlos Baca-Flor (1937) and several photographs. Among the articles on Hillman, see Charles A. Madison in the *Am. Scholar*, Autumn 1949; and Moses Rischin, "From Gompers to Hillman: Labor Goes Middle Class," *Antioch Rev.*, June 1953. There is a major obituary in the *N.Y. Times*, July 11, 1946.]

DAVID BRODY

HIRSCHBEIN, PERETZ (Nov. 7, 1880–Aug. 16, 1948), Yiddish dramatist and novelist, was born near the Russian village of Klestchel (or Kleszczele), in the province of Grodno. The youngest of seven children, he was the son of Lippe Hirschbein and Sheine (Hollander) Hirschbein. Although the father owned a water mill, the family was poor and without formal education. From an early age, Peretz absorbed the folklore and superstitions of his rural Jewish surroundings. He entered the village heder (religious school) when he was seven, a late age for those times, and made such rapid progress that his parents were encouraged to think he might become a rabbi. At twelve he was sent to various yeshivas (Talmudic schools) to continue his education. For five years he lived the hard life of a poor yeshiva student, eating at a different house each day of the week. In the process, he learned a great deal about the life of the Jews in the Russian Pale and came in contact with secular books in Yiddish. It was not long before he began to study Russian and German secretly, and, under the influence of Haskalah (the enlightenment movement) and Zionism, he discarded all notions of a rabbinic career.

In 1898 Hirschbein went to Vilna, a center of Jewish culture, where he met other Jewish writers, to whom he showed his first efforts: verses in Hebrew and some stories in Yiddish. He supported himself by giving Hebrew lessons, and teaching history to some yeshiva students. In 1904 he moved to Warsaw, where the great Jewish writers of the day lived: the Hebrew poet H. N. Bialik, Abraham Reisen, Sholem Asch, and Jacob Dineson, who en-

couraged him to write drama. *Miriam,* written in Hebrew and published in 1905 in the periodical *Ha-Zeman,* is the tragic story of a poor Jewish girl who, after having been seduced by a rich man, becomes a prostitute. Several short plays in Hebrew followed, naturalistic portrayals of life, in which the themes of poverty and helplessness prevail: *The Carcass* (1905), *Where Life Passes* (1906), and *Lonely People* (1906). (Because of their settings in dingy, dark cellars, the Hebrew writer Reuben Brainin called them "cellar dramas.")

His first drama in Yiddish, *Oif Yenner Sait Taikh* ("On the Other Side of the River," 1906), marked the beginning of a new phase in another respect as well. Hirschbein discarded naturalism in favor of symbolism, and his work showed the influence of both Maurice Maeterlinck and Leonid Andreyev. The play was translated into Russian and successfully produced in Odessa. *Die Erd* ("Earth," 1907), written during a brief stay in Berlin, expressed a dislike of city life—another recurrent theme. *Tkias Kaf* ("The Contract," 1907), written in St. Petersburg, foreshadows S. Anski's famous play *The Dybbuk.* It is the tragedy of a young girl pledged by her father to a young man who dies before releasing her from the pledge, and whose spirit prevents her from marrying another man.

In 1908, Hirschbein formed a theatrical company in Odessa, the Hirschbein Troupe, which for two years toured the Ukraine and White Russia in productions of his own plays and those of Asch, Issak Peretz, Sholom Aleichem and Jacob Gordin. The Hirschbein Troupe made a significant contribution to Yiddish theater by raising its artistic level and by attracting Russian Jewish intellectual circles to its performances. Its influence made itself felt on the establishment of the famous Vilna Yiddish Troupe and, later still, on the New York Yiddish Art Theatre.

Restlessness drove Hirschbein from city to city: Odessa, Vilna, St. Petersburg, Kiev, Vienna, Paris, London, and finally New York, where he arrived in November 1911. There, he completed in a few months *Die Puste Kretshme* ("The Haunted Inn"), the first of a series of folk dramas that evoked the rural atmosphere of his childhood. *A Farvorfen Vinkel* ("A Forsaken Corner," 1912) blended realistic and mystical elements, and was followed in the same year by the symbolic drama *Dos Kindt vun der Velt* ("A Child of the World"). Unable to get his plays produced, Hirschbein returned to Russia in 1913.

In 1914, Hirschbein went to Argentina to visit the colonies established by Baron de Hirsch and his Jewish Colonization Association. At the outbreak of World War I, he embarked for New York, by way of Brazil, where he arrived in November 1914 after an eventful voyage (the English steamer he sailed on was sunk by a German warship). He became a contributor to the newly founded daily newspaper *Der Tog,* which serialized his travel experiences, later published under the title *Fun Veite Lender* ("From Distant Lands"). In the summer of 1915, the newspaper sent him to San Francisco to cover the Panama-Pacific-International Exposition. His impressions of places and people encountered went into his book *Travels in America* (1918), in which he exhibited a sensitive understanding of the problems faced by the diverse ethnic groups of the country: Indians, Negroes, European immigrants, and Jews. During the war years, Hirschbein wrote several one-act plays: *The Prophet Elijah; Bebele; Raisins and Almonds* (all of which were published in 1915 in the periodical *Die Zukunft*). *The Blacksmith's Daughters,* a comedy, appeared in 1915 as well, and a year later he completed *Green Fields* (the first of a trilogy of plays based on the character of Levi Isaak), his best and most popular work. This tender love story in a pastoral setting was preserved in a filmed version. The two plays that completed the trilogy were *Two Towns* (1919) and *Levi Isaak* (1923). In 1916 a five-volume edition of his works was published. On a lecture tour through Western Canada in 1918, Hirschbein met, in Calgary, the Yiddish poet Esther Shumiatcher, whom he married on Dec. 11, 1918, after a brief courtship. The income he derived from his plays, the newspaper *Der Tog,* and the lectures (especially in North and South America) enabled the Hirschbeins to travel extensively.

During 1920-1923, they journeyed through Australia, New Zealand, Tahiti, and South Africa. Descriptions of this trip were serialized in *Der Tog,* and later incorporated in his book *Arum der Velt* ("Around the World," 1927). *Spirits Know Why* (1922) and *The Mouse with the Bell* (1924) were two symbolist dramas; the latter, written in free verse and set in an American steel foundry, showed expressionist influences. In 1924-1929, the Hirschbeins traveled through India (where they met Gandhi and Tagore, the Hindu poet, and lived for some time on the Tibetan border), Israel, and the Crimea (where they spent an entire year with Jews who had settled in the agri-

cultural communes there). His experiences are documented in *India* and *Eretz Israel,* both published in 1929, and in the novel *Roite Felder* ("Red Fields," 1935), a realistic treatment of life on the Jewish collective farms in the Crimea. The novel's value lay in its contribution to our understanding of the social and historical implications of the unusual experiment, rather than in its artistic merit. More successful from a literary point of view was the first volume of his memoirs, *Years of Childhood.* A moving account of the first eighteen years of his life, it was published in 1932. The trilogy *Bovel* ("Babylon"), a massive novel serialized in *Der Tog* over a number of years before its publication in 1942, traced the fortunes of a family from their arrival in the United States in 1883 to the outbreak of World War II. Hirschbein touched on nearly every aspect of the American Jewish experience as it affected the first and second generations of immigrants.

In 1940, Hirschbein, his wife, and their six-year-old son, Amos (or Omus), moved to Los Angeles. There he continued to work on his memoirs, preparing the second volume, *In the Process of Life* (1948). The book records the author's difficulties in establishing a literary career. He also began a novel of Jewish life in America, *Oif Fremde Vegen* ("Strange Roads"), which appeared in installments in *Der Tog* from 1947 to his death in 1948. He died in Los Angeles after three years of intense suffering from aminotropic lateral sclerosis and is buried in Beth Olam Cemetery in Hollywood.

Hirschbein's greatest contribution lies in his portrayal of the ordinary Jew, the *folksmentsh,* and his innate humane qualities, his *mentshlekhkait.* Valuable, too, are Hirschbein's travel books and memoirs, revealing an enormous range of interests. The fiction, though competently written, is artistically less successful. Still, the sum total of Hirschbein's work, especially his contributions to the emerging Yiddish theater, have assured him an honored place in the front ranks of Yiddish writers of the first half of the twentieth century.

[Principal English sources are the chapter on Hirschbein in Charles Madison, *Yiddish Literature: Its Scope and Major Writers* (1968) and an article by Madison, "Peretz Hirschbein," in *Poet Lore,* Spring 1927; Sol Liptzin, *The Flowering of Yiddish Literature* (1963); David S. Lifson, *The Yiddish Theatre in America* (1965). None of the English sources includes a bibliography; only a few of his plays have been translated into English, and English material on Hirschbein is sparse. The literature on Hirschbein in Yiddish is vast, but there is no systematic bibliography available. A lengthy biographical article, in Yiddish, in the *Lexicon fun der Naier Yiddisher Literatur,* vol. III, cols. 147–158 (1960), includes a substantial listing of publications by and about Hirschbein in Yiddish. A bibliography of the various editions of his plays, in Yiddish as well as in Hebrew, Russian, German, and English translations, can be found in S. Zilbercwaig's *Lexicon fun Yiddishen Theater,* I, 613–628 (1931). A volume of Hirschbein's writings, *Drames, Weltraizes, Zichroines* ("Drama, World Travels, Memoirs," Buenos Aires, 1967), which is vol. 32 in a series of *Masterworks of Yiddish Literature,* includes some critical articles on Hirschbein and a selected bibliography. This book also contains a photograph showing the author with his wife and infant son in 1938, and one of the author taken in 1940.]

ROBERT S. ROSEN

HISCOCK, FRANK HARRIS (Apr. 16, 1856-July 2, 1946), lawyer and judge, was born in Tully, N.Y., the son of Luther Harris Hiscock and Lucy (Bridgman) Hiscock, both of whom died when he was young. The Hiscock family, originally of Massachusetts, had moved to Onondaga County in New York after the American Revolution. Hiscock's father practiced law and became active in local politics, serving two terms in the state legislature and as a member of the state constitutional convention of 1867. Hiscock's uncle, with whom he lived for most of his youth, was Frank Hiscock, a lawyer prominent in the Republican party and for a time United States senator from New York. Hiscock attended Cornell University, receiving his B.A. with honors in 1875. After studying law under the preceptorship of his uncle, he was admitted to the bar in 1878 and began practice in Syracuse with Hiscock, Gifford and Doheny. A year later, on Oct. 22, 1879, he married Mary Elizabeth Barnes, the daughter of a Syracuse businessman; they had four children. For almost two decades he dabbled in Republican politics and practiced law, until Gov. Levi P. Morton appointed him a trial judge on the state supreme court in January 1896. In the fall of that year he was elected for a fourteen-year term.

Hiscock's rise within the New York judicial hierarchy was rapid. In 1901 he was elevated to the Appellate Division, Fourth Department, and five years later he was appointed an auxiliary member of the Court of Appeals, the highest state tribunal, located in Albany. In 1913, at a Republican state convention in which old-guard elements lost control, Hiscock was nominated for a full term as associate judge of the Court of Appeals. Despite the failure of bar association leaders in the state to persuade the Democrats to give him their endorsement, Hiscock was easily elected, drawing strong support from independent voters. Three years later, amid a Republican sweep of the state,

he was elected to a ten-year term as chief judge.

As the head of one of the country's most respected courts, Hiscock soon acquired a reputation for administrative efficiency and cautious progressivism. Faced at the outset with nearly 1,000 cases awaiting disposition, he speeded the processing of appeals until by the end of his tenure the court calendar was clear. In all he wrote 468 opinions, 184 as chief judge. As might have been expected from his early career on the bench, he was willing to expand the doctrine of police power to allow restraints on personal liberty not only to promote "safety, health and morals" but also to ensure "the greatest welfare of the people" by increasing "public convenience or general prosperity" (*Wulfsohn* v. *Burden,* 1925). Hiscock and his colleagues tended toward a "liberal" interpretation of remedial statutes in the direction of upholding the legislative function. In the field of torts, the Hiscock court moved gradually to establish new rules on the basis of "social utility," leaning towards the doctrine of liability without fault. He was noticeably more reluctant to defer to social needs in private than in public law, especially in commercial and banking cases, being fearful to exercise the "power of embarrassing or confusing widespread processes of commercial life" (*Laudisi* v. *American Exchange National Bank,* 1924).

As Hiscock himself explained his philosophy of law, it was difficult to classify. As chief judge he fretted over what he perceived to be "the clamor for paternalism and regulation" and "the dangers of hysteria, partisanship, radicalism, and class legislation," fomented by Samuel Gompers and Robert La Follette. Nor was he much intrigued by what he called the "rather mystic" theories being advanced within the law schools of his day. Yet, seeing law as a practical matter, he wanted to adjust it where possible to new and changing conditions and thus try "to solve the problems of life in a well-ordered, fair, and reasonable way which will secure the approval of well-informed and intelligent opinion" (see Hiscock's article, "Progressiveness of New York Law," *Cornell Law Quarterly,* 9 [1923-1924], 371-387). It was his assumption that a thorough understanding of the facts of a case allowed a court to diminish areas of controversy and sharpen the issues up for resolution. Leaving office, to be succeeded as chief judge by the more adventurous Benjamin Cardozo, he went so far as to pay tribute to the ghost of Theodore Roosevelt and assured a gathering of the New York City Bar Association that the Court of

Appeals had made "substantial progress" in bringing the law closer to "common sense and justice" (*New York Times,* Dec. 19, 1926; Jan. 9, 1927).

Returning to the private practice of law in Syracuse, which he conducted well into his eighties, Hiscock seemed to retreat from the tentatively innovative approach to jurisprudence that had characterized his service on the bench. Called on to undertake a state law survey and elected first in 1929 and then for two successsive years as president of the State Bar Association, he had little new in the way of advice for his profession. In his farewell address to the state bar, delivered in January 1932, he cautioned that criticism of delay in the courts was "much overdrawn" and made a point of belittling "doctrinaire and opinionated reformers." He also had harsh words for what he called "those selfish and foreign-minded classes and groups" who were willing to violate the Constitution to achieve "some new nostrum or some selfish and un-American benefit" (*New York Times,* Jan. 22, 1932).

Having left the bench, Hiscock resumed activity within the Republican party. In 1927 he was expected to give the keynote address at the state convention but at the last moment had to decline for medical reasons. Three years later, he was selected to be permanent chairman of the party convention and was mentioned as a possible candidate for governor. In the middle of the 1930s, he led a $60 million Onondaga County relief bond drive and waged a successful campaign against legislation to forbid private law practice by official court referees. He remained a loyal alumnus of Cornell, finally retiring as chairman of the board of trustees in 1938, after more than twenty years of service. He continued to be active in Unitarian affairs. After an uneventful final decade, he died in his home in Syracuse.

Hiscock impressed his contemporaries not by brilliant or audacious legal reasoning but by hard work and patient good sense. Modest in manner and soberly deferential to all, he joined the Court of Appeals at a time of rising popular discontent with the American judicial system. As chief judge, he encouraged his court to modify the law without giving alarm to wary spirits within the profession. What qualified him for this role, particularly, was his willingness to admit that a court might change its mind. He could not assume any group of men to be "so superhuman and wise," he once said, that their decisions might never need revision ("Progressiveness of New York Law," p. 385).

In that spirit, step by step, he played a part in modernizing early twentieth-century American law.

[See *N.Y. Times* obituary, July 3, 1946. Much of Hiscock's career may be traced in the *Times* and of course in his opinions. Also helpful is Leonard C. Crouch, "Judicial Tendencies of the Court of Appeals During the Incumbency of Chief Judge Hiscock," *Cornell Law Quarterly,* 12 (1926–1927), 137–152. See also brief personal recollections by Horace E. Whiteside and Edmund H. Lewis, *Cornell Law Quarterly,* 32 (1946–1947), 1–3, 133–136.]

STEPHEN BOTEIN

HOAGLAND, CHARLES LEE (June 6, 1907–Aug. 2, 1946), physician and biochemist, was born in Benkelman, Nebr. He did not know who his parents were, although he had some hint that his mother was of French extraction. There is no record of his early life and schooling. In 1927, while working as a busboy in a Missouri hotel, he volunteered to do some typing for a guest, Alfred L. McCawley, an influential lawyer and member of the state senate. Because of the young man's competence and winning personality, Senator McCawley offered him employment and took him into his own household; a few years later, he formally adopted him. Hoagland was thus able to obtain further education: a year at Southwest Missouri State Teachers College, three years (1928–1931) at Washington University, St. Louis, where he received the B.S. degree, and four years at the medical school of Washington University, from which he was graduated, M.D., in 1935.

Hoagland's record as a medical student was brilliant, as was his work during two additional years at Washington University as assistant in medicine. As a result, he received an appointment in 1937-1938 as assistant resident physician at the Hospital of the Rockefeller Institute for Medical Research in New York City (later the Rockefeller University). The following year he returned to Washington University Medical School as instructor in medicine and assistant in pathology; Hoagland then returned to Rockefeller Institute in 1939 as assistant in the laboratory group headed by Oswald T. Avery, working on the immunochemistry of the pneumococcus. He was transferred a year later to the laboratory of Thomas M. Rivers and Joseph S. Smadel, who were making a pioneer study of the vaccinia (cowpox) virus. Hoagland's part in this work, in which by masterly insight and ingenuity he showed that the virus is an organized biological entity, containing such complex substances as (for example) the vitamin riboflavin, was one of the earliest adequate studies of the chemical structure of an animal virus.

This success, together with Hoagland's obvious clinical skill, led to his rapid promotion (1942) to the rank of associate member of the Rockefeller Institute. Rivers, now director of the institute's hospital, supported Hoagland's desire to study certain little-understood diseases characterized by grave changes in metabolism possibly related to vitamin deficiencies or to failure of enzyme action. Choosing to study, first, progressive muscular dystrophy, Hoagland and his assistants made some progress with regard to the biochemical disturbance characteristic of the disease, but his search for its cause was interrupted when the United States entered World War II.

Volunteering for a field research unit being organized by Rivers for the navy, Hoagland was rejected because of abnormally high blood pressure. He had never complained of symptoms resulting from this condition, which must already have caused him much discomfort. He threw himself intensely, as a civilian, into a wartime undertaking of the Rockefeller Institute hospital to study and treat naval personnel suffering from infectious hepatitis. In 1944 and 1945 the navy sent about 400 patients to the institute, which provided Hoagland with facilities for hospital care and laboratory study of the disease. In 1945 he was promoted to full membership in the institute. All of the eight or nine young physicians who worked with him on this project went on, after the war, to posts as professors in other institutions or as members of the institute.

As leader of this able group Hoagland undertook to work out biochemical tests by which the extent of liver damage and the rate of repair of the liver during convalescence could be measured and to test various methods of treatment. He and his associates found, contrary to previous opinion, that patients with livers damaged by hepatitis or cirrhosis tolerate a relatively high proportion of fats in the diet, and that it is best to treat them by rest and a well-balanced general diet rather than by limiting the intake of fats.

Hoagland proved himself so obviously capable of leading a large program of medical research that his reputation began to spread beyond the Rockefeller Institute. He was offered professorships of internal medicine, physiology, and biochemistry in leading medical schools. His intelligence and charm won him personal regard and recognition in high social circles of New York, which he appreciated and sought all the more

because of his rootless childhood. Had his health not deteriorated he would almost surely have gone on to continued success in research and probably also in institutional administration. Giving himself no rest from the burden of his heavy wartime program, he developed, in June 1946, severe symptoms of malignant hypertension and became a patient in the hospital where he had cared for so many young men. After two months of painful, agitated illness, he died at the age of thirty-nine.

Hoagland did not marry, and because of the circumstances of his infancy no surviving relatives were known. He did not have time in his brief career to summarize his scientific findings in books; his numerous journal articles are listed in *Index Medicus,* 1938-1947.

[Obituaries in *N.Y. Sun,* Aug. 2, 1946, *N.Y. Times,* Aug. 3, 1946, and *Jour. Am. Medic. Assoc.,* Aug. 17, 1946; George W. Corner, *Hist. of the Rockefeller Inst. for Medical Research,* pp. 464-465, 477-480 (1964); unpublished biog. memoir by Thomas M. Rivers in minutes of the Board of Scientific Directors of the Rockefeller Inst., Jan. 1947.]

        GEORGE W. CORNER

HOAGLAND, DENNIS ROBERT (Apr. 2, 1884-Sept. 5, 1949), plant physiologist and soil chemist, was born in Golden, Colo., the son of Charles Breckenridge Hoagland and Lillian May (Burch) Hoagland. Golden, where he spent the first eight years of his life, was, in his own words, "a small town, with all the narrowness of small-town life. Something of the frontier spirit remained, however.... The foothills and mountains were near and familiar. My home was one of moderate comfort according to the standards of the time and place." (From an unpublished autobiographical sketch.)

All of his later childhood was passed in the city of Denver, where he received his primary and secondary education, graduating from East Denver High School in 1903. He then entered Stanford University, where he specialized in chemistry. In 1907 he was elected to Phi Beta Kappa and graduated with a B.A. degree.

After one semester of graduate study in chemistry at Stanford, Hoagland accepted employment as a chemist in the Laboratory of Animal Nutrition at the University of California at Berkeley and later with the Department of Agriculture in Philadelphia. In 1912 Hoagland became the first graduate student of E. V. McCollum at the University of Wisconsin, whose research in animal nutrition was later to become world-famous. Hoagland's work under McCollum resulted in several publications and a thesis for which he received an M.A. degree in 1913.

In later years, Hoagland looked back on his year with McCollum as his inspiration for a career devoted to scientific research. McCollum regarded Hoagland highly, and one would have expected Hoagland to continue in the field of animal nutrition, which was then on the eve of revolutionary advances. In 1913, however, Hoagland accepted an appointment as assistant professor of agricultural chemistry at the University of California at Berkeley and began a lifelong concentration on the field of plant and soil interrelations, in which he made notable advances and earned international renown.

Hoagland's orderly and critical mind recognized early that the complex problems of soil and plant interrelations must be studied by techniques that permitted rigid experimental control and the isolation of individual variables. To this end, he perfected the water-culture technique for growing plants without soil. Hoagland's nutrient solution is used to this day in laboratories of plant physiology throughout the world. In the late 1930's Hoagland's expert knowledge in this area did much to restore balance and rationality to debates, fueled by public enthusiasm, about the commercial possibilities of growing crops by soilless, or "hydroponic," methods.

One of Hoagland's main areas of research was the process of absorption and accumulation of ions by plants. (The nutrient elements that plants absorb from soils carry an electrical charge and are known chemically as ions.) His early work with the freshwater alga *Nitella* demonstrated that ion absorption is a metabolic process in which ions are accumulated within the plant at concentrations many times greater than those in the external medium.

Next, he turned to the system that was uppermost in his mind—the absorption of nutrients by the roots of higher plants. The broad outlines of a theory were already available from his earlier work. He decided that the fundamental questions of ion absorption by roots could be studied most effectively when the roots were severed, during a brief experimental period, from their shoots. Over the years he amassed an impressive array of data on the influence of oxygen, temperature, light, and other factors on ion absorption. In the late 1930's, when radioactive isotopes from the Berkeley cyclotron became available, he recognized at once their serviceability and used them in resolving some of the hitherto perplexing problems of ion absorption by higher plants. A solid scientific foundation was thus laid for the understanding of the factors that govern the activity of roots in soils and for interpreting and predicting a multiplicity of plant responses to fertilization and other chemical changes in the soil.

Throughout his life as a productive scientist, Hoagland sought principles in the laboratory to help in solving the practical problems of the farmer in the field but was aware that facile generalizations from laboratory observations can seldom solve field problems with dazzling simplicity. When necessary, he worked directly with soils and crops in the field. His field-work on problems of soil chemistry was especially concerned with zinc, potassium, and phosphate deficiencies of fruit trees in California. In collaboration with W. H. Chandler, he identified the important "little-leaf" disease of fruit trees as a zinc deficiency and reproduced it under controlled conditions. It was also under Hoagland's influence that intensive studies into other aspects of micronutrients (trace elements) were successfully pursued by his associates and students.

Hoagland was a tall man of dignified appearance, somewhat reserved in manner but of kindly disposition, always ready to lend friendly advice and help. Hoagland's chief personal characteristic was his integrity and objectivity of outlook. He was the uncommon scientist who carried the scientific mode of thinking outside his own specialty and even to contemporary social and political questions, in which he always maintained a keen interest.

Hoagland's qualities of mind and character and his scientific achievements gained him wide recognition and many honors. His counsel was sought and valued within his own university, where he held the position of professor of plant nutrition from 1926 and was chairman of the Division of Plant Nutrition from 1922 to 1949. In 1934 he was elected a member of the National Academy of Sciences. The American Society of Plant Physiologists bestowed upon him in 1929 its highest honor, the first Stephen Hales Award, and in 1932 elected him president. In 1942, Harvard University invited him to give the Prather Lectures, which were later published in book form as *Lectures on the Inorganic Nutrition of Plants* (1944).

On May 1, 1920, Hoagland married Jessie A. Smiley, who died of pneumonia in 1933, leaving him the responsibility of bringing up three sons, Robert Charles, Albert Smiley, and Charles Rightmire. He never remarried. The last four years of his life were marred by partial disability that resulted from a stroke. He fulfilled his responsibilities with determination and courage up to within the last few months of his life, when his eyesight failed him almost completely. He died in Berkeley.

Hoagland's scientific influence went beyond his own accomplishments. He made a deep impression on the minds and hearts of his friends and students who were inspired to continue his work.

[Biographical material includes *Who's Who in America 1948–1949*; W. P. Kelley, in *Nat. Acad. Sci., Biog. Mem.*, XXIX (1956); D. I. Arnon, in *Plant Physiol.*, (1950), v–xvi; a complete bibliography of his many articles will be found in Kelley.]
DANIEL I. ARNON

HODGKINSON, FRANCIS (June 16, 1867-Nov. 4, 1949), mechanical engineer, was born in London, England, the only child of Francis Otter Hodgkinson and Margaret (Thompson) Hodgkinson. After he received his education at the Royal Naval School, New Cross, London, he attended night courses at Durham University and worked during the day. Hodgkinson was apprenticed in 1882 as a machinist with Clayton and Shuttleworth of Lincoln, England, who were agricultural engineers and builders of steam engines. In 1885 he went to work for Clarke, Chapman, Parsons and Company, where some of the earliest Parsons turbines were built. That same year, after Sir Charles Parsons had formed his own company, Hodgkinson joined it, traveling widely as guarantee engineer at turbine-driven electrical plants and rising to superintendent of field construction. He served as second engineer on a destroyer for the Chilean navy from 1890 to 1892, including the period of the civil war of 1891. Then, after two years of work on telephone lines and electric power plants for a Peruvian company, he returned to the Parsons firm in 1894. Shortly after that, George Westinghouse acquired United States rights to the Parsons patents, and, in 1896, by which time he had become shop superintendent, Hodgkinson went to Pittsburgh on Parsons' recommendation to supervise the design and construction of steam turbines for Westinghouse.

The next year, Hodgkinson made a return visit to England to marry Edith Marion Kate Piercy in Bedford, on June 1, 1897. They had three sons, Francis Piercy, George Arthur, and William Sampson.

Hodgkinson continued as chief turbine engineer for Westinghouse until 1916, when he became chief engineer, a position he held until 1927. After that, he served as consulting engineer, and, during the 1930's, spent many months in Japan as the Westinghouse consultant on

turbines bought by the Japanese navy. He was also consulted on the mountings of the 200-inch reflecting telescope at Mount Palomar, Calif. After his retirement in 1936, he remained a consultant for Westinghouse Electric and Manufacturing Company.

In the tradition of that less celebrated but more constructive breed of empire-builders who for more than a century carried British industrial technology to the United States and other parts of the world, Hodgkinson braved skepticism and hostility toward the use of steam turbines in electric power plants. He overcame opposition by the success of his designs and by his skill and persistence in educating both suppliers and workmen, an achievement much aided by his solid background in shop work. Practically all commercial steam turbines built by Westinghouse were originated by him and designed under him; the first commercial steam turbine generating station was designed by him and installed in the Westinghouse Air Brake Co. in 1899-1900. Around him there developed a group of young engineers, many of whom became leaders in their profession. Although well-grounded in mathematical theory, Hodgkinson remained a thoroughly practical steam engineer, always ready to argue details of design and construction on grounds of both theory and practical experience. Eventually, he took out more than a hundred patents in steam turbine design.

Often called the dean of turbine engineering in the United States, Hodgkinson nevertheless remained a man of international ties and reputation. Besides contributing a number of papers on steam power plants, turbines, nozzles, and boiler tubes as a member of the American Society of Mechanical Engineers (ASME), he delivered notable papers before the British Institution of Mechanical Engineers, including "Theoretical and Practical Considerations in Steam Turbine Work" (1904) and "Journal Bearing Practice" (1929). For the latter paper, which he considered his most important, he received the institution's Willans Premium in 1931. In the late 1920's and early 1930's, as United States representative on the International Electrotechnical Commission, he was the chief force behind the initiation and development of international codes for the testing of steam turbines and internal combustion engines.

As the chairman, in 1937, of ASME's Power Test Codes Committee, Hodgkinson was responsible for the form and completion of many codes. The society awarded him its Holley Medal in 1938. In 1939 he was made a fellow of the society and elected to a two-year term as vice-president. His other honors included a silver medal from the 1904 Louisiana Purchase Exhibition, the Elliott Cresson Medal of the Franklin Institute in 1925, an honorary degree from Stevens Institute in 1935, and an appointment as honorary professor of mechanical engineering by Columbia University in 1936.

For all his plainspoken practicality, Hodgkinson had a ready and pungent wit and a facility for debate. He was well-read and loved music, especially Wagner. Originally an Anglican, he eventually became a Roman Catholic. Not until after his retirement did he and his wife exchange their British citizenship for that of the United States. In 1948 he moved from New York City to the home of his son Francis in Toledo, Ohio, where he died of cancer. He was buried in Toledo.

[Obituaries appeared in *N.Y. Times*, Nov. 6, 1949 (with photograph); *Mechanical Engineering*, Dec. 1949, p. 986; *Toledo Blade*, Nov. 5, 1949; *Engineering*, Nov. 18, 1949. A biographical sketch is to be found in *Institution of Mechanical Engineers Proc.*, 172 (1950): 475–476. See also *Nat. Cyc. Am. Biog.*, Current Vol. E. Personal information was graciously supplied by F. Piercy Hodgkinson and George A. Hodgkinson.]

ROBERT V. BRUCE

HOFFMAN, FREDERICK LUDWIG (May 2, 1865-Feb. 23, 1946), statistician and writer on public health, was born in Varel, a small town near Bremen in northwestern Germany. His parents were Augustus Franciscus Hoffman, a lawyer, and Antoinette (von Laar) Hoffman. Hoffman attended school only until 1880, when, at the age of fifteen, he began work as a clerk in a rural general store near Bremen. After four years, frustrated by poor economic conditions, he immigrated to the United States. He was naturalized in 1892.

Although Hoffman arrived in America with scanty means, few friends, and little knowledge of English, he eventually overcame these handicaps through ability, an enormous capacity for work, and some luck. After a few months as a grocery clerk in Cleveland, Ohio, he traveled through the West and South for about two years, studying on his own and supporting himself by odd jobs. In 1887 he became an agent for the Metropolitan Life Insurance Company in Waltham and Watertown, Mass., locations which enabled him to pursue his self-education in Boston libraries. The Metropolitan sent him to Chicago in 1890, but ill health soon compelled him to move south, where he joined the Life Insurance Company of Virginia, advancing within four years to superintendent of their

Newport News office. On July 15, 1891, Hoffman married Ella George Hay of Americus, Ga. They had six children: Ella Antoinette, Frances Armstrong, Virginia, Gilbert Hay, Barbara, and Victoria.

During his years in Virginia, Hoffman made extensive statistical studies of the Negro population, its diseases, and its mortality. His first report of these studies, published in the *Arena* magazine of April 1892, attracted wide attention in both the South and the North. Negro mortality rates, he found, were nearly double those of the white population. This difference he attributed, in the light of contemporary medical and ethnological writings, primarily to the "inferior constitution and vitality of the colored race," as seen in the Negro's supposed decline in morality and health since emancipation. Hoffman developed his theories more fully in his *Race Traits and Tendencies of the American Negro*, published by the American Economic Association in 1896.

American life insurance companies, which had begun in the 1880's to set higher premiums for Negroes, found "scientific" justification in Hoffman's reports. More immediately, his *Arena* article brought him a job offer from the Prudential Insurance Company. He began work as statistical assistant in the company's home office in Newark, N.J., in October 1894. He was promoted to statistician in 1901 and in 1918 was also made third vice-president. Although he resigned both posts in 1922, he remained with the firm as a part-time consultant until his retirement in 1934. Meanwhile he served as dean of advanced research at the Babson Institute, Wellesley Hills, Mass. (1922-1927), and then as a consultant with the Biochemical Research Foundation of the Franklin Institute (1934-1938), living first in Wellesley Hills and then in Philadelphia.

Methodical, energetic, and a compulsive collector of information, Hoffman had rapidly built up at the Prudential the most comprehensive library in the United States of statistical works, health reports, and demographic data. His analyses of these materials, together with data from his own special investigations and from the Prudential's mortality experience, resulted in a phenomenal outpouring of personal publications on actuarial, public health, and demographic subjects.

A Republican in politics and a Unitarian in religion, Hoffman shared some of the prevalent ideas of the era. He became a vigorous exponent of private enterprise, a staunch advocate of Anglo-Saxon racial purity, and a zealous guardian of the traditional elements of American society and life. His *Race Traits and Tendencies of the American Negro* was used in the South to justify Negro disenfranchisement. In the 1920's Hoffman conducted a comparable survey of disease and mortality risks among the American Indians. Affecting an even broader segment of society, however, was Hoffman's antagonism toward public medical care and health insurance. This emerged after 1910 and made him the most effective and uncompromising voice of the American life insurance industry in its successful early campaign against compulsory health insurance legislation.

Yet much of Hoffman's career was strongly humanitarian. Immersing himself early in the public health movement, he made statistical analyses of many ills, ranging from malaria to leprosy to industrial health hazards. One of the most important of these, his study of "The Mortality from Consumption in the Dusty Trades" (U.S. Bureau of Labor, *Bulletin*, no. 79, 1908), together with later supplemental works, had an impact not only on the tuberculosis-control campaign but also on American labor legislation. His reports on suicide and murder rates were widely read. Hoffman's most sustained health contribution was his work against cancer. He was directly responsible for the founding, in 1913, of the American Society for the Control of Cancer (later the American Cancer Society). He wrote and lectured widely in furtherance of the society's educational work and, during the 1920's, conducted the extensive San Francisco cancer survey. Throughout his career, his technical publications helped to upgrade the quality of vital statistics registration and reporting, as well as to improve the professional standing of health statisticians.

Insatiable curiosity helped make Hoffman an inveterate traveler. During the 1920's he conducted surveys of health conditions in Mexico and other Latin American countries. Much of his travel was done by air, earning him considerable publicity as the "flying actuary." As an offshoot of this interest, he made in 1928 the first thorough survey of aerial transport in the United States, covering such matters as safety problems, plane construction, and pilot qualifications.

Hoffman was active in many professional organizations, including the American Statistical Association, of which he was president in 1911. He was delegate to a host of national and international congresses, was in demand as a speaker on many subjects, and wrote dozens of letters to newspapers. His principal formal honors

were the award in 1911 of an honorary LL.D. from Tulane University and in 1943 of the Clement Cleveland Medal of the New York City Cancer Committee. Hoffman spent his retirement after 1938 in San Diego, Calif. For the last two decades of his life he suffered from Parkinson's disease. He died in San Diego of pneumonia at the age of eighty, a few days after a fall, and was buried in Greenwood Mausoleum in that city.

[No personal papers of Hoffman's have come to light, and relatively few unpublished professional papers, save for a collection at the Nat. Lib. of Medicine, Bethesda, Md. Hoffman published some sixteen books and many reports and papers; bound collections of these shorter works have been deposited at the Nat. Lib. of Medicine and the Lib. of Cong. Most of his large statistical library was given before his death to the Nat. Lib. of Medicine (then the Army Medical Lib.). Surprisingly little has been written about Hoffman: brief obituaries in the *Jour. of the Am. Statistical Assoc.*, June 1946, and the *N.Y. Times*, Feb. 25, 1946 (with photograph); a sketch in the *Nat. Cyc. Am. Biog.*, XXXIV, 66–67 (also with photograph); short résumés in *Who Was Who in America*, II (1950) and in several editions of *Am. Men of Sci.* For an analysis of his writings on the Negro, see John S. Haller, Jr., "Race, Mortality, and Life Insurance," *Jour. of the Hist. of Medicine and Allied Sciences*, July 1970. Death record from Calif. Dept. of Public Health.]

JAMES H. CASSEDY

HOKINSON, HELEN ELNA (June 29, 1893–Nov. 1, 1949), artist, was born in Mendota, Ill. She was the only child of Adolph Hokinson, a farm-machinery salesman whose family (originally named Haakonson) had emigrated from Sweden, and Mary (Wilcox) Hokinson, an Arkansas native of English descent. Their daughter attended the Mendota public schools and, during her high school years, began to sketch her friends and other townspeople without their knowledge and solely for her own enjoyment. In 1914, the year following her high-school graduation, her parents grudgingly allowed her to undertake a two-year course at the Chicago Academy of Fine Arts, which in those days guaranteed to produce commercial artists who could make a living. She lived modestly at the Three Arts Club and specialized in fashion illustration and design. Eventually Miss Hokinson managed to secure assignments from various department stores and art service agencies.

In 1920 she moved to New York, intending to continue the same sort of work. The next year she and the artist Alice Harvey, with whom she had shared a small Chicago studio, took rooms at the Smith College Club, an inexpensive haven that had just opened and had some space available for girls who were not Smith alumnae. Miss Hokinson did fashion illustrations for such stores as Lord and Taylor, B. Altman and Company, and John Wanamaker, while Miss Harvey contributed humorous drawings to *Life* magazine. Both young women attempted comic strips for the *Daily Mirror,* but Miss Hokinson's "Sylvia in the Big City" was the only one that actually appeared, and then only for a few months. In 1924 the two friends enrolled in a course at the School of Fine and Applied Art. Miss Hokinson's studies under Howard Giles, who taught the Jay Hambidge theory of dynamic symmetry, wholly altered her career.

Never a caricaturist, she had based her high school sketches on nothing more than a selective observation of the truth. They had been funny only because something about the individuals themselves had been innately funny. Giles, recognizing Miss Hokinson's talent for "drawing true," encouraged her to devote herself more and more to this form of expression but with a design basis. Soon she was doing so with authority and dispatch and working in watercolor as well, combining dynamic symmetry with the Denman Ross color theory. The artist's newfound joy resulted in her losing all interest in fashion illustrating, until then her only means of support.

The founding of the *New Yorker* early in 1925 was most fortuitous, for to its editors the fact that Miss Hokinson was not a cartoonist in the accepted sense mattered not at all. They were interested in mirroring the life of the city, and Miss Hokinson's drawings did exactly that. The earliest of these, done in the magazine's very first year, were unaccompanied by captions. Presently, however, the editors (and sometimes, the readers) began to caption her work themselves, often originating ideas for her to work out and every month or so sending her on "covering art" assignments to sketch assorted metropolitan phenomena.

In 1931 a chance meeting with James Reid Parker, one of the *New Yorker*'s short-story writers, led to a professional association that lasted for the next eighteen years, with Parker devising the situations and writing the captions for most of Miss Hokinson's drawings. In a *Saturday Review of Literature* essay John Mason Brown wrote, "Theirs was the happiest of collaborations. Without any of the friction of the lords of the Savoy, they found themselves as perfectly matched as Gilbert and Sullivan. If Miss Hokinson's was the seeing eye, Mr. Parker's was the hearing ear." And in discussing the subjects of the drawings, Brown added, "Miss Hokinson's fondness for them was transparent and contagious. Hers was the rarest of satiric gifts. She had no contempt for human failings. She approached foibles with affection. She could ridicule without wounding. She could give fun by making fun and in the process make no enemies."

Her best-known sketches were of pleasantly plump, middle-aged suburban clubwomen. Most, but certainly not all, of these women were unself-consciously charming, kind, self-indulgent, ingenuous to a degree, and generally addicted to short-lived enthusiasms. But Miss Hokinson confounds us because she drew so very many women (and men), each a true individual. The nearest thing to a Helen Hokinson stereotype was the helpless lady phoning her husband from a police station and saying, "George, I've just done something wrong on the George Washington Bridge." Another typical character was the thin, angular, elderly woman made of sterner stuff, who remarks in a crisp aside to her pewmate at a church wedding, "Personally, I *like* to see a nervous bride." It is true, however, that many of Miss Hokinson's admirers were inclined to think of her women as a type, an amalgam of women exemplified by the women's club treasurer who declines to submit her monthly report "because there is a deficit." Miss Hokinson herself thought of her characters only as individuals, which in fact they are.

Helen Hokinson worked very quickly, due in part to her huge file of rough sketches, and often completed a fine drawing within an hour. Two days usually sufficed for her weekly work, a fact she slyly concealed from the editors throughout her career.

Although she tended to be shy and monosyllabic with strangers, with people she liked and trusted, she was joyful and spontaneous.

As early as 1929, Miss Hokinson, who never married, had formed the habit of dividing her time between a New York apartment and cottages in Connecticut, first in Silvermine and then in Wilton. On Nov. 1, 1949, she was invited to Washington to speak at the opening of the capital's annual Community Chest drive; she was killed with all others aboard her plane in a collision that took place as the craft approached National Airport. She was buried in Mendota.

[Articles on Helen Hokinson are John Mason Brown, "Helen Hokinson," *Sat. Rev. of Lit.,* Dec. 10, 1949; James Reid Parker, "Helen" (1950); Dale Kramer, "Those Hokinson Women," *Sat. Evening Post,* Apr. 7, 1951; and "Editorial," *N.Y. Herald Tribune,* Nov. 2, 1949. Books by Miss Hokinson, with her drawings, include *So You're Going to Buy a Book!* (1931); *My Best Girls* (1941); *When Were You Built?* (1948), and *There Are Ladies Present* (1952). *The Hokinson Festival* (1956), an omnibus collection of drawings, and *The Ladies, God Bless*

'Em! (1950) include the Brown essay cited earlier and the memoir "Helen" by James Reid Parker. Personal recollection was the primary source.]

JAMES REID PARKER

HOLT, EDWIN BISSELL (Aug. 21, 1873-Jan. 25, 1946), psychologist, was born in Winchester, Mass., the youngest, apparently, of the seven children of Stephen Abbott Holt and Nancy Wyman (Cutter) Holt. His father, a graduate of Bowdoin College and of the Andover (Mass.) Theological Seminary, was ordained a Congregational minister but, because of poor health, went into his father-in-law's lumber business in Boston and "accumulated a large fortune." Ned, as Edwin was called, was a precocious child, and his mother strongly encouraged his early interest in the processes of plant and animal life. He attended school in Winchester and in 1892 entered Amherst College, but transferred after a year to Harvard, where he received his B.A. degree, magna cum laude, in 1896.

After studying medicine for two semesters at Freiburg in Germany, Holt returned to Harvard to begin graduate work in psychology under William James, whom he deeply admired. His study was interrupted by the Spanish-American War, when he volunteered for six months' service in the 1st Massachusetts Artillery, followed by a sojourn of travel in Mexico. He returned to psychology in 1899, this time under James McKeen Cattell at Columbia, where he took an M.A. degree in 1900. Moving back to Harvard, Holt received the Ph.D. in 1901, with a thesis on "The Motor Element in Vision," and remained to serve as instructor (1901-1905) and assistant professor (1905-1918) of psychology.

As a teacher Holt was closely associated with James and with the work of the psychological laboratory directed by Hugo Münsterberg. In 1910 Holt, with a few philosophical friends, among them Edward G. Spaulding of Princeton and Ralph Barton Perry, founded a discussion group known as the "Six Little Realists," who in general opposed the concepts of idealism and advocated a realism based on the facts of natural science. In their resulting book, *The New Realism* (1912), Holt's chapter dealt with the place of illusory experience in a realistic world. His *Concept of Consciousness* (1914) is a product of this same interest. In 1915 appeared his most popular book, *The Freudian Wish and Its Place in Ethics*. In a highly original manner this essay harmonizes the new discoveries of Freud with the motor theory of consciousness. Not for many years did psychologists (chiefly those at Yale) undertake a similar synthesis of psychoanalytic theory and behaviorism.

Unlike James, whose brilliant writing is marked by paradox and inconsistency, Holt held steadfastly to a narrow but firm position that is best called philosophic behaviorism. He took the view that the phenomena of consciousness did not require the concept of a separate psyche but could be accounted for wholly in terms of physical and physiological processes and adduced the work of Ivan Pavlov in Russia and S. T. Bok in Holland in support of his stand. To Holt the reflex circle, the motor theory, the tendency of all organisms to approach most objects in the environment (adience), and the process of piecemeal integration supplied the necessary building blocks of a science of psychology. His mature views on this matter are lucidly stated in *Animal Drive and the Learning Process* (1931).

Holt, who never married, devoted himself to the care of his mother. When she died in 1919 he resigned from Harvard and spent a few years living in New England and in the West, sometimes with a friend, sometimes alone. In 1926, he was persuaded to accept a visiting professorship at Princeton on a part-time basis. This post he held until 1936, when he retired to a quiet life at Tenants Harbor, Maine. He died in Rockland, Maine, a decade later and was buried in Wildwood Cemetery, Winchester, Mass.

All his life Holt took great pleasure in the theater. He disliked attending scientific meetings and made no effort to publish a large number of papers. He had flashing eyes and a barbed wit, and his attacks upon sham were sharp. He was regarded by all as a colorful and, by some, as a profane personality. He was especially impatient with the lack of scholarship and insight displayed by contemporary trends in psychological writing. The flavor of his irony is suggested by the title of one of his infrequent essays, "On the Whimsical Condition of Social Psychology and the World" (in Horace M. Kallen and Sidney Hook, eds., *American Philosophy, Today and Tomorrow*, 1935). In spite of the acid in his speech, his nature was basically kind; he was an excellent teacher and was known for his generous devotion to his students and loyalty to his friends.

Holt's place in the history of American psychology, although limited, is significant. As a realist, positivist, and behaviorist he strongly favored objective experimental methods; he himself, however, did little research of this type. His fame will rest rather on his ability to give depth and philosophical sophistication to his various behavioral theories.

[The best accounts of Holt are the obituaries by his friend and colleague Herbert S. Langfeld in *Psychological Rev.*, Sept. 1946, and by his pupil and short-term colleague Leonard Carmichael, in *Am. Jour. of Psychology*, July 1946. See also: *Reports* of Harvard College Class of 1896, especially obituary in *Fiftieth Anniversary Report* (1946); obituary in *Science*, May 17, 1946; and, on Holt's father, Bowdoin College alumni records and the Bowdoin *Obituary Record*, 1895–1896.]

GORDON W. ALLPORT

HOMER, LOUISE DILWORTH BEATTY (Apr. 30, 1871–May 6, 1947), contralto, was born in Shadyside, Pa. (a suburb of Pittsburgh), the third daughter and fourth of eight children of William Trimble Beatty and Sarah Colwell (Fulton) Beatty. The father was a Presbyterian clergyman; the mother's family included a Revolutionary War officer and the inventor Robert Fulton.

When Louise was seven, the Beattys moved to Minneapolis. After her husband's death in 1882 Sarah Beatty and the children moved to West Chester, Pa. Louise graduated from high school with honors, trained as a stenographer, and worked first in the office of a Quaker school and then as a court stenographer, at the same time studying voice in Philadelphia with Abbie Whinnery, an able oratorio singer of an earlier day, and Alice Groff. At the age of twenty-one Louise resolved to make music her career and went to Boston, where she studied voice with William L. Whitney and musical theory with Sidney Homer. At the First Universalist Church, she sang in what was then considered Boston's finest choir, directed by George Chadwick. Sidney Homer, six years her senior, took his attractive pupil to her first opera. They were married on Jan. 9, 1895, and began housekeeping on Boylston Street, where their first child was born.

Borrowing a sum of money, the couple went to Paris in 1896, where Mme Homer, as she was thereafter known, studied voice with Fidèle Koenig and stage movement with Paul Lhérie, making her first appearance in concert under Vincent d'Indy. A successful debut as Leonora in *La Favorita* at Vichy (June 5, 1898) led to other European engagements—the winter season at Angers in 1898-1899; performances at Covent Garden, London, beginning the following May; eight months at the Théâtre de la Monnaie, Brussels, the next winter; a second engagement at Covent Garden for the spring season of 1900—in the course of which the young artist gained much valu-

able experience. During this period Mme Homer's voice increased in volume and range; naturally well placed, it was full and rich, evenly distributed, with a wide compass, having neither the sepulchral tones in the lower register nor the shrillness in the upper range that are common to many contraltos. Although she seemed not to have a strong dramatic temperament, her voice had a powerful impact. She sang fluently in Italian, German, and French, often the same role in each.

Given a three-year contract by Maurice Grau, the Metropolitan Opera Company's general manager, Mme Homer made her American debut on Nov. 14, 1900, on tour in San Francisco, singing Amneris in *Aïda*. She opened in New York on December 22 in the same role. She was thus successfully launched on a long career that embraced many of the Metropolitan's most memorable performances. She sang Maddalena in *Rigoletto* at Enrico Caruso's American debut in 1903. She was Suzuki in *Madama Butterfly*, with Geraldine Farrar, Caruso, and Antonio Scotti, at the Metropolitan's first performance (not the American premiere) on Feb. 11, 1907, in the presence of the composer; and was Amneris at Toscanini's first appearance in America on Nov. 16, 1908. While Azucena, Orfeo, and Amneris were her favorite roles, she was qualified for every contralto part in the standard repertoire. Public demand was greatest for her Dalila, with Caruso singing Samson. Combining an ability to learn quickly with profound musicianship, Mme Homer was valued as a dependable associate in an era of unpredictable divas, missing only two scheduled performances in a career that spanned the administrations of Grau, Conried, and Gatti-Casazza.

She learned Wagnerian roles quickly, singing Brangäne in December 1901 in San Francisco, Venus in *Tannhäuser* in St. Louis in 1901 without orchestral rehearsal, and Fricka on one day's notice in 1903. Toscanini showed his admiration by inviting her to sing Orfeo in the Metropolitan's revival in New York and on tour in Paris in 1909-1910. By virtue of her artistry as Amneris, Mme Homer stilled a demonstration in Paris in support of a French singer who her admirers felt had been slighted in favor of the American.

These accomplishments would have rendered Mme Homer's career no more celebrated than that of other singers of genuine ability had it not been for her early and continuing association with the phonograph. By means of the new invention, music of high quality entered millions of American homes, and the name Louise Homer was soon widely known. Her recordings, beginning in 1902 with cylinder recordings of quartets, covered an extensive range of arias from works by Handel, Gluck, Meyerbeer, Gounod, Saint-Saëns, Verdi, and others, as well as ensembles with Caruso, Scotti, Farrar, Johanna Gadski, Emma Eames, and Bessie Abott. By 1909 she had made fifty-one recordings. It was in the next decade, however, that her record sales under the Victor label, often in duet with Alma Gluck, soared into tens of thousands. A copy of the Victor Talking Machine Company's royalty statement for 1919 may be taken as representative: 332,576 recordings were sold of sixty-nine selections available (including ensembles), of which twenty-five were operatic; nine were from oratorios; eight were hymns; and the remainder included folk songs and ballads, which by the simplicity of their message had the widest appeal. Few recording artists sustained so great a popularity.

Increasing fame led her to concert halls in major cities, where her radiant presence established a warm rapport with audiences, who greeted return engagements with the same enthusiasm as the first; in recitals, she invariably included a group of her husband's songs. For festivals, such as those in Cincinnati and Worcester, she was available for the great oratorios, with their vital sacred themes. Each season demanded extensive—and exhausting—tours under the scrutiny of the press, but Mme Homer stood forth as a splendid example of the American singer, with unblemished personal and domestic virtues. Her years before the public strongly parallel those of Annie Louise Cary, a generation earlier.

While relishing standard roles, Mme Homer also sang in new works: the first Metropolitan productions of Paderewski's *Manru* (Feb. 14, 1902) and Humperdinck's *Königskinder* (Dec. 28, 1910). Among the American productions in which she appeared were Frederick Converse's *Pipe of Desire* (Mar. 18, 1910) and Horatio Parker's *Mona* (Mar. 14, 1912). Not often lasting successes, they were worthwhile efforts. She also sang in a revival of Boeildieu's *La Dame Blanche*, which "achieved a run of one consecutive performance."

Following her last regular season with the Metropolitan (1918-1919), Mme Homer sang three seasons with the Chicago Opera and included guest performances there in concert tours from 1922-1926. Similarly she sang with the San Francisco and Los Angeles opera companies in 1926. A return to the Metropolitan as Amneris in December 1927 was warmly received. Her final appearances there were in *Il Trovatore* in December 1928 and March 1929. Mme Homer's career, begun in the days of Jean and Edouard de Reszke and Nordica, spanned those of Caruso and Farrar and ended in those of Giacomo Lauri-Volpi and Rosa Ponselle. Associates in the contralto roster included Ernestine Schumann-Heink (debut 1899), Margarete Matzenauer (debut 1911), and Marion Telva (debut 1920).

The *New York Times* noted in 1947 that Mme Homer had been trained "in a school that concentrated on diction, musical compass and refinement, and, equally important, that stressed dramatic power. The operatic realm has known few contraltos who could do justice as she could to such roles as Amneris, Suzuki, Azucena and Dalila." An editorial added, "Hers was long the voice of America."

The Homers had six children: Louise Homer (Mrs. Ernest V. R.) Stires gave many recitals with her mother; Sidney; Katharine and Anne Marie (twins); Hester Makepeace; and Helen Joy. The composer Samuel Barber is a son of Mme Homer's sister Marguerite. In 1923 a League of Women Voters poll chose Mme Homer one of Twelve Eminent American Women; five honorary degrees were conferred on her: Tufts, 1925; Smith, 1932; Russell Sage, 1932; Middlebury, 1934; and Miami University (Oxford, Ohio), 1933. In later years the Homers spent summers in Bolton, N.Y., and, after retirement, winters in Winter Park, Fla. Interested in various religious beliefs and generous in many humanitarian causes, she professed no adherence to any particular orthodoxy. Her retirement was occasioned by the state of her husband's health and not by any impairment of her voice. Mme Homer died of a heart ailment in Winter Park and was buried in Bolton. Her husband survived until July 10, 1953.

[Sidney Homer chronicled his life with Mme. Homer in *My Wife and I* (1939); see also Anne Homer's biography of her mother, *Louise Homer and the Golden Age of Opera* (1973). Various facets of the singer's career and personality are noted in Irving Kolodin, *The Metropolitan Opera, 1883–1935* (1936); Oscar Thompson, *The American Singer* (1937); *Notable Am. Women*, II (1971); Willa Cather, "Three American Singers," *McClure's Mag.*, Dec. 1913; Frederick H. Martens, *The Art of the Prima Donna and Concert Singer* (1923); Robert Bauer, *The New Catalogue of Historical Records, 1898–1908/09* (London, 1947); *Le Grandi Voci* (Istituto per la Collaborazione Culturale, Rome, 1964). An obituary appeared in the *N.Y. Times*, May 7, 1947. Personal information was provided by Katharine Homer (Mrs. Douglas) Fryer.]

H. EARLE JOHNSON

HOOKER, DONALD RUSSELL (Sept. 7, 1876-Aug. 1, 1946), physiologist and scientific editor, was born in New Haven, Conn., the second son and youngest of three children of Frank Henry Hooker and Grace (Russell) Hooker. His father, a carriage manufacturer, was a direct descendant of Rev. Thomas Hooker, founder of the Connecticut Colony. Donald Hooker attended the Hopkins Grammar School in New Haven and followed his father to Yale, gaining the degrees of B.A. in 1899 and M.S. in 1901. He then studied medicine at the Johns Hopkins University and in 1905 became an M.D. After a year at the University of Berlin, he joined the faculty of the Johns Hopkins Medical School as assistant in physiology under Prof. William Henry Howell, rising by 1910 to the rank of associate professor. He gave up this teaching post in 1920 because of the pressure of the editorial duties he had assumed for the *American Journal of Physiology*, but in 1926 accepted an appointment in the School of Hygiene and Public Health at Johns Hopkins as lecturer in social hygiene—after 1935, in physiology.

During this part of his career, which was devoted chiefly to research and teaching, Hooker worked almost exclusively on the physiology of the circulatory system. Alone or with collaborators he published more than forty journal articles, between 1907 and 1935, on the factors controlling blood pressure in the arteries, veins, and capillaries, on the regulation of the tone of the blood vessel walls, on the contractile activity of the blood capillaries, and on the role of calcium, potassium, and sodium ions in the activity of cardiac muscle. His work was of the kind that adds precision to the measurement or understanding of phenomena previously comprehended only in part, and much of it became incorporated in the general literature of physiology. For his study of venous pressure Hooker is recognized as a pioneer. Jointly with J. A. E. Eyster he devised in 1908 a practical instrument for measuring the pressure of the blood within superficial veins (e.g., of the back of the hand) by noting the height of a column of mercury required to collapse the vein by pressing upon it a soft rubber membrane. With this apparatus Hooker made an extensive study of venous pressure under various conditions. In a series of experimental observations published 1930-1933 he made fundamental observations of a type of irregularity of the heart beat known as ventricular fibrillation. His discovery that the rhythm of the fibrillating heart can be restored by properly graduated electric shock has resulted in effective methods for the treatment of cardiac fibrillation and "standstill" in human patients.

Hooker's editorial duties began in 1914, when the *American Journal of Physiology* was turned over to the American Physiological Society by its founder and first editor, William T. Porter. Hooker was appointed managing editor and served effectively in that post for thirty-two years. For a large part of that time he received no financial remuneration. He made the *Journal* not only self-supporting, but the source of a substantial reserve fund for the society. As editor, Hooker maintained high standards of accuracy, clarity, and brevity, and was at the same time considerate of the stylistic preferences of those fellow scientists who submitted articles for publication. In 1921 he helped found and served as managing editor of a second periodical newly inaugurated by the society, *Physiological Reviews*, which reported on current research. Still further duties came in 1935, when Hooker was chosen as the first permanent secretary of the Federation of American Societies for Experimental Biology (founded in 1912), of which the American Physiological Society was one of the constituents. He held this post until a few months before his death, adding the editorship of the federation's administrative *Proceedings* to his already heavy editorial tasks. This new appointment virtually terminated his research career. During World War I, he was a member of the subcommittee on surgical shock and of the committee on physiology of the National Research Council.

On June 14, 1905, Hooker married Edith Houghton of Buffalo, N.Y. They had five children: Donald Houghton; Russell Houghton; twins, Elizabeth Houghton and Edith Houghton; and Beatrice Houghton. Edith Hooker, a graduate of Bryn Mawr, had studied medicine for four years at Johns Hopkins, but gave up a medical career for marriage. She was an active and prominent worker for woman suffrage and for those social reforms in which the woman's movement was interested, particularly the establishment of neighborhood educational and recreational centers and the cause of social hygiene, i.e. the suppression of prostitution and its attendant evil, venereal disease. Hooker joined his wife in taking a leading role in these reforms. He was active in the social hygiene movement as early as 1908, organizing a society in Maryland and cooperating on the national level in the work of William F. Snow and others; he became secretary of the American Social Hygiene Association in 1928 and was a member of the board of directors. Together with his wife he established the Planned Parenthood Association of Baltimore and in 1907 the Guild of St. George, a home for unmarried mothers. The Hookers also founded in 1916 the Roosevelt Recreation Center in Hampden, a north Baltimore community; Hooker also took part in promoting the Maryland old-age pension program.

Hooker enjoyed outdoor life, especially fishing, and in his younger days was an excellent tennis player. He died of pulmonary edema in Baltimore at the age of sixty-nine. Following cremation, his ashes were buried in Evergreen Cemetery, New Haven, Conn.

[Obituaries in Federation of Am. Societies for Experimental Biology, *Proc.*, 1946, pp. 439–440 (by A. J. Carlson); and, more briefly, in *Jour. of Social Hygiene*, Oct. 1946; *Jour. Am. Medical Assoc.*, Aug. 17, 1946; and Yale Univ. *Obituary Record*, 1946–1947; *Am. Men of Sci.*, 7th ed. (1944); personal information from Dr. Donald R. Hooker, Jr. There are brief references to Hooker in Charles W. Clarke, *Taboo: The Story of the Pioneers of Social Hygiene* (1961). A sketch of Edith Hooker's career is in Margie H. Luckett, ed., *Md. Women*, I, 203–205 (1931). For Hooker's scientific articles, see *Index Medicus*, 1906–1942.]

GEORGE W. CORNER

HOPKINS, HARRY LLOYD (Aug. 17, 1890-Jan. 29, 1946), social worker, federal administrator, and diplomat, was born in Sioux City, Iowa, the fourth child of four sons and one daughter of David Aldona Hopkins and Anna (Pickett) Hopkins. His father, born in Bangor, Maine, ran a harness shop, after an erratic career as a salesman, prospector, storekeeper and bowling-alley operator; but his real passion was bowling, and he eventually returned to it as a business. Anna Hopkins, born in Hamilton, Ontario, had moved at an early age to Vermillion, S. Dak., where she married David. She was deeply religious and active in the affairs of the Methodist church. Shortly after Harry was born, the family moved successively to Council Bluffs, Iowa, and Kearney and Hastings, Nebr. They spent two years in Chicago, and finally settled in Grinnell, Iowa.

Hopkins was an unexceptional child. Always thin, he was called "Skinny" or "Hi." At Grinnell High School he was a mediocre right fielder but a good basketball player; his team won the Missouri Valley championship. He entered Grinnell College in the fall of 1908, working summers on farms or in the local brickyard. He loved campus politics and became president of the class of 1912. He also organized the Woodrow Wilson League in Grinnell. He wrote awkwardly and remained an average student.

In 1912, uncertain about a career but intent upon getting out of the Midwest, he took a summer camp job for a New York settlement house. He attended both Republican and Democratic national conventions. Fascinated by social work, by the politics and activity of Manhattan, he stayed on, for $40 a month, with the Association for Improving the Condition of the Poor (AICP). Its director, Dr. John A. Kingsbury, became his sponsor. Hopkins became immediately involved in city politics. In January 1914, Kingsbury helped him become executive secretary of the Board of Child Welfare in the reform administration of Mayor John P. Mitchel. In 1917, Hopkins supported Socialist Morris Hillquit for mayor. When a detached retina disqualified him for military service in World War I, he became director of the Gulf division of the American Red Cross in New Orleans, and later of its southeastern division in Atlanta. In 1922, Kingsbury made him director of a new subdivision of the AICP for the study of health conditions. In 1924, Hopkins became executive director of the New York Tuberculosis Association. He amalgamated his group with the New York Heart Committee and changed its name to New York Tuberculosis and Public Health Association. He soon developed relationships with a number of other organizations interested in problems ranging from silicosis to child welfare, and he set up a special Committee on Social Hygiene.

As a social worker, Hopkins earned a reputation for integrity, as well as for ambition and forthrightness. His major interest was always his work. He made a good salary, ultimately $10,000 a year, but he had little concern for personal wealth. He did enjoy life vigorously and expansively. He was addicted to bridge; he also cultivated interests as varied as poetry, tennis, and the study of fungi. He loved horseracing and betting and frequented the New York speakeasies. On Oct. 21, 1913, he married a colleague in social work, Ethel Gross. They had three sons, David, Robert, and Stephen, and a daughter, Barbara. In 1927, however, Hopkins fell in love with Barbara Duncan, a secretary from Michigan. After divorcing his first wife, he married Barbara in 1929. A daughter, Diana, was born in 1932.

In the wake of the 1929 stock market crash, Hopkins operated a Red Cross-financed work-relief program that became the model for the New York State Temporary Emergency Relief Administration. Set up by Gov. Franklin D. Roosevelt in 1931, this organization stressed the value of providing jobs instead of dole. Hopkins became its executive director, and then its chairman. Financed by two $30 million bond issues, Hopkins' organization provided relief for over a million New Yorkers during the worst years of the depression.

On May 22, 1933, President Roosevelt appointed Hopkins director of the New Deal Federal Emergency Relief Administration. FERA, modeled on the New York experiment, provided grants to the states to supplement their relief activities, coordinating these activities through regional and state offices. The administrative problems of creating an instant operating agency on a national scale were immense. Hopkins put much energy into spending the money quickly and stressing some new lines of policy. He tried to provide work not dole. Relief was viewed as a right not a privilege. Payment was in cash rather than kind, and relief was provided to cover shelter, clothing, and medical care. Meanwhile, President Roosevelt expected Harold Ickes' Public Works Administration (PWA) to become the major stimulus to economic recovery by promoting heavy construction projects, but it was slow in getting under way. In the fall of 1933, Hopkins persuaded the president to permit the development of an additional Civil Works Authority (CWA), whose purpose was to provide extensive work relief for unskilled and semiskilled people, and to do so quickly. It put four million people to work within thirty days. Within four months there were 180,000 work projects and $933 million in expenditures to stimulate the economy. By January 1934, twenty million people were being helped by the combination of federal relief programs. CWA expired in May 1934, but its objectives were served by a broadened FERA.

Hopkins worked—and spent money—quickly. His principal objective was to provide immediate relief, rather than to guarantee the quality of the work. His programs were criticized for boondoggling and inefficiency. And they were an inviting target for political interference. Although there were many local problems, there were no major scandals at the federal level. Hopkins expected that the jobs he created would help win elections, but he stoutly resisted the demands of the political organizations that the vast, decentralized work programs be turned into patronage troughs. There were also administrative frictions in Washington, especially with Harold Ickes, whose PWA stressed quality but resulted in a slow rate of expenditure and amount of relief provided. On the president's orders, Hopkins, Ickes, and Postmaster General Frank Walker joined in the fall of 1934 to develop a unified work relief program. This was designed to put an end to the rivalries. Ickes assumed that he would manage most of the actual operations, but by the end of the winter, Hopkins and Roosevelt had shifted most of the emphasis and the money to the Works Progress (Projects) Administration (WPA) which Hopkins managed.

Although Hopkins wore many hats, his central job until 1938 was Federal Emergency Relief Administrator. He was constantly in controversy. Many projects were indeed inefficient, because they had to hire the most marginal of workers as well as many who were fully employable. Programs were often hastily planned and loosely managed, and criticism frequently arose because Hopkins insisted on using the federal relief programs to set new standards for the states. Although most projects involved manual labor, he recognized the legitimacy of varied occupations and provided work for seamstresses, writers, artists, actors, ballet dancers, and college students. WPA and related Hopkins-dominated agencies, such as the Federal Surplus Relief Corporation, the Rural Rehabilitation Division, and the National Youth Administration, had a direct impact upon more individuals than did any other antidepression program. There was an enormous permanent result: new schools, post offices, libraries, town halls, swimming pools, bridges, and roads by the hundreds. At the end of the 1930's, relief expenditures helped to accelerate national defense plans.

Eventually Hopkins supervised the expenditure of more than $9 billion in federal relief money and did more than any other person to change the attitudes of Americans toward relief programs. He played a significant role, as a member of the Committee on Economic Security, in the development of the Social Security system. His personal attention, however, was increasingly directed toward presidential politics. He had hopes for the White House as early as the winter of 1935-1936. By the spring of 1938, he believed he was Roosevelt's personal choice for 1940. The tides ran against him: his health was bad, and in the summer of 1937 part of his stomach was removed at the Mayo Clinic because of cancer; in that same year, his wife died. He suffered complicated and lingering nutritional problems. In September 1939, it was expected that he would die within weeks. But his national image was also a problem. While he was well-known as a champion of the poor, many thought of him as a careless and wasteful administrator, who frequented the racetracks and signed million-dollar vouchers between bridge hands. He had made enemies: rival bureaucrats and many of the politicians who would control the nomination. He had become the butt of all the angry humor about make-work projects. He lacked charisma. When Roosevelt appointed him secretary of commerce in December 1938, the confirmation hearings were difficult and lengthy.

Hopkins was often ill while he was secretary of commerce, but he very quickly became Roosevelt's special projects man. In 1938, he did a secret survey of the aircraft production capacity of the nation. In 1940, he helped develop the Selective Service system and the National Defense Advisory Committee. From May until late August 1940, he lived in the White House. In June, he managed Roosevelt's interests at the Democratic National Convention, promoting the vice-presidential nomination of Henry A. Wallace. From that time on, Hopkins was likely to describe his White House function as that of a glorified office boy. On Aug. 22, 1940, he resigned as secretary of commerce and went to live in New York. But he was soon involved with the president's speechwriting team. Roosevelt sent him to England to catalogue British military needs, and in March 1941, he was given responsibility for the whole lend-lease program. In the fall of 1941, he turned this task over to Edward R. Stettinius, Jr. Hopkins was now called assistant to the president, but he quickly emerged as "Roosevelt's own personal foreign office" (Sherwood, p. 268). During 1941 he worked as the president's special representative in all the complicated negotiations with the British, and in everything involving the production, transportation, and allocation of military goods.

Throughout the war, Hopkins was the president's alter ego, advising on all matters, discussing everything, and carrying Roosevelt's authority in direct negotiations with Churchill, de Gaulle, Stalin, and Molotov. In July 1941, he went to Moscow to make personal contact with Stalin. Hopkins recommended, and the president accepted, the inclusion of the Russians in lend-lease. Hopkins accompanied Churchill to the Atlantic Conference. W. Averell Harriman frequently traveled for him, and together they maintained the personal linkage between Roosevelt and his generals and allies that made it possible for the White House to dominate both diplomacy and strategy. He was Roosevelt's aide at every major conference. He had the president's absolute confidence; when he exercised power, he did so by speaking for the president and by seeing that certain ideas and men received access to the president. He proved an outstanding representative of Roosevelt's views and commanded the great respect of both Churchill and Stalin.

Hopkins frequently lived in the White House with his daughter, Diana. He became a member of the president's private family. His marriage to Louise Macy on July 30, 1942, brought him a new measure of stability and comfort, but it did not weaken his ties with Roosevelt. When the president died in April 1945, Hopkins was near death himself. He had long been an emaciated wreckage of a man; his surprising energy at moments of crisis was often followed by long periods of desperate debilitation. He worked briefly and hard at maintaining the continuity between presidencies. He had Truman's confidence and used it to strengthen the administration's determination to build the United Nations and to negotiate with Stalin. Hopkins returned to New York in July 1945 to become impartial chairman of the Women's Cloak and Suit Industry, a job that provided both $50,000 a year and a significant challenge. At the age of fifty-five, he died of hemachromatosis; his remains were cremated.

Hopkins was one of the principal architects and managers of the New Deal, a major American policy maker in World War II. First brought to Washington to administer relief programs, he became one of Roosevelt's closest advisors. He commanded the president's personal confidence as no one else had done. Because of his much-valued bluntness and clarity, Churchill called him "Lord Root of the Matter." Oxford made him a doctor of civil laws. President Truman awarded him the Distinguished Service Medal. Having exercised immeasurable influence and supervised the spending of billions of dollars, Harry Hopkins died without wealth.

[The very extensive papers of Hopkins are at the Franklin D. Roosevelt Lib. in Hyde Park, N.Y., and in the National Archives, Washington, D.C. The best, and most readily available source, is the book Robert Sherwood wrote based on the Hopkins Papers, *Roosevelt and Hopkins* (1948). Hopkins himself wrote *Spending to Save* (1936). An excellent brief study, done from primary sources, is Searle F. Charles, *Minister of Relief: Harry L. Hopkins and the Depression* (1963). See also Lewis Meriam, *Relief and Social Security* (1946) and Donald Howard, *The W.P.A. and Federal Relief Policy* (1943). Hopkins figures prominently in all the extensive literature of the New Deal and World War II. Particularly recommended for a broad survey are James M. Burns, *Roosevelt: The Lion and the Fox* (1956) and *Soldier of Freedom*

(1970), and William E. Leuchtenburg, *Franklin D. Roosevelt and the New Deal, 1932–1940* (1963); Josephine C. Brown, *Public Relief, 1929–1939* (1940) is a good approach to the general history; Edward R. Stettinius, Jr., *Lend Lease* (1944) is useful. Among the many works which throw light upon Hopkins' activities in diplomacy and war are Herbert Feis, *Churchill, Roosevelt, Stalin* (1957) and William L. Lenger and S. Everett Gleason, *The Undeclared War, 1940–1941* (1953).]

ALFRED B. ROLLINS, JR.

HOPSON, HOWARD COLWELL (May 8, 1882-Dec. 22, 1949), utilities executive and financier, was born in Fort Atkinson, Wis., the firstborn and only son of the five children of Edgar Delos Hopson and Mary (Colwell) Hopson. His father was a teacher who, on occasion, took financial risks in local businesses. Both parents were Methodists and Republicans, and they raised their children to follow them in both persuasions.

After attending local public schools, Hopson entered the University of Wisconsin in 1901, at the time a center of reformist thought in America. Like many others of his generation, he was drawn to the study of economics and finance under the direction of John R. Commons and Thomas Adams, and he assisted them in editing several works on the subject, while at the same time serving as assistant editor of a Fort Atkinson newspaper, the *Jefferson County Union*. For a while it appeared Hopson was headed for an academic career, but his work with Commons led him to an interest in law, and in 1904 he began to study law at Wisconsin.

With Commons' help, Hopson obtained a position with the Interstate Commerce Commission in 1907, and while in Washington he attended George Washington University, from which he received his law degree in 1908. In the same year, he not only was admitted to the bar of the District of Columbia but also joined the newly formed Public Service Commission of New York. Continuing his studies at George Washington, he received his M.A. in 1910 and, three years later, was admitted to practice before the United States Supreme Court. In that year, 1913, the Public Service Commission of New York named him head of its Division of Capitalization, which was concerned with the structure of public utilities and their capitalizations. By then, he was considered one of the nation's leading experts in the public utilities area and a conservative: his father's beliefs had vanquished those of John Commons insofar as Hopson was concerned.

Hopson left the Public Service Commission in 1915 to open a private practice as consultant to the public utilities industry. Within a short period of time, H. C. Hopson and Co. became a leading advisor not only to utilities, but also to railroads and manufacturing businesses. In 1921, Hopson decided to enter the business world directly, through the acquisition of the Associated Gas and Electric Co. of New York, which at the time was controlled by the J. G. White Management Co. Together with his sisters, Hopson paid $125,000 for controlling interest; his personal investment in the firm was $12,500.

That same year, on Aug. 5, 1921, Hopson married Eleanor Evans of Binghamton, N.Y. They had no children.

Associated Gas and Electric was a minor force in the industry. It was a holding company —that is, a management operation whose assets consisted of shares in operating firms. The Ithaca Gas Light Co., founded in 1852, was the oldest of these and the direct ancestor. In 1906, Ithaca's directors had formed Associated to acquire control of neighboring utilities, which would then be united to form a single firm that would benefit from centralized management and economies of scale. This was a common development at the time, and when Associated took control of small properties in upper New York state, it was deemed a progressive move, one that would benefit users of gas and electricity through better service at lower prices. By 1913, Associated had moved into new areas, by acquiring control of electric companies, first in Kentucky, and then in Tennessee. This was done through the purchase of shares, usually from insiders or management. In this way, the parent company could control large utilities through ownership of a relatively small amount of their equity. The operating companies paid dividends to the parent firm, which used the new funds to purchase additional operating units. This, at least, was the situation when Hopson arrived to take command at Associated in 1921.

It was a propitious time to enter the field. The use of electricity rose sharply in the 1920's, a time when most of the nation's houses and factories were being converted to electric power. Utility stocks and bonds were among the darlings of Wall Street, where securities prices were also rising because of speculation and as a reflection of economic growth. Holding companies, like Associated, controlled some 4,000 operating firms in the nation. Eventually United Corporation, organized by J. P. Morgan and Co., controlled firms producing 23 percent of the nation's electricity, while the two Insull holding companies held interest in firms producing 11 percent of America's electricity. Hopson's Associated Gas and Electric, with some 9 percent of the total, was the third of the great utilities holding companies.

Hopson began acquiring operating companies in 1923 and continued at a rapid rate throughout the rest of the decade. In 1923, also, he obtained control of firms in Massachusetts. In 1924, additional units in New York were acquired, and Associated moved into New Hampshire and Maine. Then, in 1925, Hopson took over firms in Maryland and Pennsylvania, and one in the Philippines. Associated thus had control over some 250 operating firms (although it was later claimed the number was as high as 522) that provided electricity, steam, water, ice, and transportation to some twenty million people in twenty-six states, the Maritime Provinces of Canada, and the Philippines.

Associated's rapid expansion was due in large part to Hopson's ability to raise funds by selling additional securities at a time when the stock markets were eager for such new paper. Later on, a congressional committee tried, without success, to unravel the operations, which it was said only Hopson fully understood. Generally speaking, Hopson sold a new bond or stock issue, and then used the money obtained to purchase control of an operating firm. Then he consolidated its earnings with those of Associated, made it pay a large dividend to the parent firm—which caused the latter's stock price to rise—and repeated the operation. In the same manner, the operating firms acquired additional companies, and some became miniature holding companies in the process.

For a time, all went well, and Hopson was deemed a genius. The reason was leverage, which works well in rising markets. In 1929, Associated showed earnings of $2.91 a share, and its stock reached a high of 61. Then came the crash. Associated's common earned $0.30 to 1930 and showed deficits thereafter. Its price fell to 11⅞ in 1930. The following year, dividends were halted on the common and preferred issues, and Associated began defaulting on its bonds as well. By 1932, the common stock was selling at ½.

In 1935, Congress passed the Public Utilities Holding Company Act, which forbade operating companies from transmitting earnings to parent firms under certain conditions. This all but shattered what remained of the Hopson empire, and he resigned from the firm soon after.

But his problems were not ended. Associated filed for bankruptcy in 1940, and in the investigation that followed dissident stockholders charged Hopson with fraud. He was indicted and, on Jan. 9, 1941, found guilty of defrauding stockholders of $20 million. Hopson was sentenced to five years in prison and later received an additional two-year sentence for income tax evasion. He was released from jail in 1943 and vanished from public view.

Hopson died on Dec. 22, 1949, in Greenwich, Conn., after a long illness, and was buried in Mount Auburn Cemetery in Cambridge, Mass.

Most accounts of American business manipulation and development in the 1920's mention Howard Hopson only in passing, if at all. Instead, stress is placed on such persons as Samuel Insull, the Van Sweringen brothers, and Ivar Kreuger, who were more glamorous and eccentric than the bland, shy Hopson. If anything, however, Hopson was more inventive than the others, he rose to as great a height of power, and his crash was as resounding as that of any tycoon of the era.

[M. L. Ramsay, *Pyramids of Power* (1937), is a good source, as is the article "Hopson's Legacy," *Business Week,* Aug. 22, 1942, pp. 86–87. Obituaries appeared in the *N.Y. Times* and the *N.Y. Herald Tribune,* both on Dec. 23, 1949.]

ROBERT SOBOL

HORMEL, GEORGE ALBERT (Dec. 4, 1860–June 5, 1946), meat packer, was born in Buffalo, N.Y., the third of twelve children and eldest of six sons of John Godfrey Hormel, a tanner, and Susanna (Decker) Hormel. Both parents were natives of the German province of Hesse and had been brought to America as children. His father was of Huguenot descent; both parents were devout members of the German Reformed church. In 1865 John Hormel moved the family to Toledo, Ohio, and started his own tanning firm. The business failed, however, during the panic of 1873, and twelve-year-old Hormel was forced to leave school and go to work. Two years later, after a succession of unskilled jobs, he went to Chicago to work in a packinghouse market that processed meat products; the company was owned by a maternal uncle. Sensing broader opportunities elsewhere, in 1880 he became a traveling wool and hides buyer for a Kansas City company, and the next year for the Chicago firm of Oberne, Hosick and Company. In 1887 he settled in Austin, Minn., where he and a partner established the firm of Friedrich and Hormel, "butchers and packers." The partnership was dissolved in 1891, and Hormel set up his own packinghouse, George A. Hormel and Company.

On Feb. 24, 1892, in Austin, he married Lillian Belle Gleason, a teacher. They had one child, Jay Catherwood.

Hormel, who brought several of his brothers into the company, served as president until 1929. In his early days he was known as something of a tyrant in the operation of his plant. He made a fetish of cleanliness, even establishing a laundry to wash the butcher's smocks. Initially, Hormel's sausages, hams, and beef products were sold through the Hormel Provision Market, a wholesale outlet. Salesmen also distributed the products locally by bicycle and horse carts. Austin proved an excellent location, convenient both to the source of supply of livestock and to the major market of Minneapolis-St. Paul. Under the leadership of Hormel, who continued to cut meat until 1899, the company prospered; its annual sales in 1900 were close to $1 million. The discovery in 1921 that the comptroller had embezzled more than $1 million dealt the company a severe blow, but Hormel arranged additional financing, and the company survived. At the time of his death Hormel and Company had annual sales of $126 million and employed more than 5,000 workers.

During the early years of the twentieth century, Hormel opened distribution branches across the country. He also expanded his sales operations into the international market. His company thus became a stiff competitor to the industry's giants, Swift, Wilson, and Armour. Many of the firm's later innovations reflected the initiative of Hormel's son, Jay Catherwood Hormel (1892-1954) to whom the elder Hormel turned over active control in 1927. In that year Hormel and Company, employing a German process, produced the first successful canned ham in the United States; the process was later used to can chicken. Further canned products were added during the 1920's: soups, which met strong competition from the established brands of Campbell and Heinz; a more successful line of "poor man's" dishes like beef stew, corned beef and cabbage, and chili con carne; and, in 1937, a canned spiced pork shoulder loaf called "Spam." The widespread distribution of Spam and similar products during World War II, both among servicemen and on the home front, made the name a byword.

Although an autocratic executive, Hormel believed in treating labor fairly. He was an industry leader in the movement for shorter hours and higher wages, maintaining that the increased productivity would more than compensate for the higher wages. During the depression year of 1931, in a paper submitted to a presidential commission, he supported unemployment relief and a federal pension for retired workers. To regularize salaries and stabilize employment in an industry with seasonal fluctuations, Hormel and Company in that year initiated a "straight-time" plan offering fifty-two equal pay checks a year despite the number of hours worked in a given week. The company later introduced incentive pay and profit-sharing programs, and in 1933, although advocating the open shop, yielded to a strike and agreed to accept an independent union.

Hormel moved in 1927 to the Bel Air section of Los Angeles. Two years later he formally relinquished the title of president to his son and became chairman of the board, a position he held until his death. Hormel was a Presbyterian in religion. He died of a cerebral hemorrhage in Los Angeles and was buried in Oakwood Cemetery, Austin, Minn.

[Richard J. Dougherty, *In Quest of Quality: Hormel's First 75 Years* (1966), a history of the company, traces Hormel's career in some detail. See also "The Name is HOR-mel," *Fortune*, Oct. 1937; "Hormel: The Spam Man," *Life*, Mar. 11, 1946 (on Jay Hormel); "One-Year Plans," *Time*, Jan. 23, 1939, pp. 39–40; *Nat. Cyc. Am. Biog.*, Current Vol. E, 84–85; *Who Was Who in America*, II (1950); Jack Chernick and George C. Hellickson, *Guaranteed Annual Wages* (1945); Fred H. Blum, *Toward a Democratic Work Process: The Hormel-Packinghouse Workers' Experiment* (1953); Richard J. Arnould, "Changing Patterns of Concentration in American Meat Packing, 1880–1963," *Business Hist. Rev.*, Spring 1961. Death record from Calif. Dept. of Public Health.]

RICHARD J. ARNOULD

HOUSTON, CHARLES HAMILTON (Sept. 3, 1895-Apr. 22, 1950), lawyer and civil rights leader, was born in Washington, D.C., the only child of William LePré Houston, a lawyer, and Mary Ethel (Hamilton) Houston. After graduating at the age of fifteen from the famous M Street (later Dunbar) High School in Washington, he entered Amherst College. An excellent student, he was elected to Phi Beta Kappa and received the B.A. degree in 1915. He spent the next two years teaching English at Howard University in Washington. In 1917, after America's entry into World War I, he enrolled in the Negro officers' training camp at Fort Des Moines, Iowa, and was commissioned a first lieutenant in the infantry. The following year he entered a field artillery school in order to disprove the popular belief that Negroes could not master the requirements for this branch of the service. Assigned to duty overseas, he was shunted from post to post because of his color, but remained in France until February 1919.

Choosing the career of his father, Houston

entered Harvard Law School in the fall of 1919, where his scholastic record won him a place on the editorial board of the *Harvard Law Review*. He received the LL.B. degree, cum laude, in 1922 and, probably at the urging of Dean Roscoe Pound, stayed on for an additional year and took the S.J.D. degree in 1923. A traveling fellowship enabled him to spend a year at the University of Madrid, from which he received the degree of doctor of civil law in 1924.

In that same year Houston was admitted to the bar of the District of Columbia and became his father's partner in the firm of Houston & Houston. In 1929 Houston's cousin by marriage, William H. Hastie, formerly dean of Howard University Law School and afterward governor of the Virgin Islands and federal judge, joined the firm. Houston gave up a lucrative practice in 1929 to accept the post of resident vice-dean and then, from 1932 to 1935, dean of the Howard Law School. In Hastie's words, "In those few years he carried the institution from the status of an unaccredited and little known—though undoubtedly useful—institution to a fully accredited nationally known and respected law school taking its place with the ranking schools of the nation."

During these years, Houston participated in important cases involving civil rights. He helped prepare the brief in *Nixon* v. *Condon* (286 U.S. 73 [1932]), in which the United States Supreme Court ruled for the second time that the Texas "white primary" was unconstitutional, and the brief in *Norris* v. *Alabama* (294 U.S. 587 [1935])—the second *Scottsboro* case—in which the Court set aside the convictions of nine young Negroes charged with rape on the grounds that Alabama's systematic exclusion of Negroes from juries was a violation of the Fourteenth Amendment. Like other Negro lawyers practicing in the South, Houston displayed physical courage. In 1933 he braved strong local hostility in Leesburg, Va., to defend a Negro accused and later convicted of raping a white woman, and five years later he encountered similar hostility when he helped investigate brutalities and racial discrimination at the Tennessee Valley Authority's Chickamauga Dam.

From 1935 to 1940 Houston served as special counsel for the National Association for the Advancement of Colored People, and although he returned to private practice in 1940, he remained for the rest of his life a member of the organization's national legal committee, serving as chairman, 1948-1950. As the N.A.A.C.P.'s special counsel, he initiated and organized its legal work in support of civil rights and argued cases before the Supreme Court. One of his most important cases was *Missouri ex rel. Gaines* v. *Canada* (305 U.S. 337 [1938]), in which Chief Justice Charles Evans Hughes, speaking for the majority, declared that Missouri must offer Gaines "within its borders facilities for legal education substantially equal to those which the State there afforded for persons of the white race." One of Houston's last cases was *Shelley* v. *Kraemer* (334 U.S. 1 [1948]), in which the Supreme Court ruled that restrictive residential covenants could not be enforced by state courts. Houston excelled both in the preparation of briefs and in the presentation of oral arguments. In court he alternated between coldly logical presentations and impassioned accounts of the indignities suffered by Negroes.

Pushing himself hard and taking little time for relaxation, Houston combined an extensive private practice with unstinting work in the public interest. He was a member of the District of Columbia Board of Education, 1933-1935, an acerbic critic of racial discrimination in the army and elsewhere, and, from 1940 to his death, a vice-president of the American Council on Race Relations. He was also vice-president of the National Lawyers Guild. An ardent supporter of the cause of labor, he served as general counsel of the Association of Colored Railway Trainmen and Locomotive Firemen and of the International Association of Railway Employees. In this capacity, he fought and won two cases (*Steele* v. *Louisville and Nashville Railroad Company*, 323 U.S. 192 [1944], and *Tunstall* v. *Brotherhood of Locomotive Firemen*, 323 U.S. 210 [1944]) that affirmed that the Railway Labor Act forbade discriminatory employment practices by the railroads and gave the federal courts jurisdiction in such cases. In 1944 President Roosevelt appointed Houston to the Fair Employment Practices Committee, but he resigned the following year in a dispute with President Truman over the discriminatory hiring practices of Washington's Capital Transit Company.

On Aug. 23, 1924, Houston married Margaret Gladys Moran of Washington, D.C. The marriage, which was childless, ended in divorce, and on Sept. 14, 1937, he married Henrietta Williams, also of Washington. They had one son, Charles Hamilton. Houston was a nominal Baptist but, like many of his contemporaries among Negro intellectuals, was not strongly religious. In the last two years of his life he suffered from a heart ailment. He died in Freedman's Hospital in Washington of a coronary occlusion at the age of fifty-four and was buried in Lincoln Memorial Cemetery, Suitland, Md. On June 25, 1950, the N.A.A.C.P. posthumously awarded him its Spingarn Medal. At the formal opening of the new Howard University Law School building in 1958, Thurgood Marshall, Houston's successor as special counsel of the N.A.A.C.P. and later a Supreme Court justice, stated that not he but Houston deserved the encomium of "The First Mr. Civil Rights." Houston wrote his own epitaph in his admonition to his students: "No tea for the weak, no crepe for the dead."

[Charles H. Houston, "Cracking Closed University Doors," in Fitzhugh Lee Styles, *Negroes and the Law* (1937); obituary by William H. Hastie and tribute by Erwin N. Griswold in *Negro Hist. Bull.*, June 1950; material in Moorland-Spingarn-Negro Collection, Howard Univ.; correspondence or interviews with Chief Judge William H. Hastie, Gladys Moran Houston, Edward P. Lovett, and Judge Joseph C. Waddy; personal acquaintance. See also *Current Biog.*, 1948; and *Who's Who in Colored America*, 1941–1944.]

RAYFORD W. LOGAN

HOVGAARD, WILLIAM (Nov. 28, 1857-Jan. 5, 1950), naval architect, university professor, and specialist in warship design, was born in Aarhus, Denmark, the second son of Ole Anton Hovgaard and Louise Charlotte (Munch) Hovgaard. His father, scholar, teacher, and historian, taught in the government-operated Aarhus Cathedral School, which William entered on graduation from grammar school in 1868. He began his studies in the arts and humanities, but did not do well and transferred to mathematics and physical science, where he excelled. William's older brother, a navy officer and an explorer, was a member of the 1878-1879 Nordenskjold expedition of discovery and navigation of the Northeast Passage to the Pacific. Perhaps influenced by his brother, William entered the Danish Naval Academy at Copenhagen. He did so well there that he won the Gerner Medal, awarded for excellence in scientific studies.

After graduation from the academy in 1879, Hovgaard served as a sub-lieutenant until 1880 when he became a first lieutenant. In 1883 he was enrolled in a three-year course in naval architecture and ship construction at the Royal Naval College, Greenwich, England. At that time, the United States Navy also assigned two young graduates of the United States Naval Academy to each class at the Royal Naval College in preparation for careers in the Construction Corps. Hovgaard's classmate, David W. Taylor, CC, USN (later rear admiral), had a

profound influence on Hovgaard's career in 1901. Still later, Hovgaard acknowledged the influence of two of his teachers, Sir W. E. Smith and W. H. Whiting, in the preface to his influential textbook *General Design of Warships* (1920).

Hovgaard's first assignment after completion of the course at Greenwich in 1886 was at the Royal Dockyard in Copenhagen. Among other duties, he served as an instructor at the school in the dockyard. In 1895, he was named general manager of the Burmeister and Wain Shipyard in Copenhagen, a position he held for two years. On Sept. 19, 1896, he married Marie Ludolphine Elisabeth Nielsen of Copenhagen. They had two children, Ole Mogens and Annette, both born in Denmark. Hovgaard returned to the Royal Dockyard in 1898.

By 1901, Hovgaard had completed the design studies for a submarine and in that year he was sent to the United States to study submarines. While there, he was persuaded by Secretary of the Navy John D. Long, Chief Constructor Rear Admiral Taylor (his former classmate), and Cecil Hobart Peabody, chairman of the department of naval architecture at Massachusetts Institute of Technology, to accept an appointment at M.I.T. as a professor of naval design and construction in charge of a new three-year course for naval constructors. Hovgaard began his lectures in January 1902 after a brief return to Europe to survey the schools there. He reported his proposal to meet the challenge of technical education for naval design in a recorded discussion in the paper "Technical Training for Shipbuilders," delivered by the fifth president of M.I.T., Dr. H. S. Pritchett, at the general meeting of the Society of Naval Architects and Marine Engineers (SNAME) in November 1902.

While lectures in theoretical naval architecture were given by Peabody, Hovgaard assigned to himself three parts of the course: design practice, lectures, and shipyard visits. The nature of Hovgaard's lectures, together with the design practice, introduced a nourishing environment for learning and practice in creative warship design. Hovgaard classified his lectures into three types: historical developments, theory of design, and structural and internal arrangements. They provided the basis for his three textbooks, which later became standard works.

Hovgaard's lectures on structural design were the basis of his text *Structural Design of Warships,* published in 1915 in London. This text so endured that a complete revision was published twenty-five years later in the United States under the supervision of the author. In the tradition of master builders and architects, Hovgaard maintained his principal technical concentration in the structural arrangement and soundness of the constructions he conceived and designed.

The lectures on theory of design developed into Hovgaard's text *General Design of Warships,* published in 1920. His purpose here was at a higher level of generality, of a broader scope, than that of his book on structural design. He arranged and described the major steps and underlying principles, always with facts and data from experience, in the general and overall design of warships. Structural arrangement was his subspecialty within his exposition of general arrangement.

His lectures on historical development were to general design as the latter were to structural design. *Modern History of Warships* was published in 1920. The manuscript, completed in 1916, suffered from long publication delays due to labor conditions and revisions to include wartime developments and previously unpublished facts, but the historical review transcended a compilation of names, numbers, and dates of ship programs. The descriptive material was intended to be the basic data from construction programs necessary for comprehension of the nature and causes of warship development. His record and analysis of the evolution of warship design was a deliberate intellectual inquiry into cause and effect in sea power instruments.

Hovgaard's study and intellectual range at the national and strategic level were reported in professional publications. His Danish origins were a source of pride and strength, which he expressed in part as an organizer and founder of the American-Scandinavian Foundation and as the author of *The Voyages of the Norsemen to America* (1914).

Following his retirement from teaching in 1933, Hovgaard moved to Brooklyn, N.Y., where he continued his professional activities. His work as consultant to the Navy Department and design agents contributed to the quality of the designs executed in the expansion of the navy beginning in the late 1930's. Most of the major ships of the American World War II fleet were designed and constructed under the supervision of Hovgaard's former students. In 1943, the Society of Naval Architects and Marine Engineers bestowed upon Hovgaard its highest award, the David W. Taylor Medal. He died in 1950, after a long illness at the Aurora Hospital in Morristown, N.J., at the age of ninety-two. He was a Lutheran.

[Hovgaard's publications not noted in the text include *Submarine Boats* (1887) and *Lectures on Technology* (1891). Numerous professional papers appear mostly in *Trans.* of the American Society of Naval Architects and Marine Engineers and in the *Trans.* of the British Institution of Naval Architects. Hovgaard's interest in airships, strategy, and disarmament, and in the American-Scandinavian Foundation is reported in Nat. Acad. Sci. *Biog. Mem.,* XXXVI, 161–191, which includes a photograph. Obituaries appeared in the *N.Y. Times,* Jan. 7, 1950, and in SNAME, *Trans.,* 1950.]

WILLIAM R. PORTER

HOWARD, LELAND OSSIAN (June 11, 1857–May 1, 1950), entomologist, was born in Rockford, Ill., the first of three sons of Ossian Gregory Howard and Lucy Dunham (Thurber) Howard. His parents were natives of central New York, and his father had studied law with a firm in Ithaca. Soon after Leland was born, his father was offered a partnership with this same firm and the family moved back to Ithaca, where the children grew up. Leland's paternal grandfather was a physician in Delhi, N.Y., as well as an amateur astronomer and founder of the local natural history society. Other relatives on his father's side included Senator Jacob M. Howard and Civil War Gen. Oliver O. Howard. On his mother's side he was related to the Federalist leader Timothy Pickering, the naturalist Charles Pickering, and the Harvard astronomer E. C. Pickering.

The Howards were active in the Presbyterian church, where Mrs. Howard and later Leland sang in the choir. As a boy, Leland spent many hours roaming the fields and woods around Ithaca, collecting natural history specimens with his friends. One day while collecting butterflies he met J. H. Comstock, professor of entomology at the new Cornell University. Leland had been given T. W. Harris' classic *Insects Injurious to Vegetation* by his father when he was ten, but Comstock soon introduced him to the writings of many other entomologists. When he entered Cornell in 1873, he spent many hours in Comstock's laboratory and heard such distinguished visiting lecturers as Louis Agassiz and Charles V. Riley. He received his B.S. from Cornell in 1877 and then did a year of premedical graduate work.

Howard received his M.S. degree from Cornell in 1883. In the meantime, in 1878, he had accepted a position as assistant to C. V. Riley, entomologist of the U.S. Department of Agriculture. The years as Riley's assistant were formative ones. Howard began his studies on the systematics of parasitic wasps and suggested the potential of these insects in the control of noxious species. He became interested in mosquitos and discovered the value of kerosene for killing the larvae. He was sent to various parts of the country to study insect outbreaks. Busy as he was, he nevertheless found time to join the Capitol Bicycle Club, cycling having supplanted an earlier interest in rowing (later in his life billiards and bridge became his favorite pastimes). He also joined the Washington Choral Society, where he met his wife, Marie Theodora Clifton. They were married on Apr. 28, 1886, and had three daughters: Lucy Thurber, Candace Leland, and Janet Moore.

When Riley retired in 1894, Howard was appointed chief of the division (later bureau) of entomology, a position he filled with distinction for thirty-three years. When he assumed this position, the division employed nine persons and had an annual budget of $30,000. Upon his retirement it employed more than 750 persons and had a budget of about $3 million. Some of this expansion was a result of the general growth of government scientific activity; some may be attributed to the several serious outbreak of pests that occurred during this period—the cotton boll weevil and the San Jose scale, for example. But much can be attributed to Howard's skill as an administrator and as a popularizer of entomology. Although his lectures and publications covered a wide variety of entomological topics, he was particularly drawn to two fields: biological control and insects as disease carriers. During Howard's regime a great many parasitic insects brought in from other countries in order to control such insects as the gypsy moth and the European corn borer, and several North American species were successfully exported to other parts of the world. Howard himself traveled widely on behalf of biological control, and in the course of his career he established friendly relationships with leading entomologists throughout the world.

Howard's early interest in medicine found expression in books on the mosquito and on the housefly (1901, 1911) and (with H. G. Dyar and F. Knab) a pioneering systematic treatment of the mosquitos of North America (1912-1917). He had earlier published a popular work, *The Insect Book* (1901), and he later presented economic entomology to the layman in a book titled *The Insect Menace* (1931). His publications altogether totaled more than 1,000 titles.

Howard was secretary of the American Association for the Advancement of Science for twenty-two years, president in 1920. He was one of the founders of the American Association of Economic Entomologists and its president in 1894. He was a delegate to many international meetings and was president of the Fourth International Congress of Entomology in 1928. He held honorary memberships in more than thirty foreign scientific societies, belonged to more than twenty societies in the United States, holding office in several of them, and was awarded six honorary degrees.

Howard was of short stature and had a short, well-trimmed beard; after middle life he was quite bald. He had an excellent sense of humor and a vast store of anecdotes, which he told with gusto and with "a charming crooked smile." As chief of the Bureau of Entomology he expected the best efforts of everyone on his staff. He was a warm, courteous, and understanding person, noted for his tact and for his ability to make and keep friends. Through the Cosmos Club of Washington, which was virtually his second home, and through his travels and memberships, he perhaps knew more scientists than anyone of his generation.

After his retirement in 1927, Howard remained a consultant to the Department of Agriculture for another four years; thus his government service totaled more than half a century. He lived still another nineteen years, dying at Bronxville, N.Y., a few weeks short of his ninety-third birthday. Cremation followed at Ferncliff Cemetery.

[L. O. Howard published an autobiography, *Fighting the Insects: The Story of an Entomologist* (1933), and many personal anecdotes are to be found in his *History of Applied Entomology* (1930). I am indebted to C. F. W. Muesebeck for sending me his personal recollections of Howard as a man. The more important tributes paid at the time of Howard's death are to be found in the *Jour. of Economic Entomology*, 43 (1950): 958–962 and the *Proc. of the Entomological Society of Washington*, 52 (1950): 224–233. An especially fine account of his personal life appeared in the Nat. Acad. of Sci. *Biog. Memoirs*, XXXIII (1959); this reference also includes a photograph of Howard at the height of his career as well as a selected bibliography. A good photograph of Howard as a younger man is to be found in the *Proc. of the Entomological Soc. of Washington*, 39 (1950), 129.]
HOWARD E. EVANS

HOWARD, WILLIE (Apr. 13, 1886–Jan. 12, 1949), comedian and impersonator on the vaudeville and musical stage, was born William Levkowitz in Neustadt, Germany, evidently a brief stopping place in the migration of his Jewish parents, Leopold Levkowitz and Pauline (Glass) Levkowitz, from Russia to New York City. The father, a cantor, settled his family of three sons and two daughters in Harlem. The oldest son, Eugene, was to lead the others into show business.

Willie, manifesting his showman's talents too soon, was expelled from public school at the age of eleven. He promptly got a job as a boy soprano, singing refrains of popular hits from the wings or balcony at Proctor's 125th Street Theatre. For many months he sang such melodies as "Sweet Sixteen" in support of the great ladies of vaudeville, Anna Held, Louise Dresser, and Bonnie Thornton. Between engagements he acted as a "song plugger," singing in the aisles during intermissions for $5 a week. When his voice began to change, he turned to low comedy at Huber's Museum, doing slapstick imitations of his stage idols, David Warfield, Sam Bernard, and Joe Welsh.

His famous partnership with his brother Eugene began in 1903. At first they emphasized singing over comedy and introduced a number of popular hits, among them "Sweet Adeline." But broad humor became the staple of their act. It was in joining the partnership that Willie assumed the name Howard, under which Eugene was already performing. From the start, it was clearly Willie who was the comic genius and the darling of the audiences. Small in stature, with large brown eyes set in a round, boyish face and a mischievous Cheshire-cat grin that appeared on cue, he had a gift for mimicry and an infinite vitality that was as poised as it was unpredictable. The scenario would cast him invariably as the "little man," the servant of classic comedy, who revenges himself for the boorishness and arrogance of his partner, a stuffy upper-class type or business tycoon. From a huge repertoire of gibes, insults, impersonations, and slapstick humiliations, Willie would endlessly improvise and ultimately prevail over his straight man. Touring the Keith and Orpheum circuits, the partnership steadily increased in popularity; by 1912 they were receiving $450 a week.

By this time they had firmly established themselves on Broadway, signing with the Shubert organization to perform in *The Passing Show of 1912* and in a Sigmund Romberg revue, *The Whirl of the World* (1914). During the years that followed they appeared at the Winter Garden in *The Show of Wonders* (1916) and in other editions of *The Passing Show,* returned for a time to vaudeville, and played in several of George White's *Scandals.* On his own, Willie acted during the 1930's in *Ballyhoo of 1932,* the *Ziegfeld Follies,* and in occasional films, including *Millions in the Air* (1935) and *Rose of the Rancho* (1936). In the 1940's, still brimming with energy and with his brother Eugene as his manager, he appeared in *Crazy with the*

Heat (1941), *My Dear Public* (1943), and *Star and Garter* (Chicago, 1944).

Willie Howard married Emily Miles of Chicago, a singer and dancer, on July 2, 1918. They lived at Great Neck, L.I., until her death in 1947. The couple had no children. Howard died in Polyclinic Hospital, New York City, of a liver ailment at the age of sixty-two. He was buried at Cedar Park Cemetery, Emerson, N.J.

Willie Howard defied the solemnities of the workaday world. By word, gesture, and extravagant costuming he invited audiences into the mazes of his eccentric imagination. Offstage as well as on, he pursued a madcap course of practical jokes, impersonations, and Rube-Goldberg-style inventions. His friend and producer George White once said of him, "Anybody who don't like Willie, don't like children."

[*N.Y. Times* obituary, Jan. 13, 1949; Murray Schumach, "Willie Howard—The World's His Straight Man," *N.Y. Times Mag.,* May 2, 1948; *Who's Who in Am. Jewry,* 1938–1939; John Parker, ed., *Who's Who in the Theatre,* 10th ed. (1947), which gives his birth year as 1883; David Ewen, *Complete Book of the Am. Musical Theatre* (1958).]

ALBERT F. McLEAN

HOWE, PERCY ROGERS (Sept. 30, 1864-Feb. 28, 1950), dentist and pioneer in dental research, was born in North Providence, R.I., the younger of two children and only son of James Albert Howe and Elizabeth Rachel (Rogers) Howe, both of English and Scottish stock. His father was a Baptist minister who became dean of the Cobb Divinity School at Bates College in Lewiston, Maine. Young Howe spent his childhood in Lewiston and attended the Nichols Latin School and Bates College, receiving the B.A. degree in 1887. Unwilling to enter the ministry, as his father would have liked, and with no other career apparently available, he accepted an offer to serve an apprenticeship with the family dentist. The work kindled his interest, and at the end of the year he entered the Philadelphia Dental College, receiving the D.D.S. degree in 1890. He established a successful practice in Lewiston and—at first, on a part-time basis—a second one in Boston. In 1903 he gave up his office in Maine and settled in Boston. His practice flourished, and he gained a reputation as a dentist who took an unusual interest in the well-being of his patients.

Endowed with a keen intellect and an independent turn of mind, Howe was troubled from the beginning of his career by the feeling that he was being asked to treat the symptoms rather than the disease and that dentistry ought not to be isolated from medicine. Dentistry at this time was essentially technique-oriented, concerned with repairing or removing diseased teeth, with little attention to the cause, cure, or prevention of dental disease. It was widely believed that pyorrhea and caries were produced by chemical or bacterial substances in the mouth, that a clean tooth would not decay, and that bad teeth could cause bodily illness. Howe questioned all these views. He had observed that bacteria was normally present even in healthy mouths, and he early became convinced that diet and nutrition were important factors in the condition of the teeth and that bad teeth were usually the result rather than the cause of poor health.

Howe was among the first to seek answers to such questions through application of the scientific method. To explore the problem of dental decay, he set up a private laboratory in connection with his office, and in his spare time he studied the chemical composition of saliva, collected from his patients, and its secretion of medicinal and other substances ingested by the body. He was conscious of having an inadequate background in physiology and biological chemistry, and so, to widen his knowledge, he formed acquaintanceships with Lawrence J. Henderson and Otto Folin at Harvard, who encouraged his investigations. Howe's work attracted considerable attention, and in 1915, at the age of fifty, he was appointed chief of research at the newly opened Forsyth Dental Infirmary for Children, in Boston. Thereafter, he gradually gave up his private practice and devoted the remainder of his long life to research and to the reform of dental education.

With a well-equipped laboratory and the assistance of a trained bacteriologist, Howe investigated the role of oral microorganisms in producing caries, and particularly the etiology of pyorrhea, a disease then widely and erroneously believed to be caused by the same oral amoebas that were responsible for dysentery. Using material from the mouths of children at the infirmary, he was able to show that the amoebas often present were harmless organisms that could exist in entirely healthy mouths. One of Howe's most important contributions, made during his early years at the Forsyth, was a method of treating diseased teeth instead of extracting them. By introducing ammoniated silver nitrate into the affected tooth and root canals and then precipitating the silver so that it formed a sterile filling, he was able to check the spread of carious lesions and save the tooth. This method, which became widely adopted, was the first chemotherapeutic treatment of dental caries.

The relation between nutrition and dental disease remained a major interest. In experiments with guinea pigs and, later, with rhesus monkeys, Howe showed that diets deficient in vitamins brought about profound deterioration in the tooth and bone structure, similar to that observed in scurvy, and that an antiscorbutic diet would initiate repair. Having demonstrated that general health could directly affect dental health, he began an intensive—and, for a long time, lonely—battle against the prevalent theory that decaying teeth could act as foci for bodily infection and against the common medical practice of ordering the wholesale extraction of teeth as a means of curing a patient's illness.

In 1927 Howe was made director of the Forsyth Infirmary, a post he held until his death. During his years as director, he oversaw the training of more than five hundred interns, many of whom came from abroad and later were instrumental in advancing the progress of dentistry in their own countries. Howe formed strong personal and professional ties with such stalwarts at the Harvard Medical School as Walter B. Cannon, Hans Zinsser, and the pathologist S. Burt Wolbach. With Wolbach he collaborated on a number of fundamental studies on the pathological consequences of deficiencies in vitamins A and C. Howe also taught at the Harvard Dental School as assistant professor of dental research (1917-1925) and as Thomas Alexander Forsyth professor of dental science (1925-1940), but he was critical of the curriculum: in his opinion it paid too much attention to dental repair and not enough to the whole man. In 1937 he was appointed to a university committee to consider the future course of dental education at Harvard and was influential in the eventual conversion of the Harvard Dental School to the School of Dental Medicine, with a four-year course of instruction equally divided between medicine and clinical dentistry— a realization of his long-cherished dream that dentistry be regarded as a branch of medicine.

A man of stocky build, with a firm set to his jaw, Howe had great courage, and no opposition could dissuade him from what he believed to be the better course. Yet he was warm and sympathetic in his relations with his associates and with the child patients at the Forsyth.

On Dec. 21, 1891, Howe married Rose Alma Hilton, a college classmate. They had two sons, James Albert and John Farwell. His wife died after a marriage of fifty years, and on Aug. 18, 1943, he married Ruth Loring White, a nutritionist who had long been his assistant. Seven years later, at the age of eighty-five, Howe died of a cerebral hemorrhage at his home in Belmont, Mass. He was buried in the Belmont Cemetery.

Among the honors that came to Howe were the presidency of the American Dental Association (1929-1930)—maverick though he had been—and election as a fellow in dental surgery of the Royal College of Surgeons in England (1948). His influence on the development of dental science was far-reaching. He firmly established the need for research, and he demonstrated, to both dentists and physicians, the close relation between oral health and the health of the body as a physiological unit.

[Rollo Walter Brown, *Dr. Howe and the Forsyth Infirmary* (1952), is the basic source. It includes a photograph of Howe taken in his later years and a complete bibliography of his publications. His archival materials are at the Forsyth Dental Infirmary for Children, Boston. See also faculty minutes in *Harvard Univ. Gazette*, Apr. 29, 1950. Additional information was supplied by Mrs. Howe.]

ROY O. GREEP

HUGHES, CHARLES EVANS (Apr. 11, 1862-Aug. 27, 1948), lawyer, governor, presidential candidate, U.S. secretary of state, and chief justice of the Supreme Court, was born in Glens Falls, N.Y., an only child. His father, David Charles Hughes, was a Welshman who had been a printer but became a licensed Methodist preacher shortly before coming to the United States at the age of twenty-three. He took a church in Eddyville, N.Y., where he met and courted Mary Catherine Connelly, a young schoolteacher. Her father was a building contractor whose family, of English and Scots-Irish descent, had lived in the Hudson Valley for several generations; her maternal ancestors were mostly Dutch. The marriage occurred in 1860, after David Hughes became a Baptist to meet her family's wishes. Hughes pursued the rigorous life of an itinerant evangelical minister, and the family lived in Glens Falls, Sandy Hills, and Oswego in upstate New York, Newark, N.J., and Brooklyn, N.Y., during young Charles's earliest years.

Charles Evans Hughes recalled a sharp contrast of temper in his parents, the father warm and impetuous, the mother prudent and reserved. Together they imposed the discipline of a striving Christian household on their son. A precocious lad with a quick, retentive mind, Hughes favored the close stimulus of his parents' teaching over the ordinary schoolroom. He studied at home until he was nine, surrounded by his father's books and his mother's concern. He emerged from childhood sober, purposeful, and filled with the belief that happiness lay in the performance of duty. After three years in the Newark public schools and another at Public School No. 35 in Manhattan (a city he was fond of exploring as a boy), he was ready to leave for college.

In the fall of 1876 he entered Madison (now Colgate) University, a tiny Baptist school in upstate New York. Freedom from hovering parental oversight proved refreshing, but the academic fare at Madison left him restless. In 1878 he transferred to Brown University. There he matured socially and intellectually, savoring the pleasures of fraternity life, discovering European fiction, editing the campus paper, and testing the convictions of his parents against his academic studies. Under the training of President Ezekiel G. Robinson in philosophy and Professor J. Lewis Diman in political economy, his outlook broadened without serious damage to his inherited beliefs. "I am intent on reforming many of your opinions," he told his father (Pusey, p. 57), but his own moral framework remained grounded in reason, obligation, and faith in the friendly auspices of Divine Providence. A half-century later he would reflect on his college experience, "first, that there was so much that we did not learn, and, second, that we learned so many things that were not so" (Frankfurter, p. 148). He graduated third in a class of forty-three.

Hughes taught school for a year at Delaware Academy in Delhi, N.Y., reading law on the side under a local lawyer. In 1882 he entered Columbia Law School. The training he received was deductive in method and conservative in tone, rooted in pre-Holmesian principles of legal certitude. Precise and thorough, Hughes was an able student. Upon graduation in 1884, he passed the bar exam with an extraordinary score of 99.5. In the fall of 1884 he entered a New York law firm under the wing of Walter S. Carter, for whom he had clerked in previous summers. Three years later he became a partner in the firm, and on Dec. 5, 1888, he married his partner's daughter, Antoinette Carter. The marriage was happy and durable. Four children were born over the next nineteen years: Charles, Jr., Helen, Catherine, and Elizabeth.

Hughes attacked his work with skill and awesome devotion, and his practice, commercial law, brought him swift prominence in the New York legal community. But the strain of single-minded perfectionism began to show on his health. In 1891 he left the city for two years to teach at the Cornell Law School. Restored, he took up practice again at his usual pace.

Solitary mountain-climbing vacations in Switzerland and elsewhere offered relief in succeeding years but his normal regimen remained austere. He grew his famous beard in 1890 to save trips to the barber and later gave up smoking to improve his personal efficiency. Aside from infrequent forays into local Republican reform politics, and a stint of Sunday School teaching at John D. Rockefeller's Fifth Avenue Baptist Church, his mind focused on the law.

In 1905, on the advice of Henry W. Taft, brother of William Howard Taft, then secretary of war, the chairman of a joint investigative committee of the state legislature asked Hughes to lead an inquiry as committee counsel into the malpractices of the New York City utilities industry. Defining the job as a civic duty and insisting on absolute freedom from political pressure, Hughes proceeded to expose gross overcapitalization in the gas trust, swollen rates charged to the city for gas and electricity, and poisonous adulteration of the gas. His suggested remedies, stressing public regulation of the giant utilities rather than enforced competition, were promptly adopted in Albany. He next applied his powers of lucid analysis to the scandal-stained complexities of the New York life insurance business. As counsel for the Armstrong Committee of the state legislature, in fifty-seven public hearings, Hughes grilled a long line of political and financial titans about the web of manipulation and profiteering that governed the insurance field. The findings were sensational and chastening. Once more a cool, implacable investigation triggered corrective legislation. Both inquiries revealed a need to impose public standards of order on these fast-growing, oligopolistic sectors of American business.

Progressive reform had a new hero. In 1906, to blunt the drive of William Randolph Hearst to become Democratic governor of New York, influential Republicans led by Theodore Roosevent urged Hughes to run for the office. Hughes accepted the nomination and waged a strenuous campaign, aware that the enthusiasm of lesser party bosses for him was well under control. He enjoyed support on Wall Street and in the press, especially Joseph Pulitzer's *New York World,* and was the only Republican that year to win statewide office, defeating Hearst by 57,897 votes out of a total of 1,452,467 cast.

Hughes brought a somewhat frosty version of progressivism to the state. Assertive, disinterested, alert to public opinion, he styled the governor's role as a tribune of the citizenry. The office was superbly administered, in line with current canons of centralized executive authority. Hughes placed New York in the vanguard of states experimenting with government by commission. He persuaded the legislature to create two new regulatory commissions, one for the utilities serving the metropolis, one for the rest of the state, each equipped with fact-finding powers, rate-setting initiative, and freedom from arbitrary judicial interference. He also gained important advances in labor law, including a workmen's compensation act, which created the first significant social insurance plan in the nation.

Impervious to the normal expediencies of professional politics, he often sacrificed partisan support to gain his ends. His hard fight to maintain the state's constitutional prohibition of racetrack gambling alienated many party regulars. In the course of a long and wounding effort to remove his superintendent of insurance from office, he rebuffed friendly intervention from the White House. This permanently chilled relations with Roosevelt, who concluded that Hughes "has a nature which resents the necessity of feeling gratitude" (*Roosevelt,* VI, p. 1240). Still, Hughes's record had moved him to the front rank of nationally eminent Republicans. Roosevelt shunned him as a presidential successor in 1908 but insisted on his renomination for governor. Hughes was reelected, though he ran well behind the ticket. His efforts thereafter to rouse public opinion behind proposals for ballot reform and a state system of direct primaries were rebuffed by the legislature. His shortcomings in the craft of party leadership stalled further reform.

When William Howard Taft offered him a seat on the Supreme Court, in 1910, Hughes accepted with alacrity. The youngest member of the Court, he contributed energy, practicality, and impressive analytical force to its work. Of the 151 opinions he wrote over the next six years, he dissented in only thirty-two cases, and in only nine cases was there dissent from his decisions. His most far-reaching decisions untangled complex issues raised by expanding federal regulation of rail transportation. In both the *Minnesota Rate* cases (230 U.S. 352 [1913]) and the *Shreveport* case (234 U.S. 342 [1914]) he asserted in his majority opinion the supreme and plenary power of Congress over interstate commerce, even when used to control intrastate traffic that was commingled with interstate operations. These decisions were vital in fostering the practical achievement of a mature and integrated national rail system. Hughes also defined more generously than any colleague the regulatory power of states and cities to curb the scope of privileged contracts, and in several cases he spoke for a unanimous court in upholding state labor laws against the claim that such laws denied freedom of contract without due process of law. He showed a bent for humanitarian realism in cases affecting the treatment of contract laborers, alien workers, Negro rail passengers, and other disadvantaged groups. In the subtle context of those years, his judicial influence was activist and liberating.

Hughes rejected feelers about a presidential nomination in 1912, declaring that "no man is as essential to his country's well being as is the unstained integrity of the courts" (*New York Times,* June 21, 1912). Four years later, in the new climate of world war, with his party out of power, he answered a fresh call by leaving the Court to run against Woodrow Wilson. His campaign was a sequence of miscalculations—badly managed, captious, and unconvincing. Responding to bellicose advice from Theodore Roosevelt, who privately called him a "bearded iceberg" (*Roosevelt,* VIII, p. 1078), Hughes demanded bolder policies against both Germany and Mexico and sterner measures of war preparation. He searched in vain for domestic issues with which to challenge Wilson's progressive record, and ended with a high-tariff, antilabor, probusiness image that obscured his own reform credentials. His failure to enlist the support of Hiram Johnson and California Progressives was the climactic error of an unhappy race. Hughes lost not only California but the Midwestern farm vote. His inability to mobilize the traditional Republican majority against Wilson ended his career in elective politics.

Returning to private practice in New York, he soon worked up an impressive practice in corporate law. His libertarian scruples were abused by postwar antiradical hysteria, and in 1920 he made an angry, futile protest against the eviction of five Socialists from the New York legislature. With little prior experience in international affairs, he emerged as a moderate critic of Wilson's plans for collective security through the League of Nations. He mistrusted the abstract universalism of Wilson's rhetoric and feared that unqualified commitment to Article X of the league covenant might bind the United States in a congealing structure of postwar obligations. He favored joining the league on terms calculated to mollify domestic sentiment, with leeway for the exercise of normal American interests. During the campaign of 1920 he joined thirty other distinguished Republicans in an appeal for Republican victory to insure American membership in an amended league.

Shortly after Warren Harding made him secretary of state in 1921, Hughes bowed to congressional intransigence and presidential inertia, dropped his advocacy of league membership, and negotiated a separate peace with Germany. Prophecy and martyrdom did not attract him; he was greatly interested in contemporary success as a manager of foreign policy. Sensitive to nationalistic public opinion and expanding boundaries of congressional assertion in the field, he tried to establish American relations with the world on narrow, legalistic, but amicable grounds. While shunning political involvement in league affairs, he favored cooperation on matters of international adjudication. Here he stood in the mainstream of historic American faith and sympathy. Nevertheless, stubborn senatorial tactics blocked his efforts to secure United States membership in the World Court.

Hughes was more successful in arranging for American participation, without congressional interference, in the work of the league's Reparations Commission. In 1923 his suggestion that the commission invite American experts to help untangle Germany's postwar fiscal problems led to the adoption of the Dawes Plan, which—backed by Wall Street loans solicited by Hughes—brought momentary relief to the German economy. Remarkably, he remained untroubled by the contradiction between his own reparations and war debt policy, on the one hand, and the Republican party's high tariff policy, on the other.

His most visible feats as secretary of state occurred at the Washington Conference (1921-1922), called mainly at his initiative to deal with naval arms competition and to stabilize relations among Pacific powers. Responding to congressional support for disarmament, anxiety over tension between the United States and Great Britain and Japan, and a vague American desire to compensate for Versailles, Hughes strove to fix the construction of capital ships at current levels by international agreement. His opening speech to the conference, stunning in its concrete formulas for stability, was the most dramatic public moment of his career. In subsequent negotiations Hughes won consent to his 5-5-3 ratio, which froze the naval arms race for a decade. A Four-Power Pact, promising security for Japan in the western Pacific, and a Nine-Power Treaty, securing multilateral observance of the Open Door in China, also emerged from the conference. The latter treaty, lacking machinery and sanctions, seemed in retrospect a paper barricade against aggression, and a 1924 congressional decision to exclude Japanese immigration to the United States went far to wipe out the ameliorating influence of the Washington Conference on Japanese-American relations, as Hughes foresaw.

In Latin America, Hughes moved American policy gradually away from Wilson's interventionism and the Roosevelt "Corollary" to the Monroe Doctrine toward the Good Neighbor Policy of the 1930's. On his advice, the United States pulled marines out of the Dominican Republic in 1924 and began withdrawal from Nicaragua, but left troops in place in Haiti. He used the weapon of diplomatic nonrecognition to protect American property rights in Mexico and later supplied the Mexican government with arms for use against revolutionary dissidents. Wrapping interventionism in the soft phrase "non-belligerent interposition," he carefully preserved the substance of unilateral American power in the Western Hemisphere, insisting in effect that the Monroe Doctrine was what the United States said it was.

His achievements at the State Department, while winning wide praise, diminished in consequence with passing time. The ultimate collapse of reparations agreements, the Washington Conference treaties, and his rationales for Latin American intervention all stamped his policies as dated transitions of the interwar era. Hughes was not an adventurous or boldly creative secretary. Serving in years of narrowed national vision under two lethargic presidents, he worked with practical conservative intelligence to shore American interests in a world of radical disorder.

Hughes left office in 1925 to rebuild his fortune in Wall Street law practice. He was the acknowledged leader of the American bar when Herbert Hoover chose him to replace Taft as chief justice in 1930. Resentment among Progressives and Southern Democrats over his partisan decision to leave the Court in 1916, as well as his corporate associations as a private lawyer, resulted in a 52-26 Senate division on his confirmation. This vote, surprising and painful to Hughes, anticipated larger troubles awaiting his tenure on the high bench. He took office, at the age of sixty-eight, at the outset of the worst and longest economic crisis in American history, one that would try the nation's governing institutions, including the Court, with a severity unmatched since the Civil War. To the task of leading a divided Court through this crisis, Hughes brought not only administrative poise and clarity of intellect, but a background of experience more varied and extensive than that of any predecessor. The stability of the Court across the 1930's owed much to his radiant personal authority.

Somewhat more conservative than in his earlier service on the Court, he responded to the legislative tumult of the New Deal years with doctrinal calm and a practiced eye for the Court's reputation. Concerned to maintain an appearance of legal continuity, he often yielded logic in a search for fine distinctions to avoid abandoning precedents outright. His liberal colleague Harlan Fiske Stone found him overly sinuous in this regard. Hughes was prepared to adapt the language of the Constitution flexibly to the harsher exigencies of the Great Depression, despite grave reservations over the technical performance of legislators and anxiety about overcentralization within the federal system. In dealing with questions of legal principle, he commented in 1936, "we do not suddenly rise into a stratosphere of icy certainty" (*American Bar Association Journal*, 22 [1936], p. 375). In this attitude he differed more often than not with the Court's conservative wing and maneuvered skillfully through the judicial revolution of the decade.

His opinion in the Minnesota mortgage moratorium case, *Home Building & Loan Ass'n* v. *Blaisdell* (290 U.S. 398 [1934]), indicated the distance Hughes seemed ready to travel in sanctioning public action to meet economic emergency, in this case the problem of widespread farm foreclosures and the attendant threat of social upheaval. In upholding the Minnesota moratorium despite a constitutional bar against such legislation, he asserted the overriding need for "a government which retains adequate authority to secure the peace and good order of society." The sweep of this language may have been misleading. A year later a unanimous Court struck down the Frazier-Lemke Act, a congressional measure to protect farm mortgage debtors, and in the celebrated "sick chicken" case, *Schechter Poultry Corp.* v. *U.S.* (295 U.S. 495 [1935]), the Court unanimously found the National Industrial Recovery Act—the New Deal's most ambitious antidepression remedy—unconstitutional on the ground that Congress had stretched the NRA's code-making power beyond the limits of the commerce clause and had delegated legislative authority over the codes to the executive branch. In Hughes's opinion the NRA pressed administrative centralization too far. New Deal efforts to stabilize farm prices sustained a hard blow in *U.S.* v. *Butler* (297 U.S. 1 [1936]), in which Hughes joined a 6-3 majority that found the Agricultural Adjustment Act invalid in its misuse of the tax power to benefit one group at the expense of others. The same year, in *Carter* v. *Carter Coal Co.* (298 U.S. 238 [1936]), the Court invalidated federal legislation to bring order to the soft coal industry; in a separate concurring opinion, Hughes resorted to a distinction between mining and commerce as support for his view that parts of the law in question overreached congressional power to regulate interstate commerce. Hughes retained, however, a generous attitude toward the police power of the states, as indicated by his dissent from the decision in *Morehead* v. *Tipaldo* (298 U.S. 587 [1936]) to strike down a New York state minimum wage law for women.

When Franklin Roosevelt, out of concern for the fate of major New Deal measures still before the Court, proposed his famous court-packing plan in February 1937, he discovered in Hughes a skilled rival in the art of timing and maneuver. At the request of Sen. Burton K. Wheeler, Hughes prepared a powerful letter of reply to Roosevelt's critique of the Court's efficiency, and thereby undercut the president's public rationale for Court reform. A week later, he triumphantly spoke for the Court in *West Coast Hotel* v. *Parrish* (300 U.S. 379 [1937]), which reversed the Morehead decision of the year before. (When Justice Owen J. Roberts, who held the swing vote in this case as in several others, told Hughes of his changed position earlier that winter, the chief justice "almost hugged" him, according to Roberts.) And on Apr. 12, 1937, speaking for a 5-4 majority in one of the most important decisions he ever wrote, *National Labor Relations Board* v. *Jones and Laughlin Steel Corp.* (391 U.S. 1 [1937]), Hughes found the Wagner Labor Relations Act constitutional. In this case, his steady concern for industrial peace and meaningful liberty in a corporate society won his assent to a crucial New Deal initiative.

Hughes denied that the Court had shifted under pressure, and later noted that his opinion in *Jones and Laughlin* was consistent with the ground he had taken twenty-four years earlier in the *Minnesota Rate* cases. Nevertheless, the 1937 decisions triggered a momentous change of judicial attitude toward the commerce power and due process. Hughes's performance in the crisis was more masterful than he acknowledged. Believing with his old friend and former colleague Oliver Wendell Holmes that the Constitution was a structure in process, responsive to felt needs, he not only maintained the integrity of the high bench under duress but, in helping to adjust the limits of public intervention in the economy, he joined the master builders of the American federal system.

As chief justice, Hughes presided with grace over the changing makeup and orientation of the Court after 1937. Throughout the decade he held positions on issues of civil liberties and civil rights that anticipated the Court's later thrust in that realm. The Bill of Rights and the Fourteenth Amendment prospered from his strong stance in favor of free speech and press and equal protection of the laws. Against a background of national and international tension over these values, he repeatedly expressed a conviction that the safety of the republic lay in "the opportunity for free political discussion to the end that government may be responsive to the will of the people and that changes may be obtained by peaceful means" (*Stromberg* v. *California*, 283 U.S. 359 [1931] and *DeJonge* v. *Oregon*, 299 U.S. 353 [1937]).

After his retirement from the Court in 1941, Hughes continued to live in Washington, dictating his autobiographical notes and preparing his record for the bar of history. Always protective of his public reputation, reserving for close companions those flashes of humor and humility that revealed the stresses in the private man, he had accepted eminence as the award of a sane society to virtuous citizens who did their best. When Hughes left the Court in 1916 in the name of duty to try for his country's highest prize, Justice Holmes wrote—"I shall miss him consumedly, for he is not only a good fellow, experienced and wise, but funny, and with doubts that open vistas through the wall of a non-conformist conscience" (*Holmes-Pollock*, p. 237). Hughes died of congestive heart failure at the age of eighty-six in Washington, D.C., and was buried beside his wife in Woodlawn Cemetery in New York.

[The Charles Evans Hughes Papers are in the Lib. of Cong. David J. Danelski and Joseph S. Tulchin, eds., *The Autobiographical Notes of Charles Evans Hughes* (1973), records Hughes's estimate of his career. Merlo J. Pusey, *Charles Evans Hughes* (2 vols., 1951), is an authorized biography, thorough and sympathetic. Dexter Perkins, *Charles Evans Hughes and American Democratic Statesmanship* (1956), is a briefer friendly interpretation. Aspects of the career are treated in Robert F. Wesser, *Charles Evans Hughes: Politics and Reform in New York, 1905–1910* (1967), Betty Glad, *Charles Evans Hughes and the Illusions of Innocence: A Study in American Diplomacy* (1966), and Samuel Hendel, *Charles Evans Hughes and the Supreme Court* (1951). Differing perspectives on the chief justice are found in Alpheus T. Mason, *The Supreme Court from Taft to Warren* (1958), Ch. 3; Paul A. Freund, "Charles Evans Hughes as Chief Justice," *Harvard Law Rev.*, 81 (1967), 4–43; and Hendel, "Charles Evans Hughes," in Leon Friedman and Fred L. Israel, eds., *The Justices of the United States Supreme Court, 1789–1969*, III, 1893–1915 (1969). Also of use were Felix Frankfurter, *Of Law and Men* (1956); *Letters of Theodore Roosevelt*, VI (1952) and VIII (1954); "Address of Chief Justice Hughes," *Am. Bar Assoc. Jour.*, June 1936; and *Holmes–Pollock Letters*, I (1941).]

GEOFFREY BLODGETT

HUGHES, EDWIN HOLT (Dec. 7, 1866–Feb. 12, 1950), Methodist Episcopal bishop, was born in Moundsville, W.Va., the third son and third of six children of Thomas Bayless Hughes and Louisa (Holt) Hughes. His father's forebears were Welshmen who had farmed in the Great Valley of Virginia since the eighteenth century; the Holts descended from English settlers of Virginia's Northern Neck. Reflecting the divided sentiments of western Virginia before the Civil War, the Hughes family generally defended slavery and advocated secession, while the Holts supported abolition and union. Thomas Hughes (1836–1918) broke family traditions: he favored freedom for the slaves, and at the age of twenty-one he forsook farming to enter the Methodist ministry. Because of the Methodist itinerant system, the family moved often. As a result, Edwin received only sporadic elementary schooling, although he did have two years in the "prep department" of West Virginia University. In 1883 he was sent to Ohio Wesleyan College; but in 1885 his family removed to Iowa and he transferred to Grinnell College, where he was admitted as a sophomore.

By 1886 Hughes had become convinced that he too should become a minister. He left college that year to serve as supply pastor for a small Methodist church at Madison, Iowa, but returned in 1887 to Ohio Wesleyan, where he was elected to Phi Beta Kappa and from which he graduated in 1889. Since his chief extracurricular activity had long been "declamation," in May 1889 he easily won an interstate oratorical contest, prompting an Ohio banker and Wesleyan trustee, Morris Sharp, to offer him financial support for seminary study. After serving a summer pastorate at Marengo, Iowa, Hughes enrolled in the School of Theology at Boston University and, upon his graduation in 1892, was ordained into the Methodist ministry. On June 8, 1892, he married Isabel Baker Ebbert, of Atlanta, Ga., to whom he had been engaged for four years. They had eight children: Margaret Rebecca, Isabel, Edwin Holt, Ebbert Magee, Caroline Robinson, Morris Sharp, Anna Louise, and Francis Montgomery.

The young couple settled first into the parsonage of the Methodist church in Newton Centre, Mass., where Hughes served from 1892 to 1896. Then he was appointed to the strongest Methodist church in New England, in Malden, Mass., for what became a ministry of seven years. In 1903 he was elected to the presidency of DePauw University, in Greencastle, Ind. The school was then bordering on bankruptcy. Refusing to accept any more salary than he had received in the pastorate, Hughes worked so hard to save DePauw that his weight dropped from 151 to 120 pounds in the first year. But save the school he did—and in the process earned appointment to the State Board of Education and the board of trustees of the Carnegie Foundation for the Advancement of Teaching. As president of the Indiana State Teachers' Association in 1904 he helped secure a state minimum-wage law for teachers.

In 1908 the Methodist Episcopal Church elected Hughes as one of its bishops. For the remainder of his active ministry he exercised his considerable administrative talents in four diverse and widely separated areas: San Francisco, 1908–1916; Boston, 1916–1924; Chicago, 1924–1932; and Washington, D.C., 1932–1940. Responding to many calls, he preached on more than fifty college campuses; held lectureships at six colleges and universities; ministered in war camps (1917–1919); served as trustee for four colleges; as acting president for Boston University (1923); as acting chancellor for American University (1933); and traveled as fraternal delegate to Methodist conferences in Ireland, England, Norway, and Finland. As chairman of the Conference Courses of Study Commission (1916–1940), he helped provide educational opportunities for thousands of Methodist ministers who lacked seminary training. Fulfilling a total abstinence pledge made at age eleven, he worked with several state antisaloon groups and served as president of the Methodist Board of Temperance (1932–1940). He played a leading role in producing *The Methodist Hymnal* (1935), which included a revised ritual and new responsive readings for public worship.

The climax of Hughes's career came when as senior bishop (since 1936) of his denomination he saw the Methodist Protestant Church and the Methodist Episcopal Church, South, re-united with the Methodist Episcopal Church in 1939. The Methodist Protestants had separated in 1828 in a dispute over lay representation in General Conference, and the Southerners in 1844 because of the unresolved issue of slavery. Long years of war, Reconstruction, and recrimination had left a legacy of bitterness that tentative efforts toward reconciliation had failed to overcome. Hughes remembered with sorrow the antebellum divisions that had reached into his own family, and in his mature years the healing of Methodist rifts became an overpowering concern. From 1922 onward he served almost continuously on various commissions seeking unification and spoke with increasing urgency on the need to bring Methodists back together. He won the confidence of all three branches, so that a fellow bishop wrote, "The Hughes oratory was the largest single personal force from the northern church in creating the sentiment for the unification movement in Methodism" (McConnell, pp. 247-248). With Hughes as prime mover, a Plan of Union was formulated, which the Northern church approved in 1936. Two years later Hughes went as fraternal delegate, along with President James H. Straughn of the Methodist Protestant Church, to the General Conference of the Methodist Episcopal Church, South, meeting under the leadership of its senior bishop, John H. Moore. After the Southerners had approved the plan, Hughes, Straughn, and Moore clasped hands and posed for a photograph that quickly became one of the most famous symbols of American Methodism. When the formal Uniting Conference was held in Kansas City in April 1939, Hughes presided and closed the historic session with a moving address on the theme "Methodists are one people."

Hughes retired in 1940 but remained active. He was recalled to become temporary bishop of the Washington (D.C.) Area in 1943 and of the Wisconsin Area in 1947. While lecturing in Muncie, Ind., in January 1950, he became ill with viral pneumonia. Returning to Washington, D.C., he entered Sibley Hospital, where he died two weeks later. Memorial services were conducted at Foundry Methodist Church, and afterward his body was carried to Greencastle, Ind., for interment on the campus of DePauw University alongside that of his wife, who had died in 1938.

[Hughes's autobiography, *I Was Made a Minister* (1943), apparently written somewhat reluctantly at the urging of friends and admirers, is in a stilted Victorian style but is generally reliable for factual data. Personal observations by a friend and colleague are in Francis J. McConnell, *By the Way, An Autobiog.* (1952). Obituaries appeared on Feb. 13, 1950, in *N.Y. Times* and *Washington Post*, both with picture.]

C. C. GOEN

HUMPHREYS, WILLIAM JACKSON (Feb. 3, 1862-Nov. 10, 1949), physicist, meteorologist, was born in a one-room log house at Gap Mills, Va. (later W.Va.), the oldest of four children (two boys and two girls) of Andrew Jackson Humphreys, a farmer and miller, and Eliza Ann (Eads) Humphreys. His father was descended from Samuel Humphreys, a Scotch-Irish immigrant who settled in Pennsylvania in 1775 and moved on to Virginia. His maternal grandfather, whose family had come to Maryland about the time of the American Revolution, was a pioneer of the Gap Mills area. Eliza Humphreys was a "firm but kind" mother whose concern for her children's education strongly influenced William's career. At her urging, the family moved in 1880 to Pomeroy, Ohio, where a college-preparatory high school was available. Humphreys attended it for two years and then entered Washington and Lee University in Lexington, Va., with financial assistance from relatives, including his uncle Milton Humphreys, a professor of Greek at Vanderbilt University. After receiving the degree of B.A. (1886) and C.E. (1888), he studied for a year at the University of Virginia, where he received "diplomas" in physics and chemistry. From 1889 to 1893 he taught physics and mathematics at the nearby Miller School and then for a year was professor of science at Washington College in Maryland.

Having paid back most of his financial debt to his family, Humphreys entered Johns Hopkins University in 1894 on a scholarship and pursued graduate work under the physicist Joseph S. Ames. With another student, he carried out extensive experiments on the effect of different gas pressures on the spectra produced by electric arcs, earning a Ph.D. in 1897. He also made significant investigations of the solution and diffusion of metals and alloys in mercury. Humphreys served for the next eight years as an instructor in physics at the University of Virginia; during this time, at the invitation of the Naval Observatory, he also accompanied two eclipse expeditions, to Georgia in 1900 and to Sumatra the following year, to photograph the solar flash spectrum.

When in 1905 the University of Virginia failed to promote Humphreys to a professorship, he reluctantly accepted an appointment with the U.S. Weather Bureau as meteorological physicist. This marked a turning point in his career from experimental physics to physical meteorology. His first assignment was as director of the newly established research observatory at Mount Weather on the crest of the Blue Ridge near Bluemont, Va. Scientists, however, ranked below forecasters in the Weather Bureau at that time, and Humphreys failed to receive promised support for his research. In 1908 he was transferred to the bureau's central office in Washington, D.C., where he remained until his retirement at the end of 1935. On Jan. 11, 1908, he married Margaret Gertrude Antrim, daughter of a prosperous merchant of Charlottesville, Va. They had no children.

Besides supervising the Weather Bureau's seismological program (1914-1924) and editing the *Monthly Weather Review* (1931-1935), Humphreys pursued independent research on problems of atmospheric physics. Among these were the composition of the atmosphere, geoclimatic changes, radiational heat balance, the physics of evaporation and condensation and condensation forms, atmospheric circulations of all kinds, notably thunderstorms and tornadoes, and electrical and optical phenomena of many kinds. His most notable contribution was his explanation (1909) of the existence of the isothermal stratosphere as a necessary consequence of radiational equilibrium rather than of the convective equilibrium of the troposphere below the tropopause. The results of Humphreys' research were published in some 250 scholarly articles and in *Physics of the Air* (1920), which went through three editions. He also wrote several popular books on weather topics.

From 1911 to 1933 Humphreys was a part-time professor of meteorological physics at George Washington University, the first college in America to offer a doctorate in meteorology as a separate discipline. He also served on the National Advisory Committee for Aeronautics. He was general secretary of the American Association for the Advancement of Science (1925-1928), president of the American Meteorological Society (1928-1929), national chairman of the American Geophysical Union (1932-1935), and president of the Cosmos Club in Washington (1936). A portly, genial man, Humphreys had a sense of humor that pervaded even his scientific writings.

He died in Washington, at the age of eighty-seven, of an infected tumor of the parotid gland and was buried in Charlottesville. His writing and teaching constituted a scientific oasis in American meteorology during two decades when there was otherwise only climatology and government forecasting.

[Humphreys' colorful but somewhat random autobiography, *Of Me* (privately printed, 1947), includes a complete bibliography of his publications and photographs of him. Useful obituaries appeared in *Science*, July 21, 1950 (by his colleagues S. A. Mitchell and E. W. Woolard) ; Am. Meteorological Soc., *Bull.*, Apr. 1950; and Franklin Inst., *Jour.*, Jan. 1950. See also *Nat. Cyc. Am. Biog.*, XXXVIII, 25–26 ; and *Who Was Who in America*, II (1950).]

HURD C. WILLETT

HUNT, REID (Apr. 20, 1870–Mar. 10, 1948), pharmacologist, was born in Martinsville, Ohio, the younger of two sons of Milton L. Hunt, a prosperous banker, and Sarah E. (Wright) Hunt. His father had moved from Virginia to Ohio before the Civil War because of his opposition to slavery; his mother was a native of Ohio. Both parents were Quakers. Both had also been schoolteachers and were interested in literature; they provided a good education for their sons.

Hunt was first introduced to chemistry by the village druggist. After graduation from the Martinsville high school in 1886, he spent a year at Wilmington College and a year at the University of Ohio (Athens) and then entered the Johns Hopkins University, receiving the B.A. in 1891. He began graduate study at Johns Hopkins in pathology under William H. Welch and in biology under H. Newell Martin. Early in 1892, Hunt went to Germany and enrolled as a medical student at the University of Bonn, but at the end of the summer he returned to Johns Hopkins, where he continued graduate work first under Martin and later under William H. Howell in physiology. In 1896 he received the Ph.D. in physiology from Johns Hopkins and the M.D. from the College of Physicians and Surgeons in Baltimore. Appointed tutor in physiology at the Columbia University College of Physicians and Surgeons in New York, he continued earlier research on the physiology of the heart. He spent two summers (1898, 1899) with Columbia zoologists in Egypt and the Sudan, in a vain quest for specimens of the African lungfish.

In 1898 Hunt returned to Johns Hopkins as a member of the department of pharmacology, headed by John J. Abel. For the next six years he taught and carried out research in the department, serving first as associate in pharmacology and becoming associate professor in 1901. In the summer and fall of 1902 and again during the second half of 1903 and into the early part of 1904, he worked at the

Institut für experimentelle Therapie at Frankfurt am Main, Germany, under Paul Ehrlich, who exercised a strong influence on Hunt's scientific interests.

In 1904 Hunt was asked to organize a division of pharmacology of the Hygienic Laboratory of the United States Public Health and Marine Hospital Service in Washington, D.C. He was made chief of this division and in 1910 was given the title of professor of pharmacology. In 1913 he accepted the chair of pharmacology at the Harvard Medical School, where he served as professor of pharmacology and head of the department until 1936, when he retired.

At the turn of the century pharmacology had begun to emerge as a medical science in the United States. Hunt was uniquely qualified for work in the new field because he had subjected himself, as did few others at the time, to rigorous training in physiology and chemistry without losing sight of the problems of medicine. His first research dealt with the relation between the inhibitory and the accelerator nerves of the vertebrate heart. Under Howell's influence he investigated the reflex decrease in blood pressure resulting from stimulation of afferent nerves, the subject of his Ph.D. thesis and of his later (1918) fundamental studies on vasodilator reactions. The scientific work that brought him international fame, discovering the powerful biological activity of acetylcholine and elucidating the relation between chemical structure and pharmacological action of choline derivatives upon the autonomic system, originated from an observation made in Abel's laboratory in 1899. Hunt noted that suprarenal extracts freed of epinephrine caused a lowering of blood pressure and identified choline as one of the responsible substances. Closer study revealed discrepancies between choline content and biological activity, and Hunt reasoned that the suprarenal gland might contain derivatives of choline more potent than choline itself. After his visits to Ehrlich's laboratory and the move to the Hygienic Laboratory in Washington, he studied the known choline esters. In 1906, with R. de M. Taveau, he described a biological method for the assay of choline, by acetylating the substance and using the blood-pressure-lowering activity to determine its biological potency. He found that acetylation increased the biological activity of choline by a factor of about 100,000, a discovery of profound biological importance. During the subsequent five years, and later at Harvard with the chemist R. R. Renshaw, he amassed a monumental body of facts on a large number of choline derivatives and analogous compounds.

Hunt's wide interests are shown by his work on a variety of physiological, pharmacological, and therapeutic problems. While working with Ehrlich, he had discovered that mice fed thyroid tolerated an amount of acetonitrile several times the lethal dose. For two decades he employed this "acetonitril reaction" to study the physiology and pharmacology of thyroid function, investigations that led to the recognition that thyroid preparations could be made therapeutically reliable by establishing a required percentage content of organically bound iodine. In a study of poisonous plants made for the Department of Agriculture in 1902, Hunt found that the death of livestock ascribed to liliaceous plants of the genus *Zygadenus* (poison camas) was caused by alkaloids similar to those of the genus *Veratrum,* work since verified by definitive chemical studies. In 1902 he also alerted the American medical profession to the toxicity of methyl alcohol, a fact earlier established in Germany. While at Harvard, Hunt became interested in the problem of cancer and the possibility of finding specific remedies; he was not successful in his own experiments on tumor-bearing mice. He was convinced, however, that for this, as for other problems of disease and effective therapy, cooperative research between the chemist, the pharmacologist, and the physician offered the only promise of success.

Hunt made important contributions to the revision of *The Pharmacopeia of the United States of America.* He served as president of the United States Pharmacopeial Convention (1920–1930) and was a member of the permanent standards commission of the League of Nations Health Committee. In 1906 he joined the council on pharmacy and chemistry of the American Medical Association and served as chairman (1927–1936). Hunt was president of the Society for Pharmacology and Experimental Therapeutics (1916–1918). He was elected to membership in the National Academy of Sciences in 1919.

As an investigator, Hunt ranks among the pioneers of American pharmacology. As an educator he was less successful. He was fundamentally an individual worker, little interested in teaching. He greatly enjoyed travel; in 1923 he held a visiting professorship at the Peking Union Medical College in China. Hunt was over six feet tall and gave the impression of physical strength. Despite his dignified appearance and retiring attitude, he was easy to approach. Although gentle and modest in manner, he fought for his principles with determination and persistence. He did not subscribe to any religious beliefs but all his life "practiced self-restraint and charity in accordance with his Quaker upbringing."

Hunt married Mary Lillie Taylor of Washington, D.C., on Dec. 12, 1908; they had no children. Still physically strong for some time after his retirement, he became incapacitated by disturbances of the circulation of the brain and spent his last years at the McLean Hospital in Belmont, Mass., where he died. After cremation, his ashes were buried in the cemetery adjoining the Church of the Messiah at Woods Hole, Mass.

[Hunt's publications include "On the Physiological Action of Certain Cholin Derivatives and New Methods for Detecting Cholin," *Brit. Med. Jour.*, 2 (1906), 1788–1791; "On the Relation Between the Toxicity and Chemical Constitution of a Number of Derivatives of Choline and Analogous Compounds," *Jour. Pharmacol. Exper. Therap.*, 1 (1909), 303–339, both with R. de M. Taveau; "Vasodilator Reactions," *Am. Jour. Physiol.*, 45 (1918), 197–230, 231–267; and the following with R. R. Renshaw: "On Some Effects of Arsonium, Stibonium, Phosphonium and Sulfonium Compounds on the Autonomic Nervous System," *Jour. Pharmacol. Exper. Therap.*, 25 (1925), 315–355; "Effects of Some Quaternary Ammonium and Analogous Compounds on the Autonomic Nervous System," *ibid.*, 48 (1933), 51–56; and "Further Studies of the Methyl Cholines and Analogous Compounds," *ibid.*, 51 (1934), 237–262. A complete list and set of Hunt's publications are in the Arch., Countway Lib., Boston.
Biographical material on Hunt includes Hans Zinsser, "Reid Hunt," *Aesculapiad*, Class of 1937, Harvard Medical School, Countway Lib.; "Reid Hunt," *Harvard Medical Alumni Bull.*, 23 (1949), 39–42; Francis B. Sumner, *The Life Hist. of an Am. Naturalist* (1945); Nat. Acad. Sci., *Biog. Memoirs*, XXVI (1949); and obituary in *N.Y. Herald Tribune*, Mar. 10, 1948.
See also letters and instruction sheets (*Blöcke*) of Paul Ehrlich and other correspondence concerning Hunt; and Otto Krayer, "Letters on Hunt," both in Arch., Countway Lib. Additional information came from Mrs. M. L. Hunt, Ross G. Harrison, E. M. K. Geiling, Torald Sollman, and E. K. Marshall.]
OTTO KRAYER

HUNTINGTON, ELLSWORTH (Sept. 16, 1876–Oct. 17, 1947), geographer, was born in Galesburg, Ill., the third of six children, and the first son of Henry Strong Huntington and Mary Lawrence (Herbert) Huntington. Henry Huntington was from New York, had attended Yale, and was graduated from Andover Seminary. He became a Congregational church minister and a man of letters.

The family moved to Gotham, Me., in 1878 and to Milton, Mass., a suburb of Boston, in 1889. Henry Huntington retained his ministry in Milton until his retirement in 1907. Ellsworth Huntington attended the Milton High School and was graduated in 1893. He then commenced an undergraduate career with the

eighteen-man class of 1897 at Beloit College, Wis. His first publication, "Experiments with Available Roadmaking Material of Southern Wisconsin," delivered before the Wisconsin Academy of Sciences in 1897, was printed in *The Transactions* of the Academy.

In 1897 Huntington was appointed assistant to the president of Euphrates College, Harpoot, Turkey. While in Turkey, he undertook much fieldwork, mapped the area around Harpoot, and journeyed down the Euphrates River in April, 1901, on a raft made of inflated sheepskins in the manner reported by Xenophon, for which the Royal Geographical Society awarded Huntington the Gill Memorial. The only other European reported to have made such a journey was the German General Von Moltke (1838).

In 1901 Huntington returned to the United States in order to study physiography under William Morris Davis at Harvard (M.A., 1902) and in 1903 joined the Carnegie-sponsored Pumpelly expedition to Transcaspia as assistant to Davis. He remained in Turkestan and Persia for fourteen months, then returned to the United States, and joined Robert L. Barrett in a journey through the Himalayas into the Tarim Basin of Inner Asia (1905-1906). He returned to Harvard as a non-resident fellow (1906-1907) and there wrote *The Pulse of Asia* (1907). In September of that year he joined Yale University as an instructor in geography, was awarded the Ph.D. degree from Yale in 1909, and was promoted to the rank of assistant professor in 1910. He departed Yale in 1915, but returned in 1919 to spend the next twenty-eight years as research associate with professorial rank.

On Dec. 22, 1917, he married Rachel Slocum Brewer, the daughter of Joseph Brewer, in Milton, Mass.; they had two sons and one daughter.

Between 1909 and 1930 he traveled considerably in Asia, Europe, Africa, and North, Central, and South America. Many of his observations recorded while on these journeys were later published. He taught geography at Yale from 1907 to 1915 primarily to undergraduate students; after 1919 he rarely lectured to undergraduates and only occasionally had a class of more than four graduate students. Nevertheless he contributed to the pedagogics of geography by writing textbooks that were used both in the United States and abroad: *Asia, a Geography Reader* (1912), *The Geography of Europe* (with H. E. Gregory, 1918), *Principles of Human Geography* (first edition with Sumner W. Cushing, 1920), *Business*

Geography (with F. E. Williams, 1922), *Modern Business Geography* (first edition with S. W. Cushing, 1924), *The Human Habitat* (1927), *Living Geography* (with C. B. Benson and F. M. McMurry, in 2 volumes, 1933), *Economic and Social Geography* (with F. E. Williams and S. Van Valkenburg, 1933), *Geography of Europe* (with S. Van Valkenburg, 1935), and *Principles of Economic Geography* (1940).

It is, however, as a scientific investigator that he will be remembered. The origin, distribution, longevity, and accomplishments of civilization early became the locus of his inquiry. In searching for "plot" (rhythm, harmony, in fact, pattern) in history, he was revealing an inquiry, not offering a philosophy. The intellectual opulence of his work (twenty-eight books, parts of twenty-nine others, and over 240 articles) does not compel assent, but the whole does induce thought. He was vitally concerned to understand the reasons for the emergence and submergence of human progress through time, to understand why history revealed periods when the creative energies of men seemed to slumber, and periods when they seemed to flower. He strode colossus-like through masses of detail, and found a triadic causation for human progress: climate, the quality of people, and culture. He sought to reveal the environmental platform whereon man had been presented with the climatic circumstances, which brought about migration, hastened the processes of selection, and facilitated or obstructed the advance of culture. This thesis of multiple causation was an epic undertaking, which encouraged correspondence with an international circle of scholars in many disciplines.

The early years of Huntington's academic life were given essentially to the study of climate and more particularly to the quest for evidence (and later causation) of climatic change in postglacial time. The themes of climatic change and the relative merits of the earth's climates appear and reappear throughout his work but are particularly evident in *The Pulse of Asia* (1907), *Palestine and Its Transformation* (1911), *Civilization and Climate* (1915, and a much revised third edition, 1924), and *World Power and Evolution* (1919).

From 1910 to 1920 Huntington's concern with the quality of people began to emerge. He was concerned that democracy itself was threatened by the rapid multiplication of the less able members of the species. He opted for restrictive United States immigration and believed that "every possible measure should be

taken to change the relative birth rates in our old Nordic population as compared with our new Mediterranean and Alpine population." He associated with Roland Dixon, Lothrop Stoddard, and Madison Grant and was a significant force in the American Eugenics Society for a quarter of a century (president, 1934-1938). His works on this include *The Character of Races* (1924), *The Builders of America* (with Leon Whitney, 1927), *Tomorrow's Children: The Goal of Eugenics* (1935), *After Three Centuries* (1935), and *Season of Birth: Its Relation to Human Abilities* (1938).

Huntington regarded culture, the third of his determinants of civilization, as the field of recorded history. He enjoyed reading history but deplored the historians' failure to consider the role of environment and biological inheritance. He was especially appreciative of the role of ideas and inventions in man's progress. Parts of several of Huntington's books accept culture as a moving force: in particular his critics should read "Climate and the Evolution of Civilization," a chapter in *The Evolution of the Earth and Its Inhabitants* (edited by Richard S. Lull, 1918), and "The March of Civilization," a chapter in *Europe* (written with S. Van Valkenburg, 1935).

Huntington attempted to synthesize his life's work in two volumes; *Mainsprings of Civilization* was published in 1945, but he died before he could complete *The Pace of History,* which he was especially anxious to finish as a foil to those who had been swift to label him an exponent of climatic or environmental determinism. In fact, Huntington's investigations produced a legacy so pervasive that he became a part of the moving force that is the culture of a nation. If he was a fellow traveler of the determinists, he was continually weighing, assaying, and reshaping his postulates. Perhaps he assessed too many value judgments and produced too much too soon, yet he emerged with a new form of determinism, more moderate, subtle, and versatile than anything that had come before. It never did receive a name.

Huntington's honors included medals from the Paris Geographical Society, the Philadelphia Geographical Society, and the Foundation for the Study of Cycles. He was president of the Ecological Society of America (1917), the Association of American Geographers (1923), and the American Eugenics Society (1934-1938). He was appointed a member of the National Research Council, in both the geology and geography (1919-1922) and biology and agriculture (1921-1924) divisions. The

Distinguished Service to Geography Award of the National Council of Geography Teachers was conferred upon him (1942). He died of a heart attack.

[Geoffrey J. Martin, *Ellsworth Huntington: His Life & Thought* (1973); "The Ellsworth Huntington Papers," *Yale Univ. Lib. Gazette*, Apr. 1971, pp. 185–195; "Ellsworth Huntington and 'The Pace of History,'" *Connecticut Review*, Oct. 1971, pp. 83–123; John E. Chappell, Jr., "Huntington and His Critics: The Influence of Climate on Civilization" (Ph.D. diss., Univ. of Kansas, 1968); "Climatic Change Reconsidered: Another Look at 'The Pulse of Asia'," *Geographical Rev.*, July 1970, pp. 347–373; O. H. K. Spate, "Toynbee and Huntington: A Study in Determinism," *Geographical Jour.*, Dec. 1952, pp. 406–424; O. H. K. Spate, "Ellsworth Huntington," *Internat. Ency. Soc. Sci.* (1968); Stephen S. Visher, "Memoir to Ellsworth Huntington, 1876–1947," *Annals of the Assoc. of Am. Geog.*, Mar. 1948, pp. 38–50.]
GEOFFREY J. MARTIN

HUSTON, WALTER (Apr. 6, 1884–Apr. 7, 1950), stage and screen actor, was born in Toronto, Canada, the youngest of four children of Scots-Irish parents, Robert Moore and Elizabeth (McGibbon) Houghston. Educated in Toronto schools until he was seventeen, he then went to work in a hardware store and prepared to follow in the footsteps of his father, a contractor. His career was determined instead by the classes he took in the dramatics department of the Toronto College of Music. He made his first stage appearance in Toronto at eighteen, and then joined a road company that reached New York, where he had his first role in 1905, a minor part in a melodrama called *In Convict Stripes*. Soon after, he won a spear-carrier's role in a production of *Julius Caesar* by Richard Mansfield but forgot his short speech and landed out on the street. When he met Rhea Gore, a strong-willed newspaperwoman, he agreed to settle down and gave up the stage for marriage (1905) and a career in engineering. He managed electrical power plants in small towns in Montana, Missouri, and Texas, and on Aug. 5, 1906, his only child, John Marcellus Huston, was born. (The spelling of the family name had been altered to simplify pronunciation.) After meeting Bayonne Whipple in 1909, he gave up a promising future as an engineer and returned with her to the stage in a song-and-dance act for which he wrote several of his own songs. They were married in 1914, following Huston's divorce the previous year, and continued headlining in the Orpheum vaudeville circuit and often played at the legendary Palace Theatre in New York City. In later years, recalling his one-night stands and big-time vaudeville, Huston felt he had played "everything but the cake of ice in *Uncle Tom's Cabin*."

His career took a new turn early in 1924 when Brock Pemberton cast him in a Broadway production of *Mr. Pitt* by Zona Gale, which enjoyed only a brief life. He fared no better in another short run with *The Easy Mark*, but in November he took the role of Ephraim Cabot in Eugene O'Neill's *Desire Under the Elms*, the play that catapulted him to stardom at the age of forty. In the *New York Times* (Nov. 12, 1924), Stark Young described Huston's old man as "everywhere trenchant, gaunt, fervid, harsh, as he should be. . . . In his ability to cover his gradations, to express the natural and convincing emotion, and to convey the harsh, inarticulate life, [Huston] proved to be the best choice possible for the role." The New York Drama Critics' Circle reflected this sentiment when it presented Huston with its award for 1924. He played in other successful roles of lesser stature in the succeeding years before turning to motion pictures in 1929 after the failure of a clumsy play, *The Commodore Marries*.

On the screen that first year, Huston appeared in *Gentlemen of the Press*, in which Charlie Ruggles stole the limelight as a boozy reporter; *The Lady Lies*, with Claudette Colbert; and *The Virginian*, in which he played Trampas, the villain, opposite Gary Cooper in the first talking version of the popular novel already filmed twice as a silent. Huston had continual employment on the screen; among his best performances was the title role in *Abraham Lincoln* (1930), the last film directed by D. W. Griffith. Huston's busiest year was 1932, when he played in eight pictures.

In 1934 he returned to the stage as the lead in the adaptation by Sidney Howard of Sinclair Lewis' *Dodsworth*, a role Huston played to the life. Brooks Atkinson commented that his acting of the part "stirs your admiration and affection. How much of it is Huston and how much Dodsworth is a question that can be answered on the day after never. In the meantime it is enough to know that a broad-gauged and first-rate actor is now in town" (*New York Times*, Feb. 26, 1934). The public's response to such praise resulted in a run of 1,238 performances in New York. Following this engagement, Huston went to England in 1935 to play the lead in the film *Rhodes*, returned home to join a road company of *Dodsworth*, and then proceeded to do a screen version of the play (1936).

In the summer of 1934 Robert Edmond Jones (husband of Huston's sister Margaret) produced *Othello* in Central City, Colo., with Huston in the title role opposite his third wife, the former Ninetta Eugenia (Nan) Sunderland, whom he had married on Nov. 9, 1931, after Bayonne Whipple Huston had won a divorce in Reno on grounds of desertion. Brought to Broadway in 1937, this production closed quickly, in spite of the high feelings of the company and the bravos of the first-night audience. The critics' mixed, but generally cool, reception brought Huston his first failure in thirteen years. He appeared the following season, however, as Peter Stuyvesant in *Knickerbocker Holiday*, a musical play by Maxwell Anderson with a score by Kurt Weill, where his fine singing voice surprised a whole generation of theatergoers unacquainted with his earlier vaudeville stint. A fuller measure of his success was taken by Brooks Atkinson, who called casting Huston as Governor Stuyvesant "a stroke of genius. For he is an actor in the grand manner with a homely brand of native wit, bold in his gestures, commanding in his periods, yet purely sardonic and mischievous in spirit" (*New York Times*, Oct. 20, 1938).

In succeeding years Huston made few appearances on stage or screen, spending a considerable time in California at his home in the San Bernardino Mountains or at his cattle ranch near Delano. He gave a memorable performance, however, as Mr. Scratch in *All That Money Can Buy* (1941), the film version of "The Devil and Daniel Webster" by Stephen Vincent Benét. He played in all his son's films, whether a bit part like the dying man who stumbles into Sam Spade's office in John Huston's first success, *The Maltese Falcon* (1941), or the grizzled prospector in *The Treasure of Sierra Madre* (1948), for which he won an Academy Award for best supporting actor.

In addition to his long list of stage and screen credits, Huston also broadcast on radio. Among his most impressive were the performances on the Theatre Guild on the Air, particularly in *On Borrowed Time* (Feb. 17, 1946) and *Our Town* (Mar. 12, 1950). During World War II he contributed his voice to a wartime documentary on Soviet Russia and to an army orientation film, *Prelude to War* (1943). Even earlier, in January 1939, he had urged members of the American theater to boycott Nazi goods. Huston continued to perform in films to the very last year of his life although he claimed he preferred to remain at his mountain home or cattle ranch until "something comes along like Sierra Madre—a good spanking story." "I guess I'm just an incurable old ham," he once confessed, although the high

pay seems also to have whetted his appetite. Huston died of a ruptured abdominal aneurysm in Beverly Hills, Calif., on the day after his sixty-sixth birthday. His remains were cremated. A rare memorial tribute of two minutes of silence was observed for him at all Hollywood studios on Apr. 11, 1950.

As his career indicates, Walter Huston believed in perseverance as an essential element for ultimate success. To this axiom he applied his own particular talents—sincerity, naturalness, and humility. His success was expressed aphoristically by a commentator in *Motion Picture Classics*, who said, "Roles fit others, but Walter Huston fits the roles." Richard Watts of the *New York Post* caught the essence of Huston's personality more graphically when he emphasized his "rugged masculinity," which symbolized the "virile pioneer virtues" deemed American. His most characteristic roles were the towering individuals, somehow a little tired, bewildered, and apart, lonely giants like Dodsworth and Ephraim Cabot, whom he brought to life with force and skill, becoming "one of the truly distinguished players of his time." Yet these qualities limited his range as an actor, preventing him from gaining conviction in the role of an evil or alienated man. Recognizing this limitation when writing for *Stage* about his failure as Othello, Huston understood that he had not moved the critics or convinced them of the truth in his rendition. He acknowledged the benefit of the reality he experienced. "It deflates the ego and brings the feet back to the ground." When his broad, six-foot figure and his indigenous American manners shone forth from stage or screen, he became a symbol to his audience of the national type, and they honored him with fame and fortune.

[No biography of Huston exists. Sources for this sketch are found chiefly in the clippings, scrapbooks, and memorabilia of the Theatre Collect. of the N.Y. Public Lib. at Lincoln Center. See also Walter Huston, "In and Out of the Bag," *Stage*, March 1937; *Current Biog.*, 1949; and William F. Nolan, *John Huston: King Rebel* (1965). Death record from Calif. Dept. of Public Health.]

H. L. KLEINFIELD

HYDE, ARTHUR MASTICK (July 12, 1877-Oct. 17, 1947), governor of Missouri, secretary of agriculture, was born in Princeton, Mo., the younger of the two sons of Ira Barnes Hyde and his second wife, Caroline Emily (Mastick) Hyde. He also had two older half-brothers by his father's previous marriage. Ira Hyde, a native of New York state and an alumnus of Oberlin College, had practiced law in Minnesota and Washington, D.C., before settling in Missouri in 1866. He was a Union Army veteran and served as Republican congressman from the state's Tenth District in 1873-1875. From his parents, both of colonial Massachusetts descent, Arthur presumably acquired his conservative and puritanical bent. Since Arthur's mother died when he was twelve, he was particularly influenced by his father. With the exception of two years following his mother's death, when Arthur lived with an aunt in Rocky River, Ohio, he attended private and public schools in Princeton. He then spent two years at Oberlin Academy in Ohio and in 1895 entered the University of Michigan, where he received the B.A. in 1899. After earning an LL.B. from the State University of Iowa and being admitted to the bar the following year, he returned to Princeton and entered into a law partnership with his father. On Oct. 19, 1904, he married Hortense Cullers of Mercer County. They had one child, Caroline Cullers.

During the following years, as he widened his circle of influence in church, civic, and business affairs, Hyde's prominence as a leader of rural Republicans increased. His work in Sunday-school organization and his speeches in behalf of prohibition made him one of the outstanding Methodist laymen in Missouri. He was a captain in the Missouri National Guard, 1905-1906. He was elected mayor of Princeton in 1908 and reelected two years later. He expanded his business activities to include an automobile distributorship, farm and lumber interests, loan and investment enterprises, and an insurance agency. He also continued to practice law, and in 1915 moved to Trenton, Mo., where he established a new firm with Judge Samuel Hill. Hyde welcomed the progressive Republicanism of Theodore Roosevelt and won nomination as the Progressive party's candidate for attorney general of Missouri in 1912. Although he lost the election and quickly returned to the Republican party, he gained statewide attention with his vigorous campaign for morality in government.

By 1920 the political stage was set for Hyde's leadership of his party and state government. The advent of national prohibition that year and political corruption in Missouri urban politics assisted the shift of Republican power from wet St. Louis to outstate rural dry areas. Hyde's reputation as a staunch prohibitionist and a friend of business carried him to the forefront of the gubernatorial aspirants. With Democrats of Missouri divided over prohibition, as well as American entry into the League of Nations, Hyde gained an easy victory, thus becoming the state's second Republican post-Reconstruction

governor. The principal accomplishments of his administration were increased appropriations and higher standards for the state's public schools, especially rural schools; increased distribution of technical information to farmers; financial stabilization of the state penal institutions; and the construction of 7,640 miles of highways.

The state constitution limited Hyde to a single four-year term, but a further limitation on his political career was his uncompromising support of prohibition. This denied him any chance of support from the state's wet urban Republicans when he sought nomination to the United States Senate in 1928. He had moved to Kansas City in 1925 to practice law and became head of the Sentinel Life Insurance Company in 1927. He seemed destined to remain out of public affairs but, in 1929, President Herbert Hoover invited him to join his cabinet as secretary of agriculture. Hyde accepted the post reluctantly, for as one columnist noted, "He isn't a dirt farmer nor yet a scientific agriculturist. He is a politician who knows more about farmers than farming" (*Collier's,* Apr. 20, 1929, p. 64).

Hyde's secretaryship was burdened with the exigencies of the Great Depression and a severe drought in 1930. His conservative principles precluded all but limited aid for agriculture, with a preference for improving marketing mechanisms for farm commodities, encouragement of farm efficiency through increased capitalization and mechanization, agricultural research, road construction and improvement to provide employment and more efficient consumer traffic, and the retirement of submarginal land through government purchase and reforestation. As secretary of agriculture, he served on the Federal Farm Board established by the Agricultural Marketing Act of 1929, an act created to promote effective merchandising of agricultural commodities, thus placing agriculture on an equal economic basis with other industries. In 1930 he organized and served as chairman of the Federal Drought Relief Committee. After leaving office with Hoover in 1933, Hyde vigorously opposed New Deal agricultural programs, and in 1937 he collaborated with Ray Lyman Wilbur, former secretary of the interior in the Hoover administration, on *The Hoover Policies,* a useful compilation of the former president's speeches and state papers and a stout defense of his philosophy and principles.

Hyde settled permanently in Trenton in 1934 and spent his final years there devoting most of his energy to his farm holdings. In 1935-1936 he helped organize and promote the Conference of Methodist Laymen, a conservative organization designed to counter the social welfare activities of some members of the Methodist clergy. His other activities included membership in the Sons of the American Revolution, the Masons (thirty-third degree, Shriner), the Elks, and the Odd Fellows; his chief recreation was fishing. He died of cancer at Memorial Hospital in New York City in 1947 and was buried in the Odd Fellows' Cemetery in Trenton, Mo. A tall, angular man, with an ingratiating sense of humor and a deep, resonant voice, Hyde was one of the master orators of Missouri. He typified that generation of old-stock conservatives who dominated American political affairs in the 1920's and who failed to make the transition to modern liberalism in the 1930's.

[An extensive collection of Hyde's papers is held jointly by the Western Hist. Manuscripts Collect., Univ. of Missouri, and the State Hist. Soc. of Missouri, both in Columbia. Articles by Hyde that express his views on agriculture are "The Agricultural Teeter Board," *Rev. of Revs.*, Oct. 1931; "A New Farmer on a New Farm," *Sat. Evening Post*, Apr. 12, 1930; "The Producer Considers Consumption," *Jour. of Home Economics*, Feb. 1933; and "Research in the U.S. Dept. of Agriculture," *Scientific Monthly*, Jan. 1933. On his social views, see his "Economics Is Not the Church's Sphere," *Forum*, Nov. 1935 and Jan. 1936; and *The Philosophy of Liberty* (1939). For biographical and interpretive data, see Florence F. Hyde, *The Hyde Family in England and America* (1967); Sarah Guitar and Floyd C. Shoemaker, eds., *The Messages and Proclamations of the Governors of the State of Missouri*, vol. XII (1930); Theodore G. Joslin in *World's Work*, Apr. 1930; Marquis W. Childs in *Am. Mercury*, May 1930; *Nat. Cyc. Am. Biog.*, XL, 501–502; obituaries in *N.Y. Times*, Oct. 18, 1947, and *Princeton* (Mo.) *Post-Telegraph*, Oct. 23, 1947. A portrait of Hyde appears in Duane Meyer, *The Heritage of Mo.* (1963).]

FRANKLIN D. MITCHELL

IRWIN, WILLIAM HENRY (Sept. 14, 1873–Feb. 24, 1948), journalist, author, known as Will Irwin, was born in Oneida, N.Y., first of the two literary sons of David Smith Irwin and Edith Emily (Greene) Irwin. The family (originally Irvin) came from Irvine's Bay, Ayrshire, Scotland. In boyhood Will played in the "fairyland of woods" of the New York lake country. Before Will was six, his father, drawn by the silver boom, moved his family to the Leadville, Colo., area "in surroundings which make the western movies seem tame." Their mother, the daughter of a painter-poet, sought to infuse her sons "with the idea that art was the really important thing." The Irwin boys were remote from educational facilities and on entering public school in Denver, found themselves graded with students several years their junior.

When Will finished high school, he enrolled in the new Leland Stanford University, where he was less interested in studying than in campus dramatics, publications and politics, musicals, fencing, and socializing in general. His behavior kept him from graduating in 1898, although his degree was granted a year later. He volunteered for the Spanish-American War but was rejected. Attracted by what he called the "artistic bunch" in San Francisco, he went to work in 1899 as assistant editor of *The Wave*, a literary weekly. When *The Wave* went bankrupt, he found work on the *San Francisco Chronicle* as a reporter in 1901. Successively he was a special writer (1902) and Sunday editor (1902-1904). Yet much as he relished the Golden Gate port and friends like Jack London, Irwin turned his eyes east. With many young journalists of the day, he looked to the New York *Sun* and the editorship of Chester S. Lord. He arrived in New York in 1904 and was soon at work on the newspaper of his dreams. In 1905 in New Hampshire, Irwin reported the Portsmouth Peace Conference, ending the Russo-Japanese War, in his words, "the most newsless news event that I ever covered" (*The Making of a Reporter*, p. 123). His most remarkable journalistic feat followed the receipt of the news of the San Francisco earthquake and fire, on April 18, 1906. His account interlarded the few bits of fact available with his intimate knowledge of the city. On that day he wrote fourteen columns and for the next week produced no fewer than eight columns a day as details emerged from the stricken city. He ate with one hand while he wrote with the other. Midway through this amazing performance he turned out a vignette of San Francisco as he had known it. "The City That Was" was an account of "the gayest, lightest-hearted, . . . most romantic, most pleasure-loving" place. He described its hills, waterfronts, bay and ocean vistas, restaurants and cafes, mansions and shanties, and diverse peoples—adventurers, drifters, immigrants, seamen—even its "coyotes that still stole in and robbed hen roosts at night." It was, he wrote, "as though a pretty, frivolous woman had passed through a great tragedy." Published quickly in a small book, "The City That Was" circulated widely throughout the country, bringing national notice to its author.

Although his future in daily journalism was assured, Irwin followed the trend of probing reporters into the mass magazine field. Later in 1906 he joined *McClure's* magazine as managing editor and undertook a supervisory rather than writing role in the muckraking movement. His work as an editor was not to his liking, and in 1907 he left *McClure's* to write for Norman Hapgood and *Collier's*. After a series on the fakery of spirit mediums, he assessed the spread of prohibition through local option. Through his research he soon perceived that a frequent explanation for government's unwillingness or inability to deal with corruption was local newspaper silence.

In 1908 President Nicholas Murray Butler of Columbia University asked Irwin to collect American and European opinions on organizing a school of journalism as proposed by Joseph Pulitzer. Irwin devoted much of 1910 to interviewing editors and publishers and to library research. His fifteen-article series "The Power of the Press," appeared in *Collier's* between January and July 1911. The articles called the practices of the press into sharp account. Taken together they did for the press what earlier muckrakers had done for other aspects of American life. In 1969 the articles were reproduced in book form under the title *The American Newspaper*.

In World War I, Irwin early established himself as among the leading battlefront correspondents. He reported for both American and English publications from the German, Belgian, and British armies in 1914-1915 and for the *Saturday Evening Post* from the French, Italian, British, and American forces in 1916-1918. His dispatch "The Splendid Story of the Battle of Ypres" (1915) depicted the "filth, mud and cold" of the trenches so vividly that Lord Northcliffe, after publication in English papers, circulated it in pamphlet form. Irwin also undertook two important wartime tasks, as a member (1914-1915) of the executive committee of the Commission for Belgian Relief, headed by Herbert Hoover, and as chief of the foreign department of the Creel Committee on Public Information in 1918. A six-month "enlistment" lasted six years. Nominally a Republican, he supported President Wilson so vigorously on the League of Nations issue that he broke with George H. Lorimer, publisher of the *Saturday Evening Post*.

If Will Irwin was not writing, he seemingly was searching for a subject. His first book was a collection of writings from his college days, *Stanford Stories* (1900), with C. K. Field. In 1903 he tried fantasy and coauthored with Gelett Burgess *The Reign of Queen Isyl* and *The Picaroons*. The next year he produced a book of verse, *The Hamadryads*. The popular interest in his description of the stricken San Francisco

led him in 1908 to issue *Old Chinatown*. Next came three novels, *The House of Mystery* (1910), a love story in a "stronghold" of spiritualism and hypnosis; *The Readjustment* (1910), whose ill-starred romantic characters were a part of San Francisco's Bohemia; and *The Red Button* (1912), one of Irwin's most successful ventures in fiction. In 1914 he told the life story of ex-convict Al Jennings in *Beating Back*. During World War I, he produced books of his experiences as well as newspaper and magazine articles. In *Men, Women and War* (1915) he portrayed the women of France as courageously bearing the brunt of the struggle, often in situations as adverse as those of their men at the front. His *Reporter at Armageddon* (1918), consisting of letters recounting life among the Allied troops, was described by the *Review of Reviews* as "a model for all reporters in vividness of description" (Oct. 1918). Irwin delivered a fervent warning in *The Next War* (1918) against "the lethal nature of future wars" and pleaded for "the elimination of warfare from civilized society." His condemnation of aerial and chemical weapons led the *Boston Evening Transcript* to say that his "vital message . . . cannot be too widely or too carefully read" (June 15, 1921).

Although he avoided partisan politics, Irwin did not shun political matters. In 1912 he developed a tract for the political times entitled *Why Edison Is a Progressive,* and in 1929 his *Herbert Hoover: A Reminiscent Biography* was published. It recalled not only "our most eminent senior" at Stanford University, but also provided Irwin's explanation of the "secret force" of Hoover in public affairs, and the author's firsthand observation of Hoover at his relief work in Belgium in World War I. In the first postwar decade, Irwin also wrote a novel of the mining camps of the 1870's, *Youth Rides West* (1925), the chronicle of a tenderfoot from Harvard, notable for its "footnotes to frontier history"; and a biography of Adolph Zukor, the moving picture magnate, *The House That Shadows Built* (1929) which was also an account of the film industry to that time. One of his most serious works was *How Red is America?* (1927). In answering the question he divided the radical forces into communists, socialists, anarchists, and still lesser groups. After a description of their purposes, methods, and activities, he concluded that "at the most liberal estimate" the "revolutionary reds" number only one-sixth of one percent of the population and that "the whole strictly radical element, revolutionary and evolutionary together, not more than 1%."

Academic critics were not impressed by Irwin's *Propaganda and the News* (1936), but Stanley Walker, writing in the *N.Y. Herald-Tribune* (Jan. 26, 1936) found merit in the recital of "methods and ruses employed by successful publicity men," while the *Christian Science Monitor* (Jan. 28, 1936) said the work "may be regarded as one of the more important volumes on the modern press, including radio, and its relation to the public." His entertaining autobiography, *The Making of a Reporter* (1942), was welcomed as a "fluent, lucid and sensible narrative" describing many of the high points in American journalism between the 1890's and Hoover's administration. With Thomas M. Johnson he wrote in 1943 *What You Should Know About Spies and Saboteurs,* in effect, a manual on espionage and counterespionage and a revelation of how spies get information and transmit it, illustrated with specific examples. In 1946 he edited *Letters to Kermit by Theodore Roosevelt.* He also wrote two plays: *The Thirteenth Chair* (1916), with Bayard Veiler; and *The Lute Song* (1930), with Sidney Howard.

France decorated Irwin with the Legion of Honor, Belgium with the King Albert Medal, and Sweden with the commemorative medal of the Olympic Games. Knox College conferred the honorary degree of doctor of humane letters in 1940. Genial, warm, companionable, Irwin delighted in exchanging stories with colleagues at the Bohemian, Players, and Dutch Treat clubs. He was married twice: on Jan. 1, 1901, to Harriet Hyde of San Francisco, by whom he had a son, William Hyde Irwin; and on Feb. 1, 1916, to Inez Haynes Gillmore (1873-1970), a successful novelist and short-story writer. His second wife, like her husband, held the presidency (1931-1933) of the Authors' League of America. From 1929 to 1931, Irwin headed the American center of P.E.N., an international organization of writers. The Irwins lived in New York City and spent summers in Scituate, Mass. He died of a cerebral occlusion in St. Vincent's Hospital, Manhattan, in his seventy-fifth year. After a Protestant Episcopal service, his remains were cremated. One of the most qualified of press critics, Oswald Garrison Villard, writing in the *Saturday Review of Literature* (Nov. 14, 1942), credited Irwin with "that sure judgment of men, women and affairs which made him for so long one of the most valued and distinguished of our popular journalists."

[Irwin supplied the essential facts of his career in *The Making of a Reporter* (1942), while many of his muckraking contemporaries cited him and his contributions in their memoirs. An extensive list of these was included by Peter Lyon in *Success Story: The Life and Times of S. S. McClure* (1963). Other sources include D. M. Chalmers, *The Social and Political Ideas of the Muckrakers* (1964); R. C. Bannister, Jr., *Ray Stannard Baker: The Mind and Thought of a Progressive* (1966); J. E. Semonche, *Ray Stannard Baker: A Quest for Democracy in Modern America, 1870-1918* (1969); H. S. Wilson, *McClure's Magazine and the Muckrakers* (1970); and J. M. Harrison and H. H. Stein, *Muckraking: Past, Present and Future* (1973). C. F. Weigle and D. G. Clark, "About Will Irwin" in *The American Newspaper by Will Irwin* (1969), containing a collection of portraits. Also *Who Was Who in America, II* (1950); *Twentieth Century Authors* (1942) and *Twentieth Century Authors, First Supplement* (1955). See also newspapers in New York and San Francisco and news magazines at the time of death, particularly *N.Y. Times* (photograph) and *N.Y. Herald-Tribune,* both, Feb. 25, 1948. Irving Dilliard, "The Old Muckrakers," *Frontier,* Apr. 1965; certain information from Mrs. A. T. Mason, Princeton, N.J.; personal recollection.]

IRVING DILLIARD

JACKSON, CLARENCE MARTIN (Apr. 12, 1875-Jan. 17, 1947), anatomist, was born on a farm at What Cheer, Iowa, the eldest of the five boys and four girls born to John Calvin Jackson, a physician, and Sonora Adeline (Hartman) Jackson. His mother was of Pennsylvania Dutch origin, and his father of colonial English descent. In Clarence's early boyhood the family moved to Harper, Iowa, where he attended a German Catholic parochial school. Earning money as a harvest hand and assistant postmaster, he finished his high school work in the preparatory department of Drake University at Des Moines. After teaching for a year in a country school in Missouri, he entered the University of Missouri in 1894, where he enrolled in a combined scientific and medical course. Majoring in biology, he held a teaching fellowship in his junior year, and spent the summers of 1896 and 1897 in marine stations at Woods Hole, Mass., and Pacific Grove, Calif. He received the B.S. degree in 1898, summa cum laude, the M.S. degree in 1899 and the M.D. in 1900. On June 21, 1898, he married Helen Clarahan. Their four children were Margaret, Helen, Dorothy Anne, and Mary Elizabeth.

Jackson had no interest in establishing a medical practice. Remaining at Missouri as assistant professor of anatomy, in 1902 he was made professor and head of the department, and in 1909 became dean of the medical school. He was attracted by research and in the summers of 1900 and 1901 he did graduate study at the University of Chicago with the neurologist Henry H. Donaldson; he spent a year's leave of absence (1903-1904) studying with

Wilhelm His and Karl Werner Spalteholz in Leipzig and Wilhelm von Hartz-Waldeyer in Berlin. Thus he learned the latest research techniques in embryology and anatomy.

In 1913 Jackson was invited to become dean of the University of Minnesota medical school, which, under the leadership of George E. Vincent, president of the university, was undergoing a major reorganization. Disliking administrative work, Jackson declined the offer but did agree to become head of the department of anatomy. In this post, which he held until his retirement, he revolutionized the medical school. A strong champion of research, he gathered around him a notable group of specialists: Richard Scammon (physical growth and development), Andrew Rasmussen (neurology), Hal Downey (hematology and histology), and Allen Boyden (embryology and gross anatomy). By 1933 all five were starred in *American Men of Science*—the largest number from any one anatomical department. His own research, reported in more than a hundred publications, dealt chiefly with the effects of chronic malnutrition on growth and development. His book *The Effects of Inanition and Malnutrition upon Growth and Structure* (1925) was for many years the definitive treatise on the subject.

Jackson emphasized the importance of a strong graduate training program at the medical school and maintained close personal relationships with his students, stressing the value of the scientific method and the need for critical, independent thinking. After medical students had finished two years of the required curriculum, he encouraged the most promising to remain in anatomy for a year and work for a master's degree. Many then returned to their medical studies, carrying their interest in research into clinical fields. Others stayed on in research. In the period 1913-1941, thirty-four students received the Ph.D. in anatomy.

Jackson was a founder of the Minnesota Embryological Collection, a member of the American Association of Anatomists (president, 1922-1924), and a member of the advisory committee of the Wistar Institute of Anatomy. He was chairman of the medical division of the National Research Council (1923-1924), chairman of the American Committee on Anatomical Nomenclature (1934-1941), associate editor of the *American Journal of Anatomy* (1921-1939), and became president of the Minnesota State Board of Examiners in Basic Sciences in 1930. He received an honorary LL.D. in 1923 from the University of Missouri; and

edited Morris' standard textbook, *Human Anatomy* (5th through 9th editions).

Toward the end of his career Jackson was progressively handicapped by Parkinson's disease, and he retired in 1941. Nevertheless, he retained the same poise and the same consideration that had characterized a lifetime of activity. An agnostic, he exemplified the dignity and worth of a life dedicated to the pursuit of knowledge in its widest implications. He died of the disease at the age of seventy-one in the University Hospital in Minneapolis and was buried in that city's Sunset Memorial Cemetery.

[A chronological listing of Jackson's publications can be found in E. A. Boyden, "Clarence Martin Jackson," *Anatomical Rec.* 98 (1947): 317–324; see also J. Arthur Myers, *Masters of Medicine: An Hist. Sketch of the Coll. of Medical Sciences, Univ. of Minn., 1888–1966* (1968); "Clarence Martin Jackson —A Great Physician," *Journal-Lancet* 62 (1942): 142–145; "Contributions in Honor of Clarence Martin Jackson, M.D.," published privately under the auspices of Phi Beta Pi medical fraternity (1942); James Gray, *The University of Minnesota* (1951); additional information was obtained from Dr. and Mrs. C. M. Jackson, family memoirs, privately circulated (1943), courtesy of Dr. Fred Jackson Jarvis, Seattle, Wash.]
                                    E. A. BOYDEN

JACKSON, DUNHAM (July 24, 1888-Nov. 6, 1946), mathematician, was born in Bridgewater, Mass. His parents, William Dunham Jackson and Mary Vose (Morse) Jackson, were graduates of the Normal School at Bridgewater, and both were descended from passengers on the *Mayflower*. William Jackson became a science and mathematics professor at the Bridgewater Normal School and was active in the Congregationalist church. At an early age Dunham Jackson joined his father for walks to study geology, botany, and zoology; he was soon reading science textbooks in the family library. At the local high school his favorite subjects were languages and literature, and he enjoyed teaching Latin and German poetry to his younger sister, Elizabeth.

Jackson entered Harvard University when he was sixteen. After receiving the B.A. degree in 1908, he held an assistantship in astronomy until he received his M.A. in 1909. His many honors included membership in Phi Beta Kappa and several fellowships to support doctoral studies abroad.

In Germany, Jackson studied at the University of Göttingen in 1909-1911 under the tutelage of Edmund Landau and spent a few months at the University of Bonn in 1911. In the spring of 1911 he contracted polio. The illness caused lameness in one foot and curtailed the athletic activities of which he was so fond.

He was awarded the Ph.D. and a prize at Göttingen in 1911 for his thesis answering the question: Would it be possible to improve on the results on approximation to functions by polynomials that had been achieved by Charles Jean de la Vallée-Poussin and Henri Lebesgue? Jackson's paper went even further and dealt also with approximation by trigonometric sums.

He became an instructor in mathematics at Harvard in 1911 and an assistant professor in 1916. On June 20, 1918, he married Harriet Spratt Hulley, whom he had met while she was a graduate student in English at Radcliffe College. They had two daughters, Anne Hulley and Mary Eloise. While Jackson served as a captain in the Ordnance Department of the U.S. Army in Washington, D.C., from November, 1918, to August, 1919, he wrote a pamphlet-text on numerical integration in exterior ballistics for the department.

In 1919 Jackson accepted a professorship of mathematics at the University of Minnesota, where he remained until his death. There, his expository writing and speaking, his persistence in continuing undergraduate teaching, his stimulus of graduate students to scholarship in his special area, and his extended participation in editorial and organizational activities all significantly extended his influence.

Jackson's greatest contribution, however, was probably his own research. William L. Hart, his academic associate and biographer, analyzed sixty-three of Jackson's publications and estimated that at least seventy-five of his works involved significant novelty in content, methods, or organization. Jackson's first mathematical research paper, published in 1909, was algebraic, dealing with transformations of bilinear forms. Most of his papers after his return from Göttingen were within the broad field related to his dissertation. He wrote extensively on orthogonal polynomials, trigonometric sums, and their relation to the theory of approximations, all important fields today. However, he showed substantial diversity in his explorations of the connections of these topics with boundary value problems, the solutions of linear differential equations, functions of several complex variables, and even mathematical statistics.

In 1930 the American Mathematical Society published Jackson's *The Theory of Approximation,* the outgrowth of the Colloquium Lectures he gave at the society's summer meeting in 1925. Jackson was also invited to lecture to the society and its Chicago Section in 1921, 1928, 1933, and 1934. In 1933 he was awarded the Mathematical Association of America's Chauvenet prize for the best expository writing over the previous three years. In 1944 the Association published his *Fourier Series and Orthogonal Polynomials* as the sixth of its Carus Mathematical Monographs. His many expository articles and notes included seventeen in the *American Mathematical Monthly.*

Jackson's concerns for teaching and exposition were also reflected in his serving in 1929-1931 as chairman of the joint Committee on Geometry of the Mathematical Association and the National Council of Teachers of Mathematics, and his work at different times as editor, associate, and assistant editor of the *Bulletin* of the American Mathematical Society (1921-1925) and the *Transactions* of the American Mathematical Society (1916-1925, 1926-1931). His other elected and appointed offices and honors included member of Sigma Xi; member of the council of the American Mathematical Society (1918-1920), vice-president (1921); governor of the Mathematical Association of America (1923-1929), vice-president (1924-1925), and president (1926). He was also vice-president of the American Association for the Advancement of Science (1927), a member of the Institute of Mathematical Statistics, and a fellow of the American Academy of Arts and Sciences and the American Physical Society. He was elected a member of the National Academy of Science in 1935.

Jackson never regained full health after a heart attack in 1940. The last eighteen months of his life were spent at home and in the hospital. However, even during this time he approved at least four theses and completed a research paper. He died in Minneapolis and is buried there in Sunset Memorial Park.

Jackson's fine research capacity was accompanied by outstanding effectiveness in exposition and a concern for education and for students and friends at all levels. He stimulated, encouraged, and passed along his intellectual heritage as advisor to nineteen doctoral students.

[William L. Hart, "Dunham Jackson, July 24, 1888–November 6, 1946," Nat. Acad. Sci. *Biog. Memoirs,* XXXIII, 142–179 (1959), contains a picture of Jackson. Hart's article in the Amer. Math. Soc. *Bulletin,* 54 (1948), 847–860, gives a more extensive analysis of his mathematical work. See also *Am. Men of Sci.* (7th ed., 1944). Data on Jackson's professional organizational responsibilities are from Raymond Clare Archibald, *A Semicentennial Hist. of the Am. Mathematical Soc., 1888–1938* (1938), and K. O. May, ed., *The Mathematical Association of America: Its First Fifty Years* (1972).]

PHILLIP S. JONES

JANSKY, KARL GUTHE (Oct. 22, 1905-Feb. 14, 1950), electrical engineer and founder of the science of radio astronomy, was born in Norman, Okla., the third of four sons and third of the six children of Cyril Methodius Jansky and Nellie (Moreau) Jansky. His mother was descended from a Franco-English family that had settled in the United States early in the eighteenth century; his paternal grandfather, a stonemason, had emigrated from Bohemia (later Czechoslovakia) in 1866 and had taken up a homestead in Richland County, Wis. Karl's father, an electrical engineer, was head of the school of applied sciences at the University of Oklahoma until 1908, when he moved to the University of Wisconsin. The children grew up in a comfortably situated family, in an atmosphere that was both warm and competitive. Their mother was gentle; their vigorous father taught them to argue and criticize, to enjoy winter sports, to play games such as chess and bridge, and to respect knowledge. Karl developed an interest in radio and built an early crystal set. He entered the University of Wisconsin, where he majored in physics and received the B.S. degree in 1927 and the M.S. in 1936. He remained at the university for a year as instructor and in 1928 began work at the Cliffwood, N.J., laboratory of the Bell Telephone Company. Two years later the laboratory was moved to Holmdel, N.J., where in 1931 he made the first of the observations that led to his discovery of radio emissions from space.

Jansky had been assigned the practical problem of tracing the source of the atmospherics, or natural static, that sometimes interfered with transoceanic radiotelephone communication. To determine the intensity of the static, the directions from which it arrived, and the time pattern of its appearance, he used a shortwave receiving system. The antenna was shaped like a boxcar, 100 feet long, connected with an automatic intensity recorder and mounted on a motor-driven rotating platform. Late in 1930 he began monitoring the reception of static, usually at a wavelength of 14.6 meters, during complete twenty-four-hour periods. His antenna was highly sensitive to signals received within a cone of maximum sensitivity that swept around the sky, ten degrees above the horizon. By the end of 1932 he had found three major types of interference: local thunderstorms, distant major storms, and a "very steady hiss type static the origin of which is not yet known." Although it was stronger than a similar electrical noise generated by the receiver, it corresponded to a very weak signal.

Jansky refused to dismiss the puzzle and persisted in trying to find an explanation. In analyzing his data, he found that the source of the background noise changed direction, going completely around the compass in a period of twenty-four hours. The noise was strongest when the antenna reception cone pointed south at noon in December 1931; it came from the west at night and from the east in the morning. He therefore theorized that the noise might have its origin in the sun. But after several false starts he made the extraordinary discovery that as the seasons progressed and the sun moved past the stars, the signal was fixed with respect to the stars, not to the sun. Thus, in June 1932 the strongest signal received when the antenna pointed south came at midnight, not noon. By the end of the year he had determined that the hiss static, which he later called star-noise, came from a direction that was fixed in space. In three papers published in 1933 he suggested the strong probability that the unidentified static originated in the center of the Milky Way, in the constellation Sagittarius, which has long been recognized as the center of our galaxy. Two years later, in 1935, he suggested that the radiation arose in interstellar space from the thermal motion of charged particles or, less probably, in stars in the crowded galactic center. Jansky's discovery attracted little attention from astronomers, and the few who did suspect its importance could find no theoretical mechanism that would account for his observations. Jansky himself recognized that further research would require larger, more expensive, highly directional antennas and receivers than those extant.

Jansky ended this type of observation in 1936, and Bell Laboratories set him to work on other problems. He turned to studying the effects of man-made sources of radio interference and helped determine the best sites for receiving transatlantic radio transmissions. With his colleague C. F. Edwards, he studied the angle of arrival and the practical usefulness of radio waves and their echoes at various locations and for antennas of various sizes and carried out experiments in radio propagation. During World War II Jansky did research on radio direction finders, for which he received an army-navy citation. Soon after the war, the advent of high-frequency radio and telephone-line transmission involved him in the technical development of sensitive and reliable amplifiers.

On Aug. 3, 1929, Jansky married Alice La Rue Knapp. Their children were Anne Moreau and David Burdick Jansky. The family lived in Little Silver, N.J., and although Jansky was often ill, because of a chronic kidney infection acquired during his college days, he enjoyed playing golf, softball, and games that involved problem-solving, such as chess. After 1945 declining health resulting from hypertensive cardiovascular disease required him to take extended leaves from work. He died at the age of forty-four in Riverview Hospital in Red Bank, N.J., of a cerebral thrombosis. His remains were cremated.

Jansky's detection of radio waves from the center of our galaxy, a distance of 30,000 light-years, was a revolutionary event in the history of astronomy. It opened the way to exploring the universe at wavelengths a million times longer than those constituting the narrow, visible spectrum of light. During Jansky's lifetime his work was taken up by Grote Reber, a radio engineer who, working in the yard of his home in Wheaton, Ill., designed and built improved antennas and in 1944 was able to publish the first crude map of radio emission from the Milky Way. The growth of radio astronomy as a science began after World War II, first in England, Australia, and the Netherlands. In 1951 the Soviet astrophysicist I. S. Shklovskii showed that the emission was produced by high-energy electrons and magnetic fields in violent explosions within our own or other galaxies. Large radio telescopes have since been built in all parts of the world; they have explored space to distances of billions of light-years and have revealed the existence of new types of celestial objects—radio galaxies, quasars, remnants of supernovae, and pulsars. A National Radio Astronomy Observatory was established at Green Bank, W.Va., in 1958; its main building was named for Jansky.

[Jansky's most important articles are "Directional Studies of Atmospherics at High Frequencies," *Proc. Inst. Radio Eng.*, Dec. 1932; "Radio Waves from Outside the Solar System," *Nature*, July 8, 1933; "Electrical Phenomena That Apparently are of Interstellar Origin," *Popular Astronomy*, Dec. 1933; "Electrical Disturbances Apparently of Extraterrestrial Origin," *Proc. Inst. Radio Eng.*, Oct. 1933; and "A Note on the Source of Interstellar Interference," *ibid.*, Oct. 1935. On Jansky, see C. M. Jansky, Jr., "The Discovery and Identification by Karl Guthe Jansky of Electromagnetic Radiation of Extraterrestrial Origin in the Radio Spectrum," *Proc. Inst. Radio Eng.*, Jan. 1958; George C. Southworth, "Early Hist. of Radio Astronomy," *Scientific Monthly*, Feb. 1956; Harold T. Friis, "Karl Jansky: His Career at Bell Telephone Laboratories," *Science*, Aug. 20, 1965; Grote Reber and Jesse L. Greenstein, "Radio-Frequency Investigations of Astronomical Interest," *Observatory*, Feb. 1947; faculty memorial resolution on Jansky's father, Mar. 7, 1960 (courtesy of Engineering Lib., Univ. of Wis.); and death record from N.J. State Dept. of Health. Information was also provided by Mrs. Alice K. Knopp, Jansky's widow; by his brothers and sister—C. Moreau Jansky, Jr., Mrs. R. G. (Helen) Dingham, and Nelson M. Jansky; and by radio scientists at Bell Telephone Laboratories.]
JESSE L. GREENSTEIN

JEFFERSON, MARK SYLVESTER WILLIAM (Mar. 1, 1863-Aug. 8, 1949), geographer, was born in Melrose, Mass., the fifth son and youngest of seven children of Daniel Jefferson and Mary (Mantz) Jefferson. His father, an English bibliophile, immigrated to the United States in 1849 with his wife and first child. After a stay in Baltimore, he found work in the editorial department of a New York publishing firm, and later with Little, Brown and Company of Boston.

Mark Jefferson attended local public schools and at the age of 17 enrolled at Boston University in the eleven-man class of 1884. There he studied languages, physics, astronomy, and mathematics, and came to know fellow student Bernard Berenson. After three years at the university, an opportunity for serious work in Argentina presented itself. Eager to hear languages spoken in the philological laboratory of the Argentine, he accepted a position as assistant computer in the National Observatory of the Republic, working under Benjamin Apthorp Gould. He scanned the Southern heavens from Cordoba for three years until bothered by eye fatigue. For a time he taught languages in Cordoba; he then accepted a position as sub-manager and treasurer of La Providencia sugar estate on Argentina's frontier in the irrigable piedmont of the Andine Northwest. In 1889 he returned to Boston, completed the requirements for a bachelor degree, then taught in the Mitchell Boys School at Billerica (1890-1891), was principal at Turners Falls High School (1891-1893), and superintendent of schools in Lexington, Mass. (1893-1896). For the next two years he studied geography and geology at Harvard (B.A., 1897; M.A., 1898), working under William Morris Davis, with whom he commenced an intellectual relationship that lasted until Davis' death in 1934. From 1898 to 1901 Jefferson taught at the Brockton High School. In 1900 he was invited to teach geography (in Spanish) at the Harvard Cuban summer school, and as a result of an admirable performance, Davis found him a position at the Michigan State Normal School, Ypsilanti, in 1901.

In the years 1901 to 1939, he taught sixty-two different courses at Ypsilanti, stimulating 15,000 students, and developed a remarkable disciple-record that won for the college the appellation "nursery of America geographers." Jefferson wrote texts for several of his courses: *Teachers Geography* (1906), *Man in Europe* (1924), *Principles of Geography* (1926), *Exercises in Human Geography* (1930), *Man in the United States* (1933). These and other texts and outline maps went through many editions.

Notwithstanding his profound admiration for Davis' work it was in his departure from Davisian physiography that Jefferson perhaps made his largest contribution. Regarding the earth science recommended by the report of the 1892 Committee of Ten of the National Education Association as an incomplete geography, he insisted that man was an important part of the discipline. He helped prepare the influential "man in geography manifesto" presented before the NEA at Denver in 1908 and published much on this theme.

A vigorous and enthusiastic fieldworker, he visited parts of four continents, taking many photographs, and making many friends. In this way he amassed a remarkable collection of 7,500 slides. Friendships created on these occasions led to a substantial correspondence. Facility in approximately thirteen languages enabled him to surmount linguistic barriers.

Jefferson contributed approximately 120 books and articles to geographic literature. He presented twenty-five papers before the Association of American Geographers (a record for the first half century of Association existence, 1904-1954), and had more articles (thirty-one) published in *The Geographical Review* and its predecessor, *The Bulletin of The American Geographical Society,* than any other geographer before or since. Many of his contributions have won for themselves a permanent and abiding place in the history of the discipline; "The Anthropography of Some Great Cities" (1909), "The Civilizing Rails" (1928), "Distribution of the World's City Folks" (1931), and "The Law of the Primate City" (1939) are perhaps his most often quoted articles. He was a pioneer in urban geography in the United States, minted the term "central place" (1931), and offered one of the first courses in urban geography in the United States ("Geography of Cities," 1931). He was chief cartographer for the American Commission to Negotiate Peace at Paris, 1918-1919, and in this capacity helped supervise the compilation of some four hundred maps; he was appointed American representative to the Geographical Commission of the Paris Peace Conference. He was president of the Michigan Academy of Science (1907) and president of the Association of American Geographers

(1916); he was awarded the Cullum Medal of the American Geographical Society (1931) and the Helen Culver Medal from the Chicago Geographical Society (1931), was elected member at large of the National Research Council (1932), and was the recipient of the Annual Distinguished Service Award of the National Council of Geography Teachers (1939). He was elected to corresponding memberships of the Belgrade Geographical Society (1920), the Anthropology and Geography Society, Stockholm (1925), and the University of Belgrade Geographical Society (1932).

Jefferson married Theodora Augusta Bohnstedt at Gilmanton, N.H., on Aug. 22, 1891. Their children were Geoffrey, Theodore, Barbara, Phoebe, and Hilary. After his wife's death in 1913, he married Clara Frances Hopkins at Holland, Mich., on June 17, 1915. Their children were Sally, Thomas, and Mary Alice. Mark Jefferson died of pneumonia at his Ypsilanti home at the age of eighty-six. Following cremation, his ashes were buried at Woodmere Cemetery in Detroit.

[The Mark Jefferson Papers are in the Eastern Michigan Univ. Lib. A collection of maps secured by Jefferson at the Paris Peace Conference is currently in the Seymour Collec. at Yale Univ. See also Geoffrey I. Martin, *Mark Jefferson: Geographer* (1968); *The Mark Jefferson Paris Peace Conference Diary* (Ann Arbor, Univ. Microfilms, 1966); and "Mark Jefferson and Geography in Michigan," *Michigan Schoolmasters Bull.,* May 12, 1961, pp. 1–18.]
GEOFFREY I. MARTIN

JENNINGS, HERBERT SPENCER (Apr. 8, 1868-Apr. 14, 1947), biologist, was born in Tonica, La Salle County, Ill., the third of six children and elder of the two sons of George Nelson Jennings, a physician, and Olive Taft (Jenks) Jennings. The couple had met while both were teaching district school. George Jennings had moved west from Connecticut; his wife was born in Illinois of Pennsylvania parents. A devout Baptist, she supervised the religious training and education of their children. Dr. Jennings, after studying at Rush Medical College in Chicago, became the village infidel, greatly excited by the contents of his growing library of literary, historical, scientific, and philosophical books. His interests were reflected in the names he gave his sons: Herbert Spencer and George Darwin.

Herbert taught himself to read before he was three, read biology at four and Shakespeare at five, but with difficulty learned to write only after he started school at eight. During his boyhood the family lived for a time (1874-1879) in California, and then returned to Tonica, where Herbert graduated from the local high school in 1886. He was a good student and already showed characteristics that he retained through life: a lively sense of humor, shyness except with intimates, orderly habits of thought, and a remarkable capacity to get straight to the root of every question. After graduation he taught in district schools in Iowa and Illinois, and between teaching stints attended Illinois State Normal School (1887-1888), where he first encountered stimulating student activities and superior teachers. In 1889 he was appointed assistant professor of botany and horticulture at Texas Agricultural and Mechanical College, but the job ended after a year.

Jennings entered the University of Michigan in 1890, intending to make literature or philology his profession, but the introductory biology course of Jacob Reighard, which he took in his first year, turned his interest in that direction; and the decision was clinched at the end of the year by the offer of an assistantship in zoology, which enabled him to continue at Michigan. He earned further funds by summer work with the Michigan Fish Commission. Later, in the summer of 1901, he was in charge of the U. S. Fish Commission's survey of the Great Lakes. On these missions he studied the unicellular organisms and rotifera of Michigan lakes and the Great Lakes and thereby became a world authority on these creatures, which he used as his chief research organisms for the rest of his career.

After receiving his B.S. degree in 1893, Jennings stayed on at Michigan for a year as a graduate assistant and then entered Harvard, where he took the M.A. degree in 1895 and the Ph.D. in 1896. His doctoral thesis, a description of the early development of a rotifer, was supervised by Edward L. Mark. He was most influenced, however, by a young instructor, Charles B. Davenport, in whose home he lived. To Davenport largely belongs the credit for transforming Jennings from a descriptive to an experimental biologist. A postdoctoral fellowship enabled Jennings to spend the year 1896-1897 in Europe. He studied physiology and psychology and began experiments on behavior in Jena, and at the Naples Biological Station he became acquainted with some of the world's leading experimental biologists. During this important year he fully matured as a scientist, acquired a permanent attachment to Europe, and began the series of experimental investigations on behavior and responses to stimuli in unicellular and other lower organisms that rapidly won him recognition as one of the leading apostles of radical experimental biology.

These investigations, published in dozens of technical papers over the course of eleven years, brought Jennings into a cross fire of attack from vitalists, psychologists, and physicochemical biologists. He fought back with public and private demonstrations of key experiments and with incisive but objective rejoinders to his critics. The work of this period was summarized and interpreted in his book *Behavior of Lower Organisms* (1906). It showed, contrary to both the current vitalistic and the simplistic physicochemical theories, that although behavior is strictly determined, a decisive role in it is played by organismic structure at higher as well as at the molecular levels of organization. The book became a classic in the history of experimental biology and behaviorist psychology and after more than six decades was still a basic text for the student of animal behavior.

While this work was in progress, Jennings was moving from post to post. He returned from Europe to become professor of botany at Montana State Agricultural and Mechanical College (1897-1898), and then successively instructor in zoology at Dartmouth (1898-1899) and instructor (1899-1901) and assistant professor (1901-1903) in zoology at the University of Michigan. With his foot at last on the academic ladder at age thirty, Jennings married an artist, Mary Louise Burridge of Tecumseh, Mich., on June 18, 1898, after a long courtship going back to his college days. They had one son, Burridge, who became a physicist. At Michigan, Jennings collaborated with Professor Reighard on a book, *Anatomy of the Cat* (1901)—illustrated by Mrs. Jennings—which long remained the standard treatise. Although there were few Ph.D. candidates in the department, they included Raymond Pearl, who had followed Jennings from Dartmouth and became one of his most distinguished pupils. In 1903 Jennings was called to the University of Pennsylvania as assistant professor of zoology, with the first year on leave in Naples under a grant from the Carnegie Institution of Washington. In 1906 he went to Johns Hopkins as associate professor and a year later became professor of experimental zoology. He remained there until his retirement in 1938, from 1910 as Henry Walters Professor and director of the zoological laboratory.

At Johns Hopkins, Jennings entered a new field of research—genetics and evolution in unicellular organisms, chiefly *Paramecium* and *Difflugia*—which he explored vigorously for ten years and returned to in later life, whenever time permitted. In this field, as in behavior, he was a pioneer, laying the foundations for all subsequent studies of genetics of unicellular organisms. With characteristic originality he showed—contrary to his own earlier views and those of his contemporaries—that the processes of heredity, development, and reproduction were fundamentally the same in unicellular as in multicellular organisms. He demonstrated the genetic constancy of the clone (the asexual progeny of a single cell), and this has remained a basic principle of genetics. Searching for the hereditary variations that provide the materials for evolution, he attempted by long-continued selection to find them as exceptions to clonal constancy. Eventually he succeeded in selecting slight differences in *Difflugia* that persisted for several generations, enough to be in his opinion a demonstration of evolution in progress. The interpretation of this result, although important for the thinking of his contemporaries, remains obscure.

His experiments on heredity at sexual reproduction (conjugation) in *Paramecium* showed that genetically diverse clones were produced, as expected on the then new Mendelian principles. Surprisingly, another expectation, the production by successive inbreedings of genetically pure (homozygous) clones, was not fulfilled. To render the expectations precise, Jennings made mathematical studies of Mendelian theory applied to various breeding systems. From these studies, among the first in population genetics, he correctly concluded that Mendelian principles alone might not account for his observations on inbreeding, but he failed to find a satisfactory explanation. The work and thought of these years were summarized in the charming book *Life and Death: Heredity and Evolution in Unicellular Organisms* (1920). During this fruitful period, Jennings directed and inspired the researches of a "school" of students, including the zoologists Robert W. Hegner and William H. Taliaferro and the psychologists Karl S. Lashley and John B. Watson.

During his last two decades at Johns Hopkins, Jennings became preoccupied with other commitments and only sporadically carried on laboratory research. Wartime work as a biometrician for the federal Food Administration in Washington took much of his time in 1917-1918. He was increasingly in demand as a public lecturer, and he performed varied duties within the university. Nevertheless, he managed to write a monumental critical review, *Genetics of the Protozoa* (1929), and to carry out and publish three laboratory studies: an analysis of fecundity and aging in a rotifer, a reinvestiga-

tion of the genetic consequences of conjugation in *Paramecium,* and an extension of his earlier studies on inheritance in *Difflugia.* The last is particularly important in its demonstration that a formed structure serves as a negative model or template for the development of the corresponding structure of a daughter cell. The significance of this finding was not appreciated until more than a quarter of a century later, after his death, when the basic process of gene (DNA) reproduction was found also to occur by a template mechanism.

After retiring in 1938, Jennings moved to Los Angeles as a research associate at the University of California. There he resumed intensive laboratory research that continued for seven years, until illness forced him to stop. This final burst of activity actually began a year before retirement, when the discovery of mating types by an associate in his laboratory for the first time made possible routine cross-breeding and proper Mendelian analysis in *Paramecium.* With this tool, Jennings discovered the first system of multiple interbreeding mating types and showed that the species *P. bursaria* consists of several such systems, each genetically isolated from the others. He also contributed abundant data on mating-type inheritance and made an exhaustive study of the factors determining clonal vigor and length of life. His observations forced him to conclude, contrary to views he had vigorously maintained some thirty years earlier in disputes with Gary N. Calkins and others, that most if not all clones of unicells went through inherently determined life cycles which, if fertilization failed to occur, went on to inevitable death.

Although Jennings' fame was solidly rooted in his accomplishments as a laboratory investigator, it flowered in his public work as lecturer and writer and as a philosopher of science. Early and permanent devotion to literature and philosophy had cultivated his talents for lucid, engaging expression and for clear thinking, and he was outstandingly successful in publicizing the major advances in genetics and biology and their bearings on human affairs. He expounded the subtle interplay between heredity and environment; the fallacy in the view that progress in technology, medicine, and public health necessarily leads to genetic deterioration; and the stringent limitations of then feasible eugenic actions for achieving human betterment. These and other themes marked many journal articles for both layman and scientist; they were incorporated in his textbook *Genetics* (1935) and in two successful popular books, *Prometheus, or*

Biology and the Advancement of Man (1925) and *The Biological Basis of Human Nature* (1930). In spite of great subsequent advances in genetics, especially at the molecular and cellular levels, these books still soundly portray major features of genetics and biology and their bearing on human affairs; indeed, they are often prophetic of the stands taken by the soundest and most imaginative later spokesmen for biology.

Jennings was highly regarded as a philosopher of biology. His early researches on cell behavior led him to formulate views on the body-mind problem and on the then current heated debates between mechanists and vitalists. He vigorously attacked both mechanists such as Jacques Loeb, whom he regarded as simplistic, and vitalists such as Hans Driesch, whom he regarded as unscientific. He saw no acceptable alternative to experience, to radical experimental analysis, as the means of acquiring knowledge and understanding; but, unlike most scientists who take into account only outer or public experience, Jennings insisted that inner experience —sensation, emotion, and thought—is also a part of reality, a natural phenomenon which, if ignored, leads to a grossly deficient conception of human nature. He concluded monistically that these inner experiences are expressions of the properties of matter at its highest known level of organization and cannot be experimentally separated from such matter. From subatomic particles to man, each successively higher level of material organization exhibits new properties which cannot in principle be predicted until the higher level manifests them.

This thoroughgoing emergentism led Jennings to important biological conclusions: The ultimate problem of biology is to account for the origin, nature, and consequences of the diversity of material structure evolved from the structure of the initial living material. The basis of the uniqueness of each human individual is ultimately traceable to the uniqueness of his initial (genetic) structure, which is determined to develop a mind that is progressively altered by its own operation, each experience extending the uniqueness of the individual and playing a part in determining later actions. The interplay between genetic constitution, mind, and experience, determined but unpredictable and unique for each individual, adds up to choice and freedom in the sense of not being bound by the determinisms operating in any other individual. Moreover, the properties and actions of each generation of man, consisting of its own array of unique individuals, are likewise essentially unpredictable. Hence, what has failed in the past need not fail in the future. Therein lies man's hope. This philosophy, extended to encompass the world and man's place in it, was beautifully expressed in his *The Universe and Life* (1933), which may prove to be his greatest and most enduring contribution.

Jennings received honorary degrees from several universities and served as president of the American Society of Zoologists (1908-1909) and of the American Society of Naturalists (1910-1911). He was elected a member of the National Academy of Sciences in 1914. He was genuinely amazed at his own success and bore his honors modestly. Highstrung, nervous, energetic, he threw himself completely into everything he did. Concentrated in conversation, hearty in laughter, a keen observer of people, including himself and his ills (to which he largely ministered without medical assistance), he focused intently on every experience of life. He greatly enjoyed good conversation but was not at ease with social banalities. His influence on his professional associates was achieved mainly by the example he set of freedom from pettiness, concentration on fundamentals, profound respect for both objective investigation and the search for meaning, and an exquisite balance in dealing with fact and thought.

Jennings' wife died in 1938, and on Oct. 21, 1939, he married his brother's widow, Lulu (Plant) Jennings. During his last years he suffered from Parkinson's disease, and he died in Santa Monica, Calif., a few days after his seventy-ninth birthday, of respiratory failure. Following cremation, his ashes were placed in Forest Lawn Memorial Park, Glendale, Calif.

[The library of the Am. Philosophical Soc., Philadelphia, possesses a rich collection of MS material pertaining to Jennings, including: diaries, 1903-1904 and 1925-1941; a MS autobiography written in 1933 for Samuel Wood Geiser; copies of extensive letters (1889-1911) by Jennings to members of his family; correspondence with Geiser, T. M. Sonneborn, Arthur O. Lovejoy, and others; and a 216-page autobiography of Jennings' father. A published article by Jennings, "On the Advantages of Growing Old," *Johns Hopkins Alumni Mag.,* June 1922, gives insight into his mental life. The same magazine contains annual reports by Jennings of his research and professional activities. The fullest biographical account is the memoir by T. M. Sonneborn in Nat. Acad. Sci., *Biog. Memoirs* (forthcoming), which includes a full list of his publications. Other published biographical material includes addresses by Arthur O. Lovejoy and Charles B. Davenport in *Johns Hopkins Alumni Mag.,* Jan. 1922; Samuel Wood Geiser in *Bios,* Mar. 1934—an excellent biography with a fine line drawing; obituaries in Am. Philosophical Soc., *Year Book,* 1947 (by Edwin Grant Conklin), *Nature,* June 21, 1947 (by Clifford Dobell), and *Am. Jour. of Psychology,* July 1947 (by T. C. Schneirla). See also Donald D. Jensen's evaluation of Jennings' work in behavior in the foreword to the 1962 edition of Jennings' *The Behavior of Lower*

Organisms; and, on the family background, Chancellor L. Jenks, "Following the Westward Star," Miss. Valley Hist. Assoc., *Proc.*, July 1920. A portrait of Jennings by Frank B. A. Linton is at the Johns Hopkins Univ.]

T. M. Sonneborn

JEPSON, WILLIS LINN (Aug. 19, 1867-Nov. 7, 1946), one of the greatest of American regional botanists, was born on a ranch near Vacaville, Calif., the first son and fourth of five children of William Lemon Jepson and Martha Ann (Potts) Jepson. His father, of Scotch-English stock, was born in rural Kentucky but brought up in Missouri; his mother, of Virginia ancestry, was a native of Missouri. William Jepson went to California in 1850 as a gold miner, returned to Missouri to marry, and then took his bride to California by covered wagon train. As a boy, Willis roamed freely on the family ranch and the unfenced slopes bordering the largely unsettled Sacramento Valley. He always reveled in his pioneer background and liked to think of himself as an explorer. His bookplate shows a desert scene with an oxen-drawn covered wagon in the foreground and a range of mountains behind. Its legend, "Something lost behind the ranges—over yonder—go you there," remained a favorite quotation.

Jepson early developed a strong interest in the flowering plants of the region, an interest encouraged by one of his teachers at the local academy. At the age of twelve, on a trip to San Francisco, he visited the California Academy of Sciences, where he first met the botanists Albert Kellogg and Edward L. Greene. He entered the University of California at Berkeley to study botany and received the Ph.B. degree in 1889. A year later, botany, previously under the aegis of agriculture, was made a separate department, with one professor (Greene), one instructor, and one assistant—Jepson. In addition to his teaching duties, Jepson undertook taxonomic research under Greene and engaged in extensive fieldwork directed toward a thesis. After being promoted to instructor in 1894, he was granted leave of absence (with salary) to study at Cornell under George F. Atkinson in the spring of 1895, and again (1896-1897) to work up his California collections at the Gray Herbarium of Harvard University under the general supervision of Benjamin L. Robinson. Jepson received his Ph.D. from Berkeley in 1899 and was promoted to assistant professor. He became associate professor in 1911, and in 1918 professor, a post he held until his retirement in 1937.

Jepson's writings are voluminous, consisting of eight books and more than two hundred scientific articles, as well as innumerable lectures and popular notes in newspapers. As an undergraduate he had edited the student literary publication; he treasured literature and the classics, and he developed a colorful literary style of his own. The two botanical journals he edited provided ample outlet for any new thought or observation: *Erythea* (1893-1900), established by Greene, and *Madroño* (1916-1933), the journal of the California Botanical Society; Jepson was the founder of both the society and its journal.

His books built neatly one upon another. His doctoral thesis yielded *A Flora of Western Middle California* (1901). *Trees of California* (1909) became a popular handbook and paved the way for his sumptuously illustrated *The Silva of California* (1910). *A Manual of the Flowering Plants of California,* completed in 1925 and reprinted several times thereafter, was the standard treatise on the vascular plants of the state for at least a quarter century. His most ambitious undertaking, however, was *A Flora of California,* begun in 1909 and published in several parts at intervals until 1943, but never completed. Because he considered California a unique botanical region, Jepson did not model the work on existing floras but conceived his own. A numbered list of particulars includes reliance upon the living plant itself and observations noted in the field, careful validation of distributional ranges and altitudes, and bibliographical thoroughness. "It matters not how much knowledge may be accumulated about a given species, how many monographs discuss it, —always botanists wish *to go back to the plant,* to authentic specimens. A flora which cites no specimens whatsoever may be a useful flora but it is not a scientific flora" (letter to author, Dec. 10, 1943).

What is unique in this concept is doubtless the emphasis on the plant as a living organism in its particular natural environment. Jepson's mentor, Greene, had been a devoted observer of plants in the field. But Greene was a philosophical opponent of Darwinian evolution, who could see in natural variation only ever-increasing products of special creation. Jepson's essentially conservative taxonomic concepts rested on full acceptance of organic evolution. His *Flora* foreshadowed later biological and biosystematic approaches to systematics, but it was also based on the conviction that one man could hope to know as living organisms a flora of more than four thousand species.

Descriptions of Jepson as a teacher differ

radically, apparently depending upon the age and personality of the describer. Some of his earlier students speak enthusiastically of the exhilaration of accompanying their professor on field trips. This pleasure was largely denied his later students, who found that graduate seminars provided almost their only contact with Jepson, and that the student was expected to work out his own salvation. Nevertheless, Jepson was unusually successful in communicating his great enthusiasm for the flora and his passion for accuracy in writing about it.

A pioneer in the conservation movement, Jepson was a founder (1918) and longtime counselor of the Save-the-Redwoods League, which sought to preserve California's redwood forests. An early crusader for better forest management, he was instrumental in the university's establishment of a division of forestry in 1914. His contacts with professional foresters, sparked by a mutual love for trees, remained strong throughout his life.

Deeply dedicated to his mission of interpreting the flora of California to scientist, student, and layman, Jepson was a single-minded, indefatigable worker. He spared neither himself nor his friends and often seemed as much driven as dedicated. He was fiercely independent and found ordinary social contacts unrewarding and abrasive, so that he tended to close them off because they distracted him from his work. Nevertheless, he was capable of strong friendships, particularly with persons who were not directly in his own field of interest or with whom he was not in daily contact. Since he possessed a highly developed sense of the dramatic, he often interpreted minor lapses or defections as evidence of personal disloyalty and betrayal; his reactions to such incidents were in turn emotionally exhausting. Deeply loved and admired by some and bitterly resented by others, he estranged himself from many well-wishers, but perhaps that was a necessary sacrifice to his prodigious and lasting accomplishments. Jepson never married, but he was fortunate in having devoted friends to the very end. In mid-1945 he suffered a coronary thrombosis, and he died the following year at his home in Berkeley, at the age of seventy-nine. He was buried in the Vacaville-Elmira Cemetery. A grove of redwoods, a stand of bishop pine, a Sierran peak, and a remarkable genus of endemic, autumn-flowering Saxifragaceous plants commemorate his name.

[Jepson willed to the university his herbarium and library, to be kept as an integrated unit. Among its most valuable assets are his series of field notes, running to sixty-three volumes, and his bound correspondence, which embraces fifty-one volumes and an index. Obituaries and memorials: Lincoln Constance in *Science*, June 13, 1947; A. R. Davis, Lincoln Constance, and George D. Lauderback in Univ. of Calif., *In Memoriam*, 1946; Joseph Ewan in Wash. Acad. Sci., *Jour.*, Nov. 5, 1947; Emanuel Fritz in Calif. Horticultural Soc., *Jour.*, Jan. 1948; Herbert L. Mason in *Madrono*, Apr. 1947; David D. Keck, *ibid.*, July, 1948; H. M. Wheeler in *Desert Plant Life*, Mar. 1947. Thomas J. Gregory et al., *Hist. of Solano and Napa Counties, Calif.* (1912), includes an account of the Jepson family almost certainly written by Jepson himself. For a bibliography of his scientific writings, see Lawrence R. Heckard, John T. Howell, and Rimo Bacigalupi in *Madrono*, Oct. 1967. An excellent portrait is in the Jepson Herbarium and Lib., Univ. of Calif.]

LINCOLN CONSTANCE

JEWETT, FRANK BALDWIN (Sept. 5, 1879-Nov. 18, 1949), telephone engineer and industrial research administrator, was born in Pasadena, Calif., then a small farming community, the older of two children and only son of Stanley P. Jewett and Phebe C. (Mead) Jewett. His parents had moved to California from Ohio after their marriage. Stanley Jewett, of seventeenth-century New England ancestry, was a civil engineering graduate of the Massachusetts Institute of Technology. He had been in railroad work in Ohio, and during the 1880's, in addition to actively managing his ranch, he helped form the Los Angeles and San Gabriel Valley Railroad; this was later bought by the Atchison, Topeka, and Santa Fe, of which he became a vice-president. His subsequent involvement in the power industry, then just beginning to install electric lighting and street railways in California, influenced his son, who decided on a career in electrical engineering. By the time Frank was eight, the family had moved to Lamanda Park, about five miles east of Pasadena. After attending a one-room school until the eighth grade in Lamanda Park, Frank entered the preparatory school of Throop Institute of Technology in Pasadena (later the California Institute of Technology) and then the institute itself, graduating with the B.A. degree in 1898. His mother's death that same year prevented him from beginning graduate work at M.I.T. as planned, but at the suggestion of a Throop professor he entered the University of Chicago in January 1899 to study physics. He received the Ph.D. in 1902.

At Chicago, Jewett worked as research assistant under Albert A. Michelson and became a friend of the young instructor Robert A. Millikan, both future Nobel Prize laureates. The high standards and achievements of Michelson and other Chicago associates undoubtedly cultivated Jewett's commitment to fundamental research, later an outstanding characteristic of his as a director of research. Jewett's concentrating upon physics at this particular time was opportune, for it allowed him to comprehend the fundamental scientific discoveries concerning atomic structure, particularly electrons, that were being made by J. A. Fleming and J. J. Thomson, and being explained by O. W. Richardson and others. During Jewett's career as a telephone engineer, research scientist, and laboratory director, many of the outstanding developments were electronic applications. From Chicago, Jewett moved to M.I.T., where he carried on advanced studies and taught physics. On Dec. 28, 1905, he married Fannie C. Frisbie of Rockford, Ill., whom he had met when both were studying physics at Chicago. They had two surviving children: Harrison Leach and Frank Baldwin, Jr.

In 1904 George A. Campbell, the leading scientist of the American Telephone and Telegraph Company in Boston, asked Jewett to join the engineering department of the company. Campbell had developed the loading coil for long-distance telephone transmission, a major invention usually attributed to Michael Pupin, the distinguished American electrical engineer and professor, but an innovation resulting also from the fundamental work in design and spacing of Campbell. Jewett considered Campbell as, beyond question, first "among his generation of theoretical workers in electric communications." Jewett's appreciation of the practical contribution that could be made by a scientist steeped in fundamentals—Campbell had done advanced study abroad and had a doctorate from Harvard University—was heightened by his awareness of the immense savings that the loading coil brought the telephone company.

After serving under Campbell as a transmission engineer, Jewett succeeded him in 1906 as head of the electrical engineering department of A.T. and T. in Boston and then moved with the engineering department to New York late in the same year, where John J. Carty was chief engineer. Under Carty, Jewett played a major role in establishing in 1915 transcontinental telephone transmission, through the use of loaded lines and the more recently developed electronic telephone repeater. In the same year, engineers working under Carty and Jewett introduced the transatlantic radio telephone.

These advances resulted in great part from the work of scientists, like Campbell, with advanced training in mathematics and physics. The commercial significance of the scientists' work was indicated by Jewett, who estimated in 1925 that it would have cost the Bell system

about $40 million more a year to provide all its service without the repeater and the loaded line. Not the least of Jewett's contributions in his first two decades with the Bell system was recruiting young scientists who were able to apply higher mathematics and the growing body of science to telephone technology.

Jewett proved to be an advocate of industrial research and a recruiter and organizer of gifted scientists and engineers at a time when the support of industry and government for research was rapidly increasing. In 1917 Jewett wrote, "that industrial research has taken a firm place in shaping the destinies of our economic future no one who is at all cognizant of the facts would for a moment deny." During the war, Jewett, who served as a lieutenant colonel in the Signal Corps, and other scientists and engineers had notable success in applying science to solve industrial and military problems, and, after the war, industries, especially the electrical, chemical, and metallurgical, established more and larger research laboratories. Jewett's company, encouraged by J. J. Carty, consolidated its industrial research facilities by establishing in 1925 the Bell Telephone Laboratories, Incorporated. Jewett, a close associate and admirer of Carty's, became first president of the laboratories, as well as vice president of the American Telephone and Telegraph Company. A. T. and T. owned the laboratories jointly with the Western Electric Company, the manufacturer of equipment for the Bell system.

The Bell Laboratories came to be known throughout the world as a leading cultivator of industrial research. Jewett defined industrial research by comparing and contrasting it with pure research. He believed that both types employed identical methods and "that the real distinction lay in the *motive* behind the research and not at all in the methods employed." Pure research, Jewett argued, was carried on for the purpose of enlarging the bounds of human knowledge and was rightly concentrated in the universities, while industrial research was utilitarian and was properly concentrated in the research laboratories of industry. Jewett, who recruited many of the scientists with advanced degrees among the 2,000 employees of his laboratories, considered industrial research as fundamental as pure research.

While Jewett headed the Bell Laboratories not only was the telephone network greatly extended and the quality of transmission substantially improved through a masterful blending of science, technology, and economics, but advances were made in the transmission of photographs by wire and the potential of television was explored. When the United States entered World War II, Jewett, with his broad experience and wide circle of scientific and industrial associates, was drawn into the effort, as a recruiter, organizer, and coordinator of scientists and engineers for government service. He was advantageously placed to fulfill this function, having been elected president of the National Academy of Sciences in 1939. This singular honor and responsibility followed upon an appointment in 1923 as chairman of the Division of Engineering and Industrial Research of the National Research Council and membership on President Franklin D. Roosevelt's Science Advisory Board in 1933.

Jewett served as president of the academy for two terms, 1939-1947, when it functioned as a principal science advisory agency to the government. Jewett also helped Vannevar Bush to found in 1940 the National Defense Research Committee, on which Jewett served and which placed government research contracts with academic institutions and industrial corporations. In addition to his responsibilities as a science advisor, Jewett headed the NDRC committee for communication, transportation, and submarine warfare.

In 1940 Jewett relinquished the presidency of the Bell Telephone Laboratories to become chairman of the Board of Directors until he retired in 1944. He died on Nov. 18, 1949, of a perforated duodenal ulcer, and after cremation, his remains were buried in Short Hills, N.J. Jewett presided over a renowned industrial laboratory during its formative years, when science-based industrial research came to be regarded as the most effective method of solving the complex technological problems of industry.

[Jewett's views on industrial research can be found in his "Industrial Research with Some Notes Concerning Its Scope in the Bell Telephone System," Am. Inst. of Electrical Engineers, Trans., XXXVI, 841–855 (1917), and "Utilizing the Results of Fundamental Research in the Communication Field," Bell Telephone Quart., Apr. 1932. For his reports and analysis of advances in telephone science and technology, see "Some Recent Developments in Telephony and Telegraphy," Smithsonian Institution, Annual Report, 1915, pp. 489–509; "Telephone Repeaters," written with Bancroft Gherardi, Am. Inst. of Electrical Engineers, Proc., XXXVIII, 1287-1345 (1919); "The Telephone Switchboard—Fifty Years of Hist.," Bell Telephone Quart., July 1928; and "Telephone Communication System of the U.S.," with Gherardi, Bell System Technical Jour., Jan. 1930. The fullest biographical account is that of Oliver E. Buckley in Nat. Acad. Sci., Biog. Memoirs, XXVII (1952), which includes a list of Jewett's publications. See also the chapter on Jewett in Maurice Holland and Henry F. Pringle, Industrial Explorers (1928); and

obituaries in Nature, Dec. 17, 1949, and Electrical Engineering, Mar. 1950. Death record from N.J. Dept. of Health.]

THOMAS PARKE HUGHES

JOHNSON, GEORGE FRANCIS (Oct. 14, 1857-Nov. 28, 1948), shoe manufacturer, was born in Milford, Mass., the third of the four sons and five children of Francis A. Johnson and Sarah Jane (Aldrich) Johnson. Both parents came of old New England working-class families; the father, recorded on his son's birth record as a teamster, had held many jobs, including that of a treer at a local boot factory. George Johnson left school at the age of thirteen and went to work for the Seaver Brothers boot factory in Ashland, Mass. In 1881, after similar jobs in other Massachusetts towns, he moved to Binghamton, N.Y., and became manager of the treeing room of the Lester Brothers Boot Factory. He soon gained a reputation as an innovative leader, and in 1890, when Henry B. Endicott, a wealthy Bostonian, secured control of the firm, Johnson was made production and sales manager. So successful was he that in 1899 Endicott allowed him to buy a half-interest in the company. The Endicott-Johnson firm was incorporated in 1919, and the following year, after Endicott's death, Johnson became president.

From his earliest working days Johnson had viewed labor and capital as partners, and as an entrepreneur he became a leading exponent of industrial democracy and "welfare capitalism." The employment policies he worked out became widely known. Johnson envisioned the ideal factory as a "shop out in the open country, with the homes of the workers around it in a little village." Thus the company built factories in the rural areas west of Binghamton and established towns which eventually became Johnson City and Endicott. The company constructed several thousand houses, which it encouraged workers to purchase by making mortgages readily available; it also supplied utilities, libraries, schools, stores, and recreational facilities like the "En-Joie Health" Golf Club. Johnson himself lived among his workers, and a democratic atmosphere prevailed at the plant. Workers had direct access to "George F." (as they called him), and within limits they could choose their own hours of work.

In terms of economic benefits, Endicott-Johnson employees enjoyed a significant advantage. Johnson, who believed the term "living wage" was often synonymous with mere subsistence, consistently paid the highest salaries in the shoe industry; even during the depression of the 1930's he could boast that his wages were competitive with those of Henry Ford. In 1916 Endicott-Johnson became the first shoe manufacturer to adopt the eight-hour day and the forty-eight-hour week, and two years later it was among the first companies in the country to institute free, comprehensive medical care for employees and their families. In 1919 Johnson inaugurated a unique profit-sharing plan in which all workers and executives benefited equally, their shares dependent solely on the number of weeks worked during the previous year. In all these actions Johnson's prime objective, as his correspondence makes clear, was the maintenance of a stable, dependable labor supply. He had a genuine belief in a "square deal" for labor, and being a benefactor to his employees was important to him, but it was secondary to business motives.

Johnson's response to labor unions was ambivalent. He regarded them as a necessary means to redress workers' grievances against unfair employers, but felt that in a community-oriented shop like Endicott-Johnson they would be a disruptive force. "Unions are good," he said; "a union of interests is better." The strength of the goodwill and loyalty generated by Johnson's paternalistic policies was revealed in 1940, when his employees voted by a five-to-one margin not to join a union. The company's approach to labor-management relations appealed to Thomas J. Watson, founder of the International Business Machines Corporation, who in 1924 was persuaded by Johnson to build his first factory in Endicott, and Watson for years followed similar policies as an employer.

Johnson was as unorthodox in his political views as he was in business. An independent, he endorsed the presidential candidacies of Woodrow Wilson and Alfred E. Smith and had little use for Calvin Coolidge. He supported Franklin D. Roosevelt as governor of New York and later favored much of the New Deal. Believing that "unholy" corporate profits and underconsumption—rather than overproduction—had caused the depression, he supported measures tending to produce a more equitable distribution of wealth. He championed the National Industrial Recovery Act of 1933 and its codes of fair practice, and was one of the first businessmen to display the NRA "Blue Eagle." During the depression he managed to keep most of his workers employed by reducing working hours, and he gave free meals to the unemployed in the company's dining rooms. Johnson's natural antipathy to compulsory collective bargaining made him a foe of the NRA's labor code and

of the National Labor Relations Act of 1935; yet in 1936 he supported Roosevelt for re-election.

Johnson married Lucy Anna Willis of Braintree, Mass., on Dec. 22, 1876. They had five children: Walter L., George W., Zaida, Irma, and Ernest. This marriage ended in divorce, and he later married Mary Ann McGlone in Binghamton, N.Y.; they had one child, Esther Lillian. Reared as a Methodist, Johnson disliked sectarian divisions and often attended Roman Catholic services with his second wife. In 1930 he relinquished the presidency of the Endicott-Johnson Corporation to his son George and took the position of chairman of the board. He suffered a heart attack in 1937 and retired two years later, but lived beyond the age of ninety, when he died in Endicott of a second heart attack. He was buried in that community's Riverhurst Cemetery.

[The George F. Johnson Papers at Syracuse Univ. offer an excellent source on his ideas and management practices. Richard S. Saul, "An American Entrepreneur: George F. Johnson" (Ph.D. diss., Syracuse Univ., 1966), though pedantic in parts, is the only scholarly treatment of Johnson and his time. William Inglis, *George F. Johnson and His Industrial Democracy* (1935), is a laudatory work commissioned by Johnson. A daughter of Johnson, Mrs. Lloyd E. Sweet of Windsor, N.Y., provided family data. Johnson's birth record (which gives his birth date as Oct. 13) and the record of his first marriage were secured from the Mass. Registrar of Vital Statistics.]

RICHARD S. SAUL

JOHNSON, JACK (Mar. 31, 1878–June 10, 1946), first Negro heavyweight boxing champion of the world, was born in Galveston, Tex., and named John Arthur Johnson. He was one of at least seven children in a poor family. His father was a school janitor and occasional exhorter at revival meetings. Accounts of Johnson's early life differ, but he apparently left school after the fifth grade and worked at a variety of jobs, including stable boy and bakery assistant, and then became a longshoreman on the Galveston docks. For a time during his teens he traveled around the country, living the life of a hobo and occasionally being arrested for vagrancy. At one point he worked as an exercise boy at a racetrack in Boston, but returned to Galveston after his leg was broken by a horse's kick.

Johnson first became interested in boxing while employed as a longshoreman—initially as a means of self-defense on the tough waterfront—and began to work out at local gyms. Increasingly determined to become a professional boxer, he made vagabond junkets throughout his teens seeking matches, and worked briefly as a sparring partner for the fighter Joe Walcott. Because of prevailing racial attitudes and fears of race friction, white fighters of that era seldom met blacks in the ring. In 1899, therefore, Johnson joined a troupe of itinerant Negro boxers who toured the country putting on exhibition fights.

In a sport that was still less than respectable and outlawed in most places, Johnson nevertheless developed into a major figure. As early as 1902 he became a contender for the heavyweight crown by defeating George Gardiner, a former world light-heavyweight champion. In the next six years Johnson fought fifty-seven bouts, most with formidable black opponents, winning all but three. Fast and nimble, Johnson emerged as a ring virtuoso, possessing a flawless defense and the ability to strike a paralyzing blow with either hand. He was also a master ring showman, taunting his opponents, joking with officials, and confidently flashing his famous "golden smile" (the result of gold fillings) at hostile crowds. To supplement his precarious income from boxing during this period, Johnson applied his showmanship to the vaudeville stage, devising an act in which he danced, played the bull fiddle, and gave improvised lectures.

Despite the color barrier, the huge, bald Johnson was determined to capture the world heavyweight championship. In 1908, after defeating all other potential contenders, he finally won the chance to face Tommy Burns, the white Canadian who then held the title. In a fight in Sydney, Australia, Johnson won an easy victory in the fourteenth round. Because of his race, however, together with his free and easy style of life, his claim to the title was widely challenged. Many experts even tortuously argued that with the defeat of Burns the heavyweight crown had reverted to James J. ("Jim") Jeffries, the great champion who had retired undefeated in 1905.

Jeffries now became the "white hope" to defeat Johnson and lay undisputed claim to the title both for himself and for the white race. As the novelist Jack London wrote: "Jim Jeffries must emerge from his alfalfa farm and remove the golden smile from Jack Johnson's face." Reluctantly, the thirty-five-year-old Jeffries came out of retirement and on July 4, 1910, met Johnson before a crowd of 16,000 at Reno, Nev. From the outset, Johnson dominated the action, scoring a knockout against the exhausted ex-champion in the fifteenth round. His victory, which netted him a record $120,000, was greeted with bitterness and violence. Clashes between blacks and whites in several communities throughout the country caused eleven deaths. Almost immediately "white hope tournaments" were inaugurated to find a new challenger capable of beating Johnson.

With Jeffries defeated, Johnson's crown was secure, and he set out on a tour of Europe with his vaudeville act. But his flamboyance, his taste for stylish clothes, fast cars, and fast women, disturbed many members of both races. Racial animosity was intensified by Johnson's open association with white women. Of his four wives, only the first, Mary Austin, whom he married in 1898, was black. They were divorced around 1903. After an affair with another black woman, Clara Kerr, Johnson decided (so he later recalled) that henceforth his lot "would be cast only with white women." He subsequently took up with Belle Schreiber, a white prostitute at Chicago's notorious Everleigh Club. On Jan. 18, 1911, he married Etta (Terry) Duryea, a divorcée from Brooklyn, who had a part in his vaudeville act. She committed suicide in September 1912, and on December 12 of the same year he married Lucile Frances Cameron, a young woman from Minneapolis, Minn., who worked as a bookkeeper at the Café de Champion, the opulent cabaret Johnson had opened in Chicago.

Already, however, Johnson had become a prime target of moral reformers at a time of hysteria over the "white slave" trade. A charge by Lucile Cameron's mother that Johnson had abducted her daughter brought a police investigation. Though Lucile stood by Johnson and refused to corroborate the accusation, the outcry led authorities to revoke the liquor license of Johnson's club. In November, Belle Schreiber agreed to testify that Johnson had paid her way to Chicago from Pittsburgh for "immoral purposes." As a result, in May 1913 Johnson was convicted by an all-white jury of violating the federal Mann Act and sentenced to one year in prison. Regarding his penalty as unjust, he jumped bail and fled to Europe, accompanied by Lucile.

From this point Johnson's fortunes declined. He appeared as an entertainer throughout Europe. Since his match with Jeffries, he had fought only once—in 1912, when he successfully defended his title against "Fireman Jim" Flynn. He now engaged in a number of exhibition matches in Europe and Latin America. On Apr. 5, 1915, in Havana, Cuba, he defended his title against Jess Willard, the best of the "white hope" contenders. The bout, fought under a burning sun, dragged on for twenty-six rounds before Johnson was knocked out. He later claimed, without substantiation, that he had thrown the fight in return for an unfulfilled pledge of amnesty by the United States government. For the next five years Johnson remained in exile, living most of the time in Spain, where he gave exhibition fights, acted in a film, and even performed as a professonal matador.

Tired of his exile, Johnson returned to the United States in 1920 and served his term at Leavenworth Prison. He was divorced from Lucile Cameron in 1924, and in the summer of the following year he married Irene Marie Pineau, a divorcée. Thereafter Johnson eked out a living in a variety of ways. He gave exhibition bouts until the end of his life (although his last serious effort was probably in 1928), and as a moral exhorter he frequently appeared as a guest lecturer at evangelical churches. He also tried his hand at selling stocks, acting as a nightclub master of ceremonies, and working as a movie extra. After the mid-1930's, however, his primary employment was as a lecturer at Hubert's Museum, a combination sideshow, penny arcade, and flea circus on New York City's 42nd Street. Johnson had never lost his love of speeding, and in 1946, at the age of sixty-eight, he was critically injured when his car hit a light pole at Franklinton, N.C.; he died at St. Agnes Hospital in nearby Raleigh. After funeral services at Pilgrim Baptist Church in Chicago, he was buried in Chicago's Graceland Cemetery.

In 1954 Johnson was among the first group of fighters selected for the newly established Boxing Hall of Fame. In forty-seven years of fighting, he had been knocked out only three times. His fighting style was regarded by many as classic, and his ring success provided a symbol for the disadvantaged Negroes among whom he had his origins. Three years after Johnson's death, the boxing historian Nat Fleischer wrote that "after years devoted to the study of heavyweight fighters, I have no hesitation in naming Jack Johnson as the greatest of them all."

[Johnson published two volumes of memoirs: *Mes Combats* (1914), published in Paris in French, and *Jack Johnson, in the Ring and Out* (1927). There is a considerable body of secondary literature. The most detailed account is Finis Farr, *Black Champion: The Life and Times of Jack Johnson* (1964); but see also John Durant, *The Heavyweight Champions* (1960); Nathaniel S. Fleischer, *The Heavyweight Championship* (rev. ed., 1961); Andrew S. ("Doc") Young, *Negro Firsts in Sports* (1963); and Denzil Batchelor, *Jack Johnson and His Times* (1956). Owing to the lack of documentary evidence on Johnson's life, these works should be used with care. There is a good two-part study of Johnson by John Lardner in the *New Yorker*, June 25 and July 2, 1949. See also *N.Y. Times* obituary, June 11, 1946; and Al-Tony Gilmore, "Jack Johnson and White Women: The National Im-

pact, 1912–13," *Jour. of Negro Hist.*, Jan. 1973. A record of Johnson's 1912 marriage was secured from the County Clerk, Cook County, Ill.]

FINIS FARR

JOHNSON, TREAT BALDWIN (Mar. 29, 1875-July 28, 1947), chemist, was born at Bethany, a village near New Haven, Conn. He was the eldest of the three sons and a daughter (who died in infancy) of Dwight Lauren Johnson and Harriet Adeline (Baldwin) Johnson. His forebears were early English settlers, successive generations of whom had lived in the vicinity of New Haven. His father was a typical farmer in a community where few had progressed beyond elementary schooling. Johnson, being both intelligent and ambitious, set out to acquire a better education. He attended the local ungraded country school and then the high school in nearby Ansonia, making a good record. In 1894 he entered the Sheffield Scientific School at Yale University, from which he received the Ph.B. in chemistry in 1898. In that same year he entered graduate school, published his first scientific paper, and was appointed laboratory assistant in chemistry, a position he held until 1901. He obtained the Ph.D. in organic chemistry in 1901, by which time he had published six more papers. Johnson spent his entire professional life at Yale, as instructor in organic chemistry (1902-1909), assistant professor (1909-1914), professor (1914-1928), and Sterling professor of chemistry (1928-1943).

Johnson's scientific contribution was in the area of synthetic organic chemistry, especially as it related to biologically important materials. He was the author of 358 papers and was nationally known for his researches in pyrimidine chemistry and the chemistry of the tubercle bacillus. The biological importance of pyrimidines had only recently been disclosed when Johnson began his studies at Yale. Beginning in 1893 Albrecht Kossel and his students in Germany discovered that the nucleic acids (DNA and RNA) present in animal and plant cells contained the pyrimidines cytosine, thymine, and uracil. Kossel proposed structural formulas for the pyrimidines, the proof of which depended on their synthesis. Henry L. Wheeler, who was also at Yale, developed a new method of synthesis for pyrimidines, using the condensation reaction of pseudothioureas with β-keto esters. He had succeeded in synthesizing thymine and uracil by this method when Johnson collaborated with him in the synthesis of cytosine. By the end of 1903 they had proved that all of Kossel's structural formulas were correct.

Pyrimidine chemistry was Johnson's major scientific interest throughout his career. He developed synthetic methods for otherwise inaccessible pyrimidines, and by the 1930's an extensive literature, largely the achievement of Johnson and his students, existed on this subject, including sensitive tests for the quantitative determination and differentiation of the natural pyrimidines in nucleic acids. For these contributions Johnson was the recipient of the William H. Nichols Medal of the New York section of the American Chemical Society in 1918.

In 1922 Johnson began an investigation of the tubercle bacillus for the National Tuberculosis Association, which provided funds and culture supplies of the bacterium. He isolated the purines and pyrimidines in the nucleic acids and in 1925 discovered the presence of 5-methylcytosine in the nucleic acid of the tubercle bacillus. His comprehensive study of the chemical composition of the bacillus, which included its proteins and liquids, enlarged the knowledge of the nucleic acid content of bacterial cells.

Another area of interest, one that proved lucrative to Johnson, was the study of germicides and antiseptics, carried out in part with paid assistants at his private laboratory in Bethany (Bethwood Research Laboratory), which he had constructed in 1932. The results of these investigations led to fifteen patents assigned to Johnson and a number of his coworkers, dealing with medicinal products. In 1921 he found that the antiseptic strength of resorcinol substituted in the 4-position with alkyl groups increased with the molecular weight of the alkyl group. He developed a synthesis for substituted resorcinols that led to the commercial production of hexylresorcinol under patent rights with considerable profit to Johnson.

Johnson belonged to numerous scientific societies. He was elected to the National Academy of Sciences in 1919, served as president of the American Institute of Chemists (1926-1928), and was a member of the National Research Council. During World War I he was director of a laboratory at Yale, conducting research in the preparation of toxic organic substances for the Chemical Warfare Service. In 1918 Johnson established a fund for annual lectures by distinguished chemists at Yale, and he bequeathed $200,000 to Yale, the income to be devoted to the support of original research in organic chemistry in the graduate school.

Johnson married Emma Estelle Amerman of Woodside, L.I., on June 29, 1904. They had no children. They lived a quiet life, first in New Haven and from 1928 in a house on what had been his father's farm in Bethany.

Johnson was active in civic affairs and in the Bethany Congregational Church. In 1936 he gave his mother's house to the church for use as a parsonage, to be known as the Harriet Baldwin Memorial Church House. He also donated a library room in the Bethany community school in memory of his mother and father. From 1930 to 1947 he served as president of the Bethany Library Association, which he had founded and which built a library and established an endowment fund for its support. Johnson, however, aroused considerable dislike in the community, as he was impatient under the authority of others and would serve on a board or committee only if he could be chairman.

Johnson died of a coronary occlusion at his Bethany home. He was buried in Westville Cemetery, New Haven.

[The most informative notice is by Hubert Bradford Vickery in Nat. Acad. Sci., *Biog. Memoirs,* XXVII (1952), with full bibliography of papers and patents and a portrait. See also *Nat. Cyc. Am. Biog.,* XXXV (1949); *World Who's Who in Science*; and obituary notices in *N.Y. Times,* July 29, 1947, *Yale University Obituary Record,* and *Carnegie Foundation for the Advancement of Teaching, Annual Report* (1947-1948). Johnson wrote the historical chapter on organic chemistry in Charles A. Browne, ed., *A Half-Century of Chemistry in America 1876-1926* (1926). A valuable historical essay and summary of his investigations is his Nichols Medal acceptance speech in *Ind. Eng. Chemistry* 10 (1918): 306-312.]

ALBERT B. COSTA

JOHNSON, WALTER PERRY (Nov. 6, 1887-Dec. 10, 1946), baseball pitcher, was born in Humboldt, Kans., the second of six children and oldest of four sons of Frank Edwin Johnson and Minnie (Perry) Johnson. His father, a moderately successful farmer from Logansport, Ohio, was of Scots-Irish and Dutch descent, and his mother, born in Indiana, was of English and Scots-Irish stock. Johnson spent his first fourteen years on his father's farm near Humboldt, where he acquired an abiding love of rural life and a commitment to Protestant, middle-class values. In 1901, the family moved to a farm in Fullerton, Calif., where he attended the Fullerton Union High School. There Johnson was inducted into the world of baseball, gaining fame as a high school and, later, a semiprofessional pitcher. After his graduation, he worked briefly in the oil fields around Olinda and attended a business college in Santa Ana.

By 1906 his pitching skills attracted a scout for the Northwestern League who signed Johnson to a contract with the Tacoma, Wash., team. But Johnson lost his opportunity when the San Francisco earthquake forced the disbandment of the Pacific Coast League, thus making available a host of proven players. Released from his contract, Johnson was hired by a semiprofessional team in Weiser, Idaho, where he also worked for $75 a month digging postholes for the local telephone company. In Weiser, Johnson's talent ripened. Early in 1907 his overpowering fast ball accounted for eighty-six consecutive scoreless innings, and his salary rose to $100 a month. Not surprisingly, his performance attracted major-league scouts, including Cliff Blankenship, a reserve catcher for the American League's Washington Senators, who signed Johnson that year to a major-league contract—with the provision, insisted upon by Johnson's father, that the young pitcher be paid return fare should he prove unsatisfactory. The provision was unnecessary: he stayed with the Senators for the remaining twenty-seven years of his playing career.

In the hierarchy of American professional baseball, the distance between an Idaho semiprofessional team and the major leagues is awesome. But Johnson's assets were astonishing. Seasoned major-league batters like Ty Cobb were amazed at the speed of his pitching; according to Cobb, his most terrifying experience in baseball was playing Washington on a cloudy day with Johnson pitching. Johnson's technique, which made the most of his long arms, was described by sportswriter Grantland Rice as "a full, smooth, half side-arm sweep that sent the ball on its way like a bullet" (Treat, *Walter Johnson*). For years Johnson needed no other pitch, since batters, although knowing a fast ball was coming, were unable to hit it.

His easy motion and his great physical strength, which included the longest arm span in the major leagues, afforded Johnson a long major-league career. His nicknames, "The Big Train" and "Big Barney" (after auto racer Barney Oldfield), reflected the image of power he presented to the public. Johnson also had remarkable stamina, and in twenty-one years as a major-league pitcher, he was hampered only by illness in 1908 and by a leg injury and a sore arm in 1920.

After four years of apprenticeship, Johnson established himself as one of baseball's superstars. From 1910 to 1919 he won twenty or more games each season and became one of only five twentieth-century pitchers to win ninety games in a three-year period. In nine of these years he led the American League in strikeouts; in four years he led pitchers in the number of innings pitched, complete games, shutouts, total

victories and earned-run average. In 1913 he pitched fifty-six consecutive scoreless innings. During his long career Johnson was credited with a total of 414 victories, second only to the great Cy Young. In all, Johnson started 802 major-league games, completed 532, relieved in many others, and amassed a total of 5,923 innings pitched. Johnson's only rival as an American League star was Ty Cobb, and Johnson's $20,000 annual salary was one of baseball's highest before the age of Babe Ruth.

Although Johnson might have fared better pitching for a stronger team, his presence in the nation's capital as the prime star of the lackluster Senators enhanced his image as an American folk hero. Since Washington ranked second only to New York as a center of mass media, local sportswriters were quick to turn the tall, blue-eyed, curly-haired athlete into a national celebrity. His honesty, rugged competitiveness, even temper, and sportsmanship were proclaimed. So was his happy family life on his farm in Germantown, Md., where he raised Guernsey cattle and Percheron horses.

His dramatic victory in his first World Series, in 1924, excited the nation's capital, prompting a California congresswoman to recommend a national holiday in his honor and leading to the naming of a Washington high school for him. Johnson was forced into retirement in 1927 by a broken leg. At that time, President Coolidge voiced a common sentiment when he hailed Johnson as "a wholesome influence on clean living and clean sport."

After Johnson's active playing career ended, he managed the Newark club in the International League, and in 1929 he returned to manage the Senators. Dismissed in 1933, he managed the Cleveland Indians until 1935, when he resigned under fire from the press and local fans. His career as a baseball manager was undistinguished, in large part because his easygoing manner made for lax discipline.

In 1936 he was voted a charter member of baseball's Hall of Fame. In his last years he worked on his farm and made brief forays into radio sports broadcasting and business ventures; he also ran unsuccessfully for Congress as a Republican.

On June 24, 1914, Johnson married Hazel Lee Roberts, daughter of Edwin Roberts, a congressman from Nevada. They had six children: Walter (who had a brief baseball career), Edwin, Eleanor, Robert, Carolyn, and Barbara. Johnson died of a brain tumor in 1946 at Georgetown Hospital in Washington, D.C. His funeral services at Washington Cathedral attracted a huge crowd. He was buried in Rockville Cemetery in Maryland.

[No adequate biography exists; the only available one is Roger Treat's juvenile biography, *Walter Johnson: King of the Pitchers* (1948). *The Baseball Encyc.* (1969) is the authoritative source of information for Johnson's major-league records and annual achievements. The sporting pages of the *Washington Post* and the weekly *Sporting News* are essential primary sources. Johnson's personal recollections appear in an article, written with Billy Evans, in *St. Nicholas,* Oct. 1914. A popular treatment of his career is in Tom Meany, *Baseball's Greatest Pitchers* (1951). For Johnson's place in the total setting of major-league baseball history, see David Q. Voigt, *Am. Baseball: From the Commissioners to Continental Expansion* (1970).]
DAVID QUENTIN VOIGT

JOHNSTON, JOHN (Oct. 13, 1881–Sept. 12, 1950), chemist and metallurgist, was born in Perth, Scotland, the eldest of the three sons of James Johnston and Christina (Leslie) Johnston. His father was a prosperous wool factor until he suffered severe losses in the financial panic of 1893. Johnston attended Perth Academy and then entered University College in Dundee, which had just been united with the University of St. Andrews. He received a bachelor's degree in chemistry in 1903 but stayed on, as a Carnegie Scholar, for two years of postgraduate study. In 1905 he was awarded an 1851 Exhibition Scholarship to work with Richard Abegg at the University of Breslau (now Wrocław, Poland).

After two years in Germany, Johnston came to the United States as a research associate in the research laboratory of physical chemistry that Arthur A. Noyes had recently established at the Massachusetts Institute of Technology. Johnston had planned to stay in the United States only a year, but in 1908, after receiving the degree of D.Sc. from St. Andrews, he joined the staff of the Geophysical Laboratory of the Carnegie Institution in Washington. There he investigated the behavior of various substances under high temperatures and pressures as a guide in interpreting geological phenomena. He became an American citizen in 1915.

Having developed an interest in the possibilities of industrial research, Johnston moved in 1916 to St. Louis to take charge of the research department of the American Zinc, Lead, and Smelting Company. But in September 1917, after America's entry into World War I, he was recalled to Washington as a consultant to the U.S. Bureau of Mines in its investigation of gas warfare. The next month he was appointed to the chemistry committee of the National Research Council, recently established as an adjunct to the National Academy of Sciences. In January 1918, he was appointed secretary of the council and chairman of the section on industrial relations. In March he also assumed the chairmanship of the division of chemistry and clerical technology. He resigned all of these posts in March 1919, but retained his chairmanship of the industrial relations section until June 1920 and remained a member of the council until 1930 and returned to it in 1932–1935 and 1941–1943.

In 1919 Johnston accepted an appointment at Yale University as Sterling professor of chemistry. In addition to teaching chemical thermodynamics, directing the work of graduate students, and holding the chairmanship of the chemistry department, he participated in the republication of the collected works of the great theoretical physicist J. Willard Gibbs, of whom Johnston considered himself a disciple. Throughout his years at Yale he maintained his industrial contacts by acting as a consultant for the Bell Telephone Laboratories.

In 1927, when the United States Steel Corporation, at the instigation of its chairman, Elbert H. Gary, created a research laboratory, Johnston was asked to organize it and to become the company's director of research. The death of Gary introduced a series of frustrating uncertainties and delays, but Johnston assembled a small, capable staff, which was housed, pending construction of a laboratory, in the office building of the Federal Shipbuilding and Drydock Company, a subsidiary of the United States Steel Corporation located in Kearny, N.J. The depression of 1929 and, later, the outbreak of World War II thwarted all plans to provide the laboratory with a home of its own. Nonetheless, under Johnston's direction, the laboratory made notable contributions to both process and physical metallurgy. Its studies of the precise temperatures at which physical and chemical changes occur in steel and its alloys and of the time required for those changes substantially improved the efficiency of steel production.

Johnston's natural reserve tended to obscure his essential friendliness and his fine sense of humor. An interviewer once aptly described him as a "quiet, keen, long-faced man with equal parts of dourness and humor, both carefully restrained" (McDowell, p. 717). His high principles and his devotion to science greatly influenced his students and colleagues. Johnston enjoyed gardening, music, and, above all, reading; he scanned a page with surprising speed but with complete comprehension and amazing retention. As a writer, he strove for precision and clarity and expected those qualities of others, often to their despair. He was an early advocate and practitioner of interdisciplinary programs in teaching and in research. Always interested in professional affairs, Johnston served on the editorial board of the International Critical Tables and was president of the American Electrochemical Society in 1933-1934. He received honorary degrees from Yale (1919), New York University (1928), and Lehigh (1929).

On July 17, 1909, Johnston married Dorothy Hopkins of Dundee, Scotland, a talented home-maker who shared his ideals and enthusiasms. They had three children: Helen Leslie, John Murray, and William Valentine. After his retirement from U.S. Steel in 1946, the family moved to Southwest Harbor, Maine, on Mt. Desert Island, where they had long had a summer place. Johnston died in Bar Harbor, Maine, of hypertensive heart disease in his sixty-ninth year. He was buried in Southwest Harbor.

[The major sources are Edward C. McDowell, in *Metal Progress*, May 1943 (with photograph); *Jour. Electrochem. Soc.*, Nov. 1950, pp. 223C–224C; memoir by Zay Jeffries, Am. Phil. Soc., *Year Book*, 1950; *Am. Men of Sci.*, 8th ed. (1949); *Who Was Who in America*, III (1960); *N.Y. Times*, Sept. 14, 1950; information from archives of the Nat. Acad. of Sciences; and, on Johnston's death, from the Town Clerk, Southwest Harbor, Maine.]

JAMES B. AUSTIN

JOHNSTONE, EDWARD RANSOM (Dec. 27, 1870-Dec. 29, 1946), pioneer educator of the feebleminded, was born in Galt, Ontario, Canada, the fifth of six sons and the eleventh of twelve children of William Johnston, who had emigrated from England and owned and operated a tailoring factory in Hamilton, Ontario, and Jane (Ransom) Johnston, the daughter of a Montreal banker. Both parents were fond of music and were active members of the Presbyterian church. During Edward's boyhood the family moved to Cincinnati, Ohio, where he finished his elementary education and in 1885 graduated from Woodward High School. During these years he developed an interest in poetry and dramatics and took part in local church activities.

After graduating from the Woodward Academy in 1889, he worked briefly in the Cincinnati House of Refuge and Juvenile Reformatory, taught for a year in the high school at North Bend, a Cincinnati suburb, and served two years as principal of a school in Hamilton County. He taught literature in a Cincinnati high school in 1892, the year he became a naturalized citizen. In 1893 at the invitation of his brother-in-law Alexander Johnson, who had just been made superintendent of the Indiana

State School for the Feeble-Minded, Edward in 1893 moved to Fort Wayne as principal of the school's education department. To avoid confusion because of the similarity between their surnames, Edward added a final "e" to his name and for the remainder of his life used the form "Johnstone."

Under the influence of his brother-in-law, Johnstone developed a deep concern for the feebleminded. Distinguished by imagination, energy and practical wisdom, he became convinced that many of the pupils could learn and that they could achieve satisfaction from the successful performance of even small tasks. Under his guidance they were taught to engage in physical exercise such as marching, dancing, and singing; to act small parts in dramatic productions written especially for them; to play games; and to participate in church services, all of which he felt aided the learning process. He also instituted a system of garden cultivation, in which each child was given his own plot to tend, and he assisted in establishing a summer camp for the more advanced children.

In 1898 Johnstone was appointed vice-principal of the privately established Vineland New Jersey Home for the Education and Care of Feeble-Minded Children. Following the death of the school's founder, S. Olin Garrison, Johnstone was appointed principal in 1901. In 1903 he was designated superintendent, the post he retained until 1921, when he was appointed executive director; he remained in that office until his retirement in 1944.

In 1901, upon returning from a professional meeting, Johnstone initiated the Feeble-Minded Club, which brought together educators and administrators from the Philadelphia-New York area and served as a forum for many ideas of the time in the treatment of the mentally retarded. At Vineland, he continued his crusade to provide better training for the feebleminded and in 1903 instituted a six-week summer course for public school teachers on special educational methods for the mentally retarded. Johnstone's efforts were directed toward supporting his belief that the feebleminded should be sequestered and provided with humane care; he opposed sexual sterilization of the feebleminded, believing that it would encourage vice, and opposed the marriage of feebleminded individuals. Arguing that schools should provide more than rudimentary custodial care, Johnstone felt they should also investigate the causes and possible prevention of mental retardation. In 1906 he established a separate department of research in the psychology of the feebleminded, the first such laboratory in the country. Directed by the psychologist Henry H. Goddard, the group, which included Elizabeth Kite, made pioneer studies in the psychology of the mentally handicapped, studied the role of heredity, and introduced to the United States the use of the Binet-Simon intelligence tests. In 1906 Johnstone also began issuing a monthly publication *The Training School,* later renamed *The Training School Bulletin,* to which he contributed many articles. He promoted the passage of the 1911 New Jersey law providing special classes for children who had fallen three years behind their normal grade in school; organized a workshop to familiarize physicians with the problems faced by mentally defective children and their families; and set up an extension division headed by Alexander Johnson, whose lectures carried knowledge of the laboratory's work to thirty-three states. Johnstone also organized colonies of older boys, who were taught to clear tracts of New Jersey forest and wasteland to ready them for cultivation. This latter work led to the opening of other colonies: Menantico, a center for the school's demonstration farming activities, and New Lisbon, which was eventually taken over by the state. In 1921 he was instrumental in founding Woodbine, a custodial colony run by the state for low-grade defective males.

Johnstone took an active part in other aspects of the state's welfare work and in penal reform. He helped reorganize the classification and parole services of the state Department of Charities and Corrections (1918), was a member of the board of managers of the New Jersey State Prison (1918-1946), and was president of the New Jersey Prison and Parole Board (1927). He served as president of the American Association on Mental Deficiency in 1902 and 1927. For his work in devising a system for the care of destitute children in Serbia after World War I he was awarded the Order of St. Sava in 1920.

On June 17, 1898, Johnstone married Olive Lehman of Waterloo, Ind. Their children were Carol, Edward Lehman (who also became a worker for the feebleminded), Earl Ransom, and Douglas Davidson. After his marriage, Johnstone became a member of the Baptist church. He spent many winter holidays in Florida, where he enjoyed his favorite sport, fishing. He wrote *Some Songs From Juniper* (1938), a collection of reminiscenses of Juniper, the hunting and fishing club in Astor, Fla., of which he was a member. An earlier book, *Dear*

Robinson: Some Letters on Getting Along With Folks (1923), contained letters written by Johnstone to an imaginary young man who was starting his career as director of an institution for feebleminded children. Johnstone died of an intestinal obstruction at the age of seventy-six and was buried in Siloam Cemetery, Vineland. He was a humane and imaginative leader among the early twentieth-century pioneers who were trying to provide for and publicize the need for better care and training of feebleminded children.

[Innumerable articles by Johnstone appear in issues of *The Training School Bulletin*; his poem "The Institution," which appeared in the Feb. 1944 issue, shows his sensitive understanding of children with mental handicaps. Collections of his papers are at Rutgers Univ. Lib., New Brunswick, N.J.; in the library and offices of the director of the Laboratory Building of the Training School Unit, American Inst. for Mental Studies, Vineland, N.J.; and in the possession of Edward Lehman Johnstone and Carol Johnstone Sharp. "Founders of the Training School at Vineland, New Jersey: S. Olin Garrison, Alexander Johnson, Edward R. Johnstone" (Ed.D. diss., Columbia Univ., 1965) by Kathrine R. McCaffrey, in part, formed the basis for this article; other references include the brochure "Honoring Edward Ransom Johnstone, 1870-1946," *The Training School Bulletin,* May 1946; Joseph P. Byers, *The Village of Happiness* (1934); Edgar A. Doll, *Clinical Studies in Feeble-Mindedness* (1917); Stanley Powell Davies, *The Mentally Retarded Society* (1959); and James Leiby, *Charity and Correction in New Jersey* (1967). An oil portrait of Johnstone is displayed in Garrison Hall at the training school; a photograph, in Leiby's book.]
                                    KATHRINE R. McCAFFREY

JOLSON, AL (May 26, 1886-Oct. 23, 1950), popular singer, was born Asa Yoelson in the Russian village of Srednike, later part of Lithuania. He was the second son and youngest of four children of Moses Reuben Yoelson, a rabbi, and Naomi (Cantor) Yoelson. Like many Russian Jews, the family was forced to immigrate in 1890 to America by the pogroms of the period. They settled in 1894 in Washington, D.C., where Moses Yoelson had secured a position as cantor in a synagogue. Al seems to have received some schooling up to the age of fifteen, but he learned much more from his life in the streets. His mother died when he was about ten years old, and he was in constant conflict with the strict, traditional views of his father. His exceptional voice and musical sense were evidenced early when he sang ballads on the street corners to earn spending money. Much influenced by his older brother, Harry, who was the first to change the family name to Jolson, young Al once ran away to New York, hoping to join his brother in show business. He first appeared on the stage in 1899 as an extra in a Jewish epic, *Children of the Ghetto.* By the age of thirteen he had sung in a Baltimore beer parlor and toured as a boy singer for a burlesque company.

At fifteen he began touring the vaudeville circuits, first with his brother and then in a three-man comedy group, Jolson, Palmer, and Jolson. Subsequently he toured with Joe Palmer alone and received valuable coaching from the veteran performer. In 1906, his apprenticeship behind him, Jolson opened in San Francisco as a "single." His sentimental interpretations of popular songs, combined with his impudent charm, immediately appealed to the public. Already in blackface, the burnt cork softening his strong facial features, he seemed to capture for his urban audiences the plight of the little man in American society, small of stature and innocently vulnerable but bursting with manic energy and hope for a better life.

Following a tour with Dockstader's Minstrels in the conventional role of end man, he struck out on his own again, this time in New York, making his debut at Hammerstein's Victoria. Always preferring improvisation to a script, he introduced new songs, sang familiar ones on request, sometimes whistled or did a buck-and-wing, and conducted a lively line of patter. His monologues might be anecdotal, homiletic, or confessional, as the spirit moved him. In 1911 the Shuberts included Jolson in a review, *La Belle Paree,* but soon found a better vehicle for him called *Vera Violetta.* In 1912 they built a runway into the orchestra of the Winter Garden and featured the blackface star in another revue, *The Whirl of Society.* Simultaneously Jolson inaugurated the Sunday Night Concerts at the Winter Garden, which gave working performers an opportunity to witness the acts of their colleagues.

In *The Whirl of Society* Jolson's blackface character acquired the name of Gus, which would follow him in future shows. In *Honeymoon Express* (1913) Jolson may have first used the fall to one knee, arms extended in pathetic appeal, which was to become his hallmark. Other productions followed: *Dancing Around* (1914); three Sigmund Romberg extravaganzas, *Robinson Crusoe, Jr.* (1916), *Sinbad* (1918), and *Bombo* (1921), and *Big Boy* (1925). While playing *Sinbad,* Jolson picked up an unsuccessful tune by George Gershwin, gave it a stepped-up tempo, and introduced "Swanee" as part of his act. In *Bombo* he sang for the first time his highly personalized version of "My Mammy" (in which some observers discern the emotional scars left on him as a boy by the loss of his mother), as well as three other tunes with which he was to be perma-nently identified; "Toot, Toot, Tootsie," "California, Here I Come," and "April Showers." As a rule, the musical shows in which he appeared, never very secure in their plot lines, would leave the last thirty minutes entirely to Jolson, who would, by the magic of his personality and showmanship, effect the climax of the performance. In the late 1920's, however, his appeal began to fade with the changing times. His last two stage shows were *Wonderbar* (1931) and *Hold on to Your Hats* (1940).

However, far from being victimized by new trends in entertainment, Jolson energetically adapted to them. Already a best seller of phonograph records, he starred in the first of the "talking" motion pictures, a sentimentalized version of his life story, *The Jazz Singer* (1927), and made a number of other films for the Warner Brothers studios. His involvement with radio began in 1932 and reached its peak four years later when he teamed with two comics, Parkyakarkas and Martha Raye, in a series of programs for the Columbia Broadcasting System. Always active in giving benefit performances (he sold Liberty Bonds during World War I), he was one of the foremost entertainers on USO circuits during World War II and the Korean conflict and was to receive posthumously the Congressional Order of Merit. His film popularity slipped during the 1930's, but the release of a film biography, *The Jolson Story* (1946), evoked new interest in him, and the sales of his phonograph records soared into the millions.

Jolson's personal life seems to have been characterized by the same restless volatility as his stage performances. An inveterate gambler, he wagered heavily at the racetracks and eventually owned his own stable of thoroughbreds. He enjoyed sports, notably golf and swimming, and was the owner of a ranch in Encino, Calif., on which he raised oranges and walnuts. He married four times, the last three in the glare of publicity. His first marriage, in 1906, to Henrietta Keller, a chorus girl whom he had met in San Francisco, ended in divorce in 1919. He married Alma Osborne, well known by her stage name of Ethel Delmar, on Aug. 18, 1922, and was divorced by her in 1926. His marriage on September 21, 1928, to Ruby Keeler, a star of the Ziegfield *Follies* and later of film musicals, created a sensation and continued to make news until they parted in 1939. They adopted a son, Al Jolson, Jr. His final marriage was to Erle Chenault Galbraith of Little Rock, Ark., on Mar. 24, 1945. He and his fourth wife adopted a son, Asa, and, less formally, a daughter, Alicia.

Jolson died of a heart attack in a San Francisco hotel, having just returned from a USO tour to Korea. He was given a Jewish funeral, which included a eulogy by his close friend George Jessel, in Los Angeles, and was buried there at Hillside Memorial Park. Most of his estate, estimated at $4 million, was left to twenty institutions, including Jewish, Catholic, and Protestant charities; the Red Cross; the Actors Fund of America; and—for the benefit of needy students—to Columbia University, New York University, and the City College of New York.

[There are two biographies: Harry Jolson and Alban Emley, *Mistah Jolson* (1951), and Pearl Sieben, *The Immortal Jolson* (1962). Accounts of his New York stage career may be found in David Ewen, *Complete Book of the Musical Theatre* (1958). See also *Current Biog.*, 1940; and *N.Y. Times*, Aug. 19, 1922, Sept. 22, 1928, and Mar. 25, 1945 (on his marriages); Oct. 24, 1950 (obituary); Oct. 27, 1950 (funeral and will). Vital information was confirmed by a Certificate of Death, Calif. Dept. of Public Health.]

ALBERT F. McLEAN, JR.

JONES, RUFUS MATTHEW (Jan. 25, 1863-June 16, 1948), philosopher, mystical scholar, Quaker historian, and social reformer, was born on a farm in South China, Maine, the second son and third child of Edwin Jones and Mary Gifford (Hoxie) Jones, who were both descended from Quaker families. Rufus attended the neighborhood school and helped his father on the farm until, at sixteen, he was enrolled in the Friends Boarding School (now Moses Brown School) in Providence, R.I.; his first cousin, Augustine Jones, was headmaster. There he prepared to enter Haverford College, from which he received a B.A. in 1885 and an M.A. in 1886. The person who made the most profound impression upon him during his undergraduate years was Prof. Pliny Earle Chase. Chase launched him in his study of mysticism by suggesting the subject for his senior thesis, "Mysticism and Its Exponents."

After teaching for a year in a Quaker school, Oakwood Seminary, Union Springs, N.Y., Jones went to Europe for a year's study. Because his uncle and aunt, Eli and Sybil Jones, were internationally known Quaker ministers, he carried letters of introduction that opened many doors for him among British Friends and on the Continent. After some months in Heidelberg, in 1887, where he attended lectures in philosophy, he returned to take a teaching post in the Friends' School in Providence. On July 3, 1888, he married Sarah Hawkshurst Coutant, whom he met while teaching at Oakwood Seminary; they had one son, Lowell Coutant. In 1889

Jones was named principal of Oak Grove Seminary, Vassalboro, Maine, ten miles from his birthplace. That same year his first book, *Eli and Sybil Jones, Their Life and Work*, was published. In 1890 he was recognized as a minister by his local meeting and by the Vassalboro Quarterly Meeting.

In 1893 Jones became the editor of the *Friends' Review*, published weekly in Philadelphia, and an instructor in philosophy at Haverford College. He enlarged his editorial work in 1894 by combining the *Friends' Review* with the *Christian Worker* (Chicago) to form the *American Friend* and continued his editorial work with this journal until 1912.

During a second trip abroad in 1897 he met John Wilhelm Rowntree of York, England; they planned a scholarly history of the Religious Society of Friends from its roots in the Reformation to the twentieth century. Although Rowntree died in 1905, Jones, assisted by the British Friend William Charles Braithwaite and others, carried the project to its conclusion in 1921. Jones wrote four of the seven volumes and part of another. These volumes have been regarded as the standard history of the Society of Friends since their publication, although revisions have been made.

The next five years were crucial; his wife Sarah died from tuberculosis in 1899, and their son Lowell died of diphtheria four years later. Jones took an important part in the founding of the Five Years Meeting of Friends, created in 1902, a conference that brought together a majority of the Quakers in the United States. After a year's sabbatical at Harvard, he received his M.A. in philosophy in 1901 and was named to fill the new T. Wistar Brown chair in philosophy at Haverford. In 1898 he began a half century of service on the board of trustees of Bryn Mawr College (chairman, 1916-1936). Jones also published several books during the period, largely collections of lectures or articles previously printed in the *American Friend*. Following another visit to England, he was invited to serve as director of studies at the new Quaker center for adult studies, called Woodbrooke, which opened in Birmingham. Although this offer tempted him, he remained at Haverford. On Mar. 11, 1902, he married Elizabeth Bartram Cadbury of Philadelphia. She was a highly intelligent and lovely young woman, who supported her husband in many ways and gave him valuable editorial assistance with his many publications. They had one daughter, Mary Hoxie, born in 1904.

Elizabeth Jones, who was related to the English Cadburys, strengthened the transatlantic ties, and the couple spent several summers in England in the following years. When the Swarthmore Lecture was introduced at London Yearly Meeting in 1908, Rufus Jones was invited to deliver the first address. In 1920 he was asked to speak again, the only person ever invited to deliver two Swarthmore Lectures.

In 1904 his most important book to date, *Social Law in the Spiritual World,* was published; it was read widely outside the Society of Friends. Five years later his first volume in the Rowntree Series appeared, *Studies in Mystical Religion* (London, 1909), which gained him immediate recognition as a scholar of mysticism. He published two additional volumes in the Rowntree Series in the next five years, *The Quakers in the American Colonies* (London, 1911) and *Spiritual Reformers in the Sixteenth and Seventeenth Centuries* (London, 1914).

When the United States entered World War I in 1917, many Friends, although opposed to the war on principle, wished to serve in a civilian capacity. In April of 1917 the American Friends Service Committee (AFSC) was formed in Philadelphia with Jones as the first chairman. A training program was started at Haverford College, and Jones negotiated with the War Department to gain approval to send conscientious objectors to France to work with English Friends. He continued to serve as chairman until 1928 and again from 1935 to 1944. In 1947, after World War II, the AFSC was awarded the Nobel Peace Prize jointly with the Friends Service Council in London. Encouraged by Herbert Hoover, a fellow Quaker, he helped the AFSC to carry out child-feeding and relief programs in Germany and Russia in the postwar years.

His two-volume *The Later Periods of Quakerism* (London) appeared in 1921, completing the Rowntree Series, and in 1927 he published *New Studies in Mystical Religion.* He also published several other volumes; some were collections of lectures, and others, like *The Church's Debt to Heretics* (1924), were based on original research. Church groups, universities, and other groups besieged him with requests to lecture. He was awarded more than a dozen honorary degrees during his career, in addition to other honors.

In 1932 he shared in an interdenominational survey of missions in the Far East and contributed two chapters to the published report, *Rethinking Missions* (1932), edited by William Ernest Hocking of Harvard. This was his second visit to China, having gone to deliver a series of lectures to the YMCA there in 1926.

He retired from Haverford College after taking an active part in the centennial celebrations at the college the previous autumn, for which he wrote *Haverford College, A History and an Interpretation* (1933). The first semester of the following academic year was spent in Europe, where he gave many lectures, interspersed with additional study of the continental mystics. *The Flowering of Mysticism* (1939), about a small group of fourteenth-century mystics called the Friends of God, was the result of this research.

In 1937 he presided at the second Friends World Conference, held at Swarthmore and Haverford colleges. Early in 1938 he and his wife traveled to South Africa, where he lectured and met with Jan Smuts; they returned by way of China and Japan. In early December of the same year he visited Nazi Germany, accompanied by two younger Friends, in an attempt to intervene on behalf of the Jews. Although he was able to speak with a high official in the Gestapo and made some arrangements for alleviating the suffering of the Jews, little came of the mission.

During the final decade of his life, he lectured all over the United States and published a number of small volumes. He wrote the fourth and final of his autobiographical essays in 1941, *A Small Town Boy.* His last book, *A Call to What is Vital,* appeared shortly after his death in 1948. On June 16 he died in his sleep during an afternoon nap. A Quaker memorial service was held at the Haverford Friends Meetinghouse, and he was interred in the meeting burial ground next to his old friend John Wilhelm Rowntree.

Jones was tall and thin and somewhat awkward in his youth. Protruding teeth were an embarrassment to him until they were replaced by artificial ones later in life. He grew a moustache before his marriage in 1888, and never removed it. While his features were plain rather than handsome or powerful, as he matured and gained poise, he became a striking figure. His natural manner, sense of humor, personal warmth, and ability to respond to others drew people to him, young and old alike. Although there were some who did not respond to him, such as Quakers who differed with him over theology, or persons who could not appreciate his simplicity of expression, many more were drawn to him as an inspiring, warm, sincere man.

Jones made his first great impact upon the Society of Friends in the 1890's, and his influence has been felt ever since. Reacting strongly against the conservative, orthodox spirit and evangelical patterns dominant in nineteenth-century Quakerism, he, along with several British Friends, attempted to revitalize the Society of Friends and bring it into the mainstream of modern religious thought. Convinced that the first generation of Friends were mystics, he called upon his fellow religionists to accept a new mystical interpretation of Quakerism for the twentieth century—not the negative, withdrawn mysticism of the early church but an affirmative mysticism that would lead to involvement in the world. He asserted that early Friends were spiritually close to the pietists and continental mystics, and that they represented a reaction against Puritanism. Coupled with this was an overly optimistic view of the goodness of man and an emphasis upon the phrase adapted from the words of George Fox, the founder of Quakerism, "that of God in every man."

Jones began to modify his views before his death, but Geoffrey F. Nuttall wrote a scholarly rebuttal to his ideas in *The Holy Spirit in Puritan Faith and Experience* (1947). Wilmer A. Cooper followed with a dissertation at Vanderbilt University in 1956, "Rufus M. Jones and the Contemporary Quaker View of Man." The debate was carried further in the autumn issue of *Quaker Religious Thought* in 1965, when J. Calvin Keene and others discussed "Historic Quakerism and Mysticism." In his effort to overcome the narrow, limiting theology of nineteenth-century Quakerism, Jones moved too far in the other direction. Optimism about man and society, accepted in the first part of the twentieth century, was struck a mortal blow by neo-orthodoxy and the excesses of the Nazis and others. Also his enthusiasm for mysticism led him to overstate his case regarding early Quakerism. Scholars also concentrated upon the mysticism of Rufus Jones, beginning with a thesis by William A. Alsobrook at Drew Theological Seminary in 1954. The British medievalist, Christopher J. Holdsworth, in a paper entitled "Mystics and Heretics in the Middle Ages: Rufus Jones Reconsidered" (*Journal, Friends Historical Society*, 1972, pp. 9-30), has pointed out that while Jones was a pioneer in his day, in the scholarly examination of mysticism, his work now needs to be reconsidered in the light of more recent scholarship. Like Father Caffrey, he stressed the enormous influence of Rufus Jones during his lifetime on the people who heard him and read his books.

Jones's inspirational volumes, some of which were translated into several languages, made a much greater impact upon his contemporaries than his scholarly works. In addition, through the spoken word, he made a lasting impression upon his listeners.

[The correspondence, lecture notes, speeches, manuscripts, and diaries of Rufus M. Jones are deposited in the Quaker Collect. of the Haverford College Lib. The Clarence Tobias Collect. of the published writings of Jones, consisting of 168 volumes and eight boxes of pamphlets, cuttings, and extracts, is housed in the same library. Several paintings of Jones are owned by Haverford College, and scores of photographs are available through the Quaker Collect.

The best biography is Elizabeth Gray Vining, *Friend of Life, The Biography of Rufus M. Jones,* (1958). See also David Hinshaw, *Rufus Jones, Master Quaker* (1951); *Rufus Jones Speaks to Our Time, An Anthology,* ed. Harry Emerson Fosdick (1951); and Mary Hoxie Jones, *Rufus M. Jones* (1955). Jones himself wrote four autobiographical volumes: *A Small Town Boy* (1941); *Finding the Trail of Life* (1926); *The Trail of Life in College* (1929); and *The Trail of Life in the Middle Years* (1934).

A complete list of the separate titles written by Jones, fifty-four in all, may be found in the back of the Vining biography. Hiram Doty, assisted by Elizabeth B. Jones, compiled a seventy-page bibliography, "A Rufus M. Jones Bibliog." (mimeographed), available from the Quaker Collect.

Dissertations written about Jones include William A. Alsobrook, "The Mysticism of Rufus M. Jones" (Drew Theological Seminary, 1954); Gordon Charles Atkins, "A Critical Examination of the Mystical Idealism of Rufus Matthew Jones" (Univ. of California, 1962); Augustine J. Caffrey, "The Affirmation Mysticism of Rufus Matthew Jones" (Catholic Univ., 1967); Glen T. Cain, "The Place of Christ in the Theology of Rufus M. Jones" (Duke Univ., 1963); Wilmer A. Cooper, "Rufus M. Jones and the Contemporary Quaker View of Man" (Vanderbilt Univ., 1956); Eddie L. Dwyer, "The Principle of Authority in the Theology of Rufus Jones" (Southwestern Baptist Theological Seminary, 1951); and J. Floyd Moore, "The Ethical Thought of Rufus M. Jones" (Boston Univ., 1960).]

EDWIN B. BRONNER

JUDD, CHARLES HUBBARD (Feb. 20, 1873-July 18, 1946), educational psychologist, was born in Bareilly, India, where his parents were serving as Methodist missionaries. He was the youngest of three children and only son of Charles Wesley Judd and Sarah Annis (Hubbard) Judd, both natives of New York state. The illness of his parents forced the family to leave India in 1879; they settled in Binghamton, N.Y., where, after the father's death in 1880 and the mother's in 1884, the older sister brought up the two younger children in straitened circumstances. Charles attended the Binghamton public schools, graduating from high school in 1890. He then entered Wesleyan University in Connecticut, where he intended to prepare for the ministry, but abandoned this plan and instead decided to become a psychologist. Andrew C. Armstrong's stimulating courses and personal interest in his students attracted Judd to psychology.

Receiving the B.A. in 1894 with first honors, Judd heeded the suggestion of Armstrong and went to Germany for graduate study. He enrolled in Wilhelm Wundt's laboratory at the University of Leipzig and earned his Ph.D. in 1896, writing a dissertation on an investigation in tactile space perception. He was also chosen to translate into English Wundt's *Grundriss der Psychologie* ("Outline of Psychology"). The translation involved weekly conferences with Wundt, which, together with his other Leipzig experiences, had a permanent effect upon Judd's psychological doctrines and research, for he adopted Wundt's concepts of voluntarism and creative synthesis, his method of laboratory experiment, and his interest in historical-social psychology. Voluntarism (mental activity consists of affective and kinesthetic as well as cognitive elements) and creative synthesis (advanced kinds of mental activity are not just summations of simpler activities but new, superior organizations of mental function) were concepts underpinning Judd's later research in nature and development in reading, number ideas and their development, writing, and the higher mental processes. His wholehearted acceptance of the value of experimentation was to make him a zealous advocate of the scientific study of education; his interest in social psychology was to lead him to stress the importance of social institutions, especially language, in shaping human thinking and behavior.

Returning to the United States, Judd became successively instructor in philosophy at Wesleyan (1896-1898), professor of psychology in the School of Pedagogy at New York University (1898-1901), professor of psychology and pedagogy at the University of Cincinnati (1901-1902), and instructor in psychology at Yale (1902). By 1907 he had become a full professor and the director of the Yale Psychological Laboratory. Judd's attention and interests turned increasingly to educational psychology, so that when in 1909 he was invited to become professor of education and director of the School of Education at the University of Chicago, he accepted the offer and joined the staff. He served in this capacity until his retirement and was chairman of the department of psychology from 1920 to 1925. His election in 1909 to the presidency of the American Psychological Association marked the culmination of the research-oriented phase of his career; the next phase was one of educational administration.

At Chicago, Judd had jurisdiction over a university elementary school and high school intended for demonstration, research, and practice; over the undergraduate College of Education, which prepared students for elementary and secondary school teaching; and over a series of graduate education courses given under the auspices of the department of philosophy to train school and college administrators and professors of pedagogy. Following John Dewey's departure to Columbia in 1904, the School of Education at Chicago operated without a director for five years. Judd thus took on the task of organizing, refining, and reorienting the various programs of study in education, of strengthening the faculties engaged in research and instruction in that field, and of bringing other departments and other scholars into cooperative and fruitful relations with the work in education. At the time of his retirement in 1938, Judd had attained his goals, the great achievement of his career.

He gradually eliminated the programs of preparation for elementary school teaching and transferred the training of secondary school teachers into the hands of a university committee. Thus stripped of its functions, the College of Education withered away and was finally abolished in 1931. Meanwhile, Judd had created the office of superintendent of the laboratory schools to coordinate the programs of the elementary school, the high school, and the department of education. Superintendents like Henry C. Morrison and William C. Reavis revitalized those schools and made them centers of experimentation. In graduate programs, Judd's first act in 1909 was to establish a distinct graduate subdepartment of education within the department of philosophy. In 1916 this became an independent department within the Graduate School of Arts, Literature, and Science; in 1931 it was placed in the Division of the Social Sciences when Robert Maynard Hutchins reorganized the University.

Even though individual research had been sacrificed for his administrative duties, Judd continued four lines of investigation using the vast resources of his department. He oversaw an analysis of reading in the department of education. In 1915 he formulated and discussed the major psychological problems of high school education in his book *Psychology of High School Subjects,* rewritten and retitled *The Psychology of Secondary Education* (1927). Experimental work with number consciousness was another project; and finally, in *The Psychology of Social Institutions* (1926), he took what he considered to be the first step in the formulation of the social psychology on which all sound education must ultimately be based.

Judd also assembled and administered one of the most talented communities of educational scholars ever to grace the campus of an American university. Their orientation was Judd's orientation: "Scientific facts about school practices and results, secured through the use of historical, statistical, and experimental methods, can be put into a form which is as specific and exact as the professional information given in schools of medicine or engineering" (School of Education, *Announcement, 1926-1927,* p. 10). This empirical view of research, scientific method, and teaching and learning left little room for the speculative, theoretical, and axiological. Judd's faculty contained no educational philosopher. For good and ill, Judd and his Chicago colleagues played a major part in moving the study of education in America out of the domain of philosophy and into the social and behavioral sciences.

Judd expected his faculty to have the same conception of the professional role that he had himself: they were to be scholars, but not cloistered scholars.

Incessantly busy, Judd governed his extensive university province, taught a full schedule of courses, guided doctoral students, engaged in research, published voluminously, edited the *Elementary School Journal* and the *School Review,* spoke frequently before diverse audiences, daily conferred and corresponded with those seeking his advice, directed school surveys in several cities, and served in many educational organizations. He was president of the National Society of College Teachers of Education in 1911 and 1915 and chairman (1929-1930) of the American Council on Education, which he had helped found. He served on the International Inquiry on School and University Examinations (1935), on the science committee of the National Resources Planning Board (1937-1940), on the advisory committee of the National Youth Administration (1935-1940); was a consultant to the U.S. War Department (1942-1943); and in 1933 made public a new plan for education that was sponsored by the President's Research Committee on Social Trends and recommended cutting education from sixteen to twelve years and replacement of the normal system. On all such groups he exercised a telling influence because of the clarity and force of his thought and expression and the assertiveness of his personality. His impact on his contemporaries derived, too, from his absolute faith in certain articles of

his own personal educational creed. To his mind, the school was society's agent for civilizing the young, by laying out a program of subject matter and formulating standards of performance for pupils that would enable them to master the problems of society and life rather than rely upon spontaneous individual activities and interests. The subject matter of the curriculum should consist of the products of social evolution (such as language, number, and the social studies), which can be altered by the application of trained human intelligence.

Many persons testified that when they were in Judd's company, they felt that they were "in the presence of greatness." He was an imposing figure, six feet tall, with steady, bright blue eyes; aquiline nose; Vandyke beard; a quick, ironic, devastating wit; and a strong, expressive voice, which he employed with calculated effect—a superb teacher and speaker, a most formidable opponent. His moral and intellectual world contained no shadows or dark places; his mind, his attention, his temperament, his views were always in sharp, hard focus. He had renounced all religion in college, yet throughout his life he exhibited a professional militancy and fervor that betrayed his evangelical, pietistic upbringing. Given these qualities, he was probably wise in deciding to subordinate his career in research to a career as educational administrator and educational statesman.

Judd was married twice: first, on Aug. 23, 1898, in Binghamton, N.Y., to Ella LeCompte, who died in 1935; and second, to his longtime research assistant, May Diehl, on Aug. 28, 1937, in Chicago. By his first marriage he had a daughter, Dorothy. Judd withdrew from his university duties in August 1937 and formally retired a year later. The demands he made upon himself and the pace of his activities did not lessen during the remaining seven years of his life. He was appointed emeritus Charles F. Grey distinguished-service professor and emeritus dean in 1938. From 1944 until his death he was a consultant on social studies for Santa Barbara city schools, California. He died of cancer of the pancreas at his home in Santa Barbara and was cremated there. The next year the board of trustees of the University of Chicago changed the name of the Graduate Education Building to Charles Hubbard Judd Hall.

[The major sources are the Judd Papers, Univ. of Chicago Arch.; Judd, in Carl A. Murchison, ed., *A Hist. of Psych. in Autobiog.,* II, 207–235 (1932); Guy T. Buswell in *Am. Jour. Psych.,* Jan. 1947; Frank N. Freeman in *Psych. Rev.,* Mar. 1947, and *Elementary School Jour.,* Jan. 1947; Douglas E. Scates in *School Rev.,* Spring 1967; Margaret W.

Clark, "Charles Hubbard Judd: Educational Leadership in Am. Secondary Education" (Ph.D. diss., Stanford Univ., 1960); *Who Was Who in America,* II 1950); obituaries in *N.Y. Times* and *Chicago Tribune,* July 19, 1946; correspondence with May Diehl Judd, Santa Barbara, Calif., and Dorothy Judd Sickels, Hamilton, N.Y.; recollections of members of Dept. of Education, Univ. of Chicago.]

ROBERT L. McCAUL

KAHN, FLORENCE PRAG (Nov. 9, 1866-Nov. 16, 1948), congresswoman from California, was born in Salt Lake City, Utah, the only daughter of Conrad Prag and Mary (Goldsmith) Prag. Her parents, both Polish Jews, had been early settlers in California but had lived in Salt Lake City for several years prior to Florence's birth. They returned to California in 1869 after the failure of Conrad Prag's business, whereupon Mary Prag became the principal breadwinner of the family as head of the history department at San Francisco's Girls' High School. She was an early advocate of pensions for state teachers and later served on the San Francisco Board of Education.

Florence attended public schools in San Francisco and was graduated in 1883 from Girls' High School and in 1887 from the University of California at Berkeley. Frustrated in her ambition to study law by family financial problems, she too entered high school teaching, concentrating in history and English.

On Mar. 19, 1899, she married Julius Kahn, the newly elected Republican congressman from San Francisco's Fourth District. They had two sons, Julius and Conrad. She took an intense interest in her husband's work, frequenting the galleries when the House was in session, discussing issues with him, meeting his associates, and, in the later years of his term, serving as his secretary. Following his death on Dec. 18, 1924, she campaigned to fill his seat and was elected to the Sixty-ninth Congress on Feb. 17, 1925. An able politician in her own right, she was reelected to five successive Congresses. She lost her seat to Frank R. Havenner, a newspaperman running on the Democratic and Progressive tickets, in the 1936 Roosevelt landslide.

Kahn balked at her initial assignment to the Committee on Indian Affairs: "The only Indians in my district are in front of cigar stores," she said, "and I can't do anything for them" (*American Mercury,* p. 159). She served for three years on the committees on the census; education; expenditures in the war department; war claims; and coinage, weights, and measures. In 1928 she realized her ambition of gaining a seat on the Committee on Military

Affairs, which her husband had chaired. Like him an "ardent advocate of adequate preparedness" (*Congressional Record,* Jan. 15, 1927, p. 1736), she discounted charges that she was a militarist: "Preparedness," she said, "never caused a war, unpreparedness never prevented one" (Chamberlin, p. 50). She supported measures for a strong national defense as well as bills providing benefits for army and navy nurses, veterans and their families, and others who made personal sacrifices for the United States during World War I.

Kahn also served on the Appropriations Committee. A believer in strict economy in public expenditures, she nevertheless favored federal support for highway construction, flood control, river and harbor improvements, and radio and aviation development. She staunchly supported funding sufficient to strengthen and broaden the law-enforcement activities of the Federal Bureau of Investigation, winning from J. Edgar Hoover the label "the Mother of the FBI."

Immediately joining the "wet" faction in Congress, Kahn became an outspoken leader of the drive against prohibition on the grounds that it was unenforceable and "a complete failure." She argued for "modification" of the Volstead Act to permit the manufacture, transportation, and sale of light wines and beer; her goal was "an enforceable temperance" (*New York Times,* Apr. 14, 1930).

Known for her wit, mimicry, and candor, Florence Kahn delighted visitors to the House gallery with unexpected remarks. When Rep. Fiorello La Guardia attacked her as "nothing but a stand-patter, following that reactionary, Senator George H. Moses of New Hampshire," she shot back, "Why shouldn't I choose Moses as my leader? Haven't my people been following him for ages?" (*New York Times,* Nov. 17, 1948). When another of her colleagues labeled opponents of a movie-censorship bill unclean, she retorted, "Don't you dare call *me* unclean." Accused by a group of women of having been influenced on the bill by a young, handsome motion picture executive, she declared, "Of course I have been. Look at him and tell me if I'm to blame" (Chamberlin, p. 50). The *Literary Digest* said that "as a wit and jester, [Kahn] has no equal in the House of Representatives" (Jan. 25, 1936, p. 29).

For all her clowning, "the gentlewoman from California" successfully served her district. She was largely responsible for legislation funding the San Francisco Bay Bridge; locating an army base in Marin County and naval air stations at Sunnyvale and the Alameda; and providing improved port facilities, a new federal office building, a post office, and a marine hospital. Asked how she had won so many votes for her favorite projects, she replied, "It's my sex appeal!" (*New York Times,* Nov. 17, 1948).

When she was first elected, some people wondered "whether or not a woman could satisfactorily represent the district" (*Congressional Record,* June 15, 1926, p. 11299). In her twelve years in the House she won over the doubtful; a reporter skeptical of women serving in that body admitted that "the case of Mrs. Kahn is exceptional. Her unusual experience matches an unusual character" (*New York Times,* Aug. 22, 1926). "Congress," a contemporary periodical stated, "treats her like a man, fears her, admires her and listens to her" (Chamberlin, p. 50). Alice Roosevelt Longworth, as shrewd an observer as any, praised her as "an all-round first-rate legislator."

Following her retirement, Florence Kahn remained active in Republican, Jewish, and women's organizations until suffering a heart attack in 1942. She died of arteriosclerotic heart disease in her Huntington Hotel apartment in San Francisco and was buried in Home of Peace Cemetery, Colma, Calif.

[Sources include *Notable Am. Women,* II (1971); Hope Chamberlin, *A Minority of Members: Women in the U.S. Congress* (1973); *Biog. Directory of the Amer. Congress* (1961); *Who's Who in Amer. Jewry* (1938); *N.Y. Times,* especially Jan. 6, Feb. 21, Apr. 30, May 6, Aug. 3, 22, 1926, Mar. 8, Nov. 27, Dec. 22, 1929, Apr. 14, 1930, Nov. 4, 1936, Nov. 17, 1948; *Cong. Rec.* 69th–74th Cong., especially May 5, June 15, 1926, Jan. 15, 1927, May 29, 1928, July 3, 1930; Gertrude Atherton, *My San Francisco* (1946); Duff Gilfond, "Gentlewomen of the House," *Amer. Mercury,* Oct. 1929; Alice Roosevelt Longworth, "What Are the Women Up To?" *Ladies' Home Journal,* Mar. 1934, which includes a photograph.]

NANCY J. WEISS

KEAN, JEFFERSON RANDOLPH (June 27, 1860–Sept. 4, 1950), military surgeon, was born in Lynchburg, Va., the second of four sons and third of five children of Robert Garlick Hill Kean and Jane Nicholas (Randolph) Kean. Garlick Kean, the great-grandson of a man who emigrated from northern Ireland to Virginia at the time of the American Revolution, was a Lynchburg lawyer who, during his studies at the University of Virginia, married a great-granddaughter of Thomas Jefferson. In April 1861 he was mustered in as a private in the 11th Virginia Infantry; ten months later, as a captain, he joined the staff of his wife's uncle, Brig. Gen. George Wythe Randolph. When Randolph became secretary of war in March 1862, he was appointed head of the Bureau of War, a post he held until the dissolution of the Confederacy.

After the war, Garlick Kean resumed the practice of law in Lynchburg. Life was difficult, for his clients had no money to pay his fees. Nevertheless Jefferson Randolph Kean attended the Episcopal High School in Alexandria and the University of Virginia. When rusticated from the university because of an excess of sociability, he taught school in a hamlet on the eastern shore of Virginia. After this exile he returned to the University of Virginia, where he received his M.D. in 1883. Following graduate study at New York Polyclinic Hospital and Medical College, he was commissioned a first lieutenant in the United States Army on Dec. 8, 1884, with the designation of assistant surgeon.

Kean's first eight years of military service in the west, as a surgeon with the Ninth Cavalry, included the winter campaign against the Sioux in 1890–1891. During his next tour of duty in Florida, he married on Oct. 10, 1894, Louise Hurlbut Young; they had a daughter and a son. Louise Kean died in 1915. At the outbreak of the Spanish-American War, Captain Kean was commissioned as brigade major of volunteers, and detailed medical inspector of the 2nd Division, 7th Army Corps, in Jacksonville. There in command of the division hospital, he cared for more than 600 typhoid patients; this he regarded as "the most arduous and trying undertaking" that came to him during forty years of active service. He went to Cuba in December 1898 with the 1st Division of the 7th Army Corps, and on Feb. 18, 1899, was promoted to lieutenant colonel (volunteers), and corps chief surgeon on the staff of Maj. Gen. Fitzhugh Lee. In 1900, being ill with yellow fever, Kean's case was the first that his friend Maj. Walter Reed saw on arrival in Cuba. Although he was not one of the most publicized of the participants of the Yellow Fever Board, Kean, by then a major, was commended for his work with it in the secretary of war's annual report for 1902. During the military governorship of Leonard Wood, Kean served as superintendent of the Department of Charities.

In 1902 Major Kean returned to Washington as executive officer of the Surgeon General's Office, but in 1906, when the United States set up a provisional government after the Cuban insurrection, he returned to the island as advisor to the department of sanitation. In this capacity he drafted laws organizing sanitary departments for Cuba and Puerto Rico, as well as extinguishing a recrudescence of yellow fever. From 1909 to 1913 he was once again in the Surgeon General's Office, this time in charge of the sanitary division. During these two tours of duty in Washington he instigated a separate system of field medical supply depots, in which field equipment was accumulated. He was also the author of the law organizing the Medical Reserve Corps, which was the first, and for eight years the only, Army reserve. During the Taft administration, Secretary of War Henry L. Stimson sent Kean to the lower Mississippi valley to avert the danger of epidemic disease among flood sufferers, and to Puerto Rico to supervise measures against bubonic plague. In 1911 he was sent to Paris as a delegate to an international conference to draw a treaty for control of epidemics of plague, cholera, and yellow fever.

In January 1916 Colonel Kean was assigned to the American Red Cross, where he became director general and organizer of the department of military relief. In that capacity he organized and equipped thirty-two base hospitals that were immediately ready for service when the United States entered the war. He soon went to France as chief of the United States Ambulance Service with the French Army, with headquarters in Paris. In February 1918 he was transferred to Tours, first as chief surgeon of the line of communications and later as deputy chief surgeon of the American Expeditionary Force. While serving at Tours, he was commissioned brigadier general (National Army). There on Mar. 24, 1919, he married Cornelia Knox, a sister of Commodore Dudley W. Knox, historian of the United States Navy.

On returning to the United States after the war, Kean's last tour of duty was at Boston as corps area surgeon, First Corps Area. When he retired on June 27, 1924, Surgeon General Ireland stated that in his opinion "General Kean has done more for the advancement of the interests of the Department than any officer who ever belonged to the Corps. He had done more to establish the present satisfactory condition of the Medical Department than any other living man. The tripod on which the success of the Medical Department of the Army rested in the World War consisted of the Medical Reserve Corps, the accumulation of field supplies for an emergency, and the organization of base hospitals, and Kean was responsible for all of these activities." He was awarded the Dis-

tinguished Service Medal, the Légion d'Honneur (officier), Cuba's Grand Cross of the Order of Merit of Carlos J. Finlay, and the Gorgas Medal of the Association of Military Surgeons of the United States.

After retirement, Kean and his wife settled in Georgetown, D.C. For the next ten years he was secretary and editor of the Association of Military Surgeons of the United States, of which he had been president in 1914-1915. Kean was the organizer and first president (1913-1920) of the Monticello Association which maintains the graveyard where are buried Thomas Jefferson and many of his descendants. As historian of the association (1920-1948), he wrote many articles for its annual reports. President Roosevelt appointed him in 1934 a member of the United States commission for the construction of the National Expansion Memorial at St. Louis and in 1938 to the commission that created the Jefferson Memorial in Washington. General Kean was particularly involved in the selection and wordings of the quotations from Jefferson in the four panels on the interior walls of the Jefferson Memorial; the dedication of this monument in 1943 gave him especial pleasure.

General Kean was, unlike many able administrators, a modest, genial, and humorous man of great charm and warmth of feeling. He was a marvelous conversationalist, and his memory was so retentive and accurate that he could recall the tents and bivouacs of Gen. P. H. Sheridan's cavalry on his grandfather Randolph's lawns and fields at Edgehill in 1865, incidents of Indian fighting on the western plains in the 1880's, or of yellow fever in Cuba, with the vividness of more recent events. For his guests he mixed an admirable whiskey toddy, served in Jeffersonian metal cups. Although lame in later years, he suffered no diminution of his mind, memory, and delight in friends. He died of pneumonia at Walter Reed Hospital soon after his ninetieth birthday and is buried at Monticello.

[The most extensive account of Kean's life is the 270-page typed autobiography that he wrote on retirement in 1924 for deposit in the Army Medical Lib. There are brief memoirs of Kean in Edgar Erskine Hume, *The Golden Jubilee & the Association of Military Surgeons of the United States, A History of its First Half-Century, 1891–1941*, pp. 237–239 (1941); the 1950 annual report of the Monticello Association; *Collected Papers to Commemorate Fifty Years of the Monticello Association of the Descendants of Thomas Jefferson*, pp. 186–188 (1965); *Who Was Who in Am., III* (1960). Other details from Edward Younger, ed., *Inside the Confederate Government, The Diary of Robert Garlick Hill Kean* (1957), and from personal conversation and correspondence with the subject.]
WALTER MUIR WHITEHILL

KEFAUVER, GRAYSON NEIKIRK
(Aug. 31, 1900-Jan. 4, 1946), educator, was
born in Middletown, Md., the son of Oliver
Henry Kefauver, a farmer, and Lillie May
(Neikirk) Kefauver. Oliver Kefauver had been
married earlier to his second wife's sister
Martha Ellen Neikirk. That marriage produced
two sons and one daughter; he and his second
wife had four sons and one daughter.

Grayson attended the Valley View School,
a one-room schoolhouse in Middletown and
later the Middletown High School, to which he
drove by horse and buggy. He received the
B.A. degree from the University of Arizona
(1921), the M.A. from Leland Stanford Junior
University in California (1925), and his Ph.D.
from the University of Minnesota (1928),
where he was an instructor 1926-1928 and
an assistant professor 1928-1929. He was an
associate professor at Teachers College, Columbia University, during 1929-1932. In the intervals between his university studies, Kefauver
served briefly as a teacher and administrator
in secondary and elementary schools in Tucson,
Ariz. (1921-1922), and Fresno, Calif. (1923-
1926). It was during his year at Tucson that
he married Anna Elizabeth Skinner on Dec.
25, 1922. They had three children, Betty La
Verne, William Henry, and Robert Elwood. He
took further graduate studies at Harvard University and the University of California. In
1931-1932 he was a member of the staff of the
National Survey of Secondary Education conducted by the U.S. Office of Education.

In 1932 Kefauver returned to Stanford as
visiting professor of education, and in 1933
he was named dean of the School of Education. In the ensuing ten years he arranged and
administered many changes in the educational
school. The student enrollment and staff were
increased, and new programs were developed.
Substantial grants from foundations were secured to augment the university funds for
special projects in guidance, the language arts,
and social education. Joint staff appointments
facilitated interdisciplinary studies and services.
Projects with the public school systems of
Santa Barbara and Palo Alto and with nearby
Menlo Junior College brought the School of
Education into closer contact with practical
problems.

An abrupt change in Kefauver's career occurred in January 1943. He took a leave of
absence from Stanford and moved to Washington, D.C., where he added his energy, enthusiasm, and intelligence to the campaign to
define and secure the proper world role for
education after the end of World War II. He
first created the Liaison Committee on International Education, which in September 1943,
under his chairmanship, held an "International
Education Assembly" at Harpers Ferry, W.Va.
The ability of sixty-three participants from
twenty-six countries to develop and agree upon
a respectable report within four days can be
credited partly to Kefauver's irresistible enthusiasm and partly to the fact that the members
were free agents, not representing their governments or the voluntary organizations to
which they belonged. The chief elements of the
program they adopted were: a permanent international organization for education and cultural development, and a temporary agency to
deal with immediate postwar educational problems; rebuilding of educational facilities and
services in war-devastated areas; the redirec-
tion of education in the Axis countries; and
long-range programs in education for world
citizenship.

In March 1944, Secretary of State Cordell
Hull announced that a United States delegation
would attend the Conference of Allied Ministers of Education (CAME) in London on
April 5. The delegation consisted of Grayson
Kefauver, Archibald MacLeish of the Library
of Congress, U.S. Commissioner of Education
John W. Studebaker, Dean C. Mildred Thompson of Vassar College, Ralph Turner of the
State Department, and, as chairman, Congressman J. William Fulbright. The delegation was
authorized to work with CAME to establish
a United Nations Educational and Cultural
Organization and to offer American assistance
in the educational reconstruction of war-torn
countries.

Following the mission in April, Kefauver
remained in London, with the rank of minister,
as the American official liaison to CAME. His
chief activity was to prepare for the Constitutional Conference for the agency ultimately
called UNESCO. Facing an unknown period
of continued absence from the United States,
Kefauver early in 1945 resigned the deanship
of Stanford but remained on the faculty list
as professor of education.

The Conference for the Establishment of the
United Nations Educational and Cultural Organization met in London Nov. 1-16, 1945.
Kefauver was one member of a rather large
United States delegation, but his previous work
made him by far its best-informed member.
The conference had to deal with a number
of problems: what UNESCO should do about
the reconstruction of educational facilities in

war-devastated areas; whether UNESCO should endeavor to contribute directly to peace and security or rather make its contribution through long-range efforts to promote human welfare through education; to what extent UNESCO should be a strictly intergovernmental agency and how, if at all, nongovernmental organizations should participate in its work; how much autonomy UNESCO should claim and secure from the United Nations; whether UNESCO activities should be those of a liaison and clearing-house agency, or an action agency to promote peace, or an agency to collect and distribute knowledge.

The London conference was undoubtedly the high point in Grayson Kefauver's career. At age forty-five he should have had at least twenty more years to assist in the development of UNESCO and its program, and he certainly would have made substantial contributions to the international organization he helped to establish. He did not even live to see the ratification of the UNESCO Charter, which was approved by the Senate and signed by President Harry S. Truman in June 1946. While on a speaking tour to develop public understanding and support for the charter, Kefauver had a cerebral hemorrhage in Los Angeles on Jan. 4, 1946, and he died almost immediately. Interment was at Acacia Gardens, Forest Lawn Memorial Cemetery, Glendale, Calif.

Grayson Kefauver's excellent mind was action-oriented. He seemed to prefer working with a committee, formal or informal, rather than spending hours in isolated contemplation or writing. He was a first-class strategist, gifted with unusual ability to anticipate the reactions of others.

[Memorial resolution adopted by the Academic Council of Stanford Univ. (Stanford Univ. Archives); Harold Bienvenu, "The Educational Career of Grayson Neikirk Kefauver" (Ph.D. diss., Stanford Univ., 1956); Walter H. C. Laves and Charles A. Thomson, *UNESCO: Purpose, Progress, Prospects* (1957); International Education Assembly, *Education for International Security* (1943). Monographs written by Kefauver, Victor H. Noll, and C. Elwood Drake for the National Survey of Secondary Education in 1932 are *The Horizontal Organization of Secondary Education, Part-time Secondary Schools,* and *Secondary School Population.* Books written by Kefauver in collaboration with others are *Appraising Guidance in Secondary Schools* (1941), with H. C. Hand; and *Foreign Languages and Cultures in American Education* (1942), with W. V. Kaulfers. The Stanford University School of Education has a comprehensive list of Kefauver's published articles.]
WILLIAM G. CARR

KELLY, EDWARD JOSEPH (May 1, 1876–Oct. 20, 1950), political boss and mayor of Chicago, was born in that city's "Back of the Yards," an area that spawned generations of political leaders. He was the oldest of nine children of Stephen Kelly and Helen (Lang) Kelly. His mother was of German origin. His father, an Irish Catholic immigrant who worked as a city fireman and then as a policeman, found it difficult to support his ever-growing family, and Edward began selling newspapers at the age of nine, left school at twelve, and over the next five years worked as a stock boy for a department store, a lawyer's messenger, a window washer, and an undertaker's apprentice. While watching a crew at work on the Columbian Exposition of 1893, he was inspired to become an engineer. His Democratic precinct captain got him a job as an axman with the Sanitary District of Chicago, the political authority controlling the city's sewage and water systems. To make up for his educational deficiencies, Kelly enrolled in night classes at the Chicago Athenaeum, a school specializing in mathematics, and later studied engineering. Quick-witted and nimble-minded, he rose in the sanitary district to surveyor, assistant engineer (1908), and chief engineer (1920).

As chief engineer, Kelly supervised projects in a twenty-year program costing $120 million and often served as a consultant on state and federal waterway planning. But the graft, mismanagement, payroll padding, nepotism, and reckless spending of this period earned it the label of the "whoopee era." In 1930 Kelly and nine other sanitary-district officials were named in a federal indictment charging conspiracy to defraud the district of $5 million. The indictment against Kelly was revoked for lack of evidence, but within two years he was cited for underpayment of income taxes between 1919 and 1929, a claim that he settled for $105,000. Meanwhile, he was cementing his relationship with Patrick A. Nash, a leader in the local Democratic party and an affluent sewer contractor, whose firm had millions of dollars in sanitary-district contracts. Kelly's political connections won him a post on Chicago's South Park Board in 1922, and he became president two years later. He initiated projects to beautify the city's lakefront, oversaw construction of the Shedd Aquarium and Adler Planetarium, and cooperated with the philanthropist Julius Rosenwald in establishing Chicago's Museum of Science and Industry.

When Mayor Anton J. Cermak was killed in 1933 by an assassin's bullet meant for President-elect Franklin D. Roosevelt, Nash, as chairman of the Cook County Democratic Central Committee, ordered a subservient city council to appoint Kelly to serve out Cermak's term. Kelly remained the city's chief executive for fourteen years, winning election easily at the polls in 1935, 1939, and 1943. Meanwhile, he built with Nash one of the nation's strongest political organizations through firm control of some 40,000 patronage jobs. He faced occasional challenges from within his own party, the most serious in 1936, when he and Nash sought to keep Gov. Henry Horner from running for a second term, reportedly because Horner had vetoed a bill to license racing handbooks. Horner denounced Kelly and Nash in the primary, defeated their candidate, and went on to win reelection.

Tall, red-haired, and robust, Kelly was a dignified mayor. Increasingly he became the dominant force in what critics called "the Kelly-Nash machine." Kelly gloried in the efficiency of his organization. "In politics," he liked to say, "the machine runs you or you run the machine. I run the machine." The difference between a politician and a statesman, he asserted, is that "a politician gets things done." A civic booster in the grand tradition, Mayor Kelly did use his powers for considerable good. Chicago was virtually bankrupt when he first took office, with "payless paydays" for many city employees and millions of dollars in delinquent taxes and unpaid bills. Through federal public works projects and the mortgaging of land owned by the Board of Education, he restored the city's financial health. He pushed through innumerable physical improvements, from the widening of State Street, "the street of the merchants," to the building of the first section of a $40 million subway system; he also developed the city's fire department into one of the nation's most efficient. He was a firm exponent of public housing, and despite political and neighborhood pressure, he insisted on a policy of nondiscrimination. He established the Chicago Recovery Administration and the Keep Chicago Ahead Committee, which worked for the development of business and industry; he initiated "Drama of Chicago on Parade," a series of civic pageants; and secured $100 million for a superhighway program. During World War II he established a group of servicemen's centers that made Chicago noted for its hospitality. On the national scene, Kelly established a rapport with President Roosevelt, who held him in esteem for his political pragmatism and vote-getting ability. As Democratic na-

tional committeeman, Kelly was listened to in high party councils, and in 1940 he spearheaded Roosevelt's third-term campaign.

For all the material improvements, Kelly's mayoral years were speckled with scandal. The city was wide open, and the police force, largely inefficient and ineffectual, made scant effort to enforce antigambling laws. Chicago's civil service system was manipulated to reward political underlings and their relatives. Despite sporadic cleanup campaigns, the streets and alleys remained the dirtiest in the world. Worst of all, the school system, run by a board and superintendent beholden to City Hall's every patronage wish, was under constant fire, principally from the National Education Association, whose 1945 report charged that "some of the personnel practices in Chicago schools are undemocratic and even fascist in nature."

Such adverse publicity, coupled with local Democratic losses in the 1946 elections, prompted party leaders led by Cook County chairman Jacob M. Arvey (Nash had died in 1943) to choose a new mayoral candidate in 1947—Martin H. Kennelly, a successful businessman and political neophyte. Kelly withdrew and, after completing his term, retired from active politics. In the last three years of his life he headed an engineering consulting firm and devoted much time to a campaign to raise $6 million for a new building for Chicago's Mercy Hospital.

Kelly was married twice: on Mar. 20, 1910, to Mary Edmunda Roche of Chicago, who died in 1918; and on Jan. 25, 1922, to Margaret Ellen Kirk of Kansas City, Mo. The only child by the first marriage, Edward Joseph, died at the age of fourteen. With his second wife, Kelly adopted three children: Patricia Anne, Joseph Michael, and Stephen Edward. Kelly died of a heart attack in Chicago at the age of seventy-four. A devout Catholic, he was buried in Calvary Cemetery, near Chicago.

[Files of the *Chicago Daily News, Chicago Sun-Times,* and *Chicago Tribune,* 1920–1950, are a basic source, especially Oct. 20–25, 1950; there is also a good obituary in the *N.Y. Times,* Oct. 21, 1950. Useful secondary sources include John T. Flynn, "These Our Rulers," *Collier's,* June 29–July 20, 1940; article on the Kelly–Nash machine in *Fortune,* Aug. 1936; Harold F. Gosnell, *Machine Politics: Chicago Model* (1937); Herman Kogan and Lloyd Wendt, *Chicago: A Pictorial Hist.* (1958); Alson J. Smith, *Syndicate City* (1954); and Ovid Demaris, *Captive City* (1969). Interviews with Matthias P. Bauler, Charles Cleveland, John Dreiske, Arthur Petacque, and William Strand were helpful.]

HERMAN KOGAN

KENT, ARTHUR ATWATER (Dec. 3, 1873–Mar. 4, 1949), inventor and radio manufacturer, was born in Burlington, Vt., the son of Prentiss Jonathan Kent, a physician who had served in the Civil War, and Mary Elizabeth (Atwater) Kent. Through his father he was descended from Joseph Kent, who came from England to Rehoboth, Mass., in 1634. Atwater Kent, as he was known, was mechanically precocious, and his family sent him to the Worcester (Mass.) Polytechnic Institute. He left after two years without obtaining a degree, to begin work with a manufacturer in Lebanon, N.H. After a brief stint selling electrical equipment for a firm in Brookline, Mass., he moved to Philadelphia, where in 1902 he established the Atwater Kent Manufacturing Works.

The firm, incorporated in 1919, was wholly owned and directed by Kent and laid the basis for his personal fortune. He began by manufacturing small voltmeters and home telephones but rapidly expanded to make a variety of electrical devices—notably, automotive ignition systems. Many of these devices were of his own invention; the unisparker, one of the first jumpspark ignition systems, brought him the John Scott Medal of the Franklin Institute in 1914. During World War I the company manufactured gunnery fire-control instruments. By 1920 Kent had become one of the major suppliers of electrical systems to the automobile industry and had achieved great success in combining the inventive and entrepreneurial functions.

Kent began receiving orders for radio parts in 1922, and the following year he devised, assembled, and sold his first five-tube receiving set. He proved phenomenally successful in this burgeoning new industry: by 1926 Atwater Kent had produced more than 1,000,000 sets, and annual sales exceeded $60 million in 1929. New factories were constructed in which 12,000 workers could turn out 6,000 receivers a day. By 1930 Atwater Kent was the leading firm in the industry.

The success of Kent's radio receivers did not rest primarily on his inventive skill. Like other manufacturers seeking to meet the booming demand, he drew on the best current technology, much of which rested on patents controlled by the Radio Corporation of America (RCA). In 1927 RCA successfully sued Kent for using its Alexanderson frequency tuner but shortly thereafter permitted him to continue manufacturing the device under a licensing agreement. The following year Kent lost a similar patent case to the Hazeltine Corporation. Kent's distinctive contribution seems to have been the ability to mass-produce receivers of high quality, a quality achieved by frequent inspections during the manufacturing process (see, e.g., *New York Times,* Sept. 18, 1927, Sec. 10). His company suffered severely, however, during the Great Depression. In 1936, with only 800 employees, Kent despaired of resuming profitable operations, closed down production permanently, and retired.

Kent's interest in radio extended to the quality of programming. Beginning in 1925, he sponsored the "Atwater Kent Hour," a network program that pioneered in presenting the best classical musicians of the era. In 1927 he set up the Atwater Kent Foundation, which over the next five years sponsored nationwide auditions to discover first-class young singers; winners were awarded cash prizes and tuition at leading conservatories of music.

As Kent's prosperity increased, so did his philanthropic activities; his contributions at one time reached $300,000 annually. In the depression winter of 1931 he set up a private relief program providing aid to 3,500 former employees. More characteristically, in 1930 he contributed $225,000 toward the construction of a new building for the Franklin Institute. Subsequently, heeding the appeal of Philadelphia's mayor, he took over the old Franklin Institute building, modernized it, and donated it as a municipal historical museum, which was given his name. In 1936-1937 he also restored the Betsy Ross House in Philadelphia.

Kent was once characterized as "suave, affable, approachable but highly individualistic." He once expressed a wish to enjoy "the simple life, on a grand scale" (*Time,* June 15, 1936). On May 24, 1906, he married a Philadelphia socialite, Mabel Lucas. They had three children, Arthur Atwater, Elizabeth Brinton, and Virginia Tucker, and adopted a fourth, Jonathan Prentiss. The family acquired estates near Philadelphia; Bar Harbor, Maine; Southampton, L.I.; and Palm Beach, Fla. They maintained membership in a large number of social clubs, and their yachts plied the waters from Maine to California. Kent launched his daughters into society with elaborate balls. He was a Congregationalist in religion, and politically a Republican who thought the New Deal a "dreadful blight" (*ibid.*). After legally separating from his wife in 1940, Kent moved to California and purchased a thirty-two-room mansion on a twelve-acre hilltop estate in Bel Air, a Los Angeles suburb, where he entertained Hollywood celebrities at elaborate social affairs. He died of cancer in Los Angeles at the age of seventy-five and was buried in Forest Lawn Memorial Park, Glendale, Calif. He left an estate estimated at $8 million (*New York Times,* Apr. 23, 1949).

[*Nat. Cyc. Am. Biog.,* XXXVIII, 57–58, includes information about Kent's ancestry. Obituaries appeared in *N.Y. Times* and *N.Y. Herald Tribune,* Mar. 5, 1949. See also *Who Was Who in America,* II (1950); *Time,* June 15, 1936, pp. 66–70; and *Life,* July 1, 1946, pp. 96–98, 101 (most of the preceding include photographs). Death record from Calif. Dept. of Public Health. Kent's career can be followed in more detail through the *N.Y. Times Index.* Information in trade journals and in histories of the radio industry is scattered and disappointing. There are no known collections of personal papers.]

KENDALL BIRR

KLEIN, AUGUST CLARENCE (Apr. 1, 1887–Feb. 3, 1948), mechanical engineer, was born in Jersey City, N.J., the eldest of four children (two sons and two daughters) of August Klein and Lillian (Gavenisch) Klein. Both his parents were of German ancestry. His father was head of the cigarette department of Liggett and Myers Tobacco Company. After attending public schools, Klein entered Stevens Institute of Technology in 1904 and graduated in 1908 with the degree of mechanical engineer. He worked as a gas engineer for the United Gas Improvement Company in Philadelphia until American entry into World War I, when he became a first lieutenant in the Army Ordnance Department, assigned to the production of toluol and nitrates. In September 1919, after his discharge, he married Maree Stone Keeling. They had one daughter, Maree L., and four sons, James H., Frederick W., August S., and John D. On Apr. 1, 1920, he joined Stone and Webster Engineering Corporation in Boston as a gas engineer in its industrial division. When that division was absorbed by the mechanical division, Klein went along as a mechanical engineer. In the course of time, his work on the design of steam power plants and chemical plants, his authoritative knowledge of depreciation and public utility rates, and his ability to make quick, correct decisions led to his promotion to chief mechanical engineer in 1929.

After the outbreak of World War II, the Army Corps of Engineers turned to Stone and Webster for a number of projects, most of them carried out under Klein's direction. When the War Department called for a rapid increase in explosives-manufacturing capacity, Klein suggested that the Du Pont Company provide technical guidelines and designs and that Stone and Webster, along with other engineer-contractors, undertake construction. Klein himself speeded the program by designing a standard power plant and stockpiling basic components.

Under Klein's direction three huge plants were built in Illinois, Pennsylvania, and Tennessee. The Illinois plant, largest of the three, began manufacturing TNT only ten months after groundbreaking.

In June 1942 the task of producing fissionable material for an atomic bomb was assigned to the Army Corps of Engineers. Its deputy chief of construction, Col. Leslie R. Groves, recommended Stone and Webster as the engineering firm best suited to the job. As Groves summed up his arguments in retrospect, "They were accustomed to working with scientific people— far more than most engineering firms; they were a large firm, capable in both engineering and construction; and they were performing well on all their contracts with the Corps of Engineers" (Groves, p. 12). In July 1942 Stone and Webster began work on Project X, later to become the Manhattan Project under General Groves.

In Boston, under the direction of Klein as project engineer, the group of design engineers and draftsmen eventually grew to about 800, and other groups were formed elsewhere under Klein's authority. An evidence of Klein's commitment to the project was his insistence from the start on the need for maximum production and year-round operation of the Canadian uranium mining operation at Great Bear Lake near the Arctic Circle. He supervised the engineering design in the building of the first uranium pile facilities in the Argonne Forest Laboratory at the University of Chicago and the heavy-water plant at Trail, British Columbia. Three ways of obtaining fissionable material seemed most promising: production of the new element plutonium in uranium-graphite piles and separation of the fissionable uranium isotope U^{235} from the more common U^{238} either by gaseous diffusion or by electromagnetism. In July 1942 Klein visited the Berkeley radiation laboratory of Ernest O. Lawrence and caught its enthusiasm for electromagnetic separation. Klein correctly forecast that the electromagnetic method would ultimately be superseded by one of the others but that meanwhile it would yield the quickest results for wartime use; he therefore urged the authorities to push forward at once toward production.

In the fall of 1942, however, it was decided to develop all three approaches concurrently. It was soon apparent that no one firm could handle all of these on the enormous scale projected. Stone and Webster had been granted the contract for all the engineering work for the Manhattan Project, and Klein had already begun organizing design work for the electromagnetic separation plant. Since, in any case, Stone and Webster's forte was electrical engineering design and construction, all concerned agreed that the firm should continue with that project, leaving the essentially chemical plutonium project to Du Pont and the gaseous diffusion project to the M. W. Kellogg Company, an engineering firm with special expertise in petroleum refineries.

Klein also participated in choosing the Knoxville area for the U^{235} project, and his group in Boston designed the new town of Oak Ridge, Tenn., as well as the electromagnetic plant, both of which were constructed by Stone and Webster. By the summer of 1943 the firm had about 25,000 men at work in Tennessee. Klein dispatched engineers to work with the scientists at Berkeley and Chicago, with manufacturers, and with others involved in the complex undertaking. Frequently on the move, visiting Washington and job sites, he was adept at catching brief naps in airports and arriving at a destination refreshed. At his headquarters in Boston, he held daily meetings at 12:30 (so that lunchtime hunger would curb longwindedness) with from twelve to twenty leaders of the engineering design group. At about one o'clock, after having led the discussion with genial adroitness, he would summarize what had been said and make the necessary decisions promptly and emphatically.

The group faced unprecedented problems. Time did not even permit a pilot plant. Construction of the enormous full-scale plant had to go on simultaneously with research on the process. New findings kept requiring complicated alterations of existing designs. Nevertheless, Klein exuded confidence. His decisions were usually right but not, of course, invariably so, and to some of his more cautious colleagues, he seemed unsettlingly flamboyant and unpredictable. But he kept the thousands of design drawings coming to the field forces. However credit may be apportioned on this vast project, "Gus" Klein (as he was always called) came as close as any other man to embodying the spirit and power of that climactic engineering enterprise, desperately harried yet boldly confident, prodigal yet productive, multifarious in activity yet masterful in organization and clear in purpose.

After the war, in 1945 he became engineering manager for Stone and Webster and a year later was elected vice-president. Klein was a dynamic, ebullient man. His visits to the field were marked by all-night poker games, and he was also a vigorous and accomplished pianist. Although heavy demands were made on his time, he maintained a warm, lively family life, full of outdoor activities, at his Newton Center home. In 1947, in recognition of his work on the atomic bomb project, Stevens Institute of Technology awarded him an honorary D.Sc. In the following winter, while vacationing at Montego Bay, Jamaica, he died of coronary thrombosis after a golf game. His manner of passing was characteristic. He lay down to rest; suddenly exclaimed, "This is all nonsense"; sprang to his feet; and fell back dead. He was buried in Mount Auburn Cemetery, Cambridge, Mass.

[Sources include Richard G. Hewlett and Oscar E. Anderson, Jr., *A Hist. of the U.S.A.E.C.*, Vol. I (1962); Leslie R. Groves, *Now It Can Be Told* (1962); Stéphane Groueff, *Manhattan Project* (1967); Herbert Childs, *An American Genius* (1968); *N.Y. Times*, Feb. 6, 1948, includes photograph, and information from Klein's son James H. Klein and from Edward S. Steinbach, T. Cortlandt Williams, Ray L. Geddes, Marjorie Howe, and other associates of Klein's at Stone and Webster.]

ROBERT V. BRUCE

KNOX, ROSE MARKWARD (Nov. 18, 1857–Sept. 27, 1950), manufacturer, was born in Mansfield, Ohio, soon after her parents moved there from Pennsylvania. The third daughter of David Markward and Amanda (Foreman) Markward, she was christened Helen Rosetta. Her father was a successful druggist until the Panic of 1873, when he lost heavily on real estate investments. Rose Markward attended public school in Mansfield. When she was in her early twenties, the family moved to Gloversville, N.Y., where she began to work in a factory sewing gloves. There she met a glove salesman, Charles Briggs Knox, and on Feb. 15, 1883, with railroad tickets and $11 in pocket, they were married; they had two sons, Charles Markward and James Elisha, and a daughter, Helen, who died in infancy. After living first in New York and then in Newark, N.J., Charles Knox, who became a knit-goods salesman, saved $5,000. The Knoxes decided to invest in manufacturing a prepared gelatin—a product readily received in an age which was lightening women's housework. For the site of his factory Charles, in 1890, chose his hometown, Johnstown, N.Y., where tanneries provided calf pates from which gelatinous protein could be extracted. While Knox advertised in ways unusual for the time—with racehorses and balloon ascensions—his wife learned the details of manufacturing and concentrated on expanding the uses of gelatin, which was so tedious to make in the home that it was used only for festivities and illnesses. In 1896 she wrote a booklet of recipes, *Dainty Desserts*.

When Charles Knox died in 1908, friends advised his widow to sell the business, but she decided to keep it for her children. After an accountant discovered dishonesty in an assistant, she concluded that she must manage the business herself. Worried about the effect of a woman president upon the trade, she announced that she was carrying on for her son Charles, who was in school. Charles died soon after, and although her son James entered the firm as her assistant in 1913, she continued as president until her ninetieth birthday in 1947.

Her first important decision was to concentrate on gelatin. She sold other businesses in which her husband had been involved—a newspaper and newsplant, a hardware store, a power plant, a new line of medicated ointments. She determined to run the business "in what I call a woman's way, because . . . after all it was women who purchased gelatine" (*Time*, Nov. 29, 1937). No more horses and advertising stunts; instead she stressed nutrition, economy, sanitary production, and attractive recipes. She published another cookbook in 1917, *Food Economy*, and printed recipes on gelatin boxes and in ads under "Mrs. Knox Says." She campaigned to convince doctors of gelatin's value for certain dietetic deficiencies. To improve her product she established an experimental kitchen and pioneered in industrial research, spending more than $500,000 in twenty years endowing fellowships at the Mellon Institute to discover new uses for gelatin. At her death, 40 percent of her company's output was sold for industrial (particularly photography) and medical purposes.

The tone of her relations with her employees was set immediately: benign but brisk. When she first assumed the presidency, she ordered the rear door of the plant closed, explaining to her employees, "We are all ladies and gentlemen working together here and we will all come in through the front door" (*Time*, Nov. 29, 1937). There were no time clocks. In 1913 she initiated the five-day week—with the proviso that workers produce as much as they had in five and a half days. The company provided two-week paid vacations, sick leave, and pensions. Knox insisted that grievances be brought to her, and in 1937, although some of her employees were terrified of crossing her, their loyalty was indicated by the fact that 85 percent of them had been in her service at least twenty-five years.

In 1911 she moved into a larger and better-designed building; by 1915 volume had tripled and the company was incorporated at $300,000. This was increased to $1 million in 1925. After World War I Argentina became the new source for calf pates. Because more Argentine beef was canned, more bones and pates were available for the manufacture of gelatin. In order to meet increasing demands, Knox began purchasing gelatin from Kind and Landesmann of Camden, N.J., a company conveniently located for importing calf pates. In 1916 she bought a 50 percent interest in the firm, and in 1930 became vice-president of Kind and Knox Gelatine Company. She also established a company in Canada. During the depression, rather than laying off employees, she continued to expand her facilities and added a new factory in Camden for the manufacture of flavored gelatin.

Knox favored the use of natural fruit juices, but, in 1935, she followed her competitors and produced artificially flavored gelatin, which was made entirely in New Jersey. The unflavored gelatin was also made in New Jersey but packaged in Johnstown—an inefficient procedure that expressed the identification she had with her community. She donated an athletic field, stadium, and clubhouse to the town, a swimming pool to the YMCA, books for school libraries, and contributions to the Presbyterian, Slovak Catholic, and African Methodist Episcopal Zion churches, She established the Willing Helpers Home for Women, helped found the Federation of Women's Clubs for Civic Improvement of Johnstown in 1920 (becoming its first president), and helped the Business and Professional Woman's Club establish a student loan fund. She induced the Johnstown Historical Society to restore the baronial mansion of Sir William Johnston, an eighteenth-century fur trader and military leader. Her hobby was raising orchids, which she soon made into a profitable business.

Frequently recognized as an outstanding businesswoman, she was the first woman to attend meetings of the American Grocery Manufacturers' Association and the first to be elected to its board (1929). She was not a militant feminist: "Motherhood comprises the future and well-being of our country" (*N.Y. Times*, Feb. 19, 1939). Yet she also wrote, "From my own experience I know it is entirely possible to happily blend home life and business life" (Howes, p. xiv).

Rose Knox expressed her formula for living: "Think about the things you can help, do not think about those you cannot" (Neely, II, 696). She died of a cerebral thrombosis and is buried in Johnstown Cemetery.

[For biographical information, see Robert Lovett, *Notable Am. Women*, II, 343–344; *Current Biog.*, 1949; Ruth Neely, ed., *Women of Ohio*, II, 696–697 (1939); Mary Mullett, "How One Man Trained His Wife to Take Care of Herself," *Am. Mag.*, Oct. 1921, p. 34, on her business training and decision-making philosophy; Edith Asbury, "Grand Old Lady of Johnstown," *Colliers*, Jan. 1, 1949, p. 20; *Time*, Nov. 29, 1937, p. 55; *Fortune*, Sept. 1935, p. 83; *Independent Woman*, Feb. 2, 1949, p. 51; *N.Y. Times*: May 23, 1937, p. 28; Feb. 19, 1939, p. 5; obit., Nov. 29, 1950, p. 27. The 1939 *Times* article gives Knox's views on women and their careers, as does the foreword for Durward Howes, ed., *Am. Women, 1935–1936*, p. xiv (1935). A letter of May 9, 1973, from her grandson-in-law, George A. Graham, was most helpful. Pictures are in *Fortune*, *Independent Woman*, *Time*, *Current Biog.*, and the *N.Y. Times* obit.]

NANCY P. NORTON

KNUDSEN, WILLIAM S. (Mar. 25, 1879–Apr. 27, 1948), automobile manufacturer, government administrator in World War II, was born in Copenhagen, Denmark, to Knud Peter Knudsen and Augusta (Zollner) Knudsen. Christened Signius Wilhelm Poul, he was the first of six children and only son of his father's second marriage; the family also included three sons and a daughter by his first marriage. The elder Knudsen had headed a family cooperage business, but went bankrupt after the financial panic of 1873 and then became a customs inspector.

Young Knudsen was reared in a household managed by a resourceful mother and shaped by the values of frugality, self-reliance, and Lutheran piety. Beginning at the age of six, he worked after school to supplement the modest family income. He completed high school with honors in mathematics and for two years was a night student at the government technical school in Copenhagen, while serving an apprenticeship in a wholesale bicycle shop managed by a brother. His interest in mechanical design and construction was further stimulated by his close study of the American machine tools and the English and German bicycles handled by an importing firm which he joined in 1898.

Immigrating to the United States early in 1900, Knudsen worked first as a riveter and reamer at the Seabury shipyards in New York City. When a timekeeper there balked at recording the young immigrant's full given name, Knudsen became "William S.," the form he used for the rest of his life. Late in 1900 he took a job as a boilermaker in the Erie Railroad shops at Salamanca, N.Y. He left in 1902 to become a bench hand in the John R. Keim Mills in Buffalo, N.Y., a factory specializing in the manufacture of bicycle parts, where he rose within a few years to assistant superintendent. Six feet three inches tall and powerfully built

(he was known for much of his career as "Big Bill"), Knudsen found himself pitted against hard-fisted men in the hurly-burly of factory life at Buffalo. By mastering his own hot temper, he learned how to persuade others to accept his leadership.

With the decline of the "bicycle craze" after 1904, the Keim plant began to manufacture automobile parts. Knudsen visited the Detroit plant of Ford Motor Company in 1906 and obtained a $75,000 order for crankcases and rear-axle housings for the future Model T. By 1910 Ford's newly opened plant at Highland Park, Mich., had become the company's largest customer. Ford purchased the Keim Mills in 1911, and thus also acquired the talents of Knudsen. On November 1 of that year Knudsen married Clara Elizabeth Euler of Buffalo, N.Y. They had four children: Semon Emil (later an executive of General Motors and Ford), Clara Augusta, Elna Louise, and Martha Ellen.

In 1913 Ford called the husky Dane to Detroit and soon put him in charge of laying out and installing manufacturing operations in fourteen Ford assembly plants then being planned, built, or enlarged in principal American cities. Knudsen was made head of the company's branch assembly operations in 1915 and, later the same year, production manager at Highland Park. He was soon earning $25,000 a year plus a 15 percent bonus. Meanwhile, he became a citizen in 1914.

In his mid-thirties, Knudsen was already a seasoned factory administrator with a far-ranging command of the arts of mass production. He became a key figure in refining and applying on a broader scale the complex techniques of the moving assembly line that made automobile manufacture the technological pacesetter of American industry in the first half of the twentieth century. In his swift rise to managerial rank, he never disguised the fact, then and later, that he was essentially a self-taught master mechanic. His natural element was the shop floor, where, surrounded by tools and blueprints, he frequently could be found solving a difficult problem by trial and error.

After the United States entered World War I, Knudsen supervised the production of army ambulances and trucks, aircraft motors, and other war matériel at Highland Park. The Ford Motor Company in 1918 received a $46 million contract for the construction of navy-designed submarine patrol vessels known as "Eagle Boats," and Knudsen was put in charge of the project. At facilities he quickly erected on the River Rouge in Dearborn, Mich., he adapted mass production methods to the progressive assembly of the 200-ton steel vessels, but the war ended before production had gone into full swing.

After the war, Knudsen went to Europe to inspect the Ford overseas organization and to revamp its administrative structure. He returned in 1920 to his post as head of manufacturing operations at Highland Park, but soon found himself in a thickening atmosphere of court intrigue, with his orders systematically countermanded by Ford and an inner circle of sycophantic executives. Personal relations between the two men had never been close, and though each respected the other's abilities, there were reservations on both sides. Early in 1921, when Knudsen was on the verge of resigning, Ford ordered his discharge.

A year later (after an interim job as general manager of a Detroit firm making automobile parts) Knudsen joined the General Motors Corporation as a staff adviser. Within three weeks he was named vice-president of the Chevrolet division in charge of operations, at a salary of $50,000 a year. With the ouster of General Motors' founder, William C. Durant, in 1920 and the rise of Alfred P. Sloan, Jr., who became president in 1923, the corporation was undergoing extensive overhauling. The Chevrolet division was languishing, but despite the report of a firm of consulting engineers that the low-priced Chevrolet could not compete with Ford's Model T and should be discontinued, Sloan decided to retain it as the popular-priced car in the General Motors line. Knudsen quickly improved the Chevrolet division's sales and profit performance. He strengthened the dealer organization, made a survey of consumer preferences, and introduced new mechanical and styling features, including an improved four-cylinder engine and semielliptic springs. With such innovations, he increased Chevrolet sales from 72,806 in 1921 to 723,104 in 1926, by which time the Chevrolet was, next to the Ford, the largest-selling car in the expanding low-priced market. Meanwhile, in January 1924, Knudsen had been made president and general manager of the Chevrolet division and a vice-president and director of General Motors.

With the support of a generous corporate expansion policy, Knudsen set out to match Ford's production facilities and overtake him in sales. Perceiving a growing consumer demand for better styling and mechanical improvements, which Ford was slow in acknowledging, Knudsen redesigned the Chevrolet between 1924 and 1926. He surpassed Ford's sales in 1927—the year

Ford was forced to discontinue in May the Model T and retool for the Model A—and in virtually every succeeding year. Knudsen's mastery of production technology was demonstrated in 1928, when, as a result of careful planning and a pilot production line, he was able in forty-five days to effect a complete changeover from the four-cylinder Chevrolet to a new six-cylinder model with a larger wheelbase. By contrast, Ford had required almost a year for the full changeover, including design and production, from the Model T to the Model A.

Although hit hard by the Great Depression, Chevrolet, under Knudsen's leadership, continued to increase its share of total automobile sales throughout the 1930's. It was the only General Motors division to earn a profit in every year in the decade 1927-1937, and during that period its combined net profit, before federal income taxes, accounted for 51.6 percent of the aggregate earnings of all General Motors automotive divisions. In 1933 Knudsen became executive vice-president of General Motors in charge of all car, truck, and body operations in the United States and Canada, a position second only to that of Sloan. In 1937 he succeeded Sloan (who became chairman of the board) as president of General Motors—by then the world's largest manufacturing corporation. With earnings in salary and bonus rising as high as $507,645 in 1936, Knudsen was for most of the 1930's one of the ten highest paid men in the United States.

During the early years of the Roosevelt administration, Knudsen contributed to the formulation of both industry-wide and corporate policy, especially on labor matters. In 1933, as chairman of the Labor Relations Committee of the National Automobile Chamber of Commerce (later the Automobile Manufacturers Association), he helped draft the automobile code of the National Recovery Administration. He was often the General Motors spokesman before the NRA's National Labor Board, and in 1937 he played a prominent part in the negotiations which ended the six-week sit-down strike that had shut down eighteen General Motors plants. The agreement signed by General Motors and the United Automobile Workers that March opened the way to the rapid unionization of the motorcar industry. Although Knudsen generally shared the business community's hostility to the New Deal, he was never closely identified with the doctrinaire conservative position.

World War II brought Knudsen a new role. In May 1940 President Roosevelt, responding to the German sweep across France and the Low

Countries, called for a program of defense production with a goal of 50,000 planes a year. To guide the program he set up a seven-man National Defense Advisory Commission, to which, on the urging of his advisors, he appointed Knudsen as the nation's foremost production specialist. Like other American industrialists, Knudsen had expressed a tactful goodwill toward the Nazi regime in the mid-1930's, and, whatever his private reservations, had been noncommittal during the early stages of the war. The German invasion of Denmark affected him profoundly, however, and his anti-Axis position crystallized with the fall of France. He accepted Roosevelt's offer and, in order to give his full time without conflict of interest, resigned all his General Motors posts in September.

The NDAC, which faced the prodigious task of correlating domestic defense needs with burgeoning British demands, was a makeshift organization with purely advisory functions. Although its members included Edward R. Stettinius, Jr., of United States Steel as commissioner of industrial materials and Sidney Hillman of the Amalgamated Clothing Workers of America as commissioner of employment, Knudsen as commissioner of industrial production held the key post. There is little doubt that Roosevelt chose him in the hope of throwing a bridge to industrial management and of winning the ready cooperation of the automotive industry and its enormous potential for rearmament. Throughout the summer of 1940 Knudsen concentrated on removing bottlenecks in the production of machine tools, aircraft engines, tanks, and other critical items, and mapped out defense needs in conjunction with a group that included Secretary of War Henry L. Stimson, Secretary of the Navy Frank Knox, and Army Chief of Staff Gen. George C. Marshall. Although Knudsen's efforts were seriously hampered by his lack of experience in Washington politics and by the organizational shortcomings of the NDAC, the commission did win the important authority to place all contracts of $500,000 or more, a power which was vested in Knudsen and another NDAC member, Donald M. Nelson, a former Sears, Roebuck executive. Knudsen, who handled ordnance, aircraft, and other "hard goods," had a decisive role in the channeling of contracts.

The huge expansion of domestic and foreign military requirements in 1940–1941 brought into focus a fundamental policy divergence within the defense production program. Conservatives like Knudsen, who for the most part were drawn from industry, preferred to superimpose the rearmament program on existing industrial resources, which, because of the slack economy, still had ample reserves of labor, machinery, and materials. Oriented to a depression market, they feared that new plants would compound the problem of excess capacity in peacetime. On the other hand, "all-outers" like Nelson and Stimson supported more energetic and sweeping measures. By the autumn of 1940, Knudsen's "business-as-usual" attitude was being criticized by liberals and labor leaders, who also charged that his distribution of contracts had favored big business at the expense of small firms whose facilities for subcontracting had hardly been tapped. He blew up a storm of controversy by his dismissal of the hotly debated Reuther plan (proposed by Walter Reuther of the United Automobile Workers) for large-scale conversion of the auto industry to aircraft manufacture on a mass-production basis.

The impending lend-lease program led President Roosevelt to create, in January 1941, the Office of Production Management, with Knudsen as director general and Sidney Hillman as associate director general. Like the NDAC, the OPM institutionalized the diffusion of authority over industrial mobilization, and its record was similarly spotty. Policy differences between Knudsen and Hillman, however, did not interfere with a cordial personal relationship. Knudsen's high standing in the administration began to decline in April, when an agreement he reached with automobile manufacturers for a 20 percent curtailment of car production was regarded by the White House as inadequate. A second blow resulted from an intense struggle with Leon Henderson, head of the Office of Price Administration and Civilian Supply, for control of the priorities system. Roosevelt, in August 1941, established the Supply Priorities and Allocation Board as the policy-making and coordinating agency for the entire defense program, thus reducing OPM to a mere operating agency. Both the OPM and the SPAB came to an end after Pearl Harbor with the creation of the War Production Board (January 1942), headed by Donald Nelson.

Knudsen prepared to return to Detroit, but instead was induced to accept an army commission as a lieutenant general (the only civilian in American history appointed directly to that rank). As special advisor to Undersecretary of War Robert P. Patterson, he spent the next two and a half years expediting production in plants with War Department contracts, an assignment congenial to his talents and interests. Secretary

Stimson hailed Knudsen as a "tower of strength" in production operations and a "master trouble-shooter." In September 1944 Knudsen became director of the Air Technical Service Command and was given the responsibility of purchasing, distributing, and maintaining all aircraft and other equipment used by the Army Air Forces. He retired from the army in May 1945.

In his later years Knudsen's pink complexion, blue eyes, silvery hair and moustache, and amiable disposition gave him the appearance of a kindly, roughhewn giant. He was simple and unpretentious in demeanor, although he retained an Old World courtliness. He was a self-taught amateur musician and a voracious reader.

After leaving the army, Knudsen was elected to the board of directors of General Motors. A year later he joined the board of the Hupp Corporation, a manufacturing firm based in Detroit and Cleveland, and became its chairman. In 1948, perhaps worn out by his wartime exertions, he died at the age of sixty-nine of a cerebral hemorrhage at his Detroit home. He was buried in Acacia Park Cemetery, Royal Oak, Mich.

Knudsen's career spanned two distinct eras in the automotive industry. Having been intimately associated with the developmental phase between 1907 and 1921, during which the principles of mass production were evolved and applied, he played a leading role in adapting those principles to the market of the 1920's, which witnessed a new departure in automobile merchandising and saw the rise of the industry's "Big Three" corporations. With Henry Ford, William Durant, Walter P. Chrysler, and a few others, Knudsen looms large among the figures who pushed America into the motor age. In his government role, hampered as he was by an unfamiliar context and by the ambiguities, before Pearl Harbor, of a transitional stage between peace and war, he yet earned a secure place as one of the architects of wartime production.

[There is no collection of Knudsen papers. Norman Beasley, *Knudsen: A Biog.* (1947), an authorized work, is eulogistic and occasionally inaccurate but has some valuable materials drawn from the subject's files. Two informative and generally accurate biographical sketches are Christy Borth, *Masters of Mass Production* (1945), chap. ii, and Matthew Josephson's *New Yorker* profile, Mar. 8, 15, and 22, 1941. See also L. C. Gray, "Defense Commissioner Knudsen," *Current Hist.*, Aug. 1940, p. 12; and *N.Y. Times*, Apr. 28 and 30, 1948. Knudsen's years with the Ford Motor Co. are best traced in Allan Nevins and Frank Ernest Hill, *Ford*, 3 vols., (1954–1963); and Mira Wilkins and Frank Ernest Hill, *Am. Business Abroad: Ford on Six Continents* (1964). There is material in the Ford Arch., Henry Ford Museum, Dearborn, Mich., especially the memorandum of an interview

with Knudsen by S. T. Miller and F. D. Jones, June 25, 1926, and the oral reminiscences of Ernest C. Kanzler and Charles E. Sorensen. See also Sorensen's *My Forty Years with Ford* (with Samuel T. Williamson, 1956). For Knudsen's career with General Motors, see articles on G.M. in *Fortune*, Dec. 1938 and Jan. 1939; E. D. Kennedy, *The Automobile Industry* (1941); John B. Rae, *The Am. Automobile* (1965); Sidney Fine, *The Automobile Under the Blue Eagle* (1963) and *Sit-Down: The General Motors Strike of 1936–1937* (1969); J. Woodford Howard, Jr., *Mr. Justice Murphy* (1968); and Walter Galenson, *The CIO Challenge to the AFL* (1960). Knudsen's role in defense and war production is illuminated by various MS holdings, such as the Henry L. Stimson Papers (Yale Univ.), Robert P. Patterson Papers (Lib. of Cong.), records of the NDAC and OPM (Nat. Arch.), and the papers of Franklin D. Roosevelt and Harry L. Hopkins, and diaries of Henry J. Morgenthau, Jr., at the Franklin D. Roosevelt Lib., Hyde Park, N.Y. The best single published source is the official history, U.S. Civilian Production Administration, *Industrial Mobilization for War* (1947); see also U.S. Bureau of the Budget, *The U.S. at War* (1946). For criticism, the files of the *Nation* and *New Republic* are indispensable, especially Jonathan Mitchell, "Is Our Defense Lagging?" *New Republic*, Aug. 26, 1940, and I. F. Stone's Washington correspondence in the *Nation*. Knudsen's activities are placed against their national and world setting in William L. Langer and S. Everett Gleason, *The Challenge to Isolation, 1937–1940* (1952), and *The Undeclared War, 1940–1941* (1953); Mark S. Watson, *Chief of Staff: Prewar Plans and Preparations* (1950); R. Elberton Smith, *The Army and Economic Mobilization* (1959); and Wesley Frank Craven and James L. Cate, eds., *The Army Air Force in World War II*, VI (1955). Bruce Catton, *The War Lords of Washington* (1948), and Eliot Janeway, *The Struggle for Survival* (1951), are partisan but illuminating interpretations. On the conversion of the automotive industry, see "War is Horsepower," *Fortune*, Nov. 1941; and Barton J. Bernstein, "The Automobile Industry and the Coming of the Second World War," *Southwestern Social Sci. Quart.*, June 1966. For portraits and appraisals of Knudsen in government service, see Edward S. Greenbaum in *Saturday Evening Post*, June 26, 1948; Donald M. Nelson, *Arsenal of Democracy* (1946): Matthew Josephson, *Sidney Hillman* (1952): John M. Blum, *From the Morgenthau Diaries: Years of Urgency, 1938–1941* (1965): Henry L. Stimson and McGeorge Bundy, *On Active Service in Peace and War* (1948); Robert E. Sherwood, *Roosevelt and Hopkins* (1948); and Samuel I. Rosenman, *Working with Roosevelt* (1952).]

WILLIAM GREENLEAF

KOCH, FRED CONRAD (May 16, 1876-Jan. 26, 1948), biochemist, was born in Chicago, Ill., the son of Frederick Koch and Louise Henrietta (Fischer) Koch. His father, a native of Gudensberg, Germany, settled in Chicago in 1865; his mother was born in Elmhurst, Ill. The Koch family, which included three daughters, Gertrude, Adelheid, and Carlotte, moved to Elmhurst in 1882, where the son received his primary education. He graduated from Oak Park High School and received his B.S. in chemistry from the University of Illinois in 1899, followed a year later by an M.S. from the same institution.

His next two years were spent as an instructor in chemistry at the University of Illinois.

On Aug. 20, 1901, Koch married Bertha Ethel Zink, the daughter of John Tilghman Zink of Lehighton, Pa. Subsequently, he took a research chemist position with Armour and Company in Chicago. In 1909, feeling the need for more fundamental training, he won a graduate fellowship at the University of Chicago; he studied under Albert P. Mathews in the department of physiological chemistry. He received the Ph.D. in 1912, for a thesis entitled, "On the Nature of the Iodine-containing Complex in Thyreoglobulin."

The next twenty-nine years were spent on the staff of the University of Chicago, where he advanced from instructor in 1912 to full professor in 1923. Koch's first wife died in 1918, and four years later, on Sept. 7, 1922, he married Elizabeth Miller, daughter of Charles Miller of East Chicago. She was also a biochemist. There were no children by either marriage. After their marriage, she became a research associate in pharmacology and pediatrics in the medical college of the University of Illinois, and from 1926 to 1941 was research instructor in biochemistry at the University of Chicago. In 1926, after having served as acting chairman since 1919, Koch was elected chairman of the department of physiological chemistry and pharmacology and served in that capacity until his retirement in 1941. Upon retirement he was named Frank P. Hixon distinguished service professor emeritus and thereupon took a position with Armour and Company as director of biochemical research.

Koch's research covered a wide range of interest, chiefly in the areas of internal secretions, including hormones, vitamins, and quantitative analytical methods. His laboratory is best known for its work during the period around 1928 on the male hormone testosterone. In collaboration with Lemuel C. McGee and others Koch prepared a potent extract from the lipid (fatty) fraction of bulls' testicles, thus obtaining a male hormone in a crude form for the first time. Injection of small quantities of the extract into capons caused accentuation of secondary sex characteristics, notably growth of the comb. Koch and Thomas F. Gallagher made comb growth the basis for bioassay of testicular hormone preparations; the "capon unit" being "the amount which, injected per day for 5 days, produces an average of 5 mm. increase in length and height of the combs on at least five brown leghorn capons."

Koch later developed methods for the extraction of male hormones from human urine. This work eventually led to the isolation and synthesis of androsterone by Adolf Butenandt at Danzig in 1931, and later of testosterone and other androgens (male hormones). Other researchers on secretions involved work on secretin and other gastrointestinal hormones, thyroid and pituitary hormones, and on the activation of pepsin, rennin, and trypsinogen. He also worked on blood chemistry and, with his second wife, was the first to observe the conversion of heat-treated cholesterol to provitamin D in 1925.

Koch is also credited with several inventions of laboratory equipment, the best known of which is the Koch pipette. Among his other apparatus were a stopcock pipette with reservoir, a modified van Slyke apparatus for determination of amino nitrogen, and a microburette. In addition to numerous research papers, he was the author of a manual, *Practical Methods in Biochemistry* (1934), the fourth edition of which was published in 1944; a fifth edition (1948) was coauthored by a departmental colleague, Martin E. Hanke.

Koch had great influence as a teacher of biochemists. Forty students received the Ph.D. under his direction, many of them going on to positions of distinction in research institutions. He was noted in the classroom for clear exposition and emphasis on the quantitative approach to biochemical problems. He was methodical and conservative and known among his friends as a refined person, with good taste and deep consideration for the interests of his students and friends. He spoke thoughtfully and with quiet good humor. He enjoyed symphonic music, golf, and fishing, and was a camera enthusiast. With his second wife he traveled extensively in the United States by automobile trailer. In his later years they built a summer home at Ephraim, Wis., and spent substantial amounts of their time there.

He received numerous honors—Harvey Society lecturer, Julius Steiglitz memorial lecturer in 1941, and president of the Association for the Study of Internal Secretions (now the Endocrine Society) from 1937-1938. In 1930 Koch was the American delegate to the Second International Congress for Sex Research in London; in 1935 he was a member of the League of Nations Committee on the Biological Standardization of Sex Hormones, meeting in London; in 1941 he was a delegate to the Pan American Congress on Endocrinology when it met in Montevideo. Koch was editor of *Archives of Biochemistry* and in 1936 became a member of the committee on endocrinology, National Research Council. After his retirement in 1941, Koch continued his research projects vigorously at Armour and Company until a stroke in 1946 dictated a decreased pace. His weakened condition, aggravated by pneumonia, led to his death; he was buried in Chicago.

[Koch's work on male hormones is treated in his review papers: "The Male Sex Hormones," *Physiological Rev.* 17 (1937): 153–238; "Hormones," *Annual Rev. of Biochemistry* 9 (1940): 327–352; and "The Steroids," *ibid.* 13 (1944): 263–294. There is reference to Koch's work in Paul De Kruif, *The Male Hormone.* Obituaries are in Thomas L. McMeekin, *Archives of Biochemistry* 17 (1948): 207–209; Martin E. Hanke, *Science* 107 (1948): 671–672; *Chemical and Engineering News,* Feb. 9, 1948, pp. 402–403; *Chicago Tribune,* Jan. 27, 1948, p. 16; *N.Y. Times,* Jan. 27, 1948, p. 26; *School and Society,* Feb. 7, 1948, p. 105. See also *Nat. Cyc. Am. Biog.,* XLVI, 388. The files of the University of Illinois archives contain some information about his life in the Alumni Association files. A partial bibliography of his publications is in J. C. Poggendorff, *Biographisch-Literarisches Handwörterbuch,* VI, 1346–1347 (1937); for those after 1930, see the author indexes of *Chemical Abstracts.*]

AARON J. IHDE

KOFOID, CHARLES ATWOOD (Oct. 11, 1865–May 30, 1947), zoologist, was born on his father's farm near Granville, in north-central Illinois, the oldest of at least four children. His father, Nelson Kofoid, had emigrated from Bornholm, Denmark, in 1860; his mother, Janette (Blake) Kofoid, was a native of Indiana. Nothing is known of Kofoid's childhood and youth until 1883, when he entered the preparatory department of Oberlin College in Ohio; he began the college course two years later, earning his expenses by working as a waiter and sawing wood. Inspired by one of his teachers, Albert Wright, Kofoid became interested in natural history and began making field trips and collecting plants. He started his teaching career by serving as an assistant in the zoology course, and after graduating with the B.A. degree in 1890, he spent an additional year at Oberlin as a teaching fellow. He then entered the graduate school at Harvard University, where he received the M.A. degree in 1892 and the Ph.D. in 1894 with an embryological study of cell lineage in the land slug *Limax,* under the direction of the zoologist Edward L. Mark.

In the fall of 1894 Kofoid became instructor in vertebrate morphology at the University of Michigan, and the following year he moved to Havana, Ill., as superintendent of the biological station of the University of Illinois. He became superintendent of the Illinois State Natural History Survey in 1898 and also taught zoology at the University of Illinois at Urbana (1897–1900). In the rivers and lakes of his native state Kofoid began his professional studies on the microorganisms of fresh water, especially the phytoplankton.

During his stay at Harvard, Kofoid met William Emerson Ritter, who became chairman of the newly established zoology department at the University of California at Berkeley. At Ritter's invitation, Kofoid moved to Berkeley in 1900 as assistant professor of histology and embryology; he was made associate professor in 1904 and, in 1910, professor of zoology and chairman of the department. The two men formed a close personal and professional association that lasted until Ritter's death.

As one of Ritter's chief collaborators, Kofoid played a major role in the development of the Marine Biological Station of San Diego at La Jolla, which from 1903 until 1912 was an adjunct of the Berkeley zoology department for summer research in marine organisms; it then became the Scripps Institution for Biological Research and in 1925 was renamed the Scripps Institution of Oceanography. In addition to his duties at Berkeley, Kofoid helped select La Jolla as the permanent site for the station, enlisted financial support, directed the first building construction, negotiated the transfer of the station to the University of California, and served as assistant director for several years. Because of his involvement in the work of the marine station, he spent his sabbatical leave (1908–1909) visiting similar laboratories in Europe, particularly the Naples Zoological Station, and bought and shipped home new equipment for the La Jolla laboratories. After his return he prepared a detailed report, *The Biological Stations of Europe* (1910), for the United States Bureau of Education.

Much of Kofoid's work in Illinois had been quantitative and statistical studies of the distribution and movement of freshwater plankton. In California he shifted to the study of marine plankton, and in 1904–1905 made a six months' collecting trip to the South Seas with Alexander Agassiz. To facilitate the work of collecting, Kofoid also devised two useful pieces of apparatus, a self-closing bucket, and a horizontal net that could be opened or closed at a chosen depth. Kofoid undertook systematic studies of plankton, particularly the tintinnoids and the dinoflagellates. Perhaps his most important contribution was his extensive work on the morphology of protozoans, carried out with one of his students, Olive Swezy, with whom he wrote *The Free-Living Unarmored Dinoflagellata* (1921).

Kofoid also engaged in research related to public health and other practical problems. He had long been interested in the intestinal protozoans of termites and some of the higher animals. During World War I he was commissioned as a major in the Army Sanitary Corps; there his interest expanded to include human parasitic protozoans, tapeworms, hookworms, and other intestinal parasites. After the war he directed a laboratory of parasitology for the California State Board of Health which provided careful training for medical technicians. Other researches in the interest of public service were a study of the marine boring organisms that were damaging waterfront installations in California harbors, another on the life history of termites, and a project to detect and control plankton organisms that could contaminate the water in the San Francisco reservoirs.

An indefatigable organizer, Kofoid had a passion for detail that may have deterred him from truly great research. His work was the accumulation and cataloguing of facts and the collection of extensive material, not synthesis. His fields of interest were broad, so that he left a large body of data to be classified later, by other workers. Although he contributed much to the taxonomy of protozoans and produced excellent descriptions of individual forms, Kofoid was widely criticized for his tendency to break groups down into too fine classes and hence to name too many new species. Because of his inexperience in parasitology, he often described as new species what others regarded as accepted variations. His abilities in coordinating and organizing research groups, however, were in themselves valuable contributions to science.

Kofoid's predominant traits, according to Goldschmidt (p. 132), were "abundance of energy, the hunger for facts, the need of putting things in order, a great sense of civic responsibility and a general Puritanic outlook on life." He was not a patient man, and as chairman of the department tended to be tyrannical, chiefly because of his impelling urge to get things done. As a professor he was at his best in seminars, for he was not a sparkling lecturer. He took a strong interest in the researches of his many graduate students, with whom he frequently collaborated in publications, and whom he conscientiously helped to find employment. Kofoid also spent much time in editing various scientific periodicals and in writing abstracts and reviews. For many years he served as an editor for *Biological Abstracts* and for the *University of California Publications in Zoology*. He was elected to the National Academy of

Sciences in 1922 and was awarded various medals and honorary degrees.

On June 30, 1894, Kofoid married an Oberlin classmate, Carrie Prudence Winter. They had no children. His wife was active in charitable work and community affairs. Both were members of the Congregational church, and Kofoid took a strong interest in its missionary and other projects. His chief recreations were traveling and collecting books, particularly books relating to the history of biology. Kofoid retired in 1936, at the age of seventy. He died in Berkeley eleven years later of a heart attack and was buried there in Sunset View Cemetery. By his will he left his vast collection of books and reprints to the University of California library, which thus received more than 40,000 volumes not then among its holdings. Through prudent investment he had built up a considerable estate, which he left to the university and to the Pacific School of Religion.

[The fullest account of Kofoid's life and work is the memoir by Richard B. Goldschmidt in Nat. Acad. Sci., *Biog. Memoirs*, XXVI (1949), which includes a portrait and a bibliography of his publications. See also Helen Raitt and Beatrice Moulton, *Scripps Institution of Oceanography: First Fifty Years* (1967); Harold Kirby in *Sci. Monthly*, Nov. 1945, and *Science*, Nov. 14, 1947; Clifford Dobell in *Nature*, July 26, 1947; *Gen. Catalogue of Oberlin College, 1833–1908* (1909). Family data from federal census of 1880, Ill. State Arch.]

ELIZABETH NOBLE SHOR

KUHN, WALT (Oct. 27, 1877–July 13, 1949), painter, whose full name was Walter Francis Kuhn, was born in the Red Hook section of Brooklyn, N.Y. He was the fourth son and fifth of eight children, but only he and a younger sister survived infancy. His parents, Francis Kuhn and Amalia (Hergenhan) Kuhn, were Bavarian Catholic immigrants who had settled in 1861 in Brooklyn, where together they became hotel proprietors and food suppliers to the shipping trade. Amalia Kuhn, half Spanish and the granddaughter of a Spanish consul to the kingdom of Bavaria, encouraged her son's first artistic attempts, and as a result Walt drew throughout his childhood. His mother also interested him in the theater, which may partially account for the essentially dramatic character of his mature paintings.

At the age of fifteen Kuhn sold his first drawing to a magazine; shortly thereafter he left high school and in 1893 took art instruction at the Brooklyn Polytechnic Institute. After working briefly in a sporting goods store and as the owner of a bicycle shop, Kuhn set out in 1899 for California, where for a time he drew cartoons for the *Wasp*, a San Francisco newspaper. Soon, however, he felt the need for more formal training, and, financed by his father, he sailed in early 1901 for Europe. Kuhn studied first at the Académie Colarossi in Paris, but his letters home reveal a distaste for both the academy and the city, and so he quickly left France for Germany. He spent the summer of 1901 at Dachau studying under Hans von Hayek, but his most intensive and sustained apprenticeship took place over the next two years at the Royal Academy in Munich as a pupil of the animal painter Heinrich von Zügel. Returning to New York in 1903, Kuhn earned his living as a cartoonist for *Puck, Judge,* and *Life* magazines and for several newspapers. On Feb. 6, 1909, he married Vera Spier of Washington, D.C., a designer of jewelry. Their only child, Brenda, was born in 1911. Two months after his marriage Kuhn quit his regular job as cartoonist on the *New York World* in order to devote more time to his painting. Despite his expressed dislike for Paris, Kuhn's art at this time was a derivative continuation of French impressionism.

In conjunction with his increased commitment to a career as a painter, Kuhn began to make social contact with the New York art world. He frequented the weekly studio receptions held by Robert Henri, taught in the winter of 1908–1909 at the New York School of Art, and about 1910 met Arthur B. Davies. He was given his first one-man show at the Madison Gallery during the winter of 1910–1911; and it was in this gallery in December 1911 that Kuhn and three other painters, Henry Fitch Taylor, Jerome Myers, and Elmer Livingston MacRae, met to discuss the possibility of creating a society to exhibit the works of progressive American and European painters.

It was thus that the Association of American Painters and Sculptors was established, and its one exhibition, the Armory Show of 1913, was a significant turning point in the history of American art. Kuhn, as executive secretary of the association, traveled to Cologne, The Hague, Munich, and Berlin in the autumn of 1912 selecting examples of the most advanced European painting and sculpture for the show. He was joined in Paris by Arthur B. Davies, who was president of the association, and together with Walter Pach they completed the task of gathering the art that was to shift the main current of painting in the United States away from American scene realism for nearly two decades. After the Armory Show, Kuhn's own style, like that of Davies, changed abruptly under the pressure to assimilate European modernism. From 1912 through the early 1920's

his art reflects, in an extremely eclectic manner, the various cubist experiments, as well as the paintings of Matisse, Cézanne, Dufy, Derain, and Signac. In these years, for financial reasons, Kuhn's energies were dispersed in a variety of directions; he designed costumes for the circus and theater, created routines for vaudeville, and acted as adviser to the art collectors John Quinn and Lizzie (later known as Lillie) Bliss. Despite his somewhat solitary nature, he maintained friendships during the 1920's with George Overbury ("Pop") Hart, Jules Pascin, and William Glackens.

In 1925 Kuhn suffered from a serious stomach ulcer, and the resulting awareness of mortality forced him to come to grips with the fact that he had not yet achieved distinction as a painter. (At about this time, apparently self-conscious about his slow artistic development, he subtracted three years from his true age.) In the spring of 1925 Kuhn set out for Europe, determined to study systematically the old masters in the Louvre and the Prado. Resolving in a letter to his wife that he would combine the styles of Greek and Egyptian art with the painting freedom and confidence of Goya, Kuhn returned from Europe, and by 1929, in such works as *The White Clown,* he succeeded in creating a fully self-expressing idiom. The decade of the 1930's brought him considerable recognition. Exhibiting regularly at the Marie Harriman Gallery in New York, and also advising the Harrimans in matters of acquisition, Kuhn was praised by critics for the frankness and power of his pictures. In 1932 the Whitney Museum bought one of his circus portraits, *The Blue Clown.* Kuhn's style and message remained virtually unchanged from this point on; he had found his formula and continued to practice it until a nervous breakdown brought about his hospitalization in November 1948. He died suddenly the following summer of a perforated stomach ulcer in White Plains, N.Y. His ashes were interred in Woodlawn Cemetery in New York.

Although Kuhn painted a considerable number of landscapes and still lifes during his career, his portraits of circus performers, and clowns in particular, were his most successful artistic achievement. The melancholy of these lonely figures derived from the portraits of Goya and, ultimately, from Rembrandt. Yet Kuhn's pictures were not without more immediate predecessors. It was Robert Henri who first made popular among earlier twentieth-century artists the dramatic power of Spanish and Dutch art. Kuhn's achievement, in this sense, was a somewhat belated although authentic continuation of the Ashcan School, with additional roots as well in the clown paintings of Picasso, Derain, and Rouault. Furthermore, Kuhn's oeuvre, although rarely flawed by sentimentality, cannot compare in the depth or range of its melancholy to that of his contemporary Edward Hopper. Like many of the realists of the 1930's and 1940's Kuhn struggled to reconcile his desire for deep characterization with the problems of aesthetic structure. Paradoxically, Kuhn himself, in his most historically significant act, bequeathed these aesthetic problems to his generation by creating and promoting the Armory Show.

[A large collection of unpublished letters and other Kuhn papers is on deposit in the Arch. of Am. Art, Smithsonian Institution, Washington, D.C. Kuhn's pamphlet, *The Story of the Armory Show* (1938), is a generally accurate account of the exhibition. Also of interest are his "Cézanne: Delayed Finale," *Art News*, Apr. 1947; "Kuhn's Advice," *Art Digest*, May 1, 1942; and his contribution to an article on Albert Ryder, *Art News*, Nov. 1947. An interview with the artist can be found in *Art Digest*, Nov. 1, 1948. Although there is no definitive biography, Milton Brown, *The Story of the Armory Show* (1963), has a complete account of Kuhn's role in the exhibition. Brown's *American Painting, from the Armory Show to the Depression* (1955), contains the most extensive analysis of the artist's style. Paul Bird, *Fifty Paintings by Walt Kuhn* (1940), contains comments on individual paintings apparently written by both the author and the artist. Also important are the following exhibition catalogues: *Walt Kuhn, 1877–1949* (Cincinnati Art Museum, 1960); *Painter of Vision* (Univ. of Ariz. Art Gallery, 1966); and *Walt Kuhn* (Kennedy Galleries, 1967). Obituaries are by Philip R. Adams, *College Art Jour.*, Autumn 1949; and Alfred M. Frankfurter, *Art News*, Sept. 1949. A photograph by Edward Weston is the frontispiece to the Cincinnati exhibition catalogue. The correct number of Kuhn's siblings and certain other facts were supplied by the artist's daughter, Brenda Kuhn.]

JOHN H. BAKER

LA GUARDIA, FIORELLO HENRY (Dec. 11, 1882–Sept. 20, 1947), congressman, mayor of New York, the eldest son and second of the three children of Achille Luigi Carlo La Guardia and Irene (Coen) La Guardia, was born in the Italian section of Greenwich Village, New York City, two years after the arrival of his immigrant parents. The product of a mixed marriage—his father, a musician from Foggia, Italy, was a lapsed Catholic; his mother, a merchant's daughter from Trieste, Austria, was Jewish—La Guardia was reared an Episcopalian, and was to marry first a Catholic and then a Lutheran. All this and much more led fellow New Yorkers to toast him as "the cosmopolite of this most cosmopolitan city." La Guardia was brought up on Western army posts, where his father served as an enlisted bandmaster (1885-1898), and he was educated through the eighth grade in the public schools of Prescott, Ariz. Upon his father's discharge, the family recrossed the Atlantic to Trieste, and La Guardia grew to manhood in the Austro-Hungarian empire. A member of the American consular service from age seventeen through twenty-three, he was stationed in Budapest, then in Fiume, with short assignments in Trieste and Croatia. When he returned in 1906 to New York, from which he had been taken as a child of three, La Guardia was fluent in Hungarian, German, Serbo-Croatian, Yiddish, and Italian.

He was also ambitious and idealistic. In 1910, after putting himself through New York University Law School by taking evening classes while working as an interpreter at Ellis Island, he began practicing law on the Lower East Side. There, too, he formed a lasting association with the emerging clothing workers' trade unions. His closest friends, known locally as the "green geniuses," were young Italian-American bohemians, each of whom vowed to make the world better. La Guardia alone chose to do so through politics. Hostile to Tammany's corruption, he joined his local Republican club, which was more hospitable to aspiring Italian-American politicians than the Irish-dominated Democrats. In 1915, three years after his debut as an election district captain in his native Greenwich Village, La Guardia was appointed a deputy state attorney general.

Thereafter his career turned on elective office, and the multilingual, Western-bred, Balkan-plated Episcopalian of Italian-Jewish descent started with the advantage of being a balanced ticket in himself. But few persons felt neutral about La Guardia the campaigner, who combined the gut-fighting tactics of a political boss from the slums with the issue-oriented politics of a "people's attorney." To his enemies, he was egotistical, strutting and power-hungry, a demagogue and a radical. To his more numerous admirers, the "Little Flower" (the English translation of Fiorello) was colorful, dynamic, contagiously self-confident, progressive, and the deadliest Tammany-killer of his day. In a habitually Democratic city, La Guardia, an irregular Republican but a Republican all the same, won eleven out of fourteen campaigns.

Unlike previous New York mayors, La Guardia rose to prominence in national politics before entering City Hall. In 1916 he became the first Republican since the Civil War to be elected to Congress from the Lower East Side. Despite the neutralism and pacifism of his district, he voted for America's entrance into

World War I in 1917. He also took a leave of absence from the House to serve as a pilot-bombardier on the Italian-Austrian front. Returning home a much decorated major in 1918, he was reelected to Congress, but resigned the following year to run for president of the New York City Board of Aldermen, a post recently vacated by the newly elected governor, Alfred E. Smith. He won, by appealing to normally Democratic nationality groups (including the Irish) who were enraged by President Wilson's Versailles Treaty. In 1921, however, La Guardia lost the Republican primary for mayor. The next year, with the support of the publisher William Randolph Hearst, he was returned to Congress, this time from the Twentieth Congressional District. Supported by a predominantly Italian and Jewish constituency, he served five consecutive terms until 1932.

In the 1920's, as his party led the country in disavowing the Progressive era, East Harlem's representative gave the impression of moving to the left. He ridiculed the hypocrisy of prohibition. He denounced the immigration laws as discriminatory. He opposed the tax plans of Secretary of the Treasury Andrew W. Mellon as favoring the rich. He inveighed against the "food trust" for raising prices beyond the reach of the poor. Blaming his own party for these and other heartless stupidities, La Guardia in 1924 supported the Progressive party presidential candidacy of Robert M. La Follette, and himself stood for reelection as a Progressive. The following year he showed further contempt for the G.O.P. by endorsing the Socialist Norman Thomas in New York's mayoral race.

Although La Guardia returned to the Republican party in 1926, he remained a maverick. The "power trusts" were one of his favorite targets; with Sen. George W. Norris he had waged a successful fight (1924-1926) to prevent the private development of Muscle Shoals by the industrialist Henry Ford. In 1928 La Guardia cosponsored with Norris a measure to permit federal development of the project; it was pocket-vetoed by President Coolidge. One newspaper in the 1920's called him "America's Most Liberal Congressman." La Guardia summed up his own image of himself when he said in 1927: "I am doomed to live in a hopeless minority for most of my legislative days."

A New Dealer before that term was coined, La Guardia came into his own during the Great Depression. In 1932 he led the House in defeating President Hoover's proposed sales tax. More significant still, the Norris-La Guardia Anti-Injunction Act, for which he and the Nebraska senator had agitated throughout the age of normalcy, was passed in the same year. Yet, at the very peak of his congressional career, La Guardia lost his bid for reelection in 1932. "I was beaten," he said bitterly, "by the importation of floaters and repeaters, together with the Puerto Rican vote." When he went back to Congress for the lame-duck session, nobody was surprised when the incoming Roosevelt administration chose him to present its initial legislation.

La Guardia had run for mayor of New York City in 1929 against the popular Democratic incumbent James J. ("Jimmy") Walker and had been defeated by nearly half a million votes. In 1933, when an anti-Tammany Fusion slate was formed under the leadership of Judge Samuel Seabury, whose investigations had led to Mayor Walker's resignation, La Guardia was its nominee. This time the Little Flower was elected. Reelected in 1937 and again in 1941, he was the first reform mayor in New York's history to succeed himself.

A mayor is supposed to be chief executive of his city. La Guardia, who liked to command (the only piece of sculpture he is known to have acquired was a bust of Napoleon), relished his role. When told in 1934 that the Democrats controlled the board of aldermen, he retorted: "I'm the majority in this administration." For the next twelve years, over the city's radio station, before the legislature at Albany, at the Board of Estimate, and elsewhere, he identified good government in New York with his name. And he dramatized it. Despite his aberrant appearance (he was fat and a mere five feet two inches tall)—or perhaps aided by his looks—the Little Flower was a popular showman. He read the Sunday comics over the radio to the "kiddies" in his tenor-alto voice, and raced his own firemen to fires. The press, chronicling his every move and antic, made him the best-known chief executive that New York had ever had.

A mayor is also supposed to be chief legislator, and here, too, the former congressman played his role to the full. In 1934 he secured enabling legislation from Albany to balance the city budget through special taxes and such structural reorganization as the consolidation of the five borough park departments into a single department. Two years later he threw his weight behind a successful referendum for a new city charter. The most advanced municipal constitution of its time, it provided for a deputy mayor, a smaller city council to replace the discredited board of aldermen, and a city planning commission. Through other legislation, La Guardia built the city's first sewage treatment plants, improved the market facilities, and by 1940 achieved both the unification and public ownership of the city's subways.

New York was vital for the New Deal's recovery program, and La Guardia's standing with the Roosevelt administration released a flow of federal funds for projects dear to him. The World War I flyer, who had testified as a defense witness at the court martial of Gen. William ("Billy") Mitchell in 1925, opened New York's first major airport in northern Queens (later named La Guardia Airport). In 1942 ground was broken for Idlewild (later John F. Kennedy International) Airport in southern Queens. La Guardia drew up still other blueprints, and received still other grants from Washington, for schools, playgrounds, swimming pools, bridges, roads, health centers, parks, and even the arts.

Besides raising the quality of urban life, La Guardia's public improvements put men and women back to work in a time of mass unemployment. Organized labor was understandably grateful to him. Further, he reformed the relief system to include rent payments, food allotments, and grants to single men. Also with the help of federal money, La Guardia realized his longstanding ideas about slum clearance. By 1942 the New York City Housing Authority, which he had brought into being eight years earlier, had constructed thirteen public housing projects. He believed in "government with a heart."

What kind of administrator was this mayor? A messy one, by the looks of his desk. Moreover, as his critics pointed out, he delegated authority ungraciously and abused cabinet members. All the same, he attracted, and retained for considerable lengths of service, men of uncommon talent—among them Robert Moses, A. A. Berle, Jr., Newbold Morris, Rexford G. Tugwell, Paul Windels, and Joseph D. McGoldrick. If La Guardia was hard to work for, he appointed first-rate administrators who worked hard for him.

La Guardia's third term fell below the standards of his first two. The truth is, as World War II approached, the anti-Fascist and former flying major no longer cared to be mayor. He hoped that President Roosevelt, in a bipartisan move, would appoint him secretary of war. But that position fell to another Republican, Henry L. Stimson. La Guardia was instead appointed director of civil defense (1941). Unhappy in this role, he applied for an army general's commission and was deeply disappointed when his application was rejected. The wartime Roosevelt administration wanted La Guardia to re-

main in command of the most important city on the home front.

As chief executive, chief legislator, and chief administrator, La Guardia was probably New York's best mayor. But the mayor of a big city, even of a city with so-called nonpartisan elections, is also supposed to be chief of his party. La Guardia thought otherwise; in fact, he was so hostile to injecting party politics into municipal government that he allowed neither himself nor his appointees to hold party office. He and his associates ran on the Republican and City Fusion tickets in 1933, and on both of them and the American Labor ticket in 1937 and 1941. On all occasions he assailed "clubhouse loafers" and "party hacks." Yet, however honored a tradition in urban reform, La Guardia's nonpartisanship (he liked to say there wasn't a Democratic or a Republican way of collecting garbage) turned out to be non-self-sustaining. When he left City Hall after twelve years, there was no party leader to succeed him and no reform machine to carry on what he had started.

An enormous drive for place and power brought La Guardia close to the top of American politics. His personal life was much less full than his public career. He did not marry until he was thirty-seven. On Mar. 8, 1919, he married Thea Almerigotti, a native of Trieste; they had one child, Fioretta Thea. Both wife and infant daughter died of tuberculosis in 1921. La Guardia's second marriage, on Feb. 28, 1929, was to Marie Fischer, a native New Yorker who had been his secretary for fifteen years; the childless couple adopted a girl, Jean, and a boy, Eric. Other than a fondness for music, La Guardia had no hobbies. Although the idol of intellectuals, he seldom read anything unrelated to his day-by-day political chores. Too competitive to get along with equals, he had many associates but few friends, and they grew fewer with the passage of the years.

La Guardia left City Hall in 1945 looking older than his sixty-two years. Unwilling to retire, he served, unhappily and unsuccessfully, as director general of the United Nations Relief and Rehabilitation Administration in 1946. In his last public appearance, a commencement address to a boys' school in June 1947, he said: "My generation has failed miserably. . . . It requires more courage to keep the peace than to go to war." Characteristically, La Guardia remained hopeful that, somehow, a rising generation would learn how to make things better. He died a few months later at his home in the Riverdale section of the Bronx of cancer of the pancreas. Funeral services were conducted at the

Episcopal Cathedral of St. John the Divine, where La Guardia had occasionally worshipped. He was buried in Woodlawn Cemetery, New York City.

[La Guardia's voluminous papers, both personal and public, along with some 300 political scrapbooks, are in the Municipal Arch. and Records Center of N.Y. City. Many of the "Reminiscences" of the Columbia Univ. Oral Hist. Collection contain important references to La Guardia. His unfinished autobiography, *The Making of an Insurgent . . . 1882–1919* (1948), is one-dimensional and unreflective. Much more rewarding is Robert Moses, *La Guardia: A Salute and a Memoir* (1957). Other colorful portraits by men who knew La Guardia are Jay Franklin, *La Guardia: A Biog.* (1947); Lowell M. Limpus and Burr Leyson, *This Man La Guardia* (1938); and Ernest Cuneo, *Life with Fiorello* (1955). For a provocative comparison by one of his associates, see Rexford G. Tugwell's *The Art of Politics as Practiced by Three Great Americans: Franklin Delano Roosevelt, Luis Muñoz Marín, and Fiorello H. La Guardia* (1958). La Guardia has been the focus of two published doctoral dissertations, Howard Zinn's *La Guardia in Congress* (1959) and Charles Garrett's *The La Guardia Years* (1961). In *Governing N.Y. City: Politics in the Metropolis* (1960), Wallace S. Sayre and Herbert Kaufman make out a brief but convincing case for La Guardia as the best mayor in the city's history. A contrasting verdict is William H. Allen's *Why Tammanies Revive: La Guardia's Mis-Guard* (1937). For the official version of La Guardia's three mayoral administrations, see Rebecca B. Rankin, ed., *N.Y. Advancing*, 3 vols. (1936–1945). The first two volumes of Arthur Mann's projected three-volume biography have been published under the titles *La Guardia, A Fighter against His Times: 1882–1933* (1959) and *La Guardia Comes to Power: 1933* (1965). For an account of La Guardia's first hundred days as mayor, see Mann, "When La Guardia Took Over," *N.Y. Times Mag.*, Jan. 2, 1966.]

ARTHUR MANN

LAKE, KIRSOPP (Apr. 7, 1872–Nov. 10, 1946), New Testament scholar, was born in Southampton, England, the elder of two surviving children and the only son of George Anthony Kirsopp Lake, a physician, and Isabel Oke (Clark) Lake. His father came from a North Country family, originally Scottish. Kirsopp was the family name of the boy's paternal grandmother. He was educated at St. Paul's School and Lincoln College, Oxford, where he was graduated (B.A., 1895) with a second class in theology.

Lake had an uncommon breadth of interests; he published definitive monographs in textual criticism of the New Testament, Greek paleography, theology, and archeology. His earliest interest was sociological, and his first manuscript (unpublished) was a history of the London dock strike. Initially intending to study law for a career in politics, he was left in delicate health by an influenza attack and he decided on the less strenuous life of a clergyman. He was ordained a deacon in the Church of England in 1895 and a priest the following year. After serving for a year as curate in

Lumley, Durham, he moved to Oxford, where he was curate of St. Mary the Virgin from 1897 until 1904. He also took an M.A. degree there in 1897. During these years he was employed as a cataloguer of Greek manuscripts at the Bodleian Library. His paleographical interests led him to write a useful outline of textual criticism, *The Text of the New Testament* (1900), which went through six revised editions by 1928, and to edit a number of Greek texts, including *Codex 1 of the Gospels and Its Allies* (1902), the group later known as "Family 1" of the "Lake Group" of New Testament manuscripts.

Becoming more interested in history and exegesis than in theology and parish duties, in 1904 Lake became professor ordinarius of early Christian literature and New Testament exegesis at the University of Leiden in Holland. While continuing to publish in paleography and textual criticism, he wrote two important books dealing with historical and exegetical matters, *The Historical Evidence for the Resurrection of Jesus Christ* (1907) and *The Earlier Epistles of St. Paul: Their Motive and Origin* (1911). These studies, particularly the latter, revealed Lake's ability to analyze and evaluate complex historical and literary data and to set forth scholarly reconstructions with clarity and a certain persuasiveness. In the volume on St. Paul, as well as in later monographs, Lake gave particular attention to the Greco-Roman background of the New Testament documents. The literature of the postapostolic age also attracted his interest, and he contributed two volumes to the Loeb Classical Library: *The Apostolic Fathers, with an English Translation* (1912) and the first volume of the Loeb edition of Eusebius' *Ecclesiastical History* (1926).

Lake visited the United States in 1913 to deliver a series of lectures at the Lowell Institute and in King's Chapel in Boston, and to teach for a year at the Episcopal Theological School in Cambridge. A few weeks before his scheduled return to Europe, he accepted the offer of a professorship in early Christian literature at Harvard Divinity School. From 1915 to 1919 he was also lecturer in New Testament at Union Theological Seminary in New York City. In 1919 Lake was appointed to the Winn chair of ecclesiastical history at Harvard on the retirement of Ephraim Emerton. He retained this chair until 1932, when he resigned to become a member of the department of history at Harvard College. One of Lake's major contributions to the understanding of the New Testament was the editing of a five-volume work on the Acts of the Apostles, entitled *The Beginnings of Christianity* (1902–1933); many scholars participated in this endeavor and Lake shared the editing responsibilities with F. J. Foakes Jackson.

Over the years Lake made repeated visits to the libraries at Mount Athos and other places in Europe and the Near East to photograph important Greek manuscripts. The fruits of such expeditions included a handsome facsimile edition of *The Codex Sinaiticus Petropolitanus,* with valuable introductions (New Testament, 1911; Old Testament, 1922). In 1932 Lake and Silva New edited *Six Collations of New Testament Manuscripts,* prepared with the help of several other scholars. Surpassing any of these projects was a magnificent series of ten large albums of facsimiles entitled *Dated Greek Minuscule Manuscripts to the Year 1200* (1934–1939). The several portfolios of reproductions were organized by location, including libraries, containing the four hundred manuscripts of which specimens were reproduced.

During the latter part of his academic career, Lake's interests broadened and he organized several archeological expeditions to the Near East. In 1927, with Robert P. Blake, he went to the Sinai Peninsula in order to investigate the proto-Semitic inscriptions of Serabit el-Khadem (published in 1927). Three trips to Samaria enabled him to renew the unfinished Harvard excavations that had been started by George H. Reisner.

Lake retired in 1938 and subsequently moved to Haverford, Pa., and later to South Pasadena, Calif. He was married twice. On Nov. 10, 1903, he married Helen Courthope Forman, daughter of a businessman of Newcastle-upon-Tyne, Northumberland. They had two children, Gerard Kirsopp and Agnes Kirsopp. The marriage was terminated by divorce in 1932. On December 16 of that year, Lake married Silva New, who had been his student; they had one child, John Anthony Kirsopp. Silva Lake collaborated not only in editing the facsimiles of dated Greek manuscripts, but also in founding in 1934 and editing a series of monographs entitled *Studies and Documents.* She also assisted him in writing *An Introduction to the New Testament* (1937), a volume that embodies the skeleton of a very popular course, the Bible in English, which Lake taught at Harvard and Radcliffe colleges. The popularity of the course, concerned with literary appreciation and ethical teaching, was due in part to his lively imagina-

tion and engaging wit. According to Lake's own considered judgment: "The most important thing in a teacher's life is not to impart the knowledge of facts—which can be found much better in books—but to encourage another generation to look steadfastly at the vision which it sees, and to face its own problems in the light of that vision, controlled and guided by an understanding of what the past has done or not done" (*Paul, His Heritage and Legacy,* 1934, p. xii).

Even though he was a pronounced individualist and highly temperamental, Lake had remarkable abilities as an organizer. His own enthusiasm spurred others to cooperate, notwithstanding differences in personality and background. He possessed an uncanny skill in finding the necessary money to finance his various undertakings. His scholastic achievements were recognized at home and abroad. The recipient of several honorary degrees, he was also Arnold essay prizeman (1902) and received the Burkitt Medal of the British Academy for distinction in biblical studies (1936). He was elected a member of the American Academy of Arts and Sciences, a corresponding member of the Preussische Akademie der Wissenschaften, and in 1941 honorary fellow of Lincoln College, Oxford. Lake died of arteriosclerotic heart failure at his home in South Pasadena, Calif., at the age of seventy-four. He was buried at Glenhaven Memorial Park, San Fernando, Calif.

In his contributions to Greek paleography and textual criticism, Lake identified a group of New Testament manuscripts, moved forward significantly the investigation of the Caesarean type of text of the Gospels, and assembled information from more than 80 percent of all known Greek minuscule manuscripts dated prior to the thirteenth century. His studies on St. Paul and primitive Christianity, though brilliant in their assessment of the influences of the Greco-Roman background on the early church, gave insufficient attention (as was true of other New Testament research during the first third of the twentieth century) to the Jewish milieu from which Christianity and important New Testament documents emerged.

["Biographical Note" by Gerard K. Lake in Robert P. Casey, Silva Lake, and Agnes K. Lake, eds., *Quantulacumque, Studies Presented to Kirsopp Lake by Pupils, Colleagues and Friends* (1937); *Dict. Nat. Biog.,* 1941–1950. Obituary notices: *Am. Jour. of Archaeology,* July–Sept. 1947; *N.Y. Times,* Nov. 12, 1946; *School and Society,* Nov. 23, 1946, p. 363; and *Harvard Divinity Sch. Bull.,* June 30, 1947, p. 73. A memorial, prepared by Lake's former colleagues

R. P. Blake, H. J. Cadbury, and G. LaPiana, appeared in the *Harvard Univ. Gazette*, Jan. 11, 1947, p. 92; another in *Jour. of Biblical Literature* 66 (1947): xvii. Personal information from Agnes K. Lake Michels. A picture is included in George Huntston Williams, ed., *The Harvard Divinity School, Its Place in Harvard University and in American Culture* (1954).]

BRUCE M. METZGER

LAMONT, THOMAS WILLIAM (Sept. 30, 1870–Feb. 2, 1948), banker, international financier, philanthropist, was born in Claverack, N.Y., near Albany, the youngest of three children (two boys and a girl) of Rev. Thomas Lamont, a Methodist minister, and Caroline Deuel (Jayne) Lamont. His father served as a pastor in a succession of Methodist churches, and Thomas spent his first dozen years in a number of small-town parsonages in the Hudson River valley. The family's limited financial means and its firm adherence to a strict Methodism that looked upon cards and dancing as sinful made for a simple and uneventful life, but one which Lamont later recalled as serene and happy. His father, a teacher of classical languages before entering the ministry, insisted that the children read extensively.

With the aid of scholarships, Lamont attended both Phillips Exeter Academy and Harvard College, which he entered in 1888. An interest in journalism, begun at Exeter, led him to an editorship on the *Harvard Crimson* and a job as Harvard correspondent for two Boston newspapers, the income from which helped pay his college expenses. The work proved so enjoyable that Lamont decided to make journalism his career. After graduating from Harvard (B.A. 1892), he became a reporter on the *New York Tribune* and rose quickly to assistant night city editor. He was eager, however, "to get on in the world, specifically to marry and raise a family" (Lamont, *Across World Frontiers,* p. 29). Business promised a better future, and in 1894—investing a borrowed $5,000 in the enterprise—he accepted the position of secretary with Cushman Brothers, a New York firm that acted as an agent for manufacturers of food products seeking to introduce their goods to the metropolitan area. On Oct. 31, 1895, he married Florence Haskell Corliss of Englewood, N.J. They had four children: Thomas Stilwell, Corliss, Austin, and Eleanor.

The Cushman firm proved shaky, and despite Lamont's best efforts, by 1898 it was in such serious financial trouble that one of its major creditors asked Lamont to reorganize and manage it. He did so, founding for the purpose (with his brother-in-law Charles Corliss) the firm of Lamont, Corliss and Company. Lamont's success in turning what had been Cushman Brothers into a profitable business won him recognition among New York bankers, including Henry P. Davison, who became a longtime friend. Other similar rescue operations boosted Lamont's reputation still further, and in 1903 Davison invited him to join the newly organized Bankers Trust Company as secretary and treasurer. Lamont protested that he know nothing of banking, having devoted all his brief business life to borrowing money, not lending it. "Fine!" Davison replied, "that's just why we want you. A fearless borrower like you ought to make a prudent lender" (Lamont, *Henry P. Davison,* p. 59). Lamont remained with Bankers Trust until 1909, rising in 1905 to a vice-presidency and a directorship. In that year he accepted similar posts with the First National Bank. He left in January 1911 to become a partner in J. P. Morgan and Company, then the most prestigious and influential private banking partnership in the country.

As a Morgan partner, Lamont accomplished his most important work. He joined the firm at a time when Wall Street's leading investment banking houses were being accused by progressive critics of having organized an all-powerful "money trust." The charge never was substantiated, and Lamont rejected it outright. His vigorous defense of the policies and practices of the firm made him one of its most articulate spokesmen. "Mr. Morgan speaks to Mr. Lamont and Mr. Lamont speaks to the people," contemporaries observed (Brooks, p. 47).

Lamont's reputation rests, in fact, upon his role in financing industry and foreign governments. His involvement in international loans began shortly after the outbreak of World War I, when Britain and France appointed the House of Morgan, then headed by the younger J. P. Morgan, as their representative and purchasing agent in the United States. Lamont participated in planning and selling the giant $500 million Anglo-French loan of October 1915. This and subsequent Allied loan operations gave him an intimate knowledge of both European and American money markets. When the United States entered the war in 1917, he served with other prominent bankers on the government's Liberty Loan committees, established to help the Treasury Department sell its bonds.

In November 1917, at the request of President Wilson, Lamont went to London and Paris to serve as "confidential unofficial advisor" on financial and economic matters to Col. Edward M. House in negotiations to coordinate the American war effort with that of Britain and France. This experience, together with Lamont's intimate knowledge of wartime finance and his friendship with many British and French leaders, in and out of government, led in 1919 to his appointment, along with Norman H. Davis, as a representative of the United States Treasury on the American delegation to the Paris Peace Conference. There Lamont worked on the complex and controversial problem of determining the amount of Germany's reparations, unsuccessfully urging a moderate and fixed reparations figure. He was a strong supporter of the League of Nations, and, although a lifelong Republican, in 1920 he endorsed the Democratic presidential candidate, James M. Cox.

Lamont returned in June 1919 to the United States and to his rolltop desk at Morgan and Company. Still the nation's leading private investment banking house, the firm between 1919 and 1933 offered the public some $6 billion in securities, approximately one-third of which were foreign government and corporate issues. No one played a more important role in negotiating these offerings than Lamont. In 1920, in Japan, he represented the American banking group on a newly reconstituted international consortium established to assist China with development loans. In 1921 he headed a commission to arrange a settlement of Mexico's external debt; in 1923 he helped negotiate a $100 million recovery loan for Austria. He was instrumental in 1924 in fixing the terms of a $100 million credit to stabilize the French franc, and in 1925 he arranged a similar loan for Italy. Lamont also participated in drafting the Dawes (1924) and Young (1929) plans for German reparations. These and other transactions with which he was associated won him an international reputation. He was considered one of the world's most influential bankers.

Lamont attracted further attention during the stock market crash of 1929. Late in October, after the stock exchanges had suffered several shocks, he organized a banking consortium to stabilize the market, but it proved of little help as millions of shares were dumped at steadily falling prices. Nor were his optimistic predictions of an early recovery any more accurate than those of other financiers and public officials. As the depression deepened, congressional committees began investigating the practices of bankers during the boom years.

Although they uncovered numerous instances of fiduciary negligence, irresponsibility, and favoritism, Lamont in his testimony demonstrated that the Morgan firm had avoided such abuses. Pressure for reform after the crash led to a series of banking and securities laws, including the Glass-Steagall Banking Act of June 1933, which required the separation of commercial and investment banking. Forced to choose between its two primary functions, Morgan and Company opted to remain a bank of deposit and discontinued underwriting securities. Lamont took an active part in reaching this decision. In 1940 when J. P. Morgan and Company became incorporated as a commercial bank and trust company, Lamont became chairman of the executive committee. On the death of J. P. Morgan in 1943 he was elected chairman of the board of the firm.

During the difficult years of depression and readjustment, Lamont remained active in international finance. He helped establish the Bank for International Settlements (1931), and he was a delegate to the World Economic Conference that met in London in June 1933. Although a critic of New Deal fiscal policies, he favored Secretary of State Cordell Hull's liberal trade program of the 1930's and in 1940 he helped organize the Committee to Defend America by Aiding the Allies.

Short and slender, Lamont, in the words of his associate Thomas S. Gates, had "unshakable poise under pressure, the ability to produce a prodigious amount of work with seeming ease, . . . gentle winning charm, with an unquestionable zest for life and love of people" (*Year Book*, p. 268). In addition to his responsibilities as a Morgan partner, he held a number of corporate directorships. He also had many outside interests, most of them concerned with art, literature, and education. He bought the *New York Evening Post* in 1918, installed Edwin F. Gay as editor, and sought to build it into an American counterpart of the *Manchester Guardian,* but had to sell out four years later, after losses estimated at more than $1 million. In 1924 he helped establish and finance the *Saturday Review of Literature,* which he continued to support until 1938. He was an officer or trustee of numerous institutions, among them the Carnegie Foundation for the Advancement of Teaching, the American School of Classical Studies (Athens), the Metropolitan Museum of Art, and the Academy of Political Science.

A generous philanthropist, Lamont gave Harvard $500,000 in 1935 to endow a chair in political economy and, ten years later, $1 million for an undergraduate library. He contributed an infirmary and other benefactions to Phillips Exeter Academy and served as president of its board of trustees (1935–1940). Other large gifts included $500,000 to restore Canterbury Cathedral in England after World War II. He died of a heart ailment at his winter home in Boca Grande, Fla., at the age of seventy-seven. He was buried at Brookside Cemetery in Englewood, N.J. In his will Lamont left nearly $10 million to various educational, cultural, and religious institutions, with the largest bequests going to Harvard ($5 million), Exeter ($2 million), and the Metropolitan Museum of Art ($1 million).

[There is no biography of Lamont. Corliss Lamont, ed., *The Thomas Lamont Family* (1962), provides a useful genealogy. Lamont's own story of his early life up to the time he entered business in New York City is covered in *My Boyhood in a Parsonage* (1946); he treats aspects of his later career in *Across World Frontiers* (1950), with photograph. Lamont's biography of his partner, *Henry P. Davison: The Record of a Useful Life* (1933), provides useful details and insights into the operations of J. P. Morgan and Co. up to 1922. For the firm's activities and Lamont's role in it since 1922, see Vincent P. Carosso, *Investment Banking in America: A Hist.* (1970); and John Brooks, *Once in Golconda: A True Drama of Wall Street, 1920–1938* (1969). A brief biographical sketch is in Am. Philosophical Soc., *Year Book*, 1948, p. 268. Important primary information is to be found in the hearings of various congressional committees before which Lamont testified, particularly U.S. Senate, Committee on Finance, 72 Cong., 1 Sess., *Sale of Foreign Bonds and Securities in the U.S.* (4 pts., 1931–1932); U.S. Senate, Special Committee on Investigating the Munitions Industry, 73 and 74 Congs., *Munitions Industry* (40 pts., 1934–1943); U.S. Senate, Committee on Interstate Commerce, 74 Cong., 2 Sess., 75 Cong., 3 Sess., *Investigation of Railroads, Holding Companies, and Affiliated Companies* (29 pts., 1937–1942); and U.S. Senate, Committee on Banking and Currency, 72 Cong., 1 and 2 Sess., 73 Cong., 1 and 2 Sess., *Stock Exchange Practices* (1933–1934). Lamont's personal and business papers are in the Baker Lib., Harvard Graduate School of Business Administration. The *N.Y. Times* reported Lamont's activities in detail (see Index) and published a lengthy obituary on Feb. 3, 1948.]

VINCENT P. CAROSSO

LAWES, LEWIS EDWARD (Sept. 13, 1883–Apr. 23, 1947), prison administrator, was born in Elmira, N.Y., the son of Harry Lewis Lawes, a native of England, and Sarah (Abbott) Lawes. He grew up within a mile of the Elmira State Reformatory, where his father was a guard, and was educated at Elmira Free Academy and other local schools. During part of his schooling he worked for the *Elmira Telegram*, an experience which may have contributed both to his later penchant for publicity and to his effectiveness at writing. In 1901 he began a three-year enlistment in the army, during which he saw duty in the Philippine Islands and gained

the physical training and discipline which he was later to value in his correctional work. He took a New York civil service examination for reformatory and prison guards prior to his army discharge, but it was not until he returned to Elmira and was working in the insurance business that he was offered a position in 1905 as a guard at Clinton Prison in the Adirondack village of Dannemora.

Lawes stayed at Dannemora only one year, during which he began to formulate his lifelong conviction that a mixture of common sense and unsentimental humanitarianism was preferable to more traditional strong-arm tactics in dealing with convicts. Early in 1906 he accepted a post as guard at Auburn prison, but, six months later, dismayed by the spirit of negativism and repression that characterized New York's penitentiaries for adult offenders, he successfully sought an assignment among younger delinquents, at Elmira Reformatory. Lawes found the liberal methods of Superintendent Joseph F. Scott to his liking and remained until 1915, rising through a variety of assignments to chief guard and head records clerk. He also used part of his spare time to study the works of Cesare Beccaria, John Howard, Cesare Lombroso, and other penal theorists. In 1912 he was granted a temporary leave of absence to attend the New York School of Philanthropy (later the New York School of Social Work), where he studied under such notable social scientists as Katharine B. Davis and Orlando F. Lewis. Through the influence of Miss Davis, Lawes was appointed in March 1915 as overseer of the New York City Reformatory for male delinquents on Hart's Island.

Taking over what had been a crowded, dissension-torn, and repressively run institution, Lawes established a firm but humane discipline and weeded out many old-line staff members, surviving a grand jury investigation which may have stemmed from their attempts to discredit his tactics. He also convinced municipal officials that sharing an island with a penitentiary for alcoholics, drug addicts, and vagrants on the one hand and a graveyard for paupers on the other was undesirable for his charges, and he gained consent to establish a new reformatory at New Hampton in Orange County. After transporting more than five hundred boys and young men to the construction site by train, Lawes supervised them in helping erect the institution. As soon as it was completed he inaugurated an honor system, extending special privileges to those whose behavior qualified them for membership. In one particularly striking manifestation of his approach, he allowed the inmates to take part in the filming of the motion picture *Brand of Cowardice,* dressed as Mexican and American soldiers, brandishing rifles and revolvers with blank cartridges, and burning a simulated village. Not one piece of equipment was stolen, and no escapes were attempted. The institution, which was entirely without surrounding walls, also established a noteworthy foodstuff production record during World War I, and many of its "alumni" fought bravely in the armed forces.

Lawes's record at New Hampton attracted widespread attention, and late in 1919 Gov. Alfred E. Smith offered him the wardenship of the state penitentiary, Sing Sing, at Ossining, N.Y., despite the fact that Lawes was a Republican. He accepted with some trepidation, for the prison was known as a "warden's graveyard" because of the short tenures of most of his predecessors. Its recent history had been marked by the controversial administration of Thomas Mott Osborne, who had established a system of inmate self-government known as the Mutual Welfare League but whose efforts had been hamstrung by political interference. In addition, the prison building was so antiquated that a grand jury had not long before recommended its abandonment. Assured a free hand by Governor Smith, Lawes assumed control on New Year's Day of 1920. Long before his retirement in 1941 he had transformed Sing Sing into what was probably the most progressive institution of its type in the United States. The extent of his achievement stood clearly revealed in 1929, when Sing Sing remained calm while both Auburn and Clinton prisons exploded in riots.

Part of Lawes's program involved extensive physical modernization. The dank and primitive cellblock, dating from the 1820's, was replaced by new living quarters. A well-equipped hospital was erected, as well as a modern industrial plant. By 1932 the prison had a library of 15,000 volumes and classrooms for more than 1,100 men, who took courses in English, mathematics, business, mechanics, and other subjects. The yard was beautified with flower gardens and shrubbery under inmate direction, and an aviary was constructed. Hating capital punishment but unable to change the laws providing for it, Lawes managed at least to secure the erection of a new death house, where the condemned would be treated more humanely prior to execution.

The chief basis for Lawes's success, however, was his skillful administration of day-to-day life at Sing Sing, which he tried to make as similar to normal outside conditions as possible. Motion pictures became a standard form of entertainment, and radios with headsets were installed in the cells. A program of organized athletics was established, including football and baseball games with extramural opponents. There was a prison band, which played as the men marched from one assignment to another, and theatrical events in which inmate thespians performed. Visiting regulations were relaxed to permit limited physical contact between convicts and their families, and inmates were allowed to leave the penitentiary under guard to attend the funerals of close relatives or to be at their bedsides in cases of critical illness.

Unlike Osborne, Lawes managed to pursue unconventional policies without arousing charges of "coddling criminals." His approach was aptly characterized by the *New York Times* as one of stretching humanitarianism as far as the law would allow but "with a stiff punch always in reserve." Although he admired the idealism underlying the Mutual Welfare League that Osborne had established, he permitted it to continue only under modifications that left the warden firmly in charge of discipline. He came down swiftly and firmly upon convicts or guards who broke the rules. In short, he was a practical reformer with a keen sense of the limits of the possible.

Through his writings Lawes had a greater impact on the American public than any warden in previous history. Beginning with *Man's Judgment of Death,* a critique of capital punishment that appeared in 1924, he wrote numerous articles and eight books, of which the most famous was the partly autobiographical *Twenty Thousand Years in Sing Sing* (1932). Lawes trenchantly analyzed society's involvement in the responsibility for crime through its toleration of poverty, outmoded educational practices, formalistic religion, parental neglect, and unethical tactics which were condoned in business life but harshly punished in other contexts. He called for judicial reforms such as the indeterminate sentence, urged a thorough revamping of the criminal law, and criticized police conduct that was predicated upon inspiring fear rather than respect. Although he presided at a total of 302 executions, he denied that capital punishment had any demonstrable deterrent effect and strongly deprecated the sensationalism which inevitably surrounded its use. Harsh treatment of prisoners, he believed, would only result in further danger to society by stimulating a desire for revenge following release. Using a variety of techniques to drive home these views, Lawes conducted elaborate statistical explorations of penal records, wrote fictional stories about inmates and their problems, gave radio broadcasts, and even coauthored a prison melodrama, *Chalked Out,* which had a short run on Broadway in 1937.

Tall and sturdy, with blue eyes and blond hair, Lawes looked (in the words of Henry F. Pringle) "a great deal like an able businessman, not a little like a priest, and something like a cop. . . . He can be as sympathetic as any cleric . . . or he can be extraordinarily hard-boiled" (*Forum,* Jan. 1938, p. 5). He was president of the Wardens' Association of America (1922) and of the American Prison Association (1923). Lawes married twice, on Sept. 30, 1905, to Kathryn Irene Stanley of Elmira, and after her death in 1937 to Elise Chisholm of Jackson, Miss., on Apr. 19, 1939. He had three children by his first wife: Kathleen, Crystal, and Joan Marie. Following his retirement Lawes served as executive president of the Boy Rangers of America. He died of a cerebral hemorrhage at his home in Garrison, N.Y., at the age of sixty-three. A Roman Catholic, he was buried at Sleepy Hollow Cemetery, Tarrytown, N.Y. The *New York Times* provided a suitable epitaph in describing him as a man who "left a healing touch on one of the sorest spots of our society."

[The best sources on Lawes's life and career are his own *Twenty Thousand Years in Sing Sing;* brief sketches in *Current Biog.,* 1941, and *Nat. Cyc. Am. Biog.,* Current Vol. F, pp. 314–315; and the *N.Y. Times* obituary, Apr. 24, 1947. See also the *Times* editorial, same issue, and tribute by Burdette G. Lewis, May 24, 1947. Lawes's views on various subjects can best be traced in his books.]

W. David Lewis

LAWRANCE, CHARLES LANIER (Sept. 30, 1882-June 24, 1950), aeronautical engineer and business executive, was born in Lenox, Mass., the older of two children and only son of Francis Cooper Lawrance and his first wife, Sarah Eggleston (Lanier) Lawrance; he had a younger half sister. His father, who came of a well-to-do family, was a graduate of Yale's Sheffield Scientific School and the Columbia Law School, but never practiced his profession. The Lawrances lived in New York City. Charles attended the Groton (Mass.) School and received the B.A. degree from Yale in 1905. On Aug. 31, 1910, Lawrance married Emily Margaret Gordon Dix, daughter of Morgan Dix, rector of Trinity Church in New York City. They had three children: Emily, Margaret Lanier, and Francis Cooper. After undertaking some experimental work with automobiles, he spent six years in Paris, where he did research in aeronautical engineering at the Eiffel Laboratory and studied architecture at the École des Beaux Arts. He received his diploma in 1914.

On his return to the United States, Lawrance resumed his automotive interests but soon turned to aeronautics. He designed an experimental air-cooled engine with two opposed cylinders and in 1917 formed the Lawrance Aero-Engine Company to develop it. With support from the navy, he next developed a three-cylinder engine and began work on a nine-cylinder, 200-horsepower engine (together with a slightly less powerful version for the army). Completed in 1921, the Lawrance J-1 later came to be regarded as the prototype of all modern radial air-cooled engines.

The navy was especially interested in Lawrance's engine because of its advantage for aircraft carrier operations. Its lack of a complicated liquid cooling system made it lighter in weight, thus allowing shorter takeoffs, a better rate of climb, and, most important, easier maintenance, factors which more than compensated for the slightly lower cruising speed resulting from the drag caused by the engine's exposed cylinders. Ease of maintenance also made the air-cooled engine attractive for commercial service. After an initial order for fifty engines in 1921, the navy's Bureau of Aeronautics ordered sixty more over the next two years.

Lawrance's company, however, lacked the capacity to manufacture on this scale, and the navy, in order to ensure an adequate supply, sought to induce the two major engine manufacturers, the Wright Aeronautical Corporation and the Curtiss Aeroplane and Motor Company, to compete with Lawrance in its production. Both companies balked, but when the navy refused to purchase any more of Wright's liquid-cooled Hispano-Suiza engines, Wright bought Lawrance's company in 1923 and began production of his air-cooled engine. Lawrance's 1921 engine thus became the ancestor of the Wright series of radial air-cooled engines, including the "Whirlwind," which powered Charles A. Lindbergh's *Spirit of St. Louis* in 1927, and the 710-horsepower "Cyclone," which powered Douglas Aircraft's DC series in the early 1930's. For his J-5 Whirlwind, Lawrance was awarded the annual Collier Trophy in 1928.

With the purchase of his firm in 1923, Lawrance joined the Wright company as a vice-president. He moved up to the presidency in 1925 when Frederick B. Rentschler left to found the Pratt and Whitney Aircraft Corporation. Lawrance represented the aircraft industry before the Morrow Board of 1925, which laid the groundwork for the nation's first systematic aviation policy and led to establishment of the Bureau of Air Commerce. He was elected president of the Aeronautical Chamber of Commerce in 1931. Meanwhile, in 1929, the Wright company merged with its old rival, Curtiss, to form the Curtiss-Wright Corporation, with Lawrance as vice-president of the new combination. He was not happy with the merger, however, and resigned in 1930 to form the Lawrance Engineering and Research Corporation (later the Lawrance Aeronautical Corporation) in Linden, N.J. He served as president and chief engineer until 1944, when he became chairman of the board and director of engine research. He made no further notable contributions to aircraft engine development, however, and his reputation rests on his pioneering achievements during and shortly after World War I.

Lawrance's business operations were all located in the New York metropolitan area, where he also made his home. From about 1925 he lived at East Islip on Long Island. Besides his aeronautical activities, he had real estate interests on Long Island. Lawrance, who was an Episcopalian, died of a coronary occlusion in East Islip and was buried in the Locust Valley (N.Y.) Cemetery.

[A brief sketch of Lawrance's career appears in the *Aeronautical Engineering Rev.*, Sept. 1950. See also Yale Univ., *Obituary Record,* 1949–1950, and, for his father, 1903–1904. Descriptions and assessments of Lawrance's contribution to aircraft power plant development can be found in John B. Rae, *Climb to Greatness: The Am. Aircraft Industry, 1920–1960* (1968); Robert Schlaifer, *Development of Aircraft Engines* (published with S. D. Heron, *Development of Aviation Fuels,* 1950); C. Fayette Taylor, "Aircraft Propulsion: A Review of the Evolution of Aircraft Powerplants," Smithsonian Institution, *Annual Report,* 1962; and Eugene E. Wilson, *Slipstream: The Autobiog. of an Aircraftsman* (1965). Lawrance's *Our National Aviation Program* (1932) is a collection of essays and speeches compiled while he was president of the Aeronautical Chamber of Commerce.]

JOHN B. RAE

LEATHERS, WALLER SMITH (Dec. 4, 1874–Jan. 26, 1946), medical educator and public health physician, was born near Charlottesville, Va., the son of James Addison Leathers, a farmer and merchant, and Elizabeth (Pace) Leathers. After attending local schools, including the Miller School of Virginia, Leathers matriculated at the University of Virginia, from which he received a diploma of graduation in the schools of biology, geology, mineralogy and chemistry in 1892, and the M.D. degree in 1895. After brief graduate study the following year at the Johns Hopkins University, he taught at the University of Mississippi, became head of the department of chemistry at the Miller School of Virginia (1896-1897),

and then from 1897 to 1906 was professor of biology at the University of South Carolina. Between 1897 and 1907, he pursued advanced study during the summer months at the University of Chicago, the Long Island Biological Laboratory, the Marine Biological Laboratory at Woods Hole, Mass., and the Harvard Medical School. In 1898 he joined the Rocky Mountain Scientific Expedition. He married Sarah Ola Price in Oxford, Miss., on Nov. 14, 1906; they had one daughter, Lucy Dell.

Leathers began a quarter of a century of leadership in the development of medicine and public health in 1899. He joined the University of Mississippi faculty as professor of biology, aiding in the organization of the medical school, which opened in 1903. He held the post of dean of the medical school from 1910 to 1924, while continuing to teach and to participate in medical and public health affairs in the state. At the university, he served as professor of physiology from 1903 to 1910 and, then, reflecting his shift of focus to public health, as professor of physiology and hygiene until 1924. From 1910 to 1917, he was university director of health for the Mississippi State Board of Health. In 1917 he was elected director of public health and executive officer of the Mississippi State Board of Health.

In these positions, he was equipped to shape Mississippi medical and public health institutions to conform to the scientific and administrative models developed in Europe and the northeastern United States. During these years, he directed campaigns against a number of diseases, including typhoid fever, malaria, and hookworm; he helped establish a state tuberculosis sanatorium and a full-time county health department; and he appointed a state inspector for factories. He also helped revise the state's medical practice act. In 1911 and 1912, for example, he helped secure legislation restricting the practice of medicine in the state to graduates of medical colleges approved by the Council of Medical Education of the American Medical Association. In 1921, he supported pellagra research and control efforts of Joseph Goldberger by working to convince physicians and prominent laymen of the need for nutritional education.

Leathers' attention increasingly turned to the regional and national levels after he moved to Vanderbilt University to become professor of preventive medicine and public health in 1924. He, subsequently, became associate dean (1927) and dean (1928) of the School of Medicine. He was a member of the National Board of

Medical Examiners from 1924 to 1946, serving as president from 1930-1934 and 1936-1942; president of the Southern Medical Association (1922-1923); vice-president of the American Association for the Advancement of Science (1928); vice-president and president of the Association of American Medical Colleges (1938-1943); chairman of the Committee on Professional Education; president (1940-1941) of the American Public Health Association; and president of the Association of American Medical Colleges (1942-1943). As an advisor on scientific and medical affairs to the Rockefeller Foundation, he helped secure funds to construct a new wing, helped to develop the associated nurses school and to raise its standards. He served as an advisor, on medical and scientific affairs for the Commonwealth Fund from 1929 until his death, the American Red Cross (1939), and the United States Public Health Service (1931-1935 and 1937-1939).

His interests—ranging from preventive medicine of such diseases as lead poisoning, tuberculosis, ascariasis, to the relationship between the health officer and the medical profession, to public health administration and personnel—were reflected in his writing. He authored or coauthored over 130 articles. He died in Nashville, Tenn., at the age of seventy-one after suffering a cerebral hemorrhage.

A Democrat and a Methodist, a Southerner and a patriot, Leathers conformed to the values of his class and region sufficiently to inspire the confidence necessary to lead men and institutions toward new goals. Described as a man of excellent judgment and of high medical ideals, he helped to nationalize innovations in medical practice and education and to raise medical standards in the South.

[A biographical obituary appeared in *Federation Bull.*, 32 (1946), 56-57; other biographical material is in the Vanderbilt *Alumnus*, Oct.–Nov. 1945 and June 1933; *Jour. of the Am. Medical Assoc.*, Feb. 9, 1946. The Leathers Manuscript Collect. is in the Medical School, Vanderbilt Univ. The best recent source for a discussion of medicine and public health in the South in the early twentieth century is Elizabeth Ethridge, *The Butterfly Caste* (1972).]
DANIEL M. FOX

LEDBETTER, HUDDIE ("LEAD-BELLY") (Jan. 21, 1885-Dec. 6, 1949), singer and composer, was born two miles from Mooringsport, La., in the Caddo Lake area near the Texas border, where his parents, Wess Ledbetter and Sallie (Pugh) Ledbetter, had managed to buy sixty-five acres of land to farm together. Wess Ledbetter's parents, who had lived in Mississippi, were both slain by the Ku Klux Klan. Huddie's maternal grandmother was a Cherokee, a fact he often mentioned. He had one adopted sister, but was his parents' only natural child.

Huddie Ledbetter was first exposed to music by his mother, who led her church choir. Two "songster" uncles, Bob and Terrell Ledbetter, encouraged him to become a musician. When Uncle Terrell rode home with an accordion for him on the back of a mule, the boy quickly mastered the instrument, which was especially popular among Cajun groups in the area.

At the age of fifteen, Huddie fathered a child by a neighbor named Margaret, whom he had known since childhood. Their daughter, Arthur Mae, was born in 1900. The community was resentful when he did not marry Margaret. He dropped out of school and went to work on the family farm. At about this time, his father bought him a pistol, which Huddie carried in a holster under his coat, and a new horse and saddle.

Huddie Ledbetter was soon known as the best guitar picker and songster in his part of Louisiana. At sixteen he started visiting Fannin Street, the red-light district of nearby Shreveport. Here he heard accomplished blues musicians and learned their style and verses. He recalls these early experiences in his song "Fannin Street." Bud Coleman and Jim Fagin were two musicians with whom he worked closely.

Ledbetter soon moved away from Mooringsport. He married a girl named Lethe, and they worked together during summers on farms near New Boston, Tex., in the blackland counties east of Dallas. In the winter they moved to Dallas, where he played his guitar and sang in the red-light district. Here he met the Texas bluesman Blind Lemon Jefferson and learned many songs from him. One night at a circus in Dallas Ledbetter heard a musician play a twelve-string guitar; he bought one like it the next morning.

He received the nickname " Lead Belly" (or "Leadbelly") because his voice was a powerful bass. A handsome, strongly built young man, he had early learned that he was attractive to women. In Marshall, Tex., he attacked a woman who rejected his advances and was sentenced to a year on a chain gang. His father hid him when he escaped three days later. In late 1917 Leadbelly became involved in another fracas over a woman. He was convicted on two counts, murder and assault to murder, on May 24, 1918. Once more he escaped from his cell, but on June 7, 1918, under the alias of Walter Boyd, he entered Shaw State Prison Farm, sentenced to thirty years at hard labor. For the third time he escaped. He was soon recaptured, and in 1920 he was transferred to the Central State Farm near Houston. He worked on labor gangs for twelve to fourteen hours a day cutting logs and hoeing cotton, and through his strength and endurance he became the lead man on the fastest work gang. He recalled his skills as a laborer in prison: "In Texas I was a number one roller, jus' flyin' all day long. I can make a ax talk, an' I can handle a hoe jus' like I can handle a guitar" (Lomax, *Negro Folk Songs,* p. 17).

Leadbelly was also known for his skill as a musician and was asked to sing when visitors came to the prison. When the governor of Texas, Pat. M. Neff, came to visit, Leadbelly sang a plea for mercy to him:

> [If I] had you, Governor Neff, like you got me,
> I'd wake up in de mornin', and I'd set you free.

The governor was impressed with the man and his song, and on Jan. 15, 1925, he pardoned Leadbelly, who had then served about six and a half years. After working for a Buick agency in Houston, Leadbelly returned to his home near Mooringsport in 1926. While he worked for the Gulf Refining Company, he continued to develop as a blues singer. In 1930 he was accosted by a group of men who wanted whiskey. Leadbelly wounded five of them with his knife and was sentenced to ten years at hard labor for assault with intent to murder.

On Feb. 28, 1930, he entered Angola Penitentiary in Louisiana and became the lead man on prison gangs, as he had in Texas. He composed another plea for mercy to Gov. O. K. Allen of Louisiana:

> [If I] had you, Governor O. K. Allen, like you had me,
> I'd wake up in de mornin', let you out on reprieve.

It was recorded (along with a song that was to become even more famous, "Irene, Good Night") by folklorists John and Alan Lomax in 1934. The Lomaxes played the record for the governor in his office and obtained a reprieve for Leadbelly on Aug. 7, 1934.

The next month Leadbelly joined John Lomax in a journey that helped make both men famous. Lomax was recording folk songs in Southern prisons, and Leadbelly accompanied him, telling of his own experiences and singing to encourage the inmates to record for Lomax. Details of these travels are graphically recalled in *Negro Folk Songs as Sung by Lead Belly,* by John and Alan Lomax. At night, after the day's recording, Leadbelly, who described himself as a "nachel rambler," would take his guitar and sing in local bars, returning early the next morning to drive Lomax to his next recording location. Lomax's tapes of Leadbelly's songs were eventually deposited in the Library of Congress.

After 6,000 miles of travel, performances, and recording, they arrived in New York City. Leadbelly described it: "Capital of all de states in de world! Run under a mile of water to git in it! Subways up in de air, on de ground and under de ground through a solid rock!" (Lomax, *Negro Folk Songs,* p. 17).

Leadbelly was given a resounding reception by the New York intellectual and literary scene, who embraced him as the "bad nigger." The *Herald Tribune* introduced him as a "powerful knife-toting Negro, a saturnine singer of the swamplands, who has killed one man and seriously wounded another. . . . A large scar which spans his neck from ear to ear bears witness to his dreadful charm and a knife that was fortuitously dull."

John Lomax promoted Leadbelly's music for white audiences rather than those of his "own color." Whites who could not understand his words were drawn by the power of his singing. He performed before the Poetry Society of Cambridge and at Harvard, where George Lyman Kittredge said to his former student, "He is a demon, Lomax."

Lomax recalled that during these performances Leadbelly "crouched over his guitar as he played, as his fingers made the incredibly swift, skillful runs; and he sang with an intensity and passion that swayed audiences who could not understand a single word of his songs." During these performances Leadbelly often introduced "talkin'" before songs and between their verses to explain his music to the audience.

Leadbelly found himself surrounded by admiring middle-class whites who often could not appreciate his life style. John Lomax arranged for Leadbelly's woman, Martha Promise, to travel north for a much publicized wedding that was held in Wilmot, Conn., on Jan. 21, 1935, so that Leadbelly could lead a "normal" life. The singer soon returned to his old life style, and Lomax commented on his efforts: "I had planned to take a former Negro criminal back to Texas, changed to a good citizen. . . . But it was I who wanted the pretty home for them, not Lead Belly."

On Mar. 26, 1935, Leadbelly went back to Shreveport, La., with his wife. He later returned to New York and continued his career as a folk singer. Large recording studios refused to issue his music because he wasn't "commercial" enough. The best selection of his music was gathered by Frederick Ramsey, Jr., who recorded ninety-four of his songs on Folkways Records.

Leadbelly visited Hollywood briefly, but he was coolly received and treated as an entertainer at parties given by celebrities. He was jokingly told to come for a screen test at "45 to 9 at Hollywood and Vine," and he recalled these bitter memories in the song "4, 5, and 9."

Returning to New York City, Leadbelly did a series of half-hour programs for WNYC radio station. During a visit to Washington, D.C., he and his wife were refused service by a number of hotels, and he immortalized the city in his "Bourgeois Blues," concluding: "Tell all the colored folks to listen to me,/ Don't try to find a home in Washington, D.C." He also sang a classic version of a ballad about the *Titanic,* whose captain, refusing passage to the famous black fighter Jack Johnson, said, "I ain't haulin' no coal."

Leadbelly's repertoire included traditional folk and children's songs, blues, and topical numbers, all of which are an important part of American folklore. His best-known songs include "Boll Weevil," "Rock Island Line," "Old Cottonfields at Home," "Take This Hammer," "Pick a Bale of Cotton," and "Midnight Special." His presence in New York City was a catalyst for writers, folk singers, and leftists who saw him as a symbol of the struggling proletariat. According to one biography of Leadbelly these admirers "considered his life their personal property, to be clutched and guarded like a family heirloom."

Tennessee Williams spoke of Leadbelly in *Orpheus Descending:* "Greatest man that ever lived on the twelve-string guitar! Played it so good he broke the stone heart out of a Texas Governor and won himself a pardon out of jail." Folk singers such as Pete Seeger learned Leadbelly's style and continue to sing his music today. The man and his music became a symbol of the strength and beauty of black culture which was accessible to whites. Leadbelly survived gunfights and prison gangs to bring a unique sound to New York and the American public. His complicated boogie-woogie runs on the twelve-string guitar have been imitated but never equaled, and few other blues musicians have been so studied and appreciated. He died

of myotrophic lateral sclerosis at Bellevue Hospital in New York.

[The most thorough biography of Leadbelly and texts of his music are in John and Alan Lomax, *Negro Folk Songs as Sung by Lead Belly* (1936) and *The Leadbelly Legend* (1965). A biographical novel about Leadbelly, by Richard Garvin and Edmond G. Addes, *The Midnight Special* (1971), develops the Lomax research. The influence of Leadbelly on the white folk-song movement is discussed by Bob Groom in *The Blues Revival* (London, 1971). Extensive recordings of interviews and music made with Leadbelly by John and Alan Lomax are at the Rec. Div. of the Lib. of Congress. Commercial recordings of Leadbelly are listed in John Godrich and Robert M. W. Dixon, *Blues and Gospel Records 1902–1942,* pp. 411–418 (London, 1969), and in Mike Leadbitter and Neil Slaven, *Blues Records: January 1943 to December, 1966,* pp. 189–190 (London, 1968). The famous last session recorded by Frederick Ramsey is available commercially on Folkways FA-2941 and FA-2942 under the title *Last Sessions.*]

WILLIAM R. FERRIS JR.

LEIBER, FRITZ (Jan. 31, 1882-Oct. 14, 1949), actor and theatrical producer, was born in Chicago, the fifth of the six children of Albrecht Leiber and Meta (von Klett) Leiber. Albrecht Leiber and his family emigrated from Germany's Ruhr district to the United States in pursuit of a politically liberal environment. He served as an officer in the Civil War and held various political appointments in Springfield and Chicago, Ill. Although he died when Fritz was only ten, his scholarly interests and Republican views shaped Fritz's penchant for oratory and debate. This became evident when he went to Chicago's Lake View High School, and in later life his Episcopalian beliefs, firm Republican politics, and conservative, methodical offstage personality also reflected some of his father's influence. While still in high school he attended a performance of Richard Mansfield's, which turned his interests from platform to stage. On Mar. 30, 1902, he made his professional debut as a "walking gentleman" and followed on Apr. 6, 1902, with his first Shakespearean role as Cinna in *Julius Caesar,* both at Chicago's Dearborn Theatre. Soon thereafter he signed with a Chicago stock company, the People's Theatre. The rigors of a stock company provided excellent testing grounds, for he learned that his stage gait in a great variety of parts was in no way hampered by his being clubfooted. He had combated this handicap in childhood by wearing a corrective iron shoe with lifts and had succeeded as a high school track star. The challenge he met in the arduous stock schedule, moreover, prepared him to champion repertory in its future waning days. His appearance until the spring of 1904 in the more than thirty roles ranging from "supers" (walk-ons) to leads in several minor stock and touring companies ripened him for more important ventures.

In April 1904, Leiber joined Ben Greet's Woodland Players. Hired initially as a "utility" actor, he eventually assumed more important roles, culminating in Prospero, which he played whenever Greet was incapacitated. In December 1907, he joined Julia Marlowe for a season as her leading juvenile. Producer William A. Brady then signed him to a three-year contract with Robert Mantell's company. From 1908 until 1915 he played second leads exclusively for Mantell, whose popularity in large cities across the United States enabled Leiber to be introduced as a significant classical actor. He supported Mantell as Edgar, Mercutio, Laertes, Macduff, Bassanio, Iago, Richmond, Antony, Falconbridge, and Jacques. When Mantell disbanded his company in 1915 to go to Hollywood, Leiber tested himself in nonclassical roles. His brief appearances that season in Edward Locke's melodrama *The Revolt* and Belasco's romantic *Van der Decken* were critical failures. His few later attempts to break from Shakespeare, as in E. Holmes Hinkley's *High Tide* (1925) and Paul Green's *The Field God* (1927), also received poor notices. After his film debut in *Primitive Call* (1916), in which he played an American Indian, he rejoined Mantell. He wanted to play leads, and Mantell, aware of Leiber's box-office appeal, agreed to star him in *Hamlet,* supported by Mantell's company. Leiber opened in New York on Dec. 18, 1918, to mixed reviews. Mantell then continued to alternate both Hamlet and Romeo with him, but critics encouraged Leiber to play on his own. On Nov. 8, 1920, he opened his own company in Chicago with a two-week repertory of *Richard III, Romeo and Juliet, The Merchant of Venice, Hamlet,* and *Macbeth*. These became staples in the Leiber repertoire; in future years he added *Julius Caesar, King Lear,* and *The Taming of the Shrew*. During the 1920's he devoted himself to touring. In 1929 the Chicago Civic Shakespeare Society, founded by Midwest industrial and cultural leaders headed by the utilities magnate Harley L. Clarke, invited him to form a resident repertory company at the Civic Theatre. It opened to highly favorable reviews on Nov. 11, 1929, and then moved to New York City for a limited engagement. Critical and financial success for the society's initial season could not halt the destructive effect of the depression and competing motion pictures. Clarke, op-posing Leiber's judgment, assembled an all-star cast in a futile attempt to revive a failing box office. The Chicago Civic Shakespeare Society folded after the 1931-1932 season. Leiber resumed touring with his own company, but by 1935 abandoned the road for the financial security of films. He made about thirty-six movies from 1935 to 1949, ranging from low-grade melodramas to historical spectacles, but he never realized his dream of acting Shakespearean leads in films. An ascetic, exotic quality, suggested by his long gaunt face, hawk nose, chiseled jaw, and high forehead, prompted producers to cast him as primitives, priests, and historical figures. Among his more successful parts were Gaspard in *A Tale of Two Cities* (1935), Father Andrew in *The Prince and the Pauper* (1936), and Dr. Charbonnet in *The Story of Louis Pasteur* (1936). He also appeared in *Cleopatra* (1917), *Champagne Waltz* (1937), *All This And Heaven Too* (1940), *Desert Song* (1944), *Another Part of the Forest* (1945), and *Adventures of Casanova* (1948).

Leiber suffered a heart attack in 1943 and died in 1949 of a coronary occlusion in Pacific Palisades, Calif. His remains were cremated by request of his wife, Virginia Bronson, an actress and often his leading lady, whom he married on Mar. 9, 1910. They had one child, Fritz Leiber, Jr., a science fiction writer.

Leiber in his younger days was an impassioned, dynamic, virile actor. He seemed freshly natural in contrast to the aging Mantell. His acting lacked studious refinement, but he held his audiences through a nervous force that later led some critics to call him too flamboyant. Critics were usually more appreciative of Leiber outside of New York, and it was to audiences in smaller cities that he made his greatest contribution. While other actors turned to movies or long runs, Leiber played the road. He chose to present Shakespeare when the contemporary hit became the trend during the 1920's. His Chicago Civic Shakespeare Society was the first and, during its time, the only resident Shakespearean repertory company in the United States. A versatile practitioner, he functioned as actor, director, designer, and producer. His productions revealed how Shakespeare's plays could successfully be molded to the new stagecraft theories which called for simplified, symbolic, nonnaturalistic productions. In *Hamlet,* for example, he used a single unit set which established locale by changing suggestive scenic pieces. His productions flowed without stopping for cumbersome shifts. He even tried *The Taming of the Shrew* in contemporary dress (1928). In an unusually long career he linked the nineteenth-century Shakespearean tradition of Edwin Booth, Mantell, and E. H. Sothern with the twentieth century's theatrical vision.

[The Fritz Leiber Collect., Univ. of Ill. Lib., Urbana, Ill., is an almost complete compilation of correspondence, business records, reviews, newspaper features, programs, promptbooks, photographs, and memorabilia covering Leiber's career. It includes an unpublished autobiographical sketch and an unpublished biographical manuscript by his wife. The only other comprehensive source for information and analysis of Leiber's career is an unpublished doctoral dissertation by Herman Henry Diers, "Fritz Leiber—Actor and Producer of Shakespeare" (Univ. of Ill., 1965). Obituary in the *N.Y. Times*, Oct. 15, 1949, includes a photograph.]

WENDY ROUDER

LEMKE, WILLIAM FREDERICK (Aug. 13, 1878-May 30, 1950), agrarian leader and Congressman, was born in Albany, Minn., the second son and fourth of ten children of Frederick William Lemke, a farmer, and Julia Anna (Klier) Lemke. His father, a native of Prussia, had immigrated with his Lutheran parents in 1851; his mother, whose Catholic family had come from Bavaria, was born in Wisconsin; the couple reared their daughters as Catholics and their sons as Lutherans. In 1881 Frederick Lemke moved his family to Dakota Territory, where he settled on a homestead near Cando in Towner County in 1883. There he prospered, acquiring 2,700 acres by the mid-1890's and winning election to the state legislature as a Republican in 1900, the year before his death.

Lemke lost an eye in a boyhood accident, but apparently suffered no great handicap as a result. He graduated from the Cando high school in 1898 and entered the University of North Dakota, from which he received the B.A. degree in 1902. He then studied law at North Dakota (1902-1903), Georgetown University (1903-1904), and Yale University (1904-1905). After receiving his LL.B. degree from Yale in 1905, he established a practice in Fargo, N. Dak. On Apr. 16, 1910, he married Isabelle McIntyre (originally McGilvray), a stenographer in his office. They had three children: William Frederick, Robert McIntyre, and Mary Eleanor.

While at Yale, Lemke's friendship with the son of a Mexican senator had aroused his interest in acquiring land in western Mexico for colonization by Americans. In 1906 he organized a company which raised $400,000 through a stock offering and purchased 550,000 acres in Sinaloa and Tepic. The Mexican revolution that broke out in 1911, however, dealt the venture a blow from which it never recovered. Desiring a strong Mexican government capable of protecting his interests, Lemke applauded the seizure of power by the dictator Victoriano Huerta in 1913 and vainly urged President Wilson to recognize the Huerta regime. Lemke expressed his bitterness toward Wilson in his book *Crimes Against Mexico* (1915).

Impoverished by his Mexican debacle, Lemke became an attorney for the Society of Equity, a manifestation of Midwestern agrarian discontent founded in North Dakota in 1907. As a boy Lemke had witnessed the local successes of the Farmers' Alliance and the Populist party and had absorbed his father's concern for their programs, and he sympathized with the society's goal of giving the farmer a greater share of his product through the creation of a cooperative exchange. One outgrowth of the Equity movement was the founding in 1915 of a vigorous new organization, the Nonpartisan League, which sought to work within the two major political parties for agrarian reform. Lemke soon became one of its leaders.

Regarding himself as a progressive in the tradition of Robert M. La Follette, Lemke soon rose to a position of great political influence; he became chairman of the Republican state committee (1916-1920) and a member of the Nonpartisan League's national executive committee (1917-1921). In the gubernatorial race of 1916 he gained league endorsement in the Republican primary for Lynn J. Frazier, who was elected for the first of three terms. More important, Lemke was the chief architect of the league's legislative program, enacted in 1919, which created the state-owned Bank of North Dakota, a state grain mill and elevator, the Workmen's Compensation Bureau, a state hail insurance program, an industrial commission to oversee state industries, and machinery for rural credit loans and the building of low-cost houses for farmers.

In 1920 Lemke was elected attorney general of North Dakota. By this time, however, both his influence and that of the Nonpartisan League had begun to wane. The league's isolationism during World War I, the socialist background of some of its leaders, the financial boycott of North Dakota, Langer's withdrawal, and the league's opposition to wartime restrictions on civil liberties had made it the object of conservative attack during the war and the subsequent red scare. The deflation of 1921, which caused numerous bank failures and halted construction of the state mill and elevator, cast doubt on the viability of the League's program. Lemke himself was criticized for using a state loan to build himself a house and was attacked as a political czar who controlled the league newspapers and the Bank of North Dakota. In 1921 a legislative audit committee disclosed evidence of favoritism in the bank's policy of redepositing funds in institutions in which Lemke had an interest. These charges, though unsubstantiated, gave impetus to a recall movement led by the anti-league Independent Voters Association, and in 1921 Lemke, Frazier, and John H. Hagan, the state agricultural commissioner, were removed from office. Serious charges against Lemke were unsubstantiated and the indictment against him was dropped.

Lemke succeeded in getting Frazier elected to the United States Senate in 1922 but was himself defeated for governor. Thereafter he engaged in several business ventures, most of them unfruitful. He had hopes of being appointed ambassador to Mexico by President Coolidge, and hence abstained from league politics in the mid-1920's. As a result, the organization was captured by his opponents, who had long regarded him as too radical. Lemke ran for the Senate in 1926 as candidate of the short-lived Farmer-Labor party, but was defeated. In the presidential election of 1928 he backed Alfred E. Smith. Lemke was an early supporter of Franklin D. Roosevelt in 1932 and led the successful campaign that gave Roosevelt North Dakota's votes in the presidential primary. The depression, his transfer of support from Smith to Roosevelt, and alliance with William Langer helped launch his second political career. That fall, with the endorsement of the league, Lemke was elected to the House of Representatives as a Republican. Save for 1940, when he ran unsuccessfully for the Senate against Langer, he was regularly returned to the House until his death.

As the depression deepened, Lemke became a supporter of the militant Farm Holiday Association led by Milo Reno. A foe of production controls, he consistently backed the association's radical proposal for a "cost of production" system in which the federal government would fix prices on various commodities. He also authored and—along with Senator Frazier—cosponsored bills to ease bankruptcy terms for farmers, create a Bank of the United States (the only state-owned bank in the country), and allow farmers to refinance their mortgages

at lower interest rates. Despite the opposition of President Roosevelt, Lemke by a tireless personal campaign lined up sufficient support to secure passage of the Frazier-Lemke Farm Bankruptcy Act (1934) and, when it was declared unconstitutional, its successor, the Farm Mortgage Moratorium Act (1935), which was upheld by the Supreme Court in 1937. Known as the Frazier bills, before Lemke's election to Congress, the latter's sole authorship has been acknowledged by Frazier; they were introduced into the Senate by Frazier and into the House by Lemke.

Embittered by Roosevelt's refusal to support his program, Lemke in 1936 accepted the presidential nomination of the vaguely agrarian-inflationary Union party, recently formed by three anti-New Deal demagogues: Father Charles E. Coughlin, the Michigan radio priest, the Rev. Gerald L. K. Smith, an ally of the recently assassinated Senator Huey P. Long, and Dr. Francis E. Townsend, campaigner for old-age pensions. Long and Coughlin had supported Lemke's bills; but his association with these fringe elements eroded his influence in liberal circles, and his presidential candidacy drew less than 900,000 votes. As World War II approached, Lemke's isolationist sentiments were rekindled, and he opposed increased armaments and spoke for the America First Committee against the Lend-Lease Bill in 1941. After the war, as a member of the House Public Lands Committee, he sponsored a number of conservation measures—land reclamation, irrigation, and flood control—and the Theodore Roosevelt Memorial Park, and a liberalization of the Alaskan homestead system. He enacted several bills for the betterment of American Indians and to repay them for land taken in the construction of Garrison Dam, which he had worked to finance.

Lemke was serious and reserved, with stern features and a manner that reflected his farm background. Although something of a deist, he accepted his wife's later Christian Science affiliation. He died in Fargo, N. Dak., of a sudden coronary attack at the age of seventy-one and was buried in that city's Riverside Cemetery. Lemke's career, unlike that of more traditional politicians, defies easy characterization. A dedicated public servant, he tenaciously pursued those policies, however radical or hopeless, which he believed to be in the best interests of his constituents. Many considered him an extremist, and his zeal sometimes narrowed his vision and led him into questionable positions or dubious alliances. Yet as architect of the Nonpartisan League's program in North Dakota and as Congressman, he introduced and achieved enactment of much responsible, liberal legislation.

[Lemke was also the author of *You and Your Money* (1938); the Lemke Papers are kept at the Univ. of N. Dak. Lib.; Nat. Nonpartisan League Papers at Minn. Hist. Soc.; Edward C. Blackorby, *Prairie Rebel: The Public Life of William Lemke* (1963) has bibliography listing other sources; David H. Bennett, *Demagogues in the Depression: Am. Radicals and the Union Party, 1932–1936* (1969); Robert L. Morlan, *Political Prairie Fire: The Nonpartisan League, 1915–1922* (1955); Theodore Saloutos and John D. Hicks, *Agricultural Discontent in the Middle West, 1900–1939* (1951). For a photograph of Lemke, see sketch in *Nat. Cyc. Am. Biog.*, XXXVIII, pp. 33–34.]

EDWARD C. BLACKORBY

LENROOT, IRVINE LUTHER (Jan. 31, 1869-Jan. 26, 1949), congressman, senator, and federal judge, was born in Superior, Wis., the third son and fourth of six children of Swedish immigrant parents, Lars and Fredrika Regina (Larsdotter or Larson) Lenroot. His father, who had simplified his original name of Linderoth after coming to America in the 1850's, was a blacksmith. He later achieved some prosperity in timber and real estate ventures.

From his family, from a dedicated Yankee schoolmaster, and from his frontier community, young Lenroot early acquired high standards of private and public morality, respect for democracy and enterprise, the habits of hard work, and Republican political views. He joined his teacher's Presbyterian church, but later became a Congregationalist. Lenroot attended public schools and completed what was the equivalent of a high school education in 1884. Over the next three years he held several jobs and shared in the logging operations of one of his brothers. In 1887 he enrolled at Parsons Business College in nearby Duluth, Minn. Becoming an expert shorthand stenographer, he worked during the 1890's for a Superior law firm and then (1893-1906) as court reporter for the superior court of Douglas County. Meanwhile he studied law on his own and was admitted to the bar in 1898. On Jan. 22, 1890, he married Clara Pamelia (Clough) McCoy, the widowed daughter of a local judge. They had two children, Katharine Fredrica and Dorothy.

Lenroot meanwhile became active in local politics as a reform Republican. When Robert M. La Follette championed reform on the state level, Lenroot joined his faction, and in 1900, when La Follette first won election as governor, Lenroot was elected to the state assembly. In the ensuing battles for a primary election law, heavier taxation of railroads, and other reforms, Lenroot's superior analytical intelligence, adroitness in drafting legislation, parliamentary and debating skill, and high integrity made him one of La Follette's principal lieutenants. He was twice reelected, and from 1903 to 1907 he served as speaker of the assembly. La Follette, now a United States senator, chose Lenroot to oppose Gov. James O. Davidson in the Republican primary of 1906; but Davidson, himself a moderate Progressive, easily withstood the challenge.

Two years later Lenroot won election to the House of Representatives, where he served until 1918. He joined George W. Norris and the Republican insurgents in curbing the powers of Speaker Joseph G. Cannon and the Rules Committee and led a prolonged campaign against "gag rule" and caucus domination. A foe of special interests, he opposed his party's commitment to a high tariff and supported progressive railroad regulatory laws.

World War I proved a turning point in Lenroot's career. He reluctantly supported American entry as the only honorable course open and helped pass the draft law; La Follette argued and voted against both measures. In 1918 Lenroot ran for the Senate in a special election to fill the seat left vacant by the death of Paul Husting. In his campaign he further demonstrated his opposition to La Follette's position on America's entry into the war and his own loyalty to the American cause. La Follette backed Lenroot's opponent in the Republican primary. Lenroot won, and with the support of the "loyalty" element, both progressive and conservative, he went on to win the general election, thus marking a new configuration in Wisconsin politics. He was reelected for a full term in 1920. Earlier that year, at the Republican national convention, he was picked by party leaders to run as the vice-presidential candidate with Warren G. Harding, but the convention, balking at further dictation and conservative in mood, chose Calvin Coolidge instead.

Lenroot disapproved both the radical and reactionary forces that swelled after the war and tried to steer a middle course. Increasingly, however, his radical enemies drove him closer to his new conservative friends. Lenroot made positive contributions in the areas of conservation and agriculture. A close friend of Gifford Pinchot and a longtime champion of regulated development of public resources, he contributed importantly to the Federal Water Power Act (1920), which established a commission to authorize and license navigation improvements and hydroelectric plants on public land; and to the Mineral Leasing Act (1920), which empowered the secretary of the interior to grant private leases to oil and mineral deposits on federal land on terms favorable to the public interest. He was chiefly responsible for the Agricultural Credits Act of 1923, which set up twelve intermediate credit banks to provide loans to farmers. As a member of the Senate Committee on Public Lands and Survey (he became chairman in January 1924), Lenroot participated in the Teapot Dome hearings, but because of his closeness to the administration, many Progressives questioned his willingness to press the investigation. Newspaper and other criticism became so severe that Lenroot's health broke down, and he resigned the chairmanship in March 1924.

Lenroot was defeated for renomination in 1926 by John J. Blaine, and after the expiration of his Senate term he entered law practice in Washington. In 1929 President Hoover appointed Lenroot a judge of the federal Court of Customs and Patent Appeals in New York City a post he held until his retirement in 1944. After the death of his first wife in 1942, Lenroot married Eleonore von Eltz of New Rochelle, N.Y., on Feb. 9, 1943. He died of cancer in Washington a few days before his eightieth birthday and was buried in Greenwood Cemetery in Superior.

Lenroot failed to gain wide recognition either from his contemporaries or from history. Though a fine public speaker, he did not capture the popular imagination. Hardworking and quiet in his friendliness, he was not hail-fellow-well-met. Balanced in view, with an eye toward the complexity of things, he increasingly preferred achieving reasonable progress through compromise to generating sharp issues. And when forces polarized and positions solidified, even his skillful mediating efforts often yielded meager results and little glory. This was true of his adroit work for United States participation in the League of Nations, and later, under President Coolidge, for United States membership in the World Court. For years Lenroot labored in the shadow of the charismatic La Follette; then he suffered from La Follette's enmity. Lacking a strong political base in Wisconsin, he never won the attention reserved for presidential prospects.

[Lenroot discarded most of his papers, but some remain at the Lib. of Cong.; they include an unpublished memoir and family information and sketches compiled by Katharine Lenroot. Other key manuscript collections include the papers of Robert M. La Follette (Lib. of Cong. and State Hist. Soc. of Wis.), Gifford Pinchot (Lib. of Cong.), and William Kent (Yale Univ.). Secondary sources that deal exten-sively with Lenroot include: J. Leonard Bates, *The Origins of Teapot Dome* (1963); Burl Noggle, *Teapot Dome* (1962); Belle Case and Fola La Follette, *Robert M. La Follette* (2 vols., 1953); Herbert F. Margulies, *The Decline of the Progressive Movement in Wis., 1890–1920* (1968); Padraic M. Kennedy, "Lenroot, La Follette, and the Campaign of 1906," *Wis. Mag. of Hist.*, Spring 1959; and Robert Griffith, "Prelude to Insurgency: Irvine L. Lenroot and the Republican Primary of 1908," *ibid.*, Autumn 1965. The longest and best obituary article is in the *Superior Evening Telegram*, Feb. 4, 1949; see also *N.Y. Times*, Jan. 27, 1949.]

HERBERT F. MARGULIES

LEOPOLD, (RAND) ALDO (Jan. 11, 1886–Apr. 21, 1948), wildlife ecologist and environmental philosopher, was born in Burlington, Iowa, the eldest of four children of Carl Leopold and Clara (Starker) Leopold. His parents were second-generation Americans of German descent; both grandfathers were graduates of German universities who came to the United States and engaged in business and banking. Leopold's father was owner and manager of a factory that manufactured office furniture. Aldo began a lifelong interest in ornithology by observing birds in the Mississippi River bottomlands near his home. After graduating from Lawrenceville (N.J.) Preparatory School in 1905, he entered Yale University's Sheffield Scientific School, where he received the B.S. in 1908 and the following year, the degree of master of forestry from the Yale School of Forestry. He then entered the U.S. Forest Service as a forest assistant on the Apache National Forest in Arizona Territory. In 1911 he became deputy supervisor of the Carson National Forest in New Mexico and was promoted to supervisor the following year. A near-fatal attack of Bright's disease incapacitated him in 1913, but he recovered to take a lead in starting the game protection movement in the Southwest. In 1917 his efforts were recognized with an appointment as assistant district forester in charge of game, fish, and recreation and a medal from the Permanent Wildlife Protection Fund.

At this stage of his career Leopold's plan for protecting valued game species was to eliminate their predators. Wolves, bears, and mountain lions had to be exterminated. Gradually, however, he adopted a more ecological view. At its core was the realization that predators played a vital role in maintaining the health of the biosphere by keeping the prey species in line with environmental carrying capacity. The tragic history of the deer herd on Arizona's Kaibab Plateau, which expanded enormously in the 1920's only to die back from starvation, shocked Leopold into the new mode of thinking.

His subsequent ideas about wildlife management were premised on the idea of balance and long-term stability.

Meanwhile Leopold interrupted his Forest Service career in 1918 to become secretary of the Albuquerque (N.Mex.) Chamber of Commerce. But he rejoined the service in the summer of 1919, hopeful that its management philosophy had become less utilitarian. Specifically, Leopold wanted the Forest Service to start preserving the wilderness for its recreational and aesthetic values. Arthur Carhart, a young landscape architect associated with the Denver office of the service, shared this interest. Together they launched what was regarded in most forestry circles as an impossible and irrelevant dream. But Leopold persisted, writing in 1921 in the *Journal of Forestry* a pioneering statement of the need for wilderness protection in the national forests. His ideas bore fruit on June 3, 1924, when the Forest Service designated 574,000 acres in New Mexico as the Gila Wilderness Area. This was the first of seventy-eight Forest Service wilderness designations totaling fourteen million acres.

For Leopold wilderness preserves did not exist merely for recreational purposes. He saw them as symbols of society's capacity for self-restraint in the matter of growth and development. At stake here was the quality of people's lives. Wildernesses also constituted reservoirs of the frontier environment where, according to Leopold, the American character was shaped and where it would be sustained in an increasingly urbanized future. "Of what avail are forty freedoms without a blank spot on the map?" ("The Green Lagoons," *American Forest,* 51 [1945], 414), he wrote. In addition, wilderness had value in Leopold's eyes as an example of an undisturbed ecosystem where environmental scientists could study the processes that sustain land health.

Leopold served as associate director and field consultant of the U.S. Forest Products Laboratory in Madison, Wis., from 1924 to July 1928, when he became game consultant for the Sporting Arms and Ammunition Manufacturers' Institute. During the next three years he made game surveys in Illinois, Indiana, Iowa, Michigan, Minnesota, and Wisconsin. His findings were published as *Report on Game Survey of the North Central States* (1931). One of the first intensive studies of game population ever undertaken in America, it was an appraisal of the possibilities of game management as a means of game restoration. During this period, he also developed a national game management policy for the American Game Protective Association.

Following a year of private practice as a consulting forester, Leopold was appointed in 1933 as professor of wildlife management at the University of Wisconsin. This chair, the first of its kind in the country, was created especially for him; he held it until his death, developing new approaches to deer management, soil conservation, and environmentally responsible agriculture. In 1935 Leopold made studies of game administration in Germany and Czechoslovakia under the auspices of the Oberlander Trust and the Carl Schurz Foundation. He was particularly concerned with preventing the wholesale adoption of European methods with their overzealous extermination of predators.

In this phase of his career Leopold's most important publication was *Game Management* (1933). A textbook that revolutionized the field, it described the art of harvesting game species in such a way as to leave their reproductive capacity unimpaired. Leopold's concepts were based on the emerging science of systems ecology; they integrated the most advanced knowledge of population dynamics, food chains, and habitat protection. Leopold's wildlife management ideas, adopted by a succession of his talented Wisconsin students, quickly dominated the profession. Basic to his whole philosophy was his belief that the environment was not a commodity for man to control but rather a community to which he belonged.

This idea stimulated the development of his most important concept: the land ethic. According to Leopold, ethics had evolved over time to include more and more of the human community. The world's great religious thinkers called on the individual to regard all men as brothers worthy of respect. The land ethic, in Leopold's words, "simply enlarges the boundaries of the community to include soils, waters, plants, and animals, or collectively the land" (*A Sand County Almanac,* 1949, p. 204). Such an ethic demanded that questions about the use of the environment be studied "in terms of what is ethically and esthetically right, as well as what is economically expedient" (*ibid.,* p. 224). An action is right, he added, when "it tends to preserve the integrity, stability, and beauty of the biotic community" (*ibid.,* pp. 224-225). Here was an entirely new way of defining conservation, one that deemphasized man's interests in relation to those of the life community as a whole.

Although Leopold published versions of his

system of environmental ethics in articles during the 1930's, full formulation awaited publication of his best-known book *A Sand County Almanac*. Published posthumously in 1949, this work has been compared to that of Henry David Thoreau and John Muir. It became, in many ways, the bible of the surging environmental movement of the 1960's and early 1970's.

Before his death at the age of sixty-two, Leopold had been active in an ever-increasing number of conservation endeavors. He served on the council of the Society of American Foresters (1927-1931) and in 1946 was elected a fellow. He was a director of the National Audubon Society and a vice-president of the American Forestry Association. He helped organize the Wilderness Society in 1935 and served on its council thereafter. He was also an organizer of the Wildlife Society in 1937, serving as its president in 1939, and he was president of the Ecological Society of America in 1947. President Franklin D. Roosevelt appointed him a member of the Special Committee on Wild Life Restoration in 1934. From 1943 until his death he served as a member of the Wisconsin Conservation Commission.

Leopold married Estella Luna Bergere on Oct. 9, 1912, in Santa Fe, N.Mex. They had five children: Aldo Starker, Luna Bergere, Adelina, Aldo Carl, and Estella Bergere, four of whom chose careers in environmental science. His death was the result of a heart attack suffered while fighting a grass fire near his cabin on the Wisconsin River. Burial was in Aspen Grove Cemetery, Burlington, Iowa. Although Leopold had no formal religious affiliation, many regard his extension of the meaning of ethics from man-man to man-land relations as a religious act of towering importance to the future of life on earth.

[A preliminary bibliography of Leopold's writings, containing over three hundred entries, appeared in the *Wildlife Research Newsletter* No. 35 published by the Department of Wildlife Management of the Univ. of Wisconsin. The largest collection of his papers, amounting to more than sixty boxes, is at the University Archives of the Univ. of Wisconsin, Madison. Some of Leopold's unpublished and, in some cases, uncompleted essays appeared in Luna B. Leopold, ed., *Round River: From the Journals of Aldo Leopold* (1953). Criticism that this volume does not represent Leopold's best work has shadowed its existence. Roderick Nash's *Wilderness and the American Mind* (1967; rev. ed., 1973) contains a chapter on the evolution of Leopold's ecological perspective and its application to wilderness preservation. For an interpretation of Leopold's role in wildlife management, see James B. Trefethen, *Crusade for Wildlife* (1961). Susan Flader's unpublished dissertation "Aldo Leopold and the Evolution of an Ecological Attitude" (Stanford Univ., 1971) is limited to Leopold's thinking regarding deer management. Flader has published

"Thinking Like a Mountain: A Biographical Study of Aldo Leopold," *Forest Hist.*, Apr. 1973. Of the several obituaries, the best is an analytical essay by Paul L. Errington, "In Appreciation of Aldo Leopold," *Jour. of Wildlife Management*, Oct. 1948. Donald Fleming has assessed Leopold's influence on the American environmental movement in a perceptive essay, "Roots of the New Conservation Movement," *Perspectives in Am. Hist.*, 1972. An oil portrait of Leopold by Owen Kampen is in the National Wildlife Federation headquarters, Washington, D.C.]

RODERICK NASH

LEWIN, KURT (Sept. 9, 1890-Feb. 12, 1947), was one of the academic psychologists who immigrated to America from Germany after Hitler came to power. He was born in Mogilno, in the province of Posen, then part of Prussia, later of Poland. His father, Leopold Lewin, who owned the general store of the town and a small farm, was a leader in the Jewish community, and at the same time part of the broader community, to the extent, for example, of celebrating holidays like Christmas as well as those of the Jewish calendar. The mother was Recha (Engle) Lewin. It was a closely knit family with four children, the eldest a daughter, followed by Kurt and then two younger brothers. In 1905 the family moved to Berlin to secure better educational advantages for the children, and Kurt completed Gymnasium there. His university years followed the usual exploratory pattern of the European student, with a semester in Freiburg in 1909, and a semester in Munich. At Freiburg he began with the study of medicine and soon shifted to natural science. In the spring of 1910 he enrolled at the University of Berlin to work for a degree under Karl Stumpf, whose relatively free approach to psychological problems had already played a part in turning Max Wertheimer and Kurt Koffka away from the current Wundtian tradition toward the work from which Gestalt psychology was to emerge. Lewin, whose interests included philosophy, spoke of Ernst Cassirer as another strong influence of his student years.

Lewin spent the war years in active military service, rising to the rank of lieutenant and receiving the Iron Cross. He received the doctorate during this period, in 1916. From 1921 until he left Germany he was at the University of Berlin, as assistant in the Psychological Institute under Stumpf and finally as "ausserordentlicher Professor" without civil service rank, the highest position open to a Jew in Prussian academic life. In 1929 he attended the New Haven meeting of the International Psychological Association, and in the summer of 1932 he went to Stanford as visiting professor. He was about to return to Germany when Hitler came to power, and realizing, before many of his contemporaries, the implications of the new regime, he decided to bring his family to America.

After two years at Cornell, Lewin went in the fall of 1935 to the Child Welfare Research Station of the University of Iowa as professor of child psychology. Here, with the support of the Laura Spelman Rockefeller Fund, he gathered an active group of young American graduate and postdoctoral students. Together they carried out pioneer work in what came to be called "action research" and "group dynamics," empirical studies of human behavior in a social context. In 1944 Lewin moved, with a group of associates and graduate students, to the Massachusetts Institute of Technology to establish the Research Center for Group Dynamics.

It is probable that Lewin had a greater influence on the development of American psychology than any other emigré of the Hitler era. He was one of the first to apply laboratory techniques to everyday behavior, always formulating a problem in terms of a theory to be tested in experiments, the experiments in turn bringing about advances in theory. One example is Bluma Zeigarnik's comparison of memory for tasks that were completed and tasks that were left incomplete (1927). It began with Lewin's observation that a waiter in a restaurant could repeat a long list of items until he had served an order, but a few minutes later could hardly recall any of them. Zeigarnik's laboratory demonstration of the advantage for memory of tasks that were interrupted before they were finished played an important part in the development of Lewinian concepts. In this case, the assumption was made that the intention to perform a task sets up a psychological tension which is released with the completion of the task, and that the release of the tension is related to the loss of memory. Interest in these new kinds of problems and the ways in which they were being studied spread, and a succession of young Americans from different academic settings went to Berlin. The influence of this group, as well as Lewin's visits to this country, meant that he had already begun to play a role in American psychology before he came to Cornell in 1933.

In his approach to psychology Lewin thought of himself as closely allied to the Gestalt psychologists, though Gestalt psychology had had its origins in problems of perception and learning, whereas Lewin's work had soon begun to emphasize forces leading to action. His dissertation was a criticism of the then current acceptance of the "associative bond" as the basis of learning and behavior, especially as it was treated in laboratories like those of G. E. Müller. Without denying the role of association in some kinds of learning, Lewin treated the intention of the person concerned and emphasized *forces* in the psychological field, describing behavior as the resultant of positive and negative forces affecting the individual at a given moment. Each piece of behavior could be seen as the outcome of two kinds of factors, those of the person and those of his psychological environment.

It was these analyses of field forces determining individual behavior that in America soon led to studies of forces affecting the behavior of groups. One of the Iowa studies was a comparison of democratic and autocratic leadership, made with groups of boys (Lippitt and White, 1943). Analyses of the structure of the social group and communication among its members under the two types of leadership raised questions that were followed up in subsequent investigations. Studies in real life situations concerning social problems were made in a wide variety of settings—for example, the factory and the housing project—and led to community studies and analyses of minority group problems. As a deeply concerned Zionist, Lewin had gone through a period of conflict deciding whether to remain in the United States or to accept a chair at the Hebrew University in Jerusalem. His decision to remain in this country was in large part determined by his belief that he could, in the end, solve problems concerning minority groups more effectively with the facilities then available for research here.

Alfred J. Marrow's biography gives a good picture, both of Lewin's life and of the short, stocky man, at once gay and serious, who threw himself into life with incredible energy. He imparted his excitement about problems of psychology to his collaborators, students and colleagues alike, and drew them into his own life pattern of intense hours of work relieved by almost equally intense hours of play and discussion. Lewin was first married in 1917 to Maria Landsberg. They had a daughter, Esther Agnes (1919), and a son, Reuben Fritz (1922). This marriage terminated in divorce in 1928. A daughter, Miriam (1931), and a son, Daniel (1933), were children of his marriage in October 1928 to Gertrud Weiss. Lewin's work at M.I.T. was cut short by his sudden death from a heart attack at the age of fifty-six. He died at his home in Newtonville, Mass., and was buried in Mount Auburn Cemetery, Cambridge.

[Alfred J. Marrow, *The Practical Theorist: The Life and Work of Kurt Lewin* (1969); J. F. Brown, "The Methods of Kurt Lewin in the Psychology of Action and Affection," *Psychological Rev.*, May 1929; Fritz Heider, "On Lewin's Methods and Theory," *Jour. of Social Issues*, Supplement Series, no. 13 (1959). Lewin's books are: *A Dynamic Theory of Personality* (1935), *Principles of Topological Psychology* (1936), *Resolving Social Conflicts: Selected Papers on Group Dynamics* (1948), and *Field Theory in Social Science: Selected Theoretical Papers* (1951). For other studies referred to, see Bluma Zeigarnik, "Uber Behalten von Erledigten und Unerledigten Handlungen," *Psychologische Forschung* 9 (1927): 1-85; and Ronald Lippitt and Ralph K. White, "The Social Climate of Children's Groups," in Roger G. Barker, Jacob S. Kounin, and Herbert F. Weight, eds., *Child Behavior and Development*, pp. 485-508 (1943).]

GRACE M. HEIDER

LEWIS, GEORGE WILLIAM (Mar. 10, 1882-July 12, 1948), aeronautical engineer and research director of the National Advisory Committee for Aeronautics, was born in Ithaca, N.Y., the son of William Henry Lewis, a machinist, and Edith (Sweetland) Lewis. His father was a native of Geneva, N.Y.; his mother of England. Early in Lewis' childhood the family moved to Scranton, Pa., where he completed high school. He returned to Ithaca, however, to attend Cornell University, from which he received the degrees of mechanical engineer in 1908 and master of mechanical engineering in 1910. He then joined the engineering faculty at Swarthmore College. In 1917 he became engineer-in-charge of Clarke-Thompson Research in Philadelphia.

Lewis' connection with the National Advisory Committee for Aeronautics began in 1917 when the committee accepted a proposal he had submitted to conduct research on the internal combustion engine. Two years later he was asked to become the committee's executive officer and to take charge of its modest research facility at Langley Field in Virginia. In 1924 he was named director of aeronautical research, a title that suitably described his responsibilities. He was to hold the post for nearly a quarter of a century.

Congress had founded the N.A.C.A. in 1915 in an attempt to bring the United States abreast of European aircraft development, for despite the pioneering work of Wilbur and Orville Wright, the United States had fallen far behind France, Germany, and England in aeronautical research and development by the outbreak of World War I. The committee members—scientists, engineers, aircraft manufac-

turers; representatives of government agencies and the military—guided policy as a sort of board of directors, with Lewis as the active executive. One of their early decisions was to expend the modest research funds available during the interwar years upon aerodynamics rather than on power-plant and structures research, for Lewis believed that the full potentialities of the airplane could not be realized without a thorough understanding of the aerodynamic problems of flight.

Thus Lewis presided over the design, construction, and use of some of the world's outstanding wind tunnels. Existing tunnels, such as the one Lewis inherited at Langley in 1919, was capable of simulating only low-speed flight. N.A.C.A. and Lewis constructed in 1921 a variable-density wind tunnel which, through the use of highly compressed air, made it possible to simulate with models the flight of full-size airplanes at normal speeds. Another major tunnel introduced during his administration was a turbulence-free one with which N.A.C.A. scientists carried on vital research on wing drag. Earlier studies of this phenomenon had been frustrated by tunnel turbulence not encountered in free air. With free air conditions simulated, it was possible to study various wing curvatures and determine the shape that would produce the maximum laminar flow and thus the minimum drag. The new wing, first applied to the army's Mustang fighter of World War II, gave that plane an unusually high speed in relation to engine power. Eventually seventeen wind tunnels were in operation at Langley Field alone, including those for full-scale, free-flight, and high-speed tests, as well as the study of wind gusts and ice formation. The wind-tunnel findings were verified by actual flight tests. From this research came other notable results, among them the introduction, in the late 1920's, of cowling to cover the exposed cylinders of air-cooled engines. In the 1930's the fairing of engine nacelles of multi-engine planes into the wings began, and later the retractable landing gear was introduced. These streamlining features of design contributed to higher landing speeds, which in turn led to the tricycle landing gear and wing flaps for braking—also introduced by researchers working under Lewis' direction.

After an inspection trip to European aeronautical research centers in 1939, Lewis urged N.A.C.A. and Congress to appropriate funds for a new facility that would stress propulsion research. Located in Cleveland, Ohio (and named, after his death, the Lewis Flight Propulsion Laboratory), it was completed in 1942. Lewis himself helped plan and design the facility, as he did the Ames Aeronautical Laboratory, named for former N.A.C.A. chairman Joseph S. Ames, which opened in 1944 at Moffett Field in California. By this time Lewis was directing a staff of some 6,000 researchers, most of whom he had recruited and trained himself.

Friendly and well liked, Lewis was adept at winning the confidence and support of the leaders of the military services, a relationship that was of critical importance to both N.A.C.A. and the armed forces. He also represented N.A.C.A. before congressional committees, where he proved a lucid and convincing advocate of research appropriations. Reluctant to delegate responsibility, Lewis made frequent visits to research facilities, military flying fields, and industrial factories to keep in direct contact with his research teams and with new developments in aviation. During World War II he drove himself unusually hard, and in 1945 he developed heart trouble. When his condition grew no better, he was relieved as director of research in 1947 and became a consultant to N.A.C.A.

Personally modest, Lewis was notable for attributing the results and reports of N.A.C.A. research to his most immediately concerned subordinates. As a result, his full professional character does not emerge from his writings or from inventions or discoveries credited to him. Nonetheless, his work was significantly recognized. He received the Daniel Guggenheim Medal in 1936 for "outstanding success in . . . aeronautical research." In 1948 he was awarded the Presidential Medal for Merit and was made an honorary officer of the British Empire. He was elected to the National Academy of Sciences in 1945. Lewis married Myrtle Harvey in Scranton, Pa., on Sept. 9, 1908. They had six children: Alfred William, Harvey Sweetland, Myrtle Norlaine, George William, Leigh Kneeland, and Armin Kessler. Lewis was a Presbyterian in religion. He died of a coronary thrombosis at his summer home in Lake Winola, Pa., near Scranton, at the age of sixty-six. His remains were cremated.

[The best accounts of Lewis and his work are the memoirs by Jerome C. Hunsaker in Am. Philosophical Soc., *Year Book*, 1948, and by William F. Durand in Nat. Acad. Sci., *Biog. Memoirs*, XXV (1949); the latter has a bibliography of Lewis' publications. See also George W. Gray, *Frontiers of Flight: the Story of NACA Research* (1948); and J. C. Hunsaker, "Forty Years of Aeronautical Research," Smithsonian Institution, *Annual Report*, 1955. Lewis' "Some Modern Methods of Research in the Problems of Flight," Royal Aeronautical Soc., *Jour.* 43 (1939): 771-798, is a technical discourse on wind-tunnel research; his "The Value of the Wind Tunnel in Aeronautical Research and Design," *U.S. Air Services*, May 1938, is a brief general summary. Death record from the Pa. Dept. of Health.]

THOMAS PARKE HUGHES

LEWIS, GILBERT NEWTON (Oct. 23, 1875-Mar. 23, 1946), physical chemist, was born in Weymouth, Mass., the second of three children of Francis Wesley Lewis and Mary Burr (White) Lewis. His father, a native of New Hampshire and a graduate of Dartmouth, was a lawyer and broker. The family moved to Lincoln, Nebr., when Lewis was nine years old. He was intellectually precocious and learned to read at the age of three. He attended school only briefly but was taught by his parents until, at the age of thirteen, he entered the preparatory school of the University of Nebraska, and later the university itself. In 1893, at the end of his sophomore year, he transferred to Harvard, where he developed a strong interest in economics but concentrated in chemistry. He graduated with the B.A. degree in 1896.

After teaching for a year in Phillips Academy, Andover, Mass., Lewis returned to Harvard for graduate work in chemistry under Theodore W. Richards and received the Ph.D. in 1899, staying on for an additional year as an instructor. He then went abroad on a traveling fellowship and studied under the physical chemists Wilhelm Ostwald at Leipzig and Walter Nernst at Göttingen. Lewis returned to Harvard as an instructor for three more years and then went to Manila (1904-1905) as superintendent of weights and measures and chemist in the Bureau of Science of the Philippine Islands, a position that gave him ample opportunity for laboratory research. In 1905 he received an appointment in the Massachusetts Institute of Technology, where he joined the group of outstanding physical chemists in the research laboratory directed by Arthur Amos Noyes. Lewis was made assistant professor in 1907, associate professor in 1908, and professor in 1911. On June 21, 1912, he married Mary Hinckley Sheldon, daughter of Edward Stevens Sheldon, professor of Romance languages at Harvard. They had a daughter, Margery, and two sons, Richard Newton and Edward Sheldon, both of whom became professors of chemistry.

Although not yet forty, Lewis was recognized as one of the ablest younger physical chemists of the United States. In 1912 he accepted an appointment as professor of chemistry and dean of the College of Chemistry in the University of California at Berkeley. Save for service in France during World War I as chief of the defense division of the army's Chemical Warfare Service, Lewis continued as dean of the College of Chemistry until 1940 and as professor of chemistry until his death.

Within a few years of his arrival at the university, Lewis had developed a chemistry department that was recognized as one of the best in the world. Under his guidance, the members showed a unity of interest in the problems of chemistry and a cooperative approach in solving them that was probably unique. The time was a fortunate one, in that there were many puzzling problems, in all fields of chemistry, awaiting solution. One of Lewis' close collaborators, Joel Hildebrand, has vividly described the stimulating spirit of inquiry and the "intense scientific activity" that characterized the department, both staff members and graduate students. At the weekly departmental conference, over which Lewis presided, informal discussion of current research projects was strongly encouraged, and Lewis himself usually had some penetrating comment to make.

In his own research, Lewis' two most important contributions were in the fields of chemical thermodynamics and of valence and the electronic structure of molecules. His first paper, based on his thesis, was published with Richards in 1898 and dealt with the electrochemical and thermochemical properties of solutions of zinc and cadmium in mercury. For some time chemists had been striving to discover the principles determining the directions in which chemical reactions could take place and the nature of chemical systems in equilibrium. Through the efforts of Josiah Willard Gibbs and others, it was demonstrated that the determining factor in each case is a quantity called the change in free energy accompanying the reaction. Lewis set for himself the task of developing a practical system of chemical thermodynamics and of formulating tables of values of the free energies of a large number of substances. With the assistance of his research students and co-workers, he attacked this problem with vigor over a period of some twenty-five years. In 1923 he and his colleague Merle Randall published *Thermodynamics and the Free Energy of Chemical Substances,* which covered the results of this work and had a vast influence on the teaching of chemistry and the practical applications of thermodynamics to chemical problems.

In his first paper on valence and electronic structure, published in 1916, Lewis introduced two important ideas relating to the mechanism of chemical combination. The first is that a chemical bond between two atoms involves two electrons, held jointly by the two atoms, and that these two shared electrons serve to complete the electron shells of each of the two atoms. The second idea is that the shared pair of electrons may be held equally strongly by the two atoms, or more strongly by one than by the other, so that a continuous series of bonds is permitted, ranging from nonpolar (normal covalent) to extremely polar (ionic) bonds. In hypothesizing the structure of such a combination, Lewis first placed the eight electrons in a completed shell of an atom at the corners of a cube, and later placed them as four electron pairs at the corners of a tetrahedron. His concept seemed to be incompatible with the picture of the atom developed by Niels Bohr, which involved electrons moving in orbits around the nucleus. Lewis vigorously supported his own theories, which were also brilliantly developed by Irving Langmuir in a series of papers published in 1919 and 1920. The apparent contradiction in the different views of the atom was resolved a decade later through the development of the theory of quantum mechanics. Lewis presented his theory of the chemical bond in greater detail in his *Valence and the Structure of Atoms and Molecules,* published in 1923. This book had an influence on the field of structural chemistry only a little less than that of the book on thermodynamics in the field of thermodynamic chemistry. The modern theory of valence and the chemical bond, which is based upon quantum mechanics and a large mass of experimental information about molecular structure that was not available to Lewis, retains the principal features of Lewis' early theory, and also the chief additions made to it by Langmuir.

Lewis made many other contributions to science, covering an extraordinarily wide range of subjects. Beginning in 1908 he published several papers on Einstein's theory of relativity, in which he presented his own derivation of the relation between mass and energy. In 1919 he discovered the tetratomic oxygen molecule, by use of an original method, the analysis of the magnetic properties of solutions of oxygen in liquid nitrogen. In 1933, shortly after the discovery of heavy hydrogen (deuterium), he made the first preparations of pure heavy water (deuterium oxide), and he collaborated with Ernest O. Lawrence in the first use of the deuteron, accelerated in the cyclotron, as a tool for the study of the properties of atomic nuclei. During the last few years of his life Lewis and his students showed that the fluorescence of organic molecules involves an excited triplet state, and measured the paramagnetism of this triplet state. Among his other publications are discussions of his concept of ultimate rational units, the nature of light quanta, the symmetry of time in physics, the biology of heavy water, neutron optics, a generalized theory of acids and bases, and the color of organic substances. He did not limit his interests to physical science, however, and his continuing concern with economics was expressed in two papers on the problem of stabilizing prices. At the age of sixty-five, after his mandatory retirement from administrative duties, Lewis began to read widely on prehistoric America, and in his last paper, "Thermodynamics of an Ice Age" (*Science*, July 19, 1946), published anonymously after his death, he explored the cause and sequence of glaciation. He also wrote on the beginning of civilization in America, and presented evidence supporting his view that civilization developed originally on the American continent and spread from there to Asia, Africa, and Europe.

Lewis was a man of striking appearance and powerful personality. Hildebrand refers to his wide interests and his sparkling sense of humor, which made him a stimulating companion and conversationalist. "He loved good company and always made it better by joining it. He was very sensitive to humbug or pretense. He shunned the crowd and squirmed under personal praise. . . . Lewis was not at ease in speaking in public and rarely accepted invitations to deliver any but a scientific address. When sufficiently aroused, however, he could be effective in debate, and few cared to cross swords with him in arguments in the Academic Senate" (*Biog. Memoirs*, XXXI, 222).

Lewis was elected to the National Academy of Sciences in 1913, but resigned in 1934 to express his disagreement with what he regarded as undue domination of its affairs by particular individuals. He was an honorary member of the Royal Institution of Great Britain, the Chemical Society of London, the Indian Academy of Sciences, the Swedish Academy, the Danish Academy, the Royal Society of London, and the Franklin Institute of Pennsylvania. He was awarded the Nichols, Gibbs, Davy, Arrhenius and Richards medals, and the medal of the Society of Arts and Sciences. He received honorary degrees from the universities of Chicago, Wisconsin, Pennsylvania, Liverpool, and Madrid. Lewis continued his re-

search until the end of his life. He died at the age of seventy of a heart attack while working in his laboratory.

[Joel H. Hildebrand in *Obituary Notices of Fellows of the Royal Soc. of London*, V (1947), reprinted with minor additions in Nat. Acad. Sci., *Biog. Memoirs*, XXXI (1958), is a full account by a faculty associate; it includes a list of Lewis' 165 published papers and books. Arthur Lachman, *Borderland of the Unknown: The Life Story of Gilbert Newton Lewis* (1955), is personal and anecdotal. See also W. F. Giauque in Am. Philosophical Soc., *Year Book*, 1946; and G. Ross Robertson in *Chemical and Engineering News*, Nov. 10, 1947. Lewis' letters and other papers are at the Univ. of Calif., Berkeley.]

LINUS PAULING

LEWIS, LLOYD DOWNS (May 2, 1891– Apr. 21, 1949), journalist and biographer, was born in Pendleton, Ind., the elder of two children and only son of J. J. ("Jay") Lewis, farmer, teacher, and onetime editor of the *Anderson* (Ind.) *Herald,* and Josephine (Downs) Lewis. Both parents were Quakers. After attending local public schools, Lewis entered Swarthmore College; he graduated with a B.A. degree in 1913. He then became a reporter for the *Philadelphia North American,* but in 1915 moved to Chicago to join the staff of the *Record-Herald.* That city, crude but vibrant, captivated him, and he remained there the rest of his life.

After the United States entered World War I, Lewis, despite his Quaker heritage, enlisted in the navy and served for one year. Upon his discharge he became a publicity man for the Chicago movie theatre chain of Balaban and Katz and worked in that capacity until 1930. Even in the high-powered world of promotion, Lewis could not put out of his mind recollections of long talks with aging Union veterans in the sleepy town of his youth. Their reminiscences, often contradictory, aroused his interest in Abraham Lincoln and the legends that clustered about his name. In his off hours he gathered material for his first book, *Myths after Lincoln,* which appeared in 1929. Wise, provocative, at times gently cynical, it was immediately successful.

That same year saw the publication of *Chicago: The History of Its Reputation*—still the best short history of the city—which Lewis wrote in collaboration with Henry Justin Smith, the scholarly, patrician editor of the *Chicago Daily News.* The *Daily News* was traditionally hospitable to serious writers, and in 1930 Lewis joined its staff. He began as a drama critic, moved up to amusement editor, and in 1936 took over the sports section. There, he gave new vitality to sports writing. Recognizing that, in the age of radio, readers already knew the results of baseball games and horse races, he played up the dramatic element in sports. Among other innovations, he transferred news of wrestling, which he knew to be rigged, to the amusement section, and he emphasized colorful personalities like baseball's Dizzy Dean, Satchel Paige, and Casey Stengel.

The Civil War still fascinated him, and he began a biography of Gen. William Tecumseh Sherman. The task was arduous, compelling him, after a full day, to spend his evenings in research in libraries and then work far into the night at home. *Sherman: Fighting Prophet* appeared in 1932 and was acclaimed a masterpiece. Lewis collaborated with Sinclair Lewis (no kin) on a Civil War play, *Jayhawker,* that had a short Broadway run in 1935. He also wrote in 1941 a commissioned biography of John S. Wright, Chicago businessman and publisher of the *Prairie Farmer.* His historical work received recognition in 1937 when he was given a year's appointment as a visiting lecturer in history at the University of Chicago.

In 1943 Lewis was made managing editor of the *Daily News,* but he found the supervisory role uncongenial. "All my life I've been a reporter, trying to find out what happened yesterday or a hundred years ago," he complained to a friend. "Now I'm supposed to know what events mean. I don't like it a damned bit." He resigned in 1945, and although he continued for a time to write a weekly column for the *Chicago Sun,* he devoted most of the rest of his life to a biography of Ulysses S. Grant.

Lewis was of medium height and trim build, with a shock of dark hair that refused to turn gray and a small moustache. He was a superb conversationalist. A vocabulary that ranged from imaginative profanity through the full range of *Webster's International* enabled him to express his ideas and opinions—sometimes iconoclastic, often unconventional, always stimulating—in ways no listener could forget. Lewis married Kathryn Dougherty of Chicago on Dec. 30, 1925. They had no children, but took into their home and reared Nancy Anderson, the daughter of a friend.

Lewis took an avid interest in contemporary politics. He was a staunch supporter of Franklin D. Roosevelt, arguing with conservative friends that the president had saved the free enterprise system. He backed Henry Horner in his successful campaigns for governor of Illinois in 1932 and 1936 and became one of his confidential advisors—a service which Horner recognized by appointing Lewis a trustee of the Illinois State Historical Library. Lewis also

supported his friend and neighbor Adlai E. Stevenson when he ran for governor in 1948.

The following year Lewis died of a coronary occlusion at his home near Libertyville, Ill. Stevenson and Marc Connelly, author of *The Green Pastures,* were the only speakers at the simple funeral held in Lewis' home, and he was buried in the family lot at Pendleton, Ind. His biography of Grant, completed to the early summer of 1861, was published posthumously under the title *Captain Sam Grant* (1950). The historian Bruce Catton later wrote a companion volume, *Grant Moves South* (1960), covering the rest of Grant's life.

[Lewis collaborated with Henry Justin Smith on a second book, *Oscar Wilde Discovers America* (1936), an account of Wilde's lecture tour of the United States. *Letters from Lloyd Lewis* (1950) is a collection of letters to his publisher describing his research in writing the Grant biography. An appreciation by Adlai Stevenson and an essay on Lewis as a historian are in the *Newberry Lib.* (Chicago) *Bull.,* July, 1950. Biographical sources include obituaries in Chicago newspapers; information from Mrs. Lloyd Lewis; and personal acquaintance.]

PAUL M. ANGLE

LEWIS, WILLIAM DRAPER (Apr. 27, 1867–Sept. 2, 1949), lawyer and scholar, was born in Philadelphia, the son of Henry Lewis and Fannie Hannah (Wilson) Lewis. Of Quaker background, Lewis was educated at Germantown Academy and then attended Haverford College, graduating with a B.S. in 1888. Three years later he received both a law degree and a Ph.D. in economics from the University of Pennsylvania, where he studied with Simon N. Patten. He lectured in economics at Haverford from 1890 to 1896, and in 1891 was an instructor in legal history at the Wharton School of the University of Pennsylvania. On June 22, 1892, he married Caroline Mary Cope; they had three children. In 1896 he joined the department of law at the university, becoming dean of the school and professor of law before he had reached the age of thirty.

He was chosen for the job, he recalled much later, because he was "perhaps the only lawyer then living who would take it and agree to give his whole time to it." Despite warnings from lawyers that teaching law was best considered not a profession but a hobby, Lewis did did not hesitate to join the growing number who taught law full time, using the case system originally developed at Harvard. Under Lewis' leadership the law school at Pennsylvania flourished, as he quickly recruited a faculty of distinction. By 1901, just five years after becoming dean, he had raised enough money to move the school out of the old criminal court buildings in Independence Square and into its own facility, integrated with the rest of the university. Lewis also arranged for the law school to take over the *American Law Register,* which he himself had edited between 1892 and 1895.

Although busy with administration and teaching, he was also an energetic scholar. Having written *Our Sheep and the Tariff* (1890) and *The Federal Power Over Commerce* (1892) before joining the law school, he turned out a variety of publications during his years as dean, including his own edition of *Blackstone's Commentaries* (1897); casebooks on such topics as interference in trade and equity jurisdiction; and an eight-volume collection of essays on *Great American Lawyers* (1907-1909), which included a study by him of John Marshall. With George Wharton Pepper he prepared a twenty-three-volume *Digest of Decisions and Encyclopaedia of Pennsylvania Law, 1754-1898* (1898-1906).

In 1914 Lewis resigned as dean of the law school (but remained ten more years as a professor) to run for governor of Pennsylvania on the Progressive ticket. The experience was an unhappy one, as his candidacy proved weak; after a two-hour talk at Oyster Bay with Theodore Roosevelt, he was persuaded to withdraw in favor of fusion behind an independent Democrat. Nevertheless, Lewis' zest for reformist politics was undiminished. An organizer of the Progressive movement in his own state, he had been chairman of the platform committee at the national Progressive party convention in 1912, where he had contributed to the confusion of the gathering by misreading a key section in the party's industrial plank. He served in the same capacity at the 1916 convention. Three years later he tried to summarize and reassert the spirit of the movement in a highly partisan, but generally well-received, *Life of Theodore Roosevelt,* for which he was able to persuade William Howard Taft to supply a substantial, if somewhat ambiguous, introduction. For Lewis, there was no need to qualify praise of "T.R." "Since Caesar," he wrote, "perhaps no one has attained among crowding duties and great responsibilities such high proficiency in so many separate fields of human activity." He was pleased to count himself among the colonel's followers, "an ever-increasing number of earnest men and women" crusading against "the reactionary element" of the Republican party, in order to war on the evils of American society (*Life,* pp. 17, 323, 369-370). Among the causes Lewis advocated at one time or another were a constitutional amendment to abolish child labor, establishment of a coal commission to enforce price and wage levels, and public health insurance.

It was, therefore, not surprising that Lewis responded to the crisis of the depression by making a full and explicit commitment to the New Deal. In October 1932, the old Bull Mooser announced his support of Franklin Roosevelt, calling him "a broad-minded Progressive" and ridiculing Hoover's "delusion" that prosperity was near. As one who had predicted forty years previously that the remaining duties of state governments would soon be transferred to Washington, there was little in the New Deal to alarm Lewis. Unlike most leaders of the legal profession, he was even enthusiastic about Roosevelt's court-packing proposals of 1937, perhaps likening them in his mind to the earlier Roosevelt's call for recall of judicial decisions, which he had also favored. Testifying before Congress in March of 1937, Lewis argued that court-packing was essentially conservative, since it responded to a justifiable resentment against the Supreme Court's attack on needed social legislation and thus would prevent "radical and regrettable" action.

By this time Lewis' own work had turned in a direction quite different from that of the first half of his career. In 1923 he left the law school at Pennsylvania to direct a new organization that he had done much to found, the American Law Institute. The institute had been conceived by a committee of distinguished lawyers, judges, and scholars, including John W. Davis, George W. Wickersham, Learned Hand, Benjamin Cardozo, and Roscoe Pound. Lewis, secretary of the committee, had recruited its chairman, Elihu Root, whom he had come to know while they worked together drafting minimum requirements for admission to the bar for the American Bar Association. Alarmed by growing dissatisfaction in the country over the administration of justice, the sponsors of the institute hoped to establish a juristic center for the improvement of American law, in accordance with a proposal advanced in 1921 by the Association of American Law Schools. Their particular goal was to combine the resources of all branches of the profession to produce a massive restatement of the common law, a critical summary and evaluation of the state of legal doctrine under different topical headings. Prepared by reporters and committees of experts, the restatement was expected to remedy the two defects of American law that most disturbed Lewis and his colleagues, its uncertainty and its complexity.

As his friend George Pepper recalled, once founded, the American Law Institute was largely "the expression of the personality of one man." According to Cardozo, Lewis' "tact and wisdom and self-sacrificing industry" were crucial to its success. Backed by the Carnegie Corporation, eventually to a total of almost $2.5 million, the institute completed its first restatement in 1944. Nine broad topics were covered, ranging from contracts, which in 1932 was the first to be finished, to property, which was the last. In all, the restatement ran to twenty-four volumes and more than seventeen thousand pages. From the beginning Cardozo had interpreted the very existence of the institute as proof that laissez-faire in law was on the wane. By 1944, there were few who would doubt the validity of his claim.

Three years after completion of the first restatement, Lewis resigned as director of the institute. He died at his summer home in Northeast Harbor, Maine, after a long illness. Even as he approached eighty, he retained the vigor and sense of adventure that marked his Bull Moose years. In 1946, as chairman of the institute's Committee on Essential Human Rights, he proclaimed the possibility of accord with the Soviet Union and expressed respect for that country's achievements on behalf of human welfare. It was always something of a mystery how Lewis, whose politics often clashed sharply with those of the practicing lawyers and judges in the institute, was able to maintain authority and harmony. It appears there was a sincerity and simplicity about "Uncle Billy," as his students had referred to him, that was disarming. He was reassuringly fallible, often awkward in oral presentation, and apt to mix metaphors and mispronounce words. He was thus well suited to bringing about what some regarded as the main achievement of the institute, an atmosphere of trust between avowedly pragmatic men of affairs and their academic brethren in the law schools.

[See *N.Y. Times* obituary, Sept. 3, 1949, *Times* articles throughout Lewis' career; recollections of Lewis by Owen J. Roberts, George Wharton Pepper, and Augustus N. Hand, *University of Pennsylvania Law Review*, 98 (1949–1950), 1–9. Also helpful are Herbert F. Goodrich and Paul A. Wonkin, *The Story of the American Law Institute, 1923–1961* (1961), the original *Report of the Committee . . . Proposing the Establishment of an American Law Institute* (1923) and Benjamin Cardozo, "The American Law Institute," in *Law and Literature and Other Essays and Addresses* (1931).]

STEPHEN BOTEIN

LEWIS, WILLIAM HENRY (Nov. 28, 1868–Jan. 1, 1949), lawyer and public official, was born in Berkeley, Va. (later part of Norfolk), the first of four children of Ashley Henry Lewis, a Baptist minister, and Josephine (Baker) Lewis. Both parents had been slaves but had been manumitted several years before the Emancipation Proclamation. William attended public schools in Portsmouth, Va., and by peddling matches and taking odd jobs, he worked his way through the Virginia Normal and Collegiate Institute for blacks in Petersburg. On the strength of his excellent academic record, he went on in 1888 to Amherst College in Massachusetts. To help pay his way, he worked as a groom in the stables of Rev. Julius H. Seelye, president of Amherst, who gave the youth both financial and moral support. In later years Lewis often took inspiration from Seelye's admonition that the uplift of the black race would result, not from protest, but from individual achievement.

At Amherst, Lewis excelled as both scholar and athlete. He was a prize-winning debater and a star football player. Widely popular with his fellow students, in his senior year he was chosen as class orator and was captain of the football team—the first black to be so honored in the Ivy League. Lewis continued his football career while at Harvard Law School, which he entered after receiving the B.A. degree from Amherst in 1892. Although weighing only 170 pounds, he anchored, at the center position, a Harvard line that averaged 200 pounds, and during his second Harvard season he served as temporary captain. In both 1892 and 1893 he was named by Walter Camp to his All-American team—again the first black to win this distinction. Lewis retained a close association with football throughout his life. He wrote *A Primer of College Football* (1896), and although in 1898 he turned down an offer to become football coach at Cornell, he assisted in coaching at Harvard for a number of years.

As a law student, Lewis gained a reputation as a promising defense attorney, particularly on the basis of his showing in the law school's mock trials. He received his LL.B. in 1895 and began practice in a Boston law office. He later became senior partner in the firm of Lewis, Fox, and Andrews. On Sept. 23, 1896, Lewis married Elizabeth Baker of Cambridge, Mass., a student at Wellesley College. They had three children: Dorothy, Elizabeth, and William Henry. Mrs. Lewis took the children to France for a time so that they could be educated there. The first daughter married a Frenchman; the second committed suicide as a young adult. William H. Lewis, Jr., became a lawyer and joined his father's firm.

While at Harvard, Lewis had shown an interest in civil rights. In 1893, when he was refused service in a local barber shop, he secured the aid of Burton R. Wilson, a talented black lawyer, and succeeded in getting the Massachusetts legislature to amend its 1865 equal rights statute. The earlier statute pertained to licensed inns, public amusement centers, public conveyances, and public meetings. The amended statute broadened its definition of public facilities to include theaters, skating rinks, barber shops, and any public place kept for hire, gain, or reward, whether it be required to be licensed or not and whether it have a license or not. Lewis gave up an active role in civil rights, however, after his marriage. One reason may have been that his wife, a fair-skinned mulatto, was uncomfortable in discussions about race and refused to allow them in their home. Even more important, perhaps, was Lewis' growing friendship with the moderate black leader Booker T. Washington. In any event, Lewis pursued a career within the established political tradition. In 1899 he was elected to the first of three one-year terms on the Cambridge common council, and in 1902 he won a seat in the Massachusetts House of Representatives. He was defeated in his bid for reelection the following year, at which point Booker Washington used his influence with President Theodore Roosevelt to secure Lewis an appointment as assistant United States attorney for Massachusetts (1903-1906). Lewis next served as assistant United States district attorney for the six New England states (1907-1911), with responsibilities for naturalization and other proceedings. In 1911 President William Howard Taft appointed him assistant attorney general of the United States, the highest federal office yet attained by a Negro.

Soon after his appointment, Lewis, on the initiative of some of his Boston associates, was made a member of the American Bar Association. When his race became known, however, the national officers, citing a "settled practice" to confine the association to whites, rescinded his election and referred the matter to the next convention. In the ensuing public controversy, Lewis had the firm support of Attorney General George W. Wickersham, who threatened to resign his own membership if Lewis was refused. In 1912 the association confirmed the membership of Lewis and two other blacks but with the proviso that no "member of the colored race" should in future be proposed without being explicitly identified as such.

Leaving office with Taft in 1913, Lewis returned to Boston and formed a new law firm with Matthew L. McGarth, a jovial Irishman more noted for his ability to find clients than for his legal skill. Lewis' football fame had assisted his start in the law, but by now he had established a reputation for his dominating courtroom style. Of medium complexion, with a face more rugged than handsome, dressed in fashionable and expensively tailored clothes, he made a strong impression. Lewis was successful in defending many clients, and when the evidence was overwhelmingly against them, he often secured less than the maximum penalty. His defense of a Providence, R. I., black accused of murdering a white physician earned Lewis praise for his "natural genius as an orator" (*New York Times,* Feb. 4, 1916) and succeeded in obtaining a sentence of life imprisonment for his client at a time when the death penalty was common. In the 1920's Lewis had a highly remunerative practice as counsel for accused bootleggers. His most celebrated case occurred in 1941, when he appeared as defense counsel in the impeachment trial of his old friend Daniel H. Coakley, who was a member of the executive council of the governor of Massachusetts and was found guilty of using the influence of his office to obtain paroles for criminals.

In 1948, at the age of seventy-nine, Lewis defended several members of the Revere, Mass., city council accused of corruption. Shortly afterward a series of heart attacks forced him to retire. In later life Lewis made his home in Dedham, Mass., but after his wife's death in 1943 he moved to Boston, where he died of a heart attack on New Year's Day, 1949. Lewis had become a convert to Roman Catholicism. After a high requiem mass attended by Gov. Robert F. Bradford, former mayor of Boston James M. Curley, Charles Francis Adams, and other Boston notables, he was buried in Mount Auburn Cemetery in Cambridge.

[Conversations with William H. Lewis, Jr., who has extensive material on his father's life and career, were the basic source. There are letters to, from, and about Lewis in the Booker T. Washington and Theodore Roosevelt papers in the Lib. of Cong. The Harvard Univ. Arch. has a useful folder of clippings on Lewis; see especially *Boston Globe,* May 26 and Dec. 12, 1893, and obituaries in the *Globe, Boston Herald,* and *Boston Post,* Jan. 2, 1949. Other published biographical material is slender: a sketch by Booker T. Washington in the *American Mag.,* June 1913 (for Lewis' tribute to Washington, see his "Armstrong and Washington," *Southern Workman,* Jan. 1917); *Outlook,* June 24, 1911, pp. 370-371; *World To-day,* Dec. 1910,

p. 1309 (with photograph); John Daniels, *In Freedom's Birthplace: A Study of the Boston Negroes* (1914); *Who Was Who in Am.*, IV (1968); obituary in *Negro Hist. Bull.*, Feb. 1949; editorial in *N.Y. Age*, Jan. 15, 1949. On his football career, see Alexander M. Weyand, *Football Immortals* (1962), and L. H. Baker, *Football: Facts and Figures* (1945). For the Am. Bar Assn. episode, see *Crisis*, Apr.–May 1912; *Nation*, May 23, 1912; *N.Y. Age*, Mar. 7 and 14, 1912; *N.Y. Times*, Aug. 28, 1912. August Meier analyzes Lewis' political career in his *Negro Thought in America, 1880–1915* (1963); and there is material on Lewis and Booker T. Washington in Stephen R. Fox, *The Guardian of Boston: William Monroe Trotter* (1970). A speech by Lewis is in Alice M. Dunbar, ed., *Masterpieces of Negro Eloquence* (1914). Marriage and death records were secured from the Mass. Registrar of Vital Statistics.]

PETER SHIVER, JR.

LIBMAN, EMANUEL (Aug. 22, 1972-June 28, 1946), cardiologist, pathologist, bacteriologist, was born in New York City to Fajbush Libman and Hulda (Spivak) Libman. He had three sisters and three brothers. Educated in the New York public school system, Libman received his B.A. from the City College of New York in 1891 and was graduated from the Columbia College of Physicians and Surgeons in 1894. For the next two years he served his internship at Mount Sinai Hospital in New York City. There he came under the guidance of the eminent diagnostician Edward G. Janeway and the influence of pediatricians Abraham Jacobi and Henry Koplik. Libman spent the years 1896–1897 studying in Berlin, Munich, Vienna, and Graz. In the laboratory of the noted bacteriologist Theodor Escherich, he studied infant diarrheas, which led him to the discovery in 1898 of the causative organism Streptococcus enteritis.

Libman returned to Mount Sinai, becoming assistant pathologist in 1897 and associate pathologist in 1898, a position he held until 1923. In addition, he was appointed adjunct physician in 1903 and promoted to attending physician status a decade later. He was a consulting physician from 1925 until his death. From these positions, Libman was able to coordinate his clinical and laboratory studies, expanding each discipline by association with the other. He continued his work on streptococci and published studies on pneumococci, meningococci, typhoid, paracolon, and pyocyaneus infections. Through this research, which required the incorporation of blood into bacteriologic media, he became interested in blood cultures and did the first extensive clinical studies on blood transfusions, a form of medical treatment then in its infancy.

Continued interest in blood cultures and heart disease culminated in Libman's classic descriptions of subacute bacterial endocarditis, an infection, generally of a heart valve, which usually has an insidious onset and protean symptoms. His important papers include the 1912 recording of six cases of coronary artery thrombosis (an entity not then recognized), studies on sprue and pernicious anemia, and a notable presentation on otitic infections. Libman's observations of suffering patients led to his development of a new test for sensitivity to pain. In 1923-1924, along with Dr. Benjamin Sacks, he isolated a form of endocarditis which he called "atypical verrucous endocarditis"; it is now known as Libman-Sacks disease.

Most of his published papers reflect clinical problems studied in the laboratory, but Libman was most noted as a diagnostician with particular interest in cardiology. He had a long list of distinguished patients in his busy practice. His interest in cardiology and postgraduate medical education encouraged physicians to seek appointments under his directorship, effecting what Dr. William H. Welch termed "the Mount Sinai School of Cardiology." Libman helped organize the Graduate Fortnight (a series of lectures and seminars) of the New York Academy of Medicine, and in 1931 he presented its first symposium on diseases of the heart. Other formal expressions of his interest in medical education include the endowment of the Noguchi Lectureship at the Medical History Institute in Baltimore, the Herbert Celler Fellowship Fund, the William H. Welch Lectureship at Mount Sinai Hospital, and the Humphry Davy Rolleston Lectureship at the Royal College of Physicians in London. Although he contributed personally to these fellowships and lectureships, he was also active in raising funds for them. He was chairman of the board of the Dazian Foundation for Medical Research, established by a former patient in appreciation of Libman. The legacy he left to the Tuskegee Institute of Alabama is indicative of his humanitarianism.

Dr. Libman had an abiding interest in Judaism. He served on the board of governors of the Hebrew University in Jerusalem, was vice-president of the American Friends of the Hebrew University, and was on the executive committee of American Jewish Physicians. A member of many medical organizations, he was president of the New York Pathological Society in 1907. He received the American Medical Association's Gold Medal in 1912 for his work on bacterial endocarditis and the Silver Medal in 1942 for his exhibit "Endocarditis and Libman-Sacks Disease." Emanuel Libman died in the Mount Sinai Hospital following a short illness; funeral services were held at the Free Synagogue.

[Obituary in *Jour. of the Mount Sinai Hospital,* 13 (1946): 215–223, contains a portrait; Introduction by William H. Welch to the three-volume set *Contributions to the Medical Science in Honor of Dr. Libman* (1932); *N.Y. Times,* June 29, 1946; July 2, 1946.]

JEFFREY A. KAHN

LIEBMAN, JOSHUA LOTH (Apr. 7, 1907-June 9, 1948), American reform rabbi, author, radio preacher, and Zionist, was born in Hamilton, Ohio, the son of Simon Liebman, a merchant, and Sabina (Loth) Liebman and the descendant of rabbis on both sides. A brilliant child, Liebman entered high school at the age of ten and college at thirteen and received the B.A. from the University of Cincinnati at nineteen (1926) and his ordination from the Hebrew Union College in Cincinnati at twenty-three (1930). It is probable that he delayed receiving the B.A., because he was studying for the rabbinate simultaneously and thus accelerated the latter program. He captained his university debating team in its victory over Oxford in 1924, was nominated for Phi Beta Kappa in his junior year, and upon graduation was awarded a fellowship, a tutorial in German, and a position as lecturer in Greek philosophy (1926-1930). In 1930 he married his first cousin, the daughter of a distinguished Cincinnati Jewish family, Fannie Loth, whom he first met as a student. In the same year, Liebman received a traveling fellowship from Hebrew Union and spent 1930-1931 studying philosophy at Harvard, Columbia, and the Hebrew University in Jerusalem; he then returned to Hebrew Union as an instructor of Bible and medieval exegesis. Between 1934 and 1939 Liebman served as rabbi of Kehilath Anshe Maarab Temple in Chicago and, for one year, as lecturer in Hebrew literature at the University of Chicago. In 1939 he received his doctoral degree at Hebrew Union for his study of the religious philosophy of Aaron ben Elijah and then accepted a call to Temple Israel in Boston, where he was to remain until his death.

Temple Israel of Boston grew from 500 families in 1939 to 1,400 in 1948, and Liebman became a prominent local and national figure. He was the first rabbi ever to become a regular faculty member of a Christian theological school in America (Andover-Newton), headed the Massachusetts Governor's Committee of Clergymen for Racial and Religious Activities (1942-1945), preached regularly on Sunday mornings over two Boston radio stations, and served actively on numerous national governmental and religious boards and commissions. Liebman's national fame rests upon *Peace of Mind* (1946), a popular statement of the psychological science of his day that had an immense appeal to a distraught generation. Selling more than 5,000 copies per week and rated either first or second on national nonfiction best-seller lists through much of 1946, *Peace of Mind* has had more than forty printings and been translated into several languages. Within two years of its publication, and after being given life tenure at Temple Israel, Liebman died suddenly at the age of 41 and was buried in the temple's cemetery. Shortly before his death, he and his wife adopted a daughter.

Liebman's earliest sermons and essays demonstrated his thorough grasp of modern Hebrew poetry; his 500-page dissertation revealed that he had mastered medieval and Jewish philosophy as well. Liebman's study compares Aaron ben Elijah, whose major philosophical work, *Tree of Life,* was composed in Hebrew in 1354, with both Jewish and Islamic philosophers and argues that his was a "rich, skillful and original synthesis of the quintessential problems of Jewish religious philosophy."

Liebman's sermons suggested the influence of Freud and a deep interest in popularizing the lessons of psychology. In Boston, Liebman preached once or twice a month on what were to become themes of *Peace of Mind,* and by 1942 some of his sermons already bore the titles of chapters of the book. Liebman's message was that religion and psychology shared a common goal: to lead the individual to inner security and maturity. Psychology would provide a proper interpretation, commitment, and perspective, while religion would achieve growth and maturity in the realm of conscience by proclaiming "what ought to be rather than what is." A proper interpretation of life is the awareness that life is hard and often defeating and that perfection is an illusion. Proper commitment means achieving moral and emotional maturity by giving to the world as much as one demands from it. Perspective is the awareness that occasional destructive feelings, moods of depression, and aggressive thoughts are quite normal, for we are an assortment of impulses, traits, and emotions.

Religion offers new hopefulness about humanity, an understanding of the problem of evil, a vision of continual human growth, and an awareness of our responsibilities and goals. Liebman's concept of God supported this optimistic vision: God was the "infinite Mind" or, more commonly, the "Power" that made for righteousness as well as personal and social salvation, through the "intangible ideals of man" and their "artistic harmonies."

Peace of Mind is the distillation of a decade of thinking about psychology and religion. Its popularity probably rested on several factors: an absorbing subject at a time of immense turmoil; its skillful synthesis of a medical treatise and a religious philosophy; its simple prescriptions for inner security taken from psychiatry and its wholesome, affirmative view of the universe taken from religion; its response to the war and prophets of despair; and its felicitous style and sure grasp of the literature and philosophy of the Western world. Notwithstanding Liebman's failure to suggest that the healing of sick souls is often a lengthy and painful process, *Peace of Mind* is, as one of Liebman's honorary degrees noted, "a bold, pioneer attempt to rediscover the psyche and to restore it to its Eternal Source of love, understanding and true happiness."

[Liebman's other works include *Hope for Man* (1964), a sequel to *Peace of Mind*; as editor, *Psychiatry and Religion* (1948); and "The Religious Philosophy of Aaron ben Elijah" (unpublished doctoral diss., Hebrew Union, 1938).
On Liebman, see Arthur Mann, ed., *Growth and Achievement: Temple Israel 1854–1954* (1954), particularly "Joshua Loth Liebman: Religio-Psychiatric Thinker" (includes photograph). The Liebman papers are at the Boston Univ. Lib. and the Am. Jewish Arch. (Cincinnati). Most useful are the "Miscellaneous Sermons 1940–1948," available from Am. Jewish Arch.]

MARC LEE RAPHAEL

LIGGETT, LOUIS KROH (Apr. 4, 1875–June 5, 1946), drugstore chain founder, was born in Detroit, Mich., the youngest of four sons. His father, John Templeton Liggett, was of Scottish ancestry; his mother, Julia Ann (Kroh) Liggett, of Dutch. Both came of Ohio families. John Liggett founded the successful Michigan Mutual Life Insurance Company in 1866, but later investments in an electric trolley failed, leaving the family in reduced circumstances, and Louis left the Detroit public schools before the age of sixteen. Over the next few years he worked as a runner in a newspaper office, as a salesman for Wanamaker's Detroit outlet, as manager of a bankrupt Michigan store (which he made profitable), and as distributor, with a partner, of a headache remedy. On June 26, 1895, Liggett married Musa Bence, daughter of George W. Bence, a drug manufacturing executive who later became first vice-president of United Drug. The couple had three children: Leigh Bence, Janice, and Musa Loraine.

In 1897 Liggett became a salesman for Chester Kent and Company, Boston, distributors of Vinol, a tonic made of cod liver oil and sherry. To increase sales, Liggett suggested that an exclusive agency be designated in each city, founded a "Vinol Club" for druggists distributing the product, and started a newsletter, *Vinol Voice*. In 1898, at the age of twenty-three, he became general manager of the company.

Liggett saw great sales potential if druggists, who were at the mercy of manufacturers and wholesalers, would combine their buying power. He presented the idea at the meeting of the Vinol Club in 1900 and the following year established Drug Merchants of America, a central buying agency for retail druggists, with one druggist in each city as a stockholder and exclusive agent. Liggett soon expanded his idea to include the manufacture of "own goods" for sale at factory prices to the stockholder-druggists. Thus, on Jan. 1, 1903, the United Drug Company was established in Boston, with Liggett as secretary and general manager; he became president the following year. The first product was a dyspepsia tablet, but in rapid order other patent medicines were added, along with spices, toilet soap, candy, and rubber goods. An office boy suggested the name Rexal (Liggett added a second "l") for the product line and the co-operating stores. Promotional schemes, which soon made Rexall a household word, included the one-cent sale and Saturday night candy specials. A house organ, *Rexall Ad-Vantages*, was started, and Liggett sent out frequent "Dear Pardner" letters to the store owners. In 1906 he organized the National Cigar Stands Company, which operated independent tobacco counters in member stores, and in 1908 the United Druggists Mutual Fire Insurance Company. Both became divisions of United Drug.

Expansion of the Rexall system was rapid. In 1910 there were 2,755 agent-stockholders; by 1914 there were 5,570. Gross annual revenues rose from $1.4 million in 1909 to $5.6 million in 1914. Canadian stores were represented by the United Drug Company, Ltd., of Canada, founded by Liggett in 1909, and Rexall agents were added in England starting in 1912. When the idea of a single outlet in a city proved impractical in large centers, Liggett in 1909 formed another subsidiary corporation, the Louis K. Liggett Company, to operate a chain of drugstores under the Liggett name.

In 1920 the gross annual income of United Drug, Inc. (the holding company formed in 1916 to control the consolidated Liggett companies), was $68,428,179. In that year also Liggett acquired the Boots Pure Drug Company of England, a prosperous manufacturing and retail chain. During the depression of 1921 Liggett experienced heavy personal financial losses when he sought to bolster the sagging price of United Drug stock through large purchases. The company remained sound, however, and loyal stockholder-druggists set up a trust that lent him the money to repay his debts. In 1928 United Drug merged with Sterling Products, manufacturers of such proprietary drugs as Bayer Aspirin, to form Drug, Inc., with Liggett as chairman of the board. The merger, however, was dissolved in 1933 in the depth of the depression; only the sale of the Boot chain in 1932 enabled the economically distressed United Drug to weather the crisis. Liggett resumed the office of president and continued to direct the company's policies. He became chairman of the board in 1941 and honorary chairman in 1944, when he was succeeded by Justin M. Dart. Liggett was president of the Boston Chamber of Commerce (1916), chairman of the Pilgrim Tercentenary celebration in 1920, chairman of the Massachusetts Calvin Coolidge Finance Committee (1924), and for several years a Republican national committeeman. His health failed during his last few years, and he lived with a daughter in Washington. He died in a Washington hospital of intestinal cancer at the age of seventy-one. After Congregational services, he was buried at Newton Center, Mass., where he had made his home.

[Samuel Merwin, *Rise and Fight Againe* (1935), is an adulatory biography by a friend. (A photograph of Liggett serves as frontispiece.) See also George F. Redmond, *Financial Giants of America*, I, 367–375 (1922); and obituaries in *Boston Herald* and *N.Y. Times*, June 7, 1946. Death record from D.C. Dept. of Human Resources.]

ROBERT W. LOVETT

LILLIE, FRANK RATTRAY (June 27, 1870-Nov. 5, 1947), biologist, investigator, teacher, and administrator of biological science, was born in Toronto, Ontario, the second of five children of George Waddell Lillie and Emily Ann (Rattray) Lillie. His forebears were Scottish and English; both of his grandfathers were pioneers in Canada and both were Congregational clergymen. His father was an accountant and wholesale druggist. Frank Lillie came to the United States in 1891 after receiving the B.A. degree that year from the University of Toronto. His interest in physiological embryology and endocrinology first developed at Toronto under the influence of R. Ramsay Wright and A. B. Macallum. In 1891, he spent the summer at the Marine Biological Laboratory in Woods Hole, Mass., then in its fourth

year, where he began his research with Charles O. Whitman. He spent the academic year 1891-1892 at Clark University, working with Whitman, then the following year he moved with Whitman to the University of Chicago, where he took his Ph.D. in zoology summa cum laude in 1894. On June 29, 1895, he married Frances Crane of Chicago. They had four daughters: Catherine Crane, Margaret Halsted, Mary Prentice, and Emily Ann; and three adopted sons: Albert Reed Trenholm, Ethan, and Karl Christopher.

His first two teaching positions were at the University of Michigan (1894-1899) and at Vassar College (1899-1900). He was then appointed assistant professor of embryology at Chicago and remained there for the rest of his life. He became professor of embryology in 1906 and he succeeded Whitman as chairman of the department of zoology in 1910, retaining this position until 1931. From 1931 until 1935 he was dean of the division of biological sciences, and concurrently the Andrew MacLeish distinguished professor of embryology. He retired in 1935.

Lillie's research was highly intuitive, raising important new questions in embryology and opening up important areas of investigation. Because of his clear and logical mind and his disciplined meticulousness in the laboratory, his specific contributions in these areas were impressive and influential. His first research, begun at Woods Hole in 1891, dealt with the development of *Unio*, a freshwater clam. At Whitman's suggestion, he undertook to trace the fate of the early cleavage cells and their progeny through to the time that they formed the larval organs. Whitman himself, in the 1870's, had begun such studies of cell lineage, and they were popular in the 1890's. Although Lillie wrote in 1944 that the subject was over, "a passing episode in embryological research" (*The Woods Hole Marine Biological Laboratory*, 1944, p. 125), the eggs most appropriate for cell lineage studies, those with so-called determinate cleavage, in which the fate of the cell is fixed early in development, again became favored material in the 1970's, when it became possible to study by biochemical methods the controlling influences of the cytoplasm over the genes.

Lillie made a number of other important studies at Woods Hole on marine organisms, some dealing with regeneration in various species, others related to his work on cell lineage. One of these described differentiation without cleavage in the egg of a marine worm,

Chaetopterus. This aroused his interest in fertilization, and in 1909 he began an important series of studies on fertilization in various marine species. Lillie emphasized that fertilization involved interaction of specific substances produced by the egg and spermatozoon, and he adopted for the first time the concepts and terminology of immunology to describe the nature and action of these interacting substances. He named the species-specific substance which he demonstrated to be produced by the egg "fertilizing"; he interpreted its action as that of a sperm-isoagglutinin. In 1919 he published *Problems of Fertilization,* elaborating his fertilizing theory. Current studies of the physiology of fertilization, particularly on species-specificity, still lean heavily on Lillie's immunological analogy, and immunological concepts have been increasingly called upon to explain varied phenomena of embryonic specificity.

While Lillie was carrying out these studies on marine forms during summers at Woods Hole, he began in the early 1900's to study and to perform experiments on the chick embryo. His first experiments were designed to test the regenerative power of the chick's limb bud and other organs. One of his most enduring influences on embryology emanated from *The Development of the Chick* (1908; 1919; 3d ed., rev. by H. L. Hamilton, 1952), which incorporated many of his discoveries and which has been basic for much subsequent work on chick embryology, normal and experimental.

Before the book on the chick was completed, Lillie was already acquiring an interest in the primary causes and the subsequent sequences of events that bring about sexual differentiation. His immediate motivation for attacking this problem came about because of the birth in a herd of purebred cattle at the family farm near Chicago of a free-martin, a sterile female born as a co-twin to a bull calf. Free-martins had been known for centuries, but their origins were not understood. Lillie's intuitive mind saw that there might be a causal relationship between the sterility and the twinning. He collected at a Chicago abattoir pregnant uteri containing twins, and he was able to demonstrate that the sterile free-martin is an original female altered in the male direction by the early action of male hormones, made possible by the fusion of the twins' placentae before sex is differentiated and before the blood circulation has begun. His discovery of embryonic sex hormones gave great impetus to the development of the then-new science of endocrinology. Lillie continued his own experimental analysis of hormone action by studying the action of one of the female sex hormones, and also of the thyroid hormone, on the development of the feather pattern of domestic fowl.

Lillie was skilled at training his students to think as logically and to work as carefully in the laboratory as he did himself. Many of them have advanced embryology greatly by continuing studies that he began. He also made significant contributions to biology as an administrator both at the Marine Biological Laboratory at Woods Hole, where he spent every summer from 1891 through 1946, and at the University of Chicago. He became assistant director of the Woods Hole laboratory in 1900 and succeeded Whitman as director in 1908. He held this position until 1925, and then became president of the board of trustees and of the corporation. He retired in 1942. During the early years of his directorship the laboratory had great financial difficulty and in 1902 its very independence was threatened. It was saved as a result of Lillie's good judgment and tact. He secured financial support from the Rockefeller Foundation, the Carnegie Corporation, the General Education Board, and from his brother-in-law Charles R. Cranc. But Lillie's contribution to the development of the laboratory far transcended money raising. Because of his high standards, it became the foremost marine laboratory in the world. Cooperation and staff democracy were and remain outstanding features of its administration.

Lillie also played an important part in initiating and developing the Woods Hole Oceanographic Institution and in securing support for it. The Oceanographic Institution was founded in 1929; Lillie was president of its corporation from 1920 to 1940. Oceanography did not enjoy, then, the popularity that it has subsequently attained, and its later burgeoning was in large part a result of Lillie's foresight.

Lillie was also a wise counselor to national organizations. He was elected to the National Academy of Sciences in 1915, and was its president from 1935 to 1939. He was also chairman of the National Research Council (1935-1936); while holding both positions simultaneously, he developed cooperative relationships between the institutions, which have grown tighter over the years. He also served as chairman of the Fellowship Board of the National Research Council during the years when its policies and procedures were being determined.

Lillie received many honors during his lifetime. "The record which he established," in the words of the president of the Academy of Sciences in 1947, "of long and able guidance of a great university department, of that of a chief builder of two great research institutions, of distinguished leadership for a period of the National Academy and the Research Council, and of the affectionate devotion of a host of pupils and colleagues ... marks a career which could well be called incomparable" (A. N. Richards, in Willier, *Biog. Memoirs,* pp. 227-228). Lillie died of a cerebral hemorrhage at the age of seventy-six, at the Billing's Hospital of the University of Chicago. He was buried in the churchyard of the Episcopal church at Woods Hole.

[The principal published source is the memoir by B. H. Willier in Nat. Acad. Sci., *Biog. Memoirs,* XXX (1957). This includes a photography of Lillie, a complete bibliography of his writings, and (p. 228) a list of other important printed sources of information about him, including an obituary by Carl R. Moore in *Science,* Jan. 9, 1948, and memorial addresses by Willier, E. G. Conklin in *Biological Bull.,* 95 (1948); 151-162. Lillie's *The Woods Hole Marine Biological Laboratory* (1944) records in detail the history of the founding and administration of the laboratory, and also of the Woods Hole Oceanographic Institution, with material on Lillie's role. His correspondence, recently discovered, has been deposited in the library of the Marine Biological Laboratory, Woods Hole.]

LILLY, JOSIAH KIRBY (Nov. 18, 1861-Feb. 8, 1948), pharmaceutical manufacturer, was born in Greencastle, Ind., the only child of Eli Lilly and Emily (Lemon) Lilly. His mother, of Scottish-Irish ancestry, was the daughter of a Greencastle merchant. His father traced his descent from Gustave Lilli, a French settler who had come with his Dutch wife to Maryland in 1789. Eli Lilly had lived in Kentucky before moving to Indiana in the 1850's. After serving in the Union Army during the Civil War, he tried growing cotton in Mississippi; but his wife died, he and his son contracted malaria, and in 1866 he returned to Indiana. Three years later he became a partner in a retail drug business in Paris, Ill. He later moved to Indianapolis, Ind., where in 1876 he set up a small business to manufacture drugs.

Josiah Lilly spent four of his childhood years with his staunch Methodist grandparents in Greencastle. He entered the preparatory department of the local Asbury College (later DePauw University) in 1875, but left the following year to join his father's new business. In 1880 he entered the Philadelphia College of Pharmacy, from which he was graduated, Ph.G. cum laude, in 1882. He returned immediately to the family firm, which had been incorporated in 1881 as Eli Lilly and Company, and was placed in

charge of the laboratory. He was named a director in 1887 and, upon the death of his father in 1898, president. He continued in that office until 1932, when he became chairman of the board.

At the time Josiah Lilly entered drug manufacturing, the industry, while an ancient one, was small-scale, its products simple. The Lilly company's twenty-four employees turned out principally sugar- and gelatin-coated pills, elixirs, fluid extracts, and syrups. From the outset the firm produced "ethical" or prescription drugs rather than the more lucrative and popular patent medicines. Lilly, with his pharmaceutical training, was particularly interested in standards of manufacturing and in scientifically developed products. With Ernest G. Eberhardt, one of the first graduates of Purdue University's College of Pharmacy, he set up a scientific division in the company in 1886. Four years later he established a botanical department, and in 1891 a company library. Thus prepared, Eli Lilly and Company both contributed to and benefited from the chemotherapy revolution in medicine during the early decades of the twentieth century.

As president, Lilly turned his attention to finances, sales, and expansion. By 1903 the firm had branch houses in Kansas City, Chicago, St. Louis, New Orleans, and New York City; by 1905 sales had reached $1 million annually. Four years later the company counted a hundred traveling representatives. In 1914 Lilly opened a biological department on a 156-acre tract of land in Greenfield, Ind. Belladonna and stramonium grown on the Greenfield farms helped relieve drug shortages during World War I.

After the war Eli Lilly and Company assisted in the development and preparation of insulin on the invitation of its discoverer, Dr. Frederick Grant Banting, marketing the first commercially produced insulin in the United States in 1923. Other products developed in the company laboratories over the next two decades included barbiturates, ephedrine preparations, and liver extracts. During World War II, Eli Lilly and Company supplied the United States government with more than two hundred different pharmaceuticals, including penicillin, vitamins, and Merthiolate, and processed and delivered without charge more than a million quarts of blood plasma. Immediately after the war the firm acquired land at Lafayette, Ind., for a plant to manufacture antibiotics. The company developed its foreign market during the interwar years, finding outlets in Mexico, Central and South America, and the Far East. Its first foreign sub-

sidiary, Eli Lilly and Company, Ltd., was organized in London in 1934. This was followed in
1938 by a Canadian subsidiary, and in 1943 and
1944 by subsidiaries in Mexico, Brazil, and Argentina.

Lilly received many honors for his contributions to pharmaceutical manufacturing, including the Remington Medal (1942), awarded by
the New York section of the American Pharmaceutical Association. He was active in civic and
philanthropic organizations, particularly in Indianapolis. In 1937 Lilly and his sons established
the Lilly Endowment, Inc., a foundation for the
"promotion and support of religious, educational
or charitable purposes." Relatively small at the
start, it had grown by the 1970's into one of the
largest foundations in America. Lilly gave to
the University of Pittsburgh his extensive collection of materials by and about the composer
Stephen Foster.

Lilly believed in close attention to business,
but he seems to have been a kindly, if paternalistic, employer. He was a Republican and a member of Christ Episcopal Church of Indianapolis.
On Nov. 18, 1882, he married Lilly Marie
Ridgely of Lexington, Ky. They had two sons,
Eli and Josiah Kirby. His wife died in 1934, and
on June 29, 1935, he married Lila Allison
Humes. Lilly died of cancer in Indianapolis in
his eighty-seventh year and was buried there in
Crown Hill Cemetery.

[Roscoe C. Clark, *Threescore Years and Ten: A
Narrative of the First Seventy Years of Eli Lilly and
Company* (privately printed, 1946) ; articles on Josiah
Lilly in *Lilly Rev.*, Feb. 1948, and, by Gene E. McCor-
mick, in *Pharmacy in Hist.*, 12 (1970) : 57–67 ; *Nat.
Cyc. Am. Biog.*, XLII, 648–649 ; information from
Gene E. McCormick, corporate historian, Eli Lilly and
Company. On the family background, see Josiah K.
Lilly, "The Name Lilly," *Lilly Rev.*, Apr., May, June,
and Aug. 1942. On the Lilly Endowment, see its publi-
cation *The First Twenty Years* (1957). Obituary ar-
ticles appeared in the *N.Y. Times* and the *Indianapolis
News Star* and *Times*, Feb. 9, 1948. Portraits of
Lilly are in Clark, above (frontispiece), and *Men of
Ind. in Nineteen Hundred and One*, p. 101 (1901).]

IRENE D. NEU

LIVINGSTON, BURTON EDWARD
(Feb. 9, 1875–Feb. 8, 1948), plant physiologist,
was born in Grand Rapids, Mich., the youngest of six children of Benjamin Livingston and
Keziah (Lincoln) Livingston. His paternal
grandfather was a native of Ballybay, Ireland;
the Lincolns were descended from early settlers
of Massachusetts. Livingston's father was a
street grading and sewer contractor in Grand
Rapids, and the boy early became adept with
tools. The family was intellectually inclined
and possessed a good library in which he read
extensively. He shared a family interest in

gardening and wild plants and knew the scientific names of many plants before he knew
their common names.

After graduating from the Grand Rapids
high school, where he obtained an unusually
broad training in science, Livingston worked
for a year with his brother in a large plant
nursery in Short Hills, N.J., before entering
the University of Michigan in 1894. At Michigan he was persuaded by Frederick C. New-
combe to turn his botanical interests to the
field of plant physiology. He received his B.S.
degree in 1898. Following a year teaching high
school science in Freeport, Ill., he began graduate study at the University of Chicago, where
he was the first laboratory assistant of the well-
known plant physiologist Charles Reid Barnes.
He was greatly influenced also by Henry C.
Cowles, who was developing the new field of
plant ecology, and by the animal physiologist
Jacques Loeb. In his research Livingston effectively combined ecology and physiology. He
received his Ph.D. in 1901, and his influential
dissertation "The Role of Diffusion and Os-
motic Pressure in Plants" was published two
years later.

Livingston remained at Chicago as assistant
and associate in plant physiology until 1905,
when he accepted a post with the Bureau of
Soils of the U.S. Department of Agriculture.
The following year he joined the new Desert
Laboratory of the Carnegie Institution of Washington at Tucson, Ariz. There, building on his
primary interest in the water relations of
plants, he investigated the complex interrelationships between plants and their environment.
He was especially concerned with the water-
supplying power of soil and the evaporating
power of the air ; and to assure accurate quantitative data he developed new measuring devices such as the porous porcelain atmometer
to gauge evaporation. Livingston visited several laboratories in the United States in 1907
and spent some time at the Missouri Botanical
Garden studying transpiration of cacti. Most of
1908 was spent at various botanical laboratories
in Europe.

In 1909 Livingston moved to the Johns Hopkins University as professor of plant physiology, and in 1913 he became director of the
university's laboratory of plant physiology, a
position which he held until his retirement in
1940. The laboratory became a center to which
both students and established scientists came
from all over the world. The experiments conducted by Livingston and his students and associates, recorded in six books and nearly 280

published papers, studied the effects of numerous environmental factors—from radiation and temperature to air movement—on the physiological functions of plants. In addition, a number of new methods and pieces of equipment were developed, including standardized black and white atmometers to measure evaporation, auto-irrigators to control the water supply of potted plants, soil point cones to measure the water-supplying power of the soil, and lithium chloride clips to measure transpiration. This equipment, which Livingston manufactured and sold to other laboratories, was used by ecologists and physiologists all over the world and played an important role in a variety of research projects.

Livingston was a clear and precise writer who spent much time editing the dissertations and papers of his students. He assisted in editing several scientific journals and exercised a strong influence on the content and style of the early volumes of *Plant Physiology*. He also edited an English translation of Vladimir I. Palladin's *Plant Physiology* in 1918. In 1921, with Forrest Shreve, he coauthored an important book, *The Distribution of Vegetation in the United States, as Related to Climatic Conditions*. Livingston was also active in the management of several scientific societies, including the American Society of Plant Physiologists (president, 1934), which granted him its Stephen Hales Award, and the American Association for the Advancement of Science, which he served as permanent secretary from 1920 until 1931 and as general secretary from 1931 to 1934.

A rather large, handsome man, Livingston was self-confident yet modest; he was exacting, yet easy to work with if one could meet his high standards in research and publication. Along with great energy and enthusiasm, he had the ability to get people to work for objectives which he regarded as important. Although he had attended a Congregational Sunday school as a boy, he was never a churchgoer, and he had little patience with fundamentalist theologians who refused to accept the truth of obvious scientific facts. Curiously, although he was a leader in many areas, he never appreciated the usefulness of statistical methods in analyzing data.

Livingston was married twice: in March 1905 to Grace Johnson of Chicago, and after their divorce in 1918, to Marguerite Anna Brennan Macphilips of Syracuse, N.Y., on July 2, 1921. He had no children by either marriage. He died in Baltimore of cardiac insufficiency one day before his seventy-third birthday and was buried in Druid Ridge Cemetery, Baltimore County, Md.

[Livingston's personal correspondence was destroyed after his death. The best published source of information is his own "auto-obituary" (written in 1937), which appeared in *Ecology* (with photograph), July 1948, with an introduction by a former student, D. B. Lawrence. See also obituaries by Charles A. Shull in *Science*, May 28, 1948, and by Warren B. Mack in *Scientific Monthly*, July 1948. Other obituaries are in *Soil Science* (with photograph), July 1948, *Nature*, July 17, 1948, and Am. Philosophical Soc., *Year Book*, 1948. See also *Nat. Cyc. Am. Biog.*, XXXVI, 334. Personal information was supplied by Mrs. Burton E. Livingston, Dr. Charles F. Swingle, and Dr. Donald B. Lawrence, former students of Livingston, and Mrs. William R. Amberson, his former secretary.]

PAUL J. KRAMER

LOMAX, JOHN AVERY (Sept. 23, 1867-Jan. 26, 1948), collector of American folk songs, was born in Goodman, Miss., one of the five sons of James Avery Lomax, a farmer, and Susan Frances (Cooper) Lomax, both natives of Georgia. Although they always worked their own land, Lomax described his family as belonging to the "upper crust of the po' white trash." In 1869 they moved to a farm on the Bosque River near Meridian, Tex. From his country childhood, Lomax acquired a love for and appreciation of the rural folklore he later captured on record. He absorbed the popular hymns he heard at the Methodist camp meetings his family attended and the songs of his cowboy friends. After attending school sporadically, he spent one year (1887-1888) at a Methodist school, Granbury (Tex.) College. He then taught for seven years, six of them at Weatherford College, another Methodist institution. Eager to advance his education, Lomax attended the summer school in Chautauqua, N.Y., for three years. In 1895, at twenty-eight, he entered the University of Texas, where he took courses with feverish enthusiasm and received his B.A. degree two years later.

Then, from 1897 to 1903, Lomax served the university simultaneously as registrar, secretary to the president, and steward of men's dormitories, among other offices, for $75 a month. Thereafter, he became instructor and then associate professor of English at Texas Agricultural and Mechanical College (1903-1910). Meanwhile, he doggedly pursued graduate studies despite financial constraints. After receiving the M.A. in literature in 1906 from the University of Texas, he was offered a leave of absence by President David F. Houston of Texas A. and M. to study English at Harvard, where he earned the M.A. degree the following year.

Since childhood Lomax had been writing down the cowboy songs he heard. His English professor at Texas had scorned such frontier literature as unworthy, but at Harvard, Barrett Wendell and George Lyman Kittredge strongly encouraged Lomax to continue his collecting. After his return to Texas, they secured him three successive fellowships that enabled him to travel through the cattle country with a notebook and a primitive recording machine. Around campfires and in saloon backrooms he persuaded cowboys to sing their songs. Among his findings were the well-known "Git Along Little Dogies" and "Home on the Range," the latter sung to him by a Negro saloonkeeper in San Antonio who had been a trail cook. The result was Lomax's first published collection, *Cowboy Songs and Other Frontier Ballads* (1910), which he dedicated to Theodore Roosevelt, a firm supporter of his efforts. The book was a landmark in the study of American folklore.

The demands of supporting a family for a time curtailed Lomax's collecting. He married Bess Baumann Brown of Austin, Tex., on June 9, 1904. They had four children: Shirley, John Avery, Alan, and Bess. In 1917, when Lomax was fired from his post at the University of Texas by Gov. James E. Ferguson, Barrett Wendell, Jr., brought him to Chicago as a bond salesman for the investment banking house of Lee, Higginson, and Company. Two years later he was called back to the University of Texas as secretary of the Ex-Students Association. In 1925 he reentered the financial world as head of the bond department of the Republic Bank in Dallas. Friends like the poet Carl Sandburg and the journalist Lloyd Lewis, whom he had met in Chicago, helped Lomax keep alive his interest in folklore even "amidst the deadening influence of the stock ticker." Beginning in 1911, when Kittredge secured a place for him on a convention program of the Modern Language Association of America, he was frequently engaged to lecture on cowboy songs at colleges and universities throughout the country. He was president of the American Folklore Society in 1912-1913. In 1919 he published a second collection, *Songs of the Cattle Trail and Cow Camp.*

Illness and the collapse of the bond market left Lomax out of work in 1932; but with a contract from the Macmillan Company for a book of American folk songs and support from the Library of Congress and the American Council of Learned Societies, he set out on the first of a series of collecting trips that were to occupy the rest of his life. He now concentrated on recording the songs of the Southern black—blues, spirituals, and work chants. Often accompanied by his son Alan, he visited remote rural black communities, lumber camps, and especially penitentiaries, where blacks were isolated and where singing softened the pain of prison life. The quality and number of the songs he recorded for the Library of Congress Archive of American Folk Song—more than 10,000 in all—reflect Lomax's unusual skill as a fieldworker. In the Arkansas Penitentiary he came upon two important songs, "Rock Island Line" and "John Henry," the rhythmic ballad of a "steel drivin' man."

Being of a warm and friendly nature, Lomax moved effectively on every level of society. On the folk level, he encouraged many rural singers to take pride in, and develop, their musical traditions. On the popular level, his two collections *American Ballads and Folk Songs* (1934) and *Our Singing Country* (1941) opened an entirely new area of American folk music to the public and were largely responsible for the folk song movement that developed in New York City and spread throughout the country. One of Lomax's discoveries was an influential figure in that movement: Huddie Ledbetter, nicknamed "Lead Belly" because of his deep bass voice. Lomax and his son Alan found Lead Belly in a Louisiana penitentiary in 1933, arranged for his freedom, brought him to Greenwich Village in New York and published *Negro Folk Songs as Sung by Lead Belly* (1936).

On the scholarly level, Lomax has been criticized for his loose and eclectic treatment of some song texts and for inadequate documentation of the sources of his songs, not only in his published collections but even in his personal files. His strength was as a field collector and popularizer. As such, he had a profound impact on the widespread appreciation of the American folk song.

Lomax's first wife died in 1931, and on July 21, 1934, he married Ruby Terrill, dean of women and associate professor of classical languages at the University of Texas. Lomax died at the age of eighty of a cerebral hemorrhage while visiting in Greenville, Miss., and was buried in Austin, Tex. In his autobiography, *Adventures of a Ballad Hunter* (1947), he summed up his career: "All my life I have been interested in the songs of the people—the intimate poetic and musical expression of unlettered people, from which group I am directly sprung."

[Lomax's *Adventures of a Ballad Hunter* includes firsthand descriptions of his collecting experiences. See also the obituary by Stith Thompson in *Jour. Am. Folklore*, July–Sept. 1948; *Nat. Cyc. Am. Biog.*, XXXVIII, 187–188, with photograph; *Who Was Who in America*, II (1950), which differs on some details from the autobiography. For a critical appraisal of Lomax's work, see Donald K. Wilgus, *Anglo-Am. Folksong Scholarship Since 1898* (1959); death record from Miss. State Registrar of Vital Statistics. See also Lomax's reports in the annual *Report* of the Librarian of Cong., 1934–1937. MSS. and recordings by Lomax are at the Univ. of Texas, Harvard, and the archives of Am. Folk Song at the Lib. of Cong. A lecture by Lomax illustrated with his field recordings is available on a Lib. of Cong. record, "The Ballad Hunter: John A. Lomax" (AAFS L53).]

WILLIAM R. FERRIS

LORD, PAULINE (Aug. 8, 1890-Oct. 11, 1950), actress, was born in Hanford, Calif., one of four children of Edward Lord, reportedly a hardware merchant, and Sarah (Foster) Lord. Reared on a fruit ranch in the San Joaquin Valley, Pauline surprised her non-theatrical family with her early and lasting passion for the theater. Although she was not a Catholic, she was educated at a nearby convent, because it was the only convenient school. She spent her childhood longing for a career on the stage. She is said to have spent her weekly allowance of twenty-five cents for the cheapest seat each Saturday afternoon at San Francisco's Alcazar Theater; since the price of the ticket was exactly that amount, she would have had to walk the long distance to the theater and back.

Pauline Lord's first appearance on the professional stage came in 1903, when she played a maid in the Belasco Stock Company production of *Are You a Mason?* at that same Alcazar Theater. Despite her youth, her parents do not seem to have opposed her ambition; neither, however, did her family display any positive interest in her acting and later achievements. Her career began in earnest when she joined Nat Goodwin's company in 1905. She had met Goodwin during her brief run at the Alcazar, and he apparently fulfilled his promise, made during that meeting, to give her a role. She toured the country in his repertory and appeared with him in New York. Engagements with stock companies in Milwaukee and Springfield, Mass., followed.

Although she had played in New York with Goodwin, Pauline Lord made her real Broadway debut on Jan. 8, 1912, as Ruth Lennox in a now-forgotten play called *The Talker,* winning some recognition from the critics. She also succeeded Mary Ryan as Mrs. Strickland

in Elmer Rice's *On Trial* (1915), but her first real success came when Arthur Hopkins, whom she revered and who later would be vitally influential in her career, cast her as Sadie in *The Deluge* (1917). Unfortunately, the critical acclaim she received was not enough to prolong the run of the essentially weak play beyond a few weeks.

She then played in a succession of mediocre vehicles, among them *Under Pressure* (1917); the all-star production of *Out There* (1917), which included George M. Cohan, Laurette Taylor, and Mrs. Fiske; *April* (1918); *Our Pleasant Sins* (1919); *Night Lodging* (1919), produced by Arthur Hopkins; and *Big Game* (1920). The long list of unfamiliar titles suggests one of Pauline Lord's professional misfortunes: with four notable exceptions, her abilities were far superior to the works in which she appeared. Critics continually praised her in unsuccessful plays: Stark Young (p. 163) called her first entrance in the obscure Clemence Dane play *Mariners* (1927) "the greatest single moment . . . in my experience of the American Theater"; Brooks Atkinson was more realistic when he deplored the waste of her talent in bad pieces (*New York Times,* Nov. 20, 1927).

After having been recognized, along with Jacob Ben-Ami, for "mystical" acting in another Arthur Hopkins production, *Samson and Delilah* (1920), Pauline Lord finally achieved the fame she deserved through her memorable performance on Nov. 2, 1921, in an enduring play—Eugene O'Neill's *Anna Christie*. O'Neill had not been pleased with producer-director Arthur Hopkins' choice of her to play a Swedish sea captain's daughter whom circumstance and weakness have turned into a prostitute, but Pauline Lord's portrayal of Anna erased his doubts, made immediate theater history, and sent the reviewers searching for words to describe the new star's particular brand of realistic acting. It could be evoked in the vocabulary of acting, by referring to gesture and vocal quality, particularly her hushed, "breathless" voice, but it did not seem like acting at all.

She had tried to study prostitutes on Tenth Avenue in preparing for her role but found that she could not penetrate *their* acting; her characterization was eventually modeled on a department store clerk who had waited on her, a "beaten soul . . . tired to death." Brooks Atkinson, referring to her work in *Anna Christie,* called her the "elusive, tremulous, infinitely gifted Pauline Lord" (*Broadway,* p. 198). Percy Hammond wrote that from her first moment on stage "she makes no gestures and utters no sound that you do not believe" (New York *Tribune,* Nov. 3, 1921). *Billboard* spoke of her "wistful appeal, . . . intensity, offset by a whimsical humor . . . something so unutterably sad about her, even when she is merry" (Dec. 31, 1921). The roles she had played and would play were tragic, but her individualistic style was far from classical; she was a realistic actress who created characters often described as vulnerable.

During 1922 and 1923, she toured in *Anna Christie* and then went with the play to London, where it opened on Apr. 10, 1923. Filled with stage fright and fear of being disliked as an American actress, she gave her all, causing the English audience to stand and stamp their feet for half an hour, singing "For She's a Jolly Good Fellow" and then mob her dressing room.

Only one insignificant role, in *Launzi* (1923), a one-week failure, intervened before Lord created another masterful characterization, again in a notable American play. As Amy, the pathetically unsure waitress who marries an old, crippled ranch owner in the Napa Valley, becomes pregnant by a young farmhand, and eventually finds redemption through the love of the old man, she made Sidney Howard's *They Knew What They Wanted* a shining theatrical experience. Writing in the *New York Sun* on Nov. 25, 1924, just after the play's opening, Alexander Woollcott said that "when Pauline Lord is summoned to the stage by some role that releases the spirit that is in her, there is no room in an understanding newspaper next day for the discussion of anything else. . . . She knows certain secret places at the very heart of acting where only one or two people of our time have been before her. She has many a limitation in the theatre, but the truth is in her and it will prevail. In a scene of terror, she is incomparable. For desolation of the spirit, for a suggestion of that kind of sickening fear which is on the edge of nausea, for a picture of a frightened human being in whirling, blinding trouble, I have seen nothing comparable to her little hour in the last act of Sidney Howard's play since that scene of dumb dread which Mrs. Fiske played in the great first act of 'Salvation Nell.'" John Mason Brown, in *Dramatis Personae,* described how her hands "fluttered about her mouth like wounded doves."

Twelve years passed before Pauline Lord created another—and her last—legendary characterization. Among the fleeting plays in which she appeared after *They Knew What They Wanted* were a revival of *Trelawny of the*

Wells (1925 and 1927), *Sandalwood* (1926), *Mariners* (1927), *Spellbound* (1927), Sidney Howard's *Salvation* (1928), *Distant Drums* (1932), and *The Truth About Blayds* (1932). Although tense, emotional parts were her forte, she scored a considerable success as the maid Abby in Sidney Howard's comedy *The Late Christopher Bean* (1932), in which she toured at intervals over the next decade. The only lasting play in which she acted during this period was O'Neill's *Strange Interlude;* she succeeded to the central role of Nina Leeds, originally created by Lynn Fontanne, and toured in the play during 1928 and 1929.

Lord's growing reputation as one of the finest American actresses of her time was enhanced by the critics' repeated assertion that her gifts were so individualistic as to render meaningless a comparison between her and other leading ladies (Young, p. 165). Brooks Atkinson touched on another common perception of her acting when he wrote, "Miss Lord does not appear to be a versatile actress. She resolves the art of acting into one livid image of a woman pursued, whipped, stung by forces beyond human control; and no doubt the narrowness of her range results naturally in her amazing depth" (*New York Times,* Nov. 20, 1927).

Pauline Lord was a private person who kept her life off the stage in shadows. She married a New York advertising executive, O.B. Winters, in 1929, but they were divorced two years later. They had no children. Beyond these few facts, commentary on her private life in newspapers and magazines seems unreliable at best. She was remarkably photogenic, her theatrical and formal portraits revealing a face of plaintive simplicity framed by a ring of soft hair, her eyebrows perpetually raised above her dark eyes as if she were asking a question to which she already knew a disappointing answer.

In 1936, after more than a decade of appearing in mediocre plays, Pauline Lord gave her last enduring stage performonce as the nagging, hypochondriac wife, Zenobia, in Owen and Donald Davis' dramatization of Edith Wharton's novel *Ethan Frome.* For Brooks Atkinson, her acting created a Zenobia who was "a frightened, lonely woman entitled more to pity than to censure. Caught in an inhuman triangle with Ruth Gordon's courageous Mattie and Raymond Massey's tenacious Ethan Frome, Miss Lord's Zenobia was the third part of a masterpiece" (*Broadway,* p. 353-354). After *Ethan Frome,* Pauline Lord never again appeared in a play worthy of her abilities; she does not seem to have been discriminating in her choice of roles. There was a break between *Ethan Frome* and performances in two insignificant pieces in Australia in 1939, followed by *Suspect* (1940), *Eight O'Clock Tuesday* (1941), and *The Walrus and the Carpenter* (1941). Her last stage role came in *Sleep, My Pretty One* (1944), a play that survived for only four days.

She also acted in films in the 1930's, among them *Mrs. Wiggs of the Cabbage Patch* (1934) and *A Feather in Her Hat* (1935). In *Mrs. Wiggs,* her best and best-received film, Elinor Hughes found her to be "an actress of particularly individual style: quiet, gentle, rather beaten, a shade plaintive, but, oddly enough, never giving an impression of weakness" (*Boston Herald,* Oct. 16, 1934).

In 1950, while traveling to Tucson, Ariz., for her health, she was admitted to Champion Memorial Hospital, Alamagordo, N.Mex., where she died of asthma and a heart ailment. During the 1920's and 1930's she had created several flawless stage portraits and indelibly etched them on the memory of those who attended the American theater in its golden age. She also had the power to induce a kind of mystical ecstasy in the respected critics of the day. Brooks Atkinson's summation of her career is just: "Pauline Lord, known as Polly to her friends, was about the least theatrical woman on the stage. Her style was shy, soft, self-effacing, and defenseless, a projection of her own modesty and misgivings. But in suitable parts, she was a powerful actress. . . . The qualities that Pauline Lord feared were lacking in herself she drew out of the audience's inexhaustible fund of compassion" (*Broadway,* p. 353-354).

[See clippings in the Harvard Theatre Collect.; Brooks Atkinson, *Broadway* (1970); Stark Young, *Immortal Shadows* (1948); John Mason Brown, *Dramatis Personae.* Excellent photographs are in the following issues of *Theatre* magazine: Mar. 1916; Feb. 1922; Dec. 1925; Sept. 1927.]

GEORGE P. BIRNBAUM

LOTKA, ALFRED JAMES (Mar. 2, 1880-Dec. 5, 1949), chief architect of mathematical principles in demography, was born in Lemberg (Lvov), a Polish city that was then a part of the Austro-Hungarian empire. He was one of at least two children of Jacques Lotka and Marie (Doebely) Lotka. Both parents were American citizens who had spent most of their lives in Europe. They were, according to Lotka's own account, missionaries, possibly of the Moravian denomination. Lotka, who spent his boyhood in France, received his higher education in England, obtaining the B.Sc. degree from Birmingham University in 1901. Already interested in physics, chemistry, and biology (especially self-renewing processes), he spent the next year at the University of Leipzig, where he developed his concept of the mathematical theory of evolution.

Entering the United States in 1902, Lotka obtained employment as an assistant chemist at the General Chemical Company, where he remained until 1908. There followed a year of graduate study in physics at Cornell University, which awarded him the M.A. degree in 1909; three years later he obtained the D.Sc. degree from Birmingham University. Lotka worked as an examiner at the U.S. Patent Office (1909) and as assistant physicist at the U.S. Bureau of Standards (1909-1911). After serving three years as editor of the *Scientific American Supplement,* he returned to General Chemical (1914-1919).

Throughout these years Lotka's active mind ranged over a broad field of investigation; indeed, the breadth of his interests was comparable to that of the seventeenth-century natural philosophers. A quiet, learned man who expressed himself with equal facility in English, French, and German, he wrote numerous articles for both scholarly and popular journals. His interest in population studies, in fact, emerged as an aspect of his broader concern with physical and especially bio-physical processes, including the evolution of organisms. Lotka was a close student of such scientists as Albert Einstein, Hendrick Lorentz, and J. J. Thompson. In "A New Conception of the Universe," published in *Harper's Monthly* in April 1920, Lotka presented perhaps the most intelligible exposition of the theory of relativity ever offered to laymen and suggested—two decades before the atomic bomb —the enormous potential inherent in knowledge about the atom. In 1922 Lotka began two years in residence at the Johns Hopkins University, pursuing independent research and codifying his earlier studies into a book, *Elements of Physical Biology* (1925).

Despite the range of Lotka's interests, his enduring reputation rests chiefly on his contributions to demography. Central to his demographic studies and subsequent mathematical demography was the analysis of the structure of a stable population, a hypothetical population formed by constant age-specific birth and death rates and unaffected by migration. This concept had been approached but never fully developed in previous studies. As early as 1760, Leonard Euler, the Swiss mathematician, had formulated the age distribution of a population with a constant schedule of mortality at successive ages and a constant ratio of births in successive years. Lotka's three earliest scientific contributions in 1907 included two significant articles on apparently unrelated topics: "Relation between Birth Rates and Death Rates" and "Studies on the Mode of Growth of Material Aggregates" (respectively in *Science* and the *American Journal of Science*). Their linkage in his approach to science is shown in the concluding sentence of the second article: "We have illustrated a statistical method which is sufficiently general in its application to comprise such widely different cases as that of the growth of a population under certain conditions, on the one hand, and that of a simple chemical reaction on the other." "A Problem in Age Distribution," coauthored with Francis R. Sharpe, which appeared in *Philosophical Magazine* in 1911, showed that a closed population, submitted to fixed female (or male) rates of mortality and fertility and a constant sex ratio at birth, would develop a stable age distribution with a characteristic rate of increase.

Lotka's concentration on demography dates from 1924, when he was appointed supervisor of mathematical research in the statistical bureau of the Metropolitan Life Insurance Company. He remained with the company until his retirement in 1947, becoming general supervisor of the statistical bureau in 1933.

Lotka's contribution to demography first attracted wide attention in the article "On the True Rate of Natural Increase" (coauthored with Louis I. Dublin), which appeared in the *Journal of the American Statistical Association* in September 1925. Written just after the United States opted for a restrictive immigration policy, the article, based on data for 1920, demonstrated that the "crude" official rate of natural increase of the population, calculated at 10.7 per 1,000, was misleading and that the "true," or "intrinsic," rate was only 5.2. It was shown that the crude rate was distorted by the age distribution of the American population, at that time with a relatively high proportion of adults in the twenty-to-forty-five age group, the central reproductive period. The authors predicted the eventual stabilization of the declining American birthrate and a decline in the rate of natural increase. Dublin later re-

called that as a result of this article, "Malthusian fears of overpopulation gave way to alarm that the Western populations were headed for great declines in numbers" (*Journal of the American Statistical Association,* March 1950).

The stable population theory developed by Lotka proved to be a key instrument of demographic research. The three major characteristics of a population—age distribution, mortality schedule, and fertility—are so interrelated that any one can (disregarding the effects of migration) be mathematically derived from knowledge of the other two. This is especially useful in the investigation of populations with incomplete or erroneous data. It proved that the major determinant of population's age distribution is the previous level of fertility rather than mortality (as earlier demographers believed). Although subsequent scholarship has pointed out certain limitations of the theory as initially presented, it has illuminated a host of demographic questions. Lotka also made many specific contributions to various aspects of population study.

At Metropolitan Life, Lotka benefited from his association with Dublin, whose socially sophisticated, outgoing personality differed sharply from his own. However, each tended to minimize the contribution of the other to their collaborative efforts on several articles and three important books: *The Money Value of a Man* (1930), *Length of Life* (1936), and *Twenty-Five Years of Health Progress* (1937). Unfortunately, he became involved in a long, sterile controversy with R. R. Kuczynski. In line with his central interest, Lotka's work in demography was directed mainly to the analysis of what he called "necessary relations," the relations inherent in the physical structure of all organisms. This philosophical concept found expression in his *Analyse démographique avec application particulière a l'espèce humaine,* published in France in 1939.

Although he lacked interest in organizational activities and rarely participated actively in scientific assemblies, Lotka belonged to several professional societies, including the Institute of Mathematical Statistics and the American Public Health Association. He was president of the Population Association of America (1938-1939) and the American Statistical Association (1942) and vice-president of the International Union for the Study of Population (1948–1949). He was generally gracious and had a lively, although wry, sense of humor. A bachelor until his fifty-fifth year, Lotka married Romola

Beattie on Jan. 5, 1935. They had no children. Lotka died of coronary disease at a hospital in Red Bank, N.J., where he made his home. After Protestant funeral services, he was buried in a cemetery in Red Bank.

Lotka's name is synonymous with stable population theory, and he is widely regarded as the father of demographic analysis. In a broader sense his contribution lay in the application of mathematical principles to the sciences. His farseeing analyses of the interrelationship of the sciences, in works like *Elements of Physical Biology*, provided important foundations for such modern concepts as cybernetics and information theory.

[A complete collection of Lotka's writings is on deposit in the Princeton Univ. Lib. Published accounts of Lotka's life and work are scarce. See Joseph J. Spengler, "Alfred James Lotka" in *Internat. Encyc. of the Social Sciences*, IX, 475–476 and Frank Lorimer, "The Development of Demography," in *The Study of Population: An Inventory and Appraisal*, eds. Philip M. Hauser and Otis Dudley Duncan (1959). Obituaries include one by Dublin in the *Jour. Am. Stat. Assn.*, Mar. 1950; Metropolitan Life Insurance Co. *Stat. Bull.*, Dec. 1949, which includes a photograph; and *Population Index*, Jan. 1950, which contains a complete bibliography of Lotka's writings. Ansley J. Coale, *The Growth and Structure of Human Population: A Mathematical Analysis* (1972), is a technical exposition of the stable population theory as initiated by Lotka and as developed thereafter.]

FRANK LORIMER

LOWER, WILLIAM EDGAR (May 6, 1867-June 17, 1948), surgeon, was born in Canton, Ohio, the younger of two sons and second of three children of Henry Lower, a farmer, and Mary (Deeds) Lower. The family presently moved to a small farm near Baltic, Ohio. This was only a few miles from Chili, the home of young Lower's cousin George W. Crile, and the two boys formed a strong friendship that continued for life. Billy (or Ed, as his cousin called him) attended the local district schools, entered the Northwestern Ohio Normal School (later Ohio Northern University), and after an interval of teaching enrolled in the medical department of Wooster University (which was later consolidated with the School of Medicine of Western Reserve University) in Cleveland; he received the M.D. degree in 1891. After a year's internship at University Hospital, he joined the surgical practice established by George Crile and Frank E. Bunts in Cleveland, and was made a partner in 1895.

Lower was one of the founders of the Lutheran Hospital, which opened in 1896. A member of its first staff, he later served for twenty-two years as president and chief of staff. He was associate surgeon at Lakeside Hospital (1910-

1931) and director of surgery at Mount Sinai Hospital (1916-1924); he also served on the staff of the St. Alexis Hospital in Cleveland.

Lower had begun his career as a general surgeon but soon developed a special interest in genito-urinary problems and in 1901 visited clinics in Berlin and Paris to learn the most advanced operative techniques. Returning to Cleveland, he developed a practice in urology. He became known as a skillful and conservative surgeon who was deeply concerned with the postoperative welfare of his patients. He was particularly interested in improving the diagnostic methods used in surgical diseases of the kidney, and helped simplify and standardize the operative procedures in his field. He was one of the first to perform suprapubic prostatectomy, and devised a number of improved surgical instruments, including a trocar and cannula for suprapubic drainage of the bladder and a pedicle clamp for use in nephrectomy. Together with Crile, he pioneered in the use of spinal anaesthesia, particularly in amputation procedures. In 1898 Lower had been appointed a lecturer at the Western Reserve medical school; he was afterward (1910-1931) associate professor of genito-urinary surgery there.

During the Philippine Insurrection, Lower served as acting assistant surgeon with the 9th Cavalry (1900-1901), and then became a major in the Medical Reserve Corps. He again saw military service during World War I, when he went to France in 1917 as assistant surgical director of the Lakeside base hospital unit organized early in the war by Crile. The unit first served in Rouen, France, as Base Hospital No. 9, with the British Expeditionary Force, where Lower and Crile introduced the use of blood transfusion in the treatment of shock. After America's entry into the war, the unit was asigned to the American Expeditionary Forces as Base Hospital No. 4. Lower was promoted to lieutenant colonel in May 1918 and was made commanding officer of the Lakeside unit.

During their period of service in France the three partners—Crile, Lower, and Bunts—had been impressed with the medical advantages offered by a base hospital, in which a patient had available the skills of a wide variety of specialists, including internists, surgeons, pathologists, radiologists, and nurses. After their return to Cleveland at the end of the war, the three undertook to establish a private institution with similar advantages: a hospital that would be independent of the university and would include provision for medical research and teaching as well as comprehensive medical care. Together with

John Phillips, an internist, they secured a charter for the Cleveland Clinic Foundation, a non-profit corporation. The clinic building was formally opened in 1921, and the first unit of the permanent hospital buildings in 1924. Lower served as an administrative officer of the clinic and head of the department of urology, work that occupied his attention for the remainder of his life. Lower's keen business sense helped the clinic survive the tragic disaster of 1929, when an explosion of nitrocellulose films caused great loss of life and a financial setback. His business ability and careful planning also helped carry the clinic through the Great Depression of the 1930's.

Genito-urinary surgery remained Lower's major interest. He published some 170 papers and collaborated with Crile in the writing of *Anoci-Association* (1914) and with B. H. Nichols in *Roentgenographic Studies of the Genito-Urinary Tract* (1933). Lower was a member of the American Surgical Association, the American Association of Genito-Urinary Surgeons (president, 1922), and the Clinical Society of Genito-Urinary Surgeons (president, 1922). He also had an active interest in the affairs of organized medicine and served as president of the Cleveland Academy of Medicine and the Ohio State Medical Society. To stimulate continuing education, he provided funds to establish an annual lecture at the Academy of Medicine.

On Sept. 6, 1909, Lower married Mabel Loring Freeman of Worcester, Mass. They had one daughter, Molly. Lower's hobby was work, but he understood the importance of relaxation and escape from daily pressures. Horseback riding was a favorite exercise at the small farm he maintained near Painesville, Ohio. Lower died of coronary heart disease at the age of eighty-one at his home in Cleveland, and was buried in Arlington National Cemetery.

[Obituaries and memorial comments in *Cleveland Clinic Quart.*, Oct. 1948; Am. Surgical Assoc., *Trans.*, 47 (1949): 563-565 (by T. E. Jones); and Am. Assoc. of Genito-Urinary Surgeons, *Trans.*, 41 (1949):3-5 (by William J. Engel); Grace Crile, ed., *George Crile: An Autobiog.*, 2 vols. (1947); files of Cleveland Clinic; personal acquaintance.]
WILLIAM J. ENGEL

LUBITSCH, ERNST (Jan. 29, 1892-Nov. 30, 1947), motion picture director, was born in Berlin, Germany, the only child of a Jewish tailor and clothing-shop owner, Simon Lubitsch, and his wife, Anna (Lindenstedt) Lubitsch. He attended the Sophien Gymnasium until he was sixteen and then worked for a short time in his father's shop. From an early age Lubitsch was

interested in a theatrical career, and after leaving school he began to study acting with a stage comedian, Victor Arnold. From 1909 to 1911 he also worked as an apprentice in the Berlin Bioscope Studios, learning the fundamentals of motion picture production. In 1911 Arnold introduced him to the stage director Max Reinhardt, who invited Lubitsch to join his Deutsches Theater as a comic actor. Lubitsch toured with the Reinhardt company to London, Paris, and Vienna and appeared in two Reinhardt films made in 1912. The following year Paul Davidson, head of Union-Film in Berlin, signed Lubitsch as an actor. He was cast as a comic Jewish stereotype, usually named Meyer or Moritz, and quickly became a featured performer in silent comedies. In 1914 he also began directing comedies in order, as he later recalled, to create good parts for himself. Lubitsch had acted in or directed at least thirty films when, in 1918, Davidson persuaded him to direct the young Polish actress Pola Negri.

Lubitsch's collaboration with Negri made them both famous throughout Europe and the United States. Departing from his earlier specialization in comedy, Lubitsch directed Negri as a femme fatale in six costume or historical dramas between 1918 and 1922. Their third film, *Madame DuBarry*, made in 1919 and released in the United States in 1920 as *Passion*, was considered the most important European motion picture made up to that time, and its influence on world cinema of the 1920's was comparable to that of Robert Wiene's *The Cabinet of Dr. Caligari* and the Soviet films of Sergei Eisenstein. In *Madame DuBarry* Lubitsch turned the French Revolution into a psychological drama of personalities, re-creating the historical epic on a human level and demonstrating the possibilities for motion pictures of a realistic treatment of a historical character. He extended the innovations of *Madame DuBarry* in another historical drama, *Anna Boleyn*, 1920 (released as *Deception* in the United States), with Emil Jannings in the role of Henry VIII. It was suggested that *Madame DuBarry* and *Anna Boleyn* were Germany's way of gaining revenge on France and Great Britain, her conquerers in World War I, by artfully deflating their histories.

In 1922 Lubitsch came to the United States at the invitation of Mary Pickford and directed her in *Rosita* (1923), a film that pleased audiences and critics more than it did the star. Thereafter, Warner Brothers signed Lubitsch to a contract for five films. At this point he saw Charles Chaplin's *A Woman of Paris*

(1923), and its influence on him was as great as the impact of his *Madame DuBarry* on other filmmakers. *A Woman of Paris,* a film drama of unusual sophistication and psychological realism about sex, inspired Lubitsch to make a film of comparable sophistication; but for his form he turned back to comedy—a genre he had continued to develop even during the 1918–1922 period in Germany, when he made several popular social satires. In 1924 he directed *The Marriage Circle,* a comedy of manners, and followed it with *Three Women* (1924), *Forbidden Paradise* (1924, with Pola Negri), *Kiss Me Again* and *Lady Windermere's Fan* (both 1925), and *So This Is Paris* (1926), films that established Lubitsch as the leading American director of sophisticated comedy and as an innovator in comic styles as influential as he had been in historical drama.

When sound came into motion pictures Lubitsch was among the first directors to use dialogue successfully without compromising the visual techniques he had developed in the silent period. In his first sound film, *The Love Parade* (1929), he assimilated music as well, revitalizing by his special comic style the Graustarkian world of the operetta. The film's popularity led to four other musicals, two of them starring the *Love Parade* team, Jeanette MacDonald and Maurice Chevalier. But Lubitsch found time as well for a classic comedy that many critics consider his masterpiece: *Trouble in Paradise* (1932), notable for its wit, playful irony, and inventive camera work.

His films of the mid-1930's, by contrast, were not so well received either by audiences or by critics, who, as Lubitsch suggested, were becoming saturated with beautiful musicals and clever comedies. He served as director of production for Paramount Pictures briefly in 1935–1936 and produced as well as directed five of the eight films he made for Paramount, Metro-Goldwyn-Mayer, United Artists, and Twentieth Century-Fox in the decade from 1937 to his death. An attempt to form his own production company in 1940 was unsuccessful. With *Ninotchka* (1939), a romantic comedy satirizing Soviet communism and featuring Greta Garbo in her first comic role, Lubitsch regained public and critical acclaim. *The Shop Around the Corner* (1940) and *To Be or Not to Be* (1942) are also significant works from his last period.

At the height of Lubitsch's success as a motion picture comedy director in the early 1930's critics began to speak of a distinctive "Lubitsch touch." His comic style emphasized brevity, quickness, insouciant wit, the comedy of surprise, and clever visual touches that remain in the memory long after the light and inconsequential plots of his films have been forgotten. Nearly all Lubitsch's American films were set in the boudoirs and drawing rooms of a disappearing, or perhaps imaginary, European upper-class world, where only wit, grace, and romance (and sometimes money) mattered, and he portrayed that world with affection even as he made it the object of his satire. The Lubitsch touch was widely emulated in Hollywood comedies of the 1930's. Lubitsch ranks along with Charles Chaplin, Buster Keaton, and René Clair as one of the masters of comedy direction in the first half-century of motion picture art.

Lubitsch was a short, stocky man with an ever-present cigar and sardonic smile. Throughout his directorial career he retained the antic manner of the comedy actor he had once been. He married Helene Krauss on Aug. 22, 1922. They were divorced on June 23, 1930. On July 27, 1935, he married Sania Bezencenet who, as a literary agent, used the professional name Vivian Gaye. They had one child, a daughter, Nicola, and were divorced in 1943. Lubitsch became an American citizen in 1933. He died of a heart attack at the age of fifty-five at his home in the Bel Air section of Los Angeles and was buried in Forest Lawn Memorial Park, Glendale, Calif.

[The essential source is Herman G. Weinberg, *The Lubitsch Touch: A Critical Study* (1968). Along with Weinberg's anecdotal account of Lubitsch's life and films, it contains interviews with associates of Lubitsch, excerpts from critical works and appreciations, a filmography, a bibliography of writings about Lubitsch, film stills, photographs of Lubitsch at all stages of his career, and other material. It also includes an important Lubitsch letter (pp. 264–267), in which the director gives his own retrospective evaluation of his career. Many Lubitsch films are available from 16 mm. motion picture rental firms.]

                                        ROBERT SKLAR

LUNCEFORD, JAMES MELVIN ("JIMMIE") (June 6, 1902-July 12, 1947), bandleader, was born in Fulton, Mo. Little is known about his parents, but before the family moved to Denver, Colo., his father was a choirmaster in Warren, Ohio. He went to high school in Denver and studied music under Wilberforce J. Whiteman, father of Paul Whiteman, whose band was soon to acquire a national reputation. During 1922, Lunceford played alto saxophone in a local band led by George Morrison and including Andy Kirk, another musician destined for fame as a bandleader.

Leaving Denver, Lunceford went to Fisk

University in Nashville. He gained further musical experience during summer vacations in bands led by Wilbur Sweatman and Elmer Snowden and at City College in New York. By 1926, when he obtained a bachelor of music degree at Fisk, he was a capable performer on saxophones, flute, trombone, and guitar. He had also been prominent in sports at the university; indeed, his ability in football, baseball, basketball, and track events eventually led to an appointment as athletic instructor at Manassa High School in Memphis. There he also began to teach music, and he soon formed a jazz band among his pupils. They included drummer Jimmy Crawford and bassist Moses Allen, who were to remain important and dependable associates for many years. Among other musicians who assisted him greatly in the formative period of this band and brought it up to professional standards were saxophonist Willie Smith and pianist Ed Wilcox, two of several young friends who joined him after they graduated from Fisk.

Lunceford credited visits to Memphis by the Texas-based band of Alphonso Trent with being a major source of inspiration, and this was reflected not only in arrangements written by Wilcox and Smith but also in those by Sy Oliver, a trumpet player who joined the band in 1933. Oliver had been a member of Trent's band for several months, and he soon proved to be an original and imaginative arranger. He was extremely resourceful in extracting a variety of orchestral colors from the limited instrumentation available to him, and he had an exceptional gift for unusual, but highly effective, tempos. Most jazz performances by this time were built on a rhythmic basis of four beats to the bar, but Oliver delighted in the emphasis of two to the bar as inherited from pioneering New Orleans groups. Although Wilcox wrote with special skill for saxophones, it was Oliver, more than anyone else, who shaped and defined the Lunceford style, making it one of the most influential in jazz history.

Unlike many other black bands of the Swing Era, Lunceford's was renowned for its discipline. Apart from his astute choice of musicians, this was the leader's most significant contribution, particularly since it did not result in a dampening of enthusiasm. A tall, well-built, serious man, Lunceford was several years older than his men, and this, added to his experience in exercising authority as a teacher, enabled him to keep firm control. He instilled a sense of responsibility at all levels, and the value of teamwork was soon acknowledged by public acclaim and critical recognition. He confined himself mostly to conducting, but the band's sections (brass, reeds, and rhythm) were rehearsed separately and then together, each vying with the other in terms of precision. Punctuality and good appearance were stressed. The band was also notable for the attention it gave to entertainment values, and it became virtually a show in itself. At one time, Lunceford featured a glee club made up of members of the band; it was very popular, but when other bands copied the idea, he discarded it. In much reduced form, however, it survived in the vocal trio that was greatly responsible for the success of his versions of "My Blue Heaven," "Ain't She Sweet?" and "Cheatin' on Me." Solo vocalists, moreover, were always an essential part of his presentation. Ballads were entrusted to male singers with high, sentimental voices, their efforts often being succeeded by ensemble passages played, in complete contrast, with a powerful rhythmic emphasis. On other material, and equally typical, musicians like the saxophonists Joe Thomas and Willie Smith, trombonist Trummy Young, and Sy Oliver were responsible for vocal choruses, which they delivered with whimsical humor and relaxed jazz phrasing.

Following its first professional engagement in Memphis in 1929, Lunceford's band knew several difficult years before it appeared at the Lafayette Theatre in New York in 1933. A few months later, it was engaged at the Cotton Club in Harlem, where Duke Ellington had previously triumphed. It also began a long series of recordings, which brought international attention, and by the time Lunceford toured Europe in 1937 his was recognized as one of the most exciting jazz bands in the United States. Sy Oliver left to join Tommy Dorsey in 1939, but the band's popularity was undiminished.

At the peak of his success, Lunceford was able to indulge in what he referred to as his only vice—his passion for flying. He owned his own plane, and both he and his wife were pilots. He married Crystal Tully of Memphis in 1937, in Sy Oliver's hometown, Zanesville, Ohio.

Although he hired other capable arrangers such as Billy Moore, Ed Inge, Don Redman, and Gerald Wilson, the established character of the band was no longer maintained. In 1941, an appearance in the film *Blues in the Night* led to a record hit of the same name, but it was the band's last. Thereafter, the exigencies of World War II were responsible for a steady decline in Lunceford's fortunes. There were problems with the drafting of band members, with transportation, with incessant one-night stands, and with grown men who, as the faithful Ed Wilcox put it, no longer wanted to be treated like the "little boys" that left Memphis with their teacher years before. One by one, Willie Smith, Jimmy Crawford, Trummy Young, and Moses Allen quit, and the band never recovered from the effect of their departure. Lunceford was taken suddenly ill with a heart attack in 1947 while autographing records in a music store in Seaside, Oreg., and died on his way to the hospital. He was buried in Memphis, Tenn.

[Material on Lunceford is scattered. See Jimmie Lunceford, "The Memphis Blues," *Esquire's Jazz Book* (1947), p. 46; Hugues Panassié, "Jimmie Lunceford and His Orchestra," *Jazz Hot*, No. 21 (Paris, 1937); Robert Goffin, *Jazz: From the Congo to the Metropolitan*, pp. 204–208 (1944); Barry Ulanov, *A History of Jazz in America*, pp. 190–193 (1952); Hugues Panassié, *The Real Jazz*, pp. 210–215 (1960); Leonard Feather, *The Book of Jazz*, p. 182 (1965); George Simon, *The Big Bands*, pp. 328–335 (1971); Ian Crosbie, "Lunceford: Message from Memphis," *Jazz Journal*, Vol. 25, Nos. 1 and 2 (London 1972); John Chilton, *Who's Who of Jazz*, p. 229 (1972); and Stanley Dance, *The World of Swing*, pp. 93–134 (1974).]

STANLEY DANCE

LUNN, GEORGE RICHARD (June 23, 1873–Nov. 27, 1948), Presbyterian minister, Socialist mayor of Schenectady, N.Y., and Democratic politician, was born near Lenox, Iowa, the second son and second of at least five children of Martin A. Lunn and Mattie (Bratton) Lunn. Both parents were natives of Ohio; his paternal grandparents had emigrated from England. Martin Lunn, a farmer, later moved into Lenox and engaged in the real estate business. George left school at the age of twelve to sell newspapers in Des Moines. At seventeen he moved to Omaha, Nebr., where he worked as a deliveryman. For a time he was an insurance salesman in Grand Island, Nebr. In 1892 he entered Bellevue College near Omaha, and during the following five years he completed the B.A. degree while supporting himself by various jobs, including teaching school and preaching in country churches. Upon graduating in 1897 he entered the Princeton Theological Seminary in New Jersey. His training was interrupted by the Spanish-American War, when he joined the unit of Nebraska volunteers led by William Jennings Bryan; it was during this period that he contracted typhoid fever in Florida. Resuming his studies after the war, Lunn entered Union Theological Seminary in New York City in 1899 and graduated with the B.D. degree in 1901. He

was ordained that year in the Presbyterian ministry and became associate pastor of the Lafayette Avenue Presbyterian Church in Brooklyn. In November 1903 he moved to Schenectady, N.Y., as pastor of the First Reformed Church.

Lunn emerged in Schenectady as a leading spokesman of reform. At first he merely preached the Social Gospel and hence did not ruffle his conservative upper-middle-class congregation. In 1907, however, he turned rather abruptly toward social action. Over the next few years he lashed out at the Schenectady county supervisors for their corruption and denounced "plutocracy," led a citizens' campaign against vice in the city, and successfully blocked rate increases by the Schenectady trolley system and the Mohawk Gas Company. Lunn's new role caused friction with his congregation; he resigned at the beginning of 1910 and, in response to popular demand, founded an independent Peoples' Church, which for a time merged with the First Congregational Church. He continued in the ministry until 1915. Meanwhile, in May 1910, Lunn began publication of the *Citizen*, a weekly newspaper designed to be "an advocate of clean government and an exponent of Christian ethics." His forthright editorials brought him overtures from the local branch of the Socialist party. Lunn was ambitious for public office as well as for reform. Since he had alienated the leaders of the two major parties, he joined the Socialists in December 1910.

The next year, as the party's mayoral candidate, Lunn led a Socialist ticket to victory in the municipal elections. He quickly instituted a number of social programs. An attempt to sell ice and coal directly to the public was blocked in the courts by the retail coal and ice dealers. Lunn and his associates did establish, however, a municipal grocery store, a municipal farm to provide work for the unemployed, a lodging house for indigents, and a municipal employment bureau. All these projects met only limited success and were eventually abandoned. Lunn's most lasting contribution, perhaps, was the reorganization of the city's office and accounting procedures. Young Walter Lippmann, then a Socialist, served as Lunn's personal secretary but left after a few months complaining that Lunn's program more nearly resembled social reform than true socialism.

From the beginning of his administration, Lunn's determination to select his own appointees caused serious friction within the local Socialist party. When he ran for reelection in

1913 he was defeated by a coalition of Republicans and Democrats. Still in control of his party, he was renominated and reelected in 1915, but the controversy over appointments continued, and in the following year the state Socialist organization expelled him.

Lunn never again professed socialism, but he continued his political career. In 1916 he was elected to Congress as a Democrat. During his single term in office (he was defeated for reelection in 1918) he served on the House Military Affairs Committee, supported American entry into World War I, and worked for a selective service act. Running now as a Democrat, he was twice returned to the office of mayor of Schenectady, in 1919 and 1921. Lunn achieved a degree of prominence in New York Democratic politics, especially among the party's upstate anti-Tammany elements. His name was put forward several times as a possible candidate for either governor or United States senator, and in 1922 he was elected lieutenant governor on the ticket headed by Alfred E. Smith. Narrowly defeated for reelection in the Coolidge landslide of 1924, Lunn was appointed by Smith the following year to a ten-year term on the state Public Utilities Commission. He was reappointed for a second term by Gov. Herbert Lehman in 1935.

Lunn married Mabel Healy of Brooklyn on May 7, 1901. They had five children: George Richard, Mabel Carrington, Elizabeth Healy, Raymond Healy, and Eleanor Peabody. His first wife died in 1931, and on Nov. 3, 1932, Lunn married Anita (Oliver) Jensen, a widow. Ill health forced him to resign from the New York Public Utilities Commission in 1942. He subsequently moved to Rancho Santa Fe, Calif., where he died of coronary thrombosis at the age of seventy-five. Following cremation, his ashes were placed in Forest Lawn Memorial Park, Los Angeles, Calif. Lunn was one of a dozen or more Socialist mayors elected in large or medium-sized American cities during the progressive period. His philosophy was closer, however, to Christian than to Marxist socialism, and after a brief period of social activism he settled down to a basically conventional political career.

[Lunn did not preserve his personal papers, but there are MS memoirs by two of his associates, Hawley B. Van Vechten and William B. Efner, at the City Hist. Center, Schenectady City Hall. Some information about Lunn's administration can be gleaned from the Socialist party papers at Duke Univ. (see reports to the party's Dept. of Public Information). See also files of Lunn's *Citizen* and the *N.Y. Times Index*, 1913-1925. Other biographical sources include Richard S. Livy, "Democracy in Religion," *Survey*, July 2, 1910, a good early account; Walter Lippmann,

"Two Months in Schenectady," *Masses*, Apr. 1912; Kenneth E. Hendrickson, Jr., "George R. Lunn and the Socialist Era in Schenectady, N.Y., 1909-1916," *N.Y. Hist.*, Jan. 1966; *Biog. Directory Am. Cong.* (1961); Union Theological Seminary, *Alumni Directory 1836-1958* (1958); *Who Was Who in America*, II (1950); *Nat. Cyc. Am. Biog.*, XXXVI, 539-540; *N.Y. Times* obituary, Nov. 28, 1948; family information from Iowa state census of 1885 (State Dept. of Hist. and Arch.); death record from Calif. Dept. of Public Health.]

KENNETH E. HENDRICKSON, JR.

LYMAN, EUGENE WILLIAM (Apr. 4, 1872-Mar. 15, 1948), teacher, philosopher of religion, and liberal Protestant spokesman, was born in Cummington, Mass. Both of his parents belonged to families long established in that region. Richard Lyman, first of the paternal line in America, had migrated from High Onger, Essex, England, to Charleston, Mass., and then had moved westward as one of the first settlers of Hartford, Conn. Eugene's father, Darwin Eugene Lyman, owned the village store in Cummington and for a time served in the Massachusetts legislature; his mother, Julia Sarah (Stevens) Lyman, ran a millinery shop as part of her husband's business.

Eugene Lyman, called upon in later life to identify the sources of his liberalism, remembered a home and community atmosphere pervaded by the liberal evangelicalism of the Hartford theologian Horace Bushnell and by the political progressivism of the Springfield *Republican*. His mother, "a stalwart Christian of conservative feeling and much moral force," was also "an awakener of intellectual ambition" who introduced Eugene and his younger sister, Laura, to a wide range of imaginative literature. The father was a man of unusually catholic temper whose influence was reinforced by that of a "succession of liberal preachers" in the Congregational church that dominated the town's religious life. In his early teens, Lyman read, and was strongly influenced by, the principal Bushnellian thinkers of the time, Theodore Munger and Washington Gladden.

Because he had no access to a public high school and no funds to attend a private one, Lyman prepared for college on his own, at the same time teaching school to earn tuition. At Amherst College he studied with the philosopher Charles Edward Garman, whose nondidactic pedagogy and personalistic idealism were important in Lyman's professional development. After graduation from Amherst in 1894, Lyman taught Latin for two years, first at Williston Seminary (Easthampton, Mass.)

and then at the Lawrenceville (N.J.) School. He then entered Yale Divinity School, from which he earned both the bachelor of divinity degree (1899) and a Hooker fellowship—the latter providing for two years of advanced theological studies at the universities of Halle, Berlin, and Marburg.

Lyman was ordained in the Congregational ministry in 1901 and in the same year became professor of philosophy at Carleton College. After leaving Carleton in 1904, he held teaching posts in theology and philosophy at the Congregational Church College of Canada in Montreal (1904-1905); at Bangor (Maine) Theological Seminary (1905-1913); and at the Oberlin School of Theology (1913-1918). In 1918 he was appointed professor of the philosophy of religion at Union Theological Seminary in New York.

Lyman, like his mentor Garman, gained renown as an unusually effective and innovative teacher who inspired a generation of teacher-scholars in the field of religious philosophy; but unlike Garman, he was also a productive scholar. Lyman wrote several short books, numerous articles, and *The Meaning and Truth of Religion* (1933), his magnum opus. When this work appeared, the *New York Times* in a lead review praised it as conveying "the working of the modernist mind in its best and latest mood." Certainly the book, like Lyman's own method and personality, expressed the characteristic liberal or modernist eagerness to effect a synthesis of varying theoretical and doctrinal emphases and also the liberal tendency to make philosophy do most of the work of theology. *Meaning and Truth* at the same time reflected modernism's "latest" mood by adopting a critical attitude toward several of the leading philosophical tenets of the movement.

Early in his career, Lyman had become dissatisfied both with the abstractness of absolute idealism and with the attempt, among followers of the theologian Albrecht Ritschl, to divorce theoretical and moral knowledge. In a notable article for a Garman festschrift of 1906 and again in his Taylor Lectures of 1910, he announced broad approval of pragmatism as a corrective influence in theology. But, unable fully to conquer his own objections to pragmatism's epistemological relativism, Lyman struggled to find firmer empirical grounding for theology than either idealism or pragmatism could supply. The synthesis that he worked out over the next two decades constituted one prominent expression of what by the 1930's was being called theological realism. In Lyman's

rendition, this realism insisted upon the independent reality of natural objects, of intuitively grasped moral values, and of divine revelation —even though each of these areas of experience was thought to "criticize and supplement" the others. Lyman came to define God as "a cosmic creative spirit" whose nature combined purposiveness and open-ended creativity.

Lyman's influence, while substantial, was limited by the growing discontent with liberalism in theological circles and also by an unspectacular personal style. The publication of *The Meaning and Truth of Religion* coincided with that of Reinhold Niebuhr's *Moral Man and Immoral Society* and with other announcements of theological change that his own work, however critical, could not match as a tract for the times. In contrast with many of his colleagues on the Union faculty and in the liberal movement, moreover, Lyman was neither a political and ecclesiastical activist nor a favorite on the college-speaking circuit nor a stirring lecturer in the classroom.

He did, however, give effective support to liberal, and sometimes radical, causes. James Robinson, a prominent black churchman, remembered Lyman as almost the only person on the Union faculty to whom a black student felt able to turn for unpatronizing support. While disavowing "theoretical pacifism," Lyman opposed American entry into World War I, joined the pacifist Fellowship of Reconciliation, and inclined toward the noninterventionist side in the disputes over American foreign policy that divided the Union faculty in the 1930's. He was a steady advocate of the Social Gospel, who, particularly after 1920, castigated the "deeply immoral" features of capitalism and generally lent his support to the more activistic social radicals among his colleagues.

Lyman's first wife was Bertha Burton Thayer, of Cincinnati, Ohio, whom he married on June 1, 1899. They adopted two children, Charles Eugene and Laura Frances. Bertha Lyman died in 1924, and on Feb. 13, 1926, the widower married Mary Redington Ely of St. Johnsbury, Vt., who had been his student and then colleague at Union. Upon Lyman's retirement in 1940, the couple moved to Sweet Briar College in Virginia, where Mary Lyman took up her new post as dean and professor of religion. Although he would accept no more official position at Sweet Briar than "dean's husband," Lyman in his remaining years made himself available and valued as a philosopher-in-residence. Having suffered a stroke in 1946 and almost fully recovered from it, Lyman died suddenly at Sweet Briar two years later, the cause of death being given as heart failure. He was buried in the Lyman plot in Cummington.

[Besides *The Meaning and Truth of Religion*, Lyman wrote *Theology and Human Problems* (his Taylor Lectures at Yale, 1910) and *The Experience of God in Modern Life* (1920). His other principal writings are listed in David E. Roberts and Henry P. Van Dusen, eds., *Liberal Theology, An Appraisal: Essays in Honor of Eugene William Lyman* (1942). Lyman wrote an intellectual autobiography for a volume edited by Vergilius Ferm, *Contemporary American Theology*, pp. 105–131 (1933). The most useful critical essays on Lyman's theology are those by Walter Marshall Horton, in *Liberal Theology*, pp. 3–44, and by Kenneth Cauthen, *The Impact of American Religious Liberalism*, pp. 127–143 (1962). The most easily accessible portrait of Lyman is that in the *Nat. Cyc. Am. Biog.*, XXXVI, 287.
The present author interviewed John Coleman Bennett, Lyman's colleague at Union Seminary, on Aug. 16, 1970; and interviewed Mary Ely Lyman on Aug. 25, 1970. Transcripts of both conversations have been deposited in the Lib. of Union Theological Seminary.]
WILLIAM R. HUTCHISON

LYON, DAVID WILLARD (May 13, 1870-Mar. 16, 1949), founder of the YMCA in China, was born on a houseboat in Ningpo, China, where his parents had recently begun their service as Presbyterian missionaries that was to last for nearly four decades. He was the oldest of their seven children. His father, Rev. David Nelson Lyon, was a native of Salisbury, N.Y.; his mother, Mandana Eliza (Doolittle) Lyon, of Townshend, Vt. Both had attended Vermillion Institute in Hayesville, Ohio, and Lyon had graduated from Western Theological Seminary in 1869.

As was customary in missionary families, young Lyon returned to the United States for his education and received the B.A. from the College of Wooster in Ohio in 1891. Expecting to become a preacher of the gospel, he spent two years at McCormick Theological Seminary in Chicago preparing for ordination. The new Student Volunteer Movement, enthusiastically abetted by the college branches of the Young Men's Christian Association, was at this point encouraging young men and women to go abroad as missionaries. Lyon served for a year (1894-1895) as educational secretary for the SVM, editing the *Student Volunteer*. Because of his Chinese experience and administrative ability, the YMCA urged him to return to China to pioneer a student movement there. Although his father wanted him to become a preacher, Lyon finally decided to become a YMCA worker instead. He was ordained to the Presbyterian ministry in 1895 and never abandoned his deep religious enthusiasm, but he spent the rest of his active professional life as an administrator in the nondenominational YMCA. He was married to Grace McCaw in 1895; they had four children: David, Scovel, Jean, and Elizabeth.

When Lyon and his wife arrived in China at the end of 1895, the country seemed ready to make some fundamental changes in its institutions because of its defeat in the Sino-Japanese War. Lyon decided to go to Tientsin, where students largely trained in mission schools were eager to learn modern skills and were curious about Western institutions. In a few months Lyon founded a student YMCA, solicited local funds to buy a lot, persuaded an American donor (Mrs. J. Livingstone Taylor) to finance a building, and organized a board of directors that soon included Chinese. He began to give classes and started a bulletin in English and Chinese, the first of several published over the years by the YMCA. During 1896 he helped organize student YMCAs throughout the country. He also began to press for a school where he could train Chinese to become YMCA secretaries. Thus Lyon set a model for the later large national organization, shaping it as a movement that was self-governing and where possible self-supporting, where young men could meet together, improve themselves, and prepare to serve as modernizers of Chinese society. In these hectic months he also studied Mandarin several hours a day by setting his face "like a flint" against other demands on his time. His fluency in the vernacular enabled him to start language training schools for American missionaries. He was buoyed in the work by a conviction that the young men of America had a special responsibility toward the young men of China because of American laws against Chinese immigration.

During the Boxer Rebellion of 1900, Lyon sought refuge in Korea and started the Korean YMCA. In China the work briefly came to a standstill, but with the humiliating Boxer defeat, Chinese businessmen and officials soon became attracted to the innovative and sympathetic work of the YMCA, and its influence began to spread. In 1901 Lyon became general secretary and then associate secretary of the new National Committee of the Chinese YMCA and served in that capacity until his retirement. In the ensuing years he was involved in many areas of countrywide planning and administration. He was keenly aware of important new movements affecting China. On a trip to Japan in 1906, for example, he saw the explosive potential lodged in Chinese students living in Tokyo. Though hardly a radical reformer himself, he helped develop in Japan a Chinese YMCA that gained the confidence of these students and enhanced the YMCA reputation in China after the 1911 revolution. In the area of written language reform, he encouraged the use of the vernacular in journals and pamphlets. Far in advance of denominational church groups, he set up training schools and institutes for Chinese secretaries. His faith in Chinese leadership was acknowledged by an invitation to be the only foreign secretary to speak at the 1920 Chinese YMCA National Convention, held when nationalist feelings were emerging strongly. In 1915 Lyon published *The Christian Equivalent of War,* and in 1927, *Confucianism Today,* and along with these produced a stream of training pamphlets, institutional memoirs, and articles for the American Oriental Society, the Institute for Pacific Relations, and the *Chinese Recorder.*

Plagued by delicate health, Lyon retired in 1930, although he remained in the Far East until 1934 recruiting workers for the YMCA On his return to America he turned his interests to translating T'ang poetry. A book of his translations, *Inside the Moon Gate,* was published posthumously in 1951. Lyon died of hypertensive heart disease at his home in Claremont, Calif., at the age of seventy-eight and was cremated at the Chapel of the Pines, Los Angeles. Lyon spoke modestly of his own achievements, and after the early years he was not associated with some of the more dramatic developments in the Chinese YMCA. He had played a key role, however, in molding the early YMCA into China's first modern youth organization.

[The bulk of Lyon's papers and reports, including his *The First Quarter Century of the Young Men's Christian Assoc. in China* (Shanghai, 1920), are at the YMCA Hist. Lib. in New York City, with a small collection at the Missionary Research Lib. at Union Theological Seminary. No personal papers have come to light. For an obituary, see *N.Y. Times,* Mar. 18, 1949. A brief biography is in C. Howard Hopkins, *Hist of the Y.M.C.A. in North America* (1951), and a larger appraisal of pioneer YMCA work in China in Shirley S. Garrett, *Social Reformers in Urban China: The Chinese YMCA, 1895–1926* (1970). Information about Lyon and his parents was supplied by the Presbyterian Hist. Soc., Philadelphia; death record from Calif. Dept. of Public Health.]

SHIRLEY S. GARRETT

McCLUNG, CLARENCE ERWIN (Apr. 5, 1870-Jan. 17, 1946), biologist, was born in Clayton, Calif., the son of Charles Livingston McClung, a mining engineer of Scots-Irish descent, and Annie Howard (Mackey) McClung, the daughter of a physician. Because his father's occupation required that the family

travel considerably, Clarence's early education was acquired in several different places. After attending high school in Columbus, Kans., he worked for two years in his uncle's drug store and studied pharmacy at the University of Kansas in Lawrence, from which he received the Ph.G. degree in 1892. He then spent several years working as a chemist in a sugar refinery in New Orleans each autumn and attending the University of Kansas each spring, to earn a liberal arts degree, which he finally received in 1896.

An exceptionally gifted student, he was immediately appointed to the staff of the University of Kansas, as a substitute instructor in histology in 1896 and in botany in 1897. During those years he also spent one term studying with the cytologist E. B. Wilson at Columbia University and was awarded the M.A. degree from that institution in 1898. By that time the University of Kansas had appointed him assistant professor of zoology. He was promoted to associate professor in 1900, to chairman of the Department of Zoology in 1901, to curator of paleontology in 1902, and to professor of zoology in 1906. While engaged in these teaching and administrative duties, he was also pursuing cytological research; that research won him a Ph.D. from the University of Chicago in 1903—but more important, it also won him a permanent place of honor in the history of genetics.

The research in question was a study of spermatogenesis (cellular division leading to the production of sperm) in the grasshopper *Xiphidium fasciatum.* McClung had spent the summer of 1898 at the University of Chicago, in the laboratory of W. M. Wheeler. Wheeler, who had just completed a study of oogenesis (cellular division leading to the production of eggs) in the female of that species, urged his student to explore the parallel process in the males. McClung noticed that in the second division of spermatogenesis there was one chromosome that did not replicate itself, with the result that half the spermatids did not possess that chromosome; he named this the *accessory chromosome,* to indicate that it seemed an addition to the normal number for the species. Several other cytologists had already noticed the additional body, but no one before McClung had realized that it was in fact a chromosome. McClung's accomplishment stemmed, in part, from the excellence of his histologic preparations. As an observational feat this discovery was remarkable, but what made it particularly crucial for the history of genetics was McClung's guess—purely hypothetical at the time—that the accessory chromosome was, in fact, a determinant of the sex of the grasshopper. McClung's guess was based upon the fact that half the grown individuals of the species would possess the additional chromosome, and that the only characteristic that roughly divides the population in half is sex.

McClung's guess was proven true three years after the publication of his paper, when in 1905 E. B. Wilson and Nettie Stevens published their extensive cytological researches into the chromosomal determination of sex. These discoveries came just a few years after the rediscovery in 1900 of Mendel's work on patterns of inheritance in sweet peas and were almost contemporaneous with the enunciation, in 1902, of the Sutton-Boveri hypothesis. This hypothesis suggested that the patterns of chromosomal division could be precisely related to the Mendelian patterns of trait distribution and that, consequently, the chromosomes must be the bearers of heredity. W. S. Sutton was a student of McClung's and of Wilson's; his hypothesis, which was stated almost simultaneously by the European biologist Theodore Boveri, is now one of the tenets of modern genetics.

In 1912 McClung moved to the University of Pennsylvania, where he remained as professor of zoology and director of the Zoological Laboratories until his retirement in 1940. During this time he continued his research into the cytological aspects of chromosome behavior. He was an extremely skillful microscopist; some of the techniques that he developed for the histologic preparation of specimens and some of the devices that he suggested for the improvement of microscopes were major contributions to biology. As part of his work in microscopy he edited an influential handbook of microscopic technique, which went through several editions before and after his death. McClung was an avid collector of grasshoppers and was also very interested in paleontology, having written several papers on fossil bisons and led several paleontological expeditions while he was still at Kansas.

As his career progressed, McClung became one of the most influential biologists in the United States. He was the first director of the Division of Biology and Agriculture of the National Research Council (1919-1921); in this position he helped to establish the pattern of governmental funding for biological research. As head of this division he also laid the

original plans for an international biological abstracting service, which, as *Biological Abstracts,* has become a crucial reference tool. McClung was also very active in the development of the Biological Experiment Station at Woods Hole, Mass., one of the leading biological research facilities in the United States; he served Woods Hole (where he and his family spent many summers) in a wide variety of executive capacities. For twenty years (1920-1940) he was also the managing editor of the *Journal of Morphology.* At the universities of Kansas and Pennsylvania he trained dozens of advanced students, many of whom went on to successful careers as biologists and teachers.

McClung married Anna Adelia Drake, an accomplished pianist, on Aug. 31, 1899; they had two daughters, Ruth Cromwell and Della Elizabeth. McClung died in Swarthmore, Pa.

[For a biography of McClung and a complete bibliography of his published works, see D. H. Wenrich, "Clarence Erwin McClung," *Jour. Morphol.,* 66 (1940), 635–688; also a biographical article in *Bios,* 6 (1935), 343–371. The article in which McClung announced the discovery of the accessory chromosome is "The Accessory Chromosome—Sex Determinant?" *Bio. Bull.,* 3 (1902), 43–84. His handbook of microscopic technique is *Microscopical Technique for Workers in Animal and Plant Tissues* (1929, 1937, 1950). A portrait of McClung can be found in *Jour. Morphol.* 70 (1946), 16.]

RUTH SCHWARTZ COWAN

McCLURE, SAMUEL SIDNEY (Feb. 17, 1857-Mar. 21, 1949) editor, social crusader, and author, was born at Frocess, County Antrim, Ireland, the oldest of the four sons of Thomas McClure and Elizabeth (Gaston) McClure. His parents were descendants of farmers who lived a God-fearing, toilsome existence on their small holdings. His father's family were Scottish Lowlanders from Galloway who settled in Ireland; his mother's ancestors were French Huguenots. At eight Samuel was a bright, eager boy, advanced beyond his years in school, when his father, a carpenter, fell to his death in a Clydeside shipyard. His widow struggled for a year on their nine-acres farm and then, to avoid scattering her family among relatives, immigrated in June 1866 to northwestern Indiana, where two of her brothers and two married sisters had already settled.

There on a farm near Valparaiso and in the town itself, the McClures battled poverty with hard work. Early in 1867, in an effort to provide her sons with a financially secure home, Elizabeth McClure married Thomas Simpson, also from Ireland, by whom she had four more children. A few years later, at her urging and with one dollar, Samuel went to the new high school in Valparaiso, where he worked for his keep. When he noted that other students gave middle names he dubbed himself Samuel Sherman, in honor of the Union general whom he admired. Later he substituted Sidney for Sherman but beginning on the first day of high school he became S. S. McClure. Almost all the clothes he owned were on his spare, wiry form. As he later said, "Speed was my overcoat." Impatiently he tried a variety of odd jobs from section hand to printer's devil. After his stepfather's death, he returned to the farm as the "man of the family." A visit from an uncle Gaston, who had studied at Knox College, in Galesburg, Ill., led to McClure's enrollment in 1874 in the college's preparatory department.

The impetuous youth avidly pursued the classical-scientific studies of the time, served as editor of the *Knox Student,* organized and issued an intercollegiate news bulletin, and formed the Western College Associated Press of which he was chosen president. He also sought the hand of Harriet Hurd, the daughter of Albert Hurd, a professor of geology and Latin. Both families thought the match unsuitable, and his mother induced him to accompany her to Ireland, intending that he remain there. Determined to return to the United States, he worked his way back on shipboard, went straight to Galesburg, and began an erratic courtship. After graduation he followed Harriet to Marcy, N.Y., where she was visiting friends. Rebuffed by her, he moved to Boston and took a job with Albert Pope, a bicycle manufacturer. His work led to the launching of a magazine, *The Wheelman,* devoted to the increasingly popular bicycle craze. When McClure as editor hustled to Beacon Street to implore Oliver Wendell Holmes to produce a poem on cycling, he was on a publishing course that would lead him far in years to come. Now a modest wage earner, he redoubled his efforts to win Harriet, with the result that they were married on Sept. 4, 1883, in a still reluctant Hurd home. They had three daughters, Eleanor, Elizabeth, and Mary; a son, Robert Louis Stevenson McClure, and an adopted son, Enrico, called Henry.

Shortly thereafter, McClure left the bicycle firm to join the prestigious DeVinne printing company in New York; bored by the routine, he soon moved to the Century Company's dictionary office where he proposed a set of changes for the management—and was politely let go. Circumstances had provided him with the opportunity and necessity to develop his own literary syndicate, not the first syndicate as he claimed, for there were others at the time. His scheme was to follow a procedure used in England, namely, to circulate a flow of novels, stories, and other literary features in serial form, to newspapers, at low cost to the individual outlet. Beginning with less than $25 in the bank, he declared that his plan would provide material by well-known authors never before published in serial form. From his New York apartment he sent out announcements, dated Oct. 4, 1884, that promised writings by such writers as Helen Hunt Jackson, William Dean Howells, E. P. Roe, and Sarah Orne Jewett. The early months were rough, and the effort came close to collapsing as he went into debt and authors failed him. But he persisted, making personal calls on newspaper editors to persuade them to subscribe.

The syndicate was well enough established by 1887 for McClure to need a reliable, full-time helper, and he engaged a Knox classmate, John S. Phillips, who had worked with him at *The Wheelman.* Thereupon McClure went abroad to contract noted writers in Europe. It was the first of eight Atlantic round trips in six years during which he also crossed the American continent an equal number of times. Stevenson, Kipling, Doyle, Meredith, Edmund Gosse, Hardy, Henley, H. Rider Haggard, Ruskin, Swinburne, Zola; Harte, Henry James, Whitman, Julia Ward Howe, Stephen Crane, Hamlin Garland, Joel Chandler Harris, O. Henry, Jack London, Gertrude Atherton, Booth Tarkington—McClure signed all of them and many others. Robert Louis Stevenson was a special case, and McClure used every resource to please the ailing author and to get him on a yacht bound for the South Seas. Stevenson was contracted to write letter essays of his travels for the syndicate. Stevenson in turn based his character Jim Pinkerton in *The Wrecker* (1892) on McClure; and William Dean Howells, in *A Hazard of New Fortunes* (1890), portrayed McClure as the aggressive Westerner Fulkerson. Appraising the effect of the literary syndicate, McClure's biographer wrote that by getting fiction into the biggest newspapers, he helped change the character of journalism and also the character of American fiction with creative writing now turned "into a new and deeper channel" (Lyon, pp. 53, 70).

The transition from McClure's syndicate to *McClure's Magazine* was a natural, if hazardous, undertaking. McClure had some 2,000 manuscripts in a safe and it made sense to begin publishing them in his own monthly. But Phillips, who joined the venture with $4,500, and McClure together had barely $10,000 in capital. Moreover the first issue appeared on May 28, almost coincidentally with the panic of 1893. Twenty thousand copies were printed, and of these 12,000 were returned by the agents. Still, one way or another money was raised and *McClure's* survived. Late in 1894 the magazine, at fifteen cents a copy, enjoyed 60,000 subscribers and sixty pages of advertising. Since the *Century* had dropped from a circulation of 200,000 to 75,000, the small staff at *McClure's* could only be highly pleased. Yet as *McClure's* had undercut the twenty-five- and thirty-five-cent magazines, some proceeded to price themselves below *McClure's*. The future remained precarious.

An unexpected plus came in contracting Ida M. Tarbell to write a biography of Napoleon, which proved to be exceedingly popular, followed by an even more successful series on Lincoln's early life. Through the 1890's the magazine offered new works by many of the celebrated writers who had produced for the syndicate. Circulation climbed steadily, and by 1900 it was close to 400,000. Then in the latter part of 1902, McClure put together the issue of January 1903 that set *McClure's* on the course that made it famous. Noting that the leading article was Lincoln Steffens' "The Shame of Minneapolis" and that two others were an installment in Tarbell's epochal history of Standard Oil and Ray Stannard Baker's "The Right to Work," McClure, in an accompanying editorial, declared that all three might well have been called "The American Contempt of Law." Although the arrangement was accidental, he called it a fortuitous warning that the price of this contempt was one which would need to be paid in the end by "every one of us."

This was not the first revelatory journalism of the period, but it was the first to be pursued with McClure's intensity. One issue after another pulled screens away and showed what ugly scandals lay behind. Along with Tarbell, Steffens, and Baker, who were already on the staff, George Kibbe Turner, Burton J. Hendrick, Will Irwin, Samuel Hopkins Adams, Christopher P. Connolly, and others either joined the magazine or wrote for it. Soon many other periodicals, following *McClure's* lead, were printing their own disclosures. In a few years the reading public had been introduced to corruption in local, state, and national government, industrial management, race relations, railroads, insurance, patent medicines, liquor and white slave traffic, slum housing, foods and drugs, adult as well as child labor, the stock and money markets, poverty, unemployment, the judicial system, and the press.

After President Theodore Roosevelt belittled these reforming efforts in 1906 with his distorted allusion to Bunyan's myopic Man With the Muck-Rake, the movement became known as muckraking and the writers and editors as the muckrakers.

Often a close companion with his staff, McClure could be hot-tempered. At the height of their muckraking, Tarbell, Phillips, Baker, and Steffens broke with him and started the *American Magazine*. *McClure's* declined, was suspended in 1914, revived, associated with the *New Smart Set*, started up again and, in 1925, was bought by Hearst's International Publications. The name continued but that was all, and it disappeared in 1930. McClure joined the idealists on Henry Ford's 1915 Peace Ship, but was dissatisfied and soon left the group. After World War I, he was charmed by fascism, became an admirer of Mussolini, and went to Italy, where he observed, as he said, that the trains ran on time. He was convinced of popular gains under the fascist rule and wrote and spoke enthusiastically about the system at controversial public meetings after he returned.

McClure's *Autobiography* (1914) was ghostwritten by Willa Cather, whose stories he had printed. His books include *Obstacles to Peace* (1917), *The Achievements of Liberty* (1935), and *What Freedom Means to Man* (1938). Assessing McClure's literary output, Peter Lyon has written: "The truth was that McClure, as a writer, was a great editor . . ." (p. 410).

Living into his ninety-third year, McClure survived nearly all his muckraking colleagues. Although his house was in Brookfield Center, Conn., he resided in later life at the Murray Hill Hotel in New York and worked among his papers at the Union League Club library. For years friends and relatives helped meet his bills. He died of a heart attack at St. Barnabas Hospital in the Bronx and was buried at Galesburg. He had gone about the world so long that his old college community was as much of a home as he had ever had. Nearly forgotten in his last years, one signal honor revived his flagging spirit. The National Institute of Arts and Letters, in 1944, awarded him its Order of Merit gold medal and $1,000 for his "furtherance of arts and letters, particularly in the recognition of new talent and in the creation of a new type of journalism."

[Peter Lyon's *Success Story: The Life and Times of S. S. McClure* (1963), is not only delightful but a full and fair biography with the minuses of his subject's complex character. Lyon also assembled photographic portraits of McClure, his family and associates in a picture section along with a list of autobiographies, memoirs and collections of letters by McClure's co-workers. Books and articles on the muckrakers and the period include Jacob A Riis, *The Making of an American* (1901); Brand Whitlock, *Forty Years of It* (1914); Lincoln Steffens, *Autobiography* (1931); C. C. Regier, *The Era of the Muckrakers* (1932); John Chamberlain, *Farewell to Reform* (1932); Irving Bacheller, *From Stores of Memory* (1938); Frank L. Mott, *A History of American Magazines* (1938–1957); Louis Filler, *Crusaders for American Liberalism* (1939); William A. White, *Autobiography* (1946); Walter Johnson, ed., *Selected Letters of William Allen White* (1947); Frank L. Mott, *Golden Multitudes: The Story of Best Sellers in the United States* (1947); Charles Madison, *Critics and Crusaders* (1947); Richard Hofstadter, *The Age of Reform* (1955); Arthur and Lila Weinberg, eds., *The Muckrakers* (1961); D. M. Chalmers, *The Social and Political Ideas of the Muckrakers* (1964); Irving Dilliard, "The Old Muckrakers," *Frontier*, Apr. 1965; R. C. Bannister, Jr., *Ray Stannard Baker: The Mind and Thought of a Progressive* (1966); J. E. Semonche, *Ray Stannard Baker: A Quest for Democracy in Modern America, 1870–1918* (1969); Theodore Peterson, *Magazines in the Twentieth Century* (2nd ed., 1964); H. S. Wilson, *McClure's Magazine and the Muckrakers* (1970); J. M. Harrison and H. H. Stein, *Muckraking: Past, Present and Future* (1973). See also newspapers and magazines at the time of his death, especially *N.Y. Times,* with portrait, and *N.Y. Herald Tribune,* both Mar. 23, 1949; *Who Was Who in Am.,* II (1950); and *Americana Encyc.* (1972). A photographic portrait by Arnold Genthe in H. and B. Cirker, *Dict. of Am. Portraits* (1967), is of interest. Assistance of a nephew, R. H. McClure, is gratefully acknowledged; personal recollection.]

IRVING DILLIARD

McCORD, JAMES BENNETT (Apr. 5, 1870–Oct. 5, 1950), medical missionary, was born in Toulon, Ill. His father, Robert L. McCord, was a Congregational minister in Illinois and Iowa, and his mother, Helen D. (Hopkins) McCord, was from an Illinois family prominent in farming and local politics. McCord was sent to the preparatory department of Oberlin College and later the college, graduating in 1891. While in college he was active in the Student Volunteer Movement; his work in this organization and the encouragement of his fiancée, Margaret Mellon, a fellow student at Oberlin and the daughter of former missionaries to South Africa, led to his interest in serving as a medical missionary in Africa. He studied medicine at Northwestern University and interned at Mercy Hospital in Chicago. After his marriage on Aug. 14, 1895, he practiced medicine in Lake City, Iowa, until the American Board of Commissioners for Foreign Missions (Congregational) sent him to Natal, South Africa, in 1899.

After spending a year studying the Zulu language and the cultural background of medical practice among the Zulus, McCord discovered that he could not be registered to practice medicine in Natal without a British medical degree. He therefore spent the next year (1901–1902) in England and obtained the necessary degree. McCord inherited a small hospital at Amanzimtoti (Adams Mission) from his predecessor but found that the inaccessibility of the mission station was a great liability. In 1904 he opened the Beatrice Street Dispensary in Greyville, a section of Durban populated by many Africans, Indians, and people of mixed race. The news of his successful work spread quickly, and people soon came from hundreds of miles away for medical and surgical care.

The need for a hospital for nonwhites in Durban was great, but finding a location for one was not easy. Each location that seemed suitable was opposed by nearby whites who feared that a hospital for Africans would endanger their peace and their health. After several court battles, a hospital was established in 1908. It was known at the Mission Nursing Home until 1935 when the name was changed to McCord Zulu Hospital, by which it is still known. The training of African nurses began soon after, although it was not until 1924 that nurses were permitted to take the examinations for government registration. Courses in midwifery were also offered.

During World War I McCord served first in the British army in Natal and then in the American army in the United States. During the latter service he met Dr. Alan B. Taylor and Dr. J. W. Morledge; he enlisted these men in his attempt to provide medical training for Africans. Their efforts were frustrated in the 1920's by the opposition of white doctors. In spite of clashes over policy, McCord was always active in the Durban Medical Society; he also served as its president (1912–1914). Taylor assumed the superintendency of the hospital, while McCord continued to work at the Beatrice Street Dispensary. Both men carried on the campaign for training Africans as either medical aides or fully qualified doctors. The final achievement came after McCord's death, when the Non-European Medical School of the University of Natal opened in 1951 with Taylor as its acting dean.

In spite of the early opposition of many of the whites of Durban, McCord and his wife persisted in publicizing the medical needs of the African people. By the 1930's many prominent businessmen, both white and Indian, were contributors to the hospital. The McCords also worked for higher wages and better treatment for Africans through the Joint Council for Europeans and Non-Europeans, the Institute of Race Relations, the Natal Missionary Conference, and the General Missionary Conference of South Africa. As chairman of the American Board Mission in South Africa for many years, McCord was greatly concerned with schools for Africans, and was especially interested in Adams College and Inanda Seminary for Girls.

Margaret McCord worked with her husband in all his enterprises, serving as matron of the hospital in its early days and assisting in the operating theater. The McCord home received visitors from all over the world passing through Durban, and she was hostess to all of these, in addition to caring for a family of six children, Jessie, Mary, Robert, Laura, William, and Margaret. Her own early years spent at the Umsunduze Mission Station in Natal enabled her to help many Zulus overcome their fear of hospitals. The love and respect of many Zulu people for the McCords is reflected in the stories, some doubtless apocryphal, told of them in Zulu homes and villages in Natal and Zululand. The African nationalist leaders of John Dube and Albert Luthuli's generation (about 1910–1950) counted McCord and some of his missionary colleagues as friends and associates in a common task; some present-day leaders have seen his work only as a part of paternalism and imperialism, but others have been appreciative of the educational and medical opportunities which McCord Zulu Hospital has provided.

In 1940 the McCords retired to Oakham, Mass. McCord, an enthusiastic chess player, was a founder and champion of the Durban Chess Club. In his later years he participated in the U.S. National Chess Championship and in 1950 was its oldest competitor. McCord died at Oakham, Mass., in his sleep and was buried in Pine Grove Cemetery there.

From his arrival in South Africa in 1899 until his retirement, McCord actively pursued the goal of better medical care for the Zulu people of Natal and all nonwhites of South Africa. For him, Christian ministry meant not only proclaiming the gospel and healing the sick but also changing the conditions that bred disease (whether the ignorance of traditional Zulu doctors or the unjust laws of the white colonists).

[The chief biographical sources are J. B. McCord and J. S. Douglas, *My Patients Were Zulus* (1946) and J. B. McCord, "The Zulu Witch Doctor and Medicine Man," *South African Jour. of Science*, Jan.–Feb. 1919, pp. 306–318; *A Century of Progress in Medical Work among the Zulus, 1835–1935: The Evolution of McCord Zulu Hospital* (1935) is a brief account of the growth of the hospital. On the mission of which McCord was a member, see A. F. Christofersen, *Adventuring With God: The Story of the Am. Board Mission in South Africa*, ed. Richard W. Sales (1967), which contains a chapter on medical mission work; F. F. Goodsell, *You Shall Be My Witnesses* (1967), gives a general picture of the American Board under which McCord worked; J. D. Taylor, *One Hundred Years of the Am. Board Mission in South Africa* (1935), provides an account of the South African mission by a contemporary of McCord.]

JANE SALES

MacCURDY, GEORGE GRANT (Apr. 17, 1863-Nov. 15, 1947), anthropologist and archaeologist, was born at Warrensburg, Mo., the son of William Joseph MacCurdy and Margaret (Smith) MacCurdy. His father, a farmer, had moved to Missouri because his objections to slavery had cost him his property in his home state of Georgia. Raised in modest circumstances, MacCurdy had to teach school to finance his education at the State Normal School in Warrensburg, from which he graduated in 1887. By 1889 he had become a superintendent of schools. When, in the same year, he visited Cambridge, Mass., as a delegate to a YMCA conference, he decided that he wanted to attend Harvard University. He was admitted to Harvard with advanced standing in 1891 and received his B.A (1893) and M.A. (1894), both in geology and biology. In 1894 he worked in the laboratory of the great zoologist Alexander Agassiz.

At about this time MacCurdy met the orientalist Edward E. Salisbury of Yale University, whose wife was a distant cousin of MacCurdy's. Salisbury recognized MacCurdy's potential and, over the next four years, paid his expenses for study in Europe. During this period MacCurdy became familiar with the German scholarly emphasis on research and high standards. In 1896 his interest in paleoanthropology was whetted by attendance at the International Zoological Congress in Leyden, where he studied Eugène Du Bois's exhibition of the bones of *Pithecanthropus*. He returned to the United States in 1898 to continue his graduate work in anthropology at Yale and received his Ph.D. in 1905.

MacCurdy spent most of his professional life at Yale, where he served as instructor in anthropology (1898-1900), lecturer (1902-1910), assistant professor of prehistoric archaeology (1910-1923), and professor (1923 until his retirement in 1931). During the same period, MacCurdy also served as curator of the anthropological collections at the Peabody Museum of Natural History at Yale, thereby assuring that prehistoric archaeology would be represented alongside the natural sciences at Yale. He was called upon to catalogue collections in Old World prehistory for the American Museum of Natural History in New York in 1910-1912, which attested to his reputation as an anthropological curator. On June 30, 1919, he married Janet Glenn Bartlett, who shared her husband's enthusiasm for prehistoric archaeology and accompanied him on his many field trips abroad. They had no children.

MacCurdy's early work was done in a period when American anthropology was just beginning to develop as a professional discipline. His connections with European scholarship helped to raise the standards of American programs, as did his continued involvement in European prehistoric archaeological research. MacCurdy was greatly concerned with the development of institutional resources for anthropology in the United States. His articles at the beginning of the twentieth century in *Science* about the development of academic programs encouraged early academic recognition of the rapid growth of anthropology in America. MacCurdy also encouraged retention of the new discipline's established ties to museums and public interest in anthropological topics, alongside the new university programs.

In 1921 MacCurdy, with his wife and Dr. Charles Peabody, founded in Paris the American School in France for Prehistoric Studies (renamed in 1926 the American School of Prehistoric Research); MacCurdy served as its director for the first year and again in 1924-1945. During the 1920's he organized summer trips for students to visit European museums and archaeological sites. His own fieldwork at Abri des Merveilles, near Sergeac, France, was important in establishing the Mousterian period in the Dordogne area. After his retirement from active fieldwork in 1930, MacCurdy continued to direct many of the school's expeditions, including one at Mount Carmel, Palestine, in 1929-1934, in collaboration with the British School of Archaeology. This excavation, directed in the field by Dorothy Garrod of the British School, discovered what were then the oldest complete skeletons of *Homo sapiens*.

MacCurdy was also a prolific contributor to the literature of anthropology. Drawn to Americanist studies in his early years at Yale, he wrote a number of articles on the art and antiquities of the Chiriqui, a region of southwest Panama, and on the skeletal finds of a Peruvian expedition. Increasingly, he wrote about Old World prehistory. His *Human Ori-*

gins: A Manual of Prehistory (1924) was one of the earliest and most thorough works on prehistory published in the United States, and it contained a gazetteer of Old World archaeological sites. His other works include *Prehistoric Man* (1928), *The Coming of Man* (1932), and, as editor, *Early Man* (1937). Although much of his work has been superseded, his influence on American anthropology remains important.

Throughout his career MacCurdy was affiliated with many professional societies in both America and Europe. He served as vice-president of the Archaeological Institute of America (1947) and was a founding member, secretary (1903-1916), and president (1930-1931) of the American Anthropological Association.

This modest, gentle man remained active to the end of his life, working at his home in Old Lyme, Conn. On his way to Florida with his wife, he was struck by a car while stopping to ask directions in Plainfield, N.J. He died the same day at Plainfield's Muhlenburg Hospital. After services at Christ Church in Cambridge, Mass., he was buried in Concord. MacCurdy's will left a bequest founding a department of Old World prehistory at the Peabody Museum of Archaeology and Ethnology at Harvard, then the major American anthropological museum; in 1954 the entire assets of the American School were transferred to the museum, according to MacCurdy's wish.

[The major sources on MacCurdy are Robert W. Ehrlich, "George Grant MacCurdy, 1863–1947," *Am. Antiquity*, 14, no. 1 (1948), 49–50; Hugh Hencken, "George Grant MacCurdy, 1863–1947," *Science*, 107 (1948), 639–640; Ernest A. Hooton, "George Grant MacCurdy, 1863–1947," *Am. Anthropol.*, 52 (1950), 513–515, which contains a complete MacCurdy bibliography; Theodore D. McCown, "George Grant MacCurdy, 1863–1947," *ibid.*, 50 (1948), 516–524; and *Nat. Cyc. Am. Biog.*, XVII.]

REGNA DARNELL

McFARLAND, JOHN HORACE (Sept. 24, 1859-Oct. 2, 1948), conservationist and horticulturist. McFarland, who consistently used only the first initial of his first name, was born in McAlisterville, Pa. His parents, Col. George F. McFarland and Adeline D. (Griesemer) McFarland, were newspaper publishers and provided the comfortable financial situation that made reform and philanthropic involvement appealing. John McFarland was privately tutored but self-taught in the printing business, and his only college degree was an honorary doctorate from Dickinson College in 1924.

His diverse interests, from horticulture to the

preservation of scenic beauty and the reform of urban government, stemmed from his printing of journals espousing these interests (he was a master printer for seventy years). He was a skilled illustrator of botanical subjects, printed over 200 annual catalogs for gardening firms, and in time became a contributor to periodicals and editor of the *American Rose Annual* and *American Rose Magazine*. His ideals and zeal mark McFarland a Progressive; he typifies the Progressive reformer. Urbane, wealthy, and refined, he was uncomfortable with the rise of big business and big labor during the nineteenth century. He sought to redress the balance of power in favor of the people, their government, and cultural amenities. McFarland also represented progressivism by espousing efficient planning. He frequently used metaphors from architecture and construction to describe the role of America's civic leaders. Their responsibility was to sketch for the nation a plan providing for a beautiful, healthful, and habitable civilization that was also morally sound and culturally refined. McFarland saw himself as such a designer, charged with the duty that superiority always connoted for the Progressive mind: to lead the people to have respect for "the finer things of life."

Good government was a primary target of Progressive reform, and on the level of city politics McFarland was a significant national force. As president of the American Civic Association (1904-1924), vice-president of the National Municipal League (1912-1928), and secretary of the Harrisburg Municipal League (1907-1945), he supported candidates and programs dedicated to cleaning up the graft-filled courthouse rings that his contemporary Lincoln Steffens labeled "the shame of the cities."

From 1904, when he began writing the "Beautiful America" column in the *Ladies' Home Journal,* McFarland took an increasingly active role in the burgeoning conservation movement. But in contrast to Chief Forester Gifford Pinchot, who made "conservation" a household word during Theodore Roosevelt's administration, McFarland stressed the aesthetic dimension of concern for the environment. In the 1908 Governors' Conference on Conservation at the White House, he made one of the few pleas for conservation's aesthetic dimension. Whereas Pinchot argued on economic grounds that conservation was important to ensure future supplies of raw materials, McFarland contended that conservation should be equally concerned with beauty and

spiritual nourishment in an increasingly urbanized and industrialized nation. In 1909 he pleaded with Pinchot: "Somehow we must get you to see that . . . the preservation of forests, water powers, minerals, and other items of national prosperity . . . must be associated with the pleasure to the eye and the mind and the generation of the spirit of man" (Nov. 26, 1909, McFarland Manuscripts, Pa. Historical Museum, Harrisburg).

The issue came to a head over the future of the Hetch Hetchy Valley in Yosemite National Park. The city of San Francisco wanted to dam the Tuolumne River and create a municipal reservoir and a hydropower generating facility. Pinchot, with his wise-use conservation philosophy, favored such development, but McFarland could not support such a utilitarian definition of the function of national parks. With John Muir, president of the Sierra Club, he helped wage a protracted struggle against the Hetch Hetchy dam and, symbolically, against needless sacrifice of scenic beauty to profit and growth. In 1913 the Woodrow Wilson administration decided in favor of the Hetch Hetchy dam. McFarland could nevertheless take considerable satisfaction from his role in having helped make Hetch Hetchy a national issue. He also lent a degree of badly needed objectivity to the aesthetic conservationist cause. Muir and his colleagues defined their struggles in somewhat hysterical terms of good and evil, but McFarland was calm, cautious, and open-minded. Particularly in his dealings with politicians and bureaucrats he took the kind of frank, fair position that bred credibility. He was not lukewarm about the cause of natural beauty, but he understood the realities of the compromise tradition in American politics. Thus it was easy for him to look beyond the Hetch Hetchy defeat and work effectively for the establishment of the National Park Service in 1916. McFarland regarded his role in the establishment of organized supervision of the national parks as his single greatest accomplishment.

McFarland's appearance was neat and brisk; a well-trimmed moustache and thin-rimmed gold glasses characterized his face. He was known as a kindly, gentle man who stiffened only when justice or beauty was at stake. On May 22, 1884, McFarland married Lydia S. Walters. The couple had three children: Helen Louise, Robert Bruce, and Katherine Sieg (who died prematurely). He became an international authority on roses, receiving the

Arthur Hoyt Scott Garden and Horticultural Award in 1939 and the highest award of the National Rose Society of England, the Dean Hole Memorial Medal, in 1942. Toward the end of his life he had the satisfaction of seeing his early causes, such as the preservation of Niagara Falls, highway beautification, playgrounds and city parks, increasingly gain public and political favor. His rose garden in Harrisburg contained 800 varieties and achieved world fame. Although the national publicity accorded to some of his conservationist colleagues did not come to McFarland, he was among the most important members of the chorus of secondary leaders who defined and advanced aesthetic conservation during its inchoate period in American environmental history. He died in Harrisburg, in the ninetieth year of a busy life.

[Secondary treatment of McFarland's life and thought may be found in Holway R. Jones, *John Muir and the Sierra Club: The Battle for Yosemite* (1965); Roderick Nash, *Wilderness and the American Mind* (1973); Walter Adams, "70 Years a Crusader For a More Beautiful America," *Better Homes and Gardens,* May 1947, pp. 41, 227–231; Alfred Runte, "The Scenic Preservation Movement in the United States, 1864–1916" (master's thesis, Illinois State Univ., 1971). Samuel P. Hays, *Conservation and the Gospel of Efficiency: The Progressive Conservation Movement, 1890–1920* (1959), analyzes the schism between the utilitarian and the aesthetic conservation movements. A succinct statement of McFarland's conservation philosophy is "Shall We Have Ugly Conservation?" *Outlook,* March 1909, pp. 594–598. He also wrote, with others, *The Preservation of Niagara Falls* (1906), *The Rose in America* (1923), and *Memoirs of a Rose Man* (1949). Many of his other publications, numbering a dozen books and numerous articles, emphasize technical aspects of horticulture, particularly rose growing. His papers, collected at the Div. of Archives and Manuscripts, Pa. Hist. Museum, Harrisburg, are rich in correspondence with the leaders of the American conservation movement on the important issues of their time. An obituary and photograph appeared in *American City,* Nov. 1949, p. 151.]

RODERICK NASH

McGRAW, JAMES HERBERT (Dec. 17, 1860–Feb. 21, 1948), book and magazine publisher, was born in Panama, Chautauqua County, N.Y., the youngest of five sons and eighth of nine children. His parents, Patrick and Catharine McGraw, had emigrated from Ireland about 1849 and after a few years in Canada had moved to western New York, where they operated a dairy farm. An ambitious and determined lad with a strong didactic streak, James was first drawn to teaching, and in 1884-1885, following his graduation from the state normal school in Fredonia, he served as a school principal in Corfu, N.Y. In 1885 he joined the American Railway Publishing Company of New York, in which one of his former teachers had an interest, and was sent first to Boston and then to Philadelphia as subscription salesman for one of its periodicals, the *American Journal of Railway Appliances.* Soon thereafter, on the strength of a $1,000 investment borrowed from a wealthy Chautauqua County farmer of his acquaintance, he became a stockholder and vice-president of the nearly bankrupt company and moved to New York City.

The strong will that was one of his dominant characteristics emerged early, and in 1888 he broke with his partners and bought them out. The clash turned in part on their conflicting estimates of the importance of the electric streetcars that were then supplanting horsecars. McGraw had at once perceived that the future lay with electricity. Now sole owner and publisher of the *American Journal of Railway Appliances* (and soon of the *Street Railway Journal,* also acquired from his former partners in 1889), he built on this slight foundation a remarkable and complex industrial and technical publishing empire. At this crucial stage of his career he received important financial support from Curtis E. Whittlesey of Corfu, N.Y., whose daughter Mildred he had married on June 8, 1887. McGraw's mode of operation was to acquire several small and competing technical publications, to consolidate them into a single periodical, and to give them the benefit of his steadily expanding editorial, production, and marketing facilities. In 1899, for example, he purchased *Electrical World,* combined it with two other electrical magazines he had bought over the preceding three years, and made it a leader in the field. In 1899 he also incorporated the McGraw Publishing Company, with himself as president and his father-in-law as treasurer.

From periodicals, McGraw moved into the field of technical and scientific books. In 1909 he merged his book list with that of a rival publisher, John Alexander Hill; in 1917, a year after Hill's death, the two firms were combined to form the McGraw-Hill Publishing Company, with the McGraw-Hill Book Company as a subsidiary. In the decade that followed, as president of both the parent firm and its book-publishing subsidiary, McGraw won unchallenged supremacy in the field of technical publishing with such periodicals as *Power, American Machinist, Coal Age, Engineering News-Record,* and the *Contractor.* The book list, comprising 250 titles in 1909, was systematically expanded under the joint direction of Martin M. Foss and Edward Caldwell. Typical of the profitable and highly respected titles bearing the McGraw-Hill imprint was *A Manual of Engineering Drawing for Students and Draftsmen* (1911), by Prof. Thomas E. French of Ohio State, which in various revisions was to sell nearly two million copies in the succeeding half-century. The textbook department, aimed initially at the college market and then at the high school market as well, also made rapid strides.

The McGraws had four sons, all of whom eventually joined the family business: Harold Whittlesey (born 1889), James Herbert (1893), Curtis Whittlesey (1895), and Donald Curtis (1897). They also had a daughter, Catharine, born in 1899. During most of McGraw's career the family lived in Madison, N.J. In 1904, while chairman of the Morris County Republican Committee (1900-1908), McGraw was a delegate to the party's national convention. In 1925 McGraw, in poor health, retired as president of the McGraw-Hill Book Company and in 1928 as president of the McGraw-Hill Publishing Company. He remained as chairman of the board, but extended vacations in the West took up more and more of his time. He was thus not intimately involved in such important McGraw-Hill developments as the founding of the highly successful magazine *Business Week* (1929), the firm's tentative entry into the trade book field under the Whittlesey House imprint (1930), or the construction (1930-1931) of the distinctive McGraw-Hill Building on 42nd Street, a Manhattan landmark. He retired completely in 1935 and spent his final years in San Francisco, where he died of bronchopneumonia in 1948 at the age of eighty-seven. He was buried in Evergreen Cemetery, Morristown, N.J.

McGraw's remarkably successful career was, from one perspective, simply a by-product of the technological revolution of the late nineteenth and early twentieth centuries in America, for he supplied the channels of communication by which the leaders of that revolution kept in touch, announced new developments, advertised their wares, and transmitted their know-how to a new generation of technocrats. But McGraw also brought a unique combination of personal qualities to his profession. He insisted that his periodicals and books conform to the highest editorial and visual standards, and that each be written or edited by a recognized specialist. He was willing to pay well for such talent, and he possessed a keen sense of when to make a major commitment to a new area. Although delegating authority did not come easily to him, he recognized its practical necessity and gave wide autonomy to subordinates, provided they could withstand the rigorous and unpredictable grillings to which he periodically subjected them. A

somewhat intimidating figure in his mature years, with stern visage and precise white goatee, he had a habit, when irritated, "of moving his jaw up and down so that his whiskers came out at you—almost like a porcupine" (Burlingame, p. 235). Above all, like so many of the industrialists whose exploits his magazines chronicled, James H. McGraw was passionately, almost obsessively, devoted to the success of the firm that bore his name.

[Roger Burlingame, *Endless Frontiers: The Story of McGraw-Hill* (1959); *Who's Who in America*, 1910-1911 and later issues; *N.Y. Times*, Jan. 25, 1916 (obituary of John A. Hill), and Feb. 22, 1948 (McGraw); information on particular points from Isabelle Loughlin, Archivist, McGraw-Hill, Inc. An extensive set of interviews pertaining to the history of McGraw-Hill are in the Oral Hist. Collection, Columbia Univ.]

                                          PAUL BOYER

MACINTOSH, DOUGLAS CLYDE (Feb. 18, 1877-July 6, 1948), Baptist theologian and philosopher of religion, was born in the Scottish settlement of Breadalbane, Ontario, Canada, one of at least five children and the second of three sons of Peter Macintosh, apparently a farmer, and Elizabeth Charlotte (Everett) Macintosh. His maternal grandfather had emigrated in about 1832 from England to Canada, where he farmed, practiced medicine, and defended with skill a version of Wesleyan Methodism. Peter Macintosh was the grandson of a Scottish Congregationalist turned Baptist, and was deacon of the local Baptist church. Douglas was reared in a home where a theologically conservative evangelical piety was practiced. Profoundly influenced by his mother, he experienced in his tenth year the expected religious awakening and, after a conversion experience at the age of fourteen, joined the church. Vital personal religion remained the center of his interest throughout life.

After graduating from a boarding high school, he taught in country schools while preparing to enter the ministry. Without any formal preparation, he took charge in 1897 of a mission church in western Ontario and later engaged in evangelical work. In 1899 he entered McMaster University, Toronto, determined to subject his orthodox beliefs to rigorous intellectual scrutiny. Natural science, including Darwin's *Origin of Species,* and philosophy were favorite subjects. In an autobiographical statement he later described his pilgrimage from traditionalism through empiricism to absolute idealism, as he sought to confirm the validity and reasonableness of Christianity. Macintosh took the B.A. degree in

1903, after which he stayed on for a year to teach logic, psychology, and the history of philosophy. Deciding that philosophy rather than pastoral labor was his métier, he began graduate work at the University of Chicago. Over the next three years he studied philosophy and logic under Addison Webster Moore and George Herbert Mead, psychology under James Rowland Angell, and theology and philosophy of religion under George Burman Foster; Foster's influence was especially important.

The young theologian now found himself a partial convert to Albrecht Ritschl's point of view, espoused by Foster, and to Chicago-style pragmatism, but later upheld the necessity for a strong metaphysical grounding to theology, much in the vein of Ernst Troeltsch, whose similar views he later encountered. Before returning to Canada to complete his doctoral dissertation ("The Reaction against Metaphysics in Theology"), Macintosh was ordained in the Hyde Park Baptist Church in Chicago, despite his frank disavowal of several major points of orthodox doctrine. From 1907 to 1909 he served as professor of biblical and systematic theology at Brandon College, Brandon, Manitoba, where he helped organize a theology department. Upon receiving the Ph.D. from Chicago in 1909, he was appointed assistant professor of systematic theology at Yale, where he remained until his death, becoming successively Dwight Professor of Theology (1916-1932) and professor of theology and the philosophy of religion (1933-1942).

On Feb. 13, 1921, Macintosh married Emily Powell, who died the following year. Her death and the loss of other close relations only confirmed his belief in "the goodness and sufficiency of God," and this "profound inner certitude" played an important part in the enunciation of his doctrine of moral optimism. In 1925 he married Hope Griswold Conklin, a teacher and head of a school for girls. There were no children by either marriage.

Religious experience was the foundation on which Macintosh built a radically modernist "empirical theology," designed to resist the threat of philosophical skepticism and historical uncertainty. His method, as set forth in *Theology as an Empirical Science* (1919), was to derive laws and theories about God from religious experience in the same way that the natural and social sciences develop hypotheses in the light of sensory and social experience. His theology had three levels. The first, an organized body of religious data, consisted of those experiences or "revelations" of the divine,

viewed as the Real Object or Power which is the source of moral transformation in human life. The second was a body of laws, based on the data of religious experience and derived in the same way as scientific hypotheses, laws which specify the ways in which God can be expected to respond faithfully to persons who make the "right religious adjustment." The third level was a body of more inclusive theories that move from what God does toward what he is. These theories have a high degree of pragmatic probability insofar as they are necessary to account for the facts of the religious life.

Closely related to Macintosh's effort to develop an empirical theology was his concern with the theory of knowledge and Christian apologetics. He devoted two large volumes to epistemology, *The Problem of Knowledge* (1915) and *The Problem of Religious Knowledge* (1940). A defender of epistemological realism, he defined his own view as critical monism. He regarded metaphysics as the synthesis of all the empirical sciences, theology included. A completed theoretical scheme requires that the results of empirical theology be incorporated into a system of metaphysics, while metaphysics depends on empirical theology for some of its most valuable data.

At one point or another four factors entered the total theoretical scheme that Macintosh proposed. First, a scientific ingredient is found in the effort to establish theology on a base of empirically verified knowledge. Second, a pragmatic element enters at the point of postulating in Kantian fashion the reality of freedom, God, and immortality, as permissible presuppositions of theology based on what is practically necessary to justify the moral intuitions of the self. Third, an appeal to history is made by referring to the life and work of Jesus as exemplifying a normative revelation of God. Fourth, a metaphysical factor appears in the effort to synthesize theology with the results of the other sciences. Macintosh's approach to apologetics embodies these same elements. In *The Reasonableness of Christianity* (1925) and *The Pilgrimage of Faith in the World of Modern Thought* (1931), he developed a "representational pragmatism," according to which postulates that seem to be reasonable and practical are taken as representations in ideas of what is actually real. His basic assumption is what he calls moral optimism—the belief that the world can be made better by human effort directed by good will, and that the cosmos supports such striving.

A further dimension of his apologetic concern is found in his attempt to establish a basis for Christian belief that is not vulnerable to the shifting and uncertain results of historical investigation. Macintosh felt keenly the problems being raised by Troeltsch in Germany and by Foster in the United States regarding the finality of Christianity and the relation of the Christian faith to history. The "history of religions" school and the uncertainties of contemporary New Testament scholarship were raising serious questions about the attempt of much liberal theology to go behind theology and faith to establish a basis of Christian theology in the life of the historical Jesus. In order to escape this relativism and skepticism, Macintosh sought to show how it is possible to discover and defend the essence of Christianity entirely apart from an appeal to particular facts of history. While the historical Jesus may be *psychologically* necessary for some people, his actual historicity is not *logically* required to establish or validate the essentials of Christian belief.

Macintosh was a grave and sometimes blunt person. He was passionately devoted to the truth as he saw it, and his debates with his students who disagreed with his position were often emotionally strained. Other facets of Macintosh's career included overseas service in the chaplaincy of the Canadian Expeditionary Force in 1916 and in the American Y.M.C.A. in 1918. Although he initially endorsed the war aims in terms of Christian sacrifice, he soon reconsidered his position and became a critic. His application for American citizenship became world news when, after lengthy litigation, it was denied by the United States Supreme Court in 1931 on the basis of his refusal to agree in advance to bear arms in the event of war. A stroke in his later years prevented him from continuing the legal battle, and he remained a Canadian citizen. He died at his home in Hamden, Conn., of a coronary thrombosis. Cremation followed at Ferncliff Crematory, Ardsley, N.Y.

Macintosh was one of the most important of the modernistic liberal theologians in American Protestantism during the first four decades of the twentieth century. With others in this school, he sought a way of preserving the abiding essence of Christian belief by using contemporary scientific and philosophical methods and by restructuring Christian doctrine to bring it into harmony with modern knowledge. A critic cannot help but notice that, however radical his method, his concerted efforts to

make theology into an empirical science yielded a "common garden variety" of convictions characteristic of the liberal Protestantism of his time.

[Macintosh provides a personal and theological autobiography in "Toward a New Untraditional Orthodoxy," in Vergilius Ferm, ed., *Contemporary Am. Theology*, I (1932). He devotes a long chapter to the religious background of his family in *Personal Religion* (1942). A brief account of his life, work, and personality is in Roland H. Bainton, *Yale and the Ministry* (1957). See also *Twentieth Century Encyc. of Religious Knowledge*, II, 691 (1955). A comprehensive list of Macintosh's writings can be found in *The Nature of Religious Experience* (1937), a volume of essays written in his honor by a group of his former students; the volume also includes a photograph of him. On Macintosh's thought, see Kenneth Cauthen, *The Impact of Am. Religious Liberalism* (1962), chap. ix. Death record from Conn. State Dept. of Health.]

KENNETH CAUTHEN

McINTYRE, ALFRED ROBERT (Aug. 22, 1886–Nov. 28, 1948), book publisher, was born in the Boston suburb of Hyde Park, Mass., the only child of James William and Harriette Frances (Bradt) McIntyre. His father, a native of Boston, was a salesman for the publishing house of Little, Brown and Company. (He became a member of the firm in 1897 and the effective head from 1908 until his death in 1913.) Alfred McIntyre attended Boston Latin School and Harvard and, upon graduation in 1907, went to work for Little, Brown, which had undergone a period of dramatic growth in the late nineteenth century. By 1911, he was a partner, by 1913 vice-president and general manager, and in 1926 president. Over the next twenty-two years he solidified the firm's already secure position as one of the country's leading trade houses. Under his leadership Little, Brown offered such notable books as Erich Maria Remarque's *All Quiet on the Western Front* (1929), John P. Marquand's *The Late George Apley* (1937), the light verse of Ogden Nash, Walter Lippmann's *An Inquiry into the Principles of the Good Society* (1937), and (in association with the Atlantic Monthly Press) Samuel Eliot Morison's Pulitzer-Prize-winning biography of Columbus, *Admiral of the Ocean Sea* (1942). McIntyre also saw to it that such Little, Brown staples as the *Fannie Farmer Cookbook* and *Bartlett's Familiar Quotations* were periodically revised and promoted among new generations of readers. A responsive editor who enjoyed personal friendships with a number of his authors, he was noted for his sustained faith in writers whose books he liked, even if the public did not at first agree. In several instances—notably with the British novelists Evelyn Waugh and C. S. Forester—this practice eventually paid handsome returns.

The business side of publishing attracted McIntyre as much as the literary. It was at his initiative that Little, Brown in 1925 entered an arrangement with the Atlantic Monthly Company whereby works which had originally appeared in the *Atlantic Monthly* or were otherwise generated by its editors would be published by Little, Brown. Through this profitable arrangement, the company's list came to include such works as James Hilton's *Good-bye, Mr. Chips* (1934) and Walter D. Edmonds' *Drums along the Mohawk* (1936). During the depression and the vagaries of the World War II period, McIntyre drastically reduced the number of new titles issued—a policy of prudent retrenchment he elevated to a rather lofty plane with the motto "Fewer and Better Books." His strength as a businessman was his ability to make decisions quickly and to stand by them. Ferris Greenslet (head of Little, Brown's Boston rival, Houghton Mifflin) said of him: "The best thing about McIntyre is you always know where to find him. He's a yes or no man, quick" (*Publishers' Weekly,* Apr. 22, 1933). In a trade where a genteel facade often masked brutal rivalries, McIntyre was genuinely and widely respected. He served as vice-president of the National Association of Book Publishers in 1921-1922 and again in 1925-1928.

Boston book publishing has traditionally had a special social cachet, and Alfred McIntyre amply fulfilled this dimension of his position. He lived on Louisburg Square, within walking distance of Little, Brown's Beacon Street offices, and was a member of the Somerset, Union, and St. Botolph clubs. He was a noted host, and the formal banquet that marked Little, Brown's centennial in 1937, personally planned by McIntyre, was an event of social as well as commercial note. The social side was always something of an effort, however, for, unlike his hearty and gregarious father, he was painfully shy, as well as "high-strung and nervous of temperament" (*One Hundred and Twenty-Five Years of Publishing,* p. 28).

McIntyre was politically a conservative. In appearance he was slender, erect, and wiry, somewhat resembling an urbane Calvin Coolidge. He married on Apr. 11, 1923, comparatively late in life, Helen Palmer Horner; they had two children: Henry Pierre and Ann Elizabeth. He died in 1948 of a subarachnoid hemorrhage following a period of nervous and physical exhaustion apparently brought on by overwork, and was buried at York Village, Maine. "Alfred McIntyre was so good that we should not have worn him out at sixty-two," wrote his friend Edward Weeks, editor of the *Atlantic.*

[*One Hundred and Twenty-Five Years of Publishing, 1837–1962* (1962), a Little, Brown house history; Wallis E. Howe, Jr., "Notes on Alfred McIntyre," *Publishers' Weekly,* Apr. 22, 1933; Bernard DeVoto, "Author and Publisher," *Saturday Rev. of Literature,* Mar. 27, 1937; Alfred R. McIntyre, " 'Birth Control' for Books," *Publishers' Weekly,* Dec. 26, 1931, and "The Crisis in Book Publishing," *Atlantic,* Oct. 1947; autobiographical comments in Harvard Class of 1907, *Fifteenth Anniversary Report* (1922) and *Fortieth Anniversary Report* (1947); obituaries in *Boston Globe,* Nov. 29, 1948, and *Publishers' Weekly,* Dec. 11, 1948, pp. 2370–2371; Edward Weeks, "A Boston Publisher in Action," *Saturday Rev. of Literature,* Dec. 25, 1948; Charles A. Madison, *Book Publishing in America* (1966), pp. 438–442; death record from Mass. Registrar of Vital Statistics. On his father, see obituaries in *Boston Herald* and *Boston Advertiser,* Jan. 11, 1913.]

PAUL BOYER

McKAY, CLAUDE (Sept. 15, 1889-May 22, 1948), poet and novelist, was important in the "Negro (or Harlem) Renaissance," a term used to identify a period of intense cultural activity and productivity among black Americans during the 1920's. He was born in Sunny Ville, Jamaica, British West Indies, the youngest of eleven children of Ann Elizabeth (Edwards) McKay and Thomas Francis McKay, a peasant sufficiently prosperous to own his land. In his early years McKay was exposed to diverse educational and religious influences. His father was an Anglican deacon who later withdrew from the church. McKay was educated by an older brother who was an agnostic, despite his positions as a schoolteacher and a lay preacher for the Anglican church. At sixteen, he was further molded by Walter Jekyll, an agnostic English folklorist, who guided his reading and encouraged him to continue writing poetry in Jamaican dialect. Receiving a Government Trade Scholarship at seventeen, McKay apprenticed himself to a cabinetmaker but quit after two years and joined the island constabulary.

In 1912, after the publication of two volumes of poetry in Jamaican dialect, *Constab Ballads* (1912) and *Songs of Jamaica* (1912), McKay migrated to the United States to study agriculture and to find a wider audience for his writing. After a few months at Tuskegee Institute, McKay transferred to Kansas State University but left after two years and, like many other black Americans of the time, moved to Harlem in New York City.

For the next few years, after failing as a restaurant owner, he supported himself by work as a longshoreman, a porter, a bartender, and a waiter. On July 30, 1914, he married Eulalie Imelda Edwards; they had one child, Ruth Hope. It is known that the marriage was short-lived, but no date of separation or divorce is available. Through these years, McKay continued writing poetry, published in *Seven Arts* (under the pseudonym "Eli Edwards"); *Pearson's,* edited by Frank Harris, who became McKay's mentor; and *The Liberator* (formerly *The Masses*), edited by Max Eastman.

In 1919, his expenses paid by a benefactor and armed with a letter of introduction to George Bernard Shaw, McKay traveled to England. Shaw helped him in obtaining a reader's ticket for the British Museum; he also expressed his surprise that McKay had decided on a career in poetry rather than in prizefighting. McKay became interested in the ideas of Karl Marx and took a job as writer for a Communist publication, *The Worker's Dreadnought*. He also published a volume of nondialect poetry, *Spring in New Hampshire* (1920).

After police arrested the editor of *Dreadnought,* McKay returned to the United States and took a position with *The Liberator* as associate editor (in his autobiography, McKay identifies his position as assistant editor). In 1922, he realized his dream of a volume of poems published in America. *Harlem Shadows* was the first major publication during the 1920's by a black in the United States.

He became coeditor of *The Liberator* in 1922, but conflicts with his fellow editor Michael Gold caused him to resign in June. He traveled to Russia, where he was lionized and named unofficial delegate to the Fourth Congress of the Communist International. After the congress ended, McKay remained in Russia for several months before wanderlust took him, in 1923, to Germany and then to France.

McKay remained in France for six years, supporting himself with work as a male model (which resulted in pneumonia), as research assistant to Rex Ingram, and free-lance writer. Turning to fiction, he completed an unpublished novel, "Color Scheme," in 1925 and a volume of stories accepted for publication in 1926; advised that novels brought greater rewards, he reworked one story into *Home to Harlem* (1928), a novel about the adventures of Jake, a black American who returns to the United States after deserting from the army, and Ray, a Haitian seeking an education in America. McKay's second novel, *Banjo: A Story Without a Plot* (1929), is a sequel that describes Ray's adventures in Marseilles. Both his novels received favorable reviews, and *Home to Harlem* was a financial success. While continuing his wanderings in Spain and Morocco, McKay completed *Gingertown* (1932), a collection of the early stories about Harlem and new ones about Jamaica.

Experiencing health problems, McKay returned to the United States in the early 1930's but did not end his traveling until the middle of the 1940's. His final books—all published in the United States—were *Banana Bottom* (1933), a novel about Jamaica (McKay had suffered a breakdown while working on the book in Morocco); *A Long Way from Home* (1937), his autobiography; and *Harlem: Negro Metropolis* (1940), a sociological study of the black community of New York City.

Influenced by the writer Ellen Terry, whom he met in 1938, McKay became interested in Catholicism, and in 1944 joined the Roman Catholic church. Through the final eight years of life, he suffered increasingly from hypertension and dropsy. He died of heart failure in Chicago. After a funeral in Chicago sponsored by the Catholic Youth Organization, for which McKay had worked, his body was transported to Harlem for a second funeral. McKay was buried in Queens, New York.

In 1929, McKay received the National Association for the Advancement of Colored People's Harmon Award for distinguished achievement (*Harlem Shadows* and *Home to Harlem*) by a Negro author. McKay's fiction, however, frequently provoked controversy: some Afro-American critics accused him of imitating Carl van Vechten by exploiting base elements of black life to please white readers. More nearly unanimous praise is accorded to his poetry. In poems on racial themes, McKay —frequently using the sonnet form—bitterly denounced oppression by whites, revealed ambivalent admiration for the Western world, and compassionately delineated black Americans. Other characteristic themes are love; nostalgia for Jamaica; and, later, devotion to Catholicism. His best known poem is "If We Must Die," which was written in 1919 to encourage black Americans to defy racial massacres. According to McKay, the poem was read during World War II by a BBC announcer. Other sources state that Winston Churchill read it to the British Parliament or read it to the United States Congress.

[A full biography of McKay is *The Passion of Claude McKay* by Wayne Cooper (1973), and an appraisal of his work is *Claude McKay: The Black Poet at War* by Addison Gayle, Jr. (1972). A useful sampling of much of his best work is *Selected Poems of*

Claude McKay (1953), with a biographical introduction by Max Eastman.

A valuable source of biographical information is Claude McKay, "Boyhood in Jamaica," *Phylon*, 14 (1953): 134–145; and a full critical study of McKay is in Stephen A. Bronz, *Roots of Negro Racial Consciousness* (1964). Another long study of McKay's life and work is Sister Mary J. Conroy, "Claude McKay: Negro Poet and Novelist" (unpublished diss., Notre Dame Univ., 1968).

Useful information about McKay as a fiction writer exists in Robert Bone, *The Negro Novel in America* (rev. ed., 1965), and Hugh M. Gloster, *Negro Voices in American Fiction* (1948). Shorter valuable commentaries about McKay's fiction are Richard K. Barksdale, "Symbolism and Irony in McKay's *Home to Harlem*," *College Language Assn. Jour.*, 15 (1972): 338–344; W. E. B. DuBois, "*Home to Harlem* and *Quicksand*," *The Crisis*, 35 (1928): 207; Marcus Garvey, "*Home to Harlem*: An Insult to the Race," *Negro World*, Sept. 29, 1928, p. 1; Jacqueline Kaye, "Claude McKay's 'Banjo,'" *Présence Africaine*, 73 (1970): 165–169; Richard Priebe, "The Search for Community in the Novels of Claude McKay," *Studies in Black Literature*, 3 (1972): 22–30; Kenneth Ramchand, *The West Indian Novel and Its Background* (1970); and Saunders Redding, *To Make a Poet Black* (1939).

Useful analyses of his poetry and thought can be seen in Sterling A. Brown, *Negro Poetry and Drama* (1937); Philip Butcher, "Claude McKay—'If We Must Die,'" *Opportunity* 26 (1948): 127; Wayne Cooper, "Claude McKay and the New Negro of the 1920's," *Phylon*, 25 (1964): 297–306; Wilfred Cartey, "Four Shadows of Harlem," *Negro Dig.*, 18 (1969): 22–25, 83–92; Eugenia Collier, "The Four-Way Dilemma of Claude McKay," *College Language Assn. Jour.*, 15 (1972): 345–353; Sister Mary J. Conroy, "The Vagabond Motif in the Writings of Claude McKay," *Negro American Literature Forum*, 5 (1971): 15–23; Mark Helbling, "Claude McKay: Art and Politics," *Negro American Literature Forum*, 8 (1972): 49–51; Nathan I. Huggins, *Harlem Renaissance* (1971); Blyden Jackson, "The Essential McKay," *Phylon*, 14 (1953), 216–217; George Kent, "The Soulful Way of Claude McKay," *Black World*, 20 (1970): 37–51; Alain Locke, "Introduction," *Four Negro Poets* (1927); Gerald Moore, "Poetry in the Harlem Renaissance," *Black American Writers*, C. W. E. Bigsby, ed. (1969), pp. 67–76; Michael B. Stoff, "Claude McKay and the Cult of Primitivism," *The Harlem Renaissance Remembered*, Arna Bontemps, ed. (1972) 121–146; and Jean Wagner, *Black Poets of the United States* (1973).]

DARWIN T. TURNER

McKEAN, JAMES WILLIAM (Mar. 10, 1860-Feb. 9, 1949), Presbyterian medical missionary to Thailand and pioneer in the treatment of leprosy, was born at Scotch Grove, Jones County, Iowa. The son of Hugh and Elizabeth McKean, he was educated at Lenox College in Iowa and took the M.D. degree at Bellevue Hospital Medical School in New York City, graduating in 1882. He was practicing medicine in Omaha, Neb., when he applied to the Board of Foreign Missions of the Presbyterian Church in the U.S.A. in 1889, and was appointed to the Siam Mission. McKean was first married to Nellie Banton; they had one child, Ethel, born at Anamosa, Iowa, in 1883. Nellie McKean died Dec. 5, 1886. McKean and Laura B. Willson of Clinton County, Iowa, were married on August 29, 1889, and sailed for their new post in September. The couple had two children: Kate P., born Oct. 30, 1890, and J. Hugh, born Nov. 18, 1893, who was also to serve in the Presbyterian Thailand Mission from 1922 to 1942 as treasurer of McCormick Hospital in Chiengmai and superintendent of the leprosarium founded by his father.

The McKeans were assigned to Chiengmai, the capital of the recently suppressed Lao or Northern Thai kingdom. It was at that time so remote and inaccessible that the journey took six weeks from Bangkok. The roads of the north were so bad generally that the doctor had to use five horses to carry his medicines and equipment when traveling on extension service. In Chiengmai he drove a bay trap pony with amazing skill and speed, until he eventually acquired a Model-T Ford. McKean first established a dispensary, and then McCormick Hospital, named for Mrs. Cyrus McCormick of Chicago, from whom he obtained a grant for the central block.

The whole north region of Thailand was then afflicted with smallpox and malaria. Vaccination had been introduced into Thailand more than half a century earlier by Dr. Dan Beach Bradley in Bangkok, but it had never reached the remote northland. Vaccine could not be imported, so McKean manufactured it. He trained and supervised more than 200 vaccinators, who were also evangelists, and sent them through the district. Smallpox was almost entirely eliminated throughout the north. When many years later the government established the Pasteur Institute, manufactured vaccine, and made vaccination compulsory, McKean stopped this activity. Badly adulterated quinine sold by profiteering traders through the area was making little impression on the endemic malaria. McKean solved this problem by importing quinine and other drugs, opening a drug manufacturing plant, and standardizing the dosages. He created a drug sales department at the hospital and sold on both the wholesale and retail level, supplying medicines for the populace as far north as China. McKean drastically reduced malaria in the north countryside.

Leprosy, however, was a scourge for which no cure was known, and the only preventive was the isolation of lepers in lonely misery and squalor. The lepers were truly the wretched ones of the land. James McKean had great love and compassion for them, and his concern was recognized as being as important as his medical service to them. His sense of humor was as great as his love, and it carried him through the grueling service he was now to perform for the lepers through the whole remainder of his missionary career. He created a leprosarium which was to become one of the most famous in the whole world. He obtained from the local governor in 1908 an island in the Menam River about five miles from Chiengmai, and the king confirmed the gift. The island was cleared and cultivated. A central clinic and, later, a hospital were erected. A model village with cottages for two persons was developed. A chapel was built, also a recreation building and a powerhouse. Eventually there were more than 150 buildings. There was a separate village for uncontaminated children of the lepers. Every successive advance in the treatment of leprosy was introduced as it became known. Chaulmoogra oil treatment was initiated by Edwin C. Cort in the 1915-1918 period, when McKean was in the United States. Plastic surgery eventually became a practice also in the leprosarium. Important also was the extension service through the countryside, which brought patients into residence in the institution and cared for others in their homes. The inmates usually became Christians soon after entering this community. The church was vigorous and active, and its benevolent offerings were applied to causes throughout Thailand and abroad. The first women elders in Presbyterian churches anywhere are said to have been elected and ordained in this church.

Dr. McKean persistently sought to interest the Thai government in the welfare of lepers, and through his influence the Siamese Red Cross began the treatment of lepers in the south in 1923 and in Bangkok in 1924. The government gave financial assistance to the Chiengmai leprosarium and its extension service. The king made a present of a paved road from the island to the city. The American Mission to Lepers was a major supporter. The king decorated Dr. McKean with several national orders in recognition of his service. An able assistant, Dr. Chanta Indhravudh, was associated with McKean for forty-two years. When the founder retired in March 1931 there were 500 inmates. After the missionary died, the institution was renamed the McKean Leprosy Hospital.

The physician was always an active churchman and was an elder of the Chiengmai church almost from his arrival. Upon his retirement, the Presbyterian Church of Upland, Calif., made him a life elder. Through his evangelistic work he personally established the churches at Ban

Den and Subnatitham. He died at Long Beach, Calif., after a lingering illness.

[Kenneth E. Wells, *History of Protestant Work in Thailand, 1828-1958*; Edward M. Dodd, "Dr. James W. McKean—Doctor and Friend," in *Answering Distant Calls*, ed. Mabel H. Erdman; James W. McKean, *In the Land of the White Elephant* (pamphlet); memorial minutes adopted by the Presbyterian Board of Foreign Missions, Feb. 15, 1949.]

R. PIERCE BEAVER

McLAUGHLIN, ANDREW CUNNING-HAM (Feb. 14, 1861-Sept. 24, 1947), historian, was born in Beardstown, Ill., the youngest of the five sons of David McLaughlin and Isabella (Campbell) McLaughlin, both from Scotland. When Andrew was a baby, the family moved to Muskegon, Mich., where his father kept a store and doubled as superintendent of schools. In 1878 Andrew entered the University of Michigan at Ann Arbor, the first boy from Muskegon to go to college. Graduating in 1882, McLaughlin returned to Muskegon as principal of the local high school; the following year he went back to Ann Arbor to take a law degree at what was then the largest and the best law school west of Harvard. There he came under the influence of Judge Thomas Cooley, author of the already classic *Constitutional Limitations*; when in 1887 Cooley went to Washington to be chairman of the new Interstate Commerce Commission, McLaughlin, who had been teaching Latin, shifted to the history department, taking over his mentor's classes in constitutional history. On June 16, 1890, he married Lois Thompson Angell, daughter of President James B. Angell of the University of Michigan. Their children were James Angell, Rowland Hazard, David Blair, Constance Winsor, Esther Lois, and Isabella Campbell.

Although from the beginning McLaughlin taught constitutional history, his early books explored the history of the Old Northwest: a biography of Lewis Cass for the American Statesman series (1899) and volumes on government and on education in Michigan. In 1893-1894 McLaughlin spent a year studying in Germany, but he was never as deeply influenced by German historical or political scholarship as were some of his future colleagues at the University of Chicago. In 1901 he became managing editor of the *American Historical Review*, a post that he held for five years, and in 1903 he moved to Washington to head up the new Bureau of Historical Research of the Carnegie Institution. It was during these busy years that he wrote for the American

Nation series *The Confederation and the Constitution* (1905), a revisionist view that sharply challenged John Fiske's interpretation of the *Critical Period of American History* and that anticipated many of the theories of the origin and nature of American federalism McLaughlin was later to make peculiarly his own. *The Confederation and the Constitution* won immediate academic acclaim, and the following year McLaughlin was confronted with a choice of professorships at his own university, Yale, Johns Hopkins, Stanford, and Chicago. The offer by President William Rainey Harper of Chicago proved irresistible; for the next thirty years, as chairman of the history department, he was instrumental in making it one of the most distinguished in the nation. Long a member of the Council of the American Historical Association, McLaughlin became president of that organization in 1914. In 1929 he retired formally from his professorship, but he continued for another decade to hold seminars and guide doctoral candidates in his chosen field. With the possible exception of Edward S. Corwin no other scholar presided over so many doctorates in the field of constitutional history or sent out so many disciples into the schools and universities of the land as did McLaughlin.

Notwithstanding a heavy burden of teaching and administration, McLaughlin kept up his research and writing in his chosen field, contributing regularly to learned journals—and occasionally to the less learned. Several of his books, including *Courts, Constitution, and Parties* (1912) and *America and Britain* (1919), were made up of previously published articles. *Foundations of American Constitutionalism* (1932), the Anson Phelps lectures at New York University, remains the most original and provocative of his books. Three years later came his magisterial *Constitutional History of the United States*, which was awarded a Pulitzer Prize. It summed up with intellectual vigor and literary grace a lifetime of research and reflection, and remained for decades the most penetrating and philosophical, although far from the most comprehensive, treatment of that subject.

As director of the Bureau of Historical Research, McLaughlin launched a systematic search for original materials in the libraries and archives of Europe as well as of the United States and inaugurated a series of editorial projects, the most important of which was an edition (carried to completion by Edmund Burnett) of the letters of members of the Continental Congress. In 1914 he associated himself with Albert Bushnell Hart in editing a three-volume *Cyclopaedia of American Government* (1914), which maintained a consistently high level of scholarly and critical acumen.

From his earliest writings to the end of his long career, McLaughlin had an instinct for the jugular vein of history and constitutional law. He was not seduced by the temptations of antiquarianism or the appeals of filiopietism, nor by the importunities of either economic or psychological interpretations. Like the British constitutionalist Frederic Maitland, whom in many respects he resembled, he presented an orderly sequence of facts in history for philosophical rather than narrative purposes; he was concerned with the consequential and the significant and with ideas and events as they found expression in practices and transformed themselves into institutions. He seized on central themes and worried them until they yielded conclusions or even laws: the theme of nation-making, of the federal character of the old British Empire, of the sacred character of the compact in Puritan political theory. And he saw in the effort to reconcile liberty and order the grand and controlling theme of politics.

McLaughlin, a child of the Victorian era and of Scottish Presbyterianism, was confident that history could teach lessons, even moral lessons, and that, rightly studied, it could trace cause and effect. In philosophy an unregenerate liberal, he saw in American history a vindication of faith in reason, of the triumph of law, and of the principle of progress. In an age that was disenchanted with the work of the Founding Fathers, he celebrated their enduring contributions; in an age when it was popular to interpret the Constitution as a conservative reaction to the American Revolution, he emphasized the unity and coherence of the whole Revolutionary era; in an age that embraced, somewhat uncritically, the Turnerian emphasis on environment, he persisted in emphasizing rather the role of inheritance, tradition, and continuity.

The loss of his son Rowland, killed in action in France in 1918, the failure of Wilsonian idealism, and the repudation of the League of Nations severely tried McLaughlin's faith and optimism, yet he did not give way to cynicism or despair. His last major work, the *Constitutional History,* revealed the same Jeffersonian faith in the reasonableness and virtue of the common man—especially the American common man—that illuminates his earliest writings. In his character, his scholarly interests, his intellectual and moral commitments, the pattern of his life was harmonious.

He died at his home in Chicago of pneumonia at the age of eighty-six and was buried in the family plot at Forest Hills Cemetery, Ann Arbor, Mich.

[On McLaughlin, see *Nat. Cyc. Am. Biog.*, XXXVI, 137–138; *Who Was Who in Am.*, II (1950); obituaries in *Am. Hist. Rev.*, Jan. 1948, pp. 432–434; Am. Antiquarian Soc., *Proceedings*, Oct. 15, 1947, p. 258; *N.Y. Times*, Sept. 25, 1947; and unpublished address by William T. Hutchinson, Univ. of Chicago, Oct. 24, 1947. Information was supplied by Isabella McLaughlin Stephens. McLaughlin's place in American historiography is briefly treated in John Higham et al., *History* (1965).]

HENRY STEELE COMMAGER

MacNAIR, HARLEY FARNSWORTH (July 22, 1891-June 22, 1947), Far East historian, was born in Greenfield, Erie County, Pa., the elder of two children and only son of Dougald Evander MacNair and Nettie Adella (Farnsworth) MacNair. He was of Scottish descent, his father's family having settled in North Carolina in 1786. MacNair's family evidently moved during his boyhood to California, for he graduated in 1909 from the Redlands, Calif., high school. He then entered the newly founded University of Redlands, from which he received a Ph.B. degree in 1912. Himself an Episcopalian, MacNair went to Shanghai, China, immediately after graduation and became an instructor of history at St. John's University (Episcopal). He remained there until 1927, becoming professor of history and government in 1916 and head of the department in 1919. During this time he managed to complete his graduate education on home leaves spent at Columbia (M.A. 1916) and at the University of California in Berkeley (Ph.D. 1922). His doctoral dissertation was published at Shanghai in 1924 as *Chinese Abroad: Their Position and Protection.*

For his Chinese students, MacNair published in 1919 a collection of Western short stories and three years later an introduction to Western history. For his more advanced classes he compiled and edited a vast and still useful collection of primary source readings on the international relations of the Far East entitled *Modern Chinese History* (published in English in 1923 and in Chinese translation in 1927). This was followed by two books of essays, some of which had previously appeared in periodicals, *China's New Nationalism and Other Essays* (1925) and *China's International Relations and Other Essays* (1926). All of these works were published in Shanghai. For a num-

ber of years MacNair worked on a one-volume summary, revision, and amplification of Hosea B. Morse's classic *The International Relations of the Chinese Empire* (3 vols., 1910-1918). This was published in Shanghai in 1928 under the title *Far Eastern International Relations.* Nationalism and antiforeignism, however, were then at a fever pitch in China, and under pressure from highly placed nationalists, MacNair's Chinese publishers withdrew the book from the market because of "errors." Three years later it was published in the United States.

The impact of the nationalist movement on scholarship led MacNair regretfully to leave China. After teaching for a year at the University of Washington in Seattle (1927-1928), he moved to the University of Chicago, where he spent the remainder of his life as professor of Far Eastern history and institutions. At Chicago, MacNair pioneered graduate instruction in the history of Far Eastern international relations. He frequently returned to China on research leaves and in 1932 aided in refugee work in north China and Manchuria. He also became involved in American groups interested in the Far East (the Friends of China, Japan Society of New York, and Institute of Pacific Relations), in writing articles on Asian subjects for periodicals and encyclopedias, and in participating regularly between 1938 and 1946 in radio forums on sensitive international topics.

A great change occurred in MacNair's personal life with his marriage to Florence (Wheelock) Ayscough, a talented translator of Chinese poetry and a sophisticated lover of Chinese art. They had originally met in China in 1916. On Sept. 7, 1935, shortly after the death of Mrs. Ayscough's first husband, she and MacNair were married in Guernsey, Channel Islands. They returned to Chicago to a beautiful home, whimsically called the House of the Wu-t'ung Trees, which became a veritable Midwestern gathering place for persons concerned with China: the diplomat Hu Shih, the authors Pearl Buck and Alice Tisdale Hobart, and many others.

In 1937, as Sino-Japanese tensions mounted, MacNair published *The Real Conflict Between China and Japan,* a study based on his preliminary research for a more extensive analysis of the Far East in the twentieth century. The larger work was interrupted by World War II, during which MacNair served for a time as a consultant to the Office of Strategic Services, but in 1950 a posthumous volume, *Modern Far*

Eastern International Relations, was published in collaboration with Donald F. Lach.

MacNair's books, important as they were, do not constitute his major claim to recognition. Because of their contemporaneity, most have become dated; they also suffer from the fact that he was not a student of the Chinese language. His greatest talent, and the one that delighted him most, lay in the training of students. Many of his undergraduates from St. John's became leading lights in Chinese government and education. The graduate students he trained at Chicago came to occupy important places in American education and government. MacNair's sharp mind, puckish humor, quiet dignity, and fearless honesty endeared him to students, colleagues, and friends on both sides of the Pacific. His career came to an early end in 1947 when he died at his home in Chicago of a heart attack.

[MacNair's substantial library was donated to the Univ. of Redlands. Materials relevant to his Chicago years may be found in the Dept. of Special Collect., Univ. of Chicago Lib. The most comprehensive study is the memoir by Maurice T. Price in *Far Eastern Quart.,* Nov. 1948, which contains a full bibliography of MacNair's writings. See also obituary in *Am. Hist. Rev.,* Oct. 1947; *Nat. Cyc. Am. Biog.,* XLII, 177–178. On his ancestry, see James B. MacNair, *McNair, Mc-Near, and McNeir Genealogies* (1923). A photograph of MacNair hangs in the History Office, Social Science Building, Univ. of Chicago.]

DONALD F. LACH

MacNEIL, HERMON ATKINS (Feb. 27, 1866–Oct. 4, 1947), sculptor, was born near Chelsea, Mass., the son of John Clinton Mac-Neil, a nurseryman, and Mary Lash (Pratt) MacNeil. His father, a native of New Hampshire, was descended from Abraham MacNeil, who came to the United States from Ireland in 1750. After attending public schools, Mac-Neil received his first formal instruction in art at the Massachusetts Normal Art School in Boston, from which he graduated in 1886. He then became an instructor in modeling for three years at Cornell University before going to Paris in 1888 to continue his studies at the Académie Julian with Henri Chapu and at the École des Beaux-Arts with Jean Falguière. In 1892 MacNeil returned to the United States and settled in Chicago to assist Philip Martiny in the numerous architectural sculptures he was making for the World's Columbian Exposition of 1893 and was awarded a designer's medal for his work. After the exposition he remained in Chicago, where he taught at the Art Institute for three years. During this period he became interested in North American Indians and made several trips

to the West to study them and their way of life. For many years, Indians remained his primary subject.

In 1896 MacNeil was the first recipient (along with A. Phimister Proctor) of the Roman Rinehart Scholarship, established by the estate of William H. Rinehart to allow American sculptors to study at the American Academy in Rome. MacNeil spent the next four years there and produced several of his finest Indian pieces, including his *Sun Vow,* a moving study of an Indian brave seated next to an Indian youth who, according to tribal ritual, has just shot an arrow toward the sun. One of his best-known works, *Sun Vow* received a silver medal at the Paris Salon of 1900. The following year MacNeil returned to the United States and set up a studio at College Point, Queens, N.Y., where he continued to live and work throughout his life. He was awarded a gold medal that same year for his sculptures at the Pan-American Exposition in Buffalo; unfortunately, his vigorously composed and modeled group *The Despotic Age,* made, as were most exposition sculptures, of plaster and straw, disintegrated soon after the fair ended. Other honors followed, including a silver medal at the Charleston (S.C.) Exposition of 1902, a commemorative medal at the Louisiana Purchase Exposition in St. Louis in 1904, and the gold medal at the Panama-Pacific Exposition in San Francisco in 1915.

These honors plus several important commissions established MacNeil as one of the leading American sculptors in the years preceding World War I. In 1905 he produced a bronze group of two Indians called *The Coming of the White Man* for the city of Portland, Ore. Although this was similar in subject to the famous equestrian series by his contemporary Cyrus Dallin, MacNeil's defiant warriors stand, one with arms folded, looking intently into the distance—presumably at the white men who moved into their land in increasing numbers. The figures are richly modeled in the manner MacNeil learned during his years of study in Paris.

MacNeil also gained fame as a portraitist, two of his most important commissions being the several figures for the McKinley Memorial in Columbus, Ohio (*c.* 1907), and the bronze full-length figure of Ezra Cornell (1915-1917) for the Cornell University campus in Ithaca. The McKinley Memorial consists of a bronze full-length sculpture of the president standing in the center of a classical exedra with bronze groups of figures personifying "Industry" and "Peace and Prosperity" at the end of either arm of the memorial. His most outstanding portraits, those of Roger Williams, James Monroe, Francis Parkman, and Rufus Choate are in the Hall of Fame at New York University. MacNeil also made soldiers' and sailors' monuments for Washington Park in Albany, N.Y., and Whitinsville, Mass. In 1916 his design was selected over fifty submitted for a twenty-five-cent piece portraying the figure of Liberty in a pose of welcome, with a flying eagle on the reverse side. The Liberty quarter was minted until 1932, when it was replaced by the Washington quarter. In 1917 MacNeil was awarded the Gold Medal of Honor by the Architectural League of New York. He spent the years 1919 and 1920 at the American Academy in Rome, where he was a visiting professor. He held other teaching positions during his career at the National Academy of Design, Pratt Institute, and the Art Students League in New York.

By the time World War I began, MacNeil reached the peak of his career, although he continued to receive large commissions and remained productive for nearly twenty more years. Among his major sculptures dating from the 1920's and 1930's are the portrait statues of Judge Ellsworth and Colonel David Humphrey for Hartford, Conn.; a war monument for Flushing, N.Y.; the Marquette Memorial, Chicago; a Pilgrim Fathers Memorial for Waterbury, Conn.; the bronze figure of George Rogers Clark for the Clark Memorial in Vincennes, Ind.; a bronze equestrian *Pony Express Rider* for St. Joseph, Mo.; and the stone figure of George Washington as a military leader for the Washington Square Arch in New York City. MacNeil also created a frieze for the Missouri state capitol in Jefferson City, the theme of which was the anthropological development of man in the United States, and he made the sculpture group for the east pediment of the United States Supreme Court Building in Washington, D.C.

In style, MacNeil's work from the beginning bore the imprint of the French manner that developed around the École des Beaux-Arts—a rich and vigorous modeling with many small facets creating the effect of light and shadow actively rippling across the surfaces of the bronze. Added to this was a vital naturalism and proclivity toward colorful details, particularly in the Indian pieces and allegorical subjects. MacNeil's first fame came with the Indian subjects, but after 1920 he was increasingly absorbed with war memorials and

portrait statues, for which his lively naturalism seemed especially appropriate to his clients. He resisted the innovative experiments of modern art, such as cubism and constructivism, and like so many of his generation attempted to perpetuate the conservative academic tradition. His last major work—the heroic, bronze Fort Sumter Memorial (1932) for Charleston, S.C. —was an attempt to merge traditional with progressive styles, and the result was unsatisfactory.

MacNeil was a member of many professional societies. He was elected to the National Academy of Design in 1906 and served as president of the National Sculpture Society (1910-1912; 1922-1924). On Dec. 25, 1895, he married Carol Louise Brooks, also a sculptor; they had three children: Claude Lash, Alden Brooks, and Joie Katherine. His first wife died in 1944, and on Feb. 2, 1946, he married Cecelia (Weick) Muench, a widow. The following year MacNeil died in College Point at the age of eighty-one.

["Some Recent Work by H. A. MacNeil," *Brush and Pencil*, Nov. 1899; Lorado Taft, *Hist. of Am. Sculpture* (1903); Jean S. Holden, "The Sculptors MacNeil," *World's Work*, Oct. 1907; Joseph McSpadden, *Famous Sculptors of America* (1927); Clement Morro, "Hermon A. MacNeil," *La Revue Moderne*, July 15, 1932; *Sculpture by Hermon Atkins MacNeil, Brookgreen Gardens* (1937); *Who Was Who in America*, II (1950); Adolph Block, "Hermon A. MacNeil," *Nat. Sculpture Rev.*, 1963-1964; Albert T. Gardner, *Am. Sculpture* (1965); Beatrice Proske, *Brookgreen Gardens, Sculpture* (1968); Wayne Craven, *Sculpture in America* (1968); obituaries in *N.Y. Times*, Oct. 4, 1947 and the *Numismatist*, Nov. 1947.]

WAYNE CRAVEN

McNICHOLAS, JOHN TIMOTHY (Dec. 15, 1877-Apr. 22, 1950), Roman Catholic archbishop of Cincinnati, Ohio, was born in a thatched cottage in Treenkeel, near Kiltimagh, County Mayo, Ireland, the second youngest of seven sons and one daughter born to Patrick J. McNicholas and Mary (Mullaney) McNicholas, landowners. In 1881, Timothy—John was his chosen name in religious life—was brought to the United States, where his parents settled in Chester, Pa. There he attended the Immaculate Heart of Mary grade school, followed by high-school training at St. Joseph's College, conducted by the Jesuits in Philadelphia. While a student at St. Joseph's, young McNicholas met the Very Reverend C. H. McKenna, O.P., an illustrious Dominican who stirred the youth's interest in the Dominican Order and in the work he was later to perpetuate as organizer and first national director of the Holy Name Society. At seventeen, Timothy entered the Dominican Order of Preachers at St. Rose's priory, Springfield, Ky. His philosophical and theological studies were made in St. Joseph's house of studies, Somerset, Ohio, where he was ordained on Oct. 10, 1901. Following ordination, he studied at the Minerva University in Rome, where he earned his lectorate in sacred theology in 1904.

Upon returning to the United States, McNicholas was named Master of Novices at Somerset, the school of philosophy and theology for the Dominican province of St. Joseph, which embraced all of the United States east of the Rocky Mountains. When the Dominican house of studies, Immaculate Conception College, was opened at the Catholic University of America, Washington, D.C., McNicholas was transferred there as regent of studies and professor of philosophy, theology, and canon law, a post he held until 1909. Named national director of the Holy Name Society, an antiprofanity organization with membership exceeding a million and a half, McNicholas established headquarters in New York City and founded and edited the *Holy Name Journal*. In 1913, he was appointed pastor of St. Catherine's parish, New York; in 1917, he was elected first prior of the convent attached to the parish. Soon after this, McNicholas was summoned to Rome to assist the Dominican master general, the Most Reverend Louis Theissling. While serving in this position as representative of the English-speaking provinces of the order, he was named master of theology, a provincial of Lithuania, an honorary office, and a professor of theology at the Angelicum University in Rome. McNicholas was the moving spirit in establishing the practice, now customary, of offering a personal Christmas gift to the pope from the dioceses of America. In a pamphlet entitled "The Holy Father at Christmas Time," he sought to advance the idea of a strictly personal gift from the Roman Catholics of America to the Holy Father that would not interfere with the Peter's Pence offering for the needs of the Holy See itself.

On July 18, 1918, Pope Benedict XV appointed McNicholas bishop of the diocese of Duluth, Minn., where he ruled for seven years, during which, in 1923, he was appointed an assistant at the Pontifical Throne by Pope Pius XI. In May 1925, he was nominated to the diocese of Indianapolis, Ind., but, on July 8, he was elevated to the archdiocese of Cincinnati and installed there as the see's archbishop on August 12.

Archbishop McNicholas furthered the tradition of renowned educators, which he inherited with the see of Cincinnati. School after school he built until the archdiocese was a model of Roman Catholic education on the grade-school, high-school, and college levels. His dynamic intellect, coupled with his zeal for social justice, won for him an important place in the field of education. His voice was raised repeatedly reaffirming the rights of God, family, church, and state in molding the mind and character of the child; warning of dangerous irreligious trends in education; upbraiding parents for compromising their rights and duties and the state for failing to support the parents impartially, irrespective of religious convictions and color of skin. McNicholas served as episcopal chairman of the department of education of the National Catholic Welfare Conference (NCWC) from 1930 to 1935, and again from 1942 to 1945. He also was a five-term president general of the National Catholic Educational Association from 1946 to 1950. His annual NCEA addresses are considered classic statements in the field of education.

Other prominent national offices McNicholas held included his ten-year chairmanship (1933-1943) of the episcopal committee on motion pictures, in which he played the major role in founding the National Legion of Decency, charged with censoring motion pictures; five terms (1945-1950) as chairman of the administrative board of the NCWC; membership on the episcopal committee for the Confraternity of Christian Doctrine (1934-1945 and 1947-1950), during which time he had a hand in the revision of the Challoner-Rheims version of the New Testament and directed the writing and editing of the revised edition of the Baltimore catechism. The annual statements issued in the name of the Catholic hierarchy of America for many years owed much of their form and forcefulness to his gifted mind. In 1928, McNicholas founded the Athenaeum of Ohio as a corporation to control the institutions of higher learning in the archdiocese, and, in 1935, he established the Institutum Divi Thomae as a postgraduate school of theology and science. A teachers' college for training priests, sisters, and laity was also created. The archbishop's scholarly interest in the history of the church, especially in the American Middle West, plus an oratorical finesse characterized by forcefulness of delivery and exactness of expression made him a much-sought-after speaker for historical occasions in the church.

The archbishop was unalterably opposed to

political totalitarianism in any form—be it in Germany, in Spain, in Russia, in Mexico, or in the United States. With all the force he could muster, he lashed out to excoriate communism. He also constantly championed the rights of labor and of minority groups, especially of the blacks, for whom he established a special apostolate in the diocese. In his appraisal of war, he was a realist who analyzed clearly the distinction between the legitimate demands of patriotism and the evils consequent on war. For twenty-five years he guided the Roman Catholic church of Cincinnati in every area of moral involvement.

McNicholas died of a heart attack at his residence and was buried in the Gate of Heaven Cemetery, Montgomery, Cincinnati, Ohio. At his death, he was acclaimed by pope, president, prelates, and people as one of America's foremost churchmen.

[The Official Arch., Archdiocese of Cincinnati, St. Mary's Seminary, Norwood, Cincinnati, Ohio, are a primary source. Biographical data may be found in the Reverend Maurice E. Reardon, *Mosaic of a Bishop* (1957), an autobiographical, biographical appreciation. *The Catholic Telegraph,* official newspaper of the Archdiocese of Cincinnati, carries much information about Archbishop McNicholas. Obituaries appeared in many of the leading newspapers.]

M. E. REARDON

McREYNOLDS, JAMES CLARK (Feb. 3, 1862–Aug. 24, 1946), justice of the United States Supreme Court, was born in Elkton, Ky., a farming region a few miles north of the Tennessee border. The second child and first son of John Oliver McReynolds and Ellen (Reeves) McReynolds, he was descended from Scots-Irish Presbyterians who had migrated to Pennsylvania in the mid-eighteenth century and moved to Virginia before settling in Kentucky, where in time they joined the Disciples of Christ. His mother was a devout, kindly, but dominating woman. His father, a graduate of Jefferson Medical College in Philadelphia, was a physician. A narrow autocrat, "Dr. John" was called "The Pope" because of his belief in his own infallibility.

After attending a private school operated by a cousin, young McReynolds matriculated at Green River Academy in Elkton. In 1879 he entered Vanderbilt, which granted him the B.S. degree with first honors in his class in 1882. Two years later he graduated from the law school of the University of Virginia; he was influenced there by John B. Minor, who emphasized fixed principles of law and the need to restrain government from infringing on property rights. Steeped in the ideas of the

Old South, McReynolds did not leave the region permanently until he was in his forties.

Following a brief period as secretary to Sen. Howell E. Jackson of Tennessee, a conservative Democrat, McReynolds went to Nashville, where he developed an extensive law practice and a profitable real estate business. A low-tariff, sound-money, limited-government Cleveland Democrat, he ran as a "Gold Democrat" nominee for Congress in 1896, but met defeat in his only bid for elective office. From 1900 to 1903 he taught at Vanderbilt law school.

In 1903 President Theodore Roosevelt appointed McReynolds assistant to the attorney general of the United States, an office in which he served diligently until 1907, when he joined the New York law firm headed by Paul D. Cravath. He returned to Washington in 1910 to take part in the antitrust prosecution of the American Tobacco Company, but left in anger the following year when the attorney general approved a dissolution decree that McReynolds thought too favorable to the old "Tobacco Trust." When an attorney for the trust accused him of favoring confiscation, McReynolds replied: "Confiscation! What if it is? Since when has property illegally and criminally acquired come to have any rights?" (Hendrick, p. 30). Once again, he moved to New York City, this time to open his own law office.

In 1913, at the urging of Col. Edward M. House, who had been impressed by McReynolds' reputation as an antitrust reformer, President Woodrow Wilson appointed the Kentuckian attorney general of the United States. McReynolds proved to be a zealous foe of the trusts. After winning a dissolution decree that ended the Union Pacific Railroad's control of the Southern Pacific, he balked the American Telephone and Telegraph Company's plan to monopolize all telephone and telegraph systems in the United States. The difficult struggle over the New York, New Haven and Hartford Railroad Company, which resulted in a consent decree, brought McReynolds censure as well as praise. His campaigns against the trusts led some to regard him as a radical; in fact, he was a tenacious conservative who regarded such prosecutions as a logical consequence of his faith in a competitive society.

In August 1914 Wilson elevated McReynolds to the Supreme Court. The Senate approved the appointment over the strenuous objections of George W. Norris and others. By then McReynolds had become, as he was to remain, a storm center of controversy, as much for his temperament as for his ideas. As attorney general, he had antagonized senators who accused him of maintaining a corps of spies who investigated federal judges to influence their decisions, a charge he vigorously denied. He also got on poorly with other members of Wilson's cabinet; a feud with Secretary of the Treasury William G. McAdoo reached such a point that communications between their departments had to be carried on through the White House. On the bench, McReynolds won a reputation for churlishness toward counsel and toward his fellow justices. Chief Justice William Howard Taft described him as "one who seems to delight in making others uncomfortable. He has a continual grouch." He was especially rude to his Jewish colleagues. On one occasion, when he refused to accompany the court on a trip to Philadelphia, he explained to Taft: "I am not always to be found when there is a Hebrew abroad."

While most of Washington thought him a crotchety, acerbic misanthrope, a small circle of friends found him gallant, courteous, sentimental, and fond of children. A man of few pleasures, he enjoyed duck hunting, golf, walking, and European travel. Slender, erect, slightly over six feet tall, he had piercing steel-blue eyes, spoke with a high-pitched voice, and carried himself like a Roman senator. McReynolds never married. Only after his death did it become known that he had resolved to remain true to the memory of Miss Will Ella Pearson, who in 1885 had died suddenly at the age of twenty-four.

Soon after joining the Supreme Court, McReynolds aligned himself with the conservative wing. He viewed the Constitution as an immutable body of principles that should be interpreted chiefly as limitations on the exercise of governmental power. A believer in *stare decisis,* he apparently never wrote an opinion that reversed a judgment. McReynolds, who rarely took a position that could be interpreted as favorable to the cause of labor, formed part of the minority of four in *Wilson* v. *New* (243 U.S. 332 [1917]), which held the Adamson Eight-Hour Act unconstitutional, and he joined the majority of five in the landmark case of *Adkins* v. *Children's Hospital* (261 U.S. 525 [1923]), which invalidated a District of Columbia minimum-wage law. Despite his determination to curb government, he was willing to sanction a limited range of regulation, especially when it aimed at promoting unrestrained competition. In the field of civil liberties, McReynolds

wrote the opinions in *Meyer* v. *Nebraska* (262 U.S. 390 [1923]), which held void a Nebraska law forbidding instruction of elementary school pupils in modern foreign languages, and *Pierce* v. *Society of Sisters* (268 U.S. 510 [1925]), which overturned an Oregon statute requiring pupils to attend public schools. More typical of McReynolds' views was his action in 1932 when he was one of two justices who opposed granting new trials to the Scottsboro defendants. Rarely assigned opinions in important cases, McReynolds in his long career on the bench averaged only nineteen opinions a year, mostly on minor questions in such fields as maritime law. These opinions were generally brief and pungent.

To a Cleveland Democrat like McReynolds, the New Deal was anathema. In every crucial New Deal case, he voted against the administration, usually as a member of the conservative bloc of justices, which also included Willis Van Devanter, George Sutherland, and Pierce Butler. Speaking for this minority of four, McReynolds early in 1935 delivered a blistering oral dissent in the gold-clause cases: "The Constitution as many of us have understood it, the Constitution that has meant so much, is gone. . . . Horrible dishonesty! . . . Shame and humiliation are upon us." When Justice Owen Roberts joined the conservatives that spring, the anti-New Deal bloc secured a majority that persisted in most cases through the end of 1936. In *Ashwander* v. *Tennessee Valley Authority* (297 U.S. 288 [1936]), however, McReynolds was the lone dissenter when the Court sustained a Tennessee Valley Authority contract. McReynolds characterized President Franklin D. Roosevelt as "a fool," "not quite sane," and "bad through and through." Roosevelt, for his part, found McReynolds obnoxious. When in 1937 the president submitted his scheme to "pack" the Supreme Court, he took particular pleasure in the fact that it was based on a similar proposal McReynolds had advanced when he was attorney general.

Although Roosevelt's court plan met defeat, the president won a substantial victory when the Supreme Court in the spring of 1937 began to uphold New Deal legislation and when the first of a series of resignations enabled him to begin reconstituting its membership. As the last survivor on the Court of the conservative "Four Horsemen," McReynolds protested in vain against the "Constitutional Revolution" which saw the Court sanction an enormous range of governmental authority over the economy at the same time that it safeguarded an ever-widening scope of civil liberties. From 1937 through 1941 he dissented 119 times; in his twenty-six years on the bench, he recorded 310 dissents, a record number. Some believed that McReynolds remained on the Court only to deny Roosevelt the opportunity to name a successor. After 1937 he refused to attend the president's annual state dinner for the Supreme Court, and when the justices paid their traditional courtesy call on the president before the opening of the October term in 1939, McReynolds did not appear.

Two days after Roosevelt was inaugurated for a third term, McReynolds wrote out his resignation in two terse sentences. He left the bench on February 1, two days before his seventy-eighth birthday. He spent his final years quietly, attracting national attention only when during World War II he "adopted" thirty-three British refugee children. McReynolds died at the age of eighty-four at Walter Reed Hospital in Washington, where he had been under treatment for "an acute exacerbation of a chronic gastro-intestinal condition"; on the day before his death, he developed indications of bronchopneumonia and a failing heart. He was buried in the family plot at Glenwood Cemetery in Elkton, Ky. After his death, it was revealed that beneficiaries of the old bachelor's bequests included a "lovely" lady, the "mother of my lively triplet girl friends," the Kentucky Female Orphans School, and Centre College, "to promote instruction of girls in domestic affairs." Born in the second year of the Civil War, he died in the first year of the cold war, a man who long ago had outlived his times.

[The basic source is the collection of McReynolds Papers at the Alderman Lib., Univ. of Va. The only full-length study is Stephen Tyree Early, Jr., "James Clark McReynolds and the Judicial Process" (Ph.D. diss., Univ of Va., 1954). Arthur S. Link, *Wilson: The New Freedom* (1956), is helpful for the attorney general period, and Alpheus T. Mason, *Harlan Fiske Stone* (1956), for the Supreme Court era. Other relevant sources are *Proc. of the Bar and Officers of the Supreme Court of the U.S., Nov. 12, 1947* (1947); *N.Y. Times*, Mar. 9, 1913, Jan. 23, 1941, Aug. 26, 28, 30, 1946; Burton J. Hendrick in *World's Work*, Nov. 1913; and Ernest Sutherland Bates, "McReynolds, Roberts, and Hughes," *New Republic*, July 1, 1936.]

WILLIAM E. LEUCHTENBURG

MAGNES, JUDAH LEON (July 5, 1877–Oct. 27, 1948), rabbi, communal leader, chancellor, and first president of the Hebrew University of Jerusalem, was born in San Francisco, Calif., the eldest of five children of David Magnes and Sophie (Abrahamson) Magnes. In 1863, at the age of fifteen, his father left

Przedborz in south-central Poland, a center of Hasidic Judaism, to join his older brother in San Francisco. In later years Magnes came to revere the religious orthodoxy and Yiddish-speaking culture of his paternal grandparents. His maternal grandparents had emigrated to Oakland, Calif. from Filehne, in East Prussia, in 1872. From his grandmother and mother he acquired an appreciation for German language and culture. Magnes was thus exposed from his earliest days to the cultural heritages of the two main groups that constituted American Jewry.

While he was still a child, the family moved across the bay to Oakland, where his father established a moderately successful dry-goods business. Family life was warm and close-knit. The language of the home was English, and the children were well integrated into the social life of the community. Magnes attended the public schools and excelled in his studies. He was active on both the high school debating and baseball teams. He received a more thorough religious education than was common, and under the influence of Rabbi Jacob Voorsanger he enrolled in the Hebrew Union College in Cincinnati, Ohio. Concurrently, Magnes pursued his secular education at the University of Cincinnati; he received the B.A. degree from the university in 1898 and two years later was ordained a Reform rabbi. From 1900 to 1902 he studied Semitics and philosophy at the universities of Berlin and Heidelberg, receiving the Ph.D. degree from Heidelberg in 1902. At the same time he attended classes at the Lehranstalt in Berlin, an institute for advanced Jewish studies. During these years Magnes established lasting ties with a circle of young Jewish intellectuals from Germany, Eastern Europe, and the United States. They were committed, like himself, to the advancement of Jewish culture and Zionism. In his later life, Magnes came to emphasize Zionism as a cultural force for group survival and was less concerned with the political aspirations of the movement.

On returning to the United States, Magnes served for a year as librarian of the Hebrew Union College. In 1904 he was called to the pulpit of Temple Israel in Brooklyn, N.Y. Two years later New York's Temple Emanu-El, one of the preeminent Reform congregations, invited him to become its associate rabbi, a remarkable distinction for a young rabbi of twenty-nine. Ministering to a congregation that drew its membership from the highly acculturated and affluent German-Jewish community did not deter Magnes from participating in the Yiddish cultural life of the Jewish quarter. In 1905, in the wake of the pogroms in Russia, Magnes organized mass protest demonstrations in New York and headed a national campaign to raise funds to arm clandestine defense units of Russian Jews. These activities won him the admiration of both immigrant and native American Jews. The same year he became secretary of the Federation of American Zionists and directed its affairs until 1908. In 1906 when the notables of the established community created the American Jewish Committee to represent Jewish interests in the United States, Magnes was coopted to the executive board. Thus his communal leadership uniquely spanned the divergencies and antagonisms that characterized the heterogeneous Jewish community of that time.

On Oct. 19, 1908, Magnes married Beatrice Lowenstein, of a German-Jewish family which had settled in Memphis, Tenn., prior to the Civil War. She was the sister-in-law of Louis Marshall, an outstanding lawyer and president of the American Jewish Committee. Three sons were born to the Magneses; David, Jonathan, and Benedict.

In 1908 Magnes directed the negotiations that led to the establishment of the Kehillah of New York City, a comprehensive communal structure for coordinating and improving Jewish philanthropic, educational, and religious services. For the next thirteen years, he played a central role in educational reform, labor arbitration, anti-crime activity, and social welfare on behalf of the Kehillah. Magnes was repeatedly elected chairman and so dominated the organization. Some critics accused him of using his position to serve the interests of the "uptown" Jews in their desire to "control" the immigrant Jews of "downtown." The Kehillah ceased to function in 1922, although some of its institutions survived. Magnes had hoped the Kehillah would serve as a model for community life in America. He approved of the perpetuation of ethnic group life as a permanent feature of a pluralistic American society, a view he expressed most succinctly in a 1909 sermon, "A Republic of Nationalities."

In the course of his chairmanship of the Kehillah, Magnes left the active rabbinate. In 1910, as a consequence of his demands that the congregation introduce a more traditional ritual, his contract with Emanu-El was not renewed. A brief tenure with Congregation B'nai Jeshurun (1911-1912) was terminated for the same reason.

With the outbreak of World War I, Magnes became active in overseas relief work. He participated in the formation of the American-Jewish Joint Distribution Committee, the leading Jewish agency for overseas relief. In 1917 Magnes became a leading spokesman for the radical pacifist position. He was the main speaker at the two largest pacifist meetings of the war, which were held in New York on May 30, 1917, and in Chicago on Sept. 2, 1917. These meetings led to the formation of the People's Council of America. Following the Russian revolution, he criticized President Wilson for his hostility toward the Soviet Union. Magnes' pacifism and his concern for civil rights led him to support the American Civil Liberties Union. In these activities he collaborated closely with Scott Nearing, Emily G. Balch, Norman Thomas, Roger Baldwin, and Oswald Garrison Villard. Magnes was criticized for his support of controversial causes by some members of the Jewish community who were concerned about possible imputations of disloyalty.

In 1922 Magnes and his family left for Palestine, which he had already visited in 1907 and 1912, intending to remain for a year or two. However, with the opening of the Hebrew University in Jerusalem in 1925, he was elected chancellor, a position he held until 1935, when he was elected president, a largely honorary office. Under his administration the university developed into a major academic center. Magnes stressed the need to establish scientific research institutes to meet the needs of the country, as well as departments of Judaic, Semitic, and Islamic studies. Following the rise of Hitler, he made strenuous efforts to bring to the university scholars forced to leave Germany. Among the largest financial supporters of the university were such philanthropists as Felix M. Warburg, whose confidence he had won in the course of his public life in America. Fundraising endeavors brought Magnes to the United States periodically, and in Jerusalem he received a steady stream of distinguished American visitors.

The 1929 anti-Jewish riots in Palestine induced Magnes to reenter political life in an effort to improve relations with the Arabs. The continued growth of the Jewish settlement, he was convinced, required an accommodation with the Arabs. He spoke and wrote widely in support of a binational state in Palestine that would guarantee the essential interests of both sides. The Zionist organization, he declared, should alleviate Arab fears of Jewish domination by agreeing to a limit on immigration. The vast majority of the Jewish community in Palestine opposed his policy as capitulation; nor did important Arab leaders respond to his overtures. In 1942 a small group of intellectuals, mainly professors at the Hebrew University, joined Magnes in creating the Ihud (Unity) Association for Jewish-Arab Rapprochement. Four years later Magnes appeared before the Anglo-American Committee of Inquiry, whose investigations marked the beginning of United States involvement in the search for a solution to the Palestine question. His testimony, given despite a decision of the duly constituted Jewish bodies that their representatives alone present the Jewish case, influenced the committee's recommendation rejecting the partition of Palestine into separate states. In April 1948, encouraged by an apparent change in American policy from support of partition to support of a temporary United Nations trusteeship for Palestine, he came to America to back trusteeship. With the establishment of the state of Israel the following month, Magnes drafted a plea calling for a confederation of sovereign Jewish and Arab states in Palestine. In the midst of efforts to rally support for his position he died in New York City of a heart attack. He was buried in Shearith Israel Cemetery, Cypress Hills, Brooklyn, and in 1955 his body was reinterred in Jerusalem.

Essentially a preacher who left the Reform pulpit to become a reformer, Magnes placed principle, as he perceived it, above institutional interest or political gain, often disregarding the immediate consequences of his action for the community. The titles of two collections of his essays—*Like All the Nations?* (1930) and *In the Perplexity of the Times* (1946)—allude to the inner tensions of the religionist turned political man, striving to translate moral compulsions into public deeds. In his work he was guided by religious and social precepts which drew upon Jewish sources and the American experience. These influences are especially evident in his *War-Time Addresses* (1923), which chronicles his opposition to the war, his civil-libertarian position, and his critique of official Zionist policy.

The inherent conflict between the man of the spirit and the man of action found expression, on the one hand, in the bold leadership he gave to such undertakings as the Kehillah and the Hebrew University and, on the other hand, in the alienation of supporters to the detriment of those institutions. Few failed to recognize

the moral fervor and generous sentiments that motivated his dissenting and frequently unpopular views. It was, however, precisely his integrity and candor that became the source of his greatest influence.

[The main collection of Judah L. Magnes' papers is located in the Central Arch. for the Hist. of the Jewish People, Jerusalem, Israel. Other collections are located in the American Jewish Arch., Cincinnati, Ohio, and the Judah L. Magnes Memorial Museum, Berkeley, Calif. Other books by Magnes are *Addresses by the Chancellor of the Hebrew Univ.* (1936) and *Arab-Jewish Unity: Testimony Before the Anglo-American Committee* (1947), with Martin Buber. Norman Bentwich, *For Zion's Sake: A Biog. of Judah L. Magnes* (1954), is comprehensive and includes photographs of Magnes. The following titles deal with particular phases of his career: Arthur A. Goren, *New York Jews and the Quest for Community: the Kehillah Experiment, 1908–1922* (1970); Zosa Szajkowski, "The Pacifism of Judah Magnes," *Conservative Judaism*, 22 (1968): 36–55; Susan L. Hattis, *The Bi-National Idea in Palestine during Mandatory Times* (1970); Herbert Parzen, "The Magnes-Weizmann-Einstein Controversy," *Jewish Social Studies* 32 (1970): 187–213. For brief accounts of Magnes' life see *N.Y. Times*, Oct. 28, 1948, p. 29; *Encyclopedia Judaica*, (1972), pp. 716–718 (1972); Louis Lipsky, *A Gallery of Zionist Profiles* (1956), Nelson Glueck, *The Lion of Judah: Judah L. Magnes* (pamphlet, 1958).]

ARTHUR A. GOREN

MAIER, WALTER ARTHUR (Oct. 4, 1893-Jan. 11, 1950), Lutheran minister and radio preacher, was born in Boston, Mass., the second son and fourth of five children of Emil William Maier (pronounced "Mire") and Anna Katharine (Schad) Maier. His parents emigrated from Germany in 1880. The father was an organ and piano builder and tuner. The mother, a remarkable, energetic woman, added to the family income by running a grocery store.

Maier was baptized in the Lutheran church and was a member of the Missouri Synod, the most German and conservative of the major Lutheran bodies of the time. His elementary education in Boston public schools rather than a Lutheran parochial school, his residence in the East, and his intellectual curiosity helped produce perspectives different from those of the Midwestern German Lutheran enclave, the synod's traditional core, and his education beyond the eighth grade included unusual detours. He graduated in 1912 from the synod's Concordia Collegiate Institute in Bronxville, N.Y., but attended Boston University to earn the B.A. (1913) before going on to Concordia Theological Seminary in St. Louis, from which he graduated in 1916. He was ordained in 1917, but found the opportunity, during part-time or temporary pastoral duties, to begin graduate work in Old Testament studies and Semitics at Harvard Divinity School (1916-

1918) and Graduate School of Arts and Sciences (1918-1920), where he earned the M.A. in 1920 and began a doctoral dissertation. The pace of his subsequent activities, and difficulties at Harvard, perhaps partly over his conservatism, delayed his completion of the Ph.D. until 1929.

In 1920 Maier became executive secretary of the Walther League, the Missouri Synod's youth organization (named for the synod's founder, Carl F. W. Walther), and editor of its *Messenger*. His involvement with the league came at a time when large numbers of Lutheran young people were still close enough to the church to desire organizational identity but sufficiently alienated from the ethnic ghetto to insist on an American idiom. Maier's outlook coincided nicely. The *Messenger*'s popularity rose sharply, and league membership doubled in two years. Maier resigned his secretaryship in 1922 (though he remained editor of the *Messenger* until 1945) to become professor of Old Testament interpretation and history at Concordia Theological Seminary, a position he held until given an indefinite leave of absence in 1944.

In the 1920's and early 1930's Maier was one of a small group influential in shifting Missouri Synod missionary orientation from German immigrants to native Americans, a development basic to the synod's later remarkable growth. His interest in evangelism, when added to his rhetorical talents, all but guaranteed his participation in early Lutheran experiments in radio broadcasting. In 1930 Maier was invited to be the series speaker for the first "Lutheran Hour," a network program sponsored by the synod's Lutheran Laymen's League. Although suspended the next year because of lack of funds, the program was reestablished in 1935. with Maier as regular speaker, and fan mail receipts thereafter underwrote its continuance. By 1950 it was using two American networks and was being broadcast in fifty-five countries in thirty-six languages. "Lutheran Hour" rallies could boast attendance of as many as 25,000 people. Estimates of the program's radio audience ran as high as 20,000,000.

Maier gained an extremely large and devoted following far beyond his own denomination. His Lutheranism prevented complete congruence with revivalism, but his style and the cast of his message were not foreign to that tradition. Much of his popularity rested on his emergence after Billy Sunday, in a period characterized by upheavals and uncertainty at home and abroad. His sermons were often denunciatory; fashionable, liberal preachers, the moral laxity of society, and communism were his favorite targets. His indictments were generally severe and unqualified, and his solutions individualistic and often simplistic. He persisted even through the late 1940's in vociferous attacks on Modernism, but usually refrained from setting himself off explicitly from Fundamentalism. When once asked to preach more of the whole of Lutheran theology, he replied characteristically that he was teaching people how to die. His rhetorical style—rapid, prolix and alliterative, tense, loud and often strident— was for many an important part of his appeal. A compactly built man with regular features, ebullient and assertive in personality, Maier possessed in addition a compelling personal charisma.

On June 14, 1924, Maier married Hulda Augusta Eickhoff of Indianapolis, Ind., a former schoolteacher whom he had hired to work for the Walther League. They had two children, Walter Arthur and Paul Luther. Maier died of congestive heart failure at Lutheran Hospital in St. Louis, Mo., and was buried at that city's Concordia Cemetery. In 1951 his body was moved to an imposing memorial in Our Redeemer Cemetery, St. Louis.

[Maier's papers are in the hands of his widow. Transcriptions of most of the Lutheran Hour programs after 1938 are stored at Concordia Hist. Inst., St. Louis. Maier wrote thirty-one books (mostly collections of his sermons), many with patriotic or hortative themes like *Christ for the Nation!* (1936) and *America, Turn to Christ!* (1944). The only book-length treatment is the popular biography, *A Man Spoke, A World Listened: The Story of Walter A. Maier and the Lutheran Hour* (1963), written by Maier's son, Paul L. Maier. This book includes photographs of Maier, a list of his books, and a basic bibliography of secondary materials. See also sections of Ralph Moellering, "The Missouri Synod and Social Problems: A Theological and Sociological Analysis of the Reactions to Industrial Tensions, War, and Race Relations" (Ph.D. diss., Harvard Univ., 1964); Alan Graebner, "The Acculturation of an Immigrant Lutheran Church: The Lutheran Church—Missouri Synod, 1917-1929" (Ph.D. diss., Columbia Univ., 1965); and Milton L. Rudnick, *Fundamentalism and the Missouri Synod* (1966).]

ALAN GRAEBNER

MALONE, DUDLEY FIELD (June 3, 1882-Oct. 5, 1950), lawyer, was born in New York City, the only child of William C. Malone and Rose (McKinney) Malone. His father was from New York state; his mother came from Ireland. Reared in a middle-class Irish Catholic home, he graduated from the College of St. Francis Xavier in 1903 and later took two courses at Fordham Law School. From 1907 to 1909 he was associated with the law firm of

Battle and Marshall. On Nov. 14, 1908, he married Mary (May) P. O'Gorman, daughter of United States Sen. James A. O'Gorman. The next year Malone became assistant corporation counsel of New York City.

In politics a progressive, anti-Tammany Democrat, Malone supported the presidential candidacy of William Jennings Bryan in 1908. By the beginning of 1912 he had become a member of Woodrow Wilson's inner council. That year Malone helped organize Wilson's presidential primary campaigns and, after Wilson won the Democratic nomination, worked to secure Tammany support. He was one of the few personal friends invited to spend election day with the candidate and his family.

Early in 1913 President Wilson appointed Malone third assistant secretary of state. Malone's eye, however, was on the patronage-rich post of collector of the Port of New York, which he hoped to use to break the political power of the Tammany boss Charles F. Murphy. Wilson, seeking a compromise between the anti-Tammany counsels of Col. Edward M. House and William Gibbs McAdoo on the one hand and the wary Senator O'Gorman, an occasional ally of Tammany, on the other, gave the post at first to John Purroy Mitchel. But Mitchel's election as mayor of New York in November 1913 on an anti-Tammany fusion ticket convinced Wilson that the time was right for reorganizing the New York Democrats, and to fill Mitchel's place as collector he chose Malone.

Emphasizing the need for honest and efficient administration, and claiming Wilson's blessing, Malone used his patronage powers against Murphy and issued a broad appeal to all progressives for support. Before long, Wilson began to fear the political effects of splitting the New York party. Influenced probably by his secretary, Joseph P. Tumulty, the president in 1914 decided not to pursue the attack on Murphy and pressured the reluctant Malone to abandon his support of anti-Tammany candidates in that summer's primary election, which the Tammany forces won. Malone, in his role as port collector, was also swept up in the controversies growing out of World War I. Although accused of being duped by both British and German interests, he defended his enforcement of the port's neutrality. After the sinking of the *Lusitania* he insisted that he had not allowed the ship to arm itself, though he acknowledged interpreting regulations liberally in order to allow the loading of ammunition.

Liberal in his sympathies, Malone was an early supporter of the National Association for the Advancement of Colored People and of the woman suffrage movement, and he became increasingly critical of the Wilson administration's seeming disregard for civil liberties. In 1917 he served as an attorney for sixteen militant suffragists jailed for picketing the White House. Although Wilson subsequently pardoned the women, the arrests and imprisonment of suffragists continued; and in September 1917 Malone resigned his federal post with a widely publicized letter of protest to Wilson. When Malone divorced his first wife in Paris in August 1921 and on December 5 of that year married Doris Stevens, one of the suffragists he had defended in 1917, many persons assumed that personal considerations had strengthened his opposition to Wilson's domestic policies.

Malone's subsequent career was erratic, reflecting his impulsive nature and perhaps also the difficulty Progressives had in finding a political home after World War I. He supported the Socialist party in the New York elections of 1917, returned to the Democrats in 1918, and then helped organize the Farmer-Labor party and ran unsuccessfully as its gubernatorial candidate in 1920. In 1924 he supported the local Democratic ticket but backed Robert La Follette for president; four years later he endorsed Alfred E. Smith.

During the 1920's Malone became more a colorful personality than a political power. He advocated recognition of the Soviet Union and toured the United States on behalf of Polish and Irish freedom. Working with the American Civil Liberties Union, he represented several indicted radicals and in 1925 cooperated with Clarence Darrow in defending John T. Scopes in the Tennessee evolution trial. There the dapper, well-groomed Malone, a witty and eloquent speaker, delivered an address to the court on freedom of education which was described by co-counsel Arthur Garfield Hays as "one of the high spots of the trial," and by the journalist H. L. Mencken as "the loudest speech I ever heard" (Hays, pp. 64, 66). Characteristically, Malone combined such efforts with the lucrative practice of international divorce law, the campaign for repeal of prohibition (he was co-founder of the Association against the Prohibition Amendment), and involvement in the glamorous sports world of the 1920's, in which he arranged matches for the prizefighter Gene Tunney and financed Gertrude Ederle's successful attempt to swim the English Channel. As many of his critics charged, he enjoyed the limelight. He divorced his second wife in October 1929 and on Jan. 29, 1930, married Edna Louise Johnson, a New York actress. His only child, Dudley Field, was born the following year.

In 1932, as a delegate to the Democratic national convention, Malone worked against the nomination of his old anti-Tammany ally Franklin D. Roosevelt and eventually campaigned for the reelection of Herbert Hoover. In spite of his anti-Tammany history, he opposed the Seabury investigation into municipal corruption and then helped his friend Mayor James J. Walker prepare answers to the removal charges brought against him in the summer of 1932. Malone soon ran into financial difficulties that led to a declaration of bankruptcy in 1935, and in the late 1930's he moved to California as counsel for the Twentieth Century-Fox film corporation. His last brush with fame typified his eclectic career. Possessing a striking similarity to Winston Churchill, Malone portrayed the British prime minister in the 1943 film *Mission to Moscow*. He died of a coronary thrombosis in Culver City, Calif., and was buried in Holy Cross Cemetery, Los Angeles.

[Malone's career is generally covered in the *N.Y. Times*; see Index, and especially Dec. 11, 1913, Jan. 5, Feb. 12, June 10, 1914, July 14, 18, 1917, Dec. 8, 11, 1921, and obituary, Oct. 6, 1950. See also Arthur S. Link, *Wilson*, vols. 1–2 (1947–1956); Doris Stevens, *Jailed for Freedom*, chap. vii (1920), with photograph; Arthur Garfield Hays, *Let Freedom Ring* (1928); *Literary Digest*, Oct. 10, 1925, pp. 31–32; and, for a personal glimpse, John Reddy, "The Most Unforgettable Character I've Met," *Reader's Digest*, Aug. 1956. The maiden name of Malone's mother is given as "McKenny" in his *Who's Who* entries, "McKinney" on his marriage application (1921) and death certificate.]

EDWARD A. PURCELL, JR.
SALLEE MCNAMARA PURCELL

MANLY, BASIL MAXWELL (Mar. 14, 1886–May 11, 1950), government official and publicist, was born in Greenville, S.C., into a distinguished family of Baptist clergymen and educators. He was the namesake of three earlier Basil Manlys—a great-grandfather who had fought in the American Revolution, a grandfather (1798-1868) who was president of the University of Alabama, and an uncle (1825-1892) who was president of Georgetown College in Kentucky. His father, Rev. Charles Manly, was president of Furman University in Greenville; his mother, Mary Esther Hellen (Matthews) Manly, came from Sumter County, Ala. Basil Maxwell Manly was the youngest of three sons and of nine children. Both of his brothers attained fame, John Matthews Manly as a philologist and head of the University of Chicago English department and Charles Matthews Manly as an inventor who contributed to the development of the airplane. Young Manly attended public schools in Lexington, Mo., where his father had accepted a pastorate after leaving Furman in 1898. He entered the University of Missouri in 1902 but transferred after a year to Washington and Lee University in Lexington, Va., where he earned the B.A. degree in 1906.

Manly's first position, like most of his later career, was in the federal government. As a special agent for the Bureau of Labor Statistics in what was then called the Department of Commerce and Labor, he investigated wages and working conditions, most notably in his four-volume report on the steel industry (1912). During this period he spent a year (1909-1910) as a fellow in political science at the University of Chicago, then a seedbed of progressive reform. His involvement with reform deepened when he joined the staff of the U. S. Commission on Industrial Relations, set up by President Wilson in 1913 to study labor unrest. Working closely with Frank P. Walsh, the head of the commission, Manly drafted what was intended to be its official report; it was, however, rejected as too radical by all the nonlabor members. The Manly Report, as it came to be called, concluded that working people did not get a fair share of national wealth, that workers believed the economic system was unjust, and that denial of the right to organize was a prime cause of unrest. The report urged such reforms as an eight-hour workday, equal pay for women, federal protection of migrant workers, and nationalization of the telephone and telegraph systems.

After completing his work for the commission in 1915, Manly turned briefly to journalism, writing a syndicated column on economics for the Newspaper Enterprise Association. Soon he returned to government as a special assistant in a Federal Trade Commission investigation of the meat-packing industry; he wrote the final report, published in 1918. In December of that year he succeeded Frank Walsh as co-chairman (with former President William H. Taft) of the National War Labor Board, which had made progress toward many of the reforms urged in the Manly Report. Manly served with the N.W.L.B. until its dissolution in August 1919.

As the Wilson era in Washington ended, Manly formed a working relationship with Sen. Robert M. La Follette, leader of the Republican progressive wing. In December 1920 he became the director of the People's Legislative Service, a national counterpart of the Legislative Reference Service that La Follette had established as reform governor of Wisconsin; the service provided Congress and the public with data on legislation and public affairs. Manly worked also as a close political aide to La Follette, accompanying him on a trip to Russia in 1923 and serving as a speech writer during La Follette's presidential campaign in 1924. After La Follette's death the following year, Manly carried on the People's Legislative Service until it was closed in 1927.

For a time Manly again mixed journalism and public affairs. By 1928 he was a special correspondent for a group of Democratic-oriented newspapers—the New York *Evening World,* the *Brooklyn Eagle,* the *Atlanta Constitution,* the *St. Louis Post-Dispatch,* and the *Omaha World-Herald.* In 1931, as special counsel to a Senate committee investigating campaign expeditures, he helped draft new corrupt-practices legislation. Manly's colleague Frank Walsh, who had been named chairman of the New York State Power Authority by Gov. Franklin D. Roosevelt, called on Manly in 1932 to represent the authority in negotiations with the federal government over use of the St. Lawrence River. When Roosevelt was nominated for president, Manly helped Walsh organize the National Progressive League among former La Follette supporters.

President Roosevelt in 1933 appointed Manly to the Federal Power Commission, where, with other New Deal appointees, he helped win the FPC new powers. Even before he was named vice-chairman in December 1933, Manly was placed in charge of a national power survey; in 1934 he supervised the first national electric rate survey. He participated as well in discussions that led to passage in 1935 of the hotly debated Public Utility Act, which imposed a "death sentence" on utility holding companies and gave the FPC new authority over interstate electrical transmission. No longer vice-chairman after 1936, Manly nonetheless was named to represent the FPC in 1938 in a joint survey with the War Department of possible wartime power needs. The survey led to the appointment of a National Defense Power Committee, with Manly as vice-chairman.

With the coming of war, Manly again was elected vice-chairman of the Federal Power Commission, as well as supervisor of wartime power contracts. Looking ahead to peacetime, he undertook a prolonged effort to bring natural-gas facilities under FPC regulation, and

after his election as chairman in 1944, he sponsored an investigation of the natural gas industry. These initiatives led to a widened FPC jurisdiction in the postwar years.

Manly left government service at the close of the war, at which time he became vice-president of the Southern Natural Gas Company and president of two associated companies in Atlanta and Birmingham. He continued to live in Washington while serving in these positions until his death. On Dec. 15, 1912, he married Marie Merriman Bradley of Medford, Ore. They had one daughter, Laura Bradley. Manly remained an "unaffiliated" Baptist. He died of an internal hemorrhage at Emergency Hospital, Washington, and was buried at Fort Lincoln Mausoleum in that city.

Over a period of three decades, Manly had moved quietly in the mainstream of American progressive liberalism. His services, never spectacular nor self-aggrandizing, nonetheless had an impact on public policy, most notably in the industrial commission report and in his advocacy of stronger federal regulation by the FPC.

[The fullest biographical sketch is in the *Nat. Cyc. Am. Biog.,* XXXVIII, 72–73, with photograph; see also *Who Was Who in America,* III (1960); and *N.Y. Times,* May 12, 1950. On his ancestry, see Louise Manly, *The Manly Family* (1930). Manly's work with the industrial commission is described fully in Graham Adams, Jr., *Age of Industrial Violence: 1910–1915* (1966); and the Manly Report is included in *Final Report of the Commission on Industrial Relations* (1916). Belle Case La Follette and Fola La Follette, *Robert M. La Follette,* II (1953), describes Manly's association with the senator. For the Federal Power Commission period, see the commission's annual reports; Robert D. Baum, *The Federal Power Commission and State Utility Regulation* (1942); and Philip J. Funigiello, *Toward a National Power Policy: The New Deal and the Electric Utility Industry, 1933–1941* (1973). Scattered references can also be found in the New Deal diaries of Harold L. Ickes and David Lilienthal.]

JAMES BOYLAN

MANNES, CLARA DAMROSCH (Dec. 12, 1869–Mar. 16, 1948), pianist and music educator, was born in Breslau, Silesia, the third child and first daughter of Leopold Damrosch and Helene (von Heimburg) Damrosch. Her brothers Frank and Walter were also born in Breslau. Her one sister, Elizabeth, was born after the family's removal to the United States in 1871. The family was Lutheran, Leopold Damrosch having converted from Judaism.

The Damrosch family settled in New York. After a brief, unhappy experience in the New York public school system Clara's education was entrusted to tutors. In 1884 she began studies at Mme Mears' private French school on Madison Avenue. Clara began the study of piano at the age of six, taking lessons with Clara Gross, who was in turn studying with Leopold Damrosch and playing the repertory of violin and piano sonatas with him. Later Clara studied with Jessie Pinney, who had been a student of Daniel Gregory Mason and Clara Schumann.

In the fall of 1888 Damrosch and her sister traveled to Europe to pursue musical and artistic studies. They settled in Dresden, where Clara studied piano with Herrmann Scholtz, theory with Johannes Schreyer, and painting with a Herr Schenker, whom she later described as "a landscape painter—the chromo kind." When the sisters returned to New York in 1889, Clara began a career as teacher of piano, giving private lessons and doing some teaching at the settlement schools. Since her future husband's experiences in teaching at the Music School Settlement were to have a profound influence on the philosophy of the music school she and her husband later founded, it is interesting to note that Clara confesses in her autobiography that she disliked her early experiences as a settlement teacher.

In 1897 Damrosch returned to Europe to study with Ferruccio Busoni in Berlin. During this stay she became engaged to David Mannes, at that time a first violinist with the New York Symphony Orchestra under Walter Damrosch and soon to be its concertmaster. They were married on June 4, 1898, in Middle Granville, N.Y. They had two children, both of whom were to have important careers: Leopold Damrosch, pianist, composer, and inventor, and Marya, author.

David and Clara Mannes had agreed not to play together in public, and after their marriage Clara went back to teaching piano. In the summer of 1901, however, they began a series of summer concerts at Seal Island, Maine, then an important summer retreat for New York musicians. In the summer of 1903 they went to Belgium to enable David to study with the violinist Eugene Ysaÿe: Clara took this opportunity to study the interpretation of violin and piano works with Ysaÿe.

On their return to New York in the fall of 1903 the Manneses agreed to give a series of sonata recitals to help the Music School Settlement, at which David Mannes was then teaching. This was the beginning of a concert career that was to involve tours through most of the United States and a set of concerts in London in the summer of 1913; a proposed European tour was canceled because of the outbreak of World War I. Clara also appeared as pianist with such artists as the Kneisel Quartet, the Barrère Ensemble, and Pablo Casals.

In 1916 David and Clara Mannes founded the David Mannes School of Music in New York City. Clara Mannes remained co-director with her husband of the school until her death. The Manneses continued their joint recitals for one year after the founding of the school, but thereafter appeared together as performers only occasionally. David Mannes was to find another performing career as a conductor, but for Clara the end of the joint recitals marks a virtual end to her performing career.

The approach of the Mannes School to the teaching of music was based mainly on David Mannes' experience at the Music School Settlement. The school was first planned primarily as a school for the young; however, so many applicants of the age to enter traditional music schools appeared that the Mannes School opened itself to students of all ages. The Manneses' ideal was to provide a musical education for all who were interested rather than for the virtuoso only, "embracing under the same roof not only the intense development of the potential professional, but the efforts of those who merely wanted to enrich themselves through a better understanding of playing of music without the responsibility of a career."

In 1926 Clara Mannes received from the French government the title of Officier de l'Instruction Publique in recognition of her contribution to the teaching of music. In 1928 the Manneses (with Louis Untermeyer) published *New Songs for New Voices,* a collection of songs for children, most of them newly composed and many commissioned for the volume. As a performer Clara Mannes belongs to the first generation of American musicians to devote its major efforts to the performance of the classics of the chamber music repertory. The Manneses were the American violin-piano team that first showed itself to be the peers of the great European chamber ensembles. Critics praised their intelligence, flexibility, and give-and-take; David Mannes himself believed that when he and Clara first met she was the better musician.

As a music educator Clara Mannes is important largely for her work in the Mannes School of Music. Her contribution was partly administrative—she was the business expert among the directors—but more important was her understanding of the proper nature of music education, particularly the education of children. She believed in the essential wholeness of musical experience and therefore of the necessity of its being taught as a whole, that music study in the classroom should be complemented by musical surroundings in the home.

Mannes died suddenly of a heart ailment in New York. She was buried in Woodlawn Cemetery.

[Most of the papers documenting Clara Mannes' earlier years were destroyed in a fire. Her unfinished autobiography, along with many family papers, is in the Music Division of the Lib. of Congress. David Mannes' autobiography, *Music is My Faith* (1938), is the most valuable published source. Marya Mannes' *Out of My Time* (1971) gives glimpses of Clara Mannes as a family member. William Dinneen's article in *Notable American Women 1607–1950* (1971) is the best brief biography; it has a short but useful bibliography as well. "Building Musicianship," an interview with David and Clara Mannes in *Etude* magazine, Apr. 1944, sums up Clara Mannes' philosophy of music education.]

WAYNE SHIRLEY

MANNING, WILLIAM THOMAS (May 12, 1866-Nov. 18, 1949), bishop of the Protestant Episcopal Church of the Diocese of New York, was born in Northampton, England, the second son of John Manning and Matilda (Robinson) Manning; there were also two younger sisters and a younger brother. William was educated at Northampton Grammar School and for two years at Moulsoe School in Buckinghamshire. He later testified that his early life was shaped by the piety of his father, an Anglican layman identified with the Oxford movement, and implied that this influence was responsible, in part, for his decision, at the age of ten, to enter the ministry. In 1882 the family moved to the United States; John Manning farmed for four years in Nebraska and then in California, where he also practiced law. He and William were active in St. Paul's Church, San Diego, as Sunday School superintendent and assistant. In 1888 William entered the theological department of the University of the South at Sewanee, Tenn. There he studied under William P. DuBose, the philosopher, theologian, and mystic, and lived for a time in his household, aiding in the writing and publication of DuBose's *Soteriology of the New Testament* (1892). From DuBose he gained his firm conviction that the Anglican faith in the Incarnation of God in Christ and its extension in the church and Sacraments was consistent with the ongoing development of scientific and historical thought. In December 1889, Manning was ordained deacon at Sewanee and served for a time as curate at Calvary Church, Memphis, while continuing his studies with DuBose, and briefly,

in 1891, at the General Theological Seminary in New York. On Dec. 12, 1891, he was ordained to the priesthood by the bishop of Los Angeles and shortly after became rector of Trinity Church, Redlands, Calif. DuBose was anxious to bring him back to Sewanee, and in 1893 Manning returned to take his B.D. and was appointed professor of systematic (later dogmatic) theology, without salary.

Feeling that his permanent vocation lay in parish work, he left in 1894 for Trinity Mission in Cincinnati. On Apr. 23, 1895, he married Florence van Antwerp of Avondale, Ohio. They had two daughters: Frances van Antwerp and Elizabeth Alice van Antwerp. Two brief rectorships followed, at the Church of St. John the Evangelist, Lansdowne, Pa. (1896-1898), and Christ Church, Nashville, Tenn., in each of which he made important contributions in unifying divided congregations and encouraging their participation in the larger work of the church. His election in 1901 as deputy to the General Convention of the Episcopal Church at San Francisco indicated his growing prominence within the church. In 1903, when he was called to be vicar of St. Agnes' Chapel, one of the associated congregations of Trinity Parish, New York, Manning's significant lifework began.

Trinity Church, on Broadway at Wall Street, was then the center of a highly organized ministry, along the lines of the English parishes inspired by the ideals of the Oxford movement. There he developed a warm relationship with the aging rector, Morgan Dix. In 1904 the Trinity vestry elected him assistant rector, and after Dix's death on Apr. 29, 1908, they elected him rector on May 4 and, by Trinity's unusual privilege, the senior warden inducted him on the following day. Serious problems immediately faced the new rector, particularly the much-publicized condition of the tenement houses owned by Trinity parish. Long under attack by the press as an unconscionably wealthy church exploiting the poor, Trinity was cleared of the worst charges in an investigation conducted by the New York Charity Organization Society at Manning's behest. He then instituted a number of reforms aimed at ameliorating unsanitary and hazardous conditions, while finding other sources of income. The closing of St. John's Chapel, Varick Street, because of dwindling attendance was another of the long series of controversies in which Manning was to be involved over the years. Notable achievements of his rectorship include the cancellation of mortgages held by Trinity on other churches, the building of the Chapel of the Intercession (designed by Cram, Goodhue, and Ferguson), and the quickening of parish life and interest in social betterment.

Outside the parish, Dr. Manning became known for his encouragement of Christian unity along the lines of historic faith and order. At the 1910 General Convention, he proposed the initiation of a faith and order conference; two years later he took part in a delegation to the British Isles in the interest of the movement. However, he felt obliged to oppose Episcopal participation in the Panama Missionary Conference of 1916 in view of its anti-Catholic slant; as a result he was not elected in that year to the General Convention, to which New York had normally sent the rector of Trinity. In 1917-1918 he served with vigor and generosity as volunteer chaplain at Camp Upton on Long Island. His high standing in the church made him a natural candidate for the episcopate, and on Jan. 26, 1921, he was elected bishop of the Diocese of New York, having previously declined election as bishop of Western New York and bishop of Harrisburg. He was consecrated on May 11.

As bishop, Manning adopted the watchword of his predecessor of a century before, John Henry Hobart, "Evangelical Faith and Apostolic Order," a standard he defended through many controversies. His insistence on doctrinal purity and strict church order quickly brought him into conflict with the liberals and mavericks among the parish clergy, but he retained the esteem and support of most of the clergy and laity, despite the storm raised in 1923 over the call for loyalty to the creed in the Dallas Pastoral of the House of Bishops, which Manning helped to draft. He was likewise a vigorous supporter of strict church laws to protect the sanctity of marriage, specifically by forbidding the remarriage of divorced persons whose former spouses were still living. However, after a new Marriage Canon was passed in 1931, he was willing to grant permission for remarriage in church when there had been a civil decree of nullity and for readmission to Communion where a similar presumption was possible and the circumstances of remarriage were not scandalous.

Bishop Manning's most conspicuous public achievement was the building of the nave of the Cathedral Church of St. John the Divine on Morningside Heights, begun in 1892 but still unfinished in 1921. In 1924-1925 an elaborate drive raised over $13,000,000 and the work was resumed. It was carried on slowly through the

difficulties of the depression until the nave was complete in 1939. Services were then held there while the choir was reconstructed to fit Ralph Adams Cram's French Gothic design, which replaced the ponderous Romanesque Byzantine style of Heins and LaFarge originally planned. The whole length of the cathedral was opened with a series of special services in December 1941. Manning maintained that the cathedral project did not conflict with but rather stimulated support of the church's mission and its social outreach, expressed by its use for such special functions as a meeting to protest racial and religious persecution in 1933 and an exhibition on behalf of housing reform in 1937. Like his great predecessor Henry Codman Potter, Manning put his influence on the side of reform movements in New York City government, which won him the esteem and friendship of Mayor Fiorello H. La Guardia. Nor did he hesitate to express opinions that were not so widely shared in the church; some felt he went too far in attacking President Roosevelt's "court-packing" proposal in an Ash Wednesday sermon in 1937, and in giving perhaps unnecessarily vigorous support to the Allied cause in 1939-1941. From early in his ministry he fought against racial segregation; at Nashville in 1900 he successfully urged the abolition of segregated opening services for the Diocesan Convention; and in New York as bishop, he used his authority to acquire church buildings in Harlem for Negro congregations, on one dramatic occasion in 1932 breaking the locks on a church whose white vestry had shut out the rector when he integrated the services.

In 1927 Bishop Manning was a member of the Episcopal delegation to the first World Conference on Faith and Order at Lausanne, but took no further active part in the movement (now part of the World Council of Churches) of which he was one of the founders. He was insistent that reunion should include Catholic and Orthodox as well as Protestant traditions and therefore opposed proposals which seemed to push the Episcopal church decisively into the Protestant camp, such as, conspicuously, the plans for reunion with Presbyterians put forward in 1937-1946. However, he welcomed Protestant preachers (and Jewish speakers) on special occasions at the cathedral, supported Trinity Parish in making redundant buildings available for Russian and Serbian congregations, and enjoyed the friendship of the Greek Archbishop Athenagoras, since 1949 patriarch of Constantinople.

In later years Bishop Manning was less active outside his diocese, but retained the office since the 1943 canon requiring retirement at the age of seventy-two was not retroactive. Still vigorous and effective, he planned to continue as bishop for several more years but the onset of cancer necessitated his retirement in 1946. He moved to the house in Washington Mews that had been occupied by Bishop Gilbert, his suffragan and now successor. Here he took an active interest in local civic affairs and continued to enjoy personal contacts. His final effort was a statement of his principles in a hopeful article, "The Turning of the Tide." On Oct. 30, 1949, he celebrated the Holy Communion for the last time in his oratory, and a few days later was taken to St. Luke's, where he died on November 18. His ashes are fittingly interred under a simple monument in the nave of the cathedral.

He was an able administrator who greatly enriched and unified parish life before being elevated to the episcopate. Although he appeared stern and austere in public, he was good-humored and charitable in his private relations. He was in some ways a voice from an older and more confident age of the Church, which some found puzzling and others, refreshing. Early identified as a high churchman, Manning nevertheless was more concerned with the wholeness of evangelical Christianity than with forms and observances.

[W. T. Manning, *Strong in the Lord* (1947) collected sermons and addresses on significant occasions; W. D. F. Hughes, *Prudently with Power, William Thomas Manning, Tenth Bishop of New York* (1964), with portrait by Griffith Coale and photographs; Charles Thorley Bridgeman, *A History of the Parish of Trinity Church in the City of New York*, Part VI, *The Rectorship of Dr. William Thomas Manning 1908–1921* (1962); relevant reports in *Trinity Church Year Book* and *New York Diocesan Convention Journal*; there are portraits at the Cathedral House and at the House of the Redeemer on East 94th Street, New York.]

E. R. HARDY

MANTLE, (ROBERT) BURNS (Dec. 23, 1873-Feb. 9, 1948), drama critic and theater annalist, was born in Watertown, N.Y., the only son of Robert Burns Mantle, a local haberdasher, and Susan (Lawrence) Mantle. His parents had Scottish and English forebears. He was christened Leroy Willis Mantle, but after his father died, he adopted his father's name. In later years he was known as Burns Mantle professionally, but he was called Robert at home.

After his father's death, his mother supported the family by giving music lessons. When he was a youth the Mantle family—

consisting of his mother, one sister, two grandparents and himself—moved successively to Denver, to a colony that failed in Mexico, and then to San Diego, Calif. In San Diego, Mantle supplemented the family income by earning $5 a week for distributing copies of the *San Diegan* with a horse and wagon to newsboys throughout the city. Later he was promoted to printer's apprentice at a salary of $9 a week. In San Diego he was tutored at home by his mother and grandmother, but the record of his education is not clear. His daughter thinks that "he was mostly self-educated."

In 1892 the family returned to Denver and he went to work setting type by hand on the *Denver Times* for $25 a week. Subsequently he learned how to set type on a linotype machine that was being introduced to newspapers throughout the nation. He shifted to the composing room of the *Denver Republican* and then to the *Denver Post,* where he had his first experience as a play reviewer under peculiar circumstances. He was already an enthusiastic theatergoer and was writing drama notes directly on the typesetting machine. One night when the deadline was approaching, the drama critic of the *Post,* Frederick W. White, handed Mantle a review in longhand. Mantle could not decipher it. Since he had seen the play, he composed his own review on the machine. As Mantle told the anecdote years later, the official reviewer exclaimed when he read the proof, "My God! There isn't a word here that I wrote. But it's all right. Let it go."

Mantle began his professional career as a drama critic on the *Denver Times* in 1898. Three years later he joined the staff of the *Chicago Inter-Ocean* as the assistant drama critic. He began his long association with the *Chicago Tribune* in 1907, first as drama critic and a year and a half later as Sunday editor. But drama criticism was still the work that interested him most. When Mantle was in New York in 1911 trying to sell some *Tribune* features, T. E. Niles, managing editor of the *New York Evening Mail,* said that he did not need any features but he did need a drama critic. Mantle accepted that appointment, serving simultaneously as correspondent for the *Chicago Tribune.*

In 1922, after Joseph Medill Patterson of the *Chicago Tribune* had established the *Daily News* in New York, he asked Mantle to become the *News* drama critic. Mantle continued in that post for the next twenty-three years and became a widely read, influential authority on the contemporary theater. At the time, the

Daily News, the *Herald Tribune,* and the *Times* dominated New York's public taste in theatergoing. During his term Mantle established the star system of rating plays by posting stars at the top of the column. Four stars was the highest rating; plays of less than first quality were rated by fewer stars, down to one-half.

Being a friendly person who radiated cheer in the theater, he was a friendly critic. He regarded himself not as a dictator but as a theatergoer. Before the *Daily News* moved in 1930 into quarters easily accessible from Broadway, Mantle wrote his reviews on the typewriter of the *Chicago Tribune* correspondent in the syndicate room of the *New York Times.* A messenger from the *Daily News* came for the copy at about midnight, and Mantle would then take ten or fifteen minutes to compare notes and gossip with the drama staff of the *Times.*

But when the *Daily News* moved, Mantle went directly to his own office. First, he would remove the padlock on his typewriter (as an old linotype operator, he did not like to have anyone else using the keyboard on which he composed), and then he would take out his father's gold watch, snap open the hunting case, and put it on his desk where he could keep track of the time. He pasted up the cast of the actors in the play and sent it to the composing room and in pencil wrote the headline, which he also sent to the composing room. With all the preliminaries out of the way, he proceeded to the writing of the review. An old newspaper man accustomed to the technique of going to press, he always conformed to the printers' schedules. He never knew the exact number of plays he reviewed, but he guessed that the number exceeded 6,000.

Burns Mantle is best remembered as the founding editor of the *Best Plays* series, which he initiated in 1919-1920. The form has become standard. After choosing the ten best plays of the season, he condensed them. The condensations were, and are, the core of each book. But the rest of the book is even more vital: reports of the theater from other producing centers; the casts, statistics, and brief summaries of all the other plays produced on Broadway that season; a list of the plays with the longest runs; lists of the Pulitzer and Drama Critics Circle awards; notes on all the theater books published during the season; and brief biographies of all the theater people who died during the season.

No theater in the world is recorded as meticulously as Broadway is in the *Best Plays.* Although Mantle's active editorship (in which he was assisted by a sister-in-law, Clara Sears Taylor) ceased after 1947, the series has continued under the editorship of other critics and retained the subtitle *The Burns Mantle Yearbook of the Theatre.* John Mason Brown, a colleague on other publications, called Mantle "the recording angel of our contemporary theatre." Joseph Wood Krutch, former critic for the *Nation,* described the series as a "labor of love for which Mr. Mantle will be remembered as long as the history of the American theatre remains interesting." After more than a half-century the *Best Plays* volumes remained the one essential theater reference in America.

Mantle would not have taken such a compliment seriously. He was a modest man of less than average height, with brown hair that never turned white, bright eyes, and a kindly mouth. He was inclined to self-deprecation. "Well, Mantle will give the matter his usual consideration," he used to say puckishly when a decision had to be made. He served two terms as president of the New York Drama Critics' Circle, and he rarely missed a session of the Dutch Treat Luncheon Club. In 1940 he became the first drama critic to be elected a member of the Players, a club composed of actors and men of the theater that had always regarded critics as alien to good fellowship.

His home in Forest Hills, which he bought in 1916, was not only the physical, but the spiritual, foundation of his life. He married Lydia Holmes Sears of Denver on Aug. 20, 1903. Over the years their home also came to be the home of his two sisters-in-law, who were both widows, and his adopted daughter, Margaret, who was the center of the family life.

In the winter of 1948 he was admitted to a hospital in Forest Hills, N.Y., for tests for cancer. Although the prospects of recovery were slender, he retained his sense of humor and amiability. Staring at the crucifix on the wall before his bed, he remarked, "I suppose they put that up there to remind me of how much better off I am." He is buried in Fairmont Cemetery, Denver, Colo.

[In addition to the *Best Plays* series from the 1919-1920 to the 1946-1947 season, Burns Mantle wrote *American Playwrights of Today* (1929) and *Contemporary American Playwrights* (1938). He collaborated with Garrison P. Sherwood on *The Best Plays of 1909-1919* and with John Gassner on *A Treasury of the Theatre* (1935).
The major biographical sources are Stanley J. Kunitz and Howard Haycraft, eds., *Twentieth-Century Authors* (1942); *Current Biog.,* 1944; John Parker, ed., *Who's Who in the Theatre* (10th ed., 1947); *N.Y. Dramatic Mirror,* Oct. 16, 1912, and Mar. 4, 1914; *N.Y. Daily News,* Aug. 15, 1943 (on Mantle's retirement), and Feb. 10, 1948 (obituary); Boyden Sparkes in the *Players Bull.,* Mar. 1948; *N.Y. Times,*

Feb. 10, 1948; and letters from Mantle's daughter, Margaret Gerard; John Chapman; Joseph F. Mc-Carthy; and Louis Rachow.]

BROOKS ATKINSON

MARBURG, THEODORE (July 10, 1862-Mar. 3, 1946), publicist, internationalist, civic leader, was born in Baltimore, Md., the youngest of six sons and two daughters. His middle name, which he never used, was Herman. His father, William August Marburg, was a native of Germany, and his mother, Christine (Munder) Marburg, was born in Pennsylvania of German parents. William Marburg, the son of a successful iron manufacturer, was already a millionaire when he immigrated to the United States in 1830 and established a tobacco importing business in Baltimore.

Theodore Marburg thus enjoyed the benefits of inherited wealth. He attended Knapp's Institute in Baltimore and the Princeton (N.J.) Preparatory School and entered Johns Hopkins University in 1880. He withdrew after one year, however, to help run Marburg Brothers Tobacco Company, a business William had purchased for his sons after the Civil War. The company was sold at a substantial profit in 1889 to what afterward became the American Tobacco Company. On Nov. 6, 1889, he married Fannie Grainger of Wilmington, N.C. They had four children: Christine, Theodore, Francis Grainger, and Charles Louis. Marburg, who cared little for business, agreed to serve for one year as a director of American Tobacco, after which he returned to his formal studies, attending Oxford University (1892-1893), the École Libre de la Science Politique in Paris (1893-1895), and later, in the summers of 1901 and 1903, Heidelberg. He did not pursue a profession but devoted his life to public service, philanthropy, and the arts.

Marburg first attained prominence as an advocate of imperialism in the debate over American policy during and after the Spanish-American War. In a small book, *Expansion* (1900), he argued that civilized nations should spread democracy and progress to backward lands. He expressed similar views as a frequent contributor to periodicals, questioning, for example, the ability of different races to mingle successfully and supporting the imposition of immigration restrictions.

Although Marburg always retained nationalistic and militaristic sentiments, he believed that constructive planning might resolve international problems and reduce the incidence of war. In 1910 he helped establish the American Society for Judicial Settlement of International Disputes and the Maryland Peace Society, serving as president of the former from 1913 to 1916 and of the latter in 1913. As chairman of an organizing committee, he planned the National Peace Congress, which met in Baltimore in 1911. Long prominent in Maryland Republican politics, Marburg in 1912 was appointed minister to Belgium by President Taft, a post he retained until January 1914.

Marburg's major contribution to the cause of peace came in 1915 when he joined with Hamilton Holt, editor of the *Independent*, the economist Irving Fisher, and other internationalists in founding the League to Enforce Peace, to work for the establishment of a postwar league of nations. They envisaged a league that would require governments to submit all disputes to specified agencies, emphasizing conciliation and judicial processes. States reluctant to follow this procedure would face the concerted military and economic force of the league's members until they did so. Within the League to Enforce Peace, Marburg served as chairman of the foreign relations committee, which sought to develop similar societies abroad and influence their thinking. The league, which enlisted among its leaders ex-President Taft and A. Lawrence Lowell of Harvard, did much to mobilize American support for the League of Nations, but ultimately found itself powerless to resolve the Senate deadlock over the Treaty of Versailles. Although some of Marburg's associates supported the Republican party in the presidential election of 1920 despite its equivocal stand on the League of Nations, Marburg was one of those who bolted to the Democrats. He remained a Democrat until his death.

An internationalist rather than a pacifist, Marburg believed that some wars were justifiable. Germany's attack on Belgium outraged him and he advocated American entry into World War I as early as 1915. (He took a similar interventionist position after the outbreak of World War II.) During the interwar years, he continued his labors for internationalism as a member of the League of Nations Non-Partisan Association and as vice-president (1925) of the International Federation of League of Nations Societies, and he supported the unsuccessful campaigns to have the United States join the Permanent Court of International Justice.

Throughout his life Marburg was active in the cultural and civil life of Baltimore. He was a vice-president of the city's Reform League, and the organizer in 1899 of the Municipal Art Society. The immediate purpose of the art society was to help beautify the city, but it quickly grew into a city planning body, even recommending solutions to such technical municipal problems as sewage treatment. On behalf of the society, Marburg hired the architectural firm of Olmsted Brothers, which in 1903 devised Baltimore's highly praised plan for park development; and he later worked with this and other architectural firms in drawing up a comprehensive city plan. Marburg was also instrumental in establishing Baltimore's Museum of Art, and was for many years a trustee of Johns Hopkins University, of which he was a generous benefactor. His many activities were recognized by honorary degrees from Johns Hopkins (1902), Dickinson College (1912), the University of Cincinnati (1917), and Rollins College (1928).

Slender of build, Marburg typified in manner and bearing the educated and cultured gentleman. He wrote poetry that reflected a romantic outlook and a classical influence. He collected paintings, with a taste toward the contemporary. He enjoyed hunting and fishing and became an accomplished horseman. Marburg had a philosophical turn of mind and a warm sense of humor, and was consistently considerate of others. Although a Unitarian, Marburg regularly attended Episcopal services after his marriage. He died of a coronary thrombosis at eighty-three while in Vancouver, British Columbia. After funeral services at the family home, his body was cremated and the ashes placed in the family mausoleum in Druid Ridge Cemetery, Baltimore County.

[A small collection of Marburg Papers is in the Lib. of Cong. Henry Atkinson, *Theodore Marburg* (1951), is a brief, uncritical, and inadequate biography; it provides personal data and photographs. See also *Nat. Cyc. Am. Biog.*, XXXIV, 86–87; and obituaries in the *N.Y. Times* and *Baltimore Sun*, Mar. 5, 1946. Save for a few volumes of verse, most of Marburg's books were reprints of magazine pieces; he also wrote frequent letters to the editor of the *N.Y. Times*. For his writings, see the Lib. of Cong. catalogue, the *Readers' Guide to Periodical Literature*, and the *N.Y. Times Index*. On the League to Enforce Peace, see John H. Satané, ed., *Development of the League of Nations Idea: Documents and Correspondence of Theodore Marburg*, 2 vols. (1932); Marburg's *League of Nations*, 2 vols. (1917–1918); and Ruhl J. Bartlett, *The League to Enforce Peace* (1944). On Marburg's civic work, see James B. Crooks, *Politics and Progress: The Rise of Urban Progressivism in Baltimore, 1895–1911* (1968). Charles L. Marburg provided information about his father.]

WARREN F. KUEHL

MARLOWE, JULIA (Aug. 17, 1866–Nov. 12, 1950), actress, was born Sarah Frances ("Fanny") Frost at Caldbeck, Cumberlandshire, England, the second of the three daughters and four children of John Frost and Sarah (Hodgson) Frost. Her father, after a drunken spree in which he mistakenly believed he had seriously injured an innocent man, fled to the United States, settled twenty-five miles west of Kansas City as a country storekeeper, and changed his name to Brough. To this frontier haven he brought his wife and children when Fanny was five years old. The family later moved to Cincinnati, where Mrs. Brough opened a small hotel and Fanny began her schooling. An apt reader, Fanny learned quickly, soon outdistancing her age group.

She was of an independent spirit, and at the age of eleven she answered an advertisement in a local paper for children to sing and act in a juvenile performance of *H.M.S. Pinafore*. The manager, Col. Robert E. J. Miles, led the company on one-night stands through the Midwest, with Fanny Brough rising from the chorus to the role of Sir Joseph Porter. By the end of the winter, when the company broke up, her interest in the stage had taken hold. But her mother thought a more dependable source of livelihood was necessary and sent her to work in a cracker factory. Having won the attention of Miles and his sister-in-law, Ada Dow, the youngster rejoined their company briefly in 1882 in *Rip Van Winkle* (not the Boucicault version made famous by Joseph Jefferson) on tour in support of Josephine Reilly. At the tour's end in the spring of 1884 a new chapter opened in Fanny Brough's career when Ada Dow determined to take her protégée in hand and train her recognizable talents. In August they headed for New York.

For two and a half years, at first in a small apartment on 36th Street near Broadway and then in Bayonne, N.J., the neophyte worked through the day to master the actor's skills: diction, inflection, interpretation, movement, gesture, position, breathing. Daily rehearsals went on by the hour for an audience of one, Ada Dow. A vocal teacher, Parsons Price, trained her voice, which, because of its faultless and rich range, would later be called "vocal velvet" by critics. The student herself explored each role and the sense she wanted to convey. Interpretation was entirely her own, but it had to meet her teacher's stern approval. By the spring of 1887 both pupil and mentor agreed the time had come for a public test of her abilities. To mark the transformation of Fanny Brough, a new name was chosen, and the young actress became Julia Marlowe.

Miles formed a company for a two-week tour before launching Julia Marlowe in New York City. She opened as Parthenia in *Ingomar* at the New London (Conn.) Opera House on Apr. 25, 1887. Audiences were small, but the theater was real, and the reviews were warm and led to a New York debut at the Bijou at a professional matinee on Oct. 19, 1887. Encouraged by the applause of a critical audience that had come to sneer at a novice, her managers gathered a supporting company for a week's engagement at the Star Theatre. During the week of December 12 she opened in the role most favored by the budding actresses of the day and most savored by the baiting critics. Her portrayal of Shakespeare's Juliet scarcely gained the palm, but it won respect and more than grudging praise. Her Viola in *Twelfth Night* had greater success, and with Parthenia she completed the week, demonstrating, in the words of one critic, "the incredible proposition that it is still possible to succeed on merit."

Accepted, but not yet established, Julia Marlowe campaigned hard in the next three seasons to win a permanent place in the American theater. She redoubled her difficulty by refusing leading managers like A. M. Palmer and Charles Frohman, who offered her a place in one of the major stock companies, for she insisted that her work must be in Shakespearean drama. As she toured Eastern cities, she added Rosalind, Beatrice, and Imogen to her earlier roles, winning heartier approval every week as she moved from Washington to Boston to Philadelphia. But although it stirred audiences deeply, serious tragedy failed at the box office, and gradually she had to add novelty to her repertoire, such as Hannah Cowley's *The Belle's Stratagem* and Sheridan Knowles's *The Love Chase.* In May 1894 she married her leading man, Robert Taber, and by the season of 1894-1895, she felt sure enough of her ability to undertake her own management. Appearing with her husband as costar, she met new resistance, for although welcome in her own right, she found her supporting players attacked. The abuse reached such heights that she felt forced to sue an Indianapolis newspaper for libel; she won the case and vindicated her company.

In 1895 Taber added Shakespeare's *Henry IV, Part I,* casting his wife as Prince Hal. It was as Juliet, however, that she now came to stand with the peers of her profession, and when she returned to New York in the spring of 1896, Sarah Bernhardt and Eleonora Duse praised her as extravagantly as the press. Even this recognition, however, did not fill the theater, but by joining an all-star cast of *The Rivals* organized by Joseph Jefferson for a four-week tour, she reaped financial benefit

enough for her and her husband to summer in Europe. The season after their return was no more successful than the previous one, despite added novelties in *Romola* and *For Bonnie Prince Charlie,* both elaborate productions; by the end of the season Julia Marlowe had to defer to the Theatrical Syndicate, playing under her own name, while her husband went to London to act. They were divorced in 1900.

Despite her command of Shakespeare's art, the Theatrical Syndicate demanded that she appear in plays of more general appeal. *The Countess Valeska,* adapted from a German play, displayed her dramatic powers in January 1898. Amid the applause of crowded houses, Charles Frohman decided she was "the greatest emotional actress in America" (Russell, p. 262). After touring in this success, she returned to New York to revive *As You Like It* and *Romeo and Juliet.* With these productions, she came into direct conflict with Augustin Daly, the dean of theatrical managers, who had early cultivated his contempt for her by disparaging remarks to the press. Staging elaborate rival productions, Daly found himself overshadowed, for his leading lady's Rosalind and Juliet paled alongside Marlowe's. Her Shakespearean successes notwithstanding, however, it was through plays like *Barbara Frietchie* (1899) by Clyde Fitch, and the adaptation by Paul Kester of the best-selling novel *When Knighthood Was in Flower* (1900) that her name became a household word, as she played everywhere to standing room only. In the latter romantic extravaganza, her Mary Tudor won her a sobriquet from James Huneker: "Julia of 'the mighty line'" (Russell, p. 307). He declared that she had no rival in the United States or England. "One must go to Paris, Berlin, Vienna, or Rome to find her peer" (*ibid.*).

For Julia Marlowe, however, popularity and profits did not compose success in the theater. Her art had its roots in Shakespeare, and in his plays alone she realized her theatrical self. In the fall of 1904 she opened a new phase of her career when, under the sponsorship of Charles Frohman and the Theatrical Syndicate, she appeared with Edward H. Sothern in *Romeo and Juliet.* After a trial run of three weeks in Chicago and a stop in Pittsburgh, the company reached New York's Knickerbocker Theatre on October 17 with a *Romeo and Juliet* that surpassed expectations. Their presentations of *Much Ado About Nothing* and *Hamlet* filled out a seven-week stay. They then moved on to other cities on the first of a series of profitable tours. For the actress the larger profit lay in having found an experienced actor who shared her devotion to Shakespeare along with her inward response that brought poetry to life. Moreover, each had found an actor to complement his skill and taste.

During their two seasons together under the syndicate, they added *The Merchant of Venice, The Taming of the Shrew,* and *Twelfth Night* to their repertoire. Although the syndicate had paid them each $115,000 a year, they now turned to the more genial management of the Shuberts, from whom they received a share of the net receipts, which promised a still greater return for their efforts. For the season of 1906 they broadened their repertoire again, offering Gerhart Hauptmann's *The Sunken Bell,* Hermann Sudermann's *John the Baptist,* and Percy MacKaye's verse drama *Jeanne d'Arc,* along with four of their Shakespearean productions. This venture into continental drama won a respectful hearing, the response varying from cordial to chilly, but only Julia Marlowe's grace and poetry preserved the audience's loyalty. In the spring of 1907 the stars led their company to London, opening in *The Sunken Bell* on Apr. 22, 1907. Neither the Hauptmann nor the MacKaye drama stirred London to applause, and with *John the Baptist* banned by the royal censor, the visitors turned to Shakespeare. In *Twelfth Night* their Olivia and Malvolio triumphed. *Romeo and Juliet* and *Hamlet* added to their renown. Although the engagement entailed a loss of $15,000, the prestige far outweighed this sum. It was best put by Arthur Symons, in an essay entitled "Great Acting in English." "Have we in our whole island two actors capable of giving so serious, so intelligent, so carefully finished, so vital an interpretation of Shakespeare, or, indeed, of rendering any form of poetic drama on the stage, as the Englishman and Englishwoman who came to us . . . from America in the guise of Americans: Julia Marlowe and Edward Sothern?" (Russell, p. 343). With her "natural genius for acting," he saw Marlowe turn Juliet from a decorative ingenue into a tragic child, raise Ophelia above the limitations of a narrow role, and through Viola reveal a complex of emotions. In other than Shakespearean roles, her vitality and gaiety, her abundant strength to make a role come to life achieved a degree of excellence unattained by England's native actors.

Returning to the United States, the stars briefly went their separate ways, but despite her success in *The Goddess of Reason* (February 1909), Marlowe determined to return to Shakespeare. Reunited with Sothern, she opened the elaborate New Theatre in New York on Nov. 8, 1909, with *Antony and Cleopatra.* Playing a new role, she gave a performance of the mortal queen marked by the same honesty and perception she brought to other roles, but the darker ladies of Shakespeare were not her métier. After completing the two stipulated performances a week for twelve weeks at the New Theatre, the pair set off with their standard repertoire on a national tour. Their partnership continued, more tightly bound by a quiet marriage in London on Aug. 17, 1911, as year after year they trouped across the country, playing large cities and small towns in weekly or nightly engagements. Upholding the classic and romantic traditions of the stage, Julia Marlowe made Shakespeare's heroines credible to a modern age. Her preeminence was recognized by the Shakespeare Memorial Association in Stratford-upon-Avon, which appointed her a permanent governor in 1914.

Poor health forced her to announce her retirement in 1916, although she gave subsequent performances. The toll of endless traveling and overnight stops had long since reduced her strength to the breaking point. In January 1911 she had written typically to a close friend, "The houses are fine—but when I finish these two weeks of one-night stands I shall have lived 'years'! They seem to stretch out to the 'crack of doom.'" Repeatedly her letters spoke of how rushed she was in her work or completely fatigued by it. She hated winter with its cold winds and snow, loving the sunshine and the Mediterranean. In retirement she spent months in Egypt, on the Riviera, and in Switzerland. During World War I she entertained at benefits for wounded troops, and in the seasons of 1919-1920 and 1923-1924 she and Sothern resumed the theatrical trail in their favorite repertory, but these farewell appearances drained her of her last energy.

In 1921 George Washington University conferred on her the honorary degree of doctor of letters; Columbia added another in 1943. In 1929 the American Academy of Arts and Letters awarded her a gold medal "for clarity and melody in the use of the English language."

Although she considered motion pictures and the lecture-recital, Julia Marlowe increasingly lived in seclusion during her last twenty-five years. After her husband's death in 1933, she made only one public appearance, in 1944, when she opened an exhibition at the Museum of the City of New York of costumes worn by Sothern and herself. In 1916, on her first retirement, they had auctioned off their costumes and stage property; as though to mark their final retirement, in 1926 they gave their scenery and costumes to the Shakespeare Theatre at Stratford-upon-Avon. Thus, the 1944 exhibition marked the curtain call. She lived quietly and in poor health at her apartment in the Plaza Hotel in New York, often confined to her bed, until her death there at the age of eighty-four. Following the funeral at St. James' Protestant Episcopal Church, in New York, her ashes were placed alongside Sothern's in Brompton Cemetery, London.

As a young actress, Julia Marlowe was exceptionally handsome, with regular features, brilliant dark brown eyes, luxuriant brown hair, and a melodious voice. To these qualities she added grace, sweetness, earnestness, and vitality. The characters she portrayed embodied the nineteenth-century ideal of womanhood: love, devotion, gentleness, beauty, courage, affection, loyalty, ardor, and charm. In an occasional interview, article, or lecture, she voiced that ideal as her personal faith. In her Shakespearean impersonations these traits were blended with the fruits of lifelong study, an expressive grasp of personal dimensions, and a perceptive power over the poetic medium. Playing Shakespearean drama more often than any other actress, she brought the womanly ideal to life in art and set a standard in the American theater that endured through successive generations.

[A large body of Julia Marlowe's papers, including promptbooks and many letters written by her and to her by distinguished people of the day are in the Marlowe-Sothern Collect. of the Museum of the City of N.Y. Additional letters are in the Theater Collect. of the N. Y. Public Lib. at Lincoln Center, along with numerous scrapbooks and newspaper clippings. The chief biography is Charles Edward Russell, *Julia Marlowe, Her Life and Art* (1926). See also Fairfax Downey, ed., *Julia Marlowe's Story*, illus. by E. H. Sothern (1954); John D. Barry, *Julia Marlowe* (1907); and William Winter, *The Wallet of Time* (1913) and *Vagrant Memories* (1915).]

H. L. KLEINFIELD

MASTERS, EDGAR LEE (Aug. 23, 1869-Mar. 5, 1950), poet and novelist, was the eldest of four children and first of three sons of Hardin Wallace Masters and Emma J. (Dexter) Masters. His father's parents, descendants of English colonists in Virginia and North Carolina, were pioneers who moved to Illinois in 1829 and settled on a farm near Petersburg and New Salem. His mother was the daughter of a Methodist minister in Vermont. Lee (as he was known until his mid-twenties) was born in Garnett, Kans., where his father attempted to establish a law practice. After this venture failed, Hardin Masters returned to Illinois a year later. Around 1872, after an unsuccessful attempt to make a living at farming, he became county prosecutor in Petersburg, trying cases with Lincoln's former partner, William H. Herndon. In 1880 he started a law practice in Lewistown. For some time the family was financially hard pressed, as Hardin Masters' reputation as a liberal, freethinker, pacifist, supposed "Copperhead," and antiprohibitionist in a community dominated by Calvinists and Republicans hindered his progress.

Lee attended public schools in Petersburg and Lewistown and spent the summers in great contentment on his paternal grandparents' farm. His lifelong nostalgia for rural America and the values of pioneer people stemmed from a close relationship with these grandparents. From the age of sixteen he worked as a printer's assistant on the *Lewistown News* after school hours, spending his earnings on books. Inspired by a high school teacher, he pored over literary classics and wrote poetry. After graduation from high school he helped his father in the law office, wrote for the *News,* and published poems. In spite of wide reading and additional studies at a local academy, deficiencies in Latin and Greek thwarted his hope of enrolling as a freshman at Knox College, but he spent a year (1889-1890) in the college's preparatory department. His father, fearful that his son's literary aspirations doomed him to poverty and anxious to have him as a partner, persuaded Lee to read law with him, and in 1891 young Masters was admitted to the bar.

A year later the slender, dark-eyed young man sought a journalistic career in Chicago. Instead, he had to take a job with the Edison Company, collecting bills from such places as tough saloons and brothels. Disgusted by this work, he opened a law office with Kickham Scanlan in 1893. He embraced Populism and warmly endorsed the liberal policies of Gov. John P. Altgeld. Involved in politics from 1896 to 1908 as a supporter of William Jennings Bryan, he attacked American imperialism in *The New Star Chamber and Other Essays* (1904) and *The Blood of the Prophets* (1905). Like Clarence Darrow, whose law firm he joined in 1903, Masters defended the poor and oppressed against powerful business interests. By 1911, however, when he left the firm to practice alone, he had lost faith in making the law an instrument of social and political reform. His personal life was similarly disillusioning. He felt mismatched to his wife, Helen M. Jenkins (the daughter of a Chicago corporation lawyer), whom he married on June 21, 1898, and none of the love affairs that preceded and followed the marriage gave him lasting happiness. He did take pleasure in his children, Hardin, Marcia, and Madeline.

Although Masters published poetry continuously, he was virtually unknown until 1914, when *Reedy's Mirror* of St. Louis published a series of 244 epitaphs in free verse, under the pseudonym Webster Ford. On November 20 the true author was revealed. These searchingly frank "autobiographical" vignettes of those who lay buried in a village cemetery near Spoon River were published by Macmillan in 1915 as *Spoon River Anthology*. The volume, which by 1940 had run into seventy editions and had been translated into eight languages, catapulted Masters to fame and fortune.

Spoon River was a composite community, drawn from Masters' knowledge of Illinois towns along the Sangamon River. With merciless candor the poet unmasked the false lives of its inhabitants—corruptible editors, unscrupulous bankers, hypocritical politicians, corporation lawyers conniving with judges and courts to defeat the claims of the helpless, clerical agents of vested interests, husbands and wives slowly destroying each other behind a false façade. Yet among the acquisitive, crafty, and cowardly were courageous and noble people like Lincoln's gentle sweetheart, Anne Rutledge, and a woman modeled on Masters' grandmother.

The "village cynic's" major work opened the floodgates of controversy. Fundamentalist ministers and civic groups condemned its alleged immorality. Traditionalist critics assailed its unconventional prosody. Other Midwestern literary rebels, fellow realists, and friends of Masters like Theodore Dreiser, Vachel Lindsay, Carl Sandburg, and Sherwood Anderson recognized its validity. Later Carl Van Doren called *Spoon River Anthology* "the essence of many novels. . . . The epitaphs seemed to send up a shout of revelation" (p. 295). A friend, the poet Kimball Flaccus, observed that Masters resembled Dreiser in being "a merciless analyst of human souls, a clever chronicler of human behavior, a prober into the dark and secret and terrible crevices of American life" (p. 44).

Masters produced many more volumes of poetry after *Spoon River Anthology,* including an extension of it, *The New Spoon River* (1924). This later verse, although remarkable for its variety, was highly uneven in quality. In 1920 he published *Domesday Book,* a poetic survey of American history. A few critics and Masters himself considered this his most profound work. In it he strayed from his Populist faith, attacking mobocracy, "the vile majority," which "set up intolerable tyrannies in America." After its publication, Masters abandoned the law and devoted himself to a literary career.

Masters was divorced in 1923 and moved to the East, spending most of the remainder of his life in New York. While living in the city, he enjoyed escaping to the country, visiting friends in the Middle West, New England, or Princeton, N. J. With those he knew well his usual pessimism vanished and his love of the ludicrous emerged. Writing humorous and ribald verse served as a release from moods of depression.

During the 1920's Masters wrote five novels, drawing on his youth in Illinois. *Mitch Miller* (1920), an idealization of his boyhood in Petersburg, reflects the frustrations of a sensitive boy growing up in America. Its sequel, *Skeeters Kirby* (1923), paralleled Masters' youth in Lewistown, with Skeeters studying law to please his father and making an unfortunate marriage after several unhappy love affairs. Skeeters Kirby's story was extended into middle age in *Mirage* (1924). In *The Nuptial Flight* (1923) Masters reiterated a familiar theme: country life brings health and happiness, while city life spells decadence. And in *Kit O'Brien* (1927) he depicted the conflict between a small town and encroaching railroad interests. Through the novels ran some of Masters' favorite themes, such as America's obsessive pursuit of material success and the abandonment of Jeffersonian ideals of freedom and democracy. Critics of Masters as a novelist felt that he was more interested in proving a thesis than in the novel as an art form.

On Nov. 5, 1926, Masters married Ellen Frances Coyne of Kansas City, thirty-one years his junior. They had one son, Hilary, who later became an author. By 1931 Masters and his wife had separated, and he had settled in the faded Victorian splendor of the Chelsea Hotel in New York City. There he led a secluded life, writing ceaselessly and occasionally relaxing with intimate friends like

Dreiser, H. L. Mencken, Percy MacKaye, A. M. Sullivan, and Kimball Flaccus at the Players Club or Luchow's restaurant.

Masters was enthralled by historical themes in poetry and biography. He lamented the passing of the agrarian society of the antebellum South, the tragically "unnecessary" Civil War, and the disappearance of America's heritage of freedom. His *Lincoln: The Man* (1931), a cynical attack on the Lincoln myth, drew the ire of critics. This acid portrait was followed by *Vachel Lindsay* (1935), a sympathetic study of another Midwestern literary rebel and close friend. Next came *Whitman* (1937), on a poet for whom Masters felt an affinity in his mystic love of freedom, pantheism, and cosmic faith. In *Mark Twain: A Portrait* (1938) Masters asserted that Twain was at his best and truly himself in *Tom Sawyer,* where he spoke from the heart of America; but Masters attacked him for becoming "Easternized."

Masters' personality was strikingly revealed in his frank autobiography, *Across Spoon River* (1936). Forever searching for the ideal woman, he was continually disappointed, and he was similarly disillusioned by the injustices he suffered and observed. He saw himself as a person "annoyed, fatigued, even degraded by inferior human contacts, by experiences, amorous and other, alive with contaminations" yet also a person "existing aloof and untouched by demoralizations" (pp. 399–400). Experience bred in him the view that "all human disaster comes from the weakness or perfidy of those who are in one's life" (p. 278). And like his fictional character Skeeters Kirby, he felt himself to be "an idealist in a materialistic world doomed to continual defeat and betrayal" (quoted in Yatron, p. 60).

He suffered, too, the frustration of never repeating his initial success. For years, he yearned for recognition comparable to the critical acclaim that had greeted *Spoon River Anthology.* Only late in life did he receive a medal from the Poetry Society of America (1942), the Shelley Memorial Award (1944), and a $5,000 fellowship from the Academy of American Poetry (1946).

After an attack of pneumonia in 1943, Masters' health was permanently impaired. Suffering from hardening of the arteries, he gradually became paralyzed. He was reunited with his wife Ellen and accompanied her to Charlotte, N.C., and Rydal, Pa., where she held teaching positions. In 1950 Masters died in his sleep at Pine Manor Convalescent Home in Melrose, Pa. He was buried beside his pioneer grandfather in Oakland Cemetery, Petersburg.

[In addition to Masters' autobiography, see Michael Yatron, *America's Literary Revolt* (1959); *Edgar Lee Masters: A Centenary Memoir-Anthology* (1972), with an introduction by his son Hardin W. Masters; Kimball Flaccus, "The Art of Edgar Lee Masters," *Voices,* Summer 1940; Gertrude Claytor, "Edgar Lee Masters in the Chelsea Years," *Princeton Univ. Lib. Chronicle,* Autumn 1952; John T. Flanagan, "The Spoon River Poet," *Southwest Rev.,* Summer 1953; *Nat. Cyc. Am. Biog.,* XXXVII, 183–184; *N. Y. Times* obituary, Mar. 6, 1950; editorial in *Sat. Rev. of Lit.,* Mar. 25, 1950; Louis Untermeyer, *Am. Poetry Since 1900* (1923); and Carl Van Doren, *The Am. Novel, 1789–1939* (1940).]

CHRISTINE GIBBONS MASON

MATHEWSON, EDWARD PAYSON (Oct. 16, 1864–July 13, 1948), metallurgist and mining engineer, was born in Montreal, Canada, one of fourteen children of James Adams Mathewson and Amelia Seabury (Black) Mathewson. His father, a native of Strabane, Northern Ireland, was a wholesale grocer; his mother was a Nova Scotian descended from Massachusetts Loyalists. Young Mathewson received a Bachelor of Applied Science degree in mining engineering from McGill University in 1885. He worked during the following summer for the Dominion Geological Survey in Ontario; then in 1886, through the influence of the geologist and chemist Thomas Sterry Hunt, he began his metallurgical career as an assayer for the Pueblo Smelting and Refining Company in Colorado, a practical training ground for numerous fledgling engineers.

In 1889 Mathewson was named superintendent of the Pueblo plant and was building a reputation; in 1897 he came to the attention of Meyer Guggenheim and his son, who were welding together a vast smelting empire; they employed him to manage lead and copper refineries, first in Pueblo, then in Perth Amboy, N.J.; Monterrey, Mexico; and Antofagasta, Chile. In 1901 after the Guggenheims merged their interest with the American Smelting and Refining Company, Mathewson was recalled to New York. He recommended closing the plant in Chile in the interest of efficiency, a decision that cost him his job.

Unemployed for six months, in June 1902 he took charge of the blast furnaces of the Amalgamated Copper Company (soon to be the Anaconda Copper Mining Company) in Montana. Of the five furnaces, never more than two had been running at one time, but Mathewson managed to keep all five in operation. In the following year he took charge of the company's new Washoe Reduction Works at Anaconda, Mont., a plant that he made the "show-place of the metallurgical world" before he left it in 1916. Not only did he increase the size of the plant, already the world's largest, but he devised a furnace system that could be lengthened indefinitely, depending upon the ore supply, and any part of which could be repaired without halting the operation of the rest of the plant. Along with expanded capacity, he brought savings in fuel consumption and slag loss. Earlier he had invented a tapping device for lead and copper furnaces. In 1905 he conducted important investigations of the damage of smelter fumes to animals and vegetation; with Frederick Laist, he made advances in the lixiviation of copper tailings, the precipitation of copper by sponge iron produced by direct reduction of iron ore, and the leaching and electrolytic precipitation of zinc. Like the old Pueblo Company, Anaconda became a kind of postgraduate school for young metallurgists who served under Mathewson and Laist, his successor. In addition, Mathewson took charge of erecting smelting and refining plants at Tooele, Utah, and East Chicago, Ind., for an Anaconda subsidiary, the International Smelting and Refining Company; he also found time to consult as far afield as India, Burma, and Japan.

Having already worked intensively in lead and copper, Mathewson in 1916 moved into nickel when he became general manager of the British America Nickel Corporation, with headquarters in Toronto. Two years later he became director and consulting metallurgist of the American Smelting and Refining Company in New York City. Soon, however, he opened his own consulting office in New York, which he maintained until 1926, when he was named professor of administration of mineral industries at the University of Arizona, a position he held until retirement in 1942.

Mathewson's stature in the profession was recognized by honorary degrees from McGill University and the Colorado School of Mines; by a decoration from the Japanese government; by gold medals of achievement from the Institution of Mining and Metallurgy (London, 1911) and the Mining and Metallurgical Society of America (1917); and by election to the presidency of the American Institute of Mining and Metallurgical Engineers in 1923. A popular man, civic-minded and moderate in his attitudes toward labor, Mathewson was a Republican and an Episcopalian. He was an amateur archaeologist and was interested in wildlife. On June 25, 1890, he married Alice Barry. They

had six children: Alice Seabury, Grace, Marymet, Gertrude, Elizabeth, and Edward Payson. Mathewson died of arteriosclerotic heart disease at his home in Tucson, Ariz. Following cremation, his ashes were scattered over Mount Lemmon near Tucson.

[On Mathewson, see *Tucson Daily Citizen*, July 14, 1948; *Arizona Daily Star*, July 14, 1948; *N.Y. Times*, July 15, 1948; *Who's Who in Eng.* (1937); *Who's Who in Am.* 1944–1945; *Mining and Metallurgy*, Sept. 1948; *Metal Progress*, Aug. 1939; *Eng. Mining Jour.*, Mar. 17, 1917, June 12, 1920; Mining and Metallurgical Soc. of America, *Bull.*, Sept. 1948; *Nat. Cyc. Am Biog.*, vol. C, pp. 41–42; Thomas A. Rickard, *Interviews with Mining Engineers*, pp. 335–353 (1922); death record from Ariz. State Dept. of Health. Pertinent information was also provided by the family. Mathewson's technical diaries are at the Western Hist. Research Center, Univ. of Wyo., Laramie.]

CLARK C. SPENCE

MATTHES, FRANÇOIS EMILE (Mar. 16, 1874-June 21, 1948), geologist, was born in Amsterdam, the Netherlands, to parents who both came of old, distinguished families. He was one of twin sons of Willem Ernst Matthes, who was a prosperous dealer in such colonial products as rubber and hemp, and Johanna Suzanna (van der Does de Bije) Matthes, a brilliant woman. At the family's stately mansion facing a canal, numerous social functions were held. They vacationed at coastal and mountain resorts in France and Spain. François and his brother, Gerard Hendrik, shared instruction in art and drafting. François's precocity, particularly in sketching animals, amazed everyone.

At about the age of ten, the twins were taken to Switzerland to recover from malaria (then endemic in the Netherlands) and to gain a cosmopolitan education. Their father taught them map-reading as together they explored in the Alps. At Chamonix, France, they marveled at the awesome glacial crevasses.

In 1887 the twins entered an *Oberrealschule* at Frankfurt am Main in preparation for an engineering course in Germany. Instead, in 1891, they immigrated to the United States, where both matriculated at the Massachusetts Institute of Technology, majoring in civil engineering. After graduating with honors in 1895, receiving B.S. degrees, they became American citizens. Gerard embarked on a successful career in hydrographic engineering, and François in topographic mapping.

François's first position was draftsman for the city of Rutland, Vt., where he made topographic surveys. In 1896 he joined the U.S. Geological Survey, with which he remained for fifty-one years. Initially a topographic assistant, in 1898 he was named party chief to survey the Cloud Peak quadrangle, in the then-trackless Big Horn Mountains of Wyoming. Promoted to full topographer (1899), he mapped other challenging areas: the Blackfoot Reservation and the Chief Mountain and Browning quadrangles in Montana; and the Bradshaw Mountains and Jerome quadrangles in Arizona. On the Cloud Peak and Chief Mountain quadrangles, Matthes delineated with consummate artistry alpine landforms resulting from severe glaciation. His work later gave telling impetus to the establishment in 1910 of Glacier National Park.

In 1902 Matthes began mapping the scenically remarkable upper half of the Grand Canyon of the Colorado River, Arizona (now Grand Canyon National Park). Two years of field-work produced the Bright Angel and Vishnu quadrangles, maps of surpassing excellence. Matthes spent the academic year 1904-1905 doing graduate work at Harvard in geomorphic studies under William Morris Davis. But he left before receiving a degree to undertake the large-scale (1:24,000) mapping of the sublime Yosemite Valley. He worked out a system to express in contour lines the overhanging curves and arches of the valley. After two years he produced the exquisite "Yosemite Special" map (1907). The San Francisco earthquake of 1906, which he witnessed, led to a unique assignment: to map the San Andreas Fault in northern California. As inspector of maps (1907-1913), he supervised other topographers and also surveyed the southwestern part of Mount Rainier National Park.

On June 7, 1911, Matthes married Edith Lovell Coyle, a librarian, who became his devoted companion and indefatigable assistant. They had no children.

Matthes' marvelous draftsmanship, exemplified by his national park maps, has probably never been equaled. His success stemmed from his keen analysis of landforms and insistent endeavor to comprehend them. Extensive writing and lecturing further contributed to a momentous decision: to devote himself wholly to geomorphology. In 1913 he was transferred to the Geologic Branch of the Survey. Fortuitously, his first geologic assignment was to study the origin of Yosemite Valley. Not until 1930 was his monograph on Yosemite published. It received immediate acclaim as a great classic. To understand Yosemite, Matthes extended his investigations throughout the Sierra Nevada. However, from 1928 to 1934 he was diverted to Mississippi Valley problems. In 1935, happily,

he was reassigned to California—to Sequoia National Park. Renewed research demonstrated that the great eastern escarpment of the Sierra Nevada had resulted from early Pleistocene faulting. He considered this discovery his foremost geological contribution.

After 1937, demanding organizational responsibilities confined Matthes largely to Washington. While chairing the Committee on Glaciers of the American Geophysical Union (1932-1946), he developed a cooperative international program for study of existing glaciers. In 1939 he was drafted as secretary of the International Association of Scientific Hydrology, because of his linguistic versatility. During both world wars, he engaged in military geology. Nevertheless, he wrote two important works, a monumental treatise on glaciers and a critical reexamination of the glacial anticyclone theory. Little time remained for Sierra studies.

Matthes was decorated by King Albert of the Belgians (1920) and was president of the Geological Society of Washington (1932) and the American Association of Geographers (1933). Two Yosemite features bear his name: Matthes Crest and Matthes Lake; the twelve-mile-long Matthes Glacier is located in the Alaska Coast Mountains. Small stature belied Matthes' remarkable capacity for rugged explorations. He was tenacious and uncompromising, impelled by a tremendous inner drive to achieve his rigorous standards. In style, his writings were distinguished by rare clarity and charm.

In 1947 Matthes retired and with his wife moved to El Cerrito, Calif. Writing was scarcely resumed when he suffered a heart attack and died at the age of seventy-four. He was cremated and his ashes were scattered in Yosemite Valley. Matthes was unique in attaining distinction in both topography and geology. Dignified and courteous, he seemed shy and aloof to some, but among kindred spirits he glowed with enthusiasm. Sharing his scientific findings with the public—as in the national parks—delighted him. He was always mindful of "those who love the mountains, particularly those who come to see, and seeing, wonder and wish to understand."

[Much information about Matthes' parents, early life, and education is given in *Memorial to Gerard Hendrik Matthes (1874-1959)*, by David E. Donley, privately published by Mrs. G. H. Matthes in 1960. François Matthes' personal papers are in the Bancroft Lib., Univ. of Calif., Berkeley. His official papers are in the archives of the U.S. Geological Survey, Federal Building, Denver, Colo. The most comprehensive biography is by Matthes' literary executor, Fritiof Fryxell, *Proceedings* volume of the Geolog. Soc. of America, Annual Report for 1955, which gives a detailed bibliography of Matthes' writings. This biography was reprinted in the posthumous volume *François Matthes and the Marks of Time* (1962). Personal mementos are in the Yosemite Museum. Marble busts of the Matthes twins at the age of five, by German sculptor Robert Cauer, are in the Denkmann Memorial Lib., Augustana College, Rock Island, Ill.]

FRITIOF FRYXELL

MATTHIESSEN, FRANCIS OTTO (Feb. 19, 1902-Apr. 1, 1950), teacher, literary critic, and scholar, was born in Pasadena, Calif., the third son and fourth and youngest child of Frederic William Matthiessen, Jr., and Lucy Orne (Pratt) Matthiessen. Matthiessen's grandfather, Frederich Wilhelm Matthiessen, arrived in New York around 1850 as a penniless German immigrant and moved to La Salle, Ill., where he married a Danish girl whose family had immigrated at about the same time; he became the leading citizen of the town and mayor for ten years. He died in 1918 in his eighties, the owner of the Big Ben alarm clock factory and approximately $10 million. Frederic William, Jr., who never settled down to a regular career, met Lucy Orne Pratt, of seventeenth-century New England descent and a distant relative of the novelist Sarah Orne Jewett, at a West Coast resort and married her soon afterward at her home in Springfield, Mass. The family moved frequently, but Lucy Matthiessen and her children often lived at the Matthiessen, Sr., house in La Salle. As an adult, F. O. Matthiessen thought of himself as a "small-town boy" and "from the mid-west."

After attending Hackley School, Tarrytown, N.Y. (1914-1918) and spending a very brief period in the Canadian Royal Air Force, Matthiessen entered Yale in 1919, where he suddenly experienced "the giddy sensation of a limitless domain opening up before" him. Nearly all his activities at Yale forecast interests that were to continue throughout his life: the *Daily News,* the *Literary Magazine,* Dwight Hall (the university religious society), the Bible Study Committee, the Liberal Club, student dramatics, the Elizabethan Club, and Skull and Bones. The class of 1923 chose him orator and deacon, and recognized him as the member of the class who had "done most" for Yale and who had worked hardest. He was also elected to Phi Beta Kappa and awarded a Rhodes scholarship, which he took at New College, Oxford, where he received a B.Litt. in English in 1925. (Despite the tradition that Rhodes scholars should show athletic prowess, Matthiessen's only sports were represented by a hard-won prep-school letter in track and some

rowing in college. He later played an aggressive game of deck tennis.)

The rapidity with which Matthiessen finished his graduate work at Harvard (M.A. 1926 and Ph.D. 1927) reflected not only his intelligence and hard work but also his impatience with the usual teaching and the official requirements for the study of English. He was not much interested in purely factual information or in technical expertise and attempts at "scientific" measurement and codification. He was primarily concerned with achieving and communicating the experience of literature, literature conceived both as works of art and as the creation of individuals living in a specific society at a particular time. He valued his study of Greek and Latin at Yale and he was inspired by the teaching of Robert French. When he was not allowed to work on Chaucer at Oxford because his linguistic training was not considered adequate, he did what he considered a "finger exercise" on Oliver Goldsmith, a study which he never considered publishing. In his doctoral dissertation at Harvard, published in a revised version as *Translation: An Elizabethan Art* (1931), he put to good use his knowledge of the classics and his enthusiasm for Elizabethan prose and the problems of communicating past experience in a new language. But the man who was to change the direction of the study of American literature took only one formal course in that area—a seminar with Kenneth B. Murdock in early American historiography.

In later years, Matthiessen claimed that he learned the most important things outside of graduate school, from, for example, his introduction by Maxwell Evarts Foster and Phelps Putnam to the sounds of T. S. Eliot's poetry and from the extraordinary insights into the life of a working artist that he received from the painter Russell Cheney; he had met Cheney on the ship on his return to England in 1924, shortly after the death of Matthiessen's mother. Their friendship was almost instantaneous; their attachment also proved to be deep and lifelong. They were together in Europe and in Santa Fe, and they later shared a house in Kittery, Maine, during the summers, until Cheney's death in 1945. *Russell Cheney, 1881-1945: A Record of His Work* (1947) concentrates on the painter and the painting, but the quoted letters give a sense of Cheney's extraordinary charm, literacy, and liveliness as well as taste. The volume was, in part, Matthiessen's tribute to the closest personal relationship of his life.

In 1927 Matthiessen returned to Yale, where for two years he was an English instructor. His first book, *Sarah Orne Jewett* (1929), an impressionistic study illustrated by Cheney, revealed both Matthiessen's reaction against traditional scholarship and his discovery of the beauties of coastal Maine. His decision to go to Harvard in 1929 was influenced by the possibilities of the undergraduate honors field of history and literature and by Harvard's commitment both to the study of literature within its cultural contexts and to the tutorial system. He remained at Harvard for the rest of his life (instructor, 1929-1930; assistant professor, 1930-1934; and associate professor, 1934-1942), both as a member of the English department and as tutor and guiding spirit (usually chairman or secretary of the Board of Tutors) in history and literature; he was made professor of history and literature in 1942. The influential Harvard doctoral program in American studies was in some respects a natural development of the undergraduate field of American history and literature, and Matthiessen was committed to it. His chief courses at Harvard were in American literature, criticism of poetry, Shakespeare, and forms of drama. He did not usually give formal lectures, but spoke more or less spontaneously on the issues that a fresh review of the primary literary texts revealed as the most important at the time. The method resulted in occasionally disorganized or tensely depressing classes and in others which were brilliant, conveying a unique sense of personal conviction and an implicit demand for response and commitment. As a tutor—he was the first senior tutor at Eliot House—Matthiessen was interested in his students' responses and insisted on their authenticity. Whether in tutorial or classes he was often formidable and had a profound influence on a large number of brilliant students, ranging from James Agee, C. L. Barber, and Harry Levin to Leo Marx, Richard Wilbur, and Robert Coles, many of whom became close personal friends.

During the late 1930's and 1940's "Matty's" elegant dinners at his Pinckney Street apartment in Boston and his summer houseparties at Kittery were central occasions for a large circle of friends. Most of the group usually had some connection with either history and literature or the Harvard Teachers' Union, but they varied widely in age and political allegiance. At the enormous annual Christmas Eve parties, where all his friends in the area appeared as for a command performance, wives of old Yale friends, graduate students, poets,

a few representatives of old Boston and Cambridge, artists and theater people from New York, godchildren, political activists, all mingled, usually pleasantly, with a few Harvard professors and their families. For most of his students and younger colleagues Matthiessen's homosexuality was suggested, if at all, only by the fact that his circle was more predominantly heterosexual than was usual in Harvard literary groups of the time and that he was unusually hostile to homosexual colleagues who mixed their academic and sexual relations.

His publications suggest the chief aesthetic and ethical concerns of Matthiessen's last fifteen years. *The Achievement of T. S. Eliot: An Essay on the Nature of Poetry* (1935; enlarged edition, 1947), stimulated in part by Eliot's appointment as Norton professor at Harvard in 1932, was the first substantial book on Eliot published in either America or England, and it helped establish Eliot's importance for modern poetry and criticism. Matthiessen's masterpiece, *American Renaissance: Art and Expression in the Age of Emerson and Whitman* (1941), attempted, as Henry Nash Smith remarked, "a synthesis of a theory of art (the organic principle), a theory of tragedy, and a thoroughgoing democratic political theory" (Sweezy and Huberman, p. 59); it also defined the major figures and works of nineteenth-century American literature and made it difficult for "American Studies" to ignore the imagination. Matthiessen was one of the leaders in the revival of interest in Henry James, as author of *Henry James: The Major Phase* (1944) and *The James Family* (1947), and editor of *Stories of Writers and Artists* (1944), *The American Novels and Stories* (1947), and, with Kenneth B. Murdock, *The Notebooks* (1947). He saw James as an artist concerned with society and ethics as well as with the individual and aesthetics. The University of Toronto's invitation to him to give the Alexander Lectures in 1944, Princeton's honorary D.Litt. in 1947, and his election to the National Institute of Arts and Letters and as a senior fellow of the Kenyon School of English (1948) were recognitions of his achievement as critic and scholar.

Most of his writings clearly reflect a life larger than the "academic"—a word which, like "gentleman," Matthiessen often used in a pejorative sense. He thought of himself as a socialist from the time he was at Oxford, and he was a leading spirit of the Harvard Teachers' Union and the Massachusetts Civil Liberties Union. He worked for or supported numbers of liberal, pacifist, or radical causes, including the National Citizens Political Action Committee of 1944 and the Progressive party of 1948, and he helped in the founding of the *Monthly Review* (1949). His memoir-journal *From the Heart of Europe* (1948) suggests that the high point of his senses of fulfillment as a teacher, of involvement in a larger world, and of political and social hope may have come in the summer and fall of 1947, when he taught in the first session of the Salzburg Seminar in American Studies and at Charles University in Prague. But the happiness was brief: before this memoir was published, the Communists had seized the government of Czechoslovakia, which he saw as trying to bridge the differences between East and West, and his friend Jan Masaryk was dead.

The last years of Matthiessen's life were saddened by the death of his father (whom he had only come really to know and like a few years before), the death of Russell Cheney in 1945, and the death of two poets, Phelps Putnam, a longtime friend of the Yale group, and Theodore Spencer, who had entered graduate school at Harvard with Matthiessen in 1925 and was later one of his most valued colleagues. Matthiessen had long been alienated from the central powers at Harvard; but with the conservatism and hysteria of the Cold War period, he came to feel increasingly isolated from both students and younger colleagues alike. Earlier, while working on *American Renaissance,* he suffered a partial breakdown; in the last years his bouts of depression became frequent and intense. He was on leave from teaching during the academic year 1949-1950, and he found oppressive both the absence of students and his work on a study of Theodore Dreiser. (He was dissatisfied with the manuscript, which was published posthumously in 1951.) On Apr. 1, 1950, he leaped to his death from the twelfth floor of the Manger Hotel in Boston. He left a note in which he wrote, "I am exhausted. I have been subject to so many severe depressions during the past few years that I can no longer believe that I can continue to be of use to my profession and my friends. . . . How much the state of the world has to do with my state of mind I do not know. But as a Christian and a socialist believing in international peace, I find myself terribly oppressed by the present tensions." Matthiessen was a communicant of the Episcopal church; his funeral was at Christ Church in Cambridge. His ashes were buried, according to his request, beside his mother in Springfield, Mass.

At the time of his death Matthiessen had just completed correcting the galleys of his edition of *The Oxford Book of American Verse* (1950), a careful and bold labor of love that both Allen Tate and e. e. cummings thought contained the best selections of their poems any anthologist had made. *The Responsibilities of the Critic: Essays and Reviews,* selected and edited by John B. Rackliffe (1952), indicates the breadth and excellence of Matthiessen's uncollected critical pieces.

[Aside from his own writings, the most important biographical source is *F. O. Matthiessen (1902–1950): A Collective Portrait,* ed. Paul M. Sweezy and Leo Huberman, originally published as the Oct. 1950 issue of *Monthly Review.* It contains essays and statements by thirty-four of Matthiessen's friends, colleagues, students, and acquaintances, as well as some good photographs. Most of his papers and letters are in the Beinecke Lib., Yale, or in the possession of Louis K. Hyde, Jr. *Who's Who in Am., 1950–1951* and *Harvard Univ. Gazette,* Nov. 18, 1950, are full and generally accurate. For details we have also drawn on personal recollections. More recent critical evaluations of Matthiessen's work and career include those of Richard Ruland in *The Rediscovery of Am. Literature* (1967), Giles Gunn, "The American Scholar at Work: The Critical Achievement of F. O. Matthiessen; a Study in Religious Interpretation" (Ph.D. diss., Univ. of Chicago, 1967), and George Abbot White, "Ideology and Literature: *American Renaissance* and F. O. Matthiessen," in *Literature in Revolution,* ed. White and Charles Newman (1972).]

JOSEPH H. SUMMERS
U. T. MILLER SUMMERS

MAURIN, PETER ARISTIDE (May 9, 1877-May 15, 1949), cofounder, with Dorothy Day, of the Catholic Worker movement, was born in the mountain village of Oultet in the Gévaudan area of Languedoc, southern France. He was the first of three surviving children of Jean Baptiste Maurin, a farmer, and Marie (Pages) Maurin. His mother died when he was seven, and two years later the father married again, his second wife bearing him nineteen children. It was a well-ordered family, secure in a tradition that came from centuries of Maurin ownership of the land on which they lived. Years later Maurin would exclaim, "I am neither a bourgeois nor a proletariat. I am a peasant. I have roots!"

At fourteen Maurin entered a boarding school near Paris run by the Christian Brothers, a Catholic teaching order. He became a novice in the order in 1893, received a teaching license two years later, and for the next eight years taught at elementary schools in and near Paris. Like many other young Catholics at the time, Maurin became increasingly interested in social questions and joined Le Sillon (The Furrow), a Catholic youth movement that sought to support the rise of democratic forces as consonant with the essential spirit of Catholicism.

On Jan. 1, 1903, at the expiration of his annual religious vow, he left the Christian Brothers and devoted himself to Le Sillon. His ardor cooled, however, after several years, a fact that his biographer attributes to Maurin's desire for a more scholarly approach to social problems, as against the Sillonist propensity for parades and oratory.

In 1909 Maurin immigrated to Saskatchewan, Canada, attracted by the prospect of free land. When his partner in a homesteading venture was accidentally killed, he gave up the undertaking and took laboring jobs such as harvesting wheat and working in a stone quarry. In 1911, nearly penniless, he entered the United States, and for the next several years "rode the rails," working occasionally in coal mines and sawmills and on railroad gangs. He finally settled in Chicago, where he became a janitor. During the 1920s he began giving French lessons and soon had a number of pupils. In 1926 he moved to Woodstock, N.Y., taught French for a time at the art colony there, and then settled as caretaker at a nearby Catholic boys' camp.

At about this time Maurin apparently underwent a religious experience that gave him a new sense of the significance of the Catholic church in his social philosophy. Although inactive in the church during his years of wandering, he had spent much time reading and pondering the question of community in a world increasingly impersonalized by technology and institutions. He now refused to accept fees for his French lessons and began to lead group discussions of his ideas. His primary aim was to restore the communal aspects of Christianity. Maurin opposed capitalism, nationalism, and other bourgeois values that emphasized competitive striving and the acquisition of "things." He was distressed by the inability of scholars and workers to communicate with each other and favored a cooperative world where ideas and labor would be shared. Influenced by the European "personalist" writers, Maurin believed that man could be made good only by change in his individual personality, not through social engineering. His philosophy has been described as a blend of medieval Catholicism, romantic agrarianism, and the anarchism of Kropotkin. He preached a "Green Revolution" and hoped to see people abandon the complexity of cities and machines and return to the simplicity of subsistence agriculture and handcrafts. "My whole scheme," he wrote, "is a Utopian, Christian Communism" (Sheehan, p. 97).

In 1932 Maurin met Dorothy Day, a Catholic convert and radical journalist, who saw in his philosophy a way to relate her social concern to her new religious faith. Maurin gave her an intensive course of religious and historical instruction, and under his inspiration she founded a monthly periodical, the *Catholic Worker,* around which grew the loose association of programs known as the Catholic Worker movement. The first issue, published on May 1, 1933, was distributed among the unemployed radicals who gathered at Union Square; by the end of the year it had reached a circulation of 100,000.

Maurin's program had three aspects: public discussion, in which a mutual interaction of ideas would lead to what he called a "clarification"; urban hospitality houses, where the poor could receive food and lodging; and communal farms, to be operated on the principles of shared capital and distribution to the needy of any surplus. By 1940 the movement had spread to most major American cities; there were then over forty houses and twelve farms in existence, all autonomously operated, and the *Catholic Worker* had reached a circulation of over 150,000. Maurin's vision of direct, personal action in meeting social problems inspired many followers, but the Catholic Worker movement by its nature had no strict organization or set of beliefs. Although Maurin opposed labor unions and liberal reform movements like the New Deal, which he felt merely served to perpetuate the capitalist system, Dorothy Day and other leaders helped in unionizing efforts and lent aid in a number of strikes, and the *Catholic Worker* gave editorial support to most of the New Deal's domestic programs. There was general agreement, however, on opposing military preparedness and war. This worker pacifism caused some loss of influence during World War II, but the movement survived, and remained a major influence on the mind and life of the Catholic church in America.

Maurin was short and stocky. He cared little for money or what it could buy, wore old and disheveled clothes, and seldom had a penny in his pocket. He never married. In 1944 he began to develop symptoms of arteriosclerosis. Complaining that "I can no longer think," he retired to a communal farm in Newburgh, N.Y., where he died five years later. He was buried in St. John's Cemetery, Queens, New York City, in a cast-off suit and in a grave provided by a Dominican priest. At the time of his death, Dorothy Day said of him: "He taught us what it meant to be sons of God, and restored us to our sense of responsibility in a chaotic world. . . . He was . . . holier than anyone we ever knew."

[Arthur Sheehan, *Peter Maurin: Gay Believer* (1959), is the only biography. Dorothy Day has extended references to Maurin in most of her books; see especially *The Long Loneliness* (1952) and *Loaves and Fishes* (1963). Maurin was not essentially a writer, but he tried to put down his thoughts in a free-verse form that he thought would call attention to his ideas. Catholic Worker people called these verses "Easy Essays"; published collections are *Easy Essays* (1936), *Catholic Radicalism* (1949), revised in 1961 under the title *The Green Revolution*, and *Radical Christian Thought,* ed. by Chuck Smith (1971). The fullest source of information on Maurin is the files of the *Catholic Worker,* which includes many interpretive essays on his thought, as well as character sketches of him. See also William D. Miller, *A Harsh and Dreadful Love: Dorothy Day and the Catholic Worker Movement* (1972); and chapters on the Catholic Worker movement in David J. O'Brien, *Am. Catholics and Social Reform* (1968), and Neil B. Betten, "Catholicism and the Industrial Worker during the Great Depression" (Ph.D. diss., Univ. of Minn., 1968).]

WILLIAM D. MILLER

MAXWELL, GEORGE HEBARD (June 3, 1860–Dec. 1, 1946), lawyer and conservationist, was born in Sonoma, Calif., the first of three children of John Morgan Maxwell and Clara Love (Hebard) Maxwell. His mother was born in Ashtabula, Ohio; her parents had been early settlers in the Western Reserve; his father, born in Stonington, Conn., spent several years in Atlanta, Ga., before going in 1849 via New Orleans and Panama to California, where he worked in the mines until 1858. He then settled on the Sonoma Valley farm where his son was born. The farm continued in the family, and Maxwell returned to it often, especially in summer.

Maxwell was educated in the public schools and at St. Matthew's Hall, a military academy in nearby San Mateo. He became an official court stenographer for the federal circuit court in San Francisco and, after reading law in the office of Judge Mesick, was admitted to the California bar in 1882. As a member of the firm of Mesick and Maxwell, he became a recognized expert on water rights. He helped farmers establish private irrigation organizations but became aware of their limitations without government assistance. Whether such assistance should be state or federal was one of the much-argued questions of the 1890's. In December 1896 Maxwell attended the seventh annual meeting of the National Irrigation Congress in Phoenix, Ariz., and there, as he later confessed, became convinced that a national program was the answer. He had started the *California Advocate,* a monthly devoted to irrigation, but soon changed its name to the *National Advocate.* In 1899 he gave up his law practice, organized and became executive direc-tor of the National Irrigation Association, and began an energetic writing and speaking campaign to enlist support for a national irrigation program.

At the National Irrigation Congress in Chicago in November 1900, Maxwell and Francis G. Newlands, then congressman from Nevada, made notable speeches outlining proposed national legislation. Maxwell and Frederick H. Newell drafted a bill that Newlands introduced in the House, and Senator Henry Clay Hansbrough in the Senate, in January 1901. Both spoke frequently in the series of hearings that followed. Congress was reluctant until President Theodore Roosevelt, using memoranda prepared by Maxwell and Newell, strongly endorsed the Newlands bill and called for speedy action. Credit for the Reclamation Act of 1902 must be divided, but Maxwell's strenuous speaking campaigns helped swing Eastern businessmen and political leaders to its support.

Maxwell's next important contribution to a national irrigation program was his organization of the Salt River Valley Water Users' Association in Arizona. The valley farmers wanted a federal project; this meant taking over existing canal corporations and smoothing out tangled and snarled water rights, which Maxwell, as an experienced lawyer, understood. Also, the federal government felt it could not deal with individuals but must deal with an organized cooperative body of water users. Maxwell carefully drafted articles of incorporation for such an organization and persuaded the water users to adopt them in 1903. The Salt River project got off to an early start and became a model. Of the first twenty-six federal irrigation projects in the West, no less than twenty-three required the formation of a water users' association, and the Salt River pattern and even Maxwell's language were freely copied.

Meanwhile, his interests had broadened to include drainage, flood-control projects, and river regulation in general, and he persuaded the National Irrigation Association to change its name to the National Reclamation Association to reflect this wider concern. He spent much time in New Orleans in 1911-1912 promoting drainage projects on the lower Mississippi and worked unsuccessfully to get legislation enacted that would permit the Bureau of Reclamation to take on drainage, as well as irrigation, projects. At the New Orleans National Drainage Congress in 1912, he insisted that to control Mississippi River floods the levee system below St. Louis must be supplemented by a great national system for head-waters control on all tributaries. As executive director of the Pittsburgh Flood Commission (1908-1911), Maxwell drafted plans for the upper Ohio tributaries that he hoped would lessen Ohio River floods and thus those of the Mississippi. Later, as a member of the Ohio State Water Conservation Board, he initiated what he regarded as a model program for the Muskingum River watershed. He fought a continuous battle with the Army Corps of Engineers, whose programs he felt were not comprehensive enough. From 1912 on, he spent much time in Washington working closely with Newlands, by then an influential senator, on river regulation legislation, but results were disappointing. In 1917 an amendment to the Rivers and Harbors Act established a National Waterways Commission with broad powers, but no appointments to the commission were made, despite many letters and conferences on Maxwell's part. The act continued inoperative until, in Maxwell's words, it was "entombed" in the Waterpower Act of 1919.

Another lifelong interest of Maxwell's was getting workers in industry into contact with the soil. He advocated municipal weekend gardens for city dwellers and suburban cooperative homecroft living, a "homecroft" being a one-acre garden home. He organized the American Homecroft Society as early as 1907 and published its monthly journal, *Talisman*. He was a strong supporter of Eleanor Roosevelt's "subsistence homesteads" program. His ideas contributed to other New Deal programs, notably the Soil Conservation Service and the Civilian Conservation Corps, but poor health after 1930 did not permit him to participate actively. His many causes were set forth in several books, the best probably being his *Golden Rivers and Treasure Valleys: Wealth From Wasted Waters* (1929).

Maxwell's last ten years were spent in retirement in Phoenix, Ariz., and a paralyzing stroke left him bedridden for several years before his death in Phoenix at eighty-six years of age. His first wife, Katharine Vaughan Lanpher of San Francisco, whom he married on Oct. 28, 1880, died in 1934. They had a son, Donald, and a daughter, Ruth. On June 3, 1935, he married Lilly Belle Richardson, who survived him. His ashes were interred in the family plot at Mountain Cemetery in Sonoma Valley in 1948.

[Certain records of the Washington, D.C., office of the Nat. Reclamation Assn. were turned over to the Bureau of Reclamation and are now with the older bureau records in the Nat. Archives. They include many boxes of Maxwell's correspondence, some thirty-two volumes of clippings, press releases, drafts of speeches, and an incomplete file of his publications. The Nat. Water Resources Assn. in Washington has important correspondence about Maxwell's later years, and a 365-page draft of an unpublished biography prepared in the Bureau of Reclamation. There are over 500 of Maxwell's letters in the papers of Francis G. Newlands at the Yale Univ. Lib., plus copies of Newlands' letters to him. See also George Wharton James, *Reclaiming the Arid West* (1917); Samuel P. Hays, *Conservation and the Gospel of Efficiency* (1959); Henry Clepper, *Leaders of American Conservation* (1971); *Who Was Who in Am.*, II (1950), and obituaries in the *Evening Star* (Washington) Dec. 2, 1946, and *N.Y. Times*, Dec. 3, 1946.]
OLIVER W. HOLMES

MAYO, GEORGE ELTON (Dec. 26, 1880-Sept. 1, 1949), teacher and researcher in the social sciences, was born in Adelaide, Australia, the second child and oldest son of seven children of George Gibbes Mayo and Henrietta Mary (Donaldson) Mayo. His father was an engineer, but other members of the family through several generations attained prominence in medicine and law. Few facts are available about Mayo's early life. That he possessed a brilliant and inquiring mind seems to have been recognized early. His schooling began at home. When he was twelve, he went to Queen's College, Adelaide, and at fourteen to St. Peter's College, his father's school, where he won the Westminster Classical Scholarship in 1895. In 1897, Mayo entered the University of Adelaide to study medicine, but after a short time the routine aspects of the training began to bore him. In 1901 his parents sent him to the medical school first at the University of Edinburgh and then at St. George's Hospital, London; however, his interest in medicine as a career did not revive. He tried journalism in London and on the Continent and later accepted a position in Obuasi on the Gold Coast in West Africa (now Ghana), but was forced to return to London because of ill health. Mayo lectured at the Working Men's College in 1904 and the following year returned to Australia and became a partner in a printing firm. In 1907 he studied philosophy and psychology under William Mitchell and in 1910 received both the B.A. with first-class honors and the M.A. from the University of Adelaide.

During the next twelve years Mayo taught logic, ethics, and psychology, first at Adelaide and then at the University of Queensland, where he became lecturer in 1911. After World War I he was intensely involved in the treatment of returned soldiers who, after long periods in the trenches, suffered from nervous and mental disorders known as shell shock. To the exacting task of treating these patients and systematically reporting his observations in his lectures he brought the traditions of his medical training, familiarity with the newest trends in European psychology, and firsthand observations of life and work in societies on three continents.

At the time European psychology was in ferment. The work of Ivan Pavlov, Jean Martin Charcot, William James, and Paul Bleuler was still fresh; that of Sigmund Freud and Pierre Janet was becoming widely known, as was also the work of the British physiologists, including K. S. Lashley and Sir Charles Sherrington. Mayo's interest was always to place the problems of individuals within the broad context of society as a whole. In line with his medical training he selected from his wide reading those authors whose ideas were based on observation: François Quesnay, Pierre LePlay, Émile Durkheim, and Bronislaw Malinowski were to him more important than better-known philosophers in the academic tradition.

Mayo's lectures and studies in Australia received recognition. In 1919 he was appointed to a newly established chair of philosophy at the University of Queensland. His first book, *Democracy and Freedom,* was published that year, and a second, *Psychology and Religion,* three years later. As a result of his work the British Red Cross made a grant to the University of Queensland to establish a chair of medical psychology, to which it seems he could have been appointed. In 1922, however, he came to the United States, attracted apparently by the greater opportunities to study social and industrial problems. With the aid of a grant from the Rockefeller Foundation, he became a research associate at the University of Pennsylvania from 1923 to 1926.

In 1924-1925 Mayo wrote a series of articles, published in *Harper's,* on the problems of life and work in industrial societies. Most such statements at the time drew primarily on the ideas of economists. On topics in the area of industrial organization the ideas of Frederick W. Taylor—the rationalization of work, efficiency, and time and motion study—had special importance. Mayo's approach was from the perspective of studies and of peripheral groups, such as the mentally disturbed, in industrial societies. Such concepts as nonlogical behavior, social structure, obsessive thinking, reverie, and dreams were prominent in his thinking.

These articles attracted the attention of Wallace Donham, dean of the Harvard University Graduate School of Business Administration, who in 1926 invited Mayo to join the faculty as associate professor of industrial research. Becoming professor in 1929, Mayo remained at Harvard until his retirement in 1947. He was active in the work of the Harvard Fatigue Laboratory, established in 1927 under the direction of Lawrence J. Henderson, a prominent physiologist. Over the next two decades the two men and their associates conducted active research on industrial working conditions; the laboratory focused on physiological problems, and Mayo and his group, on the psychological, organizational, and social aspects.

Shortly after his appointment at Harvard, Mayo became interested in a study of working conditions at the Western Electric Company's Hawthorne plant in Chicago. Company officials were puzzled by the results of an earlier study that revealed that worker productivity increased when plant lighting was either increased or decreased. Mayo suggested that the major variable was not the intensity of the light but the attention that the workers—normally ignored and anonymous—received from those studying them.

This groundbreaking study, which established a pattern for the examination of group behavior, led to a series of studies about the feelings and attitudes of workers and supervisors in relation to their output. Mayo's insights and interpretations guided the development of these studies. He published the first extensive report of them in *The Human Problems of an Industrial Society* (1933). Whether directing studies of factory workers, student mental health problems, or the changes wrought by technology on communities, the intense, chain-smoking Mayo had a strong impact on the social sciences through the numerous colleagues and students he influenced. His belief in the study of social organization as the basis for understanding workers' attitudes, for example, provided the inspiration for the pioneering series, *Yankee City,* which became a five-volume study of a Massachusetts industrial city published between 1941 and 1959 by W. Lloyd Warner and others.

Mayo's best-known book, *The Social Problems of an Industrial Society* (1945), was written toward the end of his professional career and contained his most forceful statement of the ills of modern society. It was a diagnosis, in the medical tradition, based on observation guided by theory. Changes in technology, he wrote, affected more than the technical aspects of work: they also affected the relations of workers with one another and their sense of identity. The managers of organizations, intent on the efficiency of operations, missed these consequences and were not aware that the foundations of cooperation were being eroded without being replaced. They failed to see a connection, Mayo suggested, between the changes they advocated and the conditions of uprootedness, anomie, and loss of identity increasingly characteristic of modern society. The results were manifest, in industrial organizations, in complaints, grievances, absences, labor turnover, and other forms of protest.

Mayo's most complete statement of his views on individual behavior is *Some Notes on the Psychology of Pierre Janet* (1948). Dominant in this book, as in his other writings, is the notion of social skill, which for Mayo began with the capacity to receive a communication from another person; thus, Mayo's interest in the interview, especially in the therapeutic setting.

The skill of listening, in the sense of understanding another's problem from that person's point of view, Mayo found of great importance in clinical work. Like Freud, he found that an understanding of how a troubled person transferred to adulthood the meanings he had learned in childhood often helped the person to change his behavior. Like Janet, Mayo conceived the childhood meanings as oversimplifications of events, overelaborated as applied in later life. So too for Mayo the abstraction of, say, the cost accountant in the factory were too-simple evaluations of the human and social complexities of work on the factory floor, which were in turn elaborated too much when they became the major determinants of action at executive levels. Mayo believed that the emphasis that higher education gave to abstract theory, unrelated to practical knowledge about how events occurred, reinforced the dysfunctional aspects of these patterns of thinking and behaving.

To correct these tendencies Mayo believed that the leaders of organizations needed social skill which could be developed like that of artisans through practice and familiarity, guided by study under the burden of responsibility for results. No concept was more central to Mayo's thought, none more misunderstood. There were many reasons. In Mayo's time and since then, skill in social affairs—especially, but not only, in academic circles—has meant manipulation of others for the leaders' self-interest. In addition, mathematics and abstract thinking, not clinical practice and relevance, were of greater interest in the social sciences. That the best known of

Mayo's studies took place in business also became a factor in the controversies that developed. The professionals who dealt with persons needing help were in many ways separated from business. Common themes in the problems that the two groups encountered and in the methods they used were lost in controversies over the topics that divided them. The Hawthorne studies in particular became a target of these discussions.

Although Mayo's reputation was established around the study of work groups in industry, his main interest was always broadly in the relationship of individuals to society. The behavior of persons, groups, and society were not different topics for him. Mayo approached these as but aspects of one problem. Few men's studies have been acclaimed in as wide a range of disciplines. This has puzzled and misled many students of Mayo's work, who failed to see that it had its own logic, on the basis, to be sure, of his own nontraditional training but also on the basis of the structure of the problems of work and workers as he observed them.

Mayo retired from Harvard in 1947 and returned to England, where he lived at Polesden-Lacey. He married Dorothea McConnel on Apr. 18, 1913. They had two daughters, Patricia and Ruth Gale. He died at a nursing home in Guildford, Surrey, at the age of sixty-eight.

[In preparing this biography I have been assisted by having access, through the courtesy of Dr. R. C. S. Trahair of Latrobe University, to biographical notes written by Elton Mayo's sister Helen, now in the archives of the State Library of South Australia, Adelaide. The most detailed published statement about Mayo's family and early life is in L. F. Urwick, *The Life and Work of Elton Mayo* (1960): however, it contains some inaccuracies. See also *Who's Who in America, 1948–1949*, and the *Harvard Univ. Gazette*, Nov. 19, 1949.

The appendix to *Social Problems* contains a good summary and bibliography of the writings of Mayo and his colleagues for the period from 1926 through 1945. The most complete report of the Hawthorne studies is in F. J. Roethlisberger and W. J. Dickson, *Management and the Worker* (1939). A history of the fatigue laboratory is S. M. Horvath and E. C. Horvath, *Harvard Fatigue Laboratory: Its History and Contributions* (1973). Statements about some of the controversies that developed in connection with Mayo's work, especially the Hawthorne studies, may be found in H. H. Landsberger, *Hawthorne Revisited* (1958); see also Reinhard Bendix and Lloyd H. Fisher, "The Perspectives of Elton Mayo," *Rev. of Economics and Statistics*, Nov. 1949, and George C. Homans, "Some Corrections," *ibid*. For other reviews and appreciations of Mayo's work, see *Fortune*, Nov. 1946, p. 181 (the issue includes a good photograph); and Roethlisberger, *Man-in-Organization* (1968), chapters 19 and 20. There are some unpublished Mayo papers and photographs in the archives of Baker Lib. at the Harvard Business School.]

GEORGE F. F. LOMBARD

MEINZER, OSCAR EDWARD (Nov. 28, 1876-June 14, 1948), geologist, was born on a farm near Davis, Stephenson County, Ill. He was the second son and fourth of six children of William Meinzer and Mary Julia (Meinzer) Meinzer, both natives of Baden, Germany. They were not related. Meinzer's interest in geology began during his boyhood with his discovery of fossil-bearing limestone and the presence of granite boulders in the overlying glacial deposits on the family farm. After attending local schools and nearby Beloit Academy in Wisconsin (1896-1897), he entered Beloit College, from which he received the B.A. degree, magna cum laude, in 1901. He spent the next two years as a school principal in Frankfort, S. Dak., and in 1903 became a teacher of physical science at Lenox College in Hopkinton, Iowa. There he met Alice Breckenridge Crawford, whom he married on Oct. 3, 1906. They had two children, Robert William (adopted in 1913) and Roy Crawford.

While teaching at Lenox College, Meinzer began graduate study in geology at the University of Chicago, at first in summer sessions and then full time for a year (1906-1907). In July 1907 he joined the U.S. Geological Survey as a junior geologist assigned to the investigation of groundwater. In Utah, New Mexico, and Arizona he located water resources that made possible the irrigation and settlement of previously arid valleys. He became chief of the Division of Ground Water in 1913, a post he was to hold until his retirement in 1946.

Meinzer was the leader in transforming the study of groundwater—a previously neglected and poorly financed field—into a science. Earlier work in this area had consisted merely of locating and defining groundwater basins. Meinzer realized that, as water became an increasingly important natural resource, it would be necessary not only to discover underground reservoirs but also to find ways of measuring their storage capacities and their rates of discharge and renewal, and thus arrive at a safe annual yield. It was clear that in some areas this yield was already being exceeded.

Meinzer had a keen, orderly mind and a capacity for hard work. Through experimental investigations in several areas he tried to develop methods of estimating the yield of a particular groundwater basin, but concluded that a better understanding was needed of the basic principles involved. His pursuit of this understanding led to two publications that became standard references, *Outline of Ground-Water Hydrology, with Definitions* (1923), in which he sought to establish a uniform terminology, and *The Occurrence of Ground Water in the United States, with a Discussion of Principles* (1923). The latter was accepted as a dissertation by the University of Chicago, which awarded Meinzer the Ph.D., magna cum laude, in 1922.

Meinzer also established a hydrologic laboratory, where, along with other experiments, he was able to prove that as long as the flow of water through granular material is laminar, the velocity is directly proportional to the hydraulic gradient—that is, the flow conforms to Darcy's law. For field investigations, he proposed and encouraged the development of geophysical techniques and such instruments as automatic water-stage recorders on wells. He was in the vanguard in urging pumping and other analytical tests on wells to obtain quantitative information on the properties of aquifers (water-bearing strata of permeable rocks). Meinzer also directed studies of the chemical quality and geochemistry of water—such as the process by which water is naturally softened and the source of such elements as fluoride—as well as problems of saltwater encroachment in aquifers. A report prepared by John S. Brown under Meinzer's supervision introduced to this country the Ghyben-Herzberg formula to estimate the extent of saltwater encroachment in aquifers in which fresh water is in dynamic equilibrium with seawater.

Meinzer's quantitative methods were put to a practical test in 1925 in Roswell, N.Mex., where a decline in pressure in the artesian basin threatened the surrounding agricultural community. It was found that his methods gave an accurate estimate of the safe annual yield. The droughts of the early 1930's and the onset of World War II greatly increased the demand for groundwater investigations. Meinzer and his assistants trained and supervised dozens of geologists and engineers, many of whom helped develop the more sophisticated tools, methodology, and techniques of modern groundwater hydrology. Meinzer was the recognized father of the science of groundwater hydrology.

Meinzer was an active member of many scientific societies, and was president of the Society of Economic Geologists (1945) and the American Geophysical Union (1947-1948), whose Bowie Medal he received in 1943. He enjoyed working with young people. For many years he taught boys' classes at Sherwood Presbyterian Church in Washington, and he was an active leader in the Boy Scouts. He found recreation in travel and in his dairy farm in Virginia. He died of a coronary occlusion at his Washington home and was buried in Fort Lincoln Cemetery.

[The fullest account of Meinzer's career is the memoir by A. Nelson Sayre in the Geological Soc. of America, *Proc.*, 1949; it includes a photograph of Meinzer and a bibliography of his more than 100 publications. Briefer obituaries by the same author appear in the Am. Geophysical Union, *Trans.*, Aug. 1948; and the Washington Acad. of Sci., *Jour.*, Apr. 15, 1949. See also *Who Was Who in America*, II (1950). Family information from the federal census of 1880 courtesy of Ill. State Arch.]

V. T. STRINGFIELD

MELLON, WILLIAM LARIMER (June 1, 1868–Oct. 8, 1949), oil entrepreneur and executive, was born in East Liberty, near Pittsburgh, Pa., the eldest of the three children of James Ross Mellon, a supplier of building materials, and Rachel Hughey (Larimer) Mellon. Both parents came of prominent Pittsburgh families. William's paternal grandfather, Judge Thomas Mellon, of Scots-Irish descent, founded in 1870 the Pittsburgh banking house that initiated the family fortune. Andrew W. Mellon, industrialist and secretary of the treasury (1921-1932), was William's uncle. The boy was educated in public and private schools in Pittsburgh and at the Pennsylvania Military Academy in Chester. He started his business career as a shipping clerk in the family's lumber business. At the age of nineteen he took advantage of this connection to build houses on speculation.

In 1889 Mellon became interested in the oil industry, which was then centered in western Pennsylvania. After briefly negotiating oil leases for his uncles Richard and Andrew, who now ran the family bank, he obtained their support to go into the business for himself at Hookstown, Pa. Within two years he was producing, buying, and selling petroleum and owned a large number of tank cars. Most of this petroleum was sold to Standard Oil, which dominated the refining business. Wishing to escape rising rail rates and dependence on Standard, Mellon decided to build his own pipeline to the seaboard, to refine his own oil, and to sell it to foreign customers. In 1892, financed by his uncles, he built a pipeline from Gregg Station near Pittsburgh to a refinery and shipping site he had acquired at Marcus Hook, Pa., on the Delaware River. By the end of 1893 he had created a small integrated oil business, catering to French and English customers. Standard Oil was anxious to eliminate this competition, and, with a sur-

plus of oil overhanging the market, the Mellons sold their oil business to the Rockefeller firm in 1895.

William Mellon then became an "outside man" for his family's bank, investigating new investment opportunities. On Mar. 11, 1896, he married May Hill Taylor, the daughter of a New York entrepreneur. They had four children: William Larimer, Matthew Taylor, Margaret, and Rachel. In the late 1890's, Mellon began building, acquiring, and developing street railway systems in the Pittsburgh area. He left this occupation in 1902 to work for his uncles, who were concerned about their oil investments in Texas.

The Spindletop field on the Texas Gulf Coast had given a new impetus to the oil industry the previous year, and the Mellons had invested in the J. M. Guffey Petroleum Company, headed by a well-known Pennsylvania oil wildcatter, Col. James M. Guffey. But Guffey was far more adept at finding oil than he was at managing oil companies. Mellon soon found that extensive changes were required to protect the investors' stake in the Guffey company and its associated refining operation, Gulf Refining Company of Texas. Appointed executive vice-president of these firms, he demonstrated a keen ability to select talented executives and weld them into an efficient management team.

The decline of the Texas Gulf oil field in 1905-1906 threatened the Guffey companies with bankruptcy for lack of crude oil. To reach the new, flush pools in Oklahoma Territory required millions of dollars in additional financing. On Mellon's recommendation, the family bank made the investment. Buying out the Guffey interests, the Mellons created the Gulf Oil Corporation in 1907 and quickly built a pipeline from the Glenn Pool near Tulsa, Okla., to the Gulf of Mexico. In 1909 Mellon became president of Gulf Oil, a post he held until 1930.

The new corporation was a success from the start, earning $1 million net profit in its first year. Under Mellon, it pioneered in several directions. In 1910-1911 Gulf Oil undertook the first successful overwater drilling operation in Ferry Lake on the Louisiana-Texas border; and in 1913 it opened the nation's first drive-in service station in Pittsburgh. Growing rapidly, the company by the early 1930's was operating 2,300 service stations; it built refining facilities throughout the United States and expanded into international oil exploration. By the mid-1920's Gulf's refinery at Port Arthur, Tex., was the largest in the world. Mellon became chairman of the board in 1930, remaining until his retirement in 1948. Despite necessary financial retrenchment during the 1930's (including divestment of the service stations), Gulf Oil under Mellon became the nation's fourth-largest oil-producing company and worldwide ranked among the top five integrated oil companies. In no small measure its success was the product of Mellon's unusual combination of entrepreneurial and managerial talents.

Throughout his life Mellon was active in the Pennsylvania Republican party, serving at one time as state chairman. From 1928 to 1941 he lived a substantial part of each year on his yacht *Vagabondia,* in which he cruised to remote parts of the world. In 1939 he established the William L. and May T. Mellon Foundation. Among its grants was one of $6 million to the Carnegie Institute of Technology to establish a graduate school of industrial administration. Mellon died of cerebral arteriosclerosis at his home in Pittsburgh and was buried in that city's Homewood Cemetery.

[The best source of information on Mellon is his book (in collaboration with Boyden Sparkes), *Judge Mellon's Sons* (1948). His role in Gulf Oil is documented in Craig Thompson, *Since Spindletop: A Human Story of Gulf's First Half-Century* (1951). See also "Gulf Oil," *Fortune,* Oct. 1937; an article about Andrew and Richard Mellon in *World's Work,* Mar. 1932; Frank R. Denton, *The Mellons of Pittsburgh* (Newcomen Soc. Pamphlet, 1948); and obituary in *N.Y. Times,* Oct. 9, 1949. Death record from the Pa. Dept. of Health.]

ARTHUR M. JOHNSON

MEYER, ADOLF (Sept. 13, 1866-Mar. 17, 1950), professor of psychiatry at the Johns Hopkins Medical School, and director of the Henry Phipps Psychiatric Clinic of the Johns Hopkins Hospital, Baltimore, Md., was born in the parish house at Niederweningen, a farming village about five miles from Zurich, Switzerland. The oldest son and second of three children of Rudolf Meyer and Anna (Walder) Meyer, Adolf grew up in an atmosphere of liberalism and reflection. The religion of his father, a Zwinglian minister, had its origins in life, enriched but not dogmatized by the Bible. This tolerance allowed a naturally curious and open-minded youth contact with Catholic and Jewish communities in adjoining cantons. In his father's library, Adolf read the works of Lange and Wundt as well as Eduard von Hartmann's *Philosophy of the Unconscious;* he relied on his impressions of his father's thoughts about imponderables like death rather than ask openly. At confirmation he accepted the creed muttering under his breath "If that is so."

The family considered themselves the spiritual heirs of the eighteenth-century folk-philosopher Kleinjogg (Jakob Gujer), a peasant who successfully dared break with ancient customs and government prescriptions to follow his own observations and reasoning. Kleinjogg believed that psychology and biology were a unity— "the reform of the farm" must begin "with the moral reform of its inhabitants." Concerned with developing healthy, happy people, he anticipated important principles of modern mental hygiene. Example was essential to all teaching and parental example to the rearing of children, which he regarded as the distinctive characteristic of the human race, to become happy, skillful adults. Adolf's grandfather Rudolf Meyer, a potter, stove builder, and local surveyor, surveyed and rented the Katzenrütihof, farmed until then by Kleinjogg's son. Adolf's cousin later married Kleinjogg's grandson.

Adolf Meyer attended the Gymnasium and the university faculty of medicine in Zurich. He chose medicine as his profession, because he believed the ministry dealt with only a part of man. "I have decided to study the whole of man," he wrote in his diary. He was more interested "in the man that I can know than in man the unknown." An excellent student in all but composition, he achieved recognition in his third year at the Gymnasium for an autobiography which substituted an account of his attitudes and feelings for the usual chronology of events. The "acceptance of this emphasis on what counted in a person . . . impressed on him the value of a biographical sketch in getting at the core of an individual" (Lief, p. 18), a method he introduced into psychiatric training. At the university he was attracted to the vivacious clinical demonstrations of Auguste Forel, chairman of psychiatry and chief at the Burghölzli Hospital for the Insane. He was influenced also by Constantin von Monakow, who taught the anatomy of the brain more as neurobiology, i.e., life-oriented, than as neurophysiology, i.e., cell- or organ-oriented. In 1890, after passing the examination to practice medicine, Meyer, who had avidly studied French and English in school, took a *Wanderjahr* of medical studies in Paris, Edinburgh, and London on funds from a fellowship and from his father. He studied with Jean-Baptiste Charcot, Pierre Potain, Jean Alfred Fournier, John Simon, George Dieulafoy, and Joseph Jules Déjerine and learned of constitutional types, neglected by the Germans in favor of the study of tissue diseases and infective agents. He attended Byrom Bramwell's clinical presentations in Edinburgh. Although uninterested in practicing psychiatry, he included the organization of the care of mental patients in Scotland in his report *Medizinische Studien in Paris, Edinburgh, and London* (1891), his first publication. At the National Hospital in London, ward rounds with J. Taylor and clinical visits with Hughlings Jackson gave him experience with neurological diseases, including epilepsy, hysteria, brain tumors, and tabes dorsalis. He observed Victor Horsley's surgical procedures involving the central nervous system.

Throughout his career Meyer continued laboratory studies on aphasia and on the occipital lobe, making a number of fundamental contributions to neuroanatomy and neuropathology, including the discovery of the temporal-lobe detour of the optic radiations (which he named Meyer's loop) and the introduction of plasticine models into the teaching of neuroanatomy. His encounter with the biological comprehensiveness of British thought, particularly that of Huxley and Hughlings Jackson, which contrasted with the cell and organ orientation on the Continent was extremely influential in his work. Among Huxley's contributions, Meyer acknowledged his definition of science as "organized common sense," for which Meyer fought in psychiatry; his "presentation of Darwin and Hume with a tendency to give a *biological* background to the human problem" and his "extreme version of parallelism which made of mind a mere epiphenomenon—a theory which later I had to reintegrate to get my full satisfaction" (Fourteenth Maudsley Lecture). These theories, together with Hughlings Jackson's "broad and inclusive concept of the hierarchy of evolution and dissolution processes, with a distinctive psychological level, called for correlations with my comparative neurological and neuropathological work and my personal human interest in the causal efficiency of suggestion and mentation generally in psychiatry" (*ibid.*). In London, Meyer watched William R. Gowers at his dispensary for epileptics take case histories in shorthand to avoid missing anything. Painstakingly detailed case histories along with autobiographies became the marks of Meyerian training.

He returned to Zurich inspired by Gowers' accurate and clear textbook on the anatomy of the spinal cord to attempt a doctoral thesis (under Forel) which would do the same for the brain. He received his doctorate in 1892 with a thesis on the forebrain of reptiles, "Über das Vorderhirn einiger Reptilien." When he was not appointed assistant to the professor of medicine at Zurich, Meyer decided to pursue his career in the United States, for the alternative of Swiss private practice seemed too limiting.

After five months at Vienna and Berlin medical centers and a month with the Déjerines in Paris, he revisited Edinburgh, where he met an American colleague, Henry H. Donaldson, with whom he had studied under von Monakow. Donaldson secured for him an unpaid honorary fellowship (1892-1893) at the new University of Chicago. After a year in this position, Meyer obtained a docentship teaching neurology and brain anatomy. In 1893 he introduced the functional study of the nervous system and in 1895, a three-dimensional developmental anatomy. In 1898 his classic "Critical Review of the Data and General Methods and Deductions of Modern Neurology" was published; it contained the essence of his integrative theory and the nucleus of his psychobiological doctrine. After a year of private neurological practice, he assumed, with the aid of Dr. Ludwig Hektoen, a post as pathologist at the new Illinois Eastern Hospital for the Insane at Kankakee (1893-1895). He tried to introduce the ideas on psychotherapy he had first presented in February 1893 to the Chicago Pathological Society. He proposed that pathologists should go beyond the laboratory into the wards, "getting the patient to do things, and getting the things going which did not work but which could with proper straightening out," i.e., occupational therapy.

When he left Switzerland, his mother, previously eminently sensible and sane, suffered the delusion he was dead and sank into a severe depression. Her recovery in spite of Forel's hopeless prognosis made Meyer skeptical about disease entities and prognostications. He became process oriented. He interviewed patients about their lives, and in so doing discovered much of why they had become ill. In *Child Study Monthly* (1895), he spoke out against the overemphasis on hereditary factors, recognizing that children of abnormal parents are "exposed from birth to acquire unconsciously habits of a morbid character." At Kankakee, he met Julia Lathrop of the Board of Charities and Correction, later first head of the Federal Children's Bureau, who introduced him to Hull House and Jane Addams. A lasting intellectual companionship also started when John Dewey came from Michigan to Chicago in 1894. Another important influence was his exposure to the writings of Charles Peirce and William James, who also rejected the mind-body dichotomy. Meyer directed the setting up of the Illinois State Pathological Laboratory, organized the medical workers into the Association of Assistant Physicians of Hospitals for the Insane, and wrote the opening article for the new journal of the Illinois Association for Child Study.

Meyer's presentation of brain sections from epilepsy cases at the 1895 American Medico-Psychological Association meeting in Denver so impressed Edward Cowles that he invited Meyer to help make the State Lunatic Hospital in Worcester, in connection with Clark University, a training school in nervous diseases. In his new position, Meyer stressed careful study of patients' symptoms and needs, using the nearby laboratory as a staff center, "not a mere mortuary nor a scientific side show" (Lief, p. 82). He introduced bedside note-taking and trained his assistants in case taking, accurate concise recording, and uniform methods of intake examinations. He became clinical director, covering the entire hospital weekly in regular rounds. At Clark, he put the clinical demonstrations of symptom complexes on a biological basis. He opened psychiatry to psychologists; his students were among the creators of the profession of clinical psychology. In 1896 Meyer visited at Turin with Cesare Lombroso, who was making a doctrine of "degeneracy," and the physiologist Angelo Mosso, who wrote on fear. After six weeks at Emil Kraepelin's small Heidelberg hospital, he introduced in the United States Kraepelin's system of classification of the manic-depressive and schizophrenic groups of mental disease. He considered this an improvement on the old system, but had serious misgivings that nosology distracted from the patients' individual constitutions and experiences. "I decided to work pragmatically with the best possible use of critical commonsense . . . to put aside all preconceived traditional classification . . . to take the facts and group them without adulteration or suppression of any available data" (Lief, p. 82). Meyer added the classification of ergasias, mentally integrated functions or behaviors of the individual. In 1897 his psychobiological concept that physiological-anatomical development and mental development are one development from one cell was a revelation. At Clark's decennial celebration, Meyer's departmental report of psychopathology looked toward closer integration of psychopathology looked toward closer integration of psychology and biology. He launched the idea of a psychiatric clinic and research station established jointly by the state

and university and envisioned psychiatry protecting the healthy by appraising the potentialities and dangers in a person's mode of living and providing proper direction.

In 1902, hoping to establish a psychopathic hospital for voluntary commitment of early stage cases, Frederick Peterson, the newly appointed president of the New York State Commission on Lunacy, invited Meyer to become director of the Pathological Institute in New York City. Meyer transformed the insane asylums into mental hospitals. He taught the established descriptive psychiatry but opened the minds of physicians, such as Abraham Brill, to the promises of dynamic psychiatry. Autopsies failed to sustain the theory of lesions in the nervous system except in profound idiocy, general paralysis, and senile and organic dementia; insanity, Meyer argued, was a pathology not of the brain but of mental functioning.

On Sept. 15, 1902, Meyer married Mary Potter Brooks, a pioneer in psychiatric social work; they had one daughter, Julia Lathrop. After he moved the institute to Ward's Island, where the Manhattan State Hospital afforded opportunity to relate clinical observation and pathological study, his wife began visiting patients and discussing cases with him. At his suggestion, she made visits to the homes of patients and obtained a clearer view of events in patients' lives and an awareness of what awaited them on release. Meyer fought for guidance for afflicted families and for continued hospital contact after discharge; in 1906 the State Commission on Lunacy approved such an aftercare system. Mary then turned to Adolf's other therapeutic concerns: recreation and occupational therapy.

As professor of clinical medicine (psychopathology) at Cornell Medical College (1904-1909), Meyer organized an outpatient service, the first mental clinic in the city; he was assisted by George H. Kirby, C. Macfie Campbell, and later by August Hoch. He also taught at Columbia University, where he presented psychology as "a study of the determining factors of the stream of mental life" and described consciousness as "an integrate of the person, not only the brain." Under his influence the Pathological Institute was renamed the Psychiatric Institute in 1908.

Meyer recognized that schools and communities as well as families were sources of mental illness and health. By then the leading psychiatrist in the United States, Meyer helped Clifford Beers establish and name the mental hygiene movement. Meyer suggested essential changes in Beers' autobiography, *A Mind that Found Itself*. He was a charter member of the National Committee for Mental Hygiene (1908) and elected honorary president (1937).

Meyer's dynamic psychology prepared the United States for psychoanalysis. With Freud and Jung, Meyer lectured and received an honorary degree at Clark's 1909 decennial celebration. He endorsed Freud's emphasis on childhood experiences and the role of symbolism and utilized Jung's word-association, although he claimed these men "too largely emphasized a portion of the situation"; he preferred a broader base with prophylactic opportunities. In 1918 Meyer's influence saved from dissolution the American Psychoanalytic Association, of which he was a charter member. He presided at its 1928 meeting as president of the American Psychiatric Association and was made an honorary member of the New York Psychoanalytic Institute and Society (1937).

In 1910, Meyer became chairman of the new department of psychiatry at Johns Hopkins Medical School and director of the Henry Phipps Clinic. There he developed the first significant teaching and research hospital integrated with a medical school and provided a model for residency training. In teaching, as in therapy, he was dedicated to the principle of spontaneity, helping each person develop and express the utmost within him. Sympathetic interest in Harvey Cushing's surgical procedures led to a study of the mental aspects of surgical and medical patients. He fought for recognition of all patients as total persons. Psychosomatic medicine evolved from his teaching psychologic awareness in medical departments and recognition of the influences of physical factors on pathological and psychopathological functions and of psychopathological reactions on physiological functions.

In May 1913 Phipps opened an inpatient service and also a dispensary under C. Macfie Campbell which included a child-guidance clinic. Meyer believed that psychiatry and sociology should understand the functionings of the community, but he could obtain only enough support to survey a single school population. In 1914 he introduced psychology into the curriculum, eventually extending it to the full four years. In 1928 he called for a specialty board. He chaired the committee that in 1934 established the American Board of Psychiatry and Neurology, winning for psychiatry status as a fixed part of medical training. He trained an extraordinary number of leaders and innovators in psychiatry, mental hygiene, and social work.

Through his students his influence extended to major psychiatric centers throughout the United States, South America, the British Empire, Europe, China, Japan, and Southeast Asia. He held honorary degrees from Glasgow (1901), Yale (1934), and Harvard (1942). Meyer died of a cerebral hemorrhage at his home on Rugby Road in Baltimore, Md., and is buried in Druid Ridge Cemetery in Pikesville, Md.

Aside from his many contributions to psychiatry, Meyer was a fascinating human being. He cultivated an air of inscrutability, reinforced both by his bearded, somewhat owlish countenance and by his unfamiliarity, despite his long residency in the United States, with many American expressions. This sometimes led to his misunderstanding of what his patients were saying. His anxiety to present all sides of complicated questions made him a terrible committee man. Meyer's university lectures were so intricately subtle that at least one student helped support himself by selling typed summaries "translated" into plain Engilsh. Yet no one could meet him without feeling in the presence of a great man.

[The largest deposit of Meyer's papers is in the Johns Hopkins Medical School; there are thirty-five items in the G. Stanley Hall Papers, University Archives, Goddard Lib., Clark Univ. Published collections of this work include *The Collected Papers of Adolf Meyer*, ed. Eunice E. Winters (1950–1952); *The Commonsense Psychiatry of Dr. Adolf Meyer*, ed., with biographical narrative, Alfred Lief (1948); and *Psychobiology: A Science of Man*, with a foreword by Nolan D. C. Lewis, comp. and ed. Eunice E. Winters and Anna Mae Bowers (1957); Adolf Meyer, M.D., Smith Ely Jelliffe, M.D., and August Hoch, *Dementia Praecox* (1911); "Bibliography of Adolf Meyer," comp. C. M. Campbell, *Arch. of Neuro. and Psych.*, 37 (1937), 724–731; *Contributions Dedicated to Dr. Adolf Meyer by his Colleagues, Friends and Pupils*, ed. S. Katzenelbogen (1938); M. Bleuler, "Early Swiss Sources of Adolf Meyer's Concepts," *Jour. Psych.*, 119 (1962), 193–196; Theodore Lidz, "Adolf Meyer and the Development of American Psychiatry," *Am. Jour. Psych.*, 123 (1966), 320–332; Saul Feierstein, *Adolf Meyer: Life and Work* (Zurich, 1965); obituaries in *Am. Jour. of Psych.*, 107 (1950), 79–80; *Jour. of Comp. Neuro.*, 92 (1950), 131–132; and *N.Y. Times*, Mar. 18, 1950. A portrait of Meyer by Hildegard Woodward is in the National Portrait Gallery of the Smithsonian Institution.]

LUCILLE B. RITVO

MICHAELIS, LEONOR (Jan. 16, 1875– Oct. 8, 1949), physical chemist and medical scientist, was born in Berlin, Germany, the son of Jewish parents, Moriz Michaelis, who operated a small business, and Hulda (Rosenbaum) Michaelis. He attended the Koellnisches Gymnasium, which offered chiefly a liberal arts curriculum, but was allowed to study physics and chemistry in addition to the regular courses.

Deciding to become a scientist, he chose medicine as the best approach and in 1893 entered the University of Berlin.

There, Michaelis studied organic chemistry under Emil Fischer and embryology and histology under Oskar Hertwig and spent his free time in embryological research under Hertwig. He wrote his doctoral thesis on the direction of the first cleavage in the frog's egg and published his first paper (1896) on the cytology of the fertilization of the ovum in *Triton*. His experience led him to write a short textbook (1898) on embryology for medical students, which eventually went through seven editions and established a pattern for a series of textbooks published in the course of the next three decades. Each reflected a new stage in the development of his own research interests and illustrated his superb ability to select the material most useful to a particular group of readers. The subjects included the chemistry of dyes, toxin-antitoxin reactions, mathematics for biologists and chemists, hydrogen ion concentration and oxidation-reduction potentials, the dynamics of surfaces, the techniques of physical and colloid chemistry, and permeability and electric phenomena in membranes.

After receiving the M.D. degree in 1896, Michaelis studied for a year at the University of Freiburg and there passed the examination that admitted him to medical practice. He next resumed work with Hertwig and then spent a year as research assistant to the biochemist Paul Ehrlich; in studying the staining properties of various new dyes, Michaelis discovered the usefulness of Janus green in the specific staining of cellular mitochondria. Since he did not possess the independent means thought necessary for a career in research, on Ehrlich's advice he turned to clinical medicine and became an assistant (1900-1904) in a municipal hospital in Berlin. In 1904 he was appointed a research assistant in a newly established institute for cancer research, where he demonstrated that different strains of mice differed in their susceptibility to Jensen's mouse carcinoma. In 1903 Michaelis was appointed privatdocent and in 1905 professor at the University of Berlin, but since neither post included a salary or laboratory facilities, in 1905 he accepted the newly created post of bacteriologist at the Berlin City Hospital, where he remained until 1922.

These years were very productive. With the chemist Peter Rona, Michaelis constructed a private laboratory in the hospital. It was small and poorly equipped, but in spite of the press of routine duties and the opposition of the city administration, Michaelis was able to carry out basic research that brought an influx of postdoctoral students of biochemistry and biophysics. The papers published during these years dealt with such subjects as the measurement and regulation of hydrogen ion concentration, the theory of ampholytes, the techniques of electrophoresis, the effects of pH on enzymes and proteins, and the nature and rate of enzyme reactions. This work led him to the concept of an "affinity constant," a measure of the affinity of an enzyme for the substance on which it acts. The existence of such a factor was not fully confirmed for many years, but the "Michaelis constant," as it has become known, has since been computed for a large number of systems.

Although Michaelis' work gained him an international reputation, he never received a good academic post in Germany, probably for reasons of anti-Semitism. After serving in army hospitals during World War I, he returned to the Berlin City Hospital. In 1921 he was given the title of professor of physical chemistry, but since the post, like the earlier ones, did not include a salary or laboratory facilities, he worked for a time with an industrial firm, which, in return for advice on making laboratory equipment, provided a salary and laboratory space for him and his students.

In 1922 Michaelis accepted an invitation to go to Japan as professor of biochemistry at the medical school in Nagoya, the first European to be offered such a post. During his three years in Japan he did research on pH and on the permeability of biological membranes. He had long been in correspondence with Jacques Loeb of the Rockefeller Institute in New York City, and in the summer of 1924, at Loeb's invitation, Michaelis made a lecture tour in the United States. The tour led to his appointment as resident lecturer at the Johns Hopkins University (1926-1929), where he continued his research on membrane permeability. In 1929 he became a member of the Rockefeller Institute, where he remained until his retirement in 1940.

At the institute, Michaelis worked chiefly on the reactions involved in the oxidation and reduction of organic substances. He proposed the theory that such reactions take place in two stages, with the temporary participation of free radicals (semiquinones) in equilibrium with their parent substances in aqueous solution. This concept was strongly opposed by most chemists, and his first paper on the subject was rejected by American journals. He obtained experimental proof in 1938, and the hypothesis thereafter was generally accepted.

Michaelis became a naturalized citizen. He was elected to the National Academy of Sciences in 1943, and received an honorary LL.D. from the University of California at Los Angeles in 1945. After his retirement he was allowed to retain his laboratory at the Rockefeller Institute, and he continued to work at his research until shortly before his death. He also gave a series of summer lectures in physiology at the Marine Biological Laboratory in Woods Hole, Mass. His interests went far beyond the bounds of science. Linguistics was a major hobby, and during his stay in Japan he learned to speak the language and also studied Chinese. Music was a lifelong avocation; a talented pianist, he was known for his ability to improvise in the style of various classical composers.

Michaelis married Hedwig Philipsthal on Apr. 12, 1905; their children were Ilse and Eva. He died of a heart ailment in the Rockefeller Hospital at the age of seventy-four and was buried at Union Fields Cemetery of Hodeph Sholom in Brooklyn, N.Y. Biochemistry and medicine owe much to Michaelis for his research both in enzyme action, which describes the mechanisms of life processes, and in oxidation, which describes the source of energy for organisms like man.

[Autobiographical statement by Michaelis, with additions by Duncan A. MacInnes and Sam Granick, in Nat. Acad. Sci. *Biog. Memoirs*, XXXI (1958), also with photograph and a complete bibliography of Michaelis' publications. Obituaries in *Nature*, Feb. 25, 1950 (by Granick); *Science*, Feb. 25, 1950; and *N.Y. Times*, Oct. 10, 1949; see also *Who Was Who In Amer.*, II (1950); George W. Corner, *A Hist. of the Rockefeller Inst.* (1964).]

MILTON LEVY

MICHELSON, CHARLES (Apr. 18, 1868-Jan. 8, 1948), journalist and political publicist, was born in Virginia City, Nev., the third son and youngest of eight children of immigrant Jewish parents, Samuel Michelson and Rosalie (Przlubska) Michelson. The oldest child, Albert A. Michelson, became a Nobel Prize-winning physicist; the next to youngest, Miriam, became a journalist and popular novelist. The family came to the United States in 1854 from Strelno, Prussia, and moved via New York, San Francisco, and the California gold fields to Nevada, where the father prospered for a time as proprietor of a dry goods store. Charles grew up in a bookish household that contrasted

sharply with the frontier setting of Virginia City. He was not an eager scholar, and at thirteen, when the family's financial situation deteriorated, he left school and went to live with a brother in Arizona. There he worked at a copper-mining camp and later became for a time what he called "a frontier tramp," until his family reclaimed him and sent him back to finish high school in Virginia City.

Michelson began newspaper work as bookkeeper and assistant reporter on the *Virginia City Chronicle*. About 1887 he moved to San Francisco as a reporter on the *Evening Post,* edited by a brother-in-law, Arthur McEwen. He was soon attracted to the livelier *San Francisco Examiner*, recently acquired by the young William Randolph Hearst, and spent several years covering sensational crime and court cases. Following a short stint at the rival *Call,* Michelson was rehired by Hearst in 1896 and sent to cover the Cuban revolt against Spanish rule and the subsequent Spanish-American War. He was briefly imprisoned in Havana's Morro Castle as a result of running afoul of the Spanish authorities; thereafter he worked from the chartered ships of Hearst's "navy," but observed no combat.

Like other Hearst talents, Michelson was shifted about frequently. He wrote editorials for the *New York American*; he covered the trial of Leon F. Czolgosz, the assassin of President McKinley; he helped in the publisher's campaigns for public office; and he served as a city editor. He was made managing editor of the *San Francisco Examiner* in 1906, just in time to restore the paper after the earthquake. Two years later he was sent to Chicago, where he alternated as managing editor of the two Hearst papers, the *Examiner* and the *American*. After an "efficiency" reduction in salary, he left Hearst and began writing movie scenarios for the Essanay Company. He rejoined Hearst in 1914, but when the publisher ignored his request to cover the war front, Michelson moved to the Washington bureau of the *Chicago Herald,* only to have Hearst buy the paper and fire him. Thus ended his thirty years in Hearst organizations.

In 1917 Michelson joined the strongly Democratic *New York World* as chief Washington correspondent. For twelve years he covered major national stories—the fight over the Versailles Treaty, the death of President Harding, the Scopes "monkey trial," the national political conventions and campaigns. He also wrote a pro-Democratic column called "The Political Undertow." After the Republican landslide of

1928, the Democratic national chairman, John J. Raskob, established a new party headquarters under Jouett Shouse, who in June 1929 hired Michelson as full-time publicity director.

Michelson immediately took the offensive against the Republicans. His office turned out a steady flow of statements and speeches. Many were attributed to Democratic politicians, and "Charley" Michelson acquired a reputation as an able ghost. His sharp phrasing, his aggressive tactics, and his sense of timing had a maximum impact on newspapers and radio and helped hearten a defeated party. These qualities also made him a center of controversy. Republicans charged that he had been hired to smear President Hoover; Michelson insisted that he was attacking only mistaken administration policies. Contemporaries, overlooking the importance of the depression, gave Michelson's publicity major credit for the Hoover administration's downfall.

Michelson worked closely with the new Democratic chairman, James A. Farley, during the 1932 presidential campaign. With Roosevelt in office, the White House tapped Michelson for several emergency chores: press secretary to Secretary of the Treasury William H. Woodin during the banking crisis of March 1933; press officer in London for the American delegation to the ill-fated World Economic Conference; and publicity director of the National Recovery Administration. By 1934 he had returned to his post as party publicist. Some New Dealers, like Secretary of the Interior Harold L. Ickes, distrusted Michelson and complained that he was not really one of their number. Yet in 1936 he rejected an offer from his old employer, Shouse, to work for the anti-Roosevelt Liberty League. The veteran journalist also weathered complaints in 1937, when he briefly took a job as publicity consultant to the Crosley Radio Corporation, and in 1939 when he openly lobbied against passage of the Hatch Act, forbidding political participation by government employees.

Michelson retired in 1942, but remained on the Democratic payroll as a part-timer into the 1944 campaign. He continued also as an elder of the Washington press community, a member of the Gridiron Club, and a domino-playing habitué of the National Press Club. In 1896 he married Lillian Sterrett of Brooklyn. They had one child, Benjamin Charles. Michelson died of congestive heart failure at his Washington apartment. An Episcopal clergyman conducted the funeral services, and his remains were cremated.

Michelson had always depicted himself as a dispassionate professional, a hired hand; yet he remained loyal to one party and presented that party's case effectively. His virtuosity and his amiability were widely esteemed. But the *Washington Post,* at his death, doubted that he had been a healthy phenomenon: "To the extent that he put words into the mouths of public servants, the principle of representative government was distinctly blurred. To the extent that he resorted to smearing, public issues were subordinated to scintillating phrases and animosities."

[Michelson's memoir, *The Ghost Talks* (1944), is informative but often indifferent to dates and details. Substantial obituaries appeared in the *Washington Post* (by Marshall Andrews), with photograph, and the *N.Y. Times,* Jan. 9, 1948. For his Cuban adventures, see Charles H. Brown, *The Correspondents' War* (1967). On his pre-Roosevelt Democratic publicity work, see articles by Thomas Barclay in the *Am. Political Science Rev.,* Feb. 1931 and Feb. 1933. Hostile appraisals include Frank R. Kent in *Scribner's,* Sept. 1930, and Alva Johnston in the *Saturday Evening Post,* May 30, 1936. A profile appeared in *Current Biog.,* 1940. Scattered material can also be found in books by Roosevelt contemporaries: Raymond Moley, *27 Masters of Politics* (1949), which includes a chapter on Michelson; James A. Farley, *Jim Farley's Story* (1948); and the first volume of *The Secret Diary of Harold L. Ickes* (1953). Michelson gave his birth year in *Who's Who in America* as 1869; but his death certificate (D.C. Dept. of Human Resources) has the year as 1868, and this is supported by the census record of 1875 and 1880; courtesy of D. T. McAllister, curator, Michelson Museum, U.S. Naval Weapons Center, China Lake, Calif.]

JAMES BOYLAN

MILLAY, EDNA ST. VINCENT (Feb. 22, 1892–Oct. 19, 1950), poet and writer, was born in Rockland, Maine, the oldest of three daughters of Henry Tolman Millay and Cora Lounella (Buzzelle) Millay; her father was a school principal and superintendent. Cora Millay traced her family's American beginnings to Ipswich, Mass., in 1634. Henry Millay was descended from French Huguenots who settled in Ireland in the seventeenth century. When Vincent (as she was known to her family) was eight, her mother divorced her father and worked as a practical nurse to support her daughters. She moved the family about New England before settling in Camden, Maine; it was there that Millay spent her childhood.

Cora Millay encouraged her daughters to study music and literature and urged them to be independent and ambitious. In a later poem, "The Courage That My Mother Had" (*Mine the Harvest,* 1954), Millay associated her mother with "rock from New England quarried."

As a young girl, Vincent studied to become

a concert pianist but thought that her hands were too small to permit her to pursue this career. Her early intimacy with music, however, survived in the musical quality of her lyrics (many of which have been set to music). She wrote a successful libretto for *The King's Henchman*, with music by Deems Taylor, first performed on Feb. 27, 1927, at the Metropolitan Opera in New York.

Her first published poem, "Forest Trees," written when she was fourteen, appeared in *St. Nicholas Magazine* (October 1906). Within the next four years, *St. Nicholas* published five more of her poems, one of which, "The Land of Romance," received a gold badge of the St. Nicholas League and later was reprinted in *Current Literature* (April 1907). In November 1912, "Renascence" was anthologized in *The Lyric Year* and met with critical acclaim.

In early 1913, with the help of Caroline Dow, her benefactress, Vincent prepared at Barnard College for entrance examinations to Vassar College and was admitted in the fall of 1913. She received the B.A. in 1917. During these years at Vassar, she wrote constantly and contributed poems and stories to such magazines as *Smart Set* and *Poetry*. She also became interested in drama and wrote two plays, *The Princess Marries the Page* and *The Wall of Dominoes*.

Her first book of poetry, *Renascence and Other Poems*, was published in 1917. At about that time, she joined the Provincetown Players, directing her own allegorical and experimental play, *Aria da Capo*, in December 1919. Under the pseudonym "Nancy Boyd," she also began a series of prose sketches and stories. During these years, she lived with her sisters, who were later joined by their mother, in the Bohemian atmosphere of Greenwich Village.

With the publication of *A Few Figs from Thistles* (1920), Edna St. Vincent Millay became the spokesman for a younger generation exuberantly defiant of convention. For young women, especially, her irreverent wit and satiric cynicism made her a "symbolic figure—the 'free woman' of her age" (Gray, p. 8). Many contemporary critics condemned *A Few Figs*—a line of condescending critical treatment typified by John Crowe Ransom's "The Poet as Woman" (*Southern Review,* Spring 1937).

From January 1921 to February 1923, Millay traveled in Europe writing for *Vanity Fair*. Her third book of poems, *Second April* (1921), received favorable reviews. The Nancy Boyd articles written during this time were collected in 1924 as *Distressing Dialogues*. While in Europe, she completed *The Lamp and the Bell,* a celebration of the friendship of two women, for the Vassar College Alumni Association and began work on *Hardigut,* a novel she never completed. In 1922, she contributed eight sonnets to *American Poetry: A Miscellany,* and *The Ballad of the Harp-Weaver* was also published that year. For these, she received the Pulitzer Prize for 1922. On July 18, 1923, she married Eugen Jan Boissevain. She then spent much of the next few years in reading engagements throughout the United States, and with her husband she toured the Orient in 1924. Boissevain, a native of the Netherlands and an importer, devoted his life to the poet. They lived at Steepletop, their rural home in Austerlitz, N.Y., and at Ragged Island, their summer home in Casco Bay, Maine. He died on Aug. 30, 1949.

Throughout the late 1920's and the 1930's, Millay published major works of poetry: *The Buck in the Snow* (1928), *Fatal Interview* (1931), *Wine from These Grapes* (1934), and *Huntsman, What Quarry?* (1939), as well as her earlier drama, *The Princess Marries the Page* (1932), and a closet drama, *Conversation at Midnight* (1937). She was elected to the National Institute of Arts and Letters (1929), was awarded the Helen Haire Levinson Prize from *Poetry* magazine (1931), was named the laureate of the General Federation of Women's Clubs (1933), and received several honorary degrees.

During the 1940's Millay's poetic talents were directed to the war effort. She had often devoted herself and her poetry to social issues, beginning with her participation in 1923 at the National Women's Party dedication ceremony, in Washington, D.C., of a statue of three early feminist leaders. At the ceremony in the Capitol, she read "The Pioneer," a sonnet later dedicated to Inez Milholland, a feminist and Boissevain's first wife. In 1927, Millay participated in the Boston protests surrounding the Sacco-Vanzetti execution and published several propagandistic poems, including "Justice Denied in Massachusetts." In the 1940's, her poems were frankly intended to arouse national patriotism and fervor. *Make Bright the Arrows; 1940 Notebook* (1940) and *The Murder of Lidice* (1942) contain a variety of these verses. She was elected to the American Academy of Arts and Letters (1940) and received the gold medal of the Poetry Society of America (1943).

Millay died of a heart attack at Steepletop and was buried there. She left in manuscript a number of current poems, as well as a number of unpublished poems from earlier periods. These were published posthumously in *Mine the Harvest* (1954). Two years later, her *Collected Poems* appeared.

Millay is generally regarded as a "minor lyricist" whose special ability lay in expressing emotion in traditional verse forms. The skill with which she employed the sonnet, developed over a number of years, perhaps most evident in "Epitaph for the Race of Man" (1928) and *Fatal Interview* (1931), can be explained in large part by the tension created between form and content: "I will put Chaos in fourteen lines," she said in *Mine the Harvest*. Moreover, it has become clear that she helped to free the poetry of American women from thematic inhibitions.

Following her successes in the 1920's and early 1930's, Millay's poetry gradually suffered a critical and popular decline. Unfortunately, her real poetic achievements were overshadowed by her image as the free (but "naughty") woman of the 1920's. Moreover, she has been considered by some to be incapable of writing "intellectual" verse. During the last two decades of her life, Millay was almost ignored critically, although her *Collected Sonnets* appeared in 1941 and *Collected Lyrics* in 1943. Since the late 1960's, however, there has been a renewed interest in Millay's works, with more sympathetic critical evaluation.

[Her other works include *The Harp-Weaver and Other Poems* (1923); *Edna St. Vincent Millay's Poems Selected for Young People* (1929); *Flowers of Evil* (1936), a translation of Baudelaire's poems, with George Dillon; *Invocation to the Muses* (1941) and *Poem and Prayer for an Invading Army* (1944). There is no definitive study of Millay. The most thorough biographical and critical work is Norman A. Brittin, *Edna St. Vincent Millay* (1967); James Gray's pamphlet, *Edna St. Vincent Millay* (1967), is judicious and perceptive. Also of value are Elizabeth Atkins, *Edna St. Vincent Millay and Her Times* (1936), and Miriam Gurko, *Restless Spirit: The Life of Edna St. Vincent Millay* (1962). Much of value is contained in Allan Ross Macdougall, ed., *Letters of Edna St. Vincent Millay* (1952). There is an excellent picture of Millay on the cover of the Grosset's Universal Library edition of the *Letters*. For primary works published before 1936, the most complete bibliography is Karl Yost, *A Bibliog. of the Works of Edna St. Vincent Millay* (1937). See also Fred B. Millet, *Contemporary Am. Authors*, pp. 133-134 and pp. 487-491 (1943); Allen Tate, ed., *Sixty Am. Poets, 1896-1944* (rev. ed., 1954), and Robert E. Spiller, Willard Thorp, Thomas H. Johnson, and Henry Seidel Canby, *Literary Hist. of the U.S.*, pp. 656-658 (1948), Supplement, pp. 169-170 (1963); and Supplement, p. 225 (1972). The most recent critical bibliography is John J. Patton, "A Comprehensive Bibliog. of Edna St. Vincent Millay," *The Serif*, 5 (1968): 10-32. Of special interest are *Edna St. Vincent Millay, Readings From Her Poetry* (Caedmon Record 1123) and, in Yost, Harold Lewis Cook's "Edna St. Vincent Millay —An Essay in Appreciation," a review which Millay herself liked.]

EMILY STIPES WATTS

MILLER, JAMES ALEXANDER (Mar. 27, 1874-July 29, 1948), physician, was born in Roselle Park, N.J., the second of seven children of Charles Dexter Miller and Julia Muirhead (Hope) Miller. His father was in the New York Cotton Exchange. His paternal grandfather, James, came from Belfast, Ireland, to New York in about 1830, lived on a farm near 86th Street, became a colonel in the Union Army, and was killed in battle. His mother was a descendant of Samuel Fuller, a physician in the Plymouth Colony. His one sister, Helen Clarkson, was an educator and author. The parents' Presbyterian and Puritan heritage imbued their children with firm and religious discipline. James's brother, Kenneth Dexter, a clergyman, directed the New York City Mission Society.

James entered Princeton at fifteen after preparation at Pingry School. He received his B.A. in 1893 and M.A. in chemistry in 1894. In college, he was tall, good-looking, cheerful, athletic, and healthy. In his junior year, he met Marion Clifton Hunt. They became engaged but did not marry until ten years later, on June 4, 1902. During the interval she worked in New York as a kindergarten teacher. They had two daughters, Constance and Marion.

After graduation from Princeton and a short stint as chemist for the New Jersey Zinc and Iron Company, Miller was appointed by William H. Park as research chemist in the Research Laboratory of the New York City Department of Health. There, Hermann M. Biggs urged him to study medicine and, while holding his job, he enrolled in the Columbia University College of Physicians and Surgeons. He received the M.D. with high honors in 1899 and was appointed intern at the Presbyterian Hospital.

After finishing his internship in 1901, Miller became associated with A. A. Smith in private practice in New York and spent his summers in the Adirondacks, where he assisted Edward Livingston Trudeau, who, despite his own debilitating symptoms of tuberculosis, was conducting research in that disease and developing his sanatorium at Saranac Lake. Trudeau's ideals and lasting friendship influenced Miller's career deeply.

The conquest of tuberculosis, then the leading cause of death, was still a dream, although Robert Koch had discovered the tuberculosis bacillus in 1882. The communicability of the infection became recognized and the prevention of its transmission was seen to be the key to control. Against opposition, the reporting of discovered cases of tuberculosis to the public health authorities became law, and a more humane attitude toward the patients followed.

In 1903, Miller organized a separate tuberculosis clinic in the outpatient department of Bellevue, New York's largest public hospital; he was appointed adjunct assistant visiting physician and delegated to look after patients who were housed in tents on the hospital grounds. Conceptually, he outlined the objectives: medical attention; investigation and amelioration of the patients' unsanitary home conditions; hygienic education to avoid the spread of infection; material relief of patients and their families when needed. During his ensuing thirty-five years at Bellevue, he pursued these objectives undeviatingly, gradually building a staff of dedicated physicians, nurses, and social workers. In 1908 he organized a ladies' auxiliary, an effective philanthropic group that helped meet the social needs of the sick.

Miller felt that more intensive education of medical students and researchers in tuberculosis was needed and, in 1927-1928, he proposed the building of a specialized hospital in the new Columbia Presbyterian Medical Center where he was professor of clinical medicine. The cost was pledged and plans were drawn, but the idea perished in the economic crash of 1929. He then saw an alternative in the Bellevue Tuberculosis Service (later the Chest Service), long used as a Columbia teaching facility. Later, with the help of Harry Hopkins, a former tuberculosis worker and a presidential advisor, Miller explained the need to President Franklin D. Roosevelt, who responded by arranging for federal funds to build a new tuberculosis pavilion at Bellevue. When this was opened in 1938, Miller retired as director of the service. As a Columbia teaching facility, the Chest Service staff, covering special fields of pathology, physiology, surgery, and clinical medicine, became distinguished for the scope and quality of its work.

Throughout his career, Miller was active in many organizations. In 1904, he helped to found the National Association for the Study and Prevention of Tuberculosis, the first voluntary health organization in the United States. He also headed the tuberculosis committee of the Charity Organization Society of New York and in 1919 became president of its offspring, the New York Tuberculosis Association; in 1921, he became president of the national association. His experience was broadened during World War I by his service as associate medical director of a special commission of the International

Health Board in helping to launch the tuberculosis program of France (1917-1918). A major in the American Red Cross, he was decorated Chevalier of the Légion d'Honneur.

His extraordinary abilities as a policy-maker and leader drew him into various offices: he was president of the American Climatological and Clinical Association (1915), the American College of Physicians (1935-1936), the New York Academy of Medicine (1937-1938), and the Trudeau Sanatorium (1927-1945), and alumni trustee, Columbia University (1945). His influence in medical practice and public health was often exercised through the public health committee of the Academy of Medicine, of which he was a leader from the beginning (1911). The recommendations of this committee were often accepted with salutary effects, for example, examination of immigrants in the country of origin to prevent the importation of communicable disease, replacement of the political office of coroner with that of a professionally competent chief medical examiner in New York, child health surveys, and industrial health studies. During its centennial celebration in 1947 the academy honored Miller as its "most distinguished and beloved fellow and one of the greatest benefactors of mankind."

Miller was held in high esteem not only because he entered an unpopular and limited field of medicine and succeeded beyond expectation but also because he had vision, administrative and clinical skill, and great humanity. This underlay his concern for his patients and their devotion to him.

Miller lived to see the discovery of specific drug therapy, the most powerful weapon against tuberculosis. He died of cancer of the pancreas at his summer home in Black Point, Conn. After a funeral service in the Brick Presbyterian Church, New York, he was buried in Fairview Cemetery, Westfield, N.J.

[J. A. Miller, "A Study of the Tuberculosis Problem in New York City," *Medical News*, May 28, 1904, p. 25, reveals the wide prevalence of tuberculosis, describes the agencies and facilities available for treatment, and emphasizes the amelioration of social conditions. Among the more than one hundred articles in the medical literature by Miller are "The Beginnings of the American Antituberculosis Movement," 48 (1943), 361; "Climate in the Treatment of Pulmonary Tuberculosis," 18 (1928), 523; both in the *Am. Rev. of Tuberculosis*. His broad philosophical and practical outlook is shown in several presidential addresses and documents: "The Power and the Spirit," *Am. Rev. of Tuberculosis*, 6 (1922), 241; "The Story of Recent Years," chapter in *The American College of Physicians, Its First Quarter Century* (1940), p. 112; "The Doctor Himself," medical addenda, related essays in *Medicine and the Changing Order* (1947); preface to *Thirty Years of Community Service, 1911–1941*, an account of the work of the Committee on Public

Health Relations of the New York Academy of Medicine.

Other sources are R. H. Shryock, *National Tuberculosis Association 1904–1954* (1957); E. L. Trudeau, *An Autobiography* (1915); and *Medical and Surgical Report of Bellevue and Allied Hospitals*, I (1904), a brief description of the opening and operation of the separate Tuberculosis Clinic. An obituary tribute by M. Goodridge and P. Van Ingen, "James Alexander Miller, 1874–1948," appeared in the New York Academy of Medicine *Bull.*, 2nd series, 24 (1948), 743.

Mrs. Constance Meredith and Mrs. Marion Lindley have kindly provided information about their father and the Miller family. John H. McClement furnished historical items about the Bellevue Chest Service, and Irving Mushlin gave me items about the New York Tuberculosis Association. James E. McCormack, director, arranged for my access to the files of the library of the New York Academy of Medicine; photographs and a portrait of Miller are preserved there.]

J. BURNS AMBERSON

MILLIS, HARRY ALVIN (May 14, 1873–June 25, 1948), labor economist and arbitrator, was born in Paoli, Orange County, Ind., the second son and third of four children of John Millis, a merchant and farmer, and Maria (Bruner) Millis. Both parents were natives of Orange County. His father's family came from North Carolina; his mother's, from Kentucky. Harry's older brother, William Alfred, became a Presbyterian minister and president of Hanover (Ind.) College. After graduating from the local high school, Harry taught in a country school for one year and then entered Indiana University. There he came in contact with the economist John R. Commons, with whom he took a course in labor problems, one of the earliest such courses to be offered in an American university. Millis completed the B.A. (1895) and M.A. (1896) degrees at Indiana and then moved to the University of Chicago, where he worked under Thorstein Veblen and received the Ph.D. in 1899. Commons and Veblen—both institutional economists—greatly influenced Millis' thought and career.

After two years on the staff of the John Crerar Library in Chicago, Millis taught economics at the University of Arkansas (1902–1903), Stanford (1903–1912)—where he shared an office with Veblen—and the University of Kansas (1912–1916). He returned to the University of Chicago in 1916 as professor of economics and remained until his retirement in 1938; from 1926 he was chairman of the department. An inspirational teacher and administrator, he brought the department to a position of international prestige.

As a scholar, Millis was an investigator, not a theorist. He had an early interest in public finance and tax reform; with E. R. A. Seligman and others, he founded the National Tax Association in 1907. In 1908–1910 Millis conducted a study of Japanese immigration for the United States Immigration (Dillingham) Commission. A subsequent study for the Federal Council of Churches resulted in his first book: *The Japanese Problem in the United States* (1915). In 1918–1919 he was director of research for the Illinois State Health Insurance Commission; the results of his work there were published in his book *Sickness and Insurance* (1937). His major work fell in the field of industrial relations, notably the three volumes published under the collective title *Economics of Labor*, on which he collaborated with Royal E. Montgomery: *Labor's Progress and Some Basic Labor Problems* (1938), *Labor's Risks and Social Insurance* (1938), and *Organized Labor* (1945). His last book, written with Emily Clark Brown, was *From the Wagner Act to Taft-Hartley: A Study of National Labor Policy and Labor Relations* (1950). Millis' writings were, like his teaching, thorough, detailed, and comprehensive.

Despite the value of his scholarship, Millis made his greatest contribution to labor relations as an arbitrator. He was the first chairman of the trade board (later the board of arbitration) of the men's clothing industry in Chicago, 1911–1923, and again in 1937–1940 and 1945–1948. From 1923 to 1940 he was on the panel of chairmen of the international board of arbitration for the International Printing Pressmen and Assistants' Union and the American Newspaper Publishers' Association. He also served on fact-finding boards under the Railway Labor Act, and in 1940 was the first permanent umpire for General Motors Corporation and the United Automobile Workers of America. As a pioneer arbitrator he did much to lay the groundwork for the grievance and arbitration procedures in settling contract disputes that have since become standard in American labor agreements.

Nevertheless, it was in public arbitration that Millis exerted his maximum influence toward orderly collective bargaining. He served as a member of the first National Labor Relations Board of 1934–1935, set up under the National Industrial Recovery Act. In over 9,000 labor cases he and his two colleagues laid down the principles of collective bargaining that were incorporated in the National Labor Relations (Wagner) Act of 1935. That act created a new National Labor Relations Board, and Millis served as its chairman from 1940 to 1945. He took over at a time when the board was under attack from both employers and the American

Federation of Labor (A.F. of L.) as guilty of bias in favor of the Congress of Industrial Organizations (C.I.O.). As the only man acceptable to all parties, Millis moved promptly to improve procedures and ensure impartiality in decisions, with the result that the complaints disappeared and the board finished the difficult war years in a strong position.

All his life Millis was a "face-to-face" man, most influential and most impressive in direct, personal contacts with students, colleagues, labor leaders, and officials. He was a big, solid, deliberate man, with a genial personality, a sly humor, endless patience, and an unlimited capacity for work. His professional standing was recognized in his election to the presidency of the American Economic Association in 1934. Millis married Alice May Schoff, daughter of a Cincinnati newspaper editor, on Jan. 1, 1901. They had three children: Savilla Schoff, who became a social work administrator; John Schoff, who became president of the University of Vermont; and Charlotte Melissa, a sculptor. Millis returned to the University of Chicago in 1945 as senior consultant to the Industrial Relations Center and remained there until his death, of bronchopneumonia following a cerebral hemorrhage, at Billings Hospital in Chicago. He was cremated at Oakwoods Cemetery, Chicago.

[Memoir by Emily Clark Brown and others in *Am. Economic Rev.*, June 1949; *Nat. Cyc. Am. Biog.*, XLI, 529–530; *Current Biog.*, 1940; *N.Y. Times*, Nov. 24, 1940, and obituary, June 26, 1948; family information from Jean E. Singleton, Ind. State Lib.; death record from Ill. Dept. of Public Health.]

ORME W. PHELPS

MINOT, GEORGE RICHARDS (Dec. 2, 1885–Feb. 25, 1950), physician and medical scientist, was born in Boston, Mass., the oldest of three sons of James Jackson Minot and Elizabeth Frances (Whitney) Minot, and a direct descendant of George Richards Minot. The forebears of each parent had been successful in business or professional careers in Boston, often in medicine. George's father was a physician and for many years a clinical teacher of medicine at the Massachusetts General Hospital. A great-uncle, Francis Minot, and a cousin, Charles Sedgwick Minot, had taught at Harvard Medical School, as had Minot's great-grandfather James Jackson, cofounder of the Massachusetts General Hospital. Young Minot was considered a delicate child. Health-seeking winter vacations in Florida and in southern California with his parents provided opportunities for outdoor activity and led to a lifelong interest in natural history. He was educated at private schools in Boston and at Harvard, where he received the B.A. degree in 1908 and the M.D. in 1912.

After graduating from medical school, he spent sixteen months as "house pupil" (intern) at the Massachusetts General Hospital under David L. Edsall at a time when an era of hospital-based clinical research was dawning in Boston. Minot had already become interested in the relation of diet to disease, and he now began his lifelong practice of taking meticulous dietary histories of patients, particularly those with anemia. Minot went next, at Edsall's suggestion, to Johns Hopkins. His initial appointment was as assistant resident physician at the hospital, but in the fall of 1914 he transferred to the physiology laboratory of William H. Howell to work on problems of blood coagulation. Minot returned to Boston early in 1915 and on June 29 married Marian Linzee Weld, a distant cousin. Their children were Marian Linzee, Elizabeth Whitney, and Charles Sedgwick.

Upon his return, Minot resumed his research in blood disorders as assistant in medicine at the Massachusetts General Hospital (1915–1918). His office was adjacent to that of the hospital pathologist, J. Homer Wright, who had discovered in the bone marrow the site of origin of the dust-sized particles of the blood, the platelets. Minot began work with Roger I. Lee, chief of the West Medical Service at the hospital, in an attempt to learn more about the role of blood platelets in normal and in defective blood coagulation. They also studied the effect of splenectomy on patients with pernicious anemia, then a fatal disease, and found that the results were beneficial for only a few weeks or months at best. From careful studies of the blood in these cases, however, Minot found that an increase in the number of newly formed filament-containing red cells (reticulocytes) was a harbinger of a lessening of the anemia and of temporary clinical improvement. Recognition of this association became basic to his later development of a permanently successful treatment for the disease.

During World War I, at the suggestion of Alice Hamilton, pioneer in industrial medicine at Harvard, Minot investigated the anemia occurring among New Jersey ammunition workers. From studies of their blood, he found that the trinitrotoluene (TNT) used to fill shells acted as a poison, causing destruction of red cells, often producing anemia. In 1917 Minot began working at the Collis P. Huntington Memorial Hospital in Boston, operated by the Cancer Commission of Harvard University, and over the next few years he transferred his research there completely; in 1923 he was appointed chief of its medical service. At Huntington, Minot became increasingly involved in the study of patients with leukemia or cancer. He published authoritative studies of chronic leukemias, their clinical course and response to X-ray therapy, and the biological effects of X rays upon blood-cell production. During these years he was also engaged in the private practice of medicine, and in 1921, in association with Edwin A. Locke and others, he established a group practice, one of the earliest such ventures.

In the same year, at the age of thirty-five, Minot developed severe diabetes. Placed under the care of Elliott P. Joslin, he began a course of rigorous dietary restriction, virtually the only treatment then known. In spite of his illness and a progressive loss in weight, Minot continued to work. The discovery of insulin, announced in 1922 by Frederick G. Banting and Charles H. Best of Toronto, saved his life. Adhering to a carefully measured diet balanced by precise injections of insulin, a treatment that continued for life, he made a good recovery. Although attention to detail suited Minot's temperament, in carrying out this regimen he was greatly aided by his wife, who was especially helpful in minimizing interruptions of his professional activities.

At about this time Minot began the study that led to his most important achievement, a cure for pernicious anemia. He had long been interested in the problem and now began urging his private patients with anemia to include more milk and meat and some liver in their diets. The immediate stimulus for this suggestion came from the work of George Hoyt Whipple, pathologist and dean at the University of Rochester School of Medicine and Dentistry, who with his principal research associate, Dr. Frieda Robscheit-Robbins, had conducted experiments on dogs rendered anemic by repeated bleeding. They studied the effect of dietary supplements such as liver, pork muscle, or spinach on the regeneration of blood hemoglobin and by 1923 concluded that liver was by far the most potent. This evidence of the value of dietary supplementation, although based on a quite different type of experimental anemia, harmonized with Minot's long-standing clinical suspicion, gained from the taking of dietary histories, that patients with pernicious anemia often had lived for many years on diets deficient in animal protein. Encouraged by signs of some improvement in a few patients who had followed his suggestions, and especially by the considerable gain in one who greatly enjoyed eating liver, Minot invited one of his assistants in the group practice, William Parry Murphy, to join him in an all-out effort to test the possible benefits of a special diet containing as much as half a pound of liver a day. In 1926 they were able to report to the annual meeting of the Association of American Physicians that all of forty-five patients, many of them treated in Boston hospitals, "became much better rather rapidly soon after commencing the diet."

The following year, a collaboration with Edwin J. Cohn, professor of physical chemistry at Harvard, led to the development of an effective liver extract for oral use, which by 1928 was being produced on a commercial scale by the pharmaceutical firm of Eli Lilly and Company. In their early demonstration of the efficacy of liver feeding, as well as in the subsequently required testing of liver extracts on patients with pernicious anemia, Minot and his associates found that a systematic increase of reticulocytes in the blood within ten days was a reliable index of activity. In 1934 Whipple, Minot, and Murphy were jointly awarded the Nobel Prize in physiology and medicine for their discovery of liver therapy in anemias. This award presumably recognized Whipple's experimental demonstration of a novel biological principle in blood formation and its dramatic application to the cure of a fatal human anemia. Later research has found that it was chiefly the iron in the liver that benefited Whipple's dogs, and its vitamin B_{12} content that abolished the anemia in the patients of Minot and Murphy. Nevertheless, these pioneer empirical observations and the subsequent development by others of effective injectable liver extracts, replaced eventually by vitamin B_{12} injections, saved the lives of countless prospective victims of pernicious anemia.

In 1928 Minot resigned from the Huntington Hospital to become director of the Thorndike Memorial Laboratory and chief of the Fourth (Harvard) Medical Service at the Boston City Hospital, succeeding his friend and colleague Francis W. Peabody. In that laboratory and its special ward, Minot had an enhanced opportunity for carrying on teaching and research. The Thorndike (opened in 1923) was the first clinical research facility of its kind to be established in a municipal hospital in this country. Young physicians, attracted by Minot's reputation and the unusual new opportunities for clinical research, eagerly sought appointments.

Under Minot's stimulating influence, discoveries in other areas of medicine were made by his junior colleagues, among them Maxwell Finland, Chester S. Keefer, and Soma Weiss. Work on the cause of pernicious anemia was already in progress under William B. Castle, with whom Minot later published his only book, *Pathological Physiology and Clinical Description of the Anemias* (1936). In collaboration with Clark W. Heath, Minot demonstrated (1931-1932) the effectiveness of iron administration in patients with chronic hypochromic anemia; with Stacy R. Mettier he showed that the frequent lack of hydrochloric acid in the stomach of these patients was a significant factor in their decreased ability to assimilate iron; and with Maurice B. Strauss and Stanley Cobb he proved (1933) the importance of dietary inadequacy in causing "alcoholic" polyneuritis. In 1936, with Minot's encouragement, Arthur J. Patek, Jr., and Richard P. Stetson began observations on hemophilia showing that transfusions of normal platelet-free blood plasma temporarily corrected the abnormal blood coagulation. This led to the discovery, in collaboration with Francis H. L. Taylor, the biochemist of the Thorndike, of a plasma globulin of great value in the later management of hemophilia.

Along with his research Minot assumed teaching duties at Harvard Medical School, where he held appointments as assistant professor (1918-1927), clinical professor (1927-1928), and professor (1928-1948). Although his academic positions, administrative duties, and reputation as a consultant always made heavy demands upon him, he published some 150 papers, most dealing with blood disorders and the effects of nutritional deficiencies. He also found time for stimulation and encouragement of his pupils, often emphasized by notes concerning their research interests, handwritten on scraps of paper. By 1956 almost fifty of more than 400 graduates of the Thorndike or its affiliated medical services had become professors in American medical schools, and sixteen occupied distinguished posts abroad.

Many honors came to Minot in addition to the Nobel Prize. In 1928 he received the honorary degree of Sc.D. from Harvard and in 1929 the Kober Medal of the Association of American Physicians, of which he became president in 1938. He received the John Scott Medal of the City of Philadelphia in 1933. He was elected to the National Academy of Sciences in 1937 and was a member of the American Philosophical Society, the American Academy of Arts and Sciences, and a number of foreign societies.

Minot was a proper Bostonian, but he went his way unconcerned when that way was not the accepted one. In his conversation the description of any event required that it first be placed in detail in its setting. This compulsion could greatly prolong a five-minute scheduled conference. Minot had hobbies in which he took pleasure and pride. He grew irises of prize-winning beauty in his flower garden in Brookline, Mass., and as a summer sailor he was familiar with the coast of Maine and the warmer waters south of Cape Cod. His private life centered on his family and friends, but on occasion students, professional associates, or foreign visitors found a warm welcome in his home.

In spite of excellent medical care, in his middle fifties Minot developed some of the vascular and neurological complications of diabetes. In 1947 he had a stroke that paralyzed his left side; he therefore resigned as director of the Thorndike Laboratory the following year. Two years later, at the age of sixty-four, he died of pneumonia at his home in Brookline. After funeral services in King's Chapel (Unitarian) in Boston, his ashes were buried in Forest Hills (N.Y.) Cemetery.

Minot's medical career coincided with the flowering of clinical research in the United States after World War I; and his studies of nutritional deficiency in anemia were in harmony with this growing concept of the causation of ill health. His work on pernicious anemia not only provided control of a formerly fatal disease but altered the study of diseases of the blood. Previously confined largely to descriptive morphological classification, this study came to include scientific evaluations by his successors of the controls and nature of the production and destruction of blood cells and plasma components. Minot was in essence a naturalist whose interests included the organic, environmental, and emotional problems of his patients. He brought to his research and to his medical practice inexhaustible curiosity, a compulsion for accuracy, and the infinite capacity for taking pains that has been called genius.

[See Francis M. Rackemann, *The Inquisitive Physician: The Life and Times of George Richards Minot* (1956), a warmly personal biography; *Lancet*, Mar. 11, 1950 (obituary, with perceptive characterization); *Blood*, 3 (1948), 6-7 (table of biographical data); W. B. Castle in *New England Jour. Med.*, Oct. 16, 1952 (evaluation of scientific contributions); memoir by Edwin J. Cohn in Am. Philosophical Soc., *Year Book*, 1950; *Nat. Cyc. Am. Biog*, XXXVIII, 548–549; *Who Was Who in Am.*, II (1950). On his major work, see presentation speech (pp. 335–345) and Minot's "The Development of Liver Therapy in Pernicious Anemia" (pp. 357–366) in *Nobel Lectures . . . Physiology or Medicine, 1922–1941* (1965). Minot's scientific publications are in bound volumes in the Countway Lib., Harvard Medical School; the library also has an oil portrait by Charles Hopkinson (1940), which is reproduced in Rackemann, above.]

W. B. CASTLE

MITCHELL, MARGARET MUNNER-LYN (Nov. 8, 1900–Aug. 16, 1949), author, was born in Atlanta, Ga., the only daughter and the second of two children of Eugene Muse Mitchell, a lawyer, and Maybelle (Stephens) Mitchell. She attended local public and private schools and grew up quietly amid the lingering evidences of a defeated South. Her father's ancestors had resided in Atlanta and the surrounding up-country since the American Revolution; her mother's family, Irish in background and Catholic in religion (the faith of Margaret's childhood), had settled in Georgia during the early nineteenth century. Both families recounted stirring tales of the Civil War era and imbued Margaret's youth with a romantic fascination for the Lost Cause.

With intentions of becoming a doctor, Margaret Mitchell left Atlanta in the fall of 1918 to enter Smith College. The sudden death of her mother in January 1919 interrupted her freshman year, and the following June she returned home to become the mistress of her father's house. A marriage to Berrien Kinnard Upshaw on Sept. 2, 1922, ended two years later in divorce. In December 1922 she joined the staff of the *Atlanta Journal* as a feature writer for the paper's Sunday magazine. On July 4, 1925, she married John Robert Marsh, who worked in the advertising department of the Georgia Power Company. They had no children.

She left the *Journal* in 1926 and began to write a novel of the Civil War and Reconstruction South, reading extensively in the newspaper files of the Atlanta Public Library. Over the next ten years a large, unwieldy manuscript accumulated in the corners and closets of her apartment, at one time serving to prop up a sagging sofa. She was unsure of the literary merit of her work and only reluctantly permitted the Macmillan Company in 1935 to examine the disorganized pages. Macmillan, mindful of the recent financial success of another long historical romance, *Anthony Adverse* (1933), by Hervey Allen, enthusiastically contracted for the publishing rights

and then launched an extensive advertising campaign while the author made final revisions and careful checks for historical accuracy.

Surprised by Macmillan's acceptance of her novel, Margaret Mitchell was completely unprepared for its incredible success. *Gone with the Wind,* published in 1936, sold a record 1,383,000 copies in its first year. Most reviewers were unrestrained in their praise, but a few commentators, although acknowledging its exceptional readability, criticized the novel for having a deleterious effect on the reading public. Her romantic portrayal of the plantation legend, they suggested, encouraged a sentimental escapism that threatened to divert the nation's attention from the pressing problems of the 1930's. Annoyed by this kind of criticism, the author wrote to Stark Young, a friendly critic: "I wish some of them would actually read the book and review the book I wrote—not the book they imagine I've written or the book they think I should have written" (Farr, p. 131). *Gone with the Wind,* she insisted, was not "a sweet lavender and old lace, Thomas Nelson Pagish story of the old South as it never was" (Farr, p. 119). The novel won the Pulitzer Prize for 1936, but the literary debate persisted.

David O. Selznick's movie version, starring Vivien Leigh as Scarlett O'Hara and Clark Gable as Rhett Butler, converted an immensely successful novel into an entertainment revolution. A gala premiere in Atlanta on Dec. 15, 1939, climaxed a three-day festival and made a national celebrity of Margaret Mitchell, who approved of the film. In less than a year an audience of 25 million had seen the movie, and Macmillan's sales continued to soar. By the twenty-fifth anniversary of the book's publication in 1961, *Gone with the Wind* had sold over 10 million copies throughout the world—replacing *Uncle Tom's Cabin* as America's all-time best-selling novel.

Uncomfortable with the burdens of fame, Margaret Mitchell made no further attempts at fiction, destroyed an unpublished earlier work, and devoted her time to answering mail and to wartime charities. In 1949, five days after being struck down by an automobile, she died in Atlanta at the age of forty-eight. She was buried in Atlanta's Oakland Cemetery.

Not a "stylist" by her own admission (Farr, p. 109), Margaret Mitchell created a powerful narrative and injected an array of lively and memorable characters into a rich and unusually accurate historical setting. Her gift was a vivid storytelling imagination; she did not share the inner turmoil or the brooding conscience that impelled William Faulkner and other Southern writers of her time to probe the depths of human nature. A historical novel in the panoramic tradition, *Gone with the Wind* entertained a worldwide audience and enchanted a nation prone to interpret its Civil War through romantic images. Inevitably, it reminded the South of its uniqueness and conveyed a view of the past that veiled America's tragic epic with nostalgia.

[The Margaret Mitchell Marsh Estate, Atlanta, holds a collection of the author's letters and unpublished memoirs by Stephens Mitchell, her brother, and other close relatives and friends. This material formed the foundation for Finis Farr's *Margaret Mitchell of Atlanta* (1965), a competent, but uncritical, biography that provides much information on family background and the novel's career, yet accepts some crucial evidence on no more than faith. The story of the novel's emergence and eventual success is well told in Frank L. Mott, *Golden Multitudes*, pp. 255–258 (1947). See also *N.Y. Times*, Aug. 17, 1949 (obituary and editorial) and *N.Y. Times Book Rev.*, Aug. 28, 1949; *Publishers' Weekly*, Aug. 20, 1949, p. 746; *Time*, Aug. 29, 1949, p. 64; two articles noting the twenty-fifth anniversary of *Gone with the Wind* in the *N.Y. Times Book Rev.*, June 25, 1961; and the sketch in *Notable Am. Women*, II, 552–554. Facts and figures on the numerical and financial success of the novel and the movie were provided by the Margaret Mitchell Marsh Estate.]

CHARLES M. HARRIS

MITCHELL, WESLEY CLAIR (Aug. 5, 1874–Oct. 29, 1948), economist, was born in Rushville, Ill., the second of seven children and the oldest of five sons of John Wesley Mitchell, a physician, and his second wife, Lucy Medora (McClellan) Mitchell. Both parents were of English ancestry and were descended from early New England families. His father, a native of Maine, served during the Civil War as a surgeon in the Union army, where he volunteered to minister to the Negro soldiers of the Fourth United States Colored Infantry. His mother, born in Illinois, to which her forebears had migrated, was the daughter of a prominent Chicago abolitionist and had for a time attended Oberlin College, a center of abolitionist sentiment. During Wesley's childhood the family moved frequently throughout Illinois and Indiana, finally settling in Decatur, Ill., about 1880. The migrations were prompted by the search for good elementary schools for the children and for more convenient professional practice conditions for John Mitchell, who had received a serious leg injury in the war. The elder Mitchell thus sought opportunities for supplementing his decreasing professional income and meager army pension by farming and various business ventures.

Wesley's youth was generally happy and comfortable, marred only by his father's precarious health and the accompanying financial strain. He was determined to obtain a good college education, an objective his mother endorsed strongly. During the spring of his senior year in high school, he was tutored in a special school in Chicago to prepare for entrance examinations to the newly formed University of Chicago. The new university was staffed by an unusual group of gifted scholars engaged in pioneering research. Mitchell, a member of the school's first entering class in 1892, initially planned to specialize in Latin and Greek, but he soon found that his educational background had not fitted him for such studies. Fortunately for the progress of American social thinking, he shifted to economics and philosophy.

At Chicago he came under the influence of Thorstein Veblen and J. Laurence Laughlin in economics and John Dewey and his disciple George H. Meade in philosophy. Of Veblen, Mitchell later recalled, "To a well-brought up scion of American culture, taking one of [his] courses meant undergoing vivisection without an anaesthetic." As for Dewey, Mitchell said that he, like Veblen, "though with a different emphasis . . . helped an economist to drag the psychological preconceptions lurking behind theories of value and distribution into consciousness and to see how they stood the light of current knowledge." But where Veblen rejected the world, the more sanguine Dewey accepted it.

The influence of Laughlin was more complex. He had a dogmatic belief in the immutable laws of classical British economics, but, as Mitchell declared in 1945, "Laughlin's pupils . . . profited by the thinking he forced them to do for themselves." Laughlin's most telling imprint on Mitchell's thinking was in the area of monetary theory. Oddly enough, Laughlin, generally the most orthodox of the orthodox, took issue with the application of the quantity theory of the value of money to the raging bimetallic, or "free silver," controversy. As a result of Laughlin's arguments, Mitchell was stimulated to question the mechanical view of the role of money espoused by the quantity theorists and to emphasize the business or institutional considerations, such as trade and market conditions, that might be more important factors in the determination of prices.

His keen interest in the subject was evidenced in his senior year (1895-1896) by his success in an important student debate on the question of free silver and by the subject of his first publication, an essay on the quantity theory. After receiving his B.A. in 1896, Mitchell accepted a fellowship at Chicago for graduate study in economics; but Dewey also wanted him, and so Mitchell minored in philosophy. A traveling fellowship (1897-1898) enabled him to hear such leaders of current European economic thought as Johannes Conrad at Halle and Carl Menger at Vienna.

For his doctoral dissertation Mitchell undertook to study the history of the greenbacks, the Civil War inconvertible paper money that, after years of controversy, was made convertible into hard money in 1879. When he began, the topic was much more than academic. Since the case for greenbacks represented a more general form of the case for free silver, it was widely held that agitation for greenbacks would be intensified whether bimetallism won or lost. After Mitchell received his Ph.D. *summa cum laude* in 1899, he accepted a post in the United States Census Office, where he prepared a valued report on occupation statistics. The difficulties of the transition of the Census Office from a temporary, politics-ridden organization to a permanent, nonpartisan office, however, discouraged Mitchell; he thus accepted Laughlin's offer of an instructorship at Chicago at less than his government salary and supplemented his income by working as an editorial writer for the Chicago *Tribune*.

At the same time, Mitchell extended his inquiry into the greenbacks issue, which he concluded required more careful statistical treatment. He published the results, *A History of the Greenbacks, with Special Reference to the Economic Consequences of Their Issue: 1862-65* in 1903. The guiding theoretical position of the study was that while the prevailing system of money payments—he later preferred the term *system of prices*—constituted an organic whole, changes or disturbances in one segment of the system did not cause almost instantaneous equivalent changes or adjustments in other segments, as posited in the most abstract versions of neoclassical theory. While working on this treatise and its sequel, *Gold, Prices, and Wages Under the Greenback Standard* (1908), he developed a significantly new technique in economic analysis. For the first time theoretical discussion of a major economic phenomenon was supported by extensive, systematic, empirical investigation.

In 1903 Mitchell became an assistant professor of economics at the University of California in Berkeley. Rising to the rank of professor by 1909, he remained at California until 1912.

Mitchell's move to California coincided with a period of waning interest in monetary standards occasioned by an influx of gold from South Africa and Alaska and the second defeat of William Jennings Bryan for the presidency in 1900. Increasingly Mitchell saw the problem of money in a larger framework than that of the passing greenback episode. Reflecting the direction of his interests, the courses he taught at California included money, banking, foreign exchange, problems of labor, economic crises and depressions, and economic psychology.

In 1905 Mitchell began a study of the economic consequences of different monetary standards but quickly shifted his aim to an analysis of changes in the price level and their consequences. As with all of his work, this somewhat limited study broadened substantially and became a project for what he called "a theory of the money economy," which he defined as a "complex of inter-relationships on a pecuniary basis which has resulted from a long process of evolution." The study occupied Mitchell for about five years, culminating in 1910 with the delivery at Stanford University of the paper "The Money Economy and Civilization."

On the groundwork of this study's mass of drafts and detailed outlines rests practically all of Mitchell's later work. While the investigation never appeared as an integrated whole, various sections were developed and published. Thus, from the discussion of economic psychology and economic theory came the essay "The Rationality of Economic Activity" (1910), a stimulating exposition of how the economic man of classical theory is a one-sided reflection of the impact of pecuniary institutions upon the activities and minds of men. From the section "The Price System and the Consumption of Wealth," which referred to the pathetic plight of the consumer, came the basic ideas of his imaginative essay "The Backward Art of Spending Money" (1912). Less scathingly than Veblen but with equal impact, he questioned the effectiveness of the simple "buyer beware" mentality as a continuing protection of the consumer in an increasingly complex and technical age. He reworked other parts of his project into his pathbreaking essay "The Role of Money in Economic Theory" (1916), a critique of the neglect of the creative importance of money by traditional economics, and into its sequel, "The Role of Money in Economic History" (1944).

The largest segment of the study was woven into the book *Business Cycles* (1913). Mitchell's interest in business cycles was greatly stimulated by the business crisis of 1907 and by a year as a visiting lecturer at Harvard (1908-1909), where he had frequent discussions with colleagues on "the ups and downs of business." Soon after his return to Berkeley he began to gather statistics and fit them into a theoretical framework. *Business Cycles* is divided into three parts. The first sketches the leading theories of business cycles then current, the organization of the modern money economy, and a year-by-year record of cyclical fluctuations in the United States, England, France, and Germany from 1908 to 1911. The second part contains the statistical data with explanatory comment. The third section is theoretical and presents Mitchell's theory that business cycles are not "natural" in the sense that they are an inevitable tendency in all forms of economic organization; rather they are the product of the institutions and habits associated with a capitalist money economy.

"My fundamental hypothesis concerning business cycles," he later explained, "is that they result from the gradual cumulation, first of like effects in many economic processes and then of stresses that ultimately disrupt the internal balances between coordinated parts of the moving system." His primary aim was to show how these technical exigencies subject economic activity to continual alternations of expansions and contraction; he rested his analysis primarily upon an extensive detailed statistical inquiry. He chose this approach because "the problem is essentially quantitative in character, involving as it does the relative importance of divers forces which are themselves the net resultants of innumerable business decisions." The main determinant in any period is the businessman's estimate of the prospect for profits, except during crisis when the mere avoidance of bankruptcy becomes the driving force of business enterprise.

Business Cycles was a landmark both in its thesis and in its systematic use of quantitative analysis of the workings of the entire economy. Mitchell treated business cycles not as a technical specialty separate from the general body of economic theory but as an integral part of economic dynamics. Perhaps the book's most important implication is that it might be possible to substantially control and reduce the worst fluctuations of economic activity. Besides its main theme the book opened up several new avenues of economic research in which Mitchell himself became a leading investigator: national income and gross national product (which have provided the basis for modern growth economics), national planning, and such special statistical tools as economic indicators used in economic forecasting.

As he approached completion of *Business Cycles,* Mitchell decided that it was essential that he move to New York City, the center of American finance, to complete the other parts of his theory of the money economy. At the time, he was engaged to Lucy Sprague of Chicago, the dean of women at Berkeley. She also thought that New York would be ideal for her pioneering experiments in progressive education for children. Both resigned their positions, and on May 8, 1912, the couple married. They had four children: John McClellan, Sprague, Marian, and Arnold. After seven months in Europe with his wife, Mitchell returned to the United States and accepted a post in 1913 as lecturer at Columbia University. The next year he was made a full professor, a post he held for all but three years until his retirement in 1944.

The single course he gave at Columbia in his first year was on types of economic theory. This offered his students a background in the work of the classical British school, from which, he maintained, current streams of economic thought, both orthodox and not quite orthodox, flowed. The course in turn became the basis for a manuscript on classical economics (parts of which were published as articles). One of the most interesting concepts in this manuscript was his unorthodox idea that particular economic theories are not universal in the sense that laws of mathematics are; rather they are largely intellectual responses to the economic conditions and issues of a particular time and setting. In his early period at Columbia, he published pioneering articles on security prices and wrote an oft-reprinted monograph, *The Making and Using of Index Numbers* (1915), which has long been a requisite for economic statisticians.

In 1919 Mitchell joined with Veblen, James Harvey Robinson, Charles A. Beard, and other eminent social scientists to found the New School for Social Research in New York. Mitchell taught there for a time, but in 1922, after urgent requests from his former colleagues, he returned to Columbia.

In 1920 Mitchell was a principal founder of that landmark institution for quantitative economics, the National Bureau of Economic Research, which he served for twenty-five years as its director of research. The object of the bureau was to "conduct quantitative investigations into subjects that affect public welfare" with the aim of ascertaining "fundamental facts within its field as accurately as may be and to make its findings widely known." The best proof of the outstanding contribution of the bureau to the advancement of economic knowledge is the remarkable number of its investigations that were taken over by federal agencies and now, in expanded and permanent form, provide the basis for much of the nation's basic economic statistics. These studies included inquiries on price index numbers, national income, capital formation, flow of funds, consumer credit, and economic indicators. The bureau, important as it is today, stands in a real sense as a living monument to his dream that quantitative research could provide the tools for rational economic policy.

The first undertaking by the bureau was a pioneering investigation of the size and distribution of national income, *Income in the United States: Its Amount and Distribution 1909-1919* (1921-1922). Beginning in the early 1920's Mitchell led the bureau's staff in a renewed study of business cycles to correspond roughly to the three sections of *Business Cycles*. The first volume, *Business Cycles: The Problem and Its Setting* (1927), was based on data covering more countries and a more extensive time period than the earlier work and was further enriched by an account of the "evolution of business economy," drawn from Mitchell's "Theory of the Money Economy." This volume was, as economic works go, a best seller. In 1946, with Arthur F. Burns, his successor as director of the bureau, Mitchell published *Measuring Business Cycles*, which, along with the posthumously published *What Happens During Business Cycles: A Progress Report* (1951), constituted a revision of the second section of his original study. Meanwhile, in 1941, doubtful that he would live to complete the revision, Mitchell reissued the original version of the third section under the title *Business Cycles and Their Causes*.

Throughout his academic career, Mitchell took time out for public service. He served in 1906 as assistant to the chief of the Red Cross mission during the great San Francisco earthquake and two years later as superintendent of fieldwork for the newly organized National Immigration Commission. During World War I, he headed the Price Section of the Division of Planning and Statistics of the War Industries Board. After the war he supervised the preparation of a *History of Prices During the War*, which preserved most of the valuable information on wartime prices and price control. Besides editing the fifty-seven bulletins in the project, he wrote two, *International Price Comparisons* and the *Summary*, which contained

one of the first proposals for a broad index for measuring the physical production of the nation.

While director of the National Bureau of Economic Research, Mitchell often served on government commissions to increase "sure knowledge of the causal interconnection of things," which he deemed essential for devising sound national policies. Under his direction and with his collaboration, the bureau prepared for committees growing out of President Harding's Conference on Unemployment, the comprehensive surveys *Business Cycles and Unemployment* (1923) and *Recent Economic Changes in the United States* (1929). In 1929 President Hoover appointed him chairman of the President's Research Committee on Social Trends, and the outcome was *Recent Social Trends in the United States* (1933). Mitchell modestly attributed its popular reception to the depression, but not a little of its great influence was his exciting introduction, which was really a preview of much of the New Deal welfare-state program.

In 1933, at the suggestion of Secretary of the Interior Harold L. Ickes, an old schoolmate from the University of Chicago, Mitchell was made a member of the National Planning Board of the Federal Emergency Administration of Public Works, the nation's first peacetime national planning agency. He served there and at its successor agency, the National Resources Board, for two years.

Finally, during World War II he served as chairman of the President's Committee on the Cost of Living, whose report, in general, defended the accuracy of the official index numbers of changes in the cost of living prepared by the United States Bureau of Labor Statistics.

Mitchell's contributions were not limited to his chosen discipline. In 1922-1923, having long held the view that most social problems required the joint action of various disciplines, he played a primary role in bringing about the organization of the Social Science Research Council, to promote interdisciplinary research. Such was Mitchell's personality and character that over and over in his career, he was able to bring together people of sharply divergent views and to get them to work effectively.

Soft-spoken and patient, Mitchell preferred to seek out the virtues in the work of his colleagues rather than the faults. Although he set high standards of scholarship, he was never arrogant or doctrinaire, and he readily and cheerfully admitted his errors. The recipient of many honorary degrees, he also served as president of the American Economic Association, the

American Statistical Association, and the Econometric Society. In 1938 he was elected to the presidency of the American Association for the Advancement of Science, an honor only held once before by a social scientist. In 1947 he was the first recipient of the American Economic Association's Francis A. Walker medal, which is awarded to a "living American economist who has made a contribution of the highest distinction." Admired by such British statistical theorists as F. Y. Edgeworth, Mitchell was made an honorary fellow of the Royal Statistical Society. By accepting, in the academic year 1931-1932, the George Eastman visiting professorship at Oxford, he played a vital role in helping the British universities to overcome their formative deficiencies in economic research. Mitchell continued to work until nearly the end of his life, despite a heart attack suffered in 1947 at his summer home in Greensboro, Vt. He suffered a second attack the following year and died at New York Hospital (New York City). His remains were cremated.

In the end, Mitchell's unwavering determination to stick to the task of arriving at fundamental facts paid handsome dividends, not the least of which was the establishment of quantitative research on an enduring foundation. Despite his tremendous contributions to the growth of empirical research and his belief in the value of that method, he continually supplied a calm, restraining voice against misinterpretation and misuse of the results of empirical investigation.

In his imaginative use of the powerful tools of history and statistics, in his concern with the problem of a valid conception of human nature, in his faith in the long-run progress of the American people, and in the consistently constructive bent of his work in the direction of improving the existing economic order lies much of the explanation of why Mitchell's advanced views received such respect, recognition, and acceptance both within and without his profession. They stamped him the most representative American economist of the first half of the twentieth century and made his name symbolic of the ushering in of the age of research in the social sciences.

[The Mitchell papers are in Special Collect., Columbia Univ. Lib. His important works in economic theory, in addition to those mentioned above, are *The Backward Art of Spending Money and Other Essays* (1937) and the posthumous *Types of Economic Theory: From Mercantilism to Institutionalism* (2 vols., 1967, 1969), both ed. by Joseph Dorfman. For writings on Mitchell, see Dorfman, *The Economic Mind in American Civilization*, III, 455-473; IV, 360-377; V, 666-669 (5 vols., 1946-1959); Allan G. Gruchy, *Modern Economic Thought: The American Contribution*, pp. 247-333 (1946); *Wesley Clair Mitchell: The Economic Scientist*, ed. Arthur F. Burns (1952), which contains a practically complete bibliography of Mitchell's publications; Lucy Sprague Mitchell, *Two Lives* (1953); Simon Kuznets, "The Contribution of Wesley C. Mitchell," in Dorfman, et al., *Institutional Economics: Veblen, Commons, and Mitchell Reconsidered*, pp. 95-122 (1963).]

JOSEPH DORFMAN

MITSCHER, MARC ANDREW (Jan. 26, 1887-Feb. 3, 1947), pioneer naval aviator and commander of the most powerful naval striking force of World War II, was born in Hillsborough (later Hillsboro), Wis., the first son and second of three children of Oscar Mitscher and Myrta (Shear) Mitscher. His paternal grandfather had emigrated from Germany in the early 1850's; his mother was of English descent. Not long after Marc's birth the family moved to Oklahoma City, where the father ran a general store and later served as mayor. In 1900, appointed Indian agent for a remote reservation, he arranged for the boy to continue his schooling in Washington, D.C., and in 1904 secured for him an appointment to the United States Naval Academy.

At Annapolis, where he acquired his nickname, "Pete," Mitscher's career was less than distinguished. Forced to resign after two years for academic and disciplinary reasons, he was readmitted, and he graduated in 1910 near the bottom of his class. For the next five years he served in a variety of junior officer billets in ships of the Pacific Fleet. Repeated requests for transfer to aviation duty finally bore fruit in 1915, when Mitscher was ordered to Pensacola for training. He completed the course in June 1916 and qualified as naval aviator no. 33.

During World War I, Mitscher served successively as head of the aviation department on the cruiser *Huntington* and as commander of naval air stations on Long Island and at Miami. Somewhat taciturn and withdrawn, in part perhaps because of his early debacle at the Naval Academy, he nevertheless proved himself in these assignments a single-minded, efficient, and even-tempered officer. He was promoted to lieutenant commander in July 1918.

In the years between the wars Mitscher's career embraced all aspects of naval aviation. In May 1919 he piloted the flying boat NC-1 on its attempted transatlantic flight; and in 1933-1934 he directed the pioneering mass long-range flights of naval patrol planes from Norfolk to the Canal Zone and from San Diego to Hawaii. He was commanding officer of the seaplane tender *Wright* (1937-1938) and commander of Patrol Wing One (1938-1939). In 1922 he commenced the first of four tours of duty at the Bureau of Aeronautics, which involved him both in matters of design, training, and procurement and in the interservice and intraservice struggles of those years over the place of the air weapon in the military establishment. Most important for the future was his work in the development of techniques of carrier air operations, as air officer and then executive officer of the experimental carrier *Langley* (1926, 1929–1930) and of the newly commissioned *Saratoga* (1926–1929, 1934–1935). He was promoted to captain in 1938; in 1941, after two years as assistant chief of the Bureau of Aeronautics in charge of aircraft procurement, he became the first commanding officer of the new carrier *Hornet*.

Mitscher's period in command of the *Hornet* encompassed the launching of the Tokyo raid of B-25 army bombers commanded by Lieutenant Colonel James A. Doolittle (Apr. 18, 1942) and participation in the crucial battle of Midway (June 4-6), in which the ship's air group suffered heavy losses. Promoted to rear admiral, Mitscher spent the next year and a half in shore-based air commands, most notably at Guadalcanal (February–August 1943), where his mixed force of army, navy, marine, and New Zealand aircraft supported the advance through the central Solomons, destroyed some seventeen ships and 470 enemy aircraft, and shot down the plane that carried Adm. Isoroku Yamamoto, Commander-in-Chief of the Japanese Combined Fleet, to his death.

Early in 1944 Mitscher was placed in command of the Fast Carrier Task Force, Pacific Fleet (Task Force 58 when operating under Adm. Raymond A. Spruance, Commander Fifth Fleet; Task Force 38 when under the control of Adm. William F. Halsey, Jr., Commander Third Fleet). With this force, which by war's end would number over a hundred ships and a thousand aircraft, he introduced a new era of naval warfare. Between January and April, as the amphibious forces advanced into Micronesia and along the New Guinea coast, Mitscher's carrier groups gained control of the central Pacific through destructive attacks on the Marshall Islands, the Japanese base at Truk, the Mariana Islands, and the Palau group. Renewed strikes on the Marianas in June cleared the way for the invasion of Saipan. In the battle of the Philippine Sea that followed (June 19–21), the destruction of some 475 enemy aircraft and, more importantly, of their pilots, effectively wrote an end to the career of the Japanese carrier striking force, which had dominated the early months of the war. Heavy attacks on Formosa, Luzon, and the Visayas in September and October inhibited Japanese air reinforcement of the Philippines and expedited the American return; and in the great battle for Leyte Gulf (Oct. 23–26), which followed the American landings, Mitscher's force sank thirteen enemy ships, including four carriers and a battleship.

Through these ten months of almost continuous operations, Mitscher demonstrated marked skill and determination in the conduct of massed carrier operations against both shore-based air forces and fleet units, as well as a noteworthy solicitude for his pilots, as seen both in the development of submarine and seaplane rescue techniques and in his willingness to illuminate his ships to facilitate night recovery of pilots. A fighter with a marked preference for the offensive, more a doer than a thinker, Mitscher yet showed sure tactical instinct: off the Marianas in June his plan to force rather than to await battle, although vetoed by Admiral Spruance for understandable reasons, would in all probability have brought a still more crushing victory; at Leyte the battle plan prepared by his staff was in all respects superior to that implemented by Admiral Halsey.

After a period devoted to leave and planning, Mitscher resumed command of the fast carrier force in early 1945. In February his aircraft struck the Tokyo area in the first attack on the Japanese homeland launched by naval units since the *Hornet* raid three years before; in March, in anticipation of the invasion of Okinawa, they attacked airfields in southern Japan. There followed two and a half months of the most intensive sustained naval operations in history. In response to the Okinawa landing, the Japanese committed their remaining surface combatant strength against the American fleet, along with repeated mass kamikaze (suicide aircraft) attacks, which by mid-April had sunk twenty-four American ships, inflicted major damage on a hundred others, and reduced Mitscher's task groups from four to three. Before his relief on May 27 he was twice forced to change flagships as a result of damage inflicted by suicide planes.

In June 1945 Mitscher assumed the post of Deputy Chief of Naval Operations for Air and soon found himself, as after the previous war, involved in political controversy over the organization of the defense establishment. Promoted to admiral in March 1946, he gladly left Washington to assume command of the Eighth Fleet and in September became Commander-in-Chief, Atlantic Fleet, the second naval aviator to hold a major fleet command. But the strain of so many months of sustained combat and the aftereffects of malaria contracted on Guadalcanal had taken their toll. Following a heart attack in January 1947, he was hospitalized at Norfolk, Va., where he died of a coronary thrombosis a week after his sixtieth birthday. He was buried in Arlington National Cemetery. His wife, Frances Smalley of Tacoma, Wash., whom he had married on Jan. 16, 1913, survived him. They had no children.

[Theodore Taylor, *The Magnificent Mitscher* (1954), is a satisfactory biography with an extensive list of sources. The *N.Y. Times*, Feb. 4, 1947, carried both an obituary and an editorial. For background on the interwar years, with some incidental mention of Mitscher, see Archibald D. Turnbull and Clifford L. Lord, *Hist. of U.S. Naval Aviation* (1949). Wartime operations are treated in detail in the appropriate volumes of Samuel Eliot Morison, *Hist. of U.S. Naval Operations in World War II* (1947–1962), and in Clark G. Reynolds, *The Fast Carriers* (1968). The best short campaign analysis is in Elmer B. Potter, ed., *The U.S. and World Sea Power* (1955). For a fine description of Mitscher's force in action, Joseph Bryan III and Philip Reed, *Mission Beyond Darkness* (1945). The Lib. of Cong. has some Mitscher papers, as does the State Hist. Soc. of Wis.; the remainder (as of 1971) are in the possession of the family.]
JAMES A. FIELD, JR.

MOHOLY-NAGY, LÁSZLÓ (July 20, 1895–Nov 24, 1946), artist and teacher, was born in Bacsbarsod, Hungary, the second of three sons of Leopold Nagy and Caroline (Csillag) Nagy. He was brought up as a Calvinist by his mother and grandmother on the maternal family's country estate after his father had gambled away a large wheat farm, abandoned his family, and left for America. Because of the family breakup, Moholy-Nagy felt in his youth that he was ostracized by the surrounding community, and he vowed to make his name known to the world. The strongest male influence on his early life was an uncle, a lawyer and intellectual, who impressed on the boy the backwardness and decay of rural society as contrasted with the vibrant progress of the new urban industrial world.

In 1913 he entered the University of Budapest to study law, but at the outbreak of World War I, he was called up to fight and spent four years as an artillery officer, mostly on the front lines. In 1916, his entire battery except for Moholy-Nagy was wiped out. A minor wound and a severe infection required him to be hospitalized for months. While he was in the hospital he turned to art to record his emotions (he had earlier written poems, some of which had been published in avant-garde journals), sketching war scenes and portraits in an expressionistic vein.

After the war he completed his undergraduate studies in law at the University of Budapest, but he was becoming increasingly committed to art. His early drawings and paintings were representational, although he soon tried nonrepresentational work, particularly experimenting with color. These paintings made use of austere, objective, noniconographic forms in pure colors and often abstracted from industrial objects. Like other artistic radicals of the time, Moholy-Nagy sought to express a complete break from the visual modes of the past, which he believed had been closely tied to social and cultural conditions that he could no longer accept.

Even though he had received no formal training in art, Moholy-Nagy decided to embark on an art career. After a few months painting in Vienna, he went to Berlin in January 1921. Soon, under the influence of Kurt Schwitters, he was involved with a dadaistic art of collage. He also took up photography and devised what he called "photograms," patterns of light made by objects placed directly on sensitized photographic paper. In 1922, he gave his first public exhibition in Berlin's Galerie der Sturm.

In 1923, Moholy-Nagy joined the faculty in the Weimar Bauhaus, founded by Walter Gropius in 1919 to encourage craftsmanship in the arts. In Weimar and later in Dessau, in an atmosphere that encouraged free artistic experimentation, he designed the typography of fourteen publications and taught the advanced foundation course and a metal workshop. Resigning from the Bauhaus in January 1928, when political pressures intensified to limit the program to specialized technical training, Moholy-Nagy returned to Berlin, where he was soon engaged in designing settings for the Piscator Theater and for opera productions at the State Opera House. At about this time, he ceased painting and threw himself into projects in advertising, typography, and photography. Among other activities, he produced experimental films, designed magazine covers and commercial exhibition displays, and devised a light-display machine for projecting abstract light patterns. His light modulator was the subject of a film, *Light Display, Black and White and Gray* (1930). By this time he had gained an international reputation as one of the outstanding innovators in modern art.

Moholy-Nagy's opposition to Nazi rule made his position in Germany increasingly difficult. Refusing to submit his earlier painting for censorship, he fled from Germany in January 1934 and settled in Amsterdam, where he became an adviser to a large Dutch printing firm. Here he also designed an important exhibition for the Dutch rayon industry. The Stedelijk Museum honored him with a one-man show in 1934.

From May 1935 to June 1937, Moholy-Nagy lived in London, where he took up painting once again, worked on commercial design projects, published three volumes of photographs (*The Street Market of London,* 1936; *Eton Portrait,* 1937; and *An Oxford University Chest,* 1939), produced films (*Life of the Lobster,* 1935; *The New Architecture at the London Zoo,* 1936; and special effects for Alexander Korda's *The Shape of Things to Come,* 1936), and held a one-man photography show.

When in 1937 the directors of the Association of Arts and Industries in Chicago unexpectedly invited him to become director of a projected New Bauhaus school there, Moholy-Nagy accepted. Coming to Chicago, he gathered together an outstanding faculty and supervised the opening of the new school in the remodeled Marshall Field Mansion on Oct. 18, 1937, with thirty-five students. Here the old Bauhaus ideals of craftsmanship and the integrity of the arts were stressed. But the New Bauhaus was plagued with financial and administration problems, and it closed after only one year.

Taking a position then as art adviser to the Spiegel mail-order company in Chicago, Moholy-Nagy moved ahead with plans for a new School of Design. In February 1939, the school opened under his directorship, aiming to provide an education in which art, science, and technology were fully integrated. He devoted himself to gathering contributions for the school as well as teaching many of the classes. The School of Design was renamed the Institute of Design in 1944 and, expanding immensely, eventually became a division of the Illinois Institute of Technology.

While carrying on tireless activity as a teacher and administrator, Moholy-Nagy continued his own painting and design work. Many of his later endeavors were free-form sculptures, often in plastic materials, and multidimensional abstract paintings. He wrote many articles and his important testament *Vision in Motion* (1947). He was honored with several one-man shows and participated in numerous group shows. In the autumn of 1945, it was discovered that he had leukemia. He died in Chicago late the following year and was buried in Graceland Cemetery, Chicago.

Moholy-Nagy was first married on Jan. 18, 1921, to Lucia Schultz, from whom he was separated in 1929. He subsequently married Dorothea Maria Pauline Alice Sibylle (Sibyl) Pietzsch, a film scenario writer, who worked closely with him, helped administer the School of Design, and wrote his biography. They had two daughters, Hattula and Claudia. Moholy-Nagy was noted for his warmth, optimism, energy, and vitality; his enthusiasm for his work; and his commitment to his artistic vision.

Probably the most versatile figure in twentieth-century modernism, Moholy-Nagy played a seminal role in the development of several of the visual arts. Not only did he do highly original work in multidimensional abstract painting, free-form plastic and kinetic sculpture, typography and book design, commercial, industrial, and theatrical design, film, and photography, in which fields his output was prolific, but also he published a substantial body of writings, setting forth his organic view of art and life and his hopes for the possibilities of the new technology. Moreover, his impact in both Europe and America as an educator of an entire generation of artists and designers was considerable. After Gropius, he was the person most influential in spreading the ideas of the Bauhaus. Above all, as a teacher and practitioner in the arts he sought to break with the past to create an open visual experience that would encourage a freer life for all persons.

[Manuscript materials by, and relating to, Moholy-Nagy are located at the Chicago Circle branch of the Univ. of Illinois and at the Arch. of Am. Art, Washington, D.C. The most complete bibliographies of writings by and about Moholy-Nagy are to be found in *Moholy-Nagy,* ed. Richard Kostelanetz (1970) and in the Museum of Contemporary Art, Chicago, *Moholy-Nagy, Exhibition Catalogue* (1939). The fullest biographical information is to be found in Sibyl Moholy-Nagy, *Moholy-Nagy: Experiment in Totality* (1950; 2d ed., 1969). Moholy-Nagy's other books include *Das Buch neuer Künstler,* with Ludwig Kassák (Vienna, 1922); *Die Bühne im Bauhaus,* with Oskar Schlemmer and Farkas Molnar (Munich, 1925), trans. *The Theater of the Bauhaus* (1961); *Malerei, Fotografie, Film* (1925), trans., *Painting, Photography, Film* (1969); and *Von Material zu Architektur* (Munich, 1929), trans., *The New Vision: From Material to Architecture* (1932). See also *Works of Art by Moholy-Nagy,* ed. John Coolidge (1950); Siegfried Giedion, "Notes on the Life and Work of László Moholy-Nagy, Painter-Universalist," *Architects' Year Book,* vol. II (1949); Edgar Kaufmann, Jr., "Moholy," *Arts and Architecture,* vol. LXIV (1947); Sibyl Moholy-Nagy, "Constructivism from Malevitch to Moholy-Nagy," *Arts and Architecture,* vol. 83 (1966); Herbert Read, "A Great Teacher," *Architectural Rev.* 103 (1947).]

PAUL R. BAKER

MONROE, PAUL (June 7, 1869–Dec. 6, 1947), educator, was born in North Madison, Ind., the older of two sons of William Y. Monroe, a Baptist clergyman of Scots-Irish ancestry, and Juliet (Williams) Monroe, a native of Indiana whom his father married after the death of his first wife, who had borne him nine children, six boys and three girls. William Monroe was a captain during the Civil War and active in local political affairs, serving as sheriff, county treasurer, and representative in the state legislature.

After Paul's freshman year at Hanover College in Madison, the family moved to Franklin, Ind., where he was graduated from Baptist Franklin College with the B.S. degree (1890). He became a high school principal in Hopewell (1890-1891) and Martinsville (1891-1894), Ind. In 1894 Monroe went to the University of Chicago to study sociology and political science; he was awarded a fellowship the following year and received his Ph.D. in 1897. He accepted a position as instructor of history at Teachers College, which had recently affiliated with Columbia University but was still virtually a small normal school. Following Dean James Earl Russell's suggestion that he concentrate on education, Monroe became adjunct professor of history of education in 1899, studied at the University of Heidelberg in 1901, and was promoted to full professor in 1902.

Monroe soon established himself as the leading historian of education in America. He published several books within a few years, his *Textbook in the History of Education* (1905) and *Brief Course in the History of Education* (1907) being the most successful and influential. They were based on primary sources and were more thorough and scholarly than earlier textbooks in the field, dealing with both theory and practice and putting education in the broader context of the history of civilization.

Monroe's most significant achievement was the comprehensive five-volume *Cyclopedia of Education* (1911-1913). As editor-in-chief, he developed the plan of organization. Articles were contributed by more than a thousand scholars, including John Dewey, the departmental editor for philosophy of education articles. The monumental work systematically organized knowledge in the field when education was emerging as a discipline and thereby contributed to its development and professionalization. It is still the best encyclopedia of education in English and remains an invaluable reference work for educational historians.

More than any other individual, Monroe established the discipline of history of education in America. He maintained high standards of scholarship in his graduate seminars, train-ing a generation of educators in methods of historical research and application of the scientific method. Many of his students became eminent historians and educators, including Ellwood P. Cubberley, Alexander Inglis, I. L. Kandel, William H. Kilpatrick, Edgar W. Knight, Jesse Sears, Henry Suzzallo, and W. Thomas Woody.

Nearly one-fourth of the doctoral dissertations at Teachers College in the years 1899-1921 were in the history of education. The products of Monroe's seminars constitute an impressive scholarly contribution. Many of the dissertations trace the development of educational institutions and focus on the public schools, reflecting the social evolutionism and institutionalism that pervaded the thought of the day.

Monroe's influence and Cubberley's successful textbook *Public Education in the United States* (1919) shaped the interpretation of American educational history for decades. Monroe did not complete his own magnum opus, *The Founding of the American Public School System*, until 1940.

Having made his pioneering contributions in the history of education, Monroe turned his attention to administration, serving as director of the School of Education at Teachers College (1915-1923), and international education. In 1913, he made a survey of the Philippine school system for the United States government and visited Chinese colleges at the request of John D. Rockefeller, Jr. After World War I, he conducted many studies of education in foreign countries for President Wilson. Monroe returned to China in 1921 to help the government modernize its educational system. An authority on China, he served on the Boxer Indemnity Board and was a cofounder and president of the China Institute of America.

Monroe always had a special interest in the foreign students in his classes and sought to better prepare them for educational leadership in their own countries. He proposed and directed (1923-1938) the International Institute of Education at Teachers College, a successful pioneering venture in international education. Several thousand foreign students attended institute courses. Monroe lectured in foreign universities and conducted numerous educational surveys at the invitation of other countries. The institute disseminated many of his studies in its annual *Educational Yearbook*. Under the auspices of the institute, the Carnegie Corporation, and the Carnegie Foundation, Monroe organized a series of international conferences on examinations (1931, 1935, 1938) and edited three volumes of conference proceedings.

Monroe was named Barnard professor of education in 1925. While on a leave of absence, he served as president of Istanbul Woman's College and Robert College in Turkey (1932–1935). He became professor emeritus at Columbia in 1935. A founder and president of the World Federation of Education Associations (1931-1933, 1935-1943), Monroe was trustee of several foreign colleges and received five honorary degrees, as well as decorations and awards from a number of foreign governments.

Of medium height, Monroe had an oval face, high forehead, gray eyes, Roman nose, and a fair complexion. In his later years glasses and gray hair contributed to a distinguished appearance. Congenial and empathetic, Paul Monroe was respected by both students and colleagues for his humanity, love of learning, and devotion to education.

Monroe married Mary Emma Ellis of Franklin on Aug. 26, 1891. They had three children: Juliet, Ellis, and Jeanette. The Monroes made their home in Yonkers, N.Y., moving after his retirement to Garrison, N.Y. Monroe died in Goshen, N.Y., of myocardial degeneration and was buried in Sleepy Hollow Cemetery in Tarrytown, N.Y.

[The major sources are Henry Suzzallo, "Paul Monroe—An Appreciation," in I. L. Kandel, ed., *Twenty-five Years of American Education*, pp. xi–xiv (1931); Edward H. Reisner, "Paul Monroe, 1869–1947," *Teachers College Record*, Jan. 1948, pp. 290–293 (includes portrait); *Nat. Cyc. Am. Biog.*, XXXVI, 336; and information from daughter Jeanette Monroe Bassett and his son. Obituary in *N.Y. Times*, Dec. 7, 1947.

Other books written by Monroe are *A Source Book of the History of Education for the Greek and Roman Period* (1901); *Thomas Platter and the Educational Renaissance of the Sixteenth Century* (1904); *Principles of Secondary Education* (editor, 1914); *The American Spirit: A Basis for World Democracy* (co-editor, 1918); *Essays on Comparative Education* (2 vols., 1927–1932); and *China: A Nation in Evolution* (1928).]

NATALIE A. NAYLOR

MONSKY, HENRY (Feb. 4, 1890-May 2, 1947), lawyer and Jewish communal leader, was born in Omaha, Neb., the oldest of the three sons and one daughter of Abraham Monsky and his second wife, Betsy (Perisnev) Monsky; there were also five children by the first marriage. Both parents were Orthodox Jews who had emigrated from Lithuania in the 1880's. The father was a cantor, and although the family was poor, Henry grew up with a respect for learning. He attended public schools and went also to *cheder*—Hebrew religious school. After

graduating from high school, he entered the law school of Creighton University, a Roman Catholic institution in Omaha, from which he received the LL.B. degree, cum laude, in 1912. He then began a practice in Omaha that he maintained for the rest of his life.

Imbued with a sense of dedication to the welfare of the Jewish people, Monsky joined the B'nai B'rith lodge in Omaha in 1911 and became its youngest president two years later. He was attracted to this oldest of American Jewish service organizations because it adhered to no political or religious dogmas and included Jews of every variety of belief. Monsky was continually dismayed at the factionalism among American Jews, growing out of differences over religious interpretation, Zionism, assimilation, and the like. The result, he felt, was duplication of programs, competition for funds, and a growing chaos that he feared was leading to a dilution of Jewish values and loyalties. His own convictions were firm but never fanatical. Brilliant and energetic, he possessed the leadership ability to get ideological opponents to work together for a common cause. Rather than identify himself with any one Jewish religious faction, he became a member of Reform, Conservative, and Orthodox congregations.

Monsky's prominence grew, and in 1923 he was elected president of B'nai B'rith's 6th district, comprising several Midwestern states. In 1933 he was elected to the organization's national executive committee, and five years later he became international president, a post he retained until his death. He was the organization's first president from an Eastern European and Orthodox background. During his tenure B'nai B'rith grew from a membership of 60,000 men and a handful of women's chapters to nearly 200,000 men and 95,000 women. Its varied programs were expanded, and Monsky served as chairman of practically all the national committees that supervised them.

In the late 1930's the threat of Nazi-inspired anti-Semitism intensified Monsky's efforts to bring about Jewish unity. Yet it was not until 1943, after the Nazi plan to murder all European Jews became known in the United States, that he was able to establish the American Jewish Conference, of which he served as chairman until his death. This conference, made up of representatives of most American Jewish groups, was designed to aid the victims of Nazi Germany and to plan for the postwar needs of world Jewry. Monsky's dedication to Jewish unity was surpassed only by his ardent Zionism. He worked tirelessly to help create a Jewish national home in Palestine. Nevertheless, as president of B'nai B'rith, he respected that organization's historic neutrality in the ongoing Zionist controversy and prevented it from officially committing itself to either side.

Besides his B'nai B'rith activities, Monsky served in many other civic roles. He was a member of the Omaha Welfare Board, the founder (1921) of the Omaha Community Chest, and president of the Nebraska Conference of Social Work, and during the 1930's he served on the national board of the Family Welfare Association of America. A close friend of Father Edward J. Flanagan, founder of Boys Town, Monsky volunteered his efforts to raise funds for that enterprise, served on its board of trustees, and handled its legal work. In 1946 he was chairman of the executive committee of the National Conference for Prevention and Control of Juvenile Delinquency. His interfaith interests brought him to the executive committee of the National Conference of Christians and Jews and to the Catholic Committee on American Citizenship. In 1941 President Roosevelt appointed Monsky to the National Voluntary Participation Committee of the Office of Civilian Defense, and four years later he was named as one of two Jewish consultants to the United States delegation to the San Francisco conference that established the United Nations.

Monsky was married twice. As a young man he had fallen in love with Daisy Hirsh, a niece of Adolf Kraus, then international president of B'nai B'rith, and the offspring of a wealthy, "Americanized" family of the Reform tradition. The couple's plans to wed, however, were thwarted by the unyielding social and religious prejudices of both families. On May 2, 1915, Monsky married Sadie Lesser. They had three children: Joy, Hubert, and Barbara. This marriage ended in divorce in the early 1930's, and on Nov. 3, 1937, Monsky married his first love, now the widow of Albert Rothschild. Monsky died of a sudden coronary thrombosis in 1947 while attending a meeting of the interim committee of the American Jewish Conference in New York City. After ceremonies in both New York and Omaha, he was buried at Fisher Farm Cemetery, Omaha.

[Nat. Jewish Monthly, June 1947, and indexed files of that magazine, 1938-1947 (available at B'nai B'rith Nat. Headquarters, Washington, D.C.); Daisy Monsky and Maurice Bisgyer, Henry Monsky: The Man and His Work (1947); Edward E. Grusd, B'nai B'rith: The Story of a Covenant (1966); Maurice Bisgyer, Challenge and Encounter (1967); Proc. of the Am. Jewish Conference; Who Was Who in America, II (1950); N.Y. Times obituary, May 8, 1947.]
EDWARD E. GRUSD

MONTGOMERY, JAMES ALAN (June 13, 1866-Feb. 6, 1949), Old Testament scholar and Episcopal clergyman, was born in Germantown, Pa., the third of nine children and the oldest of five boys. His father, Thomas Harrison Montgomery, a successful insurance executive associated with several insurance companies in the Philadelphia area, had scholarly and literary interests and did a considerable amount of writing. James's mother, Anna (Morton) Montgomery, was of a prominent Philadelphia family whose forebears had come from Ireland. His father's lineage was dominated by Episcopalian clergymen, and his mother's by physicians.

There was a natural confluence of theological and scholarly interests in Montgomery's career. He graduated from the Episcopal Academy in Philadelphia and went on to the University of Pennsylvania, from which he received the B.A. degree in 1887 and a Phi Beta Kappa key. He continued his studies at the Philadelphia Divinity School (Episcopal), completing the course of study in 1890. In the same year, he was appointed a deacon in the Protestant Episcopal church.

Before commencing his career as a clergyman, however, he spent two years as a traveling fellow at the University of Greifswald and the University of Berlin. On his return to the United States in 1892, he was appointed curate of the Church of the Holy Communion in New York City.

He was ordained a priest in the Protestant Episcopal church in 1893 and was installed as rector of St. Paul's in West Philadelphia. On August 1 of the same year, he married Mary Frank Owen of County Derry, Ireland, whom he had met in Berlin while pursuing studies at the university.

In 1895, he transferred to St. Peter's in Philadelphia. In 1899 Montgomery became the first rector of the Church of the Epiphany in Germantown, and at the same time accepted a position as instructor in Old Testament studies at the Philadelphia Divinity School.

His first marriage ended tragically with the death of his wife on Mar. 24, 1900. There were no children. Two years later, on June 17, 1902, he married Edith Thompson, a member of a local family. From this union came five children, all boys: James Alan, Jr.; Newcomb Thompson; George Morton; and two others who died in infancy.

While serving as both rector and teacher, Montgomery also pursued graduate studies at the University of Pennsylvania, earning the

Ph.D. in 1904. His dissertation was on the Samaritans and served as the basis of his first book, which appeared in 1907. By that time he had resigned from his post as rector of the Church of the Epiphany; he did not undertake an active ministry for the church again. The rest of his career was devoted to scholarly interests in his capacity as professor, editor, and author.

He progressed rapidly to the rank of full professor at the Philadelphia Divinity School and continued to teach there until his retirement in 1935. He also taught in the Semitics department of the graduate school of the University of Pennsylvania, being appointed lecturer in 1909 and later advancing to the rank of professor. He continued to teach there until 1939, although he retired officially in 1935.

At both institutions, Montgomery trained many students who became distinguished scholars in their own right. He was elected an honorary member of the British Society for Old Testament Study and for years was the only American scholar so honored. He was also elected to the American Philosophical Society (1925).

In addition to his academic duties, Montgomery accepted a full share of administrative and editorial responsibilities in the major professional societies to which he belonged. He was invited in 1892 to join the Society of Biblical Literature, of which he was president in 1918, and served as editor of the prestigious *Journal of Biblical Literature* (1909-1913). He was a member of the American Oriental Society, edited its *Journal* (1916-1921, 1924), and was elected president for the year 1926-1927.

Of at least equal importance was his long association with the American Schools of Oriental Research. He was director of the school in Jerusalem during the critical year 1914-1915, the first editor of the *Bulletin of the American Schools of Oriental Research* (1919-1930), and president of the American Schools of Oriental Research from 1921 to 1934.

Perhaps his greatest accomplishment was to recognize, encourage, and promote the brilliant young Semitist William Foxwell Albright, who ultimately succeeded Montgomery as editor of the *Bulletin*. From the first, Montgomery recognized in Albright a man of extraordinary abilities, and became his advocate and defender. It was characteristic of the older man that he encouraged the younger one in every possible way. Albright's estimate of his mentor and sponsor is especially significant in view of their

lifelong relationship: "Eminent as scholar and teacher, Montgomery was first and last an exceptionally kind, humane, and broad-minded person, and a Christian of profound piety and dignity. It is impossible to imagine him as guilty of a breach of the severest code of conduct or of any unkind or uncouth act. The qualities denoted by the words 'gentleman' and 'scholar' have probably never been combined more harmoniously in a single man than in James Alan Montgomery" (*Journal of Biblical Literature*, 69 [1950], xviii-xix). He dedicated his book *Archaeology and the Religion of Israel* (1942) to Montgomery.

In spite of onerous editorial and administrative duties and his teaching obligations, Montgomery published eight books (a ninth appeared posthumously), well over a hundred learned articles and notes, and scores of book reviews and occasional pieces in religious publications.

Montgomery's main scholarly interest was the Old Testament. His academic pursuit, however, was inspired and informed by his religious convictions—a happy coalescence of interests that resulted in contributions of solid and enduring worth. In him and his work there was no tension or conflict between the spiritual and intellectual but a harmonious interplay of rigorous intellectual probity and unwavering commitment of faith, united by a constant devotion to, and persistent quest for, the truth.

In spite of this concentration of interests, and a scholarly career devoted to the analysis and exposition of the Old Testament, it was not until 1927 that he published a volume on that subject. Previously, he had written books and monographs on a variety of related topics, including *The Samaritans* (1907), *Aramaic Incantation Texts from Nippur* (1913), *The Origin of the Gospel According to Saint John* (1923), and *The History of Yaballaha III* (1927). Each exhibited a different aspect of his research and expertise, and the latter three mentioned show in particular his special skills and interests in Aramaic dialects.

His commentary on the Book of Daniel was part of the *International Critical Commentary,* undoubtedly the most ambitious and important series ever undertaken in the English-speaking world. This commentary on Daniel is widely regarded as a model for the series; it has not been superseded in the half-century since its publication. New discoveries (e.g., the Dead Sea scrolls) and new insights (e.g., the theories of H. H. Rowley, H. L. Ginsberg, and others) have altered the picture somewhat, but Montgomery's work remains nearly indispensable for scholar and student alike. His double mastery of Hebrew and Aramaic shows to special advantage in the study of Daniel, since half of it was written in Hebrew and half in Aramaic.

Montgomery's stature as a scholar and his permanent place in the history of biblical research depend finally upon this book and a second work, the volume on the *Books of Kings* in the same series. The manuscript of the latter was completed in 1944, but it did not appear until 1950, a year after Montgomery's death. It was seen through publication by H. S. Gehman, a former student of Montgomery and his collaborator, who contributed certain sections of the introduction, brought the bibliography up to date, and added notes here and there.

His openness to archaeological discovery and his persistent interest in exploring new areas of research are nowhere more evident than in his enthusiastic response to the discovery of the famed Ugaritic tablets at Ras Shamrah in 1929. The impact of this discovery on biblical studies has been of major proportions, both in the realm of ideas (since the tablets contain substantial segments of the long-lost Canaanite mythological literature) and in the area of linguistics (with particular attention to vocabulary, morphology, and syntax). Other results of his investigations were published in *The Ras Shamra Mythological Texts* (1955), written in collaboration with Z. Harris.

He rounded out his literary career with two semipopular works: *Arabia and the Bible* (1934) and *The Bible: The Book of God and Man* (1948). Montgomery died in Philadelphia and was buried in the cemetery of the Church of St. James the Less in that city.

James Alan Montgomery was a man of distinction and integrity. He was an aristocrat in the best sense of that much abused term. As a scholar, his skills were primarily linguistic, and his strong points, accuracy and good judgment. His work was solid, not sensational. Much of it was occasional and belongs to the ongoing history of scholarship, but a substantial amount is part of the permanent repository of hard-won knowledge of the Bible.

[The principal sources for the life and career of James Alan Montgomery are his autobiographical sketches in *Who's Who in Am. 1946–1947*; the obituary notices in the Philadelphia newspapers, Feb. 7, 1949, and in the *N.Y. Times*, Feb. 8, 1949; and the tributes and memorial notices in various scholarly journals: *Bull. Am. Schools Oriental Res.*, 115 (1949), 4–8; *Am. Jour. Archaeol.*, 53 (1949), 388–389; *Jour. Bibl. Lit.*, 69 (1950), xviii–xix. Additional information has been provided to the writer by J. A. Montgomery, Jr. Montgomery's bibliography was prepared by E. A. Speiser with assistance from J. A. Montgomery, Jr., and is to be found in the *Bull. Am. Schools Oriental Res.*, 117 (1950), 8–13. A good photograph of Montgomery is on the front cover of the *Bulletin*, 115 (1949).]

DAVID NOEL FREEDMAN

MOORE, GRACE (Dec. 5, 1901–Jan. 26, 1947), opera and popular singer, was born in Slabtown, Tenn., the first of four children of Richard L. Moore, a Scots-Irish traveling salesman from Murphy, N.C., and Tessie Jane (Stokely) Moore. Four years after the birth of Mary Willie Grace Moore, the family moved to Knoxville and then to Jellico, Tenn., where her father was a partner in a dry goods company. Influenced by the fervent religiosity of her Southern Baptist surroundings, she determined to become a missionary. Her "impetuosity" was responsible for her being forced at the age of fourteen to apologize publicly for an innocent dance. In her autobiography, *You're Only Human Once* (1944), she attributes to this embarrassing experience her resolve to become a singer and to minister through music.

Moore studied music at Ward-Belmont College in Nashville but was expelled for attending a dance. Despite her father's conviction that music and the stage were unsuitable pursuits for a woman, he was persuaded to let her attend the Wilson-Greene School of Music in Chevy Chase, Md. In 1919 she made her recital debut at the National Theater in Washington, D.C., singing "Ritorna vincitor" from *Aida* on a program with the tenor Giovanni Martinelli. Encouraged by a critic's report that she "showed promise," she ran away to New York before finishing her two-year course. Her first singing job was at the Black Cat, a Greenwich Village nightclub. On a friend's recommendation she studied voice with a teacher who was "good and cheap," subsequently injuring her voice. With the help of Dr. Marafioti, a noted voice teacher and physician, she recovered and was cast in the musicals *Suite Sixteen, Just a Minute,* and *Up in the Clouds,* but never reached Broadway. She subsequently appeared in the successful *Hitchy-Koo* (1920), with music by Jerome Kern. When *Town Gossip* closed in Boston she sailed for France, which soon became her second home.

Still aspiring to an operatic career, Moore studied singing in Paris while increasing her circle with such friends as Elsa Maxwell, the Cole Porters, Noel Coward, Alexander Woollcott, and Condé Nast. She returned to New York to head the cast of the 1923 and 1924 productions of Irving Berlin's *Music Box Revue* but gave up a Broadway career to continue serious study in Europe. Through the favor of Mary Garden, she was coached by Richard Barthélemy and studied acting with Alfred Carré of the Opéra-Comique in Paris. In Milan for her third audition for the Metropolitan Opera, she was offered a contract.

On Feb. 7, 1928, in a Metropolitan Opera matinee performance of *La Bohème*, Moore made her operatic debut in the role of Mimi to enthusiastic audiences but mixed critical notices. She also sang Juliette in Gounod's *Roméo et Juliette* that season before touring Europe, where she made her debut in that opera at Deauville and scored a triumph as Mimi at the Opéra-Comique. After her second Metropolitan season she accepted a Hollywood contract and starred in two relatively unsuccessful films, *A Lady's Morals* (1930), based on the life of Swedish soprano Jenny Lind, and *New Moon* (also 1930), which costarred Lawrence Tibbett.

While on vacation in Europe she married the Spanish movie star Valentin Parera on July 15, 1931. She returned to the Metropolitan and again to Broadway in the operetta *The Dubarry* in 1932. Lured once more to Hollywood, she achieved wide acclaim for her starring role in *One Night of Love* (1934), which was pioneering in its use of operatic excerpts. In 1935 she received the annual gold medal fellowship of the American Society of Arts and Sciences "for conspicuous achievement in raising the standard of cinema entertainment." A series of unsuccessful formula films followed: *Love Me Forever* (1935), *The King Steps Out* (1936), *When You're in Love* (1937), and *I'll Take Romance* (1937). In France she appeared in the title role of the movie version of Charpentier's *Louise* (1938). Coached in the role by both the composer and Mary Garden, she sang with acclaim at the Metropolitan Opera in 1939.

Film success increased her operatic appeal, although critical appraisal of her work remained mixed throughout her career. Ovations were accorded her in the United States and on a European tour during which she broke records at her Covent Garden debut. Among her other notable operatic roles were Manon, Marguerite, Madama Butterfly, Tosca, and Fiora in *L'amore dei tre re*, which she performed on Feb. 7, 1941, at the Metropolitan with the composer, Italo Montemezzi, conducting.

Moore's enormous public appeal was responsible for her many radio appearances and the un-

precedented success of her engagement at New York's Roxy Theater (1943). She appeared in August 1944 before an audience of 22,000 at Lewisohn Stadium. During World War II, she toured Latin and South America, sang in hospitals, canteens, and USO camp shows, and did benefit concerts for relief funds. She was decorated by the governments of France, Mexico, Denmark, Norway, and Cuba.

A beautiful blonde, accused of extremes of temperament, she lived a zesty life with determination. Her singing varied greatly in quality, but she was irrefutably celebrated. *So This Is Love* (1953), a film starring Kathryn Grayson, chronicled her life until her Metropolitan debut. Her hobbies included collecting homes and friends, and she was said to know everyone worth knowing.

Her autobiography, an episodic travelogue both revelatory and reverent, represents her as often at the mercy of publicity and the conflicts of several careers. She died in an airplane crash in Copenhagen on Jan. 26, 1947.

[*Current Biog.* 1944; *Who Was Who in Am.,* II (1950); Georg Pluck, "Grace Moore," *Hobbies,* Oct. 1958, pp. 26–28, with biography and portraits; K. Roberts, "Go the Limit," *Collier's* Aug. 21, 1937. p. 22; A. Favia-Artsay, "Grace Moore," *Hobbies,* Jan. 1963, pp. 30–31, which includes a discography; "Uproar for Grace Moore," *Newsweek,* Apr. 28, 1941, pp. 68–69; and V. Sheean, "Toujours La Moore," *Opera News,* Dec. 20, 1969, pp. 15–16, an irreverent reminiscence. Obituaries are in *N.Y. Times,* Jan. 27, 1947, p. 1; *Opera News,* with many pictures, Feb. 10, 1947, pp. 4–7; and *Newsweek,* Feb. 3, 1947, p. 70.]

WILLIAM E. BOSWELL

MOORE, JOHN BASSETT (Dec. 3, 1860–Nov. 12, 1947), international lawyer and jurist, was born in Smyrna, Del., the only child of John Adams Moore and Martha Anne (Ferguson) Moore. His father, whose ancestors had settled in Delaware before the Revolution, served the community both as a physician and as a state legislator (1861). His mother's family came originally from Maryland, where his uncle, Rev. Colin Ferguson, was president of Washington College, Chestertown. A frail youth, John was tutored by his parents, then enrolled in a private school in Felton, Del. Thus provided with a background in classics, history, and literature, Moore was admitted to the University of Virginia in 1877. There he continued his studies in the liberal arts and took up the discipline that would become his life's work—law.

In 1880, Moore left the university for reasons of health without receiving a degree. But he continued his legal education as an apprentice in the office of former Delaware State

District Attorney Edward G. Bradford and was admitted to the bar in 1883. Two years later, urged by United States Senator George Gray and Secretary of State Thomas F. Bayard, Moore successfully took the examination for a clerkship in the Department of State. In the small, closely knit department of veterans including assistant secretaries William Hunter and Alvey A. Adee, Chief Clerk Sevellon A. Brown and Solicitor Francis Wharton, Moore received unique tutelage and experience. As Adee's clerk in the Diplomatic Bureau (1885-1886), and as third assistant secretary (1886-1891), Moore was exposed to every major item of American diplomatic and consular business. In addition, he developed his scholarly talents by helping Wharton compile *A Digest of the International Law of the United States* (3 vols., 1886) and edit *The Revolutionary Diplomatic Correspondence of the United States* (6 vols., 1889), which was completed by Moore after Wharton's death.

Although offered an assistant secretaryship in 1891, Moore was prompted by his increasing editorial commitments and his marriage, on Apr. 9, 1890, to Helen Frances Toland of Philadelphia, to seek more permanent and remunerative employment. (Subsequently, they had three children: Phyllis Elwyn, Anne Ferguson, and Angela Turner.) He thus accepted an offer to become, at thirty-one, the first Hamilton Fish professor of law and diplomacy at Columbia University. Moore then began a career pattern of scholarship interspersed with public service that was to last for more than thirty years. A charmingly brilliant man with a tolerant nature and a gift for witty repartee, he was a popular and inspiring teacher. In his courses on international law and American diplomacy, he emphasized the importance of historical origins and evolutionary trends as a prerequisite to understanding both subjects. Moore's continuous research in the State Department archives resulted in many published works, including articles on extraterritoriality, extradition, and consular rights and duties. His *History and Digest of International Arbitrations* (6 vols., 1898) was followed by the *Digest of International Law* (8 vols., 1906). Originally planned as a revision of Wharton's *Digest,* Moore's work grew into an authoritative history of the origin, nature, and resolution of the cases involved. It became the standard legal compendium for the next generation. His interest in American foreign policy led to the publication of *American Diplomacy: Its Spirit and Achievements* (1905) and *Four*

Phases of American Development (1908), both of which traced the evolution of trends and principles in diplomatic history.

As a prolific and trenchant commentator on American diplomacy, Moore consistently counseled a policy of practical internationalism. Seeing the emerging world role of the United States, he stressed the need for a concurrent expansion of its diplomatic machinery and urged abandonment of isolationism in favor of participation in a variety of world legal, economic, and cultural associations. Yet, while he applied humanitarian and ethical standards to intergovernmental relations, he abhorred the tendency to view international affairs in absolute moral terms of right and wrong. A lifelong realist in diplomacy, he warned against following both the advocates of self-interest in imperialism and the proponents of utopian solutions to world problems through international agencies.

Moore's role in public service continued almost unabated even after he entered academic life. Nominally a Democrat, he served presidents of both parties. He often conferred unofficially during the 1890's with secretaries of state Walter Q. Gresham and William R. Day, and from the latter in 1898 he accepted appointment as assistant secretary of state. Taking office on the eve of the Spanish-American War, Moore quickly organized the staff and applied his expertise to maintaining the legality of America's belligerent activities and insuring the strict neutrality of the major powers. After helping to draft the armistice terms, he was named secretary and counsel to the Paris Peace Commission. In this role he was principally responsible for drawing up the peace treaty that compelled Spain to relinquish Cuba and to cede Puerto Rico, Guam, and the Philippine archipelago to the United States. Although the treaty reflected the wishes of the McKinley administration, Moore apparently justified the absorption of former Spanish colonies as an acceptable outcome of war rather than a naked act of imperialism.

As an official foreign policy advisor during the early 1900's, Moore was forced by events to reconcile his belief in international legality with the realities of international politics, especially in regard to Latin America. For example, while he accepted the time-honored principle of nonintervention in the affairs of sovereign states, he supported Theodore Roosevelt's limited intervention in the Caribbean as a reflection of America's legitimate interest in preventing economic chaos and forestalling more drastic intervention by European powers. Likewise his belief in the need for an isthmian canal led him to support American efforts to achieve it. He helped draft the first Hay-Pauncefote Treaty (1900) with England, giving the United States sole right to construct a canal; and in 1903, when the government of Colombia balked, he provided Theodore Roosevelt with legal justification for a planned seizure of the Isthmus of Panama by pointing to an 1846 treaty with New Grenada (Colombia), granting the United States the authority to guarantee the neutrality and free transit of the isthmus. In 1910, he accepted limited assignments as delegate to the Fourth International Conference of American States, and, in 1912, as head of the American delegation to the International Commission of Jurists. President Taft's recognition of Moore's preeminence in the field of law and diplomacy came in 1912, when he named Moore a member of the Permanent Court of Arbitration, The Hague. The election of Woodrow Wilson seemed to offer Moore an opportunity for significant service, and he returned to the State Department as counselor in 1913. Unfortunately, he found himself frustrated by the president's conduct of diplomacy, culminating in what he regarded as unwarranted intervention in the Mexican revolution. He resigned after one year and, although he continued to advise the administration publicly and privately, his influence on Wilsonian policies was minimal. Moore increasingly saw the perils inherent in Wilson's idealistic approach to foreign affairs. A strict advocate of the historic duties of neutral nations, he opposed the president's modification of this policy in the early years of World War I to favor the allies, and he regarded the German response as justifiable. Moore's efforts during the war years were devoted primarily to organizations concerned with international cooperation and justice. He served as president of both the Lake Mohonk Conference on International Arbitration (1914) and the Pan-American Society (1916-1921), as delegate to the Pan-American Financial Conferences of 1915 and 1919, and as officer in the New York and World Peace Societies and International Red Cross Relief Board.

The postwar years produced the strongest challenge to Moore's philosophy of practical internationalism. Maintaining his faith in the value of international adjudication, he supported the establishment of the Permanent Court of International Justice (the World Court) at The Hague. Yet he opposed its parent

organization, the League of Nations, as an instrument of idealistic futility incongruously designed to impose world peace through the threat of collective force. Furthermore, he did not believe the world balance of power had been permanently altered by World War I, and thus saw no need for the balancing influence of the United States in such an international compact.

Moore received the ultimate recognition of his professional stature in 1921, when he was selected the first American judge of the World Court. He served with distinction until 1928, presiding over the court's Commission of Jurists as it formulated rules of international conduct in time of war, 1922-1923. Continuing to urge the extension and use of traditional forms of international association, arbitration, and conciliation, and to resist such novel interpretations of international law as the Kellogg-Briand Pact, he also worked to preserve the court's freedom from league political pressures and recommended American abstention until such independence could be won.

In 1928, Moore retired from the court (he had retired from Columbia University in 1924) in order to devote full time to the preparation of his last major editorial work, the *International Adjudications* (1936), which he envisioned as the initial portion of a comprehensive international law library composed of adjudications, treaties, and state papers. Infrequently, in the 1930's, he wrote publicly in opposition to what he considered capricious alterations of American neutrality policy and dangerous expansion of executive prerogatives by Franklin D. Roosevelt.

A distinguished-looking man with white hair and beard, Moore received several honorary degrees and was an active member of many professional organizations. In his practice, he occasionally handled private cases for clients involved in international litigation.

Moore died after a series of strokes at his home in New York City and was buried there in Woodlawn Cemetery.

[Important works by John Bassett Moore, in addition to his legal treatises, are his edition of *The Works of James Buchanan* (12 vols., 1908-1911) and *International Law and Some Current Illusions, and Other Essays* (1924). The remainder of his published papers, and a portrait, may be found in Edwin Borchard, Joseph F. Chamberlain, and Stephen Duggan, eds., *The Collected Papers of John Bassett Moore* (7 vols., 1944). The Moore Papers comprise a vast collection of letters, diaries, scrapbooks, and speeches held by the Lib. of Cong. Bibliographical accounts are limited to Richard Megargee, "Realism in American Foreign Policy; The Diplomacy of John Bassett Moore" (unpublished Ph.D. diss., Northwestern Univ., 1963), and brief portraits and memorials in the *Am.*

Bar. Assoc. Jour., 32 (1946), 575–582, Am. Jour. of Internat. Law, Jan. 1948, Am. Philosophical Soc. Yearbook (1947), Political Science Quart., 63 (1948), 159–160, Nat. Cyc. Amer. Biog., Current Vol. A, Who Was Who in Am., II (1950), and N.Y. Times, Nov. 13, 1947. Moore's daughter, Mrs. Anne Frederick, provided additional information.]

RICHARD MEGARGEE

MOORE, JOSEPH HAINES (Sept. 7, 1878–Mar. 15, 1949), astronomer, was born in Wilmington, Ohio, the only child of John Haines Moore and Mary Ann (Haines) Moore, distant cousins. John Moore, of Irish descent, was a native of Clinton County, Ohio. He worked successively as a weaver, cabinetmaker, miller, and merchant and during his later years owned and operated a large farm. Mary Moore, of English ancestry, was born in Lancaster County, Pa. Both were members of the Society of Friends. Joseph was brought up in that faith and throughout his life attended Quaker meetings whenever possible. The family was in comfortable though not affluent circumstances.

Moore attended public schools in Wilmington and the local Wilmington College, founded in 1870 by the Society of Friends. He took the classical course, but a class in astronomy in his senior year stirred his interest in scientific research, and after receiving the B.A. degree in 1897 he enrolled in the graduate school of the Johns Hopkins University, planning to work under the astronomer Simon Newcomb. Although he took one graduate course in astronomy, Moore's deficiencies in mathematics and physics forced him to spend most of his first two years in undergraduate courses. By the end of that time the graduate department in astronomy had been discontinued, and he shifted his major to physics, studying under Henry A. Rowland, Joseph S. Ames, and Robert W. Wood. He received the Ph.D. in 1903 with a dissertation on the fluorescence and absorption spectra of sodium vapor. Moore was offered several posts in physics and chose to go to the Lick Observatory of the University of California as an assistant in spectroscopy to the director, William Wallace Campbell. He remained at Lick for more than forty years, becoming assistant director in 1936 and director in 1942. On June 12, 1907, he married Fredrica Chase of Payette, Idaho, a Vassar graduate and computing assistant at the observatory, who throughout their married life aided in her husband's astronomical work. They had two daughters, Mary Kathryn and Margaret Elizabeth.

At the Lick Observatory, Moore was first assigned to work in Campbell's extensive and pioneering program of using spectroscopic methods to measure the radial velocities of all the brighter stars, a collaborative project that continued for the next twenty-five years. During the period 1909-1913 he served as astronomer in charge of the observatory's D. O. Mills station in Chile. There, working under conditions that called for exceptional skill and ingenuity, he extended the radial velocity study to include stars of the southern hemisphere. The project culminated in 1928 in the publication, with Campbell, of the Lick catalogue of *Radial Velocities of Stars Brighter than Visual Magnitude 5.51*.

Moore was solely or in part responsible for several other catalogues of fundamental value in astronomy. In 1913, with Campbell, he began measuring the velocities and internal motions of the gaseous nebulae. The results, published as "The Spectroscopic Velocities of Bright-Line Nebulae" (Lick Observatory, *Publications*, 13 [1918], 75-183), included all such objects that could be observed with the means then available. He also prepared and published three catalogues of spectroscopic binaries, the last (1948) with the collaboration of Ferdinand J. Neubauer, and, in 1932, a comprehensive catalogue of all the radical velocities of stars, nebulae, star clusters, and galaxies that had been determined up to that time.

Moore was active in other fields of astronomy. Between 1918 and 1932 he took part in five Lick Observatory expeditions to observe solar eclipses, and was in charge of the last two. His particular interest was in photographing and analyzing the spectrum of the solar corona. With J. F. Chappell, photographer at the Lick Observatory, he prepared a widely used photographic atlas of the moon. He studied the spectra of novae, or temporary stars, including the remarkable southern nova Eta Carinae. He determined the orbits of numerous spectroscopic binaries and, with Donald H. Menzel, the rotation of Uranus and Neptune. Moore served as vice-president of the American Association for the Advancement of Science (1931) and was twice president of the Astronomical Society of the Pacific (1920, 1928). He was elected to the National Academy of Sciences in 1931.

A man of unfailing good humor, Moore had a store of colorful anecdotes, founded on his wide scientific acquaintance over many years, that made his companionship particularly delightful. Although his research was largely confined to spectroscopic problems, he was well informed on a wide range of astronomical subjects and never tired of discussing current astronomical developments, especially with students. A heart condition required him to leave the altitude of Mount Hamilton in 1945. He moved to Oakland and taught courses in astronomy at the University of California in Berkeley until his retirement in 1948. He died in his home six months later of a coronary occlusion and was buried at Oak Hill Cemetery, San Jose, Calif.

[Memoir by W. H. Wright in Nat. Acad. Sci., *Biog. Memoirs,* XXIX (1956), with photograph of Moore and a list of his publications; obituary by Robert G. Aitken in Astronomical Soc. of the Pacific, *Publications,* June 1949; notes assembled by Moore's daughter, Margaret E. Gulliford; close personal association. See also obituaries in *Sky and Telescope,* June 1949 (by F. J. Neubauer), and *Popular Astronomy,* Oct. 1949.]

C. D. SHANE

MORGAN, JOHN HARCOURT ALEXANDER (Aug. 31, 1867-Aug. 25, 1950), agricultural entomologist, college president, and administrator of the Tennessee Valley Authority, was born in Kerrwood, Ontario, Canada, the second son and fourth of eight children of John Morgan, a prosperous livestock farmer, and Rebecca (Truman) Morgan. The grandparents of Harcourt Morgan (he did not use his first name) were Irish Protestants who had come to North America in search of economic opportunity. Morgan attended Strathroy Collegiate Institute, a nearby preparatory school, and Ontario Agricultural College at Guelph, an institution affiliated with the University of Toronto, from which he received the B.S. degree in agriculture in 1889.

Immediately after graduating, Morgan moved to Louisiana State University in Baton Rouge, to teach entomology and work in the university's agricultural experiment station. In his special fields, entomology and crop pest control, he soon became one of the region's leading experts, gaining wide recognition for his campaigns against the boll weevil, the cattle tick, and the army worm. Later, in 1907, he served as president of the American Association of Economic Entomologists. For several summers during the 1890's Morgan pursued graduate work at Cornell University under John Henry Comstock, but he did not receive an advanced degree. He married Sara Elizabeth Fay in Baton Rouge, La., on June 25, 1895. They had five children: Fay, John Elmore, Lucy Shields (who herself became a well-known educator and international authority on public health), Evelyn Cameron, and Harcourt Alexander.

Morgan moved in 1905 to the University of Tennessee, as professor of entomology and zoology and as director of the local agricultural experiment station. Rising rapidly in the school's administration, he became dean of the college of agriculture in 1913 and president of the university in 1919. His election in 1927 as president of the Association of Land Grant Colleges and Universities reflected a widening reputation. In Morgan's fourteen years as chief executive of the University of Tennessee, its enrollment grew from fewer than eight hundred to more than five thousand students. He himself excelled as a manager of the university's external relations, rather than as a leader of faculty or students. He made the institution favorably known throughout the state, especially among farmers, and established a relationship with successive governors and legislators that brought generous state appropriations.

Morgan's evolving convictions about farming and people led him to work out a broad, elusive philosophy he called "the common mooring." In his view, mankind had begun to interfere dangerously with the earth's ecosystems, through excessive cultivation of soil-depleting cash crops, excessive consumption of finite natural resources, and excessive migration into congested cities. For Morgan, the root sin in this ominous process was man's failure to perceive the essential and delicate unity of nature—the interdependence ("common mooring") of all life. To this concept and its ramifications he devoted much of his time as a teacher.

The opportunity to put his ideas into practice came in 1933, when President Franklin D. Roosevelt appointed Morgan to the board of directors of the new Tennessee Valley Authority. Chosen as a progressive Southern agriculturist, he took his place on the three-man board alongside David E. Lilienthal, an able young lawyer who had served on the Wisconsin Public Service Commission; and the chairman, Arthur E. Morgan (who was no relation), a well-known engineer and the president of Antioch College. Together the three men set out to fulfill the exceptionally broad mandate of Congress concerning the development of the river valley.

The only one of the directors resident in Tennessee before 1933, Harcourt Morgan occupied a pivotal position. He assumed the burden of persuading his many friends in the state that the new agency was a great benefit and not a threat. He took personal charge of the agricultural portion of the authority's program, and shaped it according to his ideas about how best to promote rural progress. Most important of all, he attempted to keep peace within the

TVA's troubled hierarchy. Tactfully but consistently he sided with the aggressive David E. Lilienthal, who directed the agency's controversial power program in its successful six-year battle with private companies for control of local markets for electricity. Morgan's support gave Lilienthal's militancy a two-to-one supremacy within the board of directors. The friction culminated in 1938, when President Roosevelt dismissed the dissenting member, Chairman Arthur E. Morgan. For the next three years, Harcourt Morgan served as chairman, finally relinquishing that post to the younger Lilienthal. Morgan remained as a director, however, until 1948, when he retired at the age of eighty. His fifteen-year tenure on TVA's board was long a record, the more remarkable because he was past sixty-five at the time of his initial appointment.

Throughout his life Morgan adhered to the principle that progress, like politics, is fundamentally the art of the possible. He practiced the art to near perfection, in many different roles: as a young agricultural scientist in Louisiana, log-rolling with like-minded New England interests to secure federal appropriations for the war against crop pests; as the driving force behind the University of Tennessee's college of agriculture, carrying in person the message of scientific cultivation to farmers at institutes conducted throughout the state; as president of the university, pragmatically refusing to take a stand against the antievolution bill that was proposed and passed in the 1920's, or in the sensational Scopes trial that followed—even though he himself had taught Darwinian biology for many years; and as the architect of TVA's farm program, deliberately allying the authority with the established agricultural interests of the region, rather than with the more innovative New Deal agencies such as the Farm Security Administration. Morgan's determination to work with the materials at hand, and with the people as they were, led to TVA's official adoption of a policy praised by Lilienthal and others as "grass roots democracy." Scholars sometimes criticized the policy as the disguised cooptation of a reform agency into the local agricultural power structure. Even Morgan's critics, however, acknowledged the wisdom of his emphasis on the test-demonstration technique and his enthusiastic promotion of a soil-enrichment program built around legume crops and phosphatic fertilizers, through which he tried to shift the agricultural economy of the region away from its historic dependence on cash row crops.

As a scholar, educator, and public official, Morgan published very little, attempting instead to communicate his ideas through personal persuasion. For all his self-effacement and inarticulateness, he succeeded remarkably well, both because of the rightness of his cause—he was ahead of his time as an ecologist—and because of the intense personal devotion he inspired in students and associates. Of the TVA's three original directors, Harcourt Morgan was by far the least conspicuous and the most beloved.

Two years after his retirement, he died of cancer, at his home in Belfast, Tenn., and was buried at Greenwood Cemetery, Knoxville.

[Morgan's private papers are in the Univ. of Tenn. Lib., Knoxville. James Rorty captured his character superbly in "TVA's H. A. Morgan," *The Commonweal*, May 28, 1948, pp. 226–230. Summaries of his life appear in Mouzon Peters, "The Story of Dr. Harcourt A. Morgan," in Louis D. Wallace, ed., *Makers of Millions* (1951); and Hugh F. Hoss, "U-T Pays Tribute to Dr. H. A. Morgan," the *Knoxville News-Sentinel*, Nov. 7, 1937; see also obituary in *Jour. of Economic Entomology*, Dec. 1950. His career as dean and president is covered in James R. Montgomery, *The Volunteer State Forges Its University: The University of Tennessee, 1887–1919* (1966) and *Threshold of a New Day: The University of Tennessee, 1919–1946* (1971). Ellis F. Hartford and others attempted to synthesize Morgan's philosophy in *Our Common Mooring* (1941). Analyses of his work in the Tennessee Valley Authority are in Philip Selznick, *TVA and the Grass Roots* (1949); Norman I. Wengert, *Valley of Tomorrow: The TVA and Agriculture* (1952); C. Herman Pritchett, *The Tennessee Valley Authority* (1943); and Thomas K. McCraw, *Morgan vs. Lilienthal: The Feud within the TVA* (1970). A photograph of Morgan hangs at the TVA offices in Knoxville, and a portrait at the Univ. of Tenn.]

THOMAS K. McCRAW

MORGENTHAU, HENRY (Apr. 26, 1856–Nov. 25, 1946), lawyer, realtor, diplomat, was born in Mannheim, Germany, the son of Lazarus Morgenthau and Babette (Guggenheim) Morgenthau and the ninth of their thirteen children, of whom six sons and five daughters survived. His early childhood was spent in comfortable circumstances, until his father, a self-made and prosperous cigar manufacturer, suffered a business failure. Immigrating to the United States in 1866, Lazarus Morgenthau became an insurance agent in New York City but gave his major interest to organizing philanthropic campaigns for various Jewish welfare organizations. Young Morgenthau attended Public School 14 while learning English and graduated in 1870 at the age of fourteen. He then entered City College in New York, intending to study toward a career in the law, but was forced to leave before the end of his first year in order to help support his family. Starting as an errand boy, he worked for four years as a clerk in a law office, acquiring special experience in title searches and, after the panic of 1873, in mortgage foreclosure sales. At nineteen he left his job to enter Columbia Law School while supporting himself by teaching in an adult night school.

The fall in family circumstances left a strong impression on him, and Morgenthau was fiercely determined to make a fortune. Admitted to the bar after his graduation in 1877, he formed with two friends the law firm of Lachman, Morgenthau, and Goldsmith in 1879. He dealt chiefly in titles and mortgages and gradually turned his major attention to buying and selling real estate, at which, over the next thirty years, he was conspicuously successful. In 1899 he left his law firm and introduced the corporate form of operation into real estate with the founding of the Central Realty Bond and Trust Company, of which he was president. Six years later he founded and headed his own real estate corporation, the Henry Morgenthau Company. Meanwhile, on May 10, 1883, he married Josephine Sykes, the daughter of Samuel Sykes, a New York merchant. Four children, Helen, Alma, Henry, and Ruth, were born to them in the next decade.

Morgenthau had a strong sense of social obligation. An optimist about human progress and an adherent of reform Judaism in religion, he was in 1907 a founder and first president of the Free Synagogue, created to provide a pulpit for the advanced ideas of Rabbi Stephen S. Wise, who was expressing in religion the spirit of the progressives and reformers of the time. In the cause of civic reform Morgenthau combatted the tenement problem in 1908 as a member of the Committee on Congestion of the Population. In 1911, after the notorious Triangle Shirtwaist Company fire, he joined Henry L. Stimson, Anne Morgan, Frances Perkins, and others to form the Committee of Safety to secure legislation for improved working conditions. He engaged actively in the settlement house movement as a supporter of the Henry Street Settlement. At the suggestion of its director, Lillian Wald, he and Mrs. Morgenthau founded in 1911 the uptown sister settlement and music school, Bronx House. Activated by his wife's love of music, Morgenthau was a moving spirit and backer of the reorganization of the Metropolitan Opera Company under the regime of Heinrich Conried. On Jewish matters, Morgenthau, fearful of divided loyalties and possessing the faith of his time in the power of democracy to eradicate religious and racial prejudice, believed that when the Jew

had thoroughly Americanized himself his problem would disappear. He therefore rejected the Zionist solution of a Jewish state. His outspoken views on this issue led to irate and abusive exchanges with Zionists; in the last decade of his life, however, he changed his mind, as a result of the experience of the Jews under Hitler, and became an advocate of an independent Jewish state in Palestine.

Woodrow Wilson's fight against social privilege at Princeton appealed to Morgenthau's democratic ideals, and in December 1911, as one of Wilson's early supporters, he pledged $5,000 a month for four months to launch his campaign for the presidential nomination; later he added another $10,000 to become one of the three largest individual contributors. As chairman of the finance committee of the Democratic National Committee during the campaign he introduced the budget system in the raising and spending of funds. Wilson's inspiration, together with the constant pressure within himself to devote his energies to some higher purpose than making money, led Morgenthau to the rare decision that he had accumulated enough wealth. In 1913, when he was fifty-seven, he closed his company's books and retired from business to begin a new career in public service.

Disappointed at not being named secretary of the treasury, he at first refused Wilson's proffered appointment as ambassador to Turkey, a post which he and his friends regarded as a minor one traditionally relegated to Jews. He was persuaded to change his mind by Rabbi Wise and reached Constantinople in November 1913. Untrained as a diplomat, Morgenthau put to work the same nerve, shrewd judgment, imagination, common sense, goodwill, and tact that he had used in business and rapidly made himself liked and respected by his staff, by his diplomatic colleagues, and, more importantly, by the difficult and dangerous leaders of the Young Turk regime. Upon the outbreak of war, Morgenthau, anticipating that Turkey would soon join the Central Powers, realized that this would cut off the Jewish settlers in Palestine (then part of the Turkish empire) from the Western sources of supply on which they were dependent. His prompt action in securing $50,000 from the American Jewish Committee in New York saved many lives threatened by starvation.

The departure of the Allied ambassadors upon Turkey's entry in the war left the interests of Britain, France, Russia, and six other countries in Morgenthau's care, while at the same time he was overwhelmed by frenzied appeals for aid or asylum. As the only buffer between the harassed foreign nationals and Turkish seizures, arrests, and deportations, the American ambassador was pressed by constant crisis. His efforts gained the passionate gratitude of many groups and decorations from the French and British governments, and he managed to remain on good terms with the Turks, who at one point offered him a cabinet minister's post. Finally, revolted by the appalling cruelty of the Turks' expulsion and massacre of the Armenians, which he tried in vain to stop, he returned home early in 1916. His report on the Armenian tragedy stirred Americans deeply. Besides raising funds for Armenian relief, he plunged, again as chairman of the finance committee, into the campaign for President Wilson's reelection. Although the United States maintained diplomatic relations with the Turks, Morgenthau resigned as ambassador, because of the Armenian situation.

In June 1917 Morgenthau embarked on an official secret mission proposed by himself and authorized by Secretary of State Robert Lansing and President Wilson to mediate a separate peace between Turkey and the Allies. British Foreign Secretary Arthur Balfour at first gave his approval, but subsequently the British had second thoughts, fearing that a possible "soft peace" negotiated by an American might interfere with their plans for the ultimate dissolution of the Turkish empire. Zionists, then negotiating with Britain for a place in Palestine, also feared that Morgenthau might offer terms that would exclude their claims. Seizing on their objections, the Foreign Office succeeded in having the mission called off when Morgenthau reached Gibraltar. So failed one more effort to shorten the war.

In February 1919, together with ex-President Taft and President A. Lawrence Lowell of Harvard, Morgenthau joined a group of eight prominent citizens on a speaking tour in behalf of American participation in the League of Nations. In March he was a delegate to the conference at Cannes for the formation of the International Red Cross. He served as technical consultant on Turkish problems at the Paris Peace Conference and was a member of the Harbord Commission, which recommended an American mandate for Armenia. His concern for the plight of the Armenians had in 1915 led to the formation of the Armenian Relief Committee, under the chairmanship of James L. Barton; its scope expanded and in 1919 it became Near East Relief, Inc., with Mor-

genthau as vice-chairman (1919-1921). President Wilson sent him to Poland (July 13-Sept. 13, 1919) as chairman of a commission to investigate the persecution of the Jews, but his recommendations, regarded as an invasion of sovereignty, proved unacceptable to the Polish government. In March 1920 Wilson appointed Morgenthau ambassador to Mexico, but owing to Sen. Albert B. Fall's special interests in that country and Mexico's then chaotic conditions, the Senate Foreign Relations Committee declined in May to confirm the appointment of an ambassador. In October 1923 Morgenthau went to Athens as chairman of the League of Nations Refugee Resettlement Commission at a time when Turkey, after the Greco-Turkish War, had forcibly deported 1,250,000 Greeks. Operating on the principle that the refugees could be an asset to the Greek economy, he showed how they could be made self-supporting and thus a source of credit for further international loans to continue the process. This successful mass resettlement, one of the major feats of international aid of the postwar period, was Morgenthau's crowning achievement.

In his later years Morgenthau's interests were bound up with the political fortunes of Franklin D. Roosevelt. His son, Henry, Jr., served in both Roosevelt's gubernatorial and presidential administrations, and later became secretary of the treasury (1934-1945). In 1933 Morgenthau, Sr., was appointed technical delegate to the World Monetary and Economic Conference in London. When almost eighty, he vigorously campaigned in defense of the New Deal and in warning of the threat of Germany under Hitler.

A small, wiry, blue-eyed man with a short beard, an amused eye, and a hovering smile, he was intensely ambitious, highly moral, and not a little vain, but saved from the weight of these qualities by his warmth, buoyancy, and human understanding, a talent for friendship, and a lively sense of humor. In his later years he was known to friends and acquaintances from New York City policemen to President Franklin D. Roosevelt as "Uncle Henry." He died seven months past his ninetieth birthday of a mesenteric thrombosis at his home in New York City and was buried at Mount Pleasant Cemetery in Hawthorne, N.Y.

[Morgenthau published an autobiography, *All in a Lifetime* (1922), and two accounts of his diplomatic work, *Ambassador Morgenthau's Story* (1918) and *I Was Sent to Athens* (1929). Other sources include the Morgenthau Papers, Lib. of Cong.; *The Life Story of Lazarus Morgenthau* (privately printed, 1933); *Who Was Who in America*, II (1950); and private information. See also Burton J. Hendrick in

World's Work, May 1916 and Apr. 1918; R. L. Duffus, "Topics of the Times," *N.Y. Times,* Apr. 26, 1931, and Apr. 27, 1946, and obituary, Nov. 26, 1946. For Morgenthau's share in the Wilson campaigns, see William F. McCombs, *Making Woodrow Wilson President* (1921); James Kerney, *The Political Education of Woodrow Wilson* (1926); Josephus Daniels, *The Wilson Era* (2 vols., 1944–1946). His Zionist views were first voiced in an article in *World's Work,* July 1921. For his assistance to the Jews of Palestine, see Cyrus Adler, *Life and Letters of Jacob H. Schiff* (1928), and correspondence in files of the Joint Distribution Committee; for mission to Poland, see Arthur L. Goodhart, *Poland and the Minority Races* (1920); on Armenian relief, see James L. Barton, *Story of Near East Relief* (1930). For the secret mission of 1917 the most complete and latest study, superseding earlier accounts, is Leonard Stein, *The Balfour Declaration* (1961). The official documents are in U.S. State Dept., *Foreign Relations, 1917, Suppl. 2,* and *The Lansing Papers.*]

ROBERT L. HEILBRONER

MORLEY, SYLVANUS GRISWOLD
(June 7, 1883–Sept. 2, 1948), archaeologist and authority on Maya civilization, was born in Chester, Pa., the eldest of six children (two of them boys) of Col. Benjamin Franklin Morley, professor of chemistry and mathematics and vice-president of Pennsylvania Military College, and Sarah Eleanor Constance (de Lannoy) Morley, daughter of a professor of languages at the college. The father was from Iowa, but of colonial New England stock; the mother was of recent Belgian descent. In 1894 Colonel Morley gave up academic pursuits and moved his family to Buena Vista, Colo., where he became part-owner and operator of the nearby Mary Murphy Mine.

Sylvanus ("Vay") was educated in public schools. As a youth he developed an interest in archaeology, particularly that of Mexico and Central America, and corresponded on the subject with Frederic W. Putnam, curator of the Peabody Museum at Harvard. Morley's father, convinced that archaeology was not a practical career, sent the boy to Pennsylvania Military College to become an engineer. He received his degree in civil engineering in 1904, but that same year (his father having died in 1903) he entered Harvard as a sophomore to study archaeology. Although he took courses in a variety of fields, including Egyptology, his lifelong enthusiasm for Maya archaeology was soon evident. He received the B.A. early in 1907, having already set out to visit Maya and Mexican ruins. The following year he received the M.A. degree from Harvard, and in January 1909, he accepted a position as a fellow of the School of American Archaeology of the Archaeological Institute of America (later the School of American Research) in Santa Fe, N.Mex., where he acquired his first field training. He never completed the Ph.D. at Harvard, apparently in part because of personality conflicts there.

Morley's assigned field work at the School of American Archaeology ranged from the American Southwest to Central America. In 1909 he returned to Yucatan for archaeological surveys, the first of forty consecutive seasons in the Maya area. He undertook his first excavations at a Maya site in 1910, when work was begun at Quiriguá, Guatemala. In 1912 Morley learned that the Carnegie Institution of Washington was considering the sponsorship of research in archaeology or anthropology. With characteristic energy and optimism, he set out to persuade the institution to enter the Maya field. Despite his youth, his efforts were successful, and in 1914 he was appointed research associate in American archaeology. He continued to work under the institution's auspices until his death.

The Carnegie Institution's support of Maya research, which involved many talented scholars and numerous projects and which was originally instigated by Morley, was the greatest single contribution to Maya archaeology. The program was initially on a modest scale, but over the next several years Morley made numerous expeditions into the tropical jungles of Central America, examining Maya sites at Copan in Honduras and in the Petén district of northern Guatemala. In the year 1924 he began extensive excavations at Chichén Itzá, a major Maya city and religious center in Yucatan, Mexico, and began preliminary work at Uaxactún, Guatemala, a site later intensively studied by the institution. Through a reorganization in 1929, the Carnegie Institution broadened its Maya program under the general supervision of Morley's old friend Alfred V. Kidder.

Although Morley remained in charge of the Chichén Itzá excavations until 1934, he was better known as an epigrapher than as an archaeologist. Most of his reseach was devoted to the study of Maya hieroglyphic texts, many uncovered on the expeditions he undertook. His work resulted in numerous papers and several lengthy monographs: *An Introduction to the Study of the Maya Hieroglyphs* (1915), a beginner's manual; "The Supplementary Series in the Maya Inscriptions" (*Holmes Anniversary Volume,* 1916), an elaborate presentation of an important recurring set of hieroglyphic phrases, which facilitated their subsequent decipherment; *The Inscriptions at Copan* (1920), an exhaustive chronological analysis of the extensive inscriptions at one of the most important Maya sites; and the monumental *The Inscriptions of Petén* (5 vols., 1937–1938).

Morley was sometimes criticized as a mere collector of data, but although the sheer immensity of raw data gathered would alone ensure his importance in Maya studies, he was also an interpreter and synthesizer. His extraordinary talent for chronology permitted him to retrieve important dates from badly eroded and fragmentary texts, and he had an uncanny shrewdness in predicting dates of texts that have been established by subsequent discoveries. The meaning of several chronological glyphs was first deciphered by Morley, and he was the first to chart the history of Maya civilization by an exhaustive study of Maya hieroglyphic dates. His last book, *The Ancient Maya* (1946), was the most ambitious and detailed presentation of Maya civilization yet produced.

Morley had a witty, warm personality and boundless energy and enthusiasm. Through his extensive public lecturing he was able to develop a large and enthusiastic popular audience to support scholarly study of the Maya, and he successfully stimulated other scholarly institutions besides Carnegie to undertake Maya projects. In the field, the force of his personality and the wide range of his friendships, which extended from remote Indian hamlets to the highest offices of government, contributed to his success.

Morley was married on Dec. 30, 1908, to Alice Gallinger Williams of Nashua, N.H. They were divorced in 1915, and on July 14, 1927, he married Frances Ann Rhoads. He had one child, Alice Virginia, by his first wife. Morley was reared an Episcopalian, became an agnostic, and finally was received into the Roman Catholic church a few days before his death. His health, always precarious, was weakened by the long years he spent in the tropics. In 1947 he was appointed director of the School of American Research, but he died in Santa Fe the following year of a heart attack at the age of sixty-five. He was buried in Santa Fe.

[R. L. Brunhouse, *Sylvanus G. Morley and the World of the Ancient Mayas* (1971), provides Morley's complete bibliography, lists the obituaries and other references (published and unpublished) to Morley's life and work, and includes numerous photographs. Robert H. and Florence C. Lister, eds., *In Search of Maya Glyphs* (1970), reproduces extracts from Morley's diaries for the years 1916, 1918, 1920, 1921, and 1932.]

JOHN A. GRAHAM

MORRISON, FRANK (Nov. 23, 1859–Mar. 12, 1949), labor leader, was born in Franktown, Ontario, Canada, the oldest son of Christopher Morrison, a farmer and sawyer, and Elizabeth (Nesbitt) Morrison, the daughter of a physician. His Scots-Irish father had emigrated from Somnes, Ireland, to Franktown in 1854. When Frank was five years old, his family moved to Walkerton, Ontario, where he received his education. In 1873, while still in high school, Morrison began learning the printer's trade in the office of the *Walkerton Telescope.*

In the late 1870's or early 1880's Morrison migrated to Madison, Wis., where he worked on the *Madison Journal.* Then, in 1881, he moved to Chicago, where he set type for the *Record,* the *Journal,* and the *Herald.* While working as a compositor, he attended Lake Forest University Law School and earned an LL.B. degree in 1894. His legal training proved a major asset in his work as a union official.

Morrison's involvement in the labor movement started in 1886, when he joined Typographical Union No. 16. Over the next decade his friendly manner, honesty, and dedication to union work helped him rise to prominence in Chicago labor circles. He served as a delegate to International Typographical Union (ITU) conventions, as a representative to the Chicago Federation of Labor, and as secretary of the 1896 Chicago Labor Congress. In 1896 the ITU sent him to the American Federation of Labor (A.F. of L.) convention, where he was elected to replace a fellow printer, August McCraith, as secretary of the organization. Morrison was reelected to this post over the next forty-two years and also held the position of treasurer from 1935 to 1939. By virtue of these offices he was a member of the federation's executive council.

Morrison's primary contribution to the labor movement was to provide the A.F. of L. with a mature administrative structure, enabling it better to cope with the complexities of bureaucratic society. During his tenure, the A.F. of L. grew from roughly 250,000 to 4 million members, creating a vastly increased clerical burden. As secretary, he kept all books and records, received all funds, prepared financial statements, convened the annual convention, of which he was ex officio secretary, and performed countless other tasks. The routine of his job kept him out of the public eye but to a large extent the federation's dynamic president, Samuel Gompers, was able to participate in labor and public affairs as a result of Morrison's efficient handling of administrative details.

For the most part, Morrison followed the "Gompers line" on policy matters. On political questions, however, he was more progressive than many Federation officers. He was a Bryan supporter, an early admirer of Theodore Roosevelt, and an avid backer of Sen. Robert La Follette in 1924. Moreover, unlike Gompers and others in the A.F. of L. executive council, he was not opposed either to aggressive political activity by the federation or to government involvement in establishing minimum wages, unemployment relief, and other social programs. Throughout his career he lobbied in Congress for laws favorable to labor, including the bill establishing the Department of Labor (1913), the Clayton Antitrust Act (1914), and the National Labor Relations (Wagner) Act (1935). The passage of the Norris-La Guardia Act in 1932 successfully concluded Morrison's long fight to curtail the use of injunctions in labor disputes. Earlier, in 1908, he, Gompers, and John Mitchell of the United Mine Workers had been found guilty of contempt for violating an injunction in the Buck's Stove and Range Company case and for years faced the threat of going to prison until the case was finally dismissed by the Supreme Court on May 11, 1914, because of the expiration of the statute of limitations. Beginning in 1906, when he became secretary of the A.F. of L. labor representation committee, which sought to promote the election to public office of candidates favorable to the views of labor, he served on a number of committees designed to carry out the A.F. of L.'s political policy of rewarding its friends and punishing its enemies. Over the years he also participated in a number of governmental boards and commissions, including the executive committee of the advisory commission to the Council of National Defense during World War I and President Wilson's 1919 Industrial Conference.

By 1939 Morrison, with his frock coat and high collar reminiscent of a frontier evangelist, was an anachronism among union executives. Moreover, his administrative practices, which were up-to-date when he assumed office, had become inadequate. Some federation members thought that his deteriorating health impaired his effectiveness. Equally important, various officials, including Daniel Tobin of the Teamsters and William L. Hutcheson of the Carpenters, preferred more vigorous and youthful leadership in the A.F. of L. in order better to meet the challenge of the Congress of Industrial Organizations. Under such pressures, the eighty-year-old Morrison declined to run for re-election and was replaced by George Meany. For the next decade, until he died of old age at his home in Washington, D.C., he served as secretary emeritus of the federation.

Morrison was married twice: first, in 1891, to Josephine Curtis, whom he later divorced, and then to Alice S. Boswell in 1908. He had two children, a daughter, Esther, by his first wife, and a son, Nesbitt, by his second.

He was active in the Congregational church and served on the executive committees of both the Federal Council of Churches of Christ and the Golden Rule Sunday Society. He was a trustee of the Near East Relief Committee and a member of the Masons, Knights of Pythias, and Order of the Moose.

[Morrison's papers are on file at the Duke Univ. Lib. and AFL–CIO headquarters in Washington. A picture of Morrison can be found in *World's Work*, Dec. 1924, pp. 150–153, along with a biographical sketch. Other biographical information can be found in *Nat. Cyc. Am. Biog.*, Current Vol. C, 177-178; *Am. Federationist*, March 1904, p. 228, and Apr. 1949, pp. 6–7; *Am. Labor Who's Who; Who Was Who in America*, II (1950); *N.Y. Times*, Mar. 13, 1949; *Wash. Post*, Mar. 13, 1949.]

WARREN R. VAN TINE

MORTON, FERDINAND QUINTIN (Sept. 9, 1881–Nov. 8, 1949), lawyer and political leader, was born in Macon, Miss., one of at least two sons of former slaves Edward James Morton and Willie Mattie (Shelton) Morton. Little is known of his early life. In 1890 his family moved to Washington, D.C., where his father was appointed a clerk in the United States Treasury Department. After attending school in Washington, Morton graduated from Phillips Exeter Academy in 1902 and entered Harvard College.

Apparently because of financial pressures, Morton left Harvard at the end of his junior year in 1905. That fall he entered Boston University Law School where, as he later said, "I pursued knowledge until the bursar interfered." From 1906 to 1908, again according to his own account, he did "practically nothing" (*Harvard Class Report*, 1931). After moving to New York City in 1908, Morton worked for a time as a butler. Determined to practice law, he passed the bar examination in 1910, after working as a law clerk for two years. He also began to take an interest in Democratic party politics, and during the 1908 presidential campaign he spoke to audiences on behalf of William Jennings Bryan.

Morton soon joined the United Colored Democracy, an organization established to attract the predominantly Republican black population of New York into the Democratic fold. (Unlike the Republican party, the New York Democratic organization, Tammany Hall, did not recruit directly into the existing political clubhouses.) Morton's intelligence and oratorical ability came to the attention of Tammany boss Charles F. Murphy, who in 1915 intervened to secure his election as leader of the UCD.

The following year Morton was appointed assistant district attorney for New York County; and by 1921 he had become head of the office's indictment bureau. He resigned that year to become the first Negro member of the New York City Municipal Civil Service Commission, a move urged on him by Murphy as a means of assuring increased black representation among city employees. With an annual salary that exceeded $10,000 by the 1930's, Morton was one of the highest paid blacks on the city's payroll. He was elected president of the Civil Service Commission on July 16, 1946, and retired on Jan. 10, 1948.

Meanwhile, Morton emerged as the leading black Democratic politician in New York City. Practical and even cynical, he played the political game well, always seeking the attainable and ignoring the impossible. Yet his belief that "politics . . . is but a theoretical bargain counter, to buy wares and get the best we can in bargains," angered many blacks who felt that he did not exert enough pressure to open the political processes of Tammany Hall to them. As one of his critics later wrote, "the Race Negroes considered him weak, afraid to demand rights, and lacking in the power to fight for the advantages of political power that would create better working conditions and more pay for the Negro masses of the districts controlled by him" (Gardner).

From his Harlem headquarters, however, Morton ruled the United Colored Democracy with an iron hand throughout the 1920's. When white Tammany district leaders sought to dissolve the UCD and absorb its members into the party's regular clubhouses, Morton resisted, in part because he felt this action would diffuse and weaken the political effectiveness of Negroes, but also—it seems clear—because he intuitively sensed the threat it posed to his authority. Yet by the early 1930's, blacks had been absorbed into the regular Democratic party organizations, and the UCD became more a social and civic than a political body. Always the political survivor, Morton resigned as head of the United Colored Democracy in 1933, when Fiorello La Guardia, the newly elected reform mayor of New York, threatened him with loss of his seat on the Civil Service Commission. In 1935 Morton

was named commissioner of the Negro National League, a largely honorary title.

Morton never married, and following his retirement he moved to Washington, D.C., where his brother Fred was a physician. In his last years he suffered from Parkinson's disease. While taking treatment at Freedmen's Hospital, he died of burns received when a lit cigarette set his bed afire as he slept. He was buried in Woodlawn Cemetery in New York City.

[Biographical details about Morton are scarce. The best sources are Harvard College, *Class Reports* for the class of 1906 (1916, 1931), which included Morton although he failed to receive a degree; *Who's Who in Colored Am.,* I (1927); and two brief typescript studies in the Schomburg Collect. of the N.Y. Public Lib.: Samuel Michelson, "Hist. of the Democratic Party in Harlem," and James Gardner, "Brief Hist. of Ferdinand Q. Morton of N.Y.," both of which are in the WPA Writers Program, *Political Life and Organizations of Negroes in N.Y.C.* (n.d.). Morton's role as Negro baseball commissioner is briefly recounted in Robert W. Peterson, *Only the Ball Was White* (1970). See also the obituaries in the *N.Y. Age,* Nov. 12, 1949; *N.Y. Times,* Nov. 9, 1949; and *N.Y. Herald-Tribune,* Nov. 9, 1949.]

                                    PHILIP DE VENCENTES

MOSS, SANFORD ALEXANDER (Aug. 23, 1872-Nov. 10, 1946), mechanical engineer, was born in San Francisco, Calif., the eldest of three children (two sons and a daughter) of Ernest Goodman Moss and Josephine (Sanford) Moss. His father's English forebears came to the United States before 1800. Ernest Moss, a mining engineer, followed that profession with indifferent success until a tropical fever in Mexico led him, on his doctor's advice, to move to San Francisco, where he became a language teacher.

At sixteen, Sanford became a San Francisco machinist's apprentice and later a draftsman for a specialist in compressed-air engineering, whom he remembered as having used an impulse waterwheel to drive an air compressor. Similar work in several gas-engine shops and a course in thermodynamics taught by Frederick G. Hesse at the University of California at Berkeley in 1895 strengthened Moss's fascination with the gas turbine. After receiving the bachelor's degree in 1896, Moss wrote his master's thesis on gas turbines at Berkeley in 1900 and continued research on them as an instructor and doctoral candidate at Cornell University's Sibley College of Engineering. At Cornell in 1902 Moss developed what he later called "the first turbine wheel actually operated by products of combustion in the United States, and possibly . . . the first such . . . ever operated" ("Gas Turbines and Turbosuperchargers").

Although the turbine lacked the power even to run its own compressor, it served as the basis of Moss's 1903 doctoral thesis.

In June 1903 Moss went to work for the General Electric Company, first under Charles Steinmetz in Schenectady, N.Y., and then, from 1904 on, in the Thomson Laboratory at Lynn, Mass. From 1904 to 1907 Moss and other company engineers worked to develop a gas turbine. Materials then known could not stand the high temperatures required, and "creep"— permanent blade distortion under prolonged stress —was unrecognized. Consequent turbine inefficiency led to abandonment of the project. But it had spawned a centrifugal compressor—a sort of turbine in reverse, imparting peripheral velocity convertible into pressure—which found a good market in blast furnaces and elsewhere. Moss continued working in steam-turbine and centrifugal-compressor operations.

World War I brought Moss into the related field for which he would later be best known: aviation turbosuperchargers. If the fuel-air mixture is compressed at intake, more oxygen can be crammed into an engine cylinder, so that more fuel can be burned and thus more power generated: this process is known as "supercharging." For lightness and compactness, airplanes use centrifugal (rather than reciprocating) compressors, either geared to the engine shaft or driven by a turbine powered by engine exhaust gases. The latter type is the turbosupercharger.

The turbosupercharger concept can be found in a Swiss article of 1909 and a German patent (for sea-level engines) of 1911. In 1917 the French engineer Auguste Rateau proposed it for airplane engines at high altitudes (where the air is thin) and successfully tested it on a mountain peak. Informed of this by the French, the American government enlisted General Electric on the strength of its large steam-turbine business. Moss, in cooperation with United States Army Air Force engineers, designed a turbosupercharger, and, in August 1918 on Pike's Peak at 14,000 feet, used it to raise a Liberty engine's horsepower from 230 to 356, slightly above the engine's sea-level power.

This success led the army to finance a program of turbosupercharger research and development under Moss at General Electric through the 1920's and 1930's. Among the problems solved were those of minimizing the drag of protruding elements, propeller and airframe design for high altitudes, prevention of exhaust leaks, carburetor design, fuel-pumping systems, and such aspects of the turbosupercharger

proper as materials and turbine-wheel design for high temperatures and devices for cooling the compressed air.

Meanwhile the British had committed themselves to the geared supercharger. By the beginning of World War II, its efficiency had been so far improved that nearly all military aircraft, British and otherwise, used it. Nevertheless, the turbosupercharger remained more flexible in adjusting to varying atmospheric pressure. It also weighed much less and used no engine shaft power. In the 1930's an alloy used for dentures solved the problems of high-temperature turbine blade operation. Moss retired from General Electric in 1938, but after the Munich crisis, he came back as a consultant for further turbosupercharger work. A triumphant test in 1939 vindicated the army's faith. By 1943 turbosuperchargers were giving American fighters and bombers, such as the P-38, P-47, B-17, and B-24, a significant advantage over the enemy in high-altitude operations.

This contribution to Allied victory in World War II would in itself have entitled Moss to historical notice. After the war, moreover, the turbosupercharger remained important for reciprocating aircraft engines of 200-500 horsepower. Moss himself wrote that he "always . . . considered the turbosupercharger as merely a step on the way to the gas turbine" ("Gas Turbines and Turbosuperchargers"). He recognized, however, that its use of otherwise largely wasted power from the exhaust tended to divert attention from the improvement of its efficiency and that consequently its chief contribution to gas-turbine development was in the materials and techniques of high-temperature operation.

Moss was a small, nervously energetic man who wore eyeglasses and a pointed beard. As might be surmised from his persistence in following what for many years seemed a blind alley of mechanical engineering, he was often pertinacious and sometimes truculent. But his opponents were usually disarmed both by the clarity and precision of his argument and by his keen humor and appreciation of it in others. The set of his mind could be seen in the militant and effective crusade he waged in later years for the standardization of symbols for scientific and engineering terms.

On Aug. 23, 1899, he married Jennie Donnelly. They had four children: Donald Ernest, Evelyn Lawrence, Ethel Davis, and Sanford Alexander, Jr.

He received forty-seven patents, wrote numerous professional articles, and won several high awards, including the Collier Aviation Trophy, the Holley Medal of the American Society of Mechanical Engineers, and the Potts Medal of the Franklin Institute. He ranked the order of his interests as family, work, and genealogical research. His religious affiliation was Unitarian. He died of a heart attack in his Lynn home and was buried in Puritan Lawn Cemetery in Lynn.

[Two of Moss's publications, *Superchargers for Aviation* (1942) and "Gas Turbines and Turbosuperchargers," *GE Rev.,* Dec. 1943, are especially useful, not only for technical but also for historical and autobiographical information. They cite or list a number of Moss's other publications, mostly dealing with turbines and superchargers. An obituary in the *N.Y. Times,* Nov. 11, 1946, includes a photograph, as does Keith Ayling, "The Turbo Boys and the Magic Hotbox," *Liberty,* Apr. 8, 1944, which also exemplifies the considerable public notice Moss's work received. Robert Schlaifer, *Development of Aircraft Engines,* and S. D. Heron, *Development of Aviation Fuels,* published together in one volume in 1950, exhaustively and objectively recount supercharger development, with special attention to the role of government. George A. Stetson, "Sanford A. Moss," *Mech. Eng.,* Dec. 1946, is a pungent character sketch. Moss's daughter Ethel, now Mrs. Frank H. Samson of Nahant, Mass., furnished much information.]

ROBERT V. BRUCE

MURPHY, FRANK (Apr. 13, 1890–July 19, 1949), mayor of Detroit, governor-general and high commissioner of the Philippine Islands, governor of Michigan, attorney general of the United States, and Supreme Court justice, enjoyed a varied public career that was intertwined with the major issues in American life from World War I until his death. Born in Sand Beach (later Harbor Beach), Huron County, Mich., and baptized William Francis Murphy, he was the third of four children and second of three sons of John F. Murphy and Mary (Brennan) Murphy. His father, born in Canada of Catholic parents who had left Ireland in 1847, moved to Sand Beach in 1882 and there developed a substantial legal practice and participated actively in Democratic politics. Frank's mother, born in Whitehall, N.Y., was also of Irish Catholic extraction, her parents having emigrated from Ireland in 1849. She was "the ruling spirit" of her son's life until her death in 1924, and his unusually strong attachment to her probably accounts for his not marrying. From his mother Frank may have derived his tolerance for views at variance with his own, and it was Mary Murphy who convinced her son that he was destined for great things. Frank's absorption in public affairs, his sense of the dramatic, and his interest in Irish nationalism probably owed something to his father.

Frank was a high-spirited and fun-loving youth, with reddish hair, blue eyes, and an oval face that later in life was punctuated by bushy eyebrows. After receiving a public school education, he attended the University of Michigan and received the LL.B in 1914. He then accepted a position with a Detroit law firm and, over the next thirty months, enjoyed considerable success. When the United States declared war on Germany, Murphy enrolled for officer's training, was commissioned a first lieutenant in the infantry, and served briefly in France at the war's end. Before returning home, he took advantage of the educational program of the American Expeditionary Force to enroll for four weeks of legal study at Lincoln's Inn, London, and then at Trinity College, Dublin, where he took an active interest in Sinn Fein affairs. While he was overseas, Democratic friends in Detroit secured him the appointment of first assistant United States attorney for the Eastern District of Michigan. He was sworn in, just three days after his discharge, on Aug. 9, 1919.

Thus began the political career that was to occupy Murphy for most of the rest of his life. Although he dissembled by depreciating his own abilities and claiming an aversion to publicity, he was in fact an extremely ambitious person who aspired to the presidency itself. An excellent political orator, able to appeal to almost any kind of audience, he sought to attain his goals through dedicated public service rather than through traditional machine politics. As a political figure, he was a consistent supporter of civil service, fiscal integrity, the welfare state, organized labor, and civil liberties.

Murphy was a self-centered person who was obsessed with the importance of whatever he was doing. Although sentimental and tenderhearted, he gloried in the strenuous life and possessed a bellicose streak. Outwardly patient, he was inwardly tense, and his mild manner concealed a fierce resolve. He eschewed alcohol and tobacco and exercised regularly, because he regarded physical fitness as essential to political success. He early came to enjoy the company of the rich and the wellborn, but he had a genuine compassion for the afflicted and unfortunate. He was unusually attractive to the opposite sex, and he craved the affection of women, but he loved his own career more. Although always his own man, he was, in his fashion, a devout Catholic and was considerably influenced by Catholic social thought.

As assistant United States attorney, Murphy was responsible for prosecuting violators of the prohibition and narcotics statutes. He also joined his chief in helping to best an impressive array of legal counsel in a major case involving conspiracy to defraud the United States government of more than $300,000 in the purchase of army salvage material, and he skillfully represented the government in the lengthy proceedings of the Ford Motor Company-River Rouge condemnation case. In 1920 Murphy was defeated when he sought election as the Democratic candidate in Michigan's First Congressional District.

After resigning his federal job in 1922, Murphy joined his friend Edward G. Kemp in private law practice, and the new firm enjoyed success almost from the start. In 1923 Murphy filed as a candidate for a judgeship on Detroit's Recorder's Court, a court with a unified criminal jurisdiction that had attracted the favorable attention of students of criminal jurisprudence. Campaigning against the court's ruling bloc of four judges who had become identified with a law-and-order approach to crime, he won election and took office on Jan. 1, 1924. During his six and a half years on the court—he was reelected in 1929—his social and political views crystallized, and he won the support of Detroit's liberal elements, blacks, and white ethnic groups. Murphy found his service "comforting in a very personal way" as he dispensed justice with mercy, reduced the jail population by the use of sensible bail procedures, and exhibited a more friendly attitude toward organized labor than was customary for the era. He won national attention with a 1925 report stemming from his one-man grand jury inquiry into irregularities in various city departments, his well-publicized use of a sentencing board in felony cases, and the fair manner in which in 1925 and 1926 he presided over the famous murder trials of a black family, the Sweets, who had defended their newly acquired home in a white neighborhood against a threatening mob.

In 1930 Mayor Charles W. Bowles of Detroit, charged with mismanagement of the city's affairs, was ousted by the voters in a recall election, and Murphy decided to seek the mayoralty. His campaign stressed the gravity of the unemployment crisis confronting the city, and he defeated four opponents in the nonpartisan election. He won reelection easily in 1931 and served until May 1933. Murphy provided Detroit with a social-minded and clean government that was committed to free speech and maintained close ties with organized labor. Although sometimes lacking in decisiveness, he

selected excellent men for administrative positions and gave them his firm support, a practice that became his hallmark as an administrator. The dominating event of his mayoralty was the Great Depression. Murphy's determined efforts to cope with Detroit's unemployment, the severest in any big city, earned him nationwide attention, but there was a good deal of criticism of the city's alleged "dole spree."

When Murphy took office, more than 100,000 persons were unemployed in Detroit. Insisting that no one should go hungry, he supplemented the relief efforts of the Department of Public Welfare by creating the Mayor's Unemployment Committee, which registered the unemployed, maintained emergency lodges for homeless men, ran an employment bureau, sponsored a highly successful thrift-garden program, and became the advocate of a variety of reforms. As the depression continued and deepened, Detroit strained its resources to the utmost, but it found itself unable to cope with the problem of relief. An effort to supplement public expenditures with private funds during the winter of 1931–1932 yielded a meager result, and since the state of Michigan was unwilling to appropriate funds for direct relief, Murphy became a zealous advocate of federal aid to meet the unemployment crisis. He called a conference of Michigan mayors on May 18, 1932, to further the cause; and in June 1932 he presided over a conference of United States mayors whose importuning may have stimulated the passage of the Emergency Relief and Construction Act later that month. Detroit staggered through the bleak winter of 1932-1933 with the aid of the Reconstruction Finance Corporation loans that the statute authorized, but Murphy clearly saw the need for still further federal assistance for the financially exhausted cities. The mayors met again in February 1933; established the United States Conference of Mayors as a permanent organization, with Murphy as its first president; and urged Congress to enact a municipal debt adjustment measure.

Faced with rising welfare costs, mounting debt service charges, and soaring tax delinquencies, Murphy sharply reduced the non-welfare portion of Detroit's budget. To refund its floating debt, the city had to pledge the bankers that it would live within its income, and this placed increasingly severe limitations on municipal activities. Murphy worked out a financial plan with the city's industrialists that promised to carry Detroit through the fiscal year 1932–1933, but the state banking holiday declared on

Feb. 14, 1933, knocked the scheme into a cocked hat and forced Detroit into technical default on its obligations.

As the mayor of nonpartisan Detroit, Murphy remained largely aloof from Democratic politics until the 1932 campaign. He was a supporter of Franklin D. Roosevelt before his nomination for the presidency and stumped the state for him after the Democratic convention. His reward was an appointment, in the spring of 1933, as governor-general of the Philippine Islands.

Murphy's three years in the Philippines were the happiest of his adult life. He enjoyed the pomp and ceremony that went with his position and the warm response that his Catholicism, his idealism, his sentimentality, his sympathy for the cause of Philippine independence, and his obvious affection for the people evoked among the Filipinos. He provided the islands with a government that was fiscally sound, infused with the social-mindedness of the New Deal, and committed to the protection of civil liberties. He secured the adoption of female suffrage and significant reforms in the administration of justice.

The transcendent issue facing the Philippines when Murphy arrived in Manila was whether the Filipinos should accept the Hare-Hawes-Cutting Act of 1933 and its promise of ultimate independence. Murphy remained officially neutral in the heated political controversy surrounding this issue, but he informed Washington that, although he believed the Filipinos capable of self-government, he thought it unwise, in view of the absolute dependence of the Filipino economy on the American market, to grant them political independence and at the same time end their existing free-trade relationship with the United States. When the Hare-Hawes-Cutting Act was rejected by the Filipinos, Murphy aided the mission of Manuel Quezon to the United States in the negotiations that led to the Tydings-McDuffie Act of 1934, which provided for independence after a ten-year commonwealth status. Murphy also helped persuade President Roosevelt to accept the new Filipino-drafted constitution without alteration, and he was instrumental in laying the groundwork for the joint trade conference that met in 1937 and recommended a more gradual imposition of United States tariff rates than was provided by the Tydings-McDuffie Act.

When the Philippine Commonwealth was inaugurated in November 1935, Murphy became the United States high commissioner; but he found the job, with its largely nominal au-thority, much less satisfying than that of governor-general. He was therefore probably less reluctant than he claimed about returning to Michigan in 1936 at Roosevelt's behest to run for governor and, it was hoped, to aid an unnecessarily worried president in carrying the state. Murphy won the Democratic primary handily, but it was the heavy Roosevelt majority that helped carry Murphy to victory in November.

When he took office, the General Motors sit-down strike was already under way. He sent National Guard units into Flint after violence erupted there on January 11, but since he wished to secure a peaceful resolution of the dispute, he refused to use the guard to eject the sit-downers even after they defied a court injunction to evacuate the occupied plants. He played the crucial mediatory role in the negotiations that brought the strike to an end on February 11 on terms that amounted to a victory for the United Automobile Workers. This was probably the high point in Murphy's public career, and he received much acclaim for his peacemaking role; but when the GM settlement was followed by a wave of sit-down strikes rather than by industrial peace, Murphy became the target of widespread criticism for having failed to enforce the law in Flint. Increasingly, he took a law-and-order approach to the strike wave, but he continued to play the part of peacemaker and succeeded in settling the Chrysler sit-down strike in April and a host of lesser strikes throughout 1937.

As governor, Murphy sought to bring the New Deal to Michigan and to strengthen and improve the state's administrative structure. He was handicapped by factionalism within his party, his tendency to rely on his own popularity and a good-government emphasis rather than on party organization, a malapportioned and inexperienced legislature, a weak reform impulse in the state, and the severe impact on Michigan of the recession of 1937–1938; but he nevertheless presided over one of the state's most notable administrations, and he raised the whole tone of state government. Not only was he responsible for the enactment and effective implementation of a model civil service statute, the most significant structural reform of his governorship, but his administration also provided the state with its first effective budget system, an efficient and nonpolitical purchasing system, an excellent corrections system, an efficiently operated Liquor Control Commission, and a well-managed Corporation and Securities Commission.

Long a proponent of social security, Murphy provided the impetus for the enactment by a lame-duck legislature in December 1936 of Michigan's liberal unemployment compensation statute, and the next year the legislature liberalized the state's old-age assistance law. The massive impact of the recession on the state led Murphy, playing a role that was painfully familiar to him, to call for increased aid from the Works Progress Administration, and the federal government responded to his importunities. His Michigan New Deal also included a substantial hospital-building program, the expansion of public health services, an occupational-disease law, rural electrification, the establishment of a Consumers Bureau in the Department of Agriculture, a consumer-minded Public Utilities Commission, and liberalized housing legislation. His ambitious plans for additional structural and social reforms were thwarted by his failure to win reelection in 1938, a major defeat for the New Deal.

Wishing to provide a post for so loyal a New Dealer, Roosevelt selected Murphy to replace the departing Homer S. Cummings as attorney general. Murphy served an eventful and exciting year (January 1939–January 1940) in this cabinet position, becoming in the process the most publicized New Deal official save the president himself. Murphy particularly attracted attention as a crusader against crime and corruption, a role that he played to the hilt. During his tenure Kansas City's Tom Pendergast was convicted of income tax evasion; a thoroughgoing federal inquiry into the machinations of the successors of Huey Long in Louisiana led to numerous indictments; Martin T. Manton, a prominent federal circuit court judge, was successfully prosecuted for receiving funds from litigants; Moses Annenberg, the publisher and racetrack news czar, was indicted for income tax evasion and for operating an illegal lottery; Louis Lepke Buchalter was indicted for violating the narcotics laws; and the Chicago gambling figure William Skidmore and the boss of Atlantic City, Enoch L. Johnson, were indicted for income tax evasion. Murphy also looked into irregularities in the Hague machine in New Jersey and the Kelly-Nash machine in Chicago. In an effort to improve the administration of justice, he devised a national program to expedite the disposition of cases by the United States attorneys, called the first nationwide conference of United States attorneys and the first nationwide parole conference, raised the standards for federal marshals and recommended that they be placed under civil service, and urged Congress to create a system of public defenders.

Believing that the federal government should seek aggressively to protect civil liberties, Murphy established a special unit for this purpose in the Criminal Division of the Department of Justice. He won the plaudits of civil libertarians, but they expressed concern after war broke out in Europe about his efforts to counter alleged espionage and seditious activities. In his most controversial act in this context, Murphy ordered the presentation to a Detroit grand jury of a case involving alleged conspiracy by a group of left-wingers to induce Americans, in violation of federal law, to fight on the side of the Spanish loyalists. Twelve of the group were arrested on Feb. 6, 1940, a day after Murphy took his seat as a U.S. Supreme Court justice, but the new attorney general dismissed the charges against them.

It was an open secret in Washington that Murphy ascended to the Supreme Court with considerable reluctance. Not only did he fear that he was being "put out to pasture" before he could realize his highest ambition, but for one who loved to be at the center of the stage, playing to an admiring audience, the cloistered life of a Supreme Court justice had little appeal. As war became a possibility and then an actuality, the work of the Court seemed to Murphy, at least at times, to be trivial by comparison. After Pearl Harbor, he would have liked to resign his post and to command troops in the field, but he was told that he was too old for such an assignment, and he had to content himself, as a lieutenant colonel on inactive status, with participation in army training activities during the court recess of 1942. Although he begged the president in 1943 and 1944 for an assignment that would take him near or into the Philippines, the best that he could arrange for himself was a mission to Latin America in 1943, and even that had to be canceled when he was compelled to undergo nasal surgery. Murphy had to be satisfied during the remainder of the war with service as president of Philippine War Relief and as chairman of the National Committee Against Persecution and Extermination of the Jews.

When Murphy took his place on the nation's highest court, he lacked confidence in his qualifications for the post, but after a period of irresolution that lasted for three or four terms, he adjusted to his new life and began to take some satisfaction in a role that permitted him to "do so much for impoverished justice, for real freedom and all of man's best hopes." As a Supreme Court justice he has been widely criticized for placing his humanitarian instincts above the law, thinking more with his heart than with his head, writing emotional opinions that ignored precedent and lacked legal subtlety, and being a crusader rather than a judge. There is some truth in these judgments, but they are not the whole truth. Murphy, to be sure, always prized the substance of justice more than its form, and he relied heavily on what his conscience told him to be right. He sometimes overstated his argument or injected "a little poetry" into his opinions, but most of his opinions were technically competent. Whatever his method, he brought a necessary moral indignation to his work and spoke eloquently for the defenseless and despised. He was not a leader on the Court and, indeed, enjoyed the role of dissenter; but some of his dissents of the 1940's were to become the opinion of the Court in the 1960's.

It is doubtful if there has ever been a more ardent defender of civil liberties on the Supreme Court than Justice Murphy. A firm believer in the "preferred position" of the First Amendment freedoms, he was a zealous advocate of freedom of religion (*Jones* v. *Opelika,* 316 U.S. 584 [1942]; *Martin* v. *Struthers,* 319 U.S. 141 [1943]; *Prince* v. *Massachusetts,* 321 U.S. 158 [1944]) and freedom of speech and of the press (*National Broadcasting Co., Inc.,* v. *United States,* 319 U.S. 190 [1943]; *Associated Press* v. *United States,* 326 U.S. 1 [1945]; *Craig* v. *Harney,* 331 U.S. 367 [1947]). He invoked the constitutional guarantees to protect racial minorities against discrimination (*Steele* v. *Louisville and Nashville Railroad Co.,* 323 U.S. 192 [1944]; *Oyama* v. *California,* 332 U.S. 633 [1948]); he became the "guardian of Indian rights" on the Court; and he was the champion of nonconformists and political dissidents (*Bridges* v. *Wixon,* 326 U.S. 135 [1945]; *Christoffel* v. *United States,* 338 U.S. 84 [1949]; *Eisler* v. *United States,* 338 U.S. 189 [1949]).

Murphy believed that the constitutional guarantees of individual liberty were as controlling in wartime as in peacetime and that the clear-and-present-danger test did not lose its validity simply because the nation was at war. He was thus more reluctant than some of his colleagues to find that treason had been committed (*Haupt* v. *United States,* 330 U.S. 631 [1947]), and he stood out against the denaturalization of both Communists and Nazis (*Schneiderman* v. *United States,* 320 U.S. 118 [1943]; *Baumgartner* v. *United States,* 322 U.S. 665 [1944]). He attacked the wartime evacuation of the Japanese as racism (*Korematsu* v. *United States,* 323 U.S. 214 [1944]), found military trials in Hawaii to have been illegal (*Duncan* v. *Kahanamoku,* 327 U.S. 304 [1946]), and wished the Supreme Court to review the military trials of war criminals to ascertain if these trials had offended constitutional guarantees (*In re Yamashita,* 327 U.S. 1 [1946]; *Homma* v. *Patterson,* 327 U.S. 759 [1946]; *Hirota* v. *MacArthur,* 338 U.S. 197 [1949]).

Murphy had the same concern for the procedural rights of defendants in criminal cases as he did for civil liberties in general, and he believed that criminal proceedings in state courts as well as in federal courts were invalid if they violated the Bill of Rights or even "fundamental ideas of justice." He applied these views in cases involving the right to counsel (*Canizio* v. *New York,* 327 U.S. 82 [1946]); the composition of juries (*Thiel* v. *Southern Pacific Co.,* 328 U.S. 217 [1946]); coerced confessions (*Lyons* v. *Oklahoma,* 322 U.S. 596 [1944]); and search and seizure (*Harris* v. *United States,* 331 U.S. 145 [1947]; *Trupiano* v. *United States,* 334 U.S. 699 [1948]; *Wolf* v. *Colorado,* 338 U.S. 25 [1949]).

It is not surprising in view of his earlier career that Murphy had a special interest in cases involving labor. In one of his most significant opinions he equated peaceful picketing, under certain circumstances, with free speech (*Thornhill* v. *Alabama,* 310 U.S. 88 [1940]), and he held that the Norris-LaGuardia Act applied to the United States government as well as to private employers (*United States* v. *United Mine Workers of America,* 330 U.S. 258 [1947]). He wrote more opinions dealing with the Fair Labor Standards Act than any of his colleagues, and the thrust of what he wrote was to give the statute the broadest possible coverage, including employee travel to and from work and preparation for work (*Tennessee Coal, Iron and Railroad Co.* v. *Muscoda Local No. 123,* 321 U.S. 590 [1944]; *Jewell Ridge Coal Corporation* v. *Local No. 6167, U.M.W.A.,* 325 U.S. 161 [1945]; *Anderson* v. *Mt. Clemens Pottery Co.,* 328 U.S. 680 [1946]).

Murphy had experienced some heart trouble in 1943, and he was hospitalized off and on with a variety of ailments during his last three years on the Court. He was fifty-nine when, in 1949, he died of a coronary thrombosis at the Ford Hospital in Detroit. He was buried in the family plot in Rock Falls Cemetery, overlooking Lake Huron just south of Harbor Beach.

[The principal source is the Frank Murphy Papers, in the Mich. Hist. Collect., Univ. of Mich. The same repository also has the papers of Murphy's parents, brothers, and sister; of his close friend, Edward G. Kemp; of his secretary, Eleanor Bumgardner Wright; and of his long-time law clerk, Eugene Gressman; as well as transcripts of interviews with a large number of persons who were associated with Murphy and innumerable photographs of him. The Joseph R. Hayden Papers and the Norman Hill Scrapbooks, also in the Mich. Hist. Collect., help illuminate Murphy's career in the Philippines. The Mayor's Office Records for 1930–1933, at the Burton Hist. Collect., Detroit Public Lib., are invaluable for Murphy's mayoralty. The Felix Frankfurter Papers at the Lib. of Cong., and the Harvard Law Lib., the Harlan Fiske Stone Papers and Harold H. Burton Papers in the Lib. of Cong., and the Wiley B. Rutledge Papers and Robert H. Jackson Papers, both privately held, contribute to an understanding of Murphy's Supreme Court career. Several of the files in the Franklin D. Roosevelt Lib., Hyde Park, N.Y., are relevant, and there is a wealth of material pertaining to Murphy in the records of the following agencies in the Nat. Arch.: Bureau of Insular Affairs, Office of the U.S. High Commissioner to the Philippine Islands, President's Organization on Unemployment Relief, Dept. of Justice, and Dept. of State. The Am. Civil Liberties Union Arch., at Princeton Univ., contain valuable information on almost every phase of Murphy's career.

Of the two published biographies—Richard D. Lunt, *The High Ministry of Government* (1965), covering his pre-Court career, and J. Woodford Howard, *Mr. Justice Murphy: A Political Biog.* (1968)—the Howard biography, written after the Murphy Papers became available, is superior. Particular aspects of Murphy's career are treated in Sidney Fine, *Frank Murphy in World War I* (Mich. Hist. Collect., *Bull. No. 17*, 1968) and *Sit-Down: The General Motors Strike of 1936–1937* (1969). For Murphy's years in the Philippines, Joseph R. Hayden, *The Philippines: A Study in National Development* (1942), is especially important. Murphy's service as attorney general is critically portrayed in Eugene C. Gerhart, *America's Advocate: Robert H. Jackson* (1958); this should be supplemented by Murphy's *Annual Reports* as attorney general for 1939 and 1940. His Supreme Court opinions are in *U.S. Reports*, vols. 310–338.

Of the numerous articles dealing with Murphy, the following merit attention: William Stidger in *The Human Side of Greatness* (1940); Blair Moody in *Survey Graphic*, Dec. 1935; Russell B. Porter in *N.Y. Times Mag.*, Feb. 21, 1937; "The Labor Governors," *Fortune*, June 1937; "Lay Bishop," *Time*, Aug. 28, 1939; articles in memorial issue of *Mich. Law Rev.*, Apr. 1950; Carl Muller in *Detroit Lawyer*, Sept., 1949; Eugene Gressman in *Columbia Law Rev.*, Jan. 1950, and *Georgetown Law Rev.*, Summer 1959; John P. Frank in *Yale Law Jour.*, Dec. 1949; John P. Roche in *Vanderbilt Law Rev.*, Feb. 1957; Sidney Fine in *Pacific Hist. Rev.*, May 1964, in *Labor Hist.*, Spring 1965, and in *Jour. of Am. Hist.*, June 1966.

There are obituaries and appraisals of Murphy in *Detroit News*, July 19 and 20, 1949; *Detroit Times*, July 20, 1949; *Detroit Free Press*, July 20, 1949; *N.Y. Times*, July 20, 1949; *New Republic*, Aug. 1, 1949; *Time*, Aug. 1, 1949; *Christian Century*, Aug. 3, 1949; *America*, July 30, 1949; and *Survey*, Aug. 1949. For resolutions of the bar of the Supreme Court honoring Murphy, see 340 U.S. v–xxv (1951).]

         SIDNEY FINE

MURPHY, JAMES BUMGARDNER (Aug. 4, 1884–Aug. 24, 1950), pathologist, cancer researcher, was born in Morganton,

N.C., the second son and third of four children of Patrick Livingston Murphy, physician and director of the Western North Carolina Insane Asylum, and Bettie Wadell (Bumgardner) Murphy. His mother was a Virginian. His father was a native of Sampson County, N.C., where the family forebear, Patrick Murphy (originally MacMurdock), had settled after coming from Scotland about 1767. As a small boy James Murphy showed the beginnings of his lifelong interest in living creatures and their ailments by keeping a collection of domestic and wild animals and birds, which he cared for with the solicitude of a future physician. He attended the Horner School in North Carolina, a preparatory school of the military type. One of his biographers has suggested that this early schooling helped give him the strong sense of discipline that characterized his scientific work and his relations with other people. From 1901 to 1905 he studied at the University of North Carolina, where he took the B.S. degree, and then entered the medical school of the Johns Hopkins University.

The skill that Murphy demonstrated in practical laboratory work won him the opportunity to participate, while still a medical student, in the investigation of two important problems. With the anatomist Franklin P. Mall he studied variations in the convolutions of the human brain and found no differences depending on race; with William G. MacCallum he carried out experiments on sheep and goats to help elucidate the development of tetany after surgical removal of the parathyroid glandules. After taking the M.D. degree at Johns Hopkins in 1909, Murphy joined the research staff of the psychiatrist Adolf Meyer at the Pathological Institute of the New York State Hospitals on Ward's Island, New York City. At the end of a year there, when Meyer was made head of the newly created Phipps Psychiatric Clinic at Johns Hopkins, Murphy was invited to join him as a resident in psychiatry, but chose instead to go to the Rockefeller Institute in New York City as an assistant to the pathologist Peyton Rous.

In his work on the cause of cancer, Rous had just discovered that a malignant tumor of fowls was transmitted by a virus present in a filtrate from which all tumor cells had been removed. By showing that the virus was still active after the cells had been killed by glycerine or ultraviolet radiation, he had proved that the virus was a separate entity. During these early years at the Institute, Murphy confirmed this result by showing that the virus remained active after the tumor cells were killed by lyophilization, a freezing and drying process that he was the first to apply to biological research.

In order to determine whether the age of the host influences the growth of implanted chicken sarcoma (as it does that of nonmalignant grafts), Rous and Murphy implanted bits of the tumor in chick embryos, where it grew much faster than in adult hosts. Murphy, perceiving that embryonic tissue is not immune to foreign cells as are adult tissues, made the audacious experiment of implanting, on the embryonic membranes of chick embryos, bits of rat and mouse tumors. Such tumors, which will not grow in adults of other species, grew well in the chick embryos. This discovery had great significance for cancer research and for the understanding of species specificity; it helped elucidate the mechanism of the body's resistance to the grafting of foreign tissues, and the role of lymphoid tissue in immunological reactions. The technique has been extensively used in screening programs for chemotherapeutic agents against cancer. This work was followed in 1914 by the elegant demonstration that bits of adult chicken spleen or bone marrow injected into the chick embryo would promote resistance to transplanted foreign tissue.

In 1915, when Rous turned to work in other fields, Murphy was put in charge of cancer research and made an associate member of the Rockefeller Institute. He undertook a program of investigation based on the observation that all tissues of the adult fowl are resistant in some degree to implanted sarcoma tissue, except the brain. Since the brain and the embryo have in common the absence of lymphocytes, Murphy formed the hypothesis that white blood cells of that kind have a specific role in resisting cancer. For many years he and his associates tested this idea by a wide range of experimental methods aimed at altering or abolishing the action of lymphocytes—by X rays, heat, and various hormones and other substances. This assiduous effort confirmed the initial hypothesis in so far as the techniques of the day made it possible, and developed a great mass of incidental information (presented in more than fifty papers) about lymphocytes, tissue immunity, the effects of X radiation on living tissues, and immunity and susceptibility to cancer, information that has been of much use to subsequent investigators.

From 1917 to 1919 Murphy served in the Army Medical Corps with the rank of major. Attached to the staff of the Surgeon General

in Washington, he directed the organization of mobile medical laboratories in France and the training of their personnel. While in Washington he met and married, on Apr. 28, 1919, Ray Slater of Boston. They had two sons, James Slater and Ray Livingston; the first became a microbiologist at the Rockefeller Institute. Shortly after his marriage, Murphy developed a duodenal ulcer which, with its sequelae, required two major operations and cost him more than a year of illness. While convalescing at Seal Harbor, Maine, where he made a complete recovery, he acquired a deep affection for Mount Desert Island and eventually bought a house there, where he regularly spent his summers.

By the end of 1920 Murphy was back at work. A compilation of most of his pioneer research on the role of the lymphocyte in resistance to cancer, to tuberculosis, and to normal tissue transplantation appeared in 1926 in a Rockefeller Institute monograph. There followed a long series of papers on tumor inhibitors and on the cause of cancer. In 1931, with prophetic insight, Murphy emphasized that the chicken sarcoma agent behaved as a "transmissible mutagen" and likened its action to that of the transforming principle in bacteria. This was years before Oswald T. Avery's pioneer work on the pneumococcus transforming principle and the much later work on the action of Rous virus.

Murphy's subsequent research emphasized the role of the endocrine glands and hormone preparations in resistance to transplanted tumors and leukemia in rats. These studies showed the particular importance of the adrenal glands in susceptibility and led to fruitful clinical investigations by other workers. Over the years, many able young researchers worked with Murphy. A generous and stimulating leader, he encouraged them to develop their own potentialities. Ten or more of them went on to professorships or the direction of research institutes in the United States and several foreign countries. In the later years men in his department produced pioneer work on cell fractionation, cellular ultrastructure, and the biochemical functions of subcellular particulates.

Murphy was made a full member of the Rockefeller Institute in 1923. At this time the attitude of the medical profession and the public toward cancer was undergoing a marked change. Research was offering promise for the future, and hopelessness was giving way to optimism based on the advance of diagnostic and surgical techniques. The public needed to be educated to seek early diagnosis and treatment; physicians had to be brought up to date, and financial support obtained for research and for therapeutic centers. When in 1929 the American Society for the Control of Cancer was reorganized to meet these needs, Murphy became a member of the board of directors and its executive committee, serving until 1945. He also became a member of the advisory council of the National Cancer Institute set up by the Cancer Act of 1937, and he served several years on the committee on growth of the National Research Council, which advised the American Cancer Society on its grants in aid of research. He had earlier (1921–1922) been president of the American Association for Cancer Research. As a member of the board of trustees of the Memorial Hospital of New York he gave constructive support to the hospital's director, his friend James Ewing, and later to Ewing's successor, Cornelius P. Rhoads. Murphy was also a trustee of the Roswell Park Memorial Institute in Buffalo, N.Y., devoted primarily to clinical problems, and the Jackson Memorial Laboratory at Bar Harbor, Maine, concerned with biological studies, including basic cancer research. To all these institutions he brought not only his great scientific experience but also statesmanlike advice on problems of organization and development; thus he had a leading role in the progress of cancer research in America.

Murphy's personal charm and integrity, his hospitality to colleagues of every rank, and his conscientious performance of the many duties he assumed, won recognition in the form of honorary degrees from his alma mater, the University of North Carolina, from Oglethorpe University, and from Louvain. He was elected to the National Academy of Sciences in 1940. Murphy retired from active work at the Rockefeller Institute in 1950. Later in the same year, at his home at Seal Harbor, he suffered a cerebral hemorrhage from which he died in Bar Harbor, Maine. A Presbyterian, he was buried in the churchyard of Bethel Church near Staunton, Va.

[George W. Corner, *A Hist. of the Rockefeller Inst., 1901–1953* (1964); Clarence C. Little in Nat. Acad. Sci., *Biog. Memoirs,* XXXIV (1960), with portrait and complete bibliography; Warfield T. Longcope in Assoc. of Am. Physicians, *Trans.* 44 (1951): 15–18. See also *Who Was Who in America,* vol. III (1960); *Nat. Cyc. Am. Biog.,* XXXVIII, 69; and, on his father, Jerome Dowd, *Sketches of Prominent Living North Carolinians,* pp. 277–279 (1888).]
GEORGE W. CORNER

MYERSON, ABRAHAM (Nov. 23, 1881-Sept. 3, 1948), neuropsychiatrist, was born in Yanova, Lithuania (then part of Russia), the third of four sons and fifth of the eight children of Morris Joseph Myerson and Sophie (Segal) Myerson. His father had been educated as a rabbi but, having developed agnostic views, had turned to teaching school. To avoid possible exile for his socialist convictions, he immigrated in 1885 to the United States and settled in New Britain, Conn., where he worked as a peddler. His wife and children soon joined him, and in 1892 they moved to Boston, where he became a junk dealer.

Although young Myerson enjoyed the free life of the waterfront slums of Boston and made a place for himself in neighborhood gangs, in the scholarly atmosphere of his home he early became attracted to books and ideas, developing a phenomenal memory and unusual speed in reading. He graduated in 1898 from Boston's English High School, where he acquired a strong interest in biology, and for the next six years worked at various jobs, saving money to enter medical school. He spent two years at the College of Physicians and Surgeons at Columbia, interrupted by a year's work as a streetcar conductor to replenish his funds, and then transferred to the Tufts Medical School in Boston, where he received the M.D. degree in 1908.

At Tufts, his interest in the human mind had been stimulated by the neurologist and psychologist Morton Prince, and after graduation Myerson served as an assistant in the department of diseases of the nervous system at the Boston City Hospital (1908-1911). This was followed by a year as resident neurologist at the Alexian Brothers Hospital in St. Louis and instructor in neuropathology at St. Louis University, and a year as a resident at the new Boston Psychopathic Hospital. From 1913 to 1917 Myerson was clinical director and pathologist at the Taunton (Mass.) State Hospital. He began a long teaching career at Tufts in 1918 as assistant professor of neurology and became professor in 1921 and professor emeritus in 1940. In 1927 he was appointed director of research at the Boston State Hospital in Mattapan, a post he retained until 1948; much of his own research was done in its laboratory. His research led also to his appointment as clinical professor of psychiatry at Harvard (1935-1945).

Myerson's early work and publications dealt primarily with classical neurology and emphasized the physical diagnostic signs of neurological disease. Although he described a number of pathological reflexes, his major contribution of this period was the popularization of the glabellar reflex, since known as "Myerson's Sign," that is indicative of disorders of the basal ganglia. He also developed a technique for obtaining blood samples from both the internal carotid artery and the internal jugular vein as a way of studying brain metabolism —work that Myerson himself considered his most important scientific contribution.

Although Myerson did not abandon classical clinical neurology, he developed a major interest in psychiatry. His approach to psychiatry was physiological rather than psychological; he distrusted psychology as insufficiently scientific. Thus he favored the then current somatic forms of treatment and was a strong proponent of electroconvulsive therapy and of the "total push" concept. He was strongly anti-Freudian, and although in later life he moderated his views, he never became a supporter of the psychoanalytic method.

Myerson had a lifelong interest in the inheritance of mental disorders, which began with his collaboration with the neuropsychiatrist William Washington Graves during the St. Louis period. At the Taunton State Hospital he studied the records of all patients admitted since 1854, examined current patients and interviewed their relatives, and found that 10 percent of the families involved had had more than one member admitted. His conclusion, as set forth in *The Inheritance of Mental Diseases* (1925), was that schizophrenia and manic-depressive psychosis seemed to run in families, but that other mental diseases showed no hereditary character. Myerson also studied the families of mental retardates in two Massachusetts schools and served as chairman of the committee on eugenics of the American Neurological Association. He believed that feeblemindedness was to some extent hereditary and favored a limited program of eugenical sterilization, but found much of the eugenics movement extreme and irrational.

Myerson was much concerned with the neuroses of women, and in *The Nervous Housewife* (1920) he attributed many of their illnesses to their dissatisfaction with the inferior position imposed on them by society. Other books intended for the lay reader were *When Life Loses Its Zest* (1925) and *The Psychology of Mental Disorders* (1927). Myerson was also interested in the social aspects of alcoholism and in legal psychiatry. He testified in a number of court cases, including that of Nicola Sacco and Bartolomeo Vanzetti; he believed their trial was unfair. Along with his teaching

and research, Myerson carried on an extensive private practice. He estimated that he had seen more than 25,000 patients during a period of thirty years.

Broad-shouldered and energetic, actively athletic in his younger days, Myerson was a man of zest and enthusiasm. He had firm convictions and was a talented speaker; at professional meetings, particularly when psychoanalysis was discussed, he was equally a master of the quip, the vitriolic comment, and logical argument. A member of many scientific societies, he served as chairman of the research committee of the American Psychiatric Association, 1939-1947, and during World War II represented the association on the National Research Council. He was president of the American Psychopathological Society in 1938-1939. Myerson married Dorothy Marion Loman on Mar. 9, 1913. Their children were Paul Graves and David John, both of whom became psychiatrists, and Anne, who became a psychiatric social worker. Myerson spent the last few years of his life as a semi-invalid, suffering from cardiac disease, and occupied himself in preparing his last book, *Speaking of Man* (1950). There he discussed the problems of human existence and expressed his conviction that, even without the solace of religion, life was worth living. He died of congestive heart failure at the age of sixty-six at his home in Brookline, Mass. His remains were cremated.

[The best account of Myerson is the biographical sketch by his daughter-in-law Mildred Ann Myerson in Myerson's *Speaking of Man*. See also obituaries in *Am. Jour. of Psychiatry*, Dec. 1948 (by I. S. Wechsler), and *Archives of Neurology and Psychiatry*, Sept. 1948; *Who Was Who in America*, II (1950). Death record from Mass. Registrar of Vital Statistics.]

RICHARD D. WALTER

NADELMAN, ELIE (Feb. 20, 1882-Dec. 28, 1946), sculptor, was born in Warsaw, Russian Poland, the last of seven children of Philip Nadelman and Hannah (Arnstan) Nadelman. Philip Nadelman, a middle-class jeweler, was a Jew of liberal intellectual interests, well read in philosophical literature. His wife came from a family of artists, writers, and musicians. As a boy Nadelman attended the Gymnasium, the High School of Liberal Arts, and the Academy of Arts in Warsaw. At eighteen he voluntarily joined the Imperial Russian Army and for a year performed the relatively insignificant duties of teaching officers' children and producing paintings for barracks. Upon demobilization he returned to the Academy of Arts. Nadelman then spent some six months in Munich, an interval that proved to be highly significant for his later career as a sculptor. There he made his first study of antique sculpture with a penetrating examination of the Glyptothek's warriors of Aegina. His questioning eye also found in Bavarian folk art an essential simplicity of form that he felt to be somehow analogous to the archaic Greek works.

At the age of twenty-one Nadelman gave up painting for sculpture. Settling in Paris, he was, for a decade, obsessed with the problem of demonstrating the formal principles he assumed to be the operational method of the Aeginian sculptors. As he became much more than a mere copyist of the antique, his art was permeated by a variety of influences, some of them seemingly irreconcilable. For example, although he followed Rodin's portrait style, he also had absorbed much from the drawings of Aubrey Beardsley. Upon analysis, the Paris work between 1903 and Nadelman's immigration to America in 1914 appears to be a twentieth-century species of neoclassicism. Nadelman fared well in Paris; even before his arrival, he received a prize given by *Sztuka,* the art journal of the city's Polish community, for his drawing for a Chopin memorial. Through the Polish brothers Thadée and Alexandre Natanson, founders of *La Revue Blanche,* he met such artistically influential persons as Octave Mirbeau and André Gide. Between 1903 and 1909 he produced a large number of works, which, when shown at the Galerie Druet in 1909, attracted a great deal of critical attention. As early as 1905 Nadelman had begun what he termed researches into the nature of physical matter with analytical drawings of the human form based upon sequences of curves. He was later to say that he had "completely revolutionized the art of our time" and that "cubism was only an imitation of the abstract form" discovered in his drawings. His now somewhat doubtful claim is based upon the similarity of Picasso's bronze portrait of Fernande Olivier to Nadelman's work. But the former, even if it was produced shortly after the Spanish artist visited Nadelman's studio in 1909, in reality culminates a phase of Picasso's own artistic evolution.

Nonetheless, Nadelman was of importance in Parisian artistic circles during those years. The deliberately innovative character of his conceptions was noticed favorably both by the sculptor Alexander Archipenko and by the critic Bernard Berenson. In an age when Rodin's expressionistic surfaces were widely imitated by younger sculptors, Nadelman's highly polished "antique" heads were a departure from sculptural norms, although their technical counterpart can be found in the contemporary work of Constantin Brancusi. In London in 1911 for an exhibition of his sculpture, Nadelman met Mme Helena Rubinstein, the wealthy Polish-born proprietor of beauty salons in the United States and Europe, who purchased the entire exhibition. Nadelman's last showing in Paris was at Druet in 1913, and although it was both smaller and less spectacular than the exhibition of 1909, it caused André Salmon to publish the first full-length article devoted to Nadelman's art. Salmon characterized Nadelman as almost Byzantine in his uncompromising sacrifice of everything to the Euclidean interrelationships of forms in the glyptic art.

Encouraged by Mme Rubinstein, Nadelman came to the United States in the fall of 1914 and began, with her help, to prepare for his first New York exhibition, held at the Alfred Stieglitz Photo-Secession Gallery ("291") in December of the following year. There his "Man in the Open Air" bespoke a new satirical approach to subject matter based in part upon a study of Seurat drawings made before he left France. His first large New York showing came in 1917 at the galleries of Scott Fowles and received high praise from Henry McBride, one of America's most perceptive critic columnists. Nadelman, now a notable force in New York's artistic life, during the next few years completed a prodigious number of works. His subjects were of three kinds: commissioned portraits elegantly stylized, concert and theatrical subjects whimsically conceived, and satirical references to drawing-room behavior.

After his marriage on Dec. 29, 1919, to a wealthy widow, Viola M. Flannery, Nadelman's career took a curious turn. His wife, a daughter of Countess Naselli of Rome, was then unwell, and she and the artist virtually retired from New York life to live in seclusion on an estate in the Riverdale section of the city. Here they amassed an important collection of American folk art numbering some 15,000 items. Nadelman continued to work, but the new pieces were nearly unknown to the art world, as he refused either to sell or to exhibit them. In the 1930's, however, he responded to commissions for two large architectural decorations, and it was probably these that caused him to think of sculpture on a new scale. The late Amazonian pairs of females, circus riders standing at rest, were seen only after his death, as were also the dozens of figurines in papier-mâché, terra cotta, and plaster. The last are modern equivalents of the Tanagra works of Hellenistic Greece, some authentic fragments of which were found in his studio. Nadelman died at his Riverdale home after a long illness on December 28, 1946. Besides his wife, he was survived by their only child, E. Jan, a vice-consul of the American embassy in Poland.

Although Nadelman's oeuvre is marked by an admirable stylistic coherence, it is still possible to distinguish in the evolution of his sculpture four shifts of formal emphasis. The figural work of c. 1909 shows a somewhat mannered concern with linearity. Yet then and during the next decade Nadelman produced heads in marble and bronze distinguished by a classical volumetric lucidity. In the earlier phase of his American career, working often in cherry wood, he used color both to clarify forms and to sharpen the satiric character of his subjects. Finally, from 1930 onward, irrespective of the actual size of pieces, he achieved an impressive monumentality by stressing the sculptural element of mass.

[Lincoln Kirstein, *The Sculpture of Elie Nadelman* (Museum of Modern Art, exhibition catalogue, 1948), is still the most complete study of Nadelman's career as a sculptor; see also Kirstein's introduction to *Elie Nadelman Drawings* (1949). Alfred Stieglitz in his *Camera Work* no. 32, Oct. 1910, published an important statement of Nadelman's notions of "significant form" before the sculptor's work was seen in America. Nadelman's *Vers la beauté plastique* (1921), containing thirty-two drawings, is the republication of an earlier (1914) statement of sculptural theory. André Salmon in *L'Art décoratif*, Mar. 1914, appraises Nadelman's significance in Paris during the Cubist era. See also *N.Y. Times*, Jan. 7, 1920 (marriage) and Dec. 30, 1946 (obituary).]

JOSEPH S. BOLT

NASH, CHARLES WILLIAMS (Jan. 28, 1864–June 6, 1948), automobile manufacturer, was born in De Kalb County, Ill., the older of two children and only son of David L. Nash and Anna (Caldwell) Nash. The family was broken up by separation of the parents in 1870, and Nash was bound out to a farmer in Genesee City, Mich. Running away when he was twelve years old, he worked as a farm laborer and later as operator of a steam hay press. On Apr. 23, 1884, he married Jessie Halleck, daughter of a Genesee County farmer. They had three daughters: Mae, Lena, and Ruth.

The step that determined Nash's future career came in 1891 when, because his wife needed more medical attention than was available on the farm, he moved to Flint, Mich. After a brief interlude in various odd jobs, he went to work for the Durant-Dort Carriage Company as an upholstery trimmer; according to one account, he had attracted Dort's attention while working as a cherry picker on Dort's farm.

Rising rapidly, Nash became plant superintendent within a few years, and when Dort's partner, William C. Durant, left the carriage business in 1904 to take charge of the Buick Motor Car Company, he picked Nash to replace him as general manager. Nash introduced the straightline belt conveyer into the assembly of carriages.

Six years later Nash again took over from Durant, but under different conditions. Durant, having built up Buick, went on to found the General Motors Company in 1908. Unsuccessfully doubling as president of both companies, he overextended himself financially and in 1910 found his companies short of funds. By this time the Durant-Dort Carriage Company's principal business was building automobile bodies for Buick; and as the troubles of General Motors mounted, the carriage company was not being paid. On Nash's suggestion, Durant put him in charge of the Buick company to try to put its affairs in order.

Two years later, after Durant had been forced out of General Motors by a bankers' trust headed by James J. Storrow, Nash was made president of General Motors. Over the next three years he restored that corporation to organizational and financial stability. Unprofitable subsidiaries were liquidated, and the $15 million loan advanced by the Storrow syndicate to save General Motors from bankruptcy was paid off by the end of 1915. In pursuit of stability, Nash curtailed expenditures and withheld dividends on the common stock; it was a course suited to his own essentially cautious temperament, and it was undoubtedly necessary, but it was not popular with stockholders. As a result, when Durant, now president of Chevrolet, sought to regain control of General Motors by offering to exchange Chevrolet shares for those of GM, he met a willing response among General Motors stockholders and took over the presidency again in 1916.

With backing from Storrow, Nash now bought the Thomas B. Jeffery Company of Kenosha, Wis., makers of the original Rambler, and renamed it the Nash Motors Company. He went to Washington in 1918, during World War I, to take over a languishing program of aircraft production. Nash was given credit for doing a difficult job well, but the war ended before his efforts could have any significant results. Back in the automobile industry, he carried the Nash Motors Company through the intense competitive struggle of the 1920's to emerge as one of the few profitable independent producers. By 1929, 75 percent of the market for motor vehicles was in the hands of the "Big Three" (General Motors, Ford, Chrysler), and 90 percent of the rest was shared by the leading independents (Hudson, Nash, Packard, Studebaker, Willys-Overland). At this time, Nash's company had assets greater than the more pretentious Durant Motors created by his former employer.

Nash concentrated primarily on a single well-designed car in the upper-medium price range. He was aware, however, that some diversification was essential in order to survive in auto-mobile manufacturing. His first move in this direction was the one unsuccessful venture that appears on his record. In 1919, in the expansive optimism that followed the end of the war, Nash acquired the Lafayette Motor Company of Indianapolis and undertook the production of an eight-cylinder car for the luxury market. This enterprise was liquidated after five years with a loss of $2 million, although the Lafayette name was preserved and used on later Nash models. Nash then moved in the opposite direction and bought the plant of the bankrupt Mitchell Motor Car Company of Racine, Wis., in 1924 and converted it to the production of a light, medium-priced car named the Ajax. This venture was more successful, and the car, renamed after two years the Nash Light Six, remained on the market through the 1930's.

Nash never attempted to compete in the mass market. He was not the type to be attracted to a very risky prospect, and events seem to have vindicated his judgment, for his company was one of the few independent automobile manu-facturers not only to survive the depression but to do so without undergoing a major financial crisis. Nash retired from the presidency in 1932 and became chairman of the board, a position he retained until shortly before his death. His outstanding achievement in this position was to bring about the merger in 1937 of Nash with the Kelvinator Company as the Nash-Kelvinator Corporation. The combination of an automobile company with a manufacturer of refrigerators and other household appliances was a conscious acknowledgment that product diversification offered the small independent producer the best chance of survival.

Nash was active in civic affairs in Kenosha and received special recognition for his services to the Boy Scouts. Retiring after World War II, he moved to Beverly Hills, Calif., where he died of a heart ailment less than a year after his wife's death. His body was placed in the mausoleum of Forest Lawn Memorial Park in Glendale. Throughout his life Nash showed the influence of his early poverty. He was cautious and conservative in his methods; his career shows no bold innovations, but methodical and sound management. It was fully in character that of his estate of over $43 million, some $12 million was in savings accounts and most of the rest in bonds.

[There is no biography of Nash. Information on his career can be found in various books dealing with personalities in the automobile industry, such as Eugene W. Lewis, *Motor Memories* (1947); Christopher G. Sinsabaugh, *Who, Me? Forty Years of Automobile Hist.* (1940); and John B. Rae, *Am. Automobile Manufacturers: The First Forty Years* (1959). See also *N.Y. Times*, June 7, 1948; *Time*, June 14, 1948, p. 87.]

JOHN B. RAE

NASH, JOHN HENRY (Mar. 12, 1871–May 24, 1947), printer, was born in Woodbridge, Ontario, Canada, the son of John Marvin Nash, a mechanical engineer, and Catherine (Cain) Nash. His father's English forebears had settled in colonial Pennsylvania but had moved to Canada after the Revolutionary War; his mother was born in Canada of Irish parents. Nash acquired an early interest in fine books from an uncle. His father wanted him to become an engineer, and after leaving public school at sixteen he worked at first in a foundry, until his father relented and let him enter the printing trade. He became an apprentice at the Toronto printing firm of James Murray and Company, but interrupted his career in the early 1890's to become a professional bicycle racer. In 1892 he returned to printing, working for firms in Toronto and Denver, Colo., before settling in San Francisco in 1895. His first employer there was the Hicks-Judd Company; in 1898 he transferred to the firm of Stanley-Taylor. The excellence of Nash's work brought him quick recognition and promotion. In 1903, after two unsuccessful ventures in a company of his own, he did design and production work for the Tomoyé Press, newly founded by the San Francisco book dealer Paul Elder, Sr., who had launched an ambitious publishing program.

With its easy opulence, San Francisco had fostered a tradition of lavish, deluxe printing, a style that suited Nash. When, however, he and Elder moved the Tomoyé Press to New York City following the San Francisco earthquake of 1906, the East proved unreceptive both to Nash's ebullient designs and to the firm's Western subjects. The press returned to San Francisco in 1909, but Nash resigned two years later to assume the directorship of the Fine

Work Department of the Stanley-Taylor Company, which was now rechristened Taylor, Nash & Taylor. There he produced some of his best work, including in 1913 an edition of *Brunelleschi,* a volume of poetry by John Galen Howard, described by Henry Lewis Bullen as "a beautiful example of chaste typography, with all the details of proportion, margins, color and workmanship perfectly arranged" (Harlan, p. 19).

Ever an individualist, Nash could not long work for others. He left Taylor, Nash & Taylor in 1915, and after a year with another firm, opened his own shop in 1916. This time he met with success. Applying his considerable talent for salesmanship, he soon achieved a broad following among book collectors seeking finely printed limited editions. His most generous patron was the wealthy William Andrews Clark, Jr., for whom he designed an impressive series of Christmas books, beginning with Shelley's *Adonais* in 1922 and concluding with Robert Louis Stevenson's *Father Damien* in 1930. The high point of the series was John Dryden's *All for Love* (1929), one of Nash's most impressive technical productions. In all his work, Nash insisted on technical perfection; he employed the best available compositors, pressmen, and engravers, and personally supervised each stage of a book's development.

His most ambitious project was a deluxe edition (1929) of Dante's *Divine Comedy,* a four-volume work that was six years in the making. The type was especially adapted to Nash's specifications. The paper was handmade for him by the Van Gelder Paper Company in the Netherlands, and the printed sheets were bound in vellum in Leipzig. The edition was extravagantly praised. Nash's most lucrative commission came in the late 1920's from the newspaper publisher William Randolph Hearst, who had him print, with all the resources of fine bookmaking, the biographies of his parents, Phoebe Apperson Hearst and Sen. George Hearst, published in 1933.

The depression of the 1930's not only reduced the private commissions on which Nash depended but also dampened critical enthusiasm for his style. Yet despite financial difficulties he continued to do excellent work, including editions of Benjamin Franklin's *Autobiography* (1931) and Ralph Waldo Emerson's *Essays* (1934) for the Limited Editions Club. Nash closed his San Francisco shop in 1938 and moved to the University of Oregon, where he had since 1926 held the title of lecturer in typography and the history of printing in the School of Journalism and, on annual visits, had supervised the Fine Arts Press. Nash married Mary Henrietta Ford on Oct. 8, 1900; they had one child, Evelyn. When his relations with the University of Oregon deteriorated, he returned to Berkeley, Calif., in 1943 to live with his daughter and died there of arteriosclerosis at the age of seventy-six. He was an Episcopalian and a member of the Masonic order, the Book Club of California, the Caxton Club of Chicago, and the Grolier Club of New York.

Nash's contributions to the development of San Francisco as a center of fine printing were substantial. The technical excellence of his work still serves as a model for other printers. Egalitarian by nature, Nash lectured widely and attracted a large audience of laymen to fine printing. A reaction to the excessive praise bestowed upon his work in the 1920's began in the following decade and has only recently been tempered by reevaluation. It was his artistic rather than his technical reputation that suffered. Although he employed a variety of materials and typefaces, he adhered rigidly to two or three archaic typographical themes. As a result his pages often lacked warmth; and since he made little attempt to correlate subject matter and design, he often failed to convey a sense of the book's "spirit." Some also thought Nash's designs too self-assertive. Nash's reply would have been that the physical makeup of a book constituted a form of art, and that the book designer, as an artist, was justified in calling attention to his work.

[Joseph FauntLeRoy, *John Henry Nash, Printer* (1948); Robert D. Harlan, *John Henry Nash: The Biog. of a Career* (1970); Nell O'Day, *A Catalogue of Books Printed by John Henry Nash* (1937), with biographical notes; Marion B. Allen, "The Tomoyé Press," Book Club of Calif., *Quart. News Letter,* Fall 1951, pp. 84–88; Charles W. Evans, "John Henry Nash: the Last Ten Years," *Calif. Librarian,* 23 (1962), 139–143, 159; Martin Schmitt, "John Henry Nash at the University of Oregon," *PMLA Quart.,* 13 (1949), 129–132; *Nat. Cyc. Am. Biog.,* XXXV, 490–491. Nash's library, papers, and correspondence and an oil portrait by Henry Raschen are in the Bancroft Lib., Univ. of Calif., Berkeley.]
ROBERT D. HARLAN

NATHAN, MAUD (Oct. 20, 1862–Dec. 15, 1946), social reformer and feminist, was known best for her work as president of the Consumers' League of the City of New York. She was born in New York, the first daughter and second of four children of Robert Weeks Nathan and Anne Augusta (Florance) Nathan. The Nathans, a wealthy, closely knit Sephardic Jewish family, had been established in New York society since the early eighteenth century. Other distinguished family members included Maud's younger sister, Annie Meyer Nathan, founder of Barnard College, and her cousin, Supreme Court Justice Benjamin Nathan Cardozo.

Maud grew up in New York and in Green Bay, Wis. As a child in New York she attended Mrs. Hoffman's School and the Gardiner Institute, both private girls' schools. When she was twelve, her father suffered business reverses, sold his seat on the New York Stock Exchange, and moved his family to Green Bay, where he worked as a railway passenger agent. Her formal education ended with her graduation from the Green Bay public high school when she was fourteen.

On Apr. 7, 1880, Maud married her cousin Frederick Nathan, a New York stockbroker, but she found married life limited in possibilities for what she called "self-expression." The birth of her daughter Annette Florance in 1887 helped alleviate her discontent but did not dispel it.

During the 1880's, she worked with the Women's Auxiliary for Civil Service and the New York Exchange for Women's Work and as a director of the Mt. Sinai Hospital's nursing school. She taught English to young Jewish immigrants at the Hebrew Free School Association. In 1890, she became one of the first members of the Consumers' League of the City of New York, an organization formed to assist women retail clerks in gaining better working conditions.

Nathan's first assignment with the league was to investigate working conditions in retail stores. She had not known that women worked standing up for over sixty hours, for two or three dollars a week. She was shocked by the filth that lay behind the elegant exteriors of New York's department stores and by the petty cruelties that marked relationships between employers and workers. This investigation transformed her from a restless, but unquestioning and sheltered, young matron into "an articulate being."

After the Nathans' only child died in 1895, Nathan devoted herself full-time to the New York City Consumers' League. In 1897, she became the league's president, an office she held for twenty-one years. In 1898, she was elected to the National Consumers' League executive board. Other organizations, notably the General Federation of Women's Clubs and the Women's Municipal League, also claimed her energies.

The New York City Consumers' League accomplished its most productive work under her leadership. It publicized the deplorable conditions under which many women worked in New York stores and factories. It compiled a "white list" of merchants who met league standards for conditions and wages, and urged the public to patronize these shops exclusively. When efforts to appeal directly to consumers did not produce dramatic results, the organization turned to the state for special legislation to protect women workers. The league led campaigns for statutory limitation of women's working hours and a minimum wage for women. Nathan encouraged league members to regard themselves as an auxiliary force of factory and mercantile inspectors. The league's work was not without limitations: The organization was never sympathetic to the labor movement. Its membership policy excluded not only employers but workers, which meant that league members could never engage in meaningful dialogue with their constituents.

In addition to being an energetic administrator and a talented speaker, Nathan helped expand traditional notions of philanthropy into a more useful conception of social service. Unlike nineteenth-century philanthropists, she realized the futility of social action that did not attempt to eradicate the basic causes of poverty; and unlike twentieth-century social workers, she did not think reform was the special province of professionals.

Nathan emphasized the power of consumers to bring about economic improvements by refusing to purchase merchandise manufactured and sold under poor conditions. When she talked about consumers, she generally meant women. By the late nineteenth century, women had become American society's primary consumers, and as such, they played a special role in the American reform movement. Signifiicantly, the majority of Consumers' League members were affluent women who had the leisure and the means to devote themselves to reform activities. By emphasizing consumer responsibility, Nathan was also working to change the image of women. Women need not be frivolous, she stressed; they could be vital, socially concerned citizens.

Nathan's work in the Consumers' League and her social philosophy led naturally to a commitment to woman suffrage. She served as a vice-president of the New York Equal Suffrage League and worked as the chairwoman of the 1912 Progressive party woman suffrage committee. In her suffrage work she emphasized that winning the vote was not an end in itself, but a necessary means for women to work more effectively for social and industrial reforms.

Nathan resigned from the Consumers' League late in 1917. By that time, she had achieved an international reputation as a social feminist and reformer and spoke frequently at international conferences. In tribute to her years of service, the Consumers' League named her honorary president. She died in New York and was buried in Cypress Hills Cemetery.

[The most accessible sources on Maud Nathan are her autobiography, *Once Upon a Time and To-Day* (1933) and her history of the Consumers' League, *The Story of an Epoch-Making Movement* (1926). The development of Nathan's social philosophy and her work in the Consumers' League are delineated in the *Annual Reports* of the Consumers' League of the City of New York. Archival materials include twelve scrapbooks at Radcliffe College's Schlesinger Lib., Cambridge, Mass. The papers of the New York Consumers' League are located at Cornell Univ. The Lib. of Congress holds papers of the National Consumers' League, but there is very little material in this collection which pertains to Nathan. See also Robert Cross's article in *Notable Am. Women*, II (1971).]

NANCY SCHROM

NEILSON, WILLIAM ALLAN (Mar. 28, 1869–Feb. 13, 1946), professor of English and college president, was born in Doune, Perthshire, Scotland, the second son and youngest of four children of David Neilson and Mary (Allan) Neilson. His father was the village schoolmaster, and Will in early childhood sometimes assisted him, standing on a chair to reach the blackboard. At his father's death, when he was eleven, he became a monitor in the school, and at thirteen, a pupil teacher. After further study at Montrose Academy, he entered Edinburgh University in 1886. Borrowing the necessary funds from his brother, he lived with the utmost frugality; several of his classmates, he later recalled, died of tuberculosis brought on by cold and insufficient food. He also worked at the University Settlement, teaching the poor of Edinburgh's slums.

After graduating, M.A., with second-class honors in philosophy in 1891, Neilson immigrated with his family to Canada, where his brother had settled. He spent four years as a resident English master in Upper Canada College, Toronto, and then began graduate work at Harvard, where he received the Ph.D. in English in 1898. After brief periods of teaching at Bryn Mawr College (1898–1900), Harvard (1900–1904), and Columbia (1904–1906), he was in 1906 appointed professor of English at Harvard, where he remained until 1917, when he accepted the presidency of Smith College. In 1904, while studying at Bonn, Germany, he spent the summer in Offenburg in the family of Oskar Muser, a lawyer and member of the Landtag of the Duchy of Baden, and he returned to Germany to marry Muser's daughter, Elisabeth, on June 25, 1906. They had three children: Margaret, Caroline, and a son, Allan, who died of rheumatic fever at the age of seventeen. Neilson became an American citizen in 1905.

At Harvard, Neilson won distinction as both teacher and scholar. He taught Chaucer, Shakespeare and other Elizabethan dramatists, Milton, and various nineteenth-century authors. His doctoral dissertation, "The Origins and Sources of the Court of Love" (1899), is still respected, as are his *Essentials of Poetry* (1912), *The Facts about Shakespeare* (1913), and *Robert Burns: How to Know Him* (1917). He joined President Charles W. Eliot as associate editor of the Harvard Classics (the 50-volume "Five-Foot Bookshelf," 1909–1910), writing the notes and introductions. His edition of Shakespeare's *Complete Dramatic and Poetic Works* (Cambridge Poets series, 1906), revised with Prof. Charles J. Hill in 1942, is a standard and important one. During his career at Smith, he served as editor-in-chief of the second edition of *Webster's New International Dictionary*, which appeared in 1934.

Neilson hesitated for some time before accepting the Smith presidency. His two predecessors, L. Clark Seelye and Marion Le Roy Burton, had both been clergymen. Neilson, although reared in the Scottish Kirk, became a liberal in religion; as he wrote the trustees, he could not promise "to offer supplication aloud in Chapel." He also insisted that he could not undertake to raise money. But, although he took up his new duties in September 1917 with some misgivings, he became one of the most influential college presidents of his time. He led the faculty and students through the most difficult period colleges had ever faced: the last years of World War I, the "boom," the depression, and the post-depression period.

Neilson had no desire to increase the size of the student body of Smith, fixed at 2,000. He was, however, determined to provide college residences for all students, many of whom were living in private dormitories, a practice felt to be undemocratic. In the course of adding ten new dormitories he greatly enlarged the physical college and built two brick quadrangles on a tract adjacent to the old campus, which preserved the college's tradition of small dormitory units. He beautified the campus by planting and landscaping. During his administration a gymnasium, a music building, and an art gallery were built and the library facilities greatly expanded. Through his efforts Smith became a leading college in theoretical and practical music, the plastic arts, the history of art, and modern foreign languages. He raised considerably the standards of admission and developed a "special honors" program, open only to the upper tenth of the junior and senior classes, which emphasized independent work. Students in the program were awarded the degree on the basis of a thesis and comprehensive examinations. He established a junior year abroad as an integral part of the curriculum, which permitted qualified students to spend a year in France, Italy, Spain, Germany, or Switzerland. The ethnic quotas then prevalent at major universities he condemned outright. In spite of his insistence that fund raising was not his province, Neilson not only balanced the budget, even during the depression, but through his great personal popularity brought sizable gifts to the college that significantly increased the endowment.

Neilson opposed the growing tendency of the times toward practical and vocational education, and insisted that the best training for women, as for men, was that in the liberal arts. He maintained a balanced faculty of men and women. Himself a teacher during the early years of his presidency, he brought to Smith many distinguished scholars and teachers from abroad as well as from the United States, with the result that he left the college well on a par with leading universities. He won the respect and loyalty of the faculty for his fairmindedness and devotion to academic freedom.

Always a fighter for liberal causes, Neilson was violently opposed by the local community and by some of the Smith faculty for his defense of Nicola Sacco and Bartolomeo Vanzetti. He was an active board member of the National Association for the Advancement of Colored People, originating in 1943 and heading the Committee of 100, which raised funds for its legal defense work. Particularly concerned with foreign relations, he maintained through the isolationism of the 1930's a strong internationalist viewpoint and early warned of the danger in the rise of fascist states. His compassion for the victims of Nazism led him to become a director of the National Refugee Service and co-chairman of the Committee for the Protection of the Foreign Born.

One of the great public speakers of his time, Neilson had a remarkable range from light to solemn. No one who heard him read Burns ever forgot the experience. Speaking usually without a manuscript and even without notes, he had an extraordinary facility for adapting himself to the occasion and the audience. Smith College students long remembered his chapel talks. He could tease and cajole, he could scold, admonish, and warn. Upon occasion he could be Moses, Jeremiah, or Isaiah, Lewis Carroll or W. S. Gilbert. As the national and international situation grew more tense through the 1930's, he devoted his Monday chapel talks to attempts to make students more aware of the issues in national and international affairs.

After his retirement in 1939, Neilson settled in Falls Village, Conn., where he had bought a remodeled farmhouse. He continued to spend part of the winters in Northampton, working on a history of Smith College, and he died there in 1946 of a coronary thrombosis. His ashes were buried on the Smith campus, appropriately in the midst of a natural garden he had planned on a hillside.

[Margaret Farrand Thorp, *Neilson of Smith* (1956); Elizabeth (Mrs. Dwight W.) Morrow in *Atlantic Monthly,* Nov. 1946; Marjorie Hope Nicolson in *Am. Scholar,* Autumn 1946. The latter two articles, with other material including memorials, were published as *William Allan Neilson: Blueprint for Biog.* by the Hampshire Bookshop, Northampton (1947). Death record from Mass. Registrar of Vital Statistics.]
MARJORIE NICOLSON

NESTOR, AGNES (June 24, 1880–Dec. 28, 1948), labor leader, was born in Grand Rapids, Mich., the second daughter and third of four children of Thomas and Anna (McEwen) Nestor. Her mother, born in upper New York state and orphaned as a child, had worked as a cotton mill operator and shopgirl. Her father, a native of County Galway, Ireland, had immigrated to the United States as a boy, had become a machinist, and, when Agnes was born, was operating a grocery store. Entering politics, he achieved local prominence as alderman and city treasurer. Agnes grew up in comfortable circumstances and attended the local grammar school and then a Catholic parochial school. In the depression of the 1890's, however, Thomas Nestor lost his bid for the sheriff's office. Having earlier sold his grocery store and not finding suitable employment in Grand Rapids, he moved to Chicago in late 1896, hoping for work as a machinist. His family joined him the following spring. "Childhood was over," Agnes wrote in her autobiography, "soon I, too, would be at work."

Agnes found a job in the Eisendrath Glove Company and soon became a skilled glove operator. There was much unrest among the girls in her shop, especially because they had to pay for the power for their machines and supply their own needles and machine oil. In the spring of 1898 the girls rebelled, encouraged by the recently organized male cutters. Agnes Nestor emerged as a leader. Never robust physically, slight for her age and quiet in manner, she was also quick-witted, articulate, and endowed with a spark of leadership that made her the natural spokesman for her fellow workers. She was, moreover, well-schooled in the principles of trade unionism by her father, a fervent union man of long standing. Amid the initial confusion and uncertainty, hers was a firm voice for the cause of organization. After ten days, the girls won their demands, including the union shop.

In 1902 Nestor contrived to separate the female glove workers from the male glove-cutters' union. She became president of the new all-female local. That same year, she went as its delegate to the founding convention of the International Glove Workers Union in Washington, D.C., and the following year she became a national vice-president. The crucial opportunity came in 1906, when she was elected secretary-treasurer, for this was a paid, full-time position. Ill health had forced her to stop work several months before, and she never returned to the factory. "That convention changed the whole course of my life," she later wrote. Already thoroughly experienced, Nestor now perfected the arts of the professional trade union leader; as negotiator fully knowledgeable of the technical aspects of the glove industry; as speaker, organizer, and administrator; and as defender of the institutional integrity of her union. For the rest of her life, she was never without a national post in the Glove Workers Union.

But Agnes Nestor was not destined for the conventional career of a trade union functionary. The crucial fact was that she was a woman in a labor system and union movement dominated by men. Thus, while she never minimized the importance of collective bargaining, she saw too the great need for social legislation for women and children. And while her first obligation was to the glove workers, she recognized a responsibility to help working women in all fields. The institutional expression of these ideas was the National Women's Trade Union League. First coming in contact with the women's trade union movement in 1904, Nestor developed a lifelong association with the Chicago league (president from 1913 to 1948) and with the national league (executive board from 1907 on). The Women's

Trade Union League not only provided a means to do union work among women on a wider scope, but also broadened Nestor's horizons still farther, for it brought her into contact with such progressives as Mary McDowell, Jane Addams, and Raymond and Margaret Dreier Robins. She moved, too, within the stream of labor progressivism, which then ran strongly in Chicago under the leadership of John Fitzpatrick.

Much of her time was spent in Springfield working for social legislation, above all for a maximum-hours law for women. Developing great skill as a lobbyist, Nestor helped bring about the Illinois Ten-Hour-Day Law of 1909, and then in 1911 a second act that extended this protection to women who worked outside of factories. Only in 1937, after many defeats, were her efforts for an eight-hour maximum crowned with success. Meanwhile, Nestor participated in major strikes and organizing drives among women in many trades in Chicago and elsewhere, including the great garment workers' strikes of 1909 and 1910-1911. She also was an eloquent advocate of the cause of women workers before middle-class audiences.

These activities, plus her unique position as a female national-union leader, opened up wider opportunities for public service. In 1914 she was appointed to the National Commission on Vocational Education. During World War I, she served on the Woman's Committee of the United States Council of National Defense and participated in a goodwill mission to England and France. In 1928 she campaigned unsuccessfully (as a dry) for the Democratic nomination to a seat in the Illinois state legislature. During the depression she sat on the Illinois Commission on Unemployment and Relief, as well as on the board of trustees of the Chicago Century of Progress Exposition (1933-1934). In 1929 she received an honorary LL.D. from Loyola University in Chicago.

Despite the larger field in which she moved, Nestor remained firmly rooted in the labor movement and, notwithstanding her own progressive inclination, loyal to the movement as she had known it in pre-World War I days. When part of the Glove Workers Union developed a sympathy for the CIO in 1937 and joined the Amalgamated Clothing Workers led by Sidney Hillman, she held the loyal elements together and, with A.F. of L. help, rebuilt the Glove Workers Union into a stronger organization than it had been before the secession.

Nestor's health began to decline in 1946 from what was subsequently diagnosed as miliary tuberculosis. She underwent an operation for a breast abscess in October 1948 in St. Luke's Hospital, Chicago, and died of uremia that December. She was buried at Mount Carmel Cemetery in Hillside, Cook County, Ill.

[Agnes Nestor's papers are at the Chicago Hist. Soc. Her autobiography, *Woman's Labor Leader* (1954), is a valuable source; it reproduces a portrait by F. Sakharov. There are obituaries in the *N.Y. Times* and *Chicago Tribune,* Dec. 29, 1948. Aspects of her career can be followed in Stella M. Franklin, "Agnes Nestor of the Glove Workers," *Life and Labor,* Dec. 1913; Gladys Boone, *The Women's Trade Union Leagues in Great Britain and the U.S.A.* (1942); Allen F. Davis, *Spearheads of Reform* (1967); Rose Schneiderman (with Lucy Goldthwaite), *All for One* (1967); and in the published memoirs and biographies of such fellow workers as Margaret Dreier Robins, Rose Schneiderman, and Mary McDowell.]

DAVID BRODY

NEWTON, JOSEPH FORT (July 21, 1876–Jan. 24, 1950), clergyman and author, was born in Decatur, Tex., the third son and fifth of eight children of Lee Newton and Sue Green (Battle) Newton. His father came from a family of migrating Tennesseans; after serving in the Confederate Army he returned to Texas and became a sometime teacher, Baptist preacher, and lawyer. His mother was descended from the Battle, Fort, and Ligon families of early Virginia; educated at Mary Sharpe College in Tennessee, she was trained to be a teacher. Joseph received most of his education from her; while he earned his own money by odd jobs and cotton farming, he studied classical languages and literature under her tutelage. On his own initiative he subscribed to the *Louisville Courier-Journal* and the *Atlanta Constitution* and tested his own literary propensities by writing articles for the *Texas Baptist and Herald.*

Newton's forebears had been Baptists for generations, and even though he began early to question their sectarian exclusiveness and evangelical doctrines, it was assumed that he would enter the Baptist ministry. Thus he was ordained on Apr. 20, 1895, and soon thereafter became pastor of a small Baptist church at Rose Hill, Tex. In the fall he enrolled in the Southern Baptist Theological Seminary at Louisville, Ky., where his horizons broadened considerably: he served as associate chaplain at a nearby prison, reported religious news for the *Courier-Journal,* and heard a variety of preachers from Rabbi Adolphus Moses to the revivalist Dwight L. Moody. He read widely, often in books frowned on by the faculty—mystics like William Penn, liberals like Frederick William Robertson, and tradi-

tionalists like John Henry Newman. Even more, he absorbed the poets and essayists— "no words can ever tell my debt to Emerson"—and testified later that such writers "have always taught me more and better theology than the theologians" (*River of Years,* pp. 57, 67). Andrew Dickson White's *History of the Warfare of Science with Theology in Christendom* (1896) confirmed Newton's predilections against reactionary dogmas; and William Henry Fremantle's *The World as the Subject of Redemption* (1885) "influenced all my thinking for years, because it talked in terms of salvation, not salvage" (*ibid.,* p. 64). Along with several other activist students, Newton came to the defense of the seminary president, William Heth Whitsitt, when the latter outraged Baptist conservatives by denying the historical continuity of Baptist churches from the time of Christ. The controversy deepened Newton's disillusionment with the Baptists. He left the seminary in 1897 to preach briefly to one faction of the First Baptist Church in Paris, Tex., which had recently divided over conflicting interpretations of the Lord's Supper. After trying unsuccessfully to unite his congregation with the First Christian Church, he left Texas and the Baptists permanently.

On June 14, 1900, at Louisville, Newton married Jennie Mai Deatherage of Sanders, Ky., a church organist whom he had met during his seminary days. They had two children, Joseph Emerson and Josephine Kate. The same year Newton accepted the invitation of Robert C. Cave, a former Disciples of Christ minister, to join him at the Nonsectarian Church in St. Louis; thus began his transition to a broad churchmanship free from creedal requirements and ritual tests of fellowship. Two years later he set out in search of new fields and "a church of my own" (*ibid.,* p. 92). He first went to Boston to prowl the haunts of Emerson, inspect historic churches, hear noted preachers, and sample the ideas of William James and Josiah Royce. Then, in March 1903, he journeyed to Dixon, Ill., where a wealthy layman backed him in organizing a nonsectarian People's Church. During his five-year pastorate in Dixon, Newton fought municipal corruption as chairman of the Law and Order League, became active in the Masonic order, lectured regularly on "Great Men and Great Books," and wrote his first book, a biography of Rev. David Swing, whom he had admired since seminary days. In 1908 he moved to the Liberal Christian Church (Universalist) in Cedar Rapids, Iowa. Here the local newspaper printed his sermons weekly, gathering them monthly into pamphlets and yearly into books (*Sermons and Lectures,* 6 vols., 1911-1917); and these, along with reprints in the *Christian Century,* were distributed in England as well as the United States. His Tuesday evening talks on "Christ in Modern Literature" soon secured for him a lectureship at the State University of Iowa. There he met Franklin B. Sanborn, who had custody of the correspondence between Theodore Parker and William H. Herndon, a former law partner of Abraham Lincoln. After studying these letters and other early Lincolniana, Newton wrote *Lincoln and Herndon* (1910). Meanwhile, he had been discovering the church fathers, especially those of mystical bent, which moved him to write *What Have the Saints to Teach Us?* (1914). His lifelong interest in Freemasonry also burgeoned in Iowa: he served as grand chaplain of the Grand Lodge, helped establish a National Masonic Research Society, and wrote *The Builders: A Story and Study of Masonry* (1914).

The circulation of Newton's sermons in England brought him an invitation from London's famed City Temple when that pulpit fell vacant in 1915. His move the following year from the comparative obscurity of Cedar Rapids to the "Cathedral of British Nonconformity" astonished other churchmen and made him "for weeks the most talked of preacher in the world" (Jones, p. 241). Newton spent three years in the limelight of churchgoing London. "If we did not have three thousand [in the congregation]," he confided, "we were disappointed" (*Churchman,* Feb. 15, 1950, p. 15). In November 1919 he returned to assume the pastorate of the Church of the Divine Paternity (Universalist) in New York City, from which base he filled a busy schedule of preaching at numerous colleges, lecturing to various cultural organizations, compiling four annual volumes of *Best Sermons* (1924-1927), editing *The Master Mason* (a monthly magazine) and contributing to *The Christian Century.* Newton had always had the broadest of ecumenical sympathies and regarded denominational peculiarities as "barbed-wire entanglements about the Altar of God" (*Time,* Feb. 6, 1950, p. 70). Thus in 1925, when Thomas J. Garland, the Episcopal bishop of Pennsylvania, suggested that he might be at home in that communion, Newton soon assented. Resigning from Divine Paternity in 1925, he explained that Episcopalianism was "midway between an arid liberalism and an

acrid literalism," occupying a "central strategic position" that promised eventually to draw all Christians together (*New York Times,* Sept. 14, 1925). Installed at the Memorial Church of St. Paul in Overbrook, Pa., he served first as lay reader and was subsequently ordained deacon on Jan. 16 and priest on Oct. 28, 1926. In 1930 he became co-rector of St. James's Church in Philadelphia, and in 1935 was designated "Special Preacher to the Associated Churches" in an attempt to unite St. James's with a neighboring church, St. Luke and the Epiphany. The union not being consummated, he assumed leadership of the latter parish in 1938 and served there until his sudden death of a heart attack in 1950, at his home in Philadelphia. He was buried at St. David's Church in Devon, Pa.

As early as 1933 an admirer wrote that "through twenty years Dr. Newton has been a more prolific producer of high-class sermons than any other preacher of the period" (Jones, p. 241). From October 1932 to January 1944 Newton wrote a newspaper column called "Everyday Living," syndicated by United Features; and from 1944 until his death he furnished the "Saturday Sermon" to the *Philadelphia Evening-Bulletin.* In 1939 a poll of 25,000 ministers voted him one of the five foremost Protestant clergymen in America. Despite his limited formal education, he received four honorary degrees and was elected to honorary membership in Phi Beta Kappa. He was a 33rd Degree Mason, member of the advisory board of the Federal Council of Churches, and sometime lecturer to the College of Preachers at the Washington (D.C.) Cathedral. But in spite of his literary gifts and popular appeal, Newton had his critics. Evangelicals complained that he quoted poets and other literati far more than Holy Scripture. *The Christian Century* (Feb. 8, 1950, p. 165) found his pastorates in New York and Philadelphia an "anticlimax" because his pulpit eloquence failed to engage the moral issues of postwar America. There were other contradictions. He recognized the horrors of war, but in numerous patriotic addresses he glorified military heroes. He preached movingly of brotherhood, but he assumed Anglo-Saxon superiority, spoke contemptuously of "Japs," and repeatedly used "black" to signify evil. His penchant for mysticism led him to a credulous acceptance of occult phenomena, while his confidence in human nature overrode his realism on the force of the demonic in history. But he maintained his faith in God during an age of growing secularism, and, to judge from thousands of responses to his newspaper devotionals, he helped many others to find a similar hopeful faith.

[Newton was the author of some half a hundred books and the editor or compiler of more than thirty others, while hundreds of his sermons, addresses, and articles were broadcast in innumerable newspapers, magazines, and separately printed pamphlets across the United States and Great Britain. More than half of his published works are either sermons or concerned with preachers and preaching. A significant number have to do with Freemasonry, and the remainder are either patriotic or devotional. Besides those mentioned elsewhere, some of his more important publications include *The Sword of the Spirit: Britain and America in the Great War* (1918), *Some Living Masters of the Pulpit* (1923), *The New Preaching* (1930), *Things I Know in Religion* (1930), *His Cross and Ours* (1941), *Where Are We in Religion?* (1945), and *The One Great Church* (1948). Newton's heirs have deposited "all significant papers" with the Pa. Hist. Soc. His autobiography, *River of Years* (1946), is an important source of information but is impressionistic and has many errors of detail. Some historical data may be gleaned from his *Preaching in London* (1922) and *Preaching in New York* (1924), both taken from his diaries, and from the prefaces to some of his books. Secondary information on Newton is surprisingly scarce, and much of it is inaccurate. (He twice changed his birth year in *Who's Who in America*.) A contemporary sketch is in Edgar DeWitt Jones, *Am. Preachers of To-Day* (1933). Obituaries appeared in a "Night Extra" of the *Phila. Evening-Bull.*, the *Phila. Inquirer*, Jan. 25, 1950, and the *N.Y. Times*, Jan. 26, 1950. Pictures are included in *River of Years* and several of his other works.]

C. C. GOEN

NICHOLSON, MEREDITH (Dec. 9, 1866-Dec. 21, 1947), author, lecturer, and diplomat, was born in Crawfordsville, Ind., the first of four children of Edward Willis Nicholson and Emily (Meredith) Nicholson. His father was a substantial farmer of Kentucky ancestry and a Union officer in the Civil War. His maternal grandfather was a printer-journalist of Centerville, Ind. The family moved to Indianapolis in 1872. Nicholson's formal schooling ended at the age of fifteen after difficulties with mathematics, whereupon he proceeded to become an exceptional example of the self-educated American man of letters. He worked at various jobs, read widely, studied law for a time, taught himself foreign languages, and began in the middle 1880's to publish poems in newspapers. A regular assignment on the Indianapolis *News* extended from 1885 to 1897. His first book of poetry, *Short Flights,* was published in 1891. The appearance of *Poems* (1906) terminated Nicholson's short and undistinguished career in this medium.

On June 16, 1896, Nicholson married the cultured and wealthy Eugenie Kountze of Omaha, Nebr. They had four children: Meredith,

Elizabeth Kountze, Eugenie (who died in infancy), and Charles Lionel. In 1898 the couple moved to Denver, Colo., where Nicholson engaged in business for about three years, an experience reflected in his first novel, *The Main Chance* (1903). During his western residence, Nicholson asserted his loyalty to Indiana in a collection of delightful essays on local history, *The Hoosiers* (1900), a book as likely to survive as anything he wrote. Returning to Indianapolis in 1901, he began a long career as popular novelist, essayist for a wide range of magazines, and leading Hoosier personality, much in demand as a speaker and lecturer. In company with Booth Tarkington, George Ade, and James Whitcomb Riley, Nicholson was considered a leader in creating a Golden Age of Indiana literature in the first quarter of the twentieth century. His second novel, *Zelda Dameron* (1904), was a realistic portrayal of Indianapolis business and social life. *The House of a Thousand Candles* (1905), a best seller and later a popular motion picture, was a Hoosier romance. Nicholson's fiction was governed by the invariable triumph of true, young love over familiar obstacles and by insistence on the virtues of wholesome, bourgeois life. The protagonist is typically an irresistible Hoosier girl who saves honor, fortune, and happiness for family and community. Within this formula Nicholson alternated between light romance and a serious "realism relieved by humor . . . and lifted by cheer and hope," to cite the author's own description of *The Lords of High Decision* (1909), a novel that depicted conflicts in industrial society. The best novel in this vein is *A Hoosier Chronicle* (1912), based on Nicholson's intimate knowledge of Indiana politics. Except for the girl's heroism and the happy endings, *The Proof of the Pudding* (1916), *Broken Barriers* (1922), *The Hope of Happiness* (1923), and *And They Lived Happily Ever After!* (1925) are convincing explorations of changing times in Indianapolis society, dealing with divorce, drinking, illicit love, corrupt business practices, and briefly with class conflicts. *Otherwise Phyllis* (1913) portrays the same elements in small-town life. Nicholson closed a successful career as a novelist with his twenty-first book, *The Cavalier of Tennessee* (1928), a competent if old-fashioned historical fiction based on the lives of Andrew Jackson and his wife Rachel (Robards) Jackson.

As *The Hoosiers* indicated early, Nicholson was at his best as an essayist. His work in this form, including much delightful autobiography, can be surveyed in a number of collections: *The Provincial American and Other Papers* (1912), *The Valley of Democracy* (1918), *The Man in the Street* (1921), and *Old Familiar Faces* (1929). Most of these essays appeared originally in *Scribner's*, the *Atlantic*, and *Harper's*. The number of his miscellaneous pieces, such as reviews, speeches, introductions to books, is considerable.

Compared with Tarkington the novelist, Riley the Hoosier poet, and Ade the humorist and satirist, Nicholson cannot be said to have produced an impressive body of writing. He was in the service of his city and state, even as a novelist, and therefore wrote much that dated quickly. Riley's own success owed much to Nicholson's speaking and writing about him, including a brief romantic novel, *The Poet* (1914). As a professional Hoosier and self-styled patriotic, stay-at-home Midwesterner, Nicholson probably scattered a modest talent too thin for permanent recognition. His personal magnetism and charm were very great. With humor and a light touch, he preached the healthy pursuit of happiness and a faith in the goodness of "folks."

To the problems and dangers faced by a democracy of the "folks," Nicholson was actively responsive. He admonished his fellow Hoosiers to clean up local government and participated in Democratic party politics as party leader, candidate, and for one term (1928-1930) as a "reform" city councilman in Indianapolis. He was a moderate Democrat with Whig-Republican antecedents but began his own political life as a Mugwump in 1884. He could not support Bryan, but his voice against the Ku Klux Klan in Indiana Republican politics of the 1920's was eloquent and much needed. He supported national candidates in sane, practical, bipartisan terms. Upon the election of Franklin Roosevelt, his service to the party was rewarded with three ministries in Latin America: Paraguay (1933-1934), Venezuela (1935-1938), and Nicaragua (1938-1941).

Earlier, Nicholson received local academic honors: master's degrees from Wabash College (1901) and Butler University (1902); Litt.D. from Wabash (1907); LL.D. from Indiana University (1928) and Butler (1929).

Nicholson's first wife died in 1931. On Sept. 20, 1933, Nicholson married Dorothy (Wolfe) Lannon, of Marion, Ind. They were divorced in 1943. Nicholson died of diabetes in Indianapolis at the age of eighty-one. He is buried in Crownhill Cemetery in Indianapolis.

[The Nicholson section of Dorothy Ritter Russo and Thelma Lois Sullivan, *Bibliographical Studies of Seven Authors of Crawfordsville, Indiana*, pp. 71–153 (1952), is exhaustive and indispensable; it also lists biographical references to date of publication. Novels not mentioned above are *The Port of Missing Men* (1907), *Rosalind at Red Gate* (1907), *The Little Brown Jug at Kildare* (1908), *The Siege of Seven Suitors* (1910), *The Madness of May* (1917), *A Reversible Santa Claus* (1917), *Lady Larkspur* (1919), and *Blacksheep! Blacksheep!* (1920)—all light romances; *Best Laid Schemes* (1922), a collection of short stories; *Honor Bright* (1923), a comedy written with Kenyon Nicholson (not related). There is no full-length biography. In addition to standard biographical sources like *Who's Who in America*, an interesting short account is in R. E. Banta, *Indiana Authors and Their Books, 1816–1916* (1949). Extended treatment of Nicholson as an author is in Arthur Shumaker, *A History of Indiana Literature* (1962). Shumaker is indebted to an unpublished thesis by Jean B. Sanders, "Meredith Nicholson: Hoosier Cavalier" (DePauw Univ., 1952), which also covers Nicholson's political activities through 1933. Earlier treatments include Jacob P. Dunn, *Indiana and Indianans*, III, 1526–1528 (1919); and an anonymous pamphlet published by Charles Scribner's Sons, *Meredith Nicholson: American Man of Letters* (c. 1925).]

WALTER L. FERTIG

NOYES, FRANK BRETT (July 7, 1863-Dec. 1, 1948), newspaper publisher, was born in Washington, D.C., the second son and second of five children of Crosby Stuart Noyes and Elizabeth S. (Williams) Noyes. Both parents were natives of Maine. The father, after moving to Washington in 1852, became a reporter for the newly founded *Evening Star*. In 1867 he and four partners purchased the *Star*, and Crosby Noyes became editor, with another partner, Samuel H. Kauffman, as president. Young Frank began working on his father's paper at the age of thirteen. After graduating from a Washington high school in 1878, he enrolled for a time in the preparatory department of Columbian (later George Washington) University and in the Spencerian Business College. In 1886 he became business manager and treasurer of the *Star*, a post he continued to hold until 1901.

The *Star* thrived under Noyes's managership, and by the early 1890's it was one of only two surviving dailies in Washington. Its news emphasis throughout his career was local—some said provincial—and the *Star* carried more small advertisements than any other paper in America. Noyes himself soon moved, however, into a national role. In 1893, when the cooperative Associated Press of Illinois, led by Victor F. Lawson and Melville E. Stone of the *Chicago Daily News*, was seeking to replace the purely commercial New York United Press as the nation's principal wire service, Noyes aided the AP's cause. He enlisted the *Star* in the AP and helped convert other newspapers in Washington, Baltimore, and Philadelphia. The Associated Press was reorganized in 1900 under New York state laws, and Noyes, recognized for his business ability, was chosen president. Reelected annually, he served in this post until his resignation in 1938 and remained a director of the AP until 1947.

Although happy in publishing, Noyes may have felt overshadowed at the *Star* by his older brother Theodore Williams Noyes, who joined the staff in 1877 and became associate editor-in-chief ten years later. When Samuel Kauffman died in 1906, Theodore Noyes became president of the publishing company, and he succeeded to the editorship as well when Crosby Noyes died in 1908. Meanwhile, in 1901, Frank Noyes had accepted Victor Lawson's invitation to take charge of the *Chicago Record-Herald*, at first as publisher, then after a year as editor also. The Chicago paper encountered financial difficulties, however, and in 1910 Frank returned to the *Star* as president of the company. He remained in this post until his retirement in 1948; his brother continued as editor-in-chief and became chairman of the corporation's board of directors. Carrying on the municipal improvement policies of their father, the Noyes brothers campaigned for a clean Potomac River, better schools, and the building of a Lincoln Memorial. In national affairs the *Star* maintained an unswerving Republican editorial outlook. With a circulation that grew from 48,000 in 1910 to 152,000 in 1940 and 211,000 in 1948, it led all other Washington papers until 1939. It consistently carried the most advertising in Washington, and through most of the 1930's in the nation as well.

It was as president of the Associated Press, however, that Noyes made his most noteworthy contribution to journalism. During his tenure the nonprofit AP became the leading American press association and a major world news agency, with a reputation for accuracy and impartiality. Its membership rose from 600 papers in 1900 to 1,300 in 1937. Although the AP's relations with labor unions were sometimes strained, Noyes was responsible for the introduction, after World War I, of improved employee benefits, including pensions, sick pay, and disability provisions. Noyes viewed as his most important act the selection in 1925 of Kent Cooper as general manager of the AP. Member papers continued to supply most of the news, with the association acting as clearinghouse and editorial center, but Cooper expanded the staff and increased the number of bureaus.

He and Noyes also stepped up the agency's foreign news coverage and in 1935 inaugurated the AP Wirephoto service.

When he retired as AP president in 1938, at the age of seventy-five, Noyes seemed the personification of an agency devoted to objective news reporting. Quiet, austere, and judicial, he studiously avoided personal publicity or any public stand that might reflect on his agency's nonpartisanship. Noyes received honorary degrees from George Washington University (1925), the University of Pennsylvania (1928), Yale (1932), and the University of Maryland (1938). He was an Episcopalian in religion. He married Janet Thruston Newbold, daughter of an army colonel, on Sept, 17, 1888. They had three children: Frances, Newbold (who served as associate editor of the *Star*, 1919-1942), and Ethel. Ten years after his retirement, Noyes died at his Washington home of arteriosclerotic cardiovascular disease. Following cremation, his ashes were buried in Washington's Rock Creek Cemetery.

A fellow editor, Oswald Garrison Villard, characterized Noyes's *Star* as "extremely prosperous and extremely dull" and its publisher as lacking vision and breadth of view. A more generally held estimate for both might be "solid if unspectacular." Members of the Kauffmann family succeeded Noyes in the *Star*'s presidency, but a grandson, Newbold Noyes, Jr., became editor in 1963 and helped reinvigorate its pages.

[Washington *Evening Star*, Dec. 1, 1948 (obituary), and later articles through Dec. 5; also centennial edition, Dec. 16, 1952; *N.Y. Times*, Dec. 1 and 4, 1948; *Editor & Publisher*, Dec. 4, 1948; *Nat. Cyc. Am. Biog.*, Current Vol. E, pp. 81–82; Oliver Gramling, *AP: The Story of News* (1940); Oswald Garrison Villard's review of the Gramling book in *Saturday Rev. of Lit.*, Nov. 2, 1940; Frank B. Noyes, "The Associated Press," *North Am. Rev.*, May 1913; article on the AP in *Fortune*, Feb. 1937; Frank L. Mott, *Am. Journalism* (3rd ed., 1962); Edwin Emery, *The Press and America* (3rd ed., 1972); Kenneth Stewart and John Tebbel, *Makers of Modern Journalism* (1952); death record from D.C. Dept. of Human Resources. The obituaries and the *Fortune* article, above, reproduce photographs of Noyes.]

EDWIN EMERY

NUTTING, MARY ADELAIDE (Nov. 1, 1858-Oct. 3, 1948), pioneer in nursing organization and education, was born in Frost Village, Quebec, Canada, the fifth of six children and the first of two surviving daughters of Vespasian Nutting and Harriet Sophia (Peaseley; earlier, Peaselee) Nutting, both of English Loyalist stock. In 1861 the family moved to nearby Waterloo, where the children attended the village academy as their parents struggled to supplement Nutting's slender income as court clerk. After two years at a convent school in St. Johns, Newfoundland, and at Bute House in Montreal, Adelaide Nutting lived at home, first in Waterloo, then, after 1881, with her mother and younger siblings in Ottawa. Having briefly studied music and design in Lowell, Mass., and in Ottawa, she taught music for a year at the Cathedral School for Girls in St. Johns, where her sister was principal. She later gave piano lessons in Ottawa.

The seeds of her interest in nursing, then in its professional infancy, lay in her absorption in the life of Florence Nightingale and in a sense of incompetence that haunted her after the months of attending her mother, who died in 1884. Nursing ripened into an ambition for her as her two closest siblings married in 1885 and 1888, while she found herself unwilling similarly to forfeit her independence. At that time student nurses needed no preliminary education and no financial assets: their status in hospital training schools was that of employees who received room, board, and a small stipend in exchange for their labor. In the summer of 1889, when a training school for nurses was opened at Johns Hopkins Hospital in Baltimore, she joined the first class of fourteen students. She graduated in 1891, fourth in the class, and worked for the next two years as head nurse on various Hopkins services. In 1893 she was appointed assistant superintendent and the following year succeeded Isabel Hampton as superintendent of nurses and principal of the training school, a position then including school administration as well as direction of hospital services.

At this critical period in the development of nursing, working alongside the great experiment in medical education marked by the opening of the Johns Hopkins Medical School in 1893, Adelaide Nutting began her efforts to transform training schools from hospital service adjuncts into educational institutions. In late 1895 she submitted to the trustees plans for a three-year nursing curriculum, calling also for an eight-hour day and no stipends for students. As justification for this proposal, she presented "A Statistical Report of Working Hours in Training Schools," which showed that training schools were largely exploitative rather then educational: without the preliminary instruction typical of other professional training, student nurses were plunged immediately into ward duties, being expected to pursue their studies outside of work hours, which ranged from 60 to 105 a week. Sometimes called the

"Magna Carta of nursing," this "Hours of Duty" paper established her leadership in nursing and unveiled the telling use of carefully compiled statistics, a Nutting hallmark.

Although she never achieved the eight-hour day for Hopkins student nurses, her three-year curriculum was adopted, together with the abolition of stipends and substitution of scholarships for worthy and needy students. In 1901 she inaugurated a six-month preliminary period of study in anatomy, physiology, materia medica, hygiene, and elements of practical nursing, one of the earliest preparatory courses in America and by far the most comprehensive at that time. Among her proudest achievements was the nursing library she assembled at Johns Hopkins, from which she drew materials for her four-volume *History of Nursing* (1907-1912), written in collaboration with Lavinia Dock.

During her Hopkins years she took part in almost every effort to establish standards for nursing and nursing education. An early member of the American Society of Superintendents of Training Schools for Nurses of the United States and Canada (later, the National League of Nursing Education), she was twice its president (1896 and 1909). She was also a founder of the *American Journal of Nursing* (1900) and of the Maryland State Association of Graduate Nurses, of which she was the first president (1903). She helped draft the Maryland Registration Act, governing the practice of nursing and was active in securing its legislative passage (1904).

Nutting believed that education for nurses, as for doctors, lawyers, and engineers, should be university-affiliated. When she was unable to implement this concept at Johns Hopkins, she helped persuade James E. Russell, dean of the newly established Teachers College at Columbia University, to institute an experimental course in hospital economics and to admit nurses to existing courses that might be useful to teachers and administrators in the nursing field. Commuting between Baltimore and New York, she taught part-time in this program from 1899 until 1907, when she assumed the duties of full professor at Teachers College, the first nurse to hold such a university appointment. Initially professor of institutional management, she eventually devoted herself solely to nursing education. As chairman of the department of nursing and health established in 1910 (according to Russell, "one of the ablest men of either sex" on the Teachers College faculty), she designed programs in hospital administration and nursing education, shaping them, as she had the Baltimore school, within her humanistic concept of nursing as a crossroads for medicine, natural science, and social service. Both schools bore the imprint of her sharp appreciation of the nurse's teaching role in the new field of public health work. At her retirement in 1925, the department of nursing and health had become an international center for nursing education, awarding bachelor of science and master's degrees, and boasting many graduates who became deans of university nursing schools and directors of graduate departments.

During World War I Adelaide Nutting led the committee on nursing of the General Medical Board of the Council of National Defense, which channeled recruitment efforts through the Vassar Training Camp, the Army School of Nursing, and the Student Nurse Reserve.

Every significant nursing study published in the early 1900's was associated in some way with Adelaide Nutting: her own *Educational Status of Nursing* (U.S. Bureau of Education, 1912), the first comprehensive study of American nursing and one of the "seven historic publications by which the nursing profession now measures its progress"; the *Standard Curriculum for Schools of Nursing* (1917), prepared by the education committee of the National League of Nursing Education, of which she was chairman 1903-1921; and the historic Winslow-Goldmark report, *Nursing and Nursing Education in the United States*, produced in 1923 by the Rockefeller Commission for the Study of Nursing Education, of which she was a member, a model for professional development. The core of her farsighted concern for nursing serves as the title of a collection of her writings, *A Sound Economic Basis for Schools of Nursing* (1926).

Among her honors were the Liberty Service Medal of the American Social Science Association (World War I); an honorary M.A. conferred by Yale University in 1922 with a citation to "one of the most useful women in the world"; the Mary Adelaide Nutting Award for leadership in nursing education, created by the National League of Nursing Education in 1944; and the honorary presidency of the Florence Nightingale International Foundation (1934). In 1906, under a commission from the Johns Hopkins nursing alumnae, Cecilia Beaux re-created her chestnut hair and dark, wide-set blue-gray eyes in a portrait revealing both the strength and the sensitivity of her early maturity; a second likeness, painted in academic

robes by Stanislav Rembski in 1932, is at Teachers College.

Physically frail and often ill, Nutting felt driven, by the trust others placed in her, to surpass what she conceived to be her natural limitations. She was self-disciplined to the point of austerity, inspiring awe—sometimes fear—in students and respect in colleagues. Although her independence and perfectionism occasionally caused friction, the broad range of her mind attracted friends from many walks of life. Conscientiously self-educated, she avidly read history and literature and pursued her interest in music and art. Although not a militant suffragist, she was a member of the Equal Franchise Society and the Woman Suffrage party. While remaining a Canadian citizen, she admired the United States and followed politics closely, describing herself in 1914 as a Progressive. Through relationships developed during numerous trips abroad, her forceful personality, like her writing, played a role in the international development of nursing. Following Anglican services after her death from pneumonia in a White Plains, N.Y., hospital, her cremated remains were released to the sea.

[Helen E. Marshall, *Mary Adelaide Nutting: Pioneer of Modern Nursing* (1972), the only full biography, contains a comprehensive bibliography of Nutting's publications. Among many biographical articles by her contemporaries, the most useful are by Virginia Dunbar in *Notable Am. Women*, II (1971); Stella Goostray in *American Journal of Nursing*, Nov. 1958, and Edna Yost in *Am. Women of Nursing* (1965). Teresa E. Christy's "Portrait of a Leader: M. Adelaide Nutting," *Nursing Outlook*, Jan. 1969, is based largely on manuscripts and contains personal information not published elsewhere. A detailed account of her Hopkins years appears in Ethel Johns and Blanche Pfefferkorn, *The Johns Hopkins Hospital School of Nursing, 1889-1949* (1954); see also the *Johns Hopkins Nurses Alumnae Mag.*, Apr. 1949, largely devoted to her and including a photograph taken early in her career, and the Mary Adelaide Nutting Anniversary Issue of *Alumnae Magazine*, Apr. 1958, with a full reproduction of the Cecilia Beaux portrait, which hangs in the William H. Welch Medical Lib. at Johns Hopkins. Full obituaries appeared in *American Journal of Nursing*, Nov. 1948, with photograph and editorial; in *Teachers College Record*, Dec. 1948, with photograph of the Stanislav Rembski portrait; see also the *N.Y. Times*, Oct. 5, 1948, and letter to editor, Oct. 16. *Woman's Who's Who of America, 1914-1915* (1915) contains information she supplied. Her voluminous papers are at Teachers College. Death certificate from the New York State Department of Health.]

PATRICIA SPAIN WARD

ODELL, GEORGE CLINTON DENSMORE (Mar. 19, 1866-Oct. 17, 1949), educator and theater historian, was born in Newburgh, N.Y., the son of Benjamin Barker Odell, a businessman, and Ophelia (Bookstaver) Odell. Both parents came from early American families; the Odell line claimed descent from an ancestor who had emigrated from Bedfordshire, England, in 1637 and settled in western Connecticut. George received his early education at the local grammar school and the Newburgh Academy (1879-1883). After a year of further study at the Siglar Preparatory School in Newburgh, he entered Columbia College in 1885, largely, as he later confessed, to be near the Broadway theaters.

Odell's obsessive interest in the stage developed early and owed little to his family surroundings. There were no theater people in the family, whose male members traditionally assumed careers in business and public service. Odell's father served as mayor of Newburgh from 1884 to 1890, while his older brother, Benjamin Barker Odell, Jr., was elected to the House of Representatives in 1895 and later became governor of New York (1901-1904). A chance encounter with one of Augustin Daly's touring productions in 1876 left ten-year-old George permanently stagestruck. Thereafter he spent his weekly allowance on pictures of actresses, initiating a collection of theatrical memorabilia that expanded over the next half-century to become one of the most impressive private holdings in the country. During his undergraduate years at Columbia, Odell regularly attended the Manhattan theaters. In retrospect he hailed the mid-1880's as a "golden age" of great performers, trained in a larger-than-life style of acting that was fast disappearing. Edwin Booth, Ada Rehan, Sarah Bernhardt, John Drew, Otis Skinner, James Lewis, Modjeska, Richard Mansfield, Lillie Langtry, Joseph Jefferson—he saw them all in their most famous roles.

Odell received his B.A. from Columbia in 1889 and took both the M.A. (1890) and Ph.D. (1892) from there also. His doctoral dissertation, "Simile and Metaphor in the English and Scottish Ballads," was published in 1892 and reflected in a modest way his continuing interest in popular culture. Meticulously researched, this study sought to identify the most frequently used figures of speech in representative popular verse, as a way of testing the authenticity of other alleged folk ballads.

. In 1895 Odell joined the English department at Columbia, where he taught until his retirement in 1939. He edited student texts of Shakespeare's *Julius Caesar* (1900) and *Henry V* (1905), with the avowed object of aiding teachers to present the material more attractively to youthful audiences. A complementary concern for the changing standards of Shakespearean performance led to his first important scholarly work, *Shakespeare from Betterton to Irving* (2 vols., 1920), a history of English productions of Shakespeare from 1660 to 1902. Besides reconstructing the physical aspects of the London theaters, Odell included a wealth of detail on casts, box office receipts, textual changes, and the evolution of scene painting and costuming. Reviewers praised his intensive research and graceful style, and in 1924 the university appointed him professor of dramatic literature, a post formerly held by the distinguished critic Brander Matthews.

Odell's crowning achievement as a historian of the theater was reserved for the last twenty-two years of his life. During that period (1927-1949) he brought out, under the aegis of the Columbia University Press, fifteen volumes of his *Annals of the New York Stage,* an encyclopedic guide to all forms of public entertainment available in metropolitan New York from the mid-eighteenth century to 1894. Drawing upon years of careful research in primary source materials—newspapers, pamphlets, diaries, letters, autobiographies, playbills, account books, and the like—Odell attempted to compile an exhaustive catalogue of every play, opera, concert, dance recital, vaudeville and minstrel show performed in the New York area, together with some notice of each performer, writer, director, and producer. Through such a panoramic survey he hoped to chart changing urban mores, to "depict the city in successive eras, with all its prejudices and all its predilections, social, artistic and dramatic." The final result was a gargantuan potpourri that struck reviewers with awe. Deftly written and prodigiously detailed, Odell's *Annals* at once superseded all previous accounts of the New York stage, none of which approached their comprehensive scope or factual accuracy. They provided students with a permanently valuable repository of raw data, and it was altogether fitting that Odell received the New-York Historical Society's coveted Gold Medal for Achievement in History on Oct. 23, 1942, in acknowledgment of his herculean labors. Yet his work, for all its excellence, fails to offer any sustained critical analysis or interpretive framework by which to measure the significance of his data. A labor of love, it is permeated by a sentimental nostalgia for the kind of theater that disappeared around 1890. Odell was too much a product of the nineteenth century to criticize its dramatic conventions effectively. He reserved his jibes for twentieth-century "comedies and smart farces," whose language, he thought, needed to be "fumigated."

A tall, thin bachelor, with silver-gray hair and deep-set blue eyes, Odell lived in a modest apartment in the Hotel Seymour, at 50 West 45th Street, near Times Square. Beginning in 1937 he suffered from anemia and was largely bedridden during the last two years of his life. He died at the age of eighty-three, and was buried in Newburgh, N.Y.

[A good account of Odell's career appears in *Current Biog.*, 1944, pp. 507–509. Additional useful data, including a portrait, may be found in his obituary notice in the *N.Y. Times*, Oct. 18, 1949, p. 27. For contemporary criticism of the *Annals* and reminiscences by Odell, see *Presentation of the New-York Historical Society's Gold Medal for Achievement in History to George Clinton Densmore Odell in the Auditorium of the Society, New York City, October 23, 1942* (1943).]

MAXWELL H. BLOOMFIELD

O'HARE, KATE (RICHARDS) CUN-NINGHAM (Mar. 26, 1877–Jan. 10, 1948), socialist lecturer and organizer, teacher, and prison reformer, was born in Ottawa County, Kans., to Andrew Richards and Lucy (Thompson) Richards. Christened Kathleen, she was the fourth of five children and the second of two daughters. Her father, a partially disabled Civil War veteran, operated a prosperous stock ranch until ruined by the drought of 1887. Thereafter, his search for work took him to Kansas City, Mo., where, after securing employment as a machinist, he brought his family. Kate obtained her public education in the Ottawa County district school, a grammar school in Minneapolis, Kans., and a rural high school in Burchard, Nebr.

Choosing an unusual ocupation for a young woman of her generation, Kate went to work in her father's shop in 1894 as an apprentice machinist and eventually became a member of the union, the International Association of Machinists. At that time in her life she was a devout Protestant (Campbellite) who devoted considerable time to temperance and to saving "fallen women." Before long, however, the reality of urban poverty, especially during the depression of 1893, made Kate realize that "prayers never fill an empty stomach or avoid a panic." She began to read Henry George and Henry Demarest Lloyd, whose writings taught her that poverty caused vice and intemperance and that the true crusader fought causes and not effects. After hearing a speech by Mary Harris "Mother" Jones, she joined the Socialist Labor party in 1899. Two years later, in common with the majority of American socialists, she left the SLP for the just-formed Socialist party of America (1901). For the next twenty-five years, she served as one of the nation's most effective socialist lecturers and organizers.

In 1901 she attended the International School of Social Economy, a Socialist party training school in Girard, Kans., where she met her first husband, Francis (Frank) Patrick O'Hare, a student-teacher at the school. She and the Iowa-born, St. Louis-educated O'Hare, a Roman Catholic by birth and belief, were married on Jan. 1, 1902. Immediately after their wedding, the O'Hares crisscrossed the Midwest on a Socialist party lecture and organizing tour. Over the next fifteen years Kate O'Hare probably covered more territory and delivered more socialist lectures than any other American, appearing in every state, as well as in Canada, Mexico, and Great Britain. Her greatest successes, however, were won in the Great Plains states of Oklahoma and Kansas, where an effective synthesis of evangelistic and socialistic rhetoric in a setting patterned on a religious camp meeting attracted thousands of small dirt farmers to the Socialist party. Like many women in the Progressive era, O'Hare also worked actively for woman's suffrage, although, like most radical women of her generation, she always believed the socialist cause more important than the woman's cause. Not only was she a popular speaker, but she was also a prolific writer. Her published pamphlets such as "Law and the White Slaves," "Common Sense and the Liquor Question," and others on the church gained wide circulation; a 1904 novel about socialism, *What Happened to Dan?* (enlarged and revised in 1911 as *The Sorrows of Cupid*), won many readers. In about 1912 O'Hare and her husband became co-editors and copublishers of the *National Rip-Saw*, a St. Louis socialist monthly that featured muckraking articles. Never a theoretical journal, the *Rip-Saw*, under their guidance, preferred exposé to analysis. (It was renamed *Social Revolution* in 1917.) Socialist party members showed their admiration for O'Hare by electing her to the party's National Women's Committee (1910-1912) and choosing her as the only female to serve as an international secretary for the party (1912-1914) during the Second International. She also ran as the party's candidate for Congress from a Kansas district in 1910. Throughout this time, she associated with the more militant and leftist elements in the party and was a close friend of Eugene Victor Debs. Within this same busy period, she gave birth to four children: Francis Richards (1904), Kathleen (1906), and twins, Eugene Robert and Victor Edwin (1908).

Like most American socialists, O'Hare opposed American involvement in World War I. In her own words: I am "not pro-English; not pro-German; not pro-American," but simply "pro-working class." Her antiwar sentiments led party members to select her as chairman of the Committee on War and Militarism at the 1917 St. Louis Emergency Convention. The committee submitted a majority report, approved by the convention delegates, that condemned United States intervention. In line with her own beliefs and the party's official position, O'Hare traveled throughout the nation in 1917 presenting an antiwar lecture, "Socialism and the World War." After delivering that speech at Bowman, N.Dak., on July 17, 1917, she was indicted by the federal government under the wartime Espionage Act, found guilty, and sentenced to a five-year term in the Missouri State Penitentiary, beginning on Apr. 15, 1919. Among her fellow prisoners was the anarchist Emma Goldman. She continued to write and participate in socialist politics in prison and published *Kate O'Hare's Prison Letters* (1919) and *In Prison* (1920), the latter reissued in 1923 to favorable reviews. In 1919 she was one of four Americans elected as international representatives to the annual conferences of the Second International of the Socialist party and the following year was a leading candidate for the party's vice-presidential nomination. In May 1920 the Justice Department commuted her sentence in response to a nationwide socialist and civil-libertarian amnesty campaign. President Calvin Coolidge later granted her a full pardon.

After her release from prison, she and her husband continued their activities for the Socialist party, resuming their lecture work and editing their monthly paper, *Social Revolution.* But the decline of socialism and the collapse of third-party politics in the election of 1924 disillusioned her. Perhaps more important, her prison experiences convinced her of the need to crusade for penal reform. In 1922 the O'Hares organized the Children's Crusade, a march on Washington by children of still imprisoned opponents of the war to demand immediate amnesty. Later she directed an investigation of prison contract labor that resulted in congressional legislation in 1929 outlawing the worst features of the convict-labor system.

The O'Hares still found time for utopian ventures; they moved to Leesville, La., in 1922 and joined the Llano Co-operative Colony, a settlement modeled after nineteenth-century utopian communities. There they resumed publication of their paper, now retitled the *American Vanguard,* and founded Commonwealth College, a school for workers' education. Sectarianism split the community and the college; the *Vanguard* was terminated and the college was moved to Mena, Ark., in 1925, where Kate O'Hare served as a teacher and dean of women.

In June 1928 she obtained a divorce and on November 28 (the same day her ex-husband also remarried) married Charles C. Cunningham, a San Francisco attorney and mining engineer. She lived in California for the remainder of her life. In 1934 she campaigned actively in Upton Sinclair's "End Poverty in California" (EPIC) movement and in his gubernatorial campaign. Appointed assistant director of the California Department of Penology by Governor Culbert L. Olson in 1939, she helped introduce a substantial prison reform program that made California's penal system one of the nation's most humane. She left the department after a year and later, at the invitation of Governor Earl Warren, attended sessions of the State Crime Commission. She died at home in Benecia, Calif., in January 1948 of a coronary thrombosis; her remains were cremated.

[The best biographical material is in Kate O'Hare, "How I Became a Socialist Agitator," *Socialist Woman,* Oct. 1908; Solon DeLeon, ed., *The Am. Labor Who's Who* (1925); and a letter from Victor E. O'Hare (Los Angeles, 1967). For her role in the socialist movement, see David A. Shannon, *The Socialist Party of America: A History* (1955); James Weinstein, *The Decline of Socialism in America, 1912–1925* (1967); and Mari Jo Buhle, "Women and the Socialist Party," *Radical Am.,* Feb. 1970. For her later career, see William H. Cobb, "Commonwealth College Comes to Arkansas, 1923–1924," *Arkansas Hist. Quart.,* Summer 1964, and San Francisco *Chronicle* (magazine section), July 7, 1940. The Calif. Department of Public Health supplied the death certificate.]

MELVYN DUBOFSKY

OLDFIELD, ("BARNEY") BERNA ELI (Jan. 29, 1878–Oct. 4, 1946), automobile racer, was born on a farm near Wauseon, Ohio, the younger child and only son of Henry Clay Oldfield and Sarah (Yarnell) Oldfield. When he was eleven years old, his family moved to Toledo, where Henry Oldfield secured employment in a mental institution. In 1893 Barney left school, and the following year, having worked briefly as a newsboy, bellhop, elevator operator, and boxer, he took up the then-popular sport of bicycle racing. Through the later 1890's, Oldfield—"Champion of Ohio" —and a partner raced in bicycle meets throughout the Midwest, working during the off-season in a factory and as a bicycle-parts salesman.

His shift to automobile racing came through his friendship with Tom Cooper, a famed bicycle racer of the day who was briefly associated with Henry Ford in constructing and testing racing cars, including the "999," an awesome 2,800-pound vehicle with a tiller-type steering mechanism and few safety features. In October 1902, racing Ford's 999 at the Grosse Pointe speedway near Detroit, Oldfield covered the five-mile course in five minutes and twenty-eight seconds. On June 15, 1903, at the Indiana State Fair in Indianapolis, again in the 999, he became the first driver to break the one-minute mile.

For the next fifteen years, Oldfield drove in organized races, at county fairs, on barnstorming tours, and in exhibitions. Sometimes performing bizarre stunts, he immersed himself in the dusty, daredevil world of pre-World War I automobile racing. At one time or another, Oldfield drove most of the automobile models that to nostalgic later generations symbolized that world: the Winton "Bullet," the Peerless "Green Dragon," the "Blitzen Benz," the Stutz, the Maxwell, the Christie, the Mercer, and the Delage. His last driving season (1917-1918) was spent behind the wheel of Harry Miller's "Golden Submarine." Along the way he established many speed records, but most of them fell very quickly as automotive technology advanced. He was also involved in many accidents. He lost control of his car in Detroit in 1903, killing a spectator; a 1904 St. Louis crash left two men dead; he was badly injured in Hartford in 1906; and his riding mechanic was killed in a 1913 crash in Corona, Calif. Through it all, however, his public reputation steadily grew. Although other drivers criticized him as foolhardy and although he was often in the bad graces of the American Automobile Association and other official bodies, his gregarious and daredevil attitude, symbolized by the jaunty cigar stub firmly clamped between his teeth during every race, endeared him to his generation. He was celebrated for his showmanship and his improbable exploits as much as for his more conventional achievements. He raced a freight train (1904), an airplane (1914), and starred in a Mack Sennett melodrama, *Barney Oldfield's Race for a Life*.

Away from the race track, however, Oldfield was only intermittently successful in capitalizing upon his fame. He retired from racing in 1918 to become titular head of Harvey Fire-

stone's Oldfield Tire and Rubber Company of Akron, Ohio, but Firestone bought him out four years later when his barroom exploits diminished the public relations value of his name. A subsequent effort to establish his own tire-manufacturing business in Detroit was likewise unsuccessful. In the early 1930's, hard hit by the depression, he was often found as a ballyhoo man at thrill shows and speed meets. For several years in the mid-1930's, by contrast, he was employed by the Plymouth Motor Corporation to promote its safe-driving campaign. None of his three ventures into the saloon business in California—Los Angeles in 1911, Van Nuys in 1937, and Beverly Hills in 1941—prospered. By 1946, he was again lecturing on auto safety, this time for the General Petroleum Corporation of California.

Oldfield's career—checkered, turbulent, but ever hopeful—was mirrored in his marital history. On Aug. 25, 1896, in Toledo, he married Beatrice Loretta Oatis, whom he had met at a bicycle race; they separated in 1901, and were divorced in 1906. His second marriage, to Rebecca (Gooby) Holland, a widow, lasted from 1907 to 1924, and his third, to Hulda Braden, from 1925 to 1945. A daughter, Elizabeth, was adopted by the Oldfields in 1931. A few months before his death he remarried his second wife, who survived him. Oldfield's later years were spent in Beverly Hills, Calif., where he died of a heart attack and where, in Holy Cross Cemetery, he was buried.

[The few readily available sources are William F. Nolan, *Barney Oldfield* (1961); *World Almanac*, 1905–1920, *passim*; and *N.Y. Times*, Oct. 5, 1946, obituary, with photograph.]

                                        PAUL BOYER

OLDS, RANSOM ELI (June 3, 1864-Aug. 26, 1950), inventor and automobile manufacturer, was born in Geneva, Ohio, the fourth son and youngest of the five children of Pliny Fisk Olds and Sarah (Whipple) Olds. Both parents came of New England stock. The father, son of a Congregational minister, owned a blacksmith and machine shop in Geneva, but gave it up in 1870 and moved his family to Cleveland, where he took a job as superintendent in an ironworks. Ill health forced his resignation four years later, and after a less-than-successful try at farming in Parma, Ohio, and a second sojourn in Cleveland he moved in 1880 to Lansing, Mich., and again opened a machine shop.

In Lansing, Ransom Olds continued his schooling through the tenth grade, and after a six months' course at Bartlett's Business College (1882-1883), undertook the bookkeeping at his father's shop. He became a partner in the firm in 1885. Stimulated by successful manufacture of a small steam engine heated by ordinary gasoline stove burners, Olds built a three-wheel self-propelled vehicle in 1887, and five years later a four-wheel, dual-engine horseless carriage powered on the locomotive principle. Increasingly interested in the internal combustion engine, Olds adopted it for his third vehicle, completed in 1896. The following year he formed the Olds Motor Vehicle Company and, to supersede the family machine shop, the Olds Gasoline Engine Works.

The engine company prospered, but the motor vehicle company did not. Thus in 1899, with financing by Samuel L. Smith, a wealthy lumberman, the assets of the latter were incorporated into a new company, the Olds Motor Works, and operations transferred to Detroit. Smith, with 95 percent of the stock, maintained control, but Olds became vice-president and general manager. After several unsuccessful box-front models, Olds designed the popular and stylish Oldsmobile, in which the floor curved upward in front to form the dashboard. Fire destroyed the Olds plant in 1901, forcing the company to rely for production on subcontractors, a stimulus that led such future automotive leaders as Henry Ford, William C. Durant, and Henry Leland into the business and established Detroit as the nation's automotive capital. The curved-dash, "merry" Oldsmobile, low-priced and easily constructed, was the first automobile produced in quantity with a progressive assembly system and pointed the way to mass production through the application of interchangeable parts. In marketing innovations, Olds introduced the policy of insisting that dealers pay cash for cars delivered to them, a practice which became standard and provided much-needed immediate capital for the fledgling industry.

In 1904, when Smith insisted on substituting a larger and more expensive touring car for the curved-dash model, Olds resigned and, with financial backing, formed the Reo Motor Car Company (a name derived from his initials) in Lansing, himself taking the position of president and general manager. To ensure a nearby and steady source of parts, he organized several subsidiary firms: the National Coil Company, Michigan Screw Company, and Atlas Drop Forge Company. By 1907 the Reo company had gross sales of $4 million and Olds was again among the leaders of the industry.

The following year William Durant proposed a merger of the Reo, Buick, Ford, and Maxwell-Briscoe companies, but the plan collapsed when first Ford and then Olds each demanded $3 million in cash. Reo continued to expand, adding the Reo Motor Car Company of Canada and, in 1910, the Reo Motor Truck Company. The company's share of the automobile market nevertheless began to decline, despite the introduction in 1911 of a new model, "Reo the Fifth," which boasted a windshield, a top, and a self-starter. Four years later Olds was replaced as general manager by Richard H. Scott, an associate of long standing.

Olds played a lesser role in Reo's affairs after 1915. He gave increasing time to other ventures, including the Ideal Power Lawn Mower Company to manufacture a mower he had invented, the Capital National Bank (forerunner of the Michigan National Bank), and R. E. Olds Company, an investment firm. His most ambitious project was Oldsmar, a Florida community on Tampa Bay, begun in 1916, which he sought to make into an agricultural and industrial settlement for people of modest means. He divided the 37,000-acre tract into rural and urban sections, provided farmland and bungalow sites, and attracted several factories, but by the early 1920's it was clear that Oldsmar was not a success, and Olds began to liquidate his $4.5 million investment.

Olds resigned the presidency of the Reo Company in 1923 for the honorary position of chairman of the board. He became concerned, later, with the severe effects of the depression on the company and successfully waged a proxy fight against Scott in 1933. Although briefly in control again, Olds failed to persuade the company's executive committee to manufacture a cheap four-cylinder car or to adopt the Hill diesel engine, in which he had a substantial stake. As a result, he resigned the chairmanship of the committee in December 1934 and, two years later, his position as chairman of the board.

In his business philosophy and career, Olds typified both the early automobile manufacturer and the traditional entrepreneur. His talents were mechanical rather than administrative, and he concerned himself primarily with technological improvements. He applied his imaginative genius to promotional schemes as well, like automobile races and cross-country trips, though not all were successful. As an employer he was benevolent and paternalistic. He provided his workers with insurance programs, medical services, recreation facilities, job training, and citizenship education; but he consistently opposed organized labor and the union shop, which he thought were detrimental to individual initiative and competitive capitalism.

A Baptist, Olds neither smoked nor drank. His philanthropies, which were modest in scale, were chiefly religious or educational. He gave an engineering building to Michigan State University in East Lansing and a science hall to Kalamazoo (Mich.) College. In 1942 he bought the Daytona Terrace Hotel in Daytona Beach, Fla., and converted it into an interdenominational home for retired ministers and missionaries. Olds married Metta Ursula Woodward on June 5, 1889. They had four children, only two of whom—Gladys Marguerite and Bernice Estelle—survived infancy. Robust and active to the end of his life, Olds died of cancer in Lansing at the age of eighty-six and was buried in the family mausoleum at Lansing's Mount Hope Cemetery.

[There are two major collections of Olds's papers: at Mich. State Univ., East Lansing, and at the R. E. Olds Company in Lansing; equally helpful is the Reo Collection at Mich. State Univ. The only scholarly biography, which includes a full account of the available sources, is Glenn A. Niemeyer, *The Automotive Career of Ransom E. Olds* (1963). An older biography, probably ghostwritten by Olds, is Duane Yarnell, *Auto Pioneering: The Remarkable Story of R. E. Olds* (1949). For the general history of the automotive industry, see John B. Rae, *Am. Automobile Manufacturers: The First Forty Years* (1959) and *The Am. Automobile: A Brief Hist.* (1965). The family lineage is traced in Edson B. Olds, ed., *The Olds (Old, Ould) Family in England and America* (1915). Death record from Mich. Dept. of Public Health.]

GLENN A. NIEMEYER

OSBORN, CHASE SALMON (Jan. 22, 1860-Apr. 11, 1949), journalist, prospector, and governor of Michigan, was born in Huntington County, Ind., the seventh of ten children (seven boys and three girls) of George Augustus Osborn and Margaret Ann (Fannon) Osborn. His father, a native of Indiana, was descended from English and French Huguenot forebears who had settled in Massachusetts in the seventeenth century; his mother, born in Ohio, was of Protestant Irish ancestry. George Osborn, originally a carpenter, received a medical degree from Indiana Medical College. He established a practice with his wife, who had also studied medicine, but during the family's frequent economic reverses he supplemented their income by working as a carpenter.

Young Chase—named for his father's abolitionist hero Salmon P. Chase—moved with the family in 1866 to Lafayette, Ind., where he attended school. He developed an uncommon knowledge of nature and a spirit of adventure

that led him frequently to run away from home; once he worked for several months as a chore boy in a Michigan lumber camp. His formal education ended with three years (1874-1877) at Purdue University in Lafayette, two in the senior preparatory class and the third as a college freshman. Osborn began his journalistic career as a reporter for a Lafayette newspaper. In 1879 he traveled to Chicago by foot and freight train, worked briefly for the *Chicago Tribune,* and then went on the following year to Milwaukee, where he became a reporter for the *Evening Wisconsin.* On May 7, 1881, he married Lillian Gertrude Jones of Milwaukee. They had seven children, four of whom—Ethel Louise, George Augustus, Chase Salmon, and Emily Fisher—survived childhood.

Osborn moved north in 1883 to the mining town of Florence, Wis., where he bought and ran a local newspaper. Over the next four years he also began prospecting for iron ore in the rich Menominee range, gaining practical geological experience. He sold his newspaper in 1887 and returned to Milwaukee as city editor of the *Sentinel.* At the same time he helped establish *Miner and Manufacturer,* a weekly dedicated to news of the state's burgeoning iron ore industry. The excitement of exploration proved irresistible, and before the end of the year he left Milwaukee to prospect for a mining syndicate. Settling with his family in Sault Ste. Marie, Mich., which remained his home for the rest of his life, he became part owner (later sole owner) and editor of a weekly newspaper there, the *News,* but spent much of his time in the wilderness searching for ore. In 1901 he discovered a rich iron deposit in Ontario, from which he realized a considerable fortune. He sold the *News* the same year but in January 1902 bought a half-interest in the *Saginaw* (Mich.) *Courier-Herald,* which he held until 1912.

Osborn early became involved in Michigan politics as a Republican. He served as postmaster of Sault Ste. Marie (1889-1893) and as state game and fish warden (1895-1899). Although he was defeated for a congressional nomination in 1896, his strong showing in this race, as well as in an unsuccessful contest for the gubernatorial nomination in 1900, established his political future. The reform governor Hazen S. Pingree appointed him in 1899 to the state railroad commission, on which he remained until 1903. Osborn's experience on the commission and his high regard for President Theodore Roosevelt helped convert him to progressivism. A tall, rugged man, Osborn possessed considerable political gifts, including exceptional oratorical powers. Although somewhat vain, he had a forceful personality that made him the focus of any gathering.

In 1910, with the deft assistance of his friend and advisor Frank Knox, Osborn secured the Republican nomination for governor and, running on a strongly progressive platform, went on to win the general election. The next two years he saw a great deal of his program enacted, including a presidential primary law, tax reform, stronger regulatory acts for business, and, most important, a workmen's compensation act. Through retrenchment, Osborn turned an inherited deficit of more than $500,000 into an equally large surplus. He vigorously championed other reforms such as conservation laws, greater government efficiency, and regulation of the banking and liquor industries; and his support for the initiative, referendum, and recall paved the way for their enactment by his successor. This strong record of reform won Osborn a national reputation and made him a lasting influence in Michigan affairs.

During the 1912 presidential campaign Osborn traveled an elliptical course. Angered by President William Howard Taft's growing conservatism, he was one of the early leaders of the National Progressive Republican League in 1911. In February 1912 he called a conference of like-minded governors who urged Roosevelt to seek the Republican presidential nomination. Osborn opposed, however, the formation of a third party, which he felt would mean abandoning the GOP to the conservatives. When Roosevelt ran as a Progressive, Osborn at first urged Republicans to vote for Woodrow Wilson while backing progressive Republicans in local and state contests. Yet his loyalty to Roosevelt remained strong, and after an assassination attempt on the former president's life in October, Osborn stumped vigorously for him.

Osborn had pledged himself to a single term as governor, and although for a time he considered reversing this position, the split in the Republican party confirmed his original decision, and he did not seek reelection in 1912. Never again did he hold public office, although he unsuccessfully sought the governorship in 1914 and nomination to the United States Senate in 1918 and 1930. He became increasingly concerned with the need for prohibition, championing it almost to the exclusion of other issues. Yet Osborn never lost his essential liberalism. He supported the third-party candidacy of Robert La Follette in 1924; and although he backed Alfred M. Landon in 1936, he switched his allegiance to Franklin D. Roosevelt in 1940. He favored much of the New Deal and in 1941 served on the advisory board of the Michigan Works Progress Administration.

After 1912 Osborn spent most of his time in world travel, lecturing, and writing. His interests in science, conservation, and folklore led him into a number of ventures. He attempted, for example, to determine the source of the firefly's light, defended the American roots of the legend of Hiawatha, theorized about glaciation, and financed a study of the feasibility of transporting people across country by vacuum tube. In his final years, he became interested in promoting world peace through an international union of western democracies. A generous, unostentatious man, Osborn gave away much of his fortune to various institutions before his death, including grants of valuable land to Purdue University, the University of Michigan, and the state of Georgia. Osborn's wife, from whom he had separated in 1923, died in 1948. In his later years he was aided by his adopted daughter, Stellanova Brunt; the adoption was annulled, and they were married on Apr. 9, 1949, two days before his death. Reared as a Methodist, Osborn became a Presbyterian after his first marriage. He died of congestive heart failure at his winter home in Poulan, Ga., at the age of eighty-nine. He was buried in the Duck Island Cemetery, Sault Ste. Marie, Mich.

[The basic source is the extensive Osborn Papers in the Mich. Hist. Collect., Univ. of Mich. Osborn's autobiography, *The Iron Hunter* (1919), is useful for his philosophy, early life, and prospecting ventures. Robert M. Warner, "Chase S. Osborn and the Progressive Movement" (Ph.D. diss., Univ. of Mich., 1958), draws on the Osborn Papers; see also the same author's *Chase Salmon Osborn, 1860–1949* (Mich. Hist. Collect., Bull. no. 10, 1960), and his articles in *Mich. Hist.*, Sept. 1959, and *Miss. Valley Hist. Rev.*, June 1959. Other secondary works are Vernon L. Beal, *Promise and Performance: The Political Record of a Mich. Governor, Chase Salmon Osborn* (Mich. Hist. Collect., *Bull.* no. 4, 1950); Stellanova Brunt Osborn, ed., *An Accolade for Chase S. Osborn* (1940), and her *Eighty and On: The Unending Adventurings of Chase S. Osborn* (1941); *N.Y. Times* obituary, Apr. 12, 1949; *Nat. Cyc. Am. Biog.*, XXXVIII, 41–43; *Who Was Who in America*, II (1950). Death record from Ga. Dept. of Human Resources.]

ROBERT M. WARNER

OWEN, ROBERT LATHAM (Feb. 2, 1856–July 19, 1947), senator from Oklahoma, was born in Lynchburg, Va., the younger of two sons of Col. Robert Latham Owen and Narcissa (Chisholm) Owen. His father, a civil engineer of Scots-Irish descent, was president of the Virginia and Tennessee Railroad from 1861 to 1867; his mother was part Cherokee. Young Owen attended private schools in Lynchburg and Baltimore. The death of his father in 1872 jeopardized his further education, but he entered Washington and Lee University the following year with the aid of a scholarship and graduated with the M.A. degree in 1877. In 1879 he and his mother moved to Salina, Indian Territory. There Owen became a citizen of the Cherokee Nation, taught in the Cherokee Orphan Asylum, and later served as secretary of the Cherokee Board of Education. On Dec. 31, 1889, he married Daisy Deane Hester, daughter of a local farmer, merchant, and missionary. They had a daughter, Dorothea, and adopted a son, Robert Latham.

Soon after coming to the Indian Territory, Owen began to study law, and in 1880 he took up practice in Tahlequah. He was the federal Indian agent for the Five Civilized Tribes from 1885 to 1889. During the next few years Owen represented the Choctaws and the Cherokees in several important court cases. He became a familiar figure in Washington and was influential in securing the congressional act of 1901 giving citizenship to Indians in the territory. Earlier he had helped extend the provisions of the National Banking Act to the Indian Territory, and under that act he organized the First National Bank of Muskogee in 1890, serving as its president until 1900. He was also involved in extensive farming and cattle-raising enterprises.

Owen's Indian background and natural abilities encouraged him to enter politics. He was a leader in organizing the Democratic party in the Indian Territory in 1892 and for the next four years served on the Democratic National Committee. He took a prominent part in the Sequoyah movement for separate statehood in 1905, but when Congress refused to approve this plan he supported joint statehood for the Indian and Oklahoma territories. When the first legislature of the new state of Oklahoma convened late in 1907, Owen was elected to the United States Senate.

A tall, handsome, and dignified man with black hair, dark eyes, and a swarthy complexion, Owen soon emerged as a skillful operator in the tedious business of legislative procedure. As a member of the Indian Affairs Committee, he labored for years to remove federal restrictions on the ownership of Indian land by individual Indians, at a time when government policy sought to keep ownership in the hands of the tribes. Because individual owners were vulnerable to land grabs by unscrupulous whites, Owen's position was criticized by Indian reformers, but he seems to have been sincerely convinced that Oklahoma could be developed only if federal restraints were removed.

Owen was easily reelected in 1912, in part because of his ardent support of progressive ideas. Although a child of the Confederate and Reconstruction South, he became identified with the Western progressivism of William Jennings Bryan. In 1913 he helped organize the National Popular Government League and served as its president until 1928. He was a strong advocate of virtually every device in the arsenal of popular democracy, including a thoroughgoing primary system, the initiative, referendum, the recall, woman suffrage, the preferential ballot, direct election of United States senators, and a simple cloture procedure for the Senate. He sponsored measures to prevent inferior federal courts from taking jurisdiction in any case alleging the unconstitutionality of an act of Congress, to simplify and democratize the process of amending the Constitution, and to establish a Department of Public Health and a Department of Education.

Long interested in providing the nation with a more elastic currency, Owen became increasingly preoccupied with banking and currency legislation. He opposed the Aldrich-Vreeland Currency Act (1908), which sought to provide greater currency elasticity by authorizing national banks to issue circulating notes. He also advocated postal savings banks and worked to commit his party to the guarantee of bank deposits. In 1913 he became chairman of the newly created Senate Committee on Banking and Currency. As such, he was cosponsor, with Congressman Carter Glass, of the Federal Reserve Act (1913). Owen's principal contributions to the act were his work as administration spokesman in the Senate and his insistence, along with other progressive Democrats, upon complete governmental (rather than banker) control of the Federal Reserve Board and upon making the Federal Reserve notes obligations of the United States. Afterward Owen sought on numerous occasions to strengthen the Federal Reserve Act by amendment. He was also a warm supporter of the Federal Farm Loan Act of 1916.

The Oklahoma senator was one of the most consistent backers of Woodrow Wilson's New Freedom. He supported the administration's tariff and antitrust bills and sponsored an unsuccessful measure to establish federal control of stock exchanges. A champion of liberal labor laws, he was a cosponsor of the Palmer-Owen and Keating-Owen child labor bills. He helped commit the administration to support of a tariff commission and endorsement of a broader program of social legislation in preparation for the national campaign of 1916. Owen firmly supported Wilson's war and foreign policies as well. After the initial defeat of the Versailles Treaty, however, he took a leading part in the abortive bipartisan conferences in January 1920 seeking a compromise and was one of the Democrats who voted for ratification with the Lodge reservations.

Owen was reelected in 1918, but the intrusion of the Ku Klux Klan disturbed Oklahoma politics in the early 1920's, and in 1924 he declined to run again. At the conclusion of his term he resumed the practice of law in Washington. He voted for Hoover in the presidential election of 1928 but supported Franklin D. Roosevelt in 1932. In 1945 he urged the Senate Foreign Relations Committee to recommend ratification of the United Nations Charter. Blind during his last years, Owen died in Washington in 1947 at the age of ninety-one, of pneumonia following a prostate operation. He was buried in Spring Hill Cemetery, Lynchburg, Va. He was a member of the Episcopal church and of many fraternal organizations.

[There is no good biography of Owen, but valuable information about his public career and political philosophy is contained in two uncritical works—Edward E. Keso, *The Senatorial Career of Robert Latham Owen* (1937), and Wyatt W. Belcher, "The Political Theory of Robert L. Owen" (M.A. thesis, Univ. of Oklahoma, 1932)—and in several articles written by Owen: "The Restoration of Popular Rule," *Arena*, June 1908; "The True Meaning of Insurgency," *Independent*, June 30, 1910; "Progressive Democracy," *ibid.*, Apr. 18, 1912; and "Cloture in the Senate," *Harper's Weekly*, Nov. 27, 1915. A critical but incomplete treatment of his position on Indian affairs is provided in Angie Debo, *And Still the Waters Run* (1940). James R. Scales, "Political Hist. of Okla., 1907–1949" (Ph.D. diss., Univ. of Oklahoma, 1949), is helpful on state politics during Owen's Senate tenure. For his contribution to the origin and passage of the Federal Reserve Act, see his *The Federal Reserve Act* (1919); Henry Parker Willis, *The Federal Reserve System: Legislation, Organization, and Operation* (1923); Carter Glass, *An Adventure in Constructive Finance* (1927); and William G. McAdoo, *Crowded Years* (1931). Owen's leadership during the Wilson administration is reflected in vols. II, IV, and V (1947–1965) of Arthur S. Link's *Wilson* and vols. IV, VII, and VIII (1927–1939) of Ray Stannard Baker's *Woodrow Wilson*. For brief sketches of Owen, see *Biog. Directory Am. Cong.* (1961); *Nat. Cyc. Am. Biog.*, XXXVII, 290-291; and *N.Y. Times* obituary, July 20, 1947. Death record from D.C. Dept. of Human Resources. A small collection of Owen Papers covering the period 1920–1941 is in the Lib. of Cong., and a considerable number of letters between Owen and Wilson are in the Woodrow Wilson Papers there.]

DEWEY W. GRANTHAM

PALMER, WALTER WALKER (Feb. 27, 1882-Oct. 28, 1950), physician, scientist, and educator, was born on a farm in Southfield, Mass. He was the fourth of five children of Henry Wellington Palmer and Almira Roxana Walker, both of Southfield. Ancestors on both sides were of English descent and settled in New England in the seventeenth century, where they were known as "the Stonington [Mass.] Palmers." The first of the family to arrive in the colonies was Walter Palmer, who emigrated in 1629 and finally settled in Stonington in 1653. Walter Walker Palmer was the ninth generation and his ancestors on both sides had all been farmers. Palmer, affectionately known as "Bill," had a career that was almost fictional in quality. The modest, gentle, soft-spoken farm boy, without early medical indoctrination and without powerful sponsorship, rose to pre-eminence in the medical field. He was an acknowledged leader during a period of epoch-making advances in diagnostic and therapeutic methods. His contributions in developing new points of view in the study of disease, in formulating the philosophy of medical training, and in broadening the scope of the modern clinic assure his position in medical history.

Palmer graduated from Mount Hermon Academy in 1901 and entered Amherst College, from which he graduated, Phi Beta Kappa, in 1905. He also was renowned as a rugged linesman and varsity captain who had no peer on the gridiron. Of more satisfaction to Palmer was his participation in the Amherst paleontological expedition during the summer of 1904, when he identified (and later, in his first publication, described) a hitherto unknown species, which now bears his name. The following year Palmer taught mathematics at Milton Academy and then entered Harvard Medical School, from which he graduated with honors (Alpha Omega Alpha) in 1910. Upon completing his medical internship in 1911 at the Massachusetts General Hospital, he was appointed Henry P. Walcott fellow there, and between 1913 and 1915 he served as medical resident at the Massachusetts General and, in addition, became instructor in physiological chemistry at Harvard. Although he intended to enter medical practice, a visit to Professor L. J. Henderson at Harvard Medical School proved to be the turning point in his life, and he embarked on a fruitful career in full-time academic medicine. His earlier research, much of it in collaboration with Henderson, was devoted to important studies of acid-base balance, particularly in diabetes and nephritis. From 1915 to 1917 Palmer was a member of the staff of the Rockefeller Institute in New York, where he extended this research and also developed the first reliable quantitative method for hemoglobin determination. His later investigation was largely concerned with the physiology of the thyroid gland. In 1917 he became associate professor of medicine at Columbia University and acting director, as well as associate attending physician, at the Presbyterian Hospital in New York. He reluctantly remained a civilian in World War I, but held a commission as 1st lieutenant in the Medical Reserve Corps.

From 1919 to 1921 Palmer was associate professor of medicine at Johns Hopkins and surrounded himself with a brilliant group of younger physicians and investigators. His stay in Baltimore was not a happy one, owing to the bitterness and ridicule to which he and his new group were often subjected by the authoritarian and reactionary attitudes of many associates. In 1921 he declined the chair of medicine at Johns Hopkins and also at Yale and Michigan and returned to Columbia as Bard professor of medicine and director of the medical service at the Presbyterian Hospital. He brought his sympathetic group with him from Hopkins, and with his vision, his shining integrity, his rare sense of values and critique, his unfailing interest in and support of those about him, and his capacity to choose capable young physicians, he built up at Columbia one of the world's renowned departments of internal medicine. He established an esprit and a record of accomplishment in his department unexcelled elsewhere. Upon his mandatory retirement at Columbia, Palmer became director of the New York Public Health Research Institute, to which he brought an enormous scientific strength and new blood in the three years prior to his sudden death from heart disease on his beloved farm in Tyringham, Mass. He was buried in the village cemetery.

Palmer received the honorary degree of Sc.D. from Amherst (1922), Columbia (1929), and Princeton (1947). His participation in local and national activities reflected his diversified interests and his full and busy life. According to a close colleague, he was not indiscriminately gregarious nor politically ambitious, nor was he a facile speaker before formal gatherings, but his clarity of vision and his idealism led to positions of honor and trust in many scientific and learned organizations. He served as president of the American College of Physicians and the Harvey Society. He was

an editor of *Journal of Biological Chemistry, Archives of Internal Medicine,* and *Archives of Medicine* and was editor-in-chief of the Nelson System of Medicine. He was also chairman of the Advisory Committee of the *American Journal of Medicine.* He served with great distinction for many years on the Council of Pharmacy and Chemistry of the AMA and the National Board of Medical Examiners. He was chairman of the Medical Advisory Committee appointed by Vannevar Bush to report to the president on establishing a national science foundation, and a member of the Advisory Committee of the Office of Scientific Research and Development in World War II. He was a member of the most distinguished medical societies in the United States. At the time of his death he was vice-president of the Century Association in New York.

A big man, both in physique and spirit, Dr. Palmer was regarded by his friends as a tower of strength. Those in need constantly sought his wise counsel, for with all his solidity he had disarming warmth and a gentle humor. He had deep human understanding and inspired complete confidence. He had rugged integrity and quiet but abiding contempt for sham, superficiality, and insincerity.

Dr. Palmer relished with buoyant enthusiasm the periods of leisure on his farm with its ancestral associations, where he became an avid cabinetmaker and an amateur vintner. He cherished his family life, which was immeasurably enriched by the musical, artistic, and literary environment created by his wife and her wide circle of distinguished friends.

Dr. Palmer married Francesca de Kay Gilder, the daughter of Richard Watson Gilder, on Oct. 22, 1922. They had three children—a daughter, Helena Francesca Gilder, and two sons, Gilder and Walter de Kay.

[The major sources are AMA Council on Pharmacy and Chemistry, "Statement on Death of Walter Walker Palmer," *Jour. AMA,* 145, no. 6 (1951), 405; Robert F. Loeb, "Resolution of Faculty of Medicine," Columbia Univ., Dec. 11, 1950, vol. IIIc; "Background Information on Starred Scientists," Ind. Univ. (autobiographical data, date not known); *N.Y. Times,* Oct. 29, 1950; *N.Y. Herald Tribune,* Oct. 29, 1950; *Am. Men of Sci.,* 1949; *Who's Who in America* 1948–1949; *Who Was Who in America,* 1951–1960; Walter W. Palmer, "The Department of Medicine, 1921–1947" (Presbyterian Hospital, 1951); portrait by R. Brachman, now in the Dept. of Medicine, Presbyterian Hospital.]

ROBERT F. LOEB

PATTERSON, ELEANOR MEDILL

(Nov. 7, 1881–July 24, 1948), newspaper editor and publisher, was born in Chicago, Ill., the second of two children and only daughter of Robert Wilson Patterson, Jr., and Elinor (Medill) Patterson, both of Scots-Irish ancestry. Her mother was a daughter of Joseph Medill, editor of the *Chicago Tribune,* the city's leading newspaper; her father succeeded Medill as editor. Her parents were not a happy pair, the father preoccupied with work, the mother intent on social position. Cissy, as her brother Joseph called her (she disliked her given name, Elinor Josephine, and later changed it to Eleanor Medill), was brought up by governesses and was educated at Miss Hersey's School in Boston and subsequently at Miss Porter's in Farmington, Conn.

Cissy became a willful, "spoiled" child, as she later admitted, and suffered the consequences all her life. Slender, copper-haired, wide-eyed, and of graceful carriage, she cut a striking figure in Chicago and Washington society at the turn of the century. Her uncle, Robert S. McCormick, ambassador to Austria-Hungary, provided entrée to Viennese society; and it was at a ball in Vienna that she met Count Josef Gizycki of Poland, a fortune hunter twice her age. She married him at the family's new mansion on Dupont Circle in Washington on Apr. 14, 1904, but left him soon after the birth of their daughter, Felicia, in Poland. There ensued a headlined struggle for custody of the child, which she finally won, and eight years of divorce litigation, settled in June 1917.

Volatile and restless, Cissy moved through the 1920's with little sense of purpose. She bought a ranch near Jackson Hole, Wyo., where she became a crack shot and imbibed a measure of Western progressivism. She presided at Dupont Circle as one of the capital's brighter hostesses and roamed the country in her private railroad car. She tried her hand as a novelist with *Glass Houses,* first published in French (in 1923), a satire on Washington society. *Fall Flight* (1928), a thinly disguised account of her harrowing marriage to Gizycki, was written after her second marriage, on Apr. 11, 1925, to Elmer Schlesinger, a New York attorney. This marriage was dissolving when he died in February 1929.

The true career of Eleanor Patterson, as she now styled herself, began in 1930, when her friend Arthur Brisbane persuaded William Randolph Hearst to try her as editor-publisher of his ailing *Washington Herald.* Although she knew of newspapering little more than she had gleaned from her brother, founder of the *New York Daily News,* she threw herself into the job with familial zeal. From Boston she lured one of Hearst's best circulation men. She covered some stories herself, with flair, walking in on Al Capone for an interview. She hired and fired editors (seven in ten years), often on impulse, and she launched campaigns for home rule in the District of Columbia, for hot lunches for schoolchildren, and for a cleaner Potomac. In the early New Deal years, the *Herald,* sympathetic within Hearst-imposed limits, brimmed with news and gossip, and by 1936 Mrs. Patterson could point to a circulation double that of 1930. In August 1937, she leased from Hearst the *Herald* and his evening *Times,* and in January 1939 she exercised options to purchase them. Against the advice of her brother and others, she combined them into a single all-day paper with six editions, the *Washington Times-Herald.* As lively and spiteful as its owner, the paper shortly became Washington's largest, turned a profit in 1943, and by 1945 was clearing $1 million a year.

The paper backed Franklin Roosevelt in the 1940 election, but his lend-lease program soon roused isolationist feelings that led Mrs. Patterson to join her brother and her cousin, Col. Robert R. McCormick of the *Chicago Tribune,* in strident opposition. Foes termed the trio "the McCormick-Patterson axis," their antagonism to Roosevelt's policies continuing for the rest of his days. If she wielded the lightest weapon of the three, she did so with such joyous malice and vituperative zest that victims at times seemed more bemused than hurt. Harold L. Ickes noted in his diary, "The President said he had known Cissy since she was a girl and that he liked her but thought she was somewhat 'cracked.'" Her paper, although readable, carried little weight in affairs of state.

Mrs. Patterson's interest in her paper dwindled after World War II, and a lifelong sense of loneliness intensified after her brother's death in 1946. She died in bed, apparently of a heart attack, at her estate near Marlboro, Md., and was buried in the Medill plot at Graceland Cemetery, Chicago. Short of capital, the *Times-Herald* executives to whom she left the paper sold it the following year to Colonel McCormick, who in turn sold it in 1954 to the *Washington Post,* with which it was merged. Quick-witted and mercurial, now arrogant, now self-deprecating, by turns kind and cruel, thoughtful of associates and suspicious of them, Cissy Patterson became one of the most conspicuous of newspaper publishers, the first to succeed with an around-the-clock daily, yet a brilliant reversion to the personal journalism of the precorporate age.

[A profile by Stanley Walker in the *Sat. Evening Post*, May 6, 1939, p. 22; *Current Biog.*, 634–636 (1940); David Denker's article in *Notable Am. Women*, III (1971); Paul F. Healy, *Cissy* (1966); and Alice Albright Hoge, *Cissy Patterson* (1966); are the chief sources. See also the Arthur Brisbane papers at Syracuse Univ. and *Washington Post* files.]
LOUIS M. STARR

PATTERSON, JOSEPH MEDILL (Jan. 6, 1879–May 25, 1946), newspaper publisher, was born in Chicago into one of America's leading newspaper dynasties. He was the first of two children and only son of Elinor (Medill) Patterson and Robert Wilson Patterson, Jr., both of Scots-Irish descent. His maternal grandfather was Joseph Medill, editor and publisher of the *Chicago Tribune*. His father, the son of a prominent Presbyterian clergyman, was managing editor of the *Tribune* anl later Medill's successor at the paper.

Joseph's sister Eleanor ("Cissy") Patterson later became owner and editor of the *Washington Times-Herald*. Although raised in a mansion on Chicago's "Gold Coast," young Patterson refused to conform to his background. Tall and athletic, he dressed casually, even sloppily, and he disliked all ostentation. He enjoyed mingling with ordinary people, and throughout his life often frequented bars and restaurants in such unsavory urban areas as Chicago's first ward and New York's Bowery. Usually charming, his personality was mercurial, and as a child he possessed a violent temper.

Patterson attended private schools in Chicago and France and Groton School in Massachusetts (1890–1896). After a year spent on a ranch in New Mexico, he entered Yale University in 1897 and received the B.A. degree in 1901. Understandably, Patterson developed an early interest in journalism. In the summer of 1900 he went to China to report on the Boxer Rebellion for the *Tribune*, and after graduating from college he joined the paper's staff as a city reporter, subsequently rising to assistant editor. Meanwhile, on Nov. 19, 1902, he married Alice Higinbotham of Chicago, daughter of a partner of Marshall Field. They had three daughters, Elinor Medill, Alicia, and Josephine Medill, and adopted a son, James.

Patterson's experience as a city reporter caused his proletarian sympathies to develop into a zeal for political reform. In 1903, running as an opponent of boss rule, he was elected to the Illinois House of Representatives, resigning from the *Tribune* after he learned that his father had used the paper's influence to aid his election. Two years later Patterson supported the successful mayoral campaign of reformer Edward F. Dunne in Chicago and was rewarded by being named commissioner of public works. In this post he fought the large department stores, which were turning their basements into female sweatshops.

But Patterson came increasingly to believe that reform of the capitalist system was impossible and that socialism must replace it. He resigned his commissionership in 1906 and joined the Socialist party. In "Confessions of a Drone," published in the *Independent* that year, he described the way that he and other members of the privileged classes lived on wealth appropriated from others and suggested that the working class had it in its power to alter the "present arrangement" (Tebbel, p. 285). Patterson was named a member of the Socialist party's executive council in 1906 but spent most of the next four years on a farm he purchased near Libertyville, Ill., where he devoted himself to writing. Among the works he produced were the plays *Dope*, which showed that drug addiction grew out of slum conditions, and *The Fourth Estate*, written in collaboration with James Keeley and Harriet Ford. He also wrote a novel, *A Little Brother of the Rich* (1908), which dramatically—and with some exaggeration—portrayed the immoral and corruptive lives of the idle rich.

By 1910, when his father died, Patterson had also become disillusioned with socialism, having learned as a working author that people will only work for a profit. Returning to Chicago, he joined his cousin Robert McCormick as coeditor of the *Tribune*, taking over the editorial side of the business. Patterson had always had a high regard for his father's insistence on unbiased reporting, but both he and McCormick felt the paper was stuffy and needed to be enlivened. Crime news appeared on the front page for the first time, Lillian Russell was hired to write beauty hints, and there were crusades against everything from loan sharks to clairvoyants. Although Patterson clashed frequently with his conservative cousin over the paper's enduring conservatism on the editorial page, McCormick's influence prevailed.

More interested in reporting than editing, Patterson personally covered the border conflict with Mexico in 1914 and the beginning of World War I in Europe. In 1916 he joined the Illinois Field Artillery and after United States entry into the war, he served in France in five major engagements, rising to the rank of captain. Before returning to the United States in 1919, Patterson stopped in London, where he was impressed by the success of the tabloid *Daily Mirror*. He was convinced that such a paper, based on photographs and mass appeal, could succeed in New York. Consequently, on June 26, 1919, he brought out the first issue of the *Illustrated Daily News* (which soon became simply the *Daily News*). Having run the *News* initially from his office in Chicago, in 1925 he gave McCormick complete control of the *Tribune* and moved to New York.

Derided by critics as the "servant-girls' Bible" and "gum-chewers' delight," the *News* at first had difficulty attracting advertisers. Within a few months, however, subway straphangers found that the tabloid size was easy to read, and Patterson's view that crime and sex were sure circulation-builders was confirmed. Advertisers soon lost their squeamishness and the paper began to show a profit. Patterson introduced editorials written in everyday English and a popular letters column called "Voice of the People." Considering the comics an important journalistic feature, he developed the idea for such strips as "The Gumps," "Dick Tracy," and "Little Orphan Annie"; indeed, the character of Mr. Bailey in "Smitty" was modeled after Patterson himself.

In 1921 Patterson added a Sunday edition, and by 1925 the *News* had a circulation of over a million. It grew steadily until by the late 1930's it had the largest daily circulation in the United States and the largest Sunday circulation (over three million) in the world. Other publishers tried to emulate Patterson's achievement, but no other tabloid was ever as successful as the *News*. Patterson was highly adept at judging the popular taste, and noting the decline of the overly lurid New York *Evening Graphic*, founded in the 1920's by Bernarr MacFadden, he realized that too much sensationalism could be as unprofitable as too little. As an editor Patterson could be ruthless, dictatorial, and suspicious. Yet he knew most of his workers by their first names and often accompanied his reporters on stories.

During the 1930's the *Daily News* became somewhat more "respectable," devoting more space to national and international affairs. The paper was an early supporter of Franklin D. Roosevelt's domestic policies, and Patterson became a frequent guest at the White House. Indeed, his series of editorials in 1940 defending Roosevelt's bid for a third term helped him win a Pulitzer Prize. Yet Patterson was a devoted isolationist, and he broke with Roosevelt immediately after this election when the president introduced the lend-lease bill. He attacked the administration bitterly in the editorial columns of the *News*, and although he unsuccessfully sought to reenlist in the army after Pearl Harbor, he continued throughout the war to question the wisdom of American involvement in Europe. Increasingly alarmed about the "Red menace," he defended right-wing critics like Father Charles Coughlin and others accused of wartime sedition and vigorously opposed the reelection of Roosevelt in 1944.

In 1938 Patterson divorced his wife, from whom he had been separated for many years, and on July 7 of that year he married Mary King, women's editor of the *News*. An avid movie fan, Patterson also enjoyed hunting and fishing. Overcoming a fear of flying, he took lessons and became a licensed pilot. Patterson died in Doctors Hospital in New York, of a liver ailment complicated by pneumonia, and was buried in Arlington National Cemetery, Washington, D.C. Patterson's grasp of the techniques of popular journalism, his touch with the common people, and his editorial instincts, combined to give the *Daily News* a vitality that made it what it remains, the widest-selling newspaper in America.

[Patterson's personal papers and other important material are in the Joseph Medill Patterson Memorial Lib. at the *Daily News* Building. Biographical information is in John William Tebbel, *American Dynasty* (1947); Paul F. Healy, *Cissy* (1966); Oswald Villard, *The Disappearing Daily*; *Time*, June 20, 1938; July 3, 1939; Aug. 24, 1942; *Newsweek*, Jan. 11, 1936; Jack Alexander, "Vox Populi," *New Yorker*, Aug. 6, 13, and 20, 1938; and *Current Biog.*, 1942. Obituaries appeared in *N.Y. Times*, May 27, 1946; *Time*, June 3, 1946; and *Newsweek*, June 3, 1946. Information was also provided by Patterson's daughter Josephine Medill Patterson Albright, and his grandson Joseph Patterson Albright.]

WILLIAM V. SHANNON

PEABODY, LUCY WHITEHEAD (Mar. 2, 1861-Feb. 26, 1949), leader in women's foreign missions organizations, was born in Belmont, Kans. She was the daughter of William McGill, a merchant born in Canada, and Sarah Jane (Hart) McGill, a native of Pittsford, N.Y. The family soon after returned to Pittsford, and in 1872 moved to Rochester. An older brother died very young, but Lucy shared the home with younger sisters and brothers: Helen, Charles, Margaret, and Edgar. She was valedictorian of her class at high school graduation and later taught in the Rochester State School for the Deaf. Then in

August 1881, she married Rev. Norman Waterbury, soon after he graduated from Rochester Theological Seminary. The American Baptist Missionary Union appointed them missionaries to India that summer, and they were stationed at Madras to minister to Telegu-speaking people rather than to the dominant Tamil-speaking population.

Her husband engaged in evangelism, church building, and Bible translation, and Lucy itinerated in the villages and initiated education for children in the Telegu area. Norman Waterbury died of dysentery late in 1886. Lucy returned to Rochester in August 1887 with two of the three children who had been born in India—Norma Rose and Howard Ernest. The third child died during the return voyage.

Lucy Waterbury became assistant secretary of the Woman's American Baptist Foreign Mission Society and moved to Boston in 1889. She succeeded the retiring secretary the next year. Her position brought into light remarkable talents in promotion and administration, made especially visible in building up an efficient voluntary system of Baptist women's societies for education and support on every level from the local to the entire Eastern half of the nation. She established the Farther Lights Society of young girls as an auxiliary in 1890. Christian literature became the subject of prime importance to her. May Leavis became her assistant in this work and remained associated with her for forty years. It was concern for literature which first brought Waterbury into the creation of agencies and organs for co-operative special services.

The World's Missionary Committee of Christian Women was founded in 1888 by Abbie B. Child, secretary of the Woman's Board of Foreign Missions (Congregational). American leaders of that body planned the women's sessions of the Ecumenical Missionary Conference in New York in 1900, in which Waterbury became known nationally and interdenominationally. The committee during the period of the conference met and established the Central Committee for the United Study of Missions. Abbie Child died in 1902, and Lucy Waterbury succeeded her as chairman. She served in that office for twenty-eight years, and then was made honorary chairman. The Central Committee each year published a mission study book used by the several women's denominational boards in the local churches. In order to provide effective teaching of the annual study book and other literature, the Central Committee developed under the personal direction of

Lucy Waterbury and Helen Barrett Montgomery summer schools of missions, eventually numbering about thirty across the nation. The most noted were at Chautauqua, N.Y., and Winona Lake, Ind. After 1910 the committee did its own publishing. The offices, headed by May Leavis, were at West Medford, Mass. The program inspired parallel publication ventures by the Foreign Missions Conference and the Home Missions Council, and eventually all three were merged into the Missionary Education Movement.

Lucy resigned as secretary of the WABFMS to marry on June 16, 1906, Henry Wayland Peabody, a widower. Peabody, a member of a prominent family, was head of an import-export firm and active in Baptist foreign missions. The couple resided at the Peabody home, Parramatta, in Beverly, Mass. Peabody died in December, 1908, leaving his widow with the wealth to devote herself to missionary causes.

The Central Committee was independent, but it reported to the Interdenominational Conference of Woman's Boards of Foreign Missions in the United States and Canada, founded in 1896; and it became the publisher for that conference.

Lucy Peabody played an influential role in developing the Interdenominational Conference into a well-structured body parallel to the Foreign Missions Conference of North America and then in leading it into cooperation with that organization. She established a mission magazine for American children, called *Everyland,* and personally edited and financed it. She then became passionately devoted to providing literature for women and children overseas. She presented to the Interdenominational Conference in 1909 the basic concept that led in 1912 to the formation of the Committee on Christian Literature for Women and Children, with herself as an ex officio member. The committee worked through a commission in the United States and Canada that solicited support from mission boards and gathered material. There were parallel commissions in each major mission land abroad. These bodies selected material, employed translators, and published vernacular magazines for women and for children, such as *Treasure Chest* in India. This committee continues as a department of Inter-media, a functional section of the Division of Overseas Ministries of the National Council of Churches in the U.S.A.

It was Lucy Peabody, with the assistance of Helen Barrett Montgomery, who promoted the jubilee celebration of the American women's foreign mission enterprise in 1910. Forty-two two-day "great jubilees" were held across the country, along with a great number of local meetings in smaller communities. The president gave a reception at the White House. A thank-offering of over $1 million was gathered. Lucy Peabody spoke at nearly all the major meetings. The momentum to cooperation generated by the jubilee led her to take the initiative in transforming the old Interdenominational Conference into the more formal and effective Federation of Woman's Boards of Foreign Missions (1916). This body joined with the Council of Women for Home Missions in creating the United World Day of Prayer, which she had suggested in the 1890's and which is now broadly international. The Central Committee's office in Medford published and distributed the literature. Much of the increasing annual offerings went to women's Christian colleges in Asia, and they were the last great new cause to which she devoted herself. She and Helen Montgomery made an around-the-world trip in 1913 to study the need for such institutions. Then in 1919-1920 the federation sent around the world a commission, chaired by Lucy Peabody, to make a thorough study of the existing schools and need for others. She was chairman of the ensuing financial campaign, and raised $2.9 million. In 1924 she became chairman of the Cooperating Committee for Women's Christian Colleges in Foreign Fields. It gave great stimulus to the development of such institutions as the Woman's Christian College of Madras and Ginling College in Nanking.

While engaged in interdenominational activity, Peabody did not neglect Baptist concerns. When the WABFMS united with its counterpart in the west (Chicago) in 1914, she was elected foreign vice-president. A new independent society, the Association of Baptists for World Evangelism, was organized to support a new mission in the Philippines in 1927. Mrs. Peabody was president during the first seven years. However, she never severed relations with the WABFMS.

During her last few years Mrs. Peabody lived in a retirement home. She died within a week of her eighty-eighth birthday and was interred at Beverly.

[Louise A. Cattan, *Lamps Are For Lighting: The Story of Helen Barrett Montgomery and Lucy Waterbury Peabody* (1972); May H. Leavis, *Henry Wayland Peabody, Merchant* (1909); R. Pierce Beaver, *All Loves Excelling: American Protestant Women in World Mission* (1968); Women's Work Files in the Div. of Overseas Ministries of the Nat. Council of Churches, N.Y.C.; Archives of the Woman's Am. Baptist Foreign Mission Soc. at Baptist headquarters, Valley Forge, Pa.; Annual Reports of the Interdenominational Conference, and its successor the Federation of Woman's Boards of Foreign Missions.]
R. PIERCE BEAVER

PEMBERTON, BROCK (Dec. 14, 1885-Mar. 11, 1950), theatrical director-producer, was born in Leavenworth, Kans., the son of Albert Pemberton and Ella (Murdock) Pemberton. His father, a shoemaker, was a native of Kentucky; his mother's family had migrated from Morgantown, W.Va., to Kansas, where they pioneered in frontier journalism. He had a younger brother, Murdock, and an older sister, Ruth; the journalist Victor Murdock was his first cousin. Although reared in a strict Methodist household, Brock early developed a passion for the forbidden theater. After graduating from the Emporia, Kans., Senior High School in 1902, in entered the College of Emporia, but his prankish behavior forced his withdrawal in 1905. He had written for the *Coffeyville* (Kans.) *Record* and for William Allen White's Emporia *Gazette* during these college years; and while attending the University of Pennsylvania, 1905-1906, he was also employed part-time on the *Philadelphia Bulletin*. White, who had once worked on a Murdock paper, gave him a job on the *Gazette* and financed his studies at the University of Kansas, where Pemberton received the B.A. degree in 1908. White then employed him as reporter and play reviewer on the *Gazette*. In 1910, again with White's encouragement, Pemberton went to New York City. He served as a drama critic on the *Evening Mail,* the *World* (assisting Louis V. DeFoe), and the *Times* (assisting Alexander Woollcott), before becoming press representative for director-producer Arthur Hopkins in 1917. Three years later he abruptly left Hopkins' employ and made his advent as an independent producer with *Enter Madame* (1920), by Gilda Varesi and Dolly Byrne. He received financial backing, chiefly from his cousin, Marcellus Murdock; helped actress-playwright Varesi revise her script; directed it, with her in the title role; and personally provided its stage furnishings —"everything in the Pemberton apartment except Mamie, the maid," according to Woollcott. *Enter Madame* ran 350 performances in New York, was produced in London, perpetuated by stock and touring companies, and reportedly netted Pemberton over $150,000.

His second production, Zona Gale's *Miss Lulu Bett* (1920), divided the New York critics but won the 1921 Pulitzer Prize for drama. Then followed a series of flops that included Sidney Howard's poetic drama *Swords* (1921, thirty-six performances); Maxwell Anderson's ambitious *White Desert* (1923, twelve performances); Zona Gale's *Mr. Pitt* (1924, eighty-seven performances); and Paul Osborn's *Hotbed* (1928, nineteen performances). Also financial failures, although artistic successes, were the plays of Luigi Pirandello, whom Pemberton introduced to the American stage: *Six Characters in Search of an Author* (1922), a "fantastic comedy"; *The Living Mask* (*Enrico IV*, 1924); and *Say It With Flowers* (*L'Uomo, la bestia e la virtu,* 1926). Luigi Chiarelli's *The Mask and the Face* (1924) also failed.

J. Frank Davis' strange reincarnation play *The Ladder* (1926) logged 264 performances to "papered" houses and empty seats. Ransom Rideout's controversial miscegenation drama *Goin' Home* (1928) marked the beginning of Pemberton's association with director Antoinette Perry, who thereafter regularly staged his productions until her death in 1948. Although the play won the Longmans, Green Prize and was cordially received by the critics, the public avoided it. Its failure proved a turning point in Pemberton's outlook: "My policy had been to do a play if I liked it—now I wouldn't do a play unless I was convinced that it would sell to an audience." The practical wisdom of this philosophy was soon made evident. His next production, Preston Sturges' comedy of love and adventure, *Strictly Dishonorable* (1929), ran for 557 performances. Other long-run comedy successes included Lawrence Riley's *Personal Appearance* (1934), Clare Boothe Luce's *Kiss the Boys Goodbye* (1938), Josephine Bentham and Herschel Williams' *Janie* (1942), and Mary Coyle Chase's *Harvey* (1944), the whimsical story of an amiable alcoholic and his friend, a six-foot-tall invisible rabbit, which ran for 1,775 performances and won a Pulitzer Prize. (Pemberton himself briefly played Elwood P. Dowd in *Harvey,* notably at Phoenix, Ariz., shortly before his death.)

"Around Broadway they never give you credit for wanting to do something fine," Pemberton complained in mid-career. "They judge you only by success. If you don't succeed you're a sap" (*Topeka Capital,* Jan. 26, 1930). Twenty years later, he concluded: "Critics now seem to favor a play with a message, while the trend with the public is toward the escapist type of play that makes them laugh and forget their troubles. It's hard to please both" (*Kansas City Times,* March 10, 1950).

Brock Pemberton, a "stoutish man, with a pair of twinkling eyes and a swell, dry sense of humor" (*Boston Globe,* Mar. 22, 1936), not only introduced new dramatists to the stage but advanced the careers of many actors, including George Brent, Joe E. Brown, Claudette Colbert, Florence Eldridge, Frank Fay, Gladys George, Miriam Hopkins, Walter Huston, Fredric March, Robert Montgomery, Osgood Perkins, and Margaret Sullavan. During the 1930's he opposed the 10 percent "nuisance tax" on theater tickets, successfully lobbied for NRA control of ticket speculation, demurred at the Federal Theatre's leftist aesthetic, and inveighed against the Hollywood film industry as "the arch-consumer and destroyer of talent." He produced USO shows and managed "stagedoor canteens" during World War II; wrote periodic Broadway theater summaries for the *New York Times* and journals; and was a lecture-circuit celebrity during 1943-1944. A Republican, he actively supported the successive political campaigns of Alfred Landon, Thomas E. Dewey, and Dwight D. Eisenhower.

On Dec. 30, 1916, Pemberton married Margaret McCoy, a dress designer for Saks and RKO Studios, and a teacher at the New York School of Applied Design, whose costumes were featured in his productions; they had no children. He died of a heart attack in New York City at the age of sixty-four and was buried in Woodlawn Cemetery in New York. For his systematic adherence to a concept of theater as commercial entertainment, he was styled the "dean of American theatrical producers."

[The primary sources are Brock Pemberton's press books, Lib. for the Performing Arts, Lincoln Center, New York City. Among Pemberton's own articles are "Broadway and Main St.," *Theatre Mag.,* Mar. 1926; "The Making of a Play-Producer," *Theatre Mag.,* Jan. 1929; "The Way of a Producer Who Walks Broadway," *Theatre Mag.,* Mar. 1934; and "Hits—And Why They Are," *N.Y. Times Mag.,* Nov. 12, 1939. For reviews of his work, see Francis L. Garside, "He Went 'Astray,'" *Topeka Journal,* Sept. 26, 1920, and "Found Broadway 'Angels' in Wichita," *Kans. City Star,* Dec. 5, 1920; "Pemberton Shows 'Em, Refusing to be a Sap," *Topeka Capital,* Jan. 26, 1930; "Legitimate Stage Is Not Doomed by the Talkies—Pemberton," *Wichita Eagle,* Jan. 1, 1932; Lucius Beebe, "Brock Pemberton and His Associates," *N.Y. Herald-Tribune,* Mar. 24, 1935; Burns Mantle, "Brock Pemberton," *N.Y. Daily News,* July 21, 1935; Elita Wilson, "Brock Pemberton, Critic Turned Producer," *Cue,* Mar. 30, 1935; Bill Doll, "Producer Pemberton's Progress," *N.Y. Times,* Apr. 29, 1945; Murdock Pemberton, "Brock Pemberton, Man of the Theatre," *N.Y. Times,* Mar. 19, 1950; and Ward Morehouse, "Broadway After Dark," *N.Y. Sun,* Feb. 20, 1933; "Producer from Emporia, Kansas," *N.Y. Sun,* Dec.

15, 1949; "Puts Blame on Critics," *Kans. City Times,* Mar. 10, 1950; and "The Man Who Came from Kansas," *N.Y. Sun,* May 15, 1950. Biography in *Current Biog.,* 1945; obituary and information on funeral service and in his will in *N.Y. Times,* Mar. 12, Mar. 13, and Mar. 25, 1950.]

PAT M. RYAN

PEPPER, WILLIAM III (May 1, 1874-Dec. 3, 1947), physician, was the third in a distinguished line of physicians intimately associated with the University of Pennsylvania. His grandfather, William Pepper, was professor of medicine there in 1860-1864; his father, William Pepper, was professor of medicine 1876-1898 and provost of the university in 1880-1894. William Pepper III was the first of four sons of William Pepper II and Frances Sergeant (Perry) Pepper, a descendant of Oliver Hazard Perry. Young Pepper took his bachelor's degree at the University of Pennsylvania in 1894 and the doctorate in medicine in 1897.

As a young physician in Philadelphia he became interested in the pathology of the white blood cells and in 1901 published two articles on the subject written with Alfred Stengel, in the *University of Pennsylvania Gazette.* Appointed assistant professor of clinical pathology in 1907, he continued for some years the study of diseases of the blood and the heart, and in 1910 published jointly with F. O. Klaer the small *Manual of Clinical Laboratory Methods* (second edition with John A. Kolmer in 1920), which was long used in the University of Pennsylvania School of Medicine. In 1912 he was appointed dean of the school.

For some years the medical schools of the United States had been going through a critical period of reform and reorganization, brought to a head by a report of Abraham Flexner to the Carnegie Foundation for the Advancement of Education, *Medical Education in the United States and Canada* (1910). The University of Pennsylvania's School of Medicine, the oldest in the country and one of the most conservative, had undergone a thorough reorganization with the advent of several brilliant young men to fill time-honored professorships. The changes had left a good deal of discontent among the older faculty members. Pepper's firmness, coupled with his kindness and sincerity, made him a suitable choice for leadership in such a situation; in the thirty-three years of his deanship he won and retained the friendship of the faculty and was loved by the students. He was a tall man of distinguished appearance, slow and slightly awkward in his movements.

Pepper taught clinical pathology until 1919 but thereafter devoted his full time to the work of the dean's office. He greatly encouraged the development of strong departments of anatomy, physiology, pathology, pharmacology, and biochemistry. During his term of office, women were admitted as students (1914). The curriculum was extensively revised and the size of medical classes reduced, in conformity with advancing educational standards. A new wing was added to the great Medical Laboratories Building, and the school's library was given new and ample quarters. The Medico-Chirurgical College and the Philadelphia Polyclinic were merged with the university and close affiliation was effected with the Children's Hospital, the Orthopedic Hospital, and the psychiatric division of the Pennsylvania Hospital (Institute of Mental Hygiene). Pepper's responsibilities for major policy-making were somewhat lightened after 1928 by a reorganization of the university that placed vice-presidents at the head of the several divisions of the faculty, one of which comprised the schools of medicine, dentistry, and veterinary medicine; but there were duties and problems enough within the medical school to employ fully Pepper's special gift for harmonious leadership under such eminent vice-presidents for medical affairs as Alfred Stengel and A. N. Richards.

During World War I, Pepper was commanding officer, with the rank of lieutenant colonel, in the United States Army Medical Corps at Base Hospital 74, organized and largely manned by the University of Pennsylvania for service in France. In 1920-1921 he was president of the Association of American Medical Colleges. He was a trustee of the University of Pennsylvania from 1942 until his death.

Always interested in the history of medicine, Pepper published several articles on historical topics, including an introduction to a 1931 reprint of Benjamin Franklin's *Proposals Relating to the Education of Youth in America* and a small but thoroughly documented book, *The Medical Side of Franklin* (1911); he was a direct descendant of Franklin. His principal hobbies were nature study and fishing; he banded thousands of wild birds to record their migratory movements and was usually absent from his office on the first day of the trout-fishing season.

On Dec. 21, 1904, Pepper married Mary Godfrey, who died in 1918; on Apr. 3, 1922, he married Phoebe S. (Voorhees) Drayton.

There were three children by the first marriage, Mrs. Mary Pepper Parker, Dr. D. Sergeant Pepper, and William Pepper, Jr. Dr. Pepper died in Philadelphia, of an arteriosclerotic disease, and was buried in East Laurel Hill Cemetery in that city.

[The major sources are Alfred N. Richards, "In Memory of William Pepper, III, *Pennsylvania Gazette,* Apr. 1948, pp. 4–7; Isaac Starr, "Memoir of William Pepper III," *Trans. Coll. of Physicians,* Phila., Ser. 4, vol. 16, 1948–1949, pp. 123–124; George W. Corner, *Two Centuries of Medicine* (1965); and *N.Y. Times,* Dec. 4, 1947.]

GEORGE W. CORNER

PERKINS, MAXWELL EVARTS (Sept. 20, 1884–June 17, 1947), editor, was born in New York City, the second of the four sons and six children of Edward Clifford Perkins and Elizabeth Hoar (Evarts) Perkins; he was christened William Maxwell Evarts Perkins. Van Wyck Brooks, a lifelong friend, once said of Perkins that he knew few other Americans in whom "so much history was palpably and visibly embodied." Perkins' great-great-grandfather, Roger Sherman, had signed the Declaration of Independence for Connecticut, and William Maxwell Evarts, the grandfather for whom he was named, was a United States senator who had been attorney general under President Andrew Johnson and secretary of state under Rutherford B. Hayes. His other grandfather, Charles Callahan Perkins, a descendant of Boston merchants, was a noted art critic and a friend of Browning, Motley, Landor, Lowell, and Longfellow. Thus Maxwell Perkins' aesthetic strain was grounded in a tradition of statesmanship, and his sense of a deep ancestral stake in his country governed his career.

Although brought up in Plainfield, N.J., a short commute from New York City, where his father practiced law, Perkins had Yankee roots. His favorite haunt was the family seat in Windsor, Vt., where his boyhood summers were spent and where he returned throughout his life for refreshment and renewal. Perkins attended Leal's School in Plainfield and then, despite his family's financial straits following his father's sudden death in 1902, managed to go on to Harvard. Characteristically, he majored in economics because he much preferred literature courses and his New England conscience told him medicine should taste bad to do him any good. After graduating in 1907, he wangled a reporting job with the *New York Times.* He loved the adventurousness of journalism but quit it in February 1910 to become book advertising manager for the old-line publishing firm of Charles Scribner's Sons. On December 31 of that year he married Louise Saunders of Plainfield, who was to bear him five daughters: Bertha Saunders, Elizabeth Evarts, Louise Elvire, Jane Morton, and Nancy Galt.

When Scribners transferred Perkins to the editorial department in 1914, it was at once apparent that he had found his métier, and before long he was made a director and secretary of the corporation. By the close of World War I he was for all intents and purposes executive editor, though he still deferred to William Crary Brownell, dean of American critics and the firm's "literary advisor." Nevertheless, Perkins had a comparatively free hand at this turning point in American letters, for the renaissance heralded by such realists as Theodore Dreiser, Sherwood Anderson, and Carl Sandburg had gained momentum with the war. A new outlook, a new energy had widened the range of artistic possibilities, and, his latent daring now asserting itself, Perkins felt it his mission to seek out the freshly emerging talents and bring them together with their public.

This phase of his career began in 1920 with F. Scott Fitzgerald, whose *This Side of Paradise* Perkins persuaded Scribners to publish against the better judgment of other editors. He overcame a similar resistance among his colleagues when Ring Lardner submitted his first book of stories and Ernest Hemingway his first novel, *The Sun Also Rises.* Perkins' clairvoyance became a legend after he accepted from Thomas Wolfe the manuscript for *Look Homeward, Angel,* considered hopeless by the other publishers who had seen it. Posterity identifies Perkins with a handful of authors whose works have become modern classics, but during his life this eclectic with the nose for good writing played ringmaster to a wide variety of talents. He found what he was looking for in the ex-cowboy Will James no less than in James Boyd, author of *Drums,* who rode to hounds. One of his coups was the former art critic Willard Huntington Wright, who as "S. S. Van Dine" broke the sales record for detective fiction with his Philo Vance series. Equally successful with women writers despite a pose of misogyny, Perkins presided over the careers of Marcia Davenport, Nancy Hale, Taylor Caldwell, Christine Weston, and Marjorie Kinnan Rawlings, to cite only the best known.

A courtly, seemingly withdrawn yet listening man of patrician good looks, Perkins was a unique blend of the Puritan and the artist, of granite and warmth, of shrewdness and imagination. He had an uncanny knack of putting himself in his authors' places and visualizing their problems from the inside, and he trusted intuition to the point of discouraging advance summaries of novels as too inhibiting. Yet for all his identification with the artist, Perkins was no visionary, but a hardheaded realist with a sound grasp of the business end of publishing and a sagacity about what would and would not sell. Though he respected solid workmanship of the popular, less durable sort and fostered the narrative gift wherever he found it, his passion was the literary art, especially fiction. He had hoped to play a role, however modest, in seeing America revealed in a novel as Tolstoy had revealed Russia in *War and Peace*—for Perkins the masterpiece of all times. His reign at Scribners coincided with a literary renaissance that turned up other excellent editors, to be sure, but none who combined his cultural quality with his fine point and touch, none who responded with such subtlety and exactness to a multiplicity of challenges. An Episcopalian in his youth, Perkins drifted away from formal religion in later years, his spirituality expressing itself in a feeling for nature and for the sublimities of great literature. He died of pneumonia in Stamford, Conn., at the age of sixty-two, and was buried at Lakeview Cemetery in New Canaan, Conn., where he had made his home for twenty-three years.

[The principal primary source is Perkins' correspondence with authors in the files of Charles Scribner's Sons, Princeton Univ. Lib. A published selection of his letters, *Editor to Author* (1950), has a perceptive introduction by his colleague John Hall Wheelock. Perkins contributed an autobiographical account to the 3rd *Report* (1913) of the Harvard College Class of 1907 and wrote three self-revealing essays on Thomas Wolfe (*Carolina Mag.*, Oct. 1938; *Wings*, Oct. 1939; *Harvard Lib. Bull.*, Autumn 1947) and one on Ernest Hemingway (*Book-of-the-Month Club News*, Oct. 1940). See also Van Wyck Brooks's chapter on Perkins in *Scenes and Portraits* (1954); Wolfe's portrayal of Perkins as Foxhall Edwards in *You Can't Go Home Again* (1940); Malcolm Cowley's profile in the *New Yorker*, Apr. 1, 8, 1944; and Struthers Burt's memoir, "Catalyst for Genius," *Saturday Rev.*, June 9, 1951. Chs. vi, viii, and x of Andrew Turnbull's *Thomas Wolfe* (1968) contain a biographical portrait of Perkins based on extensive interviews.]

ANDREW TURNBULL

PERRY, ANTOINETTE (June 27, 1888-June 28, 1946), actress and stage director, was born in Denver, Colo., the only child of William Russell Perry, an attorney, and Minnie Betsy (Hall) Perry; she was named

Mary Antoinette. Her maternal grandfather, Charles L. Hall, a native of Sherman, N.Y., had come to Colorado by wagon train during the Pike's Peak gold rush of 1859; he was a member of the territorial legislature and, later, the state senate and amassed a fortune from mining and investments in gas utilities. Her grandmother Mary Melissa (Hill) Hall initiated the teaching of Christian Science in Colorado in 1886.

During holidays from high school studies at Miss Wolcott's School in Denver, Antoinette gained introduction to the professional stage by traveling with an aunt, the actress Mildred Hall, and the latter's actor husband, George Wessells, on cross-country tours. She made her acting debut as Dorothy, supporting William Morris, in *Mrs. Temple's Telegram* at Powers' Theatre, Chicago, on June 26, 1905, and was first seen in New York as Mrs. Frank Fuller in the same play at the Madison Square Theatre later that season. She subsequently supported Hilda Spong in *Lady Jim* (1906) and David Warfield in *The Music Master* (1906-1907, 1908-1909) and *A Grand Army Man* (1907-1908).

Following her marriage on Nov. 30, 1909, to Frank Wheatcroft Frueauff, president of the Denver Gas and Electric Company, Antoinette Perry retired from the stage for over fourteen years. Frueauff's junior partnership in Henry L. Doherty and Company (he was also vice-president of Cities Service Company and a director of 141 corporations) called the couple eastward to reside in Manhattan, where Mrs. Frueauff became a prominent patron of the arts and was an active promoter of World War I liberty bond campaigns. The marriage produced three daughters: Margaret Hall, Virginia Day (who died in infancy), and Elaine Storrs. Both surviving daughters early followed stage careers, Margaret Perry making her debut at the age of sixteen in the ingenue lead of *Strictly Dishonorable* and Elaine Perry gaining eminence for her production of *Anastasia* (1954-1955).

In January 1924, eighteen months after Frank Frueauff's death, Antoinette Perry returned to the New York stage as Rachel Arrowsmith, supporting Walter Huston, in Zona Gale's *Mr. Pitt*. She afterward played Lil Corey in *Minick* (1924); Ma Huckle in *The Dunce Boy* (1925); Belinda Treherne in the Stagers' updated revival of *Engaged* (1925); Judy Ross in *Caught* (1925), Sophia Weir in *The Masque of Venice* (1926); Margaret in the long-running—with "papered" houses—reincarnation drama *The Ladder* (1926-1927); and Clytemnestra, supporting Margaret Anglin, in Sophocles' *Electra* (1927). Recapitulating these years, Alan Downer characterized the actress as "a small, fair woman with a patrician profile, her gentle, feminine manner complemented by a beautiful speaking voice and spiced by a wicked sense of humor" (vol. III, p. 53).

Perry is best remembered for her gifted and versatile stage direction, an art she contemplated "in terms of architecture, which is movement—of ballet, of music, of emphasis" (*New York Times,* March 14, 1937). Her directing work, during nearly two decades, was principally in association with Brock Pemberton, the producer-director of *Mr. Pitt, The Masque of Venice,* and *The Ladder.* Their cordial collaboration began with Ransom Rideout's miscegenation drama *Goin' Home* (of which Pemberton was producer and codirector), premiered at the Hudson Theatre, New York, Aug. 23, 1928. Their first joint success was Preston Sturges' "saucy little comedy of youth and speakeasies," *Strictly Dishonorable,* which opened Sept. 18, 1929, scored a New York run of 557 performances, and dispatched several touring companies. Notably successful among more than a score of additional Perry-Pemberton enterprises were *Personal Appearance* (1934), *Ceiling Zero* (1935), *Kiss the Boys Goodbye* (1938), *Lady in Waiting* (1940), *Janie* (1942), and *Harvey* (1944).

Through skillful rewriting and resourceful stagecraft, Mary Coyle Chase's fantasy-comedy *Harvey* was nurtured from an unready, unpromising script—which Perry at first despaired of staging—into a triumph for its author (who won the Pulitzer Prize for drama), director, producer, and principals. It played 1,775 consecutive performances at the Forty-eighth Street Theatre, New York; achieved a forty-three-week run in Chicago; and was later to receive admirable productions on film and television. Under American Theatre Wing auspices, Perry's restaging of *The Barretts of Wimpole Street,* featuring Katharine Cornell and Brian Aherne, played to Allied military audiences in Europe during 1944-1945.

Pemberton recalled Perry as "an individualist who met life head on, who dramatized life, who gave of a great and generous nature" (*New York Times,* July 7, 1946). As chairman of the American Theatre Council's Committee of the Apprentice Theatre (1937-1939) and president of Actors Equity's Experimental Theatre (1941), she auditioned and advanced many young performing-arts aspirants, including Montgomery Clift, Hugh Marlowe, and David Wayne. She was also a founder and chairman (1941-1944) of the American Theatre Wing War Service, which sponsored hospital entertainment and maintained servicemen's stagedoor canteens in several cities; a trustee of the Actors' Fund; a supporter of the Musicians Emergency Fund; and a member of the Daughters of the American Revolution, the Dramatists Guild, the League of New York Theatres, the Society of Mayflower Descendants, the Republican party, and other organizations. She remained a lifelong Christian Scientist.

She died of a heart attack at her home, 510 Park Avenue, New York, and was buried in Woodlawn Cemetery, New York, beside her husband. In 1947, in commemoration of her generous service to the profession and its younger members, the American Theatre Wing inaugurated its annual presentation of Antoinette Perry Awards ("Tonys") for distinguished performances, stage direction, production, and design, dramatic and musical composition, and other achievements. These ceremonies, telecast nationwide, have since become the culminating event of each Broadway season.

[The Theatre Collection of the Lib. of the Performing Arts at Lincoln Center (N.Y.) is the principal repository of Perry materials; the same collection's Brock Pemberton papers are an important auxiliary resource. Most useful are Perry's "You Want to Go on the Stage," in Bernard Sobel, ed., *The Theatre Handbook* (1940); Wilbur F. Stone, *Hist. of Colo.,* IV, 206–212 (1919), on the Hall family; *N.Y. Times,* Aug. 1, 1922 (obituary of Frueauff); Mar. 14, 1937; June 29, 1946 (obituary of Perry); July 7, 1946 (Pemberton, "Memories of Antoinette"); Percy N. Stone, in *N.Y. Herald Tribune,* July 12, 1925; Helen Ormsbee, *ibid.,* June 12, 1938; *Who Was Who in Am.* (1950); *Nat Cyc. Amer. Biog.* XXXVII, 107; Alan S. Downer, in *Notable Am. Women,* III (1971).]

PAT M. RYAN

PERSHING, JOHN JOSEPH (Sept. 13, 1860-July 15, 1948), general of the armies of the United States, commander of the American Expeditionary Force in World War I, was born near Laclede, Mo., the first of six children of John Frederick Pershing and Anne (Thompson) Pershing. His father, descended from Alsatian Huguenots (the family name originally was Pfoershing), was a member of the Methodist Episcopal church. After working as a railroad sectionman, John Frederick Pershing became a minor merchant in Laclede.

Young John's early days were filled with alarms of the Civil War, since Missouri was sundered along ideological lines, causing friends to become enemies even in the smallest communities. Confederate partisans attacked Laclede in June 1864, and John watched the raiders pillage and terrorize his neighbors. After the war some prosperity eased life for the Pershings, but education for the growing family was piecemeal. Mrs. Pershing taught as best she could, her efforts supplemented by good books and an occasional teacher who took pupils at home. Young Pershing ("Jack" to his family) proved a selective learner, doing well in subjects he liked; but he did absorb something of his mother's respect for learning. Furthermore, education was a passport to the world beyond Missouri, and the possibility of escape lent incentive to his studies. Jack soon found himself teaching in country schools—when, that is, he was not obligated to work on the farm that his father had bought after selling his store. The panic of 1873 virtually broke the Pershings. Even with Jack helping his father in the fields and teaching, the family fortunes dwindled. At last, all but the house was gone; Jack's father became a traveling salesman and left his oldest son to hold the family intact. Jack's dreams of a college education went with the savings, and little beyond country teaching and odd-jobbing loomed in his future. Yet he managed to save tuition money from his $35 monthly wage and in 1879 entered the State Normal School in Kirksville, Mo.

Normal schools then offered solid work in mathematics, Latin, and other formal subjects, along with lessons in methods and classroom discipline. A year's study renewed his zest for learning. Introduced to systematic reading, he found a stern beauty in Blackstone and Kent; they touched a yearning in a precise and questing mind and made the law a lasting ambition. He went back to teaching to earn tuition money and then returned to Kirksville in 1881 for a full year's study. But the year was suddenly cut short by opportunity: a newspaper announcement of competitive examinations for admission to the United States Military Academy opened a new avenue toward college education and perhaps a new life.

To his own surprise, the tall, sober Missourian won admission to the plebe (freshman) class in 1882. Once through the storied gates of "the Point," Pershing changed. The challenge of soldiering intrigued him, and the routines of ragging, regimentation, marching, studying, riding, and learning the courtesies and rights of rank became second nature to him. He did well in things military and became probably the most soldierly man in his class. Mathematics came easily enough, and even the vagaries of English grammar. History and law were consumed with gusto. French and Spanish lessons were definitely not to his taste, but he finally struggled through them.

Each of his years at the Point found him rewarded with cadet offices—corporal; sergeant; and then for his first class year, the most coveted rank of all, first captain. This office came to the best man in general faculty and cadet esteem and, coupled with election to life presidency of his class, left a lasting mark on him. The responsibility was never forgotten.

Pershing stood thirtieth in a class of seventy-seven. Following graduation in June 1886, he joined the Sixth Cavalry at Fort Bayard, N.Mex., in the wake of Geronimo's capture, just in time for ragtag little skirmishes with a disappearing foe. Five years of service at remote stations in harsh plains country stretched into vast boredom broken rarely by alarm, by some random Indian "breakout," by maneuver or training patrol, or by "hops" and hunts. Pershing often was bored, sometimes doubted his future in an army that was ridden with politics and plagued by public mistrust, and rarely granted promotions.

In 1891 the Sixth Cavalry joined in Gen. Nelson A. Miles's campaign to prevent a great Sioux war; although not in the fight at Wounded Knee Creek, Pershing participated in mopping up after the battle. In the wake of that shabby finish to the independent history of a proud people, Pershing took command of a company of Sioux scouts—it was one of the army's "noble experiments" that worked. Both the Sioux and Pershing learned affection and respect for each other; the experience taught the young officer that men should be judged for what they do.

A brief stay at Fort Niobrara, Nebr., ended with Pershing's appointment, on Sept. 25, 1891, as professor of military science and tactics, commandant of the university battalion, and teacher of fencing at the University of Nebraska, in Lincoln. He coveted the Lincoln assignment. The university town was unusually cosmopolitan for a frontier community. Chancellor James H. Canfield liked his new officer, gave him extra work as a mathematics teacher, and invited him often to a stimulating household. There, as well as in his mathematics classes, Pershing became increasingly impressed with the chancellor's daughter, Dorothy, and her friend, Willa Cather. There, too, Roscoe

Pound and others of a sprightly intellectual group gathered. In Lincoln, Pershing also met Charles Dawes, a struggling young businessman soon destined for a high place in the Republican party; was given free use of William Jennings Bryan's library; and talked law with his friend Charles Magoon. He also used his time at the university to take a law degree in 1893, an achievement that tempted him briefly to consider resigning from the army. But Dawes, Magoon, and others talked him into staying in uniform—he had special talents for soldiering.

Pershing's success with the Nebraska Cadet Battalion became legendary after he carried them to victory in national drill competition in Omaha in June 1892. So strictly did he train his men that the Nebraska contingent won recognition as second only to West Point's cadets in proficiency. Pershing reaped official credit but no promotion. He left Nebraska for field duty in October 1895, in time to help round up scattered groups of Cree Indians in Montana 'and deport them to Canada.

Luck helped him again. In 1896, while at Fort Assiniboine, Mont., he took Gen. Miles and some friends on a hunting trip in the Bear Paw Mountains. Friendship began and endured. Miles called him to duty at the headquarters of the army in December, where a handsome, educated aide could be politically and socially useful. From Washington, Pershing went to West Point as instructor of tactics in June 1897.

In the confines of barracks, the old ramrod stiffness returned to Pershing, and he became disliked as a "tac," or instructor. So poor was his reputation that cadets sought derisive names for him and hit on "Black Jack." It stemmed from his service with the Negro Tenth Cavalry in Montana and his obvious devotion to the regiment. But it also meant uncommon toughness to restive young men. The name stuck.

Unhappy at West Point, Pershing sought help from George D. Meiklejohn, a Lincoln friend who had become assistant secretary of war. Meiklejohn listened willingly to a plea for field service in the coming war with Spain.

On May 5, 1898, 1st Lt. Pershing (he had been promoted by reassignment to the Tenth Cavalry in October 1892) received orders to join his regiment at Chickamauga, Ga. He went with it to Cuba, where he took a prominent part in the battles of San Juan and Kettle hills and in operations around Santiago. Reckless bravery under repeated exposure to enemy fire won him praise from Col. T. A. Baldwin,

Tenth Cavalry commander, as "the coolest man under fire I ever saw." Baldwin unsuccessfully recommended a brevet promotion for "personal gallantry, untiring energy and faithfulness in battle."

Upon Pershing's return to the United States in August, he was shifted to the volunteers with the rank of major and assigned to army headquarters. Soon his law degree brought him a call to the office of the assistant secretary of war. Meiklejohn wrestled with problems of governing the United States' newly won colonial empire and asked Pershing to take charge of the Bureau of Insular Affairs, a new division within the War Department. In that post Pershing shaped early policies of military government and set the tone of American occupation in foreign lands. By the time the assignment ended in September 1899 with his request for Philippine duty, he had gained wide experience in managing foreign peoples and governments and in assimilating strange customs and legal codes.

As adjutant general of the District of Zamboanga and of the Department of Mindanao, Philippines, in the twilight of the Filipino insurrection, Pershing encountered at first hand the problems he had handled by proxy from Washington. His competence and tact impressed superiors. Promoted to captain in the regular army on Feb. 2, 1901, and dropped from volunteer rolls, Pershing soon had an independent command on Mindanao. There the fierce Moros controlled most of the interior and had successfully resisted all opposition for generations. Operations against them had wrecked many careers, and regular officers diligently shunned the territory. But Pershing used his appreciation of Indians and blacks to win the trust of Moros, fought them when he had to—especially around Lake Lanao— with Moro-like tenacity, and in fighting and in governing this warlike people won the admiration of his superiors and the public.

Called home for service with the General Staff in 1903, Pershing attended the Army War College in 1904-1905. In February 1905, after a much-publicized marriage to Frances Warren, daughter of Sen. Francis Warren of Wyoming (a member of the Senate Committee on Military Affairs) on Jan. 26, Pershing was named military attaché in Japan and hence became official American observer of the Russo-Japanese War. His dispatches from the war zone won President Theodore Roosevelt's admiration; these, combined with his Philippine achievements, induced Roosevelt to nominate

Captain Pershing for promotion to brigadier general. Pershing was promoted on Sept. 20, 1906, over more than 800 superiors in the army.

Promotion took him again to the Philippines, where he remained, with some time out for home and European service, until 1914. As commander of the Department of Mindanao and governor of the Moro Province, he fought hard battles at Bagsak Mountain and won, and encouraged internal improvements and agricultural innovations. No other American administrator displayed affection and understanding to equal Pershing's, and when he was recalled to permanent assignment in the United States in 1914, the Moros mourned his departure.

After being stationed briefly in San Francisco, until April 1914, he was assigned to Fort Bliss, Tex., and became entangled in Mexican border problems. While he was at Fort Bliss, he left his family—now consisting of Frances; three daughters, Helen, Anne, Mary; and a son, Warren—at the Presidio (headquarters of the 8th Brigade) in San Francisco. A fire swept their quarters on Aug. 27, 1915, and all but Warren died. This tragedy quenched much of Pershing's spirit, and made him a stiffly taciturn man. Crisis on the border helped him turn from his loss to concern with Pancho Villa.

Villa raided Columbus, N.Mex., in March 1916, and President Wilson ordered retribution. Gen. Frederick Funston, in charge of the United States Southern Department, selected Pershing to command a punitive expedition to pursue Villa into Mexico and destroy him and his bandits. No American general ever commanded under tighter restrictions. Americans were permitted to use only north-south highways; railroads were not to be used. Entry into Mexican towns depended on approval by local government officials. Engagements were to be avoided except when faced by Villa's men. Nothing was to disturb the uneasy stability of relations between the United States and Venustiano Carranza's government.

Pershing led a force of infantry, cavalry, and artillery bolstered by such innovations as airplanes, a field radio unit, and machine-gun companies. He tested untried American weapons in untried combinations—tests that took on new urgency in the shadow of war in Europe. Although privately restive he kept firmly to proscriptions, talked to avoid confrontations with government troops—war could have followed such episodes as Carrizal, Parral, or Ojos Azules—and minimized tension. From

Mar. 16, 1916, until Feb. 6, 1917, United States troops sought Villa. He was never caught, but the relentless quest broke his power.

Pershing's ability to subordinate himself to his duty caught President Wilson's and Secretary of War Newton Baker's notice. Strict obedience, professional competence, and unswerving loyalty were essential in a general, especially in one considered for high command. Upon Funston's death in mid-February 1917, Pershing took command of the Southern Department, with headquarters at San Antonio. In April the United States declared war on the Central Powers, and in May 1917 Pershing received orders to go to Washington. Senator Warren hinted to him that an important assignment was in the offing. Arrival in the capital and hasty conferences with the chief of staff and Secretary Baker led at last to a curiously brief interview with the president, who said, "General, we are giving you some very difficult tasks these days." Pershing replied, "Perhaps so, Mr. President, but that is what we are trained to expect."

Even Pershing did not expect the command he received. On May 26, 1917, he was made commander of the American Expeditionary Forces (AEF), with authority to use them as he saw fit under one restriction: they were to constitute a separate American army.

Reaching England in early June, Pershing found the Allies virtually defeated. The curtailment of shipping had cut all supplies to dangerously low levels; morale had sagged among civilians, although it seemed good among the troops. Pershing's presence lifted French morale, but American divisions were needed immediately. Three years of stalemate in the trenches, three years of a seesaw struggle along 400 miles of pocked, mud-sogged ditches had killed whole armies, devastated huge areas, and, at last, brought mutiny in French ranks. Fresh German divisions freed from the eastern front by the withdrawal of Russia from the war might suddenly win the war. Pershing recognized trench fatigue, the malaise of being constantly on the defensive. He insisted on training his men for open field operations; he insisted that victory came with initiative.

British commander Sir Douglas Haig joined French Marshal Henri Pétain in urging the stern American general to put his men into existing Allied divisions, where they could be trained while helping to hold the line; but Pershing resisted all such efforts. Following orders, he insisted on a separate American army against rising pressure in France. Nothing moved the stubborn Missourian. But he offered his troops to French commanders without restriction in the March crisis of 1918, and in the hard drives of the spring, American units played a crucial role in halting the Germans at the Marne. Bloody fighting at Cantigny, in Belleau Wood, and Château Thierry baptized Americans in the realities of modern warfare, and they acquitted themselves well. German observers noted American marksmanship an art all but lost in the hail of firepower along the western front. Accurate rifle fire killed infantry at long range in great numbers.

Slowly Pershing organized, and on Sept. 12, 1918, the United States First Army launched an attack against the powerful Saint-Mihiel salient. In late September the salient was gone, and Pershing shifted his army to join the giant Allied offensive in the Meuse-Argonne —in a logistical triumph. On September 26 the American attack—using planes, infantry, tanks, and artillery in novel concert—began. It ran into bitter resistance. While the Americans ground forward, the Allied forces struggled on until the German line collapsed. With the armistice on Nov. 11, 1918, active fighting ended.

Pershing wanted to drive the enemy to Berlin, to show no mercy. He voiced his views before the Supreme Allied War Council, was ignored and somewhat resented, realized that diplomacy was not a soldier's province, and devoted himself to getting the AEF home. Remaining with remnants of his army for a year, he visited departing divisions and insisted on good discipline until the last.

In September 1919 he returned to the United States as America's most famous general. Rank had come swiftly (major general, Sept. 26, 1916; general, Oct. 6, 1917) but the crowning glory he knew en route home: on Sept. 3 he was named general of the armies. This rank, once held by George Washington, conferred honor as well as power. And when, on July 1, 1921, he became chief of staff, his military achievements exceeded those of anyone before him.

Pershing retired (as much as a general of the armies could retire) on Sept. 13, 1924— his sixty-fourth birthday. As chairman of the American Battle Monuments Commission, he devoted himself to maintaining the memory of his "boys." President Calvin Coolidge appointed him, in 1925, head of the Tacna-Arica Plebiscitary Commission, whose dubious task it was to settle a lingering boundary dispute between Peru and Chile. Almost a year he struggled there without success; at length ill health called him from a rare defeat.

In 1931 he published *My Experiences in the World War,* which won the Pulitzer Prize for history. Honors were heaped lavishly on him, and he bore them as befitted a West Point first captain, whose entire life typified the motto of his school—"Duty, Honor, Country." When war came anew in Europe, Pershing addressed the people of the United States in support of President Roosevelt's destroyers-for-bases plan with England and watched in anguish as his old friend Pétain was ostracized for collaboration with the Nazis. From invalid quarters at Walter Reed Hospital in Washington, D.C., he counseled his old staff officer, George Marshall, on the conduct of global war. With pride he saw American arms succeed again. He died of old age and heart failure and was buried at Arlington National Cemetery.

As a strategist, Pershing rarely attempted grand combinations but practiced the art with a close eye to objective, surprise, concentration, and rigid devotion to logistics. As a tactician, he ably worked grand tactics in the Philippines, in Mexico, and especially in France: his use of the Third Division at Château Thierry, his combined arms and limited attack at Saint-Mihiel, and the well-organized general assault he launched in the Meuse-Argonne reflect mastery of tactics at all levels.

Perhaps he cannot be measured entirely as a field commander. He came to prominence with a new breed of war leaders. Managers of personnel, supply, money, and firepower were needed more than bold and dashing battle commanders. Already tested in combat, Pershing knew its challenges. When combat grew to international dimensions, he grew with the demand into the first of the really modern generals. Methods he instituted were models for Marshall, MacArthur, and Eisenhower in World War II. Pershing's career spanned sixty years of military change. He was an architect and a product of that change. From him came ideas of officer education that molded the modern staff school system. From him came concepts of integrity of force, of overall command, which solved some coalition problems for his successors. His greatest achievement is the modern American army—an army he molded, trained, tested in its infancy; nurtured in its adolescence; and watched proudly in its fullest triumph, an army he loved always. He ranks as one of America's greatest generals but especially as one of her greatest soldiers.

[Pershing's extensive collection of papers is housed in the Lib. of Cong. Important biographies are Avery DeLano Andrews, *My Friend and Classmate, John J. Pershing* (1939); editors of the *Army Times, The Yanks Are Coming: The Story of General John J. Pershing* (1960); George MacAdam, "The Life of General Pershing," in *The World's Work*, vols. XXXVII-XXXIX (1918–1919); Richard O'Connor, *Black Jack Pershing* (1961); Frederick Palmer, *John J. Pershing, General of the Armies* (1948); Donald Smythe, *Guerilla Warrior* (1973); and Everett T. Tomlinson, *The Story of General Pershing* (1919).

Pershing's role in the Philippines is covered in W. Cameron Forbes, *The Philippine Islands* (2 vols., 1928), and T. J. Fleming, "Pershing's Island War," *Am. Heritage*, 19 (1968). Pershing's command of the punitive expedition against Pancho Villa is covered in Clarence C. Clenenden, *The United States and Pancho Villa* (1961); Herbert Molloy Mason, Jr., *The Great Pursuit* (1970); William H. Nelson and Frank E. Vandiver, *Fields of Glory* (1960); Frank Tompkins, *Chasing Villa* (1934); and H. A. Toulmin, *With Pershing in Mexico* (1935).

Pershing's memoirs are the best source for his own part in World War I, even though Pershing is characteristically nonautobiographical there. His *Final Report* (1920) is officially laconic. Details of his activities are left to other chroniclers. Perhaps the best summary of Pershing's role as commander of the AEF is contained in Laurence Stallings, *The Doughboys* (1963). Important recent additions to the story are Edward M. Coffman, *The War to End All Wars* (1968); and Harvey A. DeWeerd, *President Wilson Fights His War* (1968). Periodical literature on Pershing's role as AEF commander bulks beyond imagination. For a recent view of Wilson-Pershing relations, see F. E. Vandiver, "Commander-in-chief-Commander Relationships: Wilson and Pershing," *Rice Univ. Studies*, 57 (1971).

Finally, a bibliography of works about John J. Pershing must include mention of the invaluable Oral History Collect. at Columbia Univ., New York, which contains interviews with many of Pershing's contemporaries who recalled him with the immediacy of association.]

FRANK E. VANDIVER

PFUND, AUGUST HERMAN (Dec. 28, 1879–Jan. 4, 1949), physicist, was born in Madison, Wis., the eldest of at least five children of Hermann Pfund and Anna (Scheibel) Pfund. His father, a prosperous attorney, had emigrated from Switzerland in 1857 and had taught school before turning to the law. August attended Madison public schools and the University of Wisconsin, from which he received a B.S. degree in 1901. He then studied physics at Johns Hopkins University under Prof. Robert W. Wood, whom he had known at Wisconsin, earning his Ph.D. in 1906. He remained at Hopkins for the rest of his professional career, beginning in 1906 as assistant in physics, rising to professor (1927), and serving as head of the physics department from 1938 until his retirement in 1947.

Pfund chose as his principal field of research the infrared region of the electromagnetic spectrum, at that time a laboratory curiosity with little or no commercial use. His task was difficult, for he faced an almost complete lack of basic data. How do you make an infrared spectrometer if you don't know how to make a prism that will work in the infrared, don't know the refractive index of the crystals available as prism material, don't know how to make a detector or how to calibrate the detector? Advancing gradually on all fronts, using simple equipment, much of which he built himself, Pfund established, year by year, new benchmarks fundamental to the growth of infrared technology. He discovered new ways of producing infrared radiation, as well as methods of measuring its intensity, wavelength, and polarization. He also explored the behaviors of a great variety of solids, liquids, and gases in absorbing, reflecting, and refracting such radiation. He measured the spectral and total emissivities of hot bodies such as hot wires and molten metals. Working with one of his students, he discovered, by infrared spectrography, two of the five main series of lines of the hydrogen spectrum—sometimes called the Pfund atomic hydrogen series.

Pfund's research established a firm foundation for the later rapid expansion of man's understanding of infrared radiation and for its application in fields as diverse as chemistry, astronomy, medicine, communications, industry, and military science. He himself took some interest in practical applications of his findings. He invented, for example, gold-coated glasses that would screen out ultraviolet and infrared radiation while remaining transparent, and he served as an industrial consultant to the Du Pont and New Jersey Zinc companies in devising quantitative techniques for studying paint pigments. For the latter company he also helped develop, during World War II, infrared devices for nighttime military use.

Most scientists prefer to work on a tightly knit, dramatic problem; Pfund chose a heterogeneous, highly technical, nondramatic set. He dared to aim directly at the heart of each major problem encountered. Instead of seeking qualitative measurements or undertaking mere comparisons, he elected the more exacting task of making absolute quantitative determinations. Although he worked for much of his life in the shadow of Robert W. Wood, one of the world's most able and ebullient scientists and a great showman, Pfund by the early 1930's had achieved worldwide renown among physicists for his basic discoveries and his absolute determinations of key physical constants. He received the Edward Longstreth Medal of the Franklin Institute of Philadelphia (1922) and the Frederic Ives Medal of the American Optical Society (1939), and was president of the latter organization in 1943.

Short and rotund, Pfund was a warm, friendly man, an accomplished raconteur with a lively sense of humor. He loved music and for many years played the viola in neighborhood string quartets. In religion he was a Lutheran. On Aug. 30, 1910, Pfund had married Nelle Fuller, daughter of a newspaperman of Lexington, Va. They had one child, Alice Elizabeth. Pfund died in a Baltimore hospital of myocardial infarction at the age of sixty-nine and was buried in Loudon Park Cemetery, Baltimore.

[Obituary in Optical Soc. of America, *Jour.*, Apr. 1949; *Nat. Cyc. Am. Biog.*, XXXVII, 284; *Who Was Who in America*, vol. II (1950); *Am. Men of Sci.* (7th ed., 1944); biographical notes compiled by Mary Elaine Puckett, Graduate School of Lib. Science, Univ. of Ill. (1971), especially letters from John Strong, Shirleigh Silverman, and W. Henry Aughey; *Biog. Rev. of Dane County, Wis.*, pp. 180–181 (1893), on Pfund's father; death record from Md. Dept. of Health and Mental Hygiene. Most of Pfund's published papers may be found in the cumulative index, 1917–1950, of the *Jour.* of the Optical Soc. of America.]

WILLIAM A. SHURCLIFF

PHILIPSON, DAVID (Aug. 9, 1862–June 29, 1949), rabbi and leader in American Reform Judaism, was born in Wabash, Ind., the oldest of the six children of Joseph Philipson and Louisa (Freudenthal) Philipson, both natives of Germany. His father, who had taught school in Sandusky, Ohio, was a mail carrier. The family moved during David's childhood to Dayton and then to Columbus, Ohio. At the age of thirteen he was sent to Cincinnati to enter the first class in the preparatory department of the new Hebrew Union College, a rabbinical seminary founded by the Reform rabbi Isaac M. Wise, an old acquaintance of his father. At the same time Philipson entered Cincinnati's Hughes High School; in 1879 he graduated as valedictorian from the high school and received the degree of Bachelor of Hebrew Letters from the Hebrew Union. For the next four years he attended classes at both the Hebrew Union College and the University of Cincinnati. Receiving the B.A. from the university in 1883, he graduated the same year from Hebrew Union and was ordained a rabbi—one of the first group of American-trained rabbis.

In January 1884, after several months of teaching at Hebrew Union, Philipson assumed the pulpit at Har Sinai Temple in Baltimore, one of the leading congregations in America and the first to have been organized on a Reform basis. Continuing his scholarly interests in Baltimore, Philipson took postgraduate work in Semitics at the Johns Hopkins University for two years and at the same time completed the requirements for the Doctor of Divinity degree at the Hebrew Union College, which he received in 1886. The following year, at the invitation of Kaufmann Kohler, a leading Reform theologian, Philipson attended the rabbinical conference in Pittsburgh at which the "Pittsburgh Platform" was adopted, a set of guiding principles that were to dominate Reform Judaism in America for half a century. Philipson was married in Baltimore on Sept. 9, 1886, to Ella Hollander. The couple had no children.

In 1888 Philipson was called to Cincinnati to assume the pulpit of Bene Israel congregation as successor to Max Lilienthal. He remained there until his retirement in 1938. The well-known Mound Street (later Rockdale Avenue) Temple housed the oldest Jewish congregation west of the Alleghenies. At the same time, Philipson began teaching Semitic languages and homiletics at the Hebrew Union College and five years later was appointed to its board of governors. In 1889 he helped found the Central Conference of American Rabbis, which became an influential force in Reform Judaism, and served as its president from 1907 to 1909. He was also a member of the editorial board that developed the Jewish Publication Society's English translation of the Hebrew Bible and served as chairman of the committee for the revision of the Reform movement's Union Prayer Book. Although not a profound thinker or thorough scholar, Philipson was a prolific writer, editor, and translator. His works include *The Jew in English Fiction* (1889), which went through five editions, and *The Reform Movement in Judaism* (1907), a valuable study. He also translated from the German the *Reminiscences of Isaac M. Wise* (1901).

Two themes permeated Philipson's thinking and were expressed repeatedly in his writings: liberal Judaism and Americanism. Philipson was deeply devoted to the principle that Jews were a faith community only, that they were Jews in religion, Americans in nationality. He continually emphasized the community of all men and sought to minimize religious and racial differences. His firm conviction that the bond of Judaism was religious, not political, national, or racial, made him a relentless opponent of Zionism. The Jews, Philipson felt, must remain members of various nationalities, a universal people with a mission to establish righteousness and justice in all parts of the world. Thus in 1922 he protested against the adoption by the United States Congress of a resolution calling for the endorsement of the Balfour Declaration, which pledged Great Britain's support for the establishment of a Jewish homeland in Palestine. He also opposed the formation of a World Jewish Congress, which he felt would supplant or weaken established agencies and replace them with an ineffective organization based on the conception of Jewish nationhood. His vision of Palestine, as he expressed it in 1937, was as a free haven for oppressed Jews, but neither a Jewish nor an Arab state.

Throughout his rabbinic career Philipson reached out to the community at large in an attempt to fulfill his sense of civic responsibility and to bring about greater cooperation among various religious faiths. He defended the separation of church and state and fought against any sectarian religious element in the Cincinnati public schools. In 1949, while attending a rabbinical conference in Boston, Philipson was accidentally scalded in the shower at his hotel. He died a week later at Beth Israel Hospital in Boston of an acute myocardial infarction and was buried in the United Jewish Cemetery in Cincinnati. A kindly, gregarious man, Philipson was a representative figure of classical American Reform Judaism. Although the positions he upheld later lost support, they were shared by the majority of American Reform Jews in the first decades of the twentieth century.

[The basic source is Philipson's autobiography, *My Life as an Am. Jew* (1941). Works that touch upon his career are Nathan Glazer, *Am. Judaism* (1957), and W. Gunther Plaut, ed., *The Growth of Reform Judaism* (1965). Also useful are a memorial article by Victor E. Reichert in the *Yearbook* of the Central Conference of Am. Rabbis, 1950; *Nat Cyc. Am. Biog.*, Current Vol. B, pp. 302–303; and *N.Y. Times*, June 30, July 2, 1949. Death record from Mass. Registrar of Vital Statistics.]

BERNARD MARTIN

PHILLIPS, FRANK (Nov. 28, 1873–Aug. 23, 1950), oil company founder and executive, was born in Scotia, Greeley County, Nebr., the first son and third of ten children of Lewis Franklin Phillips and Lucinda Josephine (Faucett) Phillips. His ancestral background lay in Massachusetts and New York. His father, of Welsh descent and a native of Ohio, was trained as a carpenter; his mother, born in Indiana, was a schoolteacher and the daughter of a Methodist minister. They had moved in 1872 from Iowa to Nebraska to take up farming. Lewis Phillips was active in the formation

of Greeley County and was elected a county judge, but the harshness of frontier life and a grasshopper plague caused the family to return in 1874 to Iowa, where they established a farm near Creston.

Frank attended country school but left at the age of fourteen to work as a ranch hand and then in a Creston barbershop. Within ten years he had a monopoly on the local barbering trade and was known as the maker and distributor of "Phillips' Mountain Sage," a rainwater-based cure for baldness. On Feb. 18, 1897, he married Jane Gibson, daughter of a Creston banker. They had one child, John Gibson, and adopted two daughters, Mary and Sara Jane. Phillips sold his three barbershops in 1898 and became a traveling bond salesman for his father-in-law. His commissions over the next few years are said to have totaled $75,000.

With money to invest, Phillips was attracted by the rich oil discoveries in Indian Territory (Oklahoma). In 1903 he moved to Bartlesville, purchased several oil leases, set up the Anchor Oil Company, and began drilling wells. The first two were dry, but the next eighty were producers. Recognizing that most banks were too conservative to finance speculative oil ventures, Phillips in 1905 founded and became president of his own Citizens Bank and Trust Company. As the bank prospered, it absorbed and took the name of first the Bartlesville National Bank (1911) and then the First National Bank (1919). Phillips remained president until he became chairman of the board in 1929, a position he held until his death.

Phillips had early brought his brothers L. E. (Lee Eldas) and Waite to Bartlesville to assist him in his various enterprises. The three remained active in the oil business until 1915, when Waite withdrew and L. E. and Frank sold most of their holdings, intending to concentrate on banking. Soaring demands for petroleum occasioned by World War I, together with the discovery of oil in the Osage Nation, where they still had leases, altered this plan. On June 13, 1917, Frank and L. E. Phillips organized and incorporated Phillips Petroleum Company, with Frank as president. The new company began with only sixteen gas and oil leases, a net total production of 384 barrels per day, twenty-seven employees, and assets of $3 million. By 1920 it was listed on the New York Stock Exchange with 660,000 shares and a value of $34 million.

Over the next three decades, under Frank Phillips' guidance, the company experienced phenomenal growth. An innovator and rugged individualist, "Uncle Frank" (as he was known to his employees) possessed a great faith in scientific research and development. As one observer put it, "Nothing sounds crazy to Frank Phillips if it comes from an intelligent mind." Experiments his company undertook beginning in 1917 led to techniques—notably the thermal polymerization process (1930)—that greatly improved the conversion rate of waste gas at oil wells into gasoline and made Phillips Petroleum a leader in this field within a decade. Other products of the company's research program included the alkylation reaction, which permitted the production of neohexane, a component of aviation fuel, and the copper sweetening process, to raise octane ratings and improve the lead susceptibility of gasoline.

Rapid diversification was a Phillips characteristic. By 1927 the addition of refineries, a marketing division, and a chain of filling stations under the "Phillips 66" trademark had converted the company from a producer of oil into an integrated operation. Purchase of the Oklahoma National Gas Company provided an outlet for natural gas, and "Philgas," which was pumped from trucks into individual storage tanks, was introduced for those not on city gas mains. Another by-product, carbon black, went on the market in 1928. Two years later Phillips Petroleum bought up Waite Phillips' Independent Oil and Gas Company, greatly increasing the parent company's production and distribution facilities. In 1931 Phillips pioneered by using his filling stations to sell tires and by laying a 681-mile pipeline between Borger, Tex., and East St. Louis, Ill., the first major "closed system" pipeline for refined products. Long interested in aviation, Phillips sponsored Col. Arthur C. Goebel in his nonstop flight of 1927 to Hawaii—the first such flight to be successfully completed. This, coupled with Phillips' support of the high-altitude research of Wiley Post, served to further the development and sales of the company's aviation fuels. After World War II, Phillips Petroleum also entered into the production of fertilizers and chemicals. When Phillips, who had become chairman of the board in 1938, retired in 1949, his company had grown into the ninth-largest oil corporation in America, with assets of $625 million and operations in many states and several foreign countries, and he had become a multimillionaire.

A large, balding man, Phillips was unpretentious and genial so long as his authority was recognized. He was a rugged individualist, with a pioneer's optimism and self-confidence.

Believing that "the great difficulty with the American people . . . is that they are getting away from the soil," he acquired 14,265 acres of ranch land near Bartlesville, and in the early 1920's he set aside 4,000 acres, named Woolaroc, as a retreat for himself and his guests. Here he constructed a lodge modeled on his log-cabin birthplace, but featuring a 300-seat dining hall. These acres also were stocked with exotic birds and animals in the futile hope of creating a profitable game ranch. His growing memorabilia led to the construction of what became an extensive museum of Southwestern art, Indian artifacts, and historical material. Phillips also felt "a debt to society, which I believe can best be paid by training and educating the youth of the nation." He thus became a generous patron of educational institutions and national scouting programs. A Methodist, he assisted churches of several denominations. The Frank Phillips Foundation, which he established in 1941 and to which he gave $1 million, continued his charitable and educational work.

For several years, Phillips suffered from arteriosclerosis. He died at the age of seventy-six in Atlantic City, N.J., of complications that followed a gallbladder operation. He was buried near his wife in the family mausoleum at Woolaroc Ranch.

[There are files dealing with Frank Phillips at the Woolaroc Museum, the Phillips Petroleum Co. (Editorial Division), and the Frank Phillips Foundation. The Foundation has the best biographical source on the family, a manuscript prepared by Phillips' cousin Lillie Moore McNulty of Scotia, Nebr. The most useful secondary sources are Story of Phillips Petroleum Co. (1960); a special edition of the company publication Philnews, Nov. 28, 1939, celebrating Phillips' sixty-sixth birthday; R. H. Hudson, "L. E. Phillips," Chronicles of Okla., winter 1946–1947; articles on Phillips Petroleum in World Petroleum, June 1942, Fortune, Aug. 1954, and Barron's, May 14, 1956; articles on Frank Phillips in Am. Business, Sept. 1937–Jan. 1938 (a series by Howard McLellan), Oil and Gas Jour., Nov. 30, 1939, and Saturday Evening Post, July 29, 1944; Nat. Cyc. Am. Biog., XXXVIII, 28–29; Who Was Who in America, vol. III (1960); obituaries in N.Y. Times, Aug. 24, 1950, Oklahoma City Daily Oklahoman, Aug. 24, 25, 1950, Tulsa Daily World, Aug. 23, 24, 1950, World Petroleum, Sept. 1950, Oil and Gas Jour., Aug. 31, 1950, Nat. Petroleum News, Aug. 30, 1950, and Newsweek, Sept. 4, 1950.]

JOHN S. EZELL

PHILLIPS, JOHN SANBURN (July 2, 1861–Feb. 28, 1949), magazine editor and publisher, was born in Council Bluffs, Iowa, the first of two sons and second of four children born to Edgar L. Phillips, a physician, and Mary Lavinia (Sanburn) Phillips. He was descended from Rev. George Phillips, an early settler of Massachusetts, through a branch of the family that had migrated to Orange County, N.Y., intermarried there with two Dutch families, and established woolen and flour mills in Phillipsburg on the Wallkill River. Edgar Phillips, a graduate of Williams College, had moved west to practice medicine; he married Mary Sanburn of Knoxville, Ill., and chose to pioneer in Iowa. After serving as an army physician during the Civil War, he settled with his family at Galesburg, Ill.

John Phillips received his early education in local schools and entered Knox College in Galesburg. The friendship he formed there with a fellow student, Samuel S. McClure, determined his future career. He received the B.A. degree in 1882, and during the next year worked briefly with McClure editing the *Wheelman* (later renamed *Outing*), a new publication for bicycle enthusiasts. Seeking wider horizons, Phillips in 1883 entered Harvard College as a junior; he studied literature under Francis J. Child and gained a second B.A. (magna cum laude) in 1885. Then he went on to study phonetics and literature for a year at the University of Leipzig.

Returning to the United States in 1886, Phillips settled in New York City and became editor and manager of the newspaper syndicate that McClure had organized two years earlier. For the next twenty years the destinies of the two men were professionally linked in a relationship that was alternately humorous and pathetic, stimulating and frustrating. Phillips filled many roles for McClure. He was one of the formal organizers of the McClure Syndicate in 1893, and became vice-president, treasurer, and a partner. In 1899 he managed Harper and Brothers during McClure's brief ownership of that publishing house, and the following year he became head of McClure, Phillips and Company, a book-publishing venture of the syndicate.

Phillips, however, made his major contribution through his longtime guidance of *McClure's Magazine,* launched in 1893. A thorough, sensitive, and steadfast editor, he provided a balance to the untidy and erratic habits of McClure. The publisher, believing that travel was necessary to snare the ideas that were the motive force of the popular magazine, spent much time away from the office, relying on Phillips as general manager and another Knox classmate, Albert Brady, as business manager to put out the journal. *McClure's,* after initial years of struggle, rose to eminence in its field, and through the contributions of Ida M. Tarbell, Ray Stannard Baker, and Lincoln Steffens be-

came the leader of a journalistic crusade labeled "muckraking" by President Theodore Roosevelt. The typical article of exposure was known as the "McClure article," but it should more justly have been called the "Phillips article," for Phillips had the intuitive feel for the journalistic methodology required. On a day-to-day basis he would sift through ideas for usable leads, and once the subject was chosen he would shepherd the effort through detailed but sympathetic criticism. His papers are filled with evidence of his fine editorial touch. Constantly he checked the tendency of his writers to editorialize and reminded them that their task was to interest and energize the reader. The writers at *McClure's* tended to become reformers, but Phillips' caution and his editorial perspective kept him more detached, though not unsympathetic to reform. The ebullient McClure took the spotlight, and the staff writers gained renown. Phillips' visibility remained low, but his editorial talents and sensitivity to authors made him essential to the success and influence of *McClure's Magazine.*

When in 1906 the *McClure's* staff broke up over the founder's grandiose plan for starting a new magazine, a "people's" bank and life insurance company, and a model social settlement, Phillips sold McClure his substantial interests in the publishing empire. Along with Tarbell, Baker, Steffens, and others he purchased the *American Illustrated Magazine* and transformed it into the *American Magazine,* a journal he hoped would carry on the best of *McClure's* tradition. The secessionists were swept along by an enthusiasm that masked a certain naïveté about the economics of magazine publishing. Their hope was that they could produce the product they desired without having to worry about advertising revenue and other business matters. But need for stopgap financing never eased, and Phillips was forced more and more into the business end of the venture, where his talent was less developed. In 1911 the *American* was sold to the Crowell Publishing Company. Four years later Phillips resigned the editorship, at which time most of the remaining staff from *McClure's* left the magazine. After reconsideration, Phillips agreed to stay on as a consulting editor of the *American,* but although he held this post until 1938, his active editorial career ended in 1915.

Even in his early days at *McClure's,* Phillips looked older than his years. His large head, receding hairline, moustache, and steel-rimmed glasses gave him a serious and imposing countenance. He was reared a Presbyterian, and although he never joined a church, he retained strong spiritual views. On Aug. 25, 1885, Phillips married Emma Delia West of Oneida, Ill. The union was evidently short-lived, for five years later, on Oct. 2, 1890, he married Jennie Beale Peterson of Boston, the sister of a Knox friend. They had five children: Ruth Beale, Dorothy Sanburn, Margaret Evertson, Elizabeth Peterson, and John Peterson. Phillips took to semiretirement and then retirement well, dividing his time between his houses in New York City and Goshen, N.Y. Although troubled since 1900 with a heart condition, he conserved his strength with periods of relaxation. He died at his home in Goshen at the age of eighty-seven, and was buried in the family plot in the Wallkill Cemetery in Phillipsburg (later a part of Middletown), N.Y.

[The Phillips Papers are housed with the McClure Papers at the Lilly Lib., Indiana Univ., Bloomington. The family holds other personal papers, including his memoir, "A Legacy to Youth," which he wrote for his children. A letter from his daughter Mrs. Dorothy P. Huntington to Mrs. Edna M. Scatterty, July 1964 (*DAB* files), was helpful in ordering the family history. There has been no biographical study of Phillips, but the following contain substantial material about him: John E. Semonche, *Ray Stannard Baker* (1969); Robert C. Bannister, *Ray Stannard Baker* (1966); Peter Lyon, *Success Story: The Life and Times of S. S. McClure* (1963); and Harold S. Wilson, *McClure's Magazine and the Muckrakers* (1970). See also the autobiographies of two of the writers he aided, Ray Stannard Baker, *Am. Chronicle* (1945); and Ida M. Tarbell, *All in the Day's Work* (1939). The difficulties that plagued the *American Mag.* during Phillips' editorship are described in John E. Semonche, "The 'American Magazine' of 1906–15: Principle vs. Profit," *Journalism Quart.*, Winter 1963. Marriage records were obtained from the County Clerk, Knox County, Ill., and Mass. Registrar of Vital Statistics. The Lyon book contains photographs of Phillips, and there is a good portrait in *Everybody's Mag.*, Jan. 1912, p. 55.]

JOHN E. SEMONCHE

PINCHOT, GIFFORD (Aug. 11, 1865-Oct. 4, 1946), forester, conservationist, governor of Pennsylvania, was born at the summer home of his mother's family in Simsbury, Conn. He was the first of four children (the youngest died in infancy) of James Wallace Pinchot, a well-to-do New York merchant, and Mary Jane (Eno) Pinchot. His only brother was Amos Richards Eno Pinchot. James Pinchot, a Republican, Presbyterian, and member of exclusive clubs, reared his family in an atmosphere of strict decorum and in a brilliant social milieu composed of people prominent in the arts and politics on both sides of the Atlantic. One of his close friends was the American landscape painter Sanford Gifford, after whom he named his son. French cultural influence was strong in the family. The children were tutored in French as well as in English, lived and traveled extensively in France, and spent much time at Grey Towers, the family's country home—modeled on a French chateau—near Milford, Pa. Gifford Pinchot was educated in a succession of private schools in New York and Paris and at Phillips Exeter Academy. He entered Yale University in 1885, determined to pursue a career in forestry.

Pinchot was influenced in this decision by his father, whose study of French history had made him aware of the importance of natural resources to a nation's welfare. Although no American university as yet offered a course of instruction in forestry, Pinchot took related courses in botany, meteorology, and other sciences. After receiving his B.A. degree in 1889, he enrolled for a year in the French National Forestry School at Nancy and examined forests under management in France, Switzerland, and Germany. The European tradition of forests maintained as a public resource captured his imagination. No such tradition existed in the United States when Pinchot returned in 1890, but, moved by a desire to make some contribution to society for the privileges he had inherited, he quickly emerged as an influential advocate of public forestry.

His first employment was in the private realm. After earlier assignments for Phelps, Dodge and Company, Pinchot in 1892 took charge of the forests at Biltmore, the North Carolina estate of George W. Vanderbilt, applying the principles of scientific forestry in the United States for the first time. He then set up an office in New York City as a consulting forester. Through commissions and on his own, he traveled extensively in the United States, and above all tramped the woods, acquiring a knowledge of the nation's forest resources that was then unmatched. He made surveys of forest lands for the state of New Jersey and drew up plans for two private tracts in the Adirondacks. Consistently utilitarian in his approach, Pinchot favored regulated commercial use of public as well as private forests, but stressed the need for properly selective cutting, planning for future growth, and the establishment of fire prevention measures. In 1896 Pinchot was appointed to the National Forest Commission of the National Academy of Sciences, created to make recommendations on the national forest reserves in the Western states. The commission's study helped bring about passage of the Forest Management Act of 1897, which became the legal authorization for commercial use of these reserves.

In 1898 Pinchot was named chief of the tiny Division of Forestry in the federal Department of Agriculture. His predecessor, Bernhard E. Fernow, had believed the country unready for applied forestry on European lines, and the division had thus confined its work to research and education. Pinchot set about immediately to take forestry out of the laboratory and into the woods. He built a dedicated, competent force intensely loyal to himself, developed a decentralized organization capable of a flexible response to local conditions, and courted the economic groups interested in commercial use of federal forest reserves. The support of these groups, together with the firm backing of President Theodore Roosevelt, gave impetus to the brilliant campaign by which Pinchot induced Congress in 1905 to transfer the forest reserves from the General Land Office of the Interior Department to his own division in the Department of Agriculture. Now renamed the Forest Service, the division was a political force to be reckoned with. Under Pinchot it spoke for a consistent philosophy: "to make the forest produce the largest amount of whatever crop or service will be most useful, and keep on producing it for generation after generation of men and trees" (*Breaking New Ground,* p. 32). Applied to natural resources in general, this practical stand won him enemies as well as friends. In 1906, for instance, he supported the efforts of the city of San Francisco to acquire the Hetch Hetchy Valley in Yosemite National Park as a reservoir, and earned the enmity of such men as the naturalist John Muir, who wanted the valley preserved for its beauty.

The Forest Service established a precedent, during the Progressive era, for federal regulation of natural resources, and pioneered in the development of administrative procedures to deal with such larger issues as the control of economic power, the resolution of conflict in the community, and the coordination and extension of governmental authority. Meanwhile, Pinchot transcended the narrow technical mission of his bureau to help plan the general conservation policies of the Roosevelt administration. Tall, lean, and hardy, with a flourishing handlebar moustache and intense eyes, Pinchot was a man of action to suit a former Rough Rider's taste, and he quickly became a close companion and adviser in Roosevelt's select circle. In several ways Pinchot acted as a catalyst to the emerging conservation move-

ment. In 1903 he served on the Committee on the Organization of Government Scientific Work, which focused attention on the lack of efficiency and the need for coordination. Similarly, his service in 1905 on the Committee on Department Methods (Keep Committee), appointed to review the government's operating procedures, gave a platform to the point of view that the federal government should act as a giant corporation to manage the affairs of the nation "along the best modern business lines." His work on the Public Lands Commission, which he initiated in 1903, led eventually to the systematic classification of the nation's natural resources by the U.S. Geological Survey, as well as to sweeping land-law reform. In 1908 the movement flowered in the proposals of the Inland Waterways Commission—again with Pinchot a member—for the regional development of the nation's river systems. These and other conservation proposals met with congressional resistance, however, and in the declining months of the Roosevelt administration the president and Pinchot launched a crusade to broaden the movement and encourage popular support. Together, in 1908, they organized both a White House Conference on the Conservation of Natural Resources, to which all the nation's governors and other leading figures were invited, and a National Conservation Commission under Pinchot's chairmanship.

This frantic activity declined significantly when Roosevelt was succeeded by William Howard Taft, who did not admit Pinchot to his inner circle of advisers. More seriously, Taft appointed Richard A. Ballinger, onetime commissioner of the General Land Office, as Secretary of the Interior. Ballinger began to attack conservation policies on many fronts. He moved directly against the Forest Service by ending interdepartmental cooperative agreements that had enabled the Service's program to function smoothly. He dismantled the federal hydroelectric power policy on the public domain and threatened changes even more sweeping. The struggle that developed between Ballinger and Pinchot split the Taft administration down the middle. In the fall of 1909 a minor official in the Land Office, Louis R. Glavis, backed by Pinchot, charged that Ballinger was attempting to abet fraudulent claims to Alaskan coal lands. In the end Taft upheld Ballinger, and in 1910 Pinchot was dismissed from government service for publicly criticizing the president's decision. A congressional investigation cleared Ballinger of wrongdoing but branded him as hostile to conservation, and Pinchot felt vindicated before the public. The controversy contributed significantly to the estrangement between Taft and Roosevelt.

If Pinchot now turned from professional forestry to politics, the shift was less abrupt than it seemed. His ideal of public service may always have included the possibility of a political career, and his years as a close presidential adviser and molder of policy had broadened his focus. In the struggle against Ballinger he had found allies among Republican insurgents in Congress, and he soon became involved with them in efforts to prevent Taft's reelection. It was Pinchot who wrote the speech that Theodore Roosevelt delivered at Osawatomie, Kans., in August 1910 calling for creation of a "New Nationalism" to guide the destiny of the country. In January 1911 Pinchot helped found the National Progressive Republican League. He initially supported the presidential ambitions of Wisconsin Sen. Robert M. La Follette, but shifted his allegiance once Roosevelt became a candidate early in 1912. When the Republican party renominated Taft, Pinchot bolted and helped form the Progressive party, which nominated Roosevelt.

At this point Pinchot shared some of the more uncompromising views of his brother Amos. He opposed the dominance of the ex-banker George W. Perkins in the Progressive national committee. In his unsuccessful race for the Senate in 1914 against Pennsylvania's Boies Penrose, he advocated government ownership of railroads, public utilities, and the coal, copper, and lumber industries—a position he was later to moderate. The campaign against Perkins strained Pinchot's relations with Roosevelt, as did the debacle of 1916, when the former president declined the nomination of the Progressive party and so killed it; but the friendship survived and remained the single most significant fact of Pinchot's long career.

Pinchot ended a long bachelorhood on Aug. 15, 1914, at the age of forty-nine, when he married Cornelia Elizabeth Bryce of Roslyn, N.Y., a great-granddaughter of Peter Cooper. A suffragist and champion of the working girl, she took an active interest in her husband's career and became his closest political adviser. They had one child, Gifford Bryce. During World War I, Pinchot served briefly in the Food Administration under Herbert Hoover, but resigned over policy differences. He fished, unsuccessfully, for a Senate nomination in 1920. That same year he became forestry commissioner of Pennsylvania under Gov. William C.

Sproul. Meanwhile, his eye was still fixed on political office. As a maverick Republican he was viewed with suspicion by party regulars, but an opportunity opened in 1922, when the death of Boies Penrose threw the boss-ridden factions of his party into confusion. Pinchot was elected governor.

The chief contributions of his first four-year term were in the areas of government reorganization and state finances. Under his leadership a new administrative code was drafted, which modernized administrative methods, strengthened the executive branch at the expense of the legislative, and provided for an annual budget. He also took aim at public utilities. He secured the appointment of a Giant Power Survey Board, which recommended tighter regulation of the state's electrical utilities. He attempted unsuccessfully to pack the Public Service Commission, which regulated utilities, with advocates of more rigorous controls. By temperament and conviction a vigorous prohibitionist, he established state enforcement machinery for the federal Volstead Act and, when the legislature refused to finance it, obtained the necessary funds from the Woman's Christian Temperance Union.

Since Pennsylvania law barred him from succeeding himself as governor, Pinchot tried again for the Senate in 1926, but lost in the primary to William S. Vare. In 1930 a break in the ranks of the party regulars opened up the opportunity to return to the governor's mansion. Pinchot's second term, scarred by a long, unremitting, and largely futile battle with the utilities, produced no large achievements comparable to the first, but he did grapple strenuously with economic problems caused by the Great Depression. Perhaps his most important accomplishment was the construction of thousands of miles of rural roads, which not only provided jobs for the unemployed but established his reputation as the governor who took Pennsylvania farmers out of the mud. His concern for the improvement of rural life had a long history, dating back to his service on President Roosevelt's Country Life Commission of 1908. Pinchot's presidential ambitions —a pale glow that tried vainly to ignite every four years after 1916—burned most intensely in 1932, a year that also witnessed another unsuccessful bid for the Senate.

Through the years, Pinchot kept a watchful eye on matters involving conservation. His principal lobby was the National Conservation Association, which he founded in 1909 and headed from 1910 until its demise in 1923.

Pinchot played an important role in the passage of the Weeks Act in 1911, which provided for expansion of the forest reserves by purchase, and the Waterpower Act of 1920, which began federal regulation of the power industry. He maintained his interest in forestry, serving as nonresident lecturer and professor at the Yale School of Forestry, established in 1900 by a grant from his father, and as a founder and president (1900–1908, 1910–1911) of the Society of American Foresters. Over the years his influence in the Forest Service declined. To his lasting disappointment, the chief forester in the 1920's, William B. Greeley, refused to support Pinchot's push for federal regulation of private forests. Pinchot nevertheless remained a towering figure among foresters.

He used this influence in the 1930s to block a proposal by Secretary of the Interior Harold L. Ickes, a longtime friend, which would have transformed the Department of the Interior into a Department of Conservation and Public Works and moved the Forest Service into the new department. Eventually their friendship turned sour, and in fury Ickes reopened the Ballinger case in 1940, publishing an article in the *Saturday Evening Post,* and a longer account at government expense, which pictured Ballinger as the victim of a conspiracy engineered by Pinchot. The latter's autobiography, *Breaking New Ground,* published posthumously in 1947, was designed in part as an answer to Ickes and a reaffirmation of Pinchot's interpretation of the celebrated controversy.

Even in his seventies, Pinchot found it difficult to slacken his pace. In 1938 he unsuccessfully sought the nomination for governor in the state primary. On the national scene he was a strong interventionist in the years before World War II, even to the point of openly supporting Franklin D. Roosevelt in 1940. A major heart attack in 1939 and a succession of smaller attacks hampered his activity, but once war began he again found the opportunity for public service. In 1942 he showed the navy how to extract drinking water from the juices of fresh fish—something he had learned on a cruise to the South Seas in 1929—and thus contributed an important technique to survival in lifeboats. He died of leukemia at the Columbia-Presbyterian Medical Center in New York City in 1946 at the age of eighty-one and was buried in the Milford (Pa.) Cemetery.

[There is a large collection of Pinchot's papers in the Lib. of Cong. His autobiography is a good introduction to his career down to 1910 but, written nearly forty years after the last events it describes, must be used with care. His book *The Fight for Con-*servation* (1910) is useful for his attitudes on conservation and other public issues. M. Nelson McGeary, *Gifford Pinchot: Forester-Politician* (1960), is a full-scale biography. Special studies on aspects of his career include: Martin L. Fausold, *Gifford Pinchot: Bull Moose Progressive* (1961); James Penick, Jr., *Progressive Politics and Conservation: The Ballinger-Pinchot Affair* (1968); and Harold T. Pinkett, *Gifford Pinchot: Private and Public Forester* (1970). Pinchot's sketch in the Yale Univ. *Obituary Record of Graduates,* 1946–1947, contains useful details. The McGeary volume includes good photographic reproductions of Pinchot at various stages of his long life. A good word portrait can be found in Owen Wister, *Roosevelt: The Story of a Friendship, 1880–1919* (1930).]

JAMES PENICK, JR.

PIPPIN, HORACE (Feb. 22, 1888–July 6, 1946), artist, was born in West Chester, Pa. His father and mother, Daniel Pippin and Christine W. Pippin, were domestic servants; his grandparents had been slaves. When Horace was three, the family, which by then included a second son, moved to Goshen, N.Y. There Horace was sent to the segregated ("colored") school, where he was constantly in trouble for drawing when he was supposed to be doing his schoolwork. Under his mother's tutelage he grew up with a firm religious faith. His father died when Horace was ten, and at fourteen he left school to help support the family. Following a succession of unskilled jobs, he worked for seven years as a hotel porter and then, after his mother died in 1911, as a packer for a moving company in Paterson, N.J.

When the United States entered World War I, the twenty-nine-year-old Pippin joined a black regiment. His unit, the 369th Infantry, was at one time under fire for 130 days without relief. The war diary that he kept, laboriously printed in capitals as he lay in the trenches, was sprinkled with sketches of doughboys, bomb bursts, and barbed wire. During one engagement he received a bullet wound in his right shoulder that left his arm crippled and numb.

On Nov. 21, 1920, the year after his discharge, Pippin married Ora Jennie (Featherstone) Wade, a West Chester widow, and returned to live in the town of his birth. There for the next decade he collected his disability pension, helped his wife deliver the laundry she took in, and worked at times as a junkman. Tall, handsome, and powerfully built, Pippin had an open, expressive face and old-fashioned, courtly manners. He was fond of children, and, lacking any of his own (except for a stepson), he served as a scoutmaster. He and his wife sang in the Methodist choir and later attended Baptist services. Pippin was also active in the American Legion and organized a band.

Nine years passed before he made his first attempt to paint. He began by drawing a series of pictures on wood panels with a red-hot poker. Turning to oils, he held the wrist of his injured right arm in his left hand, thus controlling the movement of his brush. He worked for three years on his first painting, *The End of the War: Starting Home* (1931), adding layer after layer of paint to convey the bitter struggle and to purge his memory of it. Two other war paintings followed, and then Pippin began to paint portraits, landscapes, and the everyday life of the hardworking people around him. In 1937, when the West Chester County Art Association held its annual show, he entered two paintings, *Cabin in the Cotton* and *Abraham Lincoln and His Father Building Their Cabin at Pigeon Creek*. They were so enthusiastically praised by the illustrator N. C. Wyeth and his son-in-law, the artist John W. McCoy, who lived in nearby Chadds Ford, that the association's president, Christian Brinton, was persuaded to give Pippin a one-man show.

Thereafter, his fortunes soared. Four of his paintings were included in 1938 in an exhibit of "Modern Primitives of Europe and America" at the Museum of Modern Art in New York, where they were seen by Robert Carlen, owner of a Philadelphia gallery. Carlen soon became Pippin's friend, mentor, and dealer. A second one-man show, at Carlen's in January 1940, was an instant success and was followed by another at the Bignou Gallery in New York. The collector Albert C. Barnes ranked Pippin with the Scottish-American painter John Kane. Critics praised his work, and customers flocked to buy.

Pippin's earlier paintings, partly because of their themes, had been somber in tone, employing a limited color range. Now, spurred perhaps by his success, his work became a bright staccato of color and design. Still lifes, flowers, and themes of peace began to emerge. He embarked upon a series of "Victorian Interiors," his own versions of the wealthy drawing rooms which he now began to frequent; upon a John Brown trilogy, tributes to the great emancipator who had helped liberate his people; and upon three "Holy Mountain" pictures, depicting wild animals being gently shepherded by children in a forest—his statement of fervid love of peace.

But along with professional success, Pippin's personal life clouded. His wife suffered a breakdown and had to be confined in Norristown State Mental Hospital, and his stepson, Richard Wade, went off to face in World War II the horrors the artist knew so much about. Pippin began to spend his evenings drinking in a local café, seeking comfort in the conversation of his neighbors. In 1946, at fifty-eight, he died in bed at his West Chester home, the victim of a coronary occlusion. He was buried in Chestnut Grove Annex Cemetery, West Chester.

Horace Pippin can properly be placed among the great "naïve" painters of the world—Henri Rousseau and Camille Bombois in France, Philomé Obin and Hector Hyppolite in Haiti, Asilia Guillén in Nicaragua. Historically, he was the first black American to produce an important body of work not limited on the one hand by an assumption of inferiority or on the other by defensive attitudes of protest or satire. His art conveyed a vision of the American scene—its history and folklore, its exterior splendor and interior pathos—uniquely his own.

[Selden Rodman and Carole Cleaver, *Horace Pippin: The Artist as a Black American* (1972); Selden Rodman, *Horace Pippin: A Negro Painter in America* (1947). See also *Current Biog.* 1945; *N.Y. Times,* July 7, 1946.]

CAROLE CLEAVER

PLOTZ, HARRY (Apr. 17, 1890-Jan. 6, 1947), bacteriologist and physician, was born in Patterson, N.J., the eldest of the three children and the only son of Joseph Plotz and Ida (Adelson) Plotz. Both parents were born in Poland; his father was superintendent of the Prudential Insurance Co. in Brooklyn, N.Y. Plotz attended Newark schools and, for a time, Boys High School in Brooklyn. He was a brilliant student and also won medals as a runner. He entered a combined undergraduate and medical course at Columbia University and that university's College of Physicians and Surgeons and was awarded his M.D. degree in 1913, graduating first in his class. During his medical education he was engrossed in bacteriology.

Upon graduation he received an internship in pathology at Mt. Sinai Hospital, in New York City, and entered into investigations to show that Brill's disease was a mild form of epidemic typhus fever. It is said that he usually worked at the laboratory bench for twenty hours each day. From materials obtained from patients with Brill's disease and from immigrants from Eastern Europe hospitalized with typhus fever he succeeded in growing an anaerobic organism which, on the basis of serologic and animal inoculation experiments, he believed to be the etiologic agent of the disease. Presumably, he was to report his exciting findings for the first time at the meeting of the Association of American Physicians at Atlantic City on May 13, 1914. On the preceding day, the front page of the *New York Times* reported the essentials and significance of his research, extolling his accomplishment. A tempest of criticism immediately arose from members of the august association who accused Plotz of unethical pre-publication in the lay press, and he was not called upon to present his results at their meeting. The controversy in the medical and lay press was intense, and the *Times* chastised his critics as "small and narrow-minded" for punishing the young investigator, who had nothing to do in any way with the premature disclosure. A preliminary report of the work was published in the *Journal of the American Medical Association* on May 16, 1914. Plotz's work continued to be supported at Mt. Sinai, and in April of the next year he reported to the New York Pathological Society the details of his findings and of the preparation of an antityphus vaccine from his organism. Hans Zinsser, president of the society, announced that he and the members of his expedition, who were soon leaving to study the typhus fever epidemic in Serbia, had been inoculated with this vaccine. At the suggestion of William H. Welch, pathologist of the Johns Hopkins School of Medicine, the organism was named *Bacillus typhi exanthematicus* but became known as Plotz bacillus. The acclamation that was accorded this presentation and the subsequent scientific publications was in sharp contrast to the attitude of the previous year.

In the summer of 1915, Plotz and his associate, Dr. George Baehr, joined the American Red Cross Sanitary Commission in Serbia to test his isolation methods and vaccine under field conditions. On his return from Europe, Zinsser reported to a meeting of the New York Academy of Medicine in October that Plotz's work had been verified in the field. Later that month the entire staff of the Lady Paget Hospital in Uskub was captured by the Bulgarians, and Plotz was interned with the others although he was allowed to continue work. Released the week before Christmas, he returned to New York in the summer of 1916, having been decorated by the Serbian and Bulgarian governments, cited by his German captors for his work with ill Austrian and German soldiers, and honored in Austria and Galicia for his work on typhus fever. He also announced the successful cultivation of the agent of relapsing fever, *Spirocheta obermeieri* (now *Borrelia recurrentis*). Plotz then entered the United States Army as a major assigned to Surgeon General Gorgas' staff in Washington to work on antityphus sanitary measures. He established procedures and designed equipment and installations for the delousing of returning troops. He was discharged in 1919 as a lieutenant colonel.

On Nov. 24, 1920, he married Ella Sachs, a member of a wealthy German-Jewish family. They sailed to Europe, where Plotz became medical advisor to the Jewish Joint Distribution Committee in charge of its relief expedition in Eastern Europe. He then worked in the laboratories of the Institut Pasteur in Paris. On Apr. 13, 1922, his wife died in childbirth in Paris. Plotz stayed on at the Institut Pasteur. By this time it had been demonstrated that typhus fever was caused by *Rickettsia prowazekii* and that the Plotz bacillus had no etiologic role in the disease.

Plotz remained at the Institut Pasteur until the fall of France in 1940, having become *chef de service* in 1931. During his productive stay in Paris he published extensively on bacteriologic, virologic, and immunologic subjects, including the culture of measles and smallpox viruses in chick embryo tissue culture in the period before impetus was given to these techniques by the use of antibiotics to control contamination. He was an officer of the Légion d'Honneur and was the official French delegate to several international congresses.

At the outbreak of World War II he came to Zinsser's laboratory at Harvard as a visiting scientist and, with Zinsser and John Enders, developed a chick embryo tissue-culture method of cultivating rickettsia for the preparation of typhus fever vaccine in quantity. In 1941 he again entered the army as lieutenant colonel and established and assumed directorship of the Division of Virus and Rickettsial Diseases at the Army Medical Center, Washington, D.C. The laboratory became a center of applied research in many military problems in infectious diseases. Here much of the development of typhus vaccines for the immunization of troops was accomplished and diagnostic tests were devised for many of the rickettsial and viral diseases. Plotz made several trips abroad in the course of these studies. He was a member of the Typhus Commission and received the Typhus Medal at the end of hostilities. By his personal warmth, his gracious manners, and his captivating charisma and charm, Plotz motivated his staff to pay court to his direction. Although he continually praised and credited his co-workers, he insisted that all communications from his laboratory emanate from himself and most of his publications bear his name as sole author. Unfortunately most of the work of this period remained unpublished due to wartime restrictions.

He retired from the service as a colonel in 1945 after a coronary attack but stayed on at the laboratory as a consultant to the secretary of war. He suffered a final heart attack at his desk in the laboratory and died several days later, on Jan. 6, 1947, at Walter Reed Hospital, Washington. He was buried in Salem Fields Cemetery, N.Y., following services at Temple Emanu-El.

[*Encyclopedia Americana* (1970); *Am. Men of Sci.* (1944); *Who's Who in Am. Jewry* (1938); *Index Medicus* (1914-1949); *N.Y. Times*, May 12, 13, 14, 15, 17, 21, 23, 1914; Feb. 1, Apr. 15, 16, 17, May 16, June 26, 27, Oct. 22, 28, Dec. 19, 1915; Apr. 2, July 7, 1916; Nov. 11, 22, Dec. 26, 1920; Apr. 14, 1922; May 31, 1938; portrait, Jan. 7, 1947; *N.Y. Times Mag.*, "Typhus, War's Dread Ally, Beaten" by Van Buren Thorne, Apr. 18, 1915; "Typhus, Scourge of Europe's Armies, Conquered," with portrait, July 23, 1916; Hans Zinsser, *As I Remember Him* (1940) pp. 217, 375; *JAMA*, 62 (1914), 1556; recollections of sister, associates, and author.]
                                    MERRILL J. SNYDER

POINDEXTER, MILES (Apr. 22, 1868-Sept. 21, 1946), United States senator from Washington, was born in Memphis, Tenn., the eldest of the six children of William Bowyer Poindexter and Josephine Alexander (Anderson) Poindexter, both of old Virginia families. His maternal grandfather, Francis T. Anderson, was a prominent Virginia lawyer, landowner, and rector of Washington and Lee University; his great-uncle was Joseph Reid Anderson, Confederate general and president of the famous Tredegar Iron Works. His father, after serving in the Confederate Army, worked briefly in Tennessee and Arkansas, where he sold insurance for a time, but he settled permanently on a farm at Elk Cliff, the Anderson estate at Greenlee near Lexington, Va., when Miles was two. The boy was educated at nearby Fancy Hill Academy and at Washington and Lee University, where he attended the academic and law departments and received the LL.B. degree in 1891. That same year, reportedly at the urging of his mother, who had relatives in Oregon, he decided to pursue his career in the West. Moving to Walla Walla, Wash., he established a law practice and, on June 16, 1892, married a local girl, Elizabeth Gale Page. They had one child, a son, Gale Aylett.

Poindexter quickly entered politics, winning election as county prosecuting attorney the year after his arrival in Walla Walla, although he was defeated when he ran again two years later. At first a Democrat, he found himself repelled by the Populist doctrines espoused by most Democrats in Washington, and after supporting the Republican presidential nominee, William McKinley, in 1896, he moved the following year to Spokane, Wash., and became a Republican. Poindexter served as an assistant prosecuting attorney for Spokane County (1899-1904) and judge of the superior court (1904-1908) and in 1908 was elected to the House of Representatives. Joining the small band of Western and Midwestern Republicans known as the Insurgents, he supported their successful challenge to the leadership of Speaker Joseph G. Cannon and backed most of their program of reform, including measures for conservation, a federal income tax, railroad regulation, and postal saving banks. On the strength of his progressive record, Poindexter swept the Republican senatorial primary in 1910 and thus secured his election to the Senate by the Washington state legislature.

In the Senate, Poindexter at first continued his outspoken advocacy of progressive reform. He vigorously criticized President William Howard Taft, supported Theodore Roosevelt in the presidential election of 1912, and became the only senator to list himself as a member of the Progressive party. He backed the domestic legislative program of Woodrow Wilson; he and Robert M. La Follette, for example, were the only non-Democrats in the Senate to vote for the Underwood Tariff. Poindexter also fought to preserve Alaska's natural resources. At this time sympathetic toward labor, he strongly criticized the millowners during the 1912 textile strike in Lawrence, Mass., led by the Industrial Workers of the World; and in the following year he offered a radical plan for a federal industrial army of the unemployed to carry on public works projects. With the decline of the Progressive party, Poindexter returned in 1915 to the Republican ranks, and the following year was reelected by a substantial popular majority.

On issues of foreign policy, however, Poindexter had already begun to differ sharply with many fellow progressives, and he now drew closer to the regular Republicans. He championed a strong army and navy and advocated increased American intervention in Latin America. He criticized Wilson's handling of the Mexican revolution and even urged annexation of Mexico's northern states. He strongly supported American entry into World War I, but he disliked Wilson's international "idealism" and bitterly criticized the president for not prosecuting the war with sufficient vigor. He was even more hostile to the opponents of the war, and enthusiastically endorsed both the Espionage Act of 1917 and the Sedition Act of 1918. After the war, reacting violently against the economic radicalism and militant union activity that he believed were inspired by the Bolshevik revolution in Russia, he became one of the leaders in the "Red Scare"—the effort in 1919 and 1920 to alert the nation to the alleged dangers of "communism"—and claimed responsibility for prodding Attorney General A. Mitchell Palmer into conducting his famous raids of 1919 and 1920. An "Irreconcilable" on the Versailles Treaty, Poindexter opposed American entry into the League of Nations largely because he thought the league represented a threat to the national independence and sovereignty of the United States. He continued to support American involvement in international affairs, however, and as the acting chairman of the Senate Committee on Naval Affairs in 1922 helped secure Senate ratification of the treaties growing out of the Washington conference on arms limitation.

By the end of his second term, Poindexter had achieved some national stature in the Senate, but he had done so at the expense of political support in his own state. His record after 1917 alienated many progressives, farmers, and workingmen, and his opposition to federal legislation to ease the economic effects of the postwar agricultural depression also lost him support among distressed farmers in eastern Washington. He was soundly defeated in 1922 by a progressive Democrat. The next year President Warren Harding appointed Poindexter ambassador to Peru, a post he held until 1928. Out of his Peruvian experience emerged two studies, *The Ayar-Incas* (2 vols., 1930) and *Peruvian Pharaohs* (1938), in which he argued that the Inca civilization was founded by the "Aryan or Proto-Aryan" race, which had migrated from central Asia, a thesis discredited by serious scholars.

Poindexter returned to the state of Washington in 1928 to make a final, unsuccessful campaign for reelection to the Senate. Shortly after the death of his wife in 1929, he moved back to the family estate in Virginia and throughout the 1930's continued to practice law in Washington, D.C. On Aug. 27, 1936, he married Mrs. Elinor Jackson (Junkin) Latané, widow of the historian John Holladay Latané; their brief marriage ended in divorce. Poindexter died in his sleep of an apparent heart attack at his home in Greenlee, Va., at the age of seventy-eight. He was buried in the Presbyterian Cemetery in Lexington, Va.

[Poindexter's papers are at the Univ. of Va., with microfilm copies at the Univ. of Wash., Seattle. Secondary studies include Howard W. Allen, "Miles Poindexter: A Political Biog." (Ph.D. diss., Univ. of Wash., 1959), and the same author's "Miles Poindexter and the Progressive Movement," *Pacific Northwest Quart.*, July 1962; and Helen O. Filson, "Miles Poindexter and the Progressive Movement in Eastern Wash., 1908–1913" (M.A. thesis, Wash. State Univ., 1944). See also *Biog. Directory Am. Cong.* (1961); *Nat. Cyc. Am. Biog.*, XV, 211; *Who Was Who in America*, II (1950); *N.Y. Times*, Sept. 22, 1946. Death record from Va. Dept. of Health.]
                                    HOWARD W. ALLEN

POLLOCK, CHANNING (Mar. 4, 1880-Aug. 17, 1946), playwright, author, and lecturer, was born in Washington, D.C., the eldest of the three surviving children—two boys and a girl—of Alexander Lyon Pollock and Verona (Larkin) Pollock. His mother was a Virginian of English descent. His father, a Jew who had emigrated from Austria in the 1870's, worked for the Weather Bureau in Washington before becoming a newspaper editor and publisher in Omaha, Nebr., and Salt Lake City, Utah. Channing's public school education in those cities was supplemented by brief attendance at an Untergymnasium during a visit to relatives in Prague; by tutors in San Salvador, where his father, while serving as United States consul, died of yellow fever in 1894; and by study at Bethel Military Academy near Warrenton, Va. Possessed of an urge to write and to dramatize and believing that these ends would be better served by experience than by formal schooling, he unceremoniously left the academy and at sixteen obtained a job as reporter, and later as assistant drama editor, on the *Washington Post*. In 1897 he went to New York City to work for the *Dramatic Mirror,* but the following year found him back in Washington, this time as drama critic of the *Washington Times*. His candid review of David Belasco's farce *Naughty Anthony,* however, lost him this post in 1900.

Once again in New York, Pollock became press agent successively for Florenz Ziegfeld, William A. Brady, and the Shuberts. Brady afforded him the opportunity to dramatize Frank Norris' novel *The Pit,* which scored a hit in 1903. Meanwhile, in his spare time he wrote *In the Bishop's Carriage* (based on the romantic novel of Miriam Michelson), which opened and collapsed in Chicago in 1905; and *The Little Gray Lady,* which toured briefly after a short New York run in 1906. In the latter year he gave up press-agentry to devote himself entirely to his own work. By 1910 he had produced, in all, nine plays without feeling he was "getting anywhere." It was then that he made what he later called "a wrong-turning that took the best ten years of my life," years devoted to "silly jingles and nonsensical stories"—years, too, in which he, as librettist, collaborated with Rennold Wolf on several musical comedies, until the failure of *The Grass Widow* in 1917.

In 1919 Al Woods produced Pollock's "gripping" melodrama *The Sign on the Door,* which was also presented abroad; in London, it ran for more than a year with Gladys Cooper in the starring role. Woods rejected, however, as religious "bunk" the first of Pollock's serious efforts and what proved to be his most successful play, *The Fool,* inspired by the life of St. Francis of Assisi. Only after twenty-seven other managers turned the play down did Archie Selwyn venture to stage it. The hero, curate of a fashionable New York church, tries to lead a Christlike life, is dismissed for his liberal views, and is cast off by his socialite fiancée. He devotes his life to work in the slums and is rewarded when a crippled girl throws aside her crutches and walks. The play opened in New York on Oct. 23, 1922. Reviewers dismissed it as "thrilling honest hokum" and "socialistic and religious melodrama," but it was loved by the public, including men of the caliber of Nicholas Murray Butler, president of Columbia University ("It is a long time since I have seen a play which seemed to me so gripping"), and John Haynes Holmes, pastor of New York's Community Church ("I feel . . . that you have written a brave, eloquent and noble play"). It eventually earned close to $1 million.

Next to *The Fool, The Enemy* was perhaps Pollock's most noteworthy play. Written in a monastery in Salzburg, Austria, it shows the effect of World War I on an ordinary Viennese family. It opened in New York in October 1925, and although it never attained the commercial success of *The Fool,* it remained popular until during World War II it was rejected as pacifist propaganda.

Pollock's last plays had a disheartening reception. *Mr. Moneypenny* (1928), the story of a man who sells himself to the devil for worldly goods—which he considered his best work—proved his "most expensive failure." *The House Beautiful* (1931), depicting the lives of a young couple who endeavor against odds to live the good and simple life, "interested and moved" Mark Van Doren (*Nation,* Apr. 1, 1931); but Brooks Atkinson, although admitting that "as a playwright Mr. Pollock is to be reckoned with," concluded that "as a poet and philosopher he is commonplace" (*New York Times,* Mar. 14, 1931).

At the age of fifty-two Pollock withdrew from the theater. Over the years he had done considerable magazine writing and lecturing; he now turned his crusading efforts to these fields. Calling himself a "reactionary," he inveighed against the "cult of sophistication," racial and religious intolerance, and subversive elements in the schools. He fought for better standards in the theater, repeal of prohibition, and aid to Great Britain against the Nazis. Among the periodicals to which he contributed were the *American Magazine, Reader's Digest,* and *American Mercury.* In politics he was an independent, and although deeply religious, he belonged to no denomination. During his latter years he read and traveled extensively, fulfilling the need for the education he had missed in his youth. In his autobiography, *Harvest of My Years* (1943), he attributed his happy life to his wife, Anna Marble, a press agent whom he married on Aug. 9, 1906; to his only child, Helen; to excellent health; and to keeping busy.

Pollock died of a cerebral thrombosis at the age of sixty-six at his Shoreham, Long Island, home.

[The main sources are his autobiography, *Harvest of My Years* (1943); *N.Y. Times,* Aug. 18–19, 1946; *Nat. Cyc. Am. Biog.,* XXXIV, 50–51; Stanley J. Kunitz and Howard Haycraft, eds., *Twentieth-Century Authors* (1942); clippings in Theatre Collect. at Lincoln Center Lib. for the Performing Arts; and *Who Was Who in Am.,* II (1950).]

ELIZABETH F. HOXIE

POOLE, ERNEST COOK (Jan. 23, 1880-Jan. 10, 1950), novelist and journalist, was born in Chicago, Ill., the second son and fifth of seven children of Mary Nevin (Howe) Poole, daughter of one of Chicago's original settlers, and Abram Poole, a wealthy grain broker of Dutch descent. The name Vanderpoel had been simplified by Ernest's great-grandfather in rural New York. His mother, an earnest Presbyterian, balanced intelligent and humane childrearing with a full life in Chicago society and charity, while his father, a hard-driving self-made capitalist, indulged a love of music and theater. An older sister, Bertha, married the liberal economist and writer Walter Weyl, and Abram, their younger brother, achieved recognition as a painter.

Ernest's ordinary active boyhood in Chicago and nearby Lake Forest was enhanced by frequent trips east. He attended the University School for Boys in Chicago. In 1898 the short, wiry youth followed his older brother Ralph to Princeton University, occupying the room in Brown Hall where the novelist Booth Tarkington, later Poole's friend, had lived ten years earlier. Hard work rather than innate genius led to graduation with the A.B. degree *cum laude* in 1902, with honors in history, jurisprudence, and politics. His sessions with Woodrow Wilson aroused a long-sustained idealism. But unlike Tarkington and F. Scott Fitzgerald, he found Princeton indifferent to his strong literary ambitions. He studied and imitated Tolstoi, Turgenev, Maupassant, and Stevenson and found in Jacob Riis's *How the Other Half Lives* an impetus to make New York slum dwellers his initial subject matter.

The capacity for wonder at things new and strange, attributed to many American writers, was conspicuous in Poole. Two years as a social worker with the University Settlement on New York's Lower East Side revealed to him the astonishing diversity and vigor of human existence in the frantic metropolis, which later became a donnée of his novels. He investigated firsthand the poverty, disease, and exploitation that awaited immigrants and sold his first piece to *McClure's* in 1903. Lincoln Steffens, Ray Stannard Baker, and Abraham Cahan taught the young writer techniques for gathering and handling his teeming materials, while his mounting social concern was nurtured by activists such as his brother-in-law Walter Weyl, Arthur Bullard, Robert Hunter, and J. G. Phelps Stokes.

Commissioned to report on labor racketeering in Chicago, Poole returned to his hometown in 1904 and soon turned into a publicist for striking stockyard workers. The 1905 St. Petersburg, Russia, massacre impelled him to seek a wider perspective on mass social movements. Secretly carrying money and messages for the revolutionaries, he made the first of numerous trips abroad as a magazine correspondent. With a congenial guide-translator, he visited remote villages, and his fresh and vigorous dispatches for the *Outlook* constitute probably his best magazine writing.

Poole then wrote and published a novel, *The Voice of the Street* (1906), inexpertly handling the grim, but fascinating, New York material that he continued to place successfully in the *Saturday Evening Post* and elsewhere. On Feb. 12, 1907, he married Margaret Winterbotham,

whom he had first met when she was a Lake Forest debutante. They settled in Greenwich Village and grew more active in reform movements. Poole finally joined the Socialist party, frequently contributing to its paper, the *New York Call*. A serious attempt at playwriting produced twelve scripts, usually with social messages. Most of them were torn up by Poole, but three had modestly successful productions.

The Harbor, Poole's semiautobiographical second novel and his only book usually noted in literary histories, appeared in 1915; it treated a young writer's successive worship of pure art and business efficiency before a seamen's strike opened the vision of a future worldwide socialist revolution. It achieved critical and popular success. Further critical success came almost immediately with *His Family* (1917), a study of three sisters exemplifying roles available to modern women: reckless high society, dull domesticity, and frenetic social service. It won the first Pulitzer Prize offered in fiction. These two novels marked the apex of Poole's career.

In 1914 he had reported World War I from the front lines. Then, breaking with the pacifism of his socialist friends, Poole switched from journalist to propagandist, joining the Committee on Public Information headed by George Creel. A 1917 visit to Russia during the Kerensky government resulted in articles assembled into short books: *The Dark People* (1918), *The Village* (1919), *The Little Dark Man* (1925).

Poole was now nearing forty and the father of three children: William Morris, Nicholas, and Elizabeth Ann. Consistently alert to changes sweeping across the world, he settled down to write novels depicting American families caught in the threatening "winds," "storms," and "avalanches" of the "age of experiments" that had begun with a war to make the world safe. Later, in his undistinguished autobiography, *The Bridge* (1940), Poole's title metaphor would represent his generation's life span, stretching from a quiet "yesterday to the vast confusion of today" (p. 49). His novels—nearly one a year through the 1920's—show that bridge in the making, a pontoon at times, drawing readers close to the swirling flow of the boom years, the Jazz Age. *Blind* (1920), *Danger* (1923), and *The Destroyer* (1931) focused on individuals psychically damaged by the war. *The Avalanche* (1924), *With Eastern Eyes* (1926), and *Silent Storms* (1927) were better books and probed, respectively, excessive ambition, the conflict between job and marriage, and Wall Street materialism. *Great Winds* (1933) effectively swept up most of the above. Poole refused to submerge readers in lust or "sneers and gloom." He regarded such contemporaries as H. L. Mencken, Sinclair Lewis, and Eugene O'Neill as too often morally adrift and engulfed in cynicism. He prided himself on realism, but a realism allowing for safe green shores beyond the maelstrom.

Although a careful reviser, achieving absolute simplicity of syntax and vocabulary, Poole cared little for subtleties of character development, stylistic experiment, or a controlled point of view. He declared in 1924, "There's no excuse for writing unless there's some great message to give" (Feld, p. 2). In Poole's New York City home, William James was frequently and energetically discussed around the family table, but Henry James never. Poole did partake of James's gift for rendering women characters (often basing them on his admired mother), and he creditably portrayed old people, such as the roving song collector in his novelette *The Hunter's Moon* (1925).

Frail in appearance, shy and nervous but possessed of a temper, Poole never tried to compete with the brilliant raconteurs of his age. He considered himself "a poor talker but a good listener." He was a clubman (Players, Century, Coffee House), and stayed aloof from the Village avant-garde and the expatriate colony, being temperamentally at home with neither. Two or three evenings a week Margaret Poole gathered for dinner various professional men and women—brokers, doctors, architects—insisting that this was her contribution to the career of her introspective husband; the conversations did generate characters and dialogue for his fiction.

From 1915 to 1924 each of Poole's seven novels sold 12,000 copies or more; but of his next seven, only one, *Silent Storms* (1927), about an unsuccessful French-American marriage, went above 8,000 copies. *One of Us* (1934), about a storekeeper's life, was set in the White Mountains of New Hampshire, where for two decades Poole spent part of each year with his family. Acknowledged as one of his better novels, it still could not offset a generation of critics' demands for another *Harbor*. He did not write another book for six years; indeed, his literary output in the 1930's dwindled to column-long letters in the *New York Times,* typically urging dollars for Bowery missions. Giving up his regular writing routine, he pursued the stock market, feeling morally obliged to recoup his depression losses

for his children, while Margaret Poole's inherited money maintained the family's comfortable existence. His perennial love of heroism stimulated a visit to the Kentucky mountains, which resulted in a successful book of nonfiction, *Nurses on Horseback* (1932), but in 1936 his publisher, for the first time in twenty-five years, rejected a novel he submitted. When World War II broke out, his offer to serve again as government propagandist was refused.

In later life he grew more conservative (although far from reactionary or closed-minded) and dug into history to discern some of the roots of his obsessive theme, fast-paced change. Two of his last three books resurrected his old journalistic talent for readable, action-filled narrative. *Giants Gone* (1943) saluted twenty big-shouldered heroes of his native city, but *The Great White Hills of New Hampshire* (1946) showed his personal roots well transplanted into the rocky soil that had nurtured many other brave lovers of hard labor and privacy. Before Robert Frost became his Grafton County neighbor and walking companion, Poole had built White Pines, a house of stone and spruce halfway between Franconia and Sugar Hill. There he wrote books, served on the school board, and listened to native lore. Additional oral material combined with serious research to produce an honest, and even racy, series of topical vignettes, and *Great White Hills* justly became a best-seller. *The Nancy Flyer* (1949) mixed leftover New Hampshire jottings with Poole's own fancy to present the fascinating story of a mountain stage line.

The former Socialist was confirmed in the Episcopal church sometime after his sixtieth year, in a three-generation ceremony at White Pines. There too his ashes were scattered by his wife after his death of pneumonia in New York.

While a certain critical obtuseness had hounded Poole, novel after novel, it remains clear that his energy and admirable awareness were unaccompanied by sufficient insight and innovation. He wanted to chronicle his times in fiction and partly succeeded, but weight and texture eluded him, while jejune moralizing took over. He squandered too many of his best working years on underdeveloped novels and failed to utilize fully his ripe talent for investigative reporting and historical narrative.

[T. Frederick Keefer's unpublished dissertation "The Literary Career and Literary Productions of Ernest Poole, American Novelist" (Duke Univ., 1960) is an exhaustive, but lucid, biographical-critical study, subsequently condensed in *Ernest Poole* (1966). Aside from this, Poole's own works are his best guide. Many of his 220 magazine pieces were first-person reactions to world affairs, so that readers rightly mistrustful of errors and imbalance in his autobiography can sample his genuine concerns. An early interview is by Rose C. Feld in the *N.Y. Times Book Rev.*, Feb. 3, 1924; see also the *Daily Princetonian*, Feb. 22, 1922, and Princeton's *Twenty-Fifth Year Record of the Class of 1902*. Later short sketches appeared in Fred B. Millett, *Contemporary American Authors* (1940); Stanley J. Kunitz and Howard Haycraft, eds., *Twentieth-Century Authors* (1942); and Harry R. Warfel, *American Novelists of Today* (1951). Placing *The Harbor* in context is Walter B. Rideout, *The Radical Novel in the United States 1900–1954* (1956). Few of Poole's letters were saved. Keefer lists only 100, to Hamlin Garland and others. Personal recollections from William Morris Poole and Poole's grandson, Robert Lanchester.]

CHARLES VANDERSEE

PORTER, RUSSELL WILLIAMS (Dec. 13, 1871-Feb. 22, 1949), explorer, optician, and telescope maker, was born in Springfield, Vt., the youngest of five children of Frederick Wardsworth Porter and Caroline (Silsby) Porter. His father, an inventor, pioneer daguerreotypist, and successful manufacturer of toy baby carriages, was of English lineage—his ancestors having immigrated to New England in the seventeenth century. His mother, a former schoolteacher, was the daughter of a skilled mechanic and stone mason whose family had settled in Charlestown, N.H., soon after the American Revolution. Porter attended the Springfield public schools and the Vermont Academy in Saxon's River (1887-1889), before going for a year to Norwich University and then to the University of Vermont for his junior year. From 1890 to 1892 he worked as a draftsman for the Associated Mutual Insurance Company and then borrowed money to study architecture at the Massachusetts Institute of Technology. A special student there from 1894 to 1898, he worked with Constant Désiré Despradelle, Rotch professor of architectural design, who had an office in Boston. In 1894, after hearing Robert Peary lecture on the Arctic, he was seized with "Arctic fever." That summer he sailed with Frederick A. Cook aboard the *Miranda*. They ran aground in Greenland and were rescued by a fishing schooner.

During the next several years Porter took part in at least ten expeditions to the Arctic. They included voyages on Peary's ship to Baffin Land in the summer of 1896 and to Greenland (1899), in which Porter led groups of M.I.T. students and thus earned money to pay his college expenses.

In 1901, as assistant scientist and artist, he went with the tyrannical Evelyn Briggs Baldwin to Franz Josef Land on an expedition financed by William Ziegler to search for the North Pole. The men mutinied, and the expedition returned home without reaching the pole. In 1903 Porter joined another Ziegler expedition, led by Anthony Fiala. The base ship, a whaler, the *America,* was crushed in the Arctic ice and sank. After being marooned for nearly two years, during which the explorers barely survived the bitter cold and devastating hunger, they were rescued by relief ships. Porter, "starved to a skeleton," had suffered permanent loss of hearing. During those long, dark months of the Arctic night, however, he made astronomical observations for the determination of time and position, discovered several new islands, and surveyed and mapped five hundred miles of coastline in the Franz Josef Archipelago. He returned to civilization, vowing to spend the rest of his life in the tropics. Nevertheless, in 1906 he joined Cook again for a trip to Alaska and thus inadvertently became part of a hoax perpetrated by Cook: after sending the rest of the party on a side expedition, Cook claimed to have reached the peak of Mount McKinley, accompanied only by one guide.

In 1907, after numerous expeditions within the Arctic Circle and three shipwrecks, Porter settled at Marshall Point, a fishing village at Port Clyde, Maine, where he earned a livelihood by designing and building cottages. From 1915 to 1918 he was an instructor of architectural design at M.I.T.

In the Arctic, however, his celestial observations had roused his interest in astronomy, and in 1911, spurred by an article in *Popular Astronomy,* he began making his own telescope, a hobby that changed the course of his life. He became fascinated by the challenge of designing and making lenses and worked for a time (1917-1919) with the optical division of the National Bureau of Standards. Meanwhile, his work had attracted the attention of James Hartness, president of Jones and Lamson Machine Company in Springfield, Vt., and himself an amateur astronomer. Through Hartness, Porter became optical research engineer with the firm. While there, he developed the screw thread comparator and the turret-type telescope mounting, devised by Hartness, and continued to follow his hobby of telescope making. After successfully completing a ten-inch mirror, he described the work in "The Poor Man's Telescope" (*Popular Astronomy*, November 1921) to show how anyone with enough time and patience could achieve similar results. His enthusiasm was contagious and soon amateurs, first in Springfield and then all over the country, were following his trail. By 1925, with the help of Albert G. Ingalls, associate editor of *Scientific American,* he had organized the Telescope Makers of Springfield and had built Stellafane, a mecca for amateur telescope makers, who considered Porter their patron saint; it is still the focus of their annual summer gatherings. The first edition of *Amateur Telescope Making,* a collection of articles and detailed drawings chiefly by Porter, appeared in 1926; edited by Ingalls, it went through a succession of expanded editions and became the bible of the nation's telescope enthusiasts.

In 1928 the course of Porter's life again changed abruptly when, through Ingalls, he met George Ellery Hale, who was then planning the construction of the 200-inch telescope on Palomar Mountain. Impressed with Porter's ideas, Hale invited him to California to assist in designing the giant instrument. Porter moved to Pasadena, an associate in optics and instrument design and remained there for the rest of his life.

Two types of mounting were at first considered, the yoke and Porter's "split equatorial ring." From these, after endless experiment, a third type, the horseshoe, evolved. Porter's chief contribution lay in his ability to visualize the complex problems and, through three-dimensional designs made to scale from blueprints, to create working models for the engineers. Thus, he helped to design, not only the 200-inch mounting but also the optical, instrument, and machine shops and the astrophysical laboratory on the California Institute of Technology campus. He also designed the dome on Palomar Mountain, after making a contour map of that region. During World War II, when work on the telescope was suspended, he applied his skills to the making of roof prisms; to the design of landing craft, rockets, and fuses; and to other projects for the navy.

In November 1907, Porter married Alice Belle Marshall, the postmistress at Port Clyde. Their two children were Marshall (who died young) and Caroline. Although Porter's family had been Swedenborgians, he considered himself a Unitarian. By nature easygoing and imperturbable, he was modest and unselfish and had great energy. Porter loved to sketch, and he painted in watercolors, in oils, and in pastels—from the Arctic to California. An enthusiastic musician, he composed "just for fun." In fact, he got fun out of everything he did. Because of the diversity of Porter's talents,

Hartness called him the "Springfield Leonardo." Porter died of a heart attack in Pasadena. According to his wish, his ashes were buried in the Turkey Ridge Cemetery in Port Clyde. A crater on the near side of the moon is now named for him.

[The chief manuscript sources for Porter's life and work are in the possession of Caroline Porter Kier of Port Clyde, Maine. These include her father's correspondence, diaries, and paintings of the Arctic, New England, and California, in addition to the original manuscript of "Arctic Fever" and other papers. A copy of this manuscript is also in the Stefansson Collect. in the Baker Lib. at Dartmouth. At present there is no book-length biography of Porter, although one is in preparation by Berton C. Willard. Biographical articles include the excellent obituary by Albert G. Ingalls, "The Amateur Astronomer," *Scientific American,* Apr. 1949; Oscar Marshall, "R. W. Porter," *Pop. Astron.,* May 1949; Leo and Margaret Scanlon, "Russell W. Porter . . . Telescope Artist," *Sky and Telescope,* Apr. 1949; James Stokley, "He Showed Thousands the Stars," *Sci. News Lett.,* Dec. 7, 1929; and Webb Waldron, "One Really Happy Man," *Am. Mag.,* Nov. 1931 (these last two articles contain good photographs of Porter). Obituaries appeared also in the *N.Y. Times,* Feb. 29, 1949, and in *Science,* Mar. 4, 1949. He is listed in *Who Was Who in Am.* (1950). Published sources for the Arctic period include "Porter's March from Cape Flora to Camp Abruzzi" (autobiographical), Appendix #3 to Anthony Fiala, *Fighting the Polar Ice* (1906); Anthony Fiala, "Two Years in the Arctic," *McClure's Mag.,* Feb. 1906; and Mar. 1906; J. A. Fleming, ed., *The Ziegler Polar Expedition, 1903–1905, Scientific Results,* containing two chapters by Porter, "Astronomical Observations and Reductions" and "Map Construction and Survey Work"; Berton C. Willard, "Russell W. Porter . . . Explorer," *Polar Notes,* Dartmouth College Lib., no. 8, June 1968. A brief autobiographical article on his experiences with amateur telescope makers, "From One A.T.M. to All the Others," appeared in *Sky and Telescope,* Dec. 1946; see also Webb Waldron, "Stars on a Mountain," *Century Mag.,* Apr. 1925. Chapters on telescope making and other problems appeared in Albert G. Ingalls, ed., "Amateur Telescope Making," a series of volumes published from 1937 to 1953, and numerous articles in *Pop. Astron.,* including "A New Mounting for a Reflecting Telescope," May 1921, and in the *Sci. Am.* Other articles by Porter include (with J. A. Anderson) "The 200-Inch Telescope," *The Telescope,* Mar.–Apr. 1940, and an account of the Palomar dedication that contains many of his drawings, *Eng. Sci. Monthly,* June 1948. Additional biographical information appears in George Pendray, *Men, Mirrors and Stars* (1935) and David O. Woodbury, *The Glass Giant of Palomar* (1939). Photographs of some of Porter's drawings are reproduced in Dennis Milon, "A Russell Porter Exhibit," *Sky and Telescope,* Oct. 1967. Material on the family background may be found in C. Horace Hubbard and Justus Dartt, *Hist. of the Town of Springfield, Vt.* (1895) and in Henry H. Saunderson, *Hist. of Charlestown, N.H.* (1876).]

HELEN WRIGHT

PORTER, WILLIAM TOWNSEND (Sept. 24, 1862-Feb. 16, 1949), physiologist, was born in Plymouth, Ohio, the second son of Frank Gibson Porter, a physician, and Martha (Townsend) Porter. His father served as a medical officer in the Union Army during the Civil War and then practiced medicine in

St. Louis, Mo. Porter's mother died when he was twelve years old, and he was orphaned at the age of seventeen. He supported himself by working nights while attending the St. Louis Medical College (later the Washington University School of Medicine). He received his medical degree in 1885 and then took a course in physiological chemistry in Philadelphia before going abroad for postgraduate studies in the universities of Kiel, Breslau, and Berlin under the tutelage of Walther Flemming, Karl Hürthle, and Martin Heidenhain. The striking contrast between the didactic methods used in teaching physiology at St. Louis and the experimental approach in the German laboratories was instrumental in shaping Porter's concepts of medical education.

Returning to St. Louis, Porter became resident physician and acting superintendent of the St. Louis City Hospital. In 1887 he was appointed assistant professor of physiology at the St. Louis Medical College; he was made professor the following year. Not only did he establish the first laboratory of physiology beyond the Eastern seaboard, but in addition to physiology he taught bacteriology, laryngology, and physiological chemistry. His journal publications on ventricular filling and pressure, control of respiration, coronary circulation, and origin of the heartbeat and his monographs on the physical and mental development of children, drew the attention of eminent scientists, such as Charles Scott Sherrington, the English physiologist, and Henry Pickering Bowditch, Higginson professor of physiology at Harvard Medical School.

In 1893 Bowditch persuaded Porter to join his department to reorganize the teaching procedures and in particular to introduce the use of laboratory experiments as part of the routine instruction. Until then, physiology had been taught almost entirely by lectures, textbook assignments, and demonstrations. Since the apparatus needed to equip such laboratories was available only from Germany and was prohibitively expensive, Porter established a machine shop in the department to make simplified, less costly models of the existing apparatus and to develop and produce new instruments. The innovative techniques he devised for production in quantity enabled him not only to supply Harvard's needs but to provide surplus apparatus for use by other schools. President Charles W. Eliot of Harvard, although sympathetic to Porter's mission, was concerned that such an enterprise would be viewed as a commercial venture operating on nontaxed property. In 1901 Eliot secured for Porter the original capital to found the Harvard Apparatus Company, which was moved off the campus.

By 1900 Bowditch had turned over to Porter essentially the entire responsibility for instruction in the physiology department. Porter planned a more extended course than medical students had ever been given. As his chief teaching associate he chose Walter B. Cannon, one of the most promising of his students, and energetically furthered Cannon's career at the medical school. Porter himself was a skilled experimenter and a master of laboratory technique. He was, however, a strict disciplinarian, and he set teaching standards for his students that were perhaps too high in view of their educational background, for the medical school at Harvard, unlike that at Johns Hopkins, did not then require a bachelor's degree for admission. In the years 1902 to 1904 roughly a third of Porter's students failed to pass the physiology course. Protesting students labeled Porter a martinet, while at the same time praising the teaching ability of Cannon. The revolt became so serious that in 1906 President Eliot appointed Cannon the Higginson professor and chairman of the department, to succeed Bowditch; Porter was made professor of comparative physiology. The resulting breach between Porter and Cannon continued for many years. Porter became professor emeritus in 1928.

Porter was elected a member of the American Physiological Society at its fourth annual meeting in 1891. Members of the society were concerned that no journal existed in the United States for the publication of research in physiology but failed to agree on plans for such a journal, whereupon Porter in 1897 single-handedly founded the *American Journal of Physiology,* assuming both editorial and financial responsibility; the first issue appeared in January 1898. As an editor, Porter set high standards in the publication of research. He continued to edit the *Journal* until 1914, when he presented it to the society, debt-free.

Porter maintained his interest in supplying specialized physiological apparatus to educational institutions at minimum cost through his Harvard Apparatus Company, which in 1934 became a nonprofit organization. He had never accepted a salary from the company, and by 1921 it was amassing an annual surplus, which he used to establish the Porter Research Fellowship, to be awarded annually by the American Physiological Society to a young postdoctoral physiologist of promise.

In 1893 Porter married Alma Canfield Sterling of St. Louis. They had one child, Hildegarde. During World War I, the Rockefeller Foundation chose Porter to do a study of the treatment of traumatic shock under combat conditions in Belgium and France; a personal account, entitled *Shock at the Front* (1918), was published for the general public. Porter received honorary degrees from the University of Maryland (1907) and Washington University (1915). The American Physiological Society in 1948 elected him an honorary member, an honor previously reserved for distinguished foreign physiologists. Physiology was Porter's religion; he had no other. In later years the Pokanoket Club in Dover, Mass., where he made his home, was his chief source of companionship. He died of bronchopneumonia in a nursing home in Framingham, Mass., and was buried in Dover.

[The chief sources are Am. Physiological Soc., *Hist. of the Am. Physiological Soc., Semicentennial, 1887–1937* (1938), pp. 78–83, 171–173, 193–194; A. J. Carlson et al., "The Harvard Apparatus Co., the *Am. Jour. of Physiology* and Dr. W. T. Porter," *Science*, Dec. 8, 1944, pp. 518–519; obituary by Carlson, *ibid.*, July 29, 1949; Eugene M. Landis in *Am. Jour. of Physiology*, 158 (1949), v–vii; A. C. Barger in *Physiologist*, 14 (1971), 277–285; and correspondence of Porter with President Charles W. Eliot, Harvard Univ. Archives. Information was provided by Harold Sossen, president of the Harvard Apparatus Co., and Hildegarde Porter Heffinger.]

A. CLIFFORD BARGER

POTT, FRANCIS LISTER HAWKS (Feb. 22, 1864–Mar. 7, 1949), college president, Episcopal priest, and missionary, was born in New York City, the son of James Pott and Josephine (Hawks) Pott. It is not known if there were other children. His father was of Scottish background. After undergraduate study at Columbia College, from which he received the L.H.B. degree in 1883, Pott enrolled in the General Theological Seminary, New York. There he became interested in China through teaching the reading and speaking of English to a class composed, in part, of Chinese laundrymen. As soon as he received his B.D. in 1886, he went to China as an Episcopal missionary to devote his life, he thought, to evangelical work. A small Episcopal college, St. John's in Shanghai, was offering courses that included English, Chinese, science, and religion; a small theological school and a medical school had been added in 1880. Soon after Pott's arrival, he was transferred to St. John's, where within two years, he was translating books on science and religion. He was not happy about leaving evangelism, but his

rapid grasp of Chinese and his administrative talents clearly qualified him for the new assignment. In the summer of 1888, on August 23, he took an unusual step for a Western missionary: he married a Chinese woman, Soo-ngo Wong (Huang Su-wu), a clergyman's daughter who was headmistress of St. Mary's school. They had four children: James Hawks, William Sumner Appleton, Walter Graham Hawks, and Olivia Hawks. That same fall, Pott was named president of the college. He immediately set to work to make St. John's a university that would compare favorably with American institutions of the time. It was said of him that he never made a trip home without returning with a building for St. John's in his pocket. At the same time, he began to reorganize and strengthen the university curriculum.

By the 1890's there was a growing demand among wealthy Chinese merchants for a modern education for their sons, then unobtainable through government auspices. Although St. John's offered a classical Chinese education of sorts, its excellence in modern subjects taught in English was appealing. By 1904 its students came from eight different provinces, Hawaii, and Hongkong, and were largely drawn from wealthy families. By 1905 Pott had the college incorporated in the United States so that it could confer academic degrees similar to those offered in American colleges. Yale, among others, allowed St. John's graduates to enter its graduate and professional schools without further examination, and in 1907 over thirty St. John's graduates were studying in America, a coveted opportunity and entrée to high position in China. These advantages overshadowed the un-Chinese and sometimes unwelcome school requirements of mandatory daily chapel and dumbbell drill.

Busy heading committees, translating and writing, presiding over his close family, Pott epitomized an era of optimism in China and in Chinese-American relations. With the coming of the republic in 1911 he saw great opportunities for modernization and the spread of Christian culture under the kind of leadership his school was producing. Western-oriented St. John's graduates through the years included W. W. Yen, Wellington Koo, Alfred Sze, David Yui, and T. Z. Koo, and press references to a St. John's clique of the Christian party were as much a tribute to the university's prestige as a hint of disaffection.

But both Pott's life and that of China were changing. In 1918 Mrs. Pott died. The following year he married a widow, Emily G.

Cooper. These changes in his personal life were accompanied by convulsions in China, signaled by the growth of nationalism, anti-Christian sentiments, and mass student movements. In 1913 Pott had pleaded in his book *The Emergency in China* that the Chinese be allowed to shape their own destiny. But the new China posed what seemed a threat to the orderly American-style institutions that missionaries had created, and Pott, like many other college presidents in China, was unhappy about the loss of control. He showed signs of growing inflexibility. During the 1925 student strikes, he met a test of his authority by closing the university in an altercation over flying American and Chinese flags. It was interpreted as a lack of sympathy for the Chinese cause. A group of students left permanently, formed a new counter-university named Kwang-hua University, and tried to close St. John's; they failed, but it was a distressing incident. Shortly, too, Pott began a long quarrel with the government over registering St. John's. The official attempt to register all missionary schools meant abandoning compulsory religious education and appointing Chinese administrators. Pott immediately agreed to the second but unlike other missionary presidents resisted registration for many years. It was clear that despite his earlier remarks he welcomed Chinese control only when it agreed with his own ideas; in 1927 he was one of a group that publicly criticized the National Christian Council for its policy of conciliation toward Chinese Nationalists. As a kind and distinguished younger contemporary said years later, Pott was a progressive early in the century, but then he got "a little stiff, a little stiff."

Pott remained president until 1940, presiding reluctantly over the admission of women to the university but resisting firmly the secularization of the school. After spending the war years in the United States, he returned to Shanghai at the end of 1946. He died there in 1947. A memorial service was held at Calvary Church, New York, on Mar. 25, 1947.

St. John's as Pott knew it did not long outlast him. Taken over by the Communist regime in 1949, it officially expired as a religious institution in 1951. Pott and his university had both served for a few generations to educate modern leaders for a new China. They were dynamic, if temporary, influences during a period when China was trying to identify and develop more indigenous institutions and leaders. They introduced China to the modern world. That the pace and direction

of history made them soon obsolete should not obscure their contribution.

[The papers of F. L. Hawks Pott are at the Church Hist. Soc., Austin, Tex. A brief biography is in Sherwood Eddy, *Pathfinders of the World Missionary Crusade* (1945), and short but not wholly accurate accounts are in *Who's Who in the Clergy*, I (1935–1936) and *Religious Leaders of America*, II (1941–1942). Pott's work at the university is in *St. John's University, Shanghai: 1879–1951* (1955), written by Mary Lamberton for the United Board for Christian Colleges in China (New York).

Pott translated into Chinese a number of religious books and science texts, as well as a life of Alexander Hamilton. He wrote *The Outbreak of China* (1900); *A Sketch of Chinese History* (1903); *Lessons in the Shanghai Dialect* (1907; revised, 1913); and *A Short History of Shanghai* (1928).

A likeness of Pott is in *A Short History of Shanghai*.]

SHIRLEY GARRETT

POWELL, JOHN BENJAMIN (Apr. 18, 1886–Feb. 28, 1947), editor, correspondent, and writer on Asia, was born in Marion County, Mo., near Palmyra, the first child among two boys and four girls of Robert Powell and Flora Belle (Pilcher) Powell. He came of a Welsh family that settled in Delaware, then migrated to northeast Missouri. His farmer parents belonged to the Christian church. Growing up in the country, he went to a rural school and helped his father with the farm chores. His father died when he was about twelve. To help pay his way through high school and the Gem City Business College, both in nearby Quincy, Ill., young Powell delivered newspapers. Then, after teaching in a country school, he became a reporter on the Quincy *Whig,* earning the money to attend the University of Missouri at Columbia, where he was one of the first students in the School of Journalism, newly established (1908) by Walter Williams. Attracted to students from the Orient, Powell joined with a Chinese colleague in organizing a campus Cosmopolitan Club for foreign students. After graduation, he worked briefly for the *St. Louis Republic* and then joined the *Hannibal* (Mo.) *Courier-Post,* where (1910–1913) he was successively circulation solicitor, advertising manager, and city editor. In 1913 he returned to the University of Missouri as an instructor in journalism. While there, he wrote *Building a Circulation* (1914), *Getting Subscribers for the Country Newspaper* (1915), and *Newspaper Efficiency in the Small Town* (1915). While in Hannibal, he married, on Mar. 20, 1913, Martha Eleanor Hinton, daughter of a Hannibal banker and descendant of Moses Bates, the Revolutionary veteran who founded Hannibal. They had two children, Martha Bates and John William.

The turning point for Powell came in 1916, when Dean Williams handed him a cable from alumnus Thomas F. F. Millard, a New York newspaper correspondent in the Far East, seeking the services of a graduate of the journalism school to assist in publishing an English-language journal in China. Powell found the invitation to exotic adventure irresistible. He arrived in Shanghai on Feb. 3, 1917, and performed much of the hard, often frustrating, work involved in bringing out the first weekly issue of *Millard's Review of the Far East,* dated June 9. Covering business, financial, and economic areas as well as politics, public life, and religion, the new weekly resembled in content the London economic journals and physically the format of the *New Republic.* Its diverse subscribers were scattered throughout the Orient, ranging from missionaries in remote areas to importers and salesmen and the English captain of a tramp steamer, who stopped at Shanghai only twice a year and took his copies in six-month bundles. Powell credited himself "with being the first foreign editor in China to discover the young English-reading Chinese subscriber" (Powell, p. 13). Accordingly, he promoted the organization of English-language study clubs and current events classes in colleges and universities, "the members of which subscribed . . . in dozen or even in hundred lots" (Powell, p. 13). Powell also taught a journalism course at one of the colleges.

Millard left Shanghai later in 1917 and did not return to the *Review,* thus placing the responsibility for its continuance on Powell. In 1922 Powell assumed full financial responsibility as well, and in that year he changed the name to the more representative *China Weekly Review.* During the years 1923-1925, he also edited an English-language daily, *The China Press* of Shanghai. Early in his Far Eastern career, Powell began to represent American and British newspapers and press associations. These connections included the *Chicago Tribune* (1918-1938), the *Manchester Guardian* (1925-1936), and the London *Daily Herald* (1937-1941). He explained that he had no trouble in representing publications with divergent viewpoints because he sought only to report "the underlying facts" and scrupulously avoided "interpreting." Powell also wrote frequently for magazines, among them *Asia, Editor & Publisher, The Living Age, The Nation, The World Tomorrow,* and *Trans-Pacific.*

Although Powell gave close attention to his Shanghai weekly and at times kept it going through income from other writings, he was frequently on the move, following developments in the Far East and elsewhere He covered the Washington Conference on Limitation of Armaments, 1921-1922. He also acted as a special representative of American commercial interests in China, 1920-1922. In that capacity he labored assiduously in Congress for adoption of the China Trade Act of 1922. He witnessed the nationalist revolution in China, 1926-1927; the Chinese-Russian conflict in Manchuria, 1929; the Chinese-Japanese outbreak also in Manchuria, 1931-1932; and the hostilities between China and Japan, 1937. Editorially he strongly supported the unification movement of Sun Yat-sen.

In 1925, following the death of her father, Martha Powell returned to Missouri. The children returned home in 1926.

Powell's views were not always popular, and he knew violence firsthand. He was captured by Chinese bandits and held for five weeks in 1923 and a hand grenade was thrown at him on a Shanghai street in 1941. At times he wore a steel vest. Powell made a major point of warning that Japanese military strength was on the rise. With the outbreak of World War II, he was advanced in Japanese eyes from "unfriendly" to a "public enemy"; when the Japanese seized Shanghai, Powell was arrested. Charged with espionage, he was held in Bridge House jail and then in Kiangwan prison, Dec. 20, 1941-May 23, 1942. He was kept in an unheated cell, sometimes in solitary confinement, and fed barely enough to sustain life. Both his feet were crippled by frostbite and gangrene. When released he was also ill with beriberi and weighed only eighty pounds. He returned to the United States on the prisoner exchange ship *Gripsholm* and was hospitalized for almost three years in New York and Washington. He lost parts of both feet through operations. While recuperating, he wrote *My Twenty-Five Years in China,* published in 1945. In that year he also wrote "Today on the China Coast" for the *National Geographic Magazine* (February) and was coauthor with Max Eastman of "The Fate of the World Is at Stake in China," *Reader's Digest* (June). In August 1946, he flew to Tokyo to testify at the war crimes trials. For his wartime heroism he was publicly commended by Generalissimo Chiang Kai-shek. From many quarters came financial assistance, part of which Powell used to establish a Far Eastern studies scholarship at the University of Missouri.

Shortly after leaving Walter Reed Hospital, Powell, standing with crutches, addressed a meeting of Missouri alumni in Washington, Feb. 28, 1947, on the importance of Asia in world affairs. He had just said "thank you" when he collapsed in his chair and died of a heart attack. He was buried in Riverside Cemetery, Hannibal.

The many honors for "J.B.," as his colleagues knew the slight, mild-mannered yet often fiery crusader, included awards from the Chinese government and the Chinese National Press Association. His alma mater, after presenting him with its medal for "distinguished service in journalism" in 1942, honored him with the LL.D. in 1945. An apt description appeared in *Newsweek*: ". . . small-town editor with a world outlook, deep curiosity and an ingrained sympathy for the underdog" (Sept. 14, 1942). Citing Powell's persistence in warning of Japan's potential for aggression, Sen. Forrest C. Donnell of Missouri told Congress (Mar. 10, 1947) that "the fighting editor" had "notably distinguished himself" by his "steadfast devotion to duty."

[Powell's files, records, and library in Shanghai were seized by the Japanese and presumably destroyed, although that was not established as a fact. Subsequently, some papers and other materials were assembled at the Univ. of Missouri School of Journalism. Although it tells little about his family and early years, the fullest source is his autobiography, *My Twenty-Five Years in China* (1945). See also *Who Was Who in America*, II (1950). Numerous newspaper articles appeared at the time of his return to the United States, and obituaries were published in newspapers in St. Louis, New York, Washington, Kansas City, and Hannibal, Mo.; especially see *St. Louis Post-Dispatch*, Feb. 28, and Mar. 1, 1947. The news weeklies of the time also carried articles about him. A biobibliography with an extensive compilation of Powell's writings and citations to articles about him was prepared by Anne W. Griffin at the Emory Univ. division of librarianship in 1963. Information and assistance were provided by Powell's daughter, Mrs. W. Stewart Hensley, of Chevy Chase, Md., and his son, John W. Powell, of San Francisco; Roy M. Fisher and William H. Taft of the Univ. of Missouri, Howard R. Long of Southern Illinois Univ., and Roy T. King, St. Louis. An oil portrait painted by Yun Gee during Powell's hospitalization was placed at the Univ. of Missouri School of Journalism in 1944.]

IRVING DILLIARD

RADIN, MAX (March 29, 1880-June 22, 1950), lawyer, philologist, philosopher, and teacher, was born in Kempen, Poland; he was the second of three sons of Adolph Moses Radin and Johanna (Theodor) Radin, of German origin. His father, born in Neustadt-Schirwindt (now Lithuania), was a rabbi, and, upon his immigration to the United States, first lived in Elmira, N.Y., and then in New York City. His father's main interests and achievements were in the area of prison reform. Max, who was brought to this country at the age of four, owed to his father his early knowledge of German, Hebrew, Greek, and Latin; his love for classic literature; his interest in history; and his respect for religious tradition. He was said to be one of the few people still able to converse in Latin.

At the age of nineteen, Radin graduated from the College of the City of New York; in 1902 he acquired the LL.B. degree from New York University and in 1909 the Ph.D. from Columbia. In that year, on July 2, he married Rose Jaffe; they had one child, Rhea. After his wife's death in 1918, he married Dorothea Prall, on June 30, 1922; she later became a translator of Russian and Polish literature.

From 1900 to 1919, Radin was a teacher in the public schools of New York City, where he became vice-principal of De Witt Clinton High School; from 1917 to 1918 he lectured on Roman law in the City College of New York; and from 1918 to 1919 was an instructor at Columbia University. In 1919 he joined the law faculty of the University of California at Berkeley, where he taught until his retirement in 1948; in 1940, he was named John Henry Boalt professor of law. After a brief interlude at the Hastings College of Law in San Francisco, he became a member of the Institute for Advanced Study at Princeton.

On June 26, 1940, California's governor announced Max Radin's appointment as an associate justice of the state's supreme court, but the Commission of Judicial Appointments refused to approve the appointment.

Radin served from 1941 to 1948 as a commissioner of Uniform State Laws. He was a member of many scholarly associations. He died in Berkeley of cancer at the beginning of the summer of 1950 after his second year at the institute. His ashes were buried in the Prall family plot at Saginaw, Michigan. His obituary in the *California Law Review* recounts the story that, every month or two, Max Radin would call in a stenographer and say, "Here, take a book." This story, kindly as it was meant, is in retrospect an ironic comment on the disheartening fact that none of his seventeen books seems to have acquired lasting fame. Radin foresaw this. Speaking of his penultimate work, *The Law and You*, he joked, "This book costs a quarter and it is worth every penny." Radin's unparalleled contributions to science and literature were published in periodicals of the most varying specialization.

Radin's most important contribution to future

generations was his historical and philosophical study of the legal sources of the United States Constitution. In his articles and books, he traced these sources through statutes and precedents, discussing the philosophical and political concepts that influenced the drafting of the Constitution. Justice William O. Douglas concluded his eulogy on the occasion of Max Radin's death with the prediction that "when his period is evaluated, it will be Radin who stands out as the one who during tumultuous and critical days brought the brightest honor to the ideals of democracy. He follows the tradition of Thomas Paine and Thomas Jefferson in his daily living. His is part of the tradition of Holmes and Cardozo in his influence on the law."

[A bibliography of more than 700 items and a selection of unpublished essays is at the Univ. of Calif. Law School. Radin's own library is at the Hebrew University in Jerusalem.]

ALBERT A. EHRENZWEIG

RASKOB, JOHN JAKOB (Mar. 19, 1879-Oct. 15, 1950), financier, Democratic national chairman, was born in Lockport, N.Y., to John Raskob and Anna Frances (Moran) Raskob. His paternal grandfather, an Alsatian cigarmaker, had come to the United States in 1845; his father carried on the family trade. His mother's parents had been born in Dublin, Ireland. The oldest of four children, two of them boys, John grew up in a close-knit, devoutly Catholic family. After leaving high school, he attended a local business college, where he learned accounting and stenography. He worked briefly as secretary to a Lockport lawyer and in 1898 joined the Holly Manufacturing Company as stenographer to the chief engineer. He subsequently worked for a short time for Arthur Moxham, head of a steel company in Nova Scotia. Moxham was a former business associate of Pierre S. du Pont, and when in 1900 Raskob decided to return to the United States, du Pont took him on first as a bookkeeper and then as a personal secretary. Du Pont, who was then managing the Johnson Company of Lorain, Ohio, which was involved in real estate and interurban railroads, was impressed by his young secretary's quick, sharp mind and his talent in the understanding and manipulating of financial data, and the two became fast friends.

Raskob soon had an opportunity to demonstrate his financial skills. In 1902 Pierre du Pont and his cousins Alfred I. and T. Coleman du Pont took control of the family firm, E. I. du Pont de Nemours and Company, which had been making explosives for one hundred years. It was still a small firm with only six stockholders, but the cousins immediately began to transform it into a modern, consolidated, vertically integrated enterprise. They bought out their largest competitor, Laflin and Rand, and merged their holdings into the E. I. du Pont de Nemours Powder Company, which through exchange of stock with many smaller companies came by 1904 to control over two-thirds of the black powder and dynamite capacity and all of the smokeless powder capacity in the United States. Raskob worked closely with Pierre du Pont in devising the complex financial arrangements for this expansion—an expansion achieved with almost no outlay of cash and with the three cousins retaining full control.

In the administrative centralization that followed, du Pont as treasurer and Raskob as his assistant concentrated on building the company's financial offices. They created a large accounting and auditing department, which for the first time brought modern financial methods to the American explosives industry. They also devised policies to assure a steady flow of working capital and rational expansion of the company's productive capacity. They favored a high dividend policy in order to encourage the stockholders, still primarily members of the large du Pont clan, to reinvest their earnings. They advocated investment in plants, mines, and offices only if a 15 percent return was assured. In working out these procedures, particularly techniques for determining return on investment, du Pont and Raskob pioneered in developing many useful tools in modern corporate finance. When Pierre du Pont became acting president of the company in 1909, Raskob became *de facto* treasurer, receiving the title officially in 1914. In this capacity he carried out the financing of the company's huge expansion after the outbreak of World War I in 1914.

Meanwhile, in 1914, Raskob had invested in the General Motors Corporation and had persuaded Pierre du Pont to do the same. A dispute in 1915 between William C. Durant, founder of General Motors, and his bankers led to the appointment of du Pont as a neutral chairman of the board and of Raskob and two other associates as neutral directors. After Durant regained control of his company in 1916 (without du Pont aid), he and Raskob began to work closely together. They had much in common. Each was small in stature and dapper in dress. Both were financiers rather than manufacturers, and both relished the building of industrial empires. During a downward swing of the stock market in 1917, Raskob joined Durant in a syndicate to maintain the price of General Motors stock; and as the market continued to fall he arranged for the Du Pont Company to buy up $25 million worth of GM stock, in return for which Durant agreed to turn over financial management to the Du Pont interests. In March, 1918, accordingly, Raskob resigned as treasurer at the Du Pont Company to become chairman of the finance committee of the General Motors Corporation.

In his new post, Raskob introduced modern accounting and auditing procedures into General Motors, and indeed into the American automobile industry. He formed the General Motors Acceptance Corporation (1919), which provided extensive credit to dealers and customers, encouraging the installment buying of automobiles. His primary interest, however, was the huge expansion program that he and Durant launched immediately after the end of World War I. To fund this expansion Raskob relied on retained earnings and sold large blocks of stock to the Du Pont Company, Nobel Explosives Trades, and J. P. Morgan and Company. When the sharp postwar recession struck in September 1920, drastically reducing the demand for automobiles, Raskob was able to prevent bankruptcy by using the newly raised funds, not for new plants and equipment but to meet current obligations. Durant once again attempted to hold up the price of General Motors stock, but soon sank more than $30 million into debt. To save both Durant and the company from financial disaster, Raskob and Pierre du Pont made arrangements by which the du Ponts and J. P. Morgan and Company raised the funds Durant needed, in return for the control of a large block of his holdings of General Motors stock and his retirement as president.

After the crisis of 1920 Raskob had less influence at General Motors. Pierre du Pont, who took Durant's place as president, turned over the management of its operations to Alfred P. Sloan, Jr., and of its finances to F. Donaldson Brown, a Raskob protégé who had succeeded him as treasurer at Du Pont. Thus Raskob played a relatively minor role in the massive reorganization that soon made General Motors the largest manufacturing company in the world; but he continued to have a major say in dividend policy and in shaping the corporation's basic financial structure. He devised

a plan to provide large stock bonuses to many senior executives through the formation of the Management Securities Company. Increasingly, however, he turned to outside investment and speculation, to accepting directorships of railroads and other corporations, and to developing an interest in politics.

The bent to politics came from his association with a group of New Yorkers, including William F. Kenny, James J. Riordan, and Gov. Alfred E. Smith, who were, like himself, successful Catholics and sons and grandsons of immigrants. In 1928 Smith, the Democratic presidential candidate, decided to aim his campaign at the Northeast by exploiting the prohibition issue and by identifying his party with business and prosperity. Raskob, an outspoken "wet" and a nationally known businessman, was thus a logical choice for Democratic national chairman. Resigning from General Motors to accept the post, he concentrated on raising funds and building an effective organization but took little part in shaping campaign strategy.

After Smith's defeat, Raskob, unlike his predecessors, maintained a permanent headquarters for the Democratic National Committee in Washington, with Jouett Shouse as director and Charles Michelson as publicity chief. Over the next four years the Committee hammered away at the failure of the Hoover administration to combat the depression and, reflecting Raskob's conservative views, advocated such policies as repeal of the Eighteenth Amendment, tax cuts, and a five-day week. Raskob remained close to Al Smith. He joined with him to build and operate the Empire State Building in New York City and to take over Riordan's County Trust Company after Riordan committed suicide in 1929. Ever loyal to Smith, Raskob sought, as the 1932 Democratic convention approached, to block the nomination of Franklin D. Roosevelt by encouraging a number of local favorite sons. But at the convention he and Shouse found themselves time and again outmaneuvered, and with Roosevelt's nomination Raskob was replaced as the party's national chairman by James A. Farley.

The years after 1932 were for Raskob ones of frustration. His investments, especially the Empire State Building, did badly, and he sold his estate, Archmere, overlooking the Delaware River at Claymont, Del. He had little understanding of the deep and complex political and economic changes going on about him. He remained a director of General Motors and Du Pont until 1946, but his ties were now much closer to Smith and other New York associates. In 1934 Raskob, with Pierre du Pont, Alfred P. Sloan, Smith, and other friends, helped found the American Liberty League to "defend and uphold the Constitution" and protect "individual and group initiative and enterprise" by vigorously combating the New Deal. Raskob, however, after arranging for Shouse to become president of the League, took little part in its affairs aside from contributing funds and making an occasional speech. Instead, he began to travel widely, to expand his investments in mining, and, as prosperity returned, to contribute to civic and Catholic causes. For such contributions he had been made Private Chamberlain in the Papal Household in 1928, and he was later twice knighted by the Pope.

On June 18, 1906, Raskob married Helena Springer Green of Galena, Md. They had thirteen children: John Jakob, William Frederick, Helena Mary, Elizabeth Ann, Robert Pierre, Inez Yvonne, Margaret Lucy, Josephine Juanita, Nina Barbara, Catharine Lorena (who died in infancy), Patsy Virginia, Mary Louise, and Benjamin Green. In later years Raskob and his wife separated but were not divorced; his wife moved to Arizona and he continued to live in New York. In 1950, at the age of seventy-one, Raskob died of a coronary occlusion at his Eastern Shore farm near Centreville, Md., where he often spent weekends; he was buried in New Cathedral Cemetery, Wilmington, Del. Most of his $5 million estate was left to the Raskob Foundation for Catholic Activities, which he had established in 1945.

[There is an extensive collection of Raskob papers at the Eleutherian Mills Hist. Lib., Greenville, Del. The Pierre S. du Pont, Irénée du Pont, and T. Coleman du Pont papers at the same library also contain Raskob material. Raskob's views on contemporary issues can be found in Samuel Crowther, "Everybody Ought to Be Rich: An Interview with John J. Raskob," *Ladies' Home Jour.*, Aug. 1929; Henry F. Pringle in the *Outlook*, Aug. 22, 1928; and two pieces by Raskob, "What Next in America," *North Am. Rev.*, Nov. 1929, and a radio address on Oct. 27, 1930, which was printed in many newspapers. There is no biography of Raskob. His career at Du Pont and General Motors is covered in detail in Alfred D. Chandler, Jr., and Stephen Salsbury, *Pierre S. du Pont and the Making of the Modern Corporation* (1971). His role in the Democratic party is suggested in Oscar Handlin, *Al Smith and His America* (1958); Arthur M. Schlesinger, Jr., *The Crisis of the Old Order, 1919–1933* (1957); and Frank Freidel, *Franklin D. Roosevelt*, vols. II and III (1954–1956). George Wolfskill, *The Revolt of the Conservatives* (1962), tells of Raskob's part in the forming and financing of the Am. Liberty League. See also feature article by Julia McCarthy in *N.Y. World*, June 24, 1928; *N.Y. Times*, Oct. 16 and 26, 1950. Death record from Md. Division of Vital Records.]

ALFRED D. CHANDLER, JR.

RAVENEL, MAZŸCK PORCHER (June 16, 1861-Jan. 14, 1946), bacteriologist, hygienist, and public health authority, was born in Pendleton, S.C., the seventh child and fourth son of Henry Edmund Ravenel and Selina (Porcher) Ravenel of Charleston and Pendleton. The Ravenel family was of special distinction in South Carolina history. Their American lineage derived from René Ravenel, sieur de la Massais, of Vitré in Brittany, France, and his wife, Charlotte, daughter of Pierre de St. Julien, sieur de Malacare, each of whom was among the Huguenots who emigrated from France after the revocation (1685) of the Edict of Nantes and settled in Charles Town (now Charleston) in the province of Carolina. Marriages among their descendants introduced other Huguenot strains, including the Porcher, Mazÿck, and Gaillard families. Eminent physicians, scientists, and businessmen were in the several combined lines.

Mazÿck Porcher Ravenel graduated from the University of the South at Sewanee, Tenn., in 1881 and from the Medical College of South Carolina in Charleston in 1884. He practiced medicine in Charleston for six years, teaching at his alma mater and carrying out medical research. His interests in the latter field were developing rapidly, and as a consequence he felt the need of additional training. He moved to Philadelphia in 1892, where he matriculated in the first class in hygiene at the University of Pennsylvania and served as Scott fellow in hygiene (1893-1894) and assistant in bacteriology (1895). He pursued further medical studies at the Pasteur Institute in Paris and at the Institute of Hygiene in Halle, Germany (1896). In 1904, during his tenure at the Henry Phipps Institute (see below), he studied at the Maragliano Institute in Genoa, Italy.

Ravenel always gave credit to John Shaw Billings, professor of hygiene at the University of Pennsylvania for his early training in that field. In 1895, well prepared for studies of infectious diseases in animals and their prevention, he became the first director of the Hygienic Laboratory of the New Jersey State Board of Health. In 1896 he was appointed instructor in bacteriology at the medical and veterinary schools of the University of Pennsylvania, and bacteriologist of the Pennsylvania State Live Stock Sanitary Board. He held this position for eight years, widening his scientific associations in the veterinary field and developing a deep understanding of the relation of animal diseases to illness in man. Prominent among his investigations were studies of bovine tuberculosis, the bacteriology of milk, anthrax, fungus infections in livestock animals and man, and rabies.

Most important at the time were his studies of tuberculosis. These led to his appointment in 1904 as assistant medical director and bacteriologist at the newly founded Henry Phipps Institute for the Study, Treatment, and Prevention of Tuberculosis, a research institution founded in Philadelphia by Henry Phipps, partner of Andrew Carnegie, and directed by the distinguished Philadelphia tuberculosis specialist Lawrence Flick. His associations there with staff and visitors eminent in clinical studies on human tuberculosis were vitally important in supplementing his understanding of bovine tuberculosis. At the Phipps Institute he was fortunate also in his close association with the veterinarian Leonard Pearson, a distinguished student of bovine diseases. Ravenel traveled abroad with him to meet many eminent tuberculosis investigators in Europe. Ravenel's numerous published papers on tuberculosis marked him as one of the leading investigators of the disease in America. He was elected president of the National Tuberculosis Association in 1911.

In 1907 Ravenel accepted an invitation to the University of Wisconsin as professor of bacteriology. Here for seven years he continued his studies of tuberculosis and added important investigations on typhoid fever, rabies, and diphtheria, largely in their public health aspects. At the British Congress on Tuberculosis in London in 1901 and particularly at the International Congress on Tuberculosis in Washington, D.C., in 1908, Ravenel opposed the views of Robert Koch, discoverer of the tubercle bacillus and most eminent tuberculosis investigator of the day. Koch believed that the bovine type of tubercle bacillus could not cause pulmonary tuberculosis in man. Ravenel's experience and that of the eminent American investigator Theobald Smith were quite to the contrary. Ravenel's refutation of Koch at the international meeting in 1908 was spectacular. It is said that Ravenel, who was naturally inclined to argument, deeply enjoyed his confrontation with Koch. In subsequent years his view of the infectiousness of the bovine tubercle bacillus for man was universally accepted.

While in Wisconsin, Ravenel served as director of the state hygienic laboratory. His Wisconsin experience with typhoid and diphtheria carriers and his various related publications established his position as a leader in public health and preventive medicine. He was presi-

dent of the Wisconsin Antituberculosis Association throughout most of his stay in the state (1907-1914).

In 1914 he was appointed professor of preventive medicine and bacteriology at the University of Missouri and director of its public health laboratory. Here he continued his earlier studies and became more deeply involved in the field of public health, fortified by close association with the American Public Health Association, of which he became a director in 1915.

During World War I, Ravenel served as major and lieutenant colonel in the Army Medical Corps, with assignments at Fort Riley and Camp Funston, Kans., and Camp Kearny, Calif. In January 1919, he was commissioned assistant surgeon general in the reserve corps of the Public Health Service.

In 1920 he was named president of the American Public Health Association. He edited a monograph on the association, *A Half Century of Public Health* (1921), which is considered a classic in the history of public health. From 1924 to the end of his life he was editor or active editor emeritus of the *American Journal of Public Health*. A colleague wrote that he took it over as an ordinary association record book and handed it on to his successor as the outstanding public health publication in the country. On his retirement from active editorship in 1941 he was widely praised for his vigor, industry, integrity, and scholarship. He insisted on accuracy and was called the "paternal castigator" of the careless and inexact.

Ravenel belonged to many scientific and scholarly societies. He was chairman of the public health section of the American Medical Association (1913) and president of the United States Live Stock Sanitary Association (1913). He was a member of the National Advisory Health Council (1931) and many American and international commissions of importance to public health. He was an honorary member of the Royal Sanitary Institute of Great Britain. He belonged to the American Philosophical Society.

He died of pneumonia in 1946 at Columbia, Mo., survived by his second wife, the former Adele Allston Vanderhorst of Charleston, S.C., a daughter of Gov. Robert Withers Allston. They were married in December 1910. He was buried near his old home in Pendleton, S.C.

[Henry Edmund Ravenel, *Ravenel Records* (2nd ed. 1971), gives in great detail the genealogical lines of American Ravenels, whose progenitors moved from France to South Carolina. It deals basically with family lines prior to 1900. Additional family data have been obtained from Dr. W. Jervey Ravenel of Charleston and Augustus T. Graydon, also of Charleston. A number of pathologists and bacteriologists who knew Ravenel personally, have helped the writer, including Dr. Kenneth M. Lynch; his secretary, Julia C. Hills; Dr. Ben H. Boltjes; Dr. Paul F. Clark; and Dr. M. Pinson Neal.

Biographical sources include "Mazÿck Porcher Ravenel," *Jour. AMA,* 130 (1946), 523; John F. Norton, "Mazÿck Porcher Ravenel (1861–1946)," *Year Book Amer. Phil. Soc.* (1947), 292–293; "The Editor Emeritus," *Amer. Jour. Public Health,* 31 (1941), 80–81; "Appreciations of the Editor Emeritus," *ibid.,* 31 (1941), 1–9; and "Mazÿck Porcher Ravenel," *ibid.,* 36 (1946), 174–175.

Ravenel's papers of special distinction include the following: "The Etiology of Tuberculosis," *Amer. Jour. Med. Sci.,* 134 (1907), 469–482; "Aetiologie der Tuberkulose: Experimentelles und Statistisches über die tuberkulöse Infektion durch Nahrungsaufnahme und Kontakte. Berliner klinische Wochenschrift," 45 (1908), 788–793; and "The Transmission of Bovine Tuberculosis to Human Beings," *Arch. Pediatrics,* 34 (1917), 137.]

ESMOND R. LONG

REEVES, JOSEPH MASON (Nov. 20, 1872–Mar. 25, 1948), naval officer, was born in Tampico, Ill., the second of the five sons of Joseph Cunningham Reeves and Frances (Brewer) Reeves. He was descended on both sides from early seventeenth-century English settlers in Massachusetts. His father, born in Newark, N.Y., and educated at Ithaca College, served in the Union Army in the Civil War, after which he moved to Illinois and engaged in farming. A scholarly man, he broadened the education of his sons.

Joseph Reeves attended the United States Naval Academy, where he became noted as an athlete. He graduated in 1894 as cadet engineer and during the Spanish-American War distinguished himself in the outstanding engineering performance of the famous battleship *Oregon.* Transferred to the line in 1899, he demonstrated remarkable ability in training gun crews. He was on duty at the Naval Academy from 1906 to 1908. His first command, in 1913, was the experimental collier *Jupiter,* the navy's first ship with electric drive. Reeves commanded the second battleship *Maine* in World War I, was naval attaché to Italy, and from 1921 to 1923 commanded the battleship *North Dakota.* Then for two years he was a student and faculty member at the Naval War College, where his study of the principles of war as reflected in the battle of Jutland added a valuable document to naval literature.

The turning point in Reeves's career came in 1925, when at the age of fifty-two he volunteered for duty as an aviation observer and took three months' intensive instruction in flying at Pensacola, Fla. A new rule specified that only naval aviators and naval aviation observers could command aviation units at sea or ashore. In October, Reeves took command of Aircraft Squadrons, Battle Fleet, based at San Diego, Calif., which included the navy's first flight-deck carrier, *Langley* (converted in 1921 from the former collier *Jupiter*). This force participated little in fleet operations but devoted itself mostly to testing, breaking records, and stunt flying. Reeves observed his new command for six weeks and then bluntly told his officers they knew nothing about the military capabilities of aircraft. Proceeding to revolutionize the force with the methods that had produced his record-breaking gun crews, he shaped these squadrons into the striking arm of the navy. In 1925 *Langley* had eight aircraft embarked; three years later she was operating thirty-six with 200 landings a day. She also trained flight crews for the giant carriers *Saratoga* and *Lexington,* and when these joined the fleet in 1928, Reeves soon demonstrated that they were naval weapons of great power. In military exercises in 1928 and 1929, he conducted successful mock attacks on Hawaii and on the Panama Canal. He thus contributed to the evolution of the carrier task force, which was to play so prominent a role in World War II.

Reeves during the summer of 1927 was given temporary duty as adviser on aviation at the Geneva Disarmament Conference. The cruiser question, however, dominated the meeting. In September 1929, before a Senate committee investigating the conference, Washington reporter Drew Pearson stated that while in Geneva he had frequently heard the fluent Reeves express the hope that the conference would fail. With his naval career in jeopardy, Reeves adeptly rebutted the allegation at the next meeting of the committee.

Except for one year, Reeves remained in fleet aviation from 1925 to 1931, advancing in rank to rear admiral in 1927. In 1933 he became commander, Battle Fleet, and then for two years was commander-in-chief, United States Fleet, the first aviation officer to hold this command. He brought to fleet operations a realism never before attained, with emergency transits of the Panama Canal, unscheduled sorties from California bases, tight security measures, and a fleet problem set far in the western Pacific. When he retired in December 1936, the fleet was as ready for war as it could be made in peacetime.

Reeves was recalled to active duty in 1940 and for the next six years served on the lend-lease and munition assignment boards. As a member of the Roberts Commission, which investigated the Pearl Harbor disaster, he was severe in his criticism of Adm. Husband E. Kimmel, commander of the Pacific Fleet at the time of the attack.

Reeves married Eleanor Merrken Watkins of New York City on July 1, 1896. They had three children: Ruth Drury, Joseph Mason, and William Cunningham. Tall, bearded, and articulate, Reeves was an impressive man; those who heard him give a speech seldom forgot it. He believed that the oral word, rather than the written, was the true means of communicating ideas and of making men perform to their utmost. Reeves died of a heart attack in the Bethesda (Md.) Naval Hospital at the age of seventy-five. Burial was at the Naval Academy.

[Adolphus Andrews, Jr., "An Admiral with Wings" (senior diss., Princeton Univ., 1943; copy in U.S. Naval Acad. Lib.), based on interviews with Reeves; Eugene E. Wilson, *Slipstream* (1950); John D. Hayes, "Admiral Joseph Mason Reeves, USN," *Naval War College Review,* Nov. 1970, Jan. 1972; Archibald D. Turnbull and Clifford L. Lord, *Hist. of U.S. Naval Aviation* (1949); *Nat. Cyc. Am. Biog.,* Current Vol. D, p. 38; obituaries in *N.Y. Times* and *Baltimore Sun;* Navy Dept. records; data from members of family and from naval officer subordinates of Reeves.]

                                    JOHN D. HAYES

REID, OGDEN MILLS (May 16, 1882–Jan. 3, 1947), newspaper editor and publisher, was born in New York City, the older of two surviving children and only son of Whitelaw Reid, editor and publisher of the *New York Tribune,* and Elisabeth (Mills) Reid. He grew up in an atmosphere of affluence and achievement. His maternal grandfather was the philanthropist Darius Ogden Mills; his cousin Ogden Mills became secretary of the treasury under Herbert Hoover. After graduating from the Browning School in New York City, Reid briefly attended the University of Bonn in Germany (1899–1900) and then Yale, from which he received the B.A. degree in 1904 and the LL.B. in 1907. On Mar. 14, 1911, he married Helen Miles Rogers of Racine, Wis., a Barnard graduate who had been his mother's social secretary. They had three children: Whitelaw, Elisabeth (who died in childhood), and Ogden Rogers.

After receiving his law degree, Reid worked for a time in a law office and was admitted to the New York bar in 1908. That fall, however, he began his real career when he joined the staff of his father's newspaper, the *Tribune.* Working as reporter, copy reader, and assistant night editor, he became managing editor and president of the Tribune Association in January 1912. Early the following year, after the death of his father, he was named editor, a post he retained until his own death. Reid chose to concentrate on news and editorial policies, and gradually turned the business responsibilities over to his wife, Helen Rogers Reid, who joined the *Tribune* staff in 1918 as advertising director.

Although an active Republican, Ogden Reid was markedly more moderate and democratic in nature than his father. He worked with his staff to increase the *Tribune*'s coverage of European news and improve its criticism of art, music, and drama. He attempted to overcome the paper's reputation for dryness by hiring colorful reporters like Richard Harding Davis and Will Irwin. The *Tribune* scored during World War I with Davis' account of the entry of the German army into Brussels, Irwin's news beat on the battle of Ypres, the military criticism of Frank H. Simonds, and the war reporting of Heywood Broun and other young staff members. Mark Sullivan became a political columnist in 1923. Franklin P. Adams' "Conning Tower" became a *Tribune* feature in 1914; equally delightful were the columns of H. I. Phillips and the cartoons of Clare Briggs and H. T. Webster. The *Tribune* began to set its headlines in graceful Bodoni type in 1918, and under Reid's guidance the paper subsequently won two Ayer cups for typographical excellence.

So successful was Reid's management that the *Tribune* increased in circulation from 50,000 in 1912 to 142,000 in 1921. Yet the morning newspaper field in New York was overcrowded. Frank Munsey, the new owner of the Bennett family's illustrious *Herald,* attempted to buy the *Tribune;* when the Reids refused, he sold them the *Herald* in 1924 for $5 million. Included in the deal was the *Paris Herald,* the paper's European edition.

The new *Herald Tribune* successfully met the competitive challenge. It achieved a circulation of 275,000 by 1925 and became the principal competitor of the *New York Times.* Reid increased the coverage of local news under city editor Stanley Walker, and during the 1930's and 1940's the paper was able to boast a distinguished assortment of reporters and columnists, including Walter Lippmann, Joseph Alsop, Homer Bigart, and Alva Johnston, with Geoffrey Parsons as chief editorial writer. Eight Pulitzer prizes were awarded to *Herald Tribune* staff members during these years. By 1947 circulation had reached 358,000 daily and 700,000 on Sunday. An internationalist in outlook, Reid took a personal interest in the Paris edition, developing it into the leading American newspaper in Europe.

Reid was an independent Republican in politics, an attitude reflected by his paper, which supported most of the foreign policies of President Franklin D. Roosevelt but backed Wendell Willkie in 1940. At the age of sixty-four, Reid died of bronchial pneumonia at the Columbia-Presbyterian Medical Center in New York City, while undergoing treatment for an ulcerous throat. Funeral services were held at St. Thomas's Church (Episcopal), and he was buried in the family vault at Sleepy Hollow Cemetery, Tarrytown, N.Y. The *Herald Tribune* continued in family hands until 1958, when a controlling interest was sold to John Hay Whitney. A citywide newspaper strike impelled the new owner to close down the paper in 1966, leaving only the *International Herald Tribune* in Paris to carry on the traditions of the *Herald* of James Gordon Bennett and the *Tribune* of Horace Greeley and the Reids.

[Harry W. Baehr, Jr., *The N.Y. Tribune since the Civil War* (1936); Kenneth Stewart and John Tebbel, *Makers of Modern Journalism* (1952); Frank L. Mott, *Am. Journalism* (3rd ed., 1962); Edwin Emery, *The Press and America* (3rd ed., 1972); Fred C. Shapiro, "The Life and Death of a Great Newspaper," *Am. Heritage*, Oct. 1967; *Nat. Cyc. Am. Biog.*, XXXIII, 34–35; obituaries, with portraits, in *N.Y. Herald Tribune*, Jan. 4-8, 1947, *N.Y. Times*, Jan. 4-5, 1947, *Editor & Publisher*, Jan. 11, 1947, and *Newsweek*, Jan. 13, 1947.]

EDWIN EMERY

REINHARDT, AURELIA ISABEL HENRY (Apr. 1, 1877-Jan. 28, 1948), college president, was born in San Francisco, Calif., the second daughter and second of six children of William Warner Henry and Mollie (Merritt) Henry. Her father traveled to California in 1858 from Bennington, Vt.; her mother's family, originally from Pennsylvania, went west from Muscatine, Iowa, in 1863. Her father ran a wholesale grocery business in San Francisco, and her mother increased the family's income by running a boardinghouse and then a small hotel.

Aurelia attended San Francisco Boys' High School, newly coeducational, from 1888 to 1890, when the family temporarily moved to San Jacinto. In 1894 Aurelia entered the University of California at Berkeley, receiving the B. Litt. degree in 1898. She led an active social life and was not a brilliant student. From 1898 to 1901 she was instructor in physical culture and elocution at the University of Idaho, where she impressed students with her unusual energy, sympathy, charm, and cultivation. She taught a wide range of subjects, played in a student orchestra, and briefly considered acting as an alternative career.

Instead she decided to undertake graduate study in English at Yale, studying under Albert S. Cook and receiving the Ph.D. in 1905. Though her work was merely competent, she enjoyed steady encouragement, publishing a translation of Dante's *De Monarchia* (1904) and her dissertation on Ben Jonson's *Epicoene*. From 1903 to 1908, interrupted by one year of travel and study in Europe, she held the chair of English at the State Normal School, Lewiston, Idaho. Lonely despite her busy, outgoing involvement in college social life, she returned to Berkeley, where her family had long since settled. She spent 1908-1909 dedicatedly nursing her brother Paul during his terminal illness and writing short stories, which she was never able to publish.

On Dec. 4, 1909, she married Dr. George Frederick Reinhardt, a longtime family acquaintance and founder and director of the University Health Service in Berkeley. Two sons, George Frederick (eventually ambassador to Italy) and Paul Henry, were born in 1911 and 1913. In 1914 her husband died of blood poisoning contracted from a patient. There is much evidence that her marriage had been a strain for her. To a great extent, the couple had led separate social lives.

The young widow was offered a position teaching English in the University of California extension division. She lectured throughout the state and made a spectacular impression upon her audiences with her vivid, energetic personality. Then Mills College in Oakland invited her to become its president. Although she had two very young boys to raise, she eagerly accepted.

Her impact upon Mills, from her arrival in August 1916 until her retirement in September 1943, was enormous. When she entered upon her duties, the institution was old-fashioned, rudderless, and faltering. By 1927, she had increased student enrollment from 212 to 624; by 1943, faculty had risen from 39 to 101.

Quickly she gathered authority into her own hands. An admirer of Oxford traditionalism, she indulged in no radical curricular experiments, but gradually began raising academic standards. Aside from emphasizing the ability of women to enter a wide variety of occupations, she upheld time-honored academic ideals of leadership and service. Strengthening the college was her central aim, rather than using the institution to demonstrate a striking educational philosophy. She retained complete control of faculty appointments and moved Mills firmly into the orbit of national academic respectability, but a great many appointments were made either to personal friends or as a result of impulsive gestures. An alternative strategy was to seek out Rhodes scholars, among them Dean Rusk, later U.S. secretary of state. Her professors were not expected to publish, but to be at her constant beck and call for local social events. She went out of her way to offer positions to European refugees in the 1930's, among them the composer Darius Milhaud. Beginning in 1921, Mills offered the M.A. degree to both men and women. In 1926 she arbitrarily restructured the previously departmentalized faculty into five divisional "schools."

In sum, the tone of her administration was intensely personal and familial. Undeniably, she was autocratic; she could be sufficiently emotional to throw a book across a room. She would unpredictably order professors to teach particular courses on short notice, and in 1934 the trustees had to intervene to prevent her from carrying out capricious dismissals. She shrewdly managed scarce financial resources, but encouraged the development of extreme inequities among faculty salaries. All but a minority of the faculty revered her despite these failings. She had no airs, casually helping wash dishes after a dinner. But the faculty had to cope with her tireless, demanding intervention in every small daily matter. Indeed, she could be called "almost overpowering." Students regarded her with a mixture of fear and admiration; she prided herself on knowing them all as individuals.

Public relations was one of her greatest strengths. On her frequent statewide tours she always made a powerful impact on her audiences. Over the years she grew increasingly garrulous, pouring forth opinions on all subjects to anyone who would listen, desperately wanting to be liked. A Republican, she remained loyal to Herbert Hoover even in 1936 but also publicly opposed Japanese relocation in 1942. Reading widely if not deeply, she impulsively embraced a great variety of causes from right to left, though her activity in behalf of woman's suffrage, which began as early as 1904, was notably consistent.

She held many local civic positions. In 1919 she was president of the Oakland City Planning Commission. She was national president of the American Association of University Women from 1923 to 1927, and in 1928-1930 chairman of the department of education of the General Federation of Women's Clubs. During the 1930's she was active in nationwide Unitarian church affairs. After retirement she traveled widely, suffering increasing heart trouble. She died at the home of her son Paul, a Palo Alto physician. Her ashes are at the Oakland Columbarium.

[An exhaustive listing of sources on the life of Dr. Reinhardt is contained in George Hedley, *Aurelia Henry Reinhardt: Portrait of a Whole Woman* (Oakland, Calif.: Mills College, 1961), Appendix D. Appendix C contains a bibliography of her writings. Her papers are at Mills College and will be open to scholars in 1977. Hedley was, however, given access to them, and he provides the flavor of her correspondence in Chapter 21 of his biography, which is meticulously researched and far less reticent than his article on her in *Notable Am. Women*. The biography provides a full documentary basis for statements concerning her personality and her marriage. Memorial booklets include *In Memoriam: Aurelia Henry Reinhardt* and *The Aurelian Way* (Eucalyptus Press, Mills College, 1948, 1956).]

LAURENCE VEYSEY

REPPLIER, AGNES (Apr. 1, 1855-Dec. 15, 1950), writer, was born in Philadelphia, Pa., the second of four children and second daughter of John George Repplier and Agnes (Mathias) Repplier. Her genial but somewhat diffident father, raised in eastern Pennsylvania by French and German parents, earned a comfortable living as a coal retailer in a mining and processing partnership with his brothers. Her mother, the second wife of John Repplier, came from Westminster, Md., of German parentage and was the dominant parental force in Repplier's life.

The private events of Repplier's childhood are much obscured by her lifelong reluctance to discuss herself. Such as are known reveal early talents and eccentricities. She was nearly ten before learning to read, but from that time on she soon exhausted a rich but unconventional family library. Her formal schooling, beginning in 1867, lasted for less than four years, during which time she was admitted to and dismissed from Eden Hall, a school directed by the Sisters of the Sacred Heart in Torresdale, Pa., and a private school in Philadelphia conducted by Agnes Irwin. Although her departure in both instances was occasioned by what her mentors called excessive willfulness, Repplier paid loving tribute to both experiences in two books and maintained close ties with the Sisters. Agnes Irwin, who later became the first dean of Radcliffe College, became a close friend and sponsor of various of Repplier's professional activities.

Returning to her home in 1871, with no prospects of further education, Repplier read widely and occasionally submitted articles to local newspapers. From this life of leisurely indirection, she was suddenly called to help support her family when John Repplier lost his money through unwise investments. Largely at her mother's urging, the fifteen-year-old girl began to write essays and short fiction for children's magazines and the Sunday newspapers. Thus was launched a career that was to extend through the next eighty years, a career marked by a constantly enlarging readership and a reputation for a constancy of quality.

Her essays and fiction first reached a national audience in 1881 through publication in the *Catholic World*; she later became a regular contributor to the *Atlantic Monthly*. As her success increased, she began to live the life of a woman of letters: lecturing, traveling, doing research, and writing at her residence in Philadelphia. On the early advice of her friend Isaac Hecker, Paulist editor of the *Catholic World*, she gave up writing fiction in the 1880's. Thereafter, except for biographies of two friends and three figures from early American Catholic history, she concentrated her literary energies on the "familiar essay." This genre won her national literary prominence for over half a century. The subjects of her essays ranged from the pleasures of tea, and her favorite cats, to the strange careers of public executioners. On such diverse subjects, she trained her wit and erudition, not to prosecute a thesis but to enlarge the reader's consciousness of the richness, variety, and continuity of human experience.

To the religious enthusiast—her constant enemy—Repplier's prose is idle and self-indulgent. Indeed, some of her fellow Roman Catholics accused her of deliberately hiding her religion by refusing the role of polemicist. In fact, however, she was a very devout Catholic, as well as a constant defender of conservative values. She often spoke of her affection for England and the past, and her essays might be said to mirror the qualities of British neoclassical prose. Their pattern is quite simple: a proposition is announced, and a wealth of historical and literary references is gathered around the subject and framed by a tone of quiet detachment. The form carries large risks, particularly the temptation to facile verbal play. However, by her exquisite selection of detail, by a reverence for verbal exactitude, and by a fine balance of thought and feeling, Repplier achieved a high level of craftsmanship.

As a child, Repplier was tortured by her mother's constant disparagement of her physical features, a habit that made her almost morbidly defensive about her appearance. This fact perhaps explains the absence of close masculine relationships in her life as well as the restraint and ironic tone of her essays and conversation. But she had friends, numerous, fond, and often famous. Her earliest school comrade was the writer Elizabeth Robins Pennell, wife of Philadelphia artist Joseph Pennell. Others were Shakespearean scholar Horace Howard Furness, English essayist Andrew Lang, and—unlikeliest of all—Walt Whitman. Although the income from her numerous books was never very large she supported her mother, sister, and a partially invalided brother, and left an estate of $100,000. Thin, angular, conspicuous only for her habit of chain-smoking cigarettes and a marvelous gift for platform repartee, Repplier moved quietly through her ninety-five years, although the cultural attitudes of the twentieth century appalled and sometimes frightened her. Outside her books, always the primary interest of her life, she maintained a conservative's disdain for the waves of progressivism that swept the country and was sharply critical of programs of legislation and education designed to remedy social inequities. Rarely, however, did she enter into debate over such issues, the two most prominent exceptions being a public exchange with Jane Addams over child labor laws and her vigorous support of the entry of the United States into World War I. In this respect, her account of Lord Byron is aptly descriptive of her own temperament: ". . . the settled order of things appealed with force to his eminently practical nature" ("Allegra," *Eight Decades*, p. 201). The triumph of advocacy journalism, however, rather than her unpopular views or a loss of literary power, best accounts for her gradual loss of popularity.

By 1940, when she published her final essay, Repplier had collected a garland of public honors. Among these were honorary doctorates from the University of Pennsylvania (1902), Yale (1925), Columbia (1927), Marquette (1929), and Princeton (1935); the Laetare Medal from the University of Notre Dame (1911), and the Gold Medal from the National Institute of Arts and Letters. At the age of ninety-five Repplier died of heart failure in Philadelphia and was buried in the family vault at the Church of St. John the Evangelist.

[Repplier's writings are difficult to distinguish by quality, the earliest essays bearing rhetorical and stylistic marks identical to the last. The following titles are therefore chosen for their variety of subject matter: *The Fireside Sphinx* (1901, essays), *A Happy*

Half-Century and Other Essays (1908, essays), Eight Decades: Essays and Episodes (1937, essays), In Our Convent Days (1905, autobiography), Pere Marquette; Priest, Pioneer and Adventurer (1929, biography). A definitive critical biography has yet to be written. Two book-length accounts of Repplier, the first based primarily on her correspondence and books and the second one on personal reminiscence are George S. Stokes, Agnes Repplier, Lady of Letters (1949) and Emma Repplier Witmer, Agnes Repplier, A Memoir (1957). Critical essays comprehensive in their range are in Notable Am. Women, III (1971); Francis Sweeney, "Miss Repplier of Philadelphia," Catholic World, 173 (1951), 278–283; John T. Flanagan, "A Distinguished American Essayist," South Atlantic Quart., 44 (1945), 162–169. The library of the Univ. of Pa. and the Am. Inst. of Arts and Letters in New York are the principal repositories of Repplier's manuscripts and correspondence. Both the N.Y. Times and the Phila. Inquirer of Dec. 16, 1950, have lengthy obituaries.]

PAUL R. MESSBARGER

RICE, GEORGE SAMUEL (Sept. 8, 1866–Jan. 4, 1950), first chief mining engineer of the Bureau of Mines, was born in Claremont, N.H., the son of George Samuel Rice and Abigail (Parker) Rice. His father, a businessman, traced his family to Thomas Rhys, a seventeenth-century settler of Kittery, Maine.

Rice attended public schools in New York City, the College of the City of New York, and Columbia University, where he studied mining engineering at the School of Mines. After graduation in 1887 with an E.M. degree, Rice worked as an assistant engineer for Colorado railroad and mining firms. In 1891 he moved to the Midwest and over the next twenty years developed a successful consulting engineering practice. His clients included railroads with coal interests, coal-mining concerns in Iowa, Illinois, and Pennsylvania and lead- and zinc-mining firms elsewhere in the country. While coal-mining became his specialty, Rice also developed new methods for mining phosphates in Florida and potashes in the West. In 1908, when he was in the midst of an active and extensive private engineering practice, Rice shifted his energies to the public sector and to what became a long crusade for mine safety.

At least three factors led to his decision. First, early in his career Rice had developed an interest in mine safety. Second, he had also become interested in the conservation movement, a concern that linked safety and efficiency. Third, and probably most important, the nation's conscience was shocked by a particularly disastrous series of coal-mine explosions in 1907 that killed over a thousand miners. When, in 1908, Joseph A. Holmes, director of the technological branch of the United States Geological Survey, urged him to undertake an investigation of the explosions, Rice joined the branch as chief engineer. Two years later, when the Bureau of Mines was established, Holmes became its director, and Rice was appointed chief mining engineer.

Rice continued in the position until his retirement in 1937. During that period the bureau emerged as a world leader in research and teaching related to mine safety. Rice designed, and was responsible for the construction at Bruceton, Pa., of the world's first experimental coal mine for conducting research on the causes of mine explosions. His most significant contribution in this area was the demonstration of the explosiveness of coal dust itself and the development of techniques of spreading rock dust in mines to lessen the hazard.

There were subsequent unanticipated benefits from the bureau's research. Rice used his experimental coal mine for a series of tests to develop an adequate ventilation system for the Holland Tunnel under the Hudson River. He also turned the bureau's expertise to wartime problems in 1917, initiating a study of poison gases and the development of gas masks.

Rice published extensively on the subject of mining safety in both technical journals and publications of the Bureau of Mines. He was also active in international cooperative efforts to promote mine safety, organizing the first international conference on that subject in Pittsburgh in 1912 and acting as the United States representative at several subsequent conferences.

He served the Canadian government as an adviser on mining problems and investigated mine disasters in Belgium, France, and Germany. His international reputation brought him many honors. He was elected to honorary membership in the major British, French, Canadian, and American mining-engineering societies and received the medal of England's Institution of Mining Engineers in 1929. His enthusiasm for reform in mining practices reflected the idealism of the Progressive Era, of which he was a part.

Rice was an energetic, robust man who enjoyed sports. He was an independent in politics and an Episcopalian in religion. Rice was married twice. His first marriage, on Dec. 23, 1891, to Julia Sessions, who died in 1934, produced three children—Abby, Katharine Peabody, and Julian Brewster. On Dec. 12, 1935, he married Sarah Marie Benson. He died at the Washington Sanitarium in Takoma Park, Md.

[The major sources are Lit. Dig., Oct. 1935, p. 15; and Mining Eng., 187 (1950), 411–413. Rice's writings include "Stabilize Industry, Conserve Coal, and

Protect Miners," *Am. Labor Legis. Rev.*, 30 (1940), 109–113; "Safety in Mines and the Research Work of the United States Bureau of Mines," *Trans. Inst. Mining Eng.*, 128 (1929–1930), 290–293; *Coal-Dust Explosibility Factors Indicated by Experimental Mine Investigations, 1911 to 1929* (1929), with H. P. Greenwald; and *Ground Movement and Subsidence Studies in Mining Coal, Ores and Nonmetallic Minerals* (1939).]

BRUCE SINCLAIR

RILEY, WILLIAM BELL (Mar. 22, 1861–Dec. 5, 1947), Baptist evangelist and fundamentalist leader, was born in Greene County, Ind., the third of five sons and sixth of eight children of Branson Radish Riley and Ruth Anna (Jackson) Riley. His father's forebears were Scots-Irish farmers in Virginia; his mother's, English and Dutch Quaker merchants in Pennsylvania. Riley's boyhood was spent in humble circumstances on farms in Boone and Owen counties in Kentucky, where his father, a proslavery Democrat, had moved at the outbreak of the Civil War. From the age of nine, Riley took his turn behind the plow; in later years he frequently praised farm life as the best moral training ground for American children. His parents were devout Baptists, and he was reared in a religious atmosphere.

Riley's formal schooling was intermittent until the age of eighteen, when he earned a teacher's certificate after a year at the normal school in Valparaiso, Ind. He entered Hanover (Ind.) College in 1881 and graduated in 1885 with the B.A. degree. Although he had been converted and baptized in 1878, he remained undecided about his profession until one afternoon when he felt himself called to the ministry. He enrolled in the Southern Baptist Theological Seminary in Louisville, Ky., from which he graduated in 1888, at the same time receiving his M.A. from Hanover. On Dec. 31, 1890, he married Lillian Howard. They had six children: Arthur Howard, Mason Hewitt, Herbert Wilde, Eunice, William Bell, and John Branson.

Riley began his ministerial career as pastor of small Baptist churches in Kentucky, Indiana, and Illinois. On Jan. 1, 1893, he moved to Chicago to head the newly formed Calvary Baptist Church. During his stay there he first became conscious of the growing split among American Protestants between the fundamentalist and modernist points of view. The weekly meetings of the Chicago Baptist Ministers' Society often ended in angry exchanges, with Riley and other fundamentalists on one side and the liberal University of Chicago theologians on the other. On Mar. 1, 1897, Riley accepted a call to the First Baptist Church in Minneapolis, Minn., where he remained until his retirement in 1942.

In Minneapolis, Riley built up a large church membership, outmaneuvered his opponents within the congregation, and gained considerable local reputation. He publicly opposed America's involvement in the Spanish-American War, used his pulpit to denounce corrupt politics, and engaged in several crusades on behalf of prohibition. He gained his greatest fame, however, as an evangelist. For many years he led highly successful campaigns throughout Minnesota and neighboring states. Standing over six feet tall, with a prominent nose and curly black hair that gradually turned white, Riley made an impressive figure on the podium. He was a persuasive public speaker, gifted with a ready wit and a flair for the dramatic. Riley did not limit himself to winning souls. He also castigated a wide variety of practices and beliefs, including divorce, dancing, and all the "isms"—socialism, Unitarianism, Mormonism, spiritualism, Catholicism, liberalism. He was one of the first Protestant clergymen in the early twentieth century to speak out consistently against the theories of Charles Darwin.

In 1902 Riley founded in Minneapolis the Northwestern Bible Training School, which added an Evangelical Seminary in 1935 and a liberal arts college in 1944. The school became the base of his operations and a bulwark of conservative evangelical Protestantism for the area. It taught the verbal inerrancy of the Bible, the necessity for individual conversion, and the belief that the physical return of Christ would usher in the millennium. Neither Riley nor his school would have anything to do with theological liberalism or the social gospel; the conversion of individuals alone would produce a just society. Affirmation and attack were both part of Riley's message from the beginning. By 1910 his concern over the rise of modernism in the Baptist denomination was such that he tried to organize a conservative protest against holding the Northern Baptist Convention on the campus of the University of Chicago. Had he succeeded, this might have begun the fundamentalist-modernist controversy ten years before its time. The move failed, however, and the disagreements had another decade to build up pressure. He ultimately severed all personal ties with the Northern Baptist Convention and persuaded the Minnesota Convention effectively to disown the parent body.

After World War I, Riley emerged as the leader in the movement among conservative churchmen that led to the founding, at a large conference in Philadelphia in 1919, of the World's Christian Fundamentals Association (WCFA). This proved to be the most important interdenominational fundamentalist organization in the 1920's. Until 1929, when he gave up its presidency, all correspondence crossed Riley's desk. In this sense he might be called the "organizer" of American fundamentalism. Although he played a large role in Baptist denominational politics and helped form the conservative Baptist Bible Union, it was his WCFA work that gave him a national reputation. Popular magazines like *Current History* and the *Independent* called on him for articles on fundamentalism, and he crossed the country in a series of widely publicized debates on the theory of evolution. Riley was responsible for securing William Jennings Bryan to help prosecute John Thomas Scopes in the famous Dayton, Tenn., "Monkey Trial" of July 1925, and when the fundamentalists began an earnest campaign to pass state antievolution laws, Riley and the WCFA helped provide speakers for all critical areas.

Although Riley continued his defense of conservative evangelical Protestantism and his attack on evolution until his death, the depression brought him two new issues. In the 1930's he began to attack communism with the same vehemence he had earlier reserved for theological liberalism. He also bitterly opposed the New Deal program of President Franklin D. Roosevelt and openly supported some of its most radical right-wing, anti-Semitic critics. By this time, however, his national reputation had faded and his views received only local attention. Although the Northwestern school was flourishing at the time of his death, it soon declined, especially after the departure of Billy Graham, Riley's anointed, but reluctant, successor.

Riley's first wife died in 1931, and on Sept. 1, 1933, he married Marie R. Acomb. He died of chronic myocarditis at his home in Golden Valley, Minn. He was buried in Lakewood Cemetery in Minneapolis.

[The only biography of Riley is an uncritical study by Marie Acomb Riley, *The Dynamic of a Dream* (1938). Three unpublished Ph.D. dissertations deal with various aspects of his career: Ferenc M. Szasz, "Three Fundamentalist Leaders: The Roles of William Bell Riley, John Roach Straton, and William Jennings Bryan in the Fundamentalist–Modernist Controversy" (Univ. of Rochester, 1969); Robert S. McBirnie, "Basic Issues in the Fundamentalism of W. B. Riley" (Univ. of Iowa, 1952); and Lloyd B. Hull, "A Rhetorical Study of the Preaching of William Bell Riley" (Wayne State Univ., 1960). See also two articles in *Minn. Hist.*: Ferenc Szasz, "Wil-

liam B. Riley and the Fight Against Teaching of Evolution in Minn.," Spring 1969; and C. Allyn Russell, "W. B. Riley, Architect of Fundamentalism," Spring 1972. The three major works on fundamentalism—Ernest R. Sandeen, *The Roots of Fundamentalism* (1970); Stewart G. Cole, *The Hist. of Fundamentalism* (1931); and Norman F. Furniss, *The Fundamentalist Controversy, 1918–1931* (1954)—all treat Riley and the activities of the WCFA. Of Riley's published works, four volumes—*The Finality of the Higher Criticism* (1909), *The Menace of Modernism* (1917), *The Only Hope of Church or World* (1936), and *Wanted—A World Leader!* (1939)—offer a good cross section of his thinking. His articles "A Square Deal for Genesis," *Independent*, Nov. 12, 1927, and "The Faith of the Fundamentalists," *Current Hist.*, June, 1927, are concise statements of his views during the 1920's. His major publishing effort was a 39-volume study, *The Bible of the Expositor and the Evangelist* (1925–1935). Death record from Minn. State Board of Health. The files of the WCFA appear to have been lost, but there is a large collection of Riley's scrapbooks, publications, sermons, and memorabilia in the library of Northwestern College, Roseville, Minn.]

FERENC M. SZASZ

RIPLEY, ROBERT LeROY (Dec. 26, 1893–May 27, 1949), newspaper feature artist and creator of "Believe It or Not," was born in Santa Rosa, Calif., the oldest of three children and first of two sons of Isaac Davis Ripley, a carpenter, and Lily Belle (Yocka or Yucca) Ripley. Preferring Christmas to the day after, he designated December 25 as his birth date. Adventure ran in his blood. His father, a native of West Virginia, had left home at fourteen and made his way to California. His part-Portuguese mother was born on the Santa Fe Trail in a covered wagon. When LeRoy (he was grown before he added the Robert) was twelve, his father died, leaving the family in straitened circumstances. The shy youth helped out by polishing tombstones and working at odd jobs; he left high school before graduating. Devoted to baseball, he played whenever he could, even trying out to be a professional pitcher. An arm injury ended his hope for a sports career, and so he concentrated on drawing, which he had begun as a schoolboy. He was much encouraged when, in 1907, he sold a humorous drawing to *Life* magazine for $8.

A San Francisco newspaperwoman, Carol Ennis, impressed by his sketches, secured a job for him on the *Bulletin* as a sports cartoonist in 1909, when he was not yet sixteen. The following year he moved to the *San Francisco Chronicle*. With notables like Thomas A. Dorgan in the field, competition in San Francisco was keen; when Ripley asked for a raise in 1913, he was discharged. He took the $100 he had received for illustrating a book and traveled to New York City, where, on the recommendation of the cartoonist Jay N. Darling, who had seen his work, he was hired as a sports cartoonist by the *Globe*.

Ripley's sports sketches were popular, and they might have been his lifework except for a turn of chance in 1918. Lacking an idea for his December 19 drawing, he grouped small sketches of nine oddities from the athletic world—among them a Canadian who ran 100 yards backwards in 14 seconds, an Australian who jumped rope 11,810 times in 4 hours, and a Frenchman who stayed under water 6 minutes and 29.8 seconds—and published them under the caption "Believe It or Not!" Thus was launched the famous series. At first a weekly drawing, "Believe It or Not!" soon was appearing daily.

Ripley remained with the *Globe* until it closed in 1923 and then joined the *Evening Post*. In 1929 Simon and Schuster published a book-length selection of his sketches. Its overnight popularity led William Randolph Hearst to order his King Features Syndicate to sign Ripley for national distribution. Although the feature had its origin in sports, Ripley quickly broadened it to the world in general. It consisted of attractive bold-line drawings accompanied by such startling assertions as "The Battle of Waterloo was not fought at Waterloo" and "George Washington was not the first president of the United States." Ripley even reported in 1927 that he had found a "one-armed paperhanger"—Albert J. Smith of Dedham, Mass. His documentation did not always convince incredulous, and sometimes outraged, readers, but it satisfied Ripley.

Despite the depression of the 1930's, Ripley's burgeoning success required him to build up a large staff of researchers (headed by Norbert Pearlroth), artists, and translators. A corps of secretaries processed the mail that flooded in from around the globe, often bearing suggestions. Ripley himself traveled a substantial part of every year, indulging his wanderlust and seeking out curiosities. The Duke of Windsor was said to have dubbed him "the modern Marco Polo"—an appropriate tag, since China above all other countries fascinated him and he made friends with many Chinese. After all his traveling, he concluded that the Grand Canyon was the greatest sight in the world.

Besides his widely syndicated feature, Ripley made twenty-six movie shorts for Warner Brothers-Vitaphone, began a popular radio version of "Believe It or Not!" in 1933, and sponsored "odditoriums," where his curiosities were displayed in a carnival-type atmosphere, at several world's fairs. These ventures, along with later collections of his drawings in book form (1931, 1935, and 1939), boosted his annual income to about $500,000. Living and entertaining lavishly, he maintained a museum-like estate, Bion (the acronym of "Believe It or Not!"), on Long Island Sound, near Mamaroneck, N.Y., and a winter home at Palm Beach, Fla. The curios at his abodes were valued at $2 million and included a Chinese junk that he enjoyed sailing.

Ripley was married to Beatrice Roberts, a New York model and *Follies* showgirl, in 1919. They lived together only a few months and were divorced in 1925. Thereafter Ripley never seemed to want for feminine companions at Bion. He did not smoke or play cards. A large, energetic man, with dimples and prominent teeth, he was superstitious, sometimes hot-tempered, fond of animals, and too fearful to drive a car or dial a telephone. What he had in quantity, as William Bolitho put it, was "the curiosity of the unlearned."

Ripley died of a heart attack at New York City's Columbia-Presbyterian Medical Center. He was buried in Odd Fellows Cemetery in his hometown of Santa Rosa. A half-century after its inception, "Ripley's Believe It or Not!" was appearing in seventeen languages in 330 newspapers in thirty-two countries. Ripley's own life story had some of the incredible quality of the oddities he sketched.

[The fullest account is Bob Considine, *Ripley: The Modern Marco Polo* (1961), which contains many photographs of Ripley. See also *Who Was Who in Am.* (1950); *Current Biog.*, 1945; Walter D. Heithaus in *Tradition*, Oct. 1962; Albert Parry in *Am. Mercury*, Jan. 1934; *Literary Digest*, June 26, 1937, pp. 28–29; Geoffrey T. Hellman, *New Yorker* profile, Aug. 31 and Sept. 7, 1940. Newspapers generally carried full reports at the time of Ripley's death; note also *Editor & Publisher*, June 4, 1949. Helpful assistance was provided by Joseph Willicombe, Jr., of King Features Syndicate, N.Y. City, where a substantial collection of Ripley materials is maintained. Twenty-five years after Ripley's death, Ripley museums were in operation in Chicago; San Francisco; St. Augustine, Fla.; Gatlinburg, Tenn.; Estes Park, Colo.; Niagara Falls, Canada; and Blackpool, England.]

IRVING DILLIARD

RITTENHOUSE, JESSIE BELLE (Dec. 8, 1869-Sept. 28, 1948), poet and critic, was born in Mount Morris, N.Y., the fifth of seven children, four of whom died in their early years. Her mother, Mary J. (MacArthur) Rittenhouse, was of Scottish descent; her father, John E. Rittenhouse, was directly descended from the Philadelphia astronomer David Rittenhouse. Jessie was an early reader, dedicated to English literature, but dreamed of becoming a prison reformer. After her mother became incapacitated by family tragedies, Jessie kept house, while attending a village school and Nunda (N.Y.) Academy. In 1890 she graduated from Genesee Wesleyan Seminary.

She taught school in Cairo, Ill., and at Akeley Institute for Girls in Grand Haven, Mich., about 200 miles from Cheboygan, to which her family had moved. Frustrated by teaching, she began to write free-lance articles, chiefly interviews, for Buffalo and Rochester newspapers. She later became a reporter for the *Rochester Democrat and Chronicle;* and in 1895, she moved to Chicago and returned to free-lance writing. Although she was well-received by such feminists as Susan B. Anthony, whose home attracted others in Rochester, and although her interview with William Jennings Bryan in 1895 was treated by her editor as a coup, she was anxious to write about poetry. In 1899 she moved to Boston, where she became acquainted with Julia Ward Howe and Louise Chandler Moulton. She also edited and published two volumes of translations of Omar Khayyam's *Rubaiyat* (1900), collating materials from various translations.

Although her work with poetry was later considered conservative and passé, it was undertaken in an era challenged by naturalistic writings and not very interested in poetry. Her *The Younger American Poets* (1904), critical essays on contemporary poets, was a pioneer attempt to treat poetry as a living topic. Few of the authors she discussed intrigued later generations of readers; they included Bliss Carman, Clinton Scollard, Edith M. Thomas, whose *Selected Poems* (1926) she later edited, and Madison Cawein. George Santayana, whose works she also included, proved more influential in other fields. But Rittenhouse's regard for their art was an early example of critical involvement in their methods and intentions.

In 1905 she moved to New York City. After the *New York Times Book Review* had praised her work, she applied to its editor for an opportunity to review poetry. For the next ten years she was able to express enthusiasm for many minor poets, as well as such major ones as Edwin Arlington Robinson. The importance she attached to conventional rhyme and meter overshadowed other qualities that distinguish great poets from lesser ones, but her attempts to give poetry more scope helped to institutionalize the poetry of her time. She aided the process further as editor of highly successful anthologies. *The Little Book of Modern Verse* (1913) and *The Little Book of American Poets* (1915)

treated past and twentieth-century authors. Her *Second Book of Modern Verse* (1919) and *Third Book of Modern Verse* (1927) reflected the expanding field of poetry and included the work of T. S. Eliot and her friend Sara Teasdale. The unusually successful sales of these works rendered them a force in defining the uses of poetry in schools and literary circles.

A major factor in the founding of the Poetry Society of America in 1910, Rittenhouse became its long-time secretary and organizer. As such she was a close friend of Vachel Lindsay and Edgar Lee Masters and cooperated with Amy Lowell in furthering imagism in poetry. Since the Pulitzer Prize endowment did not originally provide a prize for poetry, the society annually honored volumes of published verse. It also sponsored poetry readings and welcomed such foreign visitors as John Masefield and William Butler Yeats.

In 1924 she married Clinton Scollard, professor of English at Hamilton College, whose prolific verses and anthologies she had long admired. Their close collaboration resulted in *The Bird-Lovers' Anthology* (1930) and *Patrician Rhymes* (1932), the latter a collection of society verse. Her own poems, published in *The Door of Dreams* (1918), *The Lifted Cup* (1921), and *The Secret Bird* (1930), were well-regarded by her numerous friends. Strong, sympathetic, and tolerant of often temperamental authors, she was awarded a bronze medal in 1931 by the Poetry Society of America for distinguished service to poetry.

Rittenhouse maintained a busy schedule, lecturing on modern poetry in extension courses at Columbia University and performing on the lecture circuit from 1914 to 1924. Until 1920 she wrote book reviews for *The Bookman,* as well as the *New York Times.* In 1924 she gave up her New York home and thereafter divided her time between the Berkshires and Winter Park, Fla., which attracted a considerable number of her literary friends. She founded the Florida Poetry Society, one of the most substantial of such organizations, and lectured on poetry at Rollins College in Winter Park. Following her husband's death in 1932, she moved from Kent, Conn., to Grosse Pointe Park, Mich. In 1934 she collected Scollard's verses in *The Singing Heart,* with a memoir. In 1940 her *The Moving Tide: New and Selected Lyrics,* published the year before, was awarded the gold medal of the National Poetry Center. She died in Detroit and was buried in Cheboygan. Her papers were left to Rollins College.

[Rittenhouse's autobiography, *My House of Life* (1934), provides many details of her growth and development, and that of the Poetry Society of America. Margaret Widdemer, *Jessie Rittenhouse: A Centenary Memoir-Anthology* (1969), comments on Rittenhouse as well as on her circle, as does Edwin Markham, comp., *The Book of American Poetry* (1934). See also *N.Y. Times,* Sept. 30, 1948; *Who Was Who in Am.,* II (1950).]

LOUIS FILLER

ROBINSON, BILL (BOJANGLES) (May 25, 1878-Nov. 25, 1949), stage and film dancer (originally Luther), was born in Richmond, Va., to Maxwell Robinson, a machine-shop worker, and Maria Robinson, a choir singer. He is believed to have had a sister and an older brother. The details of his early life are known only through legend, much of it perpetuated by Robinson himself. At the age of six he was appearing as a "hoofer," or song-and-dance man, in local beer gardens and, two years later, in Washington, D.C. While still a child, he toured with Mayme Remington's troupe as a "pick"—as black child actors were then known. In 1891, at the age of twelve, he joined a traveling company in *The South Before the War,* and in 1905 he worked with George Cooper as a vaudeville team. Not until he was fifty did he dance for white audiences, having devoted his early career exclusively to appearances on the black theater circuit.

In 1908 in Chicago he met Marty Forkins, who became his lifelong manager. Under Forkins' tutelage Robinson matured, moderated his penchant for gambling, and began working as a solo act in nightclubs, increasing his earnings to an estimated $3,500 per week. The publicity that gradually came to surround him included the creation of his famous "stair dance," his successful gambling exploits, his prodigious charity, his ability to run backward at great speed and to consume ice cream by the quart, his argot—most notably the neologism "copasetic"—and such stunts as dancing down Broadway in 1939 from Columbus Circle to 44th Street in celebration of his sixty-first birthday. Because his public image became preeminent, little is known of his first marriage, to Fannie S. Clay in Chicago shortly after World War I, his divorce in 1943, or his marriage to Elaine Plaines on Jan. 27, 1944, in Columbus, Ohio.

Toward the end of the vaudeville era a white impresario, Lew Leslie, produced *Blackbirds of 1928,* a black revue for white audiences featuring Robinson and other black stars. From then on his public role was that of a dapper, smiling, plaid-suited ambassador to the white world, maintaining a tenuous connection with black show-business circles through his continuing patronage of the Hoofers' Club, an entertainers' haven in Harlem. Consequently, blacks and whites developed differing opinions of him. To whites, for example, his nickname "Bojangles" meant happy-go-lucky, while the black variety artist Tom Fletcher claimed it was slang for "squabbler." Political figures and celebrities appointed him an honorary mayor of Harlem, a lifetime member of policemen's associations and fraternal orders, and a mascot of the New York Giants baseball team. Robinson reciprocated with openhanded generosity and frequently credited the white dancer James Barton for his contribution to Robinson's dancing style.

After 1930 black revues waned in popularity, but Robinson remained in vogue with white audiences for more than a decade in motion pictures produced by such companies as RKO, Twentieth Century-Fox, and Paramount. Most of them had musical settings, in which he played old-fashioned roles in nostalgic romances. His most frequent role was that of an antebellum butler opposite Shirley Temple or Will Rogers in such films as *The Little Colonel, The Littlest Rebel,* and *In Old Kentucky* (all released in 1935). Rarely did he depart from the stereotype imposed by Hollywood writers. In a small vignette in *Hooray for Love* (1935) he played a mayor of Harlem modeled on his own ceremonial honors; in *One Mile from Heaven* (1937) he played a policeman; and in the war-time musical *Stormy Weather* (1943) he played a romantic lead opposite the singer Lena Horne after Hollywood had relaxed its taboo against such roles for blacks. Audiences enjoyed his style, which eschewed the frenetic manner of the jitterbug. In contrast, Robinson always remained cool and reserved, rarely using his upper body and depending on his busy, inventive feet and his expressive face. He appeared in one film for black audiences, *Harlem Is Heaven* (1931), a financial failure that turned him away from independent production.

In 1939 he returned to the stage in *The Hot Mikado,* a jazz version of the Gilbert and Sullivan operetta produced at the New York World's Fair. His next appearance, in *All in Fun* (1940), failed to attract audiences. His last theatrical project was to have been *Two Gentlemen from the South* with James Barton, in which black and white roles reverse and eventually come together as equals, but the show did not open.

Robinson died of a chronic heart condition,

at Columbia Presbyterian Medical Center in New York City. His body lay in state at an armory in Harlem, schools were closed, thousands lined the streets waiting for a glimpse of his bier, and he was eulogized by politicians, black and white—perhaps more lavishly than any other Afro-American of his time. "To his own people," wrote Marshall and Jean Stearns, "Robinson became a modern John Henry, who instead of driving steel, laid down iron taps" (Stearns and Stearns, p. 184). He was buried in the Cemetery of the Evergreens in New York City.

[There are clipping files on Robinson in the Gumby Collect., Columbia Univ.; George P. Johnson Collect., Univ. of Calif. at Los Angeles; James Weldon Johnson Collect., Yale Univ.; and A. A. Schomburg Collect. and the Performing Arts Collect., both of the N.Y. Public Lib. Other sources are *N.Y. Times*, Nov. 15, 26, 28, 29, 1949; St. Clair McKelway, "Profiles—Bojangles," *New Yorker*, Oct. 6, 1934, and Oct. 13, 1934; Joe Laurie, Jr., "Bill 'Bojangles' Robinson," *Variety*, Nov. 30, 1949; the obituary in *Billboard*, Dec. 3, 1949; James Weldon Johnson, *Black Manhattan* (1930, 1968); Marshall Stearns and Jean Stearns, *Jazz Dance: The Story of American Vernacular Dance* (1968), Loften Mitchell, *Black Drama: The Story of the American Negro in the Theatre* (1967); Edith J. R. Isaacs, *The Negro in the American Theatre* (1947); and Charlemae Rollins, *Famous Negro Entertainers of Stage, Screen, and TV* (1967), an account for children.]

THOMAS CRIPPS

ROCKEFELLER, ABBY GREENE ALDRICH (Oct. 26, 1874-Apr. 5, 1948), philanthropist, was born in Providence, R.I., the second of three daughters and third of eight children of Nelson Wilmarth Aldrich and Abby (Chapman) Aldrich. The warm family environment of her childhood was dominated by her father, a self-made businessman who later became an influential United States senator. She was educated by a private teacher at home and then attended Miss Abbott's School in Providence, graduating in 1893. As a debutante, she traveled frequently in the United States and Europe, often accompanying her father, who stimulated her interests in art collecting and public affairs.

Abby Aldrich was married to John Davison Rockefeller, Jr., son of John D. Rockefeller, the founder of the Standard Oil Company, on Oct. 9, 1901, following a long courtship begun when the younger Rockefeller was an undergraduate at Brown University. The marriage was a successful union of his reserved personality and her more impulsive and outgoing temperament. They had six children: Abigail, John Davison, Nelson Aldrich, Laurance Spelman, Winthrop, and David.

Enormous wealth and efforts to spend it

wisely conditioned Mrs. Rockefeller's life, both within and outside her family. She managed the family's nine-story house in New York City and homes at Pocantico Hills, N.Y., and Seal Harbor, Maine. Her warmth, articulateness, scrupulousness, and vivid sense of detail are exemplified in her letters to her children and the extensive published correspondence with her sister Lucy. In a revealing letter published anonymously in the *Atlantic Monthly* in 1920, she declared, "The rich are given what they are expected to want. . . . It may be flattering but it is not stimulating or wholesome" (Chase, p. 54).

She was a prominent committeewoman and organizer in various social welfare causes. Among her most important affiliations were the Young Women's Christian Association (YWCA), the Girl Scouts, and the American Red Cross. Notable projects under her leadership included planning and organizing a model-home and community-center project for Standard Oil employees in New Jersey, helping to build and furnish International House near Columbia University, and sparking the housing and community service efforts of the YWCA during World War I. Her projects were characterized by the union of social and aesthetic concerns. The model home, for example, was designed to be both attractive and economical and was coupled with such services as a baby clinic and organized social activities.

She lent energy and prestige to carefully selected, and not always popular, causes; the improvement of working conditions for women, the defense of civil liberties for minority groups, the legitimacy of birth control within marriage, and the rehabilitation of war veterans. Although reared as a Congregationalist, some of her activities were extensions of her membership in the Park Avenue Baptist Church, which she joined after her marriage.

Her most notable public role was that of a patroness of art. With her husband, she participated in planning the restoration of colonial Williamsburg, and she initiated the unique collection of American folk art later housed in the Abby Aldrich Rockefeller Collection there. She developed a personal art collection, mainly of drawings and watercolors, purchased almost entirely with her own funds. This collection began with works of European and Chinese art but after 1920 was extended to American artists. The collection included works by Renoir, Cézanne, Picasso, Matisse, and Toulouse-Lautrec among Europeans; the Mexicans Orozco and Rivera; and the Americans Bellows, Sloan, and Weber. In addition, she commissioned works by American artists—for instance, Charles Sheeler and Ben Shahn. Most of this collection was given to colleges and, more important, to the Museum of Modern Art.

Mrs. Rockefeller's central role in the founding (in 1929) and early history of the Museum of Modern Art made her one of the small number of creators of a new cultural institution, the patronage museum. Unlike traditional art museums, patronage museums aim to stimulate and justify investment in the works of living artists. Helping to form the committee to organize the museum, she worked to develop the institution in collaboration with, among others, Lizzie P. Bliss, Mrs. W. Murray Crane, Frank Crowninshield, A. Conger Goodyear, Mrs. Cornelius Sullivan, and Paul Sachs; she served as its treasurer, first vice-president, and vice-chairman of the board. With her son Nelson, she set up an unrestricted purchase fund. Moreover, she donated more than 2,000 art objects from her personal collection to the museum, including some 190 paintings and 1,600 prints.

In the last years of her life, she spent considerable time with her seventeen grandchildren and in travel for pleasure and health. After several years of poor health, she suffered a heart attack and died in New York City, at the age of seventy-three. Following cremation, her ashes were buried in the family plot at Sleepy Hollow Cemetery, Tarrytown, N.Y.

Abby Aldrich Rockefeller united concern for art and life in her philanthropic career. Like other wealthy Americans of her generation, many but not all of them women, she saw the conjunction of social welfare and aesthetics as logical and necessary, the result of a sense of duty in which desires for sensory and spiritual satisfaction were unified and embodied in activities and institutions intending to improve the quality of citizens' lives.

[The major sources are Mary Ellen Chase, *Abby Aldrich Rockefeller* (1950); *Abby Aldrich Rockefeller's Letters to her Sister Lucy* (1957); *Notable Am. Women,* III (1971); and *N.Y. Times,* Apr. 6, 1948 (obituary). On her husband and family, see Raymond B. Fosdick, *John D. Rockefeller, Jr.* (1956), and Joe Alex Morris, *Nelson Rockefeller* (1960). On her art philanthropy, see A. Conger Goodyear, *The Museum of Modern Art: The First Ten Years* (1943), and Aline B. Saarinen, *The Proud Possessors* (1958).]
                                    DANIEL M. FOX

ROGERS, JAMES GAMBLE (Mar. 3, 1867-Oct. 1, 1947), architect, was born in Bryants Station, near Louisville, Ky., the second of five children, all of them sons. His father, Joseph Martin Rogers, a descendant of central Kentucky families, had attended Union College in Barbourville, Ky., and began his career in the law but within a few years moved to Chicago, where he eventually became the manager of an insurance brokerage. James Rogers' mother was Katherine Mary Gamble, whose family had also been natives of the central Kentucky area. James was educated in Louisville and Chicago public schools, graduating from West Division High School in the latter city in 1885. He enrolled in the School of Fine Arts at Yale University in the same year and graduated with the B.A. degree in 1889. Returning to Chicago, he began his architectural career in the office of William Le Baron Jenney, but in little more than a year he took the position of superintendent of construction for the Ashland Block, an early steel-and-iron-framed skyscraper. The architectural milieu of the city, however, was apparently uncongenial to the young man, very likely because his training at Yale had given him a strongly European orientation. After four years in Chicago, Rogers went to Paris in 1893 to enroll in the École des Beaux-Arts, where he was to remain for six years, leaving with a diploma *par excellence* in 1899.

This long apprenticeship would have provided an adequate preparation for most architects but events of the succeeding decade suggest that Rogers was still not ready to play his own creative role in the profession. He returned to Chicago a second time and established an independent office but left once again after five years and moved to New York, where, with Herbert D. Hale, he entered into the short-lived partnership of Hale and Rogers in 1905. The dissolution of their joint venture in 1908 marked the true inception of Rogers' own architectural career. In the quarter-century that followed he was to establish himself as the nation's leading designer of college and university buildings. He retained an active office in New York very nearly to the time of his death in 1947. The firm that he founded in 1908, having grown to one of the largest in the country, was transformed into a corporation in 1926, under the title of James Gamble Rogers, Inc., and this was in turn superseded by the partnership of Rogers and Jonathan F. Butler, established in early 1947, a few months before the older architect's death.

The beginning of Rogers' rise to prominence came in 1911, when he won the competition for the design of a new post office at New Haven, Conn. This work was closely followed by commissions for other public and commercial buildings, most notably for the New Orleans Post Office; the Shelby County Court House and Brooks Memorial in Memphis, Tenn.; and the office headquarters of the Aetna Life Insurance and General Life Insurance companies of Hartford, Conn. In style, these buildings were mostly variations on the Roman or Renaissance classicism fashionable at the time.

In 1920 Rogers began an eleven-year association with Yale University, first as consulting architect (1920-1924) and then as architect-in-charge of the university's general plan (1924-1931), for which position he was appointed to the rank of professor. The chief buildings that he designed for the New Haven campus were the Harkness Tower, the Harkness Memorial Quadrangle, the Sterling Memorial Library, the Sterling Law School, the Sterling School of Graduate Studies, and six residential colleges—Berkeley, Davenport, Timothy Dwight, Jonathan Edwards, Pierson, and Trumbull. They brought him the reputation of the foremost authority on the modern "collegiate Gothic" style, a term—whether used pejoratively or in praise—with which his name was for years virtually synonymous.

During the early part of his Yale association, beginning in 1922, Rogers received equally generous commissions from Northwestern University, including all the classroom and library buildings of the Chicago campus (Gary Law Library; Mayer Law School; and Thorne, Ward, and Wieboldt halls), Deering Library, Scott Hall, the sorority and women's dormitory quadrangles, and Dyche Stadium of the Evanston campus. The various buildings were constructed over the years from 1924 to 1932. Another major commission was the Columbia-Presbyterian Medical Center in New York City (1924-1928).

Other lesser commissions fell into this same general period: the Butler Library (completed 1934) for Columbia's main campus; extensive parts of the campuses of Southern Baptist College in Louisville, Ky.; Colgate-Rochester Divinity School in Rochester, N.Y.; Sophie Newcomb College in New Orleans; the School of Education of New York University; and dormitories for Atlanta University. Outside the collegiate work the largest building from Rogers' firm was Memorial Hospital in New York (completed 1938).

The three major institutions he served awarded him honorary degrees: Yale in 1922, Northwestern in 1927, and Columbia in 1928.

Rogers' social, organizational, and domestic life was perfectly characteristic of a celebrated upper-class architect in an extravagant age. He married Anne Tift Day of Lake Forest, Ill., on Oct. 12, 1901. Four children were born of this union: Katherine, Albert Day (who died in infancy), James Gamble, and Francis Day. Rogers held office in various organizations connected with his church, university, and professional associations: he was president of the Society of Beaux Arts Architects (1921-1923); associate fellow of Saybrook College at Yale (1933-1943); and trustee of the Madison Avenue Presbyterian Church, New York (1936-1938, 1940-1942). He belonged to a great many social and cultural organizations, notably the Société des Architectes Diplômés par le Gouvernement Français (Paris); the Chicago Art Institute; the Century, Pilgrims, University, Uptown, and Yale clubs of New York; the Onwentsia Country Club of Lake Forest, Ill.; and the Yeoman's Hall Club of Charleston, S.C.

Rogers died at the Harkness Pavilion of the Columbia-Presbyterian Medical Center after what the obituary notices designated simply as an illness of five days. To a very great extent, his major work was concentrated in a short period of time, coinciding with the building boom of the 1920's, and he never regained the authoritative position he had once held. Depression, war, and postwar adjustments brought a twenty-year hiatus to large-scale public and commercial building, and when the construction industry revived, changing architectural fashions had relegated much of Rogers' work to a discredited past. This fate grew out of modernist dogma and was wholly undeserved: although he was extensively dependent on late medieval forms, he adapted them with considerable skill to the complex requirements of large public buildings. His university designs continue to serve their respective campuses well, and some are distinguished by an innovative spirit working effectively within a traditional approach.

[The major sources are Henry F. and Elsie Withey, *Biog. Dict. of Amer. Architects* (1956); *Who Was Who in Amer.* (1950); obituaries in *N.Y. Times,* Oct. 2, 1947; and *Architectural Record,* Nov. 1947, p. 14; Yale Univ. *Obituary Record of Graduates,* 1947-1948. The Yale Univ. Portrait Collect. includes an oil portrait of Rogers by Frank O. Salisbury (1935).]

CARL W. CONDIT

ROSEN, JOSEPH A. (Feb. 15, 1878-Apr. 2, 1949), agronomist and resettlement expert, was born in Moscow. It is believed that he grew up in Tula, Russia. Little is known of his early life. He entered Moscow University in 1894 and, suspected of revolutionary activities, he was exiled to Siberia. Like many other dissidents of his generation, he escaped and made his way to Germany. Other than his claim to have studied for two years at Heidelberg, nothing is known of the six years he presumably spent in Germany before his move to the United States in 1903.

Rosen's life as agronomist and resettlement expert combined the contributions of his Russian experiences, Jewish origin, and American assimilation. As an emancipated young Jew in late nineteenth-century Russia he was torn between the attractions of revolution and Western liberalism. He flirted briefly with the former, only to dedicate his life to the latter. He clearly rejected the ever more powerful third alternative of secular or religious Zionism.

By his actions, Rosen defined Jewish emancipation as the integration of the Jews into the larger society. This support of the so-called territorial rather than Zionist solution to the Jewish problem was shared, until World War II, by the leadership of the American Jewish Committee and its major philanthropic arm, the Joint Distribution Committee (J.D.C.). Thus, while Rosen and the wealthy supporters of the J.D.C. could scarcely be suspected of sympathy with Bolshevism, Rosen was able to harness the efforts of the J.D.C. and the Soviet state in the 1920's and 1930's for an almost revolutionary project of Jewish agricultural resettlement and training, while a similar process, under Zionist inspiration, produced the kibbutz movement in Palestine.

Rosen shared little more than a common Russian Jewish origin and poverty with contemporary Russian immigrants. He came alone; he was educated; and he avoided urban areas. He worked his way to Michigan, became a farmhand for two years, and then enrolled at Michigan Agricultural College in 1905, graduating in 1908. While a student, he wrote a series of articles for Russian journals on aspects of American agriculture. These articles prompted the provincial *zemstvo* of Ekaterinoslav (Dnepropetrovsk) to engage him as head of a branch office in Minneapolis for the collection and distribution in Russia of relevant American agricultural information. Rosen effectively performed this task, with one interruption, until the 1917 Revolution. He also resumed his education at the University of Minnesota, but the claim of a Ph.D. in agricultural chemistry and the source of the subsequent use of the title doctor cannot be substantiated.

In March 1909, Rosen presented to Michigan Agricultural College a pound of Russian rye seeds, which were named Rosen rye in his honor. Due to its high yield, Rosen rye soon gained dominance over other strains in the Midwest.

During World War I Rosen headed the Baron de Hirsch Agricultural School in Woodbine, N.J.,, and became New York representative of a Russian bank. In 1921, Felix M. Warburg and James N. Rosenberg persuaded him to join Herbert Hoover's American Relief Administration in Russia as representative of the J.D.C. He had found his true mission. He recruited a staff of young Jewish agricultural specialists and was the first to introduce tractors into the famine-stricken USSR for the rehabilitation of destroyed Jewish farms. His system of centralized repair facilities later served as a prototype for the tractor stations of collectivized Soviet agriculture.

The successful application of massive relief to destitute Jewish peasants spawned the revolutionary idea of a mass transformation of déclassé, petty-bourgeois Jews into a self-reliant peasantry. Political and economic deprivation and traditional Russian peasant anti-Semitism could at last be banished within the compulsory socialist framework. While the cure of past ills had to be socialist in content, the means were found in traditional Jewish appeals to wealthy Western Jews for financial support. J.D.C. appointed Rosen as head of a subsidiary, the American Joint Agricultural Society (Agro-Joint), to cooperate with the Soviet Society for Settlement of Jewish Toilers (KOMZET) in the task of resettlement and training. Between 1924 and 1936, 250,000 Jews were sucessfully settled on three million acres in the Ukraine and the Crimea. J.D.C. contributed $16 million, largely subscribed by a few wealthy individuals, because of mass apathy toward a non-Zionist or assimilationist effort. Long before the Soviet government rejected further outside help in 1938, the Jewish collective farms had become models of productivity and organization. Herbert Hoover hailed Rosen's achievement as an amazing feat of "social engineering." During World War II, the farms were destroyed and their inhabitants were annihilated by the Germans. After the war, the Soviet government forbade reconstruction by the survivors.

After returning to the United States in 1937, Rosen joined the Anglo-American commission to study British Guiana as a potential haven for German Jewish refugees. Lack of support from the American Jewish community and Rosen's own environmental objections led to a rejection of the proposal. In 1940, he became vice-president of the J.D.C.-sponsored Dominican Resettlement Association (DORSA), which eventually succeeded in settling 500 of a projected 28,000 Jews in the area of Sosua. While Rosen himself had doubts about the future of the Dominican experiment, the holocaust of World War II would make this and all other purely territorial solutions irrelevant.

Rosen died of a stroke in New York City on Apr. 2, 1949, leaving behind his wife, the former Katherine N. Shoubine, and two sons, Eugene and Leo.

[Rosen's biographical materials at the Am. Joint Distribution Committee are very incomplete. Considerable materials on his activities for J.D.C. can be found in vols. 12, 19, 27, 30, 37, 41–43, and 73 of the *Am. Jewish Yearbook* (Jewish Publication Society). Rosen himself wrote only one article on his resettlement activities, "New Neighbors in Sosua," *Survey Graphic*, Sept. 1941, pp. 474–478, which presents the Dominican effort in an overly optimistic light. The best insight into his Russian successes by one who knew him and observed his actions on the spot can be gained from Boris Smolar, *Soviet Jewry Today and Tomorrow*, pp. 97–106 (1971). Dana G. Dalrymple in "Joseph A. Rosen and Early Russian Studies of American Agriculture," *Agricultural Hist.*, 38 (1964), 157–160, is most informative on his early American activities; and in "The American Tractor Comes to Soviet Agriculture," *Technology and Culture*, Spring 1964, pp. 193, 203, he notes the implications of Rosen's importation of tractors into the USSR. Merle Curti, *American Philanthropy Abroad: A History*, pp. 293, 365–368, 372 (1963), and Herbert Agar, *The Saving Remnant: An Account of Jewish Survival*, pp. 48–51 (1960), place Rosen's efforts in the historical context of American and Jewish philanthropy. Henry L. Feingold, *The Politics of Rescue: The Roosevelt Administration and the Holocaust, 1938–1945* (1970), emphasizes the anachronism of the Guianan and Dominican plans on the eve of World War II.]

HANS HEILBRONNER

ROSENAU, MILTON JOSEPH (Jan. 1, 1869–Apr. 9, 1946), epidemiologist and pioneer in public health and preventive medicine, was born in Philadelphia, Pa., the son of Matilda (Blitz) Rosenau and Nathan Rosenau, a Jewish merchant who emigrated from Bavaria in 1852, settled first in Louisville, Ky., and then moved to Philadelphia. Rosenau received his early education in the local public schools, graduating from Central High School. He then entered the University of Pennsylvania and received the M.D. degree in 1889. After completing an internship at the Philadelphia General Hospital (1889–1890), he became assistant surgeon with the U.S. Marine Hospital Service (now the U.S. Public Health Service). In the years that followed, he broadened his knowledge of public health work by studying at the Hygienic Institute in Berlin (1892–1893) and by serving as quarantine officer at San

Francisco (1895–1898) and in Cuba (1898). In 1899 he was appointed director of the Hygienic Laboratory of the U.S. Public Health and Marine Hospital Service (which later became the nucleus of the present National Institutes of Health) and in 1900 again went abroad for further study at the Pasteur Institute in Paris and the Pathological Institute in Vienna.

The Hygienic Laboratory, established in 1887 as essentially a one-man operation, received official recognition in 1901, when Congress appropriated $35,000 for the construction of a building to house it. As the research facility of the Public Health and Marine Hospital Service, the laboratory dealt with problems relating to foreign and interstate quarantine and with the medical inspection of immigrants; thus the service required accurate knowledge of the causes, sources, modes of spread, and means for diagnosis and prevention of major communicable diseases. As the responsibilities of the service increased, the laboratory entered a period of rapid growth; during the ten years of Rosenau's directorship the laboratory developed into a more complex organization with separate divisions of bacteriology, chemistry, pathology, pharmacology, and zoology. When Congress enacted a Biologics Control Law in 1902, a separate division was set up within the laboratory to administer it.

The expansion of the laboratory reflected Rosenau's talents as a planner and administrator, as well as his high scientific standards. During these years Rosenau made his most important contributions to basic medical research. In collaboration with John F. Anderson, his successor as director of the laboratory, he pioneered in the study of anaphylaxis, the severe and sometimes fatal reaction that occurs when an animal or a human being sensitized to a foreign substance by ingestion or injection receives this material again in the same or even smaller dosage. He not only discovered that bacterial proteins could sensitize but established the time necessary for the development of sensitization and shock. He publicized the use of the Schick test for determining the degree of immunity to diphtheria and, with Joseph Goldberger, established the official unit for standardization of diphtheria antitoxin. He also carried out investigations on the epidemiology of typhoid fever and acute respiratory infections; yellow fever; malaria; plague; the tubercle bacillus; botulism; and disinfection and disinfectants. He studied the germicidal properties of glycerin and determined what concentration was necessary to prevent bacterial contamination of vaccine virus. Rosenau's studies on milk sanitation were an important factor in procuring a clean, safe milk supply in the United States. In 1906 he gave great impetus to the use of pasteurization by determining what degree of heat was required to kill the more important pathogens in milk and showed that heating to 60°C for twenty minutes would make milk safe without damaging its quality. He also served as a part-time lecturer on tropical diseases at Georgetown University in Washington, D.C. (1905-1909), and taught bacteriology at the Army and Navy Medical School (1904-1909).

In 1909 Rosenau entered the second major phase of his career when he was appointed Charles Wilder professor of preventive medicine at Harvard Medical School, where he served until his retirement in 1935. His intimate knowledge of public health problems gave him a solid basis on which to build a teaching program and enabled him to illustrate the practical application of theoretical principles. To provide experience, he required each student to study the public health problems of a specific community and to prepare a written report offering suggestions for improvement. In association with W. T. Sedgwick and George C. Whipple, he was instrumental in establishing in 1913 the first school of public health in the United States, the Harvard and Massachusetts Institute of Technology School for Health Officers. When the joint school was discontinued in 1922 and Harvard created its own school of public health, Rosenau became its professor of epidemiology, a post he held until 1935. He also served (1914-1921) as chief of the Division of Biologic Laboratories of the Massachusetts State Board of Health and as director of the Antitoxin and Vaccine Laboratory.

In 1935, at the age of sixty-six, Rosenau retired from his posts at Harvard, and the following year moved to the University of North Carolina, at Chapel Hill, as director of the Division of Public Health and professor of epidemiology in the School of Medicine, where he spent the last ten years of his life developing a school of public health.

Rosenau exercised great influence through his publications. His *Disinfection and Disinfectants: A Practical Guide for Sanitarians, Health and Quarantine Officers* appeared in 1902. In the same year he issued a laboratory manual for students of pathology and bacteri-

ology. He summarized his work on milk sanitation in *The Milk Question* (1912). His most important book, *Preventive Medicine and Hygiene* (1913), became the standard text on the subject, was translated into several foreign languages, and went through many editions.

As an outstanding authority in public health and preventive medicine, Rosenau received many honors. He was awarded the Gold Medal of American Medicine for service to humanity, for 1912-1913; in 1933 he received the Sedgwick Memorial Medal for distinguished service in public health, and in 1935 the Pirquet Gold Medal of the Annual Forum on Allergy. He served as president of several professional organizations, including the Society of American Bacteriologists (1934) and the American Public Health Association (1944). As a Jew, Rosenau was called upon to assist in health problems involving fellow Jews. Following World War I, he served as a consultant to the Joint Distribution Committee and traveled to Europe to observe the health situation of the Jews in Central and Eastern Europe and to recommend the most appropriate course of action to take.

Rosenau was a vigorous man who enjoyed sports; he was an exceptionally good tennis player as well as a competent golfer. At Chapel Hill his garden became one of his prime interests. Dignified in appearance, kindly in manner, he was always ready to go out of his way to help his colleagues and friends.

On July 16, 1900, Rosenau married Myra F. Frank of Allegheny, Pa. Their three children were William Frank, Milton Joseph, and Bertha Pauline. His wife died in 1930 and on Jan. 13, 1935, he married Maud (Heilner) Tenner, a widow with one son, Leonard P. Tenner. In the spring of 1946 Rosenau suffered a heart attack and died a few weeks later, in Chapel Hill, of a coronary occlusion.

Rosenau's pioneer work in public health was of the greatest importance. In the period from the turn of the century to the 1930's an increasing knowledge of microbiology and immunology made possible the prevention of communicable diseases on a large scale, but few competent health officers were available to apply the new knowledge. Through his teaching, his publications, and his creation of the first school of public health, Rosenau made possible an ample supply of professionally trained workers in the field.

[The major biographical sources are L. D. Felton, "Milton J. Rosenau, 1869-1946," *Jour. Bacteriol.*,

53 (1947); 1–3 (with photograph of Rosenau); S. B. Wolbach, "Milton Joseph Rosenau, 1869–1946." *Trans. Assn. Amer. Physicians,* 59 (1946), 32–33; C.-E. A. Winslow, "Milton Joseph Rosenau," *Amer. Jour. Public Health,* 36 (1946), 530–531, which has some inaccurate dates; Ralph C. Williams, *The United States Public Health Service, 1798–1950,* pp. 250–251 (1951); *Nat. Cyc. Am. Biog.,* XLII, 690–692; Solomon R. Kagan, "Milton J. Rosenau," *Med. Rec.,* 146 (1937), 138–141; *Jewish Contributions to Medicine in America,* pp. 387–389, 764–765 (2nd ed., 1939); *Am. Jewish Physicians of Note,* pp. 29–35 (1942), which has several inaccurate dates; "Sedgwick Memorial Medal," *Amer. Jour. Public Health,* 24 (1934), 139–140; *Annual Report, Carnegie Foundation for the Advancement of Teaching,* pp. 124–125 (1945–1946); and Wilson G. Smillie, *Public Health: Its Promise for the Future* (1955), passim. Obituaries appeared in *Jour. AMA,* 130 (1946), 1185; *N.C. Med. Jour.,* 7 (1946), 233; *N.Y. Times,* Apr. 10, 1946; and *School and Society,* 63 (1946), 282–283.]

GEORGE ROSEN

ROSENFELD, PAUL LEOPOLD (May 4, 1890-July 21, 1946), music, art, and literary critic, was born in New York City, the elder of two children and only son of German-Jewish parents. His father, Julius S. Rosenfeld, a prosperous manufacturer of braids, was a native of Germany; his mother, Clara (Liebmann) Rosenfeld, was the daughter of immigrants. They were cultured and idealistic; he was a devoted reader, she a talented pianist. The family lived in the prosperous brownstone neighborhood of Mount Morris Park near Harlem and often traveled to Europe.

Rosenfeld's childhood was marred by the hysterias and depressions of his mother, related in his autobiographical novel, *The Boy in the Sun* (1928), which tells also of the painful anti-Semitism of neighbors. After his mother's death in 1900, his father went into an emotional decline, and Paul and his sister were taken in by their maternal grandmother. At thirteen Rosenfeld left the New York public schools for Riverview Military Academy in Poughkeepsie, N.Y. Neither very military nor very academic, he edited and wrote for the school magazine, read with adolescent passion, and continued the piano lessons he had begun at six. His piano teacher and the local music-store owner were, to him, oases in the cultural deserts of the world. His father died, impoverished and exhausted, in 1908. In his novel, Rosenfeld described how the ability of a boy to care for his dying father (aided by an inheritance from his mother's family) brought him to manhood and to a new sympathy with people and nature.

Rosenfeld entered Yale in 1908, spent an unremarkable four years studying literature and writing some criticism for a student magazine and a local newspaper, and graduated with the B.A. in 1912. He next attended the Columbia School of Journalism, where he received his Litt.B. degree in 1913. For six months he was a reporter on the *New York Press,* but he found the work "morally distasteful." With the security of a large personal inheritance, he determined to pursue his interests in music and art. After a European trip, he joined the New York circle that determined his career. The musician Leo Ornstein, the novelist Waldo Frank, the literary critic Van Wyck Brooks, the photographer Alfred Stieglitz, and particularly the brilliant social critic Randolph Bourne became his friends, and he shared in their projects to urge high culture and intellect upon a sluggish America.

Rosenfeld's first publications, outspoken essays on the arts, appeared in 1916 in the *New Republic* and *Seven Arts,* a short-lived but influential journal. He served briefly in the army in 1918. In 1920 he became music critic of the *Dial* and published his first book, *Musical Portraits,* which to Edmund Wilson "seemed at the time absolutely dazzling" (Mellquist and Wiese, p. 3). During the following decade, Rosenfeld wrote hundreds of articles for *Vanity Fair,* the *Nation, Modern Music,* and other journals, and six more collections of his essays appeared. *Port of New York* (1924), although not primarily concerned with music, is probably his best and most characteristic book. Here he presents portraits of "fourteen American moderns," including Bourne; Stieglitz; the composer Roger Sessions; the painters Albert P. Ryder, John Marin, Marsden Hartley, Arthur G. Dove, and Georgia O'Keeffe; and the authors Van Wyck Brooks, William Carlos Williams, and Sherwood Anderson. To Rosenfeld they manifested in this country the great modern movement in the arts represented in Europe by Stravinsky, Picasso, and Joyce; and they made New York an exciting place in which to be.

As a critic, Rosenfeld used his knowledge of history, of musical performances, of museums and studios, of the cities of Europe; he knew enough of the techniques of music and painting and writing to understand what the artist had done to get his effects. He used the life, the looks, the personality of his subject, and felt free to employ psychoanalytic concepts. Yet these things were likely to be introductory or merely explanatory in his criticism. His real point was to say what the sounds or the forms or the words were like—that is, what extended analogy to them could be found in another realm of experience. Thus, in an essay on Stravinsky he explains the composer's "intellectual" music for *Les Noces* as a result of exile, which causes cerebral rather than emotional development; but most of the essay is taken up with metaphors like "the firm rich quality of white metals, nickel, silver, and steel, felt through the score." Sherwood Anderson's words are a "gray driven throng" of drab people, but he freshens them, makes them starched and fragrant again. Ryder's paintings have dark areas in the foreground because that part of the canvas's torso represents the genitals, which Ryder dared not form.

Rosenfeld's style has often been called overblown and eccentric. He wrote in the exuberance of his period, sometimes with odd results: "Experienced once again was the spirit morning." Yet most of his prose is clear and lively, and he could be funny. Van Wyck Brooks's Harvard photograph reveals "features of a slightly virginal jack-rabbit cast [that] manage somehow to adumbrate the distinguished head of the future stiff little colonel of literature." Interest in Rosenfeld's work has continued, as seen in reprintings; yet a critic who devotes himself to interpreting new art of his time cannot expect his own work to remain important when that art has become either familiar or forgotten. Few of those he championed are now regarded as the peers of their great European forebears, although they did, like Rosenfeld himself, do much to change the cultural climate of America.

Throughout the 1920's Rosenfeld kept a kind of salon, where at quiet evening parties poets read or musicians played. Among them might be Ornstein, Darius Milhaud, Edgard Varèse, e. e. cummings, Hart Crane, Marianne Moore, the Stieglitzes, and all their group. Rosenfeld was a quiet benefactor of young artists. *American Caravan,* which he founded in 1927 with Lewis Mumford and Alfred Kreymborg as an annual anthology, was particularly hospitable to new writers. Of Rosenfeld as a person, Edmund Wilson has testified, "With his fair reddish hair and mustache, his pink cheeks and his limpid brown eyes [and] his good clothes which always followed the Brooks-cut college model, his presence, short though he was, had a certain authority and distinction" (*ibid.,* pp. 5-6). He was a good cook; he never married but was fond of women, and it is said they responded to him.

The 1930's brought Rosenfeld severe reversals: he became diabetic, his income dwindled, *American Caravan* closed, the jour-

nals he had written for died or changed. He undertook a novel, an autobiography, and, aided by a Bollingen grant in 1943, a study of literary genres, all unfinished. During World War II he wrote for the *Kenyon Review* and other academic quarterlies then becoming cultural forces. He died of a heart attack in St. Vincent's Hospital, New York City, at the age of fifty-six.

[Jerome Mellquist and Lucie Wiese, eds., *Paul Rosenfeld, Voyager in the Arts* (1948), includes memoirs and tributes and has a full bibliography of Rosenfeld's writings, a check list of reviews of his works, and a photograph by Alfred Stieglitz. Rosenfeld's *Port of New York* was reprinted in 1961 with an extended biographical and critical introduction by Sherman Paul. Herbert A. Leibowitz has edited a selection of Rosenfeld's *Musical Impressions* (1969). See also Alfred Kazin, *The Inmost Leaf* (1955); Rosenfeld's autobiographical essay, "All the World's Poughkeepsie!" *Musical Quart.,* Oct. 1943; Stanley J. Kunitz and Howard Haycraft, eds., *Twentieth-Century Authors* (1942); Yale Univ., *Obituary Record of Graduates,* 1946–1947. Rosenfeld's papers are in the Beinecke Lib. at Yale. A number of friends, among them Lewis Mumford and Dorothy Norman, provided memories of Rosenfeld.]

JOHN THOMPSON

ROSS, CHARLES GRIFFITH

ROSS, CHARLES GRIFFITH (Nov. 9, 1885–Dec. 5, 1950), newspaper correspondent, editor, and presidential press official, was born in Independence, Mo., the only son and third of the nine children of James Bruce Ross and Ella (Thomas) Ross. His Scottish forebears had come to America in colonial times. Charles's grandfather, Griffith Ross, who owned a prosperous cotton plantation in Henderson, Tenn., served as a captain in the army of the Confederacy as well as in its congress. His son, "J.B." Ross, who prospected in Colorado, married into a Campbellite Virginia family on a stop in Independence, settled there, and became Jackson County marshal. Prospecting remained in his blood and at intervals he was lured west by visions of silver and gold.

"Charlie" Ross attended public school in Independence, enjoyed the attractions of the county seat square, read every book he could put his hands on, and thrilled to his grandmother Thomas' stories of border warfare between the Kansas Jayhawkers and the Missouri Bushwhackers. Although only fifteen, he stood at the top of the 1901 high school class which included a quiet, musically inclined boy named Harry Truman. Ross then entered the University of Missouri, where as a sophomore he helped organize a society to promote writing, already a major interest. He won Phi Beta Kappa honors and worked as a part-time cam-

pus reporter for the Columbia (Mo.) *Herald,*
whose editor was Walter Williams.

After graduation, Ross spent a year on the
Herald (1905-1906), and then went to Victor,
Colo., to join his father and report briefly for
the *Victor Daily Record.* At the first opportunity, he moved to St. Louis to take a position
on the *Post-Dispatch* (1906-1907) under the
expert tutelage of Oliver K. Bovard. Then,
in 1907 he moved on to the *St. Louis Republic*
for the experience of editing news copy. He
was chief of the *Republic's* copy desk when
Walter Williams, having persuaded the University of Missouri curators to establish an
academic school of journalism, chose Ross as
his first faculty member. For the next decade
(1908-1918) Ross helped shape the curriculum
and teach the courses that made Missouri's
pioneering journalism school known worldwide.
He also produced one of the earliest books on
journalistic practice, *The Writing of News*
(1911).

On Aug. 20, 1913, Ross married Florence
Griffin, the daughter of John J. Griffin, circulation manager of the *St. Louis Republic.* They
had two sons, John Bruce and Walter Williams.

For a sabbatical year (1916-1917), Ross
went to Australia as subeditor on the *Mel-
bourne Herald.* In 1918, Bovard engaged him
to be the *Post-Dispatch's* first Washington
correspondent. Ross rose steadily in the esteem
of the capital newspaper corps. His devotion
to thorough investigation, accurate and lucid
writing, and thoughtful analysis fitted him admirably for interpretive reporting. His own
political and economic philosophy was drawn
from the thinking of Supreme Court justices
Oliver W. Holmes and Louis D. Brandeis and
senators Robert M. La Follette and George W.
Norris, whom he frequently quoted.

On a carefully directed assignment from
Bovard, Ross wrote, in the depths of the depression, a detailed examination of the collapse,
its causes, and recommended solutions (*Post-
Dispatch,* Nov. 29, 1931). Entitled "The Country's Plight—What Can Be Done About It?"
this article found American capitalism at fault,
due to its uneven distribution of wealth and
income, and called on both business enterprise
and the federal government to join in correcting the imbalance. In response to demand, it
was reprinted as a pamphlet and distributed
nationally prior to being awarded the Pulitzer
Prize for distinguished newspaper correspondence in 1932. *Editor & Publisher* described
the project as "the most thorough, scholarly

and candid roundup of the national depression
that it has ever been our fortune to read in
any newspaper, magazine or book" (Dec. 19,
1931).

Starting in the second Wilson administration,
Ross chronicled official Washington in the
Harding, Coolidge, Hoover, and early Roosevelt years. His overseas assignments included
the London Naval Conference of 1930 and
the world economic conference in London
(1933). He was one of the few foresighted
correspondents who accompanied Harding to
Alaska in 1923. He rode Harding's funeral
train from San Francisco to Washington and
reported that solemn experience with a vivid
dignity. His colleagues elected him head of
the Overseas Writers Club (1927) and president of the Gridiron Club (1933). His Washington years—he resided in Chevy Chase, Md.,
so he could have a voter's part in the electoral
process—were broken when in 1934 Joseph Pulitzer, editor and publisher of the *Post-Dispatch,*
gave him the choice between editing the editorial page and searching for a successor to
Clark McAdams, whose enthusiastic support of
Roosevelt's policies exceeded Pulitzer's restraints. Not wanting to sponsor an outsider,
Ross reluctantly went to St. Louis. It was a
difficult time to take over, for when his old
schoolmate Harry S. Truman ran for the
Senate in 1934, the *Post-Dispatch* was strenuously opposed to candidates developed by Kansas City boss Thomas J. Pendergast, of whom
Truman was one.

As editorial page editor for five years, Ross
called for Roosevelt's defeat in 1936 and campaigned against the Roosevelt proposal to enlarge the Supreme Court. He also reversed the
paper's long advocacy of the proposed child-
labor amendment. His editorials were well
written but generally and understandably lacked
characteristic *Post-Dispatch* spirit and vigor.
Supplanted in 1939 by Ralph Coghlan, he returned to Washington as contributing editor.
In this capacity he wrote a signed column of
opinion not subject to editing in St. Louis.
He also prepared and edited special projects,
such as a symposium on the nation's war aims
in 1943 and "Men and Jobs After the War,"
a major series on postwar employment, in
1944. He compiled a history of the *Post-Dispatch* for its fiftieth anniversary (1928) and
edited the sixtieth anniversary issue. The latter,
with emphasis on the state of the press, led
to an extensive inventory of the views of 120
representative Americans on press freedom that
Ross conducted.

When Truman assumed the presidency in 1945, he promptly drafted Ross for his press secretary. The selection was widely applauded, and again with reluctance Ross accepted, being sworn in on May 15. Clearly Ross's chief purpose was to help his friend; his White House compensation would be $10,000 as against a salary of more than $35,000 at the newspaper. His duties included writing and editing presidential speeches, handling much of the chief executive's mail, and counseling Truman on myriad matters. Within a few weeks he was at Potsdam directing the preparation of the final communiqué issued by Truman, Attlee, and Stalin at the Allied conference necessitated by the Nazi surrender. Although his sympathies often were with his former press associates, Ross helped train Truman to say, "No comment." After Truman's surprise victory in the 1948 election, Ross wrote for *Collier's* (Dec. 25) an article entitled "How Truman Did It." As a major White House staff member, Ross worked long, straining hours and engaged in fatiguing travel with the president, as when they flew to Wake Island in 1950 to confer with Gen. Douglas Mac-Arthur.

Many honors came to Ross. George Washington University granted him an honorary doctorate of laws in 1935. His alma mater awarded him its medal for outstanding work in journalism in 1933 and the LL.D. degree in 1936. He was national honorary president of journalism's Sigma Delta Chi in 1933.

Usually mild mannered, Ross could take up the cudgels and did successfully, for example, in 1928 against the admission of Mussolini to membership in the National Press Club. His face, long and sober-looking, often lighted up with wit and humor. Arthritis caused him almost continuous pain in his last years, and in 1949 he sought relief through a wrist operation. After briefing newsmen on the Truman-Attlee conference of Dec. 5, 1950, Ross collapsed at his desk and died of a coronary occlusion. He was buried in Mount Olivet Cemetery, Washington, D.C. The nation's newspapers paid him generous tribute as a journalistic craftsman of high order.

[Ronald T. Farrar, *Reluctant Servant: The Story of Charles G. Ross* (1969), a thorough, trustworthy report of his career, catches much of the quality and character of Ross; it contains an extensive list of sources. See also James W. Markham, *Bovard of the Post-Dispatch* (1954); Frank L. Mott, *American Journalism* (3rd. ed., 1962); *Who Was Who in Am.*, vol. III (1963); Bert Cochran, *Harry Truman and the Crisis Presidency* (1973); Harry S. Truman, *Memoirs* (1958); *Editor & Publisher*, Dec. 9, 1950;

and newspapers generally at the time of death, especially the St. Louis *Post-Dispatch*, Dec. 6, 1950, including editorial. The assistance of Roy T. King of St. Louis and *Post-Dispatch* colleagues is gratefully acknowledged. Personal recollection.]

IRVING DILLIARD

ROWE, LEO STANTON (Sept. 17, 1871-Dec. 5, 1946), political scientist and diplomat, was born at McGregor, Iowa, the second son and youngest of the four children of Louis U. Rowe and Katherine (Raff) Rowe. Both parents were natives of Germany; the father was a dry-goods merchant of considerable means. Rowe received his education in Philadelphia, to which the family moved when he was young. After graduating from Central High School in 1887, he entered the University of Pennsylvania as a sophomore, transferred after a year to the university's Wharton School of Finance and Commerce, and received a Ph.B. degree in 1890.

A fellowship from the Wharton School enabled Rowe to spend the next four years in study and travel abroad, in the course of which he earned the Ph.D. from the University of Halle in 1892. Upon his return to the United States, he studied law at the University of Pennsylvania and was awarded the LL.B. degree in 1895. Although he was admitted to the bar the same year, Rowe's interest in contemporary political questions led him to accept an appointment at his alma mater as an instructor in municipal government; the next year (1896) he became assistant professor of political science. Rising to the rank of professor in 1904, Rowe remained at the university until 1917, teaching both political science and international law. He published *Problems of City Government* in 1908. In 1900 he helped found the American Society of International Law. He was president of the American Academy of Political and Social Sciences from 1902 to 1930 and of the American Political Science Association in 1921.

Rowe's long involvement with Latin America began in 1900, when, taking a two-year leave from his teaching duties, he accepted an appointment from President McKinley to the Commission to Revise and Compile the Laws of Porto [now Puerto] Rico. The following year he served as chairman of the Insular Code Commission and coauthored its voluminous reports. In 1906 President Theodore Roosevelt named Rowe a delegate to the Third International Conference of American States at Rio de Janeiro, Brazil. Seizing the opportunity afforded by the conference, Rowe toured

South America, lecturing at various universities. He also began the research that led to his later book *The Federal System of the Argentine Republic* (1921), long a standard work.

Rowe's diplomatic reputation grew rapidly. In 1907 Secretary of State Elihu Root named him chairman of the executive committee of the Pan-American Committee, which sought to foster closer relations between the United States and Latin America. Appointments followed as chairman of the United States delegation to the First Pan American Scientific Congress in Santiago, Chile (1908-1909); as a member of the United States-Panama Land (Mixed Claims) Commission (1913); and as secretary general of the First Pan American Financial Conference in Washington, D.C. (1915) and of the United States Section of the Inter-American High Commission created by the conference. He also served in the delicate post of secretary of the United States-Mexico Mixed Claims Commission (1916-1917).

Rowe so impressed President Wilson and Secretary of the Treasury William G. McAdoo with his knowledge and tact that in 1917 he was appointed assistant secretary of the treasury. In that post he supervised Latin American affairs and international loans in general. World War I presented the United States with an opportunity to expand its economic influence in the Western hemisphere, but the many demands on limited resources made it imperative to impose some form of coordination on private American activities in Latin America. Rowe quickly became the government's top Latin American expert, and after the war, in 1919, when the Treasury Department withdrew from active involvement in international trade, he moved to the State Department as chief of its Latin American Division. Here he was instrumental in giving effect to Wilson's still vague efforts to end United States interventions in the Caribbean and to salvage United States-Latin American relations from nearly two decades of friction and misunderstanding. He brought to his task his usual efficiency and extraordinary capacity for work.

In 1920 Rowe was appointed director general of the Pan American Union, the permanent organization of the International Conferences of American States; he was to remain in this position until his death. With headquarters in Washington, D.C., the union was supposed to further hemispheric commerce, but until Rowe's appointment the director general had been little more than a public relations man

for American business. Rowe rebuilt the image of his office and of the union by following a policy of absolute respect for cultural and political differences and sincere belief in fraternal equality. These principles, when translated in the 1930's into a policy of nonintervention and juridical equality among nations, became the essence of President Franklin D. Roosevelt's Good Neighbor Policy. In a very real sense the years of patient labor by the Pan American Union under Rowe's leadership paved the way for Roosevelt's policy and facilitated whatever success it enjoyed in Latin America.

A slight, scholarly, courteous man, Rowe was fluent in Spanish and Portuguese. He traveled extensively throughout Latin America and used his influence to encourage cultural exchanges, the improvement of education, and the establishment of libraries. In 1946, while on his way to a reception at the Bolivian embassy in Washington, Rowe was struck and killed by a car. By his request, his body was cremated and the ashes placed in the headquarters building of the Pan American Union. Rowe, who never married, left the bulk of his estate, nearly half a million dollars, to the union to foster education in Latin America. Symbolically, Rowe's death marked the end of the Good Neighbor era in inter-American relations and the beginning of the Cold War. The Pan American Union soon afterward became the secretariat of the Organization of American States and part of the cold war struggle.

[There is no biography of Rowe. Some of his papers are in the Columbus Lib. of the Pan-American Union. His speeches and the work of the Pan American Union under his direction can be followed in the pages of its *Bull.*; a special issue, Apr. 1947, devoted to Rowe is the best single source of biographical information. Other useful sources are a pamphlet written by Rowe, *The Pan American Union, 1890-1940* (1940); *Nat. Cyc. Am. Biog.*, XVIII, 316-317; and obituaries in the *N.Y. Times*, Dec. 6, 1946; *Am. Political Sci Rev.*, Feb. 1947; and *Hispanic Am. Hist. Rev.*, May 1947. Joseph S. Tulchin, *The Aftermath of War* (1971), considers Rowe's work in the Treasury and State departments and on the Inter-American High Commission. Family data from federal census schedules for 1870, courtesy of Betty J. Stephenson, who prepared a helpful biobibliography on Rowe at the Univ. of Wis. Lib. School.]
JOSEPH S. TULCHIN

ROWELL, CHESTER HARVEY (Nov. 1, 1867-Apr. 12, 1948), California journalist and progressive politician, was born in the prairie town of Bloomington, Ill. He was the eldest of five children and one of three sons of Jonathan Harvey Rowell and Maria Sanford (Woods) Rowell. His father, a native of New Hampshire, had moved west as a boy; his mother was born in Illinois. Jonathan Rowell, a lawyer, served as a Republican congressman from Illinois, 1883-1891; originally a member of the Disciples of Christ, he was a Unitarian during his son's boyhood. From his parents and from his early life in the Midwest, Chester Rowell derived certain values that remained with him throughout his public career: an admiration for the enterprising individual, a commitment to the welfare of the community, a high standard of personal integrity, and a critical but not radical assessment of the American economic and political systems.

A highly motivated student, Rowell completed the four-year course in Bloomington's public high school in three years and then spent a year in the high school department of the state college at Normal. He next entered the University of Michigan, where he specialized in languages and graduated after three years (Ph.B., 1888). Drawn toward both scholarship and the law, he stayed on at Michigan for a year of graduate work in philosophy and then went to Washington to assist his father and serve as clerk of a congressional committee. Disillusioned with politics and the law, he embarked in 1891 for Europe, where he studied philology and philosophy at the universities of Halle and Berlin and traveled extensively on the Continent. Having exhausted his financial resources before completing his planned Ph.D., he returned to the United States in 1894. For the next four years Rowell taught a variety of subjects, including several foreign languages, at small schools and colleges in Kansas, Wisconsin, California, and Illinois. On Aug. 1, 1897, having been appointed instructor in German at the University of Illinois, he married Myrtle Marie Lingle of Webb City, Mo. They had five children, three of whom survived infancy: Cora Winifred, Barbara Lois, and Jonathan Harvey.

Although Rowell had long desired a career in college teaching, his wife's poor health compelled him to seek a change of climate, and in 1898 he accepted an offer from an uncle, Chester Rowell, the founder and owner of the Fresno (Calif.) Republican, to become the paper's editor and manager. The decision launched Rowell on a long and distinguished career in journalism. Although he had no previous newspaper experience, his intelligent and penetrating editorials soon attracted nationwide attention.

Rowell's role as a progressive editor drew him inevitably into municipal and state politics. He fought for regulation of Fresno's rampant liquor, prostitution, and gambling establish-

ments, and he backed a new city charter under which he unsuccessfully sought the mayoralty in 1901. Rowell was particularly angered by the political dominance in California of the Southern Pacific Railroad. In 1907 he was a leader in founding the Lincoln-Roosevelt League, which sought to convert the state Republican party to progressive principles and to emancipate California from Southern Pacific domination. Building up strength in key cities, the league elected a substantial number of the delegates to the Republican state convention of 1908, and two years later secured the nomination of Hiram Johnson for governor on a progressive platform. Rowell played a crucial role in persuading the reluctant Johnson to run and, through the editorial pages of the Republican, in garnering support for his election, which was achieved by a narrow margin.

Rowell served as a close friend and personal advisor of the energetic and often irascible governor. He played an active part in the passage of the California workmen's compensation laws of 1911 and 1913. Like other California progressives, he also endorsed the state's Alien Land Act (1913), which forbade the ownership of agricultural land by aliens (meaning Japanese), arguing that the welfare of the community must supersede individual rights. In 1914, at Johnson's request, Rowell sought the Progressive party nomination for United States senator in an attempt to thwart the ambitions of Johnson's rival Francis J. Heney, but lost after a lackluster campaign. He served on the Progressive National Committee, 1912-1916, and was chairman of the Republican State Central Committee, 1916-1918. In 1916 he managed Johnson's successful campaign for the United States Senate.

The friendship of the two men was seriously impaired during World War I, when Rowell strongly championed the League of Nations, which Johnson, one of the "irreconcilable" senators, strongly opposed. Regarding Johnson as having strayed from the progressive faith, Rowell unsuccessfully opposed his renomination to the Senate in 1922. Although he served on the federal Shipping Board in 1920 and on the State Railroad Commission, 1921-1923, Rowell was never again intimately involved in politics. The Fresno Republican, of whose ownership he had inherited a major share, was sold in 1920.

During the next twelve years Rowell traveled, lectured on educational, civic, and political subjects, and wrote a syndicated newspaper column and many magazine articles. He then served as editor (1932-1935) and editorial columnist (1935-1947) of the *San Francisco Chronicle.* He opposed the New Deal program of President Franklin D. Roosevelt as incipient "liberal revolution" (*Yale Review,* Spring 1936, p. 443). Rowell's principal interests of later years were international cooperation and world affairs. Sharply critical of isolationists in the mid-1930's, including Hiram Johnson, he was active in the Institute of Pacific Relations and served as president of the California League of Nations Association (1927-1939) and as a trustee of the World Peace Federation (1932-1939). He was also president of the California Conference on Social Work (1928-1929) and a longtime regent (1914-1948) of the University of California. A mildly religious man, Rowell did not attend any church regularly but upheld high ethical standards. He died at his home in Berkeley, Calif., at the age of eighty, of a cerebral vascular thrombosis. Following cremation, his ashes were placed in Mountain View Cemetery, Oakland, Calif.

[The papers of Rowell, Hiram Johnson, and other leading Calif. progressives are in the Bancroft Lib., Univ. of Calif., Berkeley. Other important collections, including the Lincoln-Roosevelt Republican Club Papers, are in the Borel Collect. at Stanford Univ. Of Rowell's numerous articles, several are of particular interest: "Chinese and Japanese Immigrants— A Comparison," Am. Acad. of Political and Social Sci., *Annals,* Sept. 1909; "The Freedom of the Press," *ibid.,* May 1936; "A Positive Programme for the Republican Party," *Yale Rev.,* Spring 1936; "What Americans Think about Post-War Reconstruction: On the Pacific Coast," *Foreign Policy Reports,* Jan. 15, 1943; and "What Is a Party?" *Forum,* May 1946. The best secondary source is Miles C. Everett, "Chester Harvey Rowell, Pragmatic Humanist and Calif. Progressive" (Ph.D. diss., Univ. of Calif., Berkeley, 1966), which covers his career only to 1913. See also George E. Mowry, *The Calif. Progressives* (1951); Spences C. Olin, Jr., *Calif.'s Prodigal Sons: Hiram Johnson and the Progressives, 1911–1917* (1968); *Current Biog.,* 1940; *San Francisco Chronicle,* Apr. 13, 14, 16, 1948; *N.Y. Times,* Apr. 13, 1948.]

SPENCER C. OLIN, JR.

RUNYON, DAMON (Oct. 3, 1880-Dec. 10, 1946), journalist and short story writer, was born in Manhattan, Kans.; christened Alfred Damon, he was the second of four children and only son of Alfred Lee Runyan and Libbie J. (Damon) Runyan. Both parents were natives of Kansas. The father was descended from a Huguenot family (originally Renoyan) that had settled in New Jersey shortly before the Revolution; the mother, from an early member of the Massachusetts Bay colony. A printer and newspaper publisher in a series of Kansas towns, Runyan was a poor provider who drank heavily and dressed flashily. When his wife became consumptive, he moved to the better climate of Pueblo, Colo., but she died within a year and the family was broken up, Runyan and the boy staying in Pueblo. Young Al (as he was then known) was expelled from the public schools after the sixth grade for "horseplay." In his early teens he became a feature writer for the *Pueblo Evening Press* and aped his father in the matter of drink and dress. Through a printer's error, Runyan became Runyon, the spelling he retained through life.

After serving a stint in the Philippines shortly after the Spanish-American War, Runyon joined the *Pueblo Chieftain* and began to put together a reputation as a political and feature writer that carried him quickly through a succession of small-town Colorado newspapers and then in 1905 to Denver. He became the star reporter on the *Rocky Mountain News,* noted for his descriptive powers. He was by then an alcoholic, but gave up drinking at the urging of his fiancée, Ellen Egan, a society writer for the *News.* He had been selling stories and verses to various magazines and in 1910 decided to go to New York to devote himself to writing fiction. The next year found him back on a newspaper, the *New York American,* where he quickly made a success as a sportswriter. He married Ellen Egan in May 1911 in Brooklyn; they had two children: Mary Elaine and Damon.

Long fascinated by athletics—he had managed a semiprofessional baseball team and promoted boxing matches in Colorado—Runyon won an immediate audience with his colorful rather than technical stories of the New York baseball clubs. The Hearst organization recognized his appeal, and in short order he became the highest salaried sportswriter of his time, a war correspondent in Mexico and France, and, after the war, a reporter of crimes and murder trials, and star feature writer of the Hearst chain. Arthur Brisbane—whom Runyon was to succeed as chief columnist of the Hearst papers—called him the world's greatest reporter.

After a long hiatus, Runyon returned to fiction in 1929 with "Romance in the Roaring Forties," his first Broadway story, based loosely on his cronies in the milieu of racetracks, gambling, and Broadway restaurants. In 1931, *Guys and Dolls,* his first collection of short stories, was published. Hiding behind an anonymous narrator, Runyon surveyed the sordidness, stupidity, and dullness of Broadway and its gangsters, chorus girls, gamblers, broken athletes, and bookies, and fashioned a fictional world that was an overnight sensation with his depression-ridden readers. He mixed the ingredients carefully—an assortment of seamy but likable "guys" and "dolls" with names like Harry the Horse, Educated Edmund, Dream Street Rose, and Benny South Street; a blend of fanciful but neatly contrived plots; a careful avoidance of the profane or the obscene; a unique style concocted of underworld argot and the present tense—and, marketing the mixture, made a reputed "half million bucks." There is occasional humor, there is an original "slanguage" (H. L. Mencken agreed that Runyon influenced American slang), and there is a watery core of sentimentality in all of the stories that appeared in the half-dozen collections published in his lifetime. We may look for signs of the literary regionalist, but we find Runyon's urban hoodlums playing house with little girls in St. Pierre, saving college girls from gigolos in New Haven, sacrificing their lives for nuns and detectives in Nicaragua, and marrying tubercular patients in charity wards in Montreal ("she looks up at me for the last time, and smiles a little smile, and then closes her eyes for good and all"). Near the end of his life, in a mock review of his *Short Takes* (1946), Runyon offered a devastatingly honest evaluation of his short stories: "As a study in the art of carrying water on both shoulders, of sophistry, of writing with tongue-in-cheek, and of intellectual dishonesty, I think it has no superior since the beginning of time. . . . It is a great pity the guy did not remain a rebel out-and-out, even at the cost of a good position at the feed trough."

Short and dapper, bespectacled in his later years, Runyon has been described by his biographer as a "shy, quiet introvert" who masked his feelings under the pose of "the professional tough guy." His children found him emotionally withdrawn. His wife, from whom he had separated, died (ironically) an alcoholic, in 1931, and on July 7, 1932, he married Patrice Amati del Grande, a dancer. They were divorced in June 1946. Although both his wives were Catholics, Runyon had no religion.

By the beginning of World War II, Runyon was one of the highest-paid writers in America. After the death of Arthur Brisbane in 1936, Hearst moved him from the sports pages and made him a general columnist, widely syndicated through King Features. Collections of his short stories continued to appear. Early in the 1930's the motion picture companies had seen the possibilities of these stories for mass audiences, and dozens of them were adapted to the screen, beginning with *Lady for a Day* (1933) and *Little Miss Marker* (1934), which starred Shirley Temple. In 1941 he went to Hollywood to produce his own motion pictures and stayed for two years.

By then his health was failing. Cancer necessitated the removal of his larynx in 1944, and its further inroads brought his death at Memorial Hospital in New York in 1946. By his own wishes, his body was cremated without funeral services and his ashes were scattered from a plane over Manhattan. After his death a large sum of money was raised for a cancer research foundation that bears his name. Thanks to this association his name is still a familiar one in a society that quickly forgets its reporters and is afraid to walk the night streets where Damon Runyon's guys and dolls once strolled for a brief and sentimental moment.

[Edwin P. Hoyt, *A Gentleman of Broadway* (1964), is the only full-scale biography, readable and based on careful research. Damon Runyon, Jr., *Father's Footsteps* (1954), dealing with the estrangement and eventual reconciliation of Runyon and his children, is a revealing study of Runyon's private life. Ed Weiner, *The Damon Runyon Story* (1948), is loose and somewhat sentimental. For a more favorable evaluation of Runyon's short stories, see the critical study (in English) by a French literary scholar: Jean Wagner, *Runyonese: The Mind and Craft of Damon Runyon* (1965). See also *Current Biog.,* 1942; *N.Y. Times,* Dec. 11, 1946; and, on Runyon's father, *Kans. Hist. Quart.,* Feb. 1940, pp. 58–61. Runyon's birthdate was confirmed by the Kans. State Hist. Soc.]

CARLIN T. KINDILIEN

RUTH, GEORGE HERMAN (BABE) (Feb. 6, 1895–Aug. 17, 1948), baseball player, was born in Baltimore, Md., the son of George Herman Ruth and Katherine (Shamborg or Schamberger) Ruth, who were both of German ancestry. He was the oldest of their eight children, but only he and a sister survived infancy. Ruth's father worked unsuccessfully at various jobs including bartending and slaughterhouse work, and young George had a deprived childhood. A swearing, stealing, tobacco-chewing boy, he ran wild in the city streets, frequenting saloons and pool halls. At the age of seven his parents had him legally committed to the St. Mary's Industrial Home for Boys in Baltimore, a Roman Catholic institution run by the Xaverian Brothers. The home became his training ground and, when the ne'er-do-well father found that he could escape tuition payments, it became his legal guardian as well. Ruth's mother died when he was seventeen, and his father four years later.

As surrogate parents, the Xaverian Brothers exerted a powerful influence on Ruth. He was taught shirtmaking, cabinetmaking, and cigar-rolling, tasks that he handled capably. Placed under a rigid regimen of shopwork and skimpy meals, he learned to finish his work quotas quickly to gain time for sports. Baseball was then the favorite at St. Mary's, and Ruth quickly became the school's star player, satiating his appetite by playing as many as two hundred games a year. At the age of twelve he was, in the opinion of one of the brothers, "a natural . . . born to the game." Physically he was big. "Not fleshy, in fact more on the wiry side. . . . He had a mop of thick dark-brown hair. He was livelier than most . . . full of mischief . . . aggressive, shouting . . . always wrestling . . ." (Weldon, p. 9). He developed a strong admiration for Brother Matthias, one of his teachers, and adopted his habit of walking with toes pointed inward, a characteristic stride that later delighted Ruth's fans.

When Ruth was nineteen, word of his prowess as a left-handed pitcher reached Jack Dunn, the highly successful owner-operator of the Baltimore club of the International League. After scouting Ruth in 1914, Dunn agreed to become his legal guardian in order to acquire his pitching services. It was one of Dunn's coaches who dubbed the young protégé with his lifelong nickname of "Babe." A financial squeeze, however, forced Dunn to sell Ruth the same year to the major-league Boston Red Sox for $2,900. In the remaining weeks of play in 1914, Ruth won two games for Boston and was sent for further seasoning to the Providence (R.I.) team of the International League. With a brilliant overall record for 1914, his major-league career was launched. On October 17 of that same year, Ruth married Helen Woodford, a Boston waitress. They had no children, but in 1920 they adopted a baby, Dorothy, from an orphanage. In 1928 Ruth and his wife were separated, and in early 1929 she died in a fire at Waterloo, Mass.

Over the next four years, as a regular Red Sox pitcher, Ruth helped Boston win three American League pennants and three World Series titles. A strong left-hander, he had speed and a good curve ball. In the World Series of 1918 he pitched a shutout; he later extended a string of scoreless pitching in World Series play into a record that held for almost fifty years. Overall, his six years as a Boston pitcher showed eighty-nine victories and forty-six losses, a pace which, if continued, would surely have ranked him as one of baseball's greatest pitchers.

But Ruth's versatility ended his pitching. His exceptional abilities as a hitter prompted Boston manager Ed Barrow in 1918 to place him full-time in the outfield, where he played thereafter. By then Ruth stood six feet two inches tall and weighed 185 pounds. He was brawny in the chest and inclined toward fatness, but he was muscular and, notwithstanding a pair of incongruously slim legs, a fast runner. Unlike Ty Cobb, who employed the "scientific" choke-hitting style, Ruth was a free swinger who gripped a heavy bat at the end and used body weight and wrist leverage to power the ball. When he connected, the ball flew far, and, even when he missed, his swing was an electrifying sight. In 1918 he batted .300 and hit eleven homers; a year later he astounded the baseball world by clubbing a record twenty-nine homers on a .322 batting average.

Such feats made him a superstar. When in 1919 Boston owner Harry Frazee, needing money to promote a musical play, sold Ruth to the New York Yankees for $125,000 and a loan, Boston fans were enraged. Ruth soon won the adulation of New York fans and the powerful New York press. During the 1920 season he hit fifty-four homers and quickly overshadowed the great Ty Cobb as the hero of baseball. In so doing he revolutionized the style of baseball play, popularizing the explosive, decisive, high-scoring game of the home run. With Ruth as the unparalleled exponent, the "big bang" style came to dominate baseball strategy. Since his rise to fame occurred soon after the "Black Sox" scandal, with its revelations of bribery and corruption, some historians give Ruth credit for reviving a flagging public interest in baseball; but attendance figures in the years 1919 and 1920 show that he merely escalated an already rising tide.

Ruth was the dominant figure in American baseball from 1920 to 1935, leading the New York Yankees to seven league pennants and five World Series championships. His salary rose from $20,000 in 1920 to a peak of $80,000 in 1930–1931. Altogether he earned $1 million in salary in twenty-two seasons, a sum that he doubled by endorsements and public appearances. He had become a national celebrity. In the fall of 1927, after hitting his all-time seasonal high of sixty homers, Ruth toured the Far West and attracted adoring crowds and banner headlines. Returning home, he signed a $100,000 vaudeville contract. Two years later, on Apr. 17, 1929, Ruth married Mrs. Claire

Merritt Hodgson, a widow who had been an actress and professional model, and whose daughter, Julia, he adopted.

As an American folk hero, Ruth found that his private life attracted attention, and his misdeeds became public knowledge. During World War I he was widely censured as a draft dodger. Later, sharp criticism focused on his high salary and his gambling, drinking, and wenching, and he was obliged to adjust his behavior somewhat to fit his public image. A lavish spender, Ruth learned to depend on financial advisors to curb his prodigality. Though unschooled and unmannered in middle-class etiquette, Ruth was no boorish lout. An idol of American boys, he was frequently photographed in their company, and often appeared at the bedsides of hospitalized youths, gestures that enriched his appeal and atoned for his crudities. One such visit elicited a vivid description from the writer Paul Gallico: "The door opened and it was God himself who walked into the room . . . God dressed in a camel's hair polo coat and flat, camel's hair cap, God with a flat nose and little piggy eyes, a big grin, and a fat black cigar sticking out of the side of it." By 1930 Ruth was said to be the most photographed hero of the day, eclipsing presidents, royalty, dictators, and prizefighters.

As a player Ruth was hard to manage, often brawling with fellow players and contending with managers and baseball officials. When he defied the ruling of Commissioner Kenesaw M. Landis against postseason barnstorming, Ruth was fined and barred from playing a third of the 1922 season, an action that cost him the home-run title that year. In 1925, stricken with what newspapers at first called a "big belly ache," he was hospitalized and underwent surgery for an intestinal abscess. Incapacitated for much of that season, he returned in a garrulous mood, quarreled with his manager, Miller Huggins, and was fined $5,000—the heaviest fine in baseball history. Sobered at last, Ruth submitted to discipline. He engaged a trainer to help him lose weight and effected a comeback that added to his luster. Over the seasons of 1926–1928 he led the Yankees to three straight pennants.

In a fifteen-year career as a Yankee, Ruth set many records. As of 1973, his lifetime slugging average of .690 still led all others, as did his lifetime total of 714 home runs, his 2,216 runs batted in, and the 2,056 bases on balls that cautious pitchers awarded him. His overall performance was the more remarkable since he had spent a quarter of his big-league career as a pitcher. His .342 lifetime batting average ranks ninth best in baseball history. But he also struck out often, and his 1,330 strikeouts put him in third place in that category. Ruth inevitably left many legends, none more famous than his "called-shot" home run in the 1932 World Series, when, after being heckled by the Chicago Cubs, he gestured toward the fence and on the next pitch hit a home run.

Despite his tremendous popularity among fans, Ruth found no secure place in major-league baseball in his later years. When his physical prowess waned, the Yankee management offered him a chance to manage in the minor leagues. Ruth spurned the offer, and the Yankees in 1935 released him to the Boston Braves. The Boston opportunity turned out to be a crude publicity stunt aimed at exploiting his drawing power; disillusioned, Ruth quit in midseason. In 1936 he was elected a charter member of the Baseball Hall of Fame. Two years later he accepted a coaching offer from the Brooklyn Dodgers, but resigned before the end of the season for the same reason that had made him leave the Boston Braves. His last years became increasingly embittered as he awaited the managerial offer that never came. Still in the public eye, he appeared in movies, sold bonds during World War II, and became director of the Ford Motor Company's junior baseball program. In 1948, shortly before his death, he saw himself portrayed in a Hollywood film, *The Babe Ruth Story*. Ruth had invested in annuities and remained well-off financially; he continued to be the favorite of baseball fans, who roared affectionate greetings at his public appearances.

In 1946 Ruth developed cancer of the throat. Despite surgical and X-ray treatment, he died two years later in New York City's Memorial Hospital at the age of fifty-three. American baseball officials gave him the equivalent of a state funeral, placing his casket in the rotunda of Yankee Stadium where a hundred thousand people passed by his bier. After services in St. Patrick's Cathedral, he was buried in the Gate of Heaven Cemetery in Westchester County, N.Y.

[The Baseball Lib. at Cooperstown, N.Y., has ten volumes of scrapbooks on Ruth's career and the official files of the N.Y. Yankees for this period. No adequate biography of Ruth exists. Of the popular works, the best is Martin Weldon, *Babe Ruth* (1948). Useful primary sources include Mrs. Babe Ruth (Claire Hodgson Ruth), Bill Slocum, *The Babe and I* (1959), and Waite Hoyt, *Babe Ruth as I Knew Him* (1948), by a Yankee teammate. *Babe Ruth's Own Book of*

Baseball (1928) is a ghosted autobiography, written by Christy Walsh. Walsh's *Adios to Ghosts!* (1937) offers recollections of his own career managing Ruth's publicity. Excellent short sketches include Roger Kahn, "The Real Babe Ruth," *Esquire*, Aug. 1959; and essays in Paul Gallico's *A Farewell to Sport* (1938) and Laurence Greene's *The Era of Wonderful Nonsense* (1939). The most authoritative guide to Ruth's seasonal records is *The Baseball Encyc.* (1969). Some popular baseball team histories are useful for background, notably Frank Graham, *The N.Y. Yankees* (1943), and Frederick G. Lieb, *The Boston Red Sox* (1947). Ruth's place in the history of American baseball is sketched in David Q. Voigt, *Am. Baseball: From the Commissioners to Continental Expansion* (1970), and in Harold Seymour, *Baseball: The Golden Age* (1971). A long obituary appeared in the *N.Y. Times*, Aug. 17, 1948. An excellent photograph of Ruth taken in 1927 by Edward Steichen may be found in the Steichen Collect. of the Museum of Modern Art, New York.]

DAVID QUENTIN VOIGT

RUTLEDGE, WILEY BLOUNT (July 20, 1894–Sept. 10, 1949), law professor and dean, and associate justice of the Supreme Court of the United States, was born in Cloverport, Breckenridge County, Ky. He was the older of two children (a third died in infancy) and the only son of Wiley Blount Rutledge, a Baptist minister, and Mary Louise (Wigginton) Rutledge. His father, a native of Tennessee, was of Scots-Irish descent; his mother, born in Kentucky, was a descendant of William Wigginton, who came from England in 1654 and settled in Virginia. Young Wiley's early upbringing and schooling were affected by his mother's illness from tuberculosis, which caused the family to travel to mountain areas in North Carolina and the Southwest in search of healthier climates; she died when he was nine. In that year he received his first formal education in a private school in Mount Washington, Ky. His youth was spent in several Southeastern communities until his father settled as minister in Maryville, Tenn. There Wiley attended the preparatory school of Maryville College and in 1912 entered the college itself. In his senior year, however, he transferred to the University of Wisconsin, from which he received a B.A. degree in 1914.

After graduating, Rutledge taught high school in Bloomington, Ind., and at the same time studied law at Indiana University. At this point he himself was stricken with tuberculosis, for which he received treatment at a sanitarium in Asheville, N.C. On Aug. 28, 1917, he married Annabel Person of Howell, Mich., whom he had met at Maryville College, where she was a young instructor of classics. They had three children: Mary Lou, Jean Ann, and Neal Person. Rutledge decided to move west for his health and in 1918 accepted a high school

teaching post in Albuquerque, N.Mex., where he also served as secretary to the board of education from 1918 to 1920. He then resumed the study of law, this time at the University of Colorado in Boulder, teaching school as a means of support. He received his LL.B. degree in 1922. After two years of private practice in Boulder, he became associate professor of law in the university. His period in the Rocky Mountain area was in many ways a formative one. Several lawyers of ability impressed him, and he was much attracted to some of the officials and teachers at the University of Colorado, including Herbert S. Hadley, then professor of law. Rutledge also acquired a transcending love of the great outdoors, particularly the mountains, to which he regularly returned in the summers for many years.

Hadley, who became chancellor of Washington University in St. Louis, was instrumental in bringing Rutledge to that institution as professor of law in 1926. Rutledge advanced to the deanship of the law school in 1931, a post he retained until he accepted a similar appointment at the State University of Iowa in 1935. In 1939 President Franklin D. Roosevelt appointed him to the United States Court of Appeals for the District of Columbia, from which, four years later, he was elevated to the Supreme Court.

Rutledge was of moderate height and stocky build. He had a vigorous, unassuming personal warmth, coupled with hearty humor, that commanded deep loyalty and affection. He was equally at home with tradesmen and with intellectuals, and he sought people out in many ways, stopping to converse frequently with storekeepers and Supreme Court guards, as well as with academic and judicial colleagues. In St. Louis he came in contact with an urbane culture that affected his outlook permanently. He became a leader in several interprofessional organizations there and achieved a reputation as a vigorous, independent spokesman on social issues. Later, at the State University of Iowa and in Washington, Rutledge maintained significant contact with a wide range of associates, including an influential Unitarian minister in Washington, A. Powell Davies, whose thought contributed to Rutledge's free and developing personal faith. Mrs. Rutledge's Universalist background supplied a continuing influence in liberal directions. During the 1930's Rutledge strongly supported the policies of President Franklin D. Roosevelt, including the proposal in 1937 to enlarge the Supreme Court. He was, however, without personal political connections and was appointed to the bench solely as a result of the recommendation of his associates.

Rutledge's method as a scholar and jurist was the opposite of facile. Painstaking in high degree and dissatisfied until he felt he had penetrated to the roots of any problem that commanded his attention, he produced only occasional professional writings during his teaching career. On the bench, he gave himself to unremitting toil which probably contributed to his early death. His opinions, which were not numerous, tended to be long and encyclopedic. Several of them are basic analyses of such technical legal problems as the scope of the subpoena powers of government agencies and the limits to judicial review of agency decisions (*Oklahoma Press Publishing Co.* v. *Walling*, 327 U.S. 186 [1946]; *National Labor Relations Board* v. *Hearst Publications*, 322 U.S. 111 [1944]). Others, such as his opinion in the Court of Appeals holding that a charitable hospital must pay damages for injury negligently caused by its personnel (*Georgetown College* v. *Hughes*, 76 U.S. App. D.C. 123; 130 F.2d 810 [1942]), are outstanding contributions to legal development.

Rutledge was a "lawyer's judge," able to expound the niceties of procedure and of doctrine, as well as a strong upholder of human freedom. The practical consequences of alternative legal holdings figured largely in his reasoning. His position in the interpretation of the Bill of Rights and the elaboration of legal principles protective of freedom was carefully considered and unequivocal. In *Thomas* v. *Collins* (323 U.S. 516 [1945]) he wrote the majority opinion, holding invalid a Texas statute that imposed a registration requirement on union organizers. Two years later, in a dissent, he firmly supported the doctrine of the separation of church and state by condemning the use of public funds to provide buses for parochial schoolchildren (*Everson* v. *Board of Education*, 330 U.S. 1 [1947]). His reasoning in this case was later drawn upon by the Court. Other notable civil liberties decisions include a dissent for himself and Justice Frank Murphy in which he contended that a federal criminal court could not be required to try an alleged violator of a government regulation unless it were empowered to judge the validity of the regulation (*Yakus* v. *United States*, 321 U.S. 414 [1944]); and an eloquent plea in dissent against the execution of the Japanese general Tomoyuki Yamashita for war crimes, on the basis of the procedure employed at the gen-

eral's trial (*In re Yamashita*, 327 U.S. 1 [1946]).

Rutledge summarized his jurisprudential thought and his views of American federalism in *A Declaration of Legal Faith* (1947). In the opening essay he asserted his belief in law and in freedom, each capable of destroying the other but basically interdependent. Justice, in his view, is an accommodation between these opposites, achieved through legislators and judges "who can catch the vision of what has come or will come and sense the moment of its common acceptance." His career on the bench ended at the age of fifty-five, when he died of a cerebral hemorrhage in York, Maine. Following cremation, his ashes were buried in Green Moutain Cemetery, overlooking Boulder, Colo.

[This sketch of Mr. Justice Rutledge is based on personal knowledge, interviews and correspondence with members of his family, and his judicial opinions (in vols. 70–77 of the *Reports* of the U.S. Court of Appeals of D.C. and 318–338 of the *U.S. Reports*) and other writings. Of the latter, see especially "Legal Personality—Legislative or Judicial Prerogative?" *St. Louis Law Rev.*, July 1929; and "Significant Trends in Modern Incorporation Statutes," *Wash. Univ. Law Quart.*, Apr. 1937. Fowler V. Harper, *Mr. Justice Rutledge and the Bright Constellation* (1965), is a full-scale biography. There is also a chapter on Rutledge by J. P. Stevens in Allison Dunham and Philip B. Kurland, eds., *Mr. Justice* (1964); and one by Fred L. Israel in Leon Friedman and Fred L. Israel, eds., *The Justices of the U.S. Supreme Court, 1789–1969*, vol. IV (1969). A useful summary of his years on the Supreme Court is Alfred O. Canon, "Mr. Justice Rutledge and the Roosevelt Court," *Vanderbilt Law Rev.*, Feb. 1957. For additional data see: *Proc. of the Bar and Officers of the Supreme Court of the U.S. in Memory of Wiley Blount Rutledge* (1951); "Mr. Justice Rutledge—A Symposium," *Ind. Law Jour.*, Summer 1950 (with a bibliography of Rutledge's writings); articles on Rutledge in *Iowa Law Rev.*, Summer 1950 (also with bibliography); Lester E. Mosher, "Mr. Justice Rutledge's Philosophy of Civil Rights," *N.Y. Univ. Law Rev.*, Oct. 1949; Ralph F. Fuchs, "The Judicial Art of Wiley B. Rutledge," *Wash. Univ. Law Quart.*, Apr. 1943, and "In Memory of Mr. Justice Wiley B. Rutledge," *Rocky Mountain Law Rev.*, Dec. 1951.]

RALPH F. FUCHS

SAARINEN, GOTTLIEB ELIEL (Aug. 20, 1873-July 1, 1950), architect, educator, and city planner, was born in Rantalsami, Finland, the second of the six children of the Lutheran pastor Juho Saarinen and his wife, Selma (Broms) Saarinen. He was two years old when the family moved to Ingermanland in the vicinity of St. Petersburg, Russia, but he went to school in Finland: his devotion to his native land was never questioned. Visits to the Hermitage Museum opened his eyes to painting, and for a time he was undecided whether to be a painter or an architect. However, before he completed his studies at the Polytechnic Institute in Helsinki, his loyalty was to the latter profession. In 1896, while still a student, he and his classmates Herman Gesellius and Armas Lindgren founded their own firm. On Mar. 6, 1904, he married sculptress Loja Gesellius, his partner's sister. She was the mother of his two children, Pipsan and Eero.

Recalling the beginning of his career, Saarinen claimed that "in those days architecture did not inspire one's fancy. Architecture was a dead art form, and it had gradually become the mere crowding of obsolete and meaningless stylistic decoration on the building surface." This was not quite fair either to the architecture of the period or its achievements in Finland. He paid no attention to the work of the Finnish classic revivalist Carl Ludvig Engel and overlooked the debt he himself owed to the ferment provided in his youth by Finnish architects like Lars Sonck, who learned a great deal from the accomplishments of the American H. H. Richardson. Saarinen was also affected by the *Jugendstil* (the German version of art nouveau) and was conscious of the importance of William Morris' struggle in England for the revival of the arts and crafts.

Saarinen was only twenty-seven when the firm of Gesellius, Lindgren, and Saarinen created the Finnish pavilion for the Paris Exposition of 1900. Its odd, proud tower proclaimed that the designers, even though Russian subjects at the time, were under the spell of their own folklore. Two years later came the commission for the National Museum in Helsinki, completed in 1910. This was a bold granite monument, but Saarinen first proved himself at Hvrittäsk, the great rambling country house that he and his partners built for themselves at Luoma, eighteen miles outside Helsinki. Begun in 1902, it was one of the remarkable houses of the western world in the early twentieth century. It was set on the shore of the White Lake, from which it derived its name and its high-pitched red-tile roof and its pine timbers and granite made the most of its romantic site. Perhaps it could best be compared to the Wedding Tower that the Austrian Joseph Maria Olbrich built in this decade for the Grand Duke of Hesse at Darmstadt. Lindgren resigned from the firm in 1905 and Gesellius two years later, leaving Saarinen the sole owner of the estate. Here he entertained the German art critic Julius Meier-Graefe, Maksim Gorki, Gustav Mahler, and Jean Sibelius, his favorite composer.

The major work of Saarinen before World War I was the superbly monumental Helsinki railroad station (1904-1914), which served as a wartime hospital before Finnish independence permitted its intended use. His last commission in Finland, and one of his most brilliant, was a seven-story bank on the Keskaterinkatu in Helsinki; the simplicity of its façade showed that in 1921 he far surpassed an American prototype, the DeVinne Press Building in New York (1885), by Babb, Cook, and Willard. In the meantime he had been active as a city planner, redesigning Reval in Estonia and in 1912 winning second prize in the competition for the layout of Canberra in Australia; the first prize was awarded to Walter Burley Griffin of Chicago, an associate of Frank Lloyd Wright.

Although Raymond Hood and John Mead Howells won first prize in 1922 in the competition for the Chicago Tribune Tower, Saarinen placed second, and Louis Sullivan was so moved by the contrast between the Finn's sketches (which pointed the way to the later work of Hood) and the prize-winning reminiscence of Rouen's Butter Tower that he called Saarinen "a voice resonant and rich, ringing amidst the wealth and joy of life." Pocketing his $20,000 award, Saarinen moved early in 1923 to Evanston, Ill., where he labored over what he thought were the necessary corrections to the Chicago plan of D. H. Burnham. Perhaps because he was an extravagant admirer of the Viennese city planner Camillo Sitte, he failed to appreciate Burnham's vision. In fact, he despaired of the Chicago plan. "One cannot help wondering," he asked, "why the face was washed while the heart remained dark and cruel."

Saarinen's project for an underground parking garage at Grant Park came to nothing, but in 1923 he was asked by Emil Lorch, head of the school of architecture at the University of Michigan and the brother-in-law of Sullivan's faithful friend George Grant Elmslie, to teach in Ann Arbor. Among his students were his future son-in-law, J. Robert F. Swanson; John Ekin Dinwiddie; and Henry S. Booth, son of George Gough Booth, publisher of the Detroit *News*.

The publisher was to be Saarinen's Maecenas for the rest of his life. An independent millionaire with a passionate interest in the revival of the arts and crafts, he was so impressed by what his son had to tell him of the Finnish visitor to Ann Arbor that he decided that here was the architect to supervise the project he had in mind for a children's school, a boys' school, a girls' school, and an art academy to be built on the 175 acres of Cranbrook, his estate in Bloomfield Hills near Detroit. In September 1925, Saarinen moved to Cranbrook, where a $12 million foundation was set up to make Booth's dreams come true.

The children's school, Brookside, was entrusted to young Henry S. Booth. The boys' school, begun in the fall of 1926 and opened to the public a year later, was Saarinen's first American commission. Following Booth's suggestion, he remodeled the old farm buildings of the estate for the boys' use, but the courtyards and the handsome brickwork, not to mention the tall tower that dominated the scene, were the marks of an artist who could bring the arts and crafts to terms with the twentieth century. Less successful was the institute of science (1931-1933) and the art academy (1926-1941). Far more eloquent, and possibly Saarinen's finest work in the United States, was Kingswood, the girls' school (1929-1930), an extraordinarily subtle achievement for the creator of the Helsinki railroad terminal. The decade had seen very little as fresh and original.

Saarinen was to make his greatest mark in America as an educator, but it would be difficult to list all the artists he engaged as head of the art academy to stimulate his students and revive the arts and crafts. When the Hungarian sculptor Géza Maróti, who collaborated on the decorative elements of the boys' school, returned to Europe in 1929, he was replaced by the Swede Carl Milles, who became sculptor in residence and designed the Orpheus Fountain in front of the art academy. The Englishman Arthur Nevill Kirk provided the silversmithing; still another Englishman, John Burnett, worked in wrought iron; the Swiss Jean Eschmann founded a bookbinding studio; the Swede Tor Berglund started a cabinetmaking shop; and Weyland Gregory, to be succeeded by the Finn Maija Grotell, headed the ceramics department. Weaving was the province of Loja Saarinen and her assistant from Stockholm, Maija Anderrson-Wirde.

Graduates of Cranbrook included city planners Carl Feiss and Edmund Bacon, architects Ralph Rapson of Minneapolis and Harry Weese of Chicago. Of course, the most distinguished of all the graduates was Eero Saarinen, who was far from being overshadowed by his father and easily won an international reputation.

Eliel Saarinen possessed the gift of encouraging individuals to realize themselves. This was perhaps most evident in the realm of furniture design. Even though Detroit was already in the 1920's a center for the fine coachwork that Raymond H. Dietrich and others were lavishing on particular Packards, the city would never have come to the front as a furniture capital if the inspiration of Cranbrook had been lacking.

Harry Bertoia, later to be celebrated as a sculptor, conceived his wire-webbed chairs not long after he was placed in charge of the metalwork department. Charles Eames was another designer who got his start at Cranbrook. Still another was Eero Saarinen, whose womb chair may be described as the most comfortable and graceful piece of furniture since the eighteenth century in France. The work of Bertoia and the younger Saarinen was marketed by the firm of Knoll Associates. Mrs. Knoll, the former Florence Schust of Saginaw, Mich., was a Cranbrook student who made her own contribution to the firm's line.

In spite of the administrative load that he carried, Eliel Saarinen remained an active architect, a partner from 1941 to 1947 in the firm of Saarinen, Swanson, and Associates, which included his daughter Pipsan, his son-in-law, and Eero and Eero's first wife, Lily Swann. From 1947 to his death he was the partner of his son in Saarinen, Saarinen, and Associates. In 1937, assisted by Eero, he designed the community center for Fenton, Mich., whose brick façade confirmed his allegiance to Scandinavian traditions. From 1938 to 1940 father and son worked on the Kleinhans Music Hall in Buffalo. Also in 1938 Eliel, at the invitation of Serge Koussevitzky, planned the Tanglewood Music Shed at Stockbridge, Mass., whose ceiling proved that he had looked more than once at the sculpture of Alexander Calder. In 1939 both Saarinens collaborated with the firm of Perkins, Wheeler, and Will on the Crow Island School at Winnetka, Ill. The efficiency of this one-story brick building won immediate respect. With J. Robert F. Swanson as their associate, both Saarinens received first prize in 1939 in the competition for the Smithsonian Art Gallery in Washington, but this was never built. Father and son again worked together on the Tabernacle Church of Christ for Columbus, Ind., in 1940. This was at once delicate and monumental and also distinguished by the tapestry woven by Eliel's wife. To the son rather than the father may be attributed the A. C. Wermuth house at Fort Wayne, Ind. (1941-1942), which indicated that Eero was well aware of the international style advocated by Walter Gropius. But Eliel's hand was evident in the Des Moines Art Center (1944-1948); the chapel for Stephens College, Columbia, Mo. (1947-1952); and Christ Lutheran Church in Minneapolis, completed just before he died at Cranbrook of a cerebral hemorrhage. His remains were cremated and buried in Finland. Five years before his death, he had become an American citizen.

Although he had no use for jazz and could not enjoy the work of modern painters as significant as Matisse and Picasso, he was a far from dogmatic teacher and loved to relax at the annual Cranbrook Ball, at which he and his wife, seated on seashell thrones, lorded it over their domain. "Youth," he believed, "is always close to the future, for in the future it discerns its actions to come. . . . It is through the young that the coming art form is to be found."

[The major sources are Wayne Andrews, *Architecture in Michigan* (1967); Henry S. Booth et al., *The Saarinen Door* (1963); Albert Christ-Janer, *Eliel Saarinen* (1948); Joy Hakanson Colby, *Art and A City* (1966); Leonard K. Eaton, *American Architecture Comes Of Age* (1972); W. Hawkins Ferry, *The Buildings of Detroit* (1969); Hugo A. Pfau, *The Custom Body Eda* (1970); Arthur Pound, *The Only Thing Worth Finding* (1964); Nancy Rivard, "Eliel Saarinen in America" (unpub. master's thesis, Wayne State Univ., 1973); Eliel Saarinen, *The City: Its Growth, Its Decay, Its Future* (1943); *Search for Form* (1948); and an interview with Pipsan Saarinen Swanson.]

WAYNE ANDREWS

SACHS, HANNS (Jan. 10, 1881-Jan. 10, 1947), psychoanalyst, training analyst, and author, was born in Vienna, Austria, the second son and youngest of four children of Samuel Sachs and Heimine (Heller) Sachs. His father was a lawyer, as were many of his forebears—indeed, he came from a family in which training in the law and in the arts was paramount. Not surprisingly, Hanns also was so trained, and for a time he practiced law. One of his sisters was a novelist, and his brother, twelve years his senior, was a playwright. Sachs's only marriage ended in divorce. There were no children.

Hanns Sachs's brother, Otto, who died when Hanns was sixteen, was deeply interested in dreams, and perhaps was the early inspiration for Hanns's later devotion to Freud's theory of dreams and his own beliefs about the community of daydreams which unites friends. Sachs was attracted to Freud and his ideas as early as 1904, probably because of *The Interpretation of Dreams*. He attended Freud's lectures faithfully and in 1910 became a member of the inner group of analysts who formed the Vienna Psychoanalytic Society; he was also one of the original circle of Freud's closest associates, later known as the "Seven Rings." In Sachs's own words, Freud was his master and friend. The former is undoubtedly true, but there is evidence that the latter was not fully reciprocated. Sachs did not have a competitive drive, and, according to Ernest Jones, was a witty, learned, loyal, but detached member of the group. There was never a break between Sachs and Freud, which would have been completely out-of-character for Sachs. Freud basked in the personal loyalty of Sachs and enjoyed their mutual interest in art and literature and the knowledge that Sachs would be faithful to psychoanalysis on Freud's own terms. It is no secret, however, that Freud found Jung and Karl Abraham more fascinating, Rank and Ferenczi more imaginative, and Jones more prolific and worldly. Nevertheless, in 1912, Freud appointed Sachs coeditor of *Imago*, along with Otto Rank. *Imago* was a journal specializing in nonmedical applications of psychoanalysis, or what has been called "applied analysis." Sachs and Rank combined to produce several classical works which showed how psychoanalytic concepts could clarify other fields of study, especially mythology and anthropology. When Rank split off from Freud in the furor over the birth trauma, Sachs remained faithful to Freud and above the battles, then and afterward. This was a quality in Sachs that Freud appreciated to the very end of his life, when Sachs came to England and bade the master a sincere but unemotional farewell shortly before Freud's death in 1938.

In 1918 Sachs's delicate health broke down and he was hospitalized for tuberculosis in Switzerland. There, in Zurich, he established a psychiatric practice, which he pursued until he was called to the Berlin Training Institute to become the "first training analyst." None of the early analysts had more than a smattering of personal psychoanalysis, ranging from none at all to a few months "psychoanalysis" with someone who was in all likelihood a friend and colleague. It was consistent with Sachs's retiring nature to absent himself from organizational activities, and his stay in the tuberculosis sanitarium had removed him still farther from close association with those who were becoming psychoanalysts. These are, however, negative characteristics. On the positive side, he was an extremely learned man who was intuitive, intelligent, cultivated, and trustworthy. He was thus the logical choice to become a training analyst.

In 1932 Sachs immigrated to the United

States, one of the first European analysts of Jewish extraction to do so. Boston became his home, and Harvard Medical School his professional base.

In Boston, he found a friend and early patient in Dr. Stanley Cobb, who, like J. J. Putnam of an earlier era of psychoanalysis, was a distinguished psychiatrist and neurologist and a member of the social and medical aristocracy of New England. Cobb's support was instrumental in the acceptance of psychoanalysis in the Boston community, and possibly in even wider circles.

In 1938 Sachs founded *The American Imago*, with himself as editor. He was not only the primary *imago* for several American psychiatrists who went into the specialty of psychoanalysis, but also an early contributor to the penetration of analytic concepts into literature, aesthetics, and art, although he wrote occasional papers about technical psychoanalysis. His mastery of English style, vocabulary, and prose was extraordinary. He wrote about Shakespeare, Poe, Kipling, Strindberg, Schiller, and even Mickey Mouse. His own experience in Germany during the rise of Adolf Hitler provided the impetus to analyze another tyrant, Caligula, so that he can be said to have another distinction, less praiseworthy, perhaps, of being an early psychobiographer.

Jones described Sachs as a "silent partner" of the early days of psychoanalysis, a statement which is probably neither wholly accurate nor totally in error. Sachs's private life is rarely alluded to, and his contemporaries seem to have little to say about him as a person. In his work he emphasized the primacy of intuition and the creative unconscious. His main theme is that life and death are linked together through beauty. Perhaps the pursuit of beauty removed Sachs from the give-and-take of everyday activities. For Sachs, the artist mastered his own anxiety and guilt by externalizing and sharing his conflicts. Producing beauty enabled the artist to reduce his sensitivity to hurts and to reconcile himself with his narcissism. Although this may epitomize Sachs's own personality, he was not alienated from his colleagues. The distance between them was decided by how he saw the artist and the analyst: scholarly, cordial, private, unaggressive, and utterly devoted.

From his Marlboro Street home, Sachs continued his teaching at Harvard and his writing and analysis of physicians until the day he died, from the ravages of combined illnesses, including a terminal myocardial infarction on Jan. 10, 1947. His remains were cremated at Mount Auburn Cemetery, Cambridge.

[Among the many and varied books Sachs wrote are *The Significance of Psychoanalysis for the Mental Sciences* (1915), with Otto Rank; *Caligula* (1931); *The Creative Unconscious* (1942); *Freud: Master and Friend* (1944); and *Masks of Love and Life* (1948; published posthumously). A fine appreciation of the man and his work, by F. Moellenhoff, is to be found in F. Alexander et al., eds., *Psychoanalytic Pioneers* (1966), pp. 180–199; see also the article in *Encyc. Judaica*, pp. 593–594; R. Loewenstein, "In Memoriam, Hanns Sachs," *Psychoanalytic Quarterly*, 16 (1947), 151–156, in which there is a complete bibliography of Sachs; and F. Deutsch, "Hanns Sachs, 1881–1947," *The American Imago*, 4 (1947), 1–14. Obituaries appeared in the *N.Y. Times*, Jan. 11, 1947; *School and Society*, Jan. 18, 1947, p. 41; *Isis*, 37, no. 3-4 (1947), 183; *Wilson Lib. Bull.*, Mar. 1947; death record, Office of the City Registrar, Boston, Mass.]

AVERY D. WEISMAN

SAMAROFF, OLGA (Aug. 8, 1882–May 17, 1948), pianist and teacher, was born in San Antonio, Tex., the first daughter of Carlos Hickenlooper and Jane (Grunewald) Hickenlooper, and was christened Lucie Mary Olga Agnes. Her maternal grandmother, Lucie Palmer, the daughter of a wealthy Louisiana planter-physician, who moved south from Stonington, Connecticut, in the 1840's, was raised a Catholic even though the family was of Protestant stock. She married George Loening at age sixteen and returned from Germany at his death six years later with two small children. A pianist of some repute, she gave music lessons in New Orleans until she married a music merchant named Grunewald and settled in Houston, Texas. Their daughter Jane, also a trained musician, eloped at the age of seventeen with Carlos Hickenlooper, who was of Dutch descent.

Lucie received her first musical training from her mother and grandmother, both of whom taught when the family moved to Galveston, Tex. At the age of twelve she was taken to Paris, over some family objections, by her grandmother. After a year of studying the piano with Antoine Marmontel, Charles Marie Widor, and Ludovic Breitner, she was in 1896 the first American girl to win a scholarship to the Paris Conservatoire, where she studied with Élie Delaborde. For the next two years she was subjected to a difficult and taxing schedule, acquiring artistic and intellectual self-discipline. Her grandmother then took her to Berlin, where she studied piano with Ernst Jedliczka and Ernest Hutcheson as well as organ with Hugo Riemann and composition with Otis Boise. Her debut recital was postponed by her marriage at the age of eighteen to a Russian engineer, Boris Loutsky. Until a papal annulment three years later, she was a subject of the czar and a resident of St. Petersburg and Berlin.

Upon her return, her family, which had suffered financial reverses because of the Galveston flood in 1900, spent their savings to hire Walter Damrosch and the New York Symphony Orchestra for her debut. On the advice of manager Henry Wolfson, she took the name of a remote Slavic ancestor and made her first public appearance as Olga Samaroff in Carnegie Hall on Jan. 18, 1905. This was a gamble, especially without having received the usual European press notices. Despite mixed reviews, however, she made enough contacts to launch a career. She was introduced to the eminent Boston impresario Charles A. Ellis, who added her to the artists under his management, and her reputation grew through European and American tours. On Apr. 24, 1911, she married Leopold Stokowski, and the following year they moved to Philadelphia, where he became famous as the conductor of that city's orchestra. Although she had forsaken her concert career upon marriage, she gradually resumed concert appearances and did pioneer recording work for the Victor Talking Machine Company. A daughter, Sonya Marie Noël, was born to the Stokowskis before their divorce in 1923.

Samaroff's concertizing was more permanently interrupted by a fall in 1925, which tore a ligament in her arm. That same year, she succeeded Ernest Newman as music critic for the *New York Evening Post,* a position which she held for two years. She had already joined the piano faculty of the Juilliard Graduate School of Music in New York City in 1925, and in 1928 she added piano classes at the Philadelphia Conservatory of Music to her teaching duties.

Preferring not to resume concert work, Samaroff continued teaching and devoted her time to such causes as the organization of the Schubert Memorial in 1928. Through contests and sponsored concerts the memorial aimed at providing debut opportunities for young American artists. The memorial flourished and within a few years was attached to the National Federation of Music Clubs. Around 1930 Samaroff created the Layman's Music Courses, and published three books on the subject (1935-1936). Her success in this field led the State Department to send her as a representative of the United States to the International Congress of Music Education in Prague in 1936.

Two years later she was a judge at the Concours Eugène Ysaÿe in Brussels, a contest similar to the Schubert Memorial, organized by Belgium's Queen Elisabeth.

An honorary Phi Beta Kappa, Samaroff was awarded honorary doctor of music degrees by the University of Pennsylvania (1931) and the Cincinnati Conservatory of Music (1943). Her autobiography, *An American Musician's Story* (1939), and her other writings present her as modest yet articulate, concerned with the creation, performance, and reception of music. She strove through influence and example to remove for others the obstacles that she had been forced to overcome in her own career, most notably the lack of instructional and performance opportunities for native Americans and the discrimination against women musicians. She died of natural causes in her New York City apartment on May 7, 1948. Among her better known students were Eugene List, William Kapell, Joseph Battista, Claudette Sorel, and Rosalyn Tureck.

[In addition to her autobiography cited above, Samaroff published *The Layman's Music Book* (1935), *A Music Manual* (1936), and *The Magic World of Music* (1936)—all a result of the Layman Music Courses. Sources include *Current Biog.* (1946); *Who Was Who in Am.,* II (1950); Olga Samaroff, "Women in Music," in *Nat. Federation of Music Clubs' Book of Proc.,* II, 31–38 (1937); and "Accuracy in Musical Performance," in *Am. Music Teacher,* contains portrait and short biography, Mar.–Apr. 1958, pp. 6–7, also in *Musical Courier,* June 1954, pp. 32–34, and *Music Jour.,* Jan. 1953, p. 46; G. M. Wilson, "Mme. Olga Samaroff," interview with pictures, in *The Musician* (Boston), Nov. 1914, pp. 727–728; and "A Sparring Match of Music Critics," in *Literary Digest,* Apr. 17, 1926, pp. 26–27. Obituaries and tributes are in *N.Y. Times,* May 18, 1948, p. 23; *Etude,* with portrait, Sept. 1948, p. 519; L. M. Spell, "In Memoriam," *Southwestern Musician,* Jan. 1949, pp. 28–29; C. Sorel, "A Great Piano Teacher," anecdotal account of her teaching by one of her students, in *Music Jour.,* Mar. 1961, pp. 24 ff.]

WILLIAM E. BOSWELL

SCHEVILL, RUDOLPH (June 18, 1874-Feb. 17, 1946), professor of Spanish, was born in Cincinnati, Ohio, the youngest of five children. His parents, Ferdinand August Schevill and Johanna (Hartmann) Schevill (originally Schwill), natives respectively of Königsberg and Heidelberg, were German émigrés. His father, a successful druggist and merchant, provided his children with an atmosphere of culture and stability and thus encouraged their strong artistic and intellectual bent. Of Rudolph's two brothers, William became a portrait painter and Ferdinand a prominent historian.

After graduating from Woodward High School in Cincinnati, Rudolph Schevill took his B.A. degree at Yale (1896) and his doctorate at the University of Munich (1898), with a dissertation on August Wilhelm Schlegel and the French theater. He also studied at the Sorbonne, the Collège de France, and the Universidad Central in Madrid. Schevill began his teaching career as an instructor in French and German at Bucknell University (1899-1900) and moved after a year to Yale, successively as instructor in German (1900-1901) and instructor in French and Spanish (1901-1902). Thereafter he taught Spanish alone, rising to assistant professor in 1907. In 1910 Schevill was invited by President Benjamin Ide Wheeler of the University of California in Berkeley to head what was then the department of Romanic languages with the rank of professor. After a reorganization in 1919, he became chairman of a separate department of Spanish, which in 1931 became the department of Spanish and Portuguese. He occupied this post for much of the period up to his retirement in 1944.

As a Hispanist, Schevill had few equals in either productiveness or quality. His monographs *Ovid and the Renascence in Spain* (1913) and *The Dramatic Art of Lope de Vega* (1918) and his important biography *Cervantes* (1919) remain indispensable. The more than ninety other entries in his bibliography show the same scope and versatility, extending far beyond his nominal specialization in Cervantes and the Spanish drama of its Golden Age to other periods, genres, and literatures. His best-known achievement, however, is his eighteen-volume edition (1914-1941) of the complete works of Cervantes, of which the first fourteen were prepared jointly with his devoted friend, the Spanish humanist Adolfo Bonilla y San Martín. Included in this collecttion is the whole of *Don Quixote* prepared by Schevill alone; this edition is still considered the authoritative text. These works of erudition largely account for the honors awarded to Schevill, including a medal from the Hispanic Society of America, corresponding membership in the Royal Spanish Academy and the Royal Academy of History, fellowship in the American Academy of Arts and Sciences, and presidency of the Modern Language Association of America (1943).

At the University of California, Schevill, aided by his friend Juan Cebrián, helped raise the library's collections in Hispanic and Latin American literature to the foremost rank. He created a department of distinction through the appointments, among others, of

S. Grisworld Morley (1914); E. C. Hills (1922), with whom instruction was expanded to include Portuguese; and Arturo Torres-Rioseco (1928), who introduced and developed the study of Spanish-American literature. Schevill's own teaching was unforgettable, perhaps not so much for its command and communication of the immediate subject in hand as for its revelation of an extraordinarily civilized mind, seeking to place that subject in the context of all Western culture. Spanish, after all, was a late acquisition for him, although he commanded both its colloquial and its traditional modes, its modern and its older writers. Schevill was a humanist, as devoted to painting, sculpture, and music as he was to letters. In later years, at a time when the Erasmian ideal was at a low ebb, he studied and taught a course in the influence of Erasmus on sixteenth-century Spain. A slight, almost shy figure, he was devoted to the Spanish people and their republic. During the Spanish Civil War he helped raise funds for Loyalist wounded and refugees.

Schevill was married twice: on May 22, 1912, to Margaret Erwin of Jersey City, N.J., an author (divorced 1939); and on June 4, 1939, to Isabel Magaña, a graduate of the University of California and later professor of modern languages at Stanford. By his first marriage Schevill had three children: Erwin (who died in childhood), Karl Erwin, and James Erwin, who became professor of English at Brown and a poet and dramatist. Schevill died of a coronary occlusion at his home in Berkeley less than two years after his retirement. Following cremation, his ashes were buried at Sunset View Cemetery in neighboring El Cerrito. He was one of the founders of modern Hispanism in the United States.

[S. Griswold Morley in *Hispanic Rev.*, July 1946, with a bibliography of Schevill's publications by his son Karl; Lesley B. Simpson in *Modern Language Jour.*, Jan. 1947; Yale Univ., *Obituary Record of Graduates*, 1945-1946; *Who Was Who in America*, II (1950); death record from Calif. Dept. of Public Health; typescript biographical report by Bettylou Rosen, Graduate Lib. School, La. State Univ., including letter of James Schevill; information from Karl E. Schevill; personal recollections.]
EDWIN S. MORBY

SCHMIDT, CARL LOUIS AUGUST (Mar. 7, 1885-Feb. 23, 1946), biochemist, was born in Brown County, S.Dak., the son of Gustav Schmidt and Fridericke (Unverzagt) Schmidt. He received his early education in local schools and entered the University of California, Berkeley, earning the B.S. degree in 1908, the M.S. in 1910, and the Ph.D. in 1916.

From 1908-1909 he was employed as a chemist by the Metropolitan Light and Power Company in San Francisco and later by the Referee Board of the U.S. Department of Agriculture (1909-1912). From 1912-1914 he worked for the city of Berkeley as a bacteriologist and chemist. In 1915 Schmidt returned to the University of California as research assistant in physiology, achieving the rank of professor of biochemistry in 1924.

Schmidt belonged to the first school of teachers and researchers in biological chemistry that was primarily American trained. His leadership in biochemistry at the Berkeley campus served to promote the educational and research facilities in the medical school as well as in biochemistry itself. His long-term interest in proteins and amino acids resulted in a definitive article, "The History of the Discovery of the Amino Acids," written with Hubert B. Vickery and published in 1931 in *Chemical Review*. This paper provided data related to the techniques of preparation of all the amino acids then known and supplied an operational definition of amino acids that is still applicable. His more than 150 papers reflect the areas of his greatest interest: the biochemistry of bile, especially with respect to its function in the absorption of fat-soluble vitamins and the consequent relationship of this property to the bleeding tendency in obstructive jaundice. Schmidt's researches in the physical chemistry of proteins and amino acids provided some of the most fundamental aspects of current knowledge in the medical regions or areas of these substances. In the conflict of ideas about proteins and amino acids, he offered a sober and detailed summation and synthesis of an enormous research and speculative literature. Schmidt's work also advanced the study of immunology. He investigated the antigenic properties of hemoglobin and hemocyanin, finding them to be negative and positive, respectively. He also conducted immunological experiments with enzymes such as catalese and with denatured and insoluble proteins. He studied red cell globulins and discerned the fact that injections of pure proteins had no noticeable effect upon the production of serum albumin or globulin (in rabbits). But his condition to immunology lies principally in his ability to transfer biochemical data into forms suitable to the practice of medicine.

From 1937-1944 Schmidt served as dean of the college of pharmacy at the university; he was also acting dean of the medical school from 1938-1939. His publications include *The Chemistry of the Amino Acids and Proteins* (1938) and, with Frank W. Allen, *Fundamentals of Biochemistry* (1938).

Through research, teaching, and guidance, Schmidt provided the energy and inspiration that was necessary to the development of biochemistry and medicine in the United States during the so-called critical years of the early and mid-twentieth century. Schmidt was not a towering figure in biochemistry. He was, however, illustrative of a *type* of researcher who did much of the "spade and grub" work necessary to the profession. He helped make biochemistry a "respectable" member of the medical sciences, and he trained many individuals who attained prominence in the field. He was a meticulous worker, a good organizer, and a competent administrator. Like many of his contemporaries, he designed and built much of his equipment. Schmidt was one of the first researchers to use radioactive tracer elements to study the complexities of intermediary metabolism.

Schmidt died in Berkeley of carcinoma; his remains were cremated.

[David M. Greenburg, "Obituary: Carl Louis August Schmidt, 1885–1946," *Science*, 104 (1946), 387. See also David M. Greenburg, *Recollections of the History of Biochemistry at the Univ. of Calif.* (unpub. ms.); *Nat. Cyc. Am. Biog.*, 1948, pp. 471–472; and *Carl L. A. Schmidt: Bibliog. of Publications* (unpub. doc. in author's possession).]

STANLEY L. BECKER

SCHUMPETER, JOSEPH ALOIS (Feb. 8, 1883-Jan. 8, 1950), one of the dozen leading economists of the first half of the twentieth century, was born in Triesch, Moravia (now Czechoslovakia), the only child of Joseph Alois Schumpeter, a cloth manufacturer, and Joanna (Grüner) Schumpeter, the daughter of a physician. The father died when Schumpeter was only four, leaving him the adored object of the beautiful and ambitious mother whom he in turn adored. When Schumpeter was ten, his mother married Lt. Gen. Sigismund von Kéler, commander of Emperor Franz Joseph's Viennese forces. This elevation from the middle class to the aristocracy left a permanent mark on Schumpeter's weltanschauung. In part he could be objective about the merits of capitalism and what he yet regarded as its certain demise, because by the end of World War I he felt that his own world was already permanently gone. A man may lose perspective about his own home; but who will fail to notice the defects of a boardinghouse? One wonders how the precocious Schumpeter was received at the aristocratic Theresianum Gymnasium, where the Viennese gentry were schooled. What did they make of the wunderkind?

As was customary, the young scholar in economics took a law degree at the University of Vienna (1906). He practiced law briefly in Cairo soon afterward. It was in this period that he was the well-rewarded advisor of a princess and the proud owner of a racehorse. But economics was his true love, and in the Vienna seminars of von Böhm-Bawerk and von Wieser, his quality was soon recognized. Since such brilliant Marxists as Otto Bauer and Rudolf Hilferding were also in those seminars, it was no accident that Schumpeter studied and, in his own patronizing way, admired Karl Marx.

By the time he was twenty-five he had written his first book. At twenty-six he became professor at Czernowitz, a rather exotic outpost on the Russian-Rumanian frontier of the empire. By twenty-eight he was professor at Graz, only three hours from Vienna; perhaps because he was regarded as more brilliant than sound, the man whom Gottfried Haberler of Vienna and Harvard has called "the greatest Austrian economist of his generation" was never offered a chair at the University of Vienna. And this despite the fact that he was not Jewish—as he sometimes felt it necessary to make clear.

Invited presumably by his old classmate Otto Bauer, Schumpeter served as finance minister (1919-1920) in the post-World War I Austrian socialist government. To use his kind of phrase, this was not a good performance: the Austrian crown followed the Hungarian crown down the drain; if there was no one to blame for what is a common occurrence after a lost war, Schumpeter provided the convenient scapegoat. A brief career as head of a small bank also ended with that bank's demise. Those who knew Schumpeter would have been surprised if he had been a cool, deft, and solid politician and financier. Later, at Harvard, he carried little weight in the university at large; within the department of economics he was often his own worst enemy at committee meetings, expressing his contempt for academic red tape by giving A's to idiots and perversely espousing unpopular causes, whatever their merits.

Ready to leave Austria, Schumpeter in 1925 accepted a call to the public finance chair at Bonn. There he attracted excellent students —among them, Hans Staehle, Erich Schneider, and Wolfgang Stolper. There he also annoyed German official opinion by writing publicly that of course Germans could pay reparations if they wanted to. When his old Austrian classmate Emil Lederer received the chair at Berlin, Schumpeter decided to accept the Harvard invitation that Frank Taussig had been pressing on him since his visiting professorship in Cambridge in 1927. He arrived at Harvard in 1932, to stay.

Schumpeter in 1925 married Annie Resinger, the twenty-one-year-old daughter of the caretaker of the Viennese apartment house where his mother lived. It was the romantic love of his life: he had sent her to schools in Paris and Switzerland to groom her to be his wife. But she died in futile childbirth within a year of their marriage, and ever after he paid homage at her grave in Bonn. The death of his mother that same year was a double blow. He was never the same man. But by his own peculiar theory, pressed upon his graduate students, marriage is a subtraction from the vital energies needed for creative scholarship. So perhaps he was blessed. After Schumpeter moved to Harvard, he lived with the elderly widower Taussig until Aug. 16, 1937, when he left this blessed state to marry Elizabeth (Boody) Firuski, the divorced wife of a radical bookseller. It was an agreeable marriage. Elizabeth Schumpeter was an economic historian in her own right. Their large, well-appointed Cambridge house and well-run Berkshire estate provided a good environment for what was actually a most important decade of Schumpeter's scholarly life.

Clearly Schumpeter lived up to his own Carlylean view that it is great men who make great history, great scholarly breakthroughs, and great entrepreneurial profits. And he partially lived up to his obsessive view that only in youth does one have great ideas, so that the roots of important original achievements, especially those of a theoretical nature, can almost always be found in the third decade of the lives of scholars, "that decade of sacred fertility." Newton's calculus and universal gravitation correspond to this timetable, as do Einstein's Brownian motions, special relativity theory, and photoelectric effect; but what Einstein himself regarded as his deepest and most significant contribution, general relativity, did not arrive until he was a doddering senior of more than thirty-five. Although Schumpeter by thirty-one had received an honorary degree from Columbia (where he had been an exchange professor in 1913-1914 and had seen the first of his only two football games), much of his most lasting work was probably that done in the last decade of his life.

On the surface gallant, gay, urbane, and vivacious, Schumpeter was nevertheless a somewhat sad man. His first marriage was in 1907 to an Englishwoman, Gladys Ricarde Seaver, twelve years his senior and daughter of a Church of England dignitary; it seems not to have been a happy match and was terminated de facto by World War I. That the official divorce did not occur until 1920 may possibly have been related to his then being a nominal Roman Catholic. Later he listed himself as a Lutheran, but his friends detected no religious interests; his funeral services were Episcopalian.

Despite his gallantry and his frivolous façade—both were legendary—Schumpeter was actually a driven scholar. He worked days, nights, and weekends. Each day he graded himself ruthlessly in his shorthand diary. There was an insecurity in his nature, perhaps typical of a precocious only child, with Napoleonic aspirations. He was a showman who strove to be number one, and number one forever. The triumph of John Maynard Keynes, few of Schumpeter's friends and students doubted, depreciated in Schumpeter's mind his own undoubted achievements. There may have been something of envy in his criticism of Keynes for an excessive preoccupation with policy, the same criticism that Schumpeter made of Ricardo.

If Schumpeter had died on the verge of his fiftieth birthday when newly arrived at Harvard, he would be remembered primarily as the enfant terrible of the Austrian school, who had the bizarre notion that the interest rate would be zero in the stationary state and who put great stress on the importance of the innovating entrepreneur both for business cycles and for capitalist development generally. Fortunately, in the final phase of his career, Schumpeter wrote his seminal *Capitalism, Socialism, and Democracy* (1942), which far transcended mere economics in its historical, political, and sociological insights. And at his death, in Cambridge from a cerebral hemorrhage in his sleep, he left behind the magnificent torso of his posthumously published *History of Economic Doctrines* (1951), a magisterial work that, for all its incompleteness and patronizing pretensions, will long stand as an inimitable monument of scholarship. During these same fruitful years at Harvard, Schumpeter's earlier works in German, not well known in the modern age of Anglo-Saxon illiteracy, were gradually translated: his 1911 classic, *The Theory of Economic Development*; his brief 1914 history of doctrines; his graceful biographical essays on economists; his work on imperialism and sociology. In 1939 he received an honorary degree from Sofia. And it was in this period that he had a host of students who were later to become leaders in American economics: they sat around his lecture rostrum in the hundreds and were bedazzled, stimulated, and occasionally informed by his brilliant, extemporaneous, and florid discourse. He founded no school because he had no school to found. But in 1948 he was elected president of the American Economic Association, the first of many economists who came to America only in their scholarly maturity. Only death kept him from being the first president of the newly founded International Economic Association.

A scholar's lasting fame comes from his contributions. Schumpeter first achieved notice in his early twenties for work of a methodological character, in which he praised the mathematical method in economics and found merit in turn-of-the-century American contributions, particularly the stationary-state notions of John Bates Clark. Then in his late twenties, he developed his theory of dynamic development and business cycles: in the absence of innovation, he claimed the system would gravitate down to a steady-state circular flow, in which the rate of interest would be zero (a low rate of interest would have avoided controversy and sufficed for his model). The importance that he attached to circular-flow equilibrium accounts for his immense admiration for Leon Walras, who in the last quarter of the nineteenth century established once and for all the concept of general equilibrium in economics; for his inordinate admiration for the physiocrat François Quesnay, who sketched a *tableau économique* of circulation between economic classes; and for his admiration of Marx's models of steady and expanded reproduction and of Marx's grandiose vision of supplying a Newton-Laplace dynamics of historical stages of development. Schumpeter's stationary state provides the backdrop and contrast for the dynamic entrepreneurial innovation that he considered to be the essence of capitalism. "A gale of creative destruction" characterizes the market system, and coupled with inflationary financing by newly created bank money, this provided him with a theory of the business cycle and of long-term development.

Except for a tendency to overshoot equilibrium, the capitalistic system was in his view inherently economically stable, even though politically and sociologically inevitably unstable, as its very successes would make this unlovable system unloved by its affluent offspring. This early prophetic strain of capitalism as dying not from Marxian malignancies but from Freudian self-hate and excess rationality was reasserted in *Capitalism, Socialism, and Democracy*: although the prophecies there concerning the limited effectiveness of capitalism in an oxygen tent and the inevitability of socialism were refuted by the history of the post-World War II period, the alienation of students and intellectuals and the confrontation of the late 1960's confirmed his insights. His perception of intellectuals as ineffective troublemakers served, as in the case of Pareto, to build up his contempt for the spineless bourgeoisie and led him toward certain shoals of fascistic thought, albeit not crude fascistic thought. The disillusionment of World War II, which he long thought Germany would win until he began to think that Russia would be the only real victor, may have interacted with his disappointment over the failure of his two-volume *Business Cycles* (1939) to attract much attention. Indeed, the nature of the business cycle was changing in the post-Keynes era, and the number of epicycles introduced by Schumpeter, in the form of forty-month minor cycles, eight-year major cycles, and half-century-long Kondratiev waves, began to smack of Pythagorean moonshine; nor did his fancy concepts, borrowed from Ragnar Frisch, of equilibria and cycle stages defined by inflection points ever catch on.

Although Schumpeter would have wished to be remembered most for some brilliant and basic breakthrough in economic analysis, it seems just as well that he devoted the last part of his career to insightful social prophecy and to recording his tremendous erudition on past economic thought in his massive *History of Economic Analysis* (1954). Although the manuscript was incomplete, his widow was able to edit it for publication in the few years by which she survived him. It is a unique reference work, one that concentrates not so much on general reform movements and philosophies as on the development of economic analysis itself. Here Schumpeter's almost mindless tolerance of differences in vision proved to be a great virtue. If some sympathetic follower were to prune and complete this great work, it would provide Schumpeter's most lasting memorial.

[A complete bibliography of Schumpeter's many writings appears in the *Quart. Jour. Econ.* 1950). Seymour Harris, ed., *Schumpeter: Social Scientist* (1951), contains twenty biographical eulogies and evaluations, notably one of Gottfried Haberler. R. V.

Clemence and Francis S. Doody, *The Schumpeterian System* (1950), provides an evaluation of Schumpeter's economics; see also the sixtieth birthday festschrift "Essays in Honor of Prof. Joseph A. Schumpeter," *Rev. of Econ. Stat.*, Feb. 1943, and the W. F. Stolper article on him in the *Internat. Encyc. Social Sci.*, vol. XIV (1968). Also noteworthy among Schumpeter's books, other than those mentioned in the text, are *Ten Great Economists from Marx to Keynes* (1952); *Essays,* Clemence and Doody, eds. (1951); *Imperialism and Social Classes* (German, 1919, 1927; English, 1951); *Economic Doctrine and Method* (German, 1914; English, 1954); and his first book, *Das Wesen und der Hauptinhalt der theoretischen Nationalökonomie* (1908).]

PAUL A. SAMUELSON

SCHWELLENBACH, LEWIS BAXTER (Sept. 20, 1894-June 10, 1948), United States senator and secretary of labor, was born in Superior, Wis., one of three sons of Francis William Schwellenbach, a machine operator of German descent, and Martha (Baxter) Schwellenbach. As a young boy he acquired from his father such a deep admiration for William Jennings Bryan that his playmates called him "Bryan," a nickname that remained with him for years. The family moved in 1902 to Spokane, Wash., where Lewis attended public school. Even in booming Spokane his father never achieved financial success. He died when Lewis was fourteen, and the boy sold newspapers and worked on railroad construction and in the wheat fields to finance further education. He later recalled his poverty-stricken youth as a "nightmare." He worked his way through the law department of the University of Washington, for the last year as an assistant instructor, and received the LL.B degree in 1917.

After serving in the army during World War I, Schwellenbach established a law practice in Seattle, Wash., in 1919. Along with his practice, he engaged in banking, brewing, and the laundry business. The ventures all failed, a fact that seemed to accentuate his liberalism; he grew particularly critical of banking procedures. These experiences, along with his early legal cases concerned with labor disputes, accentuated the pro-labor sympathies he had developed during his adolescence.

Schwellenbach early became active in the Democratic party. He was chairman of the state Democratic convention in 1924 and of the King County Democratic committee from 1928 to 1930. He made an unsuccessful bid for the Democratic nomination for governor in 1932. Two years later he won election to the United States Senate, defeating Clarence C. Dill, his former high school oratory teacher. In this campaign, Schwellenbach ran on a platform pledging to end poverty in Washington.

Entering the Senate in 1935, Schwellenbach

quickly became the acknowledged leader of the freshman Democratic senators, among them Harry S Truman of Missouri. For the following six years he consistently supported the New Deal program of President Franklin D. Roosevelt, breaking with Roosevelt only once to oppose peacetime conscription in 1940. Especially interested in the problems of labor, he was an active member of the La Follette Civil Liberties Committee, which investigated instances of interference with labor's rights to organize and bargain collectively. Roosevelt rewarded Schwellenbach's loyalty by appointing him judge of the eastern district of the state of Washington; he took office in December 1940. While a senator, Schwellenbach married Anne J. Duffy, his longtime confidential secretary, on Dec. 30, 1935. They had no children.

When Truman became president in 1945, he chose the Washington judge as his secretary of labor. Schwellenbach's three-year tenure coincided with a period of postwar labor-management disputes, an unprecedented series of strikes, and a strong movement in Congress to curb the power of unions. Schwellenbach believed, with Truman, that action was necessary to mitigate this strife and helped organize a labor-management conference in Washington. He strongly opposed antiunion legislation, however, and in 1946 lent his voice in opposition to the restrictive Case Bill, which Truman vetoed. The Taft-Hartley Act, which Congress passed the following year over the president's veto, created problems of adjustment for both organized labor and the Labor Department. Schwellenbach dealt with these difficulties with considerable ability, attempting, despite increasing ill health, to protect the rights of workers. During the last nineteen months of his life he was hospitalized several times. He died of heart disease at the age of fifty-three in Walter Reed Hospital, Washington, D.C., and was buried in Washelli Cemetery, Seattle. He was an Episcopalian in religion.

[Schwellenbach Papers, Lib. of Cong.; Truman Papers, Harry S. Truman Lib., Independence, Mo.; Biog. Directory Am. Cong. (1961); Who Was Who in America, II (1950); N.Y. Times, May 24, 1945, June 11, 1948; Newsweek, June 4, 1945, June 21, 1948; Time, June 4, 1945; Nation, June 19, 1948; Arthur F. McClure, The Truman Administration and the Problems of Postwar Labor, 1945–1948 (1969); R. Alton Lee, Truman and Taft-Hartley: A Question of Mandate (1966).]

R. ALTON LEE

SCHWIMMER, ROSIKA (Sept. 11, 1877–Aug. 3, 1948), writer, editor, lecturer, feminist, pacifist, and pioneer advocate of world government, was born in Budapest, Hungary, the oldest of three children of Max B. Schwimmer and Bertha (Katscher) Schwimmer. Her father, an experimental farmer who raised highly prized seed corn, dealt in agricultural produce and horses. The parents were of upper middle-class Jewish background; the father was an agnostic, the mother, a freethinker.

Born two months prematurely, Schwimmer had an invalid childhood, suffering from bouts of scarlet fever, diphtheria, rheumatic fever, and rheumatic heart disease. There was little provision for the higher education of girls, especially in the provincial cities of Temesvár, Hungary (now Timisoara, Rumania), and Szabadka (now Subotica, Yugoslavia), where she grew up, and attended convent and public schools, supplemented with private tutoring in foreign languages and music. She had only eight years of formal schooling, but by special permission— and properly chaperoned—she also attended a six-month commercial course for young men. She was highly gifted in music and an accomplished pianist; her beautiful and powerful alto voice was the pride of Szabadka's Cathedral Choir.

At eighteen, her father's business reverses compelled her to seek employment. Until 1904 she worked for a variety of firms as bookkeeper or office manager. Concurrently she was becoming known as a writer and within a few years achieved international popularity as a lecturer. When in 1897 her family returned to Budapest, Schwimmer began her organizing efforts to improve the economic, social, and political status of women. In 1897 she organized the National Association of Women Office Workers (Nőtisztviselők Országos Egyesülete) and served as its president until 1912. In 1903 she founded the first Hungarian Association of Working Women (Munkásnő Egyesület), which soon came under complete socialist control; and, at the opposite extreme, she helped found the conservative Hungarian Council of Women (Nőegyesületek Szövetsége) in 1904. In the same year, together with her Hungarian coleader, the high school teacher Vilma Glücklich (1872-1927), she organized the Hungarian Feminist Association (Feministák Egyesülete), which launched and won in 1920 the struggle for woman suffrage in one of the shortest campaigns in history. Unique among suffrage organizations because of its membership of men and women, the Feminists tried to represent in a coherent way a host of issues of concern to women, including coeducation, admission to all forms of educational and vocational training, and the right to equal employment and remuneration. Land reform and the establishment of village industries became a concern when peasant women joined the association. During World War I, the Feminists worked boldly for peace and the association became the Hungarian Section of the Women's International League for Peace and Freedom. Rosika Schwimmer edited the association monthly *A Nő és a Társadalom* (Woman and Society), which in 1914 became *A Nő* (Woman) and was published from 1907-1928. Her organizing efforts in Hungary reached their peak in June 1913, when the International Woman Suffrage Alliance held its most brilliant congress in Budapest. In 1914 she moved to London, where she served briefly as press secretary of the International Alliance. Freed from the incessant demands of organizing, she hoped to resume her private life and her journalistic and other literary work.

But with the outbreak of World War I, all interests other than stop-the-war action paled into insignificance for her. During the night of the British declaration of war, she drafted her plan for continuous offers of mediation by a conference of neutrals, addressed "to all men, women and organizations who want to stop the international massacre at the earliest possible moment." It was printed in English, German, French, Italian, and Swedish. Schwimmer mobilized international suffragist support for a petition to President Woodrow Wilson urging that he lead the neutral nations in such peace action. Secretary of State William J. Bryan and the president received her shortly after her arrival in the United States in September 1914. A second interview with Bryan in December 1914 and with President Wilson in November 1915 was still inconclusive. Determined even before her arrival that if the president did not act quickly, she would try to rouse women to force him to do so, she embarked on a fifteen-month crusade to persuade the American people that it was their moral duty to help end the war. By December 1914 she had spoken in some sixty of the largest American cities. Formerly known for her "high-spirited humor and irreverent statements," she had now no "humorous gleam" in her eye, "as if the pain that millions . . . now endure had suddenly acquired a voice that through her spoke its own desperate language" (Mia Leche, *Den Kinesiska Muren*, 1917, pp. 82-89).

The first phase of Schwimmer's European and American peace campaign culminated in the Hague Congress of Women (Apr. 28-May 1, 1915), organized by Dutch, Belgian, British, and German suffrage leaders. Although the British government prevented the attendance of 180 English delegates and only three escaped this blockade, 1,136 delegates from twelve neutral and belligerent nations attended. Public meetings drew thousands. The congress adopted a series of resolutions for postwar reorganization of the world and for stop-the-war action through neutral mediation. It supported Schwimmer's proposal to dispatch "peace deputations" to deliver and discuss its resolutions with the neutral and belligerent governments (*Hague Congress Report,* 1915, pp. 169-176). The delegation to the belligerents was led by Jane Addams, chairman of the congress; the one to the neutrals, by Schwimmer. After visits to fourteen capitals, involving thirty-five interviews with prime ministers, foreign ministers, and President Wilson, the two delegations, meeting in the United States to compare their findings, concluded that "while no belligerent could ask for mediation, the creation of a continuous conference of neutral nations might provide the machinery which would lead to peace." They found that the European neutral governments "stand ready to cooperate with others in mediation" (*Manifesto Issued by Envoys of the International Congress of Women,* Oct. 15, 1915).

The movement continued to be stalled by President Wilson's fear, diligently nourished by Col. Edward M. House and Secretary of State Robert Lansing, that if he acted prematurely he would lose his influence for the future (Ray Stannard Baker, *Woodrow Wilson, Life and Letters,* VI, pp. 119-124). Because Colonel House reported entirely opposite findings from his missions, the account of the women pacifists tended to be dismissed. Since the Ford Peace Expedition was also based on these confidential interviews, the campaign to discredit them took more virulent forms, such as ridicule of Henry Ford and attacks on Schwimmer's motives. Concerted neutral action, however, was not solely a pacifist obsession. It was also urged upon Wilson by Bryan and in frequent frantic appeals by European and Latin American neutrals. These were invariably rebuffed by a standardized form letter (Bryan to Wilson, Sept. 19, 1914, *Bryan Papers* no. 30, Lib. of Cong.; Bryan to Wilson, Oct. 7, Dec. 1, 17, 1914; Apr. 23, 28, 1915; *Lansing Papers,* I, pp. 9, 18-23, 378-380; See *U.S. Foreign Relations, 1914 Supplement* for European and Latin American mediation appeals).

Despondent over continued inaction by the United States, Schwimmer was about to return to Europe to urge the neutral governments to act alone when in November 1915 she met Henry Ford. She had begun thinking in terms of unofficial neutral action in late 1914; by March 1915 she urged a Women's Peace Ship and tried to raise funds for it. The concept of nongovernmental action appealed to Ford; a peace ship to take the American delegates to an unofficial neutral conference fired his imagination. On Dec. 4, 1915, eighteen days after her first meeting with him, the Scandinavian-American liner *Oscar II* sailed with 168 Americans (including reformers, college students, journalists, photographers, business staff, and three children) on a peace pilgrimage of the European neutral countries. Schwimmer was in charge of the expedition as unpaid expert advisor; Louis P. Lochner was general secretary. Undaunted by ridicule and growing personal attacks, she secured unofficial delegations from five European neutrals: Holland, Switzerland, Sweden, Denmark, and Norway. The American delegation, unfortunately, was a very poor one. Despite obstacles, the Ford Neutral Conference, the main purpose of the expedition, held its first meeting in Stockholm on Feb. 8, 1916. Ford's wife and business associates, hostile from the first, were anxious to shut down the entire undertaking. American attacks and intrigues against Schwimmer reached such a pitch that she resigned early in March 1916. A steady reduction and crippling of the entire enterprise followed although Ford continued to support it in some form until February 1917. In June 1916, Schwimmer and some former members of the Ford Neutral Conference organized the International Committee for Immediate Mediation to continue private efforts. During 1916 and 1917 the committee sent private missions to the British prime minister, David Lloyd George, to German Chancellor Bethmann-Hollweg, and to Alexander Kerensky in Russia. Further efforts were impeded by lack of funds.

While the Ford Expedition achieved none of Schwimmer's high hopes for mediation, the Peace Ship, "launched, to the undying shame of American journalism, upon one vast wave of ridicule" (Walter Millis, *The Road to War*, pp. 243, 245), succeeded as nothing else could have in breaking through Europe's censorship of peace news. And in retrospect, the Ford Neutral Conference can be seen as the first peace conference of the war, one, moreover, that pioneered in having also women delegates.

Its mere existence galvanized much peace activity in all the neutral countries, which helped keep these small nations out of the war. Despite Ford's initial offer of millions to help end the war, and the so-called "barbaric splendor" of Schwimmer's management, the entire cost of the Peace Ship, the Peace Pilgrimage, and the Neutral Conference from November 1915 to February 1917, was only $600,000.

When in mid-November 1918 Hungary became a republic with Count Michael Károlyi as prime minister, Schwimmer was appointed Hungarian Minister to Switzerland (November 1918-March 1919). Her mandate was to contact American and other Allied statesmen. She managed to establish good relations with the French, Italian, and American special missions, although not with their legations, and with their assistance sent numerous appeals on behalf of Hungary to the Peace Conference. Her successor in the post was one of Hungary's few liberal career diplomats. She returned to Hungary shortly before the Károlyi regime was overthrown by the communist dictatorship of Béla Kun, which she refused to serve. Because of her opposition, Kun refused her permission to leave the country. When the dictatorship was ousted in August 1919, a regime of "white terror" followed. In physical danger because of her participation in the Károlyi regime and her feminist and pacifist activities, she escaped to Vienna in 1920 with the help of several prominent foreigners and immigrated to the United States in 1921.

She was immediately confronted with the libels with which her reputation had been smeared and her motives impugned on American entry into the war. The three-volume *Lusk Report on Revolutionary Radicalism* (1920), the output of various military intelligence groups and patrioteer publications, and blacklists made her their special target of attack. One described her as "a German spy . . . who came here to prevent preparedness . . ." (Fred R. Marvin, *Bootlegging Mind Poison*). At the same time she was accused of being "an agent of the bolshevist organizations of Europe and Asia" and "of a far more dangerous organization, the political-economic movement of Jewry" (Ralph E. Duncan's report to Military Intelligence Association of Chicago, Apr. 7, 1925). Convinced that Ford was determined to take revenge on all Jews because she had "duped" him into the Peace Ship "fiasco," prominent Jews attacked her as the cause of his anti-Semitic campaign waged through *The Dear-*

born Independent. Pacifist and suffragist leaders and organizations, attacked during and after the war for association with her, tried to clear themselves by turning their backs on her. Deprived of her ability to earn her living by writing and lecturing, she could not have survived without the support of her sister, Franciska Schwimmer, and of her closest American associate, Lola Maverick Lloyd. Her victory in a 1929 libel suit and the award of $17,000 against a leading blacklister, Fred R. Marvin of the Keymen of America, did not deter other detractors, including the film magnate William Fox and the writer Upton Sinclair. In the 1930's she was again featured on new blacklists, such as Elizabeth Dilling's *The Red Network* (1934).

When her application for American citizenship became known, the American Legion and other patrioteer groups deluged the government with appeals to reject it because of her "un-American utterances and unpatriotic character" (Scranton, Pa. *Scrantonian,* June 22, 1924). Denied citizenship in the federal district court in Chicago, she won in the court of appeals on the ground that "a petitioner's rights are not to be determined by putting conundrums to her." But she lost in the Supreme Court in May 1929 in a six-to-three decision. Her only compensation was the overwhelming revulsion of press and public opinion evoked by the decision and the eloquent dissenting opinion of Oliver Wendell Holmes, in which Louis D. Brandeis concurred. In this dissent, Holmes found her to be "a woman of superior character and intelligence, obviously more than ordinarily desirable as a citizen. . . ." And while he agreed that "some of her answers might excite popular prejudice," he warned that "if there is any principle of the Constitution that more imperatively calls for attachment than any other it is the principle of free thought—not free thought for those who agree with us but freedom for the thought that we hate." Congressman Anthony J. Griffin failed in determined efforts to undo the effects of the court's decision through legislation. Although, in 1946, this seventeen-year-old ruling was at last reversed in the Girouard Case, Schwimmer made no further effort to win citizenship and remained stateless.

Her chief concern in later life was the establishment of world government. She considered the League of Nations and its successor, the United Nations, devoid of the needed authority to prevent war. Together with Lola Maverick Lloyd and the latter's children, she launched the Campaign for World Government in 1937, to promote the establishment of an all-inclusive, democratic, nonmilitary federation of nations. Between 1938 and 1942 the campaign sponsored a series of memorials and congressional resolutions that proposed the calling of a world constitutional convention and joint action with other neutrals to bring an armistice and to supervise the cessation of hostilities. During World War II she returned to experiments with parallel governmental and unofficial action in proposals to create an unofficial provisional world government and, at the end of the war, to hold a privately financed people's world constitutional convention.

In 1948 she was nominated for the Nobel Peace Prize by members of the parliaments of Great Britain, Sweden, France, Italy, and Hungary. She died from bronchial pneumonia before the award could be made, and no prize was given that year. Her ashes were scattered in Lake Michigan by Mrs. Lloyd's children, near their mother's Winnetka, Ill., home, in memory of their friendship.

Tall by European standards, she seemed even taller when she spoke in public because of her stately carriage. Until her early twenties she was quite thin. Thick, dark brown hair (which she bobbed in 1929) worn in a bun on top of her head or at the nape of the neck, nearsighted but sparkling brown eyes behind pince-nez, a round face and pink complexion gave her a striking appearance. Her reticence about her private life was characteristic of the women leaders of her generation, for among her papers there is no trace—other than in her 1924 application for citizenship and similar documents— of her marriage on Jan. 16, 1911, and her divorce on Jan. 4, 1913. She had no children.

A strong reform leader capable of brilliant original concepts of great scope, Schwimmer possessed the ability to carry out her plans. Her courage and determination were based not only on her deep knowledge of the political situation but also on her strong intuition and prescience. She attracted the strongest devotion and bitterest detestation. Her physical and emotional stamina, relentless energy, and ruthless perseverance were legendary. Warm and boundlessly sympathetic, she placed great trust in people, especially the young, on very short acquaintance and was often bitterly disappointed. But her confidence in even quite average persons often helped motivate them to accomplish the supposedly impossible. In her hands an ordinary cabbage leaf could blossom like a rose.

[Schwimmer's feminist and political articles are scattered in European periodicals and newspapers. In German and Hungarian her style could be devastatingly satiric as in editorial gibes in *A Nö* when slashing at masculine, militarist, and political foibles. Her searing wartime peace editorials were often either badly mutilated or completely cut by the censor. Hungarian newspapers for which she wrote important political and peace articles included *Pester Lloyd, Világ,* and *Magyarország.* Especially important are her 1917 and 1918 articles on Henry Ford, Woodrow Wilson, Edward M. House, and David Lloyd George. Her Hungarian translation of Charlotte Perkins Gilman's *Women and Economics* was published in 1906. After her return to the United States in 1921 very little of her writing was published. The exception was a book of Hungarian legends for children, *Tisza Tales* (1928). Her world government pamphleteering fared better: *Chaos, War or a New World Order?* (1937), written with Lola Maverick Lloyd, had several editions; *Union Now for Peace or War? The Danger in the Plan of Clarence Streit* (1939) became something of a best seller and had several printings. But her serial on the Ford Expedition, "When Henry Ford Was a Pacifist," despite high praise, found no publisher and "Women's Peace Efforts" remained uncompleted.

Thousands of newspaper and periodical articles about her work in English, German, Hungarian, and the Scandinavian languages have been microfilmed by The N.Y. Public Lib. The books most likely to be cited, such as those of Jane Addams, Louis Lochner, Emmeline Pethick-Lawrence, Ethel Snowden, omit, suppress, or distort her role. Ironically, despite their fantasies about her, the patrioteers and militarists in some ways understood better than her associates how powerful her challenge had been to the war system.

The Schwimmer Lloyd Collec. of The N.Y. Public Lib. contains the voluminous papers of Schwimmer and Lola Maverick Lloyd, their books, pamphlets, periodicals, leaflets, clippings, cartoons, and photographs, and a 1914 watercolor portrait of her by Willy Pogány.

Some Schwimmer papers are in the Hoover Institution, Stanford Univ.; Jane Addams, Emily Balch, and Woman's Peace Party Papers, Swarthmore College; Lillian Wald and Carrie Chapman Catt Papers, N.Y. Public Lib.; Louis P. Lochner and Julia Grace Wales Papers, Wisconsin State Hist. Soc.; Bryan and Ford Expedition Papers, Lib. of Cong.; Ford Archives, Dearborn, Mich.; Justice Dept. Files, Nat. Archives; Feminist Assoc. Archives, Országos Levéltár, Budapest; Swiss Bundesarchiv, Berne; World War I Foreign Office Archives, Public Record Office, London; German Foreign Office Archives on Peace Moves and Mediation, on film, Nat. Archives, Washington.

Printed sources include *Rosika Schwimmer, World Patriot* (1947), biographical sketch revised and enlarged; Edith Wynner, *World Federal Government: Why? What? How?* (1954); Edith Wynner, "Out of the Trenches by Christmas," *The Progressive,* December 1065; International Woman Suffrage Alliance *Reports* (1904–20); Peter Veres, *Falusi Krónika* (1941), about Hungarian peasant feminists, 231–43; N. K. Szegvári, *A Nők Művelödési jogáiért folytatott harc hazánkban* (1969), on feminists and women's education in Hungary; Marie Louise Degen, *History of the Woman's Peace Party* (1939); Addams, Balch, Hamilton, *Women at the Hague* (1915); Jane Addams, *Peace and Bread* (1922); Mercedes M. Randall, *Improper Bostonian—Emily Greene Balch* (1964); Vira B. Whitehouse, *A Year as a Government Agent* (1920); Mark Sullivan, *Our Times,* vol. V (1933); H. G. Wells, *The Shape of Things to Come* (1933); Louis Lochner, *Henry Ford—America's Don Quixote* (1925); Allen Nevins and Frank Hill, *Ford: Expansion and Challenge 1915–1932* (1957); Harry Bennett, *We Never Called Him Henry* (1951): Burnet Hershey, *The Odyssey of Henry Ford and the Great Peace Ship* (1967), a good example of reporters' Peace Ship fantasies; Charles Reznikoff, ed., *Louis Marshall, Champion of Liberty,* vol. I (1957), Ford's anti-Semitic campaign and apology; *U.S.* v. *Rosika Schwimmer,* 279 U.S. 644; *Griffin Bill Hearings: House Committee on Immigration and Naturalization,* H.R. 3547, May 8–9, 1930; H.R. 297 and 298, Jan. 26, 27, 1932; *Senate Subcommittee of Committee on Immigration,* S. 3275 Mar. 22, 26, 1932; Alpheus T. Mason, *Harlan Fiske Stone* (1956); Arthur and Lila Weinberg, *Instead of Violence* (1963); Lilian Schlissel, ed., *Conscience in America* (1968); N.Y. supreme court, *Schwimmer* v. *Commercial Newspaper Co. et al.* (Marvin Case), Mar. 1928; Mary G. Kilbreth, *The Woman Patriot;* Joseph P. Kamp, *We Must Abolish the United States. The Hidden Facts Behind the Crusade for World Government* (1950).

EDITH WYNNER

SCOTT, JOHN ADAMS (Sept. 15, 1867–Oct. 27, 1947), classicist, was born in Fletcher, Ill., a small town in McLean County. He was the first son of seven children born to James Sterling Scott and Henrietta P. (Sutton) Scott. His father, born in Nova Scotia, had worked in Boston for a while in the carriage-making shop managed by his brother John. Because of ill health, James Scott moved to the Midwest and became a farmer. At a very early age, John Adams and his younger brother Walter Dill (later president of Northwestern University, 1920-1939) worked on their father's 120-acre farm, and by 1880 they were managing it almost completely. Scott's early education was provided by his older sister Louise, who tutored both him and Walter at home. He graduated from the high school section of the Illinois State Normal School at Normal, Ill., in 1887 and entered Northwestern University, from which he graduated in 1895.

From 1891-1893 Scott was instructor in Greek in the academy of Northwestern University, and during 1891-1892 he was also a graduate student at Northwestern. On Sept. 1, 1892, he married Matilda Jane Spring of Centralia, Ill.; they had a daughter, Dorothy Louise, and a son, Frederick Sterling.

In 1893 he began graduate work in Greek, Latin, and Sanskrit at the Johns Hopkins University, where he held the university scholarship in Greek in 1895 and a fellowship in 1895-1896. He was a pupil of Basil Lanneau Gildersleeve, who in 1885 had edited *The Olympian and Pythian Odes of Pindar.* Scott received his doctorate from Johns Hopkins in June 1897; his dissertation, "A Comparative Study of Hesiod and Pindar," was published in 1898. He returned to Northwestern as an instructor (1897), became professor of Greek (1901), and in 1904 he was named chairman of the department of classical languages.

With the exception of his dissertation, *The Unity of Homer* (the Sather Classical Lectures he delivered in 1921) was his first book.

From it stemmed *Homer and His Influence* (1925) and *The Poetic Structure of the Odyssey,* the Martin Classical Lectures, published in 1931. *The Unity of Homer* was influential in turning the direction of Homeric studies in the United States from the German school of separatists to a new school of unitarians. Scott was by nature partisan, and he devoted himself to the uncompromising defense of Homer as the author of the two great poems. Appraisals of Scott as a scholar vary greatly. In Maurice Platinauer's *Fifty Years of Classical Scholarship* (1954), there is the following statement:

A skilful if unscrupulous controversialist, he succeeded by a careful choice of examples in conveying the impression that the greatest scholars of Germany were not only pedants but fools. . . . He certainly revealed the inaccuracy of some earlier statistics; but it may be questioned whether in matters of vocabulary and grammar a statistical approach is the right one.

One must balance against this opinion Sterling Dow's evaluation:

Scott's *The Unity of Homer* did more than any other book to defeat, though it did not annihilate, those who believed the epics were a patch-work of different poems. In fact it has been the most influential book in the whole Sather series. . . . Although many of his arguments, on the contradictions and other seeming difficulties in Homer, can now be seen differently, they still have major importance.

His other three books were of a religious nature. They contained lectures given by Scott under the auspices of the John C. Shaffer Foundation of Northwestern for promotion of the appreciation of the life, character, teachings, and influence of Jesus: *Socrates and Christ* (1928), *Luke, Greek Physician and Historian* (1930), and *We Would Know Jesus* (1936). A similar theme is represented in his article entitled, "The Church's Debt to Homer," in *Classical Essays Presented to J. A. Kleist,* edited by R. E. Arnold and published in 1946. As indicated by these writings, Scott was deeply involved with religious and intellectual questions. He tried to reconcile in some way pagan antiquity and Christianity, for both of which he had an unabashed and militant passion.

He was an active member of the First Presbyterian Church. He enjoyed golfing and was a member of the Gull Lake Country Club, of which he was at one time president. His was an energetic and vibrant personality.

In 1923 Scott was named John C. Shaffer

professor of Greek. He was a member of the American Philological Association (president, 1916) and of the Archaeological Institute of America. He was associate editor of the *Classical Journal* and edited its notes from 1910-1933. From 1926-1927, Scott was councillor to the American School in Athens. On his retirement in 1938, he was Northwestern's senior professor in length of service.

At the age of eighty, he died in his sleep at his summer home in Augusta, Mich.

[Sources include *Nat. Cyc. Am. Biog.,* XXXV; Am. Philological Assn., *Proc.* and *Trans.* (1925); *Classical Jour.,* Index vols. 1–25, 19 (1923–1924), 307, and vol. 43, p. 298; Sterling Dow, *Fifty Years of Sathers* (1965); obituary in *N.Y. Times,* Oct. 28, 1947.]
ALBERT B. LORD

SCOTT, WILLIAM BERRYMAN (Feb. 12, 1858–Mar. 29, 1947), geologist and paleontologist, was born in Cincinnati, Ohio, to William McKendree Scott, a Presbyterian minister, and Mary Elizabeth (Hodge) Scott; he was the youngest of their three sons who survived infancy. His father, the son of an immigrant from northern Ireland, had graduated from Jefferson College (later Washington and Jefferson) in Pennsylvania and had attended the Princeton Theological Seminary. William's mother was a daughter of a professor at the seminary, Charles Hodge. His older brother Hugh Lenox Scott became superintendent of West Point and the army's chief of staff. The family moved in William's infancy to Chicago, where the father taught at the Northwestern (later McCormick) Theological Seminary until his declining health caused the family to return to Princeton. After his death, when William was three, they remained in Princeton, living with Mrs. Scott's parents.

Reared chiefly among adults in an intellectual and religious household, Scott had a lonely but stimulating childhood. He was tutored at home until he was nine, spent much time in reading, and at first planned to become a clergyman. After attending a series of inadequate private schools, where he became attracted to chemistry, he entered the College of New Jersey (Princeton) at the age of fifteen, intending to prepare for a career in medicine, but a course in geology under Arnold Guyot shifted his interest to the study of geology and fossils. He received the B.A. degree in 1877. That summer, with his classmates Henry Fairfield Osborn and Francis Speir, Jr., he went to the Bridger Basin of Wyoming to collect fossil mammals, the first of ten such collecting trips he made during the period 1877-1893 to Wyoming, South Dakota, Oregon, and Montana.

Scott spent a year (1877-1878) in graduate study at Princeton, during which he became a strong partisan of the paleontologist Edward D. Cope in his bitter feud with Othniel C. Marsh, and then went to Europe for a two-year stay. He did biological research in the laboratory of Thomas H. Huxley at the Royal College of Science in London, studied embryology under Francis M. Balfour at Cambridge, and then went on to Heidelberg, where he worked under Carl Gegenbaur and received the Ph.D. in zoology in 1880, summa cum laude, with a dissertation on the embryology of the lamprey. He returned to Princeton as instructor in geology, and in 1884, at the age of twenty-six, was appointed professor. In 1909 he became chairman of the newly established department of geology. At his retirement in 1930, he had served fifty years on the Princeton faculty.

Scott was an excellent teacher and writer, and his textbook, *An Introduction to Geology,* went through three editions (1897, 1907, 1932). His major interest, however, was fossil mammals. Like his lifelong friend Osborn, he became one of the most important vertebrate paleontologists of his era. He had a phenomenal memory and produced sound and thorough research. Though he made little contribution to basic theory or methodology, he was preeminent in his descriptive and taxonomic studies of fossil vertebrates and in the mammalian paleontology of the Tertiary period. Of his publications, numbering over 170, perhaps the most important was *A History of Land Mammals in the Western Hemisphere* (1913; 2nd ed., 1937), which covered the history and distribution of species of both American continents. Another important project, which occupied Scott for more than thirty years, was editing the reports of Princeton's fossil-collecting expeditions (1896-1899) to Patagonia; the last of the fifteen volumes appeared in 1932.

Scott did not limit his research to description and classification but, particularly in the early stages of his career, attacked the problem of evolution. Taught in his boyhood that Darwinism was "atheism," he learned from his study of fossils to accept evolution as a fact, and in the period of 1890-1900 he published several perceptive discussions of evolutionary theory, in which he set forth some of the basic questions relating to species origin and differentiation. Later he became doubtful of Mendelism as an adequate explanation and concluded that the basic processes operating in evolution-

ary change had yet to be discovered, a view reflected in his *The Theory of Evolution* (1917).

Scott was active in many professional organizations. He was elected to the National Academy of Sciences in 1906 and served as president of the Paleontological Society (1911), the American Philosophical Society (1918-1925), and the Geological Society of America (1925). His several honorary degrees included the Sc.D. from Oxford (1912), and among his other honors were the Mary Clark Thompson and the Daniel Giraud Elliot medals of the National Academy.

On Dec. 15, 1883, Scott married Alice Adeline Post of New York City. Their seven children were Charles Hodge, Adeline Mitchill (who married author Herbert Agar), Mary Blanchard, Anne Kneeland, Hugh Lenox, Sarah Post, and Angelina Thayer. A lifelong Presbyterian, Scott was unassuming but somewhat formal in manner. He enjoyed music and travel, was fond of the sea, and usually spent his vacations at his summer home in Cataumet on Cape Cod.

At the age of seventy-seven, four years after his retirement, Scott undertook another large project and with two assistants prepared a five-part monograph (1936-1941) on the Oligocene mammalian fauna of the White River Group. He then began a new work, a revision of the late Eocene Uinta fauna, which occupied him until the last weeks of his life. He died of a heart attack at Princeton in his ninetieth year.

[Scott's autobiography, *Some Memories of a Palaeontologist* (1939), with portrait ; memoirs by George Gaylord Simpson in Am. Philosophical Soc., *Year Book,* 1947, and Nat. Acad. Sci., *Biog. Memoirs,* vol. XXV (1949) ; memorial by Glenn L. Jepson in Geological Soc. of America, *Proc.,* 1948 ; *N.Y. Times,* Mar. 30, 1947.]

CAROLINE HEMINWAY KIERSTEAD

SEASHORE, CARL EMIL (Jan. 28, 1866-Oct. 16, 1949), psychologist, was born Carl Emil Sjöstrand in Mörlunda, Sweden, the eldest of the three sons and two daughters of Carl Gustaf Sjöstrand and Emily Charlotta (Borg) Sjöstrand, holders of a small farming homestead. His father added to the family's financial resources and community standing as a carpenter and Lutheran lay preacher. In 1869, he followed his brothers to the United States, settling near them on an eighty-acre farm in Boone County, Iowa, and anglicizing the family name.

His parents taught him to read and write Swedish, and by the age of ten he knew large sections of the Bible by heart. His education in English began at the age of eight when the first district school, with a professional English-speaking teacher, was organized for the Swedish community of Boone County. Seashore's major boyhood interest, however, was music, to which he had been formally introduced in Sunday school. To finish his early education, his father boarded him with the pastor of a nearby church to learn formal manners and to improve his musical abilities. After a year, at the age of fourteen, Seashore became organist at the church.

In 1884, Seashore entered the second year of the preparatory department of Gustavus Adolphus College, St. Peter, Minn., a Lutheran Institution with strong ties to the midwestern Swedish community. He earned most of his expenses as a church organist and developed interests in Greek, mathematics, and, through a classmate, philosophy. In 1891, after graduating as valedictorian with the B.A., Seashore went to Yale to study philosophy with George Trumbull Ladd.

Finding a totally different world of scholarship at Yale, Seashore followed Ladd's courses with great interest and began working in the psychological laboratory under the direction of Edward Wheeler Scripture. At first he resented Scripture's instrumental approach to psychology, which reminded him of telegraphy, rather than a branch of philosophy. But, like other members of his generation who left philosophy for psychology, he gradually grew disenchanted with Ladd's reliance on textual authority and became impressed with Scripture's stress on individual initiative. Seashore later said that Scripture had greatly influenced his career in psychology, and much of his career illustrates this influence.

In 1895, Seashore was awarded the Ph.D. for a dissertation based on experiments performed under Scripture's direction. One of the few psychologists of his generation who was neither native-born nor a member of an upper-middle-class family, he served for the next two years as assistant in the Yale Psychological Laboratory, sharpening his experimental skills. In 1897, he returned to the Midwest as assistant professor at the State University of Iowa, and for the rest of his life his name was linked with this school. From his first appointment, he was in charge of the psychological laboratory, and five years later he was promoted to professor. In 1905, he became head of the department of philosophy and psychology and, in 1908, dean of the Graduate College. In 1937, at the age of seventy-one, he retired from these posts, but he was recalled during

World War II and served as dean *pro tem* from 1942 through 1946. During his long career at Iowa, Seashore made his most characteristic and important contributions to psychology and education.

At Iowa in 1897, Seashore considered his first task to be the development of the existing psychological laboratory program into an important factor in the education of both undergraduate and graduate students. In doing so, he built his department into one of the first large-scale psychology departments in the Midwest, following Scripture's lead in many ways. The formal laboratory training course that Seashore developed to drill undergraduates in the fundamentals of psychology and scientific experimentation led to the publication of *Elementary Experiments in Psychology* in 1908. For graduate students, Seashore stressed the design and manufacture of special instruments, and for many years he annually reviewed recent developments in the design of apparatus for the *Psychological Bulletin*.

Like Scripture and many of his contemporaries, Seashore was concerned with the applications of psychology, and as early as 1901 he wrote on the use of general psychological tests by educators. Probably his most important contribution was to relate testing to his earlier interest in music through the development of methods for the measurement of musical aptitude and talent. Like many of his contemporaries, he broke down what he was studying into what he felt were its elements, such as the ability to discriminate differences in pitch, time, and rhythm. In 1899, he began to publish articles in various psychological journals on tests to measure such abilities. By 1906, he was called upon to write for such journals as *The Musician, Musical Quarterly,* and *Etude,* and many of the instruments he designed for these tests became standard apparatus in physicians' offices and music schools, as well as in psychological laboratories. Seashore's interest in this area culminated in 1919 with the publication of *The Psychology of Musical Talent* and the issuance of phonograph records with standardized tones so that his tests could be performed without special equipment; in 1937, with the publication of his *Psychology of Music*; and in 1940, with his revision, with some of his students, of what is now known as the Seashore Measures of Musical Talents.

As dean of the Graduate College at Iowa, Seashore directly applied some of his psychological ideas to education and influenced others through his position, which he did not hesitate to use. His concern, throughout his career, with the differences between individuals led to a deep interest in gifted children. In 1921, he urged the sectioning of classes according to the students' ability in order to free the talented child from the reins of standard education, and for the next six years he led a National Research Council project to disseminate this idea. As an educational administrator he helped develop strong programs in most areas relating to science and stressed their interrelationships. He was proud that his department of psychology worked closely with other units of the school, operating, for example, the Psychological Clinic in connection with the Psychopathic Hospital. Under his leadership, the Graduate College accelerated its growth, and the university developed into a major institution with a well-deserved national reputation.

Seashore was a member of the American Psychological Association, which elected him president in 1911, and of the American Association for the Advancement of Science, of which, in 1926-1927, he was vice-president for the Section of Psychology. During World War I, as ex-president of the American Psychological Association, he was a member of a committee to organize his science's contribution to the war effort. His major role was as chairman of the Committee on Acoustic Problems, which applied much of his earlier research to the problems of submarine detection. After the war, he was elected to the National Academy of Sciences, and during the 1920-1921 academic year he served in Washington, D.C., as resident chairman of its Division of Anthropology and Psychology. Seashore belonged to many other professional organizations in psychology, education, and music and received numerous honorary degrees.

Raised a conservative Lutheran, Seashore later abandoned the strict theology of his father and gradually adopted a conventional Protestantism centering around the Congregational Church. On June 7, 1900, he married Mary Roberta Holmes of Iowa City, Iowa; they had four sons: Robert Holmes, who also became a psychologist, Carl Gustav, Marion Dubois, and Sigfrid Holmes. Warm, friendly, and generous, Seashore remained dapper and spry through his last years, when his moustache turned white and his thick head of hair had receded to a gray fringe above his ears. Tall and slender, he was proud of his career and his family and undertook all of his projects with confidence. He played golf into his

eighties, enjoyed the outdoors, was called The Dean, and was admired and well-liked by his colleagues and students. Two months after his wife's death, Seashore died of a stroke, at the age of eighty-three, while visiting his son Sigfrid in Lewiston, Idaho. He was buried in Iowa City, Iowa.

[At Seashore's death, the bulk of his professional papers were stored at the Univ. of Iowa, and most of his personal papers were distributed among members of his family. The personal papers remain dispersed, and all efforts to recover the professional papers have been unsuccessful. However, manuscript materials relating to Seashore and his career may be found elsewhere. The university president's files and the papers of the Inst. of Child Welfare in the Univ. of Iowa Archives contain such material, as do the papers of a number of Seashore's contemporary psychologists. Especially important are the papers of Edwin G. Boring, at the Harvard Univ. Archives (particularly for Seashore's work with the Nat. Research Council); James McKeen Cattell, at the Lib. of Cong.; Walter Bowers Pillsbury, at the Univ. of Mich. Hist. Collect.; Edward Bradford Titchener, at the Cornell Univ. Archives; and Robert Mearns Yerkes, at the Yale Univ. School of Medicine Hist. Collect.

Each of Seashore's three autobiographies overlaps the others to some degree but is revealing in its own way. The first, published as part of the *Hist. of Psychology in Autobiography* series (1930), pp. 225-297, is the most general and gives an overview of his life, as well as many insights into his personality. *Pioneering in Psychology* (1942) was issued as vol. 70 of the Univ. of Iowa Series on Aims and Progress of Research and deals most directly with his psychological work at Iowa. *Psychology and Life in Autobiography*, privately issued (1964), is primarily a rearrangement and expansion of his published articles, including his first autobiography, and emphasizes his career as an educational administrator.

An annotated bibliography of Seashore's publications through 1926, by two of his students, is "Seashore Commemorative Number," *Univ. of Iowa Studies in Psychology* (1928); more complete bibliographies appear in *Pioneering in Psychology*, and in the obituary by Walter R. Miles in *Biog. Memoirs* of the Nat. Acad. of Sciences, XXIX (1956). See also the obituaries by Milton J. Metfessel, in *Science*, June 30, 1950, pp. 713-717; Joseph Tiffin, in the *Psychological Rev.*, Jan. 1950, pp. 1-2; and George D. Stoddard in the *Am. Jour. of Psychology*, July 1950, pp. 456-462.

Seashore's most important publications include "Measurements of Illusions and Hallucinations in Normal Life," *Studies from the Yale Psychological Laboratory* 3 (1895), 1-67, his doctoral dissertation; *Elementary Experiments in Psychology* (1908, 1935); *Psychology in Daily Life* (1914); *The Psychology of Musical Talent* (1919); and *Psychology of Music* (1937). Assistance of Marjorie Seashore, Carl Gustav Seashore, Charles N. Seashore, Stanley N. Seashore, Grace Helen Kent, and Albert T. Poffenberger gratefully acknowledged.]

MICHAEL M. SOKAL

SEIDEL, GEORGE LUKAS EMIL (Dec. 13, 1864-June 24, 1947), socialist politician, reformer, and mayor of Milwaukee, was born in Ashland, Pa., the eldest of nine sons and two daughters of Otto Carl Ferdinand Seidel and Henrietta Christine Friederika (Knoll) Seidel. His father, a carpenter from Golchen in the Demmin district of western Pomerania in Prussia, had immigrated to eastern Pennsylvania. A year after Emil's birth the family moved to Prairie du Chien, Wis., then to Madison in 1867 and to Milwaukee two years later. Seidel completed elementary school in Milwaukee and began work at the age of thirteen. He was apprenticed as a woodcarver in the furniture factory that employed his father as a cabinetmaker. In his teens he participated in a woodcarver's strike over piecework rates, helped organize the Wood Carvers Association of Milwaukee, and represented the association as the Minerva Assembly in the Knights of Labor District Assembly. In 1886 Seidel left for a six-year stay in Germany, visiting relatives in Pomerania, working to improve his craft, and studying nights at the Berlin Kunstgewerbe Schule. In Berlin he chaired a woodcarver's strike committee for the eight-hour day and was converted to the radical wing of German socialist thought.

In August 1892 Seidel returned to Milwaukee and worked at his trade for the next decade in various capacities. While employed as a designer and pattern-maker for a stove company he married, on May 8, 1895, Lucy Geissel, a native Milwaukeean. The had two children, Lucius Julian, who died in infancy, and Viola Emeline.

About 1893 Seidel became involved with the Milwaukee socialists, a group of thirty-five to forty persons loosely organized by Victor L. Berger, who had recently founded the Wisconsin *Vorwärts* as a labor and socialist weekly. Although he had previously supported Daniel de Leon's Socialist Labor party, in 1897 Seidel joined the Milwaukee Branch (Number 1) of the Social Democracy of America, which had been formed by Eugene V. Debs and Berger. As a native American who spoke German, Seidel rose rapidly among the Germanic Social-Democrats. After running unsuccessfully for governor in 1902, he was one of nine members elected to the Milwaukee Common Council in 1904. He was reelected in 1906 and lost the mayoralty election of 1908 to incumbent Democrat David S. Rose by only 2,219 votes. The following spring he became the first Social-Democratic alderman-at-large.

In the Common Council the honesty and integrity of Seidel and his fellow socialists contrasted with Democratic and Republican corruption. Seidel emphasized such everyday needs as parks, public baths, street lighting, and an improved water supply, and championed wider educational opportunities. Again his party's candidate for mayor in 1910, he won easily with 27,608 votes to the Democrat's 20,530 and the Republican's 11,346. The socialists swept all citywide races, gained 21 of the 35 council seats, elected Berger alderman, and chose Edmund D. Melms, who had organized the party's campaign, as council president. The Social-Democrats also won control of the County Board.

As the first socialist mayor of a major American city, Seidel carried the hopes of thousands of optimistic party supporters throughout the nation. He introduced modern, scientific methods of government, insisted upon municipal economy, and launched programs for child welfare, public health, housing, city planning, and harbor development. Seidel and Berger brought in John R. Commons from the University of Wisconsin in Madison to organize a Bureau of Economy and Efficiency, staffed by university personnel and outside municipal experts, who investigated government organization and social welfare problems. Limitations of the municipal charter, state control of the city, socialist sectarianism, and scramble for public office, mounting public concern for the "red menace," and deepening newspaper hostility, however, frustrated Seidel's plans. Despite a valiant effort at public education, the Social-Democrats gradually lost public esteem, and Seidel was defeated in 1912 by a nonpartisan fusion candidate, former health commissioner Dr. Gerhard Bading. The party also lost control of the council and other citywide offices.

Seidel campaigned actively as the vice-presidential candidate of the Socialist Party of America in 1912, traveling more than 25,000 miles in ninety days. The 901,062 votes for Debs and Seidel constituted the highwater mark for the socialists. The following year Seidel toured the country for the socialist lyceum department and, after losing to Bading again in the 1914 campaign, lectured for the Redpath Chautauqua. When City Attorney Daniel W. Hoan began a twenty-four-year term as Milwaukee's second socialist mayor in 1916, Seidel again became alderman-at-large. His outspoken views against World War I in Horicon and Theresa caused trouble for him, but, unlike Berger, he was not indicted.

From 1920 to 1923 Seidel toured Wisconsin as state secretary of the Socialist party in a vain effort to regain the party's prewar momentum. Continued absorption in socialist politics (he ran for United States senator in 1914, governor in 1918, and city treasurer in 1920) strained his marriage; and following a separation, his wife won an uncontested divorce on Apr. 28, 1924, on grounds of desertion. Sickly as a child, never robust, Seidel suffered a serious breakdown, from which he gradually recovered through outdoor activity on a brother's farm in northern Wisconsin. Back in Milwaukee, he purchased a residence in Garden Homes, a Hoan experiment in municipal housing, which he shared for a time with his daughter and then with friends. Hoan appointed him to the City (Civil) Service Commission in 1926, a post he held until 1932. He ran again unsuccessfully for United States senator in 1932 but was returned to the Common Council for the last time in the socialist surge of 1932. He refused to run for reelection in 1936.

Seidel sustained a lifelong optimism about mankind and a vision of man's unlimited potential. Largely self-educated, modest, and self-effacing, of unquestioned sincerity and integrity, he perfectly exemplified the "sewer" socialists who set Milwaukee's movement apart in the early twentieth century. He died in Milwaukee of a heart condition and the complications of old age and was cremated at Forest Home Cemetery.

[Manuscript autobiography in collections of the State Hist. Soc. of Wis. (Milwaukee Area Research Center); *Milwaukee Jour.*, Dec. 3, 14, 1939, June 25, 1947; *Who's Who in America*, 1916–1917; Marvin Wachman, *Hist. of the Social-Democratic Party of Milwaukee, 1897–1910* (1945); Frederick I. Olson, "Milwaukee's First Socialist Administration, 1910–1912: A Political Evaluation," in *Mid-America*, July 1961, pp. 197–207.]

FREDERICK I. OLSON

SELIG, WILLIAM NICHOLAS (Mar. 14, 1864–July 15, 1948), early motion picture producer, was born in Chicago, Ill., the fourth son and fifth of seven children of Joseph Francis and Antonia (Lunsky) Selig. His father, a shoemaker, had come to Chicago in the mid-1850's from Bohemia; his mother was a native of Prussia. William Selig attended Chicago public schools and in his youth worked as an upholsterer. Around 1888 he turned to the theatre, and for most of the next ten years, sporting the title "Colonel," he toured as an actor and theatrical manager, specializing in parlor magic and minstrel shows.

Already conversant with photography, in 1895 Selig saw an Edison kinetoscope while in Dallas, Tex., and undertook to develop a motion picture projector. The result was the Selig Polyscope, which he began marketing the following year, forming a company by that name. Between 1902 and 1918 he took out ten patents on motion picture devices, none of any great originality. The first, the Selig Standard Camera, was a copy of the machine built by

the Lumière brothers of France and was substantially identical to the Warwick camera used by the American Mutoscope and Biograph Company (later the Biograph Company) of New York. Nonetheless, in this germinal stage of the film industry, suppliers of equipment, with only a modest cash investment, were able to garner a substantial return. Several, like Selig, George K. Spoor of Chicago, and Sigmund Lubin of Philadelphia, moved into film production soon after the advent of nickelodeons (small five-cent movie theaters) in 1905.

Selig had begun photographing primitive movies around 1900—extremely short incidents, filmed in the streets of Chicago, that served as novelty fillers in vaudeville theatres. Like other producers, he turned to story films after the success in 1903 of Edwin S. Porter's *The Great Train Robbery*. Three years later, lured by reports of southern California's abundant sunshine, Selig sent a crew to Los Angeles to complete the filming of the one-reel *The Count of Monte Cristo* (1908), the first commercial film made in California. Selig established in 1909 what has been called the first permanent studio in the Los Angeles area, housed in a small downtown building behind a Chinese laundry. This was two years before the Nestor Film Company opened the first studio in Hollywood. Selig soon moved to outlying Edendale, where he set up a studio. Occupying a full city block, it was surrounded by a high brick wall with an ornate Spanish-style gate. The bulk of the several hundred pictures he released between 1912 and 1917 under the "Diamond-S" label were made either in Edendale or in his large plant in Chicago, which he continued to operate until 1914.

One element in the exodus of filmmakers to California was the desire to escape litigation. A prolonged "patent war" swept the industry beginning in 1897, as pioneer companies like Edison and Vitagraph sought to enforce their patents against interlopers. A federal court in Chicago held in 1907 that Selig's camera infringed on the Edison claims. In December 1908, in a compromise settlement, the contending interests joined forces in a patent-pooling trust, the Motion Picture Patents Company, with the Selig Polyscope Company as one of the ten members. The combination encountered serious opposition from independents within the industry beginning in 1912 and was dissolved as a result of federal antitrust action in 1917.

Meanwhile, Selig was prospering in California. One of his early discoveries was the cowboy star Tom Mix. Mix made his first film appearance in Selig's *Ranch Life in the Great Southwest* in 1910 and remained with the Company until 1917. Selig was the first to specialize in films using wild animals as part of the dramatic action, and for years he maintained his own menagerie. His first such film, *Big Game Hunting in Africa* (1909), was inspired by former President Theodore Roosevelt's expedition and featured the actual killing of a superannuated lion. In conjunction with the *Chicago Tribune*, Selig made the first motion picture serial, *The Adventures of Kathlyn* (1913-1914). Starring Kathlyn Williams, it was the predecessor of the more famous *The Perils of Pauline,* which immortalized Pearl White.

Selig joined the trend toward longer "feature" films with *The Coming of Columbus* (1912). To assure an adequate supply of story material, he signed contracts with such popular authors as Zane Grey and Rex Beach. His production of Beach's *The Spoilers* (1914) opened the 3,300-seat Strand Theatre in New York City, the first of the large new metropolitan movie houses with a graduated admission scale. The film's success made Selig a substantial fortune.

After 1917 the motion picture industry was vastly transformed by large aggregations of capital and integrated control, and Selig's company went into eclipse. He made only a handful of films between 1920 and 1922 and then dropped out altogether.

Selig married Mary H. Pinkham of Stockton, Calif., on Sept. 7, 1900. They apparently had no children. He was an Episcopalian in religion and a Republican in politics. He died of a coronary thrombosis at his Los Angeles home at the age of eighty-four; his remains were cremated.

Among movie pioneers, Selig ranks high for his part in elevating the industry's technical standards. Before 1915, he had few peers in the use of studio and natural environments to achieve realistic effects, with a fidelity to detail that satisfied increasingly sophisticated audiences.

[Information about Selig's career has been pieced together from a variety of sources. On his background and early life, see city directory listings, 1856-1900 (courtesy of Larry A. Viskochil, Chicago Hist. Soc.); census of 1880 (Ill. State Archives); death record of Selig's father (Jan. 18, 1890, Cook County records). On his film career: Benjamin B. Hampton, *A Hist. of the Movies* (1931); Terry Ramsaye, *A Million and One Nights* (2 vols., 1926); Kenneth Macgowan, *Behind the Screen* (1965); Lewis Jacobs, *The Rise of the Am. Film* (1939); Kevin Brownlow, *The Parade's Gone By* (1968); Kalton C. Lahue, *Continued Next Week* (1964); George N. Fenin and William K. Ever-

son, *The Western* (1962); Fred J. Balshofer and Arthur C. Miller, *One Reel a Week* (1967); Frederick A. Talbot, *Moving Pictures* (rev. ed., 1912); *Moving Picture World,* Aug. 21, 1909, pp. 247-248; *Motography,* July 1911, pp. 7-19; Robinson Locke Scrapbook Collect., Theatre Collect. of N.Y. Public Lib. at Lincoln Center; information from Margaret Herrick, executive director, Acad. of Motion Picture Arts and Sciences, Los Angeles. See also: *Who Was Who in America,* vol. II (1950), which transposes the given names of Selig's father; *N.Y. Times* obituary, July 17, 1948; death certificate, Calif. Dept. of Public Health. A photograph of Selig is in *Photoplay,* Feb. 1923, p. 49.]

WILLIAM GREENLEAF

SETON, ERNEST THOMPSON (Aug. 14, 1860–Oct. 23, 1946), naturalist, writer, illustrator and lecturer, was born in South Shields, Durham, England. He was the twelfth of fourteen children of Joseph Logan and Alice (Snowdon) Thompson, and was christened Ernest Evan. Directly descended from Alan Cameron, a Jacobite who assumed the name Thompson upon fleeing Scotland in 1746, his father also claimed collateral descent from George Seton, Earl of Winton, an expatriate Jacobite who died without legitimate issue in 1749. In his published work, Ernest used the names Ernest E. Thompson and Ernest Seton-Thompson as well as his recognized name, legally adopted in 1901.

The Thompson family was dominated by a stern Calvinism whose "dreadful doctrines" Ernest came to despise and repudiate. Late in life he recalled his mother as gentle, ineffectual, and rigidly pious, his father as indolent, tightfisted, and a fierce disciplinarian. Bankruptcy of the family shipping business in 1866 forced an immigration to Canada, where Joseph Thompson settled his family on a farm near Lindsay, Ontario. Finding he had little aptitude or taste for farming, in 1870 Joseph sold his place to one William Blackwell and moved the family to Toronto, where he became an accountant.

But in these four years in the country Ernest had discovered his goal in life, to become a naturalist. As a schoolboy in Toronto he managed to pursue his interests despite his father's opposition, and when his health broke under the strain of studies at Toronto Collegiate High School in 1875, he was sent to the Blackwell farm to recover. On this and later visits Seton had many of the outdoor adventures he fictionalized in the famous boys' book *Two Little Savages* (1903).

With his father determined that he become an artist, Ernest was apprenticed to a hack portrait painter in 1876, studied for a time at the Ontario School of Art, and in 1879 went to London to learn figure drawing and mammalian anatomy. Late in 1880 he won a substantial scholarship to the Royal Academy of Painting and Sculpture, but attended classes for less than a year. He received little from his family and again declined in health, suffering not only from undernourishment, but also from neurotic fears of sex, which produced exhausting strains. He returned to Toronto in November 1881, thin, weak, and dispirited. Seton had attained his full six-foot height as early as sixteen, but he had not yet developed the spare and sinewy physique which later served him so well in strenuous outdoor activities.

The following March, Seton set out for his brother Arthur's farm near Carberry, Manitoba. He helped to build a house on the property, prospected for other homestead land, and in October 1883 staked his own claim, but occupied it only briefly. Except for periods in Toronto and two lengthy visits to New York, Seton spent the better part of five years in rural Manitoba, exploring, hunting, sketching, collecting—an experience which ended late in 1886 with an arthritic seizure that crippled his right knee, and only much later responded to treatment.

These prairie years matured Seton's talents for field research and discovery, and produced his first scientific publications, in particular "Mammals of Manitoba" (1886), *The Birds of Manitoba* (1891), and a number of bird articles in *The Auk,* journal of the American Ornithologists' Union. While in New York he secured a contract to make a thousand drawings for *The Century Dictionary* (1889-1891), and his meeting with Frank M. Chapman led to his work as illustrator and textual contributor for that noted ornithologist's *Handbook of Birds of Eastern North America* (1895) and *Bird-Life* (1897). Ultimately Seton's scientific reputation rested on his two-volume *Life Histories of Northern Animals* (1909) and his four-volume *Lives of Game Animals* (1925-1928), imposing works that aspired to both accurate presentation and popular format and style. The latter work won Seton the coveted John Burroughs Memorial Medal in 1926 and the Daniel Giraud Elliot medal in 1928.

Much of the appeal of his books lay in the illustrations, almost invariably his own. After a brief period in 1884 at the Art Students' League in New York, Seton went to Paris in 1890 for further training and independent anatomical study. His success in academic work was shown the following year by the selection for Grand Salon display of his oil painting of a sleeping wolf, and his anatomical researches at length bore fruit in his book *Art Anatomy of Animals* (1896).

Seton returned in ill health from Paris in 1892, and the next year took a job as wolf killer on a cattle ranch in New Mexico, using both poisoned bait and steel traps. From these experiences came his most famous story, "The King of Currumpaw," first published in *Scribner's Magazine* in 1894. It dealt with Lobo, a gray wolf of unusual size, strength, and cunning who finally fell victim to Seton's traps only because of loyalty to his mate, the white wolf Blanca. A similar pattern marks other successful stories: a particular animal or bird, named and endowed by Seton with special strength and understanding, triumphs over a series of perils and in the end, perhaps, perishes bravely. The aptly titled *Wild Animals I Have Known* (1898) demonstrated the wide appeal of such tales; the book quickly became a best seller, and founded, according to Seton, "the modern school of animal stories."

Aboard ship on his way to Paris in 1894 to resume his art studies, Seton met twenty-two-year-old Grace Gallatin, daughter of the California financier Albert Gallatin. Often together during the next two years, they returned to be married in New York, June 1, 1896. Grace Seton assisted her husband with many editorial tasks, and also had her own career as a writer, feminist reformer, and social leader. But their lives tended soon to diverge, although they were not divorced until 1935. Despite her willingness to share his interests, by his own admission Seton did not take easily to the settled and socially established ways his wife seemed to prefer. His travels took him to the Yellowstone in 1897, to the Wind River and Jackson Hole in 1898, to Norway in 1900, and nearly to the Arctic Circle on a 2,000-mile canoe trip in 1907. Meanwhile he had begun an arduous schedule of public lecturing, which earned him as much as $12,000 yearly. By 1909 Seton had traveled in nearly every state of the Union and most of the provinces of Canada, and had published nineteen works in book form, ranging from *The Wild Animal Play for Children* (1900) through *Animal Heroes* (1905), a collection of typical stories, to such slim juveniles as *Biography of a Grizzly* (1900) and *Biography of a Silver Fox* (1909).

This period saw Seton become both financially secure and well established as one of America's foremost nature writers and illustrators. He made the acquaintance of Theodore Roosevelt, and listed among his scientific friends or associates Chapman, William Brewster, C. Hart Merriam, Florence Merriam Bailey, Elliott Coues, and Spencer F. Baird. His literary acquaintances included Mark Twain, William Dean Howells, Hamlin Garland, and John Burroughs, the most famous nature essayist of his time. But the gravest public challenge ever offered to Seton came in a Burroughs article, "Real and Sham Natural History," in the March 1903 issue of the *Atlantic*. Burroughs cast serious doubt on some of the more remarkable actions of Seton's wild creatures, finding that he both humanized and fictionalized them for dramatic effect.

Decades later, in his autobiography, Seton claimed he had so thoroughly confounded Burroughs at a dinner party that a "public apology" appeared in the *Atlantic* soon afterward. But this was at best an imprecise account. Mentioning Seton only once in a six-page essay, in July 1904, Burroughs said: "Mr. Thompson Seton, as an artist and *raconteur*, ranks by far the highest [among the new group of nature students], and to those who can separate the fact from the fiction in his animal stories, he is truly delightful." Both in its praise and its caveat, this remains a perceptive estimate of Seton as a writer.

When Burroughs used the word "artist" he might better have said illustrator. In general Seton's paintings were inferior to his pen and ink or brush sketches, his marginal drawings, even his quick field impressions or preliminary studies for more formal work. In drawing mammals he could impart an acute sense of life, and even with plants he showed a like sensitivity to the living structure of his subjects. Though his commissioned illustrations were often of birds, Seton seldom mastered the look of flight, and again his most evocative bird work was likely to be the swift sketch.

Usually Seton was best served when his graphic art worked to complement the pages of his stories. At such times Seton the writer and illustrator merged with Seton the prophet and propagandist for nature, the teller of outdoor tales that finally depended for their effect not on accuracy or plausibility but on their power to evoke excitement and wonder and belief. To a society rapidly herding itself into cities, and losing its ancient touch with the natural world, Seton brought beguiling fictions of places and wild creatures left behind.

In 1910 Seton was instrumental in founding the Boy Scouts of America, serving as chief scout until December 1915, when he resigned in protest to Theodore Roosevelt's idea that the scouts should be "trained to arms." Scouting for Seton had less to do with uniforms and mottoes than with camping, woodcraft, and Indian lore. After founding the Woodcraft Indians in 1902, he wrote a dozen books on outdoor activities to interest younger readers, and for many years edited the *Totem Board*, organ of the Woodcraft League of America. No writer since Cooper was more responsible for celebrating and perhaps idealizing the American Indian, and Seton's interest was reinforced by his long association with Julia M. Buttree, a student of Indian lore.

In 1930, the year he applied for United States citizenship, Seton sold his eastern holdings and moved to New Mexico. His enduring interest in architecture and landscaping was reflected in Seton Castle, built to his own specifications on a 2,500-acre tract near Santa Fe. This thirty-room stone and adobe structure housed his library of 13,000 books, nearly 8,000 of his paintings and drawings, and his collection of 3,000 bird and animal skins.

On Jan. 22, 1935, four days after his divorce was granted, Seton married Julia M. Buttree, a woman almost thirty years his junior. Three years later a daughter, Beulah, was adopted by the couple. Meanwhile Seton's daughter Ann, only child of his first marriage, was beginning a successful career as a novelist, writing under the name of Anya Seton.

Seton died of pancreatic cancer at his home near Santa Fe. The funeral on October 25 was followed by cremation at Albuquerque.

[Seton's autobiography, *Trail of an Artist-Naturalist* (1940)—from which unattributed quotations above are taken—tells much about his early and middle periods but little of his later years. Anya Seton, who has been most helpful in providing essential data, states that the definitive biography of Seton is being prepared by John Henry Wadland of Trent University, Peterborough, Ontario, Canada. Seton's bibliography, assembled by Bonnie Stecher at the University of Wisconsin in 1964, includes books widely disparate in length, quality, and relevance to his major work. Nearly fifty titles appeared in the United States and Canada between 1891 and 1945, a few published by governmental bodies, institutions, or Seton himself, the rest by commercial publishers. Many were composed of pieces published earlier in magazines such as *Scribner's*, *The Century*, *Ladies' Home Journal*, *Country Life* and *St. Nicholas*. *A Handbook of Woodcraft, Scouting, and Life-Craft*, issued for the Boy Scouts in 1910, was followed by a series of manuals on outdoor lore, with *The Forester's Manual* (1912), a well-executed example. *The Arctic Prairies* (1911), a substantial account of Seton's Canadian canoe trip, reveals among other things his ambivalent response to the Indians he encountered.

A great deal of Setoniana may be found at the Ernest Thompson Seton Memorial Museum, Philmont Boy Scout Reservation, Cimarron, N.Mex. Seton Castle, now owned by Beulah Seton Barbour, contains many of Seton's best paintings. At the instruction of his widow, thirty-eight of the fifty-odd volumes of Seton's journal were sold at auction in 1965, and are now in the Rare Book Room of the Am. Museum of Natural History, New York.]

ROBERT H. WELKER

SHAW, ALBERT (July 23, 1857-June 25, 1947), journalist and reformer, was born in Paddy's Run (later renamed Shandon), Ohio, the youngest child and sole surviving son of Griffin Shaw and his second wife, Susan (Fisher) Shaw. His father was a physician who was also active in local Republican politics. His Vermont-bred mother, whose forebears had arrived in Massachusetts in the 1630's, had come west to teach school. Although his childhood was marred by the death of his father in 1863, Shaw's youth was not unhappy and was in fact characterized by above-average standards of comfort and refinement. Raised in his mother's Congregationalist tradition of respect for education, and influenced by Roger Williams, a young newspaper owner of Oxford, Ohio, and his cousin, Murat Halstead, a Cincinnati newspaperman of national stature, Shaw assiduously prepared himself for college and ultimately for a career in journalism. After graduating from high school in 1874, his family and he moved the following year to Grinnell, Iowa. There he entered Iowa College (renamed Grinnell in 1909), from which he received the B.A. degree in 1879.

Shortly after his graduation, Shaw became a junior partner and editor of the biweekly *Grinnell Herald*. Two years later he left the paper to undertake a semester's graduate work in history and political economy at the Johns Hopkins University. Selling his interest in the *Herald*, Shaw next secured employment as an editorial writer on the *Minneapolis Tribune* with the understanding that he could complete his graduate studies before commencing full-time work. The time he spent at Johns Hopkins was perhaps the most influential in his life. There he not only received superb academic preparation for his editorial career but also made lifelong friendships with fellow-student Woodrow Wilson, historian Herbert Baxter Adams, visiting British scholar James Bryce, and Richard T. Ely, a reform-minded political economist, who made a great intellectual impact upon Shaw. In 1884, after completing his dissertation, a study of an Icarian socialist settlement located near Corning, Iowa, he was awarded the Ph.D. with very high honors. Shaw then returned to Minneapolis as the *Tribune*'s chief editorial writer, a position which he held throughout his association with the paper. (He later received the title of as-

sociate editor.) A Republican in national politics, Shaw was most creative when discussing municipal affairs, a field in which several of Ely's disciples distinguished themselves through their intelligent advocacy of reform, and in 1888 he took a year's leave of absence to go abroad to study the great cities of England and continental Europe. Returning home, he lectured on his findings at several universities, put in a final year on the *Tribune*, and moved to New York City in 1891 to become the editor of the American edition of the *Review of Reviews*, a periodical recently established in London by the English journalist, William T. Stead. In 1892, Shaw acquired the controlling financial interest in the American *Review of Reviews*. The following year, on September 5, Shaw married Elizabeth Leonard (Bessie) Bacon, in Reading, Pa. They had two sons, Albert, Jr., and Roger.

In his editorials and other writings, Shaw revealed his continuing interest in municipal reform. Demanding though his new responsibilities were, he was able to complete a number of learned articles on the governments of the several cities he had recently visited and to culminate his work in urban affairs with the preparation of two widely applauded monographs, *Municipal Government in Great Britain* and *Municipal Government in Continental Europe*, both published in 1895. Shaw's approach throughout was didactic, his purpose being to show Americans how cities like Glasgow, Hamburg, and Paris had successfully coped with such familiar urban problems as housing, public health, and transportation through both direct municipal ownership and strict regulation of private enterprise. Politically, Shaw believed European cities were successful because of their greater reliance on professional civil servants. A resolute foe of political "bossism," he was a member of several civic organizations, such as the City Club and the Citizens Union, which sought to rationalize municipal administration. Blaming urban corruption in large measure on the influx of "new" immigrants from southern Europe, Shaw was an early advocate of immigration restriction, although he later tempered his sometimes extreme ethnocentric opinions.

Shaw balanced his concern for urban affairs with a growing interest in the problems of the countryside. As a member of the Southern Education Board (1901-1914) and General Education Board (1902-1929), which received funds from John D. Rockefeller, Shaw participated in the movement to improve rural education for the Southern whites. A believer in white supremacy, he supported the South's Jim Crow laws, including those designed to disenfranchise the Negroes. Shaw was also concerned with maintaining the viability of the family farm and purchased a 1,600-acre farm in Virginia, on which he applied scientific techniques to the raising of livestock and crops.

With the accession to the presidency of his friend Theodore Roosevelt, Shaw began devoting much time to national politics. A longtime Republican, he supported Roosevelt editorially and gave him counsel as well. The two men agreed on the need for an assertive foreign policy, while on domestic matters they favored conservation programs, giving labor a square deal, and regulating big business to ensure its social responsibility. Although he favored a moderately high tariff, Shaw opposed the excessive Payne-Aldrich tariff of 1909. Shaw thus fitted comfortably into what has become known as the New Nationalist wing of progressivism and followed Roosevelt into the Bull Moose movement of 1912.

Active also as a public speaker and as a member of numerous civic and charitable organizations, Shaw in 1912 was in the midst of a distinguished career as editor and publisher of the American *Review of Reviews*. In format the periodical still bore considerable resemblance to its English prototype, but in personality it had long since become identified with the studious Shaw. One of the first American periodicals to devote itself exclusively to the discussion of events of current interest, the *Review of Reviews* enjoyed outstanding success for a generation prior to 1920. Shaw's thoughtful and wide-ranging editorials, collected in a section of twenty or more pages titled "The Progress of the World," a selection of cartoons, reviews of features in other magazines, and as many as a dozen informative articles all contributed to its popularity. Although circulation usually hovered about 200,000 monthly, estimates were that a million or more people (many of them professional persons and students) read each issue.

As scholars of journalism have pointed out, however, magazines have a life cycle of their own, and, beginning in the 1920's, the now staid old *Review* had begun to incur deficits. In 1937 in a last fruitless effort to compete with sprightly young magazines like *Time* and *Newsweek*, the *Review* merged with its old rival, the *Literary Digest,* and converted to a weekly. Shaw's illness and the prospects of even steeper deficits soon killed the experiment.

The weekly itself was carried on under new management until early 1938, but both in name and spirit the *Review of Reviews* had died with the merger.

At the time of his retirement Shaw was a bitter old man, disturbed not only by the death of his wife in 1931, by his own debilitating illness, and by the demise of his cherished *Review,* but by the events of the last two decades. During World War I, Shaw had served as an official for the Near East relief program, and after the war he had urged American entrance into the League of Nations. During the 1920's, however, he became increasingly critical of government bureaucracy and organized labor. He grew nostalgic for the America of his youth and for such ancestral values as individualism and self-reliance. Although a concern for national unity influenced him to support the New Deal in 1933, his break with it was inevitable.

Shaw's customary optimism eventually returned, however. His second wife, his secretary Virginia McCall, whom he married on May 4, 1933, in Gainesville, Fla., did much to lighten the burdens of his last years. A self-made millionaire, he remained comfortable financially, and once his illness abated he was able to proceed with several long-deferred writing projects. The only one of the various undertakings to be completed and published was *International Bearings of American Policy* (1943), an obviously dated plea for a return to the international ideals of his old friend Wilson. Shaw died in St. Luke's Hospital, New York, one month before his ninetieth birthday and was buried in the Sleepy Hollow Cemetery in Tarrytown, N.Y.

[See Lloyd J. Graybar, "Albert Shaw's Ohio Youth," *Ohio History,* 74 (1965), 29–34, 72–73, "Albert Shaw's Search for the Ideal City," *The Historian,* 34 (1972), 421–436, "Albert Shaw and the Founding of the *Review of Reviews,* 1891–97," *Journalism Quart.,* 49 (1972), 692–696, 716, and *Albert Shaw of the Review of Reviews: An Intellectual Biography* (1974). Frank Luther Mott, *A History of American Magazines,* IV, 657–664 (1957); *Grinnell Herald,* June 1, 1934; *N.Y. Times,* June 26, 28, 1947; *Am. Hist. Rev.,* 53 (1947), 220–221; *Who Was Who in Am.;* and the Albert Shaw Papers at the N.Y. Public Lib.]
LLOYD J. GRAYBAR

SHEAN, ALBERT (May 12, 1868-Aug. 12, 1949), burlesque and vaudeville comedian, later a character actor, was born, according to most accounts, in Dornum, Germany, near Hannover, the son of Louis (or Lafe) Schoenberg and Fanny Schoenberg. Before immigrating to the United States about 1876, his Jewish parents had been beergarden performers, his father a magician and ventriloquist and his mother a harpist. All four children, two boys and two girls, were to perform on stage at some time, but only Albert was to have a full career. His sister Minna, however, was to pass on the family tradition to her sons, the Marx Brothers, and to become their promoter and business manager.

While growing up on New York City's Lower East Side, Albert worked as an usher and pants presser. At sixteen he organized the Manhattan Comedy Four and began touring the five-and-ten-cent burlesque houses and museums. It was at this time that he dropped his family name and billed himself as "Al Shean," a name he later adopted legally. When, after fourteen years, the quartet disbanded, he joined with one Charles L. Warren to romp through the cheap theatres in a two-act burlesque entitled *Quo Vadis, Upside Down*.

Shean was over forty before he teamed up with Ed Gallagher in 1910 to form the famous act of Gallagher and Shean. For four years they played together in vaudeville, burlesque, and a musical revue, *The Big Banner Show*, with considerable success, but then broke up with unexplained ill feeling on both sides. In 1920, however, under pressure from Shean's sister and sometimes business manager, Minna Marx, and attracted by a generous offer from the Shuberts to star at the Winter Garden in the revue *Cinderella on Broadway*, Gallagher and Shean reunited and went on to tremendous success. They signed for the Ziegfeld *Follies* of 1922, which was to run into the following year, an unprecedented sixty-seven weeks. Primarily responsible for this success was their theme song ("Absolutely, Mr. Gallagher?" "Positively, Mr. Shean!"), which caught the fancy of audience after audience. Shean had composed the melody, later picked up by dance bands across the country, while the patter-song lyrics had been written by Bryan Foy. The Victor company quickly turned out a best-selling record of the song, new verses to fit the refrain were improvised by the score, and so many imitations of Gallagher and Shean appeared in vaudeville that the Keith circuit prohibited more than one on any single bill. In spite of this popular following, Gallagher and Shean dissolved their act in 1925, four years before Gallagher's death.

Although Shean continued for several years in vaudeville with other straight men, he began to develop a solid reputation as a character actor. Among his stage roles were those of Stonewall Moskowitz in *Betsy* (1926), Hans Wagner in *The Prince of Pilsen* (1930), Dr.

Walther Lessing in the Oscar Hammerstein–Jerome Kern musical *Music in the Air* (1932), and the title role in *Father Malachy's Miracle* (1937). Of his performance as the simple priest —his first straight part—Brooks Atkinson wrote, "Al Shean, graduate of vaudeville and the revue rowdy-dowdies, plays the part with a warmth and sincerity that make this imaginative comedy something to be cherished" (*New York Times*, Sept. 18, 1937). Short and apple-cheeked, with expressive brown eyes, Shean also appeared in more than twenty-five motion pictures, including the film version of *Music in the Air* (1934), *Hitch Hike to Heaven* (1936), *The Prisoner of Zenda* (1937), *Too Hot to Handle* (1938), and *Ziegfeld Girl* (1941).

On Feb. 15, 1891, Shean married Johanna Davidson; they had one child, Lawrence. Toward his eminently successful nephews, the Marx Brothers, Shean played the role of benevolent uncle, giving freely of his support, both financial and theatrical, during their early years in show business. He had a comfortable home in Mount Vernon, N.Y., and a summer fishing camp at Haines Landing, Maine. He died of a heart condition at the age of eighty-one in New York City. His funeral was conducted by a rabbi at the Riverside Memorial Chapel, and he was buried in Mount Pleasant Cemetery, Hawthorne, N.Y.

[*N.Y. Times* obituary, Aug. 13, 1949; *Internat. Motion Picture Almanac*, 1942–1943; *Who's Who in the Theatre* (10th ed., 1947); Abel Green and Joe Laurie, Jr., *Show Biz* (1951); Harpo Marx and Rowland Barber, *Harpo Speaks!* (1961); Kyle Crichton, *The Marx Brothers* (1950); *Life*, Jan. 3, 1938, pp. 20–21; *N.Y. Herald Tribune*, Feb. 9, 1941 (on his fiftieth wedding anniversary).]

ALBERT F. MCLEAN

SHELDON, CHARLES MONROE (Feb. 26, 1857–Feb. 24, 1946), clergyman and author, was born in Wellsville, N.Y., the son of Stewart Sheldon, a Congregational minister, and Sarah (Ward) Sheldon, both of Scots-Irish ancestry. In the bracing moral atmosphere of the Congregational parsonage, Charles had a peripatetic boyhood as his father served successive churches in New York, Missouri, Rhode Island, and Michigan. When he was ten the family moved to a farm near Yankton, S.Dak. In later years, Sheldon fondly recalled his adolescent years on the farm, with its hard work, self-reliance, close family life, and clear-cut moral verities. Following the example of a much admired maternal uncle (also a Congregational minister), he entered Phillips Academy, Andover, Mass., and graduated in 1879; he received his degree from Brown University in 1883. He worked his way through both preparatory school and college, in part through teaching night school in a working-class section of Providence. Although he was strongly attracted to a career in journalism and received a tempting job offer from Lyman Abbott of the *Outlook,* he decided in favor of his father's vocation, entered Andover Theological Seminary, and received the B.D. in 1886.

His first pastorate, following his ordination in 1886, was a Congregational church in Waterbury, Vt. In January 1889, Sheldon became minister of the newly formed Central Congregational Church of Topeka, Kans. On May 20, 1891, he married Mary Abby Merriam, a banker's daughter whom he had met during his Waterbury days and whose family had also moved to Topeka. Their son and only child, Merriam Ward Sheldon, was born in 1897.

Topeka, originally settled by Yankee abolitionists, was in the 1890's a mirror of the stresses confronting American society in this era of industrialization and urban growth. As an important rail and shipping center, the city included a large immigrant and working-class population as well as a black ghetto called "Tennesseetown." Feeling intensely his isolation from what he called "the great world of labor," Sheldon dramatized the problems and moral challenges of the modern industrial city in a series of stories which he read to his Sunday evening congregation and which were later published serially in the *Advance,* a small Congregational paper in Chicago. Two of these series appeared in book form as *Richard Bruce* (1892) and *The Crucifixion of Philip Strong* (1894). These efforts attracted little notice until the appearance, in 1897, of Sheldon's novel *In His Steps.*

Serialized in the *Advance* and then published in paperback form, *In His Steps* sold well from the beginning, and when a copyright defect opened the door to competing editions, both in the United States and abroad, sales soared into the millions. Although Sheldon's own later estimate of 30,000,000 was exaggerated, the more likely figure of 6,000,000 still places the book among the all-time best sellers. (Only one publisher, Grosset and Dunlap, ever paid Sheldon more than token royalties.) The book was made into a movie in 1936, and over seventy years after its first publication it still appeared on several publisher's lists.

The remarkable success of *In His Steps,* all the more surprising because of the book's lack of literary merit, seems linked to its appearance at a moment when the Social Gospel movement was at its apogee, and when millions of native-born middle-class Americans were deeply disturbed by the dislocations that were transforming their world. Within a simple narrative framework—several members of a comfortable Protestant church in a Midwestern railroad town pledge to guide their lives by the question "What Would Jesus Do?"—the novel dealt with such issues as slums, class tensions, political corruption, corporate dishonesty, and labor injustice. The most deeply felt passages describe the efforts of the emotionally pent-up middle-class characters to establish vital human contact with a working class that is portrayed as at once menacing and vivifying. *In His Steps* touched an exposed nerve, and the sales statistics testified to the intensity of the concerns it articulated.

Though Sheldon never repeated the success of *In His Steps,* his fame as an author provided a stepping-stone to a long and productive career as a religious publicist. Of his lifetime total of more than fifty books, most were inspirational and rather superficial works of social comment from a liberal Protestant point of view. He also wrote occasionally for secular periodicals such as the *Independent* and the *Atlantic.* In March 1900, at the invitation of the publisher, he edited the *Topeka Daily Capital* for one week, stressing uplifting news and banning stories and advertisements he considered objectionable. Through shrewd national promotion the paper's circulation rose to more than 300,000 during this week, but efforts to continue the experiment met the united resistance of the newspaper's business and reportorial staffs.

From the 1890's on, Sheldon was also in demand as a lecturer, particularly on the theme of prohibition, which figured prominently in *In His Steps.* He toured the British Isles on behalf of this reform in 1900 and again in 1917-1918. In 1914-1915, completing a three years' leave of absence from his Topeka pulpit, he was a member of a prohibition "Flying Squadron" that spoke in 247 American cities in 243 days. He resigned from his Topeka pastorate in 1919 following a severe illness and for five years (1920-1925) was editor-in-chief of the *Christian Herald,* a nondenominational Protestant monthly published in New York City; later he was a contributing editor. After 1933 he turned his attention from prohibition to pacifism and the Protestant ecumenical movement. In 1936 he endorsed his fellow Kansan Alfred M. Landon for president.

Snowy-haired and erect, Charles Sheldon enjoyed a vigorous and active old age, with winters in Florida his only concession to advancing years. His death in Topeka's Starmont Hospital two days before his eighty-ninth birthday was the result of a cerebral hemorrhage. He and his wife, who survived to 1950, were buried in Mount Hope Cemetery, Topeka.

[The autobiography, *Charles M. Sheldon: His Life Story* (1925), is genial but vague. See also Sheldon's *The Hist. of "In His Steps"* (privately printed, 23 pp., 1938); C. Howard Hopkins, *The Rise of the Social Gospel in Am. Protestantism, 1865–1915,* pp. 141–144 (1940); Frank L. Mott, *Golden Multitudes: The Story of Best Sellers in the U.S.,* pp. 193–197 (1947); Paul S. Boyer, *"In His Steps*: A Reappraisal," *Am. Quart.,* Spring 1971; John W. Ripley, "Another Look at the Rev. Mr. Charles M. Sheldon's Christian Daily Newspaper," *Kans. Hist. Quart.,* Spring 1965, and "The Strange Story of . . . *In His Steps,*" *ibid.,* Autumn 1968; L. H. Robbins, "Militant Pacifism," *N.Y. Times,* Dec. 3, 1939, sec. 7; see obituaries, *ibid.,* Feb. 25, 1946, *Topeka Daily Capital,* Feb. 25, 1946, and *Publishers' Weekly,* Mar. 2, 1946; *Nat. Cyc. Am. Biog.,* XXXIV, 367–368; information from John W. Ripley, Shawnee County Hist. Soc., Topeka. Of the many editions of *In His Steps,* the most useful is a reprint of the original serial version, with supplementary articles and photographs, published by the Shawnee County Hist. Soc. as no. 44 of its *Bull.* (1967).]

PAUL BOYER

SHEPARD, JAMES EDWARD (Nov. 3, 1875–Oct. 6, 1947), college president, was born in Raleigh, N.C., the eldest of the twelve children of Augustus Shepard and Harriet E. (Whitted) Shepard. His father was pastor of the White Rock Baptist Church in Raleigh, an active community leader, and lifelong Republican, loyalties that his son would retain throughout his life.

Shepard graduated from Shaw University in 1894 as a registered pharmacist and worked for a year in a pharmacy in Damill, Va., before returning to Durham. In 1898 he founded, with John Merrick, Dr. A. M. Moore, and W. G. Pearson, an insurance company later called the North Carolina Mutual Life Insurance Company. Some years later, he also founded and became a trustee of the Mechanics and Farmers Bank of Durham. During 1899–1900 Shepard served as a clerk in the recorder's office in Washington, D.C., and then moved to Raleigh, where he was deputy collector of the Internal Revenue Service until 1905. His real vocation began to emerge between 1905 and 1910 while serving as field superintendent of the International Sunday School Association.

In the course of his work with Negro ministers throughout the South in organizing Sunday schools, Shepard realized that the ministers did not fully comprehend their potential for leadership, because of their lack of education. In 1910 he founded the National Religious Training School and Chatauqua "for the colored race," to give six-week courses to ministers and teachers. By 1915, however, the school had run so deeply into debt that it was sold at auction but was purchased by Mrs. Russell Sage and was reorganized as the National Training School for teachers, still under Shepard's leadership. In 1923 Shepard won state support, and the school again changed its name, to Durham State Normal School. In 1925 it became the first state-supported liberal arts college for Negroes and was renamed North Carolina College for Negroes (now North Carolina Central University). Shepard served as president until his death in 1947. During his tenure, he increased the physical plant to an estimated value of $2 million and annual appropriations of an equivalent amount. In 1939 he won approval from the legislature for a graduate program, and added the School of Law in 1940 and the School of Library Science in 1941.

In leadership and ideology, Shepard more closely resembled Booker T. Washington than W. E. B. DuBois. Like Washington, he was a leader who functioned well in both black and white communities, in state and nation, acting as liaison between the races. Although a proponent of self-help, he did not believe that Negroes should concentrate only on achieving agricultural and industrial skills; like DuBois, he was a champion of liberal and higher education for the "talented tenth," a phrase he himself would never use. He was neither an integrationist nor a crusader for civil rights, and if he belonged to the NAACP, he did not publicize the fact.

Shepard was nationally recognized for his contributions to education and was honored by degrees of D.D., Muskingum College (1910); M.A., Selma University (1912); and Litt.D., Howard University (1925). His campus office was a focal point for Negro education in North Carolina and was visited by the foremost educational and political leaders. Active in numerous community, state, and national organizations, he was for many years Grand Master of the Negro Masons in North Carolina, Grand Patron of the Eastern Star, secretary of Finances for the Knights of Pythias, a trustee of the Lincoln Hospital, and a trustee of the Lincoln School for Nurses in Durham. He belonged to the North Carolina Medical Association and, from 1909 to 1914, was president of the Interdenominational Sunday School Association. He traveled in Europe, Africa, and Asia in his capacity as educator and Sunday school leader.

Although distinguished in appearance and of serious mien, Shepard was "a master of human relations." On Nov. 7, 1895, he married Annie Day Robinson, the daughter of a Seattle, Wash., cabinetmaker; they had two daughters, Marjorie Augusta and Annie Day. Shepard died of a stroke in Durham, N.C., four weeks before his seventy-second birthday. He had won the love of his students, and the respect of the community and state was evidenced by the eulogies in the General Assembly of the state of North Carolina and the tributes in state and local newspapers.

[*Who's Who in Am.*, 1942–1943; Charles F. Helson, "Life of Doctor James E. Shephard," *Durham* (N.C.) *Morning Herald*, Apr. 14, 1940; *Nat. Cyc. Am. Biog.*, XXXIII, 33; *School and Society*, Oct. 18, 1947; Elizabeth Irene Seay, "A History of a North Carolina College for Negroes" (unpublished master's thesis, Duke Univ., 1941).]
DAVID D. VAN TASSEL

SHEPPARD, SAMUEL EDWARD (July 29, 1882–Sept. 29, 1948), chemist and photographic scientist, was born at Hither Green, Kent, England, the son of Samuel Sheppard, a market gardener, and Emily Mary (Taplin) Sheppard. He attended a preparatory school at Deal, in Kent, and later a technical school, St. Dunstan's College, at Catford, Kent. There he was a classmate of Charles Edward Kenneth Mees, with whom he was to maintain a close professional relationship for most of his life. The two went on in 1900 to University College, London, where they worked under the chemist Sir William Ramsay. Ramsay was a strong advocate of granting degrees for research, and Sheppard and Mees were the first students admitted on this basis. Since both were interested in the theory of photographic processes, Ramsay suggested that they undertake a joint program of research. They began by repeating and extending the investigations of Ferdinand Hurter and Vero Charles Driffield, who had carried on pioneering research on the sensitivity of photographic plates. Sheppard centered his efforts on the chemical dynamics of development, latent image formation, and the structure of the image. Their preliminary results earned each man a B.Sc. degree in 1903, and, following three years of further research, each received the D.Sc. in 1906. Their findings were published as *Investigations on the Theory of the Photographic Process* (1907).

With the aid of an 1851 Exhibition Scholarship, Sheppard continued his research in photochemistry at Marburg University in Germany, under Franz Richarz and Karl Schaum, and at the Sorbonne in Paris under Victor Henri. At both institutions he studied the sensitizing action of dyes, particularly the new isocyanine and carbocyanine dyes. Henri stimulated his interest in colloid chemistry, and Sheppard was the first to apply spectrophotometry to differentiating true and colloidal solutions.

Meanwhile, Mees had joined the photographic manufacturing firm of Wratten and Wainwright in Croydon, in Surrey, and in 1910 Sheppard joined him there. Both men left in 1912, Mees to head the new Kodak Research Laboratory at Rochester, N.Y., at the invitation of George Eastman, and Sheppard to enter the School of Agriculture at Cambridge University in pursuit of an earlier interest in agricultural chemistry. The following year, however, Mees called Sheppard to Rochester to join the new laboratory as a colloid and physical chemist. He was to remain with the Kodak Laboratory until his retirement in 1948, becoming chief of the departments of physical, inorganic, and analytical chemistry in 1920, and, four years later, assistant director of research.

Sheppard's work can be grouped into nonphotographic and photographic categories. In the former, one of his notable contributions was the development of colloidal fuels during World War I. He found that coal powder, a waste product from handling coal, could be dispersed as a stable suspension in fuel oil, by the use of resin soaps, to the extent of 40 percent, adding its fuel value to that of the oil. In 1921 he turned his attention to the electroplating of rubber and rubber compounds; his patents and processes were consolidated with those of others in the American Anode Company. Sheppard also developed concepts on the relationship between chemical constitution and colloidal behavior which involved studies of the viscosity, plasticity, and elasticity of solvated colloids, such as cellulose esters, gelatin, and rubber; studies on the work of adhesion at solid-liquid interfaces; and studies on thin film formation. These researches contributed to the notion of molecular individuality in high-molecular bodies, showing that colloidal behavior depended on the size and constitution of the molecules rather than on degrees of mechanical dispersion.

In the photographic field, Sheppard was responsible more than any other single person for elucidating the theory of the photographic process. In his first five years at the Kodak Laboratory, he was mainly concerned with the physicochemical properties of gelatin, the medium that contains the sensitive materials in photography. He measured the viscosity of gelatin in solution, its strength, elastic properties, setting and melting points, and drying and swelling of gelatin in the jelly and dry states. This work led in 1929 to a procedure for making a standardized gelatin.

But it was in his research on the factors determining photographic sensitivity in silver halide–gelatin "emulsions" that Sheppard made his most significant contribution. He started with an attempt to find a relation between the distribution of sizes of the silver halide crystals and the response of the sensitive material; from this his research led him to seek the nature of the action of light on the halides and the reasons for their special response. He developed a "concentration speck" theory that related sensitivity to discontinuities in the lattice of the crystal, presumably caused by some foreign substance. It was known that different gelatins produced emulsions with differing sensitivity. By systematic study and painstaking analysis, Sheppard found that traces of labile organic sulfur bodies in gelatin were the cause of high sensitivity. This led to direct sensitizing of the emulsion by means of a related compound, allylthiourea, and to the discovery that the "foreign substance" produced and giving the sensitivity was silver sulfide as minute specks in the silver halide crystals.

Sheppard's discovery had a profound effect on the photographic industry, influencing all subseqent investigations of how film exposure works and contributing to the development of higher film speeds. The discovery won him immediate recognition; he was the recipient of the Progress Medal of the Royal Photographic Society in England (1928), the Adelsköld Medal of the Swedish Photographic Society (1929), and the Nichols Medal of the American Chemical Society (1930). Sheppard's later research dealt with a wide range of matters, including photovoltaic effects (the electrical response of silver halide to light), the physicochemical properties of film supports, the nature of development and of dye sensitizing, and absorption of dyes to crystals and their absorption spectra in relation to the resonance structure of the dyes.

The rich diversity of Sheppard's work has been credited by his associate, Mees, to the combination of his driving curiosity and the challenge of the complex field of photography,

replete with facts for which the current knowledge provided no explanation. Alone or with co-authors, he published nearly 200 scientific papers and nine books, beginning with *Photo-Chemistry* (1914), and took out more than sixty patents. Sheppard was fluent in several languages, including Latin. Socially, he was a charming, tolerant companion. On Nov. 27, 1912, he married Eveline Lucy Ground, of Wisbech, Cambridgeshire, England. They had one child, Samuel Roger. In his last few years, Sheppard lost the sight of one eye from glaucoma and suffered from heart trouble. He resigned his laboratory post in January 1948, and died later that year in Rochester, at the age of sixty-six. His remains were cremated.

[C. E. K. Mees in *Jour. of the Chemical Soc.* (London), Jan. 1949; John I. Crabtree in *Jour. of the Photographic Soc. of America*, Nov. 1946; *Photographic Jour.*, Jan. 1949; Louis W. Sipley, *Photography's Great Inventors* (Am. Museum of Photography, Phila., 1965); *Who's Who in America*, 1946–1947.]

WALTER CLARK

SHORT, WALTER CAMPBELL (Mar. 30, 1880–Sept. 3, 1949), army officer, was born in Fillmore, Ill., the third son and fifth of six children of Hiram Spait Short, a physician, and Sarah Minerva (Stokes) Short. Both parents were Scots-Irish, the father having migrated from North Carolina before the Civil War. Walter was reared a Methodist, his mother's faith. After preliminary education in public schools, he entered the University of Illinois, from which he received a B.A. degree in 1901. He then taught mathematics at Western Military Academy until, in 1902, he accepted a commission in the United States Army.

Short's army career began with the 25th Infantry at Fort Reno, Okla., where he first met another new officer, George C. Marshall, with whom he later served in France. Between tours in Alaska and into Mexico with the punitive expedition of 1916-1917, Short served as secretary of the School of Musketry at Fort Sill, Okla., and while there married, on Nov. 4, 1914, Isabel Dean of Oklahoma City. They had one child, Walter Dean.

With America's entry into World War I, Short went to France with the 1st Division in June 1917. He held a series of increasingly responsible training positions while rising to the temporary rank of colonel. He won the Distinguished Service Medal for "conspicuous service in inspecting and reporting upon front-line conditions" and for his efficiency in training machine-gun units behind the lines. Returning to the United States in 1919, Short taught at the General Service Schools at Fort Leavenworth, Kans., where he wrote a textbook, *Employment of Machine Guns* (1922). He was later co-inventor of a low-slung machine-gun carrier.

Short was graduated from the School of the Line in 1921, and from the Army War College four years later. Following various troop and staff assignments and another tour at Leavenworth, he obtained his first regimental command, that of the 6th Infantry, when he was fifty-four. He was promoted to the rank of brigadier general in 1936 during a brief assignment as assistant commandant of the Infantry School at Fort Benning, Ga.; in 1939 he took command of a division. As America mobilized in 1940, Short stood out as one of the army's best training men, a reputation Chief of Staff Marshall recognized by assigning him to command provisional corps in maneuvers during 1940 and the 1st Corps later the same year. In February 1941 Short took charge of the army's Hawaiian Department, with the rank of lieutenant general.

In Hawaii, Short exerted himself with his customary industry and thoroughness, giving particular attention to improving air defenses. Serious concern in early 1941 over a possible surprise attack on the Pacific Fleet and its Pearl Harbor base gradually faded during the year. Both in Washington and in Hawaii it was generally assumed that the Japanese would not dare risk a strong carrier-based air attack on Oahu while the American fleet was based there. The real danger seemed to Short and others to lie in the half of Oahu's population that was of Japanese descent. Actually, the Japanese attacked on Dec. 7, 1941, with such force that a full alert of the army defenders would not have made much difference in the amount of damage done, although merely establishing a full alert might have warned off the enemy's striking force and probably would have saved General Short from much blame.

After the attack Short quickly instituted a tight military control of Hawaii and set in motion measures that greatly strengthened the army's defenses. The success of the surprise attack had stunned the nation. President Roosevelt, on December 15 and 16, appointed an investigating commission headed by Supreme Court Justice Owen J. Roberts and on December 17 directed the relief from duty of both Short and the fleet commander, Admiral Husband E. Kimmel. The commission's report, in January 1942, accused the Hawaiian com-

manders of poor judgment and dereliction of duty. Short submitted a request for retirement that Chief of Staff Marshall could use if he wished, and at the president's order Short and Kimmel were retired on Feb. 28, 1942, "without condonation of any offense or prejudice to any future disciplinary action"—a phrase leaving open the way to court-martial. While awaiting his day in court, Short worked as traffic manager for the Ford Motor Company in Dallas, Tex., which remained his home thereafter.

Short finally received the opportunity to testify publicly in early 1946 before the congressional committee investigating Pearl Harbor. He readily acknowledged, as he had in earlier secret testimony, that he had made the wrong decision about an alert before the attack; but he denied that his estimate of the situation was the result of any carelessness on his part or on the part of his military associates in Hawaii. He also believed that he had acted in accordance with his instructions, that Washington had withheld significant information from him that might have persuaded him to act differently, and that in effect the army had made him its scapegoat for the disaster. In retrospect it appears that General Short's chief failing was that he shared the general blindness of all Americans in authority to Japan's military potential in 1941. Heart trouble led to Short's complete retirement after the congressional inquiry, and he died in Dallas three years later, at the age of sixty-nine, of heart failure brought on by emphysema. He was buried in Arlington National Cemetery.

[The Nat. Arch. and Records Service has custody of Short's official army correspondence; material in the reference collection of the Office of the Chief of Military Hist., Dept. of the Army, records his military service. Among biographical reference works the most useful accounts are those in the *Nat. Cyc. Am. Biog.*, XL, 14, and *Current Biog.*, 1946, which has a portrait. Short's Hawaiian assignment and its aftermath are covered in Stetson Conn et al., *Guarding the U.S. and Its Outposts* (1964); Forrest C. Pogue, *George C. Marshall: Ordeal and Hope, 1939–1942* (1966); and the many volumes of *Pearl Harbor Attack* (1946), including voluminous testimony by Short himself. In a letter of Nov. 19, 1972, Col. Walter D. Short (USA Ret.), the general's son, furnished useful personal and family data.]

STETSON CONN

SIMONS, ALGIE MARTIN (Oct. 9, 1870–Mar. 11, 1950), socialist theorist, journalist, and politician; personnel management expert; medical economist, was born in North Freedom, Wis., the oldest of the three sons and a daughter of Horace Buttoph Simons and Linda (Blackman) Simons. His father was a farmer, as were many of his forebears, of English and Scottish stock, who had settled in America in colonial times and had moved westward through succeeding generations. Facing the hardships of the frontier, none of them, including his father, met with prosperity. The family's religious background was Baptist.

Simons attended the public schools of Sauk County, Wis., graduating from the Baraboo High School in 1891. He entered the University of Wisconsin, where he became a student of Frederick Jackson Turner, a research assistant to the economist Richard T. Ely, and a well-known and able campus debater. While at the university, Simons also served as a reporter for the *Madison Democrat* and as the local correspondent for the *Chicago Record*. He received a B.L. degree from the university in 1895 and was subsequently elected to Phi Beta Kappa.

Immediately after his graduation, Simons was employed as a social worker for the University of Cincinnati Settlement. A year later (1896) he went to work for the Stockyards District of the United (later Associated) Charities in Chicago, which assigned him the task of organizing relief efforts for the stockyards district, then in its third winter of severe economic depression. His pamphlet, *Packingtown* (1899), which vividly described the abominable conditions he discovered, attracted little public attention, but provided a major source for Upton Sinclair's muckraking novel, *The Jungle* (1904).

In June 1897, Simons married (Eleanor) May Wood of Baraboo. They had two children: Laurence Wood, who died in infancy, and Miriam Eleanor. That same year, discouraged by the difficulty of bringing about reform through conventional political means, Simons joined the Chicago local of the Socialist Labor party (SLP), and in 1899 he became editor of the *Worker's Call,* a weekly newspaper of the SLP. Over the next decade in Chicago, besides being elected a member of the Socialist party's National Executive Committee (1905), he successively edited the *International Socialist Review* (1900-1906) and the *Chicago Daily Socialist* (1906-1910). But his attempt in 1910—along with other moderate Socialists—to effect an alliance between the Socialist party and the left wing of the American trade union movement caused a furor that cost him both his seat on the National Executive Committee and his editorship of the *Daily Socialist.*

Abandoning political activity, Simons moved to Girard, Kans., where he became editor of the *Coming Nation* (1910-1913), a socialist literary magazine. In 1911 he published *Social Forces in American History,* the first Marxist interpretation of the American past. Elaborating upon ideas he had first presented in party pamphlets and articles several years before, Simons declared that the American nation, far from being a democracy of, by, and for the people, was really designed to exalt capitalists at the expense of the working class. It is for *Social Forces* that historians have chiefly remembered Simons.

The years before World War I were the most productive of Simons' life. During this period he moved from the extreme left wing of the Socialist movement, the Marxism of Daniel DeLeon, to the right wing, exemplified by Victor Berger and the Social Democracy of Milwaukee. In 1913, Simons moved to Milwaukee, where the Socialists were enjoying considerable success, and became editor of the *Milwaukee Leader* (1913-1916). In addition to his editing, he was one of the principal theoreticians and political leaders of the socialist movement. He was especially convinced of the need to develop a socialism suited to the American environment and responsive to the distinctive needs of the American proletariat. which he defined to include land-owning farmers as well as industrial labor. In articles in *The American Farmer* (1902) and in the Socialist party platform's planks on agriculture, Simons had, over the years, attempted to make the Socialist party a desirable political alternative for rural Americans. In 1917, along with many other Socialists, Simons broke with the party over the issue of World War I. He viewed the war's outbreak as demonstrating the ineffectiveness of internationalism, and he fully supported America's entry into it, a position that led to his expulsion from the Socialist party. Simons thereupon became an organizer for the Wisconsin Defense League and when, a few months later, this organization transformed itself into the ultra-patriotic Wisconsin Loyalty Legion, he was named head of its literature department. In that year, also, he helped weld other pro-war Socialists into the Social Democratic League, and the following year he led the league-sponsored American Socialist and Labor Mission to Europe. Modeled after a similar undertaking by Samuel Gompers and the American Federation of Labor, the mission sought to rekindle waning enthusiasm for the war among Allied radicals and set up the framework for a new Socialist international.

By the time of the armistice, Simons' disenchantment with politics was complete. The exigencies of war, he believed, had done more to fulfill socialist goals than all that the propaganda efforts, election campaigns, and Socialist officeholders had done in twenty years. His valedictory to radical politics, "The Uselessness of Protest Parties," appeared in the *American Federationist* for April 1920. The keys to the future, Simons concluded in *The Vision for Which We Fought* (1919), lay in administration and efficiency, not in parliaments and class struggles. He therefore turned his interests to scientific management and industrial psychology. In 1920 he began teaching a course in industrial management in the extension division of the University of Wisconsin, and he took a position as personnel management expert for Leffingwell-Ream, management engineers. In 1921 he published his first book based on his new career, *Personnel Relations in Industry*. When Leffingwell-Ream dissolved in 1921, he became secretary of the American School in Chicago and remained there until the onset of the depression in 1929. From 1930 until his retirement in 1944, Simons did research on the economic aspects of medical care, first for the American College of Dentists, and then as assistant director of the Bureau of Medical Economics of the American Medical Association (AMA). His writings for the AMA had a single theme: health insurance of any kind, under any direction but that of private insurance companies, must be fought tirelessly.

Simons died from complications of injuries sustained in an automobile accident, in New Martinsville, W.Va., where he had gone to live with his daughter and son-in-law. He was buried in the family plot in Baraboo, Wis.

Publicly, Simons, who was of medium height and build and wore a dark mustache and beard for much of his life, was a vain and irascible man. He had great intellectual ability and physical energy, which he enlisted totally in whatever cause he was pleading at any particular time. He grew extraordinarily angry with people who disagreed with him. Privately, he was a kind, loving husband and father, who worried about the conflicts among his family responsibilities, his social conscience, and his political ambitions.

Simons never entirely repudiated the values of midwestern rural America. He retained a distrust of "the East" that erupted at Socialist party conventions as it did among Wisconsin farmers whom he had doubtless heard curse the evil bankers of Wall Street. Frederick Jackson Turner and Richard T. Ely did the most to shape Simons' thinking, but Simons' own background had prepared him to share Turner's appreciation of the pioneer farmers' role in American development. Simons was correct in his assessment that Marxism, to attain success in America, had to be tied to traditions and institutions that were characteristically American. But he underestimated the vigor of the life to which he sought to attach this foreign graft. Socialism was choked out, and Simons went on to other careers.

Although Simons played a major role in developing the agricultural policies of the Socialist party, he was not parochial in his interests. He wrote many articles designed to familiarize Americans with the main developments of European socialism, and for thirty years maintained contacts with leading British and continental Socialists. He translated several of the works of Karl Kautsky into English. Simons also was, throughout his life, concerned with the ways industrial and urban forces were altering political and social relationships. His interest in industrial psychology and personnel management exemplified that concern in the 1920's, just as his writings on urban slums and working conditions in the stockyards had done twenty years before.

[The Algie M. and May Simons papers are at the State Hist. Soc. of Wis. The collection also contains a portrait photograph of Simons and several newspaper photos that include him. Important Simons letters are also to be found in the papers of Daniel DeLeon, Richard T. Ely, Morris Hillquit, Henry Demarest Lloyd and the Loyalty Legion, all at the State Hist. Soc. of Wis. The Milwaukee Socialist party papers at the Milwaukee County Hist. Soc. and the Socialist Party Collect. at Duke Univ. Lib. also contain relevant material. Many articles by Simons appear in the *International Socialist Review*, the *Coming Nation*, and other Socialist periodicals. In addition to the books mentioned above, Simons wrote eight pamphlets in the Pocket Library of Socialism, and *Class Struggles in American History* (1903), *Production Management*, 2 vols. (1922), *Success through Vocational Guidance*, written with James McKinney (1922), and *The Way of Health Insurance*, written with Nathan Sinai (1932). Kent Kreuter and Gretchen von Loewe Kreuter, *An American Dissenter, the Life of Algie Martin Simons, 1870–1950* (1969), is a full biography. William Glaser, "Algie Martin Simons and Marxism in America," *Miss. Valley Hist. Rev.*, 41 (1954), 419-434, deals with that aspect of his career. Samuel Haber, *Efficiency and Uplift* (1964), has a long section on Simons' role in the movement for scientific management.]

KENT KREUTER
GRETCHEN VON LOEWE KREUTER

SIMONS, HENRY CALVERT (Oct. 9, 1899-June 19, 1946), economist, was born in Virden, Ill., the younger of two children and only son of Henry Calvert Simons, a lawyer, and Mollie Willis (Sims) Simons. The boy's paternal grandfather, George W. Simons, had come from Brighton, England, in the early nineteenth century; after studying music in Cincinnati and marrying Sarah Calvert of Kentucky he had settled in Virden. Originally a church organist, he became a successful grain miller and merchant. Mollie Sims was also of Kentucky background, although born in Illinois.

Simons graduated from the Virden high school and the University of Michigan (B.A. 1920), where he specialized in economics. For the next seven years he taught at the University of Iowa, initially as teaching assistant, then as instructor and assistant professor. During summers and the academic year 1925-1926 he pursued graduate study, first at Columbia (1922) and then at the University of Chicago. At Iowa Simons came under the influence of Frank H. Knight, and he followed that economist to the University of Chicago faculty in 1927. There Simons remained for the rest of his life, becoming associate professor in 1942 and professor in 1945.

Until 1933 Simons was leading a life that could surely be called dilatory. Of undisputed intellectual brilliance, he had not completed his doctorate (and never did); a distinguished writer, he had published only three book reviews in a decade. Yet it is obvious from the range and depth of his subsequent writings, beginning with a famous, unpublished memorandum on antidepression policy (1933), that the main lines of his thought were fully developed in the 1920's. The Great Depression, which destroyed so many careers, galvanized Simons'. Aroused by the nation's calamity and by the threat to political liberty he saw in the New Deal's economic planning, he devised a highly personal program of economic reform.

The initial, yet most comprehensive, formulation of this program was a powerfully written pamphlet, *A Positive Program for Laissez Faire: Some Proposals for a Liberal Economic Policy* (1934). Simons advocated a strong, decentralized economy, achieved by a vigorous antitrust policy and statutory limitations on corporate size and reinforced by free international trade. Where competition was unattainable, industries were socialized (preferably by local governments). He was as strongly egalitarian as most socialists, and he proposed a radical reform of the tax system under which highly progressive personal income taxes would become the mainspring of the revenue system.

The details of Simons' tax proposals were spelled out in a work that has become a classic of public finance, *Personal Income Taxation* (1938), subsequently elaborated in *Federal Tax Reform* (1950). Although he viewed personal income taxation primarily as a means of reducing income inequality, he made proposals that transcended this approach. He had a comprehensive income concept (including in income capital gains, gifts, etc.), and he made an influential case for income averaging. This program was the intellectual source of the famous Carter Commission on Taxation in Canada, whose proposals led to a restructuring of that nation's federal taxation much along Simons' recommendations.

Simons also argued with great force for the guidance of monetary policy by fixed rules rather than by administrative discretion, with the goal of establishing a stable price level. Under the gold standard, the rules were provided by the system itself. With a managed currency, the same goal could be achieved by restructuring and simplifying monetary institutions and thus strengthening control over money flows. He proposed that the federal government take primary responsibility for determining the money supply, reducing commercial banks to money warehouses through a 100 percent reserve requirement. He also suggested reducing the variety of private forms of ownership and debt, as well as eliminating short-term governmental debt. Simons' natural antagonism to such nationalistic devices as tariffs, quotas, and exchange controls made him an internationalist in outlook. He was an early interventionist during World War II, and he envisioned a postwar federation of nations bound together by a commitment to both peace and free trade.

Simons does not fit neatly into the traditional categories of reform. His profound fear of the coercive propensities of an all-powerful state was shared by others as different as conservatives and anarchists. Yet he had a large faith in the competence and fairness of the state, as witnessed by his willingness to grant it ownership of public utilities, regulation of advertising, and administration of an egalitarian tax system. The greatest gap in his whole system, indeed, was the absence of a coherent, empirically testable theory of the state, although his posthumous essay, "Political Credo," has brilliant political hypotheses.

Simons was a major contributor (along with Frank Knight) to the formation of the "Chicago School" of economists, whose members share a belief in the importance of free markets and the need for quasi-constitutional rules to achieve stable monetary policy. On May 30, 1941, he married Marjorie Kimball Powell; they had one child, Mary Powell. Simons died in

Chicago at the age of forty-six of an accidental overdose of sleeping pills.

[The facts of Simons' life were derived from relatives, university records, and his correspondence and memoranda, which are at the School of Law of the Univ. of Chicago. A posthumous collection of his essays, *Economic Policy for a Free Society* (1948), contains his complete bibliography. His monetary theories are discussed by Milton Friedman in *Jour. of Law and Economics,* Oct. 1967. A photograph and a general survey is in John Davenport, "The Testament of Henry Simons," *Fortune,* Sept. 1946; see also obituary by H. G. Lewis in *Am. Economic Rev.,* Sept. 1946.]

GEORGE J. STIGLER

SMEDLEY, AGNES (1894–May 6, 1950), radical journalist and author, known mainly for her reporting on China, was probably born in rural northern Missouri, perhaps in Osgood, although the facts of her birth and upbringing are obscure. The Smedley genealogy can be traced to pre-Revolutionary Quaker stock in Pennsylvania, but her father was a little-known itinerant laborer and her mother was a washerwoman. She was the second daughter and the second of the five children of Charles H. Smedley and Sarah (Ralls) Smedley. Like their parents, none of the Smedley children went to high school, and Agnes did not even finish grade school.

Smedley grew up in the coal-mining town of Trinidad, Colo. To supplement the family's meager income, she worked as a hired girl and waitress, struggling in the meantime to gain an education through irregular attendance at school and reading in her spare time. After her mother's death, when Agnes was sixteen, she left her family. For many years her life was a series of disappointments. She became, for a short period, a schoolteacher in a remote county school in New Mexico. She spent a year (1911–1912) studying at the Tempe Normal School in Arizona, and some time before 1916 she moved to California, where she attended a summer session at the University of California at Berkeley and taught in a state normal school. A brief early marriage to an undergraduate at the University of California, Ernest Walfred Brundin, ended in divorce.

Before moving to New York City in 1916 or 1917, she met the anarchist Emma Goldman and participated with her in the free speech movement in San Diego. In New York she continued her haphazard attempts to improve herself by going to evening lectures at New York University and worked during the day. Increasingly active in political affairs, she opposed American entry into World War I. On Mar. 18, 1918, she was arrested and charged with violating the Espionage Act by failing to register as an agent for the Indian Nationalist party, which she belatedly learned had accepted German funds. The charges were dismissed, but not until Smedley had spent several weeks in prison and had become thoroughly disenchanted with her native land. Thereafter, as Upton Sinclair wrote, "Nobody could ever persuade her that there was either freedom or justice in her country" (Sinclair, "The Red Dragon," p. 5).

Late in 1919 Smedley left the United States and spent most of the rest of her life abroad. Until 1928 she lived in Berlin with the Indian nationalist leader Virendranath Chattopadhyaya. The complexities of their life led her to a nervous breakdown and an attempted suicide. After her recovery she began teaching English to university students and took up again the study of Indian history, briefly doing graduate study at the University of Berlin. She also helped organize Germany's first public birth-control clinic and continued her political efforts in behalf of Indian nationalism.

Daughter of Earth (1929), Smedley's first book and in effect her fictionalized autobiography, was drafted as part of a case history for her psychoanalyst in Germany. The book is a vivid indictment of an America that taught its author that the life of a hillbilly family promised little more than hunger and uncertainty. "We belonged to the class," Smedley wrote, "who have nothing and from whom everything is always taken away" (rev. ed., 1935, p. 58). Like the heroine of *Daughter of Earth,* Smedley never forgot the humiliations that were part of the daily existence of a second-class citizen in a land of plenty, and she bitterly resented being deprived of an adequate education. Her family background and brutalized personal life instilled in her a spirit of defiance against all constituted authority and a sympathy for the poor. Thus, when she arrived in China in 1928 as special correspondent for the liberal *Frankfurter Zeitung,* Smedley immediately identified herself with the Chinese Communists, who were in rebellion against the government of Chiang Kai-shek.

In China, Smedley found a measure of fulfillment. As correspondent for the *Zeitung* and, after about 1930, for the *Manchester Guardian,* she began a career as a journalist and free-lance writer and reported about the Chinese Communist movement. In Shanghai she made the acquaintance of such leading antigovernment intellectuals as the novelist Lu Hsün and established contacts with members of the out-

749

lawed Chinese Communist party (CCP). Although Smedley did not enter Communist-controlled areas of China until 1937 or view the Chinese Communist movement at firsthand, she was covertly supplied with exclusive information by CCP agents in Shanghai, a fact that between 1928 and 1936 gave her writings a notoriety that surpassed their intrinsic merits.

Her books *Chinese Destinies: Sketches of Present-Day China* (1933) and *China's Red Army Marches* (1934) are based on her clandestine encounters with Chinese Communists. *Chinese Destinies* is a stereotype-ridden collection of unconnected anecdotes in which Communists are always lean and unselfish, and landlords, fat and grasping. *China's Red Army Marches* was more specific about CCP developments and personnel, but it too displayed an extreme bias against the Nationalist, or Kuomintang (KMT), government of Chiang Kai-shek. Attacked by the Chinese press and placed under police surveillance, Smedley went to a rest sanatorium in the Soviet Union in 1933 and in 1934 returned for a short visit to the United States. By late 1935, however, she was back in China, serving the cause that gave her life purpose and meaning.

In July 1936 Edgar Snow made a major journalistic coup by slipping through the KMT military blockade of Mao Tse-tung's stronghold in Shensi, thereby providing Westerners with their first authoritative view of the Chinese Communist movement. Infuriated that Snow and not she herself had been the first to gain access, Smedley immediately set out for north China. Fortuitously, she happened to be in Sian in December 1936 when Chiang Kai-shek was kidnapped and briefly held captive by rebellious Manchurian troops of the Tungpei Army under Marshal Chang Hsüeh-liang. Probably the only Western journalist in Sian at the time of Chiang's abduction, she conducted English-language radio broadcasts for the Tungpei Army until January 1937, when she journeyed to Mao's headquarters at Yenan.

The years from 1937 to 1940 were the happiest of Smedley's life. While in Yenan she energetically promoted visits to the Communist areas by such journalistic colleagues as Victor Keen of the *New York Herald Tribune* and even directed a rat-extermination campaign. When the Sino-Japanese War erupted in July 1937, she devoted herself to the war effort. From October 1937 to January 1938, she traveled with the roving headquarters of the Eighth Route Army (the designation given the Red Army when it joined in a united front with

Chiang's forces against the Japanese) in Shansi. *China Fights Back: An American Woman with the Eighth Route Army* (1938) is the diary of her experiences with the Red Army in Shansi.

In January 1938 Smedley went to Hankow, where she organized a committee to collect money and supplies for the Eighth Route Army; joined the Chinese Red Cross Medical Corps; and also served as an intermediary between such CCP officials as Chou En-lai and the foreign diplomatic and news communities. When Hankow fell to the advancing Japanese in October 1938, she made her way south to the areas in the lower Yangtze region controlled by the recently formed Communist New Fourth Army. From late 1938 to mid-1940, she roamed through central China with units of the New Fourth Army, distributing Red Cross supplies, establishing medical stations, and periodically filing reports with the *Manchester Guardian*. Ravaged by malnutrition and malaria, she was compelled to seek medical care in Chungking and Kweiyama in June 1940. Despite further medical treatment in Hong Kong. she remained ill and unable to rejoin the Communist partisans, so Smedley returned to the United States in the summer of 1941.

After more than twenty years, America seemed "entirely foreign" to her (*Battle Hymn of China,* p. 526). From 1941 to 1949, when she left the United States for the last time, she made radio appearances, lectured, and continued to write. *Battle Hymn of China,* an account of her experiences from 1938 to 1941, was published in 1943.

Smedley's last years were tragic. Her unflagging support of the CCP and criticism of the KMT was not well received in a postwar America that was hardening into a rigid anti-Communist mold. In February 1949, a 32,000-word report, prepared by Gen. Douglas MacArthur's intelligence staff, among other things, identified Smedley as a secret agent for the Soviet Union. When she denounced the accusation as a "despicable lie" and threatened to institute legal proceedings, the secretary of the army publicly admitted that there was no evidence against her and withdrew the charge. The damage, however, had been done. Finding it increasingly difficult to obtain speaking engagements, to sell articles, or even to rent a place in which to live, avoided by some friends and fearful that others would be deemed guilty by association with her, in November 1949 she sought refuge in England, hoping to complete a biography of Gen. Chu Teh, commander-in-chief of the Communist military forces, *The Great Road: The Life and Times of Chu Teh,* published posthumously. In May 1950, after several unsuccessful attempts to return to her beloved China, Smedley died in an Oxford nursing home of bronchopneumonia, following surgery for stomach ulcers. Her last request was to have her ashes buried with the revolutionary dead of China.

Her last request was granted. Agnes Smedley is one of two foreigners whose ashes are buried in the National Revolutionary Martyrs Memorial Park, the People's Republic of China's equivalent of Arlington Cemetery. The simple inscription placed to honor her reads: "Agnes Smedley, revolutionary writer and friend of the Chinese people" (Snow, *The Other Side of the River,* p. 77).

By any standard, Agnes Smedley was extraordinary. Largely self-educated, she became a prominent author by virtue of native ability and indomitable effort. Her radicalism was not of foreign derivation; it can be traced directly to a wretched childhood and unhappy personal experiences in the United States. Agnes Smedley was a malcontent long before she had heard of Karl Marx or Mao Tse-tung. She was more radical than most Chinese Communists, a fact which even they recognized. Besides rejecting capitalism, she opposed marriage, the family, and all constituted authority. She even disliked the "intellectual arrogance" of certain Chinese Communists, and refused in her own words to become "a mere instrument in the hands of men who believed that they held the one and only key to truth" (*Battle Hymn,* pp. 251, 10). Driven by a Quaker heritage that prompted her to elevate conscience above institutions, this rebel against all kinds of authority could never accept the discipline of membership in a Communist party. Although often accused of being a Communist, at heart Agnes Smedley was, as Freda Utley put it, "more of an anarchist than anything else" (*China at War,* pp. 215-216).

Her peppery character embroiled her in frequent disputes with CCP officials and many others. She was an irreverent woman, blunt in her appraisals. An avid partisan, Smedley gave unstintingly of herself to the cause of the CCP because it was striving to alleviate the destitute Chinese people—a destitution that was paralleled by the grinding poverty of her own youth.

In part because of her intemperate partisanship, little of what she wrote about China has much value for historians. Her writings do provide, however, considerable insight into the mentality of the American left in the 1930's and 1940's, and *Daughter of Earth* remains one of the few major primary sources which offers a glimpse into what has been called the "underside" of American society.

[The most important sources of information about Smedley are her own books, all of which are to a substantial extent autobiographical. Valuable insights also have been gained from correspondence and conversations with those who knew her, especially James M. Bertram, Owen Lattimore, Edgar Snow, and Helen Foster Snow. The enrollment date for Smedley's year at Tempe Normal School was provided by the Special Collections Librarian of Arizona State Univ. at Tempe, and her death certificate by the General Register Office, Somerset House, London.

Memoirs and other works by her contemporaries that shed light on Smedley's personality and career include James M. Bertram, *Beneath the Shadow* (1947) and *Unconquered* (1939); Evans F. Carlson, *Twin Stars of China* (1940); Paul Frillmann and Graham Peck, *China: The Remembered Life* (1968); Mark Gayn, "Thirteen Years in China," *Sat. Rev. of Lit.,* Sept. 18, 1943, p. 22; Harold L. Ickes, "Death by Association," *New Republic,* May 29, 1950, pp. 16–17; Hilda Selwyn-Clarke, "Agnes Smedley," *New Statesman and Nation,* May 20, 1950, p. 571; Upton Sinclair, "The Red Dragon: The Story of Agnes Smedley in America and China" (unpublished manuscript, Upton Sinclair papers, Ind. Univ.); Edgar Snow, *Journey to the Beginning* (1958), "MacArthur's Fantasy," *Nation,* Feb. 19, 1949, pp. 202–203, and *The Other Side of the River: Red China Today* (1962); Hollington K. Tong, *Dateline: China* (1950); Freda Utley, *China at War* (1939), and *Odyssey of a Liberal: Memoirs* (1970).

The following secondary works are useful: John Paton Davies, Jr., *Dragon by the Tail* (1972); Ronald Gottesman, "Agnes Smedley," *Notable Am. Women, 1607–1950,* III (1971); Chalmers A. Johnson, *An Instance of Treason* (1964); Stanley J. Kunitz and Howard Haycraft, eds., *Twentieth-Century Authors* (1942); and Kenneth E. Shewmaker, *Americans and Chinese Communists, 1927–1945* (1971), which contains a photograph of Smedley attired in a Red Army uniform.]

KENNETH E. SHEWMAKER

SMITH, FRANK LESLIE (Nov. 24, 1867-Aug. 30, 1950), Illinois politician, both elected and appointed to, but not seated in, the United States Senate, was born in Dwight, Ill., the second of the three sons of John Jacob Smith and Jane E. (Ketcham) Smith. His mother was from New York state. His father, whose family name had originally been Schmidt, was a native of Baden, Germany, who had grown up in America. In Dwight he was the village blacksmith. Energetic and aggressive, Frank Smith completed high school and, after a year of teaching at a nearby country school, began work in the freight department of the Chicago and Alton Railroad at Dwight. A similar job with the Rock Island line took him to Chicago in 1887, but he returned four years later to Dwight and began a profitable real estate and insurance business. A chief client for productive farm land was Dr. Leslie E. Keeley, developer and promoter of the "Keeley cure" for alcoholics, whose thriving business was situated at Dwight. Smith shared in this prosperity, and by 1904, with Keeley's backing, he established the First National Bank of Dwight.

Long interested in politics, Smith had already gained a foothold in state Republican circles. He was elected village clerk in 1894, and his campaign support, two years later, for Gov. John R. Tanner won him appointment to the governor's staff with the rank of colonel. In 1904 Smith sought the Republican nomination for lieutenant governor, but lost, despite the support of the Chicago Republican boss William Lorimer. Later that year, United States Sen. Shelby M. Cullom secured Smith a presidential appointment as collector of internal revenue for the Springfield district, a post he held until 1909. Smith managed President Taft's reelection campaign in Illinois in 1912. His ambition was to be governor, and he sought the nomination in 1916, only to lose to Frank O. Lowden. Two years later he was named to the first of three terms as chairman of the Republican state committee (1918–1920, 1920–1922, 1924–1926), a post that gave him new power in party councils.

In 1918 Smith won election from his district to a seat in Congress. Instead of seeking reelection in 1920, he set his eye on higher office. He was generally regarded as a Lowden man, but in his successful attempt to retain the state party chairmanship in 1920 he accepted support from the Republican faction led by Fred Lundin and Mayor William Hale Thompson of Chicago. As a result, Lowden refused to back Smith's bid for the governorship, and Smith turned instead toward the United States Senate. Although he lost the senatorial primary to William B. McKinley, congressman and head of an extensive electric traction system, Smith's prestige in the party remained high. His name was urged on President Harding for a cabinet post, and early in 1921 Gov. Len Small, one of the few successful Lundin candidates, appointed Smith to the important office of chairman of the Illinois Commerce Commission, responsible for regulating public utilities.

Smith again entered the senatorial primary against McKinley in 1926, and this time, running in opposition to American participation in the World Court, he won by 100,000 votes. Along with William S. Vare of Pennsylvania, Smith quickly became identified with campaign expenditures on a scale so lavish as to cause 1926 to be called the year of the "golden primaries." An even more damaging factor in

the Smith case was the disclosure that, while still chairman of the Commerce Commission, he received a contribution of $125,000 from the utility magnate Samuel Insull, as well as lesser amounts from two other utilities industrialists, Ira C. Copley and Clement Studebaker, Jr. Smith's acceptance of such funds, which boosted his campaign total to $500,000, was a direct violation of state law. These facts, brought out by a special Senate investigating committee headed by Sen. James A. Reed, engendered a public outcry and led to the independent Senate candidacy of reformer Hugh S. Magill.

Smith won the three-way race in November, but he was never to sit in the Senate. Ironically, Senator McKinley died in December 1926, and Smith was appointed to fill out the remainder of McKinley's term. Although there was no connection between this term and the one to which Smith had been elected, the Senate refused to seat him. When the Seventieth Congress convened in late 1927, the matter was again taken up by the Reed committee. On Jan. 19, 1928, after extended debate, the committee's resolution, describing Smith's credentials as tainted with "fraud and corruption" and declaring him "not entitled to membership in the Senate," passed by a vote of 61 to 23 (the majority including 21 Republicans).

Smith formally "resigned" his seat on February 9. He quickly sought vindication in the special April primary by running again for the Senate, but was resoundingly defeated. His attempt to win nomination as congressman-at-large in 1930 was also rejected at the polls. The party organization was more kind. He was elected to the Republican national committee in 1932 and continued as a regular delegate to the party's national conventions. He also carried on his banking activities until his death. On Feb. 8, 1893, Smith married Erminie Ahern, a Dwight classmate and teacher. They had no children. She was a Roman Catholic; he, a Methodist. Smith died of pneumonia in his eighty-third year at his home in Dwight. He was buried in that town's Oak Lawn Cemetery.

[Newspapers and magazines, 1926–1928, recorded the Smith case in voluminous detail, as did the proceedings of the Reed committee. Carroll H. Wooddy turned the affair into an extended "study in representative government" in *The Case of Frank L. Smith* (1931). See also Wooddy's *The Chicago Primary of 1926* (1926). Other works touching on Smith's career include Louise Overacker, *Money in Elections* (1932); William T. Hutchinson, *Lowden of Ill.*, 2 vols. (1957); and Forrest McDonald, *Insull* (1962). A useful sketch of Smith in his early business career appears in *The Biog. Record of Livingston and Woodford Counties, Ill.* (1900). See also *Biog. Directory Am. Cong.* (1961); *Who Was Who in America*, III (1960). Among obituary accounts, see *Pontiac* (Ill.) *Daily Leader*, Aug. 30, 1950, *Chicago Tribune* and *Chicago Sun-Times*, both Aug. 31, 1950, and *Dwight* (Ill.) *Star and Herald*, Sept. 2, 1950. Assistance of Clarence A. Berdahl of Urbana, Ill., is gratefully acknowledged.]

IRVING DILLIARD

SMITH, HAROLD DEWEY (June 6, 1898-Jan. 23, 1947), public administrator, was born on his family's farm near Haven, Kans., the eldest of five children of James William Smith and Miranda (Ebling) Smith. His father was of Scots-Irish ancestry, his mother of "Pennsylvania Dutch" (German); they met in Indiana before settling in Kansas. After high school and service in the navy during World War I, Smith entered the University of Kansas, where in 1922 he earned a B.S. degree in electrical engineering. He soon decided instead on a career in public administration and began graduate study at the University of Michigan, from which he received the M.A. degree in 1925. On Apr. 18, 1926, he married Lillian Mayer, daughter of a Kansas farmer. They had five children: James Winston, Lawrence Byron, Mary Ann, Sally Jane, and Virginia Lee.

Over the next decade Smith developed a special interest in the field of budgetary and fiscal management. As a graduate student he had worked on the staff of the Detroit Bureau of Municipal Research, and after a similar position with the League of Kansas Municipalities (1925-1928), he became director of the Michigan Municipal League (1928-1937). There he worked with city administrators to increase efficiency and effect economies. At the same time he edited the *Michigan Municipal Review* (1928-1937) and headed the Bureau of Government at the University of Michigan (1934-1937). In 1937 Gov. Frank Murphy of Michigan selected Smith as state budget director. In that capacity he helped modernize accounting procedures and sponsored studies of the state's long-range fiscal prospects. President Franklin D. Roosevelt in April 1939 named Smith director of the federal Bureau of the Budget, an agency that had been created in 1921 within the Treasury Department.

Smith took over just as the federal establishment was undergoing a profound administrative transformation, one in which the Bureau of the Budget would figure heavily. Congress in April 1939 granted the president limited power to reorganize the government. That summer, with Europe moving inexorably toward war, several of Roosevelt's advisors—including Smith, Louis Brownlow, Charles E. Merriam, and Luther Gulick—sought some means to enhance the president's administrative authority. The plan they drafted, approved by Roosevelt in September, created the Executive Office of the President. The new office housed several agencies, but by far the most important was the Bureau of the Budget, which, transferred out of the Treasury Department, in effect became the president's administrative arm. The bureau examined each department's proposed annual budget; it supervised departmental spending with a view toward eliminating waste; and it analyzed every bill and proclamation submitted for the president's signature and recommended a source of action to him.

As the first chief of the renovated bureau, Smith did much to set its tone and direction. His role derived not only from his formal powers, but also from the informal powers Roosevelt entrusted to him, particularly during World War II. After 1941, as foreign affairs came to dominate Roosevelt's mind, he gave Smith broad latitude in making budgetary decisions. The mushroom growth of wartime agencies made Smith's task of coordination at once more difficult and more important. In discharging these responsibilities, the Bureau of the Budget itself grew from fewer than fifty employees in 1939 to nearly 600 in 1944. For one who prided himself on what New Dealers termed a "passion for anonymity," Smith even achieved a measure of fame. On June 14, 1943, his picture made the cover of *Time* magazine over the caption: "Czars may come and czars may go, but he goes on forever."

Smith did his best to steer clear of partisan politics, but he believed that the budgetary process could never be divorced from broad social concerns; nor did he hesitate to advance his own point of view. In 1942 he urged Roosevelt to accept a "drastic" wartime anti-inflation program involving compulsory savings, firm wage-price controls, and a stiff excess profits tax. In 1944 Smith sided with those who challenged the army's position on reconversion. He reasoned that a gradual reduction in military output along with an expansion in civilian production would minimize dislocations in the return to a peacetime economy. Smith, while himself a forceful advocate, always insisted that he attempted to give the president "all the facts and both sides of the story."

A deliberate, methodical man—critics occasionally accused him of moving too slowly—Smith possessed an impressive knowledge of administrative structure that more than compensated for his lack of economic expertise. After Roosevelt's death in 1945, he continued to serve for a time under President Truman. In February 1946, however, he complained to Truman that "while you, yourself, are an orderly person, there is disorder all around you and it is becoming worse." He also found federal salaries inadequate, and four months later he resigned to become vice-president of the International Bank for Reconstruction and Development, better known as the World Bank. He became acting head of the bank in December 1946 on the resignation of Eugene Meyer. Dedicated to privacy in his personal life, Smith enjoyed the hobbies of carpentry and farming. Early in 1947, at the age of forty-eight, he died of a heart attack at his farm in Culpepper, Va. He was buried in Arlington National Cemetery.

[No biography of Smith has yet appeared. The most important source for understanding his public career remains the sizable collection of his papers at the Franklin D. Roosevelt Lib., Hyde Park, N.Y. Also valuable are the records of the Bureau of the Budget in the Nat. Arch. Smith wrote one book, *The Management of Your Government* (1945), and many articles, among which the most important are: "Management in a Democracy," *Nat. Municipal Rev.*, Oct. 1942; "Our 300 Billion Dollar Headache," *American Mag.*, June 1945; "National Unity in Fiscal Policy," *Am. City*, Oct. 1945; and "Government Must Have and Pay for Good Men," *N.Y. Times Mag.*, July 14, 1946. Several other sources shed some light on Smith's role as budget director: Louis Brownlow, *A Passion for Anonymity* (1958); Edward H. Hobbs, *Behind the President: A Study of Executive Office Agencies* (1954); Richard Polenberg, *Reorganizing Roosevelt's Government, 1936–1939* (1966); Louis Brownlow, ed., "The Executive Office of the President: A Symposium," *Public Administration Rev.*, Winter 1941; George A. Graham, "The Presidency and the Executive Office of the President," *Jour. of Politics*, Nov. 1, 1950. Two informative obituaries of Smith appeared, one by Louis Brownlow in the *Am. Political Sci. Rev.*, May 1947; the other, more critical, by Paul H. Appleby in *Public Administration Rev.*, Spring 1947. See also *Current Biog.*, 1940; *N.Y. Times*, Jan. 24, 1947.]

RICHARD POLENBERG

SMITH, HORATIO ELWIN (May 8, 1886–Sept. 9, 1946), professor of French, was born in Cambridge, Mass., the only child of Elwin Hartley Smith, an organ tuner, and Eliza Burroughs (Taylor) Smith, a piano teacher. His father was a native of Vermont, his mother of Cambridge. Smith grew up and attended public schools in Cambridge and Somerville, Mass., and in Brattleboro, Vt. His musical heritage appears to have been of limited significance, but the imprint of New England upon his character and physical presence proved well-nigh indelible. Although he was urbane and thoroughly urbanized, he displayed at times and indeed cultivated the rigid exterior, the reticence, and the dry humor traditionally associated with Vermont. Imbued with the teachings of French *moralistes* from Montaigne to Renan, tolerant and free-thinking, he nevertheless remained committed to a set of ethical principles as binding and unchanging as that of his forefathers. The respect, not unmixed with awe, which he knew how to inspire was the basis of his authority; and only at some length did the twinkle in his eye, or the reassuring sight of his familiar pipe, afford a suggestion of benignity and betray the abiding generosity of his mind and heart.

Horatio Smith entered Amherst College in 1904, and upon his graduation four years later, entered the Johns Hopkins University, where he obtained his Ph.D. in 1912. In the latter institution he came under the influence of two prestigious masters, Edward Cooke Armstrong and Henry Carrington Lancaster, both of whom helped develop his interest in French studies. Neither, however, won him over to his specialty. Himself a critic—an admirer of Sainte-Beuve—rather than a philologist or factual historian, he was to make his contribution to teaching and scholarship mainly as a keen analyst of French critical thought or narrative art, as in his doctoral dissertation, "The Literary Criticism of Pierre Bayle" (1912), and in his book, *Masters of French Literature* (1937).

Horatio Smith's major achievements, however, lay in the administrative field and in the completion of long-range projects that called into play his exceptional gifts as a builder and organizer. Seven years of teaching at Yale (1911–1918) were followed by service as a regional director of the Foyers du Soldat of the French army in the final year of World War I. Upon his return to the United States in 1919 he joined the faculty of Amherst College. In 1925 Brown University appointed him to the chairmanship of its Romance languages department, until then rather modestly nestled in the shadow of Yale and Harvard. Within a few years Smith succeeded in making his department an important center of graduate studies. Final recognition occurred in 1936 when President Nicholas Murray Butler of Columbia invited him to head and restructure the French section of the university's Romance languages department. Smith's discharge of this responsibility proved to be a model of quiet strength and diplomacy. He earned the loyalties of his colleagues, old and new, steered a safe course through the difficult war years, and bequeathed to his successors a solid and efficient department, long rated first nationally and referred to as his personal "creation."

The same talents served him in good stead during his tenure as general editor of the *Romanic Review* (1937-1946); in the preparation of the *Columbia Dictionary of Modern European Literature* (1947), a monumental undertaking that he edited almost singlehandedly but did not live to see published; and in at least the partial realization of his last project: the reconstitution, by means of American donations of books and money, of the library of the University of Caen, thoroughly destroyed in the wake of the Allied landing in Normandy. France recognized Smith's contributions to her culture by making him a knight of the Legion of Honor (1934) and a doctor *honoris causa* of the universities of Grenoble (1939) and Paris (1945). The city of Caen named an avenue after him.

Smith was the victim of a massive heart attack in 1939, but for the next seven years, he carried out his multiple tasks despite serious ill health. After his death in New York City, his remains were cremated, and the ashes scattered in the brook of the Vermont farm, near Londonderry, where he had spent his summer vacations.

On July 3, 1911, he married Ernestine Failing, a native of Portland, Oreg.; they had two daughters, Eliza Alvord and Mary Hilliard.

[*Who Was Who in Am.,* II (1950); *Amherst College Biog. Record,* 1951; vita in Smith's doctoral diss.; *Directory of Am. Scholars* (1942); obituary in *French Rev.,* Dec. 1946; personal recollections; information from Mary Smith Johnson and from Smith's birth record (Mass. Registrar of Vital Statistics).]

JEAN-ALBERT BÉDÉ

SMITH, LLOYD LOGAN PEARSALL (Oct. 18, 1865-Mar. 2, 1946), essayist and philologist, was born in Millville, N.J., the second son and fourth of six children of Robert Pearsall Smith and Hannah Tatum (Whitall) Smith. As a member of a distinguished Quaker family whose paternal roots went back to James Logan, William Penn's secretary, and whose prosperity was assured by the glassworks founded by his maternal grandfather, young Smith would have led the unruffled life of the son of a manufacturer had his father not experienced an ecstatic conversion to the Higher Life evangelical movement and become, with his wife, an international revivalist. When disillusionment with evangelical Christianity returned the family to their origins in Germantown, Pa., where they had lived prior to their move to New Jersey, Logan entered the Quaker

Penn Charter School. His early bookishness, encouraged by the expectation that Logan would succeed his grandfather John Jay Smith and his uncle, Lloyd Pearsall Smith, as librarian of Philadelphia, was soon overshadowed by the social interests he pursued through Haverford College (1881-1884) and one year at Harvard (1884-1885), but it revived under the influence of his older sister, Mary. She induced him to read Ruskin and took him on a pilgrimage to see Walt Whitman. Awakened to his literary vocation, Logan abandoned the family business in 1888 after a trial year and, with an annuity provided by his father, followed his sister to England, entering Balliol College, Oxford. The Smiths's decision to join their children that same year ended what Pearsall Smith would later call his family's three-hundred-year exile in America.

At Oxford Smith found in Walter Pater's aestheticism a way to reconcile his skepticism with his capacity for passionate attachment. The pursuit of artistic perfection, which seemed to him at once an ironic comment on the limitations of life and a victory over them, became his lifelong concern. Although his family only tolerated this new enthusiasm, preferring the social millenarianism of Fabian circles, Logan persisted in his interest, moving first to Paris, where he met Whistler and produced a volume of stories in the manner of Maupassant entitled *The Youth of Parnassus* (1895), and then to a cottage in England, where he devoted years to the perfection of his literary style. He published a few of his finely wrought capsule essays in *The Golden Urn,* a review he produced in 1897-1898 with his sister Mary and Bernard Berenson, later her husband, but waited until 1902 to assemble a collection. Its title, *Trivia,* sounded an ironic note of affirmation for beauty and leisure in a morally pretentious and frantic world. Unsuccessful at first, *Trivia* was enlarged and revised in 1918 and enjoyed a vogue in war-weary Europe and America. It was followed by *More Trivia* (1922) and the aphoristic *Afterthoughts* (1931); the three were united in *All Trivia* (1933) and supplemented in 1945 by *Last Words.*

Pearsall Smith's interests as a student, as well as a stylist, of English led to his transformation from literary apprentice to—in Christopher Morley's phrase—"the most perfect Mandarin of English letters." Brought by his polished writing and his work on *The English Language* (1912) to the attention of the poet Robert Bridges, he joined with Bridges and others to form in 1913 the Society for Pure English, formally launched in 1919. Although Smith recognized, and was amused by, his growing reputation as a fusty traditionalist, he directed his sharpest attacks in his many tracts for the society against those who had confused pedantry with purity, compromising thereby the vitality and simplicity of the language. For models of vigorous style, he turned to the sixteenth and seventeeth centuries, producing among other books *The Life and Letters of Sir Henry Wotton* (1907), *Donne's Sermons: Selected Passages* (1920), and *The Golden Grove* (1930), an anthology of Jeremy Taylor's sermons. Smith also presented, as the views of a passionate reader rather than of a critic, numerous essays collected in his *Reperusals and Re-Collections* (1936). He enjoyed his greatest success with his autobiography, *Unforgotten Years* (1939).

An unrepentant expatriate, Smith adopted British citizenship in 1913. Unlike many of his contemporaries abroad, he rarely looked back, confining his criticism of Americans to an occasional comment on their disinterest in literary style and to an attack in *Milton and His Modern Critics* (1940) on the critical presumptions of T. S. Eliot and Ezra Pound. He was close to George Santayana, with whom he collaborated on *Little Essays* (1920), drawn from the philosopher's writings, and to Henry James, whose adoption of British citizenship he encouraged.

Smith's personal life was overshadowed by his intellectual interests. "People say life's the thing," he wrote in *Afterthoughts,* "but I prefer reading." He never married, living first alone; then with his widowed mother, whose introspective temperament and penchant for writing he shared; and for over thirty years thereafter with his sister Alys, Bertrand Russell's first wife. Outside of his family, he was closest to his three disciples, Cyril Connolly, Robert Gathorne-Hardy, and John Russell. Although moody at times, Pearsall Smith was wonderful company and a generous teacher. In his later years he looked the part of the mandarin, his boyish looks and agility replaced by an imposing stoutness. He died in his eighty-first year at his home in London. A memorial service was held at St. Margaret's Church in Westminster.

[A number of the tracts Smith prepared for the Society for Pure English are collected in his *Words and Idioms* (1925). Others are "Needed Words," Tract No. XXXI (1928) and "Fine Writing," Tract No. XLVI (1936). Smith in the role of the cultivated reader is best represented by his *On Reading Shake-*

speare (1933). There is no full-length biography, but one can turn to the somewhat ambivalent reminiscence by Robert Gathorne-Hardy, *Recollections of Logan Pearsall Smith* (1950) and John Russell, ed., *Portrait of Logan Pearsall Smith, Drawn from His Letters and Diaries* (1951), as well as Smith's tribute to his mother, *A Religious Rebel* (1949). See also Robert Allerton Parker, *The Transatlantic Smiths* (1959). The most interesting discussion of Smith's career and style is Edmund Wilson, "Logan Pearsall Smith," *The Bit Between My Teeth* (1965). Pearsall Smith's papers are at the Lib. of Congress. Four portraits of him have been reproduced in Gathorne-Hardy's *Recollections;* the one by Roger Fry is at Haverford College. His photograph appeared in the *Sat. Rev. of Lit.,* May 18, 1935.]

MARC PACHTER

SNOW, JESSIE BAKER (May 26, 1868–June 16, 1947), civil engineer, was born in Nantucket, Mass., one of the five children of Charles Earl Snow and Emily Jane (Carpenter) Snow. His father was in the packet trade, following the tradition of his ancestors, who were early settlers on the New England coast. His maternal great-grandfather was a Macy, one of the R. H. Macy department store family in New York.

Snow's early education was obtained in public schools in Nantucket; he then studied engineering and took his bachelor's degree in civil engineering from Union College, Schenectady, N.Y. in 1889. Soon after graduation, he launched his career, at a time of enormous growth in the number and size of North American cities, largely due to the effects of the industrial revolution. By 1890, three-fifths of the population of the Northeast region of the United States were living in centers of 4,000 or more inhabitants. The crowding of people into small space brought with it demands for public facilities—paved streets, public water supply, sewerage and transportation systems, and, especially, rapid transit. These needs presented great challenges to men like Snow. Since most cities were located on waterways, the solution to transportation problems had often involved the construction of bridges and subaqueous tunnels.

During the early years of his career, from 1889 until the turn of the century, Snow undertook a variety of general municipal works projects, such as surveying and designing streets, sewers, waterworks, bridges, and street railways. The results of his work were evident in the cities of Goshen, N.Y.; West Superior, Wis.; Long Island City and Tonawanda, N.Y. For the next decade his activities were confined to railroad engineering. He was responsible for a section of line of the single-track Jamestown, Chautauqua, and Lake Erie Railroad at Westfield, N.Y. He also served, for a short period, as resident engineer for the construction of a street railroad in Kitchener, Ontario. From 1902 until 1904, he was chief engineer of the Jersey City Transit Company.

During these years, Snow was married twice, first, in 1894, to Eleanor Curtis Harman, of Schenectady, N.Y., who died within a few years, and second, to May Purdy, the daughter of William Henry Purdy of New York, on Aug. 1, 1903. She died in the summer of 1945. He had two children, Annette W. and Charles G., by his first wife, and one son, Edgar P., by his second.

From 1904 to 1910, Snow aided in the construction of cross-town tunnels and a railroad tube under the North River from Manhattan to Jersey City for the Pennsylvania Tunnel and Terminal Railroad Co. Having entered the field of tunneling and, specifically, construction under compressed-air conditions, Snow spent the next five years, from 1910 until 1915, using his knowledge of tunneling in dam construction, first at the Hauser Lake dam, Montana, for the Foundation Company, then as field engineer for a proposed hydroelectric development near Port Jervis, N.Y., sponsored by the Canada Syndicate Company of Montreal.

The final, and most impressive, phase of his career was spent engineering sections of the New York subway network, particularly the underwater tunnels. In all, he played an active part in the construction of twenty-three rapid transit railroad and vehicular tunnels out of a total of forty-one constructed along the periphery of Manhattan Island. From 1914 until his reluctant retirement on May 31, 1945, he held positions with the New York Public Service Commission (1914-1919) as supervisor of the Old Slip-Clark St., the Whitehall St.-Montague St., and the 14th St.-North 7th St. tunnels; the New York, New Jersey Interstate Tunnel Commission (1919-1921) as principal assistant to the engineer for the two Holland vehicular tubes under the Hudson River; the Board of Estimate and Apportionment of New York City (1921-1925) as tunnel engineer for the proposed combined railroad and rapid transit tunnels under the Narrows between Staten Island and Brooklyn; the Board of Transportation of New York City (1925-1933) as division engineer in charge of the 53rd St., Manhattan-Nott Ave., Queens tunnels (two) and the Fulton St., Manhattan-Cranberry St., Brooklyn tunnels (two), as well as the Rutgers St., Manhattan-Jay St., Brooklyn tunnels (two), and three tunnels from 157th St. in Manhattan, under the Harlem River to the Bronx, and two tunnels under Newtown Creek, in Queens.

Snow then became chief engineer for the Board of Transportation and was responsible for consolidating the city's three subway systems as they were brought under municipal ownership, for its expansion and for the razing of some of Brooklyn's, and much of Manhattan's, elevated railway lines. In addition to his permanent responsibilities, he acted as consulting engineer for the Queens-Midtown, East River vehicular tunnels (1930-1939) and the Brooklyn-Battery tunnel (1940-1943). Snow's ability was greatest in the field of subaqueous tunnel construction. According to his engineering colleagues, he is to be credited with displaying ingenuity in a number of areas such as river shields, and he improved upon the design of cast iron tunnel rings by the insertion of a third, intermediate flange, a feature that provided greater stiffness and thus increased the allowable width of tunnels.

His engineering talent was combined with a capacity for hard work. Even in the final years of his career he was reputed to have frequently tramped through subway construction tunnels, swinging a lantern and keeping a close eye on workmen and contractors alike. His retirement itself was extended several times, with the result that he worked practically until his death, in Great Neck, N.Y., after a long illness, at the age of seventy-nine. At that time he was hailed as "the outstanding compressed air tunnel engineer."

Devoting most of his life to engineering, Snow had little time for extracurricular activities. At college he had been a member of the Delta Upsilon fraternity and the honorary society of Sigma Xi and, during his career, he belonged to the Railroad and Engineer's clubs in New York City. A licensed engineer in New York state, Snow joined the American Society of Civil Engineers in 1902 and became a life member in 1939. He received an honorary D.Sc. from Union College in 1930. In politics he was an independent and in religion a Congregationalist.

[Articles about Snow include Louis E. Robbe, "Memoir of Jessie Baker Snow," Trans. of the Am. Soc. of Civil Engineers, 113 (1948), 1550–1555; "Jessie Baker Snow," Nat. Cyc. Am. Biog., 34 (1948), 65–66, which includes a photograph, probably taken toward the end of Snow's career; and an obituary in the N.Y. Times, June 18, 1947. The James Forgie Collect. of manuscripts and publications, Smithsonian Institution, Div. of Mechan. and Civil Engineering, contains materials pertinent to Snow and Forgie, who was a prominent consulting tunnel engineer working in the New York City area at the same time as Snow.]
DIANNE NEWELL MACDOUGALL

SNOW, WILLIAM FREEMAN (July 13, 1874–June 12, 1950), public health administrator and leader in the social hygiene movement, was the younger of two children, both of them boys, of William Snow and Emily M. (Streeter) Snow. He was born in Quincy, Ill., but the family soon afterward moved to Biggs, Calif., where the father kept a small store. Snow went to high school in Oakland and to Stanford University, where he majored in chemistry, receiving his B.A. in 1896. After taking an M.A. in physiology from Stanford in 1897, he entered Cooper Medical College, San Francisco, and graduated, M.D., in 1900. He studied ophthalmology at Johns Hopkins in 1901-1902, and then returned to Stanford as assistant professor of hygiene. Snow married Blanche Malvina Boring of Palo Alto, Calif., on Aug. 15, 1899. They had two sons, William Boring and Richard Boring.

Snow's increasing interest in public health was reflected in his promotion at Stanford to professor of hygiene and public health in 1909. To lend authority to his investigations, he had early taken positions as deputy county health officer and volunteer epidemiologist for the state board of health. The cases he encountered of individuals and families devastated by venereal diseases aroused his interest in social and educational means to control these preventable infections. Although they were a leading cause of disability and death, ignorance of their true extent and effect was all but universal, and because they were associated with illicit sex they could scarcely be mentioned in public. As president of the California Public Health Association, Snow in 1909 helped form the California Association for the Study and Prevention of Syphilis and Gonococcus Infections.

He left Stanford that June (on a leave that was to be renewed yearly until 1920) to become secretary and executive officer of the California State Board of Health. There he demonstrated the concerns and methods that were to dominate the rest of his career: attacking the venereal diseases through education of the public, through interorganizational coordination, and through patient, persistent committee work. Under Snow's direction the Board of Health greatly expanded health information programs, and in 1910 California became the first state to require physicians to report cases of syphilis and gonorrhea. That same year Snow was a founder and first secretary of the California Public Health League, designed to coordinate the activities of various groups fighting tuberculosis and other health problems. By 1912, when he was elected

president of the Association of State and Provincial Boards of Health, he was deeply committed to the social hygiene movement.

That movement represented a merging of two earlier ones: the attack on prostitution as a moral and social evil, and the attack on venereal disease as a public health problem. The outstanding leader in the latter cause prior to 1913 was Prince A. Morrow, founder of the American Society for Sanitary and Moral Prophylaxis (1905). This grew in 1910 into the American Federation for Sex Hygiene (with Snow a member of the committee that formulated the constitution and bylaws). Three years later, leaders of the Federation and of the antivice American Vigilance Association joined together to form the American Social Hygiene Association. That December, Snow was called to New York City to become general secretary (later general director) of the new association. Partly on the basis of firsthand investigation in Europe in 1912, he had already concluded that both medical and moral approaches were necessary for any long-term attack on venereal diseases, and that regulated prostitution served only to increase their spread. With his public health background, high standards of personal conduct, and moral courage, Snow proved an ideal leader for this medico-moral cause. His moral fervor had no religious dimension; as a young scientist and physician he had turned strongly against the accepted dogmas of his Protestant upbringing.

Snow and the ASHA saw that their first task was to change public attitudes toward venereal disease. They issued leaflets, published articles, arranged symposia, and instituted the quarterly journal Social Hygiene. When American troops were mobilized on the Mexican border in 1916, Snow, representing the ASHA, was one of those who urged Secretary of War Newton D. Baker to eliminate prostitution and alcohol from the environs of military camps and to carry out moral education among the troops. This prepared the way for an intensive and unprecedentedly successful campaign against venereal disease instituted within weeks after the United States entered World War I. Snow himself served as secretary of the general medical board of the Council of National Defense and as chairman of its Committee on Civilian Cooperation in Combating Venereal Diseases. In 1918, by the Chamberlain-Kahn Act, Congress created the Interdepartmental Social Hygiene Board and provided funds to aid state venereal disease control programs and to support scientific and social research. Snow, by now a lieutenant colonel in the Medical Corps, was the army's representative on the board and chairman of its executive committee until it expired in 1922.

Snow participated in a meeting of Red Cross societies at Cannes, France, in April 1919, and was largely responsible for the report of the section on venereal diseases, which outlined a comprehensive program. Later conferences sponsored by the League of Red Cross Societies led to the formation in 1923 of the International Union against the Venereal Diseases, designed to serve as a propaganda and coordinating agency for national societies. Snow played an active role in the new organization and was its president from 1946 until his death. He is also credited with having strongly influenced President Wilson to insist on including in the League of Nations covenant a clause giving it supervision over agreements for the suppression of traffic in women and children. Snow served as chairman of the League's body of experts to investigate this traffic from 1924 to 1928.

In the United States during the 1920's Snow and the American Social Hygiene Association continued their campaign against commercialized prostitution and fostered education in sex hygiene. Snow took a leading role in the formation of the National Health Council in 1921 and served as its president from 1927 to 1934. A prolific author of journal articles throughout his career, he published his only book, *The Venereal Diseases: Their Medical, Nursing, and Community Aspects,* in 1924. At the White House Conference on Child Health and Protection in 1930, he was chairman of a subcommittee that issued a report favoring sex education in schools.

Although as late as 1935 the word "syphilis" could not be spoken over the radio, barriers against reporting and discussing the venereal diseases thereafter fell rapidly. With the Venereal Disease Control Act of 1938, the federal government again actively entered the campaign with grants to states through the Public Health Service. As always, Snow and the ASHA fostered the legislation and gained support for it through a network of cooperating societies, through public education, and through skillful lobbying. Snow became chairman of the executive committee of the Association in 1940 and of its board of directors in 1944. Active until the end, he died suddenly in Bangor, Maine, of a coronary occlusion at the age of seventy-five. He was buried in Silver Lake Cemetery, Bucksport, Maine, near his summer home at East Orland.

Snow was a dedicated worker in an unpopular cause. Short in stature, modest and gracious in manner, he had a cheerful disposition and was generous to his co-workers and subordinates. He was never a polished public speaker but was formidable in private debate, persuasive in small groups, and highly effective in working behind the scenes. Guiding the social hygiene movement from just before World War I to the late 1930's, Snow as much as any individual was responsible for the change in American attitudes toward syphilis, which converted it from a sin that could not be discussed to an infectious disease that could be openly attacked as a problem of public health.

[In addition to Snow's own writings, the chief sources for his life are the reports and other publications issued by the numerous organizations in which he played a part. Biographical accounts may be found in two special issues of the *Jour. of Social Hygiene*: Dec. 1937, containing the proceedings of a testimonial dinner, and Dec. 1950, containing a series of commemorative articles. Snow and others are covered in Charles W. Clarke, *Taboo: The Story of the Pioneers of Social Hygiene* (1961). Family information from Richard B. Snow, Bronxville, N.Y.]

JOHN B. BLAKE

SOUTHERN, JULIA MARLOWE. See MARLOWE, JULIA.

SPEAKS, OLEY (June 28, 1874-Aug. 27, 1948), song composer, was born in Canal Winchester near Columbus, Ohio. He was the last of eleven children—five girls and six boys (one of each died in infancy)—of Charles W. Speaks and Sarah Ann (Hesser) Speaks. His father, descended from English colonists, was a contractor in the building of the Ohio Canal and then a grain merchant in Canal Winchester. His mother was Pennsylvania "Dutch." His brother John Charles became a congressman and brigadier general in the United States Army. Oley was named for William and Henry Oley, family friends. His father died when Oley was ten years old, but the boy was able to finish high school in Canal Winchester. When his family moved to Columbus, he found a job there in the office of the Cleveland, Akron and Columbus Railroad.

Music, however, had already claimed his attention. His family on both sides were interested in music, singing in the church choir and in local performances of such works as Gilbert and Sullivan's *H.M.S. Pinafore.* In Columbus he soon had a succession of church positions as baritone soloist. There is no record of his teachers, but since he was described as often playing his own accompaniments, it seems likely that his older sisters or brothers provided piano lessons as well as instruction in singing. In the *Columbus Dispatch* in 1891 Josiah R. Smith described him as "a musician to his fingertips. His voice is singularly sweet and flexible, clear and melodious, and he sings as if singing were a delight instead of work." He also began writing songs, and two were published, "In Maytime" and "When Mabel Sings." In 1898 his railroad pass got him to New York City, and there his fine voice won him the position of bass soloist over seventy-five other candidates at the Universalist Church of the Divine Paternity. Four years later he moved to St. Thomas Church. Meanwhile, he made recital tours and received formal instruction in voice from Carl Dufft, J. Armour Galloway, and the coloratura soprano Emma Thursby and in composition from Max Spicker and Will C. Macfarlane. Around 1906 he went home to a church job in Columbus. Soon, however, his steady output of successful songs made it possible for him to return to New York, where he lived until his death.

He seems to have been a shy, modest, friendly man, neither recluse nor bon vivant; he never married. Whatever his vocal ability, he would today almost certainly be forgotten but for his songs. All of the 200 to 250 he is estimated to have written would almost certainly be forgotten were it not for "On the Road to Mandalay" (text by Rudyard Kipling, 1907), "Morning" (text by Frank L. Stanton, 1912), and the Schubertian "Sylvia" (text by Clinton Scollard, 1914). The first is said to have sold over a million copies and is still selling; the third has gone over the half-million mark. A published list of Speaks's compositions gives 119 songs published by G. Schirmer, Inc. (New York) and thirty-one published by John Church Company (Cincinnati). One can soon spot other familiar items in this list: "Hark! Hark, My Soul" (a 1923 setting of F. W. Faber's hymn); "Let Not Your Heart Be Troubled" (John 14: 1, 27; 1918); "The Prayer Perfect" (James Whitcomb Riley, 1930, a song praised by John McCormack and Louise Homer); the simple, beautiful "To You" (Marie Beatrice Gannon, 1910, sung by Lillian Nordica); and the once trumpeted patriotic "When the Boys Come Home" (a Civil War poem by John Hay, 1911). His reputation, however, rests on the three famous songs.

Speaks's songs are mostly either sacred or sentimental. They were clearly intended to be sung in church or at the piano for a live and uncritical audience. They belong to a past era, when radio was nascent and television nonexistent. They reflect not the world of the movies but that of the parlor piano, not the concert stage but the organizational banquet and the school entertainment. To sing them one must have not a great technique but utter sincerity. To analyze their poetical or musical content is perhaps unfair. Their composer, like his audience, whom he knew very well, was uncritical about poetry. He seldom reached for drama (the Easter song "In the End of the Sabbath," with a text from Matthew 28, is an exception). He rather offered melodious, tuneful musical translation of verses that had kindled his creative spark. Rhythmically and formally, the songs are all uncomplicated. Harmonically they are unadventurous—a few mildly colored chords, no more. Melodically they are instantly accessible. They are always solicitous of the singer: stepwise movement or easy leaps, high notes carefully prepared, comfortable declamation (important words receive correct musical emphasis: Speaks does not accent *and*'s or *the*'s)—such are the hallmarks. They are singers' songs, they ask nothing but modest skill of the pianist, they appeal directly to the heart of the listener. Speaks himself said that when he sat down to compose, a song either came at once or it came not at all. This lack of struggle, lack of intellectuality, is responsible for the blandness and banality that are now undeniable. In one song after another, however, Speaks has written a piece that amateur musicians, those who gather around the piano, can perform well and that amateur audiences, those for whom he clearly wrote, can understand. Whether he chose a poem by Emily Dickinson ("Charity," 1911) or one by his old pastor, Washington Gladden ("Oh, Master Let Me Walk with Thee," 1917), he wrote not as a member of the Beethoven Society or the Mendelssohn Glee Club (to both of which he belonged in New York City) but as the Methodist, Republican Ohio boy that he appears to have remained all his life. Few of the poems have survived. Few deserve to. Clinton Scollard wrote: "Sylvia's hair is like the night,/Touched with glancing starry beams;/Such a face as drifts thro' dreams,/This is Sylvia to the sight." The vague imprecision of this observation is forgettable. The melody that Speaks found to go with it, however, seems to be immortal at some level of American musical consciousness. The composer still speaks, a claim that may be asserted on the basis of sales records alone without recourse to aesthetic justification.

Following a period of declining health and a short stay at Columbia-Presbyterian Medical Center, he died at the age of seventy-four and was buried in the Speaks family plot in Union Grove Cemetery in Canal Winchester.

[The best sources of information are the interview-article by Nelson H. Budd in the *Columbus Sunday Dispatch* of July 7, 1940, and the pamphlet published for a dedication on Dec. 11, 1949, at Canal Winchester, Ohio, *The Oley Speaks Music Library*. This fifteen-page brochure is illustrated and lists the songs in print. A portrait by Howard Chandler Christy will be found in the library, housed at the Canal Winchester High School. The *N.Y. Times*, Aug. 28, 1948, and the *Canal Winchester Times*, Sept. 2, 1948, contain obituary articles. The often cited birth date of 1876 is incorrect.]

VERNON GOTWALS

SPECK, FRANK GOULDSMITH (Nov. 8, 1881-Feb. 6, 1950), ethnologist, was born in Brooklyn, N.Y., the elder of the two sons of Frank Gouldsmith Speck and Hattie L. (Staniford) Speck. His parents came from the old seafaring, whaling, mercantile communities of the lower Hudson Valley and were descended from Dutch settlers and the Mahican peoples of the area. With the nineteenth-century collapse of the upriver economy, his father moved his business to New York City. As a small child, Speck's health was precarious, and a rural environment was suggested. Since family removal was impossible, he was placed, about 1888, in the care of a family friend, Mrs. Fidelia A. Fielding, at Mohegan, Conn.; she became the most important formative influence of his life.

Speck's health improved rapidly. He attended a local grammar school and found companions among Indian children. Mrs. Fielding, a conservative Indian widow who had raised her own family, was one of the last native speakers of any American Indian language of southern New England, and Speck soon learned Mohegan. Mrs. Fielding was a gardener and an herbalist who lived an isolated rural life in close integration with nature. Her love of natural history greatly influenced Speck and always remained one of his lifelong passions. She introduced him to the nonconformity and social rebellion of her heritage and tutored him in both English and traditional Mohegan writing; his oldest fieldnotes which survive are Mohegan spelling exercises of 1892. He thus acquired the basis for his later studies and also his sense of irony toward history and society, tools which he was to continue improving for the rest of his life.

At about the age of fourteen, he returned to his family's new home at Hackensack, N.J.

Here he obtained a cedar dugout canoe and spent much of his free time exploring the salt marshes and the shoreline. After graduating from the Hackensack High School, he entered Columbia University. Beset with doubts about his own future, he embarked upon a theological program. Already proficient in French, German, and Algonkian, he plunged into the study of classical languages. As a sophomore, he enrolled in a course on philology taught by John Dyneley Prince, a noted orientalist who was studying the surviving languages of northern New England. Prince introduced his student to Franz Boas, and they both encouraged him toward a career in anthropological linguistics. This seemed an impossible dream, and he was plunged into depression, but with his father's approval and support he was able to proceed.

He coauthored articles on Algonkian speech with Prince. In 1904 he graduated from Columbia and received his M.A. in anthropology there in 1905. At the same time he began ethnographic fieldwork among the Yuchi of Oklahoma in 1904, eventually leading to his doctoral thesis in 1908. After further graduate study at Columbia, he moved to the University of Pennsylvania in 1907 when he was offered a George Leib Harrison Research Fellowship there and obtained his Ph.D. at Pennsylvania in 1908. His close friend, Edward Sapir, joined him there briefly in 1909. He was attached to the University Museum of the University of Pennsylvania, which had been constituted a department of the university in 1891. In 1908 he was appointed instructor and assistant in general ethnology, in which capacity he taught, worked in the museum, and traveled to American Indian communities at every opportunity, beginning his work with the Penobscot in 1907. His intellectual interests also attracted many visitors, the beginning of a long pattern. A wandering South African Bushman, Amgoza, visited him for several weeks in 1911, and Speck spent his spare time studying Khoisan (a southern African language group) texts, which apparently have not survived.

On Sept. 15, 1910, Speck married Florence Insley of Nanuet, N.Y.; they had three children, Frank Staniford, Alberta Insley, and Virginia Colfax. The Specks traveled to Labrador, where he began extended fieldwork that led to many publications and to his major book, *Naskapi: Savage Hunters of the Labrador Peninsula* (1935). Florence Speck always shared as much field research with him as possible.

George Byron Gordon, the autocratic director

of the University Museum, fired Speck in 1911 because of some unknown conflict. He put the contents of Speck's office in the museum courtyard and locked up the finished manuscript on the Penobscot which had been submitted for publication. The manuscript was not recovered for many years and was finally published in 1940 under the title *Penobscot Man*. Speck was immediately rehired by the university as an assistant professor, essentially filling the place of Daniel Garrison Brinton, who had originally taught anthropology in the department of comparative religion; he held this position until 1925. In 1913 he was appointed acting chairman of the department of anthropology and chairman in 1925.

All of Speck's professional life was devoted to research and teaching. His pattern of research was notable in that he maintained close contacts with so many communities over so many decades, working slowly through one fundamental paper after another on so many fronts. All of his work was fresh; no study was ever revised or imbedded in a later publication. His ability to learn languages and his phonetic ear were remarkable. He used recording equipment over many years for speech and song, beginning with Yuchi in 1904, and he pioneered in ethnomusicology in collaboration with the Cantor Jacob Sapir in his *Ceremonial Songs of the Creek and Yuchi Indians* (1911). Few of these cylinder recordings have survived, most having been reused after transcription. He also normally transcribed music in the field, checking tone with a pitch pipe. He considered the field of American Indian ethnology to be inexhaustible, seeing every stage in the culture change of native communities as presenting new challenges to anthropology, and he looked forward to a time when students might deal with communities of their own culture in the same objective manner.

He believed in a simple and uncluttered life and was most at home under primitive conditions. His fieldnotes consisted chiefly of hard data such as language texts, vocabulary, abstracts and compressions, and highly abbreviated narrative material, mostly on scrap paper. As this material was transcribed, most of the original notes were discarded; only unused material was saved. As the transcriptions were reworked into finished manuscript, they in turn were discarded; thus his archival remains contain little correspondence and a residue of unused original material. He experimented with cinematography in the 1920's, but was not impressed with the results, and few film pieces

survive. He did his own photography with simple equipment, using an old Kodak folding camera with postcard-sized film in his later years.

He had a love for material objects, the crafts, and for primitive art, collecting wherever he found specimens, being most concerned with recording their contexts and lore. The quantity of significant material that passed through his hands was enormous. His main interest in collecting was to record associated data and to have a chance to enjoy and study the object for a time. Beyond that, he believed the specimens were better stored elsewhere, and he sold practically every object he had ever found, no matter how precious, preferably to public museums. His sale of these objects was an important source of funds for his field studies. Grants were scant, and Speck financed most of his own work; he never earned more than $6,000 a year. He never paid fees to linguistic informants, but was extremely generous with gifts. He feared commercialization of ethnographic field studies.

Speck, who was fiercely democratic, identified strongly with American Indians and their values; while himself highly cultured, he condemned the values of the elite and always took the position of the common man. Curiosity and the compulsion to understand were his deepest drives. He carried Darwinism, classical philosophy, cultural relativism, social altruism, and an identification with the underdog in the most delicate balance, only seen between the lines in his publications but ever-emerging in his teaching, where he appeared to many students to be a major philosopher. He sometimes jokingly referred to himself as a vulgarian, and to some he seemed an amusing and appealing eccentric, but no intelligent person ever mistook him for an eccentric. As a scholar and as a man, he forever remained true to his family heritage of pioneer and native origin, and to the insights he gained from Fidelia Fielding. His love and respect for mankind extended everywhere. As a teacher, he touched many people with ideas and emotions that led them on to fulfillment, but none is ever likely to reach the level of understanding of the fate of man that he achieved.

His last years were spent in combating the problems of a failing heart muscle compounded with the kidney disease produced by it. He continued working at compelling problems of the recording and understanding of cultural material, and at least six American Indian communities were invoking their gods and using their religious traditions for his well-being. He collapsed in the field with his wife, at Allegheny Reservation in western New York, where he was both observer and participant in the Great Annual Renewal Ceremony of the Seneca people and a patient of their priests; he died soon after in University Hospital in Philadelphia.

[Speck's formal obituary and bibliography is by A. Irving Hallowell, *Am. Anthropologist*, 53 (1951), 67–87. His surviving field notes and personal papers are at the Am. Philos. Soc. in Philadelphia, with minor materials in the archives of the Univ. of Pennsylvania. An autobiographical sketch is reputed to be at the Peabody Museum at Salem, Mass. His photographic negative files are at the Heye Foundation, Museum of the Am. Indian, New York City. Musical and language recordings that survive are at the Archives of Folk Music, Indiana Univ. Experimental cinema reels are at the Univ. Museum, Univ. of Pennsylvania. His collections are scattered through innumerable museums, most of them accompanied by field notes and linguistic glosses. The only known photographic portrait of Speck is in the Archives of the Univ. of Pennsylvania; a published photograph (proof) appears with his formal obituary.]

JOHN WITTHOFT

SPEER, ROBERT ELLIOTT (Sept. 10, 1867-Nov. 23, 1947), Presbyterian churchman and foreign missions administrator, was born in Huntingdon, Pa., the second of the three sons and five children of Robert Milton Speer and Martha Ellen (McMurtie) Speer. His father, of Swiss, Scots-Irish, and English ancestry, was a lawyer and leader of the local Democratic party, who served two terms in Congress (1871-1875). His mother died when Robert was nine, leaving the care of the children to the father, who never remarried, and to a maternal great-aunt. A kindly, generous man of strong principles, the elder Speer was a devout Presbyterian. Young Robert grew up a hardy, athletic boy with a cheerful, uncomplicated temperament. After attending public school at home he prepared for two years (1883-1885) at Phillips Academy, Andover, Mass., to enter the College of New Jersey (now Princeton University).

While playing on the football team and participating fully in college life, Speer was a serious-minded undergraduate, and, like many of his fellow students, he came under the influence of the evangelist Dwight L. Moody. In his sophomore year, moved by a missionary's appeal, Speer decided on a career of missionary service. He graduated in 1889 with the B.A. degree, and spent the following year visiting colleges as traveling secretary of the Student Volunteer Movement for Foreign Missions. In 1890 he entered Princeton Theological Seminary but left during his second year (1891) to become secretary of the Board of Foreign

Missions of the Presbyterian Church in the U.S.A., a position he held for nearly half a century. He was never ordained to the ministry. On Apr. 20, 1893, he married Emma Doll Bailey, a student at Bryn Mawr College. They had five children: Elliott, Margaret Bailey, Eleanor McMurtrie, Constance Sophea, and William. His wife was also active in church work and shared her husband's travels, including a trip around the world in 1896.

Speer was one of the world leaders of the Protestant missionary movement in the generation when that movement reached its climax. He was a culminating product of nineteenth-century evangelicalism at a time of transition to evangelical liberalism, although he himself did not make that transition. He had a much deeper interest in historical and political forces than in metaphysics, and although throughout his life he held to the basic tenets of orthodoxy, he disparaged debate about such matters in the face of the world's pressing spiritual and social needs. Speer envisaged whole nations and their cultures being transformed by the missionary movement. Foreign missions were part of an irresistible "projection of the West upon the East," a projection which, he fully acknowledged, was accompanied by numerous economic and moral evils, but which he was convinced was predominantly beneficial, for it brought Christianity and, in its wake, "progress and free government." The primary object of missions, he insisted, was the salvation of individuals, but the winning of souls must be accompanied by the formation in each land of a native church rooted in the culture and experience of its people, yet surrendering "nothing that is essential and universal" in Christianity. It was these native churches that would transform the nation's life and culture.

Speer's duties as secretary took him to many foreign countries, particularly in the Far East and South America. He had a remarkably retentive memory, a tough constitution, and a capacity for mastering minute administrative details while never losing sight of long-range problems and opportunities. These qualities, as well as his personal kindliness and charity, enabled him to function both as an able executive and as a counselor and friend to individual missionaries. Besides being chief administrator for the Board of Foreign Missions, he was its chief spokesman, fund raiser, and publicist. He was in great demand as a speaker and influenced a great number of persons to enter missionary careers. With his world outlook, wide reading, concrete and logical thought, clear literary style, and overwhelming physical vitality, he dominated large audiences. An earnestness bordering at times on severity was softened by touches of humor and by warmly human anecdotes. In his addresses and his numerous Bible studies he emphasized the winsomeness of Jesus Christ; following the theologian Horace Bushnell, whose writings greatly influenced him, Speer frequently argued that the very perfection of Christ's humanity proved him to be more than a man. Speer's tremendous dynamism found frequent expression in his emphasis on Christ's living power. He quoted Pascal: "It is the heart that feels God, not the reason"; yet he always insisted that true spiritual experience must go beyond feelings to ethical commitment. His biographies of missionaries stressed the heroic and sacrificial aspect of Christian life.

Speer was critical of those aspects of liberalism that he deemed shallow and unrealistic. He believed firmly in the absoluteness of Christianity. Christianity does not learn new truths from non-Christian religions, he said, but is stimulated by them to discover truths in its own gospel that it has not seen before. Thus in 1933 he sharply rejected the "humanistic this-world" presuppositions underlying the laymen's report *Re-Thinking Missions,* which argued for religious syncretism, reduced or ignored the supernatural element of Christianity, and predicted a further evolution of religious truths. Although he acknowledged the positive features of the report, Speer dismissed its theological basis as that of an outmoded nineteenth-century liberalism, pointing to the modern countermovement of Karl Barth, William Visser 't Hooft, and others.

On social issues Speer was in agreement with the liberal temper. He endorsed World War I as "a just and necessary war," but did so with a restraint and Christian self-judgment that was in advance of its day and incurred bitter denunciation: he warned that the war was no panacea, and that behind the loudly professed ideals, political forces were jockeying for power. At the end of the war he declared race to be one of the world's most pressing problems, for which the solution was to be found in the gospel, with social justice and political equality for all; but he neither favored nor foresaw early racial amalgamation. He also denounced the brutality implicit in social Darwinism. Speer early favored interdenominational cooperation in the foreign mission enterprises among the evangelical churches—he even envisaged the division of the Roman Catholic church into national units that would coalesce with Protestant churches—but he always gave greater emphasis to cooperation than to organic mergers. He was particularly forward-looking in his insistence that women have an equal role in the work of the church.

Dr. Speer received honorary doctorates from eight institutions, including the University of Edinburgh, Rutgers, and Princeton. He was prominent in the World Missionary Conference in Edinburgh in 1910 and in the International Missionary Council, and was chairman (1910-1936) of the Committee on Co-operation in Latin America. During World War I he was chairman of the General Wartime Commission of the Churches. Subsequent years saw his election as president of the Federal Council of the Churches of Christ in America (1920-1924), president of the Foreign Missions Conference of North America (1937), and moderator of the General Assembly of the Presbyterian Church in the U.S.A. (1927). Probably no man of his generation represented more authentically his church's theological stance and its most deeply cherished aspirations. Speer retired from his secretaryship of the Board of Foreign Missions in 1937. Ten years later, at the age of eighty, he died of leukemia at the Bryn Mawr (Pa.) Hospital and was buried in the family plot in Brookside Cemetery, Englewood, N.J.

[Speer's extensive papers are in the Robert E. Speer Lib. of Princeton Theological Seminary. Among his sixty-nine books are *Studies of the Man Christ Jesus* (1896) ; *Missions and Politics in Asia* (1898) ; *Missions and Modern History* (2 vols., 1904) ; *Christianity and the Nations* (1910) ; *The Christian Man, the Church and the War* (1918) ; *The Finality of Jesus Christ* (1933) ; and *"Re-Thinking Missions" Examined* (1933). For biographical material, see W. Reginald Wheeler, *A Man Sent From God: A Biog. of Robert E. Speer* (1956) ; John A. Mackay in *Princeton Seminary Bull.,* Summer 1948 (an issue that contains other articles on Speer) and June 1967 ; Kenneth S. Latourette in the *Moravian,* Sept. 1967 ; and, for ecclesiastical background, Lefferts A. Loetscher, *The Broadening Church: A Study of Theological Issues in the Presbyterian Church since 1869* (1954).]
LEFFERTS A. LOETSCHER

SPURR, JOSIAH EDWARD (Oct. 1, 1870-Jan. 12, 1950), mining geologist, was born in Gloucester, Mass., the youngest of three sons of Alfred Sears Spurr and Oratia Eliza (Snow) Spurr. Both parents were Nova Scotians of colonial Massachusetts descent; his father and brothers operated a fishing schooner. Small and frail, Josiah was reared in a strict religious household (presumably Unitarian, his denomination as an adult) and in straitened circumstances. He attended the Gloucester high school, where he developed literary skills and a strong interest in poetry, and entered Harvard in

1888 on a scholarship. Although he reached the head of the freshman class, his means were limited, and out of pride he left college in 1889 to take a succession of odd jobs. Reasoning that he wanted a career as useful as that of his father, and encouraged by the geologist Nathaniel S. Shaler, Spurr returned to Harvard two years later, determined to become a geologist. He gained his first field experience as assistant to William M. Davis in mapping glacial features in New England. Spurr graduated, B.A. magna cum laude, in 1893. He received a Harvard M.A.—his highest degree—the next year, in absentia.

After leaving Harvard in 1893, Spurr joined the Minnesota Geological Survey and, for Horace V. and Newton H. Winchell, made the first geological map of the Mesabi iron range. He identified a new mineral species (grunerite) and published a well-received monograph on the iron-bearing rocks of the Mesabi. On the strength of this work, he was made a fellow of the Geological Society of America in 1894 and was appointed to the U.S. Geological Survey. Assigned to assist Samuel F. Emmons in Colorado, Spurr taught himself how to do underground mapping by candlelight at Leadville, went on to Mercur, Utah, in the Oquirrh Range, and in 1895 rejoined Emmons at Aspen. In the following year he headed the survey's first expedition to Alaska and afterward published a geologic report on the Yukon gold fields. On leave in 1897, Spurr tried to complete his education at Friedrich Wilhelm University in Berlin, but rebelled against the autocratic atmosphere and after a few months joined Alfred H. Brooks and Horace Winchell, who were studying in Paris with Alfred Lacroix at the Sorbonne. After returning to Alaska with the Klondike gold rush in 1898, Spurr was offered the task of heading an Alaskan Geological Survey, but passed it on to Brooks in order to marry (on Jan. 18, 1899) Sophie Clara Burchard. Their protracted honeymoon was a geological reconnaissance of Nevada and parts of California. In 1900 Spurr went to Turkey for a year as geological advisor to Sultan Abdul Hamid. There he studied the gold gravel deposits of Macedonia, helped revise the Turkish mining laws, and wrote a textbook, *Geology Applied to Mining* (1904). It was typical of Spurr that he refused the offer of a princely salary in Turkey in order to return to the survey, and then resigned in 1906 when his request for a $300 raise was refused.

At thirty-five, Spurr was probably as experienced as any mining expert in the world. For two years he served the American Smelting and Refining Company of Daniel Guggenheim as chief geologist. Sent to the company's Esperanza mine in Mexico, he promptly located the faulted-off extension of the main gold vein. After four years as an independent mining consultant, Spurr joined the Tonopah Mining Company of Nevada in 1912, and later carried out mining ventures in Manitoba and in Nicaragua. During World War I he served in Washington as chairman of the committee to investigate mineral needs and resources. At the close of the war he joined the McGraw-Hill Publishing Company as editor of its *Engineering and Mining Journal*. He retired in 1927.

In *The Ore Magmas* (1923), a massive two-volume work, Spurr tried to convey all of his vast experience in mining geology. As early as 1898 he had arrived at a theory of the magmatic origin of ore veins. He had observed that gold quartz veins could frequently be traced into pegmatites and these in turn into alaskites and granites. By extension he considered that even veins of sulphides are true vein-dikes, intruding under great pressure in a "viscous or gelatinous state . . . a condition between solution and crystallization." Spurr wrote knowledgeably of zoning, of metallogenetic provinces and epochs, telescoping, and magmatic differentiation. He accounted for localization of ores by an originally "heterogeneous underearth" and dealt boldly with global tectonics. Everything that he wrote had the immediacy of firsthand observation, but Spurr shared with his rivals Waldemar Lindgren and Grove K. Gilbert a fundamental discomfort in the presence of the exact sciences. His writing was discursive, polemic, ingenious, but sparing of references to the work of others, and he showed little awareness of the thermodynamic and crystallographic evidences that were then revolutionizing geology. Later, with the introduction of phase equilibria studies at high pressure, inferences that Spurr had drawn from his wide experience were in part validated—his repeated references to the "gelatinous" nature of the ore-forming fluid, for example. Spurr's inability to relate his ideas to the concepts of physical chemistry prevented their acceptance, and his lack of an academic research position prevented their further development.

Spurr earned his share of contention and dispute. Early in his career with the survey, he was invited by the director Charles D. Walcott to comment on G. K. Gilbert's interpretation of the Basin and Range Structure; he entered a controversy that pitted him with Walcott and

Emmons against Gilbert as well as against Davis, his former classmate. Believing that the Geological Society of America had become too undemocratic, he helped form the Society of Economic Geologists in 1905 and served as its president in 1923. He found similar fault with the Mining and Metallurgical Society, resigning its presidency after one year (1921).

At the time of their controversy, Gilbert was writing on the origin of topographic features on the moon. Many years later, a photograph of the lunar surface stimulated Spurr to develop a theory contradicting Gilbert's ideas. His first paper on this subject was rejected by the Geological Society's *Bulletin,* but during the years 1944-1949 he published, at his own expense, four volumes on *Geology Applied to Selenology.* His methodology was essentially that of his generation—a discursive reasoning-out of the genesis of lunar morphology by analogy with the surface of the earth and its volcanic processes. The strength of Spurr's lunar work lay in its originality and daring in applying geologic reasoning to the moon, and also in the half-century of firsthand observation of geology that he could bring to bear. Its weakness was that of *The Ore Magmas*—a basic lack of scientific sophistication. Modern students sharing views akin to those of Gilbert's paper consider Spurr's work as worthless, but the vulcanist school of selenologists consider Spurr's principal ideas to have been confirmed by actual exploration. The disputes over his ideas on this and other subjects did not end with his death. Not until two decades had passed did the Geological Society of America publish a memorial of him.

After his retirement in 1927 and some travel, Spurr settled in Winter Park, Fla., where for several years he taught at Rollins College. He died of uremia in Winter Park at the age of seventy-nine; after cremation, his ashes were buried near his summer home at East Alstead, N.H. He was survived by his wife and their five children: Edward Burchard, John Constantine, William Alfred, Robert Anton, and Stephen Hopkins. Mount Spurr in the Aleutians was named for him, as was the mineral spurrite.

[Memorial by Jack Green in Geological Soc. of America, *Proc.,* 1968, with photograph and bibliography; Harvard College Class of 1893, *Twenty-fifth Anniversary Report* (1918); *Who Was Who in America,* III (1960); death record from Fla. Bureau of Vital Statistics; obituary in *N.Y. Times,* Jan. 13, 1950. A MS. autobiography is in family possession. Some of Spurr's papers are at the West. Hist. Research Center, Univ. of Wyoming.]

CECIL J. SCHNEER

STARBUCK, EDWIN DILLER (Feb. 20, 1866-Nov. 19, 1947), pioneer psychologist of religion and innovator in character education, was born Edwin Eli Starbuck in Bridgeport, Ind. (now part of Indianapolis), the youngest of seven boys and two girls of Samuel Starbuck and Luzena (Jessup) Starbuck. His family was of Nordic stock. In 1660 his father's family had immigrated to Nantucket, where they engaged in whaling. Starbuck was educated at Union High School in Westfield, Ind.; Indiana University (B.A., 1890); Harvard University (M.A., 1895); and Clark University (Ph.D., 1897). He was assistant professor of education at Stanford University (1897-1903), professor of education at Earlham College (1904-1906), and professor of philosophy at the State University of Iowa (1906-1930) and the University of Southern California (1930-1943).

Although Starbuck was the author of the first book to be formally entitled *The Psychology of Religion* (1899), he was by no means the only pioneer applying to religious experience the methods and perspectives of the new science of psychology; George Coe and James Leuba published similar studies of conversion at about the same time, and William James's *The Varieties of Religious Experience* was to follow three years later—all these authors were in communication with each other during their writing. Starbuck's work was distinctive. It was based on the most thorough and painstaking collection of empirical data, and Starbuck made it clear that a new science was being launched. Calling it the "last step in the growth of empiricism," he spelled out its charter with unsurpassed vigor and clarity:

> The psychology of religion is a purely inductive study into the phenomena of religion as shown in individual experience. . . . The end in view is not to classify and define the phenomena of religion, but to see into the laws and processes at work in the spiritual life. The fundamental assumption is that religion is a real fact of human experience and develops according to law (p. 16).

Before becoming a Harvard graduate student in 1893, Starbuck was already committed to this program. After devising elaborate open-ended questionnaires, he began collecting several hundred lengthy statements on personal religious development, determined the units by which they could be analyzed, and organized these components into patterns. He continued during his two years at Harvard and the two years at Clark. His findings, first reported to a class at the Harvard Divinity School, later provided the basis for his doctoral dissertation (1897), two journal articles (1897), and *Psychology of Religion,* published in Havelock Ellis's Contemporary Science series. Starbuck patiently charted religion as a response to the psychic conflict and distress that James and Freud were soon to dramatize. (Starbuck's commencement oration at Indiana had been drawn from Hegel and entitled "The Unity of Opposites.")

The historical and literary study of religion was already maturing, as Starbuck eagerly discovered, first at Indiana University and then in the reading program that he prepared for himself during three years as a teacher of Latin and mathematics. Starbuck regarded such "higher criticism" and his own psychological version of it as an ally, not an antagonist, of religion. He expected such efforts to restore meaning and intellectual respectability to religion in the wake of Darwin's assaults on former orthodoxies. His own psychological study was clearly intended to preserve the intelligibility of religion, rather than to attack its credibility, as was the case with other contemporary psychologists of religion, most notably James Leuba. Starbuck's Quaker heritage endowed him with a permanent respect for religious experience but left him relatively unencumbered by dogmas to defend or to renounce. Quakerism also gave him much training in and respect for spiritual introspection—the method he later relied on for his empirical data.

Starbuck provided no research beyond his dissertation, although he continued to speak out vigorously on the need for empirical study, to teach courses in the psychology of religion, and to guide doctoral candidates. "Psychology is to religion what the science of medicine is to health," he wrote. Starbuck chose to devote most of his career to the application of his science, to encourage religious health. In the context of his humanistic, behavioristic, and nondoctrinal orientation, this outlook almost of necessity meant paying attention to character education. He argued vigorously against trying to develop character by indoctrination. One must induce character by "intriguing [the child's] imagination, eliciting his active, creative interest, and stirring his impulses" (Ferm, p. 243). He tried to persuade Unitarians to adopt such an approach, during a two-year leave (1912-1914) as a consultant to that denomination, but he regarded this venture as unsuccessful. By 1921, however, his approach had achieved wide recognition, and Starbuck's career began its most productive period. In that

year, the Character Education Institution of Washington, D.C., in a national competition awarded a $20,000 prize to the nine-member committee, of which Starbuck was chairman, that developed the "Iowa Plan" for character education. Lecture invitations followed and in 1923 the Institute of Character Research was established at Iowa. Starbuck headed it and took it with him to the University of Southern California in 1930; he retired thirteen years later. The institute, which survived until 1939, published several doctoral dissertations and many volumes of literary anthologies and bibliographies of works selected for their effectiveness in character education.

On Aug. 5, 1896, Starbuck married Anna M. Diller, whose name he took as his middle name. They had eight children, six of whom survived infancy.

[Starbuck's pioneer research on religious conversion was *The Psychology of Religion* (1899), previously published as two articles in the *Am. Jour. of Psychology:* "A Study of Conversion," Jan. 1897, pp. 268–308; and "Some Aspects of Religious Growth," Oct. 1897, pp. 70-124. Perhaps the most accessible and definitive of his writings on character education is "Methods of a Science of Character," *Religious Education,* Sept. 1927. He wrote on various subjects for the *Encyc. of Religion and Ethics* (1917), from "Backsliding" to "Self-expression"—most lengthily on "Female Principle," a survey of the role of female figures and of sex in religion. The many volumes of literature on character education were published between 1928 and 1930, and in 1936. An autobiographical account is "Religion's Use of Me," in Vergilius Ferm, ed., *Religion in Transition,* pp. 201–260 (1937). Some information on Starbuck's middle name and on other matters was kindly supplied by the registrars of Harvard and Indiana Univ.]

JAMES E. DITTES

STEIN, GERTRUDE (Feb. 3, 1874-July 27, 1946), author, liked the homely exoticism of having Allegheny, Pa., for her birthplace. Her earliest memories, however, were of Vienna, where her father, Daniel Stein, moved for business reasons in 1875, and then Paris. Her mother, Amelia (Keyser) Stein, was an invalid before dying of cancer in 1888 and figured only remotely and negatively in Gertrude's preadolescence. The family returned to America in 1879, settling the next year in Oakland, Calif. Gertrude had thus heard three different languages before fully acquiring one—the background of her fascination with words detached from common meanings. Her privileged position as second daughter and youngest of five children also had bearing on her development, particularly on her solipsism as a writer. Her belief that, after two siblings had died, she and her brother Leo had been conceived only in order to make up the quota of five children that their parents had agreed upon made life seem precarious and gave emotional impetus to her speculations on time and identity.

When her father died suddenly in 1891, it was a relief; irascible, tyrannical, and capricious, he occasioned her generalization, "Fathers are depressing." Her closest relationship was with Leo, with whom she shared not only the bond of accidental life but intellectual interests that set them apart from their schoolmates in Oakland. The Philistine do-goodism of the public school atmosphere isolated them more than their German-Jewish background. In her childhood the absence of any mention of an afterlife in the Old Testament caused Gertrude anxiety. Her lifelong search for a timeless state may be viewed as an effort to escape the blankness of nonexistence. Without religious belief, she also eventually disclaimed emotional and social identification with Judaism.

Following his father as an executive of a street railway company in San Francisco and as head of the family after his death, Michael Stein, the oldest son, managed to provide each child with an income sufficient for a modestly scaled bourgeois life. At Radcliffe College, which she attended from 1893 to 1897 (B.A., 1898), Gertrude's primary interest was the psychology of William James; his theory of consciousness forms the basis of her thought. Her name first appeared in print as coauthor of a report on normal motor automatism. Later, probably to discredit B. F. Skinner's explanation of her experimental writing as similarly "automatic," she repudiated relevant aspects of the report. Her chief interest in her single-handed experiments on automatism was in classifying the "bottom nature" of her subjects, not in their tested reactions. To prepare for a career in psychology, she entered Johns Hopkins Medical School in 1897. Her research on the brain was solid, but bored by routine courses, she failed final examinations and preferred traveling abroad with Leo to retaking them. After a period in London at the British Museum systematically reading English narratives from the Elizabethans to the present, she joined Leo in Paris in 1903 at 27 Rue de Fleurus.

Leo, although he was never to succeed in translating his aesthetic intellections into tangible achievement, was among the first to recognize the genius of postimpressionist painters. He and Gertrude began to cover their walls with masters of the Paris school, which Leo expounded to the uninitiated who streamed through their soon-famous flat. Gertrude Stein's taste in art has been challenged, but unlike Leo, who rejected cubism, she grasped its aesthetic purposes; and in her friendships, especially with Pablo Picasso, Juan Gris, and Francis Picabia, she promoted modern art. Picasso's portrait of her was a crucial step toward cubism. Massive in figure, with delicate hands, the head of a Roman emperor, and enigmatic eyes, she also sat for the sculptors Jacques Lipschitz and Jo Davidson. Cézanne's portrait of his wife in the Stein collection had a seminal effect on her thought, and her writings on Picasso contain some of her most penetrating statements on modernism. Michael Stein and his wife, Sarah, perhaps even more creatively sponsored the new art, especially that of Matisse and Le Corbusier. The four Steins have an indisputable place as patrons and publicists in the history of postimpressionism, not the least for their influence on Etta and Claribel Cone, whose collection, now in the Baltimore Museum of Art, includes many works bought on their advice or once owned by them.

Gertrude Stein's literary achievement is more problematic, partially because her work was published only sporadically, in fugitive periodicals, and out of compositional order. Her earliest fiction, Q.E.D., completed in 1903, first appeared posthumously in 1950 under the title *Things as They Are.* Supposedly "forgotten," it was more probably withheld, like E. M. Forster's *Maurice,* because of its homoeroticism. It shows adeptness in assimilation of Henry James's late techniques; despite its mixture of pseudoliterary and colloquial styles, it effectively communicates the pain of emotional entrapment. In "Melanctha," the last of three long stories published by a vanity press in 1909 as *Three Lives* (echoing Flaubert's *Trois Contes*), the central love affair between a Negro doctor and a mulatto girl is more paradigmatic, the characters existing almost entirely as mental processes. To create the illusion of experience as felt moment by moment— the "continuous present"—she heightened the inherent repetition that she observed in speech patterns and increased the incidence of present participles and gerunds. Often cited as a minor classic, its racial clichés justified or denied, "Melanctha" is stylistically original but at the expense of fictional reality as created in the cruder *Q.E.D.* or in the similarly experimental and minor *Pilgrimage,* by Dorothy Richardson.

The Making of Americans, probably written between 1903 and 1911 and published in 1925, which she considered equal in innovativeness to Proust's and Joyce's masterpieces, marks a stage in Gertrude Stein's development parallel to cubism in its incorporation of random events and the process of composition itself. Begun as a history of a representative family, it was expanded into a history of the human race. It belongs, however, to no recognizable genre except the American gigantesque—a Mount Rushmore shrouded in fog. Even leaving aside its length (550,000 words), its unpunctuated syntactic dislocations, incremental repetitions, and lack of fictional amenities make it difficult to read and indeed require a redefinition of verbal cognition. *Tender Buttons,* published in 1914, was her work most resembling verbal collage. From this book onward, narrative, with its assumption of a causal ordering of events, an assumption that she believed falsified the complexities of experience, mostly disappears. In the antinomian American tradition, she wanted to show "things as they are," not as they are known to be. Since words are residua of memory and association, she declined to use them except as counters for whatever came into her own purview.

The obvious fallacy is that words, unlike sounds in music or paint on canvas, cannot be entirely separated from generally accepted meanings. Without a frame of reference other than her own consciousness, Gertrude Stein's most extreme works make excessive demands on a reader's tolerance for mystification and tedium. Her rejection of traditional literary structures for the sake of authenticity—which makes her plays, portraits, novels, and poems virtually indistinguishable in manner and content—was not redeemed by her constant search for psychological or philosophical laws subsuming the multitudinous particulars of life. Owing to her speculative bent and scientific training, her work is thus also characterized by oversimplified schemata, relentlessly pursued classifications of minutiae, and abstractness, or a striking absence of "felt life." Fragments have wit, beauty, and aphoristic power, but her importance as a creative mind is not as an artist—certainly not an artist equal to Pound, Eliot, or Joyce, with whom some contemporaries erroneously linked her as a symbolist—but rather as an author of epistemological meditations, happenings, or enactments and for the continuing catalytic effect of her language games and theories, which first came to influence Americans who flocked to Paris after World War I.

Although in middle life she was still largely unpublished, Gertrude Stein was sought after as a savant of the new. Her lectures given at Cambridge and Oxford in 1926 and published as *Composition as Explanation* represent one of her earliest efforts to elucidate her practice and formulate theoretical principles. Other important efforts are *Lectures in America* and *Narration* (both published in 1935) and *What Are Masterpieces* (1940). Through her influence on Sherwood Anderson and, more significantly, on Ernest Hemingway, she made a decisive contribution to modern American literature and prose style, although assessments of this contribution tend to be colored by responses to her personality. Her "hearty humanity," forthrightness, shrewd picturesque pronouncements, and other less definable qualities—a reverberent voice, an infectious laugh, a mixed aura of Buddha, Wise Child, and Earth Mother—gave her a magnetism apart from the respect her work elicited. Leo having left in 1913, and with Alice B. Toklas from 1909 as her companion, amanuensis, and shield against bores and wives of geniuses, she enjoyed a Johnsonian eminence in her salon, where the roster of visitors was an index to the distinguished artists and intellectuals of her time. The poem titled "Before the Flowers of Friendship Faded Friendship Faded" epitomizes the ephemeral character of many of her friendships, but she did have warm, lasting ones, as with Anderson, Carl Van Vechten, and Thornton Wilder, and cordial ones with others, including the Sitwells and Alfred North Whitehead; but her reputation for quarrelsomeness was founded on more than the bitter personal and literary feud with Hemingway, which they both pursued in print. Other former friends and those who immediately disliked or had reason to resent her childishly absolute egotism have exposed this side of her profile in memoirs of the legendary 1920's.

She created her own legend in *The Autobiography of Alice B. Toklas,* using the persona of her friend to write about herself in a communicable style. Of permanent interest as an anecdotal history rich in personalities and period flavor, the autobiography was a best seller in 1933. The next year her esoteric opera *Four Saints in Three Acts,* with music by Virgil Thomson, was premiered with fanfare in Hartford, Conn., and moved to New York City. Of the other dramatic works produced with some critical success, the most notable are the ballet *A Wedding Bouquet* (1937), choreographed by Frederick Ashton and scored by Lord Gerald Berners, *Yes Is for a Very Young Man* (1946), and the opera *The Mother of Us All* (1947) in collaboration with Virgil Thomson. The texts, flat notations in print, come alive when spoken or staged, in some instances creating an effect comparable to the dramatic inconsequences of Harold Pinter or Eugene Ionesco.

After thirty years, Gertrude Stein returned to America for a triumphant lecture tour in 1934. Her reacquaintance with the country—and first view of it from the air—led to insights into American character and landscape in *The Geographical History of America* (1936). Although she courted public success and effectively used her grasp of modern publicity techniques, being a headlined celebrity disturbed her sense of identity, as she revealed in *Everybody's Autobiography* (1937), written in her easy-reading vein. Philosophical and exemplary like Whitman in "Song of Myself," she was, however, divided here between searching for, and egregiously celebrating, herself.

Throughout World War II, she lived in seclusion with Alice Toklas in occupied France, near Belley, where they had summered since the 1920's. With the liberation, Gertrude Stein entered her last phase as an American monument in Paris, holding open house for GI's. *Wars I Have Seen* (1945), begining with the Spanish-American, had immediate journalistic appeal in its account of daily life during her last war. She died of cancer in the American Hospital at Neuilly-sur-Seine and was buried in Père-Lachaise Cemetery, Paris. On her gravestone her birthplace is spelled "Allfghany."

[The standard bibliography is Robert B. Haas and Donald C. Gallup, *A Catalogue of the Published and Unpublished Writings of Gertrude Stein* (1941). Its chronology of composition has been revised by Richard Bridgman in *Gertrude Stein in Pieces* (1970), a balanced, comprehensive study of her works, invaluable biographically and critically. James R. Mellow's *Charmed Circle, Gertrude Stein & Company* (1974) succeeds admirably in evoking her world and the texture of her life and is rich in photographs and quotations from memoirs and letters. Also of biographical interest are John Malcolm Brinnin, *The Third Rose: Gertrude Stein and Her World* (1959), Elizabeth Sprigge, *Gertrude Stein: Her Life and Work* (1957), and Alice B. Toklas's own autobiography, *What Is Remembered* (1963), and letters, *Staying on Alone, Letters of Alice B. Toklas*, ed. Edward Burns (1973). For a brief general critical introduction, see Frederick J. Hoffman, *Gertrude Stein* (Univ. of Minn. Pamphlets on Am. Writers, 1961). More specialized studies are Allegra Stewart, *Gertrude Stein and the Present* (1967), and Michael J. Hoffman, *The Development of Abstractionism in the Writings of Gertrude Stein* (1966). Benjamin L. Reid, *Art by Subtraction: A Dissenting Opinion of Gertrude Stein* (1958), is countered by Norman Weinstein, *Gertrude Stein and the Literature of the Modern Consciousness* (1970), an interpretation in the light of recent linguistics and poetry. For her American literary relations, see Mark Schorer, *The World We Imagine* (1968), and Tony Tanner, *The Reign of Wonder* (1965). *Four Americans in Paris: The Collections of Gertrude Stein and Her Family* (1970), a catalogue of the partially reassembled collections exhibited that year at the Museum of Modern Art (N.Y.), also contains essays on the Steins as collectors and photographs of the Stein salons and works. A useful introduction to the range of her works is *Selected Writings of Gertrude Stein*, ed. Carl Van Vechten (1946); the 1962 edition contains an essay by F. W. Dupee. Other collections are *Writings and Lectures, 1911–1945*, ed. Patricia Meyerowitz (1967); *Gertrude Stein on Picasso*, ed. Edward Burns (1970); *Selected Operas and Plays of Gertrude Stein*, ed. John Malcolm Brinnin (1970); *Fernhurst, Q.E.D. and Other Early Writings*, ed. Leon Katz (1971); and *Previously Uncollected Writings of Gertrude Stein*, vols. I and II, ed. Robert Bartlett Haas (1973). The Barrett Collection of the Univ. of Va. has letters, rare editions, and contemporary newspaper clippings. The manuscripts bequeathed to Yale Univ. have been published under the general editorship of Carl Van Vechten as *The Yale Edition of the Unpublished Writings of Gertrude Stein* (8 vols., 1951–1958).]

VIOLA HOPKINS WINNER

STEIN, LEO DANIEL (May 11, 1872-July 29, 1947), author and art critic, was born in Allegheny, Pa., son of Daniel Stein and Amelia Keyser Stein, both of German-Jewish extraction, who, at the time of their marriage in Baltimore in 1864, agreed to produce five children. This they accomplished by 1871; the deaths of two older children, however, necessitated the production of two more, Leo in 1872, and Gertrude in 1874. Along with his brother Solomon, Daniel Stein was then proprietor of a prosperous wholesale woolen business. The filial partnership became strained, however, and was dissolved shortly after Gertrude's birth. The rift sent Daniel to Vienna, where he moved his family in 1875. After three years in Vienna and another in Paris, the Steins returned to the United States, eventually settling in East Oakland, Calif.

Subjected to a multitude of unusual experiences at an early age, the two youngest Stein children became close, precocious, inward, and bookish. Leo's ambition was to become a historian, on the model of Gibbon, and he occupied himself memorizing enormous numbers of dates, dynasties, and royal lineages. Later, he studied history at the University of California and at Harvard, where he also became a pupil and dévot of William James.

After two years at Harvard (1892-1894), however, Stein concluded that history dealt only with superficialities, and abandoned it as a professional objective. After a year at Harvard Law School and a trip around the world, he entered the Johns Hopkins University (1897) to study biology. Soon disenchanted, his ambitions took another erratic swing, sending him to Europe to write a book on the Renaissance painter, Mantegna. It shortly became evident that his real interest in art was "esthetic and not historical," and he next decided to live in Paris and become a painter.

Gertrude joined her brother in Paris in 1903; together they took a flat at 27 rue de Fleurus and began filling it with furniture and paintings. Stein purchased his first modern painting in London the previous year and was eager to expand his collection. Finding nothing suitable in Paris, he complained to his friend Bernard Berenson, who replied by asking "Do you know Cézanne?" Stein's introduction to Cézanne launched him as a serious collector. He bought one of Cézanne's landscapes, studied many others, and then discovered Matisse, whose Fauve-period *La Femme au Chapeau* scandalized Paris in 1905; Stein thought it "a nasty smear of paint" but "brilliant and powerful" and bought it immediately for his collection. He bought his first Picasso in the same year, making the acquaintance of the artist as well, thereby becoming perhaps the first collector to appreciate both Matisse and Picasso.

Stein also acquired canvases by Gauguin, Renoir, Manet, Daumier, Delacroix, Maurice Denis, and Toulouse-Lautrec, giving the Stein apartment the appearance and attraction of a radical museum. People from everywhere came to visit, and Stein blossomed as a messianic guide to his collection, aggressively propagandizing both the new art and his opinions about it. Visitors were impressed, irritated, often both, but their numbers and credentials multiplied. The Steins became legend on both sides of the Atlantic.

Amid the fame, however, the pair had begun to, in Leo's words, "disaggregate," and by 1912, open warfare broke out. The causes were numerous: eclipsed for years by her brother, Gertrude began to assert herself as a personality and as an artist, and demanded recognition as such. Her brother, on the other hand, could abide neither her "stuff," as he called it, nor her thirst for *la gloire*. Picasso was another factor. With his discovery of cubism, he replaced Stein as his sister's mentor, and Stein was never able to forgive either offense. In Stein's estimation, Picasso was a great illustrator, "perhaps the greatest ever born," who possessed a powerful imagination, but "intellect, never." Cubism seemed to him the "intellectual product of the unintellectual," and he found its underlying ideas "silly and boring." Stein was never able, in fact, to digest the basic modernist principle through which both his sister and Picasso achieved distinction; the idea that rules were made to be broken was completely alien to his ordered, essentially classical, mentality. Leo's personality, furthermore, had become more and more that of a neurotic, for although his intellect was remarkable, he was able neither to accept his limitations nor to capitalize upon his talents. The coup de grace for Gertrude, however, was Stein's affair with Nina Auzias, a model well known in the artists' quarter. It was, according to Gertrude, "just too much."

Leaving the apartment in rue de Fleurus, Stein spent the war years in the United States, turning out a steady flow of articles for the *New Republic*. In March 1921, he married Nina Auzias and settled in Settignano (near Florence), Italy, where he remained the rest of his life. Until 1927, he contributed frequently to American publications, and in that year his first book, *The ABC's of Aesthetics,* was published. Its lukewarm critical acceptance and his increasing deafness deepened his neuroses, and he accomplished little for the next several years. When nearly seventy, Stein began to feel that twenty years of self-analysis had finally succeeded, and he returned happily to painting and writing. In 1947 his book *Appreciation: Painting, Poetry, and Prose* was published in the United States. Its timing and critical success confirmed Leo's belief that he had finally been able to build something substantial upon his intelligence, but that it was late, "too damned late." He died of cancer and was buried in Settignano, Italy.

Evaluations of Leo Stein's achievements will always be made with difficulty. Bernard Berenson saw him as "the sort of man who was always inventing the umbrella," while the critic Alfred Barr observed that during the years 1905-1907, Stein was perhaps the world's most discriminating connoisseur of twentieth-century painting. Leo himself defined genius as "the capacity to get into a biographical dictionary"; genius or not, his intelligent recollections have increased substantially our insights into the origins of modern art.

[Leo Stein, *Journey into the Self, Being the Letters, Papers, of Leo Stein,* ed. Edmund Fuller (1950); Leo Stein, *Appreciation: Painting, Poetry, and Prose* (1947); Leo Stein, *The ABC's of Aesthetics* (1927); John M. Brinnin, *The Third Rose,* (1952); Elizabeth Sprigge, *Gertrude Stein: Her Life and Work* (1957). Several photographs of Stein, his wife, and of his famous art collection may be found in *Journey into the Self.*]

PATRICIA STIPE FAILING

STEINHARDT, LAURENCE ADOLPH (Oct. 6, 1892–Mar. 28, 1950), lawyer and diplomat, was born in New York City, the second of three children and only son of Adolph

Max Steinhardt, head of a steel enameling and stamping company, and Addie (Untermyer) Steinhardt. Both parents were of German-Jewish ancestry. His paternal grandparents had emigrated from Hamburg in 1844. His mother's family was from Bavaria; the prominent New York attorney Samuel Untermyer was his uncle. After attending private schools, Steinhardt entered Columbia University, from which he received the B.A. degree in 1913 and the M.A. and LL.B. in 1915. He was admitted to the New York bar the following year. During World War I he served in the army field artillery and as a sergeant on the Provost Marshal General's staff. In 1920 he joined his uncle's law firm, Guggenheimer, Untermyer and Marshall. He married Dulcie Yates Hofmann in New York City on Jan 15, 1923. They had one child, Dulcie Ann.

A liberal Democrat, Steinhardt became interested in politics and in 1932 joined the preconvention presidential campaign committee of Franklin D. Roosevelt, to which he was one of the largest financial contributors. Following Roosevelt's election Steinhardt sought a prestigious position for a year or two to enhance his career. He turned down an offer to become an assistant secretary of state but accepted an appointment in 1933 as United States minister to Sweden. He was the youngest chief of a diplomatic mission, and he negotiated one of the administration's first reciprocal trade agreements. Finding the diplomatic life congenial, Steinhardt sought a higher position after the 1936 presidential election, in which he once again played an active role. He was named ambassador to Peru in 1937, and worked intensively to strengthen trade and cultural relations. His efforts impressed Secretary of State Cordell Hull, who two years later recommended Steinhardt's appointment as ambassador to the Soviet Union.

Steinhardt arrived in Moscow on the eve of the Nazi-Soviet Non-Aggression Pact of 1939, and he kept Washington remarkably well informed on the progress of the Russo-German negotiations. Grasping well the realities of Soviet policies, he stressed the solidarity of the agreement with Berlin and maintained that, for the time being at least, the two nations could not afford to quarrel. Steinhardt worked closely with an extremely able staff, and the prestige of the American embassy in Moscow reached a new high within the State Department. After the Russian invasion of Finland late in 1939, when pressure grew in the United States for the recall of the American ambassador as a form of protest, Steinhardt wrote: "The only language [the Soviets] understand is that of action, retaliation, and force and one might as well strike an elephant with a feather as to believe that the Kremlin is responsive to gestures."

As Soviet-American relations continued to erode, Soviet harassment of American citizens in Russia increased. Steinhardt accordingly advocated the "reciprocal application of unpleasant measures," and on one occasion persuaded the State Department to delay processing the request of a Soviet ship seeking passage through the Panama Canal. He made no distinction between ambassadorial and consular functions and often intervened directly to defend the personal and property rights of American nationals; occasionally he used his full influence for rather minor ends. After the fall of France to the Germans in 1940, the United States sought to improve Soviet-American relations by granting unilateral concessions, despite Steinhardt's repeated warnings that America's prestige would be harmed by not demanding a quid pro quo. As the anticipated improvement in relations did not occur, Washington moved closer to Steinhardt's policy of reciprocity during the spring of 1941. Despite confidential information from the German ambassador, Steinhardt failed to foresee the German invasion of the Soviet Union in 1941. Although he thought Moscow would fall quickly, he reported Russia's determination to resist and encouraged immediate American assistance; later he facilitated the lend-lease talks in Moscow.

With the Soviet Union actively at war, Steinhardt's continued insistence on reciprocity seemed out of place. Shortly after Pearl Harbor, therefore, Roosevelt sent him as ambassador to neutral Turkey, in spite of the informal request from the late President Ataturk not to appoint a Jewish ambassador. Recognizing the strategic importance of Turkey, Steinhardt helped influence that country's decision not to fulfill its trade commitment with Germany, particularly in delivering chrome metal, thereby achieving what one State Department officer (Livingston Merchant) called "the most complete and important victory in the field of economic warfare." Steinhardt used his personal influence with Ankara officials to increase the flow of refugees from the Nazi-controlled Balkans to Palestine, and also obtained the release of interned American fliers, for which he received the Legion of Merit. He afterward described his work in Turkey as his "most useful job."

Late in 1944 Roosevelt named Steinhardt

ambassador to Czechoslovakia. That central European country, ruled by a Communist-dominated coalition government, was a sensitive and critical spot in postwar Europe. Steinhardt maintained a firm position against the Communists' strong anti-American campaign during these years. After the announcement in 1947 of the Marshall Plan for the rebuilding of Europe, he successfully urged Washington to delay action on the Czech government's loan application until the campaign ended and American claims in Czechoslovakia were settled. As the Czech elections approached, Steinhardt saw the Communists' popularity declining, but he misjudged the party's ability, abetted by Moscow, to effect the coup d'état that took place in February 1948; still, it is doubtful that earlier action on the loan could have preserved the coalition government.

In the summer of 1948 President Harry S. Truman appointed Steinhardt ambassador to Canada, where he looked forward to living under normal conditions for the first time in a decade. The Canadians appreciated the appointment of so experienced a diplomat and were quickly impressed by his opposition to "the missionary spirit" toward Canada still found in some American circles. Election to high office in New York state was Steinhardt's greatest ambition, although during his diplomatic career he did not court publicity. Early in 1950, while flying to New York to attend a political dinner, he was killed in a plane crash near Ottawa, Ontario. He was fifty-seven years old. After funeral services in Ottawa and at Temple Emanu-El in New York City, Steinhardt was buried in the family mausoleum at Washington Cemetery in Brooklyn.

A complex and controversial person, Steinhardt earned the respect if not the strong personal loyalty of his subordinates. Fluent in a number of languages, he grew with his increasingly difficult assignments and became by the late 1930's a perceptive and analytical reporter. A colleague (George V. Allen) called him an "unusually effective Ambassador."

[Steinhardt's papers, in the Lib. of Cong.; State Dept. records; interviews and correspondence with a number of Steinhardt's colleagues and friends; files of the *N.Y. Times*, 1933–1950, especially editorial, obituary, and photograph, Mar. 29, 1950. See also *Who Was Who in America*, II (1950); and *Nat. Cyc. Am. Biog.*, XL, 70–71. No published work has assessed Steinhardt's diplomatic career, but there are two Ph.D. dissertations: Joseph O'Connor, "Laurence A. Steinhardt and Am. Policy toward the Soviet Union, 1939–1941" (Univ. of Virginia, 1968), and Ralph R. Stackman, "Laurence A. Steinhardt: New Deal Diplomat, 1933–1945" (Michigan State Univ., 1967).]

TRAVIS BEAL JACOBS

STELLA, JOSEPH (June 13, 1877–Nov. 5, 1946), painter, was born Giuseppe Stella in Muro Lucano, a village in the mountains near Naples, Italy. He was the fourth of five sons of Michele Stella, a lawyer, and Vicenza (Cerone) Stella. A lonely child, fat, clumsy, and introspective, Joseph felt an early dedication to art. A picture of the village's patron saint he painted for the parish church in his early teens made him something of a local celebrity. Although Stella hated school, his father insisted on educating all his sons through the higher levels. After attending the village school, Stella entered a classical *liceo,* probably in Naples, and received a *licenza liceale* (diploma).

In 1896 he left Italy for the United States; his elder brother Antonio, a physician who was to have a distinguished career as an expert on the public health problems of immigrants, had emigrated two years earlier. His brother wanted him to study medicine or pharmacy, but Stella balked at the discipline required. He enrolled instead in the Art Students League for a few months in 1897–1898, and later (probably between 1900 and 1902) studied at the New York School of Art under its founder, William Merritt Chase.

In the following decade Stella produced some of the finest figure drawings ever made in the United States. He did a set of sketches of immigrants for *Outlook* magazine in 1905, and in 1908 was commissioned by the social work journal *Charities and the Commons* (later renamed *Survey*) to provide a pictorial dimension to the historic "Pittsburgh Survey" of the lives of miners and steelworkers. His Pittsburgh portfolio included depictions of workers' houses and the bleak city landscape. Stylistically and thematically related to the work of the contemporary New York Realists led by Robert Henri (the group later called the "Ash Can School"), Stella's art at this time was more traditional in its draftsmanship, less sketchy and journalistic than that of the native-born Americans. Presumably, his first style was largely formed before his arrival in the United States, influenced alike by the Renaissance masters (especially Rembrandt) and by the late nineteenth-century realist art he would have seen in Naples.

Stella returned to Italy in 1909 to study and, as he said, "to renew and rebuild the base and structure of my art." In Rome he met and formed a lasting friendship with the Italian artist Antonio Mancini, whose representational style, which combined a heavy impasto with the light, bright hues and broken strokes of impressionism, influenced Stella to abandon the "old master" technique of his first decade. But it was not until 1911, on a trip to Paris, that he became aware of the modernist schools of fauvism, cubism, and especially futurism, whose credo demanded the sweeping aside of traditional forms and subjects in order to celebrate on canvas the frenetic, whirling speed of modern industrial society. Struck suddenly by the impact of these movements, Stella was unable to work for several months. He studied the works of Matisse, Picasso, Robert Delaunay, and others, became a particular friend of Modigliani, and attended the first futurist exhibition in Paris in February 1912, with, as he later recalled, "the bandages of stale prejudice torn from my eyes."

Returning to New York later that year, Stella participated in the Armory Show of 1913—a major milestone in American art history—although his contribution was stylistically modest. Before the year was out, however, he had composed his *Battle of Lights, Coney Island* (1913), a highly successful and original synthesis of futurism with elements learned from Delaunay and the other modern masters. This semiabstract work was widely discussed by critics and earned Stella a leading place in the American avant-garde.

The entry of the United States into World War I focused attention on American industry. A second *Survey* commission sent Stella back to Pittsburgh in 1917, this time to report on the war effort. His renewed contact with the industrial world stimulated the most creative period in his career, a period in which he produced *The Gas Tank* (1918), the critically acclaimed *Brooklyn Bridge* (c. 1919), and *New York Interpreted* (1920-1922), the great five-part polyptych that expresses all of the ambivalence of Stella's complex, contradictory personality, and that probably inspired the major poem of Hart Crane, "The Bridge." These works are all semiabstract, making use, in an original way, of futuristic lines of force and of cubist faceting and *passage*. They are related in subject matter to the American precisionist movement, which developed at the same time, but Stella's paintings express a quite different sensibility—darkly romantic in contrast to the classical surface clarity of Charles Sheeler and Charles Demuth.

Stella spent most of the years between 1922 and 1934 in Italy and France, with visits to North Africa. Influenced by Carlo Carra's shift to a classical-archaic realism rooted in Italian tradition, he abandoned abstraction in favor of a primitivizing style that reflected his study of Giotto. He painted a number of nudes and madonnas, but his major effort of the period was *The Holy Manger* (1933), an unsuccessful attempt to fuse twentieth-century realism with fourteenth-century naturalism. Stella returned to New York in 1935 and continued to paint until the end of his life, but the last decade saw only a few paintings of real value. These were produced in 1938 on the West Indies island of Barbados and evinced the surrealist quality characteristic of much of his work from its beginning, especially in his still-life and flower paintings. Beginning in the 1920's, Stella also produced superb collages, strange and delicate, put together from odd bits of cardboard and city debris with extraordinary fantasy—as a group among the most imaginative and skillful of all his works.

Those who knew Stella invariably commented on his dual personality. Mercurial in temperament, he could be both gentle and given to sudden rages, both refined and vulgar, friendly, yet suspicious that people were trying to cheat him. Even his large, heavy-set bulk contrasted with his graceful movements. These unresolved conflicts produced a tension that was reflected in his paintings. Details of his personal life are scanty. He is supposed to have married around 1902 Mary Geraldine Walter French, a young Philadelphian who came originally from Barbados, but he later affirmed when taking out American citizenship in 1923 that he was unmarried. In the early 1920's he established a ménage with Helen Walser, a young social worker with two children (Stella had no children of his own), who acted as his manager in some of his art dealings. In the mid-1930's he lived again with Mary French, whom he accompanied to Barbados in 1937. When she died there in 1939, Stella had already returned to New York.

Bedridden for the last three years of his life, Stella died of heart failure in New York City at the age of sixty-nine. After Roman Catholic services at a church in Greenwich Village, where he had long had a studio, he was buried in New York's Woodlawn Cemetery. Although his reputation had declined as his creative power waned in the 1930's, for two decades (1913-1933) Stella's work was exhibited regularly at the leading New York galleries, and at exhibitions in Italy and France as well. He was at the center of the first heroic struggle for modern art in America, and he produced some of its finest achievements.

[Irma B. Jaffe, *Joseph Stella* (1970), is a detailed account of the artist's life and work, with full bibliography, a checklist of 785 paintings, watercolors, drawings, and collages, and an annotated catalogue of the 114 works illustrated. See also John I. H. Baur, *Joseph Stella* (1971), a sensitive appreciation of Stella's art, based on the retrospective exhibition at the Whitney Museum of Am. Art in 1963; William Gerdts, *Drawings of Joseph Stella* (1962); and Irma B. Jaffe, "Joseph Stella and Hart Crane: The Brooklyn Bridge," *Am. Art Jour.*, Fall 1969. Stella left a collection of jottings and autobiographical notes (in the possession of his nephew Sergio Stella). A selection of these are printed in the Jaffe book; some have been microfilmed by the Arch. of Am. Art, Smithsonian Inst., Washington, D.C. Stella's "Discovery of America: Autobiog. Notes," written in 1946, appeared in *Art News*, Nov. 1960.]

IRMA B. JAFFE

STERLING, ROSS SHAW (Feb. 11, 1875-Mar. 25, 1949), oilman and governor of Texas, was born on a farm near Anahuac, Chambers County, Tex., on Galveston Bay. He was the eighth child in a family of eight boys and four girls. His father, Benjamin Franklin Sterling, a native of Mississippi and a carpenter, had settled in Texas in 1848 and, after service in the Confederate army, had prospered as a farmer and storekeeper, shipping produce to Galveston and returning with merchandise. His mother, Mary Jane (Bryan) Sterling, of Scots-Irish ancestry, was a native of Liberty County, Tex. Both her father and her paternal grandfather had fought in the war for Texas independence, and she named her son for a Texan hero, Lawrence Sullivan Ross. Ross Sterling left school at about the age of twelve, when his mother died, and went to work for his father. By the time he was seventeen he was managing his father's store. On Oct. 10, 1898, he married Maud Abbie Gage, an Illinois-born schoolteacher. They had five children: Walter Gage, Mildred, Ruth, Ross Shaw, and Norma.

After his marriage Sterling built a second store, but around the turn of the century he entered the produce business in Galveston. The great Texas oil boom set off by the Spindletop discovery in 1901 gave him a fresh opportunity. The new oil field lay to the north of Galveston Bay, and beginning in 1903 Sterling opened feed stores at Sour Lake, Saratoga, Humble, and Dayton to supply the needs of the teams that hauled pipe and timbers and scooped out the great earthen storage tanks. Sterling, a handsome, massively built man with an air of confidence, was both shrewd and hardworking, and his company soon had a virtual monopoly of the feed business in its communities. Since the oil industry also needed lumber, Sterling bought an interest in the Dayton Lumber Company and in timber properties. In 1906 he joined in forming a corporation to build a

railroad from Dayton to Cleveland, Tex., and the next year, shortly after the panic of 1907, he bought four small oil-field banks for $1,000 each. Later, he organized others. He used his feed stores and banks to finance one another and both to finance other Sterling enterprises; although his methods sometimes troubled bank commissioners, his creditors were always paid sooner or later and none of his banks failed.

Sterling began to invest directly in oil properties in 1909, when he bought two producing wells in the Humble field and gave G. Clint Wood, an experienced oilman, a half-interest for operating them. Once launched, Sterling continued to acquire oil properties. Early in 1911 he and other operators in the Humble field pooled their interests to form the Humble Oil Company, with a capitalization of $150,000 and with Sterling as president. In 1912 the company headquarters were moved to Houston, which thereafter remained Sterling's home. Sterling used company surpluses over the next few years to acquire new leases and drill new wells. Six years after incorporation Humble's properties were estimated as worth between $1 million and $4 million. Although the company's success owed much to such practical oilmen as Wood, Charles B. Goddard, and, particularly, Walter W. Fondren, Sterling's managerial capacity, knowledge of oil properties, bargaining skill, and financial ability were principal factors.

In 1916 Humble and several other companies decided to merge their properties in order to bargain more effectively in selling their oil to the larger companies. The new Humble Oil and Refining Company was incorporated in June 1917 with a capitalization of $4 million; Ross Sterling continued as president. The company promptly moved in the direction of greater integration, expanding existing refineries, selling oil to retail outlets, and planning a large refinery near the prolific Goose Creek field. It was also obliged to buy extensive new leases to keep up its oil reserves. Such steps required more funds than Sterling could raise locally, and in 1919 Humble agreed to sell 50 percent of its stock to the Standard Oil Company (New Jersey) for $17 million. In return, Jersey Standard, which had been stripped of most of its producing capacity by the antitrust decision of 1911, gained a major source of crude oil. A new situation had been created, however, in which Sterling's unique abilities as promoter and financier were of less importance, and in 1922 William S. Farish—who had been largely responsible for both the new Humble company's organization and the negotiations with Jersey Standard—became president, with Sterling relegated to nominal duties as chairman of the board.

Sterling was now free to seek new outlets for his enthusiasm and daring. He engaged in real estate development in Houston, including the construction of the twenty-two-story Sterling Building, and invested in a bank, several corporations, and a large ranch. By 1929 he was reportedly worth $80 million. Increasingly, however, he was drawn into politics. His involvement was primarily inspired by his passionate hostility toward James E. Ferguson, idol of white Texas small farmers and opponent of prohibition, whose governorship had ended in impeachment in 1917.

Sterling, a convinced "dry" and a rigid advocate of honest government, bought the *Houston Dispatch* in 1923 and in the following year the *Houston Post,* combining them into the *Post-Dispatch.* Through its columns he threw his support to the Republican candidate for governor in 1924, in opposition to Miriam A. ("Ma") Ferguson, the stand-in for her ineligible husband. The Fergusons countered by accusing both Sterling and the oil companies of supporting the Ku Klux Klan, and Miriam Ferguson was elected. Jersey Standard, already alarmed by state antitrust threats against Humble's charter and wishing to avoid any appearance of political involvement, bought out most of Sterling's stockholdings early in 1925, at which time he resigned his board chairmanship. In 1926 Dan Moody, an anti-Ferguson candidate Sterling had backed, was elected governor. Moody appointed Sterling chairman of the Texas Highway Commission, and during his four-year tenure the ex-oilman restored honest administration to the department. When, in 1930, Moody declined to run for a third term and Miriam Ferguson entered the race, Sterling reluctantly announced his own candidacy for governor. He won the Democratic nomination easily in a runoff and went on to win the election.

Although he became governor in the midst of the depression, Sterling took a narrow view of his powers. He supported both economy in government and additional taxes to supplement declining revenues. He did, however, establish a state child welfare department and a commission for unemployment relief. Sterling's most important and controversial action was aimed at curbing production in the recently discovered East Texas oil field, where a vast output was ruining prices and causing great waste. In a

special session of the legislature in 1931, Sterling forced through a conservation act—but one which, to the disappointment of more farseeing oilmen like Farish, forbade any attempt to restrict production of oil to market demand. When overproduction continued in defiance of even the limited regulatory measures allowed under the new act, Sterling on Aug. 17, 1931, declared martial law in four East Texas counties, but was overruled on Feb. 18, 1932, by the federal district court. "Ma" Ferguson opposed Sterling again in 1932. On the defensive against a master rabble-rouser, Sterling—an inept speaker who disliked campaigning—this time was narrowly defeated in the runoff primary.

Ross Sterling's remaining years were primarily devoted to recouping his personal fortune, most of which he had lost early in his governorship. He became manager of Miramar Oil and Refining Company, which became Sterling Oil and Refining Company in 1935, serving as president (1933–1946) and chairman of the board (1946–1949). Although never approaching his former wealth, he built a fortune that enabled him to live comfortably in Houston's exclusive River Roads district. Sterling contributed $100,000 to Texas Christian University and lesser amounts to other philanthropies, including the South End Christian Church, of which he was a deacon. He died of a heart attack in Fort Worth, Tex., at the age of seventy-four and was buried in Houston. Ross Shaw Sterling is remembered as one of the greatest of self-made Texas oilmen, as a principal founder of Humble Oil and Refining Company, and as a highly efficient chairman of the Texas Highway Commission. As a governor, despite his honesty, public spirit, and stubbornness, he proved unable to cope effectively with the double problems of the depression and the runaway East Texas oil field.

[The principal sources are Warner E. Mills, Jr., "The Public Career of a Texas Conservative: A Biog. of Ross Shaw Sterling" (Ph.D. diss., Johns Hopkins Univ., 1956), which emphasizes Sterling's political career; and Henrietta M. Larson and Kenneth W. Porter, *Hist. of Humble Oil and Refining Co.* (1959), which focuses on his early life and his business career up to 1925. A MS. biography of Sterling by the Houston journalist Ed Kilman is in that author's possession; it was used extensively by Mills. Published biographical sketches are in *The Handbook of Texas*, II, 688–669 (1952), and *Nat. Cyc. Am. Biog.,* XXXVIII, 46–47. The latter and Larson and Porter reproduce photographs of Sterling. An unpublished biobibliography prepared at Emory Univ. in 1967 by Phyllis C. Gillikin was detailed and helpful.]
KENNETH WIGGINS PORTER

STETTINIUS, EDWARD REILLY (Oct. 22, 1900–Oct. 31, 1949), corporation executive, and United States secretary of state, was born in Chicago, Ill., the younger of two sons and third of four children of Edward Reilly (Riley, Rilley) and Judith (Carrington) Stettinius. His mother was a Virginian of colonial English ancestry. His father, of German descent, was a native of St. Louis; active in many business enterprises, he became president of the Diamond Match Company (1909–1915), a partner in the banking house of J. P. Morgan and Company, and a War Department official during World War I. Young Edward grew up in Chicago and in Staten Island, N.Y. After graduating from the Pomfret School in Connecticut, he entered the University of Virginia in 1919. An indifferent student, he neglected his studies for YMCA work, Sunday school teaching, and missionary work among the poor in Albemarle County, Va., and left college without a degree in 1924. On May 15, 1926, he married Virginia Gordon Wallace, daughter of a prominent family of Richmond, Va. They had three children: Edward Reilly, and the twins Wallace and Joseph.

Stettinius, an Episcopalian, considered becoming a minister, but he was persuaded by John Lee Pratt, a University of Virginia alumnus and vice-president of General Motors, to apply his humanitarian ideals to a business career. He began after college as a stockroom clerk at GM's Hyatt roller-bearing division and soon rose to employment manager. In 1926, as special assistant to Pratt, he instituted one of the automobile industry's first group insurance plans, improved working and sanitary conditions, and helped formulate advertising policy. He became assistant to President Alfred P. Sloan, Jr., in 1930 and, a year later, vice-president in charge of industrial and public relations. Stettinius moved in 1934 to the United States Steel Corporation as a vice-president. He was influential in the company's decision to recognize the steel workers' union in 1937. The following year he became chairman of the board of U.S. Steel.

Stettinius supported the basic economic goals of the New Deal. His liberal social views early came to the attention of President Franklin D. Roosevelt, who in 1933 appointed him to the Industrial Advisory Board to act as a liaison officer with the National Recovery Administration. Affable and informal, Stettinius proved himself a patient and effective administrator. Roosevelt called Stettinius into government service again in 1939 as chairman of the War Resources Board, established to survey potential American war needs, and the following year placed him on the new National Defense Advisory Commission, at which point Stettinius resigned from U.S. Steel to devote full time to government service. He became director of priorities of the Office of Production Management in January 1941 and, nine months later, administrator of lend-lease. The smoothness with which this vital program functioned under his direction won him acclaim both at home and abroad.

In September 1943 Roosevelt appointed Stettinius undersecretary of state and charged him with the task of reorganizing the State Department, whose structure had failed to adapt to its expanded functions during World War II. Among other changes, Stettinius eliminated administrative duplication, created a set of offices to deal with daily problems, thus giving the undersecretary and the assistant secretaries more time for broad policy questions, and established two top-level committees, one on policy and one on postwar programs. He also strengthened the department's relations with the White House, Congress, and the public. On Dec. 1, 1944, after the resignation of the ailing Cordell Hull, Roosevelt named Stettinius secretary of state.

Stettinius' tenure coincided with the crucial period at the close of World War II during which the Allied powers began to plot the course of the postwar world. It was clear that Roosevelt planned to keep most foreign policy decisions in his own hands and to negotiate personally with other heads of state. Stettinius, it was generally agreed, was selected primarily for his talents as a harmonizer, his effectiveness in implementing policy decisions, and his commitment to the ideals of a world security organization. He did not originate substantive foreign policy, and at times seemed to lack the confidence to deal with major policy perplexities; yet he selected strong men for key positions in the department, displayed a talent for getting them to work together, and often recommended forcefully to the president the ideas of these aides.

Stettinius' most notable contributions as secretary of state centered on his vigorous efforts to establish the United Nations. As undersecretary he had headed the American delegation to the seminal Dumbarton Oaks Conference in 1944, at which the Allies accepted as a basis for negotiation the State Department's proposals for structure of the United Nations. In February 1945 he accompanied Roosevelt to the Yalta Conference with Churchill and Stalin, at which it was decided to call a conference in San Francisco at the end of April to form the new organization. Stettinius subsequently attended the Inter-American Conference in Mexico City to reassure the nations of Latin America that the creation of the United Nations would not prevent the development of a hemispheric security system. The resulting Act of Chapultepec laid the foundation for the Organization of American States in 1948.

After Roosevelt's death in April 1945, President Truman asked Stettinius to continue in office and head the American delegation to the San Francisco Conference. Its successful outcome owed much to his dedication of purpose, which communicated itself to other delegations and to the American public, and to his skills as a conciliator, both within an American delegation made up of strong individualists and in the private meetings of representatives of the Big Five powers. When the Russians demanded unanimous consent in the Security Council to consider disputes, Stettinius sent word to Stalin that the United States would never agree to this proposal and succeeded in having it withdrawn. President Truman, who did not fully share Roosevelt's confidence in Stettinius, accepted his resignation as secretary of state at the close of the San Francisco Conference, but appointed him chairman of the United States delegation to the United Nations Preparatory Commission and, in January 1946, chairman of the American delegation to the first session of the U.N. General Assembly, as well as American representative on the Security Council. He resigned in June of that year.

Prematurely white-haired, with dark eyebrows, blue eyes, tanned face, and a quick smile, Stettinius was striking in appearance and inspired goodwill. For three years after his return to private life he served as rector of the University of Virginia. A longtime friend of William Tubman, the president of Liberia, he helped form (1947) and headed as board chairman the Liberia Company, a partnership between the Liberian government and American financiers to provide funds for the development of that African nation. He lived during his retirement at his estate on the Rapidan River, Va. He died of a coronary thrombosis at the home of a sister in Greenwich, Conn., at the age of forty-nine, and was buried in the family plot at Locust Valley, L. I.

[Stettinius' diaries and other unpublished papers are at the Alderman Lib. of the Univ. of Va. He was the author of *Lend-Lease: Weapon for Victory* (1944) and, with Walter Johnson, *Roosevelt and the Russians: The Yalta Conference* (1949). For his activities in the State Dept., see Walter Johnson in Norman A. Graebner, ed., *An Uncertain Tradition: Am. Secretaries of State in the Twentieth Century* (1961); Richard L. Walker in Robert H. Ferrell, ed., *The Am. Secretaries of State and Their Diplomacy*, vol. XIV (1965); Thomas M. Campbell, Jr., "The Role of Edward R. Stettinius, Jr., in the Founding of the United Nations" (Ph.D. diss., Univ. of Va., 1964); Arthur H. Vandenberg, Jr., and Joe Alex Morris, eds., *The Private Papers of Senator Vandenberg* (1952); Ruth B. Russell and Jeannette E. Muther, *A Hist. of the United Nations Charter: The Role of the U.S., 1940–1945* (1958); Graham H. Stuart, *The Dept. of State: A Hist. of Its Organization, Procedure, and Personnel* (1949); Walter H. C. Laves and Francis O. Wilcox, "The Reorganization of the Dept. of State" and "The State Dept. Continues Its Reorganization," *Am. Political Sci. Rev.*, Apr. 1944 and Apr. 1945. Useful contemporary journalistic articles include "Managers of Steel," *Fortune*, Mar. 1940; Charles Wertenbaker, "White-Haired Boy, Stettinius," *Sat. Evening Post*, July 26, 1941; John H. Crider, "Diplomat from Industry's School," *N.Y. Times Mag.*, Oct. 17, 1943; and George Creel, "The Size of Stettinius," *Collier's*, Jan. 12, 1946. See also tributes in *United Nations Bull.*, Nov. 15, 1949; and obituary in *N.Y. Times*, Nov. 1, 1949. Though Stettinius always spelled his middle name "Reilly," earlier family usage varied. His father's death certificate has "Rilley"; some accounts have "Riley."]

WALTER JOHNSON

STIEGLITZ, ALFRED (Jan. 1, 1864–July 13, 1946), photographer, art gallery proprietor, publisher, and patron of the arts, was a native of Hoboken, N.J., the first of six children born to Edward Stieglitz and Hedwig (Werner) Stieglitz. One of his brothers, Julius Stieglitz, became a noted chemist. His father had immigrated to New York City from Hannover, Germany, about 1850, and after serving as a lieutenant in the Civil War he married and settled in Hoboken, where he became an importer of woolen goods. Both parents came from a cultured middle-class German-Jewish background but were not outwardly religious. Independence, honesty, and good sportsmanship were stressed in the Stieglitz home, and Alfred learned from his father, an amateur painter, an appreciation of art, music, literature, and the theater. Edward Stieglitz' success in business enabled him to provide his family with the better things in life, and in 1871 he bought a spacious house on East 60th Street in New York, where Alfred spent much of his boyhood. Alfred attended the Charlier Institute, an exclusive private school, but in 1877 his father transferred him to public school. Stieglitz was a precocious boy, and early in life he demonstrated the inventiveness, drive, and ability to lead for which he later became famous.

Stieglitz entered the College of the City of New York in 1879, but after two years of study, he still had no definite ideas about what he wanted to do. His father, believing that the future lay in engineering and chemistry, encouraged him to become a mechanical engineer and in 1881 took the family to Germany so that the children could enjoy the advantages of a Continental education. Alfred first enrolled at the Karlsruhe Realgymnasium and then, in 1882, entered the Technische Hochschule in Berlin as a student of mechanical engineering. However, he was diverted from this subject by a course he had elected in photochemistry taught by Hermann Wilhelm Vogel. Thereafter, Stieglitz gave most of his attention to photochemistry and photography, continuing his studies from 1887 to 1890 at the University of Berlin. He became an indefatigible experimenter in the medium and produced many photographs in Berlin and during his frequent trips throughout Europe. In 1887 he won first prize in a London exhibition, the first official recognition of his skill as a photographer; in later years he was to win more than 150 medals for photography.

When Stieglitz returned to New York after eight years of study and travel in Europe, his father supported him in the photoengraving business, which he operated for five years without any great enthusiasm. On Nov. 16, 1893, Stieglitz married Emmeline Obermeyer, sister of one of his business partners. They had one child, a daughter, Katherine, before they were divorced in 1924.

Because Stieglitz had few customers, he was able to spend much of his time taking and exhibiting photographs. In the 1890's he became a renowned photographer, respected in Europe as well as the United States; he has been called, with good reason, the "father of modern photography." He became a frequent exhibitor and jury member in the most prominent American and international photographic exhibitions and the editor of two influential journals, the *American Amateur Photographer* (1893-1896) and *Camera Notes* (1897-1902), the organ of the Camera Club of New York. Stieglitz used *Camera Notes* and the exhibitions sponsored by the Camera Club to champion the idea that photography should be recognized as an artistic medium on a par with painting and sculpture. To be sure, its basic technical premises were different, but Stieglitz believed photography was as valid a means of aesthetic expression as the other fine arts. To achieve his ends, he fought for a new aesthetic (also evident in advanced European circles) that would encourage artistic control of the formal elements of the medium, in contrast to the unimaginative, descriptive records and sentimental story-telling typical of much of the photography of the 1870's and 1880's.

Growing dissatisfied with the conservative policies of the Camera Club of New York, Stieglitz organized, in 1902, the Photo-Secession, a group of photographers who were sympathetic to his advanced ideas about creative "pictorial photography." Taking its name from the antiacademic secession art movements in Munich and Vienna, the Photo-Secession became a vital force for reform in American photography. The members—including such noted photographers as Edward Steichen, Alvin Langdon Coburn, Clarence White, and Gertrude Käsebier—did not follow any fixed aesthetic doctrines, but they shared most, if not all, of Stieglitz' views about the artistic value of photography. Stieglitz gave the organization direction and financial support and arranged a series of influential photographic exhibitions in Europe and the United States under the banner of the Photo-Secession.

Although many of his colleagues were accused of seeking excessively painterly effects in their photographs, Stieglitz himself usually did not go to these extremes, preferring to work within the optical limits of his medium. In such well-known early works as *The Terminal* (1892), *The Hand of Man* (1902), and *The Steerage* (1907), he dealt with everyday subjects, but these photographs were far more than impersonal descriptive records. He was careful to select views that had an inherently interesting composition, framed the subject matter to achieve pictorial balance and relationship, and controlled the tone and color of the image in the course of making the print. Respecting the nature of his medium, he rarely retouched his negatives and prints. When his compositions were praised, he said he had never taken any formal studies in art; but his photographs show that he was endowed with a fine instinctive sense of design.

To serve the ideals of the Photo-Secession, Stieglitz established a quarterly magazine, *Camera Work,* which he issued from 1903 to 1917. The journal promoted not only the kind of photography he valued but also the newest trends in art, literature, and criticism. Later issues of *Camera Work* contained information about current developments in European and American painting, and for many years it was the most advanced American periodical devoted to the arts. It was also the most attractive journal of its day. A perfectionist in typography and printing, Stieglitz personally supervised the production of every issue.

From 1903 to 1905, Stieglitz used *Camera Work* as his primary medium to promote the

Photo-Secession. In 1905, however, he and his friend Edward Steichen discussed the prospect of converting the top floor of 291 Fifth Avenue into a gallery for the Photo-Secession group. They agreed to work together on this project, and with Stieglitz' financial backing, Steichen redecorated three small attic rooms (later two more, across the hall) to form the Little Galleries of the Photo-Secession, usually known simply as "291." The galleries opened in November 1905, with a show of photographs by members of the Photo-Secession group, and for more than a year the rooms were dedicated exclusively to the art of photography. But early in 1907 Stieglitz staged the first in a series of exhibitions of paintings, drawings, and sculptures. Nonphotographic art gradually overshadowed photographic exhibitions, and as early as 1908, 291 had become the most advanced center for the fine arts in America. The gallery was influential because Stieglitz here presented the first American exhibitions of such noted modern European artists as Matisse (1908), Henri Rousseau (1910), Cézanne (1911), Picasso (1911), Picabia (1913), and Brancusi (1914). These exhibitions were of prime importance for the development of art in America, because they gave many native artists their first glimpse of radical new directions in European painting and sculpture. Some American artists, of course, had already been to Europe and had witnessed these new styles firsthand; when they came back to this country, the shows at 291 helped them to keep the spark alive and seggested fresh points of departure. It is safe to say that American painting would not have developed as it did without the exhibitions at 291. In his work as a gallery director lies much of Stieglitz' historical importance.

Besides serving as a showcase for advanced European art, 291 played still another important role: it became a meeting place for young experimental artists and critics, who exchanged ideas with Stieglitz and each other and received encouragement that could be had nowhere else in the United States at that time. Almost every avant-garde American artist who had been exposed to European modernism (or who wished to be) was drawn to Stieglitz and 291. They were few in number, but those who valued the spirit of 291—Steichen, John Marin, Arthur G. Dove, Marsden Hartley, Alfred Maurer, Max Weber (briefly), Oscar Bluemner, Abraham Walkowitz, and later Georgia O'Keeffe, and Charles Demuth—became stronger through their association with Stieglitz. He frequently displayed their work,

too, giving them a chance to address the public in their own terms, without worrying about commercial success.

Stieglitz placed his personal stamp on 291 from the very beginning. He was present in the galleries from early in the morning until late in the evening, and if a visitor showed genuine interest in the works on view, the proprietor might engage him in a conversation that could be probing, often revealing, and sometimes insulting. His niece described him as "a black-haired, black-eyed handsome man—vibrant, impatient, passionate, yet full of humor and kindness. . . . In his serious moods he was darkly melancholy, a typical figure of the romantic age, but when he smiled, Pan smiled at you" (Engelhard, p. 8). He was renowned for his noncommercial approach to works of art. He viewed paintings as sacred objects, the product of man's priceless gift of creativity, on which it was therefore impossible to place a dollar value. Stieglitz liked to challenge his customers to offer what they were willing to sacrifice for a picture they desired; he had no time for those who saw art in financial terms or who bought for investment. One dared not haggle over the price of a painting.

Stieglitz established himself quite early in his career as a vocal philosopher of art. Believing generally in progressive causes, he was antiacademic and antidescriptive in his views on art. He managed to reconcile late nineteenth-century ideals of beauty with early twentieth-century concepts of intuitive self-expression. He was thoroughly devoted to the standards of fine craftsmanship, which he followed in his own photography and demanded of all who worked with him. For Stieglitz, art was a sacred mission to be undertaken only by the initiated, by those intellectually and spiritually worthy of the quest. Unlike his influential contemporary Robert Henri, he refused to spread the doctrine of art to everyone, to spoil the purity of its message by delivering it to an untutored audience. Stieglitz believed in a cultural oligarchy, a group of enlightened individuals exchanging ideas and discoveries among themselves. The artistic products of this group would in turn serve as tangible models, as sources of inspiration for those who were worthy of receiving their message.

By 1917, after fourteen years of intense activity, Stieglitz seemed to have exhausted himself. He closed the gallery in that year, and no further issues of *Camera Work* were published. This left him free to pursue his own photography, which he had curtailed while he was working for the advancement of other artists. His association with Georgia O'Keeffe, beginning in 1916, helped to renew his creative life. This talented young painter, whom he married on Dec. 11, 1924, served as a model for a series of superb photographic portraits and figure studies dating from the late teens and the 1920's. From this period into the 1930's he also used his camera to explore the stark geometry of skyscrapers in New York, and during his summers at Lake George he recorded, ever more abstractly, the informal aspects of the natural environment. The prints of these years, particularly his cloud studies, include many landmarks in the history of photography. Declining physical strength compelled Stieglitz to abandon photography in 1937, but not before he had executed a group of striking portraits of his friend and associate Dorothy Norman.

Although Stieglitz closed 291 in 1917, his battle for modern art was not over. He continued to sell paintings and promote his circle of artists at the Intimate Gallery (1924–1929) and at An American Place (1929–1946). In these galleries, he held exhibitions primarily of Marin, O'Keeffe, Demuth, Hartley, and Dove, abandoning almost entirely his earlier commitment to avant-garde European art. In the 1920's, moreover, he was adopted as a kind of patriarch, an American culture hero, by an emerging generation of writers and critics including Sherwood Anderson, Lewis Mumford, Paul Rosenfeld, and Waldo Frank. Stieglitz' passionate devotion to freedom and vitality of expression in contemporary art, to distinctly American values, and to fine craftsmanship inspired these younger men, although he had not made a conscious effort to do so.

In the 1920's, 1930's, and 1940's Stieglitz continued to fight many of his old battles but without significantly changing his strategies. His early crusade for avant-garde and experimental art had won so many converts among collectors and museums that in his later years he could no longer be considered a unique, prophetic figure. Admirable, however, was his determination to fight on to the very end, despite financial troubles, desertion by many of his friends, and failing health. He remained intensely loyal to the few artists who remained with his gallery, and he took great pride in serving their interests until a few days before his death.

Troubled by a heart condition in his later years, Stieglitz died of a stroke in New York. His body was cremated at Fresh Pond Crematory, Queens, N.Y.

[An archive of Stieglitz' extensive papers is housed in the Beinecke Rare Book and Manuscript Lib., Yale Univ. The only full-length books on him are Waldo Frank, Lewis Mumford, Dorothy Norman, Paul Rosenfeld, and Harold Rugg, eds., *America and Alfred Stieglitz: A Collective Portrait* (1934), a collection of essays and tributes now largely out of date, and Dorothy Norman, *Alfred Stieglitz: An American Seer* (1973). Useful references, emphasizing his photography, are Doris Bry, *Alfred Stieglitz, Photographer* (1965), and Dorothy Norman, *Alfred Stieglitz: Introduction to an American Seer* (1960). Some of his conversations are recorded in *Alfred Stieglitz Talking* (1966). See also the obituary in *N.Y. Times*, July 14, 1946; Georgia Engelhard, "Alfred Stieglitz, Master Photographer," *Am. Photography*, April 1945; Herbert J. Seligmann, "Burning Focus," *Infinity*, Dec. 1967 and Jan. 1968; Georgia O'Keeffe, "Stieglitz: His Pictures Collected Him," *N.Y. Times Mag.*, Dec. 11, 1949; Oliver Larkin, "Stieglitz and '291,'" *Mag. of Art*, May 1947; and William I. Homer, "Stieglitz and 291," *Art in Am.*, July–Aug. 1973. Information also came from interviews with Georgia O'Keeffe and Dorothy Norman.]

WILLIAM I. HOMER

STILWELL, JOSEPH WARREN (Mar. 19, 1883–Oct. 12, 1946), army officer, was the second of four children and elder of two sons of Benjamin Watson Stilwell and Mary Augusta (Peene) Stilwell. Both parents came of well-to-do families long resident in Yonkers, N.Y.; his father was a seventh-generation descendant of Nicholas Stilwell, who had come from England in 1638 and settled a decade later in New Amsterdam. Benjamin Stilwell, a prosperous and imposing dilettante, held degrees in both law and medicine but practiced neither. Instead, he engaged in a number of business ventures, including a short-lived lumber plantation at Palatka, Fla., where his son was born.

Young Stilwell grew up in Yonkers and attended public schools. Quick-witted and intelligent, he was a good student with a special proficiency in languages; but he put his heart into athletics, which remained a lifelong interest. He planned to enter Yale when he graduated from high school at sixteen, but his father, believing him too young to go to college, had him go back to high school for an additional year. The bored and highly energized youth engaged in a series of pranks that ended in disgrace, and his father, convinced that he needed discipline, secured him an appointment to West Point. Thus inadvertently Stilwell began his military career.

Graduating thirty-second out of 124 in the class of 1904, he served for the next two years with the Twelfth Infantry in the Philippines, where he saw combat against the Moros. Save for later regimental duty in the Philippines and in Monterey, Calif. (1911–1913), Stilwell spent the rest of the decade before World War I at West Point as an instructor in modern languages (French and Spanish), tactics, English, and history. He also coached basketball and football and was promoted to captain in 1916. On Oct. 18, 1910, he married Winifred Alison Smith of Syracuse, N.Y. They had five children: Joseph Warren, Nancy, Winifred, Alison, and Benjamin Watson.

Stilwell joined the American Expeditionary Forces in France in December 1917. As chief of the intelligence section (G-2) of the American IV Corps under Gen. Joseph T. Dickman, he played a major role in organizing G-2 operations for the American offensive at Saint-Mihiel, winning the Distinguished Service Medal and promotion to the temporary rank of colonel.

His first postwar assignment established the connection with China that was to dominate his future career. By a combination of lucky timing and qualifications as an intelligence officer with a gift for languages, he secured appointment, under a new program opened by the Military Intelligence Division, as the army's first language officer in China. The duty took him for a three-year tour to Peking (1920-1923), where he learned to speak Chinese. During this time, he also served the International Famine Relief Committee of the Red Cross as chief engineer on road-building projects in Shensi and Shansi provinces. Here he lived and worked in the field with Chinese laborers and village officials, marched with the warlord armies, and came to know a China far beyond the foreigner's usual ken. His immense curiosity and powers of observation found expression, then and later, in his diary, where he recorded his impressions in vivid and voluminous detail, although with little, if any, philosophic comment.

After attending the army's Infantry and Command and General Staff schools, at Fort Benning and Leavenworth, Stilwell returned to China (1926-1929) as battalion commander and later executive officer of the Fifteenth Infantry an American regiment stationed in Tientsin as a result of the Boxer Rebellion. He was thus in China during the period when the Kuomintang under Chiang Kai-shek achieved national power, and he assessed the historic turn of events he was witnessing in a series of weekly articles written through 1928 for the *Sentinel*, journal of the Fifteenth Infantry. His third China duty came in 1935-1939, when he returned as United States military attaché to observe, judge, and report in a time tragic and critical for China and the world. These were the years of increasing Japanese penetration of China and outright war, and Stilwell formed both a low opinion of Kuomintang leadership and a settled conviction that Chinese soldiers, properly led, trained, nourished, and equipped, could become the equal of any in the world.

From 1929 to 1933, Stilwell served as chief of the tactical section at the Infantry School, Fort Benning, Ga., under the direction of Col. George C. Marshall. In Marshall's opinion Stilwell had "a genius for instruction," was "ahead of his time in tactics and technique," and, although personally unassuming, was one of the "exceptionally brilliant and cultured men of the army." But Stilwell, instantly antagonized by incompetence or pretentiousness, could be cantankerous. A man of utter integrity, he was a fighter and a doer, whose too-quick disgust for anything less in others made him at times, as Marshall said, "his own worst enemy." At the Infantry School his unsparing and often acid critiques earned him the nickname "Vinegar Joe," and Marshall three times had to resist the demand of the commandant for Stilwell's relief.

In 1939 Marshall, now the army's chief of staff and determined, in the shadow of approaching conflict, to improve the quality of the officer corps, picked Stilwell for one of his first two promotions to brigadier general. By the time of Pearl Harbor, Stilwell had commanded the Third Infantry Brigade in Texas (1939), the Seventh Division in California (1940), and the III Corps (1940-1941) and had been promoted to major general (September 1940). By virtue of his training of troops and his mastery of tactics in troop maneuvers, he was rated the army's best corps commander. In December 1941 he was picked to command the planned landing in North Africa, but that operation was postponed. Meanwhile, the Asian situation was growing desperate. Japanese forces had swept through the Philippines and the East Indies, had occupied Indochina and Thailand, and were threatening Burma, vital as a protective barrier for India and as the avenue through which American lend-lease supplies were reaching beleaguered China. An American general was needed to strengthen the Asian front and tie together the discordant British and Chinese, and Stilwell's background made him the man. In February 1942 he was appointed commanding general of United States Army forces (at this time only air units) in the China-Burma-India theater, chief of staff to Generalissimo Chiang Kai-shek of China, and supervisor of lend-lease in the area; the appointment carried the rank of lieutenant general.

With no American combat troops planned for the mainland of Asia, Stilwell's command centered upon the primary mission of improving "the combat efficiency of the Chinese army." His task became a ceaseless struggle against frustrations imposed more by his allies than by the enemy. The basic difficulty was a divergence of aims. The United States considered it essential to keep China in the war, both to retain a military base for use against Japan and to ensure that a strong China would emerge from the war; this in turn meant saving Burma as the only access to China. The British, who did not share the Americans' estimate of China, saw no need to invest their weakened resources in sustaining Chiang Kai-shek, and preferred to regain Burma with ultimate victory rather than wage a bitter fight in its terrible terrain. The Chinese, for their part, sought as great a flow as possible of American supplies, not to use against the Japanese, whom they considered it the duty of the Western powers to defeat, but to hoard for eventual use against their internal enemies, the Communists. The problem was exacerbated by a shortage of means resulting from the top-level policy decision giving priority to the European front. Secretary of War Henry L. Stimson called Stilwell's mission in China "the most difficult task assigned to any American in the entire war."

Arriving at his new post in early March 1942, Stilwell took up the defense of Burma, but his command of the two Chinese divisions nominally under his direction was hamstrung by Chiang's remote control. When Burma fell to the Japanese, Stilwell, declining evacuation for himself by air, chose to lead an endangered remnant of 114 men on a 140-mile march across the mountains to India. His frank assessment on arrival, "I claim we got a hell of a beating," stirred the American consciousness.

Stilwell encountered further frustration in his subsequent program to train Chinese troops in India; in efforts to consolidate, train, and equip sixty divisions in China; and in his struggle to obtain British and Chinese forces for the fight back into north Burma. His command status was further complicated in mid-1943 when, besides his other titles, he became deputy supreme allied commander in Southeast Asia under Britain's Admiral Lord Louis Mountbatten. Yet Stilwell doggedly pressed construction of the Ledo Road (afterward named for him), which eventually linked up with the Burma Road to provide a land supply route from India to China, supplementing the air route over the Himalayas (the "Hump"); and in the first seven months of 1944 Stilwell led Chinese troops in the successful battle to retake northern Burma. Throughout, he found himself in competition for supplies with Gen. Claire Chennault, head of the Air Transport Command operating over the Hump, an ardent apostle of air power, and a close and uncritical friend of Chiang Kai-shek. But Stilwell's most enduring frustration was his long struggle to bring about a reform of the Chinese army, an effort doomed by the resistance of Chiang, who feared reform as a danger to his control. Stilwell's persistence and his unconcealed contempt for the generalissimo caused three attempts by Chiang to bring about his recall. Although President Roosevelt sometimes wavered, Marshall, as chief of staff, steadfastly stood by Stilwell.

In 1944, when a renewed Japanese offensive in China made the situation desperate, Roosevelt, persuaded by Marshall, officially requested that Stilwell be appointed to command the Chinese armed forces (promoting him to four-star rank for the assignment). This proposal, which Chiang feared might lead to American contact with the Communists and which was unacceptable to him in any event, precipitated the final crisis, which culminated in Stilwell's recall in October 1944. His mission failed in its object because the goal was unattainable. Historically, it demonstrated the limits of American influence in Asia.

Physically Stilwell was lean and wiry, with short-cropped gray-black hair; a hard, lined, decisive face; quizzical eyes behind steel-rimmed spectacles; and the shrewd, skeptical look of a down-East Yankee farmer. At the front he shed insignia of rank and made himself comfortable in nonregulation sweater, GI boots, and his old stiff-brimmed campaign hat from World War I. In China he was a liberal, at home by family habit a Republican, by upbringing a Methodist, by choice a nonbeliever and nonchurchgoer. Not ambitious for high place per se, he could not speak out for himself or his cause nor ever ingratiate himself with someone he did not respect.

In June 1945, after the death of Gen. Simon Bolivar Buckner, Jr., Stilwell was given command of the Tenth Army on Okinawa, scheduled for the invasion of Japan, but that ultimate campaign was precluded two months later by the enemy's surrender. His last command was of the Sixth Army in charge of the United States Western Defense Command. In October 1946, five months before he was due to retire, Stilwell died at Letterman General Hospital, San Francisco, following an operation for cancer of the stomach. Before his death, by his special wish, he was awarded the Combat Infantryman Badge, usually reserved for the enlisted foot soldier who has proved himself under fire. He had previously received the Distinguished Service Cross for action in Burma and the Legion of Merit for high command. According to his directions, his body was cremated and the ashes scattered over the Pacific. There is a memorial stone at West Point.

[Unpublished sources include Stilwell's diaries and papers, in the possession of the family and at the Hoover Institution, Stanford Univ.; the Chennault Papers, Hoover Institution; the Henry L. Stimson Papers, Yale Univ.; military records, including Stilwell's 201 file; and information from family and colleagues. Useful published articles by Stilwell can be found in the *Sentinel* (journal of the Fifteenth Infantry, Tientsin; file in N.Y. Public Lib.), 1927–1929; *Infantry Jour.*, Apr. 1928, Nov.–Dec. 1932, July–Aug. 1933; *Cavalry Jour.*, Mar.–Apr. 1933; *Asia*, July 1924. Excerpts from his wartime diaries and letters are in Theodore H. White, ed., *The Stilwell Papers* (1958). See also John E. Stilwell, *Stilwell Genealogy*, vol. III (1930); Charles Romanus and Riley Sunderland, *Stilwell's Mission to China* (1953) and *Stilwell's Command Problems* (1956); Jack Belden, *Retreat with Stilwell* (1943); Frank Dorn, *Walkout: With Stilwell in Burma* (1971); Fred Eldridge, *Wrath in Burma* (1946); Gordon Seagrave, *Burma Surgeon* (1943) and *Burma Surgeon Returns* (1946); Barbara W. Tuchman, *Stilwell and the American Experience in China, 1911–1945* (1971), which includes a fuller bibliography. For a pro-Chiang view, see Chin-Tun Liang, *Gen. Stilwell in China, 1942–1944* (1972).]

BARBARA W. TUCHMAN

STIMSON, HENRY LEWIS (Sept. 21, 1867–Oct. 20, 1950), statesman, was born in New York City, the first of two children and only son of Lewis Atterbury Stimson and Candace (Wheeler) Stimson. On both sides of his family the lines run back to the Massachusetts Bay Colony of the early seventeenth century. He described his ancestors as sturdy, middle-class people, religious, thrifty, energetic, and long-lived. In that stock the sense of election postulated by John Calvin was qualified by the austerity of his vision of life and by his stern injunction that it was necessary not only to know but to do the will of God. The circumstances of Stimson's youth served to confirm many of these ancestral attitudes.

His mother, the daughter of a well-to-do New York merchant, had grown up in circles both here and abroad that included such varied talents and spirits as Mark Twain, Oscar Wilde, Albert Bierstadt, Lily Langtry, and George Eliot. She was intelligent and fascinating and devoted to her children. When Stimson was eight years old, she died. Thereafter, her husband gave himself over to "years of constant grinding work." He was a very able man, "a rugged militant character" who had fought in the Civil War before he took a seat on the stock exchange. Soon bored with money matters he turned to the study of medicine, spent a year with Pasteur, and took a surgical internship in Paris. At the time of his wife's death he had just begun work in the surgical service of the Presbyterian Hospital in New York. By his ceaseless endeavors he soon rose to the top of his profession in the city.

Young Henry and his sister, Candace, went, after their mother's death, to live with their grandparents, but Dr. Stimson remained for his son the greatest influence upon the ideals and purposes of his early life. Secondary influences of great force in those circumstances of broken family life were institutions—Andover (1880-1884), Yale (1884-1888), and Harvard Law School (1888-1890). In New Haven he found a "corporate spirit and democratic energy," and in Cambridge, an exercise in "independent thinking unlike anything I had met before." At Harvard, he said near the end of his life, he discovered how the power of the mind could be used in support of the faith in mankind he had acquired in college.

When his education ended, he entered the law firm of Root and Clarke in 1891. Elihu Root, a friend of Stimson's father, was at the time one of the great men of the New York bar. For the next eight years, Stimson worked hard in the service of clients who were prime movers in the world of American finance and corporate enterprise. From Root, he learned much in those years about how to try a case, but he also learned something else of greater interest and significance for his future: Root, by example, brought home to his young law clerk the importance of the active performance of his public duties by a citizen of New York. So Stimson started his exploration of politics in something smaller than a ward, an election district, and in time worked his way up to a seat on the powerful New York County Republican Committee. Along the way, finding himself frequently in conflict with the lieutenants of Thomas Collier Platt, he discovered a great deal about the aims and methods of political bosses.

When Root went to Washington in 1899

to become secretary of war, Stimson and another member of the firm, Bronson Winthrop, started their own partnership. They remained together for the rest of their lives. It was a remarkable combination of talents: Stimson was at home in the open conflicts of the courtroom; Winthrop had the sharp, subtle mind and temperament of a legal scholar. Neither was much interested in what Stimson called the green goods business (that is, big corporations and large fees). Amid the great firms that were being built up under forced draft around them, they established a substantial, interesting practice in which even the law clerks worked at humane tempos under civilized conditions. In such circumstances Stimson developed into an excellent trial lawyer. His principal resources were painstaking preparation, an instinct for the crucial point, a simplicity of presentation, and the power to convey the sense that he was speaking the absolute truth. When he said, "This must be so," juries tended to think so too.

These assets Stimson put in the service of the government when in 1906 Theodore Roosevelt appointed him the United States attorney for the Southern District of New York. Insufficiently staffed and badly managed at the time, the office was totally reconstituted by Stimson in the next two years. First, he created a staff of such able young men as Emory Buckner, Thomas Thacher, Goldthwaite Dorr, and Felix Frankfurter. With them he prepared, argued, and won a series of cases against companies that were systematically evading the terms of the Sherman Antitrust and Elkins Railroad acts. By his successful prosecutions he obtained the dissolution of a paper trust, the conviction of the American Sugar Refining Company on the charge of extracting rebates from railroads, and a judgment against the Havemeyer interests for evading duties on imported sugar. By his work in the Southern District, which ended in 1909, he gave one of the earliest demonstrations that the power of large corporations could be sensibly controlled by the action of a determined government. As time went on, he looked back upon those years as his first love.

There followed an interlude in the law firm and some interesting cases. His service as district attorney, however, stirred up his concern over the dislocations produced in the society by the excesses of corporate enterprise. He began to seek for ways to manage a more orderly and socially useful development of American industrial energy. In 1910 he was persuaded by Root and Roosevelt to run for governor, in the hope that he might be able to put some of his ideas in effect from Albany. But 1910 was not a good Republican year, and Stimson was not as good at the whistle stops as he was in court. He sounded, as Roosevelt said, too much like a professor of government. In the election, running behind most of his ticket, he was soundly defeated.

In the following year, President William Howard Taft appointed him secretary of war. For two years thereafter he struggled to make a modern army out of a force that still was preparing itself, not very well, to fight the Indian wars of the previous century. Failing, because of congressional opposition, to abolish or consolidate all the army posts that were scattered around the country in disregard of economics and strategic need, he did succeed in two very important endeavors. First, he obtained a "tactical reorganization" of the troop units that ensured more useful training for the modern art of war. He also resolved, after painful difficulties, the ancient immobilizing conflict between the staff and line. When he left office, the army had for the first time a general staff that was a source of competent military direction. He left the War Department in 1913, but he soon returned to the army to render a different kind of service. Almost from the moment the war started in Europe in 1914, he began to take an active part in the effort to prepare the country for the conflict that he had hoped could be avoided. A persistent advocate of universal military service, he applied for active duty in 1917 on the grounds that, having proposed service for others, he had, as he said, to prove his "faith by works." That same year he went to France as a lieutenant colonel in the field artillery to fight along the Chemin des Dames in Lorraine.

On his return home at the end of the war, one part of his remarkable career came to a close. He had learned from Root that public service was a citizen's duty; he had learned from Theodore Roosevelt that it was exciting and, indeed (in a word he never would have used), fun; and from his own experience he had learned that such service most completely satisfied the requirements and desires of his personality. He had found out how to exercise power in controlled situations. Using authority bounded and defined by legal systems, bureaucratic structures, and those ancestral sanctions that worked within him, he had contributed to the general welfare. Besides, he was good at it; his years in the Southern District and the War Department were models of enlightened public administration. So it was natural that he should again be sought for further public service and that he should accept the opportunities offered.

But the times had changed. Up to now the way to Progress, as Theodore Roosevelt said, had been by calculable small next steps. After the war it often seemed that such steps led in no intended direction. In 1927, for instance, Stimson was sent to Nicaragua by President Calvin Coolidge. In a month of negotiation, he arranged a peace between the liberals and conservatives, who were at civil war. It was a neat piece of business, but the day after he left the country, fighting broke out and continued for half a decade. In the next year, Coolidge sent Stimson to the Philippines as governor-general. There, amid a population that was earnestly seeking independence, he sought to stabilize the precarious economy and restore the confidence of the people—badly damaged by his predecessor, Leonard Wood—in the United States as a concerned protector of its island possessions. In the twelve months before he was called home, he took some first steps toward economic development and made himself respected and trusted by the people and their leaders. But on his departure, agitation for independence began again, and in a few more years the great aim was actually achieved.

Stimson came home in 1929 to become secretary of state in President Herbert Hoover's cabinet. In this office he was in a position to consider the state of the world. In each month of his tenure, it seemed, matters went from bad to worse. As he wrote to Ramsey MacDonald, he often felt that he was "looking at a great flood breaking through a dam and having nothing but a hand shovel with which to make repairs" (Morison, p. 373). There was first the worldwide economic depression. Some part of the general situation was attributable to the structure of international debt created by World War I. As the principal creditor, the United States had a considerable role to play. Both Stimson and Hoover realized this and strove together to find ways for the country to make some constructive contribution. On the whole, Stimson always wanted to go a little further than the president—to extend the 1931 moratorium on debt payments from one to two years; to follow the "standstill" agreements, which postponed the collection of short-term credits, with an extension of further credits; to hold our former allies to a less strict accounting in their actual debt payments. But nothing that was done by either man served to bring more than temporary relief; conditions steadily deteriorated.

Then there was the effort to reduce tensions between nations by readjusting the structure of international armaments. At the London Naval Conference of 1930, called to seek a satisfactory balance of naval forces between the United States, England, Japan, France, and Italy, Stimson was the principal negotiator for the United States and a leading figure in the discussions; as such, he can be given much credit for the resulting agreement, which seemed on paper to eliminate "further naval competition" among the chief signatories. But in fact the written terms did nothing to stay the course of naval construction.

And then there was Manchuria. The problem was how to get the Japanese out of the province, which they had entered on Sept. 18, 1931. Hoover and Stimson tried first the soft impeachment, expressions of great "regret" and "concern." To give more bite to such words, Stimson then sought to mobilize world opinion in support of such indictments. When that failed, he and the president tried to invoke the doctrine of "nonrecognition," warning the Japanese that any territorial acquisition not in accord with existing treaties would not be recognized by the United States. Again they sought the support of world opinion and again without success. For one thing the Western nations, distracted by the depression, were in no mood to take any kind of positive position against Japan, which, as the French foreign minister Tardreu said, was "a long ways off"; for another, the obvious place to express whatever world opinion existed was in the League of Nations, to which the United States did not belong.

Searching in his frustration for some more effective instrument, Stimson proposed the application of economic sanctions. This the president rejected as, in his words, sticking pins in tigers. Deprived of other means, Stimson wrote a long letter to Sen. William E. Borah (Feb. 24, 1932), summarizing American relations with the Orient from the time of the open-door policy and restating the doctrine of nonrecognition. By this procedure he hoped, once again, to bring world opinion to the support of the rule of law. The letter was described as a master stroke and a most important utterance. But nothing happened. The Japanese remained in Manchuria, unresponsive alike to Stimson's strictures and a later condemnatory finding by the League of Nations.

In 1933 Stimson returned to private life, but he continued his active interest in a world that seemed to be falling apart. From his previous experiences he had been led to conclude that in such a world the customary measures—discussion, conference, admonition, negotiated agreement, the force of moral suasion—would no longer serve. As the decade progressed, he came increasingly to believe that the developing power of the fascist states would have to be contained by other means. The great ambiguities of that time, he argued in articles, speeches, and appearances before congressional committees, would not be resolved by the wish to avoid war or by a policy of neutrality that was simply an expression of that wish. The way to keep the peace was to choose actions that would convince others that to remain at peace was to their advantage. When in 1939 the war came, he spoke out increasingly for the support by all moral and material means of those nations opposing Germany and Italy.

Such views, which set him at odds with many of his countrymen in the last years of the decade, became the compelling reasons that he was appointed the secretary of war by President Franklin Roosevelt in June 1940. For the next five years he devoted himself with single-minded determination to the discharge of the affairs of this office.

The first thing he had to do was to give order and direction to a department that was in a state of total confusion. The second thing was to secure the orderly provision of training and matériel for the new troops. In the tangled state of affairs these were not simple tasks, and nothing moved as easily and rapidly as Stimson wished. But in his first fifteen months in office he laid sound foundations for future developments. For one thing, he surrounded himself with able, energetic, purposeful men— Robert Patterson, John McCloy, Harvey Bundy, and Robert Lovett. With George C. Marshall, the chief of staff, he established in those months a harmony of civil and military interests within the War Department that is without other example in the direction of an American armed force in time of war.

One further thing he did in those times: He took an active part in the deliberations of the administration on how to deal with the other nations in that distracted world. In these discussions he maintained that the United States should give all aid possible to Great Britain short of actually entering the war and accept no further accommodations to the actions of either the Germans or the Japanese.

This often publicly stated position and the fact that as secretary of war he was directly involved in framing the instructions that were subject to misinterpretation by commanders in the field in the last days and hours before Pearl Harbor have persuaded certain students of the situation that he was one of those who insinuated the country into a war that could have been avoided.

When the war began, Stimson had, as he said, to make decisions every hour, seven days a week. One of the first had to do with the evacuation of all Japanese—alien and citizen alike—from the coastal regions of California. After much anguish of spirit, reacting to the requests of many thoroughly frightened residents and of the greatly distressed commanding general of the area and recognizing that his decision would put, as he said, an awful hole in the Constitution, Stimson ordered the evacuation on the grounds of the safety of the nation and military necessity.

The decisions that interested Stimson most had to do with military matters. In the first year of the war he tried to use radar-equipped army planes to assist in the fight against the German submarines that were sinking so much of the indispensable merchant shipping in the Atlantic. In this effort he was thwarted by the resistance of the navy. Also in the first year Stimson did everything he could (and rather more than the president wished) to convince Roosevelt and Churchill of the necessity for, and possibility of, an early landing in Europe from British bases. His plan was to start with a small attack in the fall of 1942 to be followed by a massive invasion ("Sledgehammer") in the spring of 1943. His objective was postponed by the landings in North Africa but fulfilled in June 1944.

Late in the war much of his time was taken up with the activities surrounding the development and manufacture of the atom bomb. In the early months of 1945 work on the weapon had proceeded far enough to permit men to think about its use. Convinced by intelligence reports that the Japanese were determined to continue the war to the point of prostration and profoundly troubled by the predicted losses that would attend any attempt to invade the home islands, he never appeared to have any doubts about the necessity of dropping the bomb.

To ensure a careful consideration of the great question and to assist the new president, Harry S. Truman, to understand the nature of the problem—about which Truman knew nothing before assuming office—Stimson appointed the Interim Committee, made up of men of science and public life, to study alternatives and make recommendations. On June 1, 1945, the committee reported its conclusion that the bomb should be used.

In those closing months of the war he searched increasingly for postwar settlements that would give some promise of extended peace. To this end he had earlier opposed the Morgenthau plan to "pastoralize" Germany, and so in 1945 he urged that the United States, England, and Russia share the secret of the atom so that they could act with a common sense of power and responsibility to stabilize by mutual action the postwar world. Soon after the coming of the peace, on Sept. 21, 1945, his seventy-eighth birthday, he retired.

Too many people, he once said, looked on public service simply as an opportunity to make interesting speeches. For him it was a matter of what one did. That is what the ancestral voices had said; that was the implied meaning of his father's example; that was what the models of Root and Roosevelt demonstrated. So for forty years he did things. What they added up to was for others to analyze in what he called the cold light of history. But in his case such balancing off of acts and consequences will fall somewhat short of full summation.

What he was seemed often more important to those who worked with him than what he did. They put it in different ways: he was a "New England conscience on legs"; he was "a moral force in the Department"; everyone from Sam Rayburn and Felix Frankfurter to Harry Hopkins and Robert Oppenheimer trusted him. But they all meant the same thing. The conduct of the public business required an atmosphere that was above suspicion and beyond self. What he had learned from earlier examples and models he passed on to public servants like McCloy, Lovett, Bush, and Patterson as they continued their work.

The presence that produced such attitudes often seemed stern, reserved, and forbidding. But when beyond the call of duty, he had satisfactions and pleasures that he was delighted to share with others. He loved almost everything one could do outdoors—climbing, tennis, hunting, fishing, and especially horseback riding. He loved his home, Highhold, on Long Island, where he spent endless hours supervising the growing of crops and the raising of animals. He had built this house shortly after he and Mabel Wellington White were married on July 6, 1893. It became the center of their private lives, the gathering point for many young people who took the place of the children they never had. After leaving the War Department in 1945 he went to live at Highhold until his death.

[The Stimson Papers, including his extensive diary, are in the Yale Univ. Lib. On Stimson, see Richard N. Current, *Secretary Stimson* (1954); Robert H. Ferrell, *Stimson* (1963); Elting E. Morison, *Turmoil and Tradition* (1960); and Stimson and McGeorge Bundy, *On Active Service in Peace and War* (1948).
On the Manchuria episode, see Stimson, *The Far Eastern Crisis* (1936), for his own account; Robert H. Ferrell, *American Diplomacy in the Great Depression* (1957), chaps. 8–11, for a balanced description of events; and F. P. Walters, *A History of the League of Nations*, XI, 472ff. (1952), for an unfavorable view of the part played by Stimson and the United States.
On the internment of Japanese-Americans, see Morison; and Morton Grodzins, *Americans Betrayed* (1956; 1969).]

ELTING E. MORISON

STIMSON, JULIA CATHERINE (May 26, 1881–Sept. 29, 1948), nursing leader and superintendent of the Army Nurse Corps, was born in Worcester, Mass., the second of four daughters and second of seven children of Henry Albert Stimson and Alice Wheaton (Bartlett) Stimson, both of seventeenth-century New England ancestry. Her father, a native of New York City, was a prominent Congregational minister and an author and journalist. Her mother, a reform-minded civic leader, was born in Manchester, N.H., the daughter of Samuel Colcord Bartlett, a minister who was president of Dartmouth College from 1877 to 1892. A cousin, Henry L. Stimson, served in the cabinets of four presidents. Julia was reared in a strong tradition of service where equal opportunities for education and careers were extended to all seven children.

In 1886, when her father moved to a pastorate in St. Louis, she attended the public schools of that city; when he became pastor of the Broadway Tabernacle in 1893, she prepared for college at the Brearley School in New York City. After receiving the B.A. from Vassar in 1901, she did graduate work in biology at Columbia and worked in medical illustration at Cornell University Medical College, where her uncle Lewis Atterbury Stimson, was professor of surgery. On his advice, she postponed a decision to study medicine and considered instead the need of the nursing profession for college graduates. During a trip abroad, she met Annie Warburton Goodrich, a dynamic young nursing leader whose influence led her, in November 1904, to enter the New York Hospital Training School for Nurses, where Annie Goodrich was superintendent. She graduated in May

1908, and from several positions offered her, she chose to become superintendent of nurses at Harlem Hospital. During three years in this underprivileged area of New York, she and a colleague created a social service department at the hospital. She received her R.N. from the Board of Regents of New York in 1909, and wrote a *Nurses' Handbook of Drugs and Solutions*, published in 1910. In 1911 she became director of social service at the hospitals of Washington University Medical School in St. Louis (Barnes and Children's) and two years later assumed the duties of superintendent of nurses and director of the Washington University Training School for Nurses, positions she held until 1917. In the latter year she received the master's degree at Washington University.

The Ohio Valley flood of March 1913 brought Stimson into active duty with the Red Cross reserve, which she had joined four years earlier. Organizing a group of St. Louis nurses to accompany her, she did emergency hospital work and public health nursing in the region of Hamilton, Ohio. In 1914 she became a member of the National Committee on Red Cross Nursing, and three years later, when Red Cross chapters began creating base hospital units for military service, she led the formation of American Base Hospital No. 21 (Washington University), and was called overseas in May 1917 to staff No. 12 General Hospital with the British Expeditionary Forces near Rouen, France. From June 1917 to April 1918 this hospital, improvised on a racecourse, cared for a stream of 800 to 2,000 sick and wounded British. Surgical cases sometimes numbered 100 a day. Her letters to her family at this time convey both the details and the spirit of hospital life near the front. They also reflect her unique qualities for leadership: administrative skill, disciplinary wisdom, adaptability, enthusiasm, and an ability to evoke the best energies of her subordinates. In April 1918, she was ordered to Paris to become chief nurse, responsible for enrollment, assignment, equipment, and direction of American Red Cross nurses throughout France. Aided by her dual status as an Army nurse and a Red Cross nurse in negotiating ill-defined lines of authority between the two organizations, she accomplished her tasks with distinction. As the war ended in November, she was appointed director of the Nursing Service of the American Expeditionary Forces, with responsibility for the demobilization of some 10,000 nurses stationed in hospitals from the German border to the Mediterranean. Among her service honors were the Royal Red Cross, First Class (British), several French decorations, the Distinguished Service Medal awarded by Gen. John J. Pershing, and a citation from the AEF by Field Marshal Douglas Haig.

Stimson represented American nursing at the International Red Cross Conference at Cannes in April and returned to the United States in July 1919 as dean of the Army School of Nursing (a position she held until the school closed in 1933) and as acting superintendent of the Army Nurse Corps. On December 30 her superintendency was made permanent, vastly enlarged in its peacetime implications by the act of Congress (March 1919) providing for the establishment of veterans' hospitals. During her eighteen years as superintendent, the Army Nurse Corps rose in standing relative to the military and to nursing organizations, while enlarged opportunities for graduate study and professional affiliation made army nursing an inviting career. In 1920, in an effort to resolve administrative problems arising from the anomalous wartime status of nurses (apparent early in World War I, when nurses first served under army orders), Congress granted them "relative" rank, carrying absolute authority second after medical officers, although without privileges or salary commensurate with commissioned rank. Under this provision, Stimson became the first woman to hold the rank of major in the United States Army. She retired May 31, 1937, but in July 1940, soon after Dunkirk, as president of the American Nurses Association (1938-1944), she convened representatives of the five national nursing organizations, the American Red Cross Nursing Service, and federal nursing agencies to form the Nursing Council on National Defense. As its chairman until 1942, she directed the first American census of registered nurses. In 1942-1943, she briefly returned to active army duty, using her formidable power as a speaker to recruit nurses in twenty-three cities. In August 1948, after a full commissioned rank was authorized for nurses, she was promoted to the rank of colonel on the retired list.

Throughout retirement, as in her early years, she was concerned with drawing college graduates into nursing, a goal she pursued through such groups as the National League of Nursing Education and the American Association of University Women. In recognition of her work in nursing education, she received an honorary Sc.D. from Mt. Holyoke College in 1921 and the Florence Nightingale Medal of the International Red Cross in 1929.

A handsome, vigorous woman nearly six feet tall, Colonel Stimson was squarely built with large, even features and striking blue eyes. Independent and openly expressive of her opinions and convictions, she also possessed a generous, compassionate nature, which readily involved her with anyone in difficulty. Although she was both mechanically and athletically adept, her favorite recreation was playing the violin; when the use of her left hand was only partially restored after an automobile accident in 1925, she devised a new fingering system to accommodate her disability. During this same period, she wrote several accounts of nursing in earlier American wars (*Military Surgeon,* February 1926 and January and February 1928), and a history of the nurse's uniform (*American Journal of Nursing,* April 1936). Apart from summers in Rockland, Maine, her home during retirement was in Briarcliff Manor, N.Y., where she served as a trustee of the library and of the Congregational Church. She died after surgery in a Poughkeepsie, N.Y., hospital, in acute circulatory collapse attributed to generalized arteriosclerosis. Her ashes were buried in the woods, beside a stream near her home.

[There is no full biography. Biographical articles appear in *Notable Am. Women, 1607–1950,* III (1971); *Biog. Cyc. of Am. Women,* III (1928); *Nat. Cyc. Am. Biog.,* Current Vol. B (1927); and *Current Biog.,* 1940. *Woman's Who's Who of Am. 1914–1915* (1915) contains entries for Julia Stimson and for her mother. Obituaries appeared in *Am. Jour. of Nursing,* Nov. 1948, with photograph and editorial; and the *N.Y. Times,* Oct. 1, 1948. Other useful newspaper materials are the obituary of her father in the *N.Y. Times,* Sept. 28, 1933, and an account of the nursing census in the *N.Y. Times,* Sept. 8, 1940. Lavinia Dock et al., *Hist. of Am. Red Cross Nursing* (1922) and Portia B. Kernodle, *The Red Cross Nurse in Action 1882–1948* (1949), contain information about Colonel Stimson and about the circumstances under which she worked. Her letters of 1917–1918 were published as *Finding Themselves: The Letters of an Am. Army Chief Nurse in a British Hospital in France* (1918), with a 1917 photograph as frontispiece. Her papers were deposited with the Army Nurse Corps in Washington and at the New York Hospital School of Nursing. Personal information from Dorothy Stimson and Dr. Barbara Bartlett Stimson. Birth record from the Mass. Div. of Vital Statistics; death record from the N.Y. State Dept. of Health.]

PATRICIA SPAIN WARD

STITT, EDWARD RHODES (July 22, 1867–Nov. 13, 1948), navy surgeon, author, and teacher, was born in Charlotte, N.C., the first son of William Edward Stitt and Mary (Rhodes) Stitt. His father was a merchant and an officer in the Confederate army. After his mother died while giving birth to a younger brother when Edward was three years old, he was reared in an environment of Southern gentility by an aunt in Rock Hill, S.C. He prepared for college in a private school, then went to the University of South Carolina, where he took his B.A. in 1885. A Ph.C. (1887) earned at the Philadelphia College of Pharmacy was followed by an M.D. (1889) at the University of Pennsylvania.

Before graduation, Stitt was accepted into the U.S. Navy Medical Corps and commissioned an assistant surgeon. He spent much of 1890 serving in the Eastern Atlantic and Mediterranean. There, and later in the South Atlantic, impressed by the prevalence of epidemic diseases, he became interested in the phenomena of disease transmission and the relatively new use of the microscope in diagnosis. Stitt was one of the first in the navy to use a microscope for the examination of microorganisms. Opposition came early from many older navy (and army) doctors who thought it an outrage to have their long experience in diagnosis overruled by young men using microscopes.

On July 19, 1892, in Philadelphia, Stitt married Emma W. Scott; they had three children: Edward Wynkoop, Mary Raguet, and Emma Scott.

Stitt's interest in diseases of the tropics led to his selection as a medical member of the commissions formed to recommend possible routes for a canal across the isthmus of Central America. In 1895, he was favorably inclined toward a route across Nicaragua; later, after mosquitoes were proved to be carriers of malaria and yellow fever, he agreed with the choice of a Panama route.

In his first twenty years in the navy, Stitt spent all his available free time acquiring as much information as possible about tropical medicine and bacteriology; he never really stopped trying to learn more. Between 1895 and 1905, in addition to his regular duties, he studied at George Washington University, the Hoagland Laboratory (Brooklyn, N.Y.), and the London School of Tropical Medicine. At the same time, he was closely associated with and studied with Walter Reed and James Carroll at the Army Medical School.

In 1902, Stitt was appointed head of the departments of bacteriology, chemistry, and tropical medicine at the Navy Medical School, Washington, D.C. For the next eighteen years, with the exception of two duty tours in the Philippines, he remained at the school. During this time his two major books were written and published: one, *Practical Bacteriology, Hematology, and Animal Parasitology* (1908), which, over the years, ran to ten editions; the other, *Diagnostics and Treatment of Tropical Diseases* (1914), which appeared in seven revised editions over the subsequent forty years. After 1916, he was made commanding officer of the Navy Medical School, and for his service in that capacity during World War I he won the Navy Cross. In 1917, he was promoted to the rank of rear admiral.

When Surgeon General W. C. Braisted—owing to ill health—abruptly resigned in 1920 with two years of his second term remaining, Admiral Stitt was chosen to replace him. His first four-year term was extended to eight years when he was reappointed in 1924.

As surgeon general, Stitt carried on the onerous duties of that office in an exemplary manner; he also lectured regularly at the Navy Medical School and at three civilian medical schools. He encouraged specialization by navy physicians and provided opportunities for postgraduate training in civilian schools. He was medical consultant to three presidents: Woodrow Wilson, Warren Harding, and Calvin Coolidge.

At the conclusion of his second term, in 1928, Stitt became Inspector General, Medical Activities, West Coast, a position he held for the next two and one-half years. Finally, on Aug. 1, 1931, he was obliged to retire from active duty, having reached the statutory retirement age of sixty-four.

In his retirement years, he maintained residence in Washington for the rest of his life; while he did not keep regular office hours, he spent almost as much time at the Navy Medical School as did some who were there on active duty. He was not only unofficial consultant for the navy, he also became consultant in tropical medicine to the secretary of war during World War II. During these years, too, he spent much of his time updating his *Practical Bacteriology* and *Tropical Diseases,* both of which had become standard textbooks, internationally used, and in contributing written and oral discourses for the edification of the profession. Those years, also, saw changes in his personal life. His first wife died in 1933, and, on June 22, 1935, in Hanover Co., Va., he married Laura A. Carter, the widow of the director of the United States Patent Office. This marriage ended in tragedy when his wife committed suicide. Four years later, on May 3, 1937, in Baltimore, he married Helen Bennett Newton, the widow of James Thornwell Newton.

Stitt was a member of many professional and social groups, several of which he presided over as president. He held four honorary doctorates

and one honorary master's degree among the many honors conferred upon him during his lifetime.

Socially, Admiral Stitt was kindly and considerate, at ease in conversation and a great raconteur of old navy tales. Physically, he was a short, slender man, distinguished by a well-trimmed goatee and a fine baritone voice often heard on Sunday mornings as he sang in the choir of St. Matthew's Episcopal Church, in Washington, where he was a member of the congregation. Professionally, he was a giant.

Admiral Stitt died on Nov. 13, 1948, at the Naval Hospital, Bethesda, Md., where he had been a patient since July of that year, when he suffered a cerebral hemorrhage. He was buried with full military honors in Arlington National Cemetery.

[Primary sources are the *Annual Reports of the Surgeon General,* 1891–1931 and Admiral Stitt's service record and other official documents, Bureau of Medicine and Surgery, Navy Department. An informative article is to be found in *Nat. Cyc. Am. Biog.,* XXXIX, 350–351. Obituary articles are in *Annals of Internal Medicine,* 30 (1949), 233–234; *Jour. of the Am. Medic. Assoc.,* 138 (1948), 1051; *Military Surgeon,* 104 (1949), 71–72; *Trans. of the Assoc. of Am. Phsyicians,* 62 (1949), 15–19; *U.S. Naval Medical Bull.,* 49 (1949), 181–183; and *Washington Acad. of Sci. Jour.,* 39 (1949), 381–382. Other information came from family sources and his navy contemporaries. A portrait of the admiral hangs in the Edward R. Stitt Medical Library, Nat. Naval Medic. Center, Bethesda, Md.]

W. KENNETH PATTON

STODDARD, THEODORE LOTHROP (June 29, 1883–May 1, 1950), publicist of nativism, was born in Brookline, Mass., the only child of Mary Hammond (Brown) Stoddard, originally of Bangor, Maine, and John Lawson Stoddard, a noted lecturer and travel writer. The Stoddards took pride in their lineage, which extended to seventeenth-century Massachusetts, where Solomon Stoddard held the pastorate in Northampton.

Although his parents separated when he was five, Lothrop (as he was known) enjoyed frequent boyhood travels with his father. In 1901, after preparatory education at Cutler's School in Newton, Mass., he entered Harvard College, where he studied history, government, and European languages. Upon graduating *magna cum laude* in 1905, he moved to Boston University to study law, and in February 1908 was admitted to the Massachusetts bar. He left immediately for an eight-month trip through Europe. The trip proved a turning point. Stoddard became convinced of the imminence of a European war; caught in the turbulence of world politics, the United States would need expert guidance. In the fall of 1909, therefore, Stoddard entered Harvard graduate school to train for a new career as publicist and advisor on world affairs. He studied under Archibald Cary Coolidge and Robert Matteson Johnston and received his M.A. in 1910 and his Ph.D. in 1914.

Six months after Stoddard completed his doctorate, the war he had predicted broke out. In public lectures, in an outpouring of magazine and newspaper articles, and in two political guidebooks—*Present-Day Europe* (1917) and *Stakes of the War* (1918, with Glenn Frank)—he earnestly sought to fulfill his mission of objectively outlining Europe's political complexities to an innocent American public. In October 1918 Stoddard took over the foreign affairs department of the magazine *World's Work,* and for two years, as the nation debated the peace settlement, he found ample scope for his chosen profession.

But these informed and balanced analyses brought Stoddard little recognition. It was in the sullen atmosphere of the early 1920's, as the country rejected international crusades and sought to safeguard itself at home, that Stoddard's four books and numerous articles on the race issue won him wide renown. Of the books, the first and most successful was *The Rising Tide of Color Against White-World-Supremacy* (1920). In the preface he stated that around 1910 he had become convinced that race relations would profoundly affect the course of world politics and history. His doctoral thesis, published in 1914 as *The French Revolution in Santo Domingo,* had dealt in part with "the first great shock between the ideals of white supremacy and race equality." Written under the inspiration of the leading race theorist, Madison Grant, *The Rising Tide of Color* was concerned less with the dangers to America of the "new immigration" than with the threat posed to all of white civilization by the debilitating effects of World War I and the new expansionist desires of the yellow and brown races. *The New World of Islam* (1921) further documented these ominous stirrings. In *The Revolt Against Civilisation* (1922) Stoddard shifted his morbid fears from the inferior races to inferior men, who were seeking to overthrow their cultured masters in the brutal, mindless guise of Bolshevism. Eugenics was his ultimate solution. The last of these hereditarian polemics, *Racial Realities in Europe* (1924), was a standard comparison of the manly, creative Nordic "race" with the lesser Alpine and Mediterranean "races."

Few of these ideas were original with Lothrop Stoddard. Like many contemporaries, he fused a crude grasp of Mendelian genetics and European anthropology with a traditional faith in Anglo-Saxon culture. But the peculiar pungency of his style, the global breadth of his vision, and his pose of informed expertise made Stoddard a most influential propagandist. Invitations to congressional hearings, praise from President Harding, and many favorable reviews of his books, all suggest that Stoddard was important in rationalizing for his country its new immigration laws. Although he frequently garbed himself in the mantle of disinterested science—especially in *Scientific Humanism* (1926)—Stoddard's fond yearnings for colonial America and his brooding fears of imminent cataclysm reveal powerful emotions. Isolated in an urban America that was increasingly cosmopolitan and equalitarian, he found relief only in the dogma of blood.

The final passage of immigration restriction in 1924 restored Lothrop Stoddard's hopes as it reduced his audience. Although he wrote two further books extolling white solidarity (*Reforging America,* 1927; *Clashing Tides of Color,* 1935), the next fifteen years saw him writing on a wide range of topics: a history of children, a chatty collection of anecdotes about luck, a well-researched biography of Tammany boss Richard Croker, travel books, and two polemical works advising the United States to stop investing in Europe and to start finding friends in the world. His fascination with world affairs induced him to move from Brookline, Mass., to Washington, D.C., in the early 1930's, but he continued to summer at West Dennis, Mass., on Cape Cod. There he busied himself with landscape gardening, outdoor sports, and stamp collecting. A tall, dignified man with a refined, angular face and clipped moustache, Stoddard was a Unitarian in religion, a Republican in politics, and a member of learned societies in history, political science, sociology, and genetics. He married Elizabeth Guildford Bates of Dorchester, Mass., on Apr. 16, 1926. There were two children, Theodore Lothrop and Mary Alice. His first wife died in 1940, and on Jan. 4, 1944, in Philadelphia, Pa., he married Zoya Klementinovskaya.

The outbreak of World War II provided new professional opportunities. Stoddard's racial theories made him *persona grata* to the Nazis, and for six months from late 1939 he served as special correspondent of the North American Newspaper Alliance in Germany. The resulting book, *Into the Darkness* (1940), was a fair and honest appraisal of the Nazi state, but not without hints of admiration for Hitler's eugenic experiments. On his return, Stoddard served for five years as a foreign policy expert for the *Washington Evening Star*. He died of cancer in the George Washington University Hospital in Washington at the age of sixty-six. His ashes were buried at West Dennis, Mass. Obituaries were rare and perfunctory: the findings of science and the sordid realities of Hitler's Germany had discredited the racial and social views that Stoddard had proclaimed.

[For the intellectual context of Stoddard's beliefs, the most useful books are Barbara Miller Solomon, *Ancestors and Immigrants* (1956); John Higham, *Strangers in the Land* (1963); Mark Haller, *Eugenics* (1963); and Thomas F. Gossett, *Race: The Hist. of an Idea in Am.* (1963). Detailed information on Stoddard can be found in the *Nat. Cyc. Am. Biog.*, XL, 370; *Who Was Who in America*, III (1960); *N.Y. Times* obituary, May 2, 1950; *Time*, Jan. 22, 1940, p. 35, with photograph; Grant M. Overton, *Authors of the Day* (1924), pp. 220–226; and the reports of Stoddard's Harvard College class.]

J. O. C. PHILLIPS

STONE, HARLAN FISKE (Oct. 11, 1872–Apr. 22, 1946), chief justice of the United States, was born in Chesterfield, N.H.., the second son and second of the four children of Frederick Lauson Stone and Anne (Butler) Stone. His father, a farmer, was the eighth generation of direct descendants of Simon Stone, who settled in the Massachusetts Bay Colony in 1635; five generations lived in the little town of Chesterfield. His mother was a former school teacher. Both his parents, like their English forebears, developed physical stamina and moral strength from tilling New Hampshire's rocky soil. In 1874, seeking greater educational opportunities for their children, Winthrop and Harlan, they moved to a farm in Mill Valley, near Amherst, Mass., where Lauson and Helen were born. Frederick Stone's activities expanded beyond farming to buying and selling real estate, auctioneering agricultural implements, and engaging in civic pursuits.

Chubby and good-natured, Harlan spent his boyhood "like that of many another New England farm boy." He roamed about the countryside and fished in a stream by an old grist mill. He excelled at the district schools and became a voracious reader. Occasionally the Stones' Sunday afternoons were enlivened by visits from old Chesterfield friends, the Hermon C. Harvey family, including their daughter Agnes, the justice's future wife.

Although Stone distinguished himself in high school, he decided at the end of his sophomore year to enter Massachusetts Agricultural College in the fall of 1888. There he developed an interest in science and acquired the nickname "Doc." A twist of fate changed the course of his life when he was expelled for joining in a chapel rush, accidentally shaking the chaplain "until his teeth rattled." After a period of profound discouragement, Stone entered Amherst College in 1890, with the help of his high school teacher, Edith Field.

Specializing in science and philosophy, he blossomed under the inspiration of Edward Garman "who taught young men to stand on their own feet intellectually and to encompass in their thinking spiritual as well as moral values." Stone excelled at public speaking and won oratorical contests. Demonstrating qualities of leadership, he became class president, business manager of the college weekly, the *Student,* and a leader in the senate where he fought for reforms in student government. Classmates predicted he would "be the most famous man in '94."

After graduation, Stone taught science at Newburyport (Mass.) High School. The superior court sessions at nearby Salem stirred an interest in the law, and he abandoned a successful teaching career and entered Columbia Law School in 1895. To defray expenses, he taught history at Adelphi Academy in Brooklyn. Dean William S. Keener's innovations, especially the case system, had turned Columbia into a hotbed of controversy. To his delight, Stone found a group of men engaged in teaching law as a science (notably Dean Keener, George W. Kirchwey, John Bassett Moore, and George F. Canfield). At a boardinghouse on Morningside Heights, Stone enjoyed the friendship of fellow students—Dwight Morrow, Grosvenor Backus, Jackson E. Reynolds, Sterling Carr, and Walter Carter. In Hamilton moot court, he distinguished himself on the bench where, as Reynolds later remarked, "his judicial attitude was a striking quality in his character."

After graduation in 1898, Stone combined law school teaching with a clerkship in the firm of Sullivan and Cromwell. A year later he shifted to Wilmer and Canfield. On Sept. 7, 1899, he married his childhood sweetheart, Agnes Harvey, and settled in New York City.

Because of policy differences with President Nicholas Murray Butler, an inadequate salary, and growing family responsibilities with the birth of two sons, Marshall Harvey and Lauson, Stone resigned his professorship in March 1905 for a full-time partnership at Wilmer and

Canfield. A year later, the family moved to Englewood, N.J. Stone's impact at Columbia remained, and in 1906 he accepted Butler's invitation to return as professor and dean, with the understanding that he would enjoy freedom in choosing the law faculty. Soon the authoritarian president and the staunchly independent dean clashed. Again, Stone resigned, evoking a concerted drive by students, faculty, and trustees on his behalf. The upshot was his unanimous appointment as dean, effective July 10, 1910.

The years 1910-1916 were marked by assiduous efforts to raise academic standards and improve the curriculum. Stone himself set an example by continuing to teach, write, and maintain a nominal law practice at Wilmer, Canfield, and Stone. As a practicing lawyer, Stone's career was brief—1905-1910 and about six months in 1923-1924. In later years, he rated his teaching more enduring than anything he did as a judge.

A firm believer in the Socratic method, he led his students inductively, case by case, to reach their own conclusions. Rigorous with himself as well as his students, he never faltered in his effort to develop responsible lawyers with disciplined minds and sensitive social consciences. For him an intellectual elite was not the antithesis of democracy but its essential bulwark. "The hope and safeguard of democracy is education," he proclaimed, "not that so-called education which would popularize learning at the cost of a sacrifice of standards, nor education in the narrow and technical sense, but the education which enlightens the masses as to the right relationship of the individual to the organization of society and inculcates a sense of individual responsibility for the preservation of that relationship on a sound basis of which law is only the outgrowth" ("Obedience to Law and Social Change"). Justice William O. Douglas remembered Stone as "one of the very best, if not the best, law teacher, we ever had."

An Anglophile and strong interventionist, Stone anxiously observed the course of World War I. He lamented his ineligibility for active service. A chance to serve his country came with his appointment to a special board of inquiry to examine cases of conscientious objectors. Passions were high, especially against those "conshies" whose objections were based on social or political grounds. In spite of his own instinctive conservatism, Stone doubted the wisdom of coerced conformity at the cost of conscience and strongly supported faculty dissenters, victims of Butler's repressive measures, thus foreshadowing his tolerant attitude on the Supreme Court toward freedom of thought and conscience. His essay "The Conscientious Objector" (*Columbia University Quarterly,* October 1919) is recognized as a classic.

Increasing dislike for administrative detail, the lure of a lucrative private practice, disaffection within the faculty, and distaste for continous wrangling with Nicholas Murray Butler led Stone to resign as dean on Feb. 21, 1923. On Apr. 1, 1924, President Coolidge, hoping to restore public confidence in the scandal-plagued Department of Justice, headed by Harry M. Daugherty, named Stone attorney general.

In trying to brighten the tarnished Justice Department, Stone's primary goal was recruitment of personnel unsullied by alliance with the underworld. William J. Burns was dismissed as head of the Federal Bureau of Investigation and replaced by twenty-nine-year-old J. Edgar Hoover on Dec. 19, 1924. "Everyone says he is too young," the attorney general commented, "but maybe that's his asset. Apparently, he hasn't learned to be afraid of politicians." Stone ordered scrupulous investigations of FBI applicants and a rigorous training period. Scotland Yard was his model, tempered by his concern lest "a secret police become a menace to free government and free institutions because it carries with it the possibility of abuses of power." FBI agents must not be "above the law or beyond its reach."

Eliminating political plums for congressional protégés, accustomed to serving as counsel for the government in cases before the Supreme Court, Stone revived the tradition of arguing cases himself. He prosecuted antitrust suits against such corporations as the Aluminum Company of America, Andrew Mellon's stronghold. He campaigned for Coolidge in 1914, defending the president's purifying role in the Justice Department. Stone's nomination to the Supreme Court (succeeding Joseph McKenna) on Jan. 5, 1925, quickly followed Coolidge's victory. Although attacked by certain senators opposed to his role in prosecuting antitrust cases, Stone was overwhelmingly confirmed, on Feb. 5, 1925, by a vote of 71 to 6 and sworn in on March 2.

Stone's law school experience helped to prepare him for the Court. At Columbia he had time and opportunity for study, research, and reflection, time to develop ideas on the nature of law and the function of courts. His law practice, although helpful, was not closely related to issues which confront a Supreme Court justice. Constitutional law had not been his specialty, either in teaching or in practice. Except as attorney general, he had argued only one case, *Ownbey* v. *Morgan* (1921), before the high Court. Here he suggested the major theme in his constitutional jurisprudence—judicial self-restraint. Correction of outmoded processes ought to be left, he argued, to legislatures rather than assumed by courts. The ideas Stone expounded in a series of lectures (later published as *Law and Its Administration,* 1915) at Columbia University have been regarded as conservative, even reactionary. But when, as a Supreme Court justice, he harshly attacked judicial distrust of social legislation, he was hailed as a liberal.

Stone's approach is revealed in his consideration of intergovernmental immunities from taxation—a vexing problem during the chief justiceships of both Taft and Hughes. Rejecting the reciprocal immunities doctrine established by *McCulloch* v. *Maryland* (1819) and *Collector* v. *Day* (1871), he held that the federal system does not establish "total want of power in one government to tax the instrumentalities of the other." No formula sufficed to resolve the issue. For him, the extent and locus of the tax burden were important considerations (*Helvoring* v. *Gerhardt* [1938] and *Graves* v. *New York* [1939]). Similarly, in cases involving government regulation of the economy and state taxation affecting interstate commerce, no question-begging formula as to "business affected with a public interest" or "direct and indirect effects" was adequate. All such legislation must be subjected to factual analysis.

Although a habitual Republican, Stone realized that increased use of government, national and state, was a necessary concomitant of twentieth-century conditions. "Law functions best only when it is fitted to the life of a people," he said. This conviction usually aligned him with justices Holmes and Brandeis. Chief among points of agreement was their dedication to a living law. As the majority's doctrinaire approach became increasingly out of tune with the times, the bond uniting the illustrious three grew tighter. Yet concurring dissenting opinions revealed significant differences among them. Holmes, a gifted essayist, liked to generalize, avoiding tough issues, failing to meet the majority on its own ground. "I wish," Stone once wrote in grudging admiration, "I could make my cases sound as easy as Holmes makes his." Stone's divergence from Brandeis was revealed when the Court

struck down legislation Brandeis thought desirable. In dissent, the erstwhile people's attorney used the Court as a forum to persuade others of its wisdom. "I think you are too much an advocate of this particular legislation," Stone told Brandeis in refusing to join Brandeis' dissenting opinion (*Liggett* v. *Lee* [1933]). "I think our dissents are more effective if we take the attitude that we are concerned with power and not with the merits of its exercise."

The notion, vigorously advanced in certain quarters, that Holmes and Brandeis were the "pacemakers" and Stone a sort of judicial "me-too" is not borne out by the record. Without minimizing the contributions of Holmes and Brandeis, Stone was the one who, in both the old Court (before 1937) and the new (after 1937), carried the Holmes-Brandeis tradition to fulfillment.

Stone's constitutional jurisprudence crystallized in 1936, the heyday of judicial resistance to Roosevelt's massive New Deal program. In *United States* v. *Butler* (1936), the Court, voting 6 to 3, outlawed the Agricultural Adjustment Act. Justice Roberts, the majority's spokesman, and Justice Stone, dissenting, were equally skeptical of the AAA. They differed on the scope of national power and the Court's role in the American system of free government. Roberts raised the forbidding spectacle of "legislative power without restriction or limitation . . . a parliament of the whole people, subject to no restrictions save such as are self-imposed." "Such suppositions," Stone countered, "are addressed to the mind accustomed to believe that it is the business of courts to sit in judgment on the wisdom of legislative action." The executive and the legislature are restrained by "the ballot box and the processes of democratic government" and "subject to judicial restraint; the only check on our own exercise of power is our own sense of self-restraint."

Stone accused the recalcitrant four (Butler, McReynolds, Sutherland, and Van Devanter, sometimes joined after 1930 by Hughes and Roberts) of "torturing" the Constitution. At the end of the 1935-1936 term, the Court had, as Stone put it, "tied Uncle Sam up in a hard knot." The mask of objectivity had been removed. In 1936-1937, "government by judiciary" became a crucial political issue.

On the heels of President Roosevelt's court-packing effort of 1937, the Court abandoned guardianship of property and contract rights as preferred freedoms. At first glance it seems paradoxical that Stone, who led the campaign for judicial self-restraint in cases involving regulation of the economy, should have articulated and rationalized another category of preferred freedoms entitled to "more exacting judicial scrutiny."

In *United States* v. *Carolene Products Company* (1938), Stone suggested in the text of the opinion that the Court would not go so far as to say that no economic regulation would violate constitutional restraints, but he did indicate that henceforth the Court's role in this area would be strictly confined. Attached to this proposition is what is considered to be the most famous footnote in the Court's history, suggesting special judicial scrutiny in three areas: legislative encroachment on First Amendment freedoms; government action impeding or corrupting the political process; and official conduct adversely affecting the rights of racial, religious, or national minorities.

The Carolene Products footnote not only set the stage for a new era of judicial activism, but it also laid the ideological foundation for the Warren Court's revolutionary decisions in race relations, reapportionment, and rules of criminal procedure.

By 1938, Stone's name was identified with two seemingly contradictory postures: judicial self-restraint and preferred freedoms, which, according to the Carolene Products footnote, merited "more exacting judicial scrutiny than . . . most other types of legislation." Although Justice Frankfurter warmly endorsed both concepts, he differed sharply with Stone in their application. Speaking for a majority of eight, Frankfurter, in *Minersville School District* v. *Gobitis* (1940), upheld Pennsylvania's law requiring all public school students to salute the American flag; the Jehovah's Witnesses had challenged the law. In doing so Frankfurter thought he was adhering to his colleague's own basic prescriptions.

Underlying this cleavage are fundamental differences as to the nature and requirements of free government. Quite correctly, Frankfurter thought of judicial review as limiting popular government. Stone considered judicial review to be one of the auxiliary precautions envisioned by the founding fathers against abuse of power. He believed that unless the Court invokes its authority to preserve the rights deemed fundamental, especially the crucial preliminaries of the political process—speech, press, assembly—no free government can exist. By standing aside, as in the flag salute case, the Court, in effect, sanctioned coercion in the delicate realm of civil rights. Three years

later, Stone's dissenting views prevailed in *West Virginia Board of Education* v. *Barnette* (1943).

On June 2, 1941, Chief Justice Hughes resigned at the age of seventy-nine. Speculation concerning Hughes' successor centered on Attorney General Robert H. Jackson and Associate Justice Stone. With the country close to the brink of World War II, the appointment of a Republican chief justice was considered good strategy. The choice of Stone seemed a fitting reward for the uphill battle he had waged, despite his strong misgivings, on behalf of the New Deal's constitutionality. "Whatever the rest of the world may think," Stone commented, "Washington is under no illusion that I am a New Dealer." Hughes and Frankfurter favored Stone. Refuting the charge that he made party loyalty the primary qualification for appointment to the Supreme Court, Roosevelt passed over his popular attorney general and sent Stone's name to the Senate on June 12, 1941. The highest judicial office in the land, which had eluded him in 1930 when his friend Herbert Hoover was in the White House, came from a Democrat toward whom he felt no political kinship.

Stone's chief justiceship, however, was unimpressive. The bench Stone headed was the most frequently divided, the most openly quarrelsome in history. Unlike his predecessors Taft and Hughes, he refused to resort to ingenious reasoning, good fellowship, the caucus, and other devices useful in keeping the Court unified. Believing profoundly in freedom of expression for others no less than for himself, he was slow to cut off conference discussions. For him the Court's function was not only to decide cases, but also, through the clash of ideas, to find solutions considerate of the past, adequate for the present, and no obstacle to the future.

Nevertheless, in his two full decades (1925–1946) on the Court, Stone left his mark on almost every type of case that came before it. It seems ironical that this peace-loving man should have been caught in the cross fires of controversy throughout his judicial career. On the Taft Court (1925-1930), as during a good part of Chief Justice Hughes' regime (especially 1930-1937), Stone differed from colleagues on the right who interposed social and economic predilections under the guise of interpreting the Constitution. During his own chief justiceship, Stone clashed with colleagues on the left who appeared equally set on using judicial office to further political or personal preference.

Stone's guiding rule was judicial self-restraint, not judicial self-abnegation. The sharp barbs of his thought were intended for the flesh of judges, right and left, who, without taking the trouble to weigh competing values, prematurely enforced personal conviction as law.

When, in 1945, he found himself pitted against judicial activists, inspired by his Carolene Products footnote, he dolefully reminisced: "My more conservative brethren in the old days enacted their own economic prejudice into law. What they did placed in jeopardy a great and useful instrument of government. . . . The Court is now in as much danger of becoming a legislative Constitution-making body, enacting into law its own predilections, as it was then."

Stone's conception of the judicial function was almost monastic. He strove to keep the Court within what he considered appropriate bounds. A judge should confine himself to the issue at hand. Each case should be dealt with in the light of facts, legislative intent, precedent, and the judge's own reason and values. The Court ought "to correct its own errors, even if I helped to make them." Stone's judicial technique stressed complexity. To oversimplify was convenient for the pedagogue, disastrous for the judge. Conflicting claims of the past must be measured against those of the present. The judge would do well to weigh all this in terms of "a considered judgment of what the community may regard as within the limits of the reasonable." The "sober second thought of the community," he said, "is the firm base on which all law must ultimately rest."

Stone had an abiding faith in free government and in judicial review as an essential adjunct to its operation. For him radical change was neither necessary nor generally desirable. He believed that it could be avoided "if fear of legislative action, which Courts distrust or think unwise, is not over-emphasized in interpreting the document." A free society requires continuity, "not of rules but of aims and ideals, which will enable government in all the various crises of human affairs to continue to function and to perform its appointed task within the bounds of reasonableness."

Stone savored leisure, family, and hobbies. He enjoyed the outdoor life with his sons at his remote Isle au Haut cottage in Maine. Sharing his wife's interest in art, he encouraged her painting career. Together they visited galleries and museums here and on their extensive travels abroad. As chairman of the board of trustees of the National Gallery, he played an important role in expanding its collections and rescuing European art treasures during World War II. Stone also served on committees of the Smithsonian Institution and the Folger Library. He was affable and cosmopolitan, a gourmet and a connoisseur of wines. Stone's charm made him a favorite companion of President Hoover, with whom he sometimes went fishing; he was also a member of the intimate group known as the Medicine Ball Cabinet.

At the age of seventy-four, Stone was stricken on the bench, while his famous dictum, "courts are not the only agency of government that must be presumed to have capacity to govern," resounded as a poignant valedictory (*Girouard* v. *United States* [1946]).

Death from a massive cerebral hemorrhage came peacefully at 6:45 P.M. After funeral services in the Washington Cathedral, he was buried in the shadow of St. Paul's Episcopal Church, in Rock Creek Park, Washington, D.C.

In 1970, a widely publicized rating of judges by sixty-five law deans and professors of law, history, and political science, ranked Stone "great" in a list of twelve which included Marshall, Holmes, Brandeis, Hughes, and Warren (Abraham, pp. 289-290).

[Stone's papers are on deposit at the Lib. of Congress. His writings include *Law and Its Administration* (1915); "The Common Law in the United States," *Harvard Law Rev.*, 50 (1936), 4; "Fifty Years' Work of the Supreme Court," *Am. Bar Assn. Jour.*, 14 (1928), 428; "Some Aspects of the Problem of Law Simplification," *Columbia Law Rev.*, 23 (1923), 319; "The Public Influence of the Bar," *Harvard Law Rev.*, 48 (1934), 1; and "Obedience to Law and Social Change," *N. H. Bar Assn. Proc.* (New Series), vol. 5, no. 3 (1925). The authorized biography is Alpheus Thomas Mason, *Harlan Fiske Stone: Pillar of the Law* (1956). More specialized aspects of Stone's thought and work are discussed in S. J. Konefsky, *Chief Justice Stone and the Supreme Court* (1945); J. P. Frank, "Harlan Fiske Stone: An Estimate," *Stanford Law Rev.*, 9 (1957), 621; N. T. Dowling, "Mr. Justice Stone and the Constitution," *Columbia Law Rev.*, 36 (1936), 351; Learned Hand, "Chief Justice Stone's Conception of the Judicial Function," *Columbia Law Rev.*, 46 (1946), 696; Herbert Wechsler, "Stone and the Constitution," *Columbia Law Rev.*, 46 (1946), 793; W. O. Douglas, "Chief Justice Stone," *Columbia Law Rev.*, 46 (1946), 764; N. T. Dowling, "The Methods of Mr. Justice Stone in Constitutional Cases," *Columbia Law Rev.*, 41 (1941), 1160; Irving Dilliard, ed., "Chief Justice Stone's Concept of the Judicial Function," in *The Spirit of Liberty: Papers and Addresses of Learned Hand* (1952). See also H. J. Abraham, *Justices and Presidents* (1974). *N.Y. Times* obituary, Apr. 23, 1946.]

ALPHEUS THOMAS MASON

STRANGE, MICHAEL (Oct. 1, 1890–Nov. 5, 1950), socialite, poet, and actress, was born Blanche Oelrichs. Her parents were a socially prominent New York couple, Charles May Oelrichs and Blanche (de Loosey) Oelrichs. In a

Roman Catholic ceremony she was christened Blanche Marie Louise Oelrichs. Her paternal grandfather had emigrated from Germany to the United States in 1832, but it was with her mother's family, more recent arrivals who clung to their roots in "gay, autocratic Vienna," that she more closely identified herself. Her maternal grandfather had served for twenty years as the Austrian consul general in New York City. Her elder sister, Lily, later returned to Austria as the Duchess of Mecklenburg-Schwerin. Blanche was the youngest of the four children in the household, Lily being ten years older than she, and her brothers being senior by six and eight years.

Her father continued the family tradition of banking and maintained his family in the affluent and genteel society of New York and Newport, R.I. His children were raised within the conservative Catholicism brought over from Europe by their forebears and were expected to acquire the charm and polish appropriate to their station. By her own account, however, Blanche was mischievous as a child, brimming with undisciplined imagination and energy. She rebelled against the primness of the schools to which she was sent, was expelled by both the Brearley School in New York and the Convent of the Sacred Heart in Manhattanville, and completed her education under private tutors.

Despite a decline in her father's financial fortunes during her early years, the balls and flirtations of Newport culminated in her debut in 1908 and her marriage two years later on Jan. 26, 1910, to a rising young diplomat, Leonard Moorhead Thomas. They had two sons, Leonard Moorhead and Robin May Thomas, but domestic life left her unfulfilled. Observing the public calumny being heaped upon the suffragettes in London, she adopted their cause. Bobbing her hair and assuming the rhetoric of a woman's emancipation, she became a temporary spokesman for the cause, and in 1915 led a march for woman's rights down Fifth Avenue, past a reviewing stand whose occupants included President Wilson.

Concurrently, her enthusiasms began to overflow in verse. From Walt Whitman she borrowed not only the majestic vers libre of her lines but also the benevolent idealism, which coincided with her own aspirations toward a free and democratic American society. Upon placing a poem in the *New York Sun,* she was approached by a publisher and agreed to collect her poetry into a book. In 1916 *Miscellaneous Poems* appeared under the pen name Michael Strange. Evidently chosen on impulse, in a

moment of dissatisfaction with the appearance of the name Blanche Thomas on the title page, the name was used in all of her ventures in the arts.

She divorced Leonard Thomas in 1919, and embarked upon a tempestuous affair with the actor John Barrymore, which eventually led to their marriage on Aug. 5, 1921. Turning her focus from poetry to the drama, she wrote several plays, the most successful of which, *Claire de Lune* (1921), was produced in New York with John, Ethel, and Lionel Barrymore in the leading roles. The reviews were sufficiently mixed to discourage her for the moment. But on advice given to her by George Bernard Shaw, she started to learn about the theater from the inside, as a journeyman actress. Joining a New England summer stock company, she performed in a Clyde Fitch play, *Barbara Frietchie* (1925), and was rewarded by offers from Broadway producers for the next season. Quite aware that she could be exploited merely as a "society woman," she selected her parts carefully: Eleanora in Strindberg's *Easter* (1926) and Chrysothemis in Sophocles' *Electra* (1927), produced by Margaret Anglin. Over the ensuing years she appeared in *Man of Destiny* (1926), *The Importance of Being Earnest* (1926), and *Richard III* (1930). The performance that brought her greatest recognition, however, was in a Broadway production of Rostand's *L'Aiglon* (1927), in which the costume of the male page set off her lithe figure and graceful mannerisms to their best advantage. She apparently overextended herself, however, by writing her own double part, male and female, in a short-lived play she called *Lord and Lady Byron* (c. 1927-1928).

After a period of separation from Barrymore, occasioned in part by his life style and her posture of feminine independence, she divorced him in 1928. Diana Blythe Barrymore was the child of this marriage. On May 23, 1929, Strange married Harrison Tweed, a prosperous lawyer and yachtsman.

Faced with the further erosion of her personal fortune by the Wall Street upheavals of the late 1920's and determined to be self-sufficient, Michael Strange supported herself and her children through a series of lecture tours. Under the vague heading of "The Stage as the Actress Sees It," she presented an evolving program of memories of her stage experiences, readings from her poetry, dramatic readings, and patriotic tributes. It made little difference what she did: the audiences paid, attended, and basked in her charm. After several such tours she developed a program of readings set to music, initially with a single harpist, but as she graduated to radio, with full orchestral accompaniment.

Her career led her into contact with Norman Thomas in 1932, and she quickly espoused his brand of socialism, explaining that to her it was merely simple democracy and common sense. In 1941, as a further gesture of egalitarian patriotism, she publicly supported the America First Committee.

She and Tweed were divorced in 1942, and from that date she led a comparatively quiet life in Easton, Conn. She fell ill from leukemia in the late 1940's and died in Boston on Nov. 5, 1950. She was buried at Woodlawn Cemetery in New York City.

[Michael Strange supplies most of the information, somewhat colored but nevertheless reliable, about her personal and public life in her autobiography, *Who Tells Me True* (1940). Somewhat different perspectives are contained in Gene Fowler's *Good Night, Sweet Prince* (1945). Factual information is corroborated in her obituary in the *N.Y. Times,* Nov. 6, 1950, and an article in the *New Yorker,* Apr. 10, 1948. Biographical articles are available in *Nat. Cyc. Am. Biog.,* XXXIX, and *Notable Am. Women,* III.]
ALBERT F. McLEAN

STRAWN, SILAS HARDY (Dec. 15, 1866-Feb. 4, 1946), lawyer and businessman, was born on a farm near Ottawa, Ill., the only son and first of three children of Abner Strawn and Eliza (Hardy) Strawn. His father was a successful grain dealer and stock breeder, whose uncle, Jacob Strawn, in the antebellum and war years, had been the largest cattle dealer in the Midwest. Of Welsh extraction, this branch of the family no longer spelled the surname Straughan. Silas Strawn's sister, Julia Clark Strawn, became a distinguished physician in Chicago.

After graduating from Ottawa High School in 1885, Strawn supported himself as a teacher and, while reading law, as a clerk and court reporter. In 1889 he was admitted to the Illinois bar, practicing initially in the office of Bull and Strawn, where Lester Strawn, his first cousin, was a junior partner. Beginning in 1892, Strawn practiced in Chicago at the offices of Winston and Meagher and, in 1894, he was made a partner. His ties with the firm, like those with Chicago, were to be lifelong.

On June 22, 1897, Strawn married Margaret Stewart, of Binghamton, N.Y.; they had two daughters, Margaret and Katherine.

Strawn's firm—Winston, Strawn, Black, and Towner—one of the oldest and one of the largest and most lucrative in Chicago, engaged in general practice. Its clientele was generally corporate, with railroads supplying a large portion of its business. At one time or another, the firm represented the Chicago Great Western Railroad Company, the Union Stock Yards & Transit Company, the Michigan Central Railroad Company, the Chicago and Alton Railroad, the Chicago, Indianapolis, and Louisville Railway Company, and the Nickel Plate Railroad. Other corporate clients of note included the Mutual Life Insurance Company of New York, Wilson and Company, the Pullman Company, and Montgomery Ward. Strawn and his firm's position in Chicago also led to other relationships with corporate interests. He was a director and chairman of the board of the Electrical Household Utilities Company, a director and member of the executive committee of the First National Bank of Chicago, and a director of the First Trust and Savings Bank of Chicago, the Chicago Corporation, the Hurley Machine Company, the Wahl Company, and Montgomery Ward. Strawn took a particular interest in Montgomery Ward, serving for twelve years on the executive board and, for a few months in 1920, as president of the corporation.

Strawn was a member of the bar of the City of New York, as well as a member, officer, and active participant in the appropriate local, state, and national bar associations. He served the Chicago Bar Association as president from 1913 to 1914, the Illinois State Bar Association from 1921 to 1922 as its president, and from 1927 to 1928 he presided over the fiftieth anniversary of the American Bar Association. His tenure in this last office was most distinguished by a continuation of his perennial campaign to raise educational requirements for admission to the bar. In line with his personal and professional interests in international law and commerce, Strawn became a member of the executive council of the American Society of International Law, a trustee of the Carnegie Endowment for International Peace, and president of the Chicago Council on Foreign Relations. He attended the foreign conventions of the International Chamber of Commerce in 1923, 1927, 1931, and 1933 as an American committee delegate, an activity that helped earn his election to an honorary vice-presidency in the United States Chamber of Commerce in 1928. From 1930 to 1933 Strawn was chairman of the American committee and during those same years he was also honored as president of the United States Chamber of Commerce, serving in that office from 1931 to 1932 and on that organization's senior council from 1932 to 1940.

Strawn's interest in international affairs also led in 1925 to his appointment, by President Calvin Coolidge, as one of the two American commissioners to represent United States interests at the Chinese tariff conferences at Peking, held in accordance with the provisions of the nine-power treaty adopted at the 1921-1922 Washington conference for the limitation of armaments. Apparently at Strawn's own suggestion, Coolidge also appointed him sole commissioner of the United States on the international commission to investigate extraterritorial jurisdiction in China. Both commissions failed in the face of the Chinese revolution, but the American delegation and Strawn acquitted themselves well at what Kellogg called an "impossible" task. Rather typically, Strawn was elected presiding officer of the Extraterritoriality Commission.

However, it was not typical of Strawn to accept the China mission. Despite acceptance of elective office in private and quasi-public associations, he did not hunger for public office, either elective or appointive. The reason he and Coolidge got on so well, he once wrote Secretary of State Frank B. Kellogg, was that the president knew that, unlike so many others he saw, Strawn had no desire for a job. The work in China seems to have been uncharacteristically accepted because of its relatively short tenure, because of a strong interest in the legal problems of Chinese governance, and because of his friendships with Coolidge and Kellogg.

Strawn much preferred to work out solutions to public problems through his established private organizations or through ad hoc committees pragmatically organized to meet specific problems. In this spirit, Strawn organized and led citizen's committees to fight organized Chicago gangsters, to straighten the Chicago River, and to provide tax relief and financial reform for Chicago citizens after the Great Depression.

Strawn's later years were marked with both personal distinction and disappointment. Many of his professional offices and honors came during this period. He received honorary LL.D. degrees from the University of Michigan (1928), Lake Forest College (1928), Knox College (1930), Northwestern University (1930), and Middlebury College (1935), became Chicago's recognized elder statesman and continued his legal activities with great success. Yet the world he knew and the values and sociopolitical relations in which he believed seemed to be crumbling about him with the advent of the depression and the New Deal.

Strawn spent his later years speaking and writing against the New Deal and its alphabetical agencies, attacking them in the courts, and assailing their intrusions, real and imaginary, into business and private affairs. Strawn was a pragmatic Republican, not a rightist ideologue. He had pushed the progressive William Borah for the vice-presidency in 1924, recommended many Democrats for appointive office, and regularly assailed lawyers and businessmen when he felt their pursuits of self-interest too greatly injured the public interest and thus their own interests. His letters from China frequently attacked shortsighted and rapacious businessmen who plundered China without any sense of the effects of their actions.

Strawn died of a heart attack while vacationing in Palm Beach, Fla., and was buried first in Ottawa, then in Lake Forest, Ill. A generous man, particularly to young people and needy students, Strawn was recognized by friends and associates as a personable man of integrity, with a fine sense of humor and a large store of anecdotes. In private life, his real passion was golf. He belonged to countless golf and country clubs and played them all with the few who could match his own vigor on the links. Although he held many offices and many presidencies, it is characteristic of the man that the presidency he most delighted in was that of the United States Golf Association, from 1911 to 1912.

[Strawn's personal papers are not collected in any one place. The bulk are in the possession of his daughter Mrs. James Cathcart of Lake Forest, Ill., and in the files of his law firm. The collected papers of Frank Kellogg, at the Minn. Hist. Soc., contain a goodly amount of correspondence from Strawn and are particularly valuable for the study of Strawn's China mission. Strawn wrote many articles and spoke out frequently on the issues and causes with which he involved himself. Most of these speeches, as well as the articles, are readily available in legal journals, particularly in the journals of the state and national bar associations. The mission to China was also covered in newspapers and popular magazines. No book or major article has been written about Strawn's career, but the most helpful capsule accounts of his life are in James Grafton Rogers, *Am. Bar Leaders* (1933); *Nat. Cyc. Am. Biog.*, XXXIV; *Who Was Who in Am.*, II (1950); the *Chicago Bar Record* (1946); and newspaper obituaries, the best of these being in the *N.Y. Times* and on the front page of the *Chicago Daily Tribune*, both on Feb. 5, 1946. The best available portrait of Mr. Strawn is in *Am. Bar Leaders* (facing p. 242).]

PAUL L. MURPHY
JAMES MCCARTHY

STREETER, GEORGE LINIUS (Jan. 12, 1873-July 27, 1948), embryologist, was born in Johnstown, N.Y., the only son and third of four children born to George Austin Streeter and Hannah Green (Anthony) Streeter. His father was a leader in the local glove-manufacturing industry. Both parents were of English descent, having migrated to Johnstown via New England. His mother was a Quaker, his father a Presbyterian, and the children were brought up in the Presbyterian belief. After preparation in the local public schools, George entered Union College, from which he was graduated in 1895. He then studied medicine at the College of Physicians and Surgeons at Columbia University, where he took his A.M. and M.D. degrees in 1899. Following an internship (1899-1900) at Roosevelt Hospital, New York, he became assistant to Dr. Henry Hun, a prominent neurologist of Albany, N.Y., and also taught the anatomy of the nervous system at Albany Medical College (1901-1902). To prepare himself for practice in the diseases of the nervous system he studied in Germany (1902-1903) with the anatomist Ludwig Edinger at Frankfurt and the embryologist Wilhelm His at Leipzig. Strongly attracted by embryological research, on his return to the United States, Streeter gave up the practice of medicine and in 1904 joined the department of anatomy of the Johns Hopkins University School of Medicine, in Baltimore, under Franklin P. Mall.

Streeter's first publications, in German and American anatomical journals, dealt with the structure and development of the nervous system. They revealed a peculiar fitness for morphological research by reason of his strong powers of visual observation, accurate draftsmanship, keen analysis, and clear descriptive writing. After a brief excursion into experimental embryology of the amphibian auditory organs, Streeter returned for the rest of his career to descriptive embryology. In 1906-1907 he was assistant professor of anatomy at the Wistar Institute, Philadelphia. From 1907 to 1914 he was professor of human anatomy at the University of Michigan, where he continued work on the development of the human brain, nerves, and auditory system. His chapter on the development of the major structures of the brain, in the *Handbook of Human Embryology* edited by Franz Keibel and Franklin P. Mall (1910), remains the most authoritative account of this complicated subject.

On Apr. 9, 1910, Streeter married Julia Allen Smith of Ann Arbor, Mich. They had three children: Sarah Frances, George Allen, and Mary Raymond. The elder daughter took her Ph.D. in chemistry; both the son and the younger daughter became physicians.

In 1914, Mall, who had just launched the department of embryology of the Carnegie Institution of Washington, located at the Johns Hopkins Medical School, called Streeter back to Baltimore as a research associate. Three years later, after Mall's untimely death, Streeter succeeded to the directorship. Under his guidance the Laboratory, already possessing one of the world's largest collections of human embryological material, was developed, and Mall's program was further expanded. Gathering a staff of outstanding investigators and highly skilled technical aides—artists, photographers, modelers, and microtomists—Streeter led and encouraged morphological and experimental work that made his department the leading center of embryological research. During his directorship its publications filled twenty-two volumes (VIII-XXIX) of the *Contributions to Embryology of the Carnegie Institution,* one of the most distinguished American scientific publications in both text and illustrations. Many advanced investigators from American and foreign institutions came to work at the laboratory, finding there not only rich materials, wise counsel, and skilled help, but also an atmosphere of friendliness and enthusiasm created by its leader. Although he was an outwardly conventional person, reserved with strangers and little known outside his own field, Streeter's characteristically indirect, whimsical, and often surprisingly iconoclastic pronouncements on embryological theory never failed to stimulate his associates.

Although his published work contains few totally new observations, he possessed superlative ability to clear up imperfectly understood phases of embryonic development, refining, integrating, and accurately depicting them. Such work calls for ample material in good condition and perfectly preserved (not easily obtained when human embryos are the object of study), expert technical handling, thorough analysis, and perceptive illustration. All Streeter's major investigations were so perfectly executed that the results superseded previous work on the same topics and defy further refinement by methods known at present.

A notable early publication was a set of charts (in *Contributions to Embryology,* vol. II, 1920) relating the principal dimensions of human embryos and fetuses to their developmental age. This is still the standard quantitative record of human prenatal growth. An account (in *Contributions to Embryology,* vol. XX, 1929) of the early embryonic development of the domestic pig, done in collaboration with Chester H. Heuser, is the most accurate and complete description of the early embryology of a mammal ever published. Streeter participated, from

1925 to 1941, with Heuser and Carl G. Hartman in a masterly study (in *Contributions to Embryology,* vol. XXIX, 1941) of the early embryology of the rhesus monkey. His encouragement of Arthur T. Hertig of Harvard University and John Rock of the Free Hospital for Women, Brookline, Mass., resulted in an extraordinary advance in human embryology. The earliest stages of human development, previously practically unknown before the third week after conception, were revealed from the first day onward, by specimens collected by Hertig and Rock and prepared by Heuser and the Carnegie laboratory's technical staff.

Streeter contributed also to the pathology of the embryo and fetus, notably by a revolutionary explanation of defects in which the loss of a limb (intrauterine amputation) or similar damage is associated with adhesions of the amnion at the site of injury. He showed that the constrictive adhesions do not cause the defect but rather result from it through the adhesion of the amnion to necrotic tissue.

After his retirement in 1940, Streeter devoted himself to the compilation of a series of papers entitled "Developmental Horizons in Human Development" (*Contributions to Embryology,* 1942-1951), a descriptive and pictorial classification of the stages of embryonic development relating the successive changes of external form to those of the internal structures. These "Horizons" provide a standard with which any embryo may be compared in order to ascertain its age or detect evidences of retardation or defective development.

All Streeter's work is marked by great clarity and independent interpretation. His training as a physician and his early experience in the experimental study of living amphibian embryos taught him to regard the human embryo not as a mere blueprint for the adult, but rather as a living organism itself, with organs and tissues that are actively functioning even while they undergo change and development. He thus avoided the errors of those who, misapplying the "law of recapitulation," thought of the embryo as modeling the adult stages of successive ancestral forms. He objected, for example, to treating the branchial bars of the mammalian embryo as rudimentary gills, preferring to see them as foundation material for the various organs and tissues to which they are to give rise, that is, gills in fish, auditory and pharyngeal structures in mammals and man. He also vigorously combated in his brilliant presidential address to the American Association of Anatomists (1927) a time-honored view that the verte-

brate brain goes through a stage of three undifferentiated vesicles. Such errors, Streeter pointed out, chiefly result from reliance on schematic diagrams reflecting preconceived ideas rather than observable anatomic details. His own diagrams and schematic drawings, rarely used, were always based on actual sections of embryos.

Streeter was elected to the National Academy of Sciences in 1931 and the American Philosophical Society in 1943. He was also a fellow of the Royal Society of Edinburgh (1928). From 1926 to 1928 he was president of the American Association of Anatomists. He held three honorary degrees: D.Sc., from Trinity College, Dublin, in 1928, and from Union College in 1930, and LL.D. from the University of Michigan in 1935. He was a prolific writer in his field, with from two to five articles published almost every year from 1903 until his death in 1948, plus two published posthumously; in the same years, he published five books.

Streeter died suddenly in 1948 from a coronary occlusion in a hospital at Gloversville, N.Y., near his summer home, and was buried at Johnstown, N.Y.

[The fullest account of Streeter, his life and work, is to be found in Nat. Acad. of Sci., *Biog. Memoirs* XXVIII (1954), which includes a portrait photograph and a complete bibliography. Other sources are *Amer. Jour. of Anatomy,* 83 (1949), 51–52; *Nat. Cyc. Am. Biog.,* XXXVII, 356–357; *Who Was Who in Am.,* II (1950).]

GEORGE W. CORNER

STRONG, RICHARD PEARSON (Mar. 18, 1872-July 4, 1948), public health physician, educator, and expert on tropical medicine, was born in Fortress Monroe, Va., the only son and eldest of two children of Lt. Col. Richard Polk Strong and Marian Beaufort (Smith) Strong. His father joined the United States Army following his graduation from City College of New York in 1862 and remained in service after the Civil War. Richard Pearson Strong attended Hopkins Grammar School and graduated from the Sheffield Scientific School of Yale University with the degree Ph.B. in biology in 1893. Strong then entered the medical school of Johns Hopkins University, a member of the first class to matriculate. He was awarded the M.D. degree in 1897 and served in the coveted position of resident physician at the Johns Hopkins Hospital in 1897 and 1898. During the Spanish-American War, he was an assistant surgeon, with the rank of first lieutenant in the United States Army. From 1899 to 1901, he established and directed the work of the Army Pathological Laboratory and served as president of the Board for the Investigation of Tropical Diseases in the Isthmus of Panama. In 1901 he went to the Philippines where he made significant contributions, as both a soldier and a civilian, to medical research and education and the management of public health activities.

Leaving the army while in Manila, he became director of the Biological Laboratories Bureau of Science (1901-1913), professor of tropical medicine at the College of Medicine and Surgery at the University of the Philippine Islands (1907-1913), and chief of medicine at the Philippine Islands General Hospital (1910-1913). He remained in the Far East throughout this period, except for brief study in Berlin, at the university and the Institute for Infectious Diseases in 1903, winning an international reputation in medical research through his studies on dysentery, plague, cholera, and other diseases. In 1911, he was acclaimed for both medical brilliance and personal courage after his work during an epidemic of pneumonic plague in Manchuria.

Strong joined the faculty of medicine of Harvard University in 1913 as the first professor of tropical medicine, a position he held until his retirement in 1938. During these years, he extended his international reputation through research, teaching, and medical administration under trying and dangerous circumstances. He led numerous expeditions to study tropical diseases in their natural habitat: to Peru (1913), the Amazon basin (1925), Liberia and the Belgian Congo (1926-1927, 1934), and Guatemala (1931-1932). Many publications by Strong and his associates resulted from these expeditions, notably his monograph on onchocerciasis in Africa and America in 1934 and his two volumes on Liberia. Strong's investigations in the Amazon foreshadowed the Hylean Research Scheme of UNESCO. In 1938, he assumed responsibility for the foremost textbook in his field, Edward Stitt's *Diagnostics and Treatment of Tropical Disease*, which he rewrote after his retirement from Harvard.

Strong also made important contributions to medical administration. In 1915, he directed the Rockefeller Institute's expedition to Serbia to combat a typhus epidemic, and coordinated medical teams from several countries. Joining the American Expeditionary Force in 1917 as a member of the chief surgeon's staff, he and his group demonstrated that trench fever was transmitted by a louse. He directed the department of medical research for the American Red Cross in Paris (1918-1919) and for the League of Red Cross Societies in Geneva (1919-1920). In 1919, he organized the Inter-Allied Medical Conference at Cannes and made plans to improve public health throughout the world in time of peace. Rejoining the Medical Reserve Corps as a colonel in 1941, he served as director of tropical medicine at the Army Medical School in Washington through World War II.

Strong was the leading specialist in tropical medicine of his generation. His publications appeared in journals and conference proceedings on three continents. He was decorated by the governments of China, Serbia, France, Great Britain, and the United States. Professional organizations throughout the world sought his leadership. In 1943 the American Foundation of Tropical Medicine named the Richard P. Strong medal in his honor and made him the first recipient of it.

Strong was a reserved man, with "a great capacity for friendship with those he liked" (*British Medical Journal*, Nov. 13, 1948, p. 880). He was married three times: in Manila, in 1900, to Eleanor E. MacKay, who died in 1914, in Ann Arbor, Mich.; in 1916 to Agnes Leas Freer, whom he divorced in 1935; and in London, in 1936, to Grace Nichols, who died in 1944. He died of a heart attack after what a colleague described as a "protracted and painful illness" and was buried in Mount Auburn Cemetery, Cambridge, Mass. After his death, the *Journal of Tropical Medicine* predicted that "posterity will link his name with those of his great contemporaries, Manson, Ross, Gorgas and Reed" (51 [1948], 242). One of the first American medical researchers and public health physicians to be trained exclusively in institutions created in or by the United States, he became an international figure early in his career, and increased his fame during almost half a century of service.

[Strong's reprints, printed biographical materials, and some letters are in the archives of the Harvard Medical School, Countway Lib., Boston. Other clippings and articles about him are in the Johns Hopkins Univ. archives and the Harvard Univ. archives, Cambridge, Mass. The most useful interpretative biographical sketch is George C. Shattuck, "RPS, 1872–1948," *New England Jour. of Med.*, 239 (1948), 489. Strong's numerous official positions, memberships, and awards are listed in the *Obituary Record of Graduates of Yale Univ. Deceased During the Year, 1947-1948*, pp. 93-94, obtained from the Yale Univ. Lib. Other useful appreciations of Strong appeared in the *Jour. of Tropical Med.* and the *British Med. Jour.* (both cited in the text) and in the *Military Surgeon*, 103 (1948), 248.]

DANIEL M. FOX

STRUNSKY, SIMEON (July 23, 1879-Feb. 5, 1948), journalist and essayist, was born in Vitebsk, Russia, of Jewish parents: Isadore

Strunsky, a grain and lumber merchant, and Pearl (Weinstein) Strunsky. The next to youngest of seven children—he had four brothers and two sisters—he was brought at the age of seven to New York City, where he grew up on the Lower East Side. He showed such precocity as a student that he was awarded one of the first Pulitzer scholarships to Columbia's Horace Mann School. This led to a scholarship in Columbia College, from which he graduated, A.B., in 1900.

Strunsky's first employment was as a department editor on the *New International Encyclopedia,* where he remained from 1900 to 1906, his services being specially prized by the editor, Frank Moore Colby. He continued to contribute to the *Encyclopedia* and to the *New International Yearbook* for some years, and thus mastered a wide knowledge of history and literature. He also began writing for magazines and newspapers. While so employed, on June 18, 1905, he married Rebecca Slobodkin of Philadelphia, who bore him one son, Robert. She died in 1906, and on Sept. 11, 1910, he married Manya Gordon, Russian-born like himself and an active supporter of the Social Revolutionary party in Russia. They had a daughter, Frances.

In 1906 Strunsky joined the staff of the *New York Evening Post,* then owned by Oswald Garrison Villard, as editorial writer and humorous commentator on current events. Many of his pieces were also reprinted in Villard's weekly *Nation.* His series of essays (1912) on Theodore Roosevelt and the Progressive party, under the title "Through the Outlooking Glass" (T.R. then being an editor of the *Outlook* magazine), attracted wide notice for their genial yet penetrating view of Roosevelt's efforts to regain the White House; Roosevelt himself read them with appreciation. Strunsky's style was clever and pungent. It showed the influence of Charles Lamb, William Hazlitt, and G. K. Chesterton—like Chesterton, he often turned ideas upside down to see what would drop out of their pockets—but had a kindly wit entirely his own. His first important book, a collection of essays, *The Patient Observer and His Friends,* was published in 1911. During 1912-1913 he contributed to the *Atlantic Monthly* a series of amusing and perceptive essays on apartment-house life in New York, which were later collected under the title *Belshazzar Court* (1914). In 1918 Strunsky turned to fiction with a book of lambent observations on the New York scene, *Prof. Latimer's Progress.* It was as much a sheaf of essays as a novel. The central character was plainly

founded upon Fabian Franklin, a member of the *Evening Post* staff.

During World War I, Strunsky, in editorials and military criticism for the *Evening Post,* strongly supported the Allied cause and advocated laissez-faire economics. A series of satirical papers on the kaiser's abortive efforts to reach the French capital attracted much attention in 1917-1918 and was republished in book form under the title *Little Journeys Towards Paris.* At the close of the war he reported on the Paris Peace Conference, and later on the Washington Disarmament Conference. Like his second wife, a socialist of the Fabian type, Strunsky was a stout opponent of Bolshevism and an upholder of the Menshevik regime in Russia, an attitude fortified by their friendship with Alexander Kerensky. Strunsky's devotion to Wilsonian liberalism was reflected in his historical novel, *King Akhnaton* (1928), tracing parallels in the stormy careers of the Egyptian reformer and the American president.

Strunsky became chief editorial writer of the *New York Evening Post* in 1920. Through his editorials he played an important part in converting the then owner of the daily, Thomas W. Lamont, to a strong belief in the League of Nations and to support of a firm internationalist policy. In 1924, when Lamont sold the *Evening Post* to the ultraconservative Cyrus H. K. Curtis, owner of the *Philadelphia Public Ledger,* Strunsky joined his old chief Rollo Ogden in moving to the *New York Times.* In addition to writing editorials, he contributed a weekly column, "About Books—More or Less," to the Sunday *Book Review* from 1924 to 1929. In 1932 he took over the daily column on the editorial page called "Topics of the Times," which he continued until his death, giving it new vigor and a highly individual touch.

As international tensions deepened and many American intellectuals showed increasing sympathy with Bolshevik Russia, Strunsky asserted his own devotion to American liberalism in several outspoken volumes. Among them were *No Mean City* (1944), a defense of the great American metropolis in which he had lived so long and which he loved, and *The Living Tradition* (1939), an earnest vindication of basic American ideas and ideals. He further expressed his devotion to New York in his book *Two Came to Town* (1947).

Strunsky's stocky figure, his large bald head with blue eyes twinkling merrily behind thick glasses, and his crisp, epigrammatic speech became familiar in newspaper circles, although he was not by temperament a ready "joiner." His increasing prominence in literary circles led to his election to the National Institute of Arts and Letters in 1946. Though he disliked speech-making and detested public dinners, many of his epigrams, written and spoken, were widely quoted; but he had a far greater predilection for the humor of Dickens and Mark Twain than for Shavian irony. Strunsky made his home in Manhattan but spent most of his summers in New Canaan, Conn. He died of cancer of the pancreas in the Princeton (N.J.) Hospital at the age of sixty-eight; his ashes were interred in New York. He had done much to revive the informal essay as a literary genre of distinction and influence.

[N.Y. Times, Nov. 1, 1931, sec. 4, Jan. 17, 1932, sec. 5, Feb. 6, 1948 (obituary and editorial), Feb. 9 (funeral), Feb. 13, 14 (tributes) ; Time, Feb. 16, 1948, pp. 54–55 ; Nat. Cyc. Am. Biog., XXXVII, 171–172 ; Who's Who in Am. Jewry, 1938–1939 ; family information from Robert Strunsky and Mrs. Frances Strunsky Lindley. Harold Phelps Stokes, ed., Simeon Strunsky's America (1956), is a collection of Strunsky's "Topics of the Times" columns.]

ALLAN NEVINS

SULLIVAN, HARRY STACK (Feb. 21, 1892-Jan. 14, 1949), psychiatrist and social scientist, best known for his theory of interpersonal relations, was born in Norwich, Chenango County, N.Y., the third and only surviving child of Timothy J. Sullivan and Ellen (Stack) Sullivan. Both parents were the children of Irish immigrants who had left at the time of the potato famine; but there was a difference in class, with the mother coming from a more professional family. When Harry was three, his father gave up his job as a laborer in a farm machinery factory in Norwich and took over the management of his wife's family's farm near Smyrna, N.Y. There Harry passed an isolated childhood, without brothers or sisters and largely cut off from the old Yankee, Protestant families that lived in the community. His loneliness allowed him to ponder on the importance of every human contact that he made. In a very real sense, his later theory contains his biography, once one has a key to the outstanding events of this period of his life. He attended the public school in the village of Smyrna, but because of his ethnic and religious differences, as well as his farm background, he never gained acceptance from the other pupils. In his adult life he tended to feel that he himself was poor at compromise and cooperation because he lacked training in these qualities in his juvenile years.

When Sullivan was eight and a half years old—an age that he adopted in his later theory as the earliest possible date for the beginning of preadolescence—he acquired a chum, Clarence Bellinger, who lived on the next farm. Clarence was five years older than Sullivan, and in many ways, by Sullivan's own later theory, was not an ideal companion for the preadolescent experience, which Sullivan considered crucial for mental health. Yet Bellinger did become a crucial person in Sullivan's development and helped to determine his choice of a career. Both men became psychiatrists, although they differed in their clinical approach and their personal qualities; and neither ever married.

Sullivan graduated from Smyrna High School, as valedictorian, at sixteen and then entered Cornell University on a state scholarship, intending to major in physics. In the middle of his second semester his performance began to falter, and he was suspended until the following January. He never went back to Cornell, and from that time (the spring of 1909) until he entered the Chicago College of Medicine and Surgery in the fall of 1911, his whereabouts are not certainly known. There are rumors in his home community that he got into trouble with a group of older boys at Cornell, ran afoul of the law, and, after being apprehended, "pretended he was crazy" in order to avoid imprisonment. A further clue is the fact that Sullivan himself in later years readily admitted to old friends that as a young man he had been hospitalized with a schizophrenic break. In his theory, Sullivan states that adolescence can be delayed until the age of seventeen because of certain deprivations in earlier experience, but that this delay often eventuates in a period of great stress. Since he was seventeen when he was suspended from Cornell, it is safe to assume that he had a severe period of adolescent stress at that time. By his own account, he never achieved an enduring heterosexual adjustment, and he always viewed this as a loss. He saw homosexuality as a miscarriage of human living and denied that it was "innate." Yet he viewed a homosexual solution as a makeshift preferable to life in a mental hospital. He defined the lack of normal early homosexual experience in the preadolescent period as a handicap for heterosexuality.

Sullivan's years at the Chicago College of Medicine and Surgery (later a part of Loyola University) are largely undocumented. He was financially under stress during the entire period and seems to have spent most of his energies in earning money for school fees. In later life he referred to the school as a "diploma mill" and reported that, with the exception of two or three teachers, he trained himself through intensive reading and hospital work. He received his M.D. degree in 1917. Near the end of this training he again seems to have suffered some psychological trauma, for there is a hiatus in his records and some inconsistencies in his own applications for army assignments; he was for a time a first lieutenant in the Medical Corps during World War I. For a time also he practiced as an industrial surgeon in Chicago, and in the winter of 1916-1917, by his own report, he underwent seventy-five hours of psychoanalysis.

After the war Sullivan undertook an army assignment that brought him into contact with veterans who were suffering psychological trauma, and in 1922 he became a liaison officer for veterans' interests at St. Elizabeth's Hospital in Washington, D.C. Here he came under the tutelage of William Alanson White, then superintendent of the hospital and an early advocate of the findings of Freud as a source of new hope for hospital patients. White encouraged Sullivan in his exploration of the schizophrenic process and seems to have been instrumental in facilitating his move to Sheppard and Enoch Pratt Hospital near Baltimore in 1923. There Sullivan established a new type of ward for young male schizophrenics, essentially a one-sex, one-class society in which treatment was provided almost exclusively through hospital attendants trained and supervised by Sullivan. He assumed that the attendants often had suffered some of the same humiliations as the patients and that social recovery could be encouraged in this classless society. Thus he tried to correct for the in-group, out-group humiliations he had himself experienced in the Smyrna school and used the attendants as trusted friends of the patients to create a therapeutic milieu.

In Baltimore, Sullivan met and formed a strong friendship with the psychiatrist Clara M. Thompson, who at his urging went to Budapest for training under Sandor Ferenczi, whom both considered as theoretically more crucial to the American experience than Freud. Sullivan moved in 1930 to New York City to begin the private practice of psychiatry and to obtain further training from Thompson. He also resumed a close association with the anthropologist Edward Sapir, whom he had first met in Chicago in 1926. Their friendship probably constituted the most satisfactory intellectual and emotional relationship in Sullivan's life. His association with Sapir and with other social scientists helped deepen Sullivan's interest in how the social environment affects personality and mental disorder. With Sapir and the political scientist Harold Lasswell, Sullivan planned the establishment of the Washington (D.C.) School of Psychiatry and the journal *Psychiatry,* both of which were realities by 1938. The William Alanson White Psychiatric Foundation was the fiscal agent for both school and journal, and Sullivan as teacher and editor became its guiding force.

Sullivan's personal life continued to be in large part lonely and isolated. He had a certain charm with old friends and a tenderness toward patients in the hospital; but many young psychiatric trainees found him scathing in his criticism. He took delight in music, in breeding day lilies, and in observing the cocker spaniels who sometimes dominated his household. In 1927 James Inscoe, then fifteen years old, came to live with Sullivan. Sullivan has described him as an "ex-patient" and as an adopted son, and he became known as James I. Sullivan, although the relationship was never legally formalized. "Jimmie," who lived with Sullivan until his death, ran the household, served as a competent secretary, and generally gave Sullivan the kind of devoted attention that allowed him to remain productive during the years when his health began to fail and when he was increasingly involved in the tasks arising from his reputation as clinician and social scientist.

Pictures of Sullivan taken by Margaret Bourke-White (a former patient) show him as thin and elegant, his eyes intent in a sidelong way. When he removed his yellow-tinted glasses, his eyes were grey-green in color, according to the artist Loren MacIver; but they seemed dark and piercing with his glasses on, and they dominated his face. He tended not to look directly at the person to whom he was talking, a characteristic he explained as a result of his years of dealing with schizophrenic patients, though in fact it reflected also his shyness. As a young man he grew a rather luxuriant moustache, and he retained a clipped-down version for the rest of his life. Though he was relatively tall (nearly five feet ten inches), most of his friends thought of him as slight and short. Yet as a critic—sharp and biting—or as a humorist par excellence, he had a commanding demeanor.

The final decade of Sullivan's life was spent in Washington, D.C., where he moved in 1939, taking up residence in nearby Bethesda, Md. Here he was increasingly engaged in quasi-governmental activities: as a consultant at the White House during World War II, as a consultant in setting up standards for psychiatric examination of draftees for the Selective Service System, and as a participant in the 1948 UNESCO study of tensions that cause wars. In addition, he carried a heavy training and teaching load and made *Psychiatry* a preeminent journal in the field of interdisciplinary thinking. He died in the Ritz Hotel in Paris, of a meningeal hemorrhage, on his way home from an executive meeting in Amsterdam of the World Federation for Mental Health. At his own request, he was buried in Arlington National Cemetery in Virginia, in a military and Catholic service, although he had moved far away from any identification with the military or with formal religion.

The significance of Sullivan's work is perhaps best summed up by the social psychologist Gordon W. Allport: ". . . Sullivan, perhaps more than any other person, labored to bring about the fusion of psychiatry and social science" (Hadley Cantril, ed., *Tensions That Cause Wars*, 1950, p. 135n). Yet his work is often viewed by these two disciplines as separate contributions. Clinicians, for instance, are apt to define Sullivan's work with schizophrenic patients at Sheppard as a prime example of therapeutic art and as his unique contribution. Social scientists view the same work as offering a new, important theory for looking at human processes in a broader spectrum. The sociologist W. I. Thomas saw the work at Sheppard as an experiment "with a small group of persons now or recently disordered, from the situational standpoint, and among other results this study reveals the fact that these persons tend to make successful adjustments in groupwise association between themselves . . ." (Edmund H. Volkart, ed., *Social Behavior and Personality: Contributions of W. I. Thomas to Theory and Social Research*, 1951, p. 65). In describing these patients as "persons," Thomas reflected a theoretical position congenial to Sullivan's theory. And Edward Sapir used Sullivan's theory in a 1938 article titled "Why Cultural Anthropology Needs the Psychiatrist" as the first article in the first issue of Sullivan's journal, *Psychiatry*. Increasingly people in related disciplines, concerned with a wide spectrum of human needs—ministers, judges, lawyers, educators—have come to look to the theory as a meaningful approach to more usual difficulties in living.

In part the catholicity of Sullivan's following stems from the new unit for study posited by his theory—the interpersonal event. In a scientific sense, this unit has a direct relation to Sullivan's early interest in physics. As the British psychoanalyst John Rickman has pointed out, Sullivan's "early acceptance of field theory —a theory incommoding to one's complacency— puts him among the pioneers" (*Tensions That Cause Wars*, p. 81n). In formalizing his field theory, Sullivan gave credit specifically to the physicist P. W. Bridgman, who differentiated between the "public" and "private" mode of each person. It is only the public mode that lends itself to scientific investigation, according to Sullivan, and this leads to the interpersonal event: ". . . the true or absolute individuality of a person is always beyond scientific grasp and invariably much less significant in the person's living than he has been taught to believe" (Sullivan, *Conceptions of Modern Psychiatry*, p. xii). The approach has important implications for a preventive psychiatry and is basically optimistic. According to Sullivan, any significant encounter throughout life, even with a stranger, may offer remedial experience—may modify earlier destructive experience or reinforce the potentially hopeful part of earlier experience. "Thirty years of work," Sullivan reported near the end of his life, "has taught me that, whenever one could be aided to foresee the reasonable probability of a better future, everyone will show a sufficient tendency to collaborate in the achievement of more adequate and appropriate ways of living" (*Tensions That Cause Wars*, p. 135). It seems obvious that such a theory has important implications for disadvantaged people—the slum child, the criminal, and so on—and is, indeed, as Rickman has noted, incommoding to the complacency of advantaged people.

Like Freud, Sullivan employed the developmental approach in his theory. But he did not stress infancy and early childhood as more important than any other era. At the threshold of each new developmental era, the person has an opportunity to correct for some of the lacks or distortions of the previous era. With the learning of language, the developing person moves from infancy into childhood, with a new skill for dealing with the world. As the child develops the capacity for dealing with compeers, he moves into the juvenile era and begins to learn something about compromise and cooperation; in American society, Sullivan posits, this is usually coincidental with the entrance of the child into school. Preadolescence is ushered in as the person acquires the capacity to create a relationship of trust and collaboration with another person of his own age-group and sex. This experience, crucial in Sullivan's theory, readies the maturing person for the appearance of the lust dynamism and the movement into early adolescence, when the delicate transition from trust in a person like oneself to trust in the biological stranger takes place, in normal development. Late adolescence arrives with the patterning of heterosexual lustful behavior. Parenthood, Sullivan posits parenthetically, is the last great life opportunity for significant change and growth. The theory, emergent as it is from the cultural and social reality of life as lived in the United States in the period of his life, shows remarkable resiliency in the process of substitution of other cultures, including societies other than Western European.

In brief, Sullivan's contribution to both psychiatry and social science can be traced in a simple form from his own life experience. When he first came into contact with schizophrenic patients in a mental hospital, he recognized their similarity to himself. He sought, first, to expand Freud's theory so as to include psychotic patients and to construct scientifically a milieu for the social recovery of patients showing schizophrenic processes. Because of the importance of the preadolescent experience for his own sanity—and he saw it as partially corrective for the ostracism he had experienced when he first went to school—he used this as a corrective model for male patients on his ward at Sheppard. He encouraged peer relationships of trust with persons of the same sex —patients and attendants—as a preliminary for social recovery. He went on to build a theoretic bridge from this group of hospital patients to his office patients in New York City, observing that their obsessional preoccupations were of a piece with the behavior of most people in this society and that such preoccupations could be necessary to avoid schizophrenic process. From there, he moved in the direction of tensions in the society in general, collaborating in the late 1930's with the Negro sociologists Charles S. Johnson and E. Franklin Frazier in studies of Negro youth in the rural South and in the Middle, or Border, States. Near the end of his life, he was moving "towards a psychiatry of peoples," as he titled one of his last papers (*The Interpersonal Theory of Psychiatry*, pp. 367-382). It is significant that his isolated early life should have eventuated in an encompassing theory that articulated the one-genus postulate: ". . . we are all much more simply human than otherwise, be we happy and successful, contented and detached, miserable and mentally disordered, or whatever" (*Conceptions of Modern Psychiatry*, p. 16).

[Before Sullivan's death, most of his writings existed as articles in professional journals, with the exception of one monograph, *Conceptions of Modern Psychiatry* (1947), originally published in the journal *Psychiatry* in 1940 and republished in 1953. After his death, three books were put together from his unpublished lectures—*The Interpersonal Theory of Psychiatry* (1953), *The Psychiatric Interview* (1954), and *Clinical Studies in Psychiatry* (1956). In 1972 *Personal Psychopathology*, a book manuscript prepared by Sullivan forty years earlier, was published. Two books of selected papers were published: on his work at Sheppard, *Schizophrenia as a Human Process* (1962) and *The Fusion of Psychiatry and Social Science* (1964) on his later work; both works contain introductions and commentaries by Helen Swick Perry that trace out the historical development of his ideas and supply the main citations for missing bibliography.

For information on his life, see Clara Thompson, "Harry Stack Sullivan, the Man" in *Schizophrenia as a Human Process*; entry for Harry Stack Sullivan in *Current Biog.*, 1942. Basic source material is in the author's possession and will be presented to a university library on the completion of a scheduled biography.]

HELEN SWICK PERRY

SUTHERLAND, EDWIN HARDIN (Aug. 13, 1883-Oct. 11, 1950), sociologist and criminologist, was born in Gibbon, Neb., the son of George Sutherland, a college president, and Elizabeth Tarr (Pickett) Sutherland. After graduating from Grand Island (Nebraska) College in 1904, he immediately began teaching at Sioux Falls (South Dakota) College, giving classes in Greek, geometry, and shorthand. In 1909 he returned to his alma mater as an instructor. Then in 1911 he enrolled in the University of Chicago's pioneering graduate program in sociology and two years later was awarded the Ph.D. His dissertation dealt with the practices of public employment agencies, and in collecting the data he disguised himself as an unemployed derelict.

From 1913 to 1919, Sutherland was professor of sociology at William Jewell College in Liberty, Mo., where he taught courses on crime and delinquency. There he met Myrtle Crews, whom he married on May, 11, 1918. They had one child, Betty Ann. In 1919 Sutherland moved to the University of Illinois as an assistant professor of sociology. He subsequently held professorships at the University of Minnesota (1926-1929), the University of Chicago (1930-1935), and Indiana University (1935-1950). He was also chairman of Indiana's department of sociology until 1949.

The book through which Sutherland became widely known in behavioral science was *Criminology*, written while he was at Illinois and published in 1924. By 1947 it had gone through four editions. (Five additional editions, with Donald R. Cressey as coauthor, have appeared posthumously in 1955, 1960, 1966, 1970, and 1974.) The subject matter of the book, Sutherland later recalled, was suggested by Edward

Carey Hayes, chairman of Illinois's sociology department, who had decreed that at least one member of his staff must write a book to enhance the department's scholarly reputation. Hayes included this text in the Lippincott Sociological Series, of which he was editor.

Sutherland's criminological theory is an extension of the basic sociological and social-psychological theory of his time. He did not consider criminology an independent scientific discipline. Neither did he think it should continue as a hodgepodge of ideas taken from various academic disciplines and from the morals of the middle class. Instead, he maintained that if criminology is to be scientific, the heterogeneous collection of "multiple factors" known to be associated with crime and criminality must be organized and integrated by means of explanatory social scientific principles. His "theory of differential association," which first appeared as a chapter in the 1939 edition of his textbook, supplied the organizing and integrating framework.

The development of this theory, like most of Sutherland's work, was greatly influenced by the writings and teachings of the sociologists William I. Thomas, John Dewey, and George Herbert Mead. For these men and for Sutherland, meaning, language, and culture were closely interrelated. One learns behavior (culture) as one is learning language and meaning. Further, Sutherland said, criminal behavior is learned through the same processes that are involved in any other learning.

In both a very specific sense and in a quite general sense, Sutherland was a severe critic. Specifically, he produced critical masterpieces such as his review of studies on "Mental Deficiency and Crime" (1931), of Sheldon and Eleanor Glueck's *Later Criminal Careers* (1937), of E. A. Hooton's *The American Criminal* (1939), and of William H. Sheldon's *Varieties of Delinquent Youth* (1951). These reviews are shattering confrontations of theoretical positions, based on carefully collected data and presented with impeccable logic.

In a more general sense, Sutherland's mastery of criticism was at once responsible for the development of his own positive contributions and for his extreme modesty about the lasting value of his own works. He was constantly looking for exceptions to theoretical explanations, and he in all modesty was confident that exceptions to his own generalizations would be found.

His *White Collar Crime* (1949) exemplified his thesis that scientific research should lay stress on a search for negative cases. He noted in *Criminology* and in various journal articles that any general explanation of criminality necessarily would be imprecise because such a wide variety of acts are crimes. Nevertheless, he insisted, if one sets for himself the task of formulating a general theory of criminal behavior, he should do a good job of it. There should be no categories of behavior standing as glaring exceptions to the general explanation. He invented the concept of "white-collar crime" specifically to stress the fact that law violations by persons of respectability and high social status were being overlooked by theoreticians and others who said crime was caused by poverty, frustration, or biological makeup: "Quite obviously, the hypothesis that crime is due to personal and social pathologies does not apply to white-collar crimes, and if pathologies do not explain these crimes they are not essential factors in crimes which ordinarily confront police departments and criminal and juvenile courts. In contrast with such explanations, the hypothesis of differential association and social disorganization may apply to white-collar crimes as well as to the crimes of the lower class" (*White Collar Crime*, p. 266).

These ideas, and the first formal statement of the concept and theory of white-collar crime, also appeared in Sutherland's presidential address to the American Sociological Association on Dec. 27, 1939 (*American Sociological Review*, February 1940).

Sutherland also invented and utilized in his research an idea and concept that directly contrasts with the logical underpinnings of his work on white-collar crime. He reasoned, as indicated above, that any theory covering all criminality would necessarily be very general—perhaps too general to be of much practical or theoretical value, even if of value as an organizing framework. Accordingly, he proposed that crime be broken down into more homogeneous units, which he called "behavior systems," and that specific explanations of each homogeneous unit be developed. His *The Professional Thief* (1937) is a study of one such behavior system. This book, like Sutherland's other writings and his classroom teaching, has had a profound influence on the direction of criminological research and theory.

Sutherland died of a stroke and serious fall in Bloomington, Ind.

[The major sources are Jerome Hall, "Edwin H. Sutherland, 1883–1950," *Jour. of Criminal Law and Criminol.*, 41, no. 4 (1950), 393–396; Alfred R. Lindesmith, "Edwin H. Sutherland's Contributions to

Criminology," *Sociol. and Social Res.*, 35, no. 4 (1951), 243–249; George B. Vold, "Edwin Hardin Sutherland: Sociological Criminologist," *Am. Sociol. Rev.*, 16, no. 1 (1951), 3–9, which contains a photograph and a bibliography; Albert Cohen, Alfred Lindesmith, and Karl Schuessler, eds., *The Sutherland Papers* (1956), which contains a photograph, a bibliography, comments by the editors, reprints of seventeen Sutherland articles or chapters, and eight previously unpublished papers. The Ely Lilly Lib. at Indiana Univ. maintains a collection of Sutherland's working papers and manuscripts.]

DONALD R. CRESSEY

SWIFT, LINTON BISHOP (July 15, 1888–Apr. 11, 1946), social welfare administrator, was born in St. Paul, Minn., the only child of George Linton Swift and Tryphena (Bishop) Swift. His father, founder of a successful local law firm, Brown and Bigelow, provided amply for the family. Linton Swift's upbringing was conventional. He graduated from the University of Minnesota and St. Paul College of Law and then practiced law in St. Paul from 1910 to 1917. Following the American entry into World War I, Swift enlisted in the engineer corps. He was later commissioned and transferred to the infantry. While serving in France, he met and on May 14, 1919 married Marie Louise Arnoux; they had no children. After the armistice, Swift remained in Europe as a translator of treaties and legal documents for the United States Peace Commission and then as the American representative to the Commission for the Protection of Minorities in the Newly Created States. In this post he observed at first-hand the war's shattering effects upon community and family relationships, especially upon the Jews in Eastern Europe, and determined to devote his life to social service.

Returning home in 1920, Swift began his career in social work as assistant general secretary of the St. Paul United Charities. In 1922, he became general secretary of the Family Service Organization of Louisville, Ky., and, three years later, he moved to New York as executive secretary of the American Association for Organizing Family Social Work (renamed the Family Welfare Association of America and then later renamed the Family Service Association of America). In this position, which he held for the rest of his life, Swift was the chief spokesman for a federation of 230 family welfare agencies in the United States and Canada. He was recognized for his ability to reconcile differences between various community charities and agencies and to articulate social work policy and the purpose and scope of family social work during a period of social and economic upheaval. Swift characterized family social work as the "mother of specialties" because its practitioners focused their energies upon securing the services of experts from the medical and social sciences according to the particular needs of individual cases. In the 1920's, however, family service groups were only beginning to differentiate themselves from their predecessors, the charity organization societies that had often held quasi-public status by functioning as a clearing agency for all local requests for relief. While not actively disputing the value of the comprehensive supervisory role, Swift urged family agencies to appeal for contributions on the basis of the services they alone could provide. Public funds, he believed, ought to support those who were unemployed through no fault of their own. Well before the Great Depression, he noted that most relief expenditures were coming from government revenues rather than charity funds.

Swift's awareness of the extent of public relief made him critical of Herbert Hoover's plea for greater philanthropic effort to combat the depression. Like many social workers of that period, however, he believed that unemployment relief should remain the responsibility of state and local governments. Terming federal relief a "ghastly business," he thought that fixed relief payments, administered on a broad scale, would threaten the existence of private agencies and make "real individualization of human needs . . . impossible." By 1933, however, Swift clearly saw the need for federal relief; with three other social work executives, Allen Burns, William Hodson, and Walter West, together known as the "Four Horsemen," he helped draft the Federal Emergency Relief Act of 1933. FERA reflected the continued influence of private agencies by designating them local administrators of federal funds. This, in turn, meant that the policies of private agency officials, principally the rigid application of the means test to restrict applications for aid, became government policy as well. As a result, conflicts arose between traditional social workers and New Dealers like Harry Hopkins, who favored "public funds expended by public agencies," an approach that became federal policy with the advent of the Civil Works Administration (1934). Swift soon recognized the permanence of a public welfare bureaucracy and promoted training in social work methods for public administrators. His analysis of changes in welfare disbursement, *New Alignments Between Public and Private Agencies in a Community Family Program* (1934), became the standard work on the subject.

Swift helped to reorient the family agencies

to meet the challenges of family and individual dislocation caused by World War II. Congested defense areas often totally lacked organizations to aid servicemen's families or to provide day care for the children of working mothers and recreation for young people. Swift advised the Federal Security Agency on these problems and served on the American War Community Services Board in order to stimulate development of public and private social services in war boom towns. He continued to promote increased recognition and benefits for trained social workers through the Social Work Vocational Bureau (1940) and to coordinate the efforts and knowledge of all social agencies through the Social Casework Council of National Agencies (1940) and the National Social Welfare Assembly (1946). Greatly concerned with war-related issues of social justice, he served on the Federal Council of Churches' Committee on Resettlement of Japanese-Americans.

Throughout his career, Swift opposed radical social workers such as Mary Van Kleeck who wished to ally social workers with other workers' groups in order to create a noncapitalistic social order. At the same time, he remained skeptical about the appropriateness and social value of psychiatric social work, which was much in vogue during the 1930's and 1940's; in 1939, he wrote, "The range of social casework treatment . . . lies between but does not include social action and psychiatry at the opposite ends of the scale."

Swift died in Park East Hospital in New York after a brief illness.

[Books and articles by Linton Swift include *New Alignments Between Public and Private Agencies in a Community Family Welfare and Relief Program* (1934); National Conference of Social Work, *Proc.*, "The Community Fund and Relief-Giving," pp. 239–240 (1930); "The Social Worker's Responsibility Toward a Changing Social Order," *The Family*, 15 (1935): 283–288; "Local and National Wartime Development in the Family Welfare Field" (Family Welfare Association of America pamphlet, 1943). Related articles by Swift appear in *Compass*, *The Family*, *Social Forces*, *Social Service Review*, *Survey*, and *Social Work Yearbook* (1933, 1939, 1943). See also Hilary M. Leyendecker, *Problems and Policy in Public Assistance* (1955).

A bibliographical source outline compiled in 1967 by Mary Elizabeth Johnson, division of librarianship, Emory University, was most helpful. Other facts were provided by the Family Welfare Association of America and the St. Paul Public Lib. Obituaries in *The Family*, May 1946, *N.Y. Times*, Apr. 12, 1946; *Social Service Rev.*, Sept. 1946, and Harry L. Lurie, ed., *Encyc. of Social Work*, pp. 791–792 (1965).]

ROBERT M. MENNEL

TAGGARD, GENEVIEVE (Nov. 28, 1894–Nov. 8, 1948), poet, was born in Waitsburg, Wash., the eldest of three children of Alta Gale (Arnold) Taggard and James Nelson Taggard. Both grandfathers, of Scots-Irish descent, had been farmers and pioneers, and fought in the Union Army before moving west. James Taggard came to Washington from Missouri for his health and became principal of the elementary school. Alta Taggard was the first-grade teacher, a self-educated, energetic, and ambitious woman, who hoped marriage would help her escape from small-town sterility. Both dreamed of going to college, but James gave their savings to his hard-pressed brother instead, and Alta Taggard found herself tied to an ineffectual man whom she was to dominate and in some measure despise. Genevieve's childhood identification with her father's romantic idealism was never completely extinguished, but she grew to place greater value on her mother's pioneer endurance. In her own life and art, she came increasingly to demand toughness and commitment along with lyric grace.

In 1896 the Taggards went as missionaries to the Hawaiian Islands, where they remained until 1914 except for two short, unhappy returns to Waitsburg in 1905 and 1910 when James's health failed. Educated at her father's public school near Honolulu and then at the missionary Punahou School, Taggard felt herself part of Hawaiian culture; she played with her father's multiracial students and heard legends of the volcano goddess along with family tales of Abraham Lincoln and the Ozarks. The returns to harsh, dusty Waitsburg, where her father scraped a marginal living as a hired hand for his now prosperous brother, were traumatic for the whole family. Accustomed to the cosmopolitan openness of Hawaiian life, they felt like aliens in their native land. Like Sinclair Lewis and Sherwood Anderson, Taggard was sickened by the brutality of small-town life, while recognizing its pathos and even its vitality. Later she thought the Waitsburg experience had been "the active source of my convictions. It told me what to work against and what to work for" ("Hawaii, Washington, Vermont," p. 250).

As members of the fundamentalist Disciples of Christ, the Taggards allowed only the Bible in their home; but Taggard secretly read Keats and Ruskin, relishing their luxurious language. She began to write poetry at the age of twelve, partly in defiance of her mother's authoritarianism; and in 1910 her first published poem, "Mitchiegawa," appeared in the Punahou school magazine, the *Oahuan*. Three months before graduation, her father fell ill, and she was forced to leave school and teach in his place. But she taught herself enough Latin to pass her exams, and in the fall of 1914 entered the University of California at Berkeley, where her mother ran a boardinghouse and Genevieve worked part-time to meet expenses. She edited the student literary magazine, *Occident,* and in December 1919, "An Hour on a Hill," her first poem to be published by a national magazine, appeared in *Harper's.*

After graduating from Berkeley in June 1920, she went to New York to work for B. W. Huebsch, publisher of the *Freeman.* By this time she had become a Socialist, contributing to radical magazines like *Liberator.* In 1921, along with Maxwell Anderson and Padraic Colum, she helped found and edit a monthly poetry journal, *The Measure,* which appeared until 1926. On Mar. 21, 1921, she married Robert L. Wolf, a journalist; their only child, Marcia Sara, was born in 1922. *For Eager Lovers* (1922), poems about marriage and pregnancy, established her as a feminine lyricist of the Millay-Teasdale school, but she soon outgrew the role. Marriage, she wrote, "is the only profound human experience . . . yet having it, it is not all I want. It is better to work hard than to be married hard" ("Poet Out of Pioneer," p. 65). She and Wolf served as contributing editors to *New Masses,* but in a 1927 symposium Taggard expressed her uneasiness with pressures for artists to join the proletarian cause.

Travelling Standing Still (1928), a selection of her poems, was a turning point in her career; critics like Edmund Wilson and William Rose Benét praised her work, although they continued to emphasize its feminine and exotic qualities. During the depression, she returned to the academic world, alternating teaching at Mt. Holyoke College (1929-1930) and Bennington (1932-1935) with European research leaves, including a 1931 Guggenheim award. *The Life and Mind of Emily Dickinson* (1930), a biographical and critical study linking Dickinson to the metaphysical tradition, won wide acclaim.

Her marriage to Wolf ended in divorce in 1934; and on Mar. 10, 1935, she married Kenneth Durant, American director of the Soviet news agency Tass. She taught at Sarah Lawrence College (1935-1946) and spent her vacations at Gilfeather, her farm in East Jamaica, Vt. Taggard felt that in New England she had found the community she sought. Her most Marxist book, *Calling Western Union* (1936), expressed indignation at the plight of Vermont workers and used colloquial diction to celebrate working-class solidarity in poems that many critics found propagandistic. The effort

to connect her poetry to the political struggles of the decade also reflected Taggard's wish to be more than a "poetess": "I think the later poems and some of the early ones hold a wider consciousness than that colored by the feminine half of the race," she wrote in *Collected Poems 1918-1938.* "I think, I hope, I have written poetry that relates to general experience and the realities of the time."

In the 1940's she worked on an unfinished prose work about her family's pioneer past. At the last congress of the left-wing League of American Writers in 1941, she defended the democratic tradition of American literature against what she considered the elitist pessimism of T. S. Eliot and Ezra Pound. Her own poetry in this decade was increasingly influenced by John Donne and Dickinson. Disillusioned by World War II and shifts in the political climate, she retired to her farm in 1946, suffering from hypertension. After her death on Nov. 8, 1948, in a New York hospital, her ashes were scattered on a hill near Gilfeather.

[The Genevieve Taggard Papers in the N.Y. Public Lib. contain correspondence, MSS., and tape recordings of her voice. The general correspondence in this collection has been sealed by Kenneth Durant until Jan. 1, 1985. The Genevieve Taggard Collect. Baker Lib., Dartmouth College, has juvenilia, copies of most of her published work, and references to her by critics and literary historians. Details about her life can be found in a Univ. of Hawaii master's thesis by Kathryn Lucille Lins, "An Interpretive Study of Selected Poetry of Genevieve Taggard," which includes three photographs; there is a carbon copy at Dartmouth. The best general summary is by Basil Rauch in *Notable Am. Women* (1971). Taggard wrote about her politics in "Are Artists People?" *New Masses* (Jan. 1927); and about her life in the anonymous "Poet Out of Pioneer," *Nation,* Jan. 19, 1927; in "Hawaii, Washington, Vermont," *Scribner's,* Oct. 1934; and in Stanley J. Kunitz and Howard Haycraft, eds., *Twentieth Century Authors* (1942). In addition to the books cited above, Taggard wrote *Hawaiian Hilltop* (1023), *Words for the Chisel* (1926), *Monologue for Mothers* (1929), *Remembering Vaughan in New England* (1933), *Falcon* (1942), *Long View* (1942), *A Part of Vermont* (1945), *Slow Music* (1946), and *Origin: Hawaii* (1947). *May Days* (1925) was an anthology of verse from *Masses* and *Liberator.* Other useful sources of information are Hortense Flexner King, "Genevieve Taggard," *Sarah Lawrence College Alumnae Magazine,* Fall 1948; Edmund Wilson, "A Poet of the Pacific," in *The Shores of Light* (1952); and Alfred Kreymborg, "Remembering Genevieve Taggard," *Masses and Mainstream,* Jan. 1949. There are obituaries in *N.Y. Times* and *N.Y. Herald-Tribune,* Nov. 9, 1948; and *Saturday Rev. of Literature,* Nov. 20, 1948.]

ELAINE C. SHOWALTER

TALMADGE, EUGENE (Sept. 23, 1884-Dec. 21, 1946), governor of Georgia, was born in Forsyth, Ga., the second of six children and oldest of three sons of Thomas Romalgues Talmadge and Carrie (Roberts) Talmadge. His father, an alumnus of the University of Georgia, was descended from early seventeenth-century settlers of New Jersey, a branch of the family having migrated to Georgia after the Revolution. He was a prominent cotton farmer and civic leader. Eugene Talmadge attended public school in Forsyth and at his father's insistence entered the University of Georgia in 1901, but left before receiving a degree. He subsequently returned to earn an LL.B. degree in 1908.

Following a year of law practice in Atlanta, where he made excellent political connections with some of his father's friends, Talmadge moved to Ailey in Montgomery County. There on Sept. 12, 1909, he married Mrs. Mattie (Thurmond) Peterson, a well-to-do widow who in addition to rearing a young son was the local railroad depot agent and telegraph operator, as well as a landowner in Telfair County near the town of McRae. Of this marriage three children were born: Vera, Herman Eugene, and Margaret. In 1912 the family moved to Telfair County, where Talmadge purchased farm property along Sugar Creek, and for the next fourteen years he engaged in farming and the law. His only involvement in politics during these years was on the local level: as solicitor for the McRae city court (1918-1920) and as county attorney (1920-1923).

Talmadge began his statewide political career in 1926 when he defeated the "machine" candidate for the office of commissioner of agriculture. He was reelected in 1928 and 1930, but his tenure was marked by controversy. Economically naive, he lobbied for a protective tariff on agricultural imports, which he felt would raise the price of Georgia farm products; and in an attempt to bolster hog prices he used $10,000 of departmental funds to speculate on the Chicago hog market. A legislative investigation into this and other accounting irregularities in his department raised the threat of impeachment, but no action was taken. Talmadge's pugnacity, however, pleased the small farmers of Georgia, and with their help he was elected governor in 1932, after defeating a field of nine in the Democratic primary. He was reelected two years later.

Talmadge proved a natural campaigner. Slight and wiry, with horn-rimmed glasses and a lock of dark hair that fell across his forehead, he would "shuck off" his coat at a political rally, exposing a pair of red "galluses," roll up his shirt sleeves, and swing into a fiery tirade against his opponents to the accompaniment of delighted cheers from the crowd. He called himself a "dirt farmer," and encouraged comparison with Sen. Tom Watson, a Georgia Populist hero. Having grown up in rural Georgia in the days of the Populist revolt, he never entirely lost the agricultural tenets of that group. At the same time, he retained a conservative Bourbon financial philosophy, detesting deficit financing, cherishing states rights, and advocating a traditional American individualism. A Baptist, he frequently obscured significant issues with biblical quotations. An innate believer in white supremacy, Talmadge in later years injected the issue of race into his campaigns, though with less virulence than demagogues like Ellison ("Cotton Ed") Smith.

Talmadge took office as governor at the same time that Franklin D. Roosevelt became president. Delighted at first by the Democratic sweep and Roosevelt's leadership, he gradually became a bitter foe of the New Deal. The chief objects of his attack were agricultural policies of acreage and poundage reduction and the WPA minimum-wage level of 30 cents per hour. As governor he vetoed three bills that would have permitted the establishment of the social security system in Georgia (1935). Determined to consolidate his authority, he suspended the entire Public Utilities Commission (1933), declared martial law to "subjugate" the Highway Commission (1933), and had the state treasurer bodily removed from office when he refused to honor the checks Talmadge drew to finance the state government after the legislature had failed to pass an appropriation bill in 1935. A determined foe of organized labor, Talmadge called out the National Guard to break strikes during attempts to unionize the state's textile mills in 1934.

By 1936 Talmadge was solidly in the "stop-Roosevelt" camp. He backed Huey Long and, after Long's assassination, with support from conservatives and reactionaries like John J. Raskob and Rev. Gerald L. K. Smith, called a "Grass Roots" convention at Macon, Ga., which formed the "Constitutional Jeffersonian Democratic" party and nominated Talmadge for president. The movement soon collapsed, and the fiasco, together with his opposition to the Agricultural Adjustment Act, temporarily cost Talmadge the support of the farmers. Ineligible to run again in 1936 for governor, he made an unsuccessful attempt to unseat incumbent United States Senator Richard B. Russell, Jr. A similar attempt against Walter F. George in 1938 also failed. Between 1936 and 1940 Talmadge practiced law in Atlanta, continued to run his farms, and published the *Statesman,* a weekly newspaper that he founded in 1932.

Talmadge was returned to the governor's chair in 1940. He wisely refrained from attacking Roosevelt, but embroiled himself in a feud with the University of Georgia while attempting to return a political favor. Unable to force reinstatement of a discharged faculty member, he attacked the dean as a champion of racial integration and pressured the board of regents into firing him, an action that led to the university's loss of accreditation. The episode was largely responsible for Talmadge's defeat by Ellis G. Arnall when he ran for a four-year term in 1942. Having discovered that his states' rights, laissez-faire position attracted the support of large corporations, Talmadge accepted their campaign contributions, thus opening himself to the charge that he had betrayed the farmers for political advancement. He was nonetheless again elected governor in 1946; but before assuming office he died in Atlanta, of cirrhosis of the liver and hemolytic jaundice, at the age of sixty-two. He was buried in Oak Grove Cemetery in McRae. His son, Herman, became governor of Georgia in 1950 and United States senator in 1956.

Talmadge's career was typical of Georgia politics in that he led a personal faction rather than a machine. He never offered a serious platform to the electorate. Through flamboyant campaigning, personal magnetism, and the rural-dominated county unit voting system, he won seven victories at the polls, but never carried the legislature with him, or any other slate of candidates. His talent for leadership was wasted in fighting against an irresistible current of social change.

[This article is based on a study of Talmadge's papers in the possession of his son, Herman (possibly no longer available), together with unpublished and published state records, files of Georgia newspapers, and interviews with Herman Talmadge, Charles D. Redwine, Tom M. Linder, and Zack D. Cravey. The author's dissertation "The Public Career of Eugene Talmadge, 1926–1936" (1952) and her three articles —"The Ideology of Eugene Talmadge," *Ga. Hist. Quart.*, Sept. 1954; "The Agricultural Policies of Eugene Talmadge," *Agricultural Hist.*, Jan. 1954; and "Gov. Eugene Talmadge and the New Deal," in J. Carlyle Sittersen, ed., *Studies in Southern Hist.* (1957) —are the principal scholarly studies. Allen L. Henson, *Red Galluses* (1945), is an admiring campaign biography. See also Reinhard H. Luthin, *Am. Demagogues* (1954); Ellis G. Arnall, *The Shore Dimly Seen* (1946); and V. O. Key, Jr., *Southern Politics in State and Nation* (1949). A statue of Talmadge adorns the southeast corner of the Capitol grounds in Atlanta. Excellent photographs may be found in the *Atlanta Constitution*, Sept. 13, 1934, and the *N.Y. Times*, Dec. 22, 1946.]

SARAH McCULLOH LEMMON

TANGUAY, EVA (Aug. 1, 1878–Jan. 11, 1947), singer and stage star, was born in Marbleton, Quebec, Canada, the second daughter and youngest of the four children of Octave Tanguay and Marie Adele (Pajeau) Tanguay. Her father, a physician, was born and educated in Paris, France; her mother, a music teacher, was Canadian by birth. Before her sixth birthday, Eva moved with her family to Holyoke, Mass., where her formal schooling began. Her studies ended abruptly, however, with the death of her father (an event that left the family destitute) and the start of her stage career shortly afterward, in 1886.

Although only eight at this time, Eva already had to her credit the winning of an amateur-night contest and several other stage appearances; she therefore stepped easily into the role of Little Lord Fauntleroy when the regular juvenile star became ill during the appearance in Holyoke of the Francesca Redding Company. Accompanied by her mother, she toured with the Redding Company for five years; later, in response to offers from other musical comedy companies, she toured in *The Merry World*, and then, in 1901, she played Gabrielle de Chalus in *My Lady* at the Victoria Theatre in New York. In 1903 Tanguay attracted wide attention, first as Phorisco in *The Chaperones*, in which she first sang "I Don't Care" (the song and her attitude in general earned her the title "The I-Don't-Care Girl"), and then as Claire de Lune, opposite Frank Daniels, in *The Office Boy*. The following year, *The Blond in Black* opened, with Tanguay in the role of Carlotta Dashington, the brash "Sambo Girl"; that the show's title was soon changed to *The Sambo Girl* acknowledged her importance as a musical comedy star.

In 1906, while still the undisputed queen of the musical comedy theater, Tanguay moved into a medium even more compatible with her style: vaudeville. Soon, on a tour of the leading vaudeville theaters, she rose to the crest of her success, commanding as much as $3,500 for a one-week run and consistently evoking greater audience enthusiasm than any other stage performer of her day. However, as suggested by a contemporary critical evaluation of Tanguay as "not beautiful, witty or graceful," the exact nature of her appeal eludes definition. Perhaps the vibrancy of her high-pitched voice as she sang her self-centered, and often self-ridiculing, songs, the refrain of most of which echoed her theme song, "I Don't Care," radiated her enthusiasm to her listeners; or perhaps her imaginative costumes, including a dress made of pennies and dollars and a Salome outfit, consisting, she said, of "two pearls," dazzled her viewers as she danced in gleeful abandon. No doubt her appearance, a sparkling composite of unruly blonde hair, large, smiling mouth; impudent deep blue eyes, turned-up nose, and trim figure, contributed to the intensity of her impact.

Probably the most comprehensive explanation of Tanguay's popularity resides in the comment by an observer that she was the "Circe of the force of advertising." The infinite cataloguing in her songs of such personal attributes as her uniqueness, her success, her wealth, and her unassailability hypnotized her audience into agreement. She herself said that her success lay entirely in the force of her personality. Contemporary newspapers recorded not only her professional activities (including many publicity stunts, typified by her selling newspapers on a street corner, accompanied by a trained elephant) but also the most minute details of her personal affairs. In one respect, her private life was a rewarding one, for, according to relatives, Tanguay (born a Roman Catholic and later a self-designated "metaphysical") was a "devoted, generous, wonderfully kind . . . religious person," who enjoyed warm contacts with her family and many friends. On the other hand, she experienced two unsuccessful marriages. The first, to John W. Ford, her dancing partner, lasted from Nov. 24, 1913, until her divorce in 1917. The second marriage, to Alexander Booke, her pianist, took place in Santa Ana, Calif., on July 22, 1927, and was annulled the same year when Tanguay charged Booke with deception for entering the marriage under the name Allan Parado when his legal name was Chandos Ksiazkewacz. (She was also erroneously reported to have married Roscoe Ails.)

In the late 1920's and the 1930's, almost as counterpoint to Tanguay's spectacular rise to fame and wealth, came her decline. Although she was reputed to have earned a $2 million fortune onstage, lavish spending, generosity to friends, and stock market speculation eventually dissipated her wealth. In addition to financial reverses, a series of health problems beset her and ultimately forced her retirement. In 1933, she underwent eye surgery for the removal of cataracts; then, her sight restored, she made plans to raise money for the endowment of a hospital for blind children. Unfortunately, in 1937, an attack of arthritis prevented the realization of these plans and caused her to spend the last decade of her life as an invalid in a modest house in Hollywood. Even in these troubled circumstances, however, she retained enough of her former enthusiasm to start work on an autobiography to be entitled "Up and Down the Ladder." Before completion of the book, she died at her home of a cerebral hemorrhage. She was buried at the Hollywood Mausoleum.

Any assessment of Eva Tanguay's achievement on the stage must admit her limitations, for she possessed few of the conventional talents. Nonetheless, she claims an important niche in American theater history. For one thing, she contributed to the relaxing of the decorous aspect of vaudeville. Many of her songs, bearing such risqué titles as "It's All Been Done Before But Not the Way I Do It," and "I Want Someone to Go Wild with Me," alarmed the censors but drew approving crowds. Moreover, her independence, perhaps more accurately designated aggressiveness, both on and off the stage, not only reflected the ferment of her era but also foreshadowed the attitudes of the women of forthcoming generations. Above all, in her flamboyance, glitter, ebullience, and generosity, Eva Tanguay epitomized a phenomenon of her time—the Star.

[The *N.Y. Times Index* contains many references to newspaper items about Tanguay, the most comprehensive of which is the Jan. 12, 1947 obituary, which includes a photograph. Other helpful sources of information are the biographical sketch by Albert F. McLean, Jr., in *Notable Am. Women*, III (1971); *Encyc. Can.* (1966); and *Who's Who in the Theatre* (4th ed., 1922). An excellent detailed description of her stage personality appears in Caroline Caffin, *Vaudeville* (1914); shorter passages, as well as two photographs, appear in Albert F. McLean, *Vaudeville as Ritual* (1965). See also Douglas Gilbert, *American Vaudeville: Its Life and Times* (1940), and Joe Laurie, Jr., *Vaudeville* (1953). Information was graciously supplied by Tanguay's niece, Mrs. Lillian Collins, of Hollywood, Calif. Six of Miss Tanguay's costumes are periodically displayed by the Museum of the City of New York; four are on display at the Los Angeles County Museum.]

DOROTHY KISH

TARKINGTON, BOOTH (July 29, 1869-May 19, 1946), novelist and playwright, was born in Indianapolis, Ind., the younger of two children and only son of John Stevenson Tarkington, a lawyer and county judge, and Elizabeth (Booth) Tarkington. His paternal grandfather, Joseph Tarkington, had come north from his native Tennessee to the free soil of Indiana, where he became a circuit-riding Methodist preacher. His mother's family traced its ancestry back to Thomas Hooker, founder of Connecticut. The boy was christened Newton Booth after his mother's brother, who served California as governor and, later, as United States senator; but he early dropped his first name. From his uncle, he may have inherited the political ambition that led him to a term in the Indiana state legislature (1902-1903).

His principal ambition, however, was to become a writer and illustrator. He cultivated both skills at Phillips Exeter Academy, where he took his last two years of high school; at Purdue University (1890-1891); and at Princeton University (1891-1893), where he studied as a special student and served as editor, writer, and illustrator for several student publications and headed the Triangle Club; but, like F. Scott Fitzgerald, he did not manage to secure a degree.

He returned to his comfortably middle-class home and for five years made little progress as a free-lance writer and illustrator. In 1899 he published his successful first novel, *The Gentleman From Indiana;* followed it the next year with the popular historical romance *Monsieur Beaucaire;* and was launched on a career as a prolific novelist and playwright.

Tarkington married Laurel Louisa Fletcher, the daughter of a prominent Indianapolis banker, on June 18, 1902, but the marriage ended in divorce. His second marriage, on Nov. 6, 1912, to the widowed Susannah (Keifer) Robinson, was by all accounts an extraordinarily happy one. Laurel, Tarkington's only child, was born in 1906 and died at seventeen. Although troubled by his eyes—and at one time precariously close to blindness—Tarkington worked steadily on a schedule that, occasionally interrupted by trips abroad, found him summering in Kennebunkport, Maine, and wintering in his native Indianapolis. His books ultimately totaled more than forty-five. He died of a lung collapse following hemiplegia in Indianapolis and was buried there at Crown Hill Cemetery.

At his death he had long since passed the peak of his reputation. In 1945, to be sure, the American Academy of Arts and Letters presented him with the William Dean Howells Medal, awarded only once every five years—an appropriate honor, since Howells took an early and helpful interest in Tarkington's fiction—and in 1933 Tarkington won the gold medal, previously awarded only to Howells and Edith Wharton among novelists, of the National Institute of Arts and Letters, to which he had been elected in 1908 (he was elected to the Academy in 1920). But Tarkington's great public and critical successes belonged to the decade 1914-1924, when he wrote his best-known books of childhood and adolescence, *Penrod* (1914), *Penrod and Sam* (1916), *Seventeen* (1916), and *Gentle Julia* (1922); his two Pulitzer Prize novels, *The Magnificent*

Ambersons (1918) and *Alice Adams* (1921); and two other mature novels, *The Turmoil* (1915) and *The Midlander* (1924), into whose fabric, as in that of the Pulitzer winners, the author threaded a satiric commentary on the American worship of bigness, of growth for growth's sake. Toward the end of this period, Tarkington's reputation reached its zenith. A 1921 *Publishers' Weekly* poll of booksellers named him the most significant of contemporary authors. In a *Literary Digest* contest in 1922 he was voted the greatest living American writer, and a *New York Times* poll of the same year put him on a list of the ten greatest contemporary Americans. Tarkington's work, however, has ill survived the test of time; half a century later, his serious novels were scarcely read at all and even his juvenile entertainments were out of favor.

In several ways, Tarkington's fiction rather more resembled that of his mentor Howells than that of younger men who were beginning, in the early 1920's, to make more durable reputations. Tarkington's writing is, for example, entirely genteel in sexual matters. Further, there is an undercurrent of good nature in even his most satirical work, so that although Tarkington lampooned the booster in the figure of *The Turmoil*'s Bibbs Sheridan well in advance of Sinclair Lewis's *Babbitt,* he sensed instinctively that Lewis, whose satire was so much more bitter and heavy-handed, was "among the people I don't want to sit down with." Similarly, a 1925 interview in Paris with F. Scott Fitzgerald and Ernest Hemingway went rather badly, for Fitzgerald arrived a little drunk (Tarkington, once a prodigious drinker, had converted to teetotaling) and both young writers looked as if they had been up all night. Tarkington also remained an optimist well past the time when optimism seemed a viable literary attitude. In 1900 he declared his preference for comedy over tragedy and his impatience with writers like Victor Hugo and Ouida, who had perfected "the trick of agony." In his own fiction, he added, he would try to make the reader feel himself "full of courage and the capacity for happiness in a brightened world"; and although Tarkington's late work hardly reflects so rosy a view of the world (he created, for example, a series of selfish, egoistic women who make life miserable for their mates), he went on to provide more than his share, by twentieth-century standards, of happy endings.

It could also be argued that Tarkington wrote too much and that too much of what he did write was ephemera designed for such popular magazines as the *Saturday Evening Post*. Furthermore, he was frequently diverted from his talent for prose fiction, most notably by the lure of the stage. In all, Tarkington wrote some twenty plays, including such successes as *The Man From Home* (first performed in 1907), *The Country Cousin* (1917), and *Clarence* (1919), which starred the young Alfred Lunt. A number of these plays Tarkington wrote in genial collaboration with Harry Leon Wilson; for *The Country Cousin* his coauthor was young Julian Street, and Tarkington with characteristic generosity shared revenues with Street equally even though Tarkington single-handedly rewrote the original script. During his summers in Maine, Tarkington exhibited similar kindness in encouraging and aiding the career of Kenneth Roberts, then making a start as a novelist. He freely donated much of his substantial earnings to such organizations as the Seeing Eye, Inc., the John Herron Art Institute in Indianapolis, the Indianapolis Symphony, Princeton, and Exeter. During both world wars, Tarkington threw himself into war work, writing propaganda gratis at the request of government departments and agencies. "An old-fashioned gentleman," as his biographer James Woodress called him, Tarkington was too amiable, too aware of his obligations not to give of himself.

The principal reason for the decline of Tarkington's reputation as a writer, however, is probably his authorial attitude of superiority. Gifted at creating the atmosphere of a particular time and place, always sensitive to nuances, keenly aware of the relationship between social class and economic success, and brilliant in his command of the spoken language, Tarkington wrote as well as anyone of the American middle class in the early decades of the twentieth century. But he rarely created a character with whom he, or the reader, could identify. Even the much-loved *Penrod* does not age well, but remains a book for boys (who may feel a certain empathy for Penrod) and not for adults (who are likely, with the author, to laugh down at the "marvelous boy" from above). Moreover, Tarkington spices his narrative with the comic relief afforded by the loutish Negroes Herman and Verman, and Penrod's semivillainous antagonist is a rich Jewish boy named Maurice Levy. In *Seventeen*, as well, the author's point of view, which the reader is invited to adopt, is that of condescending amusement at the trials of Willie Baxter in the midst of his awkward adolescence. Nor did Tarkington shift his authorial attitude in the Indiana novels of his major period, when he traced the rise and fall of the Sheridan and Amberson families. In *The Turmoil*, Tarkington had indeed succeeded, as Howells remarked, in casting off the spell of his early romanticism, but he did not go on, as the older writer had written him that he must, to "be one of the greatest." Even in the best of his novels, the fine *Alice Adams*, Tarkington takes up a position above and slightly to the right of his characters, and as he manipulates them, however gently, one detects the strings of the puppet master. Perhaps it was this quality of remote amusement that Scott Fitzgerald was determined to avoid when he warned himself, at the end of his final notes for *The Last Tycoon*, "Don't wake the Tarkington ghosts."

[The standard biography is James Woodress, *Booth Tarkington: Gentleman from Indiana* (1954), based on the Tarkington papers at the Princeton Univ. Lib. Dorothy R. Russo and Thelma L. Sullivan published *A Bibliog. of Booth Tarkington* in 1949. Since that time, although Tarkington's work has suffered from a lack of critical interest, there have been a few excellent articles, including Winfield T. Scott, "Tarkington and the 1920's" (mostly about *Alice Adams*), *Am. Scholar*, Spring 1957; John D. Seelye, "That Marvelous Boy—Penrod Once Again," *Va. Quart. Rev.*, Autumn 1961, and William E. Wilson's comparison of Tarkington and Theodore Dreiser, "The Titan and the Gentleman," *Antioch Rev.*, Spring 1963. Carl D. Bennett's master's thesis, "The Literary Development of Booth Tarkington" (Emory Univ., 1944), argues the case for Tarkington as a social satirist, especially in *The Turmoil*.]

SCOTT DONALDSON

TATE, JOHN TORRENCE (July 28, 1889–May 27, 1950), physicist, was born in Lenox, Adams County, Iowa, the younger of the two sons of Samuel Aaron Tate, a physician, and Minnie Maria (Ralston) Tate. As a child he lived in several Iowa towns, including Keokuk. His mother died when he was about twelve, and he was sent to live with an uncle in New York City while his father practiced medicine on an Indian reservation in South Dakota. After graduating from DeWitt Clinton High School in New York, Tate entered the University of Nebraska, from which he received the degrees of B.S. (1910) and M.A. (1912). He then pursued graduate study at the University of Berlin, working under the noted physicist James Franck, and was awarded the Ph.D. in 1914.

Returning to the United States, Tate taught physics for two years at the University of Nebraska before becoming an instructor at the University of Minnesota in 1916. Immediately successful, he rose through the ranks to become a full professor in 1920 at the age of thirty-one, despite having spent a year as a first lieutenant in the Army Signal Corps. He remained at Minnesota for the rest of his life.

In 1919 Tate developed an introductory graduate course in theoretical classical physics, which he continued to teach until 1937. Few of Tate's students would dispute the assertion of Henry A. Erikson, the department chairman who first brought Tate to Minnesota, that they owed their success "in a large measure to his influence in this course." Tate's remarkable ability to extract and spontaneously present the essence of a scientific paper with clarity and precision, thereby opening up still unexplored vistas for his students, coupled with his personal generosity, modesty, and high standards, made him an outstanding teacher and an esteemed colleague. In contrast to almost every other American university, quantum theory flourished at Minnesota in the mid-1920's, under the leadership of Tate and J. H. Van Vleck. By the time of World War II, well over half of the students who had received Ph.D. degrees in physics at Minnesota—many of them destined for future eminence—had had Tate as their thesis advisor.

Tate's experimental researches at the University of Minnesota grew naturally out of his interest in electron collision and ionization phenomena, an interest first stimulated by Franck at Berlin. Tate and his students concentrated principally on the electron bombardment of numerous gaseous molecules and compounds, studying the efficiency and other aspects of the attendant ionization and dissociation processes. These studies not only yielded a great deal of specific information on the structure and internal force fields of the molecules in question; they also led to the refinement of such precision experimental techniques as those of mass spectroscopy, which in 1940 enabled Alfred O. C. Nier, a student of Tate's, to separate the uranium isotopes at Minnesota. In the late 1930's Tate was instrumental in securing a grant from the Rockefeller Foundation for the construction of the university's 4 Mev accelerator, and in 1946 he helped obtain funds from the navy to establish its distinguished cosmic ray program.

Tate influenced the direction of physics in this country and abroad not only through his teaching and research, but also through his work in professional associations. The American Physical Society chose him in 1926 as managing editor of the *Physical Review,* a post

he held until his death. Under his leadership, the journal grew steadily in size, circulation, and prominence. He was directly responsible for founding two additional publications of the society: the successful and respected *Reviews of Modern Physics* in 1929, which he also edited until his death, and *Physics* (later the *Journal of Applied Physics*) in 1931, which he edited for six years. With Karl T. Compton, Tate helped found in 1932 the American Institute of Physics, serving from the beginning on its governing board and as chairman, 1936–1939. He was president of the American Physical Society in 1939 and in 1942 was elected to the National Academy of Sciences.

Tate was appointed dean of the College of Science, Literature, and the Arts at the University of Minnesota in 1937. Despite his scientific background, he continually stressed the importance of the humanities and social sciences to a liberal education, and as dean he was in full accord with the academic reforms that were effected by Minnesota's president Lotus Delta Coffman. With the onset of World War II, Tate's special talents were enlisted by the United States government. His position as chief of Division 6 (on subsurface warfare) of the National Defense Research Committee (1941–1945) kept him away from campus on a full-time basis, and in 1944 he resigned his deanship. For his and his division's achievements, which greatly improved the Allies' defenses against submarines, Tate received the United States Presidential Medal of Merit (1947) and, from Britain, King George's Medal for Service in the Cause of Freedom. He returned to the University of Minnesota after the war as research professor, but he continued his government service as chairman of the board of governors of the Argonne National Laboratory of the Atomic Energy Commission from 1946 to 1949.

Tate married Lois Beatrice Fossler of Lincoln, Nebr., on Dec. 28, 1917. Their only child, John Torrence, became a distinguished mathematician. Tate's first wife died in 1939, and on June 30, 1945, he married Madeline Margarite Mitchell, manager of publications of the American Institute of Physics. A Presbyterian by upbringing, he had no religious affiliation in later life. Tate died in Minneapolis at the age of sixty of a cerebral hemorrhage. After cremation his ashes were scattered. The Tate Laboratory of Physics at the University of Minnesota, dedicated in 1966, was named in his honor, as was the John

Torrence Tate International Gold Medal of the American Institute of Physics.

[The principal published sources are obituary articles and memoirs of Tate in the *Physical Rev.*, July 1, 1950; *Revs. of Modern Physics*, July 1951 (by A. O. C. Nier); Am. Philosophical Society, *Year Book*, 1950 (by Karl K. Darrow); *Am. Jour. of Physics*, Sept. 1950 (by E. L. Hill); and *Physics Today*, Aug. 1950 (by George B. Pegram). On his deanship, see James Gray, *The Univ. of Minn., 1851–1951* (1951). Complete references to Tate's scientific papers may be obtained by consulting *Science Abstracts* and the *Physical Rev.* Unpublished materials include: Henry A. Erikson, "Hist. of the Dept. of Physics, Univ. of Minn.," in the Univ. of Minn. Archives and in the Center for Hist. of Physics, Am. Inst. of Physics, N. Y. City; remarks by (and in the possession of) W. G. Shepherd, J. H. Van Vleck, E. U. Condon, and A. O. C. Nier on the occasion of the dedication of the Tate Laboratory of Physics; and information from John Torrence Tate at Harvard. A compilation of references on Tate's life and work prepared by Gail Schlachter at the Univ. of Wis. Lib. School (1966) was helpful.]

ROGER H. STUEWER

TATLOCK, JOHN STRONG PERRY (Feb. 24, 1876-June 24, 1948), medievalist and professor of English, was born in Stamford, Conn. He was the third son and the fourth of five children of William Tatlock, rector of St. John's Episcopal Church in Stamford, and Florence (Perry) Tatlock. Both parents were of English origin. His mother, of seventeenth-century colonial descent, was from Albany, N.Y.; his father had come to the United States at the age of twenty from Liverpool, England, and had graduated from Williams College. J. S. P. Tatlock (as he was known professionally) prepared for college at the Cathedral School of St. Paul in Garden City, Long Island. He graduated from Harvard (B.A. magna cum laude) in 1896 and went on to receive a Harvard M.A. in 1897 and Ph.D. in 1903. He began his teaching as an instructor in English at the University of Michigan in 1897, and save for an interim of two years, 1901-1903, during which he completed requirements for the doctorate, he remained there until 1915, with increasing reputation as a teaching and publishing scholar. The rest of his career took him as a professor of English to three universities: Stanford, 1915-1925; Harvard, 1925-1929; and the University of California at Berkeley, 1929-1946.

On June 17, 1908, Tatlock married Marjorie Fenton. She died in 1937, after becoming well-known in Berkeley for a private school she conducted. The children of that marriage were three: Percival (died in infancy), Hugh, and Jean Frances. During World War II, Tatlock married Dr. Elizabeth Goodrich Whitney of San Francisco. Their marriage ended in divorce.

As a scholar Tatlock was born for his time.

It was a time that generously recognized what he and others of his quality could give to a university world in which the long-established Greco-Roman foundation for teaching of the humanities had lost general acceptance. The need was nevertheless still felt for some grounding upon a development of culture from the past. Opinion was strong that in the study and teaching of English, as both language and literature, the Celto-Germanic culture which rose after the fall of the Greco-Roman could serve as grounding with special aptness.

At Harvard, Tatlock encountered this approach to English studies. Under the direction of George Lyman Kittredge he gave himself to it fully. In 1903, his article "The Dates of Chaucer's *Troilus and Criseyde* and *Legend of Good Women*" appeared in the first volume of *Modern Philology*. This article placed him from the beginning as a literary historian and was the first of a procession of over a hundred shorter pieces of writing that issued from his hand. He was called an austere scholar, but he also possessed a sharp wit and an abiding comic sense. It is wholly characteristic that the last of his shorter writings, published in *Speculum* two years before his death, bore the title "Mediaeval Laughter."

In 1907 Tatlock published his first book, *The Development and Chronology of Chaucer's Works*, which after two-thirds of a century is still the most authoritative comprehensive treatment of the Chaucer chronology. Among other major publications that followed was *A Concordance to the Complete Works of Geoffrey Chaucer and to the "Romaunt of the Rose"* (1927), an indispensable reference work of which Arthur G. Kennedy was coauthor.

After retirement from teaching in 1946, Tatlock arduously devoted himself to completion of major writing he had undertaken. He did so first in Berkeley and then beginning in 1947 in Northampton, Mass., where he spent the last months of his life near his son Hugh, a physician. He died in Northampton of a coronary thrombosis at the age of seventy-two and was buried in the Rural Cemetery at Albany, N.Y. He was a member of the Episcopal church. His last works appeared posthumously in 1950, *The Mind and Art of Chaucer* and the book that Tatlock quite obviously considered his magnum opus, *The Legendary History of Britain: Geoffrey of Monmouth's Historia Regum Britanniae and its Early Vernacular Versions*. He had worked upon the latter for nearly fifteen years and had just completed it when he died. In exploring the legends in Geoffrey's twelfth-century history, which had the Arthurian matter at their center, Tatlock proved himself strongly attracted to heroic beginnings on the Celtic, rather than the Germanic, side of the post-classical culture to which he had directed his scholarship. How strongly attracted is indicated in the emphatic sentence with which he opens his book: "Geoffrey of Monmouth's *Historia Regium Britanniae* is one of the most influential books ever written, certainly one of the most influential in the middle ages."

Besides serving in many other capacities in professional organizations, Tatlock was president of the Modern Language Association of America (1938) and the Mediaeval Academy of America (1942-1945). He was a fellow of the American Academy of Arts and Sciences. Always a supporter of the institutions by which mankind has ordered its living, he looked back with learned interest to the religious organization of life in the Middle Ages. He was in character when he said at the end of a Rockford College commencement address: "Whatever respectable substitutes there may be for traditional religion, country-clubs and motoring are not among them. The wise and good man and woman remains loyal to his religion, to his institutional religion, unless he has been compelled to do otherwise."

[*Who's Who in America, 1948–1949* and previous editions; memoir by W. M. Hart, I. M. Linforth, and B. H. Lehman in Univ. of Calif., *In Memoriam,* 1948; *Class Report* of Harvard College Class of 1896; material in the archives of the Bancroft Lib., Univ. of Calif., Berkeley; interview with Hugh Tatlock of Northampton, Mass.; complete bibliography of Tatlock's publications appended to his *The Mind and Art of Chaucer* by Germaine Dempster.]

WILLARD FARNHAM

TAUSSIG, JOSEPH KNEFLER (Aug. 30, 1877-Oct. 29, 1947), naval officer, the third of the five sons of Edward David Taussig and Ellen (Knefler) Taussig, was born in Dresden, Germany, while his father, an American naval officer, was serving in the European squadron. A cousin of civic leader William Taussig and of economist Frederick William Taussig, he came of a talented St. Louis, Mo., family whose members had emigrated in the 1840's from Prague. After graduating from the Western High School in Washington, D.C., Joseph Taussig attended the United States Naval Academy, where he was an outstanding athlete, and graduated in 1899. Early in his service he saw duty in the Boxer Rebellion in China, where, as part of a multinational landing force,

he was severely wounded and was advanced in grade for "conspicuous conduct in battle." In World War I he commanded the first division of six destroyers sent overseas in May 1917, to help protect the western approaches to England. After a stormy crossing, he reported to his British superior and was asked when his ships would be ready for service. His reply, "I will be ready as soon as fueled," has become part of U.S. Navy tradition.

Taussig was early recognized as a talented officer, but his career was marred by a feud with Assistant Secretary of the Navy Franklin D. Roosevelt over conditions at the Portsmouth Naval Prison, then under the charge of Roosevelt's friend, the prison reformer Thomas Mott Osborne. Osborne's shift of emphasis from punishment to rehabilitation and his policy of returning convicted men to the fleet were resented by senior naval officers as harmful to discipline in wartime. Taussig, as head of the enlisted personnel division of the Navy Department, was the center of the opposition. When this opposition failed, Taussig in 1919 successfully requested transfer to the Naval War College. In January 1920 Roosevelt placed an unsigned article in the *Army and Navy Journal* praising Osborne's methods and stating that younger officers in destroyers approved the rehabilitation of prisoners. Taussig, in a signed letter, denied this, and further charged that many homosexual convicts had been restored to active duty. Roosevelt's reply implied that Taussig made false statements, whereupon the naval officer requested a court of inquiry to clear his name. Roosevelt attempted to reconcile their differences, but Taussig would accept nothing short of a full retraction. His request for an inquiry was not granted.

Taussig graduated from the Naval War College in 1920, and except for three years in commands at sea, he remained on duty there until 1931, rising to the rank of rear admiral. These were the war college's productive years, when the naval task force concept was formulated and general plans developed for an advance across the Pacific in the event of war with Japan. In 1931 Taussig appeared to be on his way to the top. After command of the battleship *Maryland,* he was successively chief of staff to the commander, Battle Fleet, and to the commander-in-chief, United States Fleet, and then assistant chief of naval operations (1933-1936). Roosevelt, however, was then president, and after 1936 Taussig held only minor flag assignment; in 1938 he was made commandant of the Fifth Naval District at Norfolk, Va., where he remained until reaching the statutory retirement age in August 1941. His final and characteristic major professional act was an appearance on Apr. 22, 1940, before a joint House-Senate committee hearing on Pacific fortifications at which he testified that because of the Far East situation he did not see how the United States could avoid being drawn into war with Japan. His statement stirred a worldwide press reaction; it was disavowed by the Navy Department, and he received a letter of reprimand, which was rescinded by presidential order on the day after the Pearl Harbor attack. Taussig was recalled to active duty in 1943 and served until 1946 as chairman of the naval clemency board. He died of a heart attack in 1947 at the Bethesda (Md.) Naval Hospital. Burial was in Arlington National Cemetery.

Despite his failure to receive a top command, Taussig had a cogent impact on the navy. He achieved this through numerous articles in the *Proceedings of the United States Naval Institute,* the navy's professional journal. His subjects included enlisted personnel, officer promotion, characteristics of ships, naval organization, and, during World War II, rehabilitation of naval prisoners, and were usually connected with the duty he was currently performing. Sincere in conviction and well written, his articles often persuaded his civilian and naval superiors to act on his recommendations. The most notable was a prize essay in the *Proceedings* of May 1939, "An Organization for the United States Fleet," in which he recommended establishment of task fleets, a practice followed in the formation of the Third and Fifth fleets of World War II and the Sixth and Seventh fleets in the postwar period. While commandant in Norfolk, Taussig built the first public housing for navy enlisted men, risking censure by diverting funds for it from pier repairs.

Short, muscular, and outspoken, Taussig was nevertheless a personable man, a popular officer, and a noted navy raconteur. His religious affiliation was Unitarian. He married Lulie Augusta Johnston of Norfolk, Va., on Oct. 18, 1911. They had three children: Emily Johnston, Margaret Stewart, and Joseph Knefler. The son followed his father into the navy and was seriously wounded in the Pearl Harbor attack.

[Sources include Navy Dept. records; data from family and from naval subordinates; *N.Y. Times,* Sept. 1, 1941, Oct. 30, 1947; *Army and Navy Jour.,* Nov. 1, 1947; *Army and Navy Register,* Nov. 1, 1947. On the controversy with Roosevelt, see Frank Friedel, *Franklin D. Roosevelt,* II (1954), and for Osborne's service at Portsmouth, Rudolph W. Chamberlain, *There Is No Time: A Life of Thomas Mott Osborne* (1935).]

JOHN D. HAYES

TAYLOR, LAURETTE (Apr. 1, 1884–Dec. 7, 1946), actress, was born Loretta Cooney in New York City, the oldest of three children of James Cooney, a harnessmaker from Ireland, and Elizabeth (Dorsey) Cooney, the daughter of Irish immigrants. She grew up with the fanatical Catholicism, violent temper, drunkenness, and shiftlessness of her father, contrasted with the ambitiousness, willfulness, and love for theatrical gaiety of her dressmaker mother. To the neglect of Loretta's younger siblings, Edward and Elizabeth, the Cooney household centered around the obstinate Loretta. Expelled from high school for misconduct in her first year, she rebelled against the reality of life in the unhappy Cooney family and lived in a make-believe world of playacting spun from her imagination, her lies, and her talents. Loretta could play the piano by ear, do impersonations, recite, sing, and dance. At the age of thirteen she made her first, disappointing vaudeville appearances as "La Belle Laurette" in Lynn and Gloucester, Mass.

Later, when she appeared at the Athenaeum in Boston, she met Charles Alonzo Taylor, a prolific writer and theatrical showman known as "the master of melodrama." On May 1, 1901, the seventeen-year-old Laurette married Taylor, who was twenty years her senior. They then toured in his new play, aptly titled *Child Wife.* The Taylors had two children, Dwight Oliver and Marguerite. Although Laurette played soubrettes and bit parts in her husband's blood-and-thunder productions on tour and in their Seattle stock company, she also acted roles that he had written for her, usually those of innocent, childlike virgins. From 1901 to 1908, although frustrated by the stereotyped characters and stiff dialogue of Taylor's plays, she nevertheless sought to bring life to her roles in such typical Taylor melodramas as *Escape from the Harem, Queen of the Highway,* and *Rags to Riches.* She disciplined herself to believe in the roles she played, to seek the sense of a scene, and to bring imagination and humor to her performances. Laurette did not demand leads, but rather parts that gave her contrast, such as Marguerite in Taylor's adaptation of *Faust* and Topsy in *Uncle Tom's Cabin.* She was reaching not for stardom, but for a versatility that she never achieved.

She deserted her philandering, abusive husband in 1907 and went to New York to further her stage career. During a brief attempt at marital reconciliation, she toured in 1908 as Mercedes in Taylor's *Yosemite.* She divorced Taylor in 1910.

In May 1909 the Broadway critics "discovered" Laurette Taylor as May Keating in *The Great John Ganton,* by John Hartley Manners, a new English playwright and director. From then until 1911 she worked hard to establish herself, appearing in such plays as *The Ringmaster, Mrs. Dakon, Alias Jimmy Valentine, The Girl in Waiting, Seven Sisters,* and *The Bird of Paradise.* These mediocre pieces, some not even financially successful, served to develop Laurette's flair for sentimental comedy.

As a comedienne, Taylor was able to project wholesomeness, warm-hearted optimism, and soft, gentle charm, coupled with bubbling mischievousness. These traits were enhanced by her upturned nose, orange-gold hair, and an impish smile that lit up her hazel eyes. Manners, attracted by these qualities, wrote *Peg O' My Heart* as a vehicle for her. *Peg,* which opened on Dec. 20, 1912, at the new Cort Theatre in New York, was a simple play about a waifish Irish lass transplanted into an aristocratic English family. Critics did not think much of the play; most plays by Manners were considered flimsy and unworthy of Taylor's great talents. As Peg, however, Taylor, with her moments of comedy and pathos and her lilting Irish brogue, provided a rare treat to theatergoers. Taylor's elevation to stardom brought tranquillity, discipline, and happiness to her personal life. In the winter of 1912 she married Manners. After giving 604 consecutive performances in New York, Taylor took *Peg* to London in 1914, accompanied by her husband. After more than a year's run in London, Taylor tired of *Peg,* but in 1921 she and Manners revived it for a brief American tour. In the minds of audiences she was destined to remain Peg for more than a decade. Companies toured with *Peg* throughout most of the world, and by 1919 the play had earned more than a million dollars.

Manners was to have great influence upon his wife's career, for she had unswerving faith in his ability as a playwright and found direction and love in his gentle temperament. As a professional team, they were most successful when Manners wrote plays whose leading character resembled the lovable Peg: Jenny in *Happiness* (December 1917) and " 'Aunted" Annie in *Out There* (April 1917). When Taylor played heroines of a different cast, the result

was usually popular and financial failure; nonetheless, most critics applauded Taylor's performances as Miss Alverstone in *The Wooing of Eve* (November 1917), Madame L'Enigme in *One Night in Rome* (December 1919), Marian Hale in *The National Anthem* (January 1922), and The Visitor in *Delicate Justice* (November 1927).

During the 1920's Taylor's career started to change. Manners was not writing successful plays and Hollywood beckoned. In 1921 Taylor made *Peg* into a hit movie. Two other Manners plays, *Happiness* and *One Night in Rome,* were made into inconsequential films in 1923 and 1924, respectively. When not in Hollywood, Taylor attempted to broaden her repertoire and lessen her dependency upon Manners by appearing in limited-engagement revivals of such outdated plays as *Sweet Nell of Old Drury* (May 1923) and *Trelawney of the Wells* (June 1925). She tried to experiment with new playwrights, appearing as Lissa Terry in Philip Barry's *In A Garden* (November 1925) and as Fifi Sands in Zoe Akins' *The Furies* (March 1928). In February 1923 Fannie Hurst's *Humoresque* provided Taylor with the type of role she hoped would break her image as a youthful heroine. As Sarah Kantor, an aggressive Jewish mother, Taylor felt that she had achieved new artistic depth, but the play was a box-office flop. Alcohol, moodiness, family disintegration, and plays that did not draw audiences made it impossible for her to regain stardom.

After twenty-five years of uninterrupted acting, her personal and professional life reached its ebb with Manners' death on Dec. 19, 1928. Alcohol became an escape from grief, a substitute for her dependency upon Manners, and a mask for her guilt (she had hurt Manners in his last years by revealing her short-lived love affair with screen star John Gilbert). Always an impetuous and sharp-tongued woman, now more than ever she lashed out at professional associates, friends, and family. Her attempts to grip reality by returning to the theater (as in her brief run in March 1932 as Mrs. Grey in *Alice Sit-by-the-Fire*) foundered. She often failed to appear for rehearsals or learn lines. In the 1930's she became known on the New York theatrical circuit as "unreliable." In her struggle for self-preservation she turned from acting to writing and authored several insignificant plays: *Enchantment, At Marian's,* and *Fun with Stella.* In the summer of 1938 she tried the straw-hat circuit, and in December 1938 she made a successful, but temporary, comeback as Mrs. Midget in a revival of *Outward Bound.* In the next six years she continued her battle with alcohol and tried to find herself professionally, waiting for the right role. She found it as Amanda Wingfield in Tennessee Williams' *The Glass Menagerie,* opening in New York on Mar. 31, 1945. As the hard-driving, faded Southern belle, Laurette Taylor presented one of the great performances in American theatrical history, for which she received the Drama Critics' Circle Award and the Donaldson Award. The public glory matched her private victory over tremendous odds. *The Glass Menagerie* was Laurette Taylor's final gift to the theater. She died in her New York City home of coronary thrombosis and was buried next to Manners in the family plot in Woodlawn Cemetery, New York City.

It is unfortunate that the heartbreak in her own life limited Taylor's contribution to the theater and cut her career short. Aside from her days in stock, she played fewer than forty roles. The number and scope of her parts were meager compared to those of such contemporaries as Margaret Anglin and Minnie Maddern Fiske. Further, her career lacked versatility, despite the fact that she was a superb actress in both youthful and mature parts. She shackled her professional growth by acting primarily in the plays of men upon whom she personally depended. When she tried to branch out, such as in a matinee series of scenes from Shakespeare (April 1918) or in the mime piece *Pierrot the Prodigal* (March 1925), her audiences wanted to see her as Peg. She failed to move with the theater of her time. She did not interest herself in the work of such experimental groups as the Provincetown Players, and she disregarded the innovative work of European directors and playwrights because they failed to fire the imagination of Manners, who was, in essence, a late Victorian writer.

Her contribution to the theater was significant in spite of these limitations. Throughout her career critics responded to her ability to create minute realistic details that gave depth to even the shallowest roles. They praised her well-defined transitions of mood, her emotion-filled pauses, her capacity to listen onstage with great intensity and, above all, to project the emotional energy of all her characters. Brooks Atkinson wrote that the virtue of her acting was "improvisation with the radiance of her personality, the chuckle in her voice, the undulation of her walking and the gesturing and kindliness of her spirit" (*New York Times,* Aug. 31, 1938). Onstage she seemed totally natural to most of her audiences, while her technique to theater critics remained an enigma. And yet, some critics believed her to be the greatest American actress of her time.

[The best and most complete single source is Marguerite Taylor Courtney's biography of her mother, *Laurette* (1968), the writing of which was complicated by the fact that Laurette Taylor burned all her personal and theatrical memorabilia when Manners died.

The numerous scrapbooks from the Robinson Locke Collect., the Chamberlain and Lyman Brown Theatrical Agency Collect., and the George C. Tyler bequest, all at the Lincoln Center Lib. of the Performing Arts, contain reviews, programs, photographs, and press clippings. The Museum of the City of N. Y. holds a large collection of photographs of Taylor in most of her major roles.

One gains an insight into Taylor's own goals as an actress in the following articles, which she wrote: "The Actor Who Would Not Be Starred," *Colliers,* Mar. 1912, pp. 18, 24–25; "The Quality Most Needed," *Green Book Mag.,* Apr. 1914, pp. 556–562; "Versatility," *Theatre,* Jan. 1918, pp. 31–32. In 1942 Miss Taylor wrote a series of articles for *Town and Country* magazine: "An Actress Talks Back to Noel Coward," May 1942, p. 65; "Lynn Fontanne," Aug. 1942, pp. 44, 60; "Mrs. Pat ad Libitum," Dec. 1942, pp. 98–99, 114.

For a critical evaluation of Taylor's career, see Norris Houghton, "Laurette Taylor," *Theatre Arts,* Dec. 1945, pp. 688–696. The *N.Y. Times* obituary (Dec. 8, 1946) provides important details about the circumstances of her death, but is often inaccurate in tracing the chronology of her career.]

WENDY ROUDER

TEGGART, FREDERICK JOHN (May 9, 1870–Oct. 12, 1946), historian and sociologist, was born in Belfast, Ireland, the sixth of eleven children of Scottish-Irish parents, William Teggart and Anna (Hume) Teggart. The father worked for a distilling and wholesale liquor firm. The family was Methodist. Following his schooling in Belfast, Teggart briefly attended Methodist College there, transferring after a year to Trinity College in Dublin. In 1889 his family immigrated to the United States, settling near San Diego, Calif., where his father engaged in citrus farming. Determined to complete college, Teggart enrolled in 1891 at Stanford University, where he followed a course with heavy emphasis on history, geography, and anthropology. A wide and insatiable reader, he haunted the Stanford library, where he became acting librarian following his graduation with the B.A. degree in 1894. On May 24, 1894, he married Adeline Margaret Barnes. They had two sons: Barnes, who died during his youth, and Richard Victor, who became a social scientist, author, and librarian. In 1898 he moved to San Francisco to become librarian of the noted Mechanics Mercantile Library.

Teggart's career as university teacher and scholar began in 1905, when he became lecturer in the extension division of the University of

California. At about this time he became acquainted with the publisher Hubert Howe Bancroft, whose vast and burgeoning private collection of documents and books in Southwestern and Western American history remains the world's greatest. Teggart was among those who urged the University of California to purchase the collection, and in 1906, when it was moved to Berkeley, Teggart became honorary custodian of the new Bancroft Library. The following year Teggart resigned his San Francisco post to become custodian. His scholarly labors were at first confined to compiling bibliographies of the collection and to editing and translating some of the material for publication. In 1911 he was appointed associate professor of Pacific Coast history, although he never held an advanced degree until 1943, when the University of California conferred the LL.D. upon him. He became associate professor of history in 1916. About this time he was succeeded as head of the Bancroft Library by Herbert Eugene Bolton. Stability in the department of history suffered because of the intense scholarly and personal rivalry between these two notable scholars; and in 1919 the university, loath to lose the services of either, allowed Teggart to found the department of social institutions at Berkeley. He remained chairman until his academic retirement in 1940, becoming full professor in 1925.

Even had other considerations of personal nature not prevailed, there would have been reason enough for Teggart's move from the field of history. His own temper of thought had become increasingly critical of conventional historiography. In 1910 his notable article, "The Circumstance or the Substance of History," appeared in the *American Historical Review*. Even today it remains relevant to the reigning issues in the discipline. A frontal attack on unilinear, narrative history as the then virtually unquestioned framework for the utilization of historical materials, this prophetic article clearly shows Teggart's critical attack on conventional history writing, his rapidly developing interest in the social sciences—particularly anthropology and historical geography, and his concern with enduring theory and method. A succession of articles and books followed, including *Prolegomena to History: The Relation of History to Literature, Philosophy, and Science* (1916), *The Processes of History* (1918), and *Theory of History* (1925). All his writings that precede *Rome and China* (1939) evidence a profound concern with the theoretical foundations of a genuine science of

society. This is the true hallmark of his career, and his manner of developing the theme has kept his writings fresh and evocative.

The central concern of Teggart's theoretical studies was the vital necessity of building a science of society based on the use of concrete historical materials, while freeing this use from the conventionalized framework of unilinear, narrative history writing. From Teggart's viewpoint, this conventionalism of method and approach dated from the ancient Greeks and their interest in historical genealogy on the one hand and timeless developmental growth on the other.

Only through a radical departure from these forms, according to Teggart, could a genuine science of society be created. Such a science, while making historical events fundamental, would take them out of simple narrative historiography. It would accept the social sciences' interest in change but would remove from it self-defeating premises of growthlike development. A comparative science, it would deal with classes of events, structures, and processes in their own terms, rather than forcing them into Western time sequences. Teggart was one of the first historians to protest the then utter neglect by Western historians of non-Western peoples, and his courses at Berkeley as early as 1911 included the Chinese, central Asians, Indians, and the people of the Middle East.

His persisting objective was the use of historical materials as science proper, rather than as an art form alone. Within this larger objective Teggart focused on the influence upon human behavior of migrations, of social and cultural collisions, and of breakups of what he termed "idea systems" in history. Believing that historians and social scientists alike failed to give proper due to crises and control periods, Teggart constantly emphasized historical discontinuities as well as continuities and the qualitative differences between large-scale and minor social changes.

Although he had only a few students, Teggart's influence became worldwide. Arnold Toynbee, among others, acknowledged prime indebtedness to his seminal ideas, particularly those in *The Processes of History*. *Rome and China* (1939), a study of political, military, social, and cultural relations between the two great societies at the time of the Caesars, was Teggart's major effort to apply his theories of comparative history and change. Despite the failings inevitable in a work of such scope, it is a remarkable study, still too little appreciated by historians and social scientists. Teggart's ample influence was limited by a temperament that tended to become increasingly solitary and reluctant to admit the value of the works of his contemporaries. Although deeply respected at Berkeley, he had almost no friends, apart from those in his own small department. With the exception of brief annual vacations with his family, he rarely left Berkeley during his last twenty-five years. Even so, his catholicity of interest, and his cosmopolitan—even univeral—cast of mind were notable to all who knew or read him. He died of cancer at his home in Berkeley, at the age of seventy-six; his remains were cremated.

[So far as is known, no MSS were left by Teggart, whose home was twice destroyed by fire. His major books have been noted in the text of this article; two of his important articles are "The Approach to the Study of Man," *Jour. of Philosophy*, 16 (1919), 151–156; and "Geography as an Aid to Statecraft," *Geographical Rev.*, 8 (1919). This article is based on the author's recollections; the minutes of the Regents of the Univ. of Calif.; a brief interview with Richard V. Teggart of Berkeley; and *Who Was Who in America*.]

ROBERT NISBET

THACHER, THOMAS DAY (Sept. 10, 1881–Nov. 12, 1950), New York lawyer, judge, and civic leader and solicitor general of the United States, was born in Tenafly, N.J., the oldest of four children and the only son of Thomas Thacher and Sarah McCulloh (Green) Thacher. His paternal grandfather was Thomas Anthony Thacher, professor of Latin at Yale and influential in its administration. His father was a prominent lawyer in New York City. After preparatory education at Taft School and Phillips Academy, Andover, young Thacher followed family tradition by attending Yale, from which he received a B.A. degree in 1904. During the next two years he studied at Yale Law School. He left without completing his degree and in 1906 was admitted to the New York bar and entered the office of his father's firm, Simpson, Thacher and Bartlett. Except during periods of public service, Thacher remained associated with the firm throughout his life, becoming a partner in 1914.

A Republican, Thacher took his first government post in 1907, when he became an assistant United States attorney for the Southern District of New York under Henry L. Stimson. Over the next three years he won recognition for his prosecution of customs frauds. Thacher's great admiration for Stimson was probably responsible, at least in part, for his subsequent dedication to public service. When the United States entered World War I, Thacher joined the American Red Cross Commission to Russia (1917–1918) with the rank of major. The commission, led by William Boyce Thompson and Raymond Robins, at first supported the Russian war effort and then, after the Treaty of Brest-Litovsk, sought to prevent German seizure of Russian resources. Like his superiors, Thacher respected the new Soviet government and vainly urged Washington to cooperate with the Bolshevik leadership.

In 1925 President Coolidge appointed Thacher to the United States district court for the Southern District of New York. He resigned five years later to become solicitor general of the United States under President Hoover, a post he held until 1933. As a federal judge, Thacher was instrumental in investigating the operation of the bankruptcy law in New York City, and as solicitor general, the nation's second highest legal officer, he directed a thorough examination into this subject. His report to Hoover was the basis for amendments to the bankruptcy law that reduced the opportunities for abuses on the part of greedy lawyers by extending the control of the courts over bankruptcy proceedings and hastening the process of settlement.

Thacher returned to his law practice in 1933. In that same year, along with such prominent New Yorkers as Samuel Seabury, Charles C. Burlingham, and Charles H. Tuttle, he fathered the Fusion movement that made possible the election of Fiorello H. La Guardia as reform mayor of New York City. The continued support of Thacher and other prominent Republicans was also vital in helping the pro-New Deal La Guardia gain the Republican nomination when he ran successfully for reelection in 1937 and 1941. La Guardia appointed Thacher in 1935 as head of a commission to write a new city charter; and Thacher took an active part in the campaign the next year, which secured voter approval of the charter, along with a proposal for the election of councilmen by proportional representation. Through the Citizens Non-Partisan Committee. whose chairman he became after Seabury stepped down, Thacher worked to elect antimachine candidates to the city council, defended proportional representation against attacks, and advanced the cause of county government reform by campaigning for the creation of citywide offices of sheriff and register (finally achieved in 1941). Thacher often acted as a referee or the head of a city fact-finding committee in cases involving possible corruption of public officials.

Though receptive to municipal reform, Thacher looked with less favor on the New

Deal program of President Franklin D. Roosevelt. Along with other eminent lawyers, he expressed doubt of the constitutionality of many New Deal measures. Yet during World War II, Thacher joined three other noted attorneys —Burlingham, George Rublee, and Dean Acheson—in an important letter to the *New York Times* (Aug. 11, 1940), which argued that ample legal authority existed for Roosevelt's plan to transfer overage naval vessels to England.

Mayor La Guardia appointed Thacher corporation counsel of New York City in January 1943, but several months later Thacher was named by Gov. Thomas E. Dewey to fill a vacancy on the New York State Court of Appeals. He was elected that fall to a full fourteen-year term, having been nominated by all major parties, and served until circulatory illness forced his retirement from the bench in 1948.

Trim and vigorous in appearance, direct and unpretentious in manner, a man of high ideals and steadfast integrity, Thacher drew and held the loyalty of his associates. He impressed those who knew him by his meticulous care for detail and his practical knowledge of how to achieve results. Among his other activities, he served as a fellow of the Yale Corporation from 1931 to 1949 and as president of the Association of the Bar of the City of New York (1933-1935). He was a Presbyterian in religion. Thacher married Eunice Booth Burrall of Waterbury, Conn., on Nov. 9, 1907. They had three children: Sarah Booth, Mary Eunice, and Thomas. His first wife died in January 1943, and on July 20, 1945, he married Eleanor Burroughs (Morris) Lloyd of Philadelphia. Thacher died of a coronary thrombosis at his home in New York City at the age of sixty-nine. He was buried in Brookside Cemetery, Englewood, N.J.

[Thacher's extensive papers are in the possession of his son, Thomas Thacher, Riverdale, N.Y. His reminiscences, in the Oral Hist. Project, Columbia Univ., must be used with care since Thacher, ill at the interviews, never had the opportunity to correct the transcript. Other biographical sources are the Raymond Robins Papers, State Hist. Soc. of Wis., which contain numerous personal and professional letters from Thacher; interview with Thomas Thacher; *N.Y. Times*, various issues, 1930–1950, especially Thacher's obituary, Nov. 13, 1950; memoir by Louis Connick and Whitney N. Seymour in Assoc. of the Bar of the City of N.Y., *Memorial Book*, 1951; Charles Garrett, *The La Guardia Years: Machine and Reform Politics in N.Y. City* (1961); George F. Kennan, *Soviet-American Relations, 1917–1920*, vols. I and II (1956–1958). Thomas D. Thacher, *Russia and the War* (1918) in the Manuscript Collect., N.Y. Public Lib., is a typewritten copy of his report, which argued futilely for the creation of an American commission

to assist the Soviet government in reorganizing and reconstructing its internal affairs. See also *Nat. Cyc. Am. Biog.*, XXIV, 229–230 (on his father), and XL, 110–111; Yale Univ., *Obituary Record*, 1950–1951. The best likeness of Thacher is a painting by Sidney E. Dickinson (1940), which hangs in the building of the Assoc. of the Bar of the City of N.Y.]

CHARLES GARRETT

THAW, HARRY KENDALL (Feb. 1, 1871– Feb. 22, 1947), whose murder of Stanford White in 1906 became a cause célèbre, was born in Pittsburgh, Pa., the son of William Thaw and Mary Sibbet (Copley) Thaw. William Thaw, whose father was of Scots-Irish and English Quaker stock and had settled in Pittsburgh in 1804, was a high official in the Pennsylvania Railroad Company, having amassed a fortune in canals, railroading, and related enterprises. The Thaw family, including ten children (five of them by William Thaw's first wife, who died in 1863), was among Pittsburgh's most prominent. After 1888 they lived at Lyndhurst, a mansion built that year at a reputed cost of $2.5 million.

William Thaw's death in 1889 left his eighteen-year-old son Harry with a fortune of $3 million plus an interest in valuable coke-producing properties. Young Thaw entered Western University of Pennsylvania (later the University of Pittsburgh) as a member of the class of 1893 but in 1892 transferred to Harvard University, where he enrolled as a special student in the arts and sciences; he never received a college degree. Although short, bespectacled, and unprepossessing in appearance, he soon attracted attention as a playboy. On frequent European jaunts he gave elaborate and expensive dinner parties, including one in Paris at which the invited guests included 100 actresses.

In New York City in 1901 Harry Thaw became infatuated with Evelyn Nesbit, a chorus girl then appearing in *Floradora,* a popular musical review of the day. The strikingly beautiful Nesbit had been brought to Manhattan from Pittsburgh two years earlier, when only fifteen, by a mother eager to launch her upon a stage career. Quickly winning a place for herself, she posed for Charles Dana Gibson, the magazine illustrator and creator of the "Gibson Girl," and was the model for one of his most famous sketches, *The Eternal Question,* in which the long tresses of a lovely young woman curl to form a question mark. She had also formed an attachment with the prominent architect Stanford White, then in his fifties and at the pinnacle of his career as a partner in the firm of McKim, Mead, and White. He had designed numerous public buildings and private mansions in New York and elsewhere. Thaw and Nesbit were married in Pittsburgh on Apr. 4, 1905.

On the evening of June 25, 1906, while on a trip to New York, Thaw and his wife encountered Stanford White sitting alone at a table on the roof garden of the Madison Square Garden —which he had designed—watching a performance of *Ma'mzelle Champagne*. With neither warning nor direct provocation, Thaw drew a pistol and shot the architect dead. In two murder trials (the first ended in a hung jury) conducted in the full glare of publicity, Thaw described his rage at his wife's stories of her earlier relationship with White; District Attorney William T. Jerome crossed swords with the prominent defense lawyers; and several psychiatrists offered conflicting testimony as to Thaw's mental state. Although Nesbit—and her mother—had apparently originally welcomed the liaison with White, at the trials she offered lurid testimony describing how he had seduced and ruined her, testimony shrewdly aimed at exploiting the "white slave" issue then much in the public mind. Thaw's mother, a strong-willed woman active in church and philanthropic causes in Pittsburgh, dedicated herself and her checkbook to her son's defense. In the second trial, concluded in 1908, Thaw was found innocent by reason of temporary insanity and was committed to Matteawan State Hospital for the Criminally Insane in Fishkill-on-Hudson, N.Y. Mrs. Thaw's continuing legal efforts included an impassioned, rambling pamphlet written in 1909 (*The Secret Unveiled*), in which she described her son as "an average young man with a chivalrous nature" who was being persecuted by a cabal of Stanford White's influential friends. Thaw received preferential treatment at Matteawan, including several vacations, and in August 1913, under suspicious circumstances, he "escaped" to Canada. In July 1915, having been extradited to New York and placed on trial on the escape charge, he was declared sane by a jury and released.

Thaw's days in the limelight were far from over, however. In 1916 he divorced Evelyn Nesbit, charging her with infidelity and denying the paternity of her son, Russell (born in 1909). In that same year a warrant for his arrest was issued in New York, on a charge of horsewhipping a youth whom he had allegedly coerced into accompanying him east from California. A suicide attempt early in 1917 led to an additional seven years in institutions for the insane in Pennsylvania. Freed again in 1926, Thaw described the vicissitudes of his life in a privately published work, *The Traitor*. A venture into the field of movie production early in the 1930's produced nothing but legal entanglements with several actresses and showgirls. Although he acquired the Philadelphia estate of the publisher J. Bertram Lippincott in 1939, he was constantly on the move between New York, California, Pennsylvania, Virginia, and Florida. He died in 1947 in Miami Beach, Fla., following a coronary thrombosis; after Presbyterian services, he was buried in the Thaw family plot in Allegheny Cemetery in Pittsburgh. In an unsparing obituary judgment, the *New York Times* characterized him as a man whose "colossal vanity" and appetite for sensation had ultimately "become monotonous to the point of nausea." In 1955 a Hollywood film, *The Girl in the Red Velvet Swing*, told again the story of the act of passion that almost half a century before had first propelled Thaw into the glare of publicity.

[The major sources are *N.Y. Times*, Feb. 23, 1947; *Pittsburgh Press*, Feb. 23 and 25, 1947; *Pittsburgh Sun-Telegraph*, Feb. 24 and 26, 1947; Gerald Langford, *The Murder of Stanford White* (1962); Adela Rogers St. John, "She Remembers Murder!" (on Evelyn Nesbit), *Am. Weekly*, Aug. 14, 1955; *Pittsburgh Bulletin*, Jan. 4, 11, and 18, 1930 (feature on Mary Copley Thaw).]

PAUL BOYER

THOMAS, WILLIAM ISAAC (Aug. 13, 1863–Dec. 6, 1947), sociologist, was born in Russell County, Va., the third of six sons and fourth of seven children of Sarah (Price) Thomas and Thaddeus Peter Thomas, a farmer and Methodist preacher. The mother came of Virginia stock that has been traced back to the eighteenth century. The father was descended from a German immigrant who settled in Lancaster County, Pa., in 1749. Typical of early American sociologists, William I. Thomas came from a rural Protestant background, but little is known of his early life beyond these simple facts. Seeking better schools for the children, the Thomases moved first to Morristown, Tenn., and then in 1874 to Knoxville, where in 1880 William entered the University of Tennessee. There he majored in literature and the classics. As an undergraduate he not only excelled scholastically but was also a "big man on campus." He won highest honors in oratory, became president of the Literary Society, and was captain of the university officer-training unit.

After graduation, he continued his studies at Tennessee in English literature and modern languages and was awarded the first doctorate that the university granted in 1886. He then shifted to teaching natural history and Greek as adjunct professor. He married Harriet Park on June 6, 1888. Typical of university professors of the period, he took the required year abroad in Germany in 1888-1889 at Göttingen and Berlin. There he was exposed to the German folk psychology of Moritz Lazarus and Hermann Steinhal and to ethnology, and as a result, his interests began to be redirected. When he returned to the United States, he accepted a professorship in English at Oberlin College and held this post until 1895.

Although established as a professor in a traditional subject at one of the outstanding undergraduate colleges in the country, he took steps to retrain himself. During the academic year 1893-1894, while on leave from Oberlin, he worked at the University of Chicago as one of the first graduate students in the newly established department of sociology. His studies were directed by Albion W. Small and Charles Henderson. In the summer of 1894 he taught sociology at the University of Chicago; during the following year, after having completed his doctorate, he became an assistant professor. Until 1918 he remained at Chicago, devoting himself to research for his central work on the Polish community.

Sociology was rapidly emerging as a full-fledged discipline at the University of Chicago, and Thomas was at the center of the nation's leading department of sociology, which both carried on research and trained graduate students. He was deeply interested in the anthropological materials and taught courses that were essentially anthropological. In 1900, he was promoted to associate professor and in 1910 to professor. From 1908 to 1919 Thomas had charge of the Helen Culver Fund for Race Psychology, which enabled him to travel extensively in Europe and collect much of the material on which *The Polish Peasant in Europe and America* (5 vols., 1918-1919) was based.

While at Chicago, Thomas expressed a deep concern with social policy, another of the central themes of the "Chicago school." He became a strong advocate of woman's rights. He and his wife maintained close connections with social-work circles, and he hoped that his work would supply a sound basis for social policy and his wife maintained close connections with the work of the Chicago Vice Commission. Thomas' connection with the University of Chicago ended abruptly in 1918 when an extramarital affair became the focus of intense publicity. Arrested for violating the Mann Act, he was dismissed from his post despite the intervention of Albion Small. It was said at the time that the arrest and ensuing scandal were actually measures of political intimidation directed against Thomas' wife, an activist in the peace movement.

He never again held a regular university post. He moved to New York City and spent the next year (1918-1919) working on the Americanization studies sponsored by the Carnegie Corporation in New York. He collaborated with Robert E. Park on the manuscript of *Old World Traits Transplanted* (1921), but the corporation chose not to acknowledge his authorship, on the grounds that the scandal attached to Thomas' name would harm the corporation. After the Americanization study he was supported from 1920 to 1923 by research funds provided by Mrs. W. F. Dummer of Chicago, a wealthy woman interested in sociological inquiry and social welfare problems. He spent the rest of his professional life engaged primarily in research projects, with occasional visiting university appointments. He lectured at the New School for Social Research from 1923 to 1928. For the Laura Spelman Rockefeller Memorial he prepared a study, *The Child in America* (1928), with Dorothy Swaine. From 1930 to 1936 he traveled regularly to Sweden and worked closely with the Social Science Institute of the University of Stockholm. He served on the Social Science Research Council in 1932-1933. His last academic appointment was as lecturer in sociology at Harvard University (1936-1937). His last book, *Primitive Behavior: An Introduction to the Social Sciences,* was published in 1937.

His marriage to Harriet Park was terminated by divorce in 1934 and on Feb. 7, 1935, he married Dorothy Swaine, who had been associated with his research work for a number of years. The final phase of his career was spent in semiretirement and independent research, first in New Haven until 1939 and then in Berkeley, Calif., where he died at the age of eighty-four of arteriosclerosis. His ashes were placed in the Old Gray Cemetery, Knoxville, Tenn.

W. I. Thomas launched into his sociological writing with a rich background in classical studies, history, and languages. His first writings relied heavily on anthropological studies. In the course of his lifetime he produced an extensive bibliography, in which he more and more explicitly formulated his conceptual framework and undertook the collection of primary data to explore and test his basic hypotheses. His career can be divided into three phases.

The first, from his initial publication, "The Scope and Method of Folk Psychology" (*American Journal of Sociology,* 1896), until he took charge of the Helen Culver Research Fund for Race Psychology in 1908, was the period in which he developed from a descriptive ethnographer into an empirical sociologist and social psychologist and in which he laid the foundation for his theoretical approach to social organization and social change. During this time, he wrote mainly on the sociological aspects of sexual behavior and on race—a field that he initially called folk psychology and that was to become the core of his social psychology. His first influential volume appeared in 1908 under the title *Source Book for Social Origins: Ethnological Materials, Psychological Standpoint, Classified and Annotated Bibliographies for the Interpretation of Savage Society.* This book represented Thomas' approach to the fusing of theory and empirical data. It contained not only a voluminous collection of essential source materials but also his careful comments on each selection and his bibliographic annotations. This format of the analytic source book was reproduced in the highly influential *Introduction to the Science of Sociology* by Robert E. Park and Ernest W. Burgess (1921) and became the standard approach for the teaching of sociology.

His second period began with the appearance in 1912 of "Race Psychology; Standpoint and Questionnaire, with Particular Reference to the Immigrant and the Negro" and included the intellectual climax of his career, *The Polish Peasant in Europe and America.* During this phase, which ended with the publication of *Old World Traits Transplanted* (1921) and *The Unadjusted Girl* (1923), Thomas demonstrated his sociological vision, conceptualizing social organization as the core of sociology and social psychology as the subjective aspect of social organization.

The final period of his work is not easily characterized, but he became interested in new techniques of research and the evaluation of other people's research.

When Thomas arrived at the University of Chicago, he was immediately exposed to the philosophical currents of the new pragmatism and empiricism, which reflected his own predilections. He had first to discover the limitations of Herbert Spencer's social evolution, which dominated the social science of the period. He also had to modify crude biological determinism in social behavior. His critiques of existing theories of racial and sexual difference

would alone have established him as a pioneer figure in sociology. Thomas was not a devotee of German philosophical sociology, particularly as represented by Ferdinand Tönnies, who conceptualized society as undergoing a linear transformation from *Gemeinschaft* to *Gesellschaft,* from the simple intimate but highly organized rural society to the large-scale impersonal and disorganized contemporary society. He did not conform to the pattern of the rural-born sociologist-moralizer who abhorred the culture of the city; he was too urbane and sophisticated to embrace the values of primitive and rural society.

Thomas also rejected simple technological and economic determinism. Instead, he formulated a normative concept of society that incorporated technological and economic factors in a more holistic system and that served as a forerunner of the "social organization and personality" framework. Social control and the process of social change were his core concerns. They were seen as the result of the "reciprocal dependence between social organization and individual life organization," or social personality, as he was prone to call it. Sociology was the study of social organization—namely, the socially systematized schemes of behavior imposed as rules upon individuals. His key concepts centered on the distinction between values and attitudes. Values were "the more or less explicit and formal rules of behavior by which the group tends to maintain, to regulate and to make more general and more frequent the corresponding type of actions among its members." The organization of these values constituted social organization. On the other hand, social personality was the pattern of attitudes that an individual holds; the subjective aspects of social organization.

In *The Polish Peasant in Europe and America* the full dimensions of Thomas' intellect are revealed. The book has a scope that was immense not only by the standards of his day but by those of later years. It took more than a dacade to gather the source materials in both the United States and Europe and to prepare the final publication, which totaled 2,244 pages. His original goals had been even more ambitious, since he had hoped to study a variety of Eastern European immigrant groups. The effort could not be duplicated in one man's lifetime. He selected the Poles for investigation because they were the largest, and therefore the most visible, ethnic group on the South Side of the Chicago area; it was not Thomas' style to select bizarre and minor themes. In addition, the Poles were a social problem in Chicago, and Thomas never segregated his intellectual interests from his social concerns. But fundamentally, Thomas was developing the comparative method in sociology, and the differences between the patterns of social change of the Polish peasant in Poland and in the United States permitted him to develop such an approach. In 1913 on one of his trips to Poland, he met the Polish philosopher Florian Znaniecki, who turned out to be his most useful source and informant and in time his collaborator.

It was of decisive importance that Thomas visited Poland during a period of the reemergence of a "larger" Polish community and the strengthening of its societywide institutions. Poland was in the throes of national liberation, seeking to become a "new nation." The tensions in Poland were those associated with the process of integration of communal life into a society experiencing industrialization and urbanization. Thomas did not observe a nationality group weakening under social change, for through its intellectuals, cooperative movements, and political agitation, it was demonstrating considerable vitality. These events sharpened the contrast with the social disruption that the Polish community was experiencing at the same time in the United States. They helped fashion Thomas' comparative outlook without forcing him to assume or to conclude that the outcome of social change was not inevitably disorganization.

Thomas made a deep impact on American sociology and on the development of the discipline. He rejected speculative and formal theory, and his achievements in linking theoretical and empirical research set a model for sociological investigation. The real world of immigrants, prostitutes, intellectuals, and the rest pervaded his scholarly writings, and the genius of the man was that he really made use of his categories and concepts in the collection of his voluminous empirical materials. His approach was broadly holistic and has come to be designated configurational analysis, in that he was concerned with the study of a society or a cultural group in its entirety. He identified a set of the basic units and objects of analysis that have come to be standard—namely, the primary group, community, large-scale organization, and total society. Thomas' major contribution to primary-group analysis, aside from his empirical studies, was his insistence on linking the study of primary groups to that of larger institutions. He contended that primary groups are essential aspects of larger social groups that were viable; primary groups are not residual categories.

At the level of community analysis, he identified both the spatial and social-psychological dimensions of community in a manner that loosely combined the ecological and normative approaches. He focused on the community of residence. He was aware that modern society separated place of work from place of residence, but he never fully developed the linkage between organization of work and the residential community in industrial society. In linking community to the larger society, Thomas presented trenchant analysis of both the educational institutions and the press; he failed, however, to concern himself sufficiently with political institutions, which was characteristic of the Chicago school of empirical sociology.

Thomas' name has been strongly associated with his social psychology, especially interactional social psychology. He sought to develop a theory of motivation and used the somewhat undifferentiated idea of wishes as the basic elements of his postulates about social personality. He was clear that the four wishes—new experience, security, response, and recognition—were arbitrary categories; but they were taken up and widely publicized by others without regard for their theoretical character. Thomas' interactional social psychology had its roots in the work of the pragmatists and especially John Dewey. He was pressed for empirical investigations, which were not grounded in an instinctual or psychoanalytical approach but which emphasized the social interaction of men and groups as the basis of human motives and social personality. His formulation of the "definition of the situation" came to be a dominant theme in social psychology as he argued that that "which men define as real is real."

At the heart of Thomas' sociological writings was a persistent interest in understanding the processes of social change. He had a systems outlook, since he saw social change continually passing through the phases of social organization, disorganization, and reorganization. Social change, however, was not a gradual, simple, or smooth process but represented the interplay of social organization with social personality as social groups were confronted by personal and social crises to which they had to respond. He was a pioneer in the study of social movements, collective outbursts, and rebellions. Of particular importance was his focus on the role of the intellectual in stimulating and guiding the process of social change.

Thomas rejected simple analogies with the natural sciences, in particular, because he emphasized the need for understanding the subjective meanings social groups placed on the external environment. He also avoided mechanical notions of causality and single variable explanations. Thomas was a "functionalist" in the sense that he believed that sociologists had to ask hypothetical questions about the conditions under which optimum social relations would occur. He believed that the accumulation of rational knowledge was to be desired as an end in itself, but its main purpose was for human betterment.

At the empirical level, Thomas' main research tool was human documents, those expressions that supply indicators of human motives and values. He used letters and other types of written materials, but the life-history document was crucial. He insisted also on the need for intensive direct observation in order to understand attitudes and values, and his outlook has remained a central theme in sociological research. His work challenges the research value of the brief interview, which he felt manipulated the respondent excessively.

Thomas was a sociologists' sociologist; his impact was immediate and direct on the key figures of his period. With the publication of *The Polish Peasant* he achieved a commanding intellectual position. His concepts, such as the "definition of the situation" and his distinction between personal and social disorganization have remained central to empirical investigation. He was also a powerful teacher and a campus figure who attracted wide attention among students because of his strong sense of objectivity and his analysis of highly controversial topics of his day, such as the sociology of sex and women. He directly trained a generation of graduate students who were to be the leading figures in the development of sociology. He recruited Robert E. Park to the University of Chicago, on whom he had a strong impact; and in turn Park was the central figure in American sociology for two decades after Thomas left the University of Chicago. Thomas maintained a sympathetic, but critical, outlook toward social work and helped formulate many of the ideas that have come to be associated with community participation and decentralization of civic life. He was highly critical of the excessive emphasis on "Americanization" and recognized the positive contribution of ethnic identifications to personal adjustment and to the vitality of a democratic society.

His work has continuing and central relevance to social scientists, professional groups, and public leaders concerned with the adaptation of community life to social change, whether the issues be those of an advanced industrial nation or a developing society. Thomas was one of the pioneer American sociologists who in the first quarter of the twentieth century converted sociology from a philosophical and speculative subject into a systematic research discipline.

[The most extensive biographic materials on Thomas are contained in Morris Janowitz, *W. I. Thomas: On Social Organization and Social Personality*, The Heritage of Sociology Series (1966), which also contains an overview and evaluation of Thomas' writings, selections from his most important works, and a complete bibliography. Thomas is the subject of Chapter 8 of Howard W. Odum, *American Sociology: The Story of Sociology in the United States* (1951). A particularly penetrating account of his work is Kimball Young, "The Contribution of William Isaac Thomas to Sociology," *Sociol. and Soc. Res.*, 47, nos. 1–4 (Oct. 1962; Jan., Apr., July, 1963).]

MORRIS JANOWITZ

THORNDIKE, EDWARD LEE (Aug. 31, 1874–Aug. 9, 1949), educational psychologist, was born in Williamsburg, Mass., the second son and second of four children of Edward Roberts Thorndike and Abby Brewster (Ladd) Thorndike. Both parents were natives of Maine, where the elder Edward Thorndike had first practiced law before embarking on a career as a Methodist clergyman in Massachusetts. The four children showed early signs of precocity, and all went on to subsequent careers in the scholarly world, Ashley and Mildred in English literature, Lynn in medieval history, and Edward in psychology.

Thorndike attended various local elementary schools in Massachusetts—the family moved through the usual succession of pastorates—and, after the age of twelve, the high schools of Lowell, Boston, and Providence (R.I.). He attended Wesleyan University in Connecticut from 1891 to 1895, where he did outstanding work in several subjects of the traditional classical curriculum and earned the B.A. but formed no firm career plans. From Wesleyan he went to Harvard, initially to study English literature; there he earned his second B.A. in 1896 and the M.A in 1897 and decided to make psychology his lifework. As recounted in an autobiographical sketch, Thorndike had neither heard nor seen the word "psychology" until his junior years at Wesleyan, when he took a required course in the subject with Andrew C. Armstrong. Neither the textbook, James Sully's *Elements of Psychology*, nor

Armstrong's excellent lectures aroused much interest, and the course itself seemed to have had little impact. As a senior, Thorndike studied parts of William James's *The Principles of Psychology* in connection with a prize examination and found them more stimulating than any book he had ever read. The opportunity to take a course with James the following year fanned the fires of his nascent interest, and as he later wrote, "by the fall of 1897, I thought of myself as a student of psychology and a candidate for the Ph.D. degree" (Murchison, p. 264).

Pioneering in the use of animals for psychological research, Thorndike began a number of experiments on instinctive and intelligent behavior in chickens, conducting them first in his own rooms and then in the basement of the James residence. ("The nuisance to Mrs. James," he later reflected, "was, I hope, somewhat mitigated by the entertainment to the two youngest children," Thorndike, p. 3). In 1897–1898 a fellowship brought Thorndike to Columbia, where he worked primarily under James McKeen Cattell, a psychologist trained in Wilhelm Wundt's laboratory at Leipzig, and Franz Boas, an anthropologist who had studied at Heidelberg, Bonn, and Kiel; he derived from both a lifelong interest in the quantitative treatment of psychological data. He completed the work for the doctorate in 1898 with his thesis, "Animal Intelligence," which inaugurated the scientific study of animal learning and at the same time laid the foundation for a dynamic psychology emphasizing stimulus-response connections (known as "S-R bonds") as the central factors in all learning.

Upon graduation, Thorndike accepted an instructorship at the College for Women of Western Reserve University, where he spent the year 1898–1899 teaching education and continuing his investigations into animal learning. It was there that James Earl Russell, the newly appointed dean of Teachers College, Columbia University, found him. "I knew of him," Russell later reminisced, "as a student who had made a study of the behavior of monkeys —a pretty good stepping-stone, it seemed to me, to a study of the nature and behavior of children. At that time neither the term nor the subject of educational psychology had been created; but I had a notion that a field of study so obviously fundamental to educational theory and practice should have both a name and a sponsor in the kind of teachers college which I was planning" (*Teachers College Record*, Feb. 1926, p. 460). Thorndike came to

Teachers College in 1899 as instructor in genetic psychology and remained there for the rest of his life, earning the title adjunct professor in 1901, professor in 1904, and professor emeritus in 1941.

From the beginning, Thorndike's work was precise, systematic, and original; and it quickly came to symbolize his generation's commitment to developing a true science of education. His initial experiments on animal learning involved an animal in a problem box, a situation in which a specific behavior, such as pressing a lever, was rewarded by a specific outcome, such as the appearance of a bit of food. The animal was placed in the box; after a period of random activity, it pressed the lever and received the reward. In subsequent trials the period between the animal's being introduced into the box and the pressing of the lever steadily decreased, to the point where it would make an immediate lunge at the lever. This process by which the animals tended to repeat ever more efficiently and economically behaviors that were rewarded, Thorndike called "learning," and out of his experiments came a new theory of learning and a series of "laws" founded on that theory. The theory maintained that learning involves the joining of a specific stimulus to a specific response through a neural bond, so that the stimulus regularly calls forth the response. In Thorndike's words, the bond between the stimulus and the response is "stamped in" by being continually rewarded. And from this followed Thorndike's primary law of learning, the "law of effect," namely, that a satisfactory outcome of any response tends to "stamp out" the bond or connection. Whereas previous associationist theories had emphasized merely practice or repetition—what Thorndike called "exercise"—Thorndike insisted upon giving equal weight to outcomes, to reward or punishment to the learner.

The implications of these propositions were nothing less than revolutionary. On the theoretical side, Thorndike was able to avoid the age-old problem of defining mind by simply eliminating it as a separate entity: mind in his view appears in the behavior of the organism as it responds to its environment. And beyond this, by confining himself to the study of *observable* behavior, Thorndike was able to discard the Biblical view that human nature is fundamentally sinful, the Rousseauean view that human nature is fundamentally good, and the Lockean view that human nature is fundamentally plastic, arguing instead that human nature is nothing more or less than a mass of "original tendencies" in man, as these are subsequently modified by learning. On the practical side, Thorndike was led to emphasize *activity* as the basic pedagogical principle, insisting that one learns by responding correctly to a given stimulus and having that correct response rewarded, and to stress the *specificity* of all learning as against the traditional notion that certain studies have general value in many realms of activity because they "discipline the faculties of the mind." Both emphases lent strong support to contemporary demands for more individualized and utilitarian approaches to education and thus served the cause of reformers who were seeking to introduce greater flexibility into elementary and secondary schooling.

During the five decades of his active career, Thorndike applied his theoretical principles and empirical techniques to a remarkable range of educational problems; indeed, he may well have been the most influential educational theorist of the early twentieth century. Holding that whatever exists at all exists in some amount and can hence be measured, he developed some of the earliest and most widely used American tests of aptitude and achievement, and subsequently, with George D. Strayer, profoundly shaped the movement to survey the efficiency and effectiveness of school systems. Thorndike himself prepared a series of arithmetics for the elementary grades, and his pioneering *Teacher's Word Book* (1921), an alphabetical list of 10,000 words that occur most frequently in the general use of the English language, provided the foundation for the most important series of school readers to appear between the two world wars. (He himself compiled a set of dictionaries for school use.) More generally, his laws of learning led to a fundamental rethinking of the entire school curriculum and affected everything from organization of course content to techniques for appraising student progress. His studies of adult learning, after 1925, opened up the field of adult education by establishing, contrary to time-honored belief, that the relative ability of men and women to learn after the age of twenty-five declines less than one percent a year. In all of this work, one might add, Thorndike made continuing contributions to more general theory and method in psychology and the social sciences. Energetic and efficient, he was highly productive; his bibliography includes more than 500 titles, of which seventy-eight were books. Prominent among the latter are his *Educational Psychology* (3 vols., 1913–1914), *The Measure-*

ment of Intelligence (1927), and two works in which he refined his earlier theories of the learning process, *The Fundamentals of Learning* (1932) and *Psychology of Wants, Interests and Attitudes* (1935).

Throughout his life, Thorndike was active in many scientific and scholarly associations, serving as president of the American Psychological Association (1912), the American Association for the Advancement of Science (1934), the New York Academy of Sciences (1919-1920), and the American Association for Adult Education (1934-1935). He was awarded honorary degrees by Wesleyan (1919), Iowa (1923), Columbia (1929), Chicago (1932), Harvard (1934), Edinburgh (1936), and Athens (1937). He was elected to the National Academy of Sciences in 1917.

William James is said to have remarked once to Cattell that more than any other man he knew, Edward Thorndike had the quality most essential to a scientist or an artist— the ability to see things apart from acquired perspective or personal preference. Florence L. Goodenough described him as "an ardent and tireless experimenter"; Robert S. Woodworth observed: "He was a rapid worker, quick to see the possibilities in a problem and select a first line of attack, willing to shift his attack as he got further into the problem, persistent in following up his leads, prompt in coming through with a published result" (*Science,* Mar. 10, 1950). Interestingly enough, by his own report Thorndike tended throughout his life to pursue work in response to outside pressure or opportunity rather than inner motivation or need. Thus he wrote in 1934: "Obviously I have not 'carried out my career,' as the biographers say. Rather it has been a conglomerate, amassed under the pressure of varied opportunities and demands" (Murchison, p. 266).

Thorndike was often at the center of controversy, with psychologists who thought his connectionist theories ill-suited to explain higher mental processes, and with liberal social scientists who saw in his rigorous scientism a defense of the social and economic status quo. Yet he was apparently able to maintain a general levelheadedness and goodwill, even under the sharpest criticism. Above all, there is widespread—though not unanimous—testimony to the vigor and excellence of his teaching. According to one former student, "'Look to the evidence' was his constant admonition. His courses were often strenuous, but they were never dull. He had a gift for lively illustration, for the well-pointed witticism" (Goodenough, p. 301).

On Aug. 29, 1900, Thorndike married Elizabeth Moulton of Boston; they had five children, four of whom lived to maturity and themselves followed scientific careers: Elizabeth Frances in mathematics, Edward Moulton in physics, Robert Ladd in educational psychology, and Alan Moulton in physics. Having enjoyed generally robust health throughout his life, Thorndike succumbed to a cerebral hemorrhage at his home in Montrose, N.Y., shortly before his seventy-fifth birthday. He was buried in Hillside Cemetery, Peekskill, N.Y.

[Geraldine Joncich, *The Sane Positivist* (1968), is a full-scale study of Thorndike and his work. Other biographical references include autobiographical sketch in Carl Murchison, ed., *A Hist. of Psychology in Autobiog.*, III, 263–270 (1936); Thorndike's *Selected Writings from a Connectionist's Psychology* (1949); *Teachers College Record*, Feb. 1926, a special issue containing appreciative essays by former students and colleagues; and the following obituaries and memoirs: Arthur I. Gates in *Psychological Rev.*, Sept. 1949; Robert S. Woodworth in *Science*, Mar. 10, 1950, and in Nat. Acad. Sci., *Biog. Memoirs*, XXVII (1952); Florence L. Goodenough in *Am. Jour. of Psychology*, Apr. 1950.]

LAWRENCE A. CREMIN

THURBER, JEANNETTE MEYER (Jan. 29, 1850–Jan. 2, 1946), patron of music, was born in New York City, the daughter of Henry Meyer and Anne Maria Coffin (Price) Meyer. The ancestry of her mother, born in Wappingers Falls, N.Y., earned her membership in the Daughters of the American Revolution. Her father was a Danish immigrant of some means and an amateur violinist. Nettie Meyer, as Jeannette was called, was privately educated and then sent to France to study music. There she became acquainted with the Paris-centered, government-funded system of musical education; her attempts to introduce the system to her native country were to make her the outstanding American nonprofessional supporter of music prior to Elizabeth Sprague Coolidge. She was encouraged in her ambition by her well-to-do husband, Francis Beatty Thurber, a wholesale grocer, later a lawyer, and an organizer of the National Anti-Monopoly League (1881), whom she married on Sept. 15, 1869.

Her ambition was to establish a government-supported musical conservatory in Washington with branches in numerous cities, where talented young Americans would receive superior musical training. Meanwhile, she supported foreign musical study for Americans and numerous New York musical activities, including Theodore Thomas' free youth concerts in 1883 and his first American Wagner festival in 1884.

She also supported the first appearance of the Boston Symphony Orchestra in New York (1887). By 1885 she had secured a New York State charter for her American School of Opera, which opened in New York City in December of that year with eighty-four voice pupils. Soon to be known as the National Conservatory of Music, it had among its trustees the August Belmonts, Andrew Carnegie, and Theodore Thomas. Its incorporators included prominent persons from such cities as Boston, Baltimore, Chicago, and San Francisco, where it was hoped branches could be established.

To forward her plans, she induced Thomas to join her in forming a company to produce operas in English, preferably with American singers (a distinct handicap), and with Thomas as musical director. Her husband joined her in contributing lavishly to her two projects. The American Opera Company, called by the *New York Times* an audacious experiment, opened in New York in January 1886 and presented, among other works, the first American performance of Delibes' *Lakmé*. Even in competition with the Metropolitan Opera Company, the new organization's productions surpassed any New York had seen, with one qualification—the capability of some of the soloists. Thurber accompanied the group's tour that spring, trying to form auxiliary organizations in the cities where it appeared. She was only moderately successful, and the whole venture, although artistically impressive, was financially disappointing. The resultant defection of several backers forced its reorganization as the National Opera Company. A second season ended as the first, and Thomas resigned; the disastrous management of Charles E. Locke caused the enterprise to collapse early in January 1888.

The National Conservatory of Music thereafter received Thurber's undivided energies. Mme. Fursch-Madi had been the conservatory's first director, and when the curriculum was expanded to include all departments of operatic production, other outstanding musicians were engaged for all positions. Thurber's dream of making it a national institution was realized when Congress, in a unique act, incorporated it, with the power to grant diplomas, in 1891. As a result, Thurber was able to persuade Antonín Dvořák to become its head in 1892. The school's pioneering policy of giving financial aid without discrimination according to sex or race enabled many blacks to receive a musical education. Among them was Harry T. Burleigh, an accomplished baritone who called Dvořák's attention to American plantation melodies. At

Thurber's suggestion the composer wrote several compositions influenced by these themes, including his Symphony No. 9 (*From the New World*). Dvořák returned to his homeland in 1895 and was succeeded by other notable directors, among them Emil Paur (1899-1902) and Vassily Safonoff (1906-1909), and the school enjoyed an international reputation. But Thurber's hopes for federal grants-in-aid to the arts were premature, and with Thomas' departure for Chicago in 1891, she lost an influential ally in her efforts to solicit private funds. Consequently, the conservatory gradually declined, a process abetted by the increasing conservatism of her musical tastes. By the 1920's the school was little more than a name, but Thurber fought on for her ideal. In a letter to the *New York Times* of Jan. 1, 1928, she reported that she was seeking from Congress a grant of land in the national capital on which to erect a conservatory.

Jeannette Thurber's commitment to bettering opportunities for women was expressed in her support of such organizations as the Woman's Art School of Cooper Union, the New York Exchange for Woman's Work, and the YWCA. A dark-eyed slight woman, she was striking in appearance, simple in tastes, courageous, persistent, and daring. Except for a skirt, she wore tailored masculine clothes. She was a devoted mother, taking her children and their nurse with her when traveling with the opera company's first tour. She was a member of the Presbyterian church. Thurber died of a cerebral hemorrhage in Bronxville, N.Y., at the home of her daughter Marianne. Her other children were Jeannette and Francis, Jr.

[The major sources are *Notable Am. Women*, III (1971); *Nat. Cyc. Am. Biog.*, vol. D (1934) which includes a portrait; "The National Conservatory of Music," *Harper's Weekly*, Dec. 13, 1890, which includes a portrait; obituary, *Musical Am.*, Jan. 10, 1946, which includes a portrait; marriage notice, *N.Y. Times*, Sept. 16, 1869; Thurber letters, *N.Y. World*, Jan. 22-24, 1887, and *N.Y. Times*, Jan. 1, 1928; and Thurber scrapbooks, at Lincoln Center Lib. of the Performing Arts. See also *N.Y. World*, Jan. 10, 1887, and *N.Y. Times*, Oct. 6, 1887; editorials, *N.Y. Times*, June 29, 1886, *N.Y. World*, Jan. 24, 1887, *N.Y. Times*, Jan. 12, 1946; Rose Fay Thomas, *Memoirs of Theodore Thomas* (1911); James G. Huneker, *Steeplejack*, 2 vols. (1921); Benjamin Brawley, *The Negro Genius* (1937); and Henry T. Finck, *My Adventures in the Golden Age of Music* (1926).]
MARY TOLFORD WILSON

TILZER, HARRY VON (July 8, 1872-Jan. 10, 1946), composer of popular songs, was born Harry Gumm in Detroit, Mich., the third of six sons of German Jewish parents, Jacob Gumm and Sarah (Tilzer) Gumm. Shortly after his birth the family moved to Indianapolis,

Ind., where his father acquired a shoe store. A theatrical stock company that rehearsed immediately above the store early lured Harry toward show business. At fourteen he left home to become a tumbler in the Cole Brothers circus, and a year later he joined a traveling repertory company and then a burlesque troupe. It was around this time that he took his mother's maiden name, adding the "Von" for distinction.

Although lacking formal musical training, Harry learned to play the piano and several other instruments by ear and soon began to write and sing his own compositions. A vaudeville star he met in Chicago, Lottie Gilson, liked his work and advised him to seek his fortune in New York City. Arriving there in 1892, he found a job as a saloon pianist and began writing songs for vaudeville performers; within a couple of years the famous Tony Pastor was featuring several Von Tilzer tunes at his Union Square Music Hall. He sold most of these songs outright for modest sums, and few were published. In 1894 he joined George Sidney in a moderately successful "double Dutch" vaudeville act.

Von Tilzer's first notably successful song was "My Old New Hampshire Home," written in 1898 with the lyricist Andrew B. Sterling, who became his most frequent collaborator. It sold more than two million copies and induced Maurice Shapiro, a leading publisher, to take the young composer into his firm, which was renamed Shapiro, Bernstein, and Von Tilzer. Two years later Von Tilzer published one of his best-known works, "A Bird in a Gilded Cage," which he later described as the "key that opened the door of wealth and fame" for him. Presenting the theme that money cannot buy happiness, the song was conceived by its lyricist, Arthur J. Lamb, as telling the story of a kept woman, but the upright Von Tilzer, insisting that the heroine be married, adjusted a crucial line to read "She married for wealth, not for love."

The year 1905 was perhaps Von Tilzer's most productive, for in that year he wrote "On a Sunday Afternoon," "Down on the Farm," "In the Sweet Bye and Bye" (not to be confused with the hymn of that title), and two widely popular songs: "The Mansion of Aching Hearts," a pathetic sequel to "A Bird in a Gilded Cage," and "Down Where the Wurzburger Flows," which Nora Bayes sang to such acclaim in her Orpheum Theatre act that she became known as the Wurzburger Girl. On the strength of these hits, Von Tilzer set up his own music publishing company on Twenty-eighth Street between Fifth and Sixth avenues, a section later known as Tin Pan Alley. (Von Tilzer himself is credited with inspiring the phrase when a music journalist noted that his piano, which had newspaper strips against the strings, made a sound like hitting a tin pan.) His success attracted four of his brothers to New York and the music business, all of whom took the name Von Tilzer. Albert became a songwriter, best known for his "Take Me Out to the Ball Game." The other three became the heads of music publishing companies (Jules headed his brother's Harry Von Tilzer Music Publishing Company). A fifth brother became a theatrical attorney.

Von Tilzer continued his rise to the top of the music industry. Sensitive to what the public wanted, he had a keen ear for the sentimental. The hits came easily: "Wait 'til the Sun Shines, Nellie" (1905), "Where the Morning Glories Twine Around the Door" (1905), "I Want a Girl Just Like the Girl That Married Dear Old Dad" (1911), "And the Green Grass Grew All Around" (1912). These were not merely tunes to be sung and forgotten; they became institutions. Where there were barbershop quartets, there were Von Tilzer ballads. His songs are as reminiscent of early vaudeville shows as straw hats and canes. Von Tilzer was equally adept at other popular styles: Negro dialect songs like "Alexander" (1904) and "What You Goin' to Do When the Rent Comes 'Round?" (1905); Irish ballads like "That Old Irish Mother of Mine" (1920); catchy melodies like "I Love, I Love, I Love My Wife, But Oh You Kid" (1909). He was one of the earliest composers to write a song based on a popular dance ("The Cubanola Glide," 1909). Von Tilzer tried his hand at several Broadway musicals, but with indifferent results, probably because of his ignorance of orchestration.

Von Tilzer's songwriting career largely ended with World War I. His decline was hastened both by the geographical dispersal of the publishing industry, which broke the monolithic influence of Tin Pan Alley, and by the unsentimental musical tastes of the Jazz Age. Although he continued in the publishing business, his only postwar song of any success was "Just Around the Corner" (1925). Early in his publishing career Von Tilzer encouraged the young Irving Berlin, and in 1916 he accepted the first song of George Gershwin.

On Aug. 10, 1906, Von Tilzer married Ida Rosenberg. They apparently had no children.

After the death of his wife in 1932, he lived at the Hotel Woodward in New York City, where he died of a heart attack at the age of seventy-three. Von Tilzer was one of Tin Pan Alley's most prolific composers; by his own estimate he wrote some eight thousand songs, about two thousand of which were published. His brothers carried on the family's musical tradition after his death.

[The letters, papers, and unpublished autobiography of Von Tilzer are in the possession of his brother Harold Gumm. On Von Tilzer, see Isaac Goldberg, *Tin Pan Alley* (1961), which contains a portrait; Sigmund Spaeth, *History of Popular Music in Am.* (1948); David Ewen, *Great Men of Am. Popular Song* (1970); and Nat Shapiro, *Popular Music* (1967), vol. V.]

HERBERT I. LONDON

TITTLE, ERNEST FREMONT (Oct. 21, 1885-Aug. 3, 1949), Methodist clergyman, was born in Springfield, Ohio, the eldest among two sons and one daughter of Clayton Darius Tittle and Elizabeth (Henry) Tittle. He was of mixed English, Scots-Irish, and German stock, his father's ancestors having immigrated to Maryland in the mid-eighteenth century. A clothing salesman in a town wracked by economic dislocation, Clayton Tittle never enjoyed more than middling success. He was jovial and good-natured, but a heavy drinker, and there are indications that his son was embittered by his father's weakness. His mother was a devout Methodist, whose invalidism and grief over the death of her infant daughter made her dependent on Ernest until her own early death. Intense, conscientious, and ambitious, the boy worked hard in and out of the classroom. He enrolled at Wittenberg College in Ohio but transferred after a year to Ohio Wesleyan, graduating in 1906 with a B.A. degree and highest academic honors. Influenced by the evangelical atmosphere of Wesleyan, by the idealism of the current progressive ferment, and by his own inner drive to seek fame, Tittle determined upon a life of service and a profession of prestige. Accordingly, he prepared for the Methodist ministry at Drew Theological Seminary in New Jersey and earned the B.D. degree in 1908; his ordination followed in 1910.

Tittle's initial appointment (1908) to a four-point country circuit near Christiansburg, Ohio, was a two-year purgatorial experience. The sottishness of the rustic place depressed him, but he gave his best and sustained both mind and faith by the prophetic writings of Walter Rauschenbusch, the Baptist apostle of the social gospel. He was sustained, too, by the love and loyalty of Glenna Myers, an attractive Springfield girl four years his senior whom he married on June 11, 1908. They had three children: John Myers, Elizabeth Ann, and William Myers.

There followed in rapid succession appointments to pastorates in Dayton, Delaware, and Columbus, Ohio, these increasingly prestigious calls being at once a tribute to Tittle's mounting youthful reputation and evidence that the currents of theological liberalism and the social gospel were running strong within Northern Methodism. When the United States entered World War I, Tittle responded to President Wilson's crusading appeal by serving as a YMCA secretary in Alabama and in France. In the trenches at Saint-Mihiel he saw the terrible cost of war. The memory of his experiences in France stiffened his later unconditional opposition to war—a conviction unshaken even by Pearl Harbor. In late 1918 he returned to the United States and to a new pastorate, the First Methodist Episcopal Church of Evanston, Ill.

Tittle's Evanston ministry of thirty-one years was one of continuing trials yet ultimate triumph. Physically, First Church was transformed into an impressive Gothic sanctuary, the "Cathedral of American Methodism." Membership mounted steadily; congregations averaging 1,500 gathered every Sunday for public worship, and each week some 6,000 individuals of all faiths or none utilized the church's recreational and educational facilities. Tittle was determined that First Church serve the community, and it came to occupy a central place in the life of Northwestern University and Garrett Biblical Institute (later Theological Seminary) and the Chicago area. The worship services were formally structured and conducted with majesty and solemnity, breaking with early American Methodism's emphasis on freedom, sentimentalism, and subjectivism. Tittle's sermons, painstakingly prepared and delivered without artful adornment, were themselves acts of worship. Acknowledged among his generation's greatest preachers, Tittle comforted the afflicted and afflicted the comfortable, confronting men and nations with God's word. As he once cautioned a class of seminarians, "The prophet is not a man before a microphone saying: 'I predict'; he is a man declaring: 'Thus saith the Lord.'"

Tittle quickly gained a national reputation and became the recognized leader of Methodism's liberal ministers. At meetings of the annual, jurisdictional, and General Conference,

few men's voices carried greater authority; and he served on countless denominational committees, most notably the World Peace Commission. He was active in the affairs of the Federal Council of Churches and many other interdenominational bodies and attended the major 1937 Oxford Conference. A popular preacher on university campuses, he was the recipient of honorary degrees from Ohio Wesleyan, Wittenberg, Garrett, and Yale. Twice he was asked to give the Lyman Beecher Lectures at Yale, the most signal honor in American Protestantism.

The significance of Tittle's career lies in the fact that he was not only a working minister with heavy parish responsibilities but also a prophet of social change. He was active in the work of the American Civil Liberties Union. No Methodist preacher labored more courageously to end racial segregation in Protestantism, and the nation. His critique of unfettered capitalism was incisive. Above all, his understanding of the New Testament compelled him to become, in the 1920's, an absolute pacifist. Consequently, throughout his ministry he faced heavy fire, both from influential churchmen such as Reinhold Niebuhr who accused him of utopianism and from envious "patriots" who branded him a traitor, "nigger-lover," and "Red." Yet the majority of his parishioners, many of conservative persuasion, consistently supported him.

A gravely dignified man, Tittle commanded respect without conscious effort. Yet he was not dour, and his dry wit and humility endeared him to men who were in profound intellectual disagreement with him. His dedication to the ministry led him to overtax his strength and nerves. He suffered a long series of coronary troubles culminating in a fatal heart attack in Evanston at the age of sixty-three. His ashes were buried in the chapel of First Church.

[The voluminous Tittle Collect. is deposited in the library of Garrett Theological Seminary. Of Tittle's twelve published volumes—mostly collections of sermons—probably the most enduring is *A Mighty Fortress* (1950); the foreword by Paul Hutchinson is the finest brief interpretation of Tittle's life. Robert Moats Miller attempts a fuller examination and more critical assessment in *How Shall They Hear Without a Preacher? The Life of Ernest Fremont Tittle* (1971), the footnotes and bibliography providing a guide to source materials. Walter G. Muelder, *Methodism and Society in the Twentieth Century* (1961), is useful on the broader setting of Tittle's career.]

ROBERT MOATS MILLER

TOLMAN, RICHARD CHACE (Mar. 4, 1881-Sept. 5, 1948), physical chemist and mathematical physicist, was born in West Newton,

Mass., the eldest son and second of three children of John Pike Tolman and Mary (Chace) Tolman, both of well-established and prosperous New England families. Edward Chace Tolman, his brother, became an eminent psychologist, and a maternal uncle, Arnold Buffum Chace, was chancellor at Brown University for many years. Richard attended local public schools and spent summers on Cape Cod, where he often went sailing by himself. His father, a graduate of the Massachusetts Institute of Technology and later a trustee, was the president of Samson Cordage Works; his mother came from a long line of Quakers. Their blend of Puritan and Quaker values, emphasizing the virtues of hard work and service to mankind, played a major role in Tolman's development as a scientist with a strong social conscience and with a personal life characterized by plain living.

Upon graduation from M. I. T. in 1903 with a B.S. degree in chemical engineering, Tolman went to Germany for a year, where he studied first at the Technische Hochschule in Berlin and then gained practical experience at an industrial chemical laboratory at Crefeld. Convinced at this point that he did not want to join the family business, Richard returned to M. I. T. as a graduate student; shortly thereafter he joined Arthur Amos Noyes's new Research Laboratory of Physical Chemistry. Noyes became both mentor and close friend; under his supervision, Tolman served as instructor in theoretical chemistry (1907-1909) and research associate (1909-1910) in physical chemistry while investigating the electrical effects produced in a rotating electrolytic solution by the action of a centrifugal force. In deriving an expression for the electromotive force produced, he used kinetic arguments, in addition to conventional thermodynamical reasoning of the day, and showed that both approaches yield the same equation. For this work he received the Ph.D in 1910. Tolman taught briefly at the University of Michigan (instructor, 1910-1911) and the University of Cincinnati (assistant professor, 1911-1912). At Cincinnati, with the aid of Earl Osgerby, he made a series of measurements on the electromotive force produced by the acceleration of electrolytes. Turning next to metallic conductors, Tolman with T. Dale Stewart, demonstrated the production of an electromotive force when a coil of wire rotating at high speed about its vertical axis is mechanically accelerated and then brought quickly to rest with suitable brakes. Working with copper, aluminum, and silver wire, they made

the first laboratory determination of the inertial mass of electrons in metals (1916). This work was done at the University of California, Berkeley, where Tolman remained (assistant professor, 1912-1916) until called to the University of Illinois in 1916 as professor of physical chemistry.

In the closing days of World War I, he resigned from the faculty to accept the rank of major in the army and serve as chief of the newly established Dispersoid Section of the Chemical Warfare Service. Charged with studying the production of toxic and nontoxic smoke screens and candles, the division also tested airplane ammunition, using the "hangfire measurer," a machine developed by Tolman. In Washington he crossed paths again with Noyes, who, as chairman of the Committee on Nitrate Supply, was pressing the government to continue a peacetime program on the nitrogen products used in explosives and fertilizers. The Fixed Nitrogen Research Laboratory of the Department of Agriculture began operations at the close of the war in the old headquarters of the Chemical Warfare Service at American University. Tolman plunged wholeheartedly into his new responsibilities (associate director, 1919-1920; director, 1920-1922); he described the place as "a great mixture of business, science and politics" and added, "I enjoy all of them." In his hands, the laboratory became a mecca for the best young physical chemists, who attacked a wide range of pure and applied scientific problems, including the chemistry of nitrogen pentoxide, the cyanamide and arc process of nitrogen fixation, the separation of helium from natural gases, the theory of catalysis, and the rate of chemical reaction. Here, Tolman worked together with Sebastian Karrer and Ernest W. Guernsey on a modified method of measuring the mass of the electric carrier in conductors; this study was completed in 1926 in Pasadena, with the aid of Lewis M. Mott-Smith.

In 1922 he joined the faculty of the new California Institute of Technology as professor of physical chemistry and mathematical physics, through the efforts of Noyes, who in 1919 had resigned from M. I. T. to become the full-time director of the Gates Chemical Laboratory at Caltech. Tolman became dean of the graduate school as well (1922-1946); in later years, he served also as a member of its executive council. A meticulous teacher, he would cover the blackboard with equations and notes before a class began. Known for his dry wit and affectionate sense of humor, Tolman quickly became Caltech's unofficial toastmaster, a job he relished as much as guiding the institute to the pinnacle of academic distinction.

Although the main thrust of his work in statistical mechanics, relativistic thermodynamics, and cosmology was mathematical and theoretical, his interests at Caltech were broad and ranged over all fields of science. In the 1920's, Tolman published a number of important papers in the field of chemical kinetics in gaseous systems. Starting from first principles in statistical mechanics, he analyzed completely the problem of accounting for the rate at which chemical reactions occur. His theoretical treatment of monomolecular thermal and photochemical reaction rates underscored the need to clarify the meaning of the loosely defined concept of the energy of activation. This done, Tolman turned to the experimental work of Farrington Daniels and his co-workers on the decomposition of nitrogen pentoxide—the best example of a first-order unimolecular reaction over a range of concentrations and temperatures—as a check on the then-current proposed mechanisms of chemical reaction. In particular, he showed in 1925 that the simple radiation theory of reaction proposed by Jean Perrin and W. C. McC. Lewis did not adequately account for known rates of reaction. These studies not only reveal Tolman's precise reasoning and great physical intuition but also his consuming interest in using statistical mechanics in dealing with quantum mechanical phenomena. In addition to a number of papers and a book on the subject, *Statistical Mechanics with Applications to Physics and Chemistry* (1927), he produced *Principles of Statistical Mechanics* (1938), a monograph that remains a classic in its field. In it, Tolman used the work of J. Willard Gibbs (*Elementary Principles in Statistical Mechanics*) as his model for refashioning statistical mechanics, using quantum, rather than classical, mechanics as the starting point for the science.

The book is dedicated to his friend and colleague, J. Robert Oppenheimer—he had come to Caltech as a national research fellow after meeting Tolman in Göttingen in the summer of 1927—who, in Tolman's words, contributed "minor suggestions and major enlightenment" in the preparation of the manuscript. Years later, in recalling their discussions, Tolman said, half-jokingly, to an audience that included Oppenheimer, "My book on statistical mechanics contains certain passages—written under his influence—that are so terribly highbrow that I can't understand them myself."

From its inception in 1905, Tolman followed closely the development of relativity theory and its application to the problems of cosmology. Together with Gilbert N. Lewis, he published the first American account of Einstein's special theory of relativity (1909); his introductory textbook *The Theory of the Relativity of Motion* appeared in 1917. This early interest in relativity theory, spurred on by Hubble's discovery that red shifts are proportional to distance, led to a series of studies at the institute in the 1930's on the applications of the general theory to the overall structure and evolution of the universe. His pioneering work on the thermodynamics and behavior of radiation in nonstatic cosmological models of the universe drew public attention because it challenged the pessimistic view required by classical thermodynamics. In particular, he derived relativistic expressions for the first two laws of thermodynamics and found that reversible processes could take place both at a finite rate and without increase in entropy. In his comprehensive treatise *Relativity, Thermodynamics, and Cosmology* (1934), Tolman presented the model of a universe expanding and contracting rhythmically like a beating heart, arguing that gravity has the effect of counteracting the influence of radiation, thus preventing the complete cessation of motion as predicted by the second law.

During World War II, he served as vice-chairman of the National Defense Research Committee, as scientific advisor to Gen. Leslie R. Groves on the Manhattan Project, and as United States advisor to the wartime Combined Policy Committee. After the war, he became scientific advisor to Bernard Baruch, United States delegate to the United Nations Atomic Energy Commission. He also served as chairman of the Declassification Committee, which prepared recommendations for the release of information about the development of the atomic bomb.

Tolman married Ruth Sherman, a psychologist, on Aug. 5, 1924; they had no children. Honors received during his lifetime include election to the National Academy of Sciences in 1923, the United States Medal for Merit, the Order of the British Empire, and the honorary degree of doctor of science from Princeton University in 1942. He suffered a cerebral hemorrhage while working in Pasadena and died in the Huntington Memorial Hospital. Cremation and burial at the Mountain View Mausoleum crematory followed. He willed the bulk of his considerable estate to the California Institute of Technology with the stipulation that the scientific research supported by it "should be of a character to extend the bounds of human knowledge without special reference to practical applications."

[Tolman published four books and over a hundred scientific papers, all of which are chronologically listed in the bibliography appended to the biographical introduction prepared by J. G. Kirkwood, O. R. Wulf, and P. S. Epstein, in Nat. Acad. Sci. *Biog. Mem.,* 27 (1952), 139–153 (with portrait). Details about his family and childhood can be gleaned from his brother's autobiographical notes, written up in B. F. Ritchie, "Edward Chace Tolman," Nat. Acad. Sci. *Biog. Mem.,* 37 (1964), 293–324. A sketch of Tolman's work habits at Caltech is provided in Bernard Jaffe, *Outposts of Science,* pp. 506–514 (1935). His World War II activities are thoroughly covered in Albert B. Christman, *Sailors, Scientists and Rockets,* vol. I (1971). Manuscript sources include letters in the papers of G. N. Lewis, now in the office of the Chemistry Department, Berkeley, and several boxes of correspondence and unpublished manuscripts in the archives at Caltech.]

JUDITH R. GOODSTEIN

TORRENCE, FREDERICK RIDGELY (Nov. 27, 1874-Dec. 25, 1950), poet, playwright, and editor, was born in Xenia, Ohio, the first of three children of Findley David Torrence, a lumber dealer, Civil War veteran, and descendant of one of the town's earliest Scots-Irish settlers, and Mary (Ridgely) Torrence, who had come to Xenia from Maryland, orphaned, at twelve. Save for a two-year sojourn in California, Ridgely (as he was known) spent his boyhood in Xenia, where he received his schooling. He was reared as a Presbyterian, though he later turned away from denominational Christianity. His parents, to whom he felt an abiding attachment, seem never to have understood their son. His father, for example, saved Ridgely's writings during his college years at Miami University in Ohio (1893-1895) and at Princeton (1895-1896) because he felt they provided evidence that his son was losing his mind; and when Ridgely left Princeton without graduating in December 1896 and went to New York City in search of his fortune, he wrote long and frequent letters to his family in Ohio in a vain attempt to justify to them his literary activity and liberated ways. In New York, Torrence found work at the public library, where he remained for six years. More importantly, he met in 1899 the poet and critic Edmund Clarence Stedman, who gave him the encouragement and the introductions necessary to launch his literary career.

Torrence first made his reputation as a poet with the publication of *The House of a Hundred Lights* (1899) and through representation in Stedman's *An American Anthology* (1900). Indeed, the British novelist May Sinclair fo-

cused her 1906 article, "Three American Poets of To-day" (*Fortnightly Review,* September 1906), on William Vaughn Moody, Edwin Arlington Robinson, and Torrence, whose work, she said, was distinguished by his "immense, if as yet somewhat indefinite, promise." It was a promise that remained largely unfulfilled by Torrence's two subsequent books of poetry, *Hesperides* (1925) and *Poems* (1941). His early work is flawed by its Swinburnean ornateness, and there are simply not enough of his later, more economical, and much more accomplished poems, mostly short lyrics, to classify Torrence as anything but a minor poet. In 1900 he had proclaimed his intention to write poetry "that above all *says something,* and that gives men something to chew on," and he wrote good poems proclaiming his pacifism ("Men and Wheat," "The Watcher") and his mysticism ("Eye-Witness"). His best poems, however, are those where an emotional invocation of a sense of loss ("The Son," "Outline," "The Apples") penetrates the poet's careful conventional craftsmanship.

Perhaps Torrence's greatest gift was for friendship. Tall, thin, elegant, a brilliant mimic, he could—and often did—exert great charm. Edwin Arlington Robinson on their first meeting was "unprepared for this sprightly, mischievous being, this incarnation of youth, so individual, yet so free of pose, so fluid, so witty, so imaginative, yet so honest, and so loyal . . . a social being to his fingertips, picking adventure from every bush; a fountain of gracefully rising and falling entertainment" (Hagedorn, p. 164). Torrence made it his regular business, during their thirty-five-year friendship, to cheer up the melancholic E.A.R. and was faithfully at the task during Robinson's final illness. Stedman, who introduced the two men, had been overwhelmed by the young poet, and Torrence later became a close friend of both William Vaughn Moody and Robert Frost, who dedicated a poem to Torrence ("A Passing Glimpse") and remarked of him that "I always keep seeing a light as I talk with him—and of course losing it as quickly; the thing is seeing it." Another writer Torrence met through Stedman was Zona Gale, with whom he had a love affair in 1902-1903, but it was not until Feb. 3, 1914, that Torrence married still another writer, Olivia Howard Dunbar, a New Englander and a graduate of Smith College. They had no children.

At the turn of the century, Torrence had joined with Moody, Percy MacKaye, Josephine Preston Peabody, and Robinson in a campaign to reinvigorate the American theater through verse drama. His own early efforts in this genre, *El Dorado* (1903) and *Abelard and Heloise* (1907), were published in book form but never produced. Nor did his subsequent prose dramas, set in his native Ohio and heavily dependent upon symbolism, reach the stage, though the distinguished actress Alla Nazimova showed an interest in *The Madstone,* written in 1907. But the switch to prose rhythms and the folk tales of his youth led to the three one-act Negro plays, *Granny Maumee, The Rider of Dreams,* and *Simon the Cyrenian,* which were printed as *Plays for a Negro Theatre* in 1917 and performed on Broadway that same year. They marked the first serious dramatic presentation of Negro life and opened the door for the Negro in the American theater. Inspired partly by the playwright's enthusiasm for Irish folk drama, particularly that of J. M. Synge, and partly by recollections of his black boyhood companions in Xenia, the plays presented their Negro characters as sympathetic human beings speaking a faithfully reproduced dialect of their own, and not as stereotypes.

None of Torrence's poems or plays achieved commercial success, and to eke out his living he served variously as assistant editor of the *Critic* (1903), fiction editor of *Cosmopolitan* (1905–1907), and—most importantly—poetry editor of the *New Republic* (1920–1933), where despite his own conservative tastes and the magazine's dearth of space for verse contributions, he printed much of the best of contemporary poetry. He later edited and wrote an introduction for *Selected Letters of Edwin Arlington Robinson* (1940). Torrence maintained his interest in Negro culture, and in 1948 published as his last book *The Story of John Hope,* a biography of the Negro educator. Two years later, on Christmas Day 1950, he died in New York City of lung cancer. He was buried in Woodland Cemetery in Xenia.

Torrence served as visiting professor at Miami University and at Antioch College, was awarded an honorary doctor of letters degree from Miami in 1937, won the Shelley Memorial Award for 1941 and the $5,000 fellowship of the Academy of American Poets in 1947. That he earned no additional honors was as much a matter of temperament as of talent. "I wish," he wrote after first encountering E. A. Robinson in 1900, "I could fix some of his fixity of effort and belief into my own life." On his deathbed fifty years later, he lamented to his wife that he had not worked

harder, accomplished more. "I have all the machinery in here that Frost has," he once told Winfield Townley Scott, "but I lack the dynamo."

[All of Ridgely Torrence's work, with the exception of a reprint edition of *The Story of John Hope,* was out of print in 1973. The only full-scale treatment of Torrence is John M. Clum, *Ridgely Torrence* (1972), a thoughtful and thorough study of his work with substantial biographical background and a brief bibliography. More limited in scope is Lyman Lee Feathers, "Ridgely Torrence and the Search for an Am. Identity" (Ph.D. diss., Univ. of Pennsylvania, 1963). Clum's book is largely based on the 125-box collection of Torrence material at Princeton; for description, see *Princeton Univ. Lib. Chronicle,* Summer 1954. There are good reminiscences of Torrence in Hermann Hagedorn, *Edwin Arlington Robinson* (1938) and Daniel Gregory Mason, *Music in My Time* (1938). On the family, see Michael A. Broadstone, *Hist. of Greene County, Ohio,* II, 20–23 (1918); and Robert M. Torrence, *Torrence and Allied Families,* pp. 76–77 (1938), courtesy of Greene Co. District Lib., Xenia.]

SCOTT DONALDSON

TOWNE, CHARLES HANSON (Feb. 2, 1877–Feb. 28, 1949), editor and author, was born in Louisville, Ky., youngest of the six children of Paul A. Towne, a professor of mathematics, and Mary Stuart (Campbell) Towne. When he was three years old, his family moved to New York City, where Towne acquired his formal education in the city's public schools and, for one year, at the College of the City of New York. In 1901, having served an apprenticeship as an assistant to John Brisben Walker, the editor of *Cosmopolitan* magazine, he joined the staff of the newly founded *Smart Set,* serving successively as editorial reader, associate editor, and finally (1904-1907) editor. Striving for a tone of modernity and sophistication, he opened the pages of *Smart Set* to O. Henry, Zona Gale, James Branch Cabell, and other recent arrivals on the literary scene.

In 1907, when Theodore Dreiser became editor of the woman's magazine *The Delineator,* he hired Towne as fiction editor. Three years later, in the editorial reshuffling that followed Dreiser's departure from Butterick Publications, Towne became editor of *Designer,* a post he held until 1915. Perhaps his most important position was as managing editor (1915-1920) of *McClure's Magazine,* no longer the muckraking journal in which Lincoln Steffens and Ida Tarbell had published their powerful exposés, but still a force in the world of popular magazines. Towne helped transform *McClure's* into an outspoken supporter of the Allied cause and a champion of American involvement in World War I. He was a founding member in 1917 of the Vigilantes, a group of writers and editors who banded together to produce and disseminate pro-war and pro-Allied propaganda in the nation's press. The anthology *For France* (1917) and *Shaking Hands With England* (1918) were products of this intensely political phase of Towne's career. These efforts won for him the warm friendship of Theodore Roosevelt, and after Roosevelt's death, Towne edited an anthology of poems in honor of the former president (*Roosevelt as the Poets Saw Him,* 1923).

In 1920 Towne left the declining *McClure's,* and for the next six years, without regular employment, he turned in earnest to varied literary endeavors, which he had long pursued as an avocation. For years he had contributed verses to such popular magazines as *The Saturday Evening Post,* occasionally collecting these fugitive poems into slim volumes. A longer effort, *Manhattan: A Poem* (1909), had won warm praise from William Dean Howells. In 1925 Towne gathered what he considered the best of his verse into a volume called *Selected Poems.* The reception was mixed: one reviewer perceived "a quiet, unostentatious beauty" in them, but another complained that "almost axiomatic statements are made with tedious solemnity" (*Outlook,* Oct. 21, 1925; *Saturday Review of Literature,* Oct. 17, 1925). Towne also wrote novels, producing in a four-year span *The Bad Man* (1921), *The Chain* (1922), *The Gay Ones* (1924), and *Tinsel* (1925). A prevailing theme, especially in *The Gay Ones,* was the neglect of the old verities and the undermining of traditional social arrangements by the younger generation. Again, the critical response was not encouraging.

Perhaps the happiest product of this period of indefatigable writing was a series of light and pleasant travel essays, a form well adapted to Towne's style and abilities. Serialized in various magazines, they were later published in book form as *Loafing down Long Island* (1921), *Ambling through Acadia* (1923), and *Jogging around New England* (1939).

In 1926 Towne returned to magazine publishing as editor of *Harper's Bazaar,* remaining in this position for three years. In 1931-1937 he contributed a regular literary column to the *New York American*; in 1939 he published an etiquette book for men, *Gentlemen Behave*; and in 1940-1941 he toured as one of the three doctors in a road-company production of *Life With Father.* His autobiography, *So Far So Good* (1943), was a good-tempered anecdotal account of his variegated career. Towne died shortly after his seventy-second

birthday and was buried in Earlville, N.Y. He never married.

[In addition to *So Far So Good,* see *N.Y. Times,* Mar. 1, 1949, p. 25; *Who Was Who in Am.,* II (1950); and Frank Luther Mott, *History of Am. Mags,* vols. 3, 4, and 5 (1938-1968), comprehensive index at the end of vol. 5. Most of Towne's nearly thirty books are listed in *Catalog of Books Represented by Lib. of Cong. Printed Cards Issued to July 31, 1942* (1945); the novels and *Selected Poems* are included in *Book Rev. Digest.* Much of Towne's autobiographical *Adventures in Editing* (1926) is to be found, often verbatim, in *So Far So Good.*]

PAUL BOYER

TYLER, GEORGE CROUSE (Apr. 13, 1867-Mar. 13, 1946), theatrical manager and producer, was born in Circleville, Ohio, and raised in nearby Chillicothe. His parents, George H. Tyler, founder and publisher of one of Chillicothe's two newspapers, and Harriet (Parkhurst) Tyler, were leading citizens in the conservative town of some 10,000 people. Frequent theatergoing in Chillicothe, Columbus, and Cincinnati was an important influence in Tyler's childhood. His formal education ended when he was twelve. After being apprenticed in his father's print shop for almost a year, he ran away from home three times during the 1880's to work as a tramp-printer, going as far west as San Francisco and as far south as Sanford, Fla.

During the winter of 1887-1888 Tyler's father rented Clough's Opera House in Chillicothe for his son to manage. The youth renamed it Clough's Grand and booked in such stars as Thomas Keene, Nat Goodwin, Clara Morris, May Irwin, and Julia Marlowe. Tyler's first theater management did not last even a full season, however, because he guaranteed any terms the touring companies requested. His idealism was far greater than the box-office receipts.

After nearly a year in the Government Printing Office in Washington, D.C., Tyler went to New York and took various jobs, such as a printer at the *World* and a reporter for the *Dramatic News* and the *Dramatic Mirror.* For the next five years he was an advance agent for, among others, the Hanlon Brothers and, in 1894, James O'Neill. After producing several financially disastrous shows and spending one more season as an advance agent, he began his first respectable theatrical venture. He obtained the financial backing of Theodore A. Liebler, a former lithographer with $3,000 to invest, for *The Royal Box,* written by and starring Charles Coghlan. That production in 1897 marks the founding of Liebler and Company, a partnership of Tyler's organizational and promotional expertise and Liebler's money. Their first play was artistically successful but financially unprofitable, but their next production, *The Christian* (1898), starring Viola Allen, established them financially. During its three years it netted the company over $500,000.

Until 1914 Liebler and Company produced or managed over 300 first-class attractions in New York and on tour. With the inevitability of financial loss on some shows, Tyler's company earned a profit of almost $3 million on seven of their productions during their first ten years. In scope their ventures were outranked only by the Theatrical Syndicate and the Shubert empire of that period. Most important were Tyler's management of Mrs. Patrick Campbell, who first toured America in 1901; he brought Eleonora Duse to this country in 1902 and managed Arnold Daly, who introduced several early George Bernard Shaw plays to America, and Madame Réjane. He brought the Abbey Theatre Company to New York in 1911, coping with the accompanying riots in objection to the image of the Irishman as seen in *Playboy of the Western World*. That tour was the first of four he managed for the company in the United States. He worked with many well-known actors and produced the works of a wide variety of playwrights during that time. In the spring of 1910 he gave Eugene O'Neill his first professional theater job—assistant company manager for *The White Sister* tour. In 1911 Tyler assumed management of the New Theatre, renaming it the Century, where he staged some of his most elaborate productions and experimented with children's theater. In 1914 he brought Joseph Urban, a leader in the new stagecraft movement, to Broadway to design *The Garden of Paradise,* one of the company's most ambitious productions. Unfortunately they had invested at a time when credit was tight and theater attendance was cut by the effects of World War I; as a result the company filed for bankruptcy.

Between 1915 and 1918 Tyler produced shows with Marc Klaw and A. L. Erlanger's backing. Although his first production, *Moloch* (1915), lost Tyler some $30,000, later productions proved successful. His *Pollyanna* (1916) starred Helen Hayes. In 1916 and 1917 he featured Laurette Taylor in three financially successful shows. Twenty-three benefit performances of one of them, *Out There,* with an all-star cast, raised $683,248 for the Red Cross.

Tyler became an independent manager in 1918, continuing to produce new plays and a few revivals. Of particular interest were Booth Tarkington's *Clarence* (1919), starring Alfred Lunt; experimental productions of Eugene O'Neill's *Chris Christopherson* (1920)—an early version of *Anna Christie* (1921)—with Lynn Fontanne as Anna, and *The Straw* (1921); *Dulcy* (1921), the first collaboration of George S. Kaufman and Marc Connelly; and *Macbeth* (1928), the only production in America that utilized the talents of the famous British designer Gordon Craig. From then until his last production, *For Valor* (1935), Tyler was most concerned with his all-star revivals. Providing the public the best of the past, he brought back such stars as Mrs. Fiske, John Drew, and William Gillette. He published his autobiography, *Whatever Goes Up,* in 1934 in collaboration with J. C. Furnas.

Tyler, known as the little Napoleon of the theater, was five feet, six inches tall, rotund and round-faced. He was a cigar-smoking gambler who thrived on the risks of theatrical production. "Compared with the call to produce," he once said, "the call of the wild is as the chirp of the bullfinch." His strong loyalties were to Booth Tarkington and James O'Neill, to fellow producers such as the Frohmans and Erlanger, and to the traditions of the nineteenth-century theater. He was a pioneer automobile sportsman. He avidly disliked the shallowness of the motion picture industry and the competitiveness of the Shubert brothers. He is best known for his introduction of European talent to America and his ability to elicit new dramatic material from other than theater sources. Some 90 percent of his 350 productions were new plays, and he was disappointed that he could not get Rudyard Kipling and O. Henry to write for the theater. As the theater began to move toward psychological realism and social radicalism, Tyler became increasingly adamant about the virtues of the past.

Tyler never married. In 1943 he suffered a cerebral hemorrhage and was admitted to McKinney Sanitarium, Yonkers, N.Y., where he remained until his death from a heart attack. He died penniless and was buried in Chillicothe, Ohio.

[Sources include Tyler's autobiography; Kenneth Harris, "George C. Tyler and the Liebler Company: A Study of the American Theatrical Producer at Work, 1897–1914" (unpublished Ph.D. diss., Univ. of Iowa, 1973); John P. Workman, "The George C. Tyler Star Revivals, 1924 to 1928" (unpublished Ph.D. diss., Univ. of Ill., 1968); Tyler's two articles "Play Producing and the Fickle Public," *Everybody's Magazine,* Sept. 1911, and "What I Think Is a Good

Play," *Theatre,* May 1916. Obituary in the *N.Y. Times,* Mar. 15, 1946. The theater collections at Princeton Univ. and the Lincoln Center Research Lib. for the Performing Arts have significant collections of Tyler documents. Paul Sheren, "Gordon Craig and *Macbeth,*" *Theatre Quart.,* July–Sept. 1971, discusses Craig's American *Macbeth;* and Alexander Woollcott, "O. Henry, Playwright," *Bookman,* Oct. 1922, speaks of Tyler's work with authors. Reminiscences by, and studies of, the actors mentioned include insights into Tyler.]

JAMES R. MILLER

U'REN, WILLIAM SIMON (Jan. 10, 1859– Mar. 8, 1949), political reformer, was born in Lancaster, Wis., the second of five children and first of three sons of William Richard U'Ren, a blacksmith, and Frances Jane (Ivey) U'Ren. Both parents were natives of Corn- wall, England. Their ancestry included Dutch and French Huguenot dissenters, and many of U'Ren's forebears were preachers; his parents were followers of John Wesley, al- though the family drifted away from formal affiliation with Methodism. The elder U'Ren had immigrated to the United States at the age of seventeen. Restless and independent, he moved frequently during his son's childhood, tried farming in Nebraska without success, and worked at his trade in various towns in Colorado and Wyoming.

Young U'Ren picked up his education in local public schools. At seventeen he left home to work in the mines of Colorado and later became a blacksmith in Denver, attending busi- ness college at night. Drawn to politics, he read law for two years in a Denver firm and in 1881 was admitted to the bar. He practiced in Aspen, Gunnison, and Tin Cup, Colo., but in 1888, ill with tuberculosis, went to Hawaii, where he worked on a sugar plantation. Upon his return he settled in Oregon, at first in Portland and then in Milwaukie, in the Wil- lamette Valley.

During his wanderings U'Ren read *Progress and Poverty* by Henry George and became a convert to the single tax. In Milwaukie he was quickly attracted to the local chapter of the Farmers' Alliance, organized by Seth and Al- fred Lewelling (Luelling), prosperous fruit growers, with whom he shared an interest in spiritualism; for a time he was a partner in their business. At a Farmers' Alliance meeting in 1892, U'Ren encountered the book *Direct Legislation by the Citizenship through the Initiative and Referendum* by James W. Sul- livan and became convinced that these measures offered the key to reform. Early in 1893 he helped organize and became the secretary of a joint committee on direct legislation, repre- senting the Farmers' Alliance, the State

Grange, the Knights of Labor, and the Port- land Federated Trades, and embarked on a campaign to pledge candidates for the legisla- ture to vote for the initiative and referendum. Tall and slender, earnest in countenance, soft- spoken but persistent and persuasive, U'Ren was an able organizer and lobbyist, and the measure came within a single vote of passing both houses in 1895.

U'Ren had meanwhile helped organize the Populist party in Oregon and was secretary of its state committee. In 1896 he and twelve other Populists were elected to the Oregon house of representatives. State politics were then controlled by United States Sen. John H. Mitchell, a Republican who was seeking reelection in the legislative session of 1897. When Mitchell balked at supporting the in- itiative and referendum, U'Ren, turning prac- tical politics to idealistic ends, formed an alliance of Populists, Democrats, and a group of dissident Republicans led by Jonathan Bourne that prevented the lower house from organizing and thus blocked Mitchell's election; in exchange he secured a pledge from his allies that they would put through the initiative and referendum at the next session of the legislature. The dramatic "hold-up session" did much to publicize the cause, and in the fall of 1897 U'Ren formed a new organization to carry it forward: the Non-Partisan Direct Legislation League.

Two successive sessions of the legislature now reluctantly passed the initiative and re- ferendum amendment, and in 1902 it was ratified by popular vote. U'Ren then moved toward the next step in the series of measures that became known as the "Oregon System." In 1903 he organized the Direct Primary Nom- ination League to secure the nomination of candidates for office by primary election rather than party convention or caucus. Taking his customary post as secretary, he enlisted a membership that ranged from the conservative editor of the Portland *Oregonian,* Harvey W. Scott, to the radical lawyer Charles Erskine Scott Wood. The direct-primary amendment passed in 1904. It included a provision, care- fully worded by U'Ren to avoid possible un- constitutionality, which in effect made possible the direct election of United States senators. Using the new law, U'Ren helped lead the campaign that elected Jonathan Bourne to the Senate in 1906.

U'Ren had meanwhile (1905) organized the People's Power League to press for further reforms in the machinery of government. Over the next few years nine of the league's measures were enacted, including a provision for the recall of state officers, a corrupt practices law, and one prohibiting railroads from giving free passes. U'Ren's influence and prestige reached their peak in 1908 when a Republican legislature, bound by the provisions of his direct primary law, dutifully elected a democratic senator, George E. Chamberlain, who had received the highest popular vote. Progressive magazines like the *American* and *McClure's* ran articles on U'Ren and the Oregon System, and by 1912 South Dakota, Oklahoma, Maine, Missouri, and California, had adopted the initiative and referendum. Woodrow Wilson, earlier critical of direct democracy, allowed himself to be tutored by U'Ren on its principles after his election as governor of New Jersey in 1910 and subsequently acknowledged his conversion and praised U'Ren's work.

With direct democracy now triumphant in Oregon, U'Ren felt the time was ripe to enact the single tax. He wanted to put before the voters a full-fledged tax on unearned land value, but the majority of his associates favored a moderate measure that would partially exempt buildings and other improvements on land from taxation. Such a measure was placed on the ballot in 1908; it polled well in the cities but lost in the countryside. Further campaigns in 1910 and 1912 found the farmers growing more suspicious of tax reform and U'Ren being increasingly branded as a "tinkerer" with "freak" ideas. In 1914, seeking to publicize the cause, he ran for governor as an independent, but he and the single tax were soundly defeated.

Save for his six years as a Populist (1892–1898), U'Ren had remained a Republican. He served on the executive committee of the National Progressive Republican League in 1911 and supported the presidential candidacy of Robert M. La Follette, switching after the 1912 Progressive party convention to Theodore Roosevelt. U'Ren's defeat in 1914 effectively ended his public career, although he ran unsuccessfully for the state legislature in 1932 and 1934. He supported Franklin D. Roosevelt in 1932 but soon became a severe critic of the New Deal, attacking its collectivism and urging instead an "industrial army" based on voluntary cooperation and self-supporting employment. On Mar. 6, 1901, U'Ren married Mary (Beharrell) Moore, a widow, in Portland, Oreg. They had no children. U'Ren died of pneumonia in Portland at the age of ninety; his cremated remains were placed in the Portland Memorial.

[The fullest account of U'Ren's political career is Robert C. Woodward, "William Simon U'Ren: In an Age of Protest" (M.A. thesis, Univ. of Oreg., 1956), from which two articles have been published: "William S. U'Ren: A Progressive Era Personality," *Idaho Yesterdays*, Summer 1960, and "W. S. U'Ren and the Single Tax in Oreg.," *Oreg. Hist. Quart.*, Mar. 1960. See also Thomas C. McClintock. "Seth Lewelling, William S. U'Ren and the Birth of the Oreg. Progressive Movement," *ibid.*, Sept. 1967; and the following contemporary accounts: articles on U'Ren or the initiative and referendum in Oregon by Lute Pease in *Pacific Monthly*, May 1907; by Lincoln Steffens in *American Mag.*, Mar. 1908 (also in Steffens's *Upbuilders*, 1909); by Frederic C. Howe in *Hampton's Mag.*, Apr. 1911; and by Burton J. Hendrick in *McClure's Mag.*, July, Aug., Sept. 1911; biographical sketch in Joseph Gaston, *Portland, Oreg.: Its Hist. and Builders*, II, 649–650 (1911); James D. Barnett, *The Operation of the Initiative, Referendum, and Recall in Oreg.* (1915).]

EDWARD T. JAMES

UTLEY, GEORGE BURWELL (Dec. 3, 1876–Oct. 4, 1946), librarian, was born in Hartford, Conn., the son of George Tyler Utley, a businessman, and Harriet Ella (Burwell) Utley. His father, a descendant of Samuel Utley, who arrived from England about 1647 and eventually settled in Stonington, Conn., was for many years the secretary of the Connecticut railroad commission. Before young George was three, his mother died and he was sent to live with her maiden sisters at their ancestral home in Pleasant Valley, twenty-five miles from Hartford. He prepared for college at the Vermont Academy, near Brattleboro, and after graduating in 1895 entered Colgate, but transferred after one year to Brown, where he prepared himself to teach English literature and received a Ph.B. degree in 1899. While waiting for a suitable teaching offer, Utley worked in the office of an insurance company in Hartford and frequented the Watkinson Library. Within a few weeks the librarian, Frank B. Gay, who was looking for an assistant, persuaded him to give up business records for books. Thus Utley entered upon a career of librarianship.

In 1901 he went to Baltimore to become librarian of the Maryland Diocesan Library of the Protestant Episcopal church, a choice collection of nearly 30,000 volumes of incunabula, theology, and local history. Its resources soon inspired him to write a series of papers on its rare books and, though Utley was a Baptist, to carry out research in its manuscript sources that eventually led to his volume *The Life and Times of Thomas John Clagett, First Bishop of Maryland* (1913). In 1905 he was appointed librarian of the nearly completed Carnegie Library at Jacksonville, Fla. The ability he displayed in organizing the library and his continued success in extending its services made his name known outside the state. Six years later the American Library Association chose him as its executive secretary, and Utley moved to Chicago in 1911.

The association, founded in 1876, had had no fixed headquarters until 1906, when one was set up in Boston. Not until 1909, when the Chicago Public Library provided free office space, could a definite program be envisioned. Utley found a two-year-old administrative organization operating with a sketchy plan. Quietly and efficiently he established the headquarters on a firm basis and guided its development along two lines: fieldwork, which included making speeches to state and regional meetings in order to increase membership, and work at headquarters, which encompassed publicity and publishing. From 1917 to 1920, while continuing as executive secretary, he gave his chief attention to duties as secretary of the association's Library War Service Committee, which, working in Washington, D.C., collected and distributed the "largest library in the world" for the armed forces during World War I and the period of demobilization.

Utley returned to Chicago after the war with an established reputation as an able administrator and a man of marked bibliographic tastes. In 1920 he was offered the librarianship of the Newberry Library. Acceptance meant continuing to live in Chicago, an idea by no means displeasing to the transplanted Connecticut Yankee of Republican party persuasion, who had come to love the city and felt proud of its literary and artistic creations, although he sometimes lamented the lack both of good government and of genuine "respect for law and order" (Utley to John M. Stahl, June 20, 1929, Allan Nevins Collection, Columbia University). Utley accepted the appointment and remained at the Newberry Library for nearly twenty-three years. During his incumbency, the library's holdings rose to 180,000 carefully selected volumes that earned it fame as a rich store of source materials in English and American literature as well as American history. The library's genealogical collection and its John M. Wing Foundation, devoted to the history of painting, were also augmented, and the staff grew from thirty-three to forty-five members. Utley found time to deliver papers and write articles on librarianship, books, and bibliography, including ten for the *Dictionary of American Biography*. He served, too, as the president of several organizations, among them

Chicago's Geographic Society (1929-1931), Literary Club (1935-1936), and Writers' Guild (1935-1936). Although flattered by election to the presidency of the American Library Association (1922-1923), he discovered the burden to be anything but light, and with memories of the battle over international copyright especially fresh in mind, confided at the end of his term, "I feel relief from the responsibility" (Utley to Richard R. Bowker, May 24, 1923, Bowker Papers, New York Public Library). He celebrated the organization's semicentennial in his graceful and informative *Fifty Years of the American Library Association* (1926).

In 1941 the Newberry Library trustees voted to adopt the sixty-five-year retirement policy prevailing in a large number of universities, and Utley, who had recovered from a slight heart attack in 1938, retired on Sept. 1, 1942. He occupied himself with reading and buying books (he collected the works of Robert Louis Stevenson), stamp collecting, and gardening. He enjoyed traveling by car in annual trips to Winter Park, Fla., and in the summer to Connecticut. He suffered a fatal heart attack at the age of sixty-nine while puttering in his garden in Pleasant Valley, Conn., and was buried in nearby Riverside Cemetery. He was survived by his wife, Lou Mabel Gilbert, whom he married on Sept. 4, 1901, in her native town of Fairfield, Vt. They had no children.

[Utley's papers, including his retirement diary, are in the Newberry Lib., Chicago. A good-sized file of mostly business letters between Utley and Lawrence C. Wroth is in the John Carter Brown Lib., Providence, R.I.; and a few Utley letters are in the N.Y. Public Lib.'s Richard Rogers Bowker Papers. An unpublished biography of Utley (1967) is in the possession of the author, Virgil F. Massman, executive director of the James Jerome Hill Reference Lib., St. Paul, Minn. Useful, too, is the brief biographical essay by Gilbert H. Doane in Utley's posthumous *The Librarians' Conference of 1853* (1951). Of briefer references, the more useful are Edwin B. Willoughby in Bibliographical Soc. of America, *News Sheet*, Apr. 15, 1948; Chalmers Hadley in Am. Lib. Assoc., *Bull.*, Nov. 1946; *Ill. Libraries*, Oct. 1942; *Who Was Who in America*, II (1950); *Nat. Cyc. Am. Biog.*, XXXIII, 100; obituaries in the *N.Y. Times*, *Hartford Courant*, and *Winsted* (Conn.) *Evening Citizen*, Oct. 5, 1946; and the *Hist. Catalogue of Brown Univ.* (1934, 1950). A photograph of Utley at his desk is in the *Newberry Lib. Bull.*, Dec. 1946.]

JOSEPH A. BOROMÉ

VAN DOREN, CARL CLINTON (Sept. 10, 1884-July 18, 1950), literary critic and biographer, was born in Hope, Ill., the son of Charles Lucius Van Doren, a country doctor, and Dora Anne (Butz) Van Doren. He was the eldest of five sons; the second youngest son was the poet and scholar Mark Van Doren. His paternal great-grandfather, Abraham Van

Doren, had been the first of his Dutch line to leave New Jersey for the Middle West; his maternal ancestors were of Pennsylvania German and English stock. He was descended on both sides from sturdy country people who had been blacksmiths, farmers, and preachers. In his determinedly cheerful autobiography, *Three Worlds* (1936), Van Doren described an idyllic nineteenth-century Midwestern boyhood.

In 1900 the family moved to Urbana, Ill., where the father retired from medical practice, farmed, and speculated in various business enterprises, often unsuccessfully. Carl attended Thorburn High School, where he played football and was president of his class. He was at the University of Illinois in Urbana from 1903 to 1907, when he received his B.A. He had been a great reader from earliest youth and expected to become a poet and novelist. But Van Doren at college was already the accomplished scholar and tall, distinctive figure whose appearance was to be so important to him on the New York literary scene in the 1920's; he seemed a natural leader. He was to feel about his college days at Urbana what he had felt about his boyhood in a country village and was to feel about Columbia and New York: that he had a gift for being in the right place at the right time.

In September 1908 Van Doren left home at twenty-three to attend Columbia University on a graduate scholarship. Columbia—and New York—were to make Van Doren's professional career. He took his Ph.D. in 1911 with a dissertation on Thomas Love Peacock; his biography of Peacock was already in type when he submitted it to his committee at Columbia. He taught at Columbia, on a part- or full-time basis, from 1911 to 1930. On Aug. 23, 1912, he married Irita Bradford of Tallahassee, Fla., who bore him three daughters, Anne, Margaret, and Barbara. Irita Van Doren was to become a prominent literary figure in her own right as editor of the *New York Herald Tribune* book section. The Van Dorens were divorced in 1935. Van Doren's second marriage, to Jean Wright Gorman on Feb. 27, 1939, ended in divorce in 1945.

Van Doren became an influential figure as literary editor (1919-1922) of the newly revitalized *Nation.* The "new," "modern" writers were now coming into their own, and Van Doren at the *Nation* was one of their great supporters. "Almost at once," he wrote in *Three Worlds,* "young writers turned to the *Nation* as to a critical friend." He was a great friend

to writers he admired. Van Doren was not a bold or venturesome critic, but he was indispensable to many writers struggling for recognition, and he knew and enjoyed the company of such writers as James Branch Cabell, Sinclair Lewis, and Elinor Wylie, because he had been among the first to appreciate them. A most elegant-looking man himself and an elegant, smooth, thoroughly acceptable writer, he bestowed his urbanity on every writer he discussed.

Van Doren was all his life to think of himself as a novelist *manqué,* and he did not take criticism seriously enough to take his own critical writing too seriously. But he lent his authority as a literary scholar and Columbia professor to his many genial, hospitable pieces about the new novelists and poets. He was to say of the 1920's that "the professors had been beaten by the journalists," but Van Doren somehow remained both. He kept a graduate course in American literature at Columbia even when he was briefly (1916-1918) headmaster of the Brearley School. He liked to boast that at Columbia he had more graduate students in American literature than any other teacher had ever had. He was managing editor of the Cambridge History of American Literature (1917-1920) and literary editor of the *Century* magazine (1922-1925). In 1921 he published *The American Novel,* which he described as "the first history of that literary form," and in 1922, *Contemporary American Novelists,* "the first systematic study of postwar American literature." He collected his literary reviews in *The Roving Critic* (1923) and *Many Minds* (1924) and did early studies of Cabell (1925) and Lewis (1933).

Van Doren was a fluent, practiced, genial writer. With his tall, rangy good looks, his dramatically close-clipped hair, his remarkably strong features, his memorably full, pleasant voice, he was a distinctive, and even "glamorous," figure. The Van Dorens were a famous literary family—Carl, his remarkably gifted brother Mark, his wife Irita, his sister-in-law Dorothy—and they lent a certain luster to each other in New York and at their country homes in Connecticut and to their many literary enterprises.

Yet Carl Van Doren was at heart a disappointed man. He had felt as a young man that "to write would be to tell stories. . . . I had lived a good part of my days in a stream of narrative." Criticism did not begin to satisfy this urge, nor did his novel *The Ninth Wave*

(1926). The most dramatic and successful narrative writing of his life was his biography of Benjamin Franklin (1938), which appeared at a time of urgent interest in the American past. It was admired by most reviewers, sold 270,000 copies in all editions, was generally considered the book of its year, and won the Pulitzer Prize for biography.

Van Doren died in a hospital in Torrington, Conn., of a heart attack complicated by pneumonia. After cremation, his ashes were scattered over Wickwire, his home in Cornwall, Conn.

Van Doren was no more profound a historian than he had been a critic. But he was a superb professional writer, and the crisis of the 1930's and World War II renewed his faith in the American Revolution and the Constitution and made him the passionate spokesman of "American scriptures." The success of *Benjamin Franklin* led him to write other studies of the Revolutionary period: *Secret History Of The American Revolution* (1941); *Mutiny in January* (1943), about an incident in the Continental Army in 1780-1781; *The Great Rehearsal* (1948), about the making and ratifying of the Constitution as a possible guide to the United Nations; and *Jane Mecom* (1950), a life of Franklin's sister. His last years were darkened by the strains in his second marriage. A gifted, yet never quite fulfilled, writer, he remains an indispensable part of American literary opinion in the vital years after World War I, which saw the triumph of modern American literature.

[Van Doren's autobiography is a charming, but unmistakably external, record. His place in American criticism is suggested in Charles I. Glicksberg, "Carl Van Doren, Scholar and Skeptic," *Sewanee Rev.*, Apr.–June, 1938; and Bernard Smith, *Forces in Am. Criticism* (1939). Other helpful sources include *Who Was Who in America*, III (1960); *Nat. Cyc. Am. Biog.*, XXXIX, 587–588; and obituaries in Am. Antiq. Soc., *Proc.*, Oct. 18, 1950, and the *N.Y. Times*, July 19, 1950. Details also drawn from the author's personal acquaintance and conversations with Mark Van Doren.]

ALFRED KAZIN

VICKERY, HOWARD LEROY (Apr. 20, 1892-Mar. 21, 1946), naval officer, director of merchant marine shipbuilding during World War II, was born in Bellevue, Ohio, the second son and youngest of three children of Willis Vickery and Anna Louise (Schneider) Vickery. His paternal grandparents had come to the United States from England in 1857. His father, a lawyer, moved in 1896 to Cleveland, where he became a county and later a state judge; he was also a noted book collector and Shakespear-

ean authority. Howard Vickery attended public schools in Cleveland and in 1911 entered the United States Naval Academy at Annapolis, from which he graduated, B.S., in 1915. Commissioned an ensign, he was assigned to the cruiser *Charleston*. While his ship was engaged in transport duty out of Boston during World War I, he met and married a Boston girl, Marguerite Blanchard, on Apr. 9, 1917. They had two children, Hugh Blanchard and Barbara Willis.

After the war Vickery was transferred to naval construction and assigned to a course of study at the Massachusetts Institute of Technology, from which he received an M.S. degree in naval architecture in 1921. Four years at the Boston Navy Yard followed, as superintendent of new construction, docking superintendent, and outside superintendent. From 1925 to 1928, on special assignment, he assisted the government of Haiti as director of its Shop, Supply, and Transportation Division. After a year with the navy's Bureau of Construction and Repair in Washington, Vickery served as technical adviser on shipping to the Governor General of the Philippines, 1929-1933. In this capacity he observed the building of Philippine ships in German yards and was the sole American to witness the launching of the German warship *Deutschland*. He returned to the Bureau of Construction and Repair in 1934 as head of the War Plans Section of the Design Branch (ships). At the same time he attended the Army Industrial College. When the ocean liner *Morro Castle* burned off the New Jersey coast in 1934 with the loss of 125 lives, Vickery was assigned to a board of investigation. The board's report substantially upgraded shipping safety by recommending measures that were subsequently put into law, among them asbestos insulation and automatic fire-sealing doors.

In 1937 Vickery, now a commander, left the Bureau of Construction and Repair to assist its former head, Rear Admiral Emory S. Land, on the newly constituted United States Maritime Commission. With Land's promotion to chairman in 1938, Vickery assumed responsibility for the supervision of all shipbuilding, design, and construction under a ten-year program to rehabilitate the American merchant marine. Vickery's position was given further authority in 1940 with his appointment (which because he was a naval officer required special legislation) to membership on the Commission. Two years later he was promoted to rear admiral and made vice-chairman of the Maritime Commission and deputy administrator of the War Shipping Administration—the wartime "czar" of American maritime construction, and responsible as well for charting the means by which the nation could maintain its merchant shipping growth after the war.

For his extraordinary feat in producing unparalleled amounts of merchant tonnage in record time during World War II, Vickery has been called the "miracle man" of the wartime shipping industry. Applying the lessons of World War I shipbuilding and his own unique and advanced construction notions, he transformed the moribund American shipbuilding industry of the late 1930's into the world's fastest, most efficient, and foremost producer of vessels. His innovations included the geographic dispersion of shipyards and the adoption and perfection of new methods of assemblage. Standardized designs permitted the simultaneous production of the same type of ship in widely scattered yards. They also made possible the multiple production of parts by various manufacturers to ensure a constant flow of supplies. Some of the parts were preassembled; this meant that less actual ship "building" occurred on the ways, thus greatly reducing the time lag from keel laying to launching. When, furthermore, it became apparent that too few established shipbuilders were equipped to carry out these new techniques, Vickery instituted the unprecedented practice of letting contracts to construction firms, like that of Henry J. Kaiser, without previous shipbuilding experience.

Vickery's acknowledged mastery of the technical aspects of ship construction was complemented by shrewd administrative capacity. He increased production through planned competition, incentive contracts, and constant personal on-site inspections of actual work. Powerfully built, five feet ten inches tall and weighing 210 pounds, Vickery had enormous vitality on and off the job. Blunt, often tactless, disposed to go through to desired objectives directly rather than circuitously, he was at the same time a warm and earthy man, and his social conviviality enhanced his relationship with the shipping industry. All told, by 1945 he had reduced the traditional time for completion of ships by 75 percent. Under Vickery's supervision, seventy shipyards produced 39,920,000 gross tons of vessels between 1939 and 1945, including the famous Liberty and Victory ships. The latter Vickery considered essential to the development and maintenance of America's postwar commercial trades.

Vickery's hard-driving effort took a personal toll. After suffering a severe heart attack in September 1944, he was forced to work on a reduced schedule the last months of the war, and in December 1945 he resigned with the rank of vice admiral. Still active, he was in the process of organizing a private tanker ship company when, in March 1946, he suffered a second and fatal coronary attack in Palm Springs, Calif., at the age of fifty-three. He was buried in Arlington National Cemetery. Vickery was a Congregationalist in religion, a Republican in politics. His wartime efforts won him the Distinguished Service Medal of the United States and the Order of the British Empire.

[Frederic C. Lane, et al., *Ships for Victory: A Hist. of Shipbuilding under the U.S. Maritime Commission in World War II* (1951); Emory S. Land, *Winning the War with Ships* (1958); correspondence or interviews with Vickery's wartime assistant, William A. Weber, Pittsburgh, Pa., and Hugh B. Vickery, Commander, USN (Ret.), Washington, D.C.; Howard L. Vickery, "Shipbuilding in World War II," *Marine Engineering and Shipping Rev.*, Apr. 1943; Milton Silverman, "Shipbuilder with Spurs," *Saturday Evening Post*, Aug. 21, 1943; *Time*, Mar. 31, 1941; *Current Biog.*, 1943; *Who Was Who in America*, vol. II (1950); obituary in Soc. of Naval Architects and Marine Engineers, *Transactions*, LIV, 478–479 (1946); *N.Y. Times*, Dec. 30, 1945, Mar. 22, 1946. On his father, see *Nat. Cyc. Am. Biog.*, Current Vol. A, 209–210.]

JEFFREY J. SAFFORD

VILLARD, OSWALD GARRISON (Mar. 13, 1872-Oct. 1, 1949), editor, reformer, and author, was born in Wiesbaden, Germany, where his parents, Henry Villard, financier, industrialist, and railroad builder, and Helen Frances (Garrison) Villard, daughter of the abolitionist William Lloyd Garrison, were sojourning in the husband's homeland for his health. Oswald was the second of three sons and the third among four children. Originally named Ferdinand Heinrich Gustav Hilgard, Henry Villard changed his name after immigrating to the United States in 1853. From his parents, Oswald Villard acquired a passionate love of liberty, an unshakable opposition to war, a resolute nonconformity, and a readiness to challenge governmental authority—characteristics that were to mark his life in journalism and public affairs. Assessing this heritage, he wrote in his autobiography: "These were the 'divergent' strains which made me what I am. These were the parents who gave me every opportunity, every benefit that wealth could bestow, and forged for me the tools that I used in my effort to mold the public opinion of my time" (*Fighting Years*, p. 23).

After returning from Germany, the Henry Villards lived in Boston until 1876. Thereafter they made their home in New York City with a summer estate, Thorwood, in Dobbs Ferry,

N.Y. As a boy, Oswald relished the seasonal activities of the city streets and parks hardly less than the natural wonders of the woods and fields of the towering hilltop that overlooked the Hudson River. Oswald attended the private school of James Herbert Morse and entered Harvard in 1889. He described his college performance as "undistinguished"—his Phi Beta Kappa key came much later through honorary membership at Howard University. After graduation in 1893, he traveled in Europe with his father and then returned to Harvard, where he earned the M.A. degree in history, serving (1894-1896) as an admiring teaching assistant to Albert Bushnell Hart. Although he enjoyed teaching, he found it "like sitting in a club window and watching the world go by outside." The classroom, he decided, was not in the mainstream.

Attracted to journalism, partly because his father in 1881 had acquired controlling interest in the *New York Evening Post* and its weekly literary supplement, the *Nation,* Oswald Villard served his apprenticeship (1896-1897) as a reporter on the *Philadelphia Press.* There he saw much that was wrong with the newspapers of his day. His tutelage under Talcott Williams was cut short after six months at the urging of Oswald's father, and he joined the *Evening Post* in May 1897. He was hardly settled in his editorial chair when the *Post,* with Edwin L. Godkin, the editor-in-chief, came out in opposition to war with Spain. It was to be the first of three major Villard stands against United States involvement in war. Although he had supported Woodrow Wilson in 1912 and the New Freedom legislation, and had called for Wilson's reelection in 1916, Villard now turned uncompromisingly against the president in 1917 over war with Germany. He reported the Paris Peace Conference and attacked the Treaty of Versailles as a "Covenant with Death," certain to bring on another European if not world war. It was much the same with respect to Franklin D. Roosevelt. Villard gave journalistic support to a large part of what became the New Deal of the 1930's. However, with the outbreak of World War II, he opposed the steps that soon began to edge the United States toward participation and again stood strongly against entering the conflict. In 1940 he reluctantly supported Wendell Willkie for president.

For his consistent pacifism, Villard paid a high price. Unwilling to alter his course as editor and with the *Evening Post* in 1918 losing both circulation and money, he seemingly had little choice other than to sell the newspaper, which he did to Thomas W. Lamont, at the height of the controversy. He retained the *Nation* and proceeded to develop it into what was probably the foremost liberal voice of the 1920's and 1930's, with a circulation that mounted from 7,200 to 38,000. Yet journalistic history was to be repeated. After having been president of The Nation Press, Inc. from 1900 to 1918 and owner and editor from 1918 to 1932, he yielded his control. Thereafter he wrote a signed weekly essay, "Issues and Men." On June 31, 1940, Villard and the *Nation's* editorial board, which did not share his views on defense preparations, parted company. He made the break with a fervent valedictory. The break hurt him deeply, for he had fought successfully against the *Nation's* suppression by the Post Office Department in 1918. He also knew what it was to be barred for his views from public halls and to speak under police protection, as in Cincinnati in 1921, and then to be hurried away from a hostile crowd. His family underwent the wartime ostracism, too; even the children were mistreated in school. Villard termed the charge of disloyalty as "absolutely absurd" and cited his writings first against the kaiser and then against Hitler, in both instances long in advance of general awareness of the German rulers' threat to world peace. After his separation from the *Nation,* he wrote for the *Christian Century* and the *Progressive.*

Villard had supported woman's rights as early as his Harvard days when he devoted his first public address, in Boston, to the suffrage movement. In 1911 he participated in the first woman's suffrage parade on Fifth Avenue in New York City—"one of a handful of men that day who braved both jeers and rotten eggs" (Humes, p. 7). His first major piece of writing, a biography of John Brown, fifty years after, completed in 1910, indicated another area of lasting interest, the status of the black race in the United States. He prepared the call for a national interracial conference as the most urgent observance of Lincoln's centennial in 1909. Out of that meeting of black and white social critics and reformers came the organization of the National Association for the Advancement of Colored People. Villard criticized Booker T. Washington as a "political boss of his race" (*Evening Post,* Apr. 1, 1910), and his thinking diverged widely from W. E. B. Du Bois; yet he worked with virtually every black leader to remove racial discrimination.

With Wilson's election in 1912, Villard hoped that he could work at the White House level to bring a measure of justice to the black minority. As chairman of the National Association for the Advancement of Colored People, he obtained an interview with the new president on May 14, 1913, at which he proposed the appointment of a national commission, under the direction of Jane Addams, to study Negro education, health, housing, employment, income, legal rights, and civic participation. Wilson took the idea under seemingly sympathetic advisement, but soon rejected it "with shame and humiliation" because he found himself "absolutely blocked by the sentiment of Senators" (*Fighting Years*, pp. 238-240). As a consequence Villard embarked on a speaking tour of major Eastern cities; speaking to large audiences, he said that although Wilson had given the country "beautiful and worthy" sentiments, "nowhere do we find any indication that his democracy is not strictly limited by the sex line and the color line" (*ibid.*, p. 240). When segregation in the federal departments became even more rigid, Villard wrote: "Not one thing was done by Woodrow Wilson or his Administration to ameliorate the condition of the Negro" (*ibid.*, p. 241). After the entry of the United States into World War I, it was the "supreme wrong," Villard asserted, for the Negroes of the South, "denied all participation in the government . . . deliberately kept illiterate and deprived of every civil right and personal liberty" to be drafted in 1917 and "forced to die for the country which was still for them what Wendell Phillips had called it in Abolition days, 'a magnificent conspiracy against justice'" (*ibid.*, pp. 240-241).

Meanwhile, in 1915, Villard went to Washington as the *Evening Post*'s capital correspondent. Notwithstanding his differences with Wilson on the race problem, he opened contact with White House secretary Joseph P. Tumulty to whom he supplied the words "too proud to fight," which Wilson used on May 10, 1915 in Philadelphia without Villard's qualification "because there are better ways of settling international disputes than by mass killings." As the "drift into war" continued (1915-1916), Villard sought to arrest it with editorials, cartoons, and interpretive news reports. Distressed by the president's course, he supported the Republican candidate for president, Charles Evans Hughes, in 1916.

The issues in which Villard became involved over the years seemed limitless in number. He advocated anti-lynching legislation, amnesty for conscientious objectors, prison reform, extension of labor unions, regulation of insurance companies and money and stock markets, birth control, mutual consent divorce, free speech for dissenters in public halls, the release of Eugene V. Debs from prison, full benefit of the doubt for Sacco and Vanzetti, Irish independence, and understanding sympathy for the Russian revolution, although later he condemned Soviet communism as totalitarian. He campaigned against Tammany Hall, Teapot Dome, and other forms of political corruption; he also attacked the Lusk dragnet investigation into so-called seditious activities in New York City, the A. Mitchell Palmer "Red raids," the Ku Klux Klan, red flag and criminal syndicalism statutes, and other means of harrassing minority groups. When Villard and others were blacklisted by the Daughters of the American Revolution, he organized a blacklist party on May 9, 1929, which was attended by 1,000 people. He opposed trusts, tariffs, corporate excesses, and legislation to regulate morals, including anti-white slave laws. Holding staunchly to Christian principles, he was a teetotaler but did not believe that constitutional prohibition was the answer to the liquor problem.

The subject on which Villard was preeminently qualified was the press, and he spoke as both high-level practitioner and informed observer in editorials, columns, magazine articles, books, and lectures. He deplored the trends toward fewer newspapers and their loss of individuality and the decline in investigative reporting and editorial comment and leadership. He called attention to the increasing influence of the business offices, once servants of the news and opinion departments, and to the growing amount of space allotted to entertainment, features, and comics. What had been a public service had become, he concluded, a business. His views, presented in part in *Newspapers and Newspaper Men* (1923) were expanded in *The Disappearing Daily* (1944) and in his autobiography, *Fighting Years* (1939).

Three of Villard's books were about Germany. The first, *Germany Embattled* (1915), reported on life there in World War I. In *The German Phoenix* (1933), he described the accomplishments of the German republic prior to Hitler. Then, after three months of firsthand observation, he wrote *Within Germany* (1940), an attack on the Nazi dictatorship. In *Prophets True and False* (1928) he sketched and evaluated twenty-seven public figures of the time, from Sen. George W. Norris whom he called "the noblest Roman of them all" to William Randolph Hearst, player of "the most unworthy role in American journalism." Villard's knowledge of United States defense policies and programs was displayed in *Our Military Chaos* (1939). With his son Henry, he edited *Lincoln on the Eve of '61* (1941). Villard told much about himself when he wrote: "It is one of my failings, I know, but I have never been able to work happily with men or women who were incapable of hot indignation at something or other—whether small or big, whether it stirred me personally or not, if only it was *something*." He stated his platform "to be opposed to war, to hold no hate for any people; to be determined to champion a better world; to believe in the equality of all men and women; and to be opposed to all tyrants and all suppression of liberty of conscience and belief" (*Fighting Years*, p. 108).

Living all his life close to the Atlantic, Villard was devoted to the sea. He was the owner of the *Nautical Gazette* from 1918 to 1935, but his other work did not allow him to give it active direction. He founded *Yachting* magazine in 1907, the outgrowth of summers of sailing his own sloop, the *Hilgarda*. He loved the peace and serenity of his country home near Watertown, Conn., and worked there on his last book, *Free Trade—Free World* (1947). After suffering a heart attack in 1944, his activities were reduced, although he continued his intense interest in current issues. On Sept. 29, 1949, he suffered a stroke at his New York residence and died there two days later, in his seventy-eighth year. After a memorial service at All Souls Unitarian Church, New York City, he was buried in Sleepy Hollow Cemetery, Tarrytown, N.Y. He was survived by his wife, the former Julia Breckinridge Sandford of Covington, Ky., whom he married on Feb. 18, 1903, in Athens, Ga., and by their daughter, Dorothea Marshall, and two sons, Oswald Garrison, Jr., and Henry Hilgard.

Appraisals of Villard ranged from the "pro-German," "Bolshevik," and "Negrophile," epithets of his American denouncers to the discerning praise of England's eminent journalist, S. K. Ratcliffe, who, in the *New Statesman and Nation* (Oct. 15, 1949) called him "extraordinarily resolute, consistent and courageous" and said that "despite the vigor and rigor of his opinions, he was a master of the difficult craft of objective reporting." Rev. John Haynes Holmes said that Villard "represented the ethical approach to life which has so strangely and alarmingly become old-fashioned" (*New York Herald Tribune*, Oct. 5, 1949). Villard put his editorial pen to work for more liberal political and social causes, in all probability, than any other American journalist. Equal rights for women and justice for racial minorities, to cite only two of his campaigns, were much advanced because of his unremitting labors.

[Villard's extensive papers and correspondence are in the Houghton Lib., Harvard Univ. His autobiography, with portrait, *Fighting Years: Memoirs of a Liberal Editor* (1939), recounts his failings and shortcomings no less than his successes and achievements. Other sources, in addition to the files of the *N.Y. Evening Post* and the *Nation* include, Michael Wreszin, *Oswald Garrison Villard: Pacifist at War* (1965), the best biography; D. Joy Humes, *Oswald Garrison Villard: Liberal of the 1920's* (1960); Allan Nevins, *The Evening Post: A Century of Journalism* (1922); Francis L. Broderick, *W. E. B. DuBois: Negro Leader in a Time of Crisis* (1959); Harold J. Laski, *The American Democracy* (1948); Max Lerner, "Liberalism of Oswald Garrison Villard," in *Ideas Are Weapons* (1939); *Who Was Who in Am.*, II (1950). See also newspapers at the time of his seventieth birthday and his death, particularly *N.Y. Times* and *N.Y. Herald Tribune*, Oct. 2, 1949. Representative articles in the voluminous periodical literature include *Independent*, Mar. 24, 1928; *Outlook*, Mar. 6, 1929; *Newsweek*, May 4, 1935; *Christian Century*, Apr. 26, 1939; *New Republic*, Apr. 26, 1939; *N.Y. Herald Tribune Books*, Apr. 9, 1939; *N.Y. Times Book Rev.*, Apr. 30, 1939; *Am. Mercury*, June 1939; *Time*, Jan. 29, 1940; *Survey Graphic*, Jan. 1940; *America*, Oct. 15, 1949; *New Statesman and Nation* (London), Oct. 15, 1949; *Jour. of Negro Hist.*, Jan. 1950. Personal recollection. Photograph of Villard appears as frontispiece in *Fighting Years*.]

IRVING DILLIARD

VOLSTEAD, ANDREW JOHN (Oct. 31, 1860–Jan. 20, 1947), congressman, was born near Kenyon, Goodhue County, Minn., one of four children of John Einersten and Dorothea Mathea (Lillo) Wraalstad or Vraalstad. His Norwegian parents, who had been market gardeners near Oslo, immigrated to Minnesota in 1854 and took up farming, in which they prospered. After a public school education, Andrew attended St. Olaf College in Northfield, Minn., before entering the Decorah (Iowa) Institute. His parents intended him for the Lutheran ministry, but after graduating in 1881 he taught school and read law in a Decorah firm. Admitted to the Minnesota bar in 1884, he practiced in Lac Qui Parle County, Minn., and in Grantsburg, Burnett County, Wis., before settling in 1886 in Granite Falls, Yellow Medicine County, Minn.

Volstead immediately entered politics as a Republican, becoming county attorney (1887–1893, 1895–1903), a member and later president of the Granite Falls board of education, city attorney, and mayor (1900–1902). In Granite Falls he also met a Scottish-born teacher, Helen Mary Osler ("Nellie") Gilruth (1868–1918), married her on Aug. 6, 1894, and began attending the Congregational Church. Their only child, Laura Ellen, was born in 1895.

In 1902 Volstead won election to Congress from Minnesota's 7th District for the first of ten terms. Thin and with a bushy moustache, a chewer of plug tobacco, he was for much of his career an unobtrusive, taciturn, and kindly congressional back bencher. He championed the homesteader and energetically guarded the interests of western Minnesota wheat farmers, strenuously opposing, for example, tariff reciprocity for Canadian wheat. He opposed big cities, big business, and big labor, and his belief in competition and his hatred of monopolies led him to support such early progressive legislation as the railroad regulatory laws; indeed, he thought they did not go far enough. In 1913 he joined the House Judiciary Committee as its ranking Republican, and during the next several years he opposed most of the domestic programs of the Wilson administration. He believed that the Underwood Tariff (1913) discriminated against the farmer; that the Federal Reserve Act (1913) benefited large city banks; and that the Clayton Anti-Trust Act (1914) legalized holding companies and exempted labor from practically every federal law. Nevertheless, he vigorously supported the administration's wartime measures during World War I.

In 1919, shortly after passage of the Eighteenth Amendment, Volstead became chairman of the Judiciary Committee. Although himself a teetotaler and a consistent supporter of prohibition, he had, up to this time, never made a prohibition speech. Working alone, Volstead drafted a bill to enforce prohibition. He staunchly maintained that his bill differed materially from an earlier measure drawn up by Wayne B. Wheeler of the Anti-Saloon League, and that it was less drastic than the Wheeler bill or either the Ohio or New York statutes. While permitting the sale of alcohol for industrial, medicinal, and sacramental purposes, the Volstead Act—passed in 1919 over Wilson's veto—outlawed any beverage containing more than one-half of one percent of alcohol (allowing near beer), provided for concurrent state and federal power over prohibition (so as not to set aside more drastic state laws), included a search-and-seizure clause, and provided for injunctions against and the padlocking of establishments selling alcoholic beverages.

For most Americans, Volstead personified prohibition, and he was reluctantly thrust into the limelight as a hero of the drys and the recipient of gibes, bitterness, and abuse from the wets. Although a convinced prohibitionist,

he was chagrined that the Volstead Act obscured his other legislative contributions. He was particularly proud of his authorship of the Capper-Volstead Cooperative Marketing Act (1922), which enabled farmers to organize marketing and bargaining cooperatives and exempted them from the antitrust laws. Volstead also supported woman's suffrage, backed a federal antilynch law, and favored extending workmen's compensation laws to longshoremen.

By 1920 Volstead faced opposition in his home district from organized labor, wets, and in particular the Farmer-Labor movement. A Lutheran minister, Ole J. Kvale, running first as a Farmer-Laborite and then as an Independent, combined these diverse elements to challenge Volstead in 1920 and, aided by low farm prices, defeated him two years later.

Spurning as unethical lucrative offers to write and lecture on prohibition, Volstead served from 1924 to 1931 as legal advisor to the Northwest Prohibition Enforcement District, with headquarters in St. Paul, and then returned to the practice of law in Granite Falls. A semi-invalid in his last years, he died of a coronary occlusion in Granite Falls and was buried in the local cemetery.

[Volstead's papers are in the Minn. Hist. Soc. His career can be traced in part through the *Cong. Record*, 1903–1923, and the *N.Y. Times Index*, 1913–1947. See also *Biog. Directory Am. Cong.* (1961); *Nat. Cyc. Am. Biog.*, XLI, 520–521; Henry F. Pringle in *World's Work*, July 1929; George L. Peterson in *Sat. Evening Post*, June 23, 1945, p. 44; Carol L. James, "Andrew J. Volstead–A Patron of Co-ops," *Midland Cooperator*, Jan. 11, 1971; Theodore Cristianson, *Minnesota*, IV, 9–11 (1935). An unpublished biobibliography prepared at the Univ. of Wis. Lib. School by Thomas Waldhart was helpful.]

ARI HOOGENBOOM

WAESCHE, RUSSELL RANDOLPH (Jan. 6, 1886–Oct. 17, 1946), Coast Guard officer, was born in Thurmont, Frederick County, Md., the second of four sons and sixth of eight children. His parents were Leonard Randolph Waesche, a mining engineer, and Mary Martha (Foreman) Waesche; his father's family had come to the United States from Germany about 1836. After attending Maryland public schools, young Waesche entered Purdue University in 1903 to study electrical engineering, but left after a year when his older brother, an instructor at Purdue, urged the youth to get some military training before continuing his studies.

Waesche entered the cadet school of the Revenue Cutter Service at Arundel Cove, Baltimore (forerunner of the Coast Guard Academy), and upon graduating in 1906 was commissioned a third lieutenant; he was promoted to second lieutenant the following year. Liking the service, he decided to make it his career.. For a decade Waesche saw duty as a line officer in cutters patrolling the Atlantic, Pacific, and Arctic oceans. The Revenue Cutter Service was merged in 1915 with the Life Saving Service to form the U. S. Coast Guard, and the next year Waesche became the first head of its Division of Communications. In this wartime post (he was promoted in 1917 to first lieutenant), he organized, modernized, and extended the coastal land lines network and completed a radio communications system.

Waesche was advanced to lieutenant commander in 1923, when Coast Guard ranks were adjusted to the equivalent navy ranks, and in 1926 to commander. During the 1920's the Coast Guard helped enforce national prohibition by operating in coastal waters against rumrunners. Waesche served on offshore patrol as commanding officer of the destroyer *Beale* (1924-1926) and, based in the flagship *Tucker*, as commander of a destroyer division (1926-1927). After a tour as the Coast Guard's chief ordnance officer, during which he reorganized the service's field forces, he became in 1932 aide to the commandant of the Coast Guard, serving concurrently as budget officer and chief of the finance division. Four years later President Roosevelt passed over many superior officers to appoint Waesche as commandant, a post he held until his retirement. The appointment brought him the rank of rear admiral. Subsequent promotions to vice admiral (1942) and admiral (1945) made him the first Coast Guard officer to attain these ranks.

As commandant, Waesche streamlined the administration of the Coast Guard, inaugurated a new system of gunnery practice that improved the service's marksmanship, and originated the Coast Guard Institute and Correspondence School for warrant officers and enlisted men. At his request the U. S. Lighthouse Service and the Bureau of Marine Inspection and Navigation were transferred to the Coast Guard (in 1939 and 1942). Known for his excellent relations with Congress, the affable Waesche was highly regarded both by his subordinates and by his civilian superiors.

With the outbreak of war in Europe in 1939, Waesche's command was charged, under the Neutrality Act, with preventing the shipment of war materials to belligerent nations and with carrying on antisabotage work in American ports. The entry of the United States into the war made the Coast Guard, while retaining its identity, temporarily an integral part of the navy, and greatly expanded its responsibilities. It patrolled the waters off Greenland, manned ocean weather stations, engaged in air patrol and rescue, set up a coastal communications network, and established and operated the Loran system for air and sea navigation. It also engaged in sea combat. As experts in the handling of small boats, Coast Guardsmen manned the landing craft of invasion fleets, taking part in every major naval landing operation in the Atlantic and Pacific. Coast Guard personnel rose from a prewar total of 10,000 to more than 171,000 by 1945. Besides its own ships, the service also operated 351 navy vessels, including twenty-two transports, and 288 army vessels.

Serving throughout the war, Waesche retired in January, 1946, because of ill health. He was awarded the Distinguished Service Medal for "exceptionally meritorious service." Somewhat above average height with a lean, athletic figure and ruddy complexion, Waesche had great drive and practical imagination. He was an Episcopalian in religion. He was married twice: on Oct. 18, 1911, to Dorothy Rebecca Luke of Seattle, Wash., and, following a divorce in 1926, on Mar. 21, 1931, to Agnes (Rizzuto) Cronin of New London, Conn., a widow. He had four children by his first wife—Harry Lee, Russell Randolph, James Mountford, and Dorothy Rebecca—and one, William Alexander, by his second. Waesche died of cancer at the age of sixty at the United States Naval Hospital at Bethesda, Md., and was buried at Arlington National Cemetery.

[Thomas H. Chamberlain, *The Generals and the Admirals* (1945); Malcolm F. Willoughby, *The U.S. Coast Guard in World War II* (1957); *Current Biog.*, 1945; *Who Was Who in America*, vol. II (1950); *Nat. Cyc. Am. Biog.*, XXXVIII, 629–630; *N.Y. Times* obituary, Oct. 18, 1946; correspondence with Rear Adm. Russell Randolph Waesche, Jr., USCG (Ret.). There are two paintings of Waesche at the U.S. Coast Guard Academy, New London, Conn.]
MALCOLM F. WILLOUGHBY

WALKER, JAMES JOHN (June 19, 1881-Nov. 18, 1946), mayor of New York City, was born of Irish Catholic parents in the Tammany-controlled ninth ward of New York's Greenwich Village. He was the second son and second of nine children (of whom only four survived infancy) of William Henry ("Billy") Walker and Ellen Ida (Roon) Walker. His father, a carpenter who had come to New York in 1857 from famine-stricken Kilkenny County, was a lumberyard owner and local Democratic politician; during Jimmy's boyhood he served as alderman of his ward and later as state assemblyman. Jimmy's mother had grown up in the large family of a prosperous Greenwich Village saloonkeeper.

Billy Walker wanted his son to go into politics and to have educational advantages he himself had lacked. But Walker, an indifferent and undisciplined student who had endured the regime of local parochial schools through high school, dropped out of Saint Francis Xavier College after a year and business school after three months. To please his still-tenacious father, Walker enrolled at the New York Law School in 1902, and was graduated two years later, but almost a decade passed before he became a member of the New York bar. He spent the intervening time in Tin Pan Alley, grinding out lyrics for such popular ballads as "Goodbye, Eyes of Blue," "Kiss All the Girls for Me," and "There's Music in the Rustle of a Skirt." In 1905 he scored a minor success with the lyrics for "Will You Love Me in December as You Do in May?" On Apr. 11, 1912, he married Janet Frances Allen, a musical comedy singer and vaudeville performer, who had left her native Chicago for the Great White Way. They had no children.

Not until the age of thirty did Walker finally give in to his father's desire that he quit song writing for politics. However, his style and values remained those of a man who had started out in show business. The world he continued to like best and frequent most was the world of Broadway musicals, vaudeville, professional sports, gambling casinos, nightclubs, and (in the 1920s) speakeasies, a world populated by celebrities and characters of the type chronicled by Damon Runyon. That world, in turn, adored the radiant little playboy. Gay and witty, a free spender and a snappy dresser, Beau James had a genius for making people feel good. "Jimmy! Jimmy!" Toots Shor, the fabled restaurateur, once exclaimed. "When you walked into the room you brightened up the joint."

In 1909, after serving under his father as a Tammany district captain, Walker received the Democratic nomination for the safe state assembly seat from Greenwich Village. Thus began a sixteen-year stint in the Albany legislature that led ultimately to City Hall. Elevated to the state senate in 1914, and the leader of his party in that body from 1921 to 1925, Walker was an effective debater, a popular colleague, an engaging vote-getter, and a loyal organization man. Tammany was then headed by Charles F. Murphy, who, beginning in the Progressive era, gave his support to a group of liberal young legislators that included Alfred E. Smith, Robert F. Wagner, and James A. Foley. Walker, joining the group, sponsored legislation for a uniform gas-rate law, a forty-eight-hour week for women and minors in industry, and an investigation of the New York Telephone Company. He needed no prodding to introduce bills legalizing Sunday baseball and professional boxing bouts of fifteen rounds. Opposed to the repressions that followed World War I, he spoke out against the Lusk antisedition bills of 1920, the Ku Klux Klan, prohibition, and censorship. Walker also supported Governor Smith in the passage of a bill to provide for an executive budget and in an unsuccessful attempt to extend the gubernatorial term from two to four years.

In 1925 Al Smith and other party leaders decided against renominating Mayor John F. Hylan and picked Walker as an attractive contrast to the blundering incumbent. In a city of awesome Democratic registrations, Walker went on to win the election by a margin of more than 400,000 votes over the Republican Frank D. Waterman, a fountain pen manufacturer. Four years later he won reelection by an even wider margin against Fiorello La Guardia, despite the latter's charges of corruption and mismanagement.

Walker's being a Democrat in a Democratic city was not the sole reason for his popularity. Although he let others do most of his work for him, it was during his tenure that a Department of Sanitation was created; that the public hospitals were brought under a single head; that a comprehensive system of subways was developed; and that construction was begun on the Queens-Midtown Tunnel, the Triborough Bridge, Manhattan's West Side Highway, and a new subway. Mayor Walker also took credit for the work of the prestigious Committee on Plan and Survey, which he appointed to study the long-range needs of the city.

But the major reason for Walker's popularity was that he embodied qualities that so many of his contemporaries admired during the Jazz Age. Neglecting the grueling chores of City Hall, he led parades, attended baseball games, played gracious and witty host to visiting dignitaries, took extended and exotic vacations abroad, and frequented New York's night spots. Bored with his wife, he had a publicized love affair with a beautiful actress, Betty (Violet Halling) Compton, the English-born daughter of an American wool merchant, who was twenty-three years his junior. To a generation that admired the fictional heroes of F. Scott Fitzgerald, Walker was Gotham's own Great

Gatsby out on "the greatest, gaudiest spree in history."

Meanwhile, a brigade of Tammany spoilsmen took over, and not even after an official investigation began to uncover graft and incompetence in his administration did the mayor think it necessary to put his municipal house in order. Initial hearings in 1930 by the appellate division of the state supreme court into the affairs of the municipal court system found evidence of corruption, and in 1931 the legislature appointed a committee to investigate the city government in general. As counsel, the committee selected the tenacious referee of the earlier hearings, Judge Samuel Seabury. Walker, when summoned to testify, failed to give a satisfactory explanation of either the chaos of his administration or the unorthodoxy of his personal finances. He used the word "beneficences" to describe the almost $300,000 he had received as stock profits from men who did business with the city, and he claimed ignorance of a safe-deposit box which had been taken out in both his own name and that of his financial agent and which at one time contained $750,000 in cash. It is still a matter of speculation whether Walker had been taking bribes or was telling Seabury the truth. Nor is it clear whether Gov. Franklin D. Roosevelt was planning to remove the mayor from office or merely to reprimand him.

Walker settled that question by resigning on Sept. 1, 1932. Divorced by his wife in early 1933, he married Betty Compton in a civil ceremony in Cannes, France, on Apr. 18 and took up residence in England. The couple later adopted two children, Mary Ann and James John. Walker returned to New York in 1935, and his appointment two years later as an assistant counsel of the New York State Transit Commission proved that he still had powerful friends. A better job, as impartial chairman of the National Cloak and Suit Industry, fell to him in 1940 through Mayor La Guardia.

But politically Walker was through, and after his lovely but erratic second wife divorced him in April 1941 and died in 1944, he underwent a private transformation that led him back to his ancestral faith. In a communion breakfast speech to the Catholic Traffic Guild in 1946, Walker said: "The glamor of other days I have found to be worthless tinsel, and all the allure of the world just so much seduction and deception. I now have found in religion and repentance the happiness and joy that I sought elsewhere in vain." He died a half year later, of a blood clot on the brain, in Doctors Hospital, New York City. After services at St. Patrick's Cathedral he was buried in Gate of Heaven Cemetery in Westchester County.

[Walker's personal papers were destroyed in a fire, but his mayoralty papers are in the Municipal Archives and Records Center of N.Y. City. The only full-length biography, Gene Fowler's Beau James: The Life and Times of Jimmy Walker (1949), is a richly detailed eulogy of the private man. For a less sympathetic view of Walker as both man and politician, see Raymond Moley, 27 Masters of Politics (1949). In their exhaustive Governing N. Y. City: Politics in the Metropolis (1960), Wallace S. Sayre and Herbert Kaufman rate Walker as one of the city's worst mayors and provide useful bibliographical leads. M. R. Werner likens Walker to a nineteenth-century Tammany predecessor in his "Jimmy Walker and Oakey Hall," New Republic, May 27, 1931. What's the Matter with New York? (1932), by Norman Thomas and Paul Blanshard, contains a devastating criticism of Tammany Hall and Walker during his mayoralty. His downfall, and the man responsible for it, can be followed in Herbert Mitgang, The Man Who Rode the Tiger: The Life and Times of Judge Samuel Seabury (1963). For one of the important consequences of the Seabury-Walker encounter, see Arthur Mann's La Guardia Comes to Power, 1933 (1965). There is a useful outline of Walker's life and career in a N.Y. Times front-page obituary of Nov. 19, 1946.]
ARTHUR MANN

WALKER, WALTON HARRIS (Dec. 3, 1889-Dec. 23, 1950), army officer, was born in Belton, Texas, the only surviving child of Sam Sims Walker, a successful merchant and real estate dealer, and Mary Lydia (Harris) Walker. Both parents were natives of Texas, and both were the children of former Confederate army officers, respectively from Virginia and Georgia. The family's religious affiliation was Methodist. Walker attended Wedemyer Military Academy in Belton, spent a year at the Virginia Military Institute, and in 1912 graduated as an infantry officer from the United States Military Academy at West Point.

For the next two years Walker served at army posts in Illinois, Oklahoma, and Texas. He was a member of the expedition, led by Gen. Frederick Funston, which occupied Veracruz, Mexico, in 1914, at a time of strained United States-Mexican relations. During World War I he served as a major with the 13th Machine Gun Battalion, took part in the St. Mihiel and Meuse-Argonne offensives, and was twice cited for gallantry in action, receiving the Silver Star with an Oak Leaf Cluster. He rose to lieutenant colonel while on duty with the army of occupation. In the interwar years Walker graduated from the Field Artillery School (1920), the Infantry School (1923), the Command and General Staff College at Fort Leavenworth, Kans. (1926), and the Army War College (1936). During the 1920's he was also an instructor at the Infantry and

Coast Artillery schools and a tactical officer at West Point. His assignments during the 1930's included three years (1930-1933) with the 15th Infantry on international railroad patrol in Tientsin, China.

In February 1941, now a colonel, Walker took command of the 36th Infantry at Camp Polk, La. That July, as brigadier general, he commanded the 3rd Armored Brigade and then the 3rd Armored Division. Promoted to major general in February 1942, he headed the IV Armored Corps at Camp Young, Calif., and in October was named to direct the vast Desert Training Center. Early in 1944 he moved his headquarters, now redesignated the XX Corps, to England. The XX Corps entered combat in France early in August as part of the Third Army led by Gen. George S. Patton. Walker, directing several divisions, seized Angers and Chartres and crossed the Seine River near Melun, where he was awarded the Distinguished Service Cross for gallantry under fire. He then took Reims and reached the Meuse River at Verdun.

Short, stocky, and pugnacious, Walker was nicknamed "Bulldog" for his determined fighting spirit; Patton called him one of his most aggressive leaders. During the severe winter combat of 1944, Walker led his forces across the Moselle River, and after more than two months of fierce German resistance, reduced the fortress complex of Metz. He liberated Thionville and plunged across the Saar. The XX Corps became known as the Ghost Corps for the speed of its advances; it crossed the Rhine in Germany, captured Kassel to encircle the Ruhr, liberated the notorious concentration camp at Buchenwald, and drove into Austria. In April 1945 Walker was promoted to lieutenant general.

After the close of the war in Europe, he returned to head the Eighth Service Command at Dallas, and later the Fifth Army Area in Chicago. In 1948 he went to Tokyo to assume command of the Eighth Army, the major ground forces headquarters in Gen. Douglas MacArthur's Far East Command. At the outbreak of the Korean conflict in 1950, MacArthur placed him in command of all American ground forces in Korea; Walker subsequently took command of South Korean and United Nations troops as well.

By the end of July, U.N. ground forces were pushed into a pocket in the southeastern corner of Korea known as the "Pusan Perimeter." With coolness, skill, and inspiring leadership, Walker fought an impressive battle against superior odds, deploying his units along the line with great dexterity. On July 29 he issued his famous "Stand or Die" order, declaring that "there will be no Dunkirk, there will be no Bataan. . . . We must fight until the end." The order drew criticism, but Walker succeeded in holding the perimeter and thus enabled MacArthur in mid-September to launch from Japan his invasion at Inchon. With the pressure against the Pusan Perimeter relieved, Walker immediately went on the offensive, linking up with the American forces that captured Seoul. For personal bravery in these actions he was awarded the Oak Leaf Cluster to his Distinguished Service Cross.

Walker's Eighth Army advanced into North Korea, captured the capital, Pyongyang, and reached the Chongchon River. The entry of Chinese Communist forces into the war made it impossible to hold, and Walker conducted a "scorched earth" withdrawal to the 38th Parallel. Two days before Christmas, he was killed when his jeep collided with a truck just north of Seoul. He was buried in Arlington National Cemetery in Washington. Walker was survived by his wife, Caroline Victoria (Emerson) Walker, whom he married on Mar. 18, 1924, and by their only child, Sam Sims, himself an army officer.

[Walker's military achievements are recorded in the campaign histories of the European theater in World War II and of the Korean War; see especially Roy E. Appleman, *South to the Naktong, North to the Yalu* (1961), in the series *U.S. Army in the Korean War*. Useful secondary works include: Ladislas Farago, *Patton: Ordeal and Triumph* (1963); Robert Leckie, *Conflict: The Hist. of the Korean War, 1950–1953* (1962); and T. R. Fehrenbach, *This Kind of War* (1963). For opinions of contemporaries, see George S. Patton, Jr., *War as I Knew It* (1948); Martin Blumenson, *The Patton Papers*, vol. II (1974); Douglas MacArthur, *Reminiscences* (1964); and Matthew B. Ridgway, *The Korean War* (1967). A chronology of Walker's career can be found in the various supplements to George W. Cullum's *Biog. Register of the Officers and Graduates of the U.S. Military Academy*. Walker's son, Brig. Gen. Sam S. Walker, furnished information on the family's antecedents.]

MARTIN BLUMENSON

WALSH, DAVID IGNATIUS (Nov. 11, 1872-June 11, 1947), governor of Massachusetts and United States senator, was born in Leominster, Mass., the fourth of five sons and ninth of ten children of James Walsh and Bridget (Donnelly) Walsh. His parents were Irish immigrants whose misfortunes thwarted their efforts to improve their modest circumstances. When Walsh was only twelve years old, his father died. As one of the younger children, however, he reaped the benefit of the sacrifices made thereafter by his mother and his older sisters, who worked in the textile mills of nearby Clinton.

Walsh graduated from Holy Cross College in Worcester in 1893; four years later he received his law degree from Boston University. With his younger brother, Thomas, he developed a successful law practice in the Clinton area. But politics exerted a stronger attraction on Walsh than did the law. He was well suited for politics, being personable, handsome, and a skillful orator; and so, the year after he finished law school he became a member of Clinton's Democratic Town Committee.

During the next decade Walsh's name became increasingly familiar in legal circles in Boston, and so did his reputation as an aspiring young Democrat. He delivered the keynote speech at the party's state convention in 1910, the year that Eugene Foss, a former Republican, captured the governorship for the Democrats. Two years later Walsh was elected lieutenant governor on the Foss slate. In the fall of 1913, after Foss had broken with his adopted party, Walsh secured the Democrats' gubernatorial nomination without opposition. A split in Republican ranks created by Theodore Roosevelt's launching of the Progressive party enabled Walsh not only to win the election but to secure reelection in 1914.

Walsh's rise to prominence took place during the Progressive Era, and so he campaigned on platforms that endorsed many typical reform measures. Aided by a coalition of Democratic, Progressive, and working-class Republican legislators, his administration compiled a considerable record of reform achievements. Walsh remained particularly proud of two: the improvement of the state's labor code and the inauguration of a system of state-supported university extension courses designed to bring higher education within the reach of the wage-earning class.

The governor's liberal leanings undoubtedly owed something to the deprivations he experienced as a child. In addition, Bay State Democratic leaders had become increasingly anxious to cement an alliance with the commonwealth's nascent labor movement. Moreover, during these same years Irish Catholics and other ethnic minorities had begun to grow restive under the hold so long exerted over state affairs by the Yankee Protestant, business-oriented Massachusetts establishment. The election of David I. Walsh as the first non-Yankee to serve as the state's chief executive was a landmark in the process whereby the minorities

sought, through politics, to open up wider avenues to security and advancement.

Although Walsh was identified with elements that were destructive of the Massachusetts status quo, he took pains to avoid unnecessarily offending the old-stock establishment. He remained aloof from the maneuverings of the Irish Democratic bosses—Curley, Fitzgerald, Lomasney, and the rest—who squabbled in Boston. Consequently, Walsh appeared to be "different" from that breed—more dignified—an asset when this son of immigrants sought to win votes among Republican and Democratic Yankees.

Nevertheless, Walsh lost his bid for a third term as governor in 1915; the breach within the GOP had healed by then. But his defeat was by a narrow margin, and when he sought his party's nomination for United States senator in 1918, it came without opposition. In the fall he defeated incumbent Sen. John W. Weeks; with that upset Massachusetts found herself represented in the upper house of Congress by a Democrat for the first time since 1851.

Walsh's debut in national politics was accompanied by a pledge of total support to President Woodrow Wilson in the pending negotiations to end World War I. As details of the Treaty of Versailles became known during 1919, however, disillusionment with the president's performance mounted, and nowhere more than among the ethnic minorities that constituted such a large part of Walsh's constituency. The Wilsonian principle of self-determination became a central issue, for the failure of various "old countries" to receive their "just rights" at the peace table turned important American nationality groups—the Irish and Italians, for example—against the president and his proposed League of Nations. For a while Walsh resisted the pressure to break with his party leader, but in a Senate speech of Oct. 9, 1919, he did so decisively.

If Walsh's stand on the league cost him any support among liberals, the voting record he compiled on domestic issues during the remainder of his first term won them back, for he sided consistently with those who sought to withstand the tide of Harding's "normalcy." In 1924 Sen. Robert M. La Follette's Progressive party endorsed his reelection, and when the veteran Wisconsin progressive toured the Bay State, he added his personal praise, declaring, "David I. Walsh stands for something more than party." But Calvin Coolidge's presence at the head of the ticket made the Republican sweep irresistible in Massachusetts in 1924, and by the narrow margin of 19,000 votes Walsh lost his Senate seat.

Just two years later, however, Walsh staged a startling comeback by overwhelming President Coolidge's closest confidant, Sen. William M. Butler, by more than 55,000 votes. In piecing together victory over such a formidable opponent Walsh drew heavily on his usual sources of support: the Irish Catholics, organized labor, and independent-minded Yankees. But most significant of all was the unparalleled support accorded him now by minority groups other than the Irish: the Italians, Jews, Poles, French Canadians, Portuguese, and Negroes, who together counted for much of the commonwealth's population. In the era of the Ku Klux Klan, prohibition, and immigration restriction, Walsh consistently spoke up for the minorities' interests and self-respect. For example, he was one of only six senators who voted against the Johnson Immigration Act of 1924, with its system of discriminatory quotas, and he prefaced his vote with a speech extolling the pluralistic nature of American society. He was instrumental, too, in seeing to it that during the 1920's the Democrats of Massachusetts extended recognition to diverse ethnic elements in the makeup of their statewide ticket. The results of his solicitude were apparent in 1926, when thousands of newer Americans who had never voted, or had been Republicans, came to the polls on his behalf.

During the 1930's Walsh supported most aspects of the New Deal; as chairman of the Senate Committee on Education and Labor, he was instrumental in paving the way for measures that were important to the urban, industrial population that he represented. Yet his relations with President Franklin D. Roosevelt were far from harmonious, in part because of Roosevelt's disposition to bolster the power in Massachusetts of James Michael Curley, who had jumped aboard the pre-1932 Roosevelt bandwagon earlier than Walsh. The president's Court reform bill of 1937 precipitated Walsh's first open break with the chief executive; thereafter, the Bay State senator also voiced apprehension over Roosevelt's anticipated departure from the two-term tradition.

Questions of foreign policy vastly widened the rift between Walsh and his party leader when, in 1939, Europe once again plunged into war. As chairman of the Senate Naval Affairs Committee, Walsh was an ardent exponent of preparedness, but he regarded the contest in Europe as "nothing but a clash of two forms of imperialism" and called for a policy of "absolute, unequivocal, unconditioned, and determined neutrality." He vigorously opposed the moves whereby President Roosevelt made the United States a virtual belligerent by the fall of 1941.

When the Japanese attacked Pearl Harbor, however, there was no doubt in Walsh's mind that "we must defend ourselves," and he gave energetic support to the war effort. Politically, nonetheless, his pre-Pearl Harbor attitudes now worked against him. When Walsh stood for reelection again in 1946, many ardent New Dealers withheld their support; he also faced that year the nationwide anti-Democratic trend that resulted in election of the Republican 80th Congress. In Massachusetts the veteran of nearly thirty years' service in Washington suffered a stinging defeat at the hands of the young Henry Cabot Lodge.

Almost immediately, Walsh's health began to fail and soon after he died of a cerebral hemorrhage in a Boston hospital. He was interred in St. John's Cemetery in Clinton. Walsh, who had remained a bachelor, was survived only by two of the sisters who had been so helpful in giving him his start.

After Walsh's death, many remembered him only as a "conservative" Democrat who had differed with Franklin Roosevelt. But that evaluation overlooked his long identification, in both Massachusetts and national politics, with the emerging economic and social aspirations of the urban, immigrant, industrial working class—a force that was hardly conservative. And if Walsh did not always give his constituents vigorous and wise leadership, especially in the realm of international affairs, he at least provided them with a spokesman who, in maturity and vision, stood several cuts above the unreconstructed machine politicians who frequently sprang from their ranks.

[The David I. Walsh Papers are at Holy Cross College. Other sources for this article were interviews with James Michael Curley, Frank Donahue, Amos Taylor, and B. Loring Young; J. Joseph Huthmacher, *Mass. People and Politics, 1919–1933* (1959); Dorothy G. Wayman, *David I. Walsh: Citizen-Patriot* (1952); *N.Y. Times*, June 12, 1947; *Boston Post*, June 13, 1947; *Cong. Record*, June 12, 1947, June 8, 1948.]

J. JOSEPH HUTHMACHER

WATSON, CHARLES ROGER (July 17, 1873–Jan. 10, 1948), theologian, missionary, and educator, was born in Cairo, Egypt, the third son of Andrew and Margaret (McVickar) Watson. His Scottish-born father had immigrated to the United States for schooling prior to a missionary career. In 1861 Watson's parents joined the United Presbyterian Church's American Mission, founded at Cairo seven years before. They devoted the remainder of their lives to missionary work in the Middle East.

As a youth Charles learned about Egypt by exploring the ancient monuments of its capital. He became fluent in Arabic and French, while learning the cautious, methodical practicality of his ancestors. Order, discipline, and thrift characterized his career; a spiritual experience persuaded him to train for the ministry.

In 1889 Watson left Egypt to continue his education in America. After a year at Lawrenceville Academy, he enrolled at Princeton University, graduating in 1894. During a year at Ohio State University he met Maria Elizabeth Powell of St. Louis, Mo., whom he married on Nov. 20, 1902. They had four children: Charles, Jr., Edward, Elizabeth, and Margaret. He taught for a year at Lawrenceville and attended graduate school at Princeton Seminary, from which he received a divinity degree in 1899. After directing a Pittsburgh mission for one year, Watson was ordained a United Presbyterian minister in 1900 and accepted the pastorate of the First United Presbyterian Church in St. Louis.

In 1902 Watson found a position that combined his interests and abilities when the United Presbyterian Board of Foreign Missions called him to direct its overseas activities. As corresponding secretary, he provided home office support for hundreds of teachers, doctors, and missionaries in Egypt, India, and the Sudan for the next fourteen years. Recruiting personnel, arranging transportation, handling correspondence, and securing materials occupied much of his time. He also kept American supporters informed of the church's worldwide activities and traveled extensively both in the United States and abroad.

Watson also demonstrated considerable literary talent. *Egypt and the Christian Crusade* (1907) outlined the work of various Christian organizations and pleaded for aid from wealthy Americans. He delivered the Princeton Seminary's annual student mission lectures, which were subsequently published as *In the Valley of the Nile* (1908). In this work, he attempted to acquaint potential visitors to the Middle East with the area's rich religious heritage. Watson described other United Presbyterian programs in *Far North in India* (1911), written with his assistant and successor, William B. Anderson, and *The Sorrow and Hope of the Egyptian Sudan* (1913).

While serving on the Board of Foreign Missions, Watson became interested in establishing a Christian university in Cairo, comparable to Robert College in Istanbul and the Syrian Protestant College (later American University) in Beirut. A 1912 educational survey of the Middle East provided him with the opportunity to develop plans for the college. After 1916 he worked full-time to found Cairo Christian University in 1919, renamed the American University in Cairo, an interdenominational institution offering preparatory and university work to an Arab student body. Watson raised money, organized a board of trustees, and recruited teachers. Several visits to Cairo were required before property could be purchased and arrangements negotiated with Egyptian and British officials. The outbreak of World War I delayed the school opening. Meanwhile, Watson helped Dr. John R. Mott establish YMCA programs and develop refugee relief plans in Europe. He also represented American missionaries at the Versailles Peace Conference.

Watson served as president of the American University in Cairo from its founding in 1920 until his retirement in 1945. One of the best-known and most respected American educators in the Middle East, he personally supervised the school, encouraging the introduction of innovative teaching methods. He sometimes taught ethics and often lectured at student assemblies. Regular visits to the United States were necessary to raise funds and recruit teachers. Watson was especially successful in persuading wealthy Americans to support the university, and he developed close friendships with philanthropists such as Frederick E. Weyerhaeuser, John D. Rockefeller, Jr., and William Bancroft Hill.

The university also suffered setbacks. Especially after a series of antimissionary attacks in 1930-1932, Watson realized the need to alter traditional missionary methods in the light of growing nationalism in the Middle East. The school's interdenominational status and independent board of trustees enabled it gradually to secularize programs, and new activities were introduced in an attempt to meet Egypt's needs. Watson's willingness to change with the times set him apart from conservative missionary educators and made possible the university's continued development.

Watson hoped to retire in 1938 but was persuaded by the trustees to remain in office. World War II prevented visits to the United States for nearly six years, and for a time Watson and the university staff took refuge in the Sudan. In 1945, after a near-fatal illness,

Watson turned the university over to his hand-picked successor, John S. Badeau. Returning to America, he died of a cerebral hemorrhage at Bryn Mawr, Pa., and was buried in Princeton, N.J.

[A large collection of Watson papers, especially for 1914–1945, is in the archives of the American University in Cairo. Personal letters are owned by Charles R. Watson, Jr., of Alexandria, Va., who granted the author an informative interview. Watson described his own work in frequent articles for *The United Presbyterian, The Internat. Rev. of Missions,* and *Muslim World.* For his work at the American University, see E. Freeman Gossett, *Foreign Higher Education in Egypt During the Nationalistic Era* (1962). Detailed obituaries appeared in the *N.Y. Times,* Jan. 12, 1948; *The Egyptian Gazette* (Cairo), Jan. 13, 1948; and *United Presbyterian,* Feb. 2, Mar. 1, 1948.]
                                    LAWRENCE R. MURPHY

WATSON, JAMES ELI (Nov. 2, 1864–July 29, 1948), congressman and senator from Indiana, was born in Winchester, Randolph County, Ind., the third son and third of six children of Enos Lindsey Watson and Mary Margaret (Judd) Watson. Both parents were natives of Ohio. The father was a self-taught lawyer and the owner-editor of the *Winchester Herald;* a staunch Republican, he was elected to the state legislature in 1867 and again in 1881. James Watson graduated from the Winchester high school in 1881 and from DePauw University in Greencastle, Ind., in 1886. After reading law for a year in his father's office, he was admitted to the bar and became his father's partner. On Dec. 12, 1893, he married Flora Miller of Winchester. They had five children: Edwin Gowdy, James Eli, Florine, Kathryn, and Joseph Cannon. The couple settled in Rushville, Ind., where Watson became the head of his own law firm.

His long association with politics began at the age of twelve when he accompanied his father to the Republican national convention of 1876. During the 1880's Watson campaigned extensively in Indiana for his party's presidential ticket. He first won public office in 1894 when he defeated the veteran Democratic incumbent, William S. Holman, for a seat in Congress. One element in Watson's victory was his facility in speaking German, a language he had learned as a boy from a neighbor, to the German portion of his constituency. He was narrowly defeated for reelection in 1896, but was returned to the House in 1898 and four times thereafter.

From the start, Watson identified himself unequivocally with the Old Guard Republicans. A close friend and protégé of Speaker Joseph G. Cannon, he was soon promoted to the position of Republican whip and was later placed on the powerful Ways and Means Committee. In 1908 he ran for governor of Indiana, but was defeated by Thomas R. Marshall. He remained in Washington after the expiration of his congressional term and served for a time as a lobbyist for manufacturing interests seeking higher tariffs; because of his former membership in the House, these activities were criticized by a congressional committee as a breach of propriety. His high standing with the regular Republicans led to his selection in 1912 as floor leader of the Taft forces during the Republican national convention, where he successfully forestalled Theodore Roosevelt's challenge for the disputed delegates.

Watson returned to Capitol Hill in 1916 as a United States senator, after winning a special election to fill the unexpired term of Benjamin F. Shively. He was reelected for full terms in 1920 and 1926. In the Senate, Watson remained the epitome of the Old Guardsman. His closest friend was Sen. Boies Penrose of Pennsylvania; and Sen. Henry Cabot Lodge chose Watson to act as floor whip in the GOP's fight against the Versailles Treaty and the League of Nations. At the 1920 Republican Convention, Watson was chairman of the resolutions committee and played an important part in drafting the party platform.

Throughout his years in the Senate, Watson spoke and labored faithfully for the railroads, the banks, and the corporations. He was untiring in his advocacy of high tariffs, and as a member of the Senate Finance Committee he helped devise and enact the Republican tariffs of the 1920's, which he eulogized as the very touchstone of American prosperity and greatness. He successfully urged the creation of a Railroad Labor Board to mediate labor disputes as part of the Esch-Cummins Act of 1920. Watson was also an exponent of a big navy and an isolationist in foreign policy, one who regretted his support of American entry into World War I. Sharing the traditional American distrust of Europe and the determination to remain aloof from its affairs, he believed also in "the rigid restriction of immigration." He was an early advocate of the literacy test, arguing that it would exclude "great hordes of Italians and Huns who come in year after year, undermining the very principle of this Republic and interfering with labor all over the country."

Only rarely did Watson take a stand that could be described as other than conservative. As chairman of the Senate Committee on Woman Suffrage, he helped steer the Nineteenth Amendment through the upper house. During the 1920's he joined his party's Midwestern insurgents in supporting the successive Mc-Nary-Haugen bills to raise farm prices. Watson actively opposed the nomination of Herbert Hoover for president in 1928, aspiring to that office himself. Instead, Hoover became president and Watson became the Senate majority leader—the beginning of a scarcely concealed antipathy between two very different personalities. The two men were at odds over Hoover's first major legislative proposal, tariff revision. Hoover had called for an upward revision limited to agricultural products only, but Watson insisted on a general revision. Eventually, after a protracted battle, a general revision was enacted. Hoover later unsuccessfully attempted to have Watson replaced as majority leader by the more congenial Sen. David A. Reed of Pennsylvania.

Among his contemporaries in the Senate, Watson was affectionately regarded for his imperturbable amiability, his colorful personality, and his zest for storytelling—qualities evident in his memoirs, *As I Knew Them* (1936). Political analysts were not so kind. The editor of the *New York Times* saw him as "a classic example of the 'glad hand' statesman"; Frank Kent characterized him as a "lovable old humbug." Clearly, Watson's talents were centered in the political arts of party loyalty and survival. A master horse trader, he once remarked that "all legislation of consequence is a series of compromises." Watson's long political tenure ended abruptly with the Democratic landslide of 1932, when he was defeated by Frederick Van Nuys. Retiring from active politics, he resumed the practice of law in Washington, D.C. A lifelong Methodist, he was also a member of many fraternal organizations. Watson died of a cerebral hemorrhage in Washington at the age of eighty-three and was buried there at Cedar Hill Cemetery.

[Watson's *As I Knew Them*; biographical sketches of Watson and his father in *A Portrait and Biog. Record of Delaware and Randolph Counties, Ind.*, pp. 996–997 (1894); Frank R. Kent in *Atlantic Monthly*, Feb. 1932; John W. Owens in *Am. Mercury*, May 1924; Jordan A. Schwarz, *The Interregnum of Despair* (1970); *Biog. Directory Am. Cong.* (1961); *Nat. Cyc. Am. Biog.*, XL, 382–383; *N.Y. Times* obituary, July 30, 1948. Although *Who's Who in America*, the *Biog. Directory Amer. Cong.*, and Watson's death certificate give his birth year as 1863, his autobiography and biographical material in the Ind. State Lib. seem to confirm 1864.]
ALBERT U. ROMASCO

WEBBER, HERBERT JOHN (Dec. 27, 1865–Jan. 18, 1946), plant physiologist, was born in Lawton, Mich., the son of John

Milton Webber and Rebecca Anna (Bradt) Webber. His father was a descendant of the Webbers of Hopkinton, Mass.; his mother, a descendant of the Bradts and Mabees of Rotterdam, near Schenectady, N.Y. In 1867, Webber's family moved to central Iowa, settling near Marshalltown. The family farmed there for fifteen years, becoming well-to-do, and then moved to Lincoln, Nebr., in 1883, primarily to educate their children.

Webber first attended Willow Hill School, between Marshalltown and Albion, Iowa, and continued in the Albion Seminary. He obtained the B.S. degree from the University of Nebraska in 1889 and the M.A. in 1890. His work as a student and as an assistant in botany with Charles Edwin Bessey inspired him with an active scientific interest that dominated his subsequent life. On Sept. 8, 1890, Webber married Lucena Anna Hardin, a fellow student in the University of Nebraska, who in subsequent years prepared many drawings for her husband's publications. Their children were Eugene Francis, Fera Ella, Herbert Earl, and John Milton.

From 1890 to 1892, Webber was assistant in botany in the Shaw School of Botany in Washington University, St. Louis, from which he received the Ph.D. degree in 1901. In 1892, Webber was appointed assistant pathologist in the U.S. Department of Agriculture, and went to Eustis, Fla., to study orange diseases in association with Walter T. Swingle. Here he developed two interests he was to continue throughout his career: the scientific study of living plants in the out-of-doors, and the study of botanical problems in subtropical regions. In Florida, Webber worked with Swingle in producing the first interspecific hybrids in *Citrus* having resistance to low temperatures, studied citrus diseases, and discovered motile antherozoids in *Zamia*. In 1897, Webber transferred to the Washington office of the Department of Agriculture. Two years later, he represented the department at the International Conference in London on hybridization and cross-breeding. In 1900 he was named physiologist in charge of the Laboratory of Plant Breeding, although he continued to work on the Florida citrus research. New investigations were undertaken in Washington, particularly in cotton breeding. Webber became an outstanding authority in this field, originating the Columbia variety, which in turn led to several long-staple Webber cottons. These were ancestors, in their turn, of several other widely grown varieties. In addition to citrus and cotton, Webber's name became linked to studies of corn, pineapples, timothy, and potatoes.

Webber moved to Cornell University in 1907. He was professor of plant biology in 1907–1908; head of the department of experimental plant biology in 1908–1912; and acting director of the New York State College of Agriculture in 1909–1910. During this period his most important research was in corn and timothy.

In 1912, Webber was appointed director of the newly created Citrus Experiment Station and dean of the Graduate School of Tropical Agriculture of the University of California at Riverside. He began work in 1913, the year in which he received the honorary degree of doctor of agriculture from the University of Nebraska, and built up the station and school. During 1920–1921, he was general manager of the Pedigreed Seed Company at Hartsville, S.C., specializing in cotton breeding. In 1921, he was appointed chairman of the division of subtropical horticulture in the College of Agriculture, University of California, Berkeley, and in 1923–1924, he served as acting dean of the college and director of the experiment station. From 1924 to 1925, Webber was special commissioner to study the citrus industry and agricultural research and education in the Union of South Africa. Following that assignment, he traveled in several parts of the world. Webber returned to Riverside in 1926 as director of the Citrus Experiment Station. In 1929, he retired from this position, but remained as professor of subtropical horticulture until 1936, when he retired and became professor emeritus. In 1943, he received an honorary LL.D. from the University of California. He continued to work with *Citrus*, however, until his death in Riverside, Calif., on Jan. 18, 1946, of a heart ailment.

Webber reported the results of his research in some three hundred monographs, bulletins, and papers, that have appeared in the publications of the U.S. Department of Agriculture, the New York State Agricultural Experiment Station, the California Agricultural Experiment Station, the Department of Agriculture of the Union of South Africa, and various scholarly journals. In the last years of his life, he collaborated with Leon D. Batchelor, his successor as director of the Citrus Experiment Station, in planning a three-volume work, *The Citrus Industry*. The first volume, *History, Botany and Breeding,* containing chapters by himself and several collaborators and published in 1943, was the culmination of Webber's

career. Volume 2, which contained chapters by Webber, appeared in 1948.

According to a longtime colleague, Webber was affable, genial, unselfish, alert, energetic, and optimistic. He was a charter member of the California Botanical Society, a founder of the Botanical Society of America and of the American Genetic Association, and a fellow of the American Association for the Advancement of Science. He was an active member in a number of additional botanical and horticultural societies. He influenced the development of a more scientific concept and practice of genetics in the U.S. Department of Agriculture and at Cornell University.

A study of Webber's life, particularly as revealed in his publications reporting the results of research, leads to the conclusion that his work, rigorously scientific as it was, was directed to the solution of practical problems of plant production, including the conquest of disease and the development of more productive varieties. Webber represented the best traits of the scientist in the public service—scholarly, yet concerned with science in the service of mankind.

[Publications of the U.S. Dept. of Agriculture, the N.Y. Agric. Experiment Sta., the Calif. Agric. Experiment Sta., and the Univ. of Calif. Citrus Experiment Sta. include numerous bulletins and articles by Webber. The *Calif. Citrograph,* 22 (1937), 162, reviewed Webber's career and used a portrait drawing of him on its front cover. The same journal, 31 (1946), 157, contains a full obituary and a photograph. The steps in Webber's career may be traced in consecutive volumes of *Am. Men of Sci.* (1910–1949) and *Who's Who in Am.* (1903–1905 to 1946–1947). The obituary by Howard S. Reed in *Madroño,* 8 (1946), 193–195, gives an unusually complete account of the man as well of his work. See also the *N.Y. Times,* Jan. 20, 1946, and the *Nat. Cyc. Am. Biog.,* XVII. Photographs appear in the *Proceedings* of the 48th Calif. Fruit Growers Convention, 1916, and in the *Report* of the Calif. Experiment Sta., 1920–1921. Some letters by Webber are in the records of the Bureau of Plant Industry and the Office of Experiment Stations, U.S. Dept. of Agriculture, National Archives, Washington, D.C.; in the Bancroft Lib., Univ. of Calif., Berkeley; and in the Walter T. Swingle papers at the Univ. of Miami, Miami, Fla. His personal papers and an unpublished autobiography are in the library of the Univ. of Calif., Riverside.]

WAYNE D. RASMUSSEN

WEDDELL, ALEXANDER WILBOURNE (Apr. 6, 1876-Jan. 1, 1948), career diplomat and philanthropist, was born in Richmond, Va., the second son and fourth of six children of Rev. Alexander Watson Weddell and Penelope Margaret (Wright) Weddell. His paternal grandfather had emigrated from Scotland, and his ancestry in other lines extended to colonial Virginia and North Carolina. His father, who had served as private secretary to the Confederate secretary of state, was rector of historic St. John's Episcopal Church in Richmond until his death in 1883.

Growing up under the salutary tutelage of his mother, who implanted in him a taste for literature, Weddell received his early education in Richmond public and private schools. To supplement family income he found part-time jobs as page in the state legislature and office boy for a wholesale grocery house. He was forced to seek full-time employment at the age of sixteen and worked at a succession of positions, including copy reader for the *Southern Churchman,* bank messenger, and secretary to a railroad president, for whom he traveled extensively along the Atlantic seaboard. In 1904, a self-styled "malcontent and rolling stone," Weddell rebelled at the "sheer materialism of the atmosphere surrounding and choking" him and abandoned the business world for a clerkship in the Library of Congress, in the Division of Copyrights. Through evening classes at George Washington University law school, he also earned an LL.B. degree in 1908.

Meanwhile chance steered Weddell to the world of diplomacy. As private secretary (1907-1910) to the recently appointed American minister to Denmark, Maurice Francis Egan, he found his life's work. Egan fed his intellectual hunger, remedied flaws in his education, and served as mentor on the skills and finesse of the diplomat. Returning to the United States in 1910, Weddell passed the examinations for the Consular Service. Successively he served as consul in Zanzibar (1910-1912) and in Catania, Italy (1912-1914), and as consul general in Athens (1914-1920), Calcutta (1920-1924), and Mexico (1924-1928). His tenure in Athens was interrupted by temporary assignment in Cairo (1917) and by several wartime commissions (1917-1918).

In 1928, Weddell resigned from the consular service to devote himself to philanthropy and civic interests. On May 31, 1923, he married Mrs. Virginia (Chase) Steedman, a wealthy St. Louis widow of Virginia ancestry, who shared his love for their native state. They had no children. Utilizing salvaged masonry from the ancient Warwick (England) Priory, in 1924 the Weddells built a stately home, "Virginia House," near Richmond; five years later, retaining only life tenure, they deeded it to the Virginia Historical Society. Weddell was a founder (1936) of the Virginia Museum of Fine Arts and a supporter of the Richmond Academy of Arts; and he served as president

of the Richmond Community Fund (1932-1933).

President Franklin D. Roosevelt called Weddell back into the diplomatic service in 1933 as ambassador to Argentina. During his six-year mission he represented the United States at several inter-American conferences, including the 7th Inter-American Conference, Montevideo (1933); Pan-American Commercial Conference (1935); the Chaco Peace Conference of 1935, which arranged an armistice in the Chaco War between Paraguay and Bolivia; and the Inter-American Conference for the Maintenance of Peace (1936). His *Introduction to Argentina* (1939) revealed his eagerness to acquaint his countrymen with a nation of which they knew little. In 1939 Weddell was transferred to Spain. His ambassadorship there embraced the aftermath of the Spanish Civil War and the growing threat of German occupation. His primary concern was to keep Gen. Francisco Franco's pro-Axis government in a state of nonbelligerency during World War II.

Ill health forced Weddell to leave federal service in October 1942. Returning to Richmond, he resumed a position of leadership in local historical and aesthetic causes, as president of the Virginia Museum of Fine Arts (1942-1947), the Virginia Historical Society (1944-1948), and St. John's Foundation. On New Year's Day, 1948, Weddell and his wife were killed in a railroad accident near Sedalia, Mo. They were buried in Hollywood Cemetery, Richmond.

[Weddell's personal papers, including a MS. autobiography, are in the Va. Hist. Soc., Richmond. His diplomatic career may be traced through Dept. of State Appointment Cards and files of correspondence in the Nat. Arch. See also, on his Argentine and Spanish missions, the appropriate volumes of the *Foreign Relations of the U.S., Diplomatic Papers.* For additional biographical details, see *Who Was Who in America,* II (1950); *Nat. Cyc. Am. Biog.,* XXXV, 449-450; the *N.Y. Times,* Jan. 2, 3, 1948 (and Index); *Richmond News,* Jan. 2, 1948; and *Richmond Times-Dispatch,* Jan. 3, 1948. See also Charles R. Halstead, "Diligent Diplomat: Alexander W. Weddell as American Ambassador to Spain, 1939-1942," *Va. Mag. of Hist. and Biog.,* Jan. 1974. On Virginia House and its relation to the Va. Hist. Soc., see Weddell's *A Description of Virginia House* (1947) and Walter Muir Whitehill, *Independent Historical Societies* (1962). The Va. Hist. Soc. has three paintings of Weddell.]

HAROLD F. PETERSON

WEEKS, JOHN ELMER (Aug. 9, 1853-Feb. 2, 1949), ophthalmologist, was born in Painesville, Ohio, the second son and second child among the six boys and two girls of Seth R. Weeks and Deborah Ann (Blydenburgh) Weeks. Both parents were natives of Long Island, the mother of Dutch ancestry, the father a descendant of Francis Weekes, an English settler of 1638 at Gravesend. Seth Weeks was a house painter in Painesville and, after 1866, in Corry, Pa. He made only a meager living, and John worked regularly in the family business. His later schooling was sporadic, and, at twenty, after completing the second year of high school, he went to work full time and became a painter and repairman in a railroad shop. With his mother's encouragement, however, he aspired to a professional career. He continued to study on his own and began reading medicine with a general practitioner. In 1879 he took his accumulated savings and entered the medical school at the University of Michigan. He completed the three-year course in two years and received his M.D. in 1881.

The discovery, during his medical study, that he suffered from astigmatism wakened Weeks's interest in eye diseases. In 1882 he went to New York for postgraduate training and enrolled in a three-month course of clinical instruction at the Ophthalmic and Aural Institute of Herman Knapp. At the same time he took courses in general surgery and pathology at Bellevue Hospital and supported himself with an internship at New York's Almshouse and Workhouse Hospital. During a residency (1883-1885) at the New York State Emigrant Hospital, Weeks spent six months in Berlin studying ophthalmic surgery, pathology, and the relatively new field of bacteriology. On his return to New York in August 1885 he began a two-year internship at the Ophthalmic and Aural Institute and, under Knapp's guidance, established and taught the first systematic course in bacteriology given in New York City. He also began research on the acute epidemic conjunctivitis known as "pink eye" and in 1886 isolated the causative organism, which, independently discovered by Robert Koch, became known as the Koch-Weeks bacillus; Weeks confirmed the identification by successfully inoculating one of his own eyes.

He began private practice in 1887. After a slow start, he overcame the aloofness of his shy nature and within a decade was able to limit his practice to diseases of the eye. He also took on increasing clinical and teaching responsibilities. In 1890, after brief appointments elsewhere, he became surgeon and pathologist at the New York Eye and Ear Infirmary, a post he held until 1920, when he became consulting surgeon. His principal teaching appointments were at the Woman's Medical College of the New York Infirmary for Women and Children (1892-1899), at the New York University, and at Bellevue Hospital Medical Col-

lege, where he served as lecturer (1890-1892), clinical professor (1900-1902), and professor of ophthalmology (1902-1920).

Weeks was one of the first to recognize the importance of the laboratory in ophthalmology. The clinical laboratory he established in 1893 at the Eye and Ear Infirmary soon became widely known for the excellence of its bacteriological and pathological studies. Here, in collaboration with Dr. George S. Dixon, Weeks worked out a method for using X rays to locate foreign bodies in the eye that remained an accepted technique for some fifty years. He also developed an operation for surgical reconstruction of the orbital socket to permit insertion of an artificial eye, devised a new instrument for cataract extraction, and contrived methods for the surgical treatment of trachoma and glaucoma. His publications, which dealt chiefly with the surgical aspects of his specialty, numbered more than 125. They included two books, *Diseases of the Eye, Ear, Throat, and Nose* (1892), a manual written in collaboration with Frank E. Miller and James P. McEvoy, and *A Treatise on Diseases of the Eye* (1910), a widely used text. Weeks was one of the founders of the American Board of Ophthalmology, served as president of the American Ophthalmological Society (1921), and in 1929 was awarded the Ophthalmic Research Medal of the American Medical Association.

Weeks married Jennie Post Parker, the daughter of a New York banker, on Apr. 29, 1890. They had one child, Eveline Parker. Despite his absorption with ophthalmology, Weeks was an astute businessman whose early poverty had made him appreciate the value of money, and under the guidance of his father-in-law he gained experience in finance and served as a director of two banks. His own successful investments gave him tremendous satisfaction, partly because they allowed him to make large contributions to charity. He also established scholarships for research in ophthalmology at the medical schools of the University of Michigan and New York University.

In 1923 Weeks began limiting his practice, spent more time in travel (one of his chief pleasures), and in 1927, having retired, moved to Portland, Oreg., to be near his daughter. There the department of ophthalmology at the University of Oregon medical school soon became his primary interest. He helped plan its research laboratory and contributed generously to its construction and to the establishment of its medical library, which was named in his honor.

Weeks was noted for his great capacity for work and his unruffled disposition. Unassuming and soft-spoken, he believed in moderation in every phase of life except work. In addition to travel, his chief hobbies were fishing and golf. He was a member of the Presbyterian Church. He died of a pulmonary embolus in San Diego, Calif., where he was spending the winter, and was buried in Portland.

[John E. Weeks, *Autobiog.* (1954), which includes a list of his publications; obituaries in *Archives of Ophthalmology,* June 1949 (also in Am. Ophthalmological Soc., *Trans.,* XLVII, 33–35), *Am. Jour. of Ophthalmology,* Apr. 1949, and *Jour. Am. Medic. Assoc.,* Apr. 2, 1949; *Nat. Cyc. Am. Biog.,* XXXVIII, 364–365; death record from Calif. Dept. of Health; information from members of the family and personal recollections.]

JOHN H. DUNNINGTON

WEIDENREICH, FRANZ (June 7, 1873-July 11, 1948), physical anthropologist, was born in Edenkoben, Germany, in the Bavarian Palatinate. He was the third son and youngest of four children of Jewish parents: Karl Weidenreich, the owner of a prosperous dry goods store, and Friederike (Edesheimer) Weidenreich.

After attending the local school, he was sent to nearby Landau to continue his education at the Gymnasium there. From Landau he went to the University at Munich, where he completed his preclinical medical course and took his physicum, which permitted him to continue his medical training. He then studied at Kiel and later at Strasbourg, where he received his M.D. in 1898. Following this, he completed the usual military service; in World War I, he was again on active military service in 1914-1915 at Braisach in southern Baden.

On Mar. 15, 1904, he married Mathilde Neuberger, to whom he was distantly related. Four daughters were born to this union: Friederike, who died shortly after birth, Elisabeth, Ruth, and Marion. Ruth followed her father's profession and practiced as a physician in New York City.

Weidenreich's academic career began in the department of anatomy at the University of Strasbourg, where he served as assistant and privatdocent from 1899 to 1901 under the distinguished anatomist and physical anthropologist Gustav Schwalbe. It is possible that Schwalbe's profound concern with fossil man and human evolution may have influenced his young assistant, for as early as 1904 Weidenreich published a paper on the evolution of the human chin. During his early career, however, his scientific investigations were largely concerned with human blood and lymph systems. In the first twenty years of his scientific career he published almost fifty papers in this field, many of great significance.

From 1901, Weidenreich worked at the University of Frankfurt am Main on the invitation of Dr. Paul Ehrlich. This relationship, however, ceased after a year and he returned to Strasbourg as prosector and in 1904 was appointed professor of anatomy.

As Weidenreich explored the ramifications of his early interest in hematology, he pursued its relationships with various tissue systems, particularly the osseous. As a result, the human skeleton, its structure, functions, and evolution, became his dominant scientific interest in the 1920's. At the same time, he published a number of basic papers on the structure and form of the human dentition. It was in this period that he wrote his influential paper on the evolution of the human foot.

This turn in his interests led him to undertake a study of a fossil human skull found at Ehringsdorf, Germany. His definitive report, published in 1927, marks the beginning of a profound and what was to be a totally dedicated interest in the fossil evidence of human evolution.

During this part of his career, Weidenreich was established at the University of Heidelberg as professor of anatomy. As a result of World War I, Strasbourg fell to the French and Weidenreich lost his post there. It was not until 1921 that he went to Heidelberg, where he remained until 1935. His scientific production had virtually ceased from 1914 at the outbreak of the war until 1921, when he was once more back in the academic and scientific world. But he was far from inactive during this period of seven years. Early in the war he saw service as a medical officer. For four years, until the city was lost to the French, he was a member of the Municipal Council of the City of Strasbourg, and until 1918, as president, he led the Democratic party of Alsace-Lorraine.

In the late 1920's and early 1930's racism, in a strongly anti-semitic orientation, became a major issue in Germany. Although it represented an attitude with deep and complex roots, it had become inflammatory in postwar Germany, to a large extent as the result of a pseudo-scientific racial literature that flourished in that period. With his Jewish tradition, Weidenreich, although not an active adherent, was nevertheless deeply concerned with the misuse of anthropological data and during this period wrote a considerable number of papers, both

Weidenreich

for scientific journals and for popular magazines, attacking the distorted racial views that were being widely promulgated. His decision to leave Germany was doubtless influenced by Hitler's rise to power, although his own academic position was apparently not threatened.

Late in 1934, while he was a visiting professor at the University of Chicago, Weidenreich accepted a professorship at the Peking Union Medical School to replace Davidson Black, who had recently died. The post carried the responsibility of continuing the researches begun by Black on the fossil human remains discovered at Chou Kou Tien, near Peking, during the previous decade. By this time Weidenreich's involvement in the problems of human evolution were a major focus of his scientific curiosity. And there is little doubt that this opportunity of making pioneer studies on what at that time was one of the earliest known hominids—Peking Man—must have played a major role in his acceptance of this new post. He resigned his Heidelberg professorship in 1935 and for the next six years continued his work in Peking. This flow of production included monographs on the endocranial casts, the mandibles, the dentition, and the long bones of Peking Man. From this brief period, there issued a series of major publications of outstanding scholarship dealing primarily with an evaluation of the fossil remains of Peking Man, but also ranging over the whole array of human fossils then known. These works and those that followed up to his death have placed Weidenreich in the very forefront of this field.

In 1941, as conditions became critical in China as a result of the Japanese invasion, Weidenreich was obliged to abandon his laboratory in Peking. Supported by the Rockefeller Foundation, he now moved to the American Museum of Natural History in New York City, where he continued his researches on Peking Man and on a series of related subjects, including reports on newly discovered remains of Pithecanthropus that had recently been discovered in Java. It was during this period that he produced his major opus, *The Skull of Sinanthropus Pekinensis*, in which he assembled one of the most detailed studies ever made on a hominid fossil.

On July 11, 1948, Weidenreich died of a coronary infarct and was interred in Westwood, New Jersey. In the century of research on the fossil record of man, Weidenreich's name is one of the most distinguished. His prescience and insight make his work masterly

Weill

and authoritative. His corpus of magisterial studies on the fossil remains of Peking Man remains today the major source of our knowledge of this significant stage of the hominid past.

[A full bibliography of Weidenreich's writings appears in the *Am. Jour. of Physical Anthropology*, June 1949. His work with fossils is described in Carleton S. Coon, *The Origin of Races* (1962). Obituary accounts appeared in the *Am. Anthropologist*, Jan.–Mar. 1949, by W. K. Gregory; *Nature*, Nov. 20, 1948; and *N.Y. Times*, July 13, 1948.]

HARRY L. SHAPIRO

WEILL, KURT (Mar. 2, 1900–Apr. 3, 1950), composer, was born in Dessau, Germany, of Jewish parents, Albert Weill and Emma (Ackermann) Weill. His mother was an amateur pianist, and his father, a cantor. His musical inclinations were encouraged, and at fourteen he began piano lessons with Albert Bing, who discerned his creative talent and urged him to study composition. At eighteen he enrolled in the Berlin Hochschule für Musik but left after less than a year to work as opera coach and conductor at Dessau and Lüdenscheid. Returning to Berlin in 1921, he studied privately with Ferruccio Busoni for the next three years. During this time he composed a number of large works in the severe and somewhat dissonant style then in vogue. Although he was on the way to recognition as a promising "modernist," this prospect failed to satisfy him.

Many factors contributed to Weill's dissatisfaction with the formalistic music he was then writing. He had grown up during World War I, had witnessed the collapse of the German empire, and was now experiencing the social unrest, the moral dissolution, and the political ferment of the 1920's. It was, moreover, the Jazz Age—not only in America, but also in Germany—where this contagiously uninhibited music, with its blues, fox-trots, charlestons, and shimmies, became the staple expression of the satirical cabarets that proliferated in postwar Berlin. Weill soon absorbed and transfigured this atmosphere in works that made him one of the most famous and successful theater composers of the twentieth century.

The first hint of a new direction came in 1922, when Weill was asked to write the music for a children's pantomime. To suit its purpose, the music had to be both simple and effective. The response from audiences of all ages convinced him that through music combined with theater he could communicate with the mass of ordinary people rather than with a restricted elite. Within a short time, Weill was fully committed to a career in the musical theater.

In 1924 two decisive events occurred: he met the dramatist Georg Kaiser, who was to be his first librettist, and the singing actress Lotte Lenya, who was to be his wife and the star of his biggest successes. They were married on Jan. 28, 1926. Weill's first opera, *The Protagonist,* was produced at Dresden on Mar. 27, 1926, to great acclaim. The one-act opera *Royal Palace* (Berlin, 1927, libretto by Ivan Goll) was less successful, perhaps because of its experimental character. It combined pantomine and film, play and opera. His opera buffa *The Tsar Has Himself Photographed* (Leipzig, Feb. 28, 1928) was a tremendous box-office success. Here Weill turned openly to jazz and other popular idioms. To those who accused him of "betraying" art, he replied, "I write for today. I don't care for posterity."

Thus, Weill identified himself with the movement known as *Zeitkunst*—"art of the present," contemporary in spirit, topical in content, popular in expression. Weill's vehicle for this was the "song-play," a contemporary version of the traditional German *Singspiel* that he developed in collaboration with the poet and playwright Berthold Brecht. They began with a one-act song-play called *Mahagonny* (July 17, 1927). This established the model for the Brecht-Weill "song-spiel": strongly satirical, at times bitterly cynical, ideologically motivated, yet artistically sophisticated and technically adroit, at once exploiting and transcending the topicality of *Zeitkunst* and both assimilating and transforming the jazz-based ensemble, the blues and cabaret-song styles, and the symbolically potent setting of an imagined America.

This is the model that we find fully developed in the expanded version of *Mahagonny*, titled *Aufstieg und Fall der Stadt Mahagonny* (*The Rise and Fall of the City of Mahagonny*), produced on Mar. 9, 1930. A Brechtian satire on the corruption of capitalistic society, its locale is a fictitious city in Alabama, where three ex-convicts are bent on establishing a new kind of society free from all moral restraints. The "Alabama Song" became one of Weill's hit tunes.

Less mordant in its satire, but more specifically evocative of the American scene—being set in the Chicago of 1919—was the Brecht-Weill song-play *Happy End* (1929), with its mock gangsters and hit tunes such as the "Bilbao Song" and "Surabaya Johnny."

The triumph of the Brecht-Weill collaboration was their freely adapted version of John Gay's *The Beggar's Opera* (1728), which they entitled *Die Dreigroschenoper* (*The Threepenny Opera*). Brecht redirected the thrust of political satire to Germany of the 1920's. Starring Lotte Lenya, it was produced in Berlin on Aug. 31, 1928, and immediately became a sweeping success, not only in Germany, where it had over 4,000 performances in one year, but throughout Europe. Strangely, the New York production in 1933 was a failure; but in 1952, in an English adaptation by Marc Blitzstein (with the setting changed to New York in the 1870's), it was successfully revived and thereafter enjoyed a phenomenal career in the United States, running into thousands of performances (its English locale was soon restored in the New York production).

The Threepenny Opera is unquestionably Weill's masterpiece and one of the most original, effective, and influential works of the modern musical theater. In style it is eclectic, ranging from jazz-derived and cabaret tunes to skillful parodies of operatic arias and choruses. It is also one of the most perfect collaborations between composer and librettist in the annals of music. It is both topical and timeless, a social satire that remains perennially fascinating for its human and musical qualities.

Weill's last two operas produced in Germany were *Die Bürgschaft* (*The Pledge,* 1932) and *Der Silbersee* (*The Silver Lake,* 1933), the former on a parable by Herder and the latter to a libretto by Georg Kaiser. *Der Silbersee* opened auspiciously with simultaneous performances in eleven German opera houses; but this success was deceptive, for Hitler and his Nazi party came into power in 1933. Weill was a marked man, not only as a Jew but also as a *Kultur-Bolshevist,* an exponent of "decadent" modernism. In February 1933, he and his wife fled Germany. Going to France, they lived for the next two years in Louveciennes near Paris, and then briefly in London. Weill's most important work of this period was a dance-play (or ballet with singing), *The Seven Deadly Sins,* in which Lotte Lenya and the dancer Tilly Losch costarred as twin sisters who venture forth amid lures and temptations of the world to earn enough money to build a home for their parents and two brothers—in Louisiana!

In 1935, Weill and his wife made the transition from an imaginary America to the reality. The famous stage director Max Reinhardt invited him to New York, to write music for a historical pageant of the Jewish people, *The Eternal Road.* Weill went, but the production was delayed for two years; meanwhile, he wrote the music for an antiwar fable, *Johnny Johnson*, by the North Carolina playwright Paul Green. Produced in New York on Nov. 19, 1936, it had a mixed reception.

With *Knickerbocker Holiday* (Oct. 19, 1938), to a libretto by Maxwell Anderson, Weill began his second career as a highly successful and critically respected composer of musical shows for Broadway. His next show, *Lady in the Dark* (1941), broke new ground as a "musical play"—that is, in the words of Moss Hart, "a show in which the music and lyrics carry the story forward dramatically and psychologically." With *One Touch of Venus* (1943), Weill returned to musical comedy, but in 1947 he collaborated with the playwright Elmer Rice and the poet Langston Hughes in a musical version of *Street Scene,* Rice's play of lower middle-class life in New York. Although labeled "an American opera," it hewed to the vernacular in both music and text and was essentially a seriosentimental musical play.

Weill evidently aimed at covering a wide spectrum of the musical theater. His next effort was a folk opera, *Down in the Valley* (1948), based on the folksong of that title (the score also used other well-known Anglo-American folksongs). Intended primarily for performance by schools and amateur groups, it proved to be very popular. Weill's last work was a musical tragedy, *Lost in the Stars* (1949), with a libretto by Maxwell Anderson based on Alan Paton's novel of racial injustice in South Africa, *Cry, the Beloved Country.*

Weill, who became an American citizen in 1943, fully adapted to the reality of life in the United States. For many years he and his wife lived on a farm in Rockland County, N.Y. He liked to read and to collect paintings. In person he was short and rather stocky, with a round face, large eyes (he wore glasses), and a very high forehead. He died in New York City.

Musically, Weill had a triple career: as a composer of instrumental and vocal works in the modern tradition of European art music; as a composer of works for the German musical theater; and as a versatile composer of works in English for the American musical theater. The first career earned him the respect of serious musicians. The second career produced his most original and universally admired works, culminating in *Die Dreigroschenoper.* The third and last was an extraordinary tour de force of adaptation and assimilation, which not only brought him immediate acclaim but

also assured him of an enduring place in the musical history of the United States.

[The only book devoted entirely to Weill (in German) is Hellmut Kotschenreuther's *Kurt Weill* (1962), a monograph. There are useful articles in various reference works, notably by Kurt Stone, in *Die Musik in Geschichte und Gegenwart,* XIV (1968), with a comprehensive list of works, bibliographical references, and a photograph of the composer taken in 1940; by David Ewen, in *Composers Since 1900,* pp. 622–626 (1969); and by Richard Jackson, in the *McGraw-Hill Encyc. of World Biog.* (1974). An early impression by Virgil Thomson, "Most Melodious Tears," appeared in *Modern Music,* Nov.–Dec. 1933, and a perceptive appreciation by H. W. Hensheimer in *Tomorrow,* Mar. 1948. A valuable study by Donald Mitchell is "Kurt Weill's *Dreigroschenoper* and German Cabaret-Opera in the 1920's" in the *Chesterian,* July 1950. For the American theater works, consult David Ewen, *Complete Book of the Am. Musical Theater* (1958), and Stanley Green, *The World of Musical Comedy* (1960). Performance data on the operas will be found in A. Loewenberg, *Annals of Opera* (1943; 2d ed., 1955).]

GILBERT CHASE

WELLING, RICHARD WARD GREENE (Aug. 27, 1858–Dec. 17, 1946), political and educational reformer, was born at his family's summer home, Pojac Point Farm, in North Kingstown, R.I. He was the younger of two sons and fourth of six children of Charles Hunt Welling, a wholesale textile merchant in Philadelphia, and Katharine Celia (Greene) Welling. His father's family, from Trenton, N.J., traced its ancestry back to a late-seventeenth-century settler on Long Island. His mother was from Rhode Island, her grandfather having been a brother of the Revolutionary War general Nathanael Greene. The boy was named for his maternal uncle Richard Ward Greene, chief justice of Rhode Island.

Charles Welling moved his family in 1863 to New York, where soon afterward his business went into bankruptcy. Though he later repaid all his debts and regained financial security, a lifelong fear of penury plagued his son Richard. Somewhat high-strung as a youth, Richard was instilled by both parents with the virtues of stoicism and self-reliance, but grew up painfully shy and self-conscious. After attending private school in New York, he entered Harvard in 1876. College proved disappointing, save for the formation of several close friendships, including one with his classmate Theodore Roosevelt. Graduating (B.A.) in 1880, he wanted to become a sheep raiser in the West, but his father vetoed this idea, and Welling spent the next two years at the Harvard Law School. After a brief stint as a clerk in a New York law firm, he was admitted to the bar in 1883 and began a private law practice.

It was, however, as a municipal reformer of the Mugwump type that Welling made his mark. Previously a Republican, he supported Grover Cleveland in the presidential election of 1884. He early joined the City Reform Club, founded in 1882 by Theodore Roosevelt and dedicated to the principles of honest, nonpartisan city government, and for the next two decades was in the forefront of every effort to purify city politics and unseat the entrenched Tammany machine. He fought against bribery in elections and—as secretary of the Commonwealth Club, founded in 1886 by Carl Schurz, E. L. Godkin, and others—for the adoption of the Australian ballot. He also arranged the meetings and speakers for the People's Municipal League, which ran a reform candidate for mayor in 1890. Beginning in 1892, he and Edmond Kelly organized Good Government Clubs in every assembly district in Manhattan; these contributed importantly to the election in 1894 of the reform mayor William L. Strong. In that same year, Welling helped establish the National Municipal League. He was active in the Citizens' Union campaign that failed in its attempt to elect Seth Low mayor in 1897, and in the successful campaigns of Low for mayor in 1901 and of William Travers Jerome for district attorney in 1905. A few years later, Mayor William J. Gaynor appointed Welling to the city Civil Service Commission, where he served from 1909 to 1913.

Discouraged by the defeat of Seth Low in 1897 and by the decline of the Good Government Clubs, upset by a growing conviction that voters supported reformers only in times of the most blatant public scandals, and worried about his declining law practice, Welling in the late 1890's began to waver in his zeal for municipal reform. At this time he became interested in the activities of the George Junior Republic, a self-governing community of young boys, which had been set up in 1895 in Freeville, N.Y., by William R. George. Welling became convinced that the real key to reform was education, and in 1904 he established the School Citizens Committee—later renamed the National Self Government Committee—to develop "a real love of democracy in the public schools of our country" (Welling to William Jay Schieffelin, Jan. 20, 1940, Welling Papers). Encouraged by his friend John Dewey, he began to lecture widely on the need for schools to adopt both civics courses, which would give a realistic picture of urban politics, and provisions for student self-government.

With America's entry into World War I, the fifty-eight-year-old Welling, who had served as an ensign during the Spanish-American War, returned to the navy and was given command of the base at Montauk Point, Long Island. There he introduced a novel program of limited self-government for his men. After the war he enthusiastically resumed his educational work. Sensitive to criticism and highly opinionated, he became involved in bitter controversies with educators like President A. Lawrence Lowell of Harvard over his belief that students should witness and participate in political activities; but he also won many adherents to his point of view. In 1932 Welling, along with Lyman Beecher Stowe, founded the Boys Brotherhood Republic, a boys' club on New York's Lower East Side, which worked to eliminate juvenile delinquency by imparting a sense of responsibility to its members through self-government.

Welling returned to municipal reform during the 1930's. He took part in each of the three successful mayoralty campaigns of Fiorello H. La Guardia, and, as president of the Civil Service Reform Association (to which he had belonged since 1897), he led the battle that deprived ex-mayor James J. Walker of his municipal pension. On the national scene, Welling voted in 1932 for the Socialist Norman Thomas, but he approved of the New Deal and cast his next three presidential ballots for Franklin D. Roosevelt. Among other interests, he was an active officeholder in the American Society for the Prevention of Cruelty to Animals, the Parks and Playgrounds Association of New York, the Symphony Society of New York, the Municipal Art Society, and the National Sculpture Society.

Welling never married. In 1946, at the age of eighty-eight, he contracted a severe cold and died at St. Luke's Hospital in New York City. After a brief Episcopalian service (his denomination throughout life), he was buried in North Kingstown, R.I. Though difficult and dogmatic at times, Richard Welling epitomized those who saw reform as a fight constantly to be waged. In this sense his contributions were symbolic as well as tangible. In the judgment of one prominent political scientist, "It was this great and good man who more than any other in the past fifty years successfully contributed to the cause of good government and the demolition of the machine" (introduction by Roy V. Peel to William L. Riordon, *Plunkitt of Tammany Hall*, 1948).

[Welling Papers, including diaries and letters, in the N.Y. Public Lib.; Welling's autobiography, *As the Twig Is Bent* (1942); autobiographical statements in *Reports* of Harvard College Class of 1880; Robert Muccigrosso, "Richard W. G. Welling: A Reformer's Life" (Ph.D. diss., Columbia Univ., 1966) and "The City Reform Club," *N.-Y. Hist. Soc. Quart.*, July 1968.]

ROBERT MUCCIGROSSO

WEST, JAMES EDWARD (May 16, 1876-May 15, 1948), social worker, lawyer, and Boy Scout leader, was born in Washington, D.C., the only child of James Robert West and Mary (Tyree) West. His father, who has been described as a Tennessee merchant, died before or shortly after the boy's birth, and his mother, who supported herself as a seamstress, died of tuberculosis before he was seven. In the Washington orphanage where he was placed he was punished as a malingerer until a medical examination revealed that he had contracted tuberculosis of the hip and knee. Sent to a hospital, where he remained nearly two years (including many months strapped to an orthopedic board), he was returned to the orphanage as an incurable. Strength of character, rooted in a Presbyterian religious faith that nurtured the will to serve others, apparently enabled the boy to surmount his bleak prospects as a physically handicapped orphan. The experience molded his life. It explains both his adoption of a career in child welfare and his preference for social work programs that stressed character building rather than environmental change.

An important episode in West's personal quest for fulfillment occurred around the age of twelve, when Mrs. Ellis Spear, a friend of his deceased mother, brought him home to play with her children and aroused his interest in literature. Gradually his consciousness extended beyond the confines of his orphanage and his handicap. His reading triggered ambitions and revealed latent qualities of leadership. West persuaded the authorities to allow him to supervise the orphanage library, and he secured permission for readers to stay up an hour later; sometimes he bribed other children to read by paying them a penny a book. The orphanage next consented to his request that a group of children be permitted to attend a regular public school. He himself, after completing grammar school at the age of sixteen, enrolled in Washington's Business High School, where he managed the football team, supervised the library, and edited the school paper. At the same time he carried out his responsibilities at the orphanage as librarian, night watchman, and laundryman.

Following his high school graduation in 1895, West secured a regular job on the orphanage staff and launched an improvement campaign that included painting, rat extermination, and exposure of mismanagement to the board of directors. He then secured a bookkeeping position at a bicycle shop (at which time he learned to walk without crutches and even to ride a bike). His urge for self-improvement led him to an attorney's office, where he read law while participating in YMCA work. West then became a student in Washington's National University; supporting himself as a YMCA employee and War Department stenographer, he received the degrees of LL.B. and LL.M. in 1901 and was admitted to the bar that same year. The influence of Theodore Roosevelt, with whom he had become acquainted and whom he admired throughout his life, helped get him an appointment to the Board of Pension Appeals in 1902. West later moved to the Department of the Interior as assistant attorney, and entered a private legal practice in 1906. He married Marion Olivia Speaks on June 19, 1907. Their first child, James Edward, died in childhood; the others were Arthur Pratt, Marion, Helen Margaret, and Robert.

During the first decade of the twentieth century West devoted his spare time to child welfare activities. He was involved in the citizens' committee that secured a juvenile court for Washington, D.C. As secretary and director of the Washington Playground Association, he assumed a major role in establishing that community's public playground system. In 1908 he collaborated with Theodore Dreiser, then editing the *Delineator Magazine,* in a "child-rescue" campaign, which succeeded in placing more than two thousand dependent children in foster homes. He interested Roosevelt in the campaign, and Roosevelt endorsed his proposal for a White House Conference on dependent children. West made the arrangements for the conference, which met in January 1909 and formally resolved in favor of placing dependent, but normal, children in homes rather than institutions; it also condemned the separation of children from natural parents for reasons of poverty alone. Representing a kind of children's Magna Carta, the White House Conference provided a major stimulus to the enactment of mothers' pension legislation in nearly every state within the next decade.

When the Boy Scouts of America was incorporated in Washington, D.C., in February 1910, prominent New York and Washington social workers recommended West for the position of executive officer. He declined at first, but finally agreed to accept a temporary assignment beginning January 1911. He remained with the organization as chief scout executive until his retirement in 1943. He also served on the nine-member International Scout Committee and edited *Boys' Life,* a scout periodical, from 1922 to 1943.

West and the Boy Scouts made an ideal combination. Scouting enabled West to devote his life to child welfare and, equally important, scouting was compatible with his personal preference for youth programs that stressed character development. The Boy Scouts, in turn, desperately needed West's idealism, dedication, and administrative talents in order to survive. During the early years they had to compete with similar organizations such as the Woodcraft Indians of Ernest Thompson Seton, the Boy Pioneers of Daniel Carter Beard, and the American Boy Scouts, which had briefly enjoyed the support of William Randolph Hearst. Under West's leadership the Boy Scouts of America devised techniques that enabled them to absorb the other groups or surpass them in prestige and membership. The combination of scout symbols and activities—uniforms and other visible insignia of membership (designed by Beard), the scout oath and laws, emphasis on the outdoors, the troop and patrol system, merit badge progression, community service ideals—were shrewdly designed to fulfill a variety of boyhood needs and drives. They appealed to a boy's quest for adventure and security, for individuality and belonging, for competitive achievement and cooperative association with his peers, and for autonomy and adult authority.

The hegemony of the Boy Scouts was rooted also in a sophisticated public relations program. West continually stressed the services of the scouting movement to the community and nation. He carefully emphasized that scouting merely supplemented other institutions such as church, home, and school, and indeed had no facilities of its own except for camping. Most important, scouting made provisions for the active participation of thousands of volunteers through its elaborate hierarchy of patrols, troops, local councils, and national council. Scouting flourished, finally, because of the image of the movement that West projected. It was an extension of his own personality and ideals—conservatism and Americanism, wholesomeness, utility, character building, and citizenship based upon religious faith.

West's view of the direction scouting should take was not unanimously endorsed by the national council. Seton and Beard, though themselves embroiled in a personal feud, publicly assailed West for his alleged preoccupation with bureaucratization, money raising, and the courting of powerful support. The English founder of the Boy Scout movement, Lord Baden-Powell, urged that the American organization not sacrifice the "jolly game" aspect of the movement for the sake of efficiency and membership gains. The removal of Seton from the national council effectively undercut his influence, but Beard remained a vigorous, and at times petty, critic of what he regarded as the downgrading of the strenuous outdoor and woodcraft tradition. West prevailed in the end.

West participated in three later White House conferences on children, called by Presidents Hoover and Roosevelt. He received many awards for his welfare services, including three honorary degrees. Five years after his retirement as chief scout executive, he died of Addison's disease in New Rochelle, N.Y., where he had made his home for a quarter of a century. He was buried in Kensico Cemetery, Valhalla, N.Y.

West was one of the outstanding child welfare workers of the twentieth century. Through the White House Conference of 1909 he helped launch a revolt against the institutionalization of normal, dependent children. He then shaped one of the major youth agencies of the United States, one that touched the lives of millions of children and adults. His perspective, to be sure, was limited. He always remained the nineteenth-century moralist, enunciating truisms about the importance of character and its ability to triumph over adversity: "With a worthwhile goal, hard work, training, and the determination to succeed, there is hardly anything that a young man today may not hope to attain." Yet one must concede, in the end, that in West's case the truisms were true.

[James E. West, *Making the Most of Yourself: The Boy Scout Trail to the Greatest of All Adventures* (1941), a compilation of editorials he prepared for *Boys' Life*, expresses his ideals and contains a biographical sketch by Theodore Roosevelt, Jr. See also, for biographical data, West's *What We Have Learned since the First White House Conference on the Care of Dependent Children* (Child Welfare Committee of America, 1928) and his "Training Young America for Citizenship," *Playground*, Apr. 1923; Myron M. Stearns, "Boys Will Be Scouts," *American Mag.*, June 1927; *Thirty Years of Service: Tributes to James E. West* (Boy Scouts of America, 1941); biographical sketch in *Recreation*, Feb. 1943; Harold A. Jambor, "Theodore Dreiser, *The Delineator Magazine*, and Dependent Children: A Background Note on the Calling of the 1909 White House Conference," *Social Service Rev.*, Mar. 1958; *Who Was Who in America*, II (1950); *Nat. Cyc. Am. Biog.*, XXXIV, 11; obituary in *N.Y. Times*, May 16, 1948. William D. Murray, *The Hist. of the Boy Scouts of America* (1937), is descriptive and contains some material on West. Specialized studies of Scouting include: Harold P. Levy, *Building a Popular Movement: A Case Study of the Public Relations of the Boy Scouts of America* (1944); Edwin Nicholson, *Education and the Boy Scout Movement in America* (1941); Ray O. Wyland, *Scouting in the Schools* (1934); and Allan R. Whitmore, "Beard, Boys, and Buckskins: Daniel Carter

Beard and the Preservation of the Am. Pioneer Tradition" (Ph.D. diss., Northwestern Univ., 1970). A death certificate was obtained from the N.Y. State Dept of Health.]

ROY LUBOVE

WESTERGAARD, HARALD MALCOLM (Oct. 9, 1888–June 22, 1950), civil engineer and engineering scientist, was born in Copenhagen, Denmark, the son of Harald Ludvig Westergaard and Thora Alvida (Koch) Westergaard. His father was professor of economics and statistics and his grandfather, professor of oriental languages, at the University of Copenhagen.

Westergaard received his first degree in engineering in 1911 at the Royal Technical College in Copenhagen, where he worked under Asger Ostenfeld, with whom he kept in close touch until his death in 1931. Westergaard pursued graduate studies at Göttingen under Ludwig Prandtl and at Munich under August Föppl until 1914, when he received a fellowship of the American Scandinavian Foundation to work toward the Ph.D. at the University of Illinois in Urbana. He received the degree in 1916 and, with a strong recommendation from Ostenfeld, became an instructor in theoretical and applied mechanics at Illinois. He was promoted successively to assistant professor in 1921, associated professor in 1924, and professor in 1927. In 1925 he received belatedly the degree of Doktor-Ingenieur from the Technische Hochschule in Munich. His work for that degree was completed in 1915, but World War I delayed the publication of his thesis for ten years. His dissertation, as explained in a letter written in 1926 to Ostenfeld, was dedicated to his former teacher "as a modest sign of the gratitude I feel toward you."

Westergaard's most productive years were the two decades he spent in Urbana. Many of his nearly forty papers and monographs published during that period are models of the lucid presentation of solutions to important practical engineering problems and are still widely referred to. The most influential of these papers include "Moments and Stresses in Slabs," written with W. A. Slater and published in *Proceedings of the American Concrete Institute,* 1921, Vol. 17, and in Reprint and Circular Series No. 32 of the National Research Council; "Buckling of Elastic Structures," in *Proceedings of the American Society of Civil Engineers,* 1921, Vol. 47; "Computation of Stresses in Bridge Slabs Due to Wheel Loads," in *Public Roads,* March 1930; and "Water Pressure on Dams During Earth-quakes," in *Proceedings of the American Society of Civil Engineers,* 1931, Vol. 57.

In 1936 Westergaard left Illinois to become Gordon McKay professor of civil engineering at Harvard. In 1937 he became dean of the Graduate School of Engineering at Harvard, in which position he served until 1946, when he returned to full-time academic and research work.

In 1936 he was commissioned a lieutenant commander in the Civil Engineers Corps, United States Naval Reserve, and served intermittently on active duty from 1942 to 1946, when he retired with the rank of captain.

On Sept. 15, 1925, Westergaard married Rachel Harriet Talbot, the daughter of Arthur Newell Talbot, who had just retired from the University of Illinois as professor and head of the department of municipal and sanitary engineering, where he also was in charge of theoretical and applied mechanics. The Westergaards had two children: a daughter, Mary Talbot, born in 1927; and a son, Peter Talbot, born in 1931.

With his unusual physical insight and his analytical ability, Westergaard was able to present in his classroom lectures as well as in his papers new and refreshing approaches to engineering mechanics. He made important contributions to engineering design as a consultant and adviser to the United States Bureau of Reclamation (work on structural and geophysical aspects of Hoover Dam and Lake Mead); the United States Navy Bureau of Yards and Docks; the Bureau of Public Roads (design of highway pavements and highway bridge slabs); and, in his later years, the Army Chief of Engineers (on airfield pavements), and the Panama Canal.

His scholarly contributions were recognized by the award of the Wason Medal from the American Concrete Institute in 1921, the J. James R. Croes Medal from the American Society of Civil Engineers in 1934, and the Thomas Fitch Rowland Prize of the American Society of Civil Engineers in 1950. His other honors included the honorary degrees of Dr. Techn. of the Royal Technical College in Copenhagen, in 1929, and D. Sc., Lehigh University, 1930, as well as election as a fellow of the American Academy of Arts and Sciences.

Although Westergaard's most notable contributions to engineering were in the areas of stress analysis, particularly of plates and slabs, he was one of the great scholars in America in engineering mechanics and the mathematical theory of elasticity. Because of his meticulous scholarship and his unwillingness to publish anything that was not complete and perfect, his publications were not as numerous as those of some of his contemporaries. He did not live to complete the latter part of *Theory of Elasticity and Plasticity,* a textbook begun early in 1949 and published posthumously in 1952 by the Harvard University Press as Harvard Monographs in Applied Science Number 3. Nevertheless, the number of his publications that are of the highest quality and influence is at least as great as that of any of his peers.

Westergaard was a striking figure, intellectually brilliant and physically strong. He once referred jokingly to his Viking heritage, when someone mentioned England, that "I have a fatherly interest in the English." He loved art and music, and although somewhat shy, he was warm and thoughtful of others. He loved to walk—striding along, swinging his cane at the dandelions, deeply immersed in thought, and completely unaware of the glances of passersby.

After a long illness, Westergaard died on June 22, 1950 and was buried in Belmont, Mass.

[The principal biographical sources are an obituary by Gordon M. Fair, Albert Haertlein, and Richard von Mises in the *Harvard Univ. Gazette,* Dec. 16, 1950; an article in Danish, "Kapitel 6, H. M. Westergaard og Hans Forbindelse Med A. Ostenfeld"—I have not been able to find where this was published, by whom, or when; and the preface and introduction to Westergaard's *Theory of Elasticity and Plasticity.*]
NATHAN M. NEWMARK

WHEELOCK, LUCY (Feb. 1, 1857–Oct. 2, 1946), kindergarten educator, was born in Cambridge, Vt., the second of six children of Edwin Wheelock, a Congregationalist minister, and Laura (Pierce) Wheelock. Lucy's early education took place at home under the tutelage of her mother and father, who owned an excellent library and taught his daughter to love and revere books and scholarship. She was graduated from high school in Reading, Mass., in 1874, and then in 1876 attended the Chauncy Hall School in Boston to prepare to enter Wellesley College. While a student at Chauncy Hall, she discovered its newly opened kindergarten and decided it would be her life's work. On the advice of Elizabeth Peabody, she enrolled in a one-year course at the Kindergarten Training School of Ella Snelling Hatch in Boston, and in 1879 she became an assistant in the Chauncy Hall kindergarten and later took charge of it.

In 1888 Lucy Wheelock opened a class to train kindergarten teachers, at a time when the kindergarten was still a very new idea to American education. There was an acute need for well-trained, qualified kindergartners, particularly in Boston, where the city council had just appropriated funds to support kindergartens in the public schools. While her first class consisted of six pupils, enrollment and the course of study expanded rapidly. The Wheelock School was unusual in that it did not fail when normal schools began to offer courses in kindergartening nor did it ever become absorbed by a collegiate education department. In 1940, when Lucy Wheelock retired as head of the school and arranged for it to become incorporated at Wheelock College, there were twenty-three faculty members, five administrators, and over three hundred students.

At the school, Wheelock acquainted future teachers with her conception of the breadth of early childhood education. In the early years, she taught almost exclusively from Froebel's *Mother Play,* but before long she added a diversity of courses with more general intellectual content and offered lectures on such subjects as Americanization, citizenship, woman suffrage, and political responsibility. Students were taught to be knowledgeable about community affairs and to understand the significance as well as the techniques of organizing mothers' meetings in order to involve mothers in the education of their young children. Wheelock felt that the two most important principles of education and life were self-activity (a child seeing, thinking, and acting for himself) and continuity (no break or gap should be allowed between kindergarten and the primary grades). As a result, the teachers of the respective grades needed acquaintance with each other's training, goals, and methods and Wheelock provided this experience for her future teachers. By 1929, all Wheelock students were taking a three-year course of study, receiving a nursery-kindergarten-primary diploma after completing courses, observation, and student teaching at all three levels.

Wheelock served as a mediator in the controversies among kindergartners by acting to maintain the best aspects of the traditional kindergarten while updating it with the most significant current educational theories. She thought that the division among kindergartners was healthy and that many of the "new" ideas and programs advocated by reformers were part of or in harmony with Froebel's original ideas. While there were vast differences, a certain core of Froebelian principles were common to all. These included an appreciation of the importance of self-activity and self-expression for the child, the concept of growth in child development from the simple to the complex, and the notion that education should take into account the three-fold nature of man: physical, social, and spiritual.

Wheelock was an energetic leader within the kindergarten movement. She was a founding member of the International Kindergarten Union, organized in 1893 to provide a focal point for the widely scattered kindergarten efforts across the country. From 1895 to 1899 she served as the I.K.U. president, and in that capacity lectured tirelessly on the kindergarten movement and the education of young children. She was a petite, well-proportioned woman with a warm smile and bright eyes and was a popular, persuasive speaker. Her active participation in many organizations included posts as chairman in 1908 of the National Congress of Mothers (later to become the National Congress of Parents and Teachers) and vice-president of the Department of Superintendence of the National Education Association. In 1929 she became a member of the educational committee of the League of Nations.

Wheelock wrote many articles for educational journals and was joint author with Elizabeth Colson of *Talks to Mothers* (1920). She translated several German works, including children's stories and some of Froebel's writings, for Henry Barnard's *Journal of Education*. She edited several books, including two important volumes sponsored by the I.K.U., *The Kindergarten* (1913) and *Pioneers of the Kindergarten in America* (1923); the five-volume *Kindergarten Children's Hour* (1924), a guide for mothers whose children could not attend kindergarten; and *The Kindergarten in New England* (1935).

In 1925 the University of Vermont awarded Wheelock an honorary degree of doctor of letters. She died at the age of eighty-nine of coronary thrombosis in her home in Boston.

[An important source of information on Wheelock's life and educational views is *The Wheel*, the fiftieth anniversary issue of the yearbook of Wheelock School. *Leadership in Education* (1964), by Winifred Bain, is a useful history of the college and Lucy Wheelock's role in shaping it. Also valuable is an unpublished manuscript by Abigail A. Eliot, "Miss Lucy Wheelock —Her Contributions to Early Childhood Education," Jan. 1959, at the Wheelock College Lib. See also *Who Was Who in Am.*, II (1950); Jean Betzner, "Lucy Wheelock," *Childhood Ed.*, Jan. 1947, p. 247; Caroline D. Aborn, "Lucy Wheelock," Nat. Council on Primary Ed., *Bull.*, 13 (1930), 1–2; and J. L. Harbour, "America's Leading Women Educators," *Harper's Bazaar*, Sept. 1, 1900, pp. 1102–1107.

For Wheelock's educational views and positions, see *The Kindergarten*, pp. 297–301 (1913), and her many articles in *Kindergarten Review*. Of particular interest are "The Changing and Permanent Elements in the Kindergarten," June 1910, pp. 603–611; "'Kindergarten It Shall Be!'," June 1911, pp. 612–615; and "Kindergarten Clubs and Parent-Teacher Associations," Dec. 1915, pp. 261–263. Two other significant articles are "The Kindergarten Spirit in the Grades," *American Childhood*, Sept. 1929, pp. 5–7, and "From the Kindergarten to the Primary School," *Childhood Educ.*, May 1942, pp. 414–416, which Wheelock felt she had originally written in 1894. One should also consult *Talks to Mothers*, a compilation of kindergarten materials and the intro. to *Kindergarten Children's Hour*, five vols. (1920).]
                                    ELIZABETH D. ROSS

WHITE, ALMA BRIDWELL (June 16, 1862-June 26, 1946), founder of the Pillar of Fire Church, was born on a farm on Kinniconick Creek, in Lewis County, Ky., the fifth daughter and seventh of eleven children of William Moncure Bridwell, a tanner and small farmer from Virginia, and Mary Ann (Harrison) Bridwell, a native of Kentucky. According to her autobiography, Alma (christened Mollie Alma) passed a blighted, toilsome childhood. Her melancholiac mother was harsh and exacting. "Deeply convicted of sin" at the age of nine, Alma White was later to recall the absence of religious guidance as the most painful burden of her early life. Though both parents were religious in a gloomy way, neither read the Bible or took the children to church. In 1878, however, Alma underwent a conversion experience in a revival conducted by W. B. Godbey, the learned holiness evangelist.

She decided to become a teacher and began in a log schoolhouse, between her studies at the nearby Vanceburg Seminary and at the Millersburg (Ky.) Female College. During 1882-1883 she taught at Bannack, Mont., where she had relatives, and where she met Kent White, a Methodist ministerial candidate and part-time book agent. She then taught at various schools in the West, with a further year of study in Millersburg. A large part of her earnings went to relieve her never prosperous family. In September 1887, having become engaged to White, she enrolled in an elocution school in Denver while he studied at the University of Denver. They were married on December 21.

As a husband White proved both improvident and unsympathetic, inviting his meddlesome, exigent mother to join the impecunious menage swelled by the birth of two sons, Arthur Kent and Ray Bridwell. Shortly after Arthur's birth, White was appointed pastor of an obscure, distressed church at Lamar, Colo. In subsequent pastorates he encouraged his wife to lead the singing, exhort, and testify. Though she verged on homeliness and was plagued by nervous and other diseases, Alma White had unusual speaking talents and a dignified appearance. At length, however, Kent White began to put a damper on his wife's enthusiasm, for she was alienating many of his friends and colleagues by her criticisms of their tepid piety and un-Methodist practices. The Whites had interminable matrimonial and theological wrangles, but Alma continued to aid in the church work and widened her contacts in the Colorado Holiness Association.

Her commitment to lead in the spread of holiness was strengthened in March 1893, when she experienced the "second blessing" of entire sanctification. Her health improved, and she openly assumed the role of a female preacher, to rescue, as she claimed, the doctrines of John Wesley, repudiated by the Methodists in their rush toward middle-class decorum and modernity. Her opponents retaliated by having White demoted to a particularly wretched circuit, but his wife became even more outspoken in exposing "the cloven hoof of the devil" both in orthodox Methodism and within the holiness movement. In 1895 White withdrew from regular ministerial duties to join his wife's endeavors.

The Whites now entered on a peripatetic life of open-air revivals and camp meetings, sustained solely by freewill offerings. Working from a base in Denver, they seeded several small churches and city missions in Colorado, Wyoming, and Montana. In December 1901 Alma White and fifty followers organized the Pentecostal Union Church, and she was ordained an elder in March 1902. That same year she published her autobiographical *Looking Back from Beulah,* explaining her course and defending the right of women to preach. Her organization was soon publishing the *Pentecostal Union Herald* (after 1904, the *Pillar of Fire*).

Like other holiness sects, this church taught the imminence of Christ's return, exercised stringent discipline in dress and conduct, banned tobacco and alcohol, and practiced divine healing. Several doctrinal peculiarities distinguished the church, but the chief point of separation from other holiness groups was its insistence on maintaining a strict Wesleyan standard. The Pillar of Fire, as it was known after 1917, tended to regard other holiness churches—including the largest, the Church of the Nazarene—as "derelict" or "counterfeit" professors of holiness. It was a church for plain people, characterized by a rapturous liberty of worship that one British reporter called "no more than old-time Methodism" (*Story of My Life,* IV,

236). Converts (among them Alma's father and several of her siblings) "shouted for joy" to the music of street organ, piano, or snare drum, while skipping and bounding in the "holy dance." But even as she encouraged this release of holy emotions, Alma White bitterly attacked a new development within the holiness movement, that of pentecostalism. Although glossolalia and associated phenomena had recurred in the historic church, she assailed the pentecostalists for practicing a "latter day sorcery." Pentecostalism thrived in spite of such opposition.

The winter of 1904-1905 saw White's first revival in England (she made nearly thirty transatlantic evangelistic tours in all). As fresh accessions came in this country, she had a "leading" to move the church's headquarters from Denver to Zarephath, N.J., which was accomplished in 1906-1908. In Zarephath, White adopted military uniforms for the evangelists and missionaries, along the lines of the Salvation Army. Over the next three decades her church launched extensive publishing and educational enterprises, including two radio stations. In these her sons, both Columbia University graduates, played a large role. She was at last consecrated bishop in 1918. Though her sons were ordained to the Pillar of Fire ministry, Kent White broke with his family and left the church after the move to Zarephath, going over to the pentecostalists. White's six-volume *The Story of My Life* (1919-1934) recounts her side of the break and reveals her sense of mission to the world, as shown through biblical prophecy and typology and the guidance of her visions and dreams. Of her other numerous books, the most interesting are *Hymns and Poems* (1931), with its emphases on the blood sacrifice of Christ and the joyous assurance of the sanctified; and *The Ku Klux Klan in Prophecy* (1925), in which she abandoned the holiness movement's traditional hostility to secret societies to endorse the Klan's populistic and no-popery aims, as a patriotism based in Scripture.

Alma White died of heart disease at Zarephath, just five months before the death of her son Ray, and was buried in Fairmont Cemetery, Denver. Her church of more than 4,000 members had established Alma White College and other preparatory and Bible schools in Denver, Zarephath, Cincinnati, and Los Angeles. Among the congregations was a branch in London, which issued a British *Pillar of Fire*. The church continued its missions to the impoverished and unschooled. Alma White's career, like that of the jaunty Aimee Semple McPherson, was one of ministry to a class of people shunned by or disaffected from the mainstream churches.

[The major biographical sources on Alma White are her own writings, which are voluminous; besides the *Story of My Life* and other works mentioned above, her books include *The New Testament Church*, 2 vols. (1911–1912), *Demons and Tongues* (1910), *Truth Stranger than Fiction* (1913), and *Klansmen: Guardians of Liberty* (1926). The *Nat. Cyc. Am. Biog.*, XXXV, 151–153, contains articles on Alma, Kent, and Ray White; Current Vol. F, p. 219, has one on Arthur Kent White. Most studies of holiness sects are heavily sociological; there are numerous popular treatments, which tend to be sensationalistic and derisive. The two best books for placing the Pillar of Fire in historical context are Timothy L. Smith's excellent history of the Nazarenes, *Called unto Holiness* (1962), and Vinson Synan, *The Holiness-Pentecostal Movement in the U.S.* (1971).]

MARIE CASKEY

WHITE, STEWART EDWARD (Mar. 12, 1873–Sept. 18, 1946), author, was born in Grand Rapids, Mich., the first of the five sons of Thomas Stewart White, a prosperous lumberman, and Mary Eliza (Daniell) White. His paternal grandfather, of English and Scottish descent, had come to Grand Haven, Mich., from Ashfield, Mass., in 1836; his mother was a native of Hoosick Falls, N.Y. Stewart White spent much of his early childhood traveling with his father through lumber towns in northern Michigan and later, between the ages of twelve and sixteen, to California, where his father held lumber interests. He passed his time on ranches and in the rapidly developing towns of the West. These early experiences whetted his appetite for the outdoors and adventure, and provided material for his later writings. He received his first formal schooling at sixteen, when he entered Central High School in Grand Rapids. After graduating two years later, he spent two years in the Michigan woods studying bird life and wrote several articles and a monograph that was published by the Ornithologists' Union. In 1891 he entered the University of Michigan, where he received the Ph.B. degree in 1895.

Following a period of six months working in a packing house in Grand Rapids, White joined the gold rush in the Black Hills of South Dakota; he soon ran out of money, and shortly afterward he resumed his education at the Columbia Law School (1896-1897). While at Columbia he took an English course under Brander Matthews, who encouraged him to seek publication of a short story based on his experiences in South Dakota. The tale, "A Man and His Dog," was sold to *Short Story* and launched White on his literary career.

His love of the outdoors and his yen for adventure led White to spend much of his life in the wilds of North America and Africa; he often worked as trapper, lumberjack, and explorer. From these experiences came much of the material for his writings. Leaving Columbia in 1897, he worked briefly in a Chicago bookstore, but soon returned to the Michigan woods as a lumberjack and then went camping and trapping in the Hudson Bay area. During this period he wrote his first two novels, *The Westerners* (1901) and *The Claim Jumpers* (1901), both based on frontier life in South Dakota. It was not, however, until the appearance of *The Blazed Trail* (1902) that White established his reputation as a member of the "red-blood school of writers" (Pattee, p. 114), which included Owen Wister, Jack London, Frank Norris, and Bret Harte. The book neared best-seller status. Presenting a vivid depiction of the rigors of the lumber frontier, this novel, like his later works, was an action-filled romance but had White's indelible stamp of verisimilitude. The hero, Harry Thorpe, through his unremitting labor, embodies the American myth of success and comes to terms with the almost mystical, supernatural elements of his surroundings. The book exemplifies the philosophy running through White's novels, that "the one great drama is that of the individual man's struggles toward perfect adjustment with his environment. According as he comes into correspondence and harmony with his environment, by that much does he succeed" (Saxton, p. 2).

Over the next forty years White wrote some thirty volumes, including novels, histories, juvenile works, travel and adventure books, essays, and short stories. *The Forest* (1903), *The Mountains* (1904), and *The Cabin* (1911) were based on his own camping experiences and offered his readers colorful descriptions and practical advice on outdoor living. *Blazed Trail Stories* (1904) and *The Riverman* (1908) were further tales of the Michigan woods, which achieved success. Among White's many novels recounting the history of the frontier West, such as *Arizona Nights* (1907) and *The Forty-Niners* (1918), perhaps his most ambitious undertaking was his three-volume history of California—*Gold* (1913), *The Gray Dawn* (1915), and *The Rose Dawn* (1920). For these novels he combined extensive research, vivid imagination, and his own experience to re-create the excitement of the gold rush for his readers. A forerunner of the prolific adventure novelists Rex Beach and Zane Grey, White wrote books that appealed to all Americans. If, in the words of Irving Bacheller, the years 1884 to 1895 made up the "highbrow decade" (as exemplified by the writings of Henry James), the early twentieth century brought a reaction against a "literature of books" and gave American readers a "literature of life." It is this period to which White's fiction belongs.

Lured by the excitement of the Dark Continent, White explored the jungles of German East Africa in 1913. For his mapping work there, he was made a fellow of the Royal Geographic Society of London. He hunted game and lived with tribesmen, gathering material for several books and essays that exposed readers to a new frontier: *African Campfires* (1913), *The Leopard Woman* (1916), and *Simba* (1918), illustrated with photographs, described the African wilderness in detail. These books were hailed as literary embodiments of the strenuous life advocated by Theodore Roosevelt. During World War I, White served in the American Expeditionary Forces as an artillery major.

White married Elizabeth Calvert Grant of Newport, R.I. on April 28, 1904; they had no children. His wife accompanied him on many of his travels; she was the guide "Billy" to whom many of his books were dedicated. White settled in Santa Barbara, Calif., and later moved to Burlingame. During the last years of his life, he became interested in psychic phenomena. As early as the 1920's, his wife had discovered, while using a ouija board, that she had psychic powers. White's initial venture into the world of parapsychological writing was *The Betty Book* (1937), a compilation of the messages his wife believed she had received from the "invisibles" of the spirit world. White wrote several books following her death in 1939, some based on what he believed his wife revealed to him in daily "meetings" with her through a medium. In *The Stars Are Still There* (1946), he attempted to deal with some of the more common questions about his wife's experiences and his own beliefs, which he was questioned about in thousands of letters from readers.

White died of cancer in the University of California Hospital, San Francisco. Following cremation, his ashes were buried at Cypress Lawn Memorial Park, San Mateo County. Although White never claimed literary distinction for his work, his depiction of the frontiers of nineteenth- and twentieth-century America placed him among that group of writers who, reacting against what they considered an earlier literary romanticism, attempted to inject more elements of naturalism and realism into their writing.

[The most complete biographical sources are the following: Eugene F. Saxton, *Stewart Edward White* (1939–1947); *Nat. Cyc. Am. Biog.*, Current Vol. F, 144–145; *N.Y. Times* obit., Sept. 19, 1946; Stanley J. Kunitz and Howard Haycraft, eds., *Twentieth Century Authors* (1942); and Van Wyck Brooks in Am. Acad. of Arts and Sciences, *Commemorative Tributes, 1942–1951* (1951). Theodore Roosevelt, Jr., *Stewart Edward White* (1940), is an over-laudatory appraisal of White's adventures. Periodical appraisals of White's career include A. B. Maurice, "The Hist. of Their Books," *Bookman*, Aug. 1921; and other articles in *Bookman*, May 1903, pp. 308–311; July 1910, pp. 486–492; Sept. 1913, pp. 9–10. See also Grant Overton, *When Winter Comes to Main Street* (1922), John C. Underwood, *Literature and Insurgency; Ten Studies in Racial Evolution* (1914), and Fred B. Millett, *Contemporary Am. Authors* (1940). Historical background is presented in Elias Lieberman, *The Am. Short Story* (1912); John M. Manly and Edith Rickert, *Contemporary Am. Literature* (1922); James D. Hart, *The Popular Book* (1950); Ernest E. Leisy, *The Am. Historical Novel* (1950); Frank L. Mott, *Golden Multitudes* (1947); and Fred L. Pattee, *The New Am. Lit., 1890–1930* (1930). For contemporary reviews of White's books, see *Book Review Digest*, 1901–1948. Death record from State of Calif., Dept. of Public Health. The Grand Rapids Public Lib. provided material on White's family.]

OLIVIA A. HAEHN

WHITEHEAD, ALFRED NORTH (Feb. 15, 1861–Dec. 30, 1947), philosopher, was born in Ramsgate, Isle of Thanet, Kent, England. He was the third son and youngest of the four children of Alfred Whitehead, an Anglican clergyman, and Maria Sarah (Buckmaster) Whitehead, daughter of a prosperous military tailor. The Whiteheads had risen to the professional middle class when the grandfather, Thomas Whitehead, made a great success of a private school he started in Ramsgate in 1815. In 1854 he turned Chatham House Academy over to his youngest son, Alfred, who in middle life gave it up for clerical duties. Thus, Alfred North Whitehead was born in a headmaster's house and spent much of his boyhood in a vicarage (St. Peter's-in-Thanet, near Broadstairs). His father was not consumed by religion and was not intellectual; he was a kindly man who rode to hounds and was popular with the people of Thanet and the clergy of East Kent.

Since the young Alfred was thought frail, his father taught him at home. His brothers adored him, but his mother does not seem to have been an influence in any positive way. At fourteen he was sent to Sherborne, in Dorset, then one of the best, if not most prestigious, public schools in England. There he was outstanding in mathematical studies and rugby. In his last year he was head prefect, responsible for all discipline outside the classroom, and a highly successful captain of games. He received the usual classical education but was excused from some Latin composition so that he might devote time to mathematics.

In 1880 Whitehead matriculated at Trinity College, Cambridge, to which he had won a scholarship. Like most of the men who were aiming at the mathematical tripos, he attended only mathematical lectures. Other interests were nourished by wide reading and incessant talk with friends and young dons; he was elected to the elite discussion society "the Apostles." Whitehead did well in the tripos and received the B.A. in 1884. In October of that year he was elected a fellow of Trinity (his dissertation was on Clerk Maxwell's theory of electricity and magnetism) and appointed an assistant lecturer in mathematics, becoming the senior lecturer in 1903. He earned the D.Sc. in 1905.

In 1890 Whitehead met Evelyn Willoughby Wade. A daughter of impoverished Irish landed gentry, she was witty, with passionate likes and dislikes, a great sense of drama, and —what was entirely lacking in his parents' household—a keen aesthetic sense. He fell in love with this vivacious, unacademic woman and adored her all his life; they were married on Dec. 16, 1890. She was a "sofa lady" with heart trouble, who lived to be ninety-five. She always had the energy to rule the family, take youngsters with problems under her wing, make friends be useful, and shield her husband from financial anxiety. Three children were born to them: Thomas North, Jessie Marie, and Eric Alfred.

Shortly before his marriage Whitehead considered joining the Roman Catholic church. Besides his father, three uncles and his brother Henry (later bishop of Madras) were priests of the Church of England; but Whitehead fell under the influence of Cardinal Newman. For about eight years he read a great many theological books. The upshot was a decision to sell the books and give up religion. Although his agnosticism did not survive World War I, Whitehead never again belonged to any church.

Whitehead wrote few papers in mathematics, although he taught that subject for thirty-nine years. He was most interested in those newer branches that went beyond the traditional notion of what mathematics was—quaternions, the Boolean algebra of logic, and Grassmann's calculus of extension. He planned a two-volume comparative study of all such systems of symbolic reasoning. The first volume of this *Treatise on Universal Algebra* (1898) secured his election to the Royal Society in 1903. He abandoned the second volume to collaborate with Bertrand Russell on *Principia Mathematica.*

Whitehead had recognized Russell's brilliance from the first. When Russell was a Trinity College freshman in 1890, Whitehead was one of his teachers. They gradually became close friends and in July 1900 went together to the First International Congress of Philosophy, which was held in Paris. There Russell was impressed by the precision with which the Italian mathematician Giuseppe Peano used symbolic logic to clarify the foundations of arithmetic. Russell now mastered Peano's ideography and extended his methods. Whitehead saw the importance of this; moreover, when Russell in the last three months of 1900 wrote the first draft of his brilliant *Principles of Mathematics,* Whitehead agreed with its thesis (anticipated by Frege) that mathematics is a part of logic. In January 1901 Russell secured Whitehead's collaboration on the second volume of his *Principles,* in which the principles of mathematics were to be deduced from those of logic alone by chains of strict symbolic reasoning. This task was much greater than they had foreseen, and their work had to be made independent of Russell's book.

Whitehead's letters show him ready to defer to Russell on questions of logical theory, while remaining somewhat the teacher on mathematical matters, involving most of the notation that was not taken from Peano and always encouraging his former pupil. Russell, who had no teaching duties, wrote out the final symbolic text; but each had made one or more recensions of the other's drafts. Russell always deplored the tendency of scholars to give him the major credit for *Principia Mathematica.* Most of the work was done by 1909, and the three huge volumes were published in 1910-1913. Whitehead began a fourth volume, but he never finished it. Still, the *Principia* is generally considered one of the great intellectual monuments of all time.

These two men could scarcely have collaborated on any other subject: their casts of mind were too different. Whitehead always called Russell the greatest logician since Aristotle but thought him simplistic in philosophy. Eventually even their views of mathematics and its relation to the world diverged. Ludwig Wittgenstein, who never influenced Whitehead, persuaded Russell that logical and mathematical truths are only tautologies, while Whitehead adopted a modified Platonism. The new introduction and appendices to the first volume of the second edition of the *Principia* (1925) were entirely Russell's work; Whitehead disclaimed them. In 1934 he finally published "Indication,

Classes, Numbers, Validation" (*Mind,* 43 [1934], 281-297, 543) a paper sketching his own revisionary ideas.

In 1910 Whitehead resigned his lectureship and moved to London. For the first of his fourteen years there he had no academic position. In this year he wrote his admirable *Introduction to Mathematics* for the Home University Library. University College in 1911 made him lecturer in applied mathematics and mechanics and in 1912 appointed him reader in geometry. In 1914 Whitehead was elected to the chair of applied mathematics at the Imperial College of Science and Technology, where he remained until 1924.

In London, Whitehead, who as a teacher fully elicited his pupils' latent abilities, became deeply concerned over the education then being offered to the English masses. He served on the governing bodies of several technical schools and was the only scientist on the committee (1919-1921) appointed by the prime minister to inquire into the position of classics in the educational system of the United Kingdom. As a member of the Senate, dean of the Faculty of Science, and chairman of the Academic Council, he helped run the University of London. From 1919 to 1924 he was chairman of the delegacy that governed Goldsmith's College, where many of England's teachers were being trained. On committees, Whitehead was a man of ideas, who by his shrewdness, tact, and graciousness got new things done without creating antagonisms. His general ideas about education were expressed in occasional addresses from 1911 onward. The most famous is "The Aims of Education: A Plea for Reform" —his presidential address to the Mathematical Association in 1916. Its chief protest was against imparting "inert ideas." "Culture," he said, "is activity of thought, and receptiveness to beauty and humane feeling. Scraps of information have nothing to do with it." Whitehead's further criticisms—of fragmented curricula and the English system of uniform examinations—had little effect on the secondary schools.

Whitehead believed that England had to enter World War I and that Russell's pacifism was naive. Their friendship cooled but did not break; according to Russell, Whitehead was the more tolerant man. His older son was in the army throughout the war; his younger son, Eric, was killed in action in March 1918. Only by an immense effort was Whitehead able to keep on with his work.

If the fourth volume of *Principia Mathe-matica* had been finished, it would have presented a complete theory of geometry, conceived as the first chapter of natural science. This theory required a great deal of thought, especially in view of Einstein's work. The development of Whitehead's thought went into three books on the foundations of natural science: *An Enquiry Concerning the Principles of Natural Knowledge* (1919), *The Concept of Nature* (1920), and *The Principle of Relativity* (1922).

In a memoir published by the Royal Society in 1906, Whitehead had expressed, in the symbolism of *Principia Mathematica,* the classical concept of the material world (as composed of particles occupying points of space at instants of time) and some theoretical alternatives to it. The main purpose of the *Enquiry* was to replace the classical concept, with its unperceivable points and instants, by a coherent set of meanings defined not, as in Einstein's special theory of relativity, by stipulations and instrument operations (operations, in Whitehead's view, were only means to secure precision) but in terms logically derived from the kinds of data and of relationships that are given in every external perception (e.g., one event is perceived to be a spatiotemporal part of another). The *Enquiry* was highly original, but it was too philosophical and the paths to the required definitions were too intricate to influence physicists. In *The Principle of Relativity,* Whitehead, insisting on distinguishing between geometry and physics, provided a substitute for Einstein's general theory; this was explored by a few mathematical physicists but could not compete with Einstein's.

Whitehead was much more successful with philosophers. He began to have frequent discussions of epistemological questions with them in 1915, when he joined the Aristotelian Society. *The Concept of Nature,* a nonmathematical companion to his *Enquiry,* made a great impression. He argued that nature (which he defined as the terminus of sense perception) is a system of events that—*pace* Russell and G. E. Moore—are necessarily significant of each other but independent of our minds; thus his position was realistic. Whitehead also emphasized the passage, or creative advance, of nature. He was impressed by Bergson's temporalism, but its influence on him is generally exaggerated; Whitehead was also something of a Platonist.

In 1920 the department of philosophy at Harvard was interested in a temporary appointment for Whitehead, but budgetary problems forestalled action. Late in 1923 two admirers, Henry Osborn Taylor and L. J. Henderson, also urged his appointment. When Taylor and his wife promised Harvard the money for Whitehead's salary, he was offered a five-year appointment, from Sept. 1, 1924, as professor of philosophy. He was sixty-three and had at most two more years in the Imperial College, and so, both the opportunity to develop his ideas and the prospect of teaching philosophy appealed to him. His wife wholeheartedly concurred in the move.

Whitehead had made a point of excluding metaphysics from his work on the basic concepts of natural science; now he felt his way into a metaphysical position that would embody that work and satisfy his convictions about value and existence. He expounded his ideas at Harvard and Radcliffe and in the course of the eight lectures on "Science and the Modern World" that he gave at the Lowell Institute, Boston, in February 1925. The subject of the Lowell lectures was three centuries of scientific thought. He emphasized the continuing disastrous effect on Western culture of "scientific materialism," the eighteenth-century view that nature at bottom consists of bits of matter whose only business is to change their spatial positions according to immutable laws, everything else that appears to happen in nature being either an accidental addition or an affection of human minds. Whitehead charged scientific materialism with committing a "fallacy of misplaced concreteness" by mistaking an efficient abstraction from nature for its concrete totality. The most striking thing in these lectures was Whitehead's appeal to his favorite poets, Wordsworth and Shelley, against the extrusion of values from nature. He held that philosophic theory must not defy, but elucidate, the unsophisticated intuitive experience of mankind and that the deepest expression of these institutions is found in great poetry.

On its publication later in 1925, *Science and the Modern World* was an instant success. Whitehead had told a story in dramatic sentences that were quoted far and wide; and he had offered a first sketch of his new ideas in pages whose difficulty corresponded to the magnitude of his purpose. In the book, four chapters were added to the Lowell lectures; in two of these he for the first time discussed religion and the concept of God. His purpose was evidently to overcome not only the dualism of matter and value but also that of science and religion. In February 1926 Whitehead gave four Lowell lectures, published as *Religion in the Making*. They were not pri-

marily historical. The setting in which Whitehead placed religion is shown in this passage: "The great rational religions are the outcome of the emergence of a religious consciousness which is universal, as distinguished from tribal, or even social. Because it is universal, it introduces the note of solitariness. Religion is what the individual does with his solitariness" (Ch. II, Sect. i). Whitehead argued that religion needs a metaphysics and makes its own contribution to metaphysics. His discussions of religious experience and expression and of the use and misuse of dogmas were short and pointed. In this very compact book he carried his ideas about God further, but he did not complete them until he wrote a full, formal statement of his metaphysical system.

He worked out much of the system in the summer of 1927 and attempted a compressed presentation of it in ten Gifford lectures at the University of Edinburgh in June 1928. Because of its complexity and the new terminology that the system required, the lectures were a fiasco, but their publication in 1920 (expanded to twenty-five chapters) under the title *Process and Reality* was an important event in the history of metaphysics.

In his opening chapter Whitehead laid it down that all claims to possess unquestionable premises or a coercive dialectic are vain; the metaphysician must speculate, by devising a self-consistent, coherent hypothesis about the nature of things that must be tested by its general success in application. Complete success would mean that every element of our experience can be seen as a particular instance of the general scheme and that every science—even logic and epistemology—finds a niche in it. Whitehead had faith—his "rationalism" —that nothing we experience is intrinsically incapable of such interpretation, but he also had intellectual humility; he insisted that neither in science nor philosophy can human imagination and language achieve final understanding.

Whitehead's preparation for this endeavor was unusual. He had much experience as a mathematician in framing sets of general concepts under which all known kinds of special cases could be subsumed. He had an expert knowledge of mathematical physics; but since his goal was a set of categories that would also apply to biology and psychology and to social, aesthetic, and religious experience, he could not have proceeded if he had not been at home in many other sciences and in the history of civilization. (He did not pay much attention to Marx or Freud.) No iconoclast,

Whitehead considered the peaks in the European philosophical tradition as partial insights, and after receiving his Harvard appointment, he studied them anew, especially the epistemology and metaphysics of Plato, Descartes, Locke, Hume, and Kant. It was fortunate that in *Process and Reality* he could compare their doctrines with his, for the chapters that elaborate his system in its own terms are formidably technical. His too generous statements of indebtedness misled some readers into thinking him an eclectic.

The central notion in Whitehead's speculative philosophy was that of a process, or becoming, and it was handled in an original way. Bergson, William James, and John Dewey were also process philosophers; that is, they took the process, or becoming, that is evident in the temporal world as fully real and more fundamental than substance or being. But no one before Whitehead had produced a full-fledged non-Hegelian theory of process; Bergson even declared that it could be grasped only by intuitive feeling, not by means of concepts. As Whitehead knew (although not in detail), some Buddhistic philosophies long ago made process ultimate; but they sought intuitive, not intellectual, understanding of it.

Whitehead's concept of a becoming was based on his analysis of an occasion of human experience, considered in its entirety and not as limited to what we are conscious of. In the little book *Symbolism: Its Meaning and Effect* (1927) he argued, against Hume, that a vague, but insistent, perception of casual efficacy underlies all our sensory impressions. In *Process and Reality,* he developed the thesis that an experience is fundamentally a process of absorbing the past and making ourselves different by actualizing some value-potentialities and rejecting others. Whitehead saw this activity as basically emotional and conceived of it as occurring in discrete pulses (although continuity usually dominates at the level of consciousness). The entire personal past, as well as the functioning of the body and of the universe beyond, enters into (is "prehended" into) the constitution of the present occasion; they comprise its causal basis. Qualities and possible forms of relatedness that are more or less new are also prehended, positively or negatively. The experiencing process is an internally free adjustment and integration of all these prehensions so as to produce an indivisible unity of feeling. This synthesis is self-created, not effected by a permanent soul or self that "has" the experience; rather, as William James had

claimed, the cumulative series of pulses of experience *is* the self.

In an experience-event, so conceived, consciousness, thought, and sense perception may be absent. The basic pattern could be ascribed to an amoeba and even to the inanimate—not to rocks, but to their molecules or to subatomic particles—by permitting novelty to be negligible or limited to alternation. Whitehead fashioned a conceptual matrix for all levels of existence with his speculative hypothesis: the ultimate units of the entire temporal world ("actual occasions") are becomings, each an individual process of appropriating (prehending) into its perspective the infinity of items ("reality") provided by the antecedent universe of finished becomings and by God, the abiding source of new potentialities. As each becoming is the achievement of an organic unity, Whitehead called his metaphysics "the philosophy of organism." According to it, living things are those organizations of becoming that show a marked degree of coordinated initiative in their reactions to the pressures of their environments, and any object that we meet in everyday life or in science is a group of interdependent series ("societies") of becomings that maintain a certain character for a certain time. The various sciences of course use their own concepts of process; Whitehead's hope was that these (e.g., wave transmission of energy, nutrition, communication) could be placed under his metaphysical theory, in accordance with the special abstractions that each science makes in delimiting its topic, and he made some suggestions toward this end. As for our laws of nature, Whitehead thought it parochial to suppose them eternal; they only express average regularities that prevail in what he called "our present cosmic epoch."

The many principles that appear in Whitehead's formal statement of his speculative hypothesis presuppose three notions implicit in that of becoming: "many," "one," and "creativity." The last is Whitehead's name for the underlying energy of process, the universal, but perfectly protean, drive toward an endless production of new syntheses. Within the system, Whitehead tried to fashion and interweave his concepts in such a way as to bridge every traditional dualism. Self-creation and efficient (external) causation have already been mentioned as respectively characterizing becoming in process and finished ("perished") becomings. Subject and object, permanence and transience, atomism and continuity, the physical and the mental, and so on, are all brought together. Nor would Whitehead allow anything in his universe the possibility of existing in independence of other things. His metaphysics is a unified monadology, much richer than Leibniz'.

The originality of Whitehead's theism stems from his way of conceiving of God and the temporal world as mutually dependent and of both as "in the grip of the ultimate metaphysical ground, the creative advance into novelty." This God is with all finite existence, not before it. (Whitehead's theoretical attribution of intrinsic value to every puff of inanimate existence depends on his conception of the universal immanence of God.) The infinity of Platonic forms, which in Whitehead's system are pure potentials, or forms of definiteness for possible realization in becomings, is embraced in God's unchanging vision. Condemning the attribution of arbitrary power to God, Whitehead instead wrote of the Divine Persuasion, of the cosmic urge toward harmony. On the other side of his being, God prehends every becoming in its living immediacy and transforms it into an everlasting element in himself. This conception of a growing God has become, thanks partly to the influence of Charles Hartshorne, the most favored and most discussed part of Whitehead's metaphysics.

In *Adventures of Ideas* (1933) Whitehead used his lifetime of reading in history to bring out the humanistic and sociological side of his philosophy. It was the third and last of his major American books, and the best for most readers. Its chief topic—among many—was the gradual effect of general ideas (always clothed in special forms) on the course of Western civilization. Whitehead emphasized the interplay of ideals and brute forces, the precariousness of every advance, and the necessity of societies stable enough to nourish adventure that is fruitful rather than anarchic. The third of the book's four parts was a summary and defense of his metaphysics. In the fourth he used the metaphysics to make a penetrating analysis of the qualities that he thought essential to civilized life: truth, beauty, art, adventure, and peace. By "peace" he meant a religious attitude, roughly describable as trust in the efficacy of beauty. *Adventures of Ideas* conveys a solid wisdom. With Whitehead's elevation of wisdom above knowledge went a tendency to elevate tolerance above righteousness, and beauty above truth; but there was no tameness in his valuations. Concerning the emphases on beauty, art, and adventure, it should be noticed that in the brief "Autobio-

graphical Notes" (1941) Whitehead said that the effect of his wife on his outlook had been fundamental.

Whitehead's published writings do not show that his metaphysics was implicit in the work he did while a mathematician; they do exhibit the same imaginative mind seeking, in each area it dealt with, a precision and a generality beyond that of familiar terms. Whitehead was a speculative thinker—indeed, one of the greatest—with a great respect for facts and a healthy disrespect for their compartmentalization and conventional expression. The rarity of such disrespect in his readers accounts for the frequency with which his philosophical writing is called deliberately obscure.

America gave Whitehead a youthful audience that was more receptive to his ideas than any in Britain could have been. Harvard revised the terms of his appointment and did not retire him until 1937. He was the greatest figure in its second golden age of philosophy—that of J. H. Woods, R. B. Perry, W. E. Hocking, C. I. Lewis, and others. (No colleague substantially influenced his philosophy, which issued from long years of meditation.) Most students found his loosely organized lectures, in which he conveyed his philosophy without presenting his system as such, a great experience. His voice was high-pitched but quiet; he spoke slowly and with conviction. Much of the content of those lectures can be got from his last, nontechnical book, *Modes of Thought* (1938). The Whiteheads were at home to his students on Sunday evenings; these well-attended occasions were skillfully managed by Mrs. Whitehead. Outside the philosophy department, he had a strong influence in the Harvard Society of Fellows; he helped to plan it, and was active as a senior fellow until he died.

Whitehead's American students remember him as a spare man who would have been of almost average height if he had not been so stooped. In Cambridge his dress was often casual, but at Harvard his wife saw to it that he wore the old-fashioned conservative clothes (with wing collar) that suited a scholarly Edwardian gentleman who had become a sage. His fine face—bright blue eyes, aquiline nose, pink cheeks—could not easily be taken as anything but English. His manner was rather formal, his courtesy perfect, his humor delightful. The dominant impression was of kindness, accompanied by wisdom and firmness. His mind was very quick, but hammer-and-tongs argument was not his style; his criticisms, often devastating, were always made with extreme gentleness, and his deafness to any hard words that came his way was amazing. He habitually passed over the bad sides of people and addressed himself to their good potentialities. Scores of students thought that Whitehead took a unique interest in their work, but it was not unique; he was helpful to all, on principle. The fact that he appears never to have broken a friendship also suggests a certain impersonality in his character. There was nothing soft about him; never contentious, he was astute, charitable, and quietly stubborn.

In his first nine years in America, Whitehead visited many Eastern and Midwestern campuses as a lecturer. He loved Americans, he said, for their warmheartedness and openness to ideas. Adulation did not affect him; he remained wholly modest and unassuming, and he did not want to have disciples.

Whitehead believed that the polemical activity of the intellectual world was largely waste motion, with much harmful simplification of ideas into targets. Advance called for the creation of new ideas and the exploration of their scope. He did not take time from his own work to write reviews of books or answer reviews of his. His concentration and self-discipline were phenomenal, but he did not live in an ivory tower. He always followed public affairs and discussed them with friends; but he made political speeches only in Cambridgeshire. His politics was that of a realistic reformer. He never thought he could better things by making a noise; quiet persuasion, based on an uncynical view of the whole situation, was his way. He had little more sympathy with what he took to be the detached superiority of Bloomsbury than with iconoclasts and utopians.

Whitehead received six honorary doctorates, and the British Academy elected him a fellow in 1931. The Crown bestowed on him the Order of Merit in 1945.

Whitehead died at his small apartment in Cambridge, Mass., near the Harvard Yard four days after a paralytic stroke. The body was cremated; there was no funeral, but a memorial service was held at Harvard.

Whitehead's books have been translated into many languages. At Harvard he wrote four essays on university education; these and the earlier ones on school education are likely always to inspire some teachers everywhere. The part of his work that seems to be of least permanent significance is the philosophical foundation for physics that he published in

1919-1922. It was done before the rise of quantum mechanics, to which Whitehead never worked out a response; and the advent of semantic approaches to scientific concepts put it out of fashion. Whitehead's work in his Harvard period is sometimes compared with the existentialist use of the whole experience of living, and not just sense perception, as the basis of philosophy; he was less dramatic but bolder, for he calmly used our casual, emotional, and social experience as the point of departure for a nondualistic cosmology. Many philosophers consider his system—the most original and capacious one ever written in English—a mere tour de force, but some natural scientists and social scientists find it useful. Among theologians it has made him the pioneer in what is called process theology. Whitehead's social and educational philosophy is at least as important as his metaphysics. The thorny paragraphs are fewer, and the vigorous expression of broad insights earns a place for him in the history of English literature.

[In addition to the books already mentioned, Whitehead published *The Function of Reason* (1929), which makes a good short preparation for studying his metaphysics; *The Aims of Education and Other Essays* (1929); and *Essays in Science and Philosophy* (1947), a miscellany including six other essays on education, three meditative essays on Whitehead's boyhood, his only article on international affairs ("An Appeal to Sanity," 1939), and the "Autobiographical Notes" written for, and published in, P. A. Schilpp, ed., *The Philosophy of Alfred North Whitehead* (1941; 2nd ed., 1951). F. S. C. Northrop and Mason W. Gross, eds., *Alfred North Whitehead: An Anthology,* is a large representative collection of Whitehead's essays and chapters from his books. There is an almost complete bibliography of Whitehead's writings in Schilpp's book, and a bibliography of secondary literature in *Process Studies,* 1, No. 4 (1971). Lucien Price, *Dialogues of Alfred North Whitehead* (1954), covers Whitehead's last thirteen years only.

For further information on Whitehead, see Dorothy Emmet, *Whitehead's Philosophy of Organism* (1932; 2nd ed., 1966); Victor Lowe, *Understanding Whitehead* (1962); Ivor Leclerc, *Whitehead's Metaphysics: An Introductory Exposition* (1958), for readers whose preparation is in the history of philosophy; J. M. Burgers, *Experience and Conceptual Activity: A Philosophical Essay Based Upon the Writings of A. N. Whitehead* (1965), for readers who come from physical science; and Charles Hartshorne, *Whitehead's Philosophy: Selected Essays 1935–1970* (1972).

Whitehead's widow, as he had asked, destroyed his unpublished manuscripts and his correspondence. He himself avoided writing letters not required by his academic duties or his collaboration with Russell; no collection of his letters has been or is likely to be published; those to Russell are preserved in the Bertrand Russell Archives at McMaster Univ. The author has drawn on personal knowledge and on private information.]

VICTOR LOWE

WHITMAN, CHARLES SEYMOUR (Aug. 28, 1868–Mar. 29, 1947), governor of New York State, was born in Hanover, Conn., the fourth child of John Seymour Whitman, a

Presbyterian minister of modest means, and Lillie (Arne) Whitman. The father was a seventh-generation descendant of John Whitman who immigrated to Massachusetts from England in 1635. He received his early education in local schools and attended Williams College for a year. In 1890 he graduated from Amherst College, taught Greek and Latin for a time at Adelphi Academy in Brooklyn, N.Y., and received his LL.B. from New York University in 1894. When a reform-minded Republican, Seth Low, became mayor of New York in 1902, he found a job in the city corporation counsel's office for Whitman, who had been active in his neighborhood Republican club while he eked out a living in private law practice. On Low's last day in office in December 1903 (Tammany Hall had ousted the reformers once again), the mayor appointed Whitman as a magistrate, the city's lowest judicial rank. As the result of a squabble between two Democratic factions, Whitman was the compromise choice for chief of the city's Board of Magistrates in March 1907, thus achieving his first real political visibility as he approached his fortieth year.

Almost immediately, he set about making headlines by conducting a drive against payoffs to local police by bail bondsman and the keepers of after-hours saloons. Members of the city's Police Department were then regarded as mere creatures of Tammany Hall, which had arranged most of their appointments and used them as collectors of graft. As the most visible examples of the evils of Tammany, it was the police who were recurrently the objects of sensational investigations by reform groups, whose leaders would then run for office on the claim of having cleaned up the city. Virtually every New York reform politician from the early 1890's through World War I had made his reputation as a crusader against police corruption. On a municipal level, the issue had the same passionate, sure-fire appeal that the pursuit of Communist subversives had for later political generations. Although Whitman was defeated when he ran for a city judgeship in 1907, he had identified himself with the right cause, and in January 1910 he took office as the successful reform candidate for district attorney of New York County. His first year in this office was uneventful, but during this period he established a mutually convenient alliance with Herbert Bayard Swope, then a young reporter for the *New York World,* who had previously shown less interest in his newspaper career than in the company of the city's leading gambling-house owners. By 1911, however, after Swope decided to take his reporting career seriously, Whitman began to feed him stories about what was going on in the district attorney's office, and, in return, Swope headlined Whitman's role as a demon crime fighter.

Late in 1911, the police commissioner appointed a lieutenant, Charles Becker (who had a long record as a grafter), to head a strong-arm squad charged with cleaning up gambling operations in the city. Anxious to make points with the commissioner, Becker raided some of the city's biggest gambling houses, including that of Arnold Rothstein, one of Swope's closest friends. During the same period, a small-time Lower East Side gambler named Herman Rosenthal was making trouble for both the police and gambling-house owners by complaining about police payoffs, thus imperiling the traditional arrangement by which the gamblers, having paid off the police, were left to conduct their business without interference. On July 14, 1912, in a front-page interview written by Swope, Rosenthal declared that Lieutenant Becker had once been his partner in a gambling house. Whitman publicly rejected Rosenthal as an unreliable witness. Early on the morning of July 16, however, after Rosenthal was shot down near Times Square by four gunmen, Swope routed Whitman out of bed and persuaded him to go to the police station and take charge of the case. It was a critical moment in both their careers. For the rest of his life, Swope would say that it was the Rosenthal murder, on which he worked hand-in-glove with Whitman for the next three years, that got him started toward his editorship of the *World.* And in 1915, the *New York Times,* then a Whitman supporter, noted that Whitman's "entire political standing is based upon the convictions in the Rosenthal murder case."

The case made Whitman a national figure. During the six months following the crime, the Rosenthal murder story was on the front page, usually in the lead position, of 75 percent of the editions of the *World.* In William Randolph Hearst's *New York American* the score was 80 percent. The story was also widely covered in other parts of the country. A murder that was the result of a quarrel among local gamblers would have attracted little interest; it was the involvement of a corrupt policeman that made it such a sensational event. Although the prosecution conceded that Becker had never laid eyes on the four gunmen before the crime, he was arrested for murder. The four gunmen, who were later electrocuted (they were known as Gyp the Blood, Whitey Lewis, Lefty Louie, and Dago Frank) had admittedly been hired to do the job by local gamblers who were Rosenthal's avowed enemies. Whitman immediately clapped four of the gamblers in jail and gave them a grant of immunity from the murder charge in return for their written agreement that they would testify that Lieutenant Becker had ordered them to arrange the murder. Becker was convicted in October 1912. Fourteen months later, in a six-to-one decision, the Court of Appeals, the state's highest court, overturned the verdict. In a scathing attack on the judge and the prosecution, the court held that Becker had not had a fair trial. In a second trial, however, before a new judge, with Whitman again handling the case, Becker was again convicted.

A few months later Whitman was elected governor of New York on the strength of his fame as the man who had brought Becker to justice. "Whitman for President" clubs sprang up around the country, and Woodrow Wilson was quoted as saying that he assumed Whitman would be his opponent in the next election. By the time the Becker case reached the Court of Appeals a second time not only was Whitman the most powerful politician in the state but the judge in the second trial was a member of the court. There was little surprise when the court declined to find that the two men had failed to conduct a fair trial. Again the vote was six-to-one with four members of the court directly reversing themselves. There was some public protest over the fact that Becker's plea for clemency or a stay of execution on the grounds of new evidence (several of the witnesses against him had now altered their stories) must be made to the governor who had been responsible for convicting him. Whitman declined to delegate his responsibility to a proposed commission of distinguished legal figures, however, and Becker was electrocuted on July 30, 1915. The plaque his wife had attached to his coffin ("Charles Becker . . . Murdered by Governor Whitman") was removed on orders of the district attorney.

During Whitman's remaining three-and-a-half years as governor, his lifelong tendency to overindulge in alcohol (although officially he was a strong supporter of the Anti-Saloon League) came increasingly to public attention, and inevitably it was said that he drank because he was haunted by the ghost of Charley Becker. During his term he made almost no mark on state government, possibly because of his continued preoccupation with his presiden-

tial aspirations. In 1917 he crossed the continent on a whistle-stop tour. Al Smith, his Democratic opponent in the 1918 gubernatorial election, charged him with "sitting in the Capitol at Albany with a telescope trained on the White House in Washington." When Smith won that election, Whitman refused for many weeks to concede the defeat that marked the end of his lofty political hopes. He then returned to New York City, where he practiced law for the next twenty-eight years, never again holding public office.

On Dec. 22, 1908, he married Olive Hitchcock; they had a daughter, Olive, and a son, Charles, Jr. Olive Whitman died in 1926, and in 1933 he married Mrs. Thelma Somerville Cudlipp Grosvenor.

[Sources include *The Whitman Family in America* (1889); E. J. Kahn, Jr., *The World of Swope* (1965); Matthew and Hannah Josephson, *Al Smith: Hero of the Cities* (1969); Herbert Mitgang, *The Man Who Rode the Tiger* (1963); Andy Logan, *Against the Evidence* (1970). See also major New York city newspapers, 1910–1915, 1918 and obituary in *N.Y. Times*, Mar. 30, 1947.]

ANDY LOGAN

WHITMAN, ROYAL (Oct. 24, 1857–Aug. 19, 1946), orthopedic surgeon, was born in Portland, Maine, the second of four sons and third of six children. His father, Royal Emerson Whitman, had married Lucretia Octavia Whitman of another branch of the family; both came from Turner, Maine. When his son was five, the elder Whitman left to join the Union Army in the Civil War, and thereafter seldom returned home. After the war he engaged briefly in business in Ohio and then joined the regular army as a cavalry lieutenant, serving in the Southwest. His friendly policy toward the Indians while in command of Camp Grant in Arizona roused local white hostility and led to the Camp Grant Massacre (1871) of Indians under his protection. After retiring in 1879 he invented the Whitman saddle and founded a prosperous company to manufacture it. He was divorced about 1875 and remarried.

Royal Whitman grew up in his mother's care on the family farm in Turner, Maine. His strict religious upbringing, he later recalled, turned him permanently against formal religion. After graduating from high school in nearby Auburn, he studied medicine—presumably as an apprentice—for nearly two years, and also worked as a pharmacist. In 1877 he entered the Harvard Medical School. The need for self-support evidently delayed his completion of the three-year course, for he did not receive his M.D. until 1882.

After a surgical internship in the Boston City Hospital, Whitman opened a practice in Boston. In the late 1880's he went to England, where he studied at Cook's School of Anatomy in London; he became a member of the Royal College of Surgeons in 1889. In that year he went to New York City, on the invitation of the orthopedic surgeon Virgil P. Gibney, to become assistant surgeon of the Hospital for the Ruptured and Crippled. He remained on its staff for four decades.

During that period Whitman originated several methods of treatment that quickly became standard. One of his earliest interests was problems of the foot. In 1889 he published observations on seventy-five cases of flat foot, and the following year he presented a paper on the rational treatment of this disorder before the orthopedic section of the New York Academy of Medicine. The technique he devised, which proved highly successful, employed a special metal plate, still known as the Whitman plate. Whitman's demonstrations of the nature and means of preventing and curing flat foot and weak foot are said to have established his reputation as an orthopedic surgeon.

His next important contribution, first described in 1901, was an astragalectomy operation for stabilizing the paralytic foot, especially the foot with calcaneus deformity. This operation became the standard for foot stabilization in most clinics until Michael Hoke and others published reports, many years later, on sub-astragalar arthrodesis. In a paper in 1904 Whitman presented his method for treating hip fractures at the neck of the femur. So superior were the results of this treatment, which involved wide abduction, internal rotation of the hip, and the application of a plaster spica cast to hold the extremity in this position, that again Whitman's technique became standard. In 1916 he did his first reconstruction operation for ununited fracture of the hip; he delayed publishing his description of the operation, however, until 1921, for Whitman seldom, if ever, reported a new technique until he had convinced himself that it was sound.

Whitman exerted an important influence also through his clinical teaching and through his textbook, *A Treatise on Orthopaedic Surgery*. First published in 1901, this comprehensive work soon replaced the earlier standard text by Edward H. Bradford and Robert W. Lovett; by 1930 it had gone through nine editions. Whitman's clinics attracted many vi-sitors, from this country and abroad. His exposition was extremely lucid, and his operations were planned for their practical value. As a surgeon he was rapid, but accurate and careful. A rigid and exacting disciplinarian to all who worked with him, Whitman oversaw the teaching of more than 140 residents. He was extremely punctual—it was said that one could tell the time of day by when he walked into the hospital—and he could not tolerate indolence or excuses. His criticism, although never personal in intent, was sharp and sometimes sarcastic, and many persons, particularly newcomers, took offense. As a result, Whitman was either adored or thoroughly disliked.

Small in stature, with a strong face and sparkling eyes, Whitman was one of the most dedicated orthopedists the specialty has produced. Ever curious and imaginative, he was always trying out new methods of treatment. He was thoroughly informed on the orthopedic literature in English, French, and German and expected his associates to be similarly up-to-date. Although he was a leading advocate in his day of surgery for the reconstruction of bone and joint conditions, he did not lose sight of manipulative or manual techniques for the correction of deformities and was a master at them. Whitman held appointments as adjunct professor of orthopedic surgery at the College of Physicians and Surgeons, Columbia University, and professor at the New York Polyclinic Medical School. He became an honorary fellow of the Royal Medical Society of England, a member of the French Academy of Surgery, and a member of the German Academy of Natural Scientists, and served as president of the American Orthopaedic Association in 1895.

On May 29, 1886, Whitman married Julia Lombard Armitage. Their only child, Armitage, also became an orthopedic surgeon. Whitman retired in 1929 and went to live in England. In 1943, during World War II, he returned to the United States. He died at his home in New York City at the age of eighty-eight, of chronic bronchitis and emphysema. In one of his last articles, Whitman credited the "emancipation" of orthopedic surgery to "the establishment of operative surgery as a dominant factor," a step that transformed "an ill-found and static specialty to an important and progressive branch of surgery." To that transformation Whitman was a leading contributor.

[Charles H. Farnam, *Hist. of the Descendants of John Whitman*, p. 223 (1889); Barry C. Johnson,

"Whitman of Camp Grant," in *English Westerners' Soc., The English Westerners' 10th Anniversary Publication* (1964), on Whitman's father; obituaries in *Jour. of Bone and Joint Surgery,* Oct. 1946, and *Jour. Am. Medic. Assoc.,* Sept. 14, 1946; Sir D'Arcy Power and W. R. Le Fanu, *Lives of the Fellows of the Royal College of Surgeons of England, 1930-1951* (1953); Fenwick Beekman, *Hospital for the Ruptured and Crippled: A Hist. Sketch* (1939); Alfred R. Shands, Jr., in *Am. Orth. Assoc. News,* Oct. 1970; *Who Was Who in Am.,* II (1950); enrollment records of Harvard Medical School; information from Rev. Robert S. S. Whitman, Lenox, Mass., a grandson.]

ALFRED R. SHANDS, JR.

WHITMORE, FRANK CLIFFORD (Oct. 1, 1887-June 24, 1947), organic chemist, was born in North Attleboro, Mass., the oldest of four children—three sons and a daughter—of Frank Hale Whitmore, a sewing machine salesman, and Lena Avilla (Thomas) Whitmore. His father was a native of Iowa, his mother of Rhode Island. The elder Whitmore's business took the family to Williamsport, Pa., and then to Atlantic City, N.J., where Frank attended public schools. In 1907 he entered Harvard. He arrived with neither friends nor funds, but with his usual vast energy and enthusiasm he supported himself by odd jobs and by tutoring the sons of the wealthy. He concentrated in chemistry, and after graduating in 1911, B.A. magna cum laude, he remained at Harvard for graduate study under the direction of Charles L. Jackson and later of Elmer P. Kohler and received his Ph.D. degree in 1914. On June 22 of that year he married Marion Gertrude Mason, a Radcliffe graduate in chemistry who provided wise counsel during Whitmore's career. They had five children: Frank Clifford, Mason Thomas, Harry Edison, Marion Mason, and Patricia Joan (who died in infancy).

For several years after receiving his doctorate, Whitmore continued his tutoring, which provided him a comfortable living; during 1916-1917 he also taught organic chemistry at Williams College on a part-time basis. The following year he was an instructor at Rice Institute in Houston, Texas. This was during World War I, and while at Rice he worked on toxic gases for the Chemical Warfare Service. After a year and a half at the University of Minnesota as assistant professor, Whitmore in January 1920 was appointed professor of organic chemistry at Northwestern University in Evanston, Ill. In 1929 he moved to Pennsylvania State College (later Pennsylvania State University) as dean of the School of Chemistry and Physics. He remained there until his death, becoming research professor of organic chemistry in 1937.

Whitmore's earliest research interests centered on the organic compounds of mercury. He devised new methods for the production of mercurials and demonstrated their use in synthesizing other types of organic compounds. He summed up his findings in his *Organic Compounds of Mercury* (1921), which became a standard reference work. After 1929 Whitmore devoted himself chiefly to discovering the nature of intramolecular rearrangements of organic molecules, a problem that had long baffled organic chemists. In a seminal article on this subject in the *Journal of the American Chemical Society* (August 1932), he formulated an electronic theory of rearrangement that gained wide acceptance among scientists. As an important factor in this process, Whitmore theorized the presence of carbonium ions, a presence that has since been verified by nuclear magnetic resonance and mass spectrometry. Whitmore's major hypotheses about the actual role of these ions in rearrangements, elimination and addition reactions, substitution reactions, olefin polymerization, and other types of organic chemical reactions are still valid decades after their formulation.

In another important article, published posthumously in *Chemical and Engineering News* (Mar. 8, 1948), Whitmore described seven different methods for generating carbonium ion reaction intermediates, and the type of reaction each undergoes, with emphasis on those that were important in petroleum chemistry. Other subjects on which Whitmore worked include steric hindrance in Grignard reactions, and fundamental research on the synthesis, reactions, and mechanisms of organosilicon compounds. In 1937 he published *Organic Chemistry,* a monumental work that emphasized the new fields of aliphatic and alicyclic chemistry.

Throughout his career, Whitmore served as a consultant to both private industry and the federal government. He was chairman of the Division of Chemistry and Chemical Technology of the National Research Council in 1927-1928. During World War II, as an advisor to the government's chemical warfare research group, he carried out research for the National Defense Research Committee on superexplosives like "RDX." His wartime research, conducted at Penn State, also included the production of penicillin, the synthesis of antimalarial drugs, and the analysis of hydrocarbons as standards for the development of aviation fuels.

A modest, friendly man, known to his friends as "Rocky," Whitmore was a tireless worker who often arrived at his office at 3 A.M. He was an inspiring teacher and administrator, well liked by both students and colleagues. Among his honors were the presidency of the American Chemical Society (1938), receipt of the William H. Nichols and Willard Gibbs medals (1937, 1945), and election to the National Academy of Sciences (1946). Whitmore died suddenly of a coronary thrombosis at his home in State College, Pa., at the age of fifty-nine; he was buried in Memorial Park, Centre, Pa.

[Memoir by Gerald Wendt in *Chemical and Engineering News*, July 21, 1947; Willard Gibbs Medal address by Whitmore, *ibid.*, Oct. 25, 1945; memoir by C. S. Marvel in Nat. Acad. Sci., *Biog. Memoirs*, XXVIII (1954), which contains a full bibliography of Whitmore's writings; *Who Was Who in America*, II (1950); *Nat. Cyc. Am. Biog.*, XXXIX, 359; Whitmore's contributions to the *Reports* of the Harvard College Class of 1911; birth record (Mass. Registrar of Vital Statistics) and death record (Pa. Dept. of Health); conversation and correspondence with Harry E. Whitmore; personal recollections.]

LEO H. SOMMER

WHITNEY, ALEXANDER FELL (Apr. 12, 1873-July 16, 1949), labor leader, was born in Cedar Falls, Iowa, the oldest of the three sons and two daughters of Joseph Leonard Whitney and Martha Wallin (Batcheller) Whitney. His father, a farmer and schoolteacher, came to Iowa from his native Ontario, Canada, where the Whitney family had lived since migrating from New York state in the early nineteenth century; Alexander's mother was born in Iowa, the daughter of settlers from New England. As a child, Whitney knew considerable poverty. In a vain attempt to make a living from farming and part-time teaching, his father moved the family to a homestead in Nebraska in 1880 and to a farm in Cherokee, Iowa, four years later. Finally, yielding to his strong desire to preach, the elder Whitney studied for the clergy and, after ordination as a Methodist minister, became a circuit rider in Iowa in 1891.

From his father, Whitney derived a hatred of oppression and a deep sympathy for the problems of the poor. He was tutored at home and later attended school for a time in Iowa. In 1888, at the age of fifteen, he went to work as a news vendor on the Illinois Central Railroad, and two years later he became a brakeman. Over the next seventeen years he worked as a brakeman for several midwestern railroads, despite the loss of parts of two fingers in an accident in 1893. The 1890's were marked by economic depression and labor strife, and Whitney was quick to sense the importance to

workingmen of collective action. Despite the considerable gains made by the "big four" railroad brotherhoods—already known as the "aristocracy of the labor movement"—their conservative leaders put greater emphasis on union insurance programs than on hard bargaining with management. Whitney joined the Brotherhood of Railroad Trainmen (BRT) in 1896 and within nine months was elected master of his local lodge. Rising in the union hierarchy, he served as chairman of the grievance committee (1901-1907), and as a member of the Grand Trustees (1905-1907).

In 1907 Whitney was elected a vice-president of the BRT, a post he held until 1928. During these years his labor philosophy grew more aggressively liberal, honed as it was in a continuous struggle against railroad bosses, political frustrations, and the intractable conservatism of the president of the trainmen's union, William G. Lee. Whitney was a member of the National Labor Committee, which urged President Wilson to support the Adamson Act of 1916 granting the eight-hour day to railroad employees; and following World War I, he strongly backed the Plumb Plan, which called for continued government management of the nation's railroads. A political independent with little interest in party labels, Whitney reserved his endorsements for candidates with prolabor records. In 1923 he was named a member of the executive committee of the Illinois Conference for Progressive Political Action, and the following year he enthusiastically supported the Progressive presidential bid of Sen. Robert M. La Follette.

After several previous attempts to unseat Lee, Whitney was finally elected president of the BRT in 1928 and was reelected thereafter until his death. He was well suited by temperament and philosophy to meet the emerging problems of depression, unemployment, and the technological changes in transportation that challenged the supremacy of the railroads. An energetic, peppery man, Whitney had a keen mind and an acute political awareness. If he brooked little opposition within his own union (some called him autocratic), he never hesitated to confront Congress or the president in defense of the interests of the rank and file.

Whitney fought vigorously, if unsuccessfully, in the 1930s to prevent carriers from effecting major salary reductions. He supported the Railroad Retirement Act of 1935, and the Harrington safety amendment to the Omnibus Transportation Act of 1940. A warm friend of New Deal labor policies, he helped launch the

Political Action Committee, headed by Sidney Hillman, which worked for the reelection of President Roosevelt in 1944. Whitney chafed at wage controls imposed during World War II, and when the hostilities ended, he determined to bring about substantial increases. This led to a celebrated confrontation with President Harry Truman in May 1946, in which Whitney and Alvanley Johnson of the Brotherhood of Locomotive Engineers refused to accept an arbitrated rail settlement and threatened a strike. An infuriated Truman went before Congress and asked for the power to draft strikers into the army, a request rendered moot by the last-minute settlement of the dispute. Whitney, who had backed Truman for the vice-presidential nomination in 1944, reacted strongly to this action; his split with the president proved temporary, however, and in 1948 he supported Truman's bid for a full presidential term.

On Sept. 7, 1893, Whitney married Grace Elizabeth Marshman of Hubbard, Iowa. They had three children: Joseph Lafeton, Everett Alexander, and Lydia Marie. His first wife died in 1923, and on July 2, 1927, he married Dorothy May Rawley of Oak Park, Ill. Whitney died of a heart attack at his home in Bay Village, Ohio, a suburb of Cleveland. After funeral services attended by many dignitaries, he was buried in Cleveland's Lakewood Cemetery.

[The principal source is Walter F. McCaleb, *Brotherhood of Railroad Trainmen, With Special Reference to the Life of Alexander F. Whitney* (1936), a laudatory, but detailed, biography. See also the official union biography, W. G. Edens, *A. F. Whitney* (1947). Joel Seidman's *The Brotherhood of Railroad Trainmen* (1962) is a social-scientific analysis of the union's structure and government rather than a history. For descriptions of Whitney's confrontation with Truman, see Cabell Phillips, *The Truman Presidency* (1966), and Arthur F. McClure, *The Truman Administration and the Problems of Postwar Labor, 1945–1948* (1969). Other sources include Wellington Roe, *Juggernaut: Am. Labor in Action* (1948); Charles A. Madison, *Am. Labor Leaders* (1950); *Current Biog.* (1946); *Who's Who in Labor* (1946); *Who Was Who in Am.*, II (1950); and an obituary in the *N.Y. Times*, July 17, 1949.]

PHILIP DE VENCENTES

WHITTEMORE, THOMAS (Jan. 2, 1871–June 8, 1950), archaeologist, leader in Russian relief, and specialist in Byzantine art, was born in Cambridge, Mass., the only child of Joseph Whittemore, a real estate and insurance dealer, and Elizabeth (St. Clair) Whittemore, and grandson of the Rev. Thomas Whittemore, a prominent Universalist minister in Cambridge. He attended local schools and Tufts College, and after receiving the B.A. degree in 1894, stayed on at Tufts as instructor in English, rising to professor in 1904. During this period he did some graduate work at Harvard (1895-1898) and reportedly also at Oxford. Whittemore's interests turned increasingly toward the history of art, which he began to teach at Tufts in 1906. In January 1911 he left Tufts to join a British archaeological expedition in Egypt under the auspices of the Egypt Exploration Society. There he continued to excavate, at Abydos and Balabish, until the winter of 1915.

With the advent of World War I, Whittemore became involved in a new activity. After service (1914-1915) with the French Red Cross, he found himself in the Balkans when the German advance of 1915 into Russia was creating thousands of homeless refugees. Whittemore hastened to Russia and embarked on a relief program. He returned to Boston in 1916 and organized a fund-raising committee, "Refugees in Russia," chaired by the wife of architect Ralph Adams Cram. Whittemore directed the committee's operations in Russia from 1916 to 1918. Continuing his work in Russia after the Bolshevik revolution, he shifted in 1919 to refugee camps outside the Russian borders. The committee's subsequent increased emphasis on education was reflected in its being renamed Committee for the Education of Russian Youth in Exile; the project continued until 1931. Whittemore also helped promising anti-Bolshevik youths reach the West, often by a clandestine route, through Sofia or Constantinople. A man of independent means, he paid his own expenses throughout his years of relief work, in which he was exclusively engaged until about 1927. In that year he began teaching art history at New York University, where he remained until 1930, becoming an assistant professor.

Whittemore's most important venture was the Byzantine Institute, which he organized in 1930. The list of sponsors, which included contributors to his Russian relief committee as well as others he had met during his frequent travels and numerous talks and lectures, reads like an international who's who of art, aristocracy, and money. Whittemore's message was that Christian art in the Near East, especially in Constantinople, was unknown, utterly magnificent, equal or superior to Western medieval art, and ought to be revealed and understood. From 1930 to 1932 he worked on and copied Coptic frescoes near the Red Sea. His principal objective, however, was to uncover the grand mosaics of the former church of the Hagia Sophia (Santa Sophia) at Constantinople, built by the emperor Justinian. The mosaics had long ago been covered by plaster and paint. In 1931 Whittemore obtained the permission of President Kemal Atatürk of Turkey to work in the building, long a mosque held in the greatest veneration; three years later it was declared a museum. There, and in other Byzantine churches in Istanbul, Whittemore worked for the rest of his life, spending half of each year raising money, publicizing his work, and building up the institute's Library of Byzantine Studies in Paris.

The glorious mosaics of Hagia Sophia were painstakingly uncovered and consolidated. No restorations were made; Whittemore was adamant about that. Casts and other reproductions were carefully created for sale in support of the work, and excellent photographs were taken and published. Operations were begun in the smaller, later, but artistically important churches of the Chora (the Kariye Camii) and the Theotokos Pammakaristos (the Fetiye Camii). Work on publication was carried out in the Paris library, and by 1950 a dozen articles had appeared, as well as three volumes of preliminary reports on the mosaics of the Hagia Sophia. Several future experts in different aspects of Byzantine art were trained on Whittemore's scaffolding, and the work in Istanbul had other important connections, including the detailed architectural survey of the Hagia Sophia begun in 1937 by William Emerson and R. L. Van Nice.

Through all this, Whittemore moved calmly and with supreme assurance. A short, slight, intense man, bespectacled and usually rather grave, he was highly intelligent and did not always keep his opinions about failings in others to himself. He was at once abstemious, mysterious, elegant, pensive, and positive. He was an aesthete with an iron will. Some found him truly charming, others did not. He "knew" everyone and had entry everywhere he went. Whittemore never married. A deeply religious Episcopalian, learned in the history and rituals of the Anglican church, he clearly connected his work with his belief. Out of that connection he fashioned a unique life and accomplished much of abiding significance. At the age of seventy-nine, Whittemore died of a heart attack while on a visit to the State Department in Washington, D.C. He was buried in Mount Auburn Cemetery, Cambridge.

[Whittemore's papers, including voluminous correspondence and some diaries, are in the library of the Byzantine Inst., now part of the Ecole des Langues Orientales Vivantes in Paris. Details of his background and pre-Byzantine career were pieced together from a variety of sources, including obituary of his father in *Boston Transcript*, Apr. 30, 1894, and city directory listings; folder on Whittemore in Tufts Univ. Arch.; faculty records of New York Univ.; Egypt Exploration Soc., *Archaeological Report*, 1909–1916, and Whittemore's preface to the society's *Balabish* (1920); and *The Rescue and Education of Russian Children and Youth in Exile, 1915–1925* (pamphlet, published by Whittemore's committee, 1925). Appreciations of Whittemore include E. W. Forbes in *Archaeology*, Autumn 1950; and Paul Lemerle in *Byzantion* 21 (1951): 281–283. See also *N.Y. Times* obituary, June 9, 1950. There are shrewd observations of him by Graham Greene in his "Convoy to West Africa," *The Mint*, no. 1 (1946), where he is identified as "X"; he appears in Lord Kinross' *Europa Minor* (1956) and in Donald Downes, *The Scarlet Thread*, p. 39 (1953); and he is "Professor W." in Evelyn Waugh's splendid account of the coronation of Haile Selassie, reprinted in *When the Going Was Good* (1946). A sense of Whittemore's own writing and convictions can be gained from his "The Rebirth of Religion in Russia," *Nat. Geographic Mag.*, Nov. 1918; and from the Byzantine Inst.'s four preliminary reports on *The Mosaics of St. Sophia at Istanbul* (1933–1952). For the nature of his Istanbul work, see *Life*, Dec. 25, 1950, and William MacDonald, "The Uncovering of Byzantine Mosaics in Hagia Sophia," *Archaeology*, Summer 1951. Matisse, a friend, painted Whittemore's portrait more than once; one is in the Fogg Museum at Harvard.]

WILLIAM L. MacDONALD

WILBUR, RAY LYMAN (Apr. 13, 1875–June 26, 1949), physician, college president, secretary of the interior, and protégé and friend of Herbert Hoover, was born in Boonesboro (later Boone), Iowa, the fourth of six children of Dwight Locke Wilbur and Edna Maria (Lyman) Wilbur. His father was descended from one of the founders of Rhode Island; the Lymans had roots in Massachusetts. Both families had moved westward during the nineteenth century. Dwight Wilbur earned an uneven living as a lawyer and partner in a local coal mine; his wife had once taught at Lake Erie Female Seminary in Ohio. Ray's only brother, Curtis Dwight Wilbur, eight years older than he, became secretary of the navy under President Coolidge and chief justice of the California supreme court.

Wilbur's boyhood was unexceptional. Early rejecting evangelical Christian orthodoxy (his family was Congregationalist), he nonetheless retained his mother's sternly moralistic outlook, including the hostility to alcohol that made him a lifelong teetotaler. He also developed a keen love of the outdoors, expressed through fishing, the observation of wildlife, and increasingly adventurous forays of travel. Within a context of close, loyal family relationships, his father deliberately fostered a spirit of independence in the two sons.

In 1883 the family moved to Jamestown, Dakota Territory, where Dwight Wilbur was general land agent for the Northern Pacific Railroad. Four years later they journeyed to

Riverside, Calif., where the developing of orange groves made them somewhat more comfortable financially. By the time Ray had graduated from the local high school in 1892 he had attained his full height of six feet four inches. Planning to study medicine, he entered Stanford University, recently founded by Senator Leland Stanford. During his freshman year he met Herbert Hoover, then a sophomore, and came to know him well by joining him in a compaign to systematize the finances of student organizations. In his senior year he was elected president of his class.

After receiving his B.A. in 1896, Wilbur remained at Stanford as a graduate assistant in physiology and obtained an M.A. in 1897. That summer he enrolled at Cooper Medical College in San Francisco. There he soon began to assist in teaching and became known as a clear, precise lecturer, abounding in homely epigrams. Unknown to him at the time, Hoover was also helping to see him through financially. Wilbur took his M.D. degree in 1899. On Dec. 5, 1898, he married Marguerite Blake, a former Stanford student and the daughter of a San Francisco physician. They had five children: Jessica Foster, Blake Colburn, Dwight Locke, Lois Proctor, and Ray Lyman.

For a brief period Wilbur practiced medicine in San Francisco, while teaching and serving in the clinic at Cooper. In 1900 he returned to Stanford as assistant professor of physiology and began working on a Ph.D. in that subject. He gave up advanced study, however, after three years, deciding that it was less congenial than full-time medical practice. Still, he remained in the Palo Alto community, serving its often socially prominent patients as a general practitioner. Since 1901 he had been a member of the new state Board of Medical Examiners, and he aligned himself with the forces seeking to upgrade medical education through the application of rigorous scientific standards. On trips to the East and to Europe he rapidly formed contacts with the worldwide medical elite of his day. His pronounced interest in public health took shape during these early years.

Wilbur resumed his direct tie with Stanford University in 1908; it would never again be broken until his death. Initially he served as clinical professor of medicine; he was appointed professor of medicine in 1909, and a year later became department chairman, which amounted to the headship of Stanford's new medical school (formerly the Cooper) in San Francisco. This position gave him his first baptism into administration. Under his direction, the school rapidly flourished and became prestigious. His title was changed to dean in 1911; at this time he gave up his remaining private practice. His election the next year as president of the American Academy of Physicians revealed the national stature he had won. Now strongly committed to the ideal of medical research, Wilbur lent his weight to promoting the research aspects of medical education during one of its most revolutionary periods, and himself undertook a small but significant amount of investigation. Herbert Hoover, who had become a trustee of the university in 1912, suggested Wilbur for the presidency of Stanford in 1915, to replace the retiring John Casper Branner (Hoover, *Memoirs*, I, 119). Wilbur accepted the trustees' offer in part to assure the strong position of the medical school in the university's overall future.

When Wilbur took office in January 1916, Stanford University was financially weak and the faculty poorly paid. One of his first acts was to raise salaries noticeably, and on a more rationalized basis. His longtime familiarity with the campus was a great initial asset, but this was somewhat offset, in the eyes of the arts and sciences faculty, by his evident partiality to the medical school. Moreover, fund-raising efforts were hampered by the widespread but erroneous impression that the Stanfords had given the institution a permanently generous endowment. Though resources did gradually improve, Wilbur's administration witnessed slow growth rather than dramatic upturn. Student enrollment increased from 2,199 in 1916 to 5,179 in 1941; during the same period, endowment doubled to reach $50 million. The number of graduate students increased sharply, from 342 to 1,670.

The coming of World War I interfered with Wilbur's plans and caused his first absence from the university to engage in national public service. Unlike the university's chancellor, David Starr Jordan, who was an outspoken pacifist, Wilbur threw himself wholeheartedly into war preparedness. In what may have been the most consequential action of his life, he played an early and forceful role in bringing Herbert Hoover's name before President Woodrow Wilson as a possible wartime food administrator. Hoover, after receiving the appointment, named Wilbur as one of his assistants, in charge of the domestic campaign to save food. Coining the slogan, "Food will win the war," Wilbur spent some months touring the country, crusading among local public officials and housewives against food waste. The results powerfully reenforced his belief in the efficacy of voluntary cooperation. Wilbur also aided in student mobilization efforts and more generally helped incite patriotic emotions. He always retained his admiration for Wilson as a war leader. Yet calmer afterthought enabled him to avoid the extremes of nationalistic conformity in viewing American history; the right teaching of it, he later believed, "would do a great deal to take a little cockiness out of the so-called '100-percent American.'"

Upon his return to Stanford, Wilbur began a program of alterations that led to several major changes. Wartime pressures, combined with his native bent toward efficiency, first produced a shift from the semester to the quarter system in the fall of 1917; this became permanent. Wilbur also engineered two departures aimed at reducing the power of the academic departments. Stanford's structure had leaned unusually far toward departmental autonomy; subject majors could begin in the freshman year, with a minimum of required general courses. In 1920 the four-year course was divided into an upper and a lower division, with majors confined to the junior and senior years and a new emphasis on common liberal education courses to precede them. Even more tellingly, departments were grouped into a number of schools (created between 1922 and 1925) that played a major role in promotions and appointments of professors. The result was the subjection of the faculty to a new degree of administrative pressure and control. Grading and attendance procedures were standardized. The chain of command was tightened from the top downward.

Further changes of the postwar period ran counter to Wilbur's inclinations. Because the founders desired that poor boys be given every opportunity to attend college, Stanford had never charged tuition. In 1920, under press of financial conditions, tuition fees were reluctantly imposed. The result was to alter the tone of Stanford in the direction of wealth and social elitism, much against Wilbur's own convictions. (As an undergraduate he had opposed fraternities, and he had refused to wear academic dress at his inauguration, so deep ran his commitment to plainness.) Finally, in 1919 alumni pressure compelled Wilbur to permit a return to intercollegiate football, reversing a policy that had existed since 1905. The appointment in 1924 of a big-time coach,

Glenn Warner, seemed in particular a betrayal of Wilbur's values. Both changes revealed the limitations upon a hard-driving university president's power to control the atmosphere of his own institution. The alumni had to be courted because their gifts were desperately needed, and they demanded a Stanford in their own image rather than Wilbur's. To counterattack, Wilbur sought during the 1920's to abolish all lower division (freshman and sophomore) instruction, encouraging junior colleges to provide a substitute. The alumni perceived that such a change would destroy the heartland of undergraduate social life, turning Stanford into an unrecognizably serious institution, and Wilbur met repeated defeat on the issue.

Wilbur's own sympathies lay with scientific research and with the sternly purposeful moralism of his boyhood. The humanities languished at Wilbur's Stanford, and his Darwinian positivism kept him remote from religion. Science connoted a specialization of effort that implied both inner discipline from an early age and a functional view of life. Dissipation was anathema. Only somewhat less obviously than James Rowland Angell at Yale, Wilbur thus revealed himself to be out of step with the high-living, clublike institution he headed. He made all the necessary compromises that enabled him to remain an outward success. But in the process he lost any chance to be remembered as an exceptional academic leader of his generation.

Herbert Hoover's rise to the presidency in 1928 gave Wilbur an opportunity in an environment beyond these limitations. Wilbur had helped promote the Hoover boom in 1920; a lifelong Republican with progressive leanings, he had said he would support Hoover even if he ran as a Democrat. In 1928 he, and most of Stanford, campaigned for Hoover openly and stridently. Hoover appointed Wilbur secretary of the interior, a post that he held for the entire four years, while Stanford marked time with an acting president.

Wilbur's policies were indistinguishable from those of his chief, except that he pushed the construction of Hoover Dam more vigorously (and named it on his own initiative, thereby sparking a protracted controversy). Like Hoover, Wilbur believed that the holding of national conferences was the best means for bringing scientific expertise to bear on the solving of social problems; by collecting and publicizing information the government had done its part. Like Hoover, Wilbur believed in minimizing federal bureaucracy; he disappointed his academic colleagues by refusing to support a cabinet-level Department of Education. In the same spirit, he played a prominent part over the years in opposing socialized medicine, and he minimized the government's role in selling electric power. He took pride in running the Department of the Interior with new efficiency, but did not believe in altering its essential functions. His approach to the problem of the Great Depression was calculatedly to ignore it.

The Interior Department had been criticized for showing a sometimes corrupt partiality to large business interests ever since the Teapot Dome oil scandals of the Harding administration. Wilbur ended any remaining aroma of corruption, but effectively allowed the partiality to continue. The leasing of oil fields (and oil shale deposits) on government land to private corporations remained a major issue during these years. Hoover's policy, which Wilbur cheerfully executed, was to restrict the granting of new leases as much as possible and to insist upon higher standards of efficiency in the way in which the lands were tapped. At a time when the future of the world's oil reserves appeared dangerously limited, this approach seemed to favor prudent conservation. But it also coincided with the interests of the existing large oil corporations, reducing their competition and keeping gasoline prices high.

Wilbur (and Hoover) genuinely favored conservation of natural resources, and Wilbur was proud of his numerous small additions to the national park system. Yet individualistic beliefs and constitutional scruples prevented as much positive movement in the direction of orderly planning as his rhetoric promised. A certain groundwork was laid for the interventionist policies of the Roosevelt administration, but in most areas so little action resulted that ardent conservationists were severely disappointed. With regard to Indian policy, which greatly interested Wilbur, congressional legislation gave him little leeway, but he personally favored complete assimilation of Indians into the mainstream of American life and the dissolution of reservations. In sum, Wilbur seems to have been a competent but not brilliant cabinet officer, perhaps somewhat noticeably beyond his depth in dealing with problems outside the Western states. His most important role in Washington, as one of Hoover's few close friends, was that of giving the lonely chief executive unflinching personal support.

Wilbur's erect, muscular body made him look even taller than he was. His eyes were penetrating, his nose and mouth unusually large. His face often seemed to wear a quizzical expression. In appearance and manners, he was formal rather than folksy. His efficient style struck many people as too abrupt. In his office he worked so rapidly, doing several things at once, that some callers came away believing he had hardly listened to them. He liked to make decisions instantly, in a machinelike fashion. As a student he had always enjoyed the punctual fulfillment of routine assignments, implicitly shunning open-endedness. Yet he was also sometimes remembered as tolerant and sympathetic, even kindly.

A joiner by temperament, Wilbur served in an unusually large number of organizations. He was at various times president of the American Medical Association (1923–1924), the California Physicians' Service, a body that established voluntary health care along the lines of his own earlier thinking (1939–1945), and the American Social Hygiene Association (1936-1948). He was American chairman of the Institute of Pacific Relations (1925-1929 and 1948-1949), a citizens' group devoted to the study of foreign relations in the Pacific area, and supported it vigorously when it was attacked as pro-Communist after World War II. In 1923-1925 Wilbur headed a major study of race relations concerning Asians on the Pacific Coast. He opposed legal restrictions against aliens and supported assimilation with full equality. (Yet, like many, he defended the Japanese relocation in 1942.)

Upon returning to the Stanford presidency in 1933, Wilbur faced the problems occasioned by the depression. He cut faculty salaries temporarily, but managed to keep the university fully staffed. In 1941 he dedicated a new building on campus to house the Hoover Library on War, Revolution, and Peace, and the following year he presided over the establishment of a broadly based School of Humanities. His long term as university head came to an end in 1943 when he moved into the honorary post of chancellor. He died of a coronary thrombosis at his home on the Stanford campus at the age of seventy-four; his remains were cremated. Like Hoover, Wilbur stood for ideals of individualism, voluntary cooperation, and scientific expertise, which seemed forward-looking until 1929, but conspicuously conservative thereafter.

[Wilbur's papers are scattered among several locations at Stanford. *The Memoirs of Ray Lyman Wilbur,*

1875–1949 (1960) is a basic source, especially helpful for his early life, garrulous and tending to avoid controversial issues in his later career. Wilbur's other books are of lesser interest; they are listed on p. 674 of the *Memoirs.* J. Pearce Mitchell, *Stanford Univ., 1916–1941* (1958), is an official history. Far more down-to-earth and helpful in some of its details, though verging on the idiosyncratic, is Edith R. Mirrielees, *Stanford: The Story of a Univ.* (1959). Harris G. Warren, *Herbert Hoover and the Great Depression* (1959), affords some insight into Wilbur's relations with the Hoover administration. Hoover's own *Memoirs* (3 vols., 1951–1952) are disappointing. Donald C. Swain, *Federal Conservation Policy, 1921–1933* (1963), is invaluable for its assessment of the Hoover administration and Wilbur's place in it. Good obituaries include the following: *N.Y. Times,* June 27, 1949; R. E. Swain in *Science,* Mar. 31, 1950; Albert Guérard in the *Nation,* July 30, 1949. Others, including Edgar E. Robinson's in the *Calif. Hist. Soc. Quart.,* Sept. 1949, say less.]

LAURENCE VEYSEY

WILKINSON, THEODORE STARK (Dec. 22, 1888–Feb. 21, 1946), naval officer, was born in Annapolis, Md., the only child of Ensign Ernest Wilkinson, USN, and Gulielma Caroline (Bostick) Wilkinson. Both parents had been born on Southern plantations, the father in Louisiana, the mother in South Carolina. The elder Wilkinson resigned from the navy shortly after his son's birth and became a patent lawyer in Washington, D.C. Even before entering St. Paul's School, Concord, N.H., in 1902, Theodore Wilkinson had decided on a naval career. He entered the United States Naval Academy in 1905 and graduated at the top of his class in 1909. He later (1912) received an M.S. degree from George Washington University.

As ensign on board the U.S.S. *Florida* in 1914, Wilkinson commanded a landing party which captured the customshouse at Veracruz, Mexico, leading his men with such skill and courage that he was awarded the Medal of Honor. During World War I he served in the Bureau of Ordnance, where he helped design antisubmarine depth charges and firing mechanisms for mines. On Dec. 17, 1918, he married Catherine Dorsey Harlow. They had three children: Ann Harlow, Joan Susannah, and Theodore Stark.

After the war, Wilkinson received his first command, that of a destroyer. He later had shore duty in ordnance, served as fleet gunnery officer to the Scouting Force, and was secretary of the navy's General Board (1931–1934), rising to the rank of captain in 1937. For the first nine months of 1941 he commanded the battleship *Mississippi.* In mid-October he was appointed director of the Office of Naval Intelligence (ONI) with the rank of rear admiral. He held that post at the time of the Pearl Harbor attack. ONI was charged with the gathering of intelligence from such sources as intercepted Japanese dispatches, but not with evaluating it; and though war seemed imminent, neither he nor any other responsible officer anticipated an attack in an area so remote from Japan as Hawaii.

In August 1942 Wilkinson became commander of Battleship Division Two, a post he left the following January, when he was named deputy commander, South Pacific Force, under Adm. William F. Halsey. Wilkinson's balance, good humor, and poise during the Solomon Islands campaigns made him indispensable to Halsey. His quick brain solved many operational problems, and his personality conciliated all and sundry, including the touchy French officials of New Caledonia and our tough allies from the Antipodes. He never used foul language and rarely lost his temper; his tact and consideration for others made him beloved by his staff.

From July 1943 Wilkinson commanded the Third Amphibious Force, set up headquarters at "Camp Crocodile," Guadalcanal, and applied his energies to amphibious warfare. In the Pacific theater he was a leading advocate of the "leapfrogging" strategy, through which American forces bypassed those islands on which the enemy was best fortified, cutting them off by air and sea, and concentrated instead on weaker targets. Leapfrogging, more successful than "island hopping," saved thousands of American lives. Wilkinson was the first to practice it, leaving the enemy out on a limb in Kolombangara while "III 'Phib" captured Vella Lavella in August 1943. Next came the landings in Empress Augusta Bay, Bougainville, a good instance of what the admiral liked to call, in baseball lingo, "hitting 'em where they ain't." Quick shifts in plans never fazed Wilkinson. In September 1944, when III 'Phib was already partly loaded for a landing on Yap, he was ordered instead to Leyte in the Philippines. His force of 250 ships landed the XXIV Army Corps at Dulag on schedule (Oct. 20, 1944). This exploit earned him promotion to vice admiral. In January 1945, against strong enemy opposition, he landed the XIV Corps at Lingayen, Luzon. His last war mission was to lift Gen. Robert L. Eichelberger's Eighth Army into Tokyo Bay, arriving the day of the Japanese surrender ceremony.

Returning to the United States, Wilkinson served as a member of the joint strategic survey committee of the Joint Chiefs of Staff. On Feb. 21, 1946, while he and his wife were boarding the Norfolk–Portsmouth ferry in Virginia, his car went out of control and plunged into the river. His wife survived, but Wilkinson was drowned. He was buried in Arlington National Cemetery. His wife subsequently married Adm. Sir Harry Moore, R.N.

[Memoir in *Alumni Horae* of St. Paul's School, XXVI (1946), 33–38; Samuel E. Morison, *Hist. of U.S. Naval Operations in World War II,* vols. III (1948), VI (1950), XII (1958), XIII (1959); Roberta Wohlstetter, *Pearl Harbor: Warning and Decision* (1962); family information from Theodore S. Wilkinson, Jr.]

SAMUEL ELIOT MORISON

WILLIS, BAILEY (May 31, 1857–Feb. 19, 1949), geologist, was born at Idlewild, his parents' country estate near Cornwall, N.Y. He was the youngest of the four children, two of them boys, of Nathaniel Parker Willis, noted journalist and poet, by his second wife, Cornelia (Grinnell) Willis; a daughter by the first marriage completed the family. Bailey Willis' mother was the niece and adopted daughter of Joseph Grinnell, Massachusetts merchant, congressman, and textile manufacturer. When Bailey was ten, his father died and his mother moved the family to Cambridge, Mass. A talented woman, she stirred her son's interest in art and culture and, through the example of her uncle Henry Grinnell, a benefactor of polar exploration, in travel and adventure. In 1870 she took her son to Europe, where he spent four years in German boarding schools. On his return in 1874 he entered Columbia University, from which he received degrees in mechanical and civil engineering (1878, 1879).

After graduation Willis was hired by Raphael Pumpelly, a prominent mining geologist and adventurer, to assist in an appraisal of iron and coal resources for the federal Tenth Census and in a private survey for the projected Northern Pacific Railroad. Both undertakings took him into remote and primitive areas of the country, often on his own. In 1884, when the railroad company went bankrupt, Willis joined the United States Geological Survey, with which he was to be associated for nearly three decades. Major John Wesley Powell, the director, and many of his chief subordinates were rough-hewn, self-educated men, with whom Willis felt out of place. He nevertheless did notable work in the Southern Appalachians, supervising surveys by younger geologists for the folios of the *Geological Atlas of the United States,* of which he was editor. He synthesized these results in his first major publication, "The Mechanics of Appalachian Structure" (United States Geological Survey, *Annual Report,* 1893), in which the field observations of

folding and faulting were interpreted by means of a series of laboratory experiments with models. The experiments revealed many important principles of geological dynamics, although it is now known that the models were far out of scale in the strength of the materials involved.

When Charles D. Walcott succeeded Powell in 1894 as director of the Geological Survey, Willis was given greater responsibilities, first as geologic map editor and then as geologic assistant to the director. The latter position, which he held from 1897 to 1902, gave him a roving assignment to observe the geology of many parts of the United States. He continued his early interest in the Pacific Northwest and studied such landmarks as Mount Rainier in Washington and the Lewis and Livingston ranges in Montana. He was influential in bringing both regions into the National Park system, the latter as Glacier National Park. Willis also collaborated with G. W. Stose on a geological map of North America which was published in 1912 to accompany Willis' monumental compilation *Index to the Stratigraphy of North America.* Both map and index endured for decades as standards of reference for North American geology.

Willis was irked, however, by the constraints of administration and longed for wider fields, so that during his last decade with the survey he was on leave and abroad for long periods. In 1903 he accepted the leadership of a geological expedition to northern China, organized under the auspices of the Carnegie Institution of Washington. In the course of a year, his party gathered enough data to fill the notable two-volume study *Research in China* (1907), which presented many new facts and interpretations regarding the geology of this hitherto poorly known region. In 1910-1914 Willis supervised an investigation for the Argentine government of the empty pioneer country of northern Patagonia. The objective was primarily an appraisal of resources and of planning for future development, rather than a geological survey. The results were attractively printed in a report, *Northern Patagonia* (1914), but the recommendations had little effect.

Willis severed his connection with the Geological Survey in 1915 to accept an invitation from President John C. Branner—himself a geologist—to head the department of geology at Stanford University. Although he officially retired from this post in 1922, Willis remained in close association with the university for the rest of his life. He developed many interests in California geology, especially in faulting, seismology, and earthquake hazards; he was president of the Seismological Society of America from 1921 to 1926. He collaborated in preparing a "Fault Map of California" (with H. O. Wood, 1922); and his short paper of 1927, "Folding or Shearing, Which?" (American Association of Petroleum Geologists, *Bulletin,* January 1927), although derided by many contemporaries, was prophetic of later tectonic concepts of the Pacific Coastal Belt in California. Willis' concern over earthquakes led him to study the engineering hazards of the Golden Gate Bridge and to fight for a more stringent municipal building code. He continued his foreign travels after his retirement especially for studies in faulting and seismology, to northern Chile (1923), to the rift valleys of East Africa (1929), and to the Philippines and other parts of the Far East (1936-1937).

Willis received many foreign honors. At home he was elected to the National Academy of Sciences (1920) and to the presidency of the Geological Society of America (1929), which in 1944 awarded him its Penrose Medal. During World War I he served as chief of the Latin American division of the Inquiry, the research group set up by Col. Edward M. House to gather geological and geographical information for use at the Paris Peace Conference.

Willis' interests were primarily in the broader aspects of physical and dynamic geology, in the formation and origin of rock structures, and in their effect on the evolution of the landscape. He had little interest in geological details, in laboratory procedures, or in biological geology. In the latter part of his career he summarized his geological philosophy in many theoretical papers. His hypotheses—of supposed "isthmian links" to explain biological and other resemblances between continents now separated by ocean basins, of compressional "ramping" rather than tensional separation to explain the rift valleys of East Africa and the Near East, and of hot fluid concentrations from the earth's interior (asthenoliths) to explain the gross tectonic features of the earth—seem in retrospect superficial and have been largely ignored.

Willis will be remembered far more for his personal influence on his contemporaries, his inspiration, and his kindly spirit. His personality is preserved in his charming books of autobiography and travel, *Living Africa* (1930), *A Yanqui in Patagonia* (1947), and *Friendly China* (1949), some of them illustrated with his own sketches and watercolors. Slight of build, but wiry and vigorous to the end, he was a notable figure on the Stanford campus, easily identifiable by his luxuriant beard.

Willis married Altona Holstein Grinnell of Yellow Springs, Ohio, on Mar. 4, 1882. They had two children: Marion (who died in infancy) and Hope. After the death of his first wife in 1896, he remarried Margaret Delight Baker of Washington, D.C., on Apr. 21, 1898; their children were Cornelius Grinnell, Robin, and Margaret. Both sons followed their father's footsteps into professional geology, and Robin was joint author of the second edition (1929) of Willis' textbook *Geologic Structures,* originally published in 1923. Willis died of myocardial failure in Palo Alto, Calif., at the age of ninety-one. His remains were cremated.

[In addition to Willis' autobiographical volumes, see Eliot Blackwelder in Geol. Soc. of London, *Quart. Jour.,* 105 (1949), lvi–lviii, and in Nat. Acad. Sci., *Biog. Memoirs,* XXXV (1961), with bibliography; Aaron C. Waters in Geol. Soc. of America, *Proc.,* 1962, with bibliography; Hope Willis Rathbun in *Cosmos Club Bull.,* Feb. 1969; and *Annual Reports* of the Geological Survey.]

PHILIP B. KING

WILSON, HUGH ROBERT (Jan. 29, 1885-Dec. 29, 1946), diplomat, was born in Evanston, Ill., the second son and third of four children of Hugh Robert Wilson and Alice (Tousey) Wilson. Both parents were Middle Westerners, respectively from Ohio and Indiana. The father was a founder and partner of Wilson Brothers, a Chicago wholesale house dealing in men's furnishings. Growing up in a well-to-do Episcopalian family, Wilson was educated at the Hill School in Pottstown, Pa., and at Yale, where he received the B.A. degree in 1906. He spent a year traveling around the world and then entered the family business. Increasingly, however, he began to find stultifying both the pursuit of wealth and the domination of his uncle, who had led the firm since his father's death in 1900. Seeking a "pleasant interval," Wilson looked to diplomatic service for greater intellectual and social stimulation, despite family misgivings about diplomacy as the "football of politics" and about the corrupting influence of European mores.

After studying at the École Libre des Sciences Politiques in Paris (1910-1911) and serving briefly as private secretary to Edwin Morgan, the American minister in Lisbon, Wilson returned to the United States and passed the Foreign Service examination. The following year (1912) he was appointed secretary of the American legation in Guatemala. A similar post followed in Buenos Aires (1914-1916), and after other brief assignments, he became first secretary in Berne, Switzerland (1917-1919). Meanwhile, on Apr. 25, 1914, he had married Katherine Bogle of Ann Arbor, Mich.; their only child, Hugh Robert, was born in 1918.

As with many of this first generation of professional American diplomats, Wilson's affluent, genteel Victorian background shaped his views of world politics. He admired British elitist traditions and was instinctively partial to England after the outbreak of World War I, but he was always wary of British motives and felt that Germany was no more responsible for the war than any other belligerent. He approved American entry into the war, but believed that President Wilson's visionary diplomacy raised hopes too high and was doomed by British and French realism. He considered the Versailles Treaty vindictive and thought it best that the United States did not join the League of Nations. He deplored the Bolshevik seizure of power in Russia, and even more the negotiations leading to the Treaty of Brest-Litovsk, which he felt ended the "scrupulous courtesy" of international affairs and inaugurated a new era of "diplomacy by vituperation."

Wilson held a variety of diplomatic posts during the 1920s: counselor of the American embassies in Berlin (1920-1921) and Tokyo (1921-1923); chief of the Division of Current Information in the State Department (1924-1927). In the controversy over the administration of the Rogers Act of 1924, which amalgamated the diplomatic and consular branches into a single foreign service, he worked actively, as chairman of the Foreign Service Personnel Board, for the more rapid promotion of diplomats, believing them to be superior to their consular counterparts. In 1927 President Coolidge appointed Wilson minister to Switzerland.

Wilson's ten years in Switzerland were probably the happiest and most fruitful of his diplomatic career. He reported ably on European events, tactfully channeled information to Washington on League of Nations affairs in Geneva, and represented the United States at conferences dealing with such subjects as tariffs, prisoners of war, and disarmament. During the Manchurian crisis of 1931-1932 he helped secure League of Nations adoption of the nonrecognition doctrine of Secretary of State Henry L. Stimson; but he soon came to question the value of nonrecognition, considering it a moral condemnation that only strengthened the bonds among unnatural allies in the community of the damned (Japan, and later Italy and Germany). While serving as a delegate to the World Disarmament Conference of 1932-1934, Wilson proposed to Washington that the United States forego its traditional position on neutrality and freedom of trade and aid collective security by not interfering with sanctions against an aggressor nation, a position briefly advanced by the Roosevelt administration but then dropped in the face of isolationist protests.

Wilson returned to Washington in August 1937 as assistant secretary of state. The following January, President Roosevelt named him to succeed William E. Dodd as ambassador to Nazi Germany. Wilson hoped to encourage reintegration of Germany into the political and economic mainstream of Europe. Like the appeasers, he believed that Hitler desired peace with the Western powers and sought only limited goals; he considered the Soviet Union a greater menace to European security. He thought the German Anschluss with Austria defensible and praised the Munich settlement as possibly opening the way to "a better Europe." President Roosevelt recalled Wilson in November 1938 to protest the Nazi pogrom against the Jews, and he was not allowed to return to his post, which he resigned at the end of August 1939.

Wilson next became an administrative officer in the State Department assigned to handle war-related problems, and in January 1940, he was appointed vice-chairman of the department's Advisory Committee on Problems of Foreign Relations, dealing with peace plans, disarmament, and international economics. He resigned from the Foreign Service at the end of 1940. During World War II he served (1941-1945) in the Office of Strategic Services, an agency for espionage and counterintelligence. A Republican, Wilson also acted during the war as a liaison between his party and the Roosevelt administration. In 1945 he became chief of the foreign affairs section of the Republican National Committee. The next year, at the age of sixty-one, Wilson died of a heart attack in Bennington, Vt., where he had a summer home. He was buried in Rosehill Cemetery, Chicago.

Highly praised by colleagues as belonging to the "realist" rather than "messianic" school of American diplomats (diary of Jay Pierrepont Moffat, Jan. 31, 1938, Moffat Papers, Houghton Library, Harvard University), Wilson was one of the first career diplomats to achieve ambassadorial rank. Inbred caution and concern for diplomatic detail and protocol sometimes limited his perspective, but he always labored competently and diligently to find paths to peace.

He is important, as well, for his autobiographical writings, which cast light on the attitudes of the Foreign Service and on the diplomacy of the interwar years.

[Wilson's personal papers are at the Herbert Hoover Presidential Lib., West Branch, Iowa. His published writings include *The Education of a Diplomat* (1938), *Diplomat between Wars* (1941), and *Diplomacy as a Career* (1941). His son, Hugh R. Wilson III, used his father's papers to compile *A Career Diplomat* (1960), *Disarmament and the Cold War in the Thirties* (1963), and *For Want of a Nail* (1959); the first contains a good likeness of Wilson. See also Waldo H. Heinrichs, Jr., *Am. Ambassador: Joseph C. Grew and the Development of the U.S. Diplomatic Tradition* (1966); and Arnold A. Offner, *Am. Appeasement: U.S. Foreign Policy and Germany, 1933–1938* (1969). Significant information concerning Wilson can be found in the State Dept.'s *Foreign Relations of the U.S.* series for the relevant years. Other biographical data from U.S. State Dept., *Register,* 1940; Yale Univ., *Obituary Record,* 1946–1947; and correspondence with Hugh R. Wilson III.]

ARNOLD A. OFFNER

WINANT, JOHN GILBERT (Feb. 23, 1889–Nov. 3, 1947), governor of New Hampshire and ambassador to Great Britain, was born in New York City, the oldest of the four sons of Frederick Winant, a successful real estate broker, and Jeanette Laura (Gilbert) Winant. His father was descended from seventeenth-century Dutch settlers in New Amsterdam. His mother, the daughter of a wealthy hardware wholesaler, was of Scottish and English stock. Reared in a conservative, financially comfortable, upper-middle-class household, "Gil" Winant nonetheless developed a keen sensitivity to human needs through extensive reading of Charles Dickens, John Ruskin, and the English Christian Socialists. Despite his interest in ideas, however, he was shy and somewhat inarticulate, and in school, was plagued by academic difficulties. After attending private elementary schools in New York City, he entered St. Paul's School, Concord, N.H. His days there were happy ones, and, although he failed several courses, he finally graduated in 1908.

Winant entered Princeton University, but continued to do poorly in his studies. Racked by insomnia and convinced of the futility of continuing his formal education, he accepted a standing offer from the rector of St. Paul's School to join its faculty, and in 1911 he became an instructor in history there. Winant quickly displayed a talent for stimulating and challenging his students; he also worked to democratize the student fraternal organizations.

During his years on the St. Paul's faculty, Winant became active in local Republican politics, and in 1916 he was elected to the lower house of the New Hampshire legislature. Tall and Lincolnesque, the freshman legislator quickly challenged the reactionary Republican politicians and industrial interests that dominated the state. He introduced bills into the 1917 session to limit the workweek for women and children to forty-eight hours, to regulate the assignment of wages, to establish a legislative drafting and reference bureau, and to adopt woman's suffrage. He interrupted his political and academic career in 1917 and joined the American Air Service, becoming the commanding officer of an observation squadron engaged in reconnaissance missions over German lines. On Dec. 20, 1919, nine months after returning to the United States, he married Constance Rivington Russell, a wealthy New York socialite whom he had first met while he was a student at St. Paul's. They had three children: Constance Russell, John Gilbert, and Rivington Russell.

Appointed second vice-rector, he returned to St. Paul's and remained there until 1920. That year, encouraged by the former progressive Republican governor Robert Perkins Bass, Winant won election to the New Hampshire state senate. Two years later, despite a Democratic trend, he was again elected to the lower house, where he and Bass organized a progressive caucus and forced through the forty-eight-hour bill, only to see it defeated in the senate. Bass had formed the New Hampshire Civic Association in 1921 in an attempt to mobilize former Bull Moosers and reduce the political influence of the ruling Republican clique led by conservative Sen. George H. Moses. With the backing of the civic association, Winant successfully opposed Frank Knox, publisher of the *Manchester Union,* in the 1924 Republican gubernatorial primary and went on to win the general election in November.

An indefatigable worker, Winant fought desperately to overcome the standpatism of the legislature and, despite many failures, he put through several measures, including automatic annual appropriations for the state college, a topographical survey to aid in the protection of the state's natural resources, and the appointment of a liberal Democrat to the state Public Service Commission. However, a split in the progressive Republican ranks, caused by Winant's failure to give an early endorsement to Bass in his race for the United States Senate, insured Winant's defeat in his bid for reelection in 1926. With his personal finances depleted by years of living beyond his means, Winant then spent most of the next four years searching for oil investments in Texas. Most of these investments failed, however, with the onset of the depression, and for the rest of his life, he was in almost constant debt, forced to borrow from friends and associates.

Returning to state politics, Winant won reelection as governor in 1930 (and again in 1932), and following the lead of Gov. Franklin D. Roosevelt of New York, he insisted that the state assume its proper role in providing relief services. He pushed through bills that afforded emergency relief to mothers and dependent children, tightened regulations on bank and stock transactions, and created an executive budget. During the early days of the New Deal he successfully proposed both an emergency credit act, which allowed the state to guarantee the debts of financially distressed political subdivisions, and a state minimum wage act for women and children. He also spearheaded the drive that resulted in an interstate compact on minimum wages by the New England states, Pennsylvania, and New York. Most important, in order to eliminate waste and duplication, he achieved centralization of the state's poor-relief activities under an administrator appointed by the governor. Cooperating closely with the federal government, Winant was the first governor to fill his enrollment quota in the Civilian Conservation Corps and the first to cooperate with the National Planning Board. Winant's reputation as a friend of labor led to his appointment by President Franklin D. Roosevelt in 1934 to head an emergency board of inquiry into a nationwide textile strike; within two weeks a temporary settlement was reached.

Upon leaving his gubernatorial office in January 1935, Winant, with the help of Roosevelt, was appointed assistant director of the International Labor Organization in Geneva, an autonomous agency of the League of Nations. Within four months, however, Roosevelt brought him back to head the newly created Social Security Board. Winant had been, in 1934, a member of the advisory council to the Committee on Economic Security, which helped draft the federal social security law, and, as chairman, he worked actively to make the program a success. Although Winant was boomed for the Republican presidential nomination in 1936, he was not a good public speaker and was never a serious candidate, and when the party's nominee, Alfred M. Landon, attacked social security, Winant resigned from the Social Security Board so that he could defend the act, thus destroying any future

possibility of winning Republican support for a national office. Winant returned to his ILO post in 1937, and two years later became the director. As the European war intensified, he sought to move the ILO to the sanctuary of the United States, but this plan was thwarted by the State Department, which feared the ILO might become a source of labor radicalism. With great difficulty, Winant finally transferred a reduced ILO staff to Canada in mid-1940.

In late 1940, Roosevelt appointed Winant ambassador to the Court of St. James's to replace the unpopular, defeatist Joseph P. Kennedy. Taking office in February 1941, the informal, compassionate Winant walked the streets of burning London at night in the midst of Luftwaffe bombings, instilling faith in the hearts of beleaguered Britishers; and although he was often bypassed in the decision-making process by Roosevelt's reliance on such personal emissaries as Averell Harriman or by direct negotiations between Roosevelt and Prime Minister Winston Churchill, Winant nevertheless made a greater impact on the British press, intellectual community, and general public than any other American ambassador of the century. A firm believer that labor must receive a greater share of the fruits of democracy when the war was over, he was a popular and familiar figure with British trade unions. In 1942, at a critical juncture of the war, he personally addressed a meeting of striking coal miners in Durham and successfully urged them to return to work.

Winant was one of the planners of the 1943 Three-Power Foreign Ministers Conference in Moscow, which paved the way for the later summit conference at Teheran. Out of the Moscow conference emerged the European Advisory Commission to study proposals for liberated areas of Europe and to draw up plans for the postwar occupation of Germany by the Allies. Winant was appointed to this commission, but his task was frustrated by an absence of directives from Washington—the result of presidential indecisiveness and the War Department's refusal to agree on policy resolutions. Only as the war in Europe drew rapidly to a close was Winant finally able to secure permission to sign a three-power agreement defining allied zones of occupation in Germany.

Having tied his political fortunes so closely to those of Roosevelt, Winant was shattered by the death of his friend and benefactor in April 1945. Early the following year he was named by President Truman as the United States representative to the Economic and Social

Council of the United Nations, a post he retained after his resignation from the ambassadorship in March 1946. At the same time he began the laborious task of writing his memoirs. Increasingly, however, he fell into a state of despondency. Relatively inactive for the first time in his life, he strongly desired the companionship of his family; yet his children were away at school, and his wife busy with social activities. Despairing of satisfying a huge financial indebtedness and isolated from political life, Winant had just completed the first volume of his memoirs—*Letter from Grosvenor Square* —when he took his own life at his home in Concord. After the funeral at St. Paul's Episcopal Church, he was buried in Concord's Blossom Hill Cemetery. Winant was a modest and humane man, with an almost messianic desire to serve, and his career was as varied as it was distinguished. His devotion to duty was universally respected. He was a man who gave the constant impression, as Winston Churchill said, of "how gladly he would give his life to see the good cause triumph."

[Winant's papers, a large collection, are in the Franklin D. Roosevelt Lib., Hyde Park, N.Y. Many Winant letters are also to be found in the Robert Perkins Bass Collect. at Dartmouth College; and thousands of diplomatic telegrams sent by Winant from Geneva and London are in the Hist. Office Files of the State Dept. in the Nat. Archives and at the State Dept. itself. Selected speeches from Winant's ambassadorial years are to be found in *Our Greatest Harvest* (1950). For a full-scale treatment, see Bernard Bellush, *He Walked Alone: A Biog. of John G. Winant* (1968). See also sketch by Montell Ogden in J. T. Salter, *Public Men In and Out of Office* (1946).]

BERNARD BELLUSH

WINLOCK, HERBERT EUSTIS (Feb. 1, 1884-Jan. 26, 1950), Egyptologist and museum director, was born in Washington, D.C., the oldest of two sons and one daughter of William Crawford Winlock and Alice (Broom) Monroe Winlock, and a grandson of Joseph Winlock, first director of the Harvard College Observatory. William Winlock, also an astronomer, served at the Naval Observatory in Washington and later as assistant secretary of the Smithsonian Institution; he died when Herbert was twelve. Through boyhood visits to the Smithsonian, Herbert developed an abiding fascination with Egyptian mummies and artifacts. He attended Western High School in Washington and then entered Harvard, where he received the B.A. degree in 1906 with "great distinction" in archaeology and anthropology.

That fall, at the invitation of Albert M. Lythgoe, his former archaeology professor, who had just been named the first curator of

Egyptian art at the Metropolitan Museum of Art in New York City, Winlock joined the museum staff as part of its Egyptian expedition. He was to remain with the museum for the rest of his professional career, becoming assistant curator of Egyptian art (1909-1922), associate curator (1922-1929), and curator (1929-1939). Until 1932—save for service in the army during World War I—Winlock spent the major part of his time excavating in Egypt. After 1919 he gradually took over the direction of this work and officially became director in 1928. Although he excavated at several sites, including the oasis of Khargeh and el Lisht, south of Memphis, the most important site was the area of Deir el Bahri on the western side of Thebes. Here the museum established its headquarters. Two of Winlock's findings cast fresh light on the ordinary citizen and the daily life of ancient Egypt. By thoroughly excavating (1919-1920) a previously explored 11th Dynasty tomb, that of Meket-Re, an official of King Mentuhotep II, he uncovered a set of painted wooden models of boats and workshops—"spirit models" designed to provide service in the afterlife. These models realistically portrayed clerks, farmers, and craftsmen at their work. At his summer home in North Haven, Maine, Winlock reconstructed one of the boats to its original scale and managed to sail in it. In another tomb of the same period a cache of papyri was found (1921-1922), later designated the Heka-nakhte papers, which proved to be family letters. They gave a rare picture of a tenant farmer's relations with his sons, and the personality of the querulous old man seemed to come alive. (The papers formed the basis for a detective novel by Agatha Christie.)

One of Winlock's major contributions was the excavation of the royal tombs at Thebes of the periods preceding and following the Middle Kingdom. Working from ancient accounts of the tomb robberies, he largely reconstructed the succession of the rulers of these times and identified the remains of their monuments. So adept was he at analysis that when he unearthed the burial place of a group of soldiers, he determined from the angle of their wounds that they had died storming a fortress, and suggested the specific battle involved. In 1923 Winlock began excavating along the causeway leading to the Nile River from the famous temple of Queen Hatshepsut in Thebes. Here he discovered numerous fragments of statues of the queen, which had been smashed by her stepson and successor, Thutmose III, and cast out of the temple. After several years of painstaking research, Winlock reconstructed many of the pieces, and in some cases was able to unite them with previously discovered fragments in various museums.

The particular qualities Winlock brought to his archaeological work were a keen and imaginative power of analysis that led him to discoveries other excavators had missed, and the ability to bring his findings vividly to life in his annual reports, monographs, and scholarly articles. He was fortunate in having associates of ability and dedication, among them Ambrose Lansing and William C. Hayes; the latter, a greater scholar than Winlock, was able to profit from Winlock's abilities as an organizer and fund raiser. These same abilities figured in Winlock's role as curator in the building up of the Metropolitan Museum's magnificent Egyptian collection. The objects found by his own expedition were, of course, major additions, but Winlock also brought to the collection, with the aid of loyal benefactors, important gifts, bequests, and purchases. Through contributions by Henry Walters and the Rogers Fund of the museum, the museum purchased in 1916, the Treasure of Lahun, a magnificent set of jewelry of the 12th Dynasty, an acquisition initiated by Lythgoe from Sir Flinders Petrie's excavations for the Egypt Exploration Society. The chief additions, however, were the collection of the noted British patron of archaeology, Lord Carnarvon, acquired with the aid of Edward S. Harkness, and the jewelry of three princesses of the reign of King Thutmose III of the 18th Dynasty.

In 1932 Winlock was named director of the Metropolitan Museum, a post he held concurrently with his Egyptian curatorship. Despite economic cutbacks caused by the depression, his tenure was marked by a significant expansion of the museum's holdings of American art, and by the opening in 1938 of The Cloisters, a museum to house the collection of medieval art assembled by the sculptor George Gray Barnard.

With his shaggy brows and balding head, Winlock has been described as resembling a Roman proconsul (Tomkins, p. 141). Lacking the academic formality of some of his colleagues, he was a witty, convivial man who once for amusement founded a Harvard Club at an oasis in the Sahara Desert. During the 1930's he received honorary degrees from Yale, Princeton, Michigan, and Harvard. Winlock suffered a stroke in 1937 and retired two years later, at the age of fifty-five, although he continued to act as a consultant and to write prolifically. He married Helen Chandler, daughter of the dean of the department of architecture at the Massachusetts Institute of Technology, on Oct. 26, 1912. They had three children: Frances, William Crawford, and Barbara. Winlock was a conservative, a Republican in politics and an Episcopalian. He died of a coronary thrombosis while on vacation in Venice, Fla., and was buried in Arlington National Cemetery.

Winlock's career as an archaeologist spanned an era of intensive exploration in Egypt on the part of three major and rival American expeditions: those of the Museum of Fine Arts of Boston and Harvard University under George Andrew Reisner, the Oriental Institute of the University of Chicago under James Henry Breasted, and the Metropolitan Museum under Winlock. This triumvirate dominated explorations into the ancient past of one of the world's most interesting civilizations and laid the groundwork for their successors.

[Winlock's major publications are *The Tomb of Queen Meryet-Amūn at Thebes* (1932); *The Treasure of El Lāhūn* (1934); *Excavations at Deir el Bahri, 1911–1931* (1942); *The Slain Soldiers of Neb-hep-et-Re Mentu-hotpe* (1945); *The Rise and Fall of the Middle Kingdom in Thebes* (1947); *The Treasure of Three Egyptian Princesses* (1948); and *Models of Daily Life in Ancient Egypt* (1955). On Winlock and his work, see John A. Wilson, *Signs and Wonders upon Pharaoh: A Hist. of Am. Egyptology* (1964); Calvin Tomkins, *Merchants and Masterpieces: The Story of the Metropolitan Museum of Art* (1970); Leo Lerman, *The Museum: One Hundred Years and the Metropolitan Museum of Art* (1969); profile by Geoffrey T. Hellman in the *New Yorker*, July 29, 1933; Ambrose Lansing in Am. Philosophical Soc., *Year Book*, 1951. Particular details were provided by the Harvard Class Reports of Winlock and his father.]
                                    WILLIAM KELLY SIMPSON

WINSHIP, BLANTON (Nov. 23, 1869–Oct. 9, 1947), army officer and governor of Puerto Rico, was born in Macon, Ga., the older of the two sons of Emory Winship, a clothing merchant, and Elizabeth (Alexander) Winship. His father, of English stock, was descended from colonial settlers of both Massachusetts and Georgia. Blanton Winship attended Mercer University in Macon, graduating with the B.A. degree in 1889. He then studied law at the University of Georgia and received the LL.B. degree in 1893. For the next five years he practiced law in Macon.

Winship began his army career in 1898 when he joined the Georgia volunteers in the Spanish-American War as a captain. Commissioned the next year as a first lieutenant in the Judge Advocate's Department of the regular army, he served for two years in the Philippine Islands and in 1904 advanced to major. In 1906 he was a member of the advisory commission headed by Gen. Enoch H. Crowder, which went to Cuba to rewrite the laws and draw up a new constitution for the insular government; he subsequently served as judge advocate of the Army of Cuban Pacification. In 1914, as a member of the American expeditionary force that occupied Veracruz, Mexico, Winship had charge of the civilian administration of the city.

With the entry of the United States into World War I, Winship, now a lieutenant colonel, was initially assigned to the staff of Gen. John J. Pershing as judge advocate of the 42nd Division. He requested front-line duty, however, and as commander of the 110th Infantry, 28th Division, participated in the battles of Aisne-Marne, St.-Mihiel, and Champagne-Marne. He was cited for extraordinary heroism in action near La Chausee and received the Distinguished Service Cross and other decorations, including an officership in the French Legion of Honor. After the Armistice, as director general of the Army Claims Settlement Commission (1918-1919), Winship promptly and efficiently handled more than 100,000 claims. He later served as judge advocate of the Army of Occupation in Germany, and on the Reparations Commission (1920-1923). He was promoted to colonel in 1920.

Winship in 1925 was given the difficult and delicate position of legal counsel on the military board that tried the case of Gen. William L. ("Billy") Mitchell, an assignment in which his dignity, integrity, and humor won the respect of both sides in the controversy. He later served as military aide to President Calvin Coolidge (1927-1928) and as legal advisor to Governor-General Henry L. Stimson of the Philippine Islands (1928-1930). In 1931 Winship was promoted to major general and named the army's judge advocate general. He retired from active duty in November 1933.

Early in 1934 President Franklin Roosevelt appointed Winship governor of Puerto Rico to replace Robert H. Gore. The conservative Winship had little sympathy for the reform programs of the New Deal, but he was one of the first to recognize and foster the tourist potential of Puerto Rico, a fact that made him popular with the island's commercial interests. In Puerto Rico's highly charged atmosphere of economic depression and rising nationalist sentiment, Winship's military background and strict belief in public order were

qualities of doubtful value. His position was made even less comfortable by the transfer of Puerto Rican affairs from the War Department to the Interior Department, since he did not have an amicable relationship with Interior Secretary Harold L. Ickes. Winship's response to the growing discontent on the island was to improve the efficiency and discipline of the insular police corps. Tensions mounted until in 1937 police tried to prevent a nationalist parade and fired into a crowd of unarmed civilians, killing seventeen and wounding over 100. Although Winship defended the police action, an investigation by the American Civil Liberties Union condemned both the police and the governor. The following year Winship himself narrowly escaped assassination in an attempt that killed three bystanders.

Winship resigned as governor in 1939. During World War II he was called back into active duty with the army and served as coordinator of the Inter-American Defense Board until his retirement in 1944. Winship never married. He was a Methodist in religion. He died in Washington, D.C., of a heart attack and was buried in Macon, Ga.

[Winship's private papers were as of 1974 held in the custody of his estate in Macon, Ga. His public papers, along with clippings and reports, are in the Nat. Archives, Washington. Favorable mention of Winship in the trial of Billy Mitchell is found in Isaac Don Levine, *Mitchell* (1943); and Emile Gauvreau and Lester Cohen, *Billy Mitchell* (1942). For Winship's activities in Puerto Rico, see Thomas G. Mathews, *Puerto Rican Politics and the New Deal* (1960). Certain details from *Nat. Cyc. Am. Biog.*, XXXVII, 246–247.]

THOMAS G. MATHEWS

WISE, STEPHEN SAMUEL (Mar. 17, 1874-Apr. 19, 1949), rabbi and communal and Zionist leader, was born in Budapest, Hungary, the eldest son of Rabbi Aaron Weiss and Sabine (Farkashazy) Weiss. He was brought to the United States at the age of seventeen months, when his father assumed the pulpit of Congregation Rodeph Shalom in New York City. The young Stephen Wise (in the United States the family changed the spelling of its name) decided very early in life to enter the rabbinate and was tutored in Jewish studies by his father. At the age of fifteen, he entered the College of the City of New York, continuing his rabbinic studies with Alexander Kohut and Gustav Gottheil. Upon his graduation from Columbia University in 1892 (to which he had transferred the year before), he pursued his studies with Adolph Jellinek, the chief rabbi of Vienna, receiving rabbinical ordination in 1893. In the fall of 1892, he was briefly at Oxford, studying the Bible with Adolph Neubauer. When he returned to New York in 1893, Wise was appointed assistant rabbi to Henry F. Jacobs at Congregation B'nai Jeshurun, and upon Jacobs' death several months later he assumed full responsibility, at the age of nineteen. On Nov. 14, 1900, Wise married Louise Waterman in New York City. They had two children, James Waterman and Justine. He resumed his graduate studies at Columbia University, where he received his Ph.D. in 1901 for a dissertation on Solomon ibn Gabirol.

Wise involved himself in social causes early in his career. In 1895 during a transit strike in Brooklyn, he announced his prolabor sympathies from the pulpit of B'nai Jeshurun. After he moved to Portland, Oreg., in 1899 to become rabbi of Temple Beth El, his involvement in social justice became a dominant motif in his ministry. Joining with other clergymen, he launched an attack upon the city's "two major industries," gambling and prostitution, and incurred the wrath of some of his congregants, whose income depended upon such business. He assisted Dr. Harry Lane in a civic reform campaign that eventually won Lane the office of mayor of Portland. Wise declined a position in the new mayor's cabinet, stating that a minister of religion should not accept public office under partisan circumstances.

Wise achieved national recognition in 1906 when he rebuffed offers to become the rabbi of the prestigious Temple Emanu-El in New York City, after having been refused his demand of a free pulpit, uncontrolled by the board of trustees. Reacting with outrage, Wise conducted a particularly sharp and angry feud with Louis Marshall, one of the most powerful and influential board members. This experience prompted Wise to return to New York a year later to found the Free Synagogue, where the pulpit would be unmuzzled and protected from any form of restriction. This pulpit served as Wise's principal forum in New York for the next forty-three years.

On returning to New York, Wise became ever more prominently identified with the cause of labor, and he consistently supported demands for improved working conditions and better pay. In some cases, as in several disputes in Pennsylvania in 1912, he served as mediator and arbitrator between labor and management; in other instances, he sided squarely with the workers. In 1911, after 146 female workers died in the Triangle Shirtwaist Company fire, Wise took up the cry against sweatshop owners and conditions in their factories. He placed his

reputation on the line in 1919, when he supported the cause of the steel workers against the powerful steel industry, headed by Judge Elbert Gary of United States Steel. In a sermon at the Free Synagogue, he charged Gary and his company with being the "most prolific breeders of Bolshevism in the United States." The ensuing response was almost overwhelming, but Wise stood firm, although the strike itself failed. He also aided and encouraged the strikers at the Passaic textile mill in 1926, supporting their demands for collective bargaining.

In the realm of politics, Wise fought to rid government of corruption. Immediately after his return to New York in 1907, he declared war against Tammany Hall and its stranglehold on New York politics. Wise wrote later in his autobiography: "To me it was clear that just as Tammany Hall strengthened and fed upon civic corruption and social injustice, I as minister could not separate the battle for civic decency and the battle for social justice." He attacked "King Richard" Croker, the head of Tammany Hall, characterizing a dinner given "in his honor" and attended by twelve justices of the city supreme court as a "night of shame." Wise's most ambitious attack on the Tammany wigwam came in 1930 with his assault against Mayor "Jimmy" Walker. Joining with John Haynes Holmes as cochairman of the City Affairs Committee, he accused Walker of corruption and malfeasance, eventually forcing Gov. Franklin D. Roosevelt to investigate. The result of this pressure was that the mayor resigned and fled to Europe. At that moment, Wise stood at the height of his power in the affairs of New York City.

Wise believed not only in getting rid of corrupt officials, but also in helping to elect honest ones. He worked for the candidacy of Woodrow Wilson in 1912 and was a member of the New York delegation to the Democratic convention of 1924, at which he supported Al Smith's bid for the presidency and endorsed the Roosevelt-Lehman state ticket in New York. He campaigned for Norman Thomas in 1932 but backed Roosevelt in the 1936, 1940, and 1944 campaigns.

Another aspect of Wise's philosophy of social justice was his fight for the rights of the individual. He was a cofounder of the National Association for the Advancement of Colored People in 1909 and of the American Civil Liberties Union in 1920. He stood steadfastly for justice and clemency for Sacco and Vanzetti in 1927. Closer to his Jewish concerns were his battles against the Ku Klux Klan and his support in 1924 and 1926 for liberal immigration laws.

Wise envisioned his congregation as a "Jewish society" that would fill the void between the "lifelessness of Reform" and "the lack of vitality" of Orthodoxy. The original Free Synagogue, however, served primarily an American Jewry of established means in an almost completely Americanized Jewish community. Wise regarded it as his duty to serve the ghetto of nearly a million Yiddish-speaking European immigrants who had settled on New York's Lower East Side. Within a year of its founding the Free Synagogue opened a branch there, where religious services of the liberal kind were held regularly every Friday night. In this pulpit Wise formed one of his strongest links with the new Jewish masses. He remained throughout his life the Reform rabbi whose political liberalism and Zionism, and whose common touch, endeared him to the Yiddish-speaking masses.

Wise made an important contribution to the training of rabbis in 1922 as founder of the Jewish Institute of Religion. The three existing rabbinical schools, which did not appear to Wise to satisfy the needs of American Jewry, were not attracting American-born Jews to the rabbinate. They accepted students at high-school age, before they were mature enough to make a life commitment, and none of the three was then even friendly to the cause of Zionism. In Wise's view, the rabbinical seminary for his time should consist of a faculty that would represent the best of *Jüdische Wissenschaft,* the scientific study of Judaism, which was the new mode of Jewish scholarship. Wise, therefore, assembled an eminent faculty for his new Institute of Religion, expecting it to prepare men for the rabbinate and to contribute to Jewish learning and to community service, "leaving the faculty and student body free, not merely in the matter of ritual observance, but intellectually free in accordance with undogmatic liberalism, which is at the heart of the genius of Judaism." The students did indeed enter all three branches of Judaism, although the large majority became Reform rabbis and helped bend that movement toward Zionism. In 1948, in the last months of Wise's life, and the final victory of pro-Zionist convictions within Reform Judaism, the Jewish Institute of Religion was merged with the Hebrew Union College.

The greatest passion of Wise's public life was Zionism. He joined with Richard Gottheil,

Harry Friedenwald, and others in 1897 to found the Federation of American Zionists, of which he became honorary secretary. The following year, he attended the Second World Zionist Congress in Basel, where he met Theodor Herzl. This encounter made a profound impression on him, and he pledged to Herzl that he would devote his life to the cause of Zionism. Wise made his first trip to Palestine in 1913. The next year, after the outbreak of World War I, he joined with Louis D. Brandeis to found the Provisional Executive Committee for Central Zionist Affairs, which led the fight for Zionism in America, and especially within the American Jewish community, in the second decade of the century. It fought the elitist leadership of such men as the banker Jacob Schiff and the American Jewish Committee. The platform of Brandeis and Wise was that the American Jewish community required "democratization" through an elected representative body. They were correct in their certainty that such a body would be pro-Zionist.

In 1918 Wise was elected president of the newly formed Zionist Organization of America. The following year, he sailed to France as delegate of the American Jewish Congress to lobby for the Jewish cause at the Paris peace conference. In 1921 the Brandeis group of the Zionist Organization of America, of which Wise was a member, was defeated in an internal power struggle, but Wise continued his Zionist activities. He was named honorary vice-president of the Palestine Development Council that year, and in 1925 he appeared at the Fourteenth Zionist Congress to fight Chaim Weizmann's plans for extending the Jewish Agency for Palestine to include non-Zionists. The same year he was elected president of the permanent American Jewish Congress, a post he held until his death.

With Hitler's rise to power in 1933, Wise immediately mobilized both Jews and non-Jews to protest against Hitler's anti-Semitic policies. Denouncing Hitler at a rally at Madison Square Garden, organized within a few weeks of the Nazi accession to power, Wise called for a boycott of German goods. The American Jewish Congress followed his lead and worked hard at organizing the boycott. In 1936, at a meeting in Geneva, Wise led in creating the World Jewish Congress, declaring that the task of this new organization was to bring "Jews together on a new plane . . . for an exchange of views touching every manner of Jewish problems with a view to their solution." He saw the new body as the democratically constituted political representative of world Jewry, and here too one of his objectives was to preempt Jewish representation from the elite, non-Zionist notables in the United States and Western Europe.

In 1939, as head of the American delegation, Wise attended the Round Table Conference of Jews and Arabs in London (St. James Conference). Despite the outcries of the Zionist representatives, the immediate result was the White Paper of 1939, which virtually shut off Jewish immigration to Palestine, at a time when European Jewry was desperately in need of refuge. Wise responded to the immigration problem both within the Zionist movement and through other channels. As a member of the President's Advisory Committee on Political Refugees, he focused attention on the Jewish immigration problem, strongly urging that refugees be allowed to enter the United States and Palestine. Within the Zionist movement, he helped to establish the American Emergency Committee for Zionist Affairs (which became the American Zionist Emergency Council in 1943), whose purpose would be to fight within the United States for the cause of the Jewish national homeland in Palestine.

Having learned in 1942 from the office of the World Jewish Congress in Geneva that Hitler was conducting an all-out campaign to exterminate European Jews, Wise continually railed against the Allied governments, demanding that something be done to save the victims of mass murder. There is an accepted opinion that Wise did not press the United States government because of his uncritical faith in President Roosevelt. This estimate was the platform on which Abba Hillel Silver displaced Wise as the leader of American Zionism. Silver believed in mounting maximal pressure on Roosevelt for immediate action to help the Jews of Europe and to gain public assent of the United States government for the Zionist war aim, the creation of a Jewish state in Palestine.

A perusal of Wise's papers and other documents of this period changes this estimate. By the 1940's Wise changed his opinion of Roosevelt, although he kept the personal and political connection. His way of dealing with Roosevelt was based on his estimate of what was possible, given the president's temperament and convictions, and the fact that the United States was engaged in a world war. In fact, the ascendancy of the Silver activist policy did not succeed in changing Roosevelt's policy, although the effort that Silver led and the resulting education of Congress and public opinion did pave the way for postwar Zionist victories.

Wise's cochairmanship of the Zionist Emergency Council with Silver (1943-1946) was thus marked by constant turmoil. Wise came to the Twenty-second Zionist Congress in 1946, the first postwar meeting, no longer the acknowledged leader of American Zionists. Other disappointments awaited him. Chaim Weizmann was repudiated by the World Zionist Congress over the issue of negotiating with the British to bring about some form of agreement and peace in Palestine. Disillusioned by the rejection of Weizmann and his policies and disheartened by the political scramblings at the congress, Wise withdrew from all the Zionist organizations. However, he did not cease his public activities. He continued to hold the presidency of the American Jewish Congress and the World Jewish Congress. He died in Lenox Hill Hospital in New York of a malignant stomach ailment, a month after his seventy-fifth birthday, and was buried in the Westchester Hills Cemetery in Hastings-on-Hudson, N.Y.

In his lifetime, Wise was the preeminent Jewish public figure in the United States. His roots were deep in the liberal, social-activist religion which was the advanced religious expression in the country at that time. In his own person, he was a bridge between part of the older, more settled Jewish community and the East European masses. Not even his enemies doubted that he was the colossus of American Zionism. Tall, majestic, and even theatrical, he was one of the greatest orators in the florid style of the early years of the century. He dominated any room that he entered. His acts of private kindness were innumerable, especially during the Nazi period, when he personally saved hundreds of persons. His political judgment could be questioned, but not the quality of his heart.

[The Stephen S. Wise Papers, Am. Jewish Hist. Soc., Waltham, Mass.; Justine Wise Polier and James W. Wise, eds., *Personal Letters of Stephen Wise* (1956); James W. Wise, *Legend of Louise: The Life Story of Mrs. Stephen S. Wise* (1949). See also Louis Lipsky, *A Gallery of Zionist Profiles* (1956); Carl Hermann Voss, *Rabbi and Minister—The Friendship of Stephen S. Wise and John Haynes Holmes* (1964) and *Servant of the People: Selected Letters of Stephen S. Wise* (1969); and *Cong. Weekly*, Mar. 17, 1944, and May 30, 1949. Wise's books include *Challenging Years: The Autobiography of Stephen Wise* (1949) and *As I See It* (1944).]

ARTHUR HERTZBERG

WISSLER, CLARK (Sept. 18, 1870-Aug. 25, 1947), anthropologist, christened Clarkson Davis Wissler, was born on a farm in Wayne County, Ind., the oldest of the seven children of Benjamin Franklin Wissler and Sylvania (Needler) Wissler. His father's "Pennsylvania Dutch" (German) forebears had moved west around 1800. Some of the Wisslers were Mennonites, but Benjamin followed the secular tradition of his namesake: starting out as a district teacher (and part-time carpenter), he later served as school superintendent, and in 1889 became publisher of a newspaper in Richmond, Ind. Clark Wissler grew up in the small-town culture of the middle border, where the livery stable was a central institution and the older inhabitants still remembered the days of Indian warfare. He loved the outdoor life, but he was also a bookish boy, and especially enjoyed accounts of the primitive horse cultures still alive beyond the frontier. After graduating from the local Hagerstown (Ind.) high school in 1887, he taught in a series of rural schools to earn the money to go to college. In 1893, after serving for a year as principal of his old high school, he entered Indiana University, where he majored in psychology, serving as assistant in charge of the laboratory one summer and spending another at Clark University under G. Stanley Hall. After graduating in 1897, he took a job as instructor in psychology and education at Ohio State University, while continuing graduate study at Indiana. On June 14, 1899, just after receiving his M.A., he married Etta Viola Gebhart, the daughter of a Hagerstown merchant; they had two children, Stanley Gebhart and Mary Viola.

Later that summer, while attending a scientific meeting in Columbus, Ohio, Wissler met James McKeen Cattell, who offered him an assistantship in psychology so that he could continue graduate study at Columbia University. His doctoral dissertation was a statistical analysis of data Cattell had collected on Columbia undergraduates, and in the course of it he came into contact with the anthropologist Franz Boas, who at that time was the most knowledgeable person in statistics in the Columbia psychology department. Although Wissler's earlier articles had reflected recapitulationist evolutionary assumptions of a kind Boas rejected, the results of his study of "The Correlation of Mental and Physical Tests" (*Psychological Review*, Monograph Supplement No. 16, 1901) were on the whole quite Boasian: despite his expectation to the contrary, he found little correlation. After receiving his doctorate in 1901, Wissler worked for a year as instructor in pedagogy at New York University, but under Boas' influence he had already shifted his major intellectual interest to anthropology.

From 1902 to 1905 Wissler served under Boas as assistant (later assistant curator) in ethnology at the American Museum of Natural History, and as assistant and then lecturer in anthropology at Columbia from 1903 to 1909. During this period he carried out most of his anthropological fieldwork, first among the Sioux and then, more systematically, among the Piegan division of the Blackfoot, who had been buffalo-hunting Plains Indians of the classic type before they were reduced to near starvation conditions on a Montana reservation in the 1880's and 1890's. Wissler's fieldwork was much in the early Boasian style: relatively short summer trips that sought to recapture the details of pre-reservation culture preserved in the memory of older informants, often through an interpreter—in Wissler's case, the half-breed blacksmith David Duvall, who also collected and sent back data to Wissler in New York. The results were embodied in a series of dryly factual monographs (1908-1918) on different aspects of Blackfoot culture (*Anthropological Papers*, American Museum of Natural History, vols. II, V, VII, XI, XVI) and, some three decades later, in Wissler's own colorful memory ethnography of "life on the old-time Indian reservations" (*Indian Cavalcade*, 1938).

Following Boas' resignation in 1905, Wissler took charge of anthropological work at the American Museum, and he continued to serve as curator of the department of anthropology until his retirement in 1942 (five years after his election as dean of the Museum's entire scientific staff). Although the circumstances of his appointment contributed to a permanent estrangement from Boas, Wissler's role at the museum for the next decade and a half may best be regarded as an elaboration of Boasian themes. Following up an approach rooted in the early work of Boas, Wissler worked out in detail the major "culture areas" of North America in the process of arranging and classifying ethnographic collections ("Material Cultures of the North American Indians," *Amer. Anthropologist*, July-Sept., 1914). Wissler also continued the tradition of areal fieldwork Boas had begun on the Northwest coast, sending out a series of investigators (mostly Boas-trained) to the Plains from 1907 to 1917 to recapture the late-flowering culture of the Indians of the "Wild West" of his boyhood. Under his direction they produced several controlled micro-comparisons of single complexes within one cultural area (e.g., "The Sun Dance of the Plains Indians," edited by Wissler,

Anthropological Papers, American Museum, vol. XVI, 1921), as well as numerous monographic studies. From 1909 on, Wissler also directed the Archer M. Huntington Survey, which combined archaeological and ethnographic researches in an attempt to establish "a chronology for the cultures of the Southwest" (*ibid.,* vol. XVIII, 1919). The culmination of this period of Wissler's work was *The American Indian* (1917; 2nd ed., 1922; 3rd ed., 1938), which drew together several decades of "ethnographic mapping" to provide a synthetic survey of American ethnology that was not to be superseded until after World War II.

During the 1920's Wissler elaborated a more systematic treatment of the genesis and development of culture areas. Tabulating and mapping distributions of cultural traits, he argued that culture complexes tended to diffuse at uniform rates in concentric circles from centers of innovation. On this basis he formulated the "age-area" concept, which assumed that these concentric circles were analogous to archaeological strata, and that the broader the distribution of an element or complex, the older it was. The basis for this uniformity of distribution was environmental: through the mechanism of food production, culture areas were correlated with ecological areas, and the distribution centers of various traits (physical, as well as cultural) tended to coincide with the geographical centers of particular faunal areas (see especially *The Relation of Nature to Man in Aboriginal America,* 1926). Although quite influential in the 1920's, these ideas, which had analogues in biology, and within anthropology were also developed by A. L. Kroeber, came rather quickly under sharp criticism from other anthropologists. Subsequent historical and archaeological evidence has shown that the age-area notion is inadequate even for Wissler's favorite case: the culture of the central Plains was in fact a recent elaboration in an area populated from the margins.

During this same period, Wissler played an important role in the promotion of anthropology and the diffusion of its concepts. In the nativist aftermath of World War I some leading scientists felt that Boas and his students—a number of whom were of immigrant background and had opposed the war—were "soft" on questions of race. Wissler, on the other hand, was a small-town American boy and an associate of Madison Grant and other influential racists. At the same time, he was generally committed

to the Boasian study of culture; furthermore, his age, his position in an important institution, and the range of his anthropological interests (which included all aspects save linquistics) made him seem to many to be the "logical successor [to Boas] in leadership of the guild." Thus ideally situated to play a mediating role, Wissler was in 1919 elected president of the American Anthropological Association, and during 1920 and 1921 he served as chairman of the Division of Anthropology and Psychology of the National Research Council. Much of Wissler's activity in this period was directed to meeting the charge that American anthropology was narrowly focused on the cultures of American Indians, and as anthropological consultant to the Bernice Pauahi Bishop Museum in Hawaii (1920-1947) he played an important role in turning the face of the discipline overseas.

At the same time, Wissler was the ideal person to "Americanize," as it were, the anthropological concept of culture. Although his *Man and Culture* (1923) ended with a paean to Nordic Americans as carriers of "the lamp of civilization," it also told Americans that they, too, like every tribal group, had "a culture." Drawing on the experience of "every American village," Wissler reduced the "dominant characteristics of our culture" to three central concepts: mechanical invention, mass education, and universal suffrage. Wissler's behaviorism, his scientism, his regional-ecological orientation, and his residual biologism were quite in tune with the sociology of the post-Social Darwinist period; and his book played a major role in disseminating anthropological thinking about culture to the other social sciences—a role facilitated by his active participation in the interdisciplinary movements of the period. When the landmark sociological study of the culture of an Indiana town appeared at the end of the decade, it was appropriately Wissler who contributed the introduction (Robert S. and Helen M. Lynd, *Middletown,* 1929); that same year he offered his *Introduction to Social Anthropology* to "the student of the social sciences desirous of securing something in the way of anthropological perspective."

In 1931 Wissler became professor of anthropology at Yale, where he had held a research position in the Institute of Psychology since 1924. Although his lectures were well attended and he was very helpful to a small group of graduate students who worked on American Indian topics, Wissler's primary energies continued to be directed to museum work (he was president of the American Association of Museums from 1938 to 1943 and vice-president of the advisory board of the National Park Commission from 1940 to 1943). His published work after 1930 consisted primarily of books and articles on the American Indian, many of them of a popular sort (e.g., *Indians of the United States,* 1940). Characteristically, they reflected an ambivalence which permeated his whole anthropological outlook: romantically identifying with pre-reservation Indians, he was wont to catalogue the elements they had contributed to American culture. But although his own demographic researches showed they were no longer vanishing ("Population Changes Among the Northern Plains Indians," *Yale Univ. Publications in Anthropology,* no. 1, 1936), he nevertheless described their "grand cavalcade" as "passing into oblivion"; and on a deeper level, he did not seriously doubt the manifest destiny of the civilization that had uprooted them.

At his death (from coronary thrombosis following an operation for cancer), Wissler was a member of various honorary societies, including the National Academy of Sciences and the American Philosophical Society. He died in a New York City hospital. A loyal Hoosier to the end, he was buried in Hagerstown, Ind.

Influential in his prime, Wissler did not cast a long historical shadow. Although his rather eclectic *Social Anthropology* reflected the development of more functional approaches to the study of whole cultures in the 1920's, his anthropology is best viewed as carrying to the sterile extreme one half of the double thrust of Boas: the positivistic attempt to reconstruct cultural history by a distributional analysis of cultural elements. True, Wissler encouraged other approaches by his research staff, and there are in his work analogues (such as the "universal pattern of culture") to theoretical approaches that still seem fruitful. But there is little evidence of direct lineage. His theoretical viewpoint was out of fashion years before his death, and a generation afterward his work was little read. Institutionally and intellectually, he was anchored in the 1910's and 1920's—the last phase of the "museum period" of American anthropology—and in the long run his major contribution, aside from his mediation of the culture concept, was probably the organization of the collection of a large amount of ethnographic data.

[A complete bibliography of Wissler's works is included in the obituary by George P. Murdock, *Am. Anthropologist,* Apr.–June 1948, which also includes a photograph. See also A. L. Kroeber, "The Culture Area and Age-Area Concepts of Clark Wissler," in Stuart A. Rice, ed., *Methods in Social Science* (1931); Robert H. Lowie, "Supplementary Facts about Clark Wissler," *Am. Anthropologist,* July–Sept. 1949; Carter A. Woods, "A Criticism of Wissler's North American Culture Areas," *ibid.,* Oct.–Dec. 1934; obituary by N. C. Nelson in *Am. Antiquity,* Jan. 1948, on his museum work; and George W. Stocking, Jr., *Race, Culture, and Evolution* (1968). There are professional papers still in the files of the Am. Museum of Natural Hist., including Wissler's MS history of the museum. According to Mary Wissler, who provided information on several points, there are also personal materials still in the hands of the family, including Wissler's reminiscences of his early years, a copy of which was made available to the author, along with his own memories of Wissler at Yale, by William Fenton. See also the papers of Franz Boas in the Am. Philosophical Soc., and those of A. L. Kroeber and R. H. Lowie in the Bancroft Lib., Univ. of Calif.]

GEORGE W. STOCKING, JR.

WOODRUFF, LORANDE LOSS (July 14, 1879-June 23, 1947) biologist, teacher, and editor, was born in New York City, the son of Charles Albert Woodruff and Eloise Clara (Loss) Woodruff. His father and grandfather, descendants of English settlers who had lived near Farmington, Conn., since 1641, were clothing merchants in New York City, where his mother was born. Woodruff was educated in New York public schools, the College of the City of New York, and, later, Columbia University, where he earned the B.A. degree in 1901, the M.A. in 1902, and the Ph.D. in 1905 under the direction of the eminent protozoologist Gary N. Calkins. He was Republican in his politics and Congregationalist in his religious affiliation.

Most of Woodruff's professional life was spent at two academic institutions: Williams College, where he served first as assistant in biology (1903-1904) and then as instructor (1904-1907); and at Yale University (instructor, 1907-1909; assistant professor, 1909-1915; associate professor, 1915-1922; professor of protozoology, 1922 until his death). He was appointed director of the Osborn Zoological Laboratory at Yale and chairman of the Department of Zoology in 1938 and continued to serve in these positions for the rest of his life. His forty-year tenure at Yale was broken only by World War I, in which he served as a consulting physiologist in the Chemical Warfare Service of the United States Army.

In the summer of 1905, Woodruff began lecturing in biology at the Marine Biological Laboratory, Woods Hole, Mass. On December 21 of that year, he married Margaret Louise Mitchell of New York City; they had two children, Margaret Eloise and Lorande Mitchell. The following summer, he returned to Woods Hole, and in the summer of 1907 he became an instructor in embryology there. Although occasionally he lectured at the summer sessions of the Mountain Lake Biology Laboratory of the University of Virginia, Woods Hole was the Woodruffs' principal summer base, and their cottage, with its charming hostess and genial host, became a meeting place for students and colleagues alike.

From the outset of his career, Woodruff was interested in the question of the potential immortality of the Protozoa. It had been contended by Weismann that old age and natural death are penalties demanded of the Metazoa because of their specialization and differentiation into somatic and germinal protoplasm, whereas the Protozoa, without this protoplasmic specialization, are potentially immortal like the germ cells. In pursuit of the solution to this problem, Woodruff made valuable contributions, including the discovery of a process, which he called endomixis, and its role in the life cycle as a substitute for conjugation. During these studies he also discovered two new species of *Paramecium*. These experiments spanned twenty-five years and involved some 15,000 generations of pedigreed cultures of *Paramecium*. Woodruff concluded that senescence is not inherent in protoplasm and that fertilization is not a necessity for continued vitality.

In addition to his numerous researches, Woodruff made outstanding contributions to the biology of his day through his writings on the history of biology. His *Foundations of Biology* (1922), which grew out of his experience as head of the elementary course in biology at Yale, became a standard text. According to one of his assistants, J. S. Nicholas, "this book did more to unify the teaching [of biology] throughout the country than had ever been done," and it possessed, as well, the unusual merit of excellent style and literary quality.

Woodruff produced a wide variety of publications—scientific papers, historical articles, and books. These number 119 and fall into several categories: (1) life history and physiology of the ciliated protozoa dealing mainly with *Paramecium*; (2) history of biology, particularly microscopy; (3) publications of which Woodruff served as editor, such as his textbooks of biology and zoology, chapters of books and general biological articles; (4) miscellaneous notices, book reviews, commemorative pieces, and joint authorships.

Woodruff belonged to many distinguished scientific societies, among them the National Academy of Sciences and the National Research Council, which he served as chairman of the Division of Biology and Agriculture in 1928-1929. In 1935, Woodruff was awarded the Townsend Harris Medal by the Associate Alumni of the College of the City of New York.

In the early 1940's Mrs. Woodruff suddenly died. This was a shock from which Professor Woodruff seemed not to recover. She had been for so long the coordinator of his home life as well as his intellectual colleague that he found it impossible to make the necessary adjustments. On June 23, 1947, Woodruff died of heart disease and pneumonia at his home in New Haven. After a funeral service in Dwight Chapel at Yale, he was buried in the cemetery of the Church of the Messiah at Woods Hole, near the place where he had spent so many productive and happy summers.

[The Woodruff Memorial Issue of the *Journal of Protozoology*, Feb. 1954, carries a good likeness of Woodruff as a frontispiece and includes a complete bibliography of his published works. *Amer. Men of Sci.* (7th ed., 1944) and *Who's Who in America, 1940–1941* contain informative articles. Woodruff's personal correspondence is in the possession of his son, Lorande Mitchell Woodruff. Other information comes from personal recollections and research notes arising from the author's sojourn at the Osborn Laboratory as a post-doctoral fellow. Obituaries appeared in the *N.Y. Times*, June 13, 1947, and in the *N.Y. Herald-Tribune*, June 24, 1947.]

WILLIAM F. DILLER

WOODSON, CARTER GODWIN (Dec. 19, 1875-Apr. 3, 1950), historian, was born in New Canton, Buckingham County, Va., the oldest of nine children of former slaves, James Henry Woodson and Anne Eliza (Riddle) Woodson. The family farm was in one of the poorest counties in the state, and the children had to work hard to help eke out a living. Carter attended the local school during only a part of its five-month term and was largely self-taught until he was seventeen. In 1892, drawn by employment opportunities for Negroes in the West Virginia coal fields and by the hope of further education, Woodson moved with a brother to Huntington, W.Va. After several years in the mines he entered the segregated Douglass High School in Huntington and earned his diploma in 1896. That winter, having read a magazine article about Berea College in Kentucky, he enrolled there. He left after his second year to take a teaching job in Winona, W.Va., and for a time was principal of Douglass High School, but he returned to Berea in 1901-1902 and received the B.Litt. degree in 1903.

Woodson had already begun further study at the University of Chicago in the summer of 1902. He returned for the autumn quarter of 1903 and shortly afterward went to the Philippine Islands as a teacher and then as a school supervisor. In 1906-1907 he made his way back around the world and, having learned French as well as Spanish, studied history for one semester at the Sorbonne. He spent the autumn quarter of 1907 at the University of Chicago and received the B.A. degree in March 1908 and his M.A. in history in August. The following year he was in residence as a graduate student at Harvard. He completed his dissertation in American history while teaching in Washington, D.C. and received the Ph.D. from Harvard in 1912.

From 1909 until 1918 Woodson taught French, Spanish, English, and history at Washington's M Street (after 1916, Dunbar) High School. After a year as principal of Armstrong Manual Training School in the same city, he was appointed professor of history and dean of the School of Liberal Arts at Howard University. He and J. Stanley Durkee—the last white president of Howard—eventually came to a parting of the ways, and Woodson left in 1920 to accept the position of dean of West Virginia Collegiate Institute (later State College).

By this time Woodson had become absorbed in the mission to which he was to devote the rest of his life: the study and dissemination of Negro history. Negro children in particular, he believed, needed to develop pride of race and a sense of their own potentialities through a knowledge of Negro contributions to history. In 1915 Woodson organized the Association for the Study of Negro Life and History. Its quarterly *Journal of Negro History,* inaugurated in January 1916, attained high professional standards under his editorship. In 1921 he founded his own publishing firm, Associated Publishers, Inc., which issued a score of volumes by and about Negroes. He began an additional periodical directed to a more popular audience, the *Negro History Bulletin,* in 1937. Most widespread in its impact, perhaps, was the annual Negro History Week—in February, to coincide with the birthdays of Lincoln and Frederick Douglass—which Woodson inaugurated in 1926. This event was widely observed in schools and other institutions throughout the country.

Woodson left West Virginia State College in 1922 to devote his full time to the Association for the Study of Negro Life and History. At first he received grants from several foundations, but his prickly independence alienated these benefactors, and by the early 1930's he was forced to rely almost wholly on contributions from individual Negroes and Negro organizations, together with profits from his publishing house. He himself wrote many articles and book reviews for the association's two journals, as well as a number of books. Among them were such scholarly studies as *The Education of the Negro prior to 1861* (1915), *A Century of Negro Migration* (1918), *The History of the Negro Church* (1921), and, with Lorenzo Greene, *The Negro Wage Earner* (1930); five editions of source materials, such as *Free Negro Heads of Families in the United States in 1830* (1925), *The Mind of the Negro as Reflected in Letters Written during the Crisis, 1800-1860* (1926), and *The Works of Francis J. Grimké* (4 vols., 1942); and a widely used college textbook, *The Negro in Our History* (1922 and later editions).

A "loner" by temperament, Woodson never married. He had few outside interests, other than his habit in later years of summering in Paris, where he exercised a gourmet's taste for fine restaurants. At home he lived simply in an apartment above the association's offices. He was a hard taskmaster to those who worked with him, and he resisted sharing responsibility; sometimes he broke with friends. Yet he contributed, often anonymously, to such organizations as the National Association for the Advancement of Colored People and gave financial assistance to a younger generation of Negro historians. Tall, hale, and erect, Woodson continued as president of the association he had founded and as editor of its journals until his death, of a heart attack, at the age of seventy-four. He died in his Washington apartment. Funeral services were held in Shiloh Baptist Church, which he had occasionally attended, and he was buried at Lincoln Memorial Cemetery, Suitland, Md. With the possible exception of William E. B. Du Bois, Woodson had done more than any other person to create and develop interest in Negro history.

[Woodson's "Annual Reports" in *Jour. of Negro Hist.,* 1916-1949; various articles in memorial issue of *Negro Hist. Bull.,* May 1950, especially John Hope Franklin, "The Place of Carter G. Woodson in Am. Historiography"; Rayford W. Logan in *Phylon,* Fourth Quarter, 1945; L. D. Reddick, *ibid.,* Second Quarter, 1950; W. E. B. Du Bois in *Masses and Mainstream,* June 1950; Earl E. Thorpe, *Black Historians* (1971), chap. v; Rayford W. Logan in *Jour. of Negro Hist.,* Jan. 1973; biographical sketch in *The Crisis*, July 1912, p. 120; *Who's Who in Colored America* (1929 and later editions); vertical file of Moorland-Spingarn Collect., Howard Univ.; records of Berea College, Univ. of Chicago, Harvard, and Howard. A collection of Woodson's papers is in the Lib. of Cong.; others are at the headquarters of the Assoc. for the Study of Afro-American Life and Hist., Washington, D.C.]

RAYFORD W. LOGAN

WOOLLEY, MARY EMMA (July 13, 1863–Sept. 5, 1947), college president and advocate of world peace and woman's rights, was born in South Norwalk, Conn., the eldest of the two daughters and two sons of Rev. Joseph Judah Woolley and his second wife, Mary Augusta (Ferris) Woolley. Both parents were descended from English settlers of Connecticut. Mary's early years were spent in Meriden, Conn., where her father, after serving in the Civil War as chaplain of the 8th Connecticut Volunteers, had become minister of the Center Congregational Church. He moved in 1871 to the Congregational church in Pawtucket, R.I., where he initiated controversial reforms.

In Pawtucket, Mary Woolley attended three private schools. The last, Mrs. Davis's Private School for Young Ladies, was an important educational influence, providing small classes and close attention to each student and offering excellent Latin instruction. She went next to the Providence (R.I.) high school, and then, forsaking the finishing school program she had initially envisioned, enrolled with advanced standing in Wheaton Seminary, Norton, Mass., in 1882. She later gratefully attributed this decisive step to the enlightened guidance of her father. After graduating from Wheaton in 1884, she taught there for four years. A European trip with a Smith College group in the summer of 1890 included Oxford and Cambridge in its itinerary and further encouraged Mary Woolley's growing educational ambitions.

Through her father's friendship with President E. Benjamin Andrews, she was in 1891 admitted to Brown University as one of the first seven women undergraduates. She took her B.A. degree after three years and stayed an additional year for her master's degree, studying with the noted historian J. Franklin Jameson. In 1895 she went to Wellesley College as instructor in biblical history and literature, advancing within four years to professor and chairman of the department. Her reputation as a teacher and humanist, together with her emerging qualities of leadership, led to an invitation to become president of Mount Holyoke College, which had been founded in 1837

by Mary Lyon as a seminary and had been chartered as a college in 1888. Before taking office in January 1901, she spent three months in England studying women's education in British universities.

Mary Woolley's thirty-six-year presidency of Mount Holyoke saw continual changes in the physical appearance and educational personality of the institution. In the first quarter-century of her tenure, the student body doubled; the curriculum was made more flexible; and new structures, including a student-alumnae center and a humanities building, were erected. She sought particularly to raise faculty salaries. Secret societies were abolished, as well as the traditional requirement of domestic work in the college. The religious life at Mount Holyoke came to center around the nondenominational college chapel rather than the local Congregational church. At chapel exercises Mary Woolley's talks, often emphasizing the value of service to others, were an inspiring influence upon generations of Mount Holyoke students.

Although not herself a militant, she was an enthusiastic supporter of the woman's suffrage movement and in her later years endorsed the proposed Equal Rights Amendment to the Constitution. She deplored the closing off of opportunities because of sex, and she came to believe that women must make a concerted effort to secure political power for themselves. She especially felt that they could play a critical role in the search for peace. Her own affiliations included the American Peace Society (vice-president, 1907–1913), the League of Nations Association, and the Institute for Pacific Relations. Mary Woolley's internationalist sympathies were recognized by her appointment in 1921 as the only woman on the China Christian Education Commission, which investigated missionary colleges, and as the only woman on the American delegation to the Geneva Disarmament Conference of 1932. In an address two years later entitled "Internationalism and Disarmament," she called for a reeducation toward international understanding on all levels.

Her later years were marked by numerous academic honors and by memberships on a variety of boards and committees with educational, social, religious, and political concerns. She was particularly active in the American Association of University Women, serving as president from 1927 to 1933, and she was recognized as one of the most distinguished educators of her time.

President Woolley's career ended in 1937

in a storm of controversy over her successor. The trustees wished to replace her with a man, but she and a substantial group of faculty and alumnae felt strongly that Mount Holyoke's unbroken tradition of women presidents should be maintained. The trustees decided otherwise, and Mary Woolley never recovered from this emotional blow. She refused ever to visit Mount Holyoke again. She continued active in her public career, living in West Port, N.Y., with Jeannette Marks, a faculty friend of Mount Holyoke days. Handicapped following a stroke at eighty-one, she died at West Port three years later after another stroke. Her ashes were buried in the family plot at Hillside Cemetery, Wilton, Conn.

Mary Woolley's philosophy of education for women is perhaps best expressed in an address on "The College Woman and the New Epoch," delivered in 1916. She deplored the prevailing belief that the feminine mind should content itself with a casual and superficial development. "Filling the mind with large interests," she contended, "applying native talent for painstaking industry to some investigation that will make the world richer, cultivating the powers of application and concentration, developing the habit of thinking *through,* not only about the edges of a subject, this is the power which the world has a right to demand of the college woman as well as of the college man."

[Essential sources are the Mary Woolley Papers in the Mount Holyoke College Lib.; Arthur C. Cole, *A Hundred Years of Mount Holyoke College* (1940); and Jeannette Marks, *Life and Letters of Mary Emma Woolley* (1955). Mary Woolley's occasional pieces include "The College Woman and the New Epoch," Randolph-Macon Woman's College, *Bull.,* Apr.–June 1916; and *Lida Shaw King: An Appreciation* (1923), honoring the seventeen-year administration of the dean of the Women's College in Brown Univ. A revealing autobiographical memoir is in *What I Owe to My Father,* ed. Sydney Strong (1931). Mary Woolley's mixture of political astuteness and idealism is conveyed in her *Internationalism and Disarmament* (Kappa Delta Pi Lecture Series, 38 pp., 1935). Her scholarly style can be sampled in "The Early Hist. of the Colonial Post-Office," R.I. Hist. Soc., *Publications,* Jan. 1894, and in "The Development of the Love of Romantic Scenery in America," *Am. Hist. Rev.,* Oct. 1897. In addition there are a variety of published essays on international politics, education, and women. See also Hugh Hawkins in *Notable Am. Women,* III, 660–663; *N.Y. Times* obituary, Sept. 6, 1947; and, for her memberships and honors, *Who Was Who in America,* II (1950). The Cole history reproduces a portrait of Mary Woolley.]

ANNETTE K. BAXTER

WRIGHT, ORVILLE (Aug. 19, 1871–Jan. 30, 1948), inventor and pioneer in aviation, was born at Dayton, Ohio. He was the youngest of the four Wright brothers, who, with their younger sister Katharine, were the surviving children of Milton Wright and Susan Catherine (Koerner) Wright. Their father was a minister of the United Brethren in Christ, serving as editor of church publications and later, for twenty years, as bishop. Their mother, although a homemaker, was a college graduate and displayed a bent for invention.

It is impossible to consider the career of Orville Wright apart from that of his brother Wilbur, four years his senior. The closeness of their association and the peculiarly complementary quality of their minds account in large measure for their phenomenal success in so short a time in a field where many brilliant minds had tried and failed. Despite this affinity, it is false to suppose that Wilbur and Orville Wright were as alike as the proverbial peas. They were in fact quite dissimilar in personal characteristics, in temperament, and in abilities. Their mastery of their chosen line of work derived from melding their individual talents and intuitions.

The gift by their father when they were children of a rubber-band-driven toy *hélicoptère* of the Pénaud type had stirred their curiosity about the dynamics of flight, but their mature attention was turned to the subject by the press reports of the gliding successes of the German engineer Otto Lilienthal. Shocked when Lilienthal died in a gliding accident in 1896, they resolved to learn all they could about flight. They hoped at first to discover where Lilienthal had gone wrong and later to try experiments of their own. Although to their family and friends they belittled the seriousness of their glider experiments, Wilbur's technical correspondence with Octave Chanute, himself a pioneer of gliding and the great chronicler of aeronautical history, proved that the Wrights' real intent was nothing less than the conquest of the air.

They began with the problem of control in the air, for lack of which, they felt, Lilienthal had lost his life. Orville led off with the idea that lateral balance could be maintained if the difference in air pressure on the right and left wings could be adjusted by the pilot by presenting the tip sections at correspondingly different angles to the wind. Wilbur then promptly demonstrated a practical mechanical arrangement for accomplishing this adjustment, by twisting or warping the wings to present equal opposing angles at the tips. This system was successfully tested in a small kite-glider in July 1899, and they decided to build a man-carrying glider the next year.

As their test grounds they chose the sand dunes and beaches near Kitty Hawk, N.C., where they made thousands of experimental flights with a series of gliders in 1900, 1901, and 1902. In September 1901, while Wilbur was in Chicago making a speech to the Western Society of Engineers, Orville built a small wind tunnel in order to verify and refine the ideas gained in practical gliding. On Wilbur's return, with a second enlarged and improved wind tunnel they began tests that ultimately yielded reliable data on lift-drag ratios and other characteristics of more than 200 different wing shapes. From these data they built a vastly more efficient glider in 1902, with which more than a thousand glides were made, some over a distance of more than 600 feet.

On some flights, however, the machine responded in a way opposite to the intent of the pilot's movement of the controls. Orville proposed that the fixed vertical tail vane be converted to a movable rudder and used to counterbalance the adverse effect of the greater speed of the positively warped wing. Wilbur at once suggested that the warping and rudder controls be interconnected to coordinate the two actions. The change to the movable rudder added the last element needed for control of the three axes of the plane. They were now ready to try for powered flight.

With their characteristic speed and direct attack, they had designed and built an engine and propellers by the following fall. A new larger and stronger plane had been constructed. The culmination of four and a half years of intensive thought and labor was attained on Dec. 17, 1903, at Kitty Hawk, when Orville made the first powered flight of 120 feet. Wilbur made the fourth and longest flight of the day, covering 852 feet over the ground, or about a half mile through the air, in 59 seconds. As Bishop Wright later put it, credit was due both of them about equally. (The article on Wilbur Wright gives the details of the Wrights' subsequent experiments near Dayton in 1904 and 1905 and of their epoch-making public demonstration flights in France and the United States in 1908 and in Italy, Germany, and the United States in 1909.)

Despite the acclaim they received on two continents, the success of the Wrights did not bring them the satisfactions they sought. In their view, they had solved the problem of mechanical flight, invented the airplane, taught others to fly, and ushered in a new age. For this they believed that they were entitled, first, to the credit for their achievement, and, second, to the material rewards that might arise from it. Instead, they found their claims to priority

challenged on every side and on every conceivable ground, and in place of financial ease, which they had hoped would enable them to devote their lives to scientific research, they were obliged to resort to capitalists for the funds to support a company sufficiently endowed to defend their pioneer patent in the courts against the challenges of infringement. Orville, who disliked writing and public speaking, left stage center to Wilbur, contenting himself with the details of manufacturing planes, exhibition flying, and training pilots. In the midst of myriad lawsuits in America and Europe and of daily encounters with the press, Wilbur was suddenly struck down by typhoid fever and died on May 30, 1912.

Orville Wright survived his brother almost thirty-six years. He did not become the recluse that some have supposed; he was always active. Until he sold the Wright Company in 1915, he personally flew and tested improvements on all Wright planes. His last flight as pilot was made in 1918. From 1915 on, he spent much time in his Dayton laboratory. In World War I, he was commissioned a major in the United States Army and did much work on aircraft design and development. He was director and engineer of the Dayton-Wright Company, connected with United States adoption of the British DH-4. In 1921, with J. M. H. Jacobs, he patented the split wing flap. For many years he served on the National Advisory Committee for Aeronautics. Although never a prompt or very willing letter-writer, he had a large correspondence with persons from every corner of the globe, much of it inevitably about the Wright story and other aviation matters. In spite of all the controversies and disappointments, when Orville Wright died he and Wilbur were almost universally recognized and revered as the inventors of the airplane. The brothers are buried with their father, mother, and sister, Katharine Wright Marshall, in Woodland Cemetery, Dayton, Ohio.

[Articles and books by Orville Wright include "The Wright Brothers' Aeroplane," *The Century Mag.,* Sept. 1908, with Wilbur Wright (although it appears under joint authorship, the article was entirely the work of Orville Wright); *How We Invented the Aeroplane,* ed., with commentary, Fred C. Kelly (1953); *Miracle at Kitty Hawk: the Letters of Wilbur and Orville Wright,* ed. Fred C. Kelly (1951). Major sources are Arthur G. Renstrom, comp., *Wilbur & Orville Wright: A Bibliog. Commemorating the Hundredth Anniversary of the Birth of Wilbur Wright, Apr. 16, 1867* (Lib. of Congress, 1968); Marvin W. McFarland and Arthur G. Renstrom, "The Papers of Wilbur and Orville Wright," *Lib. of Congress Quart. Jour. of Current Acquisitions,* Aug. 1950, pp. 23–34; Fred C. Kelly, *The Wright Brothers: A Biog. Authorized by Orville Wright* (1943); *The Pa-*

pers of Wilbur and Orville Wright, Including the Chanute-Wright Letters and Other Papers of Octave Chanute, ed. Marvin W. McFarland (1953).]
MARVIN W. McFARLAND

WRIGHT, RICHARD ROBERT (May 16, 1853-July 2, 1947), educator and banker, was born a slave on a plantation near Dalton, Whitfield County, Ga., the only child of Robert and Harriet Waddell. His mother was a house servant; his father, of partial Cherokee descent, was the family coachman. When Wright was two years old, his father fled to freedom, and he and his mother were moved to Cuthbert, Ga. There his mother married Alexander Wright and had two more children. Alexander Wright escaped during the Civil War to join the Union army.

After emancipation, Harriet Wright, hearing of a "Yankee school" for Negroes in Atlanta, took her children there and opened a boardinghouse. Richard, undersized but bright, attended Storr's School, operated by the American Missionary Association. In 1868 General O. O. Howard of the Freedmen's Bureau spoke at the school and asked, "What shall I tell the children up north about you?" Richard's reply —"Tell 'em we're rising!"—was celebrated in a poem by John Greenleaf Whittier. In 1869 Wright was chosen as a preparatory student at the recently established Atlanta University, a pioneering institution of higher learning for Negroes. To help finance his education, he taught school during the summers. He graduated as valedictorian of the university's first class in 1876. (He later served as a trustee of the university from 1887 to 1929.) That summer, on June 7, he married Lydia Elizabeth Howard of Columbus, Ga. They had nine children: Edmund (who died in childhood), Richard Robert, Jr., Julia Ophelia, Essie Ware, Lillian Mathilda, Whittier Howard, Edwina, Harriet Beecher Stowe, and Emanuel Crogman.

Wright's first job after graduation was as principal of an elementary school in Cuthbert, Ga., his childhood home. Working with the local black community, he organized cooperatives through which the farmers could market their own produce and conducted Georgia's first Negro county fair. In 1878 he called a convention of Negro teachers and organized the Georgia State Teachers' Association, serving as its first president. At the same time he began publishing the *Weekly Journal of Progress,* originally the organ of the teachers' association, but later, renamed the *Weekly Sentinel,* a newspaper of modest circulation. On the strength of his growing reputation as an organizer, he was invited to Augusta in 1880 to establish and head Ware High School, the state's first public high school for Negroes.

Wright was an ambitious young man, concerned with making his way as a black within the post-Reconstruction social order in Georgia; he had acquired considerable influence with his extension work, teachers' organization, and newspaper. Both his ambition and his wideranging contacts led him logically to politics, which for a black in Georgia meant the Republican party. Traditionally a minority party in the South with a black base and a white leadership, the GOP in Georgia was split in 1880 by the insurgency of able young black men looking for rewards commensurate with the voting power of their race. Wright aided in this temporarily successful revolt and was sent as an alternate delegate to the Republican National Convention of that year. Continuing as a member of the state Central Committee even after white leadership was resumed in 1882, Wright was active in party affairs for the rest of the century and was chosen as a delegate to the national conventions through 1896. In return for his influence with black voters he received patronage positions. Some he accepted, such as the office of special paymaster in the army during the Spanish-American War, from which he received the rank of major; others, such as that of United States deputy marshal for Southern Georgia, he declined. His appointment to the presidency of the newly organized, federally supported State Industrial College in Savannah was probably not unrelated to his political activities.

Some of his more significant rewards came under McKinley, shortly before Wright left politics. In addition to the paymaster's job, he had accepted a postmastership for his daughter but declined a census supervisor's position for himself after white protest. Acting as a liaison for McKinley with blacks who were piqued at being snubbed, in 1898 Wright gave a dinner for the president at the Georgia State Industrial College to help heal the breach that was growing between blacks and the Republican organization. But soon he himself was among those who felt rejected. Caught in a feud with members of the state organization, both black and white, experiencing the growing disfranchisement restrictions placed on blacks in Georgia politics, Wright abandoned politics, though he remained a Republican throughout the rest of his life.

The Second Morrill Act of 1890 provided federal money for black as well as white state colleges. In response to the act, the State Industrial College for Negroes was established in Savannah in 1891 with Wright as its first president. He was a logical choice, having spent fifteen years as a teacher and administrator. As an advocate of black self-help he believed in the need for agricultural and industrial as well as academic training, and his work in politics had demonstrated his ability and willingness to work with white leaders. He led the school for thirty years until he retired in 1921, building its campus and setting its educational philosophy.

The role of black colleges in the South was not an easy one. Responsible to white trustees who often were not eager to advance black education, dedicated to educating students who entered with poor training because of the inadequate educational systems of the South, these institutions faced a difficult task in establishing and maintaining adequate college standards. Georgia State Industrial College found itself in this predicament. Never ranked among the best Negro colleges, the institution came under fire from the Phelps-Stokes Report in 1916 and a federal government survey in 1921 as being inadequate in its plant and curriculum.

During his years as president Wright was also active in commercial activities, especially in real estate dealings in and around Savannah. His college paper stressed the values of business and thrift. Thus there was a continuity in his entrepreneurial activity when he retired from the college at the age of sixty-seven in 1921 and moved to Philadelphia, the home of his son, Richard Wright, Jr., to establish a bank. Banking had been a field both attractive and perilous to black entrepreneurs. Too often such banks had invested in high-risk loans in so large a proportion to total deposits that they were rendered vulnerable to failure during economic fluctuation. However, buoyed up by his natural optimism and the prosperity of the time, and possessed of a shrewd business sense, Wright determined to enter banking despite his lack of previous experience.

Initially accumulating the requisite capital mainly from his family, Wright opened the Citizens and Southern Banking Company as a private venture in 1921. Despite the failure of a larger black-owned bank in Philadelphia, he applied for a state charter in 1926 as the Citizens and Southern Bank and Trust Company. His success was noteworthy. Wright's own cautious, prudent nature, which had seen him through the vicissitudes of black life in Georgia, coupled with his financial acumen, caused him to eschew speculative banking and to concentrate instead on security and liquidity in preference to a higher rate of earnings. The bank's funds were invested in short-term loans, conservative bonds, and other such securities. Its initial years of slow but sound growth caused a financial historian to note in 1936 that ". . . it is perhaps one of the strongest and best managed of Negro financial institutions in existence. . . . Perhaps it is the type of bank best suited to the needs of the Negro community" (Harris, p. 143). At the time of his death in 1947 the Citizens and Southern Bank and Trust Company had over $3 million in deposits.

Richard Wright remained sprightly and vigorous throughout his long life. Organizing was one of his talents, from the early days of the Georgia Teachers' Association through the National Association of Teachers in Negro Schools in 1908 to the National Association of Negro Bankers (now the National Bankers Association) in 1926. In a highly symbolic role of the black success story in the eyes of the white world he often represented the aspirations of the black community, in such instances as when he fought successfully for the commemorative stamp of Booker T. Washington, the first honoring a black, issued in 1940. By current standards Wright might be classified racially anywhere from a moderate member of the black bourgeoisie to a Bookerite accommodationist. An advocate of integration, he was not, however, actively involved in the vanguard of such racial organizations as the NAACP. He believed that if blacks proved themselves to whites educationally and economically, political and social rights were bound to follow.

Wright was a long-time member of the African Methodist Episcopal Church. He died of circulatory failure on July 2, 1947, and was buried in Mt. Lawn Cemetery in Sharon Hill, Pa.

[The bulk of Wright's papers are in the possession of Emanuel C. Wright of Philadelphia; the remainder are held by Mrs. Harriet B. S. Hines, his daughter, of Glenarden, Md. His printed monographs and speeches are in the Trevor Arnett Lib., Atlanta Univ. See also, for his radio addresses, Harriet S. B. Lemon, ed., *Radio Speeches of Major R. R. Wright, Sr.* (privately printed, 1949). The only full-length biography of Wright is the informal account by Elizabeth Ross Haynes, *Black Boy of Atlanta* (1952). For assessments of his educational, financial, and political accomplishments, there are Willard Range, *Rise and Progress of Negro Colleges in Georgia, 1865–1949* (1951); Abram Harris, *The Negro as Capitalist* (1936; rev. ed., 1969); Olive H. Shadgett, *Republican Party in Georgia from Reconstruction through 1900* (1964). His obituary appeared in the *N.Y. Times* for July 3, 1947; his death certificate is from the state of Pennsylvania.]
ANDREW BUNI

YOST, FIELDING HARRIS (Apr. 30, 1871–Aug. 20, 1946), football coach and university athletic director, was born in Fairview, W.Va., the oldest of the four children of Permenus Wesley Yost and Elzena Jane (Ammons) Yost. His father, a farmer, came of a family that had settled in West Virginia about 1825. Fielding attended local schools, and during his teens worked as a deputy marshal in Fairview. After a short course at the Fairmont (W.Va.) Normal School, he taught school for a year (1889–1890) in Patterson Creek, W.Va., and then enrolled in Ohio Normal University (later Ohio Northern) in Ada. He left after three years, however, before completing the course, and returned to Fairview to work in the West Virginia oil fields. Attracted by the lucrative possibilities of practicing petroleum law, he entered West Virginia University in 1895 and two years later received the LL.B. degree.

Yost had enjoyed playing the newly developing game of football in Ohio, and at West Virginia he was for two years a member of the university's intercollegiate team. After graduating he accepted the post of football coach at Ohio Wesleyan University. This was the first in a series of such positions that took him to the University of Nebraska (1898), the University of Kansas (1899), and Stanford (1900); at each he led the football team to a conference championship. Yost's success, coupled with his assiduous courting of officials at the University of Michigan, resulted in his call to Ann Arbor in 1901. He remained at Michigan for the rest of his career, as head football coach (1901–1923 and 1925–1927) and as director of intercollegiate athletics (1921–1941).

Yost was one of the earliest members of the "profession" of intercollegiate football coach, and one of the most successful. His Michigan teams compiled a record of 165 games won, twenty-nine lost, and eleven tied. They were undefeated for eight seasons, and eight times they won the championship of the Intercollegiate Conference of Faculty Representatives, commonly called the Western Conference or the "Big Ten." Yost's "point-a-minute" teams of 1901-1905 were the most remarkable, averaging 49.8 points per game to 0.7 points for their opponents in the fifty-five games played. An athletic entrepreneur rather than a gridiron theoretician, Yost based his success primarily upon his abilities at personnel recruitment and management. As early as 1905, he referred appropriately to his team as his "beautiful machine." His habit of requiring swift execution of his plays on the practice field earned him the nickname "Hurry-up." Yost was a precursor of the superb managers Percy Haughton at Harvard and Knute Rockne at Notre Dame rather than the creative peer of Amos Alonzo Stagg, Henry L. Williams, or Glenn S. Warner.

Until 1921 Yost worked only during the ten-week football season, for which he was paid more than the annual salary of a full professor. This left the rest of the year free for an active business career. Yost sought out natural resource deposits for development companies, sold oil and gas leases, and supervised the construction of a hydroelectric project in Tennessee (1907–1914). So lucrative were these ventures that he was loath to give them up when in 1906 the Intercollegiate Conference resolved that coaches in member schools should have full-time academic appointments. Michigan stood by its coach, and after two years of debate left the conference, remaining out until 1917. The controversy continued, however, and in 1921 Yost's position at Michigan was finally legitimized with his appointment as director of intercollegiate athletics; two years later he was also named professor of the theory and practice of athletic coaching in the School of Education. Yost's new duties involved him in a wide range of activities, including the development of athletic curricula and the construction of such facilities as a new stadium and the Yost Field House; as a result, he gave up coaching the football team after 1927. All told, he built at Ann Arbor the largest collegiate athletic enterprise in America.

The place and style of the early twentieth-century football coach on the American campus was not unlike that of the nineteenth-century college chaplain. Yost claimed that his job gave him a "pulpit" from which to preach his message of football as a "sanctified instrument for good." He opposed smoking, drinking, and swearing. A typically long-winded speech on "football's four cornerstones of success" addressed "brains, heart, courage, and character." Yet not everyone regarded Yost as a positive moral force. As a zealous proselyter of player talent, he sometimes recruited high school boys before they had graduated. As early as 1903 President David Starr Jordan of Stanford denounced such aberrations and named Yost as a practitioner of the "kind of corruption" in intercollegiate athletics that colleges should eschew (North Central Association of Colleges and Secondary Schools, *Proceedings of the Eighth Annual Meeting*, 1903, pp. 150-151).

Yost married Eunice Josephine Fite on Mar. 12, 1906; they had one child, Fielding Harris. In 1946, five years after his retirement at the age of seventy, he died in Ann Arbor of a gallbladder condition. He was buried at Forest Hill Cemetery, Ann Arbor. Yost exemplified the success story of Middle America. Tall and ruddy, abstemious, garrulous, with a self-help anecdote always at hand, he was a personification of the self-made man. His funeral service was an appropriate conclusion to his life. Boy Scouts formed a color guard, politicians and All-Americans served as pallbearers, and his fraternity brothers sang his favorite song, "The Sweetheart of Sigma Chi."

[The papers of the Univ. of Mich. Athletic Assoc., in the Mich. Hist. Collect., Univ. of Mich., are a major primary source, dealing largely with Yost. The best source for Intercollegiate Conference proceedings, including files on Yost and Michigan, is the A. A. Stagg Papers, Univ. of Chicago. Yost's syndicated newspaper memoirs, running to fifty-three chapters, were carried by many newspapers, including the *Chicago Herald-Examiner* and *Detroit Times,* in late 1925 and early 1926. Yost wrote one book, *Football for Player and Spectator* (1905), and numerous speeches and articles; for examples, see speech in *Barnwell Bull.,* VIII, 5–16 (1931), and articles in *Athletic Jour.,* Apr. 1925, and *Jour. of Health and Physical Education,* June 1931. The most extensive study of his career is John R. Behee, "Fielding H. Yost's Legacy to the Univ. of Mich." (Ph.D. diss., Dept. of Physical Education, Univ. of Mich., 1970). J. Fred Lawton, *"Hurry Up" Yost in Story and Song* (1947), is a brief, anecdotal memoir. The *N.Y. Times,* Aug. 21 and 22, 1946, and the *Detroit News,* Aug. 22 and 23, 1946, have excellent editorials and obituaries; the *Ann Arbor News,* Jan. 11, 1937, gives financial details of the growth of Michigan athletic facilities under Yost. The 1880 federal census lists the family, spelling the name as "Youst" (courtesy of W.Va. Dept of Archives and Hist., Charleston). A portrait by Roy C. Gamble (1935) hangs in the Michigan Union.]
ROBIN D. LESTER

YOUMANS, VINCENT MILLIE (Sept. 27, 1898–Apr. 5, 1946), composer and theatrical producer, was born in New York City, the son of Vincent M. Youmans and Lucy Gibson (Millie) Youmans. He was of Anglo-Irish heritage, his mother having come from a socially prominent family. Youmans' father and his uncle Daniel operated prosperous stores along Broadway that set the style in silk hats and derbies for fashionable turn-of-the-century New Yorkers. At age four, Youmans began the privileged child's obligatory piano lessons, but his parents did not expect that the lessons would amount to more than an extra social grace. As befit his background, Youmans attended private schools in Mamaroneck and Rye, N.Y., and planned, at his parents' urging, to study engineering at Yale. Instead, he clerked for a Wall Street broker's office until enlisting in the navy upon the outbreak of World War I.

Assigned to an entertainment unit at the Great Lakes Training Station, Youmans was fortunate enough to spend his service years composing musical shows; one joyous song that attracted the navy bandmaster's attention survived to become "Hallelujah!" in *Hit the Deck* (1927).

Upon leaving the service, he went to work for the Harms Music Company in New York as a "song-plugger." His duties included rehearsing singers in Victor Herbert's musicals, and he later acknowledged Herbert's influence on his own development by saying, "I got something in less than a year that money could not buy."

In 1920 Youmans published his first song and made his first stage contributions for *Two Little Girls in Blue* (1921), with lyrics by Ira Gershwin; the particularly popular song was "Oh Me! Oh My! Oh You!" The producer of *Two Little Girls* was persuaded by composer George Gershwin, another former Harms employee, to hire Youmans, his friend and close contemporary.

The year 1923 saw two Youmans' shows: the short-lived *Mary Jane McKane,* distinguished only in that one of its melodies would, with minor variations, become the title song for *No, No, Nanette* one year later; and *Wildflower,* one of the greatest successes of the 1920's. The *New York World* described the songs from the latter show, which included the title song and "Bambalina," as "really gorgeous." With lyrics by Oscar Hammerstein II, *Wildflower* ran for over 400 performances, the longest Broadway run enjoyed by any Youmans' show.

Only three years after Youmans' first produced show, he composed the music for *No, No, Nanette,* a fluffball farce that captured the gaiety of the 1920's in the United States and quickly became "probably the biggest international hit of any of the conventional musical comedies of the decade" (Green, p. 129).

Skillfully managed by producer H. H. Frazee, *Nanette* survived a less than overwhelming first few weeks of its Detroit tryout to take Chicago by siege as longer and longer lines formed outside the box office. It eventually did so well there that Frazee kept the show running for over a year before moving it to New York. This turnabout in public opinion stemmed in part from the addition of Louise Groody and Charles Winninger to the cast but also in part from several new songs added by Youmans and lyricist Irving Caesar, two of which have become American standards, "Tea for Two" and "I Want to Be Happy."

Alec Wilder classes Youmans as one of the "great innovators" but believes that his tunes, although written for the theater, are really "better-than-average pop songs" rather than "theatre songs" (Wilder, p. 311). In "theatre songs," claims Wilder, "the canvas is larger, the line broader, the intensity greater" (p. 312). Nowhere is Wilder's point better demonstrated than in "Tea for Two" and "I Want to Be Happy," both of which contain bouncy, almost tinkling, repetitions of a short musical phrase, the effect of which makes them sound as if they were composed for an elegant society party.

No, No, Nanette opened in London in March 1925 and in New York that same September. Although *Wildflower* ran longer on Broadway, within months seventeen companies were performing *Nanette* around the world, and the urbane simplicity of "Tea for Two" floated over audiences in Europe, South America, China, New Zealand, the Philippines, and Java. The show reputedly earned the astronomical amounts of $2 million for Frazee and $500,000 for Youmans.

Oh, Please! (1926) contained one song that has remained popular, "I Know That You Know," called by Wilder "a rousing rhythm song" (p. 297). By the following year, Youmans' stature as a musical-theater composer was secure, but he was artistically unsatisfied with the performance of his songs, having been unable to work steadily with any one producer or lyricist. As a result, he became his own producer at the age of twenty-eight to present *Hit the Deck* (1927), a Herbert Fields adaptation of a Broadway comedy. Wilder called *Hit the Deck* "one of Youmans' best scores" (p. 298); it held two hit songs, the jubilant "Hallelujah!" and the sophisticated rhythm ballad "Sometimes I'm Happy" (originally sung in *A Night Out,* a 1925 Youmans show that never reached Broadway).

Rainbow (1928) closed approximately one month after it opened, but its Youmans score, Oscar Hammerstein lyrics, and book by Laurence Stallings and Hammerstein have been praised by subsequent critics as forward-looking in their integration of music and spoken dialogue to achieve a coherent dramatic effect. David Ewen praises Youmans' "fresh approach" and comments, "Here was a romantic play almost in the folk style later made popular by Rodgers and Hammerstein. Had *Rainbow* come in the 1940's it would surely have enjoyed a far greater audience response" (Ewen, *Popular American Composers,* pp. 140-141).

Youmans had production difficulties with *Rainbow* and with *Great Day!* (1929), which he conceived, scored, and produced at the former Cosmopolitan Theatre, purchased by Youmans and renamed Youmans' Cosmopolitan. *Great Day!* lasted scarcely longer than *Rainbow* but contributed a substantial number of songs to Youmans' enduring catalogue: the lilting "Happy Because I'm in Love"; the shout-and-clap-your-hands title song; and two of his best-known songs, the understated ballad "More Than You Know" and the stirring "Without a Song." This last piece has been called "virtually an art song . . . most certainly a favorite of concert singers" (Wilder, p. 305).

Youmans composed several songs for Florenz Ziegfeld's *Smiles* (1930), although his best effort, "Time on My Hands," became popular only after being removed from the show because the star refused to sing it. Youmans himself produced *Through the Years* (1932), a failure whose title song was reputedly the composer's favorite. *Take A Chance* (1932) was his last Broadway contribution, with five Youmans songs supplementing the basic score by Nacio Herb Brown. The young Ethel Merman shone brightly in the latter show, and the song "Rise 'n' Shine" joined the earlier "Hallelujah!", "Great Day!" and "Drums in My Heart" (from *Through the Years*) to reveal Youmans' predilection for up-tempo, inspirational, almost gospel (albeit patently "white" gospel) songs.

His final work of any substance was the film score for *Flying Down to Rio* (1933). The film's South American settings and its stars, Fred Astaire and Ginger Rogers in their first picture together, shaped the Latin dance qualities of its two biggest hits, "Carioca" and "Orchids in the Moonlight."

Illness and worry claimed the remainder of Youmans' relatively short life. Tuberculosis abruptly terminated his Broadway career in 1933. Forced to spend the next eleven years resting in Colorado and California, he studied classical music when able and reportedly composed show songs, a symphony, and an opera. The extent to which any of these works were ever completed and whether they survive has been inconclusively debated by musical-theater scholars. Youmans' retirement furthered his reputation for being aloof, which derived from real shyness.

He married Anne Varley, a dancer in *Hit the Deck,* on Feb. 7, 1927, and twins named Vincent and Cecily were born in the same year; this first marriage ended in divorce in

1933. His October 1935 marriage to Mildred Boots, a former *Follies* girl, lasted until 1946, when it too resulted in divorce three months before Youmans died.

Having gone bankrupt in 1936, Youmans returned to New York in 1943-1944 in an attempt to reestablish himself as a producer with the *Vincent Youmans Ballet Review,* a spectacular large-cast potpourri of modern dance, classical ballets (staged by Leonide Massine), and puppets, with music by the Cuban composer Ernesto Lecuona and financed by Doris Duke Cromwell. Sadly, but predictably, it closed before reaching Broadway.

Youmans entered Doctors Hospital in New York in early 1945 and returned to Colorado in January of 1946. Only forty-seven years old, he died of tuberculosis at the Park Lane Hotel in Denver. After services in New York's St. Thomas (Episcopal) Church, he was cremated and his ashes scattered near the Ambrose lightship off the New Jersey coast. His forced retirement from the world of musical theater and his early death remind one of George Gershwin's youthful passing; if Gershwin's talent was a greater loss and his even earlier, more sudden death a greater shock, Youmans' lingering end was perhaps more pathetic.

Alec Wilder offered a precise appreciation of Youmans when he wrote, "His interest in using ideas from his main strains in his releases was definitely an innovation and . . . his search for new ways to make simple, direct statements was almost always present. There is no doubt that his good songs are unforgettable. . . . In his constancy toward the American musical point of view and his rhythmic and harmonic inventiveness he was . . . one of the truest of the believers in the new musical world around him" (p. 312).

[The basic material for this article was provided by clippings in the files of the Harvard Theatre Collect., the *N.Y. Herald-Tribune* obituary of Apr. 6, 1946, and the biographical outline prepared by Larry Millsap of the Univ. of Ill. Lib. School. Two invaluable works for any student of American musical theater were also heavily drawn upon for this article: Alec Wilder, *Am. Popular Song* (1972) and Stanley Green, *The World of Musical Comedy* (1960). Also useful are David Ewen, *The Complete Book of the Am. Musical Theater* (1970) and David Ewen, ed., *Popular Am. Composers* (1962). For an excellent photograph of Youmans, with a characteristically winning grin, see Green, p. 124.]

GEORGE PHILIP BIRNBAUM

DICTIONARY

OF

AMERICAN BIOGRAPHY

INDEX GUIDE
TO THE
SUPPLEMENTS

INDEX GUIDE
TO THE SUPPLEMENTS

Index Guide to the Supplements

Index Guide to the Supplements

Index Guide to the Supplements

Index Guide to the Supplements

Index Guide to the Supplements

Index Guide to the Supplements

Index Guide to the Supplements

Index Guide to the Supplements

Index Guide to the Supplements

Index Guide to the Supplements

Index Guide to the Supplements

Index Guide to the Supplements

Index Guide to the Supplements

Index Guide to the Supplements

Index Guide to the Supplements

Index Guide to the Supplements

Index Guide to the Supplements

Index Guide to the Supplements

Index Guide to the Supplements

Index Guide to the Supplements

Index Guide to the Supplements

Index Guide to the Supplements

Index Guide to the Supplements

Index Guide to the Supplements

Index Guide to the Supplements

Index Guide to the Supplements

Index Guide to the Supplements

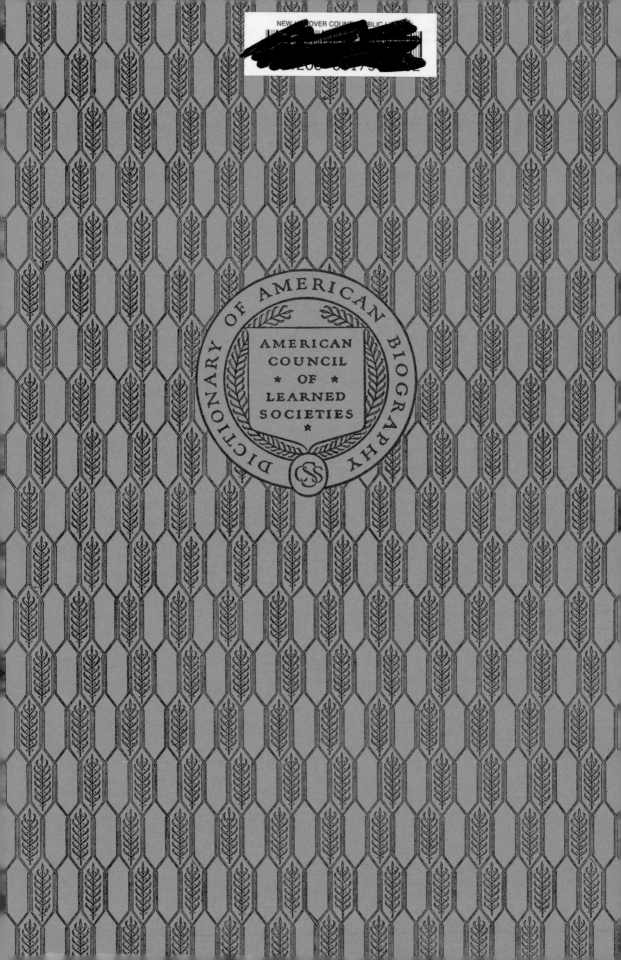

DICTIONARY OF AMERICAN BIOGRAPHY

AMERICAN
COUNCIL
* OF *
LEARNED
SOCIETIES